THE INDEX LIBRARY

PROBATE ACCOUNTS OF ENGLAND AND WALES K–Z

Issued by
THE BRITISH RECORD SOCIETY

[113]

THE INDEX LIBRARY

INDEX

TO THE

PROBATE ACCOUNTS

OF

ENGLAND AND WALES
K–Z

Edited by

Peter Spufford

with the assistance of

Matthew Brett and Amy Louise Erickson

Compiled by

Jacqueline Bower, Matthew Brett

and Nesta Evans

With an Introductory Essay by

Jacqueline Bower

LONDON :

Issued to Subscribers by

THE BRITISH RECORD SOCIETY LIMITED

1999

Published by The British Record Society Limited
c/o Patric Dickinson
The College of Arms
Queen Victoria Street
London EC4V 4BT

ISBN Part I 0 901505 38 2
ISBN Part II 0 901505 39 0
ISBN for the set 0 901505 40 4

Printed in Great Britain by
Progressive Printing (UK) Limited, Leigh-on-Sea, Essex

CONTENTS

Volume II

Guide to the Indexes

The main part of this index is arranged by the names of the deceased man or woman whose moveable goods were being accounted for. For speed of use the first surname on each page is repeated in the top outside corner. The entries give, in order, surname, christian name, status or occupation where known, place or residence, county, date of the account (not date of death which can be several years earlier), the record office in which the account is now kept, and its reference. Some record offices do not yet give very precise references to probate accounts. For example they give a general reference and ask the reader to add the name and date of the account. This has been indicated in the index.

Most of the names of record offices will be easily recognisable. RO has been used as a general abbreviation for either Record Office or Archives. So Herts RO means Hertfordshire Record Office, Oxon RO means Oxfordshire Archives and Lincs RO means Lincolnshire Archives Office. There are some which may be less obvious to some users:

Bodleian for the Oxford University Archives in the Bodleian Library
Borthwick for the Borthwick Institute, York
CKS for the Centre for Kentish Studies at Maidstone
CUL for the Cambridge University Archives in the Cambridge University Library
Greater London RO for the Greater London Record Office, now London Metropolitan Archive
Lambeth for Lambeth Palace Library
LJRO for the Lichfield Joint Record Office
NLW for the National Library of Wales in Aberystwyth
PRO for the Public Record Office.

There are two supplementary indexes:

The first of these supplemetary indexes is for status and occupation. All occupations or status for which large numbers of accounts survive have not been indexed separately since they appear on virtually every page: widow (2058 accounts); yeoman (1981 accounts); husbandman (1094 accounts); and gentleman (985 accounts). Some entries have been grouped together, like different sorts of clergy, but the cross references should make these easy to find.

The second supplementary index is for places. Entries have been arranged according to the ancient counties of England, followed by the ancient counties of Wales, followed by European countries, and then by countries elsewhere in the world. At the end are a small number of ships. Those places for which no county is given or otherwise recognisable, are listed under a 'no county' heading after Yorkshire. Within counties, places are arranged by parishes, with any place within a parish shown in brackets. The index takes the form of Chievely (Snelsmore) rather than Snelsmore in Chievely. In places with more than one parish, the index takes the form of Abingdon St Helen rather than St Helen's Abingdon.

Kadwell, John, Biddenden, Kent, 1676 CKS PRC2/37/55
Kadwell, Mary, Nackington, Kent, 1669 CKS PRC1/14/65
Kadwell, Thomas, Rolvenden, Kent, 1633 CKS PRC20/11/67
Kadwell, Thomas, esquire, Rolvenden, Kent, 1682 CKS PRC2/40/51
Kain, Isabell, widow, Ragdale, Leics, 1665 Leics RO Administrators Accounts C17th f9
Karslake, George, Chart, Great, Kent, 1596 CKS PRC2/8/7
Kay, Abraham, 1618 Lancs RO (Name of Deceased) D.R.C.H. 1618
Kay, Dionysius, Middleton (Thornham), Lancs, 1616 Lancs RO (Name of Deceased) D.R.C.H. 1616
Kay, Francys, clergy: 'clerk', Sutton, Lincs, 1601 Lincs RO Ad/Ac/5/250
Kay, James, clergy: 'mr/clerk', Selling, Kent, 1679 CKS PRC2/38/48
Kay, Thomas, farmer, Hovingham (Wath), Yorks, 1777 Borthwick Test C.P. 1777/5
Kay, Thomas, surgeon, Lymm, Ches, 1780 Cheshire RO (Name) W.C. 1780
Kay, William, currier, Sheffield, Yorks, 1812 Borthwick Test C.P. 1812/5
Kay, William, currier, Sheffield, Yorks, 1815 Borthwick Test C.P. 1815/6
Kaye, Joseph, Tetford, Lincs, 1618 Lincs RO Ad/Ac/14/292
Kaye, Paul, butcher, Thornhill, Yorks, 1822 Borthwick Test C.P. 1822/6
Kayne, Thomas, Storrington, Sussex, 1676 W. Suss RO EpI/33/1676/18
Kayser, Ennigoe, Mawgan, Corn, 1612 Cornwall RO AP/K43/2
Keable, Richard, St Laurence Thanet, Kent, CKS PRC1/12/52a
Keable, Richard, St Laurence Thanet, Kent, 1668 CKS PRC1/12/52
Keagle, Richard, Teddington, Beds, 1625 Lincs RO Ad/Ac/19B/81a
Keal, Ann, widow, Strubby, Lincs, 1682 Lincs RO Ad/Ac/42/91
Keale, Henry, Chislet, Kent, 1617 CKS PRC2/22/86
Keale, Margarett, widow, Smeeth, Kent, 1618 CKS PRC20/4/218
Keale, Reiginold, Smeeth, Kent, 1639 CKS PRC20/11/33
Keale, Thomas, Boothby Graffoe, Lincs, 1638 Lincs RO Ad/Ac/25/210
Keale, Thomas, Moorby, Lincs, 1674 Lincs RO Ad/Ac/34/32
Kealle, Ame, Strubby, Lincs, 1682 Lincs RO Ad/Ac/42/108
Keam, William, husbandman, Chislet, Kent, 1676 CKS PRC2/37/52
Keame, George, yeoman, Brightwell, Berks, 1618 Berks RO D/A1/200/92A

Keamishe, Richard, Abingdon, Berks, 1608 Berks RO D/A1/200/74A
Kearse, Edward, yeoman, Cogges, Oxon, 1641 Oxon RO MSS Wills 298/4/16
Keat, John, Frilford, Berks, 1612 Berks RO D/A1/200/79A
Keate, Awdryan, Culham, Oxon, 1627 Oxon RO MSS Wills 298/4/3
Keate, Benjamin, carpenter, Bristol, Glos, Bristol RO 1779/CP
Keate, Gregory, Ilsley, West, Berks, 1604 Berks RO D/A1/200/72D
Keate, Henry, husbandman, Lambourn (Isbury), Berks, 1680 Berks RO D/A1/201/2C
Keate, John, Drayton, Berks, 1596 Berks RO D/A1/200/61A
Keate, John, Harwell, Berks, 1596 Berks RO D/A1/200/62C
Keate, John, husbandman, Milton, Berks, 1627 Berks RO D/A1/200/102C
Keate, John, Long Wittenham, Berks, 1631 Berks RO D/A1/200/109C
Keate, John, Fovant, Wilts, 1690 Wilts RO Arch. Sarum(+ name and date)
Keate, Marian, spinster, Childrey, Berks, 1626 Berks RO D/A1/200/101A
Keate, Nicholas, chandler, Harwell, Berks, 1681 Berks RO D/A1/201/7C
Keate, Richard, Woodchurch, Kent, 1685 CKS PRC20/13/438
Keate, Simon, husbandman, Bradfield, Berks, 1620 Berks RO D/A1/200/91A
Keate, Thomas, Clifton, Oxon, 1636 Oxon RO MSS Wills Pec 69/4/5
Keate, William, weaver, Newbury, Berks, 1615 Berks RO D/A1/200/83A
Keate, William, yeoman, Harwell, Berks, 1621 Berks RO D/A1/200/94C
Keates, Edward, yeoman, Bucklebury, Berks, 1679 Berks RO D/A1/201/1C
Keay, Randle, gentleman, Burslem, Staffs, 1827 LJRO/B/C/5/1827/19b
Kebble, Richard, Stodmarsh, Kent, 1617 CKS PRC2/22/96
Kebitt, Richard, Faversham, Kent, 1640 CKS PRC1/4/71
Kedge, Margarett, widow, St Alban, London & Middlesex, 1700 PRO PROB5/1608
Kedyell, William, Hurstbourne Priors, Hants, 1623 Hants RO 21M65 D8/26
Keele, Roberte, Faversham, Kent, 1592 CKS PRC2/6/338
Keeler, Austen, Blean, Kent, 1585 CKS PRC2/3/292
Keeler, John, Herne, Kent, 1604 CKS PRC21/17/9
Keeler, John, Stelling, Kent, 1611 CKS PRC2/16/47
Keeler, Stephen, Hythe St Leonard, Kent, 1671 CKS PRC20/12/17
Keeling, Thomas, yeoman, Rolleston, Staffs, 1663 LJRO:cards/1663/38
Keen, Susannah, Bleadon, Som, 1711 Somerset RO D/D/Cta/K9
Keene, Andrew, Weston Zoyland, Som, 1681 Somerset RO D/D/Cta/K11
Keene, Emma, widow, Redbourn, Herts, 1627 Herts RO ASA25/2596
Keene, Thomas, Kingston Seymour, Som, 1623 Somerset RO D/D/Cta/K3
Keepe, Richard, yeoman, Peasemore, Berks, 1678 Berks RO D/A1/200/150C
Keepe, Thomas, shepherd, Compton, Berks, 1663 Berks RO D/A1/200/131A
Keepe, William, Goxhill, Lincs, 1632 Lincs RO Ad/Ac/23/8
Keere, Richard, Crowle, Worcs, 1680 Worcs RO 008.7 BA3585/837/bdl 2
Keete, Henry, New Romney, Kent, 1618 CKS PRC20/4/216
Keete, John, yeoman, Lyminge, Kent, 1623 CKS PRC20/6/332
Keete, John, Lydd, Kent, 1637 CKS PRC20/11/31
Keete, John, husbandman, Sittingbourne, Kent, 1692 CKS PRC2/42/41
Keete, Robert, Hollingbourne, Kent, 1585 CKS PRC21/7/116
Keete, Robert, Harwell, Berks, 1592 Berks RO D/A1/200/53A
Keete, Thomas, Reculver, Kent, 1679 CKS PRC20/12/311
Keete, Woolforne, Tenterden, Kent, 1598 CKS PRC2/9/477
Keeton, John, Kirton, Lincs, 1607 Lincs RO Ad/Ac/8a/105
Keeyes, John, Sandwich, Kent, 1625 CKS PRC2/25/80
Keighley, John, gentleman, Bretforton, Worcs, 1684 Worcs RO 008.7 BA3585/837/bdl 4
Keighley, Margerie, widow, Frampton, Lincs, 1619 Lincs RO Ad/Ac/15/79
Keightley, Giles, Bretforton, Worcs, 1680 Worcs RO 008.7 BA3585/837/bdl 2
Keightley, John, esquire, Littleton, South, Worcs, 1648 Worcs RO 008.7 BA3585/837/bdl 1
Keigwyn, see Martyn,
Keile, Robarte, Chislet, Kent, 1593 CKS PRC2/6/148

[Kekewich:]
Kekewich, Samuel, merchant, Hackney St John, London & Middlesex, 1703 Lambeth Palace Arches G53/2
Kelfill, Robert, yeoman, Sutton St Edmunds, Lincs, 1664 Lincs RO Ad/Ac/43/35
Kelham, Thomas, Gonerby, Lincs, 1638 Lincs RO Ad/Ac/25/326
Kelk, William, joiner/cabinet maker, Newark on Trent, Notts, 1829 Borthwick Test C.P. 1829/1
Kelk, William, joiner/cabinet maker, Newark on Trent, Notts, 1829 Borthwick Test C.P. 1829/4
Kelke, Francis, Markby, Lincs, 1646 Lincs RO Ad/Ac/28/237
Kelke, Nicholas, Killingholme, Lincs, 1637 Lincs RO Ad/Ac/25/643
Kelke, Richard, Stainton le Vale, Lincs, 1570 Lincs RO Ad/Ac/2b/29
Kelke, William, Huttoft, Lincs, 1679 Lincs RO Ad/Ac/43/113
Kellam, Mary, Leicester St Mary, Leics, 1639 Leics RO PR/I/41A/30
Kellam, William, Barkston, Lincs, 1639 Lincs RO Ad/Ac/26/47
Kellame, Johnne, Grantham, Lincs, 1597 Lincs RO Ad/Ac/4/133
Kellaway, Richard, Wilton, Wilts, 1684 Wilts RO Arch. Sarum(+ name and date)
Kellett, Addam, Skirbeck, Lincs, 1638 Lincs RO Ad/Ac/25/220
Kellett, Thomas, Boston, Lincs, 1626 Lincs RO Ad/Ac/20b/90
Kellett, Thomas, Boston, Lincs, 1637? Lincs RO Ad/Ac/24/556
Kellett, William, Rippingale, Lincs, 1605 Lincs RO Ad/Ac/6/87
Kelsall, Elizabeth, widow, Lymm, Ches, 1786 Cheshire RO (Name) W.C. 1786
Kelsall, Joseph, Audley, Staffs, 1728 LJRO/B/C/5/1728/132
Kelsey, Anne, Haxey, Lincs, 1607 Lincs RO Ad/Ac/37/253
Kelsey, Grace, Benington, Lincs, 1629 Lincs RO Ad/Ac/22/113
Kelsey, Gregorye, Haxey, Lincs, 1615 Lincs RO Ad/Ac/8b/222
Kelsey, Henry eld, fisherman, Ringwould, Kent, 1669 CKS PRC1/13/67
Kelsey, John, Broughton, Hants, 1598 Hants RO 1595 AD39/3
Kelsey, John, Frieston, Lincs, 1638 Lincs RO Ad/Ac/25/143
Kelsey, Margarett, Haxey (Graizelound), Lincs, 1663 Lincs RO Ad/Ac/41/76
Kelsey, Roberte, Haxey (East Lound), Lincs, 1607 Lincs RO Ad/Ac/37/232
Kelsey, Thomas, Haxey, Lincs, 1631? Lincs RO Ad/Ac/39/236
Kelsey, William, Herne, Kent, 1616 CKS PRC20/3/246
Kelsoe/Buckeridge, Ann, Tilehurst, Berks, 1598 Berks RO D/A1/200/66A
Kelson, John, Camerton, Som, 1621 Somerset RO D/D/Cta/K1
Kelson, William, Melksham, Wilts, 1669 Wilts RO Arch. Sarum(+ name and date)
Kelvin, Edward, Whaplode, Lincs, 1623 Lincs RO Ad/Ac/18/70
Kember, Joane, Hawkinge, Kent, 1639 CKS PRC1/3/1
Kember, Joane, Hawkinge, Kent, 1639 CKS PRC1/3/1a
Kember, John, mason, Abingdon, Berks, 1614 Berks RO D/A1/200/81A
Kember, Thomas, yeoman, Cookham, Berks, 1619 Berks RO D/A1/89/110D
Kember, William, Lydden, Kent, 1600 CKS PRC2/11/245
Kemble, John, Milston, Wilts, 1615 Wilts RO Miscellaneous Index (name + date)
Kemble, Richard, clothier, Newbury, Berks, 1627 Berks RO D/A1/200/104C
Kemp, John, Dover, Kent, 1625 CKS PRC20/7/299
Kemp, John, Chapel, North, Sussex, 1643 W. Suss RO EpI/33/1643/4
Kemp, Leonard, Havant, Hants, 1612 Hants RO 1612 AD56/3
Kempe, Edwarde, mayor/esquire, Dover, Kent, 1613 CKS PRC20/2/553
Kempe, Henry, weaver: 'linen weaver', Smarden, Kent, 1684 CKS PRC2/40/210
Kempe, James + Joanne, Hose, Leics, 1673 Leics RO Administrators Accounts 1667-72 f125
Kempe, John, Birchington, Kent, 1582 CKS PRC21/6/14
Kempe, John, Ringwould, Kent, 1614 CKS PRC2/17/15
Kempe, John, Ash next Sandwich, Kent, 1635 CKS PRC20/11/49
Kempe, John, St Thomas Isle of Harty, Kent, 1638 CKS PRC2/34/228
Kempe, John, yeoman, Brookland, Kent, 1672 CKS PRC2/35/64
Kempe, John, mr, St James Westminster, London & Middlesex, 1708 PRO PROB32/51/14
Kempe, Richard, yeoman, Harbledown, Kent, 1675 CKS PRC2/36/255
Kempe, Roger, Horsham, Sussex, 1624 W. Suss RO EpI/33/1624/14

Kempe, Thomas, Sidlesham, Sussex, 1635 W. Suss RO EpI/33/1635/15
Kempe, William, gentleman, Wye, Kent, 1599 CKS PRC2/11/83
Kempe, William, Sidlesham, Sussex, 1669 W. Suss RO EpI/33/1669/12
Kempe, William + Joane, Birchington, Kent, 1597 CKS PRC21/14/268
Kempson, Richard, Binton, Warks, 1685 Worcs RO 008.7 BA3585/837/bdl 4
Kempster, Richard, Canterbury St Dunstan Without, Kent, 1605 CKS PRC2/13/262
Kempster, Sarah, spinster, Prees, Shrops, 1797 LJRO/B/C/5/1797/40
Kempster, Thomas, Appleton, Berks, 1621 Wilts RO CC Sarum(+ name and date)
Kempt, Henry, bachelor, Marden, East, Sussex, 1673 W. Suss RO EpI/33/1673/19
Kemsley, John, Bredhurst, Kent, 1631 CKS PRC20/9/265
Kemslie, Sydrach, High Halstow, Kent, 1612 CKS PRC2/17/305
Kemsly, Thomas, basket maker, Headcorn, Kent, 1615 CKS PRC2/22/85
Kemsly, William, Rainham, Kent, 1619 CKS PRC2/22/91
Kenaday, Thomas, Hackington, Kent, 1599 CKS PRC2/10/442
Kenard, Thomas, Rainham, Kent, 1605 CKS PRC2/13/260
Kencham, John, Headcorn, Kent, 1615 CKS PRC2/22/89
Kencham, Robert, Aldington, Kent, 1627 CKS PRC20/7/11
Kencham, Thomas, husbandman, Bilsington, Kent, 1694 CKS PRC2/42/84
Kenchington,
Wilts 1640? Wilts RO Arch. Sarum(+ name and date)
Kendall, Catherine, widow, Witney, Oxon, 1635 Oxon RO MSS Wills 298/4/8
Kendall, Elizabeth, widow, St Blazey, Corn, 1609 Cornwall RO AP/K27/4
Kendall, John, Lanlivery, Corn, 1604 Cornwall RO AP/K7
Kendall, Joseph, basket maker, Birmingham, Warks, 1773 LJRO/B/C/5/1773/31
Kendall, Richard, Somercoates, Lincs, 1622 Lincs RO Ad/Ac/17/83
Kendall, Richard, Flixborough, Lincs, 1662 Lincs RO Ad/Ac/41/108
Kendall, Robert, Bardney, Lincs, 1605 Lincs RO Ad/Ac/6/89
Kendall/Medam, John, Devizes St John the Baptist, Wilts, 1614 Wilts RO CC Sarum(+ name and date)
Kendericke, Dorothy, Somersby, Lincs, 1612 Lincs RO Ad/Ac/11/171
Kenet, Robart, Crundale, Kent, 1582 CKS PRC2/2/138
Kenett, John, Dover, Kent, 1619 CKS PRC20/4/222
Kenfild, William, Reading, Berks, 1565 Berks RO D/A2/C5/327R
Kenn, John?, yeoman, Aldington, Kent, 1672 CKS PRC20/12/53
Kennard, Edward, Canterbury St Mary-Magdalen Burgate, Kent, 1606 CKS PRC2/14/284
Kennard, Elizabeth, Ulcombe, Kent, 1676 CKS PRC2/37/59
Kennard, James, grocer, Milton next Sittingbourne, Kent, 1639 CKS PRC1/1/80
Kennard, John, Minster in Sheppey, Kent, 1611 CKS PRC2/15/208
Kennard, John, Hucking, Kent, 1699 CKS PRC19/5/64
Kennard, Sampson, Canterbury St Paul, Kent, 1627 CKS PRC2/28/75
Kennard, Sampson, Borden, Kent, 1635 CKS PRC2/33/73
Kennard, Sampson, clergy: 'mr/vicar', Canterbury, Kent, 1636 CKS PRC20/11/27
Kennard, Thomas, Aldington, Kent, 1629 CKS PRC20/8/305
Kennet, Christofer, Ebony, Kent, 1597 CKS PRC2/9/481
Kennet, Isaac, Birchington, Kent, 1617 CKS PRC20/4/224
Kennet, John, Eastchurch, Sheppey, Kent, 1636 CKS PRC2/33/69
Kennet, John, yeoman, Wye, Kent, 1671 CKS PRC2/35/63
Kennet, Margaret, widow, Hoath, Kent, 1583 CKS PRC21/6/268
Kennett, Cyprian, Sevington, Kent, 1611 CKS PRC2/17/408
Kennett, Edward, yeoman, Elkstone, Glos, 1709 GRO GDR/B4/2/K24
Kennett, Godden, Folkestone, Kent, 1628 CKS PRC2/29/60
Kennett, Henry, Folkestone, Kent, 1600 CKS PRC2/11/241
Kennett, Henry, Herne, Kent, 1627 CKS PRC20/8/307
Kennett, John, Littlebourne, Kent, 1594 CKS PRC2/11/62
Kennett, John, New Romney, Kent, 1598 CKS PRC21/15/5

[Kennett:]
Kennett, John, Monks Horton, Kent, 1603 CKS PRC2/14/297
Kennett, John, Chilham, Kent, 1637 CKS PRC2/34/75
Kennett, John, husbandman, Stone in Oxney, Kent, 1662 CKS PRC1/9/33
Kennett, John, butcher, Monks Horton, Kent, 1666 CKS PRC1/11/130
Kennett, John, yeoman, Wye, Kent, 1696 CKS PRC2/42/117
Kennett, Margarett, widow, Lydd, Kent, 1668 CKS PRC19/4/22
Kennett, Marie, widow, Ashford, Kent, 1597 CKS PRC2/9/479
Kennett, Richard, St Laurence Thanet, Kent, 1626 CKS PRC2/27/90
Kennett, Richard, Bromfield, Kent, 1633 CKS PRC2/32/73
Kennett, Richard, Folkestone, Kent, 1635 CKS PRC2/33/71
Kennett, Sampson, Ulcombe, Kent, 1604 CKS PRC2/14/295
Kennett, William, Sandwich St Bartholomew's Hospital, Kent, 1618 CKS PRC20/4/220
Kennett, William, Lyminge, Kent, 1623 CKS PRC20/6/330
Kennett, William, Folkestone, Kent, 1624 CKS PRC20/6/114
Kennett, William, cooper, Folkestone, Kent, 1675 CKS PRC2/36/254
Kennett, William, yeoman, Sheldwich, Kent, 1686 CKS PRC2/41/36
Kennett, William, Folkestone, Kent, 1721 CKS PRC1/18/41
Kennington, John, Sandford, Oxon, 1636 Oxon RO MSS Wills 298/4/10
Kenrick, Jeffrey, Somerby, Lincs, 1600 Lincs RO Ad/Ac/5/80
Kensham, John, Tenterden, Kent, 1636 CKS PRC2/33/72
Kent, Alice, widow, Radway, Warks, 1672 LJRO:cards/1672/32
Kent, Henry, Maer, Staffs, 1663 LJRO:cards/1663/39
Kent, James, yeoman, Leeds (Pitthills, Beeston), Yorks, Borthwick Test C.P. 1733/7
Kent, John, Lydiard Tregoze, Wilts, 1631 Wilts RO Arch. Wilts.(name + date)
Kent, John, yeoman, Aston, Herts, 1635 Herts RO AHH23/1407
Kent, John, Faversham, Kent, 1646 CKS PRC1/7/87
Kent, John, Eling, Hants, 1678 Hants RO 21m65 D8/290
Kent, Philip, yeoman, Enstone, Oxon, 1627 Oxon RO MSS Wills 298/4/1
Kent, Philip, yeoman, Enstone, Church (Neat Enstone), Oxon, 1627 Oxon RO MSS Wills 298/4/1
Kent, Richard, Durrington, Sussex, 1638 W. Suss RO EpIV/10/2/16
Kent, Thomas, Wallop, Nether, Hants, 1625 Hants RO 21M65 D8/119
Kent, Thomas, husbandman, Donington on Bain, Lincs, 1637 Lincs RO Ad/Ac/24/407
Kent, Thomas, Bersted, South, Sussex, 1639 W. Suss RO EpIV/10/2/20
Kent, Thomas, Eling, Hants, 1642 Hants RO 1642 A37/2
Kent, Walter, husbandman, Wargrave, Berks, 1678 Berks RO D/A1/200/146A
Kent, William, yeoman, Middlewich, Ches, 1746 Cheshire RO (Name) W.C. 1746
Kent, William, blacksmith, Rotherham (The Wheel), Yorks, 1769 Borthwick Test C.P. 1769/2
Kentche, Richard, yeoman, Hurst, Berks, 1631 Wilts RO Miscellaneous Index (name + date)
Kente, Margaret, Powick, Worcs, 1607 Worcs RO 008.7 BA3585/839/422
Kentish, Thomas, St Albans St Michaels, Herts, 1628 Herts RO ASA25/4857
Kentishe, John,
Herts 1597 Herts RO ASA25/1625
Kentishe, Robert, yeoman, St Albans St Stephens, Herts, 1583 Herts RO ASA25/4130
Kenton, John, Dover, Kent, 1604 CKS PRC21/17/143
Kenton, John, brewer: 'beerbrewer', Dover, Kent, 1669 CKS PRC19/4/55
Kenton, John, Dover, Kent, 1679 CKS PRC20/12/309
Kenton, Richard, yeoman, Woodnesborough, Kent, 1666 CKS PRC1/11/49
Kenton, Richard, surgeon, Dover, Kent, 1676 CKS PRC20/12/205
Kentysh, Robert, St Albans St Stephens, Herts, 1563 Herts RO ASA25/565
Kenward, John, Molash, Kent, 1587 CKS PRC2/4/71
Kenward, John, Aldington, Kent, 1640 CKS PRC19/1/56
Kenward, Richard, Dymchurch, Kent, 1626 CKS PRC2/27/89
Kenwarde, William, Chilham, Kent, 1596 CKS PRC2/8/220
Kenwicke, Robert, gentleman, Sutton, Kings, Northants, 1617 Oxon RO MSS Wills Pec 44/3/14
Kenwood, Thomsyn,

Kent 1579 CKS PRC21/4/36
Kenworthe, John, Aldington, Kent, 1583 CKS PRC21/6/348
Kenyon, Richard, clergy: 'rector/clerk/sir', Stockport, Ches, 1615 Cheshire RO (Name) W.C. 1615
Kerbey, William, Gedney, Lincs, 1623 Lincs RO Ad/Ac/18/28
Kerbie, John, Birchington, Kent, 1632 CKS PRC20/11/71
Kerby, George, tin plate worker, Bristol, Glos, Bristol RO 1717/34
Kerby, John, Birchington, Kent, 1630 CKS PRC20/8/301
Kerby, Thomas, Stockbury, Kent, 1625 CKS PRC2/25/81
Kerbye, Elizabeth, widow, Wootton, Kent, 1619 CKS PRC2/22/94
Kerchian/Christian, Valentine, husbandman, Pinchbeck, Lincs, 1668 Lincs RO Ad/Ac/33/42
Kerchiver, Roger, gentleman, Stamford, Lincs, 1638 Lincs RO Ad/Ac/25/402
Kerison, John, gentleman, Marlingford, Norf, 1746 Norfolk RO ANF/11/4/77
Kerle, Thomas, Lyminster, Sussex, 1632 W. Suss RO EpI/33/1631/18
Kerley, William, Donhead St Mary, Wilts, 1677 Wilts RO Arch. Sarum(+ name and date)
Kerne, Thomas,
Wilts 1611 Wilts RO Arch. Sarum(+ name and date)
Kersby, John, Mersham, Kent, 1677 CKS PRC2/37/170
Kersby, Richard, Mersham, Kent, 1676 CKS PRC2/37/58
Kerse, John, husbandman/yeoman, Kencott, Oxon, 1676 Oxon RO MSS Wills 39/4/22
Kersey, John, gentleman, Ormsby, South, Lincs, 1624 Lincs RO Ad/Ac/19A/91
Kersfield/Chrisfield, Robert, Milsted, Kent, 1679 CKS PRC2/38/151
Kershaw, Robert, Haxey, Lincs, 1617 Lincs RO Ad/Ac/8b/282
Kershawe, John, Irnham, Lincs, 1639? Lincs RO Ad/Ac/26/86
Kerton, Eliazer, Dover, Kent, 1625 CKS PRC20/7/301
Kerton, John, woodmonger, Auckland, St Andrew (Hamsterley), Dur, 1752 Borthwick Test C.P. 1752/3
Kestin, Richard, Bowden, Great, Leics, 1673 Leics RO Administrators Accounts 1667-72 f116
Ketcherell, David, Sandwich St Clement, Kent, 1638 CKS PRC2/34/225
Ketlewell, Seth, university: 'Fellow of Trinity College, Cambridge/M.A.', Cambridge (Trinity College), Cambs, 1636 CUL V.C. Acc./Box2/43
Kettle, Christofer, Huttoft, Lincs, 1608 Lincs RO Ad/Ac/8a/147
Kettle, John, Sibsey, Lincs, 1623 Lincs RO Ad/Ac/18/64
Kettle, John, St Ives, Hunts, 1676 Hunts RO/Acc58/35(167)
Kettle, Mary, widow, Wilbraham, Little, Cambs, 1774 Cambs RO 1773/Inv
Kettle, William, Northfield, Worcs, 1684 Worcs RO 008.7 BA3585/837/bdl 4
Kettlewel, Thomas, Bolton Percy, Yorks, Borthwick Test C.P. 1741/1
Kew, Richard, yeoman, Avebury, Wilts, 1679 Wilts RO Miscellaneous Index (name + date)
Kewe, William, Calne, Wilts, 1679 Wilts RO Dean Sarum (name + date)
Kewell, Elizabeth, widow, Chichester St Andrew, Sussex, 1619 W. Suss RO EpIII/9/1/17
Kewell, Elizabeth, widow, Rustington, Sussex, 1672 W. Suss RO EpI/33/1672/5
Kewell, John, Chichester, Sussex, 1618 W. Suss RO EpIII/9/1/26
Kewell, John eld, Rustington, Sussex, 1635 W. Suss RO EpI/33/1635/13
Kewell, Mary, widow, Littlehampton, Sussex, 1682 W. Suss RO EpI/33/1682/15
Kewell, Susan, widow, Faversham, Kent, 1662 CKS PRC1/9/34
Kewell, Thomas, Lyminster (Wick), Sussex, 1648 W. Suss RO EpI/33/1648/1
Kewupp, Peter, Bearsted, Kent, 1667 CKS PRC1/12/53
Key, Thomas, labourer, Winteringham, Lincs, 1616 Lincs RO Ad/Ac/8b/125
Keyes, William, Mundham, North, Sussex, 1648 W. Suss RO EpI/33/1648/8
Keyler, Wylliam, Graveney, Kent, 1605 CKS PRC2/14/292
Keylock, John, Painswick, Glos, GRO GDR/B4/2/K2a
Keyme, mistress, Bushey, Herts, Herts RO ASA25/8
Keyme, Joane, widow, Cranbrook, Kent, 1613 CKS PRC2/16/177
Keynes, Samuel, husbandman, Box, Wilts, 1619 Wilts RO Arch. Wilts.(name + date)
Keys, Reignold, gentleman, Hythe St Leonard, Kent, 1593 CKS PRC21/12/463
Kibble, Joan, St Pauls Walden, Herts, 1617 Herts RO ASA25/4829

[Kibley:]
Kibley, Thomas, Sidlesham, Sussex, 1684 W. Suss RO EpI/33/1684/38
Kidd, Thomas, Hallington, Lincs, 1599 Lincs RO Ad/Ac/5/227
Kidd, William, Cambridge, Cambs, CUL V.C. Acc./Box3/65
Kidder, George, Stamford, Lincs, 1626 Lincs RO Ad/Ac/20/65
Kidgell, Henry, St Vedast (Foster), London & Middlesex, 1690 PRO PROB32/31/150
Kidman, William, Waresley, Hunts, Hunts RO/Acc58/88(17)
Kighley, Richard, Ewerby, Lincs, 1652 Lincs RO Ad/Ac/29/11
Kight, Richard, Stockbury, Kent, 1682 CKS PRC2/40/50
Kightly, John, Lockington, Leics, 1639 Leics RO PR/I/41A/28
Kilburne, Abraham, Louth, Lincs, 1677 Lincs RO Ad/Ac/42/80
Kilbye, William, wheelwright, Redbourn, Herts, 1585 Herts RO ASA25/1128
Kill, Christopher, Laverstock, Wilts, 1632 Wilts RO Arch. Sarum(+ name and date)
Killam, Thomas, fellmonger, Charing, Kent, 1676 CKS PRC20/12/206
Killingworth, John, Folksworth, Hunts, 1684 Hunts RO/Acc58/209(202)
Kilmister, Elizabeth, widow, Cherington, Glos, 1791 GRO GDR/B4/2/K13
Kilner, Henry, Wye, Kent, 1669 CKS PRC1/14/66
Kilner, Henry, Wye, Kent, 1669 CKS PRC1/14/66a
Kilsby, Edward, Haddon, West, Northants, 1680 Northants RO NWill A/C/37
Kilsby, Robert, Long Buckby, Northants, 1682 Northants RO NWill A/C/59
Kimbel, William, Daventry, Northants, 1676 Northants RO NWill A/C/143
Kimbell, Thomas, Cropredy (Great Bourton), Oxon, 1662 Oxon RO MSS Wills Pec 44/4/10
Kimber, John, blacksmith, Kintbury, Berks, 1680 Berks RO D/A1/201/9C
Kimble, Sarah, widow, Banbury (Calthorpe), Oxon, 1681 Oxon RO MSS Wills Pec 44/5/1
Kime, Hellen, widow, Stickford, Lincs, 1649 Lincs RO Ad/Ac/30/215
Kime, John, esquire, Boston, Lincs, 1670 Lincs RO Ad/Ac/32/210
Kinaston, John, gentleman, Leigh, Shrops, 1682 LJRO/B/C/5/1681/24
Kinder, John, St Albans, Herts, 1632 Herts RO ASA25/4877
Kine, William, cordwainer, Wittersham, Kent, 1670 CKS PRC19/4/84
King, Alexander, Biddenden, Kent, 1593 CKS PRC2/6/162
King, Ambrose, Sturry, Kent, 1626 CKS PRC2/27/85
King, Daniel, Whitminster (Wheatenhurst), Glos, 1685 GRO GDR/B4/2/K25
King, Dorothy, Hammersmith, London & Middlesex, 1706 PRO PROB32/49/50
King, Edward, husbandman, Merton, Oxon, 1638 Oxon RO MSS Wills 298/4/11
King, Edward, husbandman, Heyford, Lower (Caulcott), Oxon, 1671 Oxon RO MSS Wills 169/1/27
King, Edward, Louth, Lincs, 1675 Lincs RO Ad/Ac/42/3
King, Edward, yeoman, Harwell, Berks, 1675 Berks RO D/A1/200/147D
King, Elizabeth, widow, Minster in Sheppey, Kent, 1638 CKS PRC2/34/230
King, George, innholder, Sittingbourne, Kent, 1674 CKS PRC2/36/83
King, George, yeoman, Searby, Lincs, 1674 Lincs RO Ad/Ac/42/32
King, George, Lymington, Hants, 1679 Hants RO 21m65 D8/313
King, Hugh, yeoman, Holbeach, Lincs, 1649 Lincs RO Ad/Ac/30/235
King, Isaac, Shrewsbury St Chad, Shrops, 1685 LJRO/B/C/5/1685/58
King, James, Rolvenden, Kent, 1628 CKS PRC2/29/58
King, James, yeoman, Ryton, Shrops, 1731 LJRO/B/C/5/1732/54
King, James, tailor, Bottisham, Cambs, 1823 Cambs RO 1823/Admon
King, Jane, Altrincham, Ches, 1638 Cheshire RO (Name) W.C. 1638
King, John, Rolvenden, Kent, 1611 CKS PRC2/15/206
King, John, Skegness, Lincs, 1640 Lincs RO Ad/Ac/27/5
King, John, schoolmaster, Faversham, Kent, 1648 CKS PRC1/8/48
King, John, Scampton, Lincs, 1663 Lincs RO Ad/Ac/41/82
King, John, Hackthorne, Lincs, 1666 Lincs RO Ad/Ac/41/180
King, John, Berrick, Oxon, 1671 Bucks R.O. MSS Wills Pec 80/1/16
King, John, labourer, Harwell, Berks, 1678 Berks RO D/A1/200/151C
King, John, husbandman, Burgh on Bain (Girsby), Lincs, 1679 Lincs RO Ad/Ac/43/106

King, John, citizen/merchant tailor, St Anne Westminster, London & Middlesex, 1689 PRO PROB32/31/39
King, John, mariner, Dover, Kent, 1689 CKS PRC20/13/634
King, John, gentleman, Rolvenden, Kent, 1694 CKS PRC2/42/82
King, John, yeoman, Ospringe, Kent, 1694 CKS PRC2/42/85
King, Margery, widow, Maidstone, Kent, 1596 CKS PRC21/14/51
King, Mary, widow, Sittingbourne, Kent, 1676 CKS PRC2/37/57
King, Mathew, Fittleworth, Sussex, 1674 W. Suss RO EpI/33/1674/2
King, Richard, Willesborough, Kent, 1597 CKS PRC2/9/144
King, Richard, Newton, South, Wilts, 1640 Wilts RO Arch. Sarum(+ name and date)
King, Richard, Ibstock, Leics, 1685 Leics RO Administrators Accounts 1682-86 f39
King, Robart, Lydd, Kent, 1607 CKS PRC20/1/243
King, Robert, Hindon, Wilts, 1690 Wilts RO Arch. Sarum(+ name and date)
King, Robert ygr, Woodford, Northants, 1672 Northants RO NWill A/C/102
King, Roger, Wishford, Great, Wilts, 1687 Wilts RO Arch. Sarum(+ name and date)
King, Salathiell, Chart, Little, Kent, 1596 CKS PRC2/8/465
King, Samuel, Chislet, Kent, 1639 CKS PRC2/34/229
King, Samuel, Kingston Seymour, Som, 1642 Somerset RO D/D/Cta/K8
King, Simon, Canterbury St Mary Northgate, Kent, 1630 CKS PRC20/9/263
King, Thomas, husbandman, Sutton, Long, Lincs, 1614 Lincs RO Ad/Ac/13/199
King, Thomas, yeoman, Knoyle, East, Wilts, 1634 Wilts RO Arch. Sarum(+ name and date)
King, Thomas, yeoman, Waterperry, Oxon, 1639 Oxon RO MSS Wills 298/4/13
King, Thomas, Winterbourne Kingston, Dors, 1689 Wilts RO Dean Sarum (name + date)
King, Thomas, husbandman, Somersham, Hunts, 1716 Hunts RO/Acc58/308
King, Thomas, weaver: 'worsted weaver', Norwich, Norf, 1742 Norfolk RO ANW/23/23/74
King, Thomas, Batley, Yorks, 1800 Borthwick Test C.P. 1800/4
King, William, Wimborne Minster, Dors, Dorset RO PE/WM CP 2/4/85
King, William, Whitstable, Kent, 1616 CKS PRC2/22/88
King, William, Chipping Barnet, Herts, 1630 Herts RO ASA25/4868
King, William, Dundry, Som, 1641 Somerset RO D/D/Cta/K7
King, William, clergy: 'clerk', Hackington, Kent, 1685 CKS PRC2/41/37
King?, Thomas, labourer, Wainfleet, Lincs, 1670 Lincs RO Ad/Ac/32/168
Kingarbie, Thomas, Sturton, Great, Lincs, 1633 Lincs RO Ad/Ac/24/102
Kingarby, Stephen, yeoman, Manby, Lincs, 1614 Lincs RO Ad/Ac/13/18
Kinge, Christopher, Broad Chalke, Wilts, 1598 Wilts RO Arch. Sarum(+ name and date)
Kinge, Daniell, Chart, Little, Kent, 1624 CKS PRC2/23/184
Kinge, Edmund, husbandman, Castle Eaton, Wilts, 1618 Wilts RO Arch. Wilts.(name + date)
Kinge, Edward, Chichester St Andrew, Sussex, W. Suss RO EpIII/9/1/5
Kinge, Edward, Marden, Kent, 1593 CKS PRC2/6/354
Kinge, Edward, St Johns Thanet, Kent, 1638 CKS PRC20/11/37
Kinge, Elizabeth, widow, Warehorne, Kent, 1599 CKS PRC2/11/66
Kinge, Francis, widow, Dover, Kent, 1593 CKS PRC21/12/125
Kinge, George, Wimborne Minster, Dors, 1675 Dorset RO PE/WM CP 2/4/79
Kinge, Henrye, Barham, Kent, 1614 CKS PRC2/17/76
Kinge, Jacob, gentleman, Huntingdon, Hunts, 1684 Hunts RO/Acc58/219(209)
Kinge, James, High Halden, Kent, 1643 CKS PRC1/6/110
Kinge, John, Bobbing, Kent, 1596 CKS PRC2/9/145
Kinge, John, gentleman, Speen, Berks, 1614 Berks RO D/A1/200/84A
Kinge, John, husbandman, Wimborne Minster (Chilbridge), Dors, 1614 Dorset RO PE/WM CP 2/4/11
Kinge, John, labourer, Newington next Sittingbourne, Kent, 1662 CKS PRC1/9/35
Kinge, John eld, Tillington, Sussex, 1635 W. Suss RO EpI/33/1635/18
Kinge, Nicholas, Old Romney, Kent, 1611 CKS PRC2/17/160
Kinge, Richard, Minster in Sheppey, Kent, 1608 CKS PRC2/14/290
Kinge, Richard, Kirdford, Sussex, 1633 W. Suss RO EpI/33/1633/25

[Kinge:]
Kinge, Robert, Sutton, Lincs, 1649 Lincs RO Ad/Ac/30/167
Kinge, Sampson, Sandford, Oxon, 1634 Oxon RO MSS Wills 298/4/7
Kinge, Thomas, Witney, Oxon, 1662 Oxon RO MSS Wills 82/3/12
Kinge, Thomas, Cherington, Warks, 1684 Worcs RO 008.7 BA3585/837/bdl 4
Kinge, William, tailor, Old Romney, Kent, 1643 CKS PRC1/6/111
Kingerbie, Henry, yeoman, Sturton, Great, Lincs, 1618 Lincs RO Ad/Ac/14/258
Kingerbie, Marie, widow, Sturton, Great, Lincs, 1611? Lincs RO Ad/Ac/10/47
Kingerby, Thomas, Wainfleet All Saints, Lincs, 1664 Lincs RO Ad/Ac/45/109
Kinges, Richard, Upton Snodsbury, Worcs, Worcs RO 008.7 BA3585/838/254
Kingesmill, Augustine, Monks Horton, Kent, 1600 CKS PRC2/11/243
Kingesnoth, George, Smarden, Kent, 1596 CKS PRC2/8/326
Kingesnoth, Jeremie, Ulcombe, Kent, 1603 CKS PRC2/12/449
Kingham, Henry, gentleman, Ashford, Kent, 1677 CKS PRC2/37/169
Kingham, Henry, innkeeper, Folkestone, Kent, 1694 CKS PRC2/42/83
Kingington, Thomas, Newton, South, Wilts, 1615 Wilts RO Miscellaneous Index (name + date)
Kingman, Walter, Wishford, Great, Wilts, 1630 Wilts RO Arch. Sarum(+ name and date)
Kingsdowne, Ann, widow, Minster in Sheppey, Kent, 1624 CKS PRC2/23/185
Kingsdowne, Robert, Eastchurch, Sheppey, Kent, 1620 CKS PRC2/22/97
Kingsdowne, Stephen, yeoman, Minster in Sheppey, Kent, 1619 CKS PRC2/22/87
Kingsfoord, John, Mersham, Kent, 1588 CKS PRC2/4/452
Kingsfoord, Robert, Nonington, Kent, 1606 CKS PRC20/1/39
Kingsford, Andrew, Northbourne, Kent, 1692 CKS PRC1/15/116
Kingsford, Bartholomew, yeoman, Northbourne, Kent, 1639 CKS PRC2/34/226
Kingsford, John, yeoman, Great Mongeham, Kent, 1666 CKS PRC1/11/131
Kingsford, Richard, Alkham, Kent, 1630 CKS PRC20/9/261
Kingsford, Thomas, maltster, Sandwich St Peter, Kent, 1623 CKS PRC2/23/183
Kingsforthe, Agnes, Sellindge, Kent, 1602 CKS PRC2/14/299
Kingsland, Rebecca, widow, Deal, Kent, 1680 CKS PRC20/13/40
Kingsland, Robert, Throwleigh, Kent, 1613 CKS PRC2/18/28
Kingslande, Henrye, Bridge, Kent, 1616 CKS PRC2/22/93
Kingsley, Alicia, widow, Maidstone, Kent, 1707 CKS PRC19/6/31
Kingsley, Grissell, Wye, Kent, 1641 CKS PRC1/4/72
Kingsmil, Thomas, clergy: 'clerk', Hythe St Leonard, Kent, 1642 CKS PRC19/2/59
Kingsmill, Joane, mrs/widow, Dover, Kent, 1664 CKS PRC19/3/55
Kingsmill, John, Canterbury St Andrew, Kent, 1624 CKS PRC2/23/188
Kingsmill, Laurans, Ivychurch, Kent, 1606 CKS PRC20/1/181
Kingsmill, William, Monks Horton, Kent, 1624 CKS PRC2/23/187
Kingsnode, John, Guston, Kent, 1630 CKS PRC20/8/299
Kingson, Robert, bachelor, Kenardington, Kent, 1665 CKS PRC1/10/58
Kingston, Robert, Skirbeck, Lincs, 1635 Lincs RO Ad/Ac/24/381
Kingston, Thomas, shepherd, Hanborough, Oxon, 1638 Oxon RO MSS Wills 298/4/12
Kingston, Thomas, Shutlanger, Northants, 1672 Northants RO NWill A/C/108
Kingswood, John, Tenterden, Kent, 1583 CKS PRC2/2/263
Kingswood, John, Folkestone, Kent, 1686 CKS PRC2/41/58
Kingswood, Richard, Cranbrook, Kent, 1593 CKS PRC2/6/198
Kingswood, Richard, yeoman, Cranbrook, Kent, 1673 CKS PRC2/35/234
Kingward, Richard, Linton, Kent, 1643 CKS PRC19/2/58
Kinnersly, Edward, Worcester St Nicholas, Worcs, 1684 Worcs RO 008.7 BA3585/837/bdl 4
Kinrosse, John, innholder, Berkhamsted St Peter, Herts, 1638 Herts RO AHH23/1411
Kinsham, see George,
Kinsmith, William, Lincoln, Lincs, 1629 Lincs RO Ad/Ac/22/77
Kinton, Joane, Kyme, South, Lincs, 1638 Lincs RO Ad/Ac/25/302
Kipping, Henry, Biddenden, Kent, 1633 CKS PRC2/32/75
Kipps, Henry, Boughton Aluph, Kent, 1628 CKS PRC2/29/57
Kirbie, Alice, Winslow, Bucks, 1621 Herts RO ASA25/2543

Kirby, Edward, Havant, Hants, 1624 Hants RO 21M65 D8/72
Kirby, Henry, Warwick St Mary, Warks, 1595 Worcs RO 008.7 BA3585/834/457
Kirby, Peter, yeoman, Yarnton, Oxon, Oxon RO MSS Wills 169/1/32
Kirby, Richard, Selsey, Sussex, 1620 W. Suss RO EpI/33/1619/2
Kirby, Thomas, Sutton, Lincs, 1626 Lincs RO Ad/Ac/20/48
Kirby, Thomas, Hammersmith, London & Middlesex, 1675 Lambeth Palace Arches G29/2
Kirby, Thomas, Ainderby (Fareham), Yorks, 1785 Borthwick Test C.P. 1784/2
Kirby, William, skinner: 'artisan skinner', York, Yorks, 1777 Borthwick Test C.P. 1777/6
Kirfoote, Robert, Eastham, Ches, 1618 Cheshire RO (Name) W.C. 1617
Kirgarth, Robert, Winteringham, Lincs, 1624 Lincs RO Ad/Ac/8c/100
Kirgarth, William, Flixborough, Lincs, 1624 Lincs RO Ad/Ac/39/194
Kirk, Elizabeth, widow, Bradford (Bowling), Yorks, 1795 Borthwick Test C.P. 1795/2
Kirkby, Allen, yeoman, Thorpe St Peter, Lincs, 1679 Lincs RO Ad/Ac/43/117
Kirkby, Frances, widow, Catton, Low (High Catton), Yorks, 1838 Borthwick Test C.P. 1838/5
Kirkby, Humphrey, Boston, Lincs, 1636 Lincs RO Ad/Ac/25/123
Kirke, Helpringham, Lincs, 1603 Lincs RO Ad/Ac/43/1
Kirke, Alexander, Gainsborough, Lincs, 1599 Lincs RO Ad/Ac/37/71
Kirke, Anne, widow, Rolleston, Leics, 1684 Leics RO Administrators Accounts 1682-86 f23
Kirke, Daniel, yeoman, Prestwold, Leics, 1684 Leics RO Administrators Accounts 1682-86 f19
Kirke, Edward, Scothorne, Lincs, 1613 Lincs RO Ad/Ac/8c/59
Kirke, Edward, Tealby, Lincs, 1639? Lincs RO Ad/Ac/26/281
Kirke, Edward, Tealby, Lincs, 1640 Lincs RO Ad/Ac/27/100
Kirke, George, yeoman, Partney, Lincs, 1680 Lincs RO Ad/Ac/34/55
Kirke, Humfrey, husbandman, Marston, Lincs, 1625 Lincs RO Ad/Ac/22/10
Kirke, James, Broughton, Lincs, 1624 Lincs RO Ad/Ac/8c/69
Kirke, James, Broughton (Castlethorpe), Lincs, 1625 Lincs RO Ad/Ac/39/241
Kirke, John, clergy: 'minister', Stonesfield, Oxon, 1627 Oxon RO MSS Wills 298/4/4
Kirke, John, Lincoln St Botolph, Lincs, 1649 Lincs RO Ad/Ac/30/70
Kirke, John, tailor, Canterbury Christchurch, Kent, 1683 CKS PRC20/13/341
Kirke, Margerie, Pickwell, Leics, 1639 Leics RO PR/I/41A/4
Kirke, Mary, spinster, Norton, Bishop (Atterby), Lincs, 1666 Lincs RO Ad/Ac/32/113
Kirke, Michael, labourer, Hale, Great, Lincs, 1636 Lincs RO Ad/Ac/24/486
Kirke, Philipp, Glentworth, Lincs, 1619 Lincs RO Ad/Ac/8b/389
Kirke, Richard, yeoman, Messingham, Lincs, 1666 Lincs RO Ad/Ac/41/175
Kirke, Robert, Glentworth, Lincs, 1594 Lincs RO Ad/Ac/5/503
Kirke, Robert, Tattershall, Lincs, 1612 Lincs RO Ad/Ac/11/108
Kirke, Robert, gentleman, Gainsborough, Lincs, 1680 Lincs RO Ad/Ac/45/101
Kirke, Thomas, Barlborough, Derby, 1680 LJRO:cards/1680/22
Kirke, William, Marston, Lincs, 1614 Lincs RO Ad/Ac/12/176
Kirke, William, Humberstone, Leics, 1641 Leics RO PR/I/41A/80
Kirke, William, Harpswell, Lincs, 1663 Lincs RO Ad/Ac/41/83
Kirke, see Duckle,
Kirkham, John, St Giles in the Fields, London & Middlesex, 1667 Lambeth Palace Arches GG22/2
Kirkland, William, Sawley, Derby, 1726 LJRO/B/C/5/1726/47
Kirkman, Dorothie, widow, Keal, East, Lincs, 1624 Lincs RO Ad/Ac/18/102
Kirkman, Robert, Gedney, Lincs, 1639? Lincs RO Ad/Ac/26/273
Kirkton, John, Leadenham, Lincs, 1601 Lincs RO Ad/Ac/5/81
Kirman, Bryan, Maltby, Lincs, 1675 Lincs RO Ad/Ac/34/16
Kirman, Robert, husbandman, Coates, Great, Lincs, 1618 Lincs RO Ad/Ac/14/283
Kirton, John, Dover, Kent, 1600 CKS PRC21/15/117
Kirton, Joshua, bookseller/printer?, Savoy, London & Middlesex, 1673 PRO PROB32/10/61
Kisby, Thomas, yeoman, Minster in Sheppey, Kent, 1684 CKS PRC2/40/211
Kitchen, Christopher, Kirkby, East, Lincs, 1611 Lincs RO Ad/Ac/10/89
Kitchen, Jone, Sonning, Berks, 1597 Wilts RO Miscellaneous Index (name + date)

[Kitchen:]
Kitchen, Mary, New Romney, Kent, 1675 CKS PRC19/4/102
Kitchin, Edward, Gainsborough, Lincs, 1662 Lincs RO Ad/Ac/41/21
Kitchin, John, Belton, Lincs, 1626 Lincs RO Ad/Ac/39/122
Kitchin, John, Leeds, Kent, 1635 CKS PRC2/33/74
Kitchin, John, Lavington (Keisby), Lincs, 1689 PRO PROB5/1399
Kitchin, Nicholas, tailor, Pinchbeck, Lincs, 1638 Lincs RO Ad/Ac/25/23
Kitchin, William, Theddlethorpe, Lincs, 1624 Lincs RO Ad/Ac/19A/42
Kitchin, William, Broughton, Lincs, 1626 Lincs RO Ad/Ac/39/40
Kitching, Robert, Althorpe (Amcotts), Lincs, 1630 Lincs RO Ad/Ac/39/295
Kite, Edward, yeoman, Reculver, Kent, 1665 CKS PRC19/3/73
Kite, John, innholder, Tenterden, Kent, 1676 CKS PRC2/37/54
Kite, John, sailmaker, Sandwich, Kent, 1684 CKS PRC2/40/212
Kite, Robert, Urchfont, Wilts, 1636 Wilts RO Arch. Sarum(+ name and date)
Kite, Robert, grocer, Staplehurst, Kent, 1684 CKS PRC20/13/343
Kite, Stephen, yeoman, Swalecliffe, Kent, 1665 CKS PRC1/11/51
Kite, Thomas, Canterbury St Paul, Kent, 1643 CKS PRC1/6/112
Kite, William, Wittersham, Kent, 1626 CKS PRC20/7/9
Kite, William, grazier, Warehorne, Kent, 1710 CKS PRC1/17/7
Kitehm, Edmund, Beckingham, Lincs, 1581 Lincs RO Ad/Ac/2C/13
Kitham, Katherine, Canterbury St Margaret, Kent, 1667 CKS PRC1/12/54
Kitham, Richard, innholder, Orlestone, Kent, 1662 CKS PRC1/9/36
Kitham, Searles, Brookland, Kent, 1662 CKS PRC1/9/37
Kitte, Ludwell + Elizabeth, Nunney, Som, 1590 Somerset RO D/D/Cta/K6
Kittham, John, Hartlip, Kent, 1640 CKS PRC1/3/2
Kittle, Thomas, St Albans, Herts, 1626 Herts RO ASA25/4838
Kittowe, William, Endellion, Corn, 1610 Cornwall RO AP/K26/4
Knackstone, Marcke, Brading, Hants, 1625 Hants RO 21M65 D8/120
Knap, Walter, Drayton, Berks, 1598 Berks RO D/A1/200/67A
Knapp, Alice, widow, Kingston Lisle, Berks, 1665 Berks RO D/A1/200/133A
Knapp, Thomas, Froxfield, Wilts, 1617 Wilts RO Arch. Wilts.(name + date)
Knappe, Richard, Compton, Berks, Berks RO D/A1/1/f47R
Knappe, Thomas, Canterbury St Dunstan Without, Kent, 1613 CKS PRC2/17/146
Knappe, William, Shellingford, Berks, 1600? Berks RO D/A1/200/69A
Knapton, Richard, Kirkby Overblow (Kirkby with Wetherby), Yorks, Borthwick Test C.P. 1721/1
Knasee, Robert, Fordwich, Kent, 1666 CKS PRC1/11/132a
Knasee, Robert, Fordwich, Kent, 1667 CKS PRC1/11/132
Knell, Elizabeth, widow, Kenardington, Kent, 1629 CKS PRC2/30/74
Knell, Gyles, Hythe St Leonard, Kent, 1602 CKS PRC21/16/37
Knell, James, Appledore, Kent, 1600 CKS PRC2/11/391
Knell, James, Kenardington, Kent, 1626 CKS PRC2/27/86
Knell, Jeames, Warehorne, Kent, 1613 CKS PRC2/17/118
Knell, Thomas, clergy: 'clerk', Kenardington, Kent, 1592 CKS PRC2/5/328
Knevet, William, Northaw, Herts, 1637 Herts RO ASA25/4941
Knewstubb, Edward, Bruton, Som, 1622 Somerset RO D/D/Cta/K2
Kngiht, Edward, yeoman, Bradfield, Berks, 1629 Berks RO D/A1/200/99A
Knibb, John, Ansley, Warks, 1681 LJRO/B/C/5/1682/56
Knibb, Richard, bachelor, Claydon, Oxon, 1684 Oxon RO MSS Wills Pec 44/5/6
Knidge, Robert, Kyme, South, Lincs, 1634 Lincs RO Ad/Ac/24/514
Knight, Abell, feltmaker, Hythe St Leonard, Kent, 1675 CKS PRC20/12/175
Knight, Anne, Woodnesborough, Kent, 1627 CKS PRC2/28/72
Knight, Anne, widow, Canterbury St Mary Bredin, Kent, 1668 CKS PRC1/13/68
Knight, Anthony, Aldingbourne, Sussex, 1630 W. Suss RO EpI/33/1629/39
Knight, Augustine, yeoman, Woodnesborough, Kent, 1672 CKS PRC2/35/149
Knight, Barnard, Winnall, Hants, 1671 Hants RO 21m65 D8/232
Knight, Beniamin, Sandhurst, Kent, 1631 CKS PRC2/31/49

[Knight:]

Knight, Dorothy, widow, Canterbury St Mildred, Kent, 1626 CKS PRC2/27/87
Knight, Edmund, Charlton, Wilts, 1637 Wilts RO Arch. Wilts.(name + date)
Knight, Edward, Hough on the Hill, Lincs, 1631 Lincs RO Ad/Ac/23/52
Knight, Edward, gentleman, Woodnesborough, Kent, 1633 CKS PRC20/11/59
Knight, Edward, gentleman, Hough on the Hill (Brandon), Lincs, 1670 Lincs RO Ad/Ac/32/160
Knight, Elizabeth, widow, Scotton, Lincs, 1665 Lincs RO Ad/Ac/41/134
Knight, Frances, Stockbury, Kent, 1669 CKS PRC1/14/67
Knight, Francis, Binstead, Hants, 1672 Hants RO 21m65 D8/249
Knight, Francis, Angmering, Sussex, 1676 W. Suss RO EpI/33/1676/20
Knight, Francis, gentleman, Cotesbach, Leics, 1684 Leics RO Administrators Accounts 1682-86 f21
Knight, Giles, Stoke Sub Hamdon, Som, 1638 Somerset RO D/D/Cta/K4
Knight, Henry, Aldington, Kent, 1642 CKS PRC19/2/60
Knight, Henry, gentleman, Canterbury St Mary Bredin, Kent, 1668 CKS PRC1/13/69
Knight, Henry, bellfounder, Reading St Lawrence, Berks, 1678 Berks RO D/A1/200/145A
Knight, Henry, goldsmith, Deal, Kent, 1681 CKS PRC20/13/157
Knight, Jerom, Woodnesborough, Kent, 1594 CKS PRC2/7/191
Knight, Joane, Farringdon, Hants, 1664 Hants RO 21M65 D8/170
Knight, John, Newchurch, Kent, 1583 CKS PRC21/6/276
Knight, John, Congresbury, Som, 1587 Somerset RO D/D/Cta/K5
Knight, John, Tenterden, Kent, 1597 CKS PRC2/9/295
Knight, John, Cranbrook, Kent, 1609 CKS PRC2/15/204
Knight, John, Netherbury, Dors, 1611 Wilts RO Dean Sarum (name + date)
Knight, John, Wilsford, Lincs, 1621 Lincs RO Ad/Ac/16/56
Knight, John, Calstock, Corn, 1622 Cornwall RO AP/K74/3
Knight, John, New Romney, Kent, 1623 CKS PRC20/6/328
Knight, John, husbandman, Bersted, South, Sussex, 1633 W. Suss RO EpIV/10/2/7
Knight, John, Canterbury St Mary-Magdalen Burgate, Kent, 1637 CKS PRC2/34/76
Knight, John, Melksham, Wilts, 1638 Wilts RO Arch. Sarum(+ name and date)
Knight, John, Droxford, Hants, 1663 Hants RO 21M65 D8/171
Knight, John, Portsmouth, Hants, 1671 Hants RO 21m65 D8/233
Knight, John, tailor: 'merchant tailor/citizen', Shoreditch St Leonard, London & Middlesex, 1674 PRO PROB5/1393
Knight, John, Boarhunt, Hants, 1679 Hants RO 21m65 D8/314
Knight, John, husbandman, Langdon, East, Kent, 1679 CKS PRC2/38/149
Knight, John, Chilham, Kent, 1680 CKS PRC2/38/150
Knight, John, musician, Newbury, Berks, 1684 Berks RO D/A1/201/14C
Knight, John, yeoman, Willesborough, Kent, 1689 CKS PRC2/41/153
Knight, John, Benington, Lincs, C16th? Lincs RO Ad/Ac/45/85
Knight, Joseph, Wolstanton, Staffs, 1736 LJRO/B/C/5/1735/52
Knight, Mary, mrs/widow, Canterbury St George Martyr, Kent, 1618 CKS PRC2/22/92
Knight, Moses, innholder, Dursley, Glos, 1753 GRO GDR/B4/2/K19
Knight, Richard, Stockbury, Kent, 1583 CKS PRC2/3/133
Knight, Richard, yeoman, Thatcham (Henwick), Berks, 1607 Berks RO D/A1/200/73A
Knight, Richard, Froyle, Hants, 1625 Hants RO 21M65 D8/73
Knight, Richard, husbandman, Enderby, Mavis, Lincs, 1637 Lincs RO Ad/Ac/25/552
Knight, Richard, Tenterden, Kent, 1676 CKS PRC2/37/53
Knight, Robert, Sherbourne, Dors, 1598 Wilts RO Miscellaneous Index (name + date)
Knight, Robert, husbandman, Lanreath, Corn, 1611 Cornwall RO AP/K31/2
Knight, Robert, Rudgwick, Sussex, 1643 W. Suss RO EpI/33/1643/2
Knight, Robert, Saxilby, Lincs, 1674 Lincs RO Ad/Ac/35/80
Knight, Rose, widow, Thatcham (Colthrop), Berks, 1614 Berks RO D/A1/200/80A
Knight, Stephen, Woodnesborough, Kent, 1606 CKS PRC2/14/288
Knight, Thomas, Lincoln St Mary le Wigford, Lincs, 1587 Lincs RO Ad/Ac/0/10
Knight, Thomas, Hythe St Leonard, Kent, 1589 CKS PRC21/10/1

[Knight:]
Knight, Thomas, Bromfield, Kent, 1613 CKS PRC2/18/49
Knight, Thomas, Cranbrook, Kent, 1616 CKS PRC20/3/405
Knight, Thomas, Porchester, Hants, 1624 Hants RO 21M65 D8/27
Knight, Thomas, Heene, Sussex, 1626 W. Suss RO EpIV/10/1/24
Knight, Thomas, Felpham (Ancton), Sussex, 1632 W. Suss RO EpI/33/1632/11
Knight, Thomas, Willesborough, Kent, 1637 CKS PRC2/34/77
Knight, Thomas, yeoman, Woodhay, West, Berks, 1680 Berks RO D/A1/201/3C
Knight, Thomas, Stockbury, Kent, 1681 CKS PRC2/39/197
Knight, William, Wilsthorpe, Lincs, 1619 Lincs RO Ad/Ac/15/247
Knight, William, husbandman, Thatcham (Henwick), Berks, 1633 Berks RO D/A1/90/2D
Knight, William, yeoman, Earnley, Sussex, 1633 W. Suss RO EpI/33/1633/29
Knight, William, Crowland, Lincs, 1638 Lincs RO Ad/Ac/25/4
Knight, William, grocer, Faversham, Kent, 1676 CKS PRC2/36/210
Knight, William, yeoman, River, Kent, 1677 CKS PRC2/37/168
Knight, William, gentleman, Hythe St Leonard, Kent, 1681 CKS PRC20/13/151
Knight/Deeds, Elizabeth, widow, Eastchurch, Sheppey, Kent, 1619 CKS PRC2/22/90
Knight, see Blinkoe,
Knighte, Anne, widow, Leake, Lincs, 1640 Lincs RO Ad/Ac/27/180
Knighte, Augustine, Worth, Kent, 1615 CKS PRC20/3/248
Knighte, Edward, Kenardington, Kent, 1613 CKS PRC2/17/237
Knighte, Gabriel, Saxilby, Lincs, 1625 Lincs RO Ad/Ac/39/178
Knighte, James, Lydd, Kent, 1613 CKS PRC20/2/555
Knighte, John, Aldingbourne, Sussex, W. Suss RO EpI/33/1609
Knighte, Richard, miller?, Ferring (Kingston), Sussex, 1614 W. Suss RO EpI/33/1613/2
Knights, Philip, innholder, Halesworth, Suff, 1748 Norfolk RO NCC INV/81C/94
Knock, Hugh, Davington, Kent, 1639 CKS PRC2/34/227
Knock, John, Hernhill, Kent, 1598 CKS PRC21/14/569
Knock, Mildred, widow, Egerton, Kent, 1634 CKS PRC20/11/53
Knock, Robert, Pluckley, Kent, 1629 CKS PRC2/30/75
Knock, William, Headcorn, Kent, 1627 CKS PRC2/28/73
Knocke, Anthony, Boughton under Blean, Kent, 1633 CKS PRC20/11/45
Knocke, Robert, butcher, Pluckley, Kent, 1676 CKS PRC2/37/56
Knocke, Samuell, St Johns Thanet, Kent, 1596 CKS PRC2/8/356
Knocke, Thomas, Marden, Kent, 1626 CKS PRC2/28/74
Knott, Elizabeth, widow, Worth, Kent, 1601 CKS PRC21/15/242
Knott, John, Gonerby, Lincs, 1623 Lincs RO Ad/Ac/17/70
Knott, John, Sholden, Kent, 1634 CKS PRC2/32/72
Knott, John, Bilsington, Kent, 1639 CKS PRC2/34/224
Knott, John, Milton next Sittingbourne, Kent, 1641 CKS PRC1/5/110
Knott, John, yeoman, Deal, Kent, 1677 CKS PRC20/12/234
Knott, Phillip, gentleman, Ashford, Kent, 1674 CKS PRC2/35/233
Knott, Richard, Bilsington, Kent, 1613 CKS PRC2/17/265
Knott, Richard sen, Salford, Lancs, 1618 Lancs RO (Name of Deceased) D.R.C.H. 1618
Knott, Stephen, Folkestone, Kent, 1672 CKS PRC2/35/148
Knott, Thomas, labourer, Eythorne, Kent, 1675 CKS PRC2/36/209
Knott, William, New Romney, Kent, 1631 CKS PRC20/9/1
Knott, William, Alkham, Kent, 1682 CKS PRC2/40/49
Knott, William, blacksmith, Elham, Kent, 1694 CKS PRC2/42/69
Knowlden, Dorothy, widow, Maidstone, Kent, 1632 CKS PRC20/11/47
Knowlden, Hugh, yeoman, Lenham, Kent, 1666 CKS PRC1/11/52
Knowlden, see Weekes,
Knowler, Edward, gentleman, Faversham, Kent, 1671 CKS PRC2/35/65
Knowler, Edward, Graveney, Kent, 1712 CKS PRC1/17/32
Knowler, Elizabeth, spinster, Herne, Kent, 1632 CKS PRC20/11/57
Knowler, George, yeoman, Herne, Kent, 1625 CKS PRC20/7/305

Knowler, Henry, Hoath, Kent, 1608 CKS PRC20/1/237
Knowler, Joane, spinster, Stourmouth, Kent, 1614 CKS PRC2/17/50
Knowler, John, St Laurence Thanet, Kent, 1596 CKS PRC2/8/236
Knowler, John, Chislet, Kent, 1634 CKS PRC2/32/74
Knowler, John, grocer, Milton next Sittingbourne, Kent, 1669 CKS PRC1/14/68
Knowler, John, gentleman, Ospringe, Kent, 1701 CKS PRC1/16/31
Knowler, Joyce, Canterbury St Andrew, Kent, 1629 CKS PRC2/29/59
Knowler, Marie, spinster, Fordwich, Kent, 1626 CKS PRC2/27/88
Knowler, Mary, spinster, Fordwich, Kent, 1632 CKS PRC2/31/125
Knowler, Richard, mariner: 'seafaring man', Milton next Sittingbourne, Kent, 1685 CKS PRC20/13/507
Knowler, Stephen, gentleman, Herne, Kent, 1677 CKS PRC20/12/235
Knowler, Thomas, yeoman, Herne, Kent, 1624 CKS PRC20/6/118
Knowler, Thomas, yeoman, Chartham, Kent, 1674 CKS PRC2/35/232
Knowler, Thomas, gentleman, Deal, Kent, 1682 CKS PRC20/13/153
Knowles, Bernard, yeoman, Ackworth (High Ackworth), Yorks, 1846 Borthwick Test C.P. 1846/5
Knowles, Elinor, widow, Burpham, Sussex, 1631 W. Suss RO EpI/33/1631/7
Knowles, Nicholas, university: 'privileged person', Oxford (University), Oxon, 1640 Bodleian HYP B9/7-8
Knowles, Oliver, Sandwich, Kent, 1626 CKS PRC2/25/82
Knowles, Robert, cutler, St Albans, Herts, 1621 Herts RO ASA25/2648
Knowles, Robert, Freshwater, Hants, 1625 Hants RO 21M65 D8/121
Knowles, Stephen, Canterbury Holy Cross Westgate, Kent, 1596 CKS PRC2/8/376
Knowles, Thomas, Stopham, Sussex, 1627 W. Suss RO EpI/33/1627/8
Knowles, Thomas, gentleman, Knaresborough, Yorks, 1818 Borthwick Test C.P. 1818/11
Knowles, William, husbandman, Pershore (The Hide), Worcs, Worcs RO 008.7 BA3585/838/203
Knowles, William, St Johns Thanet, Kent, 1599 CKS PRC2/11/247
Knowles, William, Bardney (Southray), Lincs, 1663 Lincs RO Ad/Ac/42/31
Knowles, William, cordwainer, Frodsham (Overton), Ches, 1766 Cheshire RO (Name) W.C. 1766
Knowls, Thomas, Felpham, Sussex, 1599 W. Suss RO EpI/33/1599/2
Knowlson, Thomas, farmer, Bramwith, Kirk (Newsome Hall), Yorks, 1811 Borthwick Test C.P. 1811/3
Knubley, Matthew, whitesmith, Wetherby, Yorks, 1748 Borthwick Test C.P. 1748/4
Knyght, Thomas, Newington next Sittingbourne, Kent, 1589 CKS PRC2/5/330
Knyghte, George, St Albans, Herts, 1565 Herts RO ASA25/603
Kreket, John, Sandwich, Kent, 1624 CKS PRC2/23/186
Kybbet, Humfrey, gentleman, Faversham, Kent, 1602 CKS PRC2/12/448
Kyllow, Thomas, Egloskerry, Corn, 1613 Cornwall RO AP/K47
Kyme, Thomas, Frittenden, Kent, 1614 CKS PRC2/18/39
Kympton, Edmund, Caldecote, Herts, 1596 Herts RO ASA25/1556
Kyne, Richard, Woodchurch, Kent, 1585 CKS PRC21/7/243
Kyng, John ygr, Tillington, Sussex, 1597 W. Suss RO EpI/33/1597
Kynge, Christian, widow, Tillington, Sussex, 1579 W. Suss RO EpI/33/1579/1
Kynge, Johane, widow, Boughton under Blean, Kent, 1585 CKS PRC21/7/238
Kynge, John, Thurlby, Lincs, 1601 Lincs RO Ad/Ac/5/328
Kynge, Thomas, Boughton under Blean, Kent, 1584 CKS PRC21/7/35
Kyngerbie, George, Sturton, Great, Lincs, 1579 Lincs RO Ad/Ac/2b/7
Kyngesforthe, Thomas, Woodnesborough, Kent, 1585 CKS PRC2/3/323
Kynton, Nicholas, Langley, Kirk, Derby, 1682 LJRO/B/C/5/1682/57
Kynvin, James, gentleman, St Thomas Apostle, London & Middlesex, 1696 PRO PROB5/1535
Kypping, Daniell, Bethersden, Kent, 1612 CKS PRC2/18/78
Kypping, John + Elizabeth, Sandhurst, Kent, 1617 CKS PRC2/22/98
Kyrbie, William, Oddington, Oxon, 1633 Oxon RO MSS Wills 298/4/6
Kyrke, John, clergy: 'minister', Stonesfield, Oxon, 1627 Oxon RO MSS Wills 298/4/4
Kyrman, Richard, Waltham, Lincs, 1607 Lincs RO Ad/Ac/8a/145

[Kyrsbye:]
Kyrsbye, William, Westwell, Kent, 1596 CKS PRC21/14/105
Kyrspy, John, Mersham, Kent, 1593 CKS PRC2/6/346
Kytchen, William, Metheringham, Lincs, 1614 Lincs RO Ad/Ac/13/155
Kytchen, Willyam, Spalding, Lincs, 1600 Lincs RO Ad/Ac/5/189
Kytchman, Christopher, Ingoldmels, Lincs, 1594 Lincs RO Ad/Ac/5/300
Kyte, Edmund, Lyminge, Kent, 1595 CKS PRC21/13/7
Kyte, Thomas, Benenden, Kent, 1596 CKS PRC2/8/360
Kyte, Thomas, Benenden, Kent, 1598 CKS PRC2/9/475
Kyte, William, mariner, Dover, Kent, 1639 CKS PRC20/11/41
Kyte, see Havert,
Kytson, Richard, Sarratt, Herts, 1576 Herts RO ASA25/837
Laborne, John, Grantham, Lincs, 1594 Lincs RO Ad/Ac/3/125
Lacey, William, Freshwater, Hants, 1641 Hants RO 1639 B48/3
Lacie,
Som 1631 Somerset RO D/D/Cta/L22
Lacie, Edmund, bachelor: 'singleman', Bicker, Lincs, 1633 Lincs RO Ad/Ac/24/173
Lacie, Elizabeth, widow, Rippingale, Lincs, 1634 Lincs RO Ad/Ac/24/37
Lacie, John, husbandman, Blagdon, Som, 1606 Somerset RO D/D/Cta/L18
Lacie, Tymothie, Rippingale, Lincs, 1634 Lincs RO Ad/Ac/24/35
Lack, John, Mere, Wilts, 1675 Wilts RO Miscellaneous Index (name + date)
Lacke, yeoman, Glatton, Hunts, C17th? Lincs RO Ad/Ac/45/94
Lackner, Peter, Biddenden, Kent, 1677 CKS PRC2/37/173
Lackner, William, gentleman, Warehorne, Kent, 1683 CKS PRC2/40/129
Laclott, Chichester, Sussex, 1648 W. Suss RO EpIII/9/1/47
Lacocke, Gregorie, Lincoln, Lincs, 1633 Lincs RO Ad/Ac/24/183
Lacon, John, Somercoates, North, Lincs, 1670 Lincs RO Ad/Ac/32/172
Lacy, John, Fisherton Anger, Wilts, 1669 Wilts RO Arch. Sarum(+ name and date)
Lacy, Richard, Aslackby, Lincs, 1614 Lincs RO Ad/Ac/13/127
Lacy, Roger, Lavington, Market, Wilts, 1621 Wilts RO CC Sarum(+ name and date)
Lad, Thomas, Herne, Kent, 1629 CKS PRC20/8/315
Ladame, George, Heckington, Lincs, 1574 Lincs RO Ad/Ac/1/13
Ladd, Edward, yeoman, Lydd, Kent, 1667 CKS PRC19/3/128
Ladd, John, Hythe West, Kent, 1665 CKS PRC1/11/53
Ladd, John, maltster, Sandwich, Kent, 1687 CKS PRC2/41/98
Ladd, John, Adisham, Kent, 1740 CKS PRC19/6/81
Ladd, Robert, Elham, Kent, 1625 CKS PRC2/25/87
Ladd, Samuel, Kingsthorpe, Northants, 1678 Northants RO NWill A/C/32
Ladd, Samuell, Chartham, Kent, 1620 CKS PRC2/22/64
Ladd, Thomas, Cranbrook, Kent, 1585 CKS PRC2/3/284
Ladd, Thomas, Dover, Kent, 1610 CKS PRC20/2/136
Ladd, Thomas, Wingham, Kent, 1635 CKS PRC20/11/75
Ladd, Thomas, yeoman, Saltwood, Kent, 1676 CKS PRC20/12/208
Ladd, Vincent, gentleman, Leysdown, Kent, 1674 CKS PRC20/12/90
Ladd/Ludd, Randolph, Canterbury, Kent, 1613 CKS PRC2/17/263
Ladds, John, Kettering, Northants, 1671 Northants RO NWill A/C/98
Ladds, William, gentleman, Godmanchester, Hunts, Hunts RO/Acc58/149(48)
Lade, Nathaniel, draper: 'woollen draper', Faversham, Kent, 1683 CKS PRC2/40/127
Lade, Nicholas eld, gentleman, Swingfield, Kent, 1672 CKS PRC2/35/69
Lade, Vincent, yeoman, Barham, Kent, 1671 CKS PRC2/35/68
Ladyman, William, husbandman, Hogsthorpe, Lincs, 1674 Lincs RO Ad/Ac/43/174
Laggas, John, Waddington, Lincs, 1570 Lincs RO Ad/Ac/2b/31
Lagoe, John, Gresley (Church), Derby, 1680 LJRO:cards/1680/23
Lagoe, Jonathan, Wolfhampcote, Warks, 1689 LJRO/B/C/5/1689/17
Laighton, Thomas, Sawtry, Hunts, 1677 Hunts RO/Acc58/110(151)
Laignell, John, Ash next Sandwich, Kent, 1684 CKS PRC20/13/444

Laigniell, John, Ash next Sandwich, Kent, 1639 CKS PRC20/11/95
Laitie, Tobias, Perranuthnoe, Corn, 1636 Cornwall RO AP/L361/3
Lake, Bartholomew, plumber, Rochester, Kent, 1683 PRO PROB32/24/16
Lake, Charles, Salisbury, Wilts, 1696 Wilts RO Miscellaneous Index (name + date)
Lake, James, baker, Canterbury St Paul, Kent, 1681 CKS PRC2/39/67
Lake, John, Hythe St Leonard, Kent, 1598 CKS PRC21/14/258
Lake, John, Salisbury, Wilts, 1637 Wilts RO Miscellaneous Index (name + date)
Lake, John, blacksmith, Abingdon, Berks, 1644 Berks RO D/A1/202/93A
Lake, John, labourer, Tunstall, Kent, 1672 CKS PRC2/35/150
Lake, John, clothier, Cranbrook, Kent, 1678 CKS PRC2/38/49
Lake, John, gentleman, Barnoldby le Beck, Lincs, 1683 Lincs RO Ad/Ac/44/97
Lake, John, gentleman, Barnoldby le Beck, Lincs, 1683 Lincs RO Ad/Ac/45/106
Lake, Martha, mrs, Ashford, Kent, 1681 CKS PRC2/39/201
Lake, Michael, blacksmith, Shrivenham, Berks, 1610 Berks RO D/A1/202/28A
Lake, Richard, Wimborne Minster (Cowgrove), Dors, 1628 Dorset RO PE/WM CP 2/4/41
Lake, Richard, Milton next Sittingbourne, Kent, 1644 CKS PRC1/6/113
Lake, Thomas, threadtwister, Maidstone, Kent, 1640 CKS PRC19/1/57
Lake, Thomas, mr, Newington next Sittingbourne, Kent, 1693 CKS PRC2/42/72
Lakes, Jeames, gentleman, Canterbury St Margaret, Kent, 1614 CKS PRC2/17/27
Lakes, John, Ashford, Kent, 1597 CKS PRC2/10/367
Lakeye, see Lakine,
Lakine/Lakeye, Thomas, St Nicholas at Wade, Kent, 1608 CKS PRC20/1/290
Laly, Edmund, Milton Lilborne, Wilts, 1622 Wilts RO Arch. Wilts.(name + date)
Lamb, John, labourer, Birmingham, Warks, 1841 LJRO/B/C/5/1841/4
Lamb, Peter, Belton, Lincs, 1664 Lincs RO Ad/Ac/41/149
Lamb, Richard, labourer, Kidlington, Oxon, 1678 Oxon RO MSS Wills 298/5/67
Lambden, see Lambin,
Lambe, Abigail, spinster, Mersham, Kent, 1618 CKS PRC2/22/67
Lambe, Alexander, Canterbury All Saints, Kent, 1614 CKS PRC20/3/91
Lambe, Alice, spinster, Egerton, Kent, 1661 CKS PRC19/3/3
Lambe, Anne, Himbleton, Worcs, 1680 Worcs RO 008.7 BA3585/837/bdl 2
Lambe, Henry, Saltwood, Kent, 1616 CKS PRC20/3/236
Lambe, Hugh, Maiden Bradley, Wilts, 1632 Wilts RO Arch. Sarum(+ name and date)
Lambe, James, yeoman, Chart nr Sutton Valence, Kent, 1683 CKS PRC2/40/53
Lambe, Jane, widow, Reading St Lawrence, Berks, 1677 Berks RO D/A1/202/144D
Lambe, John, Frome Selwood, Som, 1637 Somerset RO D/D/Cta/L15
Lambe, Mathew, Billinghay, Lincs, 1683 Lincs RO Ad/Ac/44/109
Lambe, Robert, Habrough, Lincs, 1623 Lincs RO Ad/Ac/18/66
Lambe, Robert, Brenzett, Kent, 1638 CKS PRC2/34/232
Lambe, Susan, spinster, Egerton, Kent, 1635 CKS PRC20/11/93
Lambe, Thomas, Canterbury All Saints, Kent, 1587 CKS PRC2/4/430
Lambe, Thomas, Sandwich St Mary, Kent, 1623 CKS PRC2/23/174
Lambe, Thomas, Otham, Kent, 1633 CKS PRC2/31/127
Lambe, William, Ashford, Kent, 1624 CKS PRC2/23/177
Lambe, William, Chart nr Sutton Valence, Kent, 1676 CKS PRC2/36/212
Lambert, James, baker, Faversham, Kent, 1628 CKS PRC2/29/65
Lambert, John, Frieston, Lincs, 1620 Lincs RO Ad/Ac/16/61
Lambert, John, Dover, Kent, 1674 CKS PRC20/12/88
Lambert, Lucie, widow, New Romney, Kent, 1680 CKS PRC20/13/44
Lambert, Marie, widow, Barkston, Lincs, 1632 Lincs RO Ad/Ac/23/34
Lambert, Thomas, Wilsthorpe, Lincs, 1624 Lincs RO Ad/Ac/19A/35
Lambert, Thomas, High Halden, Kent, 1641 CKS PRC1/5/111
Lamberte, Edmond, Thurlby, Lincs, 1607 Lincs RO Ad/Ac/7/84
Lamberte, Philip, Hareby, Lincs, 1611 Lincs RO Ad/Ac/10/131
Lamberte, Richard, Wootton, Kent, 1599 CKS PRC2/11/253

[Lambin:]
Lambin, Peter, Canterbury St Dunstan Without, Kent, 1675 CKS PRC2/36/88
Lambin, Thomas, Hothfield, Kent, 1635 CKS PRC2/33/79
Lambin/Lambden, Stephen, Egerton, Kent, 1615 CKS PRC20/3/230
Lambkin, Robert, Hawkhurst, Kent, 1641 CKS PRC19/2/24
Lambley, William, yeoman, Bloxham, Oxon, 1679 Oxon RO MSS Wills 83/1/30
Lamborne, Thomas, husbandman, Stanford in the Vale, Berks, 1627 Berks RO D/A1/202/72A
Lambyn, John, Tenterden, Kent, 1601 CKS PRC2/12/240
Lambyn, Wyllyam, clergy: 'clerk', Chislet, Kent, 1587 CKS PRC2/4/243
Laming, Jeremiah, Eythorne, Kent, 1679 CKS PRC2/38/156
Laming, John, Seasalter, Kent, 1611 CKS PRC2/16/115
Laming, John, Owersby, Lincs, 1627 Lincs RO Ad/Ac/20b/17
Laming, Thomas, Evedon, Lincs, 1673 Lincs RO Ad/Ac/34/15
Laminge, Anthony, Rasen, West, Lincs, 1629 Lincs RO Ad/Ac/22/24
Laminge, Issabell, Doddington, Lincs, 1607 Lincs RO Ad/Ac/7/138
Laminge, John, Kirton, Lincs, 1623 Lincs RO Ad/Ac/39/17
Laminge, Margaret, Lissington, Lincs, 1619 Lincs RO Ad/Ac/14/156
Laminge, Thomas, yeoman, Whitstable, Kent, 1646 CKS PRC1/7/54
Laminge, William, Kirkby cum Osgodby, Lincs, 1607 Lincs RO Ad/Ac/8a/117
Lamkyn, Anne, widow, Hawkhurst, Kent, 1620 CKS PRC2/22/70
Lamley, Francis, Horbling, Lincs, 1620 Lincs RO Ad/Ac/16/58
Lamming, William, farmer, Boston, Lincs, 1825 Lincs RO Ad/Ac/45/77
Lamper, Edward, miller, Charlton nr Dover, Kent, 1679 CKS PRC2/38/152
Lamper, Edward, miller, Bethersden, Kent, 1696 CKS PRC2/42/119
Lamperne, William, yeoman, Linton, Kent, 1646 CKS PRC1/7/55
Lampley, Robert, Sandridge, Herts, 1582 Herts RO ASA25/1039
Lamprey, Bartholomew, Boston, Lincs, 1642 Lincs RO Ad/Ac/28/41
Lampson, Robert, Boston, Lincs, 1648 Lincs RO Ad/Ac/30/279
Lamyman, William, husbandman, Covenham St Mary, Lincs, 1611 Lincs RO Ad/Ac/10/7
Lamyman, see Fisher,
Lamyng, Rachael, Willingham, South, Lincs, 1635 Lincs RO Ad/Ac/24/235
Lamynge, William, Cammeringham, Lincs, 1596 Lincs RO Ad/Ac/37/24
Lancaster, Edward, barber, Newbury, Berks, 1610 Berks RO D/A1/202/30A
Lancaster, John, Willoughby, Lincs, 1597 Lincs RO Ad/Ac/4/63
Lancaster, John, Grinstead, West, Sussex, 1678 W. Suss RO EpI/33/1678/10
Lancaster, John, bachelor, Lancing, Sussex, 1685 W. Suss RO EpI/33/1684/27
Lancaster, Nicholas, Eccleston, Lancs, 1590 Lancs RO (Name of Deceased) D.R.C.H. 1590
Lancaster, Thomas, yeoman, New Romney, Kent, 1614 CKS PRC20/3/87
Lancefield, Thomas, Crundale, Kent, 1635 CKS PRC2/33/77
Lancfeild, Thomas, Bircholt, Kent, 1627 CKS PRC2/27/96
Lande, Philip, Worcester St Martin, Worcs, 1592 Worcs RO 008.7 BA3585/834/459
Landeere, John, Lanreath, Corn, 1606 Cornwall RO AP/L9/3
Landen, Abraham, Chart, Little, Kent, 1681 CKS PRC2/39/199
Landen, Edward, blacksmith, Maidstone, Kent, 1636 CKS PRC20/11/87
Landen, Jane, Maidstone, Kent, 1641 CKS PRC19/2/25a
Landen, Jane, widow, Maidstone, Kent, 1641 CKS PRC19/2/25
Lander, John, clothier, Rolvenden, Kent, 1674 CKS PRC2/36/89
Lander, Richard eld, Coventry, Warks, 1704 LJRO/B/C/5/1704/39
Landere, John, groom, Pelynt, Corn, 1622 Cornwall RO AP/L196/3
Landman, Henry, Canterbury, Kent, 1690 CKS PRC2/41/179
Landy, John, Eastry, Kent, 1617 CKS PRC20/4/234
Lane, Agnes, widow, St Albans St Stephens, Herts, 1598 Herts RO ASA25/1683
Lane, Edmund eld, yeoman, Brightwell Baldwin, Oxon, 1629 Oxon RO MSS Wills 298/5/45
Lane, Edward, yeoman, Cumnor, Berks, 1627 Berks RO D/A1/202/71A
Lane, Edward, Westbury, Wilts, 1675 Wilts RO Chantor Sarum Bundle 10/8
Lane, Edward, Westbury, Wilts, 1675? Wilts RO Chantor Sarum Bundle 10/8

Lane, Elizabeth, widow, Marlborough, Wilts, 1624 Wilts RO CC Sarum(+ name and date)
Lane, Jacob, gentleman, Faversham, Kent, 1680 CKS PRC2/38/153
Lane, Jane, widow, Cumnor, Berks, 1687 Berks RO D/A1/203/21C
Lane, John, Cholsey (Winterbrook), Berks, 1595 Berks RO D/A1/201/190C
Lane, John, Lydiard Tregoze, Wilts, 1675 Wilts RO Miscellaneous Index (name + date)
Lane, John, husbandman, Kingstone, Staffs, 1719 LJRO/B/C/5/1719/21
Lane, Margarett, widow, Moulton, Lincs, 1639 Lincs RO Ad/Ac/26/215
Lane, Margarett, widow, St Johns Thanet, Kent, 1668 CKS PRC1/13/70
Lane, Margarett, widow, Charing, Kent, 1682 CKS PRC20/13/161
Lane, Richard, gentleman,
Som 1611 Somerset RO D/D/Cta/L17
Lane, Richard, Winchester St Clement, Hants, 1624 Hants RO 21M65 D8/28
Lane, Richard, yeoman, Besselsleigh (Rockley), Berks, 1662 Berks RO D/A1/202/123C
Lane, Richard, Whitstable, Kent, 1673 CKS PRC2/35/236
Lane, Richard, Earith, Hunts, 1679 Hunts RO/Acc58/131(3)
Lane, Robert, St Albans St Stephens, Herts, 1638 Herts RO ASA25/4960
Lane, Robert, Sopley, Hants, 1663 Hants RO 21M65 D8/172
Lane, Robert, yeoman, Sopley, Hants, 1663 Hants RO 1662 AD61/1
Lane, Thomas, innholder, Watlington, Oxon, 1746 Oxon RO MSS Wills 303/3/14
Lane, William, Salisbury St Martin, Wilts, 1616 Wilts RO Miscellaneous Index (name + date)
Lane, William, Rodney Stoke, Som, 1703 Somerset RO D/D/Cta/L20
Lanes, Anne, widow, Whitstable, Kent, 1665 CKS PRC1/11/54
Lanes, Anne, widow, New Romney, Kent, 1675 CKS PRC20/12/176
Lanes, Peter, yeoman, New Romney, Kent, 1675 CKS PRC20/12/177
Lanfeire, Thomas, Lyneham, Wilts, 1635 Wilts RO CC Sarum(+ name and date)
Lanfrey, Thomas, Calne, Wilts, 1638 Wilts RO Miscellaneous Index (name + date)
Lang, Obadiah, innkeeper, Wakefield, Yorks, Borthwick Test C.P. 1757/4
Langbridge, John, Crewkerne, Som, 1592 Somerset RO D/D/Cta/L32
Langdale, Thomas, Sutton St Edmunds, Lincs, 1638 Lincs RO Ad/Ac/25/144
Langdell, Thomas, mason, Coventry, Warks, 1788 LJRO/B/C/5/1788/78
Langdon, Thomas, Camel, West, Som, 1620 Somerset RO D/D/Cta/L6
Lange, John, Stamford, Lincs, 1609 Lincs RO Ad/Ac/8a/349a
Langer, Anne, Boston, Lincs, 1638 Lincs RO Ad/Ac/25/271
Langfeild, John, miller, Thimbleby, Lincs, 1632 Lincs RO Ad/Ac/23/61
Langford, Edward, yeoman, Graveney, Kent, 1717 CKS PRC1/18/9
Langford, John, husbandman, Chart, Little, Kent, 1667 CKS PRC1/12/55
Langford, John, Rothersthorpe, Northants, 1684 Northants RO NWill A/C/72
Langford, Luke, Graveney, Kent, 1688 CKS PRC2/41/125
Langford, Luke ygr, Whitstable, Kent, 1677 CKS PRC2/37/174
Langford, Richard, Doynton, Glos, GRO GDR/B4/2/L3
Langford, Richard, Ashurst, Sussex, 1596 W. Suss RO EpI/33/1596/12
Langford, Robert, courier, Oxford St Peter in the East, Oxon, 1674 Oxon RO MSS Wills 83/1/27
Langford, Samuell, esquire, St Margaret Westminster, London & Middlesex, 1693 PRO PROB32/35/265
Langford/Oliver, Henry, Droitwich, Worcs, 1604 Worcs RO 008.7 BA3585/839/370
Langham, Richard, clergy: 'clerk', Canterbury Christchurch, Kent, 1676 CKS PRC20/12/207
Langley, Abraham, Horsley, Glos, 1685 GRO GDR/B4/2/L62
Langley, Alice, widow, Tillington, Sussex, 1626 W. Suss RO EpI/33/1625/1
Langley, Andrew, St Laurence Thanet, Kent, 1633 CKS PRC2/32/77
Langley, Christopher, Stone in Oxney, Kent, 1621 CKS PRC2/22/82
Langley, Cicely, lady/widow, Lancs RO (Name of Deceased) D.R.C.H. 1572
Langley, Edward, Sutton, Sussex, 1607 W. Suss RO EpI/33/1607/12
Langley, Henry, gentleman, Irby, Lincs, 1668 Lincs RO Ad/Ac/33/60
Langley, James, Prestbury (Butley), Ches, 1613 Cheshire RO (Name) W.C. 1613
Langley, James, Maidstone, Kent, 1679 CKS PRC20/12/267

[Langley:]
Langley, John, New Romney, Kent, 1677 CKS PRC20/12/236
Langley, Ralph, Cumnor (Whitley), Berks, 1605 Berks RO D/A1/202/13B
Langley, Ralph, Appleton (Eaton), Berks, 1619 Berks RO D/A1/202/49A
Langley, Richard, yeoman, Whitacre, Nether, Warks, 1669 LJRO:cards/1669/9
Langley, Robert, Linwood, Lincs, 1635? Lincs RO Ad/Ac/24/559
Langley, Robert, Linwood, Lincs, 1636 Lincs RO Ad/Ac/24/301
Langley, Thomas, Norton Bavant, Wilts, 1617 Wilts RO Miscellaneous Index (name + date)
Langley, Thomas, Warminster, Wilts, 1674 Wilts RO Arch. Sarum(+ name and date)
Langley, William, Hackthorne, Lincs, 1633 Lincs RO Ad/Ac/40/2
Langley, William, Lissington, Lincs, 1636 Lincs RO Ad/Ac/24/88
Langlie, John, clergy: 'mr/clerk', Smarden, Kent, 1615 CKS PRC2/22/68
Langlie, Martha, widow, Minster in Thanet, Kent, 1610 CKS PRC2/15/218
Langlie, Mary, widow, Marston, Oxon, 1630 Oxon RO MSS Wills 298/5/44
Langly, Hawker, Heytesbury, Wilts, 1681 Wilts RO Dean Sarum (name + date)
Langly, Joane, Dover, Kent, 1638 CKS PRC20/11/101
Langly, Richard, tailor, St Johns Thanet, Kent, 1674 CKS PRC2/35/237
Langrack, Piercy, gentleman, Stony Stratford, Bucks, 1692 PRO PROB5/934
Langrish, Christopher, gentleman, Funtington, Sussex, 1682 W. Suss RO EpI/33/1682/39
Langrish, Susan, widow, Funtington, Sussex, 1684 W. Suss RO EpI/33/1684/45
Langton, Charles, Boston, Lincs, 1602 Lincs RO Ad/Ac/5/551
Langton, John, Pinchbeck, Lincs, 1614 Lincs RO Ad/Ac/12/175
Langton, Peter, Hindley (Lowe), Lancs, 1574 Lancs RO (Name of Deceased) D.R.C.H. 1574
Langtree, Gilbert, esquire, Standish (Langtree), Lancs, 1597 Lancs RO (Name of Deceased) D.R.C.H. 1596
Langwith, Henry, Broughton, Brant, Lincs, 1641 Lincs RO Ad/Ac/27/266
Langwith, John, gentleman, St Margaret Westminster, London & Middlesex, 1693 PRO PROB32/35/47
Langwith, Willyam, Brant Broughton, Lincs, 1605 Lincs RO Ad/Ac/6/127
Lanison, John, Hursley, Hants, 1625 Hants RO 21M65 D8/122
Lankford, Stephen, weaver: 'broad weaver', Cranbrook, Kent, 1667 CKS PRC1/12/56
Lankford, William, Faversham, Kent, 1635 CKS PRC2/33/78
Lanman, John, innholder, Bristol St Thomas, Glos, Bristol RO 1678/77
Lanning, Phillip, Hythe St Leonard, Kent, 1641 CKS PRC19/1/58
Lannsfeilde, Robart, Ickham, Kent, 1590 CKS PRC21/10/190
Lansdell, George, Rolvenden, Kent, 1686 CKS PRC2/41/59
Lansdon, John, Cloford, Som, 1611 Somerset RO D/D/Cta/L7
Lansdon, Thomas, Camerton, Som, 1672 Somerset RO D/D/Cta/L21
Lansell, Jorine, widow, Canterbury St Alphege, Kent, CKS PRC21/16/43
Lansell, Jorrine, Canterbury St Alphege, Kent, 1602 CKS PRC21/16/39
Lanxon, Humphrey, yeoman, Blisland, Corn, 1645 Cornwall RO AP/L419/3
Lanyne, Ralph, Madron, Corn, 1607 Cornwall RO AP/L28/4
Lapish, William, cordwainer, Malton, New, Yorks, 1840 Borthwick Test C.P. 1841/3
Lapworth, Edward, Stowe, Staffs, 1684 LJRO/B/C/5/1684/46
Lapworth, Michael, Warwick St Mary, Warks, 1604 Worcs RO 008.7 BA3585/839/369
Lapworth, Thomad, Ryton on Dunsmore, Warks, 1680 LJRO:cards/1680/24
Larance, George, Hythe St Leonard, Kent, 1620 CKS PRC20/4/226
Larckham, Christian, widow, Ufton Nervet, Berks, Berks RO D/A1/202/1A
Larder, Richard, Hutton, Som, 1640 Somerset RO D/D/Cta/L33
Lardge, Richard, Aldington, Kent, 1671 CKS PRC20/12/18
Large, Edward, Derby, Derby, 1664 LJRO:cards/1664/7
Large, George, Westwell, Kent, 1632 CKS PRC20/11/73
Large, Richard, Cranbrook, Kent, 1626 CKS PRC2/27/91
Large, Stephen, Charing, Kent, 1603 CKS PRC21/17/15
Large, Thomas, Biddenden, Kent, 1637 CKS PRC2/34/78
Largman, Sampson, Pluckley, Kent, 1675 CKS PRC2/36/211

Larke, Henry, yeoman, Minster in Sheppey, Kent, 1625 CKS PRC2/25/83
Larke, Richard, Gainsborough, Lincs, 1624 Lincs RO Ad/Ac/39/135
Larke, Richard, Burgh le Marsh, Lincs, 1637 Lincs RO Ad/Ac/25/435
Larker, Robert, yeoman, Swarby, Lincs, 1670 Lincs RO Ad/Ac/32/233
Larkin, Mary, widow, Sittingbourne, Kent, 1674 CKS PRC2/36/85
Larrance, Richard, fellmonger, Ducklington, Oxon, 1664 Oxon RO MSS Wills 169/3/19
Lash, George, Rolvenden, Kent, 1605 CKS PRC2/13/274
Lasker, Henry, Hawkhurst, Kent, 1674 CKS PRC20/12/134
Laslett, Stephen, blacksmith, Deal, Kent, 1694 CKS PRC19/5/26
Lassells, Charles, Chichester St Peter the Great, Sussex, 1610 W. Suss RO EpIII/9/1/6
Lassels, John, Horbling, Lincs, 1615 Lincs RO Ad/Ac/13/9
Lassheford, Edward, Linsted, Kent, 1596 CKS PRC2/9/297
Last, Thomas, university: 'scholar's servant/privileged person', Cambridge (Barnwell), Cambs, 1644 CUL V.C. Acc./Box2/44
Lasy, James, Ash next Sandwich, Kent, 1624 CKS PRC20/6/132
Latchford, Thomas, Sandwich St Clement, Kent, 1705 CKS PRC19/6/13
Latham, George, gentleman, Belton All Saints, Lincs, 1622 Lincs RO Ad/Ac/8c/29
Latham, Henry, Betley, Staffs, 1663 LJRO:cards/1663/40
Lathbury, Richard, victualler, Gayton, Staffs, 1802 LJRO/B/C/5/1802/43
Lathbury, Samuel, Keynsham, Som, 1674 Somerset RO D/D/Cta/L23
Lathorp, William, Horncastle, Lincs, 1683 Lincs RO Ad/Ac/44/52
Lathorpe, Marie, Toft Next Newton, Lincs, 1638 Lincs RO Ad/Ac/25/340
Lathropp, Robert, Grimsby, Lincs, 1623 Lincs RO Ad/Ac/19A/43
Lathropp, Thomas,
Lincs 1649 Lincs RO Ad/Ac/30/406
Lathroppe, Richard, husbandman, Aisthorpe (Thorpe in the Fallows), Lincs, 1626 Lincs RO Ad/Ac/20/23
Lathroppe, Thomas, Hatcliffe, Lincs, 1629 Lincs RO Ad/Ac/22/117
Latimer, Francis, Paul, Corn, 1634 Cornwall RO AP/L355/1
Latter, Adam, yeoman, Hawkhurst, Kent, 1675 CKS PRC2/36/214
Latter, Ann, widow, Hawkhurst, Kent, 1675 CKS PRC2/36/216
Laugeton, William, gentleman, Winterton, Lincs, 1599 Lincs RO Ad/Ac/37/73
Laugham, Robert, husbandman, Whaplode Drove, Lincs, 1670 Lincs RO Ad/Ac/32/204
Laugham, William, Martin, Wilts, 1630 Wilts RO Arch. Sarum(+ name and date)
Laughorne, Richard, Clifton, Beds, 1622 Lincs RO Ad/Ac/17/102
Laughton, Beniamin, tanner, Lincoln, Lincs, 1642 Lincs RO Ad/Ac/28/57
Laughton, Edward, Owston, Lincs, 1628 Lincs RO Ad/Ac/39/96
Laughton, Edward, tanner, Gainsborough, Lincs, 1676 Lincs RO Ad/Ac/35/109
Laughton, Elizabeth, Lincoln St Benedict, Lincs, 1645 Lincs RO Ad/Ac/28/187
Laughton, William, Spalding, Lincs, 1606 Lincs RO Ad/Ac/7/145
Laughton, William, Owston, Lincs, 1607 Lincs RO Ad/Ac/37/248
Laughton, William, Owston, Lincs, 1669 Lincs RO Ad/Ac/33/151
Laugton, John, victualler, Pinchbeck, Lincs, 1683 Lincs RO Ad/Ac/34/103
Laugton, Roger, gentleman, Laughton, Lincs, 1626 Lincs RO Ad/Ac/20/72
Launder, John, Tenterden, Kent, 1591 CKS PRC2/5/320
Launder, Thomas, Lodsworth, Sussex, 1682 W. Suss RO EpI/33/1682/9
Launder, Thomas, Shenstone, Staffs, 1685 LJRO/B/C/5/1685/59
Laundrey, John, St Neot, Corn, 1633 Cornwall RO AP/L357/2
Laundrie, Edward, husbandman, Hill, North, Corn, 1607 Cornwall RO AP/L58/2
Laurance, Jervace, Canterbury St Dunstan Without, Kent, 1617 CKS PRC2/22/77
Laurance, John, Rainham, Kent, 1685 CKS PRC2/40/214
Laurance, Richard, St Andrew Holborn (Portpool), London & Middlesex, 1707 PRO PROB32/50/113
Laurans, Elizabeth, Acrise, Kent, 1598 CKS PRC2/10/266
Laurence, Elizabeth, Pluckley, Kent, 1678 CKS PRC2/37/171

[Laurence:]
Laurence, Gilbert, yeoman, Leadenham, Lincs, 1632 Lincs RO Ad/Ac/23/63
Laurence, Henry, Bodmin, Corn, 1627 Cornwall RO AP/L287/3
Laurence, John, St Albans, Herts, Herts RO ASA25/4780
Laurence, John, Winthorpe, Lincs, 1633 Lincs RO Ad/Ac/24/121
Laurence, Nicholas, yeoman, Stondon, Upper, Beds, 1602 Lincs RO Ad/Ac/5/580
Laurence, Peter, tanner, Charlton nr Dover, Kent, 1587 CKS PRC2/4/293
Lauriman, Nicholas, Graveney, Kent, 1683 CKS PRC2/40/52
Lavard, Richard, husbandman, St Nicholas at Wade, Kent, 1617 CKS PRC20/4/243
Lavender, Thomas, Ramsey, Hunts, Hunts RO/Acc58/120(38)
Lavington, John, Beechingstoke, Wilts, 1620 Wilts RO Arch. Wilts.(name + date)
Lavington, Robert, husbandman, Marden, Wilts, 1626 Wilts RO CC Sarum(+ name and date)
Lavor, Alice, Martock, Som, 1625 Somerset RO D/D/Cta/L12
Lavor, Edward, Load, Long, Som, 1622 Somerset RO D/D/Cta/L10
Law, Bartholomew, yeoman, Stalisfield, Kent, 1674 CKS PRC2/36/84
Law, James, Faversham, Kent, 1638 CKS PRC20/11/105
Law, Moses, husbandman, Hernhill, Kent, 1671 CKS PRC20/12/19
Law, Richard, Upchurch, Kent, 1626 CKS PRC2/27/94
Laward, William, Birchington, Kent, 1621 CKS PRC20/5/119
Lawd, William, clothworker, Reading St Lawrence, Berks, 1594 Berks RO D/A1/201/188C
Lawder, Alexander, clergy: 'clerk/rector', Broom, Worcs, 1684 Worcs RO 008.7 BA3585/837/bdl 4
Lawe, John, Bobbing, Kent, 1583 CKS PRC2/3/75
Lawe, Launcelott, gentleman, Candlesby, Lincs, 1626 Lincs RO Ad/Ac/20/66
Lawe, Mary, widow, Faversham, Kent, 1640 CKS PRC1/4/73
Lawe, Pawle, Doddington, Kent, 1627 CKS PRC2/28/78
Lawe, Richard, Borden, Kent, 1607 CKS PRC2/15/212
Lawe, Thomas, labourer, Holbeach, Lincs, 1623 Lincs RO Ad/Ac/18/21
Lawe, William, Linsted, Kent, 1638 CKS PRC2/34/236
Lawe, Willyam, Borden, Kent, 1617 CKS PRC2/22/73
Lawes, Anthonie, Fleet, Lincs, 1597 Lincs RO Ad/Ac/4/137
Lawes, David, yeoman, Wishford, Great, Wilts, 1664 Wilts RO Arch. Sarum(+ name and date)
Lawes, James, plumber, Lincoln, Lincs, 1649 Lincs RO Ad/Ac/30/169
Lawes, William, Milston, Wilts, 1635 Wilts RO CC Sarum(+ name and date)
Lawes, William, Ebbesbourne Wake, Wilts, 1670 Wilts RO Arch. Sarum(+ name and date)
Lawis, Anthonye, Frieston, Lincs, 1619 Lincs RO Ad/Ac/15/266
Lawles, Richard, Rolvenden, Kent, 1604 CKS PRC2/13/272
Lawless, William, Lydd, Kent, 1584 CKS PRC21/6/432
Lawley, Henry, Milton, Berks, 1680? Wilts RO Miscellaneous Index (name + date)
Lawley, Joseph, victualler, Swinford, Old (Wollaston), Worcs, 1779 Worcs RO 008.7 BA3585/835/bdl 2
Lawley, William, husbandman, Thatcham, Berks, 1692 Berks RO D/A1/203/36C
Lawman, Thomas, Norton, Herts, 1602 Herts RO ASA25/1842
Lawnder, George, mercer, Stafford, Staffs, 1667 LJRO:cards/1667/52
Lawnder, John, Osgodby, Lincs, 1646 Lincs RO Ad/Ac/28/172
Lawne, William, Maddington, Wilts, 1673 Wilts RO Arch. Sarum(+ name and date)
Lawrance, Richard, Lydd, Kent, 1637 CKS PRC19/1/8
Lawrance, Thomas, St Johns Thanet, Kent, 1626 CKS PRC2/27/95
Lawrence, Adam, yeoman, Buckland (Buckland Marsh), Berks, 1670 Berks RO D/A1/202/137B
Lawrence, Chrystopher, Hernhill, Kent, 1588 CKS PRC21/9/68
Lawrence, Daniel, mariner, Faversham, Kent, 1661 CKS PRC1/8/107
Lawrence, Edward, St Nicholas at Wade, Kent, 1592 CKS PRC21/11/224
Lawrence, Edward, Whitstable, Kent, 1666 CKS PRC1/11/133
Lawrence, Edward, weaver, Petherton, North, Som, 1680 Somerset RO D/D/Cta/L24
Lawrence, Henry, husbandman, Bovingdon, Herts, Herts RO AHH23/1525
Lawrence, Henry, Kingston Seymour, Som, 1595 Somerset RO D/D/Cta/L31

Lawrence, John, Eastry, Kent, 1595 CKS PRC21/13/56
Lawrence, John, St Albans, Herts, 1610 Herts RO ASA25/4781
Lawrence, John, jurat/gentleman, Faversham, Kent, 1630 CKS PRC20/8/311
Lawrence, John, yeoman, Aston, Herts, 1639 Herts RO AHH23/1503
Lawrence, John, Mumby, Lincs, 1648 Lincs RO Ad/Ac/30/364
Lawrence, John, mariner: 'seaman', Oare, Kent, 1663 CKS PRC1/9/125
Lawrence, John, clergy: 'clerk', Saltfleetby St Peter, Lincs, 1666 Lincs RO Ad/Ac/32/74
Lawrence, Margaret, widow, Leadenham, Lincs, 1632 Lincs RO Ad/Ac/23/44
Lawrence, Marke, Elmsted, Kent, 1586 CKS PRC2/4/249
Lawrence, Mathew, Catworth, Great, Hunts, 1684 Hunts RO/Acc58/229(229)
Lawrence, Richard, butcher, Abingdon, Berks, 1608 Berks RO D/A1/202/24B
Lawrence, Richard, waterman, Nocton, Lincs, 1623 Lincs RO Ad/Ac/18/8
Lawrence, Richard, gentleman, Faversham, Kent, 1629 CKS PRC2/29/63
Lawrence, Richarde, Hernhill, Kent, 1602 CKS PRC21/17/71
Lawrence, Robert, Brauncewell, Lincs, 1622 Lincs RO Ad/Ac/17/13
Lawrence, Robert, husbandman, Frodingham, Lincs, 1669 Lincs RO Ad/Ac/33/156
Lawrence, Roger, Ripon, Yorks, Borthwick Test C.P. 1740/8
Lawrence, Roger, yeoman, Calceby, Lincs, 1629 Lincs RO Ad/Ac/22/110
Lawrence, Thomas, Bray, Berks, Berks RO D/A1/202/11A
Lawrence, Thomas, Goodnestone next Wingham, Kent, 1597 CKS PRC21/14/195
Lawrence, Thomas, Hampstead Norris, Berks, 1606 Berks RO D/A1/202/18A
Lawrence, Thomas, St Albans, Herts, 1626 Herts RO ASA25/2962
Lawrence, Thomas, husbandman, Toynton, Low, Lincs, 1679 Lincs RO Ad/Ac/43/128
Lawrence, Thomas, Rainham, Kent, 1688 Lambeth Palace Arches G39/1
Lawrence, Thomas, labourer, Lapley (Wheaton Aston), Staffs, 1828 LJRO/B/C/5/1828/22
Lawrence, Thomas ygr, yeoman, Barham, Kent, 1632 CKS PRC2/31/126
Lawrence, William, St Albans, Herts, 1582 Herts RO ASA25/1012
Lawrence, William, Felpham, Sussex, 1619 W. Suss RO EpI/33/1619/5
Lawrence, William, clergy: 'rector', Cambridge (Queens' College)/Stretham, Cambs, 1623 c. CUL V.C. Acc./Box2/45
Lawrence, William, yeoman, Frilsham, Berks, 1641 Berks RO D/A1/202/97A
Lawrence, William, Barham, Kent, 1664 CKS PRC1/10/59
Lawrence, William, Hethe, Oxon, 1679 Oxon RO MSS Wills 83/2/1
Lawrence, William, Belton (Beltoft), Lincs, 1682 Lincs RO Ad/Ac/44/3
Lawrence/Bunniard, Afra, Canterbury All Saints, Kent, 1676 CKS PRC2/37/61
Lawrence/Runacre, Thomas, Letcombe Regis, Berks, 1596 Berks RO D/A1/201/189C
Lawrence/Runaker, Mary, widow, Letcombe Regis, Berks, 1678 Berks RO D/A1/94/77A
Lawrence, see Trenchmore,
Lawrett, Mathew, husbandman, Gedney, Lincs, 1639 Lincs RO Ad/Ac/26/267
Lawse, John, Altarnun, Corn, 1612 Cornwall RO AP/L104/3
Lawse, William, Canterbury St George Martyr, Kent, 1642 CKS PRC1/5/112
Lawsen, Edward, Brading, Hants, 1623 Hants RO 21M65 D8/29
Lawson, Anne, widow, Whitby, Yorks, 1724 Borthwick Test C.P. 1721/2
Lawson, George, degrees: 'B.A.', Oxford (Christ Church College), Oxon, 1598 Bodleian HYP B9/9-10
Lawson, John, Donington, Lincs, 1622 Lincs RO Ad/Ac/17/86
Lawson, John, yeoman, York (Gillygate), Yorks, 1800 Borthwick Test C.P. 1800/2
Lawson, Richard, gentleman, Bucknall (Eaves), Staffs, 1664 LJRO:cards/1664/8
Lawson, Thomas, Queenborough, Kent, 1579 CKS PRC2/1/251
Lawson, Thomas, Immingham, Lincs, 1638 Lincs RO Ad/Ac/25/530
Lawson, Thomas, Kingsnorth, Kent, 1663 CKS PRC1/9/126
Lawton, Thomas, clothmaker, Wardleworth, Lancs, 1690 Lancs RO (Name of Deceased) D.R.C.H.
Lawton, William, Chester, Ches, 1612 Cheshire RO (Name) W.C. 1612
Laxton, Robert, Hemingford Abbots, Hunts, 1702 Hunts RO/Acc58/294

[Laycock:]
Laycock, Thomas, Christchurch, London & Middlesex, 1743 Greater London RO DL/C/550/85
Laye, John, Hythe St Leonard, Kent, 1617 CKS PRC20/4/240
Layne, Edward, Torksey, Lincs, 1614 Lincs RO Ad/Ac/8b/49
Laynson, William, Hursley, Hants, 1673 Hants RO 21m65 D8/248
Laythwaite, William, tanner, Wigan, Lancs, 1600 Lancs RO (Name of Deceased) D.R.C.H. 1599-1600
Layton, Anne, widow, Boston, Lincs, 1638 Lincs RO Ad/Ac/25/268
Layton, Hughe, Herne, Kent, 1576 CKS PRC21/2/381
Layton, James, yeoman, Boston, Lincs, 1638 Lincs RO Ad/Ac/25/396
Layton, Richard, Keal, East, Lincs, 1599 Lincs RO Ad/Ac/5/185
Layton, Richard, Bonnington, Kent, 1611 CKS PRC2/16/50
Lazinby, Richard, Covent Garden, St Paul, London & Middlesex, 1692 Greater London RO AM/PP/Box 1685-1694 pt (uncatalogued)
Le Blan/White, John, Canterbury, Kent, 1638 CKS PRC20/10/140
Le Burgue, Simon, Belton All Saints, Lincs, 1650 Lincs RO Ad/Ac/40/221
Le Clark, Claudius, stranger, Canterbury, Kent, 1595 CKS PRC2/7/429
Le Clercq, James, Canterbury St Peter, Kent, 1645 CKS PRC19/2/100
Le Fever, Scipio, Canterbury All Saints, Kent, 1598 CKS PRC2/10/96
Le Gellon, Peter, 1628 CKS PRC2/29/61
Le Pepre, Paule, Canterbury, Kent, 1598 CKS PRC2/10/104
Le Sedt, Samuel, weaver: 'silk weaver', Canterbury St Alphege, Kent, 1668 CKS PRC19/4/23
Le Vasseur, see Planquett,
Lea, Elizabeth, spinster, Kettlethorpe, Lincs, 1675 Lincs RO Ad/Ac/35/140
Lea, Henery, Newton on Trent, Lincs, 1639 Lincs RO Ad/Ac/40/283
Lea, John, bachelor, 1678 PRO PROB5/781
Lea, John, Shifnal, Shrops, 1685 LJRO/B/C/5/1685/60
Lea, Joseph, Walsall, Staffs, 1681 LJRO/B/C/5/1682/58
Lea, Richard, butcher, Boston, Lincs, 1633 Lincs RO Ad/Ac/24/124
Lea, Thomas, Malmesbury, Wilts, 1620 Wilts RO Arch. Wilts.(name + date)
Leach, Edward, Longstock, Hants, 1679 Hants RO 21m65 D8/291
Leach, Henry, husbandman, Coleshill, Berks, 1610 Berks RO D/A1/202/33A
Leach, John, blacksmith, Tarring, West (Salvington), Sussex, 1640 W. Suss RO EpIV/10/2/34
Leach, Nicholas, yeoman, Ranby, Lincs, 1683 Lincs RO Ad/Ac/44/56
Leach, Richard, Chard, Som, 1619 Somerset RO D/D/Cta/L4
Leach, William, Tangley, Hants, 1608 Hants RO 1608 AD35/2
Leach, William, Theddlethorpe, Lincs, 1773 Lincs RO Ad/Ac/45/35
Leache, Margery, widow, Coleshill, Berks, 1619 Berks RO D/A1/202/51B
Leache, Robert, Martin, Lincs, 1649 Lincs RO Ad/Ac/30/237
Leache, Thomas, Wokingham, Berks, 1597 Wilts RO Miscellaneous Index (name + date)
Leachman, John, apothecary, Horncastle, Lincs, 1622 Lincs RO Ad/Ac/17/12
Leachman, Thomas, Lincoln St Swithin, Lincs, 1625 Lincs RO Ad/Ac/19B/83
Leacroft, Thomas, Stone, Staffs, 1684 LJRO/B/C/5/1684/48
Leadall, John, Somersby, Lincs, 1671 Lincs RO Ad/Ac/33/183
Leadbeater, John, mercer, Grantham, Lincs, 1620 Lincs RO Ad/Ac/16/57
Leadbeater, Rafe, Sandbach (Cranage), Ches, 1625 Cheshire RO (Name) W.C. 1625
Leadbrooke, William, yeoman, Dassett, Burton, Warks, 1707 LJRO/B/C/5/1707/114
Leader, William, Highworth, Wilts, 1678 Wilts RO Preb Court Highworth Bundle 3/36
Leafe, James, Bourne, Lincs, 1651 Lincs RO Ad/Ac/29/109
Leake, 1662 Lincs RO Ad/Ac/32/1
Leake, Gabriell, yeoman, Haceby, Lincs, 1611 Lincs RO Ad/Ac/10/121
Leake, John, Heckington, Lincs, 1640 Lincs RO Ad/Ac/27/177
Leake, Thomas, Ewerby, Lincs, 1640 Lincs RO Ad/Ac/27/150
Leakes, Margaret, Maidstone, Kent, 1605 CKS PRC20/1/33
Lealy, Ambrose, Devizes, Wilts, 1732? Wilts RO Miscellaneous Index (name + date)
Leaman, John, Dowsby, Lincs, 1650 Lincs RO Ad/Ac/29/91

Learie, Phillip, yeoman, Bassingham, Lincs, 1620 Lincs RO Ad/Ac/16/62
Learie, William, Winthorpe, Lincs, 1627 Lincs RO Ad/Ac/20/100
Learie, William, Scothorne, Lincs, 1649 Lincs RO Ad/Ac/40/190
Leary, Robert, Haltham on Bain, Lincs, 1642 Lincs RO Ad/Ac/28/39
Lease, Edward, Hothfield, Kent, 1586 CKS PRC2/5/57
Leathe, John, Halesowen, Worcs, 1680 Worcs RO 008.7 BA3585/837/bdl 2
Leather, George, Disley, Ches, 1751 Cheshire RO (Name) W.C. 1751
Leaven/Lewen, William, Newington next Sittingbourne, Kent, 1638 CKS PRC2/34/79
Leaver, Denise, widow, Moreton, North, Berks, 1626 Berks RO D/A1/202/70A
Leaver, Richard, Moreton, North, Berks, 1601 Berks RO D/A1/202/8A
Leaver, William, Hurst, Berks, 1630 Wilts RO Miscellaneous Index (name + date)
Leaves, John, Pinchbeck, Lincs, 1619 Lincs RO Ad/Ac/14/118
Leaves, Robert, mercer, Pinchbeck, Lincs, 1645 Lincs RO Ad/Ac/28/217
Leband, Henry, Morton, Lincs, 1613 Lincs RO Ad/Ac/12/5
Ledbeter, Jane, widow, Stockport, Ches, 1587 Cheshire RO (Name) W.C. 1587
Ledgard, Susanna, Kelsey, South, Lincs, 1639 Lincs RO Ad/Ac/26/207
Ledgegood, Gyles, Faversham, Kent, 1614 CKS PRC2/18/86
Ledger, see Heath,
Ledgerd, John, Kelsey, North, Lincs, 1668 Lincs RO Ad/Ac/42/33
Ledgingham, Edmund, Stainton by Langworth, Lincs, 1612 Lincs RO Ad/Ac/11/106
Lednam, George, Ingoldsby, Lincs, 1650 Lincs RO Ad/Ac/29/95
Ledner, Phillip, weaver, Stowting, Kent, 1640 CKS PRC1/4/74
Lee, Anthony, Burpham, Sussex, W. Suss RO EpI/33/1612/5
Lee, Augustine, Snitterby, Lincs, 1649 Lincs RO Ad/Ac/40/165
Lee, Charles, Croft, Lincs, 1662 Lincs RO Ad/Ac/32/36
Lee, Daniel, Blean, Kent, 1680 CKS PRC2/39/66
Lee, Edmund, Stopham, Sussex, 1640 W. Suss RO EpI/33/1640/2
Lee, Edward, pewterer, Salisbury, Wilts, 1633 Wilts RO Miscellaneous Index (name + date)
Lee, Edward, carpenter, Ashford, Kent, 1673 CKS PRC2/35/152
Lee, Edward, Itchenor, West, Sussex, 1674 W. Suss RO EpI/33/1673/12
Lee, Edward, Harley, Shrops, 1685 LJRO/B/C/5/1685/61
Lee, Elizabeth, Sandwich, Kent, 1601 CKS PRC2/12/234
Lee, Elizabeth, Deal, Kent, 1673 CKS PRC20/12/89
Lee, George, yeoman, Skirbeck, Lincs, 1653 Lincs RO Ad/Ac/29/18
Lee, George, farmer, Tankersley (Cundy House), Yorks, 1801 Borthwick Test C.P. 1801/6
Lee, George, bricklayer, York St Denis, Yorks, 1802 Borthwick Test C.P. 1802/11
Lee, Honor, St Minver, Corn, 1604 Cornwall RO AP/L24
Lee, Humfrey, Sonning, Berks, 1627 Wilts RO Miscellaneous Index (name + date)
Lee, Irael, Faversham, Kent, 1629 CKS PRC2/30/95
Lee, James, clothier, Calverley (Idle), Yorks, 1824 Borthwick Test C.P. 1824/5
Lee, Jarvice, Cheadle, Staffs, 1682 LJRO/B/C/5/1681/25
Lee, Joacim, Horncastle, Lincs, 1628 Lincs RO Ad/Ac/20b/66
Lee, John, Fareham, Hants, 1663 Hants RO 21M65 D8/173
Lee, John, yeoman, Hythe West, Kent, 1677 CKS PRC2/37/62
Lee, John, Harley, Shrops, 1684 LJRO/B/C/5/1684/47
Lee, John, Thakeham, Sussex, 1684 W. Suss RO EpI/33/1684/23
Lee, Margaret, widow, Itchingfield, Sussex, 1628 W. Suss RO EpI/33/1627/14
Lee, Mary, widow, Denton, Hunts, 1701 Hunts RO/Acc58/291
Lee, Mathewe, husbandman, Holbeach, Lincs, 1623 Lincs RO Ad/Ac/18/24
Lee, Moses, clergy: 'rector', Biddenden, Kent, 1682 CKS PRC2/40/55
Lee, Nicholas, Newport, Hants, 1664 Hants RO 21M65 D8/187
Lee, Richard, yeoman, Bisham, Berks, Berks RO D/A1/92/160C
Lee, Richard, Kenilworth, Warks, 1685 LJRO/B/C/5/1685/62
Lee, Robert, Sandwich St Mary, Kent, 1635 CKS PRC2/33/75
Lee, Roger, Lincoln St Peter at Arches, Lincs, 1575 Lincs RO Ad/Ac/1/18

[Lee:]
Lee, Stephen, Smarden, Kent, 1639 CKS PRC1/3/3
Lee, Thomas, yeoman, Westborough, Lincs, 1622 Lincs RO Ad/Ac/17/98
Lee, Thomas, victualler, Watford, Herts, 1624 Herts RO ASA25/2792
Lee, Thomas, Catthorpe, Leics, 1625 Lincs RO Ad/Ac/19B/90
Lee, Thomas, butcher, Youlgreave (Winster), Derby, 1776 LJRO/B/C/5/1776/58
Lee, Thomas, butcher, Youlgreave (Winster), Derby, 1776 LJRO/B/C/5/1776/59
Lee, Thomas sen, Kilsby, Northants, 1672 Northants RO NWill A/C/111
Lee, William, Fleet, Lincs, 1611 Lincs RO Ad/Ac/10/90
Lee, William, Bisham, Berks, 1616 Berks RO D/A1/202/45B
Lee, William, husbandman, Bersted, South, Sussex, 1631 W. Suss RO EpIV/10/2/1
Lee, William, yeoman, Bisham, Berks, 1632 Berks RO D/A1/202/83C
Lee, William, Brothertoft, Lincs, 1648 Lincs RO Ad/Ac/30/285
Lee, William, yeoman, Westborough, Lincs, 1670 Lincs RO Ad/Ac/32/229
Lee, see Cooke & Lye,
Leech, Henry, mason, Ramsden, Oxon, 1626 Oxon RO MSS Wills 298/5/38
Leech, Joane, widow, Ashton Keynes, Wilts, 1621 Wilts RO Arch. Wilts.(name + date)
Leech, Robert, Cheriton, Kent, 1670 CKS PRC1/14/71
Leech, Thomas, Ashton Keynes, Wilts, 1625 Wilts RO Arch. Wilts.(name + date)
Leeche, Thomas, Bobbing, Kent, 1612 CKS PRC2/16/2
Leeche, William, gentleman, Thimbleby, Lincs, 1626 Lincs RO Ad/Ac/20/44
Leedam, William, husbandman, Belton, Lincs, 1665 Lincs RO Ad/Ac/41/135
Leede, Joane, Headcorn, Kent, 1613 CKS PRC2/18/122
Leede, Stephen, Marden, Kent, 1586 CKS PRC2/4/152
Leede, William, Headcorn, Kent, 1612 CKS PRC2/16/3
Leede/Basden, Elizabeth, Rolvenden, Kent, 1604 CKS PRC2/14/315
Leedes, Nicholas, Goudhurst, Kent, 1596 CKS PRC2/8/47
Leedes, Noe, Canterbury St Mildred, Kent, 1598 CKS PRC2/10/82
Leedes, Stephen, Benenden, Kent, 1607 CKS PRC2/15/231
Leedes, William, Cranbrook, Kent, 1598 CKS PRC2/10/123
Leedes, Wylliam, Benenden, Kent, 1598 CKS PRC2/9/445
Leeds, Arthur, husbandman, Benenden, Kent, 1624 CKS PRC2/23/178
Leeds, Edward, Winterton, Lincs, 1620 Lincs RO Ad/Ac/8b/405
Leeds, Edward, husbandman, Biddenden, Kent, 1683 CKS PRC2/40/128
Leeds, James, Goudhurst, Kent, 1639 CKS PRC2/34/234
Leeds, James, Milton next Sittingbourne, Kent, 1682 CKS PRC2/40/56
Leeds, Richard, Cranbrook, Kent, 1617 CKS PRC2/22/78
Leeds, Stephen, cordwainer, Benenden, Kent, 1669 CKS PRC1/14/72
Leeds, Thomas, innholder, Milton next Sittingbourne, Kent, 1662 CKS PRC1/9/38
Leeds, Walter, Benenden, Kent, 1586 CKS PRC2/4/349
Leeds, Walter, Bethersden, Kent, 1679 CKS PRC2/38/155
Leeds, William, yeoman, Staplehurst, Kent, 1646 CKS PRC1/7/88
Leedum, George, Whitton, Lincs, 1615 Lincs RO Ad/Ac/8b/141
Leeke, Gabriell, yeoman, Wymeswold, Leics, 1684 Leics RO Administrators Accounts 1682-86 f30
Leeke, George, Canterbury St Mary Bredman, Kent, 1589 CKS PRC2/4/521
Leeming, Elizabeth, Frampton, Lincs, 1612 Lincs RO Ad/Ac/11/87
Leeming, Henry, husbandman, Barnetby le Wold, Lincs, 1606 Lincs RO Ad/Ac/7/76
Leeming, Thomas, yeoman, Ponton, Little, Lincs, 1597 Lincs RO Ad/Ac/4/61
Leeny, John, Brookland, Kent, 1678 CKS PRC2/37/172
Lees, Abraham, Ashford, Kent, 1682 CKS PRC20/13/163
Lees, Arthur, mercer, Maidstone, Kent, 1688 CKS PRC20/13/612
Lees, James, Oldham, Lancs, 1673 Lancs RO (Name of Deceased) D.R.C.H. 1673
Lees, James, 1676 Lancs RO (Name of Deceased) D.R.C.H. 1676
Lees, John, draper: 'woollen draper', Sandbach, Ches, 1775 Cheshire RO (Name) W.C. 1775-6
Lees, Ralph, Uttoxeter, Staffs, 1672 LJRO:cards/1672/34

Lees, Ralph, Lillington, Warks, 1684 LJRO/B/C/5/1684/51
Lees, Richard, Bapchild, Kent, 1617 CKS PRC2/22/71
Lees, Samuel, Throwleigh, Kent, 1626 CKS PRC2/27/97
Lees, Samuel, gentleman, Bapchild, Kent, 1668 CKS PRC1/13/71
Lees, Thomas, Brabourne, Kent, 1605 CKS PRC2/13/267
Lees, Thomas, mercer, Uttoxeter, Staffs, 1667 LJRO:cards/1667/53
Lees, Thomas, Stone, Staffs, 1685 LJRO/B/C/5/1684/50
Lees, William, Scotton, Lincs, 1632 Lincs RO Ad/Ac/39/253
Lees, William, Alton, Staffs, 1684 LJRO/B/C/5/1684/49
Leese, Clement, Eastling, Kent, 1631 CKS PRC2/30/96
Leete, Simon, Milton, Cambs, CUL V.C. Acc./Box3/66
Leeves, William, Wimborne Minster, Dors, 1636 Dorset RO PE/WM CP 2/4/50
Leeves, William + Dorothy, Wimborne Minster, Dors, 1619 Dorset RO PE/WM CP 2/4/22
Leeves/Mullens, John, Sherbourne, Dors, 1598 Wilts RO Miscellaneous Index (name + date)
Lefryth, Samuell, Dover, Kent, 1616 CKS PRC20/3/454
Leg, Grace, widow, Henbury, Glos, Bristol RO 1752/CP
Legard, Thomas, Kelsey, South, Lincs, 1644 Lincs RO Ad/Ac/28/63
Legat, Robert, Pluckley, Kent, 1606 CKS PRC2/13/268
Legatt, Edward, Selham, Sussex, 1670 W. Suss RO EpI/33/1670/5
Legatt, Richard, Cocking, Sussex, 1679 W. Suss RO EpI/33/1678/1
Legatt, Robert, bachelor, Sutton, Sussex, 1674 W. Suss RO EpI/33/1674/3
Legden, Nicholas, Woodnesborough, Kent, 1594 CKS PRC2/7/395
Legeante, William, Dover, Kent, 1581 CKS PRC21/5/152
Legg, Anne, widow,
Glos 1735 GRO GDR/B4/2/L61
Legg, Cantrell, university: 'university printer/stationer', Cambridge St Mary the Great, Cambs, 1625 CUL V.C. Acc./Box2/47
Legg, Samuell, yeoman, Eastington, Glos, 1720? GRO GDR/B4/2/L60
Legg, see Rodway,
Leggatt, Thomas, Muchelney, Som, 1640 Somerset RO D/D/Cta/L1
Leggett, Thomas, Queenborough, Kent, 1611 CKS PRC2/16/67
Legitt, Richard,
Leics 1672 Leics RO Administrators Accounts 1667-72 f60
Legram, Abraham, Iwade, Kent, 1639 CKS PRC1/3/4
Legram, Robert, Iwade, Kent, 1617 CKS PRC2/22/79
Legrum, Robert, Iwade, Kent, 1640 CKS PRC1/4/75
Leife, Henry, innholder, Faversham, Kent, 1666 CKS PRC1/11/134
Leife, Samuel, cordwainer, Cranbrook, Kent, 1639 CKS PRC2/34/233
Leigh, Francis, clothier, Cranbrook, Kent, 1670 CKS PRC1/14/73
Leigh, Jane, widow, Quethiock, Corn, 1615 Cornwall RO AP/L105/4
Leigh, John, Quethiock, Corn, 1606 Cornwall RO AP/L25/2
Leigh, John, mercer, Knutsford (Nether Knutsford), Ches, 1665 Cheshire RO (Name) W.C. 1665
Leigh, John, farmer, Pulford, Ches, 1781 Cheshire RO (Name) W.C. 1781
Leigh, Thomas, Habrough, Lincs, 1613 Lincs RO Ad/Ac/12/50
Leigh, Thomas, Goudhurst, Kent, 1672 CKS PRC2/35/151
Leighe, Elizabeth, widow, Croston, Lancs, Lancs RO (Name of Deceased) D.R.C.H. 1593-94
Leighe, Henry, Boyton, Corn, 1606 Cornwall RO AP/L34
Leighe, John, knight, Ingoldsby, Lincs, 1606 Lincs RO Ad/Ac/7/74
Leight, Richard, Lilleshall, Shrops, 1674 LJRO:cards/1674/28
Leightfoot, Frances, Wolford, Little, Warks, 1685 Worcs RO 008.7 BA3585/830/10
Leightfoote, John, Bourne, Lincs, 1627 Lincs RO Ad/Ac/20b/9
Leister, Henry, baker, Canterbury, Kent, 1626 CKS PRC2/25/85
Leister, Susann, widow, Milton next Sittingbourne, Kent, 1693 CKS PRC2/42/70
Lelew, Mary, widow, Stainton, Market, Lincs, 1730 Lincs RO Ad/Ac/45/19
Lellisden, Edmond, Faversham, Kent, 1596 CKS PRC2/8/439

[Lemon:]
Lemon, Arnold, Sandwich, Kent, 1595 CKS PRC2/7/177
Lemon, Catherine, Sandwich, Kent, 1602 CKS PRC2/14/317
Len, John, Littlehampton, Sussex, 1583 W. Suss RO EpI/33/1583/6
Len, Thomas, Yapton, Sussex, 1592 W. Suss RO EpI/33/1591
Lenham, Dorothy, widow, Goudhurst, Kent, 1665 CKS PRC1/11/55
Lenham, John, Goudhurst, Kent, 1665 CKS PRC1/11/56
Lenn, John, Littlehampton, Sussex, 1629 W. Suss RO EpI/33/1629/42
Lenn, Richard, Littlehampton, Sussex, 1600 W. Suss RO EpI/33/1600/12
Lennard, Alice, widow, Chester, Ches, 1691 Cheshire RO (Name) W.C. 1690/1
Lenne, Joan, widow, Lyminster, Sussex, 1618 W. Suss RO EpI/33/1618/4
Lenne, Richard, Littlehampton, Sussex, 1600 W. Suss RO EpI/33/1600/2
Lent, Catharyne, widow, Sandwich, Kent, 1596 CKS PRC2/8/278
Lenton, Alice, widow, Holbeach, Lincs, 1632 Lincs RO Ad/Ac/23/115
Lenton, Nicholas, Moulton, Lincs, 1597 Lincs RO Ad/Ac/0/12
Lenton, Richard, Corby, Lincs, 1613 Lincs RO Ad/Ac/12/9
Leny, Thomas, New Romney, Kent, 1631 CKS PRC20/9/281
Leonard, John, yeoman, Pluckley, Kent, 1697 CKS PRC2/42/131
Leonard, Robert, Saxilby, Lincs, 1632 Lincs RO Ad/Ac/39/315
Leonard, see Edmonds,
Leonardson/Dericke, Edmund, Arundel, Sussex, W. Suss RO EpI/33/1606/11
Leopard, Robert, Egerton, Kent, 1631 CKS PRC20/9/17
Lermitt, Noah, Crowle, Lincs, 1651 Lincs RO Ad/Ac/40/235
Lernoult, Philip, Canterbury St Margaret, Kent, 1672 CKS PRC2/35/67
Lessam, Richard, Basingstoke, Hants, 1594 Hants RO 1593 AD055
Lester, Edward, tawer: 'white tawer', Shirland, Derby, 1790 LJRO/B/C/5/1790/49
Lester, John, husbandman, Whatton, Long, Leics, 1671 Leics RO Administrators Accounts 1667-72 f35
Lester, William, Milton next Sittingbourne, Kent, 1697 CKS PRC2/42/118
Lettinge, William, Leadenham, Lincs, 1614 Lincs RO Ad/Ac/12/170
Lettis, John, St Neots, Hunts, 1685 Hunts RO/Acc58/252(247)
Lettis, William, Sittingbourne, Kent, 1683 CKS PRC2/40/54
Leugar, Wyllyam, Detling, Kent, CKS PRC21/3/47
Levendale, Frauncis, St Johns Thanet, Kent, CKS PRC21/11/347
Levendale, Frauncis, St Johns Thanet, Kent, 1589 CKS PRC21/11/344
Levens, Richard, Scawby, Lincs, 1622 Lincs RO Ad/Ac/8c/25
Lever, Joseph, yeoman, Moreton, South, Berks, 1663 Berks RO D/A1/202/122B
Lever, William, Abbots Langley, Herts, 1573 Herts RO ASA25/750
Leverat, Edmond, Stamford, Lincs, 1612 Lincs RO Ad/Ac/11/77
Levers, William, Boston, Lincs, 1612 Lincs RO Ad/Ac/10/133
Leverseche, Nicholas, Coningsby, Lincs, 1629 Lincs RO Ad/Ac/22/105
Leversedge, Walter, Compton Dando, Som, 1674 Somerset RO D/D/Cta/L26
Leverton, Robert, Croft, Lincs, 1649 Lincs RO Ad/Ac/30/83
Leverton, William, yeoman, Scarle, North, Lincs, 1627 Lincs RO Ad/Ac/20/88
Levett, Margarett, wife, Canterbury St Peter, Kent, 1611 CKS PRC2/15/220
Levett, William, Petworth, Sussex, 1640 W. Suss RO EpI/33/1640/30
Levingston, William, Shadwell, St Paul, London & Middlesex, 1753 Greater London RO DL/C/553/35
Levit, Peter, Canterbury, Kent, 1618 CKS PRC20/4/230
Levnize, Richard, gentleman, Cumnor (Botley), Berks, 1666 Berks RO D/A1/202/128B
Lewdon, Charles, Winscombe, Som, 1723 Somerset RO D/D/Cta/L27
Lewen, Henry, weaver: 'broad weaver', Staplehurst, Kent, 1640 CKS PRC1/4/76
Lewen, John, husbandman, Garsdon, Wilts, 1630 Wilts RO Arch. Wilts.(name + date)
Lewen, John, Devizes, Wilts, 1633 Wilts RO CC Sarum(+ name and date)
Lewen, see Leaven,
Lewendon, Lawrence, Boxford, Berks, 1641 Berks RO D/A1/202/96B

Lewens, Edward, Canterbury St Mary-Magdalen Burgate, Kent, 1640 CKS PRC1/3/5
Lewer, William, Madron, Corn, 1615 Cornwall RO AP/L147
Lewes, John, husbandman,
Herts 1587 Herts RO ASA25/1202
Lewes, John, Abbots Langley, Herts, 1597 Herts RO ASA25/1628
Lewes, Leonard, Burmarsh, Kent, 1628 CKS PRC2/28/79
Lewes, Lodwicke, clergy: 'clerk/parson', Sutton, Sussex, 1613 W. Suss RO EpI/33/1613/13
Lewes, Thomas, Brecon, Breck, NLW BR 1639/3 Ac
Lewes, Thomas, New Romney, Kent, 1604 CKS PRC21/17/1
Lewes, William, Winscombe, Som, 1635 Somerset RO D/D/Cta/L13
Lewes Apprice, Thomas, Cleeve, Old, Som, 1607 Somerset RO D/D/Cta/K10
Lewes, see Tydder & Wooddall,
Lewington, William, yeoman, Wargrave, Berks, 1636 Berks RO D/A1/202/90A
Lewis, Humphrey, Tardebigge, Worcs, 1681 Worcs RO 008.7 BA3585/830/70
Lewis, John, Rowde, Wilts, 1680? Wilts RO Miscellaneous Index (name + date)
Lewis, John, Poplar, London & Middlesex, 1685 PRO PROB32/25/125
Lewis, Mary, Defford, Worcs, 1682 Worcs RO 008.7 BA3585/837/bdl 3
Lewis, William, Newborough, Ang, NLW B 1682-9 Ac
Lewis, William, mariner, Hewelsfield, Glos, 1711 GRO GDR/B4/2/L43
Lewkmer/Rodes/Fymeux, Elizabeth, wife, Newington next Hythe, Kent, 1617 CKS PRC2/22/81
Lewkner, Richard, gentleman, Fordwich, Kent, 1611 CKS PRC2/17/178
Lewknor, Alexander, gentleman, Headcorn, Kent, 1610 CKS PRC2/15/216
Lewknor, Joan, widow, Tenterden, Kent, 1597 CKS PRC2/9/150
Lewknor, Roger, Tenterden, Kent, 1611 CKS PRC2/16/91
Lewyn, John, mariner: 'seafaring man', Deal, Kent, 1613 CKS PRC20/2/366
Lewyn, Robert, St Botolph without Aldgate, London & Middlesex, PRO PROB5/1782
Ley, Elizabeth, widow, Swineshead, Lincs, 1612 Lincs RO Ad/Ac/11/16
Ley, Thomas, Hythe St Leonard, Kent, 1591 CKS PRC21/11/26
Ley, Thomas, yeoman, Mollington, Ches, 1784 Cheshire RO (Name) W.C. 1784
Leyton, Roberte, Westenhanger, Kent, 1600 CKS PRC2/11/403
Libbard, Richard, Chichester, Sussex, 1667 W. Suss RO EpIII/9/1/52
Libbe, John, gentleman, Sulham, Berks, 1627 Berks RO D/A1/202/64A
Libbye, see Lyvell,
Libert, Peter, yeoman, Ash next Sandwich, Kent, 1675 CKS PRC20/12/209
License, William, Toft, Lincs, 1612 Lincs RO Ad/Ac/11/159
Lichell, see Lyvell,
Lickfold, John, Lurgashall, Sussex, 1635 W. Suss RO EpI/33/1635/4
Liddell, John, gentleman, Sandal Magna (New Miller Dam), Yorks, 1810 Borthwick Test C.P. 1810/1
Lidden, Henry, Molash, Kent, 1621 CKS PRC2/22/84
Lidden, Margery, widow, Stone in Oxney, Kent, 1620 CKS PRC2/22/83
Liddington, George, Ebony, Kent, 1622 CKS PRC1/1/32
Liddington, George, Ebony, Kent, 1625 CKS PRC2/25/84
Lide, John, Bradley, North, Wilts, 1629 Wilts RO Arch. Sarum(+ name and date)
Lidgeard, Robert, Rasen, West, Lincs, 1670 Lincs RO Ad/Ac/32/207
Lidgeard, Robert, Rasen, West, Lincs, 1670 Lincs RO Ad/Ac/32/208
Lidgeat, Thomas, Broughton, Lincs, 1613 Lincs RO Ad/Ac/8b/15
Lidgiter, Thomas, Steyning, Sussex, 1682 W. Suss RO EpI/33/1682/1
Lidham, Sampson, Upchurch, Kent, 1618 CKS PRC2/22/80
Lidiard, William, husbandman, Enborne, Berks, 1600 Berks RO D/A1/92/120C
Liffett, John, Hernhill, Kent, 1598 CKS PRC21/15/7
Ligham, Timothy, Stourmouth, Kent, 1619 CKS PRC2/22/65
Light, Henry, husbandman, Tollard Royal, Wilts, 1638 Wilts RO Arch. Sarum(+ name and date)
Light, Joane, Wraxall, North, Wilts, 1620 Wilts RO Arch. Wilts.(name + date)
Light, Robert, Marston, Lincs, 1624 Lincs RO Ad/Ac/18/103

[Lightfoot:]
Lightfoot, Israel, bricklayer, Dereham, East, Norf, 1757 Norfolk RO ANF/11/5/21
Lightfoot, John, yeoman, Scawby, Lincs, 1669 Lincs RO Ad/Ac/33/161
Lightfoote, John, blacksmith, Bourne, Lincs, 1632 Lincs RO Ad/Ac/23/70
Lightfoote, Richard, Althorpe (Amcotts), Lincs, 1602 Lincs RO Ad/Ac/37/105
Lightfoote, Thomas, Canterbury St Mary-Magdalen Burgate, Kent, 1612 CKS PRC20/2/368
Lightfoote, Thomas, Canterbury, Kent, 1625 CKS PRC2/25/86
Lightley, Robert, Wrawby, Lincs, 1607 Lincs RO Ad/Ac/8a/121
Lightwood, Edward, gentleman, Birmingham, Warks, 1807 LJRO/B/C/5/1807/43
Lill, John, Hemingby, Lincs, 1620 Lincs RO Ad/Ac/16/60
Lill, John, Mareham on the Hill, Lincs, 1641 Lincs RO Ad/Ac/27/265
Lilley, Thomas, Ickham, Kent, 1617 CKS PRC20/4/238
Lilley, William, Bethersden, Kent, 1670 CKS PRC1/14/74
Lilley, William, Morton, Lincs, 1682 Lincs RO Ad/Ac/44/4
Lilliatt, John, Bersted, South, Sussex, 1625 W. Suss RO EpIV/10/1/31
Lilliatt, Mary, widow, Chichester, Sussex, 1632 W. Suss RO EpIII/9/1/38
Lilliatt, Richard, Bersted, South, Sussex, 1614 W. Suss RO EpIV/10/1/56
Lilliatt, Robert, Aldingbourne, Sussex, 1600 W. Suss RO EpI/33/1598/8
Lillie, Joan, Stoke Prior, Worcs, 1600 Worcs RO 008.7 BA3585/838/188
Lillie, John, Sandwich, Kent, 1612 CKS PRC2/17/164
Lillie, Richard, Canterbury Old Castle, Kent, 1672 CKS PRC2/35/66
Lilly, Alexander, Sandwich, Kent, 1706 CKS PRC19/6/21
Lilly, George, husbandman, Huttoft, Lincs, 1612 Lincs RO Ad/Ac/10/156
Lilly, John, Sheldwich, Kent, 1701 CKS PRC1/16/32
Lilly, John, Ruckinge, Kent, 1715 CKS PRC1/17/73
Lilly, Joseph, Pytchley, Northants, 1671 Northants RO NWill A/C/109
Lilly, Nicholas, gentleman, Donhead St Mary, Wilts, 1641 Wilts RO Arch. Sarum(+ name and date)
Lilly, Thomas, Ashford, Kent, 1604 CKS PRC2/14/313
Lilly, William, Brookland, Kent, 1616 CKS PRC2/22/76
Lillyatt, William, Bersted, South, Sussex, 1644 W. Suss RO EpIV/10/2A/4
Limber, Thomas, parchment maker, Crowle, Lincs, 1624 Lincs RO Ad/Ac/39/192
Limbrick, Joseph, yeoman, Wickwar, Glos, 1813 GRO GDR/B4/2/L47
Linacre, Thomas, Huntingdon, Hunts, 1684 Hunts RO/Acc58/215(224)
Linche, Davin, St Erth, Corn, 1616 Cornwall RO AP/L154/2
Lincoln, John, Keal, West, Lincs, 1607 Lincs RO Ad/Ac/8a/119
Lincoln, John, Enderby, Mavis, Lincs, 1650 Lincs RO Ad/Ac/29/105
Lincoln, William, Bottesford, Lincs, 1681 Lincs RO Ad/Ac/34/74
Lindley, Nathanael, clergy: 'clerk', Ruckinge, Kent, 1633 CKS PRC2/32/81
Lindley, William, victualler, Killamarsh, Derby, 1777 LJRO/B/C/5/1777/20
Lindon, Daniel, Cannington, Som, Somerset RO D/D/Cta/L3
Lindon, Laurence, Moorlinch, Som, 1641 Somerset RO D/D/Cta/L2
Lindsell, Daniel, university: 'scholar's servant', Cambridge (Barnwell), Cambs, 1617 CUL V.C.Acc./Box1/33
Lindsey, John, victualler, Bourne, Lincs, 1674 Lincs RO Ad/Ac/34/30
Lindsey, Thomas, Cogges, Oxon, 1807 Oxon RO MSS Wills 306/6/3
Lingard, Edward, smith: 'jobbing smith', Birmingham, Warks, 1829 LJRO/B/C/5/1829/24a
Linge, John, husbandman, Abingdon St Helen (Shippon), Berks, 1611 Berks RO D/A1/202/34A
Linge, Richard, Abingdon, Berks, 1565 Berks RO D/A2/C5/f291R
Linley, Frances, spinster, Ashford, Kent, 1625 CKS PRC2/25/88
Linsey, Marie, widow, Moulton, Lincs, 1634? Lincs RO Ad/Ac/24/540
Linsey, Peter, St Giles in the Fields, London & Middlesex, 1609? Lambeth Palace Arches GG24/1
Linsey, Symon, Borden, Kent, 1675 CKS PRC2/36/87
Linsley, Jonathan, skinner, Malton, New St Leonard, Yorks, 1766 Borthwick Test C.P. 1766/1
Linthwaite, Joane, widow, Glen, Great, Leics, 1641 Leics RO PR/I/41A/71

Lintot, Edmund, gentleman, Lydd, Kent, 1632 CKS PRC20/9/282
Lion, Thomas, Potter Hanworth, Lincs, 1612 Lincs RO Ad/Ac/11/196
Lipps, Edward, butcher, Faversham, Kent, 1685 CKS PRC2/40/213
Lipscomb, Robert, Medstead, Hants, 1624 Hants RO 21M65 D8/74
Liptroft?, Gilbert, Barkby, Leics, 1666 Leics RO Administrators Accounts C17th f48
Lisie, James, Canterbury St Mildred, Kent, 1612 CKS PRC2/16/165
Lisle, John, Paddington, London & Middlesex, 1682 PRO PROB32/21/18
Lisle, John, 1683 PRO PROB32/22/9
Lisle, Thomas, Steyning, Sussex, 1682 W. Suss RO EpI/33/1682/49
Lissett, William, innkeeper, Bampton, Oxon, 1793 Oxon RO MSS Wills 303/3/48
Lister, Christopher, clergy: 'clerk', Theddlethorpe St Helen, Lincs, 1619 Lincs RO Ad/Ac/15/223
Lister, Henry, Leverington, Cambs, 1635 c. CUL V.C. Acc./Box3/67
Lister, John, St Peter in Thanet, Kent, 1596 CKS PRC2/8/427
Lister, John, victualler, Donington, Lincs, 1678 Lincs RO Ad/Ac/34/117
Lister, Martha, widow, Addingham, Yorks, 1827 Borthwick Test C.P. 1827/1
Lister, Richard, St Peter in Thanet, Kent, 1629 CKS PRC2/30/93
Lister, Thomas, yeoman, Halifax, Yorks, 1822 Borthwick Test C.P. 1822/2
Lister, William, yeoman, Halifax, Yorks, 1852 Borthwick Test C.P. 1852/2
Lithabye, John, Altarnun, Corn, 1648 Cornwall RO AP/L508
Lithabye, John + Anne, husbandman, St Ive, Corn, 1606 Cornwall RO AP/L49/2
Lithered, Robert, labourer, St Johns Thanet, Kent, 1675 CKS PRC2/36/86
Litherowe, Hellen, St Laurence Thanet, Kent, 1606 CKS PRC2/14/305
Litle, John, yeoman, Reepham, Lincs, 1640 Lincs RO Ad/Ac/40/266
Littilfyld/Parker, George, yeoman, Aldermaston, Berks, 1593 Berks RO D/A1/201/184C
Little, Elizabeth, widow, Hythe St Leonard, Kent, 1681 CKS PRC20/13/159
Little, Jane, widow, Nunthorpe, Yorks, 1802 Borthwick Test C.P. 1801/14
Little, John, Keevil, Wilts, 1639 Wilts RO Arch. Sarum(+ name and date)
Little, John, tanner, Hythe St Leonard, Kent, 1679 CKS PRC20/12/268
Little, Peter, tanner, Hythe St Leonard, Kent, 1684 CKS PRC20/13/346
Little, Ralph, Deeping St James, Lincs, 1714 Lincs RO Ad/Ac/45/4
Little, Samuel, weaver: 'linen weaver', Ashford, Kent, 1728 CKS PRC1/18/42
Little, Thomas, Chichester, Sussex, 1679 W. Suss RO EpIII/9/1/60
Littleboy, John, oilman, Covent Garden, St Paul, London & Middlesex, 1685 Greater London RO AM/PP/Box 1685-1694 pt (uncatalogued)
Littleburie, Edward, gentleman, Winceby, Lincs, 1605 Lincs RO Ad/Ac/6/133
Littlebury, John, gentleman, Ruskington, Lincs, 1625 Lincs RO Ad/Ac/19A/3
Littlee, Martha, widow, Swalcliffe (Sibford Gower), Oxon, 1670 Oxon RO MSS Wills 83/1/19
Littlepage, Christopher, husbandman, Lewknor, Oxon, 1638 Oxon RO MSS Wills 169/3/4
Littlepage, John,
Herts 1610 Herts RO ASA25/4771
Littlepage, Thomas, bookbinder, Oxford All Saints, Oxon, 1678 Bodleian HYP B9/11-14
Littleton, Humphrey, gentleman, Naunton Beauchamp, Worcs, 1695 Worcs RO 008.7 BA3585/836/bdl 1
Littleton, Richard, Cookham, Berks, 1602 Berks RO D/A1/202/7A
Littleton, see Griffin,
Littlewood, Daniel, yeoman, Ecclesfield (Bolsterstone), Yorks, 1772 Borthwick Test C.P. 1772/2
Littlewood, John, victualler/barber, Coventry, Warks, 1779 LJRO/B/C/5/1779/38
Littlweood, Thomas, Hathersage (Toother Hill), Derby, 1667 LJRO:cards/1667/54
Lively, Edward, university: 'Regius Professor of Hebrew/M.A.', Cambridge St Edward, Cambs, 1611 CUL V.C.Acc./Box1/34
Liverpoole, Edward, 1635 Lancs RO (Name of Deceased) D.R.C.H. 1634-35
Liversage, Robert, Newcastle under Lyme, Staffs, 1684 LJRO/B/C/5/1684/52
Livesey, Henrie, Blackburn (Darwen Hall), Lancs, 1622 Lancs RO (Name of Deceased) D.R.C.H. 1622
Livesley, Ralph, gentleman, Minster in Sheppey, Kent, 1621 CKS PRC20/5/115

[Livesley:]
Livesley, Roger, Church Minshull, Ches, 1598 Cheshire RO (Name) W.C. 1598
Lloyd, Edward, mariner: 'purser', Chatham, Kent, 1674 PRO PROB5/1242
Lloyd, John, innholder, Worcester St Helen, Worcs, 1756 Worcs RO 008.7 BA3585/835/bdl 1
Lloyd, Sarah, Mangotsfield (Downend), Glos, Bristol RO 1748/CP
Lloyd, Thomas, Cheswardine (Sowdley), Shrops, 1667 LJRO:cards/1667/55
Lloyd, see Fludd,
Lloyde, Robert, yeoman, Frankley, Worcs, 1602 Worcs RO 008.7 BA3585/838/242
LLoyde, see Barlowe,
Loader, Anthony, yeoman, Harwell, Berks, 1631 Berks RO D/A1/202/78A
Loader, Anthony, husbandman, Tilehurst, Berks, 1640 Berks RO D/A1/202/95A
Loader, Edward, Nuneaton, Warks, 1683 LJRO/B/C/5/1682/59
Loader, John, cutter, Kintbury, Berks, 1680 Berks RO D/A1/202/150B
Loadsman, Thomas, gentleman, Garford, Berks, 1614 Berks RO D/A1/202/40A
Lobb, Agnes, Talland, Corn, 1613 Cornwall RO AP/L115/2
Lobb, Hannibal, yeoman, St Kew, Corn, 1647 Cornwall RO AP/L466/3
Lobb, John, St Botolph without Aldersgate, London & Middlesex, 1685 PRO PROB5/1559
Lobb, William, Salisbury Cathedral (The Close), Wilts, 1627 Wilts RO Miscellaneous Index (name + date)
Lobbe, Elizabeth, Liskeard, Corn, 1606 Cornwall RO AP/L52
Lobell, William, Brenzett, Kent, 1606 CKS PRC2/13/270
Lobill, William eld, Warehorne, Kent, 1642 CKS PRC1/6/71
Lobill, William ygr, Warehorne, Kent, 1642 CKS PRC1/6/72
Lock, Henry, Wylye, Wilts, 1774? Wilts RO Miscellaneous Index (name + date)
Lock, Robert, husbandman, Sherbourne, Dors, 1614 Wilts RO Dean Sarum (name + date)
Lock, Thomas, Candover, Brown, Hants, 1625 Hants RO 21M65 D8/123
Lock, see Crossingham,
Locke,
Norf Norfolk RO ANW/23/13/3
Locke, George, Stoulton, Worcs, 1625 NLW BR 1625/99 Ac
Locke, Henry, Greatford, Lincs, 1626 Lincs RO Ad/Ac/19B/55
Locke, Ralph, Warningcamp, Sussex, 1596 W. Suss RO EpI/33/1596/7
Locke, Richard, Tintagel, Corn, 1606 Cornwall RO AP/L53
Locke, Richard, Rolvenden, Kent, 1610 CKS PRC2/15/214
Locke, Richard, Buscot, Berks, 1636 Berks RO D/A1/202/89A
Locke, William, Lyminster, Sussex, 1624 W. Suss RO EpI/33/1624/8
Locket, John, Muclane, Staffs, 1682 LJRO/B/C/5/1681/26
Lockett, Anne, widow, Spalding, Lincs, 1636? Lincs RO Ad/Ac/24/331
Lockett, Thomas, Moreton Corbet, Shrops, 1685 LJRO/B/C/5/1685/92
Lockey, Oliver, yeoman, Uffington, Berks, 1634 Berks RO D/A1/202/87A
Lockier, see Lockoe,
Lockley, John, Covent Garden, St Paul, London & Middlesex, 1674 Lambeth Palace Arches G28/1
Lockoe/Lockier, Francis, Sheepy Magna, Leics, 1665 Leics RO Administrators Accounts C17th f24
Lockton, John, gentleman, Boston, Lincs, 1619 Lincs RO Ad/Ac/15/245
Lockton, Protosia, widow, Brothertoft, Lincs, 1624 Lincs RO Ad/Ac/19A/46
Lockwood, John, clothier, Emley, Yorks, 1725 Borthwick Test C.P. 1723/8
Lockwood, Thomas eld, farmer, Bolton upon Dearne (Goldthorpe), Yorks, 1823 Borthwick Test C.P. 1821/7
Lockwood, William, Huttoft, Lincs, 1619 Lincs RO Ad/Ac/15/35
Lockyn, Thomas, gentleman, Laughton, Lincs, 1666 Lincs RO Ad/Ac/32/65
Locton, Elizabeth, widow, Swineshead, Lincs, 1635 Lincs RO Ad/Ac/24/307
Lodder, John, Shadoxhurst, Kent, 1621 CKS PRC2/23/175
Loder, John, gentleman, Shellingford, Berks, 1671 Berks RO D/A1/202/138B
Loder, Richard, yeoman, Harwell, Berks, 1682 Berks RO D/A1/202/152C

Lodge, Catherine, spinster, Canterbury Holy Cross Westgate, Kent, 1610 CKS PRC2/15/223
Lodge, Christopher, mercer, Donington, Lincs, 1637 Lincs RO Ad/Ac/25/358
Lodge, James, Wells, Som, 1621 Somerset RO D/D/Cta/L9
Lodge, Joane, widow, Chart, Great, Kent, 1613 CKS PRC2/18/87
Lodger, Clement, Chichester St Bartholomew, Sussex, 1622 W. Suss RO EpIII/9/1/28
Lodington, Alexander, Toft Next Newton, Lincs, 1601 Lincs RO Ad/Ac/5/549
Lodington, Myles, Winteringham, Lincs, 1604 Lincs RO Ad/Ac/5/415
Lodowicke, John, Sandwich, Kent, 1606 CKS PRC2/14/301
Loe, Bennet, baker, Yardley, Worcs, 1600 Worcs RO 008.7 BA3585/838/158
Loe, John, mr, St Botolph without Bishopsgate, London & Middlesex, 1683 PRO PROB32/21/203
Loe, Lancelott, Linsted, Kent, 1642 CKS PRC1/6/73
Lofte, Henry, Shorne, Kent, 1683 PRO PROB5/1230
Loftie, Robert, gentleman, Smeeth, Kent, 1684 CKS PRC20/13/442
Loftie, Thomas, Frinstead, Kent, 1634 CKS PRC2/32/79
Loftus, Francis, farmer, Badsworth (Thorpe Audlin), Yorks, 1809 Borthwick Test C.P. 1809/11
Logins, Silvester, gentleman, Bray, Berks, 1598 Berks RO D/A1/202/4A
Lokyer, Robert, Yeovilton, Som, 1621 Somerset RO D/D/Cta/L8
Loman, Peter, Chilham, Kent, 1694 CKS PRC2/42/71
Lomas, Edward, cordwainer, Newenden, Kent, 1673 CKS PRC2/35/235
Lomas, James, Smarden, Kent, 1605 CKS PRC2/14/307
Lomax, Richard, Tottington, Lancs, 1669 Lancs RO (Name of Deceased) D.R.C.H. 1669
London, Ralph, yeoman, Hampton Poyle, Oxon, 1627 Oxon RO MSS Wills 298/5/31
London, see Ruth,
Lone, John, Marden, Up, Sussex, 1613 W. Suss RO EpI/33/1613/16
Long, Agnes, widow, Egerton, Kent, CKS PRC21/6/409
Long, Elizabeth, spinster, Herne, Kent, 1681 CKS PRC20/13/167
Long, George, St Laurence Thanet, Kent, 1666 CKS PRC1/11/135
Long, Gilbarte, Harrietsham, Kent, 1602 CKS PRC2/12/242
Long, Henry, Linsted, Kent, 1597 CKS PRC2/10/12
Long, Henry, esquire, Wraxall, South, Wilts, 1695? Wilts RO Arch. Sarum(+ name and date)
Long, Joan, widow, Abbots Langley, Herts, Herts RO ASA25/4942
Long, John, Netheravon, Wilts, 1635 Wilts RO Preb Court Netheravon Box 1/29
Long, John, husbandman, Lyminge, Kent, 1641 CKS PRC19/2/26
Long, John, Lymington, Hants, 1668 Hants RO 21M65 D8/205
Long, John, St Albans, Herts, 1712 Herts RO ASA25/4636
Long, Mary, widow, Covent Garden, St Paul, London & Middlesex, 1675 PRO PROB32/12/22
Long, Nicholas, St Laurence Thanet, Kent, 1710 CKS PRC1/17/33
Long, Robert, Linsted, Kent, 1611 CKS PRC2/16/104
Long, Robert, Pluckley, Kent, 1633 CKS PRC2/32/80
Long, Robert, Eastchurch, Sheppey, Kent, 1635 CKS PRC2/33/76
Long, Thomas, Birchington, Kent, 1589 CKS PRC21/9/252
Long, Thomas, gentleman, Canterbury, Kent, 1617 CKS PRC2/22/74
Long, Thomas, clothier, Semington, Wilts, 1647 Wilts RO Arch. Sarum(+ name and date)
Long, Ursula, Ashton, Steeple, Wilts, 1673 Wilts RO Arch. Sarum(+ name and date)
Long, William, husbandman, Seasalter, Kent, 1677 CKS PRC2/37/60
Long, William, Arundel, Sussex, 1682 W. Suss RO EpI/33/1682/14
Long, William, gentleman, Keevil, Wilts, 1740? Wilts RO Arch. Sarum(+ name and date)
Long, William eld, tailor, Stratfield Mortimer, Berks, 1628 Berks RO D/A1/202/75B
Long/Wareing, Frances, widow, Blankney, Lincs, 1672 Lincs RO Ad/Ac/43/63
Longe, Andrew, Milton next Sittingbourne, Kent, 1614 CKS PRC2/18/46
Longe, Francis, bachelor, Lyminge, Kent, 1663 CKS PRC19/3/33
Longe, George, Thornton Curtis, Lincs, 1635 Lincs RO Ad/Ac/24/292
Longe, Henry, Melksham, Wilts, 1615 Wilts RO Miscellaneous Index (name + date)
Longe, Humfrey, Sonning, Berks, 1630 Wilts RO Miscellaneous Index (name + date)
Longe, John, Compton Abbas, Dors, 1598 Somerset RO D/D/Cta/L29

[Longe:]
Longe, John, Trowbridge, Wilts, 1612 Wilts RO CC Sarum(+ name and date)
Longe, John, St Albans, Herts, 1621 Herts RO ASA25/2722
Longe, John, yeoman, Baldon, Toot, Oxon, 1624 Oxon RO MSS Wills Pec 69/5/2
Longe, John, Tilshead, Wilts, 1634 Wilts RO Arch. Sarum(+ name and date)
Longe, Nicholas, Horsham, Sussex, 1613 W. Suss RO EpI/33/1613/15
Longe, Nicholas, Bonnington, Kent, 1631 CKS PRC2/31/50
Longe, Nicholas, university: 'Fellow of Trinity College, Cambridge/M.A.', Cambridge (Trinity College), Cambs, 1642 CUL V.C. Acc./Box2/48
Longe, Robert, Chichester St Peter (near Guildhall), Sussex, 1627 W. Suss RO EpIII/9/1/33
Longe, Rosamond, widow, Iwade, Kent, 1670 CKS PRC1/15/41
Longe, Thomas, Blockley, Worcs, 1684 Worcs RO 008.7 BA3585/837/bdl 4
Longe, William, Gorran, Corn, 1613 Cornwall RO AP/L117/2
Longe, Wyllyam, Woodchurch, Kent, 1579 CKS PRC21/4/30
Longe, see Beckingham,
Longei, Rafe, Sonning, Berks, 1600 c. Wilts RO Miscellaneous Index (name + date)
Longford, John, esquire, Chester, Ches, 1706 Cheshire RO (Name) W.C. 1706
Longhorne, Stephen, Broughton, Lincs, 1624 Lincs RO Ad/Ac/39/159
Longhurst, Walter, Horsham, Sussex, 1678 W. Suss RO EpI/33/1678/3
Longland, Humphrey, Farley Chamberlayne, Hants, 1680 Hants RO 21m65 D8/324
Longland, Mary, widow, St Giles in the Fields, London & Middlesex, 1683 PRO PROB32/22/45
Longland, William, Paxton, Little, Hunts, 1684 Hunts RO/Acc58/237(210)
Longley, James, Lurgashall, Sussex, 1636 W. Suss RO EpI/33/1635/16
Longley, John, Stone in Oxney, Kent, 1632 CKS PRC2/31/128
Longley, John, clergy: 'clerk', Firsby, Lincs, 1639 Lincs RO Ad/Ac/26/152
Longley, John, Cranbrook, Kent, 1675 CKS PRC2/36/213
Longley, Richard, Westwell, Kent, 1575 CKS PRC21/2/247
Longley, Richard, Canterbury Holy Cross Westgate, Kent, 1627 CKS PRC2/28/77
Longley, Richard, bachelor, Minster in Sheppey, Kent, 1675 CKS PRC2/36/215
Longley, Robert, clergy: 'clerk', Sulham, Berks, 1605 Berks RO D/A1/202/19A
Longley, Robert, Lydd, Kent, 1626 CKS PRC20/7/207
Longley, Thomas, husbandman, New Romney, Kent, 1667 CKS PRC19/3/98
Longlie, Anthonie, Goudhurst, Kent, 1612 CKS PRC2/16/65
Longly, George, Staplehurst, Kent, 1645 CKS PRC19/2/101
Longly, John, Ashford, Kent, 1628 CKS PRC2/29/66
Longly, John, Stone in Oxney, Kent, 1668 CKS PRC1/13/74
Longly, John, yeoman, Marden, Kent, 1668 CKS PRC1/13/73
Longman, Thomas, Rainham, Kent, 1581 CKS PRC2/2/1
Longrove, John ygr, Long Wittenham, Berks, 1683 Berks RO D/A1/203/5C
Longstaffe, Jasper, Edlington, Lincs, 1624 Lincs RO Ad/Ac/18/99
Longyeare, William, Mere, Wilts, 1636 Wilts RO Miscellaneous Index (name + date)
Lonney, Agnes, Boston, Lincs, Lincs RO Ad/Ac/2C/119
Looker, John, blacksmith, Aldbourne, Wilts, 1713 Wilts RO Arch. Wilts.(name + date)
Looker, Stephan, Baydon, Wilts, 1686 Wilts RO Dean Sarum (name + date)
Loope, Joane, widow, Bere Regis, Dors, 1641 Wilts RO Miscellaneous Index (name + date)
Loosely/Eversley, Matilda, widow, Chinnor (Oakley), Oxon, 1639 Oxon RO MSS Wills 169/3/10
Loote, Thomas, Watford, Herts, 1562 Herts RO ASA25/483
Loozely, Rowland, yeoman, Lockinge, East, Berks, 1644 Berks RO D/A1/202/104A
Lopsett, Thomas, Horncastle, Lincs, 1646 Lincs RO Ad/Ac/28/229
Lorande, Christopher, waterman, Bardney (Nocton Fen), Lincs, 1673 Lincs RO Ad/Ac/35/4
Lord, Anthony, Walesby, Lincs, 1638 Lincs RO Ad/Ac/25/310
Lord, James, Spotland, Lancs, 1637 Lancs RO (Name of Deceased) D.R.C.H. 1636-37
Lord, Joan, widow, Colne, Hunts, 1681 Hunts RO/Acc58/155(14)
Lord, Joseph, Ivychurch, Kent, 1631 CKS PRC20/9/275
Lord, Ralph, gentleman, Haugham, Lincs, 1637 Lincs RO Ad/Ac/25/651
Lord, Robert, Owersby, Lincs, 1636 Lincs RO Ad/Ac/24/449

Lorde, Henrie, Grimsby, Great, Lincs, 1606 Lincs RO Ad/Ac/6/119
Lorde, Thomas, Norton, Herts, 1586 Herts RO ASA25/1130
Lorde, Thomas, Norton, Herts, 1594 Herts RO ASA25/1484
Lording, Henry, Lydd, Kent, 1601 CKS PRC21/16/99
Lording, John, Lydd, Kent, 1631 CKS PRC20/9/269
Lording, Margaret, New Romney, Kent, 1634 CKS PRC20/11/81
Lording, Margery, New Romney, Kent, 1634 CKS PRC20/11/79
Lording, Mary, Lydd, Kent, 1639 CKS PRC20/11/103
Lording, Thomas, New Romney, Kent, 1631 CKS PRC20/9/279
Loridon, Pasqui, Canterbury St Mary Bredman, Kent, 1613 CKS PRC2/17/98
Lorkin, William, Headcorn, Kent, 1597 CKS PRC2/9/146
Lorman, Edward, miller, Newnham, Kent, 1668 CKS PRC1/12/57
Lorriman, John, Hucking, Kent, 1640 CKS PRC19/1/59
Lorryman, Nicholas eld, Challock, Kent, 1627 CKS PRC20/7/209
Lorryman, Robert, Benenden, Kent, 1595 CKS PRC2/7/425
Lorte, Thomas, degrees: 'M.A.', Oxford (Jesus College), Oxon, 1597 Bodleian HYP B9/15-16
Loryman, Richard, Challock, Kent, 1640 CKS PRC19/1/60
Losebye, Daniel, Owston, Leics, 1641 Leics RO PR/I/41A/58
Loskton, John, Aslackby, Lincs, 1642 Lincs RO Ad/Ac/28/5
Lother, Henry, Bethersden, Kent, 1586 CKS PRC2/4/57
Lotherington, Richard, Whitby, Yorks, Borthwick Test C.P. 1739/10
Lothian, John, university: 'Fellow of St Catherine's College, Cambridge/M.A.' Cambridge (St Catherine's College), Cambs, 1639 CUL V.C. Acc./Box2/49
Lott, Catherine, mrs/widow, Brenzett, Kent, 1663 CKS PRC1/9/127
Lott, Edmond, Godmersham, Kent, 1625 CKS PRC20/7/303
Lott, Ewstace, husbandman, Lydd, Kent, 1582 CKS PRC21/6/41
Lott, John, Milton next Sittingbourne, Kent, 1612 CKS PRC2/17/326
Lott, John, alderman, Canterbury, Kent, 1683 CKS PRC20/13/348
Lott, Thomas, Stockbury, Kent, 1598 CKS PRC2/10/118
Lott, William, Sevington, Kent, 1626 CKS PRC2/27/93
Lott, William eld, Stockbury, Kent, 1598 CKS PRC2/10/204
Lotte, John, Stockbury, Kent, 1594 CKS PRC2/7/379
Loud, John, Boughton under Blean, Kent, 1680 CKS PRC20/13/46
Loud, see Bettison,
Lovatt, Cicely, widow, Britwell Salome, Oxon, 1624 Oxon RO MSS Wills 298/5/33
Love, Elizabeth, Harbledown, Kent, 1638 CKS PRC2/34/231
Love, Elizabeth, widow, Terwick, Sussex, 1684 W. Suss RO EpI/33/1684/50
Love, Ellen, Badlesmere, Kent, 1624 CKS PRC2/23/180
Love, Fitten, blacksmith, Spalding, Lincs, 1775 Lincs RO Ad/Ac/36/12
Love, George, yeoman, Boston, Lincs, 1638 Lincs RO Ad/Ac/25/151
Love, George, Goodnestone next Faversham, Kent, 1650 CKS PRC1/8/74
Love, John, gentleman, Cranbrook, Kent, 1591 CKS PRC2/5/324
Love, John, Donington, Lincs, 1632 Lincs RO Ad/Ac/23/83
Love, John, Lyme Regis, Dors, 1805? Wilts RO Miscellaneous Index (name + date)
Love, Martyn, Elmsted, Kent, 1583 CKS PRC2/3/105
Love, Richard, Donington, Lincs, 1598 Lincs RO Ad/Ac/4/69
Love, Thomas, Rolvenden, Kent, CKS PRC19/5/55
Love, Thomas, yeoman, Donington, Lincs, 1615 Lincs RO Ad/Ac/13/6
Love, Tobias, Bradford on Avon, Wilts, 1637 Wilts RO Arch. Sarum(+ name and date)
Love, William, Cranbrook, Kent, 1679 CKS PRC2/38/154
Love, William, Rolvenden, Kent, 1684 CKS PRC2/40/215
Love, Wyllyam, Goudhurst, Kent, 1583 CKS PRC2/3/5
Loveday, John, Carlby, Lincs, 1612 Lincs RO Ad/Ac/11/128
Lovegrove, Abraham, blacksmith, Tilehurst, Berks, 1681 Berks RO D/A1/202/153B
Lovegrove, John eld, husbandman, Brimpton, Berks, 1618 Berks RO D/A1/202/47A

[Lovegrove:]
Lovegrove, Richard, Stratfield Mortimer, Berks, 1617 Berks RO D/A1/202/46A
Lovegrove, Robert, husbandman, Stanford Dingley, Berks, 1613 Berks RO D/A1/202/37B
Lovegrove, Thomas, Ardington, Berks, 1619 Berks RO D/A1/202/50A
Lovejoy, Roger, yeoman, Stoke, South (Exlade), Oxon, 1676 Oxon RO MSS Wills 83/1/28
Lovejoy, William, husbandman, Hurley, Berks, 1627 Berks RO D/A1/202/68C
Lovel, Daniel, Herne, Kent, 1634 CKS PRC20/11/83
Lovelace, John, bachelor, Woodchurch, Kent, 1639 CKS PRC20/11/109
Loveland, Thomas, Stockbury, Kent, 1634 CKS PRC2/32/76
Loveless, Mary, Salisbury, Wilts, 1804 Wilts RO Miscellaneous Index (name + date)
Lovell, Augustine, Batcombe (Allum), Som, 1619 Somerset RO D/D/Cta/L25
Lovell, John, Dover, Kent, 1600 CKS PRC21/15/208
Lovell, Roberte, Horncastle, Lincs, 1597 Lincs RO Ad/Ac/4/77
Lovell, Samuell, Stickney, Lincs, 1664 Lincs RO Ad/Ac/43/28
Lovell, Solomon, Dover, Kent, 1615 CKS PRC20/3/242
Lovell, Thomas, Racton, Sussex, 1648 W. Suss RO EpI/33/1648/5
Lovell, William, Dover, Kent, 1586 CKS PRC21/7/384
Lovell/Mitchell, Arnold + Martha, Hythe St Leonard, Kent, 1606 CKS PRC20/1/116
Lovell, see Michaell & Myhell,
Lovelock, Edward, husbandman, Boxford, Berks, 1631 Berks RO D/A1/202/77A
Lovering, Christian, widow, Martock, Som, Somerset RO D/D/Cta/L16
Lovering, Thomas,
Som 1623 Somerset RO D/D/Cta/L11
Loveringe, Nicholas, Langley, Kent, 1624 CKS PRC2/23/182
Lovett, Henry, Abbots Langley, Herts, 1610 Herts RO ASA25/4782
Lovett, John + Martha, Hythe St Leonard, Kent, 1603 CKS PRC21/17/82
Lovett, Katherine, Sarratt, Herts, 1584 Herts RO ASA25/1093
Lovett, Nicolas, Sandwich St Bartholomew's Hospital, Kent, 1589 CKS PRC21/10/5
Lovett, Richard, Allington, Lincs, 1627 Lincs RO Ad/Ac/20b/93
Lovett, Thomas, Hythe St Leonard, Kent, 1616 CKS PRC20/3/238
Lovett, Thomas, Myddle, Shrops, 1685 LJRO/B/C/5/1685/63
Lovys, John, Boyton, Corn, 1624 Cornwall RO AP/L251/3
Lowd, Anne, widow, Adisham, Kent, 1605 CKS PRC20/1/75
Lowde, John, Barham, Kent, 1594 CKS PRC2/7/339
Lowden, Thomas, Coningsby, Lincs, 1603 Lincs RO Ad/Ac/5/213
Lowder, John, yeoman, Croft, Lincs, 1640 Lincs RO Ad/Ac/27/120
Lowdon, Alexander, Tattershall, Lincs, 1635 Lincs RO Ad/Ac/24/431
Lowe, Elizabethe, widow, Borden, Kent, 1596 CKS PRC2/8/238
Lowe, Humphrey, Maulden, Beds, 1625 Lincs RO Ad/Ac/19B/92
Lowe, James, Canterbury, Kent, 1612 CKS PRC2/17/214
Lowe, James, farmer, Blymhill, Staffs, 1813 LJRO/B/C/5/1813/86
Lowe, John, Frittenden, Kent, 1606 CKS PRC2/15/229
Lowe, Mary, widow, Newcastle under Lyme, Staffs, 1747 LJRO/B/C/5/1748/232
Lowe, Richard, Blackburn, Lancs, Lancs RO (Name of Deceased) D.R.C.H. 1580
Lowe, Richard, Stallingborough, Lincs, 1594 Lincs RO Ad/Ac/3/129
Lowe, Robert, husbandman, Humberstone, Lincs, 1627 Lincs RO Ad/Ac/20b/50
Lowe, Tymothie, Whitstable, Kent, 1600 CKS PRC2/11/249
Lowe, William, Leverton, Lincs, 1624 Lincs RO Ad/Ac/19A/86
Lowen, William, Edlesborough (Northall), Bucks, 1560 Herts RO ASA25/482b
Lower, Thomas, Ashington, Sussex, 1606 W. Suss RO EpI/33/1606/12
Lowes, Henrye, Newenden, Kent, 1584 CKS PRC2/3/193
Lowes, Margaret, widow, Old Romney, Kent, 1594 CKS PRC2/7/313
Lowes, Marye, Maidstone, Kent, 1612 CKS PRC20/2/372
Lowgey, Ralfe, Sonning, Berks, 1567 Wilts RO Miscellaneous Index (name + date)
Lowick, Hellen, Baston, Lincs, 1607 Lincs RO Ad/Ac/7/3
Lowicke, Barbara, widow, Sandwich St Peter, Kent, 1624 CKS PRC20/6/122

Lowis, Mathew, Wainfleet All Saints, Lincs, 1611 Lincs RO Ad/Ac/10/95
Lowks, Richard, Budbrooke, Warks, 1685 Worcs RO 008.7 BA3585/830/8
Lown, Alice, Louth, Lincs, 1629 Lincs RO Ad/Ac/22/9
Lownd, Robert, gentleman, Winterton, Lincs, 1631 Lincs RO Ad/Ac/39/243
Lownes, Henry, gentleman, Ashford, Kent, 1692 CKS PRC2/42/42
Lowther, George, husbandman, Appleby, Lincs, 1617 Lincs RO Ad/Ac/8b/117
Lowther, John, mariner: 'master mariner', Rotherhithe (St Mary), Surrey, 1708 Lambeth Palace Arches G58/3
Lowther, Marmaduke, yeoman, Burton on Stather, Lincs, 1664 Lincs RO Ad/Ac/41/132
Lowton, Margaret, widow, Stanton upon Hine Heath (Hatton H), Shrops, 1731 LJRO/B/C/5/1732/67
Lowys, Henry, Wittersham, Kent, 1574 CKS PRC21/2/126
Loye, William, St Nicholas at Wade, Kent, 1616 CKS PRC20/3/401
Lucas, Anthony, esquire, Beckingham, Lincs, 1613 Lincs RO Ad/Ac/12/129
Lucas, Edward, Fovant, Wilts, 1679 Wilts RO Arch. Sarum(+ name and date)
Lucas, James, Mere, Wilts, 1635 Wilts RO Miscellaneous Index (name + date)
Lucas, John, jurat, Dover, Kent, 1581 CKS PRC21/5/1
Lucas, John, Aldington, Kent, 1614 CKS PRC20/3/93
Lucas, John, Pulborough, Sussex, 1635 W. Suss RO EpI/33/1635/14
Lucas, John, Bitteswell, Leics, 1641 Leics RO PR/I/41A/83
Lucas, John, Laughton, Leics, 1672 Leics RO Administrators Accounts 1667-72 f91
Lucas, Julian, Clapham, Sussex, 1604 W. Suss RO EpI/33/1603/1
Lucas, Margaret, St Cleer, Corn, 1617 Cornwall RO AP/L118/3
Lucas, Richard, husbandman, Lench, Church, Worcs, 1605 Worcs RO 008.7 BA3585/839/395
Lucas, Robert, Rustington, Sussex, 1631 W. Suss RO EpI/33/1631/26
Lucas, Thomas, Godmersham, Kent, 1576 CKS PRC21/2/380
Lucas, Thomas, Berwick St John, Wilts, 1691 Wilts RO Arch. Sarum(+ name and date)
Lucas, William, Horsham (Bishopric), Sussex, 1632 W. Suss RO EpIV/10/2/5
Lucas, William, Ospringe, Kent, 1644 CKS PRC1/6/114
Lucas, William, St Marylebone (Edgeware Road), London & Middlesex, 1815 Greater London RO DL/C/575/87
Lucas, William, St Marylebone (Edgeware Road), London & Middlesex, 1815 Greater London RO DL/C/575/89
Lucas/Harte, Joan, widow, Dover, Kent, 1613 CKS PRC20/2/551
Lucas/Luccas, William, Selling, Kent, 1604 CKS PRC2/13/265
Luccas, see Lucas,
Luce, Henry, blacksmith, Langdon, East, Kent, 1682 CKS PRC2/39/198
Luce, John, Sandwich, Kent, 1618 CKS PRC2/22/72
Luck, Giles, Thornham, Kent, 1647 CKS PRC1/8/21
Luckas, Thomas, Stelling, Kent, 1617 CKS PRC2/22/75
Lucke, Christopher, yeoman, Goudhurst, Kent, 1639 CKS PRC1/3/6
Lucke, Michael, Bobbing, Kent, 1617 CKS PRC2/22/69
Lucke, Richard, Alkborough, Lincs, 1596 Lincs RO Ad/Ac/2b/140
Lucke, Richard, Sittingbourne, Kent, 1598 CKS PRC2/9/449
Lucke, Richard, Sandwich, Kent, 1627 CKS PRC2/28/76
Lucke, Stephen, Sutton Valence, Kent, 1623 CKS PRC2/23/176
Lucke, Stephen, Thornham, Kent, 1681 CKS PRC2/39/68
Lucke, William, Ashford, Kent, 1633 CKS PRC2/32/78
Lucke, William, labourer, Cranbrook, Kent, 1643 CKS PRC19/2/61
Lucken, Richard, Shipley, Sussex, 1627 W. Suss RO EpI/33/1627/6
Luckett, Henry, Reculver, Kent, 1619 CKS PRC20/4/228
Luckett, John, yeoman, Kenardington, Kent, 1680 CKS PRC2/39/69
Luckett, Mark, Reculver, Kent, 1617 CKS PRC20/4/232
Luckett, Richard, Preston next Wingham, Kent, 1608 CKS PRC2/14/303
Luckett, Richard, St Swithin, London & Middlesex, 1666 PRO PROB5/1446

[Luckett:]
Luckett, William ygr, yeoman, Chilham, Kent, 1681 CKS PRC2/39/65
Luckhurst, Thomas, Rolvenden, Kent, 1639 CKS PRC1/3/7
Luckin, William, clergy: 'minister/M.A.', Cambridge (St Catherine's College), Cambs, 1666 CUL V.C. Acc./Box3/32
Lucus, John, gardener, Oxford St Thomas, Oxon, 1675 Oxon RO MSS Wills 298/5/64
Lucy, Mary, widow, Rotherfield Greys, Oxon, 1677 Oxon RO MSS Wills 298/5/68
Ludd, see Ladd,
Luddington, Chrofer, tailor, Winteringham, Lincs, 1608 Lincs RO Ad/Ac/37/257
Luddington, John, Winteringham, Lincs, 1620 Lincs RO Ad/Ac/8b/421
Luddington, Nicholas, Scotter, Lincs, 1632 Lincs RO Ad/Ac/39/311
Luddington, Richard, Normanby, Lincs, 1597 Lincs RO Ad/Ac/37/44
Luddington, Robert, Winteringham, Lincs, 1627 Lincs RO Ad/Ac/39/62
Luddington, William, Scotter, Lincs, 1641 Lincs RO Ad/Ac/40/112
Luddington, William, Scotter, Lincs, 1641 Lincs RO Ad/Ac/40/289
Ludgate, Robart, Lydd, Kent, 1584 CKS PRC21/7/50
Ludlam, James, brewer: 'beerbrewer', Leicester St Martin, Leics, Leics RO Administrators Accounts 1682-86 f36
Ludlo, Thomas, Rickmansworth, Herts, 1595 Herts RO ASA25/1487
Ludlow, Thomas, Warminster, Wilts, 1673 Wilts RO Arch. Sarum(+ name and date)
Ludlowe, Edmonde, knight, Maiden Bradley, Wilts, 1625 Wilts RO CC Sarum(+ name and date)
Luendon, Joane, widow, Buttermere, Wilts, 1619 Wilts RO Arch. Wilts.(name + date)
Luffe, Alice, widow, Easebourne, Sussex, 1624 W. Suss RO EpI/33/1624/4
Luffe, Henry, Fernhurst, Sussex, 1640 W. Suss RO EpI/33/1640/28
Luffe, Richard, Fernhurst, Sussex, 1629 W. Suss RO EpI/33/1629/30
Lukas, Margaret, Petham, Kent, 1639 CKS PRC1/3/8a
Lukas, Margaret, spinster, Petham, Kent, 1640 CKS PRC1/3/8
Luke, John, Roche, Corn, 1625 Cornwall RO AP/L276/2
Lukey, Austine, dyer, Truro, Corn, 1613 Cornwall RO AP/L96/3
Lukin, Thomas eld, Brookland, Kent, 1664 CKS PRC1/10/60
Lukine, Mary, spinster, Sandwich, Kent, 1646 CKS PRC1/7/89
Lukyn, Roger, esquire, Wingham, Kent, 1682 CKS PRC20/13/265
Lull, James, Old Romney, Kent, 1639 CKS PRC1/3/9
Lull, John, Sandwich, Kent, 1602 CKS PRC2/14/311
Lull, Vyncent, Sandwich, Kent, 1597 CKS PRC2/9/453
Lullham, Richard, Dover, Kent, 1639 CKS PRC20/11/97
Lumbe, Pauwle, Althorpe, Lincs, 1638 Lincs RO Ad/Ac/40/248
Lumbe, Robert, Epworth, Lincs, 1673 Lincs RO Ad/Ac/35/57
Lumpkin, John, Burgh, Lincs, 1669 Lincs RO Ad/Ac/33/101
Lunce, Robarte, Swalecliffe, Kent, 1606 CKS PRC2/13/263
Lund, John, Leeds, Yorks, 1638 Borthwick Prob. Ex. 1638/6
Lunde, George, Snelland, Lincs, 1587 Lincs RO Ad/Ac/2C/18
Lundy, William, Beverley St John (Woodmansey), Yorks, Borthwick Test C.P. 1737/9
Lunn, Lettice, widow, Hatford, Berks, 1683 Berks RO D/A1/203/4C
Lunn, Richard, Pinchbeck, Lincs, 1670 Lincs RO Ad/Ac/32/174
Lunne, John, husbandman, Boothby Pagnell, Lincs, 1646 Lincs RO Ad/Ac/28/190
Lunne, Richard, Tattershall, Lincs, 1625? Lincs RO Ad/Ac/19B/115
Lupton, John, Coates, North, Lincs, 1602 Lincs RO Ad/Ac/5/364
Lupton, Thomas, Laughton, Lincs, 1626 Lincs RO Ad/Ac/39/200
Lurchine, Thomas, Upchurch, Kent, 1609 CKS PRC2/15/227
Lusby, Thomas, yeoman, Humberstone, Lincs, 1680 Lincs RO Ad/Ac/34/40
Lushington, Agnes, River, Kent, 1640 CKS PRC1/3/10
Lushington, Ann, widow, St Nicholas at Wade, Kent, 1622 CKS PRC20/6/320
Lushington, Edward, Dymchurch, Kent, 1704 CKS PRC1/16/50
Lushington, Elizabeth, Stowting, Kent, 1600 CKS PRC2/11/251
Lushington, Elizabeth, Hastingleigh, Kent, 1628 CKS PRC2/29/62

Lushington, John, yeoman, Petham, Kent, 1681 CKS PRC2/39/200
Lushington, Robert, butcher, Barham, Kent, 1638 CKS PRC2/34/235
Lushington, Robert, yeoman, Lympne, Kent, 1661 CKS PRC1/8/108
Lushington, William, Lympne, Kent, 1687 CKS PRC2/41/97
Luson, Richard, St Thomas Isle of Harty, Kent, 1628 CKS PRC2/29/64
Lussenton, Michaell, River, Kent, 1627 CKS PRC2/27/92
Lusshington, William, Hawkinge, Kent, 1591 CKS PRC2/5/314
Lusshyngton, John, Sturry, Kent, 1590 CKS PRC2/5/312
Lusshyngton, Thomas, St Johns Thanet, Kent, 1590 CKS PRC2/5/318
Lussingden, see Lussington,
Lussington/Lussingden, Richard, Hougham, Kent, 1624 CKS PRC2/23/181
Lussington/Lussingden, Thomas, Hougham, Kent, 1623 CKS PRC2/23/179
Lusted, Samuell, Goudhurst, Kent, 1596 CKS PRC2/9/299
Lutley, Humfry, Uffculme, Devon, 1628 Wilts RO Miscellaneous Index (name + date)
Lutley, Humphrey, Uffculme, Devon, 1628 Wilts RO Miscellaneous Index (name + date)
Lutman, William, basket maker, Cookham, Berks, 1607 Berks RO D/A1/202/23A
Lutman, William ygr, Cookham, Berks, 1614 Berks RO D/A1/202/38A
Lutwick, Clement, Maidstone, Kent, 1592 CKS PRC21/11/250
Luxford, George, yeoman, Woodchurch, Kent, 1687 CKS PRC20/13/597
Lyarde/Jerom, Robart, East Sutton, Kent, 1602 CKS PRC2/12/450
Lychepoole, Frances, Appledore, Kent, 1587 CKS PRC2/4/359
Lydall, John, Wootton Bassett, Wilts, 1675 Wilts RO Miscellaneous Index (name + date)
Lydden, Arthure, Stone in Oxney, Kent, 1610 CKS PRC2/15/225
Lyddon, Nicholas, Kilve, Som, 1596 Somerset RO D/D/Cta/L30
Lyde, Jane, widow, St Mary Abchurch, London & Middlesex, 1666 PRO PROB5/1772
Lyde, William, Stanton Drew, Som, 1644 Somerset RO D/D/Cta/L28
Lydiard, Clement, Enborne, Berks, 1614 Berks RO D/A1/202/39A
Lye, Elizabeth, Erlestoke, Wilts, 1630 Wilts RO Arch. Sarum(+ name and date)
Lye, George, husbandman, Bradfield, Berks, 1620 Berks RO D/A1/92/192D
Lye, John, Corsley, Wilts, 1603 Wilts RO Arch. Sarum(+ name and date)
Lye, Nicholas, Lympne, Kent, 1596 CKS PRC2/8/145
Lye/Lee, Arthur, Goudhurst, Kent, 1599 CKS PRC2/11/103
Lye, see Cooke,
Lyevarte, John, Canterbury All Saints, Kent, 1608 CKS PRC2/15/221
Lyford, John, Steventon, Berks, 1669 Berks RO D/A1/202/132A
Lyford, Robert, Newington next Sittingbourne, Kent, 1640 CKS PRC1/4/77
Lyford, Thomas, clothier, Bucklebury, Berks, 1611 Berks RO D/A1/202/35A
Lyforde, Richard, gentleman, Peasemore, Berks, 1640 Berks RO D/A1/202/91A
Lyforde, William, husbandman, Finchampstead, Berks, 1634 Berks RO D/A1/202/88A
Lylley, Thomas, Egerton, Kent, 1627 CKS PRC20/8/309
Lyllie, Isaac, Wingham, Kent, 1679 CKS PRC20/12/310
Lyllie, James, Brenzett, Kent, 1597 CKS PRC2/9/152
Lylly, Thomas, husbandman, Lydd, Kent, 1584 CKS PRC21/6/452
Lyllye, John, Detling, Kent, 1614 CKS PRC20/3/89
Lylyat, Henry, Aldingbourne, Sussex, 1595 W. Suss RO EpI/33/1595/3
Lynage, William, hatter, Canterbury Holy Cross Westgate, Kent, 1585 CKS PRC2/3/259
Lyncolne, Richard, Hundleby, Lincs, 1602 Lincs RO Ad/Ac/5/23
Lyndsey, Henry, Queenborough, Kent, 1675 CKS PRC2/36/217
Lyne, Joane, Boughton Malherbe, Kent, 1630 CKS PRC2/30/94
Lyne, Richard, Newton, South, Wilts, 1630 Wilts RO Arch. Sarum(+ name and date)
Lyne, Richard, Preshute, Wilts, 1635 Wilts RO CC Sarum(+ name and date)
Lyne, William, Stert, Wilts, 1628 Wilts RO CC Sarum(+ name and date)
Lynold, Anthony, Bromsgrove, Worcs, 1686 Worcs RO 008.7 BA3585/830/22
Lynsey, John eld, chandler, Wimborne Minster, Dors, 1616 Dorset RO PE/WM CP 2/4/18
Lynsey, Myles, Hough on the Hill (Gelston), Lincs, 1618 Lincs RO Ad/Ac/14/286

[Lynsey:]
Lynsey, Simon, husbandman, Wimborne Minster, Dors, 1615 Dorset RO PE/WM CP 2/4/15
Lynwood, Richard, Sittingbourne, Kent, 1627 CKS PRC2/27/1
Lyon, John, St Nicholas at Wade, Kent, 1600 CKS PRC21/15/153
Lyon, John, Burnham, Som, 1620 Somerset RO D/D/Cta/L5
Lyon, Josias, blacksmith, St Nicholas at Wade, Kent, 1685 CKS PRC20/13/440
Lyon, Robert, victualler, Dover St James, Kent, 1641 CKS PRC19/2/27
Lyon, Robert, Laughton, Lincs, 1673 Lincs RO Ad/Ac/35/65
Lyon, Thomas, Ewerby, Lincs, 1685 Lincs RO Ad/Ac/44/144
Lyon, William, Aisthorpe, Lincs, 1618 Lincs RO Ad/Ac/8b/121
Lyons, William, Compton Dando, Som, 1635 Somerset RO D/D/Cta/L14
Lysle, see Parsons,
Lyson, Thomas, labourer, Ashby cum Fenby, Lincs, 1680 Lincs RO Ad/Ac/34/54
Lytherer, Solomon, St Nicholas at Wade, Kent, 1615 CKS PRC20/3/226
Lyttylwood, Nicolas, Whitstable, Kent, 1590 CKS PRC2/5/316
Lyvell/Libbye/Lichell, Edward, Boughton Aluph, Kent, 1602 CKS PRC2/12/236
Lyving, Peter, Sandwich St Peter, Kent, 1619 CKS PRC2/22/66
Lyvsey/Sharman, Roger, Worcester, Worcs, 1594 Worcs RO 008.7 BA3585/838/115
Lyytelton, Edmonde, clergy: 'vicar', Sittingbourne, Kent, 1604 CKS PRC2/14/309
Mabancke, James, Chichester All Saints, Sussex, 1624 W. Suss RO EpIV/10/1/33
Mabb, Thomas, Bearsted, Kent, 1628 CKS PRC2/29/69
Mabberley, Thomas, Oxford St Toles, Oxon, 1594 Bodleian HYP B9/17
Maber, Sarah, Milton next Sittingbourne, Kent, 1680 CKS PRC2/39/74
Mableson, Adam, Brothertoft, Lincs, 1638 Lincs RO Ad/Ac/25/304
Mableson, George, Kirton, Lincs, 1638 Lincs RO Ad/Ac/25/253
Mableson, George, Kirton, Lincs, 1639 Lincs RO Ad/Ac/26/224
Mableson, John, Algarkirk, Lincs, 1606 Lincs RO Ad/Ac/7/6
Mableson, Robert, Kirton in Lindsey, Lincs, 1625 Lincs RO Ad/Ac/19B/94
Mableson, William, Kirton, Lincs, 1638 Lincs RO Ad/Ac/25/208
Mablesone, George, Brothertoft, Lincs, 1597 Lincs RO Ad/Ac/4/19
Mabson, Walter, mason, Wroughton, Wilts, 1637 Wilts RO Arch. Wilts.(name + date)
Mace, Agathie, widow, Chart, Great, Kent, 1611 CKS PRC2/16/68
Mace, Alice, Molash, Kent, 1603 CKS PRC2/14/343
Mace, George, Norton, Kings, Worcs, 1681 Worcs RO 008.7 BA3585/830/47
Mace, Peter, merchant/mr, Sandwich, Kent, 1639 CKS PRC1/3/11
Mace, Richard, Wye, Kent, 1598 CKS PRC2/10/246
Mace, Stephen ygr, yeoman, Wellingborough, Northants, 1680 Northants RO NWill A/C/17
Mace, William, Boughton, Northants, 1672 Northants RO NWill A/C/106
Mace/Grig, Thomas, Milton next Sittingbourne, Kent, 1574 CKS PRC2/1/102
Macey, Richard, Chilmark, Wilts, 1635 Wilts RO Arch. Sarum(+ name and date)
Macey, Robert, Shepton Mallet, Som, 1716 Somerset RO D/D/Cta/M14
Macham, Caleb, Sandwich, Kent, 1638 CKS PRC19/1/13
Macham, Daniel, barber, Windsor, New, Berks, 1639 Berks RO D/A1/204/58A
Machell, Richard, Minster in Thanet, Kent, 1596 CKS PRC2/8/380
Machin, John, Stoke-upon-Trent, Staffs, 1684 LJRO/B/C/5/1684/53
Machon, Francis, Staveley, Derby, 1684 LJRO/B/C/5/1683/10
Machon, Godfrey, Barlborough, Derby, 1674 LJRO:cards/1674/30
Mackarell, William, Holbeach, Lincs, 1622 Lincs RO Ad/Ac/19A/120
Mackarnesse, William ygr, St Laurence Thanet, Kent, 1666 CKS PRC1/11/136
Mackeny, Jane, widow, Old Romney, Kent, 1685 CKS PRC2/41/1
Mackeny, Jane, widow, Old Romney, Kent, 1685 CKS PRC2/41/25
Mackenzie, Hector, Covent Garden, St Paul, London & Middlesex, 1731 Greater London RO AM/PP/Box 1726-1732 pt (uncatalogued)
Mackett, Elizabeth eld, widow, Lydd, Kent, 1645 CKS PRC19/2/102
Mackett, William, husbandman, Lydd, Kent, 1679 CKS PRC20/12/269
Macklesfeild, Thomas, Maer, Staffs, 1672 LJRO:cards/1672/35

Mackley, John, Hawkhurst, Kent, 1615 CKS PRC2/22/46
Mackley, Robert, Freeby, Leics, 1673 Leics RO Administrators Accounts 1667-72 f103
Macklin, Thomas, gentleman, Woodchurch, Ches, 1777 Cheshire RO (Name) W.C. 1777
Mackly, Edward, Chart, Great, Kent, 1684 CKS PRC2/40/222
Mackney, John, Old Romney, Kent, 1682 CKS PRC2/40/62
Mackney, Richard, Hurst, Kent, 1688 CKS PRC2/41/126
Mackrell, Joan, widow, Wimborne Minster (Barnsley), Dors, Dorset RO PE/WM CP 2/4/91
Mackrell, Richard, gentleman, Shifnal, Shrops, 1809 LJRO/B/C/5/1809/45
Mackrill, Jane, Holbeach, Lincs, 1648 Lincs RO Ad/Ac/30/309
Macrell, Simon, Hythe St Leonard, Kent, 1585 CKS PRC21/7/258
Macris, Francys, tanner, Horncastle, Lincs, 1632 Lincs RO Ad/Ac/23/27
Maddison, Elizabeth, Mablethorpe, Lincs, 1637 Lincs RO Ad/Ac/25/57
Maddison, John, Mablethorpe, Lincs, 1637 Lincs RO Ad/Ac/25/645
Maddison, Richard, Grimsby, Great, Lincs, 1625 Lincs RO Ad/Ac/19B/72
Maddison, Thomas, gentleman, Trusthorpe, Lincs, 1646 Lincs RO Ad/Ac/28/171
Maddock, Edward, cordwainer, Maidstone, Kent, 1667 CKS PRC19/3/129
Maddock, Thomas, Snelston, Derby, 1683 LJRO/B/C/5/1682/62
Maddocke, Edward, clothier, Hothfield, Kent, 1613 CKS PRC2/18/128
Maddocks, gentleman, Hanley Castle, Worcs, 1604 Worcs RO 008.7 BA3585/839/371
Maddocks, Richard, weaver: 'linen weaver', Hothfield, Kent, 1677 CKS PRC2/37/175
Maddocks, William, Upham, Hants, 1673 Hants RO 21m65 D8/249a
Maddox, John, tailor, Sandwich, Kent, 1675 CKS PRC2/36/91
Maddox, William, Whitchurch, Shrops, 1675 LJRO:cards/1675/38
Madehurst, John, Rustington (West Preston), Sussex, 1671 W. Suss RO EpI/33/1671/10
Maden, Richard, husbandman, Frieston, Lincs, 1614 Lincs RO Ad/Ac/13/54
Madisone, Thomas, Marsh Chapel, Lincs, 1593 Lincs RO Ad/Ac/3/127
Madocke, Roger, Herne, Kent, 1615 CKS PRC20/3/168
Madox, John, Leeds, Kent, 1633 CKS PRC2/31/138
Madox, William, Harrow on the Hill, London & Middlesex, 1678 PRO PROB32/15/86
Maeuse, see Horsefeild,
Maffey, William, Stoneham, South, Hants, Hants RO 1686 AD65/2
Magewick, William, Kirdford, Sussex, 1649 W. Suss RO EpI/33/1649/2
Magges, Agnes, Chew Magna, Som, 1588 Somerset RO D/D/Cta/M41
Magges, Thomas, Cadbury, North, Som, 1662 Somerset RO D/D/Cta/M25
Maggs, John, butcher, Bristol St Nicholas, Glos, Bristol RO 1764/CP
Magson, Thomas, Newton on Trent, Lincs, 1674 Lincs RO Ad/Ac/35/72
Maide, Thomas, Shipham, Som, 1623 Somerset RO D/D/Cta/M6
Maidestone, Christopher, dyer, Godmanchester, Hunts, Hunts RO/Acc58/89(31)
Maidstone, William, yeoman, Kisland, Norf, 1729 Norfolk RO ANF/11/3/57
Maie, Dennis, widow, Worth, Kent, 1592 CKS PRC21/12/318
Maie, Nicholas, Deal, Kent, 1609 CKS PRC20/1/340
Maiee, Johnne, Nettleton, Lincs, 1579 Lincs RO Ad/Ac/2b/49a
Maighley, Tobias, Willingham, Lincs, 1632 Lincs RO Ad/Ac/40/39
Maighley, Tobias, Willingham, Lincs, 1632 Lincs RO Ad/Ac/40/49
Mainerd, John, husbandman, Old Romney, Kent, 1680 CKS PRC2/39/75
Mainwaring, Barbara, mrs/widow, Canterbury St Mary-Magdalen Burgate, Kent, 1626 CKS PRC2/27/106
Maior, Joane, widow, Charing, Kent, 1681 CKS PRC20/13/175
Maior, Steven, Corsley, Wilts, 1642 Wilts RO Arch. Sarum(+ name and date)
Mair, John, brewer: 'common brewer', Beverley, Yorks, 1809 Borthwick Test C.P. 1809/7
Maister, William, Willesborough, Kent, 1594 CKS PRC2/7/349
Major, Arthur, mariner, Faversham, Kent, 1683 CKS PRC2/40/133
Major, William, Messingham, Lincs, 1683 Lincs RO Ad/Ac/44/41
Makenay, Robert, Saltwood, Kent, 1620 CKS PRC20/4/282
Makender, James, Branston, Lincs, 1664 Lincs RO Ad/Ac/43/37

[Makender:]
Makender, John, Timberland, Lincs, 1620 Lincs RO Ad/Ac/15/125
Makernes, Edmond, Beelsby, Lincs, 1638 Lincs RO Ad/Ac/25/218
Makernesse, Thomas, Irnham, Lincs, 1613 Lincs RO Ad/Ac/12/104
Makerys, Christopher, Horncastle, Lincs, 1600 Lincs RO Ad/Ac/5/545
Makey, Alexander, Tilmanstone, Kent, 1592 CKS PRC2/6/292
Makinder, Barnerd, Timberland, Lincs, 1633 Lincs RO Ad/Ac/24/179
Makinder, Elizabeth, widow, Aubourn, Lincs, 1669 Lincs RO Ad/Ac/33/132
Makridge, Richard, Heckington, Lincs, 1639 Lincs RO Ad/Ac/26/293
Malam, Robert, yeoman, Chisledon, Wilts, 1616? Wilts RO Arch. Wilts.(+ name and date)
Malbane, Robert, Lancs RO (Name of Deceased) D.R.C.H. 1576
Malborow, Abraham eld, husbandman, Throwleigh, Kent, 1669 CKS PRC1/13/75
Malger, Thomas, labourer, Osgodby, Lincs, 1627 Lincs RO Ad/Ac/20b/111
Malin, Gregory, Hollingbourne, Kent, 1639 CKS PRC20/11/127
Malkin, Robert, Adderley, Shrops, 1675 LJRO:cards/1675/39
Mallard, Thomas, Farringdon, Berks, 1613 Wilts RO CC Sarum(+ name and date)
Mallinson, Abraham, clothier, Huddersfield (Lockwood), Yorks, 1786 Borthwick Test C.P. 1786/5
Mallpas, Thomas, Hythe St Leonard, Kent, 1667 CKS PRC19/3/130
Maltbie, Humfrey, Upton, Lincs, 1610 Lincs RO Ad/Ac/8a/318
Maltby, Anne, widow, Manton, Lincs, 1674 Lincs RO Ad/Ac/35/48
Maltby, Christopher, Aswarby, Lincs, 1606 Lincs RO Ad/Ac/7/150
Maltby, Henry, yeoman, Crowland, Lincs, 1679 Lincs RO Ad/Ac/43/120
Maltby, Thomas, Belshford, Lincs, 1615 Lincs RO Ad/Ac/13/219
Maltby, William, Scrivelsby, Lincs, 1646 Lincs RO Ad/Ac/28/169
Malyn, Roger, Herne, Kent, 1611 CKS PRC20/2/280
Man, Agnes, widow, Newington next Hythe, Kent, 1611 CKS PRC2/17/406
Man, George, Canterbury St Dunstan Without, Kent, 1637 CKS PRC2/34/80
Man, Helen, widow, St Albans, Herts, 1602 Herts RO ASA25/4758
Man, John, Newington next Hythe, Kent, 1627 CKS PRC2/28/81
Man, John, mr, Newington next Hythe, Kent, 1664 CKS PRC1/10/61
Man, John, Gidding, Great, Hunts, 1682 Hunts RO/Acc58/178(34)
Man, John, Hunningham, Warks, 1682 LJRO/B/C/5/1682/63
Man, Richard, St Albans St Stephens, Herts, Herts RO ASA25/4862
Man, Thomas, Cheriton, Kent, 1590 CKS PRC2/5/285
Man, William, Radford, Warks, 1682 LJRO/B/C/5/1682/64
Manage, Hughe, Borden, Kent, 1596 CKS PRC2/9/154
Manby, John, Boston, Lincs, 1676 Lincs RO Ad/Ac/43/179
Manby, Samuell, Boston, Lincs, 1638 Lincs RO Ad/Ac/25/219
Mandefeilde, Joan, widow, St Pauls Walden, Herts, 1612 Herts RO ASA25/4799
Mander, Franncis, Hothfield, Kent, 1603 CKS PRC2/12/452
Mandy, John, gentleman, Sandwich St Mary, Kent, 1671 CKS PRC20/12/22
Manfeild, Thomas, husbandman, Sherbourne, Dors, 1627 Wilts RO Miscellaneous Index (name + date)
Manfild, Andrew, Wargrave, Berks, 1573 Berks RO D/A2/C10/f123V
Manger, Daniell, Folkestone, Kent, 1614 CKS PRC2/17/7
Manger, Elizabeth, spinster, Folkestone, Kent, 1626 CKS PRC2/27/99
Manger, Isaack, Hythe St Leonard, Kent, 1640 CKS PRC19/1/18
Manger, Jeremye, Folkestone, Kent, 1613 CKS PRC2/17/267
Manger, Susan, spinster, Folkestone, Kent, 1626 CKS PRC2/27/104
Manger, William, yeoman, Stelling, Kent, 1667 CKS PRC1/12/58
Manger, William, yeoman, Acrise, Kent, 1686 CKS PRC2/41/61
Manifold, Richard, Chesterfield, Derby, 1663 LJRO:cards/1663/41
Maningham, Thomas, clergy: 'clerk', Swavesey, Cambs, 1604 CUL V.C.Acc./Box1/35
Manings, Thomas, Sandwich St Clement, Kent, 1625 CKS PRC2/25/99
Manistee, Clement, Watford, Herts, 1640 Herts RO ASA25/4967
Manley, see Mauley,

Manly, Wyllyam eld, Ash next Sandwich, Kent, 1582 CKS PRC21/6/5
Mann, Ann, widow, Selsey, Sussex, 1676 W. Suss RO EpI/33/1676/3
Mann, Jane, widow, Osbournby, Lincs, 1620 Lincs RO Ad/Ac/16/70
Mannering, Robert, Selling, Kent, 1629 CKS PRC2/30/102
Mannering, Robert, tailor, Headcorn, Kent, 1673 CKS PRC2/35/241
Mannerly, Jeremiah ygr, baker, Yaxley, Hunts, 1720 Hunts RO/Acc58/310
Manners, Barnard, yeoman, Pinchbeck, Lincs, 1637 Lincs RO Ad/Ac/25/312
Manners, Christopher, Somercoates, South, Lincs, 1611 Lincs RO Ad/Ac/10/22
Manners, Richard, Horsham, Sussex, 1673 W. Suss RO EpI/33/1673/20
Manners, Robert, Alkborough, Lincs, 1623 Lincs RO Ad/Ac/8c/47
Manners, Robert, Somercoates, North, Lincs, 1626 Lincs RO Ad/Ac/20/37
Mannfield, Thomas, St Pauls Walden, Herts, 1595 Herts RO ASA25/1519
Manning, Ashton, Belton, Lincs, 1650 Lincs RO Ad/Ac/40/203
Manning, Edward, Brington (Little Brington), Northants, 1681 Northants RO NWill A/C/11
Manning, John, husbandman, Hartlebury, Worcs, 1604 Worcs RO 008.7 BA3585/839/372
Manning, John, Hardingstone (Cotton-End), Northants, 1670 Northants RO NWill A/C/94
Manning, William, yeoman, Malpas (Cholmondeley), Ches, 1663 Cheshire RO (Name) W.C. 1663
Manninge, Michael, Yaxley, Hunts, 1677 Hunts RO/Acc58/115(32)
Mannooch, Daniel, yeoman, Chart, Little, Kent, 1705 CKS PRC1/16/66
Mannooch, James, Biddenden, Kent, 1709 CKS PRC1/17/8
Mannooch, Valentine, mariner: 'sailor', Upchurch, Kent, 1672 CKS PRC2/35/155
Mannory, Robert, Tarring, West, Sussex, 1622 W. Suss RO EpIV/10/1/28
Mannsell, Susannah, Blockley, Worcs, 1681 Worcs RO 008.7 BA3585/830/49
Manochie, Edward, mr, Ulcombe, Kent, 1649 CKS PRC1/8/49
Manock, Stephen, Benenden, Kent, 1586 CKS PRC2/4/38
Mans, Lawrence, Hernhill, Kent, 1599 CKS PRC21/15/39
Mansell, Francis, bachelor/gentleman, St Margaret Westminster, London & Middlesex, 1710 PRO PROB32/53/121
Mansell, Richard, husbandman, Hanborough, Oxon, 1664 Oxon RO MSS Wills 83/4/7
Manser, Thomas, Warblington (Emsworth), Hants, 1693 Hants RO 21m65 D8/358
Manser, William, Rainham, Kent, 1624 CKS PRC2/24/23
Mansfelde, George, Sandwich, Kent, 1588 CKS PRC21/9/213
Mansforth, William + Alice, Sempringham (Pointon), Lincs, 1633 Lincs RO Ad/Ac/24/198
Manshipp, Samuel, Locking, Som, 1664 Somerset RO D/D/Cta/M48
Mansley/Maseley, Richard, Bethersden, Kent, 1626 CKS PRC2/27/108
Mantell, Richard eld, husbandman, Cheriton, Kent, 1666 CKS PRC1/11/137
Mantle, Ann, widow, Newington next Hythe, Kent, 1671 CKS PRC2/35/70
Mantle, Edward, bachelor, Stodmarsh, Kent, 1674 CKS PRC2/36/100
Mantle, Humphrey, brewer: 'beerbrewer', Dover, Kent, 1665 CKS PRC19/3/74
Mantle, John, Tonge, Kent, 1622 CKS PRC2/24/11
Mantle, Peter, Elham, Kent, 1623 CKS PRC2/24/16
Mantle, Ralfe, Ringwould, Kent, 1601 CKS PRC2/12/250
Mantle, Reginold, yeoman, Bilsington, Kent, 1640 CKS PRC1/5/1
Mantle, Richard, butcher, Hythe St Leonard, Kent, 1676 CKS PRC20/12/212
Mantle, Robert, Sandwich St Bartholomew's Hospital, Kent, 1587 CKS PRC21/8/227
Mantle, Thomas, Throwleigh, Kent, 1626 CKS PRC2/27/110
Mantle, William, Biddenden, Kent, 1682 CKS PRC2/40/61
Manton, Thomas, Tenterden, Kent, 1637 CKS PRC2/34/82
Manuell, Edmund, labourer, Althorpe (Burringham), Lincs, 1627 Lincs RO Ad/Ac/39/58
Manuell, John, Bottesford, Lincs, 1626 Lincs RO Ad/Ac/39/170
Manwareing(e), Ercall, High (Roewood), Shrops, 1667 LJRO:cards/1667/56
Manwaring, Nathaniel, gentleman, Kingsnorth, Kent, 1679 CKS PRC2/38/163
Manwaringe, John, gentleman, Canterbury, Kent, 1622 CKS PRC20/6/316
Manwearing, William, victualler, Eastchurch, Sheppey, Kent, 1668 CKS PRC1/13/76
Manyfold, Henry, Wednesbury, Staffs, 1675 LJRO:cards/1675/40

[Maple:]
Maple, Henry, Staple next Wingham, Kent, 1620 CKS PRC20/4/276
Maple, Margarett, widow, Bridge, Kent, 1619 CKS PRC2/22/36
Maple, Nicholas, Canterbury St Mary Bredman, Kent, 1620 CKS PRC2/22/29
Maple, Richard, Bridge, Kent, 1600 CKS PRC2/11/123
Maple, Stephen, Bishopsbourne, Kent, 1591 CKS PRC2/5/290
Maplesden, Henry, gentleman, Marden, Kent, 1637 CKS PRC2/33/81
Maplesden, Mildmay, brewer/gentleman, Faversham, Kent, 1662 CKS PRC1/9/39
Maplesden, Samuell, Headcorn, Kent, 1616 CKS PRC2/22/45
Maplesden, Wyllyam, Wye, Kent, 1592 CKS PRC2/6/400
Mapletofte, Matthew, Syston, Lincs, 1607 Lincs RO Ad/Ac/7/4
Mapletofte, William, Beckingham, Lincs, 1597 Lincs RO Ad/Ac/4/101
Maplisden, Agnes, widow, Marden, Kent, 1626 CKS PRC2/27/107
Maplisden, Francis, clergy: 'curate', Barham, Kent, 1684 CKS PRC2/40/225
Maplisden, John, husbandman, Chart, Little, Kent, 1695 CKS PRC2/42/105
Maplisden, Mildmatt, Maidstone, Kent, 1673 CKS PRC20/12/93
Maplisden, Paule, Graveney, Kent, 1624 CKS PRC2/24/24
Maplisden, Peeter, Snargate, Kent, 1621 CKS PRC2/22/34
Maplisden, Richard, Wye, Kent, 1640 CKS PRC1/3/12
Maplisden, Richard, Chislet, Kent, 1679 CKS PRC2/38/53
Maplisden, Thomazine, widow, Benenden, Kent, 1634 CKS PRC2/32/160
Maplisden, Walter, Canterbury St George Martyr, Kent, 1673 CKS PRC2/35/154
Mapson, Robert, Brinkworth, Wilts, 1773 Wilts RO Miscellaneous Index (name + date)
Marable, see Marble,
Marbacke, Nicholas, Ospringe, Kent, 1626 CKS PRC2/25/94
Marberow, Richard, Mickleover, Derby, 1683 LJRO/B/C/5/1682/68
Marble/Marable, John, St Margarets At Cliffe, Kent, 1575 CKS PRC21/2/237
Marbrooke, John, husbandman, Ash next Sandwich, Kent, 1699 CKS PRC19/5/59
Marbrooke, John, Ash next Sandwich, Kent, 1700 CKS PRC19/5/59a and b
Marbrooke, Stephen, Kennington, Kent, 1612 CKS PRC2/16/44
Marburie, William, esquire, Reston, South, Lincs, 1633 Lincs RO Ad/Ac/24/132
Marburrow, Abraham, Sheldwich, Kent, 1634 CKS PRC2/32/159
March, Edward, Fareham, Hants, 1669 Hants RO 21m65 D8/218
March, James, grocer, Faversham, Kent, 1674 CKS PRC2/36/93
March, Thomas, Wye, Kent, 1598 CKS PRC2/10/395
Marchall, Alexander, Cranbrook, Kent, 1598 CKS PRC2/10/423
Marchall, Robert, Milton next Sittingbourne, Kent, 1627 CKS PRC2/28/83
Marchall/Harryson, Alyce, Newington next Hythe, Kent, 1586 CKS PRC2/4/253
Marcham, Nicholas, Abingdon, Berks, 1602 Berks RO D/A1/203/254B
Marchant, Frances, Stanground, Hunts, 1682 Hunts RO/Acc58/176(36)
Marchant, James, yeoman, Kilmersdon, Som, 1679 PRO PROB5/1132
Marchant, Robarte ygr, Maidstone, Kent, 1578 CKS PRC21/3/260
Marchant, Robert, husbandman, Goudhurst, Kent, 1670 CKS PRC1/15/42
Marchant/Butcher, John, Warminster, Wilts, 1614 Wilts RO Arch. Sarum(+ name and date)
Marchant, see Jenings,
Marchaunt, William, Rainham, Kent, 1591 CKS PRC2/5/308
Marche, John, Cucklington, Som, 1624 Somerset RO D/D/Cta/M7
Marche, Ralphe, Stone in Oxney, Kent, 1622 CKS PRC2/24/5
Marchent, Robert, Tilshead, Wilts, 1619 Wilts RO Miscellaneous Index (name + date)1
Marckes, Thomas, Ruckinge, Kent, 1594 CKS PRC2/7/89
Marckham, Nicholas, beadman, Gainsborough, Lincs, 1606 Lincs RO Ad/Ac/37/217
Marden, Agnes, widow, Smarden, Kent, 1592 CKS PRC2/6/67
Marden, Christopher, Smarden, Kent, 1626 CKS PRC2/25/93
Marden, Elizabeth, Egerton, Kent, 1636 CKS PRC20/11/121
Marden, James, Egerton, Kent, 1696 CKS PRC19/5/44
Marden, John, Egerton, Kent, 1628 CKS PRC20/8/337

Marden, Mary, Lydd, Kent, 1636 CKS PRC20/11/111
Marden, Robert, butcher, Tenterden, Kent, 1613 CKS PRC2/16/185
Marden, William, Staplehurst, Kent, 1616 CKS PRC2/22/48
Marden, William, Pendock, Worcs, 1685 Worcs RO 008.7 BA3585/830/9
Marflete, George, Panton, Lincs, 1593 Lincs RO Ad/Ac/3/55
Margerie, John, Donington, Lincs, 1649 Lincs RO Ad/Ac/30/100
Margerom, Richard, Deeping St James, Lincs, 1618 Lincs RO Ad/Ac/14/271
Margerome, Robert, Ashton, Steeple, Wilts, 1691 Wilts RO Arch. Sarum(+ name and date)
Margetson, William, Buxton, Norf, 1757 Norfolk RO ANW/23/25/22A
Margetts, John, yeoman, Bury, Hunts, 1685 Hunts RO/Acc58/260(252)
Marichurch, Charles, Dover, Kent, 1616 CKS PRC20/3/360
Mariner, John, Headley, Hants, 1679 Hants RO 21m65 D8/292
Markame, Edward, Irby, Lincs, 1579 Lincs RO Ad/Ac/2b/11
Marke, Henry, Liskeard, Corn, 1606 Cornwall RO AP/M77/2
Markebe, Thomas, Hogsthorpe, Lincs, 1669 Lincs RO Ad/Ac/33/122
Markernesse, John, Saltby, Leics, 1673 Leics RO Administrators Accounts 1667-72 f137
Markes, John, mariner, Herne, Kent, 1684 CKS PRC20/13/446
Markes, William, yeoman, Duncton, Sussex, 1682 W. Suss RO EpI/33/1682/25
Marketman, Benham, Minster in Sheppey, Kent, 1701 CKS PRC1/16/33
Marketman, Ceraphin, Lydd, Kent, 1613 CKS PRC20/2/470
Marketman, Clement, Pluckley, Kent, 1638 CKS PRC2/34/238
Marketman, Henry, Bromfield, Kent, 1684 CKS PRC2/40/221
Marketman, Henry, Bromfield, Kent, 1685 CKS PRC1/15/99
Marketman, Susan, Lydd, Kent, 1640 CKS PRC19/1/61
Markhall, Thomas, labourer, Bassingham, Lincs, 1673 Lincs RO Ad/Ac/35/13
Markham, Edward, Thornton Curtis, Lincs, 1606 Lincs RO Ad/Ac/7/36
Markham, Edward, Wold Newton, Lincs, 1620 Lincs RO Ad/Ac/16/68
Markham, Francis, Louth, Lincs, 1613 Lincs RO Ad/Ac/12/123
Markham, George, clergy: 'vicar/D.D.', Carlton, Yorks, 1818 Borthwick Test C.P. 1818/9
Markham, Henrie, Irby on Humber, Lincs, 1613 Lincs RO Ad/Ac/12/36
Markham, Richard, Laughton, Lincs, 1624 Lincs RO Ad/Ac/8c/67
Markham, Thomas, gentleman, Donington on Bain, Lincs, 1619 Lincs RO Ad/Ac/15/201
Markham, William, Keelby, Lincs, 1619 Lincs RO Ad/Ac/14/122
Marks, Joseph, Bristol, Glos, Bristol RO 1747/26
Marks, Robert, Lympne, Kent, 1590 CKS PRC2/5/292
Marks, William, Lyminge, Kent, 1678 CKS PRC20/12/271
Marks/Body, John, Perrot, North, Som, 1626 Somerset RO D/D/Cta/M8
Marleton, Abraham, Saltwood, Kent, 1604 CKS PRC21/16/27
Marleton, Edmund, Dover, Kent, 1639 CKS PRC20/11/133
Marley, Jonathan, brazier, Horncastle, Lincs, 1679 Lincs RO Ad/Ac/43/102
Marley, Thomas, clergy: 'clerk', Louth, Lincs, 1666 Lincs RO Ad/Ac/42/36
Marlin, Robert, Brookland, Kent, 1632 CKS PRC2/31/129
Marloe, John, Bucklebury, Berks, 1625 Berks RO D/A1/204/14C
Marloe, Margaret, widow, Herne, Kent, 1665 CKS PRC19/3/75
Marlow, Henry, Herne, Kent, 1681 CKS PRC20/13/171
Marlow, Valentine, yeoman, Burmarsh, Kent, 1674 CKS PRC2/36/99
Marlowe, George, Wyberton, Lincs, 1611 Lincs RO Ad/Ac/10/116
Marlowe, James, Marston, Lincs, 1603 Lincs RO Ad/Ac/5/111
Marlowe, Thomas, Gedney, Lincs, 1627 Lincs RO Ad/Ac/20/105
Marlowe, William, Gedney, Lincs, 1629 Lincs RO Ad/Ac/22/120
Marlton, Edmund, Elham, Kent, 1605 CKS PRC2/13/279
Marlyman, John, Canterbury St Mary Northgate, Kent, 1585 CKS PRC2/3/298
Marner, Elizabeth, Midhurst, Sussex, 1640 W. Suss RO EpI/33/1640/1
Marner, John, Steyning, Sussex, 1670 W. Suss RO EpI/33/1670/6
Marner, see Rogers,

[Marr:]
Marr, John, Eastchurch, Sheppey, Kent, 1702 CKS PRC1/16/51
Marrable, John, St Margarets At Cliffe, Kent, 1601 CKS PRC21/15/238
Marrall, Richard, Sutton Cheney, Leics, 1665 Leics RO Administrators Accounts C17th f7
Marre, Robert, labourer, Haxey, Lincs, 1635 Lincs RO Ad/Ac/40/51
Marriat, Richard, Sibsey, Lincs, 1620 Lincs RO Ad/Ac/16/99
Marriot, John, husbandman, Bagworth, Leics, 1641 Leics RO PR/I/41A/60
Marriott, Elizabeth, spinster, Sutton, Long, Lincs, 1640 Lincs RO Ad/Ac/27/60
Marriott, Sarah, Glossop, Derby, 1681 LJRO/B/C/5/1682/65
Marriott, Thomas, Godmanchester, Hunts, 1681 Hunts RO/Acc58/158(12)
Marriott, Walter, Pershore, Worcs, 1682 Worcs RO 008.7 BA3585/837/bdl 3
Marriott, William, gentleman, Normanton, South, Derby, 1698 LJRO/B/C/5/1692/37
Marrowe, Thomas, Rippingale, Lincs, 1593 Lincs RO Ad/Ac/3/87
Marrowes, William, Spalding, Lincs, 1613 Lincs RO Ad/Ac/11/62
Marrynell, William, Southampton, Hants, 1624 Hants RO 21M65 D8/75
Marryner, Richard, Minster in Thanet, Kent, 1598 CKS PRC2/10/282
Marryot, William, Himley, Staffs, 1676 LJRO:cards/1676/36
Marsden, Christopher, Bolton, Lancs, 1637 Lancs RO (Name of Deceased) D.R.C.H. 1637
Marsden, John, Eyam, Derby, 1737 LJRO/B/C/5/1737/42
Marsh, Anne, Canterbury St Margaret, Kent, 1667 CKS PRC1/12/59
Marsh, Edward, husbandman, River, Kent, 1683 CKS PRC2/40/130
Marsh, Evan, Southwark, St Saviour, Surrey, 1750 Greater London RO DW/OP/(Ac.73.79 pt) Box 27/1 (uncatalogued)
Marsh, Francis, yeoman, Eastchurch, Sheppey, Kent, 1671 CKS PRC2/35/71
Marsh, George, Upper Hardres, Kent, 1640 CKS PRC1/5/2
Marsh, Henry, yeoman, Watchfield, Berks, 1638 Berks RO D/A1/204/50A
Marsh, Henry, Deal, Kent, 1666 CKS PRC19/3/99
Marsh, Henry, husbandman, Upper Hardres, Kent, 1667 CKS PRC1/12/60
Marsh, James, Hindley, Lancs, 1632 Lancs RO (Name of Deceased) D.R.C.H. 1631-32
Marsh, John, Ripple, Kent, 1629 CKS PRC2/29/67
Marsh, John, mariner: 'seaman', Seasalter, Kent, 1677 CKS PRC2/37/63
Marsh, John, yeoman, Eythorne, Kent, 1682 CKS PRC2/40/58
Marsh, Katherine, Chipping Barnet, Herts, 1629 Herts RO ASA25/4863
Marsh, Nicholas, husbandman, Folkestone, Kent, 1661 CKS PRC1/8/109
Marsh, Nicholas, yeoman, Swingfield, Kent, 1693 CKS PRC2/42/45
Marsh, Peter, grocer, Ashford, Kent, 1675 CKS PRC2/36/221
Marsh, Rose, widow, Hendon, London & Middlesex, 1720 Greater London RO DL/C/547/39
Marsh, Sarah, widow, Warminster, Wilts, 1771 Wilts RO Miscellaneous Index (name + date)
Marsh, Thomas, Fordwich, Kent, 1634 CKS PRC2/33/87
Marsh, Thomas, bachelor, Canterbury St Mary Bredin, Kent, 1663 CKS PRC1/9/128
Marsh, Thomas, bachelor, Eastry, Kent, 1682 CKS PRC20/13/169
Marsh, Vincent, grocer, Canterbury St Mildred, Kent, 1684 CKS PRC2/40/220
Marsh, William, Bourne, Lincs, 1607 Lincs RO Ad/Ac/8a/127
Marsh, William, gentleman, Edenham (Grimsthorpe), Lincs, 1627 Lincs RO Ad/Ac/20/97
Marsh, William, husbandman, Challock, Kent, 1679 CKS PRC20/12/312
Marshall, Anne, widow, Binbrook St Mary, Lincs, 1667 Lincs RO Ad/Ac/32/117
Marshall, Christopher, Kirmington, Lincs, 1632 Lincs RO Ad/Ac/23/94
Marshall, Christopher, Winterton, Lincs, 1668 Lincs RO Ad/Ac/33/81
Marshall, Digory, pewterer, Lostwithiel, Corn, 1645 Cornwall RO AP/M729/2
Marshall, Dorothe, widow, Graveney, Kent, 1603 CKS PRC2/13/296
Marshall, Edward, Bedwin, Little, Wilts, 1615? Wilts RO CC Sarum(+ name and date)
Marshall, Edward, carpenter, Boughton under Blean, Kent, 1666 CKS PRC19/3/100
Marshall, Edward, Idmiston, Wilts, 1684 Wilts RO Arch. Sarum(+ name and date)
Marshall, Elizabeth, spinster, Doddington, Kent, 1644 CKS PRC1/7/1
Marshall, Elizabeth, spinster, Newington next Hythe, Kent, 1681 CKS PRC2/39/207
Marshall, Francis, Derby, Derby, 1683 LJRO/B/C/5/1682/66

Marshall, Henry, yeoman, Davington, Kent, 1684 CKS PRC2/40/224
Marshall, Isaac, tailor, Hinckley, Leics, 1673 Leics RO Administrators Accounts 1667-72 f117
Marshall, Jane, Upchurch, Kent, 1611 CKS PRC2/16/70
Marshall, John, Ashford, Kent, 1592 CKS PRC2/6/280
Marshall, John, Urchfont, Wilts, 1616 Wilts RO Miscellaneous Index (name + date)
Marshall, John, clergy: 'clerk', Bassingham, Lincs, 1618 Lincs RO Ad/Ac/14/36
Marshall, John, mariner: 'sailor', Milton next Sittingbourne, Kent, 1627 CKS PRC2/28/85
Marshall, John, Appleby, Lincs, 1630s? Lincs RO Ad/Ac/40/279
Marshall, John, Milton next Sittingbourne, Kent, 1634 CKS PRC2/32/86
Marshall, John, yeoman, Tydd St Mary, Lincs, 1634 Lincs RO Ad/Ac/24/321
Marshall, John, Seasalter, Kent, 1637 CKS PRC2/33/84
Marshall, John, Theddlethorpe, Lincs, 1637 Lincs RO Ad/Ac/25/572
Marshall, John, labourer, Orgarswick, Kent, 1664 CKS PRC1/10/62
Marshall, John, Deal, Kent, 1669 CKS PRC19/4/24
Marshall, John, gentleman, Temple, Inner, London & Middlesex, 1670 PRO PROB5/839
Marshall, John, Brinklow, Warks, 1683 LJRO/B/C/5/1682/67
Marshall, Mary, spinster, Acrise, Kent, 1640 CKS PRC1/5/3
Marshall, Mary, St Neots, Hunts, 1676 Hunts RO/Acc58/46(11)
Marshall, Myles, Hough on the Hill, Lincs, 1587? Lincs RO Ad/Ac/2C/6
Marshall, Ralph, High Halstow, Kent, 1664 CKS PRC1/10/63
Marshall, Richard, Eastwell, Kent, 1603 CKS PRC2/14/349
Marshall, Richard, Faversham, Kent, 1612 CKS PRC2/16/40
Marshall, Richard, Sandgate Castle, Lieutenant of/gentleman, Folkestone, Kent, 1648 CKS PRC1/8/75
Marshall, Robert, husbandman, Bicker, Lincs, 1620 Lincs RO Ad/Ac/15/270
Marshall, Thomas, Rainham, Kent, 1609 CKS PRC2/15/241
Marshall, Thomas, Quadring, Lincs, 1620 Lincs RO Ad/Ac/16/63
Marshall, Thomas, labourer, Willian, Herts, 1640 Herts RO AHH23/1600
Marshall, Thomas, butcher, Alford, Lincs, 1642 Lincs RO Ad/Ac/28/17
Marshall, Thomas, jurat/mr, Maidstone, Kent, 1714 CKS PRC19/6/64
Marshall, Thomazine, Winthorpe, Lincs, 1640 Lincs RO Ad/Ac/27/151
Marshall, Walter, Teynham, Kent, CKS PRC2/1/204
Marshall, William, clothier, Reading, Berks, 1600 Berks RO D/A1/203/251A
Marshall, William, Tydd St Mary, Lincs, 1613 Lincs RO Ad/Ac/12/159
Marshall, William, Oare, Kent, 1637 CKS PRC2/33/83
Marshall, William, labourer, Frieston, Lincs, 1638 Lincs RO Ad/Ac/25/350
Marshall, William, yeoman, Kennington, Kent, 1639 CKS PRC1/3/13
Marshall, William, Milton next Sittingbourne, Kent, 1641 CKS PRC1/6/1
Marshall, William, Laughton, Lincs, 1662 Lincs RO Ad/Ac/41/47
Marshall, William,
Leics 1665 Leics RO Administrators Accounts C17th f13
Marshall, William, husbandman, Lenton, Lincs, 1673 Lincs RO Ad/Ac/35/10
Marshall, William, High Halstow, Kent, 1681 CKS PRC2/39/205
Marshall, William eld, gentleman, Saltwood, Kent, 1632 CKS PRC20/11/143
Marshall/Osborne, Susanne, widow, Canterbury St George Martyr, Kent, 1668 CKS PRC1/13/77
Marshall/Sumpter, Thomas, Redbourn, Herts, 1598 Herts RO ASA25/1687
Marshall, see Aubie & Berling,
Marshe, Davyd, Langdon, East, Kent, 1596 CKS PRC2/8/157
Marshe, Edward, clergy: 'clerk', Swayfield, Lincs, 1575 Lincs RO Ad/Ac/1/11
Marshe, Edward, clergy: 'clerk', Swayfield, Lincs, 1575 Lincs RO Ad/Ac/2b/43
Marshe, Elizabeth, Biddestone, Wilts, 1621 Wilts RO Arch. Wilts.(+ name and date)
Marshe, Henry, Sholden, Kent, 1591 CKS PRC2/5/304
Marshe, Joane, Hannington, Wilts, 1622 Wilts RO Arch. Wilts.(+ name and date)
Marshe, John, Acrise, Kent, 1593 CKS PRC2/6/372
Marshe, John, Lyminge, Kent, 1603 CKS PRC21/15/337

[Marshe:]
Marshe, John, Bruton, Som, 1625 Somerset RO D/D/Cta/M10
Marshe, Nicholas, Sutton Valence, Kent, 1635 CKS PRC2/33/91
Marshe, Stephen, Maiden Bradley, Wilts, 1620 c. Wilts RO Miscellaneous Index (name + date)
Marshe, Thomas, Barham, Kent, 1597 CKS PRC2/9/301
Marshe, Thomas, Dover, Kent, 1624 CKS PRC20/6/134
Marshe, Walter, Whitfield alias Beauxfield, Kent, 1614 CKS PRC2/17/11
Marshe, William, Bridge, Kent, 1604 CKS PRC2/13/298
Marshment, John, Warminster (Boreham), Wilts, 1733 Wilts RO Miscellaneous Index (name + date)
Marson, Henry, baker, Boston, Lincs, 1670 Lincs RO Ad/Ac/32/231
Marston, Joan, widow, St Albans St Michaels, Herts, Herts RO ASA25/4888
Marston, John, St Albans, Herts, 1574 Herts RO ASA25/780
Marston, John, glazier, Birmingham, Warks, 1672 LJRO:cards/1672/37
Marston/Tomlin, Catherine, Farndon, East, Northants, 1671 Northants RO NWill A/C/92
Mart, Thomas, yeoman, Bradbourne (Ballidon), Derby, 1817 LJRO/B/C/5/1817/61
Marten, Alice, widow, Ebony, Kent, 1666 CKS PRC1/11/138
Marten, Christopher, Lenham, Kent, 1604 CKS PRC2/13/294
Marten, Edmund, Lydd, Kent, 1668 CKS PRC19/3/131
Marten, Elizabeth, widow, Tidcombe, Wilts, 1614 Wilts RO CC Sarum(+ name and date)
Marten, Frances, widow,
Oxon 1628 Oxon RO MSS Wills 83/3/34
Marten, John, St Blazey, Corn, 1647 Cornwall RO AP/M760/2
Marten, John, St Laurence Thanet, Kent, 1679 CKS PRC2/38/159
Marten, Margaret, widow, Longworth, Berks, 1683 Berks RO D/A1/204/133D
Marten, Richard eld, mariner/fisherman, St Laurence Thanet, Kent, 1649 CKS PRC1/8/76
Marten, Thomas, Boughton Monchelsea, Kent, 1604 CKS PRC2/13/290
Marten, William, St Nicholas at Wade, Kent, 1592 CKS PRC21/12/195
Marten, William, Wellington, Som, 1617 Somerset RO D/D/Cta/M39
Martin, Ann, Walsall, Staffs, 1684 LJRO/B/C/5/1684/54
Martin, Bartholomewe, Gedney, Lincs, 1620 Lincs RO Ad/Ac/16/64
Martin, Edward, Donington, Lincs, 1637 Lincs RO Ad/Ac/25/470
Martin, Edward, university: 'Master of Queens' College, Cambridge/D.D.', Cambridge, Cambs, 1665 CUL V.C. Acc./Box3/33
Martin, George, Ewell, Kent, 1620 CKS PRC2/22/32
Martin, George, labourer, Aubourn, Lincs, 1670 Lincs RO Ad/Ac/32/152
Martin, George, butcher, Appledore, Kent, 1683 CKS PRC2/40/131
Martin, Henry, yeoman, Checkendon, Oxon, 1680 Oxon RO MSS Wills 83/4/35
Martin, Jeames, Lydd, Kent, 1613 CKS PRC20/2/541
Martin, John, Stogursey, Som, 1590 Somerset RO D/D/Cta/M43
Martin, John, Leigh, Dors, 1597 Wilts RO Miscellaneous Index (name + date)
Martin, John, St Columb Minor, Corn, 1613 Cornwall RO AP/M217/2
Martin, John, Liddington, Wilts, 1631 Wilts RO Arch. Wilts.(+ name and date)
Martin, John, Climping, Sussex, 1644 W. Suss RO EpI/33/1644/2
Martin, John, Whetstone, Leics, 1665 Leics RO Administrators Accounts C17th f28
Martin, John, yeoman, Ramsbury, Wilts, 1667 Lambeth Palace Arches GG19/1
Martin, John, mason: 'freemason', Boughton Monchelsea, Kent, 1675 CKS PRC2/36/92
Martin, John, Hurst, Berks, 1679 Wilts RO Dean Sarum (name + date)
Martin, John, Diddington, Hunts, 1682 Hunts RO/Acc58/181(27)
Martin, John, hay dealer, Birmingham, Warks, 1822 LJRO/B/C/5/1822/15
Martin, Joseph, Deal, Kent, 1674 CKS PRC20/12/92
Martin, Joseph, farmer, West Bromwich (Hill Top), Staffs, 1823 LJRO/B/C/5/1823/23
Martin, Joshua, Stonesfield, Oxon, 1630 Oxon RO MSS Wills 170/2/1
Martin, Laurence, Quadring, Lincs, 1637 Lincs RO Ad/Ac/25/603
Martin, Michael, yeoman, St Johns Thanet, Kent, 1671 CKS PRC2/35/72
Martin, Philip, Rickling, Essex, 1808 Greater London RO DL/C/567/207

[Martin:]

Martin, Richard, weaver: 'broad weaver', Cranbrook, Kent, 1646 CKS PRC1/7/90
Martin, Richard, Boxley, Kent, 1669 CKS PRC1/13/78
Martin, Richard, innholder, Oxford (University), Oxon, 1694 Bodleian HYP B9/18-19
Martin, Robert, Havant, Hants, 1623 Hants RO 21M65 D8/30
Martin, Robert, Blewbury, Berks, 1627 Wilts RO Miscellaneous Index (name + date)
Martin, Robert, Fovant, Wilts, 1635 Wilts RO Arch. Sarum(+ name and date)
Martin, Thomas, Lanreath, Corn, 1605 Cornwall RO AP/M41/2
Martin, Thomas, Shipley, Sussex, 1618 W. Suss RO EpI/33/1618/7
Martin, Thomas, Buckland, Bucks, 1684 Oxon RO MSS Wills Pec 46/3/4
Martin, Thomas, gentleman, Salisbury, Wilts, 1747? Wilts RO CC Sarum(+ name and date)
Martin, William, Norton Disney, Lincs, 1619 Lincs RO Ad/Ac/15/37
Martin, William, Boxley, Kent, 1620 CKS PRC2/22/55
Martin, William, Tintagel, Corn, 1621 Cornwall RO AP/M326/3
Martin, William, miller, Boston, Lincs, 1640 Lincs RO Ad/Ac/27/182
Martin, William, Northorpe, Lincs, 1667 Lincs RO Ad/Ac/33/9
Martin, William, tanner, Godmanchester, Hunts, 1676 Hunts RO/Acc58/50(3)
Martin/Drury, John, Blyton, Lincs, 1662 Lincs RO Ad/Ac/41/41
Martin/Drury, Robert, Blyton, Lincs, 1667 Lincs RO Ad/Ac/33/22
Martin, see Bartholomew,
Martindale, John, Bucknall, Lincs, 1649 Lincs RO Ad/Ac/30/89
Martine, Christopher, Ramsbury, Wilts, 1693 Wilts RO Dean Sarum (name + date)
Martine, Ellis, Bapchild, Kent, 1609 CKS PRC2/15/237
Martine, Francis, labourer, Ponton, Little, Lincs, 1670 Lincs RO Ad/Ac/32/220
Martine, Thomas, cordwainer: 'shoemaker', Kintbury, Berks, 1622 Wilts RO CC Sarum(+ name and date)
Martis, William, Oving, Sussex, 1625 W. Suss RO EpI/33/1625/9
Martyn, Agnes, widow, St Albans St Peters, Herts, 1599 Herts RO ASA25/1732
Martyn, Anne, mrs, Langley, Kent, 1689 CKS PRC2/41/155
Martyn, Francis, mr, Langley, Kent, 1689 CKS PRC2/41/154
Martyn, Henry, St Laurence Thanet, Kent, 1586 CKS PRC2/4/200
Martyn, Henry, Yapton, Sussex, 1607 W. Suss RO EpI/33/1607/13
Martyn, Henry, St Laurence Thanet, Kent, 1621 CKS PRC2/22/57
Martyn, Henry, mason: 'freemason', Boughton Monchelsea, Kent, 1621 CKS PRC2/24/3
Martyn, John, Wingham, Kent, 1596 CKS PRC21/14/89
Martyn, John, Wye, Kent, 1597 CKS PRC2/10/32
Martyn, John, Wye, Kent, 1623 CKS PRC2/24/18
Martyn, Richard, St Giles on the Heath, Corn, 1605 Cornwall RO AP/M39/2
Martyn, Richard eld, St Laurence Thanet, Kent, 1612 CKS PRC2/16/11
Martyn, Robert, yeoman, Burford (Upton), Oxon, 1626 Oxon RO MSS Wills 170/1/27
Martyn, Thomas, Blyborough, Lincs, 1587 Lincs RO Ad/Ac/2C/146
Martyn, Thomas, Rickmansworth, Herts, 1613 Herts RO ASA25/4812
Martyn, Thomas, mercer, Angmering, Sussex, 1618 W. Suss RO EpI/33/1617/13
Martyn/Drewry, Margaret, Blyton, Lincs, 1634 Lincs RO Ad/Ac/40/97
Martyn/Drewry, William, Blyton, Lincs, 1634 Lincs RO Ad/Ac/40/29
Martyn/Keigwyn, John, St Just in Penwith, Corn, 1613 Cornwall RO AP/M184/2
Martyne, Robert, Immingham, Lincs, 1618 Lincs RO Ad/Ac/14/230
Martyne, Thomas, Maidstone, Kent, 1596 CKS PRC21/14/115
Martyne, Thomas, plumber, Alconbury, Hunts, 1676 Hunts RO/Acc58/59(169)
Marwicke, Dorcas, widow, Lincoln, Lincs, 1649 Lincs RO Ad/Ac/30/220
Marwicke, Henrie, Killingholme, Lincs, 1639 Lincs RO Ad/Ac/26/205
Marwicke, Thomas, Immingham, Lincs, 1606 Lincs RO Ad/Ac/7/8
Marychurch, Joane, widow, Dover, Kent, 1623 CKS PRC20/6/312
Marychurch, John, Dover, Kent, 1572 CKS PRC21/1/126
Marychurche, Stephen, Dover, Kent, 1592 CKS PRC21/11/234
Mascall, Edmund, yeoman, Kingston Seymour, Som, 1634 Somerset RO D/D/Cta/M11

[Mascall:]
Mascall, Henry, Kingston Seymour, Som, 1619 Somerset RO D/D/Cta/M23
Mascall, Humfrey, Feckenham, Worcs, Worcs RO 008.7 BA3585/839/375
Mascall, James, innholder, Ashford, Kent, 1625 CKS PRC2/25/
Mascall, James, innholder, Ashford, Kent, 1625 CKS PRC2/25/162
Mascall, John, Chart nr Sutton Valence, Kent, 1616 CKS PRC2/22/49
Mascall, John, Deal, Kent, 1670 CKS PRC19/4/85
Mascall, Nicholas, labourer, Kingsnorth, Kent, 1674 CKS PRC2/36/98
Mascall, Robert, Chart nr Sutton Valence, Kent, 1627 CKS PRC20/8/317
Mascall, Wynefride, widow, Canterbury St Paul, Kent, 1599 CKS PRC2/10/159
Masefield, Benjamin, victualler, Birmingham, Warks, 1777 LJRO/B/C/5/1777/26
Maseley, see Mansley,
Maselyne, Robert, Lydd, Kent, 1592 CKS PRC21/11/165
Masengarbe, Phillip, bachelor, Canterbury St Alphege, Kent, 1694 CKS PRC19/5/21
Masey, John, Holte, Worcs, Worcs RO 008.7 BA3585/838/181
Mashborne, Edward, bachelor, Brackley St Peter, Northants, Northants RO NWill A/C/118
Maskall, John, Chart nr Sutton Valence, Kent, 1594 CKS PRC2/7/67
Maslin, Edward, Cannings, All, Wilts, 1617 Wilts RO Arch. Wilts.(+ name and date)
Maslin, John, Durrington, Wilts, 1621 Wilts RO Arch. Wilts.(+ name and date)
Mason, Ann, widow, St Martin in the Fields, London & Middlesex, 1728 Greater London RO AM/CP/Box 1671-1728 pt (uncatalogued)
Mason, Anne, widow, Maidstone, Kent, 1620 CKS PRC20/4/280
Mason, Arthur, East Sutton, Kent, 1627 CKS PRC20/8/333
Mason, Arthure, Gonerby, Lincs, 1611 Lincs RO Ad/Ac/10/10
Mason, Edward, Marden, Kent, 1630 CKS PRC2/30/103
Mason, Frances, widow, Milton next Sittingbourne, Kent, 1675 CKS PRC2/36/94
Mason, Francis, Bredon, Worcs, 1685 Worcs RO 008.7 BA3585/837/bdl 4
Mason, George, husbandman, Bosworth, Market, Leics, 1672 Leics RO Administrators Accounts 1667-72 f69
Mason, George, bachelor, Brabourne, Kent, 1682 CKS PRC2/40/60
Mason, Isaac, Hampton in Arden, Warks, 1672 LJRO:cards/1672/38
Mason, Jane, Stafford, Staffs, 1684 LJRO/B/C/5/1684/55
Mason, John, St Johns Thanet, Kent, 1585 CKS PRC2/3/301
Mason, John, Aldermaston, Berks, 1605 Berks RO D/A1/203/264B
Mason, John, Eastwell, Kent, 1622 CKS PRC2/24/10
Mason, John, Stickney, Lincs, 1637 Lincs RO Ad/Ac/25/398
Mason, John, Lincoln St Peter at Gowts, Lincs, 1638 Lincs RO Ad/Ac/25/73
Mason, John, Pinnalls, Leics, 1672 Leics RO Administrators Accounts 1667-72 f90
Mason, John, yeoman, Boughton under Blean, Kent, 1683 CKS PRC20/13/358
Mason, John, Hemingford Abbots, Hunts, 1700 Hunts RO/Acc58/288
Mason, Margaret, widow, Leake, Lincs, 1632 Lincs RO Ad/Ac/23/128
Mason, Margaret, spinster, St Neot, Corn, 1634 Cornwall RO AP/M523/1
Mason, Mary, widow, Tottenham (High Cross), London & Middlesex, 1756 Greater London RO DL/C/554/25/1
Mason, Nicholas, Petworth, Sussex, 1673 W. Suss RO EpI/33/1673/11
Mason, Phillip, Lydd, Kent, 1585 CKS PRC21/7/256
Mason, Richard, Kirton, Lincs, 1613 Lincs RO Ad/Ac/12/149
Mason, Richard, clergy: 'clerk', Bighton, Hants, 1623 Hants RO 21M65 D8/32
Mason, Richard, Leake, Lincs, 1632 Lincs RO Ad/Ac/23/18
Mason, Richard, Chislet, Kent, 1638 CKS PRC2/34/241
Mason, Richard, victualler, Herne, Kent, 1676 CKS PRC20/12/211
Mason, Robert, Mumby, Lincs, 1620 Lincs RO Ad/Ac/15/217
Mason, Robert, husbandman, Toft, Lincs, 1620 Lincs RO Ad/Ac/16/65
Mason, Robert, husbandman, Horsington, Lincs, 1640 Lincs RO Ad/Ac/27/58
Mason, Samuel, Faldingworth, Lincs, 1663 Lincs RO Ad/Ac/41/79
Mason, Thomas, weaver: 'worsted weaver', Morston, Norf, Norfolk RO ANW/23/11/27

Mason, Thomas, Marden, Kent, 1612 CKS PRC2/17/344
Mason, Thomas, Boothby, Lincs, 1645 Lincs RO Ad/Ac/28/193
Mason, Thomas, Legbourne, Lincs, 1645 Lincs RO Ad/Ac/28/146
Mason, Thomas, Sutton Coldfield, Warks, 1669 LJRO:cards/1669/10
Mason, Thomas, Quadring, Lincs, 1670? Lincs RO Ad/Ac/32/187
Mason, Thomas, Ulceby, Lincs, 1712 Lincs RO Ad/Ac/45/23
Mason, Walter, Shrewsbury St Mary, Shrops, 1664 LJRO:cards/1664/11
Mason, William, Goxhill, Lincs, 1636 Lincs RO Ad/Ac/24/504
Mason, William, Sutton in the Marsh, Lincs, 1638 Lincs RO Ad/Ac/25/351
Mason, William, yeoman, Leeds, Kent, 1662 CKS PRC1/9/40
Mason/Alderson/Thompson, Thomasin, widow, Moulton, Lincs, 1612 Lincs RO Ad/Ac/11/10
Mason/Cassildine, Nicholas, Somerby, Lincs, 1639? Lincs RO Ad/Ac/26/116
Mason, see Redman,
Masselin, Richard, Windsor, New, Berks, 1612 Berks RO D/A1/203/284B
Massey, Alice, widow, Barrow, Ches, 1661 Cheshire RO (Name) W.C. 1661
Massey, George, gentleman, Woodhall, Lincs, 1669 Lincs RO Ad/Ac/33/98
Massey, Hugh, Aldford (Edgerley), Ches, 1625 Cheshire RO (Name) W.C. 1624
Massey, Robert, gentleman, Northampton, Northants, 1679 Northants RO NWill A/C/49
Massie, George, Drayton, Market, Shrops, 1674 LJRO:cards/1674/31
Massie, William, Stoke upon Tern, Shrops, 1674 LJRO:cards/1674/32
Massinger, Robert, gentleman, Lincoln St Michael, Lincs, 1672 Lincs RO Ad/Ac/34/7
Master, Dionys, Ashford, Kent, 1605 CKS PRC2/15/245
Master, Edward, gentleman, Lydd, Kent, 1642 CKS PRC19/2/62
Master, Edward eld, esquire, Willesborough, Kent, 1669 CKS PRC1/14/75
Master, Elizabeth, widow, Langley, Kent, 1676 CKS PRC2/37/65
Master, Elizabeth, spinster, Yarmouth, Great, Norf, 1735 Norfolk RO ANW/23/21/58
Master, John, Newington next Hythe, Kent, 1615 CKS PRC2/22/43
Master, Nicolas, Staplehurst, Kent, 1592 CKS PRC2/6/272
Master, Peter, mercer, Cranbrook, Kent, 1669 CKS PRC1/14/76
Master, Phillip, butcher, Ivychurch, Kent, 1618 CKS PRC20/4/246
Master, Thomas, gentleman, Deal, Kent, 1629 CKS PRC20/8/345
Master, William, Tenterden, Kent, 1597 CKS PRC2/11/115
Master, William, Chart nr Sutton Valence, Kent, 1598 CKS PRC2/9/395
Master, William, Willesborough, Kent, 1633 CKS PRC2/32/84
Masterman, John, mr, Ripon, Yorks, 1780 Borthwick Test C.P. 1780/6
Masters, Edward, Rustington (West Preston), Sussex, 1673 W. Suss RO EpI/33/1673/9
Masters, James, clergy: 'clerk', Bath, Som, 1667 Somerset RO D/D/Cta/M26
Masters, John, Ferring, Sussex, 1614 W. Suss RO EpI/33/1613/9
Masters, John, Hartlip, Kent, 1663 CKS PRC19/3/15
Masters, John, yeoman, Broadwater, Sussex, 1673 W. Suss RO EpI/33/1673/10
Masters, Thomas, Ilchester, Som, 1620 Somerset RO D/D/Cta/M3
Masters, Thomas, Hartlip, Kent, 1628 CKS PRC2/29/70
Masterson, John, Sandwich, Kent, 1620 CKS PRC2/22/30
Mastin, Robert, Moulton, Lincs, 1613 Lincs RO Ad/Ac/12/19
Maston, John, Frodingham, Lincs, 1652 Lincs RO Ad/Ac/40/182
Matcham, Agnes, Shepherdswell alias Sibertswold, Kent, 1605 CKS PRC2/14/319
Matcham, Roger, Coldred, Kent, 1638 CKS PRC1/1/81
Matchett, Thomas, innholder, Norwich St Gregory, Norf, 1723 Norfolk RO NCC INV/74A/281
Mather, Georg, Bonsall, Derby, 1683 LJRO/B/C/5/1682/69
Mather, John, yeoman, Mackworth, Derby, 1816 LJRO/B/C/5/1816/27
Mather, Thomas, maltster, Abingdon, Berks, 1712 Berks RO D/A1/99/80D
Mathew, Edward, Winchfield, Hants, 1673 Hants RO 1670 AD113/2
Mathew, Elizabeth, widow, Sonning, Berks, 1631 Wilts RO Miscellaneous Index (name + date)
Mathew, Jane, widow, Hampstead Norris, Berks, 1635 Berks RO D/A1/204/41A
Mathew, Joane, widow, Hannington, Wilts, 1677 Wilts RO Miscellaneous Index (name + date)

[Mathew:]
Mathew, William, Upchurch, Kent, 1598 CKS PRC2/9/393
Mathew, see Davies,
Mathewe, Alexander, Habrough, Lincs, 1597 Lincs RO Ad/Ac/4/113
Mathewe, Humfry, Wokingham, Berks, 1637 Wilts RO Unlisted Fragment
Mathewe, James, yeoman, Hampstead Norris, Berks, 1596 Berks RO D/A1/96/258C
Mathewe, James, Ebony, Kent, 1611 CKS PRC2/17/356
Mathewe, John, Queenborough, Kent, 1608 CKS PRC2/15/239
Mathewe, John, Dean, East, Sussex, 1612 W. Suss RO EpI/33/1612/7
Mathewe, Stephen, New Romney, Kent, 1609 CKS PRC20/2/45
Mathewe, William, Wickhambreaux, Kent, 1603 CKS PRC2/14/348
Mathewe, William, yeoman, Hampstead Norris, Berks, 1629 Berks RO D/A1/204/29D
Mathewes, Allan, Linsted, Kent, 1622 CKS PRC2/24/6
Mathewes, Casshiamerus, Sandwich St Peter, Kent, 1668 CKS PRC1/13/79
Mathewes, James, Herne, Kent, 1632 CKS PRC20/9/288
Mathewes, John, Detling, Kent, 1634 CKS PRC20/11/157
Mathews, Israel, Chilham, Kent, 1680 CKS PRC2/39/71
Mathews, John, yeoman, Smarden, Kent, 1674 CKS PRC2/36/97
Mathews, John, Chilham, Kent, 1690 CKS PRC2/41/181
Mathews, Mary, widow, Oxford St Thomas, Oxon, 1678 Oxon RO MSS Wills 45/2/9
Mathews, Robert, Detling, Kent, 1631 CKS PRC20/9/11
Mathews, Robert, carpenter: 'ships carpenter', Dover, Kent, 1680 CKS PRC20/13/48
Mathewson, Thomas, St Thomas Isle of Harty, Kent, 1643 CKS PRC1/6/74
Matkin, Robert, Grantham, Lincs, 1638 Lincs RO Ad/Ac/25/96
Maton, Thomas, Stockton, Wilts, 1639 Wilts RO Arch. Sarum(+ name and date)
Matrevers, Gerard, Downton, Wilts, 1636 Wilts RO Arch. Sarum(+ name and date)
Matson, John, yeoman, Bircholt, Kent, 1686 CKS PRC2/41/62
Matson, Nicholas, Sandwich St Clement, Kent, 1600 CKS PRC2/11/119
Matthew, Richard, Wytham, Berks, 1594 Berks RO D/A1/203/241C
Matthew, Thomas, Atworth, Wilts, 1632 Wilts RO Arch. Sarum(+ name and date)
Matthew/Davis, Thomas, husbandman, Speen, Berks, 1633 Berks RO D/A1/204/36A
Matthewe, William, Wilton, Wilts, 1669 Wilts RO Arch. Sarum(+ name and date)
Matthewes, Edwarde, Bracebridge, Lincs, 1627 Lincs RO Ad/Ac/20b/22
Matthewes, Gregory, victualler, Dover, Kent, 1640 CKS PRC19/1/62
Matthews, Jeremiah, Marlborough, Wilts, 1692 Wilts RO CC Sarum(+ name and date)
Matthews, John, Morton, Lincs, 1627 Lincs RO Ad/Ac/20b/109
Matthews, John, yeoman, Oxford St Martin, Oxon, 1635 Oxon RO MSS Wills 83/3/41
Matthews, Richard, Rolvenden, Kent, 1638 CKS PRC2/34/237
Matthews, Simon, Hothfield, Kent, 1639 CKS PRC1/1/82
Matthews, Thomas/Jane, shipwright, Bristol St Mary Redcliffe, Glos, Bristol RO 1764/CP
Matthews, William, mason: 'freemason', Balscott, Oxon, 1730 Oxon RO MSS Wills 170/4/7
Matthews, William, farmer, Pattingham, Staffs, 1817 LJRO/B/C/5/1817/62
Matthews, William, farmer, Pattingham, Staffs, 1817 LJRO/B/C/5/1817/64
Matticke, Robert, Cheverell, Great, Wilts, 1672 Wilts RO Arch. Sarum(+ name and date)
Mattingley, Joan, widow, Binfield, Berks, 1663 Berks RO D/A1/204/85A
Mattingley, Marian, widow, Windsor, New, Berks, 1621 Berks RO D/A1/204/6C
Mattingley, Richard, yeoman, Waltham St Lawrence, Berks, 1640 Berks RO D/A1/204/56C
Mattinglie, Jone, widow, Wokingham, Berks, 1596 Wilts RO Miscellaneous Index (name + date)
Mattocke, Thomas, Westbourne (Aldsworth), Sussex, 1643 W. Suss RO EpI/33/1643/6
Mattrys, Robarte, Cranbrook, Kent, 1586 CKS PRC2/4/366
Mattson, George, Sotwell, Berks, 1614 Wilts RO CC Sarum(+ name and date)
Maude, Charles, clergy: 'mr/rector', Sandhurst, Kent, 1723 CKS PRC1/18/43
Maukham/Nicholas, John, Sandwich, Kent, 1667 CKS PRC1/12/61
Mauley/Manley, William, Dudley, Worcs, 1684 Worcs RO 008.7 BA3585/837/bdl 4
Maultbie, Agnes, Willoughton, Lincs, 1624 Lincs RO Ad/Ac/8c/81
Maultbie, Thomas, milliner, Ashby, Lincs, 1632 Lincs RO Ad/Ac/23/37

Maulton, Roger, Toft Next Newton, Lincs, 1639 Lincs RO Ad/Ac/26/324
Maund, Anthony, clergy: 'parson', Wheatfield, Oxon, 1630 Oxon RO MSS Wills 83/3/36
Maund, Nicholas, gentleman, Wendlebury, Oxon, 1669 Oxon RO MSS Wills 83/4/23
Maunder, George, carpenter, Claydon, Oxon, 1692 Oxon RO MSS Wills Pec 46/3/17
Maunder, Richard, clergy: 'clerk', Norton Malreward, Som, 1741 Somerset RO D/D/Cta/M17
Maundey, William, Folkestone, Kent, 1598 CKS PRC2/10/290
Maundey, William, jurat/mr, Sandwich, Kent, 1663 CKS PRC1/9/129
Maundrell, Richard, Compton Basset, Wilts, 1627 Wilts RO Arch. Wilts.(+ name and date)
Maunt, Martin, Pulborough, Sussex, W. Suss RO EpI/33/1617/3
Maunton, Richard, Waithe, Lincs, 1559 Lincs RO Ad/Ac/1/1
Maunton, William, Saxilby, Lincs, 1608 Lincs RO Ad/Ac/37/261
Maure, William, Spilsby, Lincs, 1680 Lincs RO Ad/Ac/34/65
Maurice, John, yeoman, Maer (Maer Heath), Staffs, 1670 LJRO:cards/1670/50
Maw, Edward, Gainsborough (Walkerith), Lincs, 1646 Lincs RO Ad/Ac/40/119
Maw, John, Epworth, Lincs, 1662 Lincs RO Ad/Ac/41/51
Maw, Robert, Belton, Lincs, 1681 Lincs RO Ad/Ac/34/99
Maw, Sarah, widow, Epworth, Lincs, 1664 Lincs RO Ad/Ac/41/142
Maw, Thomas, Butterwick, Lincs, 1681 Lincs RO Ad/Ac/34/70
Mawde, James, labourer, Spridlington, Lincs, 1625 Lincs RO Ad/Ac/39/202
Mawe, Robert, Epworth, Lincs, 1616 Lincs RO Ad/Ac/8b/296
Mawe, Thomas, husbandman, Haxey, Lincs, 1666 Lincs RO Ad/Ac/41/176
Mawer, Augustin, labourer, Withern, Lincs, 1670 Lincs RO Ad/Ac/32/170
Mawer, Edward, Thornton, Lincs, 1642 Lincs RO Ad/Ac/28/51
Mawer, Francis, Torksey, Lincs, 1683 Lincs RO Ad/Ac/44/22
Mawer, George, Anderby, Lincs, 1600 Lincs RO Ad/Ac/5/501
Mawer, John, husbandman, Burgh le Marsh, Lincs, 1623 Lincs RO Ad/Ac/18/41
Mawer, Margarett, widow, Trusthorpe, Lincs, 1638 Lincs RO Ad/Ac/25/341
Mawer, Richard, Tattershall, Lincs, 1595 Lincs RO Ad/Ac/5/268
Mawer, Steven, Frieston, Lincs, 1649 Lincs RO Ad/Ac/30/163
Mawer, Thomas, Mumby, Lincs, 1614 Lincs RO Ad/Ac/13/147
Mawer, William, Willoughby, Lincs, 1612 Lincs RO Ad/Ac/11/120
Mawer, Willyam, Cumberworth, Lincs, 1645 Lincs RO Ad/Ac/28/127
Mawle, John, Hawkhurst, Kent, 1636 CKS PRC2/33/90
Mawlum, Robert, yeoman, Sibsey, Lincs, 1614 Lincs RO Ad/Ac/13/115
Mawson, Christopher, yeoman, Luddington, Lincs, 1625 Lincs RO Ad/Ac/39/154
Maxefield, Edmunde, Chart, Great, Kent, 1592 CKS PRC2/5/281
Maxey, John, Wyberton, Lincs, 1637 Lincs RO Ad/Ac/24/409
Maxoile, John, Hogsthorpe, Lincs, 1624 Lincs RO Ad/Ac/19A/113
Maxrell, Samuell, Firsby, Lincs, 1637 Lincs RO Ad/Ac/25/563
Maxted, Agnes, widow, Chilham, Kent, 1584 CKS PRC2/3/212
Maxted, Alice, Boughton under Blean, Kent, 1639 CKS PRC20/11/123
Maxted, Arnold, Blean, Kent, 1594 CKS PRC2/6/438
Maxted, Edmond, Minster in Thanet, Kent, 1616 CKS PRC2/22/58
Maxted, Edward, yeoman, Herne, Kent, 1676 CKS PRC20/12/214
Maxted, Henry, yeoman, Chartham, Kent, 1641 CKS PRC1/5/4
Maxted, Henry, yeoman, Stowting, Kent, 1681 CKS PRC2/39/206
Maxted, John, Reculver, Kent, 1637 CKS PRC20/11/113
Maxted, John, yeoman, Faversham, Kent, 1693 CKS PRC2/42/46
Maxted, John, Chart, Great, Kent, 1701 CKS PRC1/16/34
Maxted, John, grazier, Eythorne, Kent, 1710 CKS PRC1/17/34
Maxted, Robert, Boughton under Blean, Kent, 1620 CKS PRC20/5/127
Maxted, Robert, husbandman, Chilham, Kent, 1692 CKS PRC2/42/44
Maxted, Thomas, Ospringe, Kent, 1596 CKS PRC2/8/91
Maxted, Thomas, yeoman, Chislet, Kent, 1672 CKS PRC2/35/153
Maxted, Thomazine, St Laurence Thanet, Kent, 1627 CKS PRC2/28/84

[Maxted:]
Maxted, William, Otterden, Kent, 1634 CKS PRC2/32/161
Maxted, William, Canterbury St Peter, Kent, 1639 CKS PRC1/3/14
Maxtede, Henry, Thanington, Kent, 1599 CKS PRC2/10/319
May, Agnes, Storrington, Sussex, 1627 W. Suss RO EpI/33/1627/1
May, Alexander, yeoman, Alvescot, Oxon, 1681 Oxon RO MSS Wills 83/4/37
May, Alice, widow, Wallingford St Leonard, Berks, 1633 Berks RO D/A1/204/37C
May, Catherine, widow, Ivychurch, Kent, 1621 CKS PRC20/5/123
May, Charles, confectioner, Hull, Yorks, 1831 Borthwick Test C.P. 1831/5
May, Daniel, Bersted, South, Sussex, 1639 W. Suss RO EpIV/10/2/19
May, Edmund, Staple next Wingham, Kent, 1620 CKS PRC20/4/274
May, Edward, Waddingham (St Mary), Lincs, 1604 Lincs RO Ad/Ac/37/188
May, George, tailor, Pluckley, Kent, 1690 CKS PRC2/41/180
May, Henry, carpenter, Canterbury St Mary Northgate, Kent, 1639 CKS PRC1/3/15
May, Israel, Malmesbury, Wilts, 1759 Wilts RO Miscellaneous Index (name + date)
May, James, Boughton Monchelsea, Kent, 1616 CKS PRC2/22/50
May, James, yeoman, Clewer, Berks, 1640 Berks RO D/A1/97/191C
May, John, Fulstow, Lincs, 1627 Lincs RO Ad/Ac/20b/58
May, John, gentleman, Canterbury St Paul, Kent, 1633 CKS PRC2/32/89
May, John, Sandwich, Kent, 1637 CKS PRC1/1/53
May, John, Stourmouth, Kent, 1663 CKS PRC1/9/130
May, John, yeoman, Bicester, Oxon, 1667 Oxon RO MSS Wills 83/4/15
May, John, St Nicholas at Wade, Kent, 1695 CKS PRC19/5/36
May, John, mercer/draper, Nottingham, Notts, 1810 Borthwick Test C.P. 1810/9
May, John + Elizabeth, Kington, West, Wilts, 1639 Wilts RO Arch. Wilts.(+ name and date)
May, John eld, Brookland, Kent, 1675 CKS PRC2/36/220
May, Mary, widow, St Johns Thanet, Kent, 1670 CKS PRC1/15/43
May, Matthew, Northbourne, Kent, 1621 CKS PRC2/26/105
May, Peter, Brookland, Kent, 1586 CKS PRC2/3/327
May, Phillip, Bicker, Lincs, 1614 Lincs RO Ad/Ac/13/78
May, Ralph, Ashford, Kent, 1622 CKS PRC2/26/113
May, Reynold, gentleman, High Halden, Kent, 1631 CKS PRC2/31/51
May, Richard, Canterbury All Saints, Kent, 1625 CKS PRC20/7/247
May, Richard, Kewstoke, Som, 1687 Somerset RO D/D/Cta/M18
May, Richard eld, Shadoxhurst, Kent, 1603 CKS PRC2/14/346
May, Robert, yeoman, Sutterton, Lincs, 1627 Lincs RO Ad/Ac/20b/113
May, Robert, Melksham, Wilts, 1634 Wilts RO Arch. Sarum(+ name and date)
May, Robert, Shadoxhurst, Kent, 1668 CKS PRC1/13/80
May, Robert, gentleman, Brookland, Kent, 1677 CKS PRC2/37/66
May, Samuel, Uphill, Som, 1611 Somerset RO D/D/Cta/M46
May, Solomon, Ulcombe, Kent, 1675 CKS PRC2/36/96
May, Thomas, Canterbury St Margaret, Kent, 1583 CKS PRC2/3/136
May, Thomas, St Johns Thanet, Kent, 1616 CKS PRC2/22/53
May, Thomas, Sutton, Lincs, 1628 Lincs RO Ad/Ac/20b/71
May, Thomas, brewer, St Johns Thanet, Kent, 1665 CKS PRC1/11/57
May, Thomas, victualler, Faversham, Kent, 1683 CKS PRC2/40/134
May, Thomas, gentleman, Rodmersham, Kent, 1693 CKS PRC2/42/43
May, Thomazine, widow, Bethersden, Kent, 1639 CKS PRC1/3/16
May, William, Woolhampton, Berks, Berks RO D/A1/204/2A
May, William, Hythe St Leonard, Kent, 1585 CKS PRC21/7/195
May, William, St Breward, Corn, 1613 Cornwall RO AP/M222/3
May, William, Boughton Monchelsea, Kent, 1619 CKS PRC2/26/117
May, William, Warehorne, Kent, 1679 CKS PRC2/38/161
May/Bottomly, Margaret, wife, Kingston Bagpuize, Berks, 1641 Berks RO D/A1/177/98A
Maydens, John, Brinkhill, Lincs, 1615 Lincs RO Ad/Ac/13/50
Maydwell, James, St Bride, London & Middlesex, 1714 Greater London RO DL/C/546/57

Maydwell, Richard, Bosworth, Market, Leics, 1672 Leics RO Administrators Accounts 1667-72 f76
Maye, Abraham, Lydd, Kent, 1583 CKS PRC21/6/339
Maye, Amye, Hothfield, Kent, 1602 CKS PRC2/12/451
Maye, Edward, Worle, Som, 1644 Somerset RO D/D/Cta/M36
Maye, Elizabeth, widow, Deal, Kent, 1591 CKS PRC21/11/44
Maye, Henry,
Wilts 1614 Wilts RO Arch. Sarum(+ name and date)
Maye, Henrye, Loose, Kent, 1613 CKS PRC20/2/545
Maye, John, Stratfield Mortimer, Berks, 1594 Berks RO D/A1/203/242C
Maye, John, Wittersham, Kent, 1594 CKS PRC21/13/22
Maye, John, St Mewan, Corn, 1611 Cornwall RO AP/M166/3
Maye, John, Sherbourne?, Dors?, early C17th? Wilts RO Miscellaneous Index (name + date)
Maye, Moses, Worth, Kent, 1605 CKS PRC20/1/49
Maye, Phillip, Potterne, Wilts, 1612 Wilts RO CC Sarum(+ name and date)
Maye, Richard, Shadoxhurst, Kent, 1618 CKS PRC2/22/37
Maye, Richard eld, Shadoxhurst, Kent, 1602 CKS PRC1/1/2
Maye, Thomas, Sholden, Kent, 1585 CKS PRC2/3/261
Maye, Thomas, Staple next Wingham, Kent, 1596 CKS PRC21/14/57
Maye, Thomas, Newchurch, Kent, 1609 CKS PRC20/2/37
Maye, Thomas, husbandman, Ashampstead, Berks, 1616 Berks RO D/A1/203/293B
Maye, Valentine, clergy: 'mr/vicar', Hackington, Kent, 1607 CKS PRC2/14/324
Maye, William, Worth, Kent, 1597 CKS PRC21/14/93
Maye/Mayowe, Edmonde, Smarden, Kent, 1586 CKS PRC2/4/23
Mayer, John, Wimborne Minster, Dors, Dorset RO PE/WM CP 2/4/90
Mayer, John, gentleman, Mareham on the Hill (Mareham Grange), Lincs, 1670 Lincs RO Ad/Ac/32/199
Mayer, Robert, Salisbury, Wilts, 1626 Wilts RO Miscellaneous Index (name + date)
Mayes, Jane, widow, Somerton, Som, 1729 Somerset RO D/D/Cta/M16
Mayes, Joseph, farmer, Hail Weston, Hunts, Hunts RO/Acc58/339
Mayham, John, Sandwich, Kent, 1612 CKS PRC2/16/172
Mayham, Richard, Canterbury St Mildred, Kent, 1640 CKS PRC1/5/5
Mayham, William, yeoman, Woodchurch, Kent, 1629 CKS PRC20/8/339
Mayho, John, husbandman, St Columb Major, Corn, 1606 Cornwall RO AP/M23/2
Mayhowe, Thomas, St Columb Minor, Corn, 1608 Cornwall RO AP/M115/3
Maylam, Thomas, Thornham, Kent, 1625 CKS PRC2/25/98
Maynard, Henry, gentleman, St Enoder, Corn, 1648 Cornwall RO AP/M716/2
Maynard, Hugh, gentleman, Leeds, Kent, 1680 CKS PRC2/38/162
Maynard, Jane, spinster, Northampton St Peter, Northants, 1673 Northants RO NWill A/C/51
Maynard, Joseph, esquire, St Anne Westminster, London & Middlesex, 1701 PRO PROB32/43/34
Maynard, Thomas, clothier ?, Tenterden, Kent, 1636 CKS PRC2/33/82
Maynarde, Jeames, Appledore, Kent, 1606 CKS PRC2/14/323
Maynarde, Lucy, widow, Appledore, Kent, 1616 CKS PRC2/22/42
Mayne, Agnes, widow, Holbeach, Lincs, 1623 Lincs RO Ad/Ac/18/2
Mayne, Francis, Weston by Welland, Northants, 1685 Northants RO NWill A/C/163
Mayne, William, Deal, Kent, 1671 CKS PRC20/12/21
Maynerd, Thomas, Compton Martin, Som, 1601 Somerset RO D/D/Cta/M47
Maynie, John, Preston next Wingham, Kent, 1595 CKS PRC2/7/148
Mayo, Rebecca, widow, Sandwich St Clement, Kent, 1626 CKS PRC2/25/90
Mayo, William, Somerford, Great, Wilts, 1622 Wilts RO Arch. Wilts.(+ name and date)
Mayot, Richard, yeoman, Norton in the Moors, Staffs, 1709 LJRO/B/C/5/1709/87
Mayott, John jun, apothecary/gentleman, Abingdon, Berks, 1692 Berks RO D/A1/98/170H
Mayott, Richard, gentleman, Abingdon, Berks, 1614 Berks RO D/A1/203/298B
Mayow, Richard, Marden, Kent, 1617 CKS PRC2/22/51
Mayowe, see Maye,

[Mayre:]
Mayre, Thomas, Dover, Kent, 1626 CKS PRC20/7/203
Maysie, John, husbandman, Langford (Grafton), Oxon, 1690 Oxon RO MSS Wills Pec 78/4/8
Maytam, Joseph, Selling, Kent, 1633 CKS PRC2/32/88
Maytam, Thomas, Chart, Great, Kent, 1611 CKS PRC2/16/209
Maytham, William, New Romney, Kent, 1583 CKS PRC21/6/344
Maythame, Henry, Woodchurch, Kent, 1573 CKS PRC21/2/52
Mazarde, John, Pickworth, Lincs, 1607 Lincs RO Ad/Ac/8a/123
McKewn, Gilbert, St Andrew Holborn, London & Middlesex, 1728 Lambeth Palace Arches G98/1
Me, Philipp, fishmonger/citizen,
London & Middlesex 1667 PRO PROB5/1730
Meacocke, John, Brailsford, Derby, 1680 LJRO:cards/1680/25
Mead, James, surgeon: 'barber-surgeon', Canterbury Holy Cross Westgate, Kent, 1716 CKS PRC1/18/10
Mead, John, Milton next Sittingbourne, Kent, 1632 CKS PRC2/31/131
Mead, Nicholas eld, Ash next Sandwich, Kent, 1617 CKS PRC20/4/272
Mead, Thomas, Langford, Steeple, Wilts, 1646 Wilts RO Arch. Sarum(+ name and date)
Mead, Thomas, St George Hanover Square, London & Middlesex, 1769 Greater London RO DL/C/555/101/2
Meade, Ann, widow, Canterbury Holy Cross Westgate, Kent, 1701 CKS PRC1/16/35
Meade, George, tailor, Tenterden, Kent, 1640 CKS PRC1/5/6
Meade, George, tailor, Tenterden, Kent, 1674 CKS PRC2/36/90
Meade, Mary, widow, Dover, Kent, 1634 CKS PRC20/11/147
Meade, Nicholas, Avebury (Beckhampton), Wilts, 1663 Wilts RO Miscellaneous Index (name + date)
Meade, Richard, Irby, Lincs, 1641 Lincs RO Ad/Ac/27/342
Meade, Robert, husbandman, Crowell, Oxon, 1644 Oxon RO MSS Wills 170/2/20
Meadewe, John, St Albans St Michaels, Herts, 1632 Herts RO ASA25/4885
Meadhop, John, clothier, Witney, Oxon, Oxon RO MSS Wills 83/3/50
Meadman, John, Whitstable, Kent, 1617 CKS PRC20/4/258
Meadman, Thomas, labourer, Bicester, Oxon, 1631 Oxon RO MSS Wills 299/1/48
Meadmar, Edward, Chislet, Kent, 1627 CKS PRC2/28/87
Meadowes, Robert, Stamford, Lincs, 1623 Lincs RO Ad/Ac/17/105
Meadowes, William, Fleet, Lincs, 1623 Lincs RO Ad/Ac/18/57
Meager, John, Poundstock, Corn, 1614 Cornwall RO AP/M236/4
Meager, Thomas, Marhamchurch, Corn, 1642 Cornwall RO AP/M665/3
Meakes, Richard, surgeon: 'barber-surgeon', Cambridge, Cambs, CUL V.C.Acc./Box1/36
Meakyn/Williamson, William, Stanton, Derby, 1683 LJRO/B/C/5/1682/61
Meanley, Robert, Heckington, Lincs, 1625 Lincs RO Ad/Ac/19B/95
Means, John, Canterbury Holy Cross Westgate, Kent, 1678 CKS PRC2/38/52
Meapham, George, St Johns Thanet, Kent, 1600 CKS PRC2/11/121
Mearce, John, Snitterfield, Warks, 1681 Worcs RO 008.7 BA3585/830/50
Meares, Anthonie, gentleman, Markby, Lincs, 1613 Lincs RO Ad/Ac/12/32
Mearly, Walter, husbandman, Swallowcliffe, Wilts, 1616? Wilts RO Dean Sarum (name + date)
Mears, John, clothier, Corsley, Wilts, 1746 Wilts RO Arch. Sarum(+ name and date)
Meas, Elizabeth, Kimbolton (Wornditch), Hunts, 1684 Hunts RO/Acc58/220(268)
Meassman, Pyrone/Parnell, widow, Canterbury, Kent, 1613 CKS PRC2/17/79
Meastday, Christopher, Canterbury, Kent, 1638 CKS PRC2/34/243
Meate, John, Ramsey, Hunts, 1676 Hunts RO/Acc58/36(137)
Medam, see Kendall,
Medames, Thomas, Broughton, Oxon, 1669 Oxon RO MSS Wills 170/2/26
Medcalf, James, Spalding, Lincs, 1612/13? Lincs RO Ad/Ac/11/84
Medcalfe, Abell, Sandwich, Kent, 1615 CKS PRC2/22/39
Medcalfe, Edmund, Benenden, Kent, 1591 CKS PRC2/5/283
Medcalfe, Mary, widow, New Romney, Kent, 1684 CKS PRC20/13/356
Medcalfe, Simon, Bapchild, Kent, 1614 CKS PRC2/18/21

[Medherst:]

Medherst, Alice, Staplehurst, Kent, 1595 CKS PRC2/7/189
Medherst, Andrewe, Headcorn, Kent, 1612 CKS PRC2/16/175
Medherst, Danyell, Sutton Valence, Kent, 1598 CKS PRC2/9/391
Medherst, Mathew, Staplehurst, Kent, 1674 CKS PRC2/36/95
Medhurst, Daniel, Maidstone, Kent, 1701 CKS PRC19/5/80
Medhurst, John, mason, Linsted, Kent, 1677 CKS PRC2/37/178
Medkins, John, husbandman, Lenham, Kent, 1679 CKS PRC2/38/158
Medley, Anthony, Louth, Lincs, 1662 Lincs RO Ad/Ac/42/35
Medley, Elizabeth, Belton, Lincs, 1682 Lincs RO Ad/Ac/44/16
Medley, John, Loose, Kent, 1631 CKS PRC20/9/284
Medley, Robert, gentleman, Haxey (East Lound), Lincs, 1664 Lincs RO Ad/Ac/41/140
Medley, Thomas, Maidenhead, Berks, 1609 Berks RO D/A1/203/271C
Medley, William, bachelor, Elsham, Lincs, 1627 Lincs RO Ad/Ac/20b/85
Medlicot, Elizabeth, widow, Bermondsey, St Mary Magdalen, Surrey, 1666 Lambeth Palace Arches G18/3
Medlicott, Richard, clergy: 'clerk', Monkton Farleigh, Wilts, 1695? Wilts RO CC Sarum(+ name and date)
Meed, George, Canterbury, Kent, 1597 CKS PRC21/14/199
Meede, Richard,
Kent 1683 CKS PRC2/40/59
Meeres, Thomas, Graveney, Kent, 1676 CKS PRC2/37/68
Meggatt, Edmund, Butterwick, Lincs, 1642 Lincs RO Ad/Ac/41/114
Meggatt, Edward, Luddington, Lincs, 1675 Lincs RO Ad/Ac/35/91
Meggott, Robert, Belton, Lincs, 1682 Lincs RO Ad/Ac/34/88
Melksham, William, Chippenham, Wilts, 1631 Wilts RO Arch. Wilts.(+ name and date)
Mell, Dorothie, Friskney, Lincs, 1615 Lincs RO Ad/Ac/13/13
Mell, John, clergy: 'clerk', Gunby, Lincs, 1640 Lincs RO Ad/Ac/26/239
Mell, Richard, Friskney, Lincs, 1638 Lincs RO Ad/Ac/25/116
Mell, William, Friskney, Lincs, 1618 Lincs RO Ad/Ac/14/28
Mellers, Robert, Bardney, Lincs, 1611 Lincs RO Ad/Ac/10/51
Mellers, William, Linch, Sussex, 1670 W. Suss RO EpI/33/1669/7
Mellersh, Richard, Fernhurst, Sussex, 1598 W. Suss RO EpI/33/1598/4
Mellinge, Grace, widow, Eccleston, Lancs, 1667 Lancs RO (Name of Deceased) D.R.C.H. 1667
Mellor, Hannah, spinster, Stockport, Ches, 1799 Cheshire RO (Name) W.C. 1799
Mellor, Henry, Alstonfield, Staffs, 1682 LJRO/B/C/5/1681/27
Mellor, William, farmer, Ashbourne (Offcoate Underwood), Derby, 1806 LJRO/B/C/5/1806/93
Mellors, Joseph, yeoman, Coningsby, Lincs, 1619 Lincs RO Ad/Ac/15/139
Mellow, John, Kennington, Kent, 1635 CKS PRC2/32/162
Mellowe, William, Old Romney, Kent, 1608 CKS PRC2/14/340
Mellowes, Richard, Gedney, Lincs, 1631 Lincs RO Ad/Ac/23/116
Melsham, Robert, Chippenham, Wilts, 1620 Wilts RO Arch. Wilts.(+ name and date)
Melson, Thomas, Hale, Great, Lincs, 1648 Lincs RO Ad/Ac/30/323
Melton, Humfrey, Coningsby, Lincs, 1629 Lincs RO Ad/Ac/22/106
Melton, John, Barkwith, East, Lincs, 1612 Lincs RO Ad/Ac/11/70
Melton, Matthew, Helpringham, Lincs, 1632 Lincs RO Ad/Ac/23/100
Melton, Philipp, Barkwith, West, Lincs, 1613 Lincs RO Ad/Ac/12/162
Melton, Richard, Kirkby on Bain (Tumby Woodside), Lincs, 1625 Lincs RO Ad/Ac/19B/111
Melton, William, Ludford, Lincs, 1622 Lincs RO Ad/Ac/17/92
Melton, William, Goulceby, Lincs, 1646 Lincs RO Ad/Ac/28/167
Mence, William, Worcester St John Bedwardine (Wick Episcopi), Worcs, 1682 Worcs RO 008.7 BA3585/837/bdl 3
Mendam, Robert, Warehorne, Kent, 1627 CKS PRC2/28/80
Menday, John, bookseller, Thame, Oxon, 1685 Oxon RO MSS Wills Pec 46/3/10
Menfeilde, Elizabeth, Graveney, Kent, 1606 CKS PRC2/13/285
Menfeilde, John ygr, Whitstable, Kent, 1614 CKS PRC2/15/246

[Menfield:]
Menfield, Stephen, Hernhill, Kent, 1614 CKS PRC20/3/75
Menis/Mennyce, Mathewe, mayor, late esquire, Sandwich, Kent, 1610 CKS PRC1/1/14
Mennas, Jeremy, Aldington, Kent, 1618 CKS PRC20/4/250
Mennes, Thomas, mr, Sandwich St Peter, Kent, 1634 CKS PRC2/32/82
Mennyce, see Menis,
Mentell, Richard, Hilton, Hunts, 1684 Hunts RO/Acc58/233(253)
Menvel, Stephen, Elmsted, Kent, 1639 CKS PRC1/3/17
Menvilde, Thomas, Whitstable, Kent, 1601 CKS PRC2/12/254
Meolls, Thomas, clergy: 'curate', Barnham, Sussex, 1617 W. Suss RO EpI/33/1617/2
Meopham, Thomas, Minster in Sheppey, Kent, 1685 CKS PRC2/40/219
Mercer, Elizabeth, widow, Goudhurst, Kent, 1636 CKS PRC2/33/89
Mercer, James, Linton, Kent, 1624 CKS PRC2/24/22
Mercer, John, Selling, Kent, 1600 CKS PRC2/11/117
Mercer, John, Dunsby, Lincs, 1608 Lincs RO Ad/Ac/8a/134
Mercer, Lawrence, Minster in Sheppey, Kent, 1613 CKS PRC2/18/135
Mercer, Richard, Hartlip, Kent, 1613 CKS PRC2/18/136
Mercer, Robert, minor, Newington next Sittingbourne, Kent, 1623 CKS PRC2/24/20
Mercer, Robert, blacksmith, Sheffield, Yorks, 1774 Borthwick Test C.P. 1774/2
Mercer, Sarah, spinster, Derby, West, Lancs, 1700 Lancs RO (Name of Deceased) D.R.C.H. 1700
Mercer, Symon, minor, Newington next Sittingbourne, Kent, 1623 CKS PRC2/24/19
Mercer, Thomas, Orlestone, Kent, 1624 CKS PRC2/24/21
Mercer, Thomas, Rodmersham, Kent, 1625 CKS PRC2/25/100
Mercer, Thomas, chandler: 'tallow chandler', Chester, Ches, 1627 Cheshire RO (Name) W.C. 1627
Mercer, Thomas, Goudhurst, Kent, 1719 CKS PRC1/18/22
Mercer, William, husbandman, Hardwick, Oxon, 1640 Oxon RO MSS Wills 170/2/13
Mercer, William, carpenter, Kenardington, Kent, 1670 CKS PRC1/15/44
Merceron, Catherine, Bethnal Green, London & Middlesex, 1815 Greater London RO DL/C/575/100/2
Merchant, John, Dover, Kent, 1600 CKS PRC21/16/160
Merchant, William, Wells St Cuthbert, Som, 1598 Somerset RO D/D/Cta/M40
Merchant, see Jennings,
Mercocke?, Ralphe, Ashby de la Zouch, Leics, 1665 Leics RO Administrators Accounts C17th f4
Meredith, David, New Romney, Kent, 1709 CKS PRC19/6/32
Meredith, William, lighterman, Brentford, Old, London & Middlesex, 1755 Greater London RO DL/C/554/17
Merell, Symon, Goudhurst, Kent, 1573 CKS PRC2/1/75
Mereweather, William, Potterne, Wilts, 1683 Wilts RO CC Sarum(+ name and date)
Merewether, Alice, Cheverell, Great, Wilts, 1596 Wilts RO Arch. Sarum(+ name and date)
Merewether, Ann, spinster, Hilperton, Wilts, 1630? Wilts RO Arch. Sarum(+ name and date)
Meriam, Judith, Sandwich, Kent, 1667 CKS PRC1/12/62
Meritt, John, Davington, Kent, 1632 CKS PRC2/31/137
Merrett, William, Bridgewater, Som, 1676 Somerset RO D/D/Cta/M22
Merriam, John, mercer, Maidstone, Kent, 1676 CKS PRC20/12/213
Merriam, William, Harrietsham, Kent, 1616 CKS PRC2/22/62
Merriam, William, Minster in Thanet, Kent, 1620 CKS PRC2/22/56
Merriam, William, 1584, St Nicholas at Wade see Forstall, John
Merricke, Jeremiah, yeoman, Charing, Kent, 1679 CKS PRC20/12/313
Merricke, John, Wimborne Minster, Dors, 1639 Dorset RO PE/WM CP 2/4/55
Merriott, John, Stockton, Wilts, 1673 Wilts RO Arch. Sarum(+ name and date)
Merriott, Richard, Portsmouth, Hants, 1663 Hants RO 21M65 D8/174
Merritt, John eld, Ash next Sandwich, Kent, 1625 CKS PRC20/7/245
Merritt, William, Saltwood, Kent, 1673 CKS PRC20/12/91
Merry, Francis, Hinckley, Leics, 1673 Leics RO Administrators Accounts 1667-72 f124
Merryam, George, carpenter, Marden, Kent, 1640 CKS PRC1/5/7a

Merryam, George, Marden, Kent, 1641 CKS PRC1/5/7
Merryam, John, Maidstone, Kent, 1609 CKS PRC20/2/104
Merryam, Thomas, Goudhurst, Kent, 1599 CKS PRC2/11/113
Merryam, William, Boughton Monchelsea, Kent, 1627 CKS PRC2/27/105
Merryman, Roger, Appledore, Kent, 1597 CKS PRC2/10/78
Mersaile, James, wool comber, Canterbury All Saints, Kent, 1710 CKS PRC1/17/35
Merser, James, St Nicholas at Wade, Kent, 1601 CKS PRC21/15/168
Merser, Thomas, Dover, Kent, 1573 CKS PRC21/1/208
Mersh, John, Brabourne, Kent, 1633 CKS PRC2/31/133
Mersh, Richard, Saltwood, Kent, 1632 CKS PRC20/11/159
Mersh, Thomas, Gosport, Hants, 1623 Hants RO 21M65 D8/31
Mersh, see Jupp,
Mershe, Augustin, husbandman, Dean, West, Wilts, 1634? Wilts RO CC Sarum(+ name and date)
Mershe, Elizabeth, widow, Coldred, Kent, 1609 CKS PRC2/14/331
Mershe, Henry, Dover, Kent, 1590 CKS PRC21/10/165
Mershe, Ingram, Great Mongeham, Kent, 1592 CKS PRC2/5/279
Mershe, Robert, miller, Patching, Sussex, 1640 W. Suss RO EpIV/10/2/25
Mershe, Winter, Wingham, Kent, 1590 CKS PRC21/10/62
Mershee, John eld, Canterbury St Peter, Kent, 1672 CKS PRC20/12/23
Mersher, Elise, Washington, Sussex, 1650 W. Suss RO EpI/33/1650/1
Mersher, George, Birdham, Sussex, 1682 W. Suss RO EpI/33/1682/37
Mersher, Henry, Midhurst, Sussex, 1679 W. Suss RO EpI/33/1678/9
Merth, see Hanmer,
Meryall, Wyllyam, Cranbrook, Kent, 1596 CKS PRC2/9/156
Merydyn, Edward, Elstree, Herts, 1561 Herts RO ASA25/502
Meryfield, George, university: 'Fellow of St John's College, Oxford', Oxford (St John's College), Oxon, 1673 Bodleian HYP B9/20-21
Meryham, William, St Nicholas at Wade, Kent, 1584 CKS PRC21/7/403
Meryman, Thomas, Alkborough, Lincs, 1592 Lincs RO Ad/Ac/37/16
Merywether, Thomas, Saxilby, Lincs, 1603 Lincs RO Ad/Ac/37/167
Mesdall, John, carpenter, Greenham, Berks, 1628 Berks RO D/A1/204/20C
Meseman, Nicholas, Sandwich, Kent, 1607 CKS PRC2/14/337
Mesman, Anthonye, Canterbury St Mildred, Kent, 1608 CKS PRC2/15/253
Messen, John, Ash next Sandwich, Kent, 1605 CKS PRC20/1/51
Messenger, Edward, Burbage, Leics, 1640 Leics RO PR/I/41A/45
Metcalfe, Agnes, Doddington, Kent, 1604 CKS PRC2/13/292
Metcalfe, Edward, Lincoln (Bail), Lincs, 1627 Lincs RO Ad/Ac/20b/36
Metcalfe, Roger, St Giles in the Fields, London & Middlesex, 1748 Greater London RO DL/C/551/124
Metford, John, Lyme Regis, Dors, 1637 Wilts RO Miscellaneous Index (name + date)
Metford, Martha, widow, Folkestone, Kent, 1590 CKS PRC2/5/288
Metheringham, Robert, Caythorpe, Lincs, 1613 Lincs RO Ad/Ac/12/78
Methurst, Thomas, Wittersham, Kent, 1634 CKS PRC20/11/151
Metrick, James, gentleman, Hinxhill, Kent, 1665 CKS PRC1/11/58
Mettcalf, Moyses, Croft, Lincs, 1632 Lincs RO Ad/Ac/23/109
Mettes, John, mariner, Bristol St Augustine, Glos, Bristol RO 1671/28
Mewdon, Reginald, Kea, Corn, 1633 Cornwall RO AP/M541/2
Mewe, John, cordwainer: 'shoemaker', Tenterden, Kent, 1617 CKS PRC2/22/59
Mewe, Richard, Horbling, Lincs, 1637 Lincs RO Ad/Ac/24/549a
Mewes, John, threadman, Canterbury Holy Cross Westgate, Kent, 1667 CKS PRC1/12/63
Meyer, Joseph eld, victualler, St Martin in the Fields, London & Middlesex, 1725 Greater London RO DL/C/547/111
Meyer see the Meyer,
Meynell, Thomas, clergy: 'clerk/rector/mr', Langley, Kirk, Derby, 1706 LJRO/B/C/5/1708/27
Michaelborne, John, Swalecliffe, Kent, 1632 CKS PRC2/31/130

[Michaell:]
Michaell, William, labourer, Wrangle, Lincs, 1673 Lincs RO Ad/Ac/35/11
Michaell/Lovell, William, Hythe St Leonard, Kent, 1594 CKS PRC21/12/507
Michaelmas, John, carpenter, Folkestone, Kent, 1696 CKS PRC2/42/120
Michelboorne, John, Harbledown, Kent, 1606 CKS PRC2/14/321
Michell, Agnes, Faversham, Kent, 1612 CKS PRC2/16/214
Michell, Charles sen, waterman, Southwark, St Olave, Surrey, 1675 Lambeth Palace Arches G29/3
Michell, John, yeoman, Newbury, Berks, 1674 Berks RO D/A1/204/115A
Michell, John, Great Stukeley, Hunts, 1677 Hunts RO/Acc58/98(142)
Michell, Richard, carpenter, Shinfield, Berks, 1629 Berks RO D/A1/204/28C
Michell, Thomas, Winteringham, Lincs, 1611 Lincs RO Ad/Ac/8a/337
Michell, Thomas, Wingham, Kent, 1630 CKS PRC20/9/294
Michell, Thomas, Hill, South, Corn, 1642 Cornwall RO AP/M682/6
Michell, William, Crewkerne, Som, 1608 Somerset RO D/D/Cta/M34
Michell, William, alderman, Lincoln, Lincs, 1625 Lincs RO Ad/Ac/19A/140
Michell, William, Maker, Corn, 1629 Cornwall RO AP/M486/3
Michell, William, Broad Chalke, Wilts, 1661 Wilts RO Arch. Sarum(+ name and date)
Micklam, Grace, widow, Littlehampton, Sussex, 1684 W. Suss RO EpI/33/1684/46
Micklam, John, Walberton, Sussex, 1671 W. Suss RO EpI/33/1671/13
Micklethwayte, George, gentleman, Lincoln (The Close), Lincs, 1671 Lincs RO Ad/Ac/42/37
Mico, Samuell, knight, St Andrew Undershaft, London & Middlesex, 1671 PRO PROB5/840
Middelton, Rafe, Bilsington, Kent, 1597 CKS PRC2/10/25
Middlemore, Henry, Lusby, Lincs, 1671 Lincs RO Ad/Ac/33/196
Middlemore, John, Norton, Kings, Worcs, 1683 Worcs RO 008.7 BA3585/837/bdl 3
Middleton, Ann, widow, Linsted, Kent, 1625 CKS PRC2/25/95
Middleton, George, Queenborough, Kent, 1625 CKS PRC2/24/1
Middleton, John, clergy: 'mr/clerk', Ivychurch, Kent, 1623 CKS PRC20/6/312
Middleton, John, earl, Governor of Tangier, 1683 PRO PROB32/24/89
Middleton, John, Deal, Kent, 1706 CKS PRC19/6/22
Middleton, John eld, Tilehurst, Berks, 1618 Berks RO D/A1/204/3A
Middleton, Myles, Barton on Humber, Lincs, 1618 Lincs RO Ad/Ac/14/106
Middleton, Susann, widow, Canterbury St Paul, Kent, 1620 CKS PRC2/22/31
Middleton, Thomas, Frampton, Lincs, 1632 Lincs RO Ad/Ac/23/145
Middleton, Thomas, yeoman, Sileby, Leics, 1673 Leics RO Administrators Accounts 1667-72 f95
Middleton, Thomas, victualler, Dover, Kent, 1675 CKS PRC20/12/178
Middleton, William, New Romney, Kent, 1603 CKS PRC21/17/53
Middleton, William, Thornham, Kent, 1637 CKS PRC2/33/85
Middleton, William, bricklayer, Tilehurst, Berks, 1640 Berks RO D/A1/97/192D
Midlebrook, William, Croydon, Kent, 1641 Lincs RO Ad/Ac/27/171
Midlebrooke, John, Swineshead, Lincs, 1674 Lincs RO Ad/Ac/34/26
Midleton, Edward, university: 'scholar's servant', Cambridge St Andrew, Cambs, 1629 CUL V.C. Acc./Box2/50
Midleton, John, High Halden, Kent, 1623 CKS PRC2/24/8
Midleton, Thomas, Canterbury, Kent, 1639 CKS PRC2/34/239
Miffin, Ambrose, Horncastle, Lincs, 1597 Lincs RO Ad/Ac/4/129
Mighill, George, yeoman, Barrow, Lincs, 1648 Lincs RO Ad/Ac/30/350
Mighill, Nicholas, Wroughton, Wilts, 1640 Wilts RO Arch. Wilts.(+ name and date)
Mighill, Walter, chandler, Newington, South, Oxon, 1666 Oxon RO MSS Wills 83/4/12
Mihill, George, Chichester, Sussex, 1616 W. Suss RO EpIII/9/1/13
Mihill, Robert, Willesborough, Kent, 1598 CKS PRC2/10/408
Milam, William, Heckfield, Hants, 1716 Hants RO 1714 B38/2
Milborne, Edward, husbandman, Charing, Kent, 1633 CKS PRC20/11/149
Milbourne, John, husbandman, Staplehurst, Kent, 1668 CKS PRC1/13/81
Mile, John, Charing, Kent, 1641 CKS PRC19/2/28
Miles, Augustine, husbandman, Sunningwell, Berks, 1639 Berks RO D/A1/204/57A

Miles, Cressant, Challow, East, Berks, 1610 Berks RO D/A1/203/276A
Miles, John, Thakeham, Sussex, 1630 W. Suss RO EpI/33/1630/29
Miles, Margaret, Molash, Kent, 1607 CKS PRC2/15/257
Miles, Richard, Kenardington, Kent, 1681 CKS PRC2/39/202
Miles, Richard, Whitstable, Kent, 1708 CKS PRC1/16/67
Miles, Thomas, Whitstable, Kent, 1726 CKS PRC1/18/44
Miles, William, Milton next Sittingbourne, Kent, 1606 CKS PRC2/13/276
Miles, William, Boston, Lincs, 1638 Lincs RO Ad/Ac/25/175
Miles, William, Bedworth, Warks, 1720 LJRO/B/C/5/1720/33b
Milford, John, Halstow, Lower, Kent, 1671 CKS PRC1/15/45
Milksted, Thomas, Herne, Kent, 1606 CKS PRC20/1/203
Mill, Walter, Stratton, Corn, 1616 Cornwall RO AP/M242/3
Mill, William, St Minver, Corn, 1648 Cornwall RO AP/M753/4
Millard, Ambrose, Chewton Mendip, Som, 1622 Somerset RO D/D/Cta/M32
Millard, Daniel, labourer, Newington, Oxon, 1683 Bucks R.O. MSS Wills Pec 80/2/8
Millard, Hannah, Brent, East, Som, 1701 Somerset RO D/D/Cta/M37
Millard, Henry, Compton Martin, Som, 1611 Somerset RO D/D/Cta/M33
Millard, Philip, Bawdrip, Som, 1640 Somerset RO D/D/Cta/M28
Millard, Thomas, Boxgrove, Sussex, 1682 W. Suss RO EpI/33/1682/52
Millard, William, innholder, Wells St Cuthbert, Som, 1644 Somerset RO D/D/Cta/M30
Millard, see Roberts,
Millen, Anne, widow, New Romney, Kent, 1687 CKS PRC20/13/561
Millen, John, Westwell, Kent, 1608 CKS PRC20/1/241
Millen, John, maltster, Ashford, Kent, 1680 CKS PRC2/39/70
Millen, Robert, Westwell, Kent, 1640 CKS PRC19/1/63
Millen, Robert, Westwell, Kent, 1692 CKS PRC19/5/3
Millen, Thomas, Orlestone, Kent, 1633 CKS PRC2/32/87
Millen, Thomas, Westwell, Kent, 1679 CKS PRC20/12/314
Millen, William, Boughton under Blean, Kent, 1613 CKS PRC20/2/362
Miller, Edward, Newchurch, Kent, 1592 CKS PRC21/12/159
Miller, Edward, carpenter, Snave, Kent, 1686 CKS PRC2/41/60
Miller, Elizabeth, Goudhurst, Kent, 1680 CKS PRC2/39/72
Miller, John, Dover, Kent, 1614 CKS PRC20/3/83
Miller, John, Rainham, Kent, 1629 CKS PRC2/30/97
Miller, John, Wimborne Minster (Barnsley), Dors, 1630 Dorset RO PE/WM CP 2/4/44
Miller, John, Crewkerne, Som, 1642 Somerset RO D/D/Cta/M24
Miller, John, clothier, Goudhurst, Kent, 1679 CKS PRC2/38/54
Miller, John, Proctor General of the Arches Court of Canterbury, 1705 Lambeth Palace Arches G55/2
Miller, Margaret, widow, Bobbing, Kent, 1675 CKS PRC2/36/224
Miller, Mary, widow, Herne, Kent, 1630 CKS PRC20/8/343
Miller, Nicholas, Fittleworth, Sussex, 1596 W. Suss RO EpI/33/1596/10
Miller, Rafe, Canterbury Holy Cross Westgate, Kent, 1593 CKS PRC2/6/262
Miller, Ralph, painter, Sparsholt (Farlow), Berks, 1617 Berks RO D/A1/203/301B
Miller, Richard, Wallop, Over, Hants, 1624 Hants RO 21M65 D8/76
Miller, Robert, carpenter, Stamford All Saints, Lincs, 1666? Lincs RO Ad/Ac/32/103
Miller, Robert, Whitacre, Over, Warks, 1682 LJRO/B/C/5/1682/70
Miller, Thomas, Rainham, Kent, 1595 CKS PRC2/7/455
Miller, Thomas, Canterbury St Alphege, Kent, 1617 CKS PRC20/4/264
Miller, Thomas, gentleman, Chart nr Sutton Valence, Kent, 1628 CKS PRC20/8/327
Miller, Thomas, yeoman, Waltham St Lawrence, Berks, 1682 Berks RO D/A1/204/139D
Miller, Valentine, yeoman, Swinford, Leics, 1672 Leics RO Administrators Accounts 1667-72 f88
Miller, William, Wye, Kent, 1607 CKS PRC2/14/333
Miller, William, clergy: 'clerk', Faversham, Kent, 1610 CKS PRC2/15/233
Miller, William, Swalecliffe, Kent, 1616 CKS PRC2/22/54

[Miller:]
Miller, William, yeoman, Sturry, Kent, 1626 CKS PRC2/25/92
Miller, William, Loddington, Leics, 1666 Leics RO Administrators Accounts C17th f56
Miller/Filles, William, yeoman, Broad Hinton, Wilts, 1650 Wilts RO CC Sarum(+ name and date)
Miller, see Wells,
Millerd, Edward, Barwick, Som, 1621 Somerset RO D/D/Cta/M1
Millerd, Elizabeth, widow, Bristol St James, Glos, Bristol RO 1665/36
Millerd, Joan, Compton Martin, Som, 1619 Somerset RO D/D/Cta/M38
Millerd, Richard, miller, Compton Martin, Som, 1621 Somerset RO D/D/Cta/M5
Milles, Andrewe, Avebury, Wilts, 1674 Wilts RO Miscellaneous Index (name + date)
Milles, Edwarde, Headcorn, Kent, 1593 CKS PRC2/6/218
Milles, Henry, Swineshead, Lincs, 1624 Lincs RO Ad/Ac/19A/8
Milles, Isaac, glazier, Petworth, Sussex, 1630 W. Suss RO EpI/33/1630/27
Milles, John, Brookland, Kent, 1611 CKS PRC2/17/168
Milles, John, Barford, Wilts, 1625? Wilts RO Miscellaneous Index (name + date)
Milles, John, Harting (Hurst), Sussex, 1632 W. Suss RO EpI/33/1632/12
Milles, John, yeoman, Coxwell, Little, Berks, 1671 Berks RO D/A3/3/142
Milles, Joseph, Canterbury St Andrew, Kent, 1670 CKS PRC1/15/46
Milles, Nicholas, husbandman, Thame (Moreton), Oxon, 1682 Oxon RO MSS Wills Pec 46/3/1
Milles, Richard, Hothfield, Kent, 1609 CKS PRC1/1/9
Milles, Richard, Petworth (Strond), Sussex, 1633 W. Suss RO EpI/33/1632/32
Milles, Robert, Marsh Chapel, Lincs, 1612 Lincs RO Ad/Ac/11/25
Milles, Robert, husbandman, Hagbourne, Berks, 1637 Berks RO D/A1/204/48C
Milles, Robert, Boxley, Kent, 1639 CKS PRC1/5/8
Milles, Stephen, miller/yeoman, Chilham, Kent, 1669 CKS PRC1/14/78
Milles, Stephen, miller/yeoman, Chilham, Kent, 1669 CKS PRC1/14/78a
Milles, Thomas, Wisborough Green, Sussex, 1640 W. Suss RO EpI/33/1640/21
Milles, William, Burpham, Sussex, 1598 W. Suss RO EpI/33/1597/14
Milles, William, St Johns Thanet, Kent, 1602 CKS PRC2/12/252
Milles, William, Brookland, Kent, 1609 CKS PRC20/2/49
Milles, William, Brookland, Kent, 1611 CKS PRC2/17/165
Milles, see Saunders,
Millet, Dorithy, widow, Bolingbroke, Old, Lincs, 1664 Lincs RO Ad/Ac/43/41
Millett, Thomas, Boarhunt, Hants, 1670 Hants RO 21m65 D8/219
Milliars, Peter, Sandwich, Kent, 1635 CKS PRC2/33/80
Millicent, Francis, Sutton St Edmunds, Lincs, 1627 Lincs RO Ad/Ac/20/91
Millicent, George, apothecary, Reading, Berks, 1641 Berks RO D/A1/204/61C
Millington, Alice, widow, Chester St Oswald (Huntington), Ches, 1636 Cheshire RO (Name) W.C. 1635/6
Millington, Anthony, Gedney, Lincs, 1611 Lincs RO Ad/Ac/10/17
Millington, Edward, Withington, Shrops, 1684 LJRO/B/C/5/1684/56
Millington, Edward, Sheffield (Owlerton), Yorks, 1767 Borthwick Test C.P. 1767/2
Millington, John, Hognaston, Derby, 1683 LJRO/B/C/5/1682/71
Millington, Thomas, Bosham, Sussex, 1676 W. Suss RO EpI/33/1676/7
Millington, Tymothy, Claxby Pluckacre, Lincs, 1651 Lincs RO Ad/Ac/29/78
Million, Anthony, Hythe St Leonard, Kent, 1606 CKS PRC20/1/101
Millner, Anne, Luddington, Lincs, 1598 Lincs RO Ad/Ac/37/90
Millner, William, Carlton, Great, Lincs, 1619 Lincs RO Ad/Ac/15/213
Millner, William, Tamworth, Staffs, 1680 LJRO:cards/1680/26
Mills, Catherine, widow, Pulborough, Sussex, 1619 W. Suss RO EpI/33/1619/12
Mills, Edward, Hawkhurst, Kent, 1603 CKS PRC2/14/345
Mills, Elizabeth, widow, Herne, Kent, 1670 CKS PRC19/4/56
Mills, Henrie, Boxley, Kent, 1612 CKS PRC2/16/41
Mills, Henry, Coldwaltham (Watersfield), Sussex, 1627 W. Suss RO EpI/33/1627/5
Mills, Hugh, Milston, Wilts, 1685 Wilts RO Arch. Sarum(+ name and date)
Mills, John, Amesbury, Wilts, 1619 Wilts RO Miscellaneous Index (name + date)

[Mills:]

Mills, John, Duncton, Sussex, 1629 W. Suss RO EpI/33/1629/18
Mills, John, Ewell, Kent, 1632 CKS PRC2/31/132
Mills, John ygr, cordwainer: 'shoemaker', Lilford (Wigthorpe), Northants, 1786 Northants RO X954/22/15
Mills, Joseph, baker, Bristol, Glos, Bristol RO 1729/26
Mills, Joseph, Minster in Sheppey, Kent, 1716 CKS PRC1/18/11
Mills, Mary, Bullington, Hants, 1663 Hants RO 21M65 D8/175
Mills, Richard, Hawkhurst, Kent, 1616 CKS PRC2/22/52
Mills, Richard, St Johns Thanet, Kent, 1636 CKS PRC2/33/93
Mills, Richard, Bethersden, Kent, 1637 CKS PRC2/34/81
Mills, Stephen, miller, Wickhambreaux, Kent, 1671 CKS PRC2/35/73
Mills, Stephen, Lodsworth, Sussex, 1676 W. Suss RO EpI/33/1676/19
Mills, Thomas, Thornham, Kent, 1620 CKS PRC2/22/63
Mills, Thomas, esquire, Davington, Kent, 1628 CKS PRC20/8/323
Mills, William, Spalding, Lincs, 1641 Lincs RO Ad/Ac/27/293
Mills, William, Claines, Worcs, 1678 Worcs RO 008.7 BA3585/830/93
Mills, William, Hardham, Sussex, 1684 W. Suss RO EpI/33/1684/31
Millsham, John, Backwell, Som, 1619 Somerset RO D/D/Cta/M31
Millward, Peter, St Albans St Peters (London Colney), Herts, 1609 Herts RO ASA25/4772
Millward, Thomas, St Giles without Cripplegate, London & Middlesex, 1712 PRO PROB5/1584
Millward, William, Doveridge, Derby, 1667 LJRO:cards/1667/58
Milner, Charles, yeoman, Normanton, Lincs, 1670 Lincs RO Ad/Ac/43/55
Milner, Henry, Gedney, Lincs, 1607 Lincs RO Ad/Ac/8a/131
Milner, Phillipp, husbandman, Metheringham, Lincs, 1670 Lincs RO Ad/Ac/32/209
Milner, Richard, gentleman, Willoughby, Lincs, 1605 Lincs RO Ad/Ac/6/101
Milner, Roberte, Luddington, Lincs, 1595 Lincs RO Ad/Ac/37/19
Milner, Thomas, High Halstow, Kent, 1676 CKS PRC2/37/67
Milner, William, Gayton le Marsh, Lincs, 1629 Lincs RO Ad/Ac/22/28
Milner, William, Gonerby, Great, Lincs, 1784 Lincs RO Ad/Ac/45/49
Milnes, Francys, chapman, Wragby, Lincs, 1614 Lincs RO Ad/Ac/13/218
Milnes, Richard, Chesterfield, Derby, 1682 LJRO/B/C/5/1682/73
Milsome, Jacob, victualler, Bristol Temple, Glos, Bristol RO 1762/CP
Milson, Eustace, Killingholme, Lincs, 1579 Lincs RO Ad/Ac/2b/61
Milson, George, Cadney, Lincs, 1648 Lincs RO Ad/Ac/30/341
Milson, Richard, Scartho, Lincs, 1612 Lincs RO Ad/Ac/10/125
Milson, Robert, Habrough, Lincs, 1630 Lincs RO Ad/Ac/22/89
Milson, Thomas, Killingholme, Lincs, 1640 Lincs RO Ad/Ac/27/124
Milsted, John, yeoman, Shadoxhurst, Kent, 1679 CKS PRC2/38/51
Milsted, Richard, Bethersden, Kent, 1638 CKS PRC2/34/244
Milton, James + Isabell, Whalley (Rough Lee), Lancs, 1626 Lancs RO (Name of Deceased) D.R.C.H. 1626
Milton, Thomas, Fordwich, Kent, 1614 CKS PRC20/3/77
Milward, Ellen, widow, Uttoxeter, Staffs, 1705 LJRO/B/C/5/1706/90
Milward, John, Chart nr Sutton Valence, Kent, 1613 CKS PRC2/18/124
Milward, John, Bassingham, Lincs, 1637 Lincs RO Ad/Ac/25/540
Milward, Thomas, Compton Chamberlain, Wilts, 1628 Wilts RO Arch. Sarum(+ name and date)
Minchin, George, baker, Leafield, Oxon, 1634 Oxon RO MSS Wills 83/3/38
Minet, Susan, widow, Dover, Kent, 1688 CKS PRC20/13/616
Minety, Walter, Imber, Wilts, 1640 Wilts RO Arch. Sarum(+ name and date)
Mingay, Henry, Wootton, Norf, 1748 Norfolk RO ANF/11/4/54
Mingay, William, gentleman, Heckingham, Norf, 1732 Norfolk RO ANF/11/3/159
Minge, Henry, Hernhill, Kent, 1694 CKS PRC19/5/27
Minge, Henrye, Milton next Sittingbourne, Kent, 1613 CKS PRC2/17/381
Minge, Thomas, husbandman, Upchurch, Kent, 1664 CKS PRC1/10/64
Minge, Thomas, yeoman, Stone next Faversham, Kent, 1667 CKS PRC1/11/139

[Minishaw:]
Minishaw, Thomas, Newchurch, Kent, 1667 CKS PRC19/3/132
Minnet, William, Gosberton, Lincs, 1618 Lincs RO Ad/Ac/14/282
Minnett, William, Worlaby, Lincs, 1627 Lincs RO Ad/Ac/20b/5
Minnis, Robert, Aldington, Kent, 1640 CKS PRC19/1/64
Minors, Isack, vintner, St John the Baptist, London & Middlesex, 1679 PRO PROB32/18/176
Minshall, William, Wellington, Shrops, 1684 LJRO/B/C/5/1684/123
Minshull, Christopher, degrees: 'M.A.', Oxford (University), Oxon, 1683 Bodleian HYP B9/22-23
Minta, John, Waltham on the Wolds, Leics, 1666 Leics RO Administrators Accounts C17th f91
Minter, Bartholomew, Folkestone, Kent, 1712 CKS PRC19/6/55
Minter, Catherine, Folkestone, Kent, 1684 CKS PRC2/40/216
Minter, Hezekiah, fisherman, Folkestone, Kent, 1676 CKS PRC2/37/69
Minter, John, fisherman, Folkestone, Kent, 1688 CKS PRC2/41/99
Minter, William, Ewell, Kent, 1628 CKS PRC2/29/68
Minter, William, fisherman, Folkestone, Kent, 1675 CKS PRC2/36/223
Minty, Susan, spinster, Wilton, Wilts, 1676 Wilts RO Arch. Sarum(+ name and date)
Mirfeild, William, Worlaby, Lincs, 1670 Lincs RO Ad/Ac/32/148
Missing, Christopher, blacksmith, Ashford, Kent, 1626 CKS PRC2/27/101
Missing, George, Charing, Kent, 1720 CKS PRC19/6/73
Missing, John, blacksmith, Westwell, Kent, 1681 CKS PRC20/13/173
Misson, Thomas, glover, Milton next Sittingbourne, Kent, 1625 CKS PRC2/25/97
Misterton, William, Gainsborough, Lincs, 1681 Lincs RO Ad/Ac/34/100
Mitchell, Agnes, St Laurence Thanet, Kent, 1639 CKS PRC1/1/83
Mitchell, Ann, widow, Chartham, Kent, 1641 CKS PRC1/6/2
Mitchell, David, Leysdown, Kent, 1709 CKS PRC19/6/33
Mitchell, Edward, Thornham, Kent, 1617 CKS PRC20/4/268
Mitchell, Elizabeth, widow, St Neots, Hunts, 1716 Hunts RO/Acc58/309
Mitchell, Henrie, Scarle, North, Lincs, 1627 Lincs RO Ad/Ac/20b/15
Mitchell, Henry, Selling, Kent, 1635 CKS PRC2/33/94
Mitchell, Henry, bachelor: 'singleman', Acrise, Kent, 1644 CKS PRC1/7/2
Mitchell, Henry, husbandman, Appleton (Eaton), Berks, 1682 Berks RO D/A1/204/135D
Mitchell, Jane, Old Romney, Kent, 1601 CKS PRC2/12/244
Mitchell, John, Smeeth, Kent, 1598 CKS PRC21/14/272
Mitchell, John, Gosberton, Lincs, 1611 Lincs RO Ad/Ac/10/52
Mitchell, John, butcher, Thorpe, Lincs, 1625 Lincs RO Ad/Ac/19B/68
Mitchell, John, Leysdown, Kent, 1673 CKS PRC2/35/239
Mitchell, John, victualler, Maidenhead, Berks, 1685 Berks RO D/A1/204/130D
Mitchell, Johnne, Scarle, North, Lincs, 1578 Lincs RO Ad/Ac/2b/22
Mitchell, Joseph, gardener, Reading St Giles, Berks, 1690 Berks RO D/A1/204/158C
Mitchell, Lawrence, Kirkby Green, Lincs, 1665 Lincs RO Ad/Ac/43/47
Mitchell, Margarett, Egerton, Kent, 1617 CKS PRC20/4/266
Mitchell, Mary, Dronfield, Derby, 1684 LJRO/B/C/5/1683/11
Mitchell, Mary, Lyng, Som, 1696 Somerset RO D/D/Cta/M19
Mitchell, Nicholas eld, tanner, Chartham, Kent, 1641 CKS PRC1/6/3
Mitchell, Richard, Stelling, Kent, 1602 CKS PRC2/12/248
Mitchell, Richard, St Laurence Thanet, Kent, 1627 CKS PRC2/28/82
Mitchell, Thomas, Lydd, Kent, 1586 CKS PRC21/8/54
Mitchell, Thomas, Lydd, Kent, 1606 CKS PRC20/1/93
Mitchell, Thomas, Minster in Sheppey, Kent, 1703 CKS PRC19/6/14
Mitchell, William, Sibsey, Lincs, 1624 Lincs RO Ad/Ac/19A/20
Mitchell, William, St Peter in Thanet, Kent, 1626 CKS PRC2/25/91
Mitchell, William, Maidstone, Kent, 1632 CKS PRC20/11/155
Mitchell, William, Hawkhurst, Kent, 1633 CKS PRC2/32/83
Mitchell, William, yeoman, Winteringham, Lincs, 1674 Lincs RO Ad/Ac/35/78
Mitchell, William eld, blacksmith, Ashford, Kent, 1626 CKS PRC2/27/103
Mitchell, see Lovell,

Mitchelson, Thomas, tanner, Gainsborough, Lincs, 1681 Lincs RO Ad/Ac/34/77
Mitten, Robert, Benenden, Kent, 1640 CKS PRC1/3/18
Mitten, Thomas, husbandman, Hawkhurst, Kent, 1675 CKS PRC2/36/222
Mitton, William, Tardebigge, Worcs, 1683 Worcs RO 008.7 BA3585/837/bdl 3
Moat, William, Ash next Sandwich, Kent, 1617 CKS PRC20/4/244
Moatar, Ann, spinster, Boughton under Blean, Kent, 1680 CKS PRC20/13/50
Moate, Jonathan, Gainsborough, Lincs, 1662 Lincs RO Ad/Ac/41/55
Mobbs, Isaac, Bugbrooke, Northants, 1678 Northants RO NWill A/C/136
Mobbs, William, hatter/hosier?, Birmingham, Warks, 1812 LJRO/B/C/5/1812/39
Mockernes, Elizabeth, St Laurence Thanet, Kent, 1614 CKS PRC2/18/73
Mockernes, Thomas, St Laurence Thanet, Kent, 1612 CKS PRC2/16/25
Mockernes, William, Sandwich St Peter, Kent, 1622 CKS PRC2/24/7
Mocket, Thomas, mr, Mersham, Kent, 1629 CKS PRC2/30/101
Mockett, John, Ash next Sandwich, Kent, 1667 CKS PRC19/3/133
Mockett, John, Deal, Kent, 1668 CKS PRC19/4/25
Mockett, Thomas, Lydd, Kent, 1637 CKS PRC20/11/115
Mockett, Thomas, husbandman, Sholden, Kent, 1684 CKS PRC2/40/218
Mockette, Richard, university: 'Warden of All Souls College, Oxford/D.D.', Oxford (All Souls College), Oxon, 1619 Bodleian HYP B9/24-26
Mockford, Edward, Sandhurst, Kent, 1708 CKS PRC1/17/9
Mockford/Pellet, Agnes, widow, Steyning, Sussex, 1619 W. Suss RO EpI/33/1618/5
Mockinesse, Mildred, widow, St Laurence Thanet, Kent, 1645 CKS PRC1/7/28
Mockness, Willyam, St Laurence Thanet, Kent, 1620 CKS PRC20/5/130
Modsley, William, innkeeper, Ospringe, Kent, 1626 CKS PRC2/27/98
Mogge, Christopher, Upton Lovell, Wilts, 1635 Wilts RO Arch. Sarum(+ name and date)
Moggerhead, Edward, Wokingham, Berks, 1633 Wilts RO Miscellaneous Index (name + date)
Moggeridge, John, Potterne, Wilts, 1634 Wilts RO CC Sarum(+ name and date)
Moggridge, Jane, widow, Thorne Falcon, Som, 1671 Somerset RO D/D/Cta/M20
Moggs, Thomas, Christchurch, Glos, Bristol RO 1678/71
Moise, William, mason, Herne, Kent, 1614 CKS PRC20/3/85
Molesey, Edward, St Albans, Herts, 1609 Herts RO ASA25/4773
Molland, John, cordwainer: 'shoemaker', Sandwich St Peter, Kent, 1619 CKS PRC2/22/33
Molleneux, William, labourer, Sefton (Ince Blundell), Lancs, 1674 Lancs RO (Name of Deceased) D.R.C.H. 1674-7
Mollett, see Phillip,
Mombrey, Walter, Coldred, Kent, 1592 CKS PRC2/5/302
Momford, Richard, Mawgan, Corn, 1611 Cornwall RO AP/M178/2
Moncke, Symon, Biddenden, Kent, 1598 CKS PRC2/9/359
Moncke, see Patridge,
Moncke?, Richard, Bowden, Great, Leics, 1673 Leics RO Administrators Accounts 1667-72 f134
Monckton, Michaell, gentleman, Belton (Beltoft), Lincs, 1671 Lincs RO Ad/Ac/33/210
Monday, George, brewer, Henley, Oxon, 1667 Oxon RO MSS Wills 170/2/24
Monday, Robert ygr, Sydenham, Oxon, 1669 Oxon RO MSS Wills Pec 46/2/27
Monde, Walter, Egerton, Kent, 1585 CKS PRC21/7/168
Monde, Wyllyam, Wye, Kent, 1579 CKS PRC2/1/206
Mondy, Clement, Edenham, Lincs, 1624 Lincs RO Ad/Ac/19A/104
Moneley, John, Liverpool, Lancs, Lancs RO (Name of Deceased) D.R.C.H. 1685-86
Money, Adam, yeoman, Kintbury (Holt), Berks, 1682 Berks RO D/A1/204/132E
Money, Ann, spinster, Bradfield, Berks, 1687 Berks RO D/A1/204/154D
Money, John, Saleby, Lincs, 1607 Lincs RO Ad/Ac/8a/5
Money, John, yeoman, Streatley, Berks, 1636 Berks RO D/A1/204/45A
Money, Richard, Hurst, Berks, 1636 Wilts RO Miscellaneous Index (name + date)
Money, Richard, yeoman, Thatcham, Berks, 1665 Berks RO D/A1/204/88A
Money, Robert, labourer, Threckingham, Lincs, 1670 Lincs RO Ad/Ac/32/217
Money, William, collar maker, Norwich St Gregory, Norf, 1775 Norfolk RO ANW/23/26/35

[Mongeham:]
Mongeham, Richard, Bethersden, Kent, 1662 CKS PRC1/9/41
Monger, Ezechiell, Folkestone, Kent, 1623 CKS PRC2/24/14
Monger, Patience, Faversham, Kent, 1682 CKS PRC2/40/57
Mongey, Wyllyam, Newington next Sittingbourne, Kent, 1590 CKS PRC2/5/294
Mongham, Joseph, tanner, Smarden, Kent, 1674 CKS PRC2/35/238
Monke, Thomas, butcher, Wye, Kent, 1673 CKS PRC2/35/243
Monke, William, Smarden, Kent, 1643 CKS PRC1/7/3
Monke, William, Appledore, Kent, 1690 CKS PRC19/4/119
Monkhouse, Joseph, gentleman, Brigham (Cockermouth), Cumb, 1772 Borthwick Test C.P. 1772/3
Monne, Rychard, Milton next Sittingbourne, Kent, 1582 CKS PRC2/2/75
Monnery, Robert, Tarring, West, Sussex, 1621 W. Suss RO EpIV/10/1/30
Monnsfell, Margaret, widow, Sandwich St Clement, Kent, 1608 CKS PRC2/14/342
Monson, John, esquire, Carlton, North, Lincs, 1641 Lincs RO Ad/Ac/42/34
Montioy, John, Hartlip, Kent, 1639 CKS PRC2/34/240
Mony, Margaret, Sandwich St Peter, Kent, 1626 CKS PRC2/27/111
Monyngs, John, esquire, Dover, Kent, 1557 Lambeth Palace Arches F 1 ff1-4
Moodey, Richard, Ellesmere, Shrops, 1674 LJRO:cards/1674/33
Moodey, William, Somborne, Kings, Hants, 1679 Hants RO 21m65 D8/315
Moodie, Anne, Manton, Lincs, 1632 Lincs RO Ad/Ac/39/278
Moodie, Charles, Haxey, Lincs, 1603 Lincs RO Ad/Ac/37/152
Moodie, Edmund, brewer, Haxey, Lincs, 1675 Lincs RO Ad/Ac/35/101
Moodie, George, Haxey (East Lound), Lincs, 1629 Lincs RO Ad/Ac/39/114
Moodie, Henrie, Owston, Lincs, 1616 Lincs RO Ad/Ac/8b/310
Moodie, James, Haxey, Lincs, 1639 Lincs RO Ad/Ac/43/4
Moodie, John, yeoman, Odstock, Wilts, 1645 Wilts RO Arch. Sarum(+ name and date)
Moodie, Nicholas, husbandman, Haxey, Lincs, 1607 Lincs RO Ad/Ac/37/241
Moodie, Robert, Belton, Lincs, 1662 Lincs RO Ad/Ac/41/22
Moodie, Thomas, Haxey, Lincs, 1617 Lincs RO Ad/Ac/8b/205
Moodie, William, Crowle, Lincs, 1664 Lincs RO Ad/Ac/41/150
Moodie, see Halliday,
Moody, Benjamine, Gainsborough, Lincs, 1645? Lincs RO Ad/Ac/40/116
Moody, Dorothie, Owston, Lincs, 1620 Lincs RO Ad/Ac/8b/381
Moody, John, husbandman, Farlesthorpe, Lincs, 1614 Lincs RO Ad/Ac/13/81
Moody, John, husbandman, Boyton, Wilts, 1634 Wilts RO CC Sarum(+ name and date)
Moody, John, Hibaldstow, Lincs, 1685 Lincs RO Ad/Ac/44/152
Moody, Richard eld, yeoman, Warwick, Warks, 1682 Worcs RO 008.7 BA3585/837/bdl 3
Moody, Robert, clergy: 'clerk', Partney, Lincs, 1632 Lincs RO Ad/Ac/23/140
Moody, Tristram, Boyton, Wilts, 1615 Wilts RO CC Sarum(+ name and date)
Moody, William, Owston, Lincs, 1619 Lincs RO Ad/Ac/8b/425
Moodye, William, Deal, Kent, 1574 CKS PRC21/2/181
Moonart, John, weaver?, Sandwich, Kent, 1635 CKS PRC2/33/88
Moonart, Mary, Sandwich, Kent, 1635 CKS PRC2/33/86
Moone, John, husbandman, Eastbridge, Kent, 1700 CKS PRC1/16/36
Moone, Margaret, spinster, Canterbury Archbishop's Palace, Kent, 1683 CKS PRC20/13/354
Moone, Marke, Gainsborough, Lincs, 1610 Lincs RO Ad/Ac/8a/316
Moone, Richard, Pulborough, Sussex, 1627 W. Suss RO EpI/33/1627/7
Moone, Richard, Shepherdswell alias Sibertswold, Kent, 1629 CKS PRC2/30/98
Moone, Richard, maltster, Sandwich, Kent, 1694 CKS PRC2/42/86
Moone, Robert, minor/bachelor, Snave, Kent, 1663 CKS PRC1/9/131
Moone, Thomas, Charlton Mackrell, Som, 1588 Somerset RO D/D/Cta/M15
Moone, William, Ruckinge, Kent, 1618 CKS PRC2/22/40
Moone, William, husbandman, Upchurch, Kent, 1641 CKS PRC1/6/4
Moonnes, Joan, widow, Ashford, Kent, 1614 CKS PRC2/18/109
Moor, Elizabeth, widow, Hedon, Yorks, 1735 Borthwick Test C.P. 1735/2

Moor, Richard, Burnham, Som, 1677 Somerset RO D/D/Cta/W33
Moorcocke, George, Cranbrook, Kent, 1665 CKS PRC1/11/59
Moorcocke, Joane, widow, Chart, Great, Kent, 1623 CKS PRC2/24/13
Moore, Alexander, esquire, Grantham, Lincs, 1641 Lincs RO Ad/Ac/27/243
Moore, Charles, gentleman, Gainsborough, Lincs, 1673 Lincs RO Ad/Ac/35/34
Moore, Edward, Ivychurch, Kent, 1638 CKS PRC20/11/131
Moore, Edwarde, Rolvenden, Kent, 1594 CKS PRC2/6/490
Moore, Francis, Burgh le Marsh, Lincs, 1634 Lincs RO Ad/Ac/24/27
Moore, Francis, Hanley Castle, Worcs, 1682 Worcs RO 008.7 BA3585/837/bdl 3
Moore, George, Halesowen, Worcs, 1607 Worcs RO 008.7 BA3585/839/435
Moore, George, Canterbury St Mary Northgate, Kent, 1626 CKS PRC2/25/89
Moore, George, Whitwick, Leics, 1673 Leics RO Administrators Accounts 1667-72 f111
Moore, Gervise, clergy: 'clerk', Skidbrooke, Lincs, 1671 Lincs RO Ad/Ac/33/212
Moore, Henry, Bath, Som, 1667 Somerset RO D/D/Cta/M27
Moore, Henry, Coker, West, Som, 1683 PRO PROB32/33/261
Moore, Humphry, gentleman, Aston upon Trent, Derby, 1817 LJRO/B/C/5/1817/65
Moore, James, Beesby, Lincs, 1626 Lincs RO Ad/Ac/20/25
Moore, John, Cranbrook, Kent, 1587 CKS PRC2/4/140
Moore, John, yeoman, Peasemore, Berks, 1635 Berks RO D/A1/204/42A
Moore, John, Dover, Kent, 1640 CKS PRC19/1/65
Moore, John, husbandman, High Halstow, Kent, 1641 CKS PRC1/6/5
Moore, John, Winteringham, Lincs, 1667 Lincs RO Ad/Ac/33/31
Moore, John, esquire/captain, Canterbury St Alphege, Kent, 1671 CKS PRC20/12/20
Moore, John, miller, Hartlip, Kent, 1677 CKS PRC2/37/177
Moore, John, husbandman, Chalgrove, Oxon, 1679 Oxon RO MSS Wills 170/2/31
Moore, John, Pillerton Priors, Worcs, 1684 Worcs RO 008.7 BA3585/837/bdl 4
Moore, Philip, gentleman, Steyning, Sussex, 1635 W. Suss RO EpI/33/1635/23
Moore, Phillipp, Durrington, Wilts, 1628? Wilts RO Arch. Sarum(+ name and date)
Moore, Ralf, Benenden, Kent, 1609 CKS PRC2/15/251
Moore, Richard, Seasalter, Kent, 1594 CKS PRC2/7/19
Moore, Richard, Lincoln St Benedict, Lincs, 1627 Lincs RO Ad/Ac/20/87
Moore, Richard, yeoman, Bexley, Kent, 1668 Lambeth Palace VH96/5397
Moore, Richard, carpenter, Rainham, Kent, 1679 CKS PRC2/38/50
Moore, Robert, Owston, Lincs, 1640 Lincs RO Ad/Ac/40/281
Moore, Robert, Faversham, Kent, 1670 CKS PRC1/15/47
Moore, Roger, Heytesbury, Wilts, 1597? Wilts RO Miscellaneous Index (name + date)
Moore, Thomas, Throwleigh, Kent, 1598 CKS PRC2/10/420
Moore, Thomas, Damerham, South, Wilts, 1630 Wilts RO Arch. Sarum/(+ name and date)
Moore, Thomas, Tamworth (Fazeley), Staffs, 1663 LJRO:cards/1663/44
Moore, Thomas, Scalford, Leics, 1664 Leics RO Administrators Accounts C17th f3
Moore, Thomas, clothier, Croscombe, Som, 1709 Somerset RO D/D/Cta/M21
Moore, Walter, gentleman, Binley (Earnsford), Warks, 1671 LJRO:cards/1671/7
Moore, William, mariner: 'master mariner', Whitby, Yorks, Borthwick Test C.P. 1756/3
Moore, William, Sandhurst, Kent, 1613 CKS PRC2/16/134
Moore, William, Bourne, Lincs, 1637 Lincs RO Ad/Ac/25/615
Moore, William, gentleman, Normanton, Lincs, 1672 Lincs RO Ad/Ac/43/73
Moore, William, husbandman, Winteringham, Lincs, 1672 Lincs RO Ad/Ac/34/2
Moore, William, butcher, Wymondham, Norf, 1749 Norfolk RO ANF/11/4/83
Moore, William, farmer/victualler, Aldridge (Great Barr), Staffs, 1819 LJRO/B/C/5/1819/82
Moore, William, Tempsford, Beds, C17th? Lincs RO Ad/Ac/45/105
Moore, Wyllyam, Sandhurst, Kent, 1590 CKS PRC2/5/296
Moore, see Awsten,
Moorecock, Daniel, Ashford, Kent, 1643 CKS PRC1/7/4
Moorecocke, John, Hawkhurst, Kent, 1622 CKS PRC2/24/15
Mooren, James, Salisbury, Wilts, 1631? Wilts RO Miscellaneous Index (name + date)

[Moores:]
Moores, John, Bierton (Broughton), Bucks, 1665 Oxon RO MSS Wills Pec 46/2/29
Moorewood, Francis, Arley, Warks, 1682 LJRO/B/C/5/1682/74
Moorey, Henry, Bosham, Sussex, 1630 W. Suss RO EpI/33/1629/37
Moorey, John, Felpham, Sussex, 1627 W. Suss RO EpI/33/1627/3
Moorey, John, Pagham, Sussex, 1681 W. Suss RO EpIV/10/2A/26
Moorey, Katherine, widow, Chidham, Sussex, 1674 W. Suss RO EpI/33/1673/6
Moorey/Cooke, Mary, Pagham, Sussex, 1686 W. Suss RO EpIV/10/2A/38
Moorfote, Nicholas, Ulcombe, Kent, 1593 CKS PRC2/6/89
Moorie, Thomas, Boxgrove, Sussex, 1618 W. Suss RO EpI/33/1618/10
Moorton, Joan, Leigh, Worcs, 1604 Worcs RO 008.7 BA3585/839/374
Moory, Anthony, Westhampnett (Westerton), Sussex, 1633 W. Suss RO EpI/33/1633/14
More, Edward, Syston, Lincs, 1611 Lincs RO Ad/Ac/10/118
More, Elyzabethe, Cranbrook, Kent, 1587 CKS PRC2/4/82
More, Henry, Orby, Lincs, 1612 Lincs RO Ad/Ac/11/166
More, John, High Halden, Kent, 1594 CKS PRC2/7/78
More, John,
Berks 1627 Berks RO D/A1/105/124C
More, Richard, Dorchester (Burcott), Oxon, Oxon RO MSS Wills Pec 70/1/4
More, Richard, Canterbury St Mary Northgate, Kent, 1583 CKS PRC2/3/24
More, Richard, Rolvenden, Kent, 1605 CKS PRC2/13/283
More, Richard, Bourne (Cawthorpe), Lincs, 1645 Lincs RO Ad/Ac/28/208
More, Robert, Edenham, Lincs, 1607 Lincs RO Ad/Ac/8a/133
More, Roberte, Cranbrook, Kent, 1599 CKS PRC2/10/305
More, Thomas, husbandman, Brent, South, Som, 1584 Somerset RO D/D/Cta/M44
More, Thomas, Eastry, Kent, 1592 CKS PRC21/11/288
More, Thomas, Tydd St Mary, Lincs, 1635 Lincs RO Ad/Ac/24/445
More, William, Carlton le Moorland, Lincs, 1605 Lincs RO Ad/Ac/6/103
More, William, Winthorpe, Lincs, 1607 Lincs RO Ad/Ac/8a/11
More, William, Syston, Lincs, 1611 Lincs RO Ad/Ac/10/67
More, William, Hawkhurst, Kent, 1616 CKS PRC2/22/60
Morecroft, Henry, 1618 Lancs RO (Name of Deceased) D.R.C.H. 1618
Morecrofte, John + Margaret, Upchurch, Kent, 1595 CKS PRC2/7/156
Morehall, Christopher, clothier, Worcester, Worcs, Worcs RO 008.7 BA3585/839/308
Morehall, John, Worcester, Worcs, Worcs RO 008.7 BA3585/838/81
Moreing, Grace, Salisbury, Wilts, 1672 Wilts RO Miscellaneous Index (name + date)
Morelay, Thomas, Claxby, Lincs, 1599 Lincs RO Ad/Ac/5/483
Moreley, Suzan, spinster, Grimsby, Great, Lincs, 1612 Lincs RO Ad/Ac/11/187
Morer, John, Midhurst, Sussex, W. Suss RO EpI/33/1612/2
Moreton, Elizabeth, widow, Birmingham, Warks, 1786 LJRO/B/C/5/1786/69
Moreton, John, Burton-upon-Trent, Staffs, 1698 LJRO/B/C/5/1698/72
Morey, Walter, Chidham, Sussex, 1628 W. Suss RO EpI/33/1627/4
Morfeild, Edward, butcher, Faversham, Kent, 1613 CKS PRC2/18/68
Morfeild, John, husbandman, Woodchurch, Kent, 1676 CKS PRC20/12/210
Morfoote, Peter, husbandman, Frieston, Lincs, 1624 Lincs RO Ad/Ac/19A/69
Morgan, Edward, Milton Clevedon, Som, 1623 Somerset RO D/D/Cta/M9
Morgan, Edward, Wootton Wawen, Worcs, 1684 Worcs RO 008.7 BA3585/837/bdl 4
Morgan, John, Warminster, Wilts, 1673 Wilts RO Arch. Sarum(+ name and date)
Morgan, John, labourer, Saleby, Lincs, 1679 Lincs RO Ad/Ac/43/98
Morgan, Lewis, mr, 1638 NLW BR 1637/56 Ac
Morgan, Mirrable, widow, Warminster, Wilts, 1638 Wilts RO Arch. Sarum(+ name and date)
Morgan, Thomas, yeoman, Upton, Ches, 1774 Cheshire RO (Name) W.C. 1774
Morgan, William, corn factor, Bristol, Glos, Bristol RO 1779/CP
Morgan, William, Upchurch, Kent, 1625 CKS PRC2/25/96
Morgan, William, gentleman, Chart nr Sutton Valence, Kent, 1665 CKS PRC1/11/60
Morgan, William, clergy: 'rector/Doctor of Physic', St Andrew Holborn, London & Middlesex,

1674 PRO PROB32/11/20
Morgane, Edward, Stanford, Kent, 1609 CKS PRC20/1/366
Morgayne, Frances, Chart nr Sutton Valence, Kent, 1610 CKS PRC2/15/235
Moriley, Richard, yeoman, Waltham, Lincs, 1624 Lincs RO Ad/Ac/19A/135
Morland, Gabriel, gentleman, Wye, Kent, 1619 CKS PRC2/22/35
Morland, John, Ilsley, East, Berks, 1604 Berks RO D/A1/203/274B
Morlay, Richard, Bucknall, Lincs, 1612 Lincs RO Ad/Ac/11/39a
Morlen, Robert, Tenterden, Kent, 1613 CKS PRC2/16/122
Morlen, Thomas, Benenden, Kent, 1624 CKS PRC2/26/114
Morley, George, Itchenor, West, Sussex, W. Suss RO EpI/33/1613/12
Morley, Hughe, Goudhurst, Kent, 1592 CKS PRC2/6/504
Morley, Marmaduke, gentleman, Bottesford, Lincs, 1680 Lincs RO Ad/Ac/43/158
Morley, Thomas, Tangmere, Sussex, 1627 W. Suss RO EpIV/10/1/21
Morley, Thomas, Aldbourne, Wilts, 1632 Wilts RO CC Sarum(+ name and date)
Morley, Thomas, Bersted, South, Sussex, 1680 W. Suss RO EpIV/10/2A/20
Morley, William, Rolvenden, Kent, 1582 CKS PRC2/2/83
Morne, Richard, Welford, Berks, 1604 Berks RO D/A1/203/261A
Morram, John, Wainfleet, Lincs, 1607 Lincs RO Ad/Ac/8a/132
Morrell, Francis, Algarkirk, Lincs, 1629 Lincs RO Ad/Ac/22/50
Morrell, Joseph, Duffield (Heage), Derby, 1710 LJRO/B/C/5/1710/43
Morrell, Joseph, Duffield (Heage), Derby, 1719 LJRO/B/C/5/1719/29
Morrell, Michael, Canterbury St Alphege, Kent, 1665 CKS PRC19/3/76
Morrell, Nicholas, smith, Warwick, Warks, 1705 Worcs RO 008.7 BA3585/837/bdl 6
Morrell, Richard, yeoman, Longcot, Berks, 1674 Berks RO D/A1/204/110C
Morrey, Leonard, mercer, Drayton in Hales, Staffs, 1691 LJRO/B/C/5/1691/12
Morreys, Mary, widow, Dover St Mary, Kent, 1614 CKS PRC20/2/539
Morrice, Edward, labourer, Coningsby, Lincs, 1612 Lincs RO Ad/Ac/11/172
Morrice, George, draper: 'linen draper', Axbridge, Som, 1612 Somerset RO D/D/Cta/M12
Morrice, Harry, Clevedon, Som, 1591 Somerset RO D/D/Cta/M45
Morrice, Richard, Ashbourne, Derby, 1674 LJRO:cards/1674/34
Morrice, Stephen, Cranbrook, Kent, 1611 CKS PRC2/16/111
Morrice, Thomas, Liss, Hants, 1679 Hants RO 21m65 D8/293
Morrice, see Stokar,
Morris, Abdy, clergy: 'clerk', Sellindge, Kent, 1682 CKS PRC2/39/204
Morris, Arthur, yeoman, Lambourn, Berks, 1638 Berks RO D/A1/204/53A
Morris, Christopher, Swaton, Lincs, 1607 Lincs RO Ad/Ac/8a/7
Morris, Edmunde, Wingham, Kent, 1596 CKS PRC21/14/33
Morris, Edward, yeoman, Preston next Wingham, Kent, 1673 CKS PRC2/35/156
Morris, Elizabeth, Tenterden, Kent, 1605 CKS PRC2/13/281
Morris, Elizabeth, widow, Sibsey, Lincs, 1627 Lincs RO Ad/Ac/20/110
Morris, Francis, Kimbolton, Hunts, 1684 Hunts RO/Acc58/216(220)
Morris, George, High Halden, Kent, 1635 CKS PRC2/33/92
Morris, Henry, Goudhurst, Kent, 1615 CKS PRC2/26/118
Morris, Henry, Graveney, Kent, 1632 CKS PRC2/31/136
Morris, Henrye, Graveney, Kent, 1614 CKS PRC2/18/1
Morris, James, labourer, Chilham, Kent, 1680 CKS PRC2/39/73
Morris, Jerome, Gainsborough, Lincs, 1681 Lincs RO Ad/Ac/34/85
Morris, Joan, spinster, Camel, Queen, Som, 1621 Somerset RO D/D/Cta/M13
Morris, John, St Nicholas at Wade, Kent, 1581 CKS PRC21/4/335
Morris, John, Dover, Kent, 1598 CKS PRC21/14/540
Morris, John, Grantham (Manthorpe), Lincs, 1612 Lincs RO Ad/Ac/10/163
Morris, John, Faversham, Kent, 1625 CKS PRC2/24/2
Morris, John, maltster, Henley, Oxon, 1632 Oxon RO MSS Wills 299/1/53
Morris, John, husbandman, Bobbing, Kent, 1640 CKS PRC1/5/9
Morris, John, Portishead, Som, 1644 Somerset RO D/D/Cta/M35

[Morris:]
Morris, John, Asfordby, Leics, 1666 Leics RO Administrators Accounts C17th f92
Morris, John, Chislet, Kent, 1716 CKS PRC1/18/12
Morris, John, Stepney, St Dunstan (Queen Street, Ratcliffe), London & Middlesex, 1798 Greater London RO DL/C/564/29/2
Morris, Nathan, Honeybourne, Worcs, 1685 GRO GDR/B4/2/M94
Morris, Olyver, Whitstable, Kent, 1613 CKS PRC2/16/123
Morris, Robert, Hodnet, Shrops, 1751 LJRO/B/C/5/1751/123
Morris, Samuel, Ivychurch, Kent, 1617 CKS PRC20/4/252
Morris, Samuel, victualler, Worcester, Worcs, 1779 Worcs RO 008.7 BA3585/835/bdl 2
Morris, Thomas, Hythe West, Kent, 1596 CKS PRC2/8/415
Morris, Thomas, Petworth, Sussex, 1617 W. Suss RO EpI/33/1617/27
Morris, Thomas, Frisby, Leics, 1666 Leics RO Administrators Accounts C17th f93
Morris, Thomas, yeoman, Woodnesborough, Kent, 1684 CKS PRC2/40/223
Morris, Thomas, Alton, Staffs, 1695 LJRO:cards/1695/3
Morris, Thomas, oatmeal maker, Birmingham, Warks, 1759 LJRO/B/C/5/1759/140
Morris, Thomas, labourer, Malpas (Cholmondeley), Ches, 1797 Cheshire RO (Name) W.C. 1797
Morris, William, Walton-on-the-Hill (Kirkby), Lancs, 1602 Lancs RO (Name of Deceased) D.R.C.H. 1602
Morris, William, Hawkinge, Kent, 1624 CKS PRC2/24/17
Morris, William, Buckland nr Dover, Kent, 1628 CKS PRC20/8/319
Morris, William, Wye, Kent, 1632 CKS PRC2/31/135
Morris, William, Todenham, Glos, 1685 GRO GDR/B4/2/M93
Morrison, George, Elsham, Lincs, 1627 Lincs RO Ad/Ac/20b/68
Morrison, Mary, spinster, Quadring, Lincs, 1668 Lincs RO Ad/Ac/33/54
Morrys, John, St Johns Thanet, Kent, 1584 CKS PRC2/3/38
Morrys, Thomas, Bretforton, Worcs, 1601 Worcs RO 008.7 BA3585/838/197
Morse, John, Hilmarton, Wilts, 1624 Wilts RO CC Sarum(+ name and date)
Morse, Mary, widow, Castle Eaton, Wilts, 1624 Wilts RO Arch. Wilts.(+ name and date)
Morse, William, Brent, South, Som, 1620 Somerset RO D/D/Cta/M4
Morse, William, Liddington, Wilts, 1629 Wilts RO Arch. Wilts.(+ name and date)
Mortemar, John eld, yeoman, Maidstone, Kent, 1671 CKS PRC19/4/86
Morter, Edward, High Halden, Kent, 1639 CKS PRC1/1/84
Mortimer, Anna, widow, Maidstone, Kent, 1713 CKS PRC19/6/65
Mortimer, Anne, widow, Maidstone, Kent, 1709 CKS PRC1/17/10
Mortimer, George, yeoman, Crowell, Oxon, 1683 Oxon RO MSS Wills 83/4/39
Mortimer, John, husbandman, Windsor, New, Berks, 1632 Berks RO D/A1/204/32C
Mortimer, Thomas, Overton, Wilts, 1617 Wilts RO Arch. Wilts.(+ name and date)
Morton, Edmund, yeoman, Normanby, Lincs, 1684 Lincs RO Ad/Ac/44/129
Morton, John, cutler, Sheffield, Yorks, 1834 Borthwick Test C.P. 1834/13
Morton, Oliver, miller, Bassingham, Lincs, 1671 Lincs RO Ad/Ac/32/206
Morton, Raphael, Kea, Corn, Cornwall RO AP/M337/3
Morton, Robert, Sutton in the Marsh, Lincs, 1613 Lincs RO Ad/Ac/11/48
Morton, Robert, knight, Chilham, Kent, 1637 CKS PRC1/1/54
Morton, Thomas, Huddersfield (Bradley), Yorks, Borthwick Test C.P. 1754/2
Morton, William, gentleman, Worcester St John Bedwardine, Worcs, 1779 Worcs RO 008.7 BA3585/835/bdl 2
Morton, see Gibbon,
Mortonne, William, Horncastle, Lincs, 1579 Lincs RO Ad/Ac/2b/20
Mortymer, Robert, Charlton, Wilts, 1640 Wilts RO Arch. Sarum(+ name and date)
Morwicke, Robert, Dunston, Lincs, 1641 Lincs RO Ad/Ac/27/245
Moryson, John, yeoman, Northaw, Herts, 1609 Herts RO ASA25/4768
Mose, Anthony, husbandman, Hagbourne, Berks, 1625 Berks RO D/A1/204/15C
Mose, Avis, widow, Wisborough Green, Sussex, 1684 W. Suss RO EpI/33/1684/44
Mose, Isabell, widow, Sandwich St Peter, Kent, 1609 CKS PRC2/15/255
Mose, John, Queenborough, Kent, 1608 CKS PRC2/15/243

Mose, John, Wisborough Green, Sussex, 1617 W. Suss RO EpI/33/1617/28
Moseden, John, Blackmanstone, Kent, 1586 CKS PRC2/4/374
Moseley, John, burgess: 'principal burgess', St Albans, Herts, 1617 Herts RO ASA25/4972
Mosgrave, Henrie, Haxey, Lincs, 1623 Lincs RO Ad/Ac/8c/70
Mosgrave, William, Haxey (Park), Lincs, 1650 Lincs RO Ad/Ac/40/168
Mosley, Francis, Althorpe (Amcotts), Lincs, 1604 Lincs RO Ad/Ac/37/169
Mosley, Robert, maltster, Newark on Trent, Notts, 1809 Borthwick Test C.P. 1809/10
Mosse, John, yeoman, Reading St Giles (Whitley), Berks, 1678 Berks RO D/A1/204/122D
Mosse, Richard, gentleman, Sandwich, Kent, 1681 CKS PRC2/39/203
Moswell, George, Brookland, Kent, 1638 CKS PRC1/1/55
Mote, John, Althorpe, Lincs, 1610 Lincs RO Ad/Ac/8a/312
Moter, Thomas eld, Bethersden, Kent, 1639 CKS PRC1/3/19
Motie, Peter, Whitstable, Kent, 1633 CKS PRC2/32/85
Mott, Humphrey, Stowe, Staffs, 1680 LJRO:cards/1680/27
Mott, John, gardener, Haseley, Great (Rycote), Oxon, 1662 Oxon RO MSS Wills 83/4/3
Mott, John, vintner, Shadwell, St Paul, London & Middlesex, 1705 PRO PROB32/48/83
Mott, Jonah, yeoman, Biddenden, Kent, 1699 CKS PRC2/42/157
Motteram, Henry, Uttoxeter, Staffs, 1685 LJRO/B/C/5/1684/57
Mottram, John, Donington, Lincs, 1787 Lincs RO Ad/Ac/45/55
Mottram, Richard, Croxden, Staffs, 1672 LJRO:cards/1672/39
Motye, Thomas, Wickhambreaux, Kent, 1597 CKS PRC2/10/381
Mould, Richard, Harrow on the Hill, London & Middlesex, 16898 PRO PROB32/28/199
Mould, Thomas, cordwainer: 'shoemaker', Windsor, New, Berks, 1636 Berks RO D/A1/204/43A
Mould, Thomas, Luddington, Lincs, 1670 Lincs RO Ad/Ac/32/136
Mould, William, Crowle, Lincs, 1664 Lincs RO Ad/Ac/41/125
Moulden, Jeffery, husbandman, Coleshill (Lint), Berks, 1618 Berks RO D/A1/203/297B
Moulden, John, labourer, Cumnor (Chawley), Berks, 1625 Berks RO D/A1/204/18C
Moulden, Robert, husbandman, Watchfield, Berks, 1622 Berks RO D/A1/204/7C
Moulden, William, husbandman, Watchfield, Berks, 1612 Berks RO D/A1/203/283B
Moulton, Hab, Wimborne Minster (Barford), Dors, 1672 Dorset RO PE/WM CP 2/4/76
Moulton, John, Boston, Lincs, 1620 Lincs RO Ad/Ac/16/69
Moulton, John, Boston, Lincs, 1620 Lincs RO Ad/Ac/19A/129
Moulton, Samuel, Lamas, Norf, Norfolk RO ANW/23/16/30
Moulton, William, Saltash, Corn, 1608 Cornwall RO AP/M106/2
Moulton, William, captain, 1695 PRO PROB32/38/91
Moulton, William, captain, St Giles in the Fields, London & Middlesex, 1697 PRO PROB32/37/38
Moulton, William, captain, St Giles in the Fields, London & Middlesex, 1698 PRO PROB32/36/67
Mouncke, John, Ashington, Sussex, 1631 W. Suss RO EpI/33/1630/1
Moundes, John, Selling, Kent, 1584 CKS PRC2/3/55
Mounioye, Margerye, widow, Faversham, Kent, 1613 CKS PRC2/16/143
Mounke, John, Broadwater, Sussex, 1632 W. Suss RO EpI/33/1631/20
Mounse, Richard, St Stephen by Launceston, Corn, 1605 Cornwall RO AP/M71
Mounsloe, Anne, widow, Chichester (Headacre), Sussex, 1684 W. Suss RO EpIV/10/2A/33
Mounson, Anthony, Northorpe, Lincs, 1684 Lincs RO Ad/Ac/44/130
Mounson, Robert, esquire, Northorpe, Lincs, 1639 Lincs RO Ad/Ac/40/249
Mount, John, Burmarsh, Kent, 1622 CKS PRC2/24/9
Mount, John, yeoman, Biddenden, Kent, 1642 CKS PRC1/6/75
Mount, John, Wye, Kent, 1684 CKS PRC2/40/217
Mount, Laurence, Boughton Aluph, Kent, 1680 CKS PRC2/38/160
Mount, Mildred, widow, Smeeth, Kent, 1639 CKS PRC20/11/129
Mount, Phillip, yeoman, Stowting, Kent, 1677 CKS PRC2/37/70
Mount, Raynold, Selling, Kent, 1604 CKS PRC2/13/277
Mount, Richard, yeoman, Wye, Kent, 1641 CKS PRC1/5/10

[Mount:]
Mount, Richard, yeoman, Canterbury St Mary Bredin, Kent, 1665 CKS PRC1/10/65
Mount, Richard eld, Ham, Kent, 1629 CKS PRC2/30/99
Mountague, Richard, Milton next Sittingbourne, Kent, 1611 CKS PRC2/16/207
Mountague, see Hanson,
Mountaine, Joan, Humberstone, Lincs, 1613 Lincs RO Ad/Ac/12/155
Mounte, Richard, Reculver, Kent, 1636 CKS PRC20/11/117
Mountford, Daniel, Hodnet, Shrops, 1674 LJRO:cards/1674/35
Mountford, John, miller, Prestbury, Ches, 1755 Cheshire RO (Name) W.C. 1755
Mountford, Samuel, Nuneaton, Warks, 1729 LJRO/B/C/5/1729/109
Mountigue, Thomas eld, Grandborough, Bucks, 1620 Herts RO ASA25/2704
Mountsteven, John, blacksmith, Minster in Thanet, Kent, 1677 CKS PRC2/37/176
Mourton, James, Ickham, Kent, 1603 CKS PRC21/16/69
Mowbray, Elizabeth, Halton Holgate, Lincs, 1649 Lincs RO Ad/Ac/30/203
Mowbray, Margrett, Boston, Lincs, 1637 Lincs RO Ad/Ac/25/517
Mowbrey, Margarett, Potter Hanworth, Lincs, 1639 Lincs RO Ad/Ac/26/283
Mowbrey, Richard, waterman, Nocton, Lincs, 1669 Lincs RO Ad/Ac/33/107
Mowbrey, Robert, Bardney, Lincs, 1639 Lincs RO Ad/Ac/26/233
Mowbrey, William, Sibsey, Lincs, 1666 Lincs RO Ad/Ac/32/123
Mower, George, Dronfield (Halsteads), Derby, 1701 LJRO/B/C/5/1701/77
Mower, Robert, Petworth, Sussex, 1607 W. Suss RO EpI/33/1607/14
Mowle, John, Swineshead, Lincs, 1614 Lincs RO Ad/Ac/13/201
Mownte, Gregorye, Boughton Aluph, Kent, 1611 CKS PRC2/15/248
Mownte, John, Ashford, Kent, 1597 CKS PRC2/12/453
Mownte, John, Ruckinge, Kent, 1608 CKS PRC2/14/325
Mownte, Rose, Dymchurch, Kent, 1601 CKS PRC2/12/246
Mowrton, Thomas, Adisham, Kent, 1584 CKS PRC21/7/138
Mowse, Thomas, Birchington, Kent, 1586 CKS PRC21/8/194
Mowsely, John, butcher, Walsall, Staffs, 1685 LJRO/B/C/5/1685/64
Moxham, Thomas, grocer, Bristol St Philip & St Jacob, Glos, Bristol RO 1773/CP
Moxsam, Thomas, yeoman, Broad Chalke, Wilts, 1638 Wilts RO Arch. Sarum(+ name and date)
Moyce, Joane, widow, Westwell, Kent, 1691 CKS PRC19/4/120
Moye, Simon, Stoke Prior, Worcs, Worcs RO 008.7 BA3585/839/408
Moyer, Robert, gentleman, Bourne, Lincs, 1666 Lincs RO Ad/Ac/32/106
Moyle, Robert, knight, Chart, Great, Kent, 1665 CKS PRC1/11/61
Moyne, Robart, Staple next Wingham, Kent, 1598 CKS PRC21/14/487
Moyse, Adrian, mariner, St Johns Thanet, Kent, 1684 CKS PRC2/40/132
Moyse, Adrian, mariner, St Johns Thanet, Kent, 1688 CKS PRC2/41/127
Moyse, Henry, victualler, Westwell, Kent, 1685 CKS PRC20/13/509
Moyse, John, Sandwich St Mary, Kent, 1668 CKS PRC1/13/82
Moyse, Josias, Woodchurch, Kent, 1630 CKS PRC20/9/290
Moyse, Lettyce, widow, Biddenden, Kent, 1592 CKS PRC2/5/27
Moyse, William, Minster in Sheppey, Kent, 1617 CKS PRC2/22/61
Moyses, George, St Laurence Thanet, Kent, 1626 CKS PRC2/27/102
Moyses, John, Lydd, Kent, 1579 CKS PRC21/3/318
Moyses, Robert, Boston, Lincs, 1632 Lincs RO Ad/Ac/23/87
Moyses, Thomas, Maltby le Marsh, Lincs, 1620 Lincs RO Ad/Ac/16/67
Mucklowe, William, Northfield, Worcs, 1648 Worcs RO 008.7 BA3585/837/bdl 1
Mudge, George, husbandman, Childrey, Berks, 1628 Berks RO D/A1/204/22C
Mudgett, John, bachelor, Shadwell, London & Middlesex, 1713 PRO PROB32/57/33
Muggleston, Brian, husbandman, Melbourne, Derby, 1672 LJRO:cards/1672/40
Mulcaster, John, gentleman, Langley Mill Houses, Northumb, 1839 Borthwick Test C.P. 1839/6
Mulgrove, James, Norton St Philip, Som, 1588 Somerset RO D/D/Cta/M42
Mullard, Dorothy, Myddle (Hadnall), Shrops, 1688 LJRO/B/C/5/1688/24b
Mullard, Robert, Berrington (Eaton Mascott), Shrops, 1688 LJRO/B/C/5/1688/25
Mullens, see Leeves,

Mullett, Edward, Deal, Kent, 1675 CKS PRC20/12/135
Mullett, Elizabeth, widow, Deal, Kent, 1711 CKS PRC19/6/44
Mullett, Hercules, Deal, Kent, 1678 CKS PRC20/12/270
Mullford, John, Burnham, Som, 1642 Somerset RO D/D/Cta/M29
Mullington, William, Bushley, Worcs, 1685 Worcs RO 008.7 BA3585/837/bdl 4
Mullins, Dorathy, widow, Wilton, Wilts, 1634 Wilts RO Arch. Sarum(+ name and date)
Mullins, Thomas, Donhead St Mary, Wilts, 1614 Wilts RO Arch. Sarum(+ name and date)
Mulward, Robert, Berrington, Shrops, 1674 LJRO:cards/1674/36
Mumbie, John, gentleman, Brocklesby, Lincs, 1620 Lincs RO Ad/Ac/16/66
Mumbray, William, baker, Deal, Kent, 1664 CKS PRC19/3/34
Mumby, Helen, Ormsby, North, Lincs, 1614 Lincs RO Ad/Ac/13/17
Mumery, Abraham, Eastry, Kent, 1618 CKS PRC20/4/256
Mumford, Robert, Deal, Kent, 1675 CKS PRC20/12/136
Mumford, William, husbandman, Hanwell, Oxon, 1662 Oxon RO MSS Wills 83/4/1
Mummery, Richard, Deal, Kent, 1626 CKS PRC20/7/201
Mummery, William, blacksmith, Folkestone, Kent, 1673 CKS PRC2/35/240
Mumrie, Abraham, Deal, Kent, 1670 CKS PRC19/4/87
Mun, James, Newnham, Kent, 1640 CKS PRC1/3/20
Mun, John, Biddenden, Kent, 1604 CKS PRC2/13/287
Mun, John, Acrise, Kent, 1638 CKS PRC2/34/242
Mun, Thomas, Sandhurst, Kent, 1582 CKS PRC2/2/100
Muncktone, Anthonie, Rasen, Middle, (Tupholme), Lincs, 1598 Lincs RO Ad/Ac/4/39
Mundaie, James, yeoman, Northmoor, Oxon, 1630 Oxon RO MSS Wills 83/3/37
Mundaie, John, yeoman, Stratfield Mortimer, Berks, 1631 Berks RO D/A1/204/30E
Munday, Henry, Highworth, Wilts, 1626 Wilts RO Dean Sarum (name + date)
Munday, John, Sandwich St Peter, Kent, 1612 CKS PRC2/17/210
Munday, John, yeoman, Shrivenham (Bourton), Berks, 1674 Berks RO D/A1/204/111A
Munday, John, Salisbury, Wilts, 1696 Wilts RO Miscellaneous Index (name + date)
Munday, John + Dionise, university: 'scholar's servants', Cambridge (University), Cambs, 1616 CUL V.C.Acc./Box1/37
Munday, Richard,
Wilts 1597? Wilts RO Miscellaneous Index (name + date)
Munday, Robert, yeoman, Aston Rowant (Chalford), Oxon, 1680 Oxon RO MSS Wills 83/4/33
Munday, William, Wootton Bassett, Wilts, 1625 Wilts RO Arch. Wilts.(+ name and date)
Mundy, Stephan, gentleman, St Dunstan in the West, London & Middlesex, 1677 PRO PROB5/1480
Munger, George, mariner: 'sailor', Faversham, Kent, 1679 CKS PRC2/38/157
Munn, Elizabeth, widow, Teynham, Kent, 1664 CKS PRC1/9/132
Munn, Godfrye, Lenham, Kent, 1599 CKS PRC2/11/101
Munn, James, yeoman, Cranbrook, Kent, 1631 CKS PRC2/31/52
Munn, James, gentleman, Frittenden, Kent, 1691 CKS PRC2/42/8
Munn, John, Chart, Great, Kent, 1611 CKS PRC2/16/69
Munn, John, yeoman, Frittenden, Kent, 1671 CKS PRC1/15/48
Munn, Joseph, yeoman, Egerton, Kent, 1672 CKS PRC20/12/54
Munn, Sara, widow, Appledore, Kent, 1715 CKS PRC1/17/75
Munn, Stephen, grazier, Woodchurch, Kent, 1717 CKS PRC19/6/66
Munnes, Clement, Brabourne, Kent, 1598 CKS PRC2/10/194
Munnes, William, Challock, Kent, 1581 CKS PRC21/5/11
Munnes, William, Hinxhill, Kent, 1608 CKS PRC2/14/327
Munns, Michael, New Romney, Kent, 1683 CKS PRC20/13/352
Muns, George, Lympne, Kent, 1627 CKS PRC2/27/109
Muns, George, Lympne, Kent, 1647 CKS PRC1/8/22
Munsey, Daniel, university: 'Fellow of St John's College, Cambridge/rector' Cambridge (St John's College), Cambs, 1620 CUL V.C.Acc./Box1/38
Murcock, Danyel ygr, Ashford, Kent, 1614 CKS PRC2/18/117

[Murfin:]
Murfin, John, Epworth, Lincs, 1610 Lincs RO Ad/Ac/8a/323
Murfin, John, Epworth, Lincs, 1627 Lincs RO Ad/Ac/39/98
Murfyn, John, Boston, Lincs, 1644 Lincs RO Ad/Ac/28/195
Murgatroid, Mary, mrs/widow, Leeds, Yorks, 1719 Borthwick Test C.P. 1719/11
Murgatroyd, John, woolworster, Nafferton (Wansworth), Yorks, 1807 Borthwick Test C.P. 1807/5
Murhall, George, Orton on the Hill, Leics, 1666 Leics RO Administrators Accounts C17th f75
Muriell, Robert, alderman/butler, Cambridge St Michael, Cambs, 1683 CUL V.C. Acc./Box3/34
Murley, Thomas, Fleet, Lincs, 1607 Lincs RO Ad/Ac/8a/125
Murphey, Francis, bachelor, Trexford, Ireland, 1706 Lambeth Palace Arches G56/1
Murrall, John, husbandman, Stratfield Mortimer, Berks, 1681 Berks RO D/A1/204/134C
Murrell, William, Chichester All Saints, Sussex, 1683 W. Suss RO EpIV/10/2A/29
Murrey, Elizabeth, Aldington, Kent, 1609 CKS PRC20/2/61
Murrie, John, yeoman, Eastbridge, Kent, 1665 CKS PRC1/11/62
Murry, Edmund, Bere Regis, Dors, 1676 Wilts RO Dean Sarum (name + date)
Murrye, Henrye, Stanford, Kent, 1584 CKS PRC21/7/81
Mursyn, Margaret, Marden, Kent, 1591 CKS PRC2/5/286
Murthall, Thomas, Deeping St James, Lincs, 1638 Lincs RO Ad/Ac/25/518
Murtin, Robert, yeoman, Epworth, Lincs, 1665 Lincs RO Ad/Ac/41/165
Murton, Isaack, jurat/woollen draper, Sandwich, Kent, 1638 CKS PRC20/11/135
Murton, John, Blean, Kent, 1632 CKS PRC2/31/134
Murvell, John, Bonnington, Kent, 1646 CKS PRC1/7/91
Musgrave, Henry, Seasalter, Kent, 1637 CKS PRC2/34/83
Musgrave, James, Haxey (East Lound), Lincs, 1682 Lincs RO Ad/Ac/44/10
Musgrave, John, husbandman, Wantage, Berks, 1646 Oxon RO MSS Wills Pec 84/1/25
Musgrave, Mark, Well, Lincs, 1629 Lincs RO Ad/Ac/22/75
Musgrave, Roger, Frampton, Lincs, 1624 Lincs RO Ad/Ac/18/94
Muson, Edward, labourer, Scremby, Lincs, 1669 Lincs RO Ad/Ac/33/141
Muspratt, Richard, Weybridge, Surrey, 1767 Greater London RO DW/OP/1767/6/2
Muspratt, Thomas, Urchfont, Wilts, 1673 Wilts RO Arch. Sarum(+ name and date)
Musred, Henry, St Nicholas at Wade, Kent, 1588 CKS PRC21/9/1
Musred, John, Worth, Kent, 1600 CKS PRC21/16/131
Musred, John eld, St Nicholas at Wade, Kent, 1581 CKS PRC21/5/237
Musred, Robarte, Herne, Kent, 1599 CKS PRC21/15/43
Musred, William, Ash next Sandwich, Kent, 1596 CKS PRC21/14/3
Musred, William, yeoman, Ash next Sandwich, Kent, 1679 CKS PRC20/12/315
Mussared, John, Sandwich, Kent, 1673 CKS PRC2/35/242
Mussared/Greneland, Jone, wife, Blean, Kent, 1594 CKS PRC2/7/289
Musse, Edward, Sittingbourne, Kent, 1615 CKS PRC2/22/47
Mussendine, Francis, esquire, Healing, Lincs, 1612 Lincs RO Ad/Ac/11/71
Mussered, Edward, Herne, Kent, 1617 CKS PRC20/4/270
Musson, Marie, Scopwick, Lincs, 1625 Lincs RO Ad/Ac/19B/106
Musson, Richard, yeoman, Bitchfield, Lincs, 1636 Lincs RO Ad/Ac/24/566
Muston, Franncis, Grantham, Lincs, 1641 Lincs RO Ad/Ac/27/285
Mutley, George, clergy: 'clerk', Bradenham, Bucks, 1622 Lincs RO Ad/Ac/17/10
Muttyer, Henry, Lymington, Hants, 1662 Hants RO 21M65 D8/188
Muzard, John, Scaldwell, Northants, 1672 Northants RO NWill A/C/135
Muzered, Nicholas, yeoman, Worth, Kent, 1608 CKS PRC20/1/330
Muzzard, John, Kimbolton, Hunts, Hunts RO/Acc58/244(238)
Mychaell, John, Owersby, Lincs, 1600 Lincs RO Ad/Ac/5/217
Mychell, Alice, Winslow, Bucks, 1602 Herts RO ASA25/4760
Mychell, John, St Albans St Peters, Herts, Herts RO ASA25/1733
Mychell, Robert, Winslow, Bucks, 1587 Herts RO ASA25/1203
Mychell, Robert, Yardley, Worcs, 1605 Worcs RO 008.7 BA3585/839/353
Mycock, George, hatter, Newcastle under Lyme, Staffs, 1811 LJRO/B/C/5/1811/60b
Mycoe, Robert, Lyme Regis, Dors, 1597 Wilts RO Miscellaneous Index (name + date)

Myers, Joseph, Leeds St Peter (Bramley), Yorks, 1807 Borthwick Test C.P. 1807/6
Myhell/Lovell, Henrye, Hythe St Leonard, Kent, 1614 CKS PRC20/2/547
Myles, Henry, Bromsgrove, Worcs, Worcs RO 008.7 BA3585/839/423
Myles, John, Petworth, Sussex, 1596 W. Suss RO EpI/33/1596/14
Myles, Roger, Wingham, Kent, 1587 CKS PRC21/8/310
Myles, Thomas, Wokingham, Berks, 1596 Wilts RO Miscellaneous Index (name + date)
Myles, Thomas, Tamworth (Amington), Staffs, 1702 LJRO/B/C/5/1701/721
Myles, William, Eastchurch, Sheppey, Kent, 1613 CKS PRC2/18/48
Myles, William, Legbourne, Lincs, 1632 Lincs RO Ad/Ac/23/114
Myller, Ingram, Wittersham, Kent, 1583 CKS PRC21/6/284
Myller, John, St Mary in the Marsh, Kent, 1590 CKS PRC2/5/300
Myller, John, Smarden, Kent, 1614 CKS PRC20/3/73
Mylles, Edwarde, gentleman, Blean, Kent, 1609 CKS PRC2/14/329
Mylles, Henry, Sandwich St Peter, Kent, 1598 CKS PRC2/10/137
Mylles, Henry, Sandwich St Mary, Kent, 1616 CKS PRC2/22/44
Mylles, John, Willesborough, Kent, 1613 CKS PRC2/16/155
Mylles, John eld, Sandwich, Kent, 1611 CKS PRC2/17/180
Mylles, Richard, Westwell, Kent, 1583 CKS PRC21/6/246
Mylls, James, Hurst, Berks, 1596 Wilts RO Miscellaneous Index (name + date)
Mylner, Richard, Metheringham, Lincs, 1602 Lincs RO Ad/Ac/5/427
Mylton, Joan, widow, Deal, Kent, 1587 CKS PRC21/8/381
Mylwaye, Richard, Upchurch, Kent, 1596 CKS PRC2/8/368
Myn, Elias, labourer/widower, Stanton Harcourt (Sutton), Oxon, 1641 Oxon RO MSS Wills 170/2/16
Mynter, Elizabeth, widow, Ewell, Kent, 1627 CKS PRC2/27/100
Myrton, James, clergy: 'clerk', Algarkirk, Lincs, 1608 Lincs RO Ad/Ac/8a/129
Mytchell, Leonard, Ebony, Kent, 1597 CKS PRC2/9/303
Mytchell, Thomas, Canterbury St Paul, Kent, 1614 CKS PRC2/17/53
Myton, John, Wargrave, Berks, 1622 Berks RO D/A1/204/5C
Nabbes, Thomas, Bury, Lancs, 1581 Lancs RO (Name of Deceased) D.R.C.H. 1581
Nah, Edward, Northaw, Herts, 1634 Herts RO ASA25/4914
Nailer, Edward, clergy: 'parson', Bigby, Lincs, 1633 Lincs RO Ad/Ac/23/158
Nailer, Marie, Halifax (Wadsworth), Yorks, 1615 Borthwick Prob. Ex. 1615/1
Nailer, William, Gainsborough, Lincs, 1594 Lincs RO Ad/Ac/5/294
Nailer, William, Marton, Lincs, 1595 Lincs RO Ad/Ac/5/292
Naill, Rebeca, Winterton, Lincs, 1681 Lincs RO Ad/Ac/34/93
Nailor, Job, labourer, Sedgley, Staffs, 1798 LJRO/B/C/5/1798/22
Nailor, Richard, Torrington, West, Lincs, 1603 Lincs RO Ad/Ac/5/21
Naish, William?, Hilperton, Wilts, 1681 Wilts RO Arch. Sarum(+ name and date)
Nalder, Robert, husbandman, Crookham, Berks, 1635 Berks RO D/A1/205/221B
Nalder, William, Kintbury, Berks, 1599 Berks RO D/A1/205/190C
Naldret, John, Kirdford, Sussex, 1594 W. Suss RO EpI/33/1594/13
Nansoge, Clement, St Clement, Corn, 1605 Cornwall RO AP/N1/1
Napleton, Anthony, Teynham, Kent, 1624 CKS PRC2/24/35
Napleton, Barbara, Boughton under Blean, Kent, 1594 CKS PRC21/13/190
Napleton, Jacob, gentleman, Canterbury St Margaret, Kent, 1668 CKS PRC1/13/83
Napleton, Joane, Teynham, Kent, 1624 CKS PRC2/24/34
Napleton, John, Graveney, Kent, 1640 CKS PRC19/1/66
Napleton, John, gentleman, Sittingbourne, Kent, 1691 CKS PRC2/42/9
Napleton, Moses, Graveney, Kent, 1602 CKS PRC2/12/268
Napleton, Nicholas, St Nicholas at Wade, Kent, 1632 CKS PRC20/9/319
Napleton, Stephen, gentleman, Faversham, Kent, 1663 CKS PRC19/3/35
Napleton, Thomas, jurat, Faversham, Kent, 1627 CKS PRC20/7/193
Napleton, Thomas eld, Warden, Kent, 1622 CKS PRC2/24/27
Napleton, William, Teynham, Kent, 1619 CKS PRC2/22/13

[Napper:]
Napper, Ann, widow, Kirdford, Sussex, 1631 W. Suss RO EpI/33/1631/25
Napper, Henry + Elizabeth, Hartley Wintney, Hants, 1664 Hants RO 21M65 D8/189
Napper, John, Marden, Up, Sussex, 1606 W. Suss RO EpI/33/1606/14
Napper, John, Selsey, Sussex, 1618 W. Suss RO EpI/33/1618/18
Napper, Thomas, Duncton, Sussex, 1633 W. Suss RO EpI/33/1633/24
Narbury, Thomas, Bozeat, Northants, 1681 Northants RO NWill A/C/68
Nash, Henry, Adisham, Kent, 1696 CKS PRC19/5/45
Nash, Hugh, mariner, St Johns Thanet, Kent, 1662 CKS PRC1/9/42
Nash, John, Burrington, Som, 1631 Somerset RO D/D/Cta/N8
Nash, John eld, yeoman, Marden, Kent, 1669 CKS PRC1/14/80
Nash, Katherine, widow, Mathon, Hfords, 1683 Worcs RO 008.7 BA3585/830/11
Nash, Katherine, widow, Mathon, Hfords, 1683 Worcs RO 008.7 BA3585/837/bdl 3
Nash, Richard, Stapleton, Shrops, 1674 LJRO:cards/1674/37
Nash, Sampson, Hollingbourne, Kent, 1664 CKS PRC19/3/36
Nash, Thomas, Murston, Kent, 1634 CKS PRC2/32/163
Nash, Thomas, Chilvers Coton, Warks, 1702 LJRO/B/C/5/1701/79
Nash, William, bachelor, Grinstead, West, Sussex, 1670 W. Suss RO EpI/33/1670/7
Nash, William, Boldre, Hants, 1676 Hants RO 21m65 D8/271
Nash, William, Hythe St Leonard, Kent, 1689 CKS PRC20/13/636
Nash/Tucker, Mary, Semington, Wilts, 1641 Wilts RO Arch. Sarum(+ name and date)
Nashe, Geoffrey, Pershore, Worcs, Worcs RO 008.7 BA3585/839/288
Nashe, Mathew, Coates, Sussex, 1632 W. Suss RO EpI/33/1632/13
Nashe, Nicholas, Whitstable, Kent, 1613 CKS PRC2/16/126
Nashe, Robarte, Monks Horton, Kent, 1611 CKS PRC2/15/261
Nashe, Thomas, Goudhurst, Kent, 1628 CKS PRC2/29/71
Nashe, William, Mimms, North, Herts, 1640 Herts RO AHH23/1723
Nation, Catherine, Cannington, Som, 1678 Somerset RO D/D/Cta/N11
Naull, John, Winterton, Lincs, 1679 Lincs RO Ad/Ac/43/133
Nayes, Robert, husbandman, Aldworth, Berks, 1621 Berks RO D/A1/205/204C
Nayler, John, Deal, Kent, 1696 CKS PRC19/5/46
Nayler, Stephen, Northorpe (Southorpe), Lincs, 1650 Lincs RO Ad/Ac/40/180
Nayler, William, St Nicholas at Wade, Kent, 1598 CKS PRC21/14/512
Nayler, William, Bridge, Kent, 1638 CKS PRC2/34/248
Naylor, Anne, widow, Childwall (Halebank), Lancs, 1663 Lancs RO (Name of Deceased) D.R.C.H. 1663
Naylor, John, Sandwich St Peter, Kent, 1588 CKS PRC2/4/275
Naylor, John, maltster, Dewsbury (Chickenley), Yorks, 1789 Borthwick Test C.P. 1789/2
Naylor, Margaret, spinster, Chilham, Kent, 1634 CKS PRC2/32/91
Naylor, Mary, spinster, Maidstone, Kent, 1674 CKS PRC20/12/137
Naylor, Matthewe, Darfield (Hemingfield), Yorks, 1622 Borthwick Prob. Ex. 1622/1
Neady, Margaret, widow, Bristol, Glos, Bristol RO 1748/CP
Neal, John, dyer, Lincoln, Lincs, 1755 Lincs RO Ad/Ac/45/28
Neale, Alice, widow, Faversham, Kent, 1582 CKS PRC2/2/154
Neale, George, New Romney, Kent, 1667 CKS PRC19/3/135
Neale, Jeriemy, Sutton Valence, Kent, 1616 CKS PRC2/22/10
Neale, John, Edenham, Lincs, 1606 Lincs RO Ad/Ac/7/170
Neale, John, upholsterer, Maidstone, Kent, 1636 CKS PRC20/11/171
Neale, John, Frodingham (Scunthorpe), Lincs, 1662 Lincs RO Ad/Ac/41/19
Neale, John, Horbling, Lincs, 1680 Lincs RO Ad/Ac/34/48
Neale, Joseph, carrier, Tenterden, Kent, 1623 CKS PRC2/24/26
Neale, Mary, widow, East Sutton, Kent, 1638 CKS PRC2/34/246
Neale, Richard, Hartlip, Kent, 1622 CKS PRC2/26/123
Neale, Richard, innholder, Newington next Sittingbourne, Kent, 1698 CKS PRC2/42/144
Neale, Robert, Thornton, Lincs, 1632 Lincs RO Ad/Ac/23/101
Neale, Sarah, widow, Pidley, Hunts, 1728 Hunts RO/Acc58/319

Neale, Stephen, gardener, market, Faversham, Kent, 1681 CKS PRC2/39/208
Neale, Thomas, Hythe St Leonard, Kent, 1595 CKS PRC21/14/215
Neale, Thomas, butcher, Banbury, Oxon, 1619 Oxon RO MSS Wills Pec 47/1/10
Neale, William, Malmesbury, Wilts, 1638 Wilts RO Arch. Wilts.(+ name and date)
Neale, William, Wye, Kent, 1639 CKS PRC1/3/21
Neale, Wyllyam, Faversham, Kent, 1586 CKS PRC2/4/170
Neale/Taylor, Anne, Sandwich, Kent, 1666 CKS PRC1/11/63
Neales, Richard, Dover, Kent, 1596 CKS PRC21/14/91
Neales, Richard, Dover, Kent, 1627 CKS PRC20/8/355
Neall, Richard, High Halstow, Kent, 1616 CKS PRC2/22/28
Neame, Daniel, maltster, Sandwich, Kent, 1639 CKS PRC1/3/22
Neame, Edmund, Teynham, Kent, 1649 CKS PRC1/8/77
Neame, Elizabeth, spinster, Canterbury Christchurch, Kent, 1700 CKS PRC19/5/75
Neame, Henrye, Monkton, Kent, 1606 CKS PRC20/1/97
Neame, James, yeoman, Worth, Kent, 1684 CKS PRC20/13/448
Neame, John, Sandwich St Mary, Kent, 1597 CKS PRC2/10/331
Neame, John, yeoman, Eastry, Kent, 1687 CKS PRC20/13/599
Neame, John eld, Staple next Wingham, Kent, 1625 CKS PRC20/7/289
Neame, Peter, Ickham, Kent, 1626 CKS PRC20/7/297
Neame, Robert, Sandwich, Kent, CKS PRC19/2/74
Neame, Robert, Ash next Sandwich, Kent, 1682 CKS PRC20/13/267
Neame, Thomas, yeoman, Goodnestone next Wingham, Kent, 1665 CKS PRC19/3/77
Neame, William, Staple next Wingham, Kent, 1586 CKS PRC21/8/94
Neame, William, Worth, Kent, 1692 CKS PRC19/5/28
Nearne, David, clergy: 'mr/curate', Swingfield, Kent, 1667 CKS PRC1/12/64
Nearne, David, clergy: 'mr/curate', Swingfield, Kent, 1667 CKS PRC1/12/64a
Nearne, Richard, yeoman, Chislet, Kent, 1670 CKS PRC1/15/49
Nearne/Nicholas, Elizabeth, Wingham, Kent, 1664 CKS PRC19/3/56
Neate?, Lucie, Pewsham, Wilts, 1675 Wilts RO Miscellaneous Index to Wills (name + date)
Neave, Edward, Chichester St Peter the Great, Sussex, 1701 W. Suss RO EpIII/9/1/58
Neave, Richard, Westhampnett, Sussex, 1676 W. Suss RO EpI/33/1676/33
Neave, William, yeoman, Hampstead Norris, Berks, 1627 Berks RO D/A1/205/211C
Neede, Richarde, Hinxhill, Kent, 1582 CKS PRC2/2/227
Needes, David, Congresbury, Som, 1611 Somerset RO D/D/Cta/N1
Needham, Edward, Chesterfield, Derby, 1684 LJRO/B/C/5/1684/58
Needham, George, throwster: 'silk throwster', Derby, Derby, 1778 LJRO/B/C/5/1778/71
Needham, John, yeoman, Boughton under Blean, Kent, 1678 CKS PRC20/12/273
Needham, John, Alton, Staffs, 1760 LJRO/B/C/5/1760/211
Needham, Lazarus, yeoman, Mickleover (Potlocks), Derby, 1793 LJRO/B/C/5/1793/36
Needham, Thomas, Humberstone, Lincs, 1602 Lincs RO Ad/Ac/5/119
Needham, Thomas, Goudhurst, Kent, 1681 CKS PRC2/39/209
Needham, William, Whaplode, Lincs, 1627 Lincs RO Ad/Ac/20b/38
Needle, James, Sutton Mandeville, Wilts, 1638 Wilts RO Arch. Sarum(+ name and date)
Neele, Nicholas, St Albans St Peters, Herts, Herts RO ASA25/4847
Neeve, William, bricklayer, Hothfield, Kent, 1674 CKS PRC2/36/101
Negall, John, Sutton, Lincs, 1620 Lincs RO Ad/Ac/15/221
Negous, William, Kyme, South (North Kyme), Lincs, 1593 Lincs RO Ad/Ac/3/39
Neild, Daniel, yeoman, Glossop (Mousley), Derby, 1748 LJRO/B/C/5/1748/250
Neild, John, Thornton (Dunham), Ches, 1590 Cheshire RO (Name) W.C. 1590
Neild, William, Tarvin, Ches, 1634 Cheshire RO (Name) W.C. 1634
Neivile, John, gentleman, Winterton, Lincs, 1667 Lincs RO Ad/Ac/33/12
Nelsey, Henry, Hackthorne, Lincs, 1682 Lincs RO Ad/Ac/44/24
Nelson, Henry, Canterbury, Kent, 1623 CKS PRC2/24/30
Nelson, John, Swaby, Lincs, 1622 Lincs RO Ad/Ac/17/32
Nelson, Richard, Northorpe, Lincs, 1615 Lincs RO Ad/Ac/8b/213

[Nelson:]
Nelson, Thomas, Marston, Lincs, 1683 Lincs RO Ad/Ac/44/70
Nelson, William, Ryhill, Yorks, 1619 Borthwick Prob. Ex. 1619/2
Nelson, see Burwash,
Nepecker, Edward, Pluckley, Kent, 1617 CKS PRC2/22/20
Nepecker, Edward, bachelor, Pluckley, Kent, 1695 CKS PRC2/42/107
Nephue, Jeremy, Dover, Kent, 1624 CKS PRC20/6/138
Nesse, Anthony, Hull, Yorks, 1626 Borthwick Prob. Ex. 1626/1
Netherall, Charles, gentleman, Spridlington, Lincs, 1680 Lincs RO Ad/Ac/43/157
Nethercoats, Frances, Nettleham, Lincs, 1617 Lincs RO Ad/Ac/8b/165
Nethercoats, Marye, Nettleham, Lincs, 1616 Lincs RO Ad/Ac/8b/161
Nethersole, Alexander, Goodnestone next Wingham, Kent, 1603 CKS PRC21/16/57
Nethersole, Henry, St Laurence Thanet, Kent, 1617 CKS PRC2/22/9
Nethersole, Hosea, Northbourne, Kent, 1635 CKS PRC2/33/98
Nethersole, James, alderman, Canterbury, Kent, 1582 CKS PRC2/2/238
Nethersole, Joane, spinster, Canterbury St Paul, Kent, 1620 CKS PRC2/22/7
Nethersole, John, Dover, Kent, 1594 CKS PRC21/12/383
Nethersole, John, Alkham, Kent, 1598 CKS PRC2/10/165
Nethersole, John, Warehorne, Kent, 1604 CKS PRC2/14/352
Nethersole, John, yeoman ?, Barham, Kent, 1644 CKS PRC1/7/5
Nethersole, John, St Peter in Thanet, Kent, 1672 CKS PRC2/35/157
Nethersole, Marke, husbandman, Ash next Sandwich, Kent, 1671 CKS PRC20/12/24
Nethersole, Nicholas, weaver, Dover, Kent, 1678 CKS PRC20/12/272
Nethersole, Robarte, Dymchurch, Kent, 1595 CKS PRC2/8/129
Nethersole, Rychard, St Peter in Thanet, Kent, 1587 CKS PRC2/4/114
Nethersole, Thomas, Nonington, Kent, 1603 CKS PRC21/16/71
Nethersole, Thomas, St Laurence Thanet, Kent, 1626 CKS PRC2/27/112
Nethersole, Thomas, yeoman, St Laurence Thanet, Kent, 1626 CKS PRC2/27/113
Nethersole, Thomas, St Laurence Thanet, Kent, 1629 CKS PRC2/30/104
Nethersole, Thomas, Hartlip, Kent, 1662 CKS PRC1/8/110
Nethersole, William, St Johns Thanet, Kent, 1598 CKS PRC2/11/13
Nethersole, William, Hawkinge, Kent, 1602 CKS PRC2/12/260
Nethersole, William, Alkham, Kent, 1630 CKS PRC20/9/304
Nethersole, William, Barham, Kent, 1650 CKS PRC1/8/78
Nethersole, William, tailor, Acrise, Kent, 1670 CKS PRC1/15/50
Nethwaie, Alice, Portbury, Som, 1594 Somerset RO D/D/Cta/N13
Nethwaie, Christopher, Bleadon, Som, 1625 Somerset RO D/D/Cta/N4
Nethwaie, John, Bleadon, Som, 1640 Somerset RO D/D/Cta/N14
Netter, Joane, widow, New Romney, Kent, 1617 CKS PRC20/4/288
Netter, Rychard, Boughton Aluph, Kent, 1582 CKS PRC2/2/193
Netter, Rychard, New Romney, Kent, 1595 CKS PRC21/14/236
Netter, Thomas, gentleman, New Romney, Kent, 1630 CKS PRC20/9/315
Netter, William, New Romney, Kent, 1596 CKS PRC21/14/21
Netter, William, Hawkhurst, Kent, 1617 CKS PRC2/22/21
Nettleship, William, Saundby, Notts, 1630 Borthwick Prob. Ex. 1630/1
Nettleshippe, George, Saundby, Notts, 1618 Borthwick Prob. Ex. 1618/1
Neutyn, Michall, Canterbury St Mildred, Kent, 1615 CKS PRC2/22/22
Nevall, Ralph, Tatenhill (Barton under Needwood), Staffs, 1663 LJRO:cards/1663/45
Nevell, John, Tenterden, Kent, 1621 CKS PRC2/24/32
Nevell, John, butcher, Welford, Berks, 1630 Berks RO D/A1/205/214C
Nevell, Thomas, haberdasher,
London & Middlesex 1577 Lambeth Palace Arches F 3a ff190-194
Nevell, see Glanfelde,
Nevet, John, Malpas (Tushingham), Ches, 1621 Cheshire RO (Name) W.C. 1621
Nevile, Catherine, widow, Thorney, Notts, 1811 Borthwick Test C.P. 1811/5
Nevill, Ann, widow, Tamworth, Staffs, 1807 LJRO/B/C/5/1807/58

Nevill, Anthony, Raithby, Lincs, Lincs RO Ad/Ac/19A/121
Nevill, Edward, university: 'Fellow of Trinity College, Cambridge/M.A.', Cambridge, Cambs, 1616 CUL V.C.Acc./Box1/39
Nevill, Edward, gentleman, Shellingford, Berks, 1633 Berks RO D/A1/205/219B
Nevill, Henry, Tenterden, Kent, 1637 CKS PRC2/33/96
Nevill, James, wheelwright, Abingdon, Berks, 1644 Berks RO D/A1/101/218B
Nevill, John, yeoman, Croxall, Derby, 1775 LJRO/B/C/5/1775/49
Nevill, Thomas, Scotton, Lincs, 1608 Lincs RO Ad/Ac/37/262
Nevill, Thomas, yeoman, Abingdon, Berks, 1644 Berks RO D/A1/205/231C
Nevill, William, Hallington, Lincs, 1644 Lincs RO Ad/Ac/28/89
Nevinson, Richard, porter: 'under porter', Deal, Kent, 1682 CKS PRC20/13/271
New, Richard, Warminster, Wilts, 1617 Wilts RO Arch. Sarum(+ name and date)
New, William, Chisenbury, Wilts, 1597 Wilts RO Miscellaneous Index (name + date)
Newark, William, butcher, Wells Next The Sea, Norf, 1749 Norfolk RO ANW/23/24/86A
Newbee, Christopher, Canterbury St Mildred, Kent, 1632 CKS PRC2/34/84
Newberry, Henry, Lillington, Warks, 1683 LJRO/B/C/5/1682/75
Newbery, John, Burlesdon, Hants, 1697 Hants RO 1696 AD64
Newbery, John eld, yeoman, Hinton Waldrist, Berks, 1672 Berks RO D/A1/206/21C
Newbery, Thomas, Tilehurst, Berks, 1596 Berks RO D/A1/205/188C
Newberye, Thomas, Cranbrook, Kent, 1598 CKS PRC2/9/383
Newbie, Thomas, Oxford (Lincoln College), Oxon, 1588 Bodleian HYP B9/27-28
Newbold, John, Seal, Nether and Over, Leics, 1666 Leics RO Administrators Accounts C17th f72
Newbold, John, yeoman, Hanbury, Staffs, 1760 LJRO/B/C/5/1761/100
Newbold, William, Seal, Nether and Over, Leics, 1666 Leics RO Administrators Accounts C17th f71
Newbold, William, farmer, Hartshorne, Derby, 1811 LJRO/B/C/5/1811/67
Newborne, Anne, spinster, Haxey, Lincs, 1635 Lincs RO Ad/Ac/40/19
Newby, Nicholas, Birchington, Kent, 1693 CKS PRC19/5/22
Newcomb, Thomas, Lincoln, Lincs, 1613 Lincs RO Ad/Ac/11/154
Newcomb, William, Worcester, Worcs, 1682 Worcs RO 008.7 BA3585/837/bdl 3
Newcombe, Thomas, coachmaker, St Giles in the Fields, London & Middlesex, 1688 PRO PROB32/27/144
Newcome, Anthonie, Gonerby, Great, Lincs, 1628 Lincs RO Ad/Ac/20b/57
Newcome, Jane, Blyton, Lincs, 1607 Lincs RO Ad/Ac/37/249
Newcome, John, Caythorpe, Lincs, 1636 Lincs RO Ad/Ac/24/327
Newcome, Robert, Welby, Lincs, 1669 Lincs RO Ad/Ac/33/128
Newcome, Thomas, Toynton, Low, Lincs, 1580 Lincs RO Ad/Ac/2b/57
Newcome, William, Saxby All Saints, Lincs, 1627 Lincs RO Ad/Ac/20b/78
Newcomen, Edward, Mareham le Fen, Lincs, 1614 Lincs RO Ad/Ac/13/62
Newcomen, John, yeoman, Aby, Lincs, 1638 Lincs RO Ad/Ac/25/251
Newcomen, Richard, gentleman, Saltfleetby, Lincs, 1619 Lincs RO Ad/Ac/15/209
Newe, Elianor, Wrockwardine, Shrops, 1682 LJRO/B/C/5/1681/28
Newe, Michaell, Chislet, Kent, 1592 CKS PRC2/6/105
Newe, Thomas, Sutton Mandeville, Wilts, 1620? Wilts RO Miscellaneous Index (name + date)
Newell, Gabriel, Southoe, Hunts, 1682 Hunts RO/Acc58/185(104)
Newell, John, Reepham, Lincs, 1618 Lincs RO Ad/Ac/8b/149
Newell, William, Northaw, Herts, 1629 Herts RO ASA25/4864
Newenden, Elizabeth, Rainham, Kent, 1592 CKS PRC2/5/251
Newenden, James, Smarden, Kent, 1701 CKS PRC1/16/37
Newenden, Mary, widow, Smarden, Kent, 1620 CKS PRC2/22/11
Newes, Barthelmew, Faversham, Kent, 1597 CKS PRC2/9/160
Newesse, Thomas, Marston, Lincs, 1606 Lincs RO Ad/Ac/7/24
Newey, Joan, Norton, Kings, Worcs, 1687 Worcs RO 008.7 BA3585/836/bdl 1
Newey, Robert, yeoman, Hampton Lovett, Worcs, 1683 Worcs RO 008.7 BA3585/837/bdl 3
Newgate, John, Kirkby on Bain, Lincs, 1619 Lincs RO Ad/Ac/15/171

[Newhook:]
Newhook, Francis, Tollard Royal, Wilts, 1744 Wilts RO Arch. Sarum(+ name and date)
Newhooks, Francis, Tollard Royal, Wilts, 1744 Wilts RO Miscellaneous Index (name + date)
Newing, John, Minster in Thanet, Kent, 1668 CKS PRC1/12/65
Newington, Zebulon, threadtwister, Maidstone, Kent, 1682 CKS PRC20/13/269
Newis, Andrew, labourer, Scopwick, Lincs, 1633 Lincs RO Ad/Ac/24/202
Newland, James, yeoman, Linsted, Kent, 1620 CKS PRC2/22/15
Newland, John, draper: 'woollen draper', Faversham, Kent, 1670 CKS PRC1/14/81
Newland, Margaret, Linsted, Kent, 1614 CKS PRC2/18/82
Newland, Margarett, widow, Canterbury St Dunstan Without, Kent, 1617 CKS PRC2/22/24
Newland, Richard, Slindon, Sussex, 1623 W. Suss RO EpIV/10/1/34
Newland, Thomas, Canterbury St Mary Northgate, Kent, 1606 CKS PRC2/14/351
Newland, William, Ashton, Long, Som, 1620 Somerset RO D/D/Cta/N2
Newlande, William, Rainham, Kent, 1582 CKS PRC2/2/59
Newlin, John, Empshott, Hants, 1624 Hants RO 21M65 D8/77
Newlove, Nicholas, Burton Pedwardine, Lincs, 1598 Lincs RO Ad/Ac/4/47
Newlove, Prudence, widow, Ewerby, Lincs, 1619 Lincs RO Ad/Ac/15/140
Newman, Abraham, Margate, Kent, 1673 CKS PRC2/35/245
Newman, Barnabas, Minster in Sheppey, Kent, 1590 CKS PRC2/5/255
Newman, Deborah, Canterbury, Kent, 1635 CKS PRC2/33/97
Newman, Elizabeth, widow, Upchurch, Kent, 1595 CKS PRC2/8/165
Newman, Ellis, Chichester St Andrew, Sussex, 1664 W. Suss RO EpIII/9/1/49
Newman, George, Downton, Wilts, 1636 Wilts RO Arch. Sarum(+ name and date)
Newman, Henry, Sandwich St Mary, Kent, 1590 CKS PRC2/5/261
Newman, Henry, Marcham, Berks, 1611 Berks RO D/A1/205/198C
Newman, Henry, tanner, Sturry, Kent, 1624 CKS PRC2/24/33
Newman, Henry, Marcham, Berks, 1637 Berks RO D/A1/205/225C
Newman, Joan, widow, Marcham, Berks, 1629 Berks RO D/A1/205/212C
Newman, John, gardener, Englefield, Berks, Berks RO D/A1/205/194C
Newman, John, Canterbury Holy Cross Westgate, Kent, 1610 CKS PRC2/15/263
Newman, John, Dover, Kent, 1621 CKS PRC20/5/132
Newman, John, Froyle, Hants, 1624 Hants RO 21M65 D8/78
Newman, John, Farringdon, Great (Chipping Farringdon), Berks, 1628 Wilts RO Miscellaneous Index (name + date)
Newman, John, Rickmansworth, Herts, 1636 Herts RO ASA25/4929
Newman, John, shepherd, Martin, Wilts, 1638 Wilts RO Arch. Sarum(+ name and date)
Newman, John, Downton (Charlton), Wilts, 1639? Wilts RO Arch. Sarum(+ name and date)
Newman, John, Dover St Mary, Kent, 1641 CKS PRC19/1/67
Newman, John, yeoman, Bampton (Cote), Oxon, 1670 Oxon RO MSS Wills 84/1/24
Newman, John, Fillongley, Warks, 1675 LJRO:cards/1675/41
Newman, John, surgeon: 'barber-surgeon/citizen/mr', St James Garlickhithe, London & Middlesex, 1685 PRO PROB32/25/423
Newman, John, Chelsea, London & Middlesex, 1754 Greater London RO AM/PI pt (uncatalogued)
Newman, John, Sherrington, Wilts, 1760 Wilts RO Miscellaneous Index (name + date)
Newman, John, glazier, Winchcombe, Glos, 1762 GRO GDR/B4/2/N20
Newman, Mary, widow, Charlton, Wilts, 1632 Wilts RO Arch. Wilts.(+ name and date)
Newman, Nicholas, Downton, Wilts, 1615 Wilts RO Miscellaneous Index (name + date)
Newman, Richard, Sutton, Sussex, 1617 W. Suss RO EpI/33/1617/14
Newman, Richard, Smarden, Kent, 1619 CKS PRC2/22/14
Newman, Richard, Canterbury, Kent, 1628 CKS PRC20/8/363
Newman, Richard, yeoman, Belleau, Lincs, 1638 Lincs RO Ad/Ac/25/520
Newman, Richard, Petworth, Sussex, 1673 W. Suss RO EpI/33/1673/8
Newman, Richard, surgeon, Wimborne Minster, Dors, 1702 Dorset RO PE/WM CP 2/4/100
Newman, Robert, Salisbury, Wilts, 1612 Wilts RO Miscellaneous Index (name + date)
Newman, Robert, smith, Kensington, London & Middlesex, 1710 Greater London RO

AM/PP/Box 1701-1710 pt (uncatalogued)
Newman, Robert, smith, Kensington, London & Middlesex, 1711 Greater London RO AM/PP/Box 1711-1714 pt (uncatalogued)
Newman, Thomas, Benenden, Kent, 1596 CKS PRC2/8/306
Newman, Thomas, Dover, Kent, 1598 CKS PRC21/14/548
Newman, Thomas, yeoman, Sutton Valence, Kent, 1612 CKS PRC20/2/285
Newman, Walter, Milton next Sittingbourne, Kent, 1610 CKS PRC2/15/259
Newman, Walter, Winterslow, Wilts, 1631? Wilts RO Arch. Sarum(+ name and date)
Newman, Walter, Winterslow, Wilts, 1640? Wilts RO Arch. Sarum(+ name and date)
Newman, Walter, innholder, Amesbury, Wilts, 1695 Wilts RO Arch. Sarum(+ name and date)
Newman, William, yeoman, Fleet, Lincs, 1620 Lincs RO Ad/Ac/16/71
Newman, William, Upchurch, Kent, 1622 CKS PRC2/24/25
Newman, William, husbandman, Marden, Kent, 1638 CKS PRC2/34/245
Newman/Newnam, Richard, Staplehurst, Kent, 1618 CKS PRC2/22/8
Newmarke, Robert, shepherd, Brocklesby (Little Limber), Lincs, 1668 Lincs RO Ad/Ac/33/57
Newnam, see Newman,
Newnham, Eleanor, Wolverley, Worcs, 1680 Worcs RO 008.7 BA3585/837/bdl 2
Newnham, see Nunam,
Newport, John, blacksmith, Eastleach Turville, Glos, 1819 GRO GDR/B4/2/N21
Newport/Pearce, Richard, blacksmith, Sparkford, Som, 1625 Somerset RO D/D/Cta/N3
Newsome, Peter, Luddington (Garthorpe), Lincs, 1611 Lincs RO Ad/Ac/8a/335
Newsted, William, gentleman, Bilsby, Lincs, 1646 Lincs RO Ad/Ac/28/233
Newstreet, Thomas, Hothfield, Kent, 1639 CKS PRC2/34/247
Newstreete, Mary, Ashford, Kent, 1598 CKS PRC2/9/385
Newstreete, Thomas ygr, Ashford, Kent, 1603 CKS PRC2/12/454
Newstreete, William, Faversham, Kent, 1620 CKS PRC2/22/18
Newstrete, Thomas, Ashford, Kent, 1589 CKS PRC2/5/277
Newton, Benjamin, Watton (Cawkeld), Yorks, 1635 Borthwick Prob. Ex. 1635/4
Newton, Caleb, clergy: 'clerk/mr', Harrington, Northants, 1674 Northants RO NWill A/C/150
Newton, Christopher, Somercoates, South, Lincs, 1650 Lincs RO Ad/Ac/29/70
Newton, Edward, Osgodby, Lincs, 1637 Lincs RO Ad/Ac/25/613
Newton, Edward, Mickleover, Derby, 1674 LJRO:cards/1674/38
Newton, Elizabeth, widow, Dover, Kent, 1627 CKS PRC20/8/359
Newton, Henry, university: 'scholar's servant', Cambridge Holy Trinity, Cambs, 1622 CUL V.C. Acc./Box2/51
Newton, James, grocer, Maidstone, Kent, 1666 CKS PRC19/3/101
Newton, John, husbandman, Hackthorne, Lincs, 1667 Lincs RO Ad/Ac/33/6
Newton, John, yeoman, Pentrich (Ripley), Derby, 1749 LJRO/B/C/5/1749/206
Newton, Laurence, goldsmith, Maidstone, Kent, 1675 CKS PRC19/4/103
Newton, Magdalen, spinster, Hereford St John Baptist, Hfords, 1701 Lambeth Palace Arches G52/2
Newton, Richard, yeoman, Crowle, Lincs, 1666 Lincs RO Ad/Ac/41/172
Newton, Robert, Kirkby on Bain (Tumby), Lincs, 1612 Lincs RO Ad/Ac/11/156
Newton, Robert, Leek, Staffs, 1684 LJRO/B/C/5/1684/59
Newton, Robert, plumber/glazier, Birmingham, Warks, 1774 LJRO/B/C/5/1774/37
Newton, Samuel, Birmingham, Warks, 1683 LJRO/B/C/5/1682/76
Newton, Seath, Sibsey, Lincs, 1624 Lincs RO Ad/Ac/19A/12
Newton, Thomas, Stubton, Lincs, 1612 Lincs RO Ad/Ac/11/188
Newton, Thomas, Beeford (Lisset), Yorks, 1619 Borthwick Prob. Ex. 1619/1
Newton, Thomas, Queniborough, Leics, 1641 Leics RO PR/I/41A/74
Newton, William, Newark on Trent, Notts, 1612 Borthwick Prob. Ex. 1609/2
Newton, William, Morton (Harmthorpe), Lincs, 1633 Lincs RO Ad/Ac/24/2
Newton, William, Grantham, Lincs, 1640 Lincs RO Ad/Ac/27/154
Niblett, William, farmer, Minchinhampton, Glos, 1798 GRO GDR/B4/2/N22
Niccals, Robert, Swayfield, Lincs, 1607 Lincs RO Ad/Ac/8a/13

[Niccoll:]
Niccoll, Robert, Dover, Kent, 1636 CKS PRC20/11/175
Niccolls, Michael, St Johns Thanet, Kent, 1638 CKS PRC20/11/181
Nicholas, Elizabeth, widow, St Keverne, Corn, 1636 Cornwall RO AP/N175
Nicholas, Frances, widow, Aldbourne, Wilts, 1699 Wilts RO Arch. Wilts.(+ name and date)
Nicholas, George, husbandman, Hatton, Lincs, 1666 Lincs RO Ad/Ac/32/118
Nicholas, John, Gwennap, Corn, 1612 Cornwall RO AP/N61/2
Nicholas, Richard,
Norf 1707 Norfolk RO ANW/23/7/98
Nicholas, Thomas, Snave, Kent, 1680 CKS PRC2/39/78
Nicholas, see Maukham & Nearne,
Nicholl, Bryan, Owston (West Kinnard's Ferry), Lincs, 1613 Lincs RO Ad/Ac/8b/14
Nicholl, Robert, Lydd, Kent, 1627 CKS PRC20/8/349
Nicholl, Roberte, Rasen, Middle, (Tupholme), Lincs, 1602 Lincs RO Ad/Ac/5/399
Nicholl, William, 1626 NLW BR 1626/4 Ac
Nicholls, Alexander, Ashford, Kent, 1601 CKS PRC2/12/264
Nicholls, Alice, widow, Bristol, Glos, Bristol RO 1723/21
Nicholls, Antony, Nettleton, Wilts, 1637 Wilts RO Arch. Wilts.(+ name and date)
Nicholls, Edward, Aldington, Kent, 1606 CKS PRC20/1/105
Nicholls, Elizabeth, 1619? Lincs RO Ad/Ac/15/299
Nicholls, John, Shrewsbury, Shrops, 1672 LJRO:cards/1672/41
Nicholls, John, Yaxley, Hunts, 1684 Hunts RO/Acc58/224(212)
Nicholls, John, Ebrington, Glos, 1685 GRO GDR/B4/2/N35
Nicholls, Joseph, coal merchant, Bromley, St Leonard, London & Middlesex, 1715 PRO PROB32/59/46
Nicholls, Josias, Deal, Kent, 1693 CKS PRC19/5/23
Nicholls, Mary, widow, Deal, Kent, 1696 CKS PRC19/5/47
Nicholls, Nicholas, husbandman, Cumnor, Berks, 1622 Berks RO D/A1/205/206C
Nicholls, Sara, Walsall, Staffs, 1680 LJRO:cards/1680/28
Nicholls, Thomas, Louth, Lincs, 1633 Lincs RO Ad/Ac/24/10
Nicholls, William, yeoman, Haceby, Lincs, 1669 Lincs RO Ad/Ac/33/133
Nicholls, William, butcher, Taynton, Glos, 1718 GRO GDR 269 (f.91)
Nicholls, William, tailor, Solihull, Warks, 1802 LJRO/B/C/5/1802/46
Nicholls, William, wheelwright, Walton upon Trent, Derby, 1831 LJRO/B/C/5/1831/21
Nichols, Benjamin, schoolmaster, Sutton Valence, Kent, 1675 CKS PRC2/36/219
Nichols, Edward, Weston (St Mary Extra), Hants, 1624 Hants RO 21M65 D8/79
Nichols, John, blacksmith, Ardington, Berks, 1670 Berks RO D/A1/206/14C
Nichols, John, Lexham, East, Norf, 1766 Norfolk RO ANW/23/25/89
Nichols, John, bachelor, Chertsey, Surrey, 1767 Greater London RO DW/OP/1767/4/1
Nichols, Joseph eld, farmer, Guiseley (Carlton), Yorks, 1801 Borthwick Test C.P. 1801/7
Nichols, Josias, gentleman, Charing, Kent, 1683 CKS PRC20/13/360
Nichols, Silvester, Claybrooke, Leics, 1666 Leics RO Administrators Accounts C17th f57
Nichols, Thomas, St Johns Thanet, Kent, 1626 CKS PRC2/27/114
Nichols, Thomas, Fawsley, Northants, 1677 Northants RO NWill A/C/144
Nicholson, Edmund, Eagle, Lincs, 1634 Lincs RO Ad/Ac/24/140
Nicholson, Humphrey, farrier, Faversham, Kent, 1640 CKS PRC1/5/12
Nicholson, James, alderman/mr, Canterbury, Kent, 1647 CKS PRC1/7/92
Nicholson, John, yeoman, Hull, Yorks, 1803 Borthwick Test C.P. 1803/9
Nicholson, Lawrence, Kirton, Lincs, 1613 Lincs RO Ad/Ac/12/53
Nicholson, Matthew, Brocklesby, Lincs, 1637 Lincs RO Ad/Ac/25/467
Nicholson, Richard, St Katherine by the Tower, London & Middlesex, Greater London RO DW/OP/1739/10/2
Nicholson, Thomas, Mablethorpe, Lincs, 1612 Lincs RO Ad/Ac/11/162
Nickson, Symon, Keal, West, Lincs, 1615 Lincs RO Ad/Ac/13/1
Nicol, see Sladden,
Nicolas, Malkham, Deal, Kent, 1574 CKS PRC21/2/94

Nicoll, William, Egloskerry, Corn, 1607 Cornwall RO AP/N30/2
Nicolls, John, Sedgeberrow, Worcs, 1602 Worcs RO 008.7 BA3585/838/258
Nicolls, John, Chislet, Kent, 1612 CKS PRC2/17/350
Nicolls/Christopher, Richard, Folkestone, Kent, 1601 CKS PRC2/12/256
Nicols, Margaret, Canterbury St Dunstan Without, Kent, 1647 CKS PRC1/8/23
Nicols, Michael, mercer, Sandwich, Kent, 1640 CKS PRC1/5/11
Nicols, Michael, mercer, Sandwich, Kent, 1640 CKS PRC1/5/11a
Nicols, Michael, Canterbury St Dunstan Without, Kent, 1647 CKS PRC1/8/50
Nid, Arthur, Greetwell, Lincs, 1625 Lincs RO Ad/Ac/39/230
Nightingale, Anthony, Rusper, Sussex, 1633 W. Suss RO EpI/33/1632/14
Nightingale, David, gentleman, Watford, Herts, 1597 Herts RO ASA25/1636
Nightingale, John, Pagham, Sussex, 1621 W. Suss RO EpIV/10/1/34
Nightscales, Simon, Pinchbeck, Lincs, 1649 Lincs RO Ad/Ac/30/51
Nightskales, Robert, Wold Newton, Lincs, 1614 Lincs RO Ad/Ac/13/173
Nine, Andrew, Boughton Aluph, Kent, 1686 CKS PRC2/41/2
Nippes, Thomas, Cambridge (Barnwell), Cambs, 1613 CUL V.C.Acc./Box1/40
Nix, Samuel, Bitchfield, Lincs, 1760 Lincs RO Ad/Ac/45/29
Nixon, Anthony, Faversham, Kent, 1617 CKS PRC2/22/16
Nixon, Ralph, innholder, Swinford, Old (Stourbridge), Worcs, 1734 Worcs RO 008.7 BA3585/836/bdl 2
Nixsam, William, Sturry, Kent, 1601 CKS PRC2/12/262
Noake, Robert, Chisledon, Wilts, 1635 Wilts RO Arch. Wilts.(+ name and date)
Noakes, Catherine, minor, Sandwich, Kent, 1623 CKS PRC2/24/29
Noakes, Joseph, Castle Morton, Worcs, 1795 Worcs RO 008.7 BA3585/835/bdl 2
Noakes, Thomas, Woodchurch, Kent, 1703 CKS PRC19/6/15
Nobes, Anne, widow, Tilehurst, Berks, Berks RO D/A1/206/5C
Noble, Anthony, Old Romney, Kent, 1636 CKS PRC2/33/99
Noble, Catherine, widow, St Peter in Thanet, Kent, 1619 CKS PRC2/22/19
Noble, Edward, mariner: 'ship master', Stepney (Stebenhythe), London & Middlesex, 1673 PRO PROB32/11/80
Noble, Francis, tailor, Shadoxhurst, Kent, 1640 CKS PRC1/3/23
Noble, Francis, husbandman, St Mary in the Marsh, Kent, 1670 CKS PRC1/14/82
Noble, John, Laughton, Lincs, 1634 Lincs RO Ad/Ac/40/69
Noble, John, Barholm, Lincs, 1639 Lincs RO Ad/Ac/26/320
Noble, John, Glentham, Lincs, 1665 Lincs RO Ad/Ac/42/38
Noble, John, Stratford-upon-Avon, Warks, 1682 Worcs RO 008.7 BA3585/837/bdl 3
Noble, John, Mattishall, Norf, 1765 Norfolk RO ANF/11/5/62
Noble, Mary, widow, York St Michael le Belfrey, Yorks, Borthwick Test C.P. 1760/3
Noble, Oliver, Kettlethorpe, Lincs, 1615 Lincs RO Ad/Ac/8c/21
Noble, Oliver, Kettlethorpe, Lincs, 1615 Lincs RO Ad/Ac/8c/22
Noble, Robert, Whiteparish, Wilts, 1613 Wilts RO Arch. Sarum(+ name and date)
Noble, Robert, Canterbury St Andrew, Kent, 1689 CKS PRC2/41/156
Noble, Thomas, yeoman, New Romney, Kent, 1691 CKS PRC19/5/4
Nock, William, carpenter, Pattingham (Westbick), Staffs, 1800 LJRO/B/C/5/1800/36
Noddle, Job, Ludford, Lincs, 1624 Lincs RO Ad/Ac/19A/88
Nodes, Charles, gentleman, Shephall, Herts, 1596 Herts RO ASA25/1562
Nodes, John, gentleman, Milton next Sittingbourne, Kent, 1640 CKS PRC19/1/68
Noell, John, Parham, Sussex, 1684 W. Suss RO EpI/33/1684/10
Noke, Richard, Hinksey, South, Berks, 1584 Berks RO D/A2/C19/f195-6
Noke, Thomas, clergy: 'mr/vicar', Goodnestone next Wingham, Kent, 1624 CKS PRC20/6/140
Nokes, George, Wye, Kent, 1634 CKS PRC2/32/92
Nole, John, gentleman, Challock, Kent, 1613 CKS PRC20/2/360
Noone, George, Northaw, Herts, 1635 Herts RO ASA25/4915
Noone, John, Northaw, Herts, 1636 Herts RO ASA25/4916
Noone, Lawrence, Barrow upon Trent, Derby, 1685 LJRO/B/C/5/1685/65

[Norborne:]
Norborne, John, Covent Garden, St Paul, London & Middlesex, 1682 PRO PROB32/19/309
Norborne, William, yeoman, Bremhill, Wilts, 1640 Wilts RO Arch. Wilts.(+ name and date)
Norbourne, Mary, spinster, Thatcham (Greenham), Berks, 1678 Berks RO D/A1/206/23C
Norclif, Jonas, Tattershall, Lincs, 1600 Lincs RO Ad/Ac/5/346
Norcott, John, husbandman, Greenham, Berks, 1595 Berks RO D/A1/205/185C
Norcott, Joyce, widow, Bierton, Bucks, 1663 Oxon RO MSS Wills Pec 47/2/12
Norcrofte, John, Shaw cum Donnington, Berks, 1617 Berks RO D/A1/205/203C
Norcrosse, Giles, Road, Som, 1611 Somerset RO D/D/Cta/N10
Norden, Henry, Rowde, Wilts, 1632 Wilts RO Arch. Wilts.(+ name and date)
Norden, John, innholder, Cranbrook, Kent, 1665 CKS PRC1/10/66
Norden, Jone, widow, Willesborough, Kent, 1586 CKS PRC2/4/180
Norden, Richard, maltster, Tenterden, Kent, 1682 CKS PRC2/40/63
Norden, Wyllyam, Ashford, Kent, 1596 CKS PRC2/9/158
Norley, Thomas, Sandhurst, Kent, 1695 CKS PRC2/42/106
Norley, William, Wittersham, Kent, 1593 CKS PRC21/12/42
Norley, William, Stone in Oxney, Kent, 1638 CKS PRC20/11/163
Norlie, Thomas, Stone in Oxney, Kent, 1596 CKS PRC2/8/254
Norly, John, Wittersham, Kent, 1622 CKS PRC20/6/298
Norly, John, husbandman, Woodchurch, Kent, 1684 CKS PRC20/13/450
Norman, Alice, widow, Spalding, Lincs, 1623 Lincs RO Ad/Ac/17/93
Norman, Augustine, Rotherfield Greys, Oxon, 1633 Oxon RO MSS Wills 299/2/7
Norman, Edward, Boughton under Blean, Kent, 1637 CKS PRC20/11/167
Norman, Edward, Ivychurch, Kent, 1637 CKS PRC20/11/177
Norman, George, Otley, Yorks, 1621 Borthwick Prob. Ex. 1621/2
Norman, Henry, Teddington, London & Middlesex, 1679 PRO PROB32/16/40
Norman, John, Hollingbourne, Kent, CKS PRC21/3/42
Norman, John, husbandman, Chadlington, Oxon, 1648 Oxon RO MSS Wills 299/2/17
Norman, John ygr, grocer, Deal, Kent, 1643 CKS PRC19/2/75
Norman, Margarett, Boughton under Blean, Kent, 1583 CKS PRC21/6/405
Norman, Richard, gentleman, Cottenham, Cambs, 1751 Cambs RO 1750/Admon
Norman, Robert, Canterbury St Mary Northgate, Kent, 1639 CKS PRC2/34/249
Norman, Saloman, Great Mongeham, Kent, 1619 CKS PRC2/22/26
Norman, Stephen, Boughton under Blean, Kent, 1583 CKS PRC21/6/186
Norman, William, Bloxholme, Lincs, 1611 Lincs RO Ad/Ac/10/113
Norman, Willyam, Brabourne, Kent, 1620 CKS PRC2/22/6
Normans, Thomas, Somerby, Lincs, 1627 Lincs RO Ad/Ac/20b/65
Normanton, Andrew, Sowerby, Yorks, 1636 Borthwick Prob. Ex. 1636/4
Normanton, Michael, yeoman, Halifax, Yorks, 1824 Borthwick Test C.P. 1824/3
Normanton, Richard, Baston, Lincs, 1646 Lincs RO Ad/Ac/28/213
Normanton, Richard, Baston, Lincs, 1646? Lincs RO Ad/Ac/28/186
Normanton, Robert, yeoman, Lincoln (The Mallandrie), Lincs, 1623 Lincs RO Ad/Ac/18/32
Norreys, Christopher, Canterbury St Mildred, Kent, 1641 CKS PRC1/6/6
Norreys, Henry, gentleman, Rainham, Kent, 1632 CKS PRC2/31/139
Norridge, Martha, widow, Fowlmere, Cambs, 1720 PRO PROB5/998
Norrington, Amy, widow, Bethersden, Kent, 1633 CKS PRC2/32/93
Norrington, Joane, widow, Bethersden, Kent, 1677 CKS PRC2/37/179
Norrington, John, Bobbing, Kent, 1621 CKS PRC2/22/17
Norrington, John, Mersham, Kent, 1680 CKS PRC2/39/76
Norrington, John ygr, Bethersden, Kent, 1633 CKS PRC2/32/90
Norrington, Matthew, High Halstow, Kent, 1683 CKS PRC2/40/136
Norrington, Michael, Bethersden, Kent, 1677 CKS PRC2/37/71
Norrington, Michel, Mersham, Kent, 1617 CKS PRC2/22/25
Norrington, Richard, husbandman, Bilsington, Kent, 1670 CKS PRC1/15/51
Norrington, William, Whitstable, Kent, 1595 CKS PRC2/7/263
Norris, Hugh, Wayford, Som, 1672 Somerset RO D/D/Cta/N7

Norris, John, Buckland, Berks, 1610 Berks RO D/A1/205/197C
Norris, John, Bradley, North, Wilts, 1614 Wilts RO Arch. Sarum(+ name and date)
Norris, John, Rolvenden, Kent, 1637 CKS PRC2/33/95
Norris, John, yeoman, Kiddington, Oxon, 1667 Oxon RO MSS Wills 84/1/22
Norris, John, labourer, Burmarsh, Kent, 1673 CKS PRC2/35/244
Norris, John, Blockley, Worcs, 1682 Worcs RO 008.7 BA3585/837/bdl 3
Norris, John, limeburner, Thornham, Kent, 1683 CKS PRC2/40/135
Norris, Katherine, widow, Wye, Kent, 1675 CKS PRC2/36/218
Norris, Nicholas, Lydd, Kent, 1627 CKS PRC20/7/189
Norris, Robert, Holbeach, Lincs, 1606 Lincs RO Ad/Ac/6/81
Norris, Silvester, gentleman, Winkfield, Berks, Berks RO D/A1/101/124C
Norris, Thomas, Burmarsh, Kent, 1622 CKS PRC2/24/31
Norris, Thomas, jurat, Burmarsh, Kent, 1668 CKS PRC1/13/84
Norris/Osburne, Anne, widow, Weston, Lincs, 1636 Lincs RO Ad/Ac/24/403
Norrish, Francis, St Thomas-by-Launceston, Corn, 1621 Cornwall RO AP/N111/2
Norrwood, Mary, widow, Bobbing, Kent, 1639 CKS PRC1/3/24
Norrys, John, Bramber, Sussex, 1618 W. Suss RO EpI/33/1618/8
Norrys, Rychard, Burmarsh, Kent, 1597 CKS PRC2/10/384
Norrys, Thomas, Brookland, Kent, 1599 CKS PRC2/11/255
Norten, Thomas, yeoman, Lydiard Millicent, Wilts, 1680? Wilts RO Arch. Wilts.(+ name and date)
North, John, Purton, Wilts, 1635 Wilts RO Arch. Wilts.(+ name and date)
North, Richard, Leake, East, Notts, 1639 Borthwick Prob. Ex. 1639/3
North, Robert, Lambourn, Berks, 1602 Berks RO D/A1/205/191L
North, Robert, Lambourn, Berks, 1606 Berks RO D/A1/205/191C
North, Thomas, Legbourne, Lincs, 1636 Lincs RO Ad/Ac/24/564
North, Thomas, yeoman, Abingdon St Helen (Shippon), Berks, 1682 Berks RO D/A1/206/28B
North, William, bachelor, Tewin, Herts, 1637 Herts RO AHH23/1715
North, see Harding,
Northall, Benjamin, yeoman, Wybunbury (Willaston), Ches, 1777 Cheshire RO (Name) W.C. 1777-8
Northam, Thomas, labourer, Purley, Berks, 1640 Berks RO D/A1/101/207C
Northe, Richard, Hawton, Notts, 1621 Borthwick Prob. Ex. 1621/1
Northe, Thomas, Hallington, Lincs, 1600 Lincs RO Ad/Ac/5/421
Northe, Thomas, Sandwich, Kent, 1606 CKS PRC1/1/4
Northe, Thomas, Bourne, Lincs, 1612 Lincs RO Ad/Ac/11/191
Northen, Thomas, Holme, Hunts, 1605 Hunts RO/Acc58/3(53)
Northend, William, gentleman, Rowley (Little Weighton), Yorks, 1774 Borthwick Test C.P. 1774/3
Northouse, William, butcher, Leeds, Yorks, 1771 Borthwick Test C.P. 1771/2
Northus, Francis, victualler/scholar's servant, Cambridge Holy Sepulchre, Cambs, 1634 CUL V.C. Acc./Box2/52
Norton, Alice, widow, Lydd, Kent, 1592 CKS PRC21/11/177
Norton, Clement, Chillenden, Kent, 1632 CKS PRC2/31/140
Norton, Daniel, bricklayer, Selling, Kent, 1678 CKS PRC2/38/55
Norton, Edward,
Som Somerset RO D/D/Cta/N5
Norton, Edward, cordwainer: 'shoemaker', Stamford, Lincs, 1622 Lincs RO Ad/Ac/17/42
Norton, Elizabeth, widow, Fleckney, Leics, 1640 Leics RO PR/I/41A/42
Norton, John, Ivychurch, Kent, 1587 CKS PRC21/8/214
Norton, John, Old Romney, Kent, 1626 CKS PRC2/25/101
Norton, John, Egerton, Kent, 1665 CKS PRC19/3/78
Norton, Joseph, Washingborough, Lincs, 1780 Lincs RO Ad/Ac/45/42
Norton, Luke, Spalding, Lincs, 1649 Lincs RO Ad/Ac/30/104
Norton, Rabydge, widow, Chislet, Kent, 1630 CKS PRC2/30/105

[Norton:]
Norton, Richard, yeoman, Hampstead Marshall, Berks, 1631 Berks RO D/A1/205/215C
Norton, Richard, Badlesmere, Kent, 1637 CKS PRC2/34/85
Norton, Robert, university: 'Fellow of University College, Oxford', Oxford (University College), Oxon, Bodleian HYP B9/29-30
Norton, Robert, tailor, Burwell, Lincs, 1613 Lincs RO Ad/Ac/12/23
Norton, Robert, St Mary in the Marsh, Kent, 1616 CKS PRC2/22/23
Norton, Simon, yeoman, Bicknoller, Som, 1588 Somerset RO D/D/Cta/N9
Norton, Stephen, gentleman, Chart nr Sutton Valence, Kent, 1612 CKS PRC2/16/38
Norton, Suzan, widow, Egerton, Kent, 1618 CKS PRC20/4/284
Norton, Thomas, Chart, Great, Kent, 1626 CKS PRC2/27/115
Norton, Thomas, gentleman, Chichester, Sussex, 1627 W. Suss RO EpIII/9/1/31
Norton, Thomas, shepherd, Markfield, Leics, 1639 Leics RO PR/I/41A/32
Norton, Thomas, Bubbenhall, Warks, 1683 LJRO/B/C/5/1682/77
Norton, Thomas ygr, bachelor, Elham, Kent, 1665 CKS PRC1/11/64
Norton, Valentine, esquire, Fordwich, Kent, 1647 CKS PRC1/8/24
Norton, William, Linwood, Lincs, 1625 Lincs RO Ad/Ac/19B/39
Norton, William, Combe (Lopper?), Warks, 1672 LJRO:cards/1672/42
Norway, Elizabeth, widow, Chippenham, Wilts, 1615 Wilts RO Arch. Wilts.(+ name and date)
Norway, Richard, husbandman, Brightwell, Berks, 1595 Berks RO D/A1/205/187C
Norwood, Alexander, gentleman, St Peter in Thanet, Kent, 1622 CKS PRC2/24/28
Norwood, Edward, St Johns Thanet, Kent, 1586 CKS PRC2/3/343
Norwood, George, Herne, Kent, 1630 CKS PRC20/9/300
Norwood, Joan, St Peter in Thanet, Kent, 1606 CKS PRC2/15/267
Norwood, John, labourer, St Nicholas at Wade, Kent, 1672 CKS PRC20/12/55
Norwood, Richard, St Peter in Thanet, Kent, 1599 CKS PRC2/10/477
Norwood, Richard, maltster, St Peter in Thanet, Kent, 1668 CKS PRC1/13/85
Norwood, Richard, bricklayer, Stourmouth, Kent, 1669 CKS PRC1/14/83
Norwood, Richarde, St Laurence Thanet, Kent, 1608 CKS PRC2/15/269
Norwood, Simon, St Peter in Thanet, Kent, 1614 CKS PRC2/18/83
Norwood, Thomas, Maidstone, Kent, 1592 CKS PRC21/11/228
Norwood, Thomas, St Johns Thanet, Kent, 1611 CKS PRC2/16/82
Norwood, Thomas, Bobbing, Kent, 1637 CKS PRC2/34/86
Norwood, William, St Johns Thanet, Kent, 1579 CKS PRC2/2/7
Norwood, William, Tonge, Kent, 1609 CKS PRC2/15/271
Norwood, William, Holme, Hunts, 1677 Hunts RO/Acc58/103(25)
Norwood, William, bachelor, St Johns Thanet, Kent, 1680 CKS PRC2/38/164
Norwood, Willyam, St Peter in Thanet, Kent, 1619 CKS PRC2/21/70
Norwoodd, George, St Johns Thanet, Kent, 1574 CKS PRC2/1/79
Norwoodd, Robert, St Peter in Thanet, Kent, 1630 CKS PRC2/30/106
Norwoodd, William, St Johns Thanet, Kent, 1613 CKS PRC2/18/2
Nosse, Joan, Petherton, North, Som, 1621 Somerset RO D/D/Cta/N6
Notingham, Robert, Herne, Kent, 1638 CKS PRC20/11/179
Nott, Daniell, Ash next Sandwich, Kent, 1683 CKS PRC20/13/362
Nott, Edmund, gentleman, Shelsey, Worcs, 1609 Worcs RO 008.7 BA3585/839/453
Nott, Edmund, gentleman, Brabourne, Kent, 1664 CKS PRC1/10/67
Nott, Elizabeth, Shelsey Beauchamp, Worcs, 1684 Worcs RO 008.7 BA3585/837/bdl 4
Nott, Fayth, Monks Horton, Kent, 1602 CKS PRC2/12/258
Nott, William, Blean, Kent, 1619 CKS PRC2/22/27
Nott, William, St James in the Fields, London & Middlesex, 1696 PRO PROB32/39/27
Nottage, Milton next Sittingbourne, Kent, 1682 CKS PRC1/15/101
Nottage, Christopher, fellmonger, Milton next Sittingbourne, Kent, 1668 CKS PRC1/13/86
Nottage, John, fellmonger, Milton next Sittingbourne, Kent, 1680 CKS PRC2/39/77
Notte, Daniell, Tilmanstone, Kent, 1616 CKS PRC20/3/397
Nottell, Thomas, Liskeard, Corn, 1606 Cornwall RO AP/N24
Notting, John, Milton next Sittingbourne, Kent, 1627 CKS PRC2/28/88

Nottingham, Thomas, bachelor: 'singleman', Leicester, Leics, 1623 Lincs RO Ad/Ac/18/76
Nowell, John, physician, Ashford, Kent, 1673 CKS PRC2/35/246
Nowell, Richard, Sandwich St Peter, Kent, 1590 CKS PRC2/5/257
Nowell, Richard, chandler: 'tallow chandler', Sandwich, Kent, 1719 CKS PRC1/18/23
Nowell, Roger, Itchenor, West, Sussex, 1583 W. Suss RO EpI/33/1583/5
Nowell, Thomas, Sandwich St Bartholomew's Hospital, Kent, 1616 CKS PRC20/3/393
Nowell, Thomas, Grayingham, Lincs, 1622 Lincs RO Ad/Ac/8c/3
Nowell, Thomas, Sandwich St Bartholomew's Hospital, Kent, 1630 CKS PRC20/9/296
Nower, Daniel, gentleman, Ashford, Kent, 1647 CKS PRC1/8/25
Nower, Daniel, Maidstone, Kent, 1673 CKS PRC20/12/94
Nower, Isake, Langdon, East, Kent, 1595 CKS PRC2/7/183
Nower, Symon, Woodchurch, Kent, 1613 CKS PRC20/2/537
Nowers, Elizabeth, Pluckley, Kent, 1679 CKS PRC2/38/165
Nowre, Henry, Benenden, Kent, 1627 CKS PRC2/28/89
Noxe, Clement, Staplehurst, Kent, 1591 CKS PRC2/5/253
Noy, John, Faversham, Kent, 1680 CKS PRC2/39/79
Noyce, Hugh, Downton, Wilts, 1615 Wilts RO Miscellaneous Index (name + date)
Noyce, Thomas, Warfield, Berks, 1615 Berks RO D/A1/205/202C
Noyce, Thomas, yeoman, Frilford, Berks, 1635 Berks RO D/A1/205/222C
Noye, Joseph, gentleman, St Buryan, Corn, 1674? PRO PROB5/1042
Noyer, Henry, yeoman, Rotherfield Greys, Oxon, 1667 Oxon RO MSS Wills 48/1/11
Noyes, George, Downton, Wilts, 1632? Wilts RO Arch. Sarum(+ name and date)
Noyes, Hugh, Downton (Charlton), Wilts, 1643 Wilts RO Arch. Sarum(+ name and date)
Noyes, Nicholas, Andover, Hants, 1664 Hants RO 21M65 D8/189a
Noyes, Thomas, Tidcombe, Wilts, 1634 Wilts RO Arch. Wilts.(+ name and date)
Nuby, James, Driby, Lincs, 1650 Lincs RO Ad/Ac/29/52
Nun, John, Ramsey, Hunts, 1684 Hunts RO/Acc58/235(236)
Nunam/Newnham, John, Ash next Sandwich, Kent, 1595 CKS PRC21/13/48
Nunn, Robert, yeoman, Lawshall, Suff, 1746 Suff RO(B) IC500/3/50/39
Nunwick, Elizabeth, widow, Normanby, Lincs, 1675 Lincs RO Ad/Ac/35/102
Nunwick, William, gentleman, Normanby, Lincs, 1686 Lincs RO Ad/Ac/44/151
Nunwicke, John, Milton next Sittingbourne, Kent, 1587 CKS PRC2/4/408
Nurss, Robert, cordwainer, Boston, Lincs, 1680 Lincs RO Ad/Ac/43/170
Nutbeame, John, Downton, Wilts, 1614 Wilts RO Arch. Sarum(+ name and date)
Nuth, John, Swindon, Wilts, 1682 Wilts RO Arch. Wilts.(+ name and date)
Nutkin, Henry, Bushey, Herts, 1611 Herts RO ASA25/4792
Nutkyn, Thomas, Rickmansworth, Herts, 1594 Herts RO ASA25/1490
Nutlinge, Jane, Lavington, West, Wilts, 1638 Wilts RO CC Sarum(+ name and date)
Nuton, Andrew, blacksmith, Lavington, Market, Wilts, 1639 Wilts RO Arch. Sarum(+ name and date)
Nuton, Prudence, Madron, Corn, 1646 Cornwall RO AP/N213/1
Nuton, William, Ash next Sandwich, Kent, 1665 CKS PRC19/3/57
Nutsam, Anthonie, Humberstone, Lincs, 1593 Lincs RO Ad/Ac/3/37
Nutt, Joseph, husbandman, Dorchester (Burcott), Oxon, 1716 Oxon RO MSS Wills Pec 79/2/12
Nutt, Richard, husbandman, Stanford in the Vale, Berks, 1625 Berks RO D/A1/205/210C
Nutt, Samuel, Nuneaton, Warks, 1794 LJRO/B/C/5/1794/75
Nutt, Thomas, butcher, Bristol St Philip & St Jacob, Glos, Bristol RO 1762/CP
Nuttall, Daniell, gentleman, Leeds St Peter (Wortley), Yorks, 1620 Borthwick Prob. Ex. 1620/1
Nuttall, Edward + Margarete, 1592 Lancs RO (Name of Deceased) D.R.C.H. 1592
Nuttall, John, Edenfield, Lancs, 1629 Lancs RO (Name of Deceased) D.R.C.H. 1628-29
Nuttell, Richard, Lanivet, Corn, 1625 Cornwall RO AP/N137/2
Nutting, Howland, university: 'registry office, employed in', Cambridge, Cambs, 1726 c. CUL V.C. Acc./Box3/35
Nutting, John, yeoman, Chislet, Kent, 1666 CKS PRC1/11/140
Nuttinge, John, St Pauls Walden, Herts, 1596 Herts RO ASA25/1563

[Nuttinge:]
Nuttinge, William, St Pauls Walden, Herts, 1629 Herts RO ASA25/4865
Nuttor, William, Hucknall, Ault, Derby, 1682 LJRO/B/C/5/1682/78
Nutwicke, Jeames, Appledore, Kent, 1609 CKS PRC2/15/265
Nycholls, Adryan, alderman, Canterbury, Kent, 1593 CKS PRC2/6/396
Nye, John, Billingshurst (Woodhouse), Sussex, 1662 W. Suss RO EpI/33/1661/1
Nye, Thomas, Billingshurst, Sussex, 1684 W. Suss RO EpI/33/1684/8
Nyghtingall, Robert, gentleman, Watford, Herts, 1581 Herts RO ASA25/1015
Nyn, George, gentleman, Bobbing, Kent, 1619 CKS PRC2/22/12
Oagle, Thomas, gentleman, Humberstone, Lincs, 1632 Lincs RO Ad/Ac/23/45
Oake, Gregory, clothworker/shearman, Goudhurst, Kent, 1671 CKS PRC2/35/74
Oake, Simon, Martin, Wilts, 1639 Wilts RO Arch. Sarum(+ name and date)
Oake, William, weaver, Salisbury, Wilts, 1681 Wilts RO Miscellaneous Index (name + date)
Oakeley, Thomas, Denton (Eastry hundred), Kent, 1648 CKS PRC1/8/51
Oakely, Samuel, gentleman, Launton, Oxon, 1639 Oxon RO MSS Wills 299/3/23
Oakes, James jun, Derby, Derby, 1684 LJRO/B/C/5/1683/12
Oakes, John, scissors maker, Sheffield, Yorks, 1853 Borthwick Test C.P. 1853/5
Oakes, William, Dorrington, Lincs, 1626 Lincs RO Ad/Ac/20/74
Oakes, William, Dawley (Dawley Greene), Shrops, 1681 LJRO/B/C/5/1681/29
Oakley, Joane, Aldershot, Hants, 1596 Hants RO 1596 B55/4
Oakshott, Mathew, Luddenham, Kent, 1684 CKS PRC2/40/227
Oaram, Richard, Castle Cary, Som, 1630 Somerset RO D/D/Cta/O4
Oateridge, Henry, Grittleton, Wilts, 1631 Wilts RO CC Sarum(+ name and date)
Oates, Alice, Mayfield, Staffs, 1702 LJRO/B/C/5/1702/21
Oates, James, cutler, Newcastle under Lyme, Staffs, 1669 LJRO:cards/1669/11
Oatley, John, Ashton, Steeple, Wilts, 1626 Wilts RO CC Sarum(+ name and date)
Oatridge, Samuel, yeoman, Oaksey, Wilts, 1695 Wilts RO CC Sarum(+ name and date)
Obbin, Thomas, labourer, Hacconby, Lincs, 1619 Lincs RO Ad/Ac/15/262
Obbinson, Thomas, yeoman, Keal, West, Lincs, 1670 Lincs RO Ad/Ac/33/135
Obinson, William, Aisthorpe (Thorpe in the Fallows), Lincs, 1645 Lincs RO Ad/Ac/28/140
Oborne, Thomas, Tisbury, Wilts, 1620 Wilts RO Miscellaneous Index (name + date)
Obrey, Edward, Spilsby, Lincs, 1611 Lincs RO Ad/Ac/10/62
Obrey, George, Donington, Lincs, 1638 Lincs RO Ad/Ac/25/342
Obrey, Joseph, yeoman, Aslackby, Lincs, 1683 Lincs RO Ad/Ac/44/78
Obrey, Robert, Sempringham, Lincs, 1641 Lincs RO Ad/Ac/27/259
Obrey, William, Donington, Lincs, 1613 Lincs RO Ad/Ac/12/117
Ockham, John, Reading St Giles, Berks, 1595 Berks RO D/A1/102/28C
Ockman, John, Canterbury St Margaret, Kent, 1684 CKS PRC2/40/228
Ockman, Simon, Brenzett, Kent, 1624 CKS PRC2/24/37
Ockman, Simon, gentleman, Canterbury St Alphege, Kent, 1675 CKS PRC20/12/179
Ockman, William, Brenzett, Kent, 1592 CKS PRC2/6/468
Ockman, Wyllyam, Brenzett, Kent, 1588 CKS PRC2/4/149
Ockold, Richard eld, Abingdon, Berks, 1597 Berks RO D/A1/206/90B
Odam, Andrew, victualler, Sandwich St Peter, Kent, 1684 CKS PRC2/40/226
Odam, William, yeoman, Lambourn (Upper Lambourn), Berks, 1612 Berks RO D/A1/206/93A
Odiarne, Gregory eld, gentleman, Leeds, Kent, 1669 CKS PRC1/14/84
Odiarne, Gregory eld, Leeds, Kent, 1670 CKS PRC1/14/84a
Odiarne, Richard, labourer, Molash, Kent, 1683 CKS PRC2/40/138
Odierne, Thomas, Harbledown, Kent, 1681 CKS PRC2/39/210
Odley, Tobyas, Bishopsbourne, Kent, 1586 CKS PRC2/3/269
Odlin, John, Baumber, Lincs, 1624 Lincs RO Ad/Ac/19A/116
Odyarne, James, New Romney, Kent, 1588 CKS PRC21/9/70
Odyarne, Thomas, Bethersden, Kent, 1631 CKS PRC2/30/107
Odye, Joane, widow, Christian Malford, Wilts, 1674 Wilts RO Miscellaneous Index (name + date)
Odye, Richard, Tockenham, Wilts, 1627 Wilts RO Arch. Wilts.(name + date)
Odymer, Edmund, Chart, Great, Kent, 1596 CKS PRC2/9/305

Offley, Thomas, esquire, St Martin in the Fields, London & Middlesex, 1679 PRO PROB32/16/115
Offley, Thomas, Holywell (Needingworth), Hunts, 1682 Hunts RO/Acc58/179(106)
Ogborne, see Taylor,
Ogden, Abraham, innkeeper, Stockport (Dukinfield), Ches, 1789 Cheshire RO (Name) W.C. 1789
Ogden, Christopher, Somerby, Leics, 1669 Leics RO Administrators Accounts 1667-72 f15
Ogden, Margaret, university: 'privileged person/widow', Cambridge, Cambs, 1634 c. CUL V.C. Acc./Box2/53
Ogle, Robert, gentleman, Pinchbeck, Lincs, 1628 Lincs RO Ad/Ac/20b/59
Oglethorpe, James, gentleman, Nocton, Lincs, 1640 Lincs RO Ad/Ac/27/130
Oglethorpe, Robert, Nocton, Lincs, 1641 Lincs RO Ad/Ac/27/255
Okeden, Anne, widow, Lenham, Kent, 1574 CKS PRC2/1/94
Okeden, Anne, widow, Lenham, Kent, 1574 CKS PRC2/1/98
Okeden, Anne, Lenham, Kent, 1579 CKS PRC2/1/254
Okeley, Edward, alderman, Lincoln, Lincs, 1638 Lincs RO Ad/Ac/25/655
Okeley, John, Hacconby, Lincs, 1580 Lincs RO Ad/Ac/2b/56
Okell, Daniel, cooper, Chester, Ches, 1736 Cheshire RO (Name) W.C. 1735
Okell, Richard, Prescot (Cruerdley), Lancs, 1630 Lancs RO (Name of Deceased) D.R.C.H. 1624-26
Okell, William, clergy: 'clerk', Canterbury St Alphege, Kent, 1595 CKS PRC21/13/44
Okely, Anthony, Woolford, Great, Warks, 1680 Worcs RO 008.7 BA3585/837/bdl 2
Okenfall, Jacob, Eastchurch, Sheppey, Kent, 1597 CKS PRC2/9/307
Okenfold, Thomas, yeoman, Hoath, Kent, 1680 CKS PRC20/12/316
Okey, John, Holbeach, Lincs, 1607 Lincs RO Ad/Ac/7/98
Okey, John, bachelor: 'singleman', Gosberton, Lincs, 1614 Lincs RO Ad/Ac/13/119
Okey, John ygr, Haddenham, Cambs, CUL V.C. Acc./Box3/68
Okey, William, Sutton St James, Lincs, 1614 Lincs RO Ad/Ac/13/139
Oland, John, Blagdon, Som, 1630 Somerset RO D/D/Cta/O1
Olberde, Elizabeth, High Halden, Kent, 1596 CKS PRC2/8/483
Oldane, Jane, widow, Leake, Lincs, 1625 Lincs RO Ad/Ac/19B/50
Olden, Martha, Fonthill Bishop, Wilts, 1682 Wilts RO Arch. Sarum(+ name and date)
Olden, Robert, surgeon: 'barber-surgeon', Warminster, Wilts, 1635 Wilts RO Arch. Sarum(+ name and date)
Older, John, husbandman, Angmering, Sussex, 1625 W. Suss RO EpI/33/1625/11
Oldes, William, Deverill, Longbridge, Wilts, 1674? Wilts RO Arch. Sarum(+ name and date)
Oldfeelde, David, Alkham, Kent, 1597 CKS PRC2/9/162
Oldfeild, John, Alkham, Kent, 1663 CKS PRC1/9/133
Oldfeild, Phillipp, Knutsford (Over Knutsford), Ches, 1635 Cheshire RO (Name) W.C. 1634-5
Oldfeild, William, Dover St Mary, Kent, 1617 CKS PRC20/4/292
Oldfeilde, see Ovill,
Oldfield, Anthony, maltster, Sandwich, Kent, 1682 CKS PRC2/40/64
Oldfield, Dorothy, widow, Chippenham, Wilts, 1678 Wilts RO Miscellaneous Index (name + date)
Oldfield, John, Alfreton, Derby, 1684 LJRO/B/C/5/1683/13
Oldfield, Michael, maltster, Deal, Kent, 1664 CKS PRC19/3/37
Oldfield, Thomas, Ewell, Kent, 1620 CKS PRC2/22/4
Oldfield, Thomas, gentleman, Stratford Tony, Wilts, 1631 Wilts RO Arch. Sarum(+ name and date)
Oldfield, William, yeoman, Wingham, Kent, 1666 CKS PRC19/3/102
Oldfield, see Baker,
Oldham, Edward, Prestbury (Butley), Ches, 1695 Cheshire RO (Name) W.C. 1695
Oldis, William, Compton, Over, Dors, 1613 Wilts RO Dean Sarum (name + date)
Oldman, Thomas, Kyme, South, Lincs, 1619 Lincs RO Ad/Ac/15/153
Oldner, George, Hinckley, Leics, 1670 Leics RO Administrators Accounts 1667-72 f23
Oldwood, John, Chart nr Sutton Valence, Kent, 1597 CKS PRC2/9/164
Olerenshawe, William, university: 'Fellow of St John's College, Cambridge/B.D.', Cambridge,

[Olerenshawe:]
Cambs, 1621 CUL V.C.Acc./Box1/41
Olfree/Alfree, Thomas, Sandhurst, Kent, 1619 CKS PRC2/20/381
Oliffe, Elizabeth, Whitchurch, Som, 1664 Somerset RO D/D/Cta/O5
Oliver, Averie, Doddington, Kent, 1594 CKS PRC2/7/327
Oliver, Christopher, Tonge, Kent, 1626 CKS PRC2/27/119
Oliver, George, Findon, Sussex, 1611 W. Suss RO EpI/33/1611/14
Oliver, Henry, Bilsington, Kent, 1683 CKS PRC2/40/137
Oliver, Isaac, mariner, Sandwich, Kent, 1675 CKS PRC2/36/102
Oliver, Jane, Tonge, Kent, 1628 CKS PRC2/29/72
Oliver, John, Gainsborough, Lincs, 1595 Lincs RO Ad/Ac/37/18
Oliver, John, Selling, Kent, 1596 CKS PRC2/8/387
Oliver, John, Canterbury Holy Cross Westgate, Kent, 1598 CKS PRC2/10/254
Oliver, John, chapman, Manaccan, Corn, 1621 Cornwall RO AP/O65/2
Oliver, John, Wiston, Sussex, 1640 W. Suss RO EpI/33/1640/11
Oliver, John, gardener, Coventry, Warks, 1768 LJRO/B/C/5/1766/102
Oliver, John eld, Mersham, Kent, 1606 CKS PRC2/13/300
Oliver, John ygr, weaver? or merchant ?, Sandwich, Kent, 1640 CKS PRC1/3/25
Oliver, Margaret, Appledore, Kent, 1592 CKS PRC2/5/13
Oliver, Mildred, Kingsnorth, Kent, 1592 CKS PRC2/5/29
Oliver, Peter, Bottesford (East Butterwick), Lincs, 1603 Lincs RO Ad/Ac/37/156
Oliver, Richard, Rolvenden, Kent, 1644 CKS PRC1/7/29
Oliver, Richard, Rolvenden, Kent, 1680 CKS PRC2/39/82
Oliver, Richard, Boughton under Blean, Kent, 1682 CKS PRC20/13/273
Oliver, Robert, Gainsborough, Lincs, 1633 Lincs RO Ad/Ac/40/71
Oliver, Robert, Maidstone, Kent, 1641 CKS PRC19/2/29
Oliver, Roger, Sandwich St Peter, Kent, 1627 CKS PRC2/28/86
Oliver, Samuel, Herne, Kent, 1712 CKS PRC19/6/56
Oliver, Sarah, Butterwick, Lincs, 1679 Lincs RO Ad/Ac/43/84
Oliver, Thomas, gentleman, Bottesford (East Butterwick), Lincs, 1669 Lincs RO Ad/Ac/33/165
Oliver, Waldram, Sandwich St Peter, Kent, 1667 CKS PRC1/12/66
Oliver, William, Boughton Malherbe, Kent, 1662 CKS PRC1/9/44
Oliver, see Becke & Langford,
Ollett, John, Swineshead, Lincs, 1636 Lincs RO Ad/Ac/24/478
Olliffe, William, cordwainer: 'shoemaker', Bierton, Bucks, 1631 Oxon RO MSS Wills Pec 47/4/6
Olliffe, William, Cocking, Sussex, 1662 W. Suss RO EpI/33/1661/4
Olliver, George, Halton, West, Lincs, 1665 Lincs RO Ad/Ac/41/136
Olliver, Henry, Lyminster (Wick), Sussex, 1650 W. Suss RO EpI/33/1649/1
Olliver, John, Steyning, Sussex, 1630 W. Suss RO EpI/33/1630/8
Olliver, John, Halton, West, Lincs, 1644 Lincs RO Ad/Ac/40/111
Olliver, John, bachelor, Angmering, Sussex, 1673 W. Suss RO EpI/33/1673/2
Olliver, Thomas, Clapham, Sussex, 1649 W. Suss RO EpI/33/1649/3
Olliver, Thomas, husbandman, Ashford, Kent, 1669 CKS PRC1/14/85
Ollow, John, husbandman, Rainham, Kent, 1692 CKS PRC2/42/47
Ollyver, William, Tortington, Sussex, 1631 W. Suss RO EpI/33/1631/5
Olyver, Isaacke, Sandwich, Kent, 1598 CKS PRC2/10/270
Olyver, John, Upchurch, Kent, 1616 CKS PRC20/3/222
Olyver, John ygr, Mersham, Kent, 1606 CKS PRC2/13/299
Olyver, John ygr, Sandwich St Clement, Kent, 1638 CKS PRC1/1/85
Olyver, Rychard, Willesborough, Kent, 1586 CKS PRC2/4/202
Olyver, Thomasine, Selling, Kent, 1610 CKS PRC2/15/274
Olyver, William, Sandwich St Clement, Kent, 1618 CKS PRC2/22/2
Omer, Alice, widow, Canterbury St Martin, Kent, 1598 CKS PRC21/14/573
Omer, Andrewe, St Laurence Thanet, Kent, 1592 CKS PRC2/6/97
Omer, Daniell, Sandwich, Kent, 1599 CKS PRC2/10/323
Omer, Ethelbert, gentleman, Canterbury St George Martyr, Kent, 1636 CKS PRC2/33/100

Omer, Fraunces, Ash next Sandwich, Kent, 1581 CKS PRC21/4/325
Omer, John, Ash next Sandwich, Kent, 1585 CKS PRC21/7/126
Omer, Richard, St Johns Thanet, Kent, 1662 CKS PRC1/9/45
Omer, Susan, spinster, Bekesbourne, Kent, 1631 CKS PRC2/31/53
Omer, Thomas, baker, Sandwich St Clement, Kent, 1640 CKS PRC1/3/26
Omer, Vincent, Staple next Wingham, Kent, 1584 CKS PRC21/6/428
Onen, see Ouen,
Ongle, Thomas, husbandman, Hurst, Kent, 1678 CKS PRC2/38/167
Onion, Alexander, Reculver, Kent, 1614 CKS PRC20/2/535
Onn, Bartholomew, husbandman, Wigtoft, Lincs, 1633 Lincs RO Ad/Ac/23/76
Onnen, Jasper, Herne, Kent, 1586 CKS PRC21/8/46
Onnen, William, St Nicholas at Wade, Kent, 1627 CKS PRC20/7/186
Onslow, Francis, mr, Canterbury St George Martyr, Kent, 1665 CKS PRC1/11/65
Onyon, William eld, yeoman, Lambourn (East Hanney), Berks, 1622 Berks RO D/A1/206/95A
Oram, Dorothie, Inglesham, Wilts, 1626 Wilts RO Arch. Wilts.(name + date)
Oram, John, vintner, Canterbury All Saints, Kent, 1670 CKS PRC1/14/86
Oram, Roger, Upavon, Wilts, 1668 Wilts RO Arch. Sarum(+ name and date)
Oram, William, Cossington, Som, 1683 Somerset RO D/D/Cta/O3
Oram/Woram, William, Baltonsborough, Som, 1596 Somerset RO D/D/Cta/O7
Oran, Robert,
Wilts 1679 Wilts RO Miscellaneous Index (name + date)
Orberie, James, Newton on Trent, Lincs, 1607 Lincs RO Ad/Ac/37/237
Orchard, John, St Clement Danes, London & Middlesex, 1673 Greater London RO AM/PP/Box 1670-1678 pt (uncatalogued)
Orchard, William, brewer, Reading St Giles, Berks, 1630 Berks RO D/A1/206/97A
Ording, George, Hale, Great, Lincs, 1615 Lincs RO Ad/Ac/13/177
Ordwey, Richard, Broadway, Worcs, 1602 Worcs RO 008.7 BA3585/838/208
Oresby, Roberte, Bilsby, Lincs, 1593 Lincs RO Ad/Ac/3/35
Oresby, William, Wrangle, Lincs, 1630 Lincs RO Ad/Ac/22/126
Orgar, Elizabethe, Cheriton, Kent, 1601 CKS PRC2/12/278
Orgill, Richard, Duffield, Derby, 1672 LJRO:cards/1672/43
Orledge, Alan, Slindon, Sussex, 1617 W. Suss RO EpIV/10/1/48
Orme, Edward, Crich (Washington), Derby, 1664 LJRO:cards/1664/13
Orme, Jane, spinster, Alderley (Upper Alderley), Ches, 1616 Cheshire RO (Name) W.C. 1616
Orme, Nicholas, Duffield, Derby, 1685 LJRO/B/C/5/1685/67
Orme, Richard, gentleman, Childwell (The Grange, Little Woolton), Lancs, 1688 Lancs RO (Name of Deceased) D.R.C.H. 1688
Orme, William, Thornton, Leics, 1671 Leics RO Administrators Accounts 1667-72 f47
Ormesbie, William, gentleman, Ormsby, North, Lincs, 1619 Lincs RO Ad/Ac/15/105
Ormesby, John, Partney, Lincs, 1594 Lincs RO Ad/Ac/3/117
Ormeshead, Ormeshead, John, Quadring, Lincs, 1598 Lincs RO Ad/Ac/4/85
Ormesheade, John, yeoman, Quadring, Lincs, 1613 Lincs RO Ad/Ac/11/44
Ormshead, Robert, Quadring, Lincs, 1632 Lincs RO Ad/Ac/23/88
Orpwood, Ralph, husbandman, Sandford, Berks, 1622 Berks RO D/A1/206/94A
Orrell, Lewis, gentleman, Wigan (Aspull), Lancs, 1683 Lancs RO (Name of Deceased) D.R.C.H. 1683
Orrell, Robert, Wigan, Lancs, 1634 Lancs RO (Name of Deceased) D.R.C.H. 1634
Orton, Dorothy, widow, Snaith, Yorks, 1779 Borthwick Test C.P. 1778/7
Orton, Edward, fisherman?, St Peter in Thanet, Kent, 1632 CKS PRC2/31/141
Orton, George, Stretton en le Field, Leics, 1683 Leics RO Administrators Accounts 1682-86 f5
Orwell, William, gentleman, Minster in Sheppey, Kent, 1627 CKS PRC2/27/116
Orwen?, Henry, Minster in Thanet, Kent, 1598 CKS PRC2/10/278
Osboorne, Robarte, Minster in Sheppey, Kent, 1610 CKS PRC2/15/273
Osbornbie, Thomas, Swaton, Lincs, 1593 Lincs RO Ad/Ac/3/5
Osborne, Alexander, butcher, Cranbrook, Kent, 1646 CKS PRC1/7/56

[Osborne:]
Osborne, Elizabeth, widow, Deal, Kent, 1586 CKS PRC21/7/362
Osborne, Elizabeth, widow, Marden, Kent, 1638 CKS PRC2/34/87
Osborne, Gabriel, Wittering, West, Sussex, 1669 W. Suss RO EpI/33/1669/27
Osborne, Geffrey, Sandwich St Mary, Kent, 1578 CKS PRC2/1/195
Osborne, Henry, Sholden, Kent, 1617 CKS PRC2/22/3
Osborne, John, draper: 'woollen draper', Canterbury St Peter, Kent, 1610 CKS PRC2/15/277
Osborne, John, baker, Sittingbourne, Kent, 1626 CKS PRC2/27/117
Osborne, John, husbandman, Brokenborough, Wilts, 1640 Wilts RO Arch. Wilts.(+ name and date)
Osborne, Margaret, widow, Leigh (Field), Staffs, 1666 LJRO:cards/1666/10
Osborne, Rhomas, Bosham, Sussex, 1618 W. Suss RO EpI/33/1618/17
Osborne, Richard, Cockerington, North, Lincs, 1586 Lincs RO Ad/Ac/2C/14
Osborne, Richard, weaver, Islip, Oxon, 1628 Oxon RO MSS Wills 299/3/17
Osborne, Richard, Egdean (Bleatham), Sussex, 1629 W. Suss RO EpI/33/1629/33
Osborne, Richard, Sittingbourne, Kent, 1634 CKS PRC2/32/164
Osborne, Thomas, vintner, Grantham, Lincs, 1603 Lincs RO Ad/Ac/5/401
Osborne, Thomas, Ramsbury, Wilts, 1628 Wilts RO Miscellaneous Index (name + date)
Osborne, Thomas, Biddenden, Kent, 1638 CKS PRC2/34/254
Osborne, Thomas, St Martin in the Fields, London & Middlesex, 1672 Greater London RO AM/PP/Box 1670-1678 pt (uncatalogued)
Osborne, Thomas, clothier, Tenterden, Kent, 1681 CKS PRC2/39/211
Osborne, Vincent, Faldingworth, Lincs, 1620 Lincs RO Ad/Ac/8b/451
Osborne, Walter, Birdham, Sussex, 1673 W. Suss RO EpI/33/1673/5
Osborne, William, Faversham, Kent, 1638 CKS PRC2/34/253
Osborne, William, Ashford, Kent, 1682 CKS PRC2/40/65
Osborne, see Marshall,
Osbourne, Joan, Ash next Sandwich, Kent, 1606 CKS PRC20/1/138
Osbourne, William, Ashbourne, Derby, 1682 LJRO/B/C/5/1682/79
Osbourne, William, clergy: 'rector', Fordwich, Kent, 1694 CKS PRC2/42/91
Osburne, John, Luddington (Garthorpe), Lincs, 1609 Lincs RO Ad/Ac/8a/305
Osburne, Katherine, Luddington (Garthorpe), Lincs, 1609 Lincs RO Ad/Ac/8a/321
Osburne, see Norris,
Osgarbie, Johnne, Stainton, Market, Lincs, 1579 Lincs RO Ad/Ac/2b/53a
Osgodby, John, chandler, Lincoln St Mary Magdalen in the Bail, Lincs, 1681 Lincs RO Ad/Ac/42/89
Osgodby, Thomas, yeoman, Waddingham, Lincs, 1673 Lincs RO Ad/Ac/35/55
Osgood, David, Wallop, Over, Hants, 1670 Hants RO 21m65 D8/220
Osgood, John, Marlborough St Peter & St Paul, Wilts, 1685 Wilts RO CC Sarum(+ name and date)
Osibrooke, Richard, Chipping Barnet, Herts, 1616 Herts RO ASA25/4826
Osmer, John, bachelor, Marden, Kent, 1711 CKS PRC1/17/36
Osmer, Matthew, blacksmith, Godmersham, Kent, 1664 CKS PRC19/3/38
Osmere, James, yeoman, High Halstow, Kent, 1680 CKS PRC2/39/80
Osmund, Martin, Othery, Som, 1593 Somerset RO D/D/Cta/O6
Osmund, Walter, Sherbourne, Dors, 1627 Wilts RO Miscellaneous Index (name + date)
Ospring, Thomas, Canterbury, Kent, 1598 CKS PRC2/10/139
Ostler, Francis, Scothorne, Lincs, 1634 Lincs RO Ad/Ac/40/52
Ostler, Francis, university: 'Fellow of Trinity College, Cambridge/B.D.', Cambridge (Trinity College), Cambs, 1637 CUL V.C. Acc./Box2/54
Ostler, George, Coningsby (Hawthorne), Lincs, 1629 Lincs RO Ad/Ac/22/122
Ostler, William, weaver, Saltfleetby St Peter, Lincs, 1634 Lincs RO Ad/Ac/24/47
Ostler, Wyllyam, High Halden, Kent, 1585 CKS PRC2/3/313
Otes, Katherine, Holywell (Needingworth), Hunts, 1674 Hunts RO/Acc58/19(207)
Ottaway, Peeter, Stalisfield, Kent, 1639 CKS PRC1/3/27
Ottenge, Alexander, Reculver, Kent, 1581 CKS PRC21/4/345

Otter, Edward, husbandman, Torksey (Brampton), Lincs, 1620s? Lincs RO Ad/Ac/8c/26
Otter, Edward, Epworth, Lincs, 1661 Lincs RO Ad/Ac/41/161
Otter, George, husbandman, Wigtoft, Lincs, 1635 Lincs RO Ad/Ac/24/542
Otter, Margarett, widow, Gainsborough, Lincs, 1679 Lincs RO Ad/Ac/43/86
Otter, Robert, Skirbeck, Lincs, 1629 Lincs RO Ad/Ac/22/107
Otter, Stephen, Owston, Lincs, 1618 Lincs RO Ad/Ac/8b/105
Otter, William, mariner, Boston, Lincs, 1670 Lincs RO Ad/Ac/32/156
Otteringham, Thomas, Aslackby, Lincs, 1613 Lincs RO Ad/Ac/12/106
Ottey, John, farmer, Wishaw, Warks, 1825 LJRO/B/C/5/1825/21
Ottey, Thomas, farmer, Ormsby St Margaret, Norf, 1779 Norfolk RO ANW/23/26/48
Ottowell, Ralph, university: 'scholar's servant', Cambridge, Cambs, 1607 CUL V.C.Acc./Box1/42
Otts, William, gentleman, St Ives, Corn, 1611 Cornwall RO AP/O25/2
Oudart, James, wool comber, Canterbury St Mary Northgate, Kent, 1663 CKS PRC1/9/134
Ouen, Richard, Sturry, Kent, 1596 CKS PRC2/8/366
Ouen/Onen, Alyce, Chislet, Kent, CKS PRC21/5/233
Oughe, Bridget, St Cleer, Corn, 1612 Cornwall RO AP/O35
Oughton, William, yeoman, Kersley, Warks, 1767 LJRO/B/C/5/1767/99
Ouldefield, Thomas, Hythe St Leonard, Kent, 1614 CKS PRC20/3/71
Ouldham, Adam, Manchester, Lancs, 1616 Lancs RO (Name of Deceased) D.R.C.H. 1616
Ouldner, William, Newbold Verdon, Leics, 1672 Leics RO Administrators Accounts 1667-72 f61
Ousnam, Andrew, Wye, Kent, 1679 CKS PRC2/38/166
Outlawe, Thomas, Bridge, Kent, 1602 CKS PRC2/13/302
Ovenden, Phillipp, yeoman, Elham, Kent, 1670 CKS PRC1/15/52
Ovenden, Samuel, yeoman, Teynham, Kent, 1695 CKS PRC2/42/87
Ovenden, Thomas, Harbledown, Kent, 1638 CKS PRC2/34/252
Ovenden, Thomas, mariner, St Johns Thanet, Kent, 1673 CKS PRC2/35/247
Over, John, Morestead, Hants, 1669 Hants RO 21m65 D8/221
Overton, Dymocke, Wycombe, Leics, 1639 Leics RO PR/I/41A/34
Overton, Thomas, Binbrook St Gabriel, Lincs, 1627 Lincs RO Ad/Ac/20b/94
Overton, Thomas, St Pauls Walden, Herts, 1651 Herts RO ASA25/3575
Overton, William, farmer, Wigtoft, Lincs, 1808 Lincs RO Ad/Ac/45/76
Overy, Edmonde, Goudhurst, Kent, 1598 CKS PRC2/10/342
Overy, Robert, Headcorn, Kent, 1615 CKS PRC2/22/5
Overye, Wylliam, Bobbing, Kent, 1604 CKS PRC2/14/354
Ovill, Thomas, Dover, Kent, 1598 CKS PRC21/14/262
Ovill/Oldfeilde, Augustine, Lympne, Kent, 1611 CKS PRC2/17/398
Owbree, Richard, Chipping Barnet, Herts, 1635 Herts RO ASA25/4917
Owden, Richard, Ivychurch, Kent, 1604 CKS PRC21/17/45
Owdy, Robert, Faversham, Kent, 1616 CKS PRC2/22/1
Owen, Benjamin, Aston, Warks, 1720 Worcs RO 008.7 BA3585/836/bdl 1
Owen, John, Chipping Barnet, Herts, 1627 Herts RO ASA25/4848
Owen, John, husbandman, Ufton Nervet, Berks, 1639 Berks RO D/A1/206/103A
Owen, John, yeoman, Tatenhill, Staffs, 1781 LJRO/B/C/5/1782/99
Owen, Katheryne, widow, Canterbury St Mary-Magdalen Burgate, Kent, 1588 CKS PRC2/4/281
Owen, Richard, yeoman, Ashbury (Kingstone Winslow), Berks, 1628 Berks RO D/A1/206/96A
Owen, Robert, Charlton nr Dover, Kent, 1637 CKS PRC2/34/251
Owen, Thomas, Smarden, Kent, 1582 CKS PRC2/2/61
Owen, Thomas, butcher, Burton-upon-Trent, Staffs, 1781 LJRO/B/C/5/1782/97
Owen/Brickenbury, Mary, widow, Ivychurch, Kent, 1663 CKS PRC19/3/39
Ower, Alexander, Canterbury, Kent, 1576 CKS PRC21/2/365
Ower, John, salter, Loughborough, Leics, 1667 Leics RO Administrators Accounts 1667-72 f5
Ower, Stephen, Maidstone, Kent, 1639 CKS PRC20/11/187
Ower, Thomas, Boughton under Blean, Kent, 1621 CKS PRC20/5/140
Owing, Edward, farmer, Normanton (Altofts), Yorks, 1779 Borthwick Test C.P. 1779/9
Owldefeeld, Nicholas, Saltwood, Kent, 1609 CKS PRC20/2/5

[Owlett:]
Owlett, George, Boughton Monchelsea, Kent, 1582 CKS PRC2/2/163
Owre, Boys, gentleman, Canterbury St Mary Northgate, Kent, 1625 CKS PRC2/24/36
Owre, Jane, widow, Maidstone, Kent, 1609 CKS PRC20/2/15
Owre, John, Chislet, Kent, 1627 CKS PRC2/27/118
Owre, Robert, gentleman, Faversham, Kent, 1662 CKS PRC1/8/111
Owre, William, Challock, Kent, 1618 CKS PRC20/4/290
Owsboorne, Jeames, Tenterden, Kent, 1601 CKS PRC2/12/280
Owsnam, Henrie, Sandwich, Kent, 1638 CKS PRC2/34/250
Owston, William, mariner: 'master mariner', Scarborough, Yorks, Borthwick Test C.P. 1735/4
Oxen/Fox, William, Chipping Barnet, Herts, 1556 Herts RO ASA25/171a
Oxenbridge, John, Stone in Oxney, Kent, 1685 CKS PRC2/41/3
Oxenbridge, Thomas eld, Stone in Oxney, Kent, 1626 CKS PRC20/7/241
Oxenden, Henry, esquire, Wingham, Kent, 1696 CKS PRC19/5/37
Oxinden, Edward, esquire, Wingham, Kent, 1622 CKS PRC20/5/144
Oxinden, Henry, gentleman, Denton (Eastry hundred), Kent, 1674 CKS PRC2/36/103
Oxinden, James, clergy: 'mr/clerk', Goodnestone next Faversham, Kent, 1663 CKS PRC1/9/135
Oxinden, Mary, lady/widow, Wingham, Kent, 1638 CKS PRC20/11/189
Oxlad, Laurence, yeoman, Stokenchurch, Oxon, 1626 Oxon RO MSS Wills 299/3/15
Oxley, Ralph, clothworker, Bethersden, Kent, 1681 CKS PRC2/39/212
Oxley, Solomon, yeoman, Bethersden, Kent, 1684 CKS PRC2/40/229
Oxman, Ralfe, Deal, Kent, 1584 CKS PRC21/7/68
Oxton, John, St Albans, Herts, 1632 Herts RO ASA25/4886
Oyle, George, Winteringham, Lincs, 1662 Lincs RO Ad/Ac/41/17
Oyler, John, Molash, Kent, 1613 CKS PRC2/16/150
Oyne, Catherine, Sholden, Kent, 1680 CKS PRC2/39/81
Oyne, Thomas, bachelor, Canterbury St Paul, Kent, 1676 CKS PRC2/37/72
Pace, John, Hodnet, Shrops, 1684 LJRO/B/C/5/1684/60
Pace, Thomas, Coventry Holy Trinity, Warks, 1682 LJRO/B/C/5/1682/81
Pacie, Richard, Lincoln St Benedict, Lincs, 1576 Lincs RO Ad/Ac/2b/41
Pacie, Richard, fishmonger, Lincoln St Benedict, Lincs, 1576 Lincs RO Ad/Ac/1/16
Pacie, Thomas, Ewerby, Lincs, 1581 Lincs RO Ad/Ac/2b/69
Pacie, Thomas, Canterbury St Paul, Kent, 1610 CKS PRC2/15/298
Pack, Margaret, widow, Loose, Kent, 1642 CKS PRC19/2/63
Pack, William, miller, Wingham, Kent, 1719 CKS PRC19/6/75
Pack, William, gentleman, Tenterden, Kent, 1726 CKS PRC19/6/74
Packe, George, Slindon, Sussex, 1627 W. Suss RO EpIV/10/1/19
Packe, George, Trotton, Sussex, 1641 W. Suss RO EpI/33/1640/14
Packe, Matthew, Faversham, Kent, 1631 CKS PRC2/31/54
Packe, Richard, Rogate, Sussex, 1623 W. Suss RO EpI/33/1623/4
Packe, Richard, yeoman, Westwell, Kent, 1680 CKS PRC20/13/54
Packe, Thomas, Ulcombe, Kent, 1629 CKS PRC2/30/111
Packe, Thomas, gentleman, Chart, Great, Kent, 1686 CKS PRC20/13/567
Packe, William, miller?, Chart, Little, Kent, 1631 CKS PRC2/31/55
Packe, William ygr, Herne, Kent, 1635 CKS PRC20/11/191
Packenham, Henrie, gentleman, Faversham, Kent, 1641 CKS PRC1/6/7
Packenham, Henry, knight, Grantham, Lincs, 1620 Lincs RO Ad/Ac/16/74
Packenham, Henrye, yeoman, Wingham, Kent, 1615 CKS PRC20/3/204
Packenham, James, Chilham, Kent, 1681 CKS PRC2/39/215
Packenham, John, yeoman, Hollingbourne, Kent, 1614 CKS PRC20/3/69
Packer, John, butcher, Purton, Wilts, 1637 Wilts RO Arch. Wilts.(+ name and date)
Packer, Ralph, Whitstable, Kent, 1628 CKS PRC2/29/97
Packham, Abraham, Wittersham, Kent, 1613 CKS PRC20/2/354
Packham, John, Boughton Malherbe, Kent, 1606 CKS PRC2/15/292
Packham, John, yeoman, Woodnesborough, Kent, 1641 CKS PRC19/1/70
Packham, Richard, Boughton Malherbe, Kent, 1609 CKS PRC2/15/315

Packham, Thomas, husbandman, Warehorne, Kent, 1663 CKS PRC1/9/136
Packharnes, Roger, Wyberton, Lincs, 1607 Lincs RO Ad/Ac/8a/113
Packman, Alice, widow, Boughton under Blean, Kent, 1632 CKS PRC20/11/206
Packman, James, Boughton under Blean, Kent, 1632 CKS PRC20/11/226
Packman, James, victualler, Thornham, Kent, 1690 CKS PRC2/41/182
Packman, John, husbandman, Leysdown, Kent, 1695 CKS PRC2/42/104
Packman, Stephen, Boughton under Blean, Kent, 1626 CKS PRC20/7/174
Packman, Stephen, Upchurch, Kent, 1638 CKS PRC2/34/109
Packman, see Pecknam,
Packnam, Christopher, Stockbury, Kent, 1604 CKS PRC2/13/314
Packnam, Laurans, St Nicholas at Wade, Kent, 1608 CKS PRC20/1/322
Packnam, Margaret,
Kent 1596 CKS PRC2/8/89
Pacy, William, Hoath, Kent, 1695 CKS PRC19/5/29
Paddison, George, Cockerington, South, Lincs, 1638 Lincs RO Ad/Ac/25/356
Paddock, John, Othery, Som, 1739 Somerset RO D/D/Cta/P29
Paddock, Richard, Rolvenden, Kent, 1618 CKS PRC2/19/144
Padget, John, yeoman, Limber Magna, Lincs, 1634 Lincs RO Ad/Ac/24/518
Padgett, Valentine, Muston, Leics, 1666 Leics RO Administrators Accounts C17th f88
Padiham, Robert, yeoman, Sandhurst, Kent, 1633 CKS PRC20/11/232
Padley, Henrie, Folkingham, Lincs, 1634 Lincs RO Ad/Ac/24/204
Padley, Henry, Quadring, Lincs, 1670 Lincs RO Ad/Ac/32/177
Padley, Thomas, husbandman, Buslingthorpe, Lincs, 1600 Lincs RO Ad/Ac/37/88
Padmore, James, yeoman, Stafford, Staffs, 1798 LJRO/B/C/5/1798/24
Page, Abraham, bachelor, Loose, Kent, 1666 CKS PRC19/3/103
Page, Alice, Biddenden, Kent, 1617 CKS PRC2/19/154
Page, Edward, innkeeper, Oxford (University), Oxon, 1640 Bodleian HYP B9/31-32
Page, Elizabeth, widow, Selling, Kent, 1684 CKS PRC2/40/232
Page, Henry, Hemingby, Lincs, 1607 Lincs RO Ad/Ac/8a/109
Page, Henrye, Biddenden, Kent, 1613 CKS PRC2/18/121
Page, Humphry, yeoman, Buckland nr Dover, Kent, 1676 CKS PRC20/12/215
Page, John, Snave, Kent, 1596 CKS PRC2/8/322
Page, John, Chilham, Kent, 1609 CKS PRC2/14/361
Page, John, Algarkirk, Lincs, 1612 Lincs RO Ad/Ac/11/110
Page, John, husbandman, Sevington, Kent, 1626 CKS PRC2/27/121
Page, John, Sandwich, Kent, 1627 CKS PRC2/27/131
Page, John, Sittingbourne, Kent, 1637 CKS PRC2/34/96
Page, John, cooper, Sittingbourne, Kent, 1676 CKS PRC2/37/79
Page, Lawrence, Hythe St Leonard, Kent, 1580 CKS PRC21/4/274
Page, Margaret, High Halden, Kent, 1608 CKS PRC2/14/356
Page, Mary, spinster, Ashford, Kent, 1620 CKS PRC2/19/125
Page, Mercye, widow, Willesborough, Kent, 1610 CKS PRC2/15/302
Page, Peter, Lympne, Kent, 1588 CKS PRC2/4/305
Page, Phillipp, tailor, Deal, Kent, 1640 CKS PRC19/1/69
Page, Ralph, Stoneham, South, Hants, 1671 Hants RO 21m65 D8/234
Page, Richard, Petham, Kent, 1668 CKS PRC1/13/87a
Page, Richard, yeoman, Petham, Kent, 1669 CKS PRC1/13/87
Page, Robert, Norwich St George at Colegate, Norf, Norfolk RO ANW/23/23/47A
Page, Robert, Canterbury St Mary Bredman, Kent, 1676 CKS PRC2/37/80
Page, Sylvester, Maidstone, Kent, 1619 CKS PRC20/4/304
Page, Thomas, Hawkhurst, Kent, 1587 CKS PRC2/4/129
Page, Thomas, butcher, Minster in Sheppey, Kent, 1681 CKS PRC2/39/214
Page, William, Harrietsham, Kent, 1589 CKS PRC2/4/525
Page, William, Staplehurst, Kent, 1596 CKS PRC2/8/69
Page, William, Maidstone, Kent, 1623 CKS PRC20/6/282

[Page:]
Page, William, Lincoln St Peter at Gowts, Lincs, 1650 Lincs RO Ad/Ac/29/58
Page, William, Rainham, Kent, 1669 CKS PRC1/14/87
Page, William, fellmonger, Lincoln, Lincs, 1680 Lincs RO Ad/Ac/34/42
Page, William, wool comber, Birmingham, Warks, 1781 LJRO/B/C/5/1781/78
Page + Rypley, William + Stephen,
Kent 1584 CKS PRC2/3/200
Pagett, John, butcher, Nuneaton, Warks, 1790 LJRO/B/C/5/1790/61
Pagy, Thomas, grocer, Yattendon, Berks, 1674 Berks RO D/A1/209/25A
Paice, William, husbandman, Stratfield Mortimer, Berks, 1680 Berks RO D/A1/209/37D
Paige, Henry, victualler, Hackney, London & Middlesex, 1677 PRO PROB32/14/125
Pain, Roberte, Dunston, Lincs, 1593 Lincs RO Ad/Ac/3/41
Pain, William, mr, Courteenhall, Northants, 1774 Northants RO X954/21/25
Paine, Anne, widow, Weston Bampfylde, Som, 1741 Somerset RO D/D/Cta/P30
Paine, Anthony, farmer, Staughton, Great, Hunts, 1600? Hunts RO/Acc58/2(160)
Paine, Benjamin, Worcester St Swithin, Worcs, 1753 Worcs RO 008.7 BA3585/835/bdl 1
Paine, Edward, Boston, Lincs, 1612 Lincs RO Ad/Ac/11/137
Paine, Edward, Lydd, Kent, 1669 CKS PRC19/4/57
Paine, Frances, widow, Bilsington, Kent, 1683 CKS PRC2/40/141
Paine, Jeames, Cranbrook, Kent, 1609 CKS PRC2/15/308
Paine, Joane, widow, Hastingleigh, Kent, 1612 CKS PRC2/17/191
Paine, John, gentleman, Wallingford, Berks, 1634 Berks RO D/A1/208/62A
Paine, John, Hastingleigh, Kent, 1639 CKS PRC2/34/104
Paine, John, Sheldwich, Kent, 1649 CKS PRC1/8/79
Paine, John, Tilshead, Wilts, 1762? Wilts RO Miscellaneous Index (name + date)
Paine, Lawrence, Biddenden, Kent, 1636 CKS PRC2/33/107
Paine, Mary, Boxley, Kent, 1663 CKS PRC1/9/137
Paine, Nathan, Berkhamsted St Peter, Herts, Herts RO AHH23/1877
Paine, Richard, Weston Zoyland, Som, 1620 Somerset RO D/D/Cta/P11
Paine, Richard, Sturry, Kent, 1637 CKS PRC2/34/94
Paine, Richard, Sturry, Kent, 1638 CKS PRC2/34/93
Paine, Richard, St Mary in the Marsh, Kent, 1675 CKS PRC2/36/229
Paine, Richard eld, Garston, East, Berks, 1612 Berks RO D/A1/207/166A
Paine, Robert, Ogbourne St Andrew, Wilts, 1641 Wilts RO Miscellaneous Index (name + date)
Paine, Stephen, Nuneaton, Warks, 1672 LJRO:cards/1672/44
Paine, Susanna, Downton, Wilts, 1681? Wilts RO Arch. Sarum(+ name and date)
Paine, Thomas, clergy: 'mr/vicar', Hernhill, Kent, 1630 CKS PRC20/9/339
Paine, Thomas, Faversham, Kent, 1662 CKS PRC1/9/46
Paine, Thomas, yeoman, Tilmanstone, Kent, 1665 CKS PRC1/10/68
Paine, William, Faversham, Kent, 1667 CKS PRC1/12/67
Paine/Harte, Julian, widow, Hawkinge, Kent, 1609 CKS PRC2/15/310
Painson, Richard, yeoman, Leake, Lincs, 1620 Lincs RO Ad/Ac/16/72
Painson, Thomas, yeoman, Leake, Lincs, 1619 Lincs RO Ad/Ac/15/215
Painter, Henry, Evenley, Northants, 1682 Northants RO NWill A/C/73
Painter, John, gentleman, Ashby, Canons, Northants, 1671 Northants RO NWill A/C/120
Painter, John, Hanbury, Staffs, 1685 LJRO/B/C/5/1685/68
Painter, Richard, Brackley St Peter, Northants, 1680 Northants RO NWill A/C/10
Painter, William, Evenley, Northants, 1681 Northants RO NWill A/C/65
Painton, Edward, yeoman, Cumnor (Botley), Berks, 1663 Berks RO D/A1/208/135B
Painton, Thomas, yeoman, Wytham, Berks, 1625 Berks RO D/A1/208/36A
Paise, Richard, Swallowfield, Berks, 1593 Berks RO D/A1/207/118A
Pakyn/Waterer, Catherine, Sittingbourne, Kent, 1614 CKS PRC2/18/47
Palfar, Anthony, wool comber, Canterbury St Margaret, Kent, 1679 CKS PRC2/38/57
Palframan, Anthonie, merchant, Lincoln St Mary le Wigford, Lincs, 1579 Lincs RO Ad/Ac/2b/51a
Palframan, Anthony, merchant, Lincoln, Lincs, 1585 Lincs RO Ad/Ac/1/28
Palfreman, Christopher, Stamford, Lincs, 1612 Lincs RO Ad/Ac/10/161

Palfreman, Francis, yeoman, Weston-upon-Trent, Derby, 1693 LJRO/B/C/5/1693/66
Palfreyman, Henry, Derby, Derby, 1679 LJRO:cards/1679/6
Palfreyman, John, yeoman, Mickleover, Derby, 1663 LJRO:cards/1663/46
Palfreyman, Nathaniel, Laughton, Lincs, 1644 Lincs RO Ad/Ac/28/71
Palin, Agnes, Bradley, Staffs, 1684 LJRO/B/C/5/1684/61
Pallfrie, William, Langford Budville, Som, 1639 Somerset RO D/D/Cta/P15
Pallmer, Francis, Yaxley, Hunts, 1684 Hunts RO/Acc58/222(222)
Pallmer, John, cordwainer: 'shoemaker', Tamworth, Warks, 1680 Worcs RO 008.7 BA3585/837/bdl 2
Pallmer, Leonard, Thimbleby, Lincs, 1597 Lincs RO Ad/Ac/4/121
Palmer, widow,
Wilts 1621 e 24 Wilts RO Unlisted Fragment
Palmer, Abraham, Maidstone, Kent, 1624 CKS PRC20/6/152
Palmer, Ann, widow, St Sepulchre, London & Middlesex, 1669 PRO PROB32/5/44
Palmer, Caleb, victualler, Sandwich St Mary, Kent, 1667 CKS PRC1/12/68
Palmer, Christopher, gentleman, Burgh le Marsh, Lincs, 1640 Lincs RO Ad/Ac/28/24
Palmer, Christopher, innkeeper, Shefford, East, Berks, 1644 Berks RO D/A1/208/98B
Palmer, Edward, yeoman, Wootton Wawen, Warks, Worcs RO 008.7 BA3585/838/259
Palmer, Edward, Holbeach, Lincs, 1622 Lincs RO Ad/Ac/17/39
Palmer, Elizabeth, Bishopstone, Wilts, 1626 Wilts RO Preb Court Bishopstone Bundle 1/2
Palmer, George, Brinkhill, Lincs, 1630 Lincs RO Ad/Ac/23/105
Palmer, James, Poulshot, Wilts, 1672 Wilts RO Arch. Sarum(+ name and date)
Palmer, James, esquire, Buttington, Mont, 1697 PRO PROB5/819
Palmer, James, yeoman, Emborrow, Som, 1735 Somerset RO D/D/Cta/P31
Palmer, John, Swallowfield, Berks, 1605 Berks RO D/A1/207/146A
Palmer, John, Seavington St Mary, Som, 1620 Somerset RO D/D/Cta/P2
Palmer, John, Aslackby, Lincs, 1632 Lincs RO Ad/Ac/23/179
Palmer, John, Nocton, Lincs, 1635 Lincs RO Ad/Ac/24/25
Palmer, John, gentleman, Bridgewater, Som, 1665 Somerset RO D/D/Cta/P49
Palmer, John, Poulshot, Wilts, 1669 Wilts RO Arch. Sarum(+ name and date)
Palmer, John, gentleman, Wingham, Kent, 1672 CKS PRC20/12/56
Palmer, John, Markby, Lincs, 1674 Lincs RO Ad/Ac/43/173
Palmer, John, clothworker, Bradford on Avon, Wilts, 1678 Wilts RO Arch. Sarum(+ name and date)
Palmer, John, St Andrew Undershaft, London & Middlesex, 1801 Greater London RO DL/C/265/18
Palmer, John, yeoman, Coombe, Wilts, 1805 Wilts RO Miscellaneous Index (name + date)
Palmer, Lawrance, Gayton, Lincs, 1595 Lincs RO Ad/Ac/4/131
Palmer, Mary, widow, Locking, Som, 1638 Somerset RO D/D/Cta/P1
Palmer, Michael, Abbots Langley, Herts, 1632 Herts RO ASA25/4878
Palmer, Peter, Chichester St Peter the Less, Sussex, 1616 W. Suss RO EpIII/9/1/15
Palmer, Peter, alderman, Chichester, Sussex, 1619 W. Suss RO EpIII/9/1/24
Palmer, Ralph, yeoman, Cumnor, Berks, Berks RO D/A1/105/116C
Palmer, Richard, Sandwich, Kent, 1583 CKS PRC2/3/7
Palmer, Richard, Chart, Great, Kent, 1595 CKS PRC2/7/95
Palmer, Richard, Rodbourne Cheney, Wilts, 1624 Wilts RO Arch. Wilts.(+ name and date)
Palmer, Richard, clergy: 'clerk', Newton on Trent, Lincs, 1639 Lincs RO Ad/Ac/40/285
Palmer, Richard, butcher, Pitsford, Northants, 1677 Northants RO NWill A/C/149
Palmer, Robert, Marsh Chapel, Lincs, 1573 Lincs RO Ad/Ac/1/8
Palmer, Robert, St Peter in Thanet, Kent, 1639 CKS PRC1/3/28
Palmer, Robert, Althorpe (Amcotts), Lincs, 1663 Lincs RO Ad/Ac/41/104
Palmer, Simon, Wantage, Berks, 1629? Wilts RO Miscellaneous Index (name + date)
Palmer, Stephen, Havant, Hants, 1668 Hants RO 21M65 D8/206
Palmer, Thomas, Coningsby, Lincs, 1640 Lincs RO Ad/Ac/27/2
Palmer, Thomas, Carlton le Moorland, Lincs, 1641 Lincs RO Ad/Ac/27/323

[Palmer:]
Palmer, Thomas, St Botolph without Aldgate, London & Middlesex, 1670 Lambeth Palace Arches G25/2
Palmer, Walter, Radway, Warks, 1682 LJRO/B/C/5/1682/80
Palmer, William, Old Romney, Kent, 1586 CKS PRC2/4/390
Palmer, William, blacksmith, Woolhampton, Berks, 1600 Berks RO D/A1/104/140C
Palmer, William, Suckley, Worcs, 1607 Worcs RO 008.7 BA3585/839/436
Palmer, William, gentleman, Carlton Scroop, Lincs, 1612 Lincs RO Ad/Ac/11/181
Palmer, William, Woolhampton, Berks, 1614 Berks RO D/A1/207/160A
Palmer, William, Boughton under Blean, Kent, 1617 CKS PRC20/4/320
Palmer, William, Sandwich St Mary, Kent, 1647 CKS PRC1/7/93
Palmer, William, Culham, Oxon, 1795 Oxon RO MSS Wills 304/1/52
Pamflett, Elias, gentleman, St Laurence Thanet, Kent, 1715 CKS PRC1/17/76
Pamphlett, Elias, yeoman, St Johns Thanet, Kent, 1667 CKS PRC1/12/69
Pamplin, Henry, victualler, Surfleet, Lincs, 1683 Lincs RO Ad/Ac/44/107
Panard, Powell, 1637 NLW BR 1636/145 Ac
Pancase, Richard, Warden, Kent, 1633 CKS PRC2/32/98
Pancase, William, Eastchurch, Sheppey, Kent, 1636 CKS PRC2/33/104
Pancke, George, Thurlby, Lincs, 1619 Lincs RO Ad/Ac/15/15
Pancke, Thomas, applemonger, Lincoln, Lincs, 1607 Lincs RO Ad/Ac/7/62
Panckhurst, Phineas, innholder, Hawkhurst, Kent, 1686 CKS PRC2/41/74
Pangborne, George, Chart, Little, Kent, 1639 CKS PRC1/3/29
Pankherst, Thomas, bricklayer, Cranbrook, Kent, 1667 CKS PRC1/12/70
Pankus, William, Eastchurch, Sheppey, Kent, 1707 CKS PRC1/16/68
Pann, Henrye, Witham on the Hill, Lincs, 1637 Lincs RO Ad/Ac/25/502
Pann, John, Aswarby, Lincs, 1641 Lincs RO Ad/Ac/27/329
Pann, Nicholas, Lincoln, Lincs, 1613 Lincs RO Ad/Ac/11/150
Pannatt, John, Stoke, North, Sussex, 1673 W. Suss RO EpI/33/1673/13
Pannatt, Judith, widow, Burpham, Sussex, 1682 W. Suss RO EpI/33/1682/19
Pannell, Henry, wheelwright, Bobbing, Kent, 1665 CKS PRC1/10/69
Pannell, Jeames, Birchington, Kent, 1616 CKS PRC20/3/381
Pannell, John, St Laurence Thanet, Kent, 1640 CKS PRC1/5/13
Pannell, Michaell, Kettlethorpe (Laughterton), Lincs, 1630 Lincs RO Ad/Ac/39/289
Pannell, Robarte, Benenden, Kent, 1601 CKS PRC2/12/296
Pannell, William, Laughton, Lincs, 1640 Lincs RO Ad/Ac/40/264
Pannell, William, wheelwright, Lympne, Kent, 1685 CKS PRC2/41/4
Panner, Robert, Blyton, Lincs, 1684 Lincs RO Ad/Ac/44/131
Pannett, Alice, Poling, Sussex, 1640 W. Suss RO EpI/33/1640/23
Pannett, Elizabeth, widow, Tarring, West (Salvington), Sussex, 1610 W. Suss RO EpIV/10/1/1
Pannett, Henry, Tarring, West (Salvington), Sussex, 1610 W. Suss RO EpIV/10/1/2
Pannett, John, yeoman, Burpham (Peppering), Sussex, 1679 W. Suss RO EpI/33/1678/11
Pannett, Michael, Patching, Sussex, 1627 W. Suss RO EpIV/10/1/20
Pannett, Richard, Burpham, Sussex, 1598 W. Suss RO EpI/33/1598/2
Pantin, Elizabeth, widow, Reading, Berks, 1663 Berks RO D/A1/208/136B
Panting, Thomas, waterman, Culham, Oxon, 1641 Oxon RO MSS Wills 171/3/19
Panting, William, Hanley Castle, Worcs, 1733 Worcs RO 008.7 BA3585/836/bdl 2
Pantinge, Alice, widow, Cumnor, Berks, 1670 Berks RO D/A1/208/176C
Panton, George, Milton next Sittingbourne, Kent, 1627 CKS PRC2/28/93
Panton, Henry, citizen/vintner, St Giles in the Fields, London & Middlesex, 1689 PRO PROB32/28/46
Panton, James, Kirkby, East, Lincs, 1649 Lincs RO Ad/Ac/30/54
Panton, John, Thimbleby, Lincs, 1670 Lincs RO Ad/Ac/32/212
Panton, Richard, Binbrook St Mary, Lincs, 1611 Lincs RO Ad/Ac/10/110
Pantrey, Alexander, Smarden, Kent, 1639 CKS PRC1/3/30
Pantrey, John, Woodchurch, Kent, 1674 CKS PRC20/12/95
Pantrie, Lawrence, Kenardington, Kent, 1593 CKS PRC2/6/201

Pantrie, Thomas, Dover, Kent, 1594 CKS PRC21/13/5
Pantrie, Thomas, Newchurch, Kent, 1604 CKS PRC21/17/365
Pantry, Henry, Wye, Kent, 1638 CKS PRC2/34/258
Pantry, Henry, husbandman, Woodchurch, Kent, 1676 CKS PRC20/12/216
Pantry, James, Kenardington, Kent, 1631 CKS PRC2/31/56
Pantry, John, St Johns Thanet, Kent, 1626 CKS PRC2/25/104
Pantry, John, Challock, Kent, 1690 CKS PRC19/4/121
Pantry, Richard, tailor, Smarden, Kent, 1666 CKS PRC1/11/141
Pantry, Thomas, Newington next Hythe, Kent, 1624 CKS PRC2/24/51
Pantry, William, St Mary in the Marsh, Kent, 1623 CKS PRC2/24/50
Pantry, William, Wye, Kent, 1671 CKS PRC1/15/53
Pantrye, John, Ruckinge, Kent, 1594 CKS PRC2/7/307
Pantrye, John, Ivychurch, Kent, 1600 CKS PRC21/15/196
Papavoine, Catherine, widow, St Stephen Coleman Street, London & Middlesex, 1800 Greater London RO DL/C/264/231
Papworth, James, jobber, Offord Cluney, Hunts, 1789 Hunts RO/Acc58/333
Papworth, Robert, St Pauls Walden, Herts, 1690 Herts RO ASA25/4321
Paramor, John, Worth, Kent, 1612 CKS PRC20/2/344
Paramor, Richard, Ash next Sandwich, Kent, 1609 CKS PRC20/2/39
Paramor, Steven, Worth, Kent, 1608 CKS PRC20/1/382
Paramor, Thomas, Eastry, Kent, 1622 CKS PRC20/5/150
Paramor, Vincent, Herne, Kent, 1592 CKS PRC21/11/270
Paramor, Wyllyam, Reculver, Kent, 1588 CKS PRC21/9/62
Paramore, Joane, widow, St Peter in Thanet, Kent, 1628 CKS PRC2/28/98
Paramore, John, Preston next Wingham, Kent, 1620 CKS PRC2/19/162
Paramore, John, Woodnesborough, Kent, 1687 CKS PRC2/41/100
Paramore, John, Hoath, Kent, 1700 CKS PRC19/5/65
Paramore, John, St Nicholas at Wade, Kent, 1711 CKS PRC19/6/45
Paramore, Joshua, Sandwich, Kent, 1692 CKS PRC2/42/12
Paramore, Susan, widow, Eastry, Kent, 1618 CKS PRC20/4/294
Paramore, Thomas, gentleman, Canterbury, Kent, 1620 CKS PRC2/19/159
Paramore, Thomas, clergy: 'clerk', Langdon, East, Kent, 1702 CKS PRC19/6/3
Paramore, William, bachelor, Borden, Kent, 1666 CKS PRC1/11/142
Paramore, see Westbeech,
Paramour, Alice, widow, Worth, Kent, 1617 CKS PRC20/4/306
Parcevall, see Percwall,
Pardo, Richard, husbandman, Ombersley, Worcs, 1597 Worcs RO 008.7 BA3585/838/124
Pardoe, John, husbandman, Ombersley, Worcs, 1594 Worcs RO 008.7 BA3585/838/123
Pardoe, John eld,
Worcs 1594 Worcs RO 008.7 BA3585/834/444
Pargate, Daniell, Sturry, Kent, 1598 CKS PRC2/10/163
Pargate, Thomas, Sturry, Kent, 1593 CKS PRC2/6/340
Pargett, Henrie, Wittersham, Kent, 1606 CKS PRC20/1/150
Pargiter, John, yeoman, Sutton, Kings, Northants, 1684 Oxon RO MSS Wills Pec 49/1/8
Parham, Thomas, yeoman, Westwell, Oxon, 1671 Oxon RO MSS Wills 84/4/2
Parie, William, labourer, Aubourn, Lincs, 1637 Lincs RO Ad/Ac/25/571
Paris, John, university: 'Fellow/Doctor of Physic', Oxford (Corpus Christi College), Oxon, 1672 Bodleian HYP B9/33-34
Paris, Robert, Woodchurch, Kent, 1679 CKS PRC20/12/317
Paris, see Taylor,
Parish, Edward, Huttoft, Lincs, 1619 Lincs RO Ad/Ac/14/148
Parish, James, Halesowen, Worcs, 1775 Worcs RO 008.7 BA3585/835/bdl 2
Parish, John, Horncastle, Lincs, 1641 Lincs RO Ad/Ac/27/287
Parish r Christchurch, Peter,

[Parish r Christchurch:]
London & Middlesex 1752 Greater London RO DL/C/552/148/1
Parkar, Gyles, Dover, Kent, 1573 CKS PRC21/2/56
Parkar, John, jurat, New Romney, Kent, 1575 CKS PRC21/2/241
Parke, John, Gosberton, Lincs, 1638 Lincs RO Ad/Ac/25/169
Parke, Nicholas, Lydd, Kent, 1618 CKS PRC20/4/316
Parke, Richard, butcher, Sleaford, Lincs, 1667 Lincs RO Ad/Ac/42/40
Parke, William, Barton on Humber, Lincs, 1578 Lincs RO Ad/Ac/2b/47
Parkehurst, Christopher, Wisborough Green, Sussex, 1641 W. Suss RO EpI/33/1640/19
Parker,
Som 1616 Somerset RO D/D/Cta/P3
Parker, Alice, widow, Dover St Mary, Kent, 1608 CKS PRC20/1/376
Parker, Anne, widow, Bourne, Lincs, 1629 Lincs RO Ad/Ac/22/32
Parker, Bernard, Portsea, Hants, 1625 Hants RO 21M65 D8/124
Parker, Dorothie, Fulstow, Lincs, 1642 Lincs RO Ad/Ac/28/25
Parker, Edmund, Spalding, Lincs, 1634 Lincs RO Ad/Ac/24/522
Parker, Edward, yeoman, Ashford, Kent, 1648 CKS PRC1/8/26
Parker, Edward, gentleman, Hough on the Hill, Lincs, 1670 Lincs RO Ad/Ac/33/136
Parker, Frances, Stoke, South (Easton), Lincs, 1670 Lincs RO Ad/Ac/43/53
Parker, Francis, Maidstone, Kent, 1632 CKS PRC20/11/236
Parker, Frauncis, St Johns Thanet, Kent, 1615 CKS PRC2/19/116
Parker, Henry, St Laurence Thanet, Kent, 1641 CKS PRC1/6/8
Parker, Henry, Chartham, Kent, 1688 CKS PRC2/41/131
Parker, Humphrey, yeoman, Algarkirk, Lincs, 1615 Lincs RO Ad/Ac/13/183
Parker, James, Goodnestone next Wingham, Kent, 1580 CKS PRC21/4/223
Parker, James, Grantham, Lincs, 1624 Lincs RO Ad/Ac/19A/127
Parker, James, Berkeley, Glos, 1685 GRO GDR/B4/2/P111
Parker, Jeremiah, Sandwich, Kent, 1699 CKS PRC1/16/9
Parker, John, St Pauls Walden, Herts, 1618 Herts RO ASA25/4831
Parker, John, Milton next Sittingbourne, Kent, 1626 CKS PRC2/25/108
Parker, John, Sandwich St Peter, Kent, 1626 CKS PRC2/27/127
Parker, John, Wrangle, Lincs, 1639 Lincs RO Ad/Ac/26/185
Parker, John, Stoke, South (Easton), Lincs, 1670 Lincs RO Ad/Ac/43/56
Parker, John, Canterbury St Peter, Kent, 1679 CKS PRC2/38/174
Parker, John, Goodnestone next Wingham, Kent, 1696 CKS PRC19/5/38
Parker, John, shopkeeper, Howden, Yorks, 1794 Borthwick Test C.P. 1794/12
Parker, Joseph, Lenham, Kent, 1635 CKS PRC2/33/108
Parker, Judith, widow, Edmonton, London & Middlesex, 1720 Greater London RO DL/C/547/37
Parker, Margaret, widow, Sandwich, Kent, 1609 CKS PRC1/1/6
Parker, Margarett, widow, Rasen, Middle, (Tupholme), Lincs, 1633 Lincs RO Ad/Ac/24/195
Parker, Mary, Woodnesborough, Kent, 1605 CKS PRC2/13/305
Parker, Mary, Derby All Saints, Derby, 1685 LJRO/B/C/5/1685/73
Parker, Mary, Alfreton, Derby, 1734 LJRO/B/C/5/1734/25
Parker, Nicholas, university: M.A. of Trinity College, Cambridge, Cambridge, Cambs, 1625 c. CUL V.C. Acc./Box3/69
Parker, Nicholas, Otterden, Kent, 1633 CKS PRC2/32/99
Parker, Nicholas, Lenham, Kent, 1666 CKS PRC1/11/143
Parker, Nicholas, Tamworth, Staffs, 1738 LJRO/B/C/5/1738/59
Parker, Peter, Staveley, Derby, 1684 LJRO/B/C/5/1683/14
Parker, Ralph, yeoman, Somersal Herbert, Derby, 1787 LJRO/B/C/5/1787/101
Parker, Richard,
Wilts Wilts RO Unlisted Fragment
Parker, Richard, Eastchurch, Sheppey, Kent, 1617 CKS PRC2/19/135
Parker, Richard, gentleman, Sandwich, Kent, 1627 CKS PRC2/28/91
Parker, Richard, Bilsington, Kent, 1632 CKS PRC2/31/145
Parker, Richard, husbandman, Leigh (Field), Staffs, 1667 LJRO:cards/1667/61

Parker, Richard, gentleman, Foston, Lincs, 1672 Lincs RO Ad/Ac/43/64
Parker, Robert, St Johns Thanet, Kent, 1598 CKS PRC2/10/116
Parker, Robert, Barham, Kent, 1635 CKS PRC2/33/102
Parker, Robert, husbandman, Rolvenden, Kent, 1681 CKS PRC2/39/222
Parker, Robert, Horsley, Derby, 1685 LJRO/B/C/5/1685/74
Parker, Robert, fishmonger/citizen,
London & Middlesex 1685 PRO PROB5/1558
Parker, Roger, cordwainer: 'shoemaker', Elham, Kent, 1674 CKS PRC2/36/111
Parker, Rychard, Brookland, Kent, 1598 CKS PRC2/9/413
Parker, Samuel, thatcher, Appledore, Kent, 1677 CKS PRC2/37/180
Parker, Samuel, clothworker, Egerton, Kent, 1685 CKS PRC20/13/517
Parker, Samuel, farmer, Heanor (Shipley), Derby, 1783 LJRO/B/C/5/1783/166
Parker, Sara, spinster, Lenham, Kent, 1612 CKS PRC2/16/24
Parker, Stephen, Stone next Faversham, Kent, 1596 CKS PRC2/8/374
Parker, Suzan, spinster, Lenham, Kent, 1612 CKS PRC2/16/21
Parker, Thomas, Westbury, Glos, GRO GDR/B4/2/P4
Parker, Thomas, Birchington, Kent, 1593 CKS PRC21/12/157
Parker, Thomas, Sandwich, Kent, 1599 CKS PRC2/10/141
Parker, Thomas, Claypole, Lincs, 1601 Lincs RO Ad/Ac/5/219
Parker, Thomas, Fulstow, Lincs, 1618 Lincs RO Ad/Ac/14/270
Parker, Thomas, Covenham St Mary, Lincs, 1622 Lincs RO Ad/Ac/17/90
Parker, Thomas, husbandman, Markfield, Leics, 1673 Leics RO Administrators Accounts 1667-72 f142
Parker, Thomas, Meriden, Warks, 1675 LJRO:cards/1675/43
Parker, Thomas, Bethersden, Kent, 1676 CKS PRC2/36/228
Parker, Thomas, yeoman, Northbourne, Kent, 1677 CKS PRC2/37/183
Parker, Thomas, yeoman, Birchington, Kent, 1686 CKS PRC20/13/563
Parker, Thomas, yeoman, Bethersden, Kent, 1696 CKS PRC2/42/121
Parker, William, Egerton, Kent, 1596 CKS PRC21/14/141
Parker, William, Toynton, High, Lincs, 1614 Lincs RO Ad/Ac/13/131
Parker, William, Colsterworth, Lincs, 1620 Lincs RO Ad/Ac/16/77
Parker, William, Bethersden, Kent, 1623 CKS PRC20/6/286
Parker, William, Folkestone, Kent, 1623 CKS PRC2/24/56
Parker, William, Wrangle, Lincs, 1626 Lincs RO Ad/Ac/20/119
Parker, William, Horncastle, Lincs, 1632 Lincs RO Ad/Ac/23/113
Parker, William, St Peter in Thanet, Kent, 1643 CKS PRC1/6/76
Parker, William, innkeeper, Canterbury St Mary Bredin, Kent, 1685 CKS PRC2/40/230
Parker, Zacheus, Minster in Thanet, Kent, 1616 CKS PRC2/19/147
Parker, see Littilfyld, Sivier & Waters,
Parkes, Henry, Cranbrook, Kent, 1680 CKS PRC2/39/89
Parkes, Margarett, Ospringe, Kent, 1681 CKS PRC2/39/216
Parkes, Richard, yeoman, Ospringe, Kent, 1673 CKS PRC2/35/250
Parkes, William, husbandman, Norton Disney, Lincs, 1673 Lincs RO Ad/Ac/35/33
Parkhurst, John, esquire, Lenham, Kent, 1640 CKS PRC1/5/14
Parkhurst, Robert, clothier, Maidstone, Kent, 1622 CKS PRC20/6/294
Parkin, Agnes, widow, Sutton St Edmunds, Lincs, 1612 Lincs RO Ad/Ac/11/11
Parkin, Francis, Fleet, Lincs, 1618 Lincs RO Ad/Ac/15/183
Parkin, Richard, farmer, Darfield (Edderthorpe), Yorks, 1809 Borthwick Test C.P. 1809/6
Parkin, Thomas, Gedney, Lincs, 1629 Lincs RO Ad/Ac/22/33
Parkine, Richard, Bottesford (Ashby), Lincs, 1600 Lincs RO Ad/Ac/5/505
Parking, John, St Columb Minor, Corn, 1615 Cornwall RO AP/P282/1
Parkins, Elizabeth, widow, Gedney, Lincs, 1641 Lincs RO Ad/Ac/27/295
Parkins, John, Ponton, Little, Lincs, 1638 Lincs RO Ad/Ac/25/155
Parkins, John, Carlton, South, Lincs, 1677 Lincs RO Ad/Ac/42/72
Parkins, Richard, Ashby, Lincs, 1591 Lincs RO Ad/Ac/37/9

[Parkins:]
Parkins, Richard, Gainsborough, Lincs, 1626 Lincs RO Ad/Ac/39/42
Parkinson, Marton, Lincs, C17th Lincs RO Ad/Ac/40/188
Parkinson, Ann, widow, Laughton en le Morthen (Throapham), Yorks, 1802 Borthwick D/C C.P. 1802/1
Parkinson, John, Thornton, Lincs, 1603 Lincs RO Ad/Ac/5/332
Parkinson, John, Althorpe, Lincs, 1609 Lincs RO Ad/Ac/8a/301
Parkinson, Reginald, 1621 Lancs RO (Name of Deceased) D.R.C.H. 1621
Parkinson, Robert, painter, Canterbury, Kent, 1620 CKS PRC2/19/163
Parkinson, Robert, Marton, Lincs, 1649 Lincs RO Ad/Ac/40/208
Parkinson, Thomas, university: 'Fellow of Clare College, Cambridge/M.A.', Cambridge (Clare College), Cambs, 1622 CUL V.C. Acc./Box2/55
Parkinson, William, Fleet, Lincs, 1623 Lincs RO Ad/Ac/18/27
Parks, John, Kenardington, Kent, 1628 CKS PRC2/29/96
Parks, Nicholas, Marden, Kent, 1619 CKS PRC20/4/300
Parks, Ralf, Westwell, Kent, 1588 CKS PRC21/9/76
Parks, Richard, Kenardington, Kent, 1611 CKS PRC2/15/293
Parks, Walter, Frittenden, Kent, 1619 CKS PRC2/19/109
Parks, William, Salisbury, Wilts, 1612 Wilts RO Miscellaneous Index (name + date)
Parlebene, Agnes, widow, Sibsey, Lincs, 1612 Lincs RO Ad/Ac/11/20
Parman/Field, Joan, widow, Moreton, North, Berks, 1591 Berks RO D/A1/207/109D
Parmentire, see Fremaux,
Parnell, John, Brookland, Kent, 1589 CKS PRC2/4/447
Parnell, Jone, Appledore, Kent, 1598 CKS PRC2/9/415
Parnell, Rawlin, Tenterden, Kent, 1630 CKS PRC2/30/114
Parnell, Richarde, Haxey, Lincs, 1678 Lincs RO Ad/Ac/35/134
Parnell, Robert, cordwainer, Sellindge, Kent, 1683 CKS PRC2/40/140
Parnell, Robert, cordwainer, Sellindge, Kent, 1689 CKS PRC2/41/157
Parnell, Robert, Lyminge, Kent, 1707 CKS PRC19/6/23
Parnell, Thomas, Chester, Ches, 1665 Cheshire RO (Name) W.C. 1665
Parnell, William, Smeeth, Kent, 1674 CKS PRC20/12/141
Parnham, William, Deeping, Market, Lincs, 1674 Lincs RO Ad/Ac/35/7
Parr, Hellen, widow, Heapham, Lincs, 1681 Lincs RO Ad/Ac/43/147a
Parr, John, yeoman, Sulhampstead Abbots, Berks, 1680 Berks RO D/A1/209/39C
Parr, Ralf, Smeeth, Kent, 1608 CKS PRC20/1/392
Parr, Richard, Avebury, Wilts, 1632 Wilts RO Arch. Wilts.(+ name and date)
Parradise, Avis, Wilton, Wilts, 1638 Wilts RO CC Sarum(+ name and date)
Parram, Thomas, Donhead St Mary, Wilts, 1639 Wilts RO Arch. Sarum(+ name and date)
Parramore, Daniel, Sheldwich, Kent, 1633 CKS PRC2/32/103
Parramore, John, Herne, Kent, 1600 CKS PRC21/15/170
Parramore, William, Herne, Kent, 1574 CKS PRC21/2/146
Parrat, Nicholas, Lyme Regis, Dors, 1628 Wilts RO Miscellaneous Index (name + date)
Parratt, Robert, Warboys, Hunts, 1686 Hunts RO/Acc58/262
Parratt, William, ironmonger, Bradford, Yorks, 1847 Borthwick Test C.P. 1847/9
Parre, Christian, widow, Reading St Giles, Berks, 1614 Berks RO D/A1/207/175A
Parre, Daniell, Twickenham, London & Middlesex, 1676 PRO PROB32/12/25
Parre, William, yeoman, Bucklebury, Berks, 1663 Berks RO D/A1/208/132B
Parrett, Robert, gentleman, St Ives, Hunts, 1682 Hunts RO/Acc58/180(25)
Parrett, Simon, Milton, Oxon, 1638 Oxon RO MSS Wills 171/3/9
Parrett, William, yeoman, Eynsham, Oxon, 1639 Oxon RO MSS Wills 84/3/18
Parrett, William, Raithby, Lincs, 1683 Lincs RO Ad/Ac/44/90
Parrey, John, St Mary le Savoy, London & Middlesex, 1670 PRO PROB32/5/29
Parrie, Peter, Stoke St Gregory, Som, 1596 Somerset RO D/D/Cta/P75
Parris, Edith, widow, Broad Hinton, Wilts, 1639 Wilts RO Arch. Wilts.(+ name and date)
Parris, John, Broad Hinton, Wilts, 1635 Wilts RO CC Sarum(+ name and date)
Parris, Roger, yeoman, Broad Hinton, Wilts, 1626? Wilts RO Arch. Wilts.(+ name and date)

Parris, William, yeoman, Sittingbourne, Kent, 1582 CKS PRC2/2/63
Parrish, Hugh, Bloxham, Oxon, 1640 Oxon RO MSS Wills 84/3/11
Parrish, Thomas, Cowbit, Lincs, 1639 Lincs RO Ad/Ac/26/285
Parrocke, Francis, Shifnal (Priors Lee), Shrops, 1675 LJRO:cards/1675/44
Parrocke, John, Inkpen, Berks, 1610 Berks RO D/A1/207/159A
Parromor, Bartholomew, Eastry, Kent, 1603 CKS PRC21/17/7
Parromor, John, Sandwich, Kent, 1604 CKS PRC2/14/365
Parromor, William, Herne, Kent, 1605 CKS PRC21/17/272
Parrot, Richard, husbandman, Holton Beckering, Lincs, 1674 Lincs RO Ad/Ac/35/24
Parrott, Richard, grocer?/freeman, St Clement Danes, London & Middlesex, 1689 PRO PROB32/28/287
Parrott, Thomas, husbandman, Hallington, Lincs, 1679 Lincs RO Ad/Ac/43/99
Parry, David, 1634 NLW BR 1634/98 Ac
Parry, Thomas, gentleman, Ogbourne St Andrew, Wilts, 1678 Wilts RO Dean Sarum (name + date)
Parry, Thomas, Ogbourne St Andrew, Wilts, 1687 Wilts RO Dean Sarum (name + date)
Parsell, Henry, shepherd, Ashwell, Herts, 1639 Herts RO AHH23/1828
Parslow, John, tailor, Beckley (Horton), Oxon, 1681 Oxon RO MSS Wills 84/4/19
Parslowe, William, husbandman, Pangbourne, Berks, 1608 Berks RO D/A1/207/153A
Parson, Joan, Tarring, West, Sussex, 1610 W. Suss RO EpIV/10/1/4
Parson, John, Grinstead, West, Sussex, 1581 W. Suss RO EpI/33/1581/1
Parson, Nicholas, Lydd, Kent, 1626 CKS PRC20/7/317
Parson, Thomas, Thornham, Kent, 1620 CKS PRC2/19/113
Parson, William, Cornelly, Corn, 1612 Cornwall RO AP/P236
Parson, William, Horsham, Sussex, 1618 W. Suss RO EpI/33/1618/1
Parsons, Edward, Rodmersham, Kent, 1636 CKS PRC2/33/109
Parsons, Francis, feltmaker, Bicester, Oxon, 1638 Oxon RO MSS Wills 171/3/12
Parsons, George, Durleigh, Som, 1596 Somerset RO D/D/Cta/P58
Parsons, Henry,
Som 1635 Somerset RO D/D/Cta/P5
Parsons, John, mercer, Oxford (University), Oxon, Bodleian HYP B9/35-36
Parsons, John, Stratford Tony, Wilts, 1617 Wilts RO Arch. Sarum(+ name and date)
Parsons, John,
Som 1621 Somerset RO D/D/Cta/P6
Parsons, John, yeoman, Shefford, East (Little Shefford), Berks, 1622 Berks RO D/A1/208/23A
Parsons, John, gentleman, Severnake, Wilts, 1676 Wilts RO Miscellaneous Index (name + date)
Parsons, John, gentleman, Sherburn (Barkston Ash), Yorks, 1783 Borthwick Test C.P. 1782/5
Parsons, John eld, Tickenham, Som, 1589 Somerset RO D/D/Cta/P77
Parsons, Joseph, Middlezoy, Som, 1648 Somerset RO D/D/Cta/P7
Parsons, Miles, Harborough, Market, Leics, 1673 Leics RO Administrators Accounts 1667-72 f122
Parsons, Robert, Worton, Nether, Oxon, 1637 Oxon RO MSS Wills 171/3/8
Parsons, Roger, Minster in Sheppey, Kent, 1638 CKS PRC2/34/110
Parsons, Thomas, Romsey, Hants, 1625 Hants RO 21M65 D8/125
Parsons, Thomas, gentleman, Newington, South, Oxon, 1649 Oxon RO MSS Wills 299/5/32
Parsons, Thomas, St Martin in the Fields, London & Middlesex, 1676 PRO PROB32/13/18
Parsons, Thomas + Jane, Wiston, Sussex, 1670 W. Suss RO EpI/33/1670/25
Parsons, William, Muchelney (Hawel), Som, 1736 Somerset RO D/D/Cta/P32
Parsons/Frowde, John, Sedgehill, Wilts, 1602 Wilts RO Miscellaneous Index (name + date)
Parsons/Lysle, Thomas, cordwainer: 'shoemaker', Steyning, Sussex, 1682 W. Suss RO EpI/33/1682/51
Partheriche, Edward, Chartham, Kent, 1613 CKS PRC2/17/100
Partheriche, Marye, widow, Newington next Hythe, Kent, 1614 CKS PRC2/19/107
Partington, William, 1692 Lancs RO (Name of Deceased) D.R.C.H. 1691
Parton, John, Cranbrook, Kent, 1677 CKS PRC2/37/184

[Parton:]
Parton, John, butcher, Wellington (Arleston), Shrops, 1818 LJRO/B/C/5/1818/26
Parton, John, butcher, Wellington (Arleston), Shrops, 1818 LJRO/B/C/5/1818/29
Parton, William, yeoman, Tenterden, Kent, 1677 CKS PRC2/37/78
Parton, William, farmer, Bromley, Abbots (Bromley Hurst), Staffs, 1793 LJRO/B/C/5/1793/43
Partredge, Elizabeth, widow, Milton next Sittingbourne, Kent, 1618 CKS PRC2/19/155
Partreeich, William, Linsted, Kent, 1640 CKS PRC1/5/15
Partriche, William, Bromfield, Kent, 1584 CKS PRC2/3/256
Partridge, Arthur, Malmesbury, Wilts, 1627 Wilts RO Arch. Wilts.(+ name and date)
Partridge, Avery, clergy: 'clerk', Scarle, North, Lincs, 1637 Lincs RO Ad/Ac/25/653
Partridge, Humfrie, Lyminge, Kent, 1612 CKS PRC20/2/342
Partridge, Idden, Newington next Hythe, Kent, 1627 CKS PRC2/28/97
Partridge, Jane, widow, Tunstall, Kent, 1620 CKS PRC2/19/122
Partridge, Nicholas, Bicker, Lincs, 1606 Lincs RO Ad/Ac/6/39
Partridge, Richard, St Botolph without Aldersgate, London & Middlesex, 1703 PRO PROB5/1603
Partridge, Robert, Bethersden, Kent, 1619 CKS PRC2/19/153
Partridge, Roger, cooper, Deal, Kent, 1678 CKS PRC20/12/279
Partridge, Thomas, Guston, Kent, 1626 CKS PRC20/7/164
Parvys, Jane, widow, Knoyle, West, Wilts, 1614 Wilts RO CC Sarum(+ name and date)
Pary, Robert, husbandman, Wilsford, Lincs, 1673 Lincs RO Ad/Ac/35/6
Pascole, William, Dover, Kent, 1635 CKS PRC20/11/197
Pascowe, John, Phillack, Corn, 1605 Cornwall RO AP/P69/2
Pashfeilde, John, Graveney, Kent, 1612 CKS PRC2/16/88
Pashley, John, Canterbury St Margaret, Kent, 1613 CKS PRC2/17/276
Pashley, Mathew, Sandwich, Kent, 1625 CKS PRC2/25/105
Pashley, Simon, Throwleigh, Kent, 1635 CKS PRC2/33/101
Pashly, John, Leysdown, Kent, 1674 CKS PRC2/36/109
Pashly, Thomas, Hythe St Leonard, Kent, 1625 CKS PRC20/7/239
Pasmore, Thomas, Cumberworth, Lincs, 1664 Lincs RO Ad/Ac/43/33
Pasmore, Thomas, Cumberworth, Lincs, 1664 Lincs RO Ad/Ac/43/43
Passell, Rowland, Nuthurst, Sussex, 1682 W. Suss RO EpI/33/1682/32
Passheley, John, Brenzett, Kent, 1591 CKS PRC2/5/243
Passheley, Willyam, thatcher, Elham, Kent, 1586 CKS PRC2/4/231
Paston, William, weaver: 'worsted weaver', Norwich St Clement, Norf, Norfolk RO NCC INV/74A/282
Patchet, Emmie, widow, Kyme, South (North Kyme), Lincs, 1627 Lincs RO Ad/Ac/20b/62
Patchett, George, Belton, Lincs, 1613 Lincs RO Ad/Ac/11/45
Patchett, Roberte, Waddington, Lincs, 1578 Lincs RO Ad/Ac/2b/27
Patchinge, John, Itchingfield, Sussex, 1640 W. Suss RO EpI/33/1640/20
Patchinge, Richarde, Rolvenden, Kent, 1615 CKS PRC2/19/128
Pate, Richard, university: 'University Registrar, Sidney Sussex College, Cambridge/scrivener' Cambridge Holy Trinity, Cambs, 1665 CUL V.C. Acc./Box3/36
Paternoster, Cicilie, Fleet, Lincs, 1618 Lincs RO Ad/Ac/14/208
Paternoster, John, Sandwich St Peter, Kent, 1584 CKS PRC2/3/172
Pateson, Jeremy, mason, Canterbury St Andrew, Kent, 1631 CKS PRC20/9/325
Patey, Timothy, Purton, Wilts, 1750 c. Wilts RO Miscellaneous Index (name + date)
Patie, Anne, widow, Chieveley, Berks, 1630 Berks RO D/A1/105/145B
Patie, Margaret, Kingston Lisle, Berks, 1605 Berks RO D/A1/207/148A
Patie, Thomas, clothworker, Reading St Giles, Berks, 1614 Berks RO D/A1/207/171C
Patland, John, Goudhurst, Kent, 1627 CKS PRC2/28/94
Patman, Richard, Woolsthorpe, Lincs, 1651? Lincs RO Ad/Ac/29/155
Patrick, Robert, Holton Beckering, Lincs, 1670 Lincs RO Ad/Ac/32/166
Patricke, Samuel, Faversham, Kent, 1625 CKS PRC2/25/107
Patridge/Moncke, Ann, widow, Alconbury, Hunts, 1679 Hunts RO/Acc58/134(187)
Patten, Robert, Chartham, Kent, 1619 CKS PRC2/19/161
Pattenden, George, Bearsted, Kent, 1633 CKS PRC2/32/102

Pattenden, William, butcher, Leeds, Kent, 1690 CKS PRC2/41/159
Pattens, Richard, Willingham, Lincs, 1639 Lincs RO Ad/Ac/40/284
Pattenson, Roger, Biddenden, Kent, 1640 CKS PRC1/5/16
Pattenson, Samuel, gentleman, Biddenden, Kent, 1663 CKS PRC1/9/138
Patteson, William, Chatham, Kent, 1697 CKS PRC2/42/134
Pattinson, Joane, Beckingham, Lincs, 1638 Lincs RO Ad/Ac/25/528
Pattison, Anthony, husbandman, Appledore, Kent, 1685 CKS PRC2/41/5
Pattison, James, yeoman, Chislet, Kent, 1692 CKS PRC2/42/48
Pattison, Robert, Appleby, Lincs, 1621 Lincs RO Ad/Ac/8c/15
Pattison, Thomas, Stone in Oxney, Kent, 1677 CKS PRC2/37/186
Pattoo, Andrew, wool comber, Canterbury St Paul, Kent, 1662 CKS PRC1/9/47
Pattrick, Dorothy, Sandiacre, Derby, 1683 LJRO/B/C/5/1683/15
Pattrick, John, Tatenhill, Staffs, 1684 LJRO/B/C/5/1684/62
Pat(t)rick(e), William, Ockbrook (Borrowash), Derby, 1663 LJRO:cards/1663/47
Pattyson, William, Frampton, Lincs, 1612 Lincs RO Ad/Ac/10/158
Paty, Edward, husbandman, Chieveley (Curridge), Berks, 1686 Berks RO D/A1/209/62C
Paty, John, victualler, Dymchurch, Kent, 1681 CKS PRC2/39/218
Paty, William, cordwainer: 'shoemaker', Farringdon, Great, Berks, 1681 Berks RO D/A3/4/20C
Patye, John, yeoman, Chieveley (Curridge), Berks, 1648 Berks RO D/A1/208/121A
Patynsonne, John, Lincoln, Lincs, 1580 Lincs RO Ad/Ac/2C/56
Paucke, Jeffrey, Bourne, Lincs, 1627 Lincs RO Ad/Ac/20b/77
Paukherst, Thomas, Cranbrook, Kent, 1671 CKS PRC2/35/75
Paul, Robert, clergy: 'clerk/vicar', Coker, East, Som, 1674 Somerset RO D/D/Cta/P33
Paul, Thomas, Norwich, Norf, 1742 Norfolk RO ANW/23/23/89A
Paul, William, Ashby Parva, Leics, 1672 Leics RO Administrators Accounts 1667-72 f68
Paule, Christopher, yeoman, Hogsthorpe, Lincs, 1619 Lincs RO Ad/Ac/15/23
Paule, Henry, Gosberton, Lincs, 1629 Lincs RO Ad/Ac/22/127
Paule, Jasper, Gulval, Corn, 1627 Cornwall RO AP/P524
Paule/Barne, Richard + Suzanne, Hannah, Lincs, 1612 Lincs RO Ad/Ac/10/149
Paulenge, Richard, Britwell Salome, Oxon, 1645 Oxon RO MSS Wills 299/5/27
Pauley, Christopher, Marden, Kent, 1601 CKS PRC2/12/300
Pauley, Richard, Horncastle, Lincs, 1614 Lincs RO Ad/Ac/13/215
Pauline, Marke, yeoman, St Johns Thanet, Kent, 1642 CKS PRC1/6/77
Paull, John, Gosberton, Lincs, 1640 Lincs RO Ad/Ac/27/64
Paunton, Marie, Swineshead, Lincs, 1634 Lincs RO Ad/Ac/24/543
Pavis, John, Sandhurst, Kent, 1617 CKS PRC2/19/140
Pavis, Robert, Sandhurst, Kent, 1628 CKS PRC2/29/95
Pavye, Andrew, Durnford, Wilts, 1628 Wilts RO Miscellaneous Index (name + date)
Pavys, Richard, Rolvenden, Kent, 1587 CKS PRC2/4/410
Pavys, Richarde, Sandhurst, Kent, 1583 CKS PRC2/3/81
Pawdy, Thomas, Montacute, Som, 1623 Somerset RO D/D/Cta/P9
Pawle, Robarte, Saltwood, Kent, 1600 CKS PRC21/15/135
Pawle, Thomas, yeoman, Helland, Corn, 1609 Cornwall RO AP/P170/2
Pawlet, William, surgeon, Pontefract, Yorks, 1804 Borthwick Test C.P. 1804/13
Pawlett, Samuel, Bytham, Little, Lincs, 1649 Lincs RO Ad/Ac/30/85
Pawley, Robert, innholder, Bromfield, Kent, 1668 CKS PRC1/13/88
Pawlin, Thomas, St Clement Danes, London & Middlesex, 1667 PRO PROB32/2/78
Pawling, Anthony, husbandman, Dorchester, Oxon, 1671 Oxon RO MSS Wills Pec 70/4/33
Pawling, Robert, Bourton, Black, Oxon, 1663 Oxon RO MSS Wills 84/3/31
Pawling, Thomas, yeoman, Hundleby, Lincs, 1666? Lincs RO Ad/Ac/32/89
Pawling, Thomas, yeoman, Standlake, Oxon, 1675 Oxon RO MSS Wills 299/5/43
Pawlinge, Richard, gentleman, Chalgrove, Oxon, 1628 Oxon RO MSS Wills 299/5/10
Pawly, July, gentleman, Croxton, South, Leics, 1666 Leics RO Administrators Accounts C17th f85
Pawmer, Robert, Stamford St Mary, Lincs, 1637 Lincs RO Ad/Ac/25/501

[Pawson:]
Pawson, Daniell, Tonge, Kent, 1596 CKS PRC2/8/457
Pawson, Ezechiel eld, Sandwich, Kent, 1626 CKS PRC2/27/124
Pawson, Henry, Fiskerton, Lincs, 1617 Lincs RO Ad/Ac/8b/266
Pawson, Henry, mr, Stockbury, Kent, 1629 CKS PRC2/30/112
Pawson, Robert, Brox-Holme, Lincs, 1614 Lincs RO Ad/Ac/8b/45
Pawson, Thomas, clergy: 'parson', Sandwich St Mary, Kent, 1597 CKS PRC2/9/170
Pawson Hargrave, George, esquire, Eslington, Northumb, 1819 Borthwick Test C.P. 1819/3
Paxton, Anne, Sulgrave, Northants, 1677 Northants RO NWill A/C/47
Paxton, Thomas, Sulgrave, Northants, 1683 Northants RO NWill A/C/80
Pay, Edmund, Elham, Kent, 1685 CKS PRC2/40/235
Pay, Mary, Elham, Kent, 1664 CKS PRC1/10/70
Pay, Nicholas, yeoman, Minster in Thanet, Kent, 1683 CKS PRC2/40/143
Pay, Richard, Elham, Kent, 1622 CKS PRC2/24/45
Pay, Willyam, Kingsnorth, Kent, 1628 CKS PRC2/29/90
Payce, John, Crondall, Hants, 1684 Hants RO 1685 AD84
Payce, John, Sherfield Upon Loddon, Hants, 1689 Hants RO 21m65 D8/352
Paycocke, William, Alvingham, Lincs, 1607 Lincs RO Ad/Ac/8a/146
Paye, John, Marden, Up, Sussex, 1594 W. Suss RO EpI/33/1594/14
Paye, Ralphe, Chawton, Hants, 1624 Hants RO 21M65 D8/81
Payen, Richard, Tickenham, Som, 1630 Somerset RO D/D/Cta/P34
Payn, George, glazier, Reading St Mary, Berks, 1678 Berks RO D/A1/209/21D
Payn, Ralph, Staughton, Great, Hunts, 1685 Hunts RO/Acc58/253(246)
Payne, 1790 Lincs RO Ad/Ac/36/16a
Payne, Agnes, Wittersham, Kent, 1588 CKS PRC21/9/33
Payne, Ann, 1662 Hants RO 21M65 D8/145
Payne, Augustine, clergy: 'clerk', Chichester, Sussex, 1665 W. Suss RO EpIII/9/1/51
Payne, Edward, Luddenham, Kent, 1601 CKS PRC2/12/282
Payne, Henrie, Langley, Kent, 1597 CKS PRC2/9/166
Payne, James, Sandwich, Kent, 1622 CKS PRC2/24/41
Payne, John, basket maker, Maidenhead, Berks, 1610 Berks RO D/A1/207/161A
Payne, John, husbandman, Whitley, Berks, 1616 Berks RO D/A1/208/3A
Payne, John, Harting, Sussex, 1631 W. Suss RO EpI/33/1630/13
Payne, John, draper: 'woollen draper', St Laurence Thanet, Kent, 1692 CKS PRC2/42/11
Payne, John, farmer, Beyton, Suff, 1804 Suff RO(B) IC500/3/53/105
Payne, Mildred, widow, Maidstone, Kent, 1615 CKS PRC20/3/160
Payne, Richard, Rolvenden, Kent, 1637 CKS PRC2/34/91
Payne, Symon, butcher, Sevenoaks (Riverhead), Kent, 1668 Lambeth Palace VH96/5632
Payne, Thomas, Stone in Oxney, Kent, 1594 CKS PRC2/7/223
Payne, Thomas, Lydd, Kent, 1604 CKS PRC21/17/148
Payne, Thomas, Rolvenden, Kent, 1617 CKS PRC2/19/146
Payne, Thomas, Ulcombe, Kent, 1627 CKS PRC2/28/92
Payne, Thomas, Eastry, Kent, 1635 CKS PRC20/11/220
Payne, Thomas, Downton, Wilts, 1672 Wilts RO Arch. Sarum(+ name and date)
Payne, Walter, St Martin in the Fields, London & Middlesex, 1676 PRO PROB32/13/171
Payne, Wyllyam, Wye, Kent, 1597 CKS PRC2/9/168
Paynter, Anne, Wimborne Minster, Dors, Dorset RO PE/WM CP 2/4/89
Paynter, Edward, Petherwin, North, Corn, 1642 Cornwall RO AP/P815/1
Paynter, John, Devizes, Wilts, 1645 Wilts RO CC Sarum(+ name and date)
Paynter, see Raynie,
Paynton, John, Wytham, Berks, 1618 Berks RO D/A1/208/15A
Payre?, Thomas, bachelor, Bighton, Hants, 1677 Hants RO 21m65 D8/278
Payse, James, labourer, Tilehurst, Berks, 1608 Berks RO D/A1/207/155A
Payse, Thomas, Watford, Herts, 1574 Herts RO ASA25/782
Peach, Mary, widow, Thirsk, Yorks, 1769 Borthwick Cons C.P. 1769/1
Peach, Thomas, Brailsford, Derby, 1682 LJRO/B/C/5/1682/82

Peach, William, Etwall, Derby, 1674 LJRO:cards/1674/39
Peacham, John, Langtoft, Lincs, 1626 Lincs RO Ad/Ac/19B/45
Peachame, Richard, Scampton, Lincs, 1595 Lincs RO Ad/Ac/5/266
Peachey, Anne, widow, Eartham, Sussex, 1674 W. Suss RO EpI/33/1674/12
Peachey, Elizabeth, widow, Yapton, Sussex, 1684 W. Suss RO EpI/33/1684/42
Peachey, Henry, Singleton, Sussex, 1684 W. Suss RO EpI/33/1684/13
Peachey, John, gentleman, Holywell (Needingworth), Hunts, Hunts RO/Acc58/186(46)
Peachey, Thomas, Singleton, Sussex, 1632 W. Suss RO EpI/33/1632/16
Peacock, William, Paxton, Little, Hunts, 1682 Hunts RO/Acc58/189(103)
Peacocke, Edward, Faversham, Kent, 1596 CKS PRC2/9/1
Peacocke, Edward, Redbourn, Herts, 1598 Herts RO ASA25/1691
Peacocke, George, gentleman, Sandwich, Kent, 1663 CKS PRC1/9/139
Peacocke, Henrie, Fulstow, Lincs, 1593 Lincs RO Ad/Ac/3/63
Peacocke, Isabel, spinster, Bray, Berks, 1638 Berks RO D/A1/208/84C
Peacocke, John, Scotter, Lincs, 1682 Lincs RO Ad/Ac/34/89
Peacocke, Richard, Covenham St Bartholomew, Lincs, 1636 Lincs RO Ad/Ac/24/456
Peacocke, Thomas, Owston, Lincs, 1662 Lincs RO Ad/Ac/41/34
Peacocke, Walter, Redbourn, Herts, 1601 Herts RO ASA25/1800
Peacok, Walter, Redbourn, Herts, 1637 Herts RO ASA25/4930
Pead, James, husbandman, Longworth, Berks, 1625 Berks RO D/A1/208/43A
Peade, Thomas, haberdasher/citizen, St Lawrence Jewry, London & Middlesex, 1685 Lambeth Palace Arches G35/3
Peak, Samuel, Seighford, Staffs, 1684 LJRO/B/C/5/1684/63
Peake, Daniel, clergy: 'clerk', Petersfield, Hants, 1679 Hants RO 21m65 D8/316
Peake, Elizabeth, Pelynt, Corn, 1610 Cornwall RO AP/P197
Peake, George, gentleman, Horncastle, Lincs, 1619 Lincs RO Ad/Ac/15/113
Peake, Lucy, widow, Stockbury, Kent, 1677 CKS PRC2/37/188
Peake, Mary, widow, Deal, Kent, 1669 CKS PRC19/4/58
Peake, Matthew, Taynton, Oxon, 1666 Oxon RO MSS Wills 171/4/1
Peake, Robert, Moulton, Lincs, 1637 Lincs RO Ad/Ac/25/455
Peake, Thomas, gentleman, Toynton, High, Lincs, 1613 Lincs RO Ad/Ac/12/89
Peake, Valentine, Eastchurch, Sheppey, Kent, 1639 CKS PRC2/34/256
Peale, Richard ygr, mariner, St Johns Thanet, Kent, 1681 CKS PRC2/39/92
Peale, Robert, Hathern, Leics, 1666 Leics RO Administrators Accounts C17th f64
Pear, Elizabeth, widow, Godshill, Hants, 1624 Hants RO 21M65 D8/82
Pearce, Bartholomew, Drayton, Berks, 1614 Berks RO D/A1/105/3C
Pearce, Edward, Egerton, Kent, 1600 CKS PRC21/15/240
Pearce, Mawde, widow, Heddington, Wilts, 1628 Wilts RO Arch. Wilts.(+ name and date)
Pearce, Richard, Monkton, West, Som, 1588 Somerset RO D/D/Cta/P26
Pearce, Robert, Rodney Stoke, Som, 1685 Somerset RO D/D/Cta/P35
Pearce, Thomas, Mundham, North, Sussex, W. Suss RO EpI/33/1613/18
Pearce, Thomas, husbandman, Chaddleworth, Berks, 1667 Berks RO D/A1/208/148C
Pearce, Thomas, baker: 'white baker', Oxford (University), Oxon, 1673 Bodleian HYP B9/37-38
Pearce, Thomas, Bridgetown, Barbados, 1683 PRO PROB32/33/6
Pearce, William,
Som Somerset RO D/D/Cta/P27
Pearce, William, Weston Zoyland, Som, 1676 Somerset RO D/D/Cta/P36
Pearce, see Newport,
Pearcie, Thomas, Epworth, Lincs, 1667 Lincs RO Ad/Ac/33/18
Pearcy, Daniel, Hallow, Worcs, Worcs RO 008.7 BA3585/835/bdl 2
Peare, Henry, Wimborne Minster, Dors, 1612 Dorset RO PE/WM CP 2/4/10
Peares, Anthonie, yeoman, Frieston, Lincs, 1639 Lincs RO Ad/Ac/26/39
Peares, Hugh, Braceby, Lincs, 1634 Lincs RO Ad/Ac/24/55
Peares, William, Kingstone, Staffs, 1685 LJRO/B/C/5/1684/64
Pearks, Thomas, Stoke Prior, Worcs, 1685 Worcs RO 008.7 BA3585/830/21

[Pearks:]
Pearks, William, yeoman, Feckenham, Worcs, 1684 Worcs RO 008.7 BA3585/837/bdl 4
Pearle, Gyles, Sandwich St Peter, Kent, 1627 CKS PRC2/28/95
Pearman, Edward, yeoman, Kintbury (Holt), Berks, 1678 Berks RO D/A1/209/28D
Pearne, John, carpenter, Inkpen, Berks, 1622 Berks RO D/A1/208/25A
Pearne, Katheryn, widow, Launcells, Corn, 1608 Cornwall RO AP/P105/2-6
Pearne, William, ploughwright, Inkpen, Berks, 1635 Berks RO D/A1/208/73A
Pears, John, bachelor, Week St Mary, Corn, 1630 Cornwall RO AP/P605/5
Pearse, Joan, Petherwin, North, Corn, 1604 Cornwall RO AP/P73
Pearse, Joane, widow, Aldbourne, Wilts, 1632 Wilts RO Arch. Wilts.(+ name and date)
Pearse, Robert, husbandman, Welford (Benham Hoe), Berks, 1633 Berks RO D/A1/208/70A
Pearse, Robert ygr, Chastleton, Oxon, 1663 Oxon RO MSS Wills 51/4/28
Pearse, Thomas, Ramsbury, Wilts, 1635 Wilts RO Miscellaneous Index (name + date)
Pearse, Ursula, widow, Deal, Kent, 1681 CKS PRC20/13/184
Pearsey, Thomas, Sutton Valence, Kent, 1619 CKS PRC2/19/114
Pearson, Edward, Droxford, Hants, 1684 Hants RO 21m65 D8/342
Pearson, Francis, husbandman, Algarkirk, Lincs, 1650 Lincs RO Ad/Ac/30/22
Pearson, Henrie, Cranwell, Lincs, 1638 Lincs RO Ad/Ac/25/71
Pearson, John, husbandman, Crowland, Lincs, 1624 Lincs RO Ad/Ac/19A/109
Pearson, John, Dover, Kent, 1625 CKS PRC20/6/154
Pearson, John, Mumby, Lincs, 1627 Lincs RO Ad/Ac/20b/29
Pearson, John, Winterton, Lincs, 1627 Lincs RO Ad/Ac/39/120
Pearson, John, Asgarby, Lincs, 1666 Lincs RO Ad/Ac/42/39
Pearson, Jonas, farmer, Bradford (Thornton), Yorks, 1833 Borthwick Test C.P. 1833/7
Pearson, Richard, Rauceby, Lincs, 1612 Lincs RO Ad/Ac/10/160
Pearson, Roger, Trotton, Sussex, 1635 W. Suss RO EpI/33/1635/28
Pearson, Sarah, Wolston, Warks, 1683 LJRO/B/C/5/1682/83
Pearson, Thomas, Bardney, Lincs, 1632 Lincs RO Ad/Ac/23/155
Pearson, Thomas, Belshford, Lincs, 1666? Lincs RO Ad/Ac/32/128
Pearson, William, yeoman, Inkpen, Berks, 1678 Berks RO D/A1/107/147C
Peart, Edward, Owston, Lincs, 1683 Lincs RO Ad/Ac/44/40
Peartree, Joshua, butcher, Edgefield, Norf, 1719 Norfolk RO ANW/23/14/4
Peartree, Richard, Holbeach, Lincs, 1607 Lincs RO Ad/Ac/7/64
Pease, John, Faversham, Kent, 1638 CKS PRC2/34/97
Pease, Michael, Lanteglos-by-Fowey, Corn, 1608 Cornwall RO AP/P131
Pease, Thomas, Hothfield, Kent, 1617 CKS PRC2/19/123
Pease, William, tailor: 'merchant tailor/citizen', St Martin in the Fields, London & Middlesex, 1677 PRO PROB5/794
Peaves?, Thomas, Ramsbury (Axford), Wilts, mid C17th? Wilts RO Miscellaneous Index (name + date)
Pebworth, Richard, Hartlip, Kent, 1630 CKS PRC20/9/323
Peck, Mary, widow, Harlaxton, Lincs, 1635 Lincs RO Ad/Ac/24/429
Pecke, Dymeon, husbandman, Sutton, Long, Lincs, 1668 Lincs RO Ad/Ac/33/67
Pecke, John, Waterbeach, Cambs, 1605 c. CUL V.C. Acc./Box3/70
Pecke, Rebecca, university: 'privileged person/widow', Cambridge All Saints, Cambs, 1662 CUL V.C. Acc./Box3/37
Pecke, Richard, tailor, Canterbury, Kent, 1633 CKS PRC2/32/96
Pecke, Thomas eld, Wells St Cuthbert, Som, 1632 Somerset RO D/D/Cta/P23
Peckenham/Pecknam, Lawrence, Ospringe, Kent, 1612 CKS PRC2/16/85
Pecker, David, Faversham, Kent, 1624 CKS PRC2/24/60
Peckerton, Thomas, Spalding, Lincs, 1613 Lincs RO Ad/Ac/12/132
Peckes or Perkes, Thomas, husbandman, Bromsgrove, Worcs, 1602 Worcs RO 008.7 BA3585/838/228
Peckham, Christopher, East Sutton, Kent, 1640 CKS PRC1/5/17
Peckham, Jane, widow, Rumboldswhyke, Sussex, 1694 W. Suss RO EpIII/9/1/63
Peckham, Joan, widow, Cocking, Sussex, 1632 W. Suss RO EpI/33/1632/15

Peckman, Hugh, Upchurch, Kent, 1594 CKS PRC2/8/311
Pecknam/Packman, Salomon, bricklayer, Hartlip, Kent, 1620 CKS PRC2/19/117
Pecknam, see Peckenham,
Pedder, Mary, spinster, Newport, Hants, 1679 Hants RO 21m65 D8/317
Pedder, Mathew, husbandman, Frieston, Lincs, 1635 Lincs RO Ad/Ac/24/357
Pedder, Richard, Frieston, Lincs, 1601 Lincs RO Ad/Ac/5/161
Pedder, Symon, Butterwick, Lincs, 1651 Lincs RO Ad/Ac/29/125
Pedder, Troughton, Sutton St James, Lincs, 1639 Lincs RO Ad/Ac/26/304
Pedder, William, St Albans St Michaels, Herts, 1638 Herts RO ASA25/4943
Pedder, William, Butterwick, Lincs, 1649 Lincs RO Ad/Ac/30/183
Peddington/Tuck, Oliver, husbandman, Malmesbury, Wilts, 1628 Wilts RO Arch. Wilts.(+ name and date)
Pedham, John,
Kent 1594 CKS PRC21/13/159
Pedington, see Tuck,
Pedley, Oliver, Paxton, Great, Hunts, 1684 Hunts RO/Acc58/238(234)
Pedley, William, butcher, Waresley, Hunts, 1677 Hunts RO/Acc58/101(40)
Peedle, Thomas, husbandman, Wardington, Oxon, 1679 Oxon RO MSS Wills Pec 49/1/1
Peeke, Martin, Muchelney (Thorney), Som, 1606 Somerset RO D/D/Cta/P64
Peeke, Mathewe, Grantham, Lincs, 1596 Lincs RO Ad/Ac/4/35
Peele, Dionice, Minster in Thanet, Kent, 1629 CKS PRC2/30/108
Peele, George, Kettlethorpe (Fenton), Lincs, 1604 Lincs RO Ad/Ac/37/183
Peeles, Anne, Horbling, Lincs, 1605 Lincs RO Ad/Ac/6/7
Peende, John, Hawkhurst, Kent, 1598 CKS PRC2/10/242
Peene, Benedict, widow, Cranbrook, Kent, 1639 CKS PRC2/34/260
Peene, John, Maidstone, Kent, 1595 CKS PRC21/14/238
Peene, John, Hawkhurst, Kent, 1617 CKS PRC2/19/151
Peene, John, Boxley, Kent, 1624 CKS PRC2/24/52
Peene, John, Boxley, Kent, 1624 CKS PRC2/24/53
Peene, Stephen, Cranbrook, Kent, 1601 CKS PRC2/12/306
Peene, Symon, Maidstone, Kent, 1603 CKS PRC21/16/31
Peene, Thomas, Maidstone, Kent, 1609 CKS PRC20/2/102
Peerce, Henry, Hougham, Kent, 1623 CKS PRC2/24/49
Peerce, Rawlin, Newton, South, Wilts, 1598? Wilts RO Arch. Sarum(+ name and date)
Peerce, Robert, Maidstone, Kent, 1614 CKS PRC20/2/531
Peerce, Thomas, Northbourne, Kent, 1596 CKS PRC2/8/292
Peerce, Thomas, Wormshill, Kent, 1610 CKS PRC2/15/290
Peerce, William, St Peter in Thanet, Kent, 1598 CKS PRC2/10/234
Peerce/Peers, Nicholas + Margaret, High Halstow, Kent, 1612 CKS PRC2/16/63
Peere, Benjamin, Waltham, Kent, 1668 CKS PRC1/13/89
Peere/VanderPeere, Marie, Canterbury St Andrew, Kent, 1622 CKS PRC2/24/39
Peers, Alexander, High Halstow, Kent, 1595 CKS PRC2/7/423
Peers, George, Canterbury, Kent, 1574 CKS PRC21/2/110
Peers, Jeames, Birchington, Kent, 1625 CKS PRC20/7/313
Peers, John, Buckland nr Dover, Kent, 1606 CKS PRC20/1/122
Peers, John, alderman/mr, Canterbury, Kent, 1628 CKS PRC2/29/94
Peers, Margaret, Challock, Kent, 1625 CKS PRC20/6/150
Peers, Mary, widow, Folkestone, Kent, 1625 CKS PRC2/25/111
Peers, Nicholas, Chart, Great, Kent, 1613 CKS PRC2/17/383
Peers, Richard, Maidstone, Kent, 1628 CKS PRC20/8/373
Peers, Richard + Thomas, St Peter in Thanet, Kent, 1595 CKS PRC2/7/193
Peers, Robert, Headcorn, Kent, 1616 CKS PRC2/19/143
Peers, Robert, Northbourne, Kent, 1616 CKS PRC2/19/137
Peers, Samuel, gentleman, Maidstone, Kent, 1633 CKS PRC20/11/238
Peers, Thomas, Hythe St Leonard, Kent, 1583 CKS PRC21/6/391

[Peers:]
Peers, Thomas, Bethersden, Kent, 1592 CKS PRC2/6/126
Peers, Thomas, St Peter in Thanet, Kent, 1596 CKS PRC2/8/103
Peers, Thomas, Woodchurch, Kent, 1612 CKS PRC20/2/348
Peers, William eld, Elham, Kent, 1594 CKS PRC2/7/343
Peers, see Peerce,
Peerse, William, Folkestone, Kent, 1638 CKS PRC2/34/98
Peerse, William, St Nicholas at Wade, Kent, 1638 CKS PRC20/11/204
Peerson, John, Canterbury St Mary Bredman, Kent, 1610 CKS PRC1/1/15
Peerson, Thomas, Rainham, Kent, 1604 CKS PRC2/14/363
Peerson, William, Steventon, Berks, 1603 Berks RO D/A1/207/143C
Peerson/Awsten, Elizabeth, Canterbury, Kent, 1619 CKS PRC2/19/104
Peet, Thomas, Southoe, Hunts, 1676 Hunts RO/Acc58/30(162)
Peeter, John, Thakeham, Sussex, 1631 W. Suss RO EpI/33/1631/2
Peeter, William, Felpham, Sussex, 1631 W. Suss RO EpI/33/1631/17
Peeters, John, husbandman, Marden, Kent, 1662 CKS PRC1/9/48
Peeters, Nicholas, Newenden, Kent, 1616 CKS PRC2/24/38
Peg, John, Normanton, South, Derby, 1683 LJRO/B/C/5/1682/84
Pegg, William, Stanton, Stoney, Leics, 1672 Leics RO Administrators Accounts 1667-72 f72
Pegler, Anthony, Berkeley, Glos, 1685 GRO GDR/B4/2/P112
Peight, George, gentleman, Denton, Lincs, 1614 Lincs RO Ad/Ac/13/129
Peike, George, clergy: 'clerk', Donington, Lincs, 1611 Lincs RO Ad/Ac/10/60
Peirce, Gabriel, gentleman, Charing, Kent, 1674 CKS PRC20/12/140
Peirce, Henry, Eythorne, Kent, 1681 CKS PRC2/39/91
Peirce, John, Minster in Thanet, Kent, 1596 CKS PRC2/8/435
Peirce, John, Sherrington, Wilts, 1641 Wilts RO Arch. Sarum(+ name and date)
Peirce, John, yeoman, Eastchurch, Sheppey, Kent, 1675 CKS PRC2/36/225
Peirce, John, yeoman, Challock, Kent, 1677 CKS PRC20/12/218
Peirce, John, Thornham, Kent, 1679 CKS PRC2/38/58
Peirce, Michael, yeoman, High Halden, Kent, 1667 CKS PRC1/12/71
Peirce, Nicholas, yeoman, Ashford, Kent, 1680 CKS PRC2/39/83
Peirce, Thomas, Minety, Wilts, 1640 Wilts RO Arch. Wilts.(+ name and date)
Peirce, Thomas, bachelor, Canterbury St Paul, Kent, 1662 CKS PRC1/9/49
Peirce, Thomas, bachelor, Mersham, Kent, 1665 CKS PRC1/11/66
Peirce/Hurd, Gyles, Potterne, Wilts, 1640 Wilts RO CC Sarum(+ name and date)
Peirce, see Robinson & Smyth,
Peircy, Richard, St Peter in Thanet, Kent, 1639 CKS PRC1/3/31
Peireson, John, Canterbury St Mary Bredman, Kent, 1610 CKS PRC2/15/295
Peirs, John, St Johns Thanet, Kent, 1664 CKS PRC1/10/71
Peirse, Edward, Biddenden, Kent, 1703 CKS PRC1/16/52
Peirse, John, Elham, Kent, 1621 CKS PRC2/24/43
Peirsey, Robert, Owston, Lincs, 1679 Lincs RO Ad/Ac/43/81
Peirson, Joane, Codford St Mary, Wilts, 1629 Wilts RO CC Sarum(+ name and date)
Peirson, John, gentleman, Bossall (Sand Hutton), Yorks, 1788 Borthwick Test C.P. 1788/6
Peirson, Robert, widow (sic), Ash next Sandwich, Kent, 1711 CKS PRC19/6/46
Peke, David, Bredgar, Kent, 1625 CKS PRC2/25/116
Pelford, John, clergy: 'clerk', Cadeby, Leics, 1666 Leics RO Administrators Accounts C17th f90
Pelham, Ann, spinster, Hull, Yorks, 1639 Lincs RO Ad/Ac/25/243
Pelham, Ann, gentlewoman, Brocklesby, Lincs, 1708 Lambeth Palace Arches G59/1
Pelham, Harbert, esquire, Boston, Lincs, 1625 Lincs RO Ad/Ac/19B/41
Pelham, Herbert, esquire, Bures St Mary (Bures Hamlet), Essex, 1683 PRO PROB32/24/100
Pelham, John, St Margarets At Cliffe, Kent, 1596 CKS PRC21/14/65
Pelham, John, Reculver, Kent, 1663 CKS PRC19/3/40
Pelham, William, Stone in Oxney, Kent, 1602 CKS PRC2/12/292
Pell, Alexander, tanner, Lincoln, Lincs, 1639 Lincs RO Ad/Ac/26/134
Pell, Bartholomew, Whaplode, Lincs, 1640 Lincs RO Ad/Ac/27/110

Pell, Edward, Hale, Great (Little Hale), Lincs, 1632 Lincs RO Ad/Ac/23/124
Pell, Edward, Smarden, Kent, 1636 CKS PRC2/33/106
Pell, Friswith, Toynton, Low, Lincs, 1636 Lincs RO Ad/Ac/25/377
Pell, Issabell, widow, Willoughby, Silk, Lincs, 1606 Lincs RO Ad/Ac/7/60
Pell, John, yeoman, Algarkirk, Lincs, 1636 Lincs RO Ad/Ac/24/287
Pell, John, yeoman, Pluckley, Kent, 1668 CKS PRC1/13/90
Pell, John, gentleman, Godmanchester, Hunts, 1708 Hunts RO/Acc58/299
Pell, Nicholas, yeoman, Witham on the Hill, Lincs, 1666 Lincs RO Ad/Ac/32/129
Pell, Paul, Bethersden, Kent, 1613 CKS PRC2/18/129
Pell, Richard, New Romney, Kent, 1592 CKS PRC21/11/314
Pell, Richard, Willoughby, Silk, Lincs, 1620 Lincs RO Ad/Ac/16/75
Pell, Thomas, Quadring, Lincs, 1640 Lincs RO Ad/Ac/26/25
Pell, Thomas, Quadring, Lincs, 1640 Lincs RO Ad/Ac/40/151
Pell, William, Quadring, Lincs, 1612 Lincs RO Ad/Ac/12/152
Pell, William, clergy: 'clerk', Tonge, Kent, 1674 CKS PRC2/36/107
Pellam, George, Tenterden, Kent, 1582 CKS PRC2/2/110
Pelland, Anne, widow, Smeeth, Kent, 1614 CKS PRC20/3/63
Pelland/Elvie, Elizabeth, Hythe St Leonard, Kent, 1615 CKS PRC20/3/216
Peller, see Jinking,
Pellet, see Mockford,
Pellett, Edward, surgeon, Dover, Kent, 1680 CKS PRC20/13/52
Pellett, James, Madehurst, Sussex, 1625 W. Suss RO EpI/33/1625/7
Pellett, John, Arundel, Sussex, 1662 W. Suss RO EpI/33/1661/6
Pember, Deveraux, St Dunstan in the East, London & Middlesex, 1634 Lambeth Palace VH95/1502
Pemble, Cherubin, Egerton, Kent, 1621 CKS PRC20/5/158
Pemble, Henry, Stelling, Kent, 1616 CKS PRC2/19/136
Pemble, Henry, Charing, Kent, 1626 CKS PRC20/7/178
Pemble, Henry, Ebony, Kent, 1667 CKS PRC1/12/72
Pemble, Jarvise, Egerton, Kent, 1636 CKS PRC20/11/193
Pemble, Joane, Molash, Kent, 1632 CKS PRC2/31/143
Pemble, John, Ebony, Kent, 1646 CKS PRC1/7/94
Pemble, Nicholas, Bethersden, Kent, 1638 CKS PRC2/34/102
Pemble, Nicholas, victualler, Appledore, Kent, 1662 CKS PRC1/9/50
Pemble, Nicolas, Folkestone, Kent, 1635 CKS PRC2/33/105
Pemble, Robert, Egerton, Kent, 1597 CKS PRC21/14/167
Pemble, Robert, Bobbing, Kent, 1631 CKS PRC2/31/57
Pemble, Stephan, Lenham, Kent, 1619 CKS PRC2/26/115
Pemble, Stephen, yeoman, Egerton, Kent, 1676 CKS PRC20/12/217
Pembrooke, James, Hackington, Kent, CKS PRC1/6/9a
Pembrooke, James, Hackington, Kent, 1641 CKS PRC1/6/9
Pembrooke, John, turner, Brimpton, Berks, 1630 Berks RO D/A1/208/55A
Pembrooke, Thomas, bookbinder/innholder, Oxford (University), Oxon, 1681 Bodleian HYP B9/39-40
Pen, Elizabeth, widow, Claydon, Oxon, 1681 Oxon RO MSS Wills Pec 48/3/14
Pen, Hughe, Wye, Kent, 1615 CKS PRC2/19/106
Pen, Thomas, Hatton (Beausale), Warks, 1606 Worcs RO 008.7 BA3585/839/410
Pencott, Richard, Wootton, Berks, 1614 Berks RO D/A1/208/1A
Pendington, see Tucke,
Pendlebury, Richard, Deane, Lancs, 1634 Lancs RO (Name of Deceased) D.R.C.H. 1634
Pendred, Robert, husbandman, Aston, Herts, 1635 Herts RO AHH23/1815
Pendreth, Charles, university: 'Fellow of Sidney Sussex College, Cambridge/B.D./priest' Cambridge (Sidney Sussex College), Cambs, 1663 CUL V.C. Acc./Box3/38
Pendrill, John, Albrighton, Shrops, 1682 LJRO/B/C/5/1681/30
Penfald, Edward, husbandman, Billingshurst, Sussex, 1662 W. Suss RO EpI/33/1661/7

[Penfold:]
Penfold, John, Shipley, Sussex, 1631 W. Suss RO EpI/33/1631/31
Penfold, John, Billingshurst, Sussex, 1647 W. Suss RO EpI/33/1647/1
Penfold, Oliver, Angmering, Sussex, 1669 W. Suss RO EpI/33/1669/11
Penfold, Thomas, Kirdford, Sussex, 1617 W. Suss RO EpI/33/1617/15
Penford, Thomas, Tilton, Leics, 1669 Leics RO Administrators Accounts 1667-72 f18
Penherst, Ann, Bromfield, Kent, 1633 CKS PRC2/32/94
Penifall, John, Woodchurch, Kent, 1583 CKS PRC21/6/238
Penithorne, Thomas, Gedney, Lincs, 1605 Lincs RO Ad/Ac/6/40
Penlington, Mary, widow, Thornton-le-Moors (Wimbolds Trafford), Ches, 1790 Cheshire RO (Name) W.C. 1790
Penlington, Thomas, miller, Warmingham, Ches, 1797 Cheshire RO (Name) W.C. 1797-8
Penn, Gervase, Hagley, Worcs, 1685 Worcs RO 008.7 BA3585/830/20
Penn, Thomas, Harting, Sussex, 1660 W. Suss RO EpI/33/1660
Penn, Thomas, saddler, Bromsgrove, Worcs, 1738 Worcs RO 008.7 BA3585/836/bdl 2
Penn, William, Sutton Coldfield, Warks, 1675 LJRO:cards/1675/45
Pennell, Andrew, Westwell, Kent, 1597 CKS PRC21/14/159
Pennell, Anne, widow, Kelsey, North, Lincs, 1683 Lincs RO Ad/Ac/42/95
Pennell, Robert, Thornton le Moor, Lincs, 1639 Lincs RO Ad/Ac/26/323
Pennell, Symon, yeoman, Kelsey, North, Lincs, 1677 Lincs RO Ad/Ac/42/74
Penney, Margarett, widow, Sherbourne, Dors, 1628 Wilts RO Miscellaneous Index (name + date)
Penney, Thomas, Detling, Kent, 1667 CKS PRC19/3/136
Penniall, Thomas, Selling, Kent, 1640 CKS PRC1/5/18
Pennie, John, Stockbury, Kent, 1606 CKS PRC2/13/316
Pennill, Isabell, Laughton, Lincs, 1632 Lincs RO Ad/Ac/39/276
Pennington, George, innkeeper, Windsor, New, Berks, 1677 Berks RO D/A1/209/22C
Pennington, Nicholas, mr, Tadcaster, Yorks, Borthwick Test C.P. 1729/13
Pennington, William, yeoman, Somercoates, South, Lincs, 1669 Lincs RO Ad/Ac/33/121
Pennock, Giles, Hackness, Yorks, Borthwick Test C.P. 1737/11
Pennock, Thomas, yeoman, Wykeham (Langdaneside), Yorks, 1777 Borthwick Test C.P. 1777/9
Penny, Ann, widow, Worth, Kent, 1627 CKS PRC20/8/367
Penny, John, Sherbourne, Dors, 1613 Wilts RO Dean Sarum (name + date)
Penny, Margarett, spinster, Compton Chamberlain, Wilts, 1681 Wilts RO Arch. Sarum(+ name and date)
Penny, Nicholas, Bower Chalke, Wilts, 1635 Wilts RO Arch. Sarum(+ name and date)
Penny, Peter, Stanford, Kent, 1671 CKS PRC20/12/26
Penny, Roger, butcher, Salisbury, Wilts, 1673 Wilts RO Miscellaneous Index (name + date)
Penny, Thomas, Worth, Kent, 1619 CKS PRC20/4/298
Pennyall, John, Maidstone, Kent, 1636 CKS PRC20/11/199
Pennycod, Alice, widow, Kirdford, Sussex, 1646 W. Suss RO EpI/33/1646/2
Pennye, Edward, Tonge, Kent, 1614 CKS PRC2/19/156
Pennye, John + Alice, Hollingbourne, Kent, 1572 CKS PRC21/1/150
Pennye, Stephen, Monkton, Kent, 1593 CKS PRC21/12/280
Pennye, Symon, Monkton, Kent, 1590 CKS PRC21/10/133
Pennye, Thomas, Faversham, Kent, 1597 CKS PRC2/9/411
Pennyfather, Thomas, St Albans St Peters, Herts, Herts RO ASA25/4806
Penquite, John, Pelynt, Corn, 1623 Cornwall RO AP/P432/2
Penrose, Richard, yeoman, Merther, Corn, 1629 Cornwall RO AP/P480/4
Penson, Richard, Seasalter, Kent, 1619 CKS PRC2/19/124
Penson, William, yeoman, Lilleshall, Shrops, 1670 LJRO:cards/1670/55
Penston, Hugh, yeoman, Langford (Radcutt), Oxon, 1678 Oxon RO MSS Wills Pec 78/4/29
Pentland, Robarte, Sandwich St Clement, Kent, 1598 CKS PRC2/9/409
Pentlow, Michael, Staughton, Great, Hunts, 1694 Hunts RO/Acc58/280
Penton, John, Overton, Hants, 1663 Hants RO 21M65 D8/177
Penvall, John, Rolvenden, Kent, 1672 CKS PRC2/35/160
Penvall, John, tailor, Rolvenden, Kent, 1693 CKS PRC2/42/73

Penvell/Rigden, Frances, Sturry, Kent, 1637 CKS PRC2/33/103
Penvill/Aldrey, Ann, widow, Seasalter, Kent, 1644 CKS PRC1/7/30
Penvold, James, yeoman, Lyminge, Kent, 1668 CKS PRC19/4/26
Penvold, James, yeoman, Lyminge, Kent, 1679 CKS PRC20/12/277
Penythorne, Peter, Bigby, Lincs, 1683 Lincs RO Ad/Ac/44/72
Pepper, Arnold, St Johns Thanet, Kent, 1639 CKS PRC1/1/86
Pepper, Joseph, maltster, Dover, Kent, 1683 CKS PRC20/13/275
Pepper, Laurence, Knowlton, Kent, 1642 CKS PRC1/6/78
Pepper, Richard, husbandman, Pinchbeck, Lincs, 1669 Lincs RO Ad/Ac/33/127
Pepper, William, Hougham, Kent, 1603 CKS PRC2/14/372
Pepson, William, Hayling, South, Hants, 1699 Hants RO 1699 AD48/3
Perce, John, bricklayer/mason/privileged person, Cambridge, Cambs, 1665 CUL V.C. Acc./Box3/39
Perce, Perone, widow, Sandwich, Kent, 1624 CKS PRC2/24/55
Perce, Stephen, Willesborough, Kent, 1605 CKS PRC2/13/312
Perce, Thomas, Lydd, Kent, 1604 CKS PRC21/17/35
Percifall, Henry, St Nicholas at Wade, Kent, 1664 CKS PRC19/3/41
Percivall, Anthony, university: 'Fellow of All Souls College, Oxford', Oxford (All Souls College), Oxon, 1676 Bodleian HYP B9/41-42
Percivall, Joseph, labourer, Frodsham, Ches, 1800 Cheshire RO (Name) W.C. 1800
Percwall/Parcevall, Henry, farmer/carpenter, Ashill, Norf, 1757 Norfolk RO ANW/23/25/36A & B
Percy, Kinnard's Ferry, Lincs, 1662 Lincs RO Ad/Ac/41/60
Percy, Elizabeth, widow, Lincoln, Lincs, 1671 Lincs RO Ad/Ac/32/213
Percy, Henry, Donington, Lincs, 1623 Lincs RO Ad/Ac/18/78
Percyfall, Robert, Sturry, Kent, 1618 CKS PRC2/19/112
Percyvall, William, Bonnington, Kent, 1597 CKS PRC2/9/174
Perdue, William, Sittingbourne, Kent, 1640 CKS PRC1/5/19
Perill, Thomas, mariner: 'seas mariner', Wapping, London & Middlesex, 1683 Lambeth Palace Arches G33/4
Perin, Mary, widow, Marden, Kent, 1662 CKS PRC1/9/51
Perin, Richard, husbandman, Marden, Kent, 1681 CKS PRC2/39/217
Perins, William, nailer, Swinford, Old (Amblecoat), Worcs, Worcs RO 008.7 BA3585/839/386
Perkin, Richard, publican, Leek, Staffs, 1818 LJRO/B/C/5/1826/29c
Perkin, Thomas, Detling, Kent, 1592 CKS PRC21/11/301
Perkins, Henrie, Hough on the Hill, Lincs, 1633 Lincs RO Ad/Ac/24/152
Perkins, John, husbandman, Stratton St Margaret, Wilts, 1622 Wilts RO Arch. Wilts.(+ name and date)
Perkins, Marie, Hayling, South, Hants, 1625 Hants RO 21M65 D8/126
Perkins, Richard, blacksmith, Banbury, Oxon, 1686 Oxon RO MSS Wills Pec 49/1/19
Perkins, Susan, Borden, Kent, 1633 CKS PRC2/32/100
Perkins, Thomas, glover, Banbury, Oxon, 1647 Oxon RO MSS Wills Pec 48/2/42
Perkins, Thomas, yeoman, Brookland, Kent, 1679 CKS PRC2/38/172
Perman, John, Kelmarsh, Northants, 1671 Northants RO NWill A/C/95
Perne, Andrew, clergy: 'clerk', Elham, Kent, 1677 CKS PRC2/37/81
Perquin, John, Canterbury St Alphege, Kent, 1641 CKS PRC19/1/71
Perrat, Edward, Erlestoke, Wilts, 1630 Wilts RO Arch. Sarum(+ name and date)
Perratt, John, Monkton Deverill, Wilts, 1640 Wilts RO Arch. Sarum(+ name and date)
Perrey, James, yeoman, Brightwell (Mackney), Berks, 1673 Berks RO D/A1/209/15A
Perrie, Henry, Wrington, Som, 1608 Somerset RO D/D/Cta/P62
Perrie, Joane, Kirton, Lincs, 1600 Lincs RO Ad/Ac/5/419
Perriman, Joane, Maidstone, Kent, 1625 CKS PRC20/7/295
Perrin, Robert, Sittingbourne, Kent, 1622 CKS PRC2/24/40
Perrin, Thomas, Boughton Aluph, Kent, 1683 CKS PRC2/40/68
Perrin/Saunders, Anne, widow, Marden, Up (West Marden), Sussex, 1635 W. Suss RO Epl/33/1635/7

[Perrins:]
Perrins, Francis, Kidderminster, Worcs, 1681 Worcs RO 008.7 BA3585/830/59
Perry, Daniel, cordwainer, Canterbury St Andrew, Kent, 1666 CKS PRC1/11/67
Perry, James, Brightwell, Berks, 1708 Wilts RO CC Sarum(+ name and date)
Perry, John, yeoman, Sotwell, Berks, 1622 Berks RO D/A1/208/27B
Perry, Margaret, widow, St Nicholas at Wade, Kent, 1685 CKS PRC20/13/513
Perry, Michael, gentleman, Aston, Warks, 1810 LJRO/B/C/5/1810/17
Perry, Nicholas, yeoman, Lyneham, Oxon, 1645 Oxon RO MSS Wills 171/3/38
Perry, Richard, Middlezoy, Som, 1639 Somerset RO D/D/Cta/P25
Perry, Richard, Glastonbury (Edgarley), Som, 1735 Somerset RO D/D/Cta/P37
Perry, Thomas, Herne, Kent, 1618 CKS PRC20/4/296
Perryam, John, yeoman, Butleigh Wootton, Som, 1640 Somerset RO D/D/Cta/P54
Perryn, Laurence, St Nicholas at Wade, Kent, 1592 CKS PRC21/11/222
Perryn/Fawkener, Joan, Chidham, Sussex, 1595 W. Suss RO EpI/33/1595/5
Persall, John, High Halstow, Kent, 1613 CKS PRC2/18/65
Persall, Judith,
Kent 1613 CKS PRC20/2/533
Perse, Edward, Egerton, Kent, 1611 CKS PRC20/2/278
Perse, Isaace, Woodchurch, Kent, 1587 CKS PRC21/8/300
Persefall, Richard, Northchurch, Herts, Herts RO AHH23/1829
Pershouse, Susanna, Kingswinford, Staffs, 1685 LJRO/B/C/5/1685/81
Persivall, Edward, university: 'scholar's servant', Cambridge, Cambs, 1610 CUL V.C.Acc./Box1/43
Persivall, John, Ambrosden (Muswell), Oxon, 1666 Oxon RO MSS Wills 51/4/31
Persivall, Jonas, Hythe West, Kent, 1612 CKS PRC2/16/158
Perye, Bennett, Wendron, Corn, 1609 Cornwall RO AP/P156/2
Peryman, Thomas, Maidstone, Kent, 1603 CKS PRC21/16/77
Peryn, Richard, Launcells, Corn, 1608 Cornwall RO AP/P135/3
Pescodd/Redwell, Joan, wife, Bosham, Sussex, 1631 W. Suss RO EpI/33/1630/30
Petch, William, yeoman, Friskney, Lincs, 1673 Lincs RO Ad/Ac/34/21
Petchell, George, Surfleet, Lincs, 1793 Lincs RO Ad/Ac/45/64
Petchell, John, Welby, Lincs, 1612 Lincs RO Ad/Ac/11/202
Petchell, Richard, Branston, Lincs, 1612 Lincs RO Ad/Ac/10/139
Petchell, Willyam, gentleman, Rippingale, Lincs, 1639 Lincs RO Ad/Ac/25/315
Peter, John, bachelor, Findon, Sussex, 1648 W. Suss RO EpI/33/1648/2
Peter, Richard, Middleton, Sussex, 1606 W. Suss RO EpI/33/1606/15
Peter, Thomas, Lancing, Sussex, W. Suss RO EpI/33/1604/6
Peters, John, Wells St Cuthbert, Som, 1588 Somerset RO D/D/Cta/P67
Peters, Thomas, cordwainer: 'shoemaker', Wells St Cuthbert, Som, 1622 Somerset RO D/D/Cta/P12
Peters, see Turner,
Peterson, Philip, Faversham, Kent, 1597 CKS PRC2/9/172
Pether, John, innholder, Cambridge St Benedict, Cambs, 1612 CUL V.C.Acc./Box1/44
Pether, William, Shinfield, Berks, 1617 Berks RO D/A1/208/12A
Pether, William, university: 'Under Bedell/scholar's servant', Cambridge St Edward, Cambs, 1640 CUL V.C. Acc./Box2/56
Petherick, Nicholas, tinner, Gwennap, Corn, 1638 Cornwall RO AP/P532/2
Petit, John, Grendon, Northants, Northants RO NWill A/C/168
Petit, Richard, Ripple, Kent, 1665 CKS PRC1/11/68
Petley, Elizabeth, widow, Ash next Sandwich, Kent, 1696 CKS PRC19/5/48
Petman, John, bachelor, Staplehurst, Kent, 1672 CKS PRC2/35/163
Pett, Andrew, Dover, Kent, 1622 CKS PRC20/6/284
Pett, Daniel, yeoman, Preston next Wingham, Kent, 1669 CKS PRC1/14/88
Pett, Daniel, Preston next Wingham, Kent, 1671 CKS PRC2/35/80
Pett, George, Wickhambreaux, Kent, 1627 CKS PRC2/27/133
Pett, Henry, Hastingleigh, Kent, 1593 CKS PRC2/6/212

Pett, Jeremy, Teynham, Kent, 1626 CKS PRC2/27/128
Pett, John, Great Mongeham, Kent, 1579 CKS PRC2/1/210
Pett, John, Borden, Kent, 1590 CKS PRC2/5/234
Pett, John, Oare, Kent, 1614 CKS PRC2/18/6
Pett, John, yeoman, Murston, Kent, 1663 CKS PRC1/9/140
Pett, John eld, Minster in Sheppey, Kent, 1603 CKS PRC2/13/319
Pett, Lore?, widow, Queenborough, Kent, 1594 CKS PRC2/7/359
Pett, Lucy, widow, Queenborough, Kent, 1618 CKS PRC2/19/145
Pett, Nicholas, mariner: 'sailor', Dover, Kent, 1621 CKS PRC20/5/148
Pett, Robert, baker, Spalding, Lincs, 1668 Lincs RO Ad/Ac/33/71
Pett, Symon, Northbourne, Kent, 1617 CKS PRC2/19/158
Pett, Symon, Teynham, Kent, 1638 CKS PRC1/1/87
Pett, Symon, Teynham, Kent, 1638 CKS PRC2/34/103
Pett, Thomas, Borden, Kent, 1582 CKS PRC2/2/175
Pett, Thomas, Borden, Kent, 1587 CKS PRC2/4/412
Pett, Thomas, mariner: 'seaman', Upchurch, Kent, 1639 CKS PRC1/3/32
Pett, Vincent, Hoath, Kent, 1583 CKS PRC21/6/289
Pett, William, Newnham, Kent, 1618 CKS PRC2/19/110
Pett, William, yeoman, Eastchurch, Sheppey, Kent, 1625 CKS PRC2/25/114
Pett, William, Upchurch, Kent, 1626 CKS PRC2/27/132
Pett, William, Wickhambreaux, Kent, 1697 CKS PRC2/42/133
Pettaway, Edward, blacksmith, Oxford, Oxon, 1707 Oxon RO MSS Wills 172/1/12
Pettenden, James, Rodmersham, Kent, 1620 CKS PRC2/19/138
Pettenden, Roberte, Milton next Sittingbourne, Kent, 1592 CKS PRC2/5/245
Petter, Elizabeth, Maidstone, Kent, 1616 CKS PRC20/3/387
Petter, Harbert, Sandhurst, Kent, 1639 CKS PRC2/34/107
Petter, Jeremy, Sandhurst, Kent, 1623 CKS PRC2/24/46
Petter, John, Sandhurst, Kent, 1631 CKS PRC20/9/331
Petter, Vincent, Hawkhurst, Kent, 1619 CKS PRC2/19/149
Petters, Vincent, Lydd, Kent, 1601 CKS PRC21/15/217
Pettet, John, maltster, Sandwich St Mary, Kent, 1681 CKS PRC20/13/179
Pettet, Roger, Newington next Sittingbourne, Kent, 1620 CKS PRC2/19/118
Pettie, William, weaver: 'broad weaver', Newbury, Berks, 1610 Berks RO D/A1/207/162C
Pettifer, Mary, widow, Hinton Waldrist, Berks, 1667 Berks RO D/A1/208/164B
Pettinger, John, yeoman, Haxey, Lincs, 1664 Lincs RO Ad/Ac/41/126
Pettinger, John, Haxey, Lincs, 1738 Lincs RO Ad/Ac/45/24
Pettinor, Edward, Grimsby, Great, Lincs, 1641 Lincs RO Ad/Ac/27/324
Pettis, John, gentleman, Pinchbeck, Lincs, 1683 Lincs RO Ad/Ac/44/62
Pettit, Edward, Graveney, Kent, 1635 CKS PRC2/32/165
Pettit, Francis, husbandman, Stone in Oxney, Kent, 1638 CKS PRC2/34/88
Pettit, Henry, gentleman, Denton (Eastry hundred), Kent, 1625 CKS PRC2/25/102
Pettit, Henry, gentleman, St Johns Thanet, Kent, 1669 CKS PRC1/14/89
Pettit, Richard, Bridge, Kent, 1664 CKS PRC1/10/72
Pettley, Thomas, Ash next Sandwich, Kent, 1692 CKS PRC19/5/9
Pettman, Thomas, butcher, Chislet, Kent, 1684 CKS PRC2/40/233
Pettman, William, Sturry, Kent, 1704 CKS PRC1/16/53
Petts, George, St Nicholas at Wade, Kent, 1682 CKS PRC20/13/186
Pettye, John, Basingstoke, Hants, 1625 Hants RO 21M65 D8/127
Pettyt, Martha, mrs, Sandwich St Clement, Kent, 1632 CKS PRC2/31/141
Petyt, William, gentleman, Chilham, Kent, 1618 CKS PRC2/19/131
Pewe, Mary, widow, Cambridge Holy Sepulchre, Cambs, 1631 CUL V.C. Acc./Box2/58
Pewe/Amerye, Thomas, Stogursey, Som, 1588 Somerset RO D/D/Cta/P71
Pewtresse, Edward, Castle Morton, Worcs, 1682 Worcs RO 008.7 BA3585/837/bdl 3
Pewtresse, Elinor, widow, Castle Morton, Worcs, 1686 Worcs RO 008.7 BA3585/830/27
Pharroe, Nicholas, Grantham, Lincs, 1605 Lincs RO Ad/Ac/6/117

[Pheasant:]
Pheasant, David, Faversham, Kent, 1682 CKS PRC2/39/223
Phelp, Thomas, Milton, Great (Blagrove), Oxon, 1649 Oxon RO MSS Wills Pec 48/2/45
Phelpe, John, yeoman, Warborough, Oxon, 1676 Oxon RO MSS Wills Pec 70/4/40
Phelpe, Thomas, husbandman, Warborough, Oxon, 1681 Oxon RO MSS Wills Pec 70/4/42
Phelps, Thomas, Cheverell, Little, Wilts, 1636 Wilts RO Arch. Sarum(+ name and date)
Phesand, Thomas, Sutton on the Hill, Derby, 1684 LJRO/B/C/5/1683/16
Phettiplace, Edward, Ringwood, Hants, 1669 Hants RO 21m65 D8/222
Philbie, Thomas, Doddington, Lincs, 1662 Lincs RO Ad/Ac/32/23
Philcock, Elizabeth, widow, Ashford, Kent, 1666 CKS PRC1/11/144
Philipe, John, Minster, Corn, Cornwall RO AP/P875/1
Philipps, Edmund, esquire, St Andrew Holborn, London & Middlesex, 1698 PRO PROB5/1507
Philips/Webb, Richard, Amesbury, Wilts, 1600? Wilts RO Miscellaneous Index (name + date)
Philipson, Richard, Worlaby, Lincs, 1593 Lincs RO Ad/Ac/3/33
Phill, Temperance, Everdon, Northants, 1680 Northants RO NWill A/C/27
Phillip, William, Milsted, Kent, 1592 CKS PRC2/6/502
Phillip/Mollett, Elizabeth, St Laurence Thanet, Kent, 1603 CKS PRC2/13/321
Phillipa/Arnet, Alice, widow, Garston, East, Berks, 1594 Berks RO D/A1/207/119D
Phillipes, George, Carlton, Great, Lincs, Lincs RO Ad/Ac/2C/122
Phillipes, Henry, Appledore, Kent, 1596 CKS PRC2/8/304
Phillipott, Timothie, Carlby, Lincs, 1637 Lincs RO Ad/Ac/25/472
Phillipp, John, Partney, Lincs, 1625 Lincs RO Ad/Ac/19B/42
Phillippe, Thomas, 1631 NLW BR 1629/7 Ac
Phillippes, Anne, widow, Donington, Lincs, 1618 Lincs RO Ad/Ac/14/164
Phillippes, Roberte, gentleman, Wispington, Lincs, 1636 Lincs RO Ad/Ac/24/94
Phillipps, Brian, Chirton, Wilts, 1636 Wilts RO Arch. Sarum(+ name and date)
Phillipps, Edmund, Donington, Lincs, 1630s Lincs RO Ad/Ac/24/320
Phillipps, George, labourer, Lenton, Lincs, 1638 Lincs RO Ad/Ac/25/139
Phillipps, Henry, Croydon (Biggin), Surrey, 1667 Lambeth Palace VH82/2
Phillipps, Henry, Cranbrook, Kent, 1671 CKS PRC2/35/79
Phillipps, John, Fleet, Lincs, 1624 Lincs RO Ad/Ac/19A/62
Phillipps, John, Preston next Wingham, Kent, 1624 CKS PRC2/24/57
Phillipps, John, Audley, Staffs, 1684 LJRO/B/C/5/1684/65
Phillipps, Mathew, Spalding, Lincs, 1639 Lincs RO Ad/Ac/26/259
Phillipps, Richard, Hythe St Leonard, Kent, 1627 CKS PRC20/8/371
Phillipps, Robert, Weston, Som, 1591 Somerset RO D/D/Cta/P73
Phillipps, Susan, Ivychurch, Kent, 1626 CKS PRC20/7/319
Phillipps, Thomas, Portbury, Som, 1668 Somerset RO D/D/Cta/T16
Phillipps, William, Claverdon, Warks, 1681 Worcs RO 008.7 BA3585/830/43
Phillipps/Fowse, Nicholas, Iffley, Oxon, 1631 Oxon RO MSS Wills 299/5/18
Phillips, Francis, yeoman, Cliffe Pypard (Bushton), Wilts, 1680 Wilts RO Arch. Wilts.(+ name and date)
Phillips, John, Halifax (North Howkins), Yorks, Borthwick Test C.P. 1736/8
Phillips, John, Sandwich, Kent, 1621 CKS PRC2/24/44
Phillips, John, husbandman, Blankney, Lincs, 1679 Lincs RO Ad/Ac/43/126
Phillips, John, Hodnet, Shrops, 1685 LJRO/B/C/5/1685/82
Phillips, Richard ygr, cordwainer, Dover, Kent, 1641 CKS PRC19/2/30
Phillips, Robert, baker, Alford, Lincs, 1639 Lincs RO Ad/Ac/26/43
Phillips, Stephen, husbandman, Snave, Kent, 1681 CKS PRC2/39/213
Phillips, Thomas, Dover, Kent, 1626 CKS PRC20/7/168
Phillips, William, Sherbourne, Dors, 1627 Wilts RO Miscellaneous Index (name + date)
Phillips, William, mariner, Faversham, Kent, 1688 CKS PRC2/41/101
Phillips/Philpe, John, Burghfield (Hartley), Berks, 1616 Berks RO D/A1/208/5A
Phillips, see Vinar,
Phillipson, George, Habrough, Lincs, 1662 Lincs RO Ad/Ac/32/28
Phillipson, Joseph, St George Hanover Square, London & Middlesex, 1742 Greater London RO

[Phillipson:]
AM/PP/Box 1739-1749 pt (uncatalogued)
Phillpott, George, St Mary Bourne, Hants, 1623 Hants RO 21M65 D8/33
Phillpott, Godfrey, Ashford, Kent, 1614 CKS PRC2/19/133
Phillpott, Henry, blacksmith, Cheriton, Kent, 1665 CKS PRC1/10/73
Phillpott, Henry, yeoman, Dymchurch, Kent, 1682 CKS PRC2/39/219
Phillpott, Philipp, Sandhurst, Kent, 1612 CKS PRC2/17/348
Phillpott, Ralph, minor: 'aged 7 yrs', St Nicholas at Wade, Kent, 1683 CKS PRC20/13/281
Phillpott, Richard, St Laurence Thanet, Kent, 1639 CKS PRC2/34/105
Phillpott, Thomas, yeoman, Cranbrook, Kent, 1676 CKS PRC2/37/74
Philp, Robert, Kirdford, Sussex, 1598 W. Suss RO EpI/33/1598/7
Philpe, John, St Mabyn, Corn, 1638 Cornwall RO AP/P535/3
Philpe, John, Petworth (Byworth), Sussex, 1711 W. Suss RO EpI/33/1710
Philpe, Margery, widow, Sulhampstead (Graisley), Berks, 1614 Berks RO D/A1/105/7C
Philpe, see Phillips,
Philpes, Henry, Heene, Sussex, 1639 W. Suss RO EpIV/10/2/21
Philpot, Ann, spinster, Ruckinge, Kent, 1671 CKS PRC2/35/76
Philpot, Edward, Faversham, Kent, 1626 CKS PRC2/27/130
Philpot, Isaac, Dover St James, Kent, 1625 CKS PRC20/7/291
Philpot, James, Lydd, Kent, 1629 CKS PRC20/8/383
Philpot, John, St Johns Thanet, Kent, 1704 CKS PRC1/16/54
Philpot, Michael, Hastingleigh, Kent, 1623 CKS PRC2/24/47
Philpot, Richarde, Faversham, Kent, 1616 CKS PRC2/19/139
Philpot, Thomas, Hawkhurst, Kent, 1606 CKS PRC2/13/303
Philpot, Thomas, minor, Kennington, Kent, 1626 CKS PRC2/25/103
Philpot, Thomas, yeoman, Stodmarsh, Kent, 1640 CKS PRC1/5/20
Philpot, Tymothie, Cliffe, West, Kent, 1609 CKS PRC2/15/312
Philpott, Alice, Faversham, Kent, 1629 CKS PRC2/29/92
Philpott, Edward, Woodchurch, Kent, 1627 CKS PRC20/7/182
Philpott, Edward, Faversham, Kent, 1645 CKS PRC1/7/57
Philpott, Edward, mariner, St Johns Thanet, Kent, 1674 CKS PRC2/36/105
Philpott, Edward, Faversham, Kent, 1678 CKS PRC2/38/59
Philpott, Edward, yeoman, St Nicholas at Wade, Kent, 1679 CKS PRC20/12/318
Philpott, Edward, yeoman, Minster in Thanet, Kent, 1710 CKS PRC1/17/37
Philpott, George, St Peter in Thanet, Kent, 1612 CKS PRC2/16/174
Philpott, Jane, Worth, Kent, 1670 CKS PRC19/4/88
Philpott, John, yeoman, Boughton Aluph, Kent, 1619 CKS PRC2/19/105
Philpott, John, Preston next Wingham, Kent, 1632 CKS PRC2/31/144
Philpott, John, St Johns Thanet, Kent, 1650 CKS PRC1/8/87
Philpott, John, Shepherdswell alias Sibertswold, Kent, 1677 CKS PRC2/37/187
Philpott, John, yeoman, Ringwould, Kent, 1678 CKS PRC2/38/56
Philpott, John ygr, Eastry, Kent, 1630 CKS PRC20/8/377
Philpott, Joseph, Worth, Kent, 1714 CKS PRC19/6/67
Philpott, Michaell, St Johns Thanet, Kent, 1589 CKS PRC2/5/239
Philpott, Richard, Canterbury Holy Cross Westgate, Kent, 1619 CKS PRC2/19/129
Philpott, Richard, Graveney, Kent, 1667 CKS PRC1/12/73
Philpott, Robart, Kennington, Kent, 1597 CKS PRC2/9/405
Philpott, Stephen, Egerton, Kent, 1620 CKS PRC20/5/154
Philpott, Thomas, Boughton Aluph, Kent, 1620 CKS PRC2/19/160
Philpott, Thomas, Boughton Aluph, Kent, 1620 CKS PRC2/19/164
Philpott, Thomas, Boughton Aluph, Kent, 1622 CKS PRC2/24/54
Philpott, William, yeoman, St Johns Thanet, Kent, 1668 CKS PRC1/13/91
Philpott, William, yeoman, Westwell, Kent, 1679 CKS PRC20/12/278
Philpott, William, yeoman, Sandwich St Mary, Kent, 1709 CKS PRC1/17/11
Phipp, Edward, Norton, Herts, 1611 Herts RO ASA25/4793
Phippen, George, Shepton Mallet, Som, 1668 Somerset RO D/D/Cta/P53

[Phipps:]
Phipps, Ralph, yeoman, Broughton, Hunts, 1676 Hunts RO/Acc58/47(170)
Phipps, Samuel, Christchurch, London & Middlesex, 1743 Greater London RO DL/C/550/99
Phipps, Willyam, Minster in Sheppey, Kent, 1600 CKS PRC2/11/363
Phoenix, Edward, St Laurence Thanet, Kent, 1667 CKS PRC1/11/145
Phountayne, Richard, clergy: 'vicar', Patrixbourne, Kent, 1592 CKS PRC2/6/266
Phyllypps, John, carrier, Canterbury, Kent, 1591 CKS PRC2/5/267
Phylpott, Wyllyam, Kennington, Kent, 1574 CKS PRC2/1/128
Phyneux, Anne, widow, Dover, Kent, 1600 CKS PRC21/16/194
Phynnis, Humfrie, Hythe St Leonard, Kent, 1605 CKS PRC20/1/9
Piball, John, Wonston, Hants, 1608 Hants RO 1608 AD44
Pibble, Thomas sen, Buckland, Bucks, 1669 Oxon RO MSS Wills Pec 48/3/10
Picard, John, clergy: 'parson', Pluckley, Kent, 1617 CKS PRC2/19/132
Picard, John, clergy: 'clerk', Bapchild, Kent, 1649 CKS PRC1/8/80
Picard, William, grocer, Sturry, Kent, 1677 CKS PRC2/37/75
Pick, Mary, Tenterden, Kent, 1672 CKS PRC2/35/162
Pickard, Daniel, Canterbury St Paul, Kent, 1713 CKS PRC1/17/61
Pickard, Richard, Tetney, Lincs, 1648? Lincs RO Ad/Ac/30/395
Picke, John, Dalby, Great, Leics, 1666 Leics RO Administrators Accounts C17th f70
Pickenden, Arthur, Murston, Kent, 1693 CKS PRC1/15/117
Pickenden, John, High Halden, Kent, 1679 CKS PRC2/38/170
Pickenden, John, husbandman, Herne, Kent, 1681 CKS PRC20/13/188
Pickerell, Robert, clothier, Goudhurst, Kent, 1672 CKS PRC2/35/159
Pickering, Isabel, widow, Wyberton, Lincs, 1632 Lincs RO Ad/Ac/23/150
Pickering, James, Bradford on Avon, Wilts, 1603 Wilts RO Arch. Sarum(+ name and date)
Pickering, James, Faversham, Kent, 1639 CKS PRC1/3/33
Pickering, Joane, widow, Deeping, Market, Lincs, 1625 Lincs RO Ad/Ac/19B/102
Pickeringe, John, Sibsey, Lincs, 1598 Lincs RO Ad/Ac/4/5
Pickeringe, Lawrence, gentleman, Wrangle, Lincs, 1669 Lincs RO Ad/Ac/33/114
Pickeringe, Richard, clergy: 'clerk', Dover St Mary, Kent, 1603 CKS PRC21/17/61
Pickeringe, Richard, Wigtoft, Lincs, 1632 Lincs RO Ad/Ac/23/80
Pickford, John, musician, Ilam, Staffs, 1779 LJRO/B/C/5/1779/64
Pickhaver, Robert, Luddington, Lincs, 1632 Lincs RO Ad/Ac/40/31
Pickin, Acton, blacksmith, Warmingham, Ches, 1774 Cheshire RO (Name) W.C. 1774
Pickle, Henry, yeoman, Herne, Kent, 1640 CKS PRC19/1/72
Pickle, John, Kingsnorth, Kent, 1679 CKS PRC2/38/171
Pickle, William, Sturry, Kent, 1615 CKS PRC2/19/150
Pickles, John, Roxby, Lincs, 1618 Lincs RO Ad/Ac/14/152
Pickman, Walter, husbandman/labourer, Stadhampton, Oxon, 1674 Oxon RO MSS Wills Pec 70/4/36
Pickmer, Elizabeth, widow, Kingsthorpe, Northants, 1684 Northants RO NWill A/C/157
Pickmer, Robert, Kingsthorpe, Northants, 1681 Northants RO NWill A/C/64
Picknall, James, yeoman, Newington next Sittingbourne, Kent, 1682 CKS PRC2/40/69
Picknall, Richard, husbandman, Hollingbourne, Kent, 1643 CKS PRC19/2/76
Pickringe, Thomas, labourer, Aby, Lincs, Lincs RO Ad/Ac/19A/25
Picks, William ygr, Hawkhurst, Kent, 1672 CKS PRC2/35/158
Pickten, Thomas, husbandman, Whitchurch, Oxon, 1679 Oxon RO MSS Wills 171/4/22
Pickwell, George, Ingham, Lincs, 1630 Lincs RO Ad/Ac/39/212
Pickworth, Henrie, Caythorpe, Lincs, 1622? Lincs RO Ad/Ac/17/36
Pickworth, Richard, bachelor, Hale, Great (Little Hale), Lincs, 1667 Lincs RO Ad/Ac/32/67
Pickworth, Thomas, husbandman, Honington, Lincs, 1632 Lincs RO Ad/Ac/23/98
Pickworth, Thomas, Kyme, South, Lincs, 1668? Lincs RO Ad/Ac/33/70
Piddington/Gunter, Thomas, husbandman, Thatcham, Berks, 1633 Berks RO D/A1/208/69A
Pidgeon, John, apothecary, Coventry, Warks, 1672 LJRO:cards/1672/45
Pidgeon, Thomas, Faversham, Kent, 1638 CKS PRC2/34/255
Pidgeon, Thomas, husbandman, Tonge, Kent, 1677 CKS PRC2/37/77

Pierce, Anne, widow, Salisbury, Wilts, 1632 Wilts RO Miscellaneous Index (name + date)
Pierce, Bennett, spinster, Chartham, Kent, 1675 CKS PRC2/36/106
Pierce, Edward, husbandman, Canning, Bishops, Wilts, 1681 Wilts RO Dean and Chapter I11
Pierce, George, Elham, Kent, 1614 CKS PRC2/17/103
Pierce, Joane, Upton Lovell, Wilts, 1638 Wilts RO Arch. Sarum(+ name and date)
Piers, Edward, Hothfield, Kent, 1593 CKS PRC2/5/263
Pigden, John, Frittenden, Kent, 1612 CKS PRC2/16/6
Pigden, Richard, Frittenden, Kent, 1609 CKS PRC2/15/280
Pigeon, Roger, husbandman, Thatcham, Berks, 1624 Berks RO D/A1/208/31A
Pigeon, Thomas, Harborough, Market, Leics, 1666 Leics RO Administrators Accounts C17th f38
Pigge, Thomas, Whaplode, Lincs, 1623 Lincs RO Ad/Ac/18/45
Piggin, William, Ockbrook, Derby, 1683 LJRO/B/C/5/1682/85
Piggot, Edward, Orby, Lincs, 1629 Lincs RO Ad/Ac/22/20
Piggott, Daniell + Dorothe, Linton, Kent, 1601 CKS PRC2/12/294
Piggott, Henry, Aldermaston, Berks, Berks RO D/A1/208/8A
Piggott, John, cordwainer: 'shoemaker', Ely Trinity, Cambs, 1743 Cambs RO 1743/Inv
Pigot, John, Oxford (University), Oxon, 1589 Bodleian HYP B9/43
Pigott, John, Stixwold, Lincs, 1611 Lincs RO Ad/Ac/10/98
Pike, Elizabeth, widow, Thatcham, Berks, 1678 Berks RO D/A1/209/32D
Pike, Geoffrey, Collingbourne Kingston, Wilts, 1620 Wilts RO Arch. Wilts.(+ name and date)
Pike, George, university: 'scholar's servant', Cambridge, Cambs, 1625 CUL V.C. Acc./Box2/61
Pike, Henry, Pewsey, Wilts, 1637 Wilts RO Arch. Wilts.(+ name and date)
Pike, Henry, Marlborough St Peter & St Paul, Wilts, 1687 Wilts RO CC Sarum(+ name and date)
Pike, Henry eld, Canterbury St George Martyr, Kent, 1625 CKS PRC2/25/109
Pike, Hugh, Stogumber, Som, 1634 Somerset RO D/D/Cta/P22
Pike, John, mason: 'freemason', Loose, Kent, 1690 CKS PRC20/13/638
Pike, Mathew, Oxford, Oxon, 1648 Oxon RO MSS Wills 299/5/30
Pike, Richard, Whiteparish, Wilts, 1619 Wilts RO Miscellaneous Index (name + date)
Pike, Robert, Bedwin, Great, Wilts, 1639 Wilts RO Pec Lord Warden Savernake Forest Bundle 1/472
Pike, Simon, Connington, Hunts, 1686 Hunts RO/Acc58/261(255)
Pike, William, Loose, Kent, 1615 CKS PRC20/3/202
Pilchar, Henry, Chart, Great, Kent, 1639 CKS PRC1/3/34
Pilchar, John, Westwell, Kent, 1600 CKS PRC21/15/221
Pilchard, Hewes, Tisbury, Wilts, 1678 Wilts RO Arch. Sarum(+ name and date)
Pilcher, Anne, widow, Wye, Kent, 1616 CKS PRC2/19/111
Pilcher, David, Hythe West, Kent, 1625 CKS PRC2/25/112
Pilcher, Edward, Hartlip, Kent, 1664 CKS PRC1/10/74
Pilcher, Francis, River, Kent, 1711 CKS PRC1/17/38
Pilcher, George, yeoman, Hougham, Kent, 1689 CKS PRC2/41/132
Pilcher, Henrie, Thornham, Kent, 1595 CKS PRC2/8/115
Pilcher, Henry, maltster, Dover, Kent, 1670 CKS PRC19/4/89
Pilcher, Ingram, Appledore, Kent, 1610 CKS PRC2/15/299
Pilcher, Jacob, Wye, Kent, 1596 CKS PRC2/8/45
Pilcher, John, Kingsnorth, Kent, 1640 CKS PRC1/5/21
Pilcher, John, yeoman/bachelor, Ewell, Kent, 1665 CKS PRC1/11/69
Pilcher, John, Ewell, Kent, 1668 CKS PRC1/13/92
Pilcher, John, Willesborough, Kent, 1678 CKS PRC2/37/185
Pilcher, Jonas, Rainham, Kent, 1616 CKS PRC2/19/142
Pilcher, Michael, Lower Hardres, Kent, 1716 CKS PRC1/17/77
Pilcher, Nicholas, Stanford, Kent, 1591 CKS PRC21/11/131
Pilcher, Nicholas, Elham, Kent, 1629 CKS PRC2/29/89
Pilcher, Richard, Ewell, Kent, 1668 CKS PRC1/13/93
Pilcher, Robert, Newington next Hythe, Kent, 1641 CKS PRC1/5/22
Pilcher, Stephen, Faversham, Kent, 1615 CKS PRC2/19/148

[Pilcher:]
Pilcher, Stephen, Upper Hardres, Kent, 1625 CKS PRC2/25/113
Pilcher, Stephen, Whitstable, Kent, 1640 CKS PRC1/3/35
Pilcher, Stephen, Smeeth, Kent, 1684 CKS PRC20/13/452
Pilcher, Thomas, Hastingleigh, Kent, 1632 CKS PRC2/31/146
Pilcher, William ygr, Denton (Eastry hundred), Kent, CKS PRC1/15/118
Pilcher, William ygr, husbandman, Denton (Eastry hundred), Kent, 1693 CKS PRC1/15/118a
Pilcher/Tree, Dorothie, Hythe St Leonard, Kent, 1641 CKS PRC19/1/73
Pile, Agnes, widow, Porton, Wilts, 1641 Wilts RO Arch. Sarum(+ name and date)
Pile, Gabriel, gentleman, Baverstock, Wilts, 1682? Wilts RO Arch. Sarum(+ name and date)
Pilgrim, John, husbandman, Thatcham (Crookham), Berks, 1629 Berks RO D/A1/208/51B
Pilgrim, Jonathan, farmer, Wattisham, Suff, 1812 Suff RO(B) IC500/3/53/117
Pilhorne, Richard, Acton Beauchamp, Worcs, 1599 Worcs RO 008.7 BA3585/838/169
Pilkington, Frances, Etwall, Derby, 1680 LJRO:cards/1680/29
Pilkington, John, St Botolph without Bishopsgate, London & Middlesex, 1677 PRO PROB5/1611
Pilkington, Thomas, yeoman, Feckenham, Worcs, 1602 Worcs RO 008.7 BA3585/838/264
Pille, John, Sandwich, Kent, 1612 CKS PRC2/17/203
Pillens, Thomas, Rippingale, Lincs, 1638 Lincs RO Ad/Ac/25/33
Pillett, Richard eld, Wandsworth, Surrey, 1690 Lambeth Palace Arches G40/2
Pillington, John, Bromborough, Ches, 1618 Cheshire RO (Name) W.C. 1618
Pillsworthe, William, Appledore, Kent, 1613 CKS PRC2/18/13
Pilmuir, William, carpenter, Northampton, Northants, 1811 Northants RO X954/21/73
Pilsworth, Joseph, Epworth, Lincs, 1678 Lincs RO Ad/Ac/35/131
Pim, Anthony, yeoman, Chilham, Kent, 1680 CKS PRC2/39/94
Pim, Richard, yeoman, Rotherfield Greys, Oxon, 1667 Oxon RO MSS Wills 84/3/37
Pimm, Richard, yeoman, Headington, Oxon, 1722 Oxon RO MSS Wills 172/1/35
Pinchbacke, Alexander, Kirton, Lincs, 1607 Lincs RO Ad/Ac/8a/136
Pinchbeck, Francis, Boston, Lincs, 1666 Lincs RO Ad/Ac/32/83
Pinchbeck, John, Butterwick, Lincs, 1637 Lincs RO Ad/Ac/25/372
Pinchbeck, Thomas, yeoman, Frieston, Lincs, 1624 Lincs RO Ad/Ac/19A/93
Pinchbecke, John, husbandman, Reepham, Lincs, 1605 Lincs RO Ad/Ac/37/215
Pinchbecke, John, Butterwick, Lincs, 1636 Lincs RO Ad/Ac/40/157
Pinchbecke, John, Frieston, Lincs, 1671 Lincs RO Ad/Ac/32/211
Pinchbecke, Thomas, Frieston, Lincs, 1632 Lincs RO Ad/Ac/23/10
Pinchen, Henry, Faversham, Kent, 1633 CKS PRC2/32/101
Pinchen, John, mason, Cheverell, Great, Wilts, 1628 Wilts RO Arch. Sarum(+ name and date)
Pinchen, William, Salisbury, Wilts, 1634 Wilts RO Miscellaneous Index (name + date)
Pincher, Charles, Coates, Lincs, 1673 Lincs RO Ad/Ac/35/37
Pinches, Alice, Manton, Lincs, 1626 Lincs RO Ad/Ac/39/15
Pinchest, Thomas, Manton, Lincs, 1618 Lincs RO Ad/Ac/8b/252
Pinchin, William, Camerton (Carlingcott), Som, 1665 Somerset RO D/D/Cta/P48
Pinckard, William, Martock, Som, 1625 Somerset RO D/D/Cta/P14
Pinckes, Joseph, Halesowen, Worcs, 1685 Worcs RO 008.7 BA3585/837/bdl 4
Pincket, Thomas, Rolvenden, Kent, 1640 CKS PRC1/5/23
Pinckney, Thomas, clergy: 'clerk', Wallingford, Berks, 1670 Berks RO D/A1/209/7C
Pincock, Roger, Whittle-le-Woods, Lancs, 1668 Lancs RO (Name of Deceased) D.R.C.H. 1668
Pindar, Robert, Eckington (Mosbrough), Derby, 1680 LJRO:cards/1680/30
Pinder, Richard, husbandman, Denton, Lincs, 1638 Lincs RO Ad/Ac/25/59
Pinder, Ursuley, widow, Tetney, Lincs, 1618 Lincs RO Ad/Ac/14/34
Pine, John, Baston, Lincs, 1599 Lincs RO Ad/Ac/5/334
Pine, Phillipp, brewer, Salisbury St Martin, Wilts, 1614 Wilts RO Miscellaneous Index (name + date)
Pine, Sarah, widow, Gainsborough, Lincs, 1685 Lincs RO Ad/Ac/44/150
Pine, William eld, Ash next Sandwich, Kent, 1696 CKS PRC19/5/39
Pines, Thomas, Dauntsey, Wilts, 1674 Wilts RO Miscellaneous Index (name + date)
Pinfold, Thomas, St Benet Paul's Wharf, London & Middlesex, 1694 PRO PROB5/1600

Pink, Richard, Catherington, Hants, Hants RO 1680 AD81/2
Pinnell, Henry, Bremhill, Wilts, 1674 Wilts RO Miscellaneous Index (name + date)
Pinnell, Margerie, Brinkworth, Wilts, 1622 Wilts RO Arch. Wilts.(+ name and date)
Pinnell, Richard, husbandman, Stanford in the Vale, Berks, 1613 Berks RO D/A1/207/178A
Pinnell, Thomas, Brinkworth, Wilts, 1623 Wilts RO Arch. Wilts.(+ name and date)
Pinniger, Edmond, husbandman, Foxley, Wilts, 1618 Wilts RO Arch. Wilts.(+ name and date)
Pinnock, Thomas, Southampton, Hants, 1623 Hants RO 21M65 D8/34
Pinnock, William, bachelor, Hanbury, Worcs, 1756 Worcs RO 008.7 BA3585/835/bdl 1
Pinnocke, Richard, Cumnor, Berks, 1666 Berks RO D/A1/208/151C
Pinnocke, William, yeoman, Hendred, West, Berks, 1615 Berks RO D/A1/208/9A
Pinsall, Richard, Wasing, Berks, 1605 Berks RO D/A1/207/145A
Pinson, Peter, Belton, Lincs, 1649 Lincs RO Ad/Ac/40/160
Pinson, William, Willoughby (Sloothby), Lincs, 1607 Lincs RO Ad/Ac/8a/115
Piper, Edward, Coldwaltham, Sussex, 1613 W. Suss RO EpI/33/1613/10
Piper, Edwarde, Stone in Oxney, Kent, 1592 CKS PRC2/6/29
Piper, Elenore, widow, Swingfield, Kent, 1600 CKS PRC2/11/361
Piper, Francis, Bearsted, Kent, 1677 CKS PRC2/37/182
Piper, Francis, Bearsted, Kent, 1683 CKS PRC2/40/142
Piper, George, yeoman, Warehorne, Kent, 1626 CKS PRC2/27/125
Piper, Henry, Goring, Sussex, 1596 W. Suss RO EpI/33/1595/2
Piper, Henry, Bury, Sussex, 1613 W. Suss RO EpI/33/1613/11
Piper, John, Poling, Sussex, 1629 W. Suss RO EpI/33/1629/24
Piper, Ruth, widow, Streatham, Surrey, 1703 Lambeth Palace Arches G52/7
Piper, Sara, widow, Rolvenden, Kent, 1632 CKS PRC20/9/9
Piper, Thomas, Kennington, Kent, 1638 CKS PRC2/34/257
Piper, Thomas, Sutton Valence, Kent, 1668 CKS PRC1/13/94
Piper, see Hopkyns,
Pipes, see Ramsey,
Pirkins, Obadiah, university: 'scholar's servant/privileged person', Cambridge St Mary the Great, Cambs, 1630 CUL V.C. Acc./Box2/63
Pirkins, Thomas, university: 'scholar's servant', Cambridge St Mary the Great, Cambs, 1632 CUL V.C. Acc./Box2/64
Pisall, John, Limber Magna, Lincs, 1594 Lincs RO Ad/Ac/3/65
Piseing, Edward, Folkestone, Kent, 1627 CKS PRC2/28/96
Pising, Henry, Sellindge, Kent, 1628 CKS PRC2/29/91
Pising, Jane, widow, Monks Horton, Kent, 1672 CKS PRC2/35/78
Pising, John, Stalisfield, Kent, 1612 CKS PRC2/16/39
Pising, John, carpenter: 'ships carpenter', Faversham, Kent, 1674 CKS PRC2/36/108
Pistall, Richard, surgeon/physician, Sandwich, Kent, 1681 CKS PRC2/39/220
Pitcher, Nicholas, yeoman, Eastry, Kent, 1685 CKS PRC20/13/511
Pitfall, Henry, yeoman, Kintbury, Berks, 1629 Berks RO D/A1/208/54C
Pitfall, William eld, Waltham, White, Berks, 1602 Berks RO D/A1/104/162B
Pither, Margery,
Wilts 1621 Wilts RO CC Sarum(+ name and date)
Pitman, Anthony, yeoman, Welford, Berks, 1680 Berks RO D/A1/209/36A
Pitman, Arthur, tanner, Salisbury, Wilts, 1623? Wilts RO Miscellaneous Index (name + date)
Pitman, John, Charlton Musgrove, Som, 1641 Somerset RO D/D/Cta/P56
Pitman, Priscilla, spinster, Bridgewater, Som, 1739 Somerset RO D/D/Cta/P40
Pitman, Robert, Weston Zoyland, Som, 1729 Somerset RO D/D/Cta/P39
Pitman, Thomas, Wimborne Minster (Leigh), Dors, 1644 Dorset RO PE/WM CP 2/4/64
Pitman, Thomas, Duntisbourne Abbots, Glos, 1685 GRO GDR/B4/2/P113
Pitt, Edward, Andover, Hants, 1624 Hants RO 21M65 D8/83
Pitt, John, Leigh, Worcs, 1681 Worcs RO 008.7 BA3585/837/bdl 2
Pitt, John, button mold turner, Birmingham St Martin, Warks, 1776 LJRO/B/C/5/1776/69
Pitt, Mark, Harting, Sussex, 1633 W. Suss RO EpI/33/1633/16

[Pitt:]
Pitt, Samuel, mason, Stroud, Glos, 1731 GRO GDR/B4/2/P65
Pitt, Thomas, Uxbridge, London & Middlesex, 1679 PRO PROB32/18/220
Pitt, Thomas, Southampton, Hants, 1694 Hants RO 21m65 D8/359
Pittman, Anthony, victualler, Norton, Chipping, Oxon, 1638 Oxon RO MSS Wills 84/3/15
Pittman, John, Charlton Musgrove, Som, 1631 Somerset RO D/D/Cta/P38
Pittman, Robert, Sandford Orcas, Som, 1619 Somerset RO D/D/Cta/P61
Pittman, Robert, Holton, Som, 1642 Somerset RO D/D/Cta/P57
Pittock, John, draper, Deal, Kent, 1670 CKS PRC19/4/90
Pittock, Martha, widow, Deal, Kent, CKS PRC20/11/201
Pittocke, John, Kingston, Kent, 1638 CKS PRC2/34/108
Pittocke, Samuel, yeoman, Great Mongeham, Kent, 1693 CKS PRC2/42/75
Pittocke, William, Canterbury, Kent, 1602 CKS PRC2/12/290
Pitts, Richard, Crowle, Lincs, 1675 Lincs RO Ad/Ac/35/90
Pitts, Robert, Chard, Som, 1676 Somerset RO D/D/Cta/P41
Pitts, Thomas, dealer, Doddington, Great, Northants, 1787 Northants RO X954/22/19
Pitts, William,
Kent 1668 CKS PRC1/13/95
Pittway, William, Shipston on Stour, Worcs, 1779 Worcs RO 008.7 BA3585/835/bdl 2
Pix, George, esquire, Hawkhurst, Kent, 1678 CKS PRC20/12/276
Pix, Joshua, gentleman, Frinstead, Kent, 1683 CKS PRC2/40/139
Pix, William, gentleman, Benenden, Kent, 1645 CKS PRC1/7/58
Pix/Seer, Elizabeth, wife, Wittersham, Kent, 1664 CKS PRC19/3/58
Pixe, Antonie, Fletton, Hunts, 1602 Lincs RO Ad/Ac/5/562
Pixe, Michaell, Elham, Kent, 1602 CKS PRC2/14/374
Place, James, Boughton under Blean, Kent, 1625 CKS PRC20/6/112
Place, Leonard, Hogsthorpe, Lincs, 1597 Lincs RO Ad/Ac/4/73
Plaisteed, Edward, Mildenhall, Wilts, 1625 Wilts RO Arch. Wilts.(+ name and date)
Plane, Ambrose, Chart, Great, Kent, 1618 CKS PRC2/19/141
Plane, Henry, Canterbury St Alphege, Kent, 1582 CKS PRC21/5/258
Planquett/Le Vasseur, Louise, widow, Canterbury St Alphege, Kent, 1616 CKS PRC20/3/383
Plant, John, Ponton, Great, Lincs, 1613 Lincs RO Ad/Ac/12/75
Plant, John, Congerstone, Leics, 1686 Leics RO Administrators Accounts 1682-86 f46
Plant, Thomas, Leek (Leekfrith), Staffs, 1676 LJRO:cards/1676/40
Plant, Thomas, Stowe, Staffs, 1684 LJRO/B/C/5/1684/66
Plaskett, James, Fareham, Hants, 1676 Hants RO 21m65 D8/272
Plasse, Willyam, Newport, Hants, 1662 Hants RO 21M65 D8/157
Platt, Edward, clergy: 'mr/vicar', Graveney, Kent, 1664 CKS PRC1/10/75
Platt, Rallfe, High Halstow, Kent, 1613 CKS PRC2/16/146
Platter, Mgart, Kirkby, East, Lincs, 1580 Lincs RO Ad/Ac/2b/53
Playce, John, Portbury, Som, 1667 Somerset RO D/D/Cta/P51
Playle, John, yeoman, Miningsby, Lincs, 1632 Lincs RO Ad/Ac/23/91
Playne, Parker, gentleman, Milton next Sittingbourne, Kent, 1618 CKS PRC20/4/312
Playne, Thomas, gentleman, Faversham, Kent, 1616 CKS PRC20/3/389
Playse, William, Boughton under Blean, Kent, 1589 CKS PRC21/10/16
Pleadall, Tobias, gentleman, Cumnor, Berks, 1633 Berks RO D/A1/208/68A
Pledger, James, Hurst, Kent, 1622 CKS PRC2/24/42
Pledger, Richard, Bonnington, Kent, 1595 CKS PRC2/7/150
Pledger, Wyllyam, Aldington, Kent, 1584 CKS PRC21/6/430
Plenty, John, Langford, Steeple, Wilts, 1669 Wilts RO Arch. Sarum(+ name and date)
Plimer, John, maltster, Wellington, Shrops, 1804 LJRO/B/C/5/1804/40
Plishare, Heaster, minor, Canterbury, Kent, 1641 CKS PRC1/6/10
Plomer, Christopher, Leverton, Lincs, 1622 Lincs RO Ad/Ac/17/75
Plomer, Sarah, spinster, Bristol, Glos, Bristol RO 1724/12
Plomer, Thomas, Canterbury St Mildred, Kent, 1680 CKS PRC2/38/173
Plott, Adam, Burbage, Wilts, 1638 Wilts RO Miscellaneous Index (name + date)

Plott, Agnes, widow, Detling, Kent, 1637 CKS PRC20/11/242
Plott, John, Murston, Kent, 1596 CKS PRC2/8/419
Plott, John, Detling, Kent, 1632 CKS PRC20/11/224
Plott, John, Detling, Kent, 1637 CKS PRC20/11/246
Plott, Robert, Ospringe, Kent, 1626 CKS PRC2/27/126
Plott, Robert, gentleman, Borden, Kent, 1670 CKS PRC1/15/54
Plott, Thomas, Faversham, Kent, 1624 CKS PRC2/24/58
Plott, William eld, Boxley, Kent, 1681 CKS PRC2/39/90
Plowman, William, Claypole, Lincs, 1662 Lincs RO Ad/Ac/32/20
Plowright, Edward, Newchurch, Kent, 1626 CKS PRC20/7/170
Plucknett, Richard, Cadbury, North, Som, 1596 Somerset RO D/D/Cta/P20
Plucknett, William eld, Charlton Horethorne, Som, 1634 Somerset RO D/D/Cta/P19
Plumb, Thomas, yeoman, Frodsham (Kingsley), Ches, 1794 Cheshire RO (Name) W.C. 1794
Plumer, Francis, Ramsbury, Wilts, 1682 Wilts RO Miscellaneous Index (name + date)
Plumer, Henry, baker, Reading St Mary, Berks, 1633 Berks RO D/A1/106/32C
Plumer, Thomas, Willoughby, Lincs, 1636 Lincs RO Ad/Ac/24/90
Plumley, Robert, mendipman, Harptree, East, Som, 1619 Somerset RO D/D/Cta/P50
Plumme, John, Lambourn (Isbury), Berks, 1618 Berks RO D/A1/105/37C
Plumme, Robert, Woodhurst, Hunts, 1677 Hunts RO/Acc58/104(129)
Plummer, Ann, Bredgar, Kent, 1641 CKS PRC1/6/11
Plummer, John, mariner: 'purser', Rotherhithe (St Mary), Surrey, 1694 Lambeth Palace Arches G44/3
Plummer, Mary, Avebury, Wilts, 1633 Wilts RO Arch. Wilts.(+ name and date)
Plummer, Thomas, Cambridge, Cambs, 1630 c. CUL V.C. Acc./Box3/71
Plummer, Thomas, yeoman, Murston, Kent, 1641 CKS PRC1/5/24
Plummer, William, Hatcliffe, Lincs, 1666 Lincs RO Ad/Ac/32/96
Plumpton, Isabell, widow, Coates, Great, Lincs, 1613 Lincs RO Ad/Ac/11/57
Plumpton, William, Trusthorpe, Lincs, 1605 Lincs RO Ad/Ac/6/38
Plumtree, Magdalen, widow, Fotherby, Lincs, 1606 Lincs RO Ad/Ac/7/146
Plymer, James, Doveridge, Derby, 1683 LJRO/B/C/5/1685/83
Plymmer, Margery, widow, Tutbury (Handbury), Staffs, 1701 LJRO/B/C/5/1701/81e, f
Pocklington, Christopher, labourer, Cumberworth, Lincs, 1669 Lincs RO Ad/Ac/33/124
Pocklington, Thomas, gentleman, Wrawby cum Brigg (Glanford Brigg), Lincs, 1618 Lincs RO Ad/Ac/14/295
Pockridge, Richard, husbandman, Foxley, Wilts, 1630 Wilts RO Arch. Wilts.(+ name and date)
Pocock, Benjamin, brickmaker, Frilsham, Berks, 1686 Berks RO D/A1/209/51C
Pocock, Edward, yeoman, Ashampstead, Berks, 1633 Berks RO D/A1/208/65B
Pocock, Edward, clergy: 'clerk/vicar', Chieveley, Berks, 1642 Berks RO D/A1/106/46B
Pocock, Richard, husbandman, Yattendon, Berks, 1674 Berks RO D/A1/209/4A
Pocock, William, yeoman, Chieveley (Oare), Berks, 1608 Berks RO D/A1/104/120C
Pococke, Anne, widow, Kintbury, Berks, 1670 Berks RO D/A1/107/63C
Pococke, Dorothy, widow, Chieveley (Snelsmore), Berks, 1628 Berks RO D/A1/208/50B
Pococke, Gregory, Hampstead Norris (Bothampstead), Berks, 1609 Berks RO D/A1/207/157A
Pococke, John, yeoman, Shaw cum Donnington, Berks, 1642 Berks RO D/A1/208/93A
Pococke, William, yeoman, Beenham, Berks, 1669 Berks RO D/A1/209/3A
Poictevin, John, widower, St James Westminster, London & Middlesex, 1711 PRO PROB32/54/30
Pointell, William, clergy: 'clerk', Carlton Scroop, Lincs, 1623 Lincs RO Ad/Ac/18/61
Pokins, Anthony, yeoman, Garsington, Oxon, 1638 Oxon RO MSS Wills 171/3/11
Poles, Edward, Bridgewater, Som, 1639 Somerset RO D/D/Cta/P16
Poley, William, Treneglos, Corn, 1624 Cornwall RO AP/P395/2
Polhill, John, Detling, Kent, 1586 CKS PRC21/8/87
Pollard, Edmond, Nonington, Kent, 1593 CKS PRC21/12/127
Pollard, John, yeoman, Lancing, Sussex, 1640 W. Suss RO EpI/33/1640/12
Pollard, John, Moorlinch, Som, 1647 Somerset RO D/D/Cta/P59

[Pollard:]
Pollard, John, esquire, Baldon, Marsh, Oxon, 1672 Oxon RO MSS Wills Pec 70/4/34
Pollard, Richard, St Columb Minor, Corn, 1624 Cornwall RO AP/P507/1
Pollard, Richard, St Johns Thanet, Kent, 1638 CKS PRC2/34/92
Pollard, Richard, gentleman, Bicknoller, Som, 1638 Somerset RO D/D/Cta/P18
Pollard, Thomas, Linsted, Kent, 1637 CKS PRC2/34/95
Pollard, William, Faversham, Kent, 1629 CKS PRC2/30/109
Pollard, William, yeoman, Hythe West, Kent, 1691 CKS PRC2/42/14
Pollarde, Mary, Aldington, Kent, CKS PRC21/15/145
Pollen, Edward, Luddenham, Kent, 1690 CKS PRC2/41/158
Pollen, George, Teynham, Kent, 1691 CKS PRC2/42/13
Pollen, Peter, husbandman, Faversham, Kent, 1666 CKS PRC1/11/146
Pollen, Valentine, yeoman, Ashford, Kent, 1682 CKS PRC2/40/67
Pollett, Marye, widow, Canterbury St Alphege, Kent, 1624 CKS PRC20/6/116
Pollett, Thomas, Bridgewater, Som, 1588 Somerset RO D/D/Cta/P69
Polley, Annis, widow, Detling, Kent, 1628 CKS PRC20/8/375
Polley, Edward, Lenham, Kent, 1629 CKS PRC2/30/110
Polley, Henry, tailor, Finchampstead, Berks, 1628 Berks RO D/A1/208/47A
Polley, Pricisen, widow, Canterbury St Mary Bredin, Kent, 1638 CKS PRC2/34/106
Pollin, William, Bushey, Herts, 1574 Herts RO ASA25/783
Pollit, Hugh, Prescot (Bold), Lancs, 1606 Lancs RO (Name of Deceased) D.R.C.H. 1606
Polly, William, Rodmersham, Kent, 1642 CKS PRC1/6/79
Polsted, Henry, mariner: 'ships mate/bachelor', Stepney (Ratcliff), London & Middlesex, 1698 PRO PROB32/36/262
Polyn, Hamond, St Johns Thanet, Kent, 1611 CKS PRC2/16/187
Polyn, Thomas, Minster in Thanet, Kent, 1596 CKS PRC2/8/107
Polyn, Thomas, St Johns Thanet, Kent, 1599 CKS PRC2/11/37
Pomery, Thomas, yeoman, St Neot, Corn, 1636 Cornwall RO AP/708/2
Pomfrett, Matthew, Clee, Lincs, 1620 Lincs RO Ad/Ac/16/76
Pomme, Peter, St Martin in the Fields, London & Middlesex, 1720 Greater London RO AM/PP/Box 1724-1727 pt (uncatalogued)
Pomphrett, William, gentleman, Clee, Lincs, 1672 Lincs RO Ad/Ac/33/197
Pond, John, shearman, Hampstead Norris (Eling), Berks, 1607 Berks RO D/A1/207/151A
Ponet, Christopher, Warehorne, Kent, 1591 CKS PRC2/5/274
Ponnett, Henry, Willesborough, Kent, 1614 CKS PRC2/17/43
Ponnier, Richard, Chart, Great, Kent, 1626 CKS PRC2/27/120
Pont, Anne, widow, Godmanchester, Hunts, Hunts RO/Acc58/340
Ponte, Francis, Frittenden, Kent, 1669 CKS PRC1/14/91
Ponte, Michaell, Wingham, Kent, 1603 CKS PRC21/17/63
Ponting, Joan, Littleton Drew, Wilts, 1636 Wilts RO Arch. Wilts.(+ name and date)
Ponting, John, wheelwright, Ashton Keynes, Wilts, 1629 Wilts RO Arch. Wilts.(+ name and date)
Ponting, Robert, Dauntsey, Wilts, 1676 Wilts RO Miscellaneous Index (name + date)
Pontinge, Nicholas, Garsdon, Wilts, 1634 Wilts RO Arch. Wilts.(+ name and date)
Pooke, William, Sturry, Kent, 1598 CKS PRC2/10/196
Poole, Agnes, widow, Ashton, Steeple, Wilts, 1632 Wilts RO Arch. Sarum(+ name and date)
Poole, Alice, Madeley, Staffs, 1676 LJRO:cards/1676/41
Poole, Anthonie, Gainsborough, Lincs, 1649 Lincs RO Ad/Ac/40/164
Poole, Charles, gentleman, Linsted, Kent, 1663 CKS PRC1/9/141
Poole, George, Orlestone, Kent, 1594 CKS PRC2/7/63
Poole, George, Folke, Dors, 1670 Wilts RO Dean Sarum (name + date)
Poole, Henry, wheelwright, Bristol, Glos, Bristol RO 1756/13
Poole, Isaac, Newnham, Herts, 1627 Herts RO ASA25/4849
Poole, James, gentleman, Keele (Fenney Green), Staffs, 1832 LJRO/B/C/5/1832/43
Poole, Jervice, esquire, Eckington, Derby, 1669 LJRO:cards/1669/12
Poole, John, Cound (Cressage?), Shrops, 1664 LJRO/B/C/5/1692/92
Poole, John, bricklayer, St Johns Thanet, Kent, 1668 CKS PRC1/13/96

Poole, John, St Johns Thanet, Kent, 1674 CKS PRC2/36/104
Poole, Joyce, widow, Ascot under Wychwood, Oxon, 1647 Oxon RO MSS Wills 299/5/28
Poole, Mychaell, Stanford, Kent, 1615 CKS PRC20/3/164
Poole, Raph, 1668 Lancs RO (Name of Deceased) D.R.C.H. 1668
Poole, Richard, husbandman, Moreton, North, Berks, 1622 Berks RO D/A1/208/28A
Poole, Richard, Elkstone, Glos, 1685 GRO GDR/B4/2/P114
Poole, Robert, Saxilby, Lincs, 1664 Lincs RO Ad/Ac/41/154
Poole, Thomas, Monks Horton, Kent, 1626 CKS PRC2/27/129
Poole, Thomas, bricklayer, St Johns Thanet, Kent, 1633 CKS PRC2/32/97
Poole, Thomas, bricklayer, Sittingbourne, Kent, 1679 CKS PRC2/38/169
Poole, Thomas eld, maltster, Sellindge, Kent, 1668 CKS PRC1/13/97
Poole, Vincent, Thimbleby, Lincs, 1664 Lincs RO Ad/Ac/43/24
Poole, William, maltster, Bristol St Philip & St Jacob, Glos, Bristol RO 1778/CP
Poole, William, St Nicholas at Wade, Kent, 1598 CKS PRC21/14/599
Poolehowse, see Portman,
Poonnet, Michaell, Warehorne, Kent, 1605 CKS PRC2/13/309
Poonnett, Joan, widow, Warehorne, Kent, 1605 CKS PRC2/13/307
Poore, Elizabeth, Ruishton, Som, Somerset RO D/D/Cta/P76
Poore, Elizabeth, Salisbury, Wilts, 1678 Wilts RO Miscellaneous Index (name + date)
Poore, Robert, Titchfield, Hants, 1663 Hants RO 21M65 D8/178
Poore, William, Longstock, Hants, 1594 Hants RO 1593 B62/4
Pope, Alice, widow, Tenterden, Kent, 1609 CKS PRC2/15/286
Pope, Edward, Tenterden, Kent, 1582 CKS PRC2/2/116
Pope, Edward, Hawkhurst, Kent, 1627 CKS PRC2/28/99
Pope, Elizabeth, Bethersden, Kent, 1637 CKS PRC2/34/100
Pope, Francis, husbandman, Upchurch, Kent, 1684 CKS PRC2/40/231
Pope, Henry, Wimborne Minster, Dors, 1682 Dorset RO PE/WM CP 2/4/92
Pope, Hugh, Herne, Kent, 1610 CKS PRC20/2/134
Pope, James, carpenter: 'ships carpenter', Maidstone, Kent, 1682 CKS PRC20/13/182
Pope, John, Glastonbury St John, Som, 1590 Somerset RO D/D/Cta/P72
Pope, John, yeoman, Harwell, Berks, 1613 Berks RO D/A1/207/167A
Pope, John, vintner, Sandwich, Kent, 1673 CKS PRC2/35/249
Pope, John + Katherine, Harwell, Berks, 1677 Berks RO D/A1/209/23C
Pope, Robert, Leeds, Kent, 1611 CKS PRC2/15/282
Pope, Robert, jurat/mr, Tenterden, Kent, 1666 CKS PRC1/11/147
Pope, Robert, yeoman, Melchet Park, Wilts, 1682 Wilts RO Arch. Sarum(+ name and date)
Pope, Robert, yeoman, Smarden, Kent, 1708 CKS PRC1/17/12
Pope, Roger, Folke, Dors, 1637 Wilts RO Miscellaneous Index (name + date)
Pope, Thomas, Burmarsh, Kent, 1680 CKS PRC2/39/93
Pope, Thomas, Canterbury St Peter, Kent, 1685 CKS PRC20/13/515
Pope, Walter, Chilmark, Wilts, 1608 Wilts RO Arch. Sarum(+ name and date)
Pope, William, St Albans St Stephens, Herts, Herts RO ASA25/4783
Pope, William, Hawkhurst, Kent, 1596 CKS PRC2/8/443
Pope, William, Chilham, Kent, 1614 CKS PRC2/17/59
Pope/Booth, Millicent, widow, Faversham, Kent, 1668 CKS PRC1/13/98b
Pope/Booth, Millicent, widow, Faversham, Kent, 1668 CKS PRC1/13/98c
Pope/Booth, Millicent, widow, Faversham, Kent, 1668 CKS PRC1/13/98d
Pope/Booth, Millicent, widow, Faversham, Kent, 1669 CKS PRC1/13/98
Pope/Booth, Millicent, widow, Faversham, Kent, 1669 CKS PRC1/13/98a
Pope/Hankin, Elizabeth, mariner, wife of, Stepney, London & Middlesex, 1692 PRO PROB32/32/251
Pope/Tritton, Martha, Leeds, Kent, 1618 CKS PRC2/19/103
Popham, Jane, spinster, Kintbury (Holt), Berks, 1688 Berks RO D/A1/209/70F
Popham, William, St Giles on the Heath, Corn, 1606 Cornwall RO AP/P123
Popioy, John, Hinxhill, Kent, 1623 CKS PRC2/24/48

[Popjoy:]
Popjoy, Edward, yeoman, Brabourne, Kent, 1680 CKS PRC2/39/88
Poplar, John, husbandman, Tunstall, Kent, 1665 CKS PRC1/11/70
Poplie, Anthony, Shellingford, Berks, 1612 Berks RO D/A1/207/168C
Popple, Deborah, Althorpe, Lincs, 1673 Lincs RO Ad/Ac/35/62
Popple, Thomas, Grainthorpe, Lincs, 1611 Lincs RO Ad/Ac/10/58
Popple, Thomas, Althorpe (Burringham), Lincs, 1626 Lincs RO Ad/Ac/39/188
Popple, William, Althorpe (Burringham), Lincs, 1650s? Lincs RO Ad/Ac/40/184
Popple, William, Althorpe, Lincs, 1679 Lincs RO Ad/Ac/43/139
Popplewell, George, Flixborough, Lincs, 1680 Lincs RO Ad/Ac/43/151
Popplewell, Mary, widow, Hartshead, Yorks, 1778 Borthwick Test C.P. 1778/8
Popplewell, Mary, widow, Batley, Yorks, 1791 Borthwick Test C.P. 1790/1
Popplewell, Robert, Belton, Lincs, 1624 Lincs RO Ad/Ac/39/162
Porch, John, Meare, Som, Somerset RO D/D/Cta/P78
Pordage, Anne, widow, Hernhill, Kent, 1639 CKS PRC20/11/248
Pordage, Francis, Preston next Faversham, Kent, 1684 CKS PRC2/40/236
Pordage, Gabriel, Woodnesborough, Kent, 1613 CKS PRC2/17/140
Pordage, Jane, widow, St Nicholas at Wade, Kent, 1683 CKS PRC20/13/365
Pordage, John, Hernhill, Kent, 1672 CKS PRC20/12/57
Pordage, Theophilus, yeoman, Preston next Wingham, Kent, 1688 CKS PRC2/41/130
Pordage, Thomas, gentleman, Sheldwich, Kent, 1688 CKS PRC2/41/128
Porrett, William, Reepham, Norf, 1744 Norfolk RO ANW/23/24/19B
Port, Thomas, innholder, Dorchester, Oxon, 1676 Oxon RO MSS Wills Pec 70/4/39
Portas, James, Clee, Lincs, 1598 Lincs RO Ad/Ac/4/107
Porte, Joane, widow, Faversham, Kent, 1618 CKS PRC20/4/310
Porter, Ann, widow, Quadring, Lincs, 1772 Lincs RO Ad/Ac/45/33
Porter, Christopher, Barkston, Lincs, Lincs RO Ad/Ac/2b/66
Porter, Edmunde, gentleman, Syston, Lincs, 1593 Lincs RO Ad/Ac/3/93
Porter, Edward, gentleman, Claines (Tapenhall), Worcs, 1604 Worcs RO 008.7 BA3585/839/324
Porter, Elizabeth, Seasalter, Kent, 1645 CKS PRC1/7/59
Porter, Francis, Lutterworth, Leics, 1665 Leics RO Administrators Accounts C17th f10
Porter, Henry, Lincoln, Lincs, 1611 Lincs RO Ad/Ac/10/77
Porter, Henry, labourer, Lydd, Kent, 1641 CKS PRC19/1/74
Porter, Jane, widow, Maidstone, Kent, 1678 CKS PRC20/12/274
Porter, Johan, widow, Charing, Kent, 1601 CKS PRC21/16/164
Porter, John, husbandman, Abingdon, Berks, 1605 Berks RO D/A1/207/147A
Porter, John, gentleman, Syston, Lincs, 1623 Lincs RO Ad/Ac/18/7
Porter, John, Weeke, Hants, 1624 Hants RO 21M65 D8/35
Porter, John, Biddulph, Staffs, 1672 LJRO:cards/1672/46
Porter, Richard, Walton, Som, 1662 Somerset RO D/D/Cta/P45
Porter, Richard, Walton, Som, 1662 Somerset RO D/D/Cta/P46
Porter, Robert, Welbourn, Lincs, 1636 Lincs RO Ad/Ac/24/565
Porter, Robert, Huntspill, Som, 1732 Somerset RO D/D/Cta/P42
Porter, Thomas, Keal, East, Lincs, 1638 Lincs RO Ad/Ac/25/125
Porter, Walter, Winthorpe, Lincs, 1611 Lincs RO Ad/Ac/10/109
Porter, Walter, yeoman, Warborough, Oxon, 1685 Oxon RO MSS Wills Pec 70/4/45
Porter, William, Boughton Malherbe, Kent, 1609 CKS PRC2/15/306
Porter, William, Burton Pedwardine, Lincs, 1636 Lincs RO Ad/Ac/24/293
Porter, William, yeoman, Boxley, Kent, 1672 CKS PRC2/35/165
Porter/Portreeve, Thomas, Tonge, Kent, 1615 CKS PRC2/19/121
Porter/Soper, John, Bedwin, Great, Wilts, 1599? Wilts RO Miscellaneous Index (name + date)
Portington, Thomas, Worlaby, Lincs, 1649 Lincs RO Ad/Ac/30/147
Portlocke, Benjamin, gentleman, St Giles in the Fields, London & Middlesex, 1689 PRO PROB32/28/213
Portman, Thomas, Snave, Kent, 1662 CKS PRC1/9/52
Portman/Poolehowse, John, yeoman, Ombersley (Sytchampton), Worcs, 1597 Worcs RO 008.7

BA3585/838/209
Portreeve, see Porter,
Portus, Christopher, Tattershall, Lincs, 1635 Lincs RO Ad/Ac/24/443
Pory, Peter, Oxford St Mary Virgin, Oxon, 1620 Bodleian HYP B9/44
Posse, Edward, Pluckley, Kent, 1679 CKS PRC2/38/168
Posse, Edward, yeoman, Pluckley, Kent, 1687 CKS PRC2/41/63
Posse, Thomas, Headcorn, Kent, 1633 CKS PRC20/11/212
Posse, William, Pluckley, Kent, 1598 CKS PRC2/10/16
Possingham, Alice, widow, Milton next Sittingbourne, Kent, 1677 CKS PRC2/37/181
Possingham, Priscilla, spinster, Sittingbourne, Kent, 1626 CKS PRC2/25/115
Possingham, Richard, Canterbury St Andrew & Harbledown, Kent, 1632 CKS PRC2/31/147
Possingham, Thomas eld, St Thomas Isle of Harty, Kent, 1669 CKS PRC1/14/92
Post, George, Smarden, Kent, 1618 CKS PRC2/19/108
Post, George, St Laurence Thanet, Kent, 1621 CKS PRC2/19/152
Post, John, High Halden, Kent, 1634 CKS PRC2/32/95
Post, John, Burmarsh, Kent, 1637 CKS PRC2/34/101
Posterne, Stephen, Sonning, Berks, 1596 Wilts RO Miscellaneous Index (name + date)
Postill, Gabriel, Chisel Borough, Som, 1588 Somerset RO D/D/Cta/P65
Pothmeare, Richard, Zennor, Corn, 1623 Cornwall RO AP/P35/2
Potier, John, Sandwich, Kent, 1625 CKS PRC2/25/106
Potier, Quintine, Canterbury St Mildred, Kent, 1613 CKS PRC2/17/109
Potle, Robert, Wimborne Minster (Chilbridge), Dors, 1621 Dorset RO PE/WM CP 2/4/25
Potman, John, Tunstall, Kent, 1620 CKS PRC2/19/127
Pott, Andrewe, Bearsted, Kent, 1594 CKS PRC2/7/301
Pott, Edward, Sturry, Kent, 1619 CKS PRC2/19/115
Pott, Ellen, widow, Macclesfield, Ches, 1766 Cheshire RO (Name) W.C. 1764-66
Pott, John, Swingfield, Kent, 1717 CKS PRC1/18/13
Pott, John, Wootton, Kent, 1718 CKS PRC1/18/24a
Pott, Nathaniell, Milton next Sittingbourne, Kent, 1612 CKS PRC2/17/307
Potten, Henry, gentleman, Lydd, Kent, 1688 CKS PRC20/13/601
Potten, Thomas, Warehorne, Kent, 1598 CKS PRC2/10/28
Potten, William, Kingsdown, Kent, 1678 CKS PRC2/38/60
Pottenger, John eld, Compton, Berks, 1614 Berks RO D/A1/207/173A
Potter, Alice, widow, Ogbourne St George, Wilts, 1677 Wilts RO Miscellaneous Index (name + date)
Potter, Ann, widow, Harrietsham, Kent, 1629 CKS PRC2/30/113
Potter, Ann, widow, Deal, Kent, 1681 CKS PRC20/13/177
Potter, George, Manchester, Lancs, 1627 Lancs RO (Name of Deceased) D.R.C.H. 1627
Potter, Henry, miller, Aston, Herts, 1636 Herts RO AHH23/1816
Potter, John, Sheldwich, Kent, 1613 CKS PRC2/16/130
Potter, John, St Just in Roseland, Corn, 1615 Cornwall RO AP/P301
Potter, John, Headcorn, Kent, 1665 CKS PRC1/11/71
Potter, Mary, widow, Wisborough Green, Sussex, 1631 W. Suss RO EpI/33/1631/6
Potter, Moses, Eastry, Kent, 1631 CKS PRC20/9/321
Potter, Moses, baker, Deal, Kent, 1667 CKS PRC19/3/104
Potter, Richard, clergy: 'clerk', Dembleby, Lincs, 1628 Lincs RO Ad/Ac/20b/69
Potter, Robert, husbandman, Appledore, Kent, 1638 CKS PRC1/1/88
Potter, Thomas, grocer, Deal, Kent, 1671 CKS PRC19/4/91
Potter, Thomas, husbandman, Limber Magna, Lincs, 1683 Lincs RO Ad/Ac/44/54
Potter, Thomas, yeoman, Oxford St Thomas (Medley), Oxon, 1770 Oxon RO MSS Wills 304/1/33
Potter, Thurston, husbandman, Tadmarton, Oxon, 1626 Oxon RO MSS Wills 299/4/74
Potter, William, butcher, Canterbury, Kent, 1589 CKS PRC2/4/501
Potter, William, clergy: 'clerk', Winteringham, Lincs, 1681 Lincs RO Ad/Ac/34/81
Potter, William, Lea, Lincs, 1682 Lincs RO Ad/Ac/44/11

[Potter:]
Potter, William, Heanor, Derby, 1683 LJRO/B/C/5/1685/84
Potterton, Thomas, Hallaton, Leics, 1641 Leics RO PR/I/41A/84
Potticary, George, Netherhampton, Wilts, 1678 Wilts RO Arch. Sarum(+ name and date)
Potticary, Richard, Teffont Ewyas, Wilts, 1687 Wilts RO Arch. Sarum(+ name and date)
Potticary, Thomas, Wylye, Wilts, 1640 Wilts RO Arch. Sarum(+ name and date)
Pottinger, James, bachelor, Basildon, Berks, 1684 Berks RO D/A1/209/52D
Pottinger, Nicholas, gentleman, Reading, Berks, 1664 Berks RO D/A1/208/153B
Pottinger, Richard, husbandman, Enborne, Berks, 1663 Berks RO D/A1/208/143B
Pottinger, Thomas, Martock, Som, 1668 Somerset RO D/D/Cta/P52
Pottle, John, Wimborne Minster, Dors, 1673 Dorset RO PE/WM CP 2/4/77
Potts, John, gentleman, Dronfield (Halfeild), Derby, 1703 LJRO/B/C/5/1703/26
Pougher, Sampson, Leicester St Martin, Leics, 1666 Leics RO Administrators Accounts C17th f60
Poulden, Thomas, Alweston, Wilts, 1647 Wilts RO CC Sarum(+ name and date)
Poulgreene, Humphrey, mariner, Bermondsey St Mary Magdalen, Surrey, 1694 PRO PROB32/34/120
Poulter, Agnes, Warboys, Hunts, 1640 Hunts RO/Acc58/10(49)
Poulter, Joseph, St Laurence Thanet, Kent, 1667 CKS PRC1/12/74
Poulter, Thomas, clergy: 'clerk', Ashford, Kent, 1602 CKS PRC2/12/455
Poulton, John, blacksmith, Harwell, Berks, 1627 Berks RO D/A1/208/45A
Poulwheele, Digory, esquire, St Erme, Corn, Cornwall RO AP/P299/2
Pound, George, Chilham, Kent, 1628 CKS PRC2/28/90
Pound, George, Milton next Sittingbourne, Kent, 1673 CKS PRC2/35/248
Pound, Rabidge, Chilham, Kent, 1676 CKS PRC2/36/227
Poute, Alice, Rolvenden, Kent, 1671 CKS PRC2/35/77
Poute, Willyam, Lydden, Kent, 1596 CKS PRC2/8/39
Povey, Anne, spinster, St Giles in the Fields, London & Middlesex, 1698 PRO PROB32/37/63
Povey, Anne, spinster, St Martin in the Fields, London & Middlesex, 1698 PRO PROB32/36/294
Povey, John, Hardwick in Bredon, Worcs, Worcs RO 008.7 BA3585/834/?
Povey, John, Shocklach, Ches, 1685 Cheshire RO (Name) W.C. 1685
Povey, Robert, yeoman, Buscot (Snowswick), Berks, 1673 Berks RO D/A1/209/5C
Povie, Thomas, husbandman, Shrivenham (Bourton), Berks, 1633 Berks RO D/A1/208/67A
Povy, Henry, Ashbury, Berks, 1610 Berks RO D/A1/207/156A
Powdich, Richard, mariner, Morston, Norf, 1708 Norfolk RO ANW/23/8/51a
Powdrell, Richard, labourer, Horncastle, Lincs, 1670 Lincs RO Ad/Ac/32/182
Powell, Abraham, Michaelchurch Esklie, 1647 NLW BR 1646/111 Ac
Powell, Agnes, widow, Henbury, Glos, Bristol RO 1635/68
Powell, Charles, yeoman, Berwick St James, Wilts, 1758 Wilts RO CC Sarum(+ name and date)
Powell, Edmund, Dover, Kent, 1605 CKS PRC21/17/264
Powell, Edmund, esquire, Sandford, Oxon, 1634 Oxon RO MSS Wills 144/2/12
Powell, Edward + Ellen, Hernhill, Kent, 1623 CKS PRC20/6/144
Powell, Hughe, Ash next Sandwich, Kent, 1596 CKS PRC21/14/73
Powell, John, yeoman, Bathampton, Som, 1640 Somerset RO D/D/Cta/P55
Powell, John, clergy: 'rector', Stourmouth, Kent, 1683 PRO PROB32/33/19
Powell, John, aledraper, York Holy Trinity, Goodramgate, Yorks, 1784 Borthwick Test C.P. 1784/4
Powell, Michaell, Dibden, Hants, 1675 Hants RO 21m65 D8/268
Powell, Raph, Mumby, Lincs, 1613 Lincs RO Ad/Ac/12/35
Powell, Richard, Ness, Great, Shrops, 1683 LJRO/B/C/5/1685/85
Powell, Robarte, Stalisfield, Kent, 1608 CKS PRC2/15/304
Powell, Robert, gentleman, Wells, Som, 1664 Somerset RO D/D/Cta/P47
Powell, Samuell, St Martin Outwich, London & Middlesex, 1679 PRO PROB32/18/189
Powell, Thomas, Collingbourne Kingston, Wilts, 1622 Wilts RO Arch. Wilts.(+ name and date)
Powell, Thomas, yeoman, Rodbourne Cheney, Wilts, 1626 Wilts RO Arch. Wilts.(+ name and date)
Powell, William, Salisbury Cathedral (The Close), Wilts, 1692 Wilts RO Dean Sarum (name +

date)
Power, Isaac, Kington St Michael, Wilts, 1674 Wilts RO Miscellaneous Index (name + date)
Power, John, hosier, Faversham, Kent, 1685 CKS PRC1/15/102
Power, Robert, Lenton, Lincs, 1646? Lincs RO Ad/Ac/28/207
Power, Thomas, Hullavington, Wilts, 1616 Wilts RO Arch. Wilts.(+ name and date)
Power, William, Faversham, Kent, 1625 CKS PRC2/24/61
Powers, Thomas eld, gunlock filer, Birmingham, Warks, 1795 LJRO/B/C/5/1795/76
Powes/Banburne, Edward, Blockley (Dorne), Worcs, 1605 Worcs RO 008.7 BA3585/839/355
Powis, John, mariner: 'purser', St Botolph without Aldgate, London & Middlesex, 1687 Lambeth Palace Arches G37/1
Powis, Richard, Upton Magna (Aston), Shrops, 1667 LJRO:cards/1667/63
Powle, Thomas, Ashcott, Som, 1588 Somerset RO D/D/Cta/P70
Powlter, Amy, widow, St Laurence Thanet, Kent, 1620 CKS PRC2/19/102
Powlter, Frances, widow, St Laurence Thanet, Kent, 1630 CKS PRC2/30/115
Powlter, Henrie, Warboys, Hunts, 1602 Lincs RO Ad/Ac/5/572
Pownall, Abdias, Barham, Kent, 1636 CKS PRC2/34/99
Pownall, Philemon, gentleman, Shepherdswell alias Sibertswold, Kent, 1663 CKS PRC1/9/142
Pownall, Ralph, Witton, Ches, 1684 Cheshire RO (Name) W.C. 1683
Pownd, Henry, gentleman, Borden, Kent, 1640 CKS PRC1/5/25
Pownd, Richard, Egerton, Kent, 1624 CKS PRC20/6/148
Pownde, John, yeoman, Drayton, Berks, 1611 Berks RO D/A1/207/165D
Pownde, William, Folkestone, Kent, 1586 CKS PRC2/4/529
Powney, Mary, spinster, Hilmarton, Wilts, 1753 Wilts RO CC Sarum(+ name and date)
Powsley, Thomas, Chichester St Martin, Sussex, 1640 W. Suss RO EpIII/9/1/40
Powte, Robert, Ash next Sandwich, Kent, 1583 CKS PRC21/6/234
Powte, Robert, Bapchild, Kent, 1635 CKS PRC2/33/110
Poyle, Elizabeth, widow, Biddenden, Kent, 1672 CKS PRC2/35/164
Poyle, Jeremye, Goudhurst, Kent, 1599 CKS PRC2/11/58
Poyle, Lawrence, Goudhurst, Kent, 1607 CKS PRC2/14/360
Poyle, Thomas, Cranbrook, Kent, 1596 CKS PRC2/8/81
Poyle, see White,
Poynett/Punnett, John, locksmith, Cranbrook, Kent, 1685 CKS PRC2/41/6
Poyntell, William, chandler: 'tallow chandler', Sleaford, New, Lincs, 1682 Lincs RO Ad/Ac/42/87
Poynter, John, husbandman, Welford, Berks, Berks RO D/A1/208/85A
Poynting, Ralph, Harptree, West, Som, 1584 Somerset RO D/D/Cta/P66
Poynton, Urban, Beoley, Worcs, 1680 Worcs RO 008.7 BA3585/837/bdl 2
Prall, Alexander, Rolvenden, Kent, 1597 CKS PRC2/9/178
Prance, Thomas, Whaplode Drove, Lincs, 1622 Lincs RO Ad/Ac/17/55
Prat, John, Eartham, Sussex, 1594 W. Suss RO EpI/33/1594/5
Prat, John, Easebourne (Ambersham), Sussex, 1594 W. Suss RO EpI/33/1594/1
Pratchett, John, Nantwich, Ches, 1619 Cheshire RO (Name) W.C. 1619
Prater, Edward, Devizes St Mary the Virgin, Wilts, 1622 Wilts RO CC Sarum(+ name and date)
Prater, Thomas, Yattendon, Berks, 1624 Wilts RO CC Sarum(+ name and date)
Pratt, Anthony, Easebourne, Sussex, 1624 W. Suss RO EpI/33/1624/1
Pratt, Barnard, Mundham, North, Sussex, W. Suss RO EpI/33/1617/16
Pratt, Christopher eld, yeoman, Lambourn (Isbury), Berks, 1636 Berks RO D/A1/105/35C
Pratt, Elizabeth, Repton, Derby, 1714 LJRO/B/C/5/1712/44
Pratt, George, victualler, Bristol, Glos, Bristol RO 1761/26
Pratt, Jeffery, cook, Bray, Berks, 1638 Berks RO D/A1/208/82B
Pratt, John eld, Rainham, Kent, 1612 CKS PRC2/17/353
Pratt, Mathew, Sandwich St Bartholomew's Hospital, Kent, 1626 CKS PRC20/7/237
Pratt, Ralph, Easebourne, Sussex, 1608 W. Suss RO EpI/33/1607/14
Pratt, Robert, Wick, Worcs, 1603 Worcs RO 008.7 BA3585/839/313
Pratt, William, Sidlesham, Sussex, 1597 W. Suss RO EpI/33/1597/11
Pratt, William, Shipley, Sussex, 1671 W. Suss RO EpI/33/1671/6

[Pratt, see Spratt:]
Pratt, see Spratt,
Pratte, Marie, Sandwich, Kent, 1614 CKS PRC2/17/17
Pratten, Robert, husbandman, Upchurch, Kent, 1695 CKS PRC2/42/88
Prattent, William eld, Chew Magna, Som, 1638 Somerset RO D/D/Cta/P17
Prebble, Bartholomew, Brookland, Kent, 1669 CKS PRC1/13/99
Prebble, Richard, Elham, Kent, 1640 CKS PRC1/5/26
Prebble, Thomas, Boughton under Blean, Kent, 1671 CKS PRC20/12/27
Preble, Elizabeth, Mersham, Kent, 1682 CKS PRC2/40/66
Preble, Thomas, Boughton under Blean, Kent, 1630 CKS PRC20/9/333
Preece, Barnabas, farmer, Ness, Great (Nesscliffe), Shrops, 1810 LJRO/B/C/5/1810/18b
Prees, David Thomas, yeoman, Llywel, Breck, NLW BR 1646/52 Ac
Prees, Thomas Lewis, Cluddock (Croswald), 1637 NLW BR 1637/257 Ac
Prees, William, Llanrug, Caern, 1674 NLW B 1673-41 Ac
Pregion, Phillip, clergy: 'clerk', Withern, Lincs, 1632 Lincs RO Ad/Ac/23/74
Pregion, Roger, Lincoln, Lincs, 1627 Lincs RO Ad/Ac/20/103
Pregion, William, Navenby, Lincs, 1650 Lincs RO Ad/Ac/29/113
Preist, Edward, yeoman, Lenton, Lincs, 1635 Lincs RO Ad/Ac/24/375
Preist, Gowin, Sutton Coldfield, Warks, 1672 LJRO:cards/1672/47
Preist, John, husbandman, Hurley, Berks, 1683 Berks RO D/A1/209/55D
Preiste, Richard, Gedney, Lincs, 1598 Lincs RO Ad/Ac/4/3
Preistland, Paul, clergy: 'clerk', Deeping, Market, Lincs, 1670 Lincs RO Ad/Ac/32/163
Preistman, Henry, Firsby, Lincs, 1639? Lincs RO Ad/Ac/26/75
Prenn, Richard, labourer, Navenby, Lincs, 1635 Lincs RO Ad/Ac/24/232
Prentice, Henry, Welwyn, Herts, 1640 Herts RO AHH23/1834
Prescot, Stephen, brother, Canterbury St John's Hospital, Kent, 1677 CKS PRC20/12/237
Prescott, Edward, wheelwright, Dover, Kent, 1678 CKS PRC20/12/275
Prescott, John, yeoman, Guston, Kent, 1646 CKS PRC19/2/108
Presgrave, William, husbandman, Scredington, Lincs, 1674 Lincs RO Ad/Ac/42/41
Presse, Francis, Hathern, Leics, 1665 Leics RO Administrators Accounts C17th f37
Presse, Richard, Norton Bavant, Wilts, 1670? Wilts RO Arch. Sarum(+ name and date)
Presse, William, Warminster, Wilts, 1632 Wilts RO Arch. Sarum(+ name and date)
Presseye, Henrye, Bishopstone, Wilts, 1600 Wilts RO Miscellaneous Index (name + date)
Pressley, Thomas, innholder, Warminster, Wilts, 1744 Wilts RO Arch. Sarum(+ name and date)
Prestman, Thomas, Leake, Lincs, 1597 Lincs RO Ad/Ac/4/123
Preston, Amos, gentleman, Glastonbury, Som, 1621 Somerset RO D/D/Cta/P24
Preston, George, Rolvenden, Kent, 1672 CKS PRC2/35/161
Preston, Hannah Elizabeth, spinster, Bridlington (Bridlington Quay), Yorks, 1833 Borthwick Test C.P. 1833/4
Preston, John, Woodchurch, Kent, 1582 CKS PRC21/6/91
Preston, John, husbandman, Stone in Oxney, Kent, 1612 CKS PRC20/2/350
Preston, Katherine, widow, Northampton (South Quarter), Northants, 1679 Northants RO NWill A/C/156
Preston, Richard, yeoman, Leigh, Glos, 1831 GRO GDR/B4/2/P87
Preston, Samuell, St Botolph without Aldgate, London & Middlesex, PRO PROB5/1637
Preston, Samuell, St Botolph without Aldgate, London & Middlesex, 1672 PRO PROB5/1637
Preston, William, Boughton under Blean, Kent, 1592 CKS PRC21/11/151
Preston, William, Weston Favell, Northants, 1680 Northants RO NWill A/C/50
Prestone, Margaret, Rolvenden, Kent, 1677 CKS PRC2/37/189
Prestwidge, John, yeoman, Alfreton, Derby, 1824 LJRO/B/C/5/1824/24
Pretious, Charles, clergy: 'clerk', Messingham, Lincs, 1680 Lincs RO Ad/Ac/43/149
Pretious, Thomas, clergy: 'clerk', Roxby, Lincs, 1679? Lincs RO Ad/Ac/43/131
Prettie, Anne, widow, Cranbrook, Kent, 1595 CKS PRC2/7/441
Prettie, Henry,
Worcs Worcs RO 008.7 BA3585/834/453
Prew, Alice, Shapwick, Som, 1622 Somerset RO D/D/Cta/P13

Prew, Richard, husbandman, Swerford, Oxon, 1663 Oxon RO MSS Wills 51/4/22
Prewett, John, Huntspill, Som, 1623 Somerset RO D/D/Cta/P4
Prewting, William eld, victualler, Thatcham, Berks, 1677 Berks RO D/A1/209/31D
Price, Bartholomew, clergy: 'clerk', Holton, Oxon, 1633 Oxon RO MSS Wills 84/3/7
Price, Edward, Condover, Shrops, 1675 LJRO:cards/1675/46
Price, Joan, Oxford, Oxon, 1636 Oxon RO MSS Wills 84/3/9
Price, John, Old Romney, Kent, 1624 CKS PRC2/24/59
Price, Marmaduke, husbandman, Holton, Oxon, 1680 Oxon RO MSS Wills 84/4/14
Price, Owen, degrees: 'M.A.', Oxford (University), Oxon, 1677 Bodleian HYP B9/45-46
Price, Peter, Biddenden, Kent, 1721 CKS PRC1/18/45
Price, Richard, Faversham, Kent, 1610 CKS PRC2/15/285
Price, Thomas, university: 'privileged person', Oxford (University), Oxon, 1640 Bodleian HYP B9/47
Price, Thomas, yeoman, Garston, East, Berks, 1680 Berks RO D/A1/209/34D
Price, Thomas, St Martin in the Fields, London & Middlesex, 1689 PRO PROB32/28/141
Price, Thomas, butcher, Birmingham, Warks, 1801 LJRO/B/C/5/1801/65
Price, Thomas, Duntisbourne Abbots, Glos, 1812 GRO GDR/B4/2/P91
Price, William, Lavant, East, Sussex, 1621 W. Suss RO EpIV/10/1/31
Prichard, Catherine, Shrewsbury, Shrops, 1683 LJRO/B/C/5/1685/86
Prichard, Thomas, 1634 NLW BR 1634/193 Ac
Prichard, William, Brecon, Breck, NLW BR 1639/5 Ac
Prichard, William, Llanllechid, Caern, NLW B 1674-26 Ac1
Prichart, John, Salisbury, Wilts, 1627? Wilts RO Miscellaneous Index (name + date)
Prichett, Joane, Wainfleet All Saints, Lincs, 1638 Lincs RO Ad/Ac/25/153
Prick/Prike, Mary, Milden, Suff, 1779 Suff RO(B) IC500/3/52/58
Prickes, John, Minster in Thanet, Kent, 1620 CKS PRC2/19/119
Prickett, Henry, Hurst, Kent, 1667 CKS PRC1/12/75
Prickett, John, Canterbury Holy Cross Westgate, Kent, 1648 CKS PRC1/8/52
Prickett, William, Oxford, Oxon, 1578 Bodleian HYP B9/48-64
Pricksmall, William, Hampstead Marshall, Berks, 1595 Berks RO D/A1/207/120C
Priddin, William, maltster, Tilston, Ches, 1775 Cheshire RO (Name) W.C. 1775-6
Pridgeon, Richard, Carlton le Moorland, Lincs, 1651 Lincs RO Ad/Ac/29/143
Pridneye, Stephen, Rolvenden, Kent, 1598 CKS PRC2/10/129
Prier, Abraham, Shipley, Sussex, 1661 W. Suss RO EpI/33/1661/11
Priest, Edward, Northfield, Worcs, 1684 Worcs RO 008.7 BA3585/837/bdl 4
Priest, Thomas, Holbeach, Lincs, 1619 Lincs RO Ad/Ac/14/280
Priestley, Thomas, Boston, Lincs, 1645? Lincs RO Ad/Ac/28/133
Prigg, Abraham, tailor, Hatford, Berks, 1682 Berks RO D/A1/209/44C
Prigg, John, saddler, Maidstone, Kent, 1675 CKS PRC20/12/139
Prike, see Prick,
Primate, Richard, clergy: 'clerk', Denton, Lincs, 1638 Lincs RO Ad/Ac/25/328
Primer, John, Bersted, South, Sussex, 1617 W. Suss RO EpIV/10/1/52
Prince, Henry, Martin, Wilts, 1782 Wilts RO Miscellaneous Index (name + date)
Prince, John, cordwainer, Abingdon, Berks, 1636 Berks RO D/A1/208/77C
Prince, Robert, yeoman, Hinksey, South, Berks, 1644 Berks RO D/A1/106A
Prince, Samuel, clothier, Reading, Berks, 1627 Berks RO D/A1/105/124C
Prince, Thomas, New Romney, Kent, 1609 CKS PRC20/2/33
Prinder, James, Mumby, Lincs, 1637 Lincs RO Ad/Ac/25/438
Prinder, Vincent, Ponton, Little, Lincs, 1646 Lincs RO Ad/Ac/28/241
Pring, John, clergy: 'clerk', Enstone, Oxon, 1627 Oxon RO MSS Wills 299/5/4
Pringle, Judith, widow, Canterbury St Margaret, Kent, 1692 CKS PRC2/42/10
Prior, Daniell, Ash next Sandwich, Kent, 1634 CKS PRC20/11/210
Prior, Edith, servant, Codford St Peter, Wilts, 1611 Wilts RO Arch. Sarum(+ name and date)
Prior, Edmund, Hanney, West, Berks, 1634 Berks RO D/A1/208/63A
Prior, Henry, Hexton, Herts, 1597 Herts RO ASA25/1568

[Prior:]
Prior, John, carrier, Biddenden, Kent, 1687 CKS PRC2/41/73
Prior, Richard, husbandman, Langford (Radcutt), Oxon, 1672 Oxon RO MSS Wills Pec 78/4/28
Prior/Amerie, Thomas, Stokechurch (sic), Som, 1588 Somerset RO D/D/Cta/P79
Pritchard, John, Lydd, Kent, 1671 CKS PRC19/4/92
Pritchard, see Pritchett,
Pritchett/Pritchard, Joseph, Madresfield, Worcs, 1789 Worcs RO 008.7 BA3585/835/bdl 2
Private, Henry, Durweston, Dors, 1665 Wilts RO Miscellaneous Index (name + date)
Prockter, John, husbandman, Evedon, Lincs, 1650 Lincs RO Ad/Ac/30/8
Procter, Marmaduke, Horton in Ribbledale (Birkwith), Yorks, 1717 Borthwick Test C.P. 1717/12
Procter, William, Scarle, North, Lincs, 1645 Lincs RO Ad/Ac/28/216
Proctor, George, innkeeper, Stone, Staffs, 1796 LJRO/B/C/5/1796/161
Proctor, John, Fosdyke, Lincs, 1622 Lincs RO Ad/Ac/17/45
Proctor, John, Bilsby, Lincs, 1641 Lincs RO Ad/Ac/27/208
Proctor, John, university: 'Fellow of Exeter College, Oxford/B.D.', Oxford (Exeter College), Oxon, 1673 Bodleian HYP B9/65-68
Proffitt, John, butcher, Walsall, Staffs, 1766 LJRO/B/C/5/1766/109
Profitt, Richard, Shustoke, Warks, 1677 LJRO:cards/1677/7
Promeque, Gyles, Sandwich, Kent, 1610 CKS PRC2/15/288
Proppers, James, Donington, Lincs, 1637 Lincs RO Ad/Ac/25/617
Prosser, John, Llanfilo, Breck, 1626 NLW BR 1626/49 Ac
Prosser, John, Bromyard, Hfords, 1675 PRO PROB5/1285
Prosser, Lewis, Marden, Kent, 1632 CKS PRC2/31/142
Proud, Daniel, yeoman, Wickhambreaux, Kent, 1697 CKS PRC2/42/132
Proud, William, Ramsey, Hunts, 1676 Hunts RO/Acc58/60(154)
Proude, Thomas, Faversham, Kent, CKS PRC1/16/10a
Proude, Thomas, Faversham, Kent, 1698 CKS PRC1/16/10
Proude, Thomas, Faversham, Kent, 1698 CKS PRC1/16/10b
Proudlove, John, husbandman, Knipton, Leics, 1672 Leics RO Administrators Accounts 1667-72 f64
Proudlove, Joseph, Harpswell, Lincs, 1663 Lincs RO Ad/Ac/41/92
Proudlove, Ralph, Manchester, Lancs, 1589 Lancs RO (Name of Deceased) D.R.C.H. 1589
Proudlove, Raphe, Metheringham, Lincs, 1612 Lincs RO Ad/Ac/11/190
Provis, Richard, Shepton Mallet, Som, 1684 Somerset RO D/D/Cta/P43
Prowd, Henry, Ash next Sandwich, Kent, 1621 CKS PRC20/5/152
Prowde, Elizabeth, widow, Canterbury, Kent, 1612 CKS PRC2/17/446
Prower, William, mariner: 'captain', Rotherhithe (St Mary), Surrey, 1704? Lambeth Palace Arches G49/1
Prowle, William, Tintagel, Corn, 1609 Cornwall RO AP/P163/3
Prudden, Robert, yeoman, Codicote, Herts, 1614 Herts RO ASA25/4816
Prudhome/De la Place, Jane, widow, Canterbury All Saints, Kent, 1626 CKS PRC2/27/123
Pruett, Edmund, Kingston, Jamaica, Bristol RO 1729/33
Pryce, Adam, 1635 NLW BR 1634/185 Ac
Pryce, Margaret, widow, Wye, Kent, 1603 CKS PRC2/14/370
Pryklove, Edward, Pulborough, Sussex, 1589 W. Suss RO EpI/33/1588
Prynn, Bridget, Swainswick, Som, 1634 Somerset RO D/D/Cta/P21
Pryor, Elizabeth, New Romney, Kent, 1599 CKS PRC21/14/508
Pryor, George, clergy: 'clerk/parson', Kilve, Som, 1593 Somerset RO D/D/Cta/P74
Pryor, George, Spaxton, Som, 1675 Somerset RO D/D/Cta/P44
Pryor, Henry, Hexton, Herts, 1590 Herts RO ASA25/1284
Pryor, Margery, Kingsclere, Hants, 1673 Hants RO 21m65 D8/261
Pryor, Thomas, Stanton, Fen, Hunts, 1685 Hunts RO/Acc58/250(258)
Pryor, William, Lyminge, Kent, 1675 CKS PRC20/12/138
Puckeridge, Richard, Romsey, Hants, 1674 Hants RO 1672 AD96/3
Puckle, John, gentleman, Brookland, Kent, 1677 CKS PRC2/37/82
Puckle, Mary, widow, Lydd, Kent, 1630 CKS PRC20/9/337

Puckle, Mathue, Ivychurch, Kent, 1579 CKS PRC21/4/126
Puckle, Robert, jurat, Lydd, Kent, 1633 CKS PRC20/11/216
Pudacket, John, Binsted, Sussex, 1663 W. Suss RO EpI/33/1662/1
Puddie, Andrew, Lympsham, Som, 1626 Somerset RO D/D/Cta/P8
Puddy, Jane, Lympsham, Som, 1640 Somerset RO D/D/Cta/P10
Pudner, John, merchant, St Johns Thanet, Kent, 1675 CKS PRC2/36/226
Pudner, Robert, merchant, St Johns Thanet, Kent, 1639 CKS PRC1/1/89
Pudsey, George, yeoman/gentleman, Yarnton, Oxon, 1661 Oxon RO MSS Wills 84/3/27
Pufford, William, yeoman, Norton, Hook (Southrope), Oxon, 1632 Oxon RO MSS Wills 171/3/3
Pugh, Humphrey, St Andrew Holborn, London & Middlesex, 1802 Greater London RO DL/C/265/145/2
Pulestone, Hugh, Canterbury St Andrew, Kent, 1601 CKS PRC2/12/286
Pulford, Henrie, Tunstall, Kent, 1612 CKS PRC2/16/20
Pulford, John, yeoman, Aldford (Churton), Ches, 1735 Cheshire RO (Name) W.C. 1735
Pull, Daniel, blacksmith, Worstead, Norf, 1774 Norfolk RO ANF/11/5/110
Pullen, Charles, Dover, Kent, 1604 CKS PRC21/16/79
Pullen, Geffrey, Tallington, Lincs, 1636 Lincs RO Ad/Ac/24/464
Pullen, George, Luddenham, Kent, 1712 CKS PRC19/6/57
Pullen, Richard, yeoman, Cranbrook, Kent, 1676 CKS PRC2/37/73
Pullen, Valentine, Shadoxhurst, Kent, 1676 CKS PRC2/37/76
Pulley, Richard, labourer, Pinchbeck, Lincs, 1615 Lincs RO Ad/Ac/13/93
Pullford, Hughe, Bearsted, Kent, 1596 CKS PRC2/8/346
Pullman, William, Chard, Som, 1598 Somerset RO D/D/Cta/P28
Pulman, John, Swalecliffe, Kent, 1619 CKS PRC2/19/126
Pulnertofte, Nicholas, Algarkirk, Lincs, 1618 Lincs RO Ad/Ac/14/14
Pulter, Roland, Covenham St Bartholomew (Cawthorpe), Lincs, 1626 Lincs RO Ad/Ac/20/27
Pulvertoft, Leonard, Algarkirk, Lincs, 1620 Lincs RO Ad/Ac/16/73
Pulvertoft, Thomas, Algarkirk, Lincs, 1607 Lincs RO Ad/Ac/8a/107
Punnett, Thomas, Cranbrook, Kent, 1669 CKS PRC1/14/93
Punnett, see Poynett,
Punter, Susan, widow, Windsor, New, Berks, 1668 Berks RO D/A1/208/169B
Purchase, William, Linsted, Kent, 1627 CKS PRC2/27/122
Purdewax, William, yeoman, Lydd, Kent, 1666 CKS PRC19/3/79
Purkase, Thomas ygr, Bluntisham, Hunts, 1676 Hunts RO/Acc58/33(135)
Purle, Anne, Withern, Lincs, 1649 Lincs RO Ad/Ac/30/37
Purser, Edward, tucker, Witney, Oxon, 1629 Oxon RO MSS Wills 299/5/9
Purser, James, husbandman, Bruntingthorpe, Leics, 1672 Leics RO Administrators Accounts 1667-72 f92
Purser/Saunders, Alice, widow, Pagham, Sussex, 1614 W. Suss RO EpIV/10/1/55
Purser/Saunders, Alice, widow, Pagham, Sussex, 1614 W. Suss RO EpIV/10/2A/1
Purvey, Robert, gentleman, Miningsby, Lincs, 1620 Lincs RO Ad/Ac/16/78
Purye, Frances, widow, Boston, Lincs, 1619 Lincs RO Ad/Ac/15/231
Purye, William, Swineshead, Lincs, 1612 Lincs RO Ad/Ac/11/146
Putham, Mary, widow, Bristol, Glos, Bristol RO 1763/CP
Putland, Thomas, Goudhurst, Kent, 1632 CKS PRC20/9/329
Putnum, Thomas, Greenwich (East Greenwich), Kent, 1713 PRO PROB5/1214
Puttock, Henry, Rudgwick, Sussex, 1670 W. Suss RO EpI/33/1670/8
Puttock, John, Binsted, Sussex, 1673 W. Suss RO EpI/33/1673/14
Puttock, Thomas, Easebourne, Sussex, 1596 W. Suss RO EpI/33/1596/11
Puttrell, John, Mumby, Lincs, 1568 Lincs RO Ad/Ac/0/4
Puxlie, William, Nailsea, Som, 1607 Somerset RO D/D/Cta/P63
Puxty, John, Warehorne, Kent, 1688 CKS PRC2/41/129
Pyborne, Elizabeth, Gainsborough, Lincs, 1620 Lincs RO Ad/Ac/8b/437
Pye, Francis, husbandman, Leigh, South, Oxon, 1637 Oxon RO MSS Wills 84/3/10
Pye, Joseph, Thornham, Kent, 1684 CKS PRC2/40/234

[Pye:]
Pye, Simon, Teynham, Kent, 1638 CKS PRC2/34/259
Pye, Symon, Teynham, Kent, 1637 CKS PRC2/34/89
Pye, Thomas, Sittingbourne, Kent, 1635 CKS PRC2/32/166
Pye, Thomas, pilot, Deal, Kent, 1671 CKS PRC20/12/25
Pye, Thomas, Alverstoke, Hants, 1684 Hants RO 21m65 D8/333
Pye, William, Gedney, Lincs, 1594 Lincs RO Ad/Ac/3/139
Pye, William, Teynham, Kent, 1614 CKS PRC2/19/120
Pye, William, gentleman, Cadney, Lincs, 1684 Lincs RO Ad/Ac/34/107
Pyecroft, Elizabeth, widow, Norwich, Norf, 1776 Norfolk RO ANW/23/26/38
Pyend, Mary, spinster, Maidstone, Kent, 1623 CKS PRC20/6/290
Pygas, Edward, yeoman, Crowle (Eastoft), Lincs, 1673 Lincs RO Ad/Ac/35/53
Pyggin, Willyam, Stamford, Lincs, 1603 Lincs RO Ad/Ac/5/403
Pyke, Dorothy, widow, Cumnor, Berks, 1613 Berks RO D/A1/207/174A
Pyke, Margery, widow, Easton, Wilts, 1674 Wilts RO Miscellaneous Index (name + date)
Pyke, Mary, Bedwin, Little, Wilts, 1641 Wilts RO Miscellaneous Index (name + date)
Pyke, Nathaniell, gentleman, Greetwell, Lincs, 1673 Lincs RO Ad/Ac/35/67
Pykett, William, Newton on Trent, Lincs, 1665 Lincs RO Ad/Ac/41/162
Pylcher, Joane, widow, Westwell, Kent, 1598 CKS PRC21/14/500
Pyleman, Thomas, Otterhampton, Som, Somerset RO D/D/Cta/P60
Pylgrim, Thomas + Eliz, Biddenden, Kent, 1595 CKS PRC2/8/161
Pylgrime, William, Beckingham, Lincs, 1607 Lincs RO Ad/Ac/7/66
Pylgrym, Thomas, Beckingham, Lincs, 1603 Lincs RO Ad/Ac/5/521
Pyman, John, surgeon: 'barber-surgeon', Herne, Kent, 1665 CKS PRC19/3/80
Pymme, Nicholas, Chilham, Kent, 1628 CKS PRC2/29/93
Pynchbecke, Alex, Fishtoft, Lincs, 1571 Lincs RO Ad/Ac/2C/61
Pynde, John, Cranbrook, Kent, 1590 CKS PRC2/5/237
Pynder, Edwarde, Doddington, Kent, 1638 CKS PRC1/1/56
Pyne, Joane, widow, Baston, Lincs, 1607 Lincs RO Ad/Ac/8a/111
Pyne, John, Wye, Kent, 1583 CKS PRC2/2/255
Pyne, Simon, Maidstone, Kent, 1682 CKS PRC20/13/277
Pyne, Thomas, Wilton, Wilts, 1615 Wilts RO Miscellaneous Index (name + date)
Pynnell, Thomas, Netherhampton, Wilts, 1629 Wilts RO Arch. Sarum(+ name and date)
Pynnell, Thomas, mason, Netherhampton, Wilts, 1637 Wilts RO Arch. Sarum(+ name and date)
Pynnock, Richard, Eling, Hants, 1578 Hants RO 1573 B110/4
Pynny, Thomas, Chardstock, Dors, 1675 Wilts RO Miscellaneous Index (name + date)
Pyper, Ann, widow, Wittersham, Kent, 1600 CKS PRC21/16/178
Pyper, Robert, Stone in Oxney, Kent, 1617 CKS PRC2/19/157
Pyper, Thomas, Wittersham, Kent, 1610 CKS PRC20/2/180
Pyrryn, John, High Halstow, Kent, 1596 CKS PRC2/8/294
Pyseing, William eld, Canterbury Christchurch, Kent, 1685 CKS PRC20/13/521
Pysing, Henry, Linsted, Kent, 1646 CKS PRC1/7/95
Pysing, John eld, Canterbury St Mary-Magdalen Burgate, Kent, 1639 CKS PRC1/3/36a
Pysing, John eld, baker, Canterbury St Mary-Magdalen Burgate, Kent, 1639 CKS PRC1/3/36
Pysing, Luke, Swalecliffe, Kent, 1611 CKS PRC2/16/77
Pysing, Richard, Canterbury St Paul, Kent, 1608 CKS PRC2/14/358
Pysing, Richard, Great Mongeham, Kent, 1637 CKS PRC2/34/90
Pysing, Robert, Rainham, Kent, 1615 CKS PRC2/19/130
Pysing, Thomas, Ringwould, Kent, 1613 CKS PRC2/17/86
Pysinge, Barnabe, Bilsington, Kent, 1587 CKS PRC2/4/229
Pysinge, James, Deal, Kent, 1581 CKS PRC21/5/148
Pytcher, Wylliam, Birchington, Kent, 1581 CKS PRC21/4/331
Pytches, Richard, Kirtling, Cambs, 1522 Suff RO(B) IC500/2/14/135
Pytham, Anne, widow, Norton, Hook, Oxon, 1630 Oxon RO MSS Wills 299/5/17
Pytham, Anthony, innholder, Deddington, Oxon, 1634 Oxon RO MSS Wills 84/3/6
Pyther, Thomas, butcher, Shinfield, Berks, 1673 Berks RO D/A1/209/16D

Pytt, William, Worcester St Andrew, Worcs, 1608 Worcs RO 008.7 BA3585/839/456
Pyttard, John, Martock, Som, 1587 Somerset RO D/D/Cta/P68
Pyttell, Nicholas, Reading St Lawrence, Berks, 1614 Berks RO D/A1/207/172C
Pyttocke, Agnes, widow, Tilmanstone, Kent, 1594 CKS PRC2/7/39
Pyxe, Henrie, Ruckinge, Kent, 1593 CKS PRC2/6/514
Quackely, Hester, Sandwich, Kent, 1686 CKS PRC2/41/75
Quackly, Abraham, Sandwich, Kent, 1682 CKS PRC2/40/70
Quaife, Michall, Goudhurst, Kent, 1630 CKS PRC2/30/116
Quakley, Peter, gardener, Sandwich, Kent, 1678 CKS PRC2/38/61
Quallett, John, Stoughton, Sussex, 1676 W. Suss RO EpI/33/1676/11
Quarrell, William, Morton, Abbots, Worcs, 1685 Worcs RO 008.7 BA3585/830/19
Quatermain, William jun, Eynsham, Oxon, 1735 Oxon RO MSS Wills 304/2/1
Quatermayne, Francis, Garsington, Oxon, 1636 Oxon RO MSS Wills 299/6/8
Quayfe, John, Benenden, Kent, 1597 CKS PRC2/9/179
Queeney, Richard, Moseley, Worcs, 1685 Worcs RO 008.7 BA3585/837/bdl 4
Queiningborrow, Mathew, clergy: 'clerk', Dowsby, Lincs, 1672 Lincs RO Ad/Ac/43/66
Quelch, Barton, miller, Rotherfield Peppard, Oxon, 1680 Oxon RO MSS Wills 172/3/2
Quelche, Mathew, mercer, Wallingford, Berks, 1603 Berks RO D/A1/210/133B
Quell, Robert, Hale, Great (Little Hale), Lincs, 1640 Lincs RO Ad/Ac/27/7
Quench, John, butcher, Standlake (Brighthampton), Oxon, 1709 Oxon RO MSS Wills 172/3/11
Quennell, Roger, Linchmere, Sussex, 1623 W. Suss RO EpI/33/1623/10
Quennell, William, Terwick, Sussex, 1632 W. Suss RO EpI/33/1632/7
Quested, Daniell, St Nicholas at Wade, Kent, 1618 CKS PRC20/4/324
Quested, George, Ashford, Kent, 1590 CKS PRC2/5/382
Quested, Henry, Ashford, Kent, 1596 CKS PRC2/8/358
Quested, Henrye, Appledore, Kent, 1607 CKS PRC2/15/317
Quested, John, Eastwell, Kent, 1618 CKS PRC2/19/101
Quested, John, Harrietsham, Kent, 1640 CKS PRC1/5/27
Quested, Peter, Mersham, Kent, 1607 CKS PRC2/15/319
Quested, Robarte, New Romney, Kent, 1589 CKS PRC21/9/325
Quested, Robert, husbandman, Sellindge, Kent, 1676 CKS PRC2/37/83
Quested, William, Mersham, Kent, 1602 CKS PRC2/12/308
Quested, Wyllyam, Mersham, Kent, 1605 CKS PRC2/14/376
Questede, John, Preston next Wingham, Kent, 1593 CKS PRC2/6/472
Quick, John, Cannington, Som, 1662 Somerset RO D/D/Cta/Q3
Quick, Nicholas, Uphill, Som, 1638 Somerset RO D/D/Cta/Q2
Quickfall, Thomas, cutler: 'travelling cutler', Norwich, Norf, 1813 Norfolk RO ANW/23/27/14A
Quilter, Simon, Stourmouth, Kent, 1593 CKS PRC2/6/506
Quincey, John, husbandman, Gosberton, Lincs, 1667 Lincs RO Ad/Ac/32/79
Quincey, Lawrence, Walcot, Lincs, 1620 Lincs RO Ad/Ac/16/79
Quinten, Robert, Shipley, Sussex, 1631 W. Suss RO EpI/33/1631/33
Quintin, see Ibbott,
Quinton, John, Wellingborough, Northants, 1681 Northants RO NWill A/C/79
Quintrell, Richard, Cuby, Corn, 1621 Cornwall RO AP/Q9/2
Quishman, Daniel, Lydd, Kent, 1677 CKS PRC20/12/238
Quoyffe, Thomas, Blean, Kent, 1591 CKS PRC2/5/380
Quynte, Marion,
Kent 1582 CKS PRC2/2/167
Quyver, John, labourer, Wigtoft, Lincs, 1629 Lincs RO Ad/Ac/22/63
Rabbett, Robert, Boughton Monchelsea, Kent, 1582 CKS PRC2/2/172
Rabey, Robert, Huntingdon, Hunts, 1683 Hunts RO/Acc58/194(33)
Rables, John, Canterbury, Kent, 1632 CKS PRC2/31/148
Rabye, Ellen, Chesterton, Cambs, 1616 c. CUL V.C. Acc./Box3/72
Race, Arthur, Hernhill, Kent, 1615 CKS PRC20/3/200
Racke, John, Hogsthorpe, Lincs, 1639 Lincs RO Ad/Ac/26/21

[Racke:]
Racke, John, Hogsthorpe, Lincs, 1639 Lincs RO Ad/Ac/26/24
Racke, John, yeoman, Keelby, Lincs, 1641 Lincs RO Ad/Ac/27/249
Rackerby, Thomas, husbandman, Langton, Lincs, 1615 Lincs RO Ad/Ac/13/46
Radbourne, William, tailor, Oxford St Aldate, Oxon, Oxon RO MSS Wills 299/7/30
Radcliffe, Anthony, clergy: 'canon/D.D.', Oxford (Christ Church College), Oxon, 1707 Bodleian HYP B9/69-70
Raddish, William, Lea, Lincs, 1681 Lincs RO Ad/Ac/34/80
Rade, Henry, Cranbrook, Kent, 1675 CKS PRC2/36/237
Rade, John, Benenden, Kent, 1595 CKS PRC2/7/115
Rade, John, Benenden, Kent, 1678 CKS PRC2/38/66
Rade, William, Benenden, Kent, 1638 CKS PRC2/34/268
Radford, Richard, Hawkhurst, Kent, 1672 CKS PRC2/35/170
Radforth, John, Alfreton, Derby, 1663 LJRO:cards/1663/49
Radley, Robert, Wigtoft, Lincs, 1629 Lincs RO Ad/Ac/22/51
Raffoote, John, Weston, Lincs, 1648 Lincs RO Ad/Ac/30/310
Ragg, Edward, Wirksworth, Derby, 1711 LJRO/B/C/5/1711/36
Ragles, Stephen, Lavant, East, Sussex, 1627 W. Suss RO EpIV/10/1/25
Rainbow, Josiah, victualler, Coventry, Warks, 1817 LJRO/B/C/5/1817/72
Rainer, Andrewe,
Kent CKS PRC2/4/21
Rainer, Henrie, Sittingbourne, Kent, 1629 CKS PRC20/8/389
Rainer, John, Milton next Sittingbourne, Kent, 1607 CKS PRC2/13/329
Rainer, John, Canterbury St Alphege, Kent, 1621 CKS PRC20/5/166
Rainer, Robert, Chart, Great, Kent, 1620 CKS PRC2/19/85
Raines, Andrew, butcher, Ashford, Kent, 1675 CKS PRC2/36/233
Raines, Thomas, Bethersden, Kent, 1665 CKS PRC1/10/76
Rainforth, Christopher, yeoman, Burton Leonard, Yorks, 1825 Borthwick Test C.P. 1825/14
Rainoldes, Richard, Sandhurst, Kent, 1605 CKS PRC2/13/325
Rainoldes, Richard, St Nicholas at Wade, Kent, 1605 CKS PRC20/1/11
Rainoldes, William, Chislet, Kent, 1596 CKS PRC2/9/339
Rains/Rainson, Abraham, Milton next Sittingbourne, Kent, 1628 CKS PRC2/29/75
Rainsbye, George, clergy: 'clerk', Kingston Bagpuize, Berks, 1625 Wilts RO CC Sarum(+ name and date)
Rainsford, Thomas, Angmering, Sussex, 1631 W. Suss RO EpI/33/1631/27
Rainson, see Rains,
Rainton, Thomas, Washingborough, Lincs, 1638 Lincs RO Ad/Ac/25/14
Raithbie, John, Hatton, Lincs, 1619 Lincs RO Ad/Ac/15/268
Raithbone, Hugh, Gainsborough, Lincs, 1662 Lincs RO Ad/Ac/41/37
Raithbye, William, Salmonby, Lincs, 1627 Lincs RO Ad/Ac/20b/47
Raithdales,
Leics 1687 Leics RO Administrators Accounts 1682-86 f51
Raithebie, Roberte, Stainfield, Lincs, 1599 Lincs RO Ad/Ac/5/53
Ralf, Christopher, Ingoldmels, Lincs, 1601 Lincs RO Ad/Ac/5/207
Ralf, Robert, Ash next Sandwich, Kent, 1605 CKS PRC20/1/21
Ralfe, Malachie, Ash next Sandwich, Kent, 1598 CKS PRC21/14/516
Ralfe, Robert, Brookland, Kent, 1694 CKS PRC2/42/90
Ralphes, John, Whitchurch, Shrops, 1674 LJRO:cards/1674/40
Ramage, David, St Katherine by the Tower, London & Middlesex, 1667 PRO PROB32/2/59
Raman, John, Holton Beckering, Lincs, 1638 Lincs RO Ad/Ac/25/252
Ramkyn, William, Kenardington, Kent, 1614 CKS PRC2/17/29
Rammage, David, St Katherine by the Tower, London & Middlesex, 1669 PRO PROB32/6/52
Rampson, John, Chardstock, Dors, 1745 Wilts RO Miscellaneous Index (name + date)
Ramsden, George, Tenterden, Kent, 1611 CKS PRC2/16/208
Ramsden, Jarvis, yeoman, Biddenden, Kent, 1684 CKS PRC2/40/238
Ramsden, John, gentleman, Bradford (Coat, Clayton), Yorks, Borthwick Test C.P. 1757/5

[Ramsden:]
Ramsden, Joseph, clothier, Almondbury (Crossland Moor), Yorks, 1808 Borthwick Test C.P. 1808/2
Ramsden, Richard, yeoman, Woodchurch, Kent, 1685 CKS PRC20/13/525
Ramsden, Richard ygr, Goudhurst, Kent, 1632 CKS PRC20/11/286
Ramsden, Thomas, husbandman, Tenterden, Kent, 1682 CKS PRC2/40/72
Ramsey, Christopher, Brington, Northants, 1673 Northants RO NWill A/C/83
Ramsey, Gertrude, mrs/widow, Linsted, Kent, 1618 CKS PRC2/19/93
Ramsey, Hugh, Sandwich, Kent, 1625 CKS PRC2/25/121
Ramsey, John, clergy: 'mr/rector', Mersham, Kent, 1639 CKS PRC2/34/263
Ramsey, John, merchant,
France, late of the City of London 1682 PRO PROB32/21/321
Ramsey, Thomas, Alkborough, Lincs, 1586 Lincs RO Ad/Ac/37/4
Ramsey, Wyllyam, Faversham, Kent, 1611 CKS PRC2/15/329
Ramsey/Pipes, Catherine, wife, Aukborough, Lincs, 1626 Lincs RO Ad/Ac/39/72
Ranby, Richard, Bleasby, Notts, 1649 Lincs RO Ad/Ac/30/404
Rance, Edward, innholder, Maidenhead, Berks, 1671 Berks RO D/A1/211/51C
Rance, John, Harrietsham, Kent, 1664 CKS PRC1/10/77
Ranckhorne, Alice, widow, St Johns Thanet, Kent, 1618 CKS PRC2/19/68
Ranckhorne/Rancone, Peter eld, Great Mongeham, Kent, 1624 CKS PRC2/24/72
Rancone, see Ranckhorne,
Rand, John, Hythe St Leonard, Kent, 1691 CKS PRC19/5/5
Randal, John, innholder, Frome Selwood, Som, 1731 Somerset RO D/D/Cta/R35
Randall, Anne, Sutterton, Lincs, 1615 Lincs RO Ad/Ac/13/14
Randall, Henry, Bristol St James, Glos, Bristol RO 1677/38
Randall, John, Salisbury, Wilts, 1619 Wilts RO Miscellaneous Index (name + date)
Randall, John, shepherd, Hornton, Oxon, 1680 Oxon RO MSS Wills Pec 50/3/3
Randall, Julyne, Eastry, Kent, 1594 CKS PRC21/12/411
Randall, Nichols, Felpham, Sussex, 1635 W. Suss RO EpI/33/1635/29
Randall, Richard, Beaulieu, Hants, 1662 Hants RO 21M65 D8/158
Randall, Robert, St Ewe, Corn, 1609 Cornwall RO AP/R18/4
Randall, Roberte, Chislet, Kent, 1600 CKS PRC2/11/269
Randall, see Everett,
Rande, George, mariner, Deal, Kent, 1612 CKS PRC20/2/340
Randell, Henry, husbandman, Minster in Sheppey, Kent, 1676 CKS PRC2/36/234
Randle, Clement, labourer, Skeffington, Leics, 1669 Leics RO Administrators Accounts 1667-72 f28
Randle, Philip, Ombersley, Worcs, 1791 Worcs RO 008.7 BA3585/835/bdl 2
Randle, William, Cirencester, Glos, 1685 GRO GDR/B4/2/R73
Randolfe, William, Allington, Lincs, 1619 Lincs RO Ad/Ac/15/302
Randoll, Alice, spinster, Nethrington, Wilts, 1632 Wilts RO Arch. Sarum(+ name and date)
Randoll, Alice, widow, Damerham, South, Wilts, 1669 Wilts RO Arch. Sarum(+ name and date)
Randoll, Elizabeth, Nethrington, Wilts, 1632 Wilts RO Arch. Sarum(+ name and date)
Randoll, Henry, Netherhampton, Wilts, 1622 Wilts RO Miscellaneous Index (name + date)
Randoll, John, Faversham, Kent, 1686 CKS PRC2/41/78
Randoll, Peter, Elsted, Sussex, 1629 W. Suss RO EpI/33/1629/26
Randoll, Sybil, widow, Hurley, Berks, 1597 Berks RO D/A1/111/113C
Randoll, Thomas, Meon, East, Hants, 1678 Hants RO 21m65 D8/294
Randolph, Elizabeth, Canterbury St Mary Bredin, Kent, 1683 CKS PRC2/40/145
Randolph/Giles/Eason, Jane, widow, St Laurence Thanet, Kent, 1669 CKS PRC1/14/94
Rands, Robert, Searby, Lincs, 1663 Lincs RO Ad/Ac/42/43
Rands, Thomas, weaver: 'silk weaver', Northampton, Northants, Northants RO NWill A/C/46
Rands, Thomas, Fleet, Lincs, 1639 Lincs RO Ad/Ac/26/211
Ranew, Nathaniel, St Faith under St Pauls, London & Middlesex, 1697 PRO PROB5/1655
Ransdalle, John, Sandwich, Kent, 1627 CKS PRC2/28/101
Ransom, John, Steeping, Great, Lincs, 1638 Lincs RO Ad/Ac/25/227

[Ranson:]
Ranson, Gabriell, yeoman, Steeping, Great, Lincs, 1624 Lincs RO Ad/Ac/19A/85
Ranson, Nicholas, Steeping, Great, Lincs, 1666 Lincs RO Ad/Ac/32/66
Ranson, Thomas, Heckington, Lincs, 1607 Lincs RO Ad/Ac/8a/9
Ranson, Thomas, yeoman, Steeping, Great, Lincs, 1670 Lincs RO Ad/Ac/32/190
Ransone, Henrie, Holbeach, Lincs, 1635 Lincs RO Ad/Ac/24/286
Rant, William, Laughton, Lincs, 1662 Lincs RO Ad/Ac/41/6
Rantum, Richard, Deal, Kent, 1670 CKS PRC19/4/93
Raphe/Adderton, John, husbandman, Churchill, Oxon, 1627 Oxon RO MSS Wills 85/2/34
Rapier, Arthur, labourer, Deeping St James, Lincs, 1634 Lincs RO Ad/Ac/24/98
Rapley, George, Northchapel, Sussex, 1674 W. Suss RO EpI/33/1674/11
Rasell, Gregorie, Westwell, Kent, 1637 CKS PRC20/11/260
Rasell, Henry, Ruckinge, Kent, 1623 CKS PRC2/24/62
Rasell, James, gentleman, Maidstone, Kent, 1635 CKS PRC20/11/250
Rasell, James, blacksmith, Westwell, Kent, 1641 CKS PRC19/2/31
Rasell, John, labourer, Ruckinge, Kent, 1641 CKS PRC1/5/28
Rasell, Ralfe, Chart, Little, Kent, 1600 CKS PRC2/11/271
Rasell, Richard, Pluckley, Kent, 1600 CKS PRC2/11/263
Rasell, Thomas, yeoman, Westwell, Kent, 1687 CKS PRC20/13/603
Raskill, Symon, yeoman, Ropsley, Lincs, 1639 Lincs RO Ad/Ac/26/69
Rasolde, Henry, Stoughton, Sussex, 1596 W. Suss RO EpI/33/1595/9
Rastell, Thomas, Ponton, Great, Lincs, 1650 Lincs RO Ad/Ac/29/66
Rastell, William ygr, yeoman, Redmarley D'Abitot, Worcs, 1649 Worcs RO 008.7 BA3585/837/bdl 1
Ratchford, Thomas, Milton next Sittingbourne, Kent, 1598 CKS PRC2/10/190
Ratclife, Edmund, Bath St James, Som, 1584 Somerset RO D/D/Cta/R31
Ratcliff, Adouwth?,
Lincs 1612 Lincs RO Ad/Ac/10/136
Ratcliff, John, St Albans St Stephens, Herts, 1612 Herts RO ASA25/4800
Ratcliffe, Christopher, Goodnestone next Wingham, Kent, 1698 CKS PRC19/5/60
Rathbone, John, clergy: 'clerk', 1577 Lancs RO (Name of Deceased) D.R.C.H. 1576
Rathbone, John, degrees: 'Doctor of Physic', St Marylebone, London & Middlesex, 1743 Greater London RO DL/C/550/103/1
Rathbone, Thomas, Astbury (Moreton with Alcumlow), Ches, 1628 Cheshire RO (Name) W.C. 1628
Rathbone, Thomas, Kirby, West (Caldey), Ches, 1647 Cheshire RO (Name) W.C. 1647
Ratleif, William, Hernhill, Kent, 1696 CKS PRC19/5/40
Ratlyfe, William, tailor, Newbury, Berks, Berks RO D/A1/210/238A
Ratsall, William, Binbrook, Lincs, 1629 Lincs RO Ad/Ac/22/58
Rattew, James, Amesbury, Wilts, 1636 Wilts RO Arch. Sarum(+ name and date)
Raughton, William, Timberland, Lincs, 1607 Lincs RO Ad/Ac/7/113
Raven, John, yeoman, Witham, North, Lincs, 1631 Lincs RO Ad/Ac/23/79
Raven, Silvester, mrs/widow, Canterbury, Kent, 1638 CKS PRC2/34/265
Raven, Thomas, Minster in Sheppey, Kent, 1593 CKS PRC2/6/142
Raven, William, Norton, Worcs, Worcs RO 008.7 BA3585/839/424
Ravens, John, Henlow, Beds, 1594 Lincs RO Ad/Ac/0/11
Ravensdale, John, Dunsby, Lincs, 1636 Lincs RO Ad/Ac/24/397
Ravense, Jane, Grimsby, Great, Lincs, 1611 Lincs RO Ad/Ac/10/105
Ravins, John, Langford (Little Faringdon), Oxon, 1614 Oxon RO MSS Wills Pec 78/4/39
Rawe, Ralph, St Hilary, Corn, 1636 Cornwall RO AP/R571/3
Rawe, Richard, yeoman, St Neot, Corn, 1623 Cornwall RO AP/R347/2
Rawe, William, Petherwin, North, Corn, 1612 Cornwall RO AP/R175/3
Rawett, Luke, St Blazey, Corn, 1627 Cornwall RO AP/R453/2
Rawkins, Edmund, labourer: 'day labourer', Newnton, North, Wilts, 1627 Wilts RO Arch. Wilts.(+ name and date)
Rawkins, Robert, Exbury, Hants, 1600 Hants RO 1599 AD46/3

[Rawkins:]
Rawkins, Robert, Newnton, North, Wilts, 1622 Wilts RO Arch. Wilts.(+ name and date)
Rawkins/Rawning?, Thomas, Canning, Bishops, Wilts, 1620 Wilts RO Dean Sarum (name + date)
Rawle, Francis, gentleman, St Juliot, Corn, 1648 Cornwall RO AP/R731/3
Rawle, William, St Juliot, Corn, 1648 Cornwall RO AP/R730/3
Rawlens, John, Maidstone, Kent, 1609 CKS PRC20/2/23
Rawlet, James, Sutton St Edmunds, Lincs, 1595 Lincs RO Ad/Ac/5/262
Rawlett, William, yeoman, Sutton St Edmunds, Lincs, 1614 Lincs RO Ad/Ac/12/193
Rawling, Thomas, Holbeach, Lincs, 1792 Lincs RO Ad/Ac/45/61
Rawlings, Elizabeth, widow, St Martin in the Fields, London & Middlesex, 1685 Greater London RO AM/PP/Box 1685-1694 pt (uncatalogued)
Rawlings, John, Dinton, Wilts, 1688 Wilts RO Arch. Sarum(+ name and date)
Rawlins, Ralph, blacksmith, Lewknor (Postcombe), Oxon, 1626 Oxon RO MSS Wills 55/4/8
Rawlins, Richard, Compton, Long, Warks, 1602 Worcs RO 008.7 BA3585/838/261
Rawlins, Thomas, husbandman, Goudhurst, Kent, 1673 CKS PRC2/35/251
Rawlins, William, Salford Priors, Warks, 1685 Worcs RO 008.7 BA3585/830/18
Rawlins, William, Madeley, Staffs, 1728 LJRO:cards/1728/18
Rawlinson, James, gentleman, Hawkhurst, Kent, 1665 CKS PRC1/11/72
Rawlinson, Richard, Greetwell, Lincs, 1650 Lincs RO Ad/Ac/40/224
Rawlyns, Alexander, clergy: 'clerk', Wigtoft, Lincs, 1614 Lincs RO Ad/Ac/13/66
Rawlyns, Thomas, gentleman, Standlake (Brighthampton), Oxon, Oxon RO MSS Wills 299/7/18
Rawlyns, William, St Albans, Herts, 1597 Herts RO ASA25/1637
Rawnce, Thomasine, Harrietsham, Kent, 1610 CKS PRC2/15/333
Rawning, see Rawkins,
Raworth, Henry, mr, Dover, Kent, 1630 CKS PRC20/9/343
Raworth, William, gentleman, Boston, Lincs, 1679 Lincs RO Ad/Ac/43/89
Rawsby, Edward, yeoman, Hykeham, North, Lincs, 1629 Lincs RO Ad/Ac/22/36
Rawson, Clement, Bury, Sussex, 1640 W. Suss RO EpI/33/1640/7
Rawson, Clement eld, Bury (West Burton), Sussex, 1632 W. Suss RO EpI/33/1632/8
Rawson, Frauncys, clergy: 'clerk', Frittenden, Kent, 1574 CKS PRC2/1/124
Rawson, John, Bury, Sussex, 1630 W. Suss RO EpI/33/1629/11
Rawson, John, yeoman, Aldbrough (Ringbrough), Yorks, 1771 Borthwick Test C.P. 1770/3
Rawson, Thomas, Stockbury, Kent, CKS PRC2/6/380
Rawson, Thomasine, widow, Bury, Sussex, 1633 W. Suss RO EpI/33/1632/9
Rawson/Rosson, Elizabeth, widow, Borden, Kent, 1627 CKS PRC2/28/104
Raxworthy, Robert, clothier, Boyton, Wilts, 1639 Wilts RO Arch. Sarum(+ name and date)
Ray, Allen, yeoman, Waterperry, Oxon, 1630 Oxon RO MSS Wills 85/2/37
Ray, Ellen, widow, Kidlington, Oxon, 1639 Oxon RO MSS Wills 172/4/41
Ray, George, Stixwold, Lincs, 1624 Lincs RO Ad/Ac/19A/115
Ray, George, Skelton, Yorks, 1724 Borthwick Test C.P. 1725/1
Ray, John, Salisbury, Wilts, 1684 Wilts RO Miscellaneous Index (name + date)
Ray, Robert, gentleman, Hartley Wintney, Hants, 1678 PRO PROB5/1300
Ray, Stephen, Dover St James, Kent, 1639 CKS PRC20/11/296
Raybie, Richard, Grantham, Lincs, 1619 Lincs RO Ad/Ac/15/93
Raye, John, Fulbeck, Lincs, 1611 Lincs RO Ad/Ac/10/63
Rayer, John eld, mason, Charney Bassett, Berks, 1634 Berks RO D/A1/211/8D
Rayer, Richard, husbandman, Sutton Courtenay, Berks, 1665 Berks RO D/A1/211/44C
Rayer, Robert, yeoman, Charney Bassett, Berks, 1694 Berks RO D/A1/211/72C
Raylton, Richard, Milton next Sittingbourne, Kent, 1625 CKS PRC2/25/123
Raylton, Robert, Canterbury St Andrew, Kent, 1612 CKS PRC1/1/20
Raymers, Joseph, Guestwick, Norf, 1750 Norfolk RO ANW/23/24/91B & C
Raymond, Thomas, Dover St James, Kent, 1627 CKS PRC20/7/158
Raymond, Thomas, fuller, Westbury, Wilts, 1644 Wilts RO CC Sarum(+ name and date)
Raymond, see Walker,
Raynales, Christopher, Mareham le Fen, Lincs, 1579 Lincs RO Ad/Ac/2b/10
Raynard, Richard, Maidstone, Kent, 1634 CKS PRC20/11/274

[Rayner:]
Rayner, Alexander, Westwell, Kent, 1617 CKS PRC20/4/326
Rayner, Augustine, upholsterer, Lincoln, Lincs, 1626 Lincs RO Ad/Ac/19B/59
Rayner, Christopher, Lenham, Kent, 1592 CKS PRC2/5/390
Rayner, Dorothy, Headcorn, Kent, 1620 CKS PRC2/19/63
Rayner, Edward, Nonington, Kent, 1618 CKS PRC20/4/342
Rayner, Francis, Canterbury Holy Cross Westgate, Kent, 1685 CKS PRC2/40/239
Rayner, Francis + Susan, Rodmersham, Kent, 1635 CKS PRC2/33/111
Rayner, George, yeoman, Boughton Malherbe, Kent, 1679 CKS PRC2/38/175
Rayner, Henry, gentleman, Beighton, Norf, 1767 Norfolk RO ANW/23/25/95A
Rayner, Hughe, yeoman, Fenton, Lincs, 1624 Lincs RO Ad/Ac/39/132
Rayner, Jacob, Canterbury St George Martyr, Kent, 1669 CKS PRC1/13/100
Rayner, Jacob/James, Canterbury St Paul, Kent, 1715 CKS PRC1/17/78
Rayner, Jeremy, Hollingbourne, Kent, 1622 CKS PRC20/6/276
Rayner, John, Ashford, Kent, 1591 CKS PRC2/5/388
Rayner, John, Boughton under Blean, Kent, 1637 CKS PRC20/11/262
Rayner, John, Newton on Trent, Lincs, 1662 Lincs RO Ad/Ac/41/10
Rayner, John, Ruckinge, Kent, 1685 CKS PRC2/41/12
Rayner, John, Littlebourne, Kent, 1723 CKS PRC1/18/46
Rayner, Mathew, Kingston, Kent, 1586 CKS PRC2/4/220
Rayner, Mathew, Lenham, Kent, 1646 CKS PRC1/7/96
Rayner, Mathewe, Gainsborough, Lincs, 1624 Lincs RO Ad/Ac/39/156
Rayner, Michael, Appledram, Sussex, 1671 W. Suss RO EpI/33/1671/1
Rayner, Michael, Iwade, Kent, 1715 CKS PRC1/17/79
Rayner, Michaell, brazier, Boston, Lincs, 1625 Lincs RO Ad/Ac/20b/84
Rayner, Nathaniell, Brookland, Kent, 1612 CKS PRC2/16/157
Rayner, Richard, Sittingbourne, Kent, 1667 CKS PRC1/12/76
Rayner, Robert, Canterbury St Alphege, Kent, 1621 CKS PRC20/5/160
Rayner, Simon, Tonge, Kent, 1625 CKS PRC2/25/119
Rayner, Simon, Kettlethorpe (Fenton), Lincs, 1627 Lincs RO Ad/Ac/39/94
Rayner, Stephen, Graveney, Kent, 1596 CKS PRC2/8/437
Rayner, Susann, Littlebourne, Kent, 1631 CKS PRC2/31/60
Rayner, Thomas,
Kent 1631 CKS PRC20/9/363
Rayner, Thomas, Newton on Trent, Lincs, 1662 Lincs RO Ad/Ac/41/23
Rayner, Thomas, Newington next Sittingbourne, Kent, 1679 CKS PRC2/38/179
Rayner, Thomas, Eastchurch, Sheppey, Kent, 1686 CKS PRC2/41/80
Rayner, Thomas, Folkestone, Kent, 1702 CKS PRC1/16/55
Rayner, William, Ashford, Kent, 1613 CKS PRC2/17/377
Rayner, William, esquire, Maidstone, Kent, 1628 CKS PRC20/8/395
Rayner, William, yeoman, Sutton Valence, Kent, 1679 CKS PRC2/38/63
Rayner, see Brooke,
Raynes, Henry,
Som 1601 Somerset RO D/D/Cta/R28
Raynes, Jeremiah, yeoman, Boughton Monchelsea, Kent, 1681 CKS PRC2/39/229
Raynes, William,
Som 1581 Somerset RO D/D/Cta/R22
Raynie/Paynter, Ralph, Bridgewater, Som, 1622 Somerset RO D/D/Cta/R2
Raynoldes, Nicholas, husbandman, Hendred, West, Berks, 1621 Berks RO D/A1/210/251D
Raynoldes, Robert, yeoman, Kingston Lisle, Berks, 1617 Berks RO D/A1/210/245C
Raynoldes, Thomas, Reading St Mary, Berks, 1587 Berks RO D/A2/C25/f15R
Raynoldes, Thomas, clergy: 'vicar', Thornham, Kent, 1599 CKS PRC2/11/257
Raynolds, Arthur, Leeds, Kent, 1582 CKS PRC21/6/117
Raynolds, Bartholmewe, Ashford, Kent, 1600 CKS PRC2/11/359
Raynolds, Edward, Tenterden, Kent, 1575 CKS PRC2/1/153
Raynolds, Frauncys, Fairfield, Kent, 1581 CKS PRC21/5/7

Raynolds, Nycholas, Petham, Kent, 1614 CKS PRC2/17/90
Raynolds, Richard, Herne, Kent, 1689 CKS PRC20/13/618
Raynolds, William, Lydd, Kent, 1584 CKS PRC21/7/142
Raynolds, Wyllyam, Sandwich, Kent, 1596 CKS PRC2/8/334
Raynouldes, Michaell, Shadoxhurst, Kent, 1613 CKS PRC2/17/297
Raynton, William, Washingborough, Lincs, 1639 Lincs RO Ad/Ac/26/309
Raysell, Thomas, yeoman, Borden, Kent, 1674 CKS PRC2/36/113
Rayson, Dorothy, widow, Stepney, London & Middlesex, 1687 PRO PROB32/26/90
Rayton, Francis, Lenham, Kent, 1680 CKS PRC2/39/97
Razell, Daniel, Tenterden, Kent, 1676 CKS PRC2/37/86
Razell, John, mariner: 'seafaring man', Queenborough, Kent, 1676 CKS PRC2/36/235
Razell, Margery, widow, Westwell, Kent, 1617 CKS PRC20/4/336
Rea, Richard, Baschurch, Shrops, 1670 LJRO:cards/1670/59
Reache, Thomas, Old Romney, Kent, 1586 CKS PRC2/4/372
Read, Alexander, clergy: 'clerk', Old Romney, Kent, 1677 CKS PRC20/12/240
Read, Alice, Knaith, Lincs, 1662 Lincs RO Ad/Ac/41/50
Read, Edward, St Peter in Thanet, Kent, 1663 CKS PRC1/9/143
Read, Edward, Faversham, Kent, 1682 CKS PRC2/39/225
Read, Elizabeth, St Johns Thanet, Kent, 1709 CKS PRC1/17/13
Read, George, New Romney, Kent, 1624 CKS PRC20/6/160
Read, George, yeoman, St Johns Thanet, Kent, 1668 CKS PRC1/13/101
Read, Henry, husbandman, Wickhambreaux, Kent, 1668 CKS PRC1/13/102
Read, James ygr, Graveney, Kent, 1681 CKS PRC2/39/227
Read, John, esquire, Abingdon St Helen (Barton), Berks, 1605 Berks RO D/A1/210/222C
Read, John, Bourne, Lincs, 1606 Lincs RO Ad/Ac/7/122
Read, John, Preston next Wingham, Kent, 1636 CKS PRC2/33/121
Read, John, Aubourn (Haddington), Lincs, 1640 Lincs RO Ad/Ac/26/219
Read, John, St Peter in Thanet, Kent, 1663 CKS PRC1/9/144
Read, John, tanner, Hythe St Leonard, Kent, 1672 CKS PRC20/12/58
Read, Laurence, yeoman, Brabourne, Kent, 1674 CKS PRC2/36/116
Read, Mary, widow, St Peter in Thanet, Kent, 1666 CKS PRC1/11/148
Read, Parslow, yeoman, Ipsden, Oxon, 1692 Oxon RO MSS Wills 172/5/28
Read, Peter, Fenton, Lincs, 1607 Lincs RO Ad/Ac/8a/35
Read, Ralph, husbandman, Wytham, Berks, 1662 Berks RO D/A1/211/31C
Read, Richard, Minster in Sheppey, Kent, 1637 CKS PRC2/33/119
Read, Richard, Arreton, Hants, 1679 Hants RO 21m65 D8/318
Read, Thomas, Edlington, Lincs, 1611 Lincs RO Ad/Ac/10/26
Read, Thomas, husbandman, Maidstone, Kent, 1667 CKS PRC19/3/137
Read, Thomas, Biddenden, Kent, 1678 CKS PRC2/38/67
Read, Thomas, Hilgay, Norf, 1779 Norfolk RO ANF/11/5/89
Read, William, Brent, East, Som, 1611 Somerset RO D/D/Cta/R27
Read, William, yeoman, Kirkstead, Lincs, 1623 Lincs RO Ad/Ac/17/67
Read, William, Marden, Up, Sussex, 1652 W. Suss RO Epl/33/1652/3
Read, see Welby,
Reade, Adrian, Lydd, Kent, 1623 CKS PRC20/6/278
Reade, Agnes, widow, Canterbury St Paul, Kent, 1610 CKS PRC2/15/355
Reade, Alexander, Aisthorpe (Thorpe in the Fallows), Lincs, 1599 Lincs RO Ad/Ac/37/69
Reade, Alexander, gentleman, Abingdon St Helen (Pomney), Berks, 1682 Berks RO D/A1/211/69C
Reade, Anne, widow, Woodnesborough, Kent, 1683 CKS PRC1/15/103
Reade, Antonie, Swaton, Lincs, 1575 Lincs RO Ad/Ac/1/17
Reade, Christopher, Marden, Kent, 1635 CKS PRC2/33/112
Reade, Dionesse, widow, Faversham, Kent, 1635 CKS PRC2/33/118
Reade, Edmond, Benenden, Kent, 1601 CKS PRC2/12/318
Reade, Edward, Wingham, Kent, 1636 CKS PRC20/11/256

[Reade:]
Reade, Francis, Shellingford, Berks, 1663 Berks RO D/A1/211/35C
Reade, James, Boughton under Blean, Kent, 1621 CKS PRC20/5/162
Reade, Joane, widow, Oare, Kent, 1634 CKS PRC2/32/106
Reade, John, Ebony, Kent, 1592 CKS PRC2/6/454
Reade, John, Sandwich St Bartholomew's Hospital, Kent, 1593 CKS PRC21/12/487
Reade, John, Lydd, Kent, 1626 CKS PRC20/7/150
Reade, John, Sandhurst, Kent, 1627 CKS PRC2/28/102
Reade, John ygr, Whitstable, Kent, 1617 CKS PRC2/19/67
Reade, Mathew, gentleman, Folkestone, Kent, 1627 CKS PRC2/27/146
Reade, Matthew ygr, clothier, Goudhurst, Kent, 1640 CKS PRC20/11/264
Reade, Nicholas, Bridge, Kent, 1606 CKS PRC2/14/381
Reade, Richard, Hothfield, Kent, 1604 CKS PRC2/13/331
Reade, Richard, yeoman, Ruckinge, Kent, 1633 CKS PRC2/32/105
Reade, Robert, St Pauls Walden, Herts, 1624 Herts RO ASA25/4836
Reade, Robert, Spalding (Wykeham), Lincs, 1626 Lincs RO Ad/Ac/20/55
Reade, Samuell, tanner, Cranbrook, Kent, 1612 CKS PRC2/16/212
Reade, Thomas, Benenden, Kent, 1597 CKS PRC2/10/44
Reade, Thomas, Brookland, Kent, 1613 CKS PRC2/17/227
Reade, Thomas, Marsh Chapel, Lincs, 1613 Lincs RO Ad/Ac/12/2
Reade, Vincent, brewer, Lydd, Kent, 1618 CKS PRC20/4/338
Reade, William, Seagrave, Leics, Leics RO PR/I/41A/3
Reade, William, Canterbury St Mildred, Kent, 1593 CKS PRC2/6/208
Reade, William, Timberland, Lincs, 1613 Lincs RO Ad/Ac/12/135
Reade/Smith, Anne, Norton Disney, Lincs, 1639 Lincs RO Ad/Ac/26/192
Reader, Abraham, yeoman, Bersted, South (Bognor), Sussex, 1626 W. Suss RO EpIV/10/1/30
Reader, Alice, widow, Bredgar, Kent, 1685 CKS PRC2/41/14
Reader, Anne, spinster, Minster in Thanet, Kent, 1664 CKS PRC1/10/78
Reader, John, Smeeth, Kent, 1579 CKS PRC21/4/51
Reader, John, Boughton Monchelsea, Kent, 1582 CKS PRC2/2/96
Reader, John, Bredgar, Kent, 1608 CKS PRC2/14/383
Reader, John, Bredgar, Kent, 1621 CKS PRC2/24/71
Reader, John, Bicknor, Kent, 1627 CKS PRC2/28/103
Reader, John, Smarden, Kent, 1674 CKS PRC2/36/112
Reader, Richard, Boughton Monchelsea, Kent, 1599 CKS PRC2/10/483
Reader, Richard, Boughton Monchelsea, Kent, 1619 CKS PRC2/19/98
Reader, Richard, Boughton Monchelsea, Kent, 1662 CKS PRC1/9/53
Reader, Richard, butcher, Canterbury Holy Cross Westgate, Kent, 1680 CKS PRC2/39/101
Reader, Robarte, Milton next Sittingbourne, Kent, 1614 CKS PRC2/18/53
Reader, Robert, clergy: 'clerk/parson', Wormshill, Kent, 1611 CKS PRC2/16/112
Reader, Robert, tanner, Faversham, Kent, 1664 CKS PRC1/10/79
Reader, Samuel, gentleman, Godmersham, Kent, 1677 CKS PRC20/12/219
Reader, Sara, widow, Frittenden, Kent, 1663 CKS PRC1/9/145
Reader, Thomas, gentleman, Hartlip, Kent, 1680 CKS PRC2/39/98
Reader, Warham, yeoman, Ulcombe, Kent, 1624 CKS PRC2/24/73
Reader, William, bachelor, Faversham, Kent, CKS PRC1/15/119
Reader, William, Lenham, Kent, 1600 CKS PRC2/11/267
Reader, William, Ulcombe, Kent, 1632 CKS PRC20/11/278
Reader, William, tanner, Faversham, Kent, 1671 CKS PRC2/35/81
Reader, William eld, Boughton Monchelsea, Kent, 1615 CKS PRC2/19/80
Reader, Wyllyam, Wormshill, Kent, 1594 CKS PRC2/7/133
Readheade, Chrofer, Luddington, Lincs, 1597 Lincs RO Ad/Ac/37/25
Reading, John, Leverton, Lincs, 1632 Lincs RO Ad/Ac/23/157
Reading, Samuel, Charing, Kent, 1688 CKS PRC20/13/605
Readinge, William, gentleman, Worcester, Worcs, 1593 Worcs RO 008.7 BA3585/838/107
Reads, Edward, butcher, New Romney, Kent, 1627 CKS PRC20/8/391

Reames, Robert, gentleman, Smeeth, Kent, 1614 CKS PRC20/3/59
Reames, Stephen, Canterbury All Saints, Kent, 1682 CKS PRC2/40/74
Reason, Edward, maltster, Faversham, Kent, 1672 CKS PRC2/35/166
Reason, John, Ewell, Kent, 1601 CKS PRC2/12/310
Reason, Thomas, husbandman, Bredgar, Kent, 1643 CKS PRC1/7/6
Rebecke, James, Wylye, Wilts, 1647 Wilts RO Arch. Sarum(+ name and date)
Recraft, Samuel, husbandman, Woodchurch, Kent, 1674 CKS PRC20/12/143
Reddatt, Richard, blacksmith, Reading St Lawrence, Berks, 1620 Berks RO D/A1/210/247C
Redding, John sen, St Giles without Cripplegate, London & Middlesex, 1668 PRO PROB5/1654
Reddinge, John, yeoman, Bucklebury, Berks, 1642 Berks RO D/A1/211/19C
Reddish, Ralph, Manchester, Lancs, 1596 Lancs RO (Name of Deceased) D.R.C.H. 1596
Rede, Philipp, Wendron, Corn, 1606 Cornwall RO AP/R71/4
Reder, William, Sutton by Dover, Kent, 1594 CKS PRC2/7/245
Redfeild, Thomas, Ashford, Kent, 1667 CKS PRC1/12/77
Redford, Edward, gentleman, Coleshill, Berks, 1669 Berks RO D/A1/211/41C
Redford, James, Sandwich, Kent, 1625 CKS PRC2/25/118
Redford, John, Dover, Kent, 1627 CKS PRC20/8/387
Redforde, Thomas, carpenter, Canterbury St Mary Northgate, Kent, 1619 CKS PRC2/19/70
Redgeway, John, Loose, Kent, 1668 CKS PRC19/4/27
Redman, Adam, Braceborough, Lincs, 1597 Lincs RO Ad/Ac/4/89
Redman, Adam, Tallington, Lincs, 1614 Lincs RO Ad/Ac/13/197
Redman, Benjamin, mariner: 'seaman', Milton next Sittingbourne, Kent, 1664 CKS PRC1/10/80
Redman, William, Bierton, Bucks, 1666 Oxon RO MSS Wills Pec 50/2/35
Redman/Mason, John, Stedham, Sussex, 1635 W. Suss RO EpI/33/1635/33
Redshawe, Thomas, Bicker, Lincs, 1612 Lincs RO Ad/Ac/11/141
Redsmyth, Oliver, cordwainer: 'shoemaker', Stamford St John Baptist, Lincs, 1666 Lincs RO Ad/Ac/32/91
Redsole, Thomas, Lympne, Kent, 1641 CKS PRC1/6/12
Redway, William, labouring man, Cookham, Berks, 1617 Berks RO D/A1/210/246C
Redwell, see Pescodd,
Redwood, John, St Peter in Thanet, Kent, 1683 CKS PRC20/13/366
Redwood, Margaret, Canterbury St Margaret, Kent, 1675 CKS PRC2/36/115
Redwood, Richard, yeoman/gentleman, Canterbury Holy Cross Westgate, Kent, 1668 CKS PRC1/13/103
Redwood, Robert, Herne, Kent, 1601 CKS PRC21/15/219
Reed, Catherine, widow, Sandhurst, Kent, 1683 CKS PRC2/40/146
Reed, Elizabeth,
Som 1619 Somerset RO D/D/Cta/R9
Reed, Robert, Manby, Lincs, 1632 Lincs RO Ad/Ac/23/26
Reede, Peter, Bickenhill, Warks, 1684 LJRO/B/C/5/1684/67
Reede, Thomas, Sandhurst, Kent, 1598 CKS PRC2/10/404
Reeder, William, labourer, Flixborough, Lincs, 1668 Lincs RO Ad/Ac/33/79
Reedinge, Thomas, Ridge, Herts, 1573 Herts RO ASA25/734
Reeks, Phillip, Dauntsey, Wilts, 1677 Wilts RO Miscellaneous Index (name + date)
Reene, Elizabeth, mrs, Westbere, Kent, 1641 CKS PRC1/6/13
Reene, Thomas eld, gentleman, Maidstone, Kent, 1623 CKS PRC20/6/274
Reeve, Agnes, widow, Queenborough, Kent, 1610 CKS PRC2/15/321
Reeve, Anne, Newcastle under Lyme, Staffs, 1675 LJRO:cards/1675/47
Reeve, Anthony, Christian Malford, Wilts, 1774 Wilts RO Arch. Wilts.(+ name and date)
Reeve, Edward, Frittenden, Kent, 1608 CKS PRC2/14/391
Reeve, Edward, farmer, Greasley (Kimberley), Notts, 1817 Borthwick Test C.P. 1817/1
Reeve, George, grocer, Milton next Sittingbourne, Kent, 1679 CKS PRC2/38/177
Reeve, Henry, Calne, Wilts, 1632 Wilts RO Miscellaneous Index (name + date)
Reeve, John, Tamerton, North, Corn, 1612 Cornwall RO AP/R189/3
Reeve, John, Sutton, Lincs, 1613 Lincs RO Ad/Ac/12/28

[Reeve:]
Reeve, John, Snave, Kent, 1616 CKS PRC2/19/71
Reeve, John, gentleman, Queenborough, Kent, 1617 CKS PRC2/19/79
Reeve, John, Basingstoke, Hants, 1624 Hants RO 21M65 D8/84
Reeve, John, Chipping Barnet, Herts, 1637 Herts RO ASA25/4944
Reeve, John, minor, Canterbury, Kent, 1645 CKS PRC19/2/103
Reeve, John, Staplehurst, Kent, 1664 CKS PRC1/10/81
Reeve, John, Ashford, Kent, 1684 CKS PRC2/40/240
Reeve, John, Painswick, Glos, 1696 GRO GDR/B4/2/R2
Reeve, John, cook, Oxford (Balliol College), Oxon, 1708 Bodleian HYP B9/71-72
Reeve, Jonathan, Griston, Norf, 1785 Norfolk RO ANW/23/26/61
Reeve, Richard, Claycoton, Northants, 1674 Northants RO NWill A/C/165
Reeve, Richard, Dauntsey, Wilts, 1677 Wilts RO Miscellaneous Index (name + date)
Reeve, Robert, Bremhill, Wilts, 1640 Wilts RO Arch. Wilts.(+ name and date)
Reeve, Sarah, widow, Yarmouth, Great, Norf, 1817 Norfolk RO ANW/23/27/19
Reeve, Thomas, Maidstone, Kent, 1625 CKS PRC20/7/259
Reeve, Thomas, carpenter, Lincoln St Swithin, Lincs, 1640 Lincs RO Ad/Ac/27/88
Reeve, Thomas, Ashford, Kent, 1681 CKS PRC2/39/226
Reeve, William, husbandman, Rickmansworth, Herts, 1694 Herts RO ASA25/4399
Reeve, see Everinge,
Reeves, John, Plaitford, Wilts, 1670 Wilts RO Arch. Sarum(+ name and date)
Reeves, Ralph, husbandman, Northbourne, Kent, 1695 CKS PRC2/42/108
Reeves, Robert, gentleman, Fittleton (Hacklestone), Wilts, 1626 Wilts RO Arch. Sarum(+ name and date)
Regimorter, Ahasuerus, Oxford (Wadham College), Oxon, 1673 Bodleian HYP B9/73-74
Reignolds, Anne, Ashford, Kent, 1606 CKS PRC2/15/347
Reignolds, Lawrence, Skirbeck, Lincs, 1598 Lincs RO Ad/Ac/4/79
Reignolds, Thomas, Deal, Kent, 1667 CKS PRC19/3/138
Reignolds, William, mariner, Sandwich St Clement, Kent, 1668 CKS PRC1/13/104
Reinold, Jane, widow, Westborough, Lincs, 1628 Lincs RO Ad/Ac/20b/70
Reinolds, Edward, labourer, Coningsby, Lincs, 1612 Lincs RO Ad/Ac/11/18
Relf, Roberte, Calceby, Lincs, 1579 Lincs RO Ad/Ac/2b/2
Rellinson, Roger, husbandman, Brothertoft, Lincs, 1620 Lincs RO Ad/Ac/16/82
Rellis, Elizabeth, Boston, Lincs, 1633 Lincs RO Ad/Ac/24/148
Rellis, Elizabeth, Boston, Lincs, 1633 Lincs RO Ad/Ac/24/158
Remington, Benjamine, Brox-Holme, Lincs, 1673 Lincs RO Ad/Ac/35/49
Remington, Georgetta, widow, Sleaford, New, Lincs, 1663 Lincs RO Ad/Ac/42/45
Remington, William, Torksey, Lincs, 1593 Lincs RO Ad/Ac/37/14
Remmington, Richard, Cranbrook, Kent, 1609 CKS PRC2/15/344
Remnant, Antony, Appledore, Kent, 1590 CKS PRC2/5/394
Remnant, John, Brenzett, Kent, 1684 CKS PRC2/40/237
Rendall, John, Creech St Michael (Ham), Som, Somerset RO D/D/Cta/R17
Reniger, Michaell, clergy: 'clerk', Ferriby, South, Lincs, 1635 Lincs RO Ad/Ac/24/417
Rennold, Roger, husbandman, Stickney, Lincs, 1618 Lincs RO Ad/Ac/14/172
Rennolds, Gyles, Bilsington, Kent, 1639 CKS PRC2/34/266
Renold, Jane, spinster, Leverton, Lincs, 1620 Lincs RO Ad/Ac/14/128
Renold, John, Winthorpe, Lincs, 1649 Lincs RO Ad/Ac/30/189
Renold, Mary, Camborne, Corn, 1609 Cornwall RO AP/R148/2
Renolds, Thomas, Stickney, Lincs, 1623 Lincs RO Ad/Ac/18/38
Renolds, Thomas, Ramsbury, Wilts, 1636 Wilts RO Miscellaneous Index (name + date)
Repington, Edward, esquire, Tamworth, Staffs, 1735 LJRO/B/C/5/1735/71
Repon, Thomas, Appledore, Kent, 1586 CKS PRC2/4/181
Restrope, Thomas, Swindon, Wilts, 1630 Wilts RO Arch. Wilts.(+ name and date)
Reve, John, victualler, Hythe St Leonard, Kent, 1675 CKS PRC20/12/144
Reve, Robert, Maidstone, Kent, 1609 CKS PRC20/1/342
Revell, William, Owston, Lincs, 1619 Lincs RO Ad/Ac/8b/343

Revell, William, Kirton, Lincs, 1632 Lincs RO Ad/Ac/23/57
Reye, Robert, Chislet, Kent, 1611 CKS PRC2/15/335
Reynard, John, bachelor, Shipley, Sussex, W. Suss RO EpI/33/1672/19
Reyner, John + Elizabeth, Egerton, Kent, 1570 CKS PRC21/1/104
Reynold, John, Sutton, Lincs, 1633 Lincs RO Ad/Ac/24/150
Reynold, John, wheelwright, Windsor, New, Berks, 1680 Berks RO D/A1/211/68C
Reynold, Thomas, Barton on Humber, Lincs, 1670 Lincs RO Ad/Ac/32/218
Reynolde, John, Bredhurst, Kent, 1596 CKS PRC21/14/69
Reynoldes, Thomas, Ashford, Kent, 1620 CKS PRC2/19/73
Reynolds, Alice, widow, Ashford, Kent, 1646 CKS PRC1/7/97
Reynolds, Catherine, widow, New Romney, Kent, 1683 CKS PRC20/13/370
Reynolds, Christopher, Wye, Kent, 1613 CKS PRC2/17/131
Reynolds, Daniel, Stone in Oxney, Kent, 1596 CKS PRC2/8/143
Reynolds, Daniel, Appledore, Kent, 1670 CKS PRC1/15/55
Reynolds, Francis, clergy: 'vicar', Crowle, Worcs, 1684 Worcs RO 008.7 BA3585/837/bdl 4
Reynolds, Henry, Tetworth (Everton), Hunts, 1676 Hunts RO/Acc58/24(194)
Reynolds, John, St Austell, Corn, 1640 Cornwall RO AP/R641
Reynolds, John, innholder, Derby, Derby, 1707 LJRO/B/C/5/1707/137
Reynolds, Margaret, widow, Boxford (Westbrook), Berks, Berks RO D/A1/211/27C
Reynolds, Richard, Burton-upon-Trent, Staffs, 1691 LJRO/B/C/5/1691/58
Reynolds, Robert, New Romney, Kent, 1679 CKS PRC20/12/320
Reynolds, Rowland, esquire, Rainham, Kent, 1641 CKS PRC19/2/32
Reynolds, Samuel, Longford (Rodsley), Derby, 1717 LJRO/B/C/5/1717/29b
Reynolds, Sara, mrs, Canterbury Christchurch, Kent, 1639 CKS PRC20/11/292
Reynolds, Thomas, yeoman, Boxford (Westbrook), Berks, Berks RO D/A1/211/28C
Reynolds, Thomas, yeoman, Rolvenden, Kent, 1639 CKS PRC1/3/37
Reynolds, Thomas, carpenter, Biddenden, Kent, 1669 CKS PRC1/14/96
Reynolds, Thomas, husbandman, Boothby, Lincs, 1671 Lincs RO Ad/Ac/33/194
Reynolds, Thomas, husbandman, Woodchurch, Kent, 1684 CKS PRC20/13/456
Reynolds, William, Maidstone, Kent, 1578 CKS PRC21/3/179
Reynolds, William, Appledore, Kent, 1615 CKS PRC20/3/196
Reynolds, William, Chart, Little, Kent, 1619 CKS PRC2/19/95
Reynolds, William, labourer, Ibstone, Oxon, 1675 Oxon RO MSS Wills 56/3/18
Reynolds/Ellis, Mary, widow, Milton next Sittingbourne, Kent, 1674 CKS PRC2/36/114
Reynton, Richard, gentleman, Sutton St James, Lincs, 1613 Lincs RO Ad/Ac/12/128
Reyson, John, Eastchurch, Sheppey, Kent, 1595 CKS PRC2/7/143
Rhodes, Robert, Hougham, Lincs, 1639? Lincs RO Ad/Ac/26/103
Ricarrd, Jeames, Canterbury St Mary Northgate, Kent, 1613 CKS PRC2/17/300
Rice, James Honeybun, St Marylebone (Queen Street, Edgeware Road), London & Middlesex, 1815 Greater London RO DL/C/575/122
Rice, Richard, baker, Stamford St John, Lincs, 1665 Lincs RO Ad/Ac/32/57
Rice, William, Brent, East, Som, 1590 Somerset RO D/D/Cta/R34
Rice, William, Bawdrip, Som, 1612 Somerset RO D/D/Cta/R12
Rich, Charles, 1693 PRO PROB32/35/356
Rich, James, yeoman, Staplehurst, Kent, 1690 CKS PRC2/41/183
Rich, John, husbandman, Bethersden, Kent, 1681 CKS PRC2/39/230
Rich, Joseph, Dover, Kent, 1626 CKS PRC20/7/251
Rich, Nicholas, Sutton St James, Lincs, 1605 Lincs RO Ad/Ac/6/5
Rich, Robert, Tunstall, Kent, 1637 CKS PRC2/33/113
Rich, Robert, yeoman, Bethersden, Kent, 1666 CKS PRC1/11/149
Rich/Ashby, Dorothy, Milton next Sittingbourne, Kent, 1675 CKS PRC2/36/232
Richard, Alexander, Camborne, Corn, 1611 Cornwall RO AP/R166/2
Richard, John, Shelford, Worcs, 1605 Worcs RO 008.7 BA3585/839/332b
Richard, Nowell, St Buryan, Corn, 1644 Cornwall RO AP/DSB/6/2
Richardby, Jane, spinster, Hirsel, Berwick, 1841 Borthwick Test C.P. 1841/2

[Richardes:]
Richardes, William, Barfreston, Kent, 1600 CKS PRC2/10/2
Richards, Edward, Cound, Shrops, 1674 LJRO:cards/1674/41
Richards, Elizabeth, mrs/widow, Goodnestone next Wingham, Kent, 1679 CKS PRC20/12/319
Richards, George, Dover, Kent, 1631 CKS PRC20/9/359
Richards, George, Stapleford, Leics, 1685 Leics RO Administrators Accounts 1682-86 f44a
Richards, Herbert, clergy: 'rector', Aldington, Kent, 1680 CKS PRC20/13/56
Richards, Isaac, Netherbury, Dors, 1679 Wilts RO Dean Sarum (name + date)
Richards, John,
Worcs Worcs RO 008.7 BA3585/834/442
Richards, John, Boxley, Kent, 1639 CKS PRC2/34/262
Richards, John, Boxley, Kent, 1639 CKS PRC2/34/267
Richards, Jonathan, St George, London & Middlesex, 1749 Greater London RO DL/C/551/115
Richards, Joseph, Lyminster, Sussex, 1650 W. Suss RO EpI/33/1649/4
Richards, Margery, widow, Lambourn (East Hanney), Berks, 1618 Berks RO D/A1/210/248C
Richards, Richard, Cocking, Sussex, 1669 W. Suss RO EpI/33/1669/10
Richards, Richard, Isleworth, London & Middlesex, 1759 Greater London RO DL/C/554/104/2
Richards, Thomas, Brent, East, Som, 1623 Somerset RO D/D/Cta/R4
Richards, Thomas, Kenilworth, Warks, 1678 LJRO:cards/1678/21
Richards, Thomas, Selborne, Hants, 1679 Hants RO 21m65 D8/295
Richards, Thomas, Kenilworth, Warks, 1683 LJRO/B/C/5/1685/88
Richards, Thomas, yeoman, Kenilworth, Warks, 1686 LJRO/B/C/5/1686/42
Richards, William, Minster in Sheppey, Kent, 1610 CKS PRC2/15/325
Richards, William, clergy: 'clerk', St Mary in the Marsh, Kent, 1617 CKS PRC2/19/74
Richards, William, St Clement Danes, London & Middlesex, 1744 Greater London RO AM/PI pt (uncatalogued)
Richards/Richardson, Averil, spinster, Pershore Holy Cross, Worcs, 1779 Worcs RO 008.7 BA3585/835/bdl 2
Richards/Rudyard, Joseph, yeoman, Ashbourne (High Finnis), Derby, 1770 LJRO/B/C/5/1770/186
Richardson, Aaron, fellmonger, King's Lynn, Norf, 1783 Norfolk RO ANW/23/26/56
Richardson, Adam, Chislet, Kent, 1611 CKS PRC2/16/108
Richardson, Arthur, miller, Headcorn, Kent, 1623 CKS PRC2/24/64
Richardson, Catherine, Laughton, Lincs, 1642 Lincs RO Ad/Ac/41/158
Richardson, Christopher, victualler, Shoreditch St Leonard, London & Middlesex, 1691 PRO PROB32/30/278
Richardson, Daniel, innholder/mr, Canterbury St Margaret, Kent, 1669 CKS PRC1/13/105
Richardson, Edward, Theddlethorpe All Saints, Lincs, 1670 Lincs RO Ad/Ac/32/159
Richardson, Edward, bachelor, Scothorne, Lincs, 1682 Lincs RO Ad/Ac/44/12
Richardson, Frances, widow, Woodhall, Lincs, 1631 Lincs RO Ad/Ac/23/103
Richardson, Francis, Halton, West, Lincs, 1626 Lincs RO Ad/Ac/39/152
Richardson, Francis, Woodstock, Oxon, 1675 Oxon RO MSS Wills 299/7/57
Richardson, George, husbandman, Bonby, Lincs, 1662 Lincs RO Ad/Ac/32/16
Richardson, Henry, Bromfield, Kent, 1619 CKS PRC2/19/86
Richardson, Hugh, Northorpe, Lincs, 1597 Lincs RO Ad/Ac/37/39
Richardson, Jeffery, labourer, Minster in Sheppey, Kent, 1642 CKS PRC1/6/80
Richardson, John, university: 'Master of Trinity College, Cambridge/Regius, Professor of Divinity' Cambridge (Trinity College), Cambs, CUL V.C. Acc./Box2/66
Richardson, John, Biddenden, Kent, 1626 CKS PRC2/27/144
Richardson, John, Ingoldmels, Lincs, 1632 Lincs RO Ad/Ac/23/71
Richardson, John, Reculver, Kent, 1635 CKS PRC20/11/254
Richardson, John, Grantham, Lincs, 1636 Lincs RO Ad/Ac/24/557
Richardson, John, Bytham, Castle, Lincs, 1646 Lincs RO Ad/Ac/28/90
Richardson, John, Stainton le Vale, Lincs, 1649 Lincs RO Ad/Ac/30/150
Richardson, John, clergy: 'clerk/M.A.', Cambridge St Benedict, Cambs, 1650 CUL V.C. Acc./Box3/40
Richardson, John, Frisby on the Wreake, Leics, 1673 Leics RO Administrators Accounts 1667-72

f105
Richardson, John, bricklayer, Chislet, Kent, 1675 CKS PRC2/36/
Richardson, John, Blackwell, Derby, 1684 LJRO/B/C/5/1683/17
Richardson, Mary, widow, Reculver, Kent, 1642 CKS PRC19/2/64
Richardson, Mary, Brookland, Kent, 1675 CKS PRC2/36/231
Richardson, Mercye, widow, St Johns Thanet, Kent, 1615 CKS PRC2/19/64
Richardson, Nicholas, Belton, Lincs, 1624 Lincs RO Ad/Ac/39/157
Richardson, Nicolas, Sandwich, Kent, 1617 CKS PRC2/19/82
Richardson, Purbeck, university: 'Fellow of Trinity College, Cambridge/Esquire, Bedell' Cambridge (Trinity College), Cambs, 1684 CUL V.C. Acc./Box3/41
Richardson, Richard, Charing, Kent, 1610 CKS PRC20/2/83
Richardson, Richard, Kirmington, Lincs, 1626 Lincs RO Ad/Ac/20/84
Richardson, Robart, Charing, Kent, 1605 CKS PRC20/1/63
Richardson, Thomas, Glentworth, Lincs, Lincs RO Ad/Ac/2b/33
Richardson, Thomas, Canterbury, Kent, 1631 CKS PRC20/9/357
Richardson, Thomas, Wootton, Lincs, 1662 Lincs RO Ad/Ac/32/41
Richardson, Thomas, husbandman, Chadlington, Oxon, 1678 Oxon RO MSS Wills 172/5/9
Richardson, Vincent, Calceby, Lincs, 1638 Lincs RO Ad/Ac/25/294
Richardson, William, Theddlethorpe, Lincs, 1568 Lincs RO Ad/Ac/2C/167
Richardson, William, Immingham, Lincs, 1620 Lincs RO Ad/Ac/15/131
Richardson, William, gentleman, Sandwich, Kent, 1622 CKS PRC2/24/67
Richardson, William, Boston, Lincs, 1628 Lincs RO Ad/Ac/22/71
Richardson, William, Minster in Sheppey, Kent, 1641 CKS PRC1/5/29
Richardson, William, butcher, Gosberton, Lincs, 1679 Lincs RO Ad/Ac/43/115
Richardson, see Jollands & Richards,
Riche, Henrye, clothier, Biddenden, Kent, 1607 CKS PRC2/14/378
Riches, widow, Belaugh, Norf, 1706 Norfolk RO ANW/23/6/10
Richinson, Josua, Belton, Lincs, 1636 Lincs RO Ad/Ac/40/79
Richman, Ambrose, clergy: 'mr' 'clerk', Wye, Kent, 1643 CKS PRC1/7/7
Richman, John, Swineshead, Lincs, 1639 Lincs RO Ad/Ac/26/70
Richman, William, gentleman, Lydiard Tregoze, Wilts, 1675 Wilts RO Arch. Wilts.(+ name and date)
Richmond, James, glazier, Milton next Sittingbourne, Kent, 1685 CKS PRC2/41/8
Richmond, John, St Clement Danes, London & Middlesex, 1715 Greater London RO AM/PP/Box 1720-1723 pt (uncatalogued)
Richmond, Richard, Warminster, Wilts, 1637 Wilts RO Arch. Sarum(+ name and date)
Richmund, John, labourer, Toynton, Lincs, 1627 Lincs RO Ad/Ac/20b/48
Rickard, Elizabeth, widow, Cranbrook, Kent, 1668 CKS PRC1/13/106
Rickard, John, Wittersham, Kent, 1603 CKS PRC21/16/81
Rickard, John + Alice, Smarden, Kent, 1596 CKS PRC2/8/280
Rickard, Samuell, Stone in Oxney, Kent, 1623 CKS PRC2/24/69
Rickard, Thomasine, Snargate, Kent, 1611 CKS PRC2/15/359
Rickard, William, Snargate, Kent, 1603 CKS PRC2/14/392
Rickard, William, Woodchurch, Kent, 1671 CKS PRC20/12/28
Rickard/Tresteyne, Adam, St Columb Major, Corn, 1606 Cornwall RO AP/T108/3
Rickarde, William, Snargate, Kent, 1595 CKS PRC2/7/195
Rickards, Joane, widow, Appledore, Kent, 1639 CKS PRC1/3/38
Rickett, Thomas, farrier, Fillingham, Lincs, 1683 Lincs RO Ad/Ac/44/31
Rickett, William, Owmby by Spital, Lincs, 1678 Lincs RO Ad/Ac/35/127
Ricketts, Edward, yeoman, Bampton (Cote), Oxon, 1678 Oxon RO MSS Wills 56/4/13
Ricketts, Robert, Charlton, Wilts, 1633 Wilts RO Arch. Sarum(+ name and date)
Ricketts, William, bachelor, Pershore St Andrew, Worcs, 1781 Worcs RO 008.7 BA3585/835/bdl 2
Rickford, John, Bersted, South, Sussex, 1648 W. Suss RO EpIV/10/2A/7
Rickford, see Upton,

[Ricquebourq:]
Ricquebourq, Nathaniel, merchant, Dover, Kent, 1682 CKS PRC20/13/196
Riddle, Francis, Staplehurst, Kent, 1636 CKS PRC2/33/120
Rider, George, yeoman, Chislet, Kent, 1619 CKS PRC2/19/94
Rider, Joane, Herne, Kent, 1619 CKS PRC20/4/330
Rider, Thomas, Wickhambreaux, Kent, 1685 CKS PRC2/41/7
Rider, William, mercer, Reading St Lawrence, Berks, 1594 Berks RO D/A1/210/211C
Rider, William, Aldbourne, Wilts, 1627 Wilts RO Arch. Wilts.(+ name and date)
Ridge, Hellen, widow, Welby, Lincs, 1637 Lincs RO Ad/Ac/25/618
Ridge, John, Bicknoller, Som, 1639 Somerset RO D/D/Cta/R1
Ridge, Thomas, Sellindge, Kent, 1596 CKS PRC2/8/33
Ridgly, Alice, Stoughton, Leics, 1672 Leics RO Administrators Accounts 1667-72 f77
Ridgway, Dionis, Maidstone, Kent, 1596 CKS PRC21/14/181
Ridgway, James, Cranbrook, Kent, 1596 CKS PRC2/8/499
Ridgway, Thomas, Ibstock, Leics, 1685 Leics RO Administrators Accounts 1682-86 f34
Ridley, George, Gosberton, Lincs, 1680 Lincs RO Ad/Ac/43/93
Ridon, Hugh, Burnham, Som, 1623 Somerset RO D/D/Cta/R3
Riedell, John, Glentham, Lincs, 1679 Lincs RO Ad/Ac/42/79
Rigat, John, Littlehampton, Sussex, 1600 W. Suss RO EpI/33/1600/11
Rigby, Gilbert, clergy: 'clerk', Standish, Lancs, 1590 Lancs RO (Name of Deceased) D.R.C.H. 1590
Rigby, Richard, Stainfield, Lincs, 1664 Lincs RO Ad/Ac/43/44
Rigby, Samuel, gentleman, Chester, Ches, 1774 Cheshire RO (Name) W.C. 1775
Rigden, Edmund, Eythorne, Kent, 1617 CKS PRC2/19/90
Rigden, Edward, yeoman, St Nicholas at Wade, Kent, 1678 CKS PRC20/12/280
Rigden, Henry, New Romney, Kent, 1627 CKS PRC20/7/146
Rigden, Henry, blacksmith, Graveney, Kent, 1677 CKS PRC2/37/194
Rigden, Joane, widow, Lyminge, Kent, 1632 CKS PRC20/9/345
Rigden, Johanna, widow, Minster in Thanet, Kent, 1715 CKS PRC1/17/80
Rigden, John, Throwleigh, Kent, 1626 CKS PRC2/27/148
Rigden, John, Selling, Kent, 1679 CKS PRC2/38/62
Rigden, Mary, widow, Chilham, Kent, 1628 CKS PRC2/29/77
Rigden, Mathew, yeoman, Petham, Kent, 1642 CKS PRC1/6/14
Rigden, Nicholas, St Nicholas at Wade, Kent, 1676 CKS PRC20/12/220
Rigden, Nicholas, yeoman, Minster in Thanet, Kent, 1686 CKS PRC2/41/76
Rigden, Roger, Barham, Kent, 1592 CKS PRC2/6/111
Rigden, Stephen, fellmonger, Milton next Sittingbourne, Kent, 1707 CKS PRC1/16/69
Rigden, Thomas, yeoman, Mersham, Kent, 1662 CKS PRC1/9/54
Rigden, Thomas, bachelor: 'singleman', Hinxhill, Kent, 1677 CKS PRC2/37/191
Rigden, Thomas, yeoman, Elmsted, Kent, 1683 CKS PRC2/40/71
Rigden, William, St Johns Thanet, Kent, 1582 CKS PRC21/5/246 and 245
Rigden, William, Throwleigh, Kent, 1621 CKS PRC2/24/68
Rigden, see Penvell,
Rigdon, Thomas, Wickhambreaux, Kent, 1601 CKS PRC2/12/312
Rigdon, William, Bekesbourne, Kent, 1595 CKS PRC2/7/131
Rigdon, Willyam eld, Elham, Kent, 1589 CKS PRC2/4/507
Rige, William, Lydd, Kent, 1584 CKS PRC21/7/66
Riggs, Charles, Newcastle under Lyme, Staffs, 1676 LJRO:cards/1676/42
Riggs, Jane, widow, High Halstow, Kent, 1671 CKS PRC2/35/85
Riggs, Jeffery, mariner: 'seaman', High Halstow, Kent, 1668 CKS PRC1/12/78
Righton, Edward, yeoman, Potter Hanworth, Lincs, 1624 Lincs RO Ad/Ac/19A/117
Righton, Mathew, Spilsby, Lincs, 1669 Lincs RO Ad/Ac/33/100
Rigley, Henrie, yeoman, Middleton (Hopwood), Lancs, 1661 Lancs RO (Name of Deceased) D.R.C.H. 1661
Rignell, Richard, Stanton, Fen, Hunts, 1685 Hunts RO/Acc58/249(256)
Riley, Henry, gentleman, Upton Lovell, Wilts, 1647 Wilts RO Arch. Sarum(+ name and date)

Riley, Martha, widow, Halifax (Slithero), Yorks, 1795 Borthwick Test C.P. 1794/8
Riley, Thomas, innkeeper, Halifax (Ovenden), Yorks, 1794 Borthwick Test C.P. 1794/13
Riley, William, gentleman, Knook, Wilts, 1687 Wilts RO Dean Sarum (name + date)
Rilie, William, Christian Malford, Wilts, 1617 Wilts RO Arch. Wilts.(+ name and date)
Rime, John, Hinton Waldrist, Berks, 1608 Berks RO D/A1/210/233C
Rimell, James, Brailes, Warks, 1684 Worcs RO 008.7 BA3585/837/bdl 4
Ring, Andrew, Patching, Sussex, 1627 W. Suss RO EpIV/10/1/22
Ring, Edward, Bishopstone, Wilts, 1615 Wilts RO Miscellaneous Index (name + date)
Ring, Isaac, vintner, Marlborough, Wilts, 1677 Wilts RO CC Sarum(+ name and date)
Ring, Joseph, potter, Bristol Temple, Glos, Bristol RO 1804/CP
Ring, Thomas, mercer, Maidenhead, Berks, 1637 Berks RO D/A1/112/99C
Ringborow, Richard, Ripton, Kings, Hunts, 1692 Hunts RO/Acc58/275
Ringe, John, Cumnor, Berks, 1616 Berks RO D/A1/210/241C
Ringe, Thomas, Hemswell, Lincs, 1622 Lincs RO Ad/Ac/39/71
Ringe, William, mercer, Maidenhead, Berks, 1640 Berks RO D/A1/211/16C
Ripingale, John, Faversham, Kent, 1599 CKS PRC2/11/81
Ripley, Francis, gentleman, Ingham, Lincs, 1677 Lincs RO Ad/Ac/35/122
Ripon, Richard, Marden, Kent, 1627 CKS PRC2/28/100
Rippen, John, Tenterden, Kent, 1609 CKS PRC2/15/349
Ripper, William, barber, Berkhamsted St Peter, Herts, 1641 Herts RO AHH23/1985
Rippington, Margaret, St Johns Thanet, Kent, 1606 CKS PRC2/13/323
Rippington, Nicholas, Canterbury St Andrew, Kent, 1598 CKS PRC2/9/437
Rippon, William, Biddenden, Kent, 1631 CKS PRC2/31/58
Risbridger/Sawyer, John, Chichester, Sussex, 1620 W. Suss RO EpIV/10/1/37
Risby, William, Hernhill, Kent, 1685 CKS PRC20/13/523
Risdale, Mary, widow, Lydd, Kent, 1618 CKS PRC20/4/328
Rise, Faldingworth, Lincs, 1594 Lincs RO Ad/Ac/5/507
Riseing, John, farmer, Witchingham, Great, Norf, Norfolk RO ANW/23/24/89
Risinge, Willyam, Boston, Lincs, 1641 Lincs RO Ad/Ac/27/270
Ritch, John, Lydford, East, Som, 1635 Somerset RO D/D/Cta/R6
Ritch, Richard, Boughton Malherbe, Kent, 1606 CKS PRC20/1/162
Rivers, John, Kintbury, Berks, 1625 Wilts RO CC Sarum(+ name and date)
Rllerby, William + Hellen, Belshford, Lincs, 1623 Lincs RO Ad/Ac/19A/131
Roach, William, haulier, Bristol St John, Glos, Bristol RO 1738/20
Road, Edward, Goudhurst, Kent, 1640 CKS PRC1/5/30
Roades, Ann, widow, Brookland, Kent, 1626 CKS PRC2/27/139
Roades, Dorothy, widow, Climping (Atherington), Sussex, 1685 W. Suss RO EpI/33/1684/43
Roades, Edmund, Goudhurst, Kent, 1669 CKS PRC1/14/97
Roades, Henry, Climping, Sussex, 1670 W. Suss RO EpI/33/1669/18
Roades, Nicholas, Normanby, Lincs, 1633 Lincs RO Ad/Ac/40/89
Roades, Robert, Sandwich, Kent, 1601 CKS PRC2/12/314
Roades, Thomas, gentleman, Leek (Bradshaw), Staffs, 1682 LJRO/B/C/5/1681/31
Roak, Thomas, Privett, Hants, 1600 Hants RO 1599 AD48/2
Roalfe, George, Monks Horton, Kent, 1621 CKS PRC2/24/66
Roanes, Anne, Metheringham, Lincs, 1624 Lincs RO Ad/Ac/19A/102
Robart, William, Linkinhorne, Corn, 1613 Cornwall RO AP/R194/2
Robartes, Elizabeth, widow, Sandwich, Kent, 1610 CKS PRC2/15/357
Robartes, Henry, Blean, Kent, 1592 CKS PRC2/6/216
Robartes, Joane, Canterbury, Kent, 1597 CKS PRC2/9/443
Robartes, John, Goudhurst, Kent, 1615 CKS PRC2/19/87
Robartes, Richarde, Bapchild, Kent, 1596 CKS PRC2/9/183
Robartes, Roger, Maidstone, Kent, 1594 CKS PRC21/12/346
Robarts, William, Bapchild, Kent, 1610 CKS PRC2/15/323
Robbens, Francis, yeoman, Lydd, Kent, 1673 CKS PRC20/12/98
Robbins, Walcot, Som, Somerset RO D/D/Cta/R8

[Robbins:]
Robbins, Andrew, St Thomas Isle of Harty, Kent, 1686 CKS PRC2/41/79
Robbins, Anthony, Dover, Kent, 1625 CKS PRC20/7/255
Robbins, Charles, Chedworth, Glos, 1784 GRO GDR/B4/2/R48
Robbins, Francis, Lydd, Kent, 1638 CKS PRC20/11/240
Robbins, John, Lydd, Kent, 1634 CKS PRC20/11/284
Robbins, Robert, yeoman, Ardington, Berks, 1663 Berks RO D/A1/211/37C
Robbins, Thomas, cordwainer, Boughton under Blean, Kent, 1665 CKS PRC19/3/81
Robbins, William, Ruckinge, Kent, 1634 CKS PRC2/32/104
Robbinson, Edward, labourer, Scotter, Lincs, 1628 Lincs RO Ad/Ac/39/1
Robbinson, Thomas, Bapchild, Kent, 1680 CKS PRC2/39/102
Robbinson, William, Horbling (Bridgend), Lincs, 1637 Lincs RO Ad/Ac/25/426
Robbyns, Nicholas, Sutton, Lincs, 1619 Lincs RO Ad/Ac/15/173
Roberds, Elizabeth, widow, Ashford, Kent, 1663 CKS PRC1/9/146
Robert, Claude, Canterbury, Kent, 1596 CKS PRC2/8/228
Robert, Michael, Sithney, Corn, 1611 Cornwall RO AP/R167/3
Robert, Richard, Barrow on Humber, Lincs, 1611 Lincs RO Ad/Ac/10/123
Robertes, John, clergy: 'vicar', Cassington, Oxon, 1547 Oxon RO MSS Wills 179 f217
Robertes, John, Ferring, Sussex, 1671 W. Suss RO Ep1/33/1671/14
Robertes, Richard, St Peter in Thanet, Kent, 1599 CKS PRC2/10/317
Robertes, Thomas, husbandman, Latton, Wilts, 1627 Wilts RO Arch. Wilts.(+ name and date)
Roberts, Alexander, Staplehurst, Kent, 1617 CKS PRC2/19/65
Roberts, Alice, Deal, Kent, 1625 CKS PRC20/7/263
Roberts, Ann, widow, Madeley, Staffs, 1746 LJRO/B/C/5/1746/344
Roberts, Christopher, St Laurence Thanet, Kent, 1597 CKS PRC2/10/36
Roberts, Drayton, gentleman, Canterbury St Dunstan Without, Kent, 1715 CKS PRC1/17/81
Roberts, Edward, Sandwich St Peter, Kent, 1610 CKS PRC2/15/353
Roberts, George, Botus Fleming, Corn, 1614 Cornwall RO AP/R206/3
Roberts, George, Bottesford, Lincs, 1650s? Lincs RO Ad/Ac/40/183
Roberts, Gilber, Owston, Lincs, 1663 Lincs RO Ad/Ac/41/98
Roberts, Henry, Bytham, Castle, Lincs, 1641 Lincs RO Ad/Ac/27/269
Roberts, Henry, husbandman, Shellingford, Berks, 1678 Berks RO D/A1/211/61C
Roberts, Henry eld, maltster, Maidstone, Kent, 1674 CKS PRC20/12/142
Roberts, Howell, New Romney, Kent, 1668 CKS PRC19/4/28
Roberts, Hugh, St Martin in the Fields, London & Middlesex, Greater London RO AM/CP/Box 1671-1728 pt (uncatalogued)
Roberts, John, St Peter in Thanet, Kent, 1627 CKS PRC2/27/145
Roberts, John, yeoman, Linkinhorne, Corn, 1647 Cornwall RO AP/R742/3
Roberts, John, husbandman, Thatcham, Berks, 1663 Berks RO D/A1/113/12C
Roberts, John, Overstone, Northants, 1672 Northants RO NWill A/C/121
Roberts, John, Bradford on Avon, Wilts, 1678 Wilts RO Arch. Sarum(+ name and date)
Roberts, John, Iwade, Kent, 1687 CKS PRC2/41/77
Roberts, John eld, Kennington, Kent, 1626 CKS PRC2/27/140
Roberts, John eld, yeoman, Iwade, Kent, 1670 CKS PRC1/15/56
Roberts, Leonard, Deal, Kent, 1622 CKS PRC20/6/272
Roberts, Mary, minor: 'infant', Maidstone, Kent, 1683 CKS PRC20/13/368
Roberts, Mathewe, Goudhurst, Kent, 1609 CKS PRC2/15/348
Roberts, Michael, degrees: 'D.D.', Oxford (University), Oxon, 1679 Bodleian HYP B9/75-76
Roberts, Richard, St Columb Minor, Corn, 1606 Cornwall RO AP/R60/2
Roberts, Richard, Rickmansworth, Herts, 1638 Herts RO ASA25/4961
Roberts, Richard, esquire, Thorpe Langton, Leics, 1666 Leics RO Administrators Accounts C17th f65
Roberts, Robert, husbandman, Marden, Kent, 1669 CKS PRC1/13/107
Roberts, Samuel, mercer, Derby, Derby, 1667 LJRO:cards/1667/64
Roberts, Sara, widow, Ashford, Kent, 1637 CKS PRC2/33/115
Roberts, Stephen, clergy: 'clerk', Dinton, Wilts, 1615 Wilts RO Miscellaneous Index (name +

date)
Roberts, Stephen, St Peter in Thanet, Kent, 1626 CKS PRC2/27/138
Roberts, Susann, Orlestone, Kent, 1671 CKS PRC20/12/29
Roberts, Thomas, Leeds, Yorks, Borthwick Test C.P. 1733/8
Roberts, Thomas, Elvaston, Derby, 1663 LJRO:cards/1663/52
Roberts, Thomas, Shawbury (Besford), Shrops, 1675 LJRO:cards/1675/48
Roberts, Thomas, baker, Canterbury Holy Cross Westgate, Kent, 1675 CKS PRC2/36/230
Roberts, Thomas, St George Hanover Square, London & Middlesex, 1726 Greater London RO AM/PP/Box 1726-1732 pt (uncatalogued)
Roberts, Thomas, clergy: 'clerk/mr', Worcester St Peter the Great, Worcs, 1736 Worcs RO 008.7 BA3585/836/bdl 2
Roberts, Walbreche, Sandwich, Kent, 1597 CKS PRC2/10/57
Roberts, William, Charley, Leics, 1669 Leics RO Administrators Accounts 1667-72 f22
Roberts, William, Youlgreave, Derby, 1684 LJRO/B/C/5/1684/68
Roberts, William, Malvern, Great, Worcs, 1685 Worcs RO 008.7 BA3585/837/bdl 4
Roberts, William, Cheltenham, Glos, 1717 GRO GDR/B4/2/R44
Roberts, William, gentleman, Cheltenham, Glos, 1717 GRO GDR/B4/2/R44
Roberts, William eld, husbandman, Bisham, Berks, 1627 Berks RO D/A1/210/257C
Roberts/Butler, Giles, Bytham, Castle, Lincs, 1624 Lincs RO Ad/Ac/19A/64
Roberts/Millard, John, Canterbury Christchurch, Kent, 1617 CKS PRC20/4/262
Roberts/Robinson, Thomas, labourer, Forest Hill, Oxon, 1637 Oxon RO MSS Wills 172/4/38
Roberts/Sye, John, husbandman, Ruan Lanihorne, Corn, 1614 Cornwall RO AP/R222/2
Roberts, see Joyner,
Robins, Edward, Tenterden, Kent, 1603 CKS PRC2/14/394
Robins, John, Dover, Kent, 1598 CKS PRC21/14/536
Robins, John, Hutton, Som, 1666 Somerset RO D/D/Cta/R15
Robins, John, blacksmith, Abingdon, Berks, 1679 Berks RO D/A1/211/65C
Robins, John, mariner, Sandwich, Kent, 1679 CKS PRC2/38/178
Robins, Richard, Sandwich, Kent, 1617 CKS PRC2/19/81
Robins, Richard, yeoman, Tintagel, Corn, 1621 Cornwall RO AP/R339/2
Robins, Richard, yeoman, Mollington, Oxon, 1681 Oxon RO MSS Wills Pec 50/3/2
Robins, Richard, Kingston Seymour, Som, 1706 Somerset RO D/D/Cta/R23
Robins, Thomas, Hythe West, Kent, 1611 CKS PRC2/17/418
Robins, Thomas, Warehorne, Kent, 1613 CKS PRC2/17/138
Robins, Thomas, Meare, Som, 1646 Somerset RO D/D/Cta/R13
Robins, Thomas, Sarre, Kent, 1712 CKS PRC19/6/58
Robins, William, Bathwick, Som, 1592 Somerset RO D/D/Cta/R20
Robins/Idlei, Thomsin, Dover, Kent, 1588 CKS PRC21/9/221
Robins/Robinson, John, Swingfield, Kent, 1626 CKS PRC2/27/143
Robinson, Adam, gentleman, Boston, Lincs, 1612 Lincs RO Ad/Ac/11/79
Robinson, Ambrose, Fosdyke, Lincs, 1614? Lincs RO Ad/Ac/13/207
Robinson, Anne, Leake, Lincs, 1627 Lincs RO Ad/Ac/20b/2
Robinson, Anne, Leake, Lincs, 1627 Lincs RO Ad/Ac/20b/3
Robinson, Anne, Owersby, Lincs, 1632 Lincs RO Ad/Ac/23/55
Robinson, David, Aisthorpe (Thorpe in the Fallows), Lincs, 1662 Lincs RO Ad/Ac/41/74
Robinson, David, Aisthorpe (Thorpe in the Fallows), Lincs, 1662 Lincs RO Ad/Ac/41/159
Robinson, Edward, yeoman, Wigtoft, Lincs, 1618 Lincs RO Ad/Ac/14/262
Robinson, Edward, blacksmith, Barham, Kent, 1622 CKS PRC2/24/70
Robinson, Edward, weaver, Chester, Ches, 1666 Cheshire RO (Name) W.C. 1666
Robinson, Elianor, spinster, St Martin in the Fields, London & Middlesex, 1700 PRO PROB32/41/92
Robinson, Ellin, widow, Kirkham (Freckleton), Lancs, 1628 Lancs RO (Name of Deceased) D.R.C.H. 1626-28
Robinson, George, Thurlby, Lincs, 1607 Lincs RO Ad/Ac/7/115
Robinson, George, Marston, Lincs, 1627 Lincs RO Ad/Ac/20b/105

[Robinson:]
Robinson, Gregorie, yeoman, Sutton, Long, Lincs, 1634 Lincs RO Ad/Ac/24/254
Robinson, Henrie, Owersby, Lincs, 1615 Lincs RO Ad/Ac/13/82
Robinson, Henry, Orlestone, Kent, 1599 CKS PRC2/11/95
Robinson, Hugh, Westbourne, Sussex, 1606 W. Suss RO EpI/33/1605/2
Robinson, Izaichar, Owersby, Lincs, 1606 Lincs RO Ad/Ac/7/121
Robinson, Joane,
Kent 1599 CKS PRC2/11/17
Robinson, Joane, Norton, Bishop, Lincs, 1649 Lincs RO Ad/Ac/42/42
Robinson, John, Sidlesham, Sussex, W. Suss RO EpI/33/1612/9
Robinson, John, Wrawby, Lincs, 1598 Lincs RO Ad/Ac/4/57
Robinson, John, Alvingham, Lincs, 1605 Lincs RO Ad/Ac/6/4
Robinson, John, Herne, Kent, 1616 CKS PRC20/3/379
Robinson, John, New Romney, Kent, 1619 CKS PRC20/4/334
Robinson, John, Hundleby, Lincs, 1623 Lincs RO Ad/Ac/19A/72
Robinson, John, Sandwich, Kent, 1638 CKS PRC2/34/261
Robinson, John, husbandman, Leckhamstead, Berks, 1638 Berks RO D/A1/211/10E
Robinson, John, Pinchbeck, Lincs, 1639 Lincs RO Ad/Ac/25/69
Robinson, John, Saxilby, Lincs, 1639 Lincs RO Ad/Ac/40/278
Robinson, John, Langtoft, Lincs, 1648 Lincs RO Ad/Ac/30/344
Robinson, John, husbandman, Gosberton, Lincs, 1650 Lincs RO Ad/Ac/29/93
Robinson, John, Althorpe (Amcotts), Lincs, 1662 Lincs RO Ad/Ac/41/35
Robinson, John, Waddingham, Lincs, 1669 Lincs RO Ad/Ac/33/167
Robinson, John, webster, Kinnard's Ferry, Lincs, 1671 Lincs RO Ad/Ac/33/208
Robinson, John, Newcastle under Lyme, Staffs, 1682 LJRO/B/C/5/1681/32
Robinson, John, yeoman, Kelsey, South, Lincs, 1684 Lincs RO Ad/Ac/44/55
Robinson, John, widower, Ardington, Berks, 1691 Berks RO D/A1/211/85C
Robinson, John, slater, Mottram in Longdendale, Ches, 1765 Cheshire RO (Name) W.C. 1765-6
Robinson, John, clergy: 'reverend', Coates, Great, Lincs, 1790 Lincs RO Ad/Ac/45/57
Robinson, Laurence, Asterby, Lincs, 1612 Lincs RO Ad/Ac/11/112
Robinson, Margaret, widow, Hucking, Kent, 1614 CKS PRC20/3/57
Robinson, Margaret, Scotter, Lincs, 1629 Lincs RO Ad/Ac/40/43
Robinson, Mary, widow, Herne, Kent, 1633 CKS PRC20/11/282
Robinson, Mary, widow, Muskham, North (Muskham Villa), Notts, 1839 Borthwick Test C.P. 1839/5
Robinson, Michael, Stockton-on-Tees, Dur, 1734 Borthwick Test C.P. 1734/7
Robinson, Peter, husbandman, Womersley, Yorks, 1788 Borthwick Test C.P. 1787/9
Robinson, Richard, Sturry, Kent, 1611 CKS PRC2/15/351
Robinson, Robert, Potter Hanworth, Lincs, 1612 Lincs RO Ad/Ac/11/142
Robinson, Robert, Mumby, Lincs, 1613 Lincs RO Ad/Ac/12/67
Robinson, Robert, Alkborough, Lincs, 1619 Lincs RO Ad/Ac/8b/403
Robinson, Robert, Bottesford (Burringham), Lincs, 1619 Lincs RO Ad/Ac/8b/372
Robinson, Robert, Epworth, Lincs, 1673 Lincs RO Ad/Ac/35/63
Robinson, Robert, Owston, Lincs, 1683 Lincs RO Ad/Ac/44/29
Robinson, Stephen, Broughton, Brant, Lincs, 1633 Lincs RO Ad/Ac/24/191
Robinson, Thomas, Sandwich St Clement, Kent, 1580 CKS PRC2/1/293
Robinson, Thomas, Owston, Lincs, 1634 Lincs RO Ad/Ac/40/73
Robinson, Thomas, Grimsby, Great, Lincs, 1639 Lincs RO Ad/Ac/26/22
Robinson, Thomas, Thornton, Lincs, 1645 Lincs RO Ad/Ac/28/131
Robinson, Thomas, Willoughton, Lincs, 1670 Lincs RO Ad/Ac/33/155
Robinson, Thomas, St Mary in the Marsh, Kent, 1672 CKS PRC2/35/167
Robinson, Thomas, yeoman, Radley, Berks, 1672 Berks RO D/A1/211/58C
Robinson, Thomas, Deal, Kent, 1696 CKS PRC19/5/49
Robinson, Thomas, shopkeeper, Malton, New, Yorks, 1783 Borthwick Test C.P. 1783/4
Robinson, Timothy, Hammersmith, London & Middlesex, PRO PROB32/15/109
Robinson, William, Owersby, Lincs, 1627 Lincs RO Ad/Ac/20b/34

Robinson, William, Mimms, North, Herts, 1637 Herts RO AHH23/1979
Robinson, William, Epworth, Lincs, 1640 Lincs RO Ad/Ac/40/256
Robinson, William, Braunstone, Leics, 1641 Leics RO PR/I/41A/70
Robinson, William, Empingham, Rut, 1668 Lincs RO Ad/Ac/42/44
Robinson, William, Wroot, Lincs, 1669 Lincs RO Ad/Ac/33/163
Robinson/Peirce, Robert, Sutton Benger, Wilts, 1629 Wilts RO Arch. Wilts.(+ name and date)
Robinson, see Bigland, Roberts & Robins,
Robinsonne, Nicholas, Warehorne, Kent, 1613 CKS PRC2/16/148
Robotham, Benjamin, cordwainer, Dover, Kent, 1683 CKS PRC20/13/283
Robotham, John, All Hallows The Great, London & Middlesex, Greater London RO AM/PP/Box 1739-1749 pt (uncatalogued)
Robotham, Robert, Hanbury (Stubby Lane), Staffs, 1673 LJRO:cards/1673/8
Robotham, Robert, Cranbrook, Kent, 1699 CKS PRC2/42/158
Robson, Edward, Gainsborough (Morton), Lincs, 1683 Lincs RO Ad/Ac/44/32
Robson, John, Gainsborough (Morton), Lincs, 1607 Lincs RO Ad/Ac/37/240
Robson, Leonard, Pinchbeck, Lincs, 1634 Lincs RO Ad/Ac/24/48
Robson, Peter, Bottesford, Lincs, 1614 Lincs RO Ad/Ac/8b/17
Robson, Robert, Covenham St Bartholomew, Lincs, 1637 Lincs RO Ad/Ac/25/551
Robson, Ruth, Scarcliffe, Derby, 1682 LJRO/B/C/5/1682/86
Robson, Simon, Chichester, Sussex, 1620 W. Suss RO EpIII/9/1/20
Robson, Thomas, Gainsborough, Lincs, 1617 Lincs RO Ad/Ac/8b/278
Robson, Thomas, Bottesford (Burringham), Lincs, 1624 Lincs RO Ad/Ac/8c/101
Robus, Elizabeth, spinster, Hythe St Leonard, Kent, 1664 CKS PRC19/3/59
Robus, Reginald, yeoman, Kenardington, Kent, 1644 CKS PRC1/7/8
Robus, Thomas, weaver, Sellindge, Kent, 1678 CKS PRC2/37/193
Robyns, John, Dover, Kent, 1581 CKS PRC21/5/140
Robyns, Thomas, Dover, Kent, 1581 CKS PRC21/5/107
Robyns, Thomas, Chart nr Sutton Valence, Kent, 1613 CKS PRC2/16/121
Robyns, Walter, Lanlivery, Corn, 1623 Cornwall RO AP/R351/2
Robyns, William, Capel le Ferne, Kent, 1596 CKS PRC2/8/272
Robyns, see Smith,
Robynson, Hughe, miller, New Romney, Kent, 1587 CKS PRC21/8/324
Robynson, William, Canterbury Holy Cross Westgate, Kent, 1606 CKS PRC2/14/388
Robynson, Wylliam, Faversham, Kent, 1586 CKS PRC2/4/98
Roche, William, clergy: 'clerk', Stickford, Lincs, 1620 Lincs RO Ad/Ac/15/129
Roche, see Rogers,
Rochester, Elizabeth, countess dowager, 1692 PRO PROB32/32/366
Rochester, John, tanner, Steyning, Sussex, 1614 W. Suss RO EpI/33/1613/1
Rochfoorthe, Symon, Milton next Sittingbourne, Kent, 1593 CKS PRC2/6/23
Rock, Henrie, Breamore, Hants, 1624 Hants RO 21M65 D8/85
Rocke, Thomas, Swinford, Old (Stourbridge), Worcs, 1647 Worcs RO 008.7 BA3585/837/bdl 1
Rocke, Thomas, Baltonsborough, Som, 1667 Somerset RO D/D/Cta/R14
Rockins, John, Faversham, Kent, 1626 CKS PRC1/1/37
Rockins, John, mariner, Faversham, Kent, 1637 CKS PRC1/1/57
Rockley, John, husbandman, Winkfield, Berks, 1663 Berks RO D/A1/211/32C
Rockley, Thomas, Harmston, Lincs, 1620 Lincs RO Ad/Ac/15/127
Rockrey, Alice, widow, Faversham, Kent, 1619 CKS PRC2/19/88
Rocliffe, James, Stallingborough, Lincs, 1636 Lincs RO Ad/Ac/24/92
Rodes, Anthonie, Brookland, Kent, 1625 CKS PRC2/25/117
Rodes, Henry, Scarcliffe, Derby, 1684 LJRO/B/C/5/1683/18
Rodes, James, Whitechapel, London & Middlesex, 1713 PRO PROB32/57/67
Rodes, Thomas, clothier, Cranbrook, Kent, 1669 CKS PRC1/14/98
Rodes, see Lewkmer,
Rodford, John, carrier, Glastonbury St John, Som, 1612 Somerset RO D/D/Cta/R32
Rodgers, Thomas, whitesmith, Chesterfield, Derby, 1785 LJRO/B/C/5/1785/78

[Rodgers:]
Rodgers, William, yeoman, Crowle, Lincs, 1669 Lincs RO Ad/Ac/33/157
Rodway/Legg, William, Limpley Stoke, Wilts, 1621 Wilts RO Miscellaneous Index (name + date)
Rodweye, John, Wellow, Som, 1644 Somerset RO D/D/Cta/H62
Roe, Ann, spinster, Ilkeston, Derby, 1752 LJRO/B/C/5/1752/237
Roe, John, baker, Kettering, Northants, 1671 Northants RO NWill A/C/116
Roe, John, yeoman, Dean, West (East Grimstead), Wilts, 1681 Wilts RO Arch. Sarum(+ name and date)
Roe, Thomas, Wrockwardine, Shrops, 1681 LJRO/B/C/5/1681/33
Roe, William, gentleman, Budworth, Great (Hartford), Ches, 1668 Cheshire RO (Name) W.C. 1668
Roe, William, husbandman, Dean, West (East Grimstead), Wilts, 1685 Wilts RO Arch. Sarum(+ name and date)
Roffe, Richard, Ripton, Kings, Hunts, 1687 Hunts RO/Acc58/268(265)
Rogeir, Bartholomew, Canterbury St Mary Northgate, Kent, 1679 CKS PRC2/38/176
Roger, John, Scotton, Lincs, 1612 Lincs RO Ad/Ac/8b/12
Roger, Nowall, Helston, Corn, 1614 Cornwall RO AP/R209/3
Rogers, Agnes, Sandwich St Clement, Kent, 1640 CKS PRC1/5/31
Rogers, Edmund, Gainsborough, Lincs, 1618 Lincs RO Ad/Ac/8b/169
Rogers, Edward, baker, Salisbury, Wilts, 1737? Wilts RO CC Sarum(+ name and date)
Rogers, Elizabeth, widow, Cranbrook, Kent, 1626 CKS PRC2/27/142
Rogers, Elizabeth, widow, Staughton, Great, Hunts, 1676 Hunts RO/Acc58/61(125)
Rogers, Gabriell, Faversham, Kent, 1623 CKS PRC2/24/63
Rogers, George, innholder, Woodstock, Oxon, 1675 Oxon RO MSS Wills 299/7/55
Rogers, Henry, butcher, Stratford-upon-Avon, Warks, Worcs RO 008.7 BA3585/838/128
Rogers, Henry, Marton, Lincs, 1612 Lincs RO Ad/Ac/8b/5
Rogers, Henry, Donhead St Andrew, Wilts, 1690 Wilts RO Arch. Sarum(+ name and date)
Rogers, James, Ruckinge, Kent, 1625 CKS PRC2/25/122
Rogers, Jasper, Hothfield, Kent, 1632 CKS PRC2/31/150
Rogers, John,
Som 1594 Somerset RO D/D/Cta/R10
Rogers, John, Weston, Som, 1594 Somerset RO D/D/Cta/R30
Rogers, John, Ruckinge, Kent, 1609 CKS PRC2/15/337
Rogers, John, Wyberton, Lincs, 1612 Lincs RO Ad/Ac/10/150
Rogers, John, glazier, Lenham, Kent, 1681 CKS PRC2/39/228
Rogers, John, bachelor, Chieveley, Berks, 1684 Berks RO D/A1/211/71C
Rogers, John, innholder, Deal, Kent, 1684 CKS PRC20/13/454
Rogers, John, university: 'President of Magdalen College, Oxford/D.D.', Oxford (Magdalen College), Oxon, 1704 Bodleian HYP B9/77-78
Rogers, John, shopkeeper, Hampton in Arden, Warks, 1762 LJRO/B/C/5/1762/81
Rogers, Margaret, spinster, Kingston Bagpuize, Berks, 1612 Berks RO D/A1/210/239C
Rogers, Mathew, Donington, Lincs, 1627 Lincs RO Ad/Ac/20b/33
Rogers, Peter, mariner, Dover, Kent, 1677 CKS PRC20/12/239
Rogers, Peter, Leaveland, Kent, 1697 CKS PRC2/42/135
Rogers, Richard, Doulting, Som, 1588 Somerset RO D/D/Cta/R33
Rogers, Robert, Banbury, Oxon, 1619 Oxon RO MSS Wills Pec 50/2/1
Rogers, Stephen, Hayling, North, Hants, Hants RO 1592 AD87/3
Rogers, Stephen, mariner, Bristol St Stephen, Glos, Bristol RO 1764/CP
Rogers, Stephen, Wymering, Hants, 1624 Hants RO 21M65 D8/36
Rogers, Thomas, Canterbury St Alphege, Kent, 1593 CKS PRC21/12/80
Rogers, Thomas, Claverdon, Warks, 1602 Worcs RO 008.7 BA3585/838/262
Rogers, Thomas, Woodchurch, Kent, 1604 CKS PRC21/16/83
Rogers, Thomas, Ringwould, Kent, 1625 CKS PRC2/25/120
Rogers, Thomas, coachman, Dover, Kent, 1675 CKS PRC20/12/181
Rogers, Thomas, Hayling, North, Hants, 1693 Hants RO 21m65 D8/360
Rogers, William, mercer, Stratford-upon-Avon, Warks, 1597 Worcs RO 008.7 BA3585/838/126

[Rogers:]

Rogers, William, Cranbrook, Kent, 1636 CKS PRC2/33/117
Rogers, William, Camel, West, Som, 1708 Somerset RO D/D/Cta/R19
Rogers, William, farmer, Shocklach (Caldecot), Ches, 1776 Cheshire RO (Name) W.C. 1776
Rogers, William sen, Heyford, Upper, Northants, 1674 Northants RO NWill A/C/140
Rogers/Cooper, Richard, Salisbury, Wilts, 1614 Wilts RO Miscellaneous Index (name + date)
Rogers/Marner, William, Farnborough, Hants, 1661 Hants RO 21M65 D8/146
Rogers/Roche, Griffin, Linton, Kent, 1617 CKS PRC2/19/91
Rogerson, Philip, Legbourne, Lincs, 1618 Lincs RO Ad/Ac/14/202
Roiston, Thomas, Thanington, Kent, 1613 CKS PRC2/17/247
Roles, Reynold, shepherd, Waterperry, Oxon, 1628 Oxon RO MSS Wills 85/2/36
Rolf, Christian, Hougham, Kent, 1602 CKS PRC2/14/398
Rolf, George, Wittersham, Kent, 1584 CKS PRC21/7/1
Rolf, Robert, Barnet, East, Herts, 1565 Herts RO ASA25/605
Rolf, Wyllyam, Wootton, Kent, 1587 CKS PRC2/4/257
Rolfe, Lavington, Wilts, 1616 Wilts RO Unlisted Fragment
Rolfe, Ann, Newington next Hythe, Kent, 1640 CKS PRC1/5/32
Rolfe, David, Minster in Thanet, Kent, 1600 CKS PRC2/11/259
Rolfe, Elias, Staplehurst, Kent, 1592 CKS PRC2/5/396
Rolfe, George, Snargate, Kent, 1617 CKS PRC2/19/78
Rolfe, George, yeoman, Chislet, Kent, 1682 CKS PRC2/40/73
Rolfe, Joan, Rickmansworth, Herts, 1613 Herts RO ASA25/4813
Rolfe, John, Lympne, Kent, 1610 CKS PRC2/15/345
Rolfe, John, clothier, Staplehurst, Kent, 1664 CKS PRC1/9/147
Rolfe, John, bricklayer, Canterbury St Mildred, Kent, 1676 CKS PRC2/37/87
Rolfe, Richard, Throwleigh, Kent, 1666 CKS PRC1/11/73
Rolfe, Richard, Ivychurch, Kent, 1709 CKS PRC19/6/39
Rolfe, Robert, Barnet, East, Herts, 1567 Herts RO ASA25/632
Rolfe, Robert, Acrise, Kent, 1635 CKS PRC2/33/116
Rolfe, Thomas, Tenterden, Kent, 1598 CKS PRC2/9/441
Rolfe, Thomas, Acrise, Kent, 1640 CKS PRC1/1/58
Rolfe, Thomas,
Kent 1677 CKS PRC2/37/190
Rolfe, William Isaac, gunmaker, Birmingham, Warks, 1818 LJRO/B/C/5/1818/32b
Roll, William, Holbeach, Lincs, 1619 Lincs RO Ad/Ac/15/219
Roll, Willyam, Kirton, Lincs, 1600 Lincs RO Ad/Ac/5/74
Rolleston, Alexander, Breedon on the Hill (Staunton Harold), Leics, 1665 Leics RO Administrators Accounts C17th f29
Rollison, Dollis, silver plater, Sheffield, Yorks, 1803 Borthwick Test C.P. 1803/10
Rolph, Henry, yeoman, Folkestone, Kent, 1672 CKS PRC2/35/168
Rolph, Mary, Lyminge, Kent, 1629 CKS PRC20/8/385
Rolph, Sara, widow, Selling, Kent, 1620 CKS PRC2/19/96
Rolph, Stephen, yeoman, Folkestone, Kent, 1630 CKS PRC20/9/355
Rolph, Thomas, pumpmaker, Bristol, Glos, Bristol RO 1752/29
Rolph, Thomas, Barham, Kent, 1624 CKS PRC2/24/74
Rolt, John, Abbots Ripton, Hunts, 1684 Hunts RO/Acc58/218(223)
Roman, Thomas, Thorney, West, Sussex, 1630 W. Suss RO EpI/33/1630/13
Romeley, Robert, Crowle, Lincs, 1683 Lincs RO Ad/Ac/44/18
Romforth, John, Fishtoft, Lincs, 1614 Lincs RO Ad/Ac/13/57
Romney, Alice, Sholden, Kent, 1677 CKS PRC2/37/195
Romney, Francis eld, gentleman, Milton next Sittingbourne, Kent, 1668 CKS PRC1/13/108
Romney, John, gentleman, Milton next Sittingbourne, Kent, 1641 CKS PRC19/1/76
Romsey, John, hosier, Marlborough, Wilts, 1595? Wilts RO CC Sarum(+ name and date)
Romyn, John, Hayling, North, Hants, Hants RO 1600 AD48/2
Romyn, Richard, Thorney, West, Sussex, 1594 W. Suss RO EpI/33/1594/12
Ronzee, Lodowick, Ashford, Kent, 1641 CKS PRC19/2/34

[Rood:]
Rood, George, Street, Som, 1665 Somerset RO D/D/Cta/R16
Rook, Thomas, Ivythorn, Som, 1730 Somerset RO D/D/Cta/R21
Rook, Thomas, shopkeeper, Cave, North, Yorks, 1804 Borthwick Test C.P. 1804/15
Rooke, Edward, yeoman, Lenham, Kent, 1681 CKS PRC2/39/99
Rooke, Elizabeth, spinster, Stalisfield, Kent, 1677 CKS PRC2/37/192
Rooke, Henry, Staplehurst, Kent, 1617 CKS PRC2/19/92
Rooke, John, Hartlip, Kent, 1666 CKS PRC1/11/150
Rooke, Katherine, widow, Coates, Sussex, 1624 W. Suss RO EpI/33/1624/5
Rooke, Lawrence, gentleman, Monks Horton, Kent, 1613 CKS PRC2/17/63
Rooke, Mary, widow, Ospringe, Kent, 1634 CKS PRC2/32/168
Rooke, Richard, Theddlethorpe St Helen, Lincs, 1671 Lincs RO Ad/Ac/33/185
Rooke, Robart, St Nicholas at Wade, Kent, 1600 CKS PRC21/16/133
Rooke, Saul, Folkingham, Lincs, 1650 Lincs RO Ad/Ac/29/117
Rooke, Stephen, Stone next Faversham, Kent, 1681 CKS PRC2/39/95
Rooke, Thomas, St Nicholas at Wade, Kent, 1589 CKS PRC21/9/264
Rooke, Thomas, Chislet, Kent, 1597 CKS PRC2/9/257
Rooke, Thomas, Normanton, Lincs, 1614 Lincs RO Ad/Ac/13/58
Rooke, William, Mumby, Lincs, 1595 Lincs RO Ad/Ac/5/254
Rooke, William, yeoman, Kintbury, Berks, 1640 Berks RO D/A1/211/13C
Rooke, William, gentleman, Petham, Kent, 1645 CKS PRC1/7/60
Rooke, William, gentleman, Petham, Kent, 1647 CKS PRC1/7/98
Rookes, Francis, Boston, Lincs, 1649 Lincs RO Ad/Ac/30/233
Rookes, Richard, husbandman, Elmlode, Worcs, Worcs RO 008.7 BA3585/838/213
Roote, Richard, Frampton, Lincs, 1642 Lincs RO Ad/Ac/28/19
Rootes, Edward, Ashford, Kent, 1614 CKS PRC2/18/118
Rootes, Richard, butcher, Frampton, Lincs, 1636 Lincs RO Ad/Ac/24/328
Roper, Christopher, peer, Linsted, Kent, 1676 CKS PRC2/37/85
Roper, Edward, husbandman, Bucklebury, Berks, Berks RO D/A1/111/99C
Roper, Edward, husbandman, Upchurch, Kent, 1663 CKS PRC1/9/56
Roper, George, weaver, Carlton Scroop, Lincs, 1666 Lincs RO Ad/Ac/32/114
Roper, Isabell, widow, Rodmersham, Kent, 1638 CKS PRC2/34/111
Roper, Jeames, Teynham, Kent, 1619 CKS PRC2/19/66
Roper, Jerman, gentleman, Sittingbourne, Kent, 1613 CKS PRC2/18/89
Roper, John, Sandwich St Peter, Kent, 1637 CKS PRC2/34/112
Roper, Margaret, widow, Thame, Oxon, 1635 Oxon RO MSS Wills Pec 50/2/21
Roper, Markes, Sandhurst, Kent, 1607 CKS PRC2/14/385
Roper, Michael, Stone next Faversham, Kent, 1628 CKS PRC2/29/76
Roper, Raynold, Rolvenden, Kent, 1626 CKS PRC20/7/160
Roper, Reignolde, Biddenden, Kent, 1592 CKS PRC2/5/398
Roper, William, Candlesby, Lincs, 1599 Lincs RO Ad/Ac/5/531
Roper, William, yeoman, Harrietsham, Kent, 1681 CKS PRC2/39/96
Roper, William, Harrietsham, Kent, 1683 CKS PRC1/15/104
Roper, see Cheyney,
Rose, Abraham, Hastingleigh, Kent, 1629 CKS PRC2/29/73
Rose, Adam, Harbledown, Kent, 1621 CKS PRC2/19/75
Rose, Agnes, widow, Brothertoft, Lincs, 1606 Lincs RO Ad/Ac/7/111
Rose, Ambrose, Chislet, Kent, 1606 CKS PRC2/13/327
Rose, Ambrose ygr, yeoman, Chislet, Kent, 1619 CKS PRC2/19/84
Rose, Ambrose ygr, yeoman, Chislet, Kent, 1640 CKS PRC1/5/33
Rose, Andrew, St Laurence Thanet, Kent, 1598 CKS PRC2/9/439
Rose, Anthonye, yeoman, Gosberton, Lincs, 1646? Lincs RO Ad/Ac/28/192
Rose, Christopher, Hernhill, Kent, 1611 CKS PRC20/2/276
Rose, Edward, Tonge, Kent, 1645 CKS PRC1/7/61
Rose, Edward, Coventry, Warks, 1672 LJRO:cards/1672/48
Rose, Edward, gentleman, Chislet, Kent, 1677 CKS PRC2/37/84

[Rose:]

Rose, Edward, yeoman, Shrivenham (Becket), Berks, 1691 Berks RO D/A1/211/84C
Rose, Francis, widower, Lympne, Kent, 1680 CKS PRC2/39/100
Rose, Harry, gentleman, Marlborough, Wilts, 1768 Wilts RO CC Sarum(+ name and date)
Rose, Henry, Reculver, Kent, 1624 CKS PRC20/6/156
Rose, Henry, tailor, Wardington (Williamscot), Oxon, 1629 Oxon RO MSS Wills Pec 50/2/15
Rose, Henry, roller of metals, Aston, Warks, 1830 LJRO/B/C/5/1830/30
Rose, James, Burmington, Warks, Worcs RO 008.7 BA3585/839/315
Rose, James ygr, yeoman, Chislet, Kent, 1617 CKS PRC20/3/374
Rose, Jervace, Chislet, Kent, 1603 CKS PRC2/12/456
Rose, Joane, Reculver, Kent, 1675 CKS PRC20/12/180
Rose, John, yeoman, Shepherdswell alias Sibertswold, Kent, 1592 CKS PRC2/6/13
Rose, John, Moulton, Lincs, 1620 Lincs RO Ad/Ac/16/81
Rose, John, Chislet, Kent, 1630 CKS PRC2/30/118
Rose, John, Chislet, Kent, 1645 CKS PRC1/7/62
Rose, John, mariner: 'seaman', Littlehampton, Sussex, 1678 W. Suss RO EpI/33/1678/12
Rose, John, bailiff, Moreton, South, Berks, 1695 Berks RO D/A1/211/93C
Rose, John, clergy: 'clerk/rector', Screveton, Notts, 1781 Borthwick Chanc C.P. 1781/1
Rose, Mary, widow, Amberley, Sussex, 1676 W. Suss RO EpI/33/1676/5
Rose, Peter, Boughton Monchelsea, Kent, 1633 CKS PRC2/32/109
Rose, Richard, mercer, Kencott, Oxon, 1681 Oxon RO MSS Wills 85/3/28
Rose, Robert, tailor, Stainton, Market, Lincs, 1607 Lincs RO Ad/Ac/8a/33
Rose, Robert, Herne, Kent, 1631 CKS PRC20/9/351
Rose, Roberte, Cockerington, South, Lincs, 1593 Lincs RO Ad/Ac/3/59
Rose, Symon, mr, Fordwich, Kent, 1636 CKS PRC2/33/114
Rose, Thomas, Newington next Sittingbourne, Kent, 1614 CKS PRC2/18/79
Rose, Thomas, Warehorne, Kent, 1626 CKS PRC2/27/134
Rose, Thomas, bachelor, Poling, Sussex, 1684 W. Suss RO EpI/33/1684/29
Rose, Thomas eld, Chislet, Kent, 1617 CKS PRC2/19/83
Rose, see Upperton,
Rosewarne, Thomas, gentleman, Gwinear, Corn, 1621 Cornwall RO AP/R321/2
Rosier/Hooper, Richard, Cliffe Pypard, Wilts, 1623 Wilts RO Arch. Wilts.(+ name and date)
Rosse, George, Crowle, Lincs, 1674 Lincs RO Ad/Ac/35/71
Rosse, Gilbert, Dover St James, Kent, 1609 CKS PRC20/1/358
Rosse, Gregory, Brothertoft, Lincs, 1648 Lincs RO Ad/Ac/30/378
Rosse, John, Sutton St Edmunds, Lincs, 1633 Lincs RO Ad/Ac/24/77
Rosse, John, cooper, Dover, Kent, 1641 CKS PRC19/2/33
Rosse, Robert, Donington, Lincs, 1637 Lincs RO Ad/Ac/25/589
Rossell, Thomas, farmer, Sandiacre, Derby, 1796 LJRO/B/C/5/1796/162
Rosseter, George, Keddington, Lincs, 1627 Lincs RO Ad/Ac/20b/54
Rossiter, Marie, widow, Keddington, Lincs, 1627 Lincs RO Ad/Ac/20b/73
Rosson, see Rawson,
Rossworm, colonel,
Glos Bristol RO 1677/55
Rosveare, Nicholas, Bodmin, Corn, 1612 Cornwall RO AP/R196/2
Rotheram, Thomas, Lea Marston, Warks, 1683 LJRO/B/C/5/1682/87
Rothwell, George, carpenter, Wispington, Lincs, 1671 Lincs RO Ad/Ac/33/177
Rothwell, James, joiner, Leyland, Lancs, 1680 Lancs RO (Name of Deceased) D.R.C.H. 1680
Rothwell, Margrett, Pinchbeck, Lincs, 1640 Lincs RO Ad/Ac/27/78
Rothwell, Richard, gentleman, Ewerby, Lincs, 1622 Lincs RO Ad/Ac/17/27
Rothwell, Thomas, Pinchbeck, Lincs, 1640 Lincs RO Ad/Ac/27/62
Rothwell, Thomas, miller, Gisburn, Yorks, 1803 Borthwick Test C.P. 1803/5
Rougan, Jane, Holbeach, Lincs, 1636 Lincs RO Ad/Ac/25/588
Roughley, Robert, Prescot (Tarbock), Lancs, 1650 Lancs RO (Name of Deceased) D.R.C.H. 1649
Roughton, Elizabeth, Coningsby, Lincs, 1662 Lincs RO Ad/Ac/45/98
Rouke, Thomas, Toynton St Peter, Lincs, 1611 Lincs RO Ad/Ac/10/44

[Rouland/Bisshoppe:]
Rouland/Bisshoppe, Robert, Sotwell, Berks, 1617 Berks RO D/A1/112/20D
Roundtree, Ralph, clergy: 'mr/clerk', Leysdown, Kent, 1670 CKS PRC1/14/99
Rouse, Agnis, Lydd, Kent, 1580 CKS PRC21/4/122
Rouse, Henry,
 Som Somerset RO D/D/Cta/R11
Rouse, John, Quadring, Lincs, 1640 Lincs RO Ad/Ac/27/181
Rouse, John, Sutton Valence, Kent, 1681 CKS PRC2/39/224
Rouse, John, Canterbury, Kent, 1712 CKS PRC19/6/47
Rouse, Thomas, baker, Deddington, Oxon, 1676 Oxon RO MSS Wills 85/3/21
Rouse, William, innholder, Lenham, Kent, 1695 CKS PRC2/42/89
Row, Isaack, Ash next Sandwich, Kent, 1639 CKS PRC20/11/290
Row, Simon, mariner: 'ship captain', Stepney, London & Middlesex, 1692 PRO PROB32/32/385
Rowbotham, Sarah, Yoxall, Staffs, 1685 LJRO/B/C/5/1685/89
Rowcliff, Thomas, clergy: 'clerk', Hardington, Som, 1738 Somerset RO D/D/Cta/R18
Rowden, Allen, Langford, Steeple, Wilts, 1619 Wilts RO Miscellaneous Index (name + date)
Rowe, Frances, widow, Donington, Lincs, 1627 Lincs RO Ad/Ac/20b/101
Rowe, John, Rainham, Kent, 1594 CKS PRC2/7/365
Rowe, John, Taunton St Mary Magdalan, Som, 1594 Somerset RO D/D/Cta/R25
Rowe, John, Milton next Sittingbourne, Kent, 1633 CKS PRC2/31/149
Rowe, Peter, Truro, Corn, 1634 Cornwall RO AP/R543/3
Rowe, Richard, Werrington, Corn, 1613 Cornwall RO AP/R210
Rowe, Robert, St Breward, Corn, 1633 Cornwall RO AP/R544/2
Rowe, Roger, Sandwich St Peter, Kent, 1595 CKS PRC2/7/173
Rowe, Thomas, husbandman, Upchurch, Kent, 1647 CKS PRC1/8/27
Rowe, William, Redbourn, Herts, 1595 Herts RO ASA25/1524
Rowe, William, Horwood, Little, Bucks, 1631 Herts RO ASA25/4879
Rowebothome, Richard, tailor, Trowbridge, Wilts, 1635? Wilts RO Misc. Wills Bk.6
Rowell, John, Hogsthorpe, Lincs, 1620 Lincs RO Ad/Ac/16/80
Rowell, Robert, Stanground, Hunts, 1685 Hunts RO/Acc58/246(240)
Roweth, Thomas, labourer, Swineshead, Lincs, 1670 Lincs RO Ad/Ac/32/178
Rowland, George, Lincoln St Martin, Lincs, 1640 Lincs RO Ad/Ac/26/102
Rowland, Richard, fisherman, Bisham, Berks, 1623 Berks RO D/A1/210/252
Rowland, Richard, husbandman, Speen, Berks, 1635 Berks RO D/A1/211/7C
Rowland, Thomas, Sparsholt, Berks, 1612 Berks RO D/A1/210/240D
Rowland, Thomas, yeoman, Sparsholt, Berks, 1662 Berks RO D/A1/211/34C
Rowld, Johnne, Gedney, Lincs, 1593 Lincs RO Ad/Ac/3/31
Rowle, Elizabeth, widow, Fiskerton, Lincs, 1685 Lincs RO Ad/Ac/44/163
Rowleright, Thomas, yeoman, Wolford, Great, Warks, 1684 Worcs RO 008.7 BA3585/837/bdl 4
Rowlett, Thomas, Monkton, Kent, 1623 CKS PRC20/6/270
Rowley, Elizabeth, widow, Betley, Staffs, 1816 LJRO/B/C/5/1816/38
Rowley, John, clothier, Worcester St Andrew, Worcs, Worcs RO 008.7 BA3585/839/425
Rowley, John, yeoman, Elmsall, North (South Elmsall), Yorks, Borthwick Test C.P. 1756/5
Rowley, Rowley, widow, Audley (Knowle Bank), Staffs, 1813 LJRO/B/C/5/1813/90b
Rowlie, Edmund,
 Som 1625 Somerset RO D/D/Cta/T10a
Rowlie, Edmund, Meare, Som, 1625 Somerset RO D/D/Cta/R5
Rowlinson, John, Lymm, Ches, 1788 Cheshire RO (Name) W.C. 1788
Rowndo, Robert, Wye, Kent, 1594 CKS PRC2/7/325
Rowne, John, husbandman, Cranbrook, Kent, 1671 CKS PRC2/35/84
Roworth, John, husbandman, Heddington, Lincs, 1684 Lincs RO Ad/Ac/44/126
Rowsberry, Elizabeth, Sandwich St Bartholomew's Hospital, Kent, 1620 CKS PRC20/5/168
Rowse, Edward, Old Romney, Kent, 1614 CKS PRC2/18/112
Rowse, Richard, St Columb Major, Corn, 1613 Cornwall RO AP/R185/3
Rowse, Richarde, Otham, Kent, 1597 CKS PRC2/9/263
Rowse, Robert, yeoman, Weston, Lincs, 1614 Lincs RO Ad/Ac/13/145

Rowse, Thomas, Hale, Great (Little Hale), Lincs, 1611 Lincs RO Ad/Ac/10/79
Rowson, William, Goodnestone next Faversham, Kent, 1668 CKS PRC1/13/109
Rowswell, Thomas, Dunkerton, Som, 1603 Somerset RO D/D/Cta/R29
Rowthe, Christopher, Sausthorpe, Lincs, 1618 Lincs RO Ad/Ac/14/96
Roy, capper, Worcester, Worcs, Worcs RO 008.7 BA3585/834/451
Royall, William, St Albans, Herts, 1632 Herts RO ASA25/4880
Royce, Richard, glover, Oxford, Oxon, Oxon RO MSS Wills 172/4/46
Roydon, John, Wingham, Kent, 1602 CKS PRC21/16/35
Royne, Robert, St Albans St Stephens, Herts, 1613 Herts RO ASA25/4801
Royse, Frances, widow, Maidstone, Kent, 1686 CKS PRC20/13/571
Royston, James, yeoman, Blackwell, Derby, 1793 LJRO/B/C/5/1793/48
Royston, Thomas, innholder, Leeds, Yorks, 1779 Borthwick Test C.P. 1779/10
Ruck, Francis, Faversham, Kent, 1710 CKS PRC1/17/39a
Ruck, Francis, Faversham, Kent, 1711 CKS PRC1/17/39
Ruck, John, Boughton under Blean, Kent, 1639 CKS PRC20/11/268
Ruck, John, Cranbrook, Kent, 1643 CKS PRC19/2/77
Ruck, Thomas, Lower Hardres, Kent, 1638 CKS PRC2/34/264
Ruck, William, Boughton under Blean, Kent, 1590 CKS PRC21/10/162
Rucke, Arthur, brother, Sandwich St Bartholomew's Hospital, Kent, 1628 CKS PRC20/8/399
Rucke, Arthur, Godmersham, Kent, 1674 CKS PRC20/12/97
Rucke, Bartholomewe, Borden, Kent, 1612 CKS PRC2/16/59
Rucke, Daniel, yeoman, Chartham, Kent, 1663 CKS PRC1/9/148
Rucke, Edward, Hythe St Leonard, Kent, 1612 CKS PRC20/2/336
Rucke, Edward, brewer, Hythe St Leonard, Kent, 1675 CKS PRC20/12/182
Rucke, John, Cranbrook, Kent, 1622 CKS PRC20/5/164
Rucke, John, yeoman, Lympne, Kent, 1685 CKS PRC2/41/11
Rucke, Josias, Norton, Kent, 1633 CKS PRC2/32/107
Rucke, Michaell, Hythe St Leonard, Kent, 1612 CKS PRC20/2/338
Rucke, Stephen, Sandwich, Kent, 1598 CKS PRC2/10/288
Rucke, Thomas, Cranbrook, Kent, 1608 CKS PRC2/15/340
Rucke, Thomas, yeoman, Dover, Kent, 1681 CKS PRC20/13/192
Rucke, William, Crundale, Kent, CKS PRC1/15/120
Rucke, Wylliam, Cranbrook, Kent, 1599 CKS PRC2/10/507
Rudd, Thomas, Beedon, Berks, 1618 Berks RO D/A1/210/249B
Ruddiard, Thomas, Coventry, Warks, 1684 LJRO/B/C/5/1684/170
Rudge, Benjamin, farmer, Sedgley, Staffs, 1817 LJRO/B/C/5/1817/74
Rudham, Richard, Gosberton, Lincs, 1618 Lincs RO Ad/Ac/14/281
Rudman, Richard, tailor, Draycot Cerne, Wilts, 1627? Wilts RO Arch. Wilts.(+ name and date)
Rudman, Samuel, Draycot Cerne, Wilts, 1640 Wilts RO Arch. Wilts.(+ name and date)
Rudrum, John, merchant, Norwich, Norf, 1791 Norfolk RO ANW/23/26/81
Rudsdale, John, farmer, Lythe (Nickleby), Yorks, 1812 Borthwick Test C.P. 1812/1
Rudston, Calverley, esquire, Hayton, Yorks, 1808 Borthwick Test C.P. 1808/3
Rudyard, Thomas, Coventry St Michael (Whitley), Warks, 1683 LJRO/B/C/5/1682/88
Rudyard, see Richards,
Ruffin, Henry, yeoman, Hinksey, North, Berks, 1674 Berks RO D/A1/211/60C
Ruffin, Joan, widow, Cumnor, Berks, 1665 Berks RO D/A1/211/42C
Ruffin, Joan, spinster, Cumnor, Berks, 1680 Berks RO D/A1/211/67C
Ruffin, Robert, yeoman, Midhurst, Sussex, 1631 W. Suss RO EpI/33/1631/40
Ruffin, Thomas, Minster in Sheppey, Kent, 1639 CKS PRC20/11/270
Ruffin, William, Cumnor, Berks, 1605 Berks RO D/A1/210/224C
Ruffin/Goddin, Alice, Stone next Faversham, Kent, 1611 CKS PRC2/16/95
Ruge, Henry, Uffculme, Devon, 1634 Wilts RO Miscellaneous Index (name + date)
Rugg, John, Weston Bampfylde, Som, 1607 Somerset RO D/D/Cta/R26
Rugley, James, Tonge, Kent, 1617 CKS PRC2/19/100
Rugley, John, Luddenham, Kent, 1617 CKS PRC2/19/97

[Rugly:]
Rugly, Robert, husbandman, Herne, Kent, 1673 CKS PRC20/12/96
Rukland, John, Friskney, Lincs, 1611 Lincs RO Ad/Ac/10/96
Rule, Christopher, Nackington, Kent, 1623 CKS PRC2/26/108
Rumbridger, John, Binderton (, Sussex, 1640 W. Suss RO EpI/33/1640/17
Rumforth, Thomas, Fishtoft, Lincs, 1649 Lincs RO Ad/Ac/30/64
Rumney, Lawrence, Maidstone, Kent, 1663 CKS PRC19/3/42
Rumney, see Runney,
Rumny, John, Milton next Sittingbourne, Kent, 1672 CKS PRC2/35/169
Rumny, John, Sholden, Kent, 1672 CKS PRC2/35/171
Rumsey, Thomas, Sandwich St Peter, Kent, 1672 CKS PRC2/35/83
Runacre, see Lawrence,
Runaker, see Lawrence,
Rundell, Henry, Edington, Wilts, 1636 Wilts RO Arch. Sarum(+ name and date)
Rundell, John, Stratton, Corn, 1638 Cornwall RO AP/R588/3
Rundle, Henry, husbandman, Edington, Wilts, 1618 Wilts RO CC Sarum(+ name and date)
Runney/Rumney, William, Portbury, Som, 1620 Somerset RO D/D/Cta/R24
Rusby, Samuel, innkeeper, Ferry Fryston, Yorks, 1840 Borthwick Test C.P. 1840/10
Ruse, Henrie, Maidstone, Kent, 1610 CKS PRC20/2/160
Rushforth, Major, gentleman, Leeds, Yorks, 1817 Borthwick Test C.P. 1817/3
Rushton, John, Shifnal, Shrops, 1769 LJRO/B/C/5/1769/132
Rushton, William, Farnworth, Lancs, 1664 Lancs RO (Name of Deceased) D.R.C.H. 1663
Rushworth, Thomas, yeoman, Steeping, Little, Lincs, 1672 Lincs Ro Ad/Ac/34/1
Rusline, Thomas, Scawby (Sturton), Lincs, 1622 Lincs RO Ad/Ac/8c/37
Russe, Walter, Christian Malford, Wilts, 1674 Wilts RO Miscellaneous Index (name + date)
Russell, David, Cranbrook, Kent, 1674 CKS PRC2/35/252
Russell, Edward, Farnham Royal, Bucks, 1622 Lincs RO Ad/Ac/17/5
Russell, Edward, Goudhurst, Kent, 1626 CKS PRC2/27/136
Russell, Elizabeth, Frittenden, Kent, 1676 CKS PRC2/37/88
Russell, George, Canterbury Holy Cross Westgate, Kent, 1625 CKS PRC2/24/65
Russell, George, Biddenden, Kent, 1631 CKS PRC2/31/59
Russell, Henry, blacksmith, Harewood (Weeton), Yorks, Borthwick Test C.P. 1756/6
Russell, Henry, servant/bachelor, Kingston, Kent, 1671 CKS PRC2/35/82
Russell, Henrye, Cranbrook, Kent, 1610 CKS PRC2/15/327
Russell, Joan, widow, Wimborne Minster, Dors, Dorset RO PE/WM CP 2/4/47
Russell, Joane, widow, Canterbury Holy Cross Westgate, Kent, 1627 CKS PRC2/27/147
Russell, John, labourer, Pinchbeck, Lincs, 1618 Lincs RO Ad/Ac/15/145
Russell, John, Wimborne Minster, Dors, 1619 Dorset RO PE/WM CP 2/4/23
Russell, John, Chale, Hants, 1624 Hants RO 21M65 D8/86
Russell, John, St Laurence Thanet, Kent, 1626 CKS PRC2/27/137
Russell, John, St Laurence Thanet, Kent, 1626 CKS PRC20/7/154
Russell, John, Marden, Kent, 1629 CKS PRC2/29/74
Russell, John, Boughton Malherbe, Kent, 1638 CKS PRC2/34/113
Russell, John, Goudhurst, Kent, 1675 CKS PRC2/36/236
Russell, John, mariner, Lymington, Hants, 1692 Hants RO 21m65 D8/357
Russell, Joshua, saddler, Maidstone, Kent, 1682 CKS PRC20/13/190
Russell, Margaret, wife, Witley, Great, Worcs, Worcs RO 008.7 BA3585/839/380
Russell, Nicholas, husbandman, Goudhurst, Kent, 1643 CKS PRC1/7/9
Russell, Nicholas + Jone, Canterbury, Kent, 1599 CKS PRC2/10/416
Russell, Richard, Tenterden, Kent, 1620 CKS PRC2/19/99
Russell, Richard, Wimborne Minster, Dors, 1625 Dorset RO PE/WM CP 2/4/34
Russell, Richard, Ashford, Kent, 1627 CKS PRC2/28/105
Russell, Richard, Smarden, Kent, 1646 CKS PRC1/7/99
Russell, Richard, Goudhurst, Kent, 1703 CKS PRC1/16/56
Russell, Robarte, Minster in Thanet, Kent, 1603 CKS PRC2/14/396
Russell, Robarte, Canterbury Holy Cross Westgate, Kent, 1609 CKS PRC2/14/390

Russell, Roger, Eling, Hants, 1663 Hants RO 21M65 D8/159
Russell, Simon, Elham, Kent, 1629 CKS PRC2/30/117
Russell, Thomas, Grantham, Lincs, 1599 Lincs RO Ad/Ac/5/348
Russell, Thomas, clothier, Tenterden, Kent, 1666 CKS PRC1/11/151
Russell, Thomas, Caverswall, Staffs, 1672 LJRO:cards/1672/49
Russell, Thomas, mariner, St Peter in Thanet, Kent, 1678 CKS PRC2/38/65
Russell, Thomas, Westburhant, Hants, 1679 Hants RO 21m65 D8/319
Russell, Thomas, chandler, Sittingbourne, Kent, 1685 CKS PRC2/41/10
Russell, William, Rowley Regis, Staffs, Worcs RO 008.7 BA3585/839/437
Russell, William, Canterbury Holy Cross Westgate, Kent, 1596 CKS PRC2/8/473
Russell, William, Bromsgrove, Worcs, 1606 Worcs RO 008.7 BA3585/839/411
Russell, William, Wye, Kent, 1619 CKS PRC2/19/69
Russell, William, Wymondham, Leics, 1626 Lincs RO Ad/Ac/20/29
Russell, William, Sutton, Bishops, Hants, 1669 Hants RO 21m65 D8/223
Russell, William, fisherman, St Johns Thanet, Kent, 1678 CKS PRC2/38/64
Russell, William, scrivener, Cambridge, Cambs, 1678 CUL V.C. Acc./Box3/42
Russell, William, butcher, Birkin (Hirst Courtney), Yorks, 1810 Borthwick Test C.P. 1810/3
Russells, Vincent, yeoman, Bassingham, Lincs, 1680 Lincs RO Ad/Ac/43/94
Russum, John, Chart, Little, Kent, 1626 CKS PRC2/27/141
Rust, Robert, Brabourne, Kent, 1665 CKS PRC1/11/74
Rutes?, John,
Leics 1666 Leics RO Administrators Accounts C17th f41
Ruth/White/London, Mary, St Albans, Herts, 1615 Herts RO ASA25/4822
Rutland, Hugh, Tenterden, Kent, 1616 CKS PRC2/19/76
Rutland, Thomas, Aswarby, Lincs, 1672? Lincs RO Ad/Ac/43/75
Rutt, Christopher, Enford, Wilts, 1701 Wilts RO Arch. Sarum(+ name and date)
Rutter, Cuthbert, husbandman, Ewerby, Lincs, 1649 Lincs RO Ad/Ac/30/66
Rutter, Henrie, Swinefleet, Yorks, 1626 Lincs RO Ad/Ac/39/74
Rutter, Henry, gentleman, Wrenbury (Bromhall), Ches, 1662 Cheshire RO (Name) W.C. 1661
Rutting, George, Chart, Little, Kent, 1618 CKS PRC2/26/131
Rutting, John, Snargate, Kent, 1596 CKS PRC2/8/288
Rutting, John, Faversham, Kent, 1668 CKS PRC1/13/110
Rutting, Nicholas, Chart, Little, Kent, 1605 CKS PRC2/15/339
Ryall, Thomas, Salisbury, Wilts, 1615 Wilts RO Miscellaneous Index (name + date)
Ryall, William, Chideock, Dors, 1714 Wilts RO Miscellaneous Index (name + date)
Ryce, Thomas, Otham, Kent, 1587 CKS PRC2/4/188
Rychardson, Lawrence, shearman, Redbourn, Herts, 1574 Herts RO ASA25/786
Rychards(on), William, Snave, Kent, 1586 CKS PRC2/5/51
Ryche, Alice, widow, Linton, Kent, 1585 CKS PRC2/3/335
Rycrafte, Robert, Lydd, Kent, 1583 CKS PRC21/6/332
Rycroft, Henry, Grappenhall, Ches, 1668 Cheshire RO (Name) W.C. 1667
Rycroft, Richard, Wem, Shrops, 1667 LJRO:cards/1667/66
Ryder, George, Herne, Kent, 1602 CKS PRC21/17/47
Ryder, Henry, grazier, Cossington, Leics, 1684 Leics RO Administrators Accounts 1682-86 f11
Ryder, Robert, Canterbury St Margaret, Kent, 1616 CKS PRC2/19/77
Ryder, Roger, Shrewsbury St Chad, Shrops, 1667 LJRO:cards/1667/67
Ryder, Thomas, Runcorn (Preston on the Hill), Ches, 1700 Cheshire RO (Name) W.C. 1699
Rye, Agnes, widow, Faversham, Kent, 1618 CKS PRC2/19/89
Rye, Jeremie, Ash next Sandwich, Kent, 1608 CKS PRC20/1/320
Rye, John, mariner: 'sailor', Faversham, Kent, 1619 CKS PRC2/19/72
Rye, Robert, mariner: 'sailor', Faversham, Kent, 1664 CKS PRC1/10/82
Rye, Thomas, Saltwood, Kent, 1604 CKS PRC21/16/73
Rye, Thomas, Faversham, Kent, 1610 CKS PRC2/15/331
Rye, Thomas, Faversham, Kent, 1722 CKS PRC1/18/47
Rye, William, Davington, Kent, 1688 CKS PRC2/41/133

[Rye (Pye ?):]
Rye (Pye ?), Joane, widow, Denton (Eastry hundred), Kent, 1614 CKS PRC2/17/34
Ryffley, Christopher, Swinstead, Lincs, 1600 Lincs RO Ad/Ac/5/101
Rygat, John, Littlehampton, Sussex, 1600 W. Suss RO EpI/33/1600/10
Ryley, Gilbert, Sibsey, Lincs, 1626 Lincs RO Ad/Ac/20/12
Ryley, Gilberte, Sibsey, Lincs, 1626 Lincs RO Ad/Ac/20/122
Ryley, John, Holbeach, Lincs, 1619 Lincs RO Ad/Ac/15/182
Ryley, Richard, Warren, Upper, Oxon, 1625 Oxon RO MSS Wills 172/4/26
Ryllam, William, Swineshead, Lincs, 1613 Lincs RO Ad/Ac/12/18
Ryman, Jane, widow, Spelsbury, Oxon, 1667 Oxon RO MSS Wills 85/3/11
Ryman, William, Oving, Sussex, 1594 W. Suss RO EpI/33/1594/1
Ryme, Thomas, joiner, Oxford (Holywell), Oxon, 1634 Oxon RO MSS Wills 172/4/36
Rypley, Gyles, Snargate, Kent, 1581 CKS PRC2/1/307
Rypley see Page + Rypley,
Ryppington, Joane, widow, Hoath, Kent, 1586 CKS PRC21/8/210
Ryppington, Roger, Fairfield, Kent, 1583 CKS PRC21/6/171
Ryvers, Joan, Singleton, Sussex, 1597 W. Suss RO EpI/33/1596/17
Ryvers, Johane, widow, Reculver, Kent, 1589 CKS PRC21/9/329
Ryves, Robert, esquire, St Clement Danes, London & Middlesex, 1693 PRO PROB32/35/76
Ryvyngton, Arthure, Woodchurch, Kent, 1588 CKS PRC21/9/47
Sabb, Thomas, Goudhurst, Kent, 1635 CKS PRC2/33/126
Sabbe, Alexander, Goudhurst, Kent, 1593 CKS PRC2/6/374
Sabie, John, husbandman, Higham Ferrers, Northants, 1671 Northants RO NWill A/C/87
Sabine, John, Wardington, Oxon, Oxon RO MSS Wills Pec 51/1/9
Sabine, Walter, Hackington, Kent, 1677 CKS PRC2/37/
Sacarye, William, Smarden, Kent, 1615 CKS PRC2/19/7
Sacker, Isaac, Yarmouth, Great, Norf, 1799 Norfolk RO ANW/23/26/94
Sacker, Thomas, Longdon, Worcs, 1685 Worcs RO 008.7 BA3585/837/bdl 4
Sackett, Elizabeth, St Johns Thanet, Kent, 1720 CKS PRC1/18/25
Sackett, John, maltster/husbandman, St Laurence Thanet, Kent, 1677 CKS PRC2/37/199
Sackett, Richard, St Johns Thanet, Kent, 1637 CKS PRC2/33/122
Sackett, Richard, St Laurence Thanet, Kent, 1694 CKS PRC2/42/93
Sackett, Thomas, St Laurence Thanet, Kent, 1635 CKS PRC2/33/129
Sackett, Thomas, Ash next Sandwich, Kent, 1673 CKS PRC20/12/103
Sacry, James, Benenden, Kent, 1675 CKS PRC2/36/246
Sacry, Thomas, Dover, Kent, 1633 CKS PRC20/11/414
Sacry, William eld, butcher, Dover St James, Kent, 1641 CKS PRC19/2/35
Sacrye, Thomas, East Sutton, Kent, 1613 CKS PRC2/16/184
Sacrye, William, Dover St Mary, Kent, 1611 CKS PRC20/2/268
Sadler, Henry, Dover, Kent, 1607 CKS PRC20/1/298
Sadler, John, Petworth, Sussex, 1645 W. Suss RO EpI/33/1645/4
Sadler, Jonathan, maltster, Rotherham, Yorks, 1756 Borthwick Test C.P. 1756/7
Sadler, Mercy, widow, Charlbury, Oxon, 1680 Oxon RO MSS Wills 174/1/36
Sadler, Philip, gentleman, Wroughton, Wilts, 1678 Wilts RO Arch. Wilts.(+ name and date)
Sadler, Robert, yeoman, Marcham, Berks, 1616 Berks RO D/A1/213/93A
Sadler, Robert, St Giles in the Fields, London & Middlesex, 1715 PRO PROB32/59/9
Sadler, Thomas, boatman, Gorleston, Suff, 1754 Suff RO(I) FE 1/31/18
Sadler, William, Gifford, Crowmarsh, Oxon, 1664 Oxon RO MSS Wills 86/2/14
Sadler, William, cooper, Wakefield, Yorks, 1814 Borthwick Test C.P. 1814/2
Sadler, see Dew,
Safery, John, yeoman, Hernhill, Kent, 1683 CKS PRC20/13/372
Safery, Richard, Hernhill, Kent, 1684 CKS PRC20/13/458
Safery, Thomas, husbandman, Faversham, Kent, 1680 CKS PRC2/38/183
Safery, William, yeoman, Hernhill, Kent, 1681 CKS PRC20/13/202
Saffery, Daniel, Ash next Sandwich, Kent, 1703 CKS PRC19/6/4
Saffery, Jeffery eld, carpenter, Deal, Kent, 1682 CKS PRC20/13/200

Saffery, Richard, Ash next Sandwich, Kent, 1694 CKS PRC19/5/30
Saffery, William, mariner?, Deal, Kent, 1673 CKS PRC20/12/102
Saffery, William, mariner?, Deal, Kent, 1674 CKS PRC20/12/101
Safferye, Stephen, Tilmanstone, Kent, 1618 CKS PRC2/19/61
Saffry, Osmund, Ash next Sandwich, Kent, 1631 CKS PRC20/9/404
Sage, Francis, Camely, Som, 1625 Somerset RO D/D/Cta/S26
Saile, Anne, widow, Horbling, Lincs, 1666 Lincs RO Ad/Ac/32/105
Sailes, John, Harworth, Notts, 1640 Borthwick Prob. Ex. 1640/3
Sailes, William, Boultham, Lincs, 1587 Lincs RO Ad/Ac/2C/156
Sainct, John, Whitstable, Kent, 1593 CKS PRC2/7/353
Saincte, Thomas, Whitstable, Kent, 1590 CKS PRC2/5/412
Saint, John, Swalecliffe, Kent, 1629 CKS PRC2/30/124
Sainte, Robert, Whitstable, Kent, 1666 CKS PRC1/11/152
Sainter, Richard, farmer, Birkin (West Haddlesey), Yorks, 1800 Borthwick Test C.P. 1800/3
Saintesbury, Thomas, Nettleton, Wilts, 1624 Wilts RO Arch. Wilts.(+ name and date)
Saintloe, John, Bishopstone, Wilts, 1683 Wilts RO Arch. Sarum(+ name and date)
Saire, Elinor, widow, Northbourne, Kent, 1596 CKS PRC2/8/53
Saire, Margery, Ash next Sandwich, Kent, 1598 CKS PRC21/14/567
Saire, Steven, Whitfield alias Beauxfield, Kent, 1603 CKS PRC2/13/360
Saker, Henry, gentleman, Faversham, Kent, 1614 CKS PRC20/3/29
Saker, Nicholas, Slinfold, Sussex, 1618 W. Suss RO EpI/33/1618/16
Sale, George, Bidford, Warks, 1721 Worcs RO 008.7 BA3585/836/bdl 1
Sale, Richard, bricklayer, Stone, Staffs, 1747 LJRO/B/C/5/1747/210
Sale, Thomas, Mucclestone, Staffs, 1684 LJRO/B/C/5/1684/69
Salisbury, Nathaniell, husbandman, Hinckley (Wykin), Leics, 1673 Leics RO Administrators Accounts 1667-72 f113
Salisbury, Nicholas, fisherman, Hythe St Leonard, Kent, 1617 CKS PRC20/4/346
Salisbury, Roger, Hythe St Leonard, Kent, 1621 CKS PRC20/5/172
Salisburye, see Strowde,
Salkyns, Richard, Chislet, Kent, 1619 CKS PRC2/19/37
Sallet, John, Wrangle, Lincs, 1612 Lincs RO Ad/Ac/11/97
Sallisbury, John, Hythe St Leonard, Kent, 1630 CKS PRC20/9/368
Salloman, Edward, Pickworth, Lincs, 1612 Lincs RO Ad/Ac/11/3
Sallway, Henry, Fivehead, Som, 1635 Somerset RO D/D/Cta/G9
Salman, Hannah, widow, Milton next Sittingbourne, Kent, 1677 CKS PRC2/37/196
Salmon, Bartholomew, Canterbury St Mary Bredman, Kent, 1605 CKS PRC2/13/370
Salmon, John, husbandman, Marksbury, Som, 1610 Somerset RO D/D/Cta/S37
Salmon, Margaret, Wyberton, Lincs, 1623 Lincs RO Ad/Ac/18/42
Salmon, Peter, Harrietsham, Kent, 1670 CKS PRC1/14/100
Salmon, Richard, Marden, Kent, 1623 CKS PRC2/24/82
Salmon, Richard, St Laurence Thanet, Kent, 1706 CKS PRC19/6/24
Salmon, Robert eld, carpenter, Maidstone, Kent, 1668 CKS PRC19/4/29
Salmon, Stephen, husbandman, Minster in Sheppey, Kent, 1666 CKS PRC1/11/153
Salmon, Thomas, Thetford, Norf, 1741 Norfolk RO ANW/23/23/48
Salmon, William, husbandman, St Albans (Childwick), Herts, 1597 Herts RO ASA25/1571
Salmon, William, yeoman, Eastchurch, Sheppey, Kent, 1713 CKS PRC1/17/63
Salmon/Hale, Richard, husbandman, Ripple, Worcs, 1601 Worcs RO 008.7 BA3585/838/210
Salomy/De Solomy, Mary, spinster, Canterbury, Kent, 1614 CKS PRC2/18/111
Salt, Stephen, victualler, Birmingham, Warks, 1821 LJRO/B/C/5/1820/48
Salt, Thomas, buttonman, Alstonfield (Flash), Staffs, 1780 LJRO/B/C/5/1780/71
Salter, Christopher, weaver: 'broad weaver', Newbury, Berks, 1685 Berks RO D/A1/215/31C
Salter, Ezra, gentleman, Holbeach, Lincs, 1692 Lincs RO Ad/Ac/44/169
Salter, John, Arreton, Hants, 1679 Hants RO 21m65 D8/320
Salter, John, yeoman, Moorlinch, Som, 1738 Somerset RO D/D/Cta/S71
Salter, Margaret, widow, Henley, Oxon, 1633 Oxon RO MSS Wills 300/1/48

[Salter:]
Salter, Robert, Saltfleetby St Clements, Lincs, 1606 Lincs RO Ad/Ac/7/174
Salter, Robert, Willoughby, Lincs, 1632 Lincs RO Ad/Ac/23/67
Salter, Robert, weaver, Buckland, West, Som, 1741 Somerset RO D/D/Cta/S82
Salter, Thomas, Willoughby (Sloothby), Lincs, 1632 Lincs RO Ad/Ac/23/127
Saltmarsh, Ellenor, Bytham, Castle, Lincs, 1637 Lincs RO Ad/Ac/25/614
Samborne, Mary, Nunney, Som, 1692 Somerset RO D/D/Cta/S73
Samborne, Momely, Nunney, Som, 1692 Somerset RO D/D/Cta/S72
Sambree, Thomas, Lymington, Hants, 1679 Hants RO 21m65 D8/321
Sammes, James, Huntingdon St Mary, Hunts, 1697 Hunts RO/Acc58/283
Sammie, Dorothy, Minster in Sheppey, Kent, 1681 CKS PRC2/39/234
Sammon, Robert, gentleman, Adderbury, Oxon, 1676 Oxon RO MSS Wills 300/2/4
Sammon, Thomas, yeoman, Shrivenham, Berks, 1618 Berks RO D/A1/213/110A
Samon, Alan, Teynham, Kent, 1595 CKS PRC2/7/109
Samon, Anthony, Canterbury St Mildred, Kent, 1682 CKS PRC2/40/76
Samon, Henry, Milton next Sittingbourne, Kent, 1613 CKS PRC2/18/75 and 74
Samon, John, Canterbury, Kent, 1598 CKS PRC2/10/448
Samon, Robarte, Tenterden, Kent, 1596 CKS PRC2/9/185
Samon, Thomas, Brook, Kent, 1620 CKS PRC2/19/2
Samon, William, chandler: 'tallow chandler', Banbury, Oxon, 1683 Oxon RO MSS Wills Pec 51/4/17
Samon, William eld, Guston, Kent, 1587 CKS PRC21/8/266
Sampford, Alexander, Lyme Regis, Dors, 1628 Wilts RO Miscellaneous Index (name + date)
Sampson, Adam, Ruan Lanihorne, Corn, 1612 Cornwall RO AP/S229
Sampson, Alexander, Faversham, Kent, 1628 CKS PRC2/29/88
Sampson, Alexander, yeoman, Minster in Sheppey, Kent, 1664 CKS PRC1/10/85
Sampson, Anne, widow, Warfield, Berks, 1639 Berks RO D/A1/214/36C
Sampson, Catherine, widow, St Laurence Thanet, Kent, 1596 CKS PRC2/8/378
Sampson, Eleanor, Pontefract, Yorks, 1833 Borthwick Test C.P. 1833/9
Sampson, Elizabeth, widow, Wye, Kent, 1624 CKS PRC2/26/126
Sampson, Emma, Milborne Port, Som, 1593 Somerset RO D/D/Cta/S42
Sampson, Isaac, Willesborough, Kent, 1612 CKS PRC2/17/439
Sampson, John, Woodchurch, Kent, 1634 CKS PRC20/11/396
Sampson, Lazarus, yeoman, St Johns Thanet, Kent, 1694 CKS PRC2/42/94
Sampson, Nehemiah, Rickmansworth, Herts, 1638 Herts RO ASA25/4945
Sampson, Nicholas, yeoman, St Peter in Thanet, Kent, 1718 CKS PRC1/18/26
Sampson, Pears, yeoman, St Columb Minor, Corn, 1617 Cornwall RO AP/S315/2
Sampson, Richard, St Peter in Thanet, Kent, 1598 CKS PRC2/10/120
Sampson, Robert, Woodchurch, Kent, 1613 CKS PRC20/2/529
Sampson, Robert, Biddenden, Kent, 1678 CKS PRC2/38/70
Sampson, Thomas, Haxey, Lincs, 1602 Lincs RO Ad/Ac/37/140
Sampson, Thomas, Haxey, Lincs, 1603 Lincs RO Ad/Ac/37/148
Sampson, Thomas, St Peter in Thanet, Kent, 1631 CKS PRC2/31/65
Sampson, William, Scotton, Lincs, 1669 Lincs RO Ad/Ac/33/150
Sampson, see Eden & Fleete,
Sampton, Henry, Staplehurst, Kent, 1601 CKS PRC2/12/345
Samson, Frances, Barkwith, East, Lincs, 1634 Lincs RO Ad/Ac/24/54
Samson, Richard, St Johns Thanet, Kent, 1631 CKS PRC20/9/398
Samson, Roberte, Hawkhurst, Kent, 1586 CKS PRC2/4/386
Samson, William, Haxey (Newbigg), Lincs, 1630s? Lincs RO Ad/Ac/39/249
Samwais, Simon, Salisbury, Wilts, 1628 Wilts RO Miscellaneous Index (name + date)
Samwayes, James, salesman, St Johns Thanet, Kent, 1681 CKS PRC2/39/105
Samyne, John, mr, Bromley, St Leonard, London & Middlesex, 1677 PRO PROB32/14/18
Sandborne, Robert, Biddenden, Kent, 1614 CKS PRC2/18/81
Sandbourne, John, Maidstone, Kent, 1619 CKS PRC20/4/350
Sandcocke, John, Bapchild, Kent, 1596 CKS PRC2/9/199

Sandcraft/Sandcroffe, William, cordwainer, Dover St Mary, Kent, 1664 CKS PRC19/3/60
Sandcroffe, see Sandcraft,
Sandell, Robert, Stourton, Wilts, 1619 Wilts RO Miscellaneous Index (name + date)
Sander, James, Sandwich St Mary, Kent, 1624 CKS PRC2/24/95
Sander, John, Catherington, Hants, 1626 Hants RO 21M65 D8/128
Sander, William, yeoman, Elham, Kent, 1662 CKS PRC1/9/57
Sandercock, John, Warbstow, Corn, 1611 Cornwall RO AP/S209/3
Sanders, David, Burlesdon, Hants, 1685 Hants RO 21m65 D8/348
Sanders, Edward, husbandman, Huttoft, Lincs, 1670 Lincs RO Ad/Ac/32/161
Sanders, Elizabeth, widow, Cranbrook, Kent, 1627 CKS PRC2/28/112
Sanders, Henry, esquire, Canterbury St Mary-Magdalen Burgate, Kent, 1638 CKS PRC2/34/276
Sanders, Henry, Alwalton, Hunts, 1685 Hunts RO/Acc58/257(247)
Sanders, Idden, Canterbury St Peter, Kent, 1629 CKS PRC2/30/121
Sanders, James, yeoman, Stoke, Ches, 1762 Cheshire RO (Name) W.C. 1760-66
Sanders, John, Otham, Kent, 1629 CKS PRC2/30/127
Sanders, John, Oxford (University), Oxon, 1639 Bodleian HYP B9/79-80
Sanders, John, Alton, Staffs, 1676 LJRO:cards/1676/43
Sanders, Richard, Leeds, Kent, 1604 CKS PRC2/13/340
Sanders, Richard, Hythe St Leonard, Kent, 1690 CKS PRC19/4/122
Sanders, Robert, Ash next Sandwich, Kent, 1707 CKS PRC19/6/34
Sanders, Thomas, St Albans, Herts, 1638 Herts RO ASA25/4962
Sanders, William, Headcorn, Kent, 1627 CKS PRC2/28/119
Sanders, William, Birdham, Sussex, 1640 W. Suss RO EpI/33/1640/6
Sanders, William, yeoman, Littlebourne, Kent, 1669 CKS PRC1/13/111
Sanders, William, glazier, Chislet, Kent, 1683 CKS PRC2/40/149
Sanders, see Burton,
Sanderson, Hanna, spinster, Crowle, Lincs, 1667 Lincs RO Ad/Ac/33/8
Sanderson, Henry, Cranbrook, Kent, 1631 CKS PRC2/31/64
Sanderson, Robert, Faldingworth, Lincs, 1620 Lincs RO Ad/Ac/8b/481
Sanderson, Robert, Faldingworth, Lincs, 1630 Lincs RO Ad/Ac/39/232
Sanderson, Thomas, cooper/privileged person, Cambridge St Edward, Cambs, 1657 CUL V.C. Acc./Box3/43
Sandes, Charles, Hollow, Worcs, 1681 Worcs RO 008.7 BA3585/830/52
Sandey, Thomas, Canterbury St Dunstan Without, Kent, 1641 CKS PRC1/6/15
Sandfoorde, Joan, St Johns Thanet, Kent, 1597 CKS PRC2/8/101
Sandford, George, gentleman, Whitchurch (Twemlows), Shrops, 1727 LJRO/B/C/5/1727/134
Sandford, William, innholder, Oxford St Martin, Oxon, 1630 Oxon RO MSS Wills 86/1/15
Sandforde, Baldwin, clergy: 'clerk/B.A.', Oxford (Magdalen College), Oxon, 1631 Bodleian HYP B9/81
Sandiford, John, Liverpool, Lancs, 1667 Lancs RO (Name of Deceased) D.R.C.H. 1667
Sandon, Suzan, widow, Bratoft, Lincs, 1648 Lincs RO Ad/Ac/30/311
Sands, John, Lydd, Kent, 1581 CKS PRC21/5/88
Sands, Robert, Hythe St Leonard, Kent, 1624 CKS PRC20/6/175
Sands, Robert, yeoman, Kintbury, Berks, 1687 Berks RO D/A1/215/46C
Sandvidge, Thomas, yeoman, Newington next Sittingbourne, Kent, 1683 CKS PRC1/15/106
Sandwell, Gefferye, St Peter in Thanet, Kent, 1612 CKS PRC2/17/362
Sandwell, Margaret, St Peter in Thanet, Kent, 1640 CKS PRC1/5/34
Sandwell, Nicholas eld, St Peter in Thanet, Kent, 1640 CKS PRC1/5/35
Sandwell, Richard, Minster in Thanet, Kent, 1613 CKS PRC2/16/196
Sandwell, Thomas, St Peter in Thanet, Kent, 1627 CKS PRC2/28/115
Sandwiche, Thomas, Tonge, Kent, 1609 CKS PRC2/15/381
Sandwill, see Tomlin,
Sandy, Samuel, Chaceley, Worcs, 1684 Worcs RO 008.7 BA3585/837/bdl 4
Saneford, Thomas, Liddington, Glos, 1826 GRO GDR/B4/2/S36
Sanford, Edmund, St Johns Thanet, Kent, 1584 CKS PRC2/3/22

[Sangar:]
Sangar, Wilts RO Unlisted Fragment
Sangar, Andrew, Sutton Mandeville, Wilts, 1613 Wilts RO Arch. Sarum(+ name and date)
Sanger, Thomas, Berwick St John, Wilts, 1621 Wilts RO Miscellaneous Index (name + date)
Sanger, William, Knoyle, East, Wilts, 1680 Wilts RO Arch. Sarum(+ name and date)
Sanger, William, Deverill, Longbridge, Wilts, 1682? Wilts RO Arch. Sarum(+ name and date)
Sangford, John, Droitwich St Peter, Worcs, 1786 Worcs RO 008.7 BA3585/835/bdl 2
Sansom, Robert, Sherbourne, Dors, 1627 Wilts RO Miscellaneous Index (name + date)
Sansom, see Bread,
Sansome, Thomas, Weston Zoyland, Som, 1641 Somerset RO D/D/Cta/S47
Santhey, John, Amesbury, Wilts, 1629 Wilts RO Arch. Sarum(+ name and date)
Santhune, Stephen, weaver: 'silk weaver', Canterbury St Mary Bredin, Kent, 1680 CKS PRC2/39/106
Sanvidge, Alice, widow, Bobbing, Kent, 1684 CKS PRC2/40/152
Sanvidge, Thomas, Newington next Sittingbourne, Kent, 1684 CKS PRC2/40/148
Sapcote, Henrie, Bracebridge, Lincs, 1632 Lincs RO Ad/Ac/23/58
Sard, Thomas, Warfield, Berks, 1618 Berks RO D/A1/213/107A
Sare, Robert, Charing, Kent, 1608 CKS PRC20/1/296
Sare, Robert, Tunstall, Kent, 1639 CKS PRC1/3/39
Sare, William, Hythe St Leonard, Kent, 1606 CKS PRC20/1/126
Sares, Robert, Warnham, Sussex, 1620 W. Suss RO EpI/33/1619/9
Sargant, Ann, widow, Chichester St Pancras, Sussex, 1626 W. Suss RO EpIV/10/1/29
Sargant, Isaac, tool maker, Birmingham, Warks, 1823 LJRO/B/C/5/1823/33
Sargeant, Robert, Marsh Chapel, Lincs, 1645 Lincs RO Ad/Ac/28/115
Sargeant, William, Barrow, Lincs, 1626 Lincs RO Ad/Ac/20/34
Sargent, Jeremy, yeoman, Liddington, Wilts, 1637 Wilts RO Arch. Wilts.(+ name and date)
Sargeson, William, Alconbury, Hunts, 1681 Hunts RO/Acc58/163(118)
Sargin, Christopher, Kirton, Lincs, 1623 Lincs RO Ad/Ac/18/44
Sarney, John, mason: 'freemason', Abingdon, Berks, 1608 Berks RO D/A1/213/49C
Sarney, Peter, Longworth, Berks, 1608 Berks RO D/A1/213/41C
Sarson, John, Frisby on the Wreake, Leics, 1673 Leics RO Administrators Accounts 1667-72 f106
Satchell, Mary, widow, St Olave Hart Street, London & Middlesex, 1682 PRO PROB32/21/55
Satchwell, Richard, St George Hanover Square (Ebury St), London & Middlesex, 1816 Greater London RO DL/C/576/121
Saul, George, Hale, Great (Little Hale), Lincs, 1652 Lincs RO Ad/Ac/29/1
Saule, Edward, gentleman, Rippingale, Lincs, 1668 Lincs RO Ad/Ac/33/75
Saule, Francis, Braceby, Lincs, 1594 Lincs RO Ad/Ac/3/141
Saule, John, yeoman, Hale, Great (Little Hale), Lincs, C17th? Lincs RO Ad/Ac/45/107
Saule, Margaret, widow, St Michael Peternoster Royal, London & Middlesex, 1635 Lambeth Palace VH95/1730
Saule, Richard, Aslackby, Lincs, 1624 Lincs RO Ad/Ac/18/100
Saule, Robert, Whaplode, Lincs, 1613 Lincs RO Ad/Ac/12/107
Saule, William, Braceby, Lincs, 1601 Lincs RO Ad/Ac/5/543
Saule, see Howett,
Saunder, Clement, Herne, Kent, 1606 CKS PRC20/1/85
Saunder, Edward, Harbledown, Kent, 1586 CKS PRC2/4/378
Saunder, John, Stanford, Kent, 1613 CKS PRC2/17/282
Saunder, Richard, Ash next Sandwich, Kent, 1609 CKS PRC20/2/59
Saunder, Thomas, Mumby, Lincs, 1605 Lincs RO Ad/Ac/6/150
Saunder, Thomas ygr, Hythe West, Kent, 1605 CKS PRC2/13/377
Saunders, Amos, Martock, Som, 1626 Somerset RO D/D/Cta/S1
Saunders, Anstis, widow, Stratton, Corn, 1631 Cornwall RO AP/S638/2
Saunders, Joan, widow, Wolstone, Berks, 1625 Berks RO D/A1/118/84B
Saunders, John, victualler, Bristol, Glos, Bristol RO 1783/CP
Saunders, John, Axbridge, Som, 1600 Somerset RO D/D/Cta/S55
Saunders, John, fuller, Loose, Kent, 1624 CKS PRC20/6/187

Saunders, John, yeoman, Shirburn, Oxon, 1627 Oxon RO MSS Wills 86/1/5
Saunders, John, gentleman, Henley, Oxon, 1635 Oxon RO MSS Wills 300/1/55
Saunders, John, Walcot, Som, 1638 Somerset RO D/D/Cta/S2
Saunders, John, carpenter, Hendred, East, Berks, 1642 Berks RO D/A1/214/56C
Saunders, John, Higham Ferrers, Northants, 1675 Northants RO NWill A/C/34
Saunders, John, Manea, Cambs, 1677? PRO PROB5/1064
Saunders, Mildred, widow, Chart nr Sutton Valence, Kent, 1620 CKS PRC2/19/32
Saunders, Nicholas, Littlehampton, Sussex, 1606 W. Suss RO EpI/33/1606/16
Saunders, Richard, St Laurence Thanet, Kent, 1596 CKS PRC2/8/495
Saunders, Richard, yeoman, Sulhampstead Bannister, Berks, 1614 Berks RO D/A1/213/90D
Saunders, Richard, St Laurence Thanet, Kent, 1618 CKS PRC2/19/20
Saunders, Robert, Brenzett, Kent, 1619 CKS PRC2/19/42
Saunders, Robert, Spalding, Lincs, 1641 Lincs RO Ad/Ac/27/283
Saunders, Robert, yeoman, Walcot, Som, 1673 Somerset RO D/D/Cta/S74
Saunders, Samuel, yeoman, Malmesbury, Wilts, 1739 Wilts RO Arch. Wilts.(+ name and date)
Saunders, Stephen, Pagham, Sussex, 1680 W. Suss RO EpIV/10/2A/23
Saunders, Thomas, Dymchurch, Kent, CKS PRC1/16/14
Saunders, Thomas, Sutton Courtenay, Berks, 1613 Berks RO D/A1/213/88A
Saunders, Thomas, butcher, Abingdon, Berks, 1613 Berks RO D/A1/213/82A
Saunders, Thomas, Weston, Som, 1669 Somerset RO D/D/Cta/S48
Saunders, Thomas, Dymchurch, Kent, 1698 CKS PRC1/16/14a
Saunders, Thomas, Dymchurch, Kent, 1699 CKS PRC1/16/14b
Saunders, Thomas eld, Wallingford, Berks, 1611 Berks RO D/A1/213/67C
Saunders, William, Odcombe, Som, 1583 Somerset RO D/D/Cta/S4
Saunders, William, yeoman, Abingdon St Helen (Shippon), Berks, 1592 Berks RO D/A1/212/149A
Saunders, William, husbandman, Warwick, Warks, 1603 Worcs RO 008.7 BA3585/839/317
Saunders, William, husbandman, Bradfield, Berks, 1616 Berks RO D/A1/213/95A
Saunders, William, Plaitford, Wilts, 1619 Wilts RO Unlisted Fragment
Saunders, William, Petherton, North, Som, 1639 Somerset RO D/D/Cta/S3
Saunders, William, Canterbury All Saints, Kent, 1665 CKS PRC1/11/76
Saunders/Burton, John eld, yeoman, Redbourn, Herts, 1631 Herts RO ASA25/4881
Saunders/Milles, Edmonde, Broad Hinton, Wilts, 1627 Wilts RO Miscellaneous Index (name + date)
Saunders, see Perrin & Purser,
Saunderson, John, esquire, Addington, Little, Northants, 1673 Northants RO NWill A/C/145
Saunderson, Richard, Cantley, Yorks, 1637 Borthwick Prob. Ex. 1637/8
Saunderson, Robert, Stow, Lincs, 1683 Lincs RO Ad/Ac/42/92
Saunderson, Thomas, Moulton, Northants, 1672 Northants RO NWill A/C/76
Saunderson, William, Bicker, Lincs, 1613 Lincs RO Ad/Ac/12/140
Saunderson, William, Dunston, Lincs, 1625 Lincs RO Ad/Ac/19A/75
Saundersone, Richard, Ramsey, Hunts, 1682 Hunts RO/Acc58/182(26)
Saundry, John, Constantine, Corn, 1615 Cornwall RO AP/S253/3
Savadge, Arnolde, St Johns Thanet, Kent, 1610 CKS PRC2/14/415
Savadge/Turner, Nicholas, bargeman, Henley, Oxon, 1640 Oxon RO MSS Wills 173/4/18
Savage, Anthony, yeoman, Uttoxeter (Crakemarsh), Staffs, 1713 LJRO/B/C/5/1713/57
Savage, Edward, Wells, Som, 1604 Somerset RO D/D/Cta/S65
Savage, Henry, Deal, Kent, 1670 CKS PRC19/4/94
Savage, James, farmer, Broadway (Gostel Farm), Worcs, 1825 Worcs RO 008.7 BA3585/835/bdl 2
Savage, John, tailor: 'merchant tailor', St Johns Thanet, Kent, 1646 CKS PRC1/7/63
Savage, John, blacksmith, Borden, Kent, 1678 CKS PRC2/37/197
Savage, Joseph, yeoman, Coaley, Glos, 1794 GRO GDR/B4/2/S42
Savage, Richard, husbandman, Norton, Worcs, 1604 Worcs RO 008.7 BA3585/839/382
Savage, Thomas,

[Savage:]
Worcs 1605 Worcs RO 008.7 BA3585/839/383
Savage, William, Newton, Wilts, 1669? Wilts RO Arch. Sarum(+ name and date)
Savedge, John, Whitstable, Kent, 1591 CKS PRC2/5/422
Savell, William, Coppingford, Hunts, 1681 Hunts RO/Acc58/162(117)
Saver, John, yeoman, Whitstable, Kent, 1619 CKS PRC2/19/34
Saver, William, Whitstable, Kent, 1618 CKS PRC2/19/12
Saver, William, Whitstable, Kent, 1626 CKS PRC2/27/156
Savery, Richard, Boughton under Blean, Kent, 1625 CKS PRC20/7/235
Savidge, Stephen, husbandman, Herne, Kent, 1641 CKS PRC19/1/77
Savile, John, knight, Sheffield (Hawley), Yorks, 1633 Borthwick Prob. Ex. 1633/1
Savile, John, knight, Sheffield (Hawley), Yorks, 1636 Borthwick Prob. Ex. 1636/3
Savill, Robert, Yelling, Hunts, 1697 Hunts RO/Acc58/284
Savin, Stephen, Challock, Kent, 1600 CKS PRC21/15/125
Savyn, John, Sellindge, Kent, 1631 CKS PRC2/31/67
Sawe, Oswald, Edington, Wilts, 1640 Wilts RO Arch. Sarum(+ name and date)
Sawe, Thomas, Edington, Wilts, 1641 Wilts RO Arch. Sarum(+ name and date)
Sawell, Richard, High Halstow, Kent, 1588 CKS PRC2/4/269
Sawer, Alicie, Fillingham, Lincs, 1614 Lincs RO Ad/Ac/8b/89
Sawer, Alicie, Fillingham, Lincs, 1615 Lincs RO Ad/Ac/8b/242
Sawer, John, Rasen, West, Lincs, 1612 Lincs RO Ad/Ac/11/78
Sawer, Richard, yeoman, Fillingham, Lincs, 1607 Lincs RO Ad/Ac/37/255
Sawer, Robert, yeoman, Nettleham, Lincs, 1681 Lincs RO Ad/Ac/34/87
Sawer, Roger, Gainsborough, Lincs, 1626 Lincs RO Ad/Ac/39/13
Sawer, Thomas, Alkborough, Lincs, 1619 Lincs RO Ad/Ac/8b/355
Sawer, William, Hykeham, North, Lincs, 1640 Lincs RO Ad/Ac/27/8
Sawier, Nicholas, Long Wittenham, Berks, 1603 Berks RO D/A1/213/27A
Sawier, Thomas, Banwell, Som, 1588 Somerset RO D/D/Cta/S45
Sawkins, James, gentleman, Lyminge, Kent, 1635 CKS PRC20/11/339
Sawkins, John, High Halstow, Kent, 1612 CKS PRC2/16/211
Sawkins, Robert, Chislet, Kent, 1628 CKS PRC2/29/86
Sawle, George, Boston, Lincs, 1619 Lincs RO Ad/Ac/15/264
Sawle, George, Legbourne, Lincs, 1623 Lincs RO Ad/Ac/18/110
Sawle, Richard, Tattershall, Lincs, 1632 Lincs RO Ad/Ac/23/43
Sawll, Thomas, Mareham le Fen, Lincs, 1611 Lincs RO Ad/Ac/10/13
Sawnder, Henrye, Elham, Kent, 1604 CKS PRC2/13/353
Sawnder, William, St Laurence Thanet, Kent, 1613 CKS PRC2/18/131
Sawnders, Bartholomew, St Laurence Thanet, Kent, 1594 CKS PRC2/6/39
Sawnders, Edmund, St Nicholas at Wade, Kent, 1624 CKS PRC20/6/181
Sawnders, Elys, Newport, Hants, 1599 Hants RO 1598 B39/3
Sawnders, John, Veryan, Corn, 1630 Cornwall RO AP/S639/2
Sawnders, Richard, Aston Abbots, Bucks, 1618 Herts RO ASA25/4832
Sawnders, Richarde, Luddenham, Kent, 1597 CKS PRC2/9/313
Sawnders, Thomas, Ash next Sandwich, Kent, 1592 CKS PRC21/12/201
Sawnders, Thomas ygr, Hythe St Leonard, Kent, 1613 CKS PRC20/2/525
Sawndry, Peter, St Enoder, Corn, Cornwall RO AP/S62/1/4
Sawyer, Amy, Hagbourne (Coscote), Berks, 1602 Berks RO D/A1/213/22C
Sawyer, Avery, husbandman, Didcot, Berks, 1622 Berks RO D/A1/213/126A
Sawyer, Elizabeth, Bristol St John, Glos, Bristol RO 1678/68
Sawyer, John, yeoman, Easton, Wilts, 1730? Wilts RO Miscellaneous Index (name + date)
Sawyer, Richard, husbandman, Hagbourne, Berks, 1603 Berks RO D/A1/213/26A
Sawyer, Stephan, River, Kent, 1615 CKS PRC2/17/39
Sawyer, Thomas, Redmarley D'Abitot, Worcs, 1604 Worcs RO 008.7 BA3585/839/385
Sawyer, William, St Clement Danes, London & Middlesex, 1684 Greater London RO AM/PP/Box 1739-1749 pt (uncatalogued)
Sawyer, William, Winteringham, Lincs, 1720 Lincs RO Ad/Ac/45/11

Sawyer, see Edmunds & Risbridger,
Saxbie, Thomas, Cranbrook, Kent, 1620 CKS PRC2/19/13 and unnumbered
Saxby, Ellen, widow, Maidstone, Kent, 1686 CKS PRC20/13/531
Saxby, Thomas, Maidstone, Kent, 1630 CKS PRC20/9/378
Saxon, John, Fulstow, Lincs, 1612 Lincs RO Ad/Ac/11/96
Saxten, Christian, widow, Ash next Sandwich, Kent, 1618 CKS PRC20/4/360
Saxten, Christian, widow, Ash next Sandwich, Kent, 1618 CKS PRC20/4/362
Saxten, Johan, Petham, Kent, 1585 CKS PRC2/3/252
Saxton, Richard, Derby, Derby, 1743 LJRO/B/C/5/1743/186
Say, Robert, clergy: 'D.D./parson', Great Mongeham, Kent, 1630 CKS PRC20/8/442
Sayer, Edward, yeoman, Bilsington, Kent, 1638 CKS PRC1/1/59
Sayer, George, Sandwich, Kent, 1633 CKS PRC2/32/119
Sayer, Hugh, Uphill, Som, 1598 Somerset RO D/D/Cta/S39
Sayer, Jeremy, Milton next Sittingbourne, Kent, 1635 CKS PRC2/33/127
Sayer, Justinian eld, husbandman, Milton, Berks, 1683 Berks RO D/A1/215/12C
Sayer, Mary, Aldington, Kent, 1641 CKS PRC19/1/78
Sayer, Mary eld, widow, Ewell, Kent, 1626 CKS PRC2/27/159
Sayer, Nicholas, Kenwyn, Corn, 1615 Cornwall RO AP/S271/2
Sayer, Sarah, widow, Lapley, Staffs, 1822 LJRO/B/C/5/1822/28
Sayer, Stephen, yeoman, St Johns Thanet, Kent, 1643 CKS PRC1/7/10
Sayer, Thomas, Milton, Berks, 1594 Berks RO D/A1/212/166D
Sayer, Thomas, Canterbury Holy Cross Westgate, Kent, 1601 CKS PRC2/12/326
Sayer, Thomas, Milton next Sittingbourne, Kent, 1672 CKS PRC2/35/175
Sayer, William, brewer: 'beerbrewer', Dover, Kent, 1675 CKS PRC20/12/188
Sayers, John, yeoman, St Faiths, Norf, 1749 Norfolk RO ANW/23/24/79
Saylbanke, Samuel, clergy: 'clerk', Wainfleet All Saints, Lincs, 1623 Lincs RO Ad/Ac/18/36
Sayre, John, Tenterden, Kent, 1631 CKS PRC20/9/384
Sayre, William, Milton next Sittingbourne, Kent, 1626 CKS PRC2/27/155
Sayre, William, Milton next Sittingbourne, Kent, 1626 CKS PRC2/27/160
Sayres, Thomas, Horsham, Sussex, 1617 W. Suss RO EpIV/10/1/44
Saywell, John, Biddenden, Kent, 1612 CKS PRC2/16/173
Scadding, Simon, Angersleigh, Som, 1638 Somerset RO D/D/Cta/S29
Scafield, John, Snitterfield, Warks, 1684 Worcs RO 008.7 BA3585/837/bdl 5
Scales, John, Belton, Lincs, 1663 Lincs RO Ad/Ac/41/67
Scales, Lancelott, yeoman, Deeping St James, Lincs, 1625 Lincs RO Ad/Ac/19B/44
Scales, Sara, spinster, Egerton, Kent, 1639 CKS PRC20/11/364
Scales, Thomas, Aisthorpe (Thorpe in the Fallows), Lincs, 1638 Lincs RO Ad/Ac/25/192
Scales, Thomas, clothier, Biddenden, Kent, 1670 CKS PRC19/4/59
Scaman, George, blacksmith, Stallingborough, Lincs, 1673 Lincs RO Ad/Ac/34/12
Scaman, Thomas, yeoman, Limber Magna, Lincs, 1673 Lincs RO Ad/Ac/35/27
Scambler, Robert, maltster, Northampton, Northants, 1671 Northants RO NWill A/C/93
Scamell, Edward,
Wilts 1625 c. Wilts RO Miscellaneous Index (name + date)
Scammell, William, Bemerton (Quidhampton), Wilts, 1680 Wilts RO Arch. Sarum(+ name and date)
Scane, Richard, Headington, Oxon, 1644 Oxon RO MSS Wills 173/4/44
Scapes, Lydia, spinster, Yarmouth, Great, Norf, 1743 Norfolk RO ANW/23/24/21
Scapeye, Gabriell, St Peter in Thanet, Kent, 1609 CKS PRC2/13/379
Scaplehorne, Fittleton, Wilts, 1624 Wilts RO Miscellaneous Index (name + date)
Scappes, Anne, widow, Wolstone, Berks, 1623 Berks RO D/A1/213/128C
Scarboroughe, Robert, Rasen, West, Lincs, 1635 Lincs RO Ad/Ac/24/451
Scarbrough, William, husbandman, Winterton, Lincs, 1607 Lincs RO Ad/Ac/37/243
Scardevill, Richard, Lavant, East, Sussex, 1636 W. Suss RO EpIV/10/2/10
Scarisbricke, Edward, esquire, Ormskirk (Scarisbrick), Lancs, 1604 Lancs RO (Name of Deceased) D.R.C.H. 1604

[Scarle:]
Scarle, William, Westbourne, Sussex, 1648 W. Suss RO EpI/33/1648/3
Scarlett, Elizabeth, widow, Deal, Kent, 1693 CKS PRC19/5/10
Scarlett, John, Deal, Kent, 1674 CKS PRC20/12/100
Scarlett, Peter, apothecary/University Appraiser/scholar's servant, Cambridge St Mary the Great, Cambs, 1613 CUL V.C.Acc./Box1/45
Scarvill, John, Ferring, Sussex, 1640 W. Suss RO EpI/33/1640/10
Scarvill, Sarah, Chichester All Saints, Sussex, 1681 W. Suss RO EpIV/10/2A/25
Scatcherd, John, maltster, Batley, Yorks, 1838 Borthwick Test C.P. 1838/3
Scawper, Jose, Sandwich, Kent, 1604 CKS PRC2/13/348
Scheeres, Adrian, Sandwich, Kent, 1617 CKS PRC2/19/47
Schoaler, Michael, Saxilby, Lincs, 1650 Lincs RO Ad/Ac/40/185
Schochie, William, Billinghay, Lincs, 1648 Lincs RO Ad/Ac/30/289
Schofield, David, cordwainer, Thornhill (Shitlington), Yorks, 1821 Borthwick Test C.P. 1821/13
Scholefield, Horsfall, esquire, Swine (Waston), Yorks, 1820 Borthwick Test C.P. 1820/2
Scholes, Abner, upholsterer, Chester, Ches, 1742 Cheshire RO (Name) W.C. 1742
Scholes, Richard, yeoman, Middleton (Thornham), Lancs, 1678 Lancs RO (Name of Deceased) D.R.C.H. 1678
Scholey, Samuel, farmer, Ardsley, East (Woodhouse Lane), Yorks, 1805 Borthwick Test C.P. 1805/5
Sciethaze, Catherine, Sandwich, Kent, 1600 CKS PRC2/11/304
Sciethaze, Joos, merchant, Sandwich, Kent, 1594 CKS PRC2/6/268
Scoffeeld, William, Graveney, Kent, 1614 CKS PRC2/18/84
Scoffing, Thomas, Buslingthorpe, Lincs, 1670 Lincs RO Ad/Ac/32/142
Scolefeild, Arthur, draper: 'woollen draper', Manchester, Lancs, Lancs RO (Name of Deceased) D.R.C.H. 1668
Scoler, Agnes/Anne, minor?, Canterbury St Paul, Kent, 1589 CKS PRC2/5/94
Scoles, Francis, Hythe St Leonard, Kent, 1591 CKS PRC21/11/36
Scoley, Robert, Coningsby, Lincs, 1646 Lincs RO Ad/Ac/28/175
Scoley, William, Donington, Lincs, 1620 Lincs RO Ad/Ac/16/85
Scolpham, Anthony, gentleman, Canterbury St Alphege, Kent, 1632 CKS PRC20/9/382
Scolpham, Anthony, gentleman, Canterbury St Alphege, Kent, 1632 CKS PRC20/11/448
Scooley, William, St Martin in the Fields, London & Middlesex, 1731 Greater London RO AM/PP/Box 1726-1732 pt (uncatalogued)
Scophine, William, Billinghay, Lincs, 1565 Lincs RO Ad/Ac/0/15
Scorge, Mary, Milton next Sittingbourne, Kent, 1674 CKS PRC2/36/117
Scot, John, Handsworth, Staffs, 1684 LJRO/B/C/5/1684/70
Scot, Peter, Caythorpe, Lincs, 1634 Lincs RO Ad/Ac/24/365
Scot, Thomas, Bobbing, Kent, 1601 CKS PRC2/12/343
Scot, William, Holbeach, Lincs, 1607 Lincs RO Ad/Ac/7/44
Scotchfoord, Walter, Cranbrook, Kent, 1614 CKS PRC2/18/29
Scotchford, Ellen, Cranbrook, Kent, 1638 CKS PRC2/34/287
Scotes, Agnes, Lyminge, Kent, 1633 CKS PRC20/11/423
Scotes, Charles, Elham, Kent, 1621 CKS PRC2/19/49
Scotreth, Agnes, Huttoft, Lincs, 1614 Lincs RO Ad/Ac/13/33
Scott, Abraham, Sutton Coldfield (Greaves), Warks, 1662 LJRO:cards/1662/10
Scott, Bennett, widow, Woodnesborough, Kent, 1671 CKS PRC1/15/58
Scott, Catherine, Bridge, Kent, 1604 CKS PRC2/13/344
Scott, Edward, Lydd, Kent, 1595 CKS PRC21/13/46
Scott, Elizabeth, widow, Hackney (Shacklewell), London & Middlesex, 1705 PRO PROB32/48/107
Scott, George, esquire, Hawkhurst, Kent, 1628 CKS PRC20/8/413
Scott, Henry, gentleman, Wootton, Lincs, 1607 Lincs RO Ad/Ac/8a/17
Scott, James, Boughton under Blean, Kent, 1594 CKS PRC21/13/26
Scott, Jeremiah, Chetwynd (Cainton Forge), Shrops, 1664 LJRO:cards/1664/14
Scott, Jervis, turner, Maidstone, Kent, 1670 CKS PRC19/4/95

[Scott:]

Scott, John, Holme, Hunts, Hunts RO/Acc58/90(50)
Scott, John, weaver, Kington St Michael, Wilts, 1626 Wilts RO Arch. Wilts.(+ name and date)
Scott, John, husbandman, Watford, Herts, 1628 Herts RO ASA25/4850
Scott, John, Ashford, Kent, 1629 CKS PRC2/30/125
Scott, John, notary public, Cambridge St Mary the Great, Cambs, 1638 c. CUL V.C. Acc./Box2/68
Scott, John, gardener, Sandwich St Clement, Kent, 1640 CKS PRC1/5/36
Scott, John, victualler, Chichester, Sussex, 1678 W. Suss RO EpIII/9/1/61
Scott, John, gentleman, Birmingham, Warks, 1780 LJRO/B/C/5/1780/78
Scott, John, corn factor, Leeds, Yorks, 1803 Borthwick Test C.P. 1803/7
Scott, John eld, gentleman, High Halden, Kent, 1643 CKS PRC1/7/11
Scott, Luke, Donington, Lincs, 1638 Lincs RO Ad/Ac/25/257
Scott, Mary, widow, Laughton, Lincs, 1684 Lincs RO Ad/Ac/44/145
Scott, Nicholas, yeoman, Westwell, Kent, 1681 CKS PRC20/13/204
Scott, Peeter, Goudhurst, Kent, 1606 CKS PRC2/14/418
Scott, Peter, Elsham, Lincs, 1662 Lincs RO Ad/Ac/32/13
Scott, Rabydge, widow, Chilham, Kent, 1593 CKS PRC2/6/384
Scott, Rebecka, widow, Canterbury St Margaret, Kent, 1668 CKS PRC1/13/112
Scott, Richard, Hundleby, Lincs, 1633 Lincs RO Ad/Ac/24/9
Scott, Richard, Gainsborough (East Stockwith), Lincs, 1662 Lincs RO Ad/Ac/32/43
Scott, Richard, Gainsborough (East Stockwith), Lincs, 1664 Lincs RO Ad/Ac/41/146
Scott, Richard, yeoman, Boughton under Blean, Kent, 1680 CKS PRC20/13/67
Scott, Robarte, Sandwich, Kent, 1598 CKS PRC2/10/108
Scott, Robert, Epworth, Lincs, 1626 Lincs RO Ad/Ac/39/31
Scott, Robert, Carlton, Great, Lincs, 1638 Lincs RO Ad/Ac/25/282
Scott, Thomas, husbandman, Sherbourne, Dors, 1605? Wilts RO Dean Sarum (name + date)
Scott, Thomas, Haxey, Lincs, 1617 Lincs RO Ad/Ac/8b/173
Scott, Thomas, Haxey (East Lound), Lincs, 1664 Lincs RO Ad/Ac/41/141
Scott, Thomas, husbandman, Alton (Spond), Staffs, 1789 LJRO/B/C/5/1789/120
Scott, Thomas ygr, gentleman, Godmersham, Kent, 1632 CKS PRC20/11/426
Scott, William, Cranbrook, Kent, 1622 CKS PRC2/26/116
Scott, William, Hallington, Lincs, 1625 Lincs RO Ad/Ac/19B/97
Scott, William, Bremhill, Wilts, 1628 Wilts RO Arch. Wilts.(+ name and date)
Scott, William, Willoughby, Scott, Lincs, 1639? Lincs RO Ad/Ac/26/144
Scotte, Henrie, yeoman, Owston, Lincs, 1596 Lincs RO Ad/Ac/37/22
Scotte, John, Rickmansworth, Herts, 1606 Herts RO ASA25/4762
Scotte, Richard, weaver, Wingham, Kent, 1582 CKS PRC21/5/189
Scotte, Thomas, Leake, Lincs, 1623 Lincs RO Ad/Ac/18/82a
Scottesford, Stephen, clergy: 'clerk', Abingdon, Berks, 1607 Berks RO D/A1/213/32A
Scotton, Nicholas, grazier, Wolvey, Warks, 1781 LJRO/B/C/5/1781/113
Scowfeild, William, Saxilby, Lincs, 1633 Lincs RO Ad/Ac/40/13
Scrace, James, gentleman, Eastchurch, Sheppey, Kent, 1670 CKS PRC1/15/59
Scrafeild, Robert, tailor, Mareham le Fen, Lincs, 1626 Lincs RO Ad/Ac/20/108
Scragg, Edward snr, baker, Yoxall, Staffs, 1698 LJRO/B/C/5/1696/101
Scranton, John, Smarden, Kent, 1612 CKS PRC2/17/313
Scranton, Richard, Smarden, Kent, 1597 CKS PRC2/9/195
Scranton, Thomas, mariner, St Laurence Thanet, Kent, 1679 CKS PRC2/38/71
Scras, Francis, Petworth, Sussex, 1684 W. Suss RO EpI/33/1684/41
Scraunton, James, Smarden, Kent, 1618 CKS PRC2/19/26
Scrill, William, mason: 'freemason', Box, Wilts, 1762 Wilts RO Miscellaneous Index (name + date)
Scrimpshire, Hugh, St Mildred Bread Street, London & Middlesex, 1705 Lambeth Palace Arches G55/1
Scrimsbye, Wylliam, Kennington, Kent, 1612 CKS PRC2/16/89
Scrimshawe, Thomas, Canterbury, Kent, 1638 CKS PRC2/34/280

[Scrimshey:]
Scrimshey, Thomas, Canterbury, Kent, 1610 CKS PRC2/15/389
Scriven, Joane, spinster, Somborne, Kings, Hants, 1625 Hants RO 21M65 D8/129
Scrivener, John, Hale, Great, Lincs, 1636 Lincs RO Ad/Ac/24/462
Scroggin, see Scrowgham,
Scrowgham/Scroggin, John, St Laurence Thanet, Kent, 1607 CKS PRC2/14/399
Scryvener, William, Wrawby, Lincs, 1602 Lincs RO Ad/Ac/5/407
Scultharpe, John, Loose, Kent, 1605 CKS PRC20/1/7
Scupholme, John, Wrangle, Lincs, 1638 Lincs RO Ad/Ac/25/200
Scupholme, William, Somercoates, Lincs, 1638 Lincs RO Ad/Ac/25/242
Scupholme/Bramby, Anne, widow, Toft Next Newton, Lincs, 1686 Lincs RO Ad/Ac/44/147
Scutt, Elias, Washington, Sussex, 1670 W. Suss RO EpI/33/1670/27
Scutt, Jane, widow, Kirdford, Sussex, 1633 W. Suss RO EpI/33/1633/3
Scutt, Richard, husbandman, Halton, West (Gunhouse), Lincs, 1684 Lincs RO Ad/Ac/44/136
Sea, Henry, Herne, Kent, 1595 CKS PRC21/13/42
Sea, John, husbandman, Herne, Kent, 1667 CKS PRC19/3/139
Sea, John, farmer, Reculver, Kent, 1678 CKS PRC20/12/282
Sea, Margaret, spinster, Eastry, Kent, 1614 CKS PRC20/3/53
Seaband, Thomas, Bluntisham, Hunts, 1684 Hunts RO/Acc58/234(235)
Seabourne, Alice, Bluntisham, Hunts, 1676 Hunts RO/Acc58/68(127)
Seabrand, John, Canterbury St Andrew, Kent, 1605 CKS PRC2/13/374
Seabrand, Robart, Lydd, Kent, 1598 CKS PRC21/14/555
Seabrook, James, silversmith, Bristol, Glos, Bristol RO 1768/CP
Seacole, Edmund, husbandman, Milton, Oxon, 1624 Oxon RO MSS Wills 173/3/14
Sead, Robert, Lydd, Kent, 1627 CKS PRC20/7/142
Seade, Elizabeth, Lydd, Kent, 1586 CKS PRC21/8/191
Seade, John, Stockbury, Kent, 1604 CKS PRC2/13/391
Seagar, Robert, Hilmarton, Wilts, 1622 Wilts RO Arch. Wilts.(+ name and date)
Seager, Anne, Tunstall, Kent, 1642 CKS PRC1/6/81
Seager, Joan, Eastchurch, Sheppey, Kent, 1605 CKS PRC2/14/414
Seager, Joseph, collier, Kingswinford, Staffs, 1749 LJRO/B/C/5/1749/221
Seager, Margaret, widow, Kingswinford, Staffs, 1695 LJRO/B/C/5/1696/104a
Seager, Margaret, widow, Kingswinford, Staffs, 1695 LJRO/B/C/5/1696/111
Seager, Stephen, yeoman, Minster in Sheppey, Kent, 1640 CKS PRC1/5/37
Seagrave, Alice, Helpringham, Lincs, 1619 Lincs RO Ad/Ac/15/71
Seagrave, Thomas, Sleaford, Lincs, 1661 Lincs RO Ad/Ac/42/48
Seagrave, William, Billingborough, Lincs, 1650 Lincs RO Ad/Ac/29/54
Seagre, Richard, Kirdford, Sussex, 1625 W. Suss RO EpI/33/1624/9
Seagrove, Thomas, Kirdford, Sussex, 1613 W. Suss RO EpI/33/1613/19
Seale, Elizabeth, widow, Cassington, Oxon, 1663 Oxon RO MSS Wills 86/2/16
Seale, Gregory, Mackworth, Derby, 1683 LJRO/B/C/5/1683/19
Seale, Henry, Upchurch, Kent, 1640 CKS PRC1/3/40
Seale, Henry, yeoman, Aylestone, Leics, 1666 Leics RO Administrators Accounts C17th f39
Seale, Thomas, Keevil, Wilts, 1626? Wilts RO CC Sarum(+ name and date)
Seale, William,
Leics 1684 Leics RO Administrators Accounts 1682-86 f14
Seale, William, bookbinder, Oxford (University), Oxon, 1720 Bodleian HYP B9/82-83
Sealy, Mary, widow, Kingston Bagpuize, Berks, 1664 Berks RO D/A1/214/109C
Sealy, Nicholas, yeoman, Kington St Michael, Wilts, 1669 Wilts RO Arch. Wilts.(+ name and date)
Seaman, Alice, widow, Long Wittenham, Berks, 1629 Berks RO D/A1/213/158C
Seaman, Creature, Preston next Wingham, Kent, 1605 CKS PRC2/13/372
Seaman, John, Rainham, Kent, 1603 CKS PRC2/15/366
Seaman, Lawrence, Gedney, Lincs, 1606 Lincs RO Ad/Ac/7/52
Seaman, Richard, Birdham, Sussex, 1629 W. Suss RO EpI/33/1629/31
Seamarke, John, Herne, Kent, 1613 CKS PRC20/2/322

Seamer, John, Reading St Giles, Berks, 1586 Berks RO D/A2/C24/f59R
Seamer, Johnne, gentleman, Lincoln, Lincs, 1580 Lincs RO Ad/Ac/2b/49
Seamor, John, yeoman, Caythorpe, Lincs, 1665 Lincs RO Ad/Ac/43/39
Searby, John, yeoman, Hackthorne, Lincs, 1680 Lincs RO Ad/Ac/43/162
Search, Elizabeth, widow, Stoke Mandeville, Bucks, 1665 Oxon RO MSS Wills Pec 51/3/17
Searche, Robert, Chipping Barnet, Herts, 1597 Herts RO ASA25/1572
Seare, Richard, Sandridge, Herts, 1635 Herts RO ASA25/4918
Seare, Robert, miller, Cumnor (Botley), Berks, 1622 Berks RO D/A1/213/125
Seare, Stephen eld, gentleman, Canterbury, Kent, 1645 CKS PRC1/7/64
Seares, Abraham, blacksmith, St Nicholas at Wade, Kent, 1667 CKS PRC19/3/140
Seares, Edward, Steyning, Sussex, 1631 W. Suss RO EpI/33/1631/29
Seares, John, St Albans St Michaels, Herts, 1559 Herts RO ASA25/439
Searle, Edward, St Neots, Hunts, 1677 Hunts RO/Acc58/102(134)
Searle, Gregory, mariner, Maker, Corn, 1637 Cornwall RO AP/S726/3
Searle, John, Ashcott, Som, 1669 Somerset RO D/D/Cta/S50
Searle, Robert, Botley, Hants, 1636 Hants RO 1635 AD82/1
Searle, Robert, Storrington, Sussex, 1648 W. Suss RO EpI/33/1648/6
Searle, Robert, Greatham, Sussex, 1685 W. Suss RO EpI/33/1684/4
Searle, Samuel, Stoke, North, Sussex, 1632 W. Suss RO EpI/33/1631/28
Searle, William, Veryan, Corn, 1614 Cornwall RO AP/S272
Searle, William, Wymering, Hants, 1625 Hants RO 21M65 D8/87
Sears, William, copperas boiler, Whitstable, Kent, 1674 CKS PRC2/36/126
Searson, John, Keal, East, Lincs, 1638 Lincs RO Ad/Ac/25/129
Seary, John, clergy: 'clerk', Lullington, Som, 1622 Somerset RO D/D/Cta/S21
Seasongle, John, Lydd, Kent, 1606 CKS PRC20/1/25
Seath, Edwarde, Throwleigh, Kent, 1596 CKS PRC2/8/479
Seath, John, Chilham, Kent, 1619 CKS PRC2/19/40
Seath, John, husbandman, Bobbing, Kent, 1680 CKS PRC2/38/189
Seath, Robert, yeoman, Bobbing, Kent, 1680 CKS PRC2/39/110
Seaton, Richard, yeoman, Sandwich St Peter, Kent, 1663 CKS PRC1/9/149
Seaton, Robert, Luddington, Lincs, 1646 Lincs RO Ad/Ac/40/129
Seaton, William, Holton le Moor, Lincs, 1660s? Lincs RO Ad/Ac/42/49
Seavell, John, Sedgebrook, Lincs, 1629 Lincs RO Ad/Ac/22/104
Seaverne, Thomas, Martley, Worcs, 1682 Worcs RO 008.7 BA3585/837/bdl 3
Sebrande, William, Lydd, Kent, 1587 CKS PRC21/8/220
Seddon, Jane, widow, Wingfield, North (Tupton Hall), Derby, 1806 LJRO/B/C/5/1806/103
Seddon, Thomas, Ormskirk (Bickerstaffe), Lancs, 1684 Lancs RO (Name of Deceased) D.R.C.H. 1685
Sedger, Henry, Leeds, Kent, 1629 CKS PRC2/30/126
Sedger, John, weaver, Folkestone, Kent, 1617 CKS PRC2/19/55
Sedger, Rychard, Maidstone, Kent, 1606 CKS PRC20/1/173
Sedger, William, millman, Leeds, Kent, 1616 CKS PRC2/19/28
Sedger, William, Canterbury St Mary-Magdalen Burgate, Kent, 1632 CKS PRC2/31/156
Sedgewick, Samuel, clothworker/citizen, St Katherine Creechurch, London & Middlesex, 1675 PRO PROB5/1685
Sedgmore, William, Talland, Corn, 1646 Cornwall RO AP/S966/4
Sedgwicke, Joane, Limber Magna, Lincs, 1611 Lincs RO Ad/Ac/10/72
Sedgworth, Edward, Hernhill, Kent, 1596 CKS PRC21/14/77
Sedweekes, Richard, Egerton, Kent, 1689 CKS PRC20/13/642
Sedwicke, Robert, Tonge, Kent, 1627 CKS PRC2/28/117
See, James, Thorney, Cambs, 1686 PRO PROB5/987
Seed, Thomas, gentleman, Hackney (Shacklewell), London & Middlesex, 1673 PRO PROB32/10/18
Seelis, Thomas, Biddenden, Kent, 1644 CKS PRC1/7/31
Seely, George, Ruckinge, Kent, 1683 CKS PRC2/40/147

[Seely:]
Seely, William, gentleman, Earith, Hunts, 1726 Hunts RO/Acc58/318
Seely, William, farmer, Hevingham, Norf, 1813 Norfolk RO ANW/23/27/15
Seer, see Pix,
Segar, Charles eld, gentleman, Tunstall, Kent, 1681 CKS PRC2/39/239
Segar, John, Reading, Berks, 1564 Berks RO D/A2/C5/f251V
Segar, Margaret, widow, Charing, Kent, 1594 CKS PRC21/12/376
Segar, Mary, widow, Borden, Kent, 1681 CKS PRC2/39/235
Segar, Richard, butcher, Chart, Great, Kent, 1681 CKS PRC2/39/232
Segood, Henry, Lympne, Kent, 1600 CKS PRC2/11/281
Segrave, Thomas, yeoman, Helpringham, Lincs, 1615 Lincs RO Ad/Ac/13/220
Seignior, George, university: 'Fellow of Trinity College, Cambridge/D.D.', Cambridge, Cambs, 1679 CUL V.C. Acc./Box3/44
Seilesse, Christopher, Biddenden, Kent, 1618 CKS PRC2/19/5
Seinteine, Peter, Canterbury Holy Cross Westgate, Kent, 1603 CKS PRC2/13/351
Selbie, Robert, Minety, Wilts, 1621 Wilts RO Arch. Wilts.(+ name and date)
Selby, Thomas, gentleman, Linwood, Lincs, 1670 Lincs RO Ad/Ac/32/151
Selden, John, yeoman, Rustington, Sussex, 1682 W. Suss RO EpI/33/1682/36
Selden, Margaret, widow, Chichester, Sussex, 1628 W. Suss RO EpIII/9/1/35
Selden, William, Tarring, West, Sussex, 1619 W. Suss RO EpIV/10/1/40
Seley, George, Burmarsh, Kent, 1682 CKS PRC2/40/75
Selfe, John, Hilperton, Wilts, 1622? Wilts RO Arch. Sarum(+ name and date)
Selherst, Christopher, Seasalter, Kent, 1583 CKS PRC2/3/145
Sellance, Marye, widow, Stowting, Kent, 1603 CKS PRC2/13/362
Sellen, William, Funtington, Sussex, W. Suss RO EpI/33/1617/18
Seller, Anne, widow, Merton, Oxon, 1684 Oxon RO MSS Wills 174/2/7
Sellers, Anthony, Wyberton, Lincs, 1635 Lincs RO Ad/Ac/24/558
Sellers, George, Nuthall, Notts, 1640 Borthwick Prob. Ex. 1640/1
Sellers, John, Youlgreave (Winster), Derby, 1733 LJRO/B/C/5/1733/98
Sellers, Richard, Wyberton, Lincs, 1632 Lincs RO Ad/Ac/23/40
Sellwood, Agnes, widow, Appleton, Berks, 1641 Berks RO D/A1/214/51C
Sellwood, Christopher, husbandman, Appleton, Berks, 1636 Berks RO D/A1/214/25C
Sellwood, Edward, cook, Oxford (University), Oxon, 1702 Bodleian HYP B9/84-85
Sellwood, Henry, Cumnor (Chawley), Berks, 1597 Berks RO D/A1/212/185A
Sellwood, John, Wittenham, Little, Berks, 1615 Berks RO D/A1/213/94A
Sellwood, Thomas, yeoman, Appleton (Eaton), Berks, 1652 Berks RO D/A1/214/86C
Sellwood, Thomas, harness maker, Dorchester (Burcott), Oxon, 1675 Oxon RO MSS Wills Pec 71/4/2
Sellyard, Josias, Biddenden, Kent, 1612 CKS PRC2/17/345
Selman, Samuell, grazier, Nibley, North, Glos, 1685 GRO GDR/B4/2/S133
Selvester, Robert, St Albans St Peters, Herts, 1559 Herts RO ASA25/351
Selye, George, Ashford, Kent, 1589 CKS PRC2/4/420
Semark, John, Herne, Kent, 1612 CKS PRC20/2/326
Semark, Thomas, Staplehurst, Kent, 1582 CKS PRC2/2/143
Semonse, Richard, Brenzett, Kent, 1609 CKS PRC2/15/377
Semper, John, Lydd, Kent, 1583 CKS PRC21/6/221
Senior, John, clothier, Dewsbury (Earlsheaton), Yorks, 1801 Borthwick Test C.P. 1801/2
Senior, John, manufacturer, Huddersfield, Yorks, 1819 Borthwick Test C.P. 1819/1
Senior, Joseph, Thornhill (Flockton), Yorks, 1719 Borthwick Test C.P. 1717/14
Senning, Richard, Marden, Kent, 1600 CKS PRC2/11/300
Sentleger, Anthonye, esquire, Leeds, Kent, 1603 CKS PRC2/12/460
Sentleger, Dudley, gentleman, St Johns Thanet, Kent, 1643 CKS PRC1/7/12
Sephton, Thomas, Wigan (Orrell), Lancs, 1663 Lancs RO (Name of Deceased) D.R.C.H. 1663
Sergeant, Henry, Beaminster, Dors, 1628 Wilts RO Miscellaneous Index (name + date)
Sergeant, Henry, Dover, Kent, 1636 CKS PRC20/11/327
Sergeant, John, Barrow on Humber, Lincs, 1605 Lincs RO Ad/Ac/6/69

Sergeant, John, Cranbrook, Kent, 1625 CKS PRC2/25/133
Sergeant, Mary, Kingsley, Staffs, 1667 LJRO:cards/1667/68
Sergeant, Thomas, Hemingby, Lincs, 1567 Lincs RO Ad/Ac/2b/44
Sergeant, William, Meare, Som, 1601 Somerset RO D/D/Cta/S33
Sergeant, William, Halton, East, Lincs, 1663 Lincs RO Ad/Ac/32/51
Serjant, Thomas, Alwalton, Hunts, 1676 Hunts RO/Acc58/72(126)
Serjeant, Gertrude, Fladbury, Worcs, 1701 Worcs RO 008.7 BA3585/837/bdl 6
Serlys, Robarte, clergy: 'clerk', Wye, Kent, 1578 CKS PRC2/1/261
Servant, Thomas, Calne, Wilts, 1638 Wilts RO Miscellaneous Index (name + date)
Servington, George, gentleman, Salisbury, Wilts, 1630 Wilts RO Miscellaneous Index (name + date)
Sessions, John, Foston, Lincs, 1638 Lincs RO Ad/Ac/25/103
Sethe, Samuell, St Peter in Thanet, Kent, 1581 CKS PRC2/2/35
Seton, William, yeoman, Harworth, Notts, 1641 Borthwick Prob. Ex. 1641/1
Sevall, Isabel, Portbury, Som, 1620 Somerset RO D/D/Cta/S16
Sevenocke, William, Harbledown, Kent, 1594 CKS PRC2/7/53
Severall, Martine, Killingholme, Lincs, 1599 Lincs RO Ad/Ac/5/65
Severn, Luke, Snelston, Derby, 1683 LJRO/B/C/5/1682/89
Sevie, John, Shepton Mallet, Som, 1625 Somerset RO D/D/Cta/S18
Sevier, Thomas, Brent, East, Som, 1710 Somerset RO D/D/Cta/S75
Sevier, see Williams,
Sewarde, John, Lyme Regis, Dors, 1591 Wilts RO Dean Sarum (name + date)
Sewarde, William, Fenton, Lincs, 1607 Lincs RO Ad/Ac/8a/37
Sewell, John, clergy: 'clerk', Shadoxhurst, Kent, 1617 CKS PRC20/4/371
Sewell, see Bauldwin,
Sewitt, Robert, Anderby, Lincs, 1614 Lincs RO Ad/Ac/13/25
Sexe, Henry, New Romney, Kent, 1584 CKS PRC21/6/369
Sexton, Helenor, widow, Faversham, Kent, 1612 CKS PRC2/17/336
Sexton, John, Ash next Sandwich, Kent, 1616 CKS PRC20/3/364
Sexton, Thomas, blacksmith, Milton, Great, Oxon, 1679 Oxon RO MSS Wills Pec 51/4/2
Sexton, William, Coxwell, Great, Berks, 1612 Berks RO D/A1/213/80A
Sexton, William, Aldbourne, Wilts, 1618 Wilts RO Arch. Wilts.(+ name and date)
Seybrooke, Thomas, St Pauls Walden, Herts, 1596 Herts RO ASA25/1493
Seyliard, Alice, Biddenden, Kent, 1641 CKS PRC1/6/16
Seyliard, Jane, spinster, Biddenden, Kent, 1646 CKS PRC1/7/100
Seyliard, John, gentleman, Biddenden, Kent, 1641 CKS PRC19/2/36
Seymer, see Halden,
Seymore, Samuel, innholder, Deal, Kent, 1681 CKS PRC20/13/62
Seymour, Daniell eld, tailor, Reading, Berks, 1693 PRO PROB5/982
Shackleton, Blanch, widow, Louth, Lincs, 1670s? Lincs RO Ad/Ac/42/102
Shackleton, John, maltster, Ripon, Yorks, Borthwick Test C.P. 1747/4
Shacklidge, Olive, Kimbolton, Hunts, 1676 Hunts RO/Acc58/62(122)
Shackspeare, Edward, Breedon on the Hill (Staunton Harold), Leics, Leics RO Administrators Accounts 1667-72 f20
Shadforth, Thomas, Hougham, Lincs, 1593 Lincs RO Ad/Ac/3/91
Shadwell, William, Bedwin, Great, Wilts, 1629 Wilts RO Miscellaneous Index (name + date)
Shafte, Andrewe, Chislet, Kent, 1612 CKS PRC2/16/61
Shafte, John, Chislet, Kent, 1595 CKS PRC2/7/209
Shakespeare, Margarete, Ruckinge, Kent, 1603 CKS PRC2/13/342
Shallard, Margaret, widow, Grafton Flyford, Worcs, 1749 Worcs RO 008.7 BA3585/835/bdl 1
Shanckster, John, Epworth, Lincs, 1668 Lincs RO Ad/Ac/33/78
Shanke, John, Acle, Norf, Norfolk RO ANW/23/21/37
Shanly, John, Swyncombe, Oxon, 1662 Oxon RO MSS Wills 86/2/10
Shareland, James, Deal, Kent, 1667 CKS PRC19/3/141
Sharfe, Anne, Southampton, Hants, 1640 Hants RO 1640 A152/3

[Sharing:]
Sharing, John, King's Lynn, Norf, Norfolk RO ANW/23/26/46A
Sharing, John, shopkeeper, King's Lynn, Norf, 1779 Norfolk RO ANW/23/26/47
Sharley, Robart, Upchurch, Kent, 1596 CKS PRC2/8/352
Sharman, see Lyvsey,
Sharnell, Thomas, mariner, Dover, Kent, 1666 CKS PRC19/3/105
Sharnell, Thomas, mariner, Dover, Kent, 1666 CKS PRC19/3/105a
Sharp, Adraham, clergy: 'clerk/rector', Londesborough, Yorks, Borthwick Test C.P. 1734/8
Sharp, Elizabeth, widow, Broughton, Brant, Lincs, 1669 Lincs RO Ad/Ac/33/120
Sharp, John, gentleman, Bethersden, Kent, 1719 CKS PRC1/18/28
Sharp, Richard, candlestick maker, brass, Birmingham, Warks, 1783 LJRO/B/C/5/1783/178
Sharp, Thomas, Lincoln (The Castle), Lincs, 1677 Lincs RO Ad/Ac/42/56
Sharp, William, Pinchbeck, Lincs, 1683 Lincs RO Ad/Ac/44/84
Sharpe, Edward, Folkestone, Kent, 1681 CKS PRC2/39/240
Sharpe, Elizabeth, spinster, Chart, Great, Kent, 1624 CKS PRC2/24/92
Sharpe, George, Gosberton, Lincs, 1665 Lincs RO Ad/Ac/43/23
Sharpe, Gregory, Scarborough, Yorks, 1638 Borthwick Prob. Ex. 1638/5
Sharpe, Hannah, widow, Cranbrook, Kent, 1719 CKS PRC1/18/27
Sharpe, Henry, Southwark, St George the Martyr, Surrey, Greater London RO DW/OP/1757/2/2
Sharpe, John, tanner, Reading, Berks, 1591 Berks RO D/A1/212/158C
Sharpe, John, gentleman, Benenden, Kent, 1629 CKS PRC20/8/421
Sharpe, John, gentleman, Brabourne, Kent, 1682 CKS PRC2/40/77
Sharpe, John, Bierton, Bucks, 1683 Oxon RO MSS Wills Pec 51/4/6
Sharpe, John, brickmaker, Waltham St Lawrence, Berks, 1686 Berks RO D/A1/215/17C
Sharpe, Margaret, widow, Frampton, Lincs, 1635 Lincs RO Ad/Ac/24/526
Sharpe, Richard, clothier, Smarden, Kent, 1610 CKS PRC20/2/85
Sharpe, Robert, Old Romney, Kent, 1624 CKS PRC2/24/96
Sharpe, Robert, Barholm, Lincs, 1646 Lincs RO Ad/Ac/28/209
Sharpe, Roger, Woolsthorpe, Lincs, 1638 Lincs RO Ad/Ac/25/284
Sharpe, Samuel, Deeping St James, Lincs, 1674 Lincs RO Ad/Ac/34/27
Sharpe, Thomas, Fladbury (Hobheath), Worcs, Worcs RO 008.7 BA3585/834/450
Sharpe, Thomas, gentleman, Warfield, Berks, 1603 Berks RO D/A1/213/21A
Sharpe, Thomas, Swineshead, Lincs, 1614 Lincs RO Ad/Ac/12/172
Sharpe, Thomas, Donington, Lincs, 1623 Lincs RO Ad/Ac/18/67
Sharpe, Valentine, Hinckley, Leics, 1642 Leics RO PR/I/41A/93
Sharpe, Vincent, husbandman, Folkestone, Kent, 1666 CKS PRC1/11/154
Sharpe, William, ?miller, Canterbury Holy Cross Westgate, Kent, 1594 CKS PRC2/7/291
Sharpe, William, Kyme, South, Lincs, 1602 Lincs RO Ad/Ac/5/17
Sharpe, William, Hurley, Berks, 1609 Berks RO D/A1/213/61C
Sharpe, William, Gosberton, Lincs, 1613 Lincs RO Ad/Ac/12/13
Sharpe, William, Fiskerton, Notts, 1638 Borthwick Prob. Ex. 1638/7
Sharpe, William, Donington, Lincs, 1648 Lincs RO Ad/Ac/30/345
Sharpe/Coller, Ann, Brookland, Kent, 1680 CKS PRC2/39/109
Sharpey, John, Whitstable, Kent, 1596 CKS PRC2/8/212
Sharpey, John, Cranbrook, Kent, 1705 CKS PRC1/16/70
Sharpey, Richard eld,
Kent 1633 CKS PRC20/11/432
Sharpie, Stephen, Rainham, Kent, 1632 CKS PRC2/31/157
Sharpis, Henry, Inkpen, Berks, 1674 Berks RO D/A1/214/161C
Sharpis, John, weaver: 'serge weaver/husbandman', Inkpen, Berks, 1681 Berks RO D/A1/214/194C
Sharples, Hugh, Ayton, Yorks, 1639 Borthwick Prob. Ex. 1639/1
Sharples, Thomas, mercer, Warwick, Warks, 1598 Worcs RO 008.7 BA3585/838/160
Sharples, William, mercer, Warwick, Warks, 1583 Worcs RO 008.7 BA3585/838/2
Sharples/Ward, Richard, Ormskirk, Lancs, 1619 Lancs RO (Name of Deceased) D.R.C.H. 1619
Sharppe, Stephen, Cranbrook, Kent, 1581 CKS PRC2/2/15

Sharpye, Stephen, yeoman, Benenden, Kent, 1664 CKS PRC1/10/86
Sharrock, Henrie, clergy: 'clerk', Bennington, Long, Lincs, 1627 Lincs RO Ad/Ac/20b/20
Sharsted, John, St Laurence Thanet, Kent, 1604 CKS PRC2/13/333
Sharsted, John, Sellindge, Kent, 1684 CKS PRC2/40/248
Sharvall, Bennett, widow, Appledore, Kent, 1620 CKS PRC2/19/57
Sharwall, Thomas eld, Appledore, Kent, 1617 CKS PRC2/19/52
Shasted, Robert, butcher, Folkestone, Kent, 1680 CKS PRC2/38/182
Shasted, William, Bearsted, Kent, 1630 CKS PRC20/9/386
Shaston, Cutbert, Lydd, Kent, 1582 CKS PRC21/5/173
Shaston, Cutbert, Lydd, Kent, 1582 CKS PRC21/5/175
Shatbolt, Thomas, husbandman, Weston, Herts, Herts RO AHH23/2148
Shaw, Anne, widow, Stainfield, Lincs, 1632 Lincs RO Ad/Ac/23/89
Shaw, Augustine, blacksmith, Sandwich, Kent, 1675 CKS PRC2/36/241
Shaw, Christopher, Filey (Gristhorpe), Yorks, 1636 Borthwick Prob. Ex. 1636/2
Shaw, Christopher, Chichester, Sussex, 1638 W. Suss RO EpIII/9/1/42
Shaw, John, Whitstable, Kent, 1629 CKS PRC2/30/128
Shaw, John, St Dunstan in the East, London & Middlesex, 1694 PRO PROB5/1578
Shaw, John, surgeon, Eckington (Mosbrough), Derby, 1785 LJRO/B/C/5/1785/87
Shaw, John, overlooker, Leeds St Peter (Holbeck), Yorks, 1825 Borthwick Test C.P. 1825/3
Shaw, Michael, butcher, Boughton under Blean, Kent, 1668 CKS PRC19/4/30
Shaw, Richard, Haxey (Burnham), Lincs, 1665 Lincs RO Ad/Ac/41/137
Shaw, Thomas, yeoman, Enderby, Mavis, Lincs, 1645 Lincs RO Ad/Ac/28/159
Shaw, William, Wyberton, Lincs, 1645? Lincs RO Ad/Ac/28/123
Shaw, William, tailor, Detling, Kent, 1682 CKS PRC20/13/287
Shawe, Henrie, Coates, Alken, Lancs, 1637 Borthwick Prob. Ex. 1637/4
Shawe, James, Horsham, Sussex, 1635 W. Suss RO EpI/33/1635/2
Shawe, Joane, widow, Sandwich, Kent, 1613 CKS PRC2/16/154
Shawe, Joane, Newcastle under Lyme, Staffs, 1685 LJRO/B/C/5/1684/71
Shawe, John, Wingham, Kent, 1574 CKS PRC21/2/179
Shawe, John, gentleman, Bottesford, Lincs, 1626 Lincs RO Ad/Ac/39/180
Shawe, John, Bottesford, Lincs, 1634 Lincs RO Ad/Ac/40/75
Shawe, John, Boston, Lincs, 1641 Lincs RO Ad/Ac/27/228
Shawe, Mary, Sibsey, Lincs, 1650 Lincs RO Ad/Ac/29/101
Shawe, Richard, Grantham, Lincs, 1638 Lincs RO Ad/Ac/25/283
Shawe, Robert, Canterbury St George Martyr, Kent, 1598 CKS PRC2/10/252
Shawe, Thomas, yeoman, Broughton (Manby), Lincs, 1602 Lincs RO Ad/Ac/37/114
Shawe, Thomas, Cranbrook, Kent, 1613 CKS PRC2/16/132
Shawe, Thomas, bricklayer, Stainfield, Lincs, 1627 Lincs RO Ad/Ac/20/111
Shawe, William, Warwick, Warks, Worcs RO 008.7 BA3585/838/91
Shawe, William, Belton All Saints, Lincs, 1612 Lincs RO Ad/Ac/8b/4
Shawe, William, yeoman, Newbury, Berks, 1615 Berks RO D/A1/117/112C
Shawe, William, Barton on Humber, Lincs, 1637 Lincs RO Ad/Ac/25/360
Shawe, William, Crosby (Crosby Grange), Yorks, 1646 Borthwick Prob. Ex. 1646/1
Shawforth, John, yeoman, Wheldrake, Yorks, 1793 Borthwick Test C.P. 1793/10
Sheafe, Alexander, Cranbrook, Kent, 1602 CKS PRC21/16/150
Sheafe, Edmund, Willesborough, Kent, 1717 CKS PRC1/18/14
Sheafe, Harman, Cranbrook, Kent, 1667 CKS PRC19/3/142
Sheafe, John, Cranbrook, Kent, 1592 CKS PRC2/5/45
Sheafe, Thomas, yeoman, Wittersham, Kent, 1680 CKS PRC20/13/60
Sheafe/Drust, Elizabeth, widow, Marden, Kent, 1623 CKS PRC2/24/87
Sheall, John, merchant, Yarmouth, Great, Norf, 1732 Norfolk RO ANW/23/20/48
Sheapheard, Ann, widow, Poulshot, Wilts, 1667 Wilts RO Arch. Sarum(+ name and date)
Sheare, John, Upton, Lincs, 1627 Lincs RO Ad/Ac/39/83
Sheareman, Thomas, Elstree, Herts, 1635 Herts RO ASA25/4919
Shearman, John, Candover, Preston, Hants, 1669 Hants RO 21M65 D8/207

[Shearme:]
Shearme, George, Marhamchurch, Corn, 1616 Cornwall RO AP/S320/2
Sheather, John, Wittersham, Kent, 1627 CKS PRC20/8/417
Sheather, Thomas, Hawkhurst, Kent, 1607 CKS PRC2/14/420
Shecrofte, Gilbert, labourer, Barkston, Lincs, 1650 Lincs RO Ad/Ac/29/82
Sheene, see Cramer,
Sheepard, Henry, husbandman, Fleet, Lincs, 1634 Lincs RO Ad/Ac/24/510
Sheepy, Thomas, Mickleover, Derby, 1680 LJRO:cards/1680/31
Sheereman, Thomas, Swineshead, Lincs, 1597 Lincs RO Ad/Ac/4/49
Shefeild, John, Broughton (Gokewell), Lincs, 1597 Lincs RO Ad/Ac/37/35
Sheffeild, John, Diseworth, Leics, 1641 Leics RO PR/I/41A/68
Sheffeild, Thomas, gentleman, Croxby, Lincs, 1645 Lincs RO Ad/Ac/28/73
Sheffeld, Vincent, esquire, Croxby, Lincs, 1618 Lincs RO Ad/Ac/14/200
Shefffeild, Thomas, Stratford-upon-Avon, Warks, 1605 Worcs RO 008.7 BA3585/839/384
Sheffield, Thomas, forgeman, Aston, Warks, 1742 LJRO/B/C/5/1742/127
Shefford, Hamlett, Wokingham, Berks, 1632 Wilts RO Miscellaneous Index (name + date)
Sheild, Thomas, grocer, Queenborough, Kent, 1680 CKS PRC2/38/186
Sheild, William, butcher, Queenborough, Kent, 1672 CKS PRC2/35/179
Shelburn, Thomas, Benington, Lincs, 1612 Lincs RO Ad/Ac/11/66
Shelburne, Edward, Caythorpe, Lincs, 1632 Lincs RO Ad/Ac/23/46
Shelburne, Thomas, clergy: 'parson/rector', Pangbourne, Berks, 1596 Berks RO D/A1/116/105C
Shelburne, Thomas, Foston, Lincs, 1613 Lincs RO Ad/Ac/12/84
Sheldon, Richard, Sherbourne, Dors, 1636 Wilts RO Miscellaneous Index (name + date)
Shelforde, Lawrence, Bourne, Lincs, 1605 Lincs RO Ad/Ac/6/149
Shell, John, Rugby, Warks, 1683 LJRO/B/C/5/1682/90
Shelley, John, gentleman, Steyning, Sussex, 1633 W. Suss RO EpI/33/1632/21
Shellitoe, Robert, butcher, Digby, Lincs, 1614 Lincs RO Ad/Ac/13/191
Shelly, Thomas, Stowe, Staffs, 1682 LJRO/B/C/5/1681/35
Shelmerdine, Anne, spinster, Manchester (Lower Ardwick), Lancs, 1609 Lancs RO (Name of Deceased) D.R.C.H. 1608
Shelston, Margarett, mrs, Wye, Kent, 1642 CKS PRC1/6/82
Shelston, Thomas, gentleman, Wye, Kent, 1640 CKS PRC19/1/79
Shelton, Hugh, Thrussington, Leics, 1684 Leics RO Administrators Accounts 1682-86 f26
Shelton, John, Atcham (Uckington), Shrops, 1691 LJRO/B/C/5/1691/63
Shelton, Robert, Lilleshall, Shrops, 1674 LJRO:cards/1674/42
Shelton, Robert, degrees: 'Bachelor of Physic', Cambridge (Gonville and Caius College), Cambs, 1683 CUL V.C. Acc./Box3/45
Shelton, Thomas, Arley, Warks, 1672 LJRO:cards/1672/50
Shelvy, John, brewer, Sandwich, Kent, 1681 CKS PRC2/39/103
Shenn, Richard, Daventry, Northants, 1685 Northants RO NWill A/C/167
Shennell, Nicholas, Grainsby, Lincs, 1626 Lincs RO Ad/Ac/20/6
Shenston, Edward, Shuckburgh, Lower, Warks, 1683 LJRO/B/C/5/1682/91
Shenton, Samuel, slater, Derby, Derby, 1817 LJRO/B/C/5/1817/78
Shepard, Richard, Chipping Barnet, Herts, 1634 Herts RO ASA25/4905
Shepard, Richard, weaver, Leigh, South, Oxon, 1673 Oxon RO MSS Wills 149/3/5
Sheparde, Richard, Pinvin, Worcs, 1600 Worcs RO 008.7 BA3585/834/445
Shepardson, Edwarde, Gainsborough, Lincs, 1589 Lincs RO Ad/Ac/37/7
Sheperd, William, Boston, Lincs, 1635 Lincs RO Ad/Ac/24/427
Shephard, James, Hothfield, Kent, 1639 CKS PRC2/34/274
Shepheard, John, Benington, Lincs, 1612 Lincs RO Ad/Ac/11/6
Shepheard, John, Brent, South, Som, 1635 Somerset RO D/D/Cta/S13
Shepheard, see Smith,
Shephearde, Roger, Dalderby, Lincs, 1612 Lincs RO Ad/Ac/11/76
Shepheare, John, Skeffling, Yorks, 1638 Borthwick Prob. Ex. 1638/11
Shepherd, Ann, widow, Repton, Derby, 1712 LJRO/B/C/5/1712/90
Shepherd, Bartholomew, Blyborough, Lincs, 1683 Lincs RO Ad/Ac/44/34

Shepherd, John, Donington, Lincs, 1619 Lincs RO Ad/Ac/15/9
Shepherd, John, innholder, Osbaldwick, Yorks, 1766 Borthwick Test C.P. 1765/3
Shepherd, Joseph, saddler, Bristol, Glos, Bristol RO 1773/CP
Shepherd, Lawrence, yeoman, Rochdale (Lee Holmes), Lancs, 1796 Lancs RO (Name of Deceased) D.R.C.H. 1796-98
Shepherd, Michael, baker, Huntingdon, Hunts, 1679 Hunts RO/Acc58/140(81)
Shepherd, Robert, Somerton, Som, 1603 Somerset RO D/D/Cta/S35
Shepherd, Robert + Mary, Somerton, Som, 1603 Somerset RO D/D/Cta/C42
Shepherd, Thomas, Wittersham, Kent, 1584 CKS PRC21/7/85
Shepherd, Thomas, Hannington, Wilts, 1605 Wilts RO CC Sarum(+ name and date)
Shepherd, Thomas, Selsey, Sussex, 1651 W. Suss RO EpI/33/1651/1
Shepley, John, Steeping, Great, Lincs, 1637 Lincs RO Ad/Ac/25/601
Sheppard, George, husbandman, Othery, Som, 1625 Somerset RO D/D/Cta/S11
Sheppard, Joane, Donington, Lincs, 1638 Lincs RO Ad/Ac/25/16
Sheppard, John, Scrivelsby, Lincs, Lincs RO Ad/Ac/1/32
Sheppard, John, Holt, Worcs, 1598 Worcs RO 008.7 BA3585/838/164
Sheppard, John, Feock, Corn, 1614 Cornwall RO AP/S256/2
Sheppard, John, Barrowby, Lincs, 1622 Lincs RO Ad/Ac/17/6
Sheppard, John, barber, Wrington, Som, 1630 Somerset RO D/D/Cta/S76
Sheppard, John, Brent, South, Som, 1635 Somerset RO D/D/Cta/S10
Sheppard, Joseph, Croscombe, Som, Somerset RO D/D/Cta/S62
Sheppard, Mary, widow, Pattishall (Dalscote), Northants, 1680 Northants RO NWill A/C/12
Sheppard, Randall, Kimbolton (Wornditch), Hunts, 1684 Hunts RO/Acc58/230(230)
Sheppard, Richard, Ferring, Sussex, 1685 W. Suss RO EpI/33/1684/34
Sheppard, Robert, yeoman, Quadring, Lincs, 1641 Lincs RO Ad/Ac/27/202
Shepparde, John, Gonerby, Lincs, 1606 Lincs RO Ad/Ac/7/42
Shepperd, Matthew, Radbourne, Derby, 1683 LJRO/B/C/5/1683/20
Shepperd, Thomas, Burton Pedwardine, Lincs, 1599 Lincs RO Ad/Ac/5/322
Sherburne, Robert, Saxilby (North Ingleby), Lincs, 1667 Lincs RO Ad/Ac/33/14
Shereshawe, Thomas, Winthorpe, Lincs, 1613 Lincs RO Ad/Ac/12/63
Sheresmyth, Thomas, yeoman, Flixborough, Lincs, 1607 Lincs RO Ad/Ac/37/242
Sherewood/Whate, Joan, widow, Beenham, Berks, 1607 Berks RO D/A1/213/36A
Shergall, John, Stratford Tony, Wilts, 1619 Wilts RO Miscellaneous Index (name + date)
Shergall, Thomas, Broad Chalke, Wilts, 1614 Wilts RO Miscellaneous Index (name + date)
Shergould, Robert, Urchfont, Wilts, 1674 Wilts RO Arch. Sarum(+ name and date)
Shergould, Robert, Urchfont (Wedhampton), Wilts, 1679? Wilts RO Arch. Sarum(+ name and date)
Sheriff, John, Martin, Lincs, 1637 Lincs RO Ad/Ac/25/565
Sheriffe, John, husbandman, Drayton, Berks, 1612 Berks RO D/A1/117/56C&D
Sherley, Francis, gentleman, Coombes, Sussex, 1621 W. Suss RO EpI/33/1621/3
Sherley, Joane, widow, Birchington, Kent, 1596 CKS PRC21/14/35
Sherley, Phillip, bachelor, Lincoln's Inn, London & Middlesex, 1674 PRO PROB32/10/39
Sherley, Richard, Birchington, Kent, 1600 CKS PRC21/15/184
Sherley, Richard, Oxford St Clement, Oxon, 1662 Oxon RO MSS Wills 86/2/4
Sherlock, Giles, Ilchester, Som, 1739 Somerset RO D/D/Cta/S77
Sherman, Anthony, husbandman, Ropsley, Lincs, 1672 Lincs RO Ad/Ac/33/195
Sherman, James, St Stephen Walbrook, London & Middlesex, 1690 PRO PROB32/31/298
Sherman, John, Coningsby, Lincs, 1666 Lincs RO Ad/Ac/32/102
Sherman, John, Bytham, Little, Lincs, 1670 Lincs RO Ad/Ac/32/181
Sherman, Marie, widow, Toft Next Newton, Lincs, 1632 Lincs RO Ad/Ac/23/29
Sherman, Richard, husbandman, Ropsley, Lincs, 1627 Lincs RO Ad/Ac/20b/80
Sherman, William, Sandwich, Kent, 1617 CKS PRC2/19/51
Sherman, William, husbandman, Toft Next Newton, Lincs, 1632 Lincs RO Ad/Ac/23/30
Sherman, William, Braceby, Lincs, 1641 Lincs RO Ad/Ac/27/226
Sherme, John, Launcells, Corn, 1608 Cornwall RO AP/S120/3

[Shermon:]
Shermon, Thomas, yeoman, Stapleton, Glos, Bristol RO 1771/CP
Shernall, William, mariner, Dover, Kent, 1665 CKS PRC19/3/82
Sherratt, Ann, spinster, Yoxall, Staffs, 1791 LJRO/B/C/5/1791/61
Sherratt, Francis, gentleman, Leigh (Nebutt), Staffs, 1679 LJRO:cards/1679/8
Sherratt, Richard, Norton in the Moors, Staffs, 1667 LJRO:cards/1667/71
Sherratt, Thomas, husbandman, Ellastone (Calwich), Staffs, 1792 LJRO/B/C/5/1792/59
Sherratt, William, yeoman, Clifton Campville, Staffs, 1779 LJRO/B/C/5/1779/85
Sherrbrook, Thomas W, Weston-upon-Trent, Staffs, 1682 LJRO/B/C/5/1681/36
Sherriff, Elizabeth, widow, Nettleham, Lincs, 1685 Lincs RO Ad/Ac/44/137
Sherwin, Elizabeth, widow, Cranbrook, Kent, 1696 CKS PRC2/42/122
Sherwin, John, Tetford, Lincs, 1620 Lincs RO Ad/Ac/16/89
Sherwin, Patience, widow, Faversham, Kent, 1668 CKS PRC1/13/113
Sherwin, Thomas, webster, Leake, Lincs, 1641 Lincs RO Ad/Ac/27/343
Sherwood, Edmond, Chippenham, Wilts, 1617 Wilts RO Arch. Wilts.(+ name and date)
Sherwood, Francis eld, Shaw cum Donnington, Berks, 1675 Berks RO D/A1/214/165C
Sherwood, Gregorie, Staplehurst, Kent, 1611 CKS PRC2/16/92
Sherwood, Henry, innholder, Oddington, Oxon, 1667 Oxon RO MSS Wills 300/2/2
Sherwood, Hugh, Ashby de la Zouch, Leics, 1673 Leics RO Administrators Accounts 1667-72 f101
Sherwood, James, Yarmouth, Great, Norf, Norfolk RO ANW/23/13/15
Sherwood, Joan, widow, Swallowfield, Berks, 1636 Berks RO D/A1/119/56C
Sherwood, John, Sevington, Kent, 1600 CKS PRC2/11/353
Sherwood, John, degrees: 'Doctor of Physic', Bath, Som, 1621 Somerset RO D/D/Cta/S34
Sherwood, John, Ashby de la Zouch, Leics, 1666 Leics RO Administrators Accounts C17th f42
Sherwood, John, gentleman, Ardington (Ardington Wick), Berks, 1679 Berks RO D/A1/121/96E
Sherwood, John, wool comber, Norwich St Martin at Oak, Norf, 1716 Norfolk RO ANW/23/12/71
Sherwood, Martha, widow, Eastchurch, Sheppey, Kent, 1613 CKS PRC2/17/375
Sherwood, Robert, Boston, Lincs, 1637 Lincs RO Ad/Ac/25/408
Sherwood, Robert, bachelor, Grinstead, West, Sussex, 1672 W. Suss RO EpI/33/1672/9
Sherwood, Thomas, tanner, Abingdon, Berks, 1667 Berks RO D/A1/214/119C
Sherwood, William, Somercoates, South, Lincs, 1635 Lincs RO Ad/Ac/24/383
Shew, Thomas, Horncastle, Lincs, 1638 Lincs RO Ad/Ac/25/67
Sheward, Richard, Inkberrow, Worcs, 1603 Worcs RO 008.7 BA3585/839/318
Sheward, Samuel, St Marylebone (Beaumont Mews High St), London & Middlesex, 1811 Greater London RO DL/C/569/110
Sheward, Samuel, St Marylebone (Beaumont Mews High St), London & Middlesex, 1815 Greater London RO DL/C/575/63
Shewry, Richard, Hinton Waldrist (Duxford), Berks, 1666 Berks RO D/A1/214/121C
Sheyler, Richard ygr, husbandman, Lyneham, Oxon, 1624 Oxon RO MSS Wills 173/3/6
Shilling, Abraham, labourer, Herne, Kent, 1677 CKS PRC20/12/242
Shilling, Elizabeth, widow, Throwleigh, Kent, 1637 CKS PRC2/34/127
Shillingford, Anne, widow, Lydd, Kent, 1639 CKS PRC20/11/368
Shillingford, see Izard,
Shilten, Alexander, Stanton Fitzwarren, Wilts, 1676 Wilts RO Miscellaneous Index (name + date)
Shilton, John eld, yeoman, Shrivenham (Bourton), Berks, 1623 Berks RO D/A1/213/129C
Shilton, Robert, Ashton Keynes, Wilts, 1618 Wilts RO Arch. Wilts.(+ name and date)
Shindler, Elizabeth, widow, Canterbury St Margaret, Kent, 1711 CKS PRC1/17/40
Shingleton, William, Marden, Kent, 1596 CKS PRC2/9/193
Shipley, Thomas, Luddington, Lincs, 1630 Lincs RO Ad/Ac/39/261
Shiplie, Ralfe, Epworth, Lincs, 1617 Lincs RO Ad/Ac/8b/201
Shipman, Margaret, widow, Cannings, All, Wilts, 1618 Wilts RO Arch. Wilts.(+ name and date)
Shipp, Edin, Careby, Lincs, 1629 Lincs RO Ad/Ac/22/103
Shipp, Henrie, Donington, Lincs, 1633 Lincs RO Ad/Ac/24/118
Shippard, William + Elizabeth, Kilkhampton, Corn, 1618 Cornwall RO AP/S319/2

Shippe, Edward, labourer, Skirbeck, Lincs, 1620 Lincs RO Ad/Ac/16/86
Shipreeve, see Shipway,
Shipton, Eleanor, widow, Shaw cum Donnington, Berks, 1681 Berks RO D/A1/214/190C
Shipton, John, apothecary, Canterbury St Mary-Magdalen Burgate, Kent, 1666 CKS PRC1/11/77
Shipton, Maurice, yeoman, Shaw cum Donnington, Berks, 1612 Berks RO D/A1/213/77A
Shipwash, Henry, Chilham, Kent, 1679 CKS PRC2/38/192
Shipway/Shipreeve, Henry, Overton, Wilts, 1633 Wilts RO Arch. Wilts.(+ name and date)
Shipwirth, John, Milton next Sittingbourne, Kent, 1638 CKS PRC2/34/281
Shires, Elizabeth, Epworth, Lincs, 1607 Lincs RO Ad/Ac/37/250
Shirfeild, John, Chichester, Sussex, 1668 W. Suss RO EpIII/9/1/53
Shirt, Margaret, Cheddleton (Cheddleton Park), Staffs, 1817 LJRO:cards/1817/2
Shobridge, Jane, widow, Appledore, Kent, 1620 CKS PRC2/19/39
Shoncke, Nicholas, Sandwich St Peter, Kent, 1606 CKS PRC2/13/365
Shonke, Thomas, fisherman, St Peter in Thanet, Kent, 1679 CKS PRC2/38/180
Shonke, see Brightwell,
Shore, Joseph, vintner, York, Yorks, 1787 Borthwick Test C.P. 1787/10
Shorie/Heathe, Robarte, Maidstone, Kent, 1609 CKS PRC20/2/21
Shorly, Robert, Winterbourne Stoke, Wilts, 1670 Wilts RO Arch. Sarum(+ name and date)
Short, Adam, Walberton, Sussex, 1682 W. Suss RO EpI/33/1682/30
Short, Ann, spinster, Birmingham, Warks, 1748 LJRO/B/C/5/1748/261
Short, Anne, widow, Canterbury All Saints, Kent, 1627 CKS PRC2/27/165
Short, Francis, yeoman, Dunholme, Lincs, 1676 Lincs RO Ad/Ac/42/55
Short, George, Poughill, Corn, 1647 Cornwall RO AP/S969/2
Short, James, Hanbury (Newborough), Staffs, 1747 LJRO/B/C/5/1747/213
Short, John, Littlehampton, Sussex, 1605 W. Suss RO EpI/33/1604/5
Short, John, Hardingstone (Cotton-End), Northants, 1685 Northants RO NWill A/C/164
Short, Jonas, Whitstable, Kent, 1672 CKS PRC2/35/174
Short, Margery, Stoke Climsland, Corn, 1605 Cornwall RO AP/S46/2
Short, Reginald, yeoman, Warehorne, Kent, 1641 CKS PRC1/6/17
Short, Richard, Bowerchalke, Wilts, 1667? Wilts RO Arch. Sarum(+ name and date)
Short, Walter, miner: 'coal miner', Mells, Som, 1717 Somerset RO D/D/Cta/S78
Short, Walton, painter, Bristol St Stephen, Glos, Bristol RO 1758/27
Short, William, cordwainer: 'shoemaker', Banbury, Oxon, Oxon RO MSS Wills Pec 51/1/5
Shorte, Grace, Ardington, Berks, 1610 Berks RO D/A1/213/65C
Shorte, Robert, Willingham, Cherry, Lincs, 1668 Lincs RO Ad/Ac/33/13
Shorte, Thomas, Smeeth, Kent, 1588 CKS PRC21/9/90
Shorth, Thomas, St Johns Thanet, Kent, 1637 CKS PRC2/33/124
Shorthoes, Henrie, Stamford St Mary, Lincs, 1606 Lincs RO Ad/Ac/6/71
Shortwilliams, Daniel, mariner?, Dover, Kent, 1634 CKS PRC20/11/418
Shosmithe, Robarte, Stelling, Kent, 1599 CKS PRC2/10/441
Shotcher, Richard, Petworth, Sussex, 1617 W. Suss RO EpI/33/1617/21
Shott, James, Bromley, Kent, 1681 PRO PROB5/1246
Shotter, Alice, spinster, Fernhurst, Sussex, 1640 W. Suss RO EpI/33/1640/15
Shotter, John ygr, Midhurst, Sussex, 1684 W. Suss RO EpI/33/1684/9
Shotwater, Anne, widow, Chartham, Kent, 1676 CKS PRC2/37/97
Shotwater, John, yeoman, Harbledown, Kent, 1639 CKS PRC2/34/279
Shotwater, Thomas, Stanford, Kent, 1662 CKS PRC19/3/16
Shotwell, Robert, Ashbourne, Derby, 1667 LJRO:cards/1667/72
Shoulder, John, Canterbury St Margaret, Kent, 1676 CKS PRC2/37/89
Shoveler, John, Minster in Sheppey, Kent, 1604 CKS PRC2/13/338
Showell, John, yeoman, Newbury, Berks, 1686 Berks RO D/A1/215/38C
Showell, Thomas, Christian Malford, Wilts, 1621 Wilts RO Arch. Wilts.(+ name and date)
Showpes, William, Whitby (Aislaby), Yorks, 1638 Borthwick Prob. Ex. 1638/10
Shrawley, Reginold, Canterbury St John's Hospital, Kent, 1638 CKS PRC20/11/318
Shreife, Thomas, blacksmith, Thame, Oxon, Oxon RO MSS Wills Pec 51/3/12

[Shrigley:]
Shrigley, Thomas, Prestbury (Hurdsfield), Ches, 1618 Cheshire RO (Name) W.C. 1617
Shrimpton, Stephen, Winchester, Hants, 1625 Hants RO 21M65 D8/130
Shroubsoll, John, yeoman, Boughton under Blean, Kent, 1631 CKS PRC20/9/402
Shrubsole, Alice, widow, Boughton under Blean, Kent, 1622 CKS PRC20/6/266
Shrubsole, Edward, yeoman, Chartham, Kent, 1673 CKS PRC2/35/177
Shrubsole, Edward, Ringwould, Kent, 1675 CKS PRC2/36/131
Shrubsole, Edward eld, Boughton under Blean, Kent, 1594 CKS PRC21/12/391
Shrubsole, John, Boughton under Blean, Kent, 1639 CKS PRC20/11/392
Shrubsole, Mary, widow, Leysdown, Kent, 1641 CKS PRC1/6/18
Shrubsole, Moses, Throwleigh, Kent, 1673 CKS PRC2/35/178
Shrubsole, Nathaniel, yeoman, Chartham, Kent, 1698 CKS PRC2/42/145
Shrubsole, Robert, Faversham, Kent, 1595 CKS PRC2/7/377
Shrubsole, Robert, Boughton under Blean, Kent, 1616 CKS PRC20/3/300
Shrubsole, Rychard, Boughton under Blean, Kent, 1596 CKS PRC21/14/143
Shrubsoll, John, yeoman, Stelling, Kent, 1666 CKS PRC1/11/155
Shuler, Robert,
Leics 1669 Leics RO Administrators Accounts 1667-72 f17
Shute, Zachary, Highgate, London & Middlesex, 1684 PRO PROB32/23/192
Shutleworth, Priscilla, Owston, Lincs, 1663 Lincs RO Ad/Ac/41/70
Shutt, William, ironmonger: 'saddlers ironmonger', Walsall, Staffs, 1831 LJRO/B/C/5/1831/28
Shuttlewood, Joell, husbandman, Thurcaston, Leics, Leics RO Administrators Accounts 1667-72 f58
Shuttlewood, Thomas, Spalding, Lincs, 1649 Lincs RO Ad/Ac/30/239
Shuttleworth, Henry, Bottesford, Lincs, 1682 Lincs RO Ad/Ac/44/14
Shyne, Nicholas, Welford/West Shefford, Berks, 1606? Berks RO D/A1/213/38A
Siar, Jo., Amesbury, Wilts, 1640 Wilts RO Arch. Sarum(+ name and date)
Sibsey, Matthew, Boston, Lincs, 1637 Lincs RO Ad/Ac/25/469
Sibsey, Peter, yeoman, Frieston, Lincs, 1620 Lincs RO Ad/Ac/15/278
Sibsey, Richard, yeoman, Skegness, Lincs, 1683 Lincs RO Ad/Ac/44/67
Sibsey, Richard, yeoman, Skegness, Lincs, 1683 Lincs RO Ad/Ac/44/116
Sicke, Thomas, Hogsthorpe, Lincs, 1593 Lincs RO Ad/Ac/3/11
Sicke, Thomas, Hogsthorpe, Lincs, 1626 Lincs RO Ad/Ac/20/21
Sicke, Thomas, Hogsthorpe, Lincs, 1632 Lincs RO Ad/Ac/23/133
Sickell, Humfrye, Ebony, Kent, 1604 CKS PRC2/13/346
Sidbirie, Thomas, weaver, Bythorn, Hunts, 1684 Hunts RO/Acc58/241(237)
Siddall, Ann, widow, Staveley, Derby, 1801 LJRO/B/C/5/1801/67
Siddall, Ann, widow, Dronfield, Derby, 1806 LJRO/B/C/5/1806/105i
Siddall, John, husbandman, Dronfield, Derby, 1799 LJRO/B/C/5/1806/105
Sidebottom, Samuel, chapman, Oldham (Hollinwood), Yorks, Borthwick Test C.P. 1738/10
Siderfin, Anne, widow, St Anne Westminster, London & Middlesex, 1707 PRO PROB32/50/71
Sigworte, Simon + Alice, St Laurence Thanet, Kent, 1616 CKS PRC2/19/38
Silcocke, Richard, Rasen, Middle, (Tupholme), Lincs, 1633 Lincs RO Ad/Ac/24/169
Silk, June, widow, Kingswinford (Brierly Hill), Staffs, 1797 LJRO/B/C/5/1797/117b
Silke, Christopher, Somersham, Hunts, 1677 Hunts RO/Acc58/113(39)
Silke, Vincent, Harbledown, Kent, 1613 CKS PRC2/17/235
Sillavant, Joan, spinster, Newlyn, East, Corn, 1642 Cornwall RO AP/S833/3
Silles, Henry, blacksmith, Kingsdown, Kent, 1682 CKS PRC2/39/236
Sillibourne, German, Canterbury St Paul, Kent, 1613 CKS PRC2/17/233
Sillver, Jacob, Godmersham, Kent, 1629 CKS PRC20/8/450
Silston, Charles, Lea, Lincs, 1662 Lincs RO Ad/Ac/41/40
Silston, Dorothie, spinster, Lea, Lincs, 1664 Lincs RO Ad/Ac/41/129
Silston, Dorothie, Lea, Lincs, 1667? Lincs RO Ad/Ac/33/5
Silver, John, yeoman, Wargrave, Berks, 1663 Berks RO D/A1/214/92C
Silverside, Thomas, fishmonger, Wrawby cum Brigg (Glanford Brigg), Lincs, 1618 Lincs RO Ad/Ac/14/108

Silversides, John, clergy: 'clerk', Calceby, Lincs, 1637 Lincs RO Ad/Ac/25/374
Silvertop, William, Sandwich, Kent, 1600 CKS PRC2/11/302
Silvester, Henrie, victualler, Canterbury St Mary Northgate, Kent, 1626 CKS PRC2/27/161
Silvester, Henry, Bletchingdon, Oxon, 1679 Oxon RO MSS Wills 86/3/23
Silvester, Michael, husbandman, Longworth, Berks, 1633 Berks RO D/A1/213/166A
Simcox, George, surgeon?, Sutton Valence, Kent, 1693 CKS PRC2/42/74
Simes, Thomas, yeoman, Chislehampton, Oxon, 1664 Oxon RO MSS Wills Pec 71/3/37
Simkins, Francis, Salisbury Cathedral (The Close), Wilts, 1640 Wilts RO Miscellaneous Index (name + date)
Simmes, John, yeoman, Speen, Berks, 1674 Berks RO D/A1/121/33C
Simmonds, Catharine, widow, Salisbury, Wilts, 1752? Wilts RO Miscellaneous Index (name + date)
Simmonds, Henry, Brook, Kent, 1712 CKS PRC19/6/59
Simmonds, William, gentleman, Boughton Aluph, Kent, 1695 CKS PRC2/42/110
Simmons, Elizabeth, Wells, Som, 1678 Somerset RO D/D/Cta/S79
Simmons, Elizabeth, widow, Stockbury, Kent, 1678 CKS PRC2/38/69
Simmons, Francis, bachelor, Deal, Kent, 1692 CKS PRC19/5/11
Simmons, George, mariner: 'ship commander', Stepney, London & Middlesex, 1708 PRO PROB32/51/69
Simmons, John, yeoman, Northbourne, Kent, 1668 CKS PRC1/13/114
Simmons, John, yeoman, Lydden, Kent, 1669 CKS PRC1/14/101
Simmons, John, Baldon, Toot, Oxon, 1795 Oxon RO MSS Wills Pec 71/5/35
Simmons, Josias, blacksmith/widow (sic), St Johns Thanet, Kent, 1675 CKS PRC2/36/125
Simmons, Margaret, Sturry, Kent, 1631 CKS PRC20/9/392
Simmons, Richard, husbandman, Chinnor, Oxon, 1692 Oxon RO MSS Wills 174/2/25
Simmons, Stephen, Hernhill, Kent, 1641 CKS PRC19/1/80
Simms, John, husbandman, Aldermaston, Berks, 1683 Berks RO D/A1/214/200C
Simon, Stephen, Antony, Corn, 1612 Cornwall RO AP/S251
Simondes, William, Halton Holgate, Lincs, 1626 Lincs RO Ad/Ac/20/40
Simonds, George, Redbourn, Herts, 1601 Herts RO ASA25/1804
Simons, Edward, husbandman, Ardington, Berks, 1694 Berks RO D/A1/215/83C
Simons, George, Reculver, Kent, 1606 CKS PRC20/1/160
Simons, John, Canterbury St John's Hospital, Kent, 1598 CKS PRC21/14/546
Simons, Robert, Dover, Kent, 1614 CKS PRC20/3/1
Simons, Robert, husbandman, Bethersden, Kent, 1664 CKS PRC1/10/87
Simons, Thomas, High Halden, Kent, 1662 CKS PRC1/8/112
Simons, Thomas, blacksmith, St Johns Thanet, Kent, 1665 CKS PRC1/11/78
Simonson, Christopher, weaver: 'linen weaver', Pluckley, Kent, 1673 CKS PRC2/35/257
Simonson, John, Headcorn, Kent, 1634 CKS PRC2/32/170
Simonson, Mercie, widow, Stanford, Kent, 1633 CKS PRC20/11/430
Simonson, Richard, Chart, Great, Kent, 1676 CKS PRC2/37/95
Simpson, Agnes, widow, Cockermouth, Cumb, 1634 Lancs RO (Name of Deceased) D.R.C.H. 1634
Simpson, Anne, widow, Sandwich St Peter, Kent, 1668 CKS PRC1/13/115
Simpson, Anne, widow, Sandwich St Peter, Kent, 1668 CKS PRC1/13/115a
Simpson, Anthony, Sotby, Lincs, 1611 Lincs RO Ad/Ac/10/78
Simpson, Edward, husbandman, Keele, Staffs, 1667 LJRO:cards/1667/73
Simpson, Edward, Toynton All Saints, Lincs, 1676 Lincs RO Ad/Ac/43/175
Simpson, Elizabeth, widow, Newbury, Berks, 1633 Berks RO D/A1/213/165C
Simpson, Elizabeth, spinster, York, Yorks, 1796 Borthwick Test C.P. 1795/6
Simpson, Francis, innholder, Gargrave, Yorks, 1786 Borthwick Test C.P. 1786/6
Simpson, Henrye, Sittingbourne, Kent, 1609 CKS PRC2/15/365
Simpson, Herbert, Gayton le Marsh, Lincs, 1605 Lincs RO Ad/Ac/7/173
Simpson, James, Dymchurch, Kent, 1641 CKS PRC1/6/19
Simpson, Jane, widow, Deptford, Kent, 1682 PRO PROB32/21/193

[Simpson:]
Simpson, John, tailor, Whitstable, Kent, 1666 CKS PRC1/11/156
Simpson, John, gentleman, Dover, Kent, 1675 CKS PRC20/12/186
Simpson, John, gentleman, Stoke-upon-Trent, Staffs, 1795 LJRO/B/C/5/1795/79
Simpson, Joseph, potter, Burslem, Staffs, 1789 LJRO/B/C/5/1789/122
Simpson, Joseph, gentleman, Saxton in Elmet, Yorks, 1823 Borthwick Test C.P. 1823/1
Simpson, Marye, widow, Wigtoft, Lincs, 1612 Lincs RO Ad/Ac/11/93
Simpson, Richard, Hunmanby, Yorks, 1610 Borthwick Prob. Ex. 1609/1
Simpson, Richard, husbandman, Milton, Great (Chilsworth), Oxon, 1664 Oxon RO MSS Wills Pec 51/3/9
Simpson, Richard, cooper: 'wine cooper', St Dunstan in the East, London & Middlesex, 1732 Lambeth Palace Arches G103/9
Simpson, Roger, Ripon (Bishopton), Yorks, 1610 Borthwick Prob. Ex. 1609/3
Simpson, Thomas, Bridlington (Buckton), Yorks, 1607 Borthwick Prob. Ex. 1607/1
Simpson, Thomas, cordwainer: 'shoemaker', Syston, Leics, 1672 Leics RO Administrators Accounts 1667-72 f54
Simpson, Thomas, yeoman, Grafham, Hunts, 1685 Hunts RO/Acc58/254(245)
Simpson, William, yeoman, Gosberton, Lincs, 1632 Lincs RO Ad/Ac/23/73
Simpson, William, Wainfleet All Saints, Lincs, 1648 Lincs RO Ad/Ac/30/335
Simpson/Tomasman, William, Saxelby, Leics, Leics RO Administrators Accounts 1667-72 f59
Sims, Christopher, Duffield (Belper), Derby, 1776 LJRO/B/C/5/1776/83
Sims, John, sergeant, Newcastle under Lyme, Staffs, 1809 LJRO/B/C/5/1809/72
Sims, Richard, yeoman, Littlebourne, Kent, 1613 CKS PRC2/17/93
Simson, Henrie, Spalding, Lincs, 1623 Lincs RO Ad/Ac/17/96
Singcombe, William, Spilsby, Lincs, 1662 Lincs RO Ad/Ac/32/35
Singer, Thomas, Broadwater, Sussex, 1648 W. Suss RO EpI/33/1647/2
Single, Thomas, Puckington, Som, 1634 Somerset RO D/D/Cta/S28
Singleton, John, esquire, Stanning, Lancs, 1589 Lancs RO (Name of Deceased) D.R.C.H. 1589
Singleton, John, Appledore, Kent, 1626 CKS PRC2/25/137
Singleton, Richard, Felpham (Ancton), Sussex, 1640 W. Suss RO EpI/33/1640/25
Sinnings, Thomas, butcher, Hollingbourne, Kent, 1679 CKS PRC20/12/321
Siseley, Henry, Rolvenden, Kent, 1631 CKS PRC20/9/388
Sisemer, John, Tunstall, Kent, 1602 CKS PRC2/12/347
Sisemore, Anthony, yeoman, Hartpury, Glos, 1687 GRO GDR/B4/2/S134
Sisley, John, Hawkhurst, Kent, 1665 CKS PRC1/11/79
Siston, George, Empingham, Rut, 1664 Lincs RO Ad/Ac/42/47
Sivers, Issabell, spinster, Kirton, Lincs, 1637 Lincs RO Ad/Ac/25/590
Sivers, Myles, husbandman, Sutterton, Lincs, 1642 Lincs RO Ad/Ac/28/43
Sivier/Parker, Sarah, Ashford, Kent, 1666 CKS PRC1/11/157
Skaife, Thomas, Ripon, Yorks, 1635 Borthwick Prob. Ex. 1635/1
Skaife, Thomas, Ripon, Yorks, 1635 Borthwick Prob. Ex. 1635/1b
Skaine, Elizabeth, widow, Chichester, Sussex, W. Suss RO EpIII/9/1/39
Skamell, John, Bemerton (Quidhampton), Wilts, 1639 Wilts RO Arch. Sarum(+ name and date)
Skamon, Edward, husbandman, Stallingborough, Lincs, 1613 Lincs RO Ad/Ac/12/14
Skarburgh, Robert, Baumber, Lincs, 1611 Lincs RO Ad/Ac/10/1
Skeath, Rowland, Greatford, Lincs, 1638 Lincs RO Ad/Ac/25/46
Skeene, Henry, mr, Boughton under Blean, Kent, 1677 CKS PRC20/12/241
Skeere, Henry, Doddington, Kent, 1601 CKS PRC2/12/349
Skeere, Jeffery, gentleman, Doddington, Kent, 1668 CKS PRC1/12/79
Skeere, Richard, Lenham, Kent, 1643 CKS PRC1/6/83
Skeete, Mabel, Heyshott, Sussex, 1629 W. Suss RO EpI/33/1629/25
Skeldinge, Thomas, Pedmore, Worcs, 1648 Worcs RO 008.7 BA3585/837/bdl 1
Skelton, Charles, Louth, Lincs, 1665 Lincs RO Ad/Ac/42/52
Skelton, Francis, Bridlington, Yorks, 1609 Borthwick Prob. Ex. 1609/5
Skelton, John, Kirton, Lincs, 1607 Lincs RO Ad/Ac/7/48
Skelton, Richard, Kirton, Lincs, 1613 Lincs RO Ad/Ac/11/43

[Skelton:]
Skelton, Sara, spinster, Lincoln St Margaret in the Close, Lincs, 1669 Lincs RO Ad/Ac/42/54
Skelton, Thomas, Wragby, Lincs, 1622 Lincs RO Ad/Ac/17/56
Skelton, Thomas, Maidstone, Kent, 1625 CKS PRC20/7/271
Skelton, Thomas, Lincoln, Lincs, 1636 Lincs RO Ad/Ac/24/268
Skelton, Thomas, husbandman, Wrangle, Lincs, 1670 Lincs RO Ad/Ac/32/175
Skelton, Thomas, wheelwright, Lichfield (Muckley Corner), Staffs, 1783 LJRO/B/C/5/1783/181
Skelton, William, Coningsby, Lincs, 1638 Lincs RO Ad/Ac/25/55
Skendlebie, James, Springthorpe, Lincs, 1628 Lincs RO Ad/Ac/39/5
Skenleby, Robert, Crowle, Lincs, 1677 Lincs RO Ad/Ac/35/124
Skeping, William, Woodchurch, Kent, 1598 CKS PRC21/14/563
Skerratt, Anne + Margarett, Weston, Ches, 1685 Cheshire RO (Name) W.C. 1685
Skerratt, Randle, bachelor, Sandbach, Ches, 1745 Cheshire RO (Name) W.C. 1745
Sketchley, Symon, Orton on the Hill, Leics, Leics RO Administrators Accounts 1667-72 f66
Sketes, Daniel, Tenterden, Kent, 1635 CKS PRC20/11/329
Skiggs, Richard, yeoman, Algarkirk, Lincs, 1614 Lincs RO Ad/Ac/12/166
Skilman, John, husbandman, Tackley (Nethercott), Oxon, 1635 Oxon RO MSS Wills 86/1/22
Skilton, Richard, Herne, Kent, 1625 CKS PRC20/7/267
Skilton, Thomas, Chartham, Kent, 1617 CKS PRC2/19/44
Skilton, Thomas, Minster in Thanet, Kent, 1638 CKS PRC2/34/270
Skimping, Mary, widow, Rustington, Sussex, 1629 W. Suss RO EpI/33/1629/29
Skingle, Robert, clergy: 'clerk', Hawkwell, Essex, 1739 Greater London RO DL/C/549/108
Skinner, Alexander, Waddingham, Lincs, 1662 Lincs RO Ad/Ac/41/39
Skinner, Catherine, Sandwich, Kent, 1674 CKS PRC2/36/124
Skinner, Golding, yeoman, Frittenden, Kent, 1666 CKS PRC1/11/80
Skinner, Grace, spinster, St John, Corn, 1646 Cornwall RO AP/S973/5
Skinner, Henry, miller, Wingham, Kent, 1675 CKS PRC20/12/149
Skinner, John, mariner, St Johns Thanet, Kent, 1673 CKS PRC2/35/255
Skinner, John, St Johns Thanet, Kent, 1693 CKS PRC2/42/77
Skinner, Rachael, Hackington, Kent, 1638 CKS PRC2/34/122
Skinner, Rachiell, Hackington, Kent, 1636 CKS PRC2/34/123
Skinner, Robert, Heckington, Lincs, 1649 Lincs RO Ad/Ac/30/219
Skinner, Robert, Raunds, Northants, 1680 Northants RO NWill A/C/14
Skinner, Thomas, Heckington, Lincs, 1636 Lincs RO Ad/Ac/24/500
Skinner, Thomas, gardener, Reading, Berks, 1640 Berks RO D/A1/214/41C
Skinner, William, Over, Cambs, 1629 c. CUL V.C. Acc./Box3/73
Skinscot, Robert, Nettleton, Wilts, 1638 Wilts RO Arch. Wilts.(+ name and date)
Skipwith, George, esquire, Keelby (Cottam), Lincs, 1602 Lincs RO Ad/Ac/5/377
Skipwith, John, Carlton, Great, Lincs, 1623 Lincs RO Ad/Ac/17/66
Skipwith, William, esquire, Ormsby, South, Lincs, 1624 Lincs RO Ad/Ac/19A/84
Skipwith, William, esquire, Kersby, Lincs, 1671 Lincs RO Ad/Ac/43/58
Skipworth, George, Saltfleetby St Peter, Lincs, 1626 Lincs RO Ad/Ac/20/35
Skipwth, John, Saltfleetby St Peter, Lincs, 1600 Lincs RO Ad/Ac/5/123
Skittell, Margaret, widow, Croft, Lincs, 1620 Lincs RO Ad/Ac/16/92
Skondifor, Thomas + Katherine, Speen (Speenhamland), Berks, 1612 Berks RO D/A1/213/79A
Skortreth, Richard, yeoman, Huttoft, Lincs, 1612 Lincs RO Ad/Ac/10/157
Skott, Henry + Anne, Grantham, Lincs, 1572 Lincs RO Ad/Ac/1/5
Skott, John, clothworker, Newbury, Berks, 1676 Berks RO D/A1/214/173C
Skott, William, Eastchurch, Sheppey, Kent, 1581 CKS PRC2/2/25
Skowing, Joseph, Stowupland, Suff, 1746 Suff RO(B) IC500/3/50/48
Skrine, Joseph, Bathford, Som, 1670 Somerset RO D/D/Cta/S80
Skriviner, Agnes, spinster, Limber Magna, Lincs, 1612 Lincs RO Ad/Ac/11/189
Skrymsby, Thomas, Eastling, Kent, 1595 CKS PRC2/7/197
Skudemore, Richard, Ashow, Warks, 1672 LJRO:cards/1672/51
Skutt, John, Rudgwick, Sussex, 1618 W. Suss RO EpI/33/1618/2
Skylton, Gylbert, Chilham, Kent, 1596 CKS PRC2/8/445

[Skyner:]
Skyner, John, Gwennap, Corn, 1605 Cornwall RO AP/S70
Skyner, William, innholder, Windsor, New, Berks, 1610 Berks RO D/A1/213/64C
Skynner, John, Burpham, Sussex, 1594 W. Suss RO EpI/33/1593/1
Skynner, John, Sandwich, Kent, 1623 CKS PRC2/24/88
Skynner, Richard, Lancing, Sussex, 1632 W. Suss RO EpI/33/1632/17
Skynner, Robert, St Laurence Thanet, Kent, 1623 CKS PRC2/24/78
Skynner, William, Bignor, Sussex, 1629 W. Suss RO EpI/33/1629/35
Slack, Abel, blacksmith, Macclesfield, Ches, 1731 Cheshire RO (Name) W.C. 1729-31
Slack, John, painter, Norwich, Norf, Norfolk RO ANW/23/25/67
Slacke, Anthony, Hogsthorpe, Lincs, 1648 Lincs RO Ad/Ac/30/251
Slacke, John, Sheen, Staffs, 1676 LJRO:cards/1676/44
Sladden, Benjamin, Elham, Kent, 1662 CKS PRC1/9/58
Sladden, George, innholder, Folkestone, Kent, 1689 CKS PRC2/41/162
Sladden, Richard, yeoman, Brabourne, Kent, 1691 CKS PRC2/41/186
Sladden, Thomas, yeoman, Folkestone, Kent, 1676 CKS PRC2/37/90
Sladden, Thomas, Mersham, Kent, 1679 CKS PRC2/38/188
Sladden, Thomas, Petham, Kent, 1687 CKS PRC2/41/104
Sladden/Nicol, Catherine, widow, Lydd, Kent, 1631 CKS PRC20/9/307
Slade, Dorothy, widow, Watlington, Oxon, 1755 Oxon RO MSS Wills 304/4/37
Slade, Henry, cooper: 'wine cooper', Hagbourne, Berks, 1647 Berks RO D/A1/214/73C
Slade, James, husbandman, Martin Hussingtree, Worcs, Worcs RO 008.7 BA3585/839/483
Slade, John, Hagbourne, Berks, 1601 Berks RO D/A1/213/15C
Slade, John, yeoman, Frilsham, Berks, 1672 Berks RO D/A1/214/147C
Slade, John, draper, Butleigh, Som, 1740 Somerset RO D/D/Cta/S29a
Slade, John, draper, Butleigh, Som, 1740 Somerset RO D/D/Cta/S81
Slade, Walter, Calstock, Corn, 1615 Cornwall RO AP/S280/3
Sladen, Thamasin, spinster, Shadoxhurst, Kent, 1608 CKS PRC2/15/384
Sladen, William, Lyminge, Kent, 1590 CKS PRC21/10/118
Slaney, John, Borden, Kent, 1640 CKS PRC1/3/41
Slaney, John, Baxterley, Warks, 1691 LJRO/B/C/5/1691/66
Slann, William, Sunninghill, Berks, 1616 Berks RO D/A1/213/100A
Slark, Edward, bachelor, Wimbledon, Surrey, 1756 Lambeth Palace VH82/132
Slater, Isaac, fellmonger, Northbourne, Kent, 1684 CKS PRC2/40/245
Slater, Joane, Newton on Trent, Lincs, 1626 Lincs RO Ad/Ac/39/37
Slater, John, yeoman, Pinchbeck, Lincs, 1627 Lincs RO Ad/Ac/20/90
Slater, John, yeoman, Pinchbeck, Lincs, 1627? Lincs RO Ad/Ac/20b/75
Slater, John, farmer, Doveridge (Doveridge Field), Derby, 1791 LJRO/B/C/5/1791/69
Slater, Richard, Ringwould, Kent, 1631 CKS PRC2/31/61
Slater, Thomas, Boughton Aluph, Kent, 1595 CKS PRC2/7/211
Slater, Thomas, Ponton, Little, Lincs, 1666 Lincs RO Ad/Ac/32/87
Slater, Thomas, fellmonger, Wye, Kent, 1666 CKS PRC1/11/158
Slater, William, waterman, Bourne, Lincs, 1650 Lincs RO Ad/Ac/29/89
Slater, William, farmer, Yoxall, Staffs, 1809 LJRO/B/C/5/1809/76
Slater, William, liquor merchant, Smisby, Derby, 1822 LJRO/B/C/5/1822/29
Slaterford, Christopher, Wisborough Green (Loxwood), Sussex, 1684 W. Suss RO EpI/33/1684/40
Slather, Daniel, Folkestone, Kent, 1667 CKS PRC1/12/80
Slatter, Decimus, cordwainer, Chadlington, Oxon, 1669 Oxon RO MSS Wills 174/1/18
Slatter, Emanuel, Thame, Oxon, 1667 Oxon RO MSS Wills Pec 51/3/13
Slatter, Jane, widow, Oxford St Martin, Oxon, 1680 Oxon RO MSS Wills 300/2/13
Slatter, John, Wolford, Warks, 1603 Worcs RO 008.7 BA3585/838/266
Slatter, John, baker, Woodstock, Oxon, 1636 Oxon RO MSS Wills 86/1/26
Slatter, Peter, husbandman, Long Wittenham, Berks, 1618 Berks RO D/A1/213/103C
Slatter, Peter, Bladon, Oxon, 1623 Oxon RO MSS Wills 173/3/4
Slatter, Thomas, husbandman, Chalgrove, Oxon, 1636 Oxon RO MSS Wills 86/1/24
Slaughter, John, Maidstone, Kent, 1584 CKS PRC21/6/365

Slaughter, John, fellmonger, Old Romney, Kent, 1695 CKS PRC2/42/92
Slaughter, William, Wiggonholt, Sussex, 1652 W. Suss RO EpI/33/1652/2
Slayney, Richard, Staplehurst, Kent, 1628 CKS PRC20/8/401
Slaynye, Frauncys, Staplehurst, Kent, 1587 CKS PRC2/4/144
Sleamaker, Christian, widow, Bletchingdon, Oxon, 1625 Oxon RO MSS Wills 173/3/10
Slee, Robert, Malton, Yorks, 1767 Borthwick Test C.P. 1766/2
Sleeford, Elizabeth, Grantham (Spittlegate), Lincs, 1619 Lincs RO Ad/Ac/15/175
Sleeman, John, Boyton, Corn, 1626 Cornwall RO AP/S566/2
Sleeman, Launcelot, St Columb Minor, Corn, 1624 Cornwall RO AP/S448/3
Sleeman, Roger, Helston, Corn, Cornwall RO AP/S173/4
Sleeper, Edmund, husbandman, Hibaldstow, Lincs, 1608 Lincs RO Ad/Ac/37/266
Sleight, Richard, husbandman, Sotby, Lincs, 1625 Lincs RO Ad/Ac/19B/110
Sleight, Thomas, Appleby, Lincs, 1646 Lincs RO Ad/Ac/40/125
Sleight, William, Coningsby, Lincs, 1664 Lincs RO Ad/Ac/43/27
Slight, Robert, labourer, Broughton, Lincs, 1623 Lincs RO Ad/Ac/8c/39
Slight, Thomas, Skirbeck, Lincs, 1645 Lincs RO Ad/Ac/28/135
Slim, Thomas, farmer, Sowe, Warks, 1786 LJRO/B/C/5/1786/88
Slingesby, Arthur, knight/baronet, Patrixbourne (Bifrous), Kent, early C18th? PRO PROB5/1179
Slingsby, Sarah, Belton All Saints, Lincs, 1681 Lincs RO Ad/Ac/43/167
Slingsby, William, Ashby, Lincs, 1680 Lincs RO Ad/Ac/43/148
Slingsby, William, farmer, Foleshill, Warks, 1826 LJRO/B/C/5/1826/43
Slodden, John, draper, Dover, Kent, 1676 CKS PRC20/12/222
Slodden, Josias, Ruckinge, Kent, 1626 CKS PRC2/27/152
Slodden, Thomas, Folkestone, Kent, 1634 CKS PRC2/32/116
Sloden, Christian, Elham, Kent, 1596 CKS PRC2/9/187
Sloden, Edwarde, Elham, Kent, 1591 CKS PRC2/5/428
Sloden, George, Lyminge, Kent, 1606 CKS PRC20/1/134
Sloden, John, St Nicholas at Wade, Kent, 1584 CKS PRC21/7/79
Slogett, John, Advent, Corn, 1613 Cornwall RO AP/S239/3
Sloman, George eld, yeoman, Hawkhurst, Kent, 1689 CKS PRC2/41/163
Sloman, James, Biddenden, Kent, 1593 CKS PRC2/6/290
Sloman, John, gentleman, Ashford, Kent, 1626 CKS PRC2/27/154
Sloman, Nycholas, Canterbury St Paul, Kent, 1578 CKS PRC2/1/191
Sloman, Thomas, Hawkhurst, Kent, 1608 CKS PRC20/1/286
Sloman, Thomas, weaver, Hawkhurst, Kent, 1639 CKS PRC1/3/42
Sloper, Henry, Canning, Bishops, Wilts, 1606 Wilts RO Dean and Chapter A41
Sloper, John, Somerford, Little, Wilts, 1674 Wilts RO Miscellaneous Index (name + date)
Sloper, Richard, weaver: 'broad weaver', Lacock, Wilts, 1625 Wilts RO CC Sarum(+ name and date)
Sloper, Richard, Calstone Wellington, Wilts, 1630 Wilts RO CC Sarum(+ name and date)
Slough, John, Daventry, Northants, 1683 Northants RO NWill A/C/19
Slow, Edward, Rothwell, Northants, 1679 Northants RO NWill A/C/40
Slow, Robert, Goudhurst, Kent, 1624 CKS PRC2/24/84
Slowe, Christopher jun, Holywell (Needingworth), Hunts, 1681 Hunts RO/Acc58/165(115)
Slowe, George, Gayton, Northants, 1685 Northants RO NWill A/C/33
Slowman, Thomas, labourer, Reading St Lawrence, Berks, 1622 Berks RO D/A1/213/127C
Slutter, George, Sompting, Sussex, 1613 W. Suss RO EpI/33/1613/17
Slutter, Jane, widow, Botolphs (Annington), Sussex, 1583 W. Suss RO EpI/33/1583/3
Sly, Henry, Bath St Peter & Paul, Som, 1664 Somerset RO D/D/Cta/S63
Slye, Richard, Boyton, Wilts, 1626 Wilts RO CC Sarum(+ name and date)
Smakergill, Henry, university: 'scholar's servant', Cambridge (King's College), Cambs, 1644 CUL V.C. Acc./Box2/69
Smalbone, Richard, Steventon, Berks, 1587 Berks RO D/A2/C24/f182R
Smalbone, Thomas, gentleman, Abingdon, Berks, Berks RO D/A1/214/6B
Smale, Humphrey sen, Bolsover, Derby, 1714 LJRO/B/C/5/1714/118

[Smale:]
Smale, Richard, Chilton, Som, 1639 Somerset RO D/D/Cta/S15
Smalebone, Thomas, Bucklebury, Berks, 1610 Berks RO D/A1/213/54
Smales, John, Maplederwell, Hants, 1625 Hants RO 21M65 D8/131
Smalewell, John, yeoman, Bradley, North, Wilts, 1619? Wilts RO Miscellaneous Index (name + date)
Small, John, Legsby, Lincs, 1721 Lincs RO Ad/Ac/45/13
Small, Thomas, Gainsborough, Lincs, 1676 Lincs RO Ad/Ac/35/110
Small, William, Manton, Lincs, 1614 Lincs RO Ad/Ac/8b/33
Small, William, bachelor, Gainsborough, Lincs, 1679 Lincs RO Ad/Ac/43/130
Small, William, Bighton, Hants, 1681 Hants RO 21m65 D8/325
Smallard, Joane, widow, Hythe St Leonard, Kent, 1619 CKS PRC20/4/375
Smallbone, Richard, Kennington, Berks, 1583 Berks RO D/A2/C19/f12-13
Smallbrooke, John, gentleman, Droitwich, Worcs, 1680 Worcs RO 008.7 BA3585/837/bdl 4
Smallpeece, James, gentleman, Cheltenham, Glos, 1716 GRO GDR/B4/2/R41
Smallpiece, Thomas, Kidderminster, Worcs, 1792 Worcs RO 008.7 BA3585/835/bdl 2
Smallwell, Robert, Wimborne Minster, Dors, Dorset RO PE/WM CP 2/4/83
Smallwoode, William, Thurlby, Lincs, 1638 Lincs RO Ad/Ac/25/269
Smalwell, Richard, Bradley, North, Wilts, 1630 Wilts RO Arch. Sarum(+ name and date)
Smalwood, Adam, gentleman, Kirmington, Lincs, 1613 Lincs RO Ad/Ac/11/153
Smarsett, Joshua, Tenterden, Kent, 1612 CKS PRC2/16/144
Smart, Edward, yeoman, Bisley, Glos, 1706 GRO GDR 269 (f.78)
Smart, Harriet, spinster, Pershore Holy Cross, Worcs, 1822 Worcs RO 008.7 BA3585/835/bdl 2
Smart, James, yeoman, Petworth (Byworth), Sussex, 1682 W. Suss RO EpI/33/1682/50
Smart, John, Prestbury, Glos, GRO GDR/B4/2/S130
Smart, John, Mersham, Kent, 1627 CKS PRC2/27/166
Smart, John, Folksworth, Hunts, 1677 Hunts RO/Acc58/106
Smart, Ralph, Faversham, Kent, 1693 CKS PRC2/42/76
Smart, Richard, Bisley, Glos, 1685 GRO GDR/B4/2/S135
Smart, Robert, Bratton, Wilts, 1639 Wilts RO Chantor Sarum Bundle 4/16
Smart, Stephen + Hannah, innholder, Holt, Wilts, 1746? Wilts RO Arch. Sarum(+ name and date)
Smart, Thomas, Winterbourne Stoke, Wilts, 1662 Wilts RO Arch. Sarum(+ name and date)
Smart, Thomas, husbandman, Ducklington (Cokethorpe), Oxon, 1664 Oxon RO MSS Wills 86/2/15
Smarte, Francis, Huddington, Worcs, Worcs RO 008.7 BA3585/839/319
Smead, John, husbandman, Newington next Sittingbourne, Kent, 1662 CKS PRC1/9/59
Smede, John, Hastingleigh, Kent, 1586 CKS PRC2/4/233
Smedley, Francis, Youlgreave, Derby, 1667 LJRO:cards/1667/74
Smedmore, John, gentleman, Salisbury, Wilts, 1670 Wilts RO Miscellaneous Index (name + date)
Smeed, John, Canterbury St Alphege, Kent, 1624 CKS PRC20/6/173
Smeed, Thomas, Biddenden, Kent, 1637 CKS PRC1/1/60
Smeede, John, yeoman, Elmsted, Kent, 1686 CKS PRC2/41/13
Smeede, Thomas, yeoman, Mersham, Kent, 1670 CKS PRC1/14/102
Smelt, William, Whitstable, Kent, 1624 CKS PRC2/24/93
Smelte, Andrewe, Whitstable, Kent, 1616 CKS PRC2/26/129
Smelte, Thomas, Seasalter, Kent, 1619 CKS PRC2/19/29
Smelter, Thomas, clergy: 'vicar', St Nicholas at Wade, Kent, 1701 CKS PRC19/5/81
Smersall, Edward, Stone in Oxney, Kent, 1638 CKS PRC2/34/118
Smethergate, John, Stibbington (Sibson), Hunts, 1682 Hunts RO/Acc58/187(197)
Smewin, Joan, widow, Waltham St Lawrence, Berks, 1634 Berks RO D/A1/213/153A
Smith, degrees: 'M.A./mr', Cambridge (Clare College), Cambs, 1633 CUL V.C. Acc./Box2/71
Smith, Abraham, Pluckley, Kent, 1632 CKS PRC2/31/66
Smith, Abraham, Steyning, Sussex, 1640 W. Suss RO EpI/33/1639/1
Smith, Abraham, weaver: 'linen weaver', Egerton, Kent, 1641 CKS PRC19/2/37
Smith, Abraham, Wrangle, Lincs, 1662 Lincs RO Ad/Ac/32/42
Smith, Abraham, carpenter, Chart, Little, Kent, 1682 CKS PRC2/40/78

Smith, Agnes, widow, Godmersham, Kent, 1616 CKS PRC20/3/194
Smith, Alexander, Willesborough, Kent, 1649 CKS PRC1/8/81
Smith, Alexander, mariner, Sandwich, Kent, 1687 CKS PRC2/41/106
Smith, Alice, Hampstead Marshall, Berks, 1616 Berks RO D/A1/213/97A
Smith, Alice, widow, Cranbrook, Kent, 1626 CKS PRC2/27/149
Smith, Allane, Stallingborough, Lincs, 1611 Lincs RO Ad/Ac/10/50
Smith, Andrew, Swingfield, Kent, 1669 CKS PRC1/14/103
Smith, Ann, widow, Tenterden, Kent, 1673 CKS PRC2/35/258
Smith, Ann, spinster, Norton Lindsey, Warks, 1792 Worcs RO 008.7 BA3585/835/bdl 2
Smith, Ann, Oxford All Saints, Oxon, 1810 Oxon RO MSS Wills 306/12/5
Smith, Anne, spinster, Queniborough, Leics, 1666 Leics RO Administrators Accounts C17th f40
Smith, Anne, Hardingstone, Northants, 1670 Northants RO NWill A/C/125
Smith, Anthony, Milton next Sittingbourne, Kent, 1641 CKS PRC1/6/20
Smith, Anthony, gentleman, Firle, Sussex, 1685 PRO PROB32/25/305
Smith, Attained eld, Goudhurst, Kent, 1668 CKS PRC1/13/116
Smith, Augustine, Lenham, Kent, 1688 CKS PRC2/41/135
Smith, Benjamin, yeoman, Tivetshall St Mary, Norf, 1755 Norfolk RO ANF/11/5/15
Smith, Bryan, Northorpe, Lincs, 1632 Lincs RO Ad/Ac/39/321
Smith, Catherine, Dover, Kent, 1641 CKS PRC19/2/38
Smith, Christopher, Belton, Lincs, 1619 Lincs RO Ad/Ac/15/75
Smith, Christopher, Blaby, Leics, 1641 Leics RO PR/I/41A/75
Smith, Christopher, Welford (Hoe Benham), Berks, 1668 Berks RO D/A1/120/153D
Smith, Christopher, Woodborough, Wilts, 1676 Wilts RO Miscellaneous Index (name + date)
Smith, Clayton, waterman/boatwright, Ely, Cambs, 1749 Cambs RO 1700/Inv
Smith, Daniel, Ousden, Suff, 1732 Suff RO(B) IC500/3/47/7
Smith, David, Minster in Thanet, Kent, 1606 CKS PRC2/14/422
Smith, Dorothy, Wrockwardine, Shrops, 1685 LJRO/B/C/5/1685/90
Smith, Dorothy, widow, Tenterden, Kent, 1701 CKS PRC1/16/39
Smith, Dorothy, widow, Canterbury St Paul, Kent, 1712 CKS PRC19/6/48
Smith, Edmund, Nunburnholme, Yorks, 1636 Borthwick Prob. Ex. 1636/1
Smith, Edmund, university: 'Fellow of Queens' College, Cambridge/M.A./priest' Cambridge (Queens' College), Cambs, 1677 CUL V.C. Acc./Box3/46
Smith, Edward, Darfield (Billingley), Yorks, Borthwick Test C.P. 1722/3
Smith, Edward, university: 'scholar's servant', Cambridge (St John's College), Cambs, 1606 CUL V.C.Acc./Box1/46
Smith, Edward, Hythe St Leonard, Kent, 1624 CKS PRC20/6/164
Smith, Edward, Sempringham (Pointon), Lincs, 1624 Lincs RO Ad/Ac/19A/137
Smith, Edward, Dover, Kent, 1628 CKS PRC20/8/407
Smith, Edward, Stallingborough, Lincs, 1637 Lincs RO Ad/Ac/25/375
Smith, Edward, High Halden, Kent, 1638 CKS PRC2/34/284
Smith, Edward, brewer: 'beerbrewer', Milton next Sittingbourne, Kent, 1669 CKS PRC1/14/104
Smith, Edward, Ashford, Kent, 1674 CKS PRC2/36/121
Smith, Edward, cordwainer, Tamworth, Staffs, 1701 LJRO/B/C/5/1701/90
Smith, Edward, Acre, West, Norf, 1801 Norfolk RO ANW/23/27/1
Smith, Edwarde, Kirkby on Bain (Toft Grange), Lincs, 1622 Lincs RO Ad/Ac/17/52
Smith, Elias, High Halstow, Kent, 1664 CKS PRC1/10/88
Smith, Elizabeth, widow, Leicester St Nicholas, Leics, Leics RO Administrators Accounts 1667-72 f26
Smith, Elizabeth, widow, Appledore, Kent, 1606 CKS PRC2/14/411
Smith, Elizabeth, widow, Scothorne, Lincs, 1626 Lincs RO Ad/Ac/39/87
Smith, Elizabeth, Wainfleet St Mary, Lincs, 1649 Lincs RO Ad/Ac/30/213
Smith, Elizabeth, wife, St Mary in the Marsh, Kent, 1664 CKS PRC1/9/150
Smith, Elizabeth, spinster, St Andrew Holborn, London & Middlesex, 1675 PRO PROB5/1686
Smith, Elizabeth, spinster, St Andrew Holborn, London & Middlesex, 1678 PRO PROB5/1686
Smith, Elizabeth, widow, Worcester St Nicholas, Worcs, 1682 Worcs RO 008.7 BA3585/837/bdl

[Smith:]
3
Smith, Elizabeth, widow, Lavenham, Suff, 1744 Suff RO(B) IC500/3/50/60
Smith, Ellen, widow, Barham, Kent, 1621 CKS PRC2/19/1
Smith, Frances, widow, Maidstone, Kent, 1641 CKS PRC19/2/39
Smith, Frances, widow, Lincoln St Mary Magdalen in the Bail, Lincs, 1661 Lincs RO Ad/Ac/42/53
Smith, Francis, Ingham, Lincs, 1620 Lincs RO Ad/Ac/8b/461
Smith, Francis, Stoke Prior, Worcs, 1682 Worcs RO 008.7 BA3585/837/bdl 3
Smith, Francis, gentleman, Chalgrove, Oxon, 1687 PRO PROB5/795
Smith, Fynch, Chislet, Kent, 1613 CKS PRC2/18/64
Smith, Georg, Derby (All Saints), Derby, 1683 LJRO/B/C/5/1682/93
Smith, George, Halton, West, Lincs, 1617 Lincs RO Ad/Ac/8b/113
Smith, George, Whalley (Cliviger), Lancs, 1637 Borthwick Prob. Ex. 1637/3
Smith, George, Heather, Leics, 1665 Leics RO Administrators Accounts C17th f16
Smith, George, Shifnal, Shrops, 1667 LJRO:cards/1667/75
Smith, George, maltster, Deal, Kent, 1684 CKS PRC20/13/460
Smith, George, blacksmith, Wetherby, Yorks, 1774 Borthwick Test C.P. 1774/4
Smith, Grace, widow, Goudhurst, Kent, 1613 CKS PRC2/16/90
Smith, Henery, husbandman, Spalding, Lincs, 1670 Lincs RO Ad/Ac/32/144a
Smith, Henrie, Brothertoft, Lincs, 1635 Lincs RO Ad/Ac/24/359
Smith, Henry, cordwainer: 'shoemaker', Thatcham (Henwick), Berks, 1612 Berks RO D/A1/213/78A
Smith, Henry, Marsh Chapel, Lincs, 1626 Lincs RO Ad/Ac/20/61
Smith, Henry, yeoman, Hagbourne, Berks, 1629 Berks RO D/A1/118/46C
Smith, Henry, shepherd, Uffington, Berks, 1667 Berks RO D/A1/120/150D
Smith, Henry,
Wilts 1677 Wilts RO Miscellaneous Index (name + date)
Smith, Henry, girdler, St Clement Danes, London & Middlesex, 1679 PRO PROB32/15/37
Smith, Henry, bachelor, St Margarets At Cliffe, Kent, 1684 CKS PRC20/13/462
Smith, Henry, victualler, Liverpool, Lancs, 1835 Borthwick Trans. C.P. 1836/1
Smith, Hobby, mr, Minster in Sheppey, Kent, 1629 CKS PRC2/30/122
Smith, Humfrey, Wainfleet All Saints, Lincs, 1632 Lincs RO Ad/Ac/23/111
Smith, Humphrey, Eastchurch, Sheppey, Kent, 1711 CKS PRC1/17/41
Smith, Isabell, Coningsby, Lincs, 1638 Lincs RO Ad/Ac/25/489
Smith, James, Steyning, Sussex, 1600 W. Suss RO EpI/33/1600/17
Smith, James, Ponton, Great, Lincs, 1618 Lincs RO Ad/Ac/14/5
Smith, James, yeoman, Ashington (Buncton), Sussex, 1632 W. Suss RO EpI/33/1632/20
Smith, James, Bredgar, Kent, 1667 CKS PRC1/12/82
Smith, James, cordwainer, Hull, Yorks, 1766 Borthwick Test C.P. 1766/3
Smith, Jane, widow, Hardham, Sussex, 1632 W. Suss RO EpI/33/1632/4
Smith, Jane, widow, Chester, Ches, 1783 Cheshire RO (Name) W.C. 1783
Smith, Jeremiah, Winterton, Lincs, 1765 Lincs RO Ad/Ac/45/30
Smith, Jeremy, Bethersden, Kent, 1639 CKS PRC2/34/285
Smith, Jeremy, Folkestone, Kent, 1708 CKS PRC1/17/14
Smith, Joan, spinster, Pyrton (Hollandridge), Oxon, 1638 Oxon RO MSS Wills 173/4/7
Smith, Joane, widow, Warehorne, Kent, 1620 CKS PRC2/19/46
Smith, Johane, widow, Alverstoke, Hants, 1625 Hants RO 21M65 D8/132
Smith, John, Norwich St Julian, Norf, Norfolk RO ANW/23/10/68
Smith, John, Stalmine, Lancs, 1600 Lancs RO (Name of Deceased) D.R.C.H. 1600
Smith, John, Belbroughton (Hollows), Worcs, 1605 Worcs RO 008.7 BA3585/839/414
Smith, John, Claines (Northwick), Worcs, 1605 Worcs RO 008.7 BA3585/839/334
Smith, John, jurat, New Romney, Kent, 1607 CKS PRC20/1/272
Smith, John, Clifton, North, Notts, 1609 Borthwick Prob. Ex. 1609/6
Smith, John, Headcorn, Kent, 1610 CKS PRC2/13/381
Smith, John, Minster in Sheppey, Kent, 1610 CKS PRC2/13/383

Smith, John, Ashby, Lincs, 1611 Lincs RO Ad/Ac/10/103
Smith, John, Chichester St Martin, Sussex, 1616 W. Suss RO EpIII/9/1/10
Smith, John, Eastwell, Kent, 1616 CKS PRC2/19/10
Smith, John, Gainsborough, Lincs, 1619 Lincs RO Ad/Ac/8b/341
Smith, John, Chinnock, West, Som, 1623 Somerset RO D/D/Cta/S7
Smith, John, Milford, Hants, 1623 Hants RO 21M65 D8/39
Smith, John, Fosdyke, Lincs, 1626 Lincs RO Ad/Ac/20/80
Smith, John, Minster in Sheppey, Kent, 1627 CKS PRC2/28/118
Smith, John, Deal, Kent, 1630 CKS PRC20/9/372
Smith, John, Cadney, Lincs, 1633 Lincs RO Ad/Ac/24/114
Smith, John, Milton next Sittingbourne, Kent, 1634 CKS PRC2/32/173
Smith, John, Hythe West, Kent, 1637 CKS PRC2/34/126
Smith, John, bachelor: 'singleman', Stone in Oxney, Kent, 1637 CKS PRC2/34/114
Smith, John, husbandman, Keal, East, Lincs, 1638 Lincs RO Ad/Ac/25/157
Smith, John, Wittersham, Kent, 1639 CKS PRC20/11/386
Smith, John, Ashton Keynes, Wilts, 1640 Wilts RO Arch. Wilts.(+ name and date)
Smith, John, Enderby, Wood, Lincs, 1645 Lincs RO Ad/Ac/28/111
Smith, John, gentleman, Sandwich, Kent, 1665 CKS PRC1/10/89
Smith, John, butcher, Ospringe, Kent, 1666 CKS PRC1/11/159
Smith, John, Gresley (Lynton), Derby, 1667 LJRO:cards/1667/76
Smith, John, gentleman, Mundham, North, Sussex, 1673 W. Suss RO EpI/33/1673/15
Smith, John, Heddington, Wilts, 1676 Wilts RO Miscellaneous Index (name + date)
Smith, John, grocer, Sittingbourne, Kent, 1677 CKS PRC2/37/98
Smith, John, labourer, Godmanchester, Hunts, 1681 Hunts RO/Acc58/157(13)
Smith, John, Knightwick, Worcs, 1682 Worcs RO 008.7 BA3585/837/bdl 3
Smith, John, Clifton Campville, Staffs, 1684 LJRO/B/C/5/1684/72
Smith, John, yeoman, Stratfield Mortimer, Berks, 1686 Berks RO D/A1/215/34C
Smith, John, chapman, Ashford, Kent, 1696 CKS PRC2/42/109
Smith, John, blacksmith, Duffield (Postern Park), Derby, 1700 LJRO/B/C/5/1700/60
Smith, John, Bermondsey, St Mary Magdalen, Surrey, 1711 PRO PROB5/943
Smith, John, Sandiacre, Derby, 1727 LJRO/B/C/5/1727/138
Smith, John, Brentford, Old, London & Middlesex, 1738 Greater London RO DL/C/549/65
Smith, John, yeoman, Wootton Bassett, Wilts, 1741 Wilts RO Arch. Wilts.(+ name and date)
Smith, John, gentleman, Watton, Norf, 1750 Norfolk RO ANW/23/24/98
Smith, John eld, Compton (Turevill), Berks, 1597 Berks RO D/A1/212/191C
Smith, Joseph, Sevenoaks (Riverhead), Kent, 1720 PRO PROB5/1178
Smith, Joyes, Kirton, Lincs, 1649 Lincs RO Ad/Ac/30/72
Smith, Jude, husbandman, Brightwell Baldwin, Oxon, 1640 Oxon RO MSS Wills 148/4/4
Smith, Laurence, Bethersden, Kent, 1629 CKS PRC2/29/81
Smith, Laurence, Legbourne, Lincs, 1662 Lincs RO Ad/Ac/32/34
Smith, Leonard, Ham, Kent, 1626 CKS PRC2/27/162
Smith, Leonard, Bilbrough, Yorks, 1640 Borthwick Prob. Ex. 1640/4
Smith, Lionel, Bucklebury (Marlston), Berks, 1617 Berks RO D/A1/117/132C
Smith, Lucy, New Romney, Kent, 1618 CKS PRC20/4/356
Smith, Margaret, spinster, Lydd, Kent, 1600 CKS PRC21/15/133
Smith, Marie, widow, Swineshead, Lincs, 1620 Lincs RO Ad/Ac/15/123
Smith, Mary, Headcorn, Kent, 1618 CKS PRC2/19/11
Smith, Mary, Sutton, Kings, Northants, 1619 Oxon RO MSS Wills Pec 51/1/20
Smith, Mary, Oxford St Aldate, Oxon, 1627 Oxon RO MSS Wills 59/4/29
Smith, Mary, widow, Boughton under Blean, Kent, 1634 CKS PRC20/11/412
Smith, Mary, Amesbury, Wilts, 1638 Wilts RO Arch. Sarum(+ name and date)
Smith, Mary, widow, Forncett St Peter, Norf, 1768 Norfolk RO ANF/11/5/77
Smith, Mathew, Sturry, Kent, 1617 CKS PRC2/19/53
Smith, Mathew, Canterbury St Mildred, Kent, 1637 CKS PRC2/34/115
Smith, Mathew, butcher, Deal, Kent, 1682 CKS PRC20/13/285

[Smith:]
Smith, Matthew, baker, Higham Ferrers, Northants, 1671 Northants RO NWill A/C/110
Smith, Michael, Upchurch, Kent, 1681 CKS PRC2/39/233
Smith, Michaell, St Johns Thanet, Kent, 1627 CKS PRC2/28/113
Smith, Mildred, Sandwich St Bartholomew's Hospital, Kent, 1611 CKS PRC20/2/264
Smith, Nathaniel, haberdasher, Dover, Kent, 1678 CKS PRC20/12/283
Smith, Nathaniel, victualler, Sandwich, Kent, 1684 CKS PRC2/40/244
Smith, Nicholas, Aylesby, Lincs, 1614 Lincs RO Ad/Ac/13/137
Smith, Nicholas, alderman, Boston, Lincs, 1627 Lincs RO Ad/Ac/20b/102
Smith, Nicholas, yeoman, Walmer, Kent, 1640 CKS PRC1/5/38
Smith, Philip, Checkley (Beamhurst), Staffs, 1663 LJRO:cards/1663/53
Smith, Ralfe, Wingham, Kent, 1635 CKS PRC20/11/402
Smith, Ralph, yeoman, Waltham St Lawrence, Berks, 1634 Berks RO D/A1/214/13C
Smith, Ralph, yeoman, Eastry, Kent, 1666 CKS PRC19/3/83
Smith, Ralph, fisherman, Wytham, Berks, 1687 Berks RO D/A1/215/49C
Smith, Randle, Newcastle under Lyme, Staffs, 1684 LJRO/B/C/5/1684/73
Smith, Reignolde, Dymchurch, Kent, 1599 CKS PRC2/11/279
Smith, Richard, gentleman, Badsey, Worcs, Worcs RO 008.7 BA3585/839/439
Smith, Richard, maltster, Alford, Lincs, 1612? Lincs RO Ad/Ac/11/4
Smith, Richard, shepherd, Shrivenham (Fernham), Berks, 1622 Berks RO D/A1/116/241C
Smith, Richard, Maidstone, Kent, 1624 CKS PRC20/6/183
Smith, Richard, Ryde, Hants, 1625 Hants RO 21M65 D8/133
Smith, Richard, degrees: 'M.A.', Cambridge (Corpus Christi College), Cambs, 1631 CUL V.C. Acc./Box2/70
Smith, Richard, Whitfield alias Beauxfield, Kent, 1632 CKS PRC2/31/154
Smith, Richard, yeoman, Compton (West Compton), Berks, 1633 Berks RO D/A1/119/19C
Smith, Richard, mason, Watlington, Oxon, 1634 Oxon RO MSS Wills 86/1/18
Smith, Richard, yeoman, Ashampstead, Berks, 1635 Berks RO D/A1/214/15C
Smith, Richard, Batheaston, Som, 1638 Somerset RO D/D/Cta/S8
Smith, Richard, Bilsington, Kent, 1638 CKS PRC2/34/273
Smith, Richard, Sandwich, Kent, 1661 CKS PRC1/8/113
Smith, Richard, cordwainer, Oxford St Mary Magdalene, Oxon, 1670 Oxon RO MSS Wills 174/1/19
Smith, Richard, Deverill, Longbridge, Wilts, 1672 Wilts RO Arch. Sarum(+ name and date)
Smith, Richard, Orton Longueville, Hunts, 1677 Hunts RO/Acc58/96(22)
Smith, Richard, Deal, Kent, 1698 CKS PRC19/5/61
Smith, Richard, farmer, Shifnal (Drayton), Shrops, 1826 LJRO/B/C/5/1826/46
Smith, Richard, clothier, Batley (Clek Green), Yorks, 1837 Borthwick Test C.P. 1837/1
Smith, Richard eld, maltster, Milton next Sittingbourne, Kent, 1667 CKS PRC1/11/160
Smith, Robert, St Albans, Herts, Herts RO ASA25/4906
Smith, Robert, clergy: 'vicar', Seasalter, Kent, 1598 CKS PRC2/10/325
Smith, Robert, husbandman, Sparsholt (Farlow), Berks, 1616 Berks RO D/A1/213/102A
Smith, Robert, Ancaster, Lincs, 1619 Lincs RO Ad/Ac/14/168
Smith, Robert, Aylesby, Lincs, 1630 Lincs RO Ad/Ac/22/125
Smith, Robert, Brattleby, Lincs, 1631 Lincs RO Ad/Ac/39/283
Smith, Robert, Goxhill, Lincs, 1635 Lincs RO Ad/Ac/24/345
Smith, Robert, husbandman, Wytham, Berks, 1635 Berks RO D/A1/214/19C
Smith, Robert, mason/privileged person, Oxford St Aldate, Oxon, 1635 Bodleian HYP B9/86-87
Smith, Robert, Lydd, Kent, 1639 CKS PRC20/11/371
Smith, Robert, grazier, Woodchurch, Kent, 1664 CKS PRC19/3/61
Smith, Robert, Thurning, Hunts, 1673 Hunts RO/Acc58/17(201)
Smith, Robert, carpenter, Hemingford Abbots, Hunts, 1680 Hunts RO/Acc58/150(19)
Smith, Robert, Wilton, Wilts, 1683 Wilts RO Arch. Sarum(+ name and date)
Smith, Samuel, Rickmansworth, Herts, 1690 PRO PROB32/31/207
Smith, Samuel eld, Stockbury, Kent, 1633 CKS PRC2/32/111
Smith, Sarah, widow, Canterbury St George Martyr, Kent, 1630 CKS PRC2/30/131

Smith, Simon, Middleton Stoney, Oxon, 1640 Oxon RO MSS Wills 173/4/9
Smith, Stephen, gentleman, Thurlby, Lincs, 1641 Lincs RO Ad/Ac/27/178
Smith, Stephen, mariner, Stepney, London & Middlesex, 1674 PRO PROB32/11/73
Smith, Thomas, Beighton, Norf, Norfolk RO ANW/23/26/11
Smith, Thomas, mariner, Bristol St Augustine, Glos, Bristol RO 1773/CP
Smith, Thomas, husbandman, Didcot, Berks, 1596 Berks RO D/A1/212/175A
Smith, Thomas, Litton, Som, 1600 Somerset RO D/D/Cta/S56
Smith, Thomas, Abingdon, Berks, 1601 Berks RO D/A1/212/171A
Smith, Thomas, Dover, Kent, 1614 CKS PRC20/3/25
Smith, Thomas, Cowbit, Lincs, 1624 Lincs RO Ad/Ac/19A/68
Smith, Thomas, Northbourne, Kent, 1625 CKS PRC2/25/128
Smith, Thomas, yeoman, Kennington, Berks, 1626 Berks RO D/A1/213/140C
Smith, Thomas, Birchington, Kent, 1627 CKS PRC20/8/405
Smith, Thomas, Roughton, Lincs, 1627 Lincs RO Ad/Ac/20b/39
Smith, Thomas, Biddenden, Kent, 1629 CKS PRC2/29/79
Smith, Thomas, Horsington, Lincs, 1633 Lincs RO Ad/Ac/24/123
Smith, Thomas, Howden (Asselby), Yorks, 1635 Borthwick Prob. Ex. 1635/5
Smith, Thomas, Wallington, Herts, 1635 Herts RO AHH23/2087
Smith, Thomas, Overton, Wilts, 1635 c. Wilts RO Miscellaneous Index (name + date)
Smith, Thomas, Hagworthingham, Lincs, 1636 Lincs RO Ad/Ac/24/453
Smith, Thomas, Saleby, Lincs, 1639 Lincs RO Ad/Ac/25/92
Smith, Thomas, yeoman, Hampstead Norris, Berks, 1640 Berks RO D/A1/214/44C
Smith, Thomas, Wroughton, Wilts, 1643 Wilts RO CC Sarum(+ name and date)
Smith, Thomas, maltster, Willesborough, Kent, 1645 CKS PRC1/7/65
Smith, Thomas, Fenton, Lincs, 1649 Lincs RO Ad/Ac/40/166
Smith, Thomas, Budworth, Great (Whitley), Ches, 1664 Cheshire RO (Name) W.C. 1664
Smith, Thomas, blacksmith, Mersham, Kent, 1664 CKS PRC1/10/90
Smith, Thomas, butcher, Watlington, Oxon, 1667 Oxon RO MSS Wills 86/2/26
Smith, Thomas, yeoman, Langton, Tur, Leics, 1668 Leics RO Administrators Accounts 1667-72 f12
Smith, Thomas, yeoman, Tenterden, Kent, 1668 CKS PRC1/13/117
Smith, Thomas, gentleman, Clanfield, Oxon, 1669 Oxon RO MSS Wills 86/2/32
Smith, Thomas, husbandman, Bethersden, Kent, 1670 CKS PRC1/14/105
Smith, Thomas, Lydd, Kent, 1672 CKS PRC20/12/61
Smith, Thomas, Wrockwardine, Shrops, 1674 LJRO:cards/1674/43
Smith, Thomas, cordwainer, Maidstone, Kent, 1675 CKS PRC20/12/145
Smith, Thomas, Rushden, Northants, 1676 Northants RO NWill A/C/131
Smith, Thomas, Cranbrook, Kent, 1679 CKS PRC2/38/193
Smith, Thomas, gentleman, Rainham, Kent, 1679 CKS PRC2/38/194
Smith, Thomas, mariner, St Laurence Thanet, Kent, 1679 CKS PRC2/38/190
Smith, Thomas, Birchington, Kent, 1684 CKS PRC20/13/466
Smith, Thomas, husbandman, Shaw cum Donnington, Berks, 1684 Berks RO D/A1/215/7C
Smith, Thomas, HMS Pearl, 1743 Greater London RO DL/C/550/82/1
Smith, Thomas eld, carpenter, St Giles in the Fields, London & Middlesex, 1717 Greater London RO DL/C/546/135
Smith, Thomas sen, Berrington, Shrops, 1674 LJRO:cards/1674/44
Smith, Thomas ygr, yeoman, Somerton, Oxon, 1640 Oxon RO MSS Wills 173/4/14
Smith, Timothy, yeoman, Deddington, Oxon, 1699 Oxon RO MSS Wills 62/4/38
Smith, Valentine, yeoman, Littleworth, Berks, 1684 Berks RO D/A3/4/69D
Smith, William, Nottingham, Notts, Borthwick Test C.P. 1757/6
Smith, William, Redmarley D'Abitot, Worcs, Worcs RO 008.7 BA3585/839/346
Smith, William, shopkeeper: 'general shopkeeper', St Andrew Holborn, London & Middlesex, PRO PROB32/53/72
Smith, William, Toft, Lincs, 1612 Lincs RO Ad/Ac/11/129
Smith, William, Ashby cum Fenby, Lincs, 1618 Lincs RO Ad/Ac/14/222

[Smith:]
Smith, William, yeoman, Godmersham, Kent, 1621 CKS PRC20/5/186
Smith, William, husbandman, Clewer, Berks, 1622 Wilts RO CC Sarum(+ name and date)
Smith, William, Elham, Kent, 1624 CKS PRC2/24/97
Smith, William, Sutton St Edmunds, Lincs, 1624 Lincs RO Ad/Ac/19A/38
Smith, William, glover, Rasen, Market, Lincs, 1624 Lincs RO Ad/Ac/18/95
Smith, William, gentleman, Hibaldstow, Lincs, 1626 Lincs RO Ad/Ac/39/75
Smith, William, Hale, Great, Lincs, 1627 Lincs RO Ad/Ac/20b/110
Smith, William, Sturry, Kent, 1628 CKS PRC2/28/107
Smith, William, Hull Sculcoates, All Saints, Yorks, 1638 Borthwick Prob. Ex. 1638/2
Smith, William, St Albans St Peters, Herts, 1638 Herts RO ASA25/4963
Smith, William, husbandman, Gedney, Lincs, 1639? Lincs RO Ad/Ac/26/294
Smith, William, Carlton Scroop, Lincs, 1648 Lincs RO Ad/Ac/30/6
Smith, William, Sixhills, Lincs, 1648 Lincs RO Ad/Ac/30/252
Smith, William, Boston, Lincs, 1649 Lincs RO Ad/Ac/30/73
Smith, William, Ilkeston, Derby, 1663 LJRO:cards/1663/54
Smith, William, Faversham, Kent, 1672 CKS PRC2/35/180
Smith, William, husbandman, Hinton Waldrist, Berks, 1673 Berks RO D/A1/214/148C
Smith, William, Stepney (Stebenhythe), London & Middlesex, 1675 PRO PROB32/12/61
Smith, William, yeoman, Eastchurch, Sheppey, Kent, 1676 CKS PRC2/37/92
Smith, William, Aldingbourne, Sussex, 1677 W. Suss RO EpI/33/1676/32
Smith, William, bachelor, St Sepulchre, London & Middlesex, 1677 PRO PROB5/1494
Smith, William, Kingswinford, Staffs, 1680 LJRO:cards/1680/32
Smith, William, Overbury (Conderton), Worcs, 1680 Worcs RO 008.7 BA3585/837/bdl 2
Smith, William, cook, Oxford (University), Oxon, 1683 Bodleian HYP B9/88-89
Smith, William, Heath, Derby, 1684 LJRO/B/C/5/1685/91
Smith, William, yeoman, Midgham, Berks, 1684 Berks RO D/A1/215/14C
Smith, William, Warboys, Hunts, 1685 Hunts RO/Acc58/255(249)
Smith, William, miller, Walsingham, Great, Norf, 1706 Norfolk RO ANW/23/6/33
Smith, William, Faversham, Kent, 1716 CKS PRC1/18/15
Smith, William, painter, Norwich, Norf, 1734 Norfolk RO ANW/23/21/46
Smith, William, gentleman, Kingswinford, Staffs, 1765 LJRO/B/C/5/1765/128a, b
Smith, William, Dilhorne, Staffs, 1767 LJRO/B/C/5/1767/117
Smith, Willyam, Spalding, Lincs, 1614 Lincs RO Ad/Ac/13/109
Smith/Browne, Symon, Smeeth, Kent, 1607 CKS PRC20/1/225
Smith/Foster, Thomas, yeoman, Thatcham (Harts Hill), Berks, 1676 Berks RO D/A1/214/171C
Smith/Robyns, Grace, widow, Bilsington, Kent, 1596 CKS PRC2/8/403
Smith/Shepheard, John eld, husbandman, Uffington, Berks, 1597 Berks RO D/A1/212/178A
Smith, see Allen, Biggs, Foster, Reade & Soare,
Smithe, Albrey, Boston, Lincs, 1620 Lincs RO Ad/Ac/16/83
Smithe, Edward, Frampton, Lincs, 1613 Lincs RO Ad/Ac/11/155
Smithe, Edward, Scothorne, Lincs, 1625 Lincs RO Ad/Ac/39/148
Smithe, Edwarde, Minster in Thanet, Kent, 1596 CKS PRC2/8/308
Smithe, Frawncis, Stone in Oxney, Kent, 1595 CKS PRC2/7/91
Smithe, George, Finchampstead, Berks, 1600 Berks RO D/A1/213/9A
Smithe, George, Dymchurch, Kent, 1608 CKS PRC1/1/7
Smithe, Gregory, husbandman, Chieveley, Berks, 1599 Berks RO D/A1/212/187A
Smithe, Helen, widow, Chieveley, Berks, 1639 Berks RO D/A1/214/37C
Smithe, Jane, widow, Sittingbourne, Kent, 1616 CKS PRC2/19/8
Smithe, Joan, widow, Tilehurst, Berks, 1609 Berks RO D/A1/117/27C
Smithe, Joane, widow, Crundale, Kent, 1614 CKS PRC2/17/25
Smithe, John, Bishops Lydeard, Som, 1587 Somerset RO D/D/Cta/S44
Smithe, John, Drayton, West, Berks, 1591 Berks RO D/A1/212/146A
Smithe, John, Lydd, Kent, 1592 CKS PRC21/11/277
Smithe, John, Devizes, Wilts, 1620 Wilts RO CC Sarum(+ name and date)
Smithe, Leonard, Sholden, Kent, 1593 CKS PRC2/6/456

Smithe, Marye, New Romney, Kent, 1612 CKS PRC20/2/270
Smithe, Ralphe, Huish, Wilts, 1628 Wilts RO Arch. Wilts.(+ name and date)
Smithe, Richard, Chilton, Berks, 1599 Berks RO D/A1/212/197A
Smithe, Richard, Headcorn, Kent, 1613 CKS PRC2/16/137
Smithe, Richarde, Ulceby, Lincs, 1611 Lincs RO Ad/Ac/10/70
Smithe, Robert, husbandman, Luddington (Garthorpe), Lincs, 1613 Lincs RO Ad/Ac/12/122
Smithe, Robert, Blankney, Lincs, 1639 Lincs RO Ad/Ac/26/223
Smithe, Thomas, Stallingborough, Lincs, 1597 Lincs RO Ad/Ac/4/17
Smithe, Thomas, Warehorne, Kent, 1597 CKS PRC2/9/343
Smithe, Thomas, Maidstone, Kent, 1605 CKS PRC20/1/45
Smithe, Thomas, Didcot, Berks, 1609 Berks RO D/A1/213/58A
Smithe, William, Norton, Worcs, Worcs RO 008.7 BA3585/839/320
Smithe, William, Hernhill, Kent, 1590 CKS PRC21/10/198
Smithe, William, weaver, Newbury, Berks, 1601 Berks RO D/A1/213/7C
Smithe, William, Appledore, Kent, 1602 CKS PRC2/12/338
Smithe, William, milliner, Cuckney (Norton), Notts, 1609 Borthwick Prob. Ex. 1609/7
Smithe, William, Ashton, Long, Som, 1619 Somerset RO D/D/Cta/S60
Smithe, William, Eastry, Kent, 1629 CKS PRC20/8/425
Smithe, Wylliam, High Halden, Kent, 1604 CKS PRC2/13/336
Smithe/Farmer, John, yeoman, Grimley, Worcs, 1602 Worcs RO 008.7 BA3585/838/216
Smithe/Farmer, Thomas, butcher, Worcester St John Bedwardine, Worcs, 1609 Worcs RO 008.7 BA3585/839/483a
Smitheat, Thomas, Buckland nr Dover, Kent, 1621 CKS PRC20/5/180
Smithes, Thomas, Heapham, Lincs, 1628 Lincs RO Ad/Ac/39/52
Smithet, Thomas, Canterbury, Kent, 1637 CKS PRC20/11/322
Smithfield, John, Wellow, Som, 1620 Somerset RO D/D/Cta/S61
Smithier, John, scrivener, St Christopher le Stock, London & Middlesex, 1675 PRO PROB5/1689
Smithley, William, Sandwich, Kent, 1638 CKS PRC2/34/286
Smithson, Ralph, carpenter, Mirfield, Yorks, 1839 Borthwick Test C.P. 1839/8
Smithson, Richard, Hernhill, Kent, 1616 CKS PRC20/3/366
Smithson, Thomas, yeoman, Lympne, Kent, 1673 CKS PRC2/35/256
Smithson, William, Shadoxhurst, Kent, 1666 CKS PRC1/11/161
Smithson, William, hackneyman, Dover, Kent, 1668 CKS PRC19/4/31
Smithson, William, Whitstable, Kent, 1670 CKS PRC1/14/106
Smithyman, Richard, Shifnal, Shrops, 1674 LJRO:cards/1674/45
Smoothing, Jonas, blacksmith, Milton next Sittingbourne, Kent, 1689 CKS PRC2/41/161
Smothing, Margaret, Harrietsham, Kent, 1595 CKS PRC2/7/271
Smothing, Stephen, Milton next Sittingbourne, Kent, 1596 CKS PRC2/8/155
Smyth, Agnes, widow, Bury, Sussex, 1595 W. Suss RO EpI/33/1594/17
Smyth, Ann, Haxey (Newbigg), Lincs, 1685 Lincs RO Ad/Ac/44/159
Smyth, Anthony, Madehurst, Sussex, 1682 W. Suss RO EpI/33/1682/13
Smyth, Dillon, innholder, Bourne, Lincs, 1679 Lincs RO Ad/Ac/43/125
Smyth, Dorothy, widow, St Albans, Herts, 1609 Herts RO ASA25/4774
Smyth, Edmund, gentleman, Stubton, Lincs, 1671 Lincs RO Ad/Ac/33/172
Smyth, Edward, Bourne, Lincs, 1593 Lincs RO Ad/Ac/3/77
Smyth, Edward, Halton, East, Lincs, 1593 Lincs RO Ad/Ac/3/27
Smyth, Edward, St Albans, Herts, 1602 Herts RO ASA25/4808
Smyth, Edward, yeoman, Habrough, Lincs, 1670 Lincs RO Ad/Ac/32/158
Smyth, Edwarde, Hareby, Lincs, 1623 Lincs RO Ad/Ac/18/34
Smyth, Elizabeth, Burghfield, Berks, 1614 Wilts RO CC Sarum(+ name and date)
Smyth, Elizabeth, widow, Grandborough, Warks, 1672 LJRO:cards/1672/52
Smyth, George, gentleman, Nettleton, Lincs, 1626 Lincs RO Ad/Ac/20/46
Smyth, Henry, baker, Chichester St Andrew, Sussex, 1619 W. Suss RO EpIII/9/1/23
Smyth, Henry, Stanton St Bernard, Wilts, 1668 Wilts RO Arch. Wilts.(+ name and date)
Smyth, Henry, Horwood, Little, Bucks, 1675 Herts RO ASA25/3965

[Smyth:]
Smyth, Hugh, Ashton-under-Lyne, Lancs, 1596 Lancs RO (Name of Deceased) D.R.C.H. 1595
Smyth, Jane, Pagham, Sussex, 1626 W. Suss RO EpIV/10/1/27
Smyth, Jeames, Deal, Kent, 1586 CKS PRC21/8/167
Smyth, Jeremy, Maidstone, Kent, 1621 CKS PRC20/5/184
Smyth, John, New Romney, Kent, 1573 CKS PRC21/2/70
Smyth, John, New Romney, Kent, 1573 CKS PRC21/2/175
Smyth, John, Horncastle, Lincs, 1612 Lincs RO Ad/Ac/11/169
Smyth, John, chapman: 'petty chapman', Rickmansworth, Herts, 1615 Herts RO ASA25/4823
Smyth, John, Bishopstoke, Hants, 1623 Hants RO 21M65 D8/38
Smyth, John, butcher, Gainsborough, Lincs, 1662 Lincs RO Ad/Ac/41/38
Smyth, John, Hordle, Hants, 1672 Hants RO 21m65 D8/250
Smyth, John, Maisemore, Glos, 1672 GRO GDR/B4/2/S38
Smyth, John, Pagham, Sussex, 1684 W. Suss RO EpIV/10/2A/31
Smyth, John, gentleman, Humberstone, Lincs, 1684 Lincs RO Ad/Ac/44/138
Smyth, Margaret, widow, Kelsey, South, Lincs, 1670 Lincs RO Ad/Ac/32/149
Smyth, Marke, yeoman, Croft, Lincs, 1671 Lincs RO Ad/Ac/32/189
Smyth, Martha, widow, Saxilby, Lincs, 1680 Lincs RO Ad/Ac/43/166
Smyth, Mildred, widow, Biddenden, Kent, 1626 CKS PRC2/25/130
Smyth, Nicholas, husbandman, Winterton, Lincs, 1686 Lincs RO Ad/Ac/44/160
Smyth, Richard, Northbourne, Kent, 1592 CKS PRC2/6/314
Smyth, Richard, husbandman, Letcombe Regis, Berks, 1628 Berks RO D/A1/213/150C
Smyth, Richard sen, Slindon, Sussex, 1680 W. Suss RO EpIV/10/2A/24
Smyth, Robert, Aisthorpe, Lincs, 1614 Lincs RO Ad/Ac/8b/37
Smyth, Robert, Worthy, Martyr, Hants, 1624 Hants RO 21M65 D8/88
Smyth, Robert, Sibsey, Lincs, 1638 Lincs RO Ad/Ac/25/202
Smyth, Robert, husbandman, Halton, East, Lincs, 1666 Lincs RO Ad/Ac/32/93
Smyth, Robert, husbandman, Ashby, West, Lincs, 1680 Lincs RO Ad/Ac/34/49
Smyth, Roberte, Dunsby, Lincs, 1593 Lincs RO Ad/Ac/3/19
Smyth, Thomas, Ashby, West, Lincs, 1579 Lincs RO Ad/Ac/2b/1
Smyth, Thomas, Deeping St James, Lincs, 1598 Lincs RO Ad/Ac/4/125
Smyth, Thomas, Tillington, Sussex, 1599 W. Suss RO EpI/33/1599/5
Smyth, Thomas, Horsham, Sussex, 1632 W. Suss RO EpI/33/1632/1
Smyth, Thomas, husbandman, Stoke, South, Oxon, 1640 Oxon RO MSS Wills 300/1/58
Smyth, Thomas, gentleman, Spalding, Lincs, 1666 Lincs RO Ad/Ac/32/111
Smyth, Thomas, gentleman, Walsall, Staffs, 1766 LJRO/B/C/5/1766/111
Smyth, Thomas ygr, Shrewsbury, Shrops, 1670 LJRO:cards/1670/63
Smyth, William, Stamford, Lincs, 1568 Lincs RO Ad/Ac/2C/31
Smyth, William, Wittering, East, Sussex, 1596 W. Suss RO EpI/33/1597/8
Smyth, William, Belbroughton, Worcs, 1605 Worcs RO 008.7 BA3585/839/310
Smyth, William, Linsted, Kent, 1626 CKS PRC2/27/157
Smyth, William, draper, Grimsby, Great, Lincs, 1627 Lincs RO Ad/Ac/20/113
Smyth, William, husbandman, Witham on the Hill, Lincs, 1666 Lincs RO Ad/Ac/32/76
Smyth, William, Torksey, Lincs, 1672 Lincs RO Ad/Ac/33/202
Smyth/Peirce, Henry, Chinnock, East, Som, 1612 Somerset RO D/D/Cta/S36
Smythe, Christopher, Cropthorne, Worcs, 1684 Worcs RO 008.7 BA3585/837/bdl 5
Smythe, Edmunde, Westwell, Kent, 1584 CKS PRC21/7/3
Smythe, Edward, Monkton, Kent, 1600 CKS PRC21/15/180
Smythe, Edward, Thatcham (Dunstan), Berks, 1636 Berks RO D/A1/214/3C
Smythe, George, gentleman, Wybunbury, Ches, 1588 Cheshire RO (Name) W.C. 1588
Smythe, Henrie, Folkingham, Lincs, 1606 Lincs RO Ad/Ac/6/65
Smythe, Henry, Sandwich St Peter, Kent, 1593 CKS PRC2/6/368
Smythe, Henry, Barnetby le Wold, Lincs, 1599? Lincs RO Ad/Ac/5/51
Smythe, John, Folkestone, Kent, 1584 CKS PRC2/3/51
Smythe, John, New Romney, Kent, 1584 CKS PRC21/7/118
Smythe, John, Wilton, Som, 1593 Somerset RO D/D/Cta/S41

Smythe, John, Waddingham (St Peter), Lincs, 1599 Lincs RO Ad/Ac/37/108
Smythe, John, Knaith, Lincs, 1601 Lincs RO Ad/Ac/5/278
Smythe, John, Goudhurst, Kent, 1613 CKS PRC2/16/210
Smythe, John, clergy: 'clerk', Coombe Bisset, Wilts, 1696 Wilts RO Miscellaneous Index (name + date)
Smythe, Leonard, Kirkby on Bain (Toft Grange), Lincs, 1611 Lincs RO Ad/Ac/10/71
Smythe, Margaret, Canterbury St George Martyr, Kent, 1597 CKS PRC2/9/197
Smythe, Margarett, Fleet, Lincs, 1614 Lincs RO Ad/Ac/13/70
Smythe, Myles, Gosberton, Lincs, 1612 Lincs RO Ad/Ac/11/38
Smythe, Thomas, Cawthorpe, Little, Lincs, 1569 Lincs RO Ad/Ac/1/2
Smythe, Thomas, Snave, Kent, 1595 CKS PRC2/7/459
Smythe, Thomas + Margery, Willesborough, Kent, 1593 CKS PRC2/6/440
Smythe, William, Stubton, Lincs, 1600 Lincs RO Ad/Ac/5/231
Smythe/Courte, John, husbandman, Oldberrow, Worcs, 1598 Worcs RO 008.7 BA3585/838/110
Snape, Thomas, Boston, Lincs, 1639 Lincs RO Ad/Ac/26/104
Snart, Johane, spinster, Dalby Chalcombe, Leics, 1642 Leics RO PR/I/41A/91
Snart, William, Linwood, Lincs, 1612 Lincs RO Ad/Ac/11/145
Snatt, William, Marden, Kent, 1619 CKS PRC2/19/6
Snawdell, John, husbandman, Caythorpe, Lincs, 1671 Lincs RO Ad/Ac/32/205
Sneath, Thomas, Deeping, Market, Lincs, 1637 Lincs RO Ad/Ac/25/628
Snelgar, Walter, Whiteparish, Wilts, 1635 Wilts RO Arch. Sarum(+ name and date)
Snelgrove, John, Codford St Peter, Wilts, 1680 Wilts RO Arch. Sarum(+ name and date)
Snell, Elizabeth, Nafferton, Yorks, 1609 Borthwick Prob. Ex. 1609/4
Snell, George, Redbourne, Lincs, 1613 Lincs RO Ad/Ac/8b/8
Snell, John, mr, Ospringe, Kent, 1623 CKS PRC2/24/90
Snell, John, Gosberton, Lincs, 1648 Lincs RO Ad/Ac/30/273
Snell, Leonard, yeoman, Spalding, Lincs, 1646 Lincs RO Ad/Ac/28/191
Snell, Lionel, bucketmaker, Bucklebury, Berks, 1612 Berks RO D/A1/117/59D
Snell, Thomas, Frampton, Lincs, 1578 Lincs RO Ad/Ac/2b/18
Snell, William,
Worcs 1601 Worcs RO 008.7 BA3585/838/205
Snellart, John, weaver: 'silk weaver', Canterbury St Dunstan Without, Kent, 1631 CKS PRC20/9/408
Snellgar, John, Downton, Wilts, 1634? Wilts RO Arch. Sarum(+ name and date)
Snelling, John, gentleman, Ferring, Sussex, 1681 W. Suss RO EpI/33/1681/2
Snelling, Thomas, Steyning, Sussex, 1620 W. Suss RO EpI/33/1619/3
Snoad, Christopher, Boughton Aluph, Kent, 1632 CKS PRC2/32/118
Snoad, Edward, Chart, Great, Kent, 1677 CKS PRC2/37/198
Snoad, John, Stonar, Kent, 1710 CKS PRC1/17/42
Snoad, Thomas, Canterbury, Kent, 1635 CKS PRC20/11/446
Snoade, James, tailor, New Romney, Kent, 1667 CKS PRC19/3/143
Snoade, Margery, widow, Ash next Sandwich, Kent, 1622 CKS PRC20/5/178
Snoath, Thomas, carpenter, Leaveland, Kent, 1675 CKS PRC2/36/240
Snode, Nicolas, Charing, Kent, 1582 CKS PRC21/6/81
Snode, Robert, Sandwich St Clement, Kent, 1610 CKS PRC2/15/392
Snode, William, yeoman, Badlesmere, Kent, 1678 CKS PRC2/38/73
Snodon, Thomas, Sandwich St Peter, Kent, 1600 CKS PRC2/11/355
Snooke, Francis, Milton next Sittingbourne, Kent, 1626 CKS PRC2/27/151
Snooke, John, Wimborne Minster, Dors, 1700 Dorset RO PE/WM CP 2/4/99
Snoth, George, cordwainer, Westwell, Kent, 1678 CKS PRC20/12/284
Snothe, Elizabeth, Throwleigh, Kent, 1600 CKS PRC2/11/294
Snothe, Richarde, Warehorne, Kent, 1592 CKS PRC2/5/43
Snow, John, Newcastle under Lyme, Staffs, 1684 LJRO/B/C/5/1684/74
Snow, Randulph, Trentham, Staffs, 1682 LJRO/B/C/5/1681/37
Snow, William, distiller, St Giles in the Fields, London & Middlesex, 1697 PRO PROB32/37/68

[Snowden:]
Snowden, Edmond, Redbourne, Lincs, 1612 Lincs RO Ad/Ac/8a/349
Snowden, Elizabeth, widow, Leeds, Yorks, 1772 Borthwick Test C.P. 1772/5
Snowden, Francis, Willingham, Lincs, 1667? Lincs RO Ad/Ac/33/7
Snowden, William, Manby, Lincs, 1650 Lincs RO Ad/Ac/29/107
Snowdon, Edmund, Redbourne, Lincs, 1611 Lincs RO Ad/Ac/8a/343
Snowe, Henry, Sittingbourne, Kent, 1579 CKS PRC2/1/216
Snowe, John, Winslow, Bucks, 1602 Herts RO ASA25/4761
Snowe, John, town clerk, Oxford, Oxon, 1629 Oxon RO MSS Wills 300/1/38
Snowe, Johnne, Dunsby, Lincs, 1593 Lincs RO Ad/Ac/3/17
Snowe, Thomas, Longparish, Hants, Hants RO 1671 AD120
Snowe, Thomas, Collingbourne Kingston, Wilts, 1621 Wilts RO Arch. Wilts.(+ name and date)
Soames, Alexander, husbandman, Mersham, Kent, 1639 CKS PRC1/3/43
Soames, Richard, labourer, Ickleford, Herts, 1610 Herts RO AHH23/2082
Soames, Richard, yeoman, Walmer, Kent, 1668 CKS PRC1/13/118
Soan, John, husbandman, Swallowfield, Berks, 1685 Berks RO D/A1/215/21C
Soane, John, Rumboldswyke, Sussex, 1615 W. Suss RO EpIII/9/1/12
Soane, Thomas, Orpington, Kent, 1670 Lambeth Palace VH96/6182
Soare, Robert, Spondon, Derby, 1680 LJRO:cards/1680/33
Soare, William, Chellaston, Derby, 1672 LJRO:cards/1672/54
Soare/Smith, Elizabeth, Coleshill, Warks, 1672 LJRO:cards/1672/53
Socke, Richard, Slindon, Sussex, 1618 W. Suss RO EpIV/10/1/41
Sockett, Thomas, Moreton Corbet, Shrops, 1685 LJRO:cards/1685/76
Sole, Andrew, yeoman, Deal, Kent, 1681 CKS PRC20/13/208
Sole, Chrystopher, Woodchurch, Kent, 1593 CKS PRC21/12/84
Sole, Cristover,
Kent CKS PRC21/12/88
Sole, Francis, Worth, Kent, 1607 CKS PRC20/1/263
Sole, George, Ickham, Kent, 1602 CKS PRC21/15/159
Sole, Richard, Mersham, Kent, 1589 CKS PRC2/4/497
Sole, Richard, Mersham, Kent, 1589 CKS PRC2/4/499
Sole, Susan, widow, Faversham, Kent, 1671 CKS PRC2/35/89
Soley, John, clergy: 'clerk/rector', Stratton St Mary, Norf, 1753 Norfolk RO ANF/11/4/93
Soley, William, Aston, Whiteladies, Worcs, 1684 Worcs RO 008.7 BA3585/837/bdl 4
Solley, George, yeoman, Westbere, Kent, 1668 CKS PRC1/13/119
Solley, Richard, yeoman, Ash next Sandwich, Kent, 1685 CKS PRC20/13/464
Solley, Stephen, St Nicholas at Wade, Kent, 1644 CKS PRC19/2/78
Solley, Stephen, yeoman, Ash next Sandwich, Kent, 1684 CKS PRC20/13/468
Solley, William, Woodnesborough, Kent, 1641 CKS PRC19/2/40
Sollis, Solomon, St Martin in the Fields, London & Middlesex, 1724 Greater London RO AM/PP/Box 1724-1727 pt (uncatalogued)
Sollomon, John, Boughton Aluph, Kent, 1665 CKS PRC1/10/91
Solly, Edward, yeoman, Wickhambreaux, Kent, 1666 CKS PRC1/11/162
Solly, Stephen, Woodnesborough, Kent, 1636 CKS PRC2/33/128
Solly, Stephen, Littlebourne, Kent, 1721 CKS PRC1/18/48
Solly, William, Sandwich, Kent, 1624 CKS PRC2/24/94
Solly, William, yeoman, Sandwich, Kent, 1625 CKS PRC2/25/132
Sollye, Stephen, Ash next Sandwich, Kent, 1613 CKS PRC20/2/527
Sollye, Thomas,
Kent 1596 CKS PRC2/8/19
Sollye, Vyncent, Ash next Sandwich, Kent, 1584 CKS PRC21/7/26
Sollye, William, Ash next Sandwich, Kent, 1612 CKS PRC20/2/332
Solman, Thomas, husbandman, Boughton Monchelsea, Kent, 1669 CKS PRC19/4/60
Solmes, Thomas, Deal, Kent, 1625 CKS PRC20/7/265
Somercoats, Edward, Scotter, Lincs, 1614 Lincs RO Ad/Ac/8b/57
Somercotes, John, Osbournby, Lincs, 1600 Lincs RO Ad/Ac/5/131

Somerland, Thomas, Curdworth, Warks, 1672 LJRO:cards/1672/55
Somers, Hugh, Canterbury St Peter, Kent, 1675 CKS PRC2/36/238
Somers, Stephen, Linton, Kent, 1611 CKS PRC2/26/133 and unnumbered
Somerseales, Henrie, Firsby, Lincs, 1611 Lincs RO Ad/Ac/12/216
Somerseales, Stephen, Firsby, Lincs, 1612 Lincs RO Ad/Ac/12/210
Somerton, Thomas, blacksmith, Norton, Chipping, Oxon, 1677 Oxon RO MSS Wills 86/3/27
Somes, Richard, Charlton nr Dover, Kent, 1625 CKS PRC2/25/134
Somes, William, husbandman, Bethersden, Kent, 1684 CKS PRC2/40/243
Sommer, Richard, Hunston, Sussex, 1618 W. Suss RO EpI/33/1617/20
Sommers, Robert, Middlezoy, Som, 1621 Somerset RO D/D/Cta/S19
Sommerscales, Stephen, Firsby, Lincs, 1611 Lincs RO Ad/Ac/10/53
Sonds, John, esquire, Throwleigh, Kent, 1672 CKS PRC2/35/172
Sonds, Michaell, knight, Throwleigh, Kent, 1618 CKS PRC2/19/27
Sone, John, innholder, Dover, Kent, 1675 CKS PRC20/12/187
Sone, William, Swallowfield, Berks, 1616 Berks RO D/A1/213/98C
Sone, William, Stoughton, Sussex, 1629 W. Suss RO EpI/33/1629/32
Sooby, Thomas, Horncastle, Lincs, 1646 Lincs RO Ad/Ac/28/170
Sooley, John, Horsington, Lincs, 1639? Lincs RO Ad/Ac/26/76
Soone, John, fishmonger, Reading, Berks, 1593 Berks RO D/A1/212/163E
Soone, William, Stafford, Staffs, 1676 LJRO:cards/1676/45
Soper, Henry, Grinstead, West, Sussex, 1608 W. Suss RO EpI/33/1607/2
Soper, Simon, Taunton St Mary Magdalan, Som, 1585 Somerset RO D/D/Cta/C37
Soper, see Porter,
Sopp, Robert, yeoman, Maddington, Wilts, 1739 Wilts RO CC Sarum(+ name and date)
Sore, Thomas, shepherd, Chew Magna, Som, 1622 Somerset RO D/D/Cta/S12
Sorie, Lawrence, Loose, Kent, 1603 CKS PRC21/16/67
Sorry, Christopher, fuller, Leeds, Kent, 1640 CKS PRC19/1/81
Sotcher, Dorothy, Petworth, Sussex, 1682 W. Suss RO EpI/33/1682/38
Sothabie, Thomas, gentleman, Bishop Wilton, Yorks, 1608 Borthwick Prob. Ex. 1607/2
Sotherden, George, Shadoxhurst, Kent, 1600 CKS PRC2/11/283
Sothernden, Gervace, Pluckley, Kent, 1599 CKS PRC2/10/527
Sotherne, Henry, Winwick, Lancs, 1592 Lancs RO (Name of Deceased) D.R.C.H. 1592
Sotherne, Richard, Wrawby cum Brigg (Glanford Brigg), Lincs, 1627 Lincs RO Ad/Ac/20b/41
Sothernwood, Thomas, Ibstock, Leics, 1665 Leics RO Administrators Accounts C17th f22
Sottby, William, Fulstow, Lincs, 1637 Lincs RO Ad/Ac/25/488
Soulby, Francis, Owersby, Lincs, 1646 Lincs RO Ad/Ac/28/247
Soundy, Anne, widow, Caversham, Oxon, 1674 Oxon RO MSS Wills 174/1/26
Soundye, Thomas, Sonning, Berks, 1596 Wilts RO Miscellaneous Index (name + date)
South, Daniell, Odiham (North Warnborough), Hants, 1684 Hants RO 21m65 D8/343
South, John, 1665 PRO PROB5/780
South, Mary, Ecchinswell, Hants, Hants RO 1605 AD72/2
South, Mary, widow, Reading St Giles (Whitley), Berks, 1640 Berks RO D/A1/119/86C
South, Thomas, Laughton, Lincs, 1663 Lincs RO Ad/Ac/41/75
South, Thomas + Isabell, Marsh Chapel, Lincs, 1633 Lincs RO Ad/Ac/24/156
South, Toby, yeoman, Reading St Giles (Whitley), Berks, 1627 Berks RO D/A1/213/143C
South, William, yeoman, Barford St Michael, Oxon, 1630 Oxon RO MSS Wills 173/3/29
South, Zache, gentleman, Somercoates, South, Lincs, 1625 Lincs RO Ad/Ac/19B/93
Southaike, Alexander, clergy: 'clerk', Waddington, Lincs, 1618 Lincs RO Ad/Ac/14/88
Southbie, Margaret, Buckland, Berks, 1613 Berks RO D/A1/213/75C
Southernwoade, Ralphe, yeoman, Bempton, Yorks, 1629 Borthwick Prob. Ex. 1629/1
Southerton, John, Bermondsey, St Mary Magdalen, Surrey, 1671 PRO PROB5/946
Southey, Steven, Stratfield Mortimer, Berks, 1601 Berks RO D/A1/213/17A
Southock, Anthony, Wilton, Wilts, 1620 Wilts RO Miscellaneous Index (name + date)
Southouse, Thomas, Faversham, Kent, 1678 CKS PRC2/38/74
Southwell, Bartholmew, Fulletby, Lincs, 1619 Lincs RO Ad/Ac/14/120

[Southwell:]
Southwell, Gregory, husbandman, Dunsby, Lincs, 1614 Lincs RO Ad/Ac/13/42
Sowdley, Edward, husbandman, Latton, Wilts, 1631 Wilts RO Arch. Wilts.(+ name and date)
Sowersbie, John, Burton on Stather, Lincs, 1629 Lincs RO Ad/Ac/39/218
Sowgate, Adam, Linsted, Kent, 1597 CKS PRC2/9/225
Sowley, Thomas, Caythorpe, Lincs, 1600 Lincs RO Ad/Ac/5/344
Sowndy, Henry, Sonning, Berks, 1639 Wilts RO Miscellaneous Index (name + date)
Sowter, John, Easebourne, Sussex, 1598 W. Suss RO EpI/33/1598/1
Sowthall, Henry, Kidderminster, Worcs, 1681 Worcs RO 008.7 BA3585/830/53
Sowthall, Richard, Kidderminster, Worcs, 1684 Worcs RO 008.7 BA3585/837/bdl 4
Sowtham, John, Hatton (Beausale), Warks, 1608 Worcs RO 008.7 BA3585/839/457
Sowthen, John, clergy: 'clerk', Langley, Kings, Herts, Herts RO AHH23/2086
Sowther, Robert, Derby, Derby, 1664 LJRO:cards/1664/15
Sowthernden, Stephen, Woodchurch, Kent, 1607 CKS PRC20/1/255
Sowthill, Robert, gentleman, Hibaldstow, Lincs, 1605 Lincs RO Ad/Ac/37/212
Sowthouse, Henrye, clergy: 'vicar', Northbourne, Kent, 1608 CKS PRC1/1/8
Sowthowse, Barbara, widow, Faversham, Kent, 1674 CKS PRC2/36/122
Sowthowse, Henrye, clergy: 'vicar', Northbourne, Kent, 1609 CKS PRC1/1/10
Sowthowsen, Joane, widow, Canterbury St Mildred, Kent, 1613 CKS PRC2/17/133
Sowthy, Thomas, Sandwich St Peter, Kent, 1599 CKS PRC2/11/275
Sowton, John, Stoke, South, Sussex, 1636 W. Suss RO EpI/33/1635/32
Sowton, John, Appledore, Kent, 1669 CKS PRC1/13/120
Spaine, Catherine, widow, Ash next Sandwich, Kent, 1627 CKS PRC20/7/136
Spaine, Stephen, Acrise, Kent, 1649 CKS PRC1/8/82
Spaine, Thomas, yeoman, Knowlton, Kent, 1629 CKS PRC2/30/119
Spaine, Thomas, yeoman, Smeeth, Kent, 1644 CKS PRC19/2/90
Spaine, Thomas, bachelor, Hernhill, Kent, 1663 CKS PRC19/3/43
Spaine, Thomas, yeoman, Preston next Wingham, Kent, 1674 CKS PRC2/36/129
Spaine, William, Winthorpe, Lincs, 1624 Lincs RO Ad/Ac/19A/124
Spaine, William, victualler, Staple next Wingham, Kent, 1664 CKS PRC19/3/62
Spaine, William, labourer, Whitstable, Kent, 1670 CKS PRC1/15/60
Spaine, William, Luddington, Lincs, 1682 Lincs RO Ad/Ac/44/6
Spalding, Christopher, Welton le Marsh, Lincs, 1593 Lincs RO Ad/Ac/3/3
Spaldinge, Johanna, Holton Beckering, Lincs, 1599 Lincs RO Ad/Ac/5/395
Spaldinge, Susan, Holton Beckering, Lincs, 1603 Lincs RO Ad/Ac/5/45
Spaldinge, William, Holton Beckering, Lincs, 1612 Lincs RO Ad/Ac/11/158
Spalton, John, yeoman, Hallam, Kirk (Mapperley), Derby, 1742 LJRO/B/C/5/1741/263
Sparepoint, John, husbandman, Preston next Wingham, Kent, 1692 CKS PRC2/42/49
Sparke, Thomas, Scotter, Lincs, 1683 Lincs RO Ad/Ac/44/35
Sparke, William, yeoman, Teffont Magna, Wilts, 1636 Wilts RO Arch. Sarum(+ name and date)
Sparkes, Mathew, Northaw, Herts, 1637 Herts RO ASA25/4946
Sparkes, Thomas, mercer, Worcester, Worcs, 1604 Worcs RO 008.7 BA3585/839/393
Sparkhall, Elizabeth, spinster, Foulsham, Norf, 1733 Norfolk RO ANW/23/21/34
Sparnall, Emme, St Minver, Corn, 1609 Cornwall RO AP/S175
Sparrow, Robert, yeoman, Oare, Kent, 1689 CKS PRC2/41/134
Sparrow, Sarah, widow, Christchurch (Cox's Square), London & Middlesex, 1808 Greater London RO DL/C/567/233
Sparrow, William, clothworker, Midgham, Berks, 1628 Berks RO D/A1/213/148D
Sparrowe, Francis, Brox-Holme, Lincs, 1604 Lincs RO Ad/Ac/37/192
Sparrowe, Stephen, carrier, Newbury, Berks, 1631 Berks RO D/A1/213/161C
Sparrowe, Thomas, Welbourn, Lincs, 1579 Lincs RO Ad/Ac/2b/9
Sparrowe, William, Tenterden, Kent, 1596 CKS PRC2/9/7
Spatchurst, John, Nuthurst, Sussex, 1623 W. Suss RO EpI/33/1623/6
Spavald, Joseph, Gainsborough (Morton), Lincs, 1685 Lincs RO Ad/Ac/44/161
Spawford, John, joiner, Gainsborough, Lincs, 1678 Lincs RO Ad/Ac/35/137
Spayne, Augustyne, Canterbury St Mildred, Kent, 1597 CKS PRC2/10/53

Spayne, John, Lympne, Kent, 1632 CKS PRC2/31/152
Spayne, Lawrence, Warehorne, Kent, 1596 CKS PRC2/8/246
Speare, William, Seal, Nether and Over, Leics, 1666 Leics RO Administrators Accounts C17th f73
Spearpoint, Robart, Shadoxhurst, Kent, 1594 CKS PRC2/6/37
Spedding, William, butcher, Batley, Yorks, 1824 Borthwick Test C.P. 1824/1
Speechley, Ralph, yeoman, Tydd St Mary, Lincs, 1669 Lincs RO Ad/Ac/33/102
Speedy, Richard, Grantham, Lincs, 1637 Lincs RO Ad/Ac/25/186
Speene, Martin, gentleman, Cumnor (Botley), Berks, 1633 Berks RO D/A1/214/1C
Speeringe, Richard, Donhead St Mary, Wilts, 1635 Wilts RO CC Sarum(+ name and date)
Speight, Jonathan, innkeeper, Ardsley, West, Yorks, 1813 Borthwick Test C.P. 1813/1
Speine, Thomas, Sandwich St Peter, Kent, 1627 CKS PRC2/27/168
Spelkes, William, yeoman, Mumby, Lincs, 1671 Lincs RO Ad/Ac/32/234
Spence, Peter, Harborough, Market, Leics, 1672 Leics RO Administrators Accounts 1667-72 f74
Spence, Thomas, upholsterer/citizen, St Clement Danes, London & Middlesex, 1671 Lambeth Palace Arches G26/1
Spence, William, Lincoln St Peter at Gowts, Lincs, 1638 Lincs RO Ad/Ac/25/182
Spencer, Alexander, Althorpe (Amcotts), Lincs, 1629 Lincs RO Ad/Ac/39/206
Spencer, Anne + Robert, Wirksworth, Derby, 1674 LJRO:cards/1674/47
Spencer, George, Tisbury, Wilts, 1806 Wilts RO Miscellaneous Index (name + date)
Spencer, Hugh, baker, St Albans, Herts, 1637 Herts RO ASA25/4947
Spencer, Isaac, Spondon, Derby, 1663 LJRO:cards/1663/56
Spencer, John, Gonerby, Great, Lincs, 1605 Lincs RO Ad/Ac/6/67
Spencer, John, Skidbrooke with Saltfleet Haven, Lincs, 1620 Lincs RO Ad/Ac/16/87
Spencer, John, mason, Abbas Combe, Som, 1622 Somerset RO D/D/Cta/S32
Spencer, John, gentleman, Faversham, Kent, 1635 CKS PRC2/33/125
Spencer, John, degrees: 'Doctor of Physic', Staughton, Great, Hunts, 1670 Hunts RO/Acc58/14(35)
Spencer, John, husbandman, Stanton St John, Oxon, 1679 Oxon RO MSS Wills 174/1/34
Spencer, John, Branston, Leics, 1683 Leics RO Administrators Accounts 1682-86 f7
Spencer, John, gentleman, Herne, Kent, 1689 CKS PRC20/13/640
Spencer, Joseph, nailer, Duffield, Derby, 1790 LJRO/B/C/5/1790/101
Spencer, Margery, widow, Boughton under Blean, Kent, 1597 CKS PRC21/14/205
Spencer, Mathew, mr, Canterbury St Mary Northgate, Kent, 1648 CKS PRC1/8/53
Spencer, Paule, Boughton under Blean, Kent, 1597 CKS PRC21/14/207
Spencer, William, Huntspill, Som, 1709 Somerset RO D/D/Cta/S66
Spencer, see Chapman,
Spender, William, Sandwich, Kent, 1576 CKS PRC2/1/178
Speney, Charles, Charminster, Dors, 1628 Wilts RO Miscellaneous Index (name + date)
Spenloe, Ambrose, Stamford, Lincs, 1637 Lincs RO Ad/Ac/25/442
Spenser, Albon, dyer, Wallingford, Berks, 1598 Berks RO D/A1/212/195A
Spenser, Amos, Biddenden, Kent, 1597 CKS PRC2/9/192
Spenser, Elizabeth, spinster, Canterbury St Dunstan Without, Kent, 1640 CKS PRC1/5/39
Spenser, Robert, fellmonger, Boughton under Blean, Kent, 1639 CKS PRC20/11/350
Spenser, Stephen, Canterbury Holy Cross Westgate, Kent, 1602 CKS PRC21/16/107
Spenser, William, Petworth, Sussex, 1599 W. Suss RO Epl/33/1599/1
Spenser, William, mariner, St Laurence Thanet, Kent, 1679 CKS PRC2/38/184
Speringe, Ann, Clanfield, Oxon, 1637 Oxon RO MSS Wills 86/1/29
Spernan, Francis, gentleman, St Erme, Corn, 1633 Cornwall RO AP/S629/2
Spice, Christopher, Whitstable, Kent, 1605 CKS PRC2/14/424
Spice, Christopher, Elmsted, Kent, 1639 CKS PRC2/34/277
Spice, Christopher, mariner: 'seaman', Seasalter, Kent, 1666 CKS PRC1/11/163
Spice, Christopher, husbandman, Boughton Monchelsea, Kent, 1677 CKS PRC2/37/94
Spice, John, Lenham, Kent, 1622 CKS PRC2/24/79
Spice, John, yeoman, Ruckinge, Kent, 1627 CKS PRC2/28/109 and unnumbered

[Spice:]
Spice, John, Smarden, Kent, 1629 CKS PRC2/29/82
Spice, John, Rainham, Kent, 1719 CKS PRC1/18/29
Spice, John eld, Bearsted, Kent, 1663 CKS PRC1/9/151
Spice, Richard, mr, Pluckley, Kent, 1627 CKS PRC2/28/116
Spice, Richard, Hawkhurst, Kent, 1632 CKS PRC2/31/155
Spice, Richard, Seasalter, Kent, 1633 CKS PRC2/32/113
Spice, Robert, Westwell, Kent, 1611 CKS PRC20/2/272
Spice, Robert, Headcorn, Kent, 1617 CKS PRC2/24/75
Spice, Robert, Ruckinge, Kent, 1641 CKS PRC1/5/40
Spice, Robert, gentleman, Old Romney, Kent, 1666 CKS PRC1/11/164
Spice, Stephan, Canterbury St Martin, Kent, 1618 CKS PRC20/4/358
Spice, Thomas, husbandman, Kennington, Kent, 1640 CKS PRC1/5/41
Spice, William, Bearsted, Kent, 1634 CKS PRC2/32/169
Spice, William, bookseller, Oxford St Mary, Oxon, 1639 Bodleian HYP B9/90-91
Spice, Willyam, Sheldwich, Kent, 1628 CKS PRC2/29/78
Spicer, Edmund, Ashford, Kent, 1629 CKS PRC2/30/129
Spicer, Edward, yeoman, Broad Hinton, Wilts, 1625 Wilts RO Arch. Wilts.(+ name and date)
Spicer, George, yeoman, Appledore, Kent, 1685 CKS PRC2/41/16
Spicer, Henrie, Newington next Hythe, Kent, 1618 CKS PRC2/19/43
Spicer, Henrie, Canterbury St Mary-Magdalen Burgate, Kent, 1620 CKS PRC2/24/80
Spicer, Henry, Beedon (Stanmore), Berks, 1632 Berks RO D/A1/213/164C
Spicer, Henry, Cheriton, Kent, 1641 CKS PRC1/6/21
Spicer, Henry ygr, yeoman, Beedon (Stanmore), Berks, 1630 Berks RO D/A1/213/160A
Spicer, John, Brabourne, Kent, 1639 CKS PRC1/3/44
Spicer, John ygr, husbandman, Goosey, Berks, 1666 Berks RO D/A1/214/110C
Spicer, Laurence, yeoman, Hendred, East, Berks, 1663 Berks RO D/A1/120/76D
Spicer, Lawrence, yeoman, Hendred, East, Berks, 1663 Berks RO D/A1/120/76D
Spicer, Margery, widow, Goosey, Berks, 1597 Berks RO D/A1/212/172C
Spicer, Phillipp, yeoman, Hythe St Leonard, Kent, 1613 CKS PRC20/2/328
Spicer, Robert, Hythe St Leonard, Kent, 1638 CKS PRC20/11/344
Spicer, Robert, Corringham, Lincs, 1663 Lincs RO Ad/Ac/42/46
Spicer, Thomas, Boxford, Berks, 1610 Berks RO D/A1/213/63C
Spicer, Thomas, Letcombe Regis, Berks, 1620 Berks RO D/A1/213/117A
Spicer, Thomas, Lyminge, Kent, 1631 CKS PRC20/9/412
Spicer, Thomas, yeoman, Lyminge, Kent, 1679 CKS PRC20/12/322
Spicer, William, Broad Hinton, Wilts, 1626 Wilts RO Arch. Wilts.(+ name and date)
Spicer, see Codham,
Spicke, John, gentleman, Dover, Kent, 1637 CKS PRC19/1/9
Spicke, Richard, Redmile, Leics, 1639 Leics RO PR/I/41A/19
Spight, Anne, widow, St Anne and St Agnes, London & Middlesex, 1703 PRO PROB5/1556
Spikeing, Thomas, Hagworthingham, Lincs, 1648 Lincs RO Ad/Ac/30/282
Spillet, John, Elham, Kent, 1593 CKS PRC2/6/308
Spillet, Thomas, kerseymaker, Charing, Kent, 1641 CKS PRC19/2/41
Spillett, John, yeoman, Ulcombe, Kent, 1614 CKS PRC2/18/133
Spillett, Mary, spinster, Faversham, Kent, 1671 CKS PRC2/35/87
Spillett, Nicholas, Challock, Kent, 1634 CKS PRC20/11/400
Spillman, Edward, St Martin in the Fields, London & Middlesex, 1669 PRO PROB32/6/24
Spillman, Edward, gentleman, Winterton, Lincs, 1682 Lincs RO Ad/Ac/44/8
Spilman, Judith, widow, Yarmouth, Great, Norf, Norfolk RO ANW/23/8/92
Spilman, Thomas, esquire, Chart nr Sutton Valence, Kent, 1601 CKS PRC2/12/339
Spinke, Alice, widow, Swillington, Yorks, 1636 Borthwick Prob. Ex. 1636/5
Spinkes, Edmund, clergy: 'clerk', Walesby, Lincs, 1624 Lincs RO Ad/Ac/19A/10
Spinnage, Michael, yeoman, Stanford in the Vale, Berks, 1665 Berks RO D/A1/214/114C
Spittle, John, yeoman, Chesterton, Oxon, 1651 Oxon RO MSS Wills 61/1/26
Spoakes, John, Wisborough Green, Sussex, 1629 W. Suss RO EpI/33/1629/15

Spolton, John, Hallam, Kirk (Mapperley Parkhall), Derby, 1741 LJRO/B/C/5/1741/252
Sponer, William, Wickhamford, Worcs, 1603 Worcs RO 008.7 BA3585/838/268
Spongue, William, turner, Chart nr Sutton Valence, Kent, 1671 CKS PRC1/15/61
Sporle, Elizabeth, widow, Norwich St Michael at Thorn, Norf, 1740 Norfolk RO ANW/23/23/10A
Sprackling, Elizabeth, Sandwich, Kent, 1639 CKS PRC1/3/45
Sprackling, John, St Johns Thanet, Kent, 1661 CKS PRC1/8/114
Sprackling, Richard, St Peter in Thanet, Kent, 1640 CKS PRC1/5/42
Spracklyng, John, St Peter in Thanet, Kent, 1591 CKS PRC2/5/414
Spragg, Edward, Alderbury, Wilts, 1793 Wilts RO Miscellaneous Index (name + date)
Sprake, Thomas, blacksmith, Bere Regis, Dors, 1630 Wilts RO Miscellaneous Index (name + date)
Spratlinge, Edward, butcher, Maidenhead, Berks, 1638 Berks RO D/A1/119/72C
Spratt, Henry, Woodchurch, Kent, 1593 CKS PRC21/12/322
Spratt, Henry, Hope All Saints, Kent, 1662 CKS PRC1/9/60
Spratt, Henry, Wye, Kent, 1670 CKS PRC1/15/62
Spratt, John, Hythe St Leonard, Kent, 1626 CKS PRC20/7/138
Spratt, Nicholas, bachelor, Elham, Kent, 1683 CKS PRC2/40/154
Spratt, Thomas, husbandman, Hothfield, Kent, 1671 CKS PRC2/35/86
Spratt/Pratt, Thomas, Pluckley, Kent, 1592 CKS PRC2/5/426
Spratte, John, Biddenden, Kent, 1582 CKS PRC2/2/221
Sprattford, Richard, Braceborough, Lincs, 1612 Lincs RO Ad/Ac/11/98
Spreckley, William, husbandman, Eaton, Leics, 1673 Leics RO Administrators Accounts 1667-72 f132
Sprie, Leonard, Lyminge, Kent, 1611 CKS PRC20/2/262
Sprigg, Samuell, Bowden, Great, Leics, Leics RO Administrators Accounts 1667-72 f84
Spright, James, clothier, Leeds St Peter (Holbeck), Yorks, 1810 Borthwick Test C.P. 1810/7
Spring, William, Birdham, Sussex, 1672 W. Suss RO EpI/33/1672/8
Springate, Christopher, Sandhurst, Kent, 1640 CKS PRC1/5/43
Springate, John, Hawkhurst, Kent, 1639 CKS PRC1/3/46
Springate, Robert, Hawkhurst, Kent, 1634 CKS PRC2/32/171
Springate, Robert, yeoman, Hawkhurst, Kent, 1643 CKS PRC1/7/13
Springe, Thomas, Congresbury, Som, 1621 Somerset RO D/D/Cta/S20
Springet, George, husbandman, Sandhurst, Kent, 1663 CKS PRC1/9/152
Springet, George, miller, Ashford, Kent, 1665 CKS PRC1/11/82
Springett, John ygr, yeoman, Stone in Oxney, Kent, 1663 CKS PRC1/9/153
Springett, Thomas, Biddenden, Kent, 1595 CKS PRC2/8/171
Sprot, Margaret, Shadoxhurst, Kent, 1593 CKS PRC2/6/109
Sprott, Christopher, clergy: 'mr/vicar', Bearsted, Kent, 1616 CKS PRC2/24/76
Sprott, Ellenor, widow, Hythe St Leonard, Kent, 1629 CKS PRC20/8/446
Sprott, Michael, Hythe St Leonard, Kent, 1634 CKS PRC20/11/404
Sprott, William, Willesborough, Kent, 1616 CKS PRC2/19/45
Spry, James, Dover, Kent, 1636 CKS PRC20/11/324
Spry, Thomas, Lympne, Kent, 1680 CKS PRC2/38/185
Spry/Cavill, Anne, wife, Lympne, Kent, 1671 CKS PRC1/15/63
Sprye, James, Lanivet, Corn, 1615 Cornwall RO AP/S286/3
Sprye, Ursula, widow, Lympne, Kent, 1666 CKS PRC1/11/83
Spryngall, William, Watford, Herts, 1560 Herts RO ASA25/532
Spuddle, John, Faversham, Kent, 1600 CKS PRC2/11/298
Spuirne, Gilbert, gentleman, Rowley Regis, Staffs, 1605 Worcs RO 008.7 BA3585/839/416
Spurge, Robert, Maidenhead, Berks, 1597 Berks RO D/A1/212/177A
Spurges, Thomas, Warehorne, Kent, 1597 CKS PRC2/9/227
Spurnell, Margaret, widow, Aldington, Kent, 1613 CKS PRC20/2/318
Spurnell, Margaret, widow, Aldington, Kent, 1615 CKS PRC20/3/192
Spurr, Henry, yeoman, Scartho, Lincs, 1680 Lincs RO Ad/Ac/34/41
Spurrier, Catharine, widow, Marston on Dove, Derby, 1811 LJRO/B/C/5/1811/82

[Spurrier:]
Spurrier, Henry, Marston on Dove, Derby, 1685 LJRO/B/C/5/1685/93
Spurrier, Thomas, gentleman, Marston on Dove, Derby, 1810 LJRO/B/C/5/1811/76
Spurryer, William, yeoman, Glatton, Hunts, 1676 Hunts RO/Acc58/84(45)
Spyce, John, Whitstable, Kent, 1589 CKS PRC2/5/408
Spyce, Thomas, Whitstable, Kent, 1596 CKS PRC2/8/131
Spycer, Chrystopher, Lyminge, Kent, 1576 CKS PRC21/2/384
Spyer, Anthony, gentleman, Dorchester (Holcombe Grange), Oxon, 1648 Oxon RO MSS Wills Pec 71/3/28
Spyer, John, tanner, Stratfield Mortimer, Berks, 1622 Berks RO D/A1/118/17C
Spykin, Michaell, Wrangle, Lincs, 1612 Lincs RO Ad/Ac/11/140
Spynner, Robert, Wittersham, Kent, 1610 CKS PRC20/2/144
Squire, David, Ruckinge, Kent, 1629 CKS PRC2/30/123
Squire, Elizabeth, Ruckinge, Kent, 1628 CKS PRC2/29/84
Squire, John, yeoman, Lewannick, Corn, 1637 Cornwall RO AP/S761/3
Squire, John, Saltfleetby St Peter, Lincs, 1649 Lincs RO Ad/Ac/30/216
Squire, Richard, Ruckinge, Kent, 1628 CKS PRC2/29/85
Squire, Thomas, yeoman, Washingborough, Lincs, 1666 Lincs RO Ad/Ac/32/94
Squire, William, Galby, Leics, 1669 Leics RO Administrators Accounts 1667-72 f24
Squire, William, Oare, Kent, 1687 CKS PRC2/41/103
Squyer, Agnes, Ruckinge, Kent, 1586 CKS PRC2/4/364
St John, Oliver, esquire, Hullavington, Wilts, 1627 Wilts RO Arch. Wilts.(+ name and date)
St Leger, Warham, knight, Ulcombe, Kent, 1633 CKS PRC20/11/438
Stables, John, stocking maker: 'framework knitter', Mickleover, Derby, 1777 LJRO/B/C/5/1777/32
Stables, Lucy, widow, Calverley (Idle), Yorks, 1723 Borthwick Test C.P. 1723/13
Stace, Catherine, Tenterden, Kent, 1596 CKS PRC2/8/338
Stace, Francis, gentleman, Edenham, Lincs, 1633 Lincs RO Ad/Ac/23/168
Stace, Godfrey, yeoman, Chislet, Kent, 1626 CKS PRC2/25/131
Stace, James, labourer, Lydd, Kent, 1638 CKS PRC20/11/348
Stace, John, gentleman, Newington next Sittingbourne, Kent, 1617 CKS PRC20/4/367
Stace, John + Suzan, Elham, Kent, 1626 CKS PRC2/27/163
Stace, Richard, Ebony, Kent, 1645 CKS PRC1/7/66
Stace, Robert, Chartham, Kent, 1613 CKS PRC2/17/129
Stace, Thomas, Tenterden, Kent, 1592 CKS PRC2/6/123
Stace, Thomas, Ebony, Kent, 1600 CKS PRC2/12/322
Stace, William, Wickhambreaux, Kent, 1603 CKS PRC2/13/356
Stacie, Roger, Stainton by Langworth (Newball), Lincs, 1619 Lincs RO Ad/Ac/15/138
Stacy, Alice, widow, Appleford, Berks, 1616 Berks RO D/A1/213/99C
Stacy, Edward, husbandman, Hagbourne, Berks, 1599 Berks RO D/A1/212/181A
Stacy, John, yeoman, Hagbourne, Berks, 1612 Berks RO D/A1/213/73C
Stacy, Thomas, miller, Watlington, Oxon, 1662 Oxon RO MSS Wills 86/2/9
Stacye, Joseph, Seasalter, Kent, 1626 CKS PRC2/27/150
Stacye, Thomas, Shrivenham (Bourton), Berks, 1592 Berks RO D/A1/212/157C
Stadder, Mathew, Sandwich St Clement, Kent, 1617 CKS PRC2/19/59
Staffoorde, Robarte, Chartham, Kent, 1592 CKS PRC2/5/19
Stafford, John, bachelor, St Botolph without Bishopsgate, London & Middlesex, 1703 Lambeth Palace Arches G54/3
Stafford, William, Denby, Derby, 1685 LJRO/B/C/5/1685/94
Stafford, William, yeoman, Ryhall, Northants, 1786 Northants RO X954/22/16
Stagg, John, Huish, Wilts, 1678 Wilts RO CC Sarum(+ name and date)
Stagg, Thomas, yeoman, Easton, Wilts, 1767? Wilts RO Miscellaneous Index (name + date)
Staggs, John, Wyberton, Lincs, 1641 Lincs RO Ad/Ac/27/204
Staincliffe, William, weaver: 'shalloon weaver', Halifax (Withings End, Richworth), Yorks, 1788 Borthwick Test C.P. 1787/12
Staine, William, Sturry, Kent, 1638 CKS PRC2/34/271
Staines, Edward, Monkton, Kent, 1672 CKS PRC20/12/60

Staines, Isaac, Faversham, Kent, 1674 CKS PRC2/36/132
Stains, John, Claxton, Norf, 1747 Norfolk RO ANF/11/4/78
Stainton, John, tanner, Broughton, Lincs, 1664 Lincs RO Ad/Ac/41/119
Stainton, Robert, Stixwold, Lincs, 1612 Lincs RO Ad/Ac/11/113
Staite, Richard, farmer, Cleeve, Bishops, Glos, 1814 GRO GDR/B4/2/S103
Staite, Thomas, Winchcombe, Glos, 1635 GRO GDR/B4/2/S136
Staker, Joan, Climping, Sussex, 1598 W. Suss RO EpI/33/1598/2
Staley, Daniel, farmer, Stapenhill (Newhall), Derby, 1807 LJRO/B/C/5/1806/126
Stalleinge, Robert, Bishops Lydeard, Som, 1639 Somerset RO D/D/Cta/S17
Stallen, John, Sandwich, Kent, 1591 CKS PRC2/5/404
Stallindge, Charles, gentleman, Laverstock, Wilts, 1639? Wilts RO Arch. Sarum(+ name and date)
Stallindge, Eululia, widow, Laverstock, Wilts, 1640 Wilts RO Arch. Sarum(+ name and date)
Stallingber, William, Tetney, Lincs, 1639 Lincs RO Ad/Ac/26/167
Stambrooke, Joan, Shaw cum Donnington, Berks, 1609 Berks RO D/A1/213/60B
Stamer, John, Broadwater (Worthing), Sussex, 1648 W. Suss RO EpI/33/1648/4
Stammer, Thomas, Appledram, Sussex, 1630 W. Suss RO EpI/33/1630/12
Stammers, Robert ygr, carpenter, Bury St Edmunds, Suff, 1711 Suff RO(B) IC500/36/13
Stamp, Robert, Newton by Toft, Lincs, 1605 Lincs RO Ad/Ac/6/148
Stamp, Thomas, draper, Rasen, Middle, (Drax), Lincs, 1637 Lincs RO Ad/Ac/25/629
Stampard, see Stampe,
Stampe, Agnes, Frodingham (Brumby), Lincs, 1610 Lincs RO Ad/Ac/8a/328
Stampe, Edmund eld, yeoman, Fifield, Oxon, 1685 Oxon RO MSS Wills Pec 71/4/9
Stampe, George, Minting, Lincs, 1612 Lincs RO Ad/Ac/10/142
Stampe, John, Brattleby, Lincs, 1662 Lincs RO Ad/Ac/41/32
Stampe, Mary, widow, Sandwich, Kent, 1632 CKS PRC2/31/153
Stampe, Paule, Sandwich, Kent, 1628 CKS PRC2/28/106
Stampe, Thomas, gentleman, Peasemore, Berks, 1636 Berks RO D/A1/214/28C
Stampe, William, Boxgrove, Sussex, 1632 W. Suss RO EpI/33/1632/22
Stampe/Stampard, John, Sandwich St Mary, Kent, 1627 CKS PRC2/27/164
Stamps, see Tewe,
Stampt, Thomas, waterman, Bardney, Lincs, 1669 Lincs RO Ad/Ac/33/139
Stanborne, Christopher, Coldred, Kent, 1602 CKS PRC2/12/336
Stanbra, Henry, publican, Compton, Fenny, Warks, 1824 LJRO/B/C/5/1824/27c
Stanbroke, John, Shaw cum Donnington, Berks, 1601 Berks RO D/A1/213/5C
Standell, William, wheelwright, Bourne, Lincs, 1632 Lincs RO Ad/Ac/23/125
Standen, Edward, Milton next Sittingbourne, Kent, 1592 CKS PRC2/6/252
Standen, Edward, hammerman, Biddenden, Kent, 1668 CKS PRC1/13/121
Standen, Francis, Ruckinge, Kent, 1622 CKS PRC1/1/29
Standen, Joane, Orlestone, Kent, 1610 CKS PRC2/15/386
Standen, Richard, Steyning, Sussex, 1634 W. Suss RO EpI/33/1633/6
Standen, Richard eld, Headcorn, Kent, 1593 CKS PRC2/6/156
Standen, Thomas, hammerman, Biddenden, Kent, 1674 CKS PRC2/36/119
Stander, Edward, Birchington, Kent, 1581 CKS PRC21/5/40
Standford, John, Queenborough, Kent, 1625 CKS PRC2/24/83
Standford, Thomas, Eastergate, Sussex, 1631 W. Suss RO EpI/33/1631/14
Standford, William, Billingshurst, Sussex, 1629 W. Suss RO EpI/33/1629/21
Standish, George, Tamworth, Staffs, 1675 LJRO:cards/1675/49
Standish, Richard, gentleman, Dorrington, Lincs, 1629 Lincs RO Ad/Ac/22/115
Standish, Robert, gentleman, Dorrington, Lincs, 1638 Lincs RO Ad/Ac/25/25
Standley, John, Lea Marston, Warks, 1672 LJRO:cards/1672/56
Standley, John, carpenter, Handsworth, Staffs, 1751 LJRO/B/C/5/1751/134
Standly, William, Bethersden, Kent, 1624 CKS PRC2/24/91
Standlye, Robarte, Tenterden, Kent, 1605 CKS PRC2/15/382
Stanforde, Alice, widow, Staple next Wingham, Kent, 1602 CKS PRC21/16/114
Stanhope, William, gentleman, Boston, Lincs, 1603 Lincs RO Ad/Ac/5/180

[Stanhopp:]
Stanhopp, Darcy, esquire, Mellwood/Axholme, Lincs, 1683 Lincs RO Ad/Ac/44/33
Stanier, Francis, surgeon, Newcastle under Lyme, Staffs, 1807 LJRO/B/C/5/1807/67
Staniford, William, Sulhampstead Bannister, Berks, 1642 Berks RO D/A1/119/12D
Staniforth, George, Eckington, Derby, 1682 LJRO/B/C/5/1682/94
Staninough, James, university: 'Fellow of Queens' College, Cambridge/M.A.', Cambridge (Queens' College), Cambs, 1639 CUL V.C. Acc./Box2/72
Stanley, Elizabeth, Fittleworth, Sussex, 1629 W. Suss RO EpI/33/1629/12
Stanley, John, Cheadle (Cheadle Hulme), Ches, Cheshire RO (Name) W.C. 1692
Stanley, John, St Giles in the Fields, London & Middlesex, 1709 Lambeth Palace Arches G59/2
Stanley, Stephen, St Peter in Thanet, Kent, 1665 CKS PRC1/11/84
Stanley, Thomas, Edlington, Lincs, 1627 Lincs RO Ad/Ac/20b/53
Stanley, Thomas, Rolvenden, Kent, 1687 CKS PRC2/41/105
Stanley, William, Harmston, Lincs, 1607 Lincs RO Ad/Ac/8a/39
Stanly, John, Stockbury, Kent, 1681 CKS PRC2/39/238
Stanly, John, gentleman, Canterbury St Mildred, Kent, 1696 CKS PRC1/16/15
Stanlye, William, Ripple, Kent, 1610 CKS PRC2/15/387
Stanmore, John, husbandman, Wilcot, Wilts, 1689 Wilts RO Arch. Wilts.(+ name and date)
Stansfield, Ely, shopkeeper, Halifax (Stansfield), Yorks, 1799 Borthwick Test C.P. 1799/6
Stansfield, Sarah, widow, Mottram in Longdendale (Stayleybridge), Ches, 1755 Cheshire RO (Name) W.C. 1756
Stanshall, William, gentleman, Nottingham, Notts, 1631 Borthwick Prob. Ex. 1631/1b
Stanton, John, Linkinhorne, Corn, 1608 Cornwall RO AP/S103/3
Stanton, John, Dover, Kent, 1629 CKS PRC20/8/419
Stanton, Samuel, Duston, Northants, 1685 Northants RO NWill A/C/161
Stanton, William, mariner: 'seaman', Dover, Kent, 1640 CKS PRC19/1/82
Stanwell, Robert, Holbeach, Lincs, 1619 Lincs RO Ad/Ac/15/99
Stanwell, William, Whaplode, Lincs, 1627 Lincs RO Ad/Ac/20/104
Staple, Elizabeth, Sidlesham, Sussex, 1626 W. Suss RO EpI/33/1626
Staple, Hugh, Chardstock, Dors, 1626 Wilts RO Miscellaneous Index (name + date)
Staple, Isabell, widow, Hucking, Kent, 1580 CKS PRC21/4/141
Staple, John, yeoman, Rolvenden, Kent, 1683 CKS PRC2/40/153
Staple, Thomas, Sandwich St Bartholomew's Hospital, Kent, 1616 CKS PRC20/3/352
Staple, Thomasyne, spinster, Borden, Kent, 1586 CKS PRC2/4/219
Staple, see Tibball,
Staplehurst, Henry, Slinfold, Sussex, 1595 W. Suss RO EpI/33/1595/6
Staples, Edmund, yeoman, Bexley, Kent, 1667 Lambeth Palace VH96/6234
Staples, Thomas, Bermondsey, St Mary Magdalen, Surrey, 1666? PRO PROB5/964
Stapleton, William, gentleman, Lacock, Wilts, 1627 Wilts RO Arch. Wilts.(+ name and date)
Stare, Robert, yeoman, Burghfield, Berks, 1640 Berks RO D/A1/214/42C
Starke, Ambrose, Chislet, Kent, 1700 CKS PRC19/5/76
Starke, Richard eld, yeoman, Westbere, Kent, 1642 CKS PRC1/6/22
Starke, Richard ygr, Chislet, Kent, 1642 CKS PRC1/6/23
Starke, Thomas, Immingham, Lincs, 1649 Lincs RO Ad/Ac/30/132
Starkes, Thomas, Fishtoft, Lincs, 1632 Lincs RO Ad/Ac/23/41
Starkey, Samuel, servant, Norwich, Norf, 1626 Norfolk RO NCC INV/33/261
Starkhill, George, Stainfield, Lincs, 1662 Lincs RO Ad/Ac/32/44
Starky, Henry, clergy: 'clerk/parson', Wytham, Berks, 1613 Berks RO D/A1/213/87A
Starky, John, Ewell, Kent, 1572 CKS PRC2/1/65
Starky, Thomas, Paddington, London & Middlesex, 1681 PRO PROB32/20/98
Starland, Ellen, Normanton, South, Derby, 1684 LJRO/B/C/5/1683/21
Starr, John, Eastchurch, Sheppey, Kent, 1625 CKS PRC2/25/135
Starr, Joy, hosier, Ashford, Kent, 1684 CKS PRC2/40/151
Starr, William, Kyme, South (North Kyme), Lincs, 1672 Lincs RO Ad/Ac/43/74
Starr/Chauntler, Jane, mrs, Canterbury St Paul, Kent, 1689 CKS PRC2/41/160
Starre, Moreguifte?, Ashford, Kent, 1619 CKS PRC2/19/19

[Start:]

Start, Edward, husbandman, St Peter in Thanet, Kent, 1634 CKS PRC2/32/172
Startup, Elizabethe, widow, Borden, Kent, 1595 CKS PRC2/7/407
Startup, William, brewer, Sittingbourne, Kent, 1676 CKS PRC2/36/244
Startupp, John, yeoman, Rainham, Kent, 1674 CKS PRC2/36/120
Startupp, Roger, yeoman ?, Linsted ?, Kent, 1672 CKS PRC2/35/173
Statham, Anne, widow, Shirland, Derby, 1698 LJRO/B/C/5/1698/104
Stather, William, labourer, Tealby, Lincs, 1634 Lincs RO Ad/Ac/24/535
Statherne, Thomas, Benington, Lincs, 1627 Lincs RO Ad/Ac/20b/82
Statte, Mathewe, Sutton Valence, Kent, 1614 CKS PRC2/18/52
Statting, William, yeoman, Messingham, Lincs, 1674 Lincs RO Ad/Ac/35/47
Staughton, Thomas, Staughton, Great, Hunts, 1676 Hunts RO/Acc58/31(173)
Staunton, Edward, clothier, Reading St Mary, Berks, 1626 Berks RO D/A1/213/139D
Stavell, Nicholas, Wittering, East, Sussex, 1671 W. Suss RO EpI/33/1670/21
Stavely, Christopher, Hurst, Berks, 1632 Wilts RO Miscellaneous Index (name + date)
Staynes, Henrie, Minster in Thanet, Kent, 1633 CKS PRC2/32/112
Stead, Thomas, Ecclesfield (Bradfield), Yorks, 1637 Borthwick Prob. Ex. 1637/1
Steaninge, see Cooper,
Steares, Emanuel, Hayling, Hants, 1699 Hants RO 1699 AD65/3
Stearne, Edward, university: 'Fellow of Pembroke College, Cambridge/M.A.', Cambridge St Mary the Less, Cambs, 1664 CUL V.C. Acc./Box3/47
Stearne, George?, university: 'Fellow of Jesus College, Cambridge/M.A.', Cambridge (Jesus College), Cambs, 1639 CUL V.C. Acc./Box2/73
Stebbing, Thomas, Woodnesborough, Kent, 1625 CKS PRC2/25/126
Stede, George, Kennington, Kent, 1637 CKS PRC2/34/125
Stede, James, Lenham, Kent, 1631 CKS PRC20/9/394
Stede, Mary, spinster, Chartham, Kent, 1668 CKS PRC1/13/122
Stede, Richard, yeoman, Chislet, Kent, 1667 CKS PRC1/12/83
Stede, Thomas, Bearsted, Kent, 1639 CKS PRC1/1/90
Stede, Thomas, Egerton, Kent, 1674 CKS PRC20/12/146
Stedman, Henry, Lenham, Kent, 1667 CKS PRC1/12/84
Stedman, Henry, tailor, Ivychurch, Kent, 1671 CKS PRC19/4/96
Stedman, Isaacke, Biddenden, Kent, 1603 CKS PRC2/12/459
Stedman, John, Biddenden, Kent, 1609 CKS PRC2/13/385
Stedman, John, blacksmith, Tenterden, Kent, 1675 CKS PRC2/36/239
Stedman, John, yeoman, Maidstone, Kent, 1677 CKS PRC20/12/221
Stedman, Samuel, Biddenden, Kent, 1595 CKS PRC2/7/413
Stedman, Thomas, Smarden, Kent, 1611 CKS PRC2/16/58
Stedman, William, yeoman, Sulhampstead Abbots, Berks, 1633 Berks RO D/A1/214/4C
Steed, George, Dover, Kent, 1628 CKS PRC20/8/411
Steed, John, Hollingbourne, Kent, 1622 CKS PRC20/6/268
Steed, Mary, widow, Harrietsham, Kent, 1668 CKS PRC1/13/123
Steed, Robert, Dover, Kent, 1641 CKS PRC19/1/83
Steed, Sarah, Canterbury St Mildred, Kent, 1675 CKS PRC2/36/245
Steed, William, yeoman, Fordwich, Kent, 1694 CKS PRC1/16/16
Steede, Francis, gentleman, Bethersden, Kent, 1671 CKS PRC1/15/64
Steede, Henry, Canterbury St Margaret, Kent, 1612 CKS PRC2/18/14
Steede, John, Lenham, Kent, 1588 CKS PRC2/9/221
Steede, John, Ashford, Kent, 1671 CKS PRC2/35/90
Steede, Mathew, Charing, Kent, 1606 CKS PRC20/1/128
Steede, Paull, Hythe St Leonard, Kent, 1605 CKS PRC20/1/77
Steede, Richard, Canterbury St Margaret, Kent, 1673 CKS PRC2/35/253
Steedes, Mathew, Gautby, Lincs, 1673 Lincs RO Ad/Ac/35/30
Steedman, John, Northaw, Herts, 1635 Herts RO ASA25/4907
Steel, Thomas, yeoman, Leighton, Ches, 1724 Cheshire RO (Name) W.C. 1724
Steele, Alice, widow, Windsor, New, Berks, 1635 Berks RO D/A1/214/5A

[Steele:]
Steele, John, gentleman, Windsor, New, Berks, 1615 Berks RO D/A1/117/106C
Steele, Richard, yeoman, Finchampstead, Berks, 1640 Berks RO D/A1/214/42C
Steele, Roberte, Billinghay, Lincs, 1593 Lincs RO Ad/Ac/5/320
Steele, Samuel, Woolsthorpe, Lincs, 1633 Lincs RO Ad/Ac/24/136
Steele, Thomas, Skirbeck, Lincs, 1605 Lincs RO Ad/Ac/6/73
Steele, Thomas, Barrowby, Lincs, 1635 Lincs RO Ad/Ac/24/298
Steeleman, Thomas, Sandwich St Clement, Kent, 1628 CKS PRC2/28/108
Steeling, John eld, Maidstone, Kent, 1610 CKS PRC20/2/90
Steeling, see Steely,
Steely/Steeling, John, Sturry, Kent, 1637 CKS PRC2/34/124
Steep, Robert, Messingham, Lincs, 1633 Lincs RO Ad/Ac/40/67
Steeper, Jane, widow, Winteringham, Lincs, 1668 Lincs RO Ad/Ac/33/83
Steephens, see West,
Steere, Peter, yeoman, Chart nr Sutton Valence, Kent, 1684 CKS PRC2/40/247
Steere, Susanna, Thorne, Yorks, 1637 Borthwick Prob. Ex. 1637/6
Steere, Thomas, husbandman, Marden, Kent, 1666 CKS PRC1/11/86
Steere, William, Sonning, Berks, 1676 Wilts RO Dean Sarum (name + date)
Steere, William eld, Rogate, Sussex, 1646 W. Suss RO EpI/33/1645/3
Steere/Stuart, Alice, Marden, Kent, 1665 CKS PRC1/11/85
Steevens, Jeremy, clergy: 'clerk', Wootton, Northants, 1670 Northants RO NWill A/C/91
Steevens, John eld, yeoman, Clanfield, Oxon, 1676 Oxon RO MSS Wills 86/3/22
Steevens, Richard, Cassington, Oxon, 1637 Oxon RO MSS Wills 173/4/1
Steevens, Thomas, Lavant, East, Sussex, 1621 W. Suss RO EpIV/10/1/35
Steevens, Thomas, Pitcombe, Som, 1622 Somerset RO D/D/Cta/S22
Steevens, Thomas, yeoman, Radley, Berks, 1639 Berks RO D/A1/214/39C
Steevens, William, husbandman, Lockinge, East, Berks, 1678 Berks RO D/A1/214/176C
Steevenson, Henry, yeoman, Sunningwell, Berks, 1636 Berks RO D/A1/214/20C
Steevenson, John, yeoman, Sunningwell, Berks, 1646 Berks RO D/A1/214/72C
Steevins, John, Salisbury St Edmund, Wilts, 1632 Wilts RO Miscellaneous Index (name + date)
Steine, John, Chislet, Kent, 1618 CKS PRC2/19/23
Stelingfleet, William, Lydd, Kent, 1586 CKS PRC21/8/123
Stempe, Robert, Lydd, Kent, 1639 CKS PRC20/11/356
Stening, James, Pulborough, Sussex, 1682 W. Suss RO EpI/33/1682/46
Stening, see Cooper,
Steninges, Alice, widow, Linsted, Kent, 1608 CKS PRC2/14/409
Stennet, Thomas, husbandman, Moulton, Lincs, 1683 Lincs RO Ad/Ac/44/61
Stennett, Elizabeth, widow, Sibsey, Lincs, 1620 Lincs RO Ad/Ac/16/91
Stennett, Michaell, Ewerby, Lincs, 1626 Lincs RO Ad/Ac/20/121
Stennett, William, Dorrington, Lincs, 1606 Lincs RO Ad/Ac/7/16
Stennings, Jeremy, clothier, Benenden, Kent, 1637 CKS PRC20/11/314
Stennitt, Eden, Ewerby, Lincs, 1632 Lincs RO Ad/Ac/23/169
Stennitt, George, yeoman, Carlton Scroop, Lincs, 1620 Lincs RO Ad/Ac/16/90
Stennytt, William, Ewerby, Lincs, 1613 Lincs RO Ad/Ac/12/27
Stente, John, Chapel, North, Sussex, 1640 W. Suss RO EpI/33/1640/16
Stephens, Agnes + Anne, Scotter, Lincs, 1652 Lincs RO Ad/Ac/40/210
Stephens, Alexander, yeoman, Goudhurst, Kent, 1619 CKS PRC2/19/16
Stephens, Benet, Crantock, Corn, 1616 Cornwall RO AP/S313/2
Stephens, Edward, Herne, Kent, 1587 CKS PRC21/8/306
Stephens, Edward, Dover, Kent, 1595 CKS PRC21/14/211
Stephens, Elizabeth, minor, Chart, Great, Kent, 1642 CKS PRC1/6/84
Stephens, Francis, yeoman, Chart, Great, Kent, 1642 CKS PRC1/6/85
Stephens, Francis jnr, Colan, Corn, 1603 Cornwall RO AP/S37
Stephens, George, gentleman, Milton Lilborne, Wilts, 1673 Wilts RO Arch. Wilts.(+ name and date)
Stephens, Henry, husbandman, Shirburn, Oxon, 1679 Oxon RO MSS Wills 86/4/1

Stephens, James, schoolmaster, Winterbourne, Glos, Bristol RO 1748/68
Stephens, James + Alice, Freshwater, Hants, 1663 Hants RO 21M65 D8/179
Stephens, John, Ruckinge, Kent, 1627 CKS PRC2/27/167
Stephens, John, Maidstone, Kent, 1634 CKS PRC20/11/408
Stephens, Joseph, mercer, Sandhurst, Kent, 1632 CKS PRC20/11/442
Stephens, Martha, spinster, West Bromwich, Staffs, 1819 LJRO/B/C/5/1819/92
Stephens, Nicholas, Chislet, Kent, 1620 CKS PRC2/19/15
Stephens, Phenice, Goudhurst, Kent, 1596 CKS PRC2/8/276
Stephens, Ralph, Hothfield, Kent, 1614 CKS PRC2/18/27
Stephens, Ralph, Bodmin, Corn, 1625 Cornwall RO AP/S485/4
Stephens, Thomas, Smarden, Kent, 1619 CKS PRC2/19/18
Stephens, Thomas, Staplehurst, Kent, 1638 CKS PRC2/34/116
Stephens, Thomas, wheelwright, Bicester, Oxon, 1688 Oxon RO MSS Wills 174/1/37
Stephens, William, yeoman, Goudhurst, Kent, 1620 CKS PRC2/19/35
Stephens, Wyllyam, Chislet, Kent, 1588 CKS PRC2/4/265
Stephens, see De Moll & Thomas,
Stephenson, Benjamin, spinner: 'worsted spinner/innkeeper', Bradford (Lingbob), Yorks, 1843 Borthwick Test C.P. 1842/9
Stephenson, Elizabeth, Tonge, Kent, 1633 CKS PRC2/32/117
Stephenson, Henry, Blackmanstone, Kent, 1639 CKS PRC2/34/278
Stephenson, John, innholder, Beverley, Yorks, Borthwick Test C.P. 1767/3
Stephenson, John, Crowle, Lincs, 1625 Lincs RO Ad/Ac/39/174
Stephenson, John, baker, Cambridge, Cambs, 1683 CUL V.C. Acc./Box3/48
Stephenson, Marmaduke, Allerthorpe, Yorks, 1639 Borthwick Prob. Ex. 1639/2
Stephenson, Matthew, yeoman, Hilston, Yorks, 1778 Borthwick Test C.P. 1778/10
Stephenson, Robert, Quarrendon, Bucks, 1622 Oxon RO MSS Wills Pec 51/1/34
Stephenson, Robert, Luddington, Lincs, 1631 Lincs RO Ad/Ac/39/263
Stephenson, Robert, clerk: 'merchant's clerk', Hull, Yorks, 1807 Borthwick Test C.P. 1807/4
Stephenson, William, yeoman, Normanby, Lincs, 1673 Lincs RO Ad/Ac/35/69
Stepto, Alexander, Wokingham, Berks, 1596 Wilts RO Miscellaneous Index (name + date)
Sterling, William, Barfreston, Kent, 1638 CKS PRC2/34/121
Steven, Robert, Morton, Lincs, 1638 Lincs RO Ad/Ac/25/272
Stevenet, Thomas, Dorrington, Lincs, Lincs RO Ad/Ac/22/121
Stevens, Ann, widow, Spalding, Lincs, 1785 Lincs RO Ad/Ac/45/50
Stevens, Christian, Brompton Regis, Som, 1611 Somerset RO D/D/Cta/S58
Stevens, Edward, yeoman, Winslow (Shipton), Bucks, 1597 Herts RO ASA25/1641
Stevens, Elizabeth, spinster, Thatcham, Berks, 1600 Berks RO D/A1/116/144C
Stevens, Francis, Fareham, Hants, 1672 Hants RO 21m65 D8/251
Stevens, George, Wittering, East, Sussex, 1676 W. Suss RO EpI/33/1676/22
Stevens, Henry, fisherman, Eaton Hastings, Berks, 1613 Berks RO D/A1/213/81C
Stevens, Henry, Chisledon, Wilts, 1623 Wilts RO Arch. Wilts.(+ name and date)
Stevens, John, Woodchurch, Kent, 1586 CKS PRC21/8/163
Stevens, John, Steventon, Berks, 1617 Berks RO D/A1/213/106C
Stevens, John, husbandman, Wittenham, Little, Berks, 1622 Berks RO D/A1/213/123C
Stevens, John, Deal, Kent, 1675 CKS PRC20/12/185
Stevens, John, Sutton Coldfield, Warks, 1740 LJRO:cards/1740/8
Stevens, John ygr, Wye, Kent, 1614 CKS PRC2/17/20
Stevens, Mark, victualler, Birmingham, Warks, 1790 LJRO/B/C/5/1790/106
Stevens, Marye, Chislet, Kent, 1597 CKS PRC2/10/379
Stevens, Mathew, Alvington, Glos, 1601 GRO GDR/B4/2/S29
Stevens, Oliver, husbandman, Kingston Bagpuize, Berks, 1602 Berks RO D/A1/213/19C
Stevens, Richard, clergy: 'clerk', Wilsford, Lincs, 1606 Lincs RO Ad/Ac/7/46
Stevens, Richard, Morton, Lincs, 1648 Lincs RO Ad/Ac/30/342
Stevens, Richard, Morton, Lincs, 1649 Lincs RO Ad/Ac/30/204
Stevens, Robert, Spalding, Lincs, 1596 Lincs RO Ad/Ac/4/9

[Stevens:]
Stevens, Robert, Midhurst, Sussex, 1604 W. Suss RO EpI/33/1604/2
Stevens, Robert, Godmanchester, Hunts, 1709 Hunts RO/Acc58/300
Stevens, Robert eld, yeoman, Aldenham, Herts, 1635 Herts RO AHH23/2085
Stevens, Samuel, mariner, St Johns Thanet, Kent, 1674 CKS PRC2/36/127
Stevens, Stephen, Holbeach, Lincs, 1629 Lincs RO Ad/Ac/22/18
Stevens, Thomas, husbandman, Windsor, New, Berks, 1620 Berks RO D/A1/213/113A
Stevens, Thomas, Woodchurch, Kent, 1639 CKS PRC20/11/354
Stevens, Thomas, Bradford on Avon, Wilts, 1678 Wilts RO Arch. Sarum(+ name and date)
Stevens, William, Bromham, Wilts, 1628 Wilts RO Arch. Wilts.(+ name and date)
Stevens, William, Chislet, Kent, 1641 CKS PRC1/6/24
Stevens/Hawkes, John, husbandman, Watchfield, Berks, 1620 Berks RO D/A1/118/3B
Stevenson, Alexander, labourer, Tatenhill (Dunstall), Staffs, 1777 LJRO/B/C/5/1777/34
Stevenson, Anne, Bainton, Yorks, 1607 Borthwick Prob. Ex. 1607/3
Stevenson, Edward, Barrow on Humber, Lincs, 1624 Lincs RO Ad/Ac/19A/79
Stevenson, George, Manton, Lincs, 1663 Lincs RO Ad/Ac/41/65
Stevenson, John, Cockerington, Lincs, 1579 Lincs RO Ad/Ac/2b/46
Stevenson, John, Goxhill, Lincs, 1633 Lincs RO Ad/Ac/24/142
Stevenson, Joshua, Walsall, Staffs, 1744 LJRO/B/C/5/1744/238
Stevenson, Katherine, widow, Thornton Curtis, Lincs, 1632 Lincs RO Ad/Ac/23/7
Stevenson, Richard, Goxhill, Lincs, 1578 Lincs RO Ad/Ac/2b/14
Stevenson, Richard, Sunningwell, Berks, 1615 Berks RO D/A1/213/91A
Stevenson, Robert, Blankney, Lincs, 1638 Lincs RO Ad/Ac/25/5
Stevenson, Thomas, Boxley, Kent, 1586 CKS PRC2/4/237
Stevenson, Thomas, Elsham, Lincs, 1620 Lincs RO Ad/Ac/15/3
Stevenson, Thomas, husbandman, Wainfleet St Mary, Lincs, C17th? Lincs RO Ad/Ac/45/108
Stevenson, William, clothier, Chichester St Bartholomew, Sussex, 1617 W. Suss RO EpIII/9/1/27
Steventon, Richard, Swynnerton (Wilkins Pleck), Staffs, 1719 LJRO/B/C/5/1719/3434
Steward, Mary, Wootton Wawen, Worcs, 1687 Worcs RO 008.7 BA3585/836/bdl 1
Steward, Richard, Norwich, Norf, 1631 Norfolk RO NCC INV/37/47
Steward, Thomas, yeoman, Buscot, Berks, 1609 Berks RO D/A1/213/55A
Steward, Thomas, husbandman, Burgh le Marsh, Lincs, 1642 Lincs RO Ad/Ac/28/61
Stewkley, Anthony, gentleman, Holbeach, Lincs, 1633 Lincs RO Ad/Ac/24/7
Steyne, Henrye, Monkton, Kent, 1616 CKS PRC20/3/368
Stibbard, John, Surfleet, Lincs, 1637 Lincs RO Ad/Ac/25/122
Stibbing, John, clergy: 'clerk', Sandwich St Peter, Kent, 1603 CKS PRC2/13/358
Stibbing, John, clergy: 'mr/curate', Ash next Sandwich, Kent, 1616 CKS PRC20/3/371
Stibbs, Elizabeth, widow, Letcombe Regis, Berks, 1609 Berks RO D/A1/213/57A
Stickland, Richard, Wimborne Minster, Dors, Dorset RO PE/WM CP 2/4/30
Stiddman, Willliam, husbandman, Ashwick, Som, 1596 Somerset RO D/D/Cta/S40
Stiff, John, St Michael Crooked Lane, London & Middlesex, 1731 Lambeth Palace VH82/99
Stiffe, Francis, Petham, Kent, 1688 CKS PRC2/41/102
Stiles, Edward, St Albans St Peters, Herts, 1638 Herts RO ASA25/4948
Stiles, Jerom, Cricklade St Sampson, Wilts, 1626 Wilts RO Arch. Wilts.(+ name and date)
Stiles, John, husbandman, Boxford, Berks, 1609 Berks RO D/A1/213/52C
Stiles, Mary, widow, Swineshead, Lincs, 1619 Lincs RO Ad/Ac/15/63
Stiles, Richard, husbandman, Rousham, Oxon, 1638 Oxon RO MSS Wills 173/4/2
Stiles, Rose, widow, Otterden, Kent, 1622 CKS PRC2/24/81
Still, Mary, spinster, Lavington, West, Wilts, 1631 Wilts RO CC Sarum(+ name and date)
Still, Robert, Wellington, Som, 1589 Somerset RO D/D/Cta/S46
Still, Thomas, butcher, Lavington, West, Wilts, 1622 Wilts RO CC Sarum(+ name and date)
Still, William, Grantham, Lincs, 1605 Lincs RO Ad/Ac/6/147
Still, William, Wittersham, Kent, 1624 CKS PRC20/6/179
Stillman, Nicholas, St Laurence Thanet, Kent, 1598 CKS PRC2/10/292
Stimpe, Thomas, husbandman, Ilsley, East, Berks, 1619 Berks RO D/A1/213/109A
Stimson, Robert, Bicker, Lincs, 1774 Lincs RO Ad/Ac/36/11

Stinnett, Nicholas, Offord Darcy, Hunts, 1680 Hunts RO/Acc58/148(120)
Stinton, Sarah, widow, Worcester St Clement, Worcs, 1767 Worcs RO 008.7 BA3585/835/bdl 1
Stippen, Silvester, Seasalter, Kent, 1668 CKS PRC1/12/85
Stirges, Ambrose, Moorlinch, Som, 1666 Somerset RO D/D/Cta/S52
Stirke, John, gentleman, Salcey Forest, Northants, 1684 Northants RO NWill A/C/22
Stoakes, George, Bristol St Stephen, Glos, Bristol RO 1684/CP
Stoakley, William eld, Warboys, Hunts, 1722 Hunts RO/Acc58/313
Stoanes, John, bachelor, Covenham St Bartholomew, Lincs, 1600 Lincs RO Ad/Ac/5/37
Stock, Daniel, Elmsted, Kent, 1626 CKS PRC2/25/138
Stock, John, Warehorne, Kent, 1665 CKS PRC1/10/92
Stock, Rebecca, Otterden, Kent, 1597 CKS PRC2/10/369
Stock, Samuel, glazier, Tewkesbury, Glos, 1744 GRO GDR/B4/2/S118
Stock, William, Cowbit (Peakhill), Lincs, 1607 Lincs RO Ad/Ac/8a/179
Stockdall, Richard, yeoman, Welford (Easton), Berks, 1641 Berks RO D/A1/214/47C
Stockden, Richard, clergy: 'clerk', Chirton, Wilts, 1615 Wilts RO Miscellaneous Index (name + date)
Stockden, Richard, Wisborough Green, Sussex, 1662 W. Suss RO EpI/33/1661/13
Stockden/Bridges, Grace, St Nicholas at Wade, Kent, 1665 CKS PRC1/11/87
Stocke, Alice, Aldington, Kent, 1585 CKS PRC21/7/376
Stocke, Edward, Ruckinge, Kent, 1615 CKS PRC20/3/154
Stocke, Edward, gentleman, Slimbridge, Glos, 1686 GRO GDR/B4/2/S132
Stocke, George, Birchington, Kent, 1624 CKS PRC20/6/189
Stocke, George, Ash next Sandwich, Kent, 1633 CKS PRC20/11/436
Stocke, Joan, Ruckinge, Kent, 1598 CKS PRC2/10/446
Stocke, John, Hythe St Leonard, Kent, 1673 CKS PRC20/12/99
Stocke, John, Springthorpe, Lincs, 1677 Lincs RO Ad/Ac/35/115
Stocke, Reginald, Orlestone, Kent, 1591 CKS PRC2/5/400
Stocke, Roberte, Nonington, Kent, 1585 CKS PRC21/7/199
Stocke, Thomas, Warehorne, Kent, 1593 CKS PRC2/6/450
Stocke, Thomas, Shadoxhurst, Kent, 1610 CKS PRC2/15/363
Stocke, Thomas, yeoman, Old Romney, Kent, 1641 CKS PRC1/6/25
Stocke, William, Ilmington, Warks, 1684 Worcs RO 008.7 BA3585/837/bdl 4
Stockell, John, Malton, New, Yorks, 1610 Borthwick Prob. Ex. 1610/1
Stocker, Robert, husbandman/yeoman, Islip, Oxon, 1633 Oxon RO MSS Wills 60/3/4
Stocker, Thomas, Grafham (East Perry), Hunts, 1676 Hunts RO/Acc58/80(139)
Stockes, Richard, Normanby, Lincs, 1626 Lincs RO Ad/Ac/39/35
Stockley, Joshua, farmer, Blymhill (Ivetsey Bank), Staffs, 1816 LJRO/B/C/5/1816/46
Stockley, William, Oxford St Michael, Oxon, 1663 Oxon RO MSS Wills 174/1/4
Stockman, Thomas, gentleman, Nunton, Wilts, 1638 Wilts RO Arch. Sarum(+ name and date)
Stocks, Hugh, Bassingham, Lincs, 1578 Lincs RO Ad/Ac/2b/34
Stocks, Robert, Bassingham, Lincs, 1635 Lincs RO Ad/Ac/24/433
Stockton, see Carpenter,
Stoddard, Thomas, Waddingham, Lincs, 1627 Lincs RO Ad/Ac/39/82
Stodder, Laurence, yeoman, Stourmouth, Kent, 1680 CKS PRC2/39/107
Stokar/Morrice, Edward, Stoke, North, Sussex, 1633 W. Suss RO EpI/33/1633/26
Stokeham, Thomas, clergy: 'clerk', Linwood, Lincs, 1618 Lincs RO Ad/Ac/14/287
Stokes, Anne, Springthorpe, Lincs, 1683 Lincs RO Ad/Ac/44/21
Stokes, Anne, widow, Sandwich, Kent, 1684 CKS PRC2/40/246
Stokes, Anthonie, yeoman, Harlaxton, Lincs, 1619 Lincs RO Ad/Ac/15/87
Stokes, Ellis, Ringwood, Hants, 1662 Hants RO 21M65 D8/160
Stokes, Francis, victualler, Sandwich, Kent, 1675 CKS PRC2/36/242
Stokes, Jeames, Linsted, Kent, 1613 CKS PRC2/18/98
Stokes, John, gentleman, Canterbury St Mildred, Kent, 1621 CKS PRC20/5/174
Stokes, John, Linsted, Kent, 1625 CKS PRC2/25/136
Stokes, John, Winscombe, Som, 1663 Somerset RO D/D/Cta/S49

[Stokes:]
Stokes, John, yeoman, Halton, Bucks, 1677 Bucks R.O. MSS Wills Pec 80/4/28
Stokes, John, hellier, Salisbury, Wilts, 1678 Wilts RO Miscellaneous Index (name + date)2
Stokes, Jonas, Hinton Blewett, Som, 1707 Somerset RO D/D/Cta/S67
Stokes, Margarett, Christchurch, Hants, 1673 Hants RO 21m65 D8/262
Stokes, Martyn, Seasalter, Kent, 1617 CKS PRC2/19/30
Stokes, Mary, Lewisham (Sydenham Green), Kent, 1663 Lambeth Palace Arches G18/1
Stokes, Nicholas, Sutton by Dover, Kent, 1628 CKS PRC2/29/87
Stokes, Suzan, spinster, Canterbury Christchurch, Kent, 1631 CKS PRC20/9/414
Stokes, Symon, Upchurch, Kent, 1600 CKS PRC2/11/357
Stokes, Thomas, shipwright, Sandwich, Kent, 1696 CKS PRC2/42/111
Stokes, William, Salisbury St Thomas, Wilts, 1625 Wilts RO Miscellaneous Index (name + date)
Stokes, William, Bilsington, Kent, 1638 CKS PRC2/34/272
Stokes/Francklin, Edith, widow, Hougham, Kent, 1625 CKS PRC2/25/125
Stokesley, Richard, Barrowby, Lincs, 1662? Lincs RO Ad/Ac/32/3
Stominge, Elizabeth, Nunton & Bodenham, Wilts, 1633 Wilts RO Arch. Sarum(+ name and date)
Stonard, Elizabeth, widow, Milton next Sittingbourne, Kent, 1642 CKS PRC1/6/86
Stonard, John, minor, Ivychurch, Kent, 1688 CKS PRC20/13/620
Stone, Ann, wife, Steventon, Berks, 1678 Berks RO D/A1/214/178C
Stone, Catharine, widow, Cerney, South, Glos, 1711 GRO GDR/B4/2/S119
Stone, George, Nuthurst, Sussex, 1682 W. Suss RO EpI/33/1682/31
Stone, Henry, Dover St Mary, Kent, 1626 CKS PRC20/7/134
Stone, James, yeoman, Steventon, Berks, 1668 Berks RO D/A1/120/134D
Stone, James, gentleman, Burgh le Marsh, Lincs, 1683 Lincs RO Ad/Ac/44/94
Stone, John, Faversham, Kent, 1582 CKS PRC2/2/196
Stone, John, Ash next Sandwich, Kent, 1586 CKS PRC21/7/366
Stone, John, Harbledown, Kent, 1596 CKS PRC2/8/411
Stone, John, yeoman, Sparsholt (Farlow), Berks, 1610 Berks RO D/A1/212/155A
Stone, John, Staplehurst, Kent, 1613 CKS PRC2/16/125
Stone, John, Nuthurst, Sussex, 1618 W. Suss RO EpI/33/1618/6
Stone, John, Tenterden, Kent, 1638 CKS PRC2/34/282
Stone, John, Shapwick, Som, 1665 Somerset RO D/D/Cta/S53
Stone, John, yeoman, Horsepath, Oxon, 1671 Oxon RO MSS Wills 86/3/6
Stone, John, Deal, Kent, 1692 CKS PRC19/5/12
Stone, Joseph, Wraxall, South, Wilts, 1673 Wilts RO Arch. Sarum(+ name and date)
Stone, Joseph, stocking maker, Stoke Lane, Som, 1742 Somerset RO D/D/Cta/S68
Stone, Peter, pilot, Deal, Kent, 1675 CKS PRC20/12/189
Stone, Richard, blacksmith, Sandwich St Clement, Kent, 1620 CKS PRC2/19/3
Stone, Richard, Staunton, Worcs, 1681 Worcs RO 008.7 BA3585/837/bdl 2
Stone, Richard, Pershore Holy Cross (Wadborough), Worcs, 1682 Worcs RO 008.7 BA3585/837/bdl 3
Stone, Richard, Hitchin, Herts, 1694 PRO PROB32/34/10
Stone, Robart, mr, Bobbing, Kent, 1607 CKS PRC20/1/312
Stone, Robert, husbandman, Denchworth, Berks, 1635 Berks RO D/A1/214/18C
Stone, Roger, St Johns Thanet, Kent, 1644 CKS PRC1/7/32
Stone, Samuel, Staplehurst, Kent, 1635 CKS PRC20/11/333
Stone, Simon, Constantine, Corn, 1612 Cornwall RO AP/S225/3
Stone, Simon, Coleshill, Warks, 1681 LJRO/B/C/5/1682/95
Stone, Somner, Dover, Kent, 1603 CKS PRC21/15/333
Stone, Symon, clergy: 'mr/vicar', St Peter in Thanet, Kent, 1617 CKS PRC2/19/33
Stone, Thomas, Letcombe Regis, Berks, 1565 Berks RO D/A2/C5/f277V
Stone, Thomas, Dymchurch, Kent, 1609 CKS PRC2/15/380
Stone, Thomas, Otterhampton, Som, 1620 Somerset RO D/D/Cta/S6
Stone, Thomas, Yapton (Bilsham), Sussex, 1625 W. Suss RO EpI/33/1625
Stone, Thomas, hardwareman, Sheffield, Yorks, 1772 Borthwick Test C.P. 1772/6
Stone, Valentine, yeoman, Minster in Thanet, Kent, 1693 CKS PRC2/42/50

Stone, William, Longworth, Berks, 1605 Berks RO D/A1/213/37C
Stone, William, Longworth, Berks, 1606 Berks RO D/A1/213/39
Stone, William, husbandman, Stoke, South, Oxon, 1680 Oxon RO MSS Wills 86/4/7
Stone, William, Perton, Worcs, 1682 Worcs RO 008.7 BA3585/830/48
Stone, Winter, gentleman, Dover, Kent, 1605 CKS PRC20/1/61
Stone, Winter, Dover, Kent, 1611 CKS PRC20/2/266
Stonebridge, Andrew, Stone in Oxney, Kent, 1606 CKS PRC2/13/388
Stonebridge, Willyam, St Mary in the Marsh, Kent, 1627 CKS PRC2/28/110
Stoneham, Henry, bachelor, Broadwater (Worthing), Sussex, 1684 W. Suss RO EpI/33/1684/33
Stoneherst, Rychard, Charing, Kent, 1588 CKS PRC21/9/110
Stonehouse, Edwarde, Ashford, Kent, 1615 CKS PRC2/19/31
Stoneman, Richard, Gorran, Corn, 1636 Cornwall RO AP/S740/3
Stoner, Henry, knight, Rotherfield Peppard (Blounts Court), Oxon, 1625 Oxon RO MSS Wills 173/3/19
Stones, Thomas, Alford, Lincs, 1650 Lincs RO Ad/Ac/29/103
Stones, William, Wainfleet All Saints, Lincs, 1606 Lincs RO Ad/Ac/7/172
Stonestreet, Damaris, Bethersden, Kent, 1628 CKS PRC2/29/80
Stonestreet, Daniell, Bethersden, Kent, 1639 CKS PRC1/3/47
Stonestreet, Elizabeth, widow, Faversham, Kent, 1637 CKS PRC1/1/61
Stonestreet, Philip, fellmonger, Kennington, Kent, 1688 PRO PROB5/1204
Stonestreet, Stephen, Ospringe, Kent, 1624 CKS PRC2/24/86
Stonestreete, Elizabeth, Boxley, Kent, 1674 CKS PRC2/36/128
Stonestrete, Thomas, Bethersden, Kent, 1613 CKS PRC2/17/392
Stonham, John, labourer, Sandhurst, Kent, 1668 CKS PRC1/13/124
Stonham, Richard, Trotton, Sussex, W. Suss RO EpI/33/1612/6
Stonherst, Margery, widow, Aldington, Kent, 1585 CKS PRC21/7/396
Stonnard, Alexander, Chart, Great, Kent, 1596 CKS PRC2/8/493
Stonnard, Daniell, Ash next Sandwich, Kent, 1593 CKS PRC21/12/275
Stonnard, John, grazier, Ivychurch, Kent, 1687 CKS PRC20/13/607
Stonnard, Robarte, Biddenden, Kent, 1604 CKS PRC2/14/412
Stonnard, Stephen, Ash next Sandwich, Kent, 1671 CKS PRC20/12/30
Stonnard, William, Rainham, Kent, 1622 CKS PRC2/24/77
Stonnarde, Joan, widow, Woodnesborough, Kent, 1618 CKS PRC2/19/41
Stonner, William, Woodnesborough, Kent, 1616 CKS PRC2/19/54
Stonstreete, Ruben, Tenterden, Kent, 1596 CKS PRC2/8/258
Stookes, Nicholas, Ringwould, Kent, 1604 CKS PRC2/13/366
Storer, John, Thrussington, Leics, 1639 Leics RO PR/I/41A/38
Storer, Joseph, labourer, Yoxall, Staffs, 1817 LJRO/B/C/5/1817/99
Storer, Margarett, Gosberton, Lincs, 1624 Lincs RO Ad/Ac/19A/40
Storer, Richard, Swineshead, Lincs, 1614 Lincs RO Ad/Ac/12/200
Storer?, John?, Barlestone, Leics, 1684 Leics RO Administrators Accounts 1682-86 f31
Storey, Anthony, mr,
Hunts Hunts RO/Acc58/286
Storey, James, captain, Stepney, London & Middlesex, 1685 PRO PROB32/25/175
Storey, William, Lincoln St Nicholas in Newport, Lincs, 1672 Lincs RO Ad/Ac/42/50
Storie, George, Glastonbury (Nyland), Som, 1623 Somerset RO D/D/Cta/S23
Storie, James, weaver, Staplehurst, Kent, 1638 CKS PRC2/34/117
Storie, Thomas, blacksmith, Spilsby, Lincs, 1619 Lincs RO Ad/Ac/15/65
Storke, William, Martin, Wilts, 1639 Wilts RO Arch. Sarum(+ name and date)
Storkes, Richard, Wyberton, Lincs, 1649 Lincs RO Ad/Ac/30/33
Storme, Alex, Whitton, Lincs, 1635 Lincs RO Ad/Ac/40/21
Storr, Frances, Kirton, Lincs, 1637 Lincs RO Ad/Ac/25/424
Storr, Walter, Somercoates, North, Lincs, 1632 Lincs RO Ad/Ac/23/97
Storr, William, Cammeringham, Lincs, 1594 Lincs RO Ad/Ac/5/318
Storr, William, Gautby, Lincs, 1602 Lincs RO Ad/Ac/5/85

[Storre, see Herne:]
Storre, see Herne,
Storrs, Thomas, jobber/farmer, Clarborough, Notts, 1851 Borthwick Test C.P. 1851/2
Storth, John, Scarcliffe, Derby, 1684 LJRO/B/C/5/1684/75
Story, Anne, widow, Pickering (Stainton), Yorks, 1635 Borthwick Prob. Ex. 1635/3
Story, Charles, Mersham, Kent, 1597 CKS PRC2/10/10
Story, Dorothy, Aslackby, Lincs, 1673 Lincs RO Ad/Ac/34/22
Story, John, cordwainer, Yaxley, Hunts, 1751 Hunts RO/Acc58/325
Story, Michael, Boston, Lincs, 1684 Lincs RO Ad/Ac/34/116
Stother, Stephen, Headcorn, Kent, 1635 CKS PRC2/32/167
Stotherd, William, Appleby, Lincs, 1619 Lincs RO Ad/Ac/8b/413
Stoughton, Francis, mr, Norwich, Norf, Norfolk RO ANW/23/21/66
Stoure, Thomas, beerseller?, Dover, Kent, 1674 CKS PRC20/12/150
Stourton, John, Gainsborough, Lincs, 1624 Lincs RO Ad/Ac/8c/65
Stoven, Martin, Miningsby, Lincs, 1638 Lincs RO Ad/Ac/25/313
Stovin, George, Crowle, Lincs, 1685 Lincs RO Ad/Ac/44/162
Stovin, Mary, Laughton, Lincs, 1662 Lincs RO Ad/Ac/41/3
Stovin, Robert, Crowle, Lincs, 1613 Lincs RO Ad/Ac/8b/9
Stow, Christopher, Kirton, Lincs, 1612 Lincs RO Ad/Ac/11/201
Stowe, Edward, yeoman, Waddingworth, Lincs, 1680 Lincs RO Ad/Ac/34/64
Stowe, John, farmer, Walden, Kings, Herts, 1640 Herts RO AHH23/2094
Stowe, Robert, Ferriby, South, Lincs, 1601 Lincs RO Ad/Ac/5/175
Stowe, Robert, gentleman, Westborough, Lincs, 1613? Lincs RO Ad/Ac/11/49
Stowe, Thomas, Fenton, Lincs, 1639 Lincs RO Ad/Ac/40/288
Stowe, William, Holbeach, Lincs, 1597 Lincs RO Ad/Ac/4/103
Stowe, see Fletcher,
Stowell, John, Sidlesham, Sussex, 1599 W. Suss RO EpI/33/1599/6
Stowell, Margaret, widow, Itchenor, West, Sussex, 1682 W. Suss RO EpI/33/1682/16
Stowell, Richard, Beaulieu, Hants, 1663 Hants RO 21M65 D8/180
Stower, Roger, Walton, Som, 1639 Somerset RO D/D/Cta/S31
Stower, Thomas, yeoman, Elmley Lovett, Worcs, 1602 Worcs RO 008.7 BA3585/838/269
Stowine, John, Scotton, Lincs, 1598 Lincs RO Ad/Ac/37/49
Stoyles, Henrie, Bloxholme, Lincs, 1637 Lincs RO Ad/Ac/25/362
Stoyt, Nicholas, gentleman, Thurlby, Lincs, 1671 Lincs RO Ad/Ac/33/188
Stpooll, Robert, Haxey (Newbigg), Lincs, 1603 Lincs RO Ad/Ac/37/158
Strachen, Alexander, mariner, Whitechapel, London & Middlesex, 1687 PRO PROB32/26/82
Straine, Nicholas, shipwright, Faversham, Kent, 1685 CKS PRC2/40/242
Strange, Catherine, widow, Buckland (Newton), Berks, 1662 Berks RO D/A1/120/112C
Strange, Thomas, yeoman, Charney Bassett, Berks, 1629 Berks RO D/A1/213/157C
Strange, William, Woodchurch, Kent, 1676 CKS PRC20/12/183
Strangewiche, Thomas, Skirbeck, Lincs, 1612 Lincs RO Ad/Ac/11/94
Strangways, Gylles, knight, Welbury Stamford, Som, 1575 Bristol RO Testamentary Misc. (+ name)
Stransham, John, Canterbury, Kent, 1613 CKS PRC1/1/17
Strapps, Nicholas, Kyme, South, Lincs, 1633 Lincs RO Ad/Ac/24/185
Stratham, William, hessian manufacturer, Leeds, Yorks, 1834 Borthwick Test C.P. 1834/4
Stratton, Edward, husbandman, Watchfield, Berks, 1625 Berks RO D/A1/213/137C
Stratton, Henry, gentleman, Seagry, Wilts, 1627 Wilts RO Arch. Wilts.(+ name and date)
Stratton, Jane, spinster, Watchfield, Berks, 1642 Berks RO D/A1/214/58C
Stratton, John, St Albans St Peters, Herts, 1631 Herts RO ASA25/4869
Stratton, John, Brinkworth, Wilts, 1678 Wilts RO Miscellaneous Index (name + date)
Stratton, Jonah, feltmaker, Letcombe Bassett, Berks, 1682 Berks RO D/A1/214/202C
Stratton, Nathaniel, tailor, Windsor, New, Berks, 1638 Berks RO D/A1/214/34C
Stratton, Richard, Chicheley, Bucks, 1622 Lincs RO Ad/Ac/17/101
Stratton, Robert, Buckland (Carswell Marsh), Berks, 1611 Berks RO D/A1/213/69A
Stratton, Thomas, Watchfield, Berks, 1642 Berks RO D/A1/214/59

Straunge, John, yeoman, Charney Bassett, Berks, 1612 Berks RO D/A1/213/76B
Straw, John, cutler, Gainsborough, Lincs, 1667 Lincs RO Ad/Ac/33/24
Straw, Richard, Mucclestone, Staffs, 1682 LJRO/B/C/5/1681/34
Strawe, Nicholas, cutler, Gainsborough, Lincs, 1640? Lincs RO Ad/Ac/40/277
Strayne, Robert, Throwleigh, Kent, 1643 CKS PRC1/6/87
Strayne, Symon, carpenter, Chilham, Kent, 1644 CKS PRC1/7/33
Streaker, Edward, Sempringham, Lincs, 1612 Lincs RO Ad/Ac/10/146
Streaker, Elizabeth, Donington, Lincs, 1637 Lincs RO Ad/Ac/25/43
Streate, Edward, husbandman, Lambourn, Berks, 1599 Berks RO D/A1/212/194C
Streate, William, Lambourn (Eastbury), Berks, 1595 Berks RO D/A1/207/120E
Streater, Edmund, Brenzett, Kent, 1669 CKS PRC1/14/107a
Streater, Edmund, Brenzett, Kent, 1669 CKS PRC1/14/107b
Streater, Edmund, yeoman, Brenzett, Kent, 1669 CKS PRC1/14/107
Streater, Edward, Pulborough, Sussex, 1670 W. Suss RO EpI/33/1670/23
Streater, Emery, Ashington, Sussex, 1631 W. Suss RO EpI/33/1631/3
Streater, John, Tarring, West, Sussex, 1621 W. Suss RO EpIV/10/1/33
Streater, John, Angmering, Sussex, 1651 W. Suss RO EpI/33/1651/4
Streater, John, youngman, Old Romney, Kent, 1692 CKS PRC2/42/51
Streater, Richard eld, Itchingfield, Sussex, 1596 W. Suss RO EpI/33/1596/13
Streater, Thomas, Pulborough, Sussex, 1667 W. Suss RO EpI/33/1666/2
Streater, William, Angmering, Sussex, 1624 W. Suss RO EpI/33/1624/13
Streating, Thomas, Saltwood, Kent, 1606 CKS PRC20/1/114
Streatley, Joan, Chieveley, Berks, 1598 Berks RO D/A1/212/186A
Stredweeke, Mary, widow, Canterbury St Mildred, Kent, 1620 CKS PRC2/26/107
Stredwicke, Elizabeth, minor: 'child', Ivychurch, Kent, 1638 CKS PRC20/11/362
Stredwicke, Henry, Fordwich, Kent, 1634 CKS PRC2/32/
Stredwicke, James, Canterbury St Paul, Kent, 1634 CKS PRC2/32/114
Stredwicke, James, maltster, Canterbury St Mildred, Kent, 1681 CKS PRC2/39/231
Stredwicke, Mary, Canterbury St Paul, Kent, 1675 CKS PRC2/36/243
Stredwicke, Thamisin, minor: 'child', Ivychurch, Kent, 1638 CKS PRC20/11/358
Streeke, Andrew, joiner, Binfield, Berks, 1626 Berks RO D/A1/213/136C
Street, George, Atworth, Wilts, 1676 Wilts RO Arch. Sarum(+ name and date)
Street, Nicholas, Martin, Wilts, 1614 Wilts RO Arch. Sarum(+ name and date)
Street, Thomas, farmer, Wirksworth, Derby, 1795 LJRO/B/C/5/1795/93
Streete, Alice, widow, Devizes, Wilts, 1626 Wilts RO CC Sarum(+ name and date)
Streete, David, Ramsgate, Kent, 1671 CKS PRC2/35/88
Streete, John, Devizes, Wilts, 1626 Wilts RO CC Sarum(+ name and date)
Streete, John, yeoman, Amesbury, Wilts, 1640 Wilts RO Arch. Sarum(+ name and date)
Streete, Symon, Milton next Sittingbourne, Kent, 1606 CKS PRC2/14/407
Streete, Thomas, boatman, Hinksey, North, Berks, 1630 Berks RO D/A1/213/155C
Streeting, William, innholder, Dover St Mary, Kent, 1640 CKS PRC19/1/84
Streetyng, Abraham, Murston, Kent, 1608 CKS PRC2/15/375
Strelley, Phillip, Wingfield, South (Oakerthorpe), Derby, 1704 LJRO/B/C/5/1704/55
Stretch, Mary, spinster, Church Hulme, Ches, Cheshire RO (Name) W.C. 1698-9
Strete, Symon, Hythe St Leonard, Kent, 1595 CKS PRC21/14/221
Strettell, Robert, yeoman, Rostherne (Marthall), Ches, 1648 Cheshire RO (Name) W.C. 1648
Streynsham, Elizabeth, Faversham, Kent, 1599 CKS PRC2/11/288
Strickland, Henry, fuller: 'walker', Worcester St Peter the Great, Worcs, 1602 Worcs RO 008.7 BA3585/838/270
Strickland, James, Toynton, High, Lincs, 1648 Lincs RO Ad/Ac/30/283
Stride, William, Barford, Wilts, 1676 Wilts RO Arch. Sarum(+ name and date)
Stridwicke, Christopher, Canterbury St Paul, Kent, 1625 CKS PRC2/25/127
Stringer, Anthony, gentleman, Borden, Kent, 1690 CKS PRC2/41/185
Stringer, Gabriel, Stowell, Som, 1723 Somerset RO D/D/Cta/S69
Stringer, Henry, gentleman, Borden, Kent, 1679 CKS PRC2/38/72

[Stringer:]
Stringer, Jane, Borden, Kent, 1679 CKS PRC2/38/
Stringer, John, Lydd, Kent, 1583 CKS PRC21/6/317
Stringer, Robert, Westminster, London & Middlesex, 1640 Lincs RO Ad/Ac/27/183
Stringer, Robert, Baston, Lincs, 1641 Lincs RO Ad/Ac/27/330
Stringer, Stephen, Little Mongeham, Kent, 1700 CKS PRC19/5/66
Strittinge, John, Selling, Kent, 1599 CKS PRC2/11/296
Strode, Richard, maltster, New Romney, Kent, 1680 CKS PRC20/13/64
Strong, Abraham, Chartham, Kent, 1611 CKS PRC2/17/400
Strong, Agnes + Thomas, Minster in Thanet, Kent, 1590 CKS PRC2/5/418
Strong, Eflett, widow, Fovant, Wilts, 1685 Wilts RO Arch. Sarum(+ name and date)
Strong, George eld, St Decumans (Watchet), Som, 1634 Somerset RO D/D/Cta/S9
Strong, Nicholas, Knoyle, West, Wilts, 1640 Wilts RO Arch. Sarum(+ name and date)
Strong, William, Northwood, Hants, 1624 Hants RO 21M65 D8/89
Stronge, Amye, Minster in Thanet, Kent, 1601 CKS PRC2/12/332
Stronge, Charles, Chartham, Kent, 1670 CKS PRC1/15/65
Stronge, George, Goodworth Clatford, Hants, Hants RO 21m65 D8/363/1
Stronge, Jespar, Fovant, Wilts, 1632 Wilts RO Arch. Sarum(+ name and date)
Stronge, Richard, Poling, Sussex, 1629 W. Suss RO EpI/33/1629/9
Stronghill, Clement, gentleman, New Romney, Kent, 1639 CKS PRC20/11/376
Stronghill, John, gentleman, Lydd, Kent, 1607 CKS PRC20/1/154
Stronghill, John, gentleman, Lydd, Kent, 1666 CKS PRC19/3/106
Strongle, Clement, Hackington, Kent, 1600 CKS PRC2/11/285
Strongle, Giles, Snargate, Kent, 1602 CKS PRC2/12/334
Strood, Henry, Mersham, Kent, 1663 CKS PRC1/9/154
Stroode, Richard, Sandwich, Kent, 1671 CKS PRC2/35/91
Strother, Martin, Barrow on Humber, Lincs, 1606 Lincs RO Ad/Ac/7/50
Stroud, Charles, Butleigh, Som, 1737 Somerset RO D/D/Cta/S70
Stroud, Martin, Fawley, Berks, 1676 Wilts RO CC Sarum(+ name and date)
Stroude, Richerd, New Romney, Kent, 1585 CKS PRC21/7/246
Stroude, Thomas, Snargate, Kent, 1602 CKS PRC2/12/328
Strout, John, gentleman, Canterbury St Margaret, Kent, 1668 CKS PRC1/13/125
Strowd, Edward, maltster, Reading St Lawrence, Berks, 1663 Berks RO D/A1/214/97C
Strowd, John, Kenardington, Kent, 1631 CKS PRC2/30/130
Strowd, John, Elham, Kent, 1642 CKS PRC1/6/26
Strowd, Richard, Smeeth, Kent, 1626 CKS PRC20/7/140
Strowd, Robert, Herne, Kent, 1625 CKS PRC20/6/169
Strowde, Elizabeth, Chilham, Kent, 1634 CKS PRC2/32/115
Strowde, Henrie, Faversham, Kent, 1605 CKS PRC2/15/373
Strowde, James, Waltham, Kent, 1584 CKS PRC2/3/207
Strowde, James, Hastingleigh, Kent, 1600 CKS PRC2/11/277
Strowde, Jeremye, Sandhurst, Kent, 1602 CKS PRC2/12/458
Strowde, John, Bircholt, Kent, 1631 CKS PRC2/31/63
Strowde, Jone, widow, Elham, Kent, 1586 CKS PRC2/4/212
Strowde, Martin, husbandman, Fawley, Berks, 1629 Berks RO D/A1/213/156C
Strowde, Stephen, Hythe St Leonard, Kent, 1616 CKS PRC20/3/358
Strowde/Salisburye, Joane, wife, Hythe St Leonard, Kent, 1617 CKS PRC20/4/365
Strowtinge, Humfrey, Grantham, Lincs, 1627 Lincs RO Ad/Ac/20b/49
Strudder, John + Ursula, Redbourn, Herts, 1626 Herts RO ASA25/2867
Strudweeke, Edward, Kirdford, Sussex, W. Suss RO EpI/33/1612/10
Strugle, Thomas, Hythe St Leonard, Kent, 1607 CKS PRC20/1/211
Strut, Thomas, Gainsborough, Lincs, 1628 Lincs RO Ad/Ac/39/84
Stryde, John, Donhead St Andrew, Wilts, 1647 Wilts RO Arch. Sarum(+ name and date)
Stuart, see Steere,
Stubber, John, Portsmouth, Hants, 1624 Hants RO 21M65 D8/90
Stubbersfeild, Richard, Goudhurst, Kent, 1620 CKS PRC2/19/24

Stubbes, Henrie, Leire, Leics, 1641 Leics RO PR/I/41A/66
Stubbes, John, clothier, Clewer, Berks, 1604 Berks RO D/A1/213/29A
Stubbes, Richard, clergy: 'clerk', Hannington, Wilts, 1628 Wilts RO Arch. Wilts.(+ name and date)
Stubbes, William, Mareham on the Hill, Lincs, 1626 Lincs RO Ad/Ac/20/18
Stubbin, Robert, butcher, Louth, Lincs, 1662 Lincs RO Ad/Ac/42/51
Stubbing, Edmund, university: 'Fellow of Trinity College, Cambridge/D.D.', Cambridge (Trinity College), Cambs, 1637 CUL V.C. Acc./Box2/74
Stubbing, Thomas, clergy: 'clerk', Marston on Dove, Derby, 1663 LJRO:cards/1663/57
Stubbs, Anne, Wainfleet St Mary, Lincs, 1635 Lincs RO Ad/Ac/24/363
Stubbs, Francis, Stainton, Lincs, 1662 Lincs RO Ad/Ac/32/21
Stubbs, John, Bicker, Lincs, 1611 Lincs RO Ad/Ac/10/86
Stubbs, John, Steeping, Little, Lincs, 1618 Lincs RO Ad/Ac/14/198
Stubbs, Josiah, Kingsley, Staffs, 1684 LJRO/B/C/5/1684/76
Stubbs, Thomas, Keele, Staffs, 1680 LJRO:cards/1680/34
Stubbs, Thomas, husbandman, Bentley, Fenny, Derby, 1724 LJRO/B/C/5/1724/29
Stubbs, William, Sibsey, Lincs, 1662 Lincs RO Ad/Ac/32/29
Stubbs, William, yeoman, Mayfield, Staffs, 1711 LJRO/B/C/5/1711/46
Stubbs, William, Mayfield, Staffs, 1712 LJRO/B/C/5/1712/96
Studman, John, Aldermaston, Berks, 1640 Berks RO D/A1/214/45C
Studman, Thomas, Downton, Wilts, 1631 Wilts RO Arch. Sarum(+ name and date)
Studsburye, John, Chart, Great, Kent, 1615 CKS PRC2/19/22
Stumble, Olyver, Ash next Sandwich, Kent, 1608 CKS PRC20/1/332
Stunt, John, husbandman, Cranbrook, Kent, 1680 CKS PRC2/39/104
Stunt, William, Appledore, Kent, 1608 CKS PRC2/14/405
Stupney, Clement, jurat/mr, Lydd, Kent, 1629 CKS PRC20/8/427
Stuppell, John, weaver, Tilmanstone, Kent, 1678 CKS PRC2/38/68
Stuppell, Michael, Eastry, Kent, 1624 CKS PRC20/6/167
Stuppell, Peeter, Woodnesborough, Kent, 1617 CKS PRC2/19/60
Stuppell, Richard, Ash next Sandwich, Kent, 1576 CKS PRC21/2/372
Stuppell, Robert, Deal, Kent, 1666 CKS PRC19/3/107
Stupple, John, Dover, Kent, 1584 CKS PRC21/7/402
Stupple, John, Ash next Sandwich, Kent, 1604 CKS PRC21/17/269
Sturdy, Amy, spinster, Kirkby Moorside, Yorks, 1838 Borthwick Test C.P. 1838/7
Sturdy, William, bachelor, Wigglesford, Warks, 1778 Worcs RO 008.7 BA3585/835/bdl 2
Sturgeon, Jude, Sittingbourne, Kent, 1625 CKS PRC2/24/98
Sturges, Anne, spinster, Wittersham, Kent, 1614 CKS PRC20/3/55
Sturges, Jeames, Maidstone, Kent, 1599 CKS PRC21/16/7
Sturges, Philip, Walgrave, Northants, 1672 Northants RO NWill A/C/130
Sturges, Richard, Collingbourne Kingston, Wilts, 1641 Wilts RO CC Sarum(+ name and date)
Sturges, Richard, yeoman, Herne, Kent, 1673 CKS PRC20/12/59
Sturges, Robert, Coldred, Kent, 1635 CKS PRC2/33/123
Sturges, Thomas, Coldred, Kent, 1627 CKS PRC2/28/111
Sturges, Thomas, husbandman, Cricklade, Wilts, 1639 Wilts RO CC Sarum(+ name and date)
Sturgion, Robert, butcher, Queenborough, Kent, 1670 CKS PRC1/15/66
Sturgis, Thomas, esquire, Temple, Middle, London & Middlesex, 1676 PRO PROB32/13/151
Sturment, Richard, St Pauls Walden, Herts, 1601 Herts RO ASA25/1806
Sturment, Richard eld, St Pauls Walden, Herts, Herts RO ASA25/4784
Sturmy, Bawldwin, Biddenden, Kent, 1587 CKS PRC2/4/325
Sturmy, John, glover, Gloucester St Michael, Glos, GRO GDR/B4/2/S25
Sturredge, William, Bath, Som, 1622 Somerset RO D/D/Cta/S25
Sturt, Anthony, Wittering, West, Sussex, 1618 W. Suss RO EpI/33/1617/17
Sturt, Richard, Storrington, Sussex, 1612 W. Suss RO EpI/33/1612/8
Sturt, Richard, Petworth, Sussex, 1620 W. Suss RO EpI/33/1619/6
Sturt, Thomas, Tillington (Parkhurst), Sussex, 1661 W. Suss RO EpI/33/1661/12

[Sturte:]
Sturte, William, Tillington, Sussex, 1618 W. Suss RO EpI/33/1618/9
Sturte, William, Angmering, Sussex, 1640 W. Suss RO EpI/33/1640/3
Sturton, George, Wyberton, Lincs, 1638 Lincs RO Ad/Ac/25/39
Sturton, John, gentleman, Ashford, Kent, 1680 CKS PRC2/38/181
Stutsburie, Frances, spinster, Fringford, Oxon, 1662 Oxon RO MSS Wills 86/2/5
Stutsbury, Richard, Winslow, Bucks, 1625 Herts RO ASA25/2868
Stuttesbery, Richard, St Albans, Herts, 1693 Herts RO ASA25/4400
Stuttinge, William, Scotter, Lincs, 1627 Lincs RO Ad/Ac/39/7
Styan, James, butcher, Newton on Ouse, Yorks, 1804 Borthwick Test C.P. 1804/6
Styant, Thomas, Merston, Sussex, 1676 W. Suss RO EpI/33/1676/31
Styant, Thomas, bachelor, Slindon, Sussex, 1680 W. Suss RO EpIV/10/2A/19
Style, Margery, widow, Overbury, Worcs, 1682 Worcs RO 008.7 BA3585/837/bdl 3
Style, Robert, Watford, Herts, 1596 Herts RO ASA25/1577
Style, Roberte, Newchurch, Kent, 1582 CKS PRC21/6/150
Style, Roger,
Som 1623 Somerset RO D/D/Cta/S14
Styleman, George, husbandman, Midgham, Berks, 1676 Berks RO D/A1/214/168C
Styles, Margarett, Sandwich, Kent, 1640 CKS PRC1/5/44
Styles, Randall, Swineshead, Lincs, 1614 Lincs RO Ad/Ac/12/202
Styles, William, Sandwich, Kent, 1617 CKS PRC2/19/48
Styll, John, Wimborne Minster, Dors, 1601 Dorset RO PE/WM CP 2/4/4
Stynings, Jeremy, Thornham, Kent, 1627 CKS PRC2/28/114
Stynninge, Robert, Smarden, Kent, 1582 CKS PRC2/2/133
Styrtonne, Thomysyn, Heckington, Lincs, 1578 Lincs RO Ad/Ac/2b/48
Succormans, Anne, Gedney, Lincs, 1611 Lincs RO Ad/Ac/10/84
Suckett, John eld, Chichester, Sussex, 1619 W. Suss RO EpIII/9/1/22
Suckling, Peter, miller, Smeeth, Kent, 1678 CKS PRC20/12/281
Suckling, Thomas, Pluckley, Kent, 1595 CKS PRC2/7/403
Sueter, Sands, Gainsborough, Lincs, 1661 Lincs RO Ad/Ac/41/109
Sugar, Henry, Charlton Adam, Som, 1611 Somerset RO D/D/Cta/S64
Sugden, John, wool stapler, Keighley (Lower Laith), Yorks, 1781 Borthwick Test C.P. 1781/6
Sugg, William, thatcher, Yeovil, Som, 1629 Somerset RO D/D/Cta/S27
Suggett, William, Sittingbourne, Kent, 1625 CKS PRC2/25/124
Sulham, Bridget, widow, Stratfield Mortimer, Berks, 1635 Berks RO D/A1/213/168E
Sumers, John, Itchenor, West, Sussex, 1682 W. Suss RO EpI/33/1682/41
Summer, Stephen, Staplehurst, Kent, 1610 CKS PRC2/15/361
Summerhill, Thomas, Siston, Glos, 1685 GRO GDR/B4/2/S137
Summers, Henry, tailor, Faversham, Kent, 1662 CKS PRC1/9/61
Sumner, Hannah, widow, St Giles in the Fields, London & Middlesex, 1754 Greater London RO DL/C/553/85/
Sumner, James, Tarring, West, Sussex, 1631 W. Suss RO EpIV/10/2/4
Sumner, Jane, widow, Budworth, Great (Aston), Ches, 1780 Cheshire RO (Name) W.C. 1780
Sumner, Peter, yeoman, Northenden, Ches, 1735 Cheshire RO (Name) W.C. 1735
Sumpter, see Marshall,
Surgood, Thomas, Hartlip, Kent, 1670 CKS PRC1/15/67
Surman, Edward, Stoulton, Worcs, 1680 Worcs RO 008.7 BA3585/837/bdl 2
Surman, William, brushmaker, Bristol, Glos, Bristol RO 1756/17
Surmon, William, Leigh, Worcs, 1681 Worcs RO 008.7 BA3585/830/51
Surr, John, yeoman, Acaster Malbis, Yorks, 1816 Borthwick Test C.P. 1817/5
Sutcliffe, William, innkeeper, Halifax (Barkisland), Yorks, 1794 Borthwick Test C.P. 1794/11
Suthons, Thomas, farmer, Dawley, Shrops, 1828 LJRO/B/C/5/1828/27
Sutliffe, Hammon, Teynham, Kent, 1641 CKS PRC1/5/45
Sutor, Walter, Kirdford, Sussex, 1617 W. Suss RO EpI/33/1617/19
Sutor, William, Lavington, Market, Wilts, 1677 Wilts RO Arch. Sarum(+ name and date)
Sutton, Benjamin eld, buttonmaker, Birmingham, Warks, 1798 LJRO/B/C/5/1798/41

Sutton, Christopher, labourer, Sutton, Long, Lincs, 1623 Lincs RO Ad/Ac/18/11
Sutton, Christopher, Hougham, Kent, 1631 CKS PRC2/31/62
Sutton, Edward, Halton Holgate, Lincs, 1640 Lincs RO Ad/Ac/27/84
Sutton, Elizabeth, Sandwich, Kent, 1642 CKS PRC1/6/88
Sutton, George, gentleman, Snarford, Lincs, 1671 Lincs RO Ad/Ac/33/203
Sutton, Humphrey, gentleman, Iffley, Oxon, 1650 Oxon RO MSS Wills 61/1/18
Sutton, Jane, spinster, Lydden, Kent, 1676 CKS PRC2/37/93
Sutton, Jane, widow, Sholden, Kent, 1683 CKS PRC2/40/155
Sutton, John, Ilsley, East, Berks, Berks RO D/A1/212/193A
Sutton, John, Hawkinge, Kent, 1604 CKS PRC2/13/369
Sutton, John, Toynton All Saints, Lincs, 1611 Lincs RO Ad/Ac/10/43
Sutton, John, yeoman, Lydden, Kent, 1676 CKS PRC2/37/96
Sutton, John, Bowden, Little, Northants, 1684 Northants RO NWill A/C/89
Sutton, Miles, clergy: 'clerk/vicar', Abingdon St Helen, Berks, 1682 Berks RO D/A1/215/4C
Sutton, Peter, Leysdown, Kent, 1572 CKS PRC2/1/67
Sutton, Richard, innkeeper, Ancaster, Lincs, 1669 Lincs RO Ad/Ac/33/110
Sutton, Robert, Shrewton, Wilts, 1611 Wilts RO Arch. Sarum(+ name and date)
Sutton, Stephen, Hythe West, Kent, 1612 CKS PRC2/16/167
Sutton, Symon, husbandman, Kelsey, South, Lincs, 1665 Lincs RO Ad/Ac/32/58
Sutton, Thomas, Fleet, Lincs, 1620 Lincs RO Ad/Ac/16/84
Sutton, Thomas, husbandman, Camel, Queen, Som, 1623 Somerset RO D/D/Cta/S24
Sutton, Thomas, Ashford, Kent, 1626 CKS PRC2/27/158
Sutton, Thomas, husbandman, Well, Lincs, 1671 Lincs RO Ad/Ac/33/211
Sutton, Valentine, innkeeper, Abingdon, Berks, 1594 Berks RO D/A1/212/168A
Sutton, William, Spalding, Lincs, 1641 Lincs RO Ad/Ac/27/341
Sutton, William, Sholden, Kent, 1673 CKS PRC2/35/176
Sutton, William, Althorpe (Amcotts), Lincs, 1684 Lincs RO Ad/Ac/44/135
Sutton, William, draper, Retford, East, Notts, 1818 Borthwick Test C.P. 1818/6
Suttone, Richard, Ropsley, Lincs, 1594 Lincs RO Ad/Ac/3/131
Sw..., Jane, Rasen, Market, Lincs, 1649 Lincs RO Ad/Ac/30/218
Swafer, John, Kenardington, Kent, 1680 CKS PRC2/39/108
Swaffer, Daniel, Mersham, Kent, 1664 CKS PRC1/10/93
Swaffer, Daniell, Sevington, Kent, 1616 CKS PRC2/19/56
Swaffer, Thomas, husbandman, Woodchurch, Kent, 1681 CKS PRC20/13/206
Swafford, John, Ashford, Kent, 1640 CKS PRC1/5/46
Swafford, Thomas, yeoman, Ash next Sandwich, Kent, 1638 CKS PRC20/11/298
Swaile, John, Westhouse, Yorks, 1606 Prob. Ex. 1606/1
Swaine, Daniel, Ulcombe, Kent, 1667 CKS PRC1/12/86
Swaine, Edmond, husbandman, Hythe West, Kent, 1673 CKS PRC2/35/254
Swaine, Jacob, Deal, Kent, 1674 CKS PRC20/12/104
Swaine, John, husbandman, Pinchbeck, Lincs, 1627? Lincs RO Ad/Ac/20b/86
Swaine, Laurance, Sandwich St Clement, Kent, 1597 CKS PRC2/10/347
Swaine, Margarett, Stowting, Kent, 1604 CKS PRC2/13/355
Swaine, Nicholas, Seasalter, Kent, 1702 CKS PRC1/16/57
Swaine, Robert, Ivychurch, Kent, 1616 CKS PRC20/3/356
Swaine, Thomas, Westwell, Kent, 1602 CKS PRC21/16/97
Swaine, Vincent, Deal, Kent, 1607 CKS PRC20/1/259
Swaine, William, Winscombe, Som, 1600 Somerset RO D/D/Cta/S54
Swaineland, John, yeoman, Sutton Valence, Kent, 1622 CKS PRC2/24/85
Swainson, John, Leeds, Yorks, 1639 Borthwick Prob. Ex. 1639/4
Swaith, Nicholas, Rotherham (Catliffe), Yorks, 1638 Borthwick Prob. Ex. 1638/8
Swale, Thomas, Eagle, Lincs, 1618 Lincs RO Ad/Ac/14/266
Swales, Thomas, Scotton, Lincs, 1608 Lincs RO Ad/Ac/37/265
Swales, William, tin plate worker, Knaresborough, Yorks, 1820 Borthwick Test C.P. 1820/4
Swallow, John, yeoman, Binbrook St Mary, Lincs, 1672 Lincs RO Ad/Ac/34/5

[Swan:]
Swan, Christopher, Minster in Thanet, Kent, 1598 CKS PRC2/10/375
Swan, Edward, Ashford, Kent, 1615 CKS PRC2/19/4
Swan, Edward, Rolvenden, Kent, 1638 CKS PRC2/34/283
Swan, John,
Hants 1684 Hants RO 21m65 D8/344
Swan, William, Wye, Kent, 1599 CKS PRC2/10/470
Swann, David, bacon factor, Wetherby, Yorks, 1813 Borthwick Test C.P. 1813/10
Swann, Thomas, Frampton, Lincs, 1627 Lincs RO Ad/Ac/20b/79
Swann, William, husbandman, Lenham, Kent, 1690 CKS PRC2/41/184
Swanne, Thomas, Digby, Lincs, 1605 Lincs RO Ad/Ac/6/75
Swanson, Brian, Worcester St Andrew, Worcs, 1681 Worcs RO 008.7 BA3585/837/bdl 2
Swanson, Richard, Spridlington, Lincs, 1621 Lincs RO Ad/Ac/8c/43
Swanton, Agnes, Alkham, Kent, 1583 CKS PRC2/3/92
Swanton, John, Alkham, Kent, 1585 CKS PRC2/3/295
Swanton, John, yeoman, Ickham, Kent, 1668 CKS PRC19/4/32
Swanton, Richard, St Johns Thanet, Kent, 1613 CKS PRC2/16/128
Swanton, Thomas, Newington next Hythe, Kent, 1610 CKS PRC2/15/369
Swanton, Thomas, mariner: 'sailor', Whitstable, Kent, 1626 CKS PRC2/27/153
Swanton, William, Whitstable, Kent, 1597 CKS PRC2/9/189
Swanton, William, Whitstable, Kent, 1600 CKS PRC2/11/290
Swanton?, Roberte, Canterbury St Margaret, Kent, 1597 CKS PRC2/9/219
Swart, Richard, Canterbury St Paul, Kent, 1593 CKS PRC2/6/458
Swarte, Jane, widow, Canterbury St Paul, Kent, 1607 CKS PRC2/15/371
Swashe, Leonard, Baumber, Lincs, 1600 Lincs RO Ad/Ac/5/155
Swate, John, Huttoft, Lincs, 1607 Lincs RO Ad/Ac/8a/41
Swayland, Richard, Smarden, Kent, 1593 CKS PRC2/6/160
Swayne, Edward, Cocking, Sussex, 1583 W. Suss RO EpI/33/1583/4
Swayne, Elizabeth, widow, Marcham, Berks, 1636 Berks RO D/A1/214/16C
Swayne, John, Deal, Kent, 1598 CKS PRC21/14/583
Swayne, John, Staple next Wingham, Kent, 1614 CKS PRC20/2/514
Swayne, Richard, New Romney, Kent, 1638 CKS PRC20/11/388
Swayne, Richard, tanner, Reading St Giles, Berks, 1639 Berks RO D/A1/214/40
Swayne, William, Brent, East, Som, 1666 Somerset RO D/D/Cta/S51
Swaysland, Richard, yeoman, Appledore, Kent, 1668 CKS PRC1/13/126
Swayton, Margaret, Faversham, Kent, 1612 CKS PRC2/17/365
Sweet, Anselme, Mumby, Lincs, 1627 Lincs RO Ad/Ac/20b/52
Sweete, Henry, Wimborne Minster, Dors, 1626 Dorset RO PE/WM CP 2/4/40
Sweete, Robert, Huttoft, Lincs, 1611 Lincs RO Ad/Ac/10/57
Sweete, Robert, Carlton, Little, Lincs, 1623 Lincs RO Ad/Ac/18/30
Sweeteaple, Richard, Andover, Hants, 1623 Hants RO 21M65 D8/40
Sweeting, Andrewe, Sandwich, Kent, 1615 CKS PRC2/19/62
Sweeting, Leonard, gentleman, Canterbury St Margaret, Kent, 1613 CKS PRC20/2/518
Sweetinge, George, gentleman, Bridge, Kent, 1629 CKS PRC2/30/120
Sweetinge, William,
Kent 1631 CKS PRC20/9/376
Swetman, Margaret, Deal, Kent, 1575 CKS PRC21/2/253
Swetnam, Roger, Deal, Kent, 1577 CKS PRC21/3/69
Swetynge, James, Sandwich St Clement, Kent, 1582 CKS PRC2/3/11
Swift, Anne, Herne, Kent, 1631 CKS PRC20/9/416
Swift, Christopher, cordwainer, Abingdon, Berks, 1643 Berks RO D/A1/214/65C
Swift, Dennis, widow, Leysdown, Kent, 1688 CKS PRC2/41/107
Swift, Godfrey, Morton, Derby, 1684 LJRO/B/C/5/1683/22
Swift, John, Newington next Sittingbourne, Kent, 1582 CKS PRC2/2/71
Swift, John, Abingdon, Berks, 1600 Berks RO D/A1/213/10C
Swift, Nicholas, Chilham, Kent, 1677 CKS PRC2/37/200

Swift, Richard, Graveney, Kent, 1601 CKS PRC2/12/351
Swift, Solomon, Leysdown, Kent, 1683 CKS PRC2/40/150
Swift/Glover, Thomasyne, Canterbury St Mildred, Kent, 1628 CKS PRC2/29/83
Swifte, Dorothie, Owston, Lincs, 1595 Lincs RO Ad/Ac/5/283
Swifte, Edward, Sompting, Sussex, 1597 W. Suss RO EpI/33/1596/15
Swifte, George, Blyton, Lincs, 1649 Lincs RO Ad/Ac/40/161
Swifte, John, Smarden, Kent, 1625 CKS PRC20/7/275
Swifte, John, Teynham, Kent, 1625 CKS PRC2/25/129
Swifte, John, Hothfield, Kent, 1632 CKS PRC2/31/151
Swifte, Richard, Patching, Sussex, 1647 W. Suss RO EpIV/10/2A/6
Swifte, Robert, Crowle, Lincs, 1626 Lincs RO Ad/Ac/39/38
Swinburn, George, yeoman, Stokesley, Yorks, 1823 Borthwick Test C.P. 1822/9
Swinburne, Mathew, Hull, Yorks, 1636 Borthwick R.VII.PU.19
Swindall, John, Whaplode Drove, Lincs, 1674 Lincs RO Ad/Ac/34/10
Swindell, Thomas, farmer, Youlgreave, Derby, 1826 LJRO/B/C/5/1826/50
Swinerton, Mary eld, Taunton St Mary Magdalan, Som, 1692 Somerset RO D/D/Cta/S57
Swinford, Alice, widow, Canterbury St George Martyr, Kent, 1612 CKS PRC2/17/219
Swinford, Dorothy, widow, St Johns Thanet, Kent, 1662 CKS PRC1/8/115
Swinford, George, Stodmarsh, Kent, 1583 CKS PRC2/2/259
Swinford, John, Sandwich, Kent, 1605 CKS PRC2/13/390
Swinford, John, Goodnestone next Faversham, Kent, 1643 CKS PRC1/6/89
Swinford, Mary, widow, Canterbury St Mary Bredin, Kent, 1641 CKS PRC1/5/47
Swinford, Nicholas, Sandwich, Kent, 1601 CKS PRC2/12/324
Swinford, Nicholas, Deal, Kent, 1674 CKS PRC20/12/147
Swinford, Peeter, St Nicholas at Wade, Kent, 1614 CKS PRC20/2/510
Swinford, Peeter, St Johns Thanet, Kent, 1638 CKS PRC2/34/288
Swinford, Thomas, Stodmarsh, Kent, 1639 CKS PRC1/3/48
Swinscoe, John, clergy: 'clerk', Swinhope, Lincs, 1601 Lincs RO Ad/Ac/5/209
Swinscote, Nicholas, Binbrook St Mary, Lincs, 1622 Lincs RO Ad/Ac/17/80
Swyderenden, Richarde, Sevington, Kent, 1582 CKS PRC2/2/152
Swyfte, Francis, Blyton, Lincs, 1607 Lincs RO Ad/Ac/37/254
Swyndell, Olyver, Dover, Kent, 1607 CKS PRC20/1/270
Swynfen, Edward, Sutton Cheney, Leics, 1685 Leics RO Administrators Accounts 1682-86 f37
Swynfen, Edward, Walsall, Staffs, 1727 LJRO/B/C/5/1727/145
Swynforde, John, Wickhambreaux, Kent, 1603 CKS PRC2/13/334
Swynnarton, Edward, Ulcombe, Kent, 1615 CKS PRC2/19/25
Swynnerton, Roberte, Marden, Kent, 1583 CKS PRC2/3/129
Sydar, John, Maidstone, Kent, 1592 CKS PRC21/12/210
Sydes, Anthony, Huncote, Leics, 1641 Leics RO PR/I/41A/86
Sye, see Roberts,
Sylam, Isabell, Benington, Lincs, 1612 Lincs RO Ad/Ac/11/81
Syllett, Lawrence, butcher, Friskney, Lincs, 1649 Lincs RO Ad/Ac/30/75
Sylver, Elizabeth, Hollingbourne, Kent, 1620 CKS PRC20/5/188
Sylvester, John, tailor, Newbury, Berks, 1686 Berks RO D/A1/215/40C
Symball, Isaac, St Anne Westminster, London & Middlesex, 1695 PRO PROB32/39/218
Symball, Isaack, St Anne Westminster, London & Middlesex, 1701 PRO PROB32/42/171
Syme, Allan, Benenden, Kent, 1596 CKS PRC2/9/311
Symes, Hannah, widow, Bristol, Glos, Bristol RO 1753/28
Symes, John, Uffington, Lincs, 1641 Lincs RO Ad/Ac/27/214
Symes, Margaret, widow, Beenham, Berks, 1600 Berks RO D/A1/212/188A
Symes, Richard, Bishopstoke, Hants, 1623 Hants RO 21M65 D8/37
Symes, Richard, Salisbury, Wilts, 1627 Wilts RO Miscellaneous Index (name + date)
Symes, Thomas, Petherton, South, Som, 1605 Somerset RO D/D/Cta/S59
Symes, William, clergy: 'clerk', Leicester St Martin, Leics, 1671 Leics RO Administrators Accounts 1667-72 f39

[Symkin:]
Symkin, Thomas, Nuneaton, Warks, 1683 LJRO/B/C/5/1682/60
Symmes, William, Moreton, North, Berks, 1593 Berks RO D/A1/212/142A
Symmes/Hayward, Avice, widow, Beechingstoke, Wilts, 1631 Wilts RO Arch. Wilts.(name + date)
Symnell, William, Bicker, Lincs, 1613 Lincs RO Ad/Ac/12/102
Symon, John, Ludgvan, Corn, 1633 Cornwall RO AP/S704
Symon, William, Worcester, Worcs, Worcs RO 008.7 BA3585/838/53
Symonds, Dorothye, Ruckinge, Kent, 1614 CKS PRC2/17/36
Symonds, John, Norwich St Clement, Norf, 1727 Norfolk RO ANW/23/17A(iii)/56
Symonds, Josias, clergy: 'clerk', Langton, Lincs, 1620 Lincs RO Ad/Ac/16/88
Symonds, Richard, Cricklade, Wilts, 1635 Wilts RO CC Sarum(+ name and date)
Symonds, Thomas, Willoughby, Lincs, 1602 Lincs RO Ad/Ac/5/159
Symonds, William, locksmith, Cambridge, Cambs, CUL V.C.Acc./Box1/48
Symons, Alexander, Tenterden, Kent, 1596 CKS PRC2/9/309
Symons, Catherine, Sandwich St Peter, Kent, 1674 CKS PRC2/36/123
Symons, John, Wittersham, Kent, 1571 CKS PRC21/1/98
Symons, John, Kingston, Kent, 1596 CKS PRC2/8/119
Symons, John, Smarden, Kent, 1596 CKS PRC2/8/37
Symons, John, Worcester, Worcs, 1603 Worcs RO 008.7 BA3585/838/273
Symons, John, Tintagel, Corn, 1606 Cornwall RO AP/S109
Symons, John, clergy: 'clerk', Teynham, Kent, 1613 CKS PRC2/18/88
Symons, John, Bethersden, Kent, 1617 CKS PRC2/19/9
Symons, John, Pangbourne, Berks, 1667 Berks RO D/A1/214/127C
Symons, John, Swingfield, Kent, 1680 CKS PRC2/38/187
Symons, John, Sandwich, Kent, 1685 CKS PRC2/41/15
Symons, Margaret, Eldersfield, Worcs, 1602 Worcs RO 008.7 BA3585/838/212
Symons, Mary, widow, Sandwich, Kent, 1675 CKS PRC2/36/118
Symons, Mary, widow, St Johns Thanet, Kent, 1676 CKS PRC2/37/91
Symons, Michael, innholder, Lenham, Kent, 1680 CKS PRC2/38/191
Symons, Moses eld, tile man, Wye, Kent, 1667 CKS PRC1/12/87
Symons, Nicholas, Woodchurch, Kent, 1605 CKS PRC21/17/282
Symons, Nicholas, Maidstone, Kent, 1618 CKS PRC20/4/352
Symons, Peter, clergy: 'mr/vicar', Sandwich St Clement, Kent, 1617 CKS PRC2/19/50
Symons, Richard, Rainham, Kent, 1615 CKS PRC2/19/36
Symons, Richard, Lydd, Kent, 1627 CKS PRC20/7/144
Symons, Richard, Ickham, Kent, 1643 CKS PRC19/2/79
Symons, Richard, yeoman, Stockbury, Kent, 1674 CKS PRC2/36/130
Symons, Rychard, Rainham, Kent, 1578 CKS PRC2/1/200
Symons, Theophilus, bricklayer, Deal, Kent, 1675 CKS PRC20/12/184
Symons, Thomas, Tenterden, Kent, 1598 CKS PRC2/10/387
Symons, see Burden,
Symonson, Richard, Maidstone, Kent, 1674 CKS PRC20/12/148
Symonson, Thomas, Chart, Little, Kent, 1630 CKS PRC2/30/132
Symonson, William + Parnell, Dover St Mary, Kent, 1597 CKS PRC21/14/169
Sympson, Anthonye, Chart, Great, Kent, 1614 CKS PRC2/18/57
Sympson, Cuthbert, husbandman, Kingsnorth, Kent, 1616 CKS PRC1/1/23
Sympson, Edward, Canterbury St Margaret, Kent, 1666 CKS PRC19/3/108
Sympson, Edward, Eastry, Kent, 1679 CKS PRC20/12/323
Sympson, George, Covent Garden, St Paul, London & Middlesex, 1729 Greater London RO AM/PP/Box 1726-1732 pt (uncatalogued)
Sympson, Jane, widow, Whitstable, Kent, 1619 CKS PRC2/19/21
Sympson, John, Bridge, Kent, 1608 CKS PRC2/14/401
Sympson, Laurence, Dorrington, Lincs, 1602 Lincs RO Ad/Ac/5/27
Sympson, Nicholas, Whitstable, Kent, 1619 CKS PRC2/19/17
Sympson, Nicholas + Jane, Whitstable, Kent, 1619 CKS PRC2/19/14

Sympson, Robert, keelman, Barton on Humber, Lincs, 1667 Lincs RO Ad/Ac/32/124
Sympson, Robert, innholder, Elham, Kent, 1684 CKS PRC2/40/241
Sympson, Thomas, blacksmith, Maidstone, Kent, 1621 CKS PRC20/5/176
Sympson, William, Hawkhurst, Kent, 1596 CKS PRC2/8/202
Sympson, William, Dover, Kent, 1638 CKS PRC20/11/341
Sympson, William, butcher, Holme, Hunts, 1738 Hunts RO/Acc58/321
Syms, John, Wick, Som, 1639 Somerset RO D/D/Cta/S30
Syndrie, Christopher, shepherd, Shellingford, Berks, 1600 Berks RO D/A1/213/1C
Synner, Tobie, Bodmin, Corn, 1639 Cornwall RO AP/S816/4-5
Syre, Richard, cordwainer: 'shoemaker', Oxford St Martin, Oxon, 1628 Oxon RO MSS Wills 86/1/7
Syseley, Peter, St Nicholas at Wade, Kent, 1581 CKS PRC21/5/81
Syseley, Thomas, Hawkhurst, Kent, 1586 CKS PRC2/4/96
Syslie, Richard, Hawkhurst, Kent, 1600 CKS PRC2/11/292
Syson, John, Quadring, Lincs, 1612 Lincs RO Ad/Ac/11/103
Taber, Dinton, Wilts, 1615 Wilts RO Miscellaneous Index (name + date)
Tabnor, William, potter, Stoke-upon-Trent, Staffs, 1809 LJRO/B/C/5/1809/86
Tabor, James, university: 'University Registrar', Cambridge (Corpus Christi College), Cambs, 1646 CUL V.C. Acc./Box2/75
Tabott, Thomas, Deal, Kent, 1626 CKS PRC20/7/132
Tabraham, see Tabram,
Tabram/Tabraham, Robert, Canterbury St Dunstan Without, Kent, 1685 CKS PRC2/41/19
Tacey, Robert, Radwell, Herts, 1638 Herts RO AHH23/2353
Tachill, George, Goxhill, Lincs, 1612 Lincs RO Ad/Ac/11/24
Tackett, Agnes, Leake, Lincs, 1624 Lincs RO Ad/Ac/19A/33
Tadd, William, Luddenham, Kent, 1641 CKS PRC1/5/48
Taddie, Alice, widow, St Johns Thanet, Kent, 1629 CKS PRC1/1/39
Taddy, Richard, St Peter in Thanet, Kent, 1674 CKS PRC2/36/133
Tadhunter, Christopher, yeoman, Chilham, Kent, 1647 CKS PRC1/8/28
Tadhunter, John, yeoman, Nackington, Kent, 1682 CKS PRC2/39/243
Taft, Robert, Cubbington, Warks, 1672 LJRO:cards/1672/57
Tagg, Ralph, Brading, Hants, 1625 Hants RO 21M65 D8/134
Tagg, Thomas, Bath, Som, 1736 Somerset RO D/D/Cta/T18
Tailbois, Margaret, Wainfleet All Saints, Lincs, 1620 Lincs RO Ad/Ac/16/98
Tailer, Edward, Sibsey, Lincs, 1649 Lincs RO Ad/Ac/30/181
Tailer, Ellis, Torksey (Brampton), Lincs, 1607 Lincs RO Ad/Ac/37/238
Tailer, George, Hainton, Lincs, 1649 Lincs RO Ad/Ac/42/59
Tailer, John, Lincoln, Lincs, 1633 Lincs RO Ad/Ac/24/175
Tailer, John, Sudbrooke, Lincs, 1637 Lincs RO Ad/Ac/25/529
Tailer, Robert, Croft, Lincs, 1639 Lincs RO Ad/Ac/26/237
Tailer, William, Killingholme, Lincs, 1640 Lincs RO Ad/Ac/27/132
Tailer, William, Apley, Lincs, 1649 Lincs RO Ad/Ac/30/217
Tailor, Edward, Swingfield, Kent, 1634 CKS PRC2/32/121
Tailor, James, gentleman, Westwell, Kent, 1643 CKS PRC19/2/80
Tailor, John, Ashby, Lincs, 1593 Lincs RO Ad/Ac/3/23
Tailor, John, clergy: 'clerk', Buckland, Kent, 1594 CKS PRC2/6/41
Tailor, John, victualler, Faversham, Kent, 1611 CKS PRC2/16/110
Tailor, Lawrence, Cranbrook, Kent, 1607 CKS PRC2/13/398
Tailor, Margaret, widow, Cranbrook, Kent, 1623 CKS PRC2/24/153
Tailor, Richard, Harrietsham, Kent, 1609 CKS PRC2/15/407
Tailor, Richard, clergy: 'clerk', Toft, Lincs, 1672 Lincs RO Ad/Ac/34/6
Tailor, Walter, Snave, Kent, 1594 CKS PRC2/7/213
Tailor, William, Shadoxhurst, Kent, 1603 CKS PRC2/14/438
Talbois, Rudulphe, clergy: 'mr/D.D.', Canterbury Christchurch, Kent, 1596 CKS PRC21/14/17
Talbot, Agnes, widow, Linsted, Kent, 1603 CKS PRC2/12/462

[Talbot:]
Talbot, John, Woodchurch, Kent, 1617 CKS PRC20/4/389
Talbot, Stephen, Salisbury, Wilts, 1616 Wilts RO Miscellaneous Index (name + date)
Talbot, William, farmer/maltster, Sedgley, Staffs, 1787 LJRO/B/C/5/1787/127
Talbott, Dorothy, spinster, Sutton Mallet, Som, 1667 Somerset RO D/D/Cta/T17
Taler, Henry, Belton, Lincs, 1629 Lincs RO Ad/Ac/39/222
Taler, Thomas, Harpswell, Lincs, 1627 Lincs RO Ad/Ac/39/220
Tall, Thomas, victualler, Willingham, Cambs, 1750s? Cambs RO
Tallant, William, Northwood, Hants, 1624 Hants RO 21M65 D8/91
Talles, William, Ivychurch, Kent, 1583 CKS PRC21/6/213
Tallette, Charles, Bromsgrove, Worcs, 1675 Worcs RO 008.7 BA3585/830/31
Talleye, Henry, St Albans, Herts, 1620 Herts RO ASA25/2661
Tallice, John, Newchurch, Kent, 1674 CKS PRC19/4/104
Tallis, Edward, yeoman, Hampton in Arden, Warks, 1762 LJRO/B/C/5/1761/147a, b
Tallis, John, Canterbury, Kent, 1633 CKS PRC2/32/123
Tallis, Lydia, widow, Bickenhill, Warks, 1795 LJRO/B/C/5/1796/217
Tallis, William, carpenter, Old Romney, Kent, 1617 CKS PRC2/24/141
Talor, John, Enderby, Wood, Lincs, 1622 Lincs RO Ad/Ac/17/84
Tame, Joan, widow, Winterbourne, Berks, 1616 Berks RO D/A1/217/109B
Tame, Ralph, Marcham, Berks, 1617 Berks RO D/A1/217/110B
Tame, Richard, weaver, Winterbourne, Berks, 1610 Berks RO D/A1/217/95B
Tame, Richard, labourer, Waltham, White, Berks, 1628 Berks RO D/A1/217/131B
Tame, Thomas, Brenzett, Kent, 1639 CKS PRC1/3/49
Tame, William, Hendred, East, Berks, 1594 Berks RO D/A1/217/62B
Tame, William, Foleshill, Warks, 1672 LJRO:cards/1672/58
Tamkin, Gabriel, Goudhurst, Kent, 1668 CKS PRC1/13/128
Tamlyn, Phillipp, husbandman, St Tudy, Corn, 1647 Cornwall RO AP/T602/3
Tandin, James, St Martin in the Fields, London & Middlesex, 1682 PRO PROB32/19/155
Tang, Anne, widow, St Johns Thanet, Kent, 1619 CKS PRC2/24/117
Tangett, Peter, Canterbury, Kent, 1621 CKS PRC2/24/146
Tangett, Symon, Canterbury St Andrew, Kent, 1642 CKS PRC1/6/90
Tangley, Samuel, clergy: 'clerk', Bosham, Sussex, 1674 W. Suss RO EpI/33/1674/5
Tannat, Robert, mariner, Bristol, Glos, Bristol RO 1739/25
Tanner, Alice, Portishead, Som, 1591 Somerset RO D/D/Cta/T43
Tanner, Alice, widow, Reculver, Kent, 1598 CKS PRC21/14/592
Tanner, David, Great Mongeham, Kent, 1593 CKS PRC2/6/132
Tanner, Elizabeth, Kington St Michael, Wilts, 1617 Wilts RO Arch. Wilts.(+ name and date)
Tanner, James, Lympne, Kent, 1613 CKS PRC2/17/144
Tanner, Joan,
Oxon Oxon RO MSS Wills 89/4/21
Tanner, John, Bilsington, Kent, 1593 CKS PRC2/6/128
Tanner, John, Fugglestone St Peter, Wilts, 1751? Wilts RO Miscellaneous Index (name + date)
Tanner, Mary, widow, Westbere, Kent, 1689 CKS PRC2/41/136
Tanner, Richard, Kingston Seymour, Som, 1640 Somerset RO D/D/Cta/T15
Tanner, Robert, labourer, Cookham, Berks, 1620 Berks RO D/A1/217/114B
Tanner, Stephen, Westbury, Wilts, 1675 Wilts RO Chantor Sarum Bundle 10/2
Tanner, Thomas, Newton Valence, Hants, 1679 Hants RO 21m65 D8/296
Tanner, William, Reculver, Kent, 1598 CKS PRC21/14/589
Tanner, William, Herne, Kent, 1600 CKS PRC21/15/166
Tanner, William, yeoman, Longcot, Berks, 1671 Berks RO D/A1/218/16D
Tanner, William,
Wilts 1679 Wilts RO Miscellaneous Index (name + date)
Tanner, William, yeoman, Beenham, Berks, 1689 Berks RO D/A1/218/67C
Tanner, William,
Wilts 1750 c. Wilts RO Miscellaneous Index (name + date)
Tanner/Grimland, Christopher, Watlington, Oxon, 1625 Oxon RO MSS Wills 300/4/27

Tanton, Henry, Norwich St Peter of Mancroft, Norf, 1708 Norfolk RO ANW/23/8/34
Tanton, John, Boughton Aluph, Kent, 1630 CKS PRC2/30/133
Tanton, John, Hull, Yorks, 1803 Borthwick Test C.P. 1803/8
Tanton, Robert, Frinstead, Kent, 1620 CKS PRC2/24/125
Tanton, Robert, Bredgar, Kent, 1630 CKS PRC20/9/422
Tanzey, Alexander, Boston, Lincs, 1632 Lincs RO Ad/Ac/23/90
Tapeley, Johane, widow, New Romney, Kent, 1590 CKS PRC21/10/196
Tapely, Mathew, Maidstone, Kent, 1682 CKS PRC20/13/289
Tapenden, Alice, Molash, Kent, 1678 CKS PRC2/38/75
Tapley, Henry, Petham, Kent, 1687 CKS PRC2/41/109
Tapley, Nicholas, Chilham, Kent, 1691 CKS PRC2/42/15
Tapley, Stephen, Milton next Sittingbourne, Kent, 1665 CKS PRC1/10/94
Tapley, Stephen, Rainham, Kent, 1675 CKS PRC2/36/
Taplin, John, Stratford-upon-Avon, Warks, 1799 Worcs RO 008.7 BA3585/835/bdl 2
Taply, Richard, Bethersden, Kent, 1673 CKS PRC2/35/92
Taplyn, Rychard, Brenzett, Kent, 1596 CKS PRC2/8/15
Taplyn, Thomas, Ivychurch, Kent, 1592 CKS PRC21/11/261
Tapp, Edmund, Benington, Herts, 1636 Herts RO AHH23/2345
Tapp, John, Higham Ferrers, Northants, 1683 Northants RO NWill A/C/23
Tappenden, Richard, Milton next Sittingbourne, Kent, 1633 CKS PRC2/32/125
Tapper, Theophilus, clergy: 'clerk', Leicester, Leics, 1684 Leics RO Administrators Accounts 1682-86 f12
Tappes, Henry, St Albans, Herts, 1596 Herts RO ASA25/1579
Tapping, William, husbandman, Drayton, West, Berks, 1594 Berks RO D/A1/217/59B
Tappinge, John, innholder, Redbourn, Herts, 1636 Herts RO ASA25/4931
Tarbocke, Elen, widow, Runcorn, Ches, 1664 Cheshire RO (Name) W.C. 1664
Tarbucke, John, Stevenage, Herts, 1635 Herts RO AHH23/2344
Targett, William, Tisbury, Wilts, 1641 Wilts RO Arch. Sarum(+ name and date)
Tarleton, Thomas, Kenardington, Kent, 1610 CKS PRC2/15/404
Tarleton, Thomas, New Romney, Kent, 1622 CKS PRC20/6/254
Tarrant, Oliver, Brinkworth, Wilts, 1640 Wilts RO Arch. Wilts.(+ name and date)
Tarrant, William, Milton, Berks, 1676 Wilts RO Miscellaneous Index to Wills (name + date)
Tarrant, see Torren,
Tarrie, Nicholas, Wyberton, Lincs, 1640 Lincs RO Ad/Ac/27/146
Tarry, Christopher, Swineshead, Lincs, 1664 Lincs RO Ad/Ac/43/25
Tarry, Thomas, Thornby, Northants, 1672 Northants RO NWill A/C/112
Tassell, James, gentleman, Faversham, Kent, 1668 CKS PRC1/12/88
Tassell, Mary, Sittingbourne, Kent, 1669 CKS PRC1/13/129
Tassell, Robert, Harrietsham, Kent, 1599 CKS PRC2/10/515
Tassell, Roberte, Egerton, Kent, 1577 CKS PRC21/3/173
Tassell, Thomas, Harrietsham, Kent, 1582 CKS PRC2/2/108
Tassell, Thomas, Rodmersham, Kent, 1604 CKS PRC21/17/136
Tassell, Thomas, Faversham, Kent, 1621 CKS PRC2/24/111
Tasset, Lucy, mistress, Walsingham, Little, Norf, 1724 Norfolk RO ANW/23/17/51
Tate, John, Canterbury St Andrew, Kent, 1623 CKS PRC2/24/151
Tate, Robert, clothier, Goudhurst, Kent, 1640 CKS PRC1/3/50
Tate, Robert eld, clothier, Rolvenden, Kent, 1669 CKS PRC1/14/109
Tatham, John, mr,
Oxon 1577 Bodleian HYP B9/92-93
Tatnoll, Richard, Sandwich, Kent, 1626 CKS PRC2/27/171
Tatone, Thomas, Willoughby (Sloothby), Lincs, 1602 Lincs RO Ad/Ac/5/265
Tattam, John, Boston, Lincs, 1577 Lincs RO Ad/Ac/1/23
Tattersole, Christopher, Graveney, Kent, 1617 CKS PRC2/24/101
Tattom, John, miller, Dorchester, Oxon, 1671 Oxon RO MSS Wills Pec 71/6/20
Tatton, William, Newcastle under Lyme, Staffs, 1676 LJRO:cards/1676/47

[Tavan:]
Tavan, Robert, university: 'scholar's servant', Cambridge, Cambs, 1643 CUL V.C. Acc./Box2/78
Tavell, Avice, Bilsington, Kent, 1598 CKS PRC2/10/112
Taverner, John, clergy: 'mr/clerk', Hackington, Kent, 1616 CKS PRC20/3/186
Taverner, Thomas, Syston, Lincs, 1619 Lincs RO Ad/Ac/14/290
Taverner, Thomas, Canterbury St Mildred, Kent, 1635 CKS PRC2/33/133
Taverner, Thomas, Gedney, Lincs, 1638 Lincs RO Ad/Ac/25/135
Taverner, Thomas, gentleman, Kingston, Kent, 1641 CKS PRC1/5/49
Tavernor, Jane, Donington, Lincs, 1639? Lincs RO Ad/Ac/26/77
Tavernor, John, innkeeper, Huddersfield, Yorks, 1814 Borthwick Test C.P. 1813/5
Tayer, Robert, clergy: 'clerk/parson', Tangmere, Sussex, 1629 W. Suss RO EpIV/10/1/15
Tayler, Agnes, widow, Englefield, Berks, 1596 Berks RO D/A1/217/72B
Tayler, Agnes, widow, Englefield, Berks, 1597 Berks RO D/A1/217/72C
Tayler, Alexander, Pinvin, Worcs, 1684 Worcs RO 008.7 BA3585/837/bdl 4
Tayler, Alice, widow, St Peter in Thanet, Kent, 1618 CKS PRC2/24/116
Tayler, Arthur, Scartho, Lincs, 1620 Lincs RO Ad/Ac/16/95
Tayler, Arthur, yeoman, Grantham (Little Gonerby), Lincs, 1633 Lincs RO Ad/Ac/24/108
Tayler, Barnerd, Maidenwell, Lincs, 1615 Lincs RO Ad/Ac/13/22
Tayler, Benjamin, Ulceby, Lincs, 1809 Lincs RO Ad/Ac/36/18
Tayler, Christopher, mariner, Dover, Kent, 1671 CKS PRC20/12/32
Tayler, Christopher, butler, Oxford (Magdalen College), Oxon, 1673 Bodleian HYP B9/94-95
Tayler, Clement, Leeds, Kent, 1618 CKS PRC2/24/118
Tayler, Daniell, Sheldwich, Kent, 1643 CKS PRC1/7/14
Tayler, Edward, Sudbrooke, Lincs, 1623 Lincs RO Ad/Ac/18/43
Tayler, Edward, Hemingby, Lincs, 1665 Lincs RO Ad/Ac/43/46 Lincs RO vk
Tayler, Edward, Bury (Hepmangrove), Hunts, 1679 Hunts RO/Acc58/137(5)
Tayler, Elenor, spinster, Salisbury, Wilts, 1676 Wilts RO Sub-Dean of Sarum (name + date)
Tayler, Elianor, St Martin in the Fields, London & Middlesex, 1679 Greater London RO AM/PP/Box 1739-1749 pt (uncatalogued)
Tayler, Elizabeth, widow, St Ives, Corn, 1602 Cornwall RO AP/T2/10
Tayler, Ellin, widow, Wrawby cum Brigg (Glanford Brigg), Lincs, 1673 Lincs RO Ad/Ac/35/142
Tayler, Francis, Chillenden, Kent, 1629 CKS PRC2/30/139
Tayler, George, Cranbrook, Kent, 1597 CKS PRC2/9/207
Tayler, George, gentleman, Scotter, Lincs, 1680 Lincs RO Ad/Ac/43/168
Tayler, Gregorie, Haxey, Lincs, 1607 Lincs RO Ad/Ac/37/259
Tayler, Gregory, Moulton, Lincs, 1612 Lincs RO Ad/Ac/11/199a
Tayler, Henry, yeoman, Englefield, Berks, 1595 Berks RO D/A1/217/64B
Tayler, Henrye, St Peter in Thanet, Kent, 1613 CKS PRC2/17/394
Tayler, Isaac, Windsor, New, Berks, 1636 Berks RO D/A1/217/149B
Tayler, James, Langley Burrell, Wilts, 1680? Wilts RO Miscellaneous Index (name + date)
Tayler, John, Kennington, Kent, 1598 CKS PRC2/9/369
Tayler, John, Canterbury St George Martyr, Kent, 1606 CKS PRC2/14/429
Tayler, John, blacksmith, Reculver, Kent, 1617 CKS PRC20/4/387
Tayler, John, Rainham, Kent, 1619 CKS PRC2/24/120
Tayler, John, Canterbury St Mildred, Kent, 1621 CKS PRC2/26/102
Tayler, John, smith, Herne, Kent, 1624 CKS PRC20/6/197
Tayler, John, Grantham, Lincs, 1625 Lincs RO Ad/Ac/19B/46
Tayler, John, Chislet, Kent, 1630 CKS PRC2/30/140
Tayler, John, Dymchurch, Kent, 1632 CKS PRC2/31/73
Tayler, John, Rainham, Kent, 1636 CKS PRC2/33/134
Tayler, John, Minster in Sheppey, Kent, 1638 CKS PRC2/34/294
Tayler, John, Searby, Lincs, 1666 Lincs RO Ad/Ac/42/57
Tayler, John, husbandman, Digby, Lincs, 1674 Lincs RO Ad/Ac/35/26
Tayler, John, butcher, St Ives, Hunts, 1682 Hunts RO/Acc58/171(17)
Tayler, John, bachelor, Croome D'Abitot, Worcs, 1760 Worcs RO 008.7 BA3585/835/bdl 1
Tayler, John eld, gentleman, Kingsnorth, Kent, 1623 CKS PRC20/6/193

Tayler, Jony, widow, Bucknall, Lincs, 1625 Lincs RO Ad/Ac/19B/67
Tayler, Laurence, yeoman, Speen (Shawbridge), Berks, 1611 Berks RO D/A1/217/97B
Tayler, Margaret, widow, Hythe West, Kent, 1619 CKS PRC2/24/134
Tayler, Marke, Marden, Kent, 1605 CKS PRC2/13/400
Tayler, Mary, Lympne, Kent, 1632 CKS PRC2/31/71
Tayler, Mary, Roughton, Lincs, 1638 Lincs RO Ad/Ac/25/303
Tayler, Mary, widow, Canterbury St George Martyr, Kent, 1671 CKS PRC20/12/31
Tayler, Nicholas, Birdham, Sussex, 1598 W. Suss RO EpI/33/1597/13
Tayler, Nicholas, Stallingborough, Lincs, 1612 Lincs RO Ad/Ac/10/155
Tayler, Nicholas, Shadoxhurst, Kent, 1620 CKS PRC2/26/109
Tayler, Nicholas, yeoman, Welford, Berks, 1635 Berks RO D/A1/217/148B
Tayler, Nicholas, Nonington, Kent, 1640 CKS PRC19/1/19
Tayler, Philip, Chebsey (Shallowford), Staffs, 1667 LJRO:cards/1667/79
Tayler, Robert, Heckington, Lincs, 1611 Lincs RO Ad/Ac/10/28
Tayler, Robert, Ashford, Kent, 1613 CKS PRC2/18/91
Tayler, Robert, Kirton, Lincs, 1614 Lincs RO Ad/Ac/13/135
Tayler, Robert, Riby, Lincs, 1618 Lincs RO Ad/Ac/14/284
Tayler, Robert, yeoman, Roxby, Lincs, 1680 Lincs RO Ad/Ac/43/155
Tayler, Roger, Wingham, Kent, 1614 CKS PRC20/3/17
Tayler, Stephen, Bishopstone, Wilts, 1630 Wilts RO Preb Court Bishopstone Bundle 1/16
Tayler, Stephen, haberdasher, Maidstone, Kent, 1641 CKS PRC19/1/85
Tayler, Sylvester, Kingston, Kent, 1612 CKS PRC2/17/187
Tayler, Thomas, Skirbeck, Lincs, 1612 Lincs RO Ad/Ac/11/185
Tayler, Thomas, Stamford, Lincs, 1612 Lincs RO Ad/Ac/12/212
Tayler, Thomas, Leeds, Kent, 1619 CKS PRC2/22/152
Tayler, Thomas, Stixwold, Lincs, 1626 Lincs RO Ad/Ac/20/11
Tayler, Thomas, Bobbing, Kent, 1627 CKS PRC2/28/120
Tayler, Thomas, Horncastle, Lincs, 1632 Lincs RO Ad/Ac/23/106
Tayler, Thomas, husbandman, Heckington, Lincs, 1633 Lincs RO Ad/Ac/24/171
Tayler, Thomas, Hollingbourne, Kent, 1637 CKS PRC20/11/476
Tayler, Thomas, Ormsby, South, Lincs, 1639 Lincs RO Ad/Ac/26/64
Tayler, Thomas, cordwainer,
Lincs 1648 Lincs RO Ad/Ac/30/347
Tayler, Thomas, Hollingbourne, Kent, 1664 CKS PRC19/3/63
Tayler, Thomas, grazier, Westwell, Kent, 1664 CKS PRC19/3/64
Tayler, Thomas, haberdasher, Ashford, Kent, 1681 CKS PRC2/39/246
Tayler, William, Boughton Monchelsea, Kent, 1609 CKS PRC2/15/414
Tayler, William, yeoman, Minety, Wilts, 1618 Wilts RO Arch. Wilts.(+ name and date)
Tayler, William, Postling, Kent, 1624 CKS PRC2/24/150
Tayler, William, Wickhambreaux, Kent, 1625 CKS PRC2/25/147
Tayler, William, Coates, Great, Lincs, 1638 Lincs RO Ad/Ac/25/339
Tayler, William, yeoman, Waltham, Lincs, 1676 Lincs RO Ad/Ac/34/33
Tayler, William, Kingsnorth, Kent, 1681 CKS PRC2/39/111
Tayler, William + Ann, Faversham, Kent, 1626 CKS PRC2/27/170
Tayler, Willyam, Queenborough, Kent, 1619 CKS PRC2/24/127
Taylor, widow, St Peter in Thanet, Kent, 1640 CKS PRC1/5/51
Taylor, Alice, Caldecote, Herts, 1591 Herts RO ASA25/1366
Taylor, Alice, Haxey (West End), Lincs, 1664 Lincs RO Ad/Ac/41/139
Taylor, Andrew eld, gentleman, Bromborough (Brimstage), Ches, 1630 Cheshire RO (Name) W.C. 1630
Taylor, Barbara, Faversham, Kent, 1637 CKS PRC2/34/138
Taylor, Charles, Stoneleigh, Warks, 1683 LJRO/B/C/5/1682/98
Taylor, Daniel, gentleman, Westwell, Kent, 1672 CKS PRC20/12/62
Taylor, Edward, Elham, Kent, 1597 CKS PRC2/9/373
Taylor, Elizabeth, Abbots Langley, Herts, 1635 Herts RO ASA25/4920

[Taylor:]
Taylor, Elizabeth, widow, Rochdale (Castleton Moor), Lancs, 1638 Lancs RO (Name of Deceased) D.R.C.H. 1637
Taylor, George, Staplehurst, Kent, 1634 CKS PRC2/32/175
Taylor, George, yeoman, Bicester, Oxon, 1641 Oxon RO MSS Wills 87/3/17
Taylor, George, Crich (Wessington), Derby, 1666 LJRO:cards/1666/14
Taylor, George, Kenilworth, Warks, 1681 LJRO/B/C/5/1682/96
Taylor, George, Staple next Wingham, Kent, 1706 CKS PRC19/6/25
Taylor, Henry, maltster, Bridlington, Yorks, Borthwick Test C.P. 1719/14
Taylor, Henry, husbandman, Ilsley, West, Berks, 1627 Berks RO D/A1/217/128B
Taylor, Henry, Haxey (Newbigg), Lincs, 1663 Lincs RO Ad/Ac/41/73
Taylor, Henry + Elizabeth, Haxey, Lincs, 1610 Lincs RO Ad/Ac/8a/322
Taylor, Hugh, yeoman, Binfield, Berks, 1614 Berks RO D/A1/127/22D
Taylor, James, yeoman, Kingsnorth, Kent, 1672 CKS PRC2/35/185
Taylor, James, husbandman, Haxey, Lincs, 1685 Lincs RO Ad/Ac/44/158
Taylor, James, yeoman, Leek (Birchall), Staffs, 1742 LJRO/B/C/5/1742/135
Taylor, Jane, widow, Murston, Kent, 1669 CKS PRC1/14/110
Taylor, John, Chillenden, Kent, CKS PRC1/6/27a
Taylor, John, Wootton, Kent, 1597 CKS PRC2/9/315
Taylor, John, Lydd, Kent, 1606 CKS PRC20/1/95
Taylor, John, Tenterden, Kent, 1613 CKS PRC2/18/93
Taylor, John, New Romney, Kent, 1615 CKS PRC20/3/150
Taylor, John, Sutton, Kings, Northants, 1619 Oxon RO MSS Wills Pec 52/3/33
Taylor, John, weaver, Compton, Berks, 1622 Berks RO D/A1/217/121B
Taylor, John, Biddenden, Kent, 1633 CKS PRC2/31/165
Taylor, John, Lympne, Kent, 1641 CKS PRC1/5/50
Taylor, John, yeoman, Chillenden, Kent, 1641 CKS PRC1/6/27
Taylor, John, yeoman, Lympne, Kent, 1641 CKS PRC1/5/50a
Taylor, John, maltster, Faversham, Kent, 1662 CKS PRC1/9/62
Taylor, John, Faldingworth, Lincs, 1663 Lincs RO Ad/Ac/41/78
Taylor, John, husbandman, Bilsington, Kent, 1665 CKS PRC1/11/88
Taylor, John,
Wilts 1675 Wilts RO Miscellaneous Index (name + date)
Taylor, John, Wolstanton, Staffs, 1678 LJRO:cards/1678/22
Taylor, John, yeoman, Farmington, Glos, 1678? GRO GDR/B4/2/T63
Taylor, John, Arundel, Sussex, 1682 W. Suss RO EpI/33/1682/34
Taylor, John, Cheddleton, Staffs, 1684 LJRO/B/C/5/1684/77
Taylor, John, Sandwich, Kent, 1684 CKS PRC2/40/249
Taylor, John, clergy: 'clerk', Nuthurst, Sussex, 1684 W. Suss RO EpI/33/1684/16
Taylor, John, innkeeper, Chester, Ches, 1684 Cheshire RO (Name) W.C. 1684
Taylor, John, yeoman, Kingsnorth, Kent, 1697 CKS PRC2/42/136
Taylor, John, mariner: 'HMS Tyger', Stepney, London & Middlesex, 1713 PRO PROB32/57/25
Taylor, John, butcher, Rotherham, Yorks, 1789 Borthwick Test C.P. 1789/3
Taylor, John, maltster, Bedworth, Warks, 1793 LJRO/B/C/5/1794/102a
Taylor, John, farmer, Hartpury, Glos, 1806 GRO GDR/B4/2/T26
Taylor, John, farmer, Ashover (The Edges), Derby, 1827 LJRO/B/C/5/1829/36
Taylor, Joseph, clothier, Huddersfield (Longroyd Bridge), Yorks, 1804 Borthwick Test C.P. 1804/7
Taylor, Laurence, Barnham, Sussex, 1674 W. Suss RO EpI/33/1674/13
Taylor, Lawrence, yeoman, St Albans St Stephens, Herts, 1609 Herts RO ASA25/4775
Taylor, Margaret, spinster, Salisbury, Wilts, 1676 Wilts RO Miscellaneous Index (name + date)
Taylor, Margaret, Stafford, Staffs, 1684 LJRO/B/C/5/1684/78
Taylor, Mary, widow, Sandwich, Kent, 1677 CKS PRC2/37/202
Taylor, Mary, widow, Ilsley, West, Berks, 1687 Berks RO D/A1/128/156C
Taylor, Mary, widow,

Glos 1748 GRO GDR/B4/2/T64
Taylor, Matthew, Emley, Yorks, 1724 Borthwick Test C.P. 1724/10
Taylor, Nicholas, Maidstone, Kent, 1611 CKS PRC20/2/254
Taylor, Nicholas, Lyminge, Kent, 1619 CKS PRC20/4/383
Taylor, Nicholas, weaver: 'broad weaver', Goudhurst, Kent, 1664 CKS PRC1/10/95
Taylor, Osmunde, Blean, Kent, 1591 CKS PRC2/5/438
Taylor, Phoebe, widow, Sheffield (Piper Houses, Brightside Bierlow), Yorks, 1788 Borthwick Test C.P. 1788/7
Taylor, Richard, Frittenden, Kent, 1629 CKS PRC2/30/137
Taylor, Richard, shepherd, Longcot, Berks, 1633 Berks RO D/A1/217/140B
Taylor, Richard, Shipley, Sussex, 1646 W. Suss RO EpI/33/1646/3
Taylor, Richard, Marhamchurch, Corn, 1649 Cornwall RO AP/T827
Taylor, Richard, Steyning, Sussex, 1669 W. Suss RO EpI/33/1669/8
Taylor, Richard eld, Teynham, Kent, 1635 CKS PRC2/33/135
Taylor, Robert, Cropredy (Coton), Oxon, 1628 Oxon RO MSS Wills Pec 52/3/43
Taylor, Robert, Spalding, Lincs, 1632 Lincs RO Ad/Ac/23/121
Taylor, Robert, Newnham, Kent, 1671 CKS PRC2/35/95
Taylor, Robert, Worthington, Leics, 1672 Leics RO Administrators Accounts 1667-72 f63
Taylor, Robert, butcher, Orlestone, Kent, 1721 CKS PRC1/18/49
Taylor, Roger, Horsham, Sussex, 1672 W. Suss RO EpI/33/1672/2
Taylor, Roger, Horsham, Sussex, 1672 W. Suss RO EpI/33/1672/18
Taylor, Samuel, Stockerston, Leics, 1673 Leics RO Administrators Accounts 1667-72 f130
Taylor, Samuel, mercer, Cheadle, Staffs, 1692 LJRO/B/C/5/1692/103
Taylor, Sarah, widow, Birmingham, Warks, 1782 LJRO/B/C/5/1782/116
Taylor, Sessely, Southoe, Hunts, 1674 Hunts RO/Acc58/20(203)
Taylor, Thomas, Leeds, Kent, 1596 CKS PRC2/8/79
Taylor, Thomas, Rainham, Kent, 1606 CKS PRC2/15/409
Taylor, Thomas, Staplehurst, Kent, 1635 CKS PRC20/11/468
Taylor, Thomas, Northbourne, Kent, 1636 CKS PRC2/33/131
Taylor, Thomas, Canterbury Holy Cross Westgate, Kent, 1639 CKS PRC1/3/51
Taylor, Thomas, Chart, Little, Kent, 1639 CKS PRC2/34/289
Taylor, Thomas, tailor, Walmer, Kent, 1642 CKS PRC1/6/91
Taylor, Thomas, husbandman, Sheldwich, Kent, 1669 CKS PRC1/14/111
Taylor, Thomas, gentleman, Claycoton, Northants, 1685 Northants RO NWill A/C/166
Taylor, Thomas, Canterbury St George Martyr, Kent, 1704 CKS PRC1/16/58
Taylor, Tymothie, Maidstone, Kent, 1600 CKS PRC21/15/139
Taylor, Vincent, Haxey, Lincs, 1663 Lincs RO Ad/Ac/41/69
Taylor, Walter, Measham, Derby, 1667 LJRO:cards/1667/81
Taylor, William, St Albans St Michaels, Herts, 1605 Herts RO ASA25/4763
Taylor, William, yeoman, Bradford, Worcs, 1607 Worcs RO 008.7 BA3585/839/426
Taylor, William, Canterbury All Saints, Kent, 1610 CKS PRC2/15/400
Taylor, William, clothier, Reading St Giles, Berks, 1618 Berks RO D/A1/126/242C
Taylor, William, Burgh, Lincs, 1663 Lincs RO Ad/Ac/43/9b
Taylor, William, Eckington, Derby, 1682 LJRO/B/C/5/1682/99
Taylor, William, bachelor, St Magnus the Martyr, London & Middlesex, 1685 PRO PROB32/25/299
Taylor, William, Brenzett, Kent, 1686 CKS PRC2/41/17
Taylor/Asherst, Frances, widow, Bilsington, Kent, 1668 CKS PRC1/13/130
Taylor/Asherst, Frances, widow, Bilsington, Kent, 1668 CKS PRC1/13/130a
Taylor/Edmonds, Margaret, wife, Midhurst, Sussex, 1635 W. Suss RO EpI/33/1635/3
Taylor/Fletcher, Christopher, Basingstoke, Hants, 1632 Hants RO 1632 ND4
Taylor/Ogborne, Frances, widow, Newbury, Berks, 1694 Berks RO D/A1/218/92C
Taylor/Paris, Robert, Banbury (Grimsbury), Oxon, 1626 Oxon RO MSS Wills Pec 52/3/42
Taylor/Tylor, William, Smarden, Kent, 1588 CKS PRC2/4/277
Taylor, see Crase & Neale,

[Taylour:]
Taylour, James, clergy: 'clerk', Sutton St Edmunds, Lincs, 1614 Lincs RO Ad/Ac/13/211
Taylour, Valentine, Horsington, Lincs, 1606 Lincs RO Ad/Ac/7/96
Teage, Alexander, Shrewsbury, Shrops, 1685 LJRO/B/C/5/1685/95
Teage, John, yeoman, Roche, Corn, 1640 Cornwall RO AP/T654/3
Teage, Nicholas, Canterbury St George Martyr, Kent, 1615 CKS PRC2/24/130
Tealby, Hughe, Theddlethorpe All Saints, Lincs, 1615 Lincs RO Ad/Ac/13/181
Teale, Richard, pilot, Deal, Kent, 1669 CKS PRC19/4/61
Tebb, John, Torksey, Lincs, 1626 Lincs RO Ad/Ac/39/27
Tebb, Raphe, mariner, St Johns Thanet, Kent, 1687 CKS PRC2/41/82
Tebbott, George, Hale, Great, Lincs, 1625 Lincs RO Ad/Ac/19A/70
Tebbott, William, yeoman, Hale, Great, Lincs, 1667 Lincs RO Ad/Ac/32/68
Tedd, John, Stoke, South, Lincs, 1601 Lincs RO Ad/Ac/5/211
Teddeman, Henry, mariner, Dover, Kent, 1679 CKS PRC20/12/324
Teeler, John, smith, Willesborough, Kent, 1646 CKS PRC1/7/67
Teenbie, Edward, husbandman, Goxhill, Lincs, 1627 Lincs RO Ad/Ac/20b/12
Teere, William, Lydd, Kent, 1614 CKS PRC20/3/21
Tegge, Thomas eld, innholder, Pangbourne, Berks, 1667 Berks RO D/A1/218/15C
Teire, John, Steep, Hants, 1639 Hants RO 21M65 D8/141
Teisdale, Thomas, Marsh Chapel, Lincs, 1613 Lincs RO Ad/Ac/12/147
Teisdale, Thomas, chapman: 'petty chapman', Lincoln St Martin, Lincs, 1619 Lincs RO Ad/Ac/15/159
Telford, Robert, gentleman, Leeds, Yorks, 1717 Borthwick Test C.P. 1717/15
Telier, William, Dunham, Stony, Ches, 1618 Cheshire RO (Name) W.C. 1617/18
Temple, John, Toynton, Low, Lincs, 1638 Lincs RO Ad/Ac/25/273
Templeman, John, Wilsthorpe, Lincs, 1646 Lincs RO Ad/Ac/28/69
Templeman, Thomas, Braceborough, Lincs, 1613 Lincs RO Ad/Ac/11/55
Templeman, Thomas, yeoman, Greatford, Lincs, 1623 Lincs RO Ad/Ac/18/91
Tems, see Wingham,
Tenby, Richard, husbandman, Goxhill, Lincs, 1669 Lincs RO Ad/Ac/33/140
Tenche, John ygr, Dover, Kent, 1614 CKS PRC20/3/13
Tenche, Richarde, gentleman, Sandwich, Kent, 1602 CKS PRC2/14/449
Tennard, William, Skirbeck, Lincs, 1634 Lincs RO Ad/Ac/24/164
Tenney, Thomas, Croft, Lincs, 1619 Lincs RO Ad/Ac/15/27
Tenpreman, Philip, Canterbury, Kent, 1735 CKS PRC19/6/80
Teptoe, John, husbandman, Gaddesden, Great, Herts, 1682 Herts RO AHH23/2376
Terell, Siprian, Durrington, Sussex, 1613 W. Suss RO EpIV/10/1/7
Terinden, John, Borden, Kent, 1594 CKS PRC2/7/283
Terrald, Robert, husbandman, Drayton, West, Berks, 1621 Wilts RO CC Sarum(+ name and date)
Terrall, Brooke, husbandman/yeoman, Farringdon, Great (Thrupp), Berks, 1681 Berks RO D/A3/4/130
Terrall, Thomas, Whaddon, Wilts, 1641 Wilts RO Arch. Sarum(+ name and date)
Terrell, Elizabeth, widow, Reading, Berks, 1675 Berks RO D/A1/128/104
Terrell, Nicholas, weaver: 'broad weaver', Reading St Giles, Berks, 1681 Berks RO D/A1/218/51C
Terrey, Thomas, Marston on Dove, Derby, 1685 LJRO/B/C/5/1685/96
Terreye, Anne, widow, Birchington, Kent, 1607 CKS PRC20/1/215
Terrie, Anthonie, Throwleigh, Kent, 1593 CKS PRC2/6/180
Terrie, Arnold, Postling, Kent, 1637 CKS PRC2/34/134
Terrie, John, Hollingbourne, Kent, 1605 CKS PRC20/1/59
Terrie, Thomas, Throwleigh, Kent, 1612 CKS PRC2/16/22
Terrill, Avery, yeoman, Hagbourne, Berks, 1641 Berks RO D/A1/217/160B
Terrold, Robert eld, yeoman, Capel le Ferne, Kent, 1637 CKS PRC2/34/135
Terroll, Richard,
Wilts 1614 Wilts RO CC Sarum(+ name and date)
Terry, Abigael, widow, Canterbury St Mary Bredin, Kent, 1662 CKS PRC1/9/63

Terry, Anthonie, Ospringe, Kent, 1595 CKS PRC2/7/121
Terry, Arnold, Faversham, Kent, 1628 CKS PRC2/29/103
Terry, Bartholomew, Blean, Kent, 1647 CKS PRC1/8/29
Terry, Charles, Somborne, Kings, Hants, 1672 Hants RO 21m65 D8/252
Terry, Edward, Linsted, Kent, 1665 CKS PRC1/10/96
Terry, Francis, Ospringe, Kent, 1669 CKS PRC1/14/112
Terry, Gabriel, Eastling, Kent, 1625 CKS PRC2/25/146
Terry, George, Throwleigh, Kent, 1670 CKS PRC1/15/68
Terry, John, Marden, Kent, 1632 CKS PRC2/31/162
Terry, John, yeoman, Herne, Kent, 1634 CKS PRC20/11/456
Terry, John, yeoman, Lydd, Kent, 1679 CKS PRC20/12/285
Terry, John, blacksmith, Marden, Kent, 1681 CKS PRC2/39/237
Terry, John, yeoman, Sutton Coldfield, Warks, 1772 LJRO/B/C/5/1772/82
Terry, John, Northampton, Northants, 1774 Northants RO X954/21/28
Terry, Joyce, Wormshill, Kent, 1668 CKS PRC1/13/131
Terry, Michael, cook, Oxford All Saints, Oxon, 1616 Bodleian HYP B9/96-97
Terry, Nathaniell, Westwell, Kent, 1620 CKS PRC20/4/377
Terry, Ralfe, yeoman, Woodnesborough, Kent, 1617 CKS PRC2/24/137
Terry, Richard, Faversham, Kent, 1623 CKS PRC2/24/144
Terry, Robert, surgeon/mr, Dover, Kent, 1665 CKS PRC19/3/84
Terry, Robert, Wye, Kent, 1700 CKS PRC2/42/160
Terry, Sara, spinster, St Laurence Thanet, Kent, 1629 CKS PRC2/30/136
Terry, Stephen, yeoman, Lydd, Kent, 1677 CKS PRC20/12/243
Terry, Thomas, Clewer, Berks, 1614 Berks RO D/A1/217/101B
Terry, Thomas, Faversham, Kent, 1622 CKS PRC2/24/143
Terry, Thomas, Preston next Wingham, Kent, 1671 CKS PRC2/35/96
Terry, William, Stone next Faversham, Kent, 1632 CKS PRC2/31/158
Terry, William, Elsted, Sussex, 1674 W. Suss RO EpI/33/1674/1
Terry, see Haggett,
Terrye, Arnold, maltster, Faversham, Kent, 1625 CKS PRC2/25/143
Terrye, Thomas, Throwleigh, Kent, 1602 CKS PRC2/12/357
Tetherden, Edward, Lydden, Kent, 1594 CKS PRC2/7/229
Tetley, Henry, Ashby de la Zouch, Leics, 1686 Leics RO Administrators Accounts 1682-86 f45
Tevelyn/Tieveline, Lewis, Canterbury St Alphege, Kent, 1600 CKS PRC21/15/236
Tew, Robert, Boscombe, Wilts, 1689 Wilts RO Arch. Sarum(+ name and date)
Tewe/Stamps, Mary, widow, Hampton Lovett, Worcs, 1647 Worcs RO 008.7 BA3585/837/bdl 1
Tewes, Richard, Purley, Berks, 1596 Berks RO D/A1/217/70B
Tewson, Richard, Pinchbeck, Lincs, 1612 Lincs RO Ad/Ac/11/26
Tey, William, yeoman, Deddington (Clifton), Oxon, 1668 Oxon RO MSS Wills 87/4/14
Teye, William, Berkhamsted St Peter, Herts, 1638 Herts RO AHH23/2350
Teynter, Gabriel, clergy: 'clerk', Barlavington, Sussex, 1633 W. Suss RO EpI/33/1633/20
Thacher, Robert, clergy: 'clerk', Pennard, East, Som, 1611 Somerset RO D/D/Cta/T37
Thackam, John, Wargrave, Berks, 1612 Berks RO D/A1/217/100B
Thacker, Christopher, Sibsey, Lincs, 1630s Lincs RO Ad/Ac/24/423
Thacker, Elizabeth, widow, Duffield (Heage), Derby, 1695 LJRO/B/C/5/1695/71
Thacker, Elizabeth, widow, Duffield (Heage), Derby, 1695 LJRO/B/C/5/1695/72
Thacker, Joane, Toynton All Saints, Lincs, 1624 Lincs RO Ad/Ac/18/105
Thacker, Ralphe, Holbeach, Lincs, 1619 Lincs RO Ad/Ac/15/229
Thacker, Samuel, brickmaker, Upton on Severn, Worcs, 1820 Worcs RO 008.7 BA3585/835/bdl 2
Thacker, Thomas eld, tailor, Coventry, Warks, 1777 LJRO/B/C/5/1777/36
Thackrah, Matthew, limeburner, Dewsbury, Yorks, 1825 Borthwick Test C.P. 1825/12
Thackray, Joseph, joiner, Wetherby, Yorks, 1774 Borthwick Test C.P. 1774/6
Thackwell, Edward, St Nicholas at Wade, Kent, 1627 CKS PRC20/7/231
Thackwray, Thomas, Crowle, Lincs, 1592 Lincs RO Ad/Ac/37/11
Thames, William, Sturton, Great, Lincs, 1639 Lincs RO Ad/Ac/26/286

[Tharpe:]
Tharpe, Richard, Tenterden, Kent, 1613 CKS PRC2/18/125
Thatcher, Amy, Sittingbourne, Kent, 1627 CKS PRC2/27/173
Thatcher, Edward, wheeler, Wolstone, Berks, 1674 Berks RO D/A1/218/33C
Thatcher, John, Goudhurst, Kent, 1587 CKS PRC2/4/398
Thatcher, John, Wolstone, Berks, 1597 Berks RO D/A1/217/77B
Thatcher, John, Rodmersham, Kent, 1625 CKS PRC2/24/119
Thatcher, John, Marden, Kent, 1638 CKS PRC2/34/131
Thatcher, John, Benenden, Kent, 1690 CKS PRC2/41/187
Thatcher, John, gentleman, Molash, Kent, 1710 CKS PRC1/17/15
Thatcher, John, Blagdon, Som, 1717 Somerset RO D/D/Cta/T19
Thatcher, Peter, clergy: 'clerk', Camel, Queen, Som, 1625 Somerset RO D/D/Cta/T1
Thatcher, Robert, Wormshill, Kent, 1616 CKS PRC2/24/147
Thatcher, Thomazine, widow, Sittingbourne, Kent, 1626 CKS PRC2/25/141
Thatcher, William, husbandman, Wolstone, Berks, 1597 Berks RO D/A1/217/73A
Thatcher, William, Abingdon, Berks, 1608 Berks RO D/A1/217/89B
Thayre, Joane, widow, Stratfield Saye, Hants, 1684 Hants RO 21m65 D8/345
the Meyer, Jacobb, merchant, Sandwich, Kent, 1594 CKS PRC2/6/296
Theaker, George, Owston, Lincs, 1663 Lincs RO Ad/Ac/41/97
Thealbie, Elizabeth, spinster, Coleby, Lincs, 1670 Lincs RO Ad/Ac/32/162
Thearle, William, Carisbrooke, Hants, 1625 Hants RO 21M65 D8/135
Theddam, Thomas, innkeeper, Wimborne Minster, Dors, 1684 Dorset RO PE/WM CP 2/4/94
Thelwall, Thomas, Coppenhall, Ches, 1618 Cheshire RO (Name) W.C. 1618
Thelwalle, Elizabeth, widow, 1592 Lancs RO (Name of Deceased) D.R.C.H. 1592
Theobald, John, Kingsnorth, Kent, 1680 CKS PRC2/39/115
Thew, Henry, Epworth, Lincs, 1679 Lincs RO Ad/Ac/43/85
Thewe, John, Greetham, Lincs, 1606 Lincs RO Ad/Ac/7/107
Thewston, Robert, Fleet, Lincs, 1650 Lincs RO Ad/Ac/30/20
Thick, Peter, Wincanton, Som, 1623 Somerset RO D/D/Cta/Q1
Thickbroome, John, Yardley, Worcs, 1681 Worcs RO 008.7 BA3585/830/54
Thickston, Thomas, Stainton by Langworth (Reasby), Lincs, 1612 Lincs RO Ad/Ac/10/127
Thimbleby, Richard, esquire, Irnham, Lincs, 1624 Lincs RO Ad/Ac/18/97
Thimielbie, John, esquire, Irnham, Lincs, 1626 Lincs RO Ad/Ac/20/81
Thirkill, William, blacksmith, Bredgar, Kent, 1667 CKS PRC1/11/165
Thirston, Thomas, Stainton by Langworth (Reasby), Lincs, 1612 Lincs RO Ad/Ac/11/164
Thirtill, Henry, blacksmith, Norwich St Julian, Norf, 1742 Norfolk RO ANW/23/23/79A
Thodell, Thomas, husbandman/widower, Redbourn, Herts, 1708 Herts RO ASA25/4609
Thodey, John, Hail Weston, Hunts, 1676 Hunts RO/Acc58/63(128)
Thomalyne, Gye, Milton next Sittingbourne, Kent, 1595 CKS PRC2/7/387
Thomas, Charles, Cury, Corn, 1612 Cornwall RO AP/T176/2
Thomas, Christopher, Teynham, Kent, 1612 CKS PRC2/16/62
Thomas, David, Llanfair-Fechan, Caern, 1693 NLW B 1693-51 Ac
Thomas, Edward, husbandman, Waithe, Lincs, 1615 Lincs RO Ad/Ac/15/301
Thomas, Edward, High Halden, Kent, 1638 CKS PRC1/1/91
Thomas, Edward, Llanfair Dyffryn Clwyd, Den, 1676 NLW B 1676-91
Thomas, Elizabeth, Hursley, Hants, 1681 Hants RO 21m65 D8/326
Thomas, Henry, Calne, Wilts, 1627 Wilts RO Miscellaneous Index (name + date)
Thomas, Henry, St Keverne, Corn, 1636 Cornwall RO AP/T290/3
Thomas, Joan, widow, Oxford, Oxon, 1623 Bodleian HYP B9/98-99
Thomas, John, Nantmel, Rad, NLW BR 1620/105 Ac
Thomas, John, cooper, Bristol St James, Glos, Bristol RO 1707/38
Thomas, John, carpenter, Linton, Kent, 1679 CKS PRC2/38/198
Thomas, John, Lenham, Kent, 1686 CKS PRC2/41/83
Thomas, John, Faversham, Kent, 1706 CKS PRC1/16/71
Thomas, Margaret, widow, Burpham, Sussex, 1677 W. Suss RO EpI/33/1677/1
Thomas, Marke, gentleman, New Romney, Kent, 1682 CKS PRC20/13/299

Thomas, Mellinie, widow, Bristol, Glos, Bristol RO 1685/CP
Thomas, Morgan, Frome Selwood, Som, 1641 Somerset RO D/D/Cta/T14
Thomas, Richard, clergy: 'clerk/vicar', Muchelney, Som, 1619 Somerset RO D/D/Cta/T29
Thomas, Richard, Potterne, Wilts, 1624 Wilts RO CC Sarum(+ name and date)
Thomas, Richard, Tenterden, Kent, 1626 CKS PRC2/25/139
Thomas, Richard, university: 'commoner/M.A.', Oxford (Lincoln College), Oxon, 1668 Bodleian HYP B9/100
Thomas, Robert, Wendron, Corn, 1615 Cornwall RO AP/T234/2
Thomas, Samuel, Norton Folgate, London & Middlesex, 1718 PRO PROB5/1732
Thomas, Thomas, Hartlip, Kent, 1632 CKS PRC2/31/159
Thomas, William, Milton next Sittingbourne, Kent, 1639 CKS PRC20/11/450
Thomas, William, innholder, Warwick, Warks, 1735 Worcs RO 008.7 BA3585/836/bdl 2
Thomas/Headach, Augustine, Reading, Berks, 1678 Berks RO D/A1/218/36C
Thomas/Headach, Frances, spinster, Reading St Giles, Berks, 1639 Berks RO D/A1/217/157B
Thomas/Stephens, Elizabeth, widow, Teynham, Kent, 1612 CKS PRC2/16/37
Thomas, ap, Richard, Cookham, Berks, 1595 Berks RO D/A1/173/55C
Thomas, ap, Richard, Maidenhead, Berks, 1596 Berks RO D/A1/217/69
Thomas, ferch, Llyky, Llanfaes, Breck, 1634 NLW BR 1634/56 Ac
Thomasman, Richard, Broughton, Nether, Leics, 1673 Leics RO Administrators Accounts 1667-72 f104
Thomingoe/Domingoe, Jacob, physician: 'rt worshipful, dr in phisicke', Canterbury St Margaret, Kent, 1628 CKS PRC2/29/99
Thomlin, John, Minster in Thanet, Kent, 1598 CKS PRC2/10/349
Thomlin, Marye, Sittingbourne, Kent, 1598 CKS PRC2/10/425
Thomlyne, Richard, Hothfield, Kent, 1598 CKS PRC2/9/363
Thompsett, John, Maidstone, Kent, 1678 CKS PRC20/12/286
Thompson, Agnes, Woodnesborough, Kent, 1597 CKS PRC2/10/68
Thompson, Alexander, Limber Magna, Lincs, 1635 Lincs RO Ad/Ac/24/341
Thompson, Alexander, cordwainer, Boston, Lincs, 1666 Lincs RO Ad/Ac/32/110
Thompson, Ambrose, Grantham, Lincs, 1618 Lincs RO Ad/Ac/14/188
Thompson, Brudnall, Kirkby Green, Lincs, 1651 Lincs RO Ad/Ac/29/131
Thompson, Christopher, labourer, Sutterton, Lincs, 1605 Lincs RO Ad/Ac/6/137
Thompson, Christopher, Fulbeck, Lincs, 1611 Lincs RO Ad/Ac/10/81
Thompson, David, Patrixbourne, Kent, 1589 CKS PRC2/5/430
Thompson, Edward, esquire, Settrington, Yorks, Borthwick Test C.P. 1739/14
Thompson, Fanny, widow, Sutton, Yorks, 1812 Borthwick Test C.P. 1812/2
Thompson, Francis, Limber Magna, Lincs, 1683 Lincs RO Ad/Ac/44/101
Thompson, George, Lincoln St Michael, Lincs, 1627 Lincs RO Ad/Ac/20b/19
Thompson, George, Rainham, Kent, 1699 CKS PRC2/42/162
Thompson, Henry, Sutton St James, Lincs, 1607 Lincs RO Ad/Ac/8a/43
Thompson, Iden, widow, Dover, Kent, 1677 CKS PRC20/12/223
Thompson, Jane, Coombes, Sussex, 1583 W. Suss RO EpI/33/1583/7
Thompson, John, Aswarby, Lincs, 1612 Lincs RO Ad/Ac/11/118
Thompson, John, Canterbury St Mary-Magdalen Burgate, Kent, 1626 CKS PRC2/27/174
Thompson, John, Stickford, Lincs, 1649 Lincs RO Ad/Ac/30/53
Thompson, John, bookseller, Lincoln St Martin, Lincs, 1650 Lincs RO Ad/Ac/29/60
Thompson, John, scrivener, St Margaret Westminster, London & Middlesex, 1696 PRO PROB32/39/68
Thompson, John, esquire, Selby, Yorks, 1822 Borthwick Test C.P. 1822/3
Thompson, Joseph, Bucknall, Lincs, 1645 Lincs RO Ad/Ac/28/75
Thompson, Lawrence, Rowley Regis, Staffs, 1684 Worcs RO 008.7 BA3585/837/bdl 4
Thompson, Margret, widow, Petham, Kent, 1596 CKS PRC2/8/487
Thompson, Martin, Boston, Lincs, 1624 Lincs RO Ad/Ac/19A/34
Thompson, Phillipp, miller, Thimbleby, Lincs, 1642 Lincs RO Ad/Ac/28/49
Thompson, Richard, Gainsborough, Lincs, 1624 Lincs RO Ad/Ac/39/196

[Thompson:]
Thompson, Robert, Owston (West Butterwick), Lincs, 1646 Lincs RO Ad/Ac/40/143
Thompson, Robert, yeoman, Normanby, Lincs, 1668 Lincs RO Ad/Ac/33/17
Thompson, Sarah, mrs/widow, Wye, Kent, 1645 CKS PRC1/7/68
Thompson, Stephen, university: 'Fellow of St John's College, Cambridge/M.A.', Cambridge (St John's College), Cambs, 1599 CUL V.C.Acc./Box1/50
Thompson, Stephen, St Laurence Thanet, Kent, 1681 CKS PRC2/39/241
Thompson, Thomas, Lyminge, Kent, 1633 CKS PRC20/11/460
Thompson, Thomas, Horbling, Lincs, 1639 Lincs RO Ad/Ac/26/201
Thompson, Thomas, baker, Denton, Lincs, 1668 Lincs RO Ad/Ac/33/52
Thompson, Thomas, Grayingham, Lincs, 1679 Lincs RO Ad/Ac/43/80
Thompson, Thomas, Warden, Kent, 1680 CKS PRC2/39/112
Thompson, Thomas William, gentleman, Selby, Yorks, 1822 Borthwick Test C.P. 1822/1
Thompson, Thomlinson, widow, Limber Magna, Lincs, 1673 Lincs RO Ad/Ac/34/8
Thompson, William, Threckingham, Lincs, 1624 Lincs RO Ad/Ac/18/101
Thompson, William, Saxilby, Lincs, 1626 Lincs RO Ad/Ac/39/130
Thompson, William, Nettleham, Lincs, 1668 Lincs RO Ad/Ac/33/77
Thompson, William, husbandman, Langton by Wragby, Lincs, 1670 Lincs RO Ad/Ac/32/153
Thompson, William, stationer, Harborough, Market, Leics, 1672 Leics RO Administrators Accounts 1667-72 f75
Thompson, William, Faversham, Kent, 1676 CKS PRC2/37/99
Thompson, see Bydall, Mason & Thorpe,
Thomson, Agnes, widow, Thimbleby, Lincs, 1579? Lincs RO Ad/Ac/2b/8
Thomson, Constance, widow, Millbrook, Hants, 1620 Hants RO 1617 AD90/3
Thomson, John, Sandwich St Clement, Kent, 1604 CKS PRC2/13/402
Thomson, Richard, university: 'Fellow of Clare College, Cambridge/rector/M.A.' Cambridge (Clare College), Cambs, 1613 CUL V.C.Acc./Box1/49
Thomson, William, Canterbury St Paul, Kent, 1617 CKS PRC2/24/139
Thorisby, Samuel, Newton St Faith, Norf, 1738 Norfolk RO ANW/23/22A/15
Thornbery, Samuell, St Matthew Friday Street, London & Middlesex, 1710 PRO PROB5/1604
Thornbury, George, Cheadle, Staffs, 1675 LJRO:cards/1675/50
Thorndyke, Francis, Croft, Lincs, 1627 Lincs RO Ad/Ac/20b/60
Thorndyke, Nicholas, Carlton, Great, Lincs, 1600 Lincs RO Ad/Ac/5/25
Thorndyke, William, Carlton, Little, Lincs, 1601 Lincs RO Ad/Ac/5/93
Thorne, Anne, Sherbourne, Dors, 1627 Wilts RO Miscellaneous Index (name + date)
Thorne, George eld, Portishead, Som, 1662 Somerset RO D/D/Cta/T31
Thorne, John, yeoman, Shiplake, Oxon, 1640 Oxon RO MSS Wills 66/2/30
Thorne, Robert, Bisham, Berks, 1678 Berks RO D/A1/218/45C
Thornebrugh, John, farmer, Corringham, Lincs, 1703? Lincs RO Ad/Ac/45/88
Thornedall, Gregory, gentleman, Eton, Bucks, 1671 PRO PROB5/917
Thornehill, Henry, colonel, Glentigh, Kent, 1691 PRO PROB5/1227
Thornell, Danyell, Sandwich, Kent, 1603 CKS PRC2/14/446
Thornell, Richard, Calcethorpe, Lincs, 1638 Lincs RO Ad/Ac/25/322
Thornell, Thomas, Appledore, Kent, 1596 CKS PRC2/9/205
Thornell, Thomas, clergy: 'clerk', Lincoln, Lincs, 1662 Lincs RO Ad/Ac/32/33
Thornes, Benjamine, Tallington, Lincs, 1639? Lincs RO Ad/Ac/26/321
Thornes, Hyppolite, gentleman, Deeping, Market, Lincs, 1613 Lincs RO Ad/Ac/11/67
Thornes, Ralph, yeoman, Shipley, Sussex, 1672 W. Suss RO EpI/33/1672/11
Thornes, Thomas, esquire, Ruyton in the Eleven Towns (Shell), Shrops, 1682 LJRO/B/C/5/1681/38
Thorneton, Jethro, Derby, Derby, 1680 LJRO:cards/1680/35
Thornhill, Edward, Willoughton, Lincs, 1681 Lincs RO Ad/Ac/34/73
Thornley, Elizabeth, widow, Bath, Som, 1729 Somerset RO D/D/Cta/T20
Thornley, Vallentine, Wainfleet All Saints, Lincs, 1638 Lincs RO Ad/Ac/25/184
Thornton, Benjamin, St Albans St Michaels, Herts, Herts RO ASA25/4968
Thornton, Edward, Winterbourne Gunner, Wilts, 1674 Wilts RO Arch. Sarum(+ name and date)

Thornton, Gregorye, Seasalter, Kent, 1599 CKS PRC2/11/308
Thornton, John,
Northants 1779 Northants RO X954/21/37
Thornton, Launcelot, Belton All Saints, Lincs, 1610 Lincs RO Ad/Ac/8a/314
Thornton, Ralph, merchant, Chester, Ches, 1585 Cheshire RO (Name) W.C. 1585
Thornton, Richard, husbandman, Althorpe (Amcotts), Lincs, 1669? Lincs RO Ad/Ac/33/162
Thornton, Robarte, Willesborough, Kent, 1594 CKS PRC2/7/287
Thornton, Roberte, Snave, Kent, 1591 CKS PRC2/5/442
Thornton, Thomas, husbandman, Hawkhurst, Kent, 1683 CKS PRC2/40/157
Thornton, William, Whitton, Lincs, 1635 Lincs RO Ad/Ac/40/103
Thornton, William, Burton Pedwardine, Lincs, 1637 Lincs RO Ad/Ac/25/120
Thorogood, see Donnell,
Thorold, Elizabeth, widow, Fulbeck, Lincs, 1671 Lincs RO Ad/Ac/33/191
Thorold, Samuell, Thoresby, North, Lincs, 1652 Lincs RO Ad/Ac/29/28
Thorold, Thomas, gentleman, Boston, Lincs, 1602 Lincs RO Ad/Ac/5/129
Thorowgood, Edward, innholder, Faversham, Kent, 1675 CKS PRC2/36/247
Thorowgood, John, Deal, Kent, 1626 CKS PRC20/7/124
Thorowgood, Robert, husbandman, Luddenham, Kent, 1683 CKS PRC2/40/156
Thorp, Henry, Stratfield Saye, Hants, 1624 Hants RO 21M65 D8/92
Thorpe, Christopher, Waddington, Lincs, 1612 Lincs RO Ad/Ac/11/198
Thorpe, Daniel, yeoman, Asgarby, Lincs, 1623 Lincs RO Ad/Ac/17/64
Thorpe, Dorothie, widow, Evedon, Lincs, 1627 Lincs RO Ad/Ac/20/83
Thorpe, George, Taynton, Oxon, 1629 Oxon RO MSS Wills 300/4/39
Thorpe, Henry, Washingborough, Lincs, 1603 Lincs RO Ad/Ac/5/167
Thorpe, Isaac, husbandman, Prestwich, Lancs, 1676 Lancs RO (Name of Deceased) D.R.C.H. 1676
Thorpe, John, High Halden, Kent, 1601 CKS PRC2/12/361
Thorpe, John, Bytham, Castle, Lincs, 1635 Lincs RO Ad/Ac/24/441
Thorpe, John, Boston, Lincs, 1648 Lincs RO Ad/Ac/30/267
Thorpe, John, yeoman, Smarden, Kent, 1674 CKS PRC2/36/134
Thorpe, John, Epworth, Lincs, 1675 Lincs RO Ad/Ac/35/89
Thorpe, John, yeoman, Benson (Roke), Oxon, 1685 Oxon RO MSS Wills Pec 71/6/23
Thorpe, Mary, widow, Taynton, Oxon, 1641 Oxon RO MSS Wills 175/1/11
Thorpe, Richard, Markby, Lincs, 1620 Lincs RO Ad/Ac/16/96
Thorpe, Richard, Bennington, Long, Lincs, 1649 Lincs RO Ad/Ac/30/115
Thorpe, Robert, Oldham, Lancs, 1664 Lancs RO (Name of Deceased) D.R.C.H. 1664
Thorpe, Thomas, Kirkby la Thorpe, Lincs, 1618 Lincs RO Ad/Ac/14/260
Thorpe, Thomas, Heckington, Lincs, 1620 Lincs RO Ad/Ac/16/93
Thorpe, William, carpenter, Ashford, Kent, 1681 CKS PRC2/39/247
Thorpe/Thompson, Awdrey, widow, Coleby, Lincs, 1627 Lincs RO Ad/Ac/20b/92
Thorppe, Robert, Ruskington, Lincs, 1601 Lincs RO Ad/Ac/5/87
Thrale, John, St Albans St Peters, Herts, 1610 Herts RO ASA25/4785
Thrale, Thomas, Sandridge, Herts, 1601 Herts RO ASA25/1808
Threed, Henry + Margaret, Chartham, Kent, 1617 CKS PRC2/24/136
Threseell, see Throstle,
Thrift, Mable, widow, St James Westminster, London & Middlesex, 1716 Greater London RO AM/PP/Box 1720-1723 pt (uncatalogued)
Thrift, Richard, Lambourn, Berks, 1592 Berks RO D/A1/217/60B
Thringe, Henry, Bemerton (Quidhampton), Wilts, 1639 Wilts RO Arch. Sarum(+ name and date)
Throckkmorton, Robert, gentleman, Offord Cluney, Hunts, 1683 Hunts RO/Acc58/200(198)
Throckly, Henry, ferryman, Queenborough, Kent, 1680 CKS PRC2/38/197
Throckmorton, Albain, gentleman, Offord Cluney, Hunts, 1682 Hunts RO/Acc58/169(111)
Throckmorton, Francis, St Martin in the Fields, London & Middlesex, 1687 Greater London RO AM/PP/Box 1685-1694 pt (uncatalogued)
Throstle/Frosle, Bridget, widow, Ellington, Hunts, 1676 Hunts RO/Acc58/48(27)

[Throstle/Threseell:]
Throstle/Threseell, Bridget, widow, Ellington, Hunts, 1667 Hunts RO/Acc58/13(25)
Throston, Thomas, St Johns Thanet, Kent, 1599 CKS PRC2/10/307
Throwley, see Drewrie,
Throwlie, see Drewry,
Thruppe, William, Wichenford, Worcs, 1675 Worcs RO 008.7 BA3585/835/bdl 3
Thunder, John, Faversham, Kent, 1616 CKS PRC2/24/114
Thunder, William, Staplehurst, Kent, 1614 CKS PRC2/18/12
Thunder, William, clothier, Marden, Kent, 1641 CKS PRC1/6/28
Thurban, Mary, Arundel, Sussex, 1629 W. Suss RO EpI/33/1629/40
Thurbarne, George, Hythe St Leonard, Kent, 1683 CKS PRC20/13/374
Thurbarne, John, minor?, Stone in Oxney, Kent, 1632 CKS PRC2/34/136
Thurbarne, Margaret, Ivychurch, Kent, 1673 CKS PRC20/12/105
Thurbarne, Martha, widow, New Romney, Kent, 1604 CKS PRC21/17/378
Thurbarne, Peter, New Romney, Kent, 1680 CKS PRC20/12/325
Thurbarne, Robert, Old Romney, Kent, 1617 CKS PRC2/24/131
Thurbarne, William, Hythe St Leonard, Kent, 1620 CKS PRC20/4/379
Thurbarne, William, yeoman, Lympne, Kent, 1676 CKS PRC2/37/100
Thurgarland, Roger, Folkingham, Lincs, 1602 Lincs RO Ad/Ac/5/554
Thurgate, Thomas, Broughton, Lincs, 1618 Lincs RO Ad/Ac/8b/133
Thurlbye, William, Ailton, Hunts, 1625 Lincs RO Ad/Ac/19B/80
Thurley, Bartholomew, Rasen, Market, Lincs, 1683 Lincs RO Ad/Ac/44/117
Thurley, Isabell, widow, Linwood, Lincs, 1636 Lincs RO Ad/Ac/24/314
Thurlie, Richard, Gainsborough, Lincs, 1623 Lincs RO Ad/Ac/40/83
Thurman, Christopher, husbandman, Burghfield, Berks, 1682 Berks RO D/A1/218/58A
Thurman, Mary, widow, Nuneaton, Warks, 1797 LJRO/B/C/5/1797/1201
Thurston, John eld, Leeds, Kent, 1616 CKS PRC2/24/122
Thurston, Robert, Faversham, Kent, 1638 CKS PRC2/34/130
Thurston, Thomas, Stalisfield, Kent, 1633 CKS PRC2/32/124
Thurstons, Richard, Covington, Hunts, 1679 Hunts RO/Acc58/135(188)
Thwayts, William, Canterbury St Dunstan Without, Kent, 1629 CKS PRC2/30/135
Thynne, Thomas, factor & Smyrna merchant, Levant Co., 1685 PRO PROB32/25/468
Tib, Elizabeth, widow, St Johns Thanet, Kent, 1678 CKS PRC2/38/80
Tibb, Jesse, mariner, St Johns Thanet, Kent, 1676 CKS PRC2/36/
Tibb, Joan, widow, Lyford, Berks, 1594 Berks RO D/A1/217/66B
Tibball, John, Ickham, Kent, 1626 CKS PRC20/7/279
Tibball/Staple/Brett, Maryan, Herne, Kent, 1593 CKS PRC21/12/329
Tibbett, Edward, Dundry, Som, 1600 Somerset RO D/D/Cta/T40
Tibbett, Richard, Farleigh Hungerford, Som, 1638 Somerset RO D/D/Cta/T5
Tiboult, see De Roo,
Tickner, Edward, St Laurence Thanet, Kent, 1685 CKS PRC20/13/470
Tickner, Mary, Stoke, North, Sussex, W. Suss RO EpI/33/1621/2
Ticknor, John, Ferring (Kingston), Sussex, 1611 W. Suss RO EpI/33/1611/7
Ticknor, Roberte, Hernhill, Kent, 1592 CKS PRC21/11/296
Tidball, John, Huntspill, Som, 1740 Somerset RO D/D/Cta/T21
Tidd, Edward, Leasingham, Lincs, 1627 Lincs RO Ad/Ac/20b/72
Tiddeman, Edward, husbandman, Chislet, Kent, 1712 CKS PRC1/17/64
Tiddeman, Edward, Chislet, Kent, 1715 CKS PRC1/17/64a
Tiddeman, Henry, Dover, Kent, 1602 CKS PRC21/16/55
Tiddiman, Henrye, Folkestone, Kent, 1610 CKS PRC20/2/172
Tidye, Richard, Rusper, Sussex, 1595 W. Suss RO EpI/33/1595/8
Tierst, John, Rainham, Kent, 1599 CKS PRC2/10/311
Tiesdall, Elizabeth, widow, Tydd St Mary, Lincs, 1619 Lincs RO Ad/Ac/15/157
Tieveline, see Tevelyn,
Tiffin, William, Sandwich, Kent, 1617 CKS PRC2/24/132
Tilberow, Richard, gentleman, Stoughton, Sussex, 1635 W. Suss RO EpI/33/1635/24

Tilby, George, butcher, Faversham, Kent, 1664 CKS PRC1/10/97
Tilby, Hugh, Hollingbourne, Kent, 1699 CKS PRC19/5/67
Tilby, Robert, yeoman, Tenterden, Kent, 1666 CKS PRC1/11/89
Tilden, Edward, Leeds, Kent, 1671 CKS PRC2/35/93
Tilden, Elizabeth, widow, Sandwich, Kent, 1638 CKS PRC2/34/292
Tilden, Henry, husbandman, Rainham, Kent, 1677 CKS PRC2/37/201
Tilden, Jeames, Birchington, Kent, 1606 CKS PRC20/1/130
Tilden, John, Newenden, Kent, 1604 CKS PRC2/13/407
Tilden, John, grocer, Sandwich, Kent, 1637 CKS PRC2/34/129
Tilden, John, Charing, Kent, 1669 CKS PRC19/4/62
Tilden, Richard, Boxley, Kent, 1611 CKS PRC2/16/193
Tilden, Samuel, Tenterden, Kent, 1625 CKS PRC20/7/285
Tilden, William, Langley, Kent, 1615 CKS PRC2/24/99
Tilden, William eld, Staplehurst, Kent, 1671 CKS PRC2/35/97
Tiler, Elizabeth ygr, Hackington, Kent, 1638 CKS PRC2/34/120
Tilghman, Ellenor, widow, Eastchurch, Sheppey, Kent, 1638 CKS PRC2/34/293
Tilghman, Richard, gentleman, Preston next Faversham, Kent, 1633 CKS PRC20/11/462
Tilgman, Edward, mariner, St Peter in Thanet, Kent, 1679 CKS PRC2/38/195
Till, James, Stone, Staffs, 1675 LJRO:cards/1675/51
Till, John, Thorney, West, Sussex, 1630 W. Suss RO EpI/33/1630/11
Till, Richard, Dean, West, Sussex, 1674 W. Suss RO EpI/33/1674/9
Till, Thomas, Thorney, West, Sussex, 1625 W. Suss RO EpI/33/1625/2
Till, William, Canterbury St John's Hospital, Kent, 1591 CKS PRC21/10/232
Till, see Boulton,
Tilladam, William, clergy: 'clerk', Edington, Wilts, 1639 Wilts RO Arch. Sarum(+ name and date)
Tilley, Joseph, Rogate, Sussex, 1684 W. Suss RO EpI/33/1684/21
Tilliard, Christopher, butcher, Oxford (University), Oxon, Bodleian HYP B9/101-102
Tillie, Richard, Sidlesham, Sussex, 1625 W. Suss RO EpI/33/1625/8
Tillie, Robert, Chewton Mendip, Som, 1619 Somerset RO D/D/Cta/T36
Tillison, John, St Gregory by St Pauls, London & Middlesex, 1688 PRO PROB5/1398
Tillman, Alice, widow, Faversham, Kent, 1678 CKS PRC2/38/78
Tillney, William, Rickmansworth, Herts, 1636 Herts RO ASA25/4921
Tillott, John, carpenter, Bury St Edmunds, Suff, 1775 Suff RO(B) IC500/3/52/4
Tillson, Thomas, Pinchbeck, Lincs, 1613 Lincs RO Ad/Ac/12/116
Tilman, Edward, Minster in Sheppey, Kent, 1621 CKS PRC2/24/149
Tilman, Isaacke, Pluckley, Kent, 1624 CKS PRC2/24/157
Tilman, John, Hythe St Leonard, Kent, 1641 CKS PRC19/2/42
Tilman, John, Borden, Kent, 1682 CKS PRC2/40/21
Tilman, Richard, Pluckley, Kent, 1606 CKS PRC2/13/397
Tilman, Robert, husbandman, Bethersden, Kent, 1662 CKS PRC1/9/64
Tilman, Stephen, Minster in Sheppey, Kent, CKS PRC1/15/123
Tilney, James, Stepney, London & Middlesex, 1704 Lambeth Palace Arches G54/4
Tilson, Richard, Minster in Thanet, Kent, 1598 CKS PRC2/10/133
Tilson, Richard, Earl Shilton, Leics, 1665 Leics RO Administrators Accounts C17th f19
Tilson, Roberte, Surfleet, Lincs, 1668 Lincs RO Ad/Ac/33/37
Tilson, William, Gedney, Lincs, 1603 Lincs RO Ad/Ac/5/387
Tilt, Joyce, widow, Birmingham, Warks, 1741 LJRO/B/C/5/1741/241
Timmins, John, gentleman, Atherstone, Warks, 1820 LJRO/B/C/5/1820/70
Timmis, Richard, Mucclestone (Aston), Staffs, 1738 LJRO/B/C/5/1738/70
Tincker, Philip, Lavington, West, Wilts, 1619 Wilts RO CC Sarum(+ name and date)
Tindall, Henry, St Giles without Cripplegate, London & Middlesex, 1702 PRO PROB5/1418
Tindall, Henry, St John Zachary, London & Middlesex, 1703 PRO PROB5/1417
Tindall, Thomas, Sandwich St Clement, Kent, 1608 CKS PRC2/14/431
Tindall, Thomas, grocer, Sutton Valence, Kent, 1641 CKS PRC19/1/86

[Tingcombe:]
Tingcombe, John, apothecary, Spilsby, Lincs, 1671 Lincs RO Ad/Ac/32/235
Tingle, Urias, Donington, Lincs, 1611 Lincs RO Ad/Ac/10/101
Tingle, Walter, Swineshead, Lincs, 1664 Lincs RO Ad/Ac/32/54
Tinley, Richard, Billingshurst, Sussex, 1682 W. Suss RO EpI/33/1682/26
Tipper, Robert, Seend, Wilts, 1633 Wilts RO Arch. Sarum(+ name and date)
Tipper, see Wadman,
Tippinge, Frances, Stokenchurch (Chequers), Oxon, 1643 Oxon RO MSS Wills 175/1/14
Tipson, Robert, husbandman, Charney Bassett, Berks, 1594 Berks RO D/A1/217/67B
Tisdale, Samuell, Minster in Thanet, Kent, 1615 CKS PRC2/24/129
Tise, James, yeoman, Bromham, Wilts, 1622 Wilts RO Arch. Wilts.(+ name and date)
Tise, Joane, Rowde, Wilts, 1631 Wilts RO Arch. Wilts.(+ name and date)
Tiser, Francis, Bridge, Kent, 1605 CKS PRC2/13/404
Tissard, Nicholas, Waltham St Lawrence, Berks, 1609 Berks RO D/A1/217/94B
Titbury, Thomas, Bucklebury (Marlston), Berks, 1647 Berks RO D/A1/217/173B
Tith/Clifford, Susanne, Blean, Kent, 1628 CKS PRC2/29/100
Titherton, James, Lydd, Kent, 1630 CKS PRC20/9/446
Titherton, Mark, Wye, Kent, 1638 CKS PRC2/34/132
Titley, Richard, Haywood, Staffs, 1685 LJRO/B/C/5/1684/79
Tittensor, Thomas, Stoke-upon-Trent, Staffs, 1675 LJRO:cards/1675/52
Tizard, Ann, Merriott, Som, Somerset RO D/D/Cta/T34
Todd, John, husbandman, Bicker, Lincs, 1619 Lincs RO Ad/Ac/15/169
Todd, John, Salisbury, Wilts, 1624 Wilts RO Miscellaneous Index (name + date)
Todd/Christopher, Alice, Barkwith, Lincs, 1671 Lincs RO Ad/Ac/33/187
Todde, Robarte, St Johns Thanet, Kent, 1597 CKS PRC2/9/201
Toddy, Sara, spinster, Sandwich St Mary, Kent, 1623 CKS PRC2/26/103
Todgoose, John, Walberton, Sussex, 1595 W. Suss RO EpI/33/1594/7
Todgose, Thomas, Walberton, Sussex, 1606 W. Suss RO EpI/33/1606/17
Todkill, Lawrence, London Thorpe, Lincs, 1600 Lincs RO Ad/Ac/5/342
Toft, John, Napton on the Hill, Warks, 1683 LJRO/B/C/5/1682/97
Toft, John, yeoman, Shuttington (Alvecote Heath), Warks, 1796 LJRO/B/C/5/1796/256
Tofte, Thomas, Torrington, West, Lincs, 1649 Lincs RO Ad/Ac/30/7
Tointon, Francis, Immingham, Lincs, 1629 Lincs RO Ad/Ac/22/55
Toke, Francis, mr, Otham, Kent, 1694 CKS PRC2/42/95
Toke, John, clergy: 'clerk', Milsted, Kent, 1670 CKS PRC1/15/69
Toke, Nicholas, clergy: 'clerk', Eastwell, Kent, 1670 CKS PRC1/15/70
Tokin, Edward, Haltham on Bain, Lincs, 1624 Lincs RO Ad/Ac/19A/61
Tokin, William, gentleman, Halton Holgate, Lincs, 1680 Lincs RO Ad/Ac/34/60
Toldervey, Walter, gentleman, Inkpen, Berks, Berks RO D/A1/217/135B
Tolfree, Olliver, Worthy Headbourn, Hants, 1663 Hants RO 21M65 D8/181
Tolfrey, Nicholas, grocer, Newbury, Berks, 1679 Berks RO D/A1/218/44C
Tolherst, Edmund ygr, Rolvenden, Kent, 1639 CKS PRC19/1/20
Tolherst, John, Rolvenden, Kent, 1595 CKS PRC2/7/416
Tolherst, Nicholas, Stone in Oxney, Kent, 1633 CKS PRC2/31/164
Tolherst, Thomas, Rolvenden, Kent, 1616 CKS PRC2/24/103
Tolherst, Thomas eld, yeoman, Rolvenden, Kent, 1670 CKS PRC1/15/71
Tolherst, William, Rolvenden, Kent, 1624 CKS PRC2/24/155
Tolherst, William, Rolvenden, Kent, 1626 CKS PRC2/25/145
Tolherst, William, butcher, Staplehurst, Kent, 1668 CKS PRC1/13/132
Tolherst, Wyllyam, Benenden, Kent, 1593 CKS PRC2/6/406
Tolkfield, Joseph, Tring (Hastoe), Herts, 1688 Herts RO AHH23/2383
Tolley, mr,
Oxon Bodleian HYP B9/103-104
Tollie, Ombersley, Worcs, Worcs RO 008.7 BA3585/839/446
Tollie, Ralph, husbandman, Upton Snodsbury, Worcs, 1601 Worcs RO 008.7 BA3585/838/214
Tolly, Thomas, Worcester St Martin, Worcs, Worcs RO 008.7 BA3585/834/439

Toly, Thomas, Langton by Wragby, Lincs, 1569 Lincs RO Ad/Ac/2C/173
Tomas, John, Stone in Oxney, Kent, 1627 CKS PRC2/28/124
Tomasman, see Simpson,
Tomkin, Guy, Milton next Sittingbourne, Kent, 1595 CKS PRC2/7/405
Tomkin, Thomas, Withiel, Corn, 1613 Cornwall RO AP/T215
Tomkin, Thomas, warrener, Ashby de la Launde, Lincs, 1639 Lincs RO Ad/Ac/26/136
Tomkin, William, Boxley, Kent, 1667 CKS PRC1/12/89
Tomkins, Mary, widow, St James Garlickhithe, London & Middlesex, 1732 Lambeth Palace Arches G103/7
Tomkinson, Joseph, yeoman, Leek (Endon, Lane Head), Staffs, 1832 LJRO/B/C/5/1832/49a
Tomlin, Christopher, Swalecliffe, Kent, 1635 CKS PRC2/33/130
Tomlin, George, maltster, Newington next Sittingbourne, Kent, 1675 CKS PRC2/36/250
Tomlin, Mary, St Peter in Thanet, Kent, 1679 CKS PRC2/38/199
Tomlin, Stephen, St Peter in Thanet, Kent, 1614 CKS PRC2/24/104
Tomlin, Stephen, gentleman, Milton next Sittingbourne, Kent, 1681 CKS PRC2/39/113
Tomlin/Sandwill, Mary, wife,
Kent 1614 CKS PRC2/24/105
Tomlin, see Marston,
Tomlinson, Henrie, Croft, Lincs, 1640 Lincs RO Ad/Ac/27/126
Tomlinson, Henrye, Althorpe (Amcotts), Lincs, 1608 Lincs RO Ad/Ac/37/264
Tomlinson, John, Blyton, Lincs, 1607 Lincs RO Ad/Ac/37/235
Tomlinson, John, Scotton, Lincs, 1611 Lincs RO Ad/Ac/8a/340
Tomlinson, John, yeoman, Blyton, Lincs, 1673 Lincs RO Ad/Ac/35/39
Tomlinson, John, farmer, Sandon (Hardewick), Staffs, 1805 LJRO/B/C/5/1805/50
Tomlinson, Robert, Walton upon Trent, Derby, 1684 LJRO/B/C/5/1685/98
Tomlinson, Robert, Walton upon Trent, Derby, 1694 LJRO/B/C/5/1694/65
Tomlinson, Samuel, farmer, Burton Joyce, Notts, 1822 Borthwick Test C.P. 1821/10
Tomlinson, Thomas, Sutterton, Lincs, 1594 Lincs RO Ad/Ac/5/515
Tomlison, John, Wednesbury, Staffs, 1684 LJRO/B/C/5/1684/80
Tomlison, Robert, Walton upon Trent, Derby, 1687 LJRO/B/C/5/1687/82
Tomlyn, George, Bobbing, Kent, 1612 CKS PRC20/2/314
Tomlyn, George, Minster in Thanet, Kent, 1637 CKS PRC2/34/137
Tomlyn, James, Sturry, Kent, 1620 CKS PRC20/5/190
Tomlyn, John, Upton Noble, Som, 1638 Somerset RO D/D/Cta/T7
Tomlyn, Mary, Maidstone, Kent, 1624 CKS PRC20/6/191
Tomlyn, Stephen, St Johns Thanet, Kent, 1616 CKS PRC2/24/109
Tomlyn, Thomas, Bobbing, Kent, 1582 CKS PRC2/2/229
Tomlyn, William, husbandman, Grandborough, Bucks, 1578 Herts RO ASA25/936
Tomlynson, Mary, widow, Mancetter, Warks, 1673 LJRO:cards/1673/11
Tomlynson, Robert, Walton upon Trent, Derby, 1666 LJRO:cards/1666/15
Tomlynson, Thomas sen, Ashbourne, Derby, 1672 LJRO:cards/1672/59
Tommes, Richard, Hilmarton, Wilts, 1631 Wilts RO Arch. Wilts.(+ name and date)
Tommes, Richard, husbandman, Dover, Kent, 1639 CKS PRC19/1/87
Tommes, Thomas, Charlton, Wilts, 1639 Wilts RO Arch. Wilts.(+ name and date)
Tomms, William, yeoman, Eythorne, Kent, 1639 CKS PRC1/3/52
Tompson, Alexander, Frodingham, Lincs, 1602 Lincs RO Ad/Ac/37/122
Tompson, Alice, Maidstone, Kent, 1629 CKS PRC20/8/452
Tompson, Cutbert, Kirkby la Thorpe, Lincs, 1646 Lincs RO Ad/Ac/28/211
Tompson, Edward, Harrietsham, Kent, 1620 CKS PRC2/24/126
Tompson, Edward, Whatton, Long, Leics, 1639 Leics RO PR/I/41A/27
Tompson, Francis, Kingsbury (Whately), Warks, 1705 LJRO/B/C/5/1705/49
Tompson, George, university: 'scholar's servant', Cambridge St Botolph, Cambs, 1645 CUL V.C. Acc./Box2/79
Tompson, George, Crowle, Lincs, 1674 Lincs RO Ad/Ac/35/82
Tompson, John, Newton on Trent, Lincs, 1626 Lincs RO Ad/Ac/39/126

[Tompson:]
Tompson, John, Bottesford (East Butterwick), Lincs, 1635 Lincs RO Ad/Ac/40/101
Tompson, John, yeoman, Dorchester, Oxon, 1673 Oxon RO MSS Wills Pec 71/6/21
Tompson, John, Warboys, Hunts, 1682 Hunts RO/Acc58/190(45)
Tompson, Richard, Donington, Lincs, 1598 Lincs RO Ad/Ac/5/455
Tompson, Robert, husbandman, Mumby, Lincs, 1639 Lincs RO Ad/Ac/25/170
Tompson, Robert, fruiterer, Norwich, Norf, 1738 Norfolk RO ANW/23/22A/43
Tompson, William, Donington, Lincs, 1612 Lincs RO Ad/Ac/11/136
Tompson, William, Kirkby cum Osgodby, Lincs, 1620 Lincs RO Ad/Ac/16/94
Tompson/Hunte, Francis, Pewsey, Wilts, 1636 Wilts RO Arch. Wilts.(+ name and date)
Tompsone, Sempringham (Pointon), Lincs, 1593 Lincs RO Ad/Ac/3/1
Toms, John, Boxgrove, Sussex, 1678 W. Suss RO EpI/33/1678/2
Toms, Margaret, widow, Longparish, Hants, 1598 Hants RO 1592 A118/5
Toms, Mathew, yeoman, Waldershare, Kent, 1643 CKS PRC1/6/92
Tomson, Margaret, Canterbury St Paul, Kent, 1627 CKS PRC2/28/123
Tomson, Robert, Hankerton, Wilts, 1677 Wilts RO Miscellaneous Index (name + date)
Tomson, Thomas, Chichester, Sussex, 1599 W. Suss RO EpIII/9/1/1
Tomson, William, Shipton under Wychwood, Oxon, 1627 Oxon RO MSS Wills 300/4/35
Tomson, William, husbandman, Stoke, South, Lincs, 1644 Lincs RO Ad/Ac/28/88
Ton, Robert, Helston, Corn, 1614 Cornwall RO AP/T237/3
Tong, Henry, Baston, Lincs, 1628 Lincs RO Ad/Ac/22/112
Tong, James, Bredgar, Kent, 1638 CKS PRC2/34/291
Tong, James, yeoman, Tonge, Kent, 1680 CKS PRC2/39/114
Tong, James eld, yeoman, Tonge, Kent, 1663 CKS PRC1/9/155
Tong, John, Smarden, Kent, 1603 CKS PRC2/14/442
Tong, John, Bredgar, Kent, 1637 CKS PRC2/34/128
Tong, Nicholas, Linsted, Kent, 1669 CKS PRC1/14/114
Tong, Robert, Iwade, Kent, 1605 CKS PRC2/13/394
Tong, Robert, carpenter: 'house carpenter', Milsted, Kent, 1684 CKS PRC2/40/250
Tong, Thomas, Headcorn, Kent, 1598 CKS PRC2/11/347
Tonge, Frances, widow, Borden, Kent, 1666 CKS PRC1/11/166
Tonge, Isaac, Boughton Malherbe, Kent, 1606 CKS PRC2/15/416
Tonge, James, Canterbury St Alphege, Kent, 1586 CKS PRC21/8/102
Tonge, James, Stapleford, Lincs, 1652 Lincs RO Ad/Ac/29/139
Tonge, John, Smarden, Kent, 1620 CKS PRC2/24/121
Tonge, John, Headcorn, Kent, 1640 CKS PRC1/3/53
Tonge, Joseph, Gainsborough, Lincs, 1677 Lincs RO Ad/Ac/35/123
Tonge, Nicholas, Gedney, Lincs, 1593 Lincs RO Ad/Ac/3/53
Tonge, Nicholas, Linsted, Kent, 1612 CKS PRC2/16/18
Tonge, Richard, tailor, Grimsby, Great, Lincs, 1633 Lincs RO Ad/Ac/24/120
Tonge, Robert, Bredgar, Kent, 1598 CKS PRC2/9/367
Tonge, Robert, Smarden, Kent, 1604 CKS PRC2/13/409
Tonge, Roger, Scarle, North, Lincs, 1613 Lincs RO Ad/Ac/11/53
Tonge, Thomas, Bapchild, Kent, 1590 CKS PRC2/5/433
Tonge, Thomas, Minster in Thanet, Kent, 1601 CKS PRC2/11/351
Tonge, Thomas, Benenden, Kent, 1625 CKS PRC2/25/140
Tonge, William, gentleman, Tunstall, Kent, 1625 CKS PRC2/25/144
Tonge, William, Dover, Kent, 1634 CKS PRC20/11/454
Tonge, Wyllyam, Sittingbourne, Kent, 1582 CKS PRC2/2/165
Tongue, John, joiner, Lincoln St Martin, Lincs, 1673 Lincs RO Ad/Ac/35/8
Tonnard, Antony, Kirton, Lincs, 1593 Lincs RO Ad/Ac/3/73
Toogood, Ann, widow, Milborne Port, Som, 1618 Somerset RO D/D/Cta/T33
Toogood, Motley, Sherbourne, Dors, 1627 Wilts RO Miscellaneous Index (name + date)
Toogood, Robert, Mere, Wilts, 1639 Wilts RO Miscellaneous Index (name + date)
Toogood, William, Mere, Wilts, 1597 Wilts RO Miscellaneous Index (name + date)
Toogood, see Druer,

Tooke, Julian, widow, Hythe St Leonard, Kent, 1608 CKS PRC20/1/388
Tooke, Thomas, gentleman, Hothfield, Kent, 1669 CKS PRC1/14/113
Tooker, Bartholomew, Glastonbury, Som, 1690 Somerset RO D/D/Cta/T22
Tooker, John, yeoman, Tilehurst, Berks, 1670 Berks RO D/A1/218/24C
Tookey, William, Lydd, Kent, 1636 CKS PRC20/11/472
Tooky, Stephen, cordwainer ?, Ashford, Kent, 1673 CKS PRC2/35/183
Toole, John, groom, Oxford (All Souls College), Oxon, 1677 Bodleian HYP B9/105-106
Tooley, Brian, Coningsby, Lincs, 1613 Lincs RO Ad/Ac/11/149
Tooley, Dorathy, widow, Buslingthorpe, Lincs, 1680 Lincs RO Ad/Ac/43/141
Tooley, Francis, Woodhall, Lincs, 1626 Lincs RO Ad/Ac/20/47
Tooley, Nicholas, goldsmith, Lincoln, Lincs, 1601 Lincs RO Ad/Ac/5/203
Tooley, Richard, Benington, Lincs, 1635 Lincs RO Ad/Ac/24/347
Tooley, Robert, Scremby, Lincs, 1645 Lincs RO Ad/Ac/28/139
Tooley, Trussell, gentleman, Roughton, Lincs, 1626 Lincs RO Ad/Ac/20/76
Tooley, William, Faversham, Kent, 1633 CKS PRC2/32/108
Tooley, William, goldsmith, Lincoln, Lincs, 1669 Lincs RO Ad/Ac/33/111
Tooly, Wyllyam, Newchurch, Kent, 1580 CKS PRC21/4/239
Toone, Henry, Derby, Derby, 1678 LJRO:cards/1678/23
Toone, Henry, bachelor, St Katherine Creechurch, London & Middlesex, 1685 PRO PROB5/1504
Toone, Marie, spinster, Belton, Leics, 1665 Leics RO Administrators Accounts C17th f17
Topcliff, Godwin, gentleman, Thanington, Kent, 1640 CKS PRC1/3/54
Topcliff, see Topley,
Topcliffe, Alice, mrs/spinster, Canterbury Christchurch, Kent, 1626 CKS PRC20/7/283
Topcliffe, Marie, mrs/spinster, Folkestone, Kent, 1629 CKS PRC2/30/134
Topenden, Wyllyam, Chart, Great, Kent, 1598 CKS PRC2/9/357
Topham, William, clergy: 'clerk', York, Yorks, Borthwick Test C.P. 1719/15
Topham, William, clergy: 'clerk', York, Yorks, 1719 Borthwick Test C.P. 1719/15
Toples, Thomas, Ireton, Kirk, Derby, 1667 LJRO:cards/1667/82
Topley, Alice, widow, Chilham, Kent, 1673 CKS PRC2/35/259
Topley, Henry, Westwell, Kent, 1582 CKS PRC21/6/34
Topley, John, Wye, Kent, 1641 CKS PRC1/6/29
Topley, Margaret, widow, Ashford, Kent, 1624 CKS PRC2/24/154
Topley, Nicholas, yeoman, Chilham, Kent, 1673 CKS PRC2/35/260
Topley, Richard, yeoman, Mersham, Kent, 1643 CKS PRC1/6/93
Topley, Richard, Mersham, Kent, 1689 CKS PRC2/41/108
Topley, Thomas, Bethersden, Kent, 1619 CKS PRC2/24/124
Topley, Thomas, Mersham, Kent, 1681 CKS PRC2/39/244
Topley/Topcliff, Robert, Ulcombe, Kent, 1646 CKS PRC1/7/69
Topliche, William, Timberland, Lincs, 1601 Lincs RO Ad/Ac/5/459
Toplie, William, Boughton Aluph, Kent, 1597 CKS PRC2/10/351
Topliffe, Peter, fletcher, Lincoln St Martin, Lincs, 1625 Lincs RO Ad/Ac/19B/66
Topliffe, Richard, Kirton, Lincs, 1648 Lincs RO Ad/Ac/30/254
Topliffe, Thomas, Ashford, Kent, 1627 CKS PRC2/28/121
Toply, Nicholas, Harrietsham, Kent, 1632 CKS PRC2/31/68
Toppam, Richard, blacksmith, Tathwell, Lincs, 1627 Lincs RO Ad/Ac/20b/107
Toppar, Thomas, Gosberton, Lincs, 1634 Lincs RO Ad/Ac/24/138
Torcksey, John, Haxey, Lincs, 1602 Lincs RO Ad/Ac/37/117
Torksey, Edmund, Scotter, Lincs, 1614 Lincs RO Ad/Ac/8b/53
Torksey, John, Haxey, Lincs, 1682 Lincs RO Ad/Ac/44/15
Torr, Gregory, Haxey (Nether Burnham), Lincs, 1663 Lincs RO Ad/Ac/41/96
Torren/Tarrant, John, mariner: 'seaman, RN?', Stepney, London & Middlesex, PRO PROB32/55/13
Tory, John, carpenter, Bytham, Little, Lincs, 1637 Lincs RO Ad/Ac/25/392
Torye, George, joiner, Deeping, Market, Lincs, 1618 Lincs RO Ad/Ac/14/42
Tottersole, Thomas, Preston next Faversham, Kent, 1673 CKS PRC2/35/261

[Tottridge:]
Tottridge, Richard, Pinchbeck, Lincs, 1618 Lincs RO Ad/Ac/14/184
Tounesend, Henry, Holywell (Needingworth), Hunts, 1683 Hunts RO/Acc58/193(47)
Tounesend, Ralph, mercer, Abingdon St Nicholas, Berks, 1629 Berks RO D/A1/217/132B
Tournay, Thomas, clergy: 'clerk', Stone in Oxney, Kent, 1647 CKS PRC1/8/30
Tourney, William, gentleman, Caenby, Lincs, 1629 Lincs RO Ad/Ac/39/108
Tourt, William, husbandman, High Halden, Kent, 1681 CKS PRC2/39/242
Tourton, William, blacksmith, Milton next Sittingbourne, Kent, 1627 CKS PRC2/28/125
Tovey, Robert, yeoman, Bredon (Hardwick), Worcs, 1686 Worcs RO 008.7 BA3585/830/24
Tovey, Thomas, Almondsbury (Rednend), Glos, Bristol RO 1680/67
Tovy, Richard, husbandman, Hinksey, South, Berks, 1620 Berks RO D/A1/217/117B
Tovye, Walter, husbandman, Norton, Worcs, Worcs RO 008.7 BA3585/838/51
Tow, Thomasin, widow, Erlestoke, Wilts, 1638 Wilts RO Arch. Sarum(+ name and date)
Towe, Elizabeth, widow, Compton, Berks, 1640 Berks RO D/A1/127/138D
Towensend, Thomas, Holywell (Needingworth), Hunts, 1678 Hunts RO/Acc58/127(9)
Towers, Clement, grocer, Norwich St George, Norf, Norfolk RO ANW/23/16/53
Towers, Edward, baker, Doddington, Dry, Lincs, 1629 Lincs RO Ad/Ac/22/11
Towers, James, innholder, Dover, Kent, 1673 CKS PRC20/12/106
Towers, John, Billingborough, Lincs, 1599 Lincs RO Ad/Ac/5/153
Towers, John, gentleman, Horkstow, Lincs, 1627 Lincs RO Ad/Ac/20/101
Towes, Anne, spinster, St Laurence Thanet, Kent, 1619 CKS PRC2/24/106
Towghton, Richard, Ospringe, Kent, 1616 CKS PRC2/24/107
Towle, Mathew, Goxhill, Lincs, 1662 Lincs RO Ad/Ac/32/17
Towle, William, carpenter, Habrough, Lincs, 1613 Lincs RO Ad/Ac/11/47
Towler, John, Lincoln St Mary Magdalen in the Bail, Lincs, 1648? Lincs RO Ad/Ac/30/329
Towler, Richard, Gainsborough, Lincs, 1624 Lincs RO Ad/Ac/39/144
Towler, Robert, Laughton, Lincs, 1580 Lincs RO Ad/Ac/2b/52
Towler, William, Winterton, Lincs, 1628 Lincs RO Ad/Ac/39/86
Towne, John, Minster in Thanet, Kent, 1691 CKS PRC2/42/16
Towne, Thomas, Leeds, Kent, 1618 CKS PRC2/24/102
Towne, William, yeoman, Staple next Wingham, Kent, 1668 CKS PRC19/4/33
Townend, Joseph, clothier, Almondbury (Hey, Meltham), Yorks, 1801 Borthwick Test C.P. 1801/4
Townend, Repentance, Manby, Lincs, 1638 Lincs RO Ad/Ac/25/53
Townend, William, labourer, Haxey, Lincs, 1674 Lincs RO Ad/Ac/35/75
Townesend, John, Woolln...dington, Warks, 1603 Worcs RO 008.7 BA3585/839/327
Townesend, Paul, bricklayer, Waltham, White, Berks, 1633 Berks RO D/A1/217/145B
Townesend, Robarte, Stamford St Michael, Lincs, 1601 Lincs RO Ad/Ac/5/71
Townesend, Robert, Bradford on Avon, Wilts, 1634 Wilts RO Arch. Sarum(+ name and date)
Townesend, Thomas, Chipping Barnet, Herts, 1601 Herts RO ASA25/1778
Towning, Edward, Torksey, Lincs, 1632 Lincs RO Ad/Ac/39/274
Towning, Thomas, Goudhurst, Kent, 1598 CKS PRC2/10/519
Townley, Richard, esquire, Norton, Lincs, 1639 Lincs RO Ad/Ac/26/319
Townrawe, John, Louth, Lincs, 1669? Lincs RO Ad/Ac/42/105
Townrowe, Thomas, clergy: 'clerk', Claypole, Lincs, 1606 Lincs RO Ad/Ac/7/125
Townsend, Ann, widow, Sheffield, Yorks, 1852 Borthwick Test C.P. 1851/3
Townsend, James, Chelsea, London & Middlesex, 1751 Greater London RO AM/PI pt (uncatalogued)
Townsend, James, gentleman, Sheffield, Yorks, 1818 Borthwick Test C.P. 1818/17
Townsend, Richard, husbandman, Longcot, Berks, 1678 Berks RO D/A1/218/41C
Townsend, Robert, Harwell, Berks, 1594 Berks RO D/A1/217/63B
Townsend, Thomas, carpenter, Bromham, Wilts, 1633 Wilts RO Arch. Wilts.(+ name and date)
Townsend, Thomas, Newbold on Avon, Warks, 1672 LJRO:cards/1672/60
Townsend, Thomas, Wolvey, Warks, 1685 LJRO/B/C/5/1685/99
Townsend, William, Badsey, Worcs, 1680 Worcs RO 008.7 BA3585/837/bdl 2
Townsend, William, yeoman, Boxwell (Leighterton), Glos, 1784 GRO GDR/B4/2/T41

Townsende, Katherine, widow, Longcot, Berks, 1608 Berks RO D/A1/217/91B
Townshend, William, Lighthorne, Warks, 1684 Worcs RO 008.7 BA3585/837/bdl 4
Townson, Thomas, Chilmark (Stockley), Wilts, 1678 Wilts RO Arch. Sarum(+ name and date)
Towrle, Thomas, Stone in Oxney, Kent, 1615 CKS PRC2/24/138
Towrte, John, Stone in Oxney, Kent, 1611 CKS PRC20/2/256
Towse, Francis, Deeping St James, Lincs, 1611 Lincs RO Ad/Ac/10/66
Towson, George, East Sutton, Kent, 1627 CKS PRC2/28/122
Towthbye, Edward, university: 'Fellow of Magdalene College, Cambridge/M.A.', Cambridge (Magdalene College), Cambs, 1615 CUL V.C.Acc./Box1/51
Toye, John, Wolverley, Worcs, 1606 Worcs RO 008.7 BA3585/839/425a
Toynby, Anne, widow, Waddington, Lincs, 1679 Lincs RO Ad/Ac/43/121
Toyne, Richard, Waddingham, Lincs, 1615 Lincs RO Ad/Ac/8b/91
Toyne, Richard, Nettleham, Lincs, 1663 Lincs RO Ad/Ac/41/105
Toynton, Thomas, Luddington (Garthorpe), Lincs, 1649 Lincs RO Ad/Ac/30/77
Tracely, Daniel, Sandwich, Kent, 1668 CKS PRC1/13/133
Tracham, Joane, widow, Dover St Mary, Kent, 1615 CKS PRC20/3/190
Trafford, Michael, Mancetter (Atherstone), Warks, 1675 LJRO:cards/1675/54
Traile, John, mariner: 'gunner/widower', Greenwich (East Greenwich), Kent, 1712 PRO PROB5/1213
Traisloe, John, Warehorne, Kent, 1607 CKS PRC2/15/423
Trapping, Benjamin,
Corn 1639 Cornwall RO AP/T617
Travaile, John, Harbledown, Kent, 1679 CKS PRC2/38/76
Travell, Nicholas, Nackington, Kent, 1639 CKS PRC2/34/290
Travell, Richard, yeoman, Gayton, Northants, 1783 Northants RO X954/22/13
Traver, Thomas, Drayton in Hales, Staffs, 1667 LJRO:cards/1667/84
Travers, Christopher, Boxley, Kent, 1594 CKS PRC2/6/460
Travers, Hugh, Compton, Sussex, 1600 W. Suss RO EpI/33/1600/5
Travers, Humphrey, Compton, Sussex, 1600 W. Suss RO EpI/33/1600/3
Travesse, Edward, Boughton under Blean, Kent, 1614 CKS PRC20/3/11
Travile, Alice, widow, Newport Pagnell, Bucks, 1682 PRO PROB5/1029
Travillian, John, Doddington, Kent, 1679 CKS PRC2/38/196
Travis, James, Haxey, Lincs, 1598 Lincs RO Ad/Ac/5/296
Travis, James, Ashton-under-Lyne, Lancs, 1648 Lancs RO (Name of Deceased) D.R.C.H. 1647
Travis, Jennett, Haxey (East Lound), Lincs, 1662 Lincs RO Ad/Ac/41/64
Travis, Robert, Crowle, Lincs, 1611 Lincs RO Ad/Ac/8a/336
Travis, Roberte, Haxey, Lincs, 1594 Lincs RO Ad/Ac/5/298
Trayhearne, Thomas, Warehorne, Kent, 1614 CKS PRC2/17/41
Trayslow, John, Barwell, Leics, 1665 Leics RO Administrators Accounts C17th f31
Treagoose, John, Walberton, Sussex, 1594 W. Suss RO EpI/33/1594/18
Tredcroft, John, clergy: 'clerk', Billingshurst, Sussex, 1671 W. Suss RO EpI/33/1671/3
Tredsothe, Samuell, Ashford, Kent, 1616 CKS PRC2/24/110
Tredway, Francis, gentleman, Baston, Lincs, 1644 Lincs RO Ad/Ac/28/206
Tree, John, Ashford, Kent, 1620 CKS PRC2/24/115
Tree, Nicholas, Stone in Oxney, Kent, 1614 CKS PRC2/17/74
Tree, see Pilcher,
Tregellest, Richard, St Enoder, Corn, 1606 Cornwall RO AP/T102
Tregonyn, Richard, yeoman, Feock/Gwennap, Corn, 1623 Cornwall RO AP/T376/9
Treham, William, Hill, South, Corn, 1646 Cornwall RO AP/T790
Tremenhere, Waren, Helston, Corn, 1611 Cornwall RO AP/T167/2
Tremer, John, Milton Chapel, Kent, 1607 CKS PRC2/15/396
Trenchmore/Lawrence, John, Itchenor, West, Sussex, 1597 W. Suss RO EpI/33/1597/5
Trender, Catherine, Gifford, Crowmarsh, Oxon, 1640 Oxon RO MSS Wills 87/3/20
Trentham, Robert, labourer, Kirby Bellars, Leics, 1641 Leics RO PR/I/41A/62
Trenwith, Henry, gentleman, St Ives, Corn, 1608 Cornwall RO AP/T106/2

[Trepe:]
Trepe, Thomas eld, Ash next Sandwich, Kent, 1614 CKS PRC20/2/502
Tresise, Nicholas, Manaccan, Corn, 1606 Cornwall RO AP/T107
Tressar, Henrie, Dover, Kent, 1628 CKS PRC20/8/456
Tresser, John, Canterbury St Dunstan Without, Kent, 1628 CKS PRC2/29/98
Tresser, Ursula, widow, Swingfield, Kent, 1648 CKS PRC1/8/54
Tressry, Abel, Oxford St Mary, Oxon, 1611 Bodleian HYP B9/107
Tresteyne, see Rickard,
Treuer, Roger, St Johns Thanet, Kent, 1638 CKS PRC2/34/133
Trevean, Stephen, Gorran, Corn, 1612 Cornwall RO AP/T207
Trevelyan, George, gentleman, Mawgan in Menage, Corn, 1641 Cornwall RO AP/T705/2
Trevewha, see John,
Trevillian, John, Kingsbury Episcopi, Som, 1664 Somerset RO D/D/Cta/T32
Trevillion, Katherine, widow, Ilton, Som, 1629 Somerset RO D/D/Cta/T4
Trevisa, Richard, St George, London & Middlesex, 1682 PRO PROB5/1762
Trevitt, Robert eld, butcher, Newport, Shrops, 1714 LJRO/B/C/5/1714/131
Trevor, John, Secretary of State, St Margaret Westminster, London & Middlesex, 1675 PRO PROB32/12/30
Trevoroe, Nicholas, Ludgvan, Corn, 1606 Cornwall RO AP/T109
Trew, Henry, St Martin in the Fields, London & Middlesex, 1696 PRO PROB32/39/260
Trewavas, John, Breage, Corn, 1603 Cornwall RO AP/T18/3
Trewe, Richard, yeoman, Croft, Lincs, 1638 Lincs RO Ad/Ac/25/98
Treweene, Joan, Trevalga, Corn, 1616 Cornwall RO AP/T265/1+3
Trewell, Thomas, Canterbury, Kent, 1630 CKS PRC20/9/418
Trewhit, Thomas, Washingborough (Heighington), Lincs, 1627 Lincs RO Ad/Ac/20b/18
Trewman, Elizabeth, Portbury, Som, 1682 Somerset RO D/D/Cta/T24
Trewman, William, Ulceby, Lincs, 1625 Lincs RO Ad/Ac/19B/91
Treworo, Peter, Ludgvan, Corn, 1608 Cornwall RO AP/T136
Tribe, Hambledon, Hants, 1682 Hants RO 21m65 D8/330
Tribe, Roger, Trotton, Sussex, 1676 W. Suss RO EpI/33/1676/28
Tribe, Thomas, Fernhurst, Sussex, 1598 W. Suss RO EpI/33/1597/6
Tribe, William, Fernhurst, Sussex, 1673 W. Suss RO EpI/33/1673/3
Trice, John, Faversham, Kent, 1617 CKS PRC2/24/113
Trice, John, Blean, Kent, 1711 CKS PRC1/17/43
Trice, Thomas, Herne, Kent, 1602 CKS PRC21/15/162
Trice, William, husbandman, Wye, Kent, 1682 CKS PRC2/39/245
Tridles, Thomas, Portsmouth, Hants, 1624 Hants RO 21M65 D8/93
Trigg, John, Maker, Corn, 1619 Cornwall RO AP/T475/2
Trigg, John, husbandman, Antony, Corn, 1631 Cornwall RO AP/T550/2
Trigott, Steephen, yeoman, Habrough, Lincs, 1632 Lincs RO Ad/Ac/23/142
Trimell, Alice, Sidlesham, Sussex, W. Suss RO EpI/33/1607/1
Trimme, Elizabeth, Wimborne Minster (Leigh), Dors, 1639 Dorset RO PE/WM CP 2/4/54
Trindale, John, Boxley, Kent, 1609 CKS PRC2/15/419
Tripland, Dyna, widow, Appledore, Kent, 1671 CKS PRC1/15/72
Triploe, John, husbandman, Colne, Hunts, 1712 Hunts RO/Acc58/306
Tripp, Charles, esquire, Wingham, Kent, 1630 CKS PRC20/9/426
Tripp, Edward, Thorton Curtis, Lincs, 1637 Lincs RO Ad/Ac/24/550
Tripp, Henrie, Barton on Humber, Lincs, 1626 Lincs RO Ad/Ac/20/9
Tripp, John, Wye, Kent, 1619 CKS PRC2/24/135
Trippe, William, Lydd, Kent, 1622 CKS PRC20/6/240
Tristram, John, clergy: 'clerk', Barrington, Som, 1619 Somerset RO D/D/Cta/T27
Tristram, Richard, Rodmersham, Kent, 1584 CKS PRC2/3/100
Tritton, Daniell, Ashford, Kent, 1615 CKS PRC2/24/108
Tritton, Henry eld, yeoman, Ashford, Kent, 1669 CKS PRC1/14/115
Tritton, Henry eld, yeoman, Ashford, Kent, 1669 CKS PRC1/14/115a
Tritton, Richard, Ewell, Kent, 1621 CKS PRC2/24/148

Tritton, Richard, Lenham, Kent, 1672 CKS PRC2/35/94
Tritton, Robert, Orlestone, Kent, 1682 CKS PRC1/15/109b
Tritton, Robert, victualler, Orlestone, Kent, 1682 CKS PRC1/15/109
Tritton, Simon, grocer, Faversham, Kent, 1678 CKS PRC2/38/79
Tritton, William, Stodmarsh, Kent, 1631 CKS PRC2/31/72
Tritton, William, yeoman, St Nicholas at Wade, Kent, 1682 CKS PRC20/13/291
Tritton/Harlestone, Ellen, Faversham, Kent, 1670 CKS PRC1/15/73
Tritton, see Pope,
Trobridge,
Som 1632 Somerset RO D/D/Cta/T23
Trothe, William, Feckenham, Worcs, Worcs RO 008.7 BA3585/839/322
Trott, Agnes, widow, St Albans St Stephens, Herts, 1610 Herts RO ASA25/4786
Trott, John, Gedney, Lincs, 1630 Lincs RO Ad/Ac/25/454
Trott, Robert, Aldingbourne, Sussex, 1677 W. Suss RO EpI/33/1677/3
Trott, Thomas, Aldingbourne, Sussex, 1630 W. Suss RO EpI/33/1629/14
Trottle, Joane, widow, Bloxworthy, Dors, 1626 Wilts RO Miscellaneous Index (name + date)
Troward, Ann, widow, St Margarets At Cliffe, Kent, 1603 CKS PRC21/15/335
Troward, Anne, widow, Waldershare, Kent, 1688 CKS PRC2/41/137
Troward, Luke, Sandwich, Kent, 1697 CKS PRC2/42/137
Troward, Mary, widow, St Laurence Thanet, Kent, 1672 CKS PRC2/35/184
Troward, Richard, St Laurence Thanet/Fordwich, Kent, 1633 CKS PRC2/32/110
Troward, Richard, St Laurence Thanet, Kent, 1642 CKS PRC1/6/30
Troward, Richard eld, St Laurence Thanet, Kent, 1640 CKS PRC1/5/52
Troward/Hewet, Helen, Minster in Thanet, Kent, 1641 CKS PRC1/5/53
Trowarde, Nicholas, St Laurence Thanet, Kent, 1609 CKS PRC2/15/411
Trowarde, William, St Laurence Thanet, Kent, 1616 CKS PRC2/24/123
Troway, Daniel, clergy: 'clerk', Croft, Leics, 1674 Leics RO Administrators Accounts 1667-72 f145
Trowd, James, Buckland, West, Som, 1619 Somerset RO D/D/Cta/T28
Trowd, James, husbandman, Buckland, West, Som, 1619 Somerset RO D/D/Cta/F18
Trowghton, Robert, innkeeper, Worcester St John Bedwardine, Worcs, 1604 Worcs RO 008.7 BA3585/839/389
Troydall, William, Kirmington, Lincs, 1665 Lincs RO Ad/Ac/43/40
Truant, Robert, Friesthorpe, Lincs, 1665 Lincs RO Ad/Ac/42/58
True, William, Kettering, Northants, 1680 Northants RO NWill A/C/2
Trueland, John, Bratton, Wilts, 1674 Wilts RO Chantor Sarum Bundle 9/44
Trueman, Jonathan, gentleman, Nottingham, Notts, 1800 Borthwick Test C.P. 1800/6
Trulocke, John eld, Radley, Berks, 1615 Berks RO D/A1/217/103B
Trulove, John, Nuthurst, Sussex, 1617 W. Suss RO EpI/33/1617/23
Trulove, John, husbandman, Easton, Wilts, 1628 Wilts RO Arch. Wilts.(+ name and date)
Trumell, John, Aldingbourne, Sussex, 1594 W. Suss RO EpI/33/1594/20
Trumplett, Richard, butcher, Aldermaston, Berks, 1628 Berks RO D/A1/217/130B
Trunnell, Richard, gentleman, Aldingbourne, Sussex, 1672 W. Suss RO EpI/33/1671/12
Truse, Thomas, drover, Coningsby, Lincs, 1668 Lincs RO Ad/Ac/33/65
Trusler, John, gentleman, Aldingbourne, Sussex, 1682 W. Suss RO EpI/33/1682/5
Trusler, Richard, Froyle, Hants, 1679 Hants RO 21m65 D8/297
Trusse, William, Billinghay, Lincs, 1625 Lincs RO Ad/Ac/19A/16
Trusser, Helene, widow, Canterbury St Dunstan Without, Kent, 1599 CKS PRC2/11/349
Trusser, John, Swingfield, Kent, 1611 CKS PRC2/15/421
Trybe, Thomas, Fernhurst, Sussex, 1594 W. Suss RO EpI/33/1594/4
Tryce, Thomas, gentleman, Godmanchester, Hunts, 1701 Hunts RO/Acc58/290
Trymnell, Michaell, Bremhill, Wilts, 1626 Wilts RO Arch. Wilts.(+ name and date)
Tryon, John, esquire, St Martin in the Fields, London & Middlesex, 1684 PRO PROB32/23/182
Tryppe, John, Brabourne, Kent, 1607 CKS PRC2/14/432
Trystram, John, Ash next Sandwich, Kent, 1608 CKS PRC20/1/362

[Tubb:]
Tubb, Francis, yeoman, Challow, East, Berks, 1670 Berks RO D/A1/218/21C
Tubb, Isabell, Washingborough, Lincs, 1606 Lincs RO Ad/Ac/7/135
Tubb, John, Stithians, Corn, 1608 Cornwall RO AP/T125/2
Tubb, Thomas, Michelmersh, Hants, Hants RO 1595 AD58/3
Tubbe, Humphrey, yeoman, Lambourn (East Hanney), Berks, 1668 Berks RO D/A1/218/17C
Tubbe, John, yeoman, Challow, East, Berks, 1669 Berks RO D/A1/218/19D
Tubbs, George, St Ives, Hunts, Hunts RO/Acc58/130(2)
Tuck, Adam, Mildenhall, Wilts, 1675 Wilts RO Miscellaneous Index (name + date)
Tuck, Henry, Westport St Mary, Wilts, 1622 Wilts RO Arch. Wilts.(+ name and date)
Tuck, Thomas, gentleman, Milsted, Kent, 1625 CKS PRC2/25/142
Tuck/Pedington, John, Hilmarton, Wilts, 1680? Wilts RO Miscellaneous Index (name + date)
Tuck, see Peddington,
Tuckar, John, yeoman, Goodnestone next Faversham, Kent, 1700 CKS PRC2/42/161
Tucke, John, Thornford, Dors, 1637 Wilts RO Miscellaneous Index (name + date)
Tucke, John, Huish, Wilts, 1676 Wilts RO Miscellaneous Index (name + date)
Tucke, Richard, Broad Hinton, Wilts, 1637 Wilts RO CC Sarum(+ name and date)
Tucke, William, Lacock, Wilts, 1622 Wilts RO Arch. Wilts.(+ name and date)
Tucke/Pendington, Christopher, Charlton, Wilts, 1631 Wilts RO Arch. Wilts.(+ name and date)
Tucker,
Som 1632 Somerset RO D/D/Cta/T25
Tucker, Benjamin, Lympne, Kent, 1723 CKS PRC1/18/50
Tucker, Elizabeth, widow, Bradford on Avon, Wilts, 1627 Wilts RO Arch. Sarum(+ name and date)
Tucker, Henry, Stapleton, Glos, Bristol RO 1609/73
Tucker, John, Elham, Kent, 1596 CKS PRC2/8/342
Tucker, John, Tresmeer, Corn, 1615 Cornwall RO AP/T238/3
Tucker, John, Bradley, West, Som, 1619 Somerset RO D/D/Cta/T35
Tucker, John, Ruckinge, Kent, 1664 CKS PRC1/10/98
Tucker, John eld, Nailsea, Som, 1667 Somerset RO D/D/Cta/T30
Tucker, Lawrence, Goodnestone next Wingham, Kent, 1703 CKS PRC19/6/16
Tucker, Martha, Folkestone, Kent, 1631 CKS PRC2/30/141
Tucker, Robert, carpenter, Staplehurst, Kent, 1672 CKS PRC2/35/182
Tucker, Roger, saddler, Canterbury St George Martyr, Kent, 1611 CKS PRC2/15/398
Tucker, Simon, Goodnestone next Wingham, Kent, 1632 CKS PRC20/11/466
Tucker, Thomas, Somerton, Som, 1610 Somerset RO D/D/Cta/T38
Tucker, Walter, Bradford on Avon, Wilts, 1614 Wilts RO Miscellaneous Index (name + date)
Tucker, William,
Som 1601 Somerset RO D/D/Cta/T8
Tucker, William, Ashford, Kent, 1624 CKS PRC2/24/156
Tucker, see Nash,
Tuckey, Francis, Abingdon, Berks, 1612 Berks RO D/A1/127/15C
Tuckie, Edmund,
Som 1613 Somerset RO D/D/Cta/T3
Tuckneis, John, Stone in Oxney, Kent, 1617 CKS PRC2/24/133
Tucknesshe, Thomas, Hawkhurst, Kent, 1587 CKS PRC2/4/138
Tuckwell, Anne, widow, Longworth, Berks, 1668 Berks RO D/A1/128/56D
Tuckwell, Jonas, Canterbury St Peter, Kent, 1675 CKS PRC2/36/249
Tuckwell, Thomas, yeoman, Longworth, Berks, 1625 Berks RO D/A1/217/126B
Tuckye, William, Kewstoke, Som, 1612 Somerset RO D/D/Cta/T39
Tuder, John, Wem, Shrops, 1681 LJRO/B/C/5/1681/39
Tue, Richard, Windsor, Old, Berks, 1594 Berks RO D/A1/126/167C
Tuesly, Thomas, Wisborough Green (Loxwood), Sussex, 1684 W. Suss RO EpI/33/1684/15
Tuesnoth, William, Bethersden, Kent, 1595 CKS PRC2/7/453
Tuesonne, Titus, Coningsby, Lincs, 1635 Lincs RO Ad/Ac/40/149
Tuffe, John, bachelor, Pagham, Sussex, 1684 W. Suss RO EpIV/10/2A/35

Tuffine, George, fisherman, Lincoln, Lincs, 1637 Lincs RO Ad/Ac/25/475
Tufton, John, miller, Lydd, Kent, 1669 CKS PRC19/4/34
Tufton, Nicholas, grocer, Lydd, Kent, 1682 CKS PRC20/13/295
Tuggett, Thomas, Brookland, Kent, 1622 CKS PRC2/24/145
Tugwell, John, Hilmarton, Wilts, 1621 Wilts RO Arch. Wilts.(+ name and date)
Tulke, Henry, Hythe St Leonard, Kent, 1594 CKS PRC21/12/509
Tulke, Nicolas, Hythe St Leonard, Kent, 1581 CKS PRC21/4/311
Tull, John, husbandman, Midgham, Berks, 1604 Berks RO D/A1/126/225C
Tull, Robert, yeoman, Midgham, Berks, 1666 Berks RO D/A1/128/48D
Tunard, Christopher, Fishtoft, Lincs, 1633 Lincs RO Ad/Ac/24/79
Tunard, Robert, Brothertoft, Lincs, 1664 Lincs RO Ad/Ac/43/11
Tunbridge, Afra, widow, Lyminge, Kent, 1611 CKS PRC20/2/252
Tunbridge, Richard, Maidstone, Kent, 1595 CKS PRC21/13/32
Tunnard, William, husbandman, Brothertoft, Lincs, 1681 Lincs RO Ad/Ac/34/69
Tunnicliff, Thomas, yeoman, Checkley, Staffs, 1814 LJRO/B/C/5/1814/42
Tunnicliffe, John, Leek, Staffs, 1682 LJRO/B/C/5/1681/40
Tunnycliffe, Roger, Alstonfield, Staffs, 1684 LJRO/B/C/5/1684/81
Tunstall, John, Bolas Magna, Shrops, 1685 LJRO/B/C/5/1685/100
Tuplin, Henry, bachelor, Halton, West/Coningsby, Lincs, 1679 Lincs RO Ad/Ac/43/87
Tuplin, Thomas, yeoman, Alkborough, Lincs, 1685 Lincs RO Ad/Ac/44/157
Tupling, John, Grimsby, Great (Wellow), Lincs, 1623 Lincs RO Ad/Ac/17/58
Tupper, Clement, Bury, Sussex, 1646 W. Suss RO EpI/33/1646/1
Turcke, John, Leeds, Kent, 1592 CKS PRC2/6/117
Turferye, John, Herne, Kent, 1611 CKS PRC20/2/248
Turfrey, Dorothy, spinster, Alvescot, Oxon, 1682 Oxon RO MSS Wills 87/4/26
Turgoose, Humfrey, Lea, Lincs, 1599 Lincs RO Ad/Ac/37/67
Turk, John, Clerkenwell St James, London & Middlesex, 1725 Greater London RO AM/PP/Box 1724-1727 pt (uncatalogued)
Turke, Azarias, Cranbrook, Kent, 1583 CKS PRC2/3/119
Turke, John, Marden, Kent, 1603 CKS PRC2/12/461
Turke, John, Cranbrook, Kent, 1641 CKS PRC1/6/31
Turke, William, Marden, Kent, 1627 CKS PRC20/8/454
Turke, William, cordwainer, Marden, Kent, 1683 CKS PRC2/40/158
Turkey/Wright, Anne,
Cambs 1675 CUL V.C. Acc./Box3/49
Turkington, Margarett, Alconbury Weston, Hunts, 1692 Lincs RO Ad/Ac/43/51
Turle, William, Salford Priors (Abbots Salford), Warks, Worcs RO 008.7 BA3585/839/328
Turley, Richard, yeoman, Hawkhurst, Kent, 1685 CKS PRC2/41/18
Turlie, Richard, Gainsborough, Lincs, 1623 Lincs RO Ad/Ac/8c/87
Turnagayne, Thomas, Broadwater, Sussex, 1652 W. Suss RO EpI/33/1652/1
Turnar, Jeniver, Dormston, Worcs, Worcs RO 008.7 BA3585/838/260
Turneagayne, Robert, Lyminster, Sussex, 1669 W. Suss RO EpI/33/1669/9
Turneley, James, Godmersham, Kent, 1630 CKS PRC20/9/420
Turnepenny, Christopher, Shenley, Herts, Herts RO AHH23/2342
Turnepenny, Thomas, St Albans St Stephens, Herts, 1599 Herts RO ASA25/4751b
Turnepenny, Thomas, St Albans St Stephens, Herts, 1603 Herts RO ASA25/4751c
Turnepeny, Thomas, St Albans St Stephens, Herts, Herts RO ASA25/4751a
Turner, Alexander, Codford St Peter, Wilts, 1614 Wilts RO CC Sarum(+ name and date)
Turner, Amon, St Laurence Thanet, Kent, 1621 CKS PRC2/24/112
Turner, Anne, spinster, Milton next Sittingbourne, Kent, 1667 CKS PRC1/12/90
Turner, Anthony, gentleman, Cumnor (Swinford), Berks, Berks RO D/A1/217/104B
Turner, Anthony, Stowey, Som, 1584 Somerset RO D/D/Cta/T44
Turner, Benjamin, fishmonger, Reading, Berks, 1599 Berks RO D/A1/217/74B
Turner, Catherine, widow, Oxford St Michael, Oxon, 1681 Oxon RO MSS Wills 87/4/25
Turner, Christopher, Ashby, Lincs, 1613 Lincs RO Ad/Ac/13/178

[Turner:]
Turner, Christopher, Grindon, Staffs, 1676 LJRO:cards/1676/49
Turner, David, Minster in Thanet, Kent, 1712 CKS PRC19/6/49
Turner, Edmond, Old Romney, Kent, 1610 CKS PRC2/15/425
Turner, Edward, Sittingbourne, Kent, CKS PRC1/16/18
Turner, Edward, cordwainer, Oxford, Oxon, 1645 Oxon RO MSS Wills 87/3/24
Turner, Elizabethe, Staple next Wingham, Kent, 1594 CKS PRC21/13/11
Turner, George, Wittersham, Kent, 1614 CKS PRC20/2/504
Turner, George, Marden, Kent, 1623 CKS PRC2/24/152
Turner, George, Swinderby (Morton Wood), Lincs, 1626 Lincs RO Ad/Ac/20/33
Turner, George, Dymchurch, Kent, 1629 CKS PRC2/30/138
Turner, George, Sutton St James, Lincs, 1803 Lincs RO Ad/Ac/45/72
Turner, Humfry,
Wilts 1580 c. Wilts RO Miscellaneous Index (name + date)
Turner, Isaac, clothier, Egerton, Kent, 1683 CKS PRC20/13/378
Turner, Jacob, Egerton, Kent, 1626 CKS PRC20/7/128
Turner, James, Chichester, Sussex, 1628 W. Suss RO EpIII/9/1/34
Turner, James, victualler, Boston, Lincs, 1673 Lincs RO Ad/Ac/35/17
Turner, James, innkeeper, Aston, Yorks, 1807 Borthwick Test C.P. 1807/3
Turner, Jarvace, Staplehurst, Kent, 1596 CKS PRC2/8/139
Turner, Jeames, Blean, Kent, 1615 CKS PRC2/24/140
Turner, John, Taunton St James, Som, 1593 Somerset RO D/D/Cta/T42
Turner, John, Hogsthorpe, Lincs, 1600 Lincs RO Ad/Ac/5/366
Turner, John, Borden, Kent, 1614 CKS PRC2/18/44
Turner, John, Folkestone, Kent, 1628 CKS PRC2/29/101
Turner, John, university: 'scholar's servant', Cambridge St Botolph, Cambs, 1628 CUL V.C. Acc./Box2/80
Turner, John, Newnham, Kent, 1632 CKS PRC2/31/160
Turner, John, Wye, Kent, 1633 CKS PRC2/32/120
Turner, John, bachelor: 'singleman', Herne, Kent, 1642 CKS PRC19/2/65
Turner, John, surgeon, Staplehurst, Kent, 1662 CKS PRC1/9/65
Turner, John, carpenter, St Johns Thanet, Kent, 1683 CKS PRC2/40/159
Turner, John, cutler: 'sword cutler', Birmingham, Warks, 1817 LJRO/B/C/5/1817/101
Turner, John eld, Canterbury St Mary Bredman, Kent, 1583 CKS PRC2/3/141
Turner, Margaret, Ivychurch, Kent, 1604 CKS PRC21/17/33
Turner, Mary, widow, Shifnal, Shrops, 1777 LJRO/B/C/5/1778/133
Turner, Nicholas, Bardney, Lincs, 1618 Lincs RO Ad/Ac/14/114
Turner, Peeter, cutler, Sandwich, Kent, 1626 CKS PRC2/27/172
Turner, Peircivall, husbandman, Upchurch, Kent, 1675 CKS PRC2/36/248
Turner, Priscilla, widow, Mersham, Kent, 1639 CKS PRC2/34/119
Turner, Richard, Surfleet, Lincs, 1605 Lincs RO Ad/Ac/6/16
Turner, Richard, weaver, St Stephen in Brannel, Corn, 1614 Cornwall RO AP/T94/5
Turner, Richard, labourer: 'day labourer', Wargrave, Berks, 1618 Berks RO D/A1/217/112B
Turner, Richard, limeburner, Pontefract (Knottingley), Yorks, 1812 Borthwick Test C.P. 1812/10
Turner, Robert, Newington next Sittingbourne, Kent, 1602 CKS PRC2/12/355
Turner, Robert, Minster in Thanet, Kent, 1629 CKS PRC2/29/102
Turner, Robert, mr, Canterbury St Alphege, Kent, 1666 CKS PRC19/3/85
Turner, Robert, Brampton, Derby, 1682 LJRO/B/C/5/1682/100
Turner, Sackvile, gentleman, Boxgrove, Sussex, 1682 W. Suss RO EpI/33/1682/33
Turner, Stephen, Kennington, Kent, 1615 CKS PRC2/24/100
Turner, Thomas, mason/mercer, Reading St Lawrence, Berks, 1596 Berks RO D/A1/217/61B
Turner, Thomas, Stockbury, Kent, 1597 CKS PRC2/10/371
Turner, Thomas, Herne, Kent, 1616 CKS PRC20/3/350
Turner, Thomas, university: 'Master of Peterhouse College, Cambridge/D.D.' Cambridge St Mary the Less, Cambs, 1618 CUL V.C.Acc./Box1/52
Turner, Thomas, Carlton le Moorland, Lincs, 1620 Lincs RO Ad/Ac/16/97

Turner, Thomas, mr, St Nicholas at Wade, Kent, 1630 CKS PRC20/9/424
Turner, Thomas, Sandwich, Kent, 1632 CKS PRC2/31/69
Turner, Thomas, bachelor, Alvescot, Oxon, 1636 Oxon RO MSS Wills 175/1/7
Turner, Thomas, husbandman, Clanfield, Oxon, 1637 Oxon RO MSS Wills 87/3/12
Turner, Thomas, bachelor, Rolvenden, Kent, 1664 CKS PRC1/10/99
Turner, Thomas, butcher, Sittingbourne, Kent, 1675 CKS PRC1/15/88
Turner, Thomas, Eckington, Derby, 1682 LJRO/B/C/5/1682/101
Turner, Thomas, Salisbury, Wilts, 1684 Wilts RO Miscellaneous Index (name + date)
Turner, Thomas, Egerton, Kent, 1699 CKS PRC19/5/68
Turner, Thomas eld, Otham, Kent, 1636 CKS PRC2/33/132
Turner, Walter, Staplehurst, Kent, 1603 CKS PRC2/14/440
Turner, William, clergy: 'vicar/Doctor of Physic', Bethersden, Kent, 1632 CKS PRC2/31/161
Turner, William, grocer, Canterbury St Andrew, Kent, 1633 CKS PRC2/31/163
Turner, William, yeoman, Herne, Kent, 1639 CKS PRC20/11/480
Turner, William, Chetwynd (Howle), Shrops, 1663 LJRO:cards/1663/58
Turner, William, Queenborough, Kent, 1673 CKS PRC2/35/181
Turner, William, Donnington, Sussex, 1683 W. Suss RO EpI/33/1682/42
Turner, William, yeoman, Warfield, Berks, 1684 Berks RO D/A1/218/62C
Turner, William, yeoman, Arksey (Bentley), Yorks, 1805 Borthwick Test C.P. 1805/6
Turner, Wyllyam, Milton next Sittingbourne, Kent, 1582 CKS PRC2/2/123
Turner/Hurleston, Margarett, Whitstable, Kent, 1617 CKS PRC2/24/128
Turner/Peters, Joane, Sittingbourne, Kent, 1674 CKS PRC2/36/110
Turner, see Savadge,
Turney, Innocent, Linslade, Bucks, 1622 Lincs RO Ad/Ac/17/104
Turnly, Thomas, yeoman, Lympne, Kent, 1679 CKS PRC2/38/77
Turnor, John, Old Romney, Kent, 1610 CKS PRC2/15/402
Turnor, Richard, Sandwich St Peter, Kent, 1576 CKS PRC2/1/156
Turnor, Robert, Ivychurch, Kent, 1569 CKS PRC21/4/252
Turpin, John, Ambrosden (Blackthorn), Oxon, 1638 Oxon RO MSS Wills 87/3/15
Turpine, Israell, Dover St Mary, Kent, 1595 CKS PRC21/13/60
Turr, George, Haxey, Lincs, 1602 Lincs RO Ad/Ac/37/144
Turr, John, Haxey, Lincs, 1618? Lincs RO Ad/Ac/8b/316
Turre, Thomas, yeoman, Haxey, Lincs, 1617 Lincs RO Ad/Ac/8b/209
Tursewell, Edmund, Gainsborough, Lincs, 1680 Lincs RO Ad/Ac/43/146
Turton, Richard, Dunstew, Oxon, 1638 Oxon RO MSS Wills 175/1/9
Turton, William, ironmaster, West Bromwich, Staffs, 1807 LJRO/B/C/5/1807/94
Turvey, Thomas, Lavant, East, Sussex, 1644 W. Suss RO EpIV/10/2A/3
Turveye, Thomas, Petham, Kent, 1611 CKS PRC2/16/57
Turvill, Henry, New Parks, Leics, 1641 Leics RO PR/I/41A/61
Tuson, Titus, Coningsby, Lincs, 1637 Lincs RO Ad/Ac/25/564
Tutchins, Margaret, Tackley, Oxon, 1631 Oxon RO MSS Wills 300/4/45
Tutchyn, Henry, Smarden, Kent, 1600 CKS PRC2/11/310
Tutt, John, Salisbury, Wilts, 1669 Wilts RO Miscellaneous Index (name + date)
Tutt, William, clothier, Benenden, Kent, 1675 CKS PRC2/36/251
Tuttey, John, Ewelme, Oxon, 1645 Oxon RO MSS Wills 87/3/23
Tutton, John, yeoman, Teynham, Kent, 1634 CKS PRC2/32/174
Tuxford, Ralfe, Coningsby, Lincs, 1633 Lincs RO Ad/Ac/24/167
Tuxford, William, Coningsby, Lincs, 1650 Lincs RO Ad/Ac/30/3
Tuxforth, Christobell, Grimoldby, Lincs, 1639 Lincs RO Ad/Ac/26/272
Tuxforth, Edward, Ludford, Lincs, 1634 Lincs RO Ad/Ac/24/246
Tuxworth, Stephen, Lissington, Lincs, 1671 Lincs RO Ad/Ac/33/186
Tuxworth, Thomas, yeoman, Ashby, Lincs, 1669 Lincs RO Ad/Ac/33/125
Twidall, William, Ingham, Lincs, 1662 Lincs RO Ad/Ac/41/4
Twiford, Edmund, Fosdyke, Lincs, 1593 Lincs RO Ad/Ac/3/45
Twiford, Katherine, Stoke-upon-Trent, Staffs, 1675 LJRO:cards/1675/55

[Twigg:]
Twigg, Henry, yeoman, Bratoft, Lincs, 1680 Lincs RO Ad/Ac/34/67
Twigge, John, Welton le Wold, Lincs, 1618 Lincs RO Ad/Ac/14/232
Twight, Phoebe, Wells Next The Sea, Norf, 1739 Norfolk RO ANW/23/23/16A
Twiney, Nicholas, shopkeeper, Melksham, Wilts, 1734? Wilts RO Arch. Sarum(+ name and date)
Twisden, Elizabeth, mrs/widow, Wye, Kent, 1626 CKS PRC2/27/169
Twisleton, Christopher, Althorpe (Amcotts), Lincs, 1627 Lincs RO Ad/Ac/39/100
Twitty, John, dyer, Coventry, Warks, 1759 LJRO/B/C/5/1759/203
Twogood, Joane, Deverill, Longbridge, Wilts, 1640 Wilts RO Arch. Sarum(+ name and date)
Twogood, Joane, Deverill, Longbridge, Wilts, 1640 Wilts RO Miscellaneous Index (name + date)
Twogood, Richard, gentleman, Newton, South, Wilts, 1683 Wilts RO Arch. Sarum(+ name and date)
Twoley, Robert, Scrivelsby, Lincs, 1639 Lincs RO Ad/Ac/26/305
Twomley, Andrew, Shenstone (Footherly), Staffs, 1683 LJRO/B/C/5/1708/43
Twomley, Charles, Ridware, Hamstall (Netherton), Staffs, 1685 LJRO/B/C/5/1685/101
Twyddall, Joane, widow, Aldington, Kent, 1600 CKS PRC21/15/188
Twyman, Henry, St Laurence Thanet, Kent, 1700 CKS PRC2/42/159
Twyman, Zacharye, St Johns Thanet, Kent, 1609 CKS PRC2/15/394
Twymer, Richard, Milton next Sittingbourne, Kent, 1603 CKS PRC2/14/444
Tybball, William + Joane, Blean, Kent, 1613 CKS PRC2/17/268
Tybbolte, John, Warwick St Nicholas, Warks, 1589 Worcs RO 008.7 BA3585/838/83
Tybbottes, Robert, baker, Warwick St Mary, Warks, Worcs RO 008.7 BA3585/838/232
Tyce, John, Luddenham, Kent, 1631 CKS PRC2/31/70
Tydder/Lewes, John, Stogursey, Som, 1587 Somerset RO D/D/Cta/T45
Tyddyman, Thomas, Dover, Kent, 1636 CKS PRC20/11/478
Tydeman, Alexander, Dover, Kent, 1599 CKS PRC21/14/524
Tydmarshe, Walter, Longcot, Berks, 1587 Berks RO D/A1/217/54B
Tyer, John, St Columb Major, Corn, 1615 Cornwall RO AP/T266
Tyer, Richarde, Panton, Lincs, 1606 Lincs RO Ad/Ac/7/92
Tyesdale, Geffrey, Tydd St Mary, Lincs, 1607 Lincs RO Ad/Ac/7/94
Tyhurst, Thomas, Steyning, Sussex, 1670 W. Suss RO EpI/33/1670/22
Tylden, Henrye + Sislie, clergy: 'mr/clerk', Leeds, Kent, 1611 CKS PRC2/16/105
Tylden, John, Westwell, Kent, 1590 CKS PRC21/10/66
Tyler, Ann, widow, Sodbury, Old, Glos, 1786 GRO GDR/B4/2/T59
Tyler, Daniell, Tockenham, Wilts, 1617 Wilts RO Arch. Wilts.(+ name and date)
Tyler, Francis, Martley, Worcs, 1684 Worcs RO 008.7 BA3585/837/bdl 4
Tyler, John, Swineshead, Lincs, 1619 Lincs RO Ad/Ac/15/227
Tyler, John, Canterbury St Dunstan Without, Kent, 1634 CKS PRC2/32/122
Tyler, John, husbandman, Crowle, Lincs, 1667 Lincs RO Ad/Ac/33/21
Tyler, Roger, Kidderminster, Worcs, 1683 Worcs RO 008.7 BA3585/837/bdl 3
Tyler, Walter, clergy: 'clerk/curate', Wick, Som, 1633 Somerset RO D/D/Cta/T26
Tylley, Richard, Thakeham, Sussex, 1597 W. Suss RO EpI/33/1597/7
Tylliard, Edward, Oxford, Oxon, 1624 Oxon RO MSS Wills 300/4/24
Tyllie, John eld, Sidlesham, Sussex, 1618 W. Suss RO EpI/33/1617/22
Tylman, Robert, Hothfield, Kent, 1607 CKS PRC2/14/434
Tylman, Thomas, Waltham, Kent, 1584 CKS PRC2/3/165
Tylman, Zacharie, Smarden, Kent, 1598 CKS PRC2/9/365
Tylor, John, Faversham, Kent, 1686 CKS PRC2/41/81
Tylor, see Taylor,
Tylson, Edward, Boughton under Blean, Kent, 1614 CKS PRC20/2/506
Tylson, Richard, Sutton St James, Lincs, 1627 Lincs RO Ad/Ac/20b/94a
Tylson, Thomas, Timberland, Lincs, 1606 Lincs RO Ad/Ac/7/105
Tymbrell, Thomas, gentleman, Bradford on Avon, Wilts, 1630 Wilts RO Arch. Sarum(+ name and date)
Tymes, Robert, blacksmith, Sandford, Oxon, 1632 Oxon RO MSS Wills 300/4/46
Tyminge, John, Stamford, Lincs, 1605 Lincs RO Ad/Ac/6/17

Tyndale, Walter, esquire, St Giles without Cripplegate, London & Middlesex, 1686 PRO PROB5/1607
Tyre, Benjamin, yeoman, Shepton Mallet, Som, 1638 Somerset RO D/D/Cta/T6
Tyrold, Richard, yeoman, Farnborough, Berks, 1617 Berks RO D/A1/217/108B
Tyrold, William, yeoman, Hagbourne (West Hagbourne), Berks, 1595 Berks RO D/A1/17/65A
Tyrrey, Anthony, Throwleigh, Kent, 1596 CKS PRC2/8/224
Tyrrey, John, Charing, Kent, 1610 CKS PRC20/2/55
Tyrrold, Edward, husbandman, Drayton, Berks, 1646 Berks RO D/A1/217/169B
Tyrrold, John, yeoman, Drayton, Berks, 1632 Berks RO D/A1/217/142B
Tyrrold, Joshua, tailor, Hendred, West (East Ginge), Berks, 1680 Berks RO D/A1/218/47C
Tyrry, Robert + Joane, Chart, Little, Kent, 1574 CKS PRC2/1/83
Tysbery, Stephen, husbandman, Speen, Berks, 1595 Berks RO D/A1/217/71B
Tysedale, Richard, Worth, Kent, 1611 CKS PRC20/2/260
Tysedale, William, husbandman, Tydd St Mary, Lincs, 1683 Lincs RO Ad/Ac/44/85
Tyser, Henrie, Nonington, Kent, 1617 CKS PRC20/4/385
Tysoe, Ambrose, Broadway, Worcs, 1687 Worcs RO 008.7 BA3585/830/23
Tyson, Peter, Mareham le Fen, Lincs, 1627 Lincs RO Ad/Ac/20b/8
Tysser, Thomas, Sandwich, Kent, 1591 CKS PRC2/6/306
Uden, John, Elmsted, Kent, 1614 CKS PRC2/17/5
Udie, Christopher, Morvah, Corn, 1606 Cornwall RO AP/U2
Uffington, Andrewe, Preston next Wingham, Kent, 1606 CKS PRC2/14/453
Uffyngton, Thomas, Chislet, Kent, 1596 CKS PRC2/8/451
Umfree, Elizabeth, widow, Maddington, Wilts, 1628 Wilts RO Arch. Sarum(+ name and date)
Ummanden, Emmanuel, Cranbrook, Kent, 1638 CKS PRC2/34/307
Umpton, Edward, yeoman, Longcot, Berks, 1639 Berks RO D/A1/219/96B
Unch, John, Brent, South, Som, 1672 Somerset RO D/D/Cta/U1
Uncle, John, Walberton, Sussex, 1595 W. Suss RO EpI/33/1595/1
Underdowne, John, Faversham, Kent, 1710 CKS PRC1/17/44
Underdowne, Richard, Faversham, Kent, 1617 CKS PRC2/24/169
Underdowne, Thomas, cooper, Sandwich, Kent, 1677 CKS PRC2/37/204
Underdowne, Vincent, bachelor, Birchington, Kent, 1663 CKS PRC19/3/45
Underhill, Elizabeth, widow, Biddenden, Kent, 1668 CKS PRC1/13/134
Underhill, John, gentleman, Whitchurch (Crimscote), Warks, 1603 Worcs RO 008.7 BA3585/839/329
Underwater, Robert, Donington, Lincs, 1612 Lincs RO Ad/Ac/11/14
Underwood, John, Hampstead Norris, Berks, 1637 Berks RO D/A1/219/95B
Underwood, Thomas, Linsted, Kent, 1622 CKS PRC20/6/244
Underwood, Thomas, yeoman, Englefield, Berks, 1630 Berks RO D/A1/219/93B
Underwood, William, Hernhill, Kent, 1677 CKS PRC20/12/244
Underwood, William, bricklayer, Hackford, Norf, 1732 Norfolk RO ANW/23/20/52
Undy, Richard, Broughton, Hants, 1669 Hants RO 21m65 D8/224
Ungleye, Dorothie, widow, Sandwich, Kent, 1609 CKS PRC2/14/460
Unglie, Mathie, Sandwich, Kent, 1606 CKS PRC2/14/459
Unsworth, Gilbert, Leigh, Lancs, 1602 Lancs RO (Name of Deceased) D.R.C.H. 1602
Unsworth, Isaac, Maidstone, Kent, 1604 CKS PRC21/16/89
Unwin, Andrew, Belton, Lincs, 1631 Lincs RO Ad/Ac/39/293
Unwin, Elizabeth, Rotherham, Yorks, 1832 Borthwick Test C.P. 1827/9
Unwin, John, Haxey, Lincs, 1671 Lincs RO Ad/Ac/32/132
Unwin, John, cordwainer/bachelor, Wadworth, Yorks, 1821 Borthwick D/C C.P. 1821/1
Up Richard, Hugh, Lenham, Kent, 1624 CKS PRC2/24/180
Uphill, John, Glastonbury (Edgarley), Som, 1728 Somerset RO D/D/Cta/U2
Uphill, John, Glastonbury St John, Som, 1738 Somerset RO D/D/Cta/U3
Upjohn, Richard, St Mary, Hants, 1673 Hants RO 1672 AD115/2
Uppecks, John, Aslackby, Lincs, 1639 Lincs RO Ad/Ac/26/31
Upperton, John, Bury (West Burton), Sussex, 1669 W. Suss RO EpI/33/1669/1

[Upperton/Rose:]
Upperton/Rose, Jane, Littlehampton, Sussex, 1669 W. Suss RO EpI/33/1669/25
Upphill, Agnes, widow, Marston Magna, Som, 1625 Somerset RO D/D/Cta/T10
Upplebie, James, Barrow, Lincs, 1612 Lincs RO Ad/Ac/11/40
Uppleby, Thomas, Langton by Wragby, Lincs, 1648 Lincs RO Ad/Ac/30/304
Uppleby, Thomas, yeoman, Thornton Curtis, Lincs, 1664 Lincs RO Ad/Ac/43/18
Upton, Anne, widow, Throwleigh, Kent, 1633 CKS PRC2/32/126
Upton, Christian, Dover St James, Kent, 1598 CKS PRC21/14/538
Upton, Christian, spinster, St Margarets At Cliffe, Kent, 1618 CKS PRC20/4/395
Upton, Henry, Donington, Lincs, 1632 Lincs RO Ad/Ac/23/146
Upton, Joanne, Throwleigh, Kent, 1601 CKS PRC2/12/365
Upton, John, Linsted, Kent, 1617 CKS PRC2/24/168
Upton, John, Ospringe, Kent, 1617 CKS PRC2/26/127
Upton, John, Faversham, Kent, 1636 CKS PRC2/33/136
Upton, John, yeoman, Lower Hardres, Kent, 1664 CKS PRC1/10/100
Upton, John, husbandman, Tenterden, Kent, 1675 CKS PRC2/36/253
Upton, Nicholas, Leaveland, Kent, 1597 CKS PRC2/9/317
Upton, Richard, Throwleigh, Kent, 1616 CKS PRC2/24/166
Upton, Robert, yeoman, Northbourne, Kent, 1682 CKS PRC2/40/79
Upton, Thomas, Headcorn, Kent, 1601 CKS PRC2/12/367
Upton, Thomas, Throwleigh, Kent, 1616 CKS PRC2/24/173
Upton, Thomas, gentleman, Faversham, Kent, 1628 CKS PRC2/29/107
Upton, Thomas, Throwleigh, Kent, 1690 CKS PRC1/15/124
Upton, Thomas, Throwleigh, Kent, 1691 CKS PRC2/42/17
Upton, Valentyne, Cliffe, West, Kent, 1590 CKS PRC2/5/444
Upton, William, weaver: 'silk weaver', Canterbury St Paul, Kent, 1692 CKS PRC2/42/52
Upton/Rickford, Elizabeth, widow, Bersted, South, Sussex, 1671 W. Suss RO EpIV/10/2A/11
Upwood, Thomas, Newnham, Herts, 1596 Herts RO ASA25/1582
Urry, Thomas, Lymington, Hants, 1674 Hants RO 1673 AD145/3
Urryck, Thomas, Ashford, Kent, 1597 CKS PRC2/10/49
Urton, John, yeoman, Mattersey, Notts, 1821 Borthwick Test C.P. 1821/3
Usboorne, Marye, widow, Ebony, Kent, 1614 CKS PRC2/17/62
Usborn, Edward, yeoman, Staplehurst, Kent, 1673 CKS PRC2/35/263
Usborne, Barricke, Bishopsbourne, Kent, 1605 CKS PRC2/13/411
Usborne, Elizabeth, widow, Staplehurst, Kent, 1617 CKS PRC2/24/170
Usborne, James, Marden, Kent, 1611 CKS PRC2/16/80
Usborne, John, Stone in Oxney, Kent, 1608 CKS PRC2/15/429
Usborne, Marie, spinster, Staplehurst, Kent, 1628 CKS PRC2/29/105
Usborne, Thomas, Staplehurst, Kent, 1680 CKS PRC2/39/117
Usborne, Thomas eld, Staplehurst, Kent, 1614 CKS PRC2/18/110
Usher, James, Snave, Kent, 1708 CKS PRC1/17/16
Usher, Peter, St Johns Thanet, Kent, 1623 CKS PRC2/24/174
Usher, Thomas, St Peter in Thanet, Kent, 1662 CKS PRC1/8/116
Usher, Thomas, yeoman, Sutton Valence, Kent, 1668 CKS PRC1/13/135
Usher, William, Maidstone, Kent, 1641 CKS PRC19/2/43
Usmer, Richard, Lenham, Kent, 1624 CKS PRC2/24/179
Usmer, Robert, yeoman, Benenden, Kent, 1679 CKS PRC2/38/200
Usmer, Thomas, Headcorn, Kent, 1644 CKS PRC1/7/34
Usser, John, Smeeth, Kent, 1602 CKS PRC21/16/102
Ussher, John, Woodnesborough, Kent, 1583 CKS PRC2/3/45
Uting, Isabell, widow, Blyborough, Lincs, 1685 Lincs RO Ad/Ac/44/165
Utterbie, William, Rasen, Middle, (Tupholme), Lincs, 1612 Lincs RO Ad/Ac/11/90
Utting, George, Benington, Lincs, Lincs RO Ad/Ac/19A/30
Utting, Thomas, Norwich, Norf, 1761 Norfolk RO ANW/23/25/72A
Uttinge, George, Benington, Lincs, Lincs RO Ad/Ac/19A/37
Uttinge, George, Benington, Lincs, 1622 Lincs RO Ad/Ac/19B/38

Uttinge, Thomas, Benington, Lincs, 1605 Lincs RO Ad/Ac/6/109
Vagg, Richard, Batcombe, Som, 1611 Somerset RO D/D/Cta/V9
Vagger, Henry, Steyning, Sussex, 1684 W. Suss RO EpI/33/1684/32
Vaham?, Silvester, St Laurence Thanet, Kent, 1620 CKS PRC2/24/172
Vahan, George, yeoman, Harbledown, Kent, 1617 CKS PRC2/24/161
Vailye, John, Dover, Kent, 1668 CKS PRC19/4/35
Vale, George, Ruckinge, Kent, 1607 CKS PRC2/14/457
Vale, Giles, Tarring, West, Sussex, 1612 W. Suss RO EpIV/10/1/10
Vale, Thomas, Tenterden, Kent, 1588 CKS PRC2/4/307
Valentine, James, university: 'Fellow of Trinity College, Cambridge/Regius, Professor of Greek/B.D.' Cambridge (Trinity College), Cambs, 1667 CUL V.C. Acc./Box3/50
Vallence, George, yeoman, Hernhill, Kent, 1690 CKS PRC19/4/123
Valler, John, yeoman, Headley, Hants, 1677 Hants RO 21m65 D8/273
Valler, Nicholas, Rogate, Sussex, 1630 W. Suss RO EpI/33/1630/10
Vallett, Mary, Southampton, Hants, 1693 Hants RO 21m65 D8/361
Vallier, Thomas, yeoman, Hougham, Kent, 1639 CKS PRC1/3/55
Vallis, George, yeoman, Shrewton, Wilts, 1645 Wilts RO Arch. Sarum(+ name and date)
Vallis, Thomas, Chichester St Bartholomew, Sussex, 1635 W. Suss RO EpIII/9/1/43
Valye, Ales, Bere Regis, Dors, 1593 Wilts RO Miscellaneous Index (name + date)
Van Acker, John, dyer, Dover, Kent, 1663 CKS PRC19/3/46
Van Acker, Peter, Sandwich, Kent, 1683 CKS PRC2/40/160
Van Buxall, Abraham, Sandwich, Kent, 1662 CKS PRC1/9/66
Van Dale, William, Maidstone, Kent, 1621 CKS PRC20/5/192
Van de glaze see Vandeglaze,
Van de velde, Jacomine, widow, Sandwich, Kent, 1625 CKS PRC2/24/181
Van de Wall, Anthony, Sandwich, Kent, 1623 CKS PRC2/24/167
Van de Waller, John, Sandwich St Clement, Kent, 1671 CKS PRC1/15/74
Van Hewle, Andrew, stranger, Sandwich, Kent, 1600 CKS PRC2/11/337
Van Niewenhuise, John, Sandwich, Kent, 1631 CKS PRC20/9/450
Van Raede, John eld, Sandwich, Kent, 1600 CKS PRC2/11/341
Van Staen/Verstaens, Margarita, widow, Sandwich, Kent, 1617 CKS PRC2/24/158
Van Wylder, Wyllyam, Dover, Kent, 1599 CKS PRC21/14/489
Vanaker, Jacob, Sandwich, Kent, 1690 CKS PRC2/41/164
Vandebrooke, Charles, Sandwich St Peter, Kent, 1621 CKS PRC2/24/175
Vandeglaze, Isaacke, Sandwich, Kent, 1639 CKS PRC2/34/306
Vandeglaze, Samuel eld, whitesmith, Sandwich, Kent, 1638 CKS PRC2/34/139
Vandepere, Magdalene, widow, Canterbury St Alphege, Kent, 1612 CKS PRC20/2/312
Vanderclitt, see Dowland,
Vanderhaghe, Garrett, Ashford, Kent, 1595 CKS PRC2/7/168
Vanderluit, Jacob, Lambeth, Surrey, 1706 PRO PROB5/1264
Vanderlure, Peter, Boston, Lincs, 1640 Lincs RO Ad/Ac/27/46
VanderPeere, see Peere,
Vanderskare, John, goldsmith, Sandwich, Kent, 1616 CKS PRC2/24/162
Vanderslate, Mary, widow, Ashford, Kent, 1677 CKS PRC2/37/205
Vanderspie, Daniell, Sandwich, Kent, 1638 CKS PRC2/34/297
Vandeslate, Peter, yeoman, Sandwich St Clement, Kent, 1673 CKS PRC2/35/264
Vandewall, John, Sandwich, Kent, 1612 CKS PRC2/17/199
Vane, William, Stone in Oxney, Kent, 1617 CKS PRC2/24/160
Vanhill, Martha, widow, Sandwich St Peter, Kent, 1611 CKS PRC2/16/48
Vanhuele, Charles, Sandwich, Kent, 1612 CKS PRC2/17/426
Vann, William, yeoman, Wittersham, Kent, 1670 CKS PRC19/4/97
Vanner, Joane, mrs/spinster, Canterbury St George Martyr, Kent, 1623 CKS PRC2/24/178
Vannos, Scarlott, husbandman, Stanground, Hunts, 1684 Hunts RO/Acc58/240(242)
Vanstaen, Charles, Sandwich, Kent, 1613 CKS PRC2/17/254
Vante, Thomas, Canterbury Holy Cross Westgate, Kent, 1612 CKS PRC2/16/166

[Varley:]
Varley, John, jobber, Pool, Yorks, 1803 Borthwick Test C.P. 1803/4
Varley, Richard, wire worker, York, Yorks, 1818 Borthwick Test C.P. 1818/12
Varley, Robert, clergy: 'clerk', Kelstern, Lincs, 1598 Lincs RO Ad/Ac/4/81
Varnam, Thomas, Canterbury St Paul, Kent, 1603 CKS PRC2/14/465
Vassell, Jane, spinster, Canterbury St Mary Northgate, Kent, 1621 CKS PRC2/24/176
Vaudrey, Margaret, widow, Bowdon (Hale), Ches, 1664 Cheshire RO (Name) W.C. 1663
Vaugham, Barbara, Hythe West, Kent, 1596 CKS PRC2/8/21
Vaughan, Edward, cooper, Watford, Herts, 1588 Herts RO ASA25/1253
Vaughan, Edward, Baschurch, Shrops, 1675 LJRO:cards/1675/56
Vaughan, Giles, Milton next Sittingbourne, Kent, 1616 CKS PRC2/24/171
Vaughan, Henry, Welford, Berks, 1613 Berks RO D/A1/219/91B
Vaughan, John, clergy: 'clerk', Butterwick, Lincs, 1625 Lincs RO Ad/Ac/19B/65
Vaughan, Roger, university: 'scholar's servant', Cambridge St Botolph, Cambs, 1613 c. CUL V.C.Acc./Box1/53
Vaughan, Thomas, cook, Cambridge (Queens' College), Cambs, 1602 c. CUL V.C.Acc./Box1/54
Vaughan, Virgill, gentleman, Paulton, Som, 1631 Somerset RO D/D/Cta/V1
Vaughan, William, carpenter, Condover, Shrops, 1799 LJRO/B/C/5/1799/58
Vaughane, Elyas, Burmarsh, Kent, 1585 CKS PRC2/3/230
Vaus, Alice, widow, Sleaford, Lincs, 1638 Lincs RO Ad/Ac/25/191
Vause, Robert, yeoman, Binbrook St Mary, Lincs, 1613 Lincs RO Ad/Ac/12/57
Vavasour, Henry, Laughton, Lincs, 1639 Lincs RO Ad/Ac/43/3
Vavaster, William, Ropsley, Lincs, 1613 Lincs RO Ad/Ac/11/51
Vawdrey, William, innholder, Watlington, Oxon, 1628 Oxon RO MSS Wills 175/4/2
Veale, Anne, Bilsby, Lincs, 1640 Lincs RO Ad/Ac/27/149
Veale, Henry, Huntspill, Som, 1665 Somerset RO D/D/Cta/V4
Veale, Thomas, clergy: 'clerk', Mablethorpe, Lincs, 1624 Lincs RO Ad/Ac/18/109
Veale, Thomas, Bilsby, Lincs, 1648 Lincs RO Ad/Ac/30/271
Veale, Walter, St Stephens by Saltash, Corn, 1619 Cornwall RO AP/V53/3
Veare, Edward, blacksmith, Watlington, Oxon, 1684 Oxon RO MSS Wills 87/6/7
Veare, Richard, husbandman, Reepham, Lincs, 1628 Lincs RO Ad/Ac/39/9
Veere, Jane, Queenborough, Kent, 1641 CKS PRC1/5/54
Veisye, Roger, Croscombe, Som, 1588 Somerset RO D/D/Cta/V8
Venables, James, Middlewich, Ches, 1649 Cheshire RO (Name) W.C. 1649
Venteman, Thomas, Blean, Kent, 1668 CKS PRC1/13/136
Venteman, Wyllyam, Sandwich, Kent, 1582 CKS PRC2/2/212
Ventyman, Thomas, Petham, Kent, 1619 CKS PRC2/24/165
Verbrugh, John, Sandwich, Kent, 1641 CKS PRC1/6/32
Verdon, Sarah, spinster, Norwich, Norf, 1713 Norfolk RO NCC INV/69D/23
Veree, Hubert, Canterbury St Mary Northgate, Kent, 1641 CKS PRC1/5/55
Verhaghe, Barbara, widow, Sandwich, Kent, 1621 CKS PRC2/24/177
Verman, George, St Just in Roseland, Corn, 1615 Cornwall RO AP/V41/2
Verman, William, Huntspill, Som, 1664 Somerset RO D/D/Cta/V5
Vernam, Robert, Bath St Michael, Som, 1621 Somerset RO D/D/Cta/T13
Vernell, Ralph, Finchampstead, Berks, 1663 Berks RO D/A1/219/103B
Vernon, George, husbandman, Wittering, West, Sussex, 1677 W. Suss RO EpI/33/1677/2
Vernon, James, clergy: 'mr/vicar', Godmersham, Kent, 1623 CKS PRC20/6/201
Vernon, John, clergy: 'clerk/vicar', Cookham, Berks, 1629 Berks RO D/A1/219/92B
Vernon, Thomas, Warwick, Warks, 1604 Worcs RO 008.7 BA3585/839/392
Vernon, William, Audley, Staffs, 1682 LJRO/B/C/5/1681/41
Vernon, William, Stoneley, Ches, 1682 Cheshire RO (Name) W.C. 1682
Veroe, Willyam, yeoman, Aswarby, Lincs, 1599 Lincs RO Ad/Ac/5/109
Verrall, Francis, Sandwich St Peter, Kent, 1664 CKS PRC1/10/101
Verrall, see Ferrall,
Verrier, Francis, Charing, Kent, 1674 CKS PRC2/35/262
Verrier, John, Sutton by Dover, Kent, 1619 CKS PRC2/24/164

Verrier, Reynold, Birchington, Kent, 1680 CKS PRC20/13/69
Verrinder, William, Cranham, Glos, 1821 GRO GDR/B4/2/V13
Verryer/Ferryer, Stephen, Sandwich, Kent, 1619 CKS PRC2/21/58
Verser, Daniel, yeoman, Rolvenden, Kent, 1686 CKS PRC2/41/84
Verser, Jervase, Wittersham, Kent, 1634 CKS PRC20/11/484
Verslate, Jacob, Sandwich, Kent, 1607 CKS PRC2/14/463
Versoll, John, Cheriton, Kent, 1619 CKS PRC2/24/163
Verstaens see Van staen/Verstaens,
Verstaens, see Van Staen,
Very, Thomas, Salisbury St Martin, Wilts, 1625 Wilts RO Miscellaneous Index (name + date)
Veryer, Rychard, Northbourne, Kent, 1595 CKS PRC2/7/385
Vessey, William, baker, St Martin in the Fields, London & Middlesex, 1670 PRO PROB32/8/18
Vessie, Nicholas, Stallingborough, Lincs, 1622 Lincs RO Ad/Ac/17/7
Vessor, John eld, Canterbury St Dunstan Without, Kent, 1590 CKS PRC2/5/49
Viall, Henry, gentleman, Ashford, Kent, 1672 CKS PRC2/35/186
Vicars, Robert, Thurlby, Lincs, 1630s? Lincs RO Ad/Ac/24/278
Vicars, William, Stragglethorpe, Lincs, 1607 Lincs RO Ad/Ac/8a/180
Vickars, Francis, Chesterfield, Derby, 1667 LJRO:cards/1667/85
Vickers, Edward, gentleman, Penn (Nether Penn), Staffs, 1781 LJRO/B/C/5/1789/129b
Vickers, Joan, widow, Baltonsborough, Som, 1627 Somerset RO D/D/Cta/T12
Videan, Ann, mrs/widow, Canterbury, Kent, 1639 CKS PRC20/11/492
Videan, Hammond, yeoman, Molash, Kent, 1664 CKS PRC1/10/102
Videan, Thomas, Woodchurch, Kent, 1689 CKS PRC20/13/622
Videan, William, Maidstone, Kent, 1630 CKS PRC20/9/448
Videan, William, Linton, Kent, 1675 CKS PRC2/36/135
Vidgean, Andrew, blacksmith, Preston next Faversham, Kent, 1694 CKS PRC2/42/96
Vidgen, Thomas, yeoman, Eastchurch, Sheppey, Kent, 1665 CKS PRC1/10/103
Vidgeon, Andrew, yeoman, Throwleigh, Kent, 1668 CKS PRC1/13/137
Vidgeon, Daniel, Ham, Kent, 1719 CKS PRC1/18/30
Vidgeon, James, Wye, Kent, 1670 CKS PRC1/14/116
Vidgeon, Richard, yeoman, Stalisfield, Kent, 1695 CKS PRC1/16/19
Vidgin, John, Eastchurch, Sheppey, Kent, 1625 CKS PRC2/25/148
Vidian, Andrew, Chilham, Kent, 1598 CKS PRC2/10/88
Vidian, Patience, spinster, Maidstone, Kent, 1634 CKS PRC20/11/488
Vidian, Thomas, Mersham, Kent, 1628 CKS PRC2/29/106
Vidian/Hills, Dorothy, Boughton Monchelsea, Kent, 1635 CKS PRC2/33/137
Vigen, John, Warehorne, Kent, 1638 CKS PRC1/1/92
Viggars, John, Norton in Hales, Shrops, 1674 LJRO:cards/1674/49
Vigor, Robert, Hemington, Som, 1634 Somerset RO D/D/Cta/T11
Vigurs, Stephen, Launceston, Corn, 1636 Cornwall RO AP/V101/5
Vinall, Edward, husbandman, Woodchurch, Kent, 1676 CKS PRC20/12/224
Vinall, John, New Romney, Kent, 1617 CKS PRC20/4/397
Vinall, Thomasine, widow, Lydd, Kent, 1612 CKS PRC20/2/310
Vinall, William, Snargate, Kent, 1616 CKS PRC2/24/159
Vinar/Phillips, Elizabeth, Bremhill, Wilts, 1615 Wilts RO Arch. Wilts.(+ name and date)
Vincent, Barbara, Fovant, Wilts, 1615 Wilts RO Miscellaneous Index (name + date)2
Vincent, Elizabeth, widow, Midhurst, Sussex, 1607 W. Suss RO EpI/33/1607/15
Vincent, John, Mareham le Fen, Lincs, 1605 Lincs RO Ad/Ac/6/50
Vincent, John, Glastonbury, Som, 1729 Somerset RO D/D/Cta/V2
Vincent, John eld, Midhurst, Sussex, 1608 W. Suss RO EpI/33/1607/3
Vincent, Martinne, tanner, Gainsborough, Lincs, 1608 Lincs RO Ad/Ac/37/268a
Vincent, Mary, widow, St Giles without Cripplegate, London & Middlesex, 1714 PRO PROB5/1388
Vincent, Mathias, knight, 1690 Lambeth Palace Arches G40/3
Vincent, Matthias, knight, Islington St Mary, London & Middlesex, 1688 PRO PROB32/27/19

[Vincent:]
Vincent, Thomas, Rippingale, Lincs, 1637 Lincs RO Ad/Ac/25/636
Vincent, Thomas, farmer, Tottenhill, Norf, 1756 Norfolk RO ANF/11/5/13
Vincomb, William, carrier, Cranbrook, Kent, 1675 CKS PRC2/36/252
Vincord, Joshua, clothier ?, Sandwich, Kent, 1639 CKS PRC2/34/298
Vine, Alexander, Cranbrook, Kent, 1676 CKS PRC2/37/101
Vine, Richard, gentleman, Threckingham, Lincs, 1670? Lincs RO Ad/Ac/32/46
Vineing, Joseph, Wells, Som, Somerset RO D/D/Cta/V7
Viner, Christopher, yeoman, Ashbury, Berks, 1705 Berks RO D/A1/219/119B
Viner, Jane, spinster, Salisbury, Wilts, 1682 Wilts RO Miscellaneous Index (name + date)
Vines, Kenelme, Stickney, Lincs, 1666 Lincs RO Ad/Ac/32/78
Viney, Elizabeth eld, Sandwich St Mary, Kent, 1668 CKS PRC1/13/138
Viney, Jeremie, Hawkhurst, Kent, 1628 CKS PRC2/29/108
Viney, Samuel, clothier, Staplehurst, Kent, 1639 CKS PRC2/34/295
Viney, Walter, Staplehurst, Kent, 1634 CKS PRC2/32/176
Viney, William, Tenterden, Kent, 1625 CKS PRC2/25/149
Vinsent, James, Berwick St John, Wilts, 1640? Wilts RO Arch. Sarum(+ name and date)
Vinsent, John, Withern, Lincs, 1624 Lincs RO Ad/Ac/19A/99
Vinter, Robert, yeoman, Firsby, Lincs, 1664 Lincs RO Ad/Ac/43/30
Vintner, Gabriell, Syston, Lincs, 1593 Lincs RO Ad/Ac/3/95
Viny, Thomas, Maidstone, Kent, 1623 CKS PRC20/6/250
Violett, Thomas, Milton next Sittingbourne, Kent, 1680 CKS PRC2/39/116
Violett, William, Oving, Sussex, 1671 W. Suss RO EpI/33/1670/18
Violett, William, tailor, Milton next Sittingbourne, Kent, 1678 CKS PRC2/37/203
Violls, John, Orton, Northants, 1673 Northants RO NWill A/C/134
Virgin, Thomas, yeoman, East Sutton, Kent, 1665 CKS PRC1/11/90
Virgin, see Hartup,
Virgo, Thomas, Faversham, Kent, 1610 CKS PRC2/15/427
Vivashe, William, Compton Basset, Wilts, 1618 Wilts RO CC Sarum(+ name and date)
Vivers, Dorothy, Shrewsbury St Chad, Shrops, 1682 LJRO/B/C/5/1681/42
Vizard, Arthur, maltster, Bristol St John, Glos, Bristol RO 1685/75
Voce, John, yeoman, Mobberley, Ches, 1782 Cheshire RO (Name) W.C. 1782
Vois, Francis, gardener, Tenterden, Kent, 1674 CKS PRC2/36/136
Voke, Edward, Compton, Sussex, 1671 W. Suss RO EpI/33/1670/19
Vokins, John, Theale, Berks, Berks RO D/A1/219/88B
Vokins, John, husbandman, Langford, Oxon, 1671 Oxon RO MSS Wills Pec 78/5/29
Vorley, Em, Brothertoft, Lincs, 1593 Lincs RO Ad/Ac/3/47
Vowe, Thomas, gentleman, Hallington, Leics, 1625 Lincs RO Ad/Ac/19B/108
Vowler, Degory, husbandman, Launcells, Corn, 1642 Cornwall RO AP/V129/4
Vowles, Grace, Pennard, West, Som, Somerset RO D/D/Cta/V6
Vowles, Mary, Blagdon, Som, 1704 Somerset RO D/D/Cta/V3
Vulckenes/Falconer, Mary, Sandwich, Kent, 1593 CKS PRC2/6/294
Vurnsey, Isaacke, Calne, Wilts, 1639 Wilts RO Miscellaneous Index (name + date)
Vyan, Antony, St Mewan, Corn, 1635 Cornwall RO AP/V106
Vydgian, John, Lyminge, Kent, 1615 CKS PRC20/3/142
Vydgian, John, Lyminge, Kent, 1615 CKS PRC20/3/146
Vydyan, Anthony, Maidstone, Kent, 1583 CKS PRC21/6/291
Vyle, Humphrey, mariner?, St Margarets At Cliffe, Kent, 1640 CKS PRC20/11/490
Vyney, Moses, Sandwich, Kent, 1665 CKS PRC1/10/104
Vyney, William, Headcorn, Kent, 1684 CKS PRC2/40/251
Vyolett, Elizabeth, spinster, Reculver, Kent, 1619 CKS PRC20/4/393
Vyrgyn, Edward, Bekesbourne, Kent, 1595 CKS PRC2/7/267
Vyrier, Richard, Little Mongeham, Kent, 1628 CKS PRC2/29/104
Waade, Allen, Boston, Lincs, 1612 Lincs RO Ad/Ac/11/9
Wabbut, Jonas, yeoman, Sutton St Edmunds, Lincs, 1684 Lincs RO Ad/Ac/44/134
Wace, Francis, cordwainer: 'shoemaker', Stanton Harcourt (Sutton), Oxon, 1673 Oxon RO MSS

Wills 88/2/38
Wacher, John, Woodchurch, Kent, 1596 CKS PRC21/14/111
Wacher, John, yeoman, Smeeth, Kent, 1619 CKS PRC20/4/442
Wacher, Robert, Goodnestone next Wingham, Kent, 1603 CKS PRC21/17/59
Wacher, Thomas, Barham, Kent, 1608 CKS PRC2/14/480
Wacher, Thomas, husbandman, Hackington, Kent, 1626 CKS PRC2/27/179
Wacher, William, yeoman, Frittenden, Kent, 1622 CKS PRC2/26/23
Wachers, Anne, widow, Milton next Sittingbourne, Kent, 1668 CKS PRC1/13/139
Wachers, John, Brookland, Kent, 1640 CKS PRC1/5/56
Wachers, Mathew, Biddenden, Kent, 1617 CKS PRC2/26/9
Wachier, Joane, widow, St Peter in Thanet, Kent, 1613 CKS PRC2/18/61
Wachier, John, Ash next Sandwich, Kent, 1599 CKS PRC21/15/41
Wachier, William, St Johns Thanet, Kent, 1601 CKS PRC2/12/375
Wachiers, Joseph, Brookland, Kent, 1619 CKS PRC2/26/74
Wachiers, Thomas, Old Romney, Kent, 1613 CKS PRC2/17/242
Wacombe, John, Merther, Corn, 1603 Cornwall RO AP/W30/3
Waddell, Elizabeth, widow, Hothfield, Kent, 1681 CKS PRC2/39/256
Waddell, John, Brabourne, Kent, 1638 CKS PRC2/34/153
Waddell, Nicholas, Sturry, Kent, 1625 CKS PRC2/25/150
Waddell, see Ireland,
Waddingham, Christopher, husbandman, Coningsby, Lincs, 1642 Lincs RO Ad/Ac/28/45
Waddingham, Richard, Stickford, Lincs, 1623 Lincs RO Ad/Ac/18/87
Waddingham, Thomas, Mareham le Fen, Lincs, 1599 Lincs RO Ad/Ac/5/177
Waddingham, William, Barton, Lincs, 1662 Lincs RO Ad/Ac/32/40
Waddington, Edward, Maidstone, Kent, 1577 CKS PRC21/3/37
Wade, Edward, cheesemonger, St Martin in the Fields, London & Middlesex, 1673 PRO PROB32/10/13
Wade, Hugh, 1626 Lancs RO (Name of Deceased) D.R.C.H. 1626
Wade, Jane,
Glos Bristol RO 1697/38
Wade, John, innholder, Stamford, Lincs, 1637 Lincs RO Ad/Ac/25/370
Wade, John, surgeon: 'barber-surgeon', Lydd, Kent, 1674 CKS PRC20/12/154
Wade, John, surgeon: 'barber-surgeon', Lydd, Kent, 1680 CKS PRC20/13/73
Wade, John, farmer, Hutton Pagnell, Yorks, 1771 Borthwick Test C.P. 1771/3
Wade, Margaret, widow, Dover, Kent, 1616 CKS PRC20/3/472
Wade, Richard, Chew Magna, Som, 1647 Somerset RO D/D/Cta/W27
Wade, Simon, Langton, Lincs, 1638 Lincs RO Ad/Ac/25/127
Wade, Thomas, Barnham, Sussex, 1610 W. Suss RO EpI/33/1610/8
Wade, Thomas, clergy: 'mr/vicar', Chislet, Kent, 1634 CKS PRC2/32/179
Wade, Valentine, Hollingbourne, Kent, 1632 CKS PRC20/9/468
Wade, William, nailer, Bristol St James, Glos, Bristol RO 1678/74
Wade, William, Steeping, Little, Lincs, 1697 Lincs RO Ad/Ac/44/170
Wadesman, William, Stamford, Lincs, 1637 Lincs RO Ad/Ac/25/574
Wadeson, Jefferey, clergy: 'clerk', Beckingham, Lincs, 1638 Lincs RO Ad/Ac/25/240
Wadeson, John, cordwainer, Grantham, Lincs, 1623 Lincs RO Ad/Ac/18/79
Wadingham, Thomas, Coningsby, Lincs, 1645 Lincs RO Ad/Ac/28/144
Wadington, John, poulterer/citizen,
London & Middlesex 1672 PRO PROB5/1445
Wadman/Tipper, William, butcher, Salisbury St Edmund, Wilts, 1644 Wilts RO CC Sarum(+ name and date)
Wadmore, Christopher, Dibden, Hants, 1626 Hants RO 21M65 D8/137
Wadsworth, Thomas, Grimsby, Great, Lincs, 1638 Lincs RO Ad/Ac/25/29
Wadwell, Thomas, Barham, Kent, 1627 CKS PRC2/27/185
Wafer, John, yeoman, Folkestone, Kent, 1682 CKS PRC2/39/251
Waffer (Swaffer?), John, Folkestone, Kent, 1710 CKS PRC1/17/45

[Wager:]
Wager, William, St Johns Thanet, Kent, 1598 CKS PRC2/10/6
Waggon, Edward, Goudhurst, Kent, 1631 CKS PRC2/31/82
Waghorn, Edward, Goudhurst, Kent, 1615 CKS PRC2/26/93
Waghorne, Joane, widow, Hawkhurst, Kent, 1592 CKS PRC2/6/488
Waghorne, John, Hawkhurst, Kent, 1612 CKS PRC2/16/23
Waghorne, Rychard, Benenden, Kent, 1587 CKS PRC2/4/456
Wagstaffe, see Grime,
Waight, Geofferie, Wootton Bassett, Wilts, 1631 Wilts RO Arch. Wilts.(+ name and date)
Waight, William, Worthy, Kings, Hants, 1667 Hants RO 21M65 D8/197
Wailesbie, Susan, widow, Leverton, Lincs, 1641 Lincs RO Ad/Ac/27/345
Wain, Sarah, widow, Alstonfield, Staffs, 1811 LJRO/B/C/5/1811/72
Wainflet, Thomas, Spilsby, Lincs, 1635 Lincs RO Ad/Ac/24/306
Wainwright, Daniel, apothecary, Stow on the Wold, Glos, 1738 GRO GDR/B4/2/W69
Wainwright, John, Nocton, Lincs, 1646 Lincs RO Ad/Ac/28/212
Waire, Arthur, Cumberworth, Lincs, 1639 Lincs RO Ad/Ac/26/191
Waite, John, Postling, Kent, 1638 CKS PRC2/34/312
Waite, Richard, mason, Oxford St Ebbe, Oxon, 1666 Oxon RO MSS Wills 88/2/5
Wake, Edward, Milton next Sittingbourne, Kent, 1638 CKS PRC2/34/142
Wake, Henry, Froyle, Hants, 1679 Hants RO 21m65 D8/298
Wake, Mathewe, yeoman, Boston, Lincs, 1626 Lincs RO Ad/Ac/20/17
Wake, Richard, tailor, Blyton, Lincs, 1673 Lincs RO Ad/Ac/35/56
Wake, Richard, yeoman, Winestead, Yorks, 1817 Borthwick Test C.P. 1817/2
Wake, Thomas, Alvediston, Wilts, 1616 Wilts RO Miscellaneous Index (name + date)
Wake, William, Chartham, Kent, 1621 CKS PRC2/26/22
Wakefeild, William, Mersham, Kent, 1629 CKS PRC2/29/109
Wakefeld, Philip, Goxhill, Lincs, 1569 Lincs RO Ad/Ac/2C/128
Wakefield, Barbara, Tutbury, Staffs, 1675 LJRO:cards/1675/57
Wakefield, Izabell, widow, Mersham, Kent, 1631 CKS PRC20/9/480
Wakefield, Josias, Dover, Kent, 1631 CKS PRC20/9/492
Wakefield, Richard, maltster/bachelor, Birmingham, Warks, 1806 LJRO/B/C/5/1806/134
Wakefield, Robert, Torksey, Lincs, 1633 Lincs RO Ad/Ac/39/309
Wakefield, Robert, Hurst, Old, Hunts, 1771 Hunts RO/Acc58/331
Wakefield, Silvester, widow, Dover, Kent, 1634 CKS PRC20/11/562
Wakeford, Elizabeth, Lurgashall, Sussex, 1640 W. Suss RO EpI/33/1640/31
Wakeham, Henry, Billingshurst, Sussex, 1633 W. Suss RO EpI/33/1633/13
Wakeham, Thomas, High Halden, Kent, 1588 CKS PRC2/5/65
Wakeley, John, yeoman, Boughton Malherbe, Kent, 1649 CKS PRC1/8/83
Wakeley/Wakeleyn, John, Swinford, Old, Worcs, Worcs RO 008.7 BA3585/838/274
Wakeleyn, see Wakeley,
Wakelin, Richard, fishmonger, Abingdon, Berks, 1641 Berks RO D/A1/222/10B
Wakelinge, Edward, Halton, East, Lincs, 1673 Lincs RO Ad/Ac/43/69
Wakely, Richard, brewer, Reading St Lawrence, Berks, 1677 Berks RO D/A1/222/139C
Wakely, Robert, Keevil, Wilts, 1627 Wilts RO Arch. Sarum(+ name and date)
Waker, Elizabeth, Goodnestone next Faversham, Kent, 1597 CKS PRC2/9/325
Waker, William, Sandwich St Mary, Kent, 1620 CKS PRC2/26/60
Waker, William, Kennington, Kent, 1626 CKS PRC2/28/132
Wakling, Thomas, Orton Longueville, Hunts, 1676 Hunts RO/Acc58/82(9)
Walbanck, Simon, Egginton, Derby, 1685 LJRO/B/C/5/1685/102
Walbancke, Bartholomewe, Luddenham, Kent, 1600 CKS PRC2/11/325
Walby, Elizabeth, St Pauls Walden, Herts, 1629 Herts RO ASA25/3029
Walcher, David, Bethersden, Kent, 1630 CKS PRC2/30/151
Walcott, Anthony, gentleman, Wickenby, Lincs, 1642 Lincs RO Ad/Ac/28/1
Walcott, Anthony, Helpringham, Lincs, 1649 Lincs RO Ad/Ac/30/52
Walcott, Henrie, Helpringham, Lincs, 1622 Lincs RO Ad/Ac/17/77
Walcott, Marie, widow, Swineshead, Lincs, 1639? Lincs RO Ad/Ac/25/86

Walden, James, Mitcheldean, Glos, 1798 GRO GDR/B4/2/W184
Walder, Jane, widow, Ferring, Sussex, 1669 W. Suss RO EpI/33/1669/24
Waldram, Matthew, Oadby, Leics, 1670 Leics RO Administrators Accounts 1667-72 f44
Waldron, Giles, Langridge, Som, 1590 Somerset RO D/D/Cta/W77
Waldron, John, yeoman, Lambourn, Berks, 1673 Berks RO D/A1/137/154B
Waldron, Mary, spinster, Bromsgrove, Worcs, 1769 Worcs RO 008.7 BA3585/835/bdl 1
Waldron, Richard, yeoman, Uffculme, Devon, 1680 Wilts RO Preb Court Uffculme Bundle 3/20
Waldron, William, yeoman, Lambourn, Berks, 1610 Berks RO D/A1/221/26B
Wale, Elizabeth, Dover, Kent, 1685 CKS PRC20/13/475
Wale, Peter, Southampton, Hants, Hants RO 21m65 D8/363
Waler, Richard, Warehorne, Kent, 1621 CKS PRC2/26/69
Wales, Isabel, Pagham, Sussex, W. Suss RO EpI/33/1610/1
Wales, Isabel, Pagham, Sussex, 1611 W. Suss RO EpIV/10/1/11
Wales, Richard, yeoman, Toft Monks, Norf, 1754 Norfolk RO ANF/11/5/2
Walford, Alexander, Stogursey, Som, 1665 Somerset RO D/D/Cta/W31
Walforde, Hugh, Watford, Herts, 1588 Herts RO ASA25/1254
Walgate, Ann, spinster, Bishop Wilton, Yorks, 1845 Borthwick Test C.P. 1845/3
Walgrave, Thomas, gentleman, Steeping, Great, Lincs, 1633 Lincs RO Ad/Ac/24/112
Walke, Thomas, Cheriton, Kent, 1691 CKS PRC2/42/21
Walker, Anne, Cranbrook, Kent, 1642 CKS PRC1/6/33
Walker, Barnard, husbandman, Welbourn, Lincs, 1612 Lincs RO Ad/Ac/10/152
Walker, Bartholomewe, Halton, Lincs, 1598 Lincs RO Ad/Ac/37/102
Walker, Benjamin, Upton on Severn, Worcs, 1765 Worcs RO 008.7 BA3585/835/bdl 3
Walker, Brian, Gainsborough, Lincs, 1645 Lincs RO Ad/Ac/40/113
Walker, Christopher, glover, Newbury, Berks, 1609 Berks RO D/A1/221/20B
Walker, Christopher, labourer, Sandwich, Kent, 1679 CKS PRC2/38/211
Walker, Cutbert, Halton, East, Lincs, 1613 Lincs RO Ad/Ac/12/88
Walker, David, Hemswell, Lincs, 1679 Lincs RO Ad/Ac/43/79
Walker, Edward, fellmonger, Canterbury All Saints, Kent, 1687 CKS PRC2/41/110
Walker, Freeman, Barford St Martin, Wilts, 1620 Wilts RO Miscellaneous Index (name + date)
Walker, George, mariner: 'master mariner', Bristol St Mary Redcliffe, Glos, Bristol RO 1772/CP
Walker, George, gentleman, Lincoln St Michael, Lincs, 1599 Lincs RO Ad/Ac/5/282
Walker, George, High Halstow, Kent, 1627 CKS PRC2/28/138
Walker, George, Cranbrook, Kent, 1638 CKS PRC20/11/548
Walker, George, Offord Cluney, Hunts, 1700 Hunts RO/Acc58/287
Walker, Henry, St Albans St Michaels, Herts, 1633 Herts RO ASA25/4897
Walker, Henry, Swinford, Leics, 1672 Leics RO Administrators Accounts 1667-72 f80
Walker, Henrye, St Laurence Thanet, Kent, 1606 CKS PRC2/13/445
Walker, Humfrey, Hartlebury, Worcs, 1599 Worcs RO 008.7 BA3585/838/166
Walker, James, St Mary in the Marsh, Kent, 1612 CKS PRC2/16/163
Walker, James, drysalter, Leeds, Yorks, 1781 Borthwick Test C.P. 1781/7
Walker, John, alderman, Congleton, Ches, 1569 Cheshire RO (Name) W.C. 1568
Walker, John, Bolingbroke, Lincs, 1603 Lincs RO Ad/Ac/5/83
Walker, John, Marden, Kent, 1614 CKS PRC2/18/40
Walker, John, butcher, Banbury, Oxon, 1614 Oxon RO MSS Wills Pec 54/1/42
Walker, John, Boston, Lincs, 1623 Lincs RO Ad/Ac/17/71
Walker, John, Deeping, Market, Lincs, 1626 Lincs RO Ad/Ac/20/107
Walker, John, tailor/scholar's servant, Cambridge St Michael, Cambs, 1667 CUL V.C. Acc./Box3/51
Walker, John, butcher, Bekesbourne, Kent, 1673 CKS PRC2/35/267
Walker, John, Wolford, Great, Warks, 1675 Worcs RO 008.7 BA3585/830/42
Walker, John, Hallam, West, Derby, 1779 LJRO/B/C/5/1792/67
Walker, Michael, Holywell, Hunts, 1683 Hunts RO/Acc58/203(49)
Walker, Owen, Holywell, Hunts, Hunts RO/Acc58/206
Walker, Peter, gentleman, Wragby, Lincs, 1624 Lincs RO Ad/Ac/18/89

[Walker:]
Walker, Richard, Kensworth, Herts, 1639 Herts RO AHH23/2492
Walker, Richard, Conisholme, Lincs, 1640 Lincs RO Ad/Ac/27/140
Walker, Richard, Edensor, Derby, 1667 LJRO:cards/1667/86
Walker, Richard, Bolas Magna, Shrops, 1681 LJRO/B/C/5/1681/43
Walker, Robert, Elkington, North, Lincs, 1594 Lincs RO Ad/Ac/3/7
Walker, Robert, Tattershall, Lincs, 1606 Lincs RO Ad/Ac/6/37
Walker, Robert, Grimoldby, Lincs, 1637 Lincs RO Ad/Ac/25/647
Walker, Rowland, carrier, Cookham, Berks, 1627 Berks RO D/A1/221/103B
Walker, Thomas, cordwainer, Bristol, Glos, Bristol RO 1739/27
Walker, Thomas, clothworker, Reading St Giles, Berks, 1602 Berks RO D/A1/220/192B
Walker, Thomas, Oare, Kent, 1612 CKS PRC2/17/361
Walker, Thomas, cordwainer, Lincoln, Lincs, 1668 Lincs RO Ad/Ac/33/48
Walker, William, Kimcote, Leics, Leics RO Administrators Accounts 1667-72 f37
Walker, William, Prescot (Cruerdley), Lancs, 1593 Lancs RO (Name of Deceased) D.R.C.H. 1592
Walker, William, Wilsford, Lincs, 1612 Lincs RO Ad/Ac/11/138
Walker, William, Grantham, Lincs, 1638 Lincs RO Ad/Ac/25/159
Walker, William, Powick, Worcs, 1676 Worcs RO 008.7 BA3585/830/40
Walker, William, butcher, Hallam, West, Derby, 1765 LJRO/B/C/5/1765/148
Walker, William, innkeeper, Halifax, Yorks, 1794 Borthwick Test C.P. 1794/9
Walker/Raymond, Priscilla, wife, Gainsborough, Lincs, 1662 Lincs RO Ad/Ac/41/20
Walkerlaye, Robert, Wickenby, Lincs, 1669 Lincs RO Ad/Ac/33/123
Walkerley, Henry, Somercoates, South, Lincs, 1650 Lincs RO Ad/Ac/29/111
Walklate, George, Glossop (Mellor), Derby, 1680 LJRO:cards/1680/37
Walkwood, John, yeoman, Crowle, Lincs, 1673 Lincs RO Ad/Ac/35/41
Walkwood, William, clergy: 'clerk', Ashby, Lincs, 1623 Lincs RO Ad/Ac/18/59
Walkwoode, John, Caythorpe, Lincs, 1600 Lincs RO Ad/Ac/5/78
Wall, Anthonie, gentleman, Preston, Lancs, 1603 Lancs RO (Name of Deceased) D.R.C.H. 1615-16
Wall, Edward, Chester St Peter, Ches, 1616 Cheshire RO (Name) W.C. 1615/16
Wall, Frances, Maidstone, Kent, 1668 CKS PRC19/4/36
Wall, Grace, mistress, Lench, Rous, Worcs, 1685 Worcs RO 008.7 BA3585/830/17
Wall, Henry, Doveridge, Derby, 1707 LJRO/B/C/5/1707/157a
Wall, Nathaniel, Lench, Church (Atch Lench), Worcs, 1682 Worcs RO 008.7 BA3585/837/bdl 3
Wall, Ralph, innholder, Rookby (Great Bridge), Westm, Borthwick Test C.P. 1763/2
Wall, Richard, Claines, Worcs, 1681 Worcs RO 008.7 BA3585/830/55
Wall, Thomas, Aston (Castle Bromwich), Warks, 1681 LJRO/B/C/5/1681/44
Wall, Thomas, Aston, Warks, 1682 LJRO/B/C/5/1682/136
Wall, Walter, Huntspill, Som, 1638 Somerset RO D/D/Cta/W17
Wallcott, Elizabeth, Boston, Lincs, 1638 Lincs RO Ad/Ac/25/531
Walle, Thomas, Brent, East, Som, 1665 Somerset RO D/D/Cta/W32
Wallell, Richard, yeoman, Standish (Welch Whittle), Lancs, 1664 Lancs RO (Name of Deceased) D.R.C.H. 1664
Wallen, William, blacksmith, Hampstead Marshall, Berks, 1633 Berks RO D/A1/221/124B
Waller, Alice, widow, Hernhill, Kent, 1701 CKS PRC19/5/82
Waller, Catherine, Newington next Hythe, Kent, 1598 CKS PRC2/9/379
Waller, Joan, widow, Snargate, Kent, 1608 CKS PRC2/15/446
Waller, John, gentleman, Dover, Kent, 1630 CKS PRC20/9/496
Waller, John, husbandman, Boughton under Blean, Kent, 1666 CKS PRC19/3/86
Waller, John, milliner, Thornton, Lincs, 1668 Lincs RO Ad/Ac/33/41
Waller, Nicholas, Titchfield, Hants, 1662 Hants RO 21M65 D8/161
Waller, Thomas, surgeon: 'barber-surgeon', Hull, Yorks, 1720 Borthwick Test C.P. 1720/10
Waller, Thomas, bachelor, Caston, Norf, 1800 Norfolk RO ANW/23/26/96A
Waller, Walter, Brenzett, Kent, 1608 CKS PRC2/14/403
Waller, Walter, yeoman, Sutton Valence, Kent, 1683 CKS PRC2/40/163
Waller, William, Thatcham, Berks, 1608 Berks RO D/A1/221/16B

Waller, William, Chart, Great, Kent, 1616 CKS PRC2/26/61
Waller, William, clergy: 'clerk', Benenden, Kent, 1640 CKS PRC1/5/57
Wallerd, Mark, Selling, Kent, 1594 CKS PRC2/7/345
Wallet, John, Witham on the Hill, Lincs, 1634 Lincs RO Ad/Ac/24/52
Wallett, Joan, Scredington, Lincs, 1662 Lincs RO Ad/Ac/42/68
Wallett, Trustram, Baston, Lincs, 1601 Lincs RO Ad/Ac/5/391
Wallett, William, gentleman, Langtoft, Lincs, 1638 Lincs RO Ad/Ac/25/137
Walley, Charles, alderman, Chester, Ches, Cheshire RO (Name) W.C. 1666
Walley, Charles, alderman, Chester, Ches, 1667 Cheshire RO (Name) W.C. 1666
Wallies, Robert, Billinghay (Dogdyke), Lincs, 1612 Lincs RO Ad/Ac/10/143
Wallington, Anthony, Speen, Berks, 1640 Berks RO D/A1/221/164B
Wallis, Alexander, Sandwich St Mary, Kent, 1670 CKS PRC1/15/75
Wallis, Brion, Goxhill, Lincs, 1637 Lincs RO Ad/Ac/25/463
Wallis, Catherine, widow, Coventry, Warks, 1785 LJRO/B/C/5/1786/109
Wallis, David, baker, Watlington, Oxon, 1684 Oxon RO MSS Wills 176/4/26
Wallis, John, bellfounder, Salisbury St Edmund, Wilts, 1628 Wilts RO Miscellaneous Index (name + date)
Wallis, Richard, glover, Letcombe Regis, Berks, 1600 Berks RO D/A1/220/189B
Wallis, Richard, husbandman, Warborough, Oxon, 1668 Oxon RO MSS Wills Pec 72/1/45
Wallis, Thomas, High Halstow, Kent, 1637 CKS PRC2/34/149
Wallis, Thomas, baker, Ramsey, Hunts, 1683 Hunts RO/Acc58/195
Wallis, Thomas, innholder, Taunton, Som, 1712 Somerset RO D/D/Cta/W34
Wallis, Thomas, yeoman, Stanton, Long, Cambs, 1773 Cambs RO
Wallis, William, Upchurch, Kent, 1610 CKS PRC2/13/451
Wallis, William, victualler, Uttoxeter, Staffs, 1774 LJRO/B/C/5/1774/70
Wallop, Thomas, Hythe St Leonard, Kent, 1598 CKS PRC21/14/544
Wallopp, John, mariner, Dover, Kent, 1679 CKS PRC20/12/247
Walloxall, Humphrey, potter, Kidderminster, Worcs, 1790 Worcs RO 008.7 BA3585/835/bdl 2
Wallpoole, Theodore, gentleman, Caistor, Lincs, 1684 PRO PROB5/1400
Walls, Edward, cordwainer/scholar's servant, Cambridge St Michael, Cambs, 1677 CUL V.C. Acc./Box3/52
Walls, John, Pagham, Sussex, 1630 W. Suss RO EpIV/10/1/13
Walls, William, Wrangle, Lincs, 1641 Lincs RO Ad/Ac/27/326
Wallsall, Godwin, university: 'Fellow of Pembroke College, Cambridge/M.A.', Cambridge (Pembroke College), Cambs, 1608 CUL V.C.Acc./Box1/55
Wallys, Garace, widow, Holbeach, Lincs, 1605 Lincs RO Ad/Ac/6/51
Wallys, Henry, Barton on Humber, Lincs, 1613 Lincs RO Ad/Ac/12/93
Wallys, James,
Lincs 1602 Lincs RO Ad/Ac/5/558
Wallys, John, Toynton, High, Lincs, 1607 Lincs RO Ad/Ac/8a/29
Wallys, John eld, yeoman, Ham, High, Som, 1588 Somerset RO D/D/Cta/W80
Wallys, Richard, Warborough, Oxon, 1624 Oxon RO MSS Wills Pec 72/1/16
Wallys, Roger, Wrawby cum Brigg (Glanford Brigg), Lincs, 1618 Lincs RO Ad/Ac/14/9
Walmesley, Elizabeth, Somercoates, South, Lincs, 1620 Lincs RO Ad/Ac/16/102
Walmsley, Step..., yeoman, Fotherby, Lincs, 1670 Lincs RO Ad/Ac/32/219
Walmsley, Thomas, labourer, Humberstone, Lincs, 1626 Lincs RO Ad/Ac/20/38
Walpoole, Thomas, Horbling, Lincs, 1648 Lincs RO Ad/Ac/30/380
Walpooll, Thomas, Horbling, Lincs, 1649 Lincs RO Ad/Ac/30/102
Walraven, Jacob, Worth, Kent, 1702 CKS PRC19/6/5
Walsall, Samuel, clergy: 'mr/vicar', Westwell, Kent, 1672 CKS PRC20/12/35
Walsham, John, yeoman, Tydd St Mary, Lincs, 1684 Lincs RO Ad/Ac/44/133
Walter, Anne, widow, Stanford in the Vale, Berks, 1671 Berks RO D/A1/222/91C
Walter, Edward, Bampton, Oxon, 1639 Oxon RO MSS Wills 300/6/23
Walter, George, tailor, Milton next Sittingbourne, Kent, 1621 CKS PRC2/26/2
Walter, John, Headcorn, Kent, 1584 CKS PRC2/3/174

[Walter:]
Walter, John, Sandwich, Kent, 1631 CKS PRC2/31/78
Walter, John, yeoman, Froxfield, Wilts, 1636 Wilts RO Arch. Wilts.(+ name and date)
Walter, John, tanner, Oxford St Ebbe, Oxon, 1645 Oxon RO MSS Wills 300/6/29
Walter, John, Ramsbury, Wilts, 1690 Wilts RO Dean Sarum (name + date)
Walter, John ygr, butcher, Marden, Kent, 1629 CKS PRC2/30/144
Walter, Mathew, yeoman, Marden, Kent, 1682 CKS PRC2/39/254
Walter, Nicholas, Bosham, Sussex, 1623 W. Suss RO EpI/33/1623/12
Walter, Richarde, Stone in Oxney, Kent, 1603 CKS PRC2/14/496
Walter, Stephen, Maidstone, Kent, 1618 CKS PRC20/4/415
Walter, Thomas, Goudhurst, Kent, 1620 CKS PRC2/26/8
Walter, Thomas, Maidstone, Kent, 1622 CKS PRC20/6/224
Walter, Thomas, Marden, Kent, 1629 CKS PRC2/29/111
Walter, Thomas, husbandman, Stanford in the Vale, Berks, 1663 Berks RO D/A1/222/46B
Walter, Thomas, Coleshill, Warks, 1684 LJRO/B/C/5/1685/106
Walter, Thomas, Waltham, Bishops, Hants, 1684 Hants RO 21m65 D8/334
Walter, William, Bruton, Som, 1584 Somerset RO D/D/Cta/W36
Walter, William, Monkton Farleigh, Wilts, 1611? Wilts RO Arch. Sarum(+ name and date)
Walter, William, Stone in Oxney, Kent, 1612 CKS PRC2/16/169
Walter, William, butcher, Maidstone, Kent, 1618 CKS PRC20/4/429
Walter, William, Cranbrook, Kent, 1623 CKS PRC20/6/236
Walter, William, Appledore, Kent, 1666 CKS PRC1/11/167
Walter/Hosier, John, Wells St Cuthbert, Som, 1628 Somerset RO D/D/Cta/W10
Walters, John, Sandwich St Peter, Kent, 1610 CKS PRC2/13/459
Walters, Robert, Curry Rivel, Som, 1636 Somerset RO D/D/Cta/W13
Walterton, William, Harborough, Great, Warks, 1674 LJRO:cards/1674/50
Walthall, Samuel, university: 'Fellow of St John's College, Cambridge/B.D./priest' Cambridge (St John's College), Cambs, 1673 CUL V.C. Acc./Box3/53
Waltham, Robert, Frampton, Lincs, 1649 Lincs RO Ad/Ac/30/165
Waltham, Thomas, labourer, Bratoft, Lincs, 1633 Lincs RO Ad/Ac/24/8
Walthew, Thomas, Wigan, Lancs, 1616 Lancs RO (Name of Deceased) D.R.C.H. 1616
Walton, Christian, St Thomas Isle of Harty, Kent, 1618 CKS PRC2/26/30
Walton, Dorothy, widow, Lincoln St Swithin, Lincs, 1758 Lincs RO Ad/Ac/36/7
Walton, Edward, Moulton, Lincs, 1611 Lincs RO Ad/Ac/10/87
Walton, John, Skellingthorpe, Lincs, 1614 Lincs RO Ad/Ac/12/184
Walton, John, captain, Dover, Kent, 1630 CKS PRC20/8/466
Walton, John, yeoman, Deeping St James, Lincs, 1669 Lincs RO Ad/Ac/33/36
Walton, John, currier/bachelor, Caldbeck, Cumb, 1815 Borthwick Test C.P. 1815/4
Walton, Margaret, Cricklade St Sampson, Wilts, 1633 Wilts RO Arch. Wilts.(+ name and date)
Walton, Richard, Leysdown, Kent, 1604 CKS PRC2/14/491
Walton, Stephan, Linsted, Kent, 1616 CKS PRC2/26/1
Walton, William, Linsted, Kent, 1596 CKS PRC2/9/319
Walton, William, yeoman, Witham on the Hill, Lincs, 1670 Lincs RO Ad/Ac/32/226
Walton, William, labourer, Gainsborough, Lincs, 1677? Lincs RO Ad/Ac/35/120
Walton, William, Oxhill, Warks, 1681 Worcs RO 008.7 BA3585/830/58
Walvens, William, miner, Youlgreave (Dudwood), Derby, 1727 LJRO/B/C/5/1727/153
Walworth, Edward, Barrow, Ches, 1664 Cheshire RO (Name) W.C. 1664
Walwyn, Richard, gentleman, Deal, Kent, 1618 CKS PRC20/4/427
Waminsley, John, Coates, Great, Lincs, 1648 Lincs RO Ad/Ac/30/392
Wamsley, Thomas, Deal, Kent, 1699 CKS PRC19/5/69
Wanderton, George, Canterbury St Margaret, Kent, 1626 CKS PRC2/27/184
Wandon, Thomas, Maidstone, Kent, 1621 CKS PRC20/5/196
Wanley, Samuell, mayor, Leicester, Leics, 1667 Leics RO Administrators Accounts 1667-72 f7
Wansborough, William, Salisbury, Wilts, 1675 Wilts RO Miscellaneous Index (name + date)
Wansbury, William, Fisherton Delamere (Bapton), Wilts, 1646? Wilts RO Arch. Sarum(+ name and date)

Wansell, Francis, Lambourn (East Hanney), Berks, 1614 Berks RO D/A1/221/43B
Wanstall, Amy, minor: 'infant', Patrixbourne, Kent, 1673 CKS PRC2/35/266
Wanstall, Henrie, Challock, Kent, 1631 CKS PRC20/9/458
Wanstall, Isbell, widow, Westwell, Kent, 1595 CKS PRC21/14/183
Wanstall, John, husbandman, Challock, Kent, 1621 CKS PRC20/5/218
Wanstall, John, Westwell, Kent, 1685 CKS PRC20/13/533
Wanstall, Michael, Goodnestone next Wingham, Kent, 1681 CKS PRC20/13/212
Wanstall, Susanna, widow, Lympne, Kent, 1693 CKS PRC2/42/56
Wantier, James, Canterbury, Kent, 1637 CKS PRC19/1/10
Wappall, Peter, Dover, Kent, 1587 CKS PRC21/8/256
Wapshott, Richard, Reading, Berks, 1615 Berks RO D/A1/221/56B
Warburton, Thomas, Bowdon, Ches, 1699 Cheshire RO (Name) W.C. 1699
Warburton, Thomas, mercer, Macclesfield, Ches, 1740 Cheshire RO (Name) W.C. 1740
Ward, Alice, widow, Solihull, Warks, 1690 LJRO/B/C/5/1690/105
Ward, Anne, widow, Wishaw, Warks, 1670 LJRO:cards/1670/68
Ward, Brian, Theddlethorpe St Helen, Lincs, 1613 Lincs RO Ad/Ac/12/6
Ward, Edward, yeoman, Fisherton Anger, Wilts, 1674 Wilts RO Arch. Sarum(+ name and date)
Ward, Elizabeth, widow, Fisherton Anger, Wilts, 1681 Wilts RO Arch. Sarum(+ name and date)
Ward, Ellen, spinster, Duffield (Holbrook), Derby, 1808 LJRO/B/C/5/1808/72
Ward, Francis, butcher, Stockbury, Kent, 1718 CKS PRC1/18/31
Ward, Isaac, mr, Appledore, Kent, 1666 CKS PRC19/3/87
Ward, Jeffery, innholder, Reading, Berks, 1644 Berks RO D/A1/222/18B
Ward, John, Grinstead, West, Sussex, 1595 W. Suss RO EpI/33/1595/4
Ward, John, clergy: 'mr/clerk', Canterbury Christchurch, Kent, 1618 CKS PRC20/4/413
Ward, John, Hythe St Leonard, Kent, 1629 CKS PRC20/8/510
Ward, John, husbandman, Nettleham, Lincs, 1638 Lincs RO Ad/Ac/40/153
Ward, John, Bolingbroke, Old, Lincs, 1648 Lincs RO Ad/Ac/27/137
Ward, John, shepherd, Galby, Leics, 1673 Leics RO Administrators Accounts 1667-72 f138
Ward, John, Burton-upon-Trent (Winsell), Staffs, 1700 LJRO/B/C/5/1700/66
Ward, John, joiner, Bury St Edmunds, Suff, 1748 Suff RO(B) IC500/3/50/3
Ward, John, yeoman, Budworth, Great (Anderton), Ches, 1800 Cheshire RO (Name) W.C. 1798-1800
Ward, Margarett, widow, Lincoln St Botolph, Lincs, 1669 Lincs RO Ad/Ac/33/96
Ward, Martha, widow, Sandhurst, Kent, 1680 CKS PRC2/39/118
Ward, Mary, Oving (Colworth), Sussex, 1630 W. Suss RO EpI/33/1629/16
Ward, Nathaniel, yeoman, Winteringham, Lincs, 1674 Lincs RO Ad/Ac/35/79
Ward, Ralf, Staplehurst, Kent, 1597 CKS PRC2/9/213
Ward, Ralph, victualler, Maidstone, Kent, 1673 CKS PRC20/12/63
Ward, Ralphe, Godmersham, Kent, 1639 CKS PRC20/11/510
Ward, Richard, Leigh (Bedford), Lancs, 1663 Lancs RO (Name of Deceased) D.R.C.H. 1663
Ward, Richard, yeoman, Claypole, Lincs, 1670? Lincs RO Ad/Ac/43/52
Ward, Robert, Hibaldstow, Lincs, 1667 Lincs RO Ad/Ac/42/65
Ward, Robert, Berkswell, Warks, 1672 LJRO:cards/1672/61
Ward, Robert, Dawley, Shrops, 1675 LJRO:cards/1675/58
Ward, Robert, labourer, Mongewell, Oxon, 1687 Oxon RO MSS Wills 176/5/15
Ward, Sara, widow, Sandhurst, Kent, 1662 CKS PRC1/9/67
Ward, Simon, Deeping St James, Lincs, 1612 Lincs RO Ad/Ac/11/193
Ward, Thomas, Berrow, Som, 1631 Somerset RO D/D/Cta/W37
Ward, Thomas, Laughton, Lincs, 1632 Lincs RO Ad/Ac/23/33
Ward, Thomas, Friskney, Lincs, 1648 Lincs RO Ad/Ac/30/280
Ward, Thomas, Godmanchester, Hunts, 1676 Hunts RO/Acc58/42(7)
Ward, Thomas, innholder, Cambridge, Cambs, 1683 CUL V.C. Acc./Box3/54
Ward, Thomas, Snargate, Kent, 1685 CKS PRC2/41/23
Ward, Thomas, yeoman, Shirley (Shirley Lodge), Derby, 1747 LJRO/B/C/5/1747/221
Ward, William, Kennington, Kent, 1627 CKS PRC2/28/126

[Ward:]
Ward, William, jurat/mr, Dover, Kent, 1629 CKS PRC20/8/516
Ward, William, Orton Longueville, Hunts, 1636 Hunts RO/Acc58/9(49)
Ward, William, Bosworth, Market, Leics, 1665 Leics RO Administrators Accounts C17th f21
Ward, William, Hampton, London & Middlesex, 1679 PRO PROB32/18/14
Ward, William, gentleman, Edlington (Poolham), Lincs, 1682 Lincs RO Ad/Ac/34/102
Ward, William, clothworker/citizen, St Matthew Friday Street, London & Middlesex, 1715 Greater London RO DL/C/546/91
Ward, William, widower, Solihull, Warks, 1750 LJRO/B/C/5/1750/236
Ward, William eld, gentleman, Sandhurst, Kent, 1669 CKS PRC1/13/140
Ward, see Sharples,
Wardall, Simon, Maltby le Marsh, Lincs, 1579 Lincs RO Ad/Ac/2b/3
Warde, Abraham, Canterbury All Saints, Kent, 1606 CKS PRC2/26/70
Warde, Anthonie, Carlton le Moorland, Lincs, 1605 Lincs RO Ad/Ac/6/111
Warde, Edward, Eagle (Eagle Hall), Lincs, 1667 Lincs RO Ad/Ac/32/125
Warde, Francis, Birstall, Leics, 1640 Leics RO PR/I/41A/51
Warde, George, husbandman, Coningsby, Lincs, 1620 Lincs RO Ad/Ac/16/106
Warde, John, Deeping St James, Lincs, 1602 Lincs RO Ad/Ac/5/423
Warde, John, Aslackby, Lincs, 1620 Lincs RO Ad/Ac/16/103
Warde, John, Claypole, Lincs, 1639 Lincs RO Ad/Ac/26/325
Warde, John, Bolingbroke, Old, Lincs, 1639? Lincs RO Ad/Ac/26/119
Warde, Richard, Stafford St Mary (Tillington), Staffs, 1555? Lambeth Palace Arches F 1A ff17-20
Warde, Robert, Lydd, Kent, 1591 CKS PRC21/11/156
Warde, Simon, Aldermaston, Berks, 1590 Berks RO D/A1/220/140B
Warde, Thomas, Sittingbourne, Kent, 1589 CKS PRC2/5/466
Warde, Thomas, Lydd, Kent, 1615 CKS PRC20/3/218
Warde, William, Boston, Lincs, 1623 Lincs RO Ad/Ac/18/74
Wardell, Anne, widow, Rickmansworth, Herts, 1585 Herts RO ASA25/1137
Wardell, James, Watford, Herts, 1621 Herts RO ASA25/2727
Wardell, Thomas, yeoman, Fulstow, Lincs, 1789 Lincs RO Ad/Ac/36/16
Warden, Thomas, innholder, Lincoln St Margaret in the Close, Lincs, 1672 Lincs RO Ad/Ac/42/62
Warden, William, Lympne, Kent, 1668 CKS PRC1/13/141
Warder, John, Chichester, Sussex, 1611 W. Suss RO EpI/33/1611/11
Wardill, Richard, Killingholme, Lincs, 1572 Lincs RO Ad/Ac/1/4
Wardle, John, Leek, Staffs, 1681 LJRO/B/C/5/1682/102
Wardle, William, farmer, Bilton (Bickerton), Yorks, 1782 Borthwick D/C C.P. 1782/2
Wardlow, Richard, Youlgreave, Derby, 1684 LJRO/B/C/5/1683/23
Wardner, Richard, Rollright, Great, Oxon, 1663 Oxon RO MSS Wills 71/3/27
Ware, Edward, clothier, Staplehurst, Kent, 1641 CKS PRC19/2/44
Ware, Lewis, Oare, Kent, 1618 CKS PRC2/26/20
Ware, Solomon eld, miller, Cranbrook, Kent, 1664 CKS PRC1/10/106
Ware, Walter, Marston Magna, Som, 1620 Somerset RO D/D/Cta/W4
Wareham, Henry, husbandman, Wimborne Minster, Dors, 1614 Dorset RO PE/WM CP 2/4/12
Wareham, John, Wimborne Minster, Dors, 1629 Dorset RO PE/WM CP 2/4/43
Wareham, Richard, Wimborne Minster (Holt), Dors, 1621 Dorset RO PE/WM CP 2/4/26
Wareing, Thomas, Stanground, Hunts, Hunts RO/Acc58/205(227)
Wareing, see Long,
Warfield, Robert, Meare, Som, 1730 Somerset RO D/D/Cta/W38
Warham, Anne, widow, Canterbury St Paul, Kent, 1685 CKS PRC2/40/260
Warham, Francis, Chilham, Kent, 1592 CKS PRC2/6/286
Warham, John, mariner: 'lieutenant, RN/widower', Stepney, London & Middlesex, 1704 PRO PROB32/44/42
Wariner, Theophilus, Washingborough, Lincs, 1638 Lincs RO Ad/Ac/25/311
Waring, Edward, Hough on the Hill, Lincs, 1662? Lincs RO Ad/Ac/32/7

Waring, Richard, Shrewsbury Holy Cross, Shrops, 1681 LJRO/B/C/5/1681/45
Warkman, John, husbandman, Upton on Severn, Worcs, 1604 Worcs RO 008.7 BA3585/839/342
Warland, Christopher, cook, Oxford (University), Oxon, 1671 Bodleian HYP B9/108-109
Warley, John, clergy: 'clerk/B.D.', Willesborough, Kent, 1680 CKS PRC2/39/127
Warley, Robert, husbandman, Tenterden, Kent, 1666 CKS PRC1/11/168
Warley, Thomas, husbandman, Marden, Kent, 1670 CKS PRC1/15/76
Warlie, John, Sutton Valence, Kent, 1598 CKS PRC2/11/23
Warman, Margery, Rodbourne Cheney, Wilts, 1621 Wilts RO Arch. Wilts.(+ name and date)
Warman, Richard, fisherman, St Peter in Thanet, Kent, 1684 CKS PRC2/40/256
Warman, Thomas, fisherman/bachelor, St Peter in Thanet, Kent, 1670 CKS PRC1/14/117
Warman, William, Liddington, Wilts, 1647 Wilts RO CC Sarum(+ name and date)
Warmoes, Marye, widow, Sandwich, Kent, 1612 CKS PRC2/17/201
Warne, John, Kenwyn, Corn, 1646 Cornwall RO AP/W747/2
Warner, Alice?, widow, Pagham, Sussex, 1650 W. Suss RO EpIV/10/2A/8
Warner, Anthonie, Ormsby, South, Lincs, 1612 Lincs RO Ad/Ac/11/126
Warner, Edward, Abbots Langley, Herts, 1613 Herts RO ASA25/4802
Warner, Edward, baker, Banbury, Oxon, 1623 Oxon RO MSS Wills Pec 54/2/27
Warner, Henry, gentleman, Streatley, Berks, 1641 Berks RO D/A1/222/8B
Warner, Hugh, Bierton, Bucks, 1614 Oxon RO MSS Wills Pec 54/1/46
Warner, Hugh, Elstree, Herts, 1635 Herts RO ASA25/4922
Warner, John, Earnley, Sussex, 1669 W. Suss RO EpI/33/1668
Warner, Morgan, Pulborough, Sussex, 1631 W. Suss RO EpI/33/1631/41
Warner, Robert, Metheringham, Lincs, 1623 Lincs RO Ad/Ac/18/112
Warner, Robert, Metheringham, Lincs, 1623 Lincs RO Ad/Ac/19A/130
Warner, Simon, Winthorpe, Lincs, 1633 Lincs RO Ad/Ac/25/441
Warner, Thomas, New Romney, Kent, 1680 CKS PRC20/13/71
Warr, Thomas ygr, Yatton, Som, 1639 Somerset RO D/D/Cta/W3
Warranne, Thomas, Harlaxton, Lincs, 1600 Lincs RO Ad/Ac/5/145
Warrell, Elizabeth, spinster, Middlewich, Ches, 1714 Cheshire RO (Name) W.C. 1714-16
Warren, Edward, Dover, Kent, 1591 CKS PRC21/11/24
Warren, Elizabeth, university: 'scholar's servant, widow of', Cambridge, Cambs, 1611 CUL V.C.Acc./Box1/56
Warren, George, surgeon, Cambridge, Cambs, 1727 CUL V.C. Acc./Box3/55
Warren, Hammon, Teynham, Kent, 1612 CKS PRC2/17/330
Warren, Henry, miller, Hendred, West, Berks, 1595 Berks RO D/A1/220/162B
Warren, John, gentleman, Chipping Barnet, Herts, 1588 Herts RO ASA25/1220
Warren, John, esquire, Poynton, Ches, 1590 Cheshire RO (Name) W.C. 1590
Warren, John, vintner/scholar's servant, Cambridge, Cambs, 1609 CUL V.C.Acc./Box1/57
Warren, John, Ashwell, Herts, 1635 Herts RO AHH23/2481
Warren, John, fellmonger, Hythe St Leonard, Kent, 1683 CKS PRC20/13/390
Warren, Maurice, carpenter, Salisbury, Wilts, 1669 Wilts RO Miscellaneous Index (name + date)
Warren, Richard, Dover, Kent, 1574 CKS PRC21/2/143
Warren, Robarte, Rippingale, Lincs, 1602 Lincs RO Ad/Ac/5/19
Warren, Robert, Beaulieu, Hants, 1663 Hants RO 21M65 D8/182
Warren, Thomas, Brookland, Kent, 1632 CKS PRC2/31/175
Warren, Tobias, husbandman, Worle, Som, 1611 Somerset RO D/D/Cta/W62
Warrener, John, cook, Oxford (University), Oxon, 1642 Bodleian HYP B9/112-113
Warriner, Ann, widow, Oxford (University), Oxon, 1642 Bodleian HYP B9/110-111
Warriner, Henry, St Laurence Thanet, Kent, 1626 CKS PRC2/27/176
Warrington, Andrew, Mucclestone (Sillinghurst), Staffs, 1690 LJRO/B/C/5/1690/46
Warry, Mary, Herne, Kent, 1639 CKS PRC20/11/504
Warry, Stephen, River, Kent, 1607 CKS PRC2/14/479
Warter, Edward, yeoman, Shrewsbury St Chad (Whelbetch), Shrops, 1705 LJRO/B/C/5/1705/51
Warter, Robert, Hameringham, Lincs, 1606 Lincs RO Ad/Ac/7/10
Wartnabie, John, Wartnaby, Leics, 1639 Leics RO PR/I/41A/24

[Warwell:]
Warwell, Robert, Sleaford, Lincs, 1612 Lincs RO Ad/Ac/11/111
Warwell, Thomas, bricklayer, New Romney, Kent, 1685 CKS PRC20/13/537
Warwick, Richard, gentleman, Milton, Hants, 1662 Hants RO 21M65 D8/162
Warwick, Robert, Timsbury, Hants, 1624 Hants RO 21M65 D8/94
Warwicke, James, Eling (Cadnam), Hants, 1625 Hants RO 21M65 D8/138
Warwicke, Richard, Messingham, Lincs, 1624 Lincs RO Ad/Ac/19A/5
Wase, Edward, husbandman, Moreton, South, Berks, 1663 Berks RO D/A1/222/64B
Wase, John, Storrington, Sussex, 1632 W. Suss RO EpI/33/1632/18
Wash, Brian, Aldermaston, Berks, 1609 Berks RO D/A1/221/23
Washborne, Robert, Minety, Wilts, 1628 Wilts RO Arch. Wilts.(+ name and date)
Washbrooke, Edward, husbandman, Norton, Hook, Oxon, 1674 Oxon RO MSS Wills 71/3/30
Washer, Richard, Eastry, Kent, 1615 CKS PRC20/3/214
Washford, Christopher, Alresford, New, Hants, 1604 Hants RO 1604 AD61
Washingborow, John, yeoman, Leasingham, Lincs, 1664 Lincs RO Ad/Ac/43/19
Washingburgh, William, Tallington, Lincs, 1640 Lincs RO Ad/Ac/27/4
Washington, Grace, mrs/widow, York, Yorks, Borthwick Test C.P. 1737/15
Washington, Jacob, Whitstable, Kent, 1612 CKS PRC2/17/325
Washwhite, William, Whaplode, Lincs, 1619 Lincs RO Ad/Ac/15/11
Wason, John,
Som Somerset RO D/D/Cta/W35
Wasse, John, yeoman, Wybunbury (Hunsterton), Ches, 1664 Cheshire RO (Name) W.C. 1664
Wassell, Isaac, blacksmith, Leeds, Kent, 1679 CKS PRC2/38/205
Wast, Francis, Boylestone, Derby, 1683 LJRO/B/C/5/1682/103
Wastcote, John, Sittingbourne, Kent, 1597 CKS PRC2/9/3
Waste, Susannah, Uttoxeter, Staffs, 1684 LJRO/B/C/5/1684/82
Wastell, Edmund, Rickmansworth, Herts, 1602 Herts RO ASA25/1809
Wastell, Henry, St Laurence Thanet, Kent, 1668 CKS PRC1/13/142
Wastell, Mildred, St Laurence Thanet, Kent, 1667 CKS PRC1/12/91
Wastell, William, Hinton Blewett, Som, 1587 Somerset RO D/D/Cta/W55
Wastfeild, Richard, merchant, Bristol, Glos, 1685 PRO PROB5/905
Wastfeild, Walter, Christian Malford, Wilts, 1681 Wilts RO Miscellaneous Index (name + date)
Wastfield, John, Biddestone, Wilts, 1763 Wilts RO CC Sarum(+ name and date)
Wastfield, Thomas, Corsham, Wilts, 1677 Wilts RO Miscellaneous Index (name + date)
Wastle, Letice, Rolvenden, Kent, 1632 CKS PRC2/31/171
Wastle, Nicholas, St Peter in Thanet, Kent, 1639 CKS PRC1/3/56
Wasty, Thomas, clothier, Broadwell (Filkins), Oxon, 1668 Oxon RO MSS Wills 176/3/15
Watchorne, Isaac, Melton Mowbray, Leics, Leics RO PR/I/41A/5
Watelyer/Havenagle, Mary, Canterbury All Saints, Kent, 1586 CKS PRC21/8/39
Wateman, Ann + Alice, Lincoln, Lincs, 1632 Lincs RO Ad/Ac/23/54
Water, Joane, widow, Headcorn, Kent, 1618 CKS PRC2/26/19
Water, John eld, yeoman, Frittenden, Kent, 1663 CKS PRC1/9/156
Water, Richarde, Staplehurst, Kent, 1583 CKS PRC2/3/79
Waterer, Henry, mercer, Wallingford, Berks, 1592 Berks RO D/A1/220/151B
Waterer, John, cordwainer, Milton next Sittingbourne, Kent, 1674 CKS PRC2/36/141
Waterer, Robert, Sittingbourne, Kent, 1639 CKS PRC20/11/574
Waterer, William, miller, Minster in Sheppey, Kent, 1640 CKS PRC1/5/58
Waterer, William eld, Milton next Sittingbourne, Kent, 1710 CKS PRC1/17/46
Waterer, see Pakyn,
Waterfeild, William, Ibstock, Leics, Leics RO Administrators Accounts 1667-72 f56
Waterhous, John, Glossop, Derby, 1685 LJRO/B/C/5/1685/107
Waterhouse, Elizabeth, widow, Lea, Lincs, 1680 Lincs RO Ad/Ac/43/140
Waterhouse, James, Waterfall, Staffs, 1681 LJRO/B/C/5/1681/46
Waterhouse, Ralph, yeoman, Glossop (High Gate), Derby, 1779 LJRO/B/C/5/1779/95
Waterhouse, Samuel, Glossop, Derby, 1680 LJRO:cards/1680/38
Waterhowse, Walter, husbandman, Buscot, Berks, 1636 Berks RO D/A1/221/148B

Wateridge, Edward, Chart, Great, Kent, 1643 CKS PRC1/7/15
Waterland, Robert, yeoman, Haxey (Nether Burnham), Lincs, 1604 Lincs RO Ad/Ac/37/181
Waterland, Thomas, husbandman, Haxey (Graizelound), Lincs, 1669? Lincs RO Ad/Ac/33/159
Waterman, Dorothe, Bethersden, Kent, 1591 CKS PRC2/5/470
Waterman, George, knight/alderman, London & Middlesex 1683 PRO PROB32/33/24
Waterman, Grace, widow, Faversham, Kent, 1640 CKS PRC1/5/59
Waterman, James, Warminghurst, Sussex, 1629 W. Suss RO EpI/33/1629/4
Waterman, Jane, Warminghurst, Sussex, 1631 W. Suss RO EpI/33/1631/8
Waterman, John, St Martin in the Fields, London & Middlesex, 1717 Greater London RO AM/CP/Box 1696-1720 pt (uncatalogued)
Waterman, Margaret, widow, Orlestone, Kent, 1612 CKS PRC2/17/1
Waterman, Peter, Sutton Valence, Kent, 1620 CKS PRC2/26/66
Waterman, Richard eld, Cranbrook, Kent, 1633 CKS PRC2/31/167
Waterman, Thomas, university: 'scholar's servant', Cambridge St Edward, Cambs, 1606 CUL V.C.Acc./Box1/58
Waterman, Thomas, gentleman, Faversham, Kent, 1641 CKS PRC1/6/34
Waterman, Thomas, High Halden, Kent, 1708 CKS PRC1/17/17
Waterman, Thomsyne, Old Romney, Kent, 1590 CKS PRC2/5/462
Waterman, William, Hants RO 1601 AD44/2
Waters, Andrew, blacksmith, Rolvenden, Kent, 1641 CKS PRC1/6/35
Waters, Andrew, blacksmith, Benenden, Kent, 1665 CKS PRC1/11/91
Waters, Elizabeth, Willesborough, Kent, 1665 CKS PRC1/11/92
Waters, Henry, Kilworth, North, Leics, 1639 Leics RO PR/I/41A/22
Waters, James, yeoman, Headcorn, Kent, 1674 CKS PRC2/36/138
Waters, Jeffrey, Spalding, Lincs, 1639 Lincs RO Ad/Ac/26/179
Waters, John, Dover St Mary, Kent, CKS PRC21/6/38
Waters, John, Staplehurst, Kent, 1628 CKS PRC2/29/115
Waters, John, Charlton, Wilts, 1630? Wilts RO Arch. Wilts.(+ name and date)
Waters, John, Witham on the Hill, Lincs, 1662 Lincs RO Ad/Ac/32/31
Waters, Katherine, widow, Uffington, Lincs, 1619 Lincs RO Ad/Ac/15/233
Waters, Katherine, widow, Uffington, Lincs, 1624 Lincs RO Ad/Ac/19A/95
Waters, Nicholas, Mersham, Kent, 1694 CKS PRC2/42/97
Waters, Peter, clergy: 'clerk/vicar', Ferring, Sussex, W. Suss RO EpI/33/1606/18
Waters, Robarte, Shadoxhurst, Kent, 1602 CKS PRC2/12/373
Waters, Robert, Witham on the Hill, Lincs, 1649 Lincs RO Ad/Ac/30/138
Waters, Robert, Deal, Kent, 1670 CKS PRC19/4/98
Waters, Roberte, Witham on the Hill, Lincs, 1612 Lincs RO Ad/Ac/11/35
Waters, Soloman, Whaplode, Lincs, 1650 Lincs RO Ad/Ac/30/24
Waters, Thomas, Tenterden, Kent, 1609 CKS PRC2/13/431
Waters, Thomas, Kirton, Lincs, 1627 Lincs RO Ad/Ac/20b/46
Waters, Thomas, Deeping St James, Lincs, 1639 Lincs RO Ad/Ac/26/17
Waters, Thomas, surgeon, Lydd, Kent, 1660 CKS PRC19/3/1
Waters, William, Bristol St Peter, Glos, Bristol RO 1677/56
Waters, William, husbandman, Charney Bassett, Berks, 1614 Berks RO D/A1/221/40B
Waters, William, Dover St Mary, Kent, 1619 CKS PRC20/4/447
Waters/Parker, Emme, Spalding, Lincs, 1642 Lincs RO Ad/Ac/28/59
Waters, see Clarke,
Watersfeilde, Thomas, Ferring, Sussex, 1605 W. Suss RO EpI/33/1604/1
Watersfeyld, Thomas, Pagham, Sussex, 1640 W. Suss RO EpIV/10/2/35
Waterson, Edward, Stallingborough, Lincs, 1612 Lincs RO Ad/Ac/10/154
Waterson, Henry, Stallingborough, Lincs, 1599 Lincs RO Ad/Ac/5/425
Waterson, William, university: 'scholar's servant/privileged person', Cambridge St Botolph, Cambs, 1643 c. CUL V.C. Acc./Box2/82
Watford, John, blacksmith, Aston Tirrold, Berks, 1615 Berks RO D/A1/221/49B

[Watham:]
Watham, John, Grainthorpe, Lincs, 1671 Lincs RO Ad/Ac/33/178
Watkin, Richard, 1637 NLW BR 1636/7 Ac
Watkin, Richard, Burbage, Leics, 1666 Leics RO Administrators Accounts C17th f46
Watkings, Thomas, Burford, Oxon, 1638 Oxon RO MSS Wills 300/6/21
Watkins, Anthony, victualler, Sutton Valence, Kent, 1670 CKS PRC1/15/77
Watkins, Christopher, Stokesley, Yorks, 1771 Borthwick Test C.P. 1771/4
Watkins, John, gentleman, Blethwaugh, Rad, 1640 NLW BR 1641/105 Ac
Watkinson, Robert, mariner, Gainsborough (East Stockwith), Lincs, 1667 Lincs RO Ad/Ac/33/10
Watkinson, Simon, Leake, Lincs, 1626 Lincs RO Ad/Ac/20/28
Watkinson, William, yeoman, Reepham, Lincs, 1683 Lincs RO Ad/Ac/44/37
Watkis, Richard, Harley, Shrops, 1667 LJRO:cards/1667/87
Watks, William, Prees, Shrops, 1675 LJRO:cards/1675/59
Watlar, William, Pagham, Sussex, 1626 W. Suss RO EpIV/10/1/28
Watler, George, husbandman, Pagham, Sussex, 1679 W. Suss RO EpIV/10/2A/16
Watlington, Valentine, Winkfield, Berks, 1611 Berks RO D/A1/221/31B
Watmer, Giles, gentleman, Canterbury St Margaret, Kent, 1677 CKS PRC2/37/207
Watmore, John, Stratfield Mortimer, Berks, 1605 Berks RO D/A1/221/3B
Watmough, Thomas, Woodchurch (Barnston), Ches, 1664 Cheshire RO (Name) W.C. 1664
Watson, Ann, widow, Chester, Ches, 1760 Cheshire RO (Name) W.C. 1768
Watson, Anne, Alton Priors, Wilts, 1678 Wilts RO Arch. Wilts.(+ name and date)
Watson, Edward, mariner, Faversham, Kent, 1664 CKS PRC1/10/107
Watson, Edward, saddler, Grantham, Lincs, 1665 Lincs RO Ad/Ac/32/62
Watson, Edward, Boughton under Blean, Kent, 1683 CKS PRC20/13/386
Watson, Elizabeth, widow, Lincoln, Lincs, 1662 Lincs RO Ad/Ac/32/12
Watson, Esther, widow, King's Lynn, Norf, 1810 Norfolk RO ANW/23/27/12
Watson, Ezechias, yeoman, Willoughby, Lincs, 1626? Lincs RO Ad/Ac/39/21
Watson, Frances, widow, Wrawby cum Brigg (Glanford Brigg), Lincs, 1664? Lincs RO Ad/Ac/45/113
Watson, Frauncis, yeoman, Skellingthorpe, Lincs, 1639 Lincs RO Ad/Ac/26/150
Watson, Hammon, bachelor, Chilham, Kent, 1663 CKS PRC1/9/157
Watson, Henrie, yeoman, Croft, Lincs, 1620 Lincs RO Ad/Ac/16/104
Watson, Henry, Anwick, Lincs, 1619 Lincs RO Ad/Ac/15/81
Watson, Henry, Owston (West Butterwick), Lincs, 1678 Lincs RO Ad/Ac/35/135
Watson, James, husbandman, Tew, Great, Oxon, 1670 Oxon RO MSS Wills 176/3/22
Watson, Jane, widow, Boughton under Blean, Kent, 1665 CKS PRC19/3/65
Watson, John, New Romney, Kent, 1588 CKS PRC21/9/210
Watson, John, Ringwould, Kent, 1593 CKS PRC2/6/270
Watson, John, Birdham, Sussex, 1596 W. Suss RO EpI/33/1596/3
Watson, John, St Johns Thanet, Kent, 1618 CKS PRC2/26/4
Watson, John, yeoman, Sibsey, Lincs, 1718 Lincs RO Ad/Ac/45/9
Watson, John, husbandman, Castle Church (Ricarscote), Staffs, 1732 LJRO/B/C/5/1732/84
Watson, John ygr, husbandman, Wye, Kent, 1665 CKS PRC1/11/93
Watson, Jonathan, mercer, Oxford St Mary Magdalene, Oxon, 1628 Oxon RO MSS Wills 88/1/55
Watson, Joseph, clergy: 'clerk', Godmanchester, Hunts, 1808 Hunts RO/Acc58/334
Watson, Margery, widow, Kenardington, Kent, 1620 CKS PRC2/26/56
Watson, Mathew, Winterton, Lincs, 1611 Lincs RO Ad/Ac/8a/331
Watson, Nicholas, Kennington, Kent, 1632 CKS PRC2/31/169
Watson, Richard, Welby, Lincs, 1670? Lincs RO Ad/Ac/32/147
Watson, Richard, gentleman, St Margaret Westminster, London & Middlesex, 1687 Lambeth Palace Arches G36/3
Watson, Robert, Donington on Bain, Lincs, 1611 Lincs RO Ad/Ac/10/88
Watson, Robert, Denton (Eastry hundred), Kent, 1617 CKS PRC2/26/65
Watson, Robert, Croft, Lincs, 1627 Lincs RO Ad/Ac/20b/1
Watson, Robert, Ash next Sandwich, Kent, 1629 CKS PRC20/8/522
Watson, Robert, Leake, Lincs, 1631 Lincs RO Ad/Ac/23/66

Watson, Robert, blacksmith, Lyminge, Kent, 1642 CKS PRC19/2/66
Watson, Robert, Witham on the Hill, Lincs, 1664 Lincs RO Ad/Ac/32/55
Watson, Samuel, Southwark, St Saviour, Surrey, 1754 Greater London RO DW/OP/(Ac.73.79 pt) Box 27/1 (uncatalogued)
Watson, Sarah, St Johns Thanet, Kent, 1639 CKS PRC2/34/300
Watson, Thomas, Sturry, Kent, 1596 CKS PRC2/8/463
Watson, Thomas, gentleman, Stamford St George, Lincs, 1639 Lincs RO Ad/Ac/26/33
Watson, Thomas, Godmersham, Kent, 1641 CKS PRC19/1/88
Watson, Thomas, Winteringham, Lincs, 1645 Lincs RO Ad/Ac/40/141
Watson, Thomas, Burton on Stather, Lincs, 1667 Lincs RO Ad/Ac/33/29
Watson, Thomas, Berkswell, Warks, 1672 LJRO:cards/1672/62
Watson, Thomas, Leigh (Field), Staffs, 1678 LJRO:cards/1678/24
Watson, Thomas, Crick, Northants, 1681 Northants RO NWill A/C/5
Watson, Thomas, Faversham, Kent, 1709 CKS PRC1/17/18
Watson, William, Surfleet, Lincs, Lincs RO Ad/Ac/2C/40
Watson, William, clergy: 'vicar', Selling, Kent, 1599 CKS PRC2/10/511
Watson, William, Winteringham, Lincs, 1605 Lincs RO Ad/Ac/37/206
Watson, William, yeoman, Godmersham, Kent, 1618 CKS PRC20/4/409
Watson, William, oatmealman, Milsted, Kent, 1640 CKS PRC1/5/60
Watson, William, yeoman, Chilham, Kent, 1669 CKS PRC1/14/118a
Watson, William, yeoman, Chilham, Kent, 1670 CKS PRC1/14/118
Watson, William, Fareham, Hants, 1682 Hants RO 21m65 D8/327
Watson, William, Hull, Yorks, 1824 Borthwick Test C.P. 1824/2
Wattam, Edward, Tetney, Lincs, 1639? Lincs RO Ad/Ac/26/122
Wattam, Robert, Willoughton, Lincs, 1662 Lincs RO Ad/Ac/41/13
Watterer, Richard, Benson, Oxon, 1635 Oxon RO MSS Wills Pec 72/1/26
Watterman, Edward, Steeping, Little, Lincs, 1602 Lincs RO Ad/Ac/5/225
Watterman, Richard, Rainham, Kent, 1597 CKS PRC2/9/209
Watters, Mary, spinster, Shrewsbury (Coleham), Shrops, 1816 LJRO/B/C/5/1816/51b
Watterson, William, Strensall, Yorks, Borthwick D/C C.P. 1755/1
Watterton, Edward, mason: 'rough mason', Lincoln St Margaret in the Close, Lincs, 1674 Lincs RO Ad/Ac/42/64
Wattes, Brian, yeoman, Woodhay, West, Berks, 1695 Berks RO D/A1/223/111C
Wattes, James, Linsted, Kent, 1600 CKS PRC2/11/333
Wattes, John, Aldington, Kent, 1599 CKS PRC21/15/55
Wattes, Margarett, widow, Ebony, Kent, 1617 CKS PRC2/26/73
Wattes, Nicholas, St Albans, Herts, 1631 Herts RO ASA25/4870
Wattes, Richard, Aldingbourne, Sussex, 1673 W. Suss RO EpI/33/1673/4
Wattes, Richard, Milton next Sittingbourne, Kent, 1684 CKS PRC2/40/259
Wattes, Roger, Wye, Kent, 1592 CKS PRC2/6/124
Wattes, Sarah, Shepton Mallet, Som, 1648 Somerset RO D/D/Cta/W28
Wattle, Henrie, Maidstone, Kent, 1622 CKS PRC20/5/204
Wattle, Thomas, St Mary in the Marsh, Kent, 1623 CKS PRC2/26/3
Wattle, Thomas, yeoman, Sellindge, Kent, 1629 CKS PRC20/8/498
Watton, John, Petworth, Sussex, W. Suss RO EpI/33/1610/4
Watton, John, Yardley, Worcs, 1603 Worcs RO 008.7 BA3585/838/276
Watton, John, smith,
Worcs 1608 Worcs RO 008.7 BA3585/839/451
Watts, widow,
Leics 1684 Leics RO Administrators Accounts 1682-86 f29
Watts, Anne, widow, Adlington, Ches, 1714 Cheshire RO (Name) W.C. 1714
Watts, Cicely, Norwich St George at Colegate, Norf, Norfolk RO NCC INV/67A/93
Watts, Edward, butcher, Sandwich, Kent, 1637 CKS PRC1/1/62
Watts, Ellen, Harrietsham, Kent, 1627 CKS PRC2/28/127
Watts, Harry, gentleman, Binley, Warks, 1803 LJRO/B/C/5/1803/97

[Watts:]
Watts, Henrie, Appledore, Kent, 1604 CKS PRC2/13/423
Watts, Henry, Hollingbourne, Kent, 1635 CKS PRC20/11/530
Watts, James, yeoman, Woodchurch, Kent, 1621 CKS PRC20/5/198
Watts, James, Bradford on Avon, Wilts, 1686 Wilts RO Arch. Sarum(+ name and date)
Watts, Jane, spinster, Mancetter (Hartshill), Warks, 1783 LJRO/B/C/5/1781/146
Watts, John, Woodchurch, Kent, 1624 CKS PRC20/6/212
Watts, John, Shepton Mallet, Som, 1625 Somerset RO D/D/Cta/W1a
Watts, John, yeoman, Kennington, Kent, 1638 CKS PRC2/34/305
Watts, John, yeoman, Shepton Mallet, Som, 1638 Somerset RO D/D/Cta/W14
Watts, John, yeoman, Speen (Woodspeen), Berks, 1682 Berks RO D/A1/223/26B
Watts, John, Canterbury St Dunstan Without, Kent, 1691 CKS PRC2/42/18
Watts, Joseph, Woodchurch, Kent, 1630 CKS PRC20/9/500
Watts, Josias, Hawkhurst, Kent, 1683 CKS PRC2/40/161
Watts, Nicholas, Rolvenden, Kent, 1630 CKS PRC2/30/148
Watts, Richard, yeoman, Warehorne, Kent, 1640 CKS PRC1/5/61
Watts, Richard, tilemaker, Boxley, Kent, 1666 CKS PRC1/11/94
Watts, Richard, Sandhurst, Kent, 1680 CKS PRC2/39/121
Watts, Richarde, Ebony, Kent, 1616 CKS PRC2/26/72
Watts, Robert, yeoman, Brampton, Derby, 1663 LJRO:cards/1663/60
Watts, Robert, Westbury, Wilts, 1676 Wilts RO Chantor Sarum Bundle 10/22
Watts, Rychard, Sandhurst, Kent, 1586 CKS PRC2/4/134
Watts, Sarah, widow, Hothfield, Kent, 1667 CKS PRC1/12/92
Watts, Susannah, widow, Yate, Glos, 1685 GRO GDR/B4/2/W188
Watts, Thomas, Ruckinge, Kent, 1636 CKS PRC2/34/154
Watts, Thomas, scrivener, St Johns Thanet, Kent, 1667 CKS PRC1/12/93
Watts, Thomas, Worcester All Saints, Worcs, 1684 Worcs RO 008.7 BA3585/837/bdl 4
Watts, William, Shepton Mallet, Som, 1684 Somerset RO D/D/Cta/W39
Watts, William, Kibworth Beauchamp, Leics, 1685 Leics RO Administrators Accounts 1682-86 f38
Watts, William, Sherbourne, Dors, 1707 Wilts RO Dean Sarum (name + date)
Watts, William, butcher, Southam, Warks, 1754 LJRO/B/C/5/1754/176
Wattson, George, Belton, Lincs, 1685 Lincs RO Ad/Ac/44/164
Wattson, John, Elham, Kent, 1639 CKS PRC1/3/57
Wattson, William, Sandwich, Kent, 1611 CKS PRC2/17/414
Wattson, William, Swineshead, Lincs, 1632 Lincs RO Ad/Ac/23/6
Waudby, Thomas, Cave, North (South Cliff), Yorks, 1764 Borthwick Test C.P. 1764/3
Waugh, John, merchant/shipowner, Stepney, London & Middlesex, 1687 PRO PROB32/26/344
Wavell, David, gentleman, Milford, Hants, 1681 Hants RO 21m65 D8/328
Way, Henry, Willesborough, Kent, 1691 CKS PRC2/42/20
Wayde, Thomas, Wainfleet All Saints, Lincs, 1618 Lincs RO Ad/Ac/14/250
Wayde, William, Croft, Lincs, 1666 Lincs RO Ad/Ac/32/71
Waye, Henry, Willesborough, Kent, 1639 CKS PRC1/1/93
Wayght, Margaret, widow, Newbury, Berks, 1633 Berks RO D/A1/221/135B
Wayhold, John, mason, Godmersham, Kent, 1641 CKS PRC19/1/89
Wayland, Elias, yeoman, Linsted, Kent, 1637 CKS PRC2/34/146
Wayland, John, Urchfont, Wilts, 1639 Wilts RO Arch. Sarum(+ name and date)
Waylande, Thomas, Frome Selwood, Som, 1592 Somerset RO D/D/Cta/W79
Wayles, Walter, Horsham, Sussex, 1623 W. Suss RO EpI/33/1623/1
Wayman, Mary, widow, Faversham, Kent, 1633 CKS PRC2/32/133
Wayman, Nicholas, Ashford, Kent, 1637 CKS PRC2/34/156
Wayman, Philip, Sutton Veny, Wilts, 1674 Wilts RO Arch. Sarum(+ name and date)
Wayman, William, Stockbury, Kent, 1597 CKS PRC2/9/484
Wayne, John, tailor, St Bride, London & Middlesex, 1683 PRO PROB32/24/126
Wayne, Ralph, Alstonfield, Staffs, 1682 LJRO/B/C/5/1681/47
Wayte, Henrie, St Nicholas at Wade, Kent, 1599 CKS PRC21/15/49

Wayte, Jeffery, Brinkworth, Wilts, 1627 Wilts RO Arch. Wilts.(+ name and date)
Wayte, John, Woolsthorpe, Lincs, 1607 Lincs RO Ad/Ac/8a/31
Wayte, John, baker, Westport St Mary, Wilts, 1614 Wilts RO CC Sarum(+ name and date)
Wayte, John, Brinkworth, Wilts, 1637 Wilts RO Arch. Wilts.(+ name and date)
Wayte, Richard, Langley Burrell, Wilts, 1617 Wilts RO Arch. Wilts.(+ name and date)
Wayte, Robert, husbandman, Purton, Wilts, 1668 Wilts RO Arch. Wilts.(+ name and date)
Wayte, Thomas, Ingoldmels, Lincs, 1612? Lincs RO Ad/Ac/11/175
Wayte, William, Knipton, Leics, 1673 Leics RO Administrators Accounts 1667-72 f131
Weale, Walter, yeoman, Sutton Courtenay (Sutton Wick), Berks, 1689 Berks RO D/A1/223/64C
Weanan, John, yeoman, Probus, Corn, 1623 Cornwall RO AP/W359/1
Weare, Andrew, tailor, Canterbury St Augustine's Monastery, Kent, 1680 CKS PRC20/12/326
Weare, Humfrey, St Clement Danes, London & Middlesex, 1664 Lambeth Palace Arches G18/5
Wearing, Edward, St Juliot, Corn, 1614 Cornwall RO AP/W197/2
Wearing, William ygr, husbandman, Wytham, Berks, 1681 Berks RO D/A1/223/22C
Wearinge, Robert, feltmaker, St Thomas-by-Launceston, Corn, 1614 Cornwall RO AP/W220/1
Weate, Walter, Seighford, Staffs, 1684 LJRO/B/C/5/1684/83
Weaver, Edward, gentleman, Stanton, Fen, Hunts, 1684 Hunts RO/Acc58/221(219)
Weaver, Sarah, Shrewsbury, Shrops, 1691 LJRO/B/C/5/1691/100
Weaver, William, Maidstone, Kent, 1678 CKS PRC20/12/287
Webb, Agnes, Harpole, Northants, 1677 Northants RO NWill A/C/66
Webb, Ambrose, gentleman, Charlton, Wilts, 1629 Wilts RO Arch. Wilts.(+ name and date)
Webb, Anne, widow, Henley, Oxon, 1683 Oxon RO MSS Wills 88/3/21
Webb, Arthur, cordwainer, Harrietsham, Kent, 1676 CKS PRC2/37/108
Webb, Christopher, nurseryman, Painswick, Glos, 1834 GRO GDR/B4/2/W98
Webb, Edith, Overton, Wilts, 1623 Wilts RO Arch. Wilts.(+ name and date)
Webb, Elizabeth, widow, Malmesbury, Wilts, 1640 Wilts RO Arch. Wilts.(+ name and date)
Webb, Elizabeth, widow, Cranmore, West, Som, 1741 Somerset RO D/D/Cta/W42
Webb, George, Stowe (Hyxon), Staffs, 1681 LJRO/B/C/5/1682/104
Webb, George, bachelor, Ashford, Kent, 1721 CKS PRC1/18/51
Webb, Henry, Ogbourne St George, Wilts, 1681 Wilts RO Dean Sarum (name + date)
Webb, Jane, widow, Bierton, Bucks, 1676 Oxon RO MSS Wills Pec 55/1/2
Webb, Joan, widow, Welford, Berks, 1607 Berks RO D/A1/221/12B
Webb, Joanna, mrs/widow, Stockbury, Kent, 1686 CKS PRC2/41/85
Webb, John, Cranbrook, Kent, 1593 CKS PRC2/6/498
Webb, John, yeoman, Abingdon, Berks, 1597 Berks RO D/A1/220/171B
Webb, John, Staplehurst, Kent, 1605 CKS PRC2/14/489
Webb, John, Ivychurch, Kent, 1627 CKS PRC20/8/458
Webb, John, kerseymaker, Harrietsham, Kent, 1668 CKS PRC1/13/143
Webb, John, Frittenden, Kent, 1677 CKS PRC2/37/206
Webb, John, husbandman, Bodicote, Oxon, 1679 Oxon RO MSS Wills 88/3/5
Webb, John, Bradden, Northants, 1680 Northants RO NWill A/C/42
Webb, John, yeoman, Charing, Kent, 1683 CKS PRC20/13/382
Webb, John, Cranbrook, Kent, 1686 CKS PRC2/41/88
Webb, John, Ash next Sandwich, Kent, 1729 CKS PRC19/6/79
Webb, Nicholas, Norton, Chipping, Oxon, 1635 Oxon RO MSS Wills 300/6/13
Webb, Nicholas, Sherborne St John, Hants, 1679 Hants RO 21m65 D8/299
Webb, Richard, Milton next Sittingbourne, Kent, 1631 CKS PRC20/9/474
Webb, Richard, bachelor, St Laurence Thanet, Kent, 1639 CKS PRC1/3/58
Webb, Robert, Chislet, Kent, 1623 CKS PRC2/26/41
Webb, Robert, gentleman, Sutton, Lincs, 1632 Lincs RO Ad/Ac/23/144
Webb, Robert, Minster in Thanet, Kent, 1635 CKS PRC2/33/141
Webb, Robert, gentleman, Sittingbourne, Kent, 1639 CKS PRC2/34/313
Webb, Roger, Downton, Wilts, 1615 Wilts RO Arch. Sarum(+ name and date)
Webb, Roger, Downton, Wilts, 1615 Wilts RO Miscellaneous Index (name + date)
Webb, Samuel, clothier, Berkeley, Glos, 1732 GRO GDR/B4/2/W100

[Webb:]
Webb, Thomas, Banbury, Oxon, Oxon RO MSS Wills Pec 54/2/6
Webb, Thomas, Monkton, Kent, 1587 CKS PRC21/8/274
Webb, Thomas, gentleman, Canterbury St Mary Bredin, Kent, 1609 CKS PRC2/15/440
Webb, Thomas, Glastonbury, Som, 1611 Somerset RO D/D/Cta/W63
Webb, Thomas, Herne, Kent, 1618 CKS PRC20/4/433
Webb, Thomas, collar maker, Abingdon, Berks, 1618 Berks RO D/A1/221/59B
Webb, Thomas, Hernhill, Kent, 1635 CKS PRC20/11/542
Webb, Thomas, gentleman, Aldenham, Herts, 1636 Herts RO AHH23/2485
Webb, Thomas, Faversham, Kent, 1672 CKS PRC2/35/98
Webb, Thomas, victualler, Banbury, Oxon, 1685 Oxon RO MSS Wills Pec 55/2/5
Webb, Thomas, gunsmith, Wrington (Haviton), Som, 1687 Somerset RO D/D/Cta/W41
Webb, William, Chewstoke, Som, Somerset RO D/D/Cta/W43
Webb, William, Brailes, Worcs, 1604 Worcs RO 008.7 BA3585/839/417
Webb, William, Elham, Kent, 1612 CKS PRC2/16/156
Webb, William, Detling, Kent, 1613 CKS PRC20/2/306
Webb, William, tanner, Finchampstead, Berks, 1615 Berks RO D/A1/134/65C
Webb, William, mercer, Newbury, Berks, 1617 Berks RO D/A1/221/63B
Webb, William, gentleman, Hollingbourne, Kent, 1618 CKS PRC20/4/403
Webb, William, Belleau, Lincs, 1626 Lincs RO Ad/Ac/19B/57
Webb, William, gentleman, Hampstead Marshall, Berks, 1648 Berks RO D/A1/222/31B
Webb, William, Canterbury St Andrew, Kent, 1669 CKS PRC1/14/119
Webb, William, mercer, Brailsford, Derby, 1674 LJRO:cards/1674/51
Webb, William, farmer, Padworth, Berks, 1677 Berks RO D/A1/222/144B
Webb, William, Mersham, Kent, 1682 CKS PRC2/40/82
Webb, William + Joan, Ruckinge, Kent, 1585 CKS PRC2/3/309
Webb/Everett, John, husbandman, Chaddleworth, Berks, 1599 Berks RO D/A1/188/30A
Webb, see Philips,
Webbe, Alane, St Nicholas at Wade, Kent, 1581 CKS PRC21/4/343
Webbe, Alice, spinster, Cliffe Pypard, Wilts, 1636 Wilts RO Arch. Wilts.(+ name and date)
Webbe, Hughe, Chislet, Kent, 1591 CKS PRC2/5/448
Webbe, Jerman, gentleman, Pluckley, Kent, 1594 CKS PRC2/7/239
Webbe, Joan, Shepton Mallet, Som, 1619 Somerset RO D/D/Cta/W52
Webbe, John, gentleman, Frittenden, Kent, 1582 CKS PRC2/2/169
Webbe, John, Teynham, Kent, 1601 CKS PRC2/12/379
Webbe, John, Tunstall, Kent, 1617 CKS PRC2/26/26
Webbe, John, Dorchester (Shillingford), Oxon, 1631 Oxon RO MSS Wills Pec 72/1/21
Webbe, John, Axbridge, Som, 1633 Somerset RO D/D/Cta/W40
Webbe, Richard, Millbrook, Beds, 1625 Lincs RO Ad/Ac/19B/104
Webbe, Richard eld, Bathford, Som, 1639 Somerset RO D/D/Cta/W1
Webbe, Robert, Windsor, New, Berks, 1636 Berks RO D/A1/221/144B
Webbe, Stephen, Woodchurch, Kent, 1621 CKS PRC20/5/216
Webbe, Thomas, cordwainer: 'shoemaker', Wallingford St Mary, Berks, 1614 Berks RO D/A1/134/105D
Webbe, Thomas, labourer, Lewannick, Corn, 1614 Cornwall RO AP/W199/2
Webbe, Thomas, grocer, Sandwich, Kent, 1640 CKS PRC1/3/59
Webbe, Tobyas, bachelor: 'singleman', Boughton Aluph, Kent, 1637 CKS PRC2/34/143
Webbe, Wylliam, Chislet, Kent, 1596 CKS PRC2/8/284
Webbe, see Barber,
Webber, Mary, widow, Langdon, East, Kent, 1684 CKS PRC2/40/252
Webdale, Thomas, husbandman, Stamford, Lincs, 1633 Lincs RO Ad/Ac/25/591
Webley, Thomas, Hanley Castle, Worcs, 1685 Worcs RO 008.7 BA3585/837/bdl 4
Webster, Anne, widow, Stepney, St Dunstan, London & Middlesex, 1732 Lambeth Palace Arches G103/10
Webster, Arthur, Stone, Staffs, 1684 LJRO/B/C/5/1684/84
Webster, John, Colsterworth, Lincs, 1612 Lincs RO Ad/Ac/11/12

Webster, John, Epworth, Lincs, 1675 Lincs RO Ad/Ac/35/96
Webster, Richard, Walmer, Kent, 1677 CKS PRC2/37/105
Webster, Richard, gentleman/brass founder/iron founder, Birmingham, Warks, 1809 LJRO/B/C/5/1809/87b
Webster, Robert, Budworth, Great (Over Whitley), Ches, 1675 Cheshire RO (Name) W.C. 1674-5
Webster, Sarah, widow, Aylsham, Norf, 1741 Norfolk RO ANW/23/23/93
Webster, Thomas, husbandman, Drayton, Oxon, 1673 Oxon RO MSS Wills Pec 72/2/1
Webster, Timothy, gentleman, Welbourn, Lincs, 1669? Lincs RO Ad/Ac/33/103
Webster, William, Epworth, Lincs, 1629 Lincs RO Ad/Ac/39/118
Wedd, John, Hawkhurst, Kent, 1618 CKS PRC2/26/13
Weddingham, Samuel, yeoman, Stone next Faversham, Kent, 1670 CKS PRC1/14/120
Wedgwood, Thomas, gentleman, Ropsley, Lincs, 1636 Lincs RO Ad/Ac/24/399
Wedgwood, Thomas, potter, Burslem, Staffs, 1698 LJRO/B/C/5/1698/114
Wedingham, Richard, Stone next Faversham, Kent, 1618 CKS PRC2/26/82
Wedmore, William, butcher, Bristol, Glos, Bristol RO 1692/CP
Wedmore, William, butcher, Bristol, Glos, Bristol RO 1695/CP
Wedon, Thomas, Watford, Herts, 1566 Herts RO ASA25/635
Wedon, William, Rickmansworth, Herts, 1594 Herts RO ASA25/1503
Weech, Eleanor, Ham, High, Som, 1663 Somerset RO D/D/Cta/W57
Weeden, Robert, wheelwright, Patching, Sussex, 1684 W. Suss RO EpIV/10/2A/32
Weedham, John, gentleman, Bosworth, Market, Leics, 1666 Leics RO Administrators Accounts C17th f67
Weedon, John, St Albans St Stephens (Tyttenhanger Green), Herts, 1616 Herts RO ASA25/4827
Weedon, Ralph, Bushey, Herts, 1635 Herts RO ASA25/4923
Weeds, Ann, widow, Norwich, Norf, 1737 Norfolk RO ANW/23/22A/28
Weekes, Wimborne Minster, Dors, Dorset RO PE/WM CP 2/4/78
Weekes, Donhead St Mary, Wilts, 1677? Wilts RO Miscellaneous Index (name + date)
Weekes, Abraham, limeburner, Salisbury, Wilts, 1780 c. Wilts RO Miscellaneous Index (name + date)
Weekes, Ann, widow, Blean, Kent, 1618 CKS PRC2/26/86
Weekes, Eliz + Richard, yeoman, Woodchurch, Kent, 1709 CKS PRC19/6/40
Weekes, James, Egerton, Kent, 1684 CKS PRC20/13/477
Weekes, Jeames, Stone in Oxney, Kent, 1594 CKS PRC2/7/371
Weekes, John, brewer: 'beerbrewer', Dover St James, Kent, 1672 CKS PRC20/12/33
Weekes, John, Ramsey, Hunts, 1676 Hunts RO/Acc58/40(121)
Weekes, Michael, husbandman, Milton, Berks, 1598 Berks RO D/A1/220/182B
Weekes, Richard, Sheldwich, Kent, 1596 CKS PRC2/8/471
Weekes, Richard, Woodchurch, Kent, 1681 CKS PRC20/13/214
Weekes, Robert, Boxley, Kent, 1687 CKS PRC2/41/87
Weekes, Roger, mason, Upavon, Wilts, 1673 Wilts RO Arch. Sarum(+ name and date)
Weekes, Thomas, gentleman, Ashbury (Kingstone Winslow), Berks, 1597 Berks RO D/A1/220/169B
Weekes, Thomas, husbandman, Buckland, Berks, 1631 Berks RO D/A1/221/121B
Weekes, William, husbandman/widow (sic), Rolvenden, Kent, 1681 CKS PRC2/39/257
Weekes, Wyllyam, Blean, Kent, 1595 CKS PRC2/7/259
Weekes/Knowlden, Elizabeth, wife, Charing, Kent, 1677 CKS PRC20/12/245
Weekes, see Browne,
Weeks, George, yeoman, Sandwich, Kent, 1616 CKS PRC2/26/71
Weeks, George, Blean, Kent, 1639 CKS PRC1/3/60
Weeks, Johnson, Broughton Gifford, Wilts, 1640? Wilts RO Arch. Sarum(+ name and date)
Weeks, Robert, Smarden, Kent, 1648 CKS PRC1/8/55
Weeks, Stephen, Linton, Kent, 1644 CKS PRC1/7/16
Weeks, Thomas, Donhead St Mary, Wilts, 1687 Wilts RO Arch. Sarum(+ name and date)
Weeks, William, Sutton Mandeville, Wilts, 1604 Wilts RO Arch. Sarum(+ name and date)
Weever, Richard, clergy: 'clerk/reverend', Wistaston, Ches, 1740 Cheshire RO (Name) W.C. 1740

[Weevill:]
Weevill, Margaret, Aldington, Kent, 1597 CKS PRC21/14/187
Weevill, Mary, spinster, Canterbury St Mildred, Kent, 1627 CKS PRC2/28/129
Weevill, Rachell, widow, Warehorne, Kent, 1627 CKS PRC2/28/133
Weevills, John, mr, Canterbury St Mildred, Kent, 1631 CKS PRC2/31/77
Weight, Richard, Ashton, Long, Som, 1728 Somerset RO D/D/Cta/A25
Weight, William, Halesowen, Shrops, 1675 Worcs RO 008.7 BA3585/830/41
Welbecke, Richard, gentleman, Hendred, East, Berks, 1594 Berks RO D/A1/220/157B
Welberry, William, Firsby, Lincs, 1672 Lincs RO Ad/Ac/43/60
Welbie, Anthony, Whitstable, Kent, 1613 CKS PRC2/16/124
Welbie, Dorothy, widow, Faversham, Kent, 1629 CKS PRC2/30/143
Welbie, Robert, labourer, Bicker, Lincs, 1639 Lincs RO Ad/Ac/26/217
Welborne, Edward, Ingham, Lincs, 1620 Lincs RO Ad/Ac/8b/429
Welburne, John, Fishtoft, Lincs, 1650 Lincs RO Ad/Ac/29/159
Welburne, Matthew, Sibsey, Lincs, 1638 Lincs RO Ad/Ac/25/256
Welburne, Robert, Woolsthorpe, Lincs, 1649 Lincs RO Ad/Ac/30/38
Welby, Henry, husbandman, Herne, Kent, 1636 CKS PRC20/11/526
Welby, John, Reculver, Kent, 1639 CKS PRC20/11/500
Welby, John, yeoman, St Johns Thanet, Kent, 1682 CKS PRC2/40/84
Welby/Read, Elizabeth, wife, Herne, Kent, 1639 CKS PRC19/1/21
Welbye, John, Leeds, Kent, 1596 CKS PRC2/8/27
Welbye, Robert, Stickney, Lincs, 1619? Lincs RO Ad/Ac/15/298
Welbye, Roberte, Herne, Kent, 1592 CKS PRC21/11/292
Welch, Elizabeth, widow, Shapwick, Som, Somerset RO D/D/Cta/W26
Welch, Richard, Chart, Great, Kent, 1624 CKS PRC2/26/52
Welch, Thomas, feltmaker, Newcastle under Lyme, Staffs, 1754 LJRO/B/C/5/1754/179
Welche, Hugh,
Worcs 1606 Worcs RO 008.7 BA3585/839/419
Welche, John, Appledore, Kent, 1593 CKS PRC2/6/442
Welche, John, clergy: 'clerk', Willingham, Cherry, Lincs, 1594 Lincs RO Ad/Ac/37/17
Welche, Robarte, Eastchurch, Sheppey, Kent, 1597 CKS PRC2/9/215
Welche, Thomas, Faversham, Kent, 1588 CKS PRC2/4/454
Welche, William, Cranbrook, Kent, 1615 CKS PRC2/26/37
Welcome, John, gentleman, Stainton, Market, Lincs, 1670 Lincs RO Ad/Ac/32/223
Welden, Bryan, yeoman, Pinchbeck, Lincs, 1683 Lincs RO Ad/Ac/44/104
Welden, George, esquire, Shottesbrook, Berks, 1672 Berks RO D/A1/222/99B
Weldish, Bartholomew, Minster in Sheppey, Kent, 1631 CKS PRC2/31/74
Weldish, Jonas, Badlesmere, Kent, 1597 CKS PRC2/9/487
Weldish, Mary, widow, Tonge, Kent, 1664 CKS PRC1/10/108
Weldish, Mary, widow, Tonge, Kent, 1664 CKS PRC19/3/66
Weldish, Richard eld, Rodmersham, Kent, 1667 CKS PRC1/12/94
Weldishe, Henrie, New Romney, Kent, 1611 CKS PRC20/2/120
Weldishe, Jeames, Hernhill, Kent, 1570 CKS PRC21/1/89
Weldishe, William, Milsted, Kent, 1585 CKS PRC2/3/282
Weldon, John, clergy: 'clerk', Newington (Butts), Surrey, 1675 PRO PROB5/1276
Weldon, John, clergy: 'clerk', Newington (Butts), Surrey, 1676 PRO PROB5/1277
Weldon, Nicholas, St Albans St Michaels, Herts, 1627 Herts RO ASA25/4851
Weldon, Thomas, Kirton, Lincs, 1612 Lincs RO Ad/Ac/11/179
Weldyshe, George, Marden, Kent, 1599 CKS PRC2/11/321
Weldyshe, John, Teynham, Kent, 1584 CKS PRC2/3/17
Wellar, Alexander ygr, Cranbrook, Kent, 1613 CKS PRC20/2/292
Welldishe, Edward, gentleman, Boughton Monchelsea, Kent, 1613 CKS PRC2/18/126
Weller, Agnes, spinster, Oxford, Oxon, 1638 Oxon RO MSS Wills 300/6/19
Weller, Alexander, clothier, Cranbrook, Kent, 1631 CKS PRC20/9/452
Weller, John, clothier, Cranbrook, Kent, 1624 CKS PRC20/6/214
Weller, John, thatcher, Cranbrook, Kent, 1686 CKS PRC2/41/86

Weller, Mary, Rolvenden, Kent, 1639 CKS PRC1/3/61
Weller, Thomas, Hanborough, Oxon, 1803 Oxon RO MSS Wills 306/14/4
Weller, see Attawaye,
Wellerd, Rychard, Biddenden, Kent, 1581 CKS PRC2/1/313
Welles, Anthonye, Benenden, Kent, 1592 CKS PRC2/5/41
Welles, Arthur, Harrietsham, Kent, 1641 CKS PRC1/6/36
Welles, Gryffyn, Appledore, Kent, 1608 CKS PRC2/14/471
Welles, John, Willesborough, Kent, 1587 CKS PRC2/4/388
Welles, John, Fairfield, Kent, 1595 CKS PRC21/13/75
Welles, John, Minster in Thanet, Kent, 1595 CKS PRC2/8/25
Welles, John, Barford St Martin, Wilts, 1613 Wilts RO Arch. Sarum(+ name and date)
Welles, John, Ulceby, Lincs, 1622 Lincs RO Ad/Ac/17/95
Welles, John, Minster in Thanet, Kent, 1623 CKS PRC2/26/28
Welles, Margaret, widow, Biddenden, Kent, 1612 CKS PRC2/16/60
Welles, Nicholas, Lydd, Kent, 1668 CKS PRC19/4/37
Welles, Rafe, Bethersden, Kent, 1607 CKS PRC2/14/467
Welles, Richard, Smarden, Kent, 1605 CKS PRC2/13/427
Welles, Richarde, Rolvenden, Kent, 1602 CKS PRC2/12/381
Welles, Robert, Branston, Lincs, 1611 Lincs RO Ad/Ac/10/74
Welles, Stephen, Hope All Saints, Kent, 1583 CKS PRC2/3/116
Welles, Susanne, widow, Lydd, Kent, 1604 CKS PRC21/17/369
Welles, Thomas, Wye, Kent, 1593 CKS PRC2/6/390
Welles, Thomas, Littlebourne, Kent, 1595 CKS PRC2/7/129
Welles, Thomas, Ruckinge, Kent, 1600 CKS PRC2/11/329
Welles, Thomas, Toft Next Newton, Lincs, 1606 Lincs RO Ad/Ac/7/12
Welles, William, yeoman, Alkborough, Lincs, 1604 Lincs RO Ad/Ac/37/178
Welles, William, Minster in Sheppey, Kent, 1611 CKS PRC2/16/190
Wellicombe, Thomas, Mixbury, Oxon, 1626 Oxon RO MSS Wills 176/2/16
Welliner, Thomas, Bassingthorpe, Lincs, 1640 Lincs RO Ad/Ac/27/176
Wellins, Thomas, bachelor, Willesborough, Kent, 1679 CKS PRC2/38/82
Wellins, William, yeoman, Willesborough, Kent, 1677 CKS PRC2/37/208
Wellman, Mary, widow, Stanford in the Vale, Berks, 1646 Berks RO D/A1/222/29B
Wellman, Richard, husbandman, Coxwell, Great, Berks, 1633 Berks RO D/A1/221/130B
Wellman, Robert, Oxford St Thomas, Oxon, 1683 Oxon RO MSS Wills 176/4/20
Wellman, William, husbandman, Coxwell, Great, Berks, 1620 Berks RO D/A1/221/75B
Wells, Alice, widow, Broughton, Hunts, 1676 Hunts RO/Acc58/38(46)
Wells, Anne, widow, Grantham, Lincs, 1626 Lincs RO Ad/Ac/20/41
Wells, Anthony, Tenterden, Kent, 1625 CKS PRC2/25/155
Wells, Anthony, Horncastle, Lincs, 1632 Lincs RO Ad/Ac/23/122
Wells, Anthony, Sandhurst, Kent, 1679 CKS PRC2/38/201
Wells, Benjamin, Wye, Kent, 1644 CKS PRC1/7/35
Wells, Benjamin, gentleman, Warminster, Wilts, 1747 Wilts RO CC Sarum(+ name and date)
Wells, Edmund, Kirton in Lindsey, Lincs, 1675 Lincs RO Ad/Ac/42/63
Wells, Edward, Harpswell, Lincs, 1597 Lincs RO Ad/Ac/37/27
Wells, Edward, Greetwell, Lincs, 1623 Lincs RO Ad/Ac/8c/55
Wells, Edward, bachelor, Langton by Wragby, Lincs, 1666 Lincs RO Ad/Ac/32/109
Wells, Francis, Luddington, Lincs, 1611 Lincs RO Ad/Ac/8a/342
Wells, George, tanner, Stoneham, North, Hants, 1678 Hants RO 21m65 D8/300
Wells, Henry, Woodhurst, Hunts, 1687 Hunts RO/Acc58/264(257)
Wells, James, Bearsted, Kent, 1671 CKS PRC2/35/101
Wells, Jane, Maidstone, Kent, 1625 CKS PRC20/6/199
Wells, Joan, widow, Oxford All Saints, Oxon, 1629 Oxon RO MSS Wills 88/1/60
Wells, Joane, widow, Benenden, Kent, 1598 CKS PRC2/11/52
Wells, Joane, widow, Lydd, Kent, 1642 CKS PRC19/2/67
Wells, John, labourer, Tealby, Lincs, 1619 Lincs RO Ad/Ac/14/234

[Wells:]
Wells, John, ploughmaker, Speen, Berks, 1619? Wilts RO CC Sarum(+ name and date)
Wells, John, Egerton, Kent, 1632 CKS PRC20/11/578
Wells, John, Northorpe, Lincs, 1632 Lincs RO Ad/Ac/39/317
Wells, John, Bowden, Great, Leics, 1667 Leics RO Administrators Accounts 1667-72 f3
Wells, John, cordwainer, Wingham, Kent, 1684 CKS PRC20/13/479
Wells, John, mariner, Whitstable, Kent, 1706 CKS PRC19/6/26
Wells, Marie, London Thorpe, Lincs, 1638 Lincs RO Ad/Ac/25/301
Wells, Mary, mrs, Shepherdswell alias Sibertswold, Kent, 1633 CKS PRC2/32/128
Wells, Michaell, St Thomas Isle of Harty, Kent, 1621 CKS PRC2/26/68
Wells, Nicholas, tailor, Washingborough, Lincs, 1638 Lincs RO Ad/Ac/25/292
Wells, Olive, widow, Garford, Berks, 1603 Berks RO D/A1/220/197B
Wells, Richard, yeoman, Kingsnorth, Kent, 1619 CKS PRC2/26/84
Wells, Richard, Benenden, Kent, 1639 CKS PRC2/34/302
Wells, Richard, Tattershall, Lincs, 1640 Lincs RO Ad/Ac/26/221
Wells, Robert, Sandridge, Herts, 1627 Herts RO ASA25/2973
Wells, Robert, Preston next Faversham, Kent, 1635 CKS PRC2/32/178
Wells, Robert, yeoman, Milton, Great, Oxon, 1677 Oxon RO MSS Wills Pec 55/1/4
Wells, Robert eld, Sandwich, Kent, 1620 CKS PRC2/26/53
Wells, Roger, Minster in Thanet, Kent, 1618 CKS PRC2/26/14
Wells, Roger, Harmston, Lincs, 1619 Lincs RO Ad/Ac/15/239
Wells, Thomas, Hinton, Little, Wilts, 1620 Wilts RO Arch. Wilts.(+ name and date)
Wells, Thomas, Ashford, Kent, 1621 CKS PRC2/26/121
Wells, Thomas, clergy: 'clerk', Stallingborough, Lincs, 1636 Lincs RO Ad/Ac/24/419
Wells, Thomas, butcher, Grimsby, Great, Lincs, 1666 Lincs RO Ad/Ac/32/92
Wells, Thomas, Chart, Great, Kent, 1668 CKS PRC1/13/144
Wells, Thomas, Horncastle, Lincs, 1669 Lincs RO Ad/Ac/33/91
Wells, Thomas, Horncastle, Lincs, 1669 Lincs RO Ad/Ac/33/137
Wells, Thomas, Brookland, Kent, 1675 CKS PRC2/36/260
Wells, Walter, Bearsted, Kent, 1633 CKS PRC2/32/134
Wells, William, Scotton, Lincs, 1619 Lincs RO Ad/Ac/8b/353
Wells, William, New Romney, Kent, 1641 CKS PRC19/1/90
Wells, William, husbandman, Upchurch, Kent, 1643 CKS PRC1/7/17
Wells, William, Willingham, Cherry, Lincs, 1673 Lincs RO Ad/Ac/35/45
Wells, William, Scothorne, Lincs, 1679 Lincs RO Ad/Ac/43/134
Wells/Den/Miller, Margarett, wife, Buckland nr Dover, Kent, 1632 CKS PRC2/31/105
Wells, see Attwell,
Wellsmyth, John, Winthorpe, Lincs, 1639 Lincs RO Ad/Ac/26/156
Welsche, Philip, Badgworth, Som, 1628 Somerset RO D/D/Cta/W11
Welshe, John, Eastchurch, Sheppey, Kent, 1609 CKS PRC2/13/441
Wenam, William, Cambridge, Cambs, 1700 Cambs RO
Wenborne, Amy, Maidstone, Kent, 1631 CKS PRC20/9/466
Wenborne, John, Maidstone, Kent, 1622 CKS PRC20/6/220
Wendover, Henry, gentleman, Winslow, Bucks, 1627 Herts RO ASA25/4852
Wengham, Stephen, Harting, Sussex, 1633 W. Suss RO EpI/33/1633/8
Wenlock, James, carpenter: 'ships carpenter', Dover, Kent, 1678 CKS PRC20/12/288
Wenman, William, Marden, Kent, 1609 CKS PRC2/13/443
Wenman, William, carpenter, Cranbrook, Kent, 1676 CKS PRC2/37/103
Wensley, Hughe, Sempringham, Lincs, 1606 Lincs RO Ad/Ac/7/148
Wentworth, John, baronet, Srayingham (Howsham), Yorks, Borthwick Test C.P. 1720/11
Wentworth, Katherine, gentlewoman/widow, Barrow, Lincs, 1635 Lincs RO Ad/Ac/24/435
Wentworth, William, Humberstone, Lincs, 1606 Lincs RO Ad/Ac/7/14
Wentworth, William, gentleman, Somercoates, North, Lincs, 1632 Lincs RO Ad/Ac/24/221
Wentworth, William, gentleman, Somercoates, North, Lincs, 1634 Lincs RO Ad/Ac/24/39
Wenwright, Margaret, widow, Storrington, Sussex, 1629 W. Suss RO EpI/33/1629/28
Wepham, Thomas, Climping, Sussex, 1631 W. Suss RO EpI/33/1630/9

Wepham, William, Bosham, Sussex, 1648 W. Suss RO EpI/33/1648/9
Weppam, Stephen, Climping, Sussex, W. Suss RO EpI/33/1617/4
Weppham, Stephen, Climping, Sussex, 1617 W. Suss RO EpI/33/1617/29
Werdnam, William, Welford (Easton), Berks, 1674 Berks RO D/A1/222/114B
Weren, Thomas, Wendron, Corn, 1609 Cornwall RO AP/W111/2
Wergg, William, grocer, Newbury, Berks, 1675 Berks RO D/A1/222/132B
Wescott, John, Hurley, Berks, Berks RO D/A1/221/25B
Wescott, Robert, Petherton, South, Som, 1620 Somerset RO D/D/Cta/W5
Weselheade, Antonie, Alford, Lincs, 1600 Lincs RO Ad/Ac/5/236
Wesilhead, John, Corby, Lincs, 1614 Lincs RO Ad/Ac/13/37
Weslye, Charles, gentleman, Grimsby, Great, Lincs, 1669 Lincs RO Ad/Ac/33/108
Wessencroft/Westerncroft, Thomas, Tarring, West, Sussex, 1685 W. Suss RO EpIV/10/2A/37
Wessenden, Christopher, Ickham, Kent, 1619 CKS PRC20/4/451
Wessenden, Elizabeth, Wickhambreaux, Kent, 1641 CKS PRC1/6/37
West, Allen, Warnham, Sussex, 1595 W. Suss RO EpI/33/1595/5
West, Ann, Stow (Stow Park), Lincs, 1649 Lincs RO Ad/Ac/42/61
West, Elizabeyh, widow, Arksey, Yorks, 1672 Lincs RO Ad/Ac/33/181
West, George, Ippollitts, Herts, 1675 Herts RO AHH23/2538
West, Grace, widow, Hilmarton, Wilts, 1627 Wilts RO Arch. Wilts.(+ name and date)
West, Hester, widow, Birchington, Kent, 1635 CKS PRC20/11/550
West, Hugh, Tetford, Lincs, 1648 Lincs RO Ad/Ac/30/286
West, Jeffery, Fittleworth, Sussex, 1613 W. Suss RO EpI/33/1613/14
West, John, Boston, Lincs, 1613 Lincs RO Ad/Ac/12/45
West, John, yeoman, Sudbrooke, Lincs, 1670? Lincs RO Ad/Ac/32/134
West, Jonathan, Oxford St Michael, Oxon, 1634 Oxon RO MSS Wills 300/6/9
West, Jone, widow, St Nicholas at Wade, Kent, 1598 CKS PRC21/14/550
West, Joseph, Welbourn, Lincs, 1619 Lincs RO Ad/Ac/15/151
West, Katherin, spinster, Saxilby, Lincs, 1614 Lincs RO Ad/Ac/13/121
West, Margaret, widow, Bishopsbourne, Kent, 1667 CKS PRC1/12/95
West, Mary, widow, Milton next Sittingbourne, Kent, 1672 CKS PRC2/35/100
West, Mathew, Canterbury St Mildred, Kent, 1632 CKS PRC20/11/572
West, Mawde, widow, Waddingham, Lincs, 1598 Lincs RO Ad/Ac/37/76
West, Nicholas, Northmoor, Oxon, 1624 Oxon RO MSS Wills 88/1/48
West, Nicholas, St Laurence Thanet, Kent, 1674 CKS PRC2/36/140
West, Oswald, Ebbesbourne Wake, Wilts, 1770 Wilts RO Miscellaneous Index (name + date)
West, Ralph, butcher, Malton, Yorks, 1786 Borthwick Test C.P. 1785/6
West, Richard, husbandman, Bradley, North, Wilts, 1579 Wilts RO Arch. Sarum(+ name and date)
West, Richard, Canterbury St Andrew, Kent, 1586 CKS PRC2/4/43
West, Richard, Benenden, Kent, 1607 CKS PRC2/13/434
West, Richard, Clee, Lincs, 1618 Lincs RO Ad/Ac/14/174
West, Richard, Sidlesham, Sussex, 1620 W. Suss RO EpI/33/1620
West, Richard, Brattleby, Lincs, 1624 Lincs RO Ad/Ac/39/136
West, Richard, Bradley, North, Wilts, 1643 Wilts RO Arch. Sarum(+ name and date)
West, Robert, Goudhurst, Kent, 1622 CKS PRC2/26/38
West, Robert, Lacock, Wilts, 1632 Wilts RO Arch. Wilts.(+ name and date)
West, Robert, Stow, Lincs, 1664 Lincs RO Ad/Ac/42/66
West, Roberte, Cowbit/Spalding, Lincs, 1598 Lincs RO Ad/Ac/4/119
West, Samuel, Kirdford, Sussex, 1661 W. Suss RO EpI/33/1661/8
West, Thomas, Wasing, Berks, 1600 Berks RO D/A1/220/186B
West, Thomas, husbandman, Sunningwell (Bayworth), Berks, 1625 Berks RO D/A1/221/97B
West, Thomas, Birchington, Kent, 1635 CKS PRC20/11/554
West, Valentyne, St Nicholas at Wade, Kent, 1592 CKS PRC21/12/161
West, William, St Nicholas at Wade, Kent, 1617 CKS PRC20/4/411
West, William, Kirkby, Lincs, 1618 Lincs RO Ad/Ac/14/40

[West:]
West, William, Pagham, Sussex, 1618 W. Suss RO EpIV/10/1/42
West, William, Monkton Farleigh, Wilts, 1623 Wilts RO Arch. Sarum(+ name and date)
West, William, gardener, Abingdon, Berks, 1639 Berks RO D/A1/221/163B
West, William, yeoman, Drayton, Berks, 1642 Berks RO D/A1/222/2B
West, William eld, Sandhurst, Kent, 1628 CKS PRC2/29/116
West, William ygr, farmer, Bawdeswell, Norf, 1758 Norfolk RO ANW/23/25/30
West/Steephens, Jane, wife, Caversham, Oxon, 1675 Oxon RO MSS Wills 86/3/18
Westaby, William, Rothwell, Lincs, 1652 Lincs RO Ad/Ac/29/7
Westall, Richard, Howell, Lincs, 1641 Lincs RO Ad/Ac/27/218
Westbeech, Thomas, St Johns Thanet, Kent, 1617 CKS PRC2/26/6
Westbeech/Paramore, Margaret, Preston next Wingham, Kent, 1685 CKS PRC2/41/20
Westbeeche, Tymothy, Canterbury St George Martyr, Kent, 1597 CKS PRC2/9/323
Westbeere, Andrew, Porton, Wilts, 1640 Wilts RO Arch. Sarum(+ name and date)
Westborne, John, Appledore, Kent, 1591 CKS PRC2/5/446
Westbourne, Thomas, Lydd, Kent, 1584 CKS PRC21/7/19
Westbroke, Richard, Challow, East, Berks, 1606 Berks RO D/A1/133/184D
Westbrook, Guy, Steep, Hants, 1625 Hants RO 21M65 D8/95
Westbrook, William, wheeler, Harting, Sussex, 1676 W. Suss RO EpI/33/1676/23
Westbrooke, Agnes, widow, Waltham, White, Berks, 1635 Berks RO D/A1/221/142B
Westcott, Robert, blacksmith, Bray, Berks, 1637 Berks RO D/A1/221/156B
Westcott, Samuel, collar maker, Bristol, Glos, Bristol RO 1772/CP
Weste, Isabell, widow, Utterby, Lincs, 1618 Lincs RO Ad/Ac/14/20
Weste, Thomas, St Mary in the Marsh, Kent, 1594 CKS PRC2/7/41
Westell, Thomas, brazier/broker, Bristol, Glos, Bristol RO 1734/52a
Westend, Richard, husbandman, Windsor, Old, Berks, 1682 Berks RO D/A1/223/13C
Westerbie, Thomas, yeoman, Boston, Lincs, 1629 Lincs RO Ad/Ac/22/64
Westerby, John, mariner: 'seafaring man', Teynham, Kent, 1679 CKS PRC2/38/83
Westerman, Thomas, Willoughby, Lincs, 1639? Lincs RO Ad/Ac/26/87
Westerncroft, see Wessencroft,
Westfeild, Henry, husbandman, Fillingham, Lincs, 1677 Lincs RO Ad/Ac/35/114
Westfield, John, Lacock, Wilts, 1621 Wilts RO CC Sarum(+ name and date)
Westgate, Charlee, Sibsey, Lincs, 1605 Lincs RO Ad/Ac/6/105
Westgates, William, Skirbeck, Lincs, 1612 Lincs RO Ad/Ac/11/173
Westland, John, Benington, Lincs, 1600 Lincs RO Ad/Ac/5/336
Westland, Susannah, Frieston, Lincs, 1672 Lincs RO Ad/Ac/43/65
Westley, Gilbarte, Frittenden, Kent, 1597 CKS PRC2/9/491
Westley, Joseph, chapman, Walsall, Staffs, 1779 LJRO/B/C/5/1779/97
Westley, Richard, Tenterden, Kent, 1639 CKS PRC1/3/62
Westmacott, Thomas, Swalcliffe, Oxon, 1637 Oxon RO MSS Wills 300/6/18
Westmells, Roberte, Thorpe, Lincs, 1579 Lincs RO Ad/Ac/2b/17
Weston, Alice, widow, Maidstone, Kent, 1613 CKS PRC20/3/470
Weston, Edward, Wherwell, Hants, 1624 Hants RO 21M65 D8/96
Weston, Edward, Tarring, West, Sussex, 1680 W. Suss RO EpIV/10/2A/18
Weston, Elizabeth, widow, Chilham, Kent, 1619 CKS PRC2/26/54
Weston, George, Pagham (Aldwick), Sussex, 1613 W. Suss RO EpIV/10/1/5
Weston, John, Durrington, Sussex, 1617 W. Suss RO EpIV/10/1/51
Weston, John, Durrington, Sussex, 1639 W. Suss RO EpIV/10/2/18
Weston, John, Burton Overy, Leics, 1666 Leics RO Administrators Accounts C17th f54
Weston, John, Drayton in Hales, Staffs, 1685 LJRO/B/C/5/1685/108
Weston, Marian, widow, Drayton, Berks, 1618 Berks RO D/A1/221/66B
Weston, Mary, widow, Hendred, East, Berks, 1677 Berks RO D/A1/222/141B
Weston, Nicholas, esquire, Canterbury, Kent, 1634 CKS PRC20/11/558
Weston, Robert, Banbury, Oxon, 1631 Oxon RO MSS Wills Pec 54/3/14
Weston, Sarah, Mackworth, Derby, 1682 LJRO/B/C/5/1682/150
Weston, Thomas, Tarring, West, Sussex, 1628 W. Suss RO EpIV/10/1/18

[Weston:]

Weston, Thomas, Banbury, Oxon, 1631 Oxon RO MSS Wills Pec 54/3/10
Weston, Thomas, yeoman, Frittenden, Kent, 1670 CKS PRC1/15/78
Weston, Thomas, carrier, Tamworth, Staffs, 1774 LJRO/B/C/5/1774/72
Weston, Walter, yeoman, Hannington, Wilts, 1634 Wilts RO CC Sarum(+ name and date)
Weston, William, Ropsley, Lincs, 1587 Lincs RO Ad/Ac/2C/30
Weston, William, clothier, Cranbrook, Kent, 1614 CKS PRC2/18/4
Weston, William, Yateley, Hants, 1624 Hants RO 21M65 D8/97
Weston, William, yeoman, Aston Tirrold, Berks, 1633 Berks RO D/A1/221/136B
Weston, William, Hannington, Wilts, 1736? Wilts RO Arch. Wilts.(+ name and date)
Westridge, see French,
Westrop, Richard, Wootton Bassett, Wilts, 1618 Wilts RO Arch. Wilts.(+ name and date)
Westwood, Samuel, Halesowen (Cradley), Worcs, 1648 Worcs RO 008.7 BA3585/837/bdl 1
Westwood, William, yeoman, Halesowen, Worcs, 1603 Worcs RO 008.7 BA3585/838/278
Wetherall, Thomas, husbandman, Bytham, Little, Lincs, 1680 Lincs RO Ad/Ac/34/46
Wethered, William, Ridge, Herts, 1591 Herts RO ASA25/1369
Wethered, William, yeoman, Sandridge, Herts, 1621 Herts RO ASA25/2610
Wetherell, Francis, Baringham (Peacock Hole), Yorks, 1724 Borthwick Test C.P. 1724/11
Wetherhead, William, Ridge, Herts, 1596 Herts RO ASA25/1584
Wetherill, Johnne, Authorpe, Lincs, 1593 Lincs RO Ad/Ac/3/121
Wetherill, William, yeoman, Rothwell (The Lodge, Thwaite), Yorks, 1779 Borthwick Test C.P. 1779/13
Wetton, Richard, Uttoxeter, Staffs, 1676 LJRO:cards/1676/50
Whaley, Henrie, Blackburn, Lancs, 1630 Lancs RO (Name of Deceased) D.R.C.H. 1630
Whaley, John, Covenham St Mary, Lincs, 1640 Lincs RO Ad/Ac/27/98
Whaley, Randall, Felpham?, Sussex, 1595 W. Suss RO EpI/33/1594/2
Whaley, Thomas, yeoman, Utterby, Lincs, 1670 Lincs RO Ad/Ac/32/227
Whall, Henry,
Norf 1738 Norfolk RO ANW/23/24/50
Whalley, Joane, widow, Aubourn (Haddington), Lincs, 1634 Lincs RO Ad/Ac/24/43
Whalley, John, Hallington, Lincs, 1611 Lincs RO Ad/Ac/10/27
Whalley, Richard, Aldford (Boughton), Ches, 1690 Cheshire RO (Name) W.C. 1690
Whalley, Thomas, labourer, Hale, Great, Lincs, 1626 Lincs RO Ad/Ac/20/2
Whaly, John, barber, Cambridge, Cambs, 1667 c. CUL V.C. Acc./Box3/56
Whaples, Samuell, St Andrew Hubbard, London & Middlesex, 1710 PRO PROB5/1726
Whapload, William, Waddingham, Lincs, 1640 Lincs RO Ad/Ac/40/280
Wharfe, Dennis, High Halstow, Kent, 1619 CKS PRC1/1/25a
Wharfe, Dennis, widow, High Halstow, Kent, 1619 CKS PRC1/1/25
Wharffe, Thomas, Mareham le Fen, Lincs, 1579? Lincs RO Ad/Ac/2b/12
Wharnsbey, James, university: 'scholar's servant', Cambridge, Cambs, 1628 CUL V.C. Acc./Box2/83
Wharrell, Henrie, Ashford, Kent, 1626 CKS PRC2/27/180
Wharrell, Thomas, bricklayer, Smeeth, Kent, 1663 CKS PRC19/3/47
Wharton, Issabell, widow, Gedney, Lincs, 1612 Lincs RO Ad/Ac/11/7
Wharton, Margaret, widow, Carlton le Moorland, Lincs, 1606 Lincs RO Ad/Ac/6/49
Wharton, William, Southampton, Hants, 1624 Hants RO 21M65 D8/98
Whassingburgh, Elizabeth, widow, Leasingham, Lincs, 1613 Lincs RO Ad/Ac/12/71
Whate, see Sherewood,
Whateley, William, collier, Wednesbury, Staffs, 1783 LJRO/B/C/5/1783/224
Whatlow, Thomas, clothier, Bethersden, Kent, 1665 CKS PRC19/3/88
Whatlowe, Ann, widow, Smarden, Kent, 1603 CKS PRC2/12/463
Whatlowe, James, Egerton, Kent, 1623 CKS PRC20/6/210
Whatlowe, Mathewe, Appledore, Kent, 1608 CKS PRC2/15/442
Whatly, Anthony, Ashton, Steeple, Wilts, 1630 Wilts RO Arch. Sarum(+ name and date)
Whatly, Jane, Bradley, North, Wilts, 1669 Wilts RO Arch. Sarum(+ name and date)
Whatly, John, Dilton, Wilts, 1639 Wilts RO Chantor Sarum Bundle 4/10

[Whatly:]
Whatly, John, Ashton, Steeple, Wilts, 1640 Wilts RO Arch. Sarum(+ name and date)
Whatman, Arthur, Chartham, Kent, 1639 CKS PRC2/34/311
Whatman, James,
Kent 1586 CKS PRC2/4/337
Whatman, James, Maidstone, Kent, 1598 CKS PRC21/14/542
Whatman, James, husbandman, Goudhurst, Kent, 1663 CKS PRC1/9/158
Whawell, Ambrose, barber, Chester St Mary on the Hill, Ches, 1744 Cheshire RO (Name) W.C. 1743-4
Wheat, Nicholas, yeoman, Tilehurst, Berks, 1633 Berks RO D/A1/221/129B
Wheat, Thomas, Tilehurst, Berks, 1625 Wilts RO CC Sarum(+ name and date)
Wheatam, John, Titchfield, Hants, 1623 Hants RO 21M65 D8/41
Wheatham, John, Titchfield, Hants, 1661 Hants RO 21M65 D8/147
Wheatland, John, Milton next Sittingbourne, Kent, 1613 CKS PRC2/16/141
Wheatland, John, Bredgar, Kent, 1638 CKS PRC2/34/299
Wheatland, Thomas, husbandman, Borden, Kent, 1678 CKS PRC2/38/88
Wheatland, William, Murston, Kent, 1672 CKS PRC2/35/190
Wheatley, Elizabeth, widow, Tarring, West, Sussex, 1671 W. Suss RO EpIV/10/2A/13
Wheatley, Humfrey, clergy: 'clerk', St Nicholas at Wade, Kent, 1632 CKS PRC20/11/566
Wheatley, Richard, Sidlesham, Sussex, 1678 W. Suss RO EpI/33/1678/13
Wheatley, William, gentleman, Tarring, West, Sussex, 1670 W. Suss RO EpIV/10/2A/9
Wheatly, Horly, gentleman, Itchingfield, Sussex, 1636 W. Suss RO EpI/33/1635/20
Wheatly, Thomas, Heckington, Lincs, 1632 Lincs RO Ad/Ac/23/139
Wheedon, Ralph, husbandman, Aldenham, Herts, 1637 Herts RO AHH23/2553
Wheelden, Thomas, Darley, Derby, 1680 LJRO:cards/1680/39
Wheeler, Elizabeth, Stratford-upon-Avon, Warks, 1602 Worcs RO 008.7 BA3585/838/279
Wheeler, John, Eastchurch, Sheppey, Kent, 1605 CKS PRC2/14/494
Wheeler, John, St Johns Thanet, Kent, 1611 CKS PRC2/16/113
Wheeler, John, Titchfield, Hants, 1625 Hants RO 21M65 D8/139
Wheeler, John, Faversham, Kent, 1639 CKS PRC1/3/63
Wheeler, John, Hamble le Rice, Hants, 1669 Hants RO 21M65 D8/208
Wheeler, John, fellmonger, Tenterden, Kent, 1674 CKS PRC2/36/139
Wheeler, Lucy, Aldingbourne, Sussex, 1678 W. Suss RO EpI/33/1678/4
Wheeler, Peter, yeoman, Besselsleigh, Berks, 1636 Berks RO D/A1/182/110C
Wheeler, Phillipp, Titchfield, Hants, 1623 Hants RO 21M65 D8/42
Wheeler, Richard, Malvern, Great, Worcs, 1607 Worcs RO 008.7 BA3585/839/440
Wheeler, Roger, Wick, Worcs, 1685 Worcs RO 008.7 BA3585/830/25
Wheeler, Samuel, Wimborne Minster, Dors, Dorset RO PE/WM CP 2/4/84
Wheeler, Sepator, Wick by Pershore, Worcs, 1685 Worcs RO 008.7 BA3585/830/26
Wheeler, Ursula, widow, Faversham, Kent, 1641 CKS PRC1/6/38
Wheeler, William, Donhead St Mary, Wilts, 1625 Wilts RO CC Sarum(+ name and date)
Wheeler, William, Horsham, Sussex, 1629 W. Suss RO EpI/33/1629/2
Wheeler, William, Sandwich, Kent, 1638 CKS PRC2/34/308
Wheeler, William, husbandman, Welford (Easton), Berks, 1677 Berks RO D/A1/222/143B
Wheelows, William, Gayton, Northants, 1682 Northants RO NWill A/C/57
Whelcombe, Thomazine, spinster, Biddenden, Kent, 1616 CKS PRC2/26/10
Wheldale, Anne, widow, Addlethorpe, Lincs, 1672 Lincs RO Ad/Ac/34/115
Wheldale, Thomas, Skirbeck, Lincs, 1632 Lincs RO Ad/Ac/23/47
Whelpdale, Elizabeth, widow, Bratoft, Lincs, 1614 Lincs RO Ad/Ac/13/153
Whetland, Thomas eld, Bredgar, Kent, 1611 CKS PRC2/16/186
Whetley, William, Queenborough, Kent, 1605 CKS PRC2/13/439
Whetnall, Richard, Hoath, Kent, 1637 CKS PRC19/1/6
Whetston, John, husbandman, Wainfleet, Lincs, 1669 Lincs RO Ad/Ac/33/145
Whetston, William, innholder, St Giles in the Fields, London & Middlesex, 1675 PRO PROB32/12/73
Whetstone, Francis, gentleman, Cadney, Lincs, 1637 Lincs RO Ad/Ac/25/412

Whetstone, Nicholas, brazier, Dover, Kent, 1610 CKS PRC20/2/142
Whetstone, William, Abingdon, Berks, 1595 Berks RO D/A1/220/165B
Whibley, Thomas, husbandman, Marden, Kent, 1672 CKS PRC2/35/188
Whichellow, Thomas, Abingdon, Berks, 1701 Berks RO D/A1/223/126E
Whicheloe, Thomas, tailor, Denchworth, Berks, 1609 Berks RO D/A1/221/27B
Whichelow, Amy, widow, Clifton, Oxon, 1674 Oxon RO MSS Wills Pec 72/1/49
Whicher, John,
Wilts 1773? Wilts RO Miscellaneous Index (name + date)
Whiffen, Richard, yeoman, Downe, Kent, 1677 Lambeth Palace VH96/6753
Whightwicke, George, clergy: 'clerk', Bradfield, Berks, 1674 Berks RO D/A1/137/188C
Whippie, Christian, Walton, Som, 1619 Somerset RO D/D/Cta/W53
Whippie, John, Whitchurch, Som, 1589 Somerset RO D/D/Cta/W81
Whiskin, John sen, yeoman, Lidgate, Suff, 1731 Suff RO(B) IC500/3/47/13a
Whison, Margery, widow, St Clement Danes, London & Middlesex, 1689 PRO PROB32/28/177
Whisson, Edmund, Newnham, Herts, 1601 Herts RO ASA25/1811
Whistler, Hugh, Haseley, Great, Oxon, 1632 Oxon RO MSS Wills 300/6/5
Whistler, Ralph, Radley, Berks, 1614 Berks RO D/A1/221/46B
Whistler, Richard, yeoman, Ardington, Berks, 1597 Berks RO D/A1/220/170B
Whistler, Thomas, Goring, Oxon, 1626 Oxon RO MSS Wills 176/2/12
Whistler, Thomas, yeoman, Chaddleworth, Berks, 1677 Berks RO D/A1/222/146B
Whistler, William, Toynton All Saints, Lincs, 1611 Lincs RO Ad/Ac/10/56
Whiston, Thomas, Cheadle (Cheadle Grange), Staffs, 1664 LJRO:cards/1664/16
Whistons, Nicholas, Bromley, Abbots, Staffs, 1669 LJRO:cards/1669/19
Whitacres, Geffery, Epworth, Lincs, 1617 Lincs RO Ad/Ac/8b/308
Whitacres, John, St Albans St Michaels, Herts, 1581 Herts RO ASA25/1024
Whitaker, John, butter factor/widower, Leeds (Woodhouse), Yorks, 1812 Borthwick Test C.P. 1812/6
Whitaker, Richard, Lenham, Kent, 1664 CKS PRC1/9/159
Whitakers, Randle, tailor, Wolstanton, Staffs, 1790 LJRO/B/C/5/1790/112
Whitbie, Augustin, Ingoldmels, Lincs, 1614 Lincs RO Ad/Ac/13/205
Whitbie, Robert, mr, Oxford, Oxon, 1618 Oxon RO MSS Wills 89/4/24
Whitborne, John, Cheriton, Hants, 1670 Hants RO 21m65 D8/228
Whitborne, John eld, weaver, Sotwell, Berks, 1672 Berks RO D/A1/222/81B
Whitby, Thomas, Doddington, Lincs, 1669 Lincs RO Ad/Ac/33/130
Whitchcote, Robert, gentleman, Dunston, Lincs, 1626 Lincs RO Ad/Ac/20/30
Whitcher, George, shipwright, Portsmouth, Hants, 1665 Hants RO 1665 A112/2
Whitcomb, Richard, 1675 LJRO:cards/1675/60
White, Alice, Croome D'Abitot, Worcs, 1682 Worcs RO 008.7 BA3585/830/56
White, Ambrose, Wimborne Minster, Dors, Dorset RO PE/WM CP 2/4/88
White, Anne, spinster, Canterbury St Peter, Kent, 1668 CKS PRC1/13/145
White, Anne, spinster, Canterbury St Peter, Kent, 1668 CKS PRC1/13/145a
White, Anne, widow, Sutton Courtenay, Berks, 1673 Berks RO D/A1/222/116B
White, Barnaby, Banbury, Oxon, 1622 Oxon RO MSS Wills Pec 54/2/2
White, Bartholomew, victualler, Canterbury St Margaret, Kent, 1624 CKS PRC2/26/48
White, Betty, widow, Bristol, Glos, 1750 GRO GDR/B4/2/W185
White, Deodatus, Maidstone, Kent, 1627 CKS PRC20/7/120
White, Edward, Highgate, London & Middlesex, 1664 Lambeth Palace Arches G18/6
White, Edward, Leysdown, Kent, 1684 CKS PRC2/40/254
White, Edwarde, Rolvenden, Kent, 1596 CKS PRC2/8/298
White, Elizabeth, mrs, Aldington, Kent, 1632 CKS PRC20/11/570
White, Elizabeth, spinster, Smeeth, Kent, 1675 CKS PRC20/12/156
White, Ellianor, widow, Thoresby, North, Lincs, 1671 Lincs RO Ad/Ac/33/198
White, Francis, plasterer/widower, Broadway, Worcs, Worcs RO 008.7 BA3585/836/bdl 1
White, Francis, Bramley, Hants, 1673 Hants RO 1673 A98/3
White, George, gentleman, Canterbury, Kent, 1613 CKS PRC2/17/250

[White:]
White, George, Branston, Lincs, 1641 Lincs RO Ad/Ac/27/267
White, George, coal dealer, Birmingham, Warks, 1832 LJRO/B/C/5/1832/51
White, Hammond, Aldington, Kent, 1671 CKS PRC20/12/34
White, Henrie + Joane, Birchington, Kent, 1629 CKS PRC20/8/478
White, Henry, yeoman, Stelling, Kent, 1617 CKS PRC2/26/92
White, Henry, Meon, East, Hants, 1624 Hants RO 21M65 D8/99
White, Henry, Stelling, Kent, 1633 CKS PRC2/31/168
White, Henry, messenger, Knoyle, West, Wilts, 1676 Wilts RO CC Sarum(+ name and date)
White, Henry, gentleman, Sandwich, Kent, 1677 CKS PRC2/37/210
White, Henry, fellmonger, Faversham, Kent, 1692 CKS PRC2/42/54
White, Isaac, St Martin in the Fields, London & Middlesex, 1673 Lambeth Palace Arches G27/1
White, Isemaell, Lydd, Kent, 1591 CKS PRC21/10/263
White, James, 1729 LJRO/B/C/5/1729/163
White, Joan, Wimborne Minster, Dors, 1623 Dorset RO PE/WM CP 2/4/29
White, Joan, Sandwich St Clement, Kent, 1667 CKS PRC1/12/96
White, Joane, Adisham, Kent, 1583 CKS PRC21/6/278
White, Joane, mrs/spinster, Canterbury St Margaret, Kent, 1640 CKS PRC1/5/62
White, Job, farmer, Wirksworth (Cromford), Derby, 1788 LJRO/B/C/5/1788/171
White, John, Funtington, Sussex, W. Suss RO EpI/33/1607/4
White, John, husbandman, Husbands Bosworth, Leics, Leics RO PR/I/41A/65
White, John, Canterbury St Mildred, Kent, 1596 CKS PRC2/8/421
White, John, Minster in Thanet, Kent, 1596 CKS PRC2/8/318
White, John, gentleman, Winchester, Hants, 1611 Hants RO 1611 A115/3
White, John, Deal, Kent, 1618 CKS PRC20/4/437
White, John, Lyminge, Kent, 1622 CKS PRC20/6/232
White, John, Findon, Sussex, 1632 W. Suss RO EpI/33/1632/6
White, John, Goudhurst, Kent, 1633 CKS PRC2/31/173
White, John, Dilton, Wilts, 1639 Wilts RO Chantor Sarum Bundle 4/11
White, John, Northmoor, Oxon, 1641 Oxon RO MSS Wills 300/6/27
White, John, Shepton Mallet, Som, 1641 Somerset RO D/D/Cta/W29
White, John, Steeping, Great, Lincs, 1641 Lincs RO Ad/Ac/27/271
White, John, Hythe West, Kent, 1646 CKS PRC1/7/101
White, John, yeoman, Waterstock, Oxon, 1662 Oxon RO MSS Wills 300/6/35
White, John, yeoman, Burnham (East Burnham), Bucks, 1663 Lambeth Palace Arches G18/2
White, John, Deal, Kent, 1668 CKS PRC19/3/144
White, John, Highworth, Wilts, 1675 Wilts RO Miscellaneous Index (name + date)
White, John, Aldington, Kent, 1681 CKS PRC19/4/113
White, John, Horsley, East, Surrey, 1681 Lambeth Palace VH96/2783
White, John, Titchfield, Hants, 1684 Hants RO 21m65 D8/346
White, John, maltster, Stanford Dingley, Berks, 1684 Berks RO D/A1/223/28C
White, John, Whitechapel, London & Middlesex, 1685 Lambeth Palace Arches G35/2
White, John, St Johns Thanet, Kent, 1692 CKS PRC2/42/53
White, John, farmer, Wragby (Saintinley), Yorks, 1796 Borthwick Test C.P. 1796/5
White, John eld, Lympne, Kent, 1609 CKS PRC2/15/435
White, Joseph, Rusper, Sussex, 1684 W. Suss RO EpI/33/1684/3
White, Joseph, miller/farmer, Stukeley, Little, Hunts, 1769 Hunts RO/Acc58/330
White, Judith, widow, Wigston Magna, Leics, 1640 Leics RO PR/I/41A/54
White, Lidia, widow, Bilsby, Lincs, 1641 Lincs RO Ad/Ac/27/225
White, Margaret, widow, Lympne, Kent, 1624 CKS PRC2/26/51
White, Moses, Salisbury, Wilts, 1674 Wilts RO Miscellaneous Index (name + date)
White, Nicholas,
Glos Bristol RO 1670/45
White, Nicholas, Sittingbourne, Kent, 1598 CKS PRC2/9/377
White, Nicholas, Dover, Kent, 1630 CKS PRC20/9/506
White, Nicodemus, glover, Banbury, Oxon, 1631 Oxon RO MSS Wills Pec 54/3/15

White, Oliver, gentleman, St Stephen by Launceston, Corn, 1645 Cornwall RO AP/W694/2
White, Paul, Lyminge, Kent, 1677 CKS PRC20/12/248
White, Peter, Stapleford, Wilts, 1684 Wilts RO Arch. Sarum(+ name and date)
White, Richard, Watford, Herts, 1583 Herts RO ASA25/1076
White, Richard, nailer, Halesowen, Worcs, 1605 Worcs RO 008.7 BA3585/839/350
White, Richard, Bapchild, Kent, 1612 CKS PRC2/16/180
White, Richard, yeoman, Bourton, Black, Oxon, 1635 Oxon RO MSS Wills 70/4/40
White, Richard, Burmarsh, Kent, 1662 CKS PRC1/8/117
White, Richard, mariner: 'seaman', Seasalter, Kent, 1664 CKS PRC1/10/109
White, Richard, mariner: 'seaman', Seasalter, Kent, 1664 CKS PRC1/10/109a
White, Robarte, Sellindge, Kent, 1591 CKS PRC2/5/458
White, Robert, Chewton Mendip (Greenwood), Som, Somerset RO D/D/Cta/W61
White, Robert, St Peter in Thanet, Kent, 1606 CKS PRC2/13/413
White, Robert, Pluckley, Kent, 1616 CKS PRC2/26/18
White, Robert, waterman, Spalding, Lincs, 1633 Lincs RO Ad/Ac/24/100
White, Robert, Stickford, Lincs, 1641 Lincs RO Ad/Ac/27/297
White, Robert, Deal, Kent, 1670 CKS PRC19/4/99
White, Robert, Winterslow, Wilts, 1676 Wilts RO Arch. Sarum(+ name and date)
White, Robert, farmer, Hayton (Thorpe Field House), Yorks, 1781 Borthwick Chanc C.P. 1781/2
White, Roger, Bethersden, Kent, 1617 CKS PRC2/26/15
White, Simon, mariner, Bristol, Glos, Bristol RO 1761/38
White, Simon, yeoman, Bucklebury, Berks, 1673 Berks RO D/A1/222/66B
White, Stephen, Hothfield, Kent, 1599 CKS PRC2/11/327
White, Stephen, carpenter, Goudhurst, Kent, 1682 CKS PRC2/40/80
White, Thomas, Bilsby (Asserby), Lincs, Lincs RO Ad/Ac/2C/70
White, Thomas, St Peter in Thanet, Kent, 1589 CKS PRC2/4/523
White, Thomas, husbandman, Fyfield, Berks, 1592 Berks RO D/A1/220/138B
White, Thomas, Queenborough, Kent, 1606 CKS PRC2/14/493
White, Thomas, Cowbit, Lincs, 1614 Lincs RO Ad/Ac/13/113
White, Thomas, mariner: 'sailor', Walton, Som, 1618 Somerset RO D/D/Cta/W54
White, Thomas, Hothfield, Kent, 1621 CKS PRC2/26/29
White, Thomas, gentleman, Hayling, South, Hants, 1625 Hants RO 21M65 D8/100
White, Thomas, Sutton St Edmunds, Lincs, 1629 Lincs RO Ad/Ac/22/22
White, Thomas, Banbury, Oxon, 1631 Oxon RO MSS Wills Pec 54/3/16
White, Thomas, Dymchurch, Kent, 1631 CKS PRC2/31/79
White, Thomas, Dover, Kent, 1636 CKS PRC20/11/524
White, Thomas, Faversham, Kent, 1639 CKS PRC1/3/64
White, Thomas, Willingham, Lincs, 1671 Lincs RO Ad/Ac/33/206
White, Thomas, chapman, Canterbury St Mary Northgate, Kent, 1673 CKS PRC2/35/269
White, Thomas, mariner, Dover, Kent, 1674 CKS PRC20/12/151
White, Thomas, Waltham, Bishops, Hants, 1684 Hants RO 21m65 D8/347
White, Thomas, caster, brass, Birmingham, Warks, 1836 LJRO/B/C/5/1836/15
White, William, Lydd, Kent, 1591 CKS PRC21/11/7
White, William, Sutton Valence, Kent, 1594 CKS PRC2/7/7
White, William, Fordington, Dors, 1596 Wilts RO Miscellaneous Index (name + date)
White, William, Lydd, Kent, 1608 CKS PRC20/1/288
White, William, Sandwich St Clement, Kent, 1611 CKS PRC2/13/457
White, William, Titchfield, Hants, 1624 Hants RO 21M65 D8/101
White, William, Selsey, Sussex, 1631 W. Suss RO EpI/33/1631/30
White, William, yeoman, Dymchurch, Kent, 1634 CKS PRC2/32/127
White, William, tailor, High Halden, Kent, 1639 CKS PRC1/3/65
White, William, St Stephen by Launceston, Corn, 1645 Cornwall RO AP/W730/3
White, William, yeoman, Boxford, Berks, 1647 Berks RO D/A1/222/25B
White, William, tailor, Streatley (Southridge), Berks, 1649 Berks RO D/A1/222/34B
White, William, Sittingbourne, Kent, 1666 CKS PRC1/11/169

[White:]
White, William, Deal, Kent, 1674 CKS PRC20/12/107
White, William, Cubbington, Warks, 1727 LJRO/B/C/5/1727/174
White/Ball, Frideswide, widow, Marcham, Berks, Berks RO D/A1/221/145B
White/Poyle, Philip,
Som 1640 Somerset RO D/D/Cta/W25
White, see Crase, Le Blan & Ruth,
Whitebread, John, Washington, Sussex, 1670 W. Suss RO EpI/33/1670/20
Whiteford, Anthony, yeoman, St Columb Major, Corn, 1640 Cornwall RO AP/W558/3
Whitehall, Anne, Ashbourne, Derby, 1681 LJRO/B/C/5/1682/105
Whitehart, Henry, Winchester, Hants, 1601 Hants RO 1600 AD63/2
Whitehead, Arthur, Iwade, Kent, 1625 CKS PRC2/26/119
Whitehead, Henry, Rochdale (Stansfield), Lancs, 1623 Lancs RO (Name of Deceased) D.R.C.H. 1623
Whitehead, Henry, Stanton, Fen, Hunts, 1681 Hunts RO/Acc58/166(114)
Whitehead, John, Warden, Kent, 1696 CKS PRC2/42/123
Whitehead, Randolph, yeoman, Minster in Sheppey, Kent, 1679 CKS PRC2/38/203
Whitehead, Thomas,
Som 1648 Somerset RO D/D/Cta/W2
Whitehead, Thomas, clothier, Birstall (Gomersal), Yorks, 1844 Borthwick Test C.P. 1844/1
Whitehead, William, Ashford, Kent, 1605 CKS PRC2/13/429
Whiteheade, John, Bury, Lancs, 1670 Lancs RO (Name of Deceased) D.R.C.H. 1670
Whitehorn, Thomas, husbandman, Broad Hinton, Wilts, 1639 Wilts RO Arch. Wilts.(+ name and date)
Whitehouse, Sarah, widow, St Botolph without Aldgate, London & Middlesex, 1673 Lambeth Palace Arches G27/2
Whiteing, Francis, Bath St James, Som, 1638 Somerset RO D/D/Cta/W15
Whiteing, George, Ascot under Wychwood, Oxon, 1677 Oxon RO MSS Wills 88/3/3
Whiteing, Mary, Fulbourn, Cambs, 1629 c. CUL V.C. Acc./Box3/74
Whiteing, Samuel, Hogsthorpe, Lincs, 1645 Lincs RO Ad/Ac/28/155
Whiteinge, William, Fishtoft, Lincs, 1619 Lincs RO Ad/Ac/15/77
Whiteside, John, Poulton (Shippoole), Lancs, 1634 Lancs RO (Name of Deceased) D.R.C.H. 1634
Whitesides, John, yeoman, Crowland, Lincs, 1726 Lincs RO Ad/Ac/45/17
Whitesides, Robert, miller, Wrawby, Lincs, 1666 Lincs RO Ad/Ac/32/77
Whiteway, William, Bedwin, Great, Wilts, 1640 Wilts RO Miscellaneous Index (name + date)
Whitewood, Elizabeth, New Romney, Kent, 1695 CKS PRC19/5/41
Whitewood, Thomas, carpenter, Dymchurch, Kent, 1689 CKS PRC2/41/112
Whitewood, William, Frome Selwood, Som, 1664 Somerset RO D/D/Cta/W59
Whitfeild, Andrew, husbandman, Whitstable, Kent, 1679 CKS PRC2/38/204
Whitfeild, Marke, Eastry, Kent, 1594 CKS PRC21/13/18
Whitfeild, Thomas, Halton Holgate, Lincs, 1638 Lincs RO Ad/Ac/25/338
Whitfeild, William, tiler/bricklayer, Stepney (Stebenhythe), London & Middlesex, 1673 Lambeth Palace Arches G27/3
Whitfield, John, husbandman, Appleford, Berks, 1627 Berks RO D/A1/221/105B
Whitfield, Robert, Westwell, Kent, 1610 CKS PRC20/2/108
Whitfield, William, yeoman, Hinksey, South, Berks, 1643 Berks RO D/A1/222/16B
Whithead, John, yeoman, Hollingbourne, Kent, 1622 CKS PRC20/5/212
Whithead, Robert, Chester, Ches, 1627 Cheshire RO (Name) W.C. 1627
Whithead, William, Lenham, Kent, 1680 CKS PRC2/39/120
Whithed, Jeames, Stalisfield, Kent, 1590 CKS PRC2/5/456
Whithorne, William, Winterbourne Stoke, Wilts, 1679 Wilts RO Arch. Sarum(+ name and date)
Whitindale, John, Clerkenwell St James, London & Middlesex, 1712 PRO PROB32/55/17
Whiting, George, Herne, Kent, 1593 CKS PRC21/12/339
Whiting, George, gentleman, Mersham, Kent, 1674 CKS PRC2/36/144
Whiting, John, Shipton under Wychwood, Oxon, 1624 Oxon RO MSS Wills 300/6/3
Whiting, John, Uffington, Berks, 1678 Berks RO D/A1/222/148B

Whiting, John, yeoman, Mersham, Kent, 1680 CKS PRC2/38/209
Whiting, John, Bilsington, Kent, 1714 CKS PRC1/17/65
Whiting, Nicholas, Ardington, Berks, 1608 Berks RO D/A1/221/14B
Whiting, William, Mersham, Kent, 1635 CKS PRC20/11/536
Whiting, William, gentleman, Canterbury, Kent, 1678 CKS PRC2/38/86
Whiting, William, Kislingbury, Northants, 1782 Northants RO X954/21/53
Whitinge, Mathewe, Brabourne, Kent, 1618 CKS PRC2/26/88
Whitinge, William, Reculver, Kent, 1632 CKS PRC20/9/462
Whitington, Christopher, Kidlington, Oxon, 1626 Oxon RO MSS Wills 176/2/8
Whitington, Edward, Goring, Sussex, 1597 W. Suss RO EpI/33/1596/19
Whitley, Arthur, Cranbrook, Kent, 1630 CKS PRC2/30/149
Whitley, Jane, widow, Ferriby, South, Lincs, 1663? Lincs RO Ad/Ac/43/9a
Whitlie, Henry, Minster Lovell, Oxon, 1633 Oxon RO MSS Wills 300/6/8
Whitlock, Joseph, Salisbury, Wilts, 1805 Wilts RO Miscellaneous Index (name + date)
Whitlock, Mary, widow, All Hallows Barking, London & Middlesex, 1697 PRO PROB5/1743
Whitlock, Thomas, Chart, Little, Kent, 1630 CKS PRC2/30/150
Whitlocke, Arthur, victualler, Faversham, Kent, 1662 CKS PRC1/9/68
Whitman, see Bayly,
Whitmill, Henry, innholder, Stoke Lyne, Oxon, 1678 Oxon RO MSS Wills 176/4/3
Whitmore, James, victualler, Coventry, Warks, 1763 LJRO/B/C/5/1763/199
Whitnall, Roger, maltster, St Johns Thanet, Kent, 1672 CKS PRC2/35/191
Whitnees, Agnes, widow, Leake, Lincs, 1611 Lincs RO Ad/Ac/10/41
Whitney, James, NLW BR 1630/66 Ac
Whitny, William, Biddenden, Kent, 1628 CKS PRC2/29/112
Whitsonton, William, Oare, Kent, 1633 CKS PRC2/31/170
Whittakers, Elizabeth, widow, Macclesfield (Long Moss), Ches, 1721 Cheshire RO (Name) W.C. 1721
Whittakers, Thomas, Whitchurch, Shrops, 1675 LJRO:cards/1675/61
Whittall, Abraham, flaxman, Faversham, Kent, 1675 CKS PRC2/36/145
Whittall, William, miller, Clifton Campville, Staffs, 1829 LJRO/B/C/5/1829/42
Whittear, John, Wallop, Over, Hants, 1673 Hants RO 21m65 D8/253
Whittell, Joseph, Sherbourne, Dors, 1628 Wilts RO Miscellaneous Index (name + date)
Whitter, John, mariner: 'sailor', Whitstable, Kent, 1619 CKS PRC2/26/24
Whitting, Joan, Nailsea, Som, 1624 Somerset RO D/D/Cta/W8
Whittingham, Jeames, Queenborough, Kent, 1604 CKS PRC2/14/485
Whittingham, John, Canterbury St Mary-Magdalen Burgate, Kent, 1666 CKS PRC1/11/170
Whittingham, Richard, Littlebourne, Kent, 1631 CKS PRC20/9/476
Whittingham, Robert, Preston upon the Weald Moors, Shrops, 1681 LJRO/B/C/5/1681/48
Whittingham, Robert, merchant, St Margaret Lothbury, London & Middlesex, 1698 PRO PROB5/1605
Whittingstowe, Edward, Doulting, Som, 1597 Somerset RO D/D/Cta/W71
Whittington, John, Ferring, Sussex, 1600 W. Suss RO EpI/33/1600/4
Whittington, John, Preston, Sussex, 1631 W. Suss RO EpI/33/1631/39
Whittington, John, Harting, Sussex, 1670 W. Suss RO EpI/33/1669/6
Whittington, Michael, Deeping St James, Lincs, 1639 Lincs RO Ad/Ac/26/251
Whittington, Thomas, Torksey, Lincs, 1662 Lincs RO Ad/Ac/41/25
Whittington, Thomas, yeoman, Burton by Lincoln, Lincs, 1675 Lincs RO Ad/Ac/35/95
Whittle, Mary, spinster, Stapleford, Lincs, 1613 Lincs RO Ad/Ac/11/50
Whittle, Richard, Stallingborough, Lincs, 1625 Lincs RO Ad/Ac/19B/37
Whittle, Thomas, Stallingborough, Lincs, 1636 Lincs RO Ad/Ac/24/555
Whittlesey, John, Hail Weston/Colne, Hunts, 1676 Hunts RO/Acc58/64(171)
Whittney, John, Drayton, Market, Shrops, 1674 LJRO:cards/1674/52
Whittocke, Nicholas, Pensford, Som, 1612 Somerset RO D/D/Cta/W65
Whitton, Jeremy, Bethersden, Kent, 1640 CKS PRC1/5/63
Whitton, John, Ringwould, Kent, 1612 CKS PRC2/17/223

[Whitton:]
Whitton, Walter, Biddenden, Kent, 1611 CKS PRC2/16/75
Whitwell, Edmund, St Mary Somerset, London & Middlesex, 1682 PRO PROB5/1766
Whitwell, Francis, husbandman, Whaplode, Lincs, 1639 Lincs RO Ad/Ac/25/90
Whitwood, Robert, husbandman, Brook, Kent, 1618 CKS PRC2/26/63
Whitwood, Thomas, Blackmanstone, Kent, 1608 CKS PRC2/15/447
Whooper, Ann, widow, Dymoke, Glos, GRO GDR/B4/2/W30
Whore, Ralphe, Stratton, Wilts, 1600 Wilts RO Dean Sarum (name + date)
Whorrall, Thomas, Westwell, Kent, 1580 CKS PRC21/4/241
Whyte, Adrian, Dover, Kent, 1584 CKS PRC21/8/133
Whyte, Alban, Remenham, Berks, 1608 Berks RO D/A1/221/18B
Whyte, Andrewe, Sellindge, Kent, 1587 CKS PRC2/4/124
Whyte, Christopher, Enborne, Berks, 1583 Berks RO D/A2/C19/f133-4
Whyte, George, Rickmansworth, Herts, 1560 Herts RO ASA25/543
Whyte, Guy, Sandwich St Mary, Kent, 1637 CKS PRC2/33/145
Whyte, Jeffery, Kintbury (Elcot), Berks, 1618 Berks RO D/A1/221/64B
Whyte, Leonard, Goodnestone next Wingham, Kent, 1586 CKS PRC21/8/56
Whyte, Richard, Canterbury, Kent, 1574 CKS PRC21/2/201
Whyte, Richard, St Peter in Thanet, Kent, 1612 CKS PRC2/17/303
Whyte, Richard, Bishopsbourne, Kent, 1621 CKS PRC2/26/91
Whyte, Richard, husbandman, Steventon, Berks, 1626 Berks RO D/A1/221/104B
Whyte, Robert, St Peter in Thanet, Kent, 1613 CKS PRC2/18/7
Whyte, Thomas, Bilsby, Lincs, Lincs RO Ad/Ac/2C/69
Whyte, William, Westwell, Kent, 1582 CKS PRC21/5/208
Whyte, William, Shadoxhurst, Kent, 1586 CKS PRC2/4/335
Whyte, see Assherst,
Whyter, John, Whitstable, Kent, 1592 CKS PRC2/6/334
Whythed, John, Smeeth, Kent, 1585 CKS PRC21/7/236
Whyting, Thomas, Dover, Kent, 1599 CKS PRC21/16/162
Whytinge, Mary, widow, Brabourne, Kent, 1618 CKS PRC2/26/87
Wiat, Thomas, Sidlesham, Sussex, 1640 W. Suss RO EpI/33/1640/22
Wiatt, Agnes, widow, Lydd, Kent, 1622 CKS PRC20/6/226
Wiatt, Thomas, Clapham, Sussex, 1623 W. Suss RO EpI/33/1623/9
Wible, Richard, Stone in Oxney, Kent, 1586 CKS PRC2/4/13
Wiblin, Thomas, Denchworth, Berks, 1610 Berks RO D/A1/221/29B
Wiborne, John, Brookland, Kent, 1594 CKS PRC2/7/373
Wiborne, Robert, Frittenden, Kent, 1612 CKS PRC2/16/147
Wickam, Henry, Warminster, Wilts, 1616 Wilts RO Miscellaneous Index (name + date)
Wicken, John, Holt, Worcs, 1647 Worcs RO 008.7 BA3585/837/bdl 1
Wickenden, John, carpenter, Rainham, Kent, 1694 CKS PRC2/42/98
Wickenden, Thomas, Newchurch, Hants, 1664 Hants RO 21M65 D8/190
Wickenden, Thomas, mr, Sevenoaks, Kent, 1670 Lambeth Palace VH96/6794
Wickens, Elizabeth, Shutlanger, Northants, 1681 Northants RO NWill A/C/82
Wickens, Stephen, Ufton, Berks, Berks RO D/A1/221/11B
Wickens, Thomas ygr, chandler: 'tallow chandler', Reading St Lawrence, Berks, 1624 Berks RO D/A1/221/90B
Wickens, William, Bampton (Cote), Oxon, 1641 Oxon RO MSS Wills 300/6/28
Wicker, John, Birdham, Sussex, 1674 W. Suss RO EpI/33/1674/10
Wickes, Richard, Aldington, Kent, 1683 CKS PRC20/13/388
Wickes, Richard, husbandman, Herne, Kent, 1722 CKS PRC19/6/76
Wickham, John, carpenter, Canterbury St Mildred, Kent, 1682 CKS PRC2/40/83
Wickham, Thomas, Bridge, Kent, 1641 CKS PRC1/5/64
Wickham, William, maltster, Sandwich, Kent, 1620 CKS PRC2/26/57
Wicking, Katherine, mrs/widow, Christchurch, London & Middlesex, 1669 PRO PROB32/4/26
Wickins, Henry, husbandman, Bampton (Cote), Oxon, 1663 Oxon RO MSS Wills 71/3/24
Wickins, William, tailor, Bradfield, Berks, 1671 Berks RO D/A1/222/100B

Wickins, William eld, yeoman, Tilehurst, Berks, 1638 Berks RO D/A1/136/54C
Wicks, William, Welford, Northants, 1674 Northants RO NWill A/C/129
Wickstead, Thomas, Shrewsbury St Chad, Shrops, 1682 LJRO/B/C/5/1681/49
Wicksted, Thomas, ironmonger, Malpas, Ches, Cheshire RO (Name) W.C. 1711
Widcombe, Charles, Chewton Mendip, Som, Somerset RO D/D/Cta/W49
Widdeatt, John, St Nicholas at Wade, Kent, 1641 CKS PRC19/2/45
Widder, Willyam, clergy: 'clerk', Harmston, Lincs, 1641 Lincs RO Ad/Ac/27/257
Widdicombe, John, Stoke St Gregory, Som, 1634 Somerset RO D/D/Cta/W12
Widdowes, Timothy, Madeley, Staffs, 1663 LJRO:cards/1663/61
Widdowes, see Johnson,
Wide, John, High Halstow, Kent, 1665 CKS PRC1/11/95
Widger, George, Ulcombe, Kent, 1602 CKS PRC2/12/385
Widgett, John, Teynham, Kent, 1614 CKS PRC2/18/104
Widgett, John, yeoman, Milton next Sittingbourne, Kent, 1646 CKS PRC1/7/102
Widhouse, John, Halesowen, Shrops, 1681 Worcs RO 008.7 BA3585/830/46
Widmar, William, Remenham, Berks, 1608 Berks RO D/A1/221/15B
Wigg, Thomas, Stratfield Turgiss, Hants, 1624 Hants RO 21M65 D8/102
Wiggen, John, Barkwith, East, Lincs, 1576 Lincs RO Ad/Ac/1/21
Wiggens, John, Rolvenden, Kent, 1634 CKS PRC2/32/177
Wiggens, William, bricklayer, Canterbury St Mary Northgate, Kent, 1663 CKS PRC1/9/69
Wiggin, Richard, husbandman, Milton, Great (Little Milton), Oxon, 1631 Oxon RO MSS Wills Pec 54/3/8
Wiggin, Samuel, innholder, Cheadle, Staffs, 1803 LJRO/B/C/5/1803/99
Wiggin, Simon, Chalgrove, Oxon, 1627 Oxon RO MSS Wills 176/2/33
Wiggins, Frances, widow, Kennington, Berks, 1674 Berks RO D/A1/222/102B
Wiggins, Nicholas, Watlington, Oxon, 1633 Oxon RO MSS Wills 300/6/7
Wiggins, William, innholder, St Albans, Herts, 1626 Herts RO ASA25/2930
Wigginton, Roger, Newington (Berrick Prior), Oxon, 1632 Bucks R.O. MSS Wills Pec 80/6/18
Wiggon, John, Mareham le Fen, Lincs, 1606? Lincs RO Ad/Ac/7/149
Wight, Thomas, grocer, Birmingham, Warks, 1788 LJRO/B/C/5/1788/172
Wight, William, Halesowen, Worcs, 1685 Worcs RO 008.7 BA3585/837/bdl 4
Wightman, George, Friskney, Lincs, 1611 Lincs RO Ad/Ac/10/2
Wightman, Henry, Maidstone, Kent, 1579 CKS PRC21/4/12
Wightwick, Robert, clothier, Biddenden, Kent, 1675 CKS PRC2/36/261
Wightwicke, Edward, gentleman, Kingsnorth, Kent, 1629 CKS PRC2/29/110
Wigmore, Edward, Reculver, Kent, 1630 CKS PRC20/9/494
Wigmore, Edward, husbandman, Woolhampton, Berks, 1687 Berks RO D/A1/223/45E
Wigmore, Laurence, Ewell, Kent, 1633 CKS PRC2/32/132
Wikes, William, yeoman, Elstree, Herts, 1583 Herts RO ASA25/1077
Wilbore, Robert, Woolsthorpe, Lincs, 1607 Lincs RO Ad/Ac/8a/27
Wilbour/Wildbore, John, husbandman, St Nicholas at Wade, Kent, 1723 CKS PRC19/6/77
Wilcock, Joseph, Thornhill (Mingley), Yorks, Borthwick Test C.P. 1738/15
Wilcock, Luce, widow, Maidstone, Kent, 1626 CKS PRC20/7/225
Wilcock, Tobie, tanner, Bourne, Lincs, C17th? Lincs RO Ad/Ac/45/110
Wilcocke, Edward, Biddenden, Kent, 1615 CKS PRC2/26/79
Wilcocke, Joane, widow, New Romney, Kent, 1615 CKS PRC20/3/206
Wilcocke, Thomas, Bekesbourne, Kent, 1633 CKS PRC2/32/130
Wilcocks, Thomas, Wroughton, Wilts, 1628 Wilts RO Arch. Wilts.(+ name and date)
Wilcox, John, Clawson, Long, Leics, 1640 Leics RO PR/I/41A/39
Wilcox, see Andrewes,
Wild, Edward, yeoman, Ash next Sandwich, Kent, 1673 CKS PRC20/12/65
Wild, James, university: 'Fellow of Corpus Christi College, Oxford/M.A.' Oxford (Corpus Christi College), Oxon, 1667 Bodleian HYP B9/114-115
Wild, John, St Peter in Thanet, Kent, 1674 CKS PRC2/36/137
Wild, Richard, St Peter in Thanet, Kent, 1692 CKS PRC2/42/55

[Wild:]
Wild, Stephen, Eyam, Derby, 1684 LJRO/B/C/5/1684/85
Wild, Thomas, Scotter, Lincs, 1662 Lincs RO Ad/Ac/41/1
Wildbore, see Wilbour,
Wilde, Barnard, Rochdale, Lancs, 1613 Lancs RO (Name of Deceased) D.R.C.H. 1612-13
Wilde, Henry, yeoman, St Peter in Thanet, Kent, 1662 CKS PRC1/9/71
Wilde, John, St Peter in Thanet, Kent, 1597 CKS PRC2/9/217
Wilde, John, St Peter in Thanet, Kent, 1606 CKS PRC2/13/419
Wilde, John, Baston, Lincs, 1639 Lincs RO Ad/Ac/26/19
Wilde, Richard, St Peter in Thanet, Kent, 1598 CKS PRC2/10/244
Wilde, Richard, yeoman, Baston, Lincs, 1670 Lincs RO Ad/Ac/32/157
Wilde, Richard, Chetwynd, Shrops, 1675 LJRO:cards/1675/62
Wilde, Robert, St Johns Thanet, Kent, 1606 CKS PRC2/13/421
Wilde, Robert, St Johns Thanet, Kent, 1623 CKS PRC2/26/16
Wilde, Roger, Chisledon, Wilts, 1622 Wilts RO Arch. Wilts.(+ name and date)
Wilde, William, Sandwich St Clement, Kent, 1678 CKS PRC2/38/89
Wildebore, Richard, Tonge, Kent, 1662 CKS PRC1/9/70
Wilder, Frances, widow, Burghfield, Berks, 1682 Berks RO D/A1/223/12C
Wilder, Henry, yeoman, Goring (Gatehampton), Oxon, 1663 Oxon RO MSS Wills 88/2/4
Wilder, John, yeoman, Shinfield, Berks, 1638 Berks RO D/A1/221/160B
Wilder, John, yeoman, Tilehurst, Berks, 1684 Berks RO D/A1/223/27C
Wilder, Nicholas, weaver: 'broad weaver', Reading, Berks, 1642 Berks RO D/A1/222/7B
Wilder, Richard, husbandman, Stoke, South, Oxon, 1675 Oxon RO MSS Wills 300/6/41
Wildes, Richard, mariner, Faversham, Kent, 1689 CKS PRC2/41/138
Wildgoos, Roger, Chalgrove, Oxon, 1640 Oxon RO MSS Wills 300/6/24
Wilding, Thomas, blacksmith, Woodchurch, Kent, 1685 CKS PRC20/13/541
Wildinge, Agnes, widow, Longton, Lancs, 1664 Lancs RO (Name of Deceased) D.R.C.H. 1664-5
Wilds, Benjamin, Sandwich, Kent, 1678 CKS PRC2/38/84
Wilds, Stephen, Dover, Kent, 1629 CKS PRC20/8/512
Wilds, Thomas, Deal, Kent, 1691 CKS PRC19/5/6
Wildsmith, Jonathan, Silkstone (Barnsley), Yorks, 1720 Borthwick Test C.P. 1721/4
Wiles, Edward, fisherman, Deal, Kent, 1640 CKS PRC19/1/91
Wiles, Nicholas, Chart, Little, Kent, 1620 CKS PRC2/26/12
Wiles, Thomas, St Peter in Thanet, Kent, 1615 CKS PRC2/26/77
Wiles, William, Dover, Kent, 1640 CKS PRC19/1/92
Wiley, Thomas, Sutton in the Marsh, Lincs, 1632 Lincs RO Ad/Ac/23/60
Wilford, Francis, university: 'Master of Corpus Christi College, Cambridge/Archdeacon of Bedford/D.D.' Cambridge (Corpus Christi College), Cambs, 1668 CUL V.C. Acc./Box3/57
Wilford, Joan, Broadwater, Sussex, 1634 W. Suss RO Epl/33/1634/2
Wilford, John, Milton next Sittingbourne, Kent, 1615 CKS PRC2/26/80
Wilford, John, Maidstone, Kent, 1629 CKS PRC20/8/460
Wilgoose, John, husbandman, Wytham, Berks, 1650 Berks RO D/A1/222/22B
Wilie, Henry, clergy: 'clerk', Glentham, Lincs, 1677 Lincs RO Ad/Ac/42/75
Wilie, Richard ygr, Cranbrook, Kent, 1634 CKS PRC20/11/560
Wilkenson, William, Canterbury St Martin, Kent, 1617 CKS PRC20/4/407
Wilkes, Alice, Bengeworth, Worcs, 1605 Worcs RO 008.7 BA3585/839/418
Wilkes, George, Reculver, Kent, 1664 CKS PRC19/3/67
Wilkes, John, Bray, Berks, 1613 Berks RO D/A1/221/33B
Wilkes, John, husbandman, Rowde, Wilts, 1617? Wilts RO Arch. Wilts.(+ name and date)
Wilkes, John, husbandman, Norton, Chipping, Oxon, 1669 Oxon RO MSS Wills 88/2/28
Wilkes, Richard, Chislet, Kent, 1612 CKS PRC2/18/127
Wilkes, Robert, Wokingham, Berks, 1678 Wilts RO Dean Sarum (name + date)
Wilkes, Roger, Bedminster, Som, 1639 Somerset RO D/D/Cta/C13a
Wilkes, William, Hoath, Kent, 1624 CKS PRC20/6/218
Wilkins, weaver, Wimborne Minster, Dors, 1655 Dorset RO PE/WM CP 2/4/101
Wilkins, Johannah, widow, St Katherine by the Tower, London & Middlesex, 1698? PRO

PROB5/1006
Wilkins, John, Dover, Kent, 1677 CKS PRC20/12/249
Wilkins, John, blacksmith, St Johns Thanet, Kent, 1679 CKS PRC2/38/207
Wilkins, Joseph, yeoman, Brightwell, Berks, 1680 Berks RO D/A1/223/3C
Wilkins, Mary eld, widow, Brightwell, Berks, 1633 Berks RO D/A1/135/86F
Wilkins, Richard, St Peter in Thanet, Kent, 1668 CKS PRC1/13/146
Wilkins, Stephen, Ashton, Steeple, Wilts, 1704 Wilts RO Arch. Sarum(+ name and date)
Wilkins, William, Nonington, Kent, 1614 CKS PRC20/2/494
Wilkinson, Alice, widow, Eastchurch, Sheppey, Kent, 1673 CKS PRC2/35/265
Wilkinson, Arthur, yeoman, Baston, Lincs, 1666 Lincs RO Ad/Ac/32/107
Wilkinson, Christopher, Snitterby, Lincs, 1624 Lincs RO Ad/Ac/39/158
Wilkinson, Eliza, spinster, Leeds, Yorks, 1845 Borthwick Test C.P. 1845/1
Wilkinson, Francis, Elkington, South, Lincs, 1620 Lincs RO Ad/Ac/16/100
Wilkinson, Francis, Withcall, Lincs, 1648 Lincs RO Ad/Ac/30/325
Wilkinson, George, Deeping, Market, Lincs, 1599 Lincs RO Ad/Ac/5/215
Wilkinson, Gilbert, butcher, St Albans, Herts, 1597 Herts RO ASA25/1654
Wilkinson, John, Benington, Lincs, 1612 Lincs RO Ad/Ac/11/122
Wilkinson, John, Borden, Kent, 1613 CKS PRC2/18/132
Wilkinson, John, Heckington, Lincs, 1640 Lincs RO Ad/Ac/26/275
Wilkinson, John, gentleman, Linsted, Kent, 1641 CKS PRC1/5/65
Wilkinson, John, Withcall, Lincs, 1662 Lincs RO Ad/Ac/32/19
Wilkinson, John, clergy: 'clerk', Thorne Coffin, Som, 1664 Somerset RO D/D/Cta/W58
Wilkinson, John, St Martin Vintry, London & Middlesex, 1725 Greater London RO DL/C/547/100
Wilkinson, John, St Marylebone, London & Middlesex, 1754 Lambeth Palace VH82/128
Wilkinson, Mathew, Stenigot, Lincs, 1641 Lincs RO Ad/Ac/27/212
Wilkinson, Mathew, husbandman, Tothill, Lincs, 1680 Lincs RO Ad/Ac/43/118
Wilkinson, Mathew, bachelor, Springthorpe, Lincs, 1683 Lincs RO Ad/Ac/44/36
Wilkinson, Peeter, Harrietsham, Kent, 1603 CKS PRC2/14/501
Wilkinson, Richard, Upton (Kexby), Lincs, 1624 Lincs RO Ad/Ac/8c/89
Wilkinson, Robert, Wigtoft, Lincs, 1620 Lincs RO Ad/Ac/16/105
Wilkinson, Robert, Scotton, Lincs, 1623 Lincs RO Ad/Ac/8c/94
Wilkinson, Robert, clothworker, Ewell, Kent, 1623 CKS PRC2/26/47
Wilkinson, Robert, Stow, Lincs, 1663 Lincs RO Ad/Ac/42/60
Wilkinson, Robert, clergy: 'rector/D.D.', Eastchurch, Sheppey, Kent, 1668 CKS PRC1/13/147
Wilkinson, Robert, chapman, Lincoln St Peter at Arches, Lincs, 1680 Lincs RO Ad/Ac/43/88
Wilkinson, Thomas, Springthorpe, Lincs, 1634 Lincs RO Ad/Ac/40/23
Wilkinson, Thomas, Tattershall, Lincs, 1636 Lincs RO Ad/Ac/24/567
Wilkinson, Thomas, husbandman, Ratcliffe on the Wreak, Leics, 1670 Leics RO Administrators Accounts 1667-72 f40
Wilkinson, Thomas, Baginton, Warks, 1685 LJRO/B/C/5/1685/109
Wilkinson, William, Barrow upon Trent, Derby, 1685 LJRO/B/C/5/1685/110
Wilkinson, William, yeoman, Silkstone (High Royd), Yorks, 1772 Borthwick Test C.P. 1772/7
Wilkinson, William, Holbeach, Lincs, 1802 Lincs RO Ad/Ac/45/69
Wilks, William, Wroughton, Wilts, 1636 Wilts RO Arch. Wilts.(+ name and date)
Wilkyns, Richard, Maidstone, Kent, 1621 CKS PRC20/5/194
Willamont, Joseph, baker, Norwich, Norf, 1734 Norfolk RO ANW/23/21/42
Willand, William, Rolvenden, Kent, 1592 CKS PRC2/6/444
Willard, David, bachelor, Tenterden, Kent, 1649 CKS PRC1/8/84
Willard, Ellinor, widow, Maidstone, Kent, 1694 CKS PRC19/5/31
Willard, John, Maidstone, Kent, 1570 CKS PRC21/1/79
Willard, John, Hawkhurst, Kent, 1630 CKS PRC2/30/153
Willard, John, Maidstone, Kent, 1681 CKS PRC20/13/210
Willard, John, blacksmith, Newington next Sittingbourne, Kent, 1684 CKS PRC2/40/261
Willard, Jonathan, Tenterden, Kent, 1639 CKS PRC1/3/66

[Willard:]
Willard, Lawrence, yeoman, Biddenden, Kent, 1669 CKS PRC1/13/148
Willard, Maryon, Maidstone, Kent, 1615 CKS PRC20/3/208
Willard, Nicholas, Maidstone, Kent, 1614 CKS PRC20/3/3
Willard, Philemon, yeoman, Minster in Sheppey, Kent, 1625 CKS PRC2/25/159
Willard, Richard, Maidstone, Kent, 1604 CKS PRC21/16/19
Willard, Stephen, blacksmith, Minster in Sheppey, Kent, 1637 CKS PRC1/1/63
Willard, Thomas, Benenden, Kent, 1612 CKS PRC2/16/200
Willard, Thomas, Hernhill, Kent, 1613 CKS PRC20/2/498
Willard, Thomas, Lenham, Kent, 1622 CKS PRC2/26/39
Willard, Thomas, Woodchurch, Kent, 1638 CKS PRC20/11/544
Willard, William, Rolvenden, Kent, 1592 CKS PRC2/5/209
Willard, William, Boxley, Kent, 1617 CKS PRC2/26/35
Willard, William, husbandman, Goudhurst, Kent, 1664 CKS PRC1/10/110
Willard, see Baseden & Clover,
Willarde, Nicholas, Wittersham, Kent, 1588 CKS PRC21/9/8
Willas, William, Irnham, Lincs, 1637 Lincs RO Ad/Ac/25/487
Willcocke, Edward, Faversham, Kent, 1613 CKS PRC2/16/33
Willcox, Christopher, Brent, East, Som, 1598 Somerset RO D/D/Cta/W21
Willcox, Thomas, plumber, Stafford, Staffs, 1728 LJRO/B/C/5/1728/282
Willcox, William, Chewton Mendip, Som, 1598 Somerset RO D/D/Cta/W69
Willes, Alice, Bredgar, Kent, 1616 CKS PRC2/26/17
Willes, Edward, Saltwood, Kent, 1661 CKS PRC19/3/4
Willes, Joane, widow, Appledore, Kent, 1590 CKS PRC2/5/472
Willes, John, Cransley, Northants, 1673 Northants RO NWill A/C/154
Willes, Thomas, Sutton Valence, Kent, 1663 CKS PRC1/9/72
Willes, Thomas, Throwleigh, Kent, 1663 CKS PRC1/9/73
Willesby, Richard, clergy: 'clerk', Benington, Lincs, 1620 Lincs RO Ad/Ac/15/290
Willet, Mathew, Appledore, Kent, 1640 CKS PRC1/5/66
Willet, Timothy, victualler, Northchurch, Herts, Herts RO AHH23/2536
Willett, Thomas, Chiltington, West, Sussex, 1643 W. Suss RO EpI/33/1643/1
Willett, Thomas, farmer, Brandon, Suff, 1773 Suff RO(B) IC500/3/51/172
Willetts, Andrew, Hagley, Worcs, 1682 Worcs RO 008.7 BA3585/837/bdl 3
Willfy, Thomas, Tenterden, Kent, 1684 CKS PRC2/40/253
Willia, Robert, Kewstoke, Som, 1639 Somerset RO D/D/Cta/W18
William, William John, Llangasty-Tal-y-llyn, Breck, 1634 NLW BR 1634/72 Ac
Williams, Albert, mercer, Longcot, Berks, 1690 Berks RO D/A1/223/67C
Williams, Daniel, jurat/gentleman, Sandwich, Kent, 1641 CKS PRC1/6/39
Williams, Daniel, mariner, Dover, Kent, 1683 CKS PRC20/13/384
Williams, Edward, clergy: 'clerk', Scopwick, Lincs, 1638 Lincs RO Ad/Ac/25/145
Williams, Edward, milliner, Witney, Oxon, 1666 Oxon RO MSS Wills 88/2/15
Williams, Elizabeth, widow, Bristol, Glos, 1697 PRO PROB5/927
Williams, Elizabeth, widow, Worcester St Clement, Worcs, 1761 Worcs RO 008.7 BA3585/835/bdl 1
Williams, Gressam, gentleman, Sandwich, Kent, 1616 CKS PRC2/26/64
Williams, Henry, clergy: 'clerk', Dalderby, Lincs, 1649 Lincs RO Ad/Ac/30/243
Williams, Henry, clothworker, Wantage, Berks, 1651 Berks RO D/A1/222/40B
Williams, Henry, Lyminster, Sussex, 1677 W. Suss RO EpI/33/1676/10
Williams, Henrye, Smarden, Kent, 1597 CKS PRC2/12/464
Williams, James, Taunton St Mary Magdalan, Som, 1594 Somerset RO D/D/Cta/W20
Williams, John, Maidstone, Kent, 1584 CKS PRC21/7/64
Williams, John, Canterbury St Mary Northgate, Kent, 1596 CKS PRC2/8/23
Williams, John, Canterbury St Paul, Kent, 1597 CKS PRC2/9/375
Williams, John, Canterbury, Kent, 1601 CKS PRC2/11/397
Williams, John, Coker, East, Som, 1612 Somerset RO D/D/Cta/W66
Williams, John, Landulph, Corn, 1616 Cornwall RO AP/W229/2

[Williams:]
Williams, John, husbandman, Windsor, New (Dedworth), Berks, 1626 Berks RO D/A1/221/99B
Williams, John, Preston Gubbals, Shrops, 1675 LJRO:cards/1675/63
Williams, John, Canterbury St Paul, Kent, 1679 CKS PRC2/38/208
Williams, John, Worcester St Andrew, Worcs, 1684 Worcs RO 008.7 BA3585/837/bdl 4
Williams, John, butcher, Kingstone, Staffs, 1835 LJRO/B/C/5/1837/26c-f
Williams, John eld, clothier, Hothfield, Kent, 1677 CKS PRC2/37/106
Williams, Joseph, Norton, Kings, Worcs, 1682 Worcs RO 008.7 BA3585/837/bdl 3
Williams, Margaret, widow, Longstock, Hants, 1596 Hants RO 1595 B68/3
Williams, Martin, St Martin in Meneage, Corn, 1623 Cornwall RO AP/W312/2
Williams, Morgan, Almondsbury, Glos, Bristol RO 1680/68
Williams, Nicholas, Canterbury St Dunstan Without, Kent, 1598 CKS PRC2/11/19
Williams, Nicholas, butcher, Canterbury St Andrew, Kent, 1681 CKS PRC2/39/255
Williams, Paul, woodmonger, Hurley, Berks, 1631 Berks RO D/A1/221/120B
Williams, Ralph, Salisbury, Wilts, 1669 Wilts RO Miscellaneous Index (name + date)
Williams, Richard, Hanley Castle, Worcs, Worcs RO 008.7 BA3585/839/331
Williams, Richard, St Stephens by Saltash, Corn, 1624 Cornwall RO AP/W404/2
Williams, Richard, Milton next Sittingbourne, Kent, 1628 CKS PRC2/29/113
Williams, Richard, Chester, Ches, 1684 Cheshire RO (Name) W.C. 1683
Williams, Rowland, Ash next Sandwich, Kent, 1594 CKS PRC21/13/28
Williams, Simon, Maidstone, Kent, 1616 CKS PRC20/3/478
Williams, Thomas, Wendron, Corn, 1612 Cornwall RO AP/W186/2
Williams, Thomas, Thanington, Kent, 1613 CKS PRC2/17/221
Williams, Thomas, yeoman, Probus/Cornelly, Corn, 1615 Cornwall RO AP/W232/2
Williams, Thomas, Henley, Oxon, 1635 Oxon RO MSS Wills 300/6/12
Williams, Thomas, Middleton Cheney, Northants, 1682 Northants RO NWill A/C/56
Williams, Thomas, Laverstock, Wilts, 1688 Wilts RO Arch. Sarum(+ name and date)
Williams, Vincent, gentleman/widower, St Martin in the Fields, London & Middlesex, 1687 PRO PROB32/26/40
Williams, William, Kingston Seymour, Som, 1588 Somerset RO D/D/Cta/W75
Williams, William, Canterbury All Saints, Kent, 1604 CKS PRC2/13/425
Williams, William, Bushey, Herts, 1623 Herts RO ASA25/4837
Williams, William, Faversham, Kent, 1625 CKS PRC2/25/152
Williams, William, Sandwich, Kent, 1638 CKS PRC2/34/150
Williams, William, Shadwell, St Paul, London & Middlesex, 1691 PRO PROB32/30/47
Williams, William, gentleman, Shadwell, St Paul, London & Middlesex, 1691 PRO PROB32/30/128
Williams, William, merchant, Bristol, Glos, 1692 PRO PROB5/928
Williams/Sevier, Nicholas, Knoyle, East, Wilts, 1625 Wilts RO Miscellaneous Index (name + date)
Williams, see Clarke & Hughes,
Williamson, Anthonie, tailor, Holbeach, Lincs, 1631 Lincs RO Ad/Ac/23/119
Williamson, Charles, Harpswell, Lincs, 1639 Lincs RO Ad/Ac/40/287
Williamson, Edward, Addlethorpe, Lincs, 1673 Lincs RO Ad/Ac/34/114
Williamson, Elizabeth, Winteringham, Lincs, 1628 Lincs RO Ad/Ac/39/59
Williamson, Francis, Newton, Lincs, 1664 Lincs RO Ad/Ac/43/16
Williamson, Francise, gentleman, Kirmington, Lincs, 1627 Lincs RO Ad/Ac/20/8
Williamson, John, clergy: 'clerk', Sparsholt, Berks, 1634 Berks RO D/A1/221/133B
Williamson, John, Appleby, Lincs, 1636 Lincs RO Ad/Ac/40/87
Williamson, John, Althorpe, Lincs, 1673 Lincs RO Ad/Ac/35/54
Williamson, John, chandler, Hull Sculcoates, All Saints, Yorks, 1771 Borthwick Test C.P. 1778/11
Williamson, Jonathan, Childwall, Lancs, 1699 Lancs RO (Name of Deceased) D.R.C.H. 1698
Williamson, Judith, widow, Somercoates, North, Lincs, 1636 Lincs RO Ad/Ac/24/466
Williamson, Mary, Winteringham, Lincs, 1622 Lincs RO Ad/Ac/8c/9
Williamson, Peter + Anne, Chichester, Sussex, 1620 W. Suss RO EpIII/9/1/21

[Williamson:]
Williamson, Richard, farmer/widower, Burnby, Yorks, 1825 Borthwick Test C.P. 1825/8
Williamson, Richarde, Crowland, Lincs, 1611 Lincs RO Ad/Ac/10/104
Williamson, Robert, Scampton, Lincs, 1680 Lincs RO Ad/Ac/43/144
Williamson, Thomas, yeoman, Winteringham, Lincs, 1625 Lincs RO Ad/Ac/39/182
Williamson, Timothy, St Andrew Holborn, London & Middlesex, 1706 Lambeth Palace Arches G56/2
Williamson, William, gentleman, Neston (Parkgate), Ches, 1782 Cheshire RO (Name) W.C. 1779-82
Williamson, see Meakyn,
Williat, John, Horwood, Little, Bucks, 1615 Herts RO ASA25/4824
Willie, James, Saltfleetby St Peter, Lincs, 1625 Lincs RO Ad/Ac/19A/96
Willies, Edward, Birmingham, Warks, 1676 LJRO:cards/1676/51
Willims, John, yeoman, Bampton (Cote), Oxon, 1680 Oxon RO MSS Wills 88/3/6
Willimson, Nicholas, Pinchbeck, Lincs, 1614 Lincs RO Ad/Ac/13/195
Willingale, Robert, Easebourne, Sussex, 1624 W. Suss RO EpI/33/1624/3
Willingham, Christopher, Bottesford, Lincs, 1620 Lincs RO Ad/Ac/8b/365
Willingham, Thomas, Keelby, Lincs, 1632 Lincs RO Ad/Ac/23/50
Willis, Annis, Bretforton, Worcs, 1603 Worcs RO 008.7 BA3585/838/257
Willis, Augustine, Canterbury Holy Cross Westgate, Kent, 1608 CKS PRC2/15/444
Willis, Edward, Clevedon, Som, 1640 Somerset RO D/D/Cta/W30
Willis, Joan, widow, Heytesbury, Wilts, 1609 Wilts RO Dean Sarum (name + date)
Willis, Joane, widow, Kintbury, Berks, 1625? Wilts RO CC Sarum(+ name and date)
Willis, Joane, Calne, Wilts, 1631 Wilts RO Miscellaneous Index (name + date)
Willis, John, Staplehurst, Kent, 1622 CKS PRC2/26/36
Willis, John, tailor, Downton, Wilts, 1641 Wilts RO Arch. Sarum(+ name and date)
Willis, John, mariner: 'captain', Stepney, London & Middlesex, 1684 PRO PROB32/23/166
Willis, Nicholas, Norton Bavant, Wilts, 1679 Wilts RO Miscellaneous Index (name + date)
Willis, Thomas, Clutton, Som, 1599 Somerset RO D/D/Cta/W68
Willis, Thomas, Kintbury (Clapton), Berks, 1615 Berks RO D/A1/221/52B
Willis, Thomas, Abbots Langley, Herts, 1694 Herts RO ASA25/4991
Willis, William, jurat, Dover, Kent, 1610 CKS PRC20/2/128
Willis, William, yeoman, Warwick, Warks, 1682 Worcs RO 008.7 BA3585/837/bdl 3
Willmot, John, yeoman, Chieveley, Berks, 1675 Berks RO D/A1/222/126B
Willmot, Peter, yeoman, Thame, Oxon, 1626 Oxon RO MSS Wills Pec 54/2/36
Willmot, Thomas ygr, Hothfield, Kent, 1614 CKS PRC2/18/76
Willmott, John, Nailsea, Som, 1590 Somerset RO D/D/Cta/W76
Willmott, John, Hollingbourne, Kent, 1600 CKS PRC21/15/192
Willmott, John, gentleman, Kidderminster (Lower Mitton), Worcs, 1684 Worcs RO 008.7 BA3585/837/bdl 5
Willmott, Richard, gentleman, Stadhampton, Oxon, 1676 Oxon RO MSS Wills Pec 72/2/5
Willmott, William, fuller, Oxford St Michael, Oxon, 1627 Oxon RO MSS Wills 70/2/33
Willmott, William, yeoman, Cholsey, Berks, 1641 Berks RO D/A1/136/94D
Willmott, William, yeoman, Cholsey (Lollingdon), Berks, 1646 Berks RO D/A1/136/94E
Willomett, William, Sandwich, Kent, 1599 CKS PRC2/11/85
Willoughby, Henry, gentleman, Knoyle, West, Wilts, 1639 Wilts RO Arch. Sarum(+ name and date)
Willoughby, John, Ingoldsby, Lincs, 1602 Lincs RO Ad/Ac/5/360
Willoughby, Peter, Kirton, Lincs, 1625 Lincs RO Ad/Ac/19B/112
Willoughby, Thomas, Stamford, Lincs, 1614 Lincs RO Ad/Ac/13/193
Willoughby, William, Evedon, Lincs, 1638 Lincs RO Ad/Ac/25/204
Willoughbye, Richard, merchant, Dover, Kent, 1613 CKS PRC20/2/500
Willoughton, Thomas, Belton, Lincs, 1601 Lincs RO Ad/Ac/5/429
Willoway, Margarett, Crondall, Hants, 1624 Hants RO 21M65 D8/103
Willowby, Edward, St Christopher le Stock, London & Middlesex, 1683 PRO PROB5/1442
Willowes, Beniamin, Ospringe, Kent, 1633 CKS PRC2/32/131

Willowes, John, Trusthorpe, Lincs, 1637 Lincs RO Ad/Ac/25/625
Willowes, Thomas, Lympne, Kent, 1619 CKS PRC2/26/59
Wills, Agnes, Haydon, Dors, 1639 Wilts RO Miscellaneous Index (name + date)
Wills, Elizabeth, Ladbroke, Warks, 1684 LJRO/B/C/5/1684/86
Wills, Isacck, Warehorne, Kent, 1620 CKS PRC2/26/104
Wills, James, Tenterden, Kent, 1637 CKS PRC1/1/64
Wills, John, Smarden, Kent, 1592 CKS PRC2/6/320
Wills, John, St Keverne, Corn, 1604 Cornwall RO AP/W59/1
Wills, John, Harvington, Worcs, 1684 Worcs RO 008.7 BA3585/837/bdl 4
Wills, Richard, Wickhambreaux, Kent, 1641 CKS PRC1/6/40
Wills, Richard, cordwainer, Appledore, Kent, 1669 CKS PRC1/14/121
Wills, Stephen, Warehorne, Kent, 1608 CKS PRC2/14/473
Wills, Thomas, Charing, Kent, 1639 CKS PRC20/11/546
Wills, Thomas, Tilmanstone, Kent, 1645 CKS PRC1/7/70
Wills, Thomas, yeoman, Chewton Mendip, Som, 1741 Somerset RO D/D/Cta/W44
Wills, William, Bugbrooke, Northants, 1782 Northants RO X954/21/56
Willsheare, William, Frittenden, Kent, 1623 CKS PRC2/26/44
Willson, Adam, draper, Worcester St Martin, Worcs, Worcs RO 008.7 BA3585/834/462
Willson, Anthony, Corby, Lincs, 1635 Lincs RO Ad/Ac/24/313
Willson, Chatherine, widow, Gainsborough, Lincs, 1632 Lincs RO Ad/Ac/39/303
Willson, Edward, Thanington, Kent, 1618 CKS PRC2/26/90
Willson, Elizabeth, widow, Whitchurch, Som, 1634 Somerset RO D/D/Cta/W16
Willson, George, Pinchbeck, Lincs, 1627 Lincs RO Ad/Ac/20b/51
Willson, John, Watford, Herts, 1639 Herts RO ASA25/4969
Willson, John, Aisthorpe (Thorpe in the Fallows), Lincs, 1645 Lincs RO Ad/Ac/28/92
Willson, John, St Andrew Holborn, London & Middlesex, 1666 PRO PROB32/1/13
Willson, Leonard, Rolvenden, Kent, 1629 CKS PRC2/30/142
Willson, Thomas, Egginton, Derby, 1683 LJRO/B/C/5/1682/107
Willson, William, Immingham, Lincs, 1641 Lincs RO Ad/Ac/27/315
Willson, William, husbandman, Bradley, Staffs, 1682 LJRO/B/C/5/1681/50
Willson, William, Eyam, Derby, 1684 LJRO/B/C/5/1683/24
Willyamson, Francis, Winthorpe, Lincs, 1639 Lincs RO Ad/Ac/26/2
Willyford, William, Upchurch, Kent, 1601 CKS PRC2/11/401
Willyns, Frances, Sittingbourne, Kent, 1608 CKS PRC2/14/475
Wilmer, William, gentleman, Reading, Berks, 1684 Berks RO D/A1/223/30C
Wilmore, John, Feckenham, Worcs, 1818 Worcs RO 008.7 BA3585/835/bdl 2
Wilmot, Arabella, widow, Hartlebury, Worcs, 1811 Worcs RO 008.7 BA3585/835/bdl 2
Wilmot, see Chambers,
Wilmott, Frances, widow, Wallingford (Rush Court), Berks, 1688 Berks RO D/A1/223/63F
Wilmott, Nathaniel, clergy: 'clerk', Canterbury St Mary Bredin, Kent, 1678 CKS PRC2/38/87
Wilner, John, Borden, Kent, 1640 CKS PRC1/5/67
Wilse, Anne, widow, Dymoke, Glos, 1685 GRO GDR/B4/2/W189
Wilse, Frances, spinster, Dymoke, Glos, 1685 GRO GDR/B4/2/W190
Wilse, Susanna, Dymoke, Glos, 1685 GRO GDR/B4/2/W191
Wilsheere, William, Sutton Poyntz, Dors, 1631 Wilts RO Miscellaneous Index (name + date)
Wilsheire, Thomas, yeoman, Rolvenden, Kent, 1647 CKS PRC1/8/31
Wilshere, Alexander, Hilperton, Wilts, 1615 Wilts RO Miscellaneous Index (name + date)
Wilshere, Robert, maltster, Bradford on Avon, Wilts, 1769? Wilts RO Miscellaneous Index (name + date)
Wilshiere, William, Wellow, Som, 1702 Somerset RO D/D/Cta/W45
Wilson, Alexander, Norton, Kent, 1626 CKS PRC2/27/182
Wilson, Alice, widow, Appleby, Lincs, 1683 Lincs RO Ad/Ac/44/38
Wilson, Alse, Ulceby, Lincs, 1614 Lincs RO Ad/Ac/13/86
Wilson, Ambrose, Queenborough, Kent, 1636 CKS PRC2/33/144
Wilson, Ann, spinster, Aldborough, Yorks, 1811 Borthwick Test C.P. 1811/15

[Wilson:]
Wilson, Anne, Bringhurst, Leics, 1666 Leics RO Administrators Accounts C17th f81
Wilson, Bartholomew, Willoughby (Sloothby), Lincs, 1644 Lincs RO Ad/Ac/28/91
Wilson, Christopher, clergy: 'clerk', Westborough, Lincs, 1611 Lincs RO Ad/Ac/10/18
Wilson, Edmund, Maidstone, Kent, 1620 CKS PRC20/5/208
Wilson, Edward, Tunstall, Kent, 1640 CKS PRC1/5/68
Wilson, Gabrill, Wyberton, Lincs, 1646 Lincs RO Ad/Ac/28/189
Wilson, George, Postling, Kent, 1598 CKS PRC2/9/381
Wilson, George, Worcester St Helen, Worcs, 1682 Worcs RO 008.7 BA3585/837/bdl 3
Wilson, Hamond, Nocton, Lincs, 1635 Lincs RO Ad/Ac/24/312
Wilson, Helen, Diseworth, Leics, 1641 Leics RO PR/I/41A/69
Wilson, Henry, Burmarsh, Kent, 1620 CKS PRC2/26/58
Wilson, James, Wigtoft, Lincs, 1637 Lincs RO Ad/Ac/25/508
Wilson, Joane, Thanington, Kent, 1634 CKS PRC2/32/129
Wilson, John, gentleman, Navenby, Lincs, Lincs RO Ad/Ac/2C/97
Wilson, John, Goudhurst, Kent, 1600 CKS PRC2/11/331
Wilson, John, Dover St Mary, Kent, 1614 CKS PRC20/2/496
Wilson, John, yeoman, Riby, Lincs, 1622 Lincs RO Ad/Ac/17/28
Wilson, John, Waddingham, Lincs, 1632 Lincs RO Ad/Ac/39/280
Wilson, John, Burmarsh, Kent, 1634 CKS PRC2/34/304
Wilson, John, Sutton St Edmunds, Lincs, 1650 Lincs RO Ad/Ac/29/64
Wilson, John, Louth, Lincs, 1672 Lincs RO Ad/Ac/42/106
Wilson, John, Berkswell, Warks, 1683 LJRO/B/C/5/1682/106
Wilson, John, Deal, Kent, 1692 CKS PRC19/5/13
Wilson, John, Edingale, Staffs, 1729 LJRO/B/C/5/1729/167
Wilson, John, clergy: 'clerk', Almondbury, Yorks, 1775 Borthwick Test C.P. 1775/1
Wilson, Joseph, Snarford, Lincs, 1674 Lincs RO Ad/Ac/35/86
Wilson, Katherine, widow, Canwick, Lincs, 1673 Lincs RO Ad/Ac/35/14
Wilson, Nathaniel, clergy: 'rector', Kingsnorth, Kent, 1678 CKS PRC2/38/81
Wilson, Nicholas, esquire, Benniworth, Lincs, 1605 Lincs RO Ad/Ac/6/107
Wilson, Peter, gentleman, Grantham, Lincs, 1620 Lincs RO Ad/Ac/16/108
Wilson, Richard, Kirkby on Bain, Lincs, 1611 Lincs RO Ad/Ac/10/15
Wilson, Roger, Minster in Sheppey, Kent, 1615 CKS PRC2/26/78
Wilson, Samuel ygr, Elmham, North, Norf, 1739 Norfolk RO ANW/23/23/18
Wilson, Sara, Canterbury, Kent, 1639 CKS PRC1/3/67
Wilson, Suzan, widow, Linsted, Kent, 1643 CKS PRC1/7/18
Wilson, Thomas, yeoman, Minster in Sheppey, Kent, 1609 CKS PRC2/13/436
Wilson, Thomas, Stixwold, Lincs, 1636 Lincs RO Ad/Ac/24/560
Wilson, Thomas, esquire, Ripple, Kent, 1673 CKS PRC2/35/192
Wilson, Thomas, Sandwich, Kent, 1689 CKS PRC2/41/166
Wilson, Thomas ygr, shipwright/carpenters mate/bachelor, Upchurch, Kent, 1663 CKS PRC1/9/160
Wilson, Walter, Kirkby on Bain (Tumby), Lincs, 1629 Lincs RO Ad/Ac/22/90
Wilson, William, Rasen, Market, Lincs, 1580 Lincs RO Ad/Ac/2b/51
Wilson, William, Donington, Lincs, 1638 Lincs RO Ad/Ac/25/161
Wilson, William, Mere, Wilts, 1638 Wilts RO Miscellaneous Index (name + date)
Wilson, William, chapman, Boston, Lincs, 1666 Lincs RO Ad/Ac/32/97
Wilson, William, Budbrooke, Warks, 1685 Worcs RO 008.7 BA3585/837/bdl 4
Wilson, William, blacksmith, Fylingdales, Yorks, 1784 Borthwick Test C.P. 1784/6
Wilson, William, apothecary/bachelor, Slaidburn, Yorks, 1836 Borthwick Test C.P. 1836/5
Wilsonn, Ambrose, Hartlip, Kent, 1637 CKS PRC2/34/140
Wilsonne, Arthure, Lincoln, Lincs, 1577 Lincs RO Ad/Ac/1/22
Wilstrapp, Robert, husbandman, Stainton le Vale, Lincs, 1625 Lincs RO Ad/Ac/19A/23
Wilton, John, Gidding, Steeple, Hunts, 1681 Hunts RO/Acc58/154(11)
Wilton, Matthew, Whitstable, Kent, 1628 CKS PRC2/28/130
Wilton, William, Warminster, Wilts, 1619 Wilts RO Miscellaneous Index (name + date)

Wilton, William, stocking maker, Bruton, Som, 1736 Somerset RO D/D/Cta/W46
Wiltone, Johne, Ulceby, Lincs, 1593 Lincs RO Ad/Ac/3/13
Wiltshire, Ellinor, widow, Lacock, Wilts, 1620? Wilts RO Arch. Wilts.(+ name and date)
Wiltshire, Richard, Warboys, Hunts, 1684 Hunts RO/Acc58/208(205)
Wiltshire, Robert, Stone in Oxney, Kent, 1679 CKS PRC2/38/206
Wilverden, Anthonye, High Halden, Kent, 1615 CKS PRC2/26/94
Wilverden, Robert, Bobbing, Kent, 1613 CKS PRC2/18/56
Wilx, Jone, widow, Minety, Wilts, 1621 Wilts RO Arch. Wilts.(+ name and date)
Wimarke, Nicholas, Woodnesborough, Kent, 1598 CKS PRC2/10/161
Wimarke, William, Goodnestone next Wingham, Kent, 1588 CKS PRC21/9/205
Wimberley, William, Witham, South, Lincs, 1648 Lincs RO Ad/Ac/30/320
Wimble, John, Rainham, Kent, 1691 CKS PRC2/42/22
Wimbleton, Nicholas, Newton, South, Wilts, 1614 Wilts RO Arch. Sarum(+ name and date)
Wimbleton, Thomas, glazier, Dover, Kent, 1643 CKS PRC19/2/81
Wimpew, Sarah, Norton, Midsomer, Som, 1695 Somerset RO D/D/Cta/W47
Wimpray, James, Brox-Holme, Lincs, 1662 Lincs RO Ad/Ac/41/56
Wimprey, William, Brox-Holme, Lincs, 1666 Lincs RO Ad/Ac/32/61
Wimprey, William, Brox-Holme, Lincs, 1666 Lincs RO Ad/Ac/41/173
Wimsherst, John, yeoman, Woodchurch, Kent, 1674 CKS PRC20/12/153
Wimsherst, Michaell, lieutenant, Dover, Kent, 1601 CKS PRC21/15/119
Wimshurst, Alexander, Woodchurch, Kent, 1606 CKS PRC20/1/165
Wimshurst, John, Woodchurch, Kent, 1694 CKS PRC19/5/32
Winborne, John, smith, Bapchild, Kent, 1684 CKS PRC2/40/262
Winboult, Ralph, blacksmith, Purley, Berks, 1605 Berks RO D/A1/221/2B
Winbrooke, John, Egerton, Kent, 1607 CKS PRC20/1/292
Winch, John, labourer, Sandwich, Kent, 1676 CKS PRC2/37/107
Winch, Richard, gentleman, Bray, Berks, 1678 Berks RO D/A1/222/149B
Winch, Robert eld, yeoman, Bray, Berks, 1648 Berks RO D/A1/135/120C
Winch, Thomas, husbandman, Bray (Hill), Berks, 1675 Berks RO D/A1/222/138D
Winchcombe, John eld, esquire, Thatcham (Henwick), Berks, 1613 Berks RO D/A1/134/79D
Winche, Sebastian, Sonning, Berks, 1597 Wilts RO Miscellaneous Index (name + date)
Winchester, Richard, Cranbrook, Kent, 1629 CKS PRC2/29/114
Winchurst, William, gentleman, St Giles without Cripplegate, London & Middlesex, 1715 Greater London RO DL/C/546/84
Winckfeelde, John, Rickmansworth, Herts, 1595 Herts RO ASA25/1528
Winckfeild, George ygr, Rickmansworth, Herts, 1612 Herts RO ASA25/4803
Winckfeild, John, husbandman, Windsor, New, Berks, 1682 Berks RO D/A1/223/15B
Winckle, George, Gosberton, Lincs, 1611 Lincs RO Ad/Ac/10/37
Winckles, John, Ashby, Castle (Chadstone), Northants, 1673 Northants RO NWill A/C/35
Winday, Thomas, St Nicholas at Wade, Kent, 1625 CKS PRC20/6/206
Winde, Richard, Killingholme, Lincs, 1642 Lincs RO Ad/Ac/28/7
Winder, John, Epworth, Lincs, 1664 Lincs RO Ad/Ac/41/128
Winder, Richard, Kingsnorth, Kent, 1681 CKS PRC2/39/253
Winder, Richard, husbandman, Rolvenden, Kent, 1687 CKS PRC2/41/
Windesor, Thomas, Biddenden, Kent, 1618 CKS PRC2/26/32
Windever, Humphrey, clothworker, Newbury, Berks, 1633 Berks RO D/A1/221/128B
Windey, Edward, Benenden, Kent, 1685 CKS PRC2/41/24
Windmills, John, Claverdon, Warks, 1684 Worcs RO 008.7 BA3585/837/bdl 5
Window, John, Haresfield, Glos, 1694 GRO GDR/B4/2/W45
Wine, Alice, widow, Lanivet, Corn, 1613 Cornwall RO AP/W207
Wines, Henry, pewterer, Chichester, Sussex, 1621 W. Suss RO EpIII/9/1/18
Winfeild, Paule, Langton, Church, Leics, 1639 Leics RO PR/I/41A/11
Winforth, Thomas, Laughton, Lincs, 1624 Lincs RO Ad/Ac/39/150
Winfrey, John, Fleet, Lincs, 1638 Lincs RO Ad/Ac/25/75
Wing, Edward, Broughton, Brant, Lincs, 1633 Lincs RO Ad/Ac/24/533

[Wing:]
Wing, Richard, Denton, Lincs, 1649 Lincs RO Ad/Ac/30/91
Wing, see Jessett,
Wingate, John, innholder, Canterbury, Kent, 1700 CKS PRC19/5/77
Wingate, John, innholder, Canterbury St Mary-Magdalen Burgate, Kent, 1702 CKS PRC19/6/
Wingate, John, innholder, Canterbury St Mary-Magdalen Burgate, Kent, 1702 CKS PRC19/6/6
Winge, John, Stoke Rochford (North Stoke), Lincs, 1635 Lincs RO Ad/Ac/24/361
Winge, John, Faversham, Kent, 1641 CKS PRC1/6/41
Winge, Thomas, cordwainer: 'shoemaker', Banbury, Oxon, 1628 Oxon RO MSS Wills Pec 54/2/45
Wingfeild, Henry + Elinor, esquire/widow, Potter Hanworth, Lincs, 1626 Lincs RO Ad/Ac/19B/101
Wingfielde, John, esquire, Potter Hanworth, Lincs, 1619 Lincs RO Ad/Ac/15/211
Wingham/Tems, Ann, Funtington, Sussex, 1661 W. Suss RO EpI/33/1661/16
Winkle, James, saddler, Wellington, Shrops, 1786 LJRO/B/C/5/1786/96a
Winkworth, John, chandler, Marlborough, Wilts, 1627? Wilts RO CC Sarum(+ name and date)
Winlowe, Richard, clergy: 'clerk/parson', Chinnor, Oxon, 1629 Oxon RO MSS Wills 176/2/40
Winn, John, Aylesby, Lincs, 1668 Lincs RO Ad/Ac/33/40
Winnington, John, yeoman, Barningham (Eastwood), Yorks, 1717 Borthwick Test C.P. 1717/13
Winshopp, Robert, Fotherby, Lincs, 1637 Lincs RO Ad/Ac/25/459
Winsor, Jeames, Rolvenden, Kent, 1618 CKS PRC2/26/11
Winsor, Roger, Fordington, Dors, 1681 Wilts RO Miscellaneous Index (name + date)
Winstone, Richard, innholder, Kingston Bagpuize, Berks, 1681 Berks RO D/A1/223/1D
Winter, Grantham, Lincs, 1648 Lincs RO Ad/Ac/30/402
Winter, Christopher, Kingston, Kent, 1599 CKS PRC2/10/492
Winter, Francis, Langley, Kirk, Derby, 1680 LJRO:cards/1680/40
Winter, Henrie, Ewell, Kent, 1635 CKS PRC2/33/142
Winter, James, Cheriton, Hants, 1624 Hants RO 21M65 D8/104
Winter, John, Whitstable, Kent, 1605 CKS PRC2/14/487
Winter, John, Chipping Barnet, Herts, 1610 Herts RO ASA25/4787
Winter, John, Witham on the Hill (Manthorpe), Lincs, 1612 Lincs RO Ad/Ac/11/102
Winter, John, Ropley, Hants, 1624 Hants RO 21M65 D8/105
Winter, John, Preston next Faversham, Kent, 1626 CKS PRC2/27/177
Winter, John, Buckland nr Dover, Kent, 1639 CKS PRC20/11/508
Winter, John, Preston (Sutton Poyntz), Dors, 1641 Wilts RO Miscellaneous Index (name + date)
Winter, John, Milton next Sittingbourne, Kent, 1716 CKS PRC19/6/68
Winter, Michael, Ewell, Kent, 1631 CKS PRC2/31/75
Winter, Richard, Donington, Lincs, 1611 Lincs RO Ad/Ac/10/117
Winter, Richard, yeoman, Ash next Sandwich, Kent, 1677 CKS PRC20/12/246
Winter, Richard, brewer: 'common brewer', York St Martin cum Gregory Micklegate, Yorks, 1784 Borthwick Test C.P. 1783/5
Winter, Sarah, Hollingbourne, Kent, 1626 CKS PRC20/7/229
Winter, Thomas, labourer, Milton, Great (Little Milton), Oxon, Oxon RO MSS Wills Pec 55/2/21
Winter, Thomas, labourer, Garston, East, Berks, 1621 Berks RO D/A1/221/76B
Winter, Thomas, Boston, Lincs, 1629 Lincs RO Ad/Ac/22/16
Winter, William, Chipping Barnet, Herts, 1630 Herts RO ASA25/4871
Winterborne, Joanne, widow, Langdon, East, Kent, 1620 CKS PRC2/26/21
Winterborne, Nicholas, husbandman, Buckland, Berks, 1665 Berks RO D/A1/222/76B
Winterborne, Richard, Wantage, Berks, 1679 Wilts RO Dean Sarum (name + date)
Winterbourne, Thomas, Buckland, Berks, 1598 Berks RO D/A1/220/183B
Winterhay, John, Glastonbury St John, Som, Somerset RO D/D/Cta/W48
Winteringham, William, Burstwick, Yorks, 1723 Borthwick Test C.P. 1723/19
Winterton, Deborah, widow, Grantham, Lincs, 1692 PRO PROB5/1336
Winterton, John, Coventry, Warks, 1683 LJRO/B/C/5/1682/108
Winterton, Thomas, Knaptoft, Leics, 1640 Leics RO PR/I/41A/43
Winterton, William, brazier, Coventry, Warks, 1774 LJRO/B/C/5/1774/75

Wintworth, John, Devizes, Wilts, 1671 Wilts RO CC Sarum(+ name and date)
Winwood, Thomas, Leigh, Worcs, 1763 Worcs RO 008.7 BA3585/835/bdl 1
Wirge, see Franklin,
Wirrall, Richard, Marden, Kent, 1676 CKS PRC2/37/102
Wisdom, John, Graffham, Sussex, 1597 W. Suss RO EpI/33/1597/10
Wisdome, Robert, weaver, Bremhill, Wilts, 1614 Wilts RO Arch. Wilts.(+ name and date)
Wisdome, William, Graffham, Sussex, 1633 W. Suss RO EpI/33/1633/21
Wise, Alexander, Shrivenham, Berks, 1617 Berks RO D/A1/221/62B
Wise, Edward, Stone next Faversham, Kent, 1618 CKS PRC2/26/7
Wise, Edward, Ospringe, Kent, 1631 CKS PRC2/30/152
Wise, Edward, painter/limner, Oxford All Saints, Oxon, 1692 Oxon RO MSS Wills 176/5/33
Wise, Henry, Sydenham, Oxon, 1622 Oxon RO MSS Wills Pec 54/2/26
Wise, James, Boxley, Kent, 1636 CKS PRC2/33/140
Wise, John, Throwleigh, Kent, 1610 CKS PRC1/1/16
Wise, John, Throwleigh, Kent, 1610 CKS PRC2/13/453
Wise, John, Acrise, Kent, 1611 CKS PRC2/17/424
Wise, John, husbandman, Dorchester, Oxon, 1668 Oxon RO MSS Wills Pec 72/1/42
Wise, John, Rochester, Kent, 1731 PRO PROB5/1228
Wise, Nathaniel, gentleman, Newington (Berrick Prior), Oxon, 1684 Bucks R.O. MSS Wills Pec 80/6/27
Wise, Thomas, Canterbury St Mary Bredin, Kent, 1637 CKS PRC2/34/158
Wise, Thomas, yeoman, Charing, Kent, 1680 CKS PRC20/13/75
Wise, Thomas, Throwleigh, Kent, 1707 CKS PRC1/16/72
Wise, William, Sandwich St Clement, Kent, 1628 CKS PRC2/28/135
Wise, William, innholder, Stokenchurch, Oxon, 1666 Oxon RO MSS Wills 88/2/17
Wise, Willyam, Sandwich, Kent, 1627 CKS PRC2/28/134
Wisedome, Thomas, husbandman, Stanton Harcourt (Sutton), Oxon, 1676 Oxon RO MSS Wills 300/6/47
Wiseman, Edward, knight, St James Westminster, London & Middlesex, PRO PROB32/48/138
Wiseman, John, grocer, Hythe St Leonard, Kent, 1623 CKS PRC20/6/242
Wiseman, Robert, Sutton St James, Lincs, 1641 Lincs RO Ad/Ac/27/229
Wiseman, Sarah, spinster, St James Westminster, London & Middlesex, 1705 PRO PROB32/48/172
Wissenden, Joane, Frittenden, Kent, 1606 CKS PRC2/13/446
Wissenden, Stephen, Canterbury, Kent, 1600 CKS PRC2/10/256
Wissenden, Thomas, Tonge, Kent, 1692 CKS PRC2/42/57
Wist, Richard eld, yeoman, Harwell, Berks, 1640 Berks RO D/A1/221/165B
Wistow, Margaret, widow, Saxilby, Lincs, 1650 Lincs RO Ad/Ac/40/238
Wistowe, Margaret, widow, Saxilby, Lincs, 1650 Lincs RO Ad/Ac/40/209
Wiswall, James, Wavertree, Lancs, 1606 Lancs RO (Name of Deceased) D.R.C.H. 1606
Witcher, William, Racton, Sussex, 1635 W. Suss RO EpI/33/1635/35
Witchingham, Susan, Norwich, Norf, 1708 Norfolk RO ANW/23/7/97
Withenbrocke, John, Headcorn, Kent, 1597 CKS PRC2/12/465
Wither, John, Wickham, Hants, 1624 Hants RO 21M65 D8/106
Wither, Nicholas, Somborne, Kings, Hants, 1677 Hants RO 21m65 D8/279
Witherden, Hester, widow, St Laurence Thanet, Kent, 1684 CKS PRC2/40/255
Witherden, Jane, widow, Sittingbourne, Kent, 1705 CKS PRC1/16/73
Witherden, Joan, widow, Bethersden, Kent, 1596 CKS PRC2/8/193
Witheredge, Robert,
Som 1601 Somerset RO D/D/Cta/W19
Witherley, Abraham, Sholden, Kent, 1624 CKS PRC2/26/50
Witherling, Thomas, Sheldwich, Kent, 1604 CKS PRC2/13/461
Withers, Anthony, Nonington, Kent, 1614 CKS PRC20/3/9
Withers, Margaret, widow, Kingsclere, Hants, 1601 Hants RO 1601 AD48/4
Withers, see Hooker,

[Witherwicke:]
Witherwicke, John, gentleman, Snelland, Lincs, 1640 Lincs RO Ad/Ac/27/122
Witherwicke, Thomas, yeoman, Manby, Lincs, 1614 Lincs RO Ad/Ac/13/163
Withey, Sarah, St Andrew Holborn (Leather Lane), London & Middlesex, 1803 Greater London RO DL/C/242/1
Withey, Susannah, widow, St Andrew Holborn (Leather Lane), London & Middlesex, 1803 Greater London RO DL/C/565/243/2
Withie, Richard, Stoke, South (Easton), Lincs, 1597 Lincs RO Ad/Ac/4/7
Withinbrooke, Christopher, Staplehurst, Kent, 1623 CKS PRC2/26/49
Withinshaw, Mary, spinster, Maer, Staffs, 1773 LJRO/B/C/5/1773/81
Withnoe, John, tailor, Farcet, Hunts, 1705 Hunts RO/Acc58/297
Withrick, Richard, Bapchild, Kent, 1617 CKS PRC2/26/42
Witt, Phillip, Broad Chalke, Wilts, 1700 Wilts RO Arch. Sarum(+ name and date)
Witt, Robert, webster, Scothorne, Lincs, 1669 Lincs RO Ad/Ac/33/154
Witt, William, Marcham, Berks, 1607 Berks RO D/A1/221/10B
Witter, Hugh, Frodsham (Manley), Ches, 1618 Cheshire RO (Name) W.C. 1618
Wittie, William, cook/privileged person, Cambridge Holy Sepulchre, Cambs, 1653 c. CUL V.C. Acc./Box3/58
Witton, Anne, widow, Bardney, Lincs, 1618 Lincs RO Ad/Ac/14/44
Witton, Robert, Horncastle, Lincs, 1626 Lincs RO Ad/Ac/19B/51
Wittone, Arthure, Bolingbroke, Lincs, 1599 Lincs RO Ad/Ac/5/221
Witts, Richard, Aldbourne, Wilts, 1750 c. Wilts RO Miscellaneous Index (name + date)
Wivill, John, Snave, Kent, 1623 CKS PRC2/26/45
Wod, William, Witley, Great, Worcs, 1602 Worcs RO 008.7 BA3585/838/252
Woddall, Congresbury, Som, 1597 Somerset RO D/D/Cta/W70
Wolfall, Richard, Derby, West, Lancs, 1576 Lancs RO (Name of Deceased) D.R.C.H. 1576
Wolfall, Richard, yeoman, Halsall (Melling), Lancs, 1625 Lancs RO (Name of Deceased) D.R.C.H. 1624-5
Wolfe, Anne, widow, Camberwell, Surrey, 1732 Lambeth Palace Arches G103/5
Wolfe, John, university: 'scholar's servant', Cambridge St Botolph, Cambs, 1627 CUL V.C. Acc./Box2/85
Wolfe, Lawrens, Smarden, Kent, 1588 CKS PRC2/4/311
Wolfe, Philip, university: 'scholar's servant/privileged person', Cambridge St Mary the Great, Cambs, 1640 c. CUL V.C. Acc./Box2/86
Wolfe, Thomas, Warehorne, Kent, 1592 CKS PRC2/6/344
Wolford, see Woollforde,
Wolgar/Hauvill, William, Appledram, Sussex, 1600 W. Suss RO EpI/33/1600/7
Wolgar/Hauvill, William, Appledram, Sussex, 1600 W. Suss RO EpI/33/1600/8
Wolgate, Mary, mrs, Borden, Kent, 1627 CKS PRC2/27/181
Wolland, Thomas, Sheldwich, Kent, 1625 CKS PRC2/25/158
Wollard, William, Kyme, South, Lincs, 1618 Lincs RO Ad/Ac/14/16
Wollaston, John, Tamworth, Warks, 1683 Worcs RO 008.7 BA3585/837/bdl 5
Wollen, Edward, Brothertoft, Lincs, 1606 Lincs RO Ad/Ac/7/147
Wollen, William, Branston, Lincs, 1601 Lincs RO Ad/Ac/5/441
Wollet, Elizabeth, Swarby, Lincs, 1627 Lincs RO Ad/Ac/20b/63
Wollet, Thomas, Headcorn, Kent, 1629 CKS PRC2/30/147
Wollett, John, Bethersden, Kent, 1632 CKS PRC2/31/176
Wollett, Michaell, Minster in Sheppey, Kent, 1600 CKS PRC2/11/399
Wollin, Edward, Brothertoft, Lincs, 1620 Lincs RO Ad/Ac/16/107
Wolline, John, Morton, Lincs, 1640 Lincs RO Ad/Ac/27/61
Wollons, Robert, Wickenby, Lincs, 1611 Lincs RO Ad/Ac/10/6
Wollridge, James, gentleman, Sherfield Upon Loddon, Hants, 1607 Hants RO 1605 AD82/9
Wolrich, Mary, Boughton under Blean, Kent, 1675 CKS PRC20/12/152
Wolton, George,
Kent 1593 CKS PRC2/6/304
Wolton, John, Thanington, Kent, 1664 CKS PRC1/9/161

Wolton, Joseph, Smarden, Kent, 1594 CKS PRC2/7/73
Wolvall, William,
Sussex W. Suss RO EpI/33/1572
Wolvins, John, Warningcamp, Sussex, 1618 W. Suss RO EpI/33/1617/25
Womack, Arthur, Mautby, Norf, Norfolk RO ANW/23/21/69
Wood, Anne, Leeds, Kent, 1596 CKS PRC2/8/187
Wood, Anne, Haxey (Graizelound), Lincs, 1662 Lincs RO Ad/Ac/41/57
Wood, Anne, Croxden, Staffs, 1676 LJRO:cards/1676/52
Wood, Anne, widow, Faversham, Kent, 1682 CKS PRC2/40/85
Wood, Anne, widow, St Johns Thanet, Kent, 1685 CKS PRC2/41/22
Wood, Avis, wife, Chartham, Kent, 1633 CKS PRC2/32/135
Wood, Beniamin, Hollingbourne, Kent, 1620 CKS PRC20/4/455
Wood, Benjamin, Hollingbourne, Kent, 1681 CKS PRC20/13/216
Wood, Betteris, widow, Charing, Kent, 1613 CKS PRC20/2/302
Wood, Catherine, Ulcombe, Kent, 1632 CKS PRC2/31/76
Wood, Christopher, Hythe St Leonard, Kent, 1626 CKS PRC20/7/114
Wood, Christopher, Boughton Monchelsea, Kent, 1641 CKS PRC1/5/70
Wood, Dorothy, widow, Canterbury St Alphege, Kent, 1693 CKS PRC19/5/24
Wood, Edward, Hothfield, Kent, 1587 CKS PRC2/4/299
Wood, Edward, Deal, Kent, 1668 CKS PRC19/4/38
Wood, Edward, Woodchurch, Kent, 1720 CKS PRC19/6/78
Wood, Elizabeth, Willoughby, Silk, Lincs, 1634 Lincs RO Ad/Ac/24/231
Wood, Elizabeth, widow, Murston, Kent, 1718 CKS PRC1/18/33
Wood, Ellen, widow, Faversham, Kent, 1619 CKS PRC2/26/31
Wood, Emmery, Worlaby, Lincs, 1612 Lincs RO Ad/Ac/11/116
Wood, George, tailor, Sutterton, Lincs, 1637 Lincs RO Ad/Ac/24/552
Wood, George, Glossop (Mellor), Derby, 1678 LJRO:cards/1678/25
Wood, George, Edlaston, Derby, 1688 LJRO/B/C/5/1688/40
Wood, Godfrey, labourer, Willoughton, Lincs, 1680 Lincs RO Ad/Ac/43/160
Wood, Grace, mrs, Boughton under Blean, Kent, 1620 CKS PRC20/5/202
Wood, Hellen, Faversham, Kent, 1612 CKS PRC2/16/31
Wood, Henry, surgeon, Deal, Kent, 1669 CKS PRC19/4/63
Wood, Henry, Ruckinge, Kent, 1698 CKS PRC2/42/146
Wood, Hester, Messingham, Lincs, 1685 Lincs RO Ad/Ac/44/139
Wood, James, Elmsted, Kent, 1627 CKS PRC20/8/482
Wood, James, Canterbury St Mildred, Kent, 1674 CKS PRC2/36/143
Wood, James, miller: 'scribbling miller', Dewsbury, Yorks, 1823 Borthwick Test C.P. 1823/3
Wood, Jane, widow, Bilsington, Kent, 1611 CKS PRC2/17/176
Wood, Jervace, Kenardington, Kent, 1611 CKS PRC2/17/416
Wood, Joane, widow, Hollingbourne, Kent, 1627 CKS PRC20/7/116
Wood, John, Chislet, Kent, 1588 CKS PRC2/4/483
Wood, John, Kennington, Kent, 1588 CKS PRC2/4/283
Wood, John, Chiltington, Sussex, 1594 W. Suss RO EpI/33/1594/4
Wood, John, Midhurst, Sussex, 1594 W. Suss RO EpI/33/1594/2
Wood, John, Hartlip, Kent, 1601 CKS PRC2/12/397
Wood, John, Halesowen, Worcs, 1604 Worcs RO 008.7 BA3585/839/336
Wood, John, Birtsmorton, Worcs, 1607 Worcs RO 008.7 BA3585/839/441
Wood, John, Wormshill, Kent, 1613 CKS PRC2/18/115
Wood, John, Lympne, Kent, 1618 CKS PRC2/26/62
Wood, John, draper, Wrawby cum Brigg (Glanford Brigg), Lincs, 1631 Lincs RO Ad/Ac/22/129
Wood, John, Wormshill, Kent, 1636 CKS PRC2/34/147
Wood, John, Ivychurch, Kent, 1637 CKS PRC19/1/11
Wood, John, husbandman, Stockbury, Kent, 1641 CKS PRC1/6/42
Wood, John, Ospringe, Kent, 1644 CKS PRC1/7/19
Wood, John, labourer, Faversham, Kent, 1681 CKS PRC2/39/250

[Wood:]
Wood, John, widower, St Lawrence Jewry, London & Middlesex, 1688 PRO PROB5/1775
Wood, John, widower, St Lawrence Jewry, London & Middlesex, 1688 PRO PROB5/1776
Wood, John, mr, Wormshill, Kent, 1689 CKS PRC2/41/139
Wood, John, Goodnestone next Wingham, Kent, 1691 CKS PRC19/5/7
Wood, John, St James Westminster (George Court, Cross Street), London & Middlesex, 1794 Greater London RO DL/C/562/209
Wood, John, gentleman, Cave, North, Yorks, 1806 Borthwick Test C.P. 1806/1
Wood, John, farmer, Glossop, Derby, 1840 LJRO/B/C/5/1840/13
Wood, John, innkeeper, Bradford, Yorks, 1841 Borthwick Test C.P. 1841/6
Wood, John eld, jurat, Faversham, Kent, 1638 CKS PRC2/34/303
Wood, Joseph, stationer, Wakefield, Yorks, 1810 Borthwick Test C.P. 1810/12
Wood, Joseph, farmer, Huddersfield (New House), Yorks, 1821 Borthwick Test C.P. 1821/8
Wood, Joshua, dealer/chapman, Kirkburton (Cumberworth Half), Yorks, 1786 Borthwick Test C.P. 1786/7
Wood, Margery, Eastchurch, Sheppey, Kent, 1639 CKS PRC2/34/309
Wood, Martine, St Mary in the Marsh, Kent, 1593 CKS PRC2/7/323
Wood, Mary, widow, Brenzett, Kent, 1684 CKS PRC2/40/257
Wood, Mathew, Chislet, Kent, 1599 CKS PRC2/10/315
Wood, Matthew, Deal, Kent, 1666 CKS PRC19/3/89
Wood, Mercye, Chart nr Sutton Valence, Kent, 1586 CKS PRC2/4/65
Wood, Michael, Sarre, Kent, 1700 CKS PRC19/5/78
Wood, Overington, Rainham, Kent, 1674 CKS PRC2/36/142
Wood, Patience, widow, Rainham, Kent, 1675 CKS PRC2/36/259
Wood, Richard, Middleton (Birtle), Lancs, 1592 Lancs RO (Name of Deceased) D.R.C.H. 1592
Wood, Richard, Hartlip, Kent, 1598 CKS PRC2/10/258
Wood, Richard, blacksmith, Warehorne, Kent, 1668 CKS PRC1/13/150
Wood, Richard, Minster in Sheppey, Kent, 1671 CKS PRC1/15/79
Wood, Richard, Leek (Leekfrith), Staffs, 1676 LJRO:cards/1676/53
Wood, Richard, cordwainer, Cranbrook, Kent, 1680 CKS PRC2/39/123
Wood, Richard, Leek, Staffs, 1682 LJRO/B/C/5/1682/182
Wood, Richard, yeoman, Dymchurch, Kent, 1682 CKS PRC2/40/81
Wood, Robert, Fairfield, Kent, 1613 CKS PRC20/2/304
Wood, Robert, Louth, Lincs, 1626 Lincs RO Ad/Ac/39/43
Wood, Robert, Hawkhurst, Kent, 1632 CKS PRC2/31/172
Wood, Robert, Hemswell, Lincs, 1639 Lincs RO Ad/Ac/40/247
Wood, Robert, baker, Cranbrook, Kent, 1666 CKS PRC1/11/171
Wood, Robert, Boughton Aluph, Kent, 1680 CKS PRC2/39/119
Wood, Robert, Adisham, Kent, 1684 CKS PRC20/13/472
Wood, Robert, husbandman, Ercall, High, Shrops, 1742 LJRO/B/C/5/1742/147
Wood, Roger, Gainsborough (Walkerith), Lincs, 1668 Lincs RO Ad/Ac/33/80
Wood, Rychard, Folkestone, Kent, 1581 CKS PRC2/1/311
Wood, Samuel, innholder, Ashford, Kent, 1680 CKS PRC2/39/124
Wood, Samuel, Allesley, Warks, 1691 LJRO/B/C/5/1691/106
Wood, Stephen, yeoman, St Nicholas at Wade, Kent, 1675 CKS PRC20/12/190
Wood, Susan, Ebony, Kent, 1618 CKS PRC2/26/89
Wood, Thomas, Milton next Sittingbourne, Kent, 1610 CKS PRC20/2/57
Wood, Thomas, yeoman, St Laurence Thanet, Kent, 1626 CKS PRC2/27/178
Wood, Thomas, Folkestone, Kent, 1627 CKS PRC2/28/136
Wood, Thomas, Minster in Sheppey, Kent, 1631 CKS PRC20/9/488
Wood, Thomas, clothworker, Thatcham, Berks, 1631 Berks RO D/A1/221/119B
Wood, Thomas, Minster in Sheppey, Kent, 1632 CKS PRC2/31/174
Wood, Thomas, Hawkhurst, Kent, 1640 CKS PRC19/1/93
Wood, Thomas, university: 'scholar's servant', Cambridge All Saints, Cambs, 1640 CUL V.C. Acc./Box2/88
Wood, Thomas, Chewton Mendip, Som, 1662 Somerset RO D/D/Cta/W56

Wood, Thomas, Croxden, Staffs, 1667 LJRO:cards/1667/90
Wood, Thomas, Lower Hardres, Kent, 1672 CKS PRC2/35/187
Wood, Thomas, Hollingbourne, Kent, 1673 CKS PRC20/12/64
Wood, Thomas, Benington, Herts, 1675 Herts RO AHH23/2537
Wood, Thomas, Hemswell, Lincs, 1675 Lincs RO Ad/Ac/35/100
Wood, Thomas, Towcester, Northants, 1680 Northants RO NWill A/C/31
Wood, Thomas, Childerditch (Tillingham Hall), Essex, 1758 Greater London RO DL/C/554/66/2
Wood, Thomas, farmer, Pauntley, Glos, 1805 GRO GDR/B4/2/W160
Wood, Thomas eld, Upper Hardres, Kent, 1592 CKS PRC2/6/57
Wood, Thomas eld, Elham, Kent, 1637 CKS PRC2/34/157
Wood, William, Marsh Chapel, Lincs, 1605 Lincs RO Ad/Ac/6/41
Wood, William, Hawkhurst, Kent, 1608 CKS PRC2/13/433
Wood, William, Brenzett, Kent, 1610 CKS PRC2/15/432
Wood, William, Elham, Kent, 1611 CKS PRC2/17/413
Wood, William, gentleman, Boughton under Blean, Kent, 1616 CKS PRC20/3/474
Wood, William, Mundham, North, Sussex, 1624 W. Suss RO EpI/33/1624/10
Wood, William, Tenterden, Kent, 1629 CKS PRC20/8/494
Wood, William, Wormshill, Kent, 1637 CKS PRC2/34/141
Wood, William, Petham, Kent, 1639 CKS PRC1/3/68
Wood, William, Ashbourne, Derby, 1685 LJRO/B/C/5/1685/111
Wood Davidson, Thomas, solicitor, Birkin (West Haddlesey), Yorks, 1832 Borthwick Test C.P. 1832/4
Wood/Atwood, Richard, Lenham, Kent, 1598 CKS PRC2/10/92
Woodall, John, yeoman, Brox-Holme, Lincs, 1673 Lincs RO Ad/Ac/35/38
Woodborne, Henry, Curry Rivel, Som, 1592 Somerset RO D/D/Cta/W73
Woodbourne, Curry Rivel, Som, 1687 Somerset RO D/D/Cta/W51
Woodbridge, Edmund, Sibsey, Lincs, 1619 Lincs RO Ad/Ac/14/46
Woodcock, Anthony, gentleman, Edgmond, Shrops, 1669 LJRO:cards/1669/20
Woodcock, Charles, farmer, Tattenhall (Rushia Hall), Ches, 1782 Cheshire RO (Name) W.C. 1782
Woodcock, John, Sutton, Long, Lincs, 1651 Lincs RO Ad/Ac/29/141
Woodcock, Richard, St Johns Thanet, Kent, 1598 CKS PRC2/10/212
Woodcock, William, Wye, Kent, 1669 CKS PRC1/14/122
Woodcocke, Agnes, widow, Reading, Berks, 1594 Berks RO D/A1/220/158B
Woodcocke, Alexander, Sandwich St Peter, Kent, 1609 CKS PRC2/14/477
Woodcocke, Alice, Seal, Nether and Over, Leics, 1665 Leics RO Administrators Accounts C17th f53
Woodcocke, Nicholas, Kingsnorth, Kent, 1594 CKS PRC2/7/1
Woodcocke, Robert, Coates, Great, Lincs, 1639 Lincs RO Ad/Ac/26/209
Woodcocke, Thomas, St Laurence Thanet, Kent, 1638 CKS PRC2/34/301
Woodd, John, blacksmith, St Albans St Michaels, Herts, Herts RO ASA25/4788
Woodd, John, Newchurch, Kent, 1611 CKS PRC20/2/244
Wooddall/Lewes, Isabel, wife, Abbots Langley, Herts, 1612 Herts RO ASA25/4804
Woodden, John, blacksmith, Oare, Kent, 1612 CKS PRC1/1/21
Wooddis, Edward, husbandman, Grindon, Staffs, 1743 LJRO/B/C/5/1743/198
Woode, Elizabeth, Sellindge, Kent, 1668 CKS PRC1/13/149
Woode, George, Charing, Kent, 1583 CKS PRC21/6/323
Woode, John, jurat, Sandwich, Kent, 1583 CKS PRC2/3/92
Woode, Richard, yeoman, Faversham, Kent, 1588 CKS PRC2/4/210
Woode, Robert, Elham, Kent, 1699 CKS PRC2/11/109
Woode, Thomas, Canterbury, Kent, 1582 CKS PRC2/2/231
Wooden, Edward, Darenth, Kent, 1673 Lambeth Palace VH96/6870
Woodes, William, Waltham, White, Berks, 1621 Berks RO D/A1/221/74B
Woodfen, Richard, 1671 Lancs RO (Name of Deceased) D.R.C.H. 1670
Woodford, Adam, Dover St Mary, Kent, 1626 CKS PRC20/7/118

[Woodford:]
Woodford, Edward, butcher, Loughborough, Leics, 1671 Leics RO Administrators Accounts 1667-72 f36
Woodforde, Richard, Ashby Folville, Leics, 1625 Lincs RO Ad/Ac/19B/87
Woodgar, Thomas, Faversham, Kent, 1627 CKS PRC2/28/128
Woodgate, Daniell, Woodchurch, Kent, 1611 CKS PRC20/2/242
Woodgate, John, Hawkhurst, Kent, 1637 CKS PRC2/34/155
Woodgate, Samuel, innholder, Lavenham, Suff, 1777 Suff RO(B) IC500/3/52/29
Woodgate, Steven, Henley, Oxon, 1630 Oxon RO MSS Wills 300/6/4
Woodger, John, Saltwood, Kent, 1602 CKS PRC21/16/103
Woodhall, Richard, Boston, Lincs, 1632 Lincs RO Ad/Ac/23/86
Woodhouse, Anthony, Dronfield (Totley), Derby, 1680 LJRO:cards/1680/41
Woodhouse, Francis ygr, coal dealer, Foleshill, Warks, 1804 LJRO/B/C/5/1804/65
Woodhouse, John, Madeley, Staffs, 1676 LJRO:cards/1676/54
Woodhouse, William, gentleman, Carlton on Trent, Notts, 1678 Lincs RO Ad/Ac/34/37
Woodinge, Randulphe, clergy: 'clerk', Roughton, Lincs, 1637 Lincs RO Ad/Ac/25/602
Woodkirke, Robert, Crowle (Ealand), Lincs, 1682 Lincs RO Ad/Ac/44/23
Woodland, Ann, widow, Smeeth, Kent, 1633 CKS PRC20/11/564
Woodland, Anthonie, Norton, Kent, 1600 CKS PRC2/12/371
Woodland, Clement, Brabourne, Kent, 1668 CKS PRC1/13/151
Woodland, Goddard, Brabourne, Kent, 1631 CKS PRC20/9/482
Woodland, John, victualler, Deal, Kent, 1599 CKS PRC21/15/47
Woodland, John, Cheriton, Kent, 1625 CKS PRC2/25/153
Woodland, John, Ashford, Kent, 1638 CKS PRC1/1/94
Woodland, John, Postling, Kent, 1672 CKS PRC2/35/99
Woodland, John, widower, Huntspill, Som, 1737 Somerset RO D/D/Cta/W50
Woodland, Joseph, Selsey, Sussex, 1632 W. Suss RO EpI/33/1632/19
Woodland, Julyan, Hythe St Leonard, Kent, 1622 CKS PRC20/6/228
Woodland, Peter, Sellindge, Kent, 1640 CKS PRC1/3/69
Woodland, Philipp, Monks Horton, Kent, 1611 CKS PRC2/15/433
Woodland, Phillip, Brookland, Kent, 1686 CKS PRC2/41/21
Woodland, Richard, Harrietsham, Kent, 1620 CKS PRC2/26/83
Woodland, Richard, Selsey, Sussex, 1630 W. Suss RO EpI/33/1630/2
Woodland, Richard, Selsey, Sussex, 1640 W. Suss RO EpI/33/1640/27
Woodland, Sara, spinster, Aldington, Kent, 1619 CKS PRC20/4/445
Woodland, Thomas, Selsey, Sussex, W. Suss RO EpI/33/1604-06/2
Woodland, William, innholder, Brabourne, Kent, 1641 CKS PRC1/6/43
Woodland, William, weaver: 'broad weaver', Cranbrook, Kent, 1645 CKS PRC1/7/36
Woodland, William ygr, Newington next Hythe, Kent, 1619 CKS PRC2/26/75
Woodley, Ralph, miller, Goring, Oxon, 1663 Oxon RO MSS Wills 88/2/3
Woodley, William, yeoman, Wootton, Berks, 1648 Berks RO D/A1/222/28B
Woodliffe, Bartholomew, Mareham le Fen, Lincs, 1626 Lincs RO Ad/Ac/20/52
Woodliffe, William, yeoman, Chilton, Berks, 1630 Berks RO D/A1/221/115B
Woodman, Christopher, Littlebourne, Kent, 1648 CKS PRC1/8/56
Woodman, John, yeoman, Woodchurch, Kent, 1632 CKS PRC20/11/586
Woodman, John, Alverstoke, Hants, 1678 Hants RO 21m65 D8/301
Woodman, Thomas, Ickham, Kent, 1664 CKS PRC19/3/49
Woodrofe, Symon, Minster in Thanet, Kent, 1602 CKS PRC2/12/391
Woodroffe, Elizabeth, widow, Henley, Oxon, 1629 Oxon RO MSS Wills 88/1/58
Woodroffe, John, fuller, Abingdon, Berks, 1604 Berks RO D/A1/220/195B
Woodrow, Jane, widow, Dereham, East, Norf, 1744 Norfolk RO ANF/11/4/76
Woodruff, Valentine, Birchington, Kent, 1636 CKS PRC20/11/528
Woodruffe, Simon, Wyberton, Lincs, 1648 Lincs RO Ad/Ac/30/307
Woodruffe, Thomas, Fordwich, Kent, 1675 CKS PRC2/36/257
Woods, Alice, widow, Grantham, Lincs, 1620 Lincs RO Ad/Ac/15/135
Woods, Edward, Kirkby, East, Lincs, 1575 Lincs RO Ad/Ac/1/15

Woods, George, Egerton, Kent, 1670 CKS PRC19/4/100
Woods, Jane, spinster, Reading St Giles, Berks, 1636 Berks RO D/A1/221/150B
Woods, John, widower, Kirton, Lincs, 1666 Lincs RO Ad/Ac/32/75
Woods, Richard, husbandman, Merton, Oxon, 1681 Oxon RO MSS Wills 176/4/12
Woods, Richard, Runcorn (Hatton), Ches, 1701 Cheshire RO (Name) W.C. 1701
Woods, Roger, Glatton, Hunts, 1691 Hunts RO/Acc58/271
Woods, William, Sandhurst, Berks, 1628 Wilts RO Miscellaneous Index (name + date)
Woods, William, Fernhurst, Sussex, 1685 W. Suss RO EpI/33/1684/2
Woodsend, George, Eagle, Lincs, 1636 Lincs RO Ad/Ac/24/488
Woodshawe, Elizabeth, Netherbury, Dors, 1597 Wilts RO Miscellaneous Index (name + date)
Woodstocke, Edward, St Neots, Hunts, 1684 Hunts RO/Acc58/232(231)
Woodstocke, Elisha, Holme, Hunts, 1684 Hunts RO/Acc58/217(206)
Woodstocke, Jane, widow, Aston Abbots, Bucks, 1612 Herts RO ASA25/4805
Woodthorpe, Thomas, yeoman, Mareham on the Hill, Lincs, 1679 Lincs RO Ad/Ac/35/1
Woodward, Christian, widow, Nonington, Kent, 1620 CKS PRC20/4/449
Woodward, Edward, Waltham, White, Berks, 1625 Berks RO D/A1/221/92B
Woodward, Elizabeth, mrs, Ashford, Kent, 1629 CKS PRC2/30/146
Woodward, Henry, Hankerton, Wilts, 1680 Wilts RO Arch. Wilts.(+ name and date)
Woodward, Joane, widow, Benington, Lincs, 1620 Lincs RO Ad/Ac/16/101
Woodward, John, Stanton, Fen, Hunts, Hunts RO/Acc58/91(195)
Woodward, John, Feckenham (Beanhall), Worcs, 1606 Worcs RO 008.7 BA3585/839/427
Woodward, John, gentleman, Wymondley, Great, Herts, 1638 Herts RO AHH23/2488
Woodward, Margaret, Watford, Herts, 1638 Herts RO ASA25/4964
Woodward, Nicholas, Kingsclere, Hants, 1678 Hants RO 21m65 D8/302
Woodward, Richard, Dassett, Avon, Warks, 1576 LJRO:cards/1576/1
Woodward, Richard, labourer, Potterspury, Northants, 1809 Northants RO X954/21/68
Woodward, Roger, yeoman, St Albans St Peters (Sleepshyde), Herts, 1578 Herts RO ASA25/941
Woodward, Thomas, Kidderminster, Worcs, 1675 Worcs RO 008.7 BA3585/830/32
Woodward, William, Waterperry, Oxon, 1623 Oxon RO MSS Wills 71/1/35
Woodward, William, Chard, Som, 1625 Somerset RO D/D/Cta/W9
Woodward, see Churden,
Woodwarde, Anne, widow, Windsor, New, Berks, 1611 Berks RO D/A1/221/32B
Woodwarde, Daniell, gentleman, Alkham, Kent, 1616 CKS PRC2/26/67
Woodwarde, Robert + Margaret, St Albans, Herts, 1596 Herts RO ASA25/1586
Woodworth, George, Belton All Saints, Lincs, 1620 Lincs RO Ad/Ac/8c/40
Woodworth, Henry, Marston on Dove, Derby, 1685 LJRO/B/C/5/1685/114
Woodyat, John, Fairfield, Kent, 1601 CKS PRC21/16/158
Woodyer, William, Pagham, Sussex, 1639 W. Suss RO EpIV/10/2/26
Wooer, Anne, spinster, Pidley, Hunts, 1716 Hunts RO/Acc58/307
Woofe, John, Broadwell (Filkins), Oxon, 1678 Oxon RO MSS Wills 300/6/48
Woofe, John, Condover, Shrops, 1685 LJRO/B/C/5/1685/115
Woolball, John, chandler: 'tallow chandler'/bachelor, Hythe St Leonard, Kent, 1664 CKS PRC19/3/48
Woolbridge, Robarte, Harrietsham, Kent, 1610 CKS PRC2/13/448
Woolby, John, gentleman, Winthorpe, Lincs, 1673 Lincs RO Ad/Ac/34/19
Wooldridge, John, Bottesford, Leics, 1683 Leics RO Administrators Accounts 1682-86 f1
Wooler, Jonathan, worsted manufacturer, Bradford (Wibsey), Yorks, 1793 Borthwick Test C.P. 1793/12
Woolestone, Richard, husbandman, Rainham, Kent, 1679 CKS PRC2/38/202
Woolfe, Mathew, Whitfield alias Beauxfield, Kent, 1595 CKS PRC2/7/253
Woolfe, Thomas, wheelwright, Hugglescote, Leics, Leics RO Administrators Accounts 1667-72 f81
Woolgar, Henry, Arundel, Sussex, 1675 W. Suss RO EpI/33/1675/5
Woolgar, Margaret, widow, Arundel, Sussex, 1682 W. Suss RO EpI/33/1682/20
Woolgate, Mary, Westwell, Kent, 1640 CKS PRC19/1/94

[Woolgate:]
Woolgate, Ralfe, Borden, Kent, 1636 CKS PRC2/33/143
Woolgate, Richard, Queenborough, Kent, 1604 CKS PRC2/13/415
Woolgate, Saferye, Borden, Kent, 1595 CKS PRC2/7/135
Woollacott, Samuel eld, farmer, Mickleover, Derby, 1800 LJRO/B/C/5/1800/56
Woollett, Catherine, widow, Elham, Kent, 1669 CKS PRC1/14/123
Woollett, Catherine, widow, Elham, Kent, 1669 CKS PRC1/14/123a
Woollett, George, Headcorn, Kent, 1619 CKS PRC2/26/81
Woollett, Henrie, Eastchurch, Sheppey, Kent, 1641 CKS PRC1/5/71
Woollett, Robert, High Halden, Kent, 1681 CKS PRC2/39/258
Woollett, Stephen, Sandwich, Kent, 1614 CKS PRC2/17/45
Woollett, William, yeoman, Boxley, Kent, 1677 CKS PRC2/37/104
Woollett, William, carpenter: 'house carpenter', Sandwich St Peter, Kent, 1678 CKS PRC2/38/90
Woolley, Adam, Youlgreave (Gratton), Derby, 1680 LJRO:cards/1680/42
Woolley, Peter, Minster in Sheppey, Kent, 1648 CKS PRC1/8/57
Woolley, Thomas, Rowley Regis, Staffs, 1685 Worcs RO 008.7 BA3585/837/bdl 4
Woollfall, Robert, clergy: 'clerk/mr', Wanstrow, Som, 1612 Somerset RO D/D/Cta/W64
Woollford, Simon, Wells St Cuthbert, Som, 1620 Somerset RO D/D/Cta/W6
Woollforde/Wolford, Richard + Cicely, Glastonbury St John, Som, 1591 Somerset RO D/D/Cta/W60
Woollmington, Henry, Barwick, Som, 1623 Somerset RO D/D/Cta/W7
Woolls, Alice, widow, Barnham, Sussex, 1633 W. Suss RO EpI/33/1633/1
Woolly, Joane, widow, Bethersden, Kent, 1619 CKS PRC2/26/40
Woolman, Nicholas, merchant, St Johns Thanet, Kent, 1641 CKS PRC1/6/44
Woolmore, Edward, Crowle, Worcs, 1673 Worcs RO 008.7 BA3585/835/bdl 1
Woolridge, Thomas, yeoman, Speen (Benham Valence), Berks, 1636 Berks RO D/A1/136/28C
Woolsey, Joane, widow, Moulton, Lincs, 1627 Lincs RO Ad/Ac/20b/21
Woolton, George, Pluckley, Kent, 1625 CKS PRC1/1/36
Woolton, John, Smarden, Kent, 1639 CKS PRC1/3/70
Woolton, Simon, Smarden, Kent, 1612 CKS PRC20/2/290
Woolvin, Mary, Grinstead, West, Sussex, 1666 W. Suss RO EpI/33/1666/3
Woolvin, Richard, Sidlesham, Sussex, 1671 W. Suss RO EpI/33/1670/24
Woolvin, Thomas, Steyning, Sussex, 1682 W. Suss RO EpI/33/1682/10
Woombell, Lawrence, cooper, Lissington, Lincs, 1680 Lincs RO Ad/Ac/34/59
Woord, Rychard, Minster in Thanet, Kent, 1596 CKS PRC2/8/332
Wooton, Elizabeth, Harpswell, Lincs, 1649 Lincs RO Ad/Ac/40/187
Wootton, Elizabeth, widow, Willoughton, Lincs, 1682 Lincs RO Ad/Ac/34/101
Wootton, John, labourer, Stockbury, Kent, 1642 CKS PRC1/6/45
Wootton, John, cordwainer, Sheldwich, Kent, 1668 CKS PRC1/13/152
Wootton, Matthew, victualler, Oxford All Saints, Oxon, 1673 Oxon RO MSS Wills 176/3/27
Wootton, Robert, Appledore, Kent, 1625 CKS PRC2/25/154
Wootton, Thomas, husbandman, Bicester, Oxon, 1667 Oxon RO MSS Wills 300/6/38
Wootton, Thomas, mariner, High Halstow, Kent, 1670 CKS PRC1/15/80
Wootton, Thomas, yeoman, Chalgrove (Rafford), Oxon, 1673 Oxon RO MSS Wills 176/3/28
Wootton, William, Marton, Warks, 1684 LJRO/B/C/5/1684/87
Wootton, William, butcher, Tamworth, Staffs, 1825 LJRO/B/C/5/1825/28
Woram, see Oram,
Worcester, Isabell, Linsted, Kent, 1608 CKS PRC2/13/455
Worceter, Elizabeth, minor: 'infant', Sandwich, Kent, 1625 CKS PRC2/25/151
Worceter, John, Sandwich St Peter, Kent, 1625 CKS PRC2/25/157
Worceter, Thomas, saddler, Sandwich St Peter, Kent, 1624 CKS PRC2/26/46
Wordly, James, yeoman, Seagry, Wilts, 1756 Wilts RO CC Sarum(+ name and date)
Worfild, Humfrey, yeoman, Powick, Worcs, 1607 Worcs RO 008.7 BA3585/839/428
Worgan, John, Newland, Glos, 1749 GRO GDR/B4/2/W187
Worgar, Nicholas, Monks Horton, Kent, 1597 CKS PRC2/9/489
Workman, Samuell, yeoman, Biddestone, Wilts, 1677 Wilts RO CC Sarum(+ name and date)

Worledge, William, Alresford, New, Hants, 1676 Hants RO 21m65 D8/274
Worley, John, Sheldwich, Kent, 1629 CKS PRC2/30/145
Worley, Marye, widow, Canterbury St Paul, Kent, 1620 CKS PRC2/26/76
Worley, Nathaniel, innholder, Henley, Oxon, 1680 Oxon RO MSS Wills 88/3/12
Worley, Stephen, Dymchurch, Kent, 1626 CKS PRC2/27/175
Worley, Thomas, gentleman, Monkton, Kent, 1614 CKS PRC20/3/5
Worley, William, Elham, Kent, 1627 CKS PRC2/27/183
Worman, John, custom house officer, King's Lynn, Norf, Norfolk RO ANW/23/25/73
Worme, George, Butterwick, Lincs, 1612 Lincs RO Ad/Ac/11/197
Worme, Joane, widow, New Romney, Kent, 1595 CKS PRC21/14/233
Worme, William, New Romney, Kent, 1592 CKS PRC21/11/240
Wormeall, Francys, clergy: 'clerk', Harbledown, Kent, 1598 CKS PRC2/11/7
Wormestone, Elizabeth, widow, Maidenhead, Berks, 1614 Berks RO D/A1/133/215D
Wormill, George, Bennington, Long, Lincs, 1615 Lincs RO Ad/Ac/13/5
Wormington, William, Wichenford, Worcs, 1682 Worcs RO 008.7 BA3585/837/bdl 3
Wormwell, Thomas, gentleman, Melton Mowbray, Leics, 1667 Leics RO Administrators Accounts 1667-72 f1
Worrall, John, Ormskirk, Lancs, 1578 Lancs RO (Name of Deceased) D.R.C.H. 1598
Worrall, John, Kinver, Staffs, 1684 LJRO/B/C/5/1684/88
Worrall, Peter, Budworth, Great (Cogshall), Ches, 1606 Cheshire RO (Name) W.C. 1606/7
Worrall, Rachell, widow, Faversham, Kent, 1675 CKS PRC2/36/258
Worrall, Robert, Adderley, Shrops, 1674 LJRO:cards/1674/53
Worsfold, John, Rusper, Sussex, 1617 W. Suss RO EpI/33/1617/24
Worshipp, Henry, Leake, Lincs, 1601 Lincs RO Ad/Ac/5/135
Worshipp, William, clergy: 'clerk/D.D./mr', Croft, Lincs, 1626 Lincs RO Ad/Ac/19B/49
Worsley, John, Stainfield, Lincs, 1627 Lincs RO Ad/Ac/20b/30
Worsley, John, Ickham, Kent, 1638 CKS PRC20/11/514
Worsley, Richard, Appledore, Kent, 1638 CKS PRC2/34/310
Worsyter/Broke, Catherine, Charing, Kent, 1598 CKS PRC21/15/29
Worte, William, Idmiston, Wilts, 1632 Wilts RO Arch. Sarum(+ name and date)
Worth, Degory, Lewannick, Corn, 1638 Cornwall RO AP/W608/2
Worthernton, John, Dover, Kent, 1629 CKS PRC20/8/464
Worthington, Francis, Budworth, Great (Dutton), Ches, 1676 Cheshire RO (Name) W.C. 1675
Worthington, James, Ropley, Hants, 1682 Hants RO 21m65 D8/331
Worthington, John, farmer, Prestbury, Ches, 1789 Cheshire RO (Name) W.C. 1789-90
Worthy, Henry, yeoman, Belvoir, Leics, 1644 Lincs RO Ad/Ac/28/83
Wotten, Antony, husbandman, Tintagel, Corn, 1646 Cornwall RO AP/W609/2
Wotton, James, knight, Boughton Malherbe, Kent, 1637 CKS PRC2/33/138
Wotton, Nicholas eld, Buckland, Berks, 1616 Berks RO D/A1/221/53B
Wotton, Thomas, Chippenham, Wilts, 1631 Wilts RO Arch. Wilts.(+ name and date)
Wotton, William, Milton next Sittingbourne, Kent, 1596 CKS PRC2/8/1
Wraie, Margarett, Fillingham, Lincs, 1619? Lincs RO Ad/Ac/8b/336
Wraight, Anthony eld, Orlestone, Kent, 1641 CKS PRC1/6/46
Wraight, Clement, Orlestone, Kent, 1631 CKS PRC2/31/81
Wraight, John, cooper, St Laurence Thanet, Kent, 1641 CKS PRC1/6/47
Wraight, Mary, widow, Canterbury St Peter, Kent, 1641 CKS PRC1/5/72
Wraight, Richard, Canterbury, Kent, 1631 CKS PRC20/9/486
Wraight, Richard, yeoman, Adisham, Kent, 1638 CKS PRC20/11/516
Wraight, Robert, Canterbury St George Martyr, Kent, 1638 CKS PRC2/34/151
Wraight, Thomas, Sandwich, Kent, 1673 CKS PRC2/35/268
Wraight, William, labourer, Dover, Kent, 1641 CKS PRC19/2/46
Wraight, William, Great Mongeham, Kent, 1680 CKS PRC2/39/126
Wraight, William, yeoman, Warehorne, Kent, 1688 CKS PRC2/41/111
Wraight, see Hall,
Wraighte, Edward, Sevington, Kent, 1613 CKS PRC2/17/240

[Wraith:]
Wraith, Edward, Tenterden, Kent, 1677 CKS PRC2/37/211
Wraith, Richard, Sarre, Kent, 1710 CKS PRC19/6/41
Wraith, Samuel, surgeon, Dover, Kent, 1685 CKS PRC20/13/539
Wraithe, John, Warehorne, Kent, 1639 CKS PRC1/3/71
Wrake, John, yeoman, Elham, Kent, 1682 CKS PRC2/39/249
Wratting, William, Faversham, Kent, 1628 CKS PRC2/29/117
Wraxworthy, Anthony, Corsley, Wilts, 1674 Wilts RO Arch. Sarum(+ name and date)
Wray, Andrew, Langton by Wragby, Lincs, Lincs RO Ad/Ac/32/47a
Wray, Barbara, spinster, Bolingbroke, Old, Lincs, 1635 Lincs RO Ad/Ac/24/387
Wray, Christopher, baronet, Glentworth, Lincs, 1668 Lincs RO Ad/Ac/33/89
Wray, Isaac, Hagworthingham, Lincs, 1652 Lincs RO Ad/Ac/29/135
Wray, John, postmaster, Hull, Yorks, 1780 Borthwick Test C.P. 1780/8
Wray, Mary, Skirbeck, Lincs, 1776 Lincs RO Ad/Ac/45/39
Wray, Nathaniel, Fillingham, Lincs, 1686 Lincs RO Ad/Ac/44/166
Wraye, John, Rainham, Kent, 1637 CKS PRC2/33/139
Wreache, William, Withycombe [Witcombe], Som, 1591 Somerset RO D/D/Cta/W74
Wread, William, Sittingbourne, Kent, 1620 CKS PRC2/26/34
Wreight, John, Preston next Wingham, Kent, 1590 CKS PRC2/5/464
Wreight, Thomas, Ruckinge, Kent, 1602 CKS PRC2/14/498
Wren, Daniel, New Romney, Kent, 1631 CKS PRC20/9/460
Wrench, Margaret, widow, Semley, Wilts, 1638 Wilts RO Arch. Sarum(+ name and date)
Wrenham, Thomas, gentleman, Sutton, Long, Lincs, 1683 Lincs RO Ad/Ac/44/89
Wrenn, William, High Halstow, Kent, 1678 CKS PRC2/37/209
Wresle, Thomas, Burton on Stather, Lincs, 1619 Lincs RO Ad/Ac/8b/433
Wrest, Alexander, Sandwich, Kent, 1615 CKS PRC2/26/85
Wreste, Samuell, Nonington, Kent, 1593 CKS PRC21/12/37
Wrett, Edward, butcher, Hedenham, Norf, 1751 Norfolk RO ANF/11/4/69
Wrigglesworth, Edmund, yeoman, Marcham, Berks, 1651 Berks RO D/A1/208/127
Wright, Agnes, Wyberton, Lincs, 1624 Lincs RO Ad/Ac/19A/51
Wright, Ann, widow, St Martin in the Fields, London & Middlesex, 1728 Greater London RO AM/CP/Box 1671-1728 pt (uncatalogued)
Wright, Anne, widow, Paxton, Little, Hunts, 1676 Hunts RO/Acc58/65(16)
Wright, Anne, widow, Aslackby, Lincs, 1679 Lincs RO Ad/Ac/43/111
Wright, Anthony, clergy: 'clerk', Owmby, Lincs, 1663 Lincs RO Ad/Ac/41/143
Wright, Charles, draper, Gainsborough, Lincs, 1606 Lincs RO Ad/Ac/37/226
Wright, Christopher, Aston upon Trent, Derby, 1672 LJRO:cards/1672/63
Wright, Cutburd, Weston, Lincs, 1618 Lincs RO Ad/Ac/14/196
Wright, Edward, husbandman, Beelsby, Lincs, 1635 Lincs RO Ad/Ac/24/447
Wright, Edward, Killingholme, Lincs, 1642 Lincs RO Ad/Ac/28/3
Wright, Edward, yeoman, Baston, Lincs, 1680 Lincs RO Ad/Ac/34/66
Wright, Edward, Faversham, Kent, 1682 CKS PRC2/39/248
Wright, Edward, yeoman, Minster in Thanet, Kent, 1690 CKS PRC2/41/165
Wright, Elizabeth, widow, Drayton, West, Notts, Borthwick Test C.P. 1762/2
Wright, Francis sen, butcher/grazier, Coventry Holy Trinity, Warks, 1666 LJRO:cards/1666/16
Wright, George, Deeping St James, Lincs, 1636 Lincs RO Ad/Ac/24/476
Wright, Giles, carpenter, Enderby, Bag, Lincs, 1674 Lincs RO Ad/Ac/34/25
Wright, Henry, Sutton, Long, Lincs, 1634 Lincs RO Ad/Ac/24/220
Wright, Isabell, Grimsby, Lincs, 1619 Lincs RO Ad/Ac/14/13
Wright, Isabell, Grimsby, Great, Lincs, 1620 Lincs RO Ad/Ac/16/110
Wright, Isabell, widow, Hemingby, Lincs, 1671 Lincs RO Ad/Ac/33/175
Wright, James, Wishaw, Warks, 1683 LJRO/B/C/5/1682/109
Wright, James, grinder: 'saw grinder', Sheffield, Yorks, 1842 Borthwick Test C.P. 1842/2
Wright, Jane, widow, Whitacre, Nether, Warks, 1708 LJRO/B/C/5/1707/160
Wright, Jane, widow, Rowley Regis, Staffs, 1794 Worcs RO 008.7 BA3585/835/bdl 2
Wright, John, merchant, Bristol, Glos, Bristol RO 1694/CP

Wright, John, Midhurst, Sussex, 1597 W. Suss RO EpI/33/1597/1
Wright, John, clergy: 'clerk', Willingham, Lincs, 1598 Lincs RO Ad/Ac/5/539
Wright, John, Canterbury St Peter, Kent, 1611 CKS PRC2/15/430
Wright, John, Whaplode, Lincs, 1613 Lincs RO Ad/Ac/12/74
Wright, John, yeoman, Hurley, Berks, 1619 Berks RO D/A1/221/68B
Wright, John, yeoman, Hale, Great (Little Hale), Lincs, 1639 Lincs RO Ad/Ac/26/297
Wright, John, Ferring, Sussex, 1645 W. Suss RO EpI/33/1645/5
Wright, John, Willoughby, Lincs, 1652 Lincs RO Ad/Ac/29/38
Wright, John, Rippingale, Lincs, 1661 Lincs RO Ad/Ac/32/15
Wright, John, yeoman, Appledore, Kent, 1669 CKS PRC1/14/124
Wright, John, yeoman, Swyncombe, Oxon, 1669 Oxon RO MSS Wills 176/3/19
Wright, John, yeoman, Tetford, Lincs, 1674 Lincs RO Ad/Ac/34/24
Wright, John, Faversham, Kent, 1680 CKS PRC2/39/122
Wright, John, St Martin in the Fields, London & Middlesex, 1706 PRO PROB32/49/2
Wright, John, victualler, Peover, Lower, Ches, 1779 Cheshire RO (Name) W.C. 1779-80
Wright, Margarett, widow, Yoxall (Morreg), Staffs, 1706 LJRO/B/C/5/1706/133
Wright, Margery, widow, Cumnor (Botley), Berks, 1641 Berks RO D/A1/221/170B
Wright, Mary, widow, Horstead, Norf, Norfolk RO ANW/23/23/91
Wright, Michael, Uffington, Lincs, 1623 Lincs RO Ad/Ac/18/12
Wright, Nicholas, Horsham, Sussex, 1611 W. Suss RO EpI/33/1611/1
Wright, Nicholas, Horsham, Sussex, 1612 W. Suss RO EpI/33/1612/1
Wright, Nicholas, Coleby, Lincs, 1618 Lincs RO Ad/Ac/8b/264
Wright, Nicolas, mariner: 'sailor', Faversham, Kent, 1640 CKS PRC1/5/73
Wright, Peter, Appleby, Leics, 1666 Leics RO Administrators Accounts C17th f89
Wright, Richard, Navenby, Lincs, 1613 Lincs RO Ad/Ac/11/63
Wright, Richard, Chester St Peter, Ches, 1615 Cheshire RO (Name) W.C. 1615
Wright, Richard, Sutton in the Marsh, Lincs, 1626 Lincs RO Ad/Ac/20/118
Wright, Richard, Horncastle, Lincs, 1633 Lincs RO Ad/Ac/24/6
Wright, Richard, husbandman, Stallingborough, Lincs, 1636 Lincs RO Ad/Ac/24/472
Wright, Richard, husbandman, Bourne, Lincs, 1638 Lincs RO Ad/Ac/25/214
Wright, Richard, Willey, Warks, 1680 LJRO:cards/1680/43
Wright, Richard, Climping, Sussex, 1684 W. Suss RO EpI/33/1684/25
Wright, Robert, Sutton St Edmunds, Lincs, 1614 Lincs RO Ad/Ac/12/208
Wright, Robert, Hibaldstow, Lincs, 1681 Lincs RO Ad/Ac/34/75
Wright, Robert, farmer, Brotherton (Sutton), Yorks, 1841 Borthwick Test C.P. 1841/4
Wright, Samuel, Scothorne, Lincs, 1639? Lincs RO Ad/Ac/40/260
Wright, Samuel, farmer, Barrow upon Trent, Derby, 1807 LJRO/B/C/5/1807/96
Wright, Sarah, widow, Barrow upon Trent, Derby, 1703 LJRO/B/C/5/1708/48
Wright, Stephen, St Johns Thanet, Kent, 1623 CKS PRC2/26/33
Wright, Thomas, victualler, Bristol St Philip & St Jacob, Glos, Bristol RO 1772/CP
Wright, Thomas, yeoman, Lutterworth, Leics, Leics RO Administrators Accounts 1667-72 f45
Wright, Thomas, Burgh on Bain (Girsby), Lincs, 1619 Lincs RO Ad/Ac/15/176
Wright, Thomas, Waltham, Lincs, 1664 Lincs RO Ad/Ac/43/20
Wright, Thomas, gentleman, Trusthorpe, Lincs, 1666 Lincs RO Ad/Ac/32/72
Wright, Thomas, yeoman, Cumnor (Botley), Berks, 1667 Berks RO D/A1/222/84B
Wright, Thomas, Leire, Leics, 1670 Leics RO Administrators Accounts 1667-72 f31
Wright, Thomas, Minster in Thanet, Kent, 1672 CKS PRC2/35/189
Wright, Thomas, Normanby, Lincs, 1675 Lincs RO Ad/Ac/35/99
Wright, Thomas, bachelor, Owmby by Spital, Lincs, 1679 Lincs RO Ad/Ac/45/100
Wright, Thomas, Draycott in the Moors, Staffs, 1684 LJRO/B/C/5/1684/89
Wright, Thomas, baker, Whitechapel, London & Middlesex, 1698 PRO PROB32/36/130
Wright, Thomas eld, husbandman, Moulsford, Berks, 1629 Berks RO D/A1/221/114B
Wright, Thomas ygr, Trusthorpe, Lincs, 1624 Lincs RO Ad/Ac/19A/74
Wright, Ursulay, spinster, Caythorpe, Lincs, 1628 Lincs RO Ad/Ac/20b/56
Wright, Valentine, Bottesford, Leics, 1618 Lincs RO Ad/Ac/14/289

[Wright:]
Wright, Will, Sheepshed, Leics, 1684 Leics RO Administrators Accounts 1682-86 f18
Wright, William, St Albans St Peters, Herts, Herts RO ASA25/4977
Wright, William, Rasen, Middle, (Tupholme), Lincs, 1599 Lincs RO Ad/Ac/5/435
Wright, William, baker, Spalding, Lincs, 1602 Lincs RO Ad/Ac/5/68
Wright, William, cook/scholar's servant, Cambridge, Cambs, 1606 CUL V.C.Acc./Box1/59
Wright, William, Hogsthorpe, Lincs, 1613 Lincs RO Ad/Ac/12/99
Wright, William, Donington, Lincs, 1619 Lincs RO Ad/Ac/15/13
Wright, William, Burton by Lincoln, Lincs, 1622 Lincs RO Ad/Ac/8c/7
Wright, William, Bicker, Lincs, 1632 Lincs RO Ad/Ac/23/156
Wright, William, weaver, Farlesthorpe, Lincs, 1637 Lincs RO Ad/Ac/25/430
Wright, William, joiner, St Giles in the Fields, London & Middlesex, 1669 PRO PROB32/3/58
Wright, Wylfryde, Canterbury St Dunstan Without, Kent, 1591 CKS PRC2/6/328
Wright/Evans, Mildred, widow, St Nicholas at Wade, Kent, 1618 CKS PRC20/4/417
Wright/Evans, Mildred, widow, St Nicholas at Wade, Kent, 1618 CKS PRC20/4/421
Wright/Hodgson, Marie, Toft Next Newton, Lincs, 1619 Lincs RO Ad/Ac/14/130
Wright, see Grantham & Turkey,
Wrighte, Anne, Surfleet, Lincs, 1649 Lincs RO Ad/Ac/30/166
Wrighte, Edward, Burgh le Marsh, Lincs, 1618 Lincs RO Ad/Ac/14/220
Wrighte, Issabell, widow, Anderby, Lincs, 1618 Lincs RO Ad/Ac/14/92
Wrighte, Marie, widow, Haxey (Nethergate), Lincs, 1640 Lincs RO Ad/Ac/40/147
Wrighte, Richard, Linsted, Kent, 1612 CKS PRC2/16/8
Wrighte, Richard, Stickney, Lincs, 1619 Lincs RO Ad/Ac/15/49
Wrighte, Richarde, Aslackby, Lincs, 1623 Lincs RO Ad/Ac/18/55
Wrighte, Robert, Heckington, Lincs, 1619 Lincs RO Ad/Ac/15/236
Wrighte, Theophile, miller, Kirkby Green, Lincs, 1639? Lincs RO Ad/Ac/26/72
Wrighte, Thomas, Kingerby, Lincs, 1601 Lincs RO Ad/Ac/5/31
Wrightson, Wyllyam, Toynton, High, Lincs, Lincs RO Ad/Ac/1/33
Writtle, John, Biddenden, Kent, 1586 CKS PRC2/4/166
Writtle, Richard, Saltwood, Kent, 1638 CKS PRC20/11/520
Wroe, John, porter: 'common porter', Leeds, Yorks, 1783 Borthwick Test C.P. 1783/1
Wroote, David, Owston, Lincs, 1613 Lincs RO Ad/Ac/8b/7
Wroote, Thomas, Epworth, Lincs, 1646 Lincs RO Ad/Ac/40/121
Wroote, William, labourer, Goxhill, Lincs, 1635 Lincs RO Ad/Ac/24/326
Wrosse, Richard, glover, Lincoln St Peter at Gowts, Lincs, 1638 Lincs RO Ad/Ac/25/37
Wryton, Edward, Barton, Steeple (Middle Barton), Oxon, 1635 Oxon RO MSS Wills 300/6/14
Wyan, John, Kirkby Underwood, Lincs, 1649 Lincs RO Ad/Ac/30/199
Wyat, Catherine, Boxley, Kent, 1622 CKS PRC20/5/220
Wyat, George, esquire, Boxley, Kent, 1626 CKS PRC2/25/160
Wyat, Robert, yeoman, Lydd, Kent, 1667 CKS PRC19/3/109
Wyat, Thomas, Leeds, Kent, 1601 CKS PRC2/12/395
Wyat, Thomas, bachelor, Hartlip, Kent, 1684 CKS PRC2/40/258
Wyatt, George, Barrowby, Lincs, 1602 Lincs RO Ad/Ac/5/147
Wyatt, George, Salisbury, Wilts, 1674 Wilts RO Miscellaneous Index (name + date)
Wyatt, Hawte, mr, Boxley, Kent, 1639 CKS PRC1/3/72
Wyatt, John, Lydd, Kent, 1602 CKS PRC21/16/124
Wyatt, John, butcher, St Johns Thanet, Kent, 1692 CKS PRC2/42/19
Wyatt, Richarde, Amesbury, Wilts, 1632 Wilts RO Miscellaneous Index (name + date)
Wyatt, Sarah, widow, Cropredy, Oxon, 1684 Oxon RO MSS Wills Pec 55/2/15
Wyatt, Stephen, Harrietsham, Kent, 1680 CKS PRC2/39/125
Wyatt, William, Wyberton, Lincs, 1607 Lincs RO Ad/Ac/8a/45
Wyatt, William, Felpham, Sussex, 1632 W. Suss RO EpI/33/1631/32
Wyboorne, John, Hawkhurst, Kent, 1602 CKS PRC2/12/393
Wyborn, John, Lenham, Kent, 1680 CKS PRC2/38/210
Wyborne, John, Smarden, Kent, 1618 CKS PRC20/4/399
Wyborne, John, yeoman, Northbourne, Kent, 1710 CKS PRC1/17/19

Wyborne, William, Quadring, Lincs, 1602 Lincs RO Ad/Ac/5/533
Wyborne, William, gentleman, Ickham, Kent, 1683 CKS PRC20/13/301
Wyborrowe, Joane, widow, East Sutton, Kent, 1613 CKS PRC2/16/194
Wycks, George, Blean, Kent, 1607 CKS PRC2/14/469
Wydgier, Henry, Canterbury Holy Cross Westgate, Kent, 1595 CKS PRC2/8/49
Wyehowse, William, Brailes, Warks, 1599 Worcs RO 008.7 BA3585/838/134
Wyer, John, 1623 Hants RO 21M65 D8/43
Wyer, Symon, Faversham, Kent, 1611 CKS PRC2/16/76
Wygmore, Edward, Reculver, Kent, 1610 CKS PRC20/2/154
Wyld, Mary, widow, Seagrave, Leics, 1684 Leics RO Administrators Accounts 1682-86 f8
Wyld, Robert, esquire, Worcester (The Commanders), Worcs, 1685 Worcs RO 008.7 BA3585/830/3
Wyld, Thomas, gentleman, Belbroughton, Worcs, 1683 Worcs RO 008.7 BA3585/837/bdl 5
Wylde, Edward, St Peter in Thanet, Kent, 1586 CKS PRC2/4/204
Wylde, George, Aldington, Kent, 1583 CKS PRC21/6/328
Wylde, John, Sandwich, Kent, 1639 CKS PRC20/11/496
Wylde, Richard, St Peter in Thanet, Kent, 1627 CKS PRC2/28/137
Wyldebore, Jeremy, Minster in Thanet, Kent, 1618 CKS PRC2/26/43
Wyldebore, William, yeoman, Holbeach, Lincs, 1614 Lincs RO Ad/Ac/12/169
Wylder, Thomas, Wokingham, Berks, 1678 Wilts RO Dean Sarum (name + date)
Wyldes, Adam, maltster, Dover St Mary, Kent, 1627 CKS PRC20/8/462
Wyleman, John, High Halstow, Kent, 1591 CKS PRC2/5/452
Wyles, Anne, widow, Woodnesborough, Kent, 1597 CKS PRC2/9/211
Wyles, Edwarde, Sandwich St Clement, Kent, 1583 CKS PRC2/3/77
Wyles, Robart, Hythe St Leonard, Kent, 1601 CKS PRC21/15/228
Wyles, Stephen, cordwainer, Dover, Kent, 1627 CKS PRC20/8/488
Wyley, Ann, widow, Leysdown, Kent, 1637 CKS PRC2/34/144
Wyley, John, Leysdown, Kent, 1637 CKS PRC2/34/145
Wyley, William, Ruckinge, Kent, 1638 CKS PRC2/34/152
Wylie, Stephen, Goudhurst, Kent, 1595 CKS PRC2/7/164
Wylie, Thomas, Lydd, Kent, 1641 CKS PRC19/1/95
Wyllard, Thomas, Benenden, Kent, 1588 CKS PRC2/4/316
Wylles, Henrie, Stamford, Lincs, 1605 Lincs RO Ad/Ac/6/115
Wylles, William, Bethersden, Kent, 1593 CKS PRC2/6/119
Wylliams, John, Dover, Kent, 1615 CKS PRC20/3/212
Wylloughbye, Percyvall, Maidstone, Kent, 1612 CKS PRC20/2/246
Wyllyams, John, vintner, Hythe St Leonard, Kent, 1583 CKS PRC21/6/256
Wyllyams, Robert, St Nicholas at Wade, Kent, 1594 CKS PRC21/12/409
Wyllyamson, John, Skegness, Lincs, Lincs RO Ad/Ac/2b/65
Wylmote, Rychard, Hollingbourne, Kent, 1582 CKS PRC21/6/64
Wylmott, John, Bearsted, Kent, 1600 CKS PRC2/11/335
Wylson, John, Rickmansworth, Herts, 1574 Herts RO ASA25/796
Wylsonn, Roberte, Egerton, Kent, 1584 CKS PRC21/7/146
Wylton, Chrystopher, Canterbury Holy Cross Westgate, Kent, 1592 CKS PRC2/6/378
Wyly, James, Faversham, Kent, 1597 CKS PRC2/9/327
Wyly, Rose, widow, Lydd, Kent, 1641 CKS PRC19/2/47
Wyman, Robert, glazier, Hythe St Leonard, Kent, 1646 CKS PRC19/2/109
Wyman, Thomas, New Romney, Kent, 1585 CKS PRC21/7/120
Wymarcke, Alice, spinster, Chillenden, Kent, 1593 CKS PRC2/5/17
Wymark, Peter, yeoman, Worth, Kent, 1640 CKS PRC19/1/96
Wymarke, Edward, Faversham, Kent, 1678 CKS PRC2/38/85
Wymarke, Peter, Worth, Kent, 1674 CKS PRC20/12/155
Wymbleby, Allice, widow, Stamford, Lincs, 1606 Lincs RO Ad/Ac/6/42
Wymon, George, New Romney, Kent, 1595 CKS PRC21/13/38
Wymont, Mary, widow, Harborough, Market, Leics, 1667 Leics RO Administrators Accounts

[Wymont:]
1667-72 f6
Wympew, John, Nunney, Som, 1646 Somerset RO D/D/Cta/W82
Wymsherst, Stephen, Cranbrook, Kent, 1625 CKS PRC2/26/5
Wyncott, Walter, Wichenford, Worcs, Worcs RO 008.7 BA3585/839/394
Wyndey, Susan, widow, Lydd, Kent, 1596 CKS PRC21/14/113
Wyndye, Thomas, Lydd, Kent, 1592 CKS PRC21/11/342
Wyniattes, Thomas, Sandwich, Kent, 1596 CKS PRC2/8/218
Wynn, Samuel, Frodsham (Helsby), Ches, 1721 Cheshire RO (Name) W.C. 1721
Wynne, Frances, mrs/widow, Canterbury St Mary Bredman, Kent, 1625 CKS PRC2/25/156
Wynne, Richard, Doddington, Lincs, 1614 Lincs RO Ad/Ac/12/198
Wynne, Thomas, Broadway, Worcs, Worcs RO 008.7 BA3585/838/280
Wynne, Thomas, miller, Brenzett, Kent, 1683 CKS PRC2/40/162
Wynnell, James, Sittingbourne, Kent, 1599 CKS PRC2/10/525
Wynsor, Francis, gentleman, Faversham, Kent, 1641 CKS PRC19/2/48
Wynter, John, Dover St Mary, Kent, 1587 CKS PRC21/8/364
Wynter, John, Maidstone, Kent, 1601 CKS PRC21/15/123
Wynter, Simon, Kelsey, South, Lincs, 1623 Lincs RO Ad/Ac/18/84
Wynter, Thomas, Sandwich St Bartholomew's Hospital, Kent, 1607 CKS PRC20/1/257
Wynter, William, Sandwich, Kent, 1592 CKS PRC2/6/115
Wynterborne, Thomas, yeoman, Canterbury St Paul, Kent, 1620 CKS PRC2/26/55
Wyres, Thomas, husbandman, Countesthorpe, Leics, 1666 Leics RO Administrators Accounts C17th f51
Wyse, George, mariner, Sandwich St Clement, Kent, 1640 CKS PRC1/5/69
Wyse, William, Felpham, Sussex, 1635 W. Suss RO EpI/33/1635/30
Wysmane, Jarmyne, Yetminster, Dors, 1600 Wilts RO Miscellaneous Index (name + date)
Wytcherling, William, Headcorn, Kent, 1615 CKS PRC2/26/27
Wythe, Elizabeth, Buckland, Berks, 1678 Berks RO D/A1/222/147B
Wythe, Walter, Bushey, Herts, 1586 Herts RO ASA25/1140
Wythers, Ann, Swineshead, Lincs, 1636? Lincs RO Ad/Ac/24/460
Wythers, John, Woodhay, East, Hants, 1625 Hants RO 21M65 D8/107
Wythers, Robert, St Johns Thanet, Kent, 1628 CKS PRC2/28/131
Wytt, Michaell, Frittenden, Kent, 1616 CKS PRC2/26/25
Wytton, Edward, Reading St Lawrence, Berks, 1593 Berks RO D/A1/220/156B
Wyxe, Richard, Selling, Kent, 1681 CKS PRC2/39/252
Yailer, Samuel, Haxey (Graizelound), Lincs, 1605 Lincs RO Ad/Ac/37/209
Yalden, Joan, widow, Meon, East, Hants, Hants RO 1687 AD99/2
Yallop, Thomas, yeoman, Braydeston, Norf, 1747 Norfolk RO ANW/23/24/67
Yanson, John, Chieveley (Curridge), Berks, 1604 Berks RO D/A1/199/58C
Yarbrough, George, clergy: 'clerk', Brattleby, Lincs, 1681 Lincs RO Ad/Ac/34/97
Yarbrough, Richard, Friskney, Lincs, 1662 Lincs RO Ad/Ac/32/25
Yarburgh, Robert, Alvingham, Lincs, 1644 Lincs RO Ad/Ac/28/65
Yarburgh, William, Yarburgh, Lincs, 1619 Lincs RO Ad/Ac/14/1
Yard, Julian, Clevedon, Som, 1591 Somerset RO D/D/Cta/Y3
Yardley, John, Farndon (Crowe), Ches, 1576 Cheshire RO (Name) W.C. 1576
Yarnton, Richard, husbandman, Bredon, Worcs, Worcs RO 008.7 BA3585/838/281
Yarram, Richard, Holme, Hunts, Hunts RO/Acc58/245(226)
Yarranton, William, Astley, Worcs, 1602 Worcs RO 008.7 BA3585/838/284
Yarwood, Abraham, wool comber, Witton (Northwich), Ches, 1794 Cheshire RO (Name) W.C. 1794
Yarwood, Timothy, yeoman, Astbury (Brookhouse Green), Ches, 1787 Cheshire RO (Name) W.C. 1787-8
Yate, Richard, clergy: 'mr/parson', Badlesmere, Kent, 1631 CKS PRC2/31/80
Yate, Thomas, gentleman, Arlingham, Glos, GRO GDR/B4/2/Y15
Yate, Thomas, Sutton, Kings, Northants, 1618 Oxon RO MSS Wills Pec 56/4/6
Yate, William, yeoman, Eynsham, Oxon, 1629 Oxon RO MSS Wills 75/3/22

Yateman, Francis, gentleman, Milton, Berks, 1669 Berks RO D/A1/225/30C
Yates, Alexander, Boston, Lincs, 1623 Lincs RO Ad/Ac/17/2
Yates, Edward, husbandman, Spalding, Lincs, 1673 Lincs RO Ad/Ac/35/19
Yates, Francis, Kingston Bagpuize, Berks, 1644 Berks RO D/A1/225/27C
Yates, Hellen, Gainsborough (Walkerith), Lincs, 1633 Lincs RO Ad/Ac/40/59
Yates, John, Wigtoft, Lincs, 1626 Lincs RO Ad/Ac/20/31
Yates, John, husbandman, Clee, Lincs, 1649 Lincs RO Ad/Ac/30/187
Yates, John, Aisthorpe (Thorpe in the Fallows), Lincs, 1682 Lincs RO Ad/Ac/44/25
Yates, John, potter, Stoke-upon-Trent (Hanley), Staffs, 1799 LJRO/B/C/5/1799/63
Yates, Marie, widow, Kirton, Lincs, 1627 Lincs RO Ad/Ac/20b/24
Yates, Peter, Egginton, Derby, 1682 LJRO/B/C/5/1682/110
Yates, Richard, Faversham, Kent, 1615 CKS PRC2/26/101
Yates, Robert, tanner, Lincoln St Peter at Gowts, Lincs, 1587 Lincs RO Ad/Ac/2C/104
Yates, Robert, Postling, Kent, 1615 CKS PRC2/26/100
Yates, Robert, Bolton, Lancs, 1696 Lancs RO (Name of Deceased) D.R.C.H. 1696
Yates, Thomas, Ulceby, Lincs, 1600 Lincs RO Ad/Ac/5/373
Yates, Thomas, carpenter, Covenham St Bartholomew, Lincs, 1668 Lincs RO Ad/Ac/33/72
Yates, Thomas, Benson (Roke), Oxon, 1673 Oxon RO MSS Wills Pec 72/5/2
Yates, Thomas, Hindon, Wilts, 1740? Wilts RO Arch. Sarum(+ name and date)
Yates, William, husbandman, Wootton Wawen, Worcs, 1586 Worcs RO 008.7 BA3585/838/63
Yates, William, Kirton, Lincs, 1627 Lincs RO Ad/Ac/20b/25
Yats, Willyam, Aisthorpe (Thorpe in the Fallows), Lincs, 1665 Lincs RO Ad/Ac/41/163
Yealie, Richard, Barrington, Som, 1622 Somerset RO D/D/Cta/W23/Y
Yearmes, Richard, Mersham, Kent, 1594 CKS PRC2/7/351
Yearwood, Thomas, Knutsford (Nether Knutsford), Ches, 1634 Cheshire RO (Name) W.C. 1634
Yeates, David, Willoughton, Lincs, 1617 Lincs RO Ad/Ac/8b/312
Yeates, John, husbandman, Moulton, Lincs, 1686 Lincs RO Ad/Ac/44/156
Yedall, Richard, Grainthorpe, Lincs, 1611 Lincs RO Ad/Ac/10/73
Yeend, James, Elmstone Hardwicke, Glos, 1790 GRO GDR/B4/2/Y8
Yeene, Jane, Elmstone Hardwicke, Glos, 1769 GRO GDR/B4/2/Y7
Yeildall, George, yeoman, Hampstead Norris, Berks, 1678 Berks RO D/A1/225/32C
Yeolland, Richard, gentleman, Helston, Corn, 1637 Cornwall RO AP/T608
Yeoman, John, bachelor, St Martin in the Fields, London & Middlesex, 1683 PRO PROB32/33/194
Yeomans, John, butcher, Queenborough, Kent, 1681 CKS PRC2/39/129
Yeomans, John,
Som 1740 Somerset RO D/D/Cta/Y1
Yeomans, Robart, Sandwich, Kent, 1597 CKS PRC2/10/216
Yeomans, William, yeoman, Norbury (Weston Jones), Staffs, 1803 LJRO/B/C/5/1803/109
Yeomanson, Ralfe, Challock, Kent, 1609 CKS PRC20/2/19
Yeomondes, William, Powick, Worcs, 1607 Worcs RO 008.7 BA3585/839/429
Yerbury, William, Bromham, Wilts, 1677 Wilts RO Arch. Wilts.(+ name and date)
Yewell, John, Ivychurch, Kent, 1632 CKS PRC20/9/508
Yewell, Thomas, Dymchurch, Kent, 1635 CKS PRC2/33/146
Yocklie, Margarett, widow, St Peter in Thanet, Kent, 1612 CKS PRC2/17/337
Yokyns, John, Goodnestone next Wingham, Kent, 1598 CKS PRC21/14/175
Yole, Henry, Luddington (Garthorpe), Lincs, 1677 Lincs RO Ad/Ac/35/126
Yong, Anthony, gentleman, Easebourne (Ambersham), Sussex, 1596 W. Suss RO EpI/33/1596/1
Yong, Isaac, Woodchurch, Kent, 1634 CKS PRC20/11/582
Yong, John eld, Godmersham, Kent, 1617 CKS PRC20/4/459
Yong, Paulina, Charing, Kent, 1636 CKS PRC20/11/588
Yong, Richard, Pluckley, Kent, 1617 CKS PRC2/26/96
Yong, Richard, yeoman, Barrow, Lincs, 1639 Lincs RO Ad/Ac/26/194
Yong, Robert, Canterbury St Peter, Kent, 1623 CKS PRC2/26/99
Yong, Thomas, Biddenden, Kent, 1649 CKS PRC1/8/58

[Yonge:]
Yonge, Edward, Boughton Monchelsea, Kent, 1634 CKS PRC2/32/180
Yonge, George, Thanington, Kent, 1600 CKS PRC2/11/345
Yonge, James, St Pauls Walden, Herts, 1560 Herts RO ASA25/550
Yonge, James, baker, Burford, Oxon, 1662 Oxon RO MSS Wills 88/6/5
Yonge, John, Selling, Kent, 1590 CKS PRC2/5/480
Yonge, John, New Romney, Kent, 1598 CKS PRC21/15/13
Yonge, John, yeoman, Wye, Kent, 1620 CKS PRC2/27/187
Yonge, John, Garford, Berks, 1639 Berks RO D/A1/225/25C
Yonge, Pawle, Selling, Kent, 1586 CKS PRC2/4/49
Yonge, Peter, miller, Hythe St Leonard, Kent, 1621 CKS PRC20/5/222
Yonge, Stephen, Saltwood, Kent, 1595 CKS PRC21/14/217
Yonge, Thomas, Gosberton, Lincs, 1586 Lincs RO Ad/Ac/2C/143
Yonge, Thomas, Kingston, Kent, 1590 CKS PRC2/5/476
Yonge, Thomas, yeoman, Cornwell, Oxon, 1625 Oxon RO MSS Wills 300/7/7
Yonge, Thomas ygr, Biddenden, Kent, 1640 CKS PRC1/5/74
Yorck/Franck, Thomas, husbandman, Winford, Som, 1625 Somerset RO D/D/Cta/W24/Y
York, Jobe, Lenham, Kent, 1615 CKS PRC2/26/97
York, John, yeoman, Wombourne, Staffs, 1779 LJRO/B/C/5/1779/109
York, Richard, yeoman, Hendred, East, Berks, 1678 Berks RO D/A1/25/35C
Yorke, Gregorie, Scampton, Lincs, 1594 Lincs RO Ad/Ac/5/519
Yorke, Humfrey, weaver, Clewer, Berks, 1642 Berks RO D/A1/142/93C
Yorke, John, Steeping, Little, Lincs, 1645 Lincs RO Ad/Ac/28/156
Yorke, Nicholas, Lincoln, Lincs, 1607 Lincs RO Ad/Ac/8a/47
Yorke, Paul, Washingborough, Lincs, 1640 Lincs RO Ad/Ac/27/172
Yorke, Richard, Scampton, Lincs, 1662 Lincs RO Ad/Ac/41/15
Yorke, Thomas, Wellesbourne, Warks, 1681 Worcs RO 008.7 BA3585/830/45
Yorkney, William, Maiden Bradley, Wilts, 1615 Wilts RO Unlisted Fragment
Yorkshire, Thomas, Bratoft, Lincs, 1606 Lincs RO Ad/Ac/7/119
Yorkton, Samuel, Cranbrook, Kent, 1667 CKS PRC1/12/98
Youicke, John, gentleman, Wigginton, Oxon, 1674 Oxon RO MSS Wills 88/6/8
Youle, John, innkeeper, St Botolph without Aldersgate, London & Middlesex, 1690 PRO PROB32/31/67
Youle, William, Luddington, Lincs, 1668 Lincs RO Ad/Ac/33/85
Young, Anne, widow, Milton next Sittingbourne, Kent, 1682 CKS PRC2/40/86
Young, Dulcibella, Alderbury, Wilts, 1687 Wilts RO Treas Sarum Box 2/10
Young, Edward, Selsey, Sussex, 1596 W. Suss RO EpI/33/1596/8
Young, Edward, mr, Mersham, Kent, 1627 CKS PRC2/28/139
Young, Francis, Greinton, Som, 1711 Somerset RO D/D/Cta/Y2
Young, Henry, Doddington, Kent, 1683 CKS PRC2/40/164
Young, Henry, Folkestone, Kent, 1692 CKS PRC19/5/14
Young, James, Petham, Kent, 1612 CKS PRC2/16/51
Young, John, Hougham, Kent, 1609 CKS PRC2/15/449
Young, John, Blean, Kent, 1629 CKS PRC2/29/118
Young, John, Ombersley, Worcs, 1675 Worcs RO 008.7 BA3585/830/29
Young, John, yeoman, Foalgate Ripon, Yorks, 1793 Borthwick Test C.P. 1793/13
Young, Martin, Belton All Saints, Lincs, 1678 Lincs RO Ad/Ac/35/132
Young, Peter, New Romney, Kent, 1586 CKS PRC21/8/125
Young, Richard, Milton next Sittingbourne, Kent, 1606 CKS PRC2/13/464
Young, Richard, Hawkhurst, Kent, 1625 CKS PRC2/25/161
Young, Robert, Downton, Wilts, 1642 Wilts RO Arch. Sarum(+ name and date)
Young, Thomas, Sandwich, Kent, 1601 CKS PRC2/12/399
Young, Thomas, Freshwater, Hants, 1624 Hants RO 21M65 D8/108
Young, Thomas, Canterbury St Dunstan Without, Kent, 1697 CKS PRC2/42/138
Young, Vincent, Kingston, Kent, 1594 CKS PRC2/7/125
Young, William, Arreton, Hants, 1595 Hants RO 1586 A95/3

Young, William, Croft, Lincs, 1662 Lincs RO Ad/Ac/32/22
Young, William, Fordwich, Kent, 1673 CKS PRC2/35/270
Young, William, Sheldwich, Kent, 1680 CKS PRC2/39/128
Young, William, yeoman, Boddington, Glos, 1715 GRO GDR/B4/2/Y14
Younge, Alice, widow, Abingdon, Berks, 1629 Wilts RO CC Sarum(+ name and date)
Younge, Elias, Preston next Faversham, Kent, 1626 CKS PRC2/27/186
Younge, Gilbert, surgeon/apothecary, Norwich, Norf, 1741 Norfolk RO ANW/23/23/53D
Younge, Joane, High Halden, Kent, 1618 CKS PRC2/26/95
Younge, John, Biddenden, Kent, 1619 CKS PRC2/26/98
Younge, John, Blean, Kent, 1629 CKS PRC20/8/526
Younge, John, Strensham, Worcs, 1681 Worcs RO 008.7 BA3585/830/44
Younge, Joseph, Deal, Kent, 1626 CKS PRC20/7/112
Younge, Mathew, Gosberton, Lincs, 1632 Lincs RO Ad/Ac/23/32
Younge, Michaell, husbandman, Anderby, Lincs, 1606 Lincs RO Ad/Ac/7/117
Younge, Nicholas, Charing, Kent, 1619 CKS PRC20/4/457
Younge, Nicholas, Kirtlington, Oxon, 1636 Oxon RO MSS Wills 88/6/1
Younge, Richard, Brook, Kent, 1594 CKS PRC2/7/9
Younge, Richard, Wye, Kent, 1611 CKS PRC2/17/428
Younge, Robart, yeoman, St Laurence Thanet, Kent, 1634 CKS PRC2/32/181
Younge, Roger, Pinchbeck, Lincs, 1642 Lincs RO Ad/Ac/27/313
Younge, Samuel, gentleman, Arundel, Sussex, 1682 W. Suss RO EpI/33/1682/8
Younge, Thomas, Milton next Sittingbourne, Kent, 1596 CKS PRC2/8/328
Younge, Thomas, gentleman, Langley, Kings (Chipperfield), Herts, 1612 Herts RO AHH23/2702
Younge, Thomas, Sandwich St Clement, Kent, 1643 CKS PRC1/7/20
Younge, Thomas, yeoman, Rolvenden, Kent, 1675 CKS PRC2/36/256
Younge, Thomas, Woodhurst, Hunts, 1684 Hunts RO/Acc58/236(232)
Younge, William, bachelor, St Pauls Walden, Herts, 1565 Herts RO ASA25/610
Younge, William, Wisborough Green, Sussex, 1632 W. Suss RO EpI/33/1632/5
Younge, William, Wisborough Green (Burchett), Sussex, 1634 W. Suss RO EpI/33/1633/19
Younger, John, Braceborough, Lincs, 1639 Lincs RO Ad/Ac/26/13
Younglove, Richard, Lincoln St Mary le Wigford, Lincs, 1598 Lincs RO Ad/Ac/4/138
Youngman, Thomas, brewer: 'beerbrewer', Dover, Kent, 1681 CKS PRC20/13/218
Yowle, Daniell, Edenham (Elsthorpe), Lincs, 1606 Lincs RO Ad/Ac/6/3
Yule, William, Yaxley, Hunts, 1676 Hunts RO/Acc58/66(138)
Zellacke, John, Tolland, Som, 1588 Somerset RO D/D/Cta/Z1
Zouch, Blanch, widow, Spelsbury (Fulwell), Oxon, 1636 Oxon RO MSS Wills 173/3/43

NO SURNAME

Henry, Frankley, Worcs, 1606 Worcs RO 008.7 BA3585/839/406
Joan, Stogursey, Som, Somerset RO D/D/Cta/S5
John, Llanfeigan, Breck, 1636 NLW BR 1636/81 Ac
John, Burgh, Lincs, 1649 Lincs RO Ad/Ac/30/407
Joseph, Wrington, Som, 1737 Somerset RO D/D/Cta/H87
Parnell, widow, Elmbridge, Worcs, 1608 Worcs RO 008.7 BA3585/839/458
Roger, Brockley, Som, 1587 Somerset RO D/D/Cta/C28
Thomas, Seend, Wilts, 1616 Wilts RO Unlisted Fragment
Thomas, All Hallows Staining, London & Middlesex, 1666 Greater London RO DL/C/(Ac 73.77 pt)/Box 85/5 (uncatalogued)
Wilkinson, Sibson, Leics, 1666 Leics RO Administrators Accounts C17th f55
William, Ulceby, Lincs, 1579 Lincs RO Ad/Ac/2b/71

NO SURNAME OR CHRISTIAN NAME

Arreton, Hants, Hants RO 21m65 D8/362a
Aswarby, Lincs, 1569 Lincs RO Ad/Ac/1/31
Bere Regis, Dors, Wilts RO Unlisted Fragment

[NO SURNAME:]
Carlton, Little, Lincs, 1648 Lincs RO Ad/Ac/30/405
Clydock, Wales, NLW BR 1622/123 Ac
Gainsborough, Lincs, 1628 Lincs RO Ad/Ac/39/50
Grimsby, Great, Lincs, 1665 Lincs RO Ad/Ac/43/172
Shepton Mallet, Som, 1712 Somerset RO D/D/Cta/A11
Stoke Prior, Worcs, 1603 Worcs RO 008.7 BA3585/834/441
Warminster, Wilts, 1614 Wilts RO Unlisted Fragment
Warminster, Wilts, 1642 Wilts RO Unlisted Fragment
Wimborne Minster, Dors, 1662 Dorset RO PE/WM CP 2/4/102

Status and Occupations

Status and occupations of which more than 300 accounts survive have not been indexed individually

Places

BEDFORDSHIRE

BERKSHIRE

BERWICKSHIRE

BUCKINGHAMSHIRE

CAMBRIDGESHIRE

CHESHIRE

CORNWALL

CUMBERLAND

DERBYSHIRE

DEVONSHIRE

DORSET

DURHAM

ESSEX

GLOUCESTERSHIRE

HAMPSHIRE

HEREFORDSHIRE

HERTFORDSHIRE

HUNTINGDONSHIRE

KENT

LANCASHIRE

LEICESTERSHIRE

LINCOLNSHIRE

LONDON & MIDDLESEX

NORFOLK

NORTHAMPTONSHIRE

NORTHUMBERLAND

Berwickshire is treated as a separate county

NOTTINGHAMSHIRE

OXFORDSHIRE

RUTLAND

SHROPSHIRE

SOMERSET

STAFFORDSHIRE

SUFFOLK

WARWICKSHIRE

WESTMORLAND

WILTSHIRE

WORCESTERSHIRE

YORKSHIRE

SHIPS

THE INDEX LIBRARY

PROBATE ACCOUNTS OF ENGLAND AND WALES A–J

Issued by
THE BRITISH RECORD SOCIETY

[112]

THE INDEX LIBRARY

INDEX

TO THE

PROBATE ACCOUNTS

OF

ENGLAND AND WALES

A–J

Edited by

Peter Spufford

with the assistance of

Matthew Brett and Amy Louise Erickson

Compiled by

Jacqueline Bower, Matthew Brett

and Nesta Evans

With an Introductory Essay by

Jacqueline Bower

LONDON :

Issued to Subscribers by

THE BRITISH RECORD SOCIETY LIMITED

1999

Published by The British Record Society Limited
c/o Patric Dickinson
The College of Arms
Queen Victoria Street
London EC4V 4BT

ISBN Part I 0 901505 38 2
ISBN Part II 0 901505 39 0
ISBN for the set 0 901505 40 4

Printed in Great Britain by
Progressive Printing (UK) Limited, Leigh-on-Sea, Essex

CONTENTS

Volume I

Figure

Tables

Preface

by Peter Spufford

The preparation of these volumes has taken well over a decade, and in the course of it I have incurred innumerable debts of gratitude.

I would firstly like to thank Dr Rosemary Rodd and Dr John Dawson of the Centre for Literary and Linguistic Computing in the Computing Service of the University of Cambridge for making the whole project possible. Without their continued and unfailing assistance and instruction over so many years this volume and the underlying database would not exist. The principal file of the database now extends to over eight megabytes, which gives some idea not only of its own enormous size, but of the enormous scale of the help they have given.

I would secondly like to thank all the archivists who have gone to so much trouble looking after me and my various assistants as we made often very prolonged visits to their Record Offices. Without their co-operation the project would also have been impossible. The Record Offices and the numbers of documents that we abstracted in each are listed in an Appendix.[1]

I would thirdly like to thank my research assistants and associates. Earliest of all there was Dr Amy Louise Erickson, who helped me set up the parameters for abstracting the documents in the first place. Next there was Dr Jacqueline Bower, who undertook the work of abstracting the largest single group of probate accounts surviving in any one place, those of the diocese of Canterbury now preserved at Maidstone. She went on to abstract some of those in London repositories. Finally she has brought the considerable expertise that she developed with probate accounts to bear in producing the splendidly useful introduction to this volume. Next came Mr Matthew Brett, who first tackled the second largest group of probate accounts in the country, those at Lincoln, and then went on to abstract the remainder of those that were looked at in detail from London archives. He also abstracted smaller groups from the National Library of Wales at Aberystwyth, and from record offices at Bristol, Chester, Exeter, Gloucester, Trowbridge, Truro, and Winchester, and from the Borthwick Institute in York, as well as part of those for Lancashire at Preston (it was unfortunate that the documents could not be produced sufficiently quickly for him to index and abstract them all in the time

1 Pp.xcv-c.

available). I was fortunate that the experienced and knowledgeable Mrs Nesta Evans, herself now General Editor of the British Record Society, was free to work her way round the rest of the country, making flying visits to Bury St Edmunds, Cambridge, Chichester, Hertford, Worcester, Huntingdon, Dorchester, Taunton, Ipswich, Northampton, Aylesbury, Norwich and Reading. The initial listing of the probate accounts at Lichfield, which is incorporated in this volume, was made by Dr Nat Alcock of the University of Warwick in conjunction with another Leverhulme Trust funded project. Mrs Evans has since been able to begin to follow up this with a fuller abstraction. These various assistants abstracted the information in the probate accounts under some thirty-six headings with the aid of lap-top computers and sent the information on disc to Cambridge where they were combined into a database on the Cambridge University's large mainframe Phoenix computer. On the demise of Phoenix, the database was transferred to the University's Unix system. I owe many thanks to Mr Brett for organising the printing out of this index from the database. Mr Brett also assisted me in using the information in the probate accounts for a study of rural debt and credit in early modern England, and Dr Bower in using it for her study of Kentish yeomen. Without their assistance I could never have undertaken this work.

The fourth essential group of partners in this enterprise were the funding bodies which paid for the research assistance, for travel to record offices and for accommodation whilst in distant places. I would like to express my warm thanks to the Economic and Social Research Council for two consecutive grants (nos.R 000 23 1749 and R 000 23 3710) from 1990 to 1991 and from 1992 to 1993, and to the Leverhulme Trust for the final stages of the operation, and for moving the project on to the use of the accounts for the light they shed on rural debt and on the lives of early modern yeomen.

I came to probate accounts quite by chance. In 1960 I became the Honorary Secretary of the British Record Society, which for over half of its lifetime has been concentrating on publishing indexes to probate records. Amongst the papers that I inherited were the notes taken by the Revd. Isham Longdon from the 165 probate accounts surviving at Northampton. I was fascinated by them, but thought that they were a peculiar Northamptonshire idiosyncrancy. I felt that were probably a unique survival, until in 1969 I met Professor David Pratt, then a young lecturer in genealogy from the Brigham Young University at Provo, who had stumbled on another equally small group in

Leicester.[2] He too had found them fascinating, but had also not known what to use them for. Over succeeding years I heard hints of more, from other people working on probate records, and, of course, also from the direction my wife's researches were taking. By the mid-1980s my wife and I were aware that small groups existed in quite a number of places. She herself had used some of them for her study of petty chapmen.[3] Mrs Clare Gittings had also recently largely based her remarkable book on the development of early modern English funeral customs on accounts surviving in the diocese of Canterbury.[4] Dr Paul Slack, Dr Barbara Todd and Mr David Vaisey had all used very small numbers of them in their work, respectively on plague, widows and retailers,[5] and Dr Holderness had also looked at a small group of Lincolnshire accounts for evidence of loans.[6] Amy Louise Erickson was finding them extraordinarily useful for her thesis on the management of property by seventeenth century English women, since the widow was usually the executrix or administratrix. They proved invaluable in demonstrating the financial and managerial competence of widows in the years immediately after their husbands' deaths. Dr Erickson was able to use accounts from seven different courts in her thesis, including my original Northamptonshire batch.[7]

By this time I was no longer the Honorary Secretary, but the General Editor of the British Record Society's *Index Library,* and it struck me that they were a suitable source for a slim index volume although I had no idea how many there were. I consequently wrote to all the record offices in England. The archivists replies revealed that

2 David Pratt has since become one of the leading authorities in North America on English probate records. He is now in the process of publishing a multi-volume reference work, *Researching British Probates* (Wilmington, Delaware, 1995, continuing).

3 Margaret Spufford, *The great reclothing of rural England. Petty chapmen and their wares in the seventeenth century* (London, 1984). She printed two accounts in her documentary appendix, pp.231-5

4 Clare Gittings, *Death burial and the individual in early modern England* (London, 1984).

5 Paul Slack, *The Impact of Plague in Tudor and Stuart England* (London, 1985); Barbara Todd, 'Widowhood in a market town: Abingdon 1540-1720', Oxford D.Phil., 1983; and David Vaisey, 'Probate inventories and provincial retailers in the seventeenth century' in Philip Riden (ed.), *Probate records and the local community* (Gloucester, 1985).

6 B.A.Holderness, 'Widows in pre-industrial society: an essay upon their economic Functions', in Richard M. Smith (ed.), *Land, Kinship and Life-Cycle* (Cambridge, 1984).

7 Amy Louise Erickson, 'The property ownership and financial decisions of ordinary women in early modern England' (University of Cambridge, Ph.D., 1990). Revised as, *Women and Property in Early Modern England* (London, 1993).

many of them knew of odd accounts in their offices, but had also thought that they were idiosyncratic, although not necessarily unique. My inquiries have made archivists 'probate account conscious', and from time to time archivists still write to me to say 'I told you that we had none, but a few have now turned up'. As the work has progressed, we have constantly had to revise our estimates of the number that have survived. Even now we can only guess at the number in the Public Record Office, which proved very much greater than we had thought. Accounts passed in the Prerogative Court of Canterbury also turned out on average to be three times as long as those passed in provincial courts. As a result we were not able to include more than a small number of them in this index, because of the limits on the available funding.

Not only have archivists become probate account conscious, but so have more early modern historians. As well as the people who had begun to use probate accounts before we embarked on this project, and the people involved in it themselves, we are aware that Dr Ralph Houlbrooke has been using them for his work on death and the seventeenth century family. Dr Margaret Pelling, Dr David Ormrod, and Dr Michael Zell used our database of abstracts from the east Kent probate accounts for their own work on medical practitioners, the economy of Kent and on clothiers respectively. Dr Nat Alcock and Ann Tarver have been working on the social structure of the west Midlands in the seventeenth century using the probate accounts at Lichfield amongst other sources. Sarah Pennell has been working on food and cooking in seventeenth and eighteenth century England. My wife has a group of people using them to work on clothing below the level of the gentry in seventeenth century England. Professor Mark Overton also has a group of people using Kent probate accounts, and Mr Anthony Poole is using them to fill out his long standing work on Cranbrook and adjacent parishes.

These volumes of index are not the first fruits of this work. We have already distributed to local record offices indexes to their own holdings of probate accounts, arranged by the name, status or occupation and place of residence of the deceased persons whose moveable goods were being accounted for. These have already proved useful for historians working on particular families, places, occupations and other topics. The Berkshire Record Society has used it as the basis for an edition of the *Berkshire Probate Accounts*. This will be the first considerable group of probate accounts ever to be published in full.

We ourselves have meanwhile used them in a number of publications. As well as revising her thesis for the press, Dr Erickson also produced a lucid introduction to the use of probate accounts for the benefit of other economic and social historians of early modern England. She outlined their potentialities in a way which has proved very effective in drawing attention to their value.[8]

I have tried to make foreign scholars aware of probate accounts by using them as a basis for lectures abroad, for example in Canada and New Zealand. I have also used them for a sequence of published conference papers on long term rural credit in Genoa,[9] Lyons[10] and Florence.[11] I am currently preparing a longer paper on rural credit which I hope to submit to the *Economic History Review* in the not too distant future.

Dr Bower, meanwhile has tried to make English scholars aware of probate accounts by using them as a basis for lectures in this country, for example at the one day conference on 'Wills and other Probate Records' in the Public Record Office in 1998. With the same end in view, she has contributed a 'short guide' to probate accounts to *History*,[12] written on them briefly for the *Local Historian*, and at greater length on their value as sources for the history of her native county, Kent.[13] She has also used them for her own research on yeomen.[14] I am delighted that she has been able to provide an extensive introduction to this volume. The purpose of her introduction is further to raise historians' awareness of probate accounts, by discussing their nature and uses at greater length, by beginning the task of analysis, and

8 Amy Louise Erickson, 'An Introduction to Probate Accounts' in G.H.Martin and Peter Spufford (eds.), *The Records of the Nation* (Woodbridge, 1990), pp.273-86. A revised version of this essay will appear as 'Using Probate Accounts'in Nesta Evans and Tom Arkell, *When Death us do Part* (Local Population Studies Supplement, 1999).

9 'Credit in Rural England before the Advent of Country Banks', in *Banchi pubblici, banchi privati e monti di pietá nell'Europa preindustriale*, Atti della Societá ligure di Storia Patria, n.s. xxxi (1991), pp.895-911.

10 'Les liens du credit au village dans l'Angleterre du XVIIe siècle', *Annales, Histoire, Sciences Sociales*, November-December 1994, vi, 1359-73. An abbreviated and revised translation of this is to appear as 'Long term rural credit in sixteenth- and seventeenth-century England the evidence of Probate Accounts', in Nesta Evans and Tom Arkell, *When Death us do Part* (Local Population Studies Supplement, 1999).

11 'Death as evidence for life' (not yet published, 1999)

12 Short Guide no.34, reprinted in K.M.Thompson (ed.), *Short Guides to Records, Second Series*, Historical Association, London, 1997, pp. 55-8.

13 Jacqueline Bower, 'Probate Accounts as a source for Early Modern Kent Economic and Social History', *Archaeologia Cantiana*, cix, 1991.

14 Jacqueline Bower, 'The Kent yeoman in the seventeenth century', *Archaeologia Cantiana*, cxiv, 1994, pp.149-63.

by attempting to indicate some of the directions future work with probate accounts might take. The whole purpose of the volume, as with all index volumes, is to make sources accessible. I trust that her introduction will aid that endeavour.

March 1999 Queens' College, Cambridge.

Introduction to Probate Accounts

by Jacqueline Bower

THE SURVIVAL OF PROBATE ACCOUNTS

Nicholas Bowden, a miller of Milton next Sittingbourne in Kent, was owed money by a number of London bakers. He was murdered while on a voyage from London to Milton in 1624 and his body thrown overboard.[1]

Thomas Hammon, a young boy of Maidstone who lost his family in an outbreak of plague in 1603, was provided with a new outfit when the infection had ceased. He was bought two and a half yards of fustian for breeches at 3s 4d, half an ell of canvas to line his doublet, two and three quarter ells of cloth at 1s 8d for a shirt, a pair of shoes for one shilling, three quarters of a yard of broadcloth at 6s 6d and two dozen buttons and a skein of silk at 10d to make a jerkin. Spinning the wool and knitting two pairs of stockings cost 2s 4d; the total cost of his outfit was 15s 8d.[2]

Catherine Symons of St Peter in Sandwich died in 1670 of stomach cancer, diagnosed as such by several physicians. She spent the last months of her life boarding at the house of John Browne in Sandwich, during which time 'she [had] such great extremity of paine by reason of her ... distemper that none would endure the roome but upon great necessity.'[3]

When Richard Estman of Canterbury died in the 1590s, he was leaseholder of a row of houses and shops evidently in need of extensive repairs. Among the materials purchased by his administrator John Illesley to do his part towards the Great Rebuilding were 3000 tiles costing 33s, 1200 bricks at 14s and several loads of sand, lime and stones. Illesley also paid wages to a pavior, carpenter and plasterer.[4]

All the episodes quoted above are taken from probate accounts surviving in the diocese of Canterbury and held at the Centre for Kentish Studies in Maidstone. Until recently, few historians have been aware of the existence of probate or administrators' accounts, although probate inventories have been extensively used by social and economic historians for the last fifty years. One reason probate accounts have been less well known is that they do not survive in such large numbers

1 Maidstone, Centre for Kentish Studies, henceforward CKS, PRC20/6/102
2 CKS PRC21/16/21; PRC21/16/370; PRC21/17/21; PRC21/17/120; PRC21/17/130
3 CKS PRC2/36/123
4 CKS PRC2/11/43

as probate inventories and their survival is unevenly spread throughout the country. In some regions, such as the diocese of Canterbury and Lincolnshire, accounts survive in large numbers; in others, especially in the north of England, few if any accounts survive. In addition, in some places, even where accounts do survive, there have been no adequate lists or calendars to guide potential users. Most surviving accounts are now in County Record Offices, but until recently few offices have even had indexes to their own holdings. An estimate of the number of surviving probate accounts is to be found in the Appendix.[5] It is arranged by record office, and within each record office, by the ecclesiastical court to which the account was rendered. Since the jurisdiction of some courts, such as the Consistory Court of the Bishop of Lichfield, extended into several counties, this list does not reveal the frequency of survival of accounts in the different counties of England and Wales. Table 1 shows the distribution of the surviving accounts rearranged according to the counties in which the deceased had property. For comparison the number of 'houses' in each county has been added from the estimates published by John Houghton in 1693. It has been suggested that these may have been derived from the Hearth Tax Returns of 1685.[6] These estimates of 'houses' give some indication of the relative frequency of the survival of probate accounts in proportion to the late seventeenth century population of the different counties.

It has not been possible to include all surviving accounts in the index. In some collections, probate accounts survive among thousands of other probate documents which have not been individually listed or indexed. It has not been possible to search through these collections to identify the probate accounts surviving among them. This has been the case with the Prerogative Court of Canterbury accounts held at the Public Record Office and with the accounts at Durham, Norwich and the City of London Guildhall Record Office. It is hoped that these record offices will at some time be able to index their probate collections as a whole, so that the probate accounts among them may be identified. In addition, among some of the collections which have been indexed, some accounts have had to be omitted because they are too fragile to be handled, including some at Lincoln, Taunton and

5 Pp.xcv-c.

6 John Houghton, *An Account of the Acres and Houses, with the Proportional Tax, &c. of each county in England and Wales* (broadsheet, London, 1693); also in John Houghton, *A Collection for the Improvement of Husbandry and Trade*, xxvi, 3 (February 1693). Republished and discussed in 'Note on the number of houses in England and Wales, 1690' as an appendix to D.V.Glass, 'Two papers on Gregory King', in D.V.Glass and E.C.Eversley (eds.), *Population in History* (London, 1965), pp.216-20.

1. Number of accounts abstracted,
arranged by county or equivalent heading
(The number of 'houses' in the mid-1680s has been added on the right)

Bedfordshire	16	12,170
Berkshire	1,765	16,906
Buckinghamshire	74	18,390
Cambridgeshire and the Isle of Ely	225	17,347
Cheshire	275	24,054
Cornwall	396	25,374
Cumberland	4	14,825
Derbyshire	367	21,155
Devon	11	56,310
Dorset	206	21,944
Durham, Northumberland and Berwick[7]	7	38,725
Essex	15	34,819
Gloucestershire	282	26,764
Hampshire	449	26,851
Herefordshire	5	15,006
Hertfordshire	519	16,569
Huntingdonshire	354	8,217
Kent	13,601	39,242
Lancashire	278	40,202
Leicestershire	379	18,702
Lincolnshire	5,989	40,590
London, Middlesex and Westminster	584	100,136
Norfolk	209	47,180
Northamptonshire	205	24,808
Nottinghamshire	37	17,554
Oxfordshire	925	19,007
Rutland	2	3,263
Shropshire	209	23,284
Somerset	929	49,808
Staffordshire	479	23,747
Suffolk	46	34,422
Surrey	51	34,218
Sussex	1,221	21,537
Warwickshire	432	21,973
Westmorland	0	6,501
Wiltshire	1,453	27,093
Worcestershire	536	20,634
Yorkshire	488	106,151

7 This is Houghton's heading - of the probate accounts abstracted 2 came from County Durham, 4 from Northumberland and 1 from Berwick upon Tweed.

Wales		25		60,473
	Anglesey		1	
	Brecknock		15	
	Caernarvon		4	
	Denbigh		1	
	Montgomery		1	
	Pembroke		1	
	Radnor		2	
Ireland		2		
	Cork		1	
	'Ireland'		1	
Overseas[8]		13		
	Barbados		3	
	France		1	
	Guinea		1	
	Jamaica		3	
	Persia		3	
	Switzerland		1	
	Tangier		1	

Bristol. In some collections, accounts seem only to have been preserved when there was some dispute surrounding the administration of the estate. This is the case with many of the accounts so far identified in the Prerogative Court of Canterbury. In classes PROB 5 and PROB 32 at the Public Record Office, accounts are preserved with inventories and cause papers. The accounts at Cambridge, Dorchester, Hertford, Huntingdon, Northampton, Oxford, Taunton and Worcester survive as loose papers. At Worcester, the accounts are mixed with other documents, chiefly administrations. At Hertford, the accounts are mixed with inventories. At Dorchester, nearly all the surviving accounts are from the Peculiar of Wimborne. This pattern of survival gives the impression that, except in cases of dispute, the survival of these accounts was random, a matter of chance rather than a conscious decision on someone's part. The result of this uneven survival is that in most counties existing accounts form only a small proportion of the possible total. These smaller collections of accounts are invaluable for anyone wishing to study the history of a particular family or locality, when that family or locality is represented among the accounts. However, they are not sufficient for a study of wealth and society over a wide area or a long period of time.

8 The British colonies in North America had their own probate jurisdictions and their probate accounts are preserved there. See below pp.xxiv-xxv.

The accounts surviving in the diocese of Canterbury are different. 13,565 accounts have been preserved in the Archdeaconry and Consistory Courts of Canterbury. The sequence begins in 1569 and ends in 1740, with just over half the accounts falling in the period 1592-1641. Keeping these accounts was evidently a conscious policy of the Canterbury authorities, for they were not preserved among inventories or other material, but bound up nearly contemporaneously in volumes, each volume normally covering two years in roughly alphabetical order of the names of the deceased, and nearly all containing only accounts. Nevertheless we suspect that, even in the diocese of Canterbury, far from all the accounts were preserved. Because of the scale of the surviving collection of probate accounts in east Kent, much of this introduction will be based on Kent examples. However, we are aware that there were strong regional differences in early modern England and that what was true of Kent was not necessarily true of Yorkshire or Somerset.

In England in the later middle ages the courts, when they made grants of probate or letters of administration, required that the executor (or administrator) should return to report how he, or, more commonly, she, had carried out the responsibility of handling the goods of the deceased. Michael Sheehan suggested that this obligation evolved in the third quarter of the thirteenth century. He pointed out that Archbishop Boniface's Lambeth Statutes of 1261 only said that accounts were to be rendered if demanded, but that later statutes all took the presentation of accounts as the regular final stage of the execution of wills.[9] After the Probate Act of 1530, the courts exacted a bond, with a substantial financial penalty, which would be forfeit if the administration was not carried out properly.[10] This demanded keeping a scrupulous record of all payments and 'casting an account' to bring back into the court.

Accounts therefore once existed as commonly as inventories, with duplicate copies in the hands of the courts and of the accountants who had rendered them. At least in the second half of the sixteenth century, and the first half of the seventeenth, one of these copies had been formally, and expensively, inscribed on parchment. It is not surprising that the accountants' copies have disappeared, like private

9 Michael M. Sheehan, *The Will in Medieval England* (Pontifical Institute of Medieval Studies, Toronto, 1963), p.218

10 21 Henry VIII c.5, *Statutes of the Realm*, iii (1817), 285-8. The later interpretation of Richard Burn in his *Ecclesiastical Law* (London, 1760), suggests that in the province of York both executors and administrators had to subscribe to a written bond, but that in the province of Canterbury executors merely had to take an oath, orally, that they would present an account.

copies of wills, inventories and letters of administration.[11] What is much more surprising is that so few of the court copies have survived, unlike wills and inventories. Like inventories, and unlike wills, they never seem to have been copied into formal registers, but kept as loose documents. The Canterbury 'registers' are loose paper copies bound up together. The only truly 'registered' accounts are a handful of copies of very early probate accounts entered, like copies of wills and other probate documents, into undifferentiated episcopal registers in the period before separate registers were kept for particular purposes.[12]

The earliest surviving loose accounts we have discovered are two accounts from the Archdeaconry Court of Sudbury from 1521 and 1522, and one from the Consistory Court of Lincoln from 1524.[13] No other loose accounts, to our knowledge, survive from before the Probate act of 1530. The hundreds of thousands of fifteenth century accounts, like the hundreds of thousands of fifteenth century wills, have vanished virtually without trace.[14] The next earliest is an Oxfordaccount of 1547. Only isolated documents have been found to survive from before the reign of Queen Elizabeth I. We have only seen nineteen survivors from the period 1555-60, and only 57 from 1561-70.

In the diocese of Canterbury the probate accounts which were drawn up before the late 1560s, were not preserved by the courts once the estate had been wound up. Had the administration not lasted so long, we would not have the account for the moveables of Edward Crayforde of Great Mongeham who died in 1558, leaving three young daughters. His administrator began to keep an account from the time of Crayforde's death, but this account was not presented to the court until 1569, when all the daughters had come of age. It is now the fourth account in the first surviving volume of the Archdeaconry Court

11 We have, however, yet to see a probate account from a collection of family papers to illustrate our supposition about the retention of sealed, parchment, copies by accountants.

12 The account-cum-inventory of 1293 printed by Sheehan, *The Will*, in his documentary appendix, pp.321-2, comes from such an indifferentiated episcopal register.

13 Margaret Baxster of Hundon, Suffolk and Richard Pytches of Kirtling, Cambs., Bury St.Edmunds, Suffolk Record Office IC500/2/14/35 and 135; and William Irchenett of Lincoln, Lincolnshire Record Office Ad/Ac/1.

14 The erratically surviving fifteenth century court books of the bishops of Hereford provide a tantalising glimpse of what once existed. M.A.Faraday and E.J.L.Cole in their Calendar of Probate and Administration Acts 1407-1541 (British Record Society, 1989), gave information about nearly twelve thousand probate and administration acts from a relatively sparsely inhabited diocese. Furthermore court books only survive for thirty years of the fifteenth century, and not even all these books are complete. With each of these grants of probate and administration the making of an account was required, except for those 'dimissus in forma pauperis' or 'dimissus quia habuit nichil de bonis'.

of Canterbury accounts.[15]

Some patterns of survival can be seen in Figure 1, overleaf, which shows the numbers surviving each year, and abstracted by us, from 1521 to the ending of the ecclesiastical probate jurisdictions in 1858. The numbers of survivors only begin to increase from the late 1570s. We have seen over a hundred survivors from each year after 1585, and two hundred survivors from each year after 1592. The increase in the number of surviving accounts from the late 1570s to the early seventeenth century parallels the increase in the number of other probate documents, but following a generation later than wills, and on a very much smaller scale.[16]

The abolition of ecclesiastical jurisdictions meant that during the Commonwealth there were neither wills proved nor accounts rendered outside the central probate court. Similarly the success of the revival in ecclesiastical probate jurisdictions after the Restoration is reflected in the numbers of surviving wills and accounts from the 1660s and 1670s.

Acts of 1671 and 1685

The requirements evolved in the third quarter of the thirteenth century were considerably eroded in the third quarter of the seventeenth. The primary requirement of the courts was that they should examine and allow the accounts. Until 1671 the courts then made *ad hoc* arrangements for a distribution of the residual assets if any. After 1671, distribution had to follow a formula laid down by the 'Act for the Better Settling of Intestates' Estates'.[17] This act nevertheless maintained the established principle that an administrator 'shall and may' be called to account, and therefore had little effect on the pattern of survival of accounts. In 1685 a general Act, misleadingly called 'for the Reviveing and Continuance of severall Acts of Parlyament',[18] far from merely extending their validity quite considerably modified a number of acts, including the Intestates' Estates Act of 1671.[19] There is a possibility that the legislation of 1685 may have been in response to judicial interpretation of the Act of

15 CKS PRC2/1/4

16 Motoyasu Takahashi, 'The Number of Wills proved in the Sixteenth and Seventeenth Centuries', in G.H. Martin and Peter Spufford (eds.), *The Records of the Nation* (London, 1990), pp. 187-213, demonstrates that it is from the 1540s that we begin to have an adequate proportion available to us, either as originals, or as registered copies, of the wills that were made. He has a revised version of this paper in preparation.

17 22 & 23 Car.II c.10

18 1 Jac.II c.17

19 See Erickson, 'An Introduction', pp.280-1 for a discussion of what lay behind these acts.

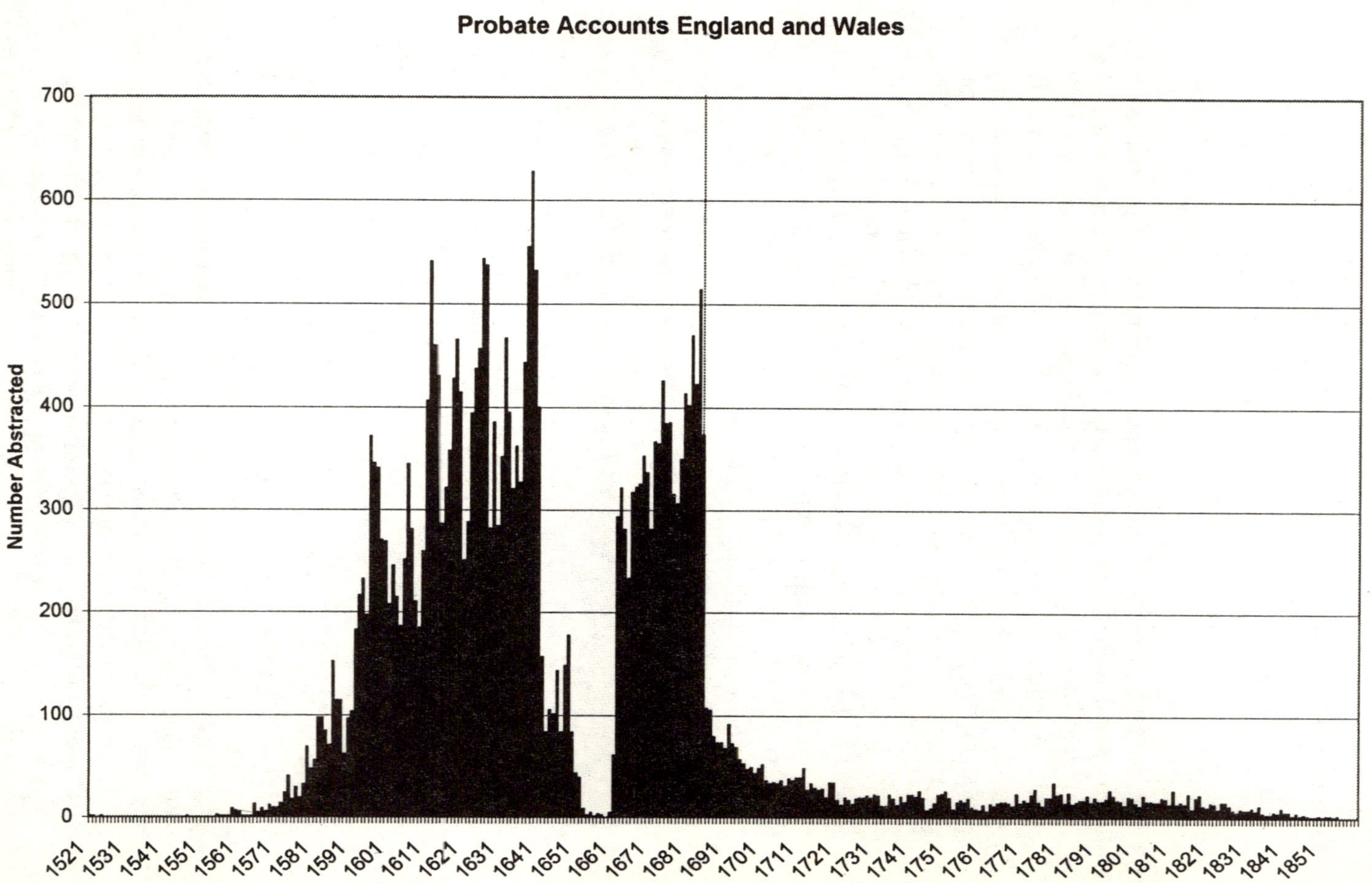
Probate Accounts England and Wales
Number Abstracted
0
100
200
300
400
500
600
700
1521
1531
1541
1551
1561
1571
1581
1591
1601
1611
1621
1631
1641
1651
1661
1671
1681
1691
1701
1711
1721
1731
1741
1751
1761
1771
1781
1791
1801
1811
1821
1831
1841
1851

1671.[20] From 24 July 1685 onwards administrators no longer needed to render account to the courts of the moveable goods they were administering, unless there was a request on behalf of a minor, from the next of kin, or from a creditor of the deceased.[21] They were still required, however, to produce an inventory of moveables before being allowed to administer them. The dotted line on Figure 1 is to indicate the passing of this Act.

The number of surviving accounts falls sharply from 1685. From the early 1680s, the years immediately before the legislation, an annual average of over 450 accounts have survived in all parts of the country. Of these around 150 were from the diocese of Canterbury. We have seen 514 surviving accounts which were exhibited in 1684, but only 373 accounts survive from 1685 itself, which suggests that in the latter part of the year many administrators were already aware that they no longer needed to render accounts. From 1685 onwards the numbers surviving drop continuously. We have seen only 107 from 1686, and never over a hundred from any year after 1687. From the late 1680s an average of only 75 accounts a year have survived from the whole country, and of these about a half come from Canterbury. By the first decade of the eighteenth century the annual rate of survival in the whole country was below forty. Although fourteen jurisdictions preserved accounts into the nineteenth century, fewer than a thousand accounts survive from the period after 1720, less than three per cent of the total. The last surviving account dates from 1855. From only two years in that period, 1735 and 1779, did more than twenty accounts survive. As a consequence there is not a large corpus of account material for use in work on eighteenth century problems in England and Wales.

Accounts even from before 1685 are now extraordinarily rare compared with wills, administrations and even inventories. Forty five to fifty thousand accounts amongst four or five million probate records is a very tiny proportion. That so many fewer accounts have survived than inventories is at first sight surprising, since, up to 1685, they were of equal, if not greater, legal importance and equally numerous. At the end of the sixteenth century Henry Swinburne had emphasised the

20 Several Gloucestershire accounts of 1685 say that the distribution was to follow Act of Parliament *as interpreted by judges*. Three of these were dated 22 April, 20 May, 18 July *before the 1685 Act came into force*, one on 24 July itself, and one a month later on 29 August. Gloucestershire Record Office GDR/B4/2/P112, B186, B185, P113, and R73.

21 Anne Tarver tells us that the Lichfield evidence (the accounts she has seen there are with cause papers) suggests that whenever there was insufficient money to pay legacies to children when they came of age, a detailed account of the costs of their upbringing had to be produced as an explanation.

subordination of inventories to accounts: 'If executors were not accountable the use of inventaris were to little purpose'.[22] It would therefore have been more logical to throw away the inventories, once the accounts had been passed. and to retain the accounts in perpetuity, but the reverse is what has generally happened. The necessity of continuing to present inventories after 1685, but not accounts, presumably meant that eighteenth century guardians of ecclesiastical court records continued to be familiar with inventories as current legal documents, but no longer routinely encountered accounts, and so disregarded and eventually destroyed them. For no apparent reason, a disproportionate number of accounts for administrators rather than executors have been retained.[23] However the survival of any particular account can sometimes seem a result of chance.[24] It is fairly clear that many of those post-1685 accounts that have survived were related to estates about which there was some dispute. Many of the Prerogative Court of Canterbury accounts which we have seen fall into this category. Some late accounts are filed with cause papers, for example many of those of the York courts in the Borthwick Institute.

Probate Accounts in the American Colonies

The legislation of 1685 had no effect in the American Colonies, where by contrast, probate accounts continued to be drawn up as a matter of course until the end of the traditional probate jurisdictions at the end of the eighteenth century.[25] In Maryland probate jurisdiction was transferred from the colony's prerogative court to county orphans' courts in 1777. The large numbers of detailed accounts preserved there have already been widely and fruitfully exploited by historians of seventeenth and eighteenth century British North America. One of the key differences between the colonies and England was that land could be left in the colonies by will as well as moveables. Land was therefore

22 Henry Swinburne, *Briefe Treatise of Testaments and last Willes* (first edition, London, 1590), Part VI, chapter xvii.

23 Of the thirty three thousand accounts we have examined, only 16% were definitely related to the estates of those who left wills, whilst 49% were definitely related to the estates of intestates. These are only minimal figures since we could not tell which was the case for 35% of them. The disproportionate survival of administrators' accounts nevertheless becomes apparent, since probates of wills were generally twice as numerous as letters of administration.

24 Erickson, 'An Introduction' cites examples. At York, for instance, over half of the 58 accounts extant from before the Civil War are for the estates of individuals whose surnames began with the letter 'S'.

25 We are much indebted to Dr Trevor Burnard of the University of Canterbury, Christchurch, New Zealand, for drawing our attention to the literatuire on probate accounts in the American colonies.

included in probate inventories and in probate accounts, so that probate records give a much more rounded picture of wealth in the American colonies than in the mother country.

The best example of the way American scholars have exploited probate accounts is in their treatment of the account of Robert and Rebecca Cole, tobacco planters of St Clements Bay in Maryland, who, when they died in 1662, left six minor children aged from thirteen down to three. In 1673 Luke Gardiner, the sole surviving executor of Robert Cole's will, presented an exceptionally detailed thirty page account to the Maryland Prerogative Court. It is the basis of the most extended study of any probate account that we know.[26]

From a period a century later, Alice Hanson Jones, in her three volume compilation for 1774, printed 919 probate inventories in full from twenty one counties ranging from Massachusetts to South Carolina 'chosen to represent an unbiased sample of all probate inventories in all thirteen colonies.'[27] Alongside these she printed in full twenty-five related probate accounts presented by executors or administrators (she calls them estate accounts), and printed abstracts of a very large number of others. Because of the time it took to wind up estates with young children, many of the accounts which began in 1774 ran on into the 1780s. When she discussed the historical implications of these documents in a separate volume, she devoted a chapter to 'Net Worth, Financial Assets and Liabilities', which relied on her probate accounts. After subtracting slaves, land formed on average 68% of the assets listed in her 1774 inventories. In other words, moveables and financial assets, which are all that appear in English inventories, formed on average only 32% of wealth. She was able to show that although financial liabilities commonly exceeded financial assets, they did not often exceed the total of moveables and financial assets, which were normally themselves under a third of individuals' gross wealth. Consequently the problem of how executors and administrators coped with negative balances at the end of their accounts does not normally plague American colonial historians.[28]

Although probate accounts survive in England, Wales and the

26 Lois Green Carr, Russell R. Menard and Lorena S.Walsh, *Robert Cole's World. Agriculture and Society in Early Maryland* (University of Carolina Press, Chapel Hill, 1991). The account itself is printed as an appendix, pp.174-207.

27 Alice Hanson Jones (ed.), *American Colonial Wealth. Documents and Methods* (New York, 1977). In her introduction she specifically discusses the accounts, which naturally only start in 1774 and consequently run on into the 1780s, pp.19-22, 31-5.

28 Alice Hanson Jones, *Wealth of a Nation to be. The American Colonies on the Eve of the Revolution* (Columbia University Press, New York, 1980). She does not, unfortunately, give any statistics for how many wills, inventories and accounts survived, or what proportion of the population was covered by them.

American colonies, they do not do so in Ireland or Scotland and it is not clear to us if there was ever a requirement to render an account in those countries.

THE PROCEDURE FOR ADMINISTRATORS AND EXECUTORS

In the sixteenth, seventeenth and eighteenth centuries, probate inventories were compiled within days of a person's death, and were supposed to list all his or her moveable assets, such as clothing, household goods and furnishings, crops, livestock and leasehold property. They also listed debts owed to the deceased. The purpose of the inventory was to provide a record of the deceased's assets to prevent dishonesty by the executor or administrator and to assist him or her in discharging the deceased's outstanding financial obligations and distributing the balance of the estate to the next of kin. After a probate inventory had been compiled, it was submitted to the appropriate ecclesiastical court, which retained a copy for its own records. These inventories, of which possibly one million survive in England and Wales, chiefly from the mid-sixteenth to the mid-eighteenth century, are mostly now in county record offices. They have been extensively used by social and economic historians for over fifty years to study wealth and standards of living in different regions during the early modern period.[29]

For the diocese of Canterbury nearly all the probate inventories that were made, some 31,000, survive from the period 1577 to 1639. We think that they are almost a complete set, because they are approximately as numerous as the entries in the probate act books of the Archdeaconry and Consistory Courts of Canterbury. We believe that this is very roughly a half of the adult men who died. This is considerably more than the 30% of adult male decedents for whom

29 For example, W.G.Hoskins, 'The Leicestershire farmer in the sixteenth century', *Transactions of the Leicestershire Archaeological Society*, xii (1945), 33-95; F.W.Steer, *Farm and cottage inventories of mid-Essex 1635-49* (Essex Record Office Publications, viii, Chelmsford, 1950); M.A.Havinden, 'Agricultural progress in open-field Oxfordshire', *Agricultural History Review*, ix (1961), 73-83; C.W.Chalklin, *Seventeenth Century Kent: A Social and Economic History* (London, 1965); Joan Thirsk (ed.), *The Agrarian History of England and Wales*, iv, 1500-1640 and v, 1640-1750 (Cambridge, 1967 and 1985); Margaret Spufford, *Contrasting Communities: English Villagers in the Sixteenth and Seventeenth Centuries* (Cambridge, 1974); Keith Wrightson and David Levine, *Poverty and Piety in an English Village, Terling 1525-1700* (New York, 1979); Lorna Weatherill, *Consumer Behaviour and Material Culture in Britain 1660-1760*, (London, 1988); David Hey, *The fiery blades of Hallamshire: Sheffield and its neighbourhood 1660-1740* (Leicester, 1991); David Levine and Keith Wrightson, *The Making of an Industrial Society: Whickham 1560-1765* (Oxford, 1991); Mark Overton *Agricultural revolution in England: the transformation of the agrarian economy 1500-1850* (Cambridge, 1996).

inventories of goods survive from the period 1660-1700 in the Vale of Berkeley in Gloucestershire. On the other hand it falls far short of the 70% of adult male decedents who had inventories made in some parts of the Chesapeake at the same period.[30]

After the probate inventory had been submitted, the court granted probate, if the deceased had left a will, or letters of administration if he had not. Published indexes suggest that, in the seventeenth century, probates of wills were approximately twice as numerous as grants of administration in both in the prerogative courts and in provincial courts.[31]

The administrator, or, more commonly, the executor, then gathered in any remaining moveable assets of the deceased and then paid as many as possible of his outstanding debts. There was a fixed order of priority for paying these, to cope with the not uncommon circumstance that there were not enough assets to meet all the liabilities. Henry Swinburne, in his *Briefe treatise of Testaments and last Willes*, explained that executors should pay the debts of the deceased according to a strict order: firstly 'debts to the Prince'; secondly recognizances 'upon statute merchant'; thirdly debts arising from court 'judgements'; fourthly obligations (on bond); fifthly debts 'due upon simple billes, or merchant bookes, or other like specialties'; and finally, if at all, those for which 'the creditor have no specialtie or writing'.[32]

The administrator also settled any expenses incurred since the deceased's death, such as the cost of the funeral, or of harvesting crops which had been sown in the deceased's lifetime. Until the estate was wound up, the administrator was also responsible for maintaining any dependents of the deceased, such as young children, or apprentices who had not yet found new masters.

A year was traditionally allowed for winding up an estate, but the process often took longer. Michael Sheehan in his work on

30 James Horn, 'Adapting to a New World: A Comparative Study of Local Society in England and Maryland 1650-1700' in Lois Green Carr et al. (eds.), *Colonial Chesapeake Society* (Chapel Hill, North Carolina, 1988), pp.133-75, and James Horn, *Adapting to a new world: English society in the seventeenth century Chesapeake* (Chapel Hill, North Carolina, 1994), pp.224-6.

31 Peter Spufford, "A Printed Catalogue of the Names of Testators", in G.H.Martin and Peter Spufford (eds.), *The Records of the Nation* (Woodbridge, 1990), pp.167-86. Documents in the process of being indexed under the aegis of English Record Collections reveal that the courts of the Archdeaconry and Consistory of Canterbury proved some 19,000 wills, and granted letters of administration for the estates of some 12,000 intestates between 1577 and 1639.

32 First edition, London, 1590, Part VI, chapter xvi. In the fourth edition, in 1677, his editor amplified all these categories, and pointed out that it was dangerous to pay debts without specialty or writing, except for servants' wages, until all other creditors had been satisfied.

medieval wills reported that the statues for the diocese of Exeter of 1287 were the earliest that he found which required accounts to be rendered within a year. It was soon realised that this was not always a reasonable time span. He noticed many examples in the registers of Archbishop Pecham (Canterbury 1279-92) in which administration lasted over several years.[33] Swinburne reminds us that by the 1590s, as in so many other things, custom had come to vary across the country according to the 'severall stiles of severall Courts'.[34] However he also said that the accountant 'ought not to be called ... before he have had sufficient time for the performance of the will which is a twelve month' and that he 'therefore may be called to a generall accompt within the year'. In the diocese of Canterbury, administrators normally took between nine months and two years to render final accounts. If an account had not been produced within two years of an inventory being exhibited, a court official known as an apparitor was sent by the court to pursue the administrator. The expenses of the apparitor would be reclaimed by the court from the estate, so it was in the administrator's interests not to delay the final settlement of the estate. During this period, the executor or administrator was supposed to keep a careful and detailed account of the money laid out from the estate. When all obligations had been discharged, and legacies paid, this account was exhibited in the court and the deceased's remaining assets, if any, distributed to his heirs.

Within the last fifteen years, historians have become increasingly aware of the limitations of probate inventories. A particular concern is that, while inventories give details of money owed to the deceased, they do not list debts owed by him, and thus often give an exaggerated idea of his wealth. Margaret Spufford has discussed the limitations of probate inventories with particular reference to her research into the financial affairs of petty chapmen and London stationers and Lincolnshire yeomen, husbandmen and labourers. She cites the example of Charles Yarwood of Macclesfield, whose probate inventory listed goods worth a total of £9226 4s 8d, but whose will showed him to be deeply in debt to Francis Dashwood of the City of London.[35] Another example is that of Henry Hougham of Graveney in Kent, who from his probate inventory appeared to be a well to do yeoman worth £875. At his death the rent he owed was £566 19s in arrears; and when this and his other debts had been paid, his estate was

33 Sheehan, *The Will*, p.218

34 In 'Of the time of the account', he tells us that it was 'left to the discretion of the Ordinarie', and therefore varied from palce to place. Swinburne, *Briefe treatise*, pt.VI cap xix.

35 Margaret Spufford, 'The limitations of the probate inventory', *English Rural Society 1500-1800*, eds. John Chartres and David Hey (Cambridge, 1990), pp.139-74.

left with a negative balance of £188 14s 11d.[36]

The deficiencies of the probate inventory can partly be compensated for by the use of probate accounts. Among other expenses, they list debts owed by the deceased, and inventory and account taken together can therefore provide a more detailed picture of an individual's wealth than the inventory alone. Accounts also contain detailed information on the day-to-day lives and business dealings of people at all levels of society from the nobility and gentry down to small craftsmen, shopkeepers and even labourers. This information is in addition to that found in wills and inventories. Yet, even putting will, inventory and account together and taking account of irrecoverable bad debts, of payments for medical care, for funeral and court expenses, the documents still do not give a snapshot of the true wealth of the individual at the time he entered his last illness, because, in England and Wales, unlike the American colonies, as we have seen, neither inventory nor account gives information on real estate.

THE FORMAT AND CONTENT OF PROBATE ACCOUNTS

Probate accounts, being legal documents, follow a set format. The format required by courts varied slightly from one jurisdiction to another. The preamble always names the administrator(s) or executor(s), that is the person or persons responsible for compiling the account.[37] Normally there was only one accountant, but occasionally there were two or even three or four.

The relationship of the accountant to the deceased was normally stated in the preamble, or can be deduced from the body of the document. For men's estates the normal accountant was the widow. Of the accounts for men's estates that we have seen, the widow was the accountant in just under 70% of cases.[38] After the widow, estates were most commonly accounted for by a son or brother of the deceased man. About 12% of accounts were exhibited by a son and about 10% by a brother, and only 8% by anyone else. These exceptional cases included a wider variety of people. In the diocese of Canterbury, the principal creditors of the deceased presented the accounts on 325 occasions, 2.4% of the total. One of the deceased's parents acted on

36 CKS PRC2/36/201

37 In the seventeenth century the use of the terms 'executor' and 'administrator' was very fluid. Accountants did not seem to know what to call themselves. In probate accounts described themselves as 'administrators' when they were the named executors of a will, or as 'executors' of the goods of intestates.

38 This proportion is almost identical with the 70% of widows who were named as executrices in seventeenth century Suffolk. Nesta Evans (ed.,), *Wills of the Archdeaconry of Sudbury 1636-1638*, Suffolk Records Society, xxxv (1993), p.viii.

225 occasions, 1.6% of the total. Where a dead man left minor children, their guardian, who was usually a relative, could also be the accountant.

Whereas the estates of men were normally accounted for by their widows, a much broader spectrum of relations accounted for the estates of women. There were no obvious accountants for their estates, since a very large proportion of them were already widows at the time of their deaths.[39] A son or a daughter acted in just under half the accounts we have seen.

It was evidently accepted that a woman was fully capable of carrying out the sometimes quite complex business of settling an estate. However, a widow sometimes renounced the right to administer her husband's estate. If the estate was heavily in debt the widow might extricate herself by renouncing the administration in favour of the principal creditor. A renunciation was also commonly made if the widow was unable to act due to age or infirmity. Susanne Oldfield renounced the administration of the account of her husband William, a yeoman of Wingham, in 1666, because she was 'very antient and helplesse.' Youth as well as age could also, occasionally, be a disadvantage. Susanna, the widow of John Kerby of Birchington, renounced her administration in 1632 because she was still under 21, and therefore counted as a minor, not legally able to act.[40]

The executor or administrator, whether woman or man, might seek assistance with the business. The estate of Richard Mills of St John's Thanet was officially administered by Mary Wastell alias Smith in 1636, but her husband 'lost two voyages to sea' while dealing with the business.[41] Marie, the widow of John Prescott, a yeoman of Guston near Dover in Kent, was named as the administrator of his estate in 1646, but she acknowledged that her father-in-law Edward had been of great help to her in the process of settling her husband's affairs.[42] Widows who were acting as executors or administrators, sometimes re-married before the account was presented, and it is occasionally apparent that the new husband had helped. Similarly when daughters and sisters acted as accountants, it is sometimes clear that the actual business was carried out by the son-in-law or brother-in-law of the deceased. In these circumstances, even if the husband went so far as to bring the accounts into court, everything was still done in the

39 See below p.xxxv.

40 Oldfield CKS PRC19/3/102; Kerby CKS PRC20/8/301.

41 Account CKS PRC2/33/93; and will CKS PRC17/69/47.

42 CKS PRC 19/2/108. Her father-in-law had perhaps already had experience of administration for an Edward Prescott had been the probate accountant for another estate in the neighbouring parish of Ewell in 1621.

wife's name.[43]

Accusations that accountants had not dealt fairly with estates, or had feathered their own nests in the process, were rare. After the death of Elizabeth Barham of Sittingbourne in Kent in 1667, Robert Barham claimed that Elizabeth's executrix Mary Jefferie had failed to pay a legacy that was due to him. John Dodson of Smarden in Kent died in 1650. His estate was not accounted for until 1675, when it was claimed that all his assets had been embezzled by his widow. Richard Lewknor of Tenterden in Kent 'spent and wasted' the estate of his mother Joan, of Tenterden, leaving the administration incomplete when he died in 1597.[44] The overall impression, however, is that the majority of administrators carried out their often onerous duties faithfully and honestly, and sometimes at considerable cost to themselves.

Requests by administrators for compensation from the deceased's estate for time and money spent on the administration are common. In 1610 the administrator of Walter Newman's estate claimed £2 to cover the cost of travelling from his home in Berkshire to Milton next Sittingbourne in Kent. The son and administrator of Henry Stephenson spent £4 travelling from Durham to Kent in 1639. Anthony Le Keux had to cross the channel to Armentières in 1614 in connection with the estate of Adam Huchon of Canterbury, perhaps a fellow Huguenot. Robert Pemble, guardian of the son of John Pemble of Ebony in Kent, claimed £80 to compensate him for five or six years spent managing the deceased's affairs in the 1640s. John Parrett, administrator of Anthony Stringer, claimed that he had lost 81 days' pay, at 2s 1d a day, from his work as a shipwright at Chatham Dockyard, while settling Stringer's estate in 1690. When the ship's captain, Benjamin Dennis, died, the owners of his ship paid for his funeral, then claimed the cost back, plus 50% interest, from his sister, who was administering the estate. The administrator of Samuel Johnston, vintner of St Martin in the Fields, London, paid bribes to butlers in various households to persuade them to buy Johnston's wines.

Sometimes there were truly tragic cases. Mary Lewis, widow and administrator of John Lewis of Poplar in Middlesex, claimed that she had had to leave her baby with a wet nurse while dealing with her husband's affairs, and that this had contributed to the death of the

43 Erickson, *Women*, p.177.

44 Barham CKS PRC1/13/7a; Dodson CKS PRC2/36/39 (possibly this was due to the breakdown of ecclesiastical administration in the 1650s, not any ill intent of the widow's); Lewknor CKS PRC2/9/150

child.[45]

Any executor or administrator forced to have dealings with any government department, but especially the Admiralty, was particularly unfortunate. Anne and Morris Rawson, sister and brother-in-law of Francis Mansell, gentleman, of St Margaret's, Westminster, had to travel from the Midlands to attend to his estate. They spent a great deal of time and money trying to recover arrears of an annuity owed to Mansell by the Treasury, to the detriment of Morris Rawson's own business, which was running a dancing school. When Henry Geary of Ospringe died he was owed £20 10s by the government for lodging sick and wounded soldiers or sailors. By the time the account of his estate was concluded in 1681, only £3 10s had been paid. In 1667 the executors of both Edward Eason and Stephen Goulding had to travel to London from Thanet to recover arrears of pay owed to the deceased men by His Majesty. The administrator of John Fitton, late of HMS Saphire, paid a shilling to the doorkeeper at the Admiralty 'to get despatch' - that is, to be attended to quickly.[46] One of Samuel Pepys' biographers believes that bribes or 'commissions' of this nature were commonplace at all levels of government at this time.[47] The fact that they were openly recorded in probate accounts, and allowed by the church courts, suggests that their payment was taken for granted.

One of the most unfortunate administrators was Jonathan Smith, executor and administrator of Isaac Murton of Sandwich in 1638.[48] At first sight Murton, a jurat and woollendraper, appears to have been a man in substantial circumstances. His estate was valued at £1523 0s 9d in his inventory. His family gave him a funeral in keeping with his status, with cakes, wine and beer served, and gloves given to the mourners, at a total cost of £15 8s 10d. Following this, however, Murton's son renounced the executorship, which passed to Murton's partner, Smith. Smith undoubtedly would not have approved the comparatively modest expenditure on Murton's funeral, for he stated repeatedly in the account that it was entered into before he took on the administration.

Murton's affairs soon proved to be in a desperate state. He

45 Newman CKS PRC 2/15/259; Stephenson CKS PRC 2/34/278; Huchon CKS PRC 20/3/174; Pemble CKS PRC 1/7/94; Stringer CKS PRC 2/38/64; Dennis, Public Record Office, henceforward PRO, PROB5/300; Johnston PRO PROB32/50/25; Lewis PRO PROB32/25/125.

46 Mansell PRO PROB32/53/121; Geary CKS PRC2/39/175; estate of Edward Eason accounted for by his widow Dorothy CKS PRC1/12/33; estate of Stephen Goulding accounted for by his widow Ann PRC1/12/42. Since Stephen Goulding had died away from home, at Faversham, Ann also had the complication of arranging his funeral there; Fitton PRO PROB5/570.

47 Richard Ollard, *Pepys; A Biography* (Oxford 1984)

48 PRC20/11/135

owed money far and wide, to London drapers, Wealden clothiers, yeomen in the countryside, tradesmen in Sandwich, even his own servant, Suzann Henneker, to whom he owed £60. He had actually procured a licence to marry Suzann shortly before his death, which would have cancelled the debt. Murton also owed £242 to Smith himself. On his deathbed, Murton asked Smith to pay three small debts, totalling £33. Smith had done this, because he had promised Murton that he would, before he knew of 'the multitude of the deceased testator his debts and the weakness of his estate.'

As Murton's administrator and former partner, Smith was imprisoned for eight weeks for the deceased's debts. When Smith and Murton became partners in the 'misterie or trade' of woollen drapery in 1635, Murton had entered into a bond, with a penalty of £1000, to pay all debts for woollen cloth incurred during the partnership. Despite this, the stock in Smith's own shop had had an execution served on it for payment of a debt of £210 for cloth due to a London draper. In order to free his stock, Smith had paid the debt, plus £10 costs, himself. Shortly after that, a group of ten drapers and clothiers forced Smith into bankruptcy over debts of Murton's totalling £371 9s and, Smith said, a few small debts of his own for which his credit had never before been questioned. For these debts, all his 'cloth and wares in his shoppe, debt books and goods to the value of one thousand pounds and upwards were seized upon and devided among the creditors aforesaid ... to his utter undoing both in the losse of his trade and disposing of his goods at farr lesser rates than they were worth.' Smith therefore claimed from Murton's estate, in compensation, the £1000 for which Murton had bound himself. Murton's estate ended in the negative by £913 10s 9d, and the unfortunate Jonathan Smith clearly felt that both his business and his creditworthiness had been ruined by his association with Isaac Murton.

Administrative costs could swallow a large proportion of a small estate. Such 'necessarie and ordinarie expenses' included drawing up the inventory, a fee to the court for the grant of probate or administration, payment for writing up the account, if the accountant was not competent to do it herself, and numerous further court fees at the final presentation of the account. These costs varied from one jurisdiction to another. In the courts of the diocese of Lincoln costs normally came to between £2 10s and £4,[49] but in the courts of the

49 A detailed breakdown of typical 'Necessarie Charges' in the archdeaconry of Lincoln is provided by the account for the estate of Nicholas Vessie of Stallingborough in 1622:
'for the l(ette)res of Administrac(i)on seale oathe and bond xvj s. ij d.
Item for the writinge and engrossinge of the Inventaries ij s.
Item for the drawinge of this Accompte iij s. iiij d.

diocese of Canterbury fees normally only came to about £1 15s. If the estate was a very small one, the court might abate all or part of its fees; whether fees were abated, and by how much, varied according to the circumstances of each case, and seems to have been left to the discretion of the court.

Sometimes, the greater part of what should have been a fairly good sized estate could be taken up by legal costs. The accountant for Stephen Benson of Linton in Kent claimed £20 spent out of his estate of £39 15s 8d in 1607 for defending a lawsuit. £220 of William Burr's estate of £1067 18s 4d was spent by his administrator in 1633 in a dispute with William's brother over the administration. Alexander Hopper's administrator spent £22 of his estate of £56 16s 10d in 1640, attempting to recover debts owed to the deceased man. All of Thomas Cole's £7 18s 10d was spent by his administrator in 1625 in connection with various lawsuits over the estate.[50]

The cumulative evidence of the experience of administrators and executors of estates is that men and women at all levels of society in the early modern period were not unsophisticated, illiterate and parochially minded. The poorest widows and labourers were accustomed to act as administrators of estates of deceased relatives. This might involve quite complex financial dealings and travel. Although legal advice and assistance was available, many people would have been unable to afford it. Most people faced with settling a deceased relative's estate would have had to rely on the voluntary help of a better informed neighbour or, from the second half of the seventeenth century, on one of the published books of legal advice available for a few pence, for example *The Countryman's Counsellor, or Everyman his own Lawyer*, or a little more expensively, at 1s.6d., George Meriton's, *Touchstone of Wills, Testaments, and Administrations*, which was aimed specifically at the 'honest countrey-

Item for engrossinge of the same iijs iiij d.
Item for Registeringe of the same iij s. iiijd.
Item for the Judges fee for the assignac(i)on of the Porc(i)ons to the Children of the said deceased vj s. viij d.
Item to the Register for his fee for the same assignac(i)ons iij s. iiij d.
Item to the Judge and Register for the l(ette)res testimoniall x s.
Item for the seale and the oathe xvj d.
Item for this Accomptants owne Charges both at the time when she came to take her le(tte)res of Administrac(i)on and also when she came to passe this Accompte xx s.
Item for expedic(i)on xij d.'
Altogether administrative charges came to more than the costs of the funeral. Lincolnshire Record Office Ad/Ac/17/7.

50 Benson CKS PRC2/13/65; Burr CKS PRC20/10/48; Hopper CKS PRC1/4/60; Cole PRC2/23/92

man' who could not afford Swinburne's *Treatise*.[51]

Although the parish of the deceased is normally given in the preamble to the account, a considerable drawback is that the status or occupation of deceased men is rarely given. Gentlemen and clergymen are usually identified as such, and so are holders of specific offices, such as mayors, aldermen and jurats. Some yeomen are also identified, and other occupations can sometimes be inferred from information in the body of the account, but since so many people in this period followed more than one occupation, caution should be used. We have been able to suggest an occupation or status for 6,461 of the men from information given directly or indirecly in their accounts. We have also been able to supply an occupation or status for a further 2,108 men from their inventories, and for 142 men from their wills. However we have not been able to discover any occupation or status for nearly 70% of the men.

On the other hand nearly two-thirds of women's accounts provide some statement of status for the dead woman. Of these, over 84% were definitely for widows. A further 14% related to single women, and most of the remainder were probably widows since they were known by such titles as 'mrs', 'mistress', 'dame'. Only one per cent of them were called 'wife'. Since married women normally had no legal control of any property, they only had any estate for the probate courts to deal with in exceptional circumstances, for example in the rare cases when their marriage settlement had been so framed that they had control of property separate from their husband's estate.[52]

Following the deceased's name and parish in the preamble is normally the date on which the account was presented to the court. It is clear that the courts worked on a seasonal basis. 44% of all known accounts were passed in the late spring/early summer months from April to July. Possibly this was the time when travel was easiest, when people were not occupied with the harvest, and when they were least likely to be discouraged from travelling by plague or some other infection. August and September were the months when court business was lightest. Ecclesiastical courts tended to observe law terms, but not rigidly. Business dropped off, but did not entirely cease, after the last day of July and only picked up again in the last week of September after Michaelmas. October was another peak month.

Much has been written about whether the preambles to wills

51 Margaret Spufford, *Small Books and Pleasant Histories* (London, 1981), pp.60-61; David Vaisey (ed.), *The Diary of Thomas Turner 1754-1765* (Oxford, 1984); Erickson, *Women*, pp.27-8.

52 Dr Erickson came across five cases of yeomen or gentry wives making wills in the seventeenth century whose marriage settlements had given them control of property. Erickson, *Women*, pp.130-1, 136-7.

can be taken as indications of testators' religious beliefs.[53] As probate accounts follow a set formula, they cannot be used in this way. One probate account preamble, however, does make a definite political statement. The account of the estate of William Norton Esq., of Fordwich, was compiled 'the thirteeth (sic) day of October in the three and twentieth yeere of the reigne of our most gracious soveraigne Lord Charles by grace of God of England Scotland France and Ireland Defender of the fayth &c Anno Domini 1647.'[54]

The second paragraph of a probate account is a statement of the 'charge'. The charge is normally a common form statement of the inventory value. A copy of the inventory itself had to be produced again with the account and is sometimes attached.[55] Occasionally there is some information as to what was in the inventory; sometimes there may be an explanation of why the administrator is now 'charging' himself or herself with more or less than the inventory value. After the statement of the charge comes the body of the account, in which the administrator 'prays' allowance of the various sums expended by him or her from the estate since the deceased's death. The great value of probate accounts to historians lies in the fact that the expenditure is normally itemised in the minutest detail.

The first item entered in the account is normally the cost of the deceased's funeral. The earliest death for which an account survives in the diocese of Canterbury is that of Edward Crayforde, who died in 1558.[56] His funeral expenses reveal a distinctly Catholic ceremony:

> 'to viii pore people for carienge tapers at his Buryall xvid
> 'to three preists and ii Clarks for Celebratinge masses and seyinge of Dyrrigs iiis viiid
> 'geven in Almes to the povertie of Mongham and other parisshes there nighe to praye for his Soule and all christen Soules xis viiid
> 'to mr preste for celebratinge masses and Dirge at hys month minde iiis

53 The most recent summary of the argument is to be found in Eric Josef Carlson, 'The Historical Value of the Ely Consistory Court Probate Records', in Elisabeth Leedham-Green and Rosemary Rodd (eds.), *Index of the Probate Records of the Consistory Court of Ely 1449-1858*, i, British Record Society (1994), pp.xxxvi-xlvii.

54 CKS PRC 1/8/24

55 We have seen 5,479 inventories filed with accounts, and also 872 of the bonds entered into by executors and administrators, which were of course cancelled when the account was accepted, besides 455 wills, 160 grants of administration and a huge range of other documents, like tuition or guardianship bonds, also cancelled when the account was accepted, cancelled bonds for debts paid, and accounts for goods sold to support claims for inventory overvaluation.

56 CKS PRC 2/1/4

Plague and other illness

Costs incurred in the deceased's last sickness normally follow. Sometimes details of specific medicines or cures are given, such as the five shillings paid for letting the blood of Henry Hall of Whitstable in 1621, or the two shillings paid to the barber in 1627 for administering two glisters to Richard Lynwood of Sittingbourne before his death, or the various apothecaries' wares, including 'unicorn's horn sucket' provided for Charles Marichurch of Dover in 1616, or the 'pidgeons and herrings' laid to the feet of John Tryon Esq. of St Martin in the Fields.[57]

Our knowledge of seventeenth century plague epidemics has chiefly been based on statistics derived from parish registers, municipal records, material arising from official responses to epidemics, and number of diarists of whom Evelyn and Pepys are the best known. Probate accounts, by listing the expenses of keeping households shut up for weeks or months at a time, plus payments for medical attention and nursing, give an additional insight into the experience of ordinary people during an epidemic.[58] While the shutting up of infected households was enforced by parish and borough authorities, the families thus confined were not completely abandoned. The Stranger communities seem to have led the way in looking after infected families. The French church at Canterbury laid out money for the support of John Dubuha and his family in 1583 (nine people may have died altogether in this household). The church also paid for 'keepers' to look after the household during the sickness and 'a poor man' who bought provisions and ran errands for the household. Towns were also introducing plague precautions by this date. Christopher Fynche, Mayor of Faversham, arranged for bread, drink and meat worth seven shillings and a further nine pounds of beef at 1s 9d to be supplied to the household of Robert Chapman in 1583.[59]

Accounts starkly illustrate the high mortality within individual families. In the 1603 epidemic, William Hammon of Maidstone died, followed by his children Thomasine, Mercie, Joseph and Ann. The only survivors were another son, Thomas, and William's apprentice. In Deal in 1665-66, Richard Rantum and seven of his children died;

57 Hall CKS PRC 2/26/132; Lynwood CKS PRC 2/27/1; Marichurch CKS PRC 20/3/360; Tryon PRO PROB32/23/182. Pickled herrings mashed with spirits of wine made a poultice for a 'straine or bruse in the bone.' Alison Revell, *A Kentish Herbal* (Maidstone, 1984), p.51.

58 Paul Slack, *The impact of Plague in Tudor and Stuart England* (London, 1985), was the first to use probate accounts for this purpose. We have now seen many more relevant accounts than he was able to use.

59 Dubuha CKS PRC21/6/367 and 368; Chapman CKS PRC2/3/1

payments for their coffins were the first items in the account of their father's estate. Eight weeks was the normal time for which an infected household might be shut up, but it could be longer. The household of Edward Harrys of Faversham, in which Harrys, his wife, two children and a maidservant died, was shut up for four months in 1580. The household of Henry Carey of Birchington was also shut up for four months in 1638.[60]

Plague was not regarded as inevitably fatal in the sixteenth and seventeenth centuries. Mortality rates are difficult to calculate, but Paul Slack has suggested that between 50% and 80% of those infected died in the early modern period.[61] Nurses could often be found to go into infected households. Thomas Brayne of Canterbury, his wife, two children and a manservant died in 1588. However, a surgeon was paid £3 for 'healing the plague sores upon the servants'. A surgeon also went into the house of Abell Garret in Sandwich in 1582 to confirm that it was plague the family was suffering from and to treat Garrett's daughter Margaret. Surgeons and nurses were professionals, but friends and neighbours were also willing to help. When Azarias Turke's family in Cranbrook was infected in 1583, seven in the household died. William Osman was 'continually in the house with the said Azarias and his household and helped them in all the time of their sickness.' Henrie Gilbert of Northbourne was cared for by his betrothed when he was ill in 1638.[62]

When the authorities judged a household to be free from infection, women would go in to clean the house. Rosin and pitch were burnt to clear the air and rosewater was also used. All linen was washed; Andrew Orgill, administrator of Mary Blacklock of St Leonard's Bromley (by Bow) in Middlesex sent her rugs and blankets to a fulling mill to be cleaned.[63] New clothing was supplied for surviving children before they were placed out as servants or apprentices.[64]

Probate accounts demonstrate the economic as well as the human costs of a plague epidemic. Money disbursed by the parish for the support of an infected family had to be repaid when the sickness was over, out of the estate if the breadwinner had died. Michael Jancocke of Minster in Thanet was out of work for three months in

60 Hammon CKS PRC21/16/21; PRC21/16/370; PRC21/17/21; PRC21/17/120; PRC21/17/130; Rantum CKS PRC19/4/93; Harrys CKS PRC2/1/269; Carey CKS PRC20/10/156.

61 Slack, *The Impact of Plague*, pp. 7, 175.

62 Brayne CKS PRC2/4/400; Garret CKS PRC2/2/39; Turke CKS PRC2/3/119; Gilbert CKS PRC1/8/16

63 PRO PROB32/6/69

64 CKS PRC2/34/269

1583; no-one would employ him for fear of infection because he had been shut up with his brother John when John was dying of plague. The family of John Page, a yeoman of Sevington in Kent, was unable to sell his cattle in 1626 due to the widespread infection. After Thomas Gruer of Westwell in Kent died of plague in 1582, his next of kin delayed going in to clear his house for fear of any lingering infection. While the house stood empty, thieves broke in and stole money, clothing and goods to the value of £5 14s 4d.[65]

Housekeeping and Prices

Probate accounts can reveal details of the food available in towns and rural districts, and much can be learned about the diet and housekeeping expenses of families of different social status. Normally, this information is only available for families of gentry status and above, who kept their own household accounts.

After the death of Davyd Croft, a yeoman or gentleman of Murston in Kent, in 1574, his household had to be maintained until the harvest had been gathered in. The account of his estate thus includes a month by month statement of the food and other necessities bought for the family, servants and harvest workers.[66] The executor's expenditure for September 1574 includes the following:

	£	s	d
Hops and seasoning			6
A loin of mutton for the house		1	2
A pound of butter and 3lb of cheese			10
For salt			4
In beef 60lb for the house		8	9
A quarter of mutton		1	3
A loin of wether's mutton			9
A quarter of barren's mutton		1	0
A pound of candles			3
Salt			4
For mutton in the house		1	0
Salt			1
Beef in the house		1	8
A quarter of mutton for the house		1	10
Another quarter of mutton		1	10
A quarter of mutton more		1	0
A pound of candles			4

65 Jancocke CKS PRC2/3/131; Page CKS PRC2/27/121; Gruer CKS PRC21/5/253.

66 CKS PRC2/4/468

Whereas the values placed on goods in probate inventories represent what the appraisors thought the goods might fetch in a sale, prices for goods in probate accounts are a statement of what was actually paid, and therefore more likely to be accurate. Detailed study of wages and prices paid for goods in the late sixteenth and seventeenth centuries as recorded in probate accounts may shed light on the local progress and effects of the 'Price Revolution' of the period. In 1596, the administrator of Thomas Maxted of Ospringe in Kent bought on one occasion 216lb of beef for his harvest workers, and on another occasion 107lb of beef. In the late 1620s, the sons of Thomas Spaine, a substantial yeoman of Knowlton in Kent, bought several quantities of beef including 170lb at one time. Through these accounts, and that of Davyd Croft already quoted, it is possible to trace a rise in the price of beef from 1 3/4d a pound in the mid 1570s to 2 1/4d a pound in the late 1620s. This is an increase of barely more than a quarter over a period of more than fifty years; hardly dramatic, considering that these fifty years cover the latter part of the price rises of the sixteenth century.[67]

In Henry Phelps-Brown and Sheila Hopkins' price indexes meat, in their case urban mutton, rose from 222 in 1572 to 555 in 1627, falling back to 544 in 1628 (there is a gap in the series in the years 1573-1580) These figures, therefore, indicate a price rise of over 50%. It is clear that detailed work on wage and price information in probate accounts will augment and amplify Phelps-Brown and Hopkins' tables, which are largely drawn from the accounts of Oxford and Cambridge colleges.[68]

Children

If the deceased left minor children, a major responsibility of the administrator was to see to their upbringing. The children's board and lodging, education, clothing and apprenticeship all had to be paid for from their deceased father's (or mother's) estate, and all expenditure was recorded in the account. The estate could not be wound up until all the children had come of age, and so some accounts ran for years. Out of more than 13,500 accounts which survive for the diocese of Canterbury, over 1500 contain details of children's

67 Maxted CKS PRC2/8/91; Spaine CKS PRC2/30/119.

68 Henry Phelps Brown and Sheila V. Hopkins, 'Seven Centuries of the Prices of Consumables, compared with Builders' Wage-rates', *Economica*, xxiii (1956), reprinted in Henry Phelps Brown and Sheila V.Hopkins, *A Perspective of Wages and Prices* (London, 1981), pp.13-59.

maintenance, food, clothing, education or apprenticeship.[69] In this respect probate accounts resemble the Orphans' Accounts kept by the Orphans' Courts in some boroughs and cities, including Sandwich in Kent and the City of London.[70]

The necessity for detailed accounts to be kept during a child's minority is demonstrated by the experiences of the Kent historian William Lambarde and his stepson Maximilian Dalison, both of whom had to resort to legal action to recover their inheritances from their guardians. As Lambarde's biographer has written, 'in the sixteenth century at least, an heir's minority often gave opportunity to even the most trusted friends and relatives to appropriate his inheritance.'[71]

As a woman's property automatically became her husband's as soon as she married, the relatives of the children of a first marriage had to take steps to ensure that those children received their rightful share of their father's goods in the event of their mother's remarriage. When the widow of Robert Saint of Whitstable remarried in the 1660s, her new husband entered into a bond to pay his stepdaughters their portions of their father's estate, £10 each, when they reached the age of 21.

In 1606 the administrators of the estate of Margaret Chese of Whitstable had to sue her former guardian in order to recover her goods. Similarly, in 1616 the administrator of Thomas Jefery of St Nicholas at Wade had trouble recovering his share of his recently deceased father's goods from his father's administrators.[72]

The Distribution of the Estate

If the deceased had left a will, legacies and bequests were normally, but not always, deducted from the charge in the body of the account. Sometimes they were not included in the charge,[73] and sometimes they were only dealt with when the account was rendered. At the end of the account, the amount spent by the administrator was totalled and the result, the discharge, deducted from the charge to give the balance. It is in the comparison of charge and balance that historians can discover to what extent probate inventories exaggerate

69 Margaret Spufford, 'The cost of apparel in seventeenth-century England', being considered for publication by the *Economic History Review* when this volume went to press, relies on probate accounts for much of her evidence for the costs of childrens' clothing.

70 CKS Sa/FOa; Thomas Dorman, 'The Sandwich Book of Orphans', *Archaeologia Cantiana*, xvi (1886); Peter Earle, *The Making of the English Middle Class ... London 1660-1730* (London, 1989).

71 Retha M. Warnicke, *William Lambarde* (Chichester, 1973), p.122.

72 Saint CKS PRC1/11/152; Chese CKS PRC 1/1/3 ; Jefery CKS PRC 20/3/414.

73 See below pp.xlvi-xlvii for a striking example of this.

or overestimate moveable wealth. This point will be discussed in detail later.[74]

When the discharge was totalled, it quite often exceeded the amount of the charge. The account then ended with a negative balance, or 'in surplussage'. In east Kent two out of every five surviving accounts ended in the negative.[75]

One cause of this was that the wife's marriage settlement had been so used that when the husband died there was a severe liquidity problem. Payment of her marriage settlement to a widow was always a considerable drain on an estate. Not every case was as bad as that of John Medley of Loose in Kent who left goods worth £37 12s 8d when he died in 1631. However, when his widow claimed her marriage settlement of £500, this caused the account to end with a negative balance of £484 7s 4d. The imbalance was on an even more substantial scale in the case of the estate of Richard Dawkes Esq. of Dover, who died in 1644. His moveables were worth £780, but when his widow's settlement of £4000 had been deducted, the estate was in the negative by £3701 14s 4d.[76]

It is not usually clear what happened when an account was 'in surplussage'. If the deceased had left a will, but had insufficient assets to pay the legacies, the court might abate or reduce the legacies proportionately. Richard Arneden's estate was left with insufficient to pay the legacies specified in his will. Legatees were paid at 10s 7d in the pound. Jane Asherste's legatees received just under half their bequests in 1596.[77]

It is just at this point that the lack of evidence for real estate is most tantalising. In the eighteenth century American colonies land was on average worth more than double the value of moveables and financial assets,[78] but we cannot know whether this was also the case in England and Wales. If the deceased did have land in addition to the moveable goods specified in the inventory, some or all could be sold or mortgaged to pay outstanding debts and legacies. However, if the deceased had nothing beyond what was specified in the inventory, either the creditors must have accepted reduced payments, or the administrator must have been left personally out of pocket. We have seen how Jonathan Smith was totally ruined and thrown into a debtor's prison because he acted as administrator of the goods of Isaac Murton.[79]

74 Below pp.xlv-liv.
75 See below pp.lix-lx.
76 Medley CKS PRC20/9/284; Dawkes CKS PRC19/2/89.
77 Arneden CKS PRC 2/11/173; Asherste CKS PRC 21/14/71.
78 See above p.xxv.
79 See above pp.xxxii-xxxiii.

If there was a positive balance, and the deceased had not left a will, it was the court's duty to distribute the balance among the deceased's next of kin. Details of the manner of the distribution were added at the foot of the account. Until 1671 this was at the discretion of the court. Everyone to whom the court apportioned a share was named and his or her relationship to the deceased was stated. Where married daughters were involved, the names of sons-in-law were also normally given, and the ages of all minor children stated. The relict (the widow of the deceased man), naturally received the greater share. She was legally entitled to one third of the residual goods, but courts normally allocated her two thirds, and sometimes even the whole of what remained after all debts had been paid.[80] The remainder was normally shared equally among surviving children. In 1671 the balance of the estate of John Adams, a yeoman of Folkestone, was distributed to his seven children John, already an adult, Elizabeth, aged eighteen, Richard, aged fifteen, Susan, aged twelve, Isaac, eight, Ann, five and Mary, two. Each received ten pounds, while the relict, Elizabeth, was allotted the remaining £74 5s 4d.[81]

Courts used their discretion to make unequal distributions under a variety of circumstances. Sons who were also to inherit land, which was not included among the assets in probate inventories or accounts, sometimes received a smaller share of moveable goods. Married daughters who had received their portions might also receive a smaller share.[82] In 1677 the distribution of the estate of John Court, a cordwainer of Stone in Oxney in Kent, was governed by the amounts already spent on the maintenance and apprenticeship of his children. The daughter of Giles Clarke received a greater share of her father's estate in 1634 because she lived with her parents 'to doe them service.'[83]

Disability or illness could influence the distribution of an estate. The youngest son of John Hull of Deal was awarded a larger share of his father's estate because he was sickly. One of the sons of Nicholas Barham of Leeds in Kent received more than his siblings in 1619 because he was blind. Special provision was made for the baseborn daughter of Christopher Ratcliffe of Goodnestone next Wingham in Kent in 1698 because she was 'small and purblind' and unlikely to be able to work to support herself. In 1600, the court awarded ten shillings to the brother of Ralf Baker of Egerton in Kent,

80 Erickson, *Women*, pp.178-9.

81 CKS PRC2/35/2

82 This applied at many social levels, from the daughter of Richard Barham, gentleman, in 1608 (account CKS PRC20/1/326) to the daughter of Samuel Collard, cordwainer, in 1684 (account CKS PRC2/40/186).

83 Court CKS PRC 2/37/127; Clarke CKS PRC 20/10/226

out of Ralf's net estate of £460 4s. The brother was a poor man and the parishioners of Headcorn, where he lived, had petitioned the court on his behalf.[84]

The custom of the particular community to which the deceased belonged might influence the distribution of his estate. Gavelkind, by which land was equally divided amongst sons, and when there were no sons, amongst daughters, or more distant relatives, obviously played a part in Kent. The Walloon custom, which operated among the 'Stranger' communities in Sandwich and Canterbury, was that a relict should receive the balance of her husband's estate for her lifetime, as did the widow of Phillipp Destrie of St Alphege in Canterbury in 1634.[85] In the City of London, the rule was that a citizen's widow should have her 'widow's chamber', a room or chamber properly furnished for her use, in addition to her legal entitlement. In Yorkshire, the custom was for the balance to be divided into three parts. The first, known as the 'widow's right,' went to the relict. The second was divided equally between surviving children. The third part was known as the 'death's part' and could be distributed at the relict's discretion. Thus in 1639 in the account of the estate of Hugh Sharples of Ayton in the North Riding, 'the last parte commonly called the Deaths parte this accomptant [the relict, Ellen] is content the same shalbe allotted unto the said two children for augmentation of their porcons.' In 1626, in Anne Aspinall's account of the estate of her late husband Anthony Nesse of Kingston upon Hull, she requested that 'in regard the children are younge and to bring up which wilbe to her a great charge', half the death's part should go to the children and the remainder to her towards their upbringing.[86]

If the deceased had neither widow nor children, the court would look more widely for his next of kin. Grandchildren, brothers, sisters, parents, nephews, nieces, uncles, aunts and cousins might all receive shares if there were no closer kin.[87] Henry Russell Kingston in Kent, was evidently not yet married when he died. He was still a servant. His estate was distributed between his brother's children Henry Russell, aged thirteen, Elizabeth Russell, aged fifteen, and Susan Russell, his sister's children Windebank, John and Jane May, and

84 Hull CKS PRC21/15/149: Barham CKS PRC2/20/346; Ratcliffe CKS PRC19/5/60; Baker CKS PRC 21/16/182.

85 CKS PRC 20/10/284

86 Sharples Borthwick Prob.Ex.1639/1; Nesse Borthwick Prob.Ex.1626/1

87 This is in line with the wider kin-universe revealed by those who had no obvious heirs who made wills. David Cressy, 'Kinship and kin interaction in early modern England', *Past and Present*, cxiii (1986), pp.41-65 and Margaret Spufford and Motoyasu Takahashi, 'Families, Will Witnesses and Economic Structure', *Albion*, xxviii (1996), pp.386-7.

another brother's son, a third Henry Russell, aged fourteen. The balance of the estate of Edward Mantle of Stodmarsh in Kent, a bachelor, was shared between his sisters Nisella, wife of Francis Larkin, and Martha, wife of Henry Churchman, and his nephews and nieces Margaret, Thomas, Nisella and John Penny, children of his late sister Mary Penny. The family of Solomon May of Ulcombe in Kent was a complicated one. His estate was shared between his brothers Henry, Abraham and Thomas and his three half brothers on his mother's side, Anthony, Thomas and William Watkins, aged fifteen, twelve and nine.[88]

The woman to whom a deceased man had been betrothed might also have a claim on his estate. Simon Rayner of Tonge died only weeks before he was due to be married; the banns had already been called twice. The court awarded ten pounds from his estate to his intended bride. Richard Harris of Bethersden was espoused 'it is thought' to Faythe Hall when he died in 1613. The court awarded Faythe £20 from his estate.[89]

Probate accounts thus follow on from wills, inventories and letters of administration and run through a year or more from the sickness of the dying man, his death and funeral, the upkeep of his household after his death, the payment of his debts and the maintenance of his children, up to the point at which there are no more expenditures to be laid out and the balance, if any, can be distributed. In doing so, probate accounts give far more detail of the expenditure of 'ordinary' households than historians have previously had available from any other source.

THE ACCURACY OF PROBATE INVENTORIES

Historians have debated the accuracy of the valuations placed on goods in probate inventories. Inventory values are the appraisors' estimates of what the deceased's goods would fetch if they were sold.[90] For shop stock and livestock, appraisors would be guided by current market prices. Household furnishings, clothing and tools were more difficult to value since they were second hand goods and prices obtainable would be governed by their age and condition. The most difficult assets to appraise were crops in the field. If a man died in spring, his appraisors would have to put a value on crops which had

88 Russell CKS PRC2/35/82; Mantle CKS PRC2/36/100; May CKS PRC2/36/96

89 Rayner CKS PRC2/25/119; Harris CKS PRC 2/18/8.

90 'The just value thereof in their judgments and consciences, that is to say at such price as the same may be sold for at that time', Swinburne, *Treatise*, Part VI, chapter ix, repeated nearly two centuries later by Burn, *Ecclesiastical Law*, p.652.

only recently been sown and which would not be ready for harvesting for several months. However experienced the farmer undertaking the appraisal, so much depended on the weather that estimating the value of the eventual yield must have involved as much guesswork as skilled judgement. It is surprising how rarely they seem to have got it wrong.[91]

Even if goods in an inventory were valued correctly, errors might be made in adding up the total which might result in over or undervaluing. Roman numerals, which implied reckoning counters, were still being used by many appraisors and administrators well into the seventeenth century, which made the task of arriving at an accurate total all the more difficult. Historians who have studied collections of inventories have concluded that appraisors' addition might often be erratic.[92]

Both Margaret Spufford and Barrie Trinder and Jeff Cox have noted that goods, particularly those bequeathed by will, might be removed from the deceased's house before an inventory was completed, especially since these bequeathed objects might well be the most highly thought of and valued.[93] Comparison of probate inventories with wills can pinpoint missing possessions and raise questions as to the completeness of inventories.

A vivid example of this is provided by the moveables of John Prescott, a yeoman of Guston in Kent, who died in the early summer of 1628. His inventory was taken on 18 July of that year. The appraisors did not add up the inventory, but the total value is £37 5s 4d. The Consistory Court Act Book which records the granting of probate gives the inventory value as £38 5s 4d. Of this sum, £3 was in ready money and wearing apparel, £4 in the value of a bed and its furnishings. There was £6 worth of household linen and two kine and a hog worth £6 10s. The remainder of the goods were chiefly household furnishings and kitchen equipment.[94]

John Prescott left a particularly detailed will, and from this one can deduce that the inventory was less than complete. He bequeathed his bed, some household linen, a cupboard, three chests, a table, a form or bench, three joined stools and some pewter and brass. When these had been deducted, the estate was probably worth only about £30, yet in addition John Prescott left £35 in cash legacies. If an account had survived for this estate, it seems likely that it would have

91 See below p.lii.

92 B.Trinder and J.Cox, *Yeomen and Colliers in Telford ... 1660-1750* (Chichester, 1980).

93 Spufford, 'Limitations', and Trinder and Cox, *Yeomen*

94 Inventory CKS PRC28/14/506; Act Book CKS PRC22/16/172

ended in the negative. The will also includes some bequests which cannot be identified in the inventory; a second brass kettle - only one is listed; two brass candlesticks - there are none in the inventory; a brass mortar - again, there is none in the inventory.[95]

The will also refers to lands in Guston, the adjoining parish of Whitfield and elsewhere in the county. The extent and tenure of these lands is not stated, but they are to bear a £10 annuity to the deceased's relict for the term of her life. Although the inventory was taken in July, it contains no mention of crops in the field or in the barn, other than one load of hay, which together with other items is valued at £1 10s. Neither does the inventory mention any livestock other than the two kine and one hog. Nor does the inventory include any carts, wagons, ploughs, harness or other farming equipment. The lands might have been let out to tenants, but the will does not use the usual formula 'now in the occupation of ...', the widow is given the right of entry into and distraint upon the lands if her annuity is not paid, and there is nothing in the will or inventory to suggest any income from rents.

Yet it can be demonstrated that John Prescott was not a poor man. Between 1614 and his death, he had recovered a total of £98 10s from the estates of six different people in repayment of loans.[96] His will describes a house with at least eight rooms and also mentions a garden, an orchard, a 'little close' and a yard used to pasture animals.

The Appraisal of Probate Inventories

The making of an inventory was the responsibility of the executor(s) or administrator(s) and had to be carried out openly in the presence of witnesses, preferably people with an interest in the proper administration of the estate. However it was 'not sufficient to make an inventory unless the same be particularly valued and praised by some honest and skilful persons', who shall 'competently understand the value of the deceased's goods'.[97] In practice the appraisal of goods for inventories was normally carried out by neighbours. However, a widow might prefer to call in outsiders, rather than her immediate neighbours to appraise her husband's goods. Members of the Dover General Baptist Church in the late seventeenth century sometimes turned to members of their own community to carry out appraisals,

95 CKS PRC32/48/227

96 CKS PRC2/25/127; PRC2/24/148; PRC2/20/241; PRC20/7/164

97 Swinburne, *Treatise*, VI,ix,1 repeated by Burn, *Ecclesiastical Law*, p.645, who attributes it to statute 21 Hen.VIII.c.5; and Swinburne, VI,ix,5 repeated and extended by Burn, p.652.

even when the chosen appraisor had to travel some distance.[98]

In a farming community, neighbours would naturally also be engaged in farming and automatically have the relevant expertise. However when a man or woman left an extensive stock in trade or complex financial dealings, the task required time and expertise that might not be available among his or her immediate neighbours. John Tavenor was a grocer in Deal in the 1690s. In addition to normal grocery wares, he stocked a wide range of vinegar and spirits, tobacco, haberdashery, stationery and marine stores. His stock was stored not only in his shop and cellar but also in his spare bedrooms. His inventory, appraised by William Bowles and John Fox, took up seven closely written pages. Even if Tavenor kept detailed books, compiling his inventory must have taken several days.[99]

The deceased's family normally supplied food and drink for the appraisors while they were carrying out their task. Sometimes cash payments were also made, particularly when a man with specialist knowledge had been called in to carry out all or part of the appraisal. In 1607 the next of kin of Valentine Maye, Vicar of Hackington, paid someone one shilling for writing a catalogue of his books. In 1569, the property of Johan Mychell, a widow of Hythe, included a boat and gear which was appraised by fishermen. The household goods of William Dollman, a cutler of Canterbury, were appraised by an upholsterer and a joiner, but his shop goods by another cutler. The leather in Mathew Downe's shop in Hythe was appraised by a glover in 1591.[100]

In some towns, professional services were available; for example, those of the 'two town prisors of Dover ... appointed and sworne for that purpose.' Many Dover inventories in the late sixteenth and early seventeenth centuries were appraised by Richard Atkins. In the 1590s, Atkins was partnered by Thomas Middleton, and in the early seventeenth century by Thomas Chalys. In the early modern period, men were not required to act as appraisors only when someone died. In Sandwich it was 'the custom of the town' for pawnbrokers who had had 'gages' or pledges in their hands for more than a year and a day to bring them before the Council to ask for a valuation to be made so that they could dispose of them. Two appraisors would then be appointed from among the jurats and common councilmen. On 30

98 J. M. Bower, The Congregation of the Dover General Baptist Church, 1660-1700, Leicester University, M.A. Dissertation 1983. Samuel Tavenor came out from Dover to Guston on the North Downs to appraise the inventory of Thomas Harrison in 1673; CKS PRC27/25/15.

99 CKS PRC27/32/282;

100 Maye CKS PRC2/14/324; Mychell CKS PRC21/1/39; Dollman CKS PRC2/39/28; Downe CKS PRC 21/11/135

April 1618, 'Peter Morard of Sandwich ... Bookebinder ... brought a bible and a childe beareing blanket of red laced about with black velvet gaged or pawned to him by one Anne Backer ... for xiis, which for that they had layen in his hands above a twelvemonth and a day he desired Mr Maior they might be appraised, which accordingly was done by Richard Pinder and Gilbert Hallywell, who appraised the same at xiiis iiiid.'[101]

Sales of deceased persons' goods were carried on with varying degrees of professionalism. In the countryside, sales of the effects of deceased people were advertised by notices given out in parish churches, or, in the provincial towns, by the town crier. In London, sales could be advertised in the *Gazette* and by notices in coffee houses. Elizabeth Symball had 400 tickets printed for the auction of part of her late husband Isaak's estate after publicising it in this manner. In parts of Kent, auctions were known as 'liefcope' sales, reflecting the Dutch influence in the county. In Canterbury and Sandwich, sales were run by professional auctioneers, 'liefcope men', who were paid a percentage of the money raised by the sale. In Canterbury in 1615, this was 1s 6d for every pound made.[102]

In Sandwich, the liefcope man was appointed by the town. The first reference to the appointment of a liefcope man in Sandwich Borough Records is for 1612. The Mayor was elected in early December each year, and at the Council meeting the following week, all borough officials for the following year were appointed. Thus on 10 December 1612, among other business, 'at this Assembly ... the cryinge of all levecopes in this Towne and benefitt to be had thereby is graunted to Robert Furner for this yere enseweinge for the rent of five pounds to be paid quarterly to the treasurers of this Town. Suerties for him truly to aunswer unto the owners for all such goods as shalbe committed to his chardge, and monyes thereof made ... he not exacting any greater Duties for the same than formerly, have bene allowed. And no other either Dutch or Englishe to intermeddle therewith.'[103]

Evidently a liefcope man had been operating in the town before 1612, but this was the first time the appointment had been made officially. The rent of £5 soon proved to be over-optimistic; in 1614 Robert Furner told the Council he had not made that much and it was agreed that he should pay the town only forty shillings for the previous year and the same for the following year. Robert Furner gave up the office in 1615, and it was re-let to Robert Ungley at forty shillings a

101 CKS PRC20/2/136; CKS PRC27/1; Sandwich Borough Records CKS Sa/Ac7 f.63.

102 Symball PRO PROB 32/42/171; CKS PRC 20/3/178.

103 CKS Sa/Ac7 f.23b

year. The profits evidently continued to decline; in 1621 Robert Furner took on the office again at thirty shillings a year for four years. In 1626 the annual farm was reduced further, to twenty shillings a year. It was let again at twenty shillings a year in 1638.[104]

So how accurate were the valuations placed on goods in probate inventories? Valuations were only tested when goods were sold. In the case of household goods and furnishings, which might pass to the heir or be divided among surviving children, there might be no sale and so no test of the accuracy of the valuations. Shop stock or crops, on the other hand, would eventually be sold, and here the appraisors' valuations would be tested. If inventories were deliberately falsified, it would only be to the accountant's advantage for the property to be undervalued, so that a larger balance would be left in his or her hands at the distribution. However, if and when a sale took place any undervaluation would become apparent and other interested parties could apply to the court for a revision of the inventory or distribution. It is also when the accounts record that the goods of the dead man or woman were sold that the modern reader has an opportunity of seeing how accurate the inventory appraisors had been.

When a sale failed to raise the amount estimated in the inventory, the administrator was entitled to claim the difference in the account. In all the 13,565 accounts in the diocese of Canterbury, only 577 contain requests by accountants for an allowance for overvaluation, less that 5% of the total. In Lincolnshire and Wiltshire, appraisers seem to have been even more accurate, for only 2% of accounts included requests for allowances for overvaluation.[105] These are extraordinarily small proportions, and in many cases there were sound reasons for the allowance being requested.

Reasons for Occasional Inaccuracy of Probate Inventories

A common cause of inventory overvaluation was goods having been included in the inventory which were later found not to have belonged to the deceased person. This most often occurred when the deceased man or woman had been in the process of administering someone else's estate and had in consequence been in possession of that person's assets also. Another commonly arising situation was that of a man dying in possession of goods brought to the marriage by his wife, which she had acquired through the death of a previous husband, and which were to be distributed among the children of that previous

104 CKS Sa/Ac7 ff. 38b, 46, 93b, 132b, 336b.

105 However among the much smaller number of Somerset accounts preserved at Taunton, 11% of accounts included such requests

marriage when they reached their majorities.

Inventories of people involved in farming were especially likely to be found to have been overvalued. Reasons put forward by administrators were usually either that crops, when harvested, had been found to be much less than had been estimated in the inventory, or that the price or one or more types of crop had fallen between appraisal and sale. In 1621 Willyam Pelham, administrator of Richard Whyte of Bishopsbourne, asked allowance of £5 16s for wheat overvalued in the inventory. It had been appraised at £25, but the price of wheat had since 'soe decayed' that it could only be sold for £19 4s. Whyte's estate still finished with a balance of £363 8s 5d, having originally been valued at £463 3s 3d. The family of Thomas Sandwell of St Peter in Thanet was less fortunate. His goods, included agricultural crops, fishing gear and household goods had initially been valued at £12 5s 2d. An acre of barley was appraised at 12s, but 'this accomptant could never make one penny profit thereof for that the same barley by reason of extraordinary dry and hot weather was utterly lost, wherefore hee craves an allowance of the same ... Also whereas vi hearing netts, one crowd (?) nett and one Lode nett are apprized at xxxs ... the same netts are still in this accompts hands and hee cannot as yett put them away as they were apprized but is like to loose by the same xiis at least.' Sandwell's bed and bedding had been appraised at £1 6s 8d, but the accountant had been offered only 18s for them; his wearing apparel had been appraised at 13s 4d but had never come to the hands of the administrator; 'lumber' had been appraised at 3s 4d, but the administrator had never made a penny from it. The miserable account ended in the negative by £1 10s 6d.[106]

John Briggs, administrator of Jane Oliver of Tong in 1628, requested allowance for 'the losse of the wheat on the ground prized in the inventory at 28li (being then at 40s a seame) but he could not make soe much of the same by at least vli for presently after the said apprizement wheat fell and soe this Accomptant was constrained to sell the same as the market went.' Edward Darknoll acted as administrator to the estate of Thomas Bennett of Newchurch, gentleman, in 1629. Darknoll 'craveth to bee allowed the summe of 30li which he lost in the sale of the said deceased's corn and malt ... he selling the same for full so much money lesse than yt was ... apprised at by reason of a great fall in the price of corne soone after the apprizing of the same.'[107] It is no coincidence that all these examples of overvalued inventories occurred in the 1620s. When all overvaluations are taken together, a pattern emerges:

106 Whyte CKS PRC2/26/91; Sandwell CKS PRC 2/28/115
107 Oliver CKS PRC 2/29/72; Bennett CKS PRC 20/8/19

2. Inventory Overvaluations in the diocese of Canterbury 1581-1700

	Overvaluations in each decade	% of accounts in each decade	Reasons for overvaluation as stated in accounts[108]
1581-1590	27	3.8	
1591-1600	22	1.4	
1601-1610	23	1.9	
1611-1620	54	2.8	Fall in corn price c.1618
1621-1630	90	5.4	Fall wheat, barley prices c.1621; plague 1626; hot dry weather 1627; fall wheat price c.1628/9
1631-1640	54	3.2	Drought, fall in prices hops, wheat, barley, 1638.
1641-1650	19	3.5	

1661-1670	68	5.8	Fall in corn, cattle prices 1666; fall in land values 1670.
1671-1680	73	5.0	Hard winter 1675; fall in corn, cattle prices 1676; heavy rain 1678; drought 1680.
1681-1690	72	8.1	Heavy rain 1684; hard winter, summer drought, 1684.
1691-1700	30	10.9	Sharp fall in corn price c.1696.
Total	532[109]		

There was a considerably higher percentage of overvaluations in the 1620s than in any other decade before the civil war. The ending of the price rise of the long sixteenth century and the fall of grain prices between 1618 and 1622 seem to have caught appraisors out more often than in earlier decades. However the 1620s and 1630s also saw some uncommonly bad harvests, followed by astonishingly high grain prices, as in 1622, 1630 and 1637. Each year seemed to have a different price régime, which made the work of appraisors the more difficult.[110]

108 The year in all cases is that of the account. The conditions described may have occurred a year or more before.

109 Plus five overvaluations, for which there is no date, and forty, which fall outside these decades, to make the 577 cited above. Over the whole period fewer than 5% of accountants made requests for allowances for overvaluation.

110 The prices of agricultural commodities year by year throughout the seventeenth century can most conveniently be found in Peter Bowden's statistical appendices to Joan Thirsk (ed.), *The Agrarian History of England and Wales*, IV, 1500-1640 and V, 1640-1750

In the generation after 1618 'the entire countryside must have felt the squeeze of poverty created by the change from inflation to uncertainty, from uncertainty to deflation and confusion.'[111] Peter Clark has noted the wide variations in the price of wheat in Kent over comparatively few years; 'at Dover the Assize of Wheat fell from a median 34s per quarter (1608-17) to 24s (1619) and 21s 6d (1620). In the winter of 1622-23 it rose as high as 50s. At Sandwich the median assize 1608-17 was 36s a quarter falling to 20s in 1619 and 18s in 1620, then rising to 51s in 1623.' He concludes 'the ten years after 1617 saw the county slide into a period of slump and depression ... a critical factor was the consecutive combination of harvest glut (1618-20) and dearth (1622,1624,1630). In these circumstances it is not surprising that appraisals were less accurate than usual. Clark identifies a number of Kent gentlemen who experienced financial difficulties, and quotes Sir Dudley Digges, who in January 1629 'was complaining that grain prices had fallen so low that unless cereal exports were permitted again farmers would not be able to pay their rents.'[112]

Because accounts might not be settled until a year or more after death, it is not possible to be certain precisely when a particular fall in prices occurred. Nevertheless it is possible to demonstrate surprisingly close correlations between requests for allowances for inventory overvaluations resulting from falls in corn prices and price falls identified by Phelps-Brown and Hopkins in their index of consumables. Phelps-Brown and Hopkins' price tables show a fall in the price of grain between 1618 and 1622; the index price fell from 750 in 1617 to 418 in 1621 before rising again in 1623. They also identify another fall in the late 1620s, from an index point of 760 in 1626 to 428 in 1628. The correlation in the 1630s is not so clear. Phelps-Brown and Hopkins' figures do show a drop in cereal prices from 1631 to 1635, but whether this is the fall complained of in Kent in 1638 is not certain.

In the post-Restoration period, accounts asking allowance for inventory overvaluations were over represented in every decade until the end of the century, most notably in 1681-90. Fewer accounts survive from this period than from before the Civil War, so it may be that the ones which were preserved were those relating to estates about which there had been some difficulty, rather than that conditions generally were especially bad at this period. In the 1660s,

(Cambridge, 1967 and 1985).

111 Charles Wilson, *England's Apprenticeship 1603-1763* (London, 1965), p.119.

112 Peter Clark, *English provincial society from the Reformation to the Revolution: religion, politics and society in Kent, 1500-1640* (Brighton, 1977), pp.466, 317, 354, and 318.

administrators in the diocese of Canterbury were complaining of a drop in corn and cattle prices in 1666 or before. Phelps-Brown and Hopkins identify a fall in cereal prices from a high in 1662 to a low point in 1667. The situation in the 1680s is not clear, but the complaint in east Kent of a sharp fall in corn prices about 1696 is reflected in Phelps-Brown and Hopkins' tables, in which cereal prices fell from an index point of 951 in 1694 to 752 in 1695. Closer study of this aspect of probate accounts may therefore shed important light on local reactions to times of economic difficulty.

In summary, the evidence of probate accounts seems to be that probate inventories were as accurate as their appraisors could make them at the time. In her assessment of eighteenth century probate inventories in the Brtitsh north American colonies, Alison Hanson Jones concluded, as we have done, that the accounts of executors or administrators indicated how accurately the valuations in inventories were a 'close approximation to the market values of the decedents' wealth.'[113] However, a cautious approach should be adopted towards inventories as a source for agricultural yields and prices, especially in periods when prices are known to have been volatile; inventories taken shortly after harvest are most likely to be accurate.

CANTERBURY AND LINCOLN ACCOUNTS

The Canterbury diocese Probate Accounts

The Canterbury diocese collection of probate accounts is by far the largest of any surviving provincial collection; the collection of Prerogative Court of Canterbury accounts in the Public Record Office, as yet unindexed, may be close to it in size. As the diocese of Canterbury covers a relatively small area, the collection of 13,500 accounts is proportionately even larger than, for example, the six thousand or so which survive for Lincolnshire. Although Kent was more densely settled than Lincolnshire, the population of the diocese of Canterbury was approximately half that of Lincolnshire.[114]

Nevertheless accounts survive for only a small part of the total population of the diocese of Canterbury in the early modern period. The population of the diocese of Canterbury aged over sixteen in 1676 was 53,538, according to the Compton Census, which Christopher

113 Jones (ed.), *American Colonial Wealth*, pp.19-22, 31-5.

114 See Table 1 above, pp.xvii-xviii and the Appendix below, pp.xcv-c. Apart from peculiars, the whole of Lincolnshire was entirely covered by the ecclesiastical jurisdictions of the Archdeaconry Court of Stow and the Consistory Court of Lincoln (for the Archdeaconry of Lincoln).

Chalklin believes was reasonably complete and accurate for Kent.[115] E.A.Wrigley and R.S.Schofield have calculated that the proportion of the population under sixteen in the late seventeenth century was a little over 30%.[116] The total population of the diocese was therefore about 80,000. The great majority of probate accounts relate to the estates of men aged 21 and over. Based on Wrigley and Schofield's figures, the proportion of the population under twenty was just under 40%. The number of people aged 21 and over was thus about 46,000-48,000, the number of men over 21 about 23,000, given that women normally outnumbered men.

Wrigley and Schofield have calculated death rates year-by-year from 1538 to 1841. They have not produced different rates for men, women and children. The whole population death rate for 1676 is 27.5 per thousand per annum. On the assumptions, certainly inaccurate, that the death rate was the same for men, women and children, and that Kent accurately reflected the overall pattern of mortality, about 630 men died in the diocese of Canterbury in 1676. Accounts survive for the estates of 107 men for 1676 in the diocese, and 135 for 1677. In addition a small proportion of the estates of those men who died would have been dealt with in the Prerogative Court of Canterbury, and thus excluded from the sample. Is it unreasonable to suggest that the accounts which survive in the diocese of Canterbury are for around one fifth of the adult men who died in the 1670s, and for an even larger proportion of those who died in the period from 1611 to 1640?

The majority of accounts from the diocese of Canterbury were for the estates of men. Only 1699, one eighth of the surviving Canterbury accounts, were for the estates of women. Canterbury was not atypical. Only twelve per cent of all the accounts we have seen were for the estates of women. In the diocese of Canterbury, the peak periods for the accounts of women's estates were 1596-98, for which there were 100 accounts (14%); 1611-20, from which 295 accounts of women's estates survive (15%), and 1637-41, from which there are 151 accounts (14%).[117]

Why, then, were accounts preserved for the moveable goods of these particular men and women? There is no evidence that these Canterbury diocese accounts were once part of a larger collection

115 Christopher W. Chalklin (ed.), 'The Compton Census of 1676 - the dioceses of Canterbury and Rochester', in *A Seventeenth-Century Miscellany*, Kent Records Series, xvii, Kent Archaeological Society (Maidstone, 1960).

116 E.A. Wrigley & R.S. Schofield, *The Population History of England 1541-1871; A Reconstruction* (London, 1981).

117 These same years also had more accounts for women's estates rendered in the country at large, but then they were also the same years that had the largest numbers of accounts rendered for men's estates.

which has disappeared during the intervening centuries. The fact that they were bound up into volumes so soon after they were made, indicates that there was a conscious decision at an early stage that these should be preserved. From the number of inventories surviving we must conclude that other accounts should have been exhibited. Although we know that in the overall business of the courts the proving of wills greatly exceeded the granting of letters of administration, amongst the accounts it is the other way round. Accounts for the estates of those without wills greatly exceed those for the estates of those who made them. One of the most important functions of the courts, the apportionment of any balance amongst surviving relatives, was not necessary if there was a will that named a residuary legatee. The accounts that were taken in and bound up were, *inter alia*, the courts' record of their actions in the apportionment of balances. Where there was a residuary legatee, the courts had only to pass the exhibited account and acquit the executor of his duties. Is it safe to assume that in such cases the courts never took in a copy of the account? If so, such accounts have not been lost or destoyed, they were never part of the courts' records.

Relatively few of the very poor are represented among the accounts. Can it be the case that many of them had so few goods that it was not worth the courts' time to call the administrators to account? We cannot tell for certain since to our knowledge nobody has yet counted up the proportion of inventories surviving for this court for estates under £5. They should not be represented at all, since in theory only executors or administrators of estates with *bona notabilia* were required to obtain probate or letters of administration.[118] However, if other accounts were duly presented, they were either not taken in by the courts, or a conscious decision must have been made to discard them at a very early stage. Probably around a half of the adult male population totally escaped the attentions of the Canterbury probate courts, presumably mostly on account of poverty.[119] There should be no accounts for those with less than £5 of goods, which we suspect was alaways the cut off point for notable goods in the diocese of Canterbury. However, there are a few accounts with charge values of less than £5 from each decade, except from the 1660s. There were 84 such accounts amongst 9092 accounts covered by Table 4 below, less

118 Swinburne, *Treatise*, VI, xi, 5 explained that in 1590 the definition of 'notable goods' varied from one ecclesiastical court to another, ranging from 40s to £23 3s 1/4d, but was generally £10. But by 1677, the editor of the new edition of the *Treatise* added 'But the Law at this day is that five pounds is the sum or value of Bona notabilia [except where] by custome in any County *bona notabilia* are rated at a greater sum, the same is to continue unaltered, as in the diocese of London it is ten pounds'

119 See above p.xxvi.

than 1% of the total. A surprisingly high proportion of the surviving accounts for very small estates, thirty, fall in the 1590s. Of the 84, 65 finished with a negative balance, but 36 of those were 'in surplussage' by less than £2. Court fees, unless waived, and the expenses of drawing up the inventory and account for presentation to the court, unless written up by the accountant herself, were in themselves enough to drive some tiny estates into debt.[120]

Greater understanding of how ecclesiastical courts worked would help to discover why and how accounts were made. Did apparitors operate on specific circuits or in specific areas? Were some more efficient than others? It is certainly the case that some parishes are far more strongly represented among the accounts than others. Table 3 shows the number of probate accounts as a percentage of the 1676 population for a selection of middling-sized towns in the diocese.

3. Population and Surviving Accounts for Selected East Kent Towns[121]

Court	Town	Population over 16, 1676	Total Number of Accounts	No. of accounts as % of 1676 population
AC	Ashford	1000	178	18%
AC	Cranbrook	1300	251	19%
CC	Deal	1450	190	13%
CC	Dover	1628	334	23%
AC	Faversham	1200	419	35%
AC	Hawkhurst	1000	115	12%
CC	Maidstone	3000	271	9%
AC	Sandwich	1416	571	40%
AC	Tenterden	1200	198	17%

Parish register evidence suggests that for these towns at least, the Compton Census was reasonably accurate. Dover, Sandwich and Faversham were old ports, whilst Deal was a new town in the seventeenth century, its population only starting to grow rapidly from the 1630s. All the other places were long established market towns. There seems to be no good reason why Faversham and Sandwich should have been so much more strongly represented among the

120 See above pp.xxxiii-xxxiv for fees.

121 AC = Accounts rendered to the Archdeaconry Court of Canterbury; CC = Accounts rendered to the Consistory Court of Canterbury. We have distinguished the two in case the differences between the numbers of accounts surviving from different towns was related to the courts to which the accounts were rendered. There was a very considerable overlap in personnel between the two courts.

surviving accounts than the other towns.[122]

The difficulty with such a large mass of material as the Canterbury diocese accounts is knowing how best to organise it so as to produce useful data. It was decided to compare gross moveable wealth (inventory values or charge) and net moveable wealth (estate after all debts and expenses had been paid) for men's accounts in the seven decades 1591-1640 and 1661-1680. This takes in the periods for which most accounts survive.

4. Range of Moveable Wealth in Accounts for Men, East Kent, 1591-1680[123]

Gross: Charge (i.e.Inventory) Values

Decade	Total Number	Highest	Median	Lowest
1591-1600	1393	£1105	£29	£2
1601-1610	1063	£1925	£33	£3
1611-1620	1611	£2169	£36	£1
1621-1630	1414	£4851	£39	15s.
1631-1640	1416	£3633	£51	18s.

1661-1670	924	£1753	£79	£10
1671-1680	1271	£3895	£80	£1

Net: Balance

Decade	Total Number	Highest	Median	Lowest
1591-1600	1393	£843	£6	-£335
1601-1610	1063	£1339	£7	-£906
1611-1620	1611	£1600	£9	-£1100
1621-1630	1414	£1550	£6	-£1048
1631-1640	1416	£2566	£9	-£1570

1661-1670	924	£1516	£11	-£1361
1671-1680	1271	£2152	£13	-£1119

Since accounts were frequently not presented until a year or

122 These figures are from Chalklin 'The Compton Census'. Slightly different figures for the diocese of Canterbury are to be found in Anne Whiteman (ed.), *The Compton Census of 1676: A critical edition*, Records of Social and Economic History, New Series, x (British Academy, 1986), pp.4-35. For Sandwich the original returns survive and total 1316, not 1416, which was an error in addition made in 1676; For Deal she has 1500, and for Dover 1950. She incidentally considers the Ashford 1000 a 'very casual estimate'. These emendations only accentuate the difference between Sandwich and Faversham on the one hand and Dover and Deal on the other.

123 Using only accounts with both charge and balance. All sums over £1 have been rounded to the nearest pound.

more after the death, it was not practical to look at a period of less than a decade. Consideration of 1591-1640 allows comparison of the bad years of the 1590s with the period after the slowing down of the price revolution after about 1610.

It must, of course, always be remembered that a considerable proportion of estates, normally, but not exclusively, those of the wealthiest men and women, was dealt with in the Prerogative Court of Canterbury, and thus not represented here.[124]

The contrast between the median inventory values, or charges, and median balances, or final account values, in each decade is immediately apparent. The median charge values increased markedly from under £30 in the 1590s to over £50 on the eve of the Civil War. In parallel, but at a much lower level, the median balance, which was under £6 in the 1590s, rose to just under £9 on the eve of the Civil War. There was not a continuous rise. The fall in median balance values from nearly £9 in the 1610s to just over £6 in the 1620s is of interest as this was the period at which the later sixteenth century inflation was levelling out; the fall may not therefore represent a fall in spending power in real terms. On the other hand, the increase again in the 1630s from £6 to nearly £9 probably does indicate a substantial increase in real terms as prices continued to level off.

The post-Civil War period saw a considerable increase in median charge values compared with the earlier decades, from about £50 to about £80 in the 1660s and 1670s. Median balance values also rose, though not by so large a percentage - from just under £9 in the 1630s to just under £11 in the 1660s and £12 11s. in the 1670s.

5. Negative Balances in Accounts for Men, East Kent 1591-1680

Decade	Total Number With Negative Balance	% of Total With Negative Balance
1591-1600	494	36%
1601-1610	397	37%
1611-1620	591	37%
1621-1630	610	43%
1631-1640	552	39%

1661-1670	380	41%
1671-1680	495	39%

124 See Takahashi, 'The Number of Wills', for the increasing proportion of wills proved and letters of administration granted by the Prerogative Court rather than the provincial courts in the seventeenth century and how far down the social scale these reached by the end of the century.

The proportion of accounts ending in the negative, that is, the deceased's debts exceeded his moveable assets, varied little over the ninety year period. Throughout the century the accountants of around two in every five men who died in east Kent had to pay out more than they received to administer. In the decade 1591-1600, 35.5% of all men's accounts ended in the negative. The 1590s are supposed to have been one of the worst decades in English history, with inflation, a succession of disastrous harvests, and epidemics. From the evidence presented here, however, it seems that the decade 1621-1630 was worse for many in east Kent. It was in this decade that the proportion of accounts ending with a negative balance reached 43.1%, its highest for the period. One of the effects of such a rise in the number of accounts ending in the negative was that the median balance value fell, having been rising since the 1590s. It has already been noted that it was in the 1620s that claims for inventory overvaluations peaked, and the reasons given for the claims indicate the difficulties that people were experiencing at the time. It is noticeable that the charge values do not suggest that the 1620s were a difficult time, demonstrating further the limitations of the probate inventory, however accurate, as an economic indicator.

Comparison of the Canterbury and Lincoln Accounts

The number of accounts from Lincolnshire available for consideration in this way is much smaller, but it is worthwhile to attempt comparison with the Canterbury diocese material.

6. Moveable Wealth in Accounts for Men, Lincolnshire 1591-1690[125]

Decade	Total Number	Median Charge Value	Median Balance
1591-1600	35	£74	£37
1601-1610	86	£65	£33
1611-1620	700	£43	£14
1621-1630	488	£41	£13
1631-1640	952	£48	£15
1641-1650	440	£64	£23

1661-1670	573	£68	£20
1671-1680	254	£80	£6
1681-1690	197	£86	£13

125 Using only accounts with both charge and balance. All sums have been rounded to the nearest pound.

The economy of Lincolnshire was of course very different from that of Kent. In Lincolnshire, the difference between median charge values and median balance values increases during the period. The pattern differs from that in east Kent in that while in Lincolnshire median charge values dip from £74 in the 1590s to just under £41 in the 1620s before rising again, median balance values fall sharply in the 1610s and remain low for the rest of the century. However, both median charge values and median balance values are generally higher in Lincolnshire than in the diocese of Canterbury, although it must be borne in mind that the Lincolnshire sample is much smaller and may be weighted towards the wealthier sections of society.[126] Unlike the Canterbury diocese accounts, median charge values in Lincolnshire do suggest some difficulty in the 1620s, while median balance values do not.

7. Negative Balances in Accounts for Men, Lincolnshire 1611-1690

Decade	Number with Negative Balance	% of Total With Negative Balance
1611-1620	166	24%
1621-1630	121	26%
1631-1640	218	24%
1641-1650	94	22%

1661-1670	127	24%
1671-1680	109	45%
1681-1690	109	56%

The proportion of accounts ending in the negative in Lincolnshire does not follow the same pattern as in the diocese of Canterbury. In the 1590s and 1600s, the Lincolnshire sample is too small for any firm conclusions to be drawn. From 1611 to 1670, only about a quarter of all Lincolnshire accounts ended with a negative balance, whilst in Kent forty per cent were doing so. From 1670, the proportion ending in surplussage increased dramatically, reaching over a half in the 1680s. However, this may reflect changes in the survival of accounts rather than changing economic conditions.

Table 8 shows the distribution of charge and balance values among different ranges of wealth in the diocese of Canterbury. The

126 The fall in Lincolnshire in both median charge value and median balance around 1620 may also relate to a change in policy over which accounts were to be retained by the court. It looks as if before 1620 only a few larger accounts were retained, but that afterwards a wider range was kept, but still far short of the Kent proportion.

charge values show a steady increase of moveable wealth in the diocese from the 1590s to the 1670s. In the 1590s, 45.4% of all men's accounts had a charge value of under £25. By the 1670s, only 12.3% of men's accounts had a charge value of less than £25. The proportion in the range £25-£50 remained steady.[127]

8. Distribution of Moveable Wealth in Accounts for Men, East Kent

Gross: Charge Value

Percentages of Total in Each Range

Range	1590s	1600s	1610s	1620s	1630s	1660s	1670s
Over £500	0.8	2.5	2.4	2.7	4.4	4.9	6.1
£250-£499.19s	3.2	3.8	4.3	5.3	7.6	10.3	10.6
£100-£249.19s	9.8	11.7	15.1	16.3	17.8	26.7	24.5
£50-£99.19s	16.6	17.6	18.2	18.9	20.6	22.2	22.8
£25-£49.19s	24.0	24.1	24.6	24.4	24.3	20.1	23.5
under £25	45.4	40.0	35.3	32.3	25.3	15.8	12.3

Net: Balance

Percentages of Total in Each Range

Range	1590s	1600s	1610s	1620s	1630s	1660s	1670s
Over £500	0.2	0.6	0.8	0.9	1.9	1.1	1.7
£250-£499.19s	0.6	1.7	1.4	1.8	1.0	3.7	3.7
£100-£249.19s	3.3	5.3	6.1	6.0	7.9	9.4	11.8
£50-£99.19s	7.5	7.2	8.4	8.2	10.2	12.2	11.0
£25-£49.19s	10.5	13.2	12.2	10.4	11.8	12.0	12.4
£0-£24.19s	42.5	34.6	34.5	29.6	26.9	20.3	20.3
above -£25	30.2	32.3	30.3	33.1	29.3	27.8	27.0
-£25- -£49.19s	2.9	2.2	2.5	4.4	4.2	5.1	4.4
below -£50	2.4	2.9	3.8	5.4	6.0	8.1	7.6
Total Accounts per Decade	1393	1063	1611	1414	1416	924	1271

There was an increase in the proportion of accounts with charge values in all ranges above £50. It is most marked in the range £100-£250. In the 1590s, under 10% of all accounts had a charge value in this range. By the 1670s, nearly a quarter of all men's accounts had a charge value between £100 and £250. Charge values in the range

127 Except for a drop in the 1660s. Figures for the 1660s should however be treated with caution, since ecclesiastical court administration remained disrupted for some time after the Restoration.

£250-£500 increased threefold, from just over 3% of the total to over 10% of the total. It is necessary to be cautious; fewer accounts survive after 1660, and it may be the poorer people's accounts that are missing. Nevertheless, it does appear that there was a steady increase in moveable wealth during the period. Neither does it appear that this increase can be accounted for solely by the effects of the price revolution. The proportion of charge values in the range £100-£250 rose from 10% in the 1590s to over 16% in the 1620s, an increase of nearly two-thirds at a time when prices generally were falling.

The evidence of charge values in Canterbury diocese probate accounts is thus of a steady increase in moveable wealth from the 1590s to the 1670s. What is the evidence of balance values? It has already been noted that the proportion of estates ending with a negative balance was 35.5% in the 1590s, rising to 43% in the 1620s, falling back to 39% in the 1670s. Most accounts which ended in the negative did so by less than £25, but a large proportion of all accounts might be found in that range. In the 1620s, a third of all men's accounts finished in the negative by up to £25. In the 1660s and 1670s, about 27% of all men's accounts finished with a negative balance of up to £25. How serious this was for each individual estate depended upon resources, primarily land, not included in the accountinf process in ecclesiastical courts. A shortfall of £25 would be less likely to be catastrophic to an estate with moveables initially worth over £500, than it would be to a estate which had only £25 of moveables to start with, since the former would be more likely to be adequately bolstered by land than the latter. It would therefore be useful to investigate the proportion of the value of each estate expended by each administrator. It is also necessary to ask whether the indebtedness of an estate came as an unwelcome surprise to an administrator or whether it was expected and planned for by the deceased. Sometimes there are clear indications within an account that an estate was in trouble. Henrie Foord of Birchington died of plague in 1638. His account concluded with a negative balance, but the creditors allowed the widow to keep her bed, worth £5. In 1612, the administrator of Thomas Browne of Hythe had to pawn a boat in order to pay his debts. Of those accounts which finished with some assets remaining in the administrators' hands, the majority in each decade were left with under £25, although the proportion fell from 41.5% of the total in the 1590s to 20.3% of the total in the 1670s. In the pre-Civil War period, there is little difference in the proportion of charge values in this range and the proportion of balance values.[128]

As with the charge values, there were increases in the

128 Foord CKS PRC20/10/362; Browne CKS PRC20/3/438

proportion of balance values in all the upper ranges, although they were less marked. The proportion of accounts with balances in the range £25-£50 remained fairly stable. There was a steady increase also in the proportion of accounts concluding with assets worth £50-£100 and also in the range £100-£250. Like the charge values, therefore, the balance values show a steady increase in net moveable wealth in the diocese from the 1590s to the 1670s, although the picture of prosperity is coloured by the large number of accounts in each decade which, whether because of poverty, miscalculation or misfortune ended with a negative balance.

9. Distribution of Moveable Wealth in Accounts for Men, Lincolnshire.

Gross: Charge Value

Percentage of Total in Each Range

Range	1610s	1620s	1630s	1640s	1660s	1670s	1680s
over £500	1.4	1.4	2.9	2.2	3.7	4.5	7.3
£250-£499.19s	6.6	3.9	6.2	7.4	7.7	9.5	14.4
£100-£249.19s	15.5	18.7	17.9	23.2	23.3	30.6	20.7
£50-£99.19s	20.6	20.6	21.3	26.7	25.3	23.1	27.9
£25-£49.19s	29.3	27.5	24.4	26.9	23.9	17.4	20.1
under £25	26.7	28.0	27.4	13.3	16.1	14.9	9.8

Net: Balance

Percentage of Total in Each Range

Range	1610s	1620s	1630s	1640s	1660s	1670s	1680s
over£500	0.8	0.6	1.0	0.9	1.3	0.8	1.6
£250-£499.19s	2.3	2.3	3.0	2.8	4.5	2.9	6.2
£100-£249.19s	7.9	6.8	8.9	11.5	8.8	12.8	8.8
£50-£99.19s	8.3	7.8	11.3	13.6	17.3	8.7	10.3
£25-£49.19s	14.6	15.5	15.2	19.3	11.6	9.5	11.3
£0-£24.19s	42.0	41.4	36.8	30.3	32.7	20.3	27.3
above -£25	20.2	21.8	19.5	15.6	17.8	30.2	24.2
-£25- -£49.19s	2.0	1.5	2.2	2.8	3.6	8.7	5.2
below -£50	2.1	2.3	2.2	3.2	2.5	6.3	5.2
Total Accounts per Decade	700	488	952	440	573	254	197

In Lincolnshire in the 1610s and 1620s, moveable wealth seems to have been more evenly distributed than in east Kent. In this period, three quarters of all Lincolnshire accounts had charge values of under

£100, but, unlike Kent, only a little over a quarter of all estates were initially worth less than £25.[129] In the 1630s, the distribution in Lincolnshire was almost identical to that in the diocese of Canterbury. In the 1660s and 1670s also, Lincolnshire and Canterbury charge values were distributed almost identically, except that in the 1670s there was a rather smaller proportion of Lincolnshire accounts in the £25-£50 range and rather more in the £100-£250 range. As in the diocese of Canterbury, the evidence of charge values in the Lincolnshire accounts is that people were becoming wealthier during the seventeenth century. Accounts with charge values of less than £25 fell from over one quarter of the total to about 15%, whereas those in the £100-£250 range rose from 15% of the total to 30%.

In Lincolnshire, more accounts ended with a balance in the £0-£25 range than in east Kent, and fewer ended in the -£25-£0 range. The picture changes in the 1670s, when only just over 20% of Lincolnshire accounts fell in to the under £25 range, and over 30% ended in the negative by less than £25. The evidence from the Lincolnshire accounts seems to be of a fairly stable economy which suffered some dislocation in the 1670s. In this decade, while the evidence of the charge values suggest that Lincolnshire men were becoming wealthier, the evidence of the balance values is that something caused a sudden increase in the proportion of accounts ending with a negative balance, and in particular may have caused the poorest groups, those with assets worth less than £25, to slip into debt.

One unexpected feature of the comparison between Canterbury diocese and Lincolnshire accounts is that for most of the period Canterbury accounts seem more likely to have ended with a negative balance. Kent, especially east Kent, is believed to have been one of the wealthier regions of England in the seventeenth century, with not only varied agriculture, much of the produce of which went to the London market, but also clothmaking both in the Weald and in towns such as Canterbury and Sandwich. One would have expected people in east Kent to have been wealthier, and less likely to die in debt, than those in Lincolnshire.

Debt and Credit

One explanation may be that the economy of east Kent was more sophisticated than that of Lincolnshire, with men in Kent having greater access to credit and being more willing to take advantage of its availability. They might therefore be more likely to find themselves in

129 This too may be an illusion created by the Lincolnshire pattern of retaining (or even demanding) fewer accounts for smaller estates than in Kent.

a position in which their obligations exceeded their assets. Just over 11,000 of the 13,585 Canterbury diocese accounts reveal that the deceased left debts to be paid. It was patently normal in east Kent in the seventeenth century to be living at least in part on other people's money. The median number of debts recorded was three. Some people, however, were indebted to quite a considerable number of people at the time of their deaths. Among the Kent accounts, 568 people, just over one in twenty, left over twenty debts to be paid after their deaths. In the country as a whole, 1674 people left twenty or more debts, again around one account in every twenty examined. There were 184 people who left fifty or more debts to be paid and even fifteen who left a hundred or more debts.

Many, probably the majority, of debts were outstanding payments for goods or services supplied, or sometimes unpaid wages. However, 26% of the Kent accounts record that the deceased owed money on a bond. Bonds were the normal written method of securing a loan in the seventeenth century. Less formal than bonds were other written records of debt, for example simple 'bills' or entries in merchant books. These were known generically as 'specialties'. In 355 of the east Kent accounts the accountants said they were paying debts 'on specialty'. In 193 cases, out of the 355, these were accounts in which there were no references to bonds, but in 162 accounts there were also references to bonds. Least formal of all were loans made for which there was no 'specialty or writing'.

The hypothesis that men in Kent had more access to credit, or were more willing to resort to borrowing, is not borne out by the evidence. Men's probate accounts in both Lincolnshire and east Kent reveal an increasing readiness to resort to borrowing from the 1610s onwards. Between 1611 and 1620, nearly 55% of all men in Lincolnshire for whose estates probate accounts survive died owing money on bills or bonds. The corresponding figure for Canterbury diocese is just over 26%. The proportion of men in Lincolnshire making use of credit fluctuates, no doubt due to the smaller samples involved, so that no definite trend can be observed. In the 1620s, nearly 52% of all men made use of credit; in the 1630s and 1640s this had fallen to around 42%. In the 1660s, a little over 40% of Lincolnshire men had bonds and bills mentioned in their accounts, while in the 1670s and 1680s the proportion rose again to around 50%. The greater use of credit in the period 1611-1630 no doubt reflects the difficult economic conditions of the time.

In the diocese of Canterbury, where the samples are much larger, a definite trend is discernible. At no time did the proportion of men owing money on bills or bonds at death equal that in Lincolnshire.

In the 1620s, nearly 35.5% of men owed money in this way. This proportion fell slightly in the next two decades and in the 1660s. There was a much more marked fall, to just over 24%, in the 1670s, but a sharp rise, to nearly 39%, in the 1680s and 1690s. Overall, it seems that credit in the form of bonds and bills was equally available in east Kent and Lincolnshire during the seventeenth century, but that Lincolnshire men were more likely to increase their borrowing in response to periods of economic difficulty, while men in east Kent maintained a more regular pattern of borrowing.

The rate of interest in England dropped continuously from the sixteenth to the eighteenth century. The rate paid on bonds was generally, but not always, the legal maximum. By the Usury Act of 1571, which re-legalised the payment of interest, the permitted maximum was 10%. The next Usury Act of 1623-24, in force from 24 June 1625, reduced the maximum rate of interest for new bonds to 8%. The Commonwealth Usury Act of 1651, confirmed by the Restoration Usury Act of 1660, reduced the maximum once more, this time to 6%.

The Usury Acts took it for granted that borrowed money was for agriculture and trade. There seem to have been a number of occasions in the life-cycle when those engaged in farming would be likely to borrow in this way. First of all in early manhood, for setting oneself up - buying or leasing land, buying stock. Further borrowings would allow for increases in the scale of farming, and later there would be marriage portions and apprenticeship premiums to be provided, and possibly portions given to sons to enable them to set themselves up rather than having to wait for their father to die before they received their inheritance. Borrowing could also take place to stave off ruin, perhaps due to individual illness or general disasters such as the harvest failures of the 1590s.[130]

The evidence from probate inventories suggests that lenders were less numerous than borrowers. Trinder and Cox, in their study of Shropshire inventories between 1660 and 1750, noted that 11%, 92 out of 846, of their probate inventories contained references to money out on bond, out at interest, or which they had some other reason to think had been invested. If the situation in Shropshire was comparable with that in east Kent, therefore, there were more borrowers than lenders.[131]

Family members seem to have been a common source of credit, at least among yeomen. In the diocese of Canterbury in the early seventeenth century, John Swaineland's goods were administered

130 Peter Spufford, 'Long term rural credit in sixteenth- and seventeenth-century England - the evidence of Probate Accounts' in T.Arkell and N.Evans, *When Death do us part* (Local Population Studies Society, in the press 1999).

131 Trinder and Cox, *Yeomen*, pp.18-19.

by Edward Prescott. Edward Prescott and John Swaineland's wives were sisters. Edward's account of John's goods included repayment of £300 which John had borrowed on bond from George Young of Canterbury, the brother of the two wives. The account of the goods of Richard Tritton, who had married Edward Prescott's sister, reveals that Edward was his principal creditor, and that he had also borrowed £7 from his father-in-law John Prescott. John Prescott's other son-in-law, Thomas Partridge, was also indebted to his father-in-law at his death. Dr Holderness in an analysis of forty two Lincolnshire accounts found that 40% of lenders could be identified as relatives by blood or marriage.[132]

Gentlemen were also providers of credit, presumably investing surplus income from rents. Robert Weedon Esq., of Bosmore, in Fawley, Buckinghamshire, illustrates the activity of one such man. At his death in 1703 he had 35 loans outstanding. Fifteen of these loans had been made in the five years before he died, eighteen were over ten years old, including four over twenty years old, and two over thirty years old. He had been investing since the 1680s to gain an income for the rest of his life.[133] Other studies have emphasised the role of widows as investors, and of 'aged' yeomen and even husbandmen who had divested themselves of their farming goods and stock and then laid out their money on loans and mortgages and, it is fair to assume, lived off the interest. One such man was Nicholas Hatton, a yeoman of Guston near Dover. He was probably a widower at his death in 1682 and may have been living with one of his married daughters; he seems to have been occupying only two rooms and had few personal possessions apart from his wearing apparel, bed and bedding. However, the total value of his inventory was £786 7s 8d. He owned '2 sixteen parts of 2 old boats belong ing to Dover', one called Five Nicholases, the other the Bartholomew. He left £68 in money, £400 due upon bonds, £220 in 'good debts likely to be received' and £45 in 'desperate debts.'[134]

There is also evidence for lending between members of small religious or ethnic groups. Dr Christopher Marsh has found evidence

132 Swaineland CKS PRC2/24/85. Edward Prescott was the son of the John Prescott referred to above, pp.xlvi-xlvii. He was a yeoman who was also Mayor of Dover twice during the 1650s. Tritton CKS PRC2/24/148; Partridge CKS PRC20/7/164; B.A.Holderness, 'Widows in pre-industrial society: an essay upon their economic Functions', in Richard M. Smith (ed.), *Land, Kinship and Life-Cycle* (Cambridge, 1984), pp.423-42.

133 Public Record Office, Chancery Lane, PROB.5.1018, printed in Michael Reed (ed.), *Buckinghamshire Probate Inventories 1661-1714* (Buckinghamshire Record Society, xxiv, 1988), no.146, pp. 280-4.

134 Holderness, 'Widows' emphasizes (pp.435-42) the role of widows as lenders, both on bond and on mortgage; Margaret Spufford, *Contrasting Communities*, p.80; Hatton CKS PRC27/29/237

for lending between members of the Family of Love in Cambridgeshire at the end of the sixteenth century and the beginning of the seventeenth.[135] Members of the Dover General Baptist Church also lent and borrowed among themselves in the post-Restoration period. The Church itself sometimes lent money from Church funds to members, or deacons might act as guarantors to enable church members to obtain credit elsewhere. At a church meeting in October 1694, it was 'agreed and concluded that the deacons Bro John Hutchens and Bro Richard Marsh should be security to the Brewers Capt Jno Hollingbery and Mr Richard Becks on behalfe of Sister Francke for due payment for such beere as she takes of them and the Church also agreed to bear ye Deacons harmless for their soe-doing.' Individual church members also made loans to each other. John Culmer had borrowed from George Hulke and Richard Hobbs, while John Lambert had borrowed from Cornelius Garrison and Widow Francke.[136]

Two of the leading figures in the Baptist congregation were Samuel Tavenor and Edward Prescott.[137] Samuel Tavenor's sister Priscilla was married to James Henry, a yeoman of Eythorne, about five miles inland from Dover, and a leading member of the Baptist congregation there. James Henry evidently felt very friendly towards Edward Prescott, since he bequeathed £10 to each of his three sons in his will. At his death in 1680, James Henry held a mortgage of lands of Edward Prescott dated 1st May 1668, a further mortgage of lands of Edward Prescott dated 28 June 1670, worth at least £100, and another mortgage of lands of Edward Prescott dated 1st April 1671. Edward Prescott had died in 1672. Unfortunately, no inventory or account survives for his estate. His will makes no mention of these mortgages, referring only to 'lands tenements hereditaments etc,' and also making bequests totalling £150 in cash legacies. In addition to the Prescott mortgages, James Henry also held a mortgage of lands in Wingham Well, a mortgage of marshland in Ash and a mortgage of lands in Eythorne valued at £100.[138]

Historians have attached some importance to changes in the law regarding mortgages in the late seventeenth century, suggesting that mortgages became more widely used as a result.[139] The number of Lincolnshire men making use of mortgages was too small for any conclusions to be drawn, but a pattern is discernible in east Kent. Until

135 Christopher W. Marsh, *The Family of Love in English Society, 1550-1630* (Cambridge, 1994).

136 J. M. Bower, The Congregation of the Dover General Baptist Church, 1660-1700, Leicester M.A. Dissertation 1983. CKS PRC20/12/73; CKS PRC20/12/88

137 Son of the Edward Prescott, Mayor of Dover, mentioned above.

138 Henry CKS PRC17/75/90; Prescott CKS PRC32/54/71

139 Wilson, *England's Apprenticeship*, p.207; Chalklin, 'Compton Census'.

the 1660s, the number of men's probate accounts mentioning-mortgages was negligible. In the 1660s, eight accounts out of 995, or 0.8%, mentioned money borrowed on mortgages by the deceased. In the 1670s eighteen accounts out of 1277, or 1.4%, mention mortgages. This increase is tiny, but corresponds to a fall in the number of men owing money on bonds and bills in the same period. Overall, however, the use of credit in the 1670s was less than that in the 1660s. The use of mortgages rose again in the 1680s and again in the 1690s, although the overall sample in this decade is too small for any firm conclusions to be reached. It seems therefore that there was a small increase in the use of mortgages after 1670, but that bonds and bills were still the preferred methods of borrowing money.

PROBATE ACCOUNTS AND ECONOMIC CONDITIONS

In summary, what do probate accounts tell us about economic conditions in the late sixteenth and seventeenth centuries? There is only space to make brief, but contrasting, case studies of the evidence that probate accounts give of conditions in the eastern parts of Kent and in London.

The Wealth of Early Modern Kent

At any time between 1591 and 1680, more than one third of men in the diocese of Canterbury had insufficient easily liquidatable assets to cover all their financial obligations. Normally this would not be a problem, as early modern society operated on long credit and all debts did not need to be repaid at once. At death, however, all creditors had to be satisfied.

Most indicators show that the 1620s were the most difficult decade in the period under discussion. During the 1590s, 1600s and 1610s, final values of estates indicate increasing prosperity, with more accounts finishing in the higher value ranges. In the 1620s, however, there was stagnation or even decline. The median value of account balances fell, the proportion of accounts with a negative balance rose, the proportion of accounts in the higher ranges of balance values fell. These conclusions agree with other historians' assessments of the 1620s. The accounts indicate that in the 1630s and especially in the post-Restoration period, there were real advances in material prosperity for the people of east Kent.

In the mid seventeenth century, Kent was the second or third wealthiest county in England, due to its nearness to the London markets and the wealth of its natural resources. The standards of living of the people of Kent were up to a hundred years ahead of the poorer counties of the north west of England. The diocese of Canterbury covers the eastern part of the county, extending for forty miles from east to west and twenty to thirty miles north to south. The River Medway divides the two dioceses of Rochester and Canterbury, except that the Medway towns of Rochester, Chatham and Gillingham, although on the eastern side of the river, are in the western diocese of Rochester. Of the two dioceses, Canterbury was larger in area, and in the early modern period outstripped Rochester in wealth and population. In 1676, some 80,000 people of the total county population of about 150,000 were in the diocese of Canterbury.[140]

Nearly all the significant towns in Kent were in the diocese of Canterbury. Several had borough status, but most had only small populations. Canterbury, with a population of five to six thousand, was the biggest town in the diocese.[141] After agriculture, the county's biggest industry in the early modern period, clothmaking, was largely concentrated in the eastern Weald and in Sandwich and Canterbury. Historians agree that early modern towns were generally poorer than the surrounding countryside due to the large numbers of subsistence migrants who moved into towns each year. However, these migrants were men and women at the very lowest levels of society, whose poverty was such that they were unlikely to feature among the probate accounts at all.

Canterbury

Most Kent towns were also ports, which may have distorted their trade and economy. In Canterbury, the church was a dominant force, and there was a significant Stranger community - perhaps a fifth of the total population of the city by 1700 - which brought with it silkweaving and papermaking. However, none of these dominated the city's economy. Canterbury was somewhat depressed, particularly in the early part of the period under discussion, when the cloth industry had been drawn away to the Weald and the newer silk and papermaking industries had yet to become established.

Table 11 demonstrates the economic condition of Canterbury in the early modern period. The median charge values for estates of

140 Chalklin, 'The Compton Census'

141 Although Maidstone is the county town, and within the diocese of Canterbury, it has been omitted from the following discussion because there are too few surviving accounts for Maidstone townspeople's estates for any useful comparisons to be made. According to the Compton Census, Deptford and Greenwich, growing rapidly with London, were already rivalling Canterbury in size. They were both in the diocese of Rochester.

Canterbury men dying between 1591 and 1670 compare favourably with those for all men's estates in the diocese. Indeed, in the 1590s, the 1610s and the critical decade of the 1620s, Canterbury men appear to be better off than those in the rest of the region.

10. Moveable Wealth in Accounts for Men, City of Canterbury, 1591-1680[142]

Decade	Number of Accounts	Median Charge Value	Median Balance
1591-1600	65	£36	£5
1601-1610	53	£33	-£2
1611-1620	76	£45	£8
1621-1630	69	£43	-£2
1631-1640	82	£43	-2s.6d

1661-1670	60	£76	-£1
1671-1680	65	£48	-2s

However, on comparing median balance values, a quite different picture emerges. In the 1590s and 1610s, Canterbury's median balances of £5 and £8 9s match almost exactly the medians of £5 14s. and £8 17s in the diocese as a whole. In the other decades, however, the median balances for Canterbury accounts are in the negative. In the post-Restoration period in particular, Canterbury lags further and further behind the rest of the region in terms of wealth.

11. Negative Balances in Accounts for Men, City of Canterbury

Decade	Total Accounts	Number in Negative	% in Negative
1591-1600	65	28	43%
1601-1610	53	34	64%
1611-1620	76	29	38%
1621-1630	69	41	59%
1631-1640	82	42	51%

1661-1670	60	31	52%
1671-1680	65	34	52%

The same impression is conveyed by the proportion of accounts

142 Using only accounts with both charge and balance. All sums over £1 rounded to nearest pound.

ending in the negative in Canterbury. In the 1610s, 38% of all Canterbury accounts concluded with a negative balance, effectively the same as the 37% of accounts in the whole diocese ending in the negative. This was Canterbury's best decade, however. In the 1600s, over 64% of all Canterbury accounts ended with a negative balance, and more than half ended in the negative in each decade after 1620. The city of Canterbury, although the principal town in east Kent, lagged behind the rest of the region in terms of wealth and prosperity. The probate accounts reveal, not only poverty among the lowest levels of urban society, but economic instability among the 'middling sort'.

Unlike most of the other towns in the diocese, Canterbury was not a sea or river port. The surrounding countryside was a fruit and corn growing area, with hopfields becoming widespread by the end of the seventeenth century. Much of the city's population was presumably occupied in marketing and processing this produce and providing goods and services for the local population, so why should the city's economy have been so weak in comparison with the surrounding rural area? Both contemporaries and later historians have noted the fact that much of the agricultural produce of east Kent went to supply the London market. Possibly because Canterbury was not a port, produce was taken to Faversham, or the Thanet ports, rather than to the Canterbury markets. It has been noted that this trade was increasingly controlled by Londoners in the seventeenth century, thus reducing still further the business opportunities for Canterbury corn merchants and fruit and hop dealers.[143]

Faversham, Sandwich and Dover

The maritime trade of east Kent was broadly based in the seventeenth century. There was fishing in the Channel and the North Sea. Kent fishermen still went to Yarmouth each autumn for the herring fair. Transporting grain and other produce to London for sale was also an important element in Kent's maritime trade. Ships from the Kent ports also carried on trade with the Low Countries and with North east England. Deal developed its victualling, piloting, and salvaging services during the seventeenth century. All Kent ports had their associated trades of boatbuilding, sailmaking and ropemaking. There were many small creeks and harbours along the Channel coast and the Thames estuary, but in east Kent Faversham, Sandwich and Dover were the principal ports. Faversham was chiefly involved in shipping grain and other agricultural produce to London, with some

143 J. H. Andrews, 'The trade of the port of Faversham 1650-1750,' *Archaeologia Cantiana*, lxix (1955).

coasting and Baltic trade. Sandwich had by the late sixteenth century declined from its medieval position as the principal port of south east England and had suffered some loss in population. However, the town still had a busy trade with the Low Countries, while Dover was the leading cross-Channel port as well as engaging in a variety of other traffic. All three towns, and especially Sandwich and Dover, were vulnerable to the repeated outbreaks of plague up to 1666. The activities of privateers in the Channel during the Thirty Years War may also have had a detrimental effect on their activities. Later, the Dutch Wars also affected trade. The late 1670s and 1680s also seem to have been a precarious time for the owners of fishing and small coasting vessels. Several accountants asked the court for allowance because the value of boats which the various deceased had owned or part owned had been overestimated in inventories.[144]

12. Moveable Wealth in Accounts for Men, Dover, Faversham, Sandwich, 1591-1680[145]

Decade	Number of Accounts	Median Charge Value	Median Balance
1591-1600	115	£23	-10s9d
1601-1610	85	£27	-£1
1611-1620	135	£30	-5s9d
1621-1630	183	£33	-8s
1631-1640	155	£39	-3s9d

1661-1670	101	£81	£8
1671-1680	124	£79	-19s3d

The median charge values of accounts from Dover, Sandwich and Faversham lagged behind the whole region except in the 1660s and 1670s. As with accounts from Canterbury, so with those from these port towns, the median balance values were only in the positive in two decades, and except in the 1660s half or more of all accounts ended with a negative balance. On this evidence, while these ports were not in so bad a position as Canterbury throughout this period, they were not doing a great deal better.

144 CKS PRC2/38/184; PRC2/39/1; PRC2/39/52; PRC20/13/99; PRC2/40/93

145 Using only accounts with both charge and balance. All sums over £1 rounded to nearest pound.

13. Negative Balances in Accounts for Men,
Dover, Faversham, Sandwich, 1591-1680

Decade	Total Accounts	Number in Negative	% in Negative
1591-1600	115	64	56%
1601-1610	85	47	55%
1611-1620	135	68	50%
1621-1630	183	92	50%
1631-1640	155	77	50%

1661-1670	101	45	45%
1671-1680	124	67	54%

Thanet

So where in east Kent does one look for the region's wealth in the seventeenth century? The corn growing parishes of the Isle of Thanet - Birchington, Minster in Thanet, Monkton, St Nicholas at Wade, St John, St Lawrence and St Peter - were the homes of some of the wealthiest men identified in these accounts, remembering always that the estates of yet wealthier men passed through the prerogative court. Of the eighty wealthiest men, in terms of net moveable assets, whose accounts were preserved by the Canterbury courts, no fewer than ten came from Thanet parishes. Five of them were described as 'yeomen'.

14. Some of the wealthiest men in East Kent
(net moveable wealth from account balance[146])

Edward Philpott, yeo.	St Nicholas at Wade	1679	£1870 7s 6d
Paul Cleaybrooke	St John Thanet	1623	£1307 12s 9d
John Bradshawe	St John Thanet	1648	£1007 11s 9d
Mathias Cauntis, yeo.	Monkton	1679	£974 0s 0d
John Curling	St Lawrence Thanet	1682	£948 11s 6d
Henry Archer, yeo.	Monkton	1679	£894 1s 0d
John Evers	St Lawrence Thanet	1692	£822 7s 6d
Ezekiel Bridges, yeo.	St Nicholas at Wade	1673	£783 11s11d
Robert Turner	Minster in Thanet	1629	£763 12s 6d
Matthias Cantis yeo.	Monkton	1664	£711 9s10d

146 Philpott CKS PRC20/12/318; Cleaybrooke PRC2/23/84; Bradshawe PRC1/8/35; Cauntis PRC20/12/295; Curling PRC2/40/13; Archer PRC 21/5/54; Evers PRC2/42/32; Bridges PRC20/12/70; Turner PRC2/29/102; Cantis PRC19/3/17

St John and St Lawrence included the ports of Margate and Ramsgate, which were largely engaged in the grain traffic with London. The two men from St Lawrence were respectively called 'mariner' and 'brewer & merchant'.

15. Moveable Wealth in Accounts for Men,
Thanet Corn Growing Parishes, 1591-1680[147]

Decade	Number of Accounts	Median Charge Value	Median Balance
1591-1600	100	£27	£5
1601-1610	60	£29	£9
1611-1620	99	£32	£9
1621-1630	84	£37	£10
1631-1640	78	£39	£11

1661-1670	54	£82	£15
1671-1680	70	£92	£35

The median charge values of the accounts from these parishes compare well with those for the whole region except in the 1630s, when Thanet fell behind, and the 1670s, when Thanet was considerably in advance of the rest of the region.

16. Negative Balances in Accounts for Men,
Thanet Corn Growing Parishes, 1591-1680

Decade	Total Accounts	Number in Negative	% in Negative
1591-1600	100	37	37%
1601-1610	60	22	37%
1611-1620	99	32	32%
1621-1630	84	31	37%
1631-1640	78	28	36%

1661-1670	54	18	33%
1671-1680	70	15	21%

On looking at median balance values, Thanet is found to be better off than the rest of the region from 1601 onwards, and the

147 Using only accounts with both charge and balance. All sums over £1 rounded to nearest pound.

difference increases throughout the seventeenth century. By the 1670s, the median balance value of Thanet accounts was £35, compared with £12.11s in the region as a whole.

Percentages of accounts ending in the negative in Thanet give a similar impression; from 1601 onwards, fewer accounts end with a negative balance in Thanet than in the whole region. By the 1670s, only 21% of Thanet accounts ended with a negative balance, compared with 39% of accounts in the diocese as a whole.

Wealden Cloth Parishes

The other principal industries of early modern Kent were ironworking and clothmaking in the Weald. The iron works were chiefly in the western Weald, and thus in the diocese of Rochester and so do not feature in the accounts. Clothmaking, however, is well represented in Canterbury and the eastern Weald. Wealden clothmaking was probably at its peak from about 1560 to 1630, and declined thereafter.[148]

Median charges of accounts from the Wealden cloth parishes are consistently ahead of those in the whole region until the 1670s, when the median charge value in the Weald dropped to under £74 compared with over £80 in the whole diocese.

17. Moveable Wealth in Accounts for Men,
Wealden Cloth Parishes[149]

Decade	Number of Accounts	Median Charge Value	Median Balance
1591-1600	125	£31	£7
1601-1610	91	£38	£9
1611-1620	136	£38	£10
1621-1630	95	£44	£8
1631-1640	120	£54	£9

1661-1670	72	£103	£24
1671-1680	97	£74	£17

On looking at the median balance values, the Weald is seen to

148 Chalklin, *Seventeenth Century Kent*, p.121.

149 Benenden, Biddenden, Cranbrook, Frittenden, Goudhurst, Hawkhurst, Marden, Staplehurst, Only using accounts with both charge and balance.

be ahead of the whole region throughout, and the difference increases during the period. In the 1660s, the median balance in the Weald was over £24, compared with under £11 in the whole region. In the 1670s the Weald slipped back a little, with a median balance of £16 10s, compared with £12 11s.

Percentages of accounts ending in the negative reveal a similar picture; until 1630, fewer Wealden accounts ended in the negative than in the whole diocese. In the 1630s, 40% of Wealden accounts had a negative balance, compared with 39% in the diocese. In the 1660s, the Weald was better off again, but in the 1670s had slipped behind once more. The evidence suggests that men in the Weald were doing as well as, or better than, men elsewhere in the region until the 1660s, although there may be some evidence of decline beginning in the 1670s.

18. Negative Balances in Accounts for Men, Wealden Cloth Parishes

Decade	Total Accounts	Number in Negative	% in Negative
1591-1600	125	38	30%
1601-1610	91	32	35%
1611-1620	136	49	36%
1621-1630	95	38	40%
1631-1640	120	48	40%

1661-1670	72	27	38%
1671-1680	97	40	41%

Occupational Structure of Selected Areas

The relative wealth of different occupational groups will be discussed below, but it may be worthwhile here to consider the occupational structures of these selected areas as revealed by the probate accounts. Although 743 accounts from the city of Canterbury have survived from between 1570 and the early eighteenth century, the occupations of only 169 of the deceased men are known. Despite the number of gentry families who used the prerogative court, the gentry were still by far the most numerous group amongst the men from the city with known occupations for whom we have surviving accounts. No fewer than 57 of the 169 were gentlemen. This is only partially a reflection of social bias in taking particular care to enter high social status in accounts. It also reflects the way that country gentlemen maintained town houses in Canterbury. Eleven of them, including

Boys, Digges and Hales, can be identified as belonging to major county gentry families, part of the 'county community'. Others may have been 'pseudo-gentry' (men with no landed estates but otherwise wealthy enough to live in the style of gentry) or successful merchants who had adopted the title 'Mr.' Fifteen Canterbury men were clergy and eight were aldermen, with no other trade specified. Eighteen were involved in wool or silk dealing or weaving. The remainder were involved in various craft and retail occupations providing services to the city's population. Thirty three different occupations are represented. Innkeepers, drapers, butchers, bakers, grocers, tailors, carpenters and medical practitioners are all present, although not in large numbers.

In Dover, Faversham and Sandwich, occupations can be discovered for 385 men for whom probate accounts survive. There is a greater range of occupations than in Canterbury; forty different occupations in Dover, 36 in Faversham and 37 in Sandwich, compared with 33 in Canterbury, although none of these towns was more than about half the size of Canterbury in this period. The gentry were less numerous in all three places than in Canterbury, a quarter of the total in Faversham, the largest single group, just over 15% in Sandwich and under 10% in Dover. In Faversham, maritime trades were the second most important economic group. In Sandwich and Dover they were the most important group. As one would expect in maritime towns, all three places had more innkeepers and victuallers proportionate to their populations than did Canterbury, and Dover and Faversham had more in absolute terms also. Sandwich had nine maltsters and Dover six brewers - both more than Canterbury had. Sandwich had a group of seven men involved in the cloth trade. Significantly, as an indication of flourishing trade, Sandwich had six 'merchants' and Dover had five, while Canterbury had only one, a woolmerchant.

In the Wealden parishes, cloth and agriculture predominated. There were only thirty different occupations. Of the 229 accounts for men whose occupations can be identified, just over a quarter were for clothiers, weavers or other clothworkers, just over a third were for yeomen or husbandmen. There were only 22 gentry, ten per cent of the total. There were fewer for retail tradesmen in the Wealden parishes than in the towns, reflecting the Weald's rural character and smaller gentry population. Seven butchers reflected the Weald's cattle grazing economy, but there was only one baker, one grocer, no brewer and no draper.

The Thanet corn growing parishes were the most successful of the four selected areas. Occupations have been identified for 162 men's accounts. There was a far smaller range of occupations, only 22 different ones. Agriculture was the most common, nine husbandmen and 55 yeomen, forty per cent of the total. Maritime trades accounted for one quarter of the total. There were only nine gentry, four brewers, six maltsters, but fewer retail services; one butcher, one salesman and one woollendraper, but no bakers or grocers.

These occupations represent only a small proportion of the populations of these towns over a long period; we cannot know how the chance of survival has influenced the pattern. The poorer classes - labourers and servants - are under-represented, and we do not know how many estates of the wealthier men in each place were dealt with in the Prerogative Court of Canterbury. However, the evidence of probate accounts suggests that prosperity in the diocese of Canterbury in the early modern period, was more likely to be found in the country rather than the town, and more probable in a corn growing area rather than a wood-pasture region.

The accounts from the diocese of Canterbury reveal what was essentially a small-scale society. The 'Stranger' communities of Sandwich and Canterbury and the maritime communities of the sea and river ports were outward looking. Some tradesmen, such as clothiers, also had dealings with Londoners, buying or selling stock there. Most people represented in the Canterbury accounts, however, restricted their business dealings to a small area around their home parishes. It obviously made sense for a man to do business as far as possible with people who were known to him personally. Work on debt and credit networks as revealed by these accounts will demonstrate this more fully.

London

Accounts dealt with in the Prerogative Court of Canterbury, in contrast, depict quite a different type of society. We were only able to abstract data from a limited number of Prerogative Court of Canterbury accounts.[150] Of these, very nearly all were from the period 1665-1725. Only three were from later in the eighteenth century. There was a strong concentration on the metropolis. Altogether 371 out of 569 were from London and Middlesex. Most of these are the accounts of the moveable goods of men and women from the City of London itself and and from Westminster. Parishes close to the City are also strongly represented, particularly Stepney, Holborn and Whitechapel. A considerable number of further accounts relate to estates of men and women from other parishes close to the City - Hackney, Clerkenwell, Shoreditch, Bromley by Bow, Islington, Marylebone, Shadwell,

150 See above p.xii and below p.xcvii.

Stratford at Bow, Southwark, Wapping and Bethnal Green. Many of the remaining accounts relate to the estates of people who still looked towards London, but lived further out. There were 27 from Kent and 23 from Surrey. Fewer than a hundred came from provincial England. The prerogative court also dealt with the estates of those who died overseas, and there were over fifty of these amongst the accounts that we saw.

Unlike the accounts from the diocese of Canterbury, the Prerogative Court of Canterbury accounts so far studied do not follow an invariable formula. Although on average three times as long, many are incomplete, with either the charge or the balance or both missing. The majority identified so far appear to relate to estates about which there was some dispute, and the executor or administrator was thus unable to conclude the account. Since most of the Prerogative Court of Canterbury accounts do not have a final total, it is impossible to use them to form any conclusions about wealth or living standards in the period they cover.

They deal with the moveable goods of people from an extremely wide social spectrum, from a Secretary of State, a Master of the Rolls and a Governor of Tangier to ordinary seamen of the Royal and Merchant navies. No one group or class is sufficiently well represented for any reliable conclusions to be drawn. The charge values range from a high of £19,431 16s 4d, the estate of John Ramsey Esq., Citizen and Grocer of London, in 1672, to a low of £1 2s 6d, the estate of John Taylor of Stepney, late of HMS Tyger, in 1713. Mr Ramsey's executor still had £19,025 6s 5d of his estate left after settling his debts, and six months later put in a supplementary account showing a further balance of £908 18s 7d. By contrast John Taylor's administrator, and principal creditor, claimed that Taylor owed him £50 and requested that Taylor's arrears of wages, when received by his next of kin, should be paid to him.[151]

Peter Earle has described the growth of the middle classes in London in the period covered by the Prerogative Court of Canterbury accounts.[152] This growth was accompanied by an expansion in the service industries which is reflected in the accounts. In the Kent countryside, as shown by the Canterbury accounts, a coffin would be supplied by the local carpenter. A woman neighbour, or perhaps a servant of the deceased, would visit friends and relatives of the deceased to invite them to the funeral. In London by 1700, the services of undertakers were available to take care of all funeral arrangements. Mourning clothes could already be hired by 1685, and by the following

151 Ramsey PRO PROB5/308; Taylor PRO PROB32/57/25.

152 Earle, *The Making of the English Middle Class*.

year admission to the funeral could be by printed ticket rather than by informal verbal invitation.[153]

Piped water supplies were unheard of in the countryside and rare in provincial towns. Londoners had the choice of two sources for their domestic water supplies. The water of the New River Company, brought by canal from Great Amwell in Hertfordshire, available in 1698 at 13s 4d a half year.[154] Twenty householders in the City, Westminster and surrounding parishes have payments for New River water recorded in the accounts of their estates. Thames water was cheaper. It was available in 1704 at 10s a half year.[155]

The late seventeenth century was a period of expansion in English overseas trade, merchant shipping and financial services; the term 'commercial revolution' to describe this period was first coined in the early eighteenth century. The expansion of England's overseas interests and the development of financial services at home is reflected in the Prerogative Court of Canterbury probate accounts.

Of those who had died outside Britain, at least eleven were Royal Navy men, and twenty more were merchant seamen or men of no stated occupation who had died at sea or overseas in a place unspecified. The remainder died in a wide variety of places, reflecting the widespread trading interests of England at this time. Four men died in Barbados, two in Jamaica, two in Antigua, two in the East Indies, one in Bengal, one in Boston, Massachusetts, one in 'Scanderoone' (Iskanderun), one in Persia, one in Moscow. Africa was also represented; one man died in Tangier, another in Algiers, one in 'Malegascoe' (Madagascar) and another in Guinea. Nearer home, one man died in France and another in Nijmegen.

The nature of the business these men were engaged in is revealed by their probate accounts. In 1692 the administrator of the estate of Thomas Dickons of Jamaica had to pay carriage and customs on his sugar and pimento. The administrator of the estate of John Carruthers of Antigua had to pay for brokerage of the deceased's sugar and cotton. Some men, although not themselves merchants, engaged in trading ventures while overseas. John Becon, a ship's surgeon, died at sea in the 1670s. His administrator had to pay carriage and excise duty on Becon's tobacco. After George Osborne of Falmouth died in Jamaica, his silver and indigo were sent back to England in 1717 for disposal. Other men, who died in England, were employees of, or investors in, one or other of the great trading companies. Christopher Hawkes, gentleman, of Hackney, had £700 of his total assets of £2599

153 PRO PROB32/41/112; PROB32/25/423; PROB32/66/34.

154 PRO PROB32/69/9.

155 PRO PROB5/531.

17s 5d in East India Company stock in 1684. In 1693 Robert Ryves Esq. of St Clement Danes had £1000 invested in Royal Africa Company stock.[156]

Participation in the overseas trade expansion was not restricted to the wealthy classes. John Hadley of the ship *Joseph and Jacob* died owing debts of £21 11s 9d from his total estate of £30, most of which debts were for cloth and other goods he had taken on his last voyage for trading. John Atkins of Stepney died in the East Indies in 1685. Much of the discharge of £1209 5s 1d from his estate of £1218 1s 0d was the repayment, with profits, of various small sums which had been 'adventured' by individuals with Atkins on his last voyage.[157]

Probate inventories and accounts also reflect a less creditable side of English trade and imperial history, with references to slaves among the property of some of the deceased. Thomas Pearce of Barbados owned a black boy worth £10. The account of his estate in 1683 records the cost of the boy's clothing and maintenance. Benjamin Dennis, a ship's captain, also had a black boy in 1708. George Simmons of Stepney, commander of the merchant ship *Rooke*, died in the East Indies. The 1708 account of his estate included payment for 'making a sea gown for the black.' [158]

Alongside the growth of overseas trade came the expansion of merchant shipping and the development of London's docks. The impression given by the probate accounts is that Stepney was a centre of maritime activity in the decades before and after 1700. Out of the 430 Prerogative Court of Canterbury accounts, 45 related to the estates of people from Stepney. 31 of these, or 69%, showed that the deceased had maritime interests. Four were in the Royal Navy, ten were merchant seamen or officers. Others died overseas or on board ship, their occupations unspecified, and others were part owners of ships or occupied in ship building.

Insurance was one of the financial services developing in England in the late seventeenth century. Charles Wilson has suggested that the Great Fire of London in September 1666 stimulated demand for insurance in this country.[159] The Great Storm of November 1703, in which damage was far more widespread, may also have led to an expansion in the insurance market. Among the Prerogative Court of Canterbury accounts, four mention payments for unspecified types of insurance. The account of the estate of William Green, innkeeper of St

156 Dickons PRO PROB5/734; Carruthers PRO PROB5/740; Becon PRO PROB32/15/94; Osborne PRO PROB32/63/75; Hawkes PRO PROB32/23/99; Ryves PRO PROB32/35/76.

157 Atkins PRO PROB32/65/125

158 Pearce PRO PROB32/33/6; Dennis PRO PROB5/300; Simmons PRO PROB32/51/69.

159 Wilson, *England's Apprenticeship*, p.334.

Dunstan in the West, mentions fire insurance in 1719 The administrators of the estates of John Sibley, gunmaker of St Botolph Aldgate and Robert Previll of St Giles in the Fields paid for house insurance. Five accounts refer to the insurance of ships. John Dore was part owner of a ship insured in Holland. The ship had sunk, but by 1695 his administrator had not been able to collect the insurance, valued in the account at £250.[160]

The contrast with eastern Kent could not be more striking.

The Wealth of Different Occupational Groups

Canterbury Consistory and Archdeaconry Court probate accounts only occasionally state the occupation of the deceased. Gentry and clergy are nearly always identified as such; other occupations are given only rarely. However, by matching accounts with their associated wills and inventories, it has been possible to discover the status or occupation of 4,223 of the 13,585 men and women for whom accounts exist. Because probate inventories in the diocese of Canterbury are more effectively indexed for the period after 1660 than before, it has been possible to discover more occupations from that period. Of the 4,223 for whom an occupation or status is known, 1,149 were women, who are identified as widows, spinsters, occasionally as wives, or as 'Mrs', implying gentry status. Otherwise, the yeomanry are by far the most strongly represented group, with 738 identified. Agriculture dominates, with 278 husbandmen, nine gardeners, six graziers, two farmers and one looker (shepherd). The gentry were the next most numerous group, with 406 men identified as gentlemen or given the suffix 'Esquire'. There are also nine knights and one peer. 44 men were also given the title 'Mr', but these have not been included among the gentry; 29 of them are found in towns and the title often goes with an occupation such as merchant or a function such as jurat (the equivalent of alderman in several Kent towns) suggesting that the man in question may not have been of true gentry status.

Maritime trades were the next most strongly represented, with 142 mariners or seamen, and 41 in associated trades such as fisherman, pilot or shipwright. There were 164 clergy of all ranks from Doctors of Divinity down to curates. 153 men were involved with clothmaking, with 63 clothiers, plus weavers of woollen, linen and silk cloth, threadtwisters, flax dressers and other associated crafts. 125 were involved in the drink trades, with 97 innholders or innkeepers and victuallers, plus brewers and vintners. There were also 41 maltsters

160 Green PRO PROB5/52; Sibley PRO PROB5/15; Previll PRO PROB32/61/45; Dore PRO PROB32/38/149

and 15 coopers, but the malt may have been for export from Kent - 28 of the maltsters were found in ports - and the coopers may have been making barrels for ships' stores, since eleven of them were found in ports.

A proportion of people, particularly, but not exclusively, from the upper ranks of society, always had their estates dealt with in the Prerogative Court of Canterbury (PCC), and therefore accounts of their estates, if they survive, are not among those in the Archdeaconry or Consistory Courts of Canterbury. It is arguable how much allowance should be made for distortion of statistics by the fact that their estates cannot be included in this discussion. Until probate accounts in the PCC are fully indexed, it will not be possible to say how many have survived there relating to men who died in the diocese of Canterbury. In the seventeenth century an increasing number of men from Kent had their wills proved in the Prerogative Court. Sixty eight such men have been identified from the period 1620-29 and 110 from the period 1671-80.[161] Their occupations or social status were as follows:

19. Status of Kent testators with wills proved in the Prerogative Court

	1620s	1670s
Titled - knighthood or above	13	8
Esquire/gentleman	19	35
Yeoman	8	9
Clothier	7	9
Mariner	4	12
Husbandman	1	4
No occupation stated	11	18
Other occupations	5[162]	23[163]

While it is probable that sufficient gentlemen's estates were being dealt with in the PCC by the post-Restoration period to distort the impression given of gentry wealth by the Archdeaconry and

161 This shift in Kent towards using the Prerogative Court rather than the Canterbury courts between the 1620s and the 1670s is typical of what was happening throughout the southern province. It was merely the acceleration of a trend that has been traced back to the middle years of Elizabeth's reign. A count of the occupational index to the *Index of Wills proved in the Prerogative Court of Canterbury* for the fifteen years from 1605 to 1619 revealed that by then the wills of over eight hundred husbandmen and even those of fifty two 'labourers' and 'day labourers' were already being taken to the Prerogative Court. Takahashi, 'The number of wills', pp.207-8.

162 Alderman, butcher, labourer, maltman and mercer.

163 Baker, blacksmith, brewer, clergy, fellmonger, innholder, joiner, jurat, labourer, medical practitioner, mercer, salter, soldier, tallowchandler, tanner, threadmaker, timber merchant and woollendraper.

Consistory Court accounts, it does not seem that the same was necessarily true of yeomen.

Margaret Spufford has suggested that one of the uses of probate accounts will be to provide a truer picture of the actual wealth of different social groups, apart from their land. She used a sample of 29 labourers' accounts, 35 husbandmen's accounts and 35 yeomen's accounts from Lincolnshire to compare the moveable wealth of these different social and occupational groups in the seventeenth century to discover 'whether the final credit sum given in the probate inventory bore any predictable relationship to the final net estate of the dead man given at the end of the probate account.'[164]

Margaret Spufford concluded that probate account evidence demonstrates how unreliable probate inventories are as a guide to wealth. She also suggested that, while the evidence of probate accounts indicates that the differences in wealth between yeomen, husbandmen and labourers might not have been so great as had been supposed, these status descriptions are still meaningful in that, among other things, they governed the amount of credit a man could expect to obtain. Since a yeoman could borrow more extensively than a labourer, he also had a the likelihood of dying in much more considerable debt if things went wrong. Her findings can be summarised as follows:

20. The Wealth of Yeomen, Husbandmen and Labourers in Lincolnshire, 1630-86

	Gross: Inventory or Charge Values		
	Yeomen	Husbandmen	Labourers
Highest	£2583	£388	£89
Median	£149	£62	£29
Lowest	£18	£9	£12
	Net: Balance		
Highest	£2580	£319	£65
Median	£26	£13	£11
Lowest	-£188	-£64	-£11
% in Negative	23	29	17

Analysis of all Lincolnshire probate accounts shows that yeomen in the county were always more likely to have borrowed money than the population as a whole. In the decades for which sufficient accounts survive for comparison to be made, the proportions

164 Spufford, 'The limitations', pp.150-72.

are as follows:

21. Borrowing on Bills and Bonds, Lincolnshire, 1611-1690, All Men

Decade	Number of Accounts	Number with Bills/Bonds	% with Bills/Bonds
1611-1620	700	383	55%
1621-1630	488	253	52%
1631-1640	952	394	41%

1661-1670	573	232	40%
1671-1680	254	122	48%
1681-1690	197	102	52%

The peak decade for borrowing in Lincolnshire was the 1610s. Possibly the prolonged period of rising prices which people had experienced at this time had given men confidence that they would always be in a position to repay loans.

22. Borrowing on Bills and Bonds, Lincolnshire, 1611-1690, Yeomen

Decade	Number of Accounts	Number with Bills/Bonds	% with Bills/Bonds
1611-1620	62	43	69%
1621-1630	30	19	63%
1631-1640	49	28	57%

1661-1670	64	33	52%
1671-1680	41	21	51%

There is not, however, any indication of a sudden dislocation in the credit market following the end of the price rises in the 1620s, rather of a steady fall in the proportion of both yeomen and all men using credit, followed by a rise later in the century.

The pattern of borrowing in Canterbury diocese is different from that found in Lincolnshire, although the Lincolnshire figures may be distorted in some decades by the smallness of the yeomen sample. The proportion of Canterbury diocese men having borrowed on bills or bonds was always smaller than in Lincolnshire. Whereas the proportion of Lincolnshire men having borrowed fell between 1611 and 1670 and then began to rise again, in east Kent the proportion rose between 1601 and 1620, then remained fairly steady for the rest of the century apart from a sudden drop in the 1670s.

23. Borrowing on Bills and Bonds, East Kent, 1591-1690.
All Men

Decade	Number of Accounts	Number with Bills/Bonds	% with Bills/Bonds
1591-1600	1393	140	10%
1601-1610	1063	186	18%
1611-1620	1611	448	28%
1621-1630	1414	523	37%
1631-1640	1416	484	34%

1661-1670	924	339	37%
1671-1680	1271	310	24%
1681-1690	794	308	39%

Until 1620, Canterbury diocese yeomen were neither more nor less likely to have borrowed than all men, but in the 1620s the proportion of east Kent yeomen having borrowed on bills or bonds rose to 45% and remained at about that level for the rest of the century. The peak decade for east Kent yeomen's borrowing was the 1630s, when nearly half of all yeomen for whom accounts have been identified had died owing money on bills or bonds.

24. Borrowing on Bills and Bonds, East Kent, 1591-1690.
Yeomen[165]

Decade	Number of Accounts	Number with Bills/Bonds	% with Bills/Bonds
1591-1600	65	2	3%
1601-1610	18	2	11%
1611-1620	61	15	25%
1621-1630	56	25	45%
1631-1640	49	24	49%

1661-1670	150	70	47%
1671-1680	190	80	42%
1681-1690	117	56	48%

165 Total numbers may differ from those given in other tables, as other tables are based on accounts giving both charge and balance, whereas this table is based on all accounts regardless of whether both charge and balance are given.

In Lincolnshire, 298 yeomen's accounts survive. In the decades for which there is a sufficiently large sample, charge and balance values are as shown in Table 25. There is a fall in the median balance values of Lincolnshire yeomen's accounts during the century, but the proportion ending with a negative balance remained at about one quarter. This is the same as the proportion of all Lincolnshire men's accounts ending with a negative balance.

25. Moveable Wealth in Accounts for Yeomen, Lincolnshire 1611-1670[166]

Decade	Median Charge Value	Median Balance	% in Negative
1611-1620	£123	£46	25%
1631-1640	£101	£38	23%
1661-1670	£80	£24	24%

The proportion of Canterbury diocese yeomen's accounts ending with a negative balance was always higher than in Lincolnshire, between 30% and 36% except in the 1620s, when the proportion rose to 46%. Recent research suggests that men described as 'yeomen' made up the largest status or occupational group by far in early modern society in Kent, and therefore one would expect their circumstances to be close to what was normal for the county.[167] It is therefore not surprising that yeomen from the diocese of Canterbury were only slightly less likely to leave an estate with a negative balance than were all men for whom accounts survive, again excepting the 1620s. As with all men's accounts, those yeomen's accounts which did end in the negative usually did so by £25 or less. Perhaps surprisingly, yeomen's accounts surviving among the records of the diocese of Canterbury do not show the steady rise in wealth over the century revealed by all men's accounts. This may be because east Kent yeomen were wealthier to begin with than other men, or because the estates of more of the wealthier yeomen were being dealt with in the Prerogative Court and so are invisible to us. Both median charge values and median balance values of yeomen's accounts were higher than those for 'all men' throughout the period, except in the 1620s.

166 Using only Accounts with both Charge and Balance. All sums have been rounded to the nearest pound.

167 Jacqueline Bower, 'The Kent Yeoman in the Seventeenth Century', *Archaeologia Cantiana*, cxiv, (1994).

26. Distribution of Moveable Wealth in Accounts for Yeomen, East Kent 1611-1690[168]

Gross: Charge i.e. Inventory Value

	1610s	1620s	1630s	1640s	1660s	1670s	1680s
Median	£81	£118	£147	£220	£174	£172	£196
Mean	£160	£284	£296	£267	£259	£276	£270
Percentages of Total in Each Range							
over £1000	2%	4%	4%	-	3%	4%	3%
£500/£999.19s	2%	4%	13%	10%	9%	10%	12%
£250/£499.19s	11%	26%	11%	40%	20%	23%	25%
£100/£249.19s	28%	30%	36%	35%	42%	36%	29%
£50/£99.19s	30%	22%	17%	8%	14%	16%	19%
£25/£49.19s	15%	8%	9%	5%	8%	10%	10%
under £25	13%	6%	11%	3%	4%	3%	3%

Net: Balance

	1610s	1620s	1630s	1640s	1660s	1670s	1680s
Median	£27	£4	£19	£71	£34	£36	£38
Mean	£41	£59	£111	£117	£80	£77	£71
Percentages of Total in Each Range							
over £1000	-	-	2%	-	-	1%	-
£500/£999.19s	-	6%	6%	5%	4%	3%	2%
£250/£499.19s	-	4%	9%	13%	7%	6%	9%
£100/£249.19s	24%	12%	15%	24%	17%	20%	17%
£50/£99.19s	11%	10%	11%	14%	17%	13%	16%
£25/£49.19s	17%	6%	6%	6%	10%	10%	13%
£0/£24.19s	17%	16%	17%	5%	9%	17%	11%
above -£25	22%	20%	26%	21%	17%	16%	17%
-£25/-£49.19s	2%	10%	-	6%	9%	5%	4%
-£50/-£99.19s	4%	4%	4%	5%	5%	4%	10%
-£100/-£249.19s	4%	6%	2%	2%	4%	2%	3%
below -£250	-	-	2%	-	1%	3%	-
Number in Negative	17	23	16	21	50	55	40
% Negative	31%	46%	34%	33%	36%	30%	33%
Total Number	54	50	47	63	139	186	120

168 Using only Accounts with both Charge and Balance. All sums have been rounded to the nearest pound. 1610s = 1611-1620 etc.

The wealthiest Canterbury diocese yeomen appear to have been wealthier than the wealthiest Lincolnshire yeomen, although allowance must be made for the smallness of the Lincolnshire sample and the yeomen in both regions whose estates were dealt with in the PCC.

Out of 298 Lincolnshire yeomen's accounts, three had inventory or charge values over £1000 and thirteen had inventory or charge values between £500 and £1000. No Lincolnshire yeoman's account had a balance of over £1000, and only four had a balance of over £500. The wealthiest Lincolnshire yeoman in this sample was Bryan Welden of Pinchbeck who in 1683 left a gross moveable estate of £1565 19s (net estate, i.e. balance £982 4s 11d). By contrast, 26 Canterbury diocese yeomen left gross estates of over £1000, while 72 left gross estates of over £500. Four Canterbury diocese yeomen's accounts finished with a balance of over £1000, while 24 finished with a balance of over £500.

The difference in wealth, if any, between yeomen and gentry has been debated for many years. Lambarde believed that, in Kent at least, many yeomen were equal to gentry in wealth. This is borne out by the evidence of the probate accounts. The five Thanet 'yeomen' listed in Table 15 are very good examples of such very prosperous Kent yeomen. It must, however, be borne in mind that land, not visible in English probate accounts, is likely to have formed a much higher proportion of the whole estates of gentry than of other social groups. Because such a high proportion of gentry estates were dealt with by the prerogative court, it is hard to make any generalisations about them from the records of provincial courts, even though they dealt with a surprisingly large number of them. The Canterbury courts, for example, preserved the probate accounts for the moveables of no fewer than 356 gentry between 1611 and 1690. The distribution of the moveable wealth of these gentry is set out in Table 28.

While the median charge values of gentlemen's accounts from the Canterbury courts were higher than those of yeomen in all but two decades, gentlemen's accounts were far more likely to end in the negative. A very large proportion of them were relying on their land to compensate for the inadequacy of their net moveable assets. More than half of all gentlemen's accounts ended with a negative balance in all decades except the 1670s and 1680s, and in these decades the proportion ending in the negative was not significantly below a half.

Gentlemen's accounts which did end in the negative were likely to have a much greater deficit than yeomen's accounts with a negative balance. Yeomen's accounts with a deficit of £100 or more peaked at 6% in, not surprisingly, the 1620s. In contrast the proportion of gentlemen's estates with a deficit of more than £100 only once fell

27. Distribution of Moveable Wealth in Gentlemen's Accounts, East Kent, 1611-90[169]

Gross: Charge i.e. Inventory Value

	1610s	1620s	1630s	1640s	1660s	1670s	1680s
Median	£103	£224	£201	£387	£140	£164	£270
Mean	£301	£371	£439	£557	£292	£324	£459
	Percentages of Total in Each Range						
over £1000	10%	6%	11%	10%	6%	7%	8%
£500-£999.99	4%	18%	14%	29%	13%	15%	24%
£250-£499.99	6%	22%	16%	19%	15%	10%	26%
£100-£249.99	33%	27%	29%	23%	33%	33%	21%
£50-£99.99	16%	13%	8%	7%	19%	21%	13%
£25-£49.99	12%	9%	11%	7%	13%	7%	5%
under £25	18%	6%	11%	7%	2%	7%	3%

Net: Balance

	1610s	1620s	1630s	1640s	1660s	1670s	1680s
Median	-14s 5d	-£4	-£1	-£5	-£14	£7	£29
Mean	£65	£49	£40	£55	£11	£34	£113
	Percentages of Total in Each Range						
over £1000	2%	4%	5%	10%	2%	1%	3%
£500/£999.19s	2%	4%	3%	7%	-	1%	5%
£250/£499.19s	2%	7%	3%	3%	-	7%	13%
£100/£249.19s	10%	9%	8%	16%	15%	15%	11%
£50/£99.19s	6%	4%	10%	3%	2%	11%	13%
£25/£49.19s	14%	4%	6%	3%	13%	7%	8%
£0/£24.19s	6%	7%	12%	3%	2%	8%	3%
above -£25	35%	20%	17%	16%	27%	18%	24%
-£25/-£49.19s	2%	9%	2%	10%	8%	6%	3%
-£50/-£99.19s	16%	15%	11%	3%	13%	11%	-
-£100/-£249.19s	4%	9%	8%	10%	13%	8%	11%
below -£250	-	9%	14%	16%	6%	6%	8%
Number in Negative	27	34	33	17	32	35	17
% Negative	55%	62%	52%	55%	67%	49%	45%
Total Number	49	55	63	31	48	72	38

169 Using only accounts with both Charge and Balance,

below 10%, in the 1610s, and was more usually about 20%. On the other hand, a higher proportion of gentlemen's accounts is likely to be found in the higher ranges of balance values. In the 1640s, for example, 16% of east Kent gentlemen's accounts ended with a balance of over £500, compared with 5% of yeomen's accounts. The highest proportion of yeomen's account to be passed with a balance of over £500 was 9% in the 1630s. However, at these levels the samples are so small that two or three accounts more or less can make a big difference. The overall evidence of the accounts that passed through the Canterbury courts is that while individual gentlemen may have been wealthier than most yeomen, as a class the yeomanry were wealthier in moveable assets and more financially stable than the gentry.

CONCLUSION

John Patten has written 'it is ...extremely difficult to illuminate the economic behaviour of individuals within cities and towns ... There are relatively few detailed sets of personal business papers. It is thus difficult to clothe the bare facts of occupation, wealth and standing with information on how individuals actually carried out their activities.'[170] The foregoing discussion demonstrates that the discovery of probate accounts means that this is no longer true. Study of probate accounts can shed light on a wide range of subjects of interest to early modern economic and social historians, such as differences in wealth from time to time and from region to region or *pays* to *pays*, wages and prices, farming practices and local industries.

There are many directions in which research using probate accounts might go. A single probate account may mention many individuals by name and often give their occupations and parishes of residence. Elizabeth Partridge's account of the estate of her husband Thomas, compiled in 1626, mentions 24 different people from the Lord Warden down to her servant Matthew Browning. The account of the estate of Davyd Croft, compiled in 1573-74, names over 60 people, including 'Capell the Smythe', 'Father Clercke the horse lyche', harvest workers, both local and from Wales, male and female farm servants, and local craftsmen and tradesmen.[171] A project to compile an index of all individuals mentioned in all accounts from a small town or group of rural parishes over a specified period could initially produce a valuable directory of local tradesmen. Combined with information from parish registers and other sources, such an index could be developed into a listing of all inhabitants of a chosen district in the

170 John Patten, *English Towns 1500-1700*, Folkestone, 1978, p.192.

171 Partridge CKS PRC20/7/164; Croft CKS PRC2/4/468.

seventeenth century.[172]

As we have seen probate accounts followed on from wills, inventories and letters of administration and run through a year or more from the sickness of the dying man, his death and funeral, the upkeep of his household after his death, the payment of his debts and the maintenance of his children, up to the point at which there are no more expenditures to be laid out and the balance, if any, can be distributed. In doing so, probate accounts give far more detail of the expenditure of 'ordinary' households than historians have previously had available from any other source.

The purpose of this introduction has been to raise historians' awareness of probate accounts by discussing their nature and uses and by beginning the task of analysis, and by attempting to indicate some of the directions future work with probate accounts might take.

172 In Kent itself there is a prospect (in 1999) of probate accounts being used in this way by a group led by Duncan Harrington for the area focussed on Faversham and by Antony Poole for the area focussed on Cranbrook.

Appendix

THE NUMBER OF SURVIVING PROBATE ACCOUNTS

The dates given are those of the first and last more or less safely dateable accounts. Many are not dated, and are not easily dateable.

Abbreviations
A = Archdeaconry Court
Comm = Commissary Court
CC = Consistory Court
D = Deanery Court
DC = Court of Dean and Chapter
PC = Prerogative Court
PCC = Prerogative Court of Canterbury
Pec = Peculiar Court

Repository and Court	Approximate Number of Documents	Period Covered
Aberystwyth, National Library of Wales		
CC Bangor	7	1674-93
A Brecon	37	1620-47
plus others filed with probate records of other Welsh courts. Inaccessible until indexes made.		
Aylesbury, Buckinghamshire Record Office		
A Buckingham, Pecs	7	1617-1684
Bedford, Bedfordshire Record Office		
A Bedford	2	1595-1677
Bristol, Bristol Record Office		
CC Bristol	133	1575-1783
plus others waiting for repair work to be undertaken.		
Bury St Edmunds, Suffolk Record Office		
A Sudbury	44	1521-1818
Cambridge, Cambridge County Record Office		
A Ely	3	1629-30
CC Ely	25	1605-1823

Cambridge, University Archives, Cambridge University Library

Vice-Chancellor's Court, Cambridge University	186	1561-1730

Chester, Cheshire Record Office

CC Chester	275	1569-1846

Chichester, West Sussex Record Office

A Chichester	1016	1578-1711
Pec Dean Chichester	200	1599-1701

Dorchester, Dorset Record Office

A Dorset	2	1663-1714
Pec Dorchester	3	1622-91
Pec Wimborne	103	1599-1702

Durham,
A considerable number filed with other probate records in 500 boxes. Inaccessible until general probate index made.

Exeter, Devon Record Office
1 or 2 14th century, plus dozens 16th and 17th centuries

Gloucester, Gloucestershire Record Office

CC Gloucester	138	1601-1834

Hertford, Hertfordshire Record Office

A Huntingdon/Hitchin	93	1610-89
A St Albans	456	1556-1753
A Bedford	1	

Huntingdon, Cambridge County Record Office

A Huntingdon	339	1597-1825

Ipswich, Suffolk Record Office

A Suffolk	1	1754

Leeds, West Yorkshire Archive Service

A Richmond (Eastern Deaneries)	A few	

Filed with wills. Inaccesible until general probate index made.

Leicester, **Wigston Magna**, Leicestershire Record Office

A Leicester	369	1639-87

Lichfield, Lichfield Joint Record Office

CC Lichfield and peculiars	1361	1576-1850

Plus others filed with 250,000 other documents, 1546-1798. Inaccessible until general probate index made - currently in progress.

Lincoln, Lincolnshire

Archives Office	6044	
with courts indicated:		
A Bedford	1	
A Stow	1158	1571-1765
CC Lincoln	4218	1524-1853
DC Lincoln	66	1605-1686
Pec Bishop Norton	1	
Pec Caister	5	
Pec Corringham	3	
Pec Kirton in Lindsey	1	
Pec Louth	11	
Pec Sleaford	5	
Pec Stow in Lindsey	1	
Lincoln Pecs	18	1619-1703
Pec?	2	1596-9

plus c.350 more, waiting for repair

London, Public Record Office

PCC	569 abstracted	1665-1754

plus 10,000-15,000 more not yet abstracted

London Metropolitan Archive (formerly Greater London Record Office)

A & Comm Surrey	12	1739-78
A Middx	71	1672-1754

Lambeth Palace Library

Court of Arches	93	1555-1733
Pec D Arches	2	1628-35
Pec D Shoreham & Croydon	21	1609-1756

City of Westminster Archives Centre
Dean and Chapter
Westminster small number

Maidstone, Centre for Kentish Studies

A Canterbury	9737	1569-1728
CC Canterbury	3822	1569-1740

Northampton, Northamptonshire Record Office

A Northampton	162	1668-85
CC Peterborough	34	1755-1816

Norwich, Norfolk Record Office

A Norfolk	40	1729-91
A Norwich	151	1701-1824
CC Norwich	15	1626-1748

More filed with inventories in 108 boxes. Not easily accessible until general probate index made.

Nottingham, Nottinghamshire
Record Office c.100-300
among 100,000 other records. Inaccessible until general probate index made.

Oxford, Oxfordshire Archives

CC & A Oxford	710	1547-1730
Pec Thame	1	1674
Pec Monks Risborough	7	1617-84
Oxfordshire Pecs	131	1614-1810

Bodleian Library

Chancellor's Court, Oxford University	96	1577-1720

Preston, Lancashire Record Office

CC Chester	307	1574-1799

Reading, Berkshire Record Office

A Berks	1657	1564-1783

Taunton, Somerset Record Office

CC Bath & Wells	925	1577-1748
Dean Wells	1	1621
Pec Wiveliscombe	1	1626
	circa 50 others	inaccessible until repaired

Trowbridge, Wiltshire Record Office

A Sarum	597	1576-1806
A Sub Dean Sarum	95	1612-1827
A Wilts	423	1600-1774
CC Sarum	189	1595-1768
Pec Dean & Canons Windsor	4	1629-1677
Pec Dean & Chapter Sarum	5	1606-81
Pec Dean Sarum	216	1567-1631
Pec Devizes	1	1732
Pec Lord Warden Savernake Forest	14	1597-1677
Pec Perpetual Vicar Corsham	2	1618-77
Pec Preb Bishopstone	4	1600-30
Pec Preb Chute & Chisenbury	1	1597
Pec Preb Coombe & Harnham	2	1696-1805
Pec Preb Durnford	2	1628-65
Pec Preb Fordington & Writhlington	6	1596-1682
Pec Preb Gillingham	1	1582
Pec Preb Highworth	4	1596-1678
Pec Preb Lyme Regis & Halstock	10	1597-1805
Pec Preb Netheravon	1	1635
Pec Preb Netherbury in Ecclesia	1	1597
Pec Preb Preston	1	1641
Pec Preb Uffculme	8	1596-1680
Pec Preb Yetminster & Grimston	1	1600
Pec Precentor Sarum	21	1609-1793
Pec Treasurer Sarum	18	1594-1793
Pec Trowbridge	2	1635-1731

Truro, Cornwall Record Office

A Cornwall	393	1600-1650

Winchester, Hampshire

Record Ofice	451	1569-1716

Worcester, County Record Office

CC Worcester	667	1583-1825

York, Borthwick Institute 536

The surviving accounts here generally related to disputes and have been filed with the cause papers. The court to which they relate is not always apparent.

Courts indicated for:

Dean & Chapter York	7	1665-1821
Exchequer C York	192	1607-1853
PC York	72	1608-1855

County archivists tell us that they believe that no accounts survive in county record offices in Carlisle, Chelmsford, Hereford, Lewes and Warwick.

Although probate accounts survive in England, Wales and the American colonies, they do not do so in Ireland or Scotland and it is not clear to us if there was ever a requirement to render an account in those countries.

Guide to the Indexes

The main part of this index is arranged by the names of the deceased man or woman whose moveable goods were being accounted for. For speed of use the first surname on each page is repeated in the top outside corner. The entries give, in order, surname, christian name, status or occupation where known, place or residence, county, date of the account (not date of death which can be several years earlier), the record office in which the account is now kept, and its reference. Some record offices do not yet give very precise references to probate accounts. For example they give a general reference and ask the reader to add the name and date of the account. This has been indicated in the index.

Most of the names of record offices will be easily recognisable. RO has been used as a general abbreviation for either Record Office or Archives. So Herts RO means Hertfordshire Record Office, Oxon RO means Oxfordshire Archives and Lincs RO means Lincolnshire Archives Office. There are some which may be less obvious to some users:

Bodleian for the Oxford University Archives in the Bodleian Library
Borthwick for the Borthwick Institute, York
CKS for the Centre for Kentish Studies at Maidstone
CUL for the Cambridge University Archives in the Cambridge University Library
Greater London RO for the Greater London Record Office, now London Metropolitan Archive
Lambeth for Lambeth Palace Library
LJRO for the Lichfield Joint Record Office
NLW for the National Library of Wales in Aberystwyth
PRO for the Public Record Office.

There are two supplementary indexes:

The first of these supplemetary indexes is for status and occupation. All occupations or status for which large numbers of accounts survive have not been indexed separately since they appear on virtually every page: widow (2058 accounts); yeoman (1981 accounts); husbandman (1094 accounts); and gentleman (985 accounts). Some entries have been grouped together, like different sorts of clergy, but the cross references should make these easy to find.

The second supplementary index is for places. Entries have been arranged according to the ancient counties of England, followed by the ancient counties of Wales, followed by European countries, and then by countries elsewhere in the world. At the end are a small number of ships. Those places for which no county is given or otherwise recognisable, are listed under a 'no county' heading after Yorkshire. Within counties, places are arranged by parishes, with any place within a parish shown in brackets. The index takes the form of Chievely (Snelsmore) rather than Snelsmore in Chievely. In places with more than one parish, the index takes the form of Abingdon St Helen rather than St Helen's Abingdon.

Abaghurste, George, Brimpton, Berks, 1596 Berks RO D/A1/173/58A
Abbatt, Richard, gentleman, Brading, Hants, 1662 Hants RO 21M65 D8/148
Abbett, Nicholas, Stelling, Kent, 1616 CKS PRC2/20/396
Abbey, Henry, Nettleton, Lincs, 1640 Lincs RO Ad/Ac/26/247
Abbot,
Som 1698 Somerset RO D/D/Cta/A10
Abbot, George, Stelling, Kent, 1588 CKS PRC2/4/460
Abbot, John, Leake, Lincs, 1611 Lincs RO Ad/Ac/10/92
Abbot, Thomas, Berkhamsted St Peter, Herts, Herts RO AHH23/30
Abbot, Thomas, Morton, Lincs, 1620 Lincs RO Ad/Ac/15/5
Abbott, Alice, Morton, Lincs, 1637 Lincs RO Ad/Ac/25/604
Abbott, Alice, widow, Sturry, Kent, 1700 CKS PRC1/16/20
Abbott, Anne, widow, St Neots, Hunts, 1682 Hunts RO/Acc58/170(110)
Abbott, Anthony, Belshford, Lincs, 1785 Lincs RO Ad/Ac/45/51
Abbott, Charles, St Neots, Hunts, 1684 Hunts RO/Acc58/225(216)
Abbott, George, Canterbury St George Martyr, Kent, 1663 CKS PRC1/9/74
Abbott, Henry, husbandman, Wimborne Minster (Barnester), Dors, 1615 Dorset RO PE/WM CP 2/4/14
Abbott, John, clergy: 'mr/D.D.', Canterbury, Kent, 1615 CKS PRC20/3/348
Abbott, John, Dover, Kent, 1678 CKS PRC20/12/251
Abbott, John, husbandman, Ruckinge, Kent, 1686 CKS PRC2/41/71
Abbott, Peter, Chinnock, East, Som, 1707 Somerset RO D/D/Cta/A13
Abbott, Richard, gentleman, Hagworthingham, Lincs, 1664 Lincs RO Ad/Ac/43/26
Abbott, Robert, Herne, Kent, 1627 CKS PRC20/8/9
Abbott, Stephen, yeoman, Sturry, Kent, 1667 CKS PRC1/12/1
Abbott, Thomas, Donhead St Mary, Wilts, 1614 Wilts RO Arch. Sarum/(+ name and date)
Abbott, William, yeoman, St Laurence Thanet, Kent, 1649 CKS PRC1/8/32
Abbotts, James, yeoman, Lee Brockhurst, Shrops, 1815 LJRO/B/C/5/1815/1
Abbyt, John, Little Mongeham, Kent, 1619 CKS PRC2/20/389
Abbytt, Richard ygr, St Peter in Thanet, Kent, 1613 CKS PRC2/18/62
Abeare, Mary, widow, Wargrave, Berks, 1637 Berks RO D/A1/174/9c
Abeare, Thomas, yeoman, Wargrave, Berks, 1637 Berks RO D/A1/174/10c
Abeere, see Beere,
Abell, Catherine, Harvington, Worcs, 1678 Worcs RO 008.7 BA3585/835/bdl 3
Abell, Henry, husbandman, Tintagel, Corn, 1622 Cornwall RO AP/A122/3
Abell, William, Blean, Kent, 1610 CKS PRC2/14/1
Abell, William, Iwade, Kent, 1631 CKS PRC2/31/1
Abell/Bullock, John, Mathon, Worcs, 1608 Worcs RO 008.7 BA3585/839/442
Aben, Allice, Wilton, Wilts, 1646 Wilts RO Arch. Sarum/(+ name and date)
Abicke, Edward, Fareham, Hants, 1639 Hants RO 21M65 D8/140
Abington, John, merchant, St Faith under St Pauls, London & Middlesex, 1694 PRO PROB32/34/108
Abington, Thomas, Woodhay, West, Berks, 1614 Berks RO D/A1/173/90A
Ablard, John, carpenter, Langton by Wragby, Lincs, 1683 Lincs RO Ad/Ac/44/92
Abney, William, Rauceby, Lincs, 1652 Lincs RO Ad/Ac/29/35
Abraham, Alice, widow, Egerton, Kent, 1644 CKS PRC19/2/82
Abraham, Bartylmewe, Minster in Thanet, Kent, 1592 CKS PRC2/5/31
Abraham, Henry, Warehorne, Kent, 1620 CKS PRC2/20/372
Abraham, John, Boughton under Blean, Kent, 1583 CKS PRC21/6/263
Abraham, John, Seasalter, Kent, 1596 CKS PRC2/8/401
Abraham, John, Stainfield, Lincs, 1792 Lincs RO Ad/Ac/45/63
Abraham, Laurance, Moulton, Lincs, 1597 Lincs RO Ad/Ac/4/65
Abraham, Moses, yeoman, Keal, East, Lincs, 1636 Lincs RO Ad/Ac/25/379
Abraham, Richard, Teynham, Kent, 1664 CKS PRC1/10/1
Abraham, Thomas, Keal, East, Lincs, 1648 Lincs RO Ad/Ac/30/333

[Abraham:]
Abraham, William, husbandman, Leake, Lincs, 1632 Lincs RO Ad/Ac/23/154
Abram, John, farmer, Scalby (Staintondale), Yorks, 1818 Borthwick Test C.P. 1818/3
Abram, Michael, Egerton, Kent, 1638 CKS PRC20/10/29
Abrathat, Edward sen, Tring, Herts, 1635 Herts RO AHH23/2
Absolon, Edward, yeoman, Cholsey, Berks, 1649 Berks RO D/A1/174/35d
Aburrow, John, Meon, East (Riplington), Hants, 1624 Hants RO 21M65 D8/44
Abyn, John, weaver: 'broad weaver', Wilton, Wilts, 1640 Wilts RO Arch. Sarum/(+ name and date)
Acham, George, gentleman, Asterby, Lincs, 1664 Lincs RO Ad/Ac/43/14
Achison, John, Stickney, Lincs, 1614 Lincs RO Ad/Ac/13/217
Achurche, Thomas, Herne, Kent, 1574 CKS PRC21/2/153
Ackworth, John, clergy: 'mr/clerk', Warehorne, Kent, 1628 CKS PRC2/29/3
Acock, Sampson, cutler: 'long cutler', Birmingham, Warks, 1663 LJRO:cards/1663/1
Aconet, Thomas, Frome Selwood, Som, 1606 Somerset RO D/D/Cta/A14
Acourte, Richard, Petham, Kent, 1591 CKS PRC2/5/223
Acreman, Robert, Lyme Regis, Dors, 1682 Wilts RO Dean Sarum (name + date)
Acres, William, Tydd St Mary, Lincs, 1639 Lincs RO Ad/Ac/26/126
Acrouch, see Crouch,
Acton, Christopher, butcher, Sutton Valence, Kent, 1616 CKS PRC2/20/393
Acton, James, Leeds, Kent, 1621 CKS PRC1/1/28
Acton, John, Stamford, Lincs, 1632 Lincs RO Ad/Ac/23/81
Acton, Randle, husbandman, Capesthorne, Ches, 1662 Cheshire RO (Name) W.C. 1662
Acton, Stephen, yeoman, Sutton Valence, Kent, 1619 CKS PRC2/20/379
Adames, Ann, widow, Stourmouth, Kent, 1619 CKS PRC2/20/400
Adames, William, Hanney, West (East Hanney), Oxon, 1596 Berks RO D/A1/173/54A
Adams, Alice, widow, St Giles without Cripplegate, London & Middlesex, 1692 PRO PROB5/1747
Adams, Arthur + Elizabeth, Petherwin, North, Corn, 1640 Cornwall RO AP/A228/2
Adams, Daniel, yeoman, Walkern, Herts, 1699 Lambeth Palace Arches G50/2
Adams, Edmund, Ashford, Kent, 1674 CKS PRC2/36/9
Adams, Edward, St Albans St Peters, Herts, 1559 Herts RO ASA25/381
Adams, Erasmus, Blean, Kent, 1597 CKS PRC2/10/22
Adams, George, Matlock, Derby, 1680 LJRO:cards/1680/1
Adams, Gylbarte, Ebony, Kent, 1602 CKS PRC2/12/5
Adams, Henry, labourer, St Nicholas at Wade, Kent, 1685 CKS PRC20/13/481
Adams, Ingram, Brookland, Kent, 1640 CKS PRC1/2/1
Adams, James, St Giles in the Fields, London & Middlesex, 1732 Greater London RO DL/C/552/124/1
Adams, Joan, Oxford St Michael, Oxon, 1627 Oxon RO MSS Wills 295/1/35
Adams, Joan, widow, Chewton Mendip, Som, 1635 Somerset RO D/D/Cta/A5
Adams, John, Chinnock, West, Som, Somerset RO D/D/Cta/A12
Adams, John, Watford, Herts, 1618 Herts RO ASA25/4830
Adams, John, Rolvenden, Kent, 1633 CKS PRC2/32/2
Adams, John, clothier, Berkhamsted St Peter, Herts, 1636 Herts RO AHH23/3
Adams, John, Clanfield, Oxon, 1639 Oxon RO MSS Wills 295/1/62
Adams, John, yeoman, Folkestone, Kent, 1671 CKS PRC2/35/2
Adams, John, yeoman, Appledore, Kent, 1680 CKS PRC2/38/91
Adams, John, yeoman, Berwick St James, Wilts, 1688 Wilts RO CC Sarum(+ name and date)
Adams, John, victualler, St Martin in the Fields (Vinegar Yard, Drury Lane), London & Middlesex, 1706 Greater London RO AM/CP/Box 1696-1720 pt (uncatalogued)
Adams, John eld, yeoman, Walmer, Kent, 1648 CKS PRC1/8/1
Adams, John eld, miller, Minster in Sheppey, Kent, 1665 CKS PRC1/10/2
Adams, John ygr, Ashford, Kent, 1615 CKS PRC2/20/374
Adams, Marke, Westwell, Kent, 1595 CKS PRC21/14/55
Adams, Mildred, Cranbrook, Kent, 1593 CKS PRC2/6/486

Adams, Nicholas, Deal, Kent, 1675 CKS PRC20/12/157
Adams, Nicolas, Lydd, Kent, 1595 CKS PRC21/13/52
Adams, Peeter, Lydd, Kent, 1608 CKS PRC20/1/239
Adams, Peter, St Columb Major, Corn, 1606? Cornwall RO AP/A40/2
Adams, Ralph, Canterbury St Andrew, Kent, 1674 CKS PRC2/36/5
Adams, Richard, Monkton, Kent, 1606 CKS PRC20/1/223
Adams, Richard, husbandman, Eastry, Kent, 1610 CKS PRC20/2/182
Adams, Richard, Aldington, Kent, 1704 CKS PRC19/6/7
Adams, Robart, Ash next Sandwich, Kent, 1592 CKS PRC21/11/161
Adams, Robert, carpenter, Clanfield, Oxon, Oxon RO MSS Wills 295/1/63
Adams, Robert, Ash next Sandwich, Kent, 1579 CKS PRC21/4/111
Adams, Robert, Leake, Lincs, 1601 Lincs RO Ad/Ac/5/481
Adams, Robert eld, Moreton, North, Berks, 1616 Berks RO D/A1/35/269C
Adams, Salomon, Lydd, Kent, 1592 CKS PRC21/11/173
Adams, Samuel, Preston Bagot, Warks, 1773 Worcs RO 008.7 BA3585/835/bdl 1
Adams, Silvanus, blacksmith, Lilleshall, Shrops, 1662 LJRO:cards/1662/1
Adams, Thomas, Oxford St Mary Virgin, Oxon, 1666 Oxon RO MSS Wills 295/1/81
Adams, William, Funtington, Sussex, W. Suss RO EpI/33/1607/7
Adams, William, Melksham, Wilts, 1612 Wilts RO Arch. Sarum/(+ name and date)
Adams, William, skinner, Belton, Lincs, 1669 Lincs RO Ad/Ac/33/160
Adams, William, wheelwright, Derby, Derby, 1745 LJRO/B/C/5/1745/192
Adams/Betty, Elizabeth, widow, Alfreton (Swanwick), Derby, 1774 LJRO/B/C/5/1774/10
Adcock, George, gentleman,
Leics 1664 Leics RO Administrators Accounts C17th f1
Adcocke, John, Faversham, Kent, 1593 CKS PRC2/6/182
Adcocke, Thomas, Packington, Great, Warks, 1672 LJRO:cards/1672/1
Adcocke, William, grocer, Hythe St Leonard, Kent, 1682 CKS PRC20/13/220
Addames, John, St Albans St Peters, Herts, 1634 Herts RO ASA25/4898
Addams, Anne, Shrewsbury, Shrops, 1685 LJRO/B/C/5/1685/2
Addams, Dorothie, Dymchurch, Kent, 1641 CKS PRC1/5/75
Addams, Edward, Haseley, Great (Little Haseley), Oxon, 1630 Oxon RO MSS Wills 295/1/48
Addams, Edward, Angmering, Sussex, 1661 W. Suss RO EpI/33/1661/5
Addams, James, Boston, Lincs, 1664 Lincs RO Ad/Ac/43/17
Addams, John, Castle Cary, Som, 1643 Somerset RO D/D/Cta/A15
Addams, Nicholas, Burslem (Sneyd Green), Staffs, 1667 LJRO:cards/1667/2
Addams, Richard, Ardley, Oxon, 1646 Oxon RO MSS Wills 295/1/66
Addams, Richard, Norton in the Moors (Bemersley), Staffs, 1662 LJRO:cards/1662/2
Addams, Richard, Angmering, Sussex, 1670 W. Suss RO EpI/33/1669/3
Addams, Roberte, Brookland, Kent, 1598 CKS PRC2/5/231
Addams, Thomas, Hagbourne, Berks, 1596 Berks RO D/A1/35/223
Addams, Thomas, Newington next Sittingbourne, Kent, 1637 CKS PRC2/34/7
Adderley, Mary, spinster, Hanbury (Fauld), Staffs, 1697 LJRO/B/C/5/1698/7
Adderton, James, Chart, Great, Kent, 1586 CKS PRC2/4/25
Adderton, see Raphe,
Addie, Bartholomew, Braceborough, Lincs, 1629 Lincs RO Ad/Ac/22/57
Addington, Maurice, Pinchbeck, Lincs, 1636 Lincs RO Ad/Ac/24/264
Addison, John, wheelwright, Marsh Chapel, Lincs, 1613 Lincs RO Ad/Ac/12/110
Addison, Robert, yeoman, Sibsey, Lincs, 1619 Lincs RO Ad/Ac/17/61
Addlesey, Thomas, Doddington, Lincs, 1619 Lincs RO Ad/Ac/15/67
Adeane, Mathew, cooper: 'wine cooper', Bristol St. Leonard, Glos, Bristol RO 1739/1
Adee, Nicholas, Faversham, Kent, 1598 CKS PRC2/10/248
Adee, Richard, Chadlington, Oxon, 1625 Oxon RO MSS Wills 295/1/33
Adey, Thomas, Eastwell, Kent, 1680 CKS PRC2/39/2
Adey, Thomas, thatcher, Uley, Glos, 1784 GRO GDR/B4/2/A23
Adie, John, butcher, Chislet, Kent, 1596 CKS PRC2/8/226

[Adie:]
Adie, Marian, widow, Sittingbourne, Kent, 1637 CKS PRC2/34/4
Adkins, Andrew, mariner, Sandwich St Clement, Kent, 1668 CKS PRC1/13/1
Adkins, Edward, husbandman, Whitstable, Kent, 1684 CKS PRC2/40/167
Adkins, George, St Peter in Thanet, Kent, 1622 CKS PRC2/23/5
Adkins, John, husbandman, Speen, Berks, 1640 Berks RO D/A1/174/17b
Adkins, Robert, Ambrosden (Blackthorn), Oxon, Oxon RO MSS Wills 295/1/58
Adkins, Thomas, Crundale, Kent, 1614 CKS PRC2/18/17
Adkins, William, husbandman, Garford, Berks, 1629 Berks RO D/A1/173/118A
Adkins, William, husbandman, Bircholt, Kent, 1666 CKS PRC1/11/96
Adkinson, John, St Antholin, London & Middlesex, 1707 PRO PROB5/1144
Adlam, South ..., Wilts, 1613 Wilts RO Arch. Sarum/(+ name and date)
Adlard, Frances, Keal, West, Lincs, 1634 Lincs RO Ad/Ac/24/233
Adlard, John, yeoman, Haltham on Bain, Lincs, 1618 Lincs RO Ad/Ac/14/244
Adlard, Michael, clergy: 'clerk', Cumberworth, Lincs, 1662 Lincs RO Ad/Ac/32/37
Adlard, Richard, Anderby, Lincs, 1642 Lincs RO Ad/Ac/28/20
Adlard, Thomas, Enderby, Wood, Lincs, 1628 Lincs RO Ad/Ac/20b/42
Adlard, William, yeoman, Theddlethorpe St Helen, Lincs, 1632 Lincs RO Ad/Ac/23/1
Adlard, William, yeoman, Huttoft, Lincs, 1641 Lincs RO Ad/Ac/27/319
Adman, George, Waltham, Kent, 1608 CKS PRC2/15/1
Adman, Robert, husbandman, Boughton Aluph, Kent, 1667 CKS PRC1/12/2
Adman, Thomas, Petham, Kent, 1624 CKS PRC2/23/17
Adman, William, Boughton under Blean, Kent, 1641 CKS PRC19/1/22
Adnam, William, husbandman, Brightwalton, Berks, 1628 Berks RO D/A1/173/114D
Adnett, Bazill, victualler, Newbold on Avon, Warks, 1769 LJRO/B/C/5/1769/60
Adnett, Richard, yeoman, Bonnington, Kent, 1667 CKS PRC1/11/97
Adnett, Thomas, Hurst, Kent, 1640 CKS PRC1/4/1
Adnett, Thomas, Hurst, Kent, 1640 CKS PRC1/4/1a
Adowne, John, Wickhambreaux, Kent, 1593 CKS PRC2/6/174
Adowne, Robert, Charing, Kent, 1596 CKS PRC21/14/133
Adren, William, Smeeth, Kent, 1600 CKS PRC21/15/234
Adrian, John, husbandman, Minster in Sheppey, Kent, 1673 CKS PRC2/35/194
Adrianson, Adrian, mariner: 'captain', Dover, Kent, 1640 CKS PRC19/1/23
Adryan, Nicholas, Sandwich, Kent, 1598 CKS PRC2/10/114
Adshad, Michael, surgeon, Abingdon, Berks, 1628 Berks RO D/A1/173/111A
Adshead, John, weaver, Stockport (Norbury), Ches, 1796 Cheshire RO (Name) W.C. 1796
Adson, Anne, widow, Sandhurst, Kent, 1620 CKS PRC2/20/376
Adsonne, George, Irby in the Marsh, Lincs, 1587 Lincs RO Ad/Ac/2C/137
Ady, Moyses, Teynham, Kent, 1623 CKS PRC2/23/8
Ady, Richard, Tenterden, Kent, 1640 CKS PRC1/4/2
Ady, Robert, Faversham, Kent, 1639 CKS PRC2/34/160
Ady, Thomas, wheeler, Newington next Sittingbourne, Kent, 1685 CKS PRC2/41/39
Adye, Henry, Faversham, Kent, 1618 CKS PRC2/20/378
Adye, Jewell, Seagry, Wilts, 1674 Wilts RO Miscellaneous Index to Wills (name + date)
Adye, John, yeoman, Borden, Kent, 1682 CKS PRC2/39/133
Adye, Peter, gentleman, Doddington, Kent, 1637 CKS PRC2/34/1
Adye, Thomas, Doddington, Kent, 1583 CKS PRC2/3/13
Aferie, William, blacksmith, Deal, Kent, 1669 CKS PRC19/4/1
Afford, Catherine, widow, Goudhurst, Kent, 1621 CKS PRC2/20/386
Afford, John, Goudhurst, Kent, 1630 CKS PRC2/30/8
Afford, Thomas, Goudhurst, Kent, 1620 CKS PRC2/20/382
Agars, Thomas, yeoman, Bempton, Yorks, 1785 Borthwick Test C.P. 1782/1
Agate, Frauncys + Pirone, strangers, Sandwich, Kent, 1588 CKS PRC2/4/289
Agates, John, Horsham, Sussex, 1601 W. Suss RO EpI/33/1600/1
Agates, John, Horsham, Sussex, 1601 W. Suss RO EpI/33/1600/9
Agates, John, Whitstable, Kent, 1630 CKS PRC2/30/4

Agbarrowe, Edward, Kidderminster, Worcs, 1587 Worcs RO 008.7 BA3585/838/57a
Agburrough, Mary, Kidderminster, Worcs, 1682 Worcs RO 008.7 BA3585/837/bdl 3
Aglen, John, carver/gilder, Cheltenham, Glos, 1825 GRO GDR/B4/2/A24
Aierst, Adam, St Laurence Thanet, Kent, 1674 CKS PRC2/36/2
Ailesburie, John, Canterbury St Paul, Kent, 1593 CKS PRC2/6/244
Ailward, John, Arundel, Sussex, 1624 W. Suss RO EpI/33/1624/11
Ainell, William, Bishopstone, Wilts, 1685 Wilts RO Arch. Sarum/(+ name and date)
Ainley, John, innkeeper, Almondbury (Armitage Bridge), Yorks, 1778 Borthwick Test C.P. 1778/1
Ainley, John, tailor, Doncaster, Yorks, 1802 Borthwick Test C.P. 1802/3
Aires, Edward, Lydd, Kent, 1674 CKS PRC20/12/108
Aiscough, Francis, Thornton le Moor, Lincs, 1611 Lincs RO Ad/Ac/10/153
Aiscoughe, John, Thornton le Moor, Lincs, 1623 Lincs RO Ad/Ac/18/18
Aiscowghe, John, esquire, Minster in Sheppey, Kent, 1603 CKS PRC2/12/409
Aishman, Henry, Kilmersdon, Som, 1706 Somerset RO D/D/Cta/A16
Aisroughe, Francis, esquire, Grimsby, Great, Lincs, 1613? Lincs RO Ad/Ac/12/151
Aistropp, Mary, Brattleby, Lincs, 1626 Lincs RO Ad/Ac/39/190
Aistropp, Troth, Brattleby, Lincs, 1626 Lincs RO Ad/Ac/39/184
Akeland, Silvester, Thurlby, Lincs, 1639 Lincs RO Ad/Ac/26/241
Akerlande, Henry, yeoman, Aylesby, Lincs, 1612 Lincs RO Ad/Ac/10/166
Akers, Mary, Milton next Sittingbourne, Kent, 1673 CKS PRC2/35/193
Alars, Richard, Selling, Kent, 1630 CKS PRC2/30/9
Alay, James, tailor, Cranbrook, Kent, 1674 CKS PRC2/36/6
Alben, Thomas, Bruton, Som, 1641 Somerset RO D/D/Cta/A18
Albot, Richard, Bromsgrove, Worcs, 1672 Worcs RO 008.7 BA3585/837/bdl 6
Alby, Charles, Dereham, East, Norf, 1767 Norfolk RO ANF/11/5/72
Alby, John, farmer, Toftrees, Norf, Norfolk RO ANW/23/21/36
Alchyn, Thomas, Stone in Oxney, Kent, 1586 CKS PRC2/4/198
Alcock, Edward, yeoman, Ruckinge, Kent, 1640 CKS PRC1/4/3
Alcock, John + Johan, Claypole, Lincs, 1611 Lincs RO Ad/Ac/10/120
Alcock, Robarte, esquire, Canterbury St Mary Bredman, Kent, 1589 CKS PRC2/5/74
Alcock, Thomas, Hemingford Abbots, Hunts, 1636 Hunts RO/Acc58/6(50)
Alcock, William, husbandman, Bennington, Long, Lincs, 1613 Lincs RO Ad/Ac/11/61
Alcock, William, Sutton Valence, Kent, 1617 CKS PRC2/20/392
Alcocke, Edwarde, Willesborough, Kent, 1618 CKS PRC2/20/403
Alcocke, Geoffrey, 1589 Lancs RO (Name of Deceased) D.R.C.H. 1589
Alcocke, Hammon, Boughton Aluph, Kent, 1593 CKS PRC2/6/144
Alcott, Joane, widow, Sandwich, Kent, 1621 CKS PRC2/23/6
Alcott, Robert, Sandwich, Kent, 1614 CKS PRC2/18/19
Alden, John, Shrewsbury, Shrops, 1678 LJRO:cards/1678/1
Alden, Richard, Cookham, Berks, 1611 Berks RO D/A1/173/87A
Alder, Francis, baker, Newbury, Berks, 1617 Berks RO D/A1/173/95A
Alder, John, husbandman, Stanford in the Vale, Berks, 1622 Berks RO D/A1/173/108A
Alder/Aldworth, Martin, Compton, Berks, 1607 Berks RO D/A1/173/78A
Alderedge, Ralph, clothier, Edington, Wilts, 1633 Wilts RO Arch. Sarum/(+ name and date)
Alderman, John, Taunton St Mary Magdalan, Som, 1620 Somerset RO D/D/Cta/A9
Alderne, Roger, husbandman,
Worcs Worcs RO 008.7 BA3585/834/431
Aldersey, John, St Thomas Isle of Harty, Kent, 1671 CKS PRC2/35/1
Aldersey, William, alderman, Chester, Ches, 1630 Cheshire RO (Name) W.C. 1630
Alderson, see Mason,
Alderstone, John, clergy: 'clerk', Stowting, Kent, 1598 CKS PRC2/10/127
Alderstone, John, Dover, Kent, 1639 CKS PRC20/10/1
Alderstone, William, Dover, Kent, 1626 CKS PRC20/7/104
Alderton, John, Pulborough, Sussex, 1632 W. Suss RO EpI/33/1632/23

[Alderton:]
Alderton, Richard eld, Wisborough Green, Sussex, 1623 W. Suss RO EpI/33/1623/14
Alderton, Thomas, Kirton, Lincs, 1649 Lincs RO Ad/Ac/30/121
Alderwick, Broughton Gifford, Wilts, 1613 Wilts RO Arch. Sarum/(+ name and date)
Aldey, Margret, widow, Tenterden, Kent, 1595 CKS PRC2/7/401
Aldey, Nycholas + Eliz, gentleman,
Kent 1580 CKS PRC21/4/101
Aldey, see Baker,
Aldey?, William, yeoman, Martley, Worcs, 1602 Worcs RO 008.7 BA3585/838/255
Aldham, Christopher, Owston, Lincs, 1636 Lincs RO Ad/Ac/40/81
Aldred, John, yeoman, Onehouse, Suff, 1790 Suff RO(B) IC500/3/53/67
Aldredge, Thomas, Herne, Kent, 1681 CKS PRC20/13/1
Aldrey, see Penvill,
Aldrich, Thomas, Canterbury St Paul, Kent, 1666 CKS PRC1/11/1
Aldridge, Andrew, Plaitford, Wilts, 1683 Wilts RO Arch. Sarum/(+ name and date)
Aldridge, Isaac, Erlestoke, Wilts, 1741 Wilts RO Arch. Sarum/(+ name and date)
Aldridge, John, husbandman, Cookham Dean, Berks, 1663 Berks RO D/A1/37/20B
Aldridge, John, Stratford Subcastle, Wilts, 1682 Wilts RO CC Sarum(+ name and date)
Aldridge, John, innholder, Amesbury, Wilts, 1748? Wilts RO Arch. Sarum/(+ name and date)
Aldridge, Mary, spinster, Thornbury, Glos, 1740 GRO GDR/B4/2/A50
Aldridge, Philadelphia, widow, Cookham, Berks, 1679 Berks RO D/A1/174/68c
Aldridge, Richard, tiler/bricklayer/citizen, St Peter Paul's Wharf, London & Middlesex, PRO PROB5/1774
Aldridge, William, Westbury, Wilts, 1609 Wilts RO Miscellaneous Index to Wills (name + date)
Aldright, James, victualler, Wednesbury, Staffs, 1773 LJRO/B/C/5/1773/2
Aldus, John, Belton, Lincs, 1627 Lincs RO Ad/Ac/39/124
Aldwine, Thomas eld, Watford, Herts, 1630 Herts RO ASA25/4866
Aldwoorth, Peeter, Compton, Berks, 1595 Wilts RO CC Sarum(+ name and date)
Aldworth, James, cordwainer, Reading, Berks, 1668 Berks RO D/A1/174/46d
Aldworth, Joan, widow, Garford, Berks, 1630 Berks RO D/A1/173/120C
Aldworth, John, yeoman, Drayton, Berks, 1601 Berks RO D/A1/173/68A
Aldworth, John, yeoman, Drayton, Berks, 1603 Berks RO D/A1/173/68D
Aldworth, Richard, tanner, Steventon, Berks, 1634 Berks RO D/A1/173/124A
Aldworth, Robert, Drayton, Berks, 1617 Berks RO D/A1/173/94C
Aldworth, Robert, husbandman, Watchfield, Berks, 1620 Berks RO D/A1/173/106C
Aldworth, William, yeoman, Drayton, Berks, 1644 Berks RO D/A1/174/24c
Aldworth, see Alder,
Aldwyn, Dorothy, Watford, Herts, 1621 Herts RO ASA25/2613
Aldwyn, Nicholas, yeoman, Rickmansworth, Herts, 1615 Herts RO ASA25/4817
Aldwyn, Thomas, Rickmansworth (Croxley Hall), Herts, 1602 Herts RO ASA25/4754
Aleburye, John, Brookland, Kent, 1596 CKS PRC2/9/13
Alee, George, Redbourn, Herts, 1611 Herts RO ASA25/4789
Alee, John, St Neot, Corn, 1638 Cornwall RO AP/A215a/2
Alegood, Frances, mistress, Norwich St Stephen, Norf, 1715 Norfolk RO ANW/23/12/23
Alen, Agnes, Lenham, Kent, 1598 CKS PRC2/10/236
Alen, Edward, Willesborough, Kent, 1584 CKS PRC2/3/65
Alen, James, Bircholt, Kent, 1582 CKS PRC2/2/53
Alen, Richard, Reculver, Kent, 1582 CKS PRC21/6/179
Alexander, Anthony, Norwich St Michael Coslany, Norf, 1722 Norfolk RO NCC INV/75A/33
Alexander, John, Waterstock, Oxon, 1627 Oxon RO MSS Wills 275/1/42
Alexander, Martin, Baltonsborough, Som, 1600 Somerset RO D/D/Cta/A20
Alexander, Thomas, Rickmansworth, Herts, 1597 Herts RO ASA25/1589
Alexander, Thomas, farmer, Ellastone (Stanton), Staffs, 1832 LJRO/B/C/5/1832/3
Alexander, see Allison,
Alexandre, Richard, Arborfield, Berks, 1598 Wilts RO Miscellaneous Index to Wills (name + date)

Alford, Edward, Lydiard Tregoze, Wilts, 1674 Wilts RO Miscellaneous Index to Wills (name + date)
Alford, John, Leverton, Lincs, 1632 Lincs RO Ad/Ac/23/84
Alford, John, Arreton, Hants, 1667 Hants RO 21M65 D8/192
Alford, Thomas, carpenter, Mere, Wilts, 1585 Wilts RO Dean Sarum (name + date)
Alforde, Thomas, Mere, Wilts, 1620 Wilts RO Miscellaneous Index to Wills (name + date)
Alfree, see Olfree,
Alies, Ralph,
Worcs 1607 Worcs RO 008.7 BA3585/834/430
Allain, William, Colsterworth, Lincs, 1618 Lincs RO Ad/Ac/14/18
Allam, Bridget, widow, Garsington, Oxon, 1682 Oxon RO MSS Wills 160/1/14
Allam, William, Eastchurch, Sheppey, Kent, 1627 CKS PRC2/27/8
Allame, Amy, widow, Dorchester (Burcott), Oxon, 1622 Oxon RO MSS Wills Pec 65/1/5
Allandbie, Ursula, widow, Immingham, Lincs, 1620 Lincs RO Ad/Ac/16/3
Allanson, James, St Martins le Grand, London & Middlesex, 1734 Lancs RO (Name of Deceased) D.R.C.H. 1734
Allanson, William, husbandman, Humberstone, Lincs, 1620 Lincs RO Ad/Ac/16/4
Allard, Edward, Warehorne, Kent, 1629 CKS PRC2/29/2
Allard, Edward, Bilsington, Kent, 1665 CKS PRC1/11/2
Allard, Francis, gentleman, Biddenden, Kent, 1639 CKS PRC1/2/2
Allard, Henry, gentleman, Biddenden, Kent, 1631 CKS PRC2/31/2
Allarde, Christopher, Mersham, Kent, 1616 CKS PRC2/20/397
Allatt, William, Barkby, Leics, 1666 Leics RO Administrators Accounts C17th f49
Allaway, Edward, Keevil (Bulkington), Wilts, 1676 Wilts RO Arch. Sarum/(+ name and date)
Allchurch, Benjamin, carpenter: 'ships carpenter', Stepney, London & Middlesex, 1702 PRO PROB32/44/54
Allchurche, William, Loose, Kent, 1611 CKS PRC20/2/238
Allderman, Benjamin, yeoman, Irthlingborough, Northants, 1764 Northants RO X954/21/7
Allderne, Edmund, yeoman, Martley, Worcs, 1599 Worcs RO 008.7 BA3585/838/132
Alldrit, John, Wednesbury, Staffs, 1685 LJRO/B/C/5/1685/14
Alleine, Sara, Stoke, South, Lincs, 1636 Lincs RO Ad/Ac/24/470
Allen, Ann, widow, Sturry, Kent, 1670 CKS PRC1/15/1
Allen, Ann, widow, Stepney, St Dunstan, London & Middlesex, 1728 Greater London RO DL/C/547/180
Allen, Ann, Stowe Nine Churches, Northants, 1780 Northants RO X954/21/46
Allen, Anthony, yeoman, Ewerby, Lincs, 1620 Lincs RO Ad/Ac/16/7
Allen, Anthony, Old Romney, Kent, 1667 CKS PRC1/12/3
Allen, Anthony, gentleman, Newington next Sittingbourne, Kent, 1682 CKS PRC20/13/77
Allen, Bennett, Bearsted, Kent, 1647 CKS PRC1/7/71
Allen, Daniell, Sturry, Kent, 1621 CKS PRC2/23/7
Allen, Dorothy, Birmingham, Warks, 1675 LJRO:cards/1675/1
Allen, Edward, yeoman, Frinstead, Kent, 1623 CKS PRC2/23/14
Allen, Edward, tailor, Oxford St Aldate, Oxon, 1644 Oxon RO MSS Wills 295/1/76
Allen, Edward, Frampton on Severn, Glos, 1829 GRO GDR/B4/2/A30
Allen, Elizabeth, Bredgar, Kent, 1679 CKS PRC2/38/96
Allen, Elizabeth, widow, Cambridge, Cambs, 1700 PRO PROB5/990 & 989
Allen, Finch, gentleman, Doddington, Kent, 1682 CKS PRC20/13/83
Allen, Frances, widow, Norton, Kent, 1676 CKS PRC2/37/1
Allen, Henry, Queenborough, Kent, 1626 CKS PRC2/27/7
Allen, Hughe, Brookland, Kent, 1605 CKS PRC2/13/13
Allen, James, gentleman, Maidstone, Kent, 1674 CKS PRC20/12/110
Allen, Joane, widow, Bredgar, Kent, 1599 CKS PRC2/10/481
Allen, John, Ickham, Kent, 1574 CKS PRC21/2/151
Allen, John, St Laurence Thanet, Kent, 1597 CKS PRC2/10/42
Allen, John, Itchenor, West, Sussex, 1598 W. Suss RO EpI/33/1598/10

[Allen:]
Allen, John, St Johns Thanet, Kent, 1600 CKS PRC2/11/419
Allen, John, Upchurch, Kent, 1607 CKS PRC2/14/3
Allen, John, Scrivelsby, Lincs, 1612/13? Lincs RO Ad/Ac/11/68
Allen, John, yeoman, Stourmouth, Kent, 1618 CKS PRC2/20/401
Allen, John, Frittenden, Kent, 1621 CKS PRC20/5/1
Allen, John, bricklayer, Sandwich, Kent, 1625 CKS PRC2/23/2
Allen, John, Barham, Kent, 1627 CKS PRC2/27/6
Allen, John, Lydd, Kent, 1629 CKS PRC20/8/1
Allen, John, Mundham, North, Sussex, 1633 W. Suss RO EpI/33/1633/22
Allen, John, yeoman, Bearsted, Kent, 1641 CKS PRC19/2/1
Allen, John, Bradford on Avon, Wilts, 1669 Wilts RO Arch. Sarum/(+ name and date)
Allen, John, Maidstone, Kent, 1674 CKS PRC20/12/109
Allen, John, miller, Milton next Sittingbourne, Kent, 1674 CKS PRC2/36/7
Allen, John, yeoman, Milsted, Kent, 1677 CKS PRC2/37/110
Allen, John, gentleman, Basildon, Berks, 1678 Berks RO D/A1/174/65c
Allen, John, yeoman, Hucking, Kent, 1681 CKS PRC20/13/81
Allen, John, Bidford, Warks, 1685 Worcs RO 008.7 BA3585/830/87
Allen, John, Biddenden, Kent, 1702 CKS PRC1/16/40
Allen, John, wheelwright, Wells Next The Sea, Norf, 1743 Norfolk RO ANW/23/24/1
Allen, Joseph, Wokingham, Berks, 1676 Wilts RO Dean Sarum (name + date)
Allen, Margaret, widow, Benenden, Kent, 1628 CKS PRC2/29/6
Allen, Matthias, Dover, Kent, 1684 CKS PRC20/13/392
Allen, Michael, St Margarets At Cliffe, Kent, 1603 CKS PRC21/16/47
Allen, Michael, Canterbury St Andrew, Kent, 1686 CKS PRC2/41/42
Allen, Nicholas, Ruckinge, Kent, 1612 CKS PRC2/17/270
Allen, Peter, Woolavington, Sussex, 1682 W. Suss RO EpI/33/1682/48
Allen, Ralph, Stockbury, Kent, 1625 CKS PRC2/25/2
Allen, Richard, Pershore, Worcs, Worcs RO 008.7 BA3585/838/175
Allen, Richard, Huntspill, Som, 1594 Somerset RO D/D/Cta/A21
Allen, Richard, Luddenham, Kent, 1622 CKS PRC2/26/122
Allen, Richard, Ashford, Kent, 1626 CKS PRC2/27/2
Allen, Richard, Bennington, Long, Lincs, 1638 Lincs RO Ad/Ac/25/101
Allen, Richard, Bennington, Long, Lincs, 1638 Lincs RO Ad/Ac/25/114
Allen, Richard, gentleman, St Margarets At Cliffe, Kent, 1670 CKS PRC19/4/64
Allen, Richard, St Johns Thanet, Kent, 1672 CKS PRC2/35/105
Allen, Richard, innkeeper, Norton, Chipping, Oxon, 1676 Oxon RO MSS Wills 76/1/31
Allen, Richard, yeoman, Compton, Berks, 1678 Berks RO D/A1/37/60C
Allen, Richard, yeoman, Spen Moor, Lancs, 1792 Lancs RO (Name of Deceased) D.R.C.H. 1792
Allen, Richarde, Whitstable, Kent, 1596 CKS PRC2/8/234
Allen, Robert, Hythe St Leonard, Kent, 1609 CKS PRC20/1/400
Allen, Robert, Stone next Faversham, Kent, 1614 CKS PRC2/20/394
Allen, Robert, St Laurence Thanet, Kent, 1624 CKS PRC2/23/15
Allen, Robert, Norton, Kent, 1626 CKS PRC2/27/10
Allen, Robert, Sutton Valence, Kent, 1629 CKS PRC2/29/4
Allen, Robert, Stretton en le Field, Derby, 1667 LJRO:cards/1667/3
Allen, Roger, Chart, Great, Kent, 1603 CKS PRC2/14/20
Allen, Samuel, victualler, Sandwich, Kent, 1686 CKS PRC2/41/72
Allen, Sara, widow, Canterbury St Paul, Kent, 1628 CKS PRC2/29/5
Allen, Sislie, Lenham, Kent, 1595 CKS PRC2/8/163
Allen, Stephan, Bapchild, Kent, 1613 CKS PRC2/18/70
Allen, Stephen, grocer, Eastchurch, Sheppey, Kent, 1672 CKS PRC2/35/104
Allen, Stephen, joiner, Milton next Sittingbourne, Kent, 1677 CKS PRC2/37/109
Allen, Stephen, husbandman, Newington next Sittingbourne, Kent, 1684 CKS PRC2/40/104
Allen, Theophylus, Boxley, Kent, 1608 CKS PRC2/13/1
Allen, Thomas, Spernall, Warks, Worcs RO 008.7 BA3585/839/376

Allen, Thomas, Rodmersham, Kent, 1582 CKS PRC2/2/80
Allen, Thomas, Quadring, Lincs, 1593 Lincs RO Ad/Ac/3/67
Allen, Thomas, Upchurch, Kent, 1608 CKS PRC2/13/3
Allen, Thomas, Wittersham, Kent, 1614 CKS PRC20/2/490
Allen, Thomas, Bredgar, Kent, 1618 CKS PRC2/20/377
Allen, Thomas, Streatley, Berks, 1618 Berks RO D/A1/36/44B
Allen, Thomas, Compton Dando, Som, 1623 Somerset RO D/D/Cta/A2
Allen, Thomas, Milton next Sittingbourne, Kent, 1634 CKS PRC2/32/136
Allen, Thomas, husbandman, Milton next Sittingbourne, Kent, 1667 CKS PRC1/11/98
Allen, Thomas, Edgmond, Shrops, 1674 LJRO:cards/1674/1
Allen, Thomas, yeoman, Challow, West, Berks, 1680 Berks RO D/A1/174/69c
Allen, Thomas, husbandman, Boughton Malherbe, Kent, 1682 CKS PRC2/40/2
Allen, Thomas, clergy: 'vicar', Hernhill, Kent, 1688 CKS PRC20/13/573
Allen, Timothie, gentleman, Hundleby, Lincs, 1634 Lincs RO Ad/Ac/24/28
Allen, Walter, clergy: 'clerk', Withcall, Lincs, 1622 Lincs RO Ad/Ac/18/71
Allen, William, Preston next Wingham, Kent, 1598 CKS PRC2/10/187
Allen, William, Boughton under Blean, Kent, 1602 CKS PRC21/17/67
Allen, William, Minster in Sheppey, Kent, 1606 CKS PRC2/15/7
Allen, William, Doddington, Kent, 1625 CKS PRC2/23/11
Allen, William, Birchington, Kent, 1631 CKS PRC20/9/23
Allen, William, Milsted, Kent, 1638 CKS PRC2/34/6
Allen, William, gentleman, Milton next Sittingbourne, Kent, 1670 CKS PRC1/14/1
Allen, William, Canterbury St Andrew, Kent, 1675 CKS PRC2/36/146
Allen, William, labourer, Upchurch, Kent, 1681 CKS PRC2/39/131
Allen, William, Doddington, Kent, 1682 CKS PRC1/15/90
Allen, William, Bridgewater (Dunwear), Som, 1683 Somerset RO D/D/Cta/A17
Allen, William, baker, Canterbury, Kent, 1724 CKS PRC1/18/34
Allen/Smith, William, butcher, St Neots, Hunts, 1710 Hunts RO/Acc58/302
Allen, see Chambers,
Allenby, John, Gainsborough, Lincs, 1683 Lincs RO Ad/Ac/44/39
Allenson, Edward, Swineshead, Lincs, 1620 Lincs RO Ad/Ac/16/8
Alley/Cocke, Thomas, Cranbrook, Kent, 1603 CKS PRC2/12/405
Alleyn, Michaell + Roger + Elizabeth, Bennington, Long, Lincs, 1607 Lincs RO Ad/Ac/8a/181
Alleyne, Elizabeth, Monks Horton, Kent, 1682 CKS PRC1/15/89
Allforde, William, Ashford, Kent, 1626 CKS PRC2/25/3
Allibone, Thomas jnr, bachelor, Ladbroke, Warks, 1711 LJRO/B/C/5/1711/3
Allibone, Thomas snr, Ladbroke, Warks, 1711 LJRO/B/C/5/1711/2
Alliley, Thomas, Scotton, Lincs, 1611 Lincs RO Ad/Ac/8a/341
Allin, Francis, clergy: 'clerk', Ponton, Great, Lincs, 1625 Lincs RO Ad/Ac/19A/26
Allin, John, gentleman, Fillingham, Lincs, 1607 Lincs RO Ad/Ac/37/239
Allin, John, Norton in Hales, Shrops, 1675 LJRO:cards/1675/2
Allin, Mary, widow, Staughton, Great, Hunts, 1679 Hunts RO/Acc58/141(180)
Allin, Richard, yeoman, Herne, Kent, 1598 CKS PRC21/14/520
Allin, Richard, Dymchurch, Kent, 1614 CKS PRC2/17/3
Allin, Robart, Staplehurst, Kent, 1592 CKS PRC2/6/81
Allin, Roger, Hernhill, Kent, 1589 CKS PRC21/10/9
Allin, Samuel, Boston, Lincs, 1673 Lincs RO Ad/Ac/35/3
Allin, Thomas, Helpringham, Lincs, 1613 Lincs RO Ad/Ac/12/144
Allin, Thomas, Bourne, Lincs, 1670 Lincs RO Ad/Ac/32/216
Allin, William, Orlestone, Kent, 1602 CKS PRC2/12/1
Alline, Alice, widow, Ash next Sandwich, Kent, 1600 CKS PRC21/16/127
Alline, Joane, widow, Dover, Kent, 1599 CKS PRC21/14/483
Allinson, Margrett, Dunston, Lincs, 1632 Lincs RO Ad/Ac/23/131
Allis, Symon, Sudbrooke, Lincs, 1662 Lincs RO Ad/Ac/41/111
Allison, George, Sandwich St Peter, Kent, 1668 CKS PRC1/13/2

[Allison:]
Aliison, William, Sandwich St Clement, Kent, 1640 CKS PRC1/4/4
Allison, William, Sandwich St Clement, Kent, 1640 CKS PRC1/4/4a
Allison/Alexander, Thomas, Lydd, Kent, 1629 CKS PRC20/8/5
Alliway, William, Keevil, Wilts, 1669 Wilts RO Arch. Sarum/(+ name and date)
Allmond, Richard, Maer, Staffs, 1685 LJRO/B/C/5/1684/1
Allott, Richard, 1663 Lambeth Palace Arches G18/7
Allott, William, nail factor, Rotherham (Park Gate, Kimberworth), Yorks, 1777 Borthwick Test C.P. 1777/1
Allpress, John eld, Stanton, Fen, Hunts, 1672 Hunts RO/Acc58/16(60)
Allred, William, Atherton, Lancs, 1688 Lancs RO (Name of Deceased) D.R.C.H. 1687-88
Allsop, Rowland, Bradbourne, Derby, 1685 LJRO/B/C/5/1685/15
Allsop, Thomas, Ashbourne, Derby, 1685 LJRO/B/C/5/1685/16
Allsop, William, Chelsea, St Luke, London & Middlesex, 1796 Greater London RO DL/C/563/72/2
Allsope, George, university: 'Fellow of Christ's College, Cambridge', Cambs 1561 CUL V.C.Acc./Box1/1
Allsopp, John, Kirby Bellars, Leics, 1668 Leics RO Administrators Accounts 1667-72 f16
Allwood, William, Glastonbury, Som, Somerset RO D/D/Cta/A19
Allwright, William, Edington, Wilts, 1762? Wilts RO Miscellaneous Index to Wills (name + date)
Allwright, William, Edington, Wilts, 1763? Wilts RO CC Sarum(+ name and date)
Allyn, Anne, widow, Dean, East, Sussex, W. Suss RO EpI/33/1607/5
Allyn, Mary, widow, Ottringham, Yorks, 1773 Borthwick Test C.P. 1773/1
Allyn, Reynold, Bonnington, Kent, 1623 CKS PRC2/23/12
Allyn, Thomas, Bodmin, Corn, 1607 Cornwall RO AP/A24
Alman, John, husbandman, Billinghay (Dogdyke), Lincs, 1627 Lincs RO Ad/Ac/20/89
Almond, Anne, widow, Blackrod, Lancs, 1764 Lancs RO (Name of Deceased) D.R.C.H. 1764
Almonson, Margerie, widow, Dover, Kent, 1597 CKS PRC21/14/246
Alnewick, Amon, clergy: 'clerk', Didcot, Berks, 1622 Wilts RO CC Sarum(+ name and date)
Alphant, John, Canterbury St Mary Northgate, Kent, 1636 CKS PRC2/33/2
Alphie, Abraham, Benenden, Kent, 1668 CKS PRC1/12/4
Alport, Edward, Tamworth, Staffs, 1674 LJRO:cards/1674/2
Alridge, Millicent, Lavington, West, Wilts, 1630 Wilts RO CC Sarum(+ name and date)
Alridge, Robert, Middleton, Warks, 1663 LJRO:cards/1663/2
Alsey, Lucy, widow, Shinfield, Berks, 1622 Berks RO D/A1/36/86D
Alsey, Richard, Cranbrook, Kent, 1674 CKS PRC2/36/10
Alsopp, John, St Helen, London & Middlesex, 1716 PRO PROB5/1778
Alwyn, Edmund, Rickmansworth, Herts, 1566 Herts RO ASA25/596
Alwyn, John, Binderton (Preston), Sussex, 1623 W. Suss RO EpI/33/1623/3
Alyes, Richard, Abberton, Worcs, 1675 Worcs RO 008.7 BA3585/830/34
Amanson, Agnes, Wigtoft, Lincs, 1606 Lincs RO Ad/Ac/7/109
Amberton, David, yeoman, Chislet, Kent, 1672 CKS PRC2/35/103
Amberton, David, Chislet, Kent, 1676 CKS PRC1/15/81
Ambrose, Isaac, Graveney, Kent, 1639 CKS PRC2/34/159
Ambrose, John, Donhead St Mary, Wilts, 1634 Wilts RO Arch. Sarum/(+ name and date)
Ambrose, Richard, Ormskirk, Lancs, 1620 Lancs RO (Name of Deceased) D.R.C.H. 1621
Ambrose, Richard, Hernhill, Kent, 1623 CKS PRC20/6/436
Ambrose, Steven, Chilham, Kent, 1607 CKS PRC2/14/10
Ambrose, William, Pinchbeck, Lincs, 1637 Lincs RO Ad/Ac/25/575
Ambrose/Amory, Robert, Milsted, Kent, 1630 CKS PRC2/30/7
Ameers, Robert, Appledram, Sussex, 1630 W. Suss RO EpI/33/1630/4
Ameres, John, Chidham, Sussex, W. Suss RO EpI/33/1604-6/1
Amerie, see Prior,
Amery, Thomas, clothier, Frittenden, Kent, 1683 CKS PRC2/40/87
Amerye, see Pewe,
Amherst, Thomas, yeoman, Chart nr Sutton Valence, Kent, 1664 CKS PRC1/9/75

Amias, John, brewer: 'beerbrewer', Abingdon, Berks, 1609 Berks RO D/A1/173/82A
Amies, John, Tong, Shrops, 1640 LJRO:cards/1640/1
Amis, Alexander, currier, Hythe St Leonard, Kent, 1668 CKS PRC19/4/2
Amis, Benjamin, yeoman, Molash, Kent, 1664 CKS PRC1/10/3
Amis, William, Herne, Kent, 1709 CKS PRC19/6/35
Amor, Thomas, Newnton, North, Wilts, 1630 Wilts RO Arch. Wilts.(name + date)
Amory, John, Stogumber, Som, 1639 Somerset RO D/D/Cta/A8
Amory, see Ambrose,
Amos, John, porter, Bristol St Philip & St Jacob, Glos, Bristol RO 1753/1
Ampleforde, John, Boston, Lincs, 1612 Lincs RO Ad/Ac/11/132
Amsden, William, Blockley, Worcs, 1682 Worcs RO 008.7 BA3585/837/bdl 3
Amsell, Edward, yeoman, Datchworth, Herts, 1637 Herts RO AHH23/5
Amy, George, Ashford, Kent, 1601 CKS PRC2/11/423
Amyas, Matthew, degrees: 'Doctor of Physic', Norwich, Norf, 1731 Norfolk RO ANW/23/20/23
Amye, John, Horsham, Sussex, 1607 W. Suss RO EpI/33/1607/6
Amys, Anne, widow, Canterbury St Mary Bredman, Kent, 1598 CKS PRC2/9/387
Amys, George, Milton next Sittingbourne, Kent, 1617 CKS PRC2/20/395
Amys, Peter, Molash, Kent, 1598 CKS PRC2/10/72
Amys, Richard, Canterbury Holy Cross Westgate, Kent, 1617 CKS PRC2/20/390
Amys, Stephen, Linton, Kent, 1591 CKS PRC2/5/374
Amys, Thomas, Tenterden, Kent, 1679 CKS PRC2/38/95
Amys, Wyllyam, Chilham, Kent, 1597 CKS PRC2/10/329
Amys, see Betts,
Ancell, Edward, yeoman, Quadring, Lincs, 1670 Lincs RO Ad/Ac/32/144
Ancell, George, Canterbury St Paul, Kent, CKS PRC1/1/40a
Anderson, Alexander, clergy: 'clerk', Wrawby, Lincs, 1597 Lincs RO Ad/Ac/4/109
Anderson, Anne, widow, Sibsey, Lincs, 1683 Lincs RO Ad/Ac/44/60
Anderson, Anthonie, Alkborough, Lincs, 1612 Lincs RO Ad/Ac/8b/3
Anderson, George, Gedney, Lincs, 1605 Lincs RO Ad/Ac/6/141
Anderson, John, Queenborough, Kent, 1594 CKS PRC2/7/357
Anderson, John, Watford, Herts, 1623 Herts RO ASA25/4835
Anderson, John, Asterby, Lincs, 1632 Lincs RO Ad/Ac/23/72
Anderson, John, mariner, St Johns Thanet, Kent, 1682 CKS PRC2/40/3
Anderson, John + Alice, Marston, Lincs, 1627 Lincs RO Ad/Ac/20b/91
Anderson, Nicholas, Roxby, Lincs, 1610 Lincs RO Ad/Ac/8a/315
Anderson, Robert, tanner, Broughton, Lincs, 1608 Lincs RO Ad/Ac/37/268
Anderson, Thomas, Tathwell, Lincs, 1627 Lincs RO Ad/Ac/20b/40
Anderson, William, mariner: 'seaman', Deal, Kent, 1681 CKS PRC20/13/79
Anderson, William,
Lincs 1797 Lincs RO Ad/Ac/45/67
Anderson, see Anderton,
Anderton/Anderson, Robert, Greenwich (East Greenwich), Kent, 1684 PRO PROB5/1212
Andeson, Edward, Sandridge, Herts, 1634 Herts RO ASA25/4899
Andrew, Ann, widow, Creaton, Northants, 1783 Northants RO X954/22/11
Andrew, Dionise, widow, Challock, Kent, 1602 CKS PRC21/16/125
Andrew, George, Nonington, Kent, 1680 CKS PRC20/12/250
Andrew, Giles, Grantham, Lincs, 1638 Lincs RO Ad/Ac/25/231
Andrew, Henry,
Hunts 1681 Hunts RO/Acc58/159
Andrew, John, Wingham, Kent, 1668 CKS PRC19/4/3
Andrew, Mathew, gentleman, Manchester, Lancs, 1795 Lancs RO (Name of Deceased) D.R.C.H. 1795-6
Andrew, Richard, gentleman, Edenham, Lincs, 1627 Lincs RO Ad/Ac/20/1
Andrew, Richard, Aston Abbots, Bucks, 1641 Herts RO ASA25/4839
Andrew, Robert, Swaton, Lincs, 1614 Lincs RO Ad/Ac/13/61

[Andrew:]
Andrew, Robert, Messingham, Lincs, 1638 Lincs RO Ad/Ac/40/246
Andrew, Robert, Gainsborough (Morton), Lincs, 1649 Lincs RO Ad/Ac/40/163
Andrew, Thomas, mariner, Kirby, West (Caldey), Ches, 1637 Cheshire RO (Name) W.C. 1637
Andrew, Thomas, Brothertoft, Lincs, 1639 Lincs RO Ad/Ac/26/261
Andrew, Thomas, bachelor, Canterbury St Andrew, Kent, 1686 CKS PRC2/41/70
Andrew, Thomas, farmer, Greaton, Northants, 1780 Northants RO X954/21/48
Andrew, William, Upper Hardres, Kent, 1630 CKS PRC2/30/5
Andrew, William, Stainton le Vale, Lincs, 1633 Lincs RO Ad/Ac/24/154
Andrew/Browne, George, Maidstone, Kent, 1583 CKS PRC21/6/385
Andrew, see Hill,
Andrewe, Henry, Caldecote, Herts, 1597 Herts RO ASA25/1590
Andrewe, John, Horbling, Lincs, 1613 Lincs RO Ad/Ac/11/46
Andrewe, John, shepherd, Kirby Bellars, Leics, 1641 Leics RO PR/I/41A/55
Andrewe, Richard, Amesbury, Wilts, 1614 Wilts RO Arch. Sarum/(+ name and date)
Andrewe, Roberte, Stapleford, Lincs, 1627 Lincs RO Ad/Ac/20b/97
Andrewe, Sampson, Northbourne, Kent, 1613 CKS PRC2/17/71
Andrewe, Thomas, Hougham, Kent, 1599 CKS PRC2/11/91
Andrewe, Thomas, husbandman, Carlby, Lincs, 1625 Lincs RO Ad/Ac/19B/82
Andrewes, Adrian, Oxford, Oxon, 1647 Oxon RO MSS Wills 295/1/78
Andrewes, Anthony, Bersted, South, Sussex, 1617 W. Suss RO EpIV/10/1/50
Andrewes, Dorothy, Capel le Ferne, Kent, 1639 CKS PRC1/2/3
Andrewes, Joane, widow, Ropley, Hants, 1624 Hants RO 21M65 D8/45
Andrewes, John, Overton, Wilts, 1627 Wilts RO Arch. Wilts.(name + date)
Andrewes, John, Tarring, West, Sussex, 1627 W. Suss RO EpIV/10/1/23
Andrewes, John, Collingbourne Kingston, Wilts, 1629 Wilts RO Arch. Wilts.(name + date)
Andrewes, John, Charing, Kent, 1631 CKS PRC20/9/29
Andrewes, John, armourer/citizen, St John Zachary, London & Middlesex, 1696 PRO PROB5/1777
Andrewes, Thomas, Sandwich, Kent, 1608 CKS PRC2/14/8
Andrewes, Thomas, yeoman, Brook, Kent, 1619 CKS PRC2/20/402
Andrewes, Thomas, Kingsdon, Som, 1640 Somerset RO D/D/Cta/A23
Andrewes/Wilcox, Thomas, Chewton Mendip, Som, 1604 Somerset RO D/D/Cta/A24
Andrews, Edmund, yeoman, Hough on the Hill, Lincs, 1624 Lincs RO Ad/Ac/19A/107
Andrews, Elizabeth, Morton, Lincs, 1796 Lincs RO Ad/Ac/45/65
Andrews, George, innholder, Hythe St Leonard, Kent, 1678 CKS PRC20/12/252
Andrews, Henry, Farcet, Hunts, 1677 Hunts RO/Acc58/94(23)
Andrews, Henry, Sawtry St Andrew, Hunts, 1682 Hunts RO/Acc58/175(99)
Andrews, John, Stretton, Little, Leics, 1666 Leics RO Administrators Accounts C17th f94
Andrews, John, Devizes, Wilts, 1676 Wilts RO CC Sarum(+ name and date)
Andrews, John, carpenter, Egerton, Kent, 1676 CKS PRC20/12/192
Andrews, Robert, Edenham, Lincs, 1635 Lincs RO Ad/Ac/24/351
Andrews, Stephen, Egerton, Kent, 1710 CKS PRC19/6/36
Andrews, Thomas, tailor, Bierton, Bucks, 1676 Oxon RO MSS Wills Pec 32/1/52
Andrews, Valentine, Patrixbourne, Kent, 1696 CKS PRC2/42/99
Andrews, William, Challock, Kent, 1675 CKS PRC20/12/158
Andrewson, Nicholas, Oare, Kent, 1680 CKS PRC2/39/1
Androwe, John, Faversham, Kent, 1593 CKS PRC2/6/226
Androwe, John, Appledore, Kent, 1607 CKS PRC2/14/5
Androwe, Stephen, Faversham, Kent, 1594 CKS PRC2/7/147
Androwes, Anne, widow, Cholsey, Berks, 1609 Berks RO D/A1/173/85D
Androwes, Thomas, gentleman, Dover, Kent, 1620 CKS PRC20/5/7
Ange, Walter, Stratford-upon-Avon, Warks, Worcs RO 008.7 BA3585/838/66
Ange, William, Alstone, Worcs, Worcs RO 008.7 BA3585/839/332
Angell, George, Rolvenden, Kent, 1608 CKS PRC2/13/5
Anger, Thomas, yeoman, Hagbourne, Berks, 1664 Berks RO D/A1/174/40c

Anglesey, Arthur, earl, 1687 PRO PROB32/26/288
Angod, Robert, shepherd, Tilshead, Wilts, 1636 Wilts RO Arch. Sarum/(+ name and date)
Anheyre, Probus, St Clement, Corn, 1615 Cornwall RO AP/A86/4
Anian, Thomas, clergy: 'D.D.', Canterbury Christchurch, Kent, 1635 CKS PRC20/10/15
Anley, Jacobi, Spilsby, Lincs, 1572 Lincs RO Ad/Ac/0/27
Annable, John, tailor, Miningsby, Lincs, 1649 Lincs RO Ad/Ac/30/149
Annable, Robert, Hognaston, Derby, 1682 LJRO/B/C/5/1682/1
Annate, William, Collingbourne Ducis, Wilts, 1632 Wilts RO Miscellaneous Index to Wills (name + date)
Anncell, Anthonye, Mersham, Kent, 1583 CKS PRC2/3/112
Anncell, George, Kirkby Underwood, Lincs, 1599 Lincs RO Ad/Ac/5/59
Anncell, John, Ash next Sandwich, Kent, 1587 CKS PRC21/8/207
Annesley, Robert, Grimsby, Great, Lincs, 1618 Lincs RO Ad/Ac/14/126
Anneson, John, Sandwich St Mary, Kent, 1669 CKS PRC1/14/2
Annetts, George, Ruardean, Glos, 1691 GRO GDR/B4/2/A7
Annis, Edmund, university: 'proctor's man/carpenter', Cambridge, Cambs, 1678 CUL V.C. Acc./Box3/1
Annis, Margery, widow, Middlezoy, Som, 1611 Somerset RO D/D/Cta/A22
Annison, Daniel, Sandwich St Peter, Kent, 1667 CKS PRC1/12/5
Annison, John, Sandwich, Kent, 1626 CKS PRC2/25/4
Annistone, William, New Romney, Kent, 1623 CKS PRC20/6/440
Annott, Peter, Canterbury St George Martyr, Kent, 1599 CKS PRC2/10/466
Annsell, Anthony, Mersham, Kent, 1586 CKS PRC2/4/321
Annsell, Richard, Chartham, Kent, 1595 CKS PRC2/7/103
Ansell, George, Kirkby Underwood, Lincs, 1618 Lincs RO Ad/Ac/14/94
Ansell, George, Westwell, Kent, 1677 CKS PRC20/12/225
Ansell, Richard, glover, Sturry, Kent, 1624 CKS PRC2/23/10
Ansell, Samuel, Harpenden, Herts, 1639 Herts RO AHH23/8
Ansloe, Richard, Bridge, Kent, 1664 CKS PRC1/10/4
Ansloe, Richard, Bridge, Kent, 1664 CKS PRC19/3/50
Ansted, Daniel, Teynham, Kent, 1633 CKS PRC20/10/33
Anstey, Mary, widow, Lavington, West, Wilts, 1631 Wilts RO CC Sarum(+ name and date)
Anstie, William, husbandman, Bisham, Berks, 1618 Berks RO D/A1/36/64C
Anstye/Feild, John, Wisborough Green, Sussex, 1632 W. Suss RO EpI/33/1631/34
Anthony, John, Shepherdswell alias Sibertswold, Kent, 1574 CKS PRC2/1/114
Anthony, William, labourer, Helpringham, Lincs, 1666 Lincs RO Ad/Ac/32/104
Anton, Benedict, Lincoln St Peter at Arches, Lincs, 1634 Lincs RO Ad/Ac/24/74
Antonie, Bennett, Halton Holgate, Lincs, 1599 Lincs RO Ad/Ac/5/205
Antonye, see Baye,
Antram, Francis, Titchfield, Hants, Hants RO 21m65 D8/303
Antram, John, Salisbury St Martin, Wilts, 1620 Wilts RO CC Sarum(+ name and date)
Antram, John, Salisbury, Wilts, 1621 Wilts RO Miscellaneous Index to Wills (name + date)
Antram, William, clothier, Salisbury, Wilts, 1671 Wilts RO Miscellaneous Index to Wills (name + date)
Antram, William, Salisbury, Wilts, 1678 Wilts RO Miscellaneous Index to Wills (name + date)
Antrobus, Robert, St Albans St Stephens, Herts, 1598 Herts RO ASA25/1659
Antrobus, Thomas,
Herts Herts RO ASA25/4986
Antrobus, Thomas, St Albans St Stephens, Herts, 1637 Herts RO ASA25/4933
Antrum, Richard, Wimborne Minster (Hillbutts), Dors, 1625 Dorset RO PE/WM CP 2/4/33
Anwicke, Thomas, Fosdyke, Lincs, 1620 Lincs RO Ad/Ac/16/2
Apeslie, George, Benenden, Kent, 1615 CKS PRC2/20/373
Apleyard, John, Grimsby, Lincs, 1606 Lincs RO Ad/Ac/7/124
Apleyard, Robert, Billinghay, Lincs, 1619 Lincs RO Ad/Ac/14/146
Apleyard, Valentyne, Kenardington, Kent, 1586 CKS PRC2/4/5

[Apleyarde:]
Apleyarde, Richarde, Mareham le Fen, Lincs, 1613 Lincs RO Ad/Ac/12/70
Apparie, John, Amport, Hants, 1624 Hants RO 21M65 D8/46
Applebee, Anne, widow, Oxford St Martin, Oxon, 1642 Oxon RO MSS Wills 295/1/74
Applebee, William, chandler, Oxford St Martin, Oxon, 1640 Oxon RO MSS Wills 295/1/67
Applebie, Henry, Bray, Berks, 1594 Berks RO D/A1/173/51B
Appleby, Ambrose, university: 'Fellow of Queens' College, Cambridge/D.D./vicar' Cambridge (Queens' College), Cambs, 1668 CUL V.C. Acc./Box3/2
Appleby, Thomas, tailor, Sutterton, Lincs, 1669 Lincs RO Ad/Ac/33/97
Appleby, William, weaver, Thoresby, North, Lincs, 1619 Lincs RO Ad/Ac/14/279
Appleford, Thomas, Ramsbury, Wilts, 1678 Wilts RO Dean Sarum (name + date)
Appleton, Henry, husbandman, Boughton Malherbe, Kent, 1682 CKS PRC2/39/132
Appleton, John, innholder, Speen (Speenhamland), Berks, 1600 Berks RO D/A1/173/66A
Appleton, John, Marton, Lincs, 1613 Lincs RO Ad/Ac/12/66
Appleton, Stephen, Boughton Malherbe, Kent, 1688 CKS PRC2/41/114
Appleton, Thomas, husbandman, Stratfield Mortimer, Berks, 1640 Berks RO D/A1/36/157C
Appleton, Thomas, cheesemonger/bachelor, Newington St Mary (Walworth), Surrey, 1814 Borthwick Test C.P. 1814/4
Appleyard, Willoughbie, Barton on Humber, Lincs, 1629 Lincs RO Ad/Ac/22/42
Apse, Robert, Appledore, Kent, 1603 CKS PRC2/14/16
Apse, Thomas, husbandman, Cranbrook, Kent, 1639 CKS PRC1/2/4
Apsley, Edward, tanner, Biddenden, Kent, 1682 CKS PRC2/40/1
Apsly, Richard, tanner, Wye, Kent, 1679 CKS PRC2/38/92
Apthorp, Henry Welch, butcher, St Ives, Hunts, 1783 Hunts RO/Acc58/332
Apthorpe, Henry, Stanton, Fen, Hunts, 1676 Hunts RO/Acc58/77(124)
Archard, Aggas, Devizes St John the Baptist, Wilts, 1628 Wilts RO CC Sarum(+ name and date)
Archard, William, Hundleby, Lincs, 1786 Lincs RO Ad/Ac/45/54
Archard/Hatchet, Edwin, labourer: 'day labourer', Lambourn (Eastbury), Berks, 1625 Berks RO D/A1/173/110C
Archard?,
Wilts 1632? Wilts RO CC Sarum(+ name and date)
Archdeacon, John, Hurst, Old, Hunts, 1684 Hunts RO/Acc58/231(225)
Archer, Edward, Fleet, Lincs, 1612 Lincs RO Ad/Ac/11/152
Archer, Edward, clergy: 'clerk', Cookham, Berks, 1675 Berks RO D/A1/174/61c
Archer, Henry eld, yeoman, Monkton, Kent, 1625 CKS PRC20/7/327
Archer, John, Boston, Lincs, 1606 Lincs RO Ad/Ac/7/123
Archer, John, Minster in Thanet, Kent, 1612 CKS PRC2/16/28
Archer, John, yeoman, Lincoln St Peter in Eastgate, Lincs, 1623 Lincs RO Ad/Ac/19A/90
Archer, John, butcher, Chartham, Kent, 1676 CKS PRC2/37/2
Archer, Mary, widow, Gillingham, Kent, 1609 Lambeth Palace VH82/143
Archer, Mary, widow, Birmingham, Warks, 1774 LJRO/B/C/5/1771/31
Archer, Richard, Gosberton, Lincs, 1623 Lincs RO Ad/Ac/18/63
Archer, Robert, Washingborough, Lincs, 1626 Lincs RO Ad/Ac/19B/61
Archer, Thomas, Cockerington, North, Lincs, 1593 Lincs RO Ad/Ac/3/69
Archer, Thomas, Frampton, Lincs, 1638 Lincs RO Ad/Ac/25/505
Archer, William, esquire, Bishopsbourne, Kent, 1618 CKS PRC2/20/399
Archer, William, Aston, Warks, 1682 LJRO/B/C/5/1682/2
Archley, Alice, widow, Wye, Kent, 1599 CKS PRC2/11/179
Archley, Samuel, yeoman, Appledore, Kent, 1688 CKS PRC2/41/113
Archley, Thomas, Lenham, Kent, 1637 CKS PRC2/34/5
Archley, Thomas, Bilsington, Kent, 1663 CKS PRC1/9/76
Archley, William, Ruckinge, Kent, 1626 CKS PRC2/25/1
Archley/Ashley, John, Canterbury, Kent, 1641 CKS PRC1/5/76
Arden, Anthony, Knaith, Lincs, 1662 Lincs RO Ad/Ac/41/53
Arden, Thomas, Canterbury, Kent, 1573 CKS PRC21/2/62
Arden, Thomas, Highworth, Wilts, 1596 Wilts RO Miscellaneous Index to Wills (name + date)

Ardern, George, alderman/gentleman, Chichester, Sussex, 1619 W. Suss RO EpIII/9/1/25
Arderne, Thomas, gentleman, Wymering, Hants, 1678 Hants RO 21m65 D8/280
Ardyn, Edward, yeoman, Horsington, Lincs, 1651? Lincs RO Ad/Ac/29/80
Argar, Robert, carpenter, Faversham, Kent, 1680 CKS PRC2/38/94
Argar, Thomas, Faversham, Kent, 1630 CKS PRC2/30/6
Argent, Robert, Whichford, Warks, 1608 Worcs RO 008.7 BA3585/839/430
Argoe/Goldfinch, Anne, widow, Harbledown, Kent, 1676 CKS PRC20/12/191
Arlett, Richard, cooper, Shaw cum Donnington, Berks, 1618 Berks RO D/A1/173/100C
Arlush, Thomas, Crowle, Lincs, 1633? Lincs RO Ad/Ac/40/11
Arlush, Thomas, Crowle, Lincs, 1633? Lincs RO Ad/Ac/40/33
Armaraz, Ellen, widow, Chipping Barnet, Herts, 1559 Herts RO ASA25/265
Armesbey, Richard, Alconbury Weston, Hunts, 1683 Hunts RO/Acc58/199(199)
Armesbie, Thomas, Weston, Lincs, 1620 Lincs RO Ad/Ac/16/1
Armested/James, Richard, Compton (West Compton), Berks, 1616 Berks RO D/A1/173/92C
Armeston, Alice, widow, Leasingham, Lincs, 1632 Lincs RO Ad/Ac/23/48
Armestronge, Grace, widow, Wyberton, Lincs, 1635 Lincs RO Ad/Ac/24/367
Armestronge, John, Ingoldsby, Lincs, 1669 Lincs RO Ad/Ac/33/117
Armestronge, Robert, yeoman, Heckington, Lincs, 1614 Lincs RO Ad/Ac/13/73
Armetrydinge, John, clergy: 'vicar', Petham, Kent, 1585 CKS PRC2/3/339
Armiger, John, Houghton, Norf, 1756 Norfolk RO ANW/23/25/48C
Arminer, William, Dibden, Hants, 1665 Hants RO 1665 AD2
Armistead, Thomas, St Anne Westminster, London & Middlesex, 1744 Greater London RO AM/PP/Box 1739-1749 pt (uncatalogued)
Armitage, Caleb, Batley (Healey), Yorks, Borthwick Test C.P. 1729/2
Armstead, Thomas, bricklayer, Somersham, Hunts, 1747 Hunts RO/Acc58/324
Armstrong, John, Wyberton, Lincs, 1637 Lincs RO Ad/Ac/25/273
Armstrong, Thomas, Leicester St Mary, Leics, Leics RO Administrators Accounts 1667-72 f83
Armstrong, Thomas, Kirkby Underwood, Lincs, 1639 Lincs RO Ad/Ac/26/140
Armstronge, William, Wyberton, Lincs, 1638 Lincs RO Ad/Ac/25/493
Armstronge, William, yeoman, Hagbourne, Berks, 1682 Berks RO D/A1/174/78c
Armytage, David, yeoman, Bradford (Great Horton), Yorks, 1840 Borthwick Test C.P. 1840/12
Arnall, Richard, Branston, Lincs, 1613 Lincs RO Ad/Ac/11/59
Arnam, Nicholas, Ansford, Som, 1623 Somerset RO D/D/Cta/A1
Arneden, Richard, Canterbury St George Martyr, Kent, 1599 CKS PRC2/11/173
Arnefield, William, yeoman, Glossop (Dinting), Derby, 1664 LJRO:cards/1664/1
Arnet, see Phillipa,
Arneway/Hawkins, Anne, Worcester, Worcs, 1681 Worcs RO 008.7 BA3585/830/82
Arnfield, Robert, Glossop, Derby, 1684 LJRO/B/C/5/1685/17
Arnold, Abraham, Alverstoke, Hants, 1662 Hants RO 21M65 D8/149
Arnold, Abraham, Shipley, Sussex, 1684 W. Suss RO EpI/33/1684/20
Arnold, Elizabeth, widow, Royston, Yorks, 1818 Borthwick Test C.P. 1818/4
Arnold, Gerard/Garret, Faversham, Kent, 1571 CKS PRC2/1/35
Arnold, Joan, widow, Pagham, Sussex, 1682 W. Suss RO EpIV/10/2A/22
Arnold, John, yeoman, Uffington, Berks, 1620 Berks RO D/A1/173/102C
Arnold, John, Rustington (West Preston), Sussex, 1631 W. Suss RO EpI/33/1631/12
Arnold, John, St Albans, Herts, 1632 Herts RO ASA25/4872
Arnold, John, Bennington, Long, Lincs, 1636 Lincs RO Ad/Ac/24/502
Arnold, John ygr, farmer, Hanbury (Newborough), Staffs, 1777 LJRO/B/C/5/1778/2
Arnold, Robert, Beeding, Upper, Sussex, 1594 W. Suss RO EpI/33/1594/19
Arnold, Robert, Timberland, Lincs, 1634 Lincs RO Ad/Ac/24/53
Arnold, Thomas, Selling, Kent, 1604 CKS PRC2/13/11
Arnold, Thomas, Smeeth, Kent, 1609 CKS PRC20/2/11
Arnold, Thomas, St Peter in Thanet, Kent, 1672 CKS PRC2/35/102
Arnold, William, Deeping, West, Lincs, 1593 Lincs RO Ad/Ac/3/79
Arnold, William, Abingdon St Nicholas, Berks, 1630 Berks RO D/A1/36/110D

[Arnold:]
Arnold, William, yeoman, Swingfield, Kent, 1697 CKS PRC2/42/124
Arnold, Zachary, bachelor, Witham, North, Lincs, 1683 Lincs RO Ad/Ac/44/63
Arnold/Grolie?, Thomas, Malmesbury, Wilts, 1674 Wilts RO Miscellaneous Index to Wills (name + date)
Arnolde, Clement, Sausthorpe, Lincs, 1607 Lincs RO Ad/Ac/8a/49
Arnolde, George, Reculver, Kent, 1609 CKS PRC20/2/67
Arnolde, Thomas, Herne, Kent, 1573 CKS PRC21/1/182
Arnolde, William, Tenterden, Kent, 1604 CKS PRC2/14/18
Arnoll, Edmund, Hutton, Som, 1626 Somerset RO D/D/Cta/A3
Arnoll, John, Newbury, Berks, 1615 Berks RO D/A1/173/93C
Arnoll, Mary, Snargate, Kent, 1675 CKS PRC2/36/148
Arnoll, Thomas, Quadring, Lincs, 1635 Lincs RO Ad/Ac/24/437
Arnot, Richard, St Mary Aldermary, London & Middlesex, 1690 PRO PROB32/31/140
Arnot, see Jacob,
Arnott, Thomas, fuller, Kinver, Staffs, 1766 LJRO/B/C/5/1766/56
Arnsby, Joseph, Kimbolton, Hunts, 1676 Hunts RO/Acc58/32(157)
Arosmith, Antony, husbandman, Doddington (Pigot), Lincs, 1679 Lincs RO Ad/Ac/43/105
Arpwood, William, yeoman, Bitteswell, Leics, 1673 Leics RO Administrators Accounts 1667-72 f121
Arrowe, Christian, Elham, Kent, 1590 CKS PRC2/5/221
Arrowes, Richard, Tenterden, Kent, 1595 CKS PRC2/7/257
Arrowsmilth, Antony, husbandman, Doddington, Lincs, C17th? Lincs RO Ad/Ac/45/102
Arrowsmith, Augustine, Belton, Lincs, 1619 Lincs RO Ad/Ac/15/91
Arrundell, John, Barton, Steeple (Middle Barton), Oxon, 1633 Oxon RO MSS Wills 295/1/55
Artenstall, Thomas, Altrincham, Ches, 1616 Cheshire RO (Name) W.C. 1616
Arter, Nicholas, Reculver, Kent, 1627 CKS PRC20/8/3
Arthrowe, Simon, Gedney, Lincs, 1626 Lincs RO Ad/Ac/20/56
Arthur, Francis, Purton, Wilts, 1615 Wilts RO Arch. Wilts.(name + date)
Arthure, John, Somborne, Kings, Hants, 1597 Hants RO 1597 AD003
Arundell, Andrew, husbandman, Enderby, Bag, Lincs, 1642 Lincs RO Ad/Ac/28/47
Arundell, John, Lydd, Kent, 1641 CKS PRC19/2/2
Arundell, Simon, Shefford, Great, Berks, 1616 Berks RO D/A1/173/91A
Asbury, John, blacksmith, Stafford St Mary, Staffs, 1681 LJRO/B/C/5/1681/1
Asbury, Maudlin, Tamworth, Staffs, 1680 LJRO:cards/1680/2
Ascoughe, Thomas, gentleman, Fulstow, Lincs, 1607 Lincs RO Ad/Ac/8a/183
Asfordby, Edward, Saltfleetby, Lincs, 1639? Lincs RO Ad/Ac/26/74
Asgarbie, Robert, Sibsey, Lincs, 1620 Lincs RO Ad/Ac/16/5
Ash, John, Uttoxeter, Staffs, 1685 LJRO/B/C/5/1684/2
Ashbie, William, Hemingby, Lincs, 1620 Lincs RO Ad/Ac/16/9
Ashbourn, John, yeoman, Bulkington, Warks, 1756 LJRO/B/C/5/1756/45
Ashbune, James, Cadney, Lincs, 1587 Lincs RO Ad/Ac/2C/120
Ashby, John, Bassingham, Lincs, 1614 Lincs RO Ad/Ac/12/177
Ashby, Richard, yeoman, Somercoates, South, Lincs, 1666 Lincs RO Ad/Ac/32/127
Ashby, William, Hollingbourne, Kent, 1614 CKS PRC20/3/140
Ashby, see Rich,
Ashbye, John, Willesborough, Kent, 1596 CKS PRC2/8/316
Ashbye, Thomas, Thornham, Kent, 1599 CKS PRC2/10/472
Ashdale, Thomas, Shadoxhurst, Kent, 1625 CKS PRC2/23/18
Ashdowne, Abraham, carpenter, Dymchurch, Kent, 1679 CKS PRC2/38/93
Ashdowne, Mathew, tailor, Staplehurst, Kent, 1667 CKS PRC1/12/6
Ashe, Roger, Grimsby, Great, Lincs, 1612 Lincs RO Ad/Ac/11/130
Ashe, William, blacksmith, Windsor, Old, Berks, 1618 Berks RO D/A1/173/97A
Ashenden, Elizabeth, widow, Tenterden, Kent, 1618 CKS PRC2/26/128 and unnumbered
Ashenden, John, Canterbury St Andrew, Kent, 1634 CKS PRC2/32/4
Ashenden, Leonard, Canterbury, Kent, 1623 CKS PRC2/23/13

Ashenden, Robarte, Ebony, Kent, 1614 CKS PRC2/18/114
Ashenden, Thomas, Hythe St Leonard, Kent, 1617 CKS PRC20/4/3
Ashepoole, Thomas, Hollingbourne, Kent, 1619 CKS PRC20/4/7
Asher, John, Wonston (Sutton Scotney), Hants, 1673 Hants RO 21m65 D8/254
Asher, Robart, Bobbing, Kent, 1586 CKS PRC2/3/341
Asherinden, Robert, Tenterden, Kent, 1633 CKS PRC2/32/1
Asherinden, Stephen, tailor, Sandwich, Kent, 1678 CKS PRC2/38/1
Asherst, Allan, Sutton Valence, Kent, 1602 CKS PRC2/12/407
Asherst, Elizabeth, widow, Ashford, Kent, 1612 CKS PRC2/16/84
Asherst, Henry, yeoman, Aldington, Kent, 1674 CKS PRC20/12/111
Asherst, Hunfrye, Kingsnorth, Kent, 1612 CKS PRC2/16/49
Asherst, Nathaniel, gentleman, Warehorne, Kent, 1674 CKS PRC2/36/4
Asherst, see Taylor,
Asherste, Joane, widow, Lydd, Kent, 1596 CKS PRC21/14/71
Asheton, Roberte, Bourne, Lincs, 1599 Lincs RO Ad/Ac/5/281
Ashinden, William, Hernhill, Kent, 1625 CKS PRC20/7/223
Ashley, Gilbert, Pinchbeck, Lincs, 1634 Lincs RO Ad/Ac/24/50
Ashley, John, university: 'scholar's servant', Cambridge St Botolph, Cambs, 1615 c. CUL V.C.Acc./Box1/2
Ashley, Joseph, Ivychurch, Kent, 1640 CKS PRC20/10/27
Ashley, Richard, tailor, Nuneham Courtenay, Oxon, 1632 Oxon RO MSS Wills 295/1/53
Ashley, Richard, Stapleton, Shrops, 1674 LJRO:cards/1674/3
Ashley, William, gunsmith, Winchcombe, Glos, 1775 GRO GDR/B4/2/A43
Ashley, see Archley,
Ashly, Richard, Salisbury, Wilts, 1674 Wilts RO Miscellaneous Index to Wills (name + date)
Ashmor, Thomas, Sandwich, Kent, 1676 CKS PRC2/36/150
Ashmore, Nicholas, husbandman, Halesowen, Worcs, 1605 Worcs RO 008.7 BA3585/839/377
Ashpoole, Alice, widow, Maidstone, Kent, 1634 CKS PRC20/10/31
Ashton, Wilts RO Unlisted Fragment
Ashton, Edward, Barton on Humber, Lincs, 1603 Lincs RO Ad/Ac/5/107
Ashton, Elizabeth, widow, Stamford, Lincs, 1623? Lincs RO Ad/Ac/18/90
Ashton, Issabell, widow, Brereton, Ches, 1618 Cheshire RO (Name) W.C. 1618
Ashton, Joane, widow, St Sepulchre, London & Middlesex, 1671 PRO PROB5/1437
Ashton, John, Mugginton (Ravensdale Park), Derby, 1663 LJRO:cards/1663/3
Ashton, Lewis, Burton by Lincoln, Lincs, 1664 Lincs RO Ad/Ac/41/133
Ashton, Luke,
Hunts 1678 Hunts RO/Acc58/129(4)
Ashton, Peter, yeoman, Sawtry All Saints, Hunts, 1703 Hunts RO/Acc58/295
Ashton, Richard, Croston (Mawdesley), Lancs, 1615 Lancs RO (Name of Deceased) D.R.C.H. 1615
Ashurst, Charles, weaver, Wigan (Haigh), Lancs, 1758 Lancs RO (Name of Deceased) D.R.C.H. 1758
Ashwell, Henrye, Bobbing, Kent, 1613 CKS PRC2/18/55
Ashwell, Richard, tailor, Gosberton, Lincs, 1633 Lincs RO Ad/Ac/24/144
Ashwell, Robert, Kenardington, Kent, 1629 CKS PRC2/29/1
Ashwell, William, Gosberton, Lincs, 1638 Lincs RO Ad/Ac/25/31
Ashwin, William, baker, Warwick, Warks, 1685 Worcs RO 008.7 BA3585/830/7
Ashwine, John, Gainsborough, Lincs, 1673 Lincs RO Ad/Ac/35/60
Ashwood, Mary, widow, Kimpton, Herts, 1635 Lambeth Palace Arches G35/1
Ashworth, George, innkeeper, Halifax, Yorks, 1787 Borthwick Test C.P. 1786/1
Ashwyn, Richard, Sullington, Sussex, 1612 W. Suss RO EpI/33/1611/15
Askam, Thomas, Stanwick, Northants, Northants RO NWill A/C/117
Askew, Addam, Minster in Sheppey, Kent, 1639 CKS PRC2/34/162
Askew, George, Faversham, Kent, 1670 CKS PRC1/14/3
Askew, James, victualler, Wingfield, South, Derby, 1791 LJRO/B/C/5/1791/1

[Askew:]
Askew, Richard, Minster in Sheppey, Kent, 1603 CKS PRC2/12/413
Askew, Robert, Lympne, Kent, 1673 CKS PRC2/35/195
Askew, Thomas, Cranford, Northants, 1681 Northants RO NWill A/C/4
Askew, Thomas, yeoman, Pinchbeck, Lincs, 1683 Lincs RO Ad/Ac/44/93
Askew, Thomas eld, gentleman, Faversham, Kent, 1641 CKS PRC1/4/5
Askewe, Adrian, Dover, Kent, 1600 CKS PRC21/15/204
Askewe, Elizabeth, widow, Minster in Sheppey, Kent, 1615 CKS PRC2/20/388
Askue, Adam, Bearsted, Kent, 1638 CKS PRC1/1/65
Aslabie, James, gentleman, Kirmington, Lincs, 1602 Lincs RO Ad/Ac/5/385
Aslene, Thomas, Aswardby, Lincs, Lincs RO Ad/Ac/2C/39
Aslett, John, Kirdford, Sussex, 1640 W. Suss RO EpI/33/1639/2
Aslett, Nicholas, yeoman, Tilehurst, Berks, 1636 Berks RO D/A1/174/6a
Aslinge, Robert, labourer, Marston, Lincs, 1638 Lincs RO Ad/Ac/25/168
Aslinge, Robert, Farcet, Hunts, 1677 Hunts RO/Acc58/95(26)
Aslocke, John, Welby, Lincs, 1649 Lincs RO Ad/Ac/30/46
Ason, Francis, Newton, Lincs, 1661 Lincs RO Ad/Ac/41/31
Aspinall, Ellis, Manchester (Reddish), Lancs, 1751 Lancs RO (Name of Deceased) W.C.W. 1750
Aspinall, Hannah, Chester, Ches, 1674 Cheshire RO (Name) W.C. 1674
Aspinall, Henrie, gentleman, Halsall (Lydiate), Lancs, 1662 Lancs RO (Name of Deceased) D.R.C.H. 1662-63
Aspinall, John, mason: 'stone mason', Dewsbury, Yorks, 1796 Borthwick Test C.P. 1796/1
Aspinwall, Christopher, gentleman, Aughton, Lancs, 1788 Lancs RO (Name of Deceased) D.R.C.H. 1788
Aspinwall, Ellis, blacksmith, Manchester (Reddish), Lancs, 1751 Lancs RO (Name of Deceased) D.R.C.H. 1751-53
Aspland, Emos, Boston, Lincs, 1805 Lincs RO Ad/Ac/45/46
Asplinge, John, Sibsey, Lincs, 1626 Lincs RO Ad/Ac/20/22
Assar, Christopher, Iwade, Kent, 1605 CKS PRC2/26/130
Asseherst, Wyllyam, Kingsnorth, Kent, 1586 CKS PRC2/4/58
Asser, Christopher, Iwade, Kent, 1605 CKS PRC2/13/9
Asshehurst, John, Preston next Faversham, Kent, 1587 CKS PRC2/4/67
Asshehurst, John, Ashford, Kent, 1590 CKS PRC2/5/226
Assherst/Whyte, Elizabeth, Tenterden, Kent, 1597 CKS PRC2/9/11
Astbury, Josias, Newcastle under Lyme, Staffs, 1684 LJRO/B/C/5/1684/3
Astell, John sen, yeoman, Tilehurst, Berks, 1681 Berks RO D/A1/174/73c
Astell, Thomas, Aldworth, Berks, 1594 Berks RO D/A1/35/229D
Astell, Timothy, baker, Kidlington, Oxon, 1634 Oxon RO MSS Wills 295/1/57
Asten, John, gentleman, Bray, Berks, 1628 Berks RO D/A1/173/115C
Astley, Merial, widow, Aston, Whiteladies, Worcs, 1756 Worcs RO 008.7 BA3585/835/bdl 1
Astley/Bell, Richard, butcher, Pershore, Worcs, 1603 Worcs RO 008.7 BA3585/839/298
Aston, John, weaver, Bradley (Wollaston), Staffs, 1663 LJRO:cards/1663/4
Aston, Richard, Acton, Ches, 1583 Cheshire RO (Name) W.C. 1582
Aston, Richard, husbandman, Aston Cantlow, Warks, 1606 Worcs RO 008.7 BA3585/839/400
Aston, Samuel, Aston Cantlow, Warks, 1675 Worcs RO 008.7 BA3585/830/35
Aston, William, currier, Birmingham, Warks, 1763 LJRO/B/C/5/1763/114
Astrey, William, Somersham, Hunts, 1676 Hunts RO/Acc58/28(12)
Astwick, Thomas, Thurlby, Lincs, 1678 Lincs RO Ad/Ac/42/78
Astwood, John, Birmingham, Warks, 1720 LJRO/B/C/5/1720/5a
Aswicke, Thomas, Thurlby, Lincs, 1662? Lincs RO Ad/Ac/42/2
Athall, Robert, Bottesford (Crosby), Lincs, 1612 Lincs RO Ad/Ac/8b/1
Athie, John, Brookland, Kent, 1617 CKS PRC2/20/398
Atkin, Alexander, Challock, Kent, 1645 CKS PRC19/2/91
Atkin, Edward, Fulbeck, Lincs, 1673 Lincs RO Ad/Ac/35/22
Atkin, Nicholas, Killamarsh, Derby, 1670 LJRO:cards/1670/3
Atkin, Nicholas, Killamarsh, Derby, 1672 LJRO:cards/1672/2

Atkin, Richard, Sotby, Lincs, 1640 Lincs RO Ad/Ac/27/152
Atkin, Thomas, Hawkhurst, Kent, 1628 CKS PRC2/28/2
Atkin, William, Bucknall, Lincs, 1666 Lincs RO Ad/Ac/32/95
Atkins, Benjamin, Holywell, Hunts, 1682 Hunts RO/Acc58/172(18)
Atkins, Christopher, Killamarsh, Derby, 1685 LJRO/B/C/5/1684/4
Atkins, James, Woodchurch, Kent, 1639 CKS PRC20/10/23
Atkins, John, clergy: 'clerk/parson', Bredon, Worcs, 1591 Worcs RO 008.7 BA3585/838/87
Atkins, John, gentleman, Sutton Benger, Wilts, 1629 Wilts RO Arch. Wilts.(name + date)
Atkins, John, Goudhurst, Kent, 1631 CKS PRC2/31/3
Atkins, Richard, Tisbury, Wilts, 1639 Wilts RO Arch. Sarum/(+ name and date)
Atkins, Robert, Wichling, Kent, CKS PRC1/9/77b
Atkins, Robert, Wichling, Kent, 1663 CKS PRC1/9/77
Atkins, Thomas, Goudhurst, Kent, 1602 CKS PRC2/12/403
Atkins, Thomas, Faversham, Kent, 1637 CKS PRC2/33/1
Atkins, William, husbandman, Woolavington, Som, 1637 Somerset RO D/D/Cta/A4
Atkinson, Alexander, Barrowby, Lincs, 1612 Lincs RO Ad/Ac/11/105
Atkinson, Ann, widow, Barrow, Lincs, 1670 Lincs RO Ad/Ac/32/155
Atkinson, George, Lancs RO (Name of Deceased) D.R.C.H. (Undated)
Atkinson, George, Belton All Saints, Lincs, 1610 Lincs RO Ad/Ac/8a/313
Atkinson, George, Gunby St Nicholas, Lincs, 1639 Lincs RO Ad/Ac/26/1
Atkinson, James, cordwainer, Tattershall, Lincs, 1627 Lincs RO Ad/Ac/20/106
Atkinson, John, shopkeeper, Huttoft, Lincs, 1853 Lincs RO Ad/Ac/45/84
Atkinson, Judith, Hogsthorpe, Lincs, 1619 Lincs RO Ad/Ac/15/47
Atkinson, Nicholas, Theddlethorpe All Saints, Lincs, 1638? Lincs RO Ad/Ac/25/656
Atkinson, Nicholas, husbandman, Norton, Bishop, Lincs, 1680s Lincs RO Ad/Ac/42/97
Atkinson, Oliver, Horncastle, Lincs, 1605? Lincs RO Ad/Ac/6/15
Atkinson, Richard, Tetney, Lincs, 1613 Lincs RO Ad/Ac/11/64
Atkinson, Richard, Epworth, Lincs, 1680 Lincs RO Ad/Ac/43/169
Atkinson, Richard, milliner, Leeds, Yorks, 1794 Borthwick Test C.P. 1794/10
Atkinson, Robert, Manton, Lincs, 1662 Lincs RO Ad/Ac/41/49
Atkinson, Thomas, Hacconby, Lincs, 1618 Lincs RO Ad/Ac/14/30
Atkinson, Thomas, carpenter, Grasby, Lincs, 1635 Lincs RO Ad/Ac/24/96
Atkinson, Thomas, Kirkby, East, Lincs, 1649 Lincs RO Ad/Ac/30/79
Atkinson, Thomas, vintner, St Clement Danes, London & Middlesex, 1691 PRO PROB32/30/216
Atkinson, Troylus, victualler/scholar's servant, Cambridge St Andrew, Cambs, 1623 CUL V.C. Acc./Box2/1
Atkyn, William, Lincoln (Bail), Lincs, 1573 Lincs RO Ad/Ac/1/9
Atkyn, William, Lincoln (Bail), Lincs, 1573 Lincs RO Ad/Ac/2b/39
Atkyne, Roberte, Challock, Kent, 1586 CKS PRC21/8/135
Atkyne, Thomas, Hawkhurst, Kent, 1604 CKS PRC2/14/14
Atkynes, Richard, Watford, Herts, 1561 Herts RO ASA25/494
Atkyns, Alice, widow, Faversham, Kent, 1602 CKS PRC2/12/401
Atkyns, George, Challock, Kent, 1623 CKS PRC20/6/444
Atkyns, John, Rickmansworth, Herts, 1565 Herts RO ASA25/580
Atkyns, John, Castle Cary, Som, 1589 Somerset RO D/D/Cta/A27
Atkyns, John, Teynham, Kent, 1592 CKS PRC2/5/229
Atkyns, John, Grandborough, Warks, 1672 LJRO:cards/1672/3
Atkyns, Richard, Sandwich St Peter, Kent, 1587 CKS PRC2/4/330
Atkyns, Robert, Newbold on Avon, Warks, 1695 LJRO:cards/1695/1
Atkyns, Thomas, Faversham, Kent, 1610 CKS PRC2/15/5
Atlee, John, yeoman, Hillingdon, London & Middlesex, 1675 PRO PROB32/12/50
Atmore, John, Trull, Som, 1698 Somerset RO D/D/Cta/A26
Atree, John, Hawkhurst, Kent, 1594 CKS PRC2/7/337
Att Wood, Nicholas, Upper Hardres, Kent, 1631 CKS PRC20/9/472
Attawaye/Weller, William, Hawkhurst, Kent, 1602 CKS PRC2/12/3

[Attenburie:]
Attenburie, Joane, widow, Woburn, Beds, 1625 Lincs RO Ad/Ac/19B/85
Atterbie, Henry, Brattleby, Lincs, 1621 Lincs RO Ad/Ac/8c/1
Atterbie, William, yeoman, Sutton, Lincs, 1618 Lincs RO Ad/Ac/14/246
Atterbury, Catherine, widow, Warwick, Warks, 1749 Worcs RO 008.7 BA3585/835/bdl 1
Atterton, Thomas, Faversham, Kent, 1626 CKS PRC2/27/3
Atthayes, John, Chewton Mendip, Som, 1638 Somerset RO D/D/Cta/A6
Atthow, Joseph, blacksmith, Norwich St Giles, Norf, Norfolk RO ANW/23/25/77
Attkin, Thomas, Keal, East, Lincs, 1638 Lincs RO Ad/Ac/25/177
Attkin, William, Leake, Lincs, 1639 Lincs RO Ad/Ac/26/213
Attkins, Thomas eld, Bathampton, Som, 1635 Somerset RO D/D/Cta/A7
Attkinson, Carlton Scroop, Lincs, 1638 Lincs RO Ad/Ac/25/12
Attkinson, George, Grantham, Lincs, 1597 Lincs RO Ad/Ac/4/13
Attkinson, Suzan, widow, Leake, Lincs, 1652 Lincs RO Ad/Ac/29/29
Attlee, Anthony, bricklayer, Winkfield, Berks, 1640 Berks RO D/A1/174/15c
Attlee, William, yeoman, Winkfield, Berks, 1639 Berks RO D/A1/174/14c
Atton, John, Kennington, Kent, 1574 CKS PRC2/1/110
Atton, Richard, butcher, Leicester St Nicholas, Leics, 1639 Leics RO PR/I/41A/31
Atton, Thomas, Stamford St Michael, Lincs, 1606 Lincs RO Ad/Ac/7/137
Attwell, Alice, Hale, Great, Lincs, 1652 Lincs RO Ad/Ac/29/39
Attwell/Wells, John, wheelwright, Thatcham, Berks, 1628 Berks RO D/A1/173/113C
Attwood, George, yeoman, Teddington, Glos, 1693 Worcs RO 008.7 BA3585/837/bdl 6
Attwood, Mary, spinster, Worcester, Worcs, 1779 Worcs RO 008.7 BA3585/835/bdl 2
Attwoodd, William, Sonning, Berks, 1596 Wilts RO Miscellaneous Index to Wills (name + date)
Atwater, John, Lenham, Kent, 1637 CKS PRC2/34/3
Atwater, John, Queenborough, Kent, 1685 CKS PRC2/41/41
Atwater, Petronell, widow, Lenham, Kent, 1620 CKS PRC2/20/383
Atwaters, Thomas, yeoman, Otterden, Kent, 1645 CKS PRC1/7/21
Atweeke, Joseph, Birdham (East Itchenor), Sussex, 1676 W. Suss RO EpI/33/1676/27
Atwell, Joane, widow, Sandwich, Kent, 1641 CKS PRC1/4/6
Atwell, John, Ickham, Kent, 1580 CKS PRC21/4/130
Atwood, Edward, yeoman, Blean, Kent, 1716 CKS PRC1/18/1
Atwood, Lawrence, Chitterne St Mary, Wilts, 1621 Wilts RO Miscellaneous Index to Wills (name + date)
Atwood, Thomas, Sittingbourne, Kent, 1595 CKS PRC2/7/391
Atwood, Thomas, Arlingham, Glos, 1667 GRO GDR/B4/2/A16
Atwood, William, Teddington, Glos, 1675 Worcs RO 008.7 BA3585/830/33
Atwood, see Wood,
Atwoods, Richard, Harting, Sussex, 1597 W. Suss RO EpI/33/1596/16
Aubie/Marshall, Mary, Crowle, Lincs, 1664 Lincs RO Ad/Ac/41/148
Aubrey, John, husbandman, Ilsley, East, Berks, 1636 Berks RO D/A1/174/5b
Aucher, Anthony, knight, Bishopsbourne, Kent, 1637 CKS PRC20/10/11
Aucher, Henry, Westwell, Kent, 1598 CKS PRC21/14/585
Aucher, James, gentleman, Cheriton, Kent, 1587 CKS PRC2/4/104
Aucher, John, Bishopsbourne, Kent, 1580 CKS PRC2/1/273
Auckland, Peter, Epworth, Lincs, 1617 Lincs RO Ad/Ac/8b/177
Audley, William, Bradford on Avon, Wilts, 1633 Wilts RO Arch. Sarum/(+ name and date)
Augar, Francis, Dover, Kent, 1621 CKS PRC20/5/3
Auger, William, Watchfield, Berks, 1618 Berks RO D/A1/173/96A
Augrom, Robert, Alford, Lincs, 1627 Lincs RO Ad/Ac/20b/27
Aunby, Henry, Belton All Saints, Lincs, 1680 Lincs RO Ad/Ac/43/153
Auncell, George, Canterbury St Paul, Kent, 1629 CKS PRC1/1/40
Auncelle, William, Watford, Herts, 1570 Herts RO ASA25/654
Aungell, John, yeoman, Reading, Berks, 1619 Berks RO D/A1/173/101C
Auste, Alice, spinster, Somerford, Great, Wilts, 1621 Wilts RO Arch. Wilts.(name + date)
Austell, Edmund, yeoman, Holbeach, Lincs, 1620 Lincs RO Ad/Ac/16/6

Austen, Alen, Rolvenden, Kent, 1597 CKS PRC2/9/331
Austen, Ann, Birchington, Kent, 1672 CKS PRC20/12/36
Austen, Ann, widow, Sandwich, Kent, 1674 CKS PRC2/36/3
Austen, David, Nonington, Kent, 1671 CKS PRC20/12/2
Austen, David, Canterbury, Kent, 1715 CKS PRC1/17/66
Austen, Edward, Chartham, Kent, 1633 CKS PRC2/32/3
Austen, Edward, Queenborough, Kent, 1675 CKS PRC2/36/149
Austen, Elizabeth, widow, Goudhurst, Kent, 1637 CKS PRC2/33/3
Austen, Francis, Bethersden, Kent, 1677 CKS PRC2/37/111
Austen, George, Woodchurch, Kent, 1584 CKS PRC21/7/31
Austen, George, Rolvenden, Kent, 1624 CKS PRC2/23/16
Austen, George, gentleman, Norton, Hook, Oxon, 1667 Oxon RO MSS Wills 76/1/16
Austen, Henry, yeoman, St Johns Thanet, Kent, 1615 CKS PRC2/20/375
Austen, Jeremye, Hythe St Leonard, Kent, 1614 CKS PRC20/2/492
Austen, John, Boughton under Blean, Kent, 1579 CKS PRC21/4/20
Austen, John, Loose, Kent, 1618 CKS PRC20/4/1
Austen, John, Northbourne, Kent, 1629 CKS PRC2/30/1
Austen, John, Ash next Sandwich, Kent, 1630 CKS PRC20/8/13
Austen, John, Goudhurst, Kent, 1631 CKS PRC2/31/4
Austen, John, Elham, Kent, 1639 CKS PRC2/34/161
Austen, John, Kingsnorth, Kent, 1668 CKS PRC1/13/5
Austen, John, Kingsnorth, Kent, 1668 CKS PRC1/13/5a
Austen, John, Kingsnorth, Kent, 1668 CKS PRC1/13/5b
Austen, John, butcher, Ashford, Kent, 1668 CKS PRC1/13/3
Austen, John, yeoman, Woodchurch, Kent, 1671 CKS PRC20/12/1
Austen, John, husbandman, Marden, Kent, 1683 CKS PRC2/40/89
Austen, John, Thornham, Kent, 1684 CKS PRC2/40/166
Austen, John eld, Goudhurst, Kent, 1668 CKS PRC1/13/4a
Austen, John eld, Goudhurst, Kent, 1668 CKS PRC1/13/4b
Austen, John eld, mercer, Goudhurst, Kent, 1669 CKS PRC1/13/4
Austen, Joseph, High Halden, Kent, 1627 CKS PRC2/28/1
Austen, Joseph, innholder, Sandwich St Peter, Kent, 1670 CKS PRC1/15/2
Austen, Leonard, Eastry, Kent, 1601 CKS PRC21/15/215
Austen, Margaret, spinster, Canterbury St Margaret, Kent, 1632 CKS PRC2/31/5
Austen, Mathew, jurat, Faversham, Kent, 1682 CKS PRC2/39/130
Austen, Nicholas, Loose, Kent, 1579 CKS PRC21/3/319
Austen, Nicholas, Sholden, Kent, 1635 CKS PRC2/34/2
Austen, Percivall, Marden, Kent, 1623 CKS PRC2/23/9
Austen, Percivall, yeoman, Ulcombe, Kent, 1683 CKS PRC2/40/88
Austen, Richard, Great Stukeley, Hunts, Hunts RO/Acc58/151(179)
Austen, Robert, butler, Holbeach, Lincs, 1629 Lincs RO Ad/Ac/22/124
Austen, Robert, Goudhurst, Kent, 1637 CKS PRC2/34/9
Austen, Robert, Cranbrook, Kent, 1715 CKS PRC1/17/67
Austen, Samuel, Eythorne, Kent, 1674 CKS PRC2/36/1
Austen, Thomas, Ash next Sandwich, Kent, 1584 CKS PRC21/6/359
Austen, Thomas, Wye, Kent, 1586 CKS PRC2/4/160
Austen, Thomas, Biddenden, Kent, 1593 CKS PRC2/6/364
Austen, Thomas, yeoman, Stone in Oxney, Kent, 1622 CKS PRC2/23/3
Austen, Thomas, Maidstone, Kent, 1636 CKS PRC20/10/19
Austen, Thomas, Warehorne, Kent, 1664 CKS PRC1/10/5
Austen, Thomas, husbandman, Headcorn, Kent, 1682 CKS PRC2/40/4
Austen, Thomas, husbandman, Snave, Kent, 1685 CKS PRC2/41/40
Austen, Thomas eld, Tenterden, Kent, 1618 CKS PRC2/20/384
Austen, William, Tenterden, Kent, 1598 CKS PRC2/9/389
Austen, William, Tenterden, Kent, 1598 CKS PRC2/10/284

[Austen:]
Austen, William, Cranbrook, Kent, 1662 CKS PRC1/9/1
Austen, William, Cranbrook, Kent, 1676 CKS PRC2/36/151
Austen, William, Sandwich, Kent, 1681 CKS PRC1/15/91
Austen, see Cooke,
Austin, Abraham, Stepney, London & Middlesex, 1699 PRO PROB32/40/65
Austin, John, Ditchampton, Wilts, 1673 Wilts RO Arch. Sarum/(+ name and date)
Austin, Ralph, yeoman, Stafford, Staffs, 1811 LJRO/B/C/5/1811/6
Austin, Solomon, Ulcombe, Kent, 1618 CKS PRC2/20/385
Austin, Susanne, widow, High Halstow, Kent, 1663 CKS PRC1/9/78
Austin, Thomas, Stukeley, Hunts, 1676 Hunts RO/Acc58/78(183)
Austin, Thomas, Keele, Staffs, 1682 LJRO/B/C/5/1681/2
Austin, see Cooper,
Austine, Christopher, Glastonbury St John, Som, 1604 Somerset RO D/D/Cta/A28
Austine, Richard, Godmersham, Kent, 1608 CKS PRC20/1/344
Austrey, Symon, Norton, Kent, 1586 CKS PRC2/4/341
Autry, Thomas, Philleigh, Corn, 1608 Cornwall RO AP/A48/2
Auty, Thomas, clothier, Dewsbury (Gawthorpe), Yorks, Borthwick Test C.P. 1746/1
Aveley, Thomas, Orton Longueville, Hunts, 1684 Hunts RO/Acc58/223(211)
Avelyn, John, labourer, Tilehurst, Berks, 1661 Berks RO D/A1/174/38c
Aven, Anne, Erlestoke, Wilts, 1669 Wilts RO Arch. Sarum/(+ name and date)
Avenell, Jane, Horsham (Bishopric), Sussex, 1636 W. Suss RO EpIV/10/2/9
Avenell, Thomas, husbandman, Tilehurst, Berks, 1618 Berks RO D/A1/173/99A
Averell, William, Wingham, Kent, 1599 CKS PRC21/15/232
Averie, William, Stone in Oxney, Kent, 1629 CKS PRC2/30/3
Averill, Henry, Chart, Little, Kent, 1627 CKS PRC2/28/4
Averill, Samuel, weaver, Ashley, Staffs, 1811 LJRO/B/C/5/1811/9
Avery, Dorothy, widow, Bramber, Sussex, 1613 W. Suss RO EpI/33/1613/4
Avery, John, Broadwater, Sussex, 1682 W. Suss RO EpI/33/1682/4
Avery, Mary, widow, Newbury, Berks, 1666 Berks RO D/A1/37/32D
Avery, Thomas, Tintagel, Corn, 1609 Cornwall RO AP/A49
Avery, William, St Stephen in Brannel, Corn, 1615 Cornwall RO AP/A96
Avery, William, gentleman, Arley, Warks, 1740 LJRO/B/C/5/1741/421
Avice, Thomas, clothworker, Wokingham, Berks, 1631 Wilts RO Miscellaneous Index to Wills (name + date)
Awbrey, Arthur, clergy: 'clerk/D.D.', Kingston Bagpuize, Berks, 1608 Berks RO D/A1/173/80C
Awbrey, Thomas, husbandman, Whichford, Warks, 1604 Worcs RO 008.7 BA3585/839/325
Awcher, Edward, Deal, Kent, 1610 CKS PRC20/2/71
Awcher, Jeames, clergy: 'clerk', Sevington, Kent, 1600 CKS PRC2/11/171
Awcocke, Richard, yeoman, Fotherby, Lincs, 1619 Lincs RO Ad/Ac/15/203
Awcocke, Robert, Bourne, Lincs, 1639? Lincs RO Ad/Ac/26/90
Awde, Elizabeth, widow, Selsey, Sussex, 1630 W. Suss RO EpI/33/1630/15
Awde, Thomas ygr, Selsey, Sussex, 1630 W. Suss RO EpI/33/1630/14
Awder, Thomas, Wyberton, Lincs, 1612 Lincs RO Ad/Ac/11/180
Awdley, Martha, widow, Littlebourne, Kent, 1665 CKS PRC1/11/3
Awdley, Richard, Billingborough, Lincs, 1646 Lincs RO Ad/Ac/28/166
Awdley, Robert, Rippingale, Lincs, 1605 Lincs RO Ad/Ac/6/143
Awdrie, John, Stickney, Lincs, 1606 Lincs RO Ad/Ac/7/133
Awdus, Stephen, Gainsborough, Lincs, 1660 Lincs RO Ad/Ac/41/52
Awgar, William, Eastchurch, Sheppey, Kent, 1620 CKS PRC2/20/380
Awghtie, Gilbert, Holbeach, Lincs, 1607 Lincs RO Ad/Ac/8a/167
Awgur, John, Lydd, Kent, 1597 CKS PRC21/14/594
Awkinson, Robert, Benington, Lincs, 1641 Lincs RO Ad/Ac/27/206
Awkinson, William, Bilsby, Lincs, 1649 Lincs RO Ad/Ac/30/118
Awkinsonne, GEorge, Mumby, Lincs, 1579 Lincs RO Ad/Ac/2b/52a
Awminson, William, husbandman, Wigtoft, Lincs, 1629 Lincs RO Ad/Ac/22/61

Awncell, Alice, Badlesmere, Kent, 1599 CKS PRC2/10/167
Awood, William, yeoman, Scalford, Leics, 1673 Leics RO Administrators Accounts 1667-72 f118
Awsten, Alice, Bethersden, Kent, 1596 CKS PRC2/8/344
Awsten, Edmund, Littlebourne, Kent, 1615 CKS PRC2/20/391
Awsten, James, Portsmouth, Hants, 1624 Hants RO 21M65 D8/47
Awsten, Jeames, Newington next Sittingbourne, Kent, 1596 CKS PRC2/9/333
Awsten, Jeremie, Smarden, Kent, 1603 CKS PRC2/14/12
Awsten, John, Ashford, Kent, 1624 CKS PRC2/23/1
Awsten, Mary, spinster, Rolvenden, Kent, 1666 CKS PRC1/9/79
Awsten, Nicholas, mariner: 'sailor', High Halstow, Kent, 1623 CKS PRC2/23/4
Awsten, Philipp, Nonington, Kent, 1611 CKS PRC20/2/240
Awsten, Robarte, Chislet, Kent, 1609 CKS PRC2/13/7
Awsten, Robert, Milton next Sittingbourne, Kent, 1610 CKS PRC2/15/3
Awsten, Robert, Postling, Kent, 1626 CKS PRC2/27/9
Awsten, Thomas, Cranbrook, Kent, 1599 CKS PRC2/11/169
Awsten, Thomas, Leeds, Kent, 1604 CKS PRC2/13/16
Awsten, Thomas, yeoman, Bray, Berks, 1604 Berks RO D/A1/173/72A
Awsten, Thomas, Goudhurst, Kent, 1626 CKS PRC2/27/5
Awsten, Thomas, Marden, Kent, 1640 CKS PRC1/2/5
Awsten, William, blacksmith, Brinkworth, Wilts, 1618 Wilts RO Arch. Wilts.(name + date)
Awsten/Moore, Constance, Rolvenden, Kent, 1628 CKS PRC2/28/3
Awsten, see Peerson,
Awstenn, Stephen, weaver: 'broad weaver', Staplehurst, Kent, 1629 CKS PRC2/30/2
Awstine, Humfrey, Reading St Giles, Berks, 1609 Berks RO D/A1/173/84C
Awstyn, John, Chislet, Kent, 1619 CKS PRC2/20/387
Axbie, Robert, Covenham St Bartholomew, Lincs, 1637 Lincs RO Ad/Ac/25/439
Axby, Richard, Rodmersham, Kent, 1684 CKS PRC2/40/165
Axford, Isaac, farmer, Erlestoke, Wilts, 1741 Wilts RO Arch. Sarum/(+ name and date)
Axtell, Robert, Reculver, Kent, 1638 CKS PRC20/10/7
Ayearst, William, Headcorn, Kent, 1626 CKS PRC2/27/4
Ayer, Elizabeth, widow, Sulhampstead (Graisley), Berks, 1598 Berks RO D/A1/173/61A
Ayer, John, Woodnesborough, Kent, 1676 CKS PRC2/37/3
Ayers, Richard, cooper, St Peter in Thanet, Kent, 1670 CKS PRC1/15/3
Ayers, Robert, Wittering, West, Sussex, 1624 W. Suss RO EpI/33/1623/8
Ayers, Thomas, university: 'scholar's servant', Cambridge St Peter, Cambs, 1617 CUL V.C.Acc./Box1/3
Ayers, William, Faversham, Kent, 1675 CKS PRC2/36/147
Ayerst, Robert, Bobbing, Kent, 1637 CKS PRC2/34/8
Ayherst, Henry, threadman, Maidstone, Kent, 1667 CKS PRC19/3/110
Ayles,
Wilts 1614 Wilts RO Arch. Sarum/(+ name and date)
Ayles, John, Felpham, Sussex, 1611 W. Suss RO EpI/33/1611/12
Ayles, John, yeoman, Felpham (Flansham), Sussex, 1631 W. Suss RO EpI/33/1630/5
Ayleward, Thomas, St Albans St Peters, Herts, 1608 Herts RO ASA25/4764
Aylewyn, William, Bighton, Hants, 1624 Hants RO 21M65 D8/49
Ayliffe, John, Downe, 1623 Hants RO 21M65 D8/2A
Ayling, Richard, Stedham, Sussex, 1594 W. Suss RO EpI/33/1593/5
Aylinge, William, Trotton (Dumpford), Sussex, 1635 W. Suss RO EpI/33/1634/1
Aylmore, Jane, widow, Chichester St Bartholomew, Sussex, 1678 W. Suss RO EpIII/9/1/64
Aylwin, John, Lurgashall, Sussex, 1643 W. Suss RO EpI/33/1643/3
Aylwin, Richard, Treyford, Sussex, 1662 W. Suss RO EpI/33/1662/2
Aylwin, William, Westbourne, Sussex, 1628 W. Suss RO EpI/33/1627/19
Aylwine, John eld, yeoman, Tillington, Sussex, 1623 W. Suss RO EpI/33/1623/11
Aylwyn, James, Duncton, Sussex, 1632 W. Suss RO EpI/33/1632/24
Aylwyn, Joan, Duncton, Sussex, W. Suss RO EpI/33/1619/13

[Aylwyn:]
Aylwyn, John, Binderton (, Sussex, 1596 W. Suss RO EpI/33/1596/5
Aynscombe, Jervase, Benenden, Kent, 1593 CKS PRC2/6/424
Aynscombe, Myldred, widow, Benenden, Kent, 1593 CKS PRC2/6/418
Aynscombe, Thomas, Headcorn, Kent, 1670 CKS PRC19/4/65
Aynscough, John, Chorley, Lancs, 1706 Lancs RO (Name of Deceased) D.R.C.H. 1705-6
Ayre, Anne, widow, Wainfleet St Mary, Lincs, 1619 Lincs RO Ad/Ac/15/238
Ayre, John, Welton le Marsh (Thwaite), Lincs, 1607 Lincs RO Ad/Ac/8a/51
Ayres, John, gardener, Wytham (Seacourt), Berks, 1661 Berks RO D/A1/174/36d
Ayres, John, tailor, Swallowfield, Berks, 1678 Berks RO D/A1/174/66c
Ayres, John, manciple, Oxford (Trinity College), Oxon, 1707 Bodleian HYP B8/1
Ayres, William, Kennington, Berks, 1618 Berks RO D/A1/36/46A
Ayres, William, victualler, Faversham, Kent, 1675 CKS PRC2/36/8
Ayrton, Matthew, manufacturer, Halifax (Ovenden), Yorks, 1834 Borthwick Test C.P. 1834/3
Ayschcombe, Oliver, esquire, Lambourn (East Hanney), Berks, 1648 Berks RO D/A1/36/192B
Ayscough, John, Osbournby, Lincs, 1674 Lincs RO Ad/Ac/34/14
Aystropp, Alexander, Brattleby, Lincs, 1649 Lincs RO Ad/Ac/40/189
B...., William, clothier, Worcester, Worcs, Worcs RO 008.7 BA3585/838/219
Bacchouse, John, Manton, Lincs, 1663 Lincs RO Ad/Ac/41/88
Bacchus, John, gentleman, Welton, Yorks, Borthwick Cons C.P. 1760/1
Baccus, William, Thornton Curtis, Lincs, 1637 Lincs RO Ad/Ac/25/366
Bach, John, Chaddesley Corbett, Worcs, 1685 Worcs RO 008.7 BA3585/837/bdl 4
Bache, Edward, Witherley, Leics, 1642 Leics RO PR/I/41A/92
Bache, Thomas, Mathon, Hfords, 1593 Worcs RO 008.7 BA3585/838/93
Bache, Thomas, Rowley Regis, Staffs, 1607 Worcs RO 008.7 BA3585/839/431
Bacheler, Agnes, Minster in Thanet, Kent, 1607 CKS PRC2/13/84
Bacheler, Boberte, Minster in Sheppey, Kent, 1601 CKS PRC2/12/54
Bacheler, Catherine, widow, Canterbury St Paul, Kent, 1606 CKS PRC2/13/58
Bacheler, John, Lenham, Kent, 1593 CKS PRC2/6/95
Bacheler, John, stapler, Canterbury St Mildred, Kent, 1669 CKS PRC1/14/6
Bacheler, Philemon, Chart, Great, Kent, 1617 CKS PRC2/20/186
Bacheler, Richard, Appledore, Kent, 1596 CKS PRC2/8/147
Bacheler/Batcheler, Samuel ygr, Minster in Sheppey, Kent, 1647 CKS PRC1/7/72
Bachelor, George, Canterbury St Margaret, Kent, 1598 CKS PRC2/10/179
Bachelor, Jonas, Newnham, Kent, 1606 CKS PRC2/13/63
Bachelor, Marie, widow, Langdon, West, Kent, 1618 CKS PRC2/20/363
Bachelor, William, Biddenden, Kent, 1641 CKS PRC1/4/7
Back, Elizabeth, widow, Sandwich St Peter, Kent, 1665 CKS PRC1/10/6
Backe, John, Faversham, Kent, 1631 CKS PRC2/31/14
Backe, Richard, Luddenham, Kent, 1615 CKS PRC20/3/340
Backe, Robert, draper: 'woollen draper', Ashford, Kent, 1638 CKS PRC2/34/174
Backe, Thomas eld, gentleman, Hinxhill, Kent, 1639 CKS PRC2/34/172
Backes, Anne, Sellindge, Kent, 1685 CKS PRC2/40/178
Backett, John, Willesborough, Kent, 1678 CKS PRC2/38/10
Backett, William, Iwade, Kent, 1613 CKS PRC2/18/63
Backhouse, Ann, widow, Wandsworth, Surrey, 1694 PRO PROB32/34/18
Backhouse, Elizabeth, widow, Stafford St Mary, Staffs, 1666 LJRO:cards/1666/1
Backhouse, James, cabinet maker, Liverpool, Lancs, 1787 Lancs RO (Name of Deceased) D.R.C.H. 1787
Backhouse, Sarah, 1675 LJRO:cards/1675/3
Backhouse, Thomas, Trusthorpe, Lincs, 1597 Lincs RO Ad/Ac/4/117
Backley, William, yeoman, Graveney, Kent, 1679 CKS PRC2/38/101
Backwist/Backwith, John, Bethersden, Kent, 1639 CKS PRC1/2/6
Backwith, Robert, Saltfleetby St Peter, Lincs, 1612 Lincs RO Ad/Ac/11/160
Backwith, see Backwist,
Bacon, Charles, Chaddesley Corbett, Worcs, 1682 Worcs RO 008.7 BA3585/837/bdl 3

Bacon, Elizabethe, widow, Linsted, Kent, 1592 CKS PRC2/5/184
Bacon, Francis, gentleman, Grantham, Lincs, 1680 Lincs RO Ad/Ac/34/50
Bacon, George, husbandman, Hough on the Hill, Lincs, 1672 Lincs RO Ad/Ac/34/4
Bacon, Henry, Billingshurst, Sussex, 1632 W. Suss RO EpI/33/1632/25
Bacon, John, wool comber, Saham Toney, Norf, 1749 Norfolk RO ANW/23/24/90A
Bacon, Mary, widow, Tutbury, Staffs, 1832 LJRO/B/C/5/1832/19
Bacon, Nicholas,
Wilts 1615 Wilts RO Arch. Wilts.(name + date)
Bacon, Richard, Grinstead, West, Sussex, 1629 W. Suss RO EpI/33/1629/8
Bacon, Robert, glover, Sittingbourne, Kent, 1616 CKS PRC2/20/237
Bacon, Robert, yeoman, Timberland, Lincs, 1639 Lincs RO Ad/Ac/26/11
Bacon, Robert, Croxton, South, Leics, 1665 Leics RO Administrators Accounts C17th f34
Bacon, Robert, Breedon on the Hill, Leics, 1666 Leics RO Administrators Accounts C17th f86
Bacon, Thomas, Rugby, Warks, 1675 LJRO:cards/1675/4
Bacon, William, Brenzett, Kent, 1629 CKS PRC2/30/11
Badcock, Henry, yeoman, Garford, Berks, 1662 Berks RO D/A1/178/54A
Badcock, John, carrier, Oxford (University), Oxon, 1709 Bodleian HYP B8/3-4
Badcock, William, yeoman, Wootton, Berks, 1649 Berks RO D/A1/178/36C
Badcocke, Adam, Sturry, Kent, 1665 CKS PRC1/10/7
Badcocke, Joan, widow, St Peter in Thanet, Kent, 1600 CKS PRC2/11/365
Badcocke, John, St Peter in Thanet, Kent, 1595 CKS PRC2/7/179
Badcocke, John, Lydd, Kent, 1670 CKS PRC19/4/66
Badcocke, Richard, husbandman, Lyminge, Kent, 1676 CKS PRC20/12/195
Badcocke, Robert, Lydd, Kent, 1587 CKS PRC21/8/308
Badcocke, Simon, yeoman, Radley, Berks, 1677 Berks RO D/A1/178/169C
Badcocke, Thomas, yeoman, Hinksey, North, Berks, 1635 Berks RO D/A1/177/53A
Badcocke, Thomas, Patrixbourne, Kent, 1681 CKS PRC2/39/9
Baddeley, Robert, gentleman, Prees, Shrops, 1675 LJRO:cards/1675/6
Baddelly, William, Norton in the Moors, Staffs, 1678 LJRO:cards/1678/3
Baddely, Anthony, Kingswinford, Staffs, 1684 LJRO/B/C/5/1684/5
Baddiley, John, husbandman, Stone, Staffs, 1667 LJRO:cards/1667/5
Baddiley, Richard, Mickleover, Derby, 1683 LJRO/B/C/5/1682/3
Baddiley, Richard, Baswich (Weeping Cross), Staffs, 1732 LJRO/B/C/5/1731/2
Baden, Margaret, Wembdon, Som, 1640 Somerset RO D/D/Cta/B106
Badge, William, Bilsby, Lincs, 1637 Lincs RO Ad/Ac/25/576
Badger, Edmund, innholder, Oxford St Martin, Oxon, 1634 Oxon RO MSS Wills 295/3/52
Badger, Joan, Cowley, Oxon, 1626 Oxon RO MSS Wills 295/3/14
Badger, John, Sutterton, Lincs, 1633 Lincs RO Ad/Ac/24/134
Badger, Thomas, Newington, South, Oxon, 1633 Oxon RO MSS Wills 295/3/49
Badger, Thomas, tailor, Sunninghill, Berks, 1678 Berks RO D/A1/47/12C
Badgshawe, Richard, Killingholme, Lincs, 1599 Lincs RO Ad/Ac/5/49
Badkyn, Richard, Boughton under Blean, Kent, 1601 CKS PRC21/17/51
Badle, Henrye, Dover, Kent, 1593 CKS PRC21/12/450
Badman, John, Congresbury, Som, 1602 Somerset RO D/D/Cta/B97
Badman, John, Wrington, Som, 1738 Somerset RO D/D/Cta/B57
Badmeringe, see Cooke,
Badnor, Christopher, Egerton, Kent, 1638 CKS PRC20/10/126
Badnor, John, Egerton, Kent, 1624 CKS PRC20/6/90
Badnor, John, yeoman, Lenham, Kent, 1648 CKS PRC1/8/33
Badnor, John eld, Lenham, Kent, 1615 CKS PRC2/20/202
Badnor, Mathew, Lenham, Kent, 1602 CKS PRC2/12/40
Badnor, Thomas, Lenham, Kent, 1614 CKS PRC2/18/36
Badnore/Barnard, Nicholas, Leeds, Kent, 1626 CKS PRC2/27/13
Badnore, see Barnard,
Baert, Peeter, Sandwich, Kent, 1596 CKS PRC2/9/55

[Bageant:]
Bageant, Giles, Folkestone, Kent, 1593 CKS PRC2/6/240
Bageant, Richard, Paddlesworth, Kent, 1599 CKS PRC21/15/51
Bagent, Thomas, Dover, Kent, 1598 CKS PRC21/14/532
Bagfoot, Christopher, Charlton nr Dover, Kent, 1628 CKS PRC2/29/18
Baggerley, Gabriel, Yaxley, Hunts, 1628 Hunts RO/Acc58/5(52)
Baggett, John, Canterbury Holy Cross Westgate, Kent, 1595 CKS PRC2/7/75
Baggett, Richard, Woodchurch, Kent, 1609 CKS PRC20/2/17
Baggfitt/Baggthwaite, Phillip, jurat, Dover, Kent, 1641 CKS PRC19/1/24
Baggthwaite, see Baggfitt,
Bagley, Humphry, Baschurch, Shrops, 1681 LJRO/B/C/5/1681/3
Bagnall, Anthony, servant, Oxford (Christ Church College), Oxon, 1666 Bodleian HYP B8/6-7
Bagnall, Hannah, widow, Newcastle under Lyme, Staffs, 1728 LJRO/B/C/5/1728/9
Bagnall, Samuel, Newcastle under Lyme, Staffs, 1675 LJRO:cards/1675/7
Bagshaw, Arthur, Crowle, Worcs, 1697 Worcs RO 008.7 BA3585/837/bdl 6
Bagshaw, Charles, gentleman, Bourne, Lincs, 1673 Lincs RO Ad/Ac/34/20
Bagster, George, Newport, Hants, 1675 Hants RO 21m65 D8/264
Baguley, John, Oldham, Lancs, 1663 Lancs RO (Name of Deceased) D.R.C.H. 1662-3
Baguley, Thomas, Belton All Saints, Lincs, 1617 Lincs RO Ad/Ac/8b/280
Baguley, William, tanner, Witton, Ches, 1764 Cheshire RO (Name) W.C. 1764
Bagust, John, husbandman, Brimpton, Berks, 1641 Berks RO D/A1/174/18c
Bagwell, Thomas, Oxford St Thomas, Oxon, 1640 Oxon RO MSS Wills 295/3/90
Bailey, Elizabeth, widow, Shenstone (Lynn), Staffs, 1781 LJRO/B/C/5/1781/4
Bailey, Henry, Carsington, Derby, 1684 LJRO/B/C/5/1685/18
Bailey, John, yeoman, Ellington, Hunts, 1724 Hunts RO/Acc58/316
Bailey, Joseph, Tatenhill, Staffs, 1684 LJRO/B/C/5/1684/6
Bailey, Thomas, Kingerby, Lincs, 1648 Lincs RO Ad/Ac/30/394
Bailey, Thomas, yeoman, Winterbourne Bassett, Wilts, 1740 Wilts RO Arch. Wilts.(name + date)
Bailey, William, cordwainer, Ashton, Steeple, Wilts, 1697 Wilts RO Arch. Sarum/(+ name and date)
Bailie, Jeremy, Tenterden, Kent, 1640 CKS PRC1/2/7
Bailie, Jeremye, Tenterden, Kent, 1638 CKS PRC1/1/66
Bailie, John, Bath, Som, 1612 Somerset RO D/D/Cta/B38
Baily, Elizabeth, Marden, Kent, 1625 CKS PRC2/25/10
Baily, Francis, Westbury, Wilts, 1648 Wilts RO CC Sarum(+ name and date)
Baily, Nicholas, Stratton, Corn, 1631 Cornwall RO AP/B798
Baily, Thomas, Frittenden, Kent, 1609 CKS PRC2/15/11
Baily, Thomas, Marden, Kent, 1617 CKS PRC2/20/345
Baily, Thomas, St Laurence Thanet, Kent, 1675 CKS PRC2/36/166
Baily, Thomas, Hackington, Kent, 1681 CKS PRC2/39/144
Bailye, Richard + Susan, yeoman, Frittenden, Kent, 1614 CKS PRC2/18/101
Bailye, Thomas, Iwade, Kent, 1609 CKS PRC2/13/28
Bailye, Thomas, St Peter in Thanet, Kent, 1610 CKS PRC2/15/13
Bailye, William, Brook, Kent, 1605 CKS PRC2/13/46
Bailye, William, Midhurst, Sussex, 1623 W. Suss RO EpI/33/1623/2
Bainton, Edward, Rowde, Wilts, 1617 Wilts RO Arch. Wilts.(name + date)
Bainton, Edward, Kettlethorpe, Lincs, 1624 Lincs RO Ad/Ac/8c/73
Bainton, Margery, Kettlethorpe (Fenton), Lincs, 1626 Lincs RO Ad/Ac/39/245
Bainton, Rebecca, spinster, St Neots, Hunts, 1753 Hunts RO/Acc58/327
Bainton, Thomas, Roxby, Lincs, 1620 Lincs RO Ad/Ac/8c/11
Bainton, Valentine, Messingham, Lincs, C17th Lincs RO Ad/Ac/40/202
Bainton, William, Deeping, West, Lincs, 1663 Lincs RO Ad/Ac/32/53
Bairstow, Robert, farmer, Halifax (Ovenden), Yorks, 1825 Borthwick Test C.P. 1825/9
Baitte, John, Willoughby, Silk, Lincs, C16th? Lincs RO Ad/Ac/45/86
Baker, Agnes, widow, Newchurch, Kent, 1609 CKS PRC20/1/368
Baker, Alexander, Westwell, Kent, 1582 CKS PRC21/6/30

Baker, Alice, widow, Newnham, Kent, 1619 CKS PRC2/20/314
Baker, Andro, Staplehurst, Kent, 1591 CKS PRC2/5/179
Baker, Arthur, Cheriton, Kent, 1619 CKS PRC2/20/353
Baker, Arthur, husbandman, High Halden, Kent, 1674 CKS PRC2/36/21
Baker, Bartholomew, Barham, Kent, 1593 CKS PRC2/6/194
Baker, Benjamin, Old Romney, Kent, 1666 CKS PRC1/11/99
Baker, Catherine, widow, Wittersham, Kent, 1613 CKS PRC20/2/472
Baker, Daniel, mariner, Queenborough, Kent, 1672 CKS PRC2/35/4
Baker, Edward, Monkton, Kent, 1639 CKS PRC19/1/14
Baker, Edward, gentleman, Chilham, Kent, 1668 CKS PRC1/12/7
Baker, Edward, shepherd, Tilshead, Wilts, 1669 Wilts RO Arch. Sarum/(+ name and date)
Baker, Edward, Berkswell, Warks, 1672 LJRO:cards/1672/4
Baker, Edward, yeoman, Saltwood, Kent, 1686 CKS PRC20/13/545
Baker, Elizabeth, widow, Barham, Kent, 1626 CKS PRC2/27/22
Baker, Elizabeth, widow, Newington next Sittingbourne, Kent, 1641 CKS PRC1/5/77
Baker, Elizabeth, Maidstone, Kent, 1673 CKS PRC20/12/69
Baker, Ely, Epsom, Surrey, 1745 Greater London RO DW/OP/1745/1b
Baker, Francis, carrier, Ashford, Kent, 1681 CKS PRC2/39/139
Baker, George, Selling, Kent, 1613 CKS PRC2/16/120
Baker, George, St Laurence Thanet, Kent, 1663 CKS PRC1/9/80
Baker, George, mariner, Upchurch, Kent, 1684 CKS PRC2/40/168
Baker, Henrie, Tydd St Mary, Lincs, 1637 Lincs RO Ad/Ac/25/587
Baker, Henry + Dorothy, St Albans, Herts, 1609 Herts RO ASA25/4765
Baker, Humphrey, butcher, St James Westminster, London & Middlesex, 1753 Greater London RO AM/PI pt (uncatalogued)
Baker, James, Cheriton, Kent, 1596 CKS PRC2/8/87
Baker, James, yeoman, Chart nr Sutton Valence, Kent, 1681 CKS PRC2/39/140
Baker, James, victualler, Atherstone, Warks, 1820 LJRO/B/C/5/1820/3
Baker, Joan, High Halden, Kent, 1627 CKS PRC2/28/10
Baker, Joane, Stapleford, Wilts, 1619 Wilts RO Miscellaneous Index to Wills (name + date)
Baker, John, St Johns Thanet, Kent, CKS PRC1/15/110
Baker, John, Folkestone, Kent, 1584 CKS PRC2/3/183
Baker, John, Canterbury St Paul, Kent, 1594 CKS PRC2/6/452
Baker, John, Staplehurst, Kent, 1596 CKS PRC2/9/33
Baker, John, Chilham, Kent, 1599 CKS PRC2/11/5
Baker, John, Woodchurch, Kent, 1599 CKS PRC21/15/35
Baker, John, Brookland, Kent, 1600 CKS PRC2/11/149
Baker, John, Fotherby, Lincs, 1601 Lincs RO Ad/Ac/5/375
Baker, John, Bethersden, Kent, 1603 CKS PRC2/14/66
Baker, John, Eythorne, Kent, 1610 CKS PRC2/15/43
Baker, John, Sandwich St Peter, Kent, 1614 CKS PRC2/17/107
Baker, John, Faversham, Kent, 1618 CKS PRC2/20/286
Baker, John, Snelland, Lincs, 1618 Lincs RO Ad/Ac/14/124
Baker, John, Bearsted, Kent, 1623 CKS PRC2/23/33
Baker, John, Warehorne, Kent, 1637 CKS PRC2/34/19
Baker, John, Portishead, Som, 1638 Somerset RO D/D/Cta/B23
Baker, John, Sutterton, Lincs, 1639 Lincs RO Ad/Ac/26/171
Baker, John, Seasalter, Kent, 1640 CKS PRC1/2/8
Baker, John, carpenter, Quadring, Lincs, 1640 Lincs RO Ad/Ac/26/146
Baker, John, Swineshead, Lincs, 1649 Lincs RO Ad/Ac/30/164
Baker, John, Stockbury, Kent, 1668 CKS PRC1/13/6
Baker, John, yeoman, Saltwood, Kent, 1672 CKS PRC20/12/40
Baker, John, cooper, Birchington, Kent, 1675 CKS PRC20/12/114
Baker, John, Barham, Kent, 1684 CKS PRC2/40/175
Baker, John, Middlezoy, Som, 1687 Somerset RO D/D/Cta/B58

[Baker:]
Baker, John, mariner, Sandwich St Mary, Kent, 1690 CKS PRC2/41/143
Baker, John, St Johns Thanet, Kent, 1693 CKS PRC1/15/110b
Baker, John, Froxfield, Hants, 1694 Hants RO 21m65 D8/362
Baker, John, Ivychurch, Kent, 1703 CKS PRC1/16/41
Baker, John, mr, Ivychurch, Kent, 1714 CKS PRC19/6/60
Baker, John,
Suff 1759 Suff RO(B) IC500/3/48/4
Baker, Leonard, apprentice, Tenterden, Kent, 1610 CKS PRC2/13/77
Baker, Luke, widower, St Stephen Walbrook, London & Middlesex, 1701 PRO PROB5/1313
Baker, Margaret, widow, Chart, Great, Kent, 1662 CKS PRC1/9/2
Baker, Margarett, widow, Cranbrook, Kent, 1627 CKS PRC2/27/23
Baker, Mary, widow, Sidlesham, Sussex, 1676 W. Suss RO EpI/33/1676/30
Baker, Michaell, Woodnesborough, Kent, 1618 CKS PRC2/20/342
Baker, Ralf, Egerton, Kent, 1600 CKS PRC21/16/182
Baker, Ralf, Egerton, Kent, 1606 CKS PRC20/1/169
Baker, Ralph, husbandman, Taynton, Oxon, 1647 Oxon RO MSS Wills 295/4/22
Baker, Randolfe, Monkton, Kent, 1602 CKS PRC21/16/156
Baker, Reginald, Windsor, New, Berks, 1610 Berks RO D/A1/176/28A
Baker, Richard, Angmering, Sussex, 1594 W. Suss RO EpI/33/1594/5
Baker, Richard, Ashford, Kent, 1605 CKS PRC2/13/99
Baker, Richard, Bearsted, Kent, 1606 CKS PRC2/13/81
Baker, Richard, Charing, Kent, 1606 CKS PRC20/1/167
Baker, Richard, Biddenden, Kent, 1615 CKS PRC2/20/146
Baker, Richard, Barham, Kent, 1625 CKS PRC2/25/29
Baker, Richard, Cowbit, Lincs, 1625 Lincs RO Ad/Ac/19B/70
Baker, Richard, Canterbury St Dunstan Without, Kent, 1632 CKS PRC2/31/84
Baker, Richard, Elham, Kent, 1664 CKS PRC1/9/81
Baker, Richard, Upper Hardres, Kent, 1674 CKS PRC2/36/24
Baker, Richard, Bristol, Glos, 1683 PRO PROB5/904
Baker, Richard, Headcorn, Kent, 1708 CKS PRC19/6/27
Baker, Robert, Goudhurst, Kent, 1572 CKS PRC2/1/53
Baker, Robert, Tenterden, Kent, 1619 CKS PRC2/20/351
Baker, Robert, Headcorn, Kent, 1630 CKS PRC2/30/24
Baker, Robert, Otham, Kent, 1632 CKS PRC2/31/9
Baker, Robert, Gainsborough (Morton), Lincs, 1662 Lincs RO Ad/Ac/41/48
Baker, Robert, husbandman, Sutterton, Lincs, 1668 Lincs RO Ad/Ac/33/38
Baker, Robert, husbandman, Minster in Sheppey, Kent, 1678 CKS PRC2/38/12
Baker, Robert, yeoman, Minster in Sheppey, Kent, 1680 CKS PRC2/39/3
Baker, Robert, Farndon, Ches, 1695 Cheshire RO (Name) W.C. 1694
Baker, Robert, St Laurence Thanet, Kent, 1705 CKS PRC1/16/59
Baker, Roberte, Thurlby, Lincs, 1599 Lincs RO Ad/Ac/5/324
Baker, Roger, Chartham, Kent, 1610 CKS PRC2/15/30
Baker, Sampson, yeoman, Wickhambreaux, Kent, 1617 CKS PRC2/20/356
Baker, Sarah, Hythe West, Kent, 1675 CKS PRC2/36/159
Baker, Sarah, Herne, Kent, 1704 CKS PRC19/6/8
Baker, Shadrach, Worcester St Nicholas, Worcs, 1769 Worcs RO 008.7 BA3585/836/bdl 2
Baker, Stephen, husbandman, Aldington, Kent, 1682 CKS PRC20/13/222
Baker, Stephen, carpenter, Milton next Sittingbourne, Kent, 1684 CKS PRC2/40/171
Baker, Stephen, blacksmith, Northbourne, Kent, 1686 CKS PRC2/41/46
Baker, Stephen, Alkham, Kent, 1692 CKS PRC2/42/24
Baker, Symonm, Hythe St Leonard, Kent, 1601 CKS PRC21/15/200
Baker, Theophilus, Spalding, Lincs, 1614 Lincs RO Ad/Ac/13/99
Baker, Thomas, Petherton, South, Som, Somerset RO D/D/Cta/B40
Baker, Thomas, Sandhurst, Kent, 1597 CKS PRC2/9/25
Baker, Thomas, Biddenden, Kent, 1598 CKS PRC2/9/403

Baker, Thomas, Rustington, Sussex, 1598 W. Suss RO EpI/33/1598/11
Baker, Thomas, Folkestone, Kent, 1599 CKS PRC2/10/437
Baker, Thomas, Sandwich, Kent, 1601 CKS PRC2/12/76
Baker, Thomas, Burgh le Marsh, Lincs, 1618 Lincs RO Ad/Ac/14/26
Baker, Thomas, Benenden, Kent, 1630 CKS PRC2/30/20
Baker, Thomas, Smeeth, Kent, 1631 CKS PRC20/9/59
Baker, Thomas, Stockbury, Kent, 1637 CKS PRC2/34/13
Baker, Thomas, innholder, St Albans, Herts, 1637 Herts RO ASA25/4924
Baker, Thomas, Corington, Hunts, 1654 Hunts RO/Acc58/12
Baker, Thomas, Barkestone, Leics, 1666 Leics RO Administrators Accounts C17th f45
Baker, Thomas, Woodnesborough, Kent, 1678 CKS PRC2/38/7
Baker, Thomas, Stockbury, Kent, 1682 CKS PRC2/40/9
Baker, Thomas, Preston, East, Sussex, 1684 W. Suss RO EpI/33/1684/7
Baker, Thomas, Wilton, Wilts, 1691 Wilts RO Arch. Sarum/(+ name and date)
Baker, Thomazine, widow, Hernhill, Kent, 1617 CKS PRC20/3/498
Baker, Walter, victualler, Deal, Kent, 1683 CKS PRC20/13/305
Baker, William,
Som 1585 Somerset RO D/D/Cta/B1
Baker, William, Sandwich, Kent, 1616 CKS PRC2/20/222
Baker, William, Cheriton, Kent, 1625 CKS PRC2/25/28
Baker, William, Warborough, Oxon, 1630 Oxon RO MSS Wills Pec 65/3/23
Baker, William, innholder, Enstone, Oxon, 1638 Oxon RO MSS Wills 295/3/63
Baker, William, Stapleford, Leics, 1641 Leics RO PR/I/41A/72
Baker, William, Dover, Kent, 1643 CKS PRC19/2/49
Baker, William, Cranwell, Lincs, 1650 Lincs RO Ad/Ac/29/74
Baker, William, Stapleford, Leics, 1674 Leics RO Administrators Accounts 1667-72 f115
Baker, William, husbandman, Maidstone, Kent, 1679 CKS PRC20/12/291
Baker, William, Chilvers Coton, Warks, 1683 LJRO/B/C/5/1682/4
Baker, William, Boughton under Blean, Kent, 1684 CKS PRC20/13/402
Baker, William, yeoman, Waltham St Lawrence, Berks, 1684 Berks RO D/A1/179/26D
Baker, William, Godmanchester, Hunts, 1687 Hunts RO/Acc58/269(264)
Baker, William, farmer, Skipsea, Yorks, 1814 Borthwick Test C.P. 1814/6
Baker/Aldey, John, Trevalga, Corn, 1623 Cornwall RO AP/B574/3
Baker/Clarke, John,
Worcs 1605 Worcs RO 008.7 BA3585/839/401
Baker/Oldfield, Richardine, wife, Ewell, Kent, 1665 CKS PRC1/11/4
Baker, see Crosse & Ellis,
Bakes, Henry, yeoman, Bradford (Eccleshill), Yorks, 1840 Borthwick Test C.P. 1840/1
Bakewell, James, farmer, Kingstone, Staffs, 1803 LJRO/B/C/5/1803/4
Balch, Robert,
Som Somerset RO D/D/Cta/B17
Balche, John, yeoman, Stoke Sub Hamdon, Som, 1640 Somerset RO D/D/Cta/B49
Balcomb, Roger, Coldwaltham (Watersfield), Sussex, 1682 W. Suss RO EpI/33/1682/44
Balden, Androw, Chart nr Sutton Valence, Kent, 1589 CKS PRC2/5/200
Balden, Catherine, widow, Boughton under Blean, Kent, 1629 CKS PRC20/8/55
Balden, Henrie, Iwade, Kent, 1604 CKS PRC2/13/103
Balden, John, Tonge, Kent, 1600 CKS PRC2/11/161
Balden, John, Pagham, Sussex, 1617 W. Suss RO EpIV/10/1/43
Balden, Leonard, Faversham, Kent, 1623 CKS PRC2/23/44
Balden, Margarett, widow, Headcorn, Kent, 1608 CKS PRC2/13/19
Balden, Mathewe, Ulcombe, Kent, 1608 CKS PRC2/14/31
Balden, Nicholas, Harrietsham, Kent, 1614 CKS PRC2/20/361
Balderston, Robert, Coningsby, Lincs, 1629 Lincs RO Ad/Ac/22/102
Balderstone, Edward, yeoman, Wigtoft, Lincs, 1637 Lincs RO Ad/Ac/25/420
Baldock, Anne, Hernhill, Kent, 1596 CKS PRC21/14/145

[Baldock:]
Baldock, Henry, yeoman, Lenham, Kent, 1676 CKS PRC2/37/14
Baldock, Nicholas, Charing, Kent, 1641 CKS PRC19/2/3
Baldock, Thomas, Oare, Kent, 1597 CKS PRC2/10/488
Baldock, William, Canterbury St Peter, Kent, 1670 CKS PRC1/14/4
Baldock, Willyam, Eastling, Kent, 1622 CKS PRC2/23/34
Baldocke, Anthony, yeoman, Charing, Kent, 1681 CKS PRC20/13/105
Baldocke, Edward, Staple next Wingham, Kent, 1598 CKS PRC21/14/504
Baldocke, Richard, Minster in Sheppey, Kent, 1629 CKS PRC2/30/19
Baldocke, Robarte, Chart, Little, Kent, 1592 CKS PRC2/6/35
Baldocke, Robert, Canterbury All Saints, Kent, 1639 CKS PRC1/2/9
Baldocke, Symon, Bethersden, Kent, 1591 CKS PRC2/5/215
Baldocke, Symon, Birchington, Kent, 1611 CKS PRC20/2/230
Baldocke, Thomas, yeoman, Goudhurst, Kent, 1664 CKS PRC1/10/8
Baldocke, William, clergy: 'clerk', Reculver, Kent, 1596 CKS PRC21/14/1
Baldon, see Hootham,
Balduck, Joseph, Sandwich St Mary, Kent, 1667 CKS PRC1/12/8
Baldwer, Robert, Sutton, Long, Lincs, 1611 Lincs RO Ad/Ac/10/99
Baldwin, Alexander, Salisbury St Martin, Wilts, 1628 Wilts RO Miscellaneous Index to Wills (name + date)
Baldwin, Alice, widow, Canterbury St Margaret, Kent, 1643 CKS PRC1/6/94
Baldwin, Giles, Canterbury, Kent, 1601 CKS PRC2/12/66
Baldwin, John, clergy: 'vicar', Aldermaston, Berks, 1618 Berks RO D/A1/176/64A
Baldwin, Ralph, clothworker, Tilehurst (Theale), Berks, 1639 Berks RO D/A1/177/80/1/C
Baldwin, Sara, spinster, Dover, Kent, 1639 CKS PRC20/10/144
Baldwin, Thomas, Walton-le-Dale, Lancs, 1666 Lancs RO (Name of Deceased) D.R.C.H. 1667
Baldwine, John, clergy: 'clerk', Crowle, Lincs, 1605 Lincs RO Ad/Ac/37/203
Baldwine, Richard, Gainsborough, Lincs, 1620 Lincs RO Ad/Ac/8b/477
Baldwyn, Agnes, Watford, Herts, 1597 Herts RO ASA25/1660
Baldwyn, Henry, Watford, Herts, 1603 Herts RO ASA25/4753
Baldwyn, Joane, spinster, Bromfield, Kent, 1648 CKS PRC1/8/2
Baldwyn, John, Rickmansworth, Herts, 1587 Herts RO ASA25/1178
Baldwyn, John, St Albans St Michaels, Herts, 1596 Herts RO ASA25/1411
Baldwyn, John, breeches maker, Cirencester, Glos, 1784 GRO GDR/B4/2/B45
Baldwyn, Mary, widow, Rickmansworth, Herts, 1598 Herts RO ASA25/1661
Baldwyn, Thomas, Rickmansworth (Pinesfield), Herts, 1602 Herts RO ASA25/1784
Bale, Samuel, degrees: 'M.A.', Cambridge, Cambs, 1675 CUL V.C. Acc./Box3/3
Balee, John, Stilton, Hunts, 1692 Hunts RO/Acc58/273
Baley, William, husbandman, Saxby, Lincs, 1613 Lincs RO Ad/Ac/11/73
Balgay, Prudence, widow, Mowsley, Leics, 1673 Leics RO Administrators Accounts 1667-72 f100
Balgey, Robert, skinner/citizen, St Botolph without Bishopsgate, London & Middlesex, 1677 PRO PROB5/1763
Balhatchet, Richard, Poughill, Corn, 1604 Cornwall RO AP/B74/2
Balie, Hellen, widow, Manton (Twigmore), Lincs, 1667 Lincs RO Ad/Ac/33/28
Ball, George, Swindon, Wilts, 1680 Wilts RO Miscellaneous Index to Wills (name + date)
Ball, John, Kilmersdon, Som, 1619 Somerset RO D/D/Cta/B86
Ball, John, yeoman, High Halstow, Kent, 1643 CKS PRC1/6/95
Ball, John, blacksmith, Billingborough, Lincs, 1666 Lincs RO Ad/Ac/32/82
Ball, John, Duffield, Derby, 1682 LJRO/B/C/5/1682/5
Ball, John, Congerstone, Leics, 1683 Leics RO Administrators Accounts 1682-86 f3
Ball, Simon, Waltham, White, Berks, 1615 Berks RO D/A1/176/47A
Ball, William, Bristol St James, Glos, Bristol RO 1678/66
Ball, William, Monkton, West, Som, 1591 Somerset RO D/D/Cta/B55
Ball, William, Norton Malreward, Som, 1641 Somerset RO D/D/Cta/B52
Ball, William, Pagham, Sussex, 1642 W. Suss RO EpIV/10/2/29
Ball, see White,

Ballan, Joane, widow, Lydd, Kent, 1620 CKS PRC20/4/17
Ballantine, James, gentleman, Castle Church (Forbridge), Staffs, 1797 LJRO/B/C/5/1797/4
Ballard, Anthony, Ramsbury, Wilts, 1674 Wilts RO Miscellaneous Index to Wills (name + date)
Ballard, Henrie, Cranbrook, Kent, 1629 CKS PRC2/30/10
Ballard, John, Boston, Lincs, 1614 Lincs RO Ad/Ac/13/90
Ballard, Jonathan, gentleman, Anstey, Warks, 1675 LJRO:cards/1675/8
Ballard, Margaret,
Worcs 1685 Worcs RO 008.7 BA3585/837/bdl 4
Ballard, Richard, Littleton, North, Worcs, 1682 Worcs RO 008.7 BA3585/837/bdl 3
Ballard, Thomas, clergy: 'mr/clerk', Ivychurch, Kent, 1625 CKS PRC20/7/335
Ballarde, Thomas, Frampton, Lincs, 1608 Lincs RO Ad/Ac/8a/182
Ballatt, Richard, gentleman, Trusthorpe, Lincs, 1684 Lincs RO Ad/Ac/44/143
Baller, William, Pennard, West, Som, 1662 Somerset RO D/D/Cta/B43
Ballinton, Robert, yeoman, Mayfield, Staffs, 1782 LJRO/B/C/5/1782/3
Ballowe, William, Huttoft, Lincs, 1648 Lincs RO Ad/Ac/30/399
Ballowe, William, merchant, St Michael Peternoster Royal, London & Middlesex, 1665 Lambeth Palace Arches G19/3
Balme, Richard, tailor, Haceby, Lincs, 1669 Lincs RO Ad/Ac/33/131
Balsarr, Willyam, Iwade, Kent, 1620 CKS PRC2/20/367
Baly, Robert, Pinchbeck, Lincs, 1670 Lincs RO Ad/Ac/32/176
Bamber, Marie, widow, Baumber, Lincs, 1637 Lincs RO Ad/Ac/25/394
Bambrigg, Elizabeth, widow, Leicester St Martin, Leics, 1664 Leics RO Administrators Accounts C17th f2
Bamford, Richard, Paxton, Great, Hunts, 1677 Hunts RO/Acc58/108(132)
Bampfield, Joan, Bath St Peter & Paul, Som, 1668 Somerset RO D/D/Cta/B48
Banaster, John, gentleman, Butterwick, Lincs, 1605 Lincs RO Ad/Ac/37/201
Banberye, Thomas, Saltwood, Kent, 1602 CKS PRC21/17/57
Banburne, see Powes,
Bance, Alexander, Bearsted, Kent, 1619 CKS PRC2/23/22
Bance, Robert, Bearsted, Kent, 1599 CKS PRC2/11/15
Banckes, Anne, widow, Coningsby, Lincs, 1629 Lincs RO Ad/Ac/22/54
Banckes, Edward, Newington next Sittingbourne, Kent, 1683 CKS PRC2/40/97
Banckes, Priscilla, mrs, Otham, Kent, 1635 CKS PRC2/33/17
Banckes, Thomas, Ulcombe, Kent, 1636 CKS PRC20/10/94
Bancks, Alice, Milton Lilborne, Wilts, 1620? Wilts RO Arch. Wilts.(name + date)
Bancks, Edward, Cranbrook, Kent, 1626 CKS PRC2/27/16
Bancks, Henry, widower, Stepney, London & Middlesex, 1702 PRO PROB32/44/43
Bancks, James, Rainham, Kent, 1622 CKS PRC2/23/26
Bancks, John, Badlesmere, Kent, 1616 CKS PRC2/20/302
Bancks, Reynold, Badlesmere, Kent, 1628 CKS PRC2/29/8
Bancks, Thomas, Cranbrook, Kent, 1636 CKS PRC2/33/20
Bancroft, Alexander, yeoman, Stockport (Etchells), Ches, 1788 Cheshire RO (Name) W.C. 1788
Bancroft, Henrie, Donington on Bain, Lincs, 1635 Lincs RO Ad/Ac/24/439
Bancroft, Thomas, Coningsby, Lincs, 1669 Lincs RO Ad/Ac/33/126
Bancus, Henry, St Mary in the Marsh, Kent, 1594 CKS PRC2/7/113
Band, Margerie, Christian Malford, Wilts, 1630 Wilts RO Arch. Wilts.(name + date)
Bandrie, see Bendrie,
Banes, Edward, Egerton, Kent, 1580 CKS PRC21/4/292
Banes, John, Sholden, Kent, 1629 CKS PRC2/30/12
Banes, Robert, gentleman, Faversham, Kent, 1601 CKS PRC2/12/9
Banes, William, Deal, Kent, 1674 CKS PRC20/12/67
Banister, Thomas, yeoman, Moulton, Lincs, 1648 Lincs RO Ad/Ac/30/327
Banister, William, Woolavington, Sussex, W. Suss RO EpI/33/1607/9
Bankes, James, clergy: 'clerk/rector', Bury, Lancs, Lancs RO (Name of Deceased) D.R.C.H. 1768-69

[Bankes:]
Bankes, John, husbandman, Biddenden, Kent, 1684 CKS PRC2/40/171
Bankes, William, Arthingworth, Northants, 1672 Northants RO NWill A/C/104
Banks, Edward, Newington next Sittingbourne, Kent, 1672 CKS PRC2/35/119
Banks, James, yeoman, Ipstones, Staffs, 1783 LJRO/B/C/5/1783/15
Banks, Thomas, York, Yorks, 1785 Borthwick Test C.P. 1785/1
Banner, Richard, Aston (Castle Bromwich), Warks, 1684 LJRO/B/C/5/1684/7
Bannidge, Hellene, High Halstow, Kent, 1626 CKS PRC2/27/19
Bannidge, Thomas, High Halstow, Kent, 1623 CKS PRC2/23/46
Bannister, Arthure, Adisham, Kent, 1606 CKS PRC20/1/199
Bannister, Edward, Wednesbury, Staffs, 1667 LJRO:cards/1667/6
Bannister, Henry, Solihull, Warks, 1683 LJRO/B/C/5/1682/6
Bannister, John, yeoman, Bampton (Shifford), Oxon, 1641 Oxon RO MSS Wills 295/4/1
Bannister, John, yeoman, Dorchester, Oxon, 1662 Oxon RO MSS Wills Pec 65/4/3
Bannister, Thomas, Deal, Kent, 1670 CKS PRC19/4/67
Bantinge, George, Northmoor, Oxon, 1626 Oxon RO MSS Wills 295/3/12
Bantinge, Margaret, Northmoor, Oxon, 1623 Oxon RO MSS Wills 295/2/79
Barber,
Sussex 1679 W. Suss RO EpI/33/1679
Barber, Cornelius, Worth, Kent, 1609 CKS PRC20/2/7
Barber, Ezechiell, Petham, Kent, 1590 CKS PRC2/5/175
Barber, John, Hernhill, Kent, 1595 CKS PRC21/14/219
Barber, John, Tilmanstone, Kent, 1595 CKS PRC2/7/80
Barber, John, Cranbrook, Kent, 1626 CKS PRC2/25/16
Barber, John, shearman, Huntingdon, Hunts, 1677 Hunts RO/Acc58/112(41)
Barber, John, Bury, Sussex, 1679 W. Suss RO EpI/33/1678/6
Barber, John, husbandman, Ewell, Kent, 1679 CKS PRC2/38/99
Barber, John, Swinford, Old (Stourbridge), Worcs, 1682 Worcs RO 008.7 BA3585/837/bdl 3
Barber, John, esquire, Nuneaton (Attleborough), Warks, 1796 LJRO/B/C/5/1796/8
Barber, Phillipp, Stone in Oxney, Kent, 1601 CKS PRC2/12/78
Barber, Rachell, widow, Witham on the Hill (Toft), Lincs, 1641 Lincs RO Ad/Ac/27/96
Barber, Richard, farmer, Tickhill, Yorks, 1824 Borthwick Test C.P. 1824/12
Barber, Robert, Ancaster, Lincs, 1611 Lincs RO Ad/Ac/10/64
Barber, Roger, Sittingbourne, Kent, 1679 CKS PRC2/38/109
Barber, Thomas, Orlestone, Kent, 1621 CKS PRC2/23/39
Barber, Thomas, Fleet, Lincs, 1641 Lincs RO Ad/Ac/27/291
Barber, Thomas, yeoman, Rolvenden, Kent, 1669 CKS PRC1/14/5
Barber, Thomas, Canterbury Christchurch, Kent, 1671 CKS PRC19/4/68
Barber, Thomas eld, mr, Sandwich, Kent, 1707 CKS PRC1/16/60
Barber, Warborow, widow, Wimborne Minster, Dors, 1632 Dorset RO PE/WM CP 2/4/48
Barber, William, St Albans St Stephens, Herts, 1629 Herts RO ASA25/4858
Barber, William, St Mary le Strand, London & Middlesex, 1740 Greater London RO AM/PP/Box 1739-1749 pt (uncatalogued)
Barber, William, yeoman, Newport, Shrops, 1818 LJRO/B/C/5/1818/3
Barber/Webbe, James, Pulborough, Sussex, 1617 W. Suss RO EpI/33/1617/34
Barber, see Butler,
Barbitt, William, Herne, Kent, 1586 CKS PRC21/8/107
Barbor, Margaret, St Johns Thanet, Kent, 1637 CKS PRC2/33/4
Barckley, Edward, Edington, Wilts, 1611 Wilts RO Arch. Sarum/(+ name and date)
Barckwith, Rauf, Burgh le Marsh, Lincs, 1614 Lincs RO Ad/Ac/13/213
Bard, Ann, widow, Mareham le Fen, Lincs, 1639 Lincs RO Ad/Ac/25/241
Bard, William, esquire, Kelsey, North, Lincs, 1677 Lincs RO Ad/Ac/42/70
Bardell, Thomas, Kirkby, East, Lincs, 1662 Lincs RO Ad/Ac/32/27
Bardney, John, Wigtoft, Lincs, 1611 Lincs RO Ad/Ac/10/14
Bardolph, James, Ardeley, Herts, 1640 Herts RO AHH23/115
Bardsey, Elizabeth, widow, Grantham (Little Gonerby), Lincs, 1650 Lincs RO Ad/Ac/29/85

Bardsley, Samuel, Ashton-under-Lyne (Woodhouses), Lancs, 1798 Lancs RO (Name of Deceased) D.R.C.H. 1798
Barefoot, William, Maidstone, Kent, 1672 CKS PRC20/12/37
Barefoote, John, yeoman, Stanton Harcourt, Oxon, 1642 Oxon RO MSS Wills 295/4/10
Barefoote, Richard, Boston, Lincs, 1633? Lincs RO Ad/Ac/24/350
Barefoott, George, Romsey, Hants, 1686 Hants RO 21m65 D8/349
Bargar, Robarte, Canterbury Holy Cross Westgate, Kent, 1588 CKS PRC2/4/502
Bargar, Thomas, Kennington, Kent, 1618 CKS PRC2/20/330
Barham, Charles, innholder, Sandwich, Kent, 1663 CKS PRC1/9/82
Barham, Elizabeth, widow, Sittingbourne, Kent, 1668 CKS PRC1/13/7
Barham, Elizabeth, widow, Sittingbourne, Kent, 1668 CKS PRC1/13/7a
Barham, Elizabeth, widow, Sittingbourne, Kent, 1668 CKS PRC1/13/7b
Barham, Isaac, Sittingbourne, Kent, 1638 CKS PRC2/34/11
Barham, Joseph, vintner, Canterbury, Kent, 1682 CKS PRC2/39/146
Barham, Mildred, widow, Boughton Monchelsea, Kent, 1598 CKS PRC2/10/345
Barham, Nicholas, Maidstone, Kent, 1603 CKS PRC21/16/62
Barham, Nicholas, Leeds, Kent, 1619 CKS PRC2/20/346
Barham, Richard, gentleman, Maidstone, Kent, 1608 CKS PRC20/1/326
Barham, Robert, clothier, Hawkhurst, Kent, 1684 CKS PRC2/40/172
Barham, Thomas, innholder, Canterbury St Margaret, Kent, 1679 CKS PRC2/38/102
Baringley, Ane, Marden, Kent, 1596 CKS PRC2/9/37
Barke, Willyam, Leadenham, Lincs, 1632 Lincs RO Ad/Ac/23/173
Barkeham, John, Beaulieu, Hants, 1674 Hants RO 21m65 D8/265
Barker, Ambrose, Rasen, West, Lincs, 1662 Lincs RO Ad/Ac/32/8
Barker, Bennett, Middlewich (Kinderton), Ches, 1701 Cheshire RO (Name) W.C. 1701
Barker, Clement, Harrietsham, Kent, 1699 CKS PRC2/42/147
Barker, Edward, Southampton, Hants, 1578 Hants RO 1576 B006/5
Barker, Edward, Huttoft, Lincs, 1619 Lincs RO Ad/Ac/15/161
Barker, Elizabethe, widow, Westwell, Kent, 1581 CKS PRC21/4/300
Barker, Henrie, Laceby, Lincs, 1639 Lincs RO Ad/Ac/26/183
Barker, Henry, Matlock, Derby, 1701 LJRO/B/C/5/1701/5
Barker, Henry, Westbury, Wilts, 1771 Wilts RO Miscellaneous Index to Wills (name + date)
Barker, James, Hackthorne, Lincs, 1683 Lincs RO Ad/Ac/44/19
Barker, John, Canterbury St Peter, Kent, 1592 CKS PRC2/5/169
Barker, John, Coningsby, Lincs, 1625 Lincs RO Ad/Ac/19B/109
Barker, John, Chipping Barnet, Herts, 1627 Herts RO ASA25/2933
Barker, John, Borden, Kent, 1639 CKS PRC1/2/10
Barker, John, clergy: 'clerk', Speen, Berks, 1661 Berks RO D/A1/178/59C
Barker, John, mercer, Louth, Lincs, 1668 Lincs RO Ad/Ac/42/9
Barker, John, mercer, Louth, Lincs, 1669 Lincs RO Ad/Ac/42/10
Barker, John, Rushden, Northants, 1671 Northants RO NWill A/C/123
Barker, Jonathan, Norwich St Mary, Norf, 1764 Norfolk RO ANW/23/25/68
Barker, Lawrence, Canterbury, Kent, 1605 CKS PRC2/13/48
Barker, Mary, widow, Thetford, Cambs, CUL V.C. Acc./Box3/59
Barker, Mary, Lutterworth, Leics, 1641 Leics RO PR/I/41A/67
Barker, Richard, Arundel, Sussex, W. Suss RO EpI/33/1611/4
Barker, Richard, Westwell, Kent, 1580 CKS PRC21/4/160
Barker, Richard, Bardney, Lincs, 1607 Lincs RO Ad/Ac/8a/55
Barker, Richard, Crowle, Lincs, 1613 Lincs RO Ad/Ac/8b/55
Barker, Robert, butcher, Worcester St Helen, Worcs, Worcs RO 008.7 BA3585/838/68
Barker, Robert, Langwith (Upper Bassett), Derby, 1663 LJRO:cards/1663/5
Barker, Robert, St James Westminster, London & Middlesex, 1749 Greater London RO AM/PI pt (uncatalogued)
Barker, Simon, Leadenham, Lincs, 1613 Lincs RO Ad/Ac/11/58
Barker, Thomas, husbandman, Sutton, Lincs, 1618 Lincs RO Ad/Ac/14/190

[Barker:]
Barker, William, clergy: 'rector', Henley, Oxon, 1581 Oxon RO MSS Wills 187.15
Barker, William, Kelsey, South, Lincs, 1598 Lincs RO Ad/Ac/5/276
Barker, William, Crowle, Lincs, 1601 Lincs RO Ad/Ac/5/479
Barker, William, Sutton, Lincs, 1612 Lincs RO Ad/Ac/11/34
Barker, William, Maidstone, Kent, 1628 CKS PRC20/8/75
Barker, William, Haxey (Nethergate), Lincs, 1663 Lincs RO Ad/Ac/41/91
Barker, William, Tarporley, Ches, 1668 Cheshire RO (Name) W.C. 1668
Barker, William, tailor, Keal, East, Lincs, 1669 Lincs RO Ad/Ac/33/94
Barker, see Carter,
Barkesdale, John ygr, gentleman, Newbury, Berks, 1626 Berks RO D/A1/176/110
Barkeworthe, Richarde, Leasingham, Lincs, 1594 Lincs RO Ad/Ac/5/302
Barkwith, Miles, yeoman, Sutton, Lincs, 1619 Lincs RO Ad/Ac/15/189
Barkwith, Phillipp, Muckton, Lincs, 1632 Lincs RO Ad/Ac/23/28
Barkwith, Thomas, Saltfleetby, Lincs, 1645 Lincs RO Ad/Ac/28/142
Barkwith, William, husbandman, Saltfleetby, Lincs, 1666 Lincs RO Ad/Ac/32/88
Barley, James, yeoman, Herne, Kent, 1625 CKS PRC20/7/343
Barling, Gilbert, Egerton, Kent, 1600 CKS PRC21/15/225
Barling, John, clothier, Ulcombe, Kent, 1644 CKS PRC1/7/22
Barling, John, Egerton, Kent, 1678 CKS PRC20/12/255
Barling, Richard eld, Egerton, Kent, 1667 CKS PRC19/3/111
Barling, Robert, husbandman, Headcorn, Kent, 1670 CKS PRC2/35/16
Barling, Stephen, bachelor, Egerton, Kent, 1668 CKS PRC19/4/4
Barling, Thomas, Charing, Kent, 1623 CKS PRC20/6/432
Barling, Walter, Brookland, Kent, 1671 CKS PRC2/35/19
Barling, William, Pluckley, Kent, 1712 CKS PRC1/17/47
Barlinge, Adryan, Headcorn, Kent, 1618 CKS PRC2/20/339
Barlinge, William ygr, Ulcombe, Kent, 1617 CKS PRC2/20/231
Barlow, Abigail, widow, Skinnand, Lincs, 1745 Lincs RO Ad/Ac/36/2
Barlow, Abigail, widow, Skinnand, Lincs, 1752 Lincs RO Ad/Ac/45/26
Barlow, Christopher, St Botolph without Aldgate, London & Middlesex, 1794 Greater London RO DL/C/562/160
Barlow, Hugh, Castle Church, Staffs, 1676 LJRO:cards/1676/2
Barlow, Humphry, clergy: 'clerk', Rand, Lincs, 1611 Lincs RO Ad/Ac/10/129
Barlow, James, chapman, Manchester, Lancs, 1759 Lancs RO (Name of Deceased) D.R.C.H. 1759
Barlow, Paule, Ashby de la Zouch, Leics, Leics RO Administrators Accounts 1667-72 f46
Barlow, Robert, 1624 e 2 Wilts RO Unlisted Fragment
Barlow, Robert, whitesmith, Manchester, Lancs, 1772 Lancs RO (Name of Deceased) D.R.C.H. 1772
Barlow, William, 1599 Lancs RO (Name of Deceased) D.R.C.H. 1598
Barlowe, Christopher, Sittingbourne, Kent, 1608 CKS PRC2/13/20
Barlowe, James, yeoman, Waddington, Lincs, 1623 Lincs RO Ad/Ac/18/39
Barlowe, James, Bury, Lancs, 1625 Lancs RO (Name of Deceased) D.R.C.H. 1625
Barlowe, Lawrence, Nettleton, Wilts, 1637 Wilts RO CC Sarum(+ name and date)
Barlowe/LLoyde, Faithe, Wragby, Lincs, 1613 Lincs RO Ad/Ac/11/151
Barlynge, John, Sutton Valence, Kent, 1582 CKS PRC2/2/157
Barman, Henry, Ruckinge, Kent, 1616 CKS PRC2/20/210
Barman, John, Woodchurch, Kent, 1592 CKS PRC21/11/268
Barman, Martha, widow, Ashford, Kent, 1677 CKS PRC2/37/112
Barman, William, Iwade, Kent, 1616 CKS PRC2/20/255
Barmbie, Thomas, Kirkby cum Osgodby, Lincs, 1623 Lincs RO Ad/Ac/18/113
Barmby, Henry, Burton Agnes (Thornholm), Yorks, Borthwick Test C.P. 1730/1
Barming, Dorothy, spinster, Faversham, Kent, 1624 CKS PRC2/23/51
Barnaby, widow, Chitterne St Mary, Wilts, 1620? c. Wilts RO Miscellaneous Index to Wills (name + date)
Barnaby, George, Boston, Lincs, 1756 Lincs RO Ad/Ac/36/6

Barnaby, John, apothecary, Boston, Lincs, 1680 Lincs RO Ad/Ac/34/47
Barnaby, Richard, Boston, Lincs, 1650 Lincs RO Ad/Ac/29/62
Barnacott, John, Madron, Corn, 1603? Cornwall RO AP/B51/2
Barnar, John, maltster, Lenham, Kent, 1697 CKS PRC19/5/50
Barnard, Anthonie, Waddingham, Lincs, 1614 Lincs RO Ad/Ac/8b/41
Barnard, Bridget, Preston, East, Sussex, 1594 W. Suss RO EpI/33/1593/2
Barnard, Charles, tailor, Warfield, Berks, 1607 Berks RO D/A1/175/194
Barnard, Daniel, Chiltington, West, Sussex, 1682 W. Suss RO EpI/33/1682/24
Barnard, Dorothy, widow, Lincoln, Lincs, 1674 Lincs RO Ad/Ac/35/16
Barnard, Edward, Goring, Sussex, 1670 W. Suss RO EpI/33/1670/17
Barnard, Francis, clergy: 'clerk', Wyton, Hunts, Hunts RO/Acc58/191(109)
Barnard, Henry, Hilmarton, Wilts, 1636 Wilts RO Arch. Wilts.(name + date)
Barnard, Henry, Angmering, Sussex, 1648 W. Suss RO EpI/33/1648/7
Barnard, Isaac, Stoke Lane, Som, 1736 Somerset RO D/D/Cta/B60
Barnard, Jeremye, Kingsnorth, Kent, 1595 CKS PRC2/7/389
Barnard, Margery, widow, Goring, Sussex, 1620 W. Suss RO EpI/33/1619/10
Barnard, Nathaniel, Caistor, Lincs, 1666 Lincs RO Ad/Ac/42/6
Barnard, Phillipp, Waddingham, Lincs, 1627 Lincs RO Ad/Ac/39/116
Barnard, Ralph, yeoman, Sutton Benger, Wilts, 1678 Wilts RO Miscellaneous Index to Wills (name + date)
Barnard, Richard, Brigsley, Lincs, 1597 Lincs RO Ad/Ac/4/55
Barnard, Roger, Stanton Harcourt, Oxon, 1581 Oxon RO MSS Wills 187.16
Barnard, Timothy, clothworker, Newbury, Berks, 1677 Berks RO D/A1/178/170
Barnard, Timothy, clothworker, Newbury, Berks, 1677 Berks RO D/A1/178/170D
Barnard, William, Goxhill, Lincs, 1627 Lincs RO Ad/Ac/20b/100
Barnard, William, Burwell, Lincs, 1662 Lincs RO Ad/Ac/32/38
Barnard/Badnore, Anne/Agnes, East Sutton, Kent, 1626 CKS PRC2/27/14
Barnard, see Badnore,
Barnarde, Thomas, Hagnaby, Lincs, 1607 Lincs RO Ad/Ac/8a/65
Barne, Mary, Kirmington, Lincs, 1645 Lincs RO Ad/Ac/28/141
Barne, see Paule,
Barnerd, William, Blisland, Corn, 1610 Cornwall RO AP/B197
Barnes, Ann, spinster, Selling, Kent, 1613 CKS PRC2/17/245
Barnes, Anthony, Teynham, Kent, 1639 CKS PRC2/34/176
Barnes, Brian, Newbury, Berks, 1628 Berks RO D/A1/177/8C
Barnes, Edward, Milton next Sittingbourne, Kent, 1633 CKS PRC2/32/5
Barnes, Edward, cutler, Wallingford, Berks, 1641 Berks RO D/A1/177/88C
Barnes, Edward, St Mildred Bread Street, London & Middlesex, 1757 Greater London RO DL/C/554/34/2
Barnes, Elizabeth, widow, Hogsthorpe, Lincs, 1632 Lincs RO Ad/Ac/23/59
Barnes, Gabriell, Chippenham, Wilts, 1695 Wilts RO Arch. Wilts.(name + date)
Barnes, George, carpenter, Wargrave, Berks, 1639 Berks RO D/A1/177/75C
Barnes, George, Nursling, Hants, 1663 Hants RO 21M65 D8/163
Barnes, Henry, Newnham, Kent, 1596 CKS PRC2/8/75
Barnes, Henrye, Maidstone, Kent, 1611 CKS PRC20/2/236
Barnes, Hugh, yeoman, Teynham, Kent, 1673 CKS PRC2/35/200
Barnes, James, yeoman, Whiteparish, Wilts, 1735 Wilts RO Arch. Sarum/(+ name and date)
Barnes, Jane, Wimborne Minster, Dors, 1672 Dorset RO PE/WM CP 2/4/75
Barnes, John, Wimborne Minster, Dors, Dorset RO PE/WM CP 2/4/80
Barnes, John, Canterbury St Andrew, Kent, 1575 CKS PRC2/1/134
Barnes, John, blacksmith, Ilsley, East, Berks, 1577 Berks RO D/A1/175/82B
Barnes, John, Toft Next Newton, Lincs, 1612 Lincs RO Ad/Ac/11/178
Barnes, John, innholder, Abingdon, Berks, 1626 Berks RO D/A1/176/103A
Barnes, John, Oving, Sussex, 1630 W. Suss RO EpI/33/1630/16
Barnes, John, Pidley, Hunts, 1676 Hunts RO/Acc58/29(18)

[Barnes:]
Barnes, John, currier/victualler, Lichfield, Staffs, 1779 LJRO/B/C/5/1779/4
Barnes, John, grinder, Ecclesfield (Stannington), Yorks, 1804 Borthwick Test C.P. 1804/5
Barnes, John + Dorothie, Cranbrook, Kent, 1607 CKS PRC2/14/22
Barnes, John + Ursula, clergy: 'clerk', Bassingham, Lincs, 1619 Lincs RO Ad/Ac/15/55
Barnes, John eld, carpenter, Hythe St Leonard, Kent, 1671 CKS PRC20/12/4
Barnes, Joseph jun, Downham, Cambs, 1764 Cambs RO 1764/Inv
Barnes, Mary, widow, St Johns Thanet, Kent, 1692 CKS PRC2/42/28
Barnes, Mawde, Halstock, Dors, 1597 Wilts RO Miscellaneous Index to Wills (name + date)
Barnes, Phylothens, Donington, Lincs, 1676 Lincs RO Ad/Ac/43/177
Barnes, Ralf, Sheldwich, Kent, 1597 CKS PRC2/9/267
Barnes, Ralph, St Martin in the Fields, London & Middlesex, 1671 PRO PROB32/8/64
Barnes, Reynold, Burmarsh, Kent, 1680 CKS PRC2/39/11
Barnes, Richard, Bobbing, Kent, 1596 CKS PRC2/8/67
Barnes, Richard, Cadbury, North, Som, 1608 Somerset RO D/D/Cta/B99
Barnes, Richard, Wimborne Minster, Dors, 1663 Dorset RO PE/WM CP 2/4/67
Barnes, Richard, Wimborne Minster, Dors, 1673 Dorset RO PE/WM CP 2/4/74
Barnes, Richard, husbandman, Blackburn (Tetleworth, Rishton), Lancs, 1749 Lancs RO (Name of Deceased) D.R.C.H. 1749
Barnes, Robarte, Wichling, Kent, 1593 CKS PRC2/6/75
Barnes, Robert, St Albans St Peters, Herts, 1637 Herts RO ASA25/4934
Barnes, Robert, Coates, Great, Lincs, 1660s? Lincs RO Ad/Ac/43/5
Barnes, Roger, Steyning, Sussex, 1627 W. Suss RO EpI/33/1627/10
Barnes, Samuel, bachelor, St Dunstan in the East, London & Middlesex, 1722 Lambeth Palace VH82/85
Barnes, Simon, husbandman, Baldon, Marsh, Oxon, 1671 Oxon RO MSS Wills Pec 65/4/19
Barnes, Stephen, Davington, Kent, 1684 CKS PRC2/40/173
Barnes, Thomas, Linton, Kent, 1583 CKS PRC2/2/48
Barnes, Thomas, Sonning, Berks, 1595 Wilts RO Miscellaneous Index to Wills (name + date)
Barnes, Thomas, Kington, West, Wilts, 1618 Wilts RO Arch. Wilts.(name + date)
Barnes, Thomas, Mildenhall (Poulton), Wilts, 1622 Wilts RO Arch. Wilts.(name + date)
Barnes, Thomas, Backwell, Som, 1666 Somerset RO D/D/Cta/B46
Barnes, William, tailor, Oare, Kent, 1620 CKS PRC2/20/312
Barnes, William, Wimborne Minster (Kingston Lacy), Dors, 1630 Dorset RO PE/WM CP 2/4/45
Barnes, William, Tenterden, Kent, 1662 CKS PRC1/9/3
Barnes, William, tailor, Abingdon, Berks, 1671 Berks RO D/A1/178/136C
Barnes, Wyllyam, Selling, Kent, 1592 CKS PRC2/5/182
Barnet, Christopher, bachelor, Codicote, Herts, 1699 Herts RO ASA25/4487
Barnet, John, butcher, Wylye, Wilts, 1742 Wilts RO Arch. Sarum/(+ name and date)
Barnett, Daniel, Brownlow, Ches, 1712 Cheshire RO (Name) W.C. 1712
Barnett, Matthew, bachelor, Whitstable, Kent, 1705 CKS PRC1/16/61
Barnett, Richard, mariner, Dover, Kent, 1669 CKS PRC19/4/39
Barnewell, Richard, Burbage, Leics, 1640 Leics RO PR/I/41A/46
Barnewell, William, Burbage, Leics, 1669 Leics RO Administrators Accounts 1667-72 f21
Barnham, Nicholas, butcher, Chart, Great, Kent, 1675 CKS PRC2/36/167
Barnsdale, Anne, widow, Bilsington, Kent, 1680 CKS PRC2/39/5
Barnsdale, John, Bilsington, Kent, 1677 CKS PRC2/37/117
Barnsley, Margaret, widow, Hythe St Leonard, Kent, 1687 CKS PRC20/13/543
Barnsley, Phillip, mariner: 'seaman', Hythe St Leonard, Kent, 1681 CKS PRC20/13/103
Barnwell, Ann, Newington next Sittingbourne, Kent, 1674 CKS PRC2/36/22
Barnwell, John, Newington next Sittingbourne, Kent, 1672 CKS PRC2/35/115
Baron, Thomas, Folkestone, Kent, 1604 CKS PRC2/13/109
Barr, David, Wye, Kent, 1721 CKS PRC1/18/35
Barraclough, Robert, yeoman, Halifax (Saltonheble), Yorks, 1739 Borthwick Test C.P. 1739/3
Barrae, Fortune, Tangmere, Sussex, 1613 W. Suss RO EpIV/10/1/3
Barraford, Mathew, gentleman, Kirkby, Lincs, 1683 Lincs RO Ad/Ac/44/113

Barraker, William, Mere, Wilts, 1598 Wilts RO Miscellaneous Index to Wills (name + date)
Barrat, Robert, husbandman, Thatcham, Berks, 1631 Berks RO D/A1/177/27A
Barratt, Philip, Shipton under Wychwood (Milton), Oxon, 1633 Oxon RO MSS Wills 295/3/44
Barre, Emme, Gedney, Lincs, 1640 Lincs RO Ad/Ac/27/66
Barre, Stephen, Fillingham, Lincs, 1673 Lincs RO Ad/Ac/35/68
Barre, William, husbandman, Lambourn, Berks, 1618 Berks RO D/A1/176/65A
Barrell, Martyn, Sandwich, Kent, 1596 CKS PRC2/8/13
Barret, John, Lydd, Kent, 1599 CKS PRC21/15/45
Barrett, Alexander, Sturry, Kent, 1628 CKS PRC2/29/11
Barrett, Anne, widow, Berrick Salome, Oxon, 1666 Oxon RO MSS Wills 6/1/40
Barrett, Helen, widow, St Albans, Herts, 1628 Herts RO ASA25/4853
Barrett, Henry, Fletton, Hunts, 1681 Hunts RO/Acc58/161(37)
Barrett, Humfry, Lydd, Kent, 1616 CKS PRC20/3/254
Barrett, John, Duloe, Corn, 1606 Cornwall RO AP/B92
Barrett, John, Chislet, Kent, 1635 CKS PRC2/32/137
Barrett, Martha, widow, Bloxham, Oxon, 1795 Oxon RO MSS Wills Pec 301/2/119
Barrett, Mary, spinster, Chieveley, Berks, 1639 Berks RO D/A1/177/82C
Barrett, Robert, Chilham, Kent, 1599 CKS PRC2/11/87
Barrett, Robert, gentleman, Droitwich, Worcs, 1604 Worcs RO 008.7 BA3585/839/287
Barrett, Robert, Surfleet, Lincs, 1634 Lincs RO Ad/Ac/24/244
Barrett, Thomas, Winteringham, Lincs, 1662 Lincs RO Ad/Ac/41/8
Barrett, Thomas, clockmaker, Canterbury St Andrew, Kent, 1666 CKS PRC1/11/100
Barrett, Thomas, Frome Selwood, Som, 1701 Somerset RO D/D/Cta/B61
Barrett, William, Algarkirk, Lincs, 1611 Lincs RO Ad/Ac/10/29
Barrett, William, Ashford, Kent, 1670 CKS PRC1/15/4
Barrett, see Cheales,
Barrey, Moyses, Chilham, Kent, 1614 CKS PRC2/18/113
Barringly, Richard, Marden, Kent, 1617 CKS PRC2/20/162
Barringon, Thomas, Newington next Sittingbourne, Kent, 1643 CKS PRC1/6/96
Barrington, John, Bowdon, Ches, 1628 Cheshire RO (Name) W.C. 1628
Barroe, Giles, stranger, Canterbury St Alphege, Kent, 1624 CKS PRC20/6/80
Barrom, see Hartt,
Barron, Elizabeth, widow, Deeping, Market, Lincs, 1668 Lincs RO Ad/Ac/33/66
Barron, Richard, Rippingale, Lincs, 1607 Lincs RO Ad/Ac/8a/53
Barrow, Edward, Haxey, Lincs, 1646 Lincs RO Ad/Ac/40/123
Barrow, Edward, Smeeth, Kent, 1674 CKS PRC20/12/118
Barrow, Henry, Brabourne, Kent, 1640 CKS PRC1/4/8
Barrow, John, St Johns Thanet, Kent, 1631 CKS PRC20/9/73
Barrow, John, mariner, St Johns Thanet, Kent, 1645 CKS PRC1/7/37
Barrow, John, yeoman, Hatherley, Down, Glos, 1732 GRO GDR/B4/2/B64
Barrow, Margery, Bowdon (Hale), Ches, 1682 Cheshire RO (Name) W.C. 1682
Barrow, Richard, gentleman, Milton next Sittingbourne, Kent, 1668 CKS PRC1/12/9
Barrow, Robert, Haxey, Lincs, 1676 Lincs RO Ad/Ac/35/106
Barrow, Robert, Whitchurch, Shrops, 1698 LJRO/B/C/5/1698/13
Barrow, Sydrach, Norton, Kent, 1627 CKS PRC2/27/18
Barrow, Thomas, Potterspury, Northants, 1685 Northants RO NWill A/C/24
Barrow, William, university: 'Fellow of Emmanuel College, Cambridge', Cambs 1614 CUL V.C.Acc./Box1/4
Barrow, William, maltster, Warrington, Lancs, 1664 Lancs RO (Name of Deceased) D.R.C.H. 1664-65
Barrowby, Richard, shipowner, Hull, Yorks, 1794 Borthwick Test C.P. 1794/14
Barrowe, Henrie, Mersham, Kent, 1605 CKS PRC2/13/56
Barrowe, John, yeoman, Kennington, Kent, 1638 CKS PRC20/10/43
Barrowe, Margarett, widow, Ashford, Kent, 1611 CKS PRC2/16/83
Barrowe, Richard, yeoman, Boughton Aluph, Kent, 1608 CKS PRC20/1/350

[Barrowe:]
Barrowe, Robarte, Boughton Aluph, Kent, 1607 CKS PRC2/15/25
Barrowe, Thomas, Lenham, Kent, 1599 CKS PRC2/10/503
Barrowe, William, gentleman, Canterbury Christchurch, Kent, 1598 CKS PRC21/14/557
Barrowe, William, Haxey, Lincs, 1624-Lincs RO Ad/Ac/8c/75
Barrowes, Christopher, Clewer, Berks, 1593 Berks RO D/A1/175/133A
Barrowes, Joan, widow, Banbury, Oxon, 1635 Oxon RO MSS Wills Pec 33/1/2
Barry, Christopher, Tickenham, Som, 1638 Somerset RO D/D/Cta/B22
Barry, John, yeoman, Sutton, Lincs, 1635 Lincs RO Ad/Ac/24/377
Barry, William, Titchfield, Hants, 1674 Hants RO 21m65 D8/266
Barson, Henrie, Swaton, Lincs, 1620 Lincs RO Ad/Ac/16/13
Barter, Edward, Bradley, North, Wilts, 1642 Wilts RO Arch. Sarum/(+ name and date)
Bartholmew, John, husbandman, Hurst, Berks, 1634 Wilts RO Miscellaneous Index to Wills (name + date)
Bartholmew, John, Sturton, Great, Lincs, 1664? Lincs RO Ad/Ac/45/114
Bartholmew, William, Gedney, Lincs, 1640 Lincs RO Ad/Ac/27/104
Bartholmewe, John, Hothfield, Kent, 1601 CKS PRC2/12/19
Bartholmewe, John, Sandwich, Kent, 1608 CKS PRC20/1/370
Bartholmewe, Richard, clergy: 'clerk', Gayton le Wold, Lincs, 1611 Lincs RO Ad/Ac/10/54
Bartholomew, John, Sandwich, Kent, 1613 CKS PRC2/17/230
Bartholomew, John, gentleman, Sandwich, Kent, 1635 CKS PRC20/10/70
Bartholomew, John, husbandman, Chaddleworth, Berks, 1663 Berks RO D/A1/178/55A
Bartholomew, Richard, shearman, Hampstead Marshall, Berks, 1611 Berks RO D/A1/176/23A
Bartholomew, Thomas, Burghfield, Berks, 1607 Berks RO D/A1/176/11
Bartholomew, Thomas, Ford, Sussex, 1678 W. Suss RO EpI/33/1678/14
Bartholomew/Burrish, Margaret, widow, Lydd, Kent, 1667 CKS PRC19/3/112
Bartholomew/Martin, Thomas, husbandman, Warborough, Oxon, 1677 Oxon RO MSS Wills Pec 65/4/31
Bartholomewe, Richard, Treyford, Sussex, 1604 W. Suss RO EpI/33/1603/2
Bartle, Francis, Belton, Lincs, 1682 Lincs RO Ad/Ac/44/27
Bartle, Stephen, Scotter, Lincs, 1681 Lincs RO Ad/Ac/34/92
Bartlet, Nicholas, Reculver, Kent, 1626 CKS PRC20/7/100
Bartlet, Richard, esquire, Stopham, Sussex, 1618 W. Suss RO EpI/33/1617/31
Bartlet, Thomas, baker, Dover, Kent, 1637 CKS PRC20/10/108
Bartlett, Ann, St Nicholas at Wade, Kent, 1678 CKS PRC20/12/256
Bartlett, Anthony, Cannings, All, Wilts, 1674 Wilts RO Miscellaneous Index to Wills (name + date)
Bartlett, John, Reading St Mary, Berks, 1600 Berks RO D/A1/175/159B
Bartlett, John, Wick, Som, 1620 Somerset RO D/D/Cta/B3
Bartlett, John, Bampton (Lew), Oxon, 1696 Oxon RO MSS Wills 295/6/17
Bartlett, Richard, St Nicholas at Wade, Kent, 1598 CKS PRC21/14/581
Bartlett, Robert, Chilham, Kent, 1638 CKS PRC2/34/14
Bartlett, Thomas, baker, Henley, Oxon, 1633 Oxon RO MSS Wills 295/3/39
Bartlett, Thomas, fellmonger, Watlington, Oxon, 1679 Oxon RO MSS Wills 161/1/6
Bartlett, Thomas, scribbler, Westbury, Wilts, 1755? Wilts RO Chantor Sarum Bundle
Bartlett, Trustram, Lavington, Market, Wilts, 1628 Wilts RO CC Sarum(+ name and date)
Bartlett, William, fellmonger, Faversham, Kent, 1677 CKS PRC2/37/17
Bartlett, William, gentleman, Sutton Courtenay, Berks, 1684 Berks RO D/A1/179/19D
Bartley, Hughe, Cheverell, Great, Wilts, 1614 Wilts RO CC Sarum(+ name and date)
Barton, Agnes, Dunston, Lincs, 1634 Lincs RO Ad/Ac/24/215
Barton, Bartholomew, Faversham, Kent, CKS PRC1/4/9b
Barton, Bartholomew, Faversham, Kent, 1640 CKS PRC1/4/9
Barton, Edward, university: 'Vice-Master & Fellow of Trinity College, Cambridge/B.D.' Cambridge (Trinity College), Cambs, 1646 CUL V.C. Acc./Box2/2
Barton, Elisabethe, widow, Hemingby, Lincs, 1580 Lincs RO Ad/Ac/2b/62
Barton, George, Solihull, Warks, 1675 LJRO:cards/1675/9

[Barton:]

Barton, Henry, yeoman, Mersham, Kent, 1641 CKS PRC1/5/78
Barton, Jeames, Maidstone, Kent, 1601 CKS PRC21/15/206
Barton, John, saddler, Abingdon St Helen, Berks, 1626 Berks RO D/A1/43/123C
Barton, John, husbandman, Welton le Marsh (Boothby), Lincs, 1631 Lincs RO Ad/Ac/23/180
Barton, John, husbandman, Welton le Marsh (Boothby), Lincs, 1632 Lincs RO Ad/Ac/23/31
Barton, John, Sittingbourne, Kent, 1637 CKS PRC2/34/22
Barton, John, Pluckley, Kent, 1666 CKS PRC1/11/101
Barton, John, Fareham, Hants, 1669 Hants RO 21m65 D8/209
Barton, John, Worth, Kent, 1695 CKS PRC19/5/33
Barton, John, butcher, Thornbury, Glos, 1730 GRO GDR/B4/2/B61
Barton, Josias, yeoman, Ashby cum Fenby, Lincs, 1683 Lincs RO Ad/Ac/44/79
Barton, Margaret, Appleby, Lincs, 1619 Lincs RO Ad/Ac/8b/367
Barton, Margarett, Welton le Wold, Lincs, 1640 Lincs RO Ad/Ac/27/94
Barton, Richard, Luddenham, Kent, 1630 CKS PRC20/9/61
Barton, Richard, yeoman, Chart nr Sutton Valence, Kent, 1712 CKS PRC1/17/48
Barton, Richard + Frances, Lancs RO (Name of Deceased) D.R.C.H. 1635
Barton, Robart, Detling, Kent, 1601 CKS PRC21/15/121
Barton, Robert, Louth, Lincs, 1675 Lincs RO Ad/Ac/42/67
Barton, Robert, Huddington, Worcs, 1685 Worcs RO 008.7 BA3585/837/bdl 4
Barton, Thomas, Horwood, Little, Bucks, 1596 Herts RO ASA25/1534
Barton, Thomas, Charing, Kent, 1602 CKS PRC21/16/141
Barton, Thomas, Thorpe St Peter, Lincs, 1662 Lincs RO Ad/Ac/32/18
Barton, Thomas, degrees: 'D.D.', Westmeston, Sussex, 1683 PRO PROB32/33/200
Barton, Thomas, Uttoxeter (Loxly), Staffs, 1713 LJRO/B/C/5/1712/2
Barton, William, baker, Canterbury, Kent, 1616 CKS PRC2/20/338
Barton, William, Ormsby, North, Lincs, 1618 Lincs RO Ad/Ac/14/226
Barton, William, Washingborough, Lincs, 1683 Lincs RO Ad/Ac/44/75
Barton, William, St Laurence Thanet, Kent, 1684 CKS PRC2/40/176
Bartonn, William, university: 'Fellow of Trinity College, Cambridge/B.D.', Cambridge, Cambs, 1629 CUL V.C. Acc./Box2/3
Bartrum, George, yeoman, Pickworth, Lincs, 1669 Lincs RO Ad/Ac/33/118
Barwick, John, mariner, Bristol St Michael the Archangel, Glos, Bristol RO 1717/5a
Barwicke, Giles, Whitstable, Kent, 1597 CKS PRC2/9/41
Barworth, Samuel, Appledore, Kent, 1641 CKS PRC1/4/10
Barworthe, Jacob, Wittersham, Kent, 1616 CKS PRC20/3/504
Basden, Arthur, Hawkhurst, Kent, 1616 CKS PRC2/20/343
Basden, John, Staplehurst, Kent, 1614 CKS PRC2/18/11
Basden, Thomas, Cranbrook, Kent, 1612 CKS PRC2/16/86
Basden, William, clothier ?, Maidstone, Kent, 1632 CKS PRC20/10/58
Basden, see Leede,
Base, Thomas, Waltham, Kent, 1592 CKS PRC2/5/39
Baseden, John, Smarden, Kent, 1582 CKS PRC2/2/136
Baseden, John, Cranbrook, Kent, 1628 CKS PRC2/28/8
Baseden, John eld, yeoman, Benenden, Kent, 1676 CKS PRC2/36/156
Baseden, Thomas, Bethersden, Kent, 1597 CKS PRC2/10/490
Baseden, Thomas, Loose, Kent, 1645 CKS PRC19/2/92
Baseden, William, Boxley, Kent, 1681 CKS PRC2/39/153
Baseden/Willard/Evenden, Dorothy, Biddenden, Kent, 1626 CKS PRC2/27/20
Baseley, James, Compton, Fenny, Warks, 1682 LJRO/B/C/5/1682/7
Baseley, John, Duston, Northants, 1674 Northants RO NWill A/C/44
Baseley, Samuel, Coventry, Warks, 1676 LJRO:cards/1676/3
Basell, George, Dunstable, Beds, 1669 PRO PROB5/985
Basely, Richard, yeoman, Wytham, Berks, 1676 Berks RO D/A1/178/149A
Basey, Anthony, fisherman, Folkestone, Kent, 1674 CKS PRC2/36/12
Baskerfeild, John, Egginton, Derby, 1683 LJRO/B/C/5/1683/1

[Baskerville:]
Baskerville, Hanibal, esquire, Sunningwell (Bayworth), Berks, 1670 Berks RO D/A1/178/117C
Basley, Thomas, husbandman, Adderbury (Milton), Oxon, 1637 Oxon RO MSS Wills 5/4/12
Basnet, George, Riby, Lincs, 1650 Lincs RO Ad/Ac/30/5
Bason, Richard, Wimborne Minster, Dors, Dorset RO PE/WM CP 2/4/87
Baspoole, Walter ygr, Wrawby cum Brigg (Glanford Brigg), Lincs, 1625? Lincs RO Ad/Ac/19B/114
Basrly, John, St John, Corn, 1641 Cornwall RO AP/B995
Bassacke, John, Walmer, Kent, 1681 CKS PRC2/39/135
Basse, Thomas, Bonnington, Kent, 1626 CKS PRC2/27/11
Basse, Thomas, Chilham, Kent, 1666 CKS PRC1/11/5
Basset, Albert, clergy: 'clerk', Boughton under Blean, Kent, 1592 CKS PRC21/12/226
Basset, Als,
Kent 1598 CKS PRC2/10/102
Basset, Elias, mariner: 'sailor', Queenborough, Kent, 1632 CKS PRC2/31/7
Basset, Robert, yeoman, Thatcham (Henwick), Berks, 1626 Berks RO D/A1/176/111A
Basset, Thomas, St Laurence Thanet, Kent, 1638 CKS PRC2/34/12
Basset, William, Whitstable, Kent, 1594 CKS PRC2/7/27
Basset, William + Helen, Whitstable, Kent, 1598 CKS PRC2/10/410
Basset, William eld, fellmonger, Stanford in the Vale, Berks, 1667 Berks RO D/A1/178/100A
Bassett, Edward ygr, Whitstable, Kent, 1612 CKS PRC2/16/30
Bassett, Elias, jurat/gentleman, Hythe St Leonard, Kent, 1684 CKS PRC20/13/408
Bassett, Gregory, Sandwich St Peter, Kent, 1667 CKS PRC1/12/10
Bassett, Hellen, widow, Whitstable, Kent, 1587 CKS PRC2/4/442
Bassett, Henrie, Ashford, Kent, 1637 CKS PRC2/34/18
Bassett, John, Whitstable, Kent, 1605 CKS PRC2/13/33
Bassett, John, Faversham, Kent, 1624 CKS PRC2/23/52
Bassett, Nicholas, St Laurence Thanet, Kent, 1614 CKS PRC2/20/176
Bassett, Robert, Hartlip, Kent, 1638 CKS PRC2/34/15
Bassett, William, Eastchurch, Sheppey, Kent, 1602 CKS PRC2/12/38
Bassock, John, Sandwich St Peter, Kent, 1593 CKS PRC2/6/416
Bassocke, John, Staplehurst, Kent, 1627 CKS PRC2/28/9
Bassocke, Ralphe, Sandhurst, Kent, 1607 CKS PRC2/13/83
Bassocke, Richard, Sandhurst, Kent, 1594 CKS PRC2/7/331
Bassocke, Richard, Headcorn, Kent, 1630 CKS PRC2/30/25
Bassocke, Robert, Maidstone, Kent, 1603 CKS PRC21/15/326
Bassocke, Stephen, Blean, Kent, 1606 CKS PRC2/14/29
Bassocke, Thomas, Smarden, Kent, 1605 CKS PRC2/14/37
Bassocke, Thomas, Wormshill, Kent, 1631 CKS PRC2/31/12
Bassocke, Thomazine, widow, Blean, Kent, 1611 CKS PRC2/17/411
Bastable, Nancy, widow, Bristol, Glos, Bristol RO 1768/CP
Bastable, Ralph, Petherton, North, Som, 1608 Somerset RO D/D/Cta/B95
Batcheler, Bartholomewe, St Laurence Thanet, Kent, 1617 CKS PRC2/20/274
Batcheler, Thomas, St Thomas Isle of Harty, Kent, 1620 CKS PRC2/20/354
Batcheler, William, Weyhill, Hants, 1677 Hants RO 21m65 D8/275
Batcheler, William, Bierton (Broughton), Bucks, 1682 Oxon RO MSS Wills Pec 33/4/7
Batcheler, see Bacheler,
Batcheller, John, Sandhurst, Kent, 1673 CKS PRC2/35/201
Batcheller, John, mr, Frittenden, Kent, 1701 CKS PRC1/16/21
Batcheller, Richard, Earls Croome, Worcs, 1602 Worcs RO 008.7 BA3585/838/223
Batcheller, Robert, Hawkhurst, Kent, 1684 CKS PRC2/40/169
Batchellers, Richard, Barwell, Leics, 1640 Leics RO PR/I/41A/44
Batchellor, Henry, Hawkhurst, Kent, 1684 CKS PRC2/40/174
Batchellor, John, Tonge, Kent, 1687 CKS PRC2/41/91
Batchellor, Thomas, Amesbury, Wilts, 1620? Wilts RO Arch. Sarum/(+ name and date)
Batchelor, John, Hawkhurst, Kent, 1665 CKS PRC1/11/6

Batchelor, Thomas, Grinstead, West, Sussex, 1670 W. Suss RO EpI/33/1670/15
Batchelor, Thomas, Grinstead, West, Sussex, 1672 W. Suss RO EpI/33/1671/2
Batchelor, William, Cranbrook, Kent, 1598 CKS PRC2/10/353
Batchelour, Ellen, widow, Maidstone, Kent, 1670 CKS PRC19/4/40
Batchelour, Thomas, Amesbury, Wilts, 1686 Wilts RO Arch. Sarum/(+ name and date)
Batchiler, Richard, Cheriton, Hants, 1623 Hants RO 21M65 D8/4
Batcock, Francis, Storrington, Sussex, 1673 W. Suss RO EpI/33/1673/23
Batcocke, Edward, Hawkhurst, Kent, 1625 CKS PRC2/23/25
Batcocke, Francis, brewer, Storrington, Sussex, 1682 W. Suss RO EpI/33/1682/29
Bate, Dyer, captain, Stepney, London & Middlesex, 1688 PRO PROB32/27/55
Bate, George, Whaplode, Lincs, 1629 Lincs RO Ad/Ac/22/30
Bate, Gregorie, Birchington, Kent, 1600 CKS PRC21/15/137
Bate, James, Orton Water Ville, Hunts, 1684 Hunts RO/Acc58/239(263)
Bate, John, Elmley, Sheppey, Kent, 1596 CKS PRC2/8/43
Bate, John, Petherwin, North, Corn, 1607 Cornwall RO AP/B147
Bate, John, Stamford, Lincs, 1636 Lincs RO Ad/Ac/24/262
Bate, John, mr, Lydd, Kent, 1644 CKS PRC19/2/83
Bate, John, bachelor/gentleman, Ashford, Kent, 1665 CKS PRC1/10/9
Bate, Margaret, widow, Newbury, Berks, 1622 Berks RO D/A1/176/80C
Bate, Margaret, widow, Maidstone, Kent, 1634 CKS PRC20/10/68
Bate, Marie, widow, Deeping, Market, Lincs, 1612 Lincs RO Ad/Ac/10/144
Bate, Richard, Minster in Sheppey, Kent, 1601 CKS PRC2/12/34
Bate, Robarte, Bearsted, Kent, 1591 CKS PRC2/5/214
Bate, Robert, Willoughby, Silk, Lincs, 1639 Lincs RO Ad/Ac/26/154
Bate, Sampson, husbandman, Petherwin, North, Corn, Cornwall RO AP/B545/3
Bate, Samuel, gentleman, Ashford, Kent, 1675 CKS PRC20/12/117
Bate, Thomas, Hythe St Leonard, Kent, 1581 CKS PRC21/5/9
Bate, Thomas, Sandwich St Mary, Kent, 1616 CKS PRC2/20/235
Bate, Thomas, Lydd, Kent, 1639 CKS PRC20/10/132
Bate, Thomas, grocer, Warrington, Lancs, 1761 Lancs RO (Name of Deceased) D.R.C.H. 1761
Bate, Thomas eld, jurat, Lydd, Kent, 1637 CKS PRC20/10/90
Bate, Willyam, Littlebourne, Kent, 1628 CKS PRC2/28/19
Bately, Ralph, yeoman, Sunningwell, Berks, 1683 Berks RO D/A1/179/8D
Bateman, Cornelia, Erith, Kent, 1704 Lambeth Palace Arches G54/3A
Bateman, Elizabeth, widow, Ash next Sandwich, Kent, 1615 CKS PRC20/3/334
Bateman, Elizabeth, widow, Ash next Sandwich, Kent, 1617 CKS PRC20/4/31
Bateman, Henry, Frinstead, Kent, 1592 CKS PRC2/6/282
Bateman, Henry, Rodmersham, Kent, 1681 CKS PRC2/39/151
Bateman, James, Glentworth, Lincs, 1594 Lincs RO Ad/Ac/5/485
Bateman, John, Bapchild, Kent, 1603 CKS PRC2/14/62
Bateman, John, Bapchild, Kent, 1612 CKS PRC2/16/4
Bateman, John, Sandwich St Mary, Kent, 1628 CKS PRC2/29/17
Bateman, John, gentleman, Lydd, Kent, 1670 CKS PRC19/4/69
Bateman, John, Bredgar, Kent, 1678 CKS PRC2/38/5
Bateman, John, gentleman, Hollingbourne, Kent, 1681 CKS PRC20/13/97
Bateman, Katherine, widow, Willingham, South, Lincs, 1680 Lincs RO Ad/Ac/43/90
Bateman, Laurence, Borden, Kent, 1672 CKS PRC2/35/7
Bateman, Luce, widow, Lydd, Kent, 1610 CKS PRC20/2/148
Bateman, Mary, Somercoates, North, Lincs, 1632 Lincs RO Ad/Ac/23/99
Bateman, Mathew, yeoman, Upwell, Cambs, 1708 PRO PROB5/993
Bateman, Thomas, Selling, Kent, 1586 CKS PRC2/4/208
Bateman, William, Bitton, Glos, late C17th? GRO GDR/B4/2/B183
Bateman, Zacharias, Lydd, Kent, 1639 CKS PRC20/10/122
Bateman/Jeakin, Elizabeth, Ospringe, Kent, 1618 CKS PRC2/20/180
Bates, James, innkeeper, Rolleston (Anslow), Staffs, 1822 LJRO/B/C/5/1821/4

[Bates:]
Bates, John, Sibsey, Lincs, 1605 Lincs RO Ad/Ac/6/95
Bates, John, miller: 'corn miller', Dewsbury (Burgh Mill), Yorks, 1815 Borthwick Test C.P. 1815/8
Bates, Jonas, weaver, Bristol, Glos, Bristol RO 1736/4
Bates, Michaell, Stainfield, Lincs, 1620? Lincs RO Ad/Ac/16/16
Bates, Nicolas, Sandwich St Peter, Kent, 1588 CKS PRC2/4/259
Bates, Simon, yeoman, Newnham, Kent, 1661 CKS PRC1/8/88
Bates, Symon, householder, East Sutton, Kent, 1682 CKS PRC2/39/142
Bates, William, cook, Cambridge (Trinity College), Cambs, 1678 CUL V.C. Acc./Box3/4
Batey, John, Yaxley, Hunts, 1680 Hunts RO/Acc58/146(30)
Bathars, Edward, copperas boiler, Whitstable, Kent, 1682 CKS PRC2/39/152
Bathe, Elizabeth, widow, Kirtlington, Oxon, 1667 Oxon RO MSS Wills 76/4/30
Bathe, Jasper, Merther, Corn, 1606 Cornwall RO AP/B77
Bathe, John, Wrington, Som, 1662 Somerset RO D/D/Cta/B42
Bathe, Richard, Wootton Bassett, Wilts, 1618 Wilts RO Arch. Wilts.(name + date)
Batherst, Anne, widow, Staplehurst, Kent, 1633 CKS PRC2/31/88
Batherst, Lancelott, Biddenden, Kent, 1609 CKS PRC2/13/26
Batherst, Thomas, Staplehurst, Kent, 1601 CKS PRC2/11/375
Batherst, Thomas, Staplehurst, Kent, 1615 CKS PRC2/20/371
Batho, David, Wrockwardine, Shrops, 1664 LJRO:cards/1664/3
Batho, Randle, maltster, Chester St John the Baptist, Ches, 1727 Cheshire RO (Name) W.C. 1727
Bathoe, William, cordwainer: 'shoemaker', Worcester, Worcs, 1610 Worcs RO 008.7 BA3585/839/485
Batholmew, Laurence, labourer, Whitstable, Kent, 1674 CKS PRC2/35/203
Bathurst, Edward, Marden, Kent, 1666 CKS PRC1/10/10
Batley, Richard, innkeeper, Huddersfield, Yorks, 1824 Borthwick Test C.P. 1824/6
Batl(e)y, Isaac, Sheinton, Shrops, 1674 LJRO:cards/1674/4
Batman, Henry, Blyton, Lincs, 1609 Lincs RO Ad/Ac/8a/304
Batmanson, John, Bersted, South, Sussex, 1631 W. Suss RO EpIV/10/1/12
Batt, Agnes, widow, Leigh on Mendip, Som, 1639 Somerset RO D/D/Cta/B25
Batt, James, Clanfield, Hants, 1680 Hants RO 1680 AD9/2
Batt, Thomas, innholder, Hindon, Wilts, 1639 Wilts RO Arch. Sarum/(+ name and date)
Battell, Robert, gentleman, Winkfield, Berks, 1591 Berks RO D/A1/175/111
Batten, Maiden Bradley, Wilts, 1615 Wilts RO Miscellaneous Index to Wills (name + date)
Batten, John, yeoman, Ardington (Ardington Wick), Berks, 1620 Berks RO D/A1/176/79A
Batten, Robert, husbandman, Ardington, Berks, 1685 Berks RO D/A1/179/37C
Batten, William, Portishead, Som, 1619 Somerset RO D/D/Cta/B103
Batter, Gyles, Winterbourne Earls, Wilts, 1619 Wilts RO Arch. Sarum/(+ name and date)
Batter, Gyles, Winterbourne Earls, Wilts, 1619 Wilts RO Miscellaneous Index to Wills (name + date)
Batteur, John, Canterbury Holy Cross Westgate, Kent, 1614 CKS PRC2/17/13
Batthurst, Thomas, esquire, Goudhurst, Kent, 1639 CKS PRC1/2/11
Battie, Joane, widow, Nocton, Lincs, 1627 Lincs RO Ad/Ac/20b/6
Battie, Robert, Gainsborough (Thonock), Lincs, 1662 Lincs RO Ad/Ac/41/63
Battin, Henry, husbandman, Appleton, Berks, 1699 Berks RO D/A1/179/120C
Battinge, Thomas, Launceston, Corn, 1613 Cornwall RO AP/B275/2
Battle, Thomas, Milton next Sittingbourne, Kent, 1680 CKS PRC2/38/103
Battye, John, Owston, Lincs, 1676 Lincs RO Ad/Ac/35/112
Baude, John, joiner, Cambridge St Andrew, Cambs, CUL V.C. Acc./Box3/60
Bauger, Henry, labourer, Horbling, Lincs, 1633 Lincs RO Ad/Ac/23/159
Baugh, Elizabeth, widow, Bristol St James, Glos, Bristol RO 1666/7
Bauldwin/Sewell, Marie, widow, Appleby, Lincs, 1631 Lincs RO Ad/Ac/39/297
Baunton, Thomas eld, Camel, West, Som, 1622 Somerset RO D/D/Cta/B9
Baverstock, Thomas, Porton, Wilts, 1629 Wilts RO Miscellaneous Index to Wills (name + date)
Bavin, Thomas, widower, Ruislip, London & Middlesex, 1694 PRO PROB32/32/107

Bawcomb, John, Goudhurst, Kent, 1675 CKS PRC2/36/13
Bawcombe, John, Stalisfield, Kent, 1594 CKS PRC2/6/47
Bawden, Richard, Ladock, Corn, 1615 Cornwall RO AP/B333
Bawden, Robert, 1591 Lancs RO (Name of Deceased) D.R.C.H. 1591
Bawden, William, Kea, Corn, 1621 Cornwall RO AP/B547
Bawdon, John, Spaxton, Som, 1611 Somerset RO D/D/Cta/B81
Bawdrie, Johnne, Leake, Lincs, 1578 Lincs RO Ad/Ac/2b/22a
Bawdrye, John, Leake, Lincs, 1577 Lincs RO Ad/Ac/2b/64
Bawerstock, Thomas, Porton, Wilts, 1629 Wilts RO Arch. Sarum/(+ name and date)
Bawler, John, Beer Hackett, Dors, 1631 Wilts RO Miscellaneous Index to Wills (name + date)
Bawtree, John, Leake, Lincs, 1626 Lincs RO Ad/Ac/20/62
Bawtree, William, Boston, Lincs, 1649 Lincs RO Ad/Ac/30/17
Bawtrie, Andrew, Whaplode, Lincs, 1640 Lincs RO Ad/Ac/27/43
Bawtry, Abraham, Skirbeck, Lincs, 1631 Lincs RO Ad/Ac/23/17
Bax, John, mariner, Rainham, Kent, 1674 CKS PRC2/36/16
Bax, John, Littlebourne, Kent, 1683 CKS PRC1/15/92
Bax, Marrian, Rainham, Kent, 1674 CKS PRC2/36/17
Bax, Raymond + Julian, Woodnesborough, Kent, 1587 CKS PRC2/4/432
Bax, Simon eld, yeoman, Woodnesborough, Kent, 1623 CKS PRC2/23/37
Bax, Thomas, St Peter in Thanet, Kent, 1626 CKS PRC2/25/15
Bax, Thomas, Ash next Sandwich, Kent, 1688 CKS PRC20/13/579
Bax, William, Ash next Sandwich, Kent, 1641 CKS PRC19/2/4
Baxe, Elizabeth, widow, Staple next Wingham, Kent, 1600 CKS PRC21/16/184
Baxley, John, Dover, Kent, 1636 CKS PRC20/10/112
Baxley, John, Whitstable, Kent, 1647 CKS PRC1/7/73
Baxster, Margaret, Hundon, Suff, 1521 Suff RO(B) RO IC500/2/14/35
Baxted, James, bricklayer, Bearsted, Kent, 1676 CKS PRC2/37/4
Baxter, Elizabeth, Wavertree, Lancs, 1666 Lancs RO (Name of Deceased) D.R.C.H. 1665-66
Baxter, Gerard, Hackthorne, Lincs, 1612 Lincs RO Ad/Ac/8a/344
Baxter, James, yeoman, Coldred, Kent, 1641 CKS PRC1/4/11
Baxter, Jane, Helpringham, Lincs, 1613 Lincs RO Ad/Ac/12/131
Baxter, John, degrees: 'M.A.',
Cambs 1619 CUL V.C.Acc./Box1/5
Baxter, John, gentleman, Ranby, Lincs, 1632 Lincs RO Ad/Ac/24/528
Baxter, John, tailor, Hale, Great, Lincs, 1639 Lincs RO Ad/Ac/26/222
Baxter, John, tailor: 'merchant tailor', York Holy Trinity, Goodramgate, Yorks, 1747 Borthwick Test C.P. 1747/1
Baxter, Richard, Sempringham (Pointon), Lincs, 1633 Lincs RO Ad/Ac/23/181
Baxter, Robert, Sempringham (Pointon), Lincs, 1670 Lincs RO Ad/Ac/32/154
Baxter, Thomas, tailor, St Laurence Thanet, Kent, 1618 CKS PRC2/20/308
Baxter, Thomas, maltster, Clewer, Berks, 1683 Berks RO D/A1/179/4D
Baxter, Thomas, miller, Wolstanton (Tunstall), Staffs, 1834 LJRO/B/C/5/1834/4b
Baxter, William, Norwich St George, Norf, 1673 Norfolk RO NCC INV/58/30
Baxter, William, Davington, Kent, 1681 CKS PRC2/39/145
Bayard, Amy, widow, Maidstone, Kent, 1578 CKS PRC21/4/119
Baye/Antonye, John, Worcester St Martin, Worcs, Worcs RO 008.7 BA3585/838/59
Bayes, John, Maidstone, Kent, 1596 CKS PRC21/14/27
Baylee, Richard, Shepton Mallet, Som, 1630 Somerset RO D/D/Cta/B59
Bayles, John, Whichford, Warks, 1608 Worcs RO 008.7 BA3585/839/443
Bayles, Philip, yeoman, Woolley, Hunts, 1681 Hunts RO/Acc58/156(15)
Bayley, Edward, Moreton Corbet, Shrops, 1663 LJRO:cards/1663/6
Bayley, George, Bishopstoke, Hants, 1664 Hants RO 21M65 D8/183
Bayley, Henry, Sellindge, Kent, 1620 CKS PRC2/20/166
Bayley, John, Crich, Derby, 1744 LJRO/B/C/5/1744/169
Bayley, John, farmer, Edgmond (Pickstock), Shrops, 1776 LJRO/B/C/5/1776/9

[Bayley:]
Bayley, Mary, spinster, Badsworth, Yorks, 1811 Borthwick Test C.P. 1811/1
Bayley, Robert, carrier, Odd Rode St Thomas, Ches, 1772 Cheshire RO (Name) W.C. 1772-3
Bayley, Thomas, Coates, Great, Lincs, 1618 Lincs RO Ad/Ac/14/99
Bayley, Thomas, Stoughton, Sussex, 1684 W. Suss RO EpI/33/1684/22
Bayley, William, Swineshead, Lincs, 1638 Lincs RO Ad/Ac/25/45
Bayley, William, butcher, Lichfield, Staffs, 1715 LJRO/B/C/5/1715/1
Bayley, William, Middleton, Lancs, 1794 Lancs RO (Name of Deceased) D.R.C.H. 1795
Bayley, see Clark,
Baylie, Avis, widow, Bobbing, Kent, 1595 CKS PRC2/8/183
Baylie, Bartholomew, yeoman, Funtington, Sussex, 1673 W. Suss RO EpI/33/1673/21
Baylie, David, yeoman, Tilehurst, Berks, 1601 Berks RO D/A1/175/172A
Baylie, Gregorye, Chilham, Kent, 1611 CKS PRC2/17/183
Baylie, Henrie, Canterbury St Alphege, Kent, 1590 CKS PRC21/10/169
Baylie, John, Benenden, Kent, 1597 CKS PRC2/9/45
Baylie, John, Upton Lovell, Wilts, 1616 Wilts RO Miscellaneous Index to Wills (name + date)
Baylie, John, gentleman, Banbury, Oxon, 1618 Oxon RO MSS Wills Pec 32/4/68
Baylie, Richard, St Albans St Stephens, Herts, 1561 Herts RO ASA25/456
Baylie, Richard, Faversham, Kent, 1612 CKS PRC2/16/87
Baylie, Richard, Slindon, Sussex, 1617 W. Suss RO EpIV/10/1/47
Baylie, Richarde, Digby, Lincs, 1603 Lincs RO Ad/Ac/5/137
Baylie, Robarte, Dover St Mary, Kent, 1603 CKS PRC21/16/122
Baylie, Robert, Newport, Hants, 1624 Hants RO 21M65 D8/2B
Baylie, Samuel eld, Cranbrook, Kent, 1667 CKS PRC1/11/102
Baylie, Thomas, Staplehurst, Kent, 1604 CKS PRC2/13/105
Baylie, Thomas, St Peter in Thanet, Kent, 1611 CKS PRC2/16/98
Baylie, William, Kidlington, Oxon, 1641 Oxon RO MSS Wills 295/3/98
Baylie, see Boys,
Baylies, John, Upton on Severn, Worcs, 1684 Worcs RO 008.7 BA3585/837/bdl 4
Baylies, Morgan, Swerford, Oxon, Oxon RO MSS Wills 295/3/59
Baylies, Richard, Powick, Worcs, 1682 Worcs RO 008.7 BA3585/837/bdl 3
Baylies, William, Warwick, Warks, 1684 Worcs RO 008.7 BA3585/837/bdl 4
Bayliffe, Matthew, Slaughterford, Wilts, 1626 Wilts RO Arch. Wilts.(name + date)
Baylis, Richard, labourer, Eydon, Northants, 1779 Northants RO X954/21/40
Bayly, Christopher, Maiden Bradley, Wilts, 1630 Wilts RO Arch. Sarum/(+ name and date)
Bayly, Edward, Godmersham, Kent, CKS PRC20/8/29
Bayly, Edward, mariner, Bristol, Glos, Bristol RO 1723/3
Bayly, Elizabeth, widow, Winterbourne (Hambrook), Glos, Bristol RO 1677/60
Bayly, George, apothecary, Milton next Sittingbourne, Kent, 1683 CKS PRC2/40/96
Bayly, John eld, Hernhill, Kent, 1582 CKS PRC21/6/183
Bayly, Michaell, Folkestone, Kent, 1663 CKS PRC1/9/83
Bayly, Nicholas, Westbourne, Sussex, 1614 W. Suss RO EpI/33/1613/29
Bayly, Thomas, Faversham, Kent, 1635 CKS PRC2/33/7
Bayly, William, Watford, Herts, 1558 Herts RO ASA25/271
Bayly, William, Saxby, Lincs, 1669 Lincs RO Ad/Ac/33/93
Bayly, William, Faversham, Kent, 1670 CKS PRC1/15/5
Bayly/Fox, Isabell, widow, Laughton, Lincs, 1632 Lincs RO Ad/Ac/39/313
Bayly/Whitman, Margaret + Thomas, Benenden, Kent, 1630 CKS PRC2/30/26
Baynes, John, Claypole, Lincs, 1613 Lincs RO Ad/Ac/12/39
Baynham, PRO PROB32/18/148
Baynton, George, Fenton, Lincs, 1623 Lincs RO Ad/Ac/8c/91
Baynton, William, Hungerford, Berks, 1638 Wilts RO Miscellaneous Index to Wills (name + date)
Baytes, Henry, Minting, Lincs, 1619 Lincs RO Ad/Ac/15/51
Baytupp, Thomas, Tenterden, Kent, 1671 Lambeth Palace Arches G26/2
Beach, Anne, Woodford (West Farndon), Northants, 1680 Northants RO NWill A/C/8

Beachman, William + Ellenore, Hythe West, Kent, 1609 CKS PRC2/15/35
Beacocke, Thomas, Torksey, Lincs, 1667 Lincs RO Ad/Ac/33/32
Beacon, Edmund, Congresbury, Som, 1592 Somerset RO D/D/Cta/B93
Beadells, John, Earith, Hunts, 1679 Hunts RO/Acc58/138(6)
Beadle, George, yeoman, Burton Coggles, Lincs, 1637 Lincs RO Ad/Ac/25/15
Beadle, John, Ivychurch, Kent, 1646 CKS PRC19/2/104
Beadle, Roberte, New Romney, Kent, CKS PRC21/4/167
Beadles, Robert, Grafham, Hunts, 1688 Hunts RO/Acc58/270(263)
Beadles, Thomas, Alconbury Weston, Hunts, 1676 Hunts RO/Acc58/76(156)
Beake, Weston, Som, 1599 Somerset RO D/D/Cta/B30
Beake, Anne, Wickhambreaux, Kent, 1604 CKS PRC2/13/42
Beake, Aphra, mrs/widow, Canterbury St Margaret, Kent, 1686 CKS PRC20/13/483
Beake, Frances, spinster, Woodnesborough, Kent, 1624 CKS PRC2/23/54
Beake, Margaret, widow, Canterbury St Mildred, Kent, 1672 CKS PRC2/35/118
Beake, Robert, yeoman, Ickham, Kent, 1679 CKS PRC20/12/254
Beake, Robert eld, mr, Canterbury St Mildred, Kent, 1665 CKS PRC1/11/7
Beake, Thomas, yeoman, Ickham, Kent, 1687 CKS PRC20/13/575
Beake, Thomas eld, Wickhambreaux, Kent, 1569 CKS PRC2/1/22
Beaker, John, Malmesbury, Wilts, 1636 Wilts RO Arch. Wilts.(name + date)
Beale, Alexander, Maidstone, Kent, 1619 CKS PRC20/4/13
Beale, Ambrose, Chewton Mendip, Som, 1625 Somerset RO D/D/Cta/B15
Beale, Angell, widow, Sandwich, Kent, 1596 CKS PRC2/9/19
Beale, Clement, Hythe St Leonard, Kent, 1604 CKS PRC21/17/275
Beale, Edward, Whitton, Lincs, 1600 Lincs RO Ad/Ac/5/489
Beale, Edward, gentleman, Faversham, Kent, 1626 CKS PRC20/7/219
Beale, Edwarde, Cranbrook, Kent, 1616 CKS PRC2/20/206
Beale, Hughe, Canterbury Holy Cross Westgate, Kent, 1586 CKS PRC2/4/84
Beale, John, Biddenden, Kent, 1632 CKS PRC2/31/91
Beale, John, clergy: 'clerk/vicar/bachelor', Bromley, London & Middlesex, 1684 PRO PROB32/23/38
Beale, Nathaniel, weaver: 'worsted weaver', Norwich St Peter per Mountgate, Norf, 1728 Norfolk RO NCC INV/78A/95
Beale, Richard, Witham, South, Lincs, 1636 Lincs RO Ad/Ac/24/261
Beale, Robert, Brinkworth, Wilts, 1619 Wilts RO Arch. Wilts.(name + date)
Beale, Robert, Lea & Cleverton, Wilts, 1630 Wilts RO Arch. Wilts.(name + date)
Beale, Robert, Quadring, Lincs, 1643 Lincs RO Ad/Ac/28/4
Beale, Robert, yeoman, Berrow, Worcs, 1646 Worcs RO 008.7 BA3585/837/bdl 1
Beale, Thomas, Cranbrook, Kent, 1614 CKS PRC2/18/96
Beale, Thomas, Sutton, Sussex, 1671 W. Suss RO EpI/33/1671/5
Beale, Thomas, surgeon, Lechlade, Glos, 1833 GRO GDR/B4/2/B76
Beale, William, Hythe St Leonard, Kent, 1614 CKS PRC20/2/468
Beale, William, Sandwich, Kent, 1645 CKS PRC1/7/38
Beamond, Thomas, Moorlinch, Som, 1590 Somerset RO D/D/Cta/B83
Beamont, John, husbandman, Hethe, Oxon, 1640 Oxon RO MSS Wills 295/3/96
Beamont, John, Stanton, Fen, Hunts, 1699 Hunts RO/Acc58/285
Beamont, see Collard,
Beane, Augustine, Lympne, Kent, 1685 CKS PRC2/40/170
Beane, Edward, Elham, Kent, 1591 CKS PRC2/5/212
Beane, Elie, widow, Folkestone, Kent, 1611 CKS PRC2/15/9
Beane, Elizabeth, widow, Aunsby, Lincs, 1622 Lincs RO Ad/Ac/17/15
Beane, Henrye, Goodnestone next Wingham, Kent, 1615 CKS PRC20/3/330
Beane, John, Newington next Hythe, Kent, 1603 CKS PRC2/14/73
Beane, John, Elham, Kent, 1617 CKS PRC2/20/253
Beane, John, Charing, Kent, 1623 CKS PRC20/6/416
Beane, John, Hythe St Leonard, Kent, 1629 CKS PRC20/8/77

[Beane:]
Beane, John, weaver, Canterbury St Mildred, Kent, 1640 CKS PRC1/2/12
Beane, John, Elham, Kent, 1667 CKS PRC1/12/11
Beane, John, bachelor, Blean, Kent, 1667 CKS PRC1/12/12
Beane, John, Hurst, Kent, 1678 CKS PRC2/38/9
Beane, Leonard, Sandon, Herts, 1639 Herts RO AHH23/112
Beane, Mary, widow, Waldershare, Kent, 1661 CKS PRC1/8/89
Beane, Robert, Stourmouth, Kent, 1603 CKS PRC2/14/80
Beane, Robert, Lyminge, Kent, 1630 CKS PRC20/8/71
Beane, Robert, Wingham, Kent, 1682 CKS PRC20/13/228
Beane, Robert, husbandman, Hernhill, Kent, 1683 CKS PRC20/13/303
Beane, Roger, Titchfield, Hants, 1679 Hants RO 21m65 D8/304
Beane, Simon, Elham, Kent, 1586 CKS PRC2/4/370
Beane, William, Sandwich, Kent, 1596 CKS PRC2/8/3
Beane, William, Cheriton, Kent, 1613 CKS PRC2/17/151
Beane, William, Canterbury St Andrew, Kent, 1674 CKS PRC2/36/19
Beane, William, Tonge, Kent, 1694 CKS PRC2/42/59
Beane, William, Folkestone, Kent, 1709 CKS PRC1/17/1
Beaney, Joseph, New Romney, Kent, 1710 CKS PRC19/6/37
Beard, George, university: 'Fellow of Exeter College, Oxford/B.D.', Oxford (Exeter College), Oxon, 1639 Bodleian HYP B8/9-11
Beard, Henry, husbandman, Preston next Wingham, Kent, 1669 CKS PRC1/14/7
Beard, James, Rolvenden, Kent, 1616 CKS PRC2/20/264
Beard, James, Henley, Oxon, 1628 Oxon RO MSS Wills 76/3/36
Beard, John, East Sutton, Kent, 1620 CKS PRC2/20/368
Beard, John, Canterbury St Paul, Kent, 1633 CKS PRC2/32/11
Beard, John, Randwick, Glos, 1685 GRO GDR/B4/2/B185
Beard, Marie, Preston next Wingham, Kent, 1670 CKS PRC1/15/6
Beard, Thomas, Youlgreave, Derby, 1684 LJRO/B/C/5/1683/2
Beard, William, husbandman, Shiplake, Oxon, 1628 Oxon RO MSS Wills 160/3/22
Beard, William, Canterbury St Mary Bredman, Kent, 1676 CKS PRC2/37/11
Beard, William, yeoman, Shiplake, Oxon, 1689 Oxon RO MSS Wills 161/2/5
Beardew, Ellen, Warboys, Hunts, 1685 Hunts RO/Acc58/258(250)
Beardmore, George, Ashley, Staffs, 1692 LJRO/B/C/5/1692/9
Beardmore, Jane, Westcroft?, 1676 LJRO:cards/1676/4
Beardow, Ralph eld, miner, Ashover (Little Moor), Derby, 1778 LJRO/B/C/5/1778/7
Beardsell, John, clothier, Almondbury (Lane), Yorks, 1818 Borthwick Test C.P. 1818/14
Beardsworth, Edward, cordwainer, Penwortham, Lancs, 1778 Lancs RO (Name of Deceased) D.R.C.H. 1776-79
Beardwood, Thomas, Leyland (Wheelton), Lancs, 1770 Lancs RO (Name of Deceased) D.R.C.H. 1770
Beare, Thomas, Padworth, Berks, 1599 Berks RO D/A1/175/157A
Bearecrofte, Christopher, Hanbury, Worcs, Worcs RO 008.7 BA3585/839/333
Bearidge, Thomas, Torksey, Lincs, 1615 Lincs RO Ad/Ac/8b/87
Bearling, Thomas, Faversham, Kent, 1669 CKS PRC1/14/8
Bearnes, Dorothie, Cranbrook, Kent, 1597 CKS PRC2/9/17
Beasley, John, Huyton, Lancs, Lancs RO (Name of Deceased) D.R.C.H. 1581
Beaton, John, Wells St Cuthbert, Som, 1612 Somerset RO D/D/Cta/B37
Beaton, John, St Martin in the Fields, London & Middlesex, 1706 Greater London RO AM/PP/Box 1695-1706 pt (uncatalogued)
Beaton, Thomas, Mudford, Som, 1588 Somerset RO D/D/Cta/B50
Beaton, Thomas, Burmarsh, Kent, 1688 CKS PRC2/41/117
Beaton, William, tailor, Wheathill, Som, 1588 Somerset RO D/D/Cta/B54
Beaumont, Francis, knight, Washingborough, Lincs, 1626 Lincs RO Ad/Ac/20/32
Beaumont, Thomas, degrees: 'Doctor of Physic', Canterbury St Andrew, Kent, 1666 CKS PRC1/11/103

[Beaumont:]
Beaumont, Thomas, baronet, Belton (Gracedieu), Leics, 1686 Leics RO Administrators Accounts 1682-86 f49
Beauty, John, Faversham, Kent, 1672 CKS PRC2/35/108
Beaver, Henry, Langtoft, Lincs, 1653 Lincs RO Ad/Ac/29/17
Beavis, Jacob, merchant, Cley next the Sea, Norf, 1736 Norfolk RO ANW/23/22/13
Becham, Henry, Whiteparish, Wilts, 1641 Wilts RO Arch. Sarum/(+ name and date)
Beche, Walter, Redbourn (Bestney End), Herts, 1602 Herts RO ASA25/4755
Beck, Edward, Winterton, Lincs, 1676 Lincs RO Ad/Ac/35/108
Beck, John, gentleman, Leigh, Little, Ches, 1807 Cheshire RO (Name) W.C. 1806-7
Beck, Robert, husbandman, Kirkby Green, Lincs, 1641 Lincs RO Ad/Ac/27/26
Beck, Thomas, Austrey, Warks, 1682 LJRO/B/C/5/1682/8
Beck, William, Dunston, Lincs, 1627 Lincs RO Ad/Ac/20/92
Beck, William, Winteringham, Lincs, 1662 Lincs RO Ad/Ac/41/27
Becke, Isabell, Anwick, Lincs, 1639 Lincs RO Ad/Ac/26/177
Becke, John, bachelor, Saxby, Lincs, 1626 Lincs RO Ad/Ac/39/73
Becke, John, yeoman, Worlaby, Lincs, 1673 Lincs RO Ad/Ac/35/9
Becke, Robert, Scotter, Lincs, 1597 Lincs RO Ad/Ac/37/33
Becke, Thomas, Longdon, Worcs, Worcs RO 008.7 BA3585/839/401a
Becke, William, Orby, Lincs, 1644 Lincs RO Ad/Ac/28/95
Becke/Oliver, Marie, Donington, Lincs, 1632 Lincs RO Ad/Ac/23/22
Becket, Abraham, Boxley, Kent, 1688 CKS PRC2/41/115
Becket, Isaac, Bearsted, Kent, 1665 CKS PRC1/11/8
Becket, John, Brailes, Warks, 1682 Worcs RO 008.7 BA3585/837/bdl 3
Beckett, Christopher, Milton next Sittingbourne, Kent, 1617 CKS PRC2/20/290
Beckett, Edward, Hartlip, Kent, 1596 CKS PRC2/8/123
Beckett, Edward, Stockbury, Kent, 1664 CKS PRC1/10/11
Beckett, Edward, Stockbury, Kent, 1664 CKS PRC19/3/51
Beckett, Edward eld, Stockbury, Kent, 1629 CKS PRC2/29/12
Beckett, John, Boxley, Kent, 1682 CKS PRC2/40/11
Beckett, John, Wootton, Northants, 1684 Northants RO NWill A/C/71
Beckett, John, gentleman, Newhall, Ches, 1747 Cheshire RO (Name) W.C. 1747
Beckett, Peter, surgeon, Davenham (Stanthorne), Ches, 1738 Cheshire RO (Name) W.C. 1737
Beckett, Robert, Faversham, Kent, 1668 CKS PRC1/13/8a
Beckett, Robert, blacksmith, Faversham, Kent, 1668 CKS PRC1/13/8
Beckett, Symon, Sittingbourne, Kent, 1579 CKS PRC2/1/230
Beckett, Thomas, Burton by Lincoln, Lincs, 1597 Lincs RO Ad/Ac/37/52
Beckett, William, Middlewich, Ches, 1593 Cheshire RO (Name) W.C. 1592
Beckett, William, Milton next Sittingbourne, Kent, 1617 CKS PRC2/20/359
Beckett, see Brockas,
Beckford, Elizabeth, Hurley, Berks, 1633 Berks RO D/A1/177/22A
Beckford, Ralph, bookbinder, Oxford (University), Oxon, 1673 Bodleian HYP B8/12-15
Beckford, Rooke, husbandman, Lewknor, Oxon, 1637 Oxon RO MSS Wills 295/3/70
Beckingham, Anthony, Blewbury, Berks, 1675 Wilts RO Miscellaneous Index to Wills (name + date)
Beckingham/Longe, William, Welbourn, Lincs, 1586 Lincs RO Ad/Ac/2C/105
Beckit, Thomas, Burton by Lincoln, Lincs, 1632 Lincs RO Ad/Ac/39/272
Beckne, Catharyne, stranger, Canterbury St Alphege, Kent, 1598 CKS PRC21/14/575
Beckwith, Thomas, mariner: 'master of a merchant ship', Bermondsey, St Mary Magdalen, Surrey, 1705 PRO PROB5/955
Becon, John, surgeon: 'ship surgeon', Stepney (Stebenhythe), London & Middlesex, 1678 PRO PROB32/15/94
Bedall, Edmund, Hackthorne, Lincs, 1594 Lincs RO Ad/Ac/5/269
Bedell, Henry, Linsted, Kent, 1597 CKS PRC2/9/63
Bedenson, Robert, husbandman, Mumby, Lincs, 1671 Lincs RO Ad/Ac/33/171
Bedenton, Jeames, Newnham, Kent, 1597 CKS PRC2/9/47

[Bedford:]
Bedford, Aman, Hibaldstow, Lincs, 1676 Lincs RO Ad/Ac/42/12
Bedford, Francis, Northmoor, Oxon, 1624 Oxon RO MSS Wills 295/2/80
Bedford, John, Bourton, Black, Oxon, 1639 Oxon RO MSS Wills 295/3/82
Bedford, John, Dover St Mary, Kent, 1640 CKS PRC19/1/15
Bedford, John, Hemingford Grey, Hunts, 1685 Hunts RO/Acc58/259(251)
Bedford, Thomas, Stanford in the Vale, Berks, 1592 Berks RO D/A1/175/132B
Bedford, William, labourer, Whitstable, Kent, 1678 CKS PRC2/37/115
Bedforde, Robert, Standlake, Oxon, Oxon RO MSS Wills 295/3/51
Bedgeant, Richard, Charlton nr Dover, Kent, 1643 CKS PRC1/6/48
Bedingfeild, Anthony, husbandman, Throwleigh, Kent, 1679 CKS PRC2/38/100
Bedingfeild, Peter, gentleman, Chart, Great, Kent, 1674 CKS PRC2/36/11
Bedingfeild, Thomas, gentleman, Smeeth, Kent, 1628 CKS PRC20/8/33
Bedingfeild, William, gentleman, Sandwich, Kent, 1675 CKS PRC2/36/153
Bedle, Mercy, widow, New Romney, Kent, 1620 CKS PRC20/5/13
Bedle, Rose, New Romney, Kent, 1597 CKS PRC21/14/179
Bedle, William, mayor, New Romney, Kent, 1594 CKS PRC21/12/364
Bedman, William, Norton Juxta Twycross, Leics, 1639 Leics RO PR/I/41A/29
Bedwell, Martin, Oxford St Michael, Oxon, 1648 Oxon RO MSS Wills 295/4/33
Bee, Alice, widow, Chichester St Andrew, Sussex, 1616 W. Suss RO EpIII/9/1/14
Bee, John, Kirton, Lincs, 1632 Lincs RO Ad/Ac/23/5
Bee, John, Coleby, Lincs, 1679 Lincs RO Ad/Ac/43/92
Bee, William, clergy: 'clerk', Newton, Lincs, 1597 Lincs RO Ad/Ac/37/98
Beech, Francis, yeoman, Barkwith, East, Lincs, 1680 Lincs RO Ad/Ac/34/57
Beech, James, tailor, Farlesthorpe, Lincs, 1628 Lincs RO Ad/Ac/22/27
Beech, James, Stallingborough, Lincs, 1641 Lincs RO Ad/Ac/27/224
Beech, James, Fotherby, Lincs, 1652 Lincs RO Ad/Ac/29/21
Beech, John, Stoke-upon-Trent, Staffs, 1676 LJRO:cards/1676/5
Beech, John, mercer, Donington, Lincs, 1717 Lincs RO Ad/Ac/45/7
Beech, Ralph, Burslem, Staffs, 1676 LJRO:cards/1676/6
Beech, Robert, Fosdyke, Lincs, 1612? Lincs RO Ad/Ac/11/100
Beeche, William, Letcombe Bassett, Berks, 1586 Berks RO D/A2/C24/f121-2
Beecher, Joseph, Sittingbourne, Kent, 1622 CKS PRC2/23/31
Beecher, Wyllyam, Headcorn, Kent, 1611 CKS PRC2/16/94
Beeching, Alice, widow, Tenterden, Kent, 1624 CKS PRC2/23/43
Beeching, Andrewe, Hawkhurst, Kent, 1600 CKS PRC2/13/52
Beeching, Arthur, bachelor, Bobbing, Kent, 1670 CKS PRC1/15/7
Beeching, Joan, widow, Ashford, Kent, 1616 CKS PRC2/20/316
Beeching, John, Cranbrook, Kent, 1625 CKS PRC2/25/5
Beeching, Nicholas, Wye, Kent, 1640 CKS PRC1/2/13
Beeching, Richard, Lydd, Kent, 1612 CKS PRC20/2/440
Beeching, Richard, cordwainer, Tenterden, Kent, 1669 CKS PRC1/14/9
Beeching, Stephen, Boxley, Kent, 1629 CKS PRC20/8/49
Beeching, Vincent, Aldington, Kent, 1614 CKS PRC20/3/132
Beechinge, Elizabeth, Newenden, Kent, 1619 CKS PRC2/20/224
Beechynge, Elizabethe, widow, Hernhill, Kent, 1598 CKS PRC21/14/252
Beedinge, William, clergy: 'rector', Burton, Sussex, 1633 W. Suss RO EpI/33/1633/15
Beedle, Edward jun, yeoman, Piddington, Oxon, 1684 Oxon RO MSS Wills 77/2/18
Beedle, Robert, Upham, Hants, 1665 Hants RO 21M65 D8/191
Beeham, William, Holbeach, Lincs, 1637 Lincs RO Ad/Ac/25/418
Beekeman, Daniel, distiller, Maidstone, Kent, 1672 CKS PRC20/12/39
Beell, John, Stickney, Lincs, 1630 Lincs RO Ad/Ac/23/102
Beeney, John + Jane, Clevedon, Som, 1590 Somerset RO D/D/Cta/B84
Beere, George, Whitfield alias Beauxfield, Kent, 1613 CKS PRC2/17/260
Beere, George, Bridge, Kent, 1614 CKS PRC2/20/188
Beere, Gregory, Sandwich St Peter, Kent, 1611 CKS PRC2/15/41

Beere, Robert, Wye, Kent, 1586 CKS PRC2/4/214
Beere/Abeere, Andrew, Sandwich, Kent, 1627 CKS PRC2/28/6
Beesby, Charles, Langton, Lincs, 1644 Lincs RO Ad/Ac/28/67
Beeseley, Mary, widow, Sunningwell (Bayworth), Berks, 1646 Berks RO D/A1/44/175C
Beesely, William, Ely, Cambs, 1680 PRO PROB5/995
Beeston, Anne, Utterby, Lincs, 1649 Lincs RO Ad/Ac/30/202
Beeston, John, Mugginton, Derby, 1680 LJRO:cards/1680/3
Beeston, John, Witchingham, Great, Norf, 1765 Norfolk RO ANW/23/25/79
Beeston, Joseph, gentleman, Mugginton (Wild Park), Derby, 1824 LJRO/B/C/5/1824/3a
Beeston, Thomas, Coningsby, Lincs, 1612 Lincs RO Ad/Ac/11/17
Beetch, John, Harpswell, Lincs, 1631 Lincs RO Ad/Ac/39/257
Beetenson, Charles, Forton, Staffs, 1719 LJRO/B/C/5/1719/4
Beety, Edward, yeoman, Stickney, Lincs, 1668 Lincs RO Ad/Ac/33/39
Beevell, Vincent, Ash next Sandwich, Kent, 1615 CKS PRC20/3/258
Begell, William, mariner: 'seafaring man', Milton next Sittingbourne, Kent, 1671 CKS PRC2/35/14
Behage, Peter, Ramsey, Hunts, 1676 Hunts RO/Acc58/25(190)
Beighton, Henry, yeoman, Chilvers Coton (Griff), Warks, 1731 LJRO/B/C/5/1733/7a
Beighton, John, Wingfield, North, Derby, 1684 LJRO/B/C/5/1683/3
Beighton, Thomas, Mildenhall, Suff, 1751 Suff RO(B) IC500/3/50/13
Bekyngham, John, Moreton, North, Berks, Berks RO D/A1/1/72R
Belbin, Nicholas, gentleman, Whitechapel, London & Middlesex, 1709 PRO PROB32/52/46
Belchamber, Richard, Lydd, Kent, 1588 CKS PRC21/9/72
Belchamber, Robert, Petworth, Sussex, 1617 W. Suss RO EpI/33/1617/32
Belchambers, Jane, widow, Linton, Kent, 1679 CKS PRC2/38/106
Belcher, John, husbandman, Thatcham, Berks, 1689 Berks RO D/A1/179/56C
Beldom, Nicholas eld, yeoman, Old Romney, Kent, 1668 CKS PRC1/13/9
Beldon, William, St Albans St Michaels, Herts, 1627 Herts RO ASA25/4840
Belfeild, Charles, gentleman, Owston, Lincs, 1600 Lincs RO Ad/Ac/37/94
Belfeild, Charles, Gainsborough, Lincs, 1609 Lincs RO Ad/Ac/8a/303
Belfeild, Mary, spinster, Belton, Lincs, 1633 Lincs RO Ad/Ac/23/165
Belhew, Francis, Minster in Thanet, Kent, 1681 CKS PRC2/39/141
Belke, George, Sheldwich, Kent, 1611 CKS PRC2/15/19
Bell, Anthony, Helpringham, Lincs, 1614 Lincs RO Ad/Ac/12/204
Bell, Catherine, Shrewsbury St Julian, Shrops, 1667 LJRO:cards/1667/7
Bell, Edward, Elsham, Lincs, 1639? Lincs RO Ad/Ac/26/274
Bell, Edward, yeoman, Kington St Michael, Wilts, 1641 Wilts RO Arch. Wilts.(name + date)
Bell, George, Ruskington, Lincs, 1611 Lincs RO Ad/Ac/10/8
Bell, Gervase, Swinderby, Lincs, 1669 Lincs RO Ad/Ac/32/56
Bell, John, Canterbury St Margaret, Kent, 1595 CKS PRC2/8/375
Bell, John, Brabourne, Kent, 1687 CKS PRC2/41/90
Bell, John, university: 'Fellow of Sidney Sussex College, Cambridge/clerk/B.D.' Cambridge (Sidney Sussex College), Cambs, 1730 CUL V.C. Acc./Box3/5
Bell, Leonard, Whaplode, Lincs, 1638 Lincs RO Ad/Ac/25/258
Bell, Margerie, Bremhill, Wilts, 1629 Wilts RO Arch. Wilts.(name + date)
Bell, Michaell, tailor, Barton on Humber, Lincs, 1633 Lincs RO Ad/Ac/23/162
Bell, Miles, clergy: 'clerk', Croston, Lancs, 1725 Lancs RO (Name of Deceased) D.R.C.H. 1725
Bell, Richard, Ruckinge, Kent, 1599 CKS PRC2/10/296
Bell, Richard, Billinghay, Lincs, 1601 Lincs RO Ad/Ac/5/409
Bell, Richard, Kirkby la Thorpe, Lincs, 1635 Lincs RO Ad/Ac/24/300
Bell, Richard, Wrawby, Lincs, 1649 Lincs RO Ad/Ac/30/168
Bell, Robert, Kirmington, Lincs, 1612 Lincs RO Ad/Ac/11/37
Bell, Robert, Benniworth, Lincs, 1637 Lincs RO Ad/Ac/25/437
Bell, Robert, Hale, Great, Lincs, 1698 Lincs RO Ad/Ac/44/171
Bell, Thomas, Garstang, Lancs, Lancs RO (Name of Deceased) D.R.C.H. 1638

[Bell:]
Bell, Thomas, Donington, Lincs, 1629 Lincs RO Ad/Ac/22/119
Bell, Thomas, baker, Norwich St Swithin, Norf, 1737 Norfolk RO ANW/23/22A/44
Bell, Tristram, innholder, Sittingbourne, Kent, 1666 CKS PRC1/11/104
Bell, Walter, Sittingbourne, Kent, 1639 CKS PRC1/2/14
Bell, William, Swinderby, Lincs, 1624 Lincs RO Ad/Ac/19A/100
Bell, William, Carlton, Great, Lincs, 1626 Lincs RO Ad/Ac/20/10
Bell, William, Algarkirk, Lincs, 1634 Lincs RO Ad/Ac/24/73
Bell, William, Kinnersley, Shrops, 1667 LJRO:cards/1667/8
Bell, see Astley,
Bellamie, Jervice, Kettlethorpe, Lincs, 1627 Lincs RO Ad/Ac/39/128
Bellamie, Nathaniel, Branston, Lincs, 1638 Lincs RO Ad/Ac/25/280
Bellamy, Thomas, Claypole, Lincs, 1613 Lincs RO Ad/Ac/12/139
Bellamy, Thomas, Rochester, Kent, late C17th? PRO PROB5/1235
Bellamy, William, Surfleet, Lincs, 1770 Lincs RO Ad/Ac/36/10
Bellamye, John, Norton, Herts, 1593 Herts RO ASA25/1662
Bellases, Elizabeth, spinster, Manchester (Winwick, Hulme), Lancs, 1799 Lancs RO (Name of Deceased) D.R.C.H. 1799
Bellewe, Steven, Theddlethorpe, Lincs, 1637 Lincs RO Ad/Ac/25/461
Bellimye, Christopher, Shadoxhurst, Kent, 1611 CKS PRC2/15/45
Bellinger, Henrye, Newington next Hythe, Kent, 1616 CKS PRC2/20/214
Bellis, Samuel, clergy: 'clerk/reverend', Aston-upon-Mersey, Ches, 1728 Cheshire RO (Name) W.C. 1726
Bellshaw, Robert, Wigan, Lancs, 1678 Lancs RO (Name of Deceased) D.R.C.H. 1678
Bellwood, John, Stepney, London & Middlesex, 1695 PRO PROB32/38/181
Belman, Elizabeth, widow, Faversham, Kent, 1622 CKS PRC20/5/27
Belsey, Roger, Monkton, Kent, 1693 CKS PRC19/5/15
Belsey, William, husbandman, Tilmanstone, Kent, 1669 CKS PRC1/14/10
Belsey, William, Minster in Thanet, Kent, 1706 CKS PRC1/16/62
Belson, John, Towersey, Bucks, 1674 Oxon RO MSS Wills Pec 33/3/22
Beltcher, Cuthbert, husbandman, Hanney, West, Berks, 1676 Berks RO D/A1/178/150A
Belton, David, Snitterby, Lincs, 1639 Lincs RO Ad/Ac/40/254
Belton, Henry, Waddingham, Lincs, 1639 Lincs RO Ad/Ac/40/262
Belton, John, Bourne, Lincs, 1613 Lincs RO Ad/Ac/11/65
Belton, John, Luddington, Lincs, 1684 Lincs RO Ad/Ac/44/132
Belton, Robert, Tealby, Lincs, 1617 Lincs RO Ad/Ac/8b/153
Belwood, Anne, Gainsborough, Lincs, 1661 Lincs RO Ad/Ac/41/14
Belwood, Roger, Gainsborough, Lincs, 1683 Lincs RO Ad/Ac/44/51
Bemrose, Richard, Rasen, Middle, Lincs, 1598 Lincs RO Ad/Ac/4/23
Bemrose, Stephen, Grayingham, Lincs, 1626 Lincs RO Ad/Ac/39/18
Ben, Peter, Wrangle, Lincs, 1612 Lincs RO Ad/Ac/11/41
Benackle, John, Sutterton, Lincs, 1606 Lincs RO Ad/Ac/7/157
Benbowe, Richard, Lydd, Kent, 1629 CKS PRC20/8/61
Bence, Wyllyam, Benenden, Kent, 1596 CKS PRC2/8/262
Benchkyn, Richard, Charing, Kent, 1598 CKS PRC21/14/587
Benchskin, Thomas, Lydd, Kent, 1621 CKS PRC20/5/25
Bend, Anthony, university: 'scholar's servant', Cambridge Holy Sepulchre, Cambs, 1605 c. CUL V.C.Acc./Box1/6
Benden, Anne, widow, Ebony, Kent, 1683 CKS PRC2/40/7
Benden, Edward, Biddenden, Kent, 1612 CKS PRC2/17/372
Benden, Elizabeth, Ashford, Kent, 1682 CKS PRC2/39/136
Benden, Francis, yeoman, Ashford, Kent, 1682 CKS PRC2/40/10
Benden, John, Ebony, Kent, 1672 CKS PRC2/35/114
Benden, Nathaniell, Rolvenden, Kent, 1618 CKS PRC2/20/348
Benden, Richard, Appledore, Kent, 1627 CKS PRC2/28/16
Benden, Thomas, Challock, Kent, 1632 CKS PRC20/10/66

Benden, William, Ebony, Kent, 1626 CKS PRC2/25/8
Bendish, Mary, widow, East Ham, Essex, 1691 Lambeth Palace Arches G41/1
Bendlowes, Catherine, Kirklington (East Tanfield), Yorks, Borthwick Test C.P. 1739/4
Bendrie/Bandrie, Francis, Christian Malford, Wilts, 1674 Wilts RO Miscellaneous Index to Wills (name + date)
Benet, John, Ivychurch, Kent, 1596 CKS PRC21/14/107
Benet, Richard, St Laurence Thanet, Kent, 1584 CKS PRC2/3/57
Benet, Richard, High Halden, Kent, 1590 CKS PRC2/5/217
Benet, Simon, Goudhurst, Kent, 1639 CKS PRC1/2/16
Benfild, John, weaver, Thatcham, Berks, 1636 Berks RO D/A1/177/54A
Benford, Baldwyn, Worcester St Nicholas, Worcs, 1597 Worcs RO 008.7 BA3585/838/121
Benford, Mathew, Ash next Sandwich, Kent, 1671 CKS PRC20/12/5
Benger, John, Dover, Kent, 1629 CKS PRC20/8/67
Benhallicke, John, St Ewe, Corn, 1614 Cornwall RO AP/B347
Benham, John, Bishopstoke, Hants, 1673 Hants RO 21m65 D8/255
Benifold, Roger, Mitcham, Surrey, 1769 Greater London RO DW/OP/1769/10/2
Benington, John, Burton on Stather, Lincs, 1682 Lincs RO Ad/Ac/34/72
Benkyn, Richard, Stone in Oxney, Kent, 1598 CKS PRC2/9/397
Benn, John, Frieston, Lincs, 1623 Lincs RO Ad/Ac/18/37
Bennet, Cutbert, husbandman, Biddestone, Wilts, 1632? Wilts RO Arch. Wilts.(name + date)
Bennet, Edward, Broad Chalke, Wilts, 1633 Wilts RO Miscellaneous Index to Wills (name + date)
Bennet, George, fisherman, St Laurence Thanet, Kent, 1663 CKS PRC1/9/4
Bennet, Henrye, Tenterden, Kent, 1606 CKS PRC20/1/87
Bennet, John, Stone next Faversham, Kent, 1599 CKS PRC2/10/439
Bennet, John, St Laurence Thanet, Kent, 1601 CKS PRC2/12/11
Bennet, John, Brookland, Kent, 1614 CKS PRC2/17/65
Bennet, John, Seend, Wilts, 1614? Wilts RO Miscellaneous Index to Wills (name + date)
Bennet, John, High Halstow, Kent, 1615 CKS PRC2/20/192
Bennet, John, labourer, Reading St Lawrence, Berks, 1626 Berks RO D/A1/176/109
Bennet, Mary, widow, Cranbrook, Kent, 1634 CKS PRC2/32/144
Bennet, Reynold, Upchurch, Kent, 1626 CKS PRC2/25/11
Bennet, Richarde + wife, Newington next Hythe, Kent, 1589 CKS PRC2/4/503
Bennet, Robarte, St Laurence Thanet, Kent, 1603 CKS PRC2/14/60
Bennet, Robert, Poling, Sussex, 1606 W. Suss RO EpI/33/1606/7
Bennet, Susan, widow, High Halstow, Kent, 1639 CKS PRC1/2/17
Bennet, Sybil, widow, Kirtlington (Northbrook), Oxon, 1627 Oxon RO MSS Wills 295/3/5
Bennet, Thomas, Evesham, Worcs, 1596 Worcs RO 008.7 BA3585/838/117
Bennet, Thomas, carpenter, Ashton Keynes, Wilts, 1639 Wilts RO Arch. Wilts.(name + date)
Bennet, Thomas, miller, Chillenden, Kent, 1667 CKS PRC1/12/13
Bennet, Thomas, baronet, Babraham, Cambs, 1675 PRO PROB5/1075
Bennet, Thomas, husbandman, Folkingham, Lincs, 1683 Lincs RO Ad/Ac/44/83
Bennet, Thomas, Morton, Abbots, Worcs, 1686 Worcs RO 008.7 BA3585/830/14
Bennett, Anne, widow, Stepney, London & Middlesex, 1705 PRO PROB32/48/43
Bennett, Arthur, Upchurch, Kent, 1634 CKS PRC2/32/141
Bennett, Charles, butcher, Catworth, Great, Hunts, 1676 Hunts RO/Acc58/79(10)
Bennett, Daniell eld, yeoman, Biddenden, Kent, 1662 CKS PRC1/8/90
Bennett, Edward, yeoman, Brighthampton, Oxon, 1629 Oxon RO MSS Wills 76/3/39
Bennett, George, St Laurence Thanet, Kent, 1612 CKS PRC2/16/15
Bennett, George, St Laurence Thanet, Kent, 1637 CKS PRC2/33/9
Bennett, Henry, Kirdford, Sussex, 1633 W. Suss RO EpI/33/1633/28
Bennett, Humfrey, Hythe St Leonard, Kent, 1619 CKS PRC20/4/21
Bennett, James, Wittersham, Kent, 1620 CKS PRC20/5/9
Bennett, James, Stone, Staffs, 1670 LJRO:cards/1670/9
Bennett, James, Dronfield, Derby, 1678 LJRO:cards/1678/4

[Bennett:]
Bennett, Jane, Cound, Shrops, 1667 LJRO:cards/1667/9
Bennett, Joan, Walberton, Sussex, W. Suss RO EpI/33/1610/7
Bennett, Joan, widow, Aldingbourne, Sussex, 1635 W. Suss RO EpI/33/1635/9
Bennett, John, Snave, Kent, 1597 CKS PRC2/9/61
Bennett, John, Upchurch, Kent, 1605 CKS PRC2/13/89
Bennett, John, St Cleer, Corn, 1608 Cornwall RO AP/B176/1
Bennett, John, Stratton, Corn, 1612 Cornwall RO AP/B294/2
Bennett, John, Bethersden, Kent, 1631 CKS PRC2/31/13
Bennett, John, surgeon, Maidstone, Kent, 1644 CKS PRC19/2/84
Bennett, John, tanner, Ashton Keynes, Wilts, 1674 Wilts RO Miscellaneous Index to Wills (name + date)
Bennett, John, Codford St Mary, Wilts, 1675? Wilts RO Miscellaneous Index to Wills (name + date)
Bennett, John, yeoman, Chislehampton, Oxon, 1676 Oxon RO MSS Wills Pec 65/4/30
Bennett, John, Tollard Royal, Wilts, 1754 Wilts RO Arch. Sarum/(+ name and date)
Bennett, John, yeoman, Taxal, Ches, 1771 Cheshire RO (Name) W.C. 1771
Bennett, Mary, widow, Chislehampton, Oxon, 1633 Oxon RO MSS Wills Pec 65/3/26
Bennett, Mary, widow, Buckland, Berks, 1668 Berks RO D/A1/178/108A
Bennett, Michael, husbandman, Mawgan-in-Pydar, Corn, 1612 Cornwall RO AP/B232/3
Bennett, Nicholas, St Laurence Thanet, Kent, 1607 CKS PRC2/14/26
Bennett, Nicholas, Faversham, Kent, 1634 CKS PRC2/32/140
Bennett, Peter, clergy: 'clerk', Ewell, Kent, 1619 CKS PRC2/20/259
Bennett, Phillipe, Maidstone, Kent, 1579 CKS PRC21/4/150
Bennett, Richard, Woodchurch, Kent, 1608 CKS PRC20/1/398
Bennett, Richard, yeoman, Bampton (Brighthampton), Oxon, 1621 Oxon RO MSS Wills 295/2/70
Bennett, Richard, mariner: 'sailor', St Laurence Thanet, Kent, 1623 CKS PRC2/17/391
Bennett, Richard, Ashington, Sussex, 1632 W. Suss RO EpI/33/1632/31
Bennett, Richard, Goudhurst, Kent, 1639 CKS PRC1/2/15
Bennett, Richard, husbandman, Barkby, Leics, 1671 Leics RO Administrators Accounts 1667-72 f38
Bennett, Richard, St Laurence Thanet, Kent, 1675 CKS PRC2/36/20
Bennett, Robert, Headcorn, Kent, 1612 CKS PRC2/16/43
Bennett, Sidrach, High Halstow, Kent, 1612 CKS PRC2/16/64
Bennett, Thomas, Tenterden, Kent, 1579 CKS PRC2/1/257
Bennett, Thomas, Coates, North, Lincs, 1625 Lincs RO Ad/Ac/19B/78
Bennett, Thomas, Neston (Willaston), Ches, 1626 Cheshire RO (Name) W.C. 1626
Bennett, Thomas, gentleman, Newchurch, Kent, 1629 CKS PRC20/8/19
Bennett, Thomas, Faversham, Kent, 1665 CKS PRC1/11/9
Bennett, Thomas, yeoman, Wroxeter, Shrops, 1675 LJRO:cards/1675/10
Bennett, Thomas, yeoman, Burghfield, Berks, 1679 Berks RO D/A1/178/178C
Bennett, Thomas, gentleman, Goudhurst, Kent, 1681 CKS PRC2/39/138
Bennett, Thomas, merchant: 'silk merchant', Derby, Derby, 1787 LJRO/B/C/5/1787/17
Bennett, William, Dover, Kent, 1607 CKS PRC20/1/217
Bennett, William, Holbeach, Lincs, 1611 Lincs RO Ad/Ac/10/82
Bennett, William, yeoman, Bray, Berks, 1616 Berks RO D/A1/176/52A
Bennett, William, Faversham, Kent, 1639 CKS PRC1/2/18
Bennett, William, Tilton, Leics, 1665 Leics RO Administrators Accounts C17th f23
Bennett, William, Bersted, South, Sussex, 1671 W. Suss RO EpIV/10/2A/10
Bennison, Benjamin, West Ham, Essex, 1796 Greater London RO DL/C/563/70/2
Bennison, Robert, Lenham, Kent, 1712 CKS PRC1/17/49
Bennitland, William, Crowle, Lincs, 1620 Lincs RO Ad/Ac/8b/377
Bensan, Thomas, clergy: 'clerk/rector', Hatford, Berks, 1574 Berks RO D/A2/C15/f100V
Benskin, John, cordwainer, Tenterden, Kent, 1676 CKS PRC2/37/9
Benskin, Nicholas, Biddenden, Kent, 1638 CKS PRC2/34/175
Benskyn, Henry, Stretton en le Field, Derby, 1683 LJRO/B/C/5/1682/9

Benson, Anthony, Swineshead, Lincs, 1638 Lincs RO Ad/Ac/25/491
Benson, Edward, vintner, All Hallows Barking, London & Middlesex, 1689 Lambeth Palace Arches G40/1
Benson, Ellen, widow, Copmanthorpe, Yorks, 1844 Borthwick Test C.P. 1844/5
Benson, John, farmer, Skipton (East Halton), Yorks, 1821 Borthwick Test C.P. 1821/2
Benson, Stephen, Linton, Kent, 1607 CKS PRC2/13/65
Benson, Thomas, yeoman, Ferry Fryston, Yorks, 1773 Borthwick Test C.P. 1773/2
Benstedd, Stephen, Sittingbourne, Kent, 1615 CKS PRC2/20/130
Benstedd, Thomas, Sandwich, Kent, 1617 CKS PRC2/20/270
Bent, George, maltster, Reading, Berks, 1682 PRO PROB32/21/282
Bent, John, Wittering, West, Sussex, 1596 W. Suss RO EpI/33/1596/9
Bent, John, Harborough, Market, Leics, 1640 Leics RO PR/I/41A/47
Bentham, Mary, widow, Croston (Mawdesley), Lancs, 1769 Lancs RO (Name of Deceased) D.R.C.H. 1769-71
Bentley, Mary, widow, Handsworth, Staffs, 1808 LJRO/B/C/5/1808/4
Bentley, Mary, widow, Handsworth, Staffs, 1808 LJRO/B/C/5/1808/5
Bentley, Peter, Helmsley, Yorks, 1748 Borthwick Test C.P. 1747/2
Bentley, Richard, St Ives, Hunts, 1677 Hunts RO/Acc58/92(14)
Bentlie, Mathew, mercer, Banbury, Oxon, 1629 Oxon RO MSS Wills Pec 33/1/4
Bently, Ann, widow, Pluckley, Kent, 1647 CKS PRC1/8/3
Bently, Phillip, Snargate, Kent, 1681 CKS PRC2/39/134
Bentlye, Michael, university: 'Fellow of Christ's College, Cambridge/priest/B.D.' Cambridge (Christ's College), Cambs, 1628 CUL V.C. Acc./Box2/4
Benton, Edmund, husbandman, Wymondley, Great (Titmore Green), Herts, 1638 Herts RO AHH23/108
Benton, Nicholas, Sandhurst, Kent, 1673 CKS PRC2/35/197
Benwell, Bridget, widow, Bucklebury, Berks, 1615 Berks RO D/A1/176/49A
Beny, Elizabeth, widow, Preston next Faversham, Kent, 1696 CKS PRC2/42/112
Berage, Alexander, Wittersham, Kent, 1608 CKS PRC20/1/328
Berche, Henry, Redbourn, Herts, 1577 Herts RO ASA25/822
Berde, William, Hurst, Berks, 1596 Wilts RO Miscellaneous Index to Wills (name + date)
Bereck, William, Burmarsh, Kent, 1626 CKS PRC2/25/14
Beresfore, 1684 LJRO/B/C/5/1684/8
Berfoote, Richard, Minster in Sheppey, Kent, 1671 CKS PRC2/35/17
Berkley, William, Upton, Waters (Waters), Shrops, 1708 LJRO/B/C/5/1708/2
Berling/Marshall, Margaret, Teynham, Kent, 1674 CKS PRC2/36/26
Bernacle, Henry, Dover, Kent, 1627 CKS PRC20/8/41
Bernard, Edward, gentleman, Crudwell, Wilts, 1678 Wilts RO Miscellaneous Index to Wills (name + date)
Bernard, Nathanael, St Andrew Holborn, London & Middlesex, 1677 PRO PROB5/793A
Bernard, Rebecca, spinster, Salisbury, Wilts, 1672 Wilts RO Miscellaneous Index to Wills (name + date)
Bernard, Thomas, yeoman, Belton, Lincs, 1671 Lincs RO Ad/Ac/33/207
Berrat, Samuel, Litton, Som, 1601 Somerset RO D/D/Cta/B98
Berrell, Margaret, spinster, Immingham, Lincs, 1641 Lincs RO Ad/Ac/27/289
Berrey, Jacob, Sandwich, Kent, 1602 CKS PRC2/12/60
Berrey, John, Elmsted, Kent, 1620 CKS PRC2/20/143
Berridge, George, Swineshead, Lincs, 1683 Lincs RO Ad/Ac/44/115
Berridge, Henry, Belgrave, Leics, 1666 Leics RO Administrators Accounts C17th f43
Berridge, John, Upton, Hunts, 1722 Hunts RO/Acc58/314
Berridge, Stanford, farmer, Farcet (Farcet Fen), Hunts, 1825 Hunts RO/Acc58/336
Berrie, Anthonie, Kirton, Lincs, 1621 Lincs RO Ad/Ac/17/38
Berrie, Roberte, Laceby, Lincs, 1595 Lincs RO Ad/Ac/5/267
Berrie, William, Messingham, Lincs, 1620 Lincs RO Ad/Ac/8b/465
Berriffe, William, gentleman, Ravely, Little, Hunts, late C17th? PRO PROB5/1299

[Berriman:]
Berriman, John, Hannington, Wilts, 1621 Wilts RO CC Sarum(+ name and date)
Berris, Thomas, Coningsby, Lincs, 1602 Lincs RO Ad/Ac/5/63
Berrow, Charles, cooper, Bristol St John Baptist, Glos, Bristol RO 1635/8
Berrowe, William, copyholder, Grimley, Worcs, 1647 Worcs RO 008.7 BA3585/837/bdl 1
Berry, Edward, husbandman, Stratton Audley, Oxon, 1641 Oxon RO MSS Wills 295/3/97
Berry, Edward, Canterbury Holy Cross Westgate, Kent, 1713 CKS PRC1/17/50
Berry, Gabriel, collar maker, Faversham, Kent, 1679 CKS PRC2/38/104
Berry, Jane, widow, Oxford St Peter in the East, Oxon, 1638 Oxon RO MSS Wills 295/3/80
Berry, John, Kenardington, Kent, 1591 CKS PRC2/5/186
Berry, John, Canterbury St Peter, Kent, 1677 CKS PRC2/37/119
Berry, John, gentleman, Faversham, Kent, 1698 CKS PRC2/42/125
Berry, Mary, Faversham, Kent, 1680 CKS PRC2/39/7
Berry, Mathew, gentleman, Faversham, Kent, 1679 CKS PRC2/38/11
Berry, Ralfe, Denton (Eastry hundred), Kent, 1621 CKS PRC2/23/36
Berry, Robert, Malmesbury, Wilts, 1629 Wilts RO Arch. Wilts.(name + date)
Berry, Robert, Hinton, Little, Wilts, 1631 Wilts RO Arch. Wilts.(name + date)
Berry, Thomas, Selling, Kent, 1621 CKS PRC2/23/20
Berry, Thomas ygr, Canterbury All Saints, Kent, 1617 CKS PRC2/20/358
Berry, William, Northaw, Herts, 1617 Herts RO ASA25/4828
Berry, William, yeoman, Tenterden, Kent, 1668 CKS PRC1/13/10
Berry, William, gentleman, Canterbury Christchurch, Kent, 1670 CKS PRC19/4/5
Berry, William, currier, Faversham, Kent, 1671 CKS PRC2/35/10
Berry, William, Canterbury St Martin, Kent, 1677 CKS PRC20/12/193
Berrye, John, Faversham, Kent, 1588 CKS PRC2/4/438
Berryworth, Richarde, Willingham, Lincs, 1590 Lincs RO Ad/Ac/37/8
Bertles, Abigail, spinster, Salford, Lancs, 1788 Lancs RO (Name of Deceased) D.R.C.H. 1788
Berwick, Thomas, Packington, Little, Warks, 1684 LJRO/B/C/5/1684/9
Berworth, Peter, Hythe St Leonard, Kent, 1616 CKS PRC20/3/502
Beryall, Thomas, Halton, East, Lincs, 1598 Lincs RO Ad/Ac/5/356
Berye, Thomas, husbandman, St Albans St Stephens, Herts, 1570 Herts RO ASA25/670
Besbeech, John, butcher, Goudhurst, Kent, 1625 CKS PRC2/25/30
Besbeech, Katherine, Faversham, Kent, 1639 CKS PRC1/2/19
Besbeech, Martha, widow, Faversham, Kent, 1635 CKS PRC2/33/11
Besbitch, John, jurat/gentleman, Faversham, Kent, 1634 CKS PRC20/10/80
Besbitche, George, Goudhurst, Kent, 1605 CKS PRC2/13/87
Besbitche, John, Faversham, Kent, 1606 CKS PRC2/13/85
Besbyche, John, Chillenden, Kent, 1592 CKS PRC2/6/312
Beson, William, Hythe St Leonard, Kent, 1599 CKS PRC21/15/17
Bessey, Thomas, blacksmith, Herne, Kent, 1681 CKS PRC20/13/89
Best, Alexander, Bersted, South, Sussex, 1619 W. Suss RO EpIV/10/1/38
Best, Christopher, Bethersden, Kent, 1586 CKS PRC2/4/162
Best, Edmund, Mere, Wilts, 1637 Wilts RO Miscellaneous Index to Wills (name + date)
Best, Edward, Potter Hanworth, Lincs, 1622 Lincs RO Ad/Ac/17/48
Best, Francis, yeoman, Leadenham, Lincs, 1615 Lincs RO Ad/Ac/13/187
Best, George, Mangotsfield, Glos, Bristol RO 1677/57
Best, Gilbarte, Linton, Kent, 1596 CKS PRC2/8/340
Best, Henry, Monkton, Kent, 1624 CKS PRC20/6/98
Best, John, Graveney, Kent, 1597 CKS PRC2/7/447
Best, John, Cotheridge, Worcs, 1678 Worcs RO 008.7 BA3585/830/4
Best, Richard, gentleman,
Kent 1634 CKS PRC20/10/86
Best, Richard, Upchurch, Kent, 1693 CKS PRC1/15/111
Best, Richard, merchant, Croydon, Surrey, 1702 Lambeth Palace Arches G52/4
Best, Stephen, yeoman, Sturry, Kent, 1619 CKS PRC2/20/318
Best, Thomas, yeoman, Cotheridge, Worcs, Worcs RO 008.7 BA3585/838/172

Best, William, Boughton Monchelsea, Kent, 1617 CKS PRC2/20/184
Best, William, Kidderminster, Worcs, 1678 Worcs RO 008.7 BA3585/830/57
Bestbech, Thomas, Goudhurst, Kent, 1600 CKS PRC2/12/21
Beste, Thomas, Cotheridge, Worcs, 1594 Worcs RO 008.7 BA3585/838/173
Bestley, Richard, yeoman, Ashbury, Berks, 1627 Berks RO D/A1/176/112C
Beswick, Hannah, spinster, Cheetwood, Lancs, 1761 Lancs RO (Name of Deceased) D.R.C.H. 1761
Bethel, Hugh, gentleman, Winteringham, Lincs, 1636 Lincs RO Ad/Ac/40/55
Bethell, Robert, husbandman, Wargrave, Berks, 1630 Berks RO D/A1/177/21
Bethwine, Nathaniel, Oxford St Martin, Oxon, 1633 Oxon RO MSS Wills 5/3/16
Betney, Alexander, Lincoln St Swithin, Lincs, 1627 Lincs RO Ad/Ac/20b/87
Betsey, Edward, Gonerby, Lincs, 1649 Lincs RO Ad/Ac/30/116
Betson, John, university: 'scholar's servant', Cambridge St Mary the Great, Cambs, 1644 CUL V.C. Acc./Box2/6
Betson, William, Chester, Ches, 1603 Cheshire RO (Name) W.C. 1602
Bett, Hamon, Ivychurch, Kent, 1622 CKS PRC20/5/23
Bett, John, Hothfield, Kent, 1612 CKS PRC2/16/199
Bett, John, Sutton, Kings, Northants, 1616 Oxon RO MSS Wills Pec 32/4/58
Bett, Thomas, Willesborough, Kent, 1627 CKS PRC2/28/5
Bett, Thomas, yeoman, Marden, Kent, 1642 CKS PRC19/2/50
Bett, Thomas, Waddingham, Lincs, 1684 Lincs RO Ad/Ac/44/125
Bett, William, Sutton, Kings, Northants, 1619 Oxon RO MSS Wills Pec 32/4/69
Bette, Robert, Marden, Kent, 1614 CKS PRC20/3/128
Bettes, William, Hythe St Leonard, Kent, 1600 CKS PRC21/15/198
Bettesworth, John, Rogate, Sussex, 1684 W. Suss RO EpI/33/1684/30
Bettison, Robert, husbandman, Glentham, Lincs, 1681 Lincs RO Ad/Ac/42/84
Bettison, William, Frampton, Lincs, 1620 Lincs RO Ad/Ac/16/14
Bettison/Loud, Agnes, Frampton, Lincs, 1616 Lincs RO Ad/Ac/19A/73
Betts, Jane, Chilham, Kent, 1632 CKS PRC2/31/6
Betts, Richard, Hilton, Hunts, 1676 Hunts RO/Acc58/43(153)
Betts, Robert, Canterbury St Mary Northgate, Kent, 1575 CKS PRC2/1/132
Betts, Thomas, Kirkby, East, Lincs, 1633 Lincs RO Ad/Ac/24/106
Betts, Thomas, Brook, Kent, 1639 CKS PRC2/34/165
Betts, William, innholder, Cambridge, Cambs, 1678 CUL V.C. Acc./Box3/6
Betts/Amys, John, Ashford, Kent, 1636 CKS PRC2/33/14
Bettson, John, Swineshead, Lincs, 1638 Lincs RO Ad/Ac/25/194
Betty, see Adams,
Beunce, John, yeoman, Goosey, Berks, 1680 Berks RO D/A1/178/180C
Beusy, Edmund, Thornford, Dors, 1600 Wilts RO Miscellaneous Index to Wills (name + date)
Bevan, Thomas, Berkeley, Glos, 1685 GRO GDR/B4/2/B186
Bevell, Catherine, widow, Minster in Thanet, Kent, 1634 CKS PRC2/32/138
Bevell, John, husbandman, Minster in Thanet, Kent, 1632 CKS PRC1/1/41
Beveridge, William, clergy: 'Lord Bishop of St Asaph', 1712 PRO PROB5/820
Beverley, John, Rasen, Middle, Lincs, 1598 Lincs RO Ad/Ac/5/242
Beverley, Richard, Leadenham, Lincs, 1622 Lincs RO Ad/Ac/18/3
Beverley, Robert, university: 'Fellow of Gonville and Caius College, Cambridge/M.A.' Cambridge (Gonville and Caius College), Cambs, 1662 CUL V.C. Acc./Box3/7
Beverley, Thomas, Rasen, West, Lincs, 1601 Lincs RO Ad/Ac/5/240
Beverley, Timothie, Weighton, Market, Yorks, 1665 Borthwick D/C C.P. 1665/3
Beverley, William, Willingham, Cherry, Lincs, 1629 Lincs RO Ad/Ac/39/210
Beverlye, Josephe, Wye, Kent, 1614 CKS PRC2/17/88
Beverton, Simon, Canterbury All Saints, Kent, 1625 CKS PRC2/25/13
Beverton, Squire, Canterbury, Kent, 1687 CKS PRC1/15/93
Beverton, Squire eld, gentleman, Canterbury, Kent, 1687 CKS PRC1/15/93a
Bevill, Bartholomew, Witham on the Hill, Lincs, 1679 Lincs RO Ad/Ac/43/91

[Bevill:]
Bevill, Thomas, St Laurence Thanet, Kent, 1597 CKS PRC2/9/65
Bevis, Edward, Bishops Hull, Som, 1639 Somerset RO D/D/Cta/B24
Bevis, Richard, Newton Tony, Wilts, 1630 Wilts RO Arch. Sarum/(+ name and date)
Bevis, Robert, Newton Tony, Wilts, 1639 Wilts RO Arch. Sarum/(+ name and date)
Bevis, William, Landford, Wilts, 1632 Wilts RO Arch. Sarum/(+ name and date)
Bevys, Henry, Clee, Lincs, 1570 Lincs RO Ad/Ac/2b/28
Bewe, Thomas, Kennington, Berks, 1610 Berks RO D/A1/176/30A
Bewle, see Bewley,
Bewley, Caleb, distiller/chandler, St Bartholomew the Great, London & Middlesex, 1739 Greater London RO DL/C/549/93
Bewley, Henry, Melbourne, Derby, 1683 LJRO/B/C/5/1682/10
Bewley, John, Bridge, Kent, 1675 CKS PRC2/36/168
Bewley, Richard, Stratton Audley, Oxon, 1626 Oxon RO MSS Wills 295/3/8
Bewley, William, Gainsborough, Lincs, 1597 Lincs RO Ad/Ac/37/29
Bewley, William, Upchurch, Kent, 1636 CKS PRC2/33/23
Bewley/Bewle, Robert, Newington next Sittingbourne, Kent, 1618 CKS PRC2/20/357
Bewly, John, husbandman, Urchfont, Wilts, 1646 Wilts RO Arch. Sarum/(+ name and date)
Bex, Raymond, Woodnesborough, Kent, 1610 CKS PRC2/15/51
Bex, William, St Peter in Thanet, Kent, 1586 CKS PRC2/4/255
Bexe, Thomas, St Margarets At Cliffe, Kent, 1591 CKS PRC21/11/63
Bexwell, Henrie, Crowland, Lincs, 1626 Lincs RO Ad/Ac/20/53
Bexworth, John, Weston, Ches, 1606 Cheshire RO (Name) W.C. 1606
Bibbesworthe, Henry, Rickmansworth, Herts, 1597 Herts RO ASA25/1595
Bibbie, Thomas, Neston, Ches, 1627 Cheshire RO (Name) W.C. 1626/7
Bibby, Alice, widow, Wigan, Lancs, 1775 Lancs RO (Name of Deceased) D.R.C.H. 1775
Bicker, Stephen, Preston next Wingham, Kent, 1688 CKS PRC2/41/89
Bickerdike, Mary, widow, Leeds St Peter (Bramley), Yorks, 1839 Borthwick Test C.P. 1839/1
Bickerdike, Richard, farmer, Spofforth, Yorks, 1801 Borthwick Test C.P. 1801/3
Bickerstaffe, Nicholas, cordwainer, Melton Mowbray, Leics, 1673 Leics RO Administrators Accounts 1667-72 f127
Bickerstaffe, William, husbandman, Norton, Chipping (Over Norton), Oxon, 1640 Oxon RO MSS Wills 295/3/86
Bickersteth, Mary, widow, Ormskirk, Lancs, 1794 Lancs RO (Name of Deceased) D.R.C.H. 1794
Bickerton, Ann, widow, Tamworth, Staffs, 1775 LJRO/B/C/5/1775/20
Bickerton, see Fox,
Bickley, George, university: 'Fellow of Magdalene College, Cambridge/M.A.', Cambridge (Magdalene College), Cambs, 1636 CUL V.C. Acc./Box2/7
Bickley, William, yeoman, Myddle, Shrops, 1699 LJRO/B/C/5/1699/43
Bicknall, Walter, servant, Aldington, Kent, 1641 CKS PRC19/2/5
Bickner, William, Bermondsey, St Mary Magdalen, Surrey, 1705 PRO PROB5/954
Biddle, Edward, Stoneleigh, Warks, 1684 LJRO/B/C/5/1684/10
Biddle, Elizabeth, Coughton, Warks, 1675 Worcs RO 008.7 BA3585/830/37
Biddle, Elizabeth, Bushley, Worcs, 1684 Worcs RO 008.7 BA3585/837/bdl 4
Biddle, Nicholas, Minster in Thanet, Kent, 1639 CKS PRC1/2/20a
Biddle, Nicholas, Minster in Thanet, Kent, 1640 CKS PRC1/2/20
Biddle, William, Newbold Verdon, Leics, 1674 Leics RO Administrators Accounts 1667-72 f97
Biden, Richard, Blendworth, Hants, 1624 Hants RO 21M65 D8/50
Bie, Walter eld, clothier, Reading St Giles, Berks, 1630 Berks RO D/A1/177/16F
Bigg, Anthony, Canterbury, Kent, 1635 CKS PRC2/32/23
Bigg, Elizabeth, widow, St Leonard Eastcheap, London & Middlesex, 1700 Lambeth Palace Arches G49/3
Bigg, John, husbandman, Sheldwich, Kent, 1667 CKS PRC1/12/14
Bigg, Richard, Wellow, Som, 1622 Somerset RO D/D/Cta/B10
Bigge, John, Canterbury Holy Cross Westgate, Kent, 1593 CKS PRC2/6/462
Bigge, John, Ebony, Kent, 1594 CKS PRC2/7/333

Bigge, John, Cranbrook, Kent, 1606 CKS PRC20/1/183
Bigge, John, Tenterden, Kent, 1613 CKS PRC2/16/26
Bigge, John, Biddenden, Kent, 1617 CKS PRC2/20/282
Bigge, Mary, widow, Loose, Kent, 1684 CKS PRC20/13/398
Bigge, Richard, yeoman, Benenden, Kent, 1683 CKS PRC2/40/98
Bigge, Walter, Harrietsham, Kent, 1669 CKS PRC1/14/11
Biggerstaffe, George, Tackley, Oxon, 1625 Oxon RO MSS Wills 295/3/1
Bigges, John, Hayling, North, Hants, Hants RO 1599 AD03/3
Bigges, John, husbandman, Stapleford, Wilts, 1602 e 5 Wilts RO Arch. Sarum/(+ name and date)
Bigges, Mary, widow, Headington, Oxon, 1675 Oxon RO MSS Wills 295/5/22
Biggins, James, yeoman, Wigan (Haigh), Lancs, 1794 Lancs RO (Name of Deceased) D.R.C.H. 1794
Biggs, Edward, yeoman, Monkton Farleigh, Wilts, 1749 Wilts RO CC Sarum(+ name and date)
Biggs, Jane, widow, Old Romney, Kent, 1625 CKS PRC2/25/22
Biggs, Thomas, Fisherton Anger, Wilts, 1686 Wilts RO Arch. Sarum/(+ name and date)
Biggs/Smith, Alice, Huncote, Leics, 1665 Leics RO Administrators Accounts C17th f33
Bigland/Robinson, Jane, Boston, Lincs, 1612 Lincs RO Ad/Ac/11/39
Bignall, Walter, Newington St Mary, Surrey, 1743 Lambeth Palace VH96/241
Bignoll, Sibell, widow, Candover, Brown, Hants, 1623 Hants RO 21M65 D8/5
Bigood, Robert, clothier, Fordington, Dors, 1633 Wilts RO Miscellaneous Index to Wills (name + date)
Bigs, Joane, Lydd, Kent, 1591 CKS PRC21/11/34
Bill, William, Lilleshall, Shrops, 1686 LJRO/B/C/5/1685/20
Billan, John, St Martin in the Fields, London & Middlesex, 1725 Greater London RO AM/PP/Box 1724-1727 pt(uncatalogued)
Billen, Francis, gardener, Sandwich, Kent, 1673 CKS PRC2/35/199
Billet, Hillary, Chichester, Sussex, 1627 W. Suss RO EpIII/9/1/32
Billett, Anthonie, Lacock, Wilts, 1631 Wilts RO Arch. Wilts.(name + date)
Billiard, Daniel, baker, Dover, Kent, 1642 CKS PRC19/2/51
Billie, James, Abingdon St Helen, Berks, 1618 Berks RO D/A1/176/58D
Billing, Hugh, innkeeper, Milton next Sittingbourne, Kent, 1692 CKS PRC2/42/26
Billing, John, Chillington, Som, 1634 Somerset RO D/D/Cta/B20
Billingburghe, John, Kyme, South (North Kyme), Lincs, 1602 Lincs RO Ad/Ac/5/370
Billinghurst, Robert, Lodsworth, Sussex, 1650 W. Suss RO EpI/33/1649/5
Billingsby, Mathew, cordwainer, Sandwich, Kent, 1684 CKS PRC2/40/181
Billingshurst, see Hull,
Billingsley, John, barber, Faversham, Kent, 1697 CKS PRC2/42/126
Billington, John, Thurlby, Lincs, 1613 Lincs RO Ad/Ac/12/40
Bills, George, Headcorn, Kent, 1637 CKS PRC2/34/16
Bills, John, Sutton Valence, Kent, 1634 CKS PRC2/32/8
Bills, Water (sic), Hothfield, Kent, 1618 CKS PRC2/20/276
Bilting, Edward, cordwainer, St Johns Thanet, Kent, 1692 CKS PRC2/42/23
Bilting, William, carpenter, Faversham, Kent, 1639 CKS PRC1/2/21
Biltinge, William, Tattershall, Lincs, 1598 Lincs RO Ad/Ac/4/29
Bilton, Walter, yeoman, Witham on the Hill, Lincs, 1670 Lincs RO Ad/Ac/32/143
Binderslaughte, Simon, Sutton, Long, Lincs, 1599 Lincs RO Ad/Ac/5/165
Bine, William, miller, Biddenden, Kent, 1681 CKS PRC2/39/155
Bine, William, miller, Biddenden, Kent, 1689 CKS PRC2/41/141
Bing, Andrew, Ash next Sandwich, Kent, 1619 CKS PRC20/4/19
Bing, Christian, widow, Canterbury St George Martyr, Kent, 1638 CKS PRC2/34/168
Bing, Christopher, yeoman, Minster in Thanet, Kent, 1625 CKS PRC2/25/23
Bing, George, Boughton under Blean, Kent, 1625 CKS PRC20/7/323
Bing, Henry, yeoman, Monkton, Kent, 1624 CKS PRC20/6/82
Bing, Henry, Canterbury Holy Cross Westgate, Kent, 1627 CKS PRC2/28/18
Bing, Henry, Wickhambreaux, Kent, 1715 CKS PRC1/17/68

[Bing:]
Bing, John, Minster in Thanet, Kent, 1627 CKS PRC2/28/17
Bing, John, Biddenden, Kent, 1699 CKS PRC2/42/148
Bing, Joseph, husbandman, Ash next Sandwich, Kent, 1700 CKS PRC19/5/70
Bing, Mary, Graveney, Kent, 1618 CKS PRC2/20/140
Bing, Richard, Buckland, Kent, 1600 CKS PRC21/16/135
Bing, Siriack, Birchington, Kent, 1616 CKS PRC20/3/500
Bing, Stephen, Canterbury St George Martyr, Kent, 1637 CKS PRC2/33/13
Bing, Thomas, Thanington, Kent, 1594 CKS PRC2/7/299
Bing, Thomas, Lower Hardres, Kent, 1603 CKS PRC2/14/85
Bing, Thomas, Canterbury St Peter, Kent, 1663 CKS PRC1/9/84
Bing, Thomasine, widow, Monkton, Kent, 1618 CKS PRC20/4/37
Bing, William, yeoman, Selling, Kent, 1624 CKS PRC2/23/49
Bing, William, Whitstable, Kent, 1635 CKS PRC2/33/10
Binge, Bartholomew, yeoman, Minster in Sheppey, Kent, 1618 CKS PRC2/20/337
Binge, Edward, Thurlby, Lincs, 1611 Lincs RO Ad/Ac/10/5
Binge, Elizabeth, Canterbury, Kent, 1600 CKS PRC2/11/379
Binge, John, Chartham, Kent, 1603 CKS PRC2/14/83
Binge, Mary, spinster, Canterbury St Mary Northgate, Kent, 1666 CKS PRC1/13/12d
Binge, Mary, Canterbury St Paul, Kent, 1667 CKS PRC1/13/12b
Binge, Mary, Canterbury St Paul, Kent, 1667 CKS PRC1/13/12c
Binge, Mary, Canterbury St Paul, Kent, 1668 CKS PRC1/13/12a
Binge, Mary, spinster, Canterbury St Mary Northgate, Kent, 1668 CKS PRC1/13/12
Binge, William, Canterbury St Dunstan Without, Kent, 1613 CKS PRC2/17/124
Binge, William, yeoman, Minster in Thanet, Kent, 1619 CKS PRC20/4/25
Binge, William, Minster in Thanet, Kent, 1623 CKS PRC2/23/19
Binge, William, Boughton under Blean, Kent, 1674 CKS PRC20/12/113
Bingham, Alice, widow, Chartham, Kent, 1610 CKS PRC2/15/37
Bingham, Charles, clergy: 'clerk', Croft, Lincs, 1600 Lincs RO Ad/Ac/5/233
Bingham, George, Crowland, Lincs, 1611 Lincs RO Ad/Ac/10/16
Bingham, John, Staplehurst, Kent, 1633 CKS PRC2/32/22
Bingham, Randolph, Linsted, Kent, 1614 CKS PRC2/18/103
Bingham, Richard, Norton, Derby, 1684 LJRO/B/C/5/1684/11
Bingham, Thomas, Upper Hardres, Kent, 1633 CKS PRC2/32/14
Bingley, John, miller, Castleford, Yorks, 1723 Borthwick Test C.P. 1724/3
Bingley, Peter, gentleman, Melton Mowbray, Leics, 1639 Leics RO PR/I/41A/9
Bingly, Thomas, Bruntingthorpe, Leics, 1666 Leics RO Administrators Accounts C17th f59
Binley, Robert, wheelwright, Braybrooke, Northants, 1787 Northants RO X954/22/21
Binley, Zephania, Hill, Derby, 1683 LJRO/B/C/5/1682/12
Binskin, George, Benenden, Kent, 1597 CKS PRC2/9/29
Birch, Bartholomew, labourer, Shadoxhurst, Kent, 1665 CKS PRC1/10/12
Birch, Henry, Petham, Kent, 1677 CKS PRC2/37/5
Birch, John, iron waiter tray maker, Wolverhampton (Bilston), Staffs, 1824 LJRO/B/C/5/1824/7
Birch, Mary, spinster, Hanney, West, Berks, 1682 Berks RO D/A1/178/193
Birch, Richard, Goudhurst, Kent, 1630 CKS PRC2/30/21
Birch, Robert, bricklayer, Derby, Derby, 1764 LJRO/B/C/5/1764/52
Birch, Robert, bricklayer, Derby, Derby, 1765 LJRO/B/C/5/1765/56
Birch, Thomas, blacksmith, Wetton, Staffs, 1782 LJRO/B/C/5/1782/9
Birch, William, Petham, Kent, 1624 CKS PRC2/23/48
Birch, William, Hothfield, Kent, 1631 CKS PRC20/9/63
Birchall, Margery, Mucklestone, Shrops, 1684 LJRO/B/C/5/1684/12
Bircham, Christopher, Ewell, Kent, 1624 CKS PRC2/23/57
Birche, James, Sedgebrook, Lincs, 1594 Lincs RO Ad/Ac/3/123
Birche, Jane, Skidbrooke, Lincs, 1625 Lincs RO Ad/Ac/19B/76
Birchett, Phillip, St Nicholas at Wade, Kent, 1686 CKS PRC20/13/547
Birchmore, Robert, St Albans St Stephens, Herts, 1614 Herts RO ASA25/4814

Bird, Alexander, Epworth, Lincs, 1617 Lincs RO Ad/Ac/8b/137
Bird, Bartholomew, husbandman, Islip, Oxon, 1666 Oxon RO MSS Wills 160/4/10
Bird, Christopher, gentleman, Goxhill, Lincs, 1670 Lincs RO Ad/Ac/32/215
Bird, Edward, Epworth, Lincs, 1630 Lincs RO Ad/Ac/39/259
Bird, Edward, Uttoxeter, Staffs, 1675 LJRO:cards/1675/11
Bird, Elinor, widow, Chichester, Sussex, 1633 W. Suss RO EpIII/9/1/45
Bird, Henry, yeoman, Epworth, Lincs, 1661 Lincs RO Ad/Ac/41/66
Bird, Henry, yeoman, Epworth, Lincs, 1661 Lincs RO Ad/Ac/41/160
Bird, John, yeoman, Welwyn, Herts, 1674 Herts RO AHH23/161
Bird, John, Canterbury St Mary Northgate, Kent, 1676 CKS PRC2/36/157
Bird, John, tanner, Horncastle, Lincs, 1683 Lincs RO Ad/Ac/44/66
Bird, John eld, Capel le Ferne, Kent, 1669 CKS PRC1/14/12
Bird, Mathew, Epworth, Lincs, 1663 Lincs RO Ad/Ac/41/68
Bird, Richard, clothworker, Reading St Mary, Berks, 1619 Berks RO D/A1/176/62C
Bird, Richard, yeoman, Saltwood, Kent, 1680 CKS PRC20/13/7
Bird, Thomas, Epworth, Lincs, 1664 Lincs RO Ad/Ac/41/118
Bird, Thomas, chandler: 'tallow chandler', Deeping, Market, Lincs, 1679 Lincs RO Ad/Ac/43/127
Bird, Thomas, Hawkhurst, Kent, 1683 CKS PRC2/40/94
Bird, Thomas, thatcher, Aldington, Kent, 1684 CKS PRC20/13/400
Bird, Thomas, gentleman, Blackbrook, Lancs, 1769 Lancs RO (Name of Deceased) D.R.C.H. 1769
Bird, Thomas, farmer, Everdon, Northants, 1780 Northants RO X954/21/42
Bird, Thomas, farmer, Everdon, Northants, 1780 Northants RO X954/21/43
Bird, William, Yoxall, Staffs, 1672 LJRO:cards/1672/5
Bird, William, esquire, Liddington, Wilts, 1694 Wilts RO CC Sarum(+ name and date)
Birde, John, butcher, Worcester, St Michael, Worcs, 1595 Worcs RO 008.7 BA3585/838/112
Birde, Jone, Elham, Kent, 1594 CKS PRC2/7/295
Birde, William, Hernhill, Kent, 1595 CKS PRC21/13/196
Birde, William, Hawkhurst, Kent, 1605 CKS PRC2/13/29
Birdie, William, Barton on Humber, Lincs, 1637 Lincs RO Ad/Ac/25/578
Birkbeck, Thomas, mercer, Orton, Westm, Borthwick Test C.P. 1723/2
Birkby, Joseph, innkeeper, Wakefield, Yorks, 1818 Borthwick Test C.P. 1818/10
Birkenhead, John, Bowdon (Partington), Ches, 1748 Cheshire RO (Name) W.C. 1749-50
Birkenhead, Thomas, mercer, Warrington, Lancs, 1668 Lancs RO (Name of Deceased) D.R.C.H. 1668
Birkes, Roberte, Skidbrooke, Lincs, 1593 Lincs RO Ad/Ac/3/9
Birkett, Amy, spinster, Eythorne, Kent, 1629 CKS PRC2/29/13
Birkhened, Susanna, widow, Sittingbourne, Kent, 1641 CKS PRC1/5/79
Birtchley/Britchley, Samuel, Sandhurst, Kent, 1636 CKS PRC2/33/18
Birte, Caundle Marsh, Dors, 1601 Wilts RO Miscellaneous Index to Wills (name + date)
Birte, Thomas, Buckland, Berks, 1616 Berks RO D/A1/41/138D
Birtwisle, Thomas, Skipton, Yorks, Borthwick Test C.P. 1739/5
Biscomb, William, wheelwright, Kippax, Yorks, 1824 Borthwick Test C.P. 1824/14
Bisham, William, Waltham, Bishops, Hants, 1677 Hants RO 21m65 D8/276
Bishop,
Wilts 1638 Wilts RO Arch. Sarum/(+ name and date)
Bishop, Alice, widow, Tring, Herts, Herts RO AHH23/98
Bishop, Avis, Boultham, Lincs, 1672 Lincs RO Ad/Ac/43/67
Bishop, Christian, widow, Cranbrook, Kent, 1602 CKS PRC2/12/424
Bishop, Edward, Hythe West, Kent, 1625 CKS PRC2/23/45
Bishop, Edward, victualler, Finchley (Finchley Common, The Old Swan with Two Necks), London & Middlesex, 1813 Greater London RO DL/C/572/49
Bishop, Elizabeth, Chart nr Sutton Valence, Kent, 1679 CKS PRC2/38/6
Bishop, George, Trowbridge, Wilts, 1764 Wilts RO CC Sarum(+ name and date)
Bishop, Jane, widow, New Romney, Kent, 1628 CKS PRC20/8/79

[Bishop:]
Bishop, John, Berwick St John, Wilts, 1617 Wilts RO CC Sarum(+ name and date)
Bishop, John + Anne, Cranbrook, Kent, 1619 CKS PRC2/20/226
Bishop, Margarett, Calne, Wilts, 1638 Wilts RO Miscellaneous Index to Wills (name + date)
Bishop, Mary, widow, Spridlington, Lincs, 1662 Lincs RO Ad/Ac/41/43
Bishop, Richard, Hemswell, Lincs, 1668 Lincs RO Ad/Ac/33/86
Bishop, Robert, Willoughton, Lincs, 1624 Lincs RO Ad/Ac/8c/99
Bishop, Samuel, Dover, Kent, 1631 CKS PRC20/9/37
Bishop, Stephen, Canterbury St Margaret, Kent, 1631 CKS PRC20/9/77
Bishop, Stephen, yeoman, High Halden, Kent, 1666 CKS PRC1/11/105
Bishop, Thomas, Frisby on the Wreake, Leics, 1683 Leics RO Administrators Accounts 1682-86 f2
Bishop, Thomas, Kirton in Lindsey, Lincs, 1683 Lincs RO Ad/Ac/42/82
Bishop, William, Egerton, Kent, 1605 CKS PRC20/1/73
Bishop, William, Melton Mowbray, Leics, 1684 Leics RO Administrators Accounts 1682-86 f16
Bishopenden/Chittenden, Sarah, widow, Biddenden, Kent, 1677 CKS PRC2/37/15
Bishopp, Alice, widow, Tring, Herts, 1637 Herts RO AHH23/102
Bishopp, Christopher, Canterbury St Margaret, Kent, 1631 CKS PRC20/9/31
Bishopp, John, Cranbrook, Kent, 1602 CKS PRC2/12/64
Bishopp, John, Sutton Valence, Kent, 1623 CKS PRC2/23/42
Bishopp, Richard, Maidstone, Kent, 1602 CKS PRC21/16/50
Bishopp, Sarah, Chart, Great, Kent, 1668 CKS PRC1/13/13
Bishopp, Thomas, Linton, Kent, 1624 CKS PRC2/23/53
Bishopp, Thomas, Lea, Lincs, 1625 Lincs RO Ad/Ac/39/172
Bishopp, Thomas, Tenterden, Kent, 1637 CKS PRC2/34/10
Bishopp, William, yeoman, Ulceby, Lincs, 1618 Lincs RO Ad/Ac/14/264
Bishopp, William, Sandwich, Kent, 1626 CKS PRC2/27/24
Bishopp/Buckler, Martha, Chickerell, Dors, 1676 PRO PROB5/1096
Bishoppe, Deverill, Brixton, Wilts, 1616 Wilts RO Miscellaneous Index to Wills (name + date)
Bishoppe, Arthur, Aston Abbots, Bucks, 1602 Herts RO ASA25/1815
Bishoppe, Giles, Sutton Valence, Kent, 1605 CKS PRC2/13/91
Bishoppe, Richard, Murston, Kent, 1617 CKS PRC2/20/336
Bishoppe, Roger, Hemswell, Lincs, 1615 Lincs RO Ad/Ac/8b/226
Bishoppe, William, husbandman, Ramsden, Oxon, 1626 Oxon RO MSS Wills 295/3/6
Bishoppenden, John, yeoman, Biddenden, Kent, 1672 CKS PRC2/35/106
Biske, William, Whitstable, Kent, 1611 CKS PRC2/16/117
Bisley, John ygr, Sunningwell (Bayworth), Berks, 1592 Berks RO D/A1/175/130A
Bisley, Robert, Abingdon, Berks, 1599 Berks RO D/A1/175/163A
Bisse, James, gentleman, Wells, Som, 1623 Somerset RO D/D/Cta/B5
Bisse, Katherine, Pensford, Som, 1623 Somerset RO D/D/Cta/B11
Bissel, William, Coughton (Sambourn), Warks, Worcs RO 008.7 BA3585/836/bdl 2
Bissell, James, mr, Canterbury St Mary Bredman, Kent, 1639 CKS PRC1/2/22
Bissell, John, yeoman, Yardley, Worcs, 1608 Worcs RO 008.7 BA3585/839/445
Bissell, John, bendwareman, Burton-upon-Trent (Bond End), Staffs, 1748 LJRO/B/C/5/1748/198
Bissell, Richard, Pinchbeck, Lincs, 1627 Lincs RO Ad/Ac/20b/114
Bissett, Sarah, widow, Canterbury St Peter, Kent, 1682 CKS PRC2/40/8
Bisshopp, Robert, Selsey, Sussex, 1607 W. Suss RO EpI/33/1607/8
Bisshoppe, see Rouland,
Bisson, Jane, widow, Faversham, Kent, 1674 CKS PRC20/12/115
Bithery, John, Irthlingborough, Northants, 1672 Northants RO NWill A/C/107
Bix, Ady, clergy: 'mr/clerk', Canterbury St Mary-Magdalen Burgate, Kent, 1645 CKS PRC1/7/39
Bix, Frances, widow, Ulcombe, Kent, 1672 CKS PRC2/35/107
Bix, John, Linsted, Kent, 1627 CKS PRC2/28/15
Bix, Richard, Canterbury St Mary Northgate, Kent, 1621 CKS PRC2/26/110
Bix, Richard, Bapchild, Kent, 1628 CKS PRC2/29/19
Bix, Stephen, Bapchild, Kent, 1633 CKS PRC2/32/9

Bix, Thomas, yeoman, Ulcombe, Kent, 1670 CKS PRC1/14/13
Bix, William, Bapchild, Kent, 1633 CKS PRC2/32/10
Bix, William, gentleman, Canterbury St Mildred, Kent, 1675 CKS PRC2/36/152
Bixe, Henry, Hernhill, Kent, 1586 CKS PRC21/8/115
Bixe, John, Linsted, Kent, 1600 CKS PRC2/11/157
Bixe, Samuell, Ulcombe, Kent, 1615 CKS PRC2/20/172
Blaby, William, Butterwick, Lincs, 1683 Lincs RO Ad/Ac/44/20
Blachley, William, tailor, Bristol, Glos, Bristol RO 1720/3
Blackamore, William, Stone in Oxney, Kent, 1640 CKS PRC1/4/12
Blackard, Issabell, widow, Aylesby, Lincs, 1614 Lincs RO Ad/Ac/12/174
Blackborne, Alexander, Ospringe, Kent, 1638 CKS PRC1/1/68
Blackborne, Edmunde, Bassingthorpe, Lincs, 1593 Lincs RO Ad/Ac/3/57
Blackborne, George, Crundale, Kent, 1606 CKS PRC2/14/58
Blackborne, John, Deal, Kent, 1684 CKS PRC20/13/412
Blackborne, Mathew, kerseymaker, Chart nr Sutton Valence, Kent, 1647 CKS PRC1/8/4
Blackborne, Michaell, Canterbury St Mildred, Kent, 1617 CKS PRC2/20/257
Blackborne, Susan, widow, Faversham, Kent, 1663 CKS PRC1/9/5
Blackborowgh, John, Axbridge, Som, 1633 Somerset RO D/D/Cta/B63
Blackbourne, Elizabeth, Staplehurst, Kent, 1674 CKS PRC2/36/23
Blackbourne, George, St Giles without Cripplegate, London & Middlesex, 1688 PRO PROB5/1389
Blackbourne, James, Lympne, Kent, 1626 CKS PRC2/27/26
Blackbourne, Thomas, Bilsington, Kent, 1640 CKS PRC1/2/23
Blackbourne, Triphena, widow, Bethersden, Kent, 1639 CKS PRC1/2/24
Blackboy, Joane, Newington next Sittingbourne, Kent, 1645 CKS PRC1/7/40c
Blackboy, Joane, widow, Newington next Sittingbourne, Kent, 1645 CKS PRC1/7/40
Blackboy, Joane, widow, Newington next Sittingbourne, Kent, 1645 CKS PRC1/7/40b
Blackboy, Simon, Newington next Sittingbourne, Kent, 1632 CKS PRC2/31/83
Blackburn, Thomas, cabinet maker, Manchester, Lancs, 1779 Lancs RO (Name of Deceased) D.R.C.H. 1779
Blackburne, John, clergy: 'clerk', Sibsey, Lincs, 1615 Lincs RO Ad/Ac/13/2
Blackburne, Richard, mercer, Staplehurst, Kent, 1670 CKS PRC1/14/14
Blackburne, Robert, Edenham, Lincs, 1637 Lincs RO Ad/Ac/25/503
Blackburne, Thomas, 1671 Lancs RO (Name of Deceased) D.R.C.H. 1671
Blacke, George, Sandhurst, Kent, 1593 CKS PRC2/6/170
Blacke, James, Tenterden, Kent, 1598 CKS PRC2/10/359
Blacke, John, Grantham, Lincs, 1606 Lincs RO Ad/Ac/7/161
Blacke, Robart, Lydd, Kent, 1599 CKS PRC21/14/485
Blacke, Robart, Warehorne, Kent, 1601 CKS PRC21/15/209
Blacke, Robert, Swineshead, Lincs, 1637 Lincs RO Ad/Ac/25/432
Blacke, Robert, Faversham, Kent, 1640 CKS PRC1/4/13
Blacke, William, Rippingale, Lincs, 1637 Lincs RO Ad/Ac/25/451
Blackemore, Henry, Weston under Lizard, Staffs, 1619 LJRO:cards/1619/1
Blacker, James, Norton, Midsomer, Som, 1707 Somerset RO D/D/Cta/B62
Blacker, John, Donhead St Mary, Wilts, 1614 Wilts RO Arch. Sarum/(+ name and date)
Blacker, Roger, Stallingborough, Lincs, 1579 Lincs RO Ad/Ac/2b/54
Blacker, Thomas, miller, Hatfield (Stainforth), Yorks, 1806 Borthwick Test C.P. 1806/2
Blacker, William, yeoman, Wickenby, Lincs, 1614 Lincs RO Ad/Ac/13/171
Blacketh, John, yeoman, Kyme, South, Lincs, 1612 Lincs RO Ad/Ac/10/122
Blackfan, Henry ygr, Ashurst, Sussex, 1676 W. Suss RO EpI/33/1676/26
Blackheathe, Thomas, Donington, Lincs, 1612 Lincs RO Ad/Ac/11/131
Blackherd, Thomas, Clee (Cleethorpes), Lincs, 1606 Lincs RO Ad/Ac/7/160
Blackleeche, Abraham, Sandwich, Kent, 1613 CKS PRC2/17/95
Blacklock, Christophr eld, husbandman, Ospringe, Kent, 1669 CKS PRC1/14/15
Blacklock, Mary, mrs/widow, Bromley, St Leonard, London & Middlesex, 1669 PRO

[Blacklock:]
PROB32/6/69
Blacklocke, Thomas, yeoman, Cheriton, Kent, 1681 CKS PRC2/39/143
Blackman, Wilts RO Unlisted Fragment
Blackman, James, Aldermaston, Berks, 1616 Berks RO D/A1/176/56C
Blackman, John, Smarden, Kent, 1627 CKS PRC2/28/7
Blackman, Richard, cordwainer, Stratfield Mortimer (Wokefield), Berks, 1633 Berks RO D/A1/177/42C
Blackman, William, Midhurst, Sussex, 1597 W. Suss RO EpI/33/1597/2
Blackman, William, cook, Oxford St John Baptist, Oxon, 1673 Bodleian HYP B8/16-17
Blackmore, Edward, yeoman, Collingbourne Kingston, Wilts, 1632 Wilts RO CC Sarum(+ name and date)
Blackmore, John, Darlaston, Staffs, 1698 LJRO/B/C/5/1698/17
Blackmore, Richard, Collingbourne Ducis, Wilts, 1625? Wilts RO Miscellaneous Index to Wills (name + date)
Blacknoll, John eld, gentleman, Abingdon, Berks, 1611 Berks RO D/A1/176/25A
Blackston, Samuel, Wainfleet All Saints, Lincs, 1618 Lincs RO Ad/Ac/14/253
Blackstone, Thomas, Fulstow, Lincs, 1597 Lincs RO Ad/Ac/4/43
Blackwell, Humphrey, yeoman, Castle Eaton, Wilts, 1685 Wilts RO Arch. Wilts.(name + date)
Blackwell, Humphry, Kemble, Wilts, 1675 Wilts RO Miscellaneous Index to Wills (name + date)
Bladen, Willyam, Sutton St James, Lincs, 1595 Lincs RO Ad/Ac/5/312
Blades, Robert, husbandman, Steeping, Great, Lincs, 1678 Lincs RO Ad/Ac/34/36
Bladesmith, William, Marston, Lincs, 1650 Lincs RO Ad/Ac/29/46
Bladworth, Marie, widow, Canterbury Christchurch, Kent, 1626 CKS PRC20/7/339
Bladwyne, John, Sutton St James, Lincs, 1602 Lincs RO Ad/Ac/5/15
Blagdon, Nicholas, Clevedon, Som, 1584 Somerset RO D/D/Cta/B53
Blagdon/Gefford, Philip, Tintagel, Corn, 1608 Cornwall RO AP/J84/1
Blagrave, Alexander, gentleman, Reading St Mary, Berks, 1640 Berks RO D/A1/177/86/2/C
Blagrove, Edward, gentleman, Reading St Giles, Berks, 1640 Berks RO D/A1/177/48C
Blagrove, Henry, yeoman, Buckland, Berks, 1627 Berks RO D/A1/176/115
Blagrove, Richard, Stepney, St Dunstan, London & Middlesex, 1685 PRO PROB32/25/150
Blagrove, Robert, Hatford, Berks, 1593 Berks RO D/A1/42/41C
Blagrove, Walter, gentleman, Tilehurst, Berks, 1669 Berks RO D/A1/178/56A
Blaidwyn, Richard, Sutton St James, Lincs, 1618 Lincs RO Ad/Ac/14/178
Blaixland, John, Minster in Thanet, Kent, 1600 CKS PRC2/11/159
Blake, Catherine, Twycross, Leics, 1625 Lincs RO Ad/Ac/19B/88
Blake, Catherine?, spinster, Wootton Rivers, Wilts, 1676 Wilts RO Miscellaneous Index to Wills (name + date)
Blake, Frances, Marhamchurch, Corn, 1616 Cornwall RO AP/B371
Blake, Henry, Warminster, Wilts, 1627 Wilts RO Arch. Sarum/(+ name and date)
Blake, Joan, Purton, Wilts, 1623 Wilts RO Arch. Wilts.(name + date)
Blake, John, husbandman, Fladbury, Worcs, 1604 Worcs RO 008.7 BA3585/839/335
Blake, John, Sherston Magna, Wilts, 1619 Wilts RO Arch. Wilts.(name + date)
Blake, John, Cheriton, Hants, 1679 Hants RO 21m65 D8/305
Blake, John, Hythe St Leonard, Kent, 1697 CKS PRC19/5/51
Blake, Richard, Overton, Hants, Hants RO 21m65 D8/335
Blake, Richard, Niton, Hants, 1673 Hants RO 21m65 D8/256
Blake, Thomas, Salisbury, Wilts, 1675 Wilts RO Miscellaneous Index to Wills (name + date)
Blake, William, 1616? Wilts RO Unlisted Fragment
Blake, William, husbandman, Graveney, Kent, 1678 CKS PRC2/38/2
Blakemore, Thomas, wheelwright, West Bromwich, Staffs, 1817 LJRO/B/C/5/1817/15
Blaketh, William, Kyme, South, Lincs, 1593 Lincs RO Ad/Ac/3/71
Blakeway, John, yeoman, Chaddesley Corbett, Worcs, 1727 Worcs RO 008.7 BA3585/829/4
Blakeway, William, Kingswinford, Staffs, 1675 LJRO:cards/1675/12
Blakey, Robert, carpenter, Ormsby, South, Lincs, 1679 Lincs RO Ad/Ac/43/97
Blakey, William eld, wool stapler, Keighley, Yorks, 1779 Borthwick Test C.P. 1779/2

Blakhaye, William, Helston, Corn, 1610 Cornwall RO AP/B209/2
Blakie, Thomas, Carlton, Castle, Lincs, 1620 Lincs RO Ad/Ac/16/15
Blanchard, John, husbandman, Wimborne Minster, Dors, 1617 Dorset RO PE/WM CP 2/4/19
Blanchard, John, husbandman, Quadring, Lincs, 1624 Lincs RO Ad/Ac/19A/81
Blanchard, John, Collingbourne Kingston, Wilts, 1626 Wilts RO Arch. Wilts.(name + date)
Blanchard, Thomas, Bradford on Avon, Wilts, 1620 Wilts RO Miscellaneous Index to Wills (name + date)
Blanchard, Walter, Bromham, Wilts, 1747 Wilts RO Miscellaneous Index to Wills (name + date)
Blanchard, William, Stixwold, Lincs, 1593 Lincs RO Ad/Ac/3/49
Blanchard, William, gentleman, Tetford, Lincs, 1637 Lincs RO Ad/Ac/25/380
Blanchard, William, Wimborne Minster (Bothenwood), Dors, 1640 Dorset RO PE/WM CP 2/4/60
Blanche, William, Stratfield Mortimer, Berks, 1610 Berks RO D/A1/176/29A
Blanckett, Richard, Faversham, Kent, 1616 CKS PRC2/20/154
Blanckney, Thomas, Sutterton, Lincs, 1605 Lincs RO Ad/Ac/6/97
Blanckney, William, Helpringham, Lincs, 1639 Lincs RO Ad/Ac/26/181
Bland, Arthur, Rainham, Kent, 1629 CKS PRC2/30/18
Bland, George, yeoman, Stoke Bruerne, Northants, 1669 Northants RO NWill A/C/133
Bland, John, Burton on Stather, Lincs, 1633 Lincs RO Ad/Ac/40/77
Bland, William, Broughton, Lincs, 1646 Lincs RO Ad/Ac/40/131
Blandford, Margaret, Martin, Wilts, 1742 Wilts RO Arch. Sarum/(+ name and date)
Blandon, John, Chewton Mendip, Som, 1594 Somerset RO D/D/Cta/B91
Blandy, Thomas eld, yeoman, Wittenham, Little, Berks, 1667 Berks RO D/A1/178/109C
Blanford, James, Tisbury, Wilts, 1681 Wilts RO Arch. Sarum/(+ name and date)
Blanke, Edward, husbandman, Aslackby, Lincs, 1672 Lincs RO Ad/Ac/33/199
Blanning, Julian, widow, Stoke Lane, Som, 1664 Somerset RO D/D/Cta/B45
Blanshard, Robert, Winteringham, Lincs, 1662 Lincs RO Ad/Ac/41/106
Blase, John, Climping, Sussex, 1599 W. Suss RO EpI/33/1598/6
Blawe, Robert, Lincoln, Lincs, 1612 Lincs RO Ad/Ac/10/162
Blaxelande, Henrye, Sturry, Kent, 1613 CKS PRC2/17/289
Blaxland, John, Northbourne, Kent, 1603 CKS PRC2/14/74
Blaxland, Margery, widow, Sturry, Kent, 1620 CKS PRC2/20/128
Blaxton, Henry, Chichester, Sussex, 1610 W. Suss RO EpIII/9/1/7
Blay, Ralph, yeoman, Dorchester (Burcott), Oxon, 1691 Oxon RO MSS Wills Pec 65/5/5
Blayden, John, Canterbury St Mary Northgate, Kent, 1599 CKS PRC2/10/294
Blayne, Henry, gentleman, Hail Weston, Hunts, 1677 Hunts RO/Acc58/100(51)
Blayney, David, clergy: 'clerk', Merston, Sussex, 1677 W. Suss RO EpI/33/1676/24
Blease, Mary, widow, Budworth, Great (Wincham), Ches, 1777 Cheshire RO (Name) W.C. 1777
Bleay, Iffley, Oxon, 1679 Oxon RO MSS Wills 160/4/6
Blechenden, John, Cranbrook, Kent, 1596 CKS PRC2/9/39
Blechenden, Thomas, High Halstow, Kent, 1592 CKS PRC2/6/79
Blechenden, Thomas, Boughton Malherbe, Kent, 1596 CKS PRC2/8/216
Blechlie,
Som Somerset RO D/D/Cta/B29
Blendover, Richard, Catherington, Hants, 1674 Hants RO 21m65 D8/257
Bleney, Martha, widow, Hornsey (Newington Green), London & Middlesex, 1752 Greater London RO DL/C/552/157/2
Bleshenden, John, High Halstow, Kent, 1618 CKS PRC2/20/341
Blessed/Blissett, Samuel, chandler: 'tallow chandler', Pinchbeck, Lincs, 1683 Lincs RO Ad/Ac/44/64
Blethyn, Francis, Llanfyrnach, Pembs, 1636 NLW BR 1635/62 Ac
Bletthoe, William, Timberland (Martin), Lincs, 1638 Lincs RO Ad/Ac/25/6
Blewet, William, brewer, Clerkenwell St James, London & Middlesex, 1695 PRO PROB32/38/166
Blewett, Timothy, yeoman, Westbury on Severn, Glos, 1803 GRO GDR/B4/2/B105
Blewick, Henrie, mariner, Dover, Kent, 1641 CKS PRC19/1/25

[Bley:]
Bley, John, Islip, Oxon, 1663 Oxon RO MSS Wills 295/5/2
Blimlowe?, Robert, Barwell, Leics, 1642 Leics RO PR/I/41A/90
Blincksopp, Thomas, widow, Laughton, Lincs, 1680 Lincs RO Ad/Ac/43/164
Blincoe, George, Ashford, Kent, 1625 CKS PRC20/6/78
Blincorn, John, Earith, Hunts, 1705 Hunts RO/Acc58/296
Blinkinsaps, Richard, Canterbury St Paul, Kent, 1597 CKS PRC2/10/363
Blinkoe/Knight, Jane, Deal, Kent, 1668 CKS PRC19/4/6
Blinston, John, Warrington, Lancs, 1701 Lancs RO (Name of Deceased) D.R.C.H. 1697-99
Blinstone, see Flintstone,
Blisse, Anne, Harborough, Market, Leics, 1674 Leics RO Administrators Accounts 1667-72 f114
Blissett, Thomas, tawer: 'white tawer', Abingdon, Berks, 1684 Berks RO D/A1/179/10C
Blissett, see Blessed,
Blisson, Charles, Geneva, Switzerland, 1707 PRO PROB5/1141
Blithman, John, Northaw, Herts, 1638 Herts RO ASA25/4949
Blizard, Thomas, lighterman, St Botolph without Bishopsgate, London & Middlesex, 1755 Greater London RO DL/C/553/112
Blocke, Elizabeth, widow, Deal, Kent, 1584 CKS PRC21/7/24
Blocke, George, Minster in Thanet, Kent, 1614 CKS PRC2/18/31
Blocke, John, Whitstable, Kent, 1596 CKS PRC2/8/461
Blockly, John, husbandman, Knaptoft, Leics, 1669 Leics RO Administrators Accounts 1667-72 f25
Blogg, William, Canterbury, Kent, 1637 CKS PRC2/34/23
Blondell, Anthony, Sandwich St Mary, Kent, 1674 CKS PRC2/36/25
Blood, Edmund eld, Duffield, Derby, 1604 LJRO:cards/1604/1
Blood, John, Leek, Staffs, 1684 LJRO/B/C/5/1684/13
Bloomer, Giles, Halesowen, Worcs, 1684 Worcs RO 008.7 BA3585/837/bdl 4
Bloore, John, yeoman, Blackburn (Wilpshire), Lancs, 1727 Lancs RO (Name of Deceased) D.R.C.H. 1727
Blount, John, knight, St Magnus the Martyr, London & Middlesex, 1696 PRO PROB5/1731
Blow, John, yeoman, Linwood, Lincs, 1680 Lincs RO Ad/Ac/34/43
Blowe, Richard, Northorpe, Lincs, 1599 Lincs RO Ad/Ac/37/60
Blowe, William, Toft Next Newton, Lincs, 1607 Lincs RO Ad/Ac/8a/59
Blownte, John, fuller: 'walker', Worcester, Worcs, 1609 Worcs RO 008.7 BA3585/839/480
Blunckett, John, Boughton under Blean, Kent, 1596 CKS PRC21/14/85
Blunckett, Thomas, Mersham, Kent, 1670 CKS PRC1/15/8
Blundell, Abraham, Carisbrooke, Hants, 1623 Hants RO 21M65 D8/7
Blundell, Elias, Dover, Kent, 1639 CKS PRC20/10/150
Blunden, Margery, Basingstoke, Hants, 1669 Hants RO 21m65 D8/210
Blunder, Roger, Faversham, Kent, 1637 CKS PRC2/34/17
Blundy, Thomas, innholder, Reading, Berks, 1692 Berks RO D/A1/179/89I
Blunt, George, Grainthorpe, Lincs, 1638 Lincs RO Ad/Ac/25/193
Blunt, George, yeoman, Bucklebury, Berks, 1678 Berks RO D/A1/178/160A
Blunt, James, Solihull, Warks, 1685 LJRO/B/C/5/1685/21
Blunt, Robert, gentleman, Berkhamsted St Peter, Herts, 1647 Herts RO AHH23/127
Blunte, William, Wymeswold, Leics, 1625 Lincs RO Ad/Ac/19B/86
Blushe, Alice, Sutton Valence, Kent, 1603 CKS PRC2/13/54
Blushe, Elizabeth, Marden, Kent, 1596 CKS PRC2/9/67
Blushe, William, Marden, Kent, 1614 CKS PRC2/18/38
Blyck, Richard, vintner, Warwick, Warks, 1602 Worcs RO 008.7 BA3585/838/225
Blye, Margerye, Faversham, Kent, 1613 CKS PRC2/18/94
Blye, Robart, Wickhambreaux, Kent, 1596 CKS PRC2/8/286
Blyth, John, husbandman, Trusthorpe, Lincs, 1670 Lincs RO Ad/Ac/32/171
Blyth, Thomas, yeoman, Bucklebury, Berks, 1639 Berks RO D/A1/177/78A
Blythe, Francis, Coventry, Warks, 1683 LJRO/B/C/5/1682/13
Blythe, Margarett, Binbrook St Mary, Lincs, 1649 Lincs RO Ad/Ac/30/133

Boade, James eld, Boughton Monchelsea, Kent, 1648 CKS PRC1/8/34
Boade, Thomas, Chart nr Sutton Valence, Kent, 1633 CKS PRC2/32/15
Boale, John, Slawston, Leics, Leics RO Administrators Accounts 1682-86 f43a
Boales, John,
Leics Leics RO Administrators Accounts 1682-86 f43
Boardman, Edmund, Witham, North, Lincs, 1620 Lincs RO Ad/Ac/16/10
Boardman, Henry, carpenter, Derby, West, Lancs, 1797 Lancs RO (Name of Deceased) D.R.C.H. 1797
Boardman, Sarah, widow, Bolton-le-Moors, Lancs, 1761 Lancs RO (Name of Deceased) D.R.C.H. 1761
Boarsley, John, Marton, Warks, 1672 LJRO:cards/1672/6
Boate, Benjamin, Deptford, Kent, 1673 PRO PROB5/1103
Boathe, John, Kenardington, Kent, 1595 CKS PRC2/7/154
Bochart, Jane, minor, Canterbury St Mildred, Kent, 1625 CKS PRC2/23/58
Bochillion, Suzan, widow, Sandwich, Kent, 1631 CKS PRC20/9/41
Bockart, George, Sandwich, Kent, 1629 CKS PRC2/30/14
Boddenham, Humfrey, Hallow, Worcs, 1685 Worcs RO 008.7 BA3585/830/88
Boddy, Thomas, husbandman, Checkendon, Oxon, 1668 Oxon RO MSS Wills 76/4/32
Bode, Edward, Langley, Kent, 1628 CKS PRC2/29/15
Bode, Francis, gentleman, Whitchurch, Oxon, 1625 Oxon RO MSS Wills 295/2/94
Bodefishe, William, Selling, Kent, 1600 CKS PRC2/11/153
Boden, Thomas, yeoman, Bunbury (Peckforton), Ches, 1780 Cheshire RO (Name) W.C. 1780
Bodfeilde/Bodfishe, Augustine, Kennington, Kent, 1606 CKS PRC2/13/36
Bodfishe, see Bodfeilde,
Bodie, Henrie, Stamford, Lincs, 1622 Lincs RO Ad/Ac/17/30
Bodkin, Anne, widow, Staplehurst, Kent, 1646 CKS PRC19/2/93
Bodkin, John, yeoman, Kenardington, Kent, 1672 CKS PRC2/35/12
Bodkin, Robert, miller, Henley, Oxon, 1631 Oxon RO MSS Wills 295/3/31
Bodkin, William, Staplehurst, Kent, 1640 CKS PRC1/2/25
Bodkin, William, yeoman, Sutton Valence, Kent, 1674 CKS PRC2/36/27
Bodkyn, Thomas, Canterbury St Dunstan Without, Kent, 1608 CKS PRC2/13/68
Bodle, Anthony, mercer, Tenterden, Kent, 1681 CKS PRC2/39/137
Bodle, Isaack, Tenterden, Kent, 1625 CKS PRC2/25/6
Bodle, John, Goudhurst, Kent, 1635 CKS PRC2/33/16
Bodman, John, Weston-Super-Mare, Som, 1584 Somerset RO D/D/Cta/B94
Body, Edith, Glastonbury, Som, 1641 Somerset RO D/D/Cta/B51
Body, see Marks,
Bogey, John, Pinchbeck, Lincs, 1634 Lincs RO Ad/Ac/24/530
Boghurst, Lazarus, Rainham, Kent, 1639 CKS PRC19/1/16
Bolande, Lionell, yeoman, Appleby, Lincs, 1640 Lincs RO Ad/Ac/27/102
Bold, Florence, widow, Tre-yr-ddol, 1677 NLW B 1676/25
Bold, John, clergy: 'clerk', Broughton Gifford, Wilts, 1622 Wilts RO CC Sarum(+ name and date)
Bold, Nicholas, yeoman, Boxford, Berks, 1604 Berks RO D/A1/175/182A
Bolden, Sara, Elmsted, Kent, 1638 CKS PRC2/34/173
Bolderson, Mary, widow, Chislet, Kent, 1636 CKS PRC2/33/6
Boldersonne, John, Chislet, Kent, 1631 CKS PRC2/30/22
Bolding, Cycelye, Canterbury St Mary Bredin, Kent, 1603 CKS PRC2/14/70
Bolgaye, Hughe, Canterbury All Saints, Kent, 1574 CKS PRC2/1/89
Boll, Richard, Ringwould, Kent, 1597 CKS PRC2/9/345
Bolland, Baron, gentleman, Leeds, Yorks, 1781 Borthwick Test C.P. 1781/1
Bolland, Robert, Lydd, Kent, 1613 CKS PRC20/2/474
Bolland, Robert, Lydd, Kent, 1689 CKS PRC20/13/626
Bolland, Thomas, innkeeper, Neston, Ches, 1735 Cheshire RO (Name) W.C. 1735
Bollande, Edmonde, Old Romney, Kent, 1594 CKS PRC2/7/231

[Bollard:]
Bollard, John, glazier, Dover, Kent, 1681 CKS PRC20/13/99
Bolle, John, Friskney, Lincs, 1611 Lincs RO Ad/Ac/10/9
Bollom, John, Skegness, Lincs, 1614 Lincs RO Ad/Ac/13/161
Bolls, Richard, gentleman, Theddlethorpe St Helen, Lincs, 1632 Lincs RO Ad/Ac/23/163
Bolt, Henry, Feckenham, Worcs, 1616 Worcs RO 008.7 BA3585/837/bdl 1
Bolt, Thomas, sexton, Bristol St Augustine the Less, Glos, Bristol RO 1766/CP
Bolt, Thomas, Wellington, Shrops, 1674 LJRO:cards/1674/6
Bolton, Elizabeth, widow, Islington (Lower Street), London & Middlesex, 1813 Greater London RO DL/C/573/86
Bolton, Hugh, potter, Stoke-upon-Trent, Staffs, 1798 LJRO/B/C/5/1798/4
Bolton, John, victualler, Abingdon, Berks, 1679 Berks RO D/A1/178/172C
Bolton, Matthewe, Barham, Kent, 1600 CKS PRC2/12/72
Bolton, Phillipp, Gosport/Alverstoke, Hants, 1673 Hants RO 1673 AD14
Bolton, Richard, Alderminster, Warks, Worcs RO 008.7 BA3585/838/176
Boman, John, Somerton, East, Norf, Norfolk RO ANW/23/10/37
Bond, Andrew, Standon, Staffs, 1708 LJRO/B/C/5/1708/8
Bond, Henry, Davington, Kent, 1583 CKS PRC2/2/243
Bond, Henry, husbandman, Cumnor, Berks, 1637 Berks RO D/A1/177/58B
Bond, Henry, yeoman, Ospringe, Kent, 1669 CKS PRC1/14/16
Bond, John, yeoman, Wootton, Berks, 1637 Berks RO D/A1/177/62A
Bond, Martha, Brent, East, Som, 1625 Somerset RO D/D/Cta/B13
Bond, Thomas, yeoman, Hendred, East, Berks, 1683 Berks RO D/A1/179/6D
Bond, William, Long Wittenham, Berks, 1619 Berks RO D/A1/176/63A
Bond, William, Madresfield, Worcs, 1685 Worcs RO 008.7 BA3585/837/bdl 4
Bonde, William, Holnest, Dors, 1600 Wilts RO Miscellaneous Index to Wills (name + date)
Bone, John, Deal, Kent, 1675 CKS PRC20/12/116
Bone, John, Deal, Kent, 1699 CKS PRC19/5/62
Bone, Nicholas, prisoner, Norwich (Castle), Norf, 1709 Norfolk RO ANW/23/9/15
Bones, Thomas, Normanton, Lincs, 1625 Lincs RO Ad/Ac/19B/47
Bones, Thomas, Normanton, Lincs, 1626? Lincs RO Ad/Ac/20/71
Bonest, John, grocer, Ellington, Hunts, 1724 Hunts RO/Acc58/315
Bongay, Mathew, Canterbury, Kent, 1620 CKS PRC20/5/15
Bonham, John, Fairfield, Kent, 1607 CKS PRC20/1/308
Bonham, John, Amesbury, Wilts, 1674 Wilts RO Arch. Sarum/(+ name and date)
Bonham, Luke, Wimborne Minster, Dors, 1685 Dorset RO PE/WM CP 2/4/95
Bonham, Luke, Wimborne Minster, Dors, 1686 Dorset RO PE/WM CP 2/4/95a
Bonham, Peeter, Tenterden, Kent, 1608 CKS PRC2/15/21
Bonne, Charles, Canterbury St Margaret, Kent, 1677 CKS PRC2/37/122
Bonner, Edward, Upavon, Wilts, 1677 Wilts RO Arch. Sarum/(+ name and date)
Bonner, Francis, Willoughby, Lincs, 1670 Lincs RO Ad/Ac/32/165
Bonner, John, Toynton, High, Lincs, 1634 Lincs RO Ad/Ac/24/214
Bonner, Joseph, Baumber, Lincs, 1642 Lincs RO Ad/Ac/28/18
Bonner, Richard sen, husbandman, Brightwalton, Berks, 1677 Berks RO D/A1/178/173C
Bonner, Robert, Holywell, Lincs, 1641 Lincs RO Ad/Ac/27/23
Bonner, Simon, Yaxley, Hunts, 1676 Hunts RO/Acc58/81(34)
Bonner, William, Barkwith, East, Lincs, 1593 Lincs RO Ad/Ac/3/75
Bonner, William, Wayford, Som, 1635 Somerset RO D/D/Cta/B17
Bonney, Joan, widow, Thorney, West, Sussex, 1635 W. Suss RO EpI/33/1635/6
Bonny, Christopher, Lenham, Kent, 1675 CKS PRC2/36/162
Bonny, John, Birdham?, Sussex, 1675 W. Suss RO EpI/33/1675/3
Bonny, Peter, clergy: 'rector', Hawkinge, Kent, 1679 CKS PRC2/38/97
Bonnye, William, High Halden, Kent, 1613 CKS PRC2/16/142
Bono, Nathaniel, Ringstead, Northants, 1674 Northants RO NWill A/C/146
Bonye, John, Lenham, Kent, 1610 CKS PRC2/15/14
Boode, John, yeoman, Steyning, Sussex, 1630 W. Suss RO EpI/33/1629/7

Booker, Agnes, Elsted, Sussex, 1629 W. Suss RO EpI/33/1629/6
Booker, Henry, Rudgwick, Sussex, 1600 W. Suss RO EpI/33/1600/14
Booker, James, Sutton, Sussex, 1671 W. Suss RO EpI/33/1670/28
Booker, John, Rudgwick, Sussex, 1696 W. Suss RO EpI/33/1696
Booker, William, maltster, St Peter in Thanet, Kent, 1689 CKS PRC2/41/140
Bookey, Joan, Grafton Flyford, Worcs, 1683 Worcs RO 008.7 BA3585/837/bdl 3
Bookey, John, St Peter Cornhill, London & Middlesex, 1703 PRO PROB5/1602
Boole, John, Deeping St James, Lincs, 1614 Lincs RO Ad/Ac/13/45
Boole, Josua, Stow in Lindsey, Lincs, 1663 Lincs RO Ad/Ac/42/8
Booles, Richard, Holme, Hunts, Hunts RO/Acc58/243(214)
Booles, Richard, Wigtoft, Lincs, 1612 Lincs RO Ad/Ac/11/109
Boone, Alyce, Biddenden, Kent, 1595 CKS PRC2/7/435
Boone, Humphry, collar maker, Maidstone, Kent, 1674 CKS PRC20/12/119
Boorder, John, Hackington, Kent, 1633 CKS PRC2/32/19
Booreman, James, husbandman, Deal, Kent, CKS PRC19/1/1
Booreman, Richard, Detling, Kent, 1644 CKS PRC19/2/69
Boorman, Abraham, Sandwich, Kent, 1599 CKS PRC2/10/456
Boorne, Bradley, North, Wilts, 1632 Wilts RO CC Sarum(+ name and date)
Boorne, Ann, widow, Herne, Kent, 1636 CKS PRC20/10/102
Boorne, Henry, Eastling, Kent, 1617 CKS PRC2/20/212
Boorne, James, Sandhurst, Kent, 1620 CKS PRC2/20/369
Boorne, Thomas, Sandhurst, Kent, 1607 CKS PRC2/14/24
Boot, Richard, victualler, Birmingham, Warks, 1781 LJRO/B/C/5/1781/11
Boot, Thomas, mason: 'stone mason', Sheffield (Cherry Tree Hill), Yorks, 1837 Borthwick Test C.P. 1836/6
Booth, Avera, widow, Barton on Humber, Lincs, 1632 Lincs RO Ad/Ac/23/36
Booth, Edward, gentleman, Barton on Humber (Fleet Hargate), Lincs, 1650 Lincs RO Ad/Ac/29/56
Booth, Elizabeth, widow, Warboys, Hunts, 1684 Hunts RO/Acc58/211(204)
Booth, Gabriell, Pickworth, Lincs, 1640 Lincs RO Ad/Ac/27/108
Booth, George, Oxcombe, Lincs, 1611 Lincs RO Ad/Ac/10/148
Booth, John, Lincoln St Peter at Gowts, Lincs, 1618 Lincs RO Ad/Ac/14/268
Booth, John, husbandman, Bobbing, Kent, 1665 CKS PRC1/11/10
Booth, John, Liverpool, Lancs, 1726 Lancs RO (Name of Deceased) D.R.C.H. 1726
Booth, John, husbandman, Middleton (Dixon Fold), Lancs, 1767 Lancs RO (Name of Deceased) D.R.C.H. 1765-67
Booth, Margerye, widow, Chislet, Kent, 1616 CKS PRC2/20/132
Booth, Mathew, husbandman, Saxilby, Lincs, 1650 Lincs RO Ad/Ac/40/207
Booth, Nicholas, yeoman, Keal, West, Lincs, 1624 Lincs RO Ad/Ac/19A/106
Booth, Richard, Barton on Humber, Lincs, 1614 Lincs RO Ad/Ac/13/53
Booth, Richard, gentleman, Sparsholt, Berks, 1625 Berks RO D/A1/176/97
Booth, Richard, yeoman, Brimpton, Berks, 1642 Berks RO D/A1/177/103C
Booth, Robert, Ramsey, Hunts, 1676 Hunts RO/Acc58/34(123)
Booth, Thomas, Goxhill, Lincs, 1666 Lincs RO Ad/Ac/32/85
Booth, Thomas, Glossop (Thorsitt), Derby, 1682 LJRO/B/C/5/1682/11
Booth, Thomas, weaver/yarn factor, Coventry, Warks, 1758 LJRO/B/C/5/1760/81
Booth, William, Goxhill, Lincs, 1626 Lincs RO Ad/Ac/19B/56
Booth, see Pope,
Boothby, John, yeoman, Hanbury (Hanbury), Staffs, 1741 LJRO/B/C/5/1741/185
Boothe, Alexander, Maidstone, Kent, 1615 CKS PRC20/3/346
Boothe, Barnabe, Faversham, Kent, 1597 CKS PRC2/9/27
Boothe, Margarett, mrs, Brocklesby, Lincs, 1606 Lincs RO Ad/Ac/7/32
Boothe, Ralphe, Swineshead, Lincs, 1623 Lincs RO Ad/Ac/18/69
Boothe, Richard, Chislet, Kent, 1612 CKS PRC2/16/204
Boothe, Robert, Hemingby, Lincs, 1611 Lincs RO Ad/Ac/10/46

[Boothe:]
Boothe, Suzan, Tenterden, Kent, 1611 CKS PRC2/16/188
Boothe, William, Deal, Kent, 1605 CKS PRC20/1/5
Boothe, William, Heckington, Lincs, 1648 Lincs RO Ad/Ac/30/343
Boothes, Henry, Congleton, Ches, 1626 Cheshire RO (Name) W.C. 1623-26
Bootie, Thomas, Tydd St Mary, Lincs, 1598 Lincs RO Ad/Ac/4/31
Booton, William, Grandborough, Bucks, Herts RO ASA25/4950
Booton, William, Grandborough, Bucks, Herts RO ASA25/4951
Border, Francis, Somersham, Hunts, 1701 Hunts RO/Acc58/292
Bordman, George, 1627 Lancs RO (Name of Deceased) D.R.C.H. 1627
Bore, Elizabeth, widow, Stilton, Hunts, 1711 Hunts RO/Acc58/304
Boreman, John, collar maker, Biddenden, Kent, 1678 CKS PRC2/38/3
Boreman, Thomas, yeoman, Claydon, Oxon, 1630 Oxon RO MSS Wills Pec 33/1/14
Borer, William, Horsham, Sussex, W. Suss RO EpI/33/1611/2
Borer, William, Horsham, Sussex, 1611 W. Suss RO EpI/33/1612/4
Borey, John, Minster in Thanet, Kent, 1633 CKS PRC2/32/12
Borne, Henrye, Marden, Kent, 1620 CKS PRC2/20/335
Borne, John, Teynham, Kent, 1586 CKS PRC2/4/356
Borne, Mathew, St Laurence Thanet, Kent, 1598 CKS PRC2/10/427
Borne, William, Seasalter, Kent, 1626 CKS PRC2/25/25
Borneforde, Marion, widow, Sittingbourne, Kent, 1613 CKS PRC2/16/136
Bornell, George, Thakeham, Sussex, 1606 W. Suss RO EpI/33/1605/1
Borrow, William, Metheringham, Lincs, 1651 Lincs RO Ad/Ac/29/133
Borslaye, John, Thorpe St Peter, Lincs, 1586 Lincs RO Ad/Ac/0/39
Borsley, John, Thorpe St Peter, Lincs, 1586 Lincs RO Ad/Ac/1/29
Borsley, Thomas, innholder, Faversham, Kent, 1673 CKS PRC2/35/196
Bortley, Francis, yeoman, Henley, Oxon, 1676 Oxon RO MSS Wills 295/5/16
Bosely, John, Oxford St Mary Magdalene, Oxon, 1624 Oxon RO MSS Wills 4/6/32
Boskewen, Mary, widow, St Columb Major, Corn, 1611 Cornwall RO AP/B266/2
Bossaert, Josse, Sandwich, Kent, 1625 CKS PRC2/25/7
Bossart, Joane, Sandwich, Kent, 1633 CKS PRC2/32/18
Bossome, Triphena, spinster, Dover, Kent, 1641 CKS PRC20/10/146
Bostock, Bettrice, widow, Abingdon, Berks, 1603 Berks RO D/A1/175/179
Bostock, Francis, yeoman, Prestbury (Harropp in Macclesfield), Ches, 1726 Cheshire RO (Name) W.C. 1726-7
Boston, Jerome, Rickmansworth, Herts, 1597 Herts RO ASA25/1598
Boston, John, Bourne, Lincs, 1605 Lincs RO Ad/Ac/6/52
Boston, Rose, widow, Staughton, Great, Hunts, 1676 Hunts RO/Acc58/51(18)
Boston, Simon, Old Romney, Kent, 1677 CKS PRC2/37/114
Boston, Thomas, Pinchbeck, Lincs, 1648 Lincs RO Ad/Ac/30/275
Boswell, William, yeoman, Cholsey, Berks, 1609 Berks RO D/A1/176/17C
Bosworth, John, grazier, Haselbech, Northants, 1757 Northants RO X954/21/4
Bote, John, weaver, Wardington (Williamscot), Oxon, 1617 Oxon RO MSS Wills Pec 32/4/59
Boteler, Edward, clergy: 'clerk', Winteringham, Lincs, 1673 Lincs RO Ad/Ac/35/66
Boteler, Henry, gentleman, Eastry, Kent, 1672 CKS PRC20/12/38
Boteler, Noel, gentleman, Boston, Lincs, 1667 Lincs RO Ad/Ac/33/2
Boteler, Richard, gentleman, Eastry, Kent, 1684 CKS PRC20/13/396
Botham, Edward, Glossop (Chalesworth), Derby, 1720 LJRO/B/C/5/1720/11
Bothe, Phillipe, gentleman, Snitterby, Lincs, 1595 Lincs RO Ad/Ac/37/21
Botlemaker, Jasper, yeoman, Coleshill, Berks, 1677 Berks RO D/A1/178/167C
Bott, Abraham, Bagworth, Leics, 1641 Leics RO PR/I/41A/85
Bott, Edward, bricklayer, Stafford, Staffs, 1779 LJRO/B/C/5/1779/10
Bott, George, yeoman, Alton (Cotton), Staffs, 1791 LJRO/B/C/5/1791/5a
Bottenden, William, yeoman, Sunningwell, Berks, 1639 Berks RO D/A1/177/81A
Botting, John, Goudhurst, Kent, 1636 CKS PRC2/33/19
Bottinge, John, Nuthurst, Sussex, 1601 W. Suss RO EpI/33/1600/13

Bottle, Thomas, yeoman, Selling, Kent, 1684 CKS PRC2/40/170
Bottley, Margaret, widow, Canterbury St Alphege, Kent, 1630 CKS PRC20/9/35
Bottomley, Sarah, widow, Halifax (Fixby), Yorks, 1795 Borthwick Test C.P. 1794/1
Bottomly, see May,
Boucher, William, Harptree, East, Som, 1624 Somerset RO D/D/Cta/B6
Boucker, John, Teynham, Kent, 1672 CKS PRC2/35/11
Boughton, Danyell, Barham, Kent, 1597 CKS PRC2/9/15
Boughton, John, yeoman, Elham, Kent, 1684 CKS PRC19/4/105
Boughton, Margaret, widow, Elham, Kent, 1662 CKS PRC1/8/91
Boughton, Margaret, Charing, Kent, 1690 CKS PRC20/13/624
Boughton, Margarett, widow, Elham, Kent, 1668 CKS PRC1/12/15
Boughton, Richard, Waltham, Kent, 1676 CKS PRC2/36/155
Boughton, Robert, Waltham, Kent, 1644 CKS PRC1/6/97
Boughton, William, Belton, Lincs, 1586 Lincs RO Ad/Ac/37/3
Boughton, William, Reading, Berks, 1586 Berks RO D/A2/C24/f78R
Boulding, Thomas, Crundale, Kent, 1683 CKS PRC2/40/6
Bouller, Frederick, yeoman, Piddington, Oxon, 1676 Oxon RO MSS Wills 295/6/3
Boulter, Hugh, Salisbury St Thomas, Wilts, 1670 Wilts RO Miscellaneous Index to Wills (name + date)
Boulter, John, Hemingby, Lincs, 1611 Lincs RO Ad/Ac/10/114
Boulter, Thomas, Wigston Magna, Leics, 1641 Leics RO PR/I/41A/77
Boulton, Anthony, Bromsgrove, Worcs, 1685 Worcs RO 008.7 BA3585/837/bdl 4
Boulton, Elizabeth, Stoke-upon-Trent, Staffs, 1777 LJRO/B/C/5/1777/3
Boulton, Henria, yeoman, Bardney, Lincs, 1632 Lincs RO Ad/Ac/23/64
Boulton, James, farmer, Lilleshall, Shrops, 1821 LJRO/B/C/5/1821/6
Boulton, John, Upper Hardres, Kent, 1625 CKS PRC2/25/20
Boulton, John eld, husbandman, Ilsley, East, Berks, 1622 Berks RO D/A1/176/85C
Boulton, Joseph, yeoman, Kellington, Yorks, 1774 Borthwick Test C.P. 1774/7
Boulton, Leon, Coningsby, Lincs, 1640 Lincs RO Ad/Ac/27/157
Boulton, Mary, widow, Upper Hardres, Kent, 1625 CKS PRC2/25/17
Boulton, Walter, Ash next Sandwich, Kent, 1581 CKS PRC21/4/327
Boulton/Till, William, Cheadle, Staffs, 1676 LJRO:cards/1676/7
Bounde, Edmund, Minster in Thanet, Kent, 1583 CKS PRC2/3/123
Boundy, John, Chirton, Wilts, 1613 Wilts RO Miscellaneous Index to Wills (name + date)
Bounsall, John, yeoman, St Ive, Corn, 1638 Cornwall RO AP/B709/2
Bourman, William, Sandwich, Kent, 1597 CKS PRC2/9/269
Bourn, Edward, Leigh, Staffs, 1684 LJRO/B/C/5/1684/14
Bourne, Anne, widow, Westwell, Kent, 1680 CKS PRC20/13/3
Bourne, Christopher, Biddenden, Kent, 1669 CKS PRC1/13/14
Bourne, Daniel, Westwell, Kent, 1674 CKS PRC20/12/66
Bourne, James, Newington next Sittingbourne, Kent, 1675 CKS PRC2/36/160
Bourne, John, Hawkhurst, Kent, 1598 CKS PRC2/10/200
Bourne, John, Sandhurst, Kent, 1631 CKS PRC20/9/13
Bourne, John, innholder, Appledore, Kent, 1677 CKS PRC2/37/113
Bourne, Nicholas, gentleman, Westwell, Kent, 1632 CKS PRC20/10/52
Bourne, Richard, weaver: 'linen weaver', Hothfield, Kent, 1675 CKS PRC2/36/158
Bourne, Thomas, Upchurch, Kent, 1628 CKS PRC2/29/9
Bourne, Thomas, gentleman, Doddington, Kent, 1629 CKS PRC2/30/17
Bourne, Thomas, Newington next Sittingbourne, Kent, 1671 CKS PRC2/35/20
Bourne, Thomas, Canterbury St Margaret, Kent, 1675 CKS PRC2/36/154
Boutcher, Edward, Alderton?, Glos, 1672 GRO GDR/B4/2/B180
Bouteler, Mathew, Sandwich, Kent, 1612 CKS PRC2/17/262
Bouthe, John, esquire, Killingholme, Lincs, 1599 Lincs RO Ad/Ac/5/463
Bovier, George, Hernhill, Kent, 1589 CKS PRC21/9/248
Bovier, John, yeoman, Preston next Faversham, Kent, 1671 CKS PRC2/35/6

[Bovier:]
Bovier, Stephen, Boughton under Blean, Kent, 1646 CKS PRC19/2/94
Bovier, Thomas, Binsted, Sussex, 1614 W. Suss RO EpI/33/1613/23
Bovier, Thomas, tanner, Bridge, Kent, 1625 CKS PRC2/25/12
Bowbanke, Robert, Minster in Sheppey, Kent, 1639 CKS PRC2/34/177
Bowbrook, Amy, widow, Cranbrook, Kent, 1626 CKS PRC2/25/27
Bowden, Gilbert, Newington next Sittingbourne, Kent, 1608 CKS PRC2/14/41
Bowden, Henry, Sherfield, Hants, 1624 Hants RO 21M65 D8/51
Bowden, Mary, Roxby, Lincs, 1673 Lincs RO Ad/Ac/35/64
Bowden, Nicholas, miller, Milton next Sittingbourne, Kent, 1624 CKS PRC20/6/102
Bowden, Robert, Nonington, Kent, 1626 CKS PRC2/25/26
Bowden, Thomas, Sutton, Lincs, 1638 Lincs RO Ad/Ac/25/41
Bowdler, Marmaduke eld, Bristol, Glos, 1714? PRO PROB5/926
Bowdon, George, degrees: 'M.A.', Oxford (Trinity College), Oxon, 1640 Bodleian HYP B8/18-19
Bowell, Rebecca, Bredgar, Kent, 1680 CKS PRC2/39/8
Boweman, John, Lympsham, Som, 1611 Somerset RO D/D/Cta/B34
Bowen, John, Bristol, Glos, Bristol RO 1714/6
Bowen, John, clergy: 'clerk', Norton, Chipping, Oxon, 1662 Oxon RO MSS Wills 76/4/2
Bowen, John, Deal, Kent, 1706 CKS PRC19/6/17
Bower, George, Coningsby, Lincs, 1645 Lincs RO Ad/Ac/28/121
Bower, Godfrey, Morton, Derby, 1680 LJRO:cards/1680/4
Bower, Jeffry, Rostherne (Mere), Ches, 1649 Cheshire RO (Name) W.C. 1649
Bower, John, Arreton, Hants, 1649 Hants RO 1647 A5/3
Bower, John, wool stapler, Bradford, Yorks, 1793 Borthwick Test C.P. 1793/3
Bower, Robert, Glossop, Derby, 1684 LJRO/B/C/5/1685/22
Bower, William, Sefton, Lancs, 1592 Lancs RO (Name of Deceased) D.R.C.H. 1592
Bowers q widow, Elizabeth, Southwark, St George the Martyr, Surrey, 1740 Greater London RO DW/OP/1740/12
Bowes, Francys, clergy: 'clerk/parson', Claxby, Lincs, 1587 Lincs RO Ad/Ac/2C/94
Bowghton, John, Otham, Kent, 1608 CKS PRC2/14/39
Bowis, John + Katherine, Horncastle, Lincs, 1633 Lincs RO Ad/Ac/24/162
Bowker, Thomas, Yaxley, Hunts, 1670? Hunts RO/Acc58/15
Bowker, Thomas, Yaxley, Hunts, 1676 Hunts RO/Acc58/52(189)
Bowland, Alexander, Withern, Lincs, 1624 Lincs RO Ad/Ac/19A/45
Bowland, Margaret, Yaxley, Hunts, 1676 Hunts RO/Acc58/21(191)
Bowland, Richard, Yaxley, Hunts, 1678 Hunts RO/Acc58/125(41)
Bowland, Robert, Yaxley, Hunts, 1683 Hunts RO/Acc58/197(44)
Bowlden, Thomas, Waltham, Kent, 1619 CKS PRC2/20/347
Bowlder, Francis, widow, Shrewsbury, Shrops, 1730 LJRO/B/C/5/1732/17
Bowldinge, Robert, Whitstable, Kent, 1617 CKS PRC2/20/300
Bowle, Alice, Brox-Holme, Lincs, 1673 Lincs RO Ad/Ac/35/36
Bowle, John, minor/gentleman?, Canterbury St Alphege, Kent, 1621 CKS PRC20/5/29
Bowle, see Horsley,
Bowler, James, clergy: 'clerk', Stamford, Lincs, 1612 Lincs RO Ad/Ac/11/199
Bowler, Robert, Bisham, Berks, 1586 Berks RO D/A2/C24/f60R
Bowles, Christofer, Hallington, Lincs, 1626? Lincs RO Ad/Ac/20/24
Bowles, Edward, husbandman, Lambourn (East Hanney), Berks, 1664 Berks RO D/A1/45/134C
Bowles, Edward eld, yeoman, Hanney, West, Berks, 1667 Berks RO D/A1/178/89A
Bowles, Henrie, Boston, Lincs, 1619 Lincs RO Ad/Ac/15/288
Bowles, Henry, mason, Fovant, Wilts, 1693 Wilts RO Arch. Sarum/(+ name and date)
Bowles, John, Idmiston (Gomeldon), Wilts, 1691 Wilts RO Arch. Sarum/(+ name and date)
Bowles, Joseph, St Mary Abchurch, London & Middlesex, 1703 PRO PROB5/1560
Bowles, William,
Wilts 1600 c. Wilts RO Miscellaneous Index to Wills (name + date)
Bowles, William, Fisherton Anger, Wilts, 1636 Wilts RO Arch. Sarum/(+ name and date)
Bowles/Cook, Catherine, wife, Kingston Bagpuize, Berks, 1676 Berks RO D/A1/178/158A

Bowley, John, Fishbourne, Sussex, 1664 W. Suss RO EpIII/9/1/50
Bowlles, John, Bracebridge, Lincs, 1602 Lincs RO Ad/Ac/5/121
Bowllesworth, Willyam, Algarkirk, Lincs, 1600 Lincs RO Ad/Ac/5/229
Bowman, Edward, Bilsington, Kent, 1594 CKS PRC2/7/311
Bowman, Edward, clergy: 'clerk', Ewerby, Lincs, 1618 Lincs RO Ad/Ac/14/22
Bowman, Lyon, Huttoft, Lincs, 1623 Lincs RO Ad/Ac/18/25
Bowman, Thomas, Grimston, Leics, 1641 Leics RO PR/I/41A/88
Bowman, William, Brookland, Kent, 1672 CKS PRC2/35/113
Bowne, Edward, Drayton, Fenny, Leics, 1666 Leics RO Administrators Accounts C17th f84
Bowne, Elizabeth, Haxey (East Lound), Lincs, 1663 Lincs RO Ad/Ac/41/72
Bowridge, William, Chard, Som, 1640 Somerset RO D/D/Cta/B26
Bowrman, Edward, Headcorn, Kent, 1601 CKS PRC2/12/48
Bowrne, John, Tenterden, Kent, 1591 CKS PRC2/5/181
Bowrne, William, Upchurch, Kent, 1602 CKS PRC2/12/423
Bowry, John, mariner: 'seaman, RN', Stepney, London & Middlesex, 1677 PRO PROB32/14/71
Bowser, John, Chilham, Kent, 1600 CKS PRC2/11/147
Bowsher, Roger, Chilton Foliat, Wilts, 1674 Wilts RO Miscellaneous Index to Wills (name + date)
Bowthe, Alice, widow, Goxhill, Lincs, 1579 Lincs RO Ad/Ac/2b/25
Bowther, Roger, Selling, Kent, 1601 CKS PRC2/12/32
Bowyer, John, yeoman, Bray, Berks, 1589 Berks RO D/A1/175/115A
Bowyer, John, yeoman, Ospringe, Kent, 1691 CKS PRC2/41/168
Bowyer, Margaret, widow, Bray, Berks, 1598 Berks RO D/A1/175/156A
Bowyer, Mathew, yeoman, Dilton, Wilts, 1639 Wilts RO Chantor Sarum Bundle 4/15
Bowyer, Thomas, Mundham, North (Vinnetrow), Sussex, 1612 W. Suss RO EpI/33/1611/9
Bowyer, William, St Martin in the Fields, London & Middlesex, 1696 Greater London RO AM/PP/Box 1695-1706 pt (uncatalogued)
Box, Henry, gentleman, Witney, Oxon, 1624 Oxon RO MSS Wills 76/3/30
Box, Richard, husbandman, Churchill, Oxon, 1684 Oxon RO MSS Wills 77/2/20
Box, Robert, Sutton Benger, Wilts, 1624 Wilts RO Arch. Wilts.(name + date)
Boxall, Anthony, Aldingbourne, Sussex, 1635 W. Suss RO EpI/33/1635/19
Boxall, John, Grinstead, West, Sussex, 1684 W. Suss RO EpI/33/1684/36
Boxall, Robert, Chapel, North, Sussex, 1650 W. Suss RO EpI/33/1650/7
Boxe, Leonard, gentleman, Ascot under Wychwood, Oxon, 1624 Oxon RO MSS Wills 295/2/92
Boxer, James, tobacco pipe maker, Maidstone, Kent, 1673 CKS PRC20/12/68
Boxley, Joan, Wimborne Minster, Dors, Dorset RO PE/WM CP 2/4/35
Boyce, John eld, Ashby St Ledgers, Northants, 1676 Northants RO NWill A/C/48
Boyce, Richard, carpenter, Wickhampton, Norf, Norfolk RO ANW/23/10/64
Boyce, William, Stawell, Som, 1611 Somerset RO D/D/Cta/B76
Boycott, Henry, Smarden, Kent, 1588 CKS PRC2/4/295
Boye/Crapon, John, Lambourn, Berks, 1612 Berks RO D/A1/176/33C
Boyer, Abraham, Glastonbury St John, Som, 1666 Somerset RO D/D/Cta/B47
Boyer, John, Morborne, Hunts, Hunts RO/Acc58/204(42)
Boyes, Edward, Burlesdon, Hants, 1686 Hants RO 21m65 D8/350
Boyes, Joseph, clergy: 'clerk/reverend/rector', York St Mary in Walmgate, Yorks, Borthwick Chanc C.P. 1765/1
Boyes, Peter, Epworth, Lincs, 1604 Lincs RO Ad/Ac/37/171
Boyfield, William, Saxby, Leics, 1673 Leics RO Administrators Accounts 1667-72 f126
Boykett, James, innholder, Dover, Kent, 1668 CKS PRC19/4/7
Boyleston, Henry, Rolleston, Staffs, 1667 LJRO:cards/1667/11
Boylston, John, Burbage, Leics, 1640 Leics RO PR/I/41A/53
Boylston, William, husbandman, Desford, Leics, 1683 Leics RO Administrators Accounts 1682-86 f6
Boynton, William, Gainsborough, Lincs, 1664 Lincs RO Ad/Ac/41/130
Boys, Alexander, chandler, Canterbury Holy Cross Westgate, Kent, 1642 CKS PRC1/6/49

[Boys:]
Boys, Alexander, Canterbury Holy Cross Westgate, Kent, 1643 CKS PRC1/6/98a
Boys, Alexander, chandler, Canterbury Holy Cross Westgate, Kent, 1643 CKS PRC1/6/98
Boys, Anthony, Borden, Kent, 1672 CKS PRC2/35/9
Boys, Cordelia, widow, Hawkhurst, Kent, 1669 CKS PRC19/4/41
Boys, Edward, esquire, Canterbury St George Martyr, Kent, 1664 CKS PRC1/10/13
Boys, Francis, Eastchurch, Sheppey, Kent, 1637 CKS PRC2/34/21
Boys, Jane, Ospringe, Kent, 1679 CKS PRC2/38/108
Boys, John, gentleman, Challock, Kent, 1614 CKS PRC20/3/134
Boys, John, Ashby St Ledgers, Northants, 1680 Northants RO NWill A/C/15
Boys, John, carpenter, Sittingbourne, Kent, 1681 CKS PRC2/39/
Boys, Richard, merchant, Dover, Kent, 1627 CKS PRC20/8/39
Boys, Steven, Canterbury St Mildred, Kent, 1579 CKS PRC2/1/233
Boys, Suzan, widow, Canterbury St Martin, Kent, 1610 CKS PRC20/2/162
Boys, Thomas, Canterbury St Martin, Kent, 1605 CKS PRC20/1/19
Boys, Vincent, Fordwich, Kent, 1624 CKS PRC2/23/55
Boys/Baylie, Mary, widow, Faversham, Kent, 1662 CKS PRC1/9/6
Boyse, Richard, shipwright, Limehouse, London & Middlesex, 1690 PRO PROB32/29/41
Boze, John, Inkberrow, Worcs, 1681 Worcs RO 008.7 BA3585/830/81
Brabhan, William, Petherton, North, Som, 1588 Somerset RO D/D/Cta/B78
Brabourne, John, clergy: 'vicar', Charlbury, Oxon, 1729 Oxon RO MSS Wills 161/4/34
Brabrooke, Steven, Carlton, Great, Lincs, 1627 Lincs RO Ad/Ac/20b/67
Brabyn, Thomas, St Columb Major, Corn, 1606 Cornwall RO AP/B134
Brace, Henry, brazier, Chichester, Sussex, 1621 W. Suss RO EpIII/9/1/19
Brace, John, Worcester St Martin, Worcs, 1792 Worcs RO 008.7 BA3585/835/bdl 2
Brace, Philip, gentleman, Dodderhill, Worcs, 1601 Worcs RO 008.7 BA3585/838/189
Bracebie, Austine, Aslackby, Lincs, 1639 Lincs RO Ad/Ac/26/53
Bracebridge, William, Kirton, Lincs, 1648 Lincs RO Ad/Ac/30/263
Bracebrigg, Thomas, Scremby, Lincs, 1599 Lincs RO Ad/Ac/5/433
Bracegirdle, William, shopkeeper, Stockport, Ches, 1751 Cheshire RO (Name) W.C. 1751-9
Bracher,
Wilts 1642 Wilts RO Arch. Sarum/(+ name and date)
Bracher, Samuel, Tisbury, Wilts, 1642 Wilts RO Arch. Sarum/(+ name and date)
Brackelbie, see Brackenbury,
Brackeley, Thomas, labourer, Cholsey (Winterbrook), Berks, 1612 Berks RO D/A1/176/43/1C
Brackenburgh, John, Belshford, Lincs, 1619 Lincs RO Ad/Ac/15/167
Brackenbury/Brackelbie, Margaret, widow, Threckingham, Lincs, 1618 Lincs RO Ad/Ac/14/176
Brackett, Thomas, Rolvenden, Kent, 1630 CKS PRC2/30/23
Brackett, see Carpenter,
Bradborne, Thomas, yeoman, Worfield (Chesterton), Shrops, 1663 LJRO:cards/1663/9
Bradbridge, William, Eartham, Sussex, 1673 W. Suss RO EpI/33/1673/22
Bradburie, Thomas, gentleman, Milton next Sittingbourne, Kent, 1605 CKS PRC2/13/95
Bradburie, see Inniotts,
Bradbury, Francis, esquire, Wicken Bonhunt, Essex, 1720 Greater London RO DL/C/547/30
Bradbury, John, Tatenhill, Staffs, 1684 LJRO/B/C/5/1684/15
Bradbury, Joseph, cordwainer: 'shoemaker?', Egginton, Derby, 1709 LJRO/B/C/5/1708/10
Bradbury, Otthowell, Holbeach, Lincs, 1607 Lincs RO Ad/Ac/8a/69
Bradd, John, husbandman, Borden, Kent, 1681 CKS PRC2/39/154
Bradeley, Humfrey, Bromsgrove, Worcs, 1599 Worcs RO 008.7 BA3585/838/135
Brader, Phebe, Utterby, Lincs, 1633 Lincs RO Ad/Ac/24/80
Braderton, William, husbandman, Oxford, Oxon, 1663 Oxon RO MSS Wills 160/4/5
Bradfeild, George, husbandman, Davington, Kent, 1678 CKS PRC2/38/8
Bradfeild, Rose, St Johns Thanet, Kent, 1601 CKS PRC2/12/26
Bradfield, John, bargeman, Reading, Berks, 1660 Berks RO D/A1/178/49/B
Bradfold, Richard, Goring, Sussex, 1594 W. Suss RO EpI/33/1594/3
Bradford,

Wilts 1585? Wilts RO Miscellaneous Index to Wills (name + date)
Bradford, Anne, widow, St Laurence Thanet, Kent, 1695 CKS PRC2/42/78
Bradford, Edwyn, Sandwich, Kent, 1598 CKS PRC2/10/135
Bradford, Humfrey, Astbury (Hulme Walfield), Ches, 1604 Cheshire RO (Name) W.C. 1604
Bradford, John, Clevedon, Som, 1595 Somerset RO D/D/Cta/B89
Bradford, John, Willesborough, Kent, 1603 CKS PRC2/14/78
Bradford, John, Clevedon, Som, 1663 Somerset RO D/D/Cta/B44
Bradford, Thomas, Abingdon, Berks, 1594 Berks RO D/A1/175/134A
Bradford, Thomas, draper: 'linen draper', Abingdon, Berks, 1625 Berks RO D/A1/176/104
Bradford, Thomas, victualler, Abingdon, Berks, 1637 Berks RO D/A1/177/56A
Bradford, William, Stoke Golding, Leics, Leics RO Administrators Accounts 1667-72 f82
Bradforthe, Thomas, Goxhill, Lincs, 1570 Lincs RO Ad/Ac/2b/32
Bradley, Alexander, clergy: 'rector', Elmstone, Kent, 1692 CKS PRC2/42/25
Bradley, Henry, Gosberton, Lincs, 1639 Lincs RO Ad/Ac/26/250
Bradley, Humfrey, Enderby, Bag, Lincs, 1611 Lincs RO Ad/Ac/10/30
Bradley, John, gentleman, Frinstead, Kent, 1635 CKS PRC1/1/43
Bradley, John, confectioner, Birmingham, Warks, 1757 LJRO/B/C/5/1757/100
Bradley, Joseph, Worcester St Helen, Worcs, 1755 Worcs RO 008.7 BA3585/835/bdl 1
Bradley, Martha, widow, Outwell, Norf, 1775 Norfolk RO ANF/11/5/114
Bradley, Robert, Grantham, Lincs, 1612 Lincs RO Ad/Ac/10/132
Bradley, Roger, Kinver, Staffs, 1682 LJRO/B/C/5/1681/4
Bradley, Thomas, Althorpe, Lincs, 1606 Lincs RO Ad/Ac/37/223
Bradley, Thomas, husbandman, Speen (Bagnor), Berks, 1638 Berks RO D/A1/177/69A
Bradley, William, bargeman, Maidenhead, Berks, 1639 Berks RO D/A1/177/70B
Bradly, Thomas, Swinford, Old, Worcs, Worcs RO 008.7 BA3585/830/15
Bradly, Thomas, mariner: 'seaman', Upchurch, Kent, 1679 CKS PRC2/38/110
Bradly, William, yeoman, Herne, Kent, 1694 CKS PRC19/5/16
Bradlye, William, Whitstable, Kent, 1601 CKS PRC2/12/23
Bradshaw, Edward, Bekesbourne, Kent, 1624 CKS PRC20/6/94
Bradshaw, Elizabeth, widow, Dover, Kent, 1684 CKS PRC20/13/404
Bradshaw, Henry, Uttoxeter, Staffs, 1684 LJRO/B/C/5/1684/16
Bradshaw, James eld, yeoman, Eccles (Crofts Bank, Barton upon Irwell), Lancs, 1796 Lancs RO (Name of Deceased) D.R.C.H. 1796-97
Bradshaw, John, yeoman, Eastham (Great Sutton), Ches, 1792 Cheshire RO (Name) W.C. 1792
Bradshaw, Richard, Dover, Kent, 1682 CKS PRC19/4/106
Bradshawe, George, Chislet, Kent, 1600 CKS PRC2/11/165
Bradshawe, John, Marston Bigot, Som, 1611 Somerset RO D/D/Cta/B80
Bradshawe, John, St Johns Thanet, Kent, 1648 CKS PRC1/8/35
Bradshewe, George, clergy: 'vicar', Aldermaston, Berks, 1627 Berks RO D/A1/176/107
Bradstowe, Grace, widow, Chart, Little, Kent, 1605 CKS PRC2/13/93
Bradstreete, Humfrey, Lincoln St Swithin, Lincs, 1597 Lincs RO Ad/Ac/4/91
Bradstreete, Margaret, widow, Horbling, Lincs, 1632 Lincs RO Ad/Ac/23/93
Bragg, George, Bristol St Philip & St Jacob, Glos, Bristol RO 1677/59
Bragg, George, Faversham, Kent, 1639 CKS PRC1/2/26
Bragg, John, Sittingbourne, Kent, 1669 CKS PRC1/14/17
Bragg, Walter, Uphill, Som, 1593 Somerset RO D/D/Cta/B92
Bragg, William, Laverstock, Wilts, 1670 Wilts RO Arch. Sarum/(+ name and date)
Bragge, Edward, Chichester, Sussex, 1603 W. Suss RO EpIII/9/1/3
Brailes, William, Sheldwich, Kent, 1597 CKS PRC2/9/273
Brain, Robert, farmer, Rothwell, Northants, 1791 Northants RO X954/22/24
Braine, Henrie, Canterbury, Kent, 1604 CKS PRC2/13/40
Braine, John, yeoman, Rainford, Lancs, 1775 Lancs RO (Name of Deceased) D.R.C.H. 1775-76
Brainford, John, clothier, Benenden, Kent, 1666 CKS PRC1/11/11
Brakenbury, William, yeoman, Toynton St Peter, Lincs, 1619 Lincs RO Ad/Ac/15/107
Bramall, Elizabeth, widow, Chester, Ches, 1582 Cheshire RO (Name) W.C. 1583

[Bramble:]
Bramble, George, Tenterden, Kent, 1586 CKS PRC2/4/17
Bramble, Stephen, Minster in Sheppey, Kent, 1592 CKS PRC2/5/196
Bramby, William, Gainsborough (Morton), Lincs, 1679 Lincs RO Ad/Ac/43/83
Bramby, see Scupholme,
Bramham, John, butcher, Clifton, Yorks, 1793 Borthwick Test C.P. 1793/4
Bramley, Edward, Pentrich, Derby, 1685 LJRO/B/C/5/1685/23
Bramly, Stephen, Smeeth, Kent, 1677 CKS PRC20/12/227
Branch, William, clergy: 'mr/vicar', Rodmersham, Kent, 1626 CKS PRC2/27/17
Branche, Thomas, clothworker, St Albans St Peters, Herts, 1576 Herts RO ASA25/823
Brand, Christopher, Enderby, Mavis, Lincs, 1674 Lincs RO Ad/Ac/34/28
Brand, Francis, Kirton, Lincs, 1623 Lincs RO Ad/Ac/18/86
Brand, James, Fosdyke, Lincs, 1722 Lincs RO Ad/Ac/45/14
Brand, Richard, husbandman, Newton Purcell, Oxon, 1662 Oxon RO MSS Wills 160/4/4
Brand, William, Marston, Lincs, 1640 Lincs RO Ad/Ac/27/6
Brand, William, Fenton, Lincs, 1641? Lincs RO Ad/Ac/27/340
Brandford, William, husbandman, Sheldwich, Kent, 1677 CKS PRC2/37/6
Brandon, John, Woodhall, Lincs, 1664 Lincs RO Ad/Ac/43/22
Brandreth, Grace, Derby, Derby, 1682 LJRO/B/C/5/1682/14
Brandreth, John, Bromley, Abbots, Staffs, 1672 LJRO:cards/1672/7
Brandwood, Margaret, widow, Altham, Lancs, 1630 Lancs RO (Name of Deceased) D.R.C.H. 1630
Branforth, Edward, Algarkirk, Lincs, 1613 Lincs RO Ad/Ac/12/114
Brangwin, Francis, Warren, Upper, Oxon, 1636 Oxon RO MSS Wills 295/3/64
Brannebie, Jhonne, Faldingworth, Lincs, 1587 Lincs RO Ad/Ac/2C/106
Brannston, William, Heapham, Lincs, 1681 Lincs RO Ad/Ac/34/95
Bransbie, Humfery, gentleman, Heapham, Lincs, 1613 Lincs RO Ad/Ac/8b/71
Bransby, Henry, Conisholme, Lincs, 1640 Lincs RO Ad/Ac/27/39
Branston, John, Bardney, Lincs, 1598 Lincs RO Ad/Ac/4/114
Branston, Margarett, Swayfield, Lincs, 1638 Lincs RO Ad/Ac/25/506
Brarne?, Robert, Stanton, Stoney, Leics, 1641 Leics RO PR/I/41A/76
Brary, John, Billingshurst, Sussex, 1651 W. Suss RO EpI/33/1651/3
Brasfeilde, Thomas, Hurst, Kent, 1611 CKS PRC2/17/169
Brasgirdle, Thomas, Walsall (Goscote Hall), Staffs, 1663 LJRO:cards/1663/10
Brasier, Edward, husbandman, Charlton nr Dover, Kent, 1639 CKS PRC2/34/171
Brasier, Henry, husbandman, St Peter in Thanet, Kent, 1666 CKS PRC1/11/106
Brasill, Thomas, Quarrendon, Bucks, 1663 Oxon RO MSS Wills Pec 33/3/21
Brassington, George, Caverswall, Staffs, 1676 LJRO:cards/1676/8
Brassington, Thomas, yeoman, Westbury, Glos, 1783 GRO GDR/B4/2/B122
Bratfeild, Robert, Birstall, Leics, 1665 Leics RO Administrators Accounts C17th f20
Brather, John, Coates, North, Lincs, 1622 Lincs RO Ad/Ac/17/16
Brathwaite, Agnes, Covent Garden, St Paul, London & Middlesex, 1694 PRO PROB32/32/68
Bratle, Jeremy, Wittersham, Kent, 1639 CKS PRC20/10/116
Brattle, Alexander, Egerton, Kent, 1619 CKS PRC20/4/23
Brattle, Nathaniel, yeoman, Ashford, Kent, 1662 CKS PRC1/9/7
Brattle, Thomas, Maidstone, Kent, 1622 CKS PRC20/6/434
Brattle, Thomas, Goudhurst, Kent, 1633 CKS PRC2/31/85
Bratton, Richard, Saxilby, Lincs, 1667 Lincs RO Ad/Ac/33/19
Braunch, Richard, clergy: 'parson', Hinton, Berks, 1595 Berks RO D/A1/175/141
Bray, Francis, husbandman, Wallington, Herts, Herts RO AHH23/118
Bray, James, clothier, Huddersfield (Deighton), Yorks, 1781 Borthwick Test C.P. 1780/1
Bray, John, Molash, Kent, 1594 CKS PRC2/7/25
Bray, John, Enderby, Wood, Lincs, 1628 Lincs RO Ad/Ac/20b/43
Bray, John, Stone in Oxney, Kent, 1641 CKS PRC1/5/80
Bray, Peter, cordwainer, Wrawby cum Brigg (Glanford Brigg), Lincs, 1645 Lincs RO Ad/Ac/28/113

Bray, Tristram, yeoman, Tamerton, North, Corn, 1647 Cornwall RO AP/B1202/4
Braybrooke, Robert, gentleman, Brightwalton, Berks, 1597 Berks RO D/A1/175/148A
Braybrooke, Thomas, Kingsnorth, Kent, 1685 CKS PRC2/41/43
Braybrooke, William, gentleman, Brightwalton, Berks, 1594 Berks RO D/A1/175/129A&C
Braye, John, yeoman, Burford, Oxon, 1626 Oxon RO MSS Wills 295/2/83
Brayles, John, Leysdown, Kent, 1600 CKS PRC2/11/369
Brayles, Richardin, widow, Leysdown, Kent, 1616 CKS PRC2/20/216
Brayles, Thomas, Iwade, Kent, 1642 CKS PRC1/6/50
Braynche, William, husbandman, Frilford, Berks, 1607 Berks RO D/A1/176/6A
Brayne, Hugh, Cricklade St Sampson, Wilts, 1616 Wilts RO Arch. Wilts.(name + date)
Brayne, Thomas, Canterbury St Andrew, Kent, 1588 CKS PRC2/4/400
Braysland, Richard, Leysdown, Kent, 1606 CKS PRC2/13/38
Brazier, Thomas, Ash next Sandwich, Kent, CKS PRC19/3/113a
Brazier, Thomas, Ash next Sandwich, Kent, 1667 CKS PRC19/3/113
Bread, Dorothy, widow, Whitstable, Kent, 1638 CKS PRC2/34/178
Bread/Sansom, Edward, Malmesbury, Wilts, 1619 Wilts RO Arch. Wilts.(name + date)
Breadon, Dionize, widow, Rustington, Sussex, 1631 W. Suss RO EpI/33/1631/37
Breakell, Richard, Hesketh (Hesketh Bank), Lancs, 1634 Lancs RO (Name of Deceased) D.R.C.H. 1634
Breakspeare, William, blacksmith, Leigh, North, Oxon, 1675 Oxon RO MSS Wills 295/5/19
Bredgate, Thomas, jurat, Dover, Kent, 1589 CKS PRC21/9/279
Bredgeland, Jeames, Lenham, Kent, 1593 CKS PRC2/6/248
Bredgeland, Martin, Cranbrook, Kent, 1635 CKS PRC20/10/104
Bredger, Henrye, Marden, Kent, 1603 CKS PRC2/12/416
Bredger, Roberte, Leeds, Kent, 1582 CKS PRC2/2/146
Bredgland, Thomas, clothworker, Goudhurst, Kent, 1678 CKS PRC2/37/120
Bredgman, Thomas, Milsted, Kent, 1683 CKS PRC2/40/90
Bredmore, John, Potterne, Wilts, 1615 Wilts RO CC Sarum(+ name and date)
Breeche, Jone, Shadoxhurst, Kent, 1593 CKS PRC2/6/446
Breeche, Roger, miller, Chart, Great, Kent, 1585 CKS PRC2/3/274
Breeding, John, brickmaker/coal merchant, Cottingham (Norland Clough), Yorks, 1826 Borthwick Test C.P. 1825/5
Breese, Henry, Itteringham, Norf, 1743 Norfolk RO ANW/23/24/15
Breese, Robert, victualler, Forton, Staffs, 1794 LJRO/B/C/5/1794/10
Bremble, Bartholomew, Wells St Cuthbert, Som, 1619 Somerset RO D/D/Cta/B104
Bremble, Jeames, Tenterden, Kent, 1601 CKS PRC2/12/44
Brems, Thomas, Bearding, 1623 Hants RO 21M65 D8/3
Brencheley, Vyncent, Whitfield alias Beauxfield, Kent, 1596 CKS PRC2/9/43
Brencheley, Wyllyam, Canterbury St Andrew, Kent, 1605 CKS PRC2/13/71
Brenchley, Nathaniel, Newington next Sittingbourne, Kent, 1726 CKS PRC1/18/36
Brenchley, Thomas, Headcorn, Kent, 1616 CKS PRC2/20/324 and 322
Brenchlie, Agnes, Whitfield alias Beauxfield, Kent, 1598 CKS PRC2/9/399
Brenchlie, Elizabeth, Otham, Kent, 1598 CKS PRC2/10/393
Brenchlie, John, Bredgar, Kent, 1605 CKS PRC2/13/60
Brenchlie, William, Bobbing, Kent, 1608 CKS PRC2/14/33
Brenchly, Alice, widow, Bredgar, Kent, 1669 CKS PRC1/14/18
Brenchly, John, Bredgar, Kent, 1625 CKS PRC2/23/59
Brenchly, Nicholas, bachelor, Bredgar, Kent, 1669 CKS PRC1/12/16
Brent, John, Milford, Hants, 1624 Hants RO 21M65 D8/52
Brent, Margaret, widow, Haydon, Dors, 1628? Wilts RO Dean Sarum (name + date)
Breres, John, 1662 Lancs RO (Name of Deceased) D.R.C.H. 1662
Brereton, Ralph, esquire, Handworth, Ches, 1581 Cheshire RO (Name) W.C. 1581
Brereton, Richard, Cheddleton, Staffs, 1684 LJRO/B/C/5/1684/17
Bret, Ann, widow, Wye, Kent, 1639 CKS PRC1/2/27
Bret, Robarte + Christopher, Petham, Kent, 1592 CKS PRC2/5/1

[Brethers:]
Brethers, Thomas, Poulshot, Wilts, 1616 Wilts RO Miscellaneous Index to Wills (name + date)
Brett, Edward, Elham, Kent, 1632 CKS PRC2/31/89
Brett, Frances, Wolstanton, Staffs, 1676 LJRO:cards/1676/9
Brett, Francis, tailor, Norwich St Andrew, Norf, 1805 Norfolk RO ANW/23/27/6
Brett, Gregorie, Smeeth, Kent, 1629 CKS PRC20/8/51
Brett, Gregory, Chart, Great, Kent, 1596 CKS PRC2/9/57
Brett, Jacob, husbandman, Ruckinge, Kent, 1626 CKS PRC2/27/27
Brett, James, Ringwould, Kent, 1629 CKS PRC2/30/13
Brett, James, mercer, Faversham, Kent, 1636 CKS PRC2/33/8
Brett, James, yeoman, St Mary in the Marsh, Kent, 1636 CKS PRC2/33/15
Brett, Jane, Wye, Kent, 1663 CKS PRC1/9/85
Brett, John, Hope All Saints, Kent, 1613 CKS PRC2/17/287
Brett, John, Bonnington, Kent, 1641 CKS PRC1/5/81
Brett, John, Wootton, North, Wilts, 1644 Wilts RO Dean Sarum (name + date)
Brett, Julyan, widow, Godmersham, Kent, 1581 CKS PRC21/5/48
Brett, Michael, Chislet, Kent, 1701 CKS PRC1/16/22
Brett, Nicholas, husbandman, Deal, Kent, 1680 CKS PRC20/12/289
Brett, Ralfe, Mersham, Kent, 1630 CKS PRC20/9/87
Brett, Richard, Woodchurch, Kent, 1627 CKS PRC20/8/25
Brett, Richard eld, Ashford, Kent, 1623 CKS PRC2/23/47
Brett, Robert, Fairfield, Kent, 1640 CKS PRC20/10/120
Brett, Robert, bachelor, Cliffe, West, Kent, 1712 CKS PRC1/17/51
Brett, Robert, bachelor, Cliffe, West, Kent, 1712 CKS PRC19/6/50
Brett, Thomas, Wye, Kent, 1632 CKS PRC2/31/90
Brett, Thomas, gentleman, Wye, Kent, 1667 CKS PRC1/11/107
Brett, William, Lydd, Kent, 1606 CKS PRC20/1/99
Brett, William, New Romney, Kent, 1638 CKS PRC20/10/134
Brett, William, baker, Maidstone, Kent, 1668 CKS PRC19/3/114
Brett, see Tibball,
Bretton, Christopher, Broughton, Lincs, 1598 Lincs RO Ad/Ac/5/306
Brew, James, cotton manufacturer, Bolton, Lancs, 1803 Borthwick Test C.P. 1802/5
Brewen, see Bruin,
Brewer, Anne, widow, Boston, Lincs, 1637? Lincs RO Ad/Ac/25/548
Brewer, Christopher, Wraxall, North, Wilts, 1620 Wilts RO Arch. Wilts.(name + date)
Brewer, Elizabeth, spinster, Rodmersham, Kent, 1681 CKS PRC2/39/147
Brewer, Francis, Potterne, Wilts, 1741 Wilts RO CC Sarum(+ name and date)
Brewer, John, Droxford, Hants, 1666 Hants RO 1669 AD19
Brewer, John, yeoman, Fleet, Lincs, 1683 Lincs RO Ad/Ac/44/68
Brewer, Sarah, Hollow, Worcs, 1681 Worcs RO 008.7 BA3585/837/bdl 2
Brewer, Thomas, Bedminster, Som, 1644 Somerset RO D/D/Cta/B39
Brewer, William, Halesowen, Worcs, 1681 Worcs RO 008.7 BA3585/830/79
Brewster, Edward, Croft, Lincs, 1632 Lincs RO Ad/Ac/23/110
Brewster, John, Bapchild, Kent, 1622 CKS PRC2/26/134
Brewster, Richard, miller, Bicker, Lincs, 1666 Lincs RO Ad/Ac/32/86
Brewster, Thomas, Teynham, Kent, 1671 CKS PRC2/35/18
Brewster, William, yeoman, Sutterton, Lincs, 1614 Lincs RO Ad/Ac/12/196
Brey, William, Somersham, Hunts, 1693 Hunts RO/Acc58/276
Briane, Johnne, Bolingbroke, Lincs, 1593 Lincs RO Ad/Ac/3/89
Briant, John, St Laurence Thanet, Kent, 1618 CKS PRC2/20/355
Briant, William, Enmore, Som, 1612 Somerset RO D/D/Cta/B35
Briant, William, husbandman, Willesborough, Kent, 1619 CKS PRC2/20/310
Briant, William, yeoman, Shrivenham (Fernham), Oxon, 1672 Berks RO D/A1/178/134C
Brice, Ciciley, Rothwell, Lincs, 1627 Lincs RO Ad/Ac/20b/99
Brice, Edward, Sandhurst, Kent, 1607 CKS PRC2/14/43
Brice, Gilbert, Chislet, Kent, 1623 CKS PRC2/23/28

Brice, Henrie, Theddlethorpe All Saints, Lincs, 1624 Lincs RO Ad/Ac/19A/89
Brice, John, Durrington, Wilts, 1624 Wilts RO Miscellaneous Index to Wills (name + date)
Brice, John, yeoman, Kintbury (Walcot Marsh), Berks, 1663 Berks RO D/A1/178/68C
Brice, John, blacksmith, Faversham, Kent, 1664 CKS PRC1/10/14
Brice, John, blacksmith, Staple next Wingham, Kent, 1681 CKS PRC20/13/9
Brice, John eld, Staple next Wingham, Kent, 1626 CKS PRC20/7/106
Brice, Jonathan, blacksmith, Sibsey, Lincs, 1683 Lincs RO Ad/Ac/44/74
Brice, Mathew, Faversham, Kent, 1690 CKS PRC2/41/169
Brice, Nicholas, gentleman, Cookham (Northtown), Berks, 1669 Berks RO D/A1/178/111A
Brice, Samson, Graveney, Kent, 1630 CKS PRC20/9/65
Brice, Simon, blacksmith, Preston next Faversham, Kent, 1664 CKS PRC1/9/86
Brice, Simon, Ash next Sandwich, Kent, 1671 CKS PRC20/12/6
Brice, Solomon, Faversham, Kent, 1699 CKS PRC1/16/3
Brice, Thomas, mariner, Faversham, Kent, 1693 CKS PRC19/5/17
Brice, Vincent, Preston next Wingham, Kent, 1633 CKS PRC2/32/20
Brice, William, Quinton, Northants, 1679 Northants RO NWill A/C/138
Brickels, Hammonde, Baumber, Lincs, 1612 Lincs RO Ad/Ac/10/134
Brickenburie, Clement, Ivychurch, Kent, 1610 CKS PRC20/2/146
Brickenbury, Stephen, yeoman, Brookland, Kent, 1671 CKS PRC2/35/15
Brickenbury, see Owen,
Brickenden, Anthony, Deal, Kent, 1674 CKS PRC20/12/112
Brickenden, John, Wye, Kent, 1612 CKS PRC2/17/205
Brickenden, John, Ruckinge, Kent, 1666 CKS PRC1/11/108
Brickenden, Richard, Cranbrook, Kent, 1648 CKS PRC1/8/5
Brickenden, Robarte, Benenden, Kent, 1604 CKS PRC2/13/101
Brickenden, Robert, High Halden, Kent, 1619 CKS PRC2/20/220
Brickenden, Thomas, Mersham, Kent, 1692 CKS PRC1/15/112a
Brickenden, Thomas, blacksmith, Mersham, Kent, 1692 CKS PRC1/15/112
Brickendenn, William eld, jurat, Tenterden, Kent, 1622 CKS PRC2/23/38
Brickinden, Elizabeth, widow, Ruckinge, Kent, 1675 CKS PRC2/36/14
Brickner, Thomas, Kidlington (Water Eaton), Oxon, Oxon RO MSS Wills 295/3/60
Bridden, John, Youlgreave, Derby, 1694 LJRO/B/C/5/1694/19
Bride, Edward, Claythorpe, Lincs, 1624 Lincs RO Ad/Ac/18/108
Bridge, Averie, husbandman, Ospringe, Kent, 1626 CKS PRC2/25/18
Bridge, George, Faversham, Kent, 1616 CKS PRC2/20/370
Bridge, Golden, groom, Newmarket, Suff, 1743 Suff RO(B) IC500/3/50/65
Bridge, James, Drayton Bassett, Staffs, 1676 LJRO:cards/1676/10
Bridge, Joane, spinster, Canterbury, Kent, 1639 CKS PRC1/2/28
Bridge, John, Canterbury, Kent, 1619 CKS PRC2/20/182
Bridge, John, Biddenden, Kent, 1631 CKS PRC2/31/15
Bridge, John, Lydd, Kent, 1682 CKS PRC20/13/230
Bridge, John, yeoman, Lydd, Kent, 1682 CKS PRC20/13/224
Bridge, Joseph, Canterbury Holy Cross Westgate, Kent, 1629 CKS PRC2/30/16
Bridge, Richard, Sturry, Kent, 1629 CKS PRC2/30/15
Bridge, Richard eld, dyer, Chester, Ches, 1635 Cheshire RO (Name) W.C. 1635/6
Bridge, Thomas, Canterbury St Alphege, Kent, 1605 CKS PRC20/1/67
Bridge, Thomas eld, Egerton, Kent, 1640 CKS PRC19/1/26
Bridge, see Gate,
Bridgeman, Richard, Sacombe, Herts, 1635 Herts RO AHH23/96
Bridger, George, Smarden, Kent, 1640 CKS PRC1/4/14
Bridger, Henry, Rudgwick, Sussex, 1670 W. Suss RO EpI/33/1670/14
Bridger, John, Pagham, Sussex, 1634 W. Suss RO EpIV/10/2/8
Bridger, John, Boughton Malherbe, Kent, 1637 CKS PRC2/34/25
Bridger, John, Storrington, Sussex, 1685 W. Suss RO EpI/33/1684/6
Bridger, Nicholas, Stedham, Sussex, 1647 W. Suss RO EpI/33/1647/3

[Bridger:]
Bridger, Richard, Yapton, Sussex, 1594 W. Suss RO EpI/33/1594/6
Bridger, Thomas, Birdham, Sussex, 1617 W. Suss RO EpI/33/1617/30
Bridger, William, Warminghurst, Sussex, 1598 W. Suss RO EpI/33/1598/3
Bridges, Elizabeth, lady/widow, Keynsham, Som, 1627 Somerset RO D/D/Cta/B4
Bridges, Ezechiel, yeoman, St Nicholas at Wade, Kent, 1673 CKS PRC20/12/70
Bridges, Gregory, Road, Som, 1588 Somerset RO D/D/Cta/B77
Bridges, John, yeoman, St Nicholas at Wade, Kent, 1669 CKS PRC19/4/42
Bridges, John, yeoman, St Nicholas at Wade, Kent, 1673 CKS PRC20/12/71
Bridges, Peter, Frittenden, Kent, 1634 CKS PRC2/32/7
Bridges, Richard, Hundleby, Lincs, 1633 Lincs RO Ad/Ac/24/146
Bridges, William, Tydd St Mary, Lincs, 1605 Lincs RO Ad/Ac/6/99
Bridges, see Stockden,
Bridgland, Mary, Goudhurst, Kent, 1680 CKS PRC2/39/6
Bridgland, Samuel, clothier, Cranbrook, Kent, 1675 CKS PRC2/36/161
Bridgman, Henrie, Tenterden, Kent, 1638 CKS PRC1/1/69
Briearley, James, cotton manufacturer, Prestwich (Hermitage, Crompton), Lancs, 1797 Lancs RO (Name of Deceased) D.R.C.H. 1797
Brierly, Jonathan, St Martin in the Fields, London & Middlesex, 1711 PRO PROB32/54/88
Brigg, Henry, Bethersden, Kent, 1673 CKS PRC2/35/202
Brigges, Cassandra, Sutton (Lutton), Lincs, 1608 Lincs RO Ad/Ac/8a/168
Brigges, Richard, Swineshead, Lincs, 1595 Lincs RO Ad/Ac/5/513
Briggs, Elizabeth, widow, Melton Mowbray, Leics, 1669 Leics RO Administrators Accounts 1667-72 f29
Briggs, Henrye, Woolsthorpe, Lincs, 1644 Lincs RO Ad/Ac/28/78
Briggs, Hugh, brickmaker, Remenham, Berks, 1678 Berks RO D/A1/178/174C
Briggs, John, Gedney, Lincs, 1626 Lincs RO Ad/Ac/20/57
Briggs, Richard, Bitchfield, Lincs, 1601 Lincs RO Ad/Ac/5/358
Briggs, Susanna, widow, Upton, Hunts, 1711 Hunts RO/Acc58/303
Briggs, Thomas, Sandwich St Peter, Kent, 1626 CKS PRC2/27/21
Briggs, Thomas, victualler, Stanton, Derby, 1791 LJRO/B/C/5/1791/7
Briggs, Thomas, victualler, Stanton, Derby, 1793 LJRO/B/C/5/1793/7
Brigham, John, gentleman, Cottenham, Cambs, 1753 Cambs RO 1750/Inv
Bright, Clement, Canterbury St Peter, Kent, 1624 CKS PRC2/23/56
Bright, John, Reculver, Kent, 1599 CKS PRC21/14/506
Bright, John, Rolvenden, Kent, 1639 CKS PRC1/2/29
Bright, John, cordwainer: 'shoemaker', Worcester St Nicholas, Worcs, 1681 Worcs RO 008.7 BA3585/830/78
Bright, Robert, Humberstone, Leics, 1666 Leics RO Administrators Accounts C17th f87
Bright, Thomas, Newent, Glos, 1819 GRO GDR/B4/2/B127
Bright, William, husbandman, Orlestone, Kent, 1684 CKS PRC2/40/179
Brightfeild, John, Stukeley, Hunts, 1676 Hunts RO/Acc58/26(193)
Brightling, Abraham, Marden, Kent, 1598 CKS PRC2/10/385
Brightman, Thomas, yeoman, Thurlby, Lincs, 1619 Lincs RO Ad/Ac/15/249
Brightwell/Shonke, Richard, husbandman, Brimpton, Berks, 1632 Berks RO D/A1/177/37C
Brigstock, Joane, widow, Husbands Bosworth, Leics, 1639 Leics RO PR/I/41A/10
Brimley, Edward, blacksmith, Hardingstone (Cotton-End), Northants, 1679 Northants RO NWill A/C/137
Brimsted, William, Leeds, Kent, 1628 CKS PRC2/29/14
Brinall, James, victualler, Gloucester, Glos, 1828? GRO GDR/B4/2/B129
Brinall, James, victualler, Gloucester, Glos, 1829 GRO GDR/B4/2/B130
Brinckle, Margarett, widow, Branston, Lincs, 1640 Lincs RO Ad/Ac/27/268
Brinckle, Robert, Swineshead, Lincs, 1639 Lincs RO Ad/Ac/25/323
Brincknell, Robert, tailor, Bromham, Wilts, 1620 Wilts RO Arch. Wilts.(name + date)
Brindley, Elizabeth, widow, Leek, Staffs, 1682 LJRO/B/C/5/1681/5
Brindley, John, Leek, Staffs, 1724 LJRO/B/C/5/1724/5

Brindley, Thomas, farmer, Aston, Warks, 1692 LJRO/B/C/5/1692/15
Brinsbury/Grantham, Mary, widow, Clapham, Sussex, 1684 W. Suss RO EpI/33/1684/47
Brinsmaid, Daniel, Messingham, Lincs, 1635 Lincs RO Ad/Ac/40/95
Brinton, Roger, Breamore, Hants, 1663 Hants RO 21M65 D8/164
Briscoe, Joseph, Cheadle, Staffs, 1680 LJRO:cards/1680/5
Briskowe, Edward, Boston, Lincs, 1612 Lincs RO Ad/Ac/11/29
Briskowe, Hugh, Reading, Berks, 1575 Berks RO D/A1/175/77
Brissenden, Isaac, Bethersden, Kent, 1614 CKS PRC2/18/120
Brissenden, Joan, Bethersden, Kent, 1597 CKS PRC2/10/20
Brissenden, John, Wittersham, Kent, 1637 CKS PRC20/10/39
Brissenden, John, Biddenden, Kent, 1703 CKS PRC1/16/42
Brissenden, William, yeoman, Bethersden, Kent, 1685 CKS PRC2/41/45
Brisseville, Anthonie, weaver: 'silk weaver', Canterbury, Kent, 1641 CKS PRC19/2/6
Bristoe, John, cordwainer, Norwich, Norf, 1708 Norfolk RO ANW/23/8/144
Bristow, Jacob, Lacock, Wilts, 1633 Wilts RO Arch. Wilts.(name + date)
Bristow, James, gentleman, Rigsby, Lincs, 1667 Lincs RO Ad/Ac/33/27
Bristow, John, Weston, Som, 1626 Somerset RO D/D/Cta/B16
Bristow, John, yeoman, Cholsey, Berks, 1647 Berks RO D/A1/178/29
Bristow, John, Liddington, Wilts, 1672 Wilts RO Arch. Wilts.(name + date)
Bristow, John, Clarendon Park, Wilts, 1685 Wilts RO Miscellaneous Index to Wills (name + date)
Bristowe, James, yeoman, Tilehurst, Berks, 1636 Berks RO D/A1/177/47E
Bristowe, Richard, Kirdford, Sussex, 1633 W. Suss RO EpI/33/1633/17
Bristowes, Johane, widow, Headcorn, Kent, 1586 CKS PRC2/4/45
Brit, Thomas, Ashurst, Sussex, 1617 W. Suss RO EpI/33/1617/35
Britcher, Alexander, Maidstone, Kent, 1675 CKS PRC20/12/160
Britcherd, Robert,
Wilts 1622 Wilts RO Miscellaneous Index to Wills (name + date)
Britchley, see Birtchley,
Brithrid, Sarah, Davington, Kent, 1676 CKS PRC2/37/16
Britridge, Simon, Rickmansworth, Herts, 1622 Herts RO ASA25/2732
Brittaine, Thomas, Bristol, Glos, Bristol RO 1687/CP
Brittayne, Francis, Coxwell, Great, Berks, 1617 Berks RO D/A1/176/61A
Britten, Nicholas, Stoke, North, Som, 1599 Somerset RO D/D/Cta/B41
Britteyne, Henry, Woodnesborough, Kent, 1598 CKS PRC2/10/260
Brixe, Richard, Harrietsham, Kent, 1601 CKS PRC2/12/52
Brixey, Rebecca, widow, Ringwood, Hants, 1665 Hants RO 1665 AD19
Brixey, Richard, Mere, Wilts, 1678 Wilts RO Dean Sarum (name + date)
Brizenden, Robert, Bethersden, Kent, 1640 CKS PRC1/2/30
Broad, Henry, Maidstone, Kent, 1624 CKS PRC20/6/110
Broad, John, Bath (Stawles), Som, 1619 Somerset RO D/D/Cta/B102
Broad, John, Sandwich, Kent, 1685 CKS PRC2/41/49
Broad, Richard, Stoke-upon-Trent (Fenton Vivian), Staffs, 1675 LJRO:cards/1675/13
Broad, Samuel, Compton Dando, Som, 1729 c. Somerset RO D/D/Cta/B88
Broad, Thomas, brewer: 'beerbrewer', St Peter in Thanet, Kent, 1683 CKS PRC2/40/91
Broadbent, George, joiner, Tong, Yorks, 1794 Borthwick Test C.P. 1794/2
Broadbridge, Gregory, Hernhill, Kent, 1679 CKS PRC20/12/292
Broade, Rychard, Rolvenden, Kent, 1590 CKS PRC2/5/219
Broade, Thomas, St Martin by Looe, Corn, 1606 Cornwall RO AP/B108
Broade, William, Maidstone, Kent, 1599 CKS PRC21/14/528
Broadhurst, John, yeoman, Kintbury (Elcot), Berks, 1675 Berks RO D/A1/178/152C
Broadley, William, yeoman, Stallingborough, Lincs, 1627 Lincs RO Ad/Ac/20/94
Broadstreete, Edward, Boughton under Blean, Kent, 1629 CKS PRC20/8/57
Broadstreete, Edward, yeoman, Minster in Sheppey, Kent, 1671 CKS PRC2/35/13
Broadwater, Giles, yeoman, Garsington, Oxon, Oxon RO MSS Wills 76/4/5
Broadway, Edward, blacksmith, Coventry, Warks, 1778 LJRO/B/C/5/1778/12

[Broadway:]
Broadway, Thomas, vintner, Bristol, Glos, 1683 PRO PROB5/906
Brock, George, Belton All Saints, Lincs, 1673 Lincs RO Ad/Ac/35/59
Brock, Laurence, maltster, Maidenhead, Berks, 1630 Berks RO D/A1/177/5C
Brock, Sarah, widow, Bristol, Glos, Bristol RO 1723/4
Brockas/Beckett, Pexall?, gentleman, Titchfield, Hants, 1672 Hants RO 21m65 D8/235
Brocke, Adam, St Albans St Peters, Herts, 1612 Herts RO ASA25/4810
Brocke, John, gentleman, Chester, Ches, 1594 Cheshire RO (Name) W.C. 1594
Brockenborrowe, William, Kington St Michael, Wilts, 1624 Wilts RO Arch. Wilts.(name + date)
Brockenshaw, Joseph, Lyndhurst, Hants, Hants RO 21m65 D8/351
Brockett, Nicholas, Tortington, Sussex, 1670 W. Suss RO EpI/33/1670/11
Brockhill, Robert, gentleman, Linsted, Kent, 1671 CKS PRC2/35/8
Brockhull, Edward, Rodmersham, Kent, 1602 CKS PRC2/12/422
Brockhull, Richard, Bredgar, Kent, 1600 CKS PRC2/11/163
Brockhull, William, Borden, Kent, 1595 CKS PRC2/8/181
Brockhurst, Edmund, degrees: 'M.A.', Oxford (University), Oxon, 1624 Bodleian HYP B8/20-21
Brockhurst, John, mercer, Bromsgrove, Worcs, 1593 Worcs RO 008.7 BA3585/838/95
Brocklesbie, Simon, Rasen, Middle, (Tupholme), Lincs, 1620 Lincs RO Ad/Ac/16/12
Brocklesby, Nathaniel, Sutton St James, Lincs, 1614 Lincs RO Ad/Ac/13/69
Brocklesby, Thomas, Stainton by Langworth (Newball), Lincs, 1640s? Lincs RO Ad/Ac/40/145
Brockman, Christopher, Whitfield alias Beauxfield, Kent, 1615 CKS PRC2/20/241
Brockman, John, Newington next Hythe, Kent, 1607 CKS PRC2/14/51
Brockman, Thomas, Swingfield, Kent, 1582 CKS PRC2/2/51
Brockman, Zouch, gentleman, Cheriton, Kent, 1682 CKS PRC20/13/226
Brockwell, Alice, Teynham, Kent, 1633 CKS PRC2/32/6
Brockwell, Henry, Milton next Sittingbourne, Kent, 1620 CKS PRC2/20/360
Brockwell, Henry, Stockbury, Kent, 1683 CKS PRC2/40/95
Brockwell, Henry, St Martin in the Fields, London & Middlesex, 1691 PRO PROB32/30/124
Brockwell, John, Sandwich St Bartholomew's Hospital, Kent, 1589 CKS PRC21/10/297
Brockwell, John, gentleman, Lenham, Kent, 1672 CKS PRC2/35/112
Brockwell, John, yeoman, Wormshill, Kent, 1684 CKS PRC2/40/177
Brockwell, John, Davington, Kent, 1701 CKS PRC1/16/23
Brockwell, Parnell, widow, Teynham, Kent, 1694 CKS PRC2/42/58
Brockwell, Richard, Boughton under Blean, Kent, 1604 CKS PRC21/17/147
Brockwell, Samuel, Teynham, Kent, 1614 CKS PRC2/18/77
Brockwell, Susanne, Canterbury St Paul, Kent, 1667 CKS PRC1/11/109
Brockwell, Thomas, physician, Sittingbourne, Kent, 1685 CKS PRC2/41/69
Brockwell, see Elwyn,
Brodbank, Thomas, Frittenden, Kent, 1587 CKS PRC2/4/426
Brodburye, John, Smeeth, Kent, 1593 CKS PRC21/12/372
Brodehed, Henry, Wingham, Kent, 1586 CKS PRC21/8/198
Brodhurst, Richard, Shifnal, Shrops, 1682 LJRO/B/C/5/1681/6
Brodhurst, William, gentleman, Lilleshall, Shrops, 1662 LJRO:cards/1662/5
Brodnax, Anthonie, gentleman, Canterbury St Mildred, Kent, 1649 CKS PRC1/8/36
Brodnax, Catheryne, spinster, Canterbury, Kent, 1620 CKS PRC2/20/138
Brodnax, Jervice, Godmersham, Kent, 1644 CKS PRC19/2/70
Brodnax, John, Godmersham, Kent, 1638 CKS PRC20/10/148
Brodnax, Thomas, esquire, Godmersham, Kent, 1673 CKS PRC20/12/3
Brodrippe, William, Berrow, Som, 1612 Somerset RO D/D/Cta/B36
Brodshawe, George, Chart, Little, Kent, 1610 CKS PRC2/15/16
Brodstreet, Alice, widow, Minster in Sheppey, Kent, 1638 CKS PRC2/34/169
Broke, Henry, Waltham, Kent, 1591 CKS PRC2/6/410
Broke, Robarte, Woodchurch, Kent, 1580 CKS PRC21/4/225
Broke, see Worsyter,
Broman, Arnold, Whitstable, Kent, 1592 CKS PRC2/6/480
Broman, Thomas, Hollingbourne, Kent, 1635 CKS PRC20/10/35

Brombie, George, Grayingham, Lincs, 1634 Lincs RO Ad/Ac/40/5
Bromby, Valentine, gentleman, Kirkby on Bain (Toft Grange), Lincs, 1623 Lincs RO Ad/Ac/18/80
Brome, Robert, husbandman, Curry Mallett, Som, 1593 Somerset RO D/D/Cta/B87
Bromefeelde, Edwarde, Tenterden, Kent, 1596 CKS PRC2/8/113
Bromeley, John, ironmonger, Chesterfield, Derby, 1684 LJRO/B/C/5/1683/4
Bromeman, Henrye, Marden, Kent, 1608 CKS PRC2/13/31
Bromfeild, Daniell, Daresbury, Ches, 1665 Cheshire RO (Name) W.C. 1664
Bromfield, Alice, Crowland, Lincs, 1638 Lincs RO Ad/Ac/25/118
Bromham, Jacob, Compton, Wilts, 1670 Wilts RO Arch. Sarum/(+ name and date)
Bromidge, Abraham, clergy: 'vicar', Sheldwich, Kent, 1662 CKS PRC1/9/8
Bromiley, Daniel, husbandman, Deane (Halliwell), Lancs, 1783 Lancs RO (Name of Deceased) D.R.C.H. 1783
Bromingham, Anne, Dalby, Little, Leics, 1672 Leics RO Administrators Accounts 1667-72 f55
Bromley, Mary, widow, Barthomley, Ches, 1746 Cheshire RO (Name) W.C. 1746
Bromley, Robert, joiner, Dover, Kent, 1683 CKS PRC20/13/307
Bromley, Thomas, Capel le Ferne, Kent, 1693 CKS PRC2/42/27
Brompton, Agnes, widow, Elham, Kent, 1605 CKS PRC2/13/50
Brompton, John, Ashby cum Fenby, Lincs, 1611 Lincs RO Ad/Ac/10/3
Brompton, Richard, Shrewsbury, Shrops, 1667 LJRO:cards/1667/12
Brompton, William, Elham, Kent, 1606 CKS PRC2/14/28
Bromwich, Arthur, Seend, Wilts, 1673 Wilts RO Arch. Sarum/(+ name and date)
Bronsell, Mary, spinster, Covent Garden, St Paul, London & Middlesex, 1730 Greater London RO AM/PP/Box 1726-1732 pt (uncatalogued)
Broockland, Christian, Abingdon St Helen (Northcourt), Berks, 1573 Berks RO D/A2/C10/f124R
Broodie, Bryan, Barton, Earls, Northants, 1674 Northants RO NWill A/C/142
Brook, John, Kingston, Kent, 1608 CKS PRC2/15/28
Brook, Thomas, Maidstone, Kent, 1623 CKS PRC20/6/430
Brookarde, Abigall, Sandwich, Kent, 1606 CKS PRC2/14/56
Brookbanckes, Christopher, Madresfield, Worcs, 1682 Worcs RO 008.7 BA3585/837/bdl 3
Brooke, Anne, widow, Milton next Sittingbourne, Kent, 1664 CKS PRC1/10/15
Brooke, Arthur, gentleman, Grimsby, Great, Lincs, 1637 Lincs RO Ad/Ac/25/549
Brooke, Edward, gentleman, Pluckley, Kent, 1620 CKS PRC2/20/334
Brooke, Elizabeth, widow, Maidstone, Kent, 1619 CKS PRC20/4/35
Brooke, Frances, St Johns Thanet, Kent, 1673 CKS PRC2/35/198
Brooke, Frances, widow, St Johns Thanet, Kent, 1680 CKS PRC1/15/95
Brooke, Gabraell, mariner, St Johns Thanet, Kent, 1662 CKS PRC1/9/9
Brooke, George, Hartlip, Kent, 1679 CKS PRC2/38/98
Brooke, Hammon, Queenborough, Kent, 1615 CKS PRC2/20/249
Brooke, Jane, mrs/widow, Preston next Faversham, Kent, 1641 CKS PRC1/5/82
Brooke, John, Lenham, Kent, 1599 CKS PRC2/10/505
Brooke, John, bricklayer, Maidstone, Kent, 1616 CKS PRC20/3/511
Brooke, John, Biddenden, Kent, 1628 CKS PRC2/28/12
Brooke, John, Rustington, Sussex, 1631 W. Suss RO EpI/33/1631/11
Brooke, John, gentleman, Thornham, Kent, 1637 CKS PRC2/34/24
Brooke, John, gentleman, Worfield (Hoccome), Shrops, 1663 LJRO:cards/1663/11
Brooke, Joseph, gentleman, Minster in Sheppey, Kent, 1643 CKS PRC19/2/71
Brooke, Josephe, Midley, Kent, 1608 CKS PRC2/14/47
Brooke, Martin eld, Woodnesborough, Kent, 1644 CKS PRC1/7/23
Brooke, Martyn, Woodnesborough, Kent, 1597 CKS PRC2/10/361
Brooke, Richard, yeoman, Eastchurch, Sheppey, Kent, 1649 CKS PRC1/8/59
Brooke, Richard, Bilsington, Kent, 1678 CKS PRC2/38/4
Brooke, Roger, vintner, Sherbourne, Dors, 1609 Wilts RO Dean Sarum (name + date)
Brooke, Samuell, Sandwich St Clement, Kent, 1638 CKS PRC2/34/167
Brooke, Thomas, Binbrook, Lincs, 1606 Lincs RO Ad/Ac/7/158

[Brooke:]
Brooke, Thomas, husbandman, Leysdown, Kent, 1626 CKS PRC2/25/19
Brooke, Thomas, Witley, Great, Worcs, 1677 Worcs RO 008.7 BA3585/837/bdl 6
Brooke, Thomas, yeoman, Lydd, Kent, 1679 CKS PRC20/12/290
Brooke, William, Powick, Worcs, 1602 Worcs RO 008.7 BA3585/838/191a
Brooke, William, esquire, Hartlip, Kent, 1632 CKS PRC2/31/87
Brooke, William, bachelor, Elham, Kent, 1664 CKS PRC1/9/88
Brooke, Wyllyam, Canterbury St Mildred, Kent, 1587 CKS PRC2/4/126
Brooke/Rayner, Susan, widow, Teynham, Kent, 1663 CKS PRC1/9/87
Brookefeild, John, Coldwaltham, Sussex, 1623 W. Suss RO EpI/33/1623/13
Brookefilede, George, Coldwaltham, Sussex, 1623 W. Suss RO EpI/33/1623/7
Brookeman, Charles, Kingston Seymour, Som, 1623 Somerset RO D/D/Cta/B7
Brooker, John, husbandman, Ilsley, East, Berks, 1610 Berks RO D/A1/176/20C
Brooker, John, Pagham, Sussex, 1626 W. Suss RO EpIV/10/1/26
Brooker, John, tanner, Staplehurst, Kent, 1681 CKS PRC2/39/150
Brooker, Robert, Stone in Oxney, Kent, 1613 CKS PRC2/17/126
Brooker, Robert, Henley, Oxon, 1631 Oxon RO MSS Wills 295/3/32
Brooker, Robert, Bethersden, Kent, 1640 CKS PRC1/4/15
Brooker, Walter, husbandman, Ilsley, East, Berks, 1637 Berks RO D/A1/177/61A
Brookes, Anthony, Kirton, Lincs, 1624 Lincs RO Ad/Ac/19A/49
Brookes, Edward, Wanlip, Leics, Leics RO Administrators Accounts 1667-72 f98
Brookes, Elline, widow, Liverpool, Lancs, 1618 Lancs RO (Name of Deceased) D.R.C.H. 1618
Brookes, James, Nettleton, Lincs, 1649 Lincs RO Ad/Ac/30/97
Brookes, John, maltster, Abingdon, Berks, 1647 Berks RO D/A1/45/20B
Brookes, John, yeoman, Shipton under Wychwood, Oxon, 1666 Oxon RO MSS Wills 76/4/21
Brookes, John, Ferring, Sussex, 1670 W. Suss RO EpI/33/1670/12
Brookes, Richard, Ascot under Wychwood, Oxon, 1638 Oxon RO MSS Wills 295/3/75
Brookes, Robert, yeoman, Bearsted, Kent, 1676 CKS PRC2/37/12
Brookes, Samuel, Cleeve Prior, Worcs, 1811 Worcs RO 008.7 BA3585/835/bdl 2
Brookes, Sarah, widow/hatter, Derby, Derby, 1714 LJRO/B/C/5/1714/7
Brookes, Thomas, husbandman, Leigh, South, Oxon, 1627 Oxon RO MSS Wills 295/3/15
Brookes, Thomas, Billingborough, Lincs, 1642 Lincs RO Ad/Ac/28/6
Brookes, William, yeoman, Searby, Lincs, 1660s? Lincs RO Ad/Ac/42/11
Brookes, William, Angmering, Sussex, 1669 W. Suss RO EpI/33/1669/2
Brookes, William, cook, Oxford (Merton College), Oxon, 1673 Bodleian HYP B8/22-25
Brookes/Hodges, William, Wells, Som, 1726 Somerset RO D/D/Cta/B65
Brookfield, John, Coldwaltham, Sussex, 1623 W. Suss RO EpI/33/1623/5
Brookfild, John, Pulborough?, Sussex, 1606 W. Suss RO EpI/33/1606/6
Brookhouse, John, Grantham, Lincs, 1671 Lincs RO Ad/Ac/33/182
Brookinge, James, St Stephens by Saltash, Corn, 1613 Cornwall RO AP/B320
Brookland, Thomasine, widow, Sunningwell, Berks, 1625 Berks RO D/A1/176/95D
Brooks, Henry, butcher, Aldermaston, Berks, 1641 Berks RO D/A1/177/101A
Brooks, John sen, yeoman, Lambourn (East Hanney), Oxon, 1672 Berks RO D/A1/178/118C
Brooks, Joseph, St Botolph without Aldersgate, London & Middlesex, 1676 PRO PROB5/1756
Brooks, Margarett, widow, St James Westminster, London & Middlesex, 1714 Greater London RO AM/PP/Box 1711-1714 pt (uncatalogued)
Brooks, see Darlinge,
Brookshaw, William, Alfreton, Derby, 1818 LJRO:cards/1818/1
Brooman, Arnold, Whitstable, Kent, 1634 CKS PRC2/32/145
Brooman, John, mariner, St Johns Thanet, Kent, 1677 CKS PRC2/37/7
Brooman, Robert, Wittering, West, Sussex, 1597 W. Suss RO EpI/33/1597/4
Brooman, Thomas, Loose, Kent, 1680 CKS PRC20/13/5
Broome, Ambrose, waterman, Reading St Lawrence, Berks, 1621 Berks RO D/A1/176/76C
Broome, Henry, Lovington, Som, 1634 Somerset RO D/D/Cta/B19
Broome, Hugh, Sandbach (Little Hassall), Ches, 1662 Cheshire RO (Name) W.C. 1662
Broome, John, Dover, Kent, 1602 CKS PRC21/16/148

Broome, Richard, Kington St Michael, Wilts, 1639 Wilts RO Arch. Wilts.(name + date)
Broome, Symon, alderman/mr, Canterbury St Andrew, Kent, 1603 CKS PRC2/13/107
Broome, Thomas, Budworth, Great (Northwich), Ches, 1596 Cheshire RO (Name) W.C. 1596
Broome, Thomas, yeoman, Elmsted, Kent, 1625 CKS PRC2/25/24
Brotherton, Geoffrey, Grantham, Lincs, 1596 Lincs RO Ad/Ac/5/511
Brotherton, Thomas, yeoman, Eastchurch, Sheppey, Kent, 1670 CKS PRC1/15/9
Brotherton, William, fishmonger, Salisbury, Wilts, 1629 Wilts RO Miscellaneous Index to Wills (name + date)
Brougar, Thomas, Dover St James, Kent, 1617 CKS PRC20/4/9
Brouger, Cycyly, Staplehurst, Kent, 1597 CKS PRC2/10/131
Brough, Robert, Measham, Derby, 1680 LJRO:cards/1680/6
Broughe, Agnes, widow, Lincoln, Lincs, 1580? Lincs RO Ad/Ac/2C/112
Broughton, Anthony, Bobbing, Kent, 1622 CKS PRC2/23/41
Broughton, Avery, Horncastle, Lincs, 1600 Lincs RO Ad/Ac/5/535
Broughton, Hughe, Witham, North, Lincs, 1622 Lincs RO Ad/Ac/17/78
Broughton, John, Rolvenden, Kent, 1582 CKS PRC2/2/73
Broughton, Leonard, Kirton, Lincs, 1622 Lincs RO Ad/Ac/17/63
Broughton, Robert, yeoman, Rooden, Lancs, 1629 Lancs RO (Name of Deceased) D.R.C.H. 1628-29
Broughton, Thomas, Brookland, Kent, 1609 CKS PRC2/15/47
Broughton, Thomas, gentleman, Englefield, Berks, 1616 Berks RO D/A1/176/53A
Broughton, William, yeoman, Cumnor (Farmoor), Berks, 1642 Berks RO D/A1/177/96A
Browkard, Martin, Sandwich, Kent, 1607 CKS PRC2/14/52
Brown, 1666 Lancs RO (Name of Deceased) D.R.C.H. 1665
Brown, Ann, widow, Aldborough, Yorks, 1817 Borthwick D/C C.P. 1816/1
Brown, Benjamin, pigkiller, Wotton under Edge, Glos, 1832 GRO GDR/B4/2/B133
Brown, Henry, yeoman, Abbots Ripton, Hunts, 1740 Hunts RO/Acc58/322
Brown, James, esquire, Westhoughton, Lancs, 1634 Lancs RO (Name of Deceased) D.R.C.H. 1634
Brown, James, Dilton, Wilts, 1750? Wilts RO Miscellaneous Index to Wills (name + date)
Brown, John, Barton on Humber, Lincs, 1598 Lincs RO Ad/Ac/5/453
Brown, John, yeoman, Thatcham, Berks, 1678 Berks RO D/A1/178/151C
Brown, John, Anderby, Lincs, 1683 Lincs RO Ad/Ac/44/87
Brown, John, yeoman, Handsworth, Staffs, 1697 LJRO/B/C/5/1698/27
Brown, John, factor, Coventry, Warks, 1774 LJRO/B/C/5/1774/16
Brown, John, cordwainer, Kenilworth, Warks, 1778 LJRO/B/C/5/1778/14b
Brown, John, husbandman, Chester St Mary on the Hill (Handbridge), Ches, 1778 Cheshire RO (Name) W.C. 1778
Brown, Richard, tailor, Newbury, Berks, 1683 Berks RO D/A1/179/20D
Brown, Robert, Boston, Lincs, 1783 Lincs RO Ad/Ac/45/45
Brown, Stephen, yeoman, Pulham St Mary the Virgin, Norf, 1771 Norfolk RO ANF/11/5/95
Brown, Thomas, labourer, Horncastle, Lincs, 1671 Lincs RO Ad/Ac/33/200
Brown, Thomas, merchant, Manchester, Lancs, 1721 Lancs RO (Name of Deceased) D.R.C.H. 1721
Brown, Thomas, mercer, Witton (Northwich), Ches, 1748 Cheshire RO (Name) W.C. 1748-50
Browne, Addam, Burton Coggles, Lincs, 1663 Lincs RO Ad/Ac/32/49
Browne, Agnes, spinster, Warnham, Sussex, 1629 W. Suss RO EpI/33/1629/17
Browne, Alyce, widow, Ashford, Kent, 1582 CKS PRC2/2/209
Browne, Andrew, Marden, Wilts, 1611 Wilts RO Arch. Sarum/(+ name and date)
Browne, Ann, widow, Winwick, Hunts, Hunts RO/Acc58/117(152)
Browne, Anne, widow, Pinchbeck, Lincs, 1666 Lincs RO Ad/Ac/32/116
Browne, Anne, widow, Cherhill, Wilts, 1689 Wilts RO Miscellaneous Index to Wills (name + date)
Browne, Anthony, gentleman, Broad Chalke, Wilts, 1641 Wilts RO Arch. Sarum/(+ name and date)

[Browne:]
Browne, Anthony, Chichester, Sussex, 1668 W. Suss RO EpIII/9/1/54
Browne, Arthur, gentleman, Gosberton, Lincs, 1634 Lincs RO Ad/Ac/24/218
Browne, Bartholomew, Horncastle, Lincs, 1630 Lincs RO Ad/Ac/23/14
Browne, Catharine, Devizes, Wilts, 1612 Wilts RO CC Sarum(+ name and date)
Browne, Christopher, Whitstable, Kent, 1618 CKS PRC2/20/196
Browne, Christopher, Horsington, Lincs, 1635 Lincs RO Ad/Ac/24/366
Browne, Clement, yeoman, Hollingbourne, Kent, 1617 CKS PRC20/3/492
Browne, Clement, Gedney, Lincs, 1626 Lincs RO Ad/Ac/20/58
Browne, Daniel, Sandwich St Peter, Kent, 1638 CKS PRC2/34/164
Browne, Dionice, widow, Barham, Kent, 1664 CKS PRC1/9/89
Browne, Edmund, Purton, Wilts, 1624 Wilts RO Arch. Wilts.(name + date)
Browne, Edmund, carpenter, Preston next Wingham, Kent, 1700 CKS PRC2/42/149
Browne, Edward, Barton on Humber, Lincs, 1579 Lincs RO Ad/Ac/2b/38
Browne, Edward, Maidstone, Kent, 1612 CKS PRC20/2/436
Browne, Edward, Sittingbourne, Kent, 1620 CKS PRC2/20/366
Browne, Edward, yeoman, Ashbury (Idstone), Berks, 1641 Berks RO D/A1/177/87/1/A
Browne, Edward, gentleman, Swineshead, Lincs, 1672 Lincs RO Ad/Ac/33/193
Browne, Edward, Deal, Kent, 1698 CKS PRC19/5/56
Browne, Edward, Preston next Wingham, Kent, 1713 CKS PRC1/17/52
Browne, Edward, yeoman, Bramham, Yorks, 1723 Borthwick Test C.P. 1723/3
Browne, Elizabeth, Hareby, Lincs, 1627 Lincs RO Ad/Ac/22/49
Browne, Francis, Nonington, Kent, 1629 CKS PRC20/8/17
Browne, Francis, Bremhill, Wilts, 1638 Wilts RO Arch. Wilts.(name + date)
Browne, Gabriel, Letcombe Regis, Berks, 1619 Berks RO D/A1/176/67C
Browne, Gabriell, Smarden, Kent, 1586 CKS PRC2/4/79
Browne, George, innholder, Barton on Humber, Lincs, 1598 Lincs RO Ad/Ac/5/330
Browne, George, Algarkirk, Lincs, 1613 Lincs RO Ad/Ac/11/75
Browne, George, Hollingbourne, Kent, 1613 CKS PRC20/2/488
Browne, George, fellmonger, Lincoln, Lincs, 1632 Lincs RO Ad/Ac/23/35
Browne, George, Crich (Wheatcroft), Derby, 1663 LJRO:cards/1663/12
Browne, George, Tisbury, Wilts, 1673 Wilts RO Arch. Sarum/(+ name and date)
Browne, Henry, Clewer, Berks, 1626 Berks RO D/A1/176/101C
Browne, Henry, Worth, Kent, 1637 CKS PRC20/10/114
Browne, Henry, Laughton, Lincs, 1662 Lincs RO Ad/Ac/41/7
Browne, Henrye, yeoman, Herne, Kent, 1617 CKS PRC20/4/39
Browne, Huon, Marton, Lincs, 1613 Lincs RO Ad/Ac/8b/65
Browne, James, yeoman, Hainford, Norf, Norfolk RO ANW/23/13/50
Browne, James, Epworth, Lincs, 1682 Lincs RO Ad/Ac/44/9
Browne, James, Duffield, Derby, 1683 LJRO/B/C/5/1683/5
Browne, James, Borden, Kent, 1706 CKS PRC19/6/18
Browne, Jeames, Lydd, Kent, 1603 CKS PRC21/15/328
Browne, Jerimie, Adisham, Kent, 1626 CKS PRC20/7/1
Browne, Joan, widow, Woodstock, Oxon, 1626 Oxon RO MSS Wills 5/2/9
Browne, Joane, widow, Ivychurch, Kent, 1641 CKS PRC19/1/27
Browne, John,
Worcs Worcs RO 008.7 BA3585/834/443
Browne, John, Worth, Kent, 1593 CKS PRC21/12/103
Browne, John, Ropsley, Lincs, 1607 Lincs RO Ad/Ac/8a/57
Browne, John, Canterbury Holy Cross Westgate, Kent, 1612 CKS PRC2/17/111
Browne, John, Kingsnorth, Kent, 1612 CKS PRC2/16/152
Browne, John, Wellington, Som, 1623 Somerset RO D/D/Cta/B8
Browne, John, Sittingbourne, Kent, 1631 CKS PRC20/9/69
Browne, John, Carlton le Moorland, Lincs, 1635 Lincs RO Ad/Ac/24/401
Browne, John, gunner, Dover, Kent, 1638 CKS PRC20/10/138
Browne, John, Calne, Wilts, 1639 Wilts RO Miscellaneous Index to Wills (name + date)

[Browne:]

Browne, John, Charlton, Wilts, 1639 Wilts RO Arch. Wilts.(name + date)
Browne, John, Holbeach, Lincs, 1641 Lincs RO Ad/Ac/27/227
Browne, John, Althorpe, Lincs, 1645 Lincs RO Ad/Ac/41/116
Browne, John, Binstead, Hants, 1666 Hants RO 21M65 D8/193
Browne, John, Monks Horton, Kent, 1673 CKS PRC2/35/204
Browne, John, Quadring, Lincs, 1673 Lincs RO Ad/Ac/25/473
Browne, John, Morley, Derby, 1681 LJRO/B/C/5/1682/15
Browne, John, yeoman, Whaddon, Glos, 1682 GRO GDR/B4/2/B184
Browne, John, Pinchbeck, Lincs, 1685 Lincs RO Ad/Ac/44/149
Browne, John, yeoman, Smarden, Kent, 1688 CKS PRC2/41/116
Browne, John, Whatley, Som, 1705 Somerset RO D/D/Cta/B67
Browne, John, Ellingham, Little, Norf, 1808 Norfolk RO ANW/23/27/10
Browne, John eld, yeoman, Chalgrove, Oxon, 1663 Oxon RO MSS Wills 76/4/14
Browne, Joseph, gentleman, Minsterworth, Glos, 1785 GRO GDR/B4/2/B139
Browne, Katherine, Grimoldby, Lincs, 1635 Lincs RO Ad/Ac/24/520
Browne, Katherine, Charlton Mackrell, Som, 1712 Somerset RO D/D/Cta/B66
Browne, Lawrence, Torksey, Lincs, 1602 Lincs RO Ad/Ac/37/126
Browne, Margery, Bucklebury, Berks, 1611 Berks RO D/A1/176/26A
Browne, Mary, spinster, Handsworth, Staffs, 1810 LJRO/B/C/5/1810/2
Browne, Mathew, clergy: 'clerk', Stainby, Lincs, 1613 Lincs RO Ad/Ac/11/52
Browne, Mathew, Bilsington, Kent, 1662 CKS PRC1/9/10
Browne, Matthew, yeoman, Harbledown, Kent, 1726 CKS PRC1/18/37
Browne, Michaell, St Johns Thanet, Kent, 1601 CKS PRC2/12/56
Browne, Mildred, widow, Boston, Lincs, 1668 Lincs RO Ad/Ac/33/58
Browne, Myles, Challock, Kent, 1578 CKS PRC21/3/184
Browne, Nicholas, Donington, Lincs, 1638 Lincs RO Ad/Ac/25/290
Browne, Peter, Canterbury, Kent, 1616 CKS PRC2/20/200
Browne, Richard, Lyneham, Wilts, 1627 Wilts RO Arch. Wilts.(name + date)
Browne, Richard, Herne, Kent, 1644 CKS PRC19/2/85
Browne, Richard, gentleman, Saltfleetby St Peter, Lincs, 1668 Lincs RO Ad/Ac/33/73
Browne, Richard, mariner, Dover, Kent, 1681 CKS PRC20/13/87
Browne, Richerde, Maidstone, Kent, 1586 CKS PRC21/8/64
Browne, Robarte, Mersham, Kent, 1616 CKS PRC2/20/228
Browne, Robert, Careby, Lincs, 1613 Lincs RO Ad/Ac/12/85
Browne, Robert, Elmsted, Kent, 1621 CKS PRC2/23/21
Browne, Robert, Bradford on Avon, Wilts, 1627 Wilts RO Arch. Sarum/(+ name and date)
Browne, Robert, Chart nr Sutton Valence, Kent, 1628 CKS PRC2/29/16
Browne, Robert, Haxey, Lincs, 1650 Lincs RO Ad/Ac/40/206
Browne, Robert, esquire, Westhoughton (Brinsop), Lancs, 1663 Lancs RO (Name of Deceased) D.R.C.H. 1663-64
Browne, Robert, Minster in Sheppey, Kent, 1677 CKS PRC2/37/118
Browne, Robert, Hankerton, Wilts, 1679 Wilts RO Miscellaneous Index to Wills (name + date)
Browne, Robert, bookbinder, Cambridge St Mary the Great, Cambs, 1682 CUL V.C. Acc./Box3/8
Browne, Robert + Helen, university: 'scholar's servant', Cambridge St Benedict, Cambs, 1622 CUL V.C. Acc./Box2/8
Browne, Roberte, Wingham, Kent, 1592 CKS PRC21/11/218
Browne, Roger, St Albans, Herts, 1609 Herts RO ASA25/4766
Browne, Roger, Ipsden, Oxon, 1630 Oxon RO MSS Wills 295/3/30
Browne, Roger, Elmsted, Kent, 1633 CKS PRC2/32/16
Browne, Samuell, Canterbury St Andrew, Kent, 1597 CKS PRC2/9/401
Browne, Simon, Shepton Mallet, Som, 1682 Somerset RO D/D/Cta/B69
Browne, Stephen, Worth, Kent, 1634 CKS PRC20/10/62
Browne, Susanne, Hythe St Leonard, Kent, 1620 CKS PRC20/5/11
Browne, Thomas, Lilbourne, Northants, Northants RO NWill A/C/158
Browne, Thomas, Boston, Lincs, 1577 Lincs RO Ad/Ac/2b/37

[Browne:]
Browne, Thomas, Godmersham, Kent, 1579 CKS PRC21/3/329
Browne, Thomas, Eastry, Kent, 1584 CKS PRC21/6/426
Browne, Thomas, Bethersden, Kent, 1592 CKS PRC2/5/192
Browne, Thomas, St Albans, Herts, 1595 Herts RO ASA25/1455
Browne, Thomas, Donington, Lincs, 1602 Lincs RO Ad/Ac/5/149
Browne, Thomas, Frampton, Lincs, 1612 Lincs RO Ad/Ac/11/167
Browne, Thomas, Hythe St Leonard, Kent, 1612 CKS PRC20/2/438
Browne, Thomas, Toynton, High, Lincs, 1613 Lincs RO Ad/Ac/11/54
Browne, Thomas, gentleman, Chester (Netherleigh), Ches, 1625 Cheshire RO (Name) W.C. 1625/6
Browne, Thomas, Patching, Sussex, 1629 W. Suss RO EpIV/10/1/16
Browne, Thomas, Hawkinge, Kent, 1637 CKS PRC2/34/20
Browne, Thomas, Witham on the Hill (Manthorpe), Lincs, 1638 Lincs RO Ad/Ac/25/104
Browne, Thomas, mariner, Dover, Kent, 1638 CKS PRC20/10/136
Browne, Thomas, Heene, Sussex, 1643 W. Suss RO EpIV/10/2/28
Browne, Thomas, grocer, Faversham, Kent, 1663 CKS PRC1/9/90
Browne, Thomas, Whaplode, Lincs, 1671 Lincs RO Ad/Ac/33/184
Browne, Thomas, Grafton Underwood, Northants, 1680 Northants RO NWill A/C/16
Browne, Thomas, High Halden, Kent, 1681 CKS PRC2/39/4
Browne, Thomas, Saltfleetby, Lincs, 1683 PRO PROB5/1353
Browne, Thomas, husbandman, Loose, Kent, 1683 CKS PRC20/13/313
Browne, Thomas, fisherman, Rochester St Margaret, Kent, 1689 PRO PROB5/1184
Browne, Thomas ygr, Canterbury St Andrew, Kent, 1639 CKS PRC1/2/31
Browne, Walter, Brading, Hants, 1664 Hants RO 21M65 D8/184
Browne, William, Boughton under Blean, Kent, 1584 CKS PRC21/7/28
Browne, William, Maidstone, Kent, 1598 CKS PRC21/14/173
Browne, William, Wells St Cuthbert, Som, 1600 Somerset RO D/D/Cta/B100
Browne, William, Minster in Sheppey, Kent, 1602 CKS PRC2/12/418
Browne, William, Boston, Lincs, 1606 Lincs RO Ad/Ac/7/34
Browne, William, Spalding, Lincs, 1606 Lincs RO Ad/Ac/7/159
Browne, William, gentleman, Newbury, Berks, 1608 Berks RO D/A1/175/196B
Browne, William, yeoman, Saltfleetby All Saints, Lincs, 1611 Lincs RO Ad/Ac/10/23
Browne, William, Baston, Lincs, 1612 Lincs RO Ad/Ac/11/177
Browne, William, Boughton Aluph, Kent, 1617 CKS PRC2/20/344
Browne, William, Ashton Keynes, Wilts, 1631 Wilts RO Arch. Wilts.(name + date)
Browne, William, butcher, Somerford, Great, Wilts, 1637 Wilts RO Arch. Wilts.(name + date)
Browne, William, Bethersden, Kent, 1671 CKS PRC2/35/5
Browne, William, innholder, Wilton, Wilts, 1673 Wilts RO Arch. Sarum/(+ name and date)
Browne, William, Canterbury St Peter, Kent, 1675 CKS PRC2/36/165
Browne, William, Dauntsey, Wilts, 1679 Wilts RO Miscellaneous Index to Wills (name + date)
Browne, William, yeoman, Moulton, Lincs, 1680 Lincs RO Ad/Ac/43/123
Browne, William, Wilton, Wilts, 1682 Wilts RO Arch. Sarum/(+ name and date)
Browne, William, fellmonger, Loose, Kent, 1684 CKS PRC20/13/394
Browne, William, Worth, Kent, 1688 CKS PRC20/13/577
Browne, Wolfran, Gainsborough (East Stockwith), Lincs, 1619? Lincs RO Ad/Ac/8b/391
Browne, Zachary, Lydd, Kent, 1585 CKS PRC21/7/166
Browne/Clement, Peter,
Wilts 1600 c. Wilts RO Miscellaneous Index to Wills (name + date)
Browne/Weekes, Grace, wife, Wrington, Som, 1697 Somerset RO D/D/Cta/B68
Browne, see Andrew, Burnett, Johnson & Smith,
Browneing, John, St Giles without Cripplegate, London & Middlesex, 1669 PRO PROB32/6/45
Brownell, Elizabeth, spinster, Bowdon (Carrington), Ches, 1768 Cheshire RO (Name) W.C. 1768
Brownerigge, Oswalde, gentleman, Kirton, Lincs, 1612 Lincs RO Ad/Ac/11/5
Browning, Arthur, cook, Cambridge St Mary the Great, Cambs, 1610 CUL V.C.Acc./Box1/7
Browning, Edward, Barham, Kent, 1641 CKS PRC1/4/16

Browning, Jane, widow, Aubourn, Lincs, 1620 Lincs RO Ad/Ac/16/18
Browning, John, Hythe St Leonard, Kent, 1631 CKS PRC20/9/57
Browning, John, Ashford, Kent, 1672 CKS PRC2/35/111
Browning, Reynold, Lydd, Kent, 1632 CKS PRC20/9/53
Browning, Richard, Sellindge, Kent, 1682 CKS PRC2/40/5
Browning, Sibill, widow, Lydd, Kent, 1634 CKS PRC20/10/84
Browning, Thomas, Alford, Som, 1594 Somerset RO D/D/Cta/B90
Browning, Thomas ygr, Postling, Kent, 1635 CKS PRC2/33/12
Browning, William, Lydd, Kent, 1636 CKS PRC20/10/100
Browning, William, gentleman, Stanford, Kent, 1641 CKS PRC19/1/28
Browning, William, yeoman, Chillenden, Kent, 1685 CKS PRC2/41/48
Browninge, George, Aslackby, Lincs, 1642 Lincs RO Ad/Ac/27/325
Browninge, Joan, widow, Wimborne Minster, Dors, 1607 Dorset RO PE/WM CP 2/4/8
Browninge, John, Elham, Kent, 1620 CKS PRC2/20/164
Browninge, Lewis, university: 'scholar's servant', Cambridge, Cambs, 1634 c. CUL V.C. Acc./Box2/9
Browninge, Richard, Wimborne Minster, Dors, 1601 Dorset RO PE/WM CP 2/4/3
Browninge, Richard, gentleman, Kilkhampton, Corn, 1613 Cornwall RO AP/B275/3
Brownlowe, Thomas, yeoman, Stainfield, Lincs, 1626 Lincs RO Ad/Ac/20/75
Brownlowe, Vincent, Belton All Saints, Lincs, 1623 Lincs RO Ad/Ac/8c/61
Brownswell, Roger, Stocklinch Magdalen, Som, 1590 Somerset RO D/D/Cta/B85
Brownyng, Clement, Postling, Kent, 1590 CKS PRC2/5/208
Brownynge, Edward, Crundale, Kent, 1585 CKS PRC2/3/311
Brownynge, Julian, clergy: 'vicar', Felpham, Sussex, 1583 W. Suss RO EpI/33/1583/2
Broxholm, Jenet, Owersby, Lincs, Lincs RO Ad/Ac/2C/50
Broxholme, Godfrey, apothecary, Lincoln, Lincs, 1633 Lincs RO Ad/Ac/24/104
Bruar, John, Fivehead, Som, 1645 Somerset RO D/D/Cta/B
Brudenell, Ellanor, widow, Stonton Wyville, Leics, 1641 Leics RO PR/I/41A/57
Bruen, Jonathan, yeoman, Alvanley, Ches, 1735 Cheshire RO (Name) W.C. 1735-6
Bruer, George, Lydd, Kent, 1626 CKS PRC20/7/337
Bruger, Ralph, Funtington, Sussex, 1598 W. Suss RO EpI/33/1598/9
Bruin/Brewen, Clement, gentleman, St Martin in the Fields, London & Middlesex, 1698 PRO PROB32/36/7
Brumbie, Elizabeth, widow, Messingham, Lincs, 1662 Lincs RO Ad/Ac/41/29
Brumbie, see Burrill,
Brumby, Anthony, Barnetby, Lincs, 1644 Lincs RO Ad/Ac/28/96
Brumby, John, Bottesford (Yaddlethorpe), Lincs, 1681 Lincs RO Ad/Ac/34/82
Brumby, William, Rasen, Middle, Lincs, 1672 Lincs RO Ad/Ac/35/141
Brumsden, Edward, Swinbrook, Oxon, 1624 Oxon RO MSS Wills 295/2/88
Brumwell, Henry, Wittersham, Kent, 1643 CKS PRC19/2/72
Brumwell, William, surgeon, Newcastle upon Tyne, Northumb, 1842 Borthwick Test C.P. 1842/6
Brunker, Ann, Bradford on Avon, Wilts, 1635 Wilts RO Arch. Sarum/(+ name and date)
Brunton, John, soap boiler, Norwich, Norf, 1760 Norfolk RO ANW/23/25/47A
Brushe, George, Swallowfield, Berks, 1612 Berks RO D/A1/176/40A
Bruton, John, yeoman, Cotheridge, Worcs, 1602 Worcs RO 008.7 BA3585/838/226
Bruton, Richard, Stixwold, Lincs, 1648 Lincs RO Ad/Ac/30/281
Bruton, see Burton,
Bruxbie, John, Canterbury All Saints, Kent, 1664 CKS PRC1/9/91
Bryan, Anthony, weaver, Reading St Lawrence, Berks, 1604 Berks RO D/A1/175/183A
Bryan, Charles, pawn broker, Chapman, Lower, London & Middlesex, 1813 Greater London RO DL/C/572/39
Bryan, Edward, Swaton, Lincs, 1673 Lincs RO Ad/Ac/35/28
Bryan, Richard, gentleman, Abingdon, Berks, 1616 Berks RO D/A1/176/48A
Bryan, Robert, gentleman, Bolingbroke, Old, Lincs, 1635 Lincs RO Ad/Ac/24/379
Bryant, Humfreye, Dover, Kent, 1606 CKS PRC20/1/189

[Bryant:]
Bryant, Humphry, Cranbrook, Kent, 1677 CKS PRC2/37/8
Bryant, John, St Mary in the Marsh, Kent, 1612 CKS PRC2/16/56
Bryant, Thomas, Ippollitts, Herts, 1637 Herts RO AHH23/100
Bryant, William, yeoman, Shrivenham (Fernham), Berks, 1664 Berks RO D/A1/178/70A
Bryantt, George, St Mary in the Marsh, Kent, 1613 CKS PRC2/17/252
Bryars, Chambers, cardmaker, Halifax, Yorks, 1833 Borthwick Test C.P. 1833/1
Bryce, Richard, Hallow, Worcs, Worcs RO 008.7 BA3585/838/70
Bryce, Thomas, Eastry, Kent, 1612 CKS PRC20/2/422
Bryce, Thomas eld, Tilmanstone, Kent, 1586 CKS PRC2/4/194
Bryce, Wyllyam, Maidstone, Kent, 1581 CKS PRC21/4/353
Brydall, Phillip, esquire, Lincoln's Inn, London & Middlesex, 1700 PRO PROB32/41/83
Brydges, John, Grimley, Worcs, 1685 Worcs RO 008.7 BA3585/830/90
Brynde, Thomas, Aldbourne, Wilts, 1638 Wilts RO Arch. Wilts.(name + date)
Bryne, Robert, Salisbury St Edmund, Wilts, 1631 Wilts RO Miscellaneous Index to Wills (name + date)
Brynker, John, Wingham, Kent, 1583 CKS PRC21/6/421
Bryson, Robarte, clergy: 'clerk/vicar', Grantham, Lincs, 1601 Lincs RO Ad/Ac/5/475
Bubb, John, Canterbury St Alphege, Kent, 1627 CKS PRC20/8/45
Buchler, Marie, spinster, Butterwick, Lincs, 1626 Lincs RO Ad/Ac/20/63
Buck, Wokingham, Berks, 1600 Wilts RO Miscellaneous Index to Wills (name + date)
Buck, Elizabeth, spinster, Stockbury, Kent, 1669 CKS PRC1/14/19
Buck, Richard, Sittingbourne, Kent, 1625 CKS PRC2/23/24
Buck, Symon + Alice, yeoman & widow, Fleet, Lincs, 1619 Lincs RO Ad/Ac/15/163
Buck, Thomas, gentleman, Surfleet, Lincs, 1619 Lincs RO Ad/Ac/15/165
Buck, Thomas, Toynton, Lincs, 1640 Lincs RO Ad/Ac/26/245
Buck, Walter, Faversham, Kent, 1599 CKS PRC2/10/313
Buck, William, Carlton, South, Lincs, 1663 Lincs RO Ad/Ac/42/4
Buck, William, merchant, Halifax, Yorks, 1800 Borthwick Test C.P. 1800/5
Buckberrie, Buckberrie, Anthonye, Billingborough, Lincs, 1598 Lincs RO Ad/Ac/4/21
Buckberry, John, Sholden, Kent, 1626 CKS PRC2/25/9
Bucke, John, Compton Martin, Som, 1587 Somerset RO D/D/Cta/B105
Bucke, John, carpenter, Canterbury St Margaret, Kent, 1662 CKS PRC1/9/11
Bucke, Peregrine, gentleman, Syston, Lincs, 1639 Lincs RO Ad/Ac/26/158
Bucke, Robert, Harmston, Lincs, 1637 Lincs RO Ad/Ac/25/519
Bucke, Samuel, gardener, Canterbury St Mary Bredin, Kent, 1668 CKS PRC1/12/17
Bucke, Sara, widow, Cranbrook, Kent, 1602 CKS PRC2/12/457
Buckeridge, Simon, husbandman, Ashampstead, Berks, 1612 Berks RO D/A1/176/41A
Buckeridge, William, Lydiard Millicent, Wilts, 1624 Wilts RO Arch. Wilts.(name + date)
Buckeridge, see Kelsoe,
Buckherst, James, Canterbury St Mary Bredman, Kent, 1597 CKS PRC2/9/21
Buckherst, Joseph, victualler, Bethersden, Kent, 1649 CKS PRC1/8/60
Buckherst, Stephen, Canterbury Holy Cross Westgate, Kent, 1598 CKS PRC2/10/332
Buckherst, Thomas, Charing, Kent, 1580 CKS PRC21/4/176
Buckherst, William, Canterbury St Mary Bredman, Kent, 1603 CKS PRC2/14/68
Buckherst, William, Stockbury, Kent, 1638 CKS PRC20/10/130
Buckhurst, Bartholomew, tailor, Herne, Kent, 1681 CKS PRC20/13/95
Buckhurst, John, labourer, Sutton Valence, Kent, 1638 CKS PRC1/1/70
Buckhurst, Michael, Staplehurst, Kent, 1678 CKS PRC2/37/116
Buckhurst, Rebecca, minor, Canterbury St Mary Bredman, Kent, 1599 CKS PRC2/10/450
Buckhurst, Thomas, gentleman, Appledore, Kent, 1686 CKS PRC2/41/68
Buckhurst, William eld, Canterbury St Andrew, Kent, 1669 CKS PRC1/13/15
Buckhurst, William eld, Stockbury, Kent, 1670 CKS PRC1/15/10
Buckingham, Anne, widow, Wye, Kent, 1618 CKS PRC2/20/280
Buckingham, Robert, husbandman, Kea, Corn, 1606 Cornwall RO AP/B110/8
Buckingham, Thomas, husbandman, Hanney, West, Berks, 1626 Berks RO D/A1/176/113A

Buckingham, Thomas eld, Sandford, Oxon, 1632 Oxon RO MSS Wills 295/3/36
Buckingham, William, Kimpton, Herts, 1639 Herts RO AHH23/113
Buckland, James, husbandman, Goudhurst, Kent, 1676 CKS PRC2/37/13
Buckland, James eld, yeoman, Goudhurst, Kent, 1643 CKS PRC1/6/51
Buckland, Jeames, Headcorn, Kent, 1614 CKS PRC2/18/5
Buckland, John, Staplehurst, Kent, 1596 CKS PRC2/8/348
Buckland, John eld, Tibshelf, Derby, 1672 LJRO:cards/1672/9
Buckland, Margery, Watlington, Oxon, 1634 Oxon RO MSS Wills 295/3/54
Buckle, Nicholas, Stratfield Mortimer, Berks, 1604 Berks RO D/A1/175/177A
Buckler, Daubeny, grocer, Bristol, Glos, Bristol RO 1721/6
Buckler, see Bishopp,
Buckley, James, Oldham (Whitfield), Lancs, 1632 Lancs RO (Name of Deceased) D.R.C.H. 1631
Buckley, Michael, yeoman, Tidmarsh, Berks, 1640 Berks RO D/A1/177/49A
Buckley, Thomas, Hodnet (Moreton Say, Longford), Shrops, 1672 LJRO:cards/1672/10
Buckly, William, Tackley (Nethercott), Oxon, 1635 Oxon RO MSS Wills 295/3/62
Bucklye, Thomas, university: 'Fellow of St John's College, Cambridge/University Appraiser/B.D.' Cambridge (St John's College), Cambs, 1632 CUL V.C. Acc./Box2/10
Buckman, Edward, carpenter, Milton next Sittingbourne, Kent, 1668 CKS PRC1/13/16
Buckman, Robert, Brent, East, Som, 1608 Somerset RO D/D/Cta/B96
Buckmer, Christopher, Murston, Kent, 1649 CKS PRC1/8/61
Buckmer, Joane, Milton next Sittingbourne, Kent, 1639 CKS PRC1/2/32
Buckmer, Nicholas, Upchurch, Kent, 1626 CKS PRC2/27/25
Buckmer, Thomas, Milton next Sittingbourne, Kent, 1590 CKS PRC2/5/206
Buckminster, Thomas, Holbeach, Lincs, 1629 Lincs RO Ad/Ac/22/34
Buckminster, Thomas, Holbeach, Lincs, 1648 Lincs RO Ad/Ac/30/269
Bucknall, Thomas, yeoman, Rolleston, Staffs, 1668 LJRO:cards/1668/1
Bucknall, William, yeoman, Solihull, Warks, 1694 LJRO/B/C/5/1694/21
Bucknam, Joane, Maidstone, Kent, 1593 CKS PRC21/12/78
Bucknell, Andrew, Thorney, West, Sussex, 1673 W. Suss RO EpI/33/1672/7
Bucknell, Edward, university: 'porter', Oxford (Merton College), Oxon, 1669 Bodleian HYP B8/26-27
Bucknell, John, Winwick, Hunts, 1676 Hunts RO/Acc58/53(140)
Buckner, Henry, Minster in Sheppey, Kent, 1600 CKS PRC2/11/373
Buckston, Edmund, Coleby, Lincs, 1614 Lincs RO Ad/Ac/13/151
Buckston, John, Kirkby Underwood, Lincs, 1619 Lincs RO Ad/Ac/15/121
Budd, Christopher, Sittingbourne, Kent, 1640 CKS PRC1/4/17
Budd, Richard, Maidstone, Kent, 1631 CKS PRC20/9/49
Budd, Robert, bellman, Oxford St Michael, Oxon, 1638 Oxon RO MSS Wills 115/2/34
Budd, William, Winchester, Hants, 1625 Hants RO 21M65 D8/109
Buddes, William, Staplehurst, Kent, 1597 CKS PRC2/9/31
Buddivant, George, Nettleton, Lincs, 1623 Lincs RO Ad/Ac/18/85
Budds, John, husbandman, Rolvenden, Kent, 1674 CKS PRC2/36/18
Budds, Mary, widow, Folkestone, Kent, 1672 CKS PRC2/35/3
Budds, Samuel, East Sutton, Kent, 1634 CKS PRC2/32/139
Budds, William, mason: 'freemason', Folkestone, Kent, 1666 CKS PRC1/11/110
Budds, William, Teynham, Kent, 1691 CKS PRC2/41/167
Budgin, Thomas, Barwick (Stoford), Som, 1638 Somerset RO D/D/Cta/B18
Budle, Francis, Aslackby (Millthorpe), Lincs, 1639 Lincs RO Ad/Ac/26/295
Buens, Francis, baymaker, Sandwich, Kent, 1614 CKS PRC2/17/105
Bugby, Vincent, yeoman, Christchurch, Hants, Hants RO 1661 HP1/3
Bugden, John, Donhead St Mary, Wilts, 1628 Wilts RO Arch. Sarum/(+ name and date)
Bugge, John, Gonerby, Great, Lincs, 1641 Lincs RO Ad/Ac/27/328
Bulbeck, Thomas, Cheriton, Hants, 1623 Hants RO 21M65 D8/8
Bulcock, Hamond, clergy: 'clerk', Harpswell, Lincs, 1670 Lincs RO Ad/Ac/32/141
Bulfell, Francis, Shadwell, St Paul, London & Middlesex, 1697 Lambeth Palace Arches G48

[Bulfinch:]
Bulfinch, Grissell, widow, Chatham, Kent, 1692 PRO PROB5/1253
Bulford, James, Deverill, Longbridge, Wilts, 1613 Wilts RO Arch. Sarum/(+ name and date)
Bulgin, John, Brent, East, Som, 1606 Somerset RO D/D/Cta/B101
Bull, Edward, Westbury, Wilts, 1681 Wilts RO Miscellaneous Index to Wills (name + date)
Bull, Elizabeth, widow, Cowes, West, Hants, 1670 Hants RO 21m65 D8/225
Bull, George, Lenham, Kent, 1616 CKS PRC2/20/134
Bull, George, Dymchurch, Kent, 1621 CKS PRC2/23/40
Bull, John, Trull, Som, 1577 Somerset RO D/D/Cta/B56
Bull, John, carpenter, Hale, Great (Little Hale), Lincs, 1634 Lincs RO Ad/Ac/24/65
Bull, John, clothier, Melksham, Wilts, 1677 Wilts RO Arch. Sarum/(+ name and date)
Bull, Peeter, Canterbury St Andrew, Kent, 1622 CKS PRC2/23/30
Bull, Richard, Hothfield, Kent, 1598 CKS PRC2/10/357
Bull, Richard, Hothfield, Kent, 1599 CKS PRC2/10/302
Bull, Richard, Hothfield, Kent, 1631 CKS PRC20/9/83
Bull, Richerde, Saltwood, Kent, 1587 CKS PRC21/8/372
Bull, Robert, weaver: 'broad weaver', Reading, Berks, 1606 Berks RO D/A1/176/2C
Bull, Robert, clothier, Hothfield, Kent, 1616 CKS PRC20/3/507
Bull, Robert, Flixborough, Lincs, 1635 Lincs RO Ad/Ac/40/27
Bull, Robert, yeoman, Hothfield, Kent, 1646 CKS PRC1/7/74
Bull, Robert, Norton Subcourse, Norf, 1754 Norfolk RO ANF/11/4/95
Bull, Roberte, Laughton, Lincs, 1607 Lincs RO Ad/Ac/37/233
Bull, Sarah, spinster, Spalding, Lincs, 1684 Lincs RO Ad/Ac/44/110
Bull, Thomas, Hothfield, Kent, 1630 CKS PRC20/9/89
Bull, Thomas, yeoman, Eynesbury, Hunts, 1676 Hunts RO/Acc58/74(164)
Buller, John, Gosberton, Lincs, 1640 Lincs RO Ad/Ac/27/19
Buller, Robert, Halford, Warks, 1682 Worcs RO 008.7 BA3585/830/77
Buller, William, yeoman, Sandford, Oxon, 1633 Oxon RO MSS Wills 5/3/45
Bullfynch, William, Elmsted, Kent, 1611 CKS PRC2/13/73
Bullie, Alexander, Bicker, Lincs, 1612 Lincs RO Ad/Ac/11/36
Bullin, Henry, blacksmith, Oxford St Clement, Oxon, 1688 Oxon RO MSS Wills 161/2/2
Bulling, John, Saham Toney, Norf, 1753 Norfolk RO ANW/23/24/140
Bullock, Richard, Minster in Sheppey, Kent, 1610 CKS PRC2/13/79
Bullock, Richard, Probus, Corn, 1636 Cornwall RO AP/B905
Bullock, Thomas, Fyfield, Berks, 1601 Berks RO D/A1/175/165A
Bullock, see Abell,
Bullocke, George, gentleman, Bristol, Glos, Bristol RO 1761/3
Bullocke, Richard, Swingfield, Kent, 1627 CKS PRC2/28/14
Bullocke, Richard, Grimley, Worcs, 1682 Worcs RO 008.7 BA3585/837/bdl 3
Bullocke, Thomas, Canterbury Holy Cross Westgate, Kent, 1628 CKS PRC2/29/10
Bullocke, Thomas, Canterbury St Mary-Magdalen Burgate, Kent, 1663 CKS PRC1/9/92
Bullocke, William, Canterbury Holy Cross Westgate, Kent, 1608 CKS PRC2/14/45
Bullough, Richard, yeoman, Deane (Little Hulton), Lancs, 1687 Lancs RO (Name of Deceased) D.R.C.H. 1686-87
Bulpan, John, Woolavington, Som, 1626 Somerset RO D/D/Cta/B31
Buly, Mary, widow, Bridge, Kent, 1666 CKS PRC1/11/12
Bumpas, Robert, Bredon, Worcs, 1675 Worcs RO 008.7 BA3585/830/36
Bunce, Ann, widow, Leaveland, Kent, 1676 CKS PRC1/15/82
Bunce, Henry, draper: 'linen draper', Milton next Sittingbourne, Kent, 1670 CKS PRC1/15/11
Bunce, James, yeoman, Northbourne, Kent, 1669 CKS PRC1/14/20
Bunce, John, Eastchurch, Sheppey, Kent, 1683 CKS PRC2/40/92
Bunce, John eld, Letcombe Regis, Berks, 1615 Berks RO D/A1/176/51A
Bunce, Matthew, yeoman, Preston next Faversham, Kent, 1640 CKS PRC1/4/18
Bunce, Richard, Warehorne, Kent, 1590 CKS PRC2/5/53
Bunce, Richard, Warehorne, Kent, 1596 CKS PRC2/9/49
Bunce, Richard, bachelor: 'singleman', Ham, Kent, 1681 CKS PRC2/39/10

Bunce, Thomas, Eastling, Kent, 1620 CKS PRC2/20/350
Bunce, Thomas, Linsted, Kent, 1639 CKS PRC1/2/33
Bunce, Thomas, yeoman, Ham, Kent, 1662 CKS PRC1/9/12
Bunce, Thomas, carpenter, Tenterden, Kent, 1674 CKS PRC2/36/15
Bunce, Thomas, Biddenden, Kent, 1685 CKS PRC2/41/44
Bunce, Thomas, tanner, Wye, Kent, 1686 CKS PRC2/41/66
Bunce, Thomas, carpenter, New Romney, Kent, 1688 CKS PRC20/13/628
Bunce, Vincent, Sandwich, Kent, 1631 CKS PRC2/31/8
Bunce, William, yeoman, Chart nr Sutton Valence, Kent, 1645 CKS PRC1/7/41
Bunce, William, Oxford St Thomas, Oxon, 1648 Oxon RO MSS Wills 295/4/32
Bunche, Richard, Lincoln St Peter [probably in Eastgate], Lincs, 1586 Lincs RO Ad/Ac/2C/134
Buncker, Alice, widow, Iwade, Kent, 1633 CKS PRC2/32/21
Bundy, John, Chirton, Wilts, 1613 Wilts RO Arch. Sarum/(+ name and date)
Bundy, Thomas, Amesbury, Wilts, 1642 Wilts RO Arch. Sarum/(+ name and date)
Bungey, John, mr, Canterbury Holy Cross Westgate, Kent, 1618 CKS PRC2/20/349
Bunn, Faith, widow, Bovingdon, Herts, Herts RO AHH23/181
Bunnes?, Abraham, Thrussington, Leics, 1640 Leics RO PR/I/41A/41
Bunney, George, Chilvers Coton, Warks, 1727 LJRO/B/C/5/1727/28
Bunniard, John, Hackington, Kent, 1675 CKS PRC2/36/163
Bunniard, see Lawrence,
Bunter, Robert, Bowerchalke, Wilts, 1674 Wilts RO Arch. Sarum/(+ name and date)
Bunting, Robert, Trusthorpe, Lincs, 1683 Lincs RO Ad/Ac/44/111
Buntinge, William, Springthorpe, Lincs, 1624 Lincs RO Ad/Ac/39/176
Bunton, Robert, High Halstow, Kent, 1613 CKS PRC2/16/182
Buntynge, Richard, jurat, New Romney, Kent, 1582 CKS PRC21/6/17
Bunworth, Elizabeth, Grantham, Lincs, 1632 Lincs RO Ad/Ac/23/78
Bunworth, William, Barkston, Lincs, 1623 Lincs RO Ad/Ac/18/53
Bunyar, Ann, Leeds, Kent, 1620 CKS PRC2/20/352
Bunyar, Frances, Leeds, Kent, 1620 CKS PRC20/5/31
Burbeigh, George, Belton, Lincs, 1637 Lincs RO Ad/Ac/25/599
Burbidge, John, yeoman, Herne, Kent, 1676 CKS PRC20/12/194
Burbidge, Robert, husbandman, Swayfield, Lincs, 1623 Lincs RO Ad/Ac/18/5
Burbotts, William, Honington, Lincs, 1578 Lincs RO Ad/Ac/0/26b
Burch, John, yeoman, Garston, East, Berks, 1661 Berks RO D/A1/178/58A
Burch, John, Mablethorpe, Lincs, 1671 Lincs RO Ad/Ac/33/176
Burch, Richard, weaver, Hernhill, Kent, 1683 CKS PRC20/13/311
Burch, Robert, gingerbread maker, Abingdon, Berks, 1725 Berks RO D/A1/180/76C
Burcham, Thomas, Fersfield, Norf, 1769 Norfolk RO ANF/11/5/80
Burchard, Richard, maltster, Abingdon, Berks, 1639 Berks RO D/A1/177/79C
Burche, John, Froxfield, Wilts, 1627 Wilts RO Arch. Wilts.(name + date)
Burche, Thomas, Fairfield, Kent, 1600 CKS PRC21/16/176
Burchett, David, Borden, Kent, 1632 CKS PRC2/31/86
Burchett, George, Hythe St Leonard, Kent, 1604 CKS PRC21/17/140
Burchett, Robart, Stone in Oxney, Kent, 1608 CKS PRC20/1/394
Burcholl, William, Chelvey, Som, 1599 Somerset RO D/D/Cta/W67
Burd, Henry, Quantoxhead, West, Som, 1680 Somerset RO D/D/Cta/B70
Burd, Stephen, husbandman, Hallington, Lincs, 1669 Lincs RO Ad/Ac/33/134
Burde, Margaret, widow, Fordington, Dors, 1596 Wilts RO Miscellaneous Index to Wills (name + date)
Burden, Elizabeth, Stallingborough, Lincs, 1627 Lincs RO Ad/Ac/20b/7
Burden, Harbert, Cranbrook, Kent, 1611 CKS PRC20/2/228
Burden, Joane, Chart nr Sutton Valence, Kent, 1599 CKS PRC2/11/155
Burden, John, Sittingbourne, Kent, 1622 CKS PRC2/23/23
Burden, John, St Mary in the Marsh, Kent, 1623 CKS PRC2/23/29
Burden, John, Biddenden, Kent, 1646 CKS PRC1/7/75

[Burden:]
Burden, Marke, Faversham, Kent, 1668 CKS PRC1/13/17
Burden, Martyne, Cranbrook, Kent, 1611 CKS PRC2/16/116
Burden, Robert, Petherwin, North, Corn, 1635 Cornwall RO AP/B864
Burden, Stephen, Faversham, Kent, 1634 CKS PRC2/32/142
Burden, Thomas, Linton, Kent, 1597 CKS PRC2/9/35
Burden, Thomas eld, grocer, Canterbury St George Martyr, Kent, 1676 CKS PRC2/37/10
Burden, William, yeoman, Bottesford, Leics, 1640 Leics RO PR/I/41A/35
Burden/Symons, Alice, widow, Reading St Lawrence, Berks, 1630 Berks RO D/A1/177/12
Burdett, Edward, yeoman, Burton Overy, Leics, 1672 Leics RO Administrators Accounts 1667-72 f57
Burdge, see Hilsdon,
Burdhead, Alex, Hough on the Hill (Brandon), Lincs, Lincs RO Ad/Ac/2C/64
Burdikinne, Robert, labourer, Bardney, Lincs, 1626 Lincs RO Ad/Ac/19B/63
Burdley, Richard, Midhurst, Sussex, 1640 W. Suss RO EpI/33/1640/8
Burdocke, Edward, Bampton, Oxon, 1626 Oxon RO MSS Wills 4/6/40
Burdon, John, Wheldrake (Messhouses), Yorks, Borthwick Test C.P. 1738/3
Burfoote, George, Marden, Kent, 1635 CKS PRC2/33/5
Burfoote, Margarett, Headcorn, Kent, 1668 CKS PRC1/13/18
Burford, Francis, clergy: 'clerk', Cliffe Pypard, Wilts, 1614 Wilts RO CC Sarum(+ name and date)
Burford, George, grocer, Sandwich, Kent, 1689 CKS PRC2/41/142
Burford, Thomas, husbandman, Headcorn, Kent, 1672 e 13 CKS PRC2/35/116
Burford, William, Rainham, Kent, 1672 e ? CKS PRC2/35/117
Burge, George, Stone Easton, Som, 1689 Somerset RO D/D/Cta/B71
Burge, John, Truro, Corn, 1605 Cornwall RO AP/B111
Burge, John, wareburner, Reading St Giles, Berks, 1606 Berks RO D/A1/176/5A
Burge, Ralph, Cricklade St Mary, Wilts, 1623 Wilts RO Arch. Wilts.(name + date)
Burge, Thomas, gentleman, Kimbolton (Stonely), Hunts, 1695 Hunts RO/Acc58/282
Burges, Clement, Ferriby, South, Lincs, 1612 Lincs RO Ad/Ac/11/174
Burges, Dane ?, Canterbury St Mary Northgate, Kent, 1672 CKS PRC2/35/110
Burges, Edward, Compton, Sussex, 1618 W. Suss RO EpI/33/1617/36
Burges, Francis, maltster, Wallingford, Berks, 1708 Berks RO D/A1/179/172C
Burges, Giles, Cranbrook, Kent, 1609 CKS PRC2/13/24
Burges, John, Marlborough, Wilts, 1616 Wilts RO CC Sarum(+ name and date)
Burges, John, blacksmith, Dover, Kent, 1624 CKS PRC20/6/106
Burges, John, Westbury, Wilts, 1674 Wilts RO Chantor Sarum Bundle 9/46
Burges, Philip, Watford, Herts, 1638 Herts RO ASA25/4952
Burges, Richard, Chilham, Kent, 1607 CKS PRC2/14/49
Burges, Richard, yeoman, Sulhampstead Abbots, Berks, 1641 Berks RO D/A1/177/102A
Burges, Richard, butcher, Faversham, Kent, 1662 CKS PRC1/9/13
Burges, Richard, Faversham, Kent, 1703 CKS PRC1/16/43
Burges, Robert, Hythe St Leonard, Kent, 1626 CKS PRC20/7/7
Burges, Robert, Chilmark, Wilts, 1636 Wilts RO Arch. Sarum/(+ name and date)
Burges, Thomas, Tenterden, Kent, 1593 CKS PRC2/6/152
Burges, Thomas, Lambourn (Woodlands), Berks, 1618 Berks RO D/A1/176/59C
Burges, Thomas, Tenterden, Kent, 1626 CKS PRC2/27/15
Burges, Thomas, husbandman, Minster in Sheppey, Kent, 1680 CKS PRC2/38/107
Burges, William, Marshall, Hampstead, Berks, 1614 Wilts RO CC Sarum(+ name and date)
Burges, William, Tenterden, Kent, 1617 CKS PRC2/20/245
Burges, William, butcher, Stone in Oxney, Kent, 1684 CKS PRC2/40/180
Burgess, Peter, clergy: 'clerk/mr', Norwich Cathedral, Norf, Norfolk RO NCC INV/78A/143
Burgess, William, Birmingham, Warks, 1684 LJRO/B/C/5/1684/19
Burgesse, Isaac, Darley (Snitterton), Derby, 1680 LJRO:cards/1680/7
Burgesse, Nicholas, Tenterden, Kent, 1615 CKS PRC2/20/251
Burgesse, William, husbandman, Ferriby, South, Lincs, 1627 Lincs RO Ad/Ac/20/4

Burgh, Edward, esquire, Gainsborough, Lincs, 1665 Lincs RO Ad/Ac/41/167
Burgh, Richard, Skidbrooke, Lincs, 1565 Lincs RO Ad/Ac/2b/42
Burgh, Stephen, Marden, Kent, 1615 CKS PRC2/20/158
Burghe, John, Saltfleetby St Peter, Lincs, Lincs RO Ad/Ac/2C/74
Burghe, Richard, Skidbrooke, Lincs, 1565 Lincs RO Ad/Ac/0/16b
Burgis, Robert, Minstead, Hants, 1670 Hants RO 21m65 D8/226
Burgis, Thomas, Eling, Hants, 1672 Hants RO 21m65 D8/236
Burheye, James, Stockbury, Kent, 1606 CKS PRC2/13/22
Burie, Frances, Loughborough, Leics, 1639 Leics RO PR/I/41A/15
Burke, William, Dymchurch, Kent, 1662 CKS PRC1/9/14
Burkett, Lambert, Bitchfield, Lincs, 1637 Lincs RO Ad/Ac/25/428
Burkham, Richard, Cranbrook, Kent, 1634 CKS PRC2/32/143
Burkill, James, Messingham, Lincs, 1667 Lincs RO Ad/Ac/33/35
Burlace, Henry, Paul, Corn, 1613 Cornwall RO AP/B304
Burleigh, Nicholas, blacksmith, Louth, Lincs, 1662 Lincs RO Ad/Ac/42/1
Burley, Hugh, clothier, Reading St Mary, Berks, 1637 Berks RO D/A1/177/65A
Burley, William, Welby, Lincs, 1598 Lincs RO Ad/Ac/4/87
Burman, John, Uphill, Som, 1677 Somerset RO D/D/Cta/B72
Burname, Richard, Hurley, Berks, 1628 Berks RO D/A1/43/156D
Burnard, George eld, coachmaker, Leeds, Yorks, 1807 Borthwick Test C.P. 1807/8
Burnard, Oliver, husbandman, St Austell, Corn, Cornwall RO AP/B735/2
Burnard, Thomas, Altarnun, Corn, 1646 Cornwall RO AP/B1107/1
Burnbie, William, gentleman, Barholm, Lincs, 1619 Lincs RO Ad/Ac/14/236
Burnby, William, clergy: 'clerk', Tothill, Lincs, 1619 Lincs RO Ad/Ac/15/32
Burnby, William, gentleman, Barholm, Lincs, 1624 Lincs RO Ad/Ac/18/93
Burnby, William, yeoman, Morton, Lincs, 1653 Lincs RO Ad/Ac/29/20
Burne, Barnaby, Holton, Oxon, 1625 Oxon RO MSS Wills 295/2/81
Burne, Bartholemew, Bodmin, Corn, 1613 Cornwall RO AP/B279/3
Burne, Richard, Somercoates, North, Lincs, 1620 Lincs RO Ad/Ac/16/11
Burne, Thomas, Althorpe (Amcotts), Lincs, 1616 Lincs RO Ad/Ac/8b/276
Burne, Thomas, Burslem, Staffs, 1684 LJRO/B/C/5/1684/18
Burneberry, Anne, Colan, Corn, 1610 Cornwall RO AP/B225/3
Burneford, John, yeoman, Stoke Prior, Worcs, 1605 Worcs RO 008.7 BA3585/839/337
Burneforde, Henrie, Sittingbourne, Kent, 1613 CKS PRC2/16/131
Burnell, John, Storrington, Sussex, 1617 W. Suss RO EpI/33/1617/33
Burnell, John, Sydmonton, Hants, 1678 Hants RO 21m65 D8/281
Burner, Henry,
Berks 1631 Berks RO D/A1/177/33
Burnet, William, victualler, Salisbury, Wilts, 1612 Wilts RO Miscellaneous Index to Wills (name + date)
Burnett, Elizabeth, Minting, Lincs, 1645 Lincs RO Ad/Ac/28/157
Burnett, John, Baltonsborough, Som, 1729 Somerset RO D/D/Cta/B73
Burnett, Richard, husbandman, Bampton (Bampton Aston), Oxon, 1633 Oxon RO MSS Wills 295/3/46
Burnett, Thomas, Holbeach, Lincs, 1612 Lincs RO Ad/Ac/11/148
Burnett, William, yeoman, Holbeach, Lincs, 1676 Lincs RO Ad/Ac/43/176
Burnett/Browne, Marie, Holbeach, Lincs, 1639 Lincs RO Ad/Ac/26/308
Burnham, John, Stoke Talmage, Oxon, Oxon RO MSS Wills 161/1/21
Burnish, William, St Martin in the Fields, London & Middlesex, 1743 Greater London RO AM/PP/Box 1739-1749 pt (uncatalogued)
Burnshawe, Thomas, Hagworthingham, Lincs, 1618 Lincs RO Ad/Ac/14/214
Burr, John, yeoman, Brookland, Kent, 1672 CKS PRC2/35/109
Burr, John, yeoman, Benenden, Kent, 1678 CKS PRC2/37/121
Burr, Joseph, innholder, St Albans St Peters, Herts, 1693 Herts RO ASA25/4975
Burr, Thomas, husbandman, Legsby, Lincs, 1670 Lincs RO Ad/Ac/32/225

[Burr:]
Burr, William, Bramfield, Herts, Herts RO AHH23/134
Burr, William, Fairfield, Kent, 1633 CKS PRC20/10/48
Burraman, William, husbandman, Caythorpe, Lincs, 1668 Lincs RO Ad/Ac/33/74
Burredge, Clement, miller, Canterbury Holy Cross Westgate, Kent, 1622 CKS PRC2/23/27
Burredge, James, Bredgar, Kent, 1596 CKS PRC2/8/61
Burredge, John, Warden, Kent, 1641 CKS PRC1/5/83
Burrell, George, Chichester All Saints, Sussex, 1623 W. Suss RO EpIV/10/1/29
Burrell, William, Skellingthorpe, Lincs, 1602 Lincs RO Ad/Ac/5/264
Burrell, William, clergy: 'clerk', Bignor, Sussex, 1606 W. Suss RO EpI/33/1606/5
Burrell, William, Waddingham, Lincs, 1632 Lincs RO Ad/Ac/39/331
Burren, Richard, husbandman, Hagbourne, Berks, 1641 Berks RO D/A1/177/71C
Burren, Thomas, Oxford St Peter in the East, Oxon, 1646 Oxon RO MSS Wills 295/4/18
Burren, Thomas, clothworker, Staplehurst, Kent, 1663 CKS PRC1/9/93
Burrett, John, Raithby, Lincs, 1611 Lincs RO Ad/Ac/10/45
Burridge, Abraham, gentleman, Kirkby on Bain, Lincs, 1633? Lincs RO Ad/Ac/40/65
Burrill, Richard, Gautby, Lincs, 1611 Lincs RO Ad/Ac/10/20
Burrill/Brumbie, Dorotie, Manton, Lincs, 1627 Lincs RO Ad/Ac/39/29
Burringham, Anne, widow, Alkborough, Lincs, 1646 Lincs RO Ad/Ac/40/137
Burrish, see Bartholomew,
Burrishe, William, Wittering, West, Sussex, W. Suss RO EpI/33/1610/5
Burrough, John, gentleman, Bradfield St George, Suff, 1726 Suff RO(B) IC500/3/45/5a
Burroughes, John, yeoman, Over, Ches, 1770 Cheshire RO (Name) W.C. 1770
Burrow, Edward, Woodford, Wilts, 1677 Wilts RO Dean Sarum (name + date)
Burrow, John, Hampstead Marshall, Berks, 1606 Berks RO D/A1/175/190A
Burrow, John, Biddisham, Som, 1621 Somerset RO D/D/Cta/B33
Burrow, John, Brington, Northants, 1678 Northants RO NWill A/C/63
Burrowe, Christopher, Kettlethorpe, Lincs, 1610 Lincs RO Ad/Ac/8a/311
Burrowe, John, Barrow, Som, 1596 Somerset RO D/D/Cta/B2
Burrowe, Nicholas, Quadring, Lincs, Lincs RO Ad/Ac/19A/31
Burrowes, George, Grimsby, Great, Lincs, 1625 Lincs RO Ad/Ac/19A/141
Burrowes, Stephen,
Leics Leics RO Administrators Accounts 1682-86 f54
Burrowes, Thomas, yeoman, Bristol, Glos, Bristol RO 1713/5
Burrowes, Thomas, Heswall, Ches, 1606 Cheshire RO (Name) W.C. 1606
Burrows, Henry, Bradley, Derby, 1683 LJRO/B/C/5/1682/16
Burrows, Robert, Icklington, Norf, 1820 Norfolk RO ANW/23/27/21
Burry, Henry, Bersted, South, Sussex, 1684 W. Suss RO EpIV/10/2A/34
Burslem, James, Newcastle under Lyme, Staffs, 1676 LJRO:cards/1676/11
Burt, Henry, Sholden, Kent, 1667 CKS PRC1/12/18
Burt, John, Oxford St Aldate, Oxon, 1634 Oxon RO MSS Wills 295/3/48
Burt, John, tailor, Brant Broughton, Lincs, 1673 Lincs RO Ad/Ac/35/29
Burt, Peter, Southwick, Hants, 1602 Hants RO 1597 AD020
Burt, Walter, Grinstead, West, Sussex, 1674 W. Suss RO EpI/33/1673/24
Burt, William, Horsham, Sussex, 1670 W. Suss RO EpI/33/1669/4
Burte, Anne, widow, Faversham, Kent, 1662 CKS PRC1/9/15
Burte, John, Newington next Sittingbourne, Kent, 1636 CKS PRC2/33/21
Burte, Thomas, Warehorne, Kent, 1615 CKS PRC2/20/340
Burten, Vincent, Sandwich, Kent, 1603 CKS PRC2/14/64
Burtham, Edward, Dalby, Lincs, 1664 Lincs RO Ad/Ac/42/5
Burtoft, Matthew, labourer, Althorpe (Burringham), Lincs, 1667 Lincs RO Ad/Ac/33/26
Burton, Anne, Haxey, Lincs, 1677 Lincs RO Ad/Ac/35/138
Burton, Anthonie, Lincoln St Swithin, Lincs, 1593 Lincs RO Ad/Ac/3/83
Burton, Christopher, clergy: 'clerk', Ripple, Kent, 1600 CKS PRC2/11/143
Burton, Edward, Great Mongeham, Kent, 1607 CKS PRC2/15/32
Burton, Elizabeth, widow, Woodchurch, Kent, 1683 CKS PRC20/13/309

[Burton:]
Burton, George, labourer, Marton, Lincs, 1626 Lincs RO Ad/Ac/39/70
Burton, George, Betteshanger, Kent, 1635 CKS PRC2/33/22
Burton, George, clothier, Ashton-under-Lyne (Alt), Lancs, 1749 Lancs RO (Name of Deceased) D.R.C.H. 1748-9
Burton, James eld, Faversham, Kent, 1627 CKS PRC2/28/13
Burton, Joane, widow, Northbourne, Kent, 1616 CKS PRC2/20/218
Burton, John, Rolvenden, Kent, 1582 CKS PRC2/2/125
Burton, John, Eastbridge, Kent, 1596 CKS PRC2/8/59
Burton, John, Barkwith, West, Lincs, 1613 Lincs RO Ad/Ac/11/42
Burton, John, Swineshead, Lincs, 1629 Lincs RO Ad/Ac/22/66
Burton, John, Owston, Lincs, 1664 Lincs RO Ad/Ac/41/127
Burton, John, baker, Bourne, Lincs, 1679 Lincs RO Ad/Ac/43/96
Burton, John, Derby, Derby, 1737 LJRO/B/C/5/1737/9
Burton, John, farmer, Shipdham, Norf, 1780 Norfolk RO ANF/11/5/118
Burton, John, farmer, Hemingbrough, Yorks, 1844 Borthwick Test C.P. 1844/4
Burton, Lancelot, gentleman, Surfleet, Lincs, 1611 Lincs RO Ad/Ac/10/76
Burton, Margaret, widow, Sandwich, Kent, 1612 CKS PRC2/17/216
Burton, Matthew, Faversham, Kent, 1631 CKS PRC2/31/10
Burton, Michael, Sandwich St Peter, Kent, 1638 CKS PRC2/34/166
Burton, Rhoda, spinster, Faversham, Kent, 1626 CKS PRC2/27/12
Burton, Richard, Quadring, Lincs, 1607 Lincs RO Ad/Ac/8a/67
Burton, Richard, Stallingborough, Lincs, 1632 Lincs RO Ad/Ac/23/143
Burton, Richard, Fishtoft, Lincs, 1649 Lincs RO Ad/Ac/30/35
Burton, Robert, Torrington, West, Lincs, 1611 Lincs RO Ad/Ac/10/119
Burton, Robert, yeoman, Owston, Lincs, 1670? Lincs RO Ad/Ac/32/135
Burton, Susanne, widow, Sandwich, Kent, 1611 CKS PRC2/15/39
Burton, Thomas, Scotton (East Kinnard's Ferry), Lincs, 1611 Lincs RO Ad/Ac/8a/345
Burton, Thomas, clergy: 'clerk', Stixwold, Lincs, 1618 Lincs RO Ad/Ac/14/186
Burton, Thomas, Woodchurch, Kent, 1621 CKS PRC20/5/19
Burton, Thomas, clergy: 'clerk', Moulton, Lincs, 1640 Lincs RO Ad/Ac/27/86
Burton, Thomas, Owston, Lincs, 1662 Lincs RO Ad/Ac/41/156
Burton, Thomas, Haxey, Lincs, 1663 Lincs RO Ad/Ac/41/71
Burton, Thomas, Eastling, Kent, 1669 CKS PRC1/14/21
Burton, Thomas, clergy: 'clerk', Sibsey, Lincs, 1684 Lincs RO Ad/Ac/44/124
Burton, Thomas Miles, cabinet maker, Birmingham, Warks, 1826 LJRO/B/C/5/1826/2
Burton, William, Keal, West, Lincs, 1603 Lincs RO Ad/Ac/5/368
Burton, William, Thoresway, Lincs, 1611 Lincs RO Ad/Ac/10/12
Burton, William, Billingborough, Lincs, 1649 Lincs RO Ad/Ac/30/42
Burton, William, Louth, Lincs, 1667 Lincs RO Ad/Ac/42/7
Burton, William, yeoman, Kinnard's Ferry, Lincs, 1669 Lincs RO Ad/Ac/33/164
Burton, William, Brome, Worcs, 1680 Worcs RO 008.7 BA3585/837/bdl 2
Burton, William, tanner, Willesborough, Kent, 1686 CKS PRC2/41/47
Burton/Bruton, Francis, Eldersfield, Worcs, 1601 Worcs RO 008.7 BA3585/838/192
Burton/Sanders, Walter, Redbourn, Herts, 1638 Herts RO ASA25/4953
Burton, see Saunders,
Burtwesle, Thomas, Belton, Lincs, 1651? Lincs RO Ad/Ac/40/236
Burueby, Thomas, Barholm, Lincs, 1626 Lincs RO Ad/Ac/19B/54
Burvell, Quintance, High Halden, Kent, 1615 CKS PRC2/20/170
Burvill, William, yeoman, Hawkinge, Kent, 1675 CKS PRC2/36/164
Burvishe, John, Snargate, Kent, 1623 CKS PRC2/23/32
Burwash, Alexander eld, glazier, Hythe St Leonard, Kent, CKS PRC19/4/8
Burwash, Margaret, Charing, Kent, 1679 CKS PRC20/12/253
Burwash, Thomas, Egerton, Kent, 1623 CKS PRC20/6/406
Burwash/Nelson, Joane, widow, Egerton, Kent, 1623 CKS PRC20/6/408
Burwashe, John, Egerton, Kent, 1584 CKS PRC21/7/42

[Burwell:]
Burwell, Thomas, Waltham, Bishops, Hants, 1625 Hants RO 21M65 D8/53
Burwell, William, wool comber, Norwich St Stephen, Norf, 1701 Norfolk RO ANW/23/5/280
Bury, Jane, widow, Linwood, Lincs, 1680 Lincs RO Ad/Ac/34/44
Bury, John, Aston, Warks, 1729 LJRO/B/C/5/1729/59
Bury, Robarte, Bitchfield, Lincs, 1600 Lincs RO Ad/Ac/5/383
Bury, Robert, Helmdon, Northants, 1680 Northants RO NWill A/C/26
Busbie, Barbara, Spelsbury, Oxon, 1630 Oxon RO MSS Wills 295/3/28
Busbridge, John, Sturry, Kent, 1597 CKS PRC2/12/425
Busby, Isaac, Boxley, Kent, 1633 CKS PRC2/32/17
Busby, Moses, yeoman, Tackley (Whitehill), Oxon, 1766 Oxon RO MSS Wills Pec 301/2/52
Busby, William, Earnley, Sussex, 1594 W. Suss RO EpI/33/1594/9
Bush, John, Keynsham, Som, 1695 Somerset RO D/D/Cta/B74
Bush, Thomas eld, yeoman, Childrey, Berks, 1669 Berks RO D/A1/178/113A
Bush, William, Sheldwich, Kent, 1633 CKS PRC2/32/13
Bushby, William, Wittering, West, Sussex, 1673 W. Suss RO EpI/33/1673/25
Bushe, Agnes, widow, Goudhurst, Kent, 1616 CKS PRC2/20/266
Bushe, John, Reading, Berks, 1608 Berks RO D/A1/176/13C
Bushell, Beniamin, Stepney, London & Middlesex, 1669 PRO PROB32/6/12
Bushell, John, Bedwin, Little, Wilts, 1677 Wilts RO Pec Lord Warden Savernake Forest Bundle 2/47b
Bushell, Mary, Hampstead Marshall, Berks, 1604 Berks RO D/A1/175/187A
Bushell, Thomas, Willesborough, Kent, 1667 CKS PRC1/12/19
Bushell, Thomas, yeoman, Birchington, Kent, 1681 CKS PRC20/13/91
Bushell, William, Willesborough, Kent, 1619 CKS PRC2/20/306
Bushell, William, Aston Cantlow, Warks, 1693 Worcs RO 008.7 BA3585/837/bdl 6
Busher, Thomas, St Johns Thanet, Kent, 1616 CKS PRC2/20/145
Busher, Thomas eld, St Johns Thanet, Kent, 1622 CKS PRC2/23/35
Bushey, Abraham, Leake, Lincs, 1600 Lincs RO Ad/Ac/5/280
Bushey, Abraham, bachelor, Sibsey, Lincs, 1683 Lincs RO Ad/Ac/44/77
Bushey, Cassander, widow, Mareham le Fen, Lincs, 1612 Lincs RO Ad/Ac/11/86
Bushey, Christopher, Sibsey, Lincs, 1639 Lincs RO Ad/Ac/26/142
Bushey, Richard, Leverton, Lincs, 1641 Lincs RO Ad/Ac/27/272
Bushey, William, Leake, Lincs, 1630s? Lincs RO Ad/Ac/24/236
Bushey, William, Leake, Lincs, 1639? Lincs RO Ad/Ac/26/91
Bushie, Richard, Leake, Lincs, 1670 Lincs RO Ad/Ac/32/188
Bushnell, John, husbandman, Yarnton, Oxon, 1674 Oxon RO MSS Wills 77/1/23
Bushnell, Richard, Sulham, Berks, 1596 Berks RO D/A1/175/96A
Busie, John, Winkfield, Wilts, 1628 Wilts RO Arch. Sarum/(+ name and date)
Buskyn, Henry, esquire, Langley, Kent, 1613 CKS PRC2/18/95
Buskyn, Joyce (sic), Sandwich, Kent, 1586 CKS PRC2/4/55
Busse, Gabraell, Cranbrook, Kent, 1631 CKS PRC2/31/11
Busse, Henrie, Canterbury St Mary Northgate, Kent, 1638 CKS PRC2/34/163
Bussey, Nicholas, Yarmouth, Great, Norf, 1750 Norfolk RO ANW/23/24/100
Busshe, Andrew, Lenham, Kent, 1587 CKS PRC2/4/192
Busshe, John, Sandwich St Mary, Kent, 1587 CKS PRC2/4/136
Busshope, George, Boxley, Kent, 1602 CKS PRC2/12/30
Bustard, Catherine, mistress/widow, Adderbury, Oxon, 1648 Oxon RO MSS Wills 295/4/20
Buste, Lawrance, Hythe St Leonard, Kent, 1610 CKS PRC20/2/43
Buswell, Henry, Leamington Hastings, Warks, 1682 LJRO/B/C/5/1682/17
Butcher, Daniell, Ulcombe, Kent, 1610 CKS PRC2/16/213
Butcher, Edward, baker, Oxford St Peter in the East, Oxon, 1636 Oxon RO MSS Wills 295/3/58
Butcher, Elizabeth, Bolas Magna, Shrops, 1685 LJRO/B/C/5/1685/24
Butcher, George, Pluckley, Kent, 1614 CKS PRC2/18/108
Butcher, George, weaver: 'linen weaver', Headcorn, Kent, 1679 CKS PRC2/38/105
Butcher, Hugh, yeoman, Kidderminster (Puxton), Worcs, Worcs RO 008.7 BA3585/838/194

Butcher, Isaac, Lydd, Kent, 1601 CKS PRC21/16/190
Butcher, James, Pluckley, Kent, 1612 CKS PRC2/16/66
Butcher, Joan, Petworth, Sussex, 1604 W. Suss RO EpI/33/1599
Butcher, Joan, widow, Petworth, Sussex, 1614 W. Suss RO EpI/33/1613/27
Butcher, John, gentleman, Selling, Kent, 1638 CKS PRC2/34/170
Butcher, John, widower, Newington next Hythe, Kent, 1712 CKS PRC1/17/20
Butcher, Leonard, Stone in Oxney, Kent, 1628 CKS PRC2/29/7
Butcher, Philip, university: 'privileged person', Oxford (University), Oxon, 1669 Bodleian HYP B8/28-29
Butcher, Richard, Bersted, South, Sussex, 1613 W. Suss RO EpIV/10/1/6
Butcher, Richard, Ashurst, Sussex, 1670 W. Suss RO EpI/33/1670/13
Butcher, William, Canterbury St Dunstan Without, Kent, 1586 CKS PRC2/3/263
Butcher, William, Sturry, Kent, 1595 CKS PRC2/7/437
Butcher, William, Cranbrook, Kent, 1631 CKS PRC20/9/79
Butcher, see James & Marchant,
Butler, Alice, widow, Hemingford Grey, Hunts, 1677 Hunts RO/Acc58/114(141)
Butler, Anthony, esquire, Coates, Lincs, 1663 Lincs RO Ad/Ac/41/86
Butler, Dorothy, widow, Taynton, Oxon, 1637 Oxon RO MSS Wills 295/3/73
Butler, Edward, Shadwell, St Paul, London & Middlesex, 1688 PRO PROB32/27/166
Butler, Elizabeth, widow, Hartlip, Kent, 1642 CKS PRC1/6/52
Butler, Hannah, widow, Darlaston, Staffs, 1777 LJRO/B/C/5/1777/5
Butler, Helen, Wimborne Minster, Dors, 1673 Dorset RO PE/WM CP 2/4/73
Butler, Henrye, Birchington, Kent, 1615 CKS PRC20/3/338
Butler, James, yeoman, Abingdon, Berks, 1664 Berks RO D/A1/178/72C
Butler, John, Keelby, Lincs, 1619 Lincs RO Ad/Ac/15/204
Butler, John, fellmonger, New Romney, Kent, 1676 CKS PRC20/12/159
Butler, John, Feltham, London & Middlesex, 1686 Greater London RO AM/PP/Box 1685-1694 pt (uncatalogued)
Butler, Joseph, slater, Abingdon St Helen, Berks, 1627 Berks RO D/A1/43/99C
Butler, Joseph ygr, Abingdon St Helen, Berks, 1630 Berks RO D/A1/177/23A
Butler, Leonard, Teynham, Kent, 1594 CKS PRC2/7/237
Butler, Luke, Canterbury Holy Cross Westgate, Kent, 1697 CKS PRC2/42/113
Butler, Mary, Wolfhampcote, Warks, 1684 LJRO/B/C/5/1684/20
Butler, Mary, widow, Seighford, Staffs, 1742 LJRO/B/C/5/1740/178
Butler, Nathaniel, Mells, Som, 1708 Somerset RO D/D/Cta/B75
Butler, Phillip, mariner, Faversham, Kent, 1683 CKS PRC2/40/93
Butler, Ralph, yeoman, Garsington, Oxon, 1641 Oxon RO MSS Wills 295/4/8
Butler, Rauf?, Grantham, Lincs, 1605 Lincs RO Ad/Ac/6/93
Butler, Richard, shepherd, Kingston Lisle, Berks, 1614 Berks RO D/A1/176/45A
Butler, Richard, husbandman, Sparsholt (Westcote), Berks, 1620 Berks RO D/A1/176/68C
Butler, Richard, glover/fellmonger, Gifford, Crowmarsh, Oxon, 1679 Oxon RO MSS Wills 7/1/30
Butler, Robert, Helpringham, Lincs, 1599 Lincs RO Ad/Ac/5/245
Butler, Robert, Fittleton, Wilts, 1625 Wilts RO CC Sarum(+ name and date)
Butler, Thomas, Ormskirk, Lancs, 1611 Lancs RO (Name of Deceased) D.R.C.H. 1611
Butler, Thomas, Bourton, Black, Oxon, 1623 Oxon RO MSS Wills 295/2/76
Butler, Thomas, Monkton Farleigh, Wilts, 1632 Wilts RO Arch. Sarum/(+ name and date)
Butler, Thomas, New Romney, Kent, 1677 CKS PRC20/12/226
Butler, William, husbandman, Aston Tirrold, Berks, 1647 Berks RO D/A1/178/26A
Butler, William, Basingstoke, Hants, 1669 Hants RO 21m65 D8/211
Butler/Barber, John, Witney, Oxon, 1664 Oxon RO MSS Wills 295/5/3
Butler, see Roberts,
Butt, Andrewe, Milton next Sittingbourne, Kent, 1610 CKS PRC2/13/75
Butt, William, Huntspill, Som, 1588 Somerset RO D/D/Cta/B76
Butter, Anne, widow, Hartpury, Glos, 1620s? GRO GDR/B4/2/B178
Butterfeild, Robert, Swineshead, Lincs, 1639 Lincs RO Ad/Ac/26/124

[Butterfield:]
Butterfield, Ralph, Cookham, Berks, 1705 Lambeth Palace Arches G54/2
Butterfield, Swithin, university: 'scholar's servant', Cambridge St Botolph, Cambs, 1612 CUL V.C.Acc./Box1/8
Butterfield, William, Barking, Essex, 1812 Greater London RO DL/C/571/116
Butterick, Alice, widow, Kingsnorth, Kent, 1678 CKS PRC2/38/13
Butteris, Christopher, Ickham, Kent, 1610 CKS PRC20/2/140
Butterwicke, William, Bersted, South, Sussex, 1644 W. Suss RO EpIV/10/2A/2
Butterworth, Abraham, husbandman, Ashton-under-Lyne, Lancs, 1623 Lancs RO (Name of Deceased) D.R.C.H. 1623
Butterworth, Richard, blacksmith, Coningsby, Lincs, 1668 Lincs RO Ad/Ac/33/69
Buttler, Gilbert, Bromsgrove, Worcs, 1682 Worcs RO 008.7 BA3585/837/bdl 3
Buttler, Henry, yeoman, Backford (Lea), Ches, 1678 Cheshire RO (Name) W.C. 1678
Buttler, James, husbandman, Standlake (Brighthampton), Oxon, 1627 Oxon RO MSS Wills 295/3/16
Button, Elizabeth, widow, Stainton le Vale, Lincs, 1671 Lincs RO Ad/Ac/43/57
Button, Francis, Abthorpe, Northants, 1676 Northants RO NWill A/C/147
Button, Joane, widow, Bishopstone, Wilts, 1669 Wilts RO Arch. Sarum/(+ name and date)
Button, John eld, yeoman, Cholsey, Berks, 1626 Berks RO D/A1/176/114
Button, Samuel, gentleman, Holborn (Staple Inn), London & Middlesex, 1685 PRO PROB32/25/84
Button, Samuell, gentleman, Holborn (Staple Inn), London & Middlesex, 1685 PRO PROB32/25/56
Button, William, Herne, Kent, 1583 CKS PRC21/6/205
Buttry, John, Kirton, Lincs, 1648 Lincs RO Ad/Ac/30/284
Buttry, Thomas, Great Mongeham, Kent, 1627 CKS PRC2/28/11
Buxell, Isaac, Sandwich, Kent, 1668 CKS PRC1/13/19
Buxie, Robert, Somborne, Kings, Hants, 1625 Hants RO 21M65 D8/110
Buxton, John, yeoman, Spalding, Lincs, 1634 Lincs RO Ad/Ac/24/49
Buxton, John, potter, Stoke-upon-Trent (Lane Delph), Staffs, 1830 LJRO/B/C/5/1827/14
Buxton, Susanna, spinster, Norwich, Norf, Norfolk RO ANW/23/24/134
By, Edward, Whitstable, Kent, 1616 CKS PRC2/20/294
Byam, William, St Nicholas at Wade, Kent, 1616 CKS PRC20/3/496
Byard, James, St Sepulchre, London & Middlesex, 1677 PRO PROB5/1770
Byard, Nicholas, Gosberton, Lincs, 1638 Lincs RO Ad/Ac/25/163
Bydaels, Philibert, Kensington, London & Middlesex, 1671 PRO PROB32/7/13
Bydall/Thompson, Alice, Boston, Lincs, 1640 Lincs RO Ad/Ac/27/173
Bydell, Anne, Bidford, Warks, 1608 Worcs RO 008.7 BA3585/839/444
Byden, Thomas, Froxfield, Hants, 1623 Hants RO 21M65 D8/6
Bye, Richard, husbandman, Uffington, Berks, 1607 Berks RO D/A1/176/1C
Bye, Thomas, Somerford, Little, Wilts, 1674 Wilts RO Miscellaneous Index to Wills (name + date)
Bye, Thomas, yeoman, Reading St Giles (Whitley), Berks, 1684 Berks RO D/A1/179/7C
Bygge, Hugh, Sandridge, Herts, 1598 Herts RO ASA25/1596
Bygges, Alexander, St Johns Thanet, Kent, 1613 CKS PRC2/18/123
Bygges, Henry, Dover, Kent, 1582 CKS PRC21/5/204
Bygrave, Richard, Newnham, Herts, 1598 Herts RO ASA25/1666
Byham, John, Cliddesden, Hants, 1598 Hants RO 1597 AD021
Byllington, Barthelmewe, Cranbrook, Kent, 1591 CKS PRC2/5/190
Bylls, George, Sutton Valence, Kent, 1596 CKS PRC2/8/240
Byng, John, St Johns Thanet, Kent, 1589 CKS PRC2/5/202
Byngham, Paule, Wingham, Kent, 1596 CKS PRC21/14/53
Bynyon, Laurens, Faversham, Kent, 1598 CKS PRC2/10/185
Byorly, Thomas, yeoman, Claxby, Lincs, 1662 Lincs RO Ad/Ac/32/33a
Byram, Repent, Kingston, Kent, 1625 CKS PRC2/25/21
Byrch, John, Bredhurst, Kent, 1601 CKS PRC21/15/211

Byrche, Patiens, Canterbury St Andrew, Kent, 1596 CKS PRC2/9/271
Byrchett, John, Wittersham, Kent, 1584 CKS PRC21/7/43
Byrckgarth, Thomas, Althorpe (Derrythorpe), Lincs, 1606 Lincs RO Ad/Ac/37/222
Byrckyn, Allane, Saltwood, Kent, 1611 CKS PRC20/2/234
Byrd, John, Watford, Herts, 1620 Herts RO ASA25/4833
Byrd, Richard, clergy: 'mr/D.D.', Canterbury Christchurch, Kent, 1610 CKS PRC20/2/150
Byrde, Richard, Elham, Kent, 1613 CKS PRC2/18/15
Byrkenhead, Thomas, clergy: 'clerk', Throwleigh, Kent, 1601 CKS PRC2/12/58
Byrkyn, Nicolas, Newchurch, Kent, 1578 CKS PRC21/3/175
Byrom, Raphe, clergy: 'clerk', Salford, Lancs, 1663 Lancs RO (Name of Deceased) D.R.C.H. 1662
Byshopp, Clemence, Bethersden, Kent, 1615 CKS PRC2/20/150
Byshopp, John, Linton, Kent, 1607 CKS PRC20/1/247
Byshopp, Thomas, Weston Bampfylde, Som, 1625 Somerset RO D/D/Cta/B14
Byssell, Richard, Cottisford, Oxon, 1633 Oxon RO MSS Wills 295/3/50
Bysshoppe, Thomas, Bethersden, Kent, 1586 CKS PRC2/4/155
Byworth, Dunstan, Grafham, Hunts, 1576 Lincs RO Ad/Ac/0/7
Cable, Mary, widow, Rothwell, Northants, 1676 Northants RO NWill A/C/153
Cable, Thomas, Whiteparish, Wilts, 1638 Wilts RO Arch. Sarum/(+ name and date)
Caborne, Christopher, Saltfleetby, Lincs, 1626 Lincs RO Ad/Ac/20/13
Caborne, Hellene, Saltfleetby, Lincs, 1664 Lincs RO Ad/Ac/43/15
Cackett, John, Hollingbourne, Kent, 1684 CKS PRC20/13/416
Cackstone, see Cason,
Cacott, William, weaver: 'broad weaver', Staplehurst, Kent, 1641 CKS PRC1/5/84
Cadbury, Matthew, Uffculme, Devon, 1627 Wilts RO Preb Court Uffculme Bundle 1/13
Cadbye, John, labourer, Kirkby, East, Lincs, 1620 Lincs RO Ad/Ac/16/27
Cade, Richard, Littlehampton, Sussex, 1618 W. Suss RO EpI/33/1617/37
Cade, William, Ludborough, Lincs, 1600 Lincs RO Ad/Ac/5/187
Cade, William, gentleman, Keddington, Lincs, 1617 Lincs RO Ad/Ac/14/274
Cadell, Philip, teaman, Bristol, Glos, Bristol RO 1776/CP
Cadell, William, yeoman, Rainham, Kent, 1623 CKS PRC2/23/72
Cadge, Richard, Faversham, Kent, 1616 CKS PRC2/21/151
Cadman, John, clergy: 'mr/clerk', Brabourne, Kent, 1619 CKS PRC2/20/122
Cadman, John, Willesborough, Kent, 1662 CKS PRC1/9/16
Cadman, Richarde, Challock, Kent, 1615 CKS PRC20/3/184
Cadman, Thomas, Reculver, Kent, 1592 CKS PRC21/12/165
Cadman, William, Hinstock, Shrops, 1684 LJRO/B/C/5/1684/21
Cadogan, Sarafina, spinster, Scarborough, Yorks, 1788 Borthwick Test C.P. 1787/4
Cadwell, Nicholas, Tetworth (Everton), Hunts, 1676? Hunts RO/Acc58/22(184)
Cadwell, Robert, Tenterden, Kent, 1600 CKS PRC2/12/98
Caesar, Joane, widow, Croydon (Waddon), Surrey, 1729 Lambeth Palace VH82/88
Caffinch, Abraham, butcher, Canterbury St Andrew, Kent, 1648 CKS PRC1/8/37
Caffinch, George, Cranbrook, Kent, 1636 CKS PRC2/33/27
Caffinch, John, Cranbrook, Kent, 1648 CKS PRC1/8/38
Caffinch, Mary, Tenterden, Kent, 1635 CKS PRC2/33/37
Caffinch, Thomas, butcher, Biddenden, Kent, 1668 CKS PRC1/13/20
Caffinch, William, yeoman, Staplehurst, Kent, 1683 CKS PRC2/40/108
Caffinche, Alexander, Ebony, Kent, 1607 CKS PRC2/14/100
Caffinche, William, Tenterden, Kent, 1619 CKS PRC2/20/17
Cage, Agnes, widow, Birchington, Kent, 1598 CKS PRC21/14/534
Cage, John, Birchington, Kent, 1591 CKS PRC21/10/272
Cain, Thomas, Buckminster, Leics, 1665 Leics RO Administrators Accounts C17th f12
Caister, Alexander, mercer, Epworth, Lincs, 1677 Lincs RO Ad/Ac/35/121
Caister, Ann, spinster, Frieston, Lincs, 1649 Lincs RO Ad/Ac/30/99
Caister, Thomas, glazier, Tenterden, Kent, 1671 CKS PRC2/35/27

[Caister, see Diconson:]
Caister, see Diconson,
Calcott, John, glover, Thame, Oxon, 1625 Oxon RO MSS Wills Pec 34/4/40
Calcott, Richard, Norton, Hook, Oxon, 1638 Oxon RO MSS Wills 296/2/71
Calcott, Richard, Norton, Hook, Oxon, 1663 Oxon RO MSS Wills 78/1/52
Calcott, Walter, Norton, Hook, Oxon, 1662 Oxon RO MSS Wills 78/1/43
Calcott/Hughes, Henry, glover, Standlake, Oxon, 1639 Oxon RO MSS Wills 296/3/11
Calcroft, John, clergy: 'clerk', Saleby, Lincs, 1680 Lincs RO Ad/Ac/34/61
Calcrofte, William, Redmile, Leics, 1674 Leics RO Administrators Accounts 1667-72 f140
Caldecote, James, Barrington, Cambs, 1675 CUL V.C. Acc./Box3/9
Caldecott, Joseph, bookbinder, Stamford St Michael, Lincs, 1629 Lincs RO Ad/Ac/22/2
Caldicott, Thomas, gentleman, Shocklach (Caldecot), Ches, 1674 Cheshire RO (Name) W.C. 1674/5
Cale, William,
Worcs 1680 Worcs RO 008.7 BA3585/837/bdl 2
Calendrine, Jane, spinster, St Michael Cornhill, London & Middlesex, 1672 PRO PROB5/1606
Calfe, John, mr, Sandwich, Kent, 1668 CKS PRC1/13/21
Calfehill, Jeames, clergy: 'clerk', Dover, Kent, 1603 CKS PRC21/17/55
Calkwell, William, husbandman, Legsby, Lincs, 1683 Lincs RO Ad/Ac/44/106
Call, Marke, Hernhill, Kent, 1639 CKS PRC20/10/172
Callant, Abraham, Maidstone, Kent, 1632 CKS PRC20/10/232
Callant, Abraham, gentleman, Maidstone, Kent, 1672 CKS PRC20/12/41
Calley, Francis, Stepney (Stebenhythe), London & Middlesex, 1678 PRO PROB32/15/105
Callis, Roger, brewer, Deal, Kent, 1692 CKS PRC19/5/8
Callis, William, Ravendale (East Randall), Lincs, 1613 Lincs RO Ad/Ac/12/31
Callow, Edmund, Pickworth, Lincs, 1639 Lincs RO Ad/Ac/26/35
Callow, Francis, clergy: 'clerk', Weston, Lincs, 1612 Lincs RO Ad/Ac/11/200
Callow, Joan, Baltonsborough, Som, Somerset RO D/D/Cta/C46
Callowaye, Alice, widow, Donnington, Sussex, 1583 W. Suss RO EpI/33/1583/1
Callowe, John, Throckmorton, Worcs, 1685 Worcs RO 008.7 BA3585/837/bdl 4
Callys, Robart, Hale, Great (Little Hale), Lincs, 1601 Lincs RO Ad/Ac/5/91
Calthorp, Thomas, husbandman, Fleet, Lincs, 1683 Lincs RO Ad/Ac/44/65
Calver/Culver, Anne, widow, Dover, Kent, 1672 CKS PRC20/12/45
Calvert, Elizabeth, Morton, Lincs, 1669 Lincs RO Ad/Ac/33/169
Calvert, James, innkeeper, Crambe (Spittle Bridge), Yorks, 1794 Borthwick Test C.P. 1793/5
Calvert, Richard, Torksey, Lincs, 1660s? Lincs RO Ad/Ac/41/24
Calvert, Robert, butcher, Ripon (Pateley Bridge), Yorks, Borthwick Test C.P. 1771/1
Calvert, Robert, Saxilby (Ingleby), Lincs, 1670? Lincs RO Ad/Ac/32/140
Cambden, Giles, Minety, Wilts, 1638 Wilts RO Arch. Wilts.(name + date)
Cambell, Rachaell, dame, 1665 Lambeth Palace Arches G19/2
Cambfeild, Joshua, St Lawrence Jewry, London & Middlesex, 1686 PRO PROB5/1506
Camborne, Robert, Shepherdswell alias Sibertswold, Kent, 1632 CKS PRC2/31/101
Came, Robert, Huntspill, Som, 1611 Somerset RO D/D/Cta/C19
Came, Thomas, Weston-Super-Mare, Som, 1612 Somerset RO D/D/Cta/C51
Camell, Christopher, Ingoldmels, Lincs, 1611 Lincs RO Ad/Ac/10/59
Camell, Thomas, husbandman, Hendred, East, Berks, 1676 Berks RO D/A1/183/106A
Camfelde, Thomas, cordwainer: 'shoemaker', St Albans, Herts, 1613 Herts RO ASA25/4811
Camish, William, Medstead, Hants, 1600 Hants RO 1595 AD10/3
Camme, William, bachelor, Burton by Lincoln, Lincs, 1677 Lincs RO Ad/Ac/35/125
Cammer?, Thomas, Branston, Lincs, 1611 Lincs RO Ad/Ac/10/75
Cammock, Richard, Stixwold, Lincs, 1683 Lincs RO Ad/Ac/44/98
Cammocke, John, Boston, Lincs, 1651 Lincs RO Ad/Ac/29/148
Camocke, William, Skirbeck, Lincs, 1627 Lincs RO Ad/Ac/20b/98
Campes, John, Chatteris, Cambs, 1626 CUL V.C. Acc./Box2/11
Campian, Rowland, Bury (Hepmangrove), Hunts, Hunts RO/Acc58/118(33)
Camping, Margaret, widow, Shelford, Cambs, 1723 Cambs RO 1723/Inv

Campion, Emanues, Hemingford Grey, Hunts, 1707 Hunts RO/Acc58/298
Campion, Richard, gentleman, St Anne Westminster, London & Middlesex, 1693 PRO PROB32/35/121
Campion, William, butcher, Coningsby, Lincs, 1629 Lincs RO Ad/Ac/22/111
Campion, William, Newington, South, Oxon, 1630 Oxon RO MSS Wills 296/2/30
Campion, William ygr, Newington, South, Oxon, 1674 Oxon RO MSS Wills 296/3/57
Camplin, James,
Som 1738 Somerset RO D/D/Cta/C80
Candy, Christopher, Bishopstrow, Wilts, 1612 Wilts RO Miscellaneous Index to Wills (name + date)
Candy, William, Bere Regis, Dors, 1676 Wilts RO Dean Sarum (name + date)
Cannon, Frances, widow, Covent Garden, St Paul, London & Middlesex, 1731 Greater London RO AM/PP/Box 1726-1732 pt (uncatalogued)
Cannon, Francis, Chartham, Kent, 1679 CKS PRC2/38/132
Cannon, John, Sutton in the Marsh, Lincs, 1645 Lincs RO Ad/Ac/28/125
Cannon, Richard, Canterbury, Kent, 1600 CKS PRC2/11/389
Cannon, Robert, yeoman, Welford (Hoe Benham), Berks, 1642 Berks RO D/A1/183/14A
Cannopp, Joane, widow, Charlton, Wilts, 1628 Wilts RO Arch. Wilts.(name + date)
Canon, John, High Halstow, Kent, 1592 CKS PRC2/6/130
Cansden, Thomas, brickmaker, Sittingbourne, Kent, 1677 CKS PRC2/37/25
Cant, Richard, Sandwich St Peter, Kent, 1584 CKS PRC2/3/53
Canting, William, Stubton, Lincs, 1648 Lincs RO Ad/Ac/30/397
Cantis, Jane, widow, Monkton, Kent, 1685 CKS PRC20/13/485
Cantis, Matthias eld, yeoman, Monkton, Kent, 1664 CKS PRC19/3/17
Cantlo, Katherine, Fonthill Gifford, Wilts, 1617 Wilts RO Arch. Sarum/(+ name and date)
Cantrill, Catharine, Melbourne, Derby, 1683 LJRO/B/C/5/1682/18
Cantwell, William, husbandman, Cumnor (Wormestall), Berks, 1664 Berks RO D/A1/183/75A
Canty, John, Hainton, Lincs, 1682 Lincs RO Ad/Ac/42/86
Cantys, Henry, Birchington, Kent, 1619 CKS PRC20/4/59
Capell, George, Haddon, West, Northants, 1675 Northants RO NWill A/C/62
Capell, Phillipp, Coventry St Michael, Warks, 1684 LJRO/B/C/5/1684/22
Capell, Thomas, Brington, Northants, 1672 Northants RO NWill A/C/96
Capell, William, Stanton Harcourt, Oxon, 1674 Oxon RO MSS Wills 163/1/17
Caplin, Walter, Selsey, Sussex, 1617 W. Suss RO EpI/33/1617/5
Capon, Elizabeth,
Som 1591 Somerset RO D/D/Cta/C24
Capon, Robert, Chipping Barnet, Herts, 1639 Herts RO ASA25/4965
Caporne, Pleasance, widow, Brimpton, Berks, 1615 Berks RO D/A1/53/114B
Cappe, John, yeoman, Fulbeck, Lincs, 1670 Lincs RO Ad/Ac/33/90
Capper, James, upholsterer, Windsor, New, Berks, 1622 Berks RO D/A1/182/36A
Capps, Henry, Reedham, Norf, 1768 Norfolk RO ANW/23/26/10
Capps, William, wool stapler, Hockering, Norf, 1736 Norfolk RO ANF/11/3/349
Capps, William, tailor, Beeston, Norf, 1766 Norfolk RO ANW/23/25/87
Capron, Anthony, bachelor, Lodsworth, Sussex, 1674 W. Suss RO EpI/33/1674/7
Captayn, Richard, innholder, Salisbury, Wilts, 1633 Wilts RO Miscellaneous Index to Wills (name + date)
Card, William, Fisherton Anger, Wilts, 1683 Wilts RO Arch. Sarum/(+ name and date)
Carden, Ambrosse, Mersham, Kent, 1638 CKS PRC2/34/183
Carden, Humphrey, Minster in Sheppey, Kent, 1641 CKS PRC1/5/85
Carden, John, Minster in Sheppey, Kent, 1616 CKS PRC2/20/9
Carden, Richard, Stone in Oxney, Kent, 1629 CKS PRC2/30/28
Carden, Robert, yeoman, Itchenor, West, Sussex, 1633 W. Suss RO EpI/33/1633/11
Carden, Stephen, Stone in Oxney, Kent, 1621 CKS PRC2/23/78
Carden, Thomas, Fordwich, Kent, 1628 CKS PRC2/28/20
Carden, Thomas, yeoman, Elham, Kent, 1647 CKS PRC1/8/6

[Carden:]
Carden, Thomas, Chislet, Kent, 1649 CKS PRC1/8/62
Carden, William, clergy: 'clerk', Elham, Kent, 1586 CKS PRC2/4/394
Cardin, William, Salisbury, Wilts, 1679 Wilts RO Miscellaneous Index to Wills (name + date)
Cardinall, Robarte, Canterbury St Mary Northgate, Kent, 1614 CKS PRC2/17/69
Care, John, Smarden, Kent, 1632 CKS PRC2/31/96
Care, Thomas, Smarden, Kent, 1628 CKS PRC20/8/137
Careless, Henry, waterman, Godmanchester, Hunts, 1720 Hunts RO/Acc58/311
Carelesse, William, Tardebigge, Worcs, 1605 Worcs RO 008.7 BA3585/839/339
Carey, Edmund, Chelsea, London & Middlesex, 1750 Greater London RO AM/PI pt (uncatalogued)
Carey, Francis, harness maker, coach, St Giles in the Fields, London & Middlesex, 1690 PRO PROB32/31/221
Carey, Henry, Birchington, Kent, 1638 CKS PRC20/10/156
Carey, Henry, victualler, Cranbrook, Kent, 1678 CKS PRC2/38/19
Carey, Thomas, Canterbury St Mary-Magdalen Burgate, Kent, 1685 CKS PRC2/41/38
Cargge, Thomas, Muston, Leics, 1665 Leics RO Administrators Accounts C17th f15
Carhill, George, Faldingworth, Lincs, 1733 Lincs RO Ad/Ac/36/5
Carie, Edward, Babcary (Foddington), Som, 1642 Somerset RO D/D/Cta/C53
Carlell, Leonard, Ash next Sandwich, Kent, 1583 CKS PRC21/6/293
Carlell, Margaret, widow, Barham, Kent, 1601 CKS PRC2/12/116
Carles, Henry, Hucking, Kent, 1672 CKS PRC20/12/44
Carles, Sarah, spinster, Handsworth, Staffs, 1794 LJRO/B/C/5/1794/17
Carless, Jonathas, Barham, Kent, 1603 CKS PRC2/14/134
Carleton, Thomas, Canterbury St George Martyr, Kent, 1610 CKS PRC2/13/127
Carley, Ann, widow, Biddenden, Kent, 1699 CKS PRC2/42/150
Carlill, Josias, Minster in Thanet, Kent, 1611 CKS PRC2/16/97
Carlton, Richard, Frampton, Lincs, 1637 Lincs RO Ad/Ac/25/600
Carme, Roger, St Columb Minor, Corn, 1605 Cornwall RO AP/K4/5
Carney, Edward, Whalley, Lancs, 1586 Lancs RO (Name of Deceased) D.R.C.H. 1586
Carpender, Nathaniell, Faversham, Kent, 1607 CKS PRC2/14/87
Carpender, Robert, Culham, Oxon, 1636 Oxon RO MSS Wills 296/2/65
Carpenter, Abraham, Wymondham, Leics, Leics RO Administrators Accounts 1682-86 f27
Carpenter, Alice, Deerhurst, Glos, early C17th GRO GDR/B4/2/C5
Carpenter, Edward, Cranbrook, Kent, 1613 CKS PRC2/16/127
Carpenter, Elizabeth, widow, Corsley, Wilts, 1614 Wilts RO Arch. Sarum/(+ name and date)
Carpenter, Francis, gentleman, Hackington, Kent, 1602 CKS PRC21/16/93
Carpenter, Frauncys, Chislet, Kent, 1619 CKS PRC2/21/154
Carpenter, Gervis, Rolvenden, Kent, 1620 CKS PRC2/20/33
Carpenter, James, Chart, Great, Kent, 1619 CKS PRC2/20/21
Carpenter, Joane eld, widow, New Romney, Kent, 1670 CKS PRC19/4/43
Carpenter, John, butcher, Canterbury, Kent, 1618 CKS PRC20/4/51
Carpenter, John, Swyncombe, Oxon, 1638 Oxon RO MSS Wills 296/3/3
Carpenter, John, Horsham, Sussex, 1684 W. Suss RO EpI/33/1684/18
Carpenter, Margaret, widow, Staplehurst, Kent, 1615 CKS PRC2/21/157
Carpenter, Margery, widow, Canterbury St George Martyr, Kent, 1597 CKS PRC2/9/81
Carpenter, Mildred, spinster, Biddenden, Kent, 1630 CKS PRC20/9/113
Carpenter, Nicholas, Edington, Wilts, 1636 Wilts RO Arch. Sarum/(+ name and date)
Carpenter, Philip, Berkley, Som, 1611 Somerset RO D/D/Cta/C50
Carpenter, Robert, Harpenden, Herts, 1640 Herts RO AHH23/413
Carpenter, Simon, yeoman, Bampton, Oxon, 1667 Oxon RO MSS Wills 78/2/4
Carpenter, Thomas, Rolvenden, Kent, 1622 CKS PRC2/23/75
Carpenter, Thomas, Newton, South, Wilts, 1638 Wilts RO Arch. Sarum/(+ name and date)
Carpenter, William, Fovant, Wilts, 1639 Wilts RO CC Sarum(+ name and date)
Carpenter, William, Marden, Kent, 1675 CKS PRC2/36/176
Carpenter, William eld, Chart, Great, Kent, 1639 CKS PRC2/34/188

Carpenter/Brackett, Ellen, wife, Rolvenden, Kent, 1620 CKS PRC2/21/149
Carpenter/Stockton, Elizabeth, Staplehurst, Kent, 1620 CKS PRC2/21/163
Carpenter, see Feldon,
Carpinter, Edmund, yeoman, St Albans St Michaels, Herts, 1597 Herts RO ASA25/1602
Carpinter, John, Chislet, Kent, 1611 CKS PRC2/13/124
Carpinter, Robert, Mersham, Kent, 1607 CKS PRC2/15/81
Carpinter, Thomas, Boughton under Blean, Kent, 1617 CKS PRC20/4/49
Carr, Agnes, widow, Ash next Sandwich, Kent, 1639 CKS PRC20/10/200
Carr, Elizabeth, widow, Chartham, Kent, 1669 CKS PRC1/13/22
Carr, Henry, Canterbury St George Martyr, Kent, 1597 CKS PRC2/9/77
Carr, James, Preston next Faversham, Kent, 1604 CKS PRC2/13/150
Carr, John, Stourmouth, Kent, 1638 CKS PRC2/34/30
Carr, John, yeoman, Ash next Sandwich, Kent, 1674 CKS PRC20/12/74
Carr, John, clergy: 'clerk', Ivychurch, Kent, 1681 CKS PRC20/13/117
Carr, John, cordwainer/spirit merchant, Corbridge, Northumb, 1834 Borthwick Test C.P. 1834/10
Carr, Margarett, Grayingham, Lincs, 1624 Lincs RO Ad/Ac/8c/79
Carr, Patricke, Goxhill, Lincs, 1598 Lincs RO Ad/Ac/4/51
Carr, Richard, Canterbury All Saints, Kent, 1634 CKS PRC2/32/25
Carr, Robert, clergy: 'mr/clerk', Maidstone, Kent, 1621 CKS PRC20/5/35
Carr, William, clergy: 'mr/vicar', Langley, Kent, 1627 CKS PRC2/27/36
Carr, William, Kingsley, Staffs, 1675 LJRO:cards/1675/14
Carr, William, Ash next Sandwich, Kent, 1696 CKS PRC19/5/34
Carr, William, Ash next Sandwich, Kent, 1700 CKS PRC19/5/71
Carraway, John, Pewsham, Wilts, 1674 Wilts RO Miscellaneous Index to Wills (name + date)
Carre, John, Goxhill, Lincs, 1607 Lincs RO Ad/Ac/8a/71
Carre, John, Staplehurst, Kent, 1639 CKS PRC1/2/34
Carre, John, yeoman, Kennington, Kent, 1681 CKS PRC2/39/159
Carre, Marie, Goxhill, Lincs, 1627 Lincs RO Ad/Ac/20b/89
Carrell, Hugh, mariner, Liverpool, Lancs, 1770 Lancs RO (Name of Deceased) D.R.C.H. 1770
Carrick, George, gentleman, Sigglesthorne, Yorks, 1782 Borthwick Test C.P. 1782/2
Carriell, Thomas, Bromborough, Ches, 1619 Cheshire RO (Name) W.C. 1619
Carrier, Stephen, Milton next Sittingbourne, Kent, 1668 CKS PRC1/12/20
Carrill, Richard, knight, Harting, Sussex, 1629 W. Suss RO EpI/33/1629/3
Carrington, Henry, Stockton (Boningale, Whiteladies), Shrops, 1667 LJRO:cards/1667/14
Carrington, James, innholder, Redbourn, Herts, 1637 Herts RO ASA25/3311
Carrington, John, Mareham le Fen, Lincs, 1613 Lincs RO Ad/Ac/12/54
Carrington, Robert, Swaton, Lincs, 1640 Lincs RO Ad/Ac/26/130
Carryer, Henry, husbandman, Milsted, Kent, 1643 CKS PRC1/6/99
Carryer, Richard, Sawtry Moyne, Hunts, 1681 Hunts RO/Acc58/164
Carter, Abigail, Louth, Lincs, 1675 Lincs RO Ad/Ac/42/104
Carter, Abraham, brewer, Henley, Oxon, 1663 Oxon RO MSS Wills 296/3/51
Carter, Andrew, Chipping Barnet, Herts, 1665 Herts RO ASA25/4973
Carter, Anne, Bushey, Herts, 1633 Herts RO ASA25/4889
Carter, Anne, widow, Wye, Kent, 1668 CKS PRC1/13/23
Carter, Charles, Sandbach (Cranage), Ches, 1638 Cheshire RO (Name) W.C. 1638
Carter, Edmund, husbandman, Thatcham (Crookham), Berks, 1640 Berks RO D/A1/183/3A
Carter, Edward, husbandman, Fyfield, Berks, 1628 Berks RO D/A1/182/65A
Carter, Faith, widow, Drayton, Oxon, 1667 Oxon RO MSS Wills Pec 66/3/39
Carter, George, Crundale, Kent, 1604 CKS PRC2/13/141
Carter, George, Brookland, Kent, 1617 CKS PRC2/20/83
Carter, George, Willesborough, Kent, 1633 CKS PRC2/32/34
Carter, Grace, Winterbourne, Wilts, 1621? Wilts RO CC Sarum(+ name and date)
Carter, Henry, Ashton Keynes, Wilts, 1631 Wilts RO Arch. Wilts.(name + date)
Carter, Henry, clothworker, Lambourn (Isbury), Berks, 1641 Berks RO D/A1/183/7C
Carter, Henry, maltster, Milton next Sittingbourne, Kent, 1669 CKS PRC1/13/24

[Carter:]
Carter, Isaac, Ulcombe, Kent, 1671 CKS PRC2/35/29
Carter, Isaac, Baginton, Warks, 1685 LJRO/B/C/5/1685/25
Carter, Joan, Wargrave, Berks, 1638 Berks RO D/A1/182/131
Carter, John, Hexton, Herts, Herts RO ASA25/4935
Carter, John, St Mary in the Marsh, Kent, 1584 CKS PRC2/3/196
Carter, John, Abbots Langley, Herts, 1588 Herts RO ASA25/1228
Carter, John, Crundale, Kent, 1597 CKS PRC2/9/423
Carter, John, Stapleford, Lincs, 1597 Lincs RO Ad/Ac/4/41
Carter, John, Boughton under Blean, Kent, 1604 CKS PRC21/16/25
Carter, John, Mareham le Fen, Lincs, 1612 Lincs RO Ad/Ac/11/163
Carter, John, yeoman, Wigtoft, Lincs, 1618 Lincs RO Ad/Ac/14/216
Carter, John, yeoman, Hornton, Oxon, 1630 Oxon RO MSS Wills Pec 34/4/50
Carter, John, Borden, Kent, 1635 CKS PRC20/10/174
Carter, John, Latches, Ches, 1664 Cheshire RO (Name) W.C. 1664
Carter, John, miller, Chesterfield, Derby, 1674 LJRO/B/C/5/1692/18
Carter, John, Salisbury, Wilts, 1675 Wilts RO Miscellaneous Index to Wills (name + date)
Carter, John, Frinstead, Kent, 1679 CKS PRC2/38/117
Carter, John, yeoman, Farndon (Churton), Ches, 1727 Cheshire RO (Name) W.C. 1727
Carter, John, Meare, Som, 1738 Somerset RO D/D/Cta/C81
Carter, John, farmer, Leigh, Staffs, 1783 LJRO/B/C/5/1783/25
Carter, Jonas, Ospringe, Kent, 1621 CKS PRC2/23/60
Carter, Mary, wife, Bampton, Oxon, 1675 Oxon RO MSS Wills 296/3/63
Carter, Mary, widow, Bewdley (Wribbenhall), Worcs, 1779 Worcs RO 008.7 BA3585/835/bdl 2
Carter, Nicholas, gentleman, Willesborough, Kent, 1631 CKS PRC2/31/19
Carter, Nicholas, Aslackby, Lincs, 1683 Lincs RO Ad/Ac/44/95
Carter, Oliffe, widow, Broad Hinton, Wilts, 1637 Wilts RO Arch. Wilts.(name + date)
Carter, Richard, bachelor: 'singleman', Sandy, Beds, 1595 Lincs RO Ad/Ac/2b/139
Carter, Richard, yeoman, Spelsbury (Dean), Oxon, 1624 Oxon RO MSS Wills 296/1/122
Carter, Richard, Weston, South, Oxon, 1684 PRO PROB32/33/231
Carter, Robert, Sompting, Sussex, 1617 W. Suss RO EpI/33/1617/39
Carter, Robert, husbandman, Chadlington, Oxon, 1636 Oxon RO MSS Wills 296/2/56
Carter, Robert, weaver, Wallingford, Berks, 1641 Berks RO D/A1/183/5A
Carter, Robert, St Benet Fink, London & Middlesex, 1685 PRO PROB32/25/318
Carter, Robert, cordwainer, Tamworth, Staffs, 1778 LJRO/B/C/5/1778/22
Carter, Samuel, yeoman, Thatcham (Crookham), Berks, 1665 Berks RO D/A1/183/74A
Carter, Samuel, clergy: 'clerk', Findon, Sussex, 1676 W. Suss RO EpI/33/1676/25
Carter, Simon, husbandman, Bucklebury, Berks, 1653 Berks RO D/A1/183/45C
Carter, Susan, St Mary in the Marsh, Kent, 1598 CKS PRC2/10/338
Carter, Thomas, yeoman, Northill, Beds, 1602 Lincs RO Ad/Ac/5/566
Carter, Thomas, Ashby by Partney, Lincs, 1603 Lincs RO Ad/Ac/5/169
Carter, Thomas, Godmersham, Kent, 1615 CKS PRC20/3/312
Carter, Thomas, clothworker, Newbury, Berks, 1668 Berks RO D/A1/56/95C
Carter, Walter, Romsey, Hants, 1624 Hants RO 21M65 D8/54
Carter, Walter, Tenterden, Kent, 1627 CKS PRC2/28/22
Carter, William, Faversham, Kent, 1594 CKS PRC2/7/235
Carter, William, Cookham, Berks, 1615 Berks RO D/A1/182/18A
Carter, William, Tetford, Lincs, 1619 Lincs RO Ad/Ac/15/25
Carter, William, Easebourne, Sussex, 1629 W. Suss RO EpI/33/1629/1
Carter, William, weaver, Sittingbourne, Kent, 1630 CKS PRC20/9/101
Carter, William, Christchurch, Hants, 1663 Hants RO 21M65 D8/150
Carter, William, yeoman, Preston next Faversham, Kent, 1663 CKS PRC1/9/94
Carter, William, East Sutton, Kent, 1669 CKS PRC1/14/22
Carter, Willyam, Gosberton, Lincs, 1599 Lincs RO Ad/Ac/5/127
Carter/Barker, Margaret, wife, Ashford, Kent, 1610 CKS PRC2/13/126
Carter/Clarke, Cicely, widow, Charing, Kent, 1639 CKS PRC20/10/162

Carterwright, William, Leamington Priors, Warks, 1683 LJRO/B/C/5/1682/19
Cartwell, Charles, blacksmith, Gainsborough, Lincs, 1664 Lincs RO Ad/Ac/41/145
Cartwright, Edward, farmer, Pattingham, Staffs, 1823 LJRO/B/C/5/1823/7a
Cartwright, George, Shadwell, St Paul, London & Middlesex, 1748 Greater London RO DL/C/551/119/1
Cartwright, John, Rufforth, Yorks, Borthwick Test C.P. 1729/3
Cartwright, Katherine, Normanby, Lincs, 1610 Lincs RO Ad/Ac/8a/319
Cartwright, Mathew, Bromsgrove, Worcs, 1675 Worcs RO 008.7 BA3585/830/28
Cartwright, Vincent, draper, Canterbury St Andrew, Kent, 1626 CKS PRC20/7/78
Cartwrighte, John, Canterbury St Andrew, Kent, 1611 CKS PRC2/17/422
Carver, James, innholder, Norwich, Norf, 1756 Norfolk RO ANW/23/25/17
Carver, Joseph, Whitwick, Leics, 1665 Leics RO Administrators Accounts C17th f25
Carver, Thomas, Hougham, Lincs, 1605 Lincs RO Ad/Ac/6/151
Cary, John, shopkeeper, Egerton, Kent, 1673 CKS PRC20/12/42
Cary, John, Maidstone, Kent, 1679 CKS PRC20/12/296
Carye, Richard, cordwainer, Abingdon St Helen, Berks, 1636 Berks RO D/A1/182/108C
Carye, Stephen, Coultin, Som, 1592 Somerset RO D/D/Cta/C75
Caryll, Mary, widow, Slindon, Sussex, 1679 W. Suss RO EpIV/10/2A/15
Case, George, clergy: 'vicar', Boxley, Kent, 1632 CKS PRC2/31/97
Case, John, Corton Denham, Som, 1622 Somerset RO D/D/Cta/C3
Casebert, Christopher, yeoman, Blewbury, Berks, 1626 Wilts RO Dean Sarum (name + date)
Caseboard, Richard, carpenter, Hagbourne, Berks, 1668 Berks RO D/A1/183/61A
Casely, William,
Som 1715 Somerset RO D/D/Cta/C17
Casey, Henrie, Chislet, Kent, 1647 CKS PRC1/8/7
Cashere, see Cole,
Cashmore, Humphrey, bucklemaker, Walsall, Staffs, 1767 LJRO/B/C/5/1767/49
Cason, Dorothy, spinster, St Mary le Savoy, London & Middlesex, 1712 PRO PROB32/56/24
Cason, Lawrence, Lydd, Kent, 1613 CKS PRC20/2/408
Cason, Rychard, Borden, Kent, 1597 CKS PRC2/10/47
Cason, Thomas, Lydd, Kent, 1607 CKS PRC20/1/300
Cason/Cackstone, Thomas, Lydd, Kent, 1601 CKS PRC21/16/192
Cass, John, farmer, Fishlake (Sykehouse), Yorks, 1813 Borthwick Test C.P. 1813/2
Casselden, Thomas, Snave, Kent, 1613 CKS PRC2/17/142
Casselman, Bulford, Wilts, 1621 Wilts RO Unlisted Fragment
Cassildine, see Mason,
Cassire, Joane, widow, Sandwich, Kent, 1609 CKS PRC2/15/85
Cassire, John, Sandwich, Kent, 1607 CKS PRC2/15/71
Castell, Benjamin, St Mary in the Marsh, Kent, 1677 CKS PRC2/37/131
Castell, Richard, cordwainer, Reading St Lawrence, Berks, 1618 Berks RO D/A1/182/26A
Castell, Suzann eld, Canterbury St Margaret, Kent, 1636 CKS PRC2/33/34
Castell, Thomas, labourer, Basildon, Berks, 1674 Berks RO D/A1/183/130A
Castell, William, St Johns Thanet, Kent, 1585 CKS PRC2/3/290
Castell, William, Coningsby, Lincs, 1649 Lincs RO Ad/Ac/30/182
Castiel, John, Canterbury St Mary Bredin, Kent, 1614 CKS PRC2/17/32
Castiel, John, Canterbury Holy Cross Westgate, Kent, 1624 CKS PRC2/23/79
Castle, Anthony, yeoman, Uffington, Berks, 1646 Berks RO D/A1/183/25A
Castle, Clement, Upchurch, Kent, 1596 CKS PRC2/9/91
Castle, Elizabethe, Upchurch, Kent, 1601 CKS PRC2/12/96
Castle, John, Upchurch, Kent, 1599 CKS PRC2/10/529
Castle, John, Upchurch, Kent, 1626 CKS PRC2/25/38
Castle, Richard, Faversham, Kent, 1625 CKS PRC2/23/91
Castle, Richard, Bridge, Kent, 1674 CKS PRC2/36/34
Castle, Richard, Shadoxhurst, Kent, 1675 CKS PRC2/36/173
Castle, Silvestra, Shepherdswell alias Sibertswold, Kent, 1666 CKS PRC1/11/111

[Castle:]
Castle, Thomas, Wye, Kent, 1598 CKS PRC2/10/272
Castleden, John, Oare, Kent, 1647 CKS PRC1/8/8
Castlen, John, Warehorne, Kent, 1586 CKS PRC2/4/382
Castleton, Humphrey, Shifnal, Shrops, 1667 LJRO:cards/1667/15
Castlocke, Alice, widow, Faversham, Kent, 1614 CKS PRC2/18/134
Castlyn, Ales, Cranbrook, Kent, 1597 CKS PRC2/10/365
Castlyn, John, Queenborough, Kent, 1599 CKS PRC2/11/105
Caswell, William, Rothersthorpe, Northants, 1680 Northants RO NWill A/C/36
Catcheside, Robert, Carisbrooke, Hants, 1672 Hants RO 21m65 D8/237
Catelyn, Laurence, university: 'Fellow of Queens' College, Cambridge/B.D./vicar' Cambridge (Queens' College), Cambs, 1682 CUL V.C. Acc./Box3/10
Cater, Francis, Tattershall, Lincs, 1622 Lincs RO Ad/Ac/17/29
Cater, John, Langton, Lincs, 1639 Lincs RO Ad/Ac/26/4
Cater, John, gentleman, Coningsby, Lincs, 1670 Lincs RO Ad/Ac/32/202
Cater, Katherine, widow, Leverton, Lincs, 1626? Lincs RO Ad/Ac/20/86
Cater, Lewis, St Laurence Thanet, Kent, 1633 CKS PRC2/32/30
Cater, Richard, gentleman, Welton le Marsh, Lincs, 1632 Lincs RO Ad/Ac/23/176
Cater, Richard, gentleman, Welton le Marsh, Lincs, 1632 Lincs RO Ad/Ac/23/177
Cater, Samuel, Scartho, Lincs, 1648 Lincs RO Ad/Ac/30/308
Cater?, Richard, Ratby, Leics, 1639 Leics RO PR/I/41A/16
Caterer, Richard, yeoman, Chislehampton, Oxon, 1765 Oxon RO MSS Wills Pec 67/1/37
Caterman, Richard, Warehorne, Kent, 1592 CKS PRC2/6/330
Catlet, Benet, Tonge, Kent, 1592 CKS PRC2/6/278
Catlet, William, Teynham, Kent, 1614 CKS PRC2/18/119
Catlet, William, Teynham, Kent, 1625 CKS PRC2/25/36
Catlett, Daniel, joiner, Faversham, Kent, 1663 CKS PRC1/9/95
Catlett, John, Tonge, Kent, 1611 CKS PRC2/16/78
Catlett, John, yeoman, Newington next Sittingbourne, Kent, 1623 CKS PRC2/23/83
Catlett, Maryon, widow, Bapchild, Kent, 1611 CKS PRC2/16/79
Catlett, Ralphe, Lenham, Kent, 1601 CKS PRC2/12/100
Catlett, Thomas, Bapchild, Kent, 1604 CKS PRC2/14/119
Catlett, William, Tonge, Kent, 1604 CKS PRC2/14/125
Catlett, William, Teynham, Kent, 1629 CKS PRC2/30/29
Catley, Richard, Messingham, Lincs, 1612 Lincs RO Ad/Ac/8b/10
Catley, Richard, Kelstern, Lincs, 1626 Lincs RO Ad/Ac/20/26
Catley, Thomas, Belton, Lincs, 1663 Lincs RO Ad/Ac/41/107
Catley, William, Willingham, Lincs, 1639 Lincs RO Ad/Ac/40/258
Catlin, Philip, Walton, Wood, Hunts, 1681 Hunts RO/Acc58/160(116)
Catlin, Thomas, Deeping St James, Lincs, 1612 Lincs RO Ad/Ac/11/104
Catlin, William, Wistow, Hunts, 1677 Hunts RO/Acc58/111(28)
Catlin, William, Wistow, Hunts, 1685 Hunts RO/Acc58/248(244)
Cator, George, clergy: 'clerk', Addlethorpe, Lincs, 1645 Lincs RO Ad/Ac/28/160
Catt, John, Wittersham, Kent, 1675 CKS PRC20/12/165
Cattell, Elizabeth, Alconbury, Hunts, 1602 Lincs RO Ad/Ac/5/578
Cattell, Steven, Deeping, Market, Lincs, 1649 Lincs RO Ad/Ac/30/87
Cattell, William, St Albans, Herts, 1628 Herts RO ASA25/4854
Cattell, William, husbandman, Cropredy, Oxon, 1635 Oxon RO MSS Wills Pec 35/1/2
Catten, Edmond, St Johns Thanet, Kent, 1607 CKS PRC2/13/159
Catten, John, Harmston, Lincs, 1815 Lincs RO Ad/Ac/36/19
Cattermoull, Thomas, Norwich St Peter of Mancroft, Norf, 1749 Norfolk RO ANW/23/24/81A
Catterowe, Christopher, Bridge, Kent, 1609 CKS PRC2/15/58
Catterton, Richard, Halton Holgate, Lincs, 1625 Lincs RO Ad/Ac/19B/40
Cattle,
Som Somerset RO D/D/Cta/C7
Cauldicott, Nicholas, Blockley, Worcs, 1685 Worcs RO 008.7 BA3585/830/12

Cauldron, Maurice, Somerby, Lincs, 1649 Lincs RO Ad/Ac/30/93
Caulton, John, Whitwell, Derby, 1684 LJRO/B/C/5/1684/24
Caulton, Joseph, Wolstanton, Staffs, 1684 LJRO/B/C/5/1684/23
Caunter, Bartholomew, esquire, Gray's Inn, London & Middlesex, 1701 PRO PROB32/43/96
Cauntis, Mathias, yeoman, Monkton, Kent, 1679 CKS PRC20/12/295
Cave, Anthony, Canterbury St Mildred, Kent, 1628 CKS PRC20/8/127
Cave, Edwarde, Doddington (Whisby), Lincs, 1611 Lincs RO Ad/Ac/10/135
Cave, John, Iwade, Kent, 1600 CKS PRC2/11/385
Cave, John, husbandman, Stratfield Saye, Hants, 1663 Hants RO 21M65 D8/151
Cave, John, gentleman, Thorpe Satchville, Leics, 1673 Leics RO Administrators Accounts 1667-72 f136
Cave, Phillipp, Willingham, North, Lincs, 1639 Lincs RO Ad/Ac/26/88
Cave, Richard, Leigh, Worcs, Worcs RO 008.7 BA3585/838/195
Cave, Robert, butcher, Woodhay, West, Berks, 1616 Wilts RO CC Sarum(+ name and date)
Cavell, Andrew, Sellindge, Kent, 1609 CKS PRC2/15/60
Cavell, John, St Laurence Thanet, Kent, 1626 CKS PRC2/27/38
Cavell, Peter, blacksmith, Sellindge, Kent, 1617 CKS PRC2/20/52
Caverley, Jenet, Crowle, Lincs, 1609 Lincs RO Ad/Ac/8a/302
Cavill, see Spry,
Cawbert, Richard, husbandman, Fillingham, Lincs, 1626 Lincs RO Ad/Ac/39/228
Cawcott, Edward, butcher, Windsor, New, Berks, 1626 Berks RO D/A1/182/53C
Cawd, Nicholas, Barlings, Lincs, 1635 Lincs RO Ad/Ac/40/107
Cawdell, Thomas, Scarle, North, Lincs, 1612 Lincs RO Ad/Ac/10/137
Cawdorne, Mary, Norwich (St Mary Maddermarket sic), Norf, Norfolk RO ANW/23/25/61
Cawdron, Robert, Halton Holgate, Lincs, 1623 Lincs RO Ad/Ac/18/20
Cawkwell, Thomas, Hainton, Lincs, 1672 Lincs RO Ad/Ac/42/19
Cawle, William, Hernhill, Kent, 1664 CKS PRC19/3/18
Cawley, Ralph, Box, Wilts, 1630 Wilts RO Arch. Wilts.(name + date)
Cawnton, Edward, gentleman, Wingham, Kent, 1617 CKS PRC20/4/41
Cawood, Edmund, Surfleet, Lincs, 1637 Lincs RO Ad/Ac/25/649
Cawrthop, Richard, Cranbrook, Kent, 1617 CKS PRC2/21/158
Cawsey, Margaret, widow, 1574 Lancs RO (Name of Deceased) D.R.C.H. 1574
Cawthorne, John, Sutton, Lincs, 1614 Lincs RO Ad/Ac/13/117
Cawthorne, John, Alconbury, Hunts, 1684 Hunts RO/Acc58/214(218)
Cawthorpe, Brian, weaver, Theddlethorpe All Saints, Lincs, 1636 Lincs RO Ad/Ac/24/570
Cayroze, Lewis, master/bachelor, St Martin in the Fields, London & Middlesex, 1677 PRO PROB32/14/47
Ceelie, John,
Som C17th Somerset RO D/D/Cta/C25
Ceney, Edmund, clergy: 'vicar', Shoebury, North, Essex, 1669 Greater London RO DL/C/(Ac 73.77 pt)/Box 85/5 (uncatalogued)
Cetchaside, Richard, Abingdon St Helen, Berks, 1610 Berks RO D/A1/182/1A
Chadderton, Thomas, shepherd, Tetney, Lincs, 1620 Lincs RO Ad/Ac/16/22
Chadwick, John, yeoman, Belton All Saints, Lincs, 1677 Lincs RO Ad/Ac/35/133
Chadwick, John, surgeon, Bromley, Abbots, Staffs, 1800 LJRO/B/C/5/1800/11b
Chadwick, Richard, innkeeper, Oldham, Lancs, 1754 Lancs RO (Name of Deceased) D.R.C.H. 1754
Chadwick, Thomas, mealman, Spotland (Woodhouse Lane), Lancs, 1760 Lancs RO (Name of Deceased) D.R.C.H. 1760
Chadwicke, John, Rochdale (Meirland), Lancs, 1616 Lancs RO (Name of Deceased) D.R.C.H. 1616
Chadwicke, Roger, clergy: 'clerk', Billinghay, Lincs, 1593 Lincs RO Ad/Ac/3/99
Chaffie, Richard, Lillington, Dors, 1691 Wilts RO Dean Sarum (name + date)
Chaimbers, Henrie, yeoman, Doddington, Lincs, 1614 Lincs RO Ad/Ac/13/157
Chaire, Thomas, Glentworth, Lincs, 1682 Lincs RO Ad/Ac/44/2

[Chalcroft:]
Chalcroft, William, Ruckinge, Kent, 1682 CKS PRC2/40/16
Chalcrofte, Thomas, Faversham, Kent, 1579 CKS PRC2/1/226
Chalcrofte, Thomas, Stedham, Sussex, 1617 W. Suss RO EpI/33/1617/38
Chalke, Anne, widow, Pulborough, Sussex, 1634 W. Suss RO EpI/33/1633/2
Chalke, Thomas, Pulborough, Sussex, 1631 W. Suss RO EpI/33/1631/9
Chalke, William, looker, Elmley, Sheppey, Kent, 1661 CKS PRC1/8/92
Chalker, Thomas, gentleman, New Romney, Kent, 1675 CKS PRC20/12/163
Chalkley, William, St Pauls Walden, Herts, 1627 Herts RO ASA25/4841
Challand, Richard, Bennington, Long, Lincs, 1613 Lincs RO Ad/Ac/11/60
Challen, Richard, Cocking, Sussex, 1640 W. Suss RO EpI/33/1640/9
Challen, Richard eld, Cocking, Sussex, 1671 W. Suss RO EpI/33/1671/8
Challen, William, Lurgashall, Sussex, 1682 W. Suss RO EpI/33/1682/28
Challice, Thomas, husbandman, Speen (Benham), Berks, 1663 Berks RO D/A1/183/59A
Challiner, Timothy, currier, Stoke-upon-Trent (Burslem), Staffs, 1835 LJRO/B/C/5/1835/5
Challis, Anne, Maidstone, Kent, 1641 CKS PRC19/1/30
Challoner, John, Cheadle, Staffs, 1684 LJRO/B/C/5/1684/25
Challoner, Thomas, gentleman, Stratford-upon-Avon, Warks, 1698 Worcs RO 008.7 BA3585/837/bdl 6
Cham, Thomas, Branston, Lincs, 1614 Lincs RO Ad/Ac/13/34
Chamber, Jeames, Lenham, Kent, 1606 CKS PRC2/14/104
Chamber, Joane, widow, Woodchurch, Kent, 1596 CKS PRC21/14/99
Chamber, Robarte, Canterbury St Dunstan Without, Kent, 1590 CKS PRC2/5/156
Chamberlain, George, Spilsby, Lincs, 1597 Lincs RO Ad/Ac/4/27
Chamberlain, John, maltster, Bromley, Abbots, Staffs, 1795 LJRO/B/C/5/1795/9
Chamberlain, Robert, husbandman, Preston Capes, Northants, 1814 Northants RO X954/21/69
Chamberlain, Walter, Melbourne, Derby, 1683 LJRO/B/C/5/1682/20
Chamberlaine, Henry, Spalding, Lincs, 1639? Lincs RO Ad/Ac/26/89
Chamberlaine, John, Bratoft, Lincs, 1626 Lincs RO Ad/Ac/20/77
Chamberlaine, Robert, Kingston Deverill, Wilts, 1628 Wilts RO Arch. Sarum/(+ name and date)
Chamberlaine, Thomas, gentleman, Broadwas, Worcs, Worcs RO 008.7 BA3585/837/bdl 1
Chamberlaine, Thomas, gentleman, Bolingbroke, Old, Lincs, 1640 Lincs RO Ad/Ac/27/116
Chamberlaine, Thomas, Clifton upon Dunsmore, Warks, 1672 LJRO:cards/1672/11
Chamberlaine, William, Barholm, Lincs, 1621 Lincs RO Ad/Ac/16/25
Chamberlaine, William, husbandman, Uffington, Berks, 1635 Berks RO D/A1/182/106C
Chamberlayne, Henry, husbandman, Sulhampstead (Graisley), Berks, 1662 Berks RO D/A1/183/58D
Chamberlayne, John, Nettleham, Lincs, 1603 Lincs RO Ad/Ac/37/163
Chamberlayne, Lawrence, Droxford, Hants, 1685 Hants RO 21m65 D8/336
Chamberlen, Emme, widow, Pinchbeck, Lincs, 1639 Lincs RO Ad/Ac/25/314
Chamberlin, Catherine, Glen, Great, Leics, 1672 Leics RO Administrators Accounts 1667-72 f93
Chamberlin, Francis, Woodnesborough, Kent, 1638 CKS PRC2/34/180
Chamberlin, John, husbandman, Claines, Worcs, 1603 Worcs RO 008.7 BA3585/839/290
Chamberlin, John, gentleman, Newton Harcourt, Leics, 1639 Leics RO PR/I/41A/12
Chamberlin, Thomas, labourer, Sempringham (Pointon), Lincs, 1670 Lincs RO Ad/Ac/32/228
Chambers, Abraham, Capel le Ferne, Kent, 1608 CKS PRC2/14/101
Chambers, Ann, widow, Bristol St Stephen, Glos, Bristol RO 1678/65
Chambers, Beniamin, Bearsted, Kent, 1620 CKS PRC2/21/169
Chambers, Benjamin, Marden, Kent, 1676 CKS PRC2/37/24
Chambers, Benjamin, Leeds (Great Woodhouse), Yorks, 1720 Borthwick Test C.P. 1720/2
Chambers, Charles, brass founder/brazier/tinman/ironmonger, Halifax, Yorks, 1799 Borthwick Test C.P. 1799/1
Chambers, Dunstane, husbandman, Lenham, Kent, 1620 CKS PRC2/23/74
Chambers, Edward, Eythorne, Kent, 1599 CKS PRC2/11/1
Chambers, Edward, Belvoir, Leics, 1684 Leics RO Administrators Accounts 1682-86 f32
Chambers, Ely, Eastwell, Kent, 1623 CKS PRC2/23/71

Chambers, Henry, yeoman, Boughton Malherbe, Kent, 1690 CKS PRC2/41/170
Chambers, Hugh, Stowting, Kent, 1641 CKS PRC1/5/86
Chambers, Humphrey, Swineshead, Lincs, 1637 Lincs RO Ad/Ac/25/492
Chambers, James, Liverpool, Lancs, 1581 Lancs RO (Name of Deceased) D.R.C.H. 1581
Chambers, James, Fillingham, Lincs, 1632 Lincs RO Ad/Ac/39/305
Chambers, Joan, widow, Poling, Sussex, 1682 W. Suss RO EpI/33/1682/18
Chambers, John, Canterbury St Margaret, Kent, 1583 CKS PRC2/3/84
Chambers, John, Bath, Som, 1620 Somerset RO D/D/Cta/C48
Chambers, John, Tenterden, Kent, 1633 CKS PRC2/32/31
Chambers, John, Eastchurch, Sheppey, Kent, 1637 CKS PRC2/34/36
Chambers, John, Bearsted, Kent, 1674 CKS PRC2/35/207
Chambers, John, Batcombe, Som, 1748 Somerset RO D/D/Cta/C82
Chambers, Mary, Pershore, Worcs, 1680 Worcs RO 008.7 BA3585/837/bdl 2
Chambers, Mary, Melbourne, Derby, 1685 LJRO/B/C/5/1685/26
Chambers, Michael, Sutton, Kings, Northants, Oxon RO MSS Wills Pec 34/4/30
Chambers, Michael, university: 'Fellow of Queens' College, Cambridge/deacon/M.A.' Cambridge (Queens' College), Cambs, 1634 CUL V.C. Acc./Box2/12
Chambers, Richard, Bearsted, Kent, 1620 CKS PRC2/21/168
Chambers, Robert, Hartlip, Kent, 1609 CKS PRC2/13/113
Chambers, Robert, Fillingham, Lincs, 1626 Lincs RO Ad/Ac/39/198
Chambers, Simon, Teynham, Kent, 1631 CKS PRC2/31/17
Chambers, Stephen, yeoman, Minster in Thanet, Kent, 1680 CKS PRC2/39/24
Chambers, Thomas, Halton, East, Lincs, 1663 Lincs RO Ad/Ac/32/48
Chambers, Thomas, Monkton, Kent, 1681 CKS PRC20/13/125
Chambers, Thomas, yeoman, Ash next Sandwich, Kent, 1687 CKS PRC20/13/582
Chambers, Thomas, gentleman, Derby, Derby, 1757 LJRO/B/C/5/1757/103
Chambers, Walter, yeoman, Horsley, Glos, 1717 GRO GDR/B4/2/C55
Chambers, William, Stockbury, Kent, 1635 CKS PRC2/33/33
Chambers, William, Harrietsham, Kent, 1637 CKS PRC2/33/31
Chambers, William, Bottesford, Leics, 1668 Leics RO Administrators Accounts 1667-72 f14
Chambers/Allen/Wilmot, Marian, wife, Lenham, Kent, 1624 CKS PRC2/23/90
Champ, John, Sittingbourne, Kent, 1627 CKS PRC2/28/29
Champe, Gregory, husbandman, Compton, Berks, 1621 Wilts RO CC Sarum(+ name and date)
Champe, Henry, yeoman, Hampstead Norris, Berks, 1640 Berks RO D/A1/182/134C
Champe, James, Stratfield Mortimer, Berks, 1608 Berks RO D/A1/53/175C
Champe, Richard, husbandman, Hendred, East, Berks, 1633 Berks RO D/A1/182/91A
Champe, Richard, yeoman, Hendred, East, Berks, 1676 Berks RO D/A1/183/100A
Champen, James, labourer, Stockbury, Kent, 1610 CKS PRC1/1/11
Champen, Jeames, Stockbury, Kent, 1610 CKS PRC2/13/117
Champion, Arnold, Reading St Giles, Berks, 1594 Berks RO D/A1/181/145A
Champion, Christopher, Biddenden, Kent, 1595 CKS PRC2/7/433
Champion, Frances, widow, Shapwick, Som, 1667 Somerset RO D/D/Cta/C65
Champion, Henry, Wisborough Green, Sussex, 1633 W. Suss RO EpI/33/1633/5
Champion, James, Bersted, South, Sussex, 1637 W. Suss RO EpIV/10/2/17
Champion, John, Wisborough Green, Sussex, 1629 W. Suss RO EpI/33/1629/19
Champion, John, Newport, Hants, 1661 Hants RO 21M65 D8/142
Champion, William, Portbury, Som, 1641 Somerset RO D/D/Cta/C72
Champion, William, Meare, Som, 1679 Somerset RO D/D/Cta/C83
Champyon, Alice, widow, Duncton, Sussex, 1627 W. Suss RO EpI/33/1627/15
Champyon, Joan, widow, Chichester St Pancras, Sussex, 1621 W. Suss RO EpIV/10/1/32
Chandelor, Martha, widow, Bovingdon, Herts, 1634 Herts RO AHH23/392
Chandler, Elizabeth, Chilham, Kent, 1667 CKS PRC1/12/21
Chandler, John, Ferring, Sussex, 1670 W. Suss RO EpI/33/1670/10
Chandler, John, yeoman, Biddenden, Kent, 1684 CKS PRC2/40/185
Chandler, John, yeoman, Otterden, Kent, 1701 CKS PRC1/16/24

[Chandler:]
Chandler, Lydia, widow, Reading St Lawrence, Berks, 1682 Berks RO D/A1/184/24C
Chandler, Mathew, Woodchurch, Kent, 1683 CKS PRC20/13/235
Chandler, Matthew, butcher, Canterbury St Andrew, Kent, 1649 CKS PRC1/8/39
Chandler, Richard, butcher, Canterbury Holy Cross Westgate, Kent, 1672 CKS PRC2/35/121
Chandler, William, Lincs RO Ad/Ac/36/8
Chandler, William, butcher, Dover, Kent, 1612 CKS PRC20/2/414
Chandler, William, cordwainer, Deeping, Market, Lincs, 1774 Lincs RO Ad/Ac/45/37
Chanertrell, Elizabeth, Peopleton, Worcs, 1606 Worcs RO 008.7 BA3585/839/402
Chanler, Lancelot, Swinford, Old (Stourbridge), Worcs, 1682 Worcs RO 008.7 BA3585/830/74
Channcelor, Adam, tailor, Harwell, Berks, 1609 Berks RO D/A1/181/211A
Channell, Thomas, Rudgwick, Sussex, 1684 W. Suss RO EpI/33/1684/17
Chanon, Richard, fuller, St Ives, Hunts, Hunts RO/Acc58/143(177)
Chant, Robert, Chilthorne Domer, Som, 1735 Somerset RO D/D/Cta/C84
Chant, Thomas, Ormsby, Lincs, 1639? Lincs RO Ad/Ac/26/85
Chantler, Richard, Cranbrook, Kent, 1644 CKS PRC1/7/24
Chapleine, William, Frittenden, Kent, 1619 CKS PRC2/21/162
Chaplin, Ebenezer, Ashcott, Som, 1744 Somerset RO D/D/Cta/C85
Chaplin, James, husbandman, Upchurch, Kent, 1637 CKS PRC2/33/28
Chaplin, Thomas, yeoman, Wistow, Hunts, 1694 Hunts RO/Acc58/281
Chapline, Thomas, Cranbrook, Kent, 1637 CKS PRC2/34/28
Chaplyn, Richard, husbandman, Upchurch, Kent, 1642 CKS PRC1/6/53
Chapman, Abraham, Ash next Sandwich, Kent, 1685 CKS PRC20/13/418
Chapman, Alexander, Sittingbourne, Kent, 1596 CKS PRC2/8/200
Chapman, Ann, widow, Canterbury St Paul, Kent, 1619 CKS PRC2/20/106
Chapman, Anne, widow, Chichester, Sussex, 1630 W. Suss RO EpIII/9/1/37
Chapman, Anne, widow, Leaveland, Kent, 1662 CKS PRC1/8/93
Chapman, Anne, spinster, Scothorne, Lincs, 1680 Lincs RO Ad/Ac/43/145
Chapman, Anthony, Willingham, North, Lincs, 1618 Lincs RO Ad/Ac/14/180
Chapman, Bridgett, Morton, Lincs, 1664 Lincs RO Ad/Ac/41/144
Chapman, Bridgitt, widow, Saltfleetby, Lincs, 1637 Lincs RO Ad/Ac/25/554
Chapman, Christopher, Boughton under Blean, Kent, 1583 CKS PRC21/6/167
Chapman, Drewe, Linton, Kent, 1619 CKS PRC2/21/170
Chapman, Edward, yeoman, Eastchurch, Sheppey, Kent, 1682 CKS PRC2/40/19
Chapman, Elizabeth, widow, Folkestone, Kent, 1636 CKS PRC2/34/33
Chapman, Elizabeth, widow, Godmersham, Kent, 1636 CKS PRC20/10/190
Chapman, Elizabeth,
Lincs 1649 Lincs RO Ad/Ac/30/403
Chapman, George, Howell, Lincs, 1739 Lincs RO Ad/Ac/45/25
Chapman, Henry, Whaplode Drove, Lincs, 1629 Lincs RO Ad/Ac/22/17
Chapman, Henry, Challock, Kent, 1630 CKS PRC20/9/91
Chapman, Henrye, Cheriton, Kent, 1602 CKS PRC2/12/106
Chapman, Hugh, Hallaton, Leics, 1639 Leics RO PR/I/41A/25
Chapman, Humphrey, Bosworth, Market, Leics, 1666 Leics RO Administrators Accounts C17th f68
Chapman, John, innholder, Hull, Yorks, Borthwick Test C.P. 1738/4
Chapman, John, gentleman, Canterbury St George Martyr, Kent, 1610 CKS PRC2/15/53
Chapman, John, Hythe St Leonard, Kent, 1634 CKS PRC20/10/252
Chapman, John, Milton next Sittingbourne, Kent, 1636 CKS PRC2/33/35
Chapman, John, Bitchfield, Lincs, 1640 Lincs RO Ad/Ac/27/22
Chapman, John, labourer, Sempringham (Pointon), Lincs, 1670 Lincs RO Ad/Ac/32/230
Chapman, John, yeoman, Epworth, Lincs, 1672 Lincs RO Ad/Ac/33/201
Chapman, John, yeoman, Panton, Lincs, 1673 Lincs RO Ad/Ac/35/15
Chapman, Julian, widow, Rolvenden, Kent, 1630 CKS PRC20/9/111
Chapman, Mary, widow, Kennington, Kent, 1664 CKS PRC1/10/16
Chapman, Mathew, Sturton, Great, Lincs, 1650 Lincs RO Ad/Ac/30/4

[Chapman:]

Chapman, Nathaniell, yeoman, Haceby, Lincs, 1642 Lincs RO Ad/Ac/28/21
Chapman, Nicholas, Shipton under Wychwood (Milton), Oxon, 1638 Oxon RO MSS Wills 296/3/5
Chapman, Peter, Whaplode Drove, Lincs, 1636 Lincs RO Ad/Ac/24/474
Chapman, Peter, Ospringe, Kent, 1684 CKS PRC2/40/191
Chapman, Richard, Kirton, Lincs, 1634 Lincs RO Ad/Ac/24/213
Chapman, Richard, Stoke Talmage, Oxon, 1637 Oxon RO MSS Wills 296/2/69
Chapman, Richard, Blockley, Worcs, 1683 Worcs RO 008.7 BA3585/837/bdl 3
Chapman, Robert, Bolingbroke, Old, Lincs, 1607 Lincs RO Ad/Ac/8a/73
Chapman, Robert, glover, Bethersden, Kent, 1622 CKS PRC2/23/65
Chapman, Robert, husbandman, Kirkby, East, Lincs, 1632 Lincs RO Ad/Ac/23/69
Chapman, Robert, Godmersham, Kent, 1712 CKS PRC19/6/51
Chapman, Roberte, Faversham, Kent, 1583 CKS PRC2/3/1
Chapman, Sara, Shifnal, Shrops, 1667 LJRO:cards/1667/16
Chapman, Stephen, Bethersden, Kent, 1677 CKS PRC2/37/128
Chapman, Symon, Godmersham, Kent, 1597 CKS PRC21/14/177
Chapman, Thomas, Paddlesworth, Kent, 1604 CKS PRC21/17/380
Chapman, Thomas, husbandman, Weston, Lincs, 1623 Lincs RO Ad/Ac/18/26
Chapman, Thomas, Whaplode Drove, Lincs, 1624 Lincs RO Ad/Ac/19A/105
Chapman, Thomas, Oxford (Holywell), Oxon, 1626 Oxon RO MSS Wills 296/1/130
Chapman, Thomas, Holbeach, Lincs, 1641 Lincs RO Ad/Ac/27/273
Chapman, Thomas, Crowle, Lincs, 1673 Lincs RO Ad/Ac/35/50
Chapman, Thomas, gentleman, Caistor, Lincs, 1675 Lincs RO Ad/Ac/42/18
Chapman, Thomas, Milton next Sittingbourne, Kent, 1681 CKS PRC2/39/163
Chapman, Thomas, Manchester, Lancs, 1721 Lancs RO (Name of Deceased) D.R.C.H. 1721
Chapman, Thomas, victualler, Derby, Derby, 1806 LJRO/B/C/5/1806/4
Chapman, Thomas + Eliz, widow, Chilham, Kent, 1594 CKS PRC2/7/35
Chapman, Timothy, husbandman, Ingoldsby, Lincs, 1672 Lincs RO Ad/Ac/34/3
Chapman, Tobias, labourer, Croxby, Lincs, 1633 Lincs RO Ad/Ac/23/170
Chapman, William, Dover, Kent, 1605 CKS PRC20/1/1
Chapman, William, Milton next Sittingbourne, Kent, 1606 CKS PRC2/14/112
Chapman, William, Hythe St Leonard, Kent, 1629 CKS PRC20/8/93
Chapman, William, miller, Shipton under Wychwood (Milton), Oxon, 1636 Oxon RO MSS Wills 296/2/58
Chapman, William, Sutterton, Lincs, 1637 Lincs RO Ad/Ac/24/551
Chapman, William, labourer, Ospringe, Kent, 1666 CKS PRC1/11/112
Chapman, William, Arundel, Sussex, 1681 W. Suss RO EpI/33/1681/3
Chapman, William, Cheriton, Kent, 1685 CKS PRC19/4/107
Chapman/Spencer, Elizabeth, Dunston, Leics, 1625 Lincs RO Ad/Ac/19B/107
Chappell, John, Muchelney, Som, 1587 Somerset RO D/D/Cta/C29
Chappell, John, Chewton Mendip, Som, 1605 Somerset RO D/D/Cta/C43
Chappell, Richard, yeoman, St Albans St Peters, Herts, 1569 Herts RO ASA25/659
Chappell, Robert, butcher, Thatcham, Berks, 1686 Berks RO D/A1/184/28C
Charder, Mychaell, Wye, Kent, 1591 CKS PRC2/5/67
Chare, Agnes, widow, Drayton, Berks, 1594 Berks RO D/A1/181/144D
Charier, Anthonye, Old Romney, Kent, 1609 CKS PRC2/15/64
Charity, Fran, husbandman, Dembleby, Lincs, 1664 Lincs RO Ad/Ac/43/31
Charles, John, St Giles in the Fields, London & Middlesex, 1674 PRO PROB32/11/39
Charles, Margarett, widow, Hackington, Kent, 1617 CKS PRC2/20/49
Charles, Richard, labourer, Aslackby, Lincs, 1669 Lincs RO Ad/Ac/33/99
Charles, Robert, yeoman, Gonerby, Great, Lincs, 1614 Lincs RO Ad/Ac/13/111
Charles, Thomas, Walcot, Lincs, 1625 Lincs RO Ad/Ac/22/128
Charles, Thomas, yeoman, Aslackby, Lincs, 1684 Lincs RO Ad/Ac/44/141
Charles, William, Donington, Lincs, 1627 Lincs RO Ad/Ac/20b/45
Charlesworth, Thomas, Minting, Lincs, 1641 Lincs RO Ad/Ac/27/222

[Charleton:]
Charleton, Abraham, Boughton Monchelsea, Kent, 1619 CKS PRC2/20/1
Charleton, Abraham, Loose, Kent, 1623 CKS PRC20/6/404
Charleton, Anne, lady, Cheveley (Cheveley Park House), Cambs, 1673 PRO PROB5/1059
Charleton, Robert, clergy: 'clerk', Owston, Lincs, 1606 Lincs RO Ad/Ac/37/225
Charlett, George, Evesham St Lawrence, Worcs, 1678 Worcs RO 008.7 BA3585/830/16
Charlett, Richard, Raveley, Hunts, 1643 Hunts RO/Acc58/11(36)
Charlton, George, yeoman, Loose, Kent, 1666 CKS PRC19/3/91
Charlton, Mary, widow, Dean (Kearsley), Lancs, 1846 Borthwick Trans. C.P. 1847/1
Charlton, Thomas, Boughton Monchelsea, Kent, 1639 CKS PRC1/2/35
Charman, John, yeoman, Warnham, Sussex, W. Suss RO EpI/33/1630/18
Charman, Thomas, cooper, Deal, Kent, 1642 CKS PRC19/2/52
Charnley, Edward, Eccleston (Wrightington), Lancs, 1581 Lancs RO (Name of Deceased) D.R.C.H. 1581
Charnock, Charles, merchant, Leeds, Yorks, 1801 Borthwick Test C.P. 1801/8
Charrier, Beniamyn, clergy: 'D.D.', Canterbury, Kent, 1615 CKS PRC20/3/322
Charvill, Randall, Canterbury Christchurch, Kent, 1638 CKS PRC20/10/152
Chase, Thomas, Worldham, East, Hants, 1623 Hants RO 21M65 D8/9
Chase, William, St Clement Danes, London & Middlesex, 1731 Greater London RO AM/PP/Box 1726-1732 pt (uncatalogued)
Chasmer, John, Ash next Sandwich, Kent, 1638 CKS PRC20/10/202
Chater, Thomas, Damerham, South, Wilts, 1634 Wilts RO CC Sarum(+ name and date)
Chater, Thomas, Shuckburgh, Lower, Warks, 1673 LJRO:cards/1673/2
Chaterton, John, Wybunbury, Ches, 1636 Cheshire RO (Name) W.C. 1635/6
Chaterton, William, Earnley, Sussex, 1596 W. Suss RO EpI/33/1596/6
Chatfeild, William, bachelor, Tangmere, Sussex, 1681 W. Suss RO EpIV/10/2A/27
Chatterton, Richard, Fiskerton, Lincs, 1651 Lincs RO Ad/Ac/40/237
Chatterton, Richard, husbandman, Snitterby, Lincs, 1675 Lincs RO Ad/Ac/35/97
Chatterton, Simon, Corringham, Lincs, 1663 Lincs RO Ad/Ac/42/16
Chatterton, Stephen, cordwainer, Walsall, Staffs, 1748 LJRO/B/C/5/1748/205
Chatterton, Thomas, Faldingworth, Lincs, 1626 Lincs RO Ad/Ac/39/186
Chatterton, William, Loughborough, Leics, 1665 Leics RO Administrators Accounts C17th f32
Chattock, Susanna, Bickenhill, Warks, 1682 LJRO/B/C/5/1682/21
Chatton, Richard, farmer, Dickleburgh, Norf, 1768 Norfolk RO ANF/11/5/76
Chaulke, Hugh, Pulborough, Sussex, 1629 W. Suss RO EpI/33/1629/10
Chaulkley, Richard, St Pauls Walden, Herts, 1566 Herts RO ASA25/616
Chaundler, Abraham, Dover, Kent, 1641 CKS PRC19/2/7
Chaundler, Ann, spinster, Mildenhall, Wilts, 1636 Wilts RO Arch. Wilts.(name + date)
Chaundler, George, Bradford on Avon, Wilts, 1606? Wilts RO CC Sarum(+ name and date)
Chaundler, Ralph, Midhurst, Sussex, 1676 W. Suss RO EpI/33/1676/16
Chaundler, Richard, Canterbury Holy Cross Westgate, Kent, 1664 CKS PRC1/10/17
Chaundler, William, Ash next Sandwich, Kent, 1664 CKS PRC19/3/19
Chauntler, Ralph, alderman, Chichester, Sussex, W. Suss RO EpIII/9/1/4
Chauntler, see Starr,
Chauntree, John, Baumber, Lincs, 1611 Lincs RO Ad/Ac/10/93
Chauntrey, Elizabeth, Sutton, Derby, 1684 LJRO/B/C/5/1684/26
Chaveney, Peter, gentleman, Quorndon, Leics, 1672 Leics RO Administrators Accounts 1667-72 f52
Chawke, Richard, yeoman, Shaw cum Donnington, Berks, 1621 Berks RO D/A1/181/188E
Chawkley, Edward, St Pauls Walden, Herts, 1591 Herts RO ASA25/1340
Chawklye, John, Hawkhurst, Kent, 1599 CKS PRC21/14/526
Chawklyne, Margerie, widow, Hawkhurst, Kent, 1598 CKS PRC2/10/198
Chawner, Rupert, surgeon, Melbourne, Derby, 1821 LJRO/B/C/5/1821/22b
Chawner, William, Spondon, Derby, 1685 LJRO/B/C/5/1685/27
Chayney, Elias, Arundel, Sussex, 1682 W. Suss RO EpI/33/1682/2
Cheaketts, Philip, Peopleton, Worcs, 1684 Worcs RO 008.7 BA3585/837/bdl 4

Cheales, Coates, Great, Lincs, 1648 Lincs RO Ad/Ac/30/337
Cheales, Richard, Ingoldmels, Lincs, 1646 Lincs RO Ad/Ac/28/173
Cheales, Roberte, Hogsthorpe, Lincs, 1580 Lincs RO Ad/Ac/2b/36
Cheales/Barrett, Alice, Lusby, Lincs, 1622 Lincs RO Ad/Ac/17/87
Chearsone, George, Hawkhurst, Kent, 1610 CKS PRC2/13/122
Checkley, Thomas, Woodford (Hinton), Northants, 1674 Northants RO NWill A/C/77
Checkley, William, Preston Capes, Northants, 1672 Northants RO NWill A/C/105
Cheese, John, Nackington, Kent, 1595 CKS PRC2/7/427
Cheese, Oliver + Eliz, Nackington, Kent, 1599 CKS PRC2/10/433
Cheese, Richard, Canterbury St Martin, Kent, 1608 CKS PRC20/1/336
Cheese, Robart, Swalecliffe, Kent, 1602 CKS PRC2/12/114
Cheese, Solomon, Sutton Valence, Kent, 1638 CKS PRC1/1/71
Cheeseman, Anne, Cheriton, Kent, 1639 CKS PRC2/34/182
Cheeseman, George, Coldred, Kent, 1637 CKS PRC2/34/37
Cheeseman, Henry, husbandman, Kenardington, Kent, 1642 CKS PRC1/5/87
Cheeseman, John, Woodchurch, Kent, 1628 CKS PRC20/8/123
Cheeseman, John, butcher, New Romney, Kent, 1674 CKS PRC20/12/122
Cheeseman, John, Newington next Sittingbourne, Kent, 1676 CKS PRC2/37/18
Cheeseman, John, weaver: 'linen weaver', Lyminge, Kent, 1700 CKS PRC19/5/63
Cheeseman, Richard, carpenter, Chart nr Sutton Valence, Kent, 1640 CKS PRC1/4/19
Cheeseman, Robert, Woodchurch, Kent, 1673 CKS PRC20/12/75
Cheeseman, Robert, yeoman, East Sutton, Kent, 1675 CKS PRC2/36/32
Cheeseman, Robert, Woodchurch, Kent, 1681 CKS PRC20/13/109
Cheeseman, Sampson, Brookland, Kent, 1629 CKS PRC2/30/34
Cheeseman, Stephen, Brabourne, Kent, 1602 CKS PRC2/14/138
Cheeseman, Stephen, Nackington, Kent, 1681 CKS PRC2/39/12
Cheeseman, Thomas, Cranbrook, Kent, 1607 CKS PRC2/14/91
Cheeseman, Thomas, flaxman, Faversham, Kent, 1682 CKS PRC2/40/14
Cheesman, Alexander, husbandman, Belton All Saints, Lincs, 1613 Lincs RO Ad/Ac/8b/13
Cheesman, John, Frittenden, Kent, 1639 CKS PRC1/2/36
Cheesman, John, Brabourne, Kent, 1641 CKS PRC1/5/88
Cheesman, John, Mersham, Kent, 1679 CKS PRC2/38/115
Cheesman, Paul, Lympne, Kent, 1638 CKS PRC2/34/186
Cheesman, Thomas, Goring, Sussex, 1671 W. Suss RO EpI/33/1671/9
Cheesman, Thomas, yeoman, Brabourne, Kent, 1677 CKS PRC2/37/19
Cheetam, Oates, Manchester (Houghton), Lancs, 1625 Lancs RO (Name of Deceased) D.R.C.H. 1625
Cheetham, Adam, Denton, Lancs, 1625 Lancs RO (Name of Deceased) D.R.C.H. 1625
Chell, Jasper, Cheadle, Staffs, 1667 LJRO:cards/1667/17
Cheltenham, Edmund, Ansford, Som, 1611 Somerset RO D/D/Cta/C34
Cheney, Thomas, Howell, Lincs, 1634 Lincs RO Ad/Ac/24/66
Chenocke, John, Whaplode, Lincs, 1580 Lincs RO Ad/Ac/2b/58
Chepman, John, Wells St Cuthbert, Som, 1633 Somerset RO D/D/Cta/C10
Chepsey, Ellen, Hemswell, Lincs, 1609 Lincs RO Ad/Ac/8a/306
Cherington, Eleazer, Englefield, Berks, 1611 Berks RO D/A1/181/213C
Cherrey, Thomas, surgeon, St Clement Danes, London & Middlesex, 1693 PRO PROB32/35/341
Cherrington/Hooper, Sarah, Kinnersley, Shrops, 1675 LJRO:cards/1675/15
Cheryton, Thomas, Sandwich, Kent, 1593 CKS PRC2/6/414
Chese, Margaret, Whitstable, Kent, 1606 CKS PRC1/1/3
Cheseman, William, St Mary in the Marsh, Kent, 1598 CKS PRC2/10/268
Cheseman, William, Chislet, Kent, 1606 CKS PRC2/13/132
Chesheire, William, Pickwell, Leics, 1639 Leics RO PR/I/41A/6
Cheshiere, Elizabeth, Oldbury, Shrops, 1681 Worcs RO 008.7 BA3585/830/76
Cheshire, Henry, Atherstone, Warks, 1680 LJRO:cards/1680/8
Chesman, Vincent, Belton All Saints, Lincs, 1676 Lincs RO Ad/Ac/35/105

[Chessell:]
Chessell, Robert, blacksmith, Titchfield, Hants, 1678 Hants RO 21m65 D8/282
Chesseman, Robert, Boughton Malherbe, Kent, 1638 CKS PRC2/34/181
Chesson, Stephen, Stelling, Kent, 1624 CKS PRC2/23/88
Chest, Emme, St Martin in the Fields, London & Middlesex, 1695 PRO PROB32/38/43
Chest, Thomas, clergy: 'clerk', Hythe St Leonard, Kent, 1622 CKS PRC20/6/400
Chester, Alexander, Algarkirk, Lincs, 1649 Lincs RO Ad/Ac/30/48
Chester, John, carpenter, Woodchurch, Kent, 1681 CKS PRC20/13/15
Cheston, Nicholas, Faversham, Kent, 1621 CKS PRC2/21/164
Chettell, Henry, tailor, Stevenage, Herts, 1640 Herts RO AHH23/415
Chettle, Henry, Caldecott, Northants, 1668 Northants RO NWill A/C/124
Cheverton, William, Boldre, Hants, 1624 Hants RO 21M65 D8/55
Chevin, Bartholomew, St George Hanover Square, London & Middlesex, 1741 Greater London RO DL/C/550/32
Chevin, Christopher, yeoman, Coleby, Lincs, 1640 Lincs RO Ad/Ac/27/18
Chewne, Peter, Sutton St Edmunds, Lincs, 1638 Lincs RO Ad/Ac/25/105
Chewney, Nicholas, clergy: 'D.D.', St Johns Thanet, Kent, 1686 CKS PRC2/41/67
Cheyney, Richard, gentleman, Canterbury St George Martyr, Kent, 1664 CKS PRC1/10/18
Cheyney, Thomas, gentleman, Tidcombe, Wilts, 1676 Wilts RO Miscellaneous Index to Wills (name + date)
Cheyney, Wyllyam, gentleman, Sittingbourne, Kent, 1586 CKS PRC2/4/7
Cheyney/Roper, Anne,
Kent 1586 CKS PRC2/4/417
Chidwick, Mary, Elham, Kent, 1632 CKS PRC2/31/99
Chidwick, Thomas, Lympne, Kent, 1630 CKS PRC20/8/105
Chidwick, Thomas, maltster, Hythe St Leonard, Kent, 1684 CKS PRC20/13/321
Chidwicke, Henry, Sandwich, Kent, 1698 CKS PRC19/5/52
Chidwicke, John, labourer, Deal, Kent, 1682 CKS PRC20/13/107
Chiffinch, Thomas, esquire, Milton, Kent, 1692 PRO PROB5/1245
Child, Elinor, widow, Washingborough, Lincs, 1667 Lincs RO Ad/Ac/32/121
Child, Joyce, Henbury (Hallen), Glos, Bristol RO 1706/CP
Child, Nicholas, Grimley, Worcs, 1593 Worcs RO 008.7 BA3585/838/97
Child, Philip, Leysdown, Kent, 1584 CKS PRC2/3/204
Child, Robert, esquire, Hayes, London & Middlesex, 1697 PRO PROB32/37/25
Child, Thomas, gentleman, Windsor, New, Berks, 1627 Berks RO D/A1/182/59D
Child, William, labourer, Chalgrove, Oxon, 1631 Oxon RO MSS Wills 296/2/36
Child, William, Leebotwood, Shrops, 1667 LJRO:cards/1667/18
Childe, John, saddler, Reading St Lawrence, Berks, 1618 Berks RO D/A1/182/29D
Childe, Roger, Barnet, East, Herts, 1567 Herts RO ASA25/639
Childe, Sylvester, Canterbury St Mildred, Kent, 1611 CKS PRC2/17/402
Childe, Thomas, Bethersden, Kent, 1597 CKS PRC2/12/421
Childe, William, joiner, Sedgebrook, Lincs, 1620 Lincs RO Ad/Ac/16/23
Childerbye, Thomas, Chipping Barnet, Herts, 1582 Herts RO ASA25/1002
Childes, Jeffery, mariner: 'seaman', St Peter in Thanet, Kent, 1680 CKS PRC2/38/118
Childes, Mary, widow, Adderbury, Oxon, 1675 Oxon RO MSS Wills 296/3/62
Childes, Michael, yeoman, Stone in Oxney, Kent, 1674 CKS PRC2/35/208
Childes, Thomas, Long Wittenham, Berks, 1609 Berks RO D/A1/181/207A
Childes, William, Bethersden, Kent, 1633 CKS PRC2/32/32
Childs, Margaret, widow, Maidstone, Kent, 1630 CKS PRC20/9/115
Childs, Thomas, Bethersden, Kent, 1604 CKS PRC2/14/118
Chiles, Thomas, Thornford, Dors, 1600 Wilts RO Miscellaneous Index to Wills (name + date)
Chillenden, Ralfe, St Nicholas at Wade, Kent, 1609 CKS PRC20/2/63
Chillenden, Thomas, Faversham, Kent, 1629 CKS PRC2/30/32
Chillenden, Thomas, Faversham, Kent, 1629 CKS PRC2/30/33
Chillenden, Thomas, Faversham, Kent, 1631 CKS PRC20/9/109
Chillenden, William, Boughton under Blean, Kent, 1599 CKS PRC21/14/510

Chillman, George, weaver, Newnham, Kent, 1672 CKS PRC2/35/123
Chillman, Henry, yeoman, Ospringe, Kent, 1681 CKS PRC2/39/162
Chilman, Henry, Chilham, Kent, 1628 CKS PRC2/29/23
Chilman, John, weaver: 'linen weaver', Newnham, Kent, 1677 CKS PRC2/37/135
Chilman, Robert, weaver: 'linen weaver', Bearsted, Kent, 1668 CKS PRC1/13/25
Chilman, Thomas, Mersham, Kent, 1605 CKS PRC2/13/137
Chilman, Thomas/Joane, Rolvenden, Kent, 1597 CKS PRC2/11/195
Chilmell, Josias, Godmersham, Kent, 1632 CKS PRC20/9/5
Chilmell, William, Boughton Aluph, Kent, 1605 CKS PRC2/14/93
Chilton, Christian, spinster, Sandwich St Clement, Kent, 1629 CKS PRC2/30/35
Chilton, John, brewer, Sandwich St Mary, Kent, 1637 CKS PRC1/1/48
Chilton, Stephen, Sandwich St Bartholomew's Hospital, Kent, 1614 CKS PRC20/2/484
Chinall, Sampson, maltster, Staines, London & Middlesex, 1667 PRO PROB32/3/62
Chinnock, Thomas, Moulton, Lincs, 1611 Lincs RO Ad/Ac/10/36
Chipman, see Greetham,
Chippingdale, Gregorie, Gainsborough, Lincs, 1612 Lincs RO Ad/Ac/8b/6
Chippinghurst, John + Annabel, Abingdon, Berks, 1610 Berks RO D/A1/181/217A
Chipsham, Edmund, Frieston, Lincs, 1662 Lincs RO Ad/Ac/32/30
Chiselden/Hellier, Thomas, Calne, Wilts, 1639 Wilts RO Miscellaneous Index to Wills (name + date)
Chissell, Edward, Tetford, Lincs, 1637 Lincs RO Ad/Ac/25/539
Chiswell, Elizabeth, widow, St Botolph without Bishopsgate, London & Middlesex, 1709 Greater London RO DL/C/545/55/1
Chittanden, Rycharde, Cranbrook, Kent, 1587 CKS PRC2/4/118
Chittenden, Agnes, widow, Tenterden, Kent, 1637 CKS PRC2/34/31
Chittenden, Edward, Stanford, Kent, 1628 CKS PRC20/8/119
Chittenden, Edward, clergy: 'clerk', Milton next Sittingbourne, Kent, 1637 CKS PRC2/33/26
Chittenden, Elizabeth, widow, Hawkhurst, Kent, 1637 CKS PRC2/34/38
Chittenden, James, yeoman, Marden, Kent, 1641 CKS PRC1/4/20
Chittenden, James, Ashford, Kent, 1673 CKS PRC2/35/209
Chittenden, James, Hinxhill, Kent, 1690 CKS PRC2/41/171
Chittenden, Joane, widow, Tenterden, Kent, 1614 CKS PRC2/18/26
Chittenden, John, Willesborough, Kent, 1602 CKS PRC2/12/110
Chittenden, John, tanner, Faversham, Kent, 1683 CKS PRC2/40/99
Chittenden, Joseph, Monks Horton, Kent, 1618 CKS PRC2/20/104
Chittenden, Mathewe ygr, Benenden, Kent, 1615 CKS PRC2/20/37
Chittenden, Peter, Wittersham, Kent, 1596 CKS PRC21/14/139
Chittenden, Richard, Wittersham, Kent, 1614 CKS PRC20/2/476
Chittenden, Richard, Wormshill, Kent, 1680 CKS PRC2/39/20
Chittenden, Stephen, Smarden, Kent, 1637 CKS PRC2/34/41
Chittenden, Stephen, Tenterden, Kent, 1662 CKS PRC1/8/94
Chittenden, Thomas, Cranbrook, Kent, 1595 CKS PRC2/7/227
Chittenden, Thomas, Stone in Oxney, Kent, 1597 CKS PRC2/9/75
Chittenden, Thomas, Hawkhurst, Kent, 1620 CKS PRC2/20/19
Chittenden, Thomas, tanner, Teynham, Kent, 1678 CKS PRC2/38/17
Chittenden, William, Hawkhurst, Kent, 1633 CKS PRC20/10/240
Chittenden, William, Ruckinge, Kent, 1681 CKS PRC2/39/164
Chittenden, see Bishopenden,
Chittie, Clarimon, Chichester, Sussex, 1613 W. Suss RO EpIII/9/1/8
Chitton, Richard, Norton in Hales, Shrops, 1675 LJRO:cards/1675/16
Chivers, Dorothy, Salisbury, Wilts, 1672 Wilts RO Miscellaneous Index to Wills (name + date)
Chivers, Roger, Shipton under Wychwood (Milton), Oxon, Oxon RO MSS Wills 296/3/36
Choppinge, Arthur, St Albans St Peters, Herts, 1616 Herts RO ASA25/4818
Chorlton, Edward, Didsbury (Hough-Head), Lancs, 1625 Lancs RO (Name of Deceased) D.R.C.H. 1625

[Chorlton:]
Chorlton, Thomas jun, Macclesfield, Ches, 1683 Cheshire RO (Name) W.C. 1683
Chowles, Robert, Welford (Hoe Benham), Berks, 1624 Berks RO D/A1/182/45A
Chowne, Robert, yeoman, Stokenchurch (Penley), Oxon, 1668 Oxon RO MSS Wills 78/2/10
Chowning, Thomas, carpenter, Harrietsham, Kent, 1667 CKS PRC1/12/22
Chrichlow, Nicholas, Sheen, Staffs, 1681 LJRO/B/C/5/1681/7
Chrisbye, John, Mersham, Kent, 1614 CKS PRC2/17/23
Chrisfeild, Walter, Lenham, Kent, 1597 CKS PRC2/9/79
Chrisfeilde, John eld, Chart nr Sutton Valence, Kent, 1625 CKS PRC2/25/45
Chrisfield, see Kersfield,
Christen, John, East Sutton, Kent, 1615 CKS PRC2/21/172
Christenwheate, John, Bluntisham, Hunts, 1681 Hunts RO/Acc58/168(29)
Christfield, Mathew, Headcorn, Kent, 1600 CKS PRC2/11/181
Christian, Benedict, Minster in Thanet, Kent, 1643 CKS PRC1/6/100
Christian, John, tailor, Faversham, Kent, 1670 CKS PRC1/15/12
Christian, Thomas, yeoman, Skillington, Lincs, 1686 Lincs RO Ad/Ac/42/98
Christian, William, Rainham, Kent, 1624 CKS PRC2/23/85
Christian, William, husbandman, Hale, Great, Lincs, 1644 Lincs RO Ad/Ac/28/81
Christian, William, weaver, Colsterworth, Lincs, 1668 Lincs RO Ad/Ac/33/76
Christian, see Kerchian,
Christmas, Andrew, Biddenden, Kent, 1618 CKS PRC2/21/160
Christmas, John, Itchenor, West, Sussex, 1683 W. Suss RO EpI/33/1682/45
Christmas, Robert, St Ives, Hunts, 1677 Hunts RO/Acc58/105(19)
Christofer, Joane, widow, Folkestone, Kent, 1615 CKS PRC2/20/71
Christopher, George, Dover St James, Kent, 1621 CKS PRC20/5/45
Christopher, John, Folkestone, Kent, 1626 CKS PRC2/27/31
Christopher, John, Gainsborough, Lincs, 1681 Lincs RO Ad/Ac/34/94
Christopher, see Nicolls & Todd,
Christopherson, William, Croston (Little Hoole), Lancs, 1617 Lancs RO (Name of Deceased) D.R.C.H. 1616-17
Chubb, Amesbury, Wilts, 1600 c. Wilts RO Miscellaneous Index to Wills (name + date)
Chubb, John, Amesbury, Wilts, 1639 Wilts RO Arch. Sarum/(+ name and date)
Chubbs, John, yeoman, Spilsby, Lincs, 1623 Lincs RO Ad/Ac/18/15
Church, Barnaby, Ash next Sandwich, Kent, 1617 CKS PRC20/4/47
Church, Edward, Hemsby, Norf, 1808 Norfolk RO ANW/23/27/13
Church, Edward + Joane, Minster in Thanet, Kent, 1632 CKS PRC2/31/16
Church, Elizabeth, widow, Dover, Kent, 1631 CKS PRC20/9/99
Church, George, Herne, Kent, 1640 CKS PRC19/1/31
Church, George, joiner, Canterbury St George Martyr, Kent, 1677 CKS PRC2/37/133
Church, James, tailor, Canterbury St George Martyr, Kent, 1676 CKS PRC2/37/21
Church, Josias, Doddington, Kent, 1635 CKS PRC2/32/147
Church, Richard, tailor, Childrey, Berks, 1628 Berks RO D/A1/182/72A
Church, Roger, St Nicholas at Wade, Kent, 1645 CKS PRC19/2/86
Church, Stephen, Walmer, Kent, 1618 CKS PRC2/20/73
Church, Thomas, Wingham, Kent, 1629 CKS PRC20/8/97
Church, Thomas, Hartwell, Northants, 1671 Northants RO NWill A/C/122
Church, Thomas, Wick, Wilts, 1675 Wilts RO Miscellaneous Index to Wills (name + date)
Church, Vallentine, Hernhill, Kent, 1626 CKS PRC20/7/92
Church, William, Amberley, Sussex, 1626 W. Suss RO EpI/33/1625/3
Church, William, yeoman, Bucklebury, Berks, 1677 Berks RO D/A1/184/5C
Church, William, Nonington, Kent, 1704 CKS PRC19/6/9
Church/Curling, Ann, St Peter in Thanet, Kent, 1674 CKS PRC2/36/36
Church/Halsnoth, Joane, Linsted, Kent, 1633 CKS PRC2/32/27
Churche, Elizabeth, Tonge, Kent, 1598 CKS PRC2/11/31
Churche, John, clergy: 'vicar', Tonge, Kent, 1596 CKS PRC2/8/405
Churche, Michaell, Whitstable, Kent, 1600 CKS PRC2/11/185

Churcheman, Thomas, Elmsted, Kent, 1586 CKS PRC2/4/392
Churcher, Isaacke, Canterbury St Mary-Magdalen Burgate, Kent, 1665 CKS PRC1/11/13
Churchill, John, yeoman, Bloxham, Oxon, 1636 Oxon RO MSS Wills 296/2/55
Churchill, Thomas, Deddington (Clifton), Oxon, 1790 Oxon RO MSS Wills Pec 301/3/91
Churchman, Christopher, Minster in Thanet, Kent, 1715 CKS PRC1/17/69
Churchman, Henry, yeoman, Minster in Thanet, Kent, 1679 CKS PRC2/38/116
Churchman, Nicholas, Sturry, Kent, 1627 CKS PRC2/28/26
Churchman, Robert, Stourmouth, Kent, 1617 CKS PRC2/20/102
Churchyard, Thomas, bucklemaker, Birmingham, Warks, 1767 LJRO/B/C/5/1767/66
Churden/Jurden, Tymothie, Stourmouth, Kent, 1591 CKS PRC2/5/134
Churden/Woodward, Ales, Cranbrook, Kent, 1600 CKS PRC2/11/383
Chysild, Sarah, spinster, Fisherton Anger, Wilts, 1760? Wilts RO Miscellaneous Index to Wills (name + date)
Chyttenden, John, Benenden, Kent, 1591 CKS PRC2/6/218
Chyvington, Thomas, Hawkhurst, Kent, 1607 CKS PRC2/13/157
Cicill, William, husbandman, Shipton on Cherwell, Oxon, 1625 Oxon RO MSS Wills 296/1/131
Clabburn, John, twisterer, Norwich St Michael Coslany, Norf, Norfolk RO NCC INV/78B/26
Clace, John, Deverill, Longbridge, Wilts, 1669 Wilts RO Arch. Sarum/(+ name and date)
Clagett, Ann, widow, Headcorn, Kent, 1678 CKS PRC2/38/16
Clagget, George, haberdasher, Ashford, Kent, 1638 CKS PRC1/1/72
Claggett, William, Headcorn, Kent, 1595 CKS PRC2/7/449
Claggett, William, yeoman, Smarden, Kent, 1647 CKS PRC1/8/9
Claie, Thomas, Gosberton, Lincs, 1634 Lincs RO Ad/Ac/24/506
Claie, Thomas, Gosberton, Lincs, 1634 Lincs RO Ad/Ac/24/516
Claiton, Jennet, Appleby, Lincs, 1604 Lincs RO Ad/Ac/37/173
Claiton, Mathew, Appleby, Lincs, 1610 Lincs RO Ad/Ac/8a/320
Claiton, Richard, clergy: 'Archdeacon of Lincoln', Lincoln, Lincs, 1612 Lincs RO Ad/Ac/11/123
Claiton, Robert, Flixborough, Lincs, 1582 Lincs RO Ad/Ac/2C/78
Clamper, William, Hawkhurst, Kent, 1624 CKS PRC2/23/86
Clapcott, Robert, Dorchester, Dors, 1684 Wilts RO Miscellaneous Index to Wills (name + date)
Clapham, Charles, Dover, Kent, 1694 CKS PRC19/5/18
Clapham, Jonathan, yeoman, Weston, Lincs, 1683 Lincs RO Ad/Ac/44/121
Clapham, Joseph, butcher, Horncastle, Lincs, 1683 Lincs RO Ad/Ac/44/99
Clapham, Walter, Boston, Lincs, 1612 Lincs RO Ad/Ac/11/134
Clapham, William, labourer, Weston, Lincs, 1684 Lincs RO Ad/Ac/34/105
Clapton, Richard, Uffington, Lincs, 1623 Lincs RO Ad/Ac/18/60
Clarabut, John, baker, Sandwich, Kent, 1676 CKS PRC2/36/180
Clarck, John, Chartham, Kent, 1617 CKS PRC2/20/60
Clarck, John, Martin, Wilts, 1632 Wilts RO Arch. Sarum/(+ name and date)
Clarck, William, Throwleigh, Kent, 1637 CKS PRC2/34/39
Clarck, William, Loose, Kent, 1641 CKS PRC19/1/32
Clarcke, Elizabeth, widow, Woodnesborough, Kent, 1597 CKS PRC2/10/110
Clarcke, Jeffrye, Newington next Sittingbourne, Kent, 1596 CKS PRC2/8/362
Clarcke, Jeffrye, High Halden, Kent, 1613 CKS PRC2/16/14
Clarcke, Joane, widow, Ivychurch, Kent, 1612 CKS PRC20/2/412
Clarcke, John, Hernhill, Kent, 1596 CKS PRC21/14/101
Clarcke, John, Sholden, Kent, 1605 CKS PRC2/13/146
Clarcke, John, High Halstow, Kent, 1615 CKS PRC2/21/155
Clarcke, John, Aldbourne, Wilts, 1626 Wilts RO Arch. Wilts.(name + date)
Clarcke, Richard, St Peter in Thanet, Kent, 1612 CKS PRC2/17/328
Clarcke, Robarte, Sandwich, Kent, 1595 CKS PRC2/7/117
Clarcke, Robert, Lydiard Millicent, Wilts, 1630 Wilts RO Arch. Wilts.(name + date)
Clarcke, William, Harrietsham, Kent, 1614 CKS PRC2/18/42
Clare, Edward, Warminster, Wilts, 1679 Wilts RO Miscellaneous Index to Wills (name + date)
Clare, Francis, Kidderminster, Worcs, 1683 Worcs RO 008.7 BA3585/837/bdl 5

[Clare:]
Clare, Jane, widow, Stoke, South (Offham), Sussex, 1681 W. Suss RO EpI/33/1681/1
Clare, Joseph, toymaker: 'steel toymaker', Birmingham, Warks, 1803 LJRO/B/C/5/1803/14
Clare, Phillipp, Wilton, Wilts, 1615 Wilts RO Miscellaneous Index to Wills (name + date)
Clare, Richard, apothecary, Ashford, Kent, 1678 CKS PRC2/38/15
Clare, Sarah, widow, Birmingham, Warks, 1806 LJRO/B/C/5/1806/8
Clare, William, Bourne, Lincs, 1639 Lincs RO Ad/Ac/26/269
Clare, see Dominick,
Clares, John,
Sussex 1600 W. Suss RO EpI/33/1599/4
Claringbole, Thomas, Saltwood, Kent, 1594 CKS PRC21/13/3
Claringboll, Edward, Saltwood, Kent, 1610 CKS PRC20/2/98
Claringboll, John, Barham, Kent, 1591 CKS PRC2/6/260
Claringboll, Thomas, Saltwood, Kent, 1610 CKS PRC20/2/96
Claringbowle, Malcombe, Chartham, Kent, 1614 CKS PRC2/20/79
Clark, Edward, Alconbury (Weybridge), Hunts, 1710 Hunts RO/Acc58/305
Clark, George, yeoman, Frodingham, Lincs, 1670 Lincs RO Ad/Ac/32/138
Clark, Gregory, Tathwell, Lincs, Lincs RO Ad/Ac/2C/59
Clark, Henry, Hythe St Leonard, Kent, 1595 CKS PRC21/14/234
Clark, Isaac, St Peter in Thanet, Kent, 1611 CKS PRC2/16/162
Clark, Joane, widow, St Peter in Thanet, Kent, 1587 CKS PRC2/4/319
Clark, Joane, widow, New Romney, Kent, 1606 CKS PRC20/1/69
Clark, John, yeoman, Luddington, Lincs, 1606 Lincs RO Ad/Ac/37/219
Clark, John eld, Boughton Monchelsea, Kent, 1621 CKS PRC20/5/39
Clark, Joseph, Aston (Saltly), Warks, 1690 LJRO/B/C/5/1690/16
Clark, Mary, widow, Wotton under Edge, Glos, 1833 GRO GDR/B4/2/C72
Clark, Nicholas, Stratton (Grimstone), Dors, 1615? Wilts RO Dean Sarum (name + date)
Clark, Samuel, Stanton, Derby, 1683 LJRO/B/C/5/1682/22
Clark, Thomas, bachelor: 'singleman', Birchington, Kent, 1607 CKS PRC20/1/268
Clark, William, Killingholme, Lincs, 1599 Lincs RO Ad/Ac/5/529
Clark/Bayley, John, clothworker, Newbury, Berks, 1681 Berks RO D/A1/184/19D
Clarke, Adam, yeoman, Harbledown, Kent, 1680 CKS PRC2/39/18
Clarke, Agnes, Doddington, Kent, 1598 CKS PRC2/9/427
Clarke, Anne, widow, Lincoln St Swithin, Lincs, 1627 Lincs RO Ad/Ac/20b/112
Clarke, Augustine, husbandman, Finchampstead, Berks, 1616 Berks RO D/A1/182/14A
Clarke, Catherine, widow, St Laurence Thanet, Kent, 1708 CKS PRC1/17/2
Clarke, Daniel, Maidstone, Kent, 1675 CKS PRC20/12/164
Clarke, Daniell, yeoman, Lydd, Kent, 1639 CKS PRC20/10/168
Clarke, Edward, Minster in Sheppey, Kent, 1622 CKS PRC2/26/120
Clarke, Edward, innholder, Lydd, Kent, 1673 CKS PRC20/12/72
Clarke, Elizabeth, mrs/widow, Bobbing, Kent, 1620 CKS PRC2/20/31
Clarke, Elizabeth, widow, Faversham, Kent, 1667 CKS PRC1/11/113
Clarke, Elizabeth, widow, Harmston, Lincs, 1674 Lincs RO Ad/Ac/34/23
Clarke, Faith, Friskney, Lincs, 1672 Lincs RO Ad/Ac/43/62
Clarke, Francis, miller, Horncastle, Lincs, 1669 Lincs RO Ad/Ac/33/115
Clarke, Gabriell, St Peter in Thanet, Kent, 1623 CKS PRC2/23/77
Clarke, George, Sandridge, Herts, 1635 Herts RO ASA25/4908
Clarke, George, yeoman, Mimms, North, Herts, 1636 Herts RO AHH23/395
Clarke, George, yeoman, Cranbrook, Kent, 1684 CKS PRC2/40/187
Clarke, Giles, Maidstone, Kent, 1634 CKS PRC20/10/226
Clarke, Hamlett, St Ethelburga, London & Middlesex, 1713 PRO PROB5/1679
Clarke, Henry, Fulstow, Lincs, 1597 Lincs RO Ad/Ac/4/70
Clarke, Henry eld, weaver: 'linen weaver', Ashford, Kent, 1663 CKS PRC1/9/96
Clarke, James, Tattenhall, Ches, 1592 Cheshire RO (Name) W.C. 1592
Clarke, James, Epworth, Lincs, 1650 Lincs RO Ad/Ac/40/223
Clarke, James, Aldersfield, Worcs, 1683 Worcs RO 008.7 BA3585/837/bdl 5

[Clarke:]
Clarke, James, clergy: 'rector', Toft Monks, Norf, 1718 Greater London RO DL/C/546/143
Clarke, James, weaver, Aston, Warks, 1781 LJRO/B/C/5/1781/21
Clarke, Jane, widow, Rasen, West, Lincs, 1605 Lincs RO Ad/Ac/6/61
Clarke, Jane, Bere Regis, Dors, 1611 Wilts RO Dean Sarum (name + date)
Clarke, Joane, widow, Old Romney, Kent, 1617 CKS PRC2/20/126
Clarke, John, Rasen, West, Lincs, 1598 Lincs RO Ad/Ac/4/15
Clarke, John, Killingholme, Lincs, 1599 Lincs RO Ad/Ac/5/260
Clarke, John, Swalecliffe, Kent, 1602 CKS PRC2/12/429
Clarke, John, Stone in Oxney, Kent, 1605 CKS PRC2/13/139
Clarke, John, tanner, Windsor, New, Berks, 1610 Berks RO D/A1/181/216A
Clarke, John, husbandman, Streatley, Berks, 1616 Berks RO D/A1/182/20A
Clarke, John, Sibsey, Lincs, 1618 Lincs RO Ad/Ac/14/84
Clarke, John, Boughton Monchelsea, Kent, 1620 CKS PRC2/21/166
Clarke, John, Holbeach, Lincs, 1621 Lincs RO Ad/Ac/16/19
Clarke, John, yeoman, Tetney, Lincs, 1623 Lincs RO Ad/Ac/18/22
Clarke, John, servant, Bradfield, Berks, 1624 Berks RO D/A1/182/44A
Clarke, John, Deal, Kent, 1626 CKS PRC20/7/90
Clarke, John, Frieston, Lincs, 1635 Lincs RO Ad/Ac/24/349
Clarke, John, clergy: 'clerk', Sapperton, Lincs, 1638 Lincs RO Ad/Ac/25/100
Clarke, John, Hungerton, Leics, 1641 Leics RO PR/I/41A/73
Clarke, John, Stamford, Lincs, 1649 Lincs RO Ad/Ac/30/44
Clarke, John, Langtoft, Lincs, 1651 Lincs RO Ad/Ac/29/157
Clarke, John, tailor, Faversham, Kent, 1663 CKS PRC1/9/97
Clarke, John, Claypole, Lincs, 1664 Lincs RO Ad/Ac/43/29
Clarke, John, gentleman, Oxford St Thomas, Oxon, 1668 Oxon RO MSS Wills 78/2/5
Clarke, John, Easton, Wilts, 1674 Wilts RO Miscellaneous Index to Wills (name + date)
Clarke, John, Glatton, Hunts, 1687 Hunts RO/Acc58/267(261)
Clarke, John, husbandman, Tring (Wilstone), Herts, 1689 Herts RO AHH23/465
Clarke, John, yeoman, Lavenham, Suff, 1727 Suff RO(B) IC500/3/45/7a
Clarke, John, baker, King's Lynn, Norf, 1787 Norfolk RO ANW/23/26/68
Clarke, John ygr, burgess: 'principal burgess/gentleman', St Albans, Herts, 1634 Herts RO ASA25/4890
Clarke, Johnne, Saleby, Lincs, 1579 Lincs RO Ad/Ac/2b/21
Clarke, Judith, widow, Dover, Kent, 1683 CKS PRC20/13/319
Clarke, Margaret, Horncastle, Lincs, 1627 Lincs RO Ad/Ac/22/4
Clarke, Margaret, widow, Boston, Lincs, 1628 Lincs RO Ad/Ac/22/1
Clarke, Martin, clergy: 'mr/curate', Bilsington, Kent, 1638 CKS PRC2/34/184
Clarke, Mary, wife, Chart, Great, Kent, 1675 CKS PRC2/36/?
Clarke, Mary, widow, Baldon, Toot, Oxon, 1685 Oxon RO MSS Wills Pec 66/4/7
Clarke, Matthew, Thoresby, North, Lincs, 1649 Lincs RO Ad/Ac/30/386
Clarke, Matthewe, clergy: 'clerk', Holbeach, Lincs, 1627 Lincs RO Ad/Ac/20b/61
Clarke, Morgan, Cowes, West, Hants, 1668 Hants RO 21M65 D8/198
Clarke, Morrice, Fleet, Lincs, 1683 Lincs RO Ad/Ac/44/91
Clarke, Nicholas, Deal, Kent, 1596 CKS PRC21/14/41
Clarke, Nicholas, Bowden, Great, Leics, 1666 Leics RO Administrators Accounts C17th f77
Clarke, Peter, Haxey, Lincs, 1614 Lincs RO Ad/Ac/8b/20
Clarke, Peter, Epworth, Lincs, 1624 Lincs RO Ad/Ac/8c/51
Clarke, Richard, Ickham, Kent, 1599 CKS PRC21/15/60
Clarke, Richard, Hythe St Leonard, Kent, 1616 CKS PRC20/3/490
Clarke, Richard, Dover St Mary, Kent, 1620 CKS PRC20/5/43
Clarke, Richard, Boughton Monchelsea, Kent, 1631 CKS PRC20/9/105
Clarke, Richard, Crundale, Kent, 1633 CKS PRC2/32/33
Clarke, Richard, butcher, Standlake, Oxon, 1635 Oxon RO MSS Wills 296/2/57
Clarke, Richard, Hogsthorpe, Lincs, 1639 Lincs RO Ad/Ac/26/193
Clarke, Richard, Biddenden, Kent, 1644 CKS PRC19/2/87

[Clarke:]
Clarke, Richard, fisherman, Folkestone, Kent, 1680 CKS PRC2/39/15
Clarke, Richard, Greinton, Som, 1711 Somerset RO D/D/Cta/C33
Clarke, Robert, Kintbury, Berks, Berks RO D/A1/1/100BV
Clarke, Robert, Dorchester, Oxon, 1620 Oxon RO MSS Wills Pec 66/3/9
Clarke, Robert, Lenham, Kent, 1625 CKS PRC2/25/43
Clarke, Robert, Minster in Sheppey, Kent, 1632 CKS PRC2/31/93
Clarke, Robert, Sibsey (Frithbank), Lincs, 1635 Lincs RO Ad/Ac/24/385
Clarke, Robert, Stamford St Michael, Lincs, 1636 Lincs RO Ad/Ac/24/549
Clarke, Robert, yeoman, Seasalter, Kent, 1665 CKS PRC1/11/14
Clarke, Robert, clergy: 'rector', Frittenden, Kent, 1667 CKS PRC1/12/23
Clarke, Robert, yeoman, Braunston, Northants, 1673 Northants RO NWill A/C/151
Clarke, Robert, Brinkworth, Wilts, 1676 Wilts RO Miscellaneous Index to Wills (name + date)
Clarke, Robert, St Clement Danes, London & Middlesex, 1679 PRO PROB32/16/91
Clarke, Robert, tailor, Goudhurst, Kent, 1684 CKS PRC2/40/189
Clarke, Robert, gentleman, Bolingbroke, Old, Lincs, 1829 Lincs RO Ad/Ac/45/81
Clarke, Roberte, Killingholme, Lincs, 1599 Lincs RO Ad/Ac/5/372
Clarke, Rychard, Hythe St Leonard, Kent, 1584 CKS PRC21/7/47
Clarke, Samuel, Chelveston cum Caldecote, Northants, 1669 Northants RO NWill A/C/90
Clarke, Stephen, butcher, Oxford, Oxon, 1666 Oxon RO MSS Wills 296/3/53
Clarke, Theophilus, grocer, Welwyn, Herts, 1635 Herts RO AHII23/394
Clarke, Thomas, Kirton, Lincs, 1612 Lincs RO Ad/Ac/11/89
Clarke, Thomas, Skirbeck, Lincs, 1612 Lincs RO Ad/Ac/11/133
Clarke, Thomas, glazier, Stamford, Lincs, 1619 Lincs RO Ad/Ac/15/103
Clarke, Thomas, Hythe St Leonard, Kent, 1626 CKS PRC20/7/76
Clarke, Thomas, Stamford, Lincs, 1627 Lincs RO Ad/Ac/20b/4
Clarke, Thomas, cook, Oxford (University), Oxon, 1635 Bodleian HYP B8/30-31
Clarke, Thomas, Wye, Kent, 1646 CKS PRC1/7/76
Clarke, Thomas, Buckland, Bucks, 1668 Oxon RO MSS Wills Pec 35/2/16
Clarke, Thomas, wheelwright, Wolstone, Berks, 1670 Berks RO D/A1/183/96A
Clarke, Thomas, Westbury, Wilts, 1674 Wilts RO Chantor Sarum Bundle 9/43
Clarke, Thomas, Chichester, Sussex, 1678 W. Suss RO EpIII/9/1/62
Clarke, Thomas, innholder, Lydd, Kent, 1680 CKS PRC20/13/13
Clarke, Thomas, Eldersfield, Worcs, 1683 Worcs RO 008.7 BA3585/837/bdl 5
Clarke, Thomas, Martin, Wilts, 1690 Wilts RO Arch. Sarum/(+ name and date)
Clarke, Vincent, Frodingham (Crosby), Lincs, 1603 Lincs RO Ad/Ac/37/165
Clarke, William, Hale, Great, Lincs, 1597 Lincs RO Ad/Ac/4/45
Clarke, William, Blankney, Lincs, 1599 Lincs RO Ad/Ac/5/541
Clarke, William, Godmanchester, Hunts, 1602 Lincs RO Ad/Ac/5/576
Clarke, William, Croft, Lincs, 1607 Lincs RO Ad/Ac/8a/61
Clarke, William, Sutton, Long, Lincs, 1607 Lincs RO Ad/Ac/8a/23
Clarke, William, Linsted, Kent, 1616 CKS PRC2/21/150
Clarke, William, husbandman, Weston, Lincs, 1623? Lincs RO Ad/Ac/18/16
Clarke, William, husbandman, Weston, Lincs, 1624 Lincs RO Ad/Ac/19A/103
Clarke, William, tailor, Washingborough (Heighington), Lincs, 1625 Lincs RO Ad/Ac/19B/64
Clarke, William, Alford, Lincs, 1629 Lincs RO Ad/Ac/22/114
Clarke, William, Leverton, Lincs, 1632 Lincs RO Ad/Ac/23/12
Clarke, William, gentleman, Boston, Lincs, 1632 Lincs RO Ad/Ac/23/120
Clarke, William, Skellingthorpe, Lincs, 1633 Lincs RO Ad/Ac/23/172
Clarke, William, Faldingworth, Lincs, 1635 Lincs RO Ad/Ac/40/24
Clarke, William, Loughborough, Leics, 1641 Leics RO PR/I/41A/81
Clarke, William, Haxey, Lincs, 1642 Lincs RO Ad/Ac/41/112
Clarke, William, Skellingthorpe, Lincs, 1649 Lincs RO Ad/Ac/30/184
Clarke, William, Friesthorpe, Lincs, 1665 Lincs RO Ad/Ac/42/15
Clarke, William, St Nicholas Acon, London & Middlesex, 1667 PRO PROB5/1769
Clarke, William, mariner, Dover, Kent, 1668 CKS PRC19/4/9

[Clarke:]

Clarke, William, Courteenhall, Northants, 1671 Northants RO NWill A/C/115
Clarke, William, gentleman, Ardington, Berks, 1672 Berks RO D/A1/183/114A
Clarke, William, Bottesford, Lincs, 1674 Lincs RO Ad/Ac/35/70
Clarke, William, bachelor, Linch, Sussex, 1674 W. Suss RO EpI/33/1673/26
Clarke, William, Bluntisham, Hunts, 1682 Hunts RO/Acc58/177(24)
Clarke, William, Frodingham (Scunthorpe), Lincs, 1683 Lincs RO Ad/Ac/44/49
Clarke, William, All Hallows Staining, London & Middlesex, 1696 Lambeth Palace Arches G46/2
Clarke, Yhomas, Yarburgh, Lincs, 1636 Lincs RO Ad/Ac/24/458
Clarke/Hiller, Roger, Crudwell, Wilts, 1633 Wilts RO Arch. Wilts.(name + date)
Clarke/Waters, Susan, Deeping St James, Lincs, 1634 Lincs RO Ad/Ac/24/200
Clarke/Williams, John, Upton Lovell, Wilts, 1597 Wilts RO Arch. Sarum/(+ name and date)
Clarke, see Baker, Carter & Gilburt,
Clarkson, John, Alford, Lincs, 1633 Lincs RO Ad/Ac/23/174
Clarkson, John, St Clement Danes, London & Middlesex, 1688 PRO PROB32/27/117
Clase, John, Ham, High, Som, Somerset RO D/D/Cta/C47
Clathe, Richard, Woodhall, Lincs, 1611 Lincs RO Ad/Ac/10/102
Clattercoates, Richard, Carlton le Moorland, Lincs, 1662 Lincs RO Ad/Ac/32/11
Claver, Richard, gentleman, Oving, Bucks, 1674 PRO PROB5/916
Clavor, Thomas, Earls Croome, Worcs, 1675 Worcs RO 008.7 BA3585/830/38
Claward, see Clement,
Clawes, Vincent, Corby, Lincs, 1571 Lincs RO Ad/Ac/2b/30
Claxon, James, husbandman, Leake, Lincs, 1669 Lincs RO Ad/Ac/33/146
Claxon, Thomas, Huttoft, Lincs, 1662 Lincs RO Ad/Ac/32/24
Clay, Elizabeth, widow, Sandwich, Kent, 1623 CKS PRC2/23/64
Clay, Humphry, yeoman, Kyme, South, Lincs, 1668? Lincs RO Ad/Ac/33/44
Clay, John, Canterbury St Mary-Magdalen Burgate, Kent, 1608 CKS PRC2/14/110
Clay, Robert, gentleman, Dalby, Lincs, 1673 Lincs RO Ad/Ac/42/90
Clay, Thomas, Hacconby, Lincs, 1674 Lincs RO Ad/Ac/43/78
Clay, William, Leverton, Lincs, 1641 Lincs RO Ad/Ac/27/210
Claye, Alexander, Skirbeck, Lincs, 1632 Lincs RO Ad/Ac/23/153
Claypool, William, Hacconby, Lincs, 1648 Lincs RO Ad/Ac/30/409
Claypoole, Adam, esquire, Deeping, West, Lincs, 1636 Lincs RO Ad/Ac/24/263
Claypoole, John, Edenham, Lincs, 1623 Lincs RO Ad/Ac/18/30b
Clayton, Henry, husbandman, Lancaster (Fulwood), Lancs, 1661 Lancs RO (Name of Deceased) D.R.C.H. 1659
Clayton, Humphrey, yeoman, Scarcliffe (Scarcliff Lanes), Derby, 1681 LJRO/B/C/5/1682/23
Clayton, John, Claypole, Lincs, 1648 Lincs RO Ad/Ac/30/370
Clayton, John, innkeeper, Thornton, Yorks, 1810 Borthwick Test C.P. 1810/8
Clayton, Richard, university: 'Master of St John's College, Cambridge', Cambridge St Botolph, Cambs, 1612 CUL V.C.Acc./Box1/9
Clayton, Thomas, Barnoldby le Beck, Lincs, 1638 Lincs RO Ad/Ac/25/84
Clayton, Thomas, Barnoldby le Beck, Lincs, 1640 Lincs RO Ad/Ac/26/249
Clayton, Thomas, yeoman, Somercoates, North, Lincs, 1671 Lincs RO Ad/Ac/34/109
Clayton, William, stocking maker: 'framework knitter', Basford (Old Basford), Notts, 1824 Borthwick Test C.P. 1824/7
Cleare, James, Canterbury St Mary Northgate, Kent, 1665 CKS PRC1/11/15
Cleare, Richard, yeoman, Wytham, Berks, 1649 Berks RO D/A1/183/38A
Cleasbie, Henrie, Bicker, Lincs, 1640 Lincs RO Ad/Ac/27/41
Cleasby, Peter, Holbeach, Lincs, 1619 Lincs RO Ad/Ac/15/111
Cleavely, John, clergy: 'rector', Sutton Veny, Wilts, 1681 Wilts RO CC Sarum(+ name and date)
Cleaver, Thomas, clergy: 'clerk', Hellidon, Northants, 1677 Northants RO NWill A/C/170
Cleaybrook, John, gentleman, St Johns Thanet, Kent, 1625 CKS PRC2/25/33
Cleaybrooke, Paule, esquire, St Johns Thanet, Kent, 1623 CKS PRC2/23/84
Cleeter, Robert, Witney (Curbridge), Oxon, 1640 Oxon RO MSS Wills 296/3/2
Cleeve, John, Hardwick, Cambs, CUL V.C. Acc./Box3/61

[Cleeve:]
Cleeve, William, Milford, Hants, 1677 Hants RO 21m65 D8/277
Cleeveland, John, Upton Noble, Som, 1641 Somerset RO D/D/Cta/C70
Cleevely, Thomas, Cheltenham, Glos, C17th? GRO GDR/B4/2/C13
Cleeves, John, Fordingbridge, Hants, 1673 Hants RO 1673 AD26
Clegg, James, Oldham (Shawside), Lancs, 1734 Lancs RO (Name of Deceased) D.R.C.H. 1734
Clegg, Richard, Kirton, Lincs, 1598 Lincs RO Ad/Ac/5/316
Clegg, Robert, shopkeeper, Rochdale, Lancs, 1788 Lancs RO (Name of Deceased) D.R.C.H. 1788
Clemens, John,
Som Somerset RO D/D/Cta/C5
Clemens, Thomas, labourer, Rainham, Kent, 1681 CKS PRC2/39/161
Clemens, William eld, husbandman, Buckland, Berks, 1630 Berks RO D/A1/182/78C
Clement, Alexander,
Kent 1605 CKS PRC2/14/106
Clement, Alice, Ewell, Kent, 1594 CKS PRC2/7/37
Clement, Amye, widow, Charing, Kent, 1614 CKS PRC20/2/482
Clement, Christopher, gentleman, Faversham, Kent, 1627 CKS PRC20/8/113
Clement, Edward, Winkfield, Wilts, 1622 Wilts RO CC Sarum(+ name and date)
Clement, James eld, Lenham, Kent, 1677 CKS PRC2/37/123
Clement, John,
Glos Bristol RO 1628/19b
Clement, John, Ewell, Kent, 1594 CKS PRC2/7/243
Clement, John eld, Bersted, South, Sussex, 1615 W. Suss RO EpIV/10/1/53
Clement, Robert, Oxford St Peter le Bailey, Oxon, 1665 Oxon RO MSS Wills 162/4/22
Clement, Stephen, bachelor, Mareham le Fen, Lincs, 1684 Lincs RO Ad/Ac/44/105
Clement, Thomas, Mersham, Kent, 1627 CKS PRC2/28/31
Clement, William, husbandman, Seasalter, Kent, 1672 CKS PRC2/35/120
Clement/Claward, Marye, widow, Sandwich, Kent, 1606 CKS PRC2/14/128
Clement, see Browne,
Clements, Christopher, Faversham, Kent, 1675 CKS PRC2/36/30
Clements, Clement, labourer, Dowdeswell, Glos, 1821 GRO GDR/B4/2/C73
Clements, George, Stanwick, Northants, Northants RO NWill A/C/128
Clements, John, Canterbury St Dunstan Without, Kent, 1599 CKS PRC2/10/304
Clements, Tristram, mason: 'freemason', Oxford St Ebbe, Oxon, 1673 Oxon RO MSS Wills 78/2/23
Clemond, Robert, Mere, Wilts, 1635 Wilts RO Dean Sarum (name + date)
Clemson, Richard, Worfield, Shrops, 1676 LJRO:cards/1676/13
Clemson, Thomas, Wroxeter (Norton), Shrops, 1674 LJRO:cards/1674/7
Clench, William + Ann, Bere Regis, Dors, 1596 Wilts RO Miscellaneous Index to Wills (name + date)
Clenche, William + Ann, Bere Regis, Dors, 1587 Wilts RO Miscellaneous Index to Wills (name + date)
Clerck, John, carrier, Benenden, Kent, 1592 CKS PRC2/6/71
Clercke, Elizabeth, widow, Rodmersham, Kent, 1596 CKS PRC2/8/268
Clercke, John, Headcorn, Kent, 1605 CKS PRC2/13/154
Clercke, Thomas, Crundale, Kent, 1594 CKS PRC2/7/55
Clercke, Willyam, Faversham, Kent, 1588 CKS PRC2/4/291
Cleridge, Richard, Mollington, Warks, 1613 Oxon RO MSS Wills Pec 34/4/15
Clerie, Peter, Kirkby on Bain, Lincs, 1612 Lincs RO Ad/Ac/11/101
Clerk, Abraham, tailor, Canterbury St Margaret, Kent, 1626 CKS PRC2/27/30
Clerk, Humphrie, Yateley, Hants, 1624 Hants RO 21M65 D8/56
Clerk, John, Rodmersham, Kent, 1580 CKS PRC2/1/279
Clerk, John, Canterbury St John's Hospital, Kent, 1584 CKS PRC21/7/11
Clerk, Richard, Hythe St Leonard, Kent, 1630 CKS PRC20/9/97
Clerk, Richard, clergy: 'mr/D.D.', Canterbury Christchurch, Kent, 1634 CKS PRC20/10/216
Clerk, Thomas, Dymchurch, Kent, 1631 CKS PRC2/31/22

Clerk, Wylyam, Ivychurch, Kent, 1586 CKS PRC21/7/388
Clerke, Abraham, mr, Maidstone, Kent, 1646 CKS PRC19/2/105
Clerke, Christopher, Boston, Lincs, 1637 Lincs RO Ad/Ac/25/47
Clerke, Cicilye, spinster, Harrietsham, Kent, 1637 CKS PRC1/1/45
Clerke, George, Braunston, Northants, 1685 Northants RO NWill A/C/25
Clerke, Henry, clergy: 'clerk/vicar', Windsor, Old, Berks, 1611 Berks RO D/A1/181/212A
Clerke, Henry, Harbledown, Kent, 1676 CKS PRC2/37/27
Clerke, John, Maidstone, Kent, 1588 CKS PRC21/9/21
Clerke, John, Weston, Lincs, 1618 Lincs RO Ad/Ac/14/182
Clerke, John, Weston, Lincs, 1623 Lincs RO Ad/Ac/18/52
Clerke, Joseph, Towcester, Northants, 1682 Northants RO NWill A/C/21
Clerke, Martha, Harrietsham, Kent, 1640 CKS PRC1/2/37
Clerke, Richard, Lyminge, Kent, 1634 CKS PRC20/10/248
Clerke, Richard, High Halden, Kent, 1699 CKS PRC2/42/151
Clerke, Roger, Stamford, Lincs, 1623 Lincs RO Ad/Ac/18/13
Clerke, Thomas, Aldworth, Berks, 1602 Berks RO D/A1/181/177A
Clerke, Thomas, Hoath, Kent, 1603 CKS PRC21/17/76
Clerke, William, Warehorne, Kent, 1628 CKS PRC2/29/28
Clerke/Cockey, Lydia, widow, Sandwich, Kent, 1678 CKS PRC2/38/18
Clerkson, John, St Clement Danes, London & Middlesex, 1688 PRO PROB32/27/181
Cleve?, Richard, Chalton, Hants, 1663 Hants RO 21M65 D8/176
Cleveland, Robarte, Wye, Kent, 1594 CKS PRC2/7/29
Clews, Elizabeth, widow, Uttoxeter (Stramshall), Staffs, 1699 LJRO/B/C/5/1699/20
Clews, Josepoh, farmer, Berrow, Worcs, 1824 Worcs RO 008.7 BA3585/835/bdl 2
Cley, Thomas, Muchelney, Som, 1599 Somerset RO D/D/Cta/T41
Cleydon, William, Reading St Lawrence, Berks, 1593 Berks RO D/A1/181/141C
Cleyland, James, clergy: 'D.D.', Canterbury St Alphege, Kent, 1629 CKS PRC20/8/111
Clif, John, clergy: 'clerk', Thorpe, Lincs, 1593 Lincs RO Ad/Ac/3/135
Clife, Henry, Sibsey, Lincs, 1669 Lincs RO Ad/Ac/33/113
Cliff, John, Swinstead, Lincs, 1568 Lincs RO Ad/Ac/0/3
Cliffe, Richard, clergy: 'clerk', Alkborough, Lincs, 1607 Lincs RO Ad/Ac/37/247
Cliffe, William, yeoman, Blithfield (Newton), Staffs, 1753 LJRO/B/C/5/1755/96
Clifford, Andrew, blacksmith, Dymchurch, Kent, 1681 CKS PRC2/39/19
Clifford, Anthony, Sonning, Berks, 1633 Wilts RO Miscellaneous Index to Wills (name + date)
Clifford, Dorothy, widow, Staple next Wingham, Kent, 1676 CKS PRC20/12/198
Clifford, Edward, Hernhill, Kent, 1679 CKS PRC20/12/298
Clifford, Francis, yeoman, Ardington, Berks, 1671 Berks RO D/A1/183/108A
Clifford, Mary, widow, Droitwich St Nicholas, Worcs, 1683 Worcs RO 008.7 BA3585/837/bdl 3
Clifford, Mathew, Whitstable, Kent, 1612 CKS PRC1/1/18
Clifford, Mathewe, Whitstable, Kent, 1613 CKS PRC2/16/176
Clifford, Rachell, widow, Canterbury St Dunstan Without, Kent, 1670 CKS PRC1/14/23
Clifford, Richard, Yeovilton, Som, 1594 Somerset RO D/D/Cta/C74
Clifford, William, yeoman, Wroughton, Wilts, 1675 Wilts RO Arch. Wilts.(name + date)
Clifford, William, Lenham, Kent, 1704 CKS PRC1/16/44
Clifford, see Tith,
Clifton, John, Humby, Lincs, 1620 Lincs RO Ad/Ac/16/26
Clifton, Katherine, widow, Buscot, Berks, 1612 Berks RO D/A1/182/9C
Clifton, Peter, Grantham, Lincs, 1642 Lincs RO Ad/Ac/27/327
Clifton, Thomas, Overton, Wilts, 1677 Wilts RO Miscellaneous Index to Wills (name + date)
Clifton, William, Waddington, Lincs, 1613 Lincs RO Ad/Ac/12/60
Climpson, Thomas, Berkhamsted St Peter, Herts, Herts RO AHH23/390
Climsoll, Edmund, Angmering, Sussex, 1644 W. Suss RO EpI/33/1644/1
Climson, Francis, tailor, Harrietsham, Kent, 1680 CKS PRC2/39/13
Clinch, Richard, St James Westminster, London & Middlesex, 1710 Greater London RO AM/PP/Box 1701-1710 pt (uncatalogued)

[Clinch:]
Clinch, Richard, St James Westminster, London & Middlesex, 1714 Greater London RO AM/PP/Box 1711-1714 pt (uncatalogued)
Clinche, Edwarde, Otterden, Kent, 1595 CKS PRC2/7/275
Clinckard, Eleanor, widow, Baldon, Toot, Oxon, 1631 Oxon RO MSS Wills Pec 66/3/19
Clinkeard, Thomas jun, Baldon, Toot, Oxon, 1721 Oxon RO MSS Wills Pec 66/4/33
Clinkett, John, St Albans St Peters, Herts, 1634 Herts RO ASA25/4900
Clintch, Thomas, Moreton, South, Berks, 1596 Berks RO D/A1/181/152A
Clintch, Thomas, Hendred, East, Berks, 1616 Berks RO D/A1/182/21A
Clinton, Bridget, Selling, Kent, 1671 CKS PRC2/35/28
Clinton, Henry, Minster in Sheppey, Kent, 1600 CKS PRC2/11/183
Clinton, John, Queenborough, Kent, 1633 CKS PRC2/31/94
Clinton, John, Canterbury St Mildred, Kent, 1635 CKS PRC2/33/24
Clinton, John, Hernhill, Kent, 1670 CKS PRC19/4/70
Clinton, Richard, baker, Bampton, Oxon, 1634 Oxon RO MSS Wills 296/2/53
Clinton, Robert, yeoman, Hernhill, Kent, 1671 CKS PRC19/4/71
Clinton, William, mariner, Queenborough, Kent, 1675 CKS PRC2/36/169
Clippingdale, Edward, Alford, Lincs, 1601 Lincs RO Ad/Ac/5/95
Clipsam, Thomas, Wigtoft, Lincs, 1625 Lincs RO Ad/Ac/19B/53
Clipsham, John, Walesby, Lincs, 1620 Lincs RO Ad/Ac/16/24
Clipsham, William, Holbeach, Lincs, 1611 Lincs RO Ad/Ac/10/38
Clipwell, William, Hartlip, Kent, 1647 CKS PRC1/8/10
Cliterbuck, Robert, gentleman, Remenham, Berks, 1590 Berks RO D/A1/181/128A
Clitter, Robert, husbandman, Inkpen, Berks, 1631 Berks RO D/A1/182/79A
Cloake, Beniamin, gentleman, Folkestone, Kent, 1633 CKS PRC2/32/29
Cloake, Edward, Folkestone, Kent, 1674 CKS PRC2/36/29
Cloake, Gyles, High Halden, Kent, 1619 CKS PRC2/20/43
Cloake, John, Elmsted, Kent, 1601 CKS PRC2/12/120
Cloake, John, husbandman, Charing, Kent, 1672 CKS PRC20/12/43
Cloake, Mary, spinster, Shadoxhurst, Kent, 1642 CKS PRC1/6/54
Cloake, Robert, Dover, Kent, 1626 CKS PRC20/7/86
Cloake, Thomas, yeoman, Elmsted, Kent, 1597 CKS PRC2/9/335
Clodd, Anthonie, Saxilby (Ingleby), Lincs, 1640 Lincs RO Ad/Ac/40/282
Cloke, Humphrey, Hythe St Leonard, Kent, 1591 CKS PRC21/11/65
Cloke, James, Kingsnorth, Kent, 1595 CKS PRC2/8/85
Cloke, Thomas, Woodnesborough, Kent, 1620 CKS PRC2/20/120
Close, Alice, Kirton, Lincs, 1612 Lincs RO Ad/Ac/11/80
Close, John, Boston, Lincs, 1641 Lincs RO Ad/Ac/27/309
Close, Thomas, Kirton, Lincs, 1611 Lincs RO Ad/Ac/10/69
Clotherell, Robert, innholder, Canterbury St Mildred, Kent, 1681 CKS PRC2/39/158
Clotterbook, Samuel, weaver: 'broad weaver', Stanley, Leonard, Glos, 1716 GRO GDR/B4/2/C78
Clotworthie, Lawrence, Monkton, West, Som, 1612 Somerset RO D/D/Cta/C32
Clough, Alexander, university: M.A. of Emmanuel College, Cambridge, Cambridge St Benedict, Cambs, 1621 c. CUL V.C.Acc./Box1/10
Clough, George, husbandman, Kelsey, South, Lincs, 1636 Lincs RO Ad/Ac/24/332
Clough, James, chapman, Manchester, Lancs, 1683 Lancs RO (Name of Deceased) D.R.C.H. 1683
Clover/Willard, Elizabeth, Minster in Sheppey, Kent, 1617 CKS PRC2/21/146
Cloves, William, Beoley, Worcs, 1685 Worcs RO 008.7 BA3585/837/bdl 4
Clowes, William, maltster, Sandwich, Kent, 1677 CKS PRC2/37/134
Clowser, John, Horsham, Sussex, 1631 W. Suss RO EpI/33/1631/1
Cluer, Thomas, maltmaker, Oxford St Thomas, Oxon, 1663 Oxon RO MSS Wills 78/1/46
Cluffe, Peeter, New Romney, Kent, 1612 CKS PRC20/2/214
Cluffe, Thomas, blacksmith, Linsted, Kent, 1676 CKS PRC2/37/20
Clun, Richard, St Laurence Thanet, Kent, 1627 CKS PRC2/28/28
Clutterbuck, Samuel, St Augustine Watling Street, London & Middlesex, late C17th? PRO PROB5/1314

Clutteringe, Edward, Wiston, Sussex, 1611 W. Suss RO EpI/33/1611/5
Clutting, Osmund, clergy: 'mr/clerk', Eastchurch, Sheppey, Kent, 1641 CKS PRC1/4/21
Cluttler, Thomas, clergy: 'clerk', Stoke St Gregory, Som, 1633 Somerset RO D/D/Cta/C9
Clyffe, Thomas, Wittersham, Kent, 1613 CKS PRC20/2/460
Clyffe, Willyam, Biddenden, Kent, 1611 CKS PRC2/16/189
Clynton, Alice, widow, Glastonbury, Som, 1601 Somerset RO D/D/Cta/C41
Clynton, Phillipp, widow,
Kent 1578 CKS PRC21/4/190
Clynton, Roger, Canterbury St Margaret, Kent, 1617 CKS PRC2/20/89
Clyve, Thomas, Faversham, Kent, 1635 CKS PRC2/32/148
Coake, Thomas, Woodchurch, Kent, 1638 CKS PRC20/10/178
Coalbrooke, Samuel, St Martin in the Fields, London & Middlesex, 1726 Greater London RO AM/PP/Box 1726-1732 pt (uncatalogued)
Coale, Ann, Fillingham, Lincs, 1673? Lincs RO Ad/Ac/35/35
Coale, John, Gainsborough, Lincs, 1629 Lincs RO Ad/Ac/22/67
Coale, John, Canterbury St Dunstan Without, Kent, 1633 CKS PRC2/32/26
Coales, Roger, Dinton, Wilts, 1631 Wilts RO Arch. Sarum/(+ name and date)
Coate, Marmaduke, Curry Rivel, Som, 1664 Somerset RO D/D/Cta/C61
Coates, Anne, widow, Shipley, Sussex, 1631 W. Suss RO EpI/33/1630/31
Coates, Christopher, weaver, Witney, Oxon, 1626 Oxon RO MSS Wills 296/1/129
Coates, Edward, Morton, Lincs, 1669 Lincs RO Ad/Ac/33/149
Coates, George, St Laurence Thanet, Kent, 1615 CKS PRC2/20/45
Coates, James, Newington, South, Oxon, 1633 Oxon RO MSS Wills 296/2/48
Coates, James, butler, Cambridge (Pembroke College), Cambs, 1665 CUL V.C. Acc./Box3/11
Coates, John, Wirksworth, Derby, 1685 LJRO/B/C/5/1685/28
Coates, Rebecca, widow, Selling, Kent, 1693 CKS PRC1/15/113
Coates, Robert, Althorpe (Burringham), Lincs, 1686 Lincs RO Ad/Ac/34/108
Coates, Thomas, Stanford, Kent, 1690 CKS PRC19/4/114
Coates, William, Aslackby (Graby), Lincs, 1625 Lincs RO Ad/Ac/19B/77
Coates, William, Stoughton, Sussex, 1666 W. Suss RO EpI/33/1666/1
Coather, John, Dover, Kent, 1677 CKS PRC20/12/228
Coats, Henry, Kidlington, Oxon, 1674 Oxon RO MSS Wills 296/3/58
Cobb, Ambrose, Petham, Kent, CKS PRC2/17/155 and 153 and 154
Cobb, Augustine, bachelor: 'singleman', Chislet, Kent, 1639 CKS PRC1/2/38
Cobb, Benjamin, Chislet, Kent, 1684 CKS PRC2/40/184
Cobb, Nicholas, Reculver, Kent, 1624 CKS PRC20/6/70
Cobb, Robert, gentleman, Reculver, Kent, 1677 CKS PRC20/12/197
Cobb, Thomas, Rogate, Sussex, 1646 W. Suss RO EpI/33/1646/4
Cobb, Thomas, alehouse keeper, Wittersham, Kent, 1682 CKS PRC20/13/233
Cobb, Thomas, carpenter, Faversham, Kent, 1693 CKS PRC2/42/60
Cobb, William, Reculver, Kent, 1611 CKS PRC20/2/224
Cobb, William, Ickham, Kent, 1676 CKS PRC20/12/161
Cobbe, Gregorye, Faversham, Kent, 1612 CKS PRC2/16/10
Cobbe, Richard, yeoman, Herne, Kent, 1616 CKS PRC20/3/328
Cobbe, Symeon eld, Wittersham, Kent, 1612 CKS PRC20/2/406
Cobbe, William, mariner, Birchington, Kent, 1646 CKS PRC19/2/95
Cobbin, Richard, Bacton, Suff, 1786 Suff RO(B) IC500/3/53/1
Cobbs, Erasmus, Appledore, Kent, 1645 CKS PRC1/7/42
Cobham, William, Sandwich, Kent, 1667 CKS PRC1/12/24
Cochran, Hugh, shipowner, Hull, Yorks, 1827 Borthwick Test C.P. 1827/3
Cock, George + John, yeoman, Alstonfield, Staffs, 1678 LJRO:cards/1678/8
Cock, John, Steyning, Sussex, 1582 W. Suss RO EpI/33/1582/2
Cock, John, Hythe St Leonard, Kent, 1583 CKS PRC21/6/272
Cock, John, husbandman, Welford (Weston), Berks, 1636 Berks RO D/A1/182/118C
Cock, Thomas, Upchurch, Kent, 1586 CKS PRC2/4/223

[Cockain:]
Cockain, Henry, mariner, Milton next Sittingbourne, Kent, 1671 CKS PRC2/35/30
Cockbould, Nicholas, Wappenham, Northants, 1674 Northants RO NWill A/C/61
Cockbould, Nicholas, Wappenham, Northants, 1676 Northants RO NWill A/C/81
Cocke, Christopher, Digby, Lincs, 1638 Lincs RO Ad/Ac/25/300
Cocke, Edmund, St Albans St Stephens, Herts, 1582 Herts RO ASA25/1003
Cocke, Edward, Walmer, Kent, 1671 CKS PRC2/35/26
Cocke, Edwarde, New Romney, Kent, 1604 CKS PRC21/17/150
Cocke, Henry, husbandman, Herne, Kent, 1640 CKS PRC19/1/33
Cocke, Jeremy, St Laurence Thanet, Kent, 1630 CKS PRC20/8/109
Cocke, John, Canterbury Christchurch, Kent, 1610 CKS PRC20/2/156
Cocke, John, Herne, Kent, 1618 CKS PRC20/4/54
Cocke, John, Swalecliffe, Kent, 1621 CKS PRC2/23/63
Cocke, John, Bilsington, Kent, 1627 CKS PRC2/27/29
Cocke, John, St Nicholas at Wade, Kent, 1634 CKS PRC20/10/224
Cocke, Josua, clergy: 'clerk', Gosberton, Lincs, 1618 Lincs RO Ad/Ac/14/206
Cocke, Leonard, Spalding, Lincs, 1593 Lincs RO Ad/Ac/3/81
Cocke, Paule, Sittingbourne, Kent, 1603 CKS PRC2/12/426
Cocke, Peter, Herne, Kent, 1608 CKS PRC20/1/384
Cocke, Samuell, Herne, Kent, 1632 CKS PRC20/10/236
Cocke, Thomas, Folkestone, Kent, 1598 CKS PRC2/10/90
Cocke, Thomas, yeoman, Deal, Kent, 1667 CKS PRC19/3/115
Cocke, Walters, Wrangle, Lincs, 1632 Lincs RO Ad/Ac/23/152
Cocke, William, Norton, Herts, 1597 Herts RO ASA25/1605
Cocke, William, Kirton, Lincs, 1611 Lincs RO Ad/Ac/10/147
Cocke, William, yeoman, Herne, Kent, 1640 CKS PRC19/1/34
Cocke, William, bachelor, Bekesbourne, Kent, 1711 CKS PRC1/17/21
Cocke, Willyam, clergy: 'mr/parson', Swalecliffe, Kent, 1612 CKS PRC2/16/13
Cocke, see Alley,
Cockell, Thomas, mercer, Wrawby cum Brigg (Glanford Brigg), Lincs, 1649 Lincs RO Ad/Ac/30/95
Cocken, Robert, St Peter in Thanet, Kent, 1611 CKS PRC2/16/102
Cocker, David, Chipping Barnet, Herts, 1595 Herts RO ASA25/1512
Cocker, Henry, Spilsby, Lincs, 1640 Lincs RO Ad/Ac/27/118
Cocker, James, husbandman, Oldham (High Crompton), Lancs, 1734 Lancs RO (Name of Deceased) D.R.C.H. 1734
Cocker, John, Budworth, Great (Over Whitley), Ches, 1598 Cheshire RO (Name) W.C. 1597
Cocker, John, Hougham, Kent, 1616 CKS PRC2/20/69
Cocker, Roger, Bilsington, Kent, 1609 CKS PRC2/15/62
Cockeram, Roger, Lincoln St Mary Magdalen in the Bail, Lincs, 1674 Lincs RO Ad/Ac/42/17
Cockerell, Ambrose, Stockton, Wilts, 1614 Wilts RO Arch. Sarum/(+ name and date)
Cockerell, Thomas, Rogate, Sussex, 1614 W. Suss RO EpI/33/1613/3
Cockerell, William, Rogate, Sussex, 1634 W. Suss RO EpI/33/1633/27
Cockerill, Thomas, innholder, Gayton, Northants, 1816 Northants RO X954/21/74
Cockes, John, innholder, Ashford, Kent, 1606 CKS PRC2/13/115
Cockes, Paull, Lyminge, Kent, 1601 CKS PRC21/15/202
Cocket, Gilbert, Elm, Cambs, 1628 CUL V.C. Acc./Box2/15
Cockey, see Clerke,
Cockin, William, bridle bit maker, Walsall (Great Bloxwich), Staffs, 1808 LJRO/B/C/5/1808/10
Cockle, John, Staplehurst, Kent, 1592 CKS PRC2/6/77
Cockle, Katherine, Codford St Peter, Wilts, 1613 Wilts RO Arch. Sarum/(+ name and date)
Cockle, Richard, Westbury, Wilts, 1763? Wilts RO Miscellaneous Index to Wills (name + date)
Cockling, John, yeoman, Cheriton, Kent, 1676 CKS PRC2/37/26
Cockling, Robert, St Peter in Thanet, Kent, 1606 CKS PRC2/13/133
Cockling, Susanne, spinster, St Peter in Thanet, Kent, 1665 CKS PRC1/10/19
Cockman, John, gentleman, Warmington, Northants, 1755 Northants RO X954/21/2

Cockman, Robert, Chart, Great, Kent, 1640 CKS PRC1/4/22
Cockman, Stephen, Blean, Kent, 1603 CKS PRC2/14/136
Cockman, William, blacksmith, Herne, Kent, 1682 CKS PRC20/13/123
Cockson, Thomas, cordwainer: 'shoemaker', Horncastle, Lincs, 1626 Lincs RO Ad/Ac/20/50
Cockup, Richard, weaver, Langley, Kings, Herts, 1624 Herts RO AHH23/389
Cod, Christopher, Northorpe (Southorpe), Lincs, 1624 Lincs RO Ad/Ac/39/160
Cod, Thomas, Norton, Bishop, Lincs, 1677 Lincs RO Ad/Ac/42/71
Codd, John, clergy: 'D.D.', Rochester, Kent, 1674? Lambeth Palace Arches G28/2
Codd, Robert, yeoman, Cadney, Lincs, 1639 Lincs RO Ad/Ac/26/231
Codd, Thomas, Springthorpe, Lincs, 1680 Lincs RO Ad/Ac/43/165
Codde, Margerie, widow, Minster in Sheppey, Kent, 1593 CKS PRC2/6/53
Codder, Richard, Branston, Lincs, 1597 Lincs RO Ad/Ac/4/99
Codder, William, Ormsby, North, Lincs, 1614 Lincs RO Ad/Ac/13/21
Coddington, Anthony, Bennington, Long, Lincs, 1645 Lincs RO Ad/Ac/28/137
Codham/Spicer, Anna, widow, Dover, Kent, 1664 CKS PRC19/3/20
Codlinge, Lawrence, Caythorpe, Lincs, 1649 Lincs RO Ad/Ac/30/135
Codwell, Daniell, Pluckley, Kent, 1620 CKS PRC20/5/47
Codwell, John, clothier, Biddenden, Kent, 1638 CKS PRC20/10/165
Codwyne, Edward, 1625 Hants RO 21M65 D8/118
Coe, Jonas, Sharrington, Norf, 1806 Norfolk RO ANW/23/27/7
Coe, Robert, farmer, Wiggenhall St German, Norf, 1824 Norfolk RO ANW/23/27/24
Coffin, Thomas, Bere Regis, Dors, 1598 Wilts RO Miscellaneous Index to Wills (name + date)
Coffyn, Gyles, Sopley, Hants, 1623 Hants RO 21M65 D8/10
Coga, Nathaniell, university: 'Master of Pembroke College, Cambridge', Cambridge (Pembroke College), Cambs, 1695 PRO PROB5/1053
Cogan, Anthony, Montacute, Som, 1598 Somerset RO D/D/Cta/C56
Cogdell, Elizabeth, St Albans St Stephens, Herts, 1631 Herts RO ASA25/4873
Cogdell, George, Abbots Langley, Herts, 1584 Herts RO ASA25/1080
Cogdell, Richard, Watford, Herts, 1560 Herts RO ASA25/463
Cogdell, Thomas, Abbots Langley, Herts, 1610 Herts RO ASA25/4769
Coggan, George, Epworth, Lincs, 1651 Lincs RO Ad/Ac/40/220
Coggan, John, Haxey, Lincs, 1615 Lincs RO Ad/Ac/8b/217
Coggan, John, Haxey, Lincs, 1663 Lincs RO Ad/Ac/41/99
Coggan, Roberte, Haxey, Lincs, 1629 Lincs RO Ad/Ac/39/214
Cogger, Thomas eld, yeoman, Stone in Oxney, Kent, 1646 CKS PRC1/7/77
Coggs, Henry, husbandman, Chieveley, Berks, 1663 Berks RO D/A1/183/56C
Coife, Richard, Goudhurst, Kent, 1626 CKS PRC2/25/37
Coke, John, Langford, Steeple, Wilts, 1605 Wilts RO Arch. Sarum/(+ name and date)
Coker, Thomas, Lenham, Kent, 1606 CKS PRC2/13/130
Colbie, Anthonie, Aswarby, Lincs, 1637 Lincs RO Ad/Ac/25/382
Colborne, Thomas, brewer, Stratford le Bow, London & Middlesex, 1676 PRO PROB32/12/85
Colbrand, Robarte, St Johns Thanet, Kent, 1598 CKS PRC2/10/202
Colbrand, William, St Peter in Thanet, Kent, 1620 CKS PRC2/21/165
Colbrand, William, Shadoxhurst, Kent, 1631 CKS PRC2/31/21
Colbrand, Wyllyam, St Laurence Thanet, Kent, 1591 CKS PRC2/5/165
Colbrand, Zacharie, St Laurence Thanet, Kent, 1593 CKS PRC2/6/519
Colbrooke, Henry, Woolavington, Sussex, 1638 W. Suss RO EpI/33/1638
Coldame, Katherine, widow, Sandwich St Bartholomew's Hospital, Kent, 1626 CKS PRC20/7/345
Colden, Susan, widow, Wittering, West, Sussex, 1676 W. Suss RO EpI/33/1676/4
Colden, William, Westbourne, Sussex, 1671 W. Suss RO EpI/33/1671/4
Coldgate, Patience, widow, Lenham, Kent, 1674 CKS PRC2/36/35
Coldwell, Richard, Glentworth, Lincs, 1610 Lincs RO Ad/Ac/8a/330
Cole, Wilts RO Unlisted Fragment
Cole, Agnes, widow, New Romney, Kent, 1599 CKS PRC21/16/196
Cole, Anthonyie, Whitchurch, Hants, 1623 Hants RO 21M65 D8/11

[Cole:]
Cole, Benjamin, Parham, Sussex, 1673 W. Suss RO EpI/33/1673/7
Cole, Daniel, butcher, Hougham, Lincs, 1683 Lincs RO Ad/Ac/44/82
Cole, Edmunde, Uffculme, Devon, 1631 Wilts RO Miscellaneous Index to Wills (name + date)
Cole, Frances, widow, St Laurence Thanet, Kent, 1626 CKS PRC2/27/41
Cole, Francis, Stamford, Lincs, 1629 Lincs RO Ad/Ac/22/5
Cole, George, Grantham, Lincs, 1636 Lincs RO Ad/Ac/24/548
Cole, Henry, clergy: 'clerk', Torksey, Lincs, 1607 Lincs RO Ad/Ac/37/236
Cole, James, gentleman, Gloucester, Glos, 1819 GRO GDR/B4/2/C82
Cole, John, Dover, Kent, 1600 CKS PRC21/15/194
Cole, John, Stamford, Lincs, 1626 Lincs RO Ad/Ac/20/120
Cole, John, Fillingham, Lincs, 1671 Lincs RO Ad/Ac/33/205
Cole, John, Weedon Beck, Northants, 1680 Northants RO NWill A/C/18
Cole, Mary, Smeeth, Kent, 1701 CKS PRC19/5/79
Cole, Nicholas, Weyhill, Hants, 1671 Hants RO 21m65 D8/227
Cole, Richard, Canterbury St Paul, Kent, 1612 CKS PRC2/17/212
Cole, Richard, Ashford, Kent, 1627 CKS PRC2/28/25
Cole, Robert, Aslackby, Lincs, 1606 Lincs RO Ad/Ac/7/40
Cole, Robert, Dover, Kent, 1629 CKS PRC20/8/133
Cole, Robert, clergy: 'clerk', Bethersden, Kent, 1667 CKS PRC1/12/25
Cole, Thomas, Sandwich, Kent, 1625 CKS PRC2/23/92
Cole, Thomas, Willingham, Lincs, 1629 Lincs RO Ad/Ac/39/208
Cole, Thomas, chandler: 'tallow chandler', Grantham, Lincs, 1634 Lincs RO Ad/Ac/24/256
Cole, Thomas, Grantham, Lincs, 1636 Lincs RO Ad/Ac/24/541
Cole, Thomas, Grantham, Lincs, 1641 Lincs RO Ad/Ac/27/175
Cole, Thomas, Fawley, Hants, 1665 Hants RO 1665 P8
Cole, William, Bourne, Lincs, 1613 Lincs RO Ad/Ac/12/79
Cole, William, Whaplode, Lincs, 1614 Lincs RO Ad/Ac/13/209
Cole, William, bachelor, Gunby, Lincs, 1678 Lincs RO Ad/Ac/34/36a
Cole, William ygr, Belbroughton, Worcs, 1695 Worcs RO 008.7 BA3585/837/bdl 6
Cole/Cashere, John, Uffculme, Devon, 1596 Wilts RO Miscellaneous Index to Wills (name + date)
Colebecke, Thomas, Bolsover, Derby, 1663 LJRO:cards/1663/14
Colebie, Richard, Boston, Lincs, 1612 Lincs RO Ad/Ac/11/194
Coleborne, Richard, Hayes, London & Middlesex, 1673 Lambeth Palace VH96/570
Colebrook, Symon, Ashford, Kent, 1683 CKS PRC2/40/101
Coleclough, Adam, gentleman, Dilhorne, Staffs, 1685 LJRO/B/C/5/1685/29
Colegate, James, wheelwright, Newnham, Kent, 1684 CKS PRC2/40/190
Coleman, Edward, Long Buckby, Northants, 1681 Northants RO NWill A/C/69
Coleman, George, Torrington, East, Lincs, 1648 Lincs RO Ad/Ac/30/376
Coleman, Joane, Hungerford, Berks, 1598 Wilts RO Miscellaneous Index to Wills (name + date)
Coleman, John, Malvern, Great (Pool Brook), Worcs, 1606 Worcs RO 008.7 BA3585/834/?
Coleman, John, Arreton, Hants, 1672 Hants RO 21m65 D8/229
Coleman, John, husbandman, Stockbury, Kent, 1675 CKS PRC2/36/171
Coleman, Richard, Birchington, Kent, 1633 CKS PRC20/10/238
Coleman, Richard, husbandman, Dymchurch, Kent, 1671 CKS PRC2/35/24
Coleman, Richard, Herne, Kent, 1677 CKS PRC20/12/229
Coleman, Robert, yeoman, Langton, Tur, Leics, 1673 Leics RO Administrators Accounts 1667-72 f110
Coleman, Roger, Foxton, Cambs, 1640 c. CUL V.C. Acc./Box3/62
Coleman, Thomas, Aldbourne, Wilts, 1623 Wilts RO Arch. Wilts.(name + date)
Coleman, Thomas, Harborough, Market, Leics, 1666 Leics RO Administrators Accounts C17th f79
Coleman, Thomas, Thorpe Langton, Leics, 1670 Leics RO Administrators Accounts 1667-72 f42
Coleman, Walter, Langley Burrell, Wilts, 1678 Wilts RO Miscellaneous Index to Wills (name + date)

Coleman, William, Tenterden, Kent, 1628 CKS PRC2/29/26
Coles, Anthony, husbandman, Fulbrook, Oxon, 1636 Oxon RO MSS Wills 12/4/26
Coles, Benjamin, innholder, Wallingford, Berks, 1682 Berks RO D/A1/184/16C
Coles, George, Amberley, Sussex, 1631 W. Suss RO EpI/33/1631/10
Coles, Jane, widow, Beenham, Berks, 1632 Berks RO D/A1/182/95C
Coles, Peter, attorney, Oxford, Oxon, 1679 Oxon RO MSS Wills 163/1/21
Coles, Richard, carpenter, Abingdon, Berks, 1627 Berks RO D/A1/182/66A
Coles, Robert, Maddington, Wilts, 1670 Wilts RO Arch. Sarum/(+ name and date)
Coles, William, St Botolph Billingsgate, London & Middlesex, 1676 PRO PROB5/1670
Coley, Richard, gentleman, Sibsey, Lincs, 1671 Lincs RO Ad/Ac/33/179
Colfe, Isack, clergy: 'clerk', Canterbury Christchurch, Kent, 1599 CKS PRC21/15/21
Colfe, Joseph, alderman, Canterbury, Kent, 1641 CKS PRC1/5/89
Colgrove, William, husbandman, Abingdon, Berks, 1684 Berks RO D/A1/184/25C
Colland, John, Tupholme, Lincs, 1633 Lincs RO Ad/Ac/24/1
Collard, Ambrose, St Nicholas at Wade, Kent, 1681 CKS PRC20/13/113
Collard, Elizabeth, Swalecliffe, Kent, 1685 CKS PRC2/40/182
Collard, Henry, Wittersham, Kent, 1589 CKS PRC21/9/237
Collard, John, Lympne, Kent, 1627 CKS PRC2/28/21
Collard, Samuel, cordwainer, Canterbury St Andrew, Kent, 1684 CKS PRC2/40/186
Collard, Thomas, Alkham, Kent, 1624 CKS PRC2/23/89
Collard/Beamont, Mary, St Mary in the Marsh, Kent, 1637 CKS PRC2/34/32
Collen, Dorothy, widow, Lurgashall, Sussex, 1624 W. Suss RO EpI/33/1624/12
Collens, Anne, widow, Wood Eaton, Oxon, 1640 Oxon RO MSS Wills 13/2/6
Collens, John, Benenden, Kent, CKS PRC1/2/39a
Collens, John, Old Romney, Kent, 1624 CKS PRC2/23/82
Collens, John, Benenden, Kent, 1640 CKS PRC1/2/39
Collens, Thomas,
Som 1588 Somerset RO D/D/Cta/C20
Collens, William, Goudhurst, Kent, 1592 CKS PRC2/6/322
Collens, William, St Nicholas at Wade, Kent, 1616 CKS PRC20/3/316
Coller, Robert, Boxley, Kent, 1613 CKS PRC2/16/118
Coller, William, Kington St Michael, Wilts, 1620? Wilts RO CC Sarum(+ name and date)
Coller, William, Dover, Kent, 1681 CKS PRC20/13/119
Coller, see Sharpe,
Colles, Thomas, yeoman, Coxwell, Great, Berks, 1621 Berks RO D/A1/182/25A
Colles, Thomas, Crowland, Lincs, 1692 PRO PROB5/810
Colleson, Mathew, gardener, Bearsted, Kent, 1683 CKS PRC2/40/105
Collet, Mathew, gentleman, Salisbury, Wilts, 1668 Wilts RO Miscellaneous Index to Wills (name + date)
Collet, William, St Johns Thanet, Kent, 1625 CKS PRC2/25/44
Collett, Sibrian, blacksmith, Candlesby, Lincs, 1637 Lincs RO Ad/Ac/25/436
Collett, Thomas, Lydd, Kent, 1613 CKS PRC20/2/352
Collett, William, carpenter, Monkton Farleigh, Wilts, 1694 Wilts RO Arch. Sarum/(+ name and date)
Colley, Gillyan, widow, Dover, Kent, 1625 CKS PRC20/7/360
Colley, Thomas, victualler, Trowbridge, Wilts, 1731? Wilts RO Miscellaneous Index to Wills (name + date)
Colliar, Jeames, Lydd, Kent, 1594 CKS PRC21/13/1
Collice, Deodate, yeoman, Cumnor (Woodend), Berks, 1666 Berks RO D/A1/56/68D
Collick, Mary, widow, Pagham, Sussex, 1681 W. Suss RO EpIV/10/2A/17
Collie, Ralph, Chester St Oswald (Newton by Chester), Ches, 1597 Cheshire RO (Name) W.C. 1596
Collier, ..., Glossop, Derby, 1684 LJRO/B/C/5/1684/27
Collier, Clement, yeoman, Lydd, Kent, 1669 CKS PRC19/4/44
Collier, Edward, Swalecliffe, Kent, 1683 CKS PRC2/40/100

[Collier:]
Collier, Edward, Sutton Veny, Wilts, 1768 Wilts RO Miscellaneous Index to Wills (name + date)
Collier, Henry, Winford, Som, 1666 Somerset RO D/D/Cta/C63
Collier, John, Maidstone, Kent, 1592 CKS PRC21/12/214
Collier, John, Milton next Sittingbourne, Kent, 1632 CKS PRC2/31/92
Collier, John, innkeeper, Burford, Oxon, 1638 Oxon RO MSS Wills 12/4/27
Collier, John, innholder, Lydd, Kent, 1670 CKS PRC19/4/72
Collier, John, yeoman, Oxford St Mary Magdalene, Oxon, 1676 Oxon RO MSS Wills 78/2/28
Collier, Rafe, Staplehurst, Kent, 1597 CKS PRC2/9/95
Collier, Robert, husbandman, Cassington, Oxon, 1683 Oxon RO MSS Wills 163/1/35
Collimore, Samuel, Lydd, Kent, 1678 CKS PRC20/12/230
Collin, Francis, tailor, Witham on the Hill (Toft), Lincs, 1627 Lincs RO Ad/Ac/20b/13
Collin, Henrie, Grantham, Lincs, 1639 Lincs RO Ad/Ac/25/255
Collin, Margery, Winwick, Hunts, 1608 Hunts RO/Acc58/4
Collin, Thomas, Surfleet, Lincs, 1620 Lincs RO Ad/Ac/16/20
Collines, Phillip, Romsey, Hants, 1596 Hants RO 1595 A15/5
Collingwood, Christopher, labourer, Somercoates, North, Lincs, 1669 Lincs RO Ad/Ac/33/95
Collingwood, George, Luddington (Garthorpe), Lincs, 1638 Lincs RO Ad/Ac/25/349
Collingwood, Nicholas, labourer, Lincoln, Lincs, 1669 Lincs RO Ad/Ac/33/105
Collingwood, William, Marsh Chapel, Lincs, 1622 Lincs RO Ad/Ac/17/49
Collins, Northshalle, Berks, 1598 Berks RO D/A1/181/156A
Collins, Aburne, Wallingford, Berks, 1596 Berks RO D/A1/181/150A
Collins, Clement, husbandman, Milton next Sittingbourne, Kent, 1677 CKS PRC2/37/22
Collins, Edward, butcher, Brewham, Som, 1599 Somerset RO D/D/Cta/C59
Collins, Edward, Biddenden, Kent, 1634 CKS PRC2/32/146
Collins, Elizabeth, Stapleford, Wilts, 1611 Wilts RO Arch. Sarum/(+ name and date)
Collins, Elizabeth, widow, Lurgashall, Sussex, 1685 W. Suss RO EpI/33/1684/48
Collins, Ellen, Dunchurch, Warks, 1684 LJRO/B/C/5/1684/28
Collins, Hercules, yeoman, Didcot, Berks, 1684 Berks RO D/A1/184/31C
Collins, Hugh, husbandman, Hinksey, South, Berks, 1630 Berks RO D/A1/182/81A
Collins, James, Farrington Curney, Som, 1743 Somerset RO D/D/Cta/C88
Collins, John, Stratford near Bow, Essex, 1705 PRO PROB5/1175
Collins, John, mr, Worcester St John Bedwardine, Worcs, 1775 Worcs RO 008.7 BA3585/835/bdl 2
Collins, John + Mary, Timsbury, Som, 1668 Somerset RO D/D/Cta/C68
Collins, Joseph, Newbury, Berks, 1632 Berks RO D/A1/182/92A
Collins, Judith, widow, Hungerford, Berks, 1626 Wilts RO Dean Sarum (name + date)
Collins, Kellam, Connington, Hunts, 1681 Hunts RO/Acc58/167(105)
Collins, Peter, husbandman, Brightwell (Mackney), Berks, 1653 Berks RO D/A1/183/42A
Collins, Philip, Wells St Cuthbert, Som, 1666 Somerset RO D/D/Cta/C64
Collins, Philippa, Bath, Som, 1691 Somerset RO D/D/Cta/C89
Collins, Richard, Shadoxhurst, Kent, 1595 CKS PRC2/7/255
Collins, Richard, Brading, Hants, 1624 Hants RO 21M65 D8/80
Collins, Robarte, Lydd, Kent, 1583 CKS PRC21/6/224
Collins, Robert, Fittleworth, Sussex, 1618 W. Suss RO EpI/33/1617/8
Collins, Robert, Earnley (Almodington), Sussex, 1626 W. Suss RO EpI/33/1625/6
Collins, Robert, Newenden, Kent, 1626 CKS PRC2/25/32
Collins, Simon, Minster in Sheppey, Kent, 1605 CKS PRC2/13/152
Collins, Thomas, Wardington, Oxon, 1613 Oxon RO MSS Wills Pec 34/4/16
Collins, Thomas, labourer, Hendred, West, Berks, 1625 Berks RO D/A1/182/56A
Collins, Thomas, Lavant, East, Sussex, 1637 W. Suss RO EpIV/10/2/13
Collins, Thomas, butcher, Cranbrook, Kent, 1677 CKS PRC2/37/129
Collins, Thomas, Wichenford, Worcs, 1780 Worcs RO 008.7 BA3585/835/bdl 2
Collins, Walter, mariner: 'ship master & part owner', Shadwell, St Paul, London & Middlesex, 1688 PRO PROB32/27/202
Collins, William, Salisbury St Martin, Wilts, 1625 Wilts RO Miscellaneous Index to Wills (name

+ date)
Collins, William, gentleman, Linsted, Kent, 1637 CKS PRC20/10/182
Collins, William, Boxford, Berks, 1638 Wilts RO CC Sarum(+ name and date)
Collins, William, Winscombe, Som, 1639 Somerset RO D/D/Cta/C15
Collins, William sen, yeoman, Lambourn (East Hanney), Berks, 1636 Berks RO D/A1/182/107A
Collinson, Henry, clergy: 'mr/clerk', Murston, Kent, 1623 CKS PRC2/23/81
Collis, William, husbandman, Wellingborough, Northants, 1672 Northants RO NWill A/C/101
Collishawe, Richard, Grantham, Lincs, 1637 Lincs RO Ad/Ac/24/425
Collison, Giles, gardener, Charing, Kent, 1681 CKS PRC20/13/121
Collyar, Thomas, Sandwich, Kent, 1581 CKS PRC2/2/29
Collye, Thomas, Buckland, Kent, 1598 CKS PRC21/14/250
Collye, Thomas, Alkham, Kent, 1613 CKS PRC2/17/272
Collyer, John, Hernhill, Kent, 1679 CKS PRC20/12/297
Collyer, Philip, Yarnton, Oxon, 1637 Oxon RO MSS Wills 296/2/75
Collyer, Philip, blacksmith, Farringdon, Great, Berks, 1671 Berks RO D/A3/2/95B
Collyer, William, Chart nr Sutton Valence, Kent, 1637 CKS PRC2/34/34
Collyer, William, Derby All Saints, Derby, 1685 LJRO/B/C/5/1685/30
Collyns, John, Hurst, Berks, 1637 Wilts RO Dean Sarum (name + date)
Collyns, Thomas, Aldbourne, Wilts, 1630 Wilts RO Arch. Wilts.(name + date)
Collyson, John, Yarburgh, Lincs, 1624 Lincs RO Ad/Ac/19A/98
Colman, Henry, St Nicholas at Wade, Kent, 1614 CKS PRC20/3/124
Colman, Jeremiah snr, farmer, Wymondham, Norf, 1749 Norfolk RO ANF/11/4/84
Colman, John, Petham, Kent, 1594 CKS PRC2/7/297
Colman, John, St Nicholas at Wade, Kent, 1661 CKS PRC19/3/1a
Colman, John, Chilham, Kent, 1675 CKS PRC2/36/174
Colman, John, blacksmith, Cranbrook, Kent, 1676 CKS PRC2/37/28
Colman, John ygr, Birchington, Kent, 1600 CKS PRC21/16/120
Colman, Pawle, clergy: 'vicar', Selling, Kent, 1581 CKS PRC2/2/31
Colman, William, Bradford on Avon, Wilts, 1694 Wilts RO Arch. Sarum/(+ name and date)
Colmer, William,
Som 1631 Somerset RO D/D/Cta/C86
Colner, Stephen, St Laurence Thanet, Kent, 1621 CKS PRC2/26/124
Colpes, John, Bosham, Sussex, 1652 W. Suss RO EpI/33/1652/5
Colpis, William, Chapel, North, Sussex, 1641 W. Suss RO EpI/33/1640/18
Colpys, Richard, Marden, Up, Sussex, 1594 W. Suss RO EpI/33/1594/15
Colson, John, Hamble le Rice, Hants, 1624 Hants RO 21M65 D8/57
Colson, Peter, Stoneham, North, Hants, 1671 Hants RO 21m65 D8/230
Colsonsacke, Joan, Patrixbourne, Kent, 1598 CKS PRC2/10/208
Coltman, Thomas, Wigston Magna, Leics, 1665 Leics RO Administrators Accounts C17th f35
Colvill, Robert, mariner, Deal, Kent, 1702 CKS PRC19/6/1
Colvill, Samuel, Cranbrook, Kent, 1621 CKS PRC2/20/23
Colwell, Luke, Seasalter, Kent, 1593 CKS PRC2/6/350
Colye, John, gentleman, Sibsey, Lincs, 1639 Lincs RO Ad/Ac/26/173
Colyer, John, yeoman, Crowland, Lincs, 1624 Lincs RO Ad/Ac/19A/108
Colyer, Roberte, Crowland, Lincs, 1613 Lincs RO Ad/Ac/11/74
Combe, Clemence, widow, Ash next Sandwich, Kent, 1613 CKS PRC20/2/424
Combe, Richard, Heyshott, Sussex, 1605 W. Suss RO EpI/33/1604/4
Combe, Thomas, Tisbury, Wilts, 1616 Wilts RO Miscellaneous Index to Wills (name + date)
Combe, Thomas, Sandwich St Clement, Kent, 1637 CKS PRC2/34/27
Combe, Tristram, Thornford, Dors, 1636 Wilts RO Miscellaneous Index to Wills (name + date)
Combe, William, Padworth, Berks, Berks RO D/A1/1/73R
Comber, John, husbandman, Maidstone, Kent, 1618 CKS PRC20/4/45
Comber, Jone, widow, Marden, Kent, 1587 CKS PRC2/4/247
Comber, Stephen, Leeds, Kent, 1618 CKS PRC2/21/153
Comber, Stephen, Leeds, Kent, 1619 CKS PRC2/21/171

[Comberworth:]
Comberworth, Thomas, Billingborough, Lincs, 1606 Lincs RO Ad/Ac/7/56
Combes, Margaret, widow, Alverstoke, Hants, 1691 Hants RO 1690 P/09/4
Combes, Richard, Wapping, London & Middlesex, 1715 PRO PROB32/59/106
Combes, see Harris,
Combey, John, husbandman, Strensham, Worcs, 1673 Worcs RO 008.7 BA3585/837/bdl 6
Combs, Robert, Wye, Kent, 1674 CKS PRC2/36/28
Comelie, Richard, gentleman, Oxford (University), Oxon, Bodleian HYP B8/32
Comin, William, Blewbury, Berks, 1677 Wilts RO Miscellaneous Index to Wills (name + date)
Comly, Robert, Somerford, Great, Wilts, 1637 Wilts RO Arch. Wilts.(name + date)
Compton, Humfrye, Chitterne All Saints, Wilts, 1628 Wilts RO CC Sarum(+ name and date)
Compton, John, Willingham, Lincs, 1662 Lincs RO Ad/Ac/41/46
Compton, Matthew, Kyme, South, Lincs, 1625 Lincs RO Ad/Ac/19B/79
Compton, Robert, Willingham, Lincs, 1662 Lincs RO Ad/Ac/41/54
Compton, William, Deverill, Brixton, Wilts, 1628 Wilts RO Arch. Sarum/(+ name and date)
Compton, William, esquire, Grasby, Lincs, 1670 Lincs RO Ad/Ac/32/146
Comyn, Edwarde, Oare, Kent, 1598 CKS PRC2/10/344
Conckers, Robert, Maidstone, Kent, 1605 CKS PRC20/1/55
Conduit, William, Hinckley, Leics, 1673 Leics RO Administrators Accounts 1667-72 f123
Condye, Jane + Liddia, Boston, Lincs, 1637 Lincs RO Ad/Ac/25/410
Conell, Grace, widow, Timberland, Lincs, 1641 Lincs RO Ad/Ac/27/25
Coney, Henry, Burton Coggles, Lincs, 1649 Lincs RO Ad/Ac/30/50
Coney, Richard, yeoman, Swineshead, Lincs, 1633 Lincs RO Ad/Ac/24/189
Coney, Tomas, Hythe St Leonard, Kent, 1603 CKS PRC21/17/65
Congreve, John, gentleman, Wolston, Warks, 1810 LJRO/B/C/5/1810/7
Coning, Robert, Deal, Kent, 1679 CKS PRC20/12/293
Coningsbie, Henry, Manton, Lincs, 1640? Lincs RO Ad/Ac/40/272
Coningsby, Thomas, Bexley, Kent, 1693 PRO PROB5/1196
Connaway, Robert, Leeds, Kent, 1597 CKS PRC2/10/45
Connell, John, Ridge, Herts, 1579 Herts RO ASA25/945
Conniar, Zacharie, gentleman, Canterbury Holy Cross Westgate, Kent, 1669 CKS PRC1/14/25
Connill, George, yeoman, Skelbrooke, Yorks, 1787 Borthwick Test C.P. 1787/5
Connoway, George, butler/scholar's servant, Cambridge (Jesus College), Cambs, 1641 CUL V.C. Acc./Box2/16
Conolly, Bartholomew, St Martin in the Fields, London & Middlesex, 1781 Greater London RO DL/C/559/116/1
Conoway, Cycely, Bearsted, Kent, 1615 CKS PRC2/20/39
Conowaye, James, Dover St Mary, Kent, 1607 CKS PRC20/1/249
Consant, Nicholas, Reculver, Kent, 1633 CKS PRC20/10/210
Consaunte, William, Chislet, Kent, 1571 CKS PRC2/1/47
Constable, John, Sandwich, Kent, 1629 CKS PRC2/30/27
Constable, Marmaduke, esquire, Rasen, West, Lincs, 1634 Lincs RO Ad/Ac/24/219
Constable, Richard, husbandman, Cogges, Oxon, 1628 Oxon RO MSS Wills 296/2/23
Constable, Robert, esquire, Hough on the Hill, Lincs, 1673 Lincs RO Ad/Ac/43/68
Constable, William, Snargate, Kent, 1596 CKS PRC2/8/270
Constable, William, gentleman, Rasen, West, Lincs, 1641 Lincs RO Ad/Ac/27/20
Constant, Ralph, St Johns Thanet, Kent, 1707 CKS PRC19/6/28
Contry, Elizabethe, Nonington, Kent, 1592 CKS PRC21/11/168
Conwaye, Robert, mason: 'freemason', Abingdon St Helen, Berks, 1606 Berks RO D/A1/181/197C
Conye, Thomas, gentleman, Burton Coggles, Lincs, 1607 Lincs RO Ad/Ac/8a/75
Conyers, John, Thimbleby, Lincs, 1619 Lincs RO Ad/Ac/15/97
Conyers, John, yeoman, Fiskerton, Lincs, 1662 Lincs RO Ad/Ac/41/62
Conyers, William, merchant, Boston, Lincs, 1729 Lincs RO Ad/Ac/36/4
Cooch, John, Milton next Sittingbourne, Kent, 1639 CKS PRC1/2/40
Cooch, John, Milton next Sittingbourne, Kent, 1639 CKS PRC1/2/40a

Coockcowe, Jane, spinster, Leigh, South, Oxon, 1633 Oxon RO MSS Wills 296/2/45
Coocu, Anthonie, Canterbury St Alphege, Kent, 1625 CKS PRC20/7/357
Cook, Henry?, Sutton Veny, Wilts, 1641 Wilts RO Miscellaneous Index to Wills (name + date)
Cook, John, Baltonsborough, Som, Somerset RO D/D/Cta/C35
Cook, John, yeoman, Sparsholt, Berks, 1673 Berks RO D/A1/183/112C
Cook, John, yeoman, Compton, Fenny, Warks, 1800 LJRO/B/C/5/1800/14
Cook, Mary, widow, Derby, Derby, 1751 LJRO/B/C/5/1751/107
Cook, Richard, Martley, Worcs, 1796 Worcs RO 008.7 BA3585/835/bdl 2
Cook, Robert, Hursley, Hants, 1624 Hants RO 21M65 D8/59
Cook, Roger, Brockley, Som, 1587 Somerset RO D/D/Cta/C76
Cook, Samuel, brazier, Derby, Derby, 1751 LJRO/B/C/5/1751/106a
Cook, Samuel, brazier, Derby, Derby, 1751 LJRO/B/C/5/1751/106b
Cook, Thomas, Cheddleton, Staffs, 1676 LJRO:cards/1676/15
Cook, Thomas, Laughton (Wildsworth), Lincs, 1685 Lincs RO Ad/Ac/44/155
Cook, William, Godshill, Hants, 1624 Hants RO 21M65 D8/60
Cook, see Bowles,
Cooke, Chippenham, Wilts, 1679 Wilts RO Miscellaneous Index to Wills (name + date)
Cooke, Adam, Appleby, Lincs, 1602 Lincs RO Ad/Ac/37/131
Cooke, Alan, Stallingborough, Lincs, 1649 Lincs RO Ad/Ac/30/151
Cooke, Anne, widow, Canterbury St Paul, Kent, 1638 CKS PRC2/34/26
Cooke, Anthony, Winterton, Lincs, 1629 Lincs RO Ad/Ac/39/255
Cooke, Anthony, Salisbury, Wilts, 1677 Wilts RO Miscellaneous Index to Wills (name + date)
Cooke, Bartholomew, Pinchbeck, Lincs, 1626 Lincs RO Ad/Ac/20/51
Cooke, Binjamyn, Bardney, Lincs, 1599 Lincs RO Ad/Ac/5/61
Cooke, Charles, Snelston, Derby, 1681 LJRO/B/C/5/1682/24
Cooke, Christofer, Barlings, Lincs, 1620 Lincs RO Ad/Ac/8b/479
Cooke, Christopher, Godmersham, Kent, 1602 CKS PRC21/15/178
Cooke, Daniel, Graveney, Kent, 1668 CKS PRC1/13/26
Cooke, David, Westwell, Oxon, 1673 Oxon RO MSS Wills 163/1/13
Cooke, Dyon, Coates, Great, Lincs, 1619 Lincs RO Ad/Ac/15/235
Cooke, Edith, widow, Wantage, Berks, 1638 Wilts RO Dean Sarum (name + date)
Cooke, Edmund, Tunstall, Kent, 1613 CKS PRC2/18/30
Cooke, Edmund, yeoman, Ulcombe, Kent, 1667 CKS PRC1/12/26
Cooke, Edward, Allington, Lincs, 1605 Lincs RO Ad/Ac/6/152
Cooke, Edward, Stockbury, Kent, 1626 CKS PRC2/27/32
Cooke, Edward, Dudley, Worcs, 1677 Worcs RO 008.7 BA3585/837/bdl 6
Cooke, Edward, husbandman, Bicker, Lincs, 1680 Lincs RO Ad/Ac/43/95
Cooke, Elizabeth, Wye, Kent, 1595 CKS PRC2/8/121
Cooke, Elizabeth, widow, Leysdown, Kent, 1613 CKS PRC2/16/138
Cooke, Elizabeth, Raithby, Lincs, 1624 Lincs RO Ad/Ac/19A/133
Cooke, Ellen, spinster, Canterbury Christchurch, Kent, 1681 CKS PRC20/13/111
Cooke, Francis, Bierton (Broughton), Bucks, 1674 Oxon RO MSS Wills Pec 35/2/22
Cooke, George, Goring, Sussex, 1606 W. Suss RO EpI/33/1606/8
Cooke, George, Timberland, Lincs, 1639 Lincs RO Ad/Ac/25/293
Cooke, George, Withern, Lincs, 1673 Lincs RO Ad/Ac/34/18
Cooke, Godfrey, Bassingham, Lincs, 1636 Lincs RO Ad/Ac/24/415
Cooke, Henry, husbandman, Hampstead Norris, Berks, 1622 Berks RO D/A1/182/39A
Cooke, Henry, flaxdresser, Faversham, Kent, 1642 CKS PRC1/6/55
Cooke, Henry, Salisbury, Wilts, 1677 Wilts RO Miscellaneous Index to Wills (name + date)
Cooke, James, Norton, Kent, 1620 CKS PRC2/21/167
Cooke, James, Brafield on the Green, Northants, 1680 Northants RO NWill A/C/30
Cooke, Jeffrey, Standlake, Oxon, 1648 Oxon RO MSS Wills 296/3/38
Cooke, Joan, widow, Redbourn, Herts, 1627 Herts RO ASA25/2942
Cooke, John, husbandman, Shapwick, Som, 1592 Somerset RO D/D/Cta/C38
Cooke, John, Dover St Mary, Kent, 1603 CKS PRC21/17/11

[Cooke:]
Cooke, John, Faversham, Kent, 1605 CKS PRC2/14/114
Cooke, John, Menheniot, Corn, 1607 Cornwall RO AP/C164
Cooke, John, Bolton-le-Moors, Lancs, 1618 Lancs RO (Name of Deceased) D.R.C.H. 1618
Cooke, John, Grimsby, Great, Lincs, 1620 Lincs RO Ad/Ac/15/276
Cooke, John, cordwainer: 'shoemaker', Newbury, Berks, 1620 Berks RO D/A1/182/31D
Cooke, John, Shalfleet, Hants, 1624 Hants RO 21M65 D8/58
Cooke, John, Goring, Sussex, 1627 W. Suss RO EpI/33/1627/18
Cooke, John, Owston, Lincs, 1628 Lincs RO Ad/Ac/39/224
Cooke, John, yeoman, Hampstead Norris (Bothampstead), Berks, 1643 Berks RO D/A1/183/24C
Cooke, John, Alresford, New, Hants, 1669 Hants RO 21m65 D8/212
Cooke, John, High Halden, Kent, 1670 CKS PRC1/14/26
Cooke, John, Salisbury, Wilts, 1670 Wilts RO Miscellaneous Index to Wills (name + date)
Cooke, John, yeoman, Smarden, Kent, 1679 CKS PRC2/38/112
Cooke, John, Bromsgrove, Worcs, 1681 Worcs RO 008.7 BA3585/830/72
Cooke, John, Glentworth, Lincs, 1682 Lincs RO Ad/Ac/44/1
Cooke, John, Ponton, Great, Lincs, 1778 Lincs RO Ad/Ac/45/40
Cooke, Julian, Elham, Kent, 1628 CKS PRC2/29/25
Cooke, Katherine, widow, Pinchbeck, Lincs, 1626 Lincs RO Ad/Ac/20/54
Cooke, Lawrence, Sutton St James, Lincs, 1640 Lincs RO Ad/Ac/27/156
Cooke, Lawrence, clergy: 'rector/bachelor', Hornsey, London & Middlesex, 1736 Greater London RO DL/C/549/5
Cooke, Magdalen, widow, Sandwich, Kent, 1619 CKS PRC2/20/110
Cooke, Margaret, Ospringe, Kent, 1593 CKS PRC2/6/310
Cooke, Martin, Faversham, Kent, 1636 CKS PRC2/33/29
Cooke, Mary, widow, Quedgeley, Glos, 1782 GRO GDR/B4/2/C144
Cooke, Matthew, Crowle, Lincs, 1675 Lincs RO Ad/Ac/35/88
Cooke, Matthew, Kelsey, North, Lincs, 1679 Lincs RO Ad/Ac/42/81
Cooke, Michael, Appleby, Lincs, 1668 Lincs RO Ad/Ac/33/84
Cooke, Michael, husbandman, Timberland, Lincs, 1668 Lincs RO Ad/Ac/33/47
Cooke, Miles, knight, 1700 PRO PROB32/41/12
Cooke, Miles, knight/Master in Chancery, 1700 PRO PROB32/41/112
Cooke, Myles, clergy: 'mr/clerk', Fordwich, Kent, 1616 CKS PRC2/20/63
Cooke, Nataniel, Lyme Regis, Dors, 1636 Wilts RO Miscellaneous Index to Wills (name + date)
Cooke, Osmund, Marden, Kent, 1610 CKS PRC2/13/119
Cooke, Peter, Heckfield, Hants, 1679 Hants RO 21m65 D8/283
Cooke, Reginald, Eckington, Worcs, Worcs RO 008.7 BA3585/839/344
Cooke, Richard, Norton, Kent, 1598 CKS PRC2/10/402
Cooke, Richard, Winterton, Lincs, 1621 Lincs RO Ad/Ac/8c/44
Cooke, Richard, Donnington, Sussex, 1650 W. Suss RO EpI/33/1650/4
Cooke, Richard, Chipping Warden, Northants, 1678 Northants RO NWill A/C/60
Cooke, Richard, Carisbrooke, Hants, 1682 Hants RO 21m65 D8/329
Cooke, Richard, chandler, Gloucester, Glos, 1684? GRO GDR/B4/2/C23
Cooke, Richard, Baltonsborough, Som, 1748 Somerset RO D/D/Cta/C87
Cooke, Richarde, Careby, Lincs, 1611 Lincs RO Ad/Ac/10/24
Cooke, Robert, Holbeach, Lincs, 1603 Lincs RO Ad/Ac/5/381
Cooke, Robert, Fulstow, Lincs, 1641 Lincs RO Ad/Ac/27/170
Cooke, Robert, Bonnington, Kent, 1647 CKS PRC1/8/11
Cooke, Robert, clothier, Newbury, Berks, 1663 Berks RO D/A1/183/48C
Cooke, Robert, Sleaford, Lincs, 1664 Lincs RO Ad/Ac/42/14
Cooke, Robert, Welton/Louth, Lincs, 1678 Lincs RO Ad/Ac/43/178
Cooke, Robert, Amesbury, Wilts, 1685 Wilts RO Arch. Sarum/(+ name and date)
Cooke, Roberte, Toynton St Peter, Lincs, 1611 Lincs RO Ad/Ac/10/126
Cooke, Roger, Brockley, Som, 1587 Somerset RO D/D/Cta/C27
Cooke, Rolland, Barton on Humber, Lincs, 1602 Lincs RO Ad/Ac/5/252
Cooke, Samuel, Tattershall, Lincs, 1636 Lincs RO Ad/Ac/24/421

Cooke, Thomas, Arundel, Sussex, W. Suss RO EpI/33/1610/6
Cooke, Thomas, yeoman, Cookham, Berks, 1601 Berks RO D/A1/181/171A
Cooke, Thomas, Coningsby, Lincs, 1618 Lincs RO Ad/Ac/14/162
Cooke, Thomas, innholder, Canterbury St Mildred, Kent, 1620 CKS PRC2/21/145
Cooke, Thomas, collar maker, Canterbury St George Martyr, Kent, 1628 CKS PRC2/29/22
Cooke, Thomas, Ash next Sandwich, Kent, 1638 CKS PRC20/10/204
Cooke, Thomas, yeoman, Ash next Sandwich, Kent, 1638 CKS PRC20/10/206
Cooke, Thomas, milliner, Horncastle, Lincs, 1652 Lincs RO Ad/Ac/29/15
Cooke, Thomas, Walton on the Wolds, Leics, 1666 Leics RO Administrators Accounts C17th f58
Cooke, Thomas, Worthy, Martyr, Hants, 1669 Hants RO 21M65 D8/199
Cooke, Thomas, Upton Magna, Shrops, 1681 LJRO/B/C/5/1681/8
Cooke, Thomas, gentleman, Nantwich, Ches, 1797 Cheshire RO (Name) W.C. 1797
Cooke, William, Hucking, Kent, 1584 CKS PRC21/7/122
Cooke, William, yeoman, Yattendon, Berks, 1598 Berks RO D/A1/181/164C
Cooke, William, Lincoln, Lincs, 1612 Lincs RO Ad/Ac/11/117
Cooke, William, wheeler, Thatcham, Berks, 1623 Berks RO D/A1/182/41C
Cooke, William, Buckland, Kent, 1626 CKS PRC2/27/37
Cooke, William, Leake, Lincs, 1626 Lincs RO Ad/Ac/20/79
Cooke, William, Heapham, Lincs, 1627 Lincs RO Ad/Ac/39/85
Cooke, William, yeoman, Conisholme, Lincs, 1629 Lincs RO Ad/Ac/22/25
Cooke, William, Canterbury St Dunstan Without, Kent, 1639 CKS PRC2/34/183
Cooke, William, Ramsbury, Wilts, 1675 Wilts RO Miscellaneous Index to Wills (name + date)
Cooke, William, Staines, London & Middlesex, 1700 PRO PROB32/41/21
Cooke/Austen, Margaret, widow, Lenham, Kent, 1627 CKS PRC2/28/30
Cooke/Badmeringe, Thomas, Wiston, Sussex, 1631 W. Suss RO EpI/33/1631/21
Cooke/Croucher, Jane, widow, Ospringe, Kent, 1679 CKS PRC2/38/111
Cooke/Farrow, Elizabeth, widow, Goxhill, Lincs, 1615 Lincs RO Ad/Ac/13/185
Cooke/Lye, John, Newenden, Kent, 1635 CKS PRC2/33/36
Cooke/Lye/Lee, Gyles, Sandhurst, Kent, 1627 CKS PRC2/28/27
Cooke, see Moorey,
Cookeman, Giles, Wimborne Minster (Barnsley), Dors, 1640 Dorset RO PE/WM CP 2/4/61
Cookes, Dorothy, Bromsgrove, Worcs, 1679 Worcs RO 008.7 BA3585/830/91
Cookes, Thomas, gentleman, Bidford (Bidford Grange), Warks, 1675 Worcs RO 008.7 BA3585/830/39
Cookes, Thomas, Bidford, Warks, 1685 Worcs RO 008.7 BA3585/837/bdl 4
Cookloe, see Johnson,
Cookman, Jane, widow, Ottringham, Yorks, 1803 Borthwick Test C.P. 1803/2
Coole, Thomas, Stodmarsh, Kent, 1617 CKS PRC2/20/95
Coolee, Thomas, Harbledown, Kent, 1662 CKS PRC1/9/17
Cooley, John, Barham, Kent, 1689 CKS PRC2/41/145
Cooling, Edward + Alice, Whaplode, Lincs, 1611 Lincs RO Ad/Ac/10/35
Coolly, Thomas, Rolvenden, Kent, 1596 CKS PRC2/8/232
Cooly, John, Shepherdswell alias Sibertswold, Kent, 1648 CKS PRC1/8/40
Coolye, Henrye, Rolvenden, Kent, 1613 CKS PRC2/16/135
Coolye, Thomas, Monkton, Kent, 1599 CKS PRC21/15/25
Coombe, John, Glastonbury, Som, 1678 Somerset RO D/D/Cta/C77
Coombe, Nicholas, Hucking, Kent, 1620 CKS PRC20/5/55
Coombe, Nicholas, Wimborne Minster (Badbury), Dors, 1626 Dorset RO PE/WM CP 2/4/38
Coombe, Thomas,
Som 1705 Somerset RO D/D/Cta/C90
Coombe, William, Wimborne Minster, Dors, 1619 Dorset RO PE/WM CP 2/4/20
Coombes, James, Mells, Som, 1712 Somerset RO D/D/Cta/C91
Coombes, John, Southampton, Hants, 1662 Hants RO 21M65 D8/152
Coombes, Thomas, Freshwater, Hants, 1662 Hants RO 21M65 D8/153
Coombs, Stephen, Ashton, Steeple, Wilts, 1791 Wilts RO Arch. Sarum/(+ name and date)

[Coombs:]
Coombs, Stephen, Ashton, Steeple, Wilts, 1793 Wilts RO Miscellaneous Index to Wills (name + date)
Coombs, William, bachelor, St Clement Danes, London & Middlesex, 1705 PRO PROB32/48/54
Coome, John, Whitstone, Corn, 1609 Cornwall RO AP/C167/1
Coomer, Elizabeth, widow, Brent, East, Som, 1727 Somerset RO D/D/Cta/C92
Coomes, John ygr, Swalecliffe, Kent, 1637 CKS PRC2/34/35
Coomes, Thomas, Rolvenden, Kent, 1635 CKS PRC20/10/192
Coomes, William, yeoman, Rolvenden, Kent, 1628 CKS PRC2/28/24
Coop, John, Tempsford, Beds, 1622 Lincs RO Ad/Ac/17/72
Coop, Robert, Melton Mowbray, Leics, 1674 Leics RO Administrators Accounts 1667-72 f143
Coope, John, Wirksworth, Derby, 1721 LJRO/B/C/5/1721/4
Coopeland, William, husbandman, Billinghay, Lincs, 1664 Lincs RO Ad/Ac/43/32
Cooper, Alexander, Andover, Hants, 1669 Hants RO 21m65 D8/213
Cooper, Alexander, mason, Lincoln St Peter in Eastgate, Lincs, 1679 Lincs RO Ad/Ac/43/107
Cooper, Alice, widow, Chichester, Sussex, 1618 W. Suss RO EpIII/9/1/16
Cooper, Andrew, webster, Appleby, Lincs, 1669 Lincs RO Ad/Ac/33/148
Cooper, Anne, widow, Ashby, Lincs, 1680 Lincs RO Ad/Ac/43/142
Cooper, Christian, widow, Boston, Lincs, 1624 Lincs RO Ad/Ac/19A/101
Cooper, Christopher, husbandman, Pangbourne, Berks, 1638 Berks RO D/A1/182/132A&C
Cooper, Dorothy, spinster, Clerkenwell St James, London & Middlesex, 1792 Greater London RO DL/C/562/129/2
Cooper, Edward, yeoman, St Laurence Thanet, Kent, 1694 CKS PRC2/42/61
Cooper, Elizabeth, widow, Canterbury Holy Cross Westgate, Kent, 1613 CKS PRC2/17/292
Cooper, Elizabeth, widow, Walsall, Staffs, 1749 LJRO/B/C/5/1781/41
Cooper, Francis, Coston, Leics, 1639 Leics RO PR/I/41A/26
Cooper, Francis + Cassander, Appleby, Lincs, 1629 Lincs RO Ad/Ac/22/123
Cooper, George, Rodmersham, Kent, 1585 CKS PRC2/3/286
Cooper, George, Glastonbury St John, Som, 1612 Somerset RO D/D/Cta/C52
Cooper, George, carpenter, Loddington, Leics, 1669 Leics RO Administrators Accounts 1667-72 f27
Cooper, George, West Ham, Essex, 1761 Greater London RO DL/C/554/127
Cooper, James, Willesborough, Kent, 1599 CKS PRC2/10/220
Cooper, James, Cadney, Lincs, 1601 Lincs RO Ad/Ac/5/89
Cooper, James, Stamford, Lincs, 1611 Lincs RO Ad/Ac/10/11
Cooper, James, Stanground, Hunts, 1681 Hunts RO/Acc58/152(31)
Cooper, John, Reculver, Kent, 1598 CKS PRC21/14/256
Cooper, John, Stourmouth, Kent, 1606 CKS PRC2/13/148
Cooper, John, clergy: 'parson', Sudbrooke, Lincs, 1619 Lincs RO Ad/Ac/8b/345
Cooper, John, Wigtoft, Lincs, 1623 Lincs RO Ad/Ac/18/9
Cooper, John, Rolvenden, Kent, 1626 CKS PRC2/27/33
Cooper, John, yeoman, Barton, Wescot, Oxon, 1637 Oxon RO MSS Wills 296/2/66
Cooper, John, Marden, Kent, 1640 CKS PRC1/4/23
Cooper, John, yeoman, Ruckinge, Kent, 1647 CKS PRC1/8/12
Cooper, John, gentleman, Rudgwick, Sussex, 1675 W. Suss RO EpI/33/1674/4
Cooper, John, labourer, Whitstable, Kent, 1682 CKS PRC2/39/156
Cooper, John, Leysdown, Kent, 1687 CKS PRC2/41/92
Cooper, John, husbandman, Nuneaton (Attleborough), Warks, 1714 LJRO/B/C/5/1714/19
Cooper, John ygr, husbandman, Bobbing, Kent, 1671 CKS PRC2/35/31
Cooper, Joseph, Haxey, Lincs, 1683 Lincs RO Ad/Ac/44/50
Cooper, Judith, widow, Stamford, Lincs, 1637 Lincs RO Ad/Ac/25/635
Cooper, Katherine,
Herts Herts RO ASA25/4988
Cooper, Martin, Charlton, Wilts, 1615 Wilts RO Miscellaneous Index to Wills (name + date)
Cooper, Mary, widow, Pishill, Oxon, 1672 Oxon RO MSS Wills Pec 66/3/47
Cooper, Peter, Desford, Leics, 1672 Leics RO Administrators Accounts 1667-72 f71

[Cooper:]
Cooper, Randolph, Loughborough, Leics, 1668 Leics RO Administrators Accounts 1667-72 f13
Cooper, Reginald, Canterbury Holy Cross Westgate, Kent, 1602 CKS PRC2/14/141
Cooper, Reignold, Minster in Sheppey, Kent, 1639 CKS PRC1/1/73
Cooper, Richard, Enborne, Berks, Berks RO D/A1/182/86
Cooper, Richard, Powick, Worcs, 1682 Worcs RO 008.7 BA3585/837/bdl 3
Cooper, Richerde, Appledore, Kent, 1586 CKS PRC2/4/9
Cooper, Robert, Chislet, Kent, 1641 CKS PRC1/5/90
Cooper, Roger, Spilsby, Lincs, Lincs RO Ad/Ac/19A/55
Cooper, Stephen, Elham, Kent, 1597 CKS PRC2/9/73
Cooper, Susanne, widow, Dover St Mary, Kent, 1610 CKS PRC20/2/100
Cooper, Thomas, Newchurch, Kent, 1617 CKS PRC20/4/63
Cooper, Thomas, husbandman, Boxford, Berks, 1669 Berks RO D/A1/183/89C
Cooper, Thomas, university: 'scholar's servant', Cambridge, Cambs, 1680 CUL V.C. Acc./Box3/12
Cooper, Timothye, Sandwich, Kent, 1607 CKS PRC2/14/98
Cooper, William, Gayton le Marsh, Lincs, Lincs RO Ad/Ac/2C/150
Cooper, William, Sutton, Sussex, 1594 W. Suss RO EpI/33/1594/16
Cooper, William, New Romney, Kent, 1596 CKS PRC21/14/25
Cooper, William, sergeant: 'town sergeant', Dover St Mary, Kent, 1606 CKS PRC20/1/146
Cooper, William, Rolvenden, Kent, 1611 CKS PRC2/16/101
Cooper, William, husbandman, Murston, Kent, 1668 CKS PRC1/13/27
Cooper, William, Boston, Lincs, 1683 Lincs RO Ad/Ac/44/57
Cooper, William, innholder, Staplehurst, Kent, 1685 PRO PROB32/25/380
Cooper, William, clergy: 'clerk', Clerkenwell St James, London & Middlesex, 1687 PRO PROB32/26/113
Cooper, William, Darlaston, Staffs, 1710 LJRO/B/C/5/1710/29
Cooper r Christchurch, Zachariah eld,
London & Middlesex 1756 Greater London RO DL/C/554/4/2
Cooper/Austin, William, dyer, Wallingford St Leonard, Berks, 1642 Berks RO D/A1/183/11A
Cooper/Fryday, Joane, widow, Luddenham, Kent, 1664 CKS PRC1/10/20
Cooper/Steaninge, John, Slinfold, Sussex, 1611 W. Suss RO EpI/33/1611/13
Cooper/Steaninge, William, Lurgashall, Sussex, 1684 W. Suss RO EpI/33/1684/14
Cooper/Stening, Richard, Lurgashall, Sussex, 1670 W. Suss RO EpI/33/1669/5
Cooper, see Higginson & Rogers,
Coote, Ambrose, Alconbury, Hunts, 1674 Hunts RO/Acc58/18(192)
Coote, Ambrose, Alconbury, Hunts, 1676 Hunts RO/Acc58/37(8)
Coote, Phillip, knight, Kilmallack (Mount Coote), Cork, Ireland, 1718 PRO PROB5/1303
Coote, William, Binsted, Sussex, 1630 W. Suss RO EpI/33/1630/17
Cootts, John, Welton le Marsh, Lincs, 1632 Lincs RO Ad/Ac/23/118
Cope, Edmund, gentleman, Thame, Oxon, 1618 Oxon RO MSS Wills Pec 34/4/26
Cope, Edmund, gentleman, Kiddington, Oxon, 1647 Oxon RO MSS Wills 296/3/35
Cope, Lettice, widow, Thame, Oxon, 1647 Oxon RO MSS Wills Pec 35/1/25
Cope, Richard sen, Norbury/Rosson, Derby, 1663 LJRO:cards/1663/15
Copeland, Thomas, Trusthorpe, Lincs, 1620 Lincs RO Ad/Ac/16/28
Copland, Joane, spinster, Stratton St Margaret, Wilts, 1639 Wilts RO Arch. Wilts.(name + date)
Copland, Richard, Herne, Kent, 1617 CKS PRC20/3/484
Copland, Robert, Deal, Kent, 1617 CKS PRC20/4/67
Copland, Thomas, Loughborough, Leics, 1665 Leics RO Administrators Accounts C17th f26
Copland, Thomas, Kenardington, Kent, 1683 CKS PRC2/40/106
Copledike, Margaret + Dorothie, Frampton, Lincs, 1639 Lincs RO Ad/Ac/25/238
Copledike, Marie, Frampton, Lincs, 1640 Lincs RO Ad/Ac/26/248
Coppen, Roger, St Johns Thanet, Kent, 1662 CKS PRC1/8/95
Copper, George, Leeds, Kent, 1689 CKS PRC2/41/144
Copperthwaith, Edmund, university: 'Fellow of Queen's College, Oxford/M.A.', Oxford (Queen's College), Oxon, 1632 Bodleian HYP B8/33-34

[Copperthwayte:]
Copperthwayte, Henry, Cranbrook, Kent, 1588 CKS PRC2/4/466
Coppie, John, labourer, Halton Holgate, Lincs, 1634 Lincs RO Ad/Ac/24/217
Coppin, George, Deal, Kent, 1600 CKS PRC21/15/131
Coppin, George, Boston, Lincs, 1639 Lincs RO Ad/Ac/26/306
Coppin, James, Canterbury St Alphege, Kent, 1626 CKS PRC20/7/349
Coppin, Jeames, St Laurence Thanet, Kent, 1595 CKS PRC2/7/105
Coppin, John, St Laurence Thanet, Kent, 1627 CKS PRC2/27/39
Coppin, John, mr, Canterbury St George Martyr, Kent, 1629 CKS PRC2/30/30
Coppin, John, St Laurence Thanet, Kent, 1664 CKS PRC1/10/21
Coppin, John eld, St Laurence Thanet, Kent, 1619 CKS PRC2/21/148
Coppin, Marye, widow, St Johns Thanet, Kent, 1630 CKS PRC2/30/38
Coppin, Nathaniel, Bekesbourne, Kent, 1671 CKS PRC2/35/25
Coppin, Robarte, Wittersham, Kent, 1609 CKS PRC20/2/27
Coppin, William, Kenardington, Kent, 1606 CKS PRC2/14/96
Coppin/Davis, Anne, St Johns Thanet, Kent, 1668 CKS PRC1/13/28
Copping, John, Cardinham, Corn, 1646 Cornwall RO AP/C1159
Copping, Matthew, husbandman, Burlingham, North, Norf, Norfolk RO ANW/23/11/84
Coppyn, John, Boughton Monchelsea, Kent, 1582 CKS PRC2/2/92
Coppyn, Nycholas, St Nicholas at Wade, Kent, 1583 CKS PRC21/6/201
Coppyn, Roger, St Laurence Thanet, Kent, 1590 CKS PRC2/5/146
Coppyn, Roger, St Laurence Thanet, Kent, 1612 CKS PRC2/17/340
Copsie, Gilbert, Sittingbourne, Kent, 1625 CKS PRC2/25/34
Coram, Agnes, widow, St Thomas-by-Launceston, Corn, 1605 Cornwall RO AP/C74/3
Corbet, Thomas, Stapenhill, Derby, 1693 LJRO/B/C/5/1693/31
Corbett, Edward, brewer: 'beerbrewer', Rickmansworth, Herts, 1621 Herts RO ASA25/2676
Corbett, Henry + Catherine, Brookland, Kent, 1610 CKS PRC2/15/55
Corbett, John, Anstey, Leics, 1639 Leics RO PR/I/41A/23
Corbett, Joseph, engineer, Handsworth, Staffs, 1831 LJRO/B/C/5/1830/24a
Corbett, Thomas, Bosworth, Market, Leics, 1665 Leics RO Administrators Accounts C17th f5
Corbin, Thomas, Kidderminster, Worcs, 1681 Worcs RO 008.7 BA3585/830/75
Corbin, Thomas, Kidderminster, Worcs, 1681 Worcs RO 008.7 BA3585/830/80
Corbitt, Arthur, Edenham (Grimsthorpe), Lincs, 1626 Lincs RO Ad/Ac/19B/58
Corbridge, Nicholas, Carlton, Great, Lincs, 1612 Lincs RO Ad/Ac/11/165
Corbridge, William, Hibaldstow, Lincs, 1664 Lincs RO Ad/Ac/42/13
Corderoy, Elizabeth, Compton Chamberlain, Wilts, 1636 Wilts RO Arch. Sarum/(+ name and date)
Corderoy, Thomas, Sulhamstead Bannister, Berks, 1635 Wilts RO CC Sarum(+ name and date)
Corderoy, William, miller, Stoke, North, Oxon, 1669 Oxon RO MSS Wills 163/1/6
Corderoy, William, clergy: 'clerk', Thakeham, Sussex, 1670 W. Suss RO EpI/33/1670/29
Cordery, Richard, Chichester St Pancras, Sussex, 1629 W. Suss RO EpIV/10/1/17
Cordewell, Thomas, Sandwich, Kent, 1617 CKS PRC2/20/56
Cordrey, Elizabeth, widow, Bradfield, Berks, 1606 Berks RO D/A1/181/191C
Cordrey, William, Bray, Berks, 1601 Berks RO D/A1/181/172A
Cordrie, William, Bradfield, Berks, 1592 Berks RO D/A1/181/126C
Cordroie, James, Basildon, Berks, 1597 Berks RO D/A1/181/157A
Cordwine, Stephen, gentleman, Elsham, Lincs, 1645 Lincs RO Ad/Ac/28/158
Core, Thomas, Sutton Valence, Kent, 1612 CKS PRC2/16/17
Corey, Robert, yeoman, Stevenage, Herts, 1674 Herts RO AHH23/449
Corey, Samuel, Harpole, Northants, 1682 Northants RO NWill A/C/52
Corfe, Richard, Winchester St Michael, Hants, 1664 Hants RO 21M65 D8/165
Corfeeld, William, Winscombe, Som, 1626 Somerset RO D/D/Cta/C8
Corfield, Thomas, Cheswardine, Shrops, 1678 LJRO:cards/1678/9
Corke, John, St Nicholas at Wade, Kent, 1679 CKS PRC20/12/294
Corker, George, Kirton, Lincs, 1606 Lincs RO Ad/Ac/7/175
Corker, Thomas, bachelor,

[Corker:]

Guinea 1703 PRO PROB5/1046
Corles, Marie, widow, Garstang (Kirkland), Lancs, 1634 Lancs RO (Name of Deceased) D.R.C.H. 1638
Corne, Henry, Headcorn, Kent, 1593 CKS PRC2/6/168
Corneford, Edward, Botolphs, Sussex, 1632 W. Suss RO EpI/33/1632/3
Cornell, Margaret, widow, Sible Hedingham, Essex, 1740 Greater London RO DL/C/549/126
Corner, Thomas, Wittersham, Kent, 1578 CKS PRC21/3/193
Cornest, Louisa, widow, Sandwich, Kent, 1637 CKS PRC1/1/49
Corning, Thomas, Gainsborough, Lincs, 1635 Lincs RO Ad/Ac/40/17
Cornish, Edward, Boughton under Blean, Kent, 1674 CKS PRC20/12/121
Cornish, John, tailor, Abingdon, Berks, 1628 Berks RO D/A1/182/63C
Cornish, Richard, Linsted, Kent, 1621 CKS PRC2/20/25
Cornish, Thomas, Northaw, Herts, 1634 Herts RO ASA25/4901
Cornish, Thomas, Ashford, Kent, 1644 CKS PRC1/7/25
Cornish, William, yeoman, Ditcheat, Som, 1640 Somerset RO D/D/Cta/C69
Cornishe, Alice, widow, Boughton under Blean, Kent, 1596 CKS PRC21/14/13
Cornishe, Phillipp, Boughton under Blean, Kent, 1588 CKS PRC21/9/36
Cornwail, Richard, Holbeach, Lincs, 1612 Lincs RO Ad/Ac/11/107
Cornwaleys, Henry, clergy: 'clerk', Stockbury, Kent, 1711 CKS PRC1/17/22
Cornwall, Gilbert, Upton on Severn, Worcs, 1647 Worcs RO 008.7 BA3585/837/bdl 1
Cornwell, Betty, Wotton under Edge, Glos, 1825 GRO GDR/B4/2/C112
Cornwell, William, Luddington, Lincs, 1607 Lincs RO Ad/Ac/37/251
Corpe, James, Edington, Som, 1611 Somerset RO D/D/Cta/C49
Correll, William, Eastry, Kent, 1591 CKS PRC21/10/277
Cort, John, Bowden, Great, Leics, 1684 Leics RO Administrators Accounts 1682-86 f13
Cory, John, mercer, Sutton, Long, Lincs, 1683 Lincs RO Ad/Ac/44/59
Cory, Thomas, butcher, Yeovil, Som, 1646 Somerset RO D/D/Cta/C54
Coryn, John, gentleman, Kenwyn, Corn, Cornwall RO AP/C465/2
Cosbie, John, Preston next Wingham, Kent, 1596 CKS PRC2/8/383
Cosby, William, Taunton St Mary Magdalan, Som, 1682 Somerset RO D/D/Cta/C97
Cosbye, John, brewer, Canterbury St Martin, Kent, 1585 CKS PRC21/7/208
Cosen, Edward, yeoman, Beesby, Lincs, 1618 Lincs RO Ad/Ac/14/251
Cosen, Frauncis, Addlethorpe, Lincs, 1635 Lincs RO Ad/Ac/24/343
Cosen, Nicholas, blacksmith, Waltham, Bishops, Hants, 1662 Hants RO 21M65 D8/143
Cosen, Thomas, Sherfield, Hants, 1623 Hants RO 21M65 D8/13
Cosen, William, Fordington, Dors, 1598 Wilts RO Miscellaneous Index to Wills (name + date)
Cosford, Robert, Maidstone, Kent, 1667 CKS PRC19/3/116
Coshe, Robert, Wimborne Minster (Hillbutts), Dors, 1622 Dorset RO PE/WM CP 2/4/27
Cosin, Thomas, husbandman, Downton (Hamptworth), Wilts, 1630 Wilts RO Arch. Sarum/(+ name and date)
Cosine, Willyam, Barnoldby le Beck, Lincs, 1601 Lincs RO Ad/Ac/5/151
Cosnett, John, husbandman, Pershore, Worcs, Worcs RO 008.7 BA3585/838/238
Cossen, Nicholas, Cheriton, Hants, 1672 Hants RO 21m65 D8/238
Cossen, Robert, Ebony, Kent, 1648 CKS PRC1/8/41
Cossens, John, Molash, Kent, 1639 CKS PRC1/2/41
Costall, Anne, widow, Foston, Lincs, 1627 Lincs RO Ad/Ac/20b/28
Costard, William, yeoman, Buckland, Berks, 1662 Berks RO D/A1/183/52
Coste, Richard, Newchurch, Kent, 1601 CKS PRC21/15/141
Coste, Thomas, Newchurch, Kent, 1597 CKS PRC21/14/149
Costow, Richard, Dowsby, Lincs, 1637 Lincs RO Ad/Ac/25/521
Cosyn, Gyles, Canterbury All Saints, Kent, 1586 CKS PRC21/8/177
Cotchett, Roger, St Albans, Herts, 1627 Herts RO ASA25/2943
Cotemore, Thomas, Leigh, North, Oxon, 1628 Oxon RO MSS Wills 296/2/17
Coten, Samuel, Wimborne Minster, Dors, 1614 Dorset RO PE/WM CP 2/4/13
Cotes, Edward, Saltfleetby, Lincs, 1593 Lincs RO Ad/Ac/3/43

[Cotes:]
Cotes, Thomas eld, Gosberton, Lincs, 1587 Lincs RO Ad/Ac/2C/107
Cotgrave, Thomas, gentleman, Chester, Ches, 1800 Cheshire RO (Name) W.C. 1800
Cotgreave, Robert, shopkeeper/innkeeper, Shenstone (Stonall), Staffs, 1803 LJRO/B/C/5/1803/19
Cotmore, Anne, widow, Bampton (Bampton Aston), Oxon, 1628 Oxon RO MSS Wills 296/2/21
Cotmore, William, Norton, Brize, Oxon, 1630 Oxon RO MSS Wills 292/2/26
Cottam, Leonard, shopkeeper, Doncaster, Yorks, 1818 Borthwick Test C.P. 1818/15
Cottam, William, publican, Retford, East, Notts, 1827 Borthwick Test C.P. 1827/4
Cottee, John, innkeeper, Dover, Kent, 1638 CKS PRC20/10/262
Cottell, George, St Keverne, Corn, 1613 Cornwall RO AP/C315
Cotten, William,
Som 1602 Somerset RO D/D/Cta/C21
Cotterell, Nicholas, Morton, Abbots, Worcs, 1601 Worcs RO 008.7 BA3585/838/198
Cottesmore, Cosine, gentleman, Culham, Oxon, 1624 Oxon RO MSS Wills 296/1/124
Cotteye, Berthrame, Sittingbourne, Kent, 1602 CKS PRC2/12/62
Cottingham, John, purveyor, Dowgate, London & Middlesex, 1561 Lambeth Palace Arches F 1a ff255-258
Cottingham, Robert, Owersby, Lincs, 1680 Lincs RO Ad/Ac/34/62
Cottmore, Francis, labourer, Harwell, Berks, 1673 Berks RO D/A1/183/86A
Cotton, Bartholomew, Canterbury St Andrew, Kent, CKS PRC1/1/12b
Cotton, Bartholomew, Canterbury St Andrew, Kent, CKS PRC1/1/12c
Cotton, Bartholomew, Canterbury St Andrew, Kent, 1610 CKS PRC1/1/12a
Cotton, Henry, clergy: 'chancellor of Salisbury Cathedral', Salisbury Cathedral (The Close), Wilts, 1626 Wilts RO Dean Sarum (name + date)
Cotton, John, wool merchant, Canterbury St Margaret, Kent, 1675 CKS PRC2/36/33
Cotton, Richard, chapman, Shepton Mallet, Som, 1609 Somerset RO D/D/Cta/C40
Cotton, Richard, Myddle, Shrops, 1674 LJRO:cards/1674/8
Cotton, Richard, cordwainer: 'shoe manufacturer', Milwich (Coton), Staffs, 1834 LJRO/B/C/5/1834/16b
Cotton, Thomas, Northampton All Saints, Northants, Northants RO NWill A/C/86
Cotton, Thomas, farmer, Bradley (Littywood), Staffs, 1811 LJRO/B/C/5/1811/16
Cotton, William, carpenter, Chester St Oswald, Ches, 1748 Cheshire RO (Name) W.C. 1747-8
Cotton, William, labourer, Tong (Meese Hill), Shrops, 1815 LJRO/B/C/5/1815/18
Cottrell, Robert, Overbury, Worcs, 1603 Worcs RO 008.7 BA3585/839/292
Cottrill, Richard, Crowle, Lincs, 1680 Lincs RO Ad/Ac/43/171
Couchman, Francis, minor, St Peter in Thanet, Kent, 1624 CKS PRC2/23/87
Couchman, John, Rolvenden, Kent, 1627 CKS PRC2/28/32
Couchman, John, Cranbrook, Kent, 1630 CKS PRC2/30/37
Couchman, John, Lydd, Kent, 1666 CKS PRC19/3/92
Couchman, John, Sittingbourne, Kent, 1683 CKS PRC2/40/109
Couchman, John, victualler, Headcorn, Kent, 1691 CKS PRC2/42/2
Couchman, Lawrence, Bethersden, Kent, 1595 CKS PRC2/8/173
Couchman, Matthew, butcher, Cranbrook, Kent, 1673 CKS PRC2/35/206
Couchman, Richard, Cranbrook, Kent, 1584 CKS PRC2/3/191
Couchman, Richard, Headcorn, Kent, 1667 CKS PRC1/12/27
Couchman, Thomas, Cranbrook, Kent, 1629 CKS PRC2/29/21
Couchman, William, fuller, Loose, Kent, CKS PRC20/10/228
Couchman, William, yeoman, Lydd, Kent, 1641 CKS PRC19/1/35
Couell, William, clergy: 'mr/parson', Mersham, Kent, 1614 CKS PRC2/18/114
Couelson, John, yeoman, Hursley, Hants, Hants RO 1663 AD25/2
Coule, George, St Cleer, Corn, 1612 Cornwall RO AP/C296
Coule, Thomas, Milton next Sittingbourne, Kent, 1626 CKS PRC2/25/42
Coulner, Christopher, Birchington, Kent, 1680 CKS PRC20/13/11
Coulner, William, Harbledown, Kent, 1592 CKS PRC2/6/466
Coulner/Coulver, William, Harbledown, Kent, 1597 CKS PRC2/10/486
Coulsey, Peter, yeoman, Themelthorpe, Norf, 1769 Norfolk RO ANW/23/26/17

Coulson, John, waterman, Timberland, Lincs, 1666 Lincs RO Ad/Ac/32/100
Coulson, Robert, yeoman, Hockerton, Notts, 1623 Lincs RO Ad/Ac/18/83
Coulson, Thomas, husbandman, Preston next Wingham, Kent, 1675 CKS PRC2/36/179
Coulson, Thomas, Crowle, Lincs, 1678 Lincs RO Ad/Ac/35/129
Coulson, William, Weston, Lincs, 1649 Lincs RO Ad/Ac/30/241
Coulston, Richard, Winterton, Lincs, 1675 Lincs RO Ad/Ac/35/92
Coulter, John, Ruckinge, Kent, 1608 CKS PRC2/14/103
Coulter, John, Bilsington, Kent, 1627 CKS PRC2/28/23
Coulter, John, grocer, Wye, Kent, 1673 CKS PRC2/35/210
Coulter, Richard eld, Bilsington, Kent, 1628 CKS PRC2/29/20
Coulthirst, William, Liverpool, Lancs, 1799 Lancs RO (Name of Deceased) D.R.C.H. 1798-99
Coultman, Robart, Biddenden, Kent, 1592 CKS PRC2/6/316
Coulton, Richard, cook, Cambridge St Benedict, Cambs, 1610 CUL V.C.Acc./Box1/11
Coulver, see Coulner,
Coumber, John, surgeon: 'barber-surgeon', Tenterden, Kent, 1675 CKS PRC2/36/31
Councer, George, gentleman, Bloxham, Oxon, 1630 Oxon RO MSS Wills 12/3/21
Counly, Edward, tennis court keeper, Cambridge, Cambs, 1671 c. CUL V.C. Acc./Box3/13
Counsell,
    Som Somerset RO D/D/Cta/C6
Counsell, John, Congresbury, Som, 1667 Somerset RO D/D/Cta/C67
Countrey, Richard, Deal, Kent, 1638 CKS PRC20/10/196
Country, Humphrey, Fordwich, Kent, 1623 CKS PRC2/23/73
Couny, Thomas, Frampton, Lincs, 1593 Lincs RO Ad/Ac/3/29
Coupe, Charles, yeoman, Gedney, Lincs, 1634 Lincs RO Ad/Ac/24/45
Coupland, John, yeoman, Mablethorpe, Lincs, 1671 Lincs RO Ad/Ac/35/20
Coupledike, Suzan, Aswarby, Lincs, 1623 Lincs RO Ad/Ac/18/29
Coupleditch, Cook, Horbling, Lincs, 1789 Lincs RO Ad/Ac/45/56
Course, Henrie, Maidstone, Kent, 1628 CKS PRC20/8/101
Court, Clement eld, yeoman, Waltham, Kent, 1661 CKS PRC1/8/96
Court, David, Goodnestone next Wingham, Kent, 1676 CKS PRC20/12/162
Court, Henry, Tamworth, Warks, 1677 Worcs RO 008.7 BA3585/837/bdl 6
Court, Joane, Stone in Oxney, Kent, 1681 CKS PRC2/39/22
Court, John, Ullenhall, Warks, Worcs RO 008.7 BA3585/837/bdl 2
Court, John, Kingston, Kent, 1603 CKS PRC2/14/132
Court, John, cordwainer, Stone in Oxney, Kent, 1677 CKS PRC2/37/127
Court, Robert, yeoman, Reculver, Kent, 1664 CKS PRC19/3/52
Court, Robert, Reculver, Kent, 1725 CKS PRC19/6/69
Court, Sampson, yeoman, Elmsted, Kent, 1671 CKS PRC2/35/32
Court, Stephen, Reculver, Kent, 1693 CKS PRC19/5/19
Court, Thomas, Boxgrove, Sussex, 1673 W. Suss RO EpI/33/1673/27
Court, Thomas, yeoman, Hunston, Sussex, 1678 W. Suss RO EpI/33/1678/7
Court, Thomas, Waltham, Kent, 1699 CKS PRC2/42/140
Court, William, Waltham, Kent, 1639 CKS PRC1/2/42
Court, William, yeoman, Elmsted, Kent, 1662 CKS PRC1/8/97
Court, William, yeoman, Waltham, Kent, 1698 CKS PRC2/42/139
Courte, Daniel, Singleton, Sussex, 1631 W. Suss RO EpI/33/1631/15
Courte, William, Studley, Worcs, 1683 Worcs RO 008.7 BA3585/837/bdl 5
Courte, see Smythe,
Courteney, George, St Michael Penkevil, Corn, 1636 Cornwall RO AP/C887/2
Courteney, Thomas, Middleton, Sussex, 1661 W. Suss RO EpI/33/1661/10
Courthop, Elizabeth, Marden, Kent, 1680 CKS PRC2/39/14
Courthop, John, gentleman, Faversham, Kent, 1590 CKS PRC2/5/159
Courthop, Paull, Hackington, Kent, 1612 CKS PRC2/16/53
Courthop, Peter eld, clothier, Cranbrook, Kent, 1641 CKS PRC19/2/8
Courthop, Richard, Cranbrook, Kent, 1616 CKS PRC20/3/480

[Courthop:]
Courthop, Stephen, innholder, Ashford, Kent, 1678 CKS PRC2/38/20
Courthop, Thomas, Sandwich St Bartholomew's Hospital, Kent, 1592 CKS PRC21/11/298
Courthope, Peter, clothier, Cranbrook, Kent, 1679 CKS PRC2/38/114
Courthopp, Alexander, Goudhurst, Kent, 1599 CKS PRC2/10/169
Courthoppe, Jerome, Sandwich, Kent, 1586 CKS PRC2/4/29
Courthoppe, Margaret, widow, Dover, Kent, 1627 CKS PRC20/8/131
Courthoppe, Thomas, Dymchurch, Kent, 1586 CKS PRC2/4/216
Courtis, William, Hallaton, Leics, 1641 Leics RO PR/I/41A/59
Courtlowe, John, Imber, Wilts, 1674 Wilts RO Arch. Sarum/(+ name and date)
Courtup, Peter, miller, Marden, Kent, 1675 CKS PRC2/36/172
Cousen, Anthony, husbandman, Bourton, Black, Oxon, 1666 Oxon RO MSS Wills 296/3/54
Cousen, Charity, widow, Molash, Kent, 1668 CKS PRC1/13/29
Cousnell/Cozener, Thomas, gentleman, Bradford on Avon, Wilts, 1634 Wilts RO Arch. Sarum/(+ name and date)
Couston, William, Fulstow, Lincs, 1603 Lincs RO Ad/Ac/5/248
Couzens, William, Staughton, Great, Hunts, Hunts RO/Acc58/337
Covell, Abraham, Sevington, Kent, 1625 CKS PRC2/25/40
Covell, Agnes, Luddenham, Kent, 1601 CKS PRC2/12/102
Covell, Alexander, innholder, Queenborough, Kent, 1675 CKS PRC2/36/170
Covell, Edward, Hogsthorpe, Lincs, 1627 Lincs RO Ad/Ac/20b/23
Covell, John, yeoman, Halton Holgate, Lincs, 1606 Lincs RO Ad/Ac/7/38
Covell, John, St Laurence Thanet, Kent, 1626 CKS PRC2/27/34
Covell, John, Croft, Lincs, 1670 Lincs RO Ad/Ac/32/164
Covell, Richard, carpenter, Swineshead, Lincs, 1631 Lincs RO Ad/Ac/23/148
Covell, Richard, yeoman, Burgh le Marsh, Lincs, 1662? Lincs RO Ad/Ac/32/6
Covell, Robert, Sandwich, Kent, 1594 CKS PRC2/7/367
Covell, Thomas, Skirbeck, Lincs, 1635 Lincs RO Ad/Ac/24/393
Coveney, John, Loose, Kent, 1580 CKS PRC21/4/231
Coveney, John, Sutton Valence, Kent, 1633 CKS PRC2/32/28
Coveney, John, gentleman, Hastingleigh, Kent, 1678 CKS PRC2/38/21
Coveney, John, Hinxhill, Kent, 1696 CKS PRC19/5/42
Coveney, William, Headcorn, Kent, 1626 CKS PRC2/27/35
Coventree, Thomas, Rodbourne Cheney, Wilts, 1679 Wilts RO Miscellaneous Index to Wills (name + date)
Coveny, Roger, husbandman, Brook, Kent, 1671 CKS PRC1/15/13
Coverley, Edmund, Faversham, Kent, 1626 CKS PRC2/25/39
Covert, Walter, knight, Maidstone, Kent, 1629 CKS PRC20/8/89
Coward, Eleanor, spinster, Chichester, Sussex, 1633 W. Suss RO EpIII/9/1/44
Coward, John, Gillingham, Dors, 1582? Wilts RO Miscellaneous Index to Wills (name + date)
Coward, John, Pennard, West, Som, 1662 Somerset RO D/D/Cta/C60
Coward, Thomas, Newton, South, Wilts, 1668 Wilts RO Arch. Sarum/(+ name and date)
Cowche, Luke, Endellion, Corn, 1603 Cornwall RO AP/C59
Cowchman, Edward, Cranbrook, Kent, 1600 CKS PRC2/11/191
Cowchman, John,
Kent 1592 CKS PRC21/11/220
Cowdale, William, Gayton, Staffs, 1667 LJRO:cards/1667/19
Cowdrye, Edward, Sidlesham, Sussex, 1622 W. Suss RO EpI/33/1622/2
Cowell, Christopher, Canterbury St George Martyr, Kent, 1677 CKS PRC2/37/23
Cowell, Jonah, draper: 'woollen draper', Faversham, Kent, 1669 CKS PRC1/14/27
Cowell, Joseph, Canterbury St Mary-Magdalen Burgate, Kent, 1624 CKS PRC2/23/80
Cowell, Ralph, Boxley, Kent, 1671 CKS PRC2/35/22
Cowell, Thomas, yeoman, Minster in Thanet, Kent, 1647 CKS PRC1/7/78
Cowell, William, clergy: 'mr/clerk', Sheldwich, Kent, 1625 CKS PRC2/25/41
Cowell, William, Minster in Thanet, Kent, 1675 CKS PRC2/36/177
Cowell, William, mariner, Deal, Kent, 1682 CKS PRC20/13/237

Cowes, James, clergy: 'clerk', Davington, Kent, 1677 CKS PRC20/12/196
Cowland, Gyles, Luddenham, Kent, 1614 CKS PRC2/18/33
Cowland, Joseph, Stalisfield, Kent, 1595 CKS PRC2/7/451
Cowland, Vyncent, Throwleigh, Kent, 1588 CKS PRC2/4/261
Cowlande, Stephen, Luddenham, Kent, 1611 CKS PRC2/16/203
Cowldwell, Thomas, clergy: 'clerk', Salisbury, Wilts, 1618? Wilts RO Miscellaneous Index to Wills (name + date)
Cowle, Elizabeth, Brenzett, Kent, 1608 CKS PRC2/15/83
Cowle, Henrie, Brenzett, Kent, 1608 CKS PRC2/14/108
Cowle, Henrye, New Romney, Kent, 1598 CKS PRC21/14/264
Cowley, George, Wingerworth, Derby, 1672 LJRO:cards/1672/12
Cowley, James, yeoman, Leven, Yorks, Borthwick Test C.P. 1760/2
Cowley, Joane, widow, Pewsey, Wilts, 1640 Wilts RO Arch. Wilts.(name + date)
Cowley, Margaret, widow, Guston, Kent, 1602 CKS PRC21/16/111
Cowley, Mary, Wingerworth, Derby, 1683 LJRO/B/C/5/1682/25
Cowling, George, Draycott in the Moors, Staffs, 1676 LJRO:cards/1676/16
Cowling, Thomas, Hale, Great, Lincs, 1624 Lincs RO Ad/Ac/19A/58
Cowlinge, Humphrey, husbandman, Chadlington, Oxon, 1639 Oxon RO MSS Wills 296/3/8
Cowlson, Thomas, Leake, Lincs, 1614 Lincs RO Ad/Ac/13/89
Cowlter, John, Ashford, Kent, 1617 CKS PRC2/20/41
Cowlye, Margerye, Benenden, Kent, 1612 CKS PRC2/16/12
Cownstabell, John, Hothfield, Kent, 1599 CKS PRC2/10/300
Cowp, Alice, widow, Preston, Lancs, 1637 Lancs RO (Name of Deceased) D.R.C.H. 1640
Cowper, Henry, Newchurch, Kent, 1621 CKS PRC20/5/53
Cowper, John, Rudgwick, Sussex, W. Suss RO EpI/33/1672/1
Cowper, John, Graveney, Kent, 1583 CKS PRC2/3/30
Cowper, John, Appledram, Sussex, 1600 W. Suss RO EpI/33/1600/6
Cowper, John, Rudgwick, Sussex, 1670 W. Suss RO EpI/33/1670/9
Cowper, Robert, physician/mr, Faversham, Kent, 1648 CKS PRC1/8/42
Cowper, Sara, widow, Kenardington, Kent, 1612 CKS PRC2/17/444
Cowper, Thomas, Crundale, Kent, 1586 CKS PRC2/4/379
Cowper, Thomas, Winslow, Bucks, 1602 Herts RO ASA25/4756
Cowper, Thomas, Ockbrook, Derby, 1685 LJRO/B/C/5/1685/31
Cowper, William, tailor, Holbeach, Lincs, 1619 Lincs RO Ad/Ac/15/181
Cowper, William, innkeeper, Sandbach, Ches, 1771 Cheshire RO (Name) W.C. 1771
Cowpere, John, Algarkirk, Lincs, 1574 Lincs RO Ad/Ac/1/12
Cowpis, William, Warblington (Emsworth), Hants, 1623 Hants RO 21M65 D8/12
Cowpledike, Thomas, Well, Lincs, 1637 Lincs RO Ad/Ac/25/627
Cowrlies, Cicelye, Sandwich, Kent, 1604 CKS PRC2/13/144
Cowrthop, Peeter, Cheriton, Kent, 1595 CKS PRC2/9/85
Cox, Alice, widow, Chelwood, Som, 1640 Somerset RO D/D/Cta/C16
Cox, Anne, widow, Wimborne Minster, Dors, 1698 Dorset RO PE/WM CP 2/4/97
Cox, Arthur, Shipton under Wychwood, Oxon, 1639 Oxon RO MSS Wills 296/2/73
Cox, Cuthbert eld, Frome Selwood, Som, 1639 Somerset RO D/D/Cta/C13
Cox, Edward, gentleman, Corston, Som, 1647 Somerset RO D/D/Cta/C55
Cox, Henry, Blagdon, Som, 1634 Somerset RO D/D/Cta/C12
Cox, Henry, Pensford, Som, 1736 Somerset RO D/D/Cta/C93
Cox, James, yeoman, Welford, Berks, 1617 Berks RO D/A1/182/23C
Cox, John, Lyford, Berks, 1602 Berks RO D/A1/181/173A
Cox, John, yeoman, Newton Regis, Warks, 1667 LJRO:cards/1667/21
Cox, John, yeoman, Uffington, Berks, 1673 Berks RO D/A1/183/105A
Cox, John, Yaxley, Hunts, 1676 Hunts RO/Acc58/54(166)
Cox, John, Raveley, Hunts, 1677 Hunts RO/Acc58/109(36)
Cox, John, Canterbury Holy Cross Westgate, Kent, 1681 CKS PRC2/39/157
Cox, John, husbandman, Hampstead Norris, Berks, 1683 Berks RO D/A1/184/29B

[Cox:]
Cox, John, Middleton, Warks, 1685 LJRO/B/C/5/1685/32
Cox, John, Bilsington, Kent, 1698 CKS PRC2/42/127
Cox, John eld, gentleman, Ardington, Berks, 1674 Berks RO D/A1/183/128A
Cox, Joseph, gentleman, Milton next Sittingbourne, Kent, 1684 CKS PRC2/40/188
Cox, Michael, Abingdon, Berks, 1597 Berks RO D/A1/181/159A
Cox, Nicholas, Wimborne Minster, Dors, 1599 Dorset RO PE/WM CP 2/4/1
Cox, Nicholas, Christchurch, Hants, 1673 Hants RO 21m65 D8/258
Cox, Richard, yeoman, Ashbury, Berks, 1670 Berks RO D/A1/183/98D
Cox, Richard, Bilsington, Kent, 1671 CKS PRC2/35/21
Cox, Richard, Brompton, 1674 LJRO:cards/1674/9
Cox, Robert, Hythe St Leonard, Kent, 1576 CKS PRC21/2/369
Cox, Robert, yeoman, Warborough, Oxon, 1669 Oxon RO MSS Wills Pec 66/3/43
Cox, Robert, Salisbury, Wilts, 1693 Wilts RO Miscellaneous Index to Wills (name + date)
Cox, Thomas, Northchapel, Sussex, W. Suss RO EpI/33/1676/15
Cox, Thomas, Congresbury, Som, 1595 Somerset RO D/D/Cta/C73
Cox, Thomas, Northchapel, Sussex, 1676 W. Suss RO EpI/33/1676/29
Cox, Thomas, Alcester, Warks, 1681 Worcs RO 008.7 BA3585/830/71
Cox, William, Mere, Wilts, 1679 Wilts RO Dean Sarum (name + date)
Cox, William, gentleman, Merston, Sussex, 1682 W. Suss RO EpI/33/1682/52
Coxall, Cavelerey, Boston, Lincs, 1683 Lincs RO Ad/Ac/44/112
Coxall, Robert, Waltham on the Wolds, Leics, 1687 Leics RO Administrators Accounts 1682-86 f52
Coxall, Sara, Boston, Lincs, 1640 Lincs RO Ad/Ac/27/90
Coxall, William, Boston, Lincs, 1638 Lincs RO Ad/Ac/25/228
Coxe, Adam, Chilton Foliat, Wilts, 1624 Wilts RO CC Sarum(+ name and date)
Coxe, George, Pillerton Hersey, Warks, 1683 Worcs RO 008.7 BA3585/837/bdl 5
Coxe, Henry, Pershore, Worcs, Worcs RO 008.7 BA3585/838/221
Coxe, Hugh, weaver: 'broad weaver', Melksham, Wilts, 1614? Wilts RO CC Sarum(+ name and date)
Coxe, Jane, Sandwich, Kent, 1625 CKS PRC2/23/50
Coxe, Joan, Hanney, West, Berks, 1603 Berks RO D/A1/181/185C
Coxe, John, Cranbrook, Kent, 1596 CKS PRC2/8/300
Coxe, John, Milton next Sittingbourne, Kent, 1596 CKS PRC2/8/501
Coxe, John, husbandman, Barkham, Berks, 1625 Berks RO D/A1/182/57A
Coxe, Jonathan, Bringhurst, Leics, 1670 Leics RO Administrators Accounts 1667-72 f32
Coxe, Katherine, widow, Moulsford, Berks, 1641 Berks RO D/A1/55/53C
Coxe, Nicholas, Reading, Berks, 1617 Berks RO D/A1/54/19D
Coxe, Nicholas, yeoman, Shrivenham (Bourton), Berks, 1635 Berks RO D/A1/182/40A
Coxe, Robert, Cranbrook, Kent, 1626 CKS PRC2/27/42
Coxe, Robert, Staplehurst, Kent, 1646 CKS PRC1/7/79
Coxe, Thomas, blacksmith, Uffington, Berks, 1633 Berks RO D/A1/182/98C
Cox(e), Thomas, Aldridge, Staffs, 1667 LJRO:cards/1667/20
Coxett, Henry, university: 'scholar's servant', Cambridge St Botolph, Cambs, 1617 CUL V.C.Acc./Box1/12
Coxhead, Anthony, yeoman, Steeping, Great, Lincs, 1619 Lincs RO Ad/Ac/15/296
Coxitor, William, carrier, Abingdon St Helen, Berks, 1607 Berks RO D/A1/181/194A
Coxon, Ellin, widow, Lea, Lincs, 1632 Lincs RO Ad/Ac/39/301
Coxon, Fitzwilliams, blacksmith, Washingborough, Lincs, 1634 Lincs RO Ad/Ac/24/252
Coxon, John, Firsby, Lincs, 1637 Lincs RO Ad/Ac/25/626
Coxon, Richard, Grainthorpe, Lincs, 1671 Lincs RO Ad/Ac/33/173
Coxon, Robert, Wainfleet All Saints, Lincs, 1649 Lincs RO Ad/Ac/30/81
Coy, Richard, Burton Coggles, Lincs, 1601 Lincs RO Ad/Ac/5/437
Coy, William, Swinstead, Lincs, 1587 Lincs RO Ad/Ac/2C/20
Coyfe, Elenor, Blean, Kent, 1607 CKS PRC2/14/97
Coyfe, Richard, Tenterden, Kent, 1582 CKS PRC2/2/148

Coytmor, Arthur, clergy: 'rector', Burmarsh, Kent, 1641 CKS PRC1/5/91
Cozbie, Elizabeth, Smeeth, Kent, 1641 CKS PRC19/2/9
Cozen, Andrew, Wilsthorpe, Lincs, 1636 Lincs RO Ad/Ac/24/568
Cozen, James, Dorrington, Lincs, 1607 Lincs RO Ad/Ac/8a/15
Cozener, Richard,
Som 1640 Somerset RO D/D/Cta/C71
Cozener, see Cousnell,
Cozens, Henry, Hound, Hants, 1624 Hants RO 21M65 D8/61
Cozens/Friend, Mary, widow, Ash next Sandwich, Kent, 1678 CKS PRC20/12/257
Crabb, Salisbury, Wilts, 1619 Wilts RO Miscellaneous Index to Wills (name + date)
Crabb, Edith, Easton, Wilts, 1638 Wilts RO Arch. Wilts.(name + date)
Crabb, Isaac, Bradley, North, Wilts, 1684 Wilts RO Arch. Sarum/(+ name and date)
Crabb, John, husbandman, Linkinhorne, Corn, 1646 Cornwall RO AP/C920/2
Crabb, Walter, Bradley, North, Wilts, 1642 Wilts RO Arch. Sarum/(+ name and date)
Crackell, John, Alkborough, Lincs, 1612 Lincs RO Ad/Ac/10/141
Crackford, John, yeoman, Holme, Hunts, C17th? Lincs RO Ad/Ac/45/95
Cracroft, John, esquire, Hackthorne, Lincs, 1669 Lincs RO Ad/Ac/33/152
Cracroft, Robert, esquire, Hackthorne, Lincs, 1678 Lincs RO Ad/Ac/34/118
Cradocke, John, Milton next Sittingbourne, Kent, 1689 CKS PRC2/41/146
Cradocke, William, Goudhurst, Kent, 1600 CKS PRC2/11/189
Craft, Robert, yeoman, St Peter in Thanet, Kent, 1619 CKS PRC2/23/61
Craft, Susanna, widow, Hoath, Kent, 1719 CKS PRC19/6/70
Crafte, Thomas, Newnham, Kent, 1607 CKS PRC2/14/89
Crafts, Adam, Lenham, Kent, 1676 CKS PRC2/36/175
Cragge, George, yeoman, Thorpe, Lincs, 1626 Lincs RO Ad/Ac/20b/74
Cragge, William, Horsham, Sussex, 1632 W. Suss RO EpI/33/1632/2
Cragge, William, clergy: 'mr/vicar', Hollingbourne, Kent, 1637 CKS PRC20/10/180
Craggill, Mark, Ripon (Winksley), Yorks, Borthwick Test C.P. 1740/2
Craggs, John, Barton, Yorks, Borthwick Test C.P. 1724/5
Cragoe, William, Liskeard, Corn, 1613 Cornwall RO AP/C298
Craicrofte, William, Aswardby, Lincs, 1586 Lincs RO Ad/Ac/2C/124
Crake, James, Ingoldmels, Lincs, 1579 Lincs RO Ad/Ac/2b/13
Crake, James, Ingoldmels, Lincs, 1579 Lincs RO Ad/Ac/2C/126
Crambrok, Henry, St Laurence Thanet, Kent, 1582 CKS PRC2/2/233
Crambroke, Henry, St Laurence Thanet, Kent, 1597 CKS PRC2/9/93
Crambrooke, John, maltster, St Johns Thanet, Kent, 1649 CKS PRC1/8/63
Crambrooke, Stephen, Great Mongeham, Kent, 1638 CKS PRC1/1/50
Cramer, Thomas, Anderby, Lincs, 1619 Lincs RO Ad/Ac/15/45
Cramer/Cramer/Sheene, Brian + Bridgett, Beelsby, Lincs, 1632 Lincs RO Ad/Ac/23/24
Cramer, see Cramer,
Cramford, Samuel, university: 'Fellow of Trinity College, Oxford/M.A.', Oxford (Trinity College), Oxon, 1646 Bodleian HYP B8/35-36
Crammer, Philip, Beaudesert, Warks, Worcs RO 008.7 BA3585/838/140
Cramp, Richard, Harbledown, Kent, 1677 CKS PRC2/37/124
Crampe, Robert, labourer, Hernhill, Kent, 1683 CKS PRC20/13/315
Crampe, William, labourer, Linsted, Kent, 1664 CKS PRC1/10/22
Crampton, Anne, Billingborough, Lincs, 1664 Lincs RO Ad/Ac/43/13
Crampton, Anthony, Willoughby, Silk, Lincs, 1606 Lincs RO Ad/Ac/7/58
Crampton, James, yeoman, Cranbrook, Kent, 1679 CKS PRC2/38/113
Crampton, John, tailor, Cranbrook, Kent, 1664 CKS PRC1/10/23
Crampton, Samuell, clothier, Cranbrook, Kent, 1672 CKS PRC2/35/122
Crampton, William, chandler, Helpringham, Lincs, 1636 Lincs RO Ad/Ac/24/562
Cramton, Thomas, yeoman, Heckington, Lincs, 1666 Lincs RO Ad/Ac/32/108
Cranbroke, Thomas, Nonington, Kent, 1591 CKS PRC21/11/71
Cranbrook, Robert, Newchurch, Kent, 1617 CKS PRC20/3/486

[Cranbrooke:]
Cranbrooke, Roger, Tilmanstone, Kent, 1673 CKS PRC2/35/205
Crane, Agnes, Chedzoy, Som, 1591 Somerset RO D/D/Cta/C22
Crane, Avery, Swinford, Old (Stourbridge), Worcs, 1683 Worcs RO 008.7 BA3585/837/bdl 3
Crane, Edward, coach painter, Bristol, Glos, Bristol RO 1764/CP
Crane, Joane, widow, Appledore, Kent, 1603 CKS PRC21/16/45
Crane, John, innholder, Watton-at-Stone, Herts, 1635 Herts RO AHH23/398
Cranford, Robert, university: 'scholar's servant', Cambridge St Andrew, Cambs, 1607 CUL V.C.Acc./Box1/13
Cranmer, Thomas, Linsted, Kent, 1667 CKS PRC19/4/45
Crann, John, Hardington Mandeville, Som, 1666 Somerset RO D/D/Cta/C66
Crannage, Katherine, widow, Speen (Speenhamland), Berks, 1606 Berks RO D/A1/181/196A
Cranston, Stephen, Holybourne, Hants, 1684 Hants RO 21m65 D8/337
Cranwell, Benedict, Colne, Hunts, 1676 Hunts RO/Acc58/55(144)
Crapon, see Boye,
Crapp, John, St Neot, Corn, 1607 Cornwall RO AP/C136
Crase/Taylor/White, Mary, Ruckinge, Kent, 1662 CKS PRC1/9/18
Crassingham, John, Wittersham, Kent, 1639 CKS PRC19/1/12
Crassingham, John, Wittersham, Kent, 1639 CKS PRC19/1/12a
Crasson, Alice, Kennington, Kent, 1608 CKS PRC2/13/111
Craven, Hammond, labourer, Boultham, Lincs, 1680 Lincs RO Ad/Ac/43/124
Craven, James, farmer, Ebberston, Yorks, 1777 Borthwick Test C.P. 1777/2
Craven, Martha, widow, Bunbury (Calverley), Ches, 1756 Cheshire RO (Name) W.C. 1756
Craven, Richard, cordwainer, Lincoln St Benedict, Lincs, 1639 Lincs RO Ad/Ac/26/57
Crawely, John, Pricklesthorne, Bucks, 1668? Lambeth Palace Arches G25/3
Crawford, Christopher, Sibsey, Lincs, 1666 Lincs RO Ad/Ac/32/122
Crawford, John, yeoman, Barton, Yorks, Borthwick Test C.P. 1729/5
Crawforth, James, Carlton, Great, Lincs, 1601 Lincs RO Ad/Ac/5/258
Crawforth, John, Coningsby, Lincs, 1620 Lincs RO Ad/Ac/16/21
Crawforth, Thomas, Coningsby, Lincs, 1639 Lincs RO Ad/Ac/26/37
Cray, Abraham, clergy: 'clerk', Reading St Lawrence, Berks, 1604 Berks RO D/A1/191/98
Cray, Jane, spinster, Deal, Kent, 1666 CKS PRC19/3/93
Cray, John, husbandman, Locking, Som, 1587 Somerset RO D/D/Cta/C98
Crayford, Edward, esquire, Great Mongeham, Kent, 1618 CKS PRC2/20/112
Crayford, Edwarde, gentleman, Great Mongeham, Kent, 1569 CKS PRC2/1/4
Crayford, Thomas, esquire, Great Mongeham, Kent, 1619 CKS PRC20/4/61
Crayforde, Edwarde, Great Mongeham, Kent, 1576 CKS PRC2/1/169
Crayle, William, Grantham, Lincs, 1618 Lincs RO Ad/Ac/14/296
Crayne, William, Wigtoft, Lincs, 1620 Lincs RO Ad/Ac/16/29
Craythorne, see Grathorne,
Creake, Nicholas, yeoman, Nonington, Kent, 1666 CKS PRC19/3/68
Creake, Percival, Rousham, Oxon, 1638 Oxon RO MSS Wills 296/3/1
Creake, Stephen, Nonington, Kent, 1634 CKS PRC20/10/244
Creake, Timothy, Rousham, Oxon, 1638 Oxon RO MSS Wills 296/2/78
Creasey, Ralph, Scawby, Lincs, 1665 Lincs RO Ad/Ac/41/168
Creckett, John, Sandwich St Mary, Kent, 1669 CKS PRC1/14/28
Creed, William, butcher, Reading St Lawrence, Berks, 1678 Berks RO D/A1/184/10C
Creed, William, yeoman, Minster in Thanet, Kent, 1680 CKS PRC2/39/17
Creffell, Thomas, Lanhydrock, Corn, Cornwall RO AP/C546/4
Cressey, Bryan, yeoman, Scawby, Lincs, 1673 Lincs RO Ad/Ac/35/44
Cressey, James, Crowle, Lincs, C17th? Lincs RO Ad/Ac/45/92
Cressey, Richard, husbandman, Crowle, Lincs, 1670 Lincs RO Ad/Ac/32/139
Cresswell, Richard + Ursula, Basingstoke, Hants, 1625 Hants RO 21M65 D8/111
Creswell, George, Bardney, Lincs, 1636 Lincs RO Ad/Ac/24/265
Creswell, John, yeoman, Wragby, Lincs, 1663 Lincs RO Ad/Ac/43/9
Creswell, John, Shenstone, Staffs, 1676 LJRO:cards/1676/18

Creswell, Thomas, Heckfield, Hants, 1624 Hants RO 21M65 D8/62
Creswell, William, yeoman, Bardney, Lincs, 1636 Lincs RO Ad/Ac/24/395
Cresweller, Francis, Chichester, Sussex, 1604 W. Suss RO EpIII/9/1/2
Cresweller, Joyce, widow, Harting, Sussex, 1635 W. Suss RO EpI/33/1635/8
Crew, Richard, mr, St Margaret Westminster, London & Middlesex, 1707 PRO PROB32/50/102
Crew, Thomas, bachelor, Rainham, Essex, 1730 Greater London RO DL/C/548/43
Cribb, William, husbandman, Martock (Stapleton), Som, 1588 Somerset RO D/D/Cta/C31
Cricke, Robert, Sywell, Northants, 1682 Northants RO NWill A/C/53
Crickett, Daniel, Sandwich, Kent, 1678 CKS PRC2/38/14
Crickman, Richard, Bishopsbourne, Kent, 1618 CKS PRC2/20/118
Cridland, Richard, Monkton, West, Som, 1620 Somerset RO D/D/Cta/C1
Crimble, Charles, gentleman, Tenterden, Kent, 1630 CKS PRC2/30/36
Cripp, William, Ilsley, East, Berks, 1594 Berks RO D/A1/181/140A
Crippen, William, Canterbury St Mary Northgate, Kent, 1666 CKS PRC1/11/114
Crippes, Andrew, Oxford St Mary Magdalene, Oxon, 1640 Oxon RO MSS Wills 296/2/77
Crippes, Thomas, Chislet, Kent, 1589 CKS PRC2/4/517
Crippin, Thomas, carpenter, Sutton Valence, Kent, 1673 CKS PRC2/35/124
Cripps, Edward, husbandman, Minster in Sheppey, Kent, 1649 CKS PRC1/8/64
Cripps, John, Huntspill, Som, 1581 Somerset RO D/D/Cta/C39
Cripps, John, Lydd, Kent, 1606 CKS PRC20/1/107
Cripps, John, Ilsley, East, Berks, 1610 Berks RO D/A1/181/215C
Cripps, Mathew, Hurst, Berks, 1632 Wilts RO Miscellaneous Index to Wills (name + date)
Cripps, Thomas, Mildenhall (Poulton), Wilts, 1631 Wilts RO Arch. Wilts.(name + date)
Crips, Richard, Hythe St Leonard, Kent, 1598 CKS PRC21/15/11
Crisp, George, wine & spirit: 'spirit merchant', Yarm, Yorks, 1826 Borthwick Test C.P. 1824/15
Crisp, Mary, widow, St Alban, London & Middlesex, 1732 Lambeth Palace Arches G103/8
Crispe, Alexander, Sandwich, Kent, 1613 CKS PRC2/17/249
Crispe, Francis, organist, Cambridge St Mary the Less, Cambs, 1680 CUL V.C. Acc./Box3/14
Crispe, Henry, St Johns Thanet, Kent, 1590 CKS PRC2/5/140
Crispe, Henrye, Sandwich St Bartholomew's Hospital, Kent, 1620 CKS PRC20/5/33
Crispe, John, merchant, Sandwich, Kent, 1609 CKS PRC2/15/66
Crispe, John, St Johns Thanet, Kent, 1611 CKS PRC20/2/218
Crispe, Nicolas, St Peter in Thanet, Kent, 1595 CKS PRC2/7/249
Crispe, Richard, Upton on Severn, Worcs, Worcs RO 008.7 BA3585/839/448
Crispe, Richard, gentleman, Lenham, Kent, 1682 CKS PRC2/40/18
Crispe, Robert, Maidstone, Kent, 1667 CKS PRC19/3/117
Crispe, Thomas, draper: 'woollen draper', Canterbury, Kent, 1617 CKS PRC2/20/116
Crispe, William, jurat, Sandwich, Kent, 1596 CKS PRC2/8/449
Crispe, William, Sandwich, Kent, 1604 CKS PRC2/14/130
Crispes, Thomas + John, Minster in Thanet, Kent, 1605 CKS PRC2/14/116
Critch, William, cordwainer, Oxford St Peter le Bailey, Oxon, 1633 Oxon RO MSS Wills 296/2/46
Critchfield, William, husbandman, Goring, Oxon, 1680 Oxon RO MSS Wills 163/1/22
Critchley, George, Maghull, Lancs, 1768 Lancs RO (Name of Deceased) D.R.C.H. 1768
Crockar, John, clergy: 'clerk', Preston next Faversham, Kent, 1684 CKS PRC2/40/103
Crockenden, Daniel, Sandwich St Clement, Kent, 1667 CKS PRC1/12/28
Crockenden, Thomas, mariner, Sandwich St Clement, Kent, 1669 CKS PRC1/14/29
Crockford, Henry, Sonning, Berks, 1596 Wilts RO Miscellaneous Index to Wills (name + date)
Crockford, John, Windsor, New, Berks, 1586 Berks RO D/A2/C24/f6R
Crockwell, Richard, yeoman, Speen (Benham), Berks, 1647 Berks RO D/A1/183/35C
Crodwyn, Erasmus, carpenter, Somerby, Leics, 1640 Leics RO PR/I/41A/36
Croft, Daniel, Boughton under Blean, Kent, 1666 CKS PRC19/3/94
Croft, Davyd, Murston, Kent, 1585 CKS PRC2/4/468
Croft, George, Glastonbury St John, Som, 1684 Somerset RO D/D/Cta/C94
Croft, James, Staveley, Derby, 1684 LJRO/B/C/5/1683/6

[Croft:]
Croft, John, Stone next Faversham, Kent, 1591 CKS PRC2/5/154
Croft, John, gentleman, Boughton under Blean, Kent, 1626 CKS PRC20/7/94
Croft, John, Stone next Faversham, Kent, 1638 CKS PRC2/34/179
Croft, Lyonell, Atherstone, Warks, 1682 LJRO/B/C/5/1682/26
Croft, Mary eld, widow, Appledore, Kent, 1668 CKS PRC1/13/30
Croft, Richard, Tilton, Leics, 1666 Leics RO Administrators Accounts C17th f52
Crofte, Katheryn, widow, Rodmersham, Kent, 1573 CKS PRC2/1/71
Crofte, Thomas, Nettleham, Lincs, 1597? Lincs RO Ad/Ac/37/32
Crofte, Thomas, Pickwell, Leics, 1673 Leics RO Administrators Accounts 1667-72 f129
Crofte, William, Oving, Sussex, 1617 W. Suss RO EpI/33/1617/9
Croftes, Gilbert, Panton, Lincs, 1606 Lincs RO Ad/Ac/7/54
Croftes, John, university: 'scholar's servant', Cambridge (High Ward), Cambs, 1608 CUL V.C.Acc./Box1/14
Crofts, Henry, apothecary, St Ives, Hunts, 1676 Hunts RO/Acc58/75(163)
Croke?, Richard, husbandman, Kidderminster (Habberley), Worcs, 1602 Worcs RO 008.7 BA3585/838/236
Crokenden, Thomas, St Johns Thanet, Kent, 1591 CKS PRC2/5/163
Croker, Michael, Barton, Steeple, Oxon, 1625 Oxon RO MSS Wills 296/2/1
Crompe, Edward, St Johns Thanet, Kent, 1596 CKS PRC2/8/431
Crompe, John, clergy: 'mr/vicar', Thornham, Kent, 1664 CKS PRC1/10/24
Crompe, Vane, Harrietsham, Kent, 1618 CKS PRC2/21/159
Crompton, Richard, merchant, Liverpool, Lancs, 1684 Lancs RO (Name of Deceased) D.R.C.H. 1684
Crompton, Robert, gentleman, Chester St Oswald (Bach), Ches, 1685 Cheshire RO (Name) W.C. 1684
Cronds, David, Denton (Eastry hundred), Kent, 1677 CKS PRC2/37/125
Croney, George, Twickenham, London & Middlesex, 1709 Greater London RO AM/PP/Box 1701-1710 pt (uncatalogued)
Crooche, William, Rodmersham, Kent, 1586 CKS PRC2/3/329
Crooke, Andrew, Aston Rowant (Kingston Blount), Oxon, 1631 Oxon RO MSS Wills 296/2/41
Crooke, Christopher, yeoman, Aston Rowant (Kingston Blount), Oxon, 1667 Oxon RO MSS Wills 162/4/26
Crooke, Edmund, victualler, Watlington, Oxon, 1633 Oxon RO MSS Wills 296/2/49
Crooke, Edmund, husbandman, Murren, Newnham, Oxon, 1673 Oxon RO MSS Wills 163/1/14
Crooke, John, gentleman, Preston, Lancs, 1634 Lancs RO (Name of Deceased) D.R.C.H. 1634
Crooke, John, husbandman, Hinton, Little, Wilts, 1639 Wilts RO Arch. Wilts.(name + date)
Crooke, Mary, Somercoates, South, Lincs, 1638 Lincs RO Ad/Ac/25/348
Crooke, Robert, Chesterfield, Derby, 1663 LJRO:cards/1663/16
Crooke, Thomas, Chisledon, Wilts, 1628 Wilts RO Arch. Wilts.(name + date)
Crooke, Thomas, blacksmith, Benson, Oxon, 1663 Oxon RO MSS Wills Pec 66/3/33
Crooke, William, mariner, Liverpool, Lancs, 1799 Lancs RO (Name of Deceased) D.R.C.H. 1798
Crookes, William, Cranbrook, Kent, 1606 CKS PRC2/13/135
Crooks, Anthony, Kirton, Lincs, 1623 Lincs RO Ad/Ac/18/58
Croom, Dioness, widow, Kelston, Som, 1726 Somerset RO D/D/Cta/C36
Croom, Joseph, Kelston, Som, 1727 Somerset RO D/D/Cta/C95
Croome, Edward, Deverill, Longbridge, Wilts, 1674 Wilts RO Arch. Sarum/(+ name and date)
Croome, Walter, Salisbury St Edmund, Wilts, 1626 Wilts RO Miscellaneous Index to Wills (name + date)
Cropley, John, esquire, Rochester St Margaret, Kent, 1694 PRO PROB5/1185
Croply, John, Newton, Cambs, CUL V.C. Acc./Box3/63
Cropper, Ralfe, Minster in Thanet, Kent, 1602 CKS PRC2/12/92
Crosbie, Francys, Bassingham, Lincs, 1640 Lincs RO Ad/Ac/27/106
Crosbie, Henry, farmer, Cadney, Lincs, 1638 Lincs RO Ad/Ac/25/27
Crosbie, Joseph, Reepham, Lincs, 1662 Lincs RO Ad/Ac/41/110
Crosbie, Robert, Hykeham, North, Lincs, 1587 Lincs RO Ad/Ac/2C/12

Crosby, James, Deal, Kent, 1663 CKS PRC19/3/21
Crosby, John, Morton, Lincs, 1683 Lincs RO Ad/Ac/44/118
Crosby, William, Halton, West, Lincs, 1626 Lincs RO Ad/Ac/39/41
Crosen, William, 1769 Lincs RO Ad/Ac/36/9
Croskhill, John, bricklayer, Caistor, Lincs, 1669 Lincs RO Ad/Ac/42/69
Crosley, Samuel, butcher, Sheffield, Yorks, 1779 Borthwick Test C.P. 1779/3
Crosman, Thomas, Kingston Seymour, Som, 1622 Somerset RO D/D/Cta/C2
Cross, George, shipwright, Liverpool, Lancs, 1769 Lancs RO (Name of Deceased) D.R.C.H. 1769
Cross, John, coachmaker, St Martin in the Fields, London & Middlesex, 1691 PRO PROB32/30/21
Cross, John, smallwareman, Manchester, Lancs, 1773 Lancs RO (Name of Deceased) D.R.C.H. 1773
Crosse, Anthony, yeoman, Norton, Hook, Oxon, 1665 Oxon RO MSS Wills 13/4/39
Crosse, Arthur, labourer, Chadlington, Oxon, 1630 Oxon RO MSS Wills 296/2/31
Crosse, Ellis, gentleman, Fringford, Oxon, 1640 Oxon RO MSS Wills 296/3/9
Crosse, Henry, Warwick St Mary, Warks, Worcs RO 008.7 BA3585/834/455
Crosse, John, Wainfleet, Lincs, 1612 Lincs RO Ad/Ac/11/143
Crosse, John, husbandman, Ambrosden (Arncott), Oxon, 1662 Oxon RO MSS Wills 78/1/44
Crosse, John, Eaton, Leics, 1673 Leics RO Administrators Accounts 1667-72 f96
Crosse, John, husbandman, Fringford, Oxon, 1685 Oxon RO MSS Wills 163/1/45
Crosse, John, weaver, Middleton (Great Lever), Lancs, 1727 Lancs RO (Name of Deceased) D.R.C.H. 1727
Crosse, Richard, Stickney, Lincs, 1634 Lincs RO Ad/Ac/24/51
Crosse, Robert, yeoman, Prees, Shrops, 1674 LJRO:cards/1674/10
Crosse, William, labourer, Shorthampton, Oxon, 1668 Oxon RO MSS Wills 163/1/1
Crosse/Baker, Thomas, husbandman, Brimpton, Berks, 1617 Berks RO D/A1/182/22A
Crossingham/Lock, Elizabeth, widow, Washington, Sussex, 1684 W. Suss RO EpI/33/1684/49
Croswell, Samuel, clergy: 'clerk', Wittersham, Kent, 1671 CKS PRC20/12/7
Croswoode, Robert, Gayton le Marsh, Lincs, 1605 Lincs RO Ad/Ac/6/63
Crottenden, Audrian, widow, St Peter in Thanet, Kent, 1596 CKS PRC2/9/83
Crottoll, Alice, widow, Tenterden, Kent, 1587 CKS PRC2/4/416
Crouch, John, Headcorn, Kent, 1677 CKS PRC2/37/130
Crouch, John eld, Aldington, Kent, 1670 CKS PRC19/4/73
Crouch, Mathew, tanner, Abingdon, Berks, 1603 Berks RO D/A1/181/176A
Crouch, Nicholas, yeoman, Barford, Wilts, 1737 Wilts RO Arch. Sarum/(+ name and date)
Crouch, Thomas, husbandman, Codford St Mary, Wilts, 1625 Wilts RO Arch. Sarum/(+ name and date)
Crouch, Thomas, yeoman, Radley, Berks, 1638 Berks RO D/A1/182/127A
Crouch, Thomas, bachelor, Sevington, Kent, 1675 CKS PRC2/36/178
Crouch, Thomas, gentleman, Rye, Sussex, 1683 PRO PROB32/33/143
Crouch, Thomas, yeoman, Binsey, Oxon, 1713 Oxon RO MSS Wills 296/3/72
Crouch, Thomas eld, Radley, Berks, 1615 Berks RO D/A1/182/15A
Crouch/Acrouch, John, Lydd, Kent, 1625 CKS PRC20/7/351
Crouch, see Gray,
Crouche, Thomas, Rolvenden, Kent, 1616 CKS PRC2/21/152
Croucher, Edward, Doddington, Kent, 1627 CKS PRC2/28/34
Croucher, James, Doddington, Kent, 1663 CKS PRC1/9/98
Croucher, Thomas, Doddington, Kent, 1620 CKS PRC2/20/7
Croucher, William, Whitstable, Kent, 1618 CKS PRC2/20/27
Croucher, William, Midhurst, Sussex, 1684 W. Suss RO EpI/33/1684/26
Croucher, see Cooke,
Crouchley, John, shopkeeper, Winwick (Haydock), Lancs, 1769 Lancs RO (Name of Deceased) D.R.C.H. 1769
Crouchman, George, Wittersham, Kent, 1637 CKS PRC20/10/188
Crouchman, Robart, Orlestone, Kent, 1606 CKS PRC2/14/95

[Crouchman:]
Crouchman, Stephan, Canterbury St George Martyr, Kent, 1616 CKS PRC2/20/97
Crouttall, Alyce, Tenterden, Kent, 1587 CKS PRC2/4/146
Crow, Nathanael, clergy: 'rector', Stoke Climsland, Corn, 1702 Lambeth Palace Arches G52/3
Crow, Roger, Ham, High, Som, 1665 Somerset RO D/D/Cta/C62
Crowch, Christopher, Rodmersham, Kent, 1611 CKS PRC2/16/72
Crowch, Elizabeth, widow, Ashford, Kent, 1616 CKS PRC2/21/147
Crowch, Thomas, Ashford, Kent, 1613 CKS PRC2/16/183
Crowcher, Edward, husbandman, Stalisfield, Kent, 1640 CKS PRC1/4/24
Crowcher, Richard, Millbrook, Hants, 1664 Hants RO 21M65 D8/166
Crowcher, Thomas, Stockbury, Kent, 1627 CKS PRC2/28/33
Crowcher, William, Midhurst, Sussex, 1684 W. Suss RO EpI/33/1684/1
Crowchman, Christopher, Woodchurch, Kent, 1586 CKS PRC21/7/372
Crowchman, Elizabethe, Snave, Kent, 1602 CKS PRC2/12/104
Crowchman, John, Warehorne, Kent, 1594 CKS PRC2/7/279
Crowden, Peter, Allexton, Leics, 1672 Leics RO Administrators Accounts 1667-72 f70
Crowly, Thomas, Milton Bryant, Beds, 1625 Lincs RO Ad/Ac/19B/81
Crowsdell, William, 1592 Lancs RO (Name of Deceased) D.R.C.H. 1592
Crowshaw, Benjamin, Measham, Derby, 1682 LJRO/B/C/5/1682/27
Crowston, Barnett, yeoman, Marsh Chapel, Lincs, 1718 Lincs RO Ad/Ac/45/8
Crowther, Agnes, Winterton, Lincs, 1612 Lincs RO Ad/Ac/8b/2
Crowther, George, clothier, Huddersfield (Longwood), Yorks, 1780 Borthwick Test C.P. 1780/2
Crowther, John, Frinstead, Kent, 1623 CKS PRC2/26/125
Crowther, John, yeoman, Glossop (New Mills), Derby, 1818 LJRO/B/C/5/1819/25
Crowther, William, Uffington, Shrops, 1674 LJRO:cards/1674/11
Croxton, John, carpenter, Godmanchester, Hunts, 1701 Hunts RO/Acc58/289
Croych, Thomas, Ludgershall, Wilts, 1685 Wilts RO Arch. Sarum/(+ name and date)
Croyden, Samuel, Deal, Kent, 1630 CKS PRC20/9/95
Croydon, George, Weston Zoyland, Som, 1639 Somerset RO D/D/Cta/C14
Croydon, Richard, husbandman, Walmer, Kent, 1585 CKS PRC2/3/321
Croydon, Robert eld, usher, Canterbury Christchurch, Kent, 1665 CKS PRC19/3/69
Cruchman, Roger, Warehorne, Kent, 1617 CKS PRC2/20/100
Crump, William, yeoman, Sutton Valence, Kent, 1681 CKS PRC2/39/165
Crumpe, Anthony, yeoman, Bretforton, Worcs, 1602 Worcs RO 008.7 BA3585/838/234
Crumpe, Christofer, St Nicholas at Wade, Kent, 1613 CKS PRC20/2/464
Crumpe, James eld, yeoman, Staplehurst, Kent, 1664 CKS PRC1/10/25
Crumpe, John, Worcester St Martin, Worcs, Worcs RO 008.7 BA3585/834/433
Crumpe, John, Birchington, Kent, 1629 CKS PRC20/8/85
Crumpe, John, Staplehurst, Kent, 1684 CKS PRC2/40/183
Crumpe, Stephen, Herne, Kent, 1608 CKS PRC20/1/302
Crumpe, William, Maidstone, Kent, 1584 CKS PRC21/7/38
Crumpe, William,
Kent 1585 CKS PRC2/3/233
Crumplehere, Richard + Marie, Winterbourne Kingston, Dors, 1597 Wilts RO Miscellaneous Index to Wills (name + date)
Crumpleshere?, Sherbourne?, Dors?, Wilts RO Unlisted Fragment
Crupe?, John, yeoman, Martley, Worcs, 1608 Worcs RO 008.7 BA3585/839/449
Crushe/Dawling, Edward, gentleman, Hythe St Leonard, Kent, 1615 CKS PRC20/3/308
Crust, Thomas, Minster in Sheppey, Kent, 1635 CKS PRC2/33/30
Crust, William, Halton, West, Lincs, 1623 Lincs RO Ad/Ac/8c/10
Cruste, Joane, widow, Minster in Sheppey, Kent, 1617 CKS PRC2/21/156
Crutall, Peter, Rainham, Kent, 1680 CKS PRC2/39/21
Crutchfeild, John, Stoke, South, Oxon, 1630 Oxon RO MSS Wills 296/2/34
Crutchloe, Robert, Rickmansworth, Herts, 1610 Herts RO ASA25/4776
Cruttall, Anthony, Chartham, Kent, 1616 CKS PRC2/20/67
Cruttall, Robert, Tenterden, Kent, 1632 CKS PRC2/31/95

Cruttall, Thomas, Canterbury St Mary Bredman, Kent, 1625 CKS PRC2/25/31
Cruttenden, Anthony, Ruckinge, Kent, 1613 CKS PRC2/17/225
Cruttenden, Elizabeth, Hope All Saints, Kent, 1637 CKS PRC1/1/46
Cruttenden, Henry, blacksmith, Cranbrook, Kent, 1683 CKS PRC2/40/107
Cruttenden, John, High Halden, Kent, 1597 CKS PRC2/9/71
Cruttenden, Josias, High Halden, Kent, 1598 CKS PRC2/9/351
Crux, Helene, High Halstow, Kent, 1598 CKS PRC2/9/425
Crux, John, gentleman, Oare, Kent, 1681 CKS PRC2/39/23
Crux, Jonas, gentleman, Faversham, Kent, 1627 CKS PRC2/28/35
Crux, Marryan, widow, Milton next Sittingbourne, Kent, 1670 CKS PRC1/15/14
Crux, Mary, minor, Borden, Kent, 1618 CKS PRC2/20/15
Crux, Richard, Maidstone, Kent, 1589 CKS PRC21/10/20
Crux, Thomas, High Halstow, Kent, 1616 CKS PRC2/20/3
Cruxe, John, Upchurch, Kent, 1591 CKS PRC2/5/144
Cruxe, John, Rainham, Kent, 1592 CKS PRC2/6/83
Cruxe, Josias, Rainham, Kent, 1602 CKS PRC1/1/1
Cruxe, William, Milton next Sittingbourne, Kent, 1606 CKS PRC2/13/161
Cryer, John, yeoman, Benenden, Kent, 1670 CKS PRC1/14/30
Cryill?, Nicholas, Norton Juxta Twycross, Leics, 1666 Leics RO Administrators Accounts C17th f61
Cryspe, Wyllyam, St Laurence Thanet, Kent, 1586 CKS PRC2/4/92
Cubberly, William, Milton next Sittingbourne, Kent, 1666 CKS PRC1/11/16
Cuckow, Daniell, fellmonger, Ashford, Kent, 1681 CKS PRC2/39/159
Cuckow, John, Charing, Kent, 1683 CKS PRC20/13/323
Cuckson, Henry, millwright, Boston, Lincs, 1666 Lincs RO Ad/Ac/32/98
Cudborne/Cutborne, Anne, widow, Ash next Sandwich, Kent, 1624 CKS PRC20/6/74
Cudbushe, Edward, Marden, Kent, 1614 CKS PRC2/18/102
Cudmore, John, Canterbury, Kent, 1633 CKS PRC2/31/98
Cuff, John, Wells St Cuthbert, Som, Somerset RO D/D/Cta/C57
Cuffe, Adam, Mere, Wilts, 1676 Wilts RO Dean Sarum (name + date)
Cuffe, Francis, Stourton, Wilts, 1674 Wilts RO Arch. Sarum/(+ name and date)
Cuffe, Nicholas, Martock, Som, 1592 Somerset RO D/D/Cta/C78
Cuffley, John, Hexton, Herts, 1621 Herts RO ASA25/2585
Culivord, William, Kingsbury Episcopi, Som, 1587 Somerset RO D/D/Cta/C26
Cull, Stephen, yeoman, Scampton, Lincs, 1681 Lincs RO Ad/Ac/34/76
Cullambine, Elizabeth, Appledore, Kent, 1637 CKS PRC2/34/29
Culledge, Andrew, Langtoft, Lincs, 1638 Lincs RO Ad/Ac/25/3
Cullen, Gregory, Fordwich, Kent, 1692 CKS PRC2/42/29
Cullen, Henry, Ospringe, Kent, 1677 CKS PRC2/37/126
Cullen, John, St Nicholas at Wade, Kent, 1675 CKS PRC20/12/120
Cullen, Marke eld, gentleman, Faversham, Kent, 1680 CKS PRC2/39/16
Cullen, Mathew, Tunstall, Kent, 1646 CKS PRC1/7/43
Cullen, Thomas, Stowting, Kent, 1619 CKS PRC2/20/114
Cullin, Raphe, Lower Hardres, Kent, 1634 CKS PRC2/32/24
Cullin, Thomas, Stone in Oxney, Kent, 1629 CKS PRC2/30/31
Culling, Edward, Harbledown, Kent, 1628 CKS PRC2/29/24
Culling, Elizabeth, widow, Newington next Hythe, Kent, 1639 CKS PRC1/2/43
Culling, Henry, yeoman, Ospringe, Kent, 1641 CKS PRC1/4/25
Culling, John, Tilmanstone, Kent, 1581 CKS PRC2/1/282
Culling, John, Orlestone, Kent, 1625 CKS PRC2/25/35
Culling, Matthew, Canterbury St Mary Northgate, Kent, 1616 CKS PRC2/20/75
Culling, Richard, husbandman, Chillenden, Kent, 1682 CKS PRC2/40/15
Culling, Thomas, Chartham, Kent, 1604 CKS PRC2/14/123
Culling, Thomas, New Romney, Kent, 1604 CKS PRC21/17/373
Culling, Thomas, Dover, Kent, 1627 CKS PRC20/8/141

[Culling:]
Culling, William, Sutton Valence, Kent, CKS PRC1/2/44a
Culling, William, Sutton Valence, Kent, 1640 CKS PRC1/2/44
Culling, William, Sutton Valence, Kent, 1641 CKS PRC1/4/26 and 26a
Cullinge, Henry, Worth, Kent, 1595 CKS PRC21/14/9
Cullinge, Henry, Upper Hardres, Kent, 1621 CKS PRC2/23/69
Cullinge, Thomas, Northbourne, Kent, 1583 CKS PRC2/2/267
Cullis, Thomas, haulier, Gloucester, Glos, 1828 GRO GDR/B4/2/C133
Culmer, Daniel, mariner, St Peter in Thanet, Kent, 1696 CKS PRC2/42/114
Culmer, Ellen, widow, St Johns Thanet, Kent, 1628 CKS PRC2/29/27
Culmer, Jeremiah, mariner, St Johns Thanet, Kent, 1689 CKS PRC2/41/118
Culmer, John, brewer, Birchington, Kent, 1669 CKS PRC19/4/46
Culmer, John, pilot, Deal, Kent, 1674 CKS PRC20/12/73
Culmer, Leonard, mariner, Sandwich, Kent, 1642 CKS PRC1/6/56
Culmer, Leonard, Sandwich, Kent, 1643 CKS PRC1/6/101
Culmer, Margaret, St Peter in Thanet, Kent, 1631 CKS PRC2/31/18
Culmer, Mary, widow, St Johns Thanet, Kent, 1691 CKS PRC2/42/1
Culmer, Stephen, Birchington, Kent, 1691 CKS PRC19/4/115
Culmer, Thomas, St Johns Thanet, Kent, 1598 CKS PRC2/10/414
Culmer, Thomas, yeoman, Birchington, Kent, 1702 CKS PRC19/6/2
Culmer, Valentine, St Peter in Thanet, Kent, 1627 CKS PRC2/27/40
Culmer, Valentine, St Peter in Thanet, Kent, 1631 CKS PRC2/31/20
Culmer, William, Monkton, Kent, 1691 CKS PRC19/5/1
Culpepper, John, Hernhill, Kent, 1625 CKS PRC20/7/355
Culver, William, Sandwich St Peter, Kent, 1674 CKS PRC2/36/37
Culver, see Calver,
Culverden, William, Fawley, Hants, 1672 Hants RO 21m65 D8/239
Culverhouse, Alice, widow, St Peter in Thanet, Kent, 1602 CKS PRC2/12/428
Culverhowse, John, Woodnesborough, Kent, 1598 CKS PRC2/10/210
Culverhowse, Thomas, Ickham, Kent, 1588 CKS PRC21/10/293
Culverhowse, Thomas, minor?, Ash next Sandwich, Kent, 1595 CKS PRC21/13/198
Cumberlage, John, Cheddleton, Staffs, 1680 LJRO:cards/1680/9
Cumberland, William, Canterbury St Andrew, Kent, 1683 CKS PRC2/40/12
Cumberpatch, John, horner, Bristol, Glos, Bristol RO 1689/CP
Cumberworth, Thomas, Hale, Great, Lincs, 1612 Lincs RO Ad/Ac/11/2
Cumfort, Thomas, Stone in Oxney, Kent, 1622 CKS PRC2/23/68
Cundey, William, Derby, Derby, 1685 LJRO/B/C/5/1685/33
Cunduit, Michaell, Ashby de la Zouch, Leics, 1673 Leics RO Administrators Accounts 1667-72 f94
Cuniworth, William, Foston, Lincs, 1644 Lincs RO Ad/Ac/28/84
Cunley, John, Smeeth, Kent, 1681 CKS PRC20/13/115
Cuntrey, Mary, Deal, Kent, 1640 CKS PRC20/10/254
Cuntrie, Marie, widow, Deal, Kent, 1640 CKS PRC19/1/29
Cuntry, Thomas, Deal, Kent, 1627 CKS PRC20/8/149
Cuppage, Joseph, tailor, Westwell, Kent, 1683 CKS PRC20/13/317
Cupper, William, Shelsey, Worcs, 1602 Worcs RO 008.7 BA3585/838/231
Curd, Edward, Hartlip, Kent, 1681 CKS PRC2/39/160
Curle, John, university: 'Fellow of Magdalen College, Oxford/M.A.', Oxford (Magdalen College), Oxon, 1672 Bodleian HYP B8/37-38
Curles, William, Canterbury St George Martyr, Kent, 1637 CKS PRC2/34/40
Curling, Edward, St Peter in Thanet, Kent, 1612 CKS PRC2/16/9
Curling, George, Lydd, Kent, 1616 CKS PRC20/3/318
Curling, Henry, Newington next Sittingbourne, Kent, 1622 CKS PRC2/23/67
Curling, John, St Laurence Thanet, Kent, 1603 CKS PRC21/17/39
Curling, John, gentleman, St Johns Thanet, Kent, 1641 CKS PRC1/5/92
Curling, John, mariner, St Laurence Thanet, Kent, 1682 CKS PRC2/40/13

Curling, Margaret, St Laurence Thanet, Kent, 1639 CKS PRC2/34/189
Curling, Robert, Headcorn, Kent, 1603 CKS PRC2/12/427
Curling, Stephen, St Laurence Thanet, Kent, 1623 CKS PRC2/23/66
Curling, William, St Laurence Thanet, Kent, 1596 CKS PRC2/8/71
Curling, William, maltster, St Peter in Thanet, Kent, 1640 CKS PRC1/2/45
Curling, see Church,
Curlinge, An, widow, St Laurence Thanet, Kent, 1623 CKS PRC2/23/76
Curlinge, Nicholas, fisherman, St Laurence Thanet, Kent, 1623 CKS PRC2/23/70
Curll, William, Acle, Norf, 1821 Norfolk RO ANW/23/27/22
Curnock, William, Freshford, Som, 1588 Somerset RO D/D/Cta/C30
Currant, William, Therfield, Herts, 1638 Herts RO AHH23/408
Curre, Anthony, husbandman, Welford (Weston), Berks, 1626 Berks RO D/A1/182/54A
Cursell, Mary, widow, Newbury, Berks, 1629 Berks RO D/A1/182/70A
Curson, Elizabeth, widow, Bampton (Brighthampton), Oxon, 1636 Oxon RO MSS Wills 296/2/64
Curson, Robert, university: 'scholar's servant', Cambridge Holy Sepulchre, Cambs, 1622 CUL V.C. Acc./Box2/17
Curteis, Mildred, widow, Ashford, Kent, 1683 CKS PRC2/40/102
Curteys, Richard, Sittingbourne, Kent, 1613 CKS PRC2/18/71
Curtice, Robert, yeoman, Torrington, West, Lincs, 1672 Lincs RO Ad/Ac/43/180
Curtice, Robert, Kingston Deverill, Wilts, 1704 Wilts RO Arch. Sarum/(+ name and date)
Curties, Barnabe, Kilkhampton, Corn, 1613 Cornwall RO AP/C303
Curties, Martha, widow, Dover, Kent, 1677 CKS PRC20/12/231
Curtin, Henry, cordwainer, Abingdon St Helen, Berks, 1635 Berks RO D/A1/182/104A
Curtin, John eld, yeoman, Sutton Courtenay, Berks, 1628 Berks RO D/A1/54/145D
Curtis, Daniell, Tenterden, Kent, 1624 CKS PRC20/6/68
Curtis, Elizabeth, widow, High Halstow, Kent, 1636 CKS PRC2/33/25
Curtis, Elizabeth, mrs, Tenterden, Kent, 1682 CKS PRC2/40/17
Curtis, Francis, gentleman, Woodchurch, Kent, 1641 CKS PRC19/2/10
Curtis, George, Winkfield, Berks, 1610 Berks RO D/A1/181/219A
Curtis, George, Downton, Wilts, 1639 Wilts RO Arch. Sarum/(+ name and date)
Curtis, Joane, widow, Seend (Seend Row), Wilts, 1609 Wilts RO Arch. Sarum/(+ name and date)
Curtis, John, Minster in Sheppey, Kent, 1620 CKS PRC2/21/161
Curtis, John, Stickney, Lincs, 1651 Lincs RO Ad/Ac/29/123
Curtis, John, mariner, Hythe St Leonard, Kent, 1669 CKS PRC19/4/47
Curtis, John, Goring, Sussex, 1670 W. Suss RO EpI/33/1670/30
Curtis, John, brewer?, St Botolph without Aldgate, London & Middlesex, 1673 PRO PROB32/10/219
Curtis, John, yeoman, Burghfield, Berks, 1673 Berks RO D/A1/183/83A
Curtis, John, Bluntisham, Hunts, 1680 Hunts RO/Acc58/153(176)
Curtis, John, Glatton, Hunts, 1680 Hunts RO/Acc58/147(32)
Curtis, Michael, cooper, Bristol St Stephen, Glos, Bristol RO 1697/82
Curtis, Peeter, New Romney, Kent, 1619 CKS PRC20/4/69
Curtis, Richard, yeoman, Sutton Courtenay, Berks, 1644 Berks RO D/A1/183/12A
Curtis, Robert, Tetford, Lincs, 1625 Lincs RO Ad/Ac/19A/21
Curtis, Robert, jurat/gentleman, Tenterden, Kent, 1641 CKS PRC19/1/36
Curtis, Samuel, Chewton Mendip, Som, 1738 Somerset RO D/D/Cta/C96
Curtis, Suzanna, minor, Dover, Kent, 1644 CKS PRC19/2/88
Curtis, Thomas, clothier, Tenterden, Kent, 1624 CKS PRC20/6/64
Curtis, Thomas, High Halstow, Kent, 1636 CKS PRC2/33/32
Curtis, William, Woodchurch, Kent, 1622 CKS PRC20/6/402
Curtis/Dynis, Elizabeth, Coates, Great, Lincs, 1637 Lincs RO Ad/Ac/25/400
Curtize, John, Kirby, West (Caldey), Ches, 1623 Cheshire RO (Name) W.C. 1623
Curtys, William, Glatton, Hunts, 1597 Hunts RO/Acc58/1(54)
Cushman, James, labourer, New Romney, Kent, 1616 CKS PRC20/3/314
Cushman, Thomas, Loose, Kent, 1625 CKS PRC20/7/347

[Cushman:]
Cushman, Thomas ygr, Cranbrook, Kent, 1638 CKS PRC2/34/187
Cusson, William, husbandman, Glentworth, Lincs, 1662 Lincs RO Ad/Ac/41/36
Cutbarte, John, Frampton, Lincs, 1600 Lincs RO Ad/Ac/5/472
Cutberde, William, Eastchurch, Sheppey, Kent, 1600 CKS PRC2/11/381
Cutbert, Catherine, widow, Friskney, Lincs, 1638 Lincs RO Ad/Ac/25/217
Cutberte, Edward, tailor, Frampton, Lincs, 1632 Lincs RO Ad/Ac/23/166
Cutborne, see Cudborne,
Cutbush, Edward, Newenden, Kent, 1671 CKS PRC2/35/23
Cutbush, Edward eld, Newenden, Kent, 1643 CKS PRC1/6/102
Cutbushe, Thomas, Maidstone, Kent, 1612 CKS PRC20/2/410
Cutforth, John, Epworth, Lincs, 1678 Lincs RO Ad/Ac/35/130
Cutforth, John, Epworth, Lincs, 1682 Lincs RO Ad/Ac/44/26
Cuthbert, John, yeoman, Friskney, Lincs, 1672 Lincs RO Ad/Ac/43/70
Cuthbert, John, husbandman, Whaplode, Lincs, 1684 Lincs RO Ad/Ac/44/146
Cutler, Edward, labourer, Upchurch, Kent, 1678 CKS PRC2/37/132
Cutler, John, Remenham (Strowdes), Berks, 1612 Berks RO D/A1/182/8A
Cutt, Simon, Sutton St James, Lincs, 1599 Lincs RO Ad/Ac/5/326
Cutte, Margaret, Donington, Lincs, 1580 Lincs RO Ad/Ac/2b/68
Cutter, Lawrence, blacksmith, Saltwood, Kent, 1585 CKS PRC21/7/189
Cutter, Stephen, Saltwood, Kent, 1613 CKS PRC20/2/416
Cutting, James, miller?, Battersea, Surrey, 1682 PRO PROB32/21/6
Cuttle, William, Calne, Wilts, 1639 Wilts RO Miscellaneous Index to Wills (name + date)
Cuttle, Zacharie, Stratfield Mortimer, Berks, 1599 Berks RO D/A1/181/168A
Cuttler, James, St Michael Bassishaw, London & Middlesex, 1688 PRO PROB5/1391
Cuttler, John, husbandman, Stourpaine, Dors, 1671 Wilts RO Dean and Chapter H7
Cuttluffe, Charles, chapman, Bardney, Lincs, 1625 Lincs RO Ad/Ac/19B/74
Cuttriss, Jeremiah, Norwich, Norf, 1806 Norfolk RO ANW/23/27/5
Dabbes, Edward, Wye, Kent, 1600 CKS PRC2/12/130
Dabbes, Elizabeth, Thornham, Kent, 1620 CKS PRC2/21/141
Dabbs, Richard, Maidstone, Kent, 1631 CKS PRC20/9/125
Daber, Richard, Newenden, Kent, 1579 CKS PRC21/4/60
Dabson, Solomon, Marden, Kent, 1615 CKS PRC2/21/121
Dacers, Martin, Brothertoft, Lincs, 1613 Lincs RO Ad/Ac/12/17
Dad, William, St Peter in Thanet, Kent, 1633 CKS PRC2/32/38
Dadd, Stephen, Selling, Kent, 1620 CKS PRC2/21/128
Dadd, Thomas, yeoman, Newington next Sittingbourne, Kent, 1671 CKS PRC1/15/15
Dadd, William, Lympne, Kent, 1679 CKS PRC2/38/119
Daddie, Helene, widow, Appleby, Lincs, 1619 Lincs RO Ad/Ac/8b/357
Daddie, Julian, Appleby, Lincs, 1634 Lincs RO Ad/Ac/40/45
Dadds, William, St Laurence Thanet, Kent, 1623 CKS PRC2/23/98
Dade, Robert, Littlebourne, Kent, 1665 CKS PRC1/11/17
Dadson, John, High Halstow, Kent, 1637 CKS PRC2/34/43
Daffern, Yestus, farmer, Nuneaton, Warks, 1807 LJRO/B/C/5/1807/13
Daffey, Anthony, mr, 1685 PRO PROB32/25/259
Dafte, Humfrey, Kirkby on Bain, Lincs, 1633 Lincs RO Ad/Ac/24/201
Daggett, William, university: 'Fellow of Sidney Sussex College, Cambridge/B.D./priest' Cambridge (Sidney Sussex College), Cambs, 1649 CUL V.C. Acc./Box3/15
Dagnall, John, Tring, Herts, 1636 Herts RO AHH23/633
Daie, Richard, Tenterden, Kent, 1617 CKS PRC2/21/132
Dailes, Richard, labourer, Bratoft, Lincs, 1626 Lincs RO Ad/Ac/20/70
Daines, George, Lenham, Kent, 1623 CKS PRC2/23/100
Daintith, William, Milton next Sittingbourne, Kent, 1632 CKS PRC2/31/23
Daives/Davis, Mary, widow, Isleworth, London & Middlesex, 1764 Greater London RO DL/C/554/159/2
Dakins, Robert, St Botolph without Aldgate, London & Middlesex, 1727 Lambeth Palace Arches

G98/4
Dakyn, Samuel, Ashbourne, Derby, 1682 LJRO/B/C/5/1682/28
Dakyn, Sarah, Ashbourne, Derby, 1682 LJRO/B/C/5/1682/29
Dalbie, Ann, Langley, Kirk, Derby, 1667 LJRO:cards/1667/23
Dalbie, John, glazier, Newbury, Berks, 1611 Berks RO D/A1/186/94C
Dalbney, Roger, husbandman, Canwick, Lincs, 1580 Lincs RO Ad/Ac/2b/60
Dalby, Francis, apothecary, Melton Mowbray, Leics, 1667 Leics RO Administrators Accounts 1667-72 f4
Dalby, Hamond, yeoman, Wainfleet St Mary, Lincs, 1668 Lincs RO Ad/Ac/33/62
Dalby, James, mariner, York, Yorks, 1830 Borthwick Test C.P. 1829/2
Dalby, John, yeoman, Wainfleet, Lincs, 1668 Lincs RO Ad/Ac/33/63
Dalby, Thomas, Appleby, Lincs, 1624 Lincs RO Ad/Ac/19A/125
Dale, Andrew, gentleman, Lincoln St Peter in Eastgate, Lincs, 1668 Lincs RO Ad/Ac/33/50
Dale, Christopher, Wimborne Minster, Dors, 1625 Dorset RO PE/WM CP 2/4/36
Dale, Christopher, Brothertoft, Lincs, 1641 Lincs RO Ad/Ac/27/221
Dale, Deborah, widow, Pinchbeck, Lincs, 1664 Lincs RO Ad/Ac/43/48
Dale, Edward, Sefton (Down Litherland), Lancs, 1723 Lancs RO (Name of Deceased) D.R.C.H. 1723
Dale, John, Wimborne Minster, Dors, 1619 Dorset RO PE/WM CP 2/4/21
Dale, John, Branston, Lincs, 1623 Lincs RO Ad/Ac/18/72
Dale, John, gentleman, Hollingbourne, Kent, 1629 CKS PRC20/8/161
Dale, John, yeoman, Staple next Wingham, Kent, 1675 CKS PRC20/12/166
Dale, John, Frampton, Lincs, 1683 Lincs RO Ad/Ac/44/88
Dale, John, clergy: 'rector', Standlake, Oxon, 1685 Oxon RO MSS Wills 124/4/17
Dale, Margery, widow, Loxton, Som, 1634 Somerset RO D/D/Cta/D23
Dale, Mary, widow, Bucknall, Staffs, 1805 LJRO/B/C/5/1805/5
Dale, Robert, Maltby le Marsh, Lincs, 1627 Lincs RO Ad/Ac/20b/88
Dale, Rowland, Smisby, Derby, 1706 LJRO/B/C/5/1708/14
Dale, Thomas, Wimborne Minster, Dors, Dorset RO PE/WM CP 2/4/39
Dale, Thomas, mariner: 'sailor', Sandwich St Clement, Kent, 1637 CKS PRC1/1/47
Dale, Thurston, yeoman, Leek, Staffs, 1783 LJRO/B/C/5/1783/59
Dale, William, Dowsby, Lincs, 1579 Lincs RO Ad/Ac/2b/63
Dale, William, Wyberton, Lincs, 1612 Lincs RO Ad/Ac/10/138
Dale, William, Swaton, Lincs, 1625 Lincs RO Ad/Ac/19B/43
Dale, William, glass merchant/widower, Yarm, Yorks, 1831 Borthwick Test C.P. 1831/6
Dale, Willyam, clergy: 'clerk', Hagworthingham, Lincs, 1639 Lincs RO Ad/Ac/26/61
Dales, John, Tothill, Lincs, 1683 Lincs RO Ad/Ac/44/122
Daliell, Robert, clergy: 'rector', St Ann Blackfriars & Chelsea, London & Middlesex, PRO PROB32/15/145
Daling, John, Sandwich St Mary, Kent, 1626 CKS PRC2/27/43
Dallifield, William, St Martin in the Fields, London & Middlesex, 1695 Greater London RO AM/CP/Box 1696-1720 pt (uncatalogued)
Dally, Edward, Edington, Som, 1619 Somerset RO D/D/Cta/D18
Dally, Thomas, Brookland, Kent, 1613 CKS PRC2/17/285
Dalmer, George, Keevil, Wilts, 1646 Wilts RO Arch. Sarum/(+ name and date)
Dalton, Henrie, joiner, Holbeach, Lincs, 1619? Lincs RO Ad/Ac/18/88
Dalton, Henry, farmer, Dronfield (Totley), Derby, 1814 LJRO/B/C/5/1814/13
Dalton, John, clergy: 'clerk', Fiskerton, Lincs, 1662 Lincs RO Ad/Ac/41/44
Dalton, Robert, Moorlinch, Som, 1642 Somerset RO D/D/Cta/D20
Dalton, Roger, Thurlby, Lincs, 1678 Lincs RO Ad/Ac/42/77
Daltone, Lancelott, Aylesby, Lincs, 1598 Lincs RO Ad/Ac/4/97
Daltonne, Robert, Horncastle, Lincs, 1587 Lincs RO Ad/Ac/2C/7
Dambrell, John, mariner, Dover St Mary, Kent, 1641 CKS PRC19/1/37
Dambrell, Robert, mariner, Dover, Kent, 1642 CKS PRC19/2/53
Damm, Henry, Edensor, Derby, 1684 LJRO/B/C/5/1685/34

[Damman:]
Damman, Henry, mariner, Dover, Kent, 1625 CKS PRC20/7/371
Dammon, William, Faversham, Kent, 1676 CKS PRC2/37/29
Damon, William, St Nicholas at Wade, Kent, 1624 CKS PRC20/6/58
Damport, Edmund, yeoman, Taynton, Oxon, 1633 Oxon RO MSS Wills 18/1/13
Damsell, William, yeoman, Bisley, Glos, 1788 GRO GDR/B4/2/D38
Dan, James, Harrietsham, Kent, 1637 CKS PRC2/34/46
Dan, James, carpenter, Marden, Kent, 1681 CKS PRC2/39/167
Dan, John, husbandman, Marden, Kent, 1677 CKS PRC2/37/138
Dan, Robart, Boughton Monchelsea, Kent, 1596 CKS PRC2/8/244
Danbie, Thomas, gentleman, Bottesford, Lincs, 1632 Lincs RO Ad/Ac/39/307
Danby, William, Rasen, Middle, Lincs, 1607 Lincs RO Ad/Ac/8a/3
Dancaster, William, Stanford in the Vale, Berks, 1611 Berks RO D/A1/186/95C
Dance, George, Carlton, South, Lincs, 1682 Lincs RO Ad/Ac/42/85
Dance, Robert, husbandman, Riby, Lincs, 1666 Lincs RO Ad/Ac/32/101
Dancer, Daniell, Fulham, London & Middlesex, 1704 Greater London RO DL/C/545/9
Danckester, Richard, St Peter in Thanet, Kent, 1626 CKS PRC2/25/48
Dand, Michael, joiner, Sheffield, Yorks, 1838 Borthwick Test C.P. 1838/2
Dandisonne, Geffrey, Wainfleet, Lincs, 1579 Lincs RO Ad/Ac/2b/5
Dando, Avis + Anne, Paulton, Som, 1600 Somerset RO D/D/Cta/D45
Dandridge, John, yeoman, Aston Tirrold, Berks, 1628 Berks RO D/A1/186/129A
Dane, John, Challock, Kent, 1584 CKS PRC21/7/7
Dane, Marie, spinster, Throwleigh, Kent, 1633 CKS PRC2/32/37
Dane, Richard, Skidbrooke, Lincs, 1593 Lincs RO Ad/Ac/3/97
Dane, Robert, Rodmersham, Kent, 1709 CKS PRC1/17/3
Dane, Sara, Fordwich, Kent, 1594 CKS PRC2/7/49
Dane, Thomas, Challock, Kent, 1594 CKS PRC21/13/30
Dane, William, Hythe St Leonard, Kent, 1606 CKS PRC20/1/140
Danes, John, Frittenden, Kent, 1692 CKS PRC2/42/31
Dangerfield, Richard, Calne, Wilts, 1597 Wilts RO Miscellaneous Index to Wills (name + date)
Daniel, Richard, Ardington, Berks, 1612 Berks RO D/A1/186/98A
Daniel, Thomas, Davington, Kent, 1675 CKS PRC2/36/38
Daniel, William, gentleman, Cheadle, Staffs, 1819 LJRO/B/C/5/1819/64
Daniell, Adam, Lockinge, East, Berks, 1614 Wilts RO CC Sarum(+ name and date)
Daniell, Christopher, Upton Scudamore, Wilts, 1640 Wilts RO Arch. Sarum/(+ name and date)
Daniell, Francis, tailor, Snargate, Kent, 1684 CKS PRC2/40/196
Daniell, James, Bridgewater (East Bower), Som, 1663 Somerset RO D/D/Cta/D26
Daniell, John, Beaminster, Dors, 1631 Wilts RO Miscellaneous Index to Wills (name + date)
Daniell, John eld, gentleman, Faversham, Kent, 1629 CKS PRC20/8/165
Daniell, Richard, Basingstoke, Hants, 1669 Hants RO 21m65 D8/214
Daniell, William, Saltwood, Kent, 1662 CKS PRC19/3/2
Danks, Thomas, Rainham, Kent, 1682 CKS PRC2/40/20
Dankyn, Mary, Canterbury St Peter, Kent, 1623 CKS PRC2/23/99
Danne, George, husbandman, Sutton Valence, Kent, 1639 CKS PRC1/2/46
Danne, Joane, widow, Marden, Kent, 1636 CKS PRC2/33/39
Danne, Richard, Chislet, Kent, 1627 CKS PRC2/28/37
Dannett, Fretzwill, yeoman, Laceby, Lincs, 1649 Lincs RO Ad/Ac/30/106
Dannot, William, Rasen, Market, Lincs, 1605 Lincs RO Ad/Ac/6/54
Dans, John, draper: 'woollen draper', Newbury, Berks, 1670 Berks RO D/A1/187/21C
Danser, John, gentleman, Doncaster, Yorks, 1805 Borthwick Test C.P. 1805/9
Danson, Elen, widow, Stalmine (Staynall), Lancs, 1631 Lancs RO (Name of Deceased) D.R.C.H. 1631
Danson, Thomas, Stayno, Lancs, 1631 Lancs RO (Name of Deceased) D.R.C.H. 1631
Danyel, Stephan, Kenwyn, Corn, 1615 Cornwall RO AP/D137/2
Danyell, Anne, Shipley, Sussex, 1640 W. Suss RO EpI/33/1640/24
Danyell, Joane, widow, Faversham, Kent, 1599 CKS PRC2/11/203

Danyell, Thomas, Iwade, Kent, 1611 CKS PRC2/16/191
Danyell, Thomas, Burslem, Staffs, 1663 LJRO:cards/1663/17
Darbie, Henrye, Upton (Kexby), Lincs, 1611 Lincs RO Ad/Ac/8a/334
Darbie, Richard, husbandman, Aswarby, Lincs, 1626 Lincs RO Ad/Ac/20/49
Darbie, Robert, husbandman, Burton by Lincoln, Lincs, 1676 Lincs RO Ad/Ac/35/103
Darbishire, John, Eccles (Worsley), Lancs, 1624 Lancs RO (Name of Deceased) D.R.C.H. 1624
Darbishire, William, mason: 'stone mason', Liverpool, Lancs, 1769 Lancs RO (Name of Deceased) D.R.C.H. 1768
Darby, Douch, gentleman, Yarmouth, Great, Norf, 1717 Norfolk RO ANW/23/12a/42
Darby, John, St Martin Vintry, London & Middlesex, 1682 PRO PROB32/21/101
Darby, John, mariner, Walton-on-the-Hill (Kirkdale), Lancs, 1730 Lancs RO (Name of Deceased) D.R.C.H. 1730
Darby, Richard, Chislet, Kent, 1712 CKS PRC19/6/52
Darby, Robert, Horncastle, Lincs, 1644 Lincs RO Ad/Ac/28/93
Darby, Thomas, Bromsgrove, Worcs, Worcs RO 008.7 BA3585/839/432a
Darby, Thomas, victualler, Wheatley, Oxon, Oxon RO MSS Wills 164/1/32
Darby, Thomas, Newington next Sittingbourne, Kent, 1638 CKS PRC2/34/190
Darby, William, Pattingham, Staffs, 1680 LJRO:cards/1680/10
Darcy, Alford, Lincs, 1649 Lincs RO Ad/Ac/30/390
Dardes, Alexander, St Mary Aldermary, London & Middlesex, 1681 PRO PROB5/1779
Dardes, Alexander, 1682 PRO PROB32/21/270
Dardes, George, husbandman, Stevenage, Herts, 1635 Herts RO AHH23/631
Darke, William, Comberton, Worcs, 1603 Worcs RO 008.7 BA3585/839/293a
Darley, Isabell, Waddingham, Lincs, 1632 Lincs RO Ad/Ac/39/299
Darling, John, mariner, Sandwich, Kent, 1721 CKS PRC19/6/71
Darling, Richard, gentleman, Potton, Beds, 1724 PRO PROB5/1122
Darlinge/Brooks, Elizabeth, widow, Merton, Oxon, 1624 Oxon RO MSS Wills 296/4/49A
Darlowe, Edward, Tysoe, Warks, 1593 Worcs RO 008.7 BA3585/834/456
Darlowe, John, tanner, Kimbolton, Hunts, 1684 Hunts RO/Acc58/226(215)
Darlye, Nicolas, Lydd, Kent, 1587 CKS PRC21/8/240
Darnell, Henry,
Suff 1741 Suff RO(B) IC500/3/49/5
Darnell, Rose, Stickford, Lincs, 1639 Lincs RO Ad/Ac/26/51
Darrell, Edward, Kenardington, Kent, 1612 CKS PRC2/16/52
Darrell, Thomas, Lenham, Kent, 1593 CKS PRC2/6/234
Dart, Jerome, St Austell, Corn, 1642 Cornwall RO AP/D426/2
Darwin, John, Boston, Lincs, 1785 Lincs RO Ad/Ac/36/15
Darwin, John,
Lincs C17th? Lincs RO Ad/Ac/45/104
Dasye, Richard, Linsted, Kent, 1612 CKS PRC2/16/7
Date, Agnes, High Halstow, Kent, 1599 CKS PRC2/11/25
Date, William, Upchurch, Kent, 1596 CKS PRC2/8/459
Daulton, Robert, husbandman, Carlton le Moorland, Lincs, 1680 Lincs RO Ad/Ac/43/101
Daunce, Henrie, Washingborough (Heighington), Lincs, 1641 Lincs RO Ad/Ac/27/114
Daunce, John, Sibsey, Lincs, 1613 Lincs RO Ad/Ac/12/24
Daunt, Nicolas, Bennington, Long, Lincs, 1644 Lincs RO Ad/Ac/28/87
Daunton, William, Eastry, Kent, 1617 CKS PRC20/3/460
Dauntrey, John, cordwainer: 'shoemaker', Lambourn, Berks, 1644 Berks RO D/A1/186/169A
Davenport, John, Steyning, Sussex, 1617 W. Suss RO EpI/33/1617/10
Davenport, John, esquire, Astbury (Davenport), Ches, 1637 Cheshire RO (Name) W.C. 1637
Davenport, John, Sandwich, Kent, 1650 CKS PRC1/8/86
Davenport, John, wheelwright, Ardwick, Lancs, 1685 Lancs RO (Name of Deceased) D.R.C.H. 1684
Davenporte, Christopher, esquire, Widford, Ches, 1593 Cheshire RO (Name) W.C. 1592
Davenporte, Samuell, yeoman, Hungerton, Leics, 1684 Leics RO Administrators Accounts 1682-

[Davenporte:]
86 f20
Davenporte, Thomas, Upton, Lincs, 1607 Lincs RO Ad/Ac/37/230
Daves, William, Sutton Cheney, Leics, 1666 Leics RO Administrators Accounts C17th f76
Daveys,
Leics 1640 Leics RO PR/I/41A/37
Daveys, George, Coningsby, Lincs, 1611 Lincs RO Ad/Ac/10/97
David, David Jenkin, Trallong, Breck, 1634 NLW BR 1633/119 Ac
David, Edward, St Davids, Breck, 1636 NLW BR 1635/6 Ac
David, Jenkin, 1631 NLW BR 1631/20 Ac
Davie, Richard, Cardinham, Corn, 1612 Cornwall RO AP/D95/3
Davie, Thomas, Westwell, Kent, 1601 CKS PRC21/15/213
Davie, Thomas, Ashurst, Sussex, 1631 W. Suss RO EpI/33/1631/36
Davies, Ann, Tisbury (Chicksgrove), Wilts, 1773 Wilts RO Miscellaneous Index to Wills (name + date)
Davies, Edmund, Bersted, South, Sussex, 1625 W. Suss RO EpIV/10/1/32
Davies, Edward, gentleman, Tothill, Lincs, 1633 Lincs RO Ad/Ac/24/160
Davies, Edward, gentleman, St Andrew Holborn, London & Middlesex, 1683 PRO PROB32/22/24
Davies, Frances, mrs, Maidenhead, Berks, 1607 Berks RO D/A1/186/83A
Davies, Henry, Tamworth, Staffs, 1676 LJRO:cards/1676/20
Davies, Job, baker, St Clement Danes, London & Middlesex, 1684 PRO PROB32/23/94
Davies, John, Beedon, Berks, 1607 Berks RO D/A1/186/86A
Davies, Richard + Bennett, Murston, Kent, 1617 CKS PRC2/21/134
Davies, Thomas, Hampton in Arden, Warks, 1676 LJRO:cards/1676/21
Davies, William, husbandman, Hinksey, North, Berks, 1652 Berks RO D/A1/186/183A
Davies/Mathew, Thomas, Speen (Bagnor), Berks, 1617 Berks RO D/A1/186/112C
Davill, Samuel, Gosberton, Lincs, 1673 Lincs RO Ad/Ac/35/25
Davington/Dawnton, Elizabeth, Bonnington, Kent, 1597 CKS PRC2/9/463
Davis, Abraham, St Giles without Cripplegate, London & Middlesex, 1686 PRO PROB5/1680
Davis, Benjamin, farmer, Wrockwardine, Shrops, 1813 LJRO/B/C/5/1813/46
Davis, Elizabeth, widow, St Martin in the Fields, London & Middlesex, Greater London RO AM/CP/Box 1696-1720 pt (uncatalogued)
Davis, Elizabeth, widow, St Martin in the Fields, London & Middlesex, 1708 Greater London RO AM/CP/Box 1696-1720 pt (uncatalogued)
Davis, Elizabeth, widow, Sutton Coldfield, Warks, 1813 LJRO/B/C/5/1813/48
Davis, Frances, draper: 'linen draper/widow', Norton, Chipping, Oxon, 1668 Oxon RO MSS Wills 164/1/33
Davis, George, Ashton, Steeple, Wilts, 1639 Wilts RO Arch. Sarum/(+ name and date)
Davis, Henry, Tisbury, Wilts, 1631 Wilts RO Arch. Sarum/(+ name and date)
Davis, Henry, maltster, Leeds, Kent, 1664 CKS PRC1/10/26
Davis, Henry, Whitstable, Kent, 1683 CKS PRC2/40/23
Davis, Henry, clergy: 'rector/D.D.', Cheam, Surrey, 1704 PRO PROB32/46/146
Davis, Hugh, Oxford (University), Oxon, 1619 Bodleian HYP B8/39-40
Davis, James, clergy: 'clerk', Shefford, Great, Berks, 1612 Berks RO D/A1/186/102C
Davis, Jane, widow, St Michael Bassishaw, London & Middlesex, 1666 Lambeth Palace Arches G21
Davis, John, Broad Hinton, Wilts, 1630 Wilts RO Arch. Wilts.(name + date)
Davis, John, Hawkhurst, Kent, 1670 CKS PRC1/15/16
Davis, John, clergy: 'mr/clerk', Maidstone, Kent, 1678 CKS PRC20/12/259
Davis, John, St Martin in the Fields, London & Middlesex, 1698 PRO PROB32/36/78
Davis, John, St Dionis Backchurch, London & Middlesex, 1710s? Lambeth Palace VH82/55
Davis, Mary, widow, Aldworth, Berks, Berks RO D/A1/186/140
Davis, Mary, spinster, Sherston Magna, Wilts, 1674 Wilts RO Miscellaneous Index to Wills (name + date)
Davis, Mathew, Faversham, Kent, 1639 CKS PRC1/2/47
Davis, Nicholas, Ditcheat, Som, 1666 Somerset RO D/D/Cta/D29

Davis, Nicholas, Stone in Oxney, Kent, 1678 CKS PRC2/37/137
Davis, Richard, Slinfold, Sussex, 1670 W. Suss RO EpI/33/1670/26
Davis, Robert, Kingston, Kent, 1610 CKS PRC2/15/87
Davis, Sarah, widow, Aldridge (Great Barr), Staffs, 1799 LJRO/B/C/5/1799/8
Davis, William, Winslow, Bucks, 1588 Herts RO ASA25/1233
Davis, see Coppin, Davies & Matthew,
Davison, Joane, widow, St Laurence Thanet, Kent, 1664 CKS PRC1/10/27
Davison, William, Weston, Lincs, 1599 Lincs RO Ad/Ac/5/143
Davy, Elizabeth, widow, Stone in Oxney, Kent, 1633 CKS PRC2/32/36
Davy, Joane, spinster, Rolvenden, Kent, 1667 CKS PRC1/12/29
Davy, John, blacksmith, Brimpton, Berks, 1685 Berks RO D/A1/187/50A
Davy, John + Joan, Wimborne Minster, Dors, 1601 Dorset RO PE/WM CP 2/4/5
Davy, Mark, cooper, Pluckley, Kent, 1664 CKS PRC1/9/99
Davy, Mathew, husbandman, Yattendon, Berks, 1648 Berks RO D/A1/62/166B
Davy, Richard, Pluckley, Kent, 1621 CKS PRC2/23/97
Davy, Richard,
Wilts 1677 Wilts RO Miscellaneous Index to Wills (name + date)
Davy, Thomas, Hythe West, Kent, 1674 CKS PRC2/36/40
Davye, Ann, Bersted, South, Sussex, 1619 W. Suss RO EpIV/10/1/39
Davye, Thomas, St Hilary, Corn, 1606 Cornwall RO AP/D38
Davye, Thomas, Oxford St Mary Virgin, Oxon, 1624 Oxon RO MSS Wills 296/4/45
Davye, Thomas, Belton All Saints, Lincs, 1683 Lincs RO Ad/Ac/44/47
Davye, William, Wimborne Minster, Dors, Dorset RO PE/WM CP 2/4/86
Davyes, Alyce, Barham, Kent, 1626 CKS PRC2/27/44
Davyes, John, Bethersden, Kent, 1596 CKS PRC2/8/336
Davyes, John, Hernhill, Kent, 1598 CKS PRC21/14/565
Davyes, John, Crowle, Worcs, 1603 Worcs RO 008.7 BA3585/839/294
Davyes, John, Wanstrow, Som, 1619 Somerset RO D/D/Cta/D44
Davyes, Robert, Canterbury St Alphege, Kent, 1623 CKS PRC20/6/386
Davyes, William, chapman, Winslow, Bucks, 1589 Herts RO ASA25/4807
Davys, Humfrey, mercer, Lambourn, Berks, 1630 Berks RO D/A1/186/142C
Davys, John, Trowbridge, Wilts, 1576 Wilts RO Arch. Sarum/(+ name and date)
Davys, Robert, Minster in Thanet, Kent, 1618 CKS PRC2/21/133
Davys, Symon, Selling, Kent, 1590 CKS PRC2/5/130
Daw, William, Rolvenden, Kent, 1638 CKS PRC2/34/191
Dawber, Richard, husbandman, Althorpe (Amcotts), Lincs, 1607 Lincs RO Ad/Ac/37/246
Dawbie, Thomas, Bapchild, Kent, 1637 CKS PRC2/33/40
Dawbrey, John, clergy: 'clerk', Scotton, Lincs, 1611 Lincs RO Ad/Ac/8a/339
Dawbrey, Phillipp, yeoman, Scotter, Lincs, 1616 Lincs RO Ad/Ac/8b/193
Dawbrey, William, Scothorne, Lincs, 1633 Lincs RO Ad/Ac/40/15
Dawes, Jarvis, Stapleton, Leics, 1665 Leics RO Administrators Accounts C17th f30
Dawes, Joseph, clergy: 'clerk', Luddenham, Kent, 1619 CKS PRC2/21/130
Dawes, Thomas, farmer, Mickleover, Derby, 1820 LJRO/B/C/5/1820/8
Dawkes, Francis, Himbleton, Worcs, 1684 Worcs RO 008.7 BA3585/837/bdl 5
Dawkes, Richard, jurat/mr, Dover, Kent, 1639 CKS PRC20/10/268
Dawkes, Richard, esquire, Dover, Kent, 1644 CKS PRC19/2/89
Dawkin, Henry, Caldecote, Warks, 1680s LJRO/B/C/5/1682/30
Dawkins, John, Enford, Wilts, 1734 Wilts RO Arch. Sarum/(+ name and date)
Dawkins, Mathew, husbandman, Bourne, Lincs, 1613 Lincs RO Ad/Ac/12/136
Dawkins, Phillip, Downton, Wilts, 1687 Wilts RO Arch. Sarum/(+ name and date)
Dawkins, Thomas, husbandman, Pinchbeck, Lincs, 1627 Lincs RO Ad/Ac/20/93
Dawlin, Nicholas, labourer, Aby, Lincs, 1633 Lincs RO Ad/Ac/24/76
Dawling, John, Owersby, Lincs, 1615 Lincs RO Ad/Ac/13/30
Dawling, Robert, Wye, Kent, 1621 CKS PRC2/23/95
Dawling, see Crushe,

[Dawlinge:]
Dawlinge, Thomas, Algarkirk, Lincs, 1650 Lincs RO Ad/Ac/30/21
Dawnce, John, yeoman, Defford, Worcs, 1604 Worcs RO 008.7 BA3585/839/296
Dawnton, see Davington,
Daws, Edward, Wrockwardine, Shrops, 1685 LJRO/B/C/5/1685/35
Dawson, Bennett, Thorpe, Lincs, 1611 Lincs RO Ad/Ac/10/32
Dawson, Christopher, Theddlethorpe, Lincs, 1640 Lincs RO Ad/Ac/27/1a
Dawson, Edmund + Margaret, alderman & widow, Lincoln, Lincs, 1619 Lincs RO Ad/Ac/14/110
Dawson, Edward, Weston-upon-Trent, Derby, 1680 LJRO:cards/1680/11
Dawson, George, Hythe St Leonard, Kent, 1579 CKS PRC21/4/136
Dawson, George, New Romney, Kent, 1612 CKS PRC20/2/432
Dawson, George, Enderby, Mavis, Lincs, 1632 Lincs RO Ad/Ac/23/160
Dawson, Isaac, butcher, Folkingham, Lincs, 1611 Lincs RO Ad/Ac/10/4
Dawson, John, Mareham on the Hill, Lincs, 1611 Lincs RO Ad/Ac/10/25
Dawson, John, Brattleby, Lincs, 1618 Lincs RO Ad/Ac/8b/101
Dawson, John, Croft, Lincs, 1622 Lincs RO Ad/Ac/17/89
Dawson, John, Swaby, Lincs, 1627 Lincs RO Ad/Ac/20b/14
Dawson, John, Skidbrooke, Lincs, 1651 Lincs RO Ad/Ac/29/146
Dawson, John, Thorpe Satchville, Leics, 1672 Leics RO Administrators Accounts 1667-72 f50
Dawson, John, Swynnerton, Staffs, 1684 LJRO/B/C/5/1684/29
Dawson, John, yeoman, Nantwich, Ches, 1773 Cheshire RO (Name) W.C. 1773
Dawson, Martin, St Mary Magdalen Old Fish Street, London & Middlesex, 1669 PRO PROB5/1447
Dawson, Matthew, Nocton, Lincs, 1624 Lincs RO Ad/Ac/18/30a
Dawson, Michael, husbandman, Kirkby on Bain, Lincs, 1625 Lincs RO Ad/Ac/19A/142
Dawson, Oliver, Stamford, Lincs, 1624 Lincs RO Ad/Ac/18/96
Dawson, Richard, blacksmith, Hanney, West, Berks, 1665 Berks RO D/A1/187/7C
Dawson, Robert, Barkwith, East, Lincs, 1578 Lincs RO Ad/Ac/2b/23
Dawson, Robert, Stainfield, Lincs, 1624 Lincs RO Ad/Ac/19A/128
Dawson, Robert, waterman, Lincoln St Swithin, Lincs, 1625 Lincs RO Ad/Ac/19B/75
Dawson, Robert, Gainsborough, Lincs, 1635 Lincs RO Ad/Ac/40/47
Dawson, Robert, clergy: 'clerk', Toynton All Saints, Lincs, 1644 Lincs RO Ad/Ac/28/214
Dawson, Robert, Somercoates, South, Lincs, 1783 Lincs RO Ad/Ac/45/47
Dawson, Roger, Holbeach, Lincs, 1619 Lincs RO Ad/Ac/15/119
Dawson, Sentley, Derby (Oosmaston), Derby, 1663 LJRO:cards/1663/18
Dawson, Thomas, mercer, Tattershall, Lincs, 1611 Lincs RO Ad/Ac/10/48
Dawson, Thomas, Ashby, West, Lincs, 1651 Lincs RO Ad/Ac/29/72
Dawson, Thomas, degrees: 'Doctor of Physic', St Alphage, London & Middlesex, 1682 PRO PROB32/21/178
Dawson, Walter, Marsh Chapel, Lincs, 1620 Lincs RO Ad/Ac/16/35
Dawson, William, Martin, Lincs, 1620 Lincs RO Ad/Ac/16/31
Dawson, William, blacksmith, Chart, Great, Kent, 1682 CKS PRC2/40/22
Dawson, William, yeoman, Boston, Lincs, 1684 Lincs RO Ad/Ac/44/108
Dawson, William, farmer, Newton on Ouse (Linton on Ouse), Yorks, 1779 Borthwick Test C.P. 1779/4
Dawson, William, husbandman, Wolvey, Warks, 1785 LJRO/B/C/5/1788/16
Dawson, William, clergy: 'clerk/rector', Weston-upon-Trent, Derby, 1809 LJRO/B/C/5/1809/22
Dawsone, Robert, Croft, Lincs, 1611 Lincs RO Ad/Ac/10/94
Dawsten, Richard eld, blacksmith, Hanney, West, Berks, 1623 Berks RO D/A1/186/123A
Dawtonne, Roberte, Owersby, Lincs, 1597 Lincs RO Ad/Ac/4/111
Dawtrey, William, Bosham, Sussex, 1630 W. Suss RO EpI/33/1629/23
Day, Barbara, spinster, Boscombe, Wilts, 1636 Wilts RO Arch. Sarum/(+ name and date)
Day, Elizabethe, widow, Tenterden, Kent, 1586 CKS PRC2/4/75
Day, Gertrude, Woolavington, Som, 1686 Somerset RO D/D/Cta/D34
Day, Hugh, Barrow, South, Som, 1634 Somerset RO D/D/Cta/D6
Day, John, Marden, Kent, 1603 CKS PRC2/14/160

Day, John, New Romney, Kent, 1635 CKS PRC20/10/288
Day, John, Kingston Seymour, Som, 1640 Somerset RO D/D/Cta/D31
Day, John, bachelor, Tenterden, Kent, 1668 CKS PRC1/13/31
Day, John eld, Worle, Som, 1604 Somerset RO D/D/Cta/D16
Day, Joseph, nailer, Kingswinford (Wordsley), Staffs, 1834 LJRO/B/C/5/1834/17
Day, Lawrence, High Halden, Kent, 1615 CKS PRC2/21/120
Day, Lawrence, High Halden, Kent, 1616 CKS PRC2/21/138
Day, Martha, widow, Tankersley (Pilley), Yorks, 1787 Borthwick Test C.P. 1787/6
Day, Nicholas, Whiteparish, Wilts, 1642 Wilts RO Arch. Sarum/(+ name and date)
Day, Peter, Kenardington, Kent, 1621 CKS PRC2/23/96
Day, Philip, Dover St Mary, Kent, 1635 CKS PRC20/10/272
Day, Richard, Gonerby, Lincs, 1674 Lincs RO Ad/Ac/34/9
Day, Robert, Ludborough, Lincs, 1606 Lincs RO Ad/Ac/7/22
Day, Thomas, Boughton under Blean, Kent, 1637 CKS PRC20/10/286
Day, Thomas, innholder, Brookland, Kent, 1640 CKS PRC1/4/27
Day, Thomas, High Halstow, Kent, 1641 CKS PRC1/5/93
Day, Thomas, Walsall, Staffs, 1684 LJRO/B/C/5/1684/30
Day, Walter, husbandman, Buckland (Buckland Marsh), Berks, 1632 Berks RO D/A1/186/146A
Day, William, yeoman, Eastchurch, Sheppey, Kent, 1668 CKS PRC1/13/32
Day, William, yeoman, Twyford, Leics, 1670 Leics RO Administrators Accounts 1667-72 f43
Daye, Bennett, Ivychurch, Kent, 1587 CKS PRC21/8/254
Daye, Edmund, Kingston Lisle, Berks, 1613 Berks RO D/A1/186/106A
Daye, Jervase, Rolvenden, Kent, 1607 CKS PRC2/14/145
Daye, Joan, widow, Shrivenham, Berks, 1637 Berks RO D/A1/62/144B
Daye, John, Ivychurch, Kent, 1585 CKS PRC21/7/219
Daye, John, Somercoates, North, Lincs, 1607 Lincs RO Ad/Ac/8a/63
Daye, Richard, Yarlington, Som, 1622 Somerset RO D/D/Cta/D3
Daye, Thomas, Kewstoke, Som, 1625 Somerset RO D/D/Cta/D10
Daye, William, Westwell, Kent, 1576 CKS PRC21/3/103
Daye, William, Tenterden, Kent, 1607 CKS PRC2/14/152
Dayle, Richard, Sutton St Edmunds, Lincs, 1619 Lincs RO Ad/Ac/15/101
Dayles, Mathew, Alvingham, Lincs, 1638 Lincs RO Ad/Ac/25/250
Daynes, Elizabeth, Marden, Kent, 1605 CKS PRC2/13/171
De Beaver, John, Canterbury St Peter, Kent, 1638 CKS PRC1/1/67
De Bettremieux, Fermine, widow, Canterbury St Mary Northgate, Kent, 1627 CKS PRC2/27/28
De Bourgh, Noell, widow, Canterbury All Saints, Kent, 1620 CKS PRC2/20/326
De Brooker, Frawnces, widow, Sandwich, Kent, 1611 CKS PRC2/17/185
De Bus, Magdaline, Sandwich, Kent, 1619 CKS PRC2/20/298
De Casteker, Francis, Sandwich, Kent, 1612 CKS PRC2/17/434
De Clopper, Israel, Sandwich, Kent, 1623 CKS PRC2/23/62
De Clopper, Jeremy, baymaker, Sandwich, Kent, 1638 CKS PRC2/34/185
De Colville, Lewis, esquire, St James Westminster, London & Middlesex, 1694 Greater London RO AM/PP/Box 1695-1706 pt (uncatalogued)
De Farvaques, Paul, Canterbury St Margaret, Kent, 1681 CKS PRC2/39/168
De Fox, John, saymaker, Sandwich St Mary, Kent, 1662 CKS PRC1/9/19
De Keuwer, Jacob, weaver, Sandwich St Mary, Kent, 1665 CKS PRC1/11/50
De Knight, Nicasius, Sandwich St Peter, Kent, 1612 CKS PRC2/17/209
De Knute, William, Sandwich St Peter, Kent, 1619 CKS PRC2/22/95
De la Clusa, Allard, wheelwright, Sandwich, Kent, 1665 CKS PRC1/11/18
De la Fond, Peter, St Anne Westminster, London & Middlesex, 1696 Greater London RO AM/PP/Box 1695-1706 pt (uncatalogued)
De la Place, see Prudhome,
De Lannoy, Anthony, Canterbury St Alphege, Kent, 1623 CKS PRC20/6/326
De Lannoy, Mary, widow, Canterbury St Alphege, Kent, 1623 CKS PRC20/6/316
De Master, Marke, merchant, Sandwich, Kent, 1621 CKS PRC2/24/12

[De Master:]
De Master, Oliver, Sandwich, Kent, 1629 CKS PRC2/30/100
De Master, Samuell, Sandwich St Mary, Kent, 1617 CKS PRC2/22/41
De Moll/Stephens, Fransyne, Sandwich, Kent, 1619 CKS PRC2/22/38
De Mona, Isaac, Canterbury St Mildred, Kent, 1673 CKS PRC2/35/212
De Monier, Peter, Sandwich, Kent, 1623 CKS PRC2/24/4
De Morie, James, weaver, Canterbury St Alphege, Kent, 1668 CKS PRC19/3/134
De New, Samuel, weaver, Canterbury St Alphege, Kent, 1686 CKS PRC20/13/491
De Par, Samuel, merchant, St Anne Westminster, London & Middlesex, 1704 PRO PROB32/47/63
De Radet, John, Sandwich, Kent, 1626 CKS PRC2/27/135
De Ricqueburge, Albaine, Canterbury St Mary Northgate, Kent, 1662 CKS PRC1/9/55
De Roo/Tiboult, Catherine, Sandwich St Mary, Kent, 1638 CKS PRC2/34/269
De Scheiter, Lieven eld, Sandwich, Kent, 1639 CKS PRC2/34/275
De Smyth, Francis, Sandwich, Kent, 1623 CKS PRC2/24/89
De Solomy, see Salomy,
De Spayne, Gerves, stranger, Canterbury St Alphege, Kent, 1595 CKS PRC21/14/227
De Toor, Rebecca, spinster, Sandwich, Kent, 1616 CKS PRC2/24/142
De Verges, see Deverges,
De Vinck, Katherine, widow, Sandwich, Kent, 1633 CKS PRC2/31/166
De Vinck, Nicholas, stranger, Canterbury, Kent, 1597 CKS PRC2/9/459
Deacon, Ann, Redbourn, Herts, 1624 Herts RO ASA25/2774
Deacon, Christopher, Manton, Lincs, 1610 Lincs RO Ad/Ac/8a/324
Deacon, Daniel, Abbots Langley, Herts, 1621 Herts RO ASA25/2586
Deacon, Edmund/Edward, Dover, Kent, 1597 CKS PRC21/14/185
Deacon, Geffery, Sturry, Kent, 1596 CKS PRC2/10/321
Deacon, Henry, Norwich St Stephen, Norf, 1732 Norfolk RO ANW/23/20/47
Deacon, John, Watford, Herts, 1633 Herts RO ASA25/4891
Deacon, Thomas, Somerton, Som, 1640 Somerset RO D/D/Cta/D32
Deacon, William, Heytesbury, Wilts, 1675 Wilts RO Miscellaneous Index to Wills (name + date)
Deacons, John, yeoman, Hatford, Berks, 1676 Berks RO D/A1/63/64D
Deakin, Hugh, Wichenford, Worcs, 1681 Worcs RO 008.7 BA3585/835/bdl 3
Deakin, James, yeoman, Swynnerton (Hatton), Staffs, 1803 LJRO/B/C/5/1803/23
Deakin, Thomas, Cropthorne (Netherton), Worcs, 1679 Worcs RO 008.7 BA3585/830/92
Deale, Anthony, Westwell, Kent, 1578 CKS PRC21/3/275
Deale, John, Boughton Aluph, Kent, 1680 CKS PRC2/39/27
Dean, Jonathan, gentleman, Ashbourne, Derby, 1788 LJRO/B/C/5/1788/20
Dean, Thomas, weaver, Rochdale (Inghams), Lancs, 1790 Lancs RO (Name of Deceased) D.R.C.H. 1790
Deane, Agnis, Chirton, Wilts, 1616 Wilts RO Unlisted Fragment
Deane, Anne, Wimborne Minster, Dors, 1638 Dorset RO PE/WM CP 2/4/51
Deane, Christopher, Stokenchurch, Oxon, 1626 Oxon RO MSS Wills 296/4/54
Deane, Edmund, Bleadon, Som, 1588 Somerset RO D/D/Cta/D43
Deane, Edward, husbandman, Hampstead Norris, Berks, 1667 Berks RO D/A1/187/15C
Deane, Jeremiah, barber, Deal, Kent, 1679 CKS PRC20/12/299
Deane, John, Brent, East, Som, 1588 Somerset RO D/D/Cta/D12
Deane, John, yeoman, Linwood, Lincs, 1620 Lincs RO Ad/Ac/16/30
Deane, John, bachelor, Whitstable, Kent, 1639 CKS PRC1/2/48
Deane, Richard, Thakeham, Sussex, 1662 W. Suss RO EpI/33/1661/3
Deane, Stephen, Boughton Malherbe, Kent, 1613 CKS PRC2/18/67
Deane, Thomas, yeoman, Waltham St Lawrence, Berks, 1661 Berks RO D/A1/187/2C
Deane, Walter, Shipley, Sussex, 1662 W. Suss RO EpI/33/1661/2
Deane, William, victualler, Gloucester, Glos, 1808 GRO GDR/B4/2/D53
Dearbarne, Henry, Marsh Chapel, Lincs, 1649 Lincs RO Ad/Ac/30/200
Deard, William, Stourmouth, Kent, 1666 CKS PRC1/11/115
Deare, Edward, Scothorne, Lincs, 1669 Lincs RO Ad/Ac/33/166

Deare, Elizabeth, Hackthorne, Lincs, 1632 Lincs RO Ad/Ac/39/234
Deare, Jonathan, Scothorne, Lincs, 1682 Lincs RO Ad/Ac/34/71
Deareling, Robert, Sidlesham, Sussex, 1607 W. Suss RO EpI/33/1607/10
Dearing, Jane, widow, Hackney, London & Middlesex, 1682 PRO PROB32/21/71
Dearing, Richard, tailor, Reading St Giles, Berks, 1634 Berks RO D/A1/186/150C
Dearing, William, husbandman, Buscot, Berks, 1635 Berks RO D/A1/186/151C
Dearle, Robert, Hampton, London & Middlesex, 1811 Greater London RO DL/C/569/139
Dearling, William, Boxgrove, Sussex, 1676 W. Suss RO EpI/33/1676/17
Dearn, John, victualler/scholar's servant, Cambridge Holy Sepulchre, Cambs, 1640 CUL V.C. Acc./Box2/18
Death, Jonathan, innholder, Spalding, Lincs, 1640 Lincs RO Ad/Ac/27/57
Deaton, William, Coningsby, Lincs, 1651 Lincs RO Ad/Ac/29/121
Debeney, Samuell, Sandwich, Kent, 1598 CKS PRC2/10/173
Debsen, William, Brightwell, Berks, 1639 Berks RO D/A1/186/158A
Dedicott, Richard, Worcester, Worcs, 1605 Worcs RO 008.7 BA3585/839/348
Dee, David, victualler, Bristol, Glos, Bristol RO 1759/6
Dee, John, Easthamstead, Berks, 1610 Berks RO D/A1/186/89A
Deeds, Daniell, Hythe St Leonard, Kent, 1610 CKS PRC20/2/92
Deeds, Hester, widow, Dover, Kent, 1675 CKS PRC20/12/168
Deeds, Robart, Egerton, Kent, 1608 CKS PRC20/1/318
Deeds, Thomas, Hythe St Leonard, Kent, 1600 CKS PRC21/15/190
Deeds, Thomas, Dover, Kent, 1640 CKS PRC19/1/38
Deeds, see Knight,
Deely, Anthony, bricklayer, Winslow, Bucks, 1693 Herts RO ASA25/4408
Deely, John, Halesowen, Worcs, 1680 Worcs RO 008.7 BA3585/837/bdl 2
Deepe, George, barber, Axbridge, Som, 1622 Somerset RO D/D/Cta/D4
Deere, John, Whitstable, Kent, 1629 CKS PRC2/30/39
Dehane, Abraham eld, Sandwich, Kent, 1607 CKS PRC2/14/150
Deighton, Frances, widow, Owmby by Spital, Lincs, 1649 Lincs RO Ad/Ac/40/155
Deighton, Thomas, Owmby by Spital, Lincs, 1649 Lincs RO Ad/Ac/40/169
Deighton, William, yeoman, Minety, Glos, 1678 Wilts RO Miscellaneous Index to Wills (name + date)
Delahay, Job, Norwich, Norf, 1751 Norfolk RO ANW/23/24/152C
Delamine, John, bachelor, HMS The Fox, 1708 Lambeth Palace Arches G57/4
Deligne, Erasmus, esquire, Harlaxton, Lincs, 1684 Lincs RO Ad/Ac/34/106
Dell, Edward, Dover, Kent, 1621 CKS PRC20/5/57
Dell, Henry, St Albans St Michaels, Herts, 1597 Herts RO ASA25/1606
Dell, Henry, Sarratt, Herts, 1637 Herts RO ASA25/4936
Dell, Hugh, St Albans St Peters, Herts, 1560 Herts RO ASA25/465
Dell, Thomas, Abbots Langley, Herts, 1559 Herts RO ASA25/396
Dell, Thomas, St Albans St Michaels, Herts, 1599 Herts RO ASA25/1712
Delman, Abraham, Newenden, Kent, 1628 CKS PRC2/29/29
Delman, Clement, Rolvenden, Kent, 1591 CKS PRC2/5/120
Den, Abraham, Sandwich, Kent, 1599 CKS PRC2/10/224
Den, Mary, widow, Canterbury St Margaret, Kent, 1634 CKS PRC2/32/35
Den, see Wells,
Denbye, Thomas, husbandman, Belton, Lincs, 1606 Lincs RO Ad/Ac/37/220
Dence, John, Brook, Kent, 1617 CKS PRC2/21/112
Dence, Mary, Blean, Kent, 1629 CKS PRC2/30/41
Dence, Michael, Seasalter, Kent, 1648 CKS PRC1/8/43
Dence, Phillip, Wye, Kent, 1613 CKS PRC2/17/117
Dence, William, Hawkhurst, Kent, 1594 CKS PRC2/7/341
Dendy, Lettice, widow, Horsham, Sussex, 1669 W. Suss RO EpI/33/1669/23
Denew, John, husbandman, Whitstable, Kent, 1684 CKS PRC2/40/193
Denham, Christopher, Woolavington, Sussex, 1640 W. Suss RO EpI/33/1640/4

[Denham:]
Denham, John, Littlebourne, Kent, 1584 CKS PRC2/3/59
Denham, John, Littlebourne, Kent, 1595 CKS PRC2/7/137
Denham, John, Tenterden, Kent, 1627 CKS PRC2/28/38
Denman, John, Cranbrook, Kent, 1628 CKS PRC2/29/30
Denman, Richard, Headcorn, Kent, 1630 CKS PRC20/9/121
Denman, Thomas, gentleman, Alkborough, Lincs, 1677 Lincs RO Ad/Ac/35/118
Denn, Anne, spinster, Bishopsbourne, Kent, 1632 CKS PRC2/31/100
Denn, Anne, widow, Hemingford Grey, Hunts, 1684 Hunts RO/Acc58/242(239)
Denn, Catherine, widow, Brookland, Kent, 1643 CKS PRC1/6/57
Denn, David, Eastry, Kent, 1704 CKS PRC19/6/10
Denn, Richard, Deal, Kent, 1626 CKS PRC20/7/74
Denn, Thomas, jurat, Sandwich, Kent, 1622 CKS PRC20/6/396
Denn, Thomas, Sandwich St Peter, Kent, 1627 CKS PRC2/28/36
Denn, Thomas, Upper Hardres, Kent, 1698 CKS PRC2/42/141
Denn, Thomas eld, yeoman, Folkestone, Kent, 1661 CKS PRC1/8/98
Denn, Valentine, Eastry, Kent, 1670 CKS PRC19/4/74
Denn, Vincent, Deal, Kent, 1671 CKS PRC19/4/75
Denn, William, yeoman, Brookland, Kent, 1643 CKS PRC1/6/58
Dennay, Robert, innholder, Abingdon, Berks, 1607 Berks RO D/A1/186/87A
Denne, Edward, Ash next Sandwich, Kent, 1687 CKS PRC20/13/584
Denne, John, gentleman, Smeeth, Kent, 1679 CKS PRC20/12/300
Denne, John, yeoman, Ash next Sandwich, Kent, 1682 CKS PRC20/13/127
Denne, John, apothecary, Ashford, Kent, 1684 CKS PRC2/40/111
Denne, John, yeoman, Littlebourne, Kent, 1691 CKS PRC2/42/3
Denne, Michael, Brookland, Kent, 1637 CKS PRC2/34/42
Dennett, Edwarde, Tenterden, Kent, 1605 CKS PRC2/13/166
Denning, Thomas, Wellington, Som, 1626 Somerset RO D/D/Cta/P8a
Dennis, Edward, Staplehurst, Kent, 1638 CKS PRC2/34/196
Dennis, Heneage, Swinhope, Lincs, 1645 Lincs RO Ad/Ac/28/143
Dennis, John, Faversham, Kent, CKS PRC2/4/41
Dennis, Richard, farmer, Glemsford, Suff, Suff RO(B) IC500/3/53/63
Dennis, William, Faversham, Kent, 1608 CKS PRC2/15/93
Dennis, William, Walsham, North, Norf, 1757 Norfolk RO ANF/11/5/26
Dennison, John, miller, Lythe (Ugthorpe), Yorks, 1805 Borthwick Test C.P. 1805/2
Dennys, James, Smeeth, Kent, 1604 CKS PRC21/17/384
Dennys, Richard, tinner, Gwennap, Corn, 1645 Cornwall RO AP/D448/3
Dennys, Thomas, Maidstone, Kent, 1627 CKS PRC20/8/157
Densell, Walter, brewer, Sittingbourne, Kent, 1645 CKS PRC1/7/44
Densham, William, Cowes, West, Hants, 1666 Hants RO 21M65 D8/194
Denston, Stephen, esquire, Shrewsbury Abbey Foregate, Shrops, 1797 LJRO/B/C/5/1797/23
Dent, Ann, widow, St Giles without Cripplegate, London & Middlesex, 1671 Lambeth Palace Arches G25/4
Dent, George, Broughton, Lincs, 1626 Lincs RO Ad/Ac/39/39
Dent, George, Burgh le Marsh, Lincs, 1637 Lincs RO Ad/Ac/25/376
Dent, John, Hibaldstow, Lincs, 1612 Lincs RO Ad/Ac/8b/11
Dent, John, Kirdford, Sussex, 1631 W. Suss RO EpI/33/1630/6
Dent, John, Gainsborough (Thonock), Lincs, 1664 Lincs RO Ad/Ac/41/151
Dent, Thomas, New Romney, Kent, 1678 CKS PRC20/12/258
Denton, Christopher, Brenzett, Kent, 1594 CKS PRC2/7/281
Denton, Henry, gentleman, Sellindge, Kent, 1679 CKS PRC2/38/121
Denton, John, yeoman, Huddersfield (Slack, Longwood), Yorks, 1795 Borthwick Test C.P. 1795/1
Denton, Nicholas, Sheffield (Brightside Bierlow), Yorks, 1614 Borthwick Prob. Ex. 1614/1
Denwood, Anne, Minster in Thanet, Kent, 1607 CKS PRC2/15/92
Denwood, Daniel, Sandwich, Kent, 1632 CKS PRC2/31/102
Denwood, John, Minster in Thanet, Kent, 1597 CKS PRC2/9/455

Denys, John, Selling, Kent, 1582 CKS PRC2/2/203
Deping, Valentine, mercer, Witham on the Hill, Lincs, 1633 Lincs RO Ad/Ac/24/86
Deratt, George, Crowle, Lincs, 1646 Lincs RO Ad/Ac/40/117
Derby, Thomas, Tenterden, Kent, 1632 CKS PRC2/31/104
Derelove, Nicholas, Canterbury St George Martyr, Kent, 1603 CKS PRC2/14/162
Dericke, see Leonardson,
Derricke, Marrian, widow, Headcorn, Kent, 1614 CKS PRC2/18/24
Derrie, John, Marston, Lincs, 1637? Lincs RO Ad/Ac/25/433
Desborrow, Susanna, widow, Whaplode Drove, Lincs, 1683 Lincs RO Ad/Ac/44/73
Desronsseau, Noelle, Canterbury Holy Cross Westgate, Kent, 1597 CKS PRC2/9/101
Destrie, Phillipp, Canterbury St Alphege, Kent, 1634 CKS PRC20/10/284
Dethe, Welcome, gentleman, Spalding, Lincs, 1674 Lincs RO Ad/Ac/34/111
Dethliefe, Mark, yeoman, Gwennap, Corn, 1649 Cornwall RO AP/D531/3
Devell, William, baker, Eynsham, Oxon, 1639 Oxon RO MSS Wills 296/4/78
Devenish, Jasper, Southampton, Hants, 1661 Hants RO 21M65 D8/144
Deverell, John, millwright, Bristol, Glos, Bristol RO 1778/CP
Deverell, John, Winsley, Wilts, 1703 Wilts RO Arch. Sarum/(+ name and date)
Deverges/De Verges, Parnell, widow, Dover, Kent, 1672 CKS PRC20/12/8
Devine, Lewis, Canterbury St Mildred, Kent, 1713 CKS PRC1/17/53
Devinson, John, Canterbury Holy Cross Westgate, Kent, 1636 CKS PRC2/33/44
Devis, John, Warwick, Warks, 1684 Worcs RO 008.7 BA3585/837/bdl 5
Devison, Alexander, surgeon, Staple next Wingham, Kent, 1675 CKS PRC20/12/167
Devison, Stephen, Lympne, Kent, 1619 CKS PRC2/26/106
Dew/Sadler, John, husbandman, Iffley, Oxon, 1636 Oxon RO MSS Wills 296/4/76
Dewarde, John, Faversham, Kent, 1593 CKS PRC2/6/188
Dewberry, Nicholas, Bonnington, Kent, 1586 CKS PRC2/4/102
Dewe, John, Shorwell, Hants, Hants RO 1597 AD030
Dewe, John, yeoman, Stanton St John, Oxon, 1624 Oxon RO MSS Wills 296/4/44
Dewe, John, gentleman, Oxford St Martin, Oxon, 1640 Oxon RO MSS Wills 296/4/85
Dewe, Thomas, husbandman, Aston Tirrold, Berks, 1627 Berks RO D/A1/186/130C
Dewe, William, Broad Chalke, Wilts, 1643 Wilts RO Arch. Sarum/(+ name and date)
Dewell, Robert, husbandman, Ickham, Kent, 1617 CKS PRC20/4/77
Dewen, Ralph, mercer, Gwinear, Corn, 1607 Cornwall RO AP/D52/2
Dewey, George, Leadenham, Lincs, 1632 Lincs RO Ad/Ac/23/23
Dewey, William, husbandman, Wimborne Minster (Leigh), Dors, 1638 Dorset RO PE/WM CP 2/4/52
Dewis, Thomas, Grimsby, Great, Lincs, 1620 Lincs RO Ad/Ac/16/33
Dewsbury, Thomas, hatter, Liverpool, Lancs, 1743 Lancs RO (Name of Deceased) D.R.C.H. 1743
Dexter, Elizabeth, widow, Bristol, Glos, Bristol RO 1714/15
Dexter, William, Belton, Leics, 1640 Leics RO PR/I/41A/52
Deyman, Hugh, Morwenstow, Corn, 1628 Cornwall RO AP/D272/3
Deyne, George, yeoman, Swineshead, Lincs, 1632 Lincs RO Ad/Ac/23/149
Diaper, Robert, husbandman, Chaddleworth, Berks, 1677 Berks RO D/A1/187/31C
Diar, Thomas + John, Sutton Courtenay, Berks, 1599 Berks RO D/A1/61/205D
Dibbs, John, innholder, Dover, Kent, 1642 CKS PRC19/2/11
Dibdale, Alexander, Eastchurch, Sheppey, Kent, 1597 CKS PRC2/9/341
Dibden, John, Luddenham, Kent, 1601 CKS PRC2/12/124
Dibley, William, husbandman, Thatcham (Colthrop), Berks, 1627 Berks RO D/A1/186/134A
Dicer, John, Bruton, Som, 1588 Somerset RO D/D/Cta/D33
Dick, William, Enford (Fyfield), Wilts, 1620 Wilts RO Miscellaneous Index to Wills (name + date)
Dickanson, Thomas, esquire, Salford, Lancs, Lancs RO (Name of Deceased) D.R.C.H. 1704-09
Dicke, John, Sandwich, Kent, 1629 CKS PRC2/30/42
Dicke, William, Crudwell, Wilts, 1629 Wilts RO CC Sarum(+ name and date)
Dickein, Joseph, husbandman, Newton Solney, Derby, 1672 LJRO:cards/1672/13

[Dicken:]
Dicken, William, Darlaston, Staffs, 1684 LJRO/B/C/5/1684/31
Dickens, Robert + Katherine, Burton Coggles, Lincs, 1619 Lincs RO Ad/Ac/15/17
Dickenson, Elizabeth, spinster, Salford, Lancs, 1778 Lancs RO (Name of Deceased) D.R.C.H. 1771-72
Dickenson, Francis, Bardney, Lincs, 1651 Lincs RO Ad/Ac/29/151
Dickenson, John, Godmanchester, Hunts, 1676 Hunts RO/Acc58/39(30)
Dickenson, Margery, Canterbury, Kent, 1631 CKS PRC2/31/24
Dickenson, Robert, yeoman, Stamford St Michael, Lincs, 1638 Lincs RO Ad/Ac/26/138
Dickenson, Roger, Canterbury St Andrew, Kent, 1618 CKS PRC2/21/116
Dickenson, Roger, cordwainer: 'shoemaker', Canterbury St Andrew, Kent, 1627 CKS PRC2/28/39
Dickenson, Thomas, Billinghay, Lincs, 1622 Lincs RO Ad/Ac/17/33
Dickenson, William, Stanground, Hunts, 1678 Hunts RO/Acc58/124(40)
Dickin, Thomas, Loppington, Shrops, 1685 LJRO/B/C/5/1685/36
Dickins, Anne, widow, Sewstern, Leics, 1673 Leics RO Administrators Accounts 1667-72 f135
Dickins, Jane, widow, Enville, Staffs, 1675 LJRO:cards/1675/17
Dickins, John, bachelor, St Gregory by St Pauls, London & Middlesex, 1677 PRO PROB5/1352
Dickins, Katherine, widow, Kensington, London & Middlesex, 1711 Greater London RO AM/PP/Box 1701-1710 pt (uncatalogued)
Dickins, Richard, Melton Mowbray, Leics, 1685 Leics RO Administrators Accounts 1682-86 f41
Dickins, Thomas, saddler, Melton Mowbray, Leics, 1673 Leics RO Administrators Accounts 1667-72 f99
Dickinson, Francis, victualler, St Clement Danes, London & Middlesex, 1677 Greater London RO AM/PP/Box 1670-1678 pt (uncatalogued)
Dickinson, James, Wainfleet St Mary, Lincs, 1639 Lincs RO Ad/Ac/26/169
Dickinson, Nicholas, Billinghay, Lincs, 1664 Lincs RO Ad/Ac/43/42
Dickinson, Robert, Canterbury, Kent, 1628 CKS PRC2/29/32
Dickinson, Thomas, grocer/chandler, Liverpool, Lancs, 1766 Lancs RO (Name of Deceased) D.R.C.H. 1766
Dickinson, William, Wigtoft, Lincs, C18th? Lincs RO Ad/Ac/45/93
Dickocks, Thomas, Collingbourne Kingston, Wilts, 1623 Wilts RO Arch. Wilts.(name + date)
Dickonson, Hugh, husbandman, Billinghay, Lincs, 1673 Lincs RO Ad/Ac/35/31
Dickonson, John, Billinghay, Lincs, 1599 Lincs RO Ad/Ac/5/397
Dickonson, John, Billinghay, Lincs, 1602 Lincs RO Ad/Ac/5/139
Dickonson, Nicholas, Bloxholme, Lincs, 1606 Lincs RO Ad/Ac/7/171
Dickonson, William, Claypole, Lincs, 1605 Lincs RO Ad/Ac/6/77
Dickonson, William, draper: 'linen draper', Stockport, Ches, 1614 Cheshire RO (Name) W.C. 1614
Diconson, William, Faversham, Kent, 1638 CKS PRC2/34/192
Diconson/Caister, Robert, Belton All Saints, Lincs, 1610 Lincs RO Ad/Ac/8a/329
Didington, Christopher, Mere, Wilts, 1689 Wilts RO Dean Sarum (name + date)
Dieen, Giles, Sandwich, Kent, 1624 CKS PRC2/23/102
Dier, John, Lansallos, Corn, 1606 Cornwall RO AP/D47/2
Dier, Robert, husbandman, Bleadon, Som, 1612 Somerset RO D/D/Cta/D19
Digbie, Kenelme, clergy: 'clerk', Old Romney, Kent, 1604 CKS PRC2/13/169
Digby, John, gentleman, Watford, Herts, 1614 Herts RO ASA25/4815
Digginson, John, Ashford, Kent, 1594 CKS PRC2/7/219
Diggle, Elizabeth, widow, Prestwich, Lancs, 1774 Lancs RO (Name of Deceased) D.R.C.H. 1774-75
Diggons, Edward, Arundel, Sussex, 1606 W. Suss RO EpI/33/1606/4
Diggons, John, Woolbeding, Sussex, 1682 W. Suss RO EpI/33/1682/7
Diggons, Thomas, clergy: 'vicar', Donnington, Sussex, 1600 W. Suss RO EpI/33/1600/1
Diggs, Thomas, gentleman, Canterbury Christchurch, Kent, 1605 CKS PRC20/1/35
Dighton, Ester, Burwell, Lincs, 1624 Lincs RO Ad/Ac/18/98
Dighton, John, Burwell, Lincs, 1601 Lincs RO Ad/Ac/5/35
Dighton, Robert, gentleman, Boston, Lincs, 1612 Lincs RO Ad/Ac/10/168

Dighton, Willyam, Fulletby, Lincs, 1646 Lincs RO Ad/Ac/28/231
Diglin, William, Stamford, Lincs, 1638 Lincs RO Ad/Ac/25/142
Digly, John, Harbledown, Kent, 1598 CKS PRC2/11/70
Digwead, Richard, husbandman, Drayton, Berks, 1597 Berks RO D/A1/186/63C
Digweed, John, labourer: 'day labourer', Sutton Courtenay, Berks, 1609 Berks RO D/A1/186/88A
Dike, Thomas, Street, Som, 1611 Somerset RO D/D/Cta/D15
Dilke, John, Kirkby Mallory, Leics, 1665 Leics RO Administrators Accounts C17th f6
Dilkes, Edward, husbandman, Thurlaston, Leics, 1672 Leics RO Administrators Accounts 1667-72 f49
Dillingham, Ann, widow, Addington, Little, Northants, 1769 Northants RO X954/21/16
Dillnett, John, St Johns Thanet, Kent, 1638 CKS PRC2/34/45
Dillnett, Richard, Blean, Kent, 1639 CKS PRC1/2/49
Dillnett, Robert, Ewell, Kent, 1620 CKS PRC2/21/119
Dilnor, William, Blean/Hackington, Kent, 1633 CKS PRC2/32/39
Dilnot, Valentine, collar maker, Ash next Sandwich, Kent, 1686 CKS PRC20/13/493
Dim, Henry, Stepney, London & Middlesex, PRO PROB32/19/324
Dimbleby, John, Scampton, Lincs, 1680 Lincs RO Ad/Ac/43/161
Dimbleby, Richard, Brattleby, Lincs, 1679 Lincs RO Ad/Ac/43/138
Dingle, Peter, Morval, Corn, 1614 Cornwall RO AP/D118/2
Dingleden, Dionis, Smarden, Kent, 1599 CKS PRC2/11/35
Dinsdale, John, Barrow, Lincs, 1641 Lincs RO Ad/Ac/27/305
Dinsdale, Robert, Winteringham, Lincs, 1652 Lincs RO Ad/Ac/40/181
Diones, John, Coates, Great, Lincs, 1619 Lincs RO Ad/Ac/15/179
Dipple, John, Isham, Northants, 1671 Northants RO NWill A/C/126
Dirkin, George, Marden, Kent, 1603 CKS PRC2/14/156
Dirkine, Thomas, Canterbury St Mary Bredman, Kent, 1599 CKS PRC2/10/464
Dirrock, William, Winford, Som, 1605 Somerset RO D/D/Cta/D42
Disborough, Anne, widow, Boughton Monchelsea, Kent, 1617 CKS PRC2/21/125
Dister, Richard, New Romney, Kent, 1626 CKS PRC20/7/70
Ditch, George, Minster in Sheppey, Kent, 1708 CKS PRC1/17/4
Ditcher, Margaret, widow, Bath, Som, 1666 Somerset RO D/D/Cta/D28
Ditcher, William, Molash, Kent, 1641 CKS PRC1/5/94a
Ditcher, William, husbandman, Molash, Kent, 1641 CKS PRC1/5/94
Dittie, John, Wincanton, Som, 1662 Somerset RO D/D/Cta/D25
Ditton, John, Wilton, Wilts, 1639 Wilts RO Arch. Sarum/(+ name and date)
Ditton, Richard, Woodchurch, Kent, 1673 CKS PRC20/12/76
Dive, Jacob, yeoman, Headcorn, Kent, 1681 CKS PRC2/39/166
Dive, Thomas, Boughton Malherbe, Kent, 1600 CKS PRC2/11/199
Dive, Thomas, Benenden, Kent, 1699 CKS PRC2/42/152
Divers, William, Hawkhurst, Kent, 1679 CKS PRC2/38/120
Divis, Thomas, Marden, Kent, 1617 CKS PRC2/21/142
Dix, John ygr, Glastonbury St John, Som, 1640 Somerset RO D/D/Cta/D30
Dixe, John, Rainham, Kent, 1599 CKS PRC2/11/47
Dixe, Ralph, Banbury, Oxon, 1619 Oxon RO MSS Wills Pec 36/3/30
Dixon, Aron, Boston, Lincs, 1618 Lincs RO Ad/Ac/14/293
Dixon, Augustine, Saxilby, Lincs, 1633 Lincs RO Ad/Ac/40/35
Dixon, Edward, gentleman, Harbledown, Kent, 1606 CKS PRC2/14/142
Dixon, Edward, cordwainer/scholar's servant, Cambridge St Benedict, Cambs, 1626 c. CUL V.C. Acc./Box2/19
Dixon, George, Hamworth, Cold, Lincs, 1663 Lincs RO Ad/Ac/41/80
Dixon, Henry, wheelwright, Gainsborough, Lincs, 1608 Lincs RO Ad/Ac/37/267
Dixon, James, Keal, East, Lincs, 1620 Lincs RO Ad/Ac/16/32
Dixon, John, Hougham, Kent, 1597 CKS PRC2/9/347
Dixon, John, St Albans, Herts, 1630 Herts RO ASA25/4859
Dixon, John, labourer,

[Dixon:]
Lincs 1648 Lincs RO Ad/Ac/30/339
Dixon, Mary, Birchington, Kent, 1616 CKS PRC20/3/462
Dixon, Oliver,
Worcs 1680 Worcs RO 008.7 BA3585/837/bdl 2
Dixon, Richard, Coates, Lincs, 1620 Lincs RO Ad/Ac/8b/379
Dixon, Richard, weaver, Newbury, Berks, 1628 Berks RO D/A1/62/84E
Dixon, Robert, husbandman, Brightwell (Mackney), Berks, 1602 Berks RO D/A1/186/74A
Dixon, Robert, Alford, Lincs, 1632 Lincs RO Ad/Ac/23/25
Dixon, Robert, Ormsby, North, Lincs, 1638 Lincs RO Ad/Ac/25/281
Dixon, Roberte, Owersby, Lincs, 1593 Lincs RO Ad/Ac/3/21
Dixon, Rowland, Canterbury St Margaret, Kent, 1630 CKS PRC2/30/40
Dixon, Stephen, Knowlton, Kent, 1612 CKS PRC2/17/193
Dixon, Thomas, Canterbury St Paul, Kent, 1596 CKS PRC2/9/97
Dixon, Thomas, Welton le Marsh (Boothby), Lincs, 1632 Lincs RO Ad/Ac/23/38
Dixon, Thomas, husbandman, Ash next Sandwich, Kent, 1641 CKS PRC19/2/12
Dixon, Thomas, Lincoln, Lincs, 1726 Lincs RO Ad/Ac/45/16
Dixon, William, Wingham, Kent, 1585 CKS PRC21/7/291
Dixon, William, maltster, Kingsbury, Warks, 1755 LJRO/B/C/5/1754/107
Dixon, William, maltster, Kingsbury, Warks, 1756 LJRO/B/C/5/1754/112
Dixon (Dixson), Richard, innholder, Aston (Deritend), Warks, 1661 LJRO:cards/1661/4
Dixson, Robert, Middleton, Warks, 1663 LJRO:cards/1663/19
Dixson, Stephen, Knowlton, Kent, 1610 CKS PRC1/1/13
Dixy, Nicholas, Holywell, Hunts, 1692 Hunts RO/Acc58/274
Dober, John, Holnest, Dors, 1627 Wilts RO Miscellaneous Index to Wills (name + date)
Dober, Mary, spinster, Milton next Sittingbourne, Kent, 1693 CKS PRC2/42/52
Dober, Simon, Minster in Sheppey, Kent, 1616 CKS PRC2/21/144
Dobin, Simon, Ashcott, Som, 1686 Somerset RO D/D/Cta/D35
Dobin, Simon, Ashcott, Som, 1702 Somerset RO D/D/Cta/D36
Dobson, Robert, clergy: 'clerk', Wroot, Lincs, 1619 Lincs RO Ad/Ac/8b/369
Dobson, Robert, butcher, Witton (Northwich), Ches, 1735 Cheshire RO (Name) W.C. 1734
Dobson, William, Sutton, Lincs, 1648 Lincs RO Ad/Ac/30/366
Docket, Christopher, Feock, Corn, 1613 Cornwall RO AP/D107/2
Dockin, Edmond, yeoman, Butterwick, Lincs, 1619 Lincs RO Ad/Ac/15/294
Dod, Elizabeth, widow, Rolvenden, Kent, 1596 CKS PRC2/9/281
Dod, George, Stockbury, Kent, 1586 CKS PRC2/4/206
Dod, Henry, Faversham, Kent, 1593 CKS PRC2/6/356
Dod, Henry, husbandman, Dassett, Avon, Warks, 1672 LJRO:cards/1672/14
Dod, John, university: 'Fellow of Jesus College, Cambridge/vicar/M.A.' Cambridge (Jesus College), Cambs, 1632 CUL V.C. Acc./Box2/20
Dod, Jonas, Cound, Shrops, 1681 LJRO/B/C/5/1681/9
Dod, Michael, Patrixbourne, Kent, 1629 CKS PRC2/29/31
Dod, Sampson, Canterbury, Kent, 1592 CKS PRC2/6/186
Dod, Stephyne, Wye, Kent, 1588 CKS PRC2/5/61
Dod, Thomas, Rainham, Kent, 1592 CKS PRC2/6/318
Dod, Thomas, Wytham, Berks, 1612 Berks RO D/A1/186/100A
Dod, William, Challock, Kent, 1592 CKS PRC21/12/174
Dodd, Elizabeth, widow, Chislet, Kent, 1617 CKS PRC2/21/126
Dodd, Francis, Coventry, Warks, 1681 LJRO/B/C/5/1682/31
Dodd, Gilbert, Milton next Sittingbourne, Kent, 1680 CKS PRC2/39/30
Dodd, Gylberte, St Peter in Thanet, Kent, 1601 CKS PRC2/12/122
Dodd, Henrye, Faversham, Kent, 1601 CKS PRC2/12/126
Dodd, John, innkeeper, Norwich St John Maddermarket, Norf, Norfolk RO ANW/23/17A(ii)/16
Dodd, John, Sevington, Kent, 1666 CKS PRC1/10/29
Dodd, John, Seasalter, Kent, 1685 CKS PRC2/40/192
Dodd, Margerye, widow, Upchurch, Kent, 1599 CKS PRC2/11/207

Dodd, Thomas, Sittingbourne, Kent, 1638 CKS PRC2/34/44
Dodd, Thomas, Lympne, Kent, 1688 CKS PRC2/41/120
Dodd, Wiliam, Brenzett, Kent, 1664 CKS PRC1/10/28
Doddes, John, Rainham, Kent, 1595 CKS PRC2/7/84
Dodding, Nicholas, cooper, Grantham, Lincs, 1632 Lincs RO Ad/Ac/23/161
Dodgson, John, gentleman, Leeds (Cross Green), Yorks, 1799 Borthwick Test C.P. 1799/3
Dodington, William, Mere, Wilts, 1596 Wilts RO Miscellaneous Index to Wills (name + date)
Dodkin, Roger, Apley, Lincs, 1638 Lincs RO Ad/Ac/26/271
Dods, Thomas, Minster in Thanet, Kent, 1639 CKS PRC1/2/50
Dodson, Elizabeth, widow, Maidstone, Kent, 1626 CKS PRC20/7/363
Dodson, George, Hallaton, Leics, Leics RO Administrators Accounts 1682-86 f24
Dodson, James, St Albans, Herts, 1584 Herts RO ASA25/1081
Dodson, James, Chart, Great, Kent, 1626 CKS PRC2/25/46
Dodson, John, Smarden, Kent, 1675 CKS PRC2/36/39
Dodson, Jonathan, bricklayer, Leeds, Kent, 1677 CKS PRC2/37/136
Dodson, Thomas, Bearsted, Kent, 1624 CKS PRC2/23/101
Dodson, Thomas, Thurlby, Lincs, 1663 Lincs RO Ad/Ac/32/50
Dodson, Thomas, attorney, Mansfield, Notts, 1804 Borthwick Test C.P. 1804/1
Doe, Brian, yeoman, Garford, Berks, 1636 Berks RO D/A1/186/154C
Doe, Ethelbert, labourer, Wootton, Oxon, 1627 Oxon RO MSS Wills 296/4/60
Doe, John, Lyford, Berks, 1587 Berks RO D/A2/C24/196V
Doe, John, Lockinge, East, Berks, 1599 Berks RO D/A1/186/69A
Doe, Leonard, Challow, West, Berks, 1595 Berks RO D/A1/186/61D
Doe, Richard, Petworth, Sussex, 1672 W. Suss RO EpI/33/1672/6
Doe, Robert, husbandman, Lyford, Berks, 1600 Berks RO D/A1/186/71C
Doe, Stephen, surgeon: 'apprentice surgeon',
Kent 1624 CKS PRC20/6/1
Doe, Thomas, shepherd, Frilford, Berks, 1681 Berks RO D/A1/187/38D
Doelittle, William, clergy: 'clerk/vicar', Wasperton, Warks, 1684 Worcs RO 008.7 BA3585/837/bdl 5
Does, Richard, Bredhurst, Kent, 1680 CKS PRC20/13/18
Does, Thomas, flaxman, Faversham, Kent, 1670 CKS PRC1/15/17
Dogget, Denyse, widow, Sholden, Kent, 1593 CKS PRC2/6/288
Dogget, George, tailor, Gaddesden, Great, Herts, 1631 Herts RO AHH23/629
Doggett,
Som 1640 Somerset RO D/D/Cta/D1
Doggett, Peter, Sholden, Kent, 1598 CKS PRC2/10/232
Doggett, Robert, Birchington, Kent, 1621 CKS PRC20/5/61
Doidge, Roger, St Stephen by Launceston, Corn, 1642 Cornwall RO AP/D455
Dolburne, William, gentleman, Rowley Regis, Staffs, 1607 Worcs RO 008.7 BA3585/839/432
Doleman, Walter, Trysull/Seisdon, Staffs, 1685 LJRO/B/C/5/1685/37
Dollin, Vincent, Canterbury, Kent, 1603 CKS PRC2/14/164
Dolling, Thomas, Warfield, Berks, 1615 Berks RO D/A1/186/110A
Dollinge, John, Redbourn, Herts, 1638 Herts RO ASA25/4937
Dollinge, John jun, Wheat Hampstead, Herts, 1715 Herts RO ASA25/4993
Dollinge, Richard, St Albans, Herts, 1621 Herts RO ASA25/2681
Dollman, William, cutler, Canterbury, Kent, 1680 CKS PRC2/39/28
Dollyn, William, yeoman, Warfield, Berks, 1618 Berks RO D/A1/186/117A
Dolphin, Ralph, Yardley, Worcs, 1604 Worcs RO 008.7 BA3585/839/349
Dolphin, Richard, Barton on Humber, Lincs, 1629 Lincs RO Ad/Ac/22/59
Dombell, John, Flixton (Newcroft), Lancs, 1580 Lancs RO (Name of Deceased) D.R.C.H. 1580
Domeney, Richard, Charing, Kent, CKS PRC20/7/365
Domingoe, see Thomingoe,
Dominick/Clare, John, clergy: 'clerk', Fonthill Bishop, Wilts, 1621 Wilts RO CC Sarum(+ name and date)

[Dominicke:]
Dominicke, Thomas, Edington, Wilts, 1614 Wilts RO Miscellaneous Index to Wills (name + date)
Dominie, George, Ditcheat, Som, 1662 Somerset RO D/D/Cta/D24
Dominique, Paul eld, merchant, Tottenham (High Cross), London & Middlesex, 1682 PRO PROB32/19/139
Dommy, Anne, widow, Wimborne Minster, Dors, 1697 Dorset RO PE/WM CP 2/4/96
Donaldson, John, Ashby de la Zouch, Leics, 1669 Leics RO Administrators Accounts 1667-72 f19
Done, John, yeoman, Coddington, Ches, 1672 Cheshire RO (Name) W.C. 1671
Done, Peter, husbandman, Weverham (Acton), Ches, 1753 Cheshire RO (Name) W.C. 1753
Done, Thomas, Milton next Sittingbourne, Kent, 1614 CKS PRC2/18/97
Done, Thomas, yeoman, Frodsham (Catten Hall), Ches, 1735 Cheshire RO (Name) W.C. 1735
Donington, John, Skendleby, Lincs, 1606 Lincs RO Ad/Ac/7/18
Doningtonne, Johnne, Anderby, Lincs, 1579 Lincs RO Ad/Ac/2b/50a
Donn, Henry, St Laurence Thanet, Kent, 1673 CKS PRC2/35/129
Donnell/Thorogood, John, St Albans, Herts, 1626 Herts RO ASA25/2944
Doo, Christopher, Eastling, Kent, 1600 CKS PRC2/11/201
Doo, Elizabeth, Orlestone, Kent, 1593 CKS PRC2/7/47
Doo, John, Hucking, Kent, 1597 CKS PRC21/14/157
Doorne, John, Chartham, Kent, 1591 CKS PRC2/6/206
Dorante, Alexander, Ebony, Kent, 1612 CKS PRC2/17/195
Dore, John, Shadwell, St Paul, London & Middlesex, 1695 PRO PROB32/38/149
Dore, William, husbandman, Welford, Berks, 1622 Wilts RO CC Sarum(+ name and date)
Dore, William, husbandman, Welford, Berks, 1628 Berks RO D/A1/186/132A
Dore, William, labourer, Reading St Lawrence, Berks, 1635 Berks RO D/A1/186/153C
Dorley, John, Staplehurst, Kent, 1615 CKS PRC2/21/137
Dorley, Wyllyam, Staplehurst, Kent, 1593 CKS PRC2/6/436
Dorly, Isaack, Wormshill, Kent, 1623 CKS PRC2/23/93
Dorman, Awsten, Minster in Sheppey, Kent, 1611 CKS PRC2/16/107
Dorman, John, Fleckney, Leics, 1673 Leics RO Administrators Accounts 1667-72 f109
Dorman, Richard, Biddenden, Kent, 1629 CKS PRC2/30/43
Dormer, John, Bicester, Oxon, 1664 Oxon RO MSS Wills 164/1/30
Dorney, Joseph, saddler, Sodbury, Chipping, Glos, 1730 GRO GDR/B4/2/D66
Dorsett, John, Wells, Som, Somerset RO D/D/Cta/D13
Dorvill, Arthur, Ansford, Som, 1665 Somerset RO D/D/Cta/D27
Dory, Thomas, Camely, Som, 1673 Somerset RO D/D/Cta/D37
Dose, Christopher, Canterbury St Mary-Magdalen Burgate, Kent, 1632 CKS PRC2/31/25
Doubling, Thomas eld, Chilham, Kent, 1685 CKS PRC2/40/194
Doubte, Reginald, Cornelly, Corn, 1606 Cornwall RO AP/D42/2
Doughtie, Edward, Halton, East, Lincs, 1612 Lincs RO Ad/Ac/10/151
Doughton, John, Datchworth, Herts, 1641 Herts RO AHH23/652
Doughty, Alice, spinster, Halton, East, Lincs, 1611 Lincs RO Ad/Ac/10/55
Doughty, Christopher, Sibsey, Lincs, 1611 Lincs RO Ad/Ac/10/31
Doughty, Epaphras, mr, Foulsham, Norf, 1753 Norfolk RO ANW/23/24/145A
Doughtye, Doughtye, Thomas, Halton, East, Lincs, 1603 Lincs RO Ad/Ac/5/141
Douglis, Elizabeth, Chipping Warden, Northants, 1680 Northants RO NWill A/C/7
Dourne, Josias, Throwleigh, Kent, 1616 CKS PRC2/21/127
Dourne, Stephen, bachelor, Faversham, Kent, 1713 CKS PRC1/17/54
Dove, Ellen, widow, Wymondley, Little, Herts, 1613 Herts RO AHH23/627
Dove, Francys, spinster, Hykeham, North, Lincs, 1600 Lincs RO Ad/Ac/5/256
Dove, Henrye, Milton next Sittingbourne, Kent, 1611 CKS PRC2/16/74
Dove, James, Aubourn (Haddington), Lincs, 1636 Lincs RO Ad/Ac/24/391
Dove, John, Boston, Lincs, 1573 Lincs RO Ad/Ac/1/6
Dove, Thomas, Lydden, Kent, 1593 CKS PRC2/6/476
Dove, Thomas, clothworker, Newbury, Berks, 1641 Berks RO D/A1/186/159C
Dover, Christopher, Gonerby, Great, Lincs, 1613 Lincs RO Ad/Ac/11/56
Doverdale, Henry, Crowle, Worcs, 1602 Worcs RO 008.7 BA3585/838/235

Doverdale, Luke, Broughton Hackett, Worcs, 1684 Worcs RO 008.7 BA3585/837/bdl 5
Doverston, John, Worcester St John Bedwardine (Wick Episcopi), Worcs, 1681 Worcs RO 008.7 BA3585/830/73
Doves, Edward, Dover, Kent, 1636 CKS PRC20/10/270
Doves, German, Dover, Kent, 1581 CKS PRC21/5/146
Doves, John, husbandman, Herne, Kent, 1674 CKS PRC20/12/123
Doves, Richard, Dover, Kent, 1625 CKS PRC20/6/54
Dovey, Richard, Kinver, Staffs, 1698 LJRO/B/C/5/1698/37
Dowce, Edward, Wrangle, Lincs, 1638 Lincs RO Ad/Ac/25/141
Dowde, John, Westwell, Kent, 1598 CKS PRC21/15/27
Dowdinge, Maude, Urchfont, Wilts, 1616 Wilts RO Miscellaneous Index to Wills (name + date)
Dowdinge, Thomas, clothier, Worcester, Worcs, 1592 Worcs RO 008.7 BA3585/838/89
Dowdswell, Thomas, gentleman, Coates, Little, Lincs, 1673 Lincs RO Ad/Ac/35/21
Dowes?, Anthony, Bennington, Long, Lincs, 1650 Lincs RO Ad/Ac/30/1
Dowglas, John, Faversham, Kent, 1616 CKS PRC2/21/135
Dowland/Vanderclitt, Judith, widow, Sandwich, Kent, 1639 CKS PRC2/34/296
Dowle, Abraham, Old Romney, Kent, 1613 CKS PRC2/17/274
Dowle, Elizabeth, Cirencester, Glos, GRO GDR/B4/2/D22
Dowle, Jeames, gentleman, Lenham, Kent, 1610 CKS PRC20/1/15
Dowle, William, yeoman, Milton next Sittingbourne, Kent, 1672 CKS PRC2/35/126
Dowling, Thomas, Harting, Sussex, 1674 W. Suss RO EpI/33/1674/6
Dowling, William, Mottisfont, Hants, 1625 Hants RO 21M65 D8/112
Dowlinge, Thomas, Petersfield, Hants, 1680 Hants RO 21m65 D8/322
Dowman, Ales, Faversham, Kent, 1593 CKS PRC2/6/300
Dowman, Cornelius, Faversham, Kent, 1590 CKS PRC2/5/132
Down, William, Viscount of Down & Baron of Cloney, Charlton, Kent, 1681 PRO PROB5/1302
Downe, Anne, widow, Linsted, Kent, 1640 CKS PRC1/4/28
Downe, Beatrice, widow, Tenterden, Kent, 1635 CKS PRC2/33/38
Downe, Beniamin eld, Woodchurch, Kent, 1626 CKS PRC20/7/64
Downe, Christopher, Rainham, Kent, 1639 CKS PRC1/2/51
Downe, Clement, Old Romney, Kent, 1626 CKS PRC2/27/45
Downe, Clement, widow, Old Romney, Kent, 1635 CKS PRC2/33/42
Downe, Daniel, husbandman, Herne, Kent, 1683 CKS PRC20/13/325
Downe, Daniell, Sandwich St Clement, Kent, 1611 CKS PRC2/15/88
Downe, George, Tenterden, Kent, 1635 CKS PRC2/33/43
Downe, Henry, Mersham, Kent, 1596 CKS PRC2/9/277
Downe, Heugh, Lenham, Kent, 1621 CKS PRC2/21/139
Downe, Jasper, Leeds, Kent, 1599 CKS PRC2/11/68
Downe, Joane, widow, Hythe St Leonard, Kent, 1617 CKS PRC20/3/464
Downe, John, Sturry, Kent, 1577 CKS PRC2/1/181
Downe, John, Godmersham, Kent, 1618 CKS PRC20/4/75
Downe, John, Faversham, Kent, 1674 CKS PRC1/15/83
Downe, John + Agnes, Smarden, Kent, 1605 CKS PRC2/13/173
Downe, Mathye, Hythe St Leonard, Kent, 1592 CKS PRC21/11/142
Downe, Richard, Biddenden, Kent, 1614 CKS PRC2/18/106
Downe, Richard, Charing, Kent, 1616 CKS PRC20/3/466
Downe, Robert, Hartlip, Kent, 1692 CKS PRC2/42/30
Downe, William, Sturry, Kent, 1614 CKS PRC2/18/16
Downe, William, yeoman, Folkestone, Kent, 1684 CKS PRC2/40/195
Downer, Edward, Littlehampton, Sussex, 1608 W. Suss RO EpI/33/1607/11
Downer, Thomas, Linsted, Kent, 1598 CKS PRC2/10/286
Downerd, Richard, Hawkhurst, Kent, 1617 CKS PRC2/21/122
Downes, John, innholder, Charlbury, Oxon, 1636 Oxon RO MSS Wills 296/4/73
Downes, John, gentleman, Speen, Berks, 1683 Berks RO D/A1/187/43C
Downes, Richard, Faversham, Kent, 1664 CKS PRC1/10/30

[Downes:]
Downes, Walter, Ingestre, Staffs, 1672 LJRO:cards/1672/15
Downing, Thomas, St Clement, Corn, 1613 Cornwall RO AP/D102/3
Downinge, Degory, yeoman, Egloskerry, Corn, 1630 Cornwall RO AP/D252/3
Downinge, William, wood seller, Dudley, Worcs, 1588 Worcs RO 008.7 BA3585/838/74
Downinge, William, gentleman, Lincoln St Peter in Eastgate, Lincs, 1626 Lincs RO Ad/Ac/20/82
Downward, John, blockmaker, Liverpool, Lancs, 1752 Lancs RO (Name of Deceased) D.R.C.H. 1752
Dowse, Elizabeth, widow, Lincoln St Mary, Lincs, 1607 Lincs RO Ad/Ac/7/20
Dowse, John, Tathwell, Lincs, 1650 Lincs RO Ad/Ac/29/115
Dowse, Peter, shepherd, Ludford, Lincs, 1623 Lincs RO Ad/Ac/18/48
Dowse, Richard, Frieston, Lincs, 1600 Lincs RO Ad/Ac/5/338
Dowse, Richard, Leverton, Lincs, 1614 Lincs RO Ad/Ac/12/206
Dowse, Robert, Dean, West, Wilts, 1636 Wilts RO Arch. Sarum/(+ name and date)
Dowse, Susan, widow, Leverton, Lincs, 1614 Lincs RO Ad/Ac/13/103
Dowse, Thomas, Birchington, Kent, 1581 CKS PRC21/5/109
Dowsett, Mercy, widow, Watton-at-Stone, Herts, 1636 Herts RO AHH23/632
Dowson, Isaac, yeoman, Drax (Newland), Yorks, 1773 Borthwick Test C.P. 1773/3
Dowson, John, Oxford (University), Oxon, 1709 Bodleian HYP B8/41-42
Dowtye, Marian, widow, Woodchurch, Kent, 1583 CKS PRC21/6/258
Dowzin, Jane, widow, St Bride, London & Middlesex, 1743 Greater London RO DL/C/550/50/1
Doy, Nicholas, Dover, Kent, 1630 CKS PRC20/8/163
Doyste, John,
Kent 1579 CKS PRC21/3/306
Doyste, John,
Kent 1579 CKS PRC21/3/310
Dracott, James, Canterbury, Kent, 1638 CKS PRC2/34/195
Drage, Stukeley, Little, Hunts, 1721 Hunts RO/Acc58/312
Drage, John, yeoman, Hemingford Abbots, Hunts, 1680 Hunts RO/Acc58/145(7)
Drake, Anthony, Truro, Corn, 1604 Cornwall RO AP/D31
Drake, Thomas, yeoman, Chadlington, Oxon, 1647 Oxon RO MSS Wills 296/4/87
Drakeford, James, carpenter, Newton Regis, Warks, 1815 LJRO/B/C/5/1815/23
Dramer, John, Sandwich, Kent, 1591 CKS PRC2/5/126
Dranner, Thomas, Biddenden, Kent, 1614 CKS PRC2/18/3
Draper, Adam, Clewer, Berks, 1610 Berks RO D/A1/186/93A
Draper, Edmund, tilemaker, Ippollitts (Maydencroft), Herts, Herts RO AHH23/628
Draper, George, wheelwright, Sulham, Berks, 1648 Berks RO D/A1/187/35D
Draper, Humfrie, Smarden, Kent, 1600 CKS PRC2/11/197
Draper, Jane, Crowle, Lincs, 1623 Lincs RO Ad/Ac/8c/63
Draper, John, gentleman, Shipton under Wychwood, Oxon, 1680 Oxon RO MSS Wills 164/1/39
Draper, John, Repton, Derby, 1682 LJRO/B/C/5/1682/33
Draper, John, Melbourne, Derby, 1683 LJRO/B/C/5/1682/32
Draper, John, mariner: 'captain', HMS Hastings,, 1701 PRO PROB5/1125
Draper, Margaret, spinster, Perrot, North, Som, 1730 Somerset RO D/D/Cta/D38
Draper, Richard, Brockenhurst, Hants, 1625 Hants RO 21M65 D8/113
Draper, Richard, gentleman, Boston, Lincs, 1640 Lincs RO Ad/Ac/27/144
Draper, Robert, Dogmersfield, Hants, 1623 Hants RO 21M65 D8/14
Draper, Robert, Weston, Herts, 1637 Herts RO AHH23/638
Draper, Robert, gentleman, Brailsford (Culland), Derby, 1696 LJRO/B/C/5/1696/16a, b
Draper, Thomas, Swarkestone, Derby, 1663 LJRO:cards/1663/20
Draper, Thomas, collier, Bolton-le-Moors, Lancs, 1771 Lancs RO (Name of Deceased) D.R.C.H. 1771
Drawbridge, Elizabeth, Brenzett, Kent, 1630 CKS PRC2/30/44
Drawbridge, James, Brenzett, Kent, 1618 CKS PRC2/21/118
Drawbridge, John, Westwell, Kent, 1619 CKS PRC20/4/79
Drawebridge, Christopher, Lenham, Kent, 1591 CKS PRC2/5/128

Drax, John,
Barbados 1679 PRO PROB32/18/18
Dray, John, Newenden, Kent, 1632 CKS PRC20/9/19
Draye, John, Wingham, Kent, 1633 CKS PRC20/10/278
Draye, Thomas, Smeeth, Kent, 1614 CKS PRC20/2/480
Drayner, John, Frittenden, Kent, 1630 CKS PRC20/9/127
Drayner, John, Headcorn, Kent, 1640 CKS PRC1/4/29
Drayner, John, Frittenden, Kent, 1648 CKS PRC1/8/13
Drayner, John, yeoman, Staplehurst, Kent, 1669 CKS PRC1/14/31
Drayner, Michael, Frittenden, Kent, 1612 CKS PRC2/17/368
Drayner, Michaell, Staplehurst, Kent, 1588 CKS PRC2/5/72
Drayner, Thomas, Frittenden, Kent, 1631 CKS PRC20/9/119
Drayner, Thomas, Appledore, Kent, 1680 CKS PRC2/39/29
Drayner, Thomas eld, Smarden, Kent, 1627 CKS PRC2/28/41
Drayson, John, Stalisfield, Kent, 1576 CKS PRC2/1/166
Drayson, Stephen, Hothfield, Kent, 1612 CKS PRC2/17/333
Drayton, James, apothecary, Maidstone, Kent, 1684 CKS PRC20/13/414
Dredforth, Lyon, Huttoft, Lincs, 1632 Lincs RO Ad/Ac/23/136
Drew, Abraham, Bulkington, Warks, 1672 LJRO:cards/1672/16
Drew, George + Jone, Dover St Mary, Kent, 1627 CKS PRC20/8/153
Drew, Margaret, widow, Christchurch, Glos, Bristol RO 1688/17
Drew, Richard, miller, Dover, Kent, 1672 CKS PRC20/12/46
Drewe, Henry, Corsham, Wilts, 1618? Wilts RO Pec the Perpetual Vicar of Corsham 1285/6/118
Drewe, Henry, Poulshot, Wilts, 1678 Wilts RO Arch. Sarum/(+ name and date)
Drewe, Joane, widow, Tenterden, Kent, 1616 CKS PRC2/21/136
Drewet, John, Patching, Sussex, 1683 W. Suss RO EpIV/10/2A/30
Drewet, Robert, Lancing, Sussex, 1684 W. Suss RO EpI/33/1684/5
Drewett, Richard, Bampton, Oxon, 1634 Oxon RO MSS Wills 296/4/72
Drewrey, James, yeoman, Eastchurch, Sheppey, Kent, 1649 CKS PRC1/8/65
Drewrie, Christopher, Minting, Lincs, 1624 Lincs RO Ad/Ac/19A/83
Drewrie, Henrie, Saxilby (North Ingleby), Lincs, 1624 Lincs RO Ad/Ac/8c/77
Drewrie, Homfrie, Wainfleet St Mary, Lincs, 1614 Lincs RO Ad/Ac/13/85
Drewrie, James, Swinhope, Lincs, 1626 Lincs RO Ad/Ac/20/16
Drewrie, John, Epworth, Lincs, 1607 Lincs RO Ad/Ac/37/252
Drewrie, Roger, Lenton, Lincs, 1599 Lincs RO Ad/Ac/5/469
Drewrie, William, Halton Holgate, Lincs, 1652 Lincs RO Ad/Ac/29/37
Drewrie/Throwley, William, Bapchild, Kent, CKS PRC1/10/31
Drewry, John, yeoman, Scotter, Lincs, 1673 Lincs RO Ad/Ac/35/46
Drewry, Theophilous, Hannah, Lincs, 1637 Lincs RO Ad/Ac/25/381
Drewry, William, Tattershall, Lincs, 1639 Lincs RO Ad/Ac/27/17
Drewry, William, grazier, Wyberton, Lincs, 1825 Lincs RO Ad/Ac/45/78
Drewry, Willyam, Tattershall, Lincs, 1601 Lincs RO Ad/Ac/5/125
Drewry/Throwlie, John, Rodmersham, Kent, 1595 CKS PRC2/7/409
Drewry, see Martyn,
Drewrye, William, Spalding, Lincs, 1612 Lincs RO Ad/Ac/10/170
Dreyton, James, alderman, Canterbury Holy Cross Westgate, Kent, 1582 CKS PRC2/2/41
Driall, John, Chewton Mendip, Som, 1607 Somerset RO D/D/Cta/D22
Driden, Mary, widow, Woodford (West Farndon), Northants, 1677 Northants RO NWill A/C/45
Drie, Henrie, husbandman, Netherbury, Dors, 1607 Wilts RO Dean Sarum (name + date)
Dringe, Daniel, St Neots, Hunts, 1676 Hunts RO/Acc58/27(130)
Drinker, Edward, yeoman, Hernhill, Kent, 1642 CKS PRC19/2/13
Drinker, Joane, widow, Hernhill, Kent, 1624 CKS PRC20/6/52
Drinker, Thomas, Lydd, Kent, 1588 CKS PRC21/9/25
Drinkewater, Edward, Sittingbourne, Kent, 1671 CKS PRC2/35/33
Drinkwater, Peter, gentleman, Massey Green, Ches, 1664 Cheshire RO (Name) W.C. 1664

[Drinkwater:]
Drinkwater, Richard, gentleman, Temple, Inner, London & Middlesex, 1700 Lambeth Palace Arches G49/2
Drinkwater, Sarah, widow, Semington, Wilts, 1757? Wilts RO Miscellaneous Index to Wills (name + date)
Drinkwater, Sarah, widow, Semington, Wilts, 1762 Wilts RO Miscellaneous Index to Wills (name + date)
Drope, James, Grimsby, Great (Wellow), Lincs, 1625 Lincs RO Ad/Ac/19B/73
Drought, John, turner, Canterbury, Kent, 1631 CKS PRC20/9/117
Drought, Richard, blacksmith, Canterbury Holy Cross Westgate, Kent, 1671 CKS PRC1/15/18
Drought, Richard, Wolston (Bretford), Warks, 1681 LJRO/B/C/5/1681/10
Drought, Ursula, Canterbury, Kent, 1639 CKS PRC2/34/194
Druce, John, Garsington, Oxon, 1675 Oxon RO MSS Wills 296/4/91
Drue, Benjamin, gentleman, Baverstock, Wilts, 1670 Wilts RO Arch. Sarum/(+ name and date)
Druer/Toogood, William, Frome Selwood, Som, 1621 Somerset RO D/D/Cta/D5
Drury, George, Aylesby, Lincs, 1639 Lincs RO Ad/Ac/26/73
Drury, James, Eastchurch, Sheppey, Kent, 1625 CKS PRC2/25/49
Drury, John, Tenterden, Kent, 1627 CKS PRC2/28/40
Drury, Mary, widow, Rainham, Kent, 1674 CKS PRC2/35/211
Drury, Thomas, esquire, Lincoln's Inn, London & Middlesex, 1673 PRO PROB32/10/164
Drury, William, Epworth, Lincs, 1632 Lincs RO Ad/Ac/39/270
Drury, see Martin,
Drust, Robert, Marden, Kent, 1640 CKS PRC1/2/52
Drust, Stephen, labourer, Wrawby cum Brigg, Lincs, 1663 Lincs RO Ad/Ac/43/9c
Drust, see Sheafe,
Dry, Abraham, Greenwich (East Greenwich), Kent, 1700 PRO PROB5/1216
Dry, Roland, Etton, Yorks, 1613 Borthwick Prob. Ex. 1613/1
Dryland, Anthony, Eastchurch, Sheppey, Kent, 1625 CKS PRC2/23/104
Dryland, Christopher, Hernhill, Kent, 1634 CKS PRC20/10/282
Dryland, Elizabeth, widow, Wye, Kent, 1616 CKS PRC2/21/113
Dryland, John, Wye, Kent, 1638 CKS PRC2/34/193
Du Forrest, John, Canterbury St Alphege, Kent, 1613 CKS PRC20/2/454
Du Lake, Lancelot, knight,
London & Middlesex 1681 PRO PROB32/20/40
Du Pree, James, Canterbury St Margaret, Kent, 1611 CKS PRC2/16/46
Dubber, Richard, husbandman, Woolvercott, Oxon, 1627 Oxon RO MSS Wills 17/4/23
Dubbin, Edward, Eastergate, Sussex, 1676 W. Suss RO EpI/33/1676/13
Dubbin, Robert, Appleby, Lincs, 1609 Lincs RO Ad/Ac/8a/300
Dubble, James, Stone in Oxney, Kent, 1586 CKS PRC2/4/47
Dubbleday, Isabell, spinster, Broughton, Nether, Leics, 1639 Leics RO PR/I/41A/18
Dubuha, John, Canterbury, Kent, 1583 CKS PRC21/6/368
Duck, John, yeoman, Wroughton, Wilts, 1681 Wilts RO Arch. Wilts.(name + date)
Ducke, Alice, Egerton, Kent, 1586 CKS PRC21/8/31
Ducke, Alice, widow, Hollingbourne, Kent, 1612 CKS PRC20/2/232
Ducke, Edward, Warminghurst, Sussex, 1631 W. Suss RO EpI/33/1631/4
Ducke, Joanne, widow, Hucking, Kent, 1603 CKS PRC21/17/266
Ducke, Thomas, Wroughton, Wilts, 1639 Wilts RO Arch. Wilts.(name + date)
Ducker, Catherine, spinster, Haxey, Lincs, 1683 Lincs RO Ad/Ac/44/48
Ducker, John, yeoman, Marr, Yorks, Borthwick Test C.P. 1717/4
Duckett, Gabriel, university: 'Fellow/University Library Keeper/M.A.', Cambridge (Trinity College/St John's College), Cambs, 1624 CUL V.C. Acc./Box2/21
Duckett, Gabriel, university: 'Fellow/University Library Keeper/M.A.', Cambridge (Trinity College/St John's College), Cambs, 1624 CUL V.C. Acc./Box2/22
Duckett, William, Selling, Kent, 1614 CKS PRC2/17/81
Duckle, Henrye, Messingham, Lincs, 1600 Lincs RO Ad/Ac/5/279
Duckle, Thomas, Winterton, Lincs, 1616 Lincs RO Ad/Ac/8b/234

Duckle/Kirke, Katherine, widow, Heapham, Lincs, 1662 Lincs RO Ad/Ac/41/26
Duckworth, James, weaver: 'cotton weaver', Tottington, Lancs, 1755 Lancs RO (Name of Deceased) D.R.C.H. 1754-55
Duckworth, Roger, Dodleston, Ches, 1680 Cheshire RO (Name) W.C. 1680
Duckworth, William, innkeeper, Manchester, Lancs, 1798 Lancs RO (Name of Deceased) D.R.C.H. 1798
Duddicke, Margarett, widow, Billinghay (Dogdyke), Lincs, 1669 Lincs RO Ad/Ac/33/142
Dudding, Margaret, widow, Durrington, Sussex, 1632 W. Suss RO EpIV/10/2/6
Duddyng, Mary + Edith,
  Som Somerset RO D/D/Cta/D9
Dudley, Edward, West Bromwich, Staffs, 1667 LJRO:cards/1667/26
Duell, Edmund, yeoman, Waltham, White, Berks, 1684 Berks RO D/A1/187/45d
Duell, John jun, bachelor, Waltham, White, Berks, 1685 Berks RO D/A1/187/51C
Duell, Richard, Newbury, Berks, 1597 Berks RO D/A1/186/62C
Duffield, Robert, fellmonger, Leeds, Kent, 1692 CKS PRC2/42/4
Duffild, Thomas, Swineshead, Lincs, 1615 Lincs RO Ad/Ac/13/95
Duffin, Edward, yeoman, Aldermaston, Berks, 1633 Berks RO D/A1/186/149D
Duffin, Elizabeth, wife, Abingdon, Berks, 1603 Berks RO D/A1/186/77A&C
Duffin, John, miller, Abingdon St Nicholas (Ock Mill), Berks, 1672 Berks RO D/A1/187/29C
Duffin, William, butcher, Woolhampton, Berks, 1630 Berks RO D/A1/186/144A
Duffy, John, tailor, Fairfield, Kent, 1687 CKS PRC20/13/586
Duffyld, Alexander, Sandwich St Peter, Kent, 1585 CKS PRC2/3/243
Duflo, James, Canterbury St Dunstan Without, Kent, 1697 CKS PRC19/5/53
Duflo, James, Canterbury St Dunstan Without, Kent, 1701 CKS PRC19/5/53a
Dugard, William, gentleman, Bebington (Tranmere), Ches, 1800 Cheshire RO (Name) W.C. 1800
Dugdale, Elizabeth, Codford St Peter, Wilts, 1640? Wilts RO Arch. Sarum/(+ name and date)
Dugleyes, William, Aylesby, Lincs, 1649 Lincs RO Ad/Ac/30/221
Duglis, William, Henley, Oxon, 1630 Oxon RO MSS Wills 296/4/55
Dugoe, John, Collingbourne Kingston, Wilts, 1677 Wilts RO Miscellaneous Index to Wills (name + date)
Dugs, Robert, husbandman, Durrington, Wilts, 1611 Wilts RO Arch. Sarum/(+ name and date) w
Duhen, Michaell, weaver: 'silk weaver', Canterbury St Margaret, Kent, 1619 CKS PRC2/21/117
Duke, Andrew, esquire,
  Wilts 1682 Wilts RO Arch. Sarum/(+ name and date)
Duke, Anthony, husbandman, Sutton (Lutton), Lincs, 1679 Lincs RO Ad/Ac/43/114
Duke, Charles, cook, Speen, Berks, 1619 Berks RO D/A1/186/114A
Duke, Francis, glover, Reading St Mary, Berks, 1597 Berks RO D/A1/186/65C
Duke, George,
  Wilts 1656 Wilts RO Miscellaneous Index to Wills (name + date)
Duke, John, Hawkhurst, Kent, 1603 CKS PRC2/14/158
Duke, John, New Romney, Kent, 1625 CKS PRC20/7/369
Duke, Nicholas, Folkestone, Kent, 1620 CKS PRC2/21/114
Duke, Richard, Amberley, Sussex, 1618 W. Suss RO EpI/33/1617/26
Duke, William, Storrington, Sussex, 1596 W. Suss RO EpI/33/1596/4
Duker, William, brewer, Elham, Kent, 1640 CKS PRC1/4/30
Dukesell, Robert, widower, Borden, Kent, 1672 CKS PRC2/35/128
Duling, John, Axbridge, Som, 1639 Somerset RO D/D/Cta/D7
Dull, Henry, Yardley, Worcs, 1605 Worcs RO 008.7 BA3585/839/346a
Dumbleton, George, Tadmarton (Lower Tadmarton), Oxon, Oxon RO MSS Wills 296/4/74
Dumper, William, cordwainer, Reading St Lawrence, Berks, 1627 Berks RO D/A1/186/128A
Dun, Edward, Barwick, Som, 1620 Somerset RO D/D/Cta/D14
Dun, Richard, Hanbury, Staffs, 1675 LJRO:cards/1675/18
Dunburie, John, Smarden, Kent, 1615 CKS PRC2/21/123
Dunch, Anne, mistress/widow, Wittenham, Little, Berks, 1633 Berks RO D/A1/62/89D
Duncke, Frances, Hawkhurst, Kent, 1603 CKS PRC2/14/154

[Duncke:]
Duncke, John, Hawkhurst, Kent, 1625 CKS PRC2/25/47
Duncke, Thomas, Tenterden, Kent, 1617 CKS PRC2/21/131
Duncke, Ursula, widow, Brabourne, Kent, 1671 CKS PRC1/15/19
Dunckin, John, Sandwich, Kent, 1598 CKS PRC2/8/250
Dunckin, John, Brabourne, Kent, 1609 CKS PRC2/14/148
Dunckin, John, mr, Canterbury, Kent, 1610 CKS PRC20/2/122
Dunckyn, John, Elmsted, Kent, 1596 CKS PRC2/8/204
Duncoft, Isaiah, yeoman, Hathershaw, Lancs, 1766 Lancs RO (Name of Deceased) D.R.C.H. 1766
Dundy, Edmund, Milton next Sittingbourne, Kent, 1617 CKS PRC2/21/143
Dungate, John, Horsham, Sussex, 1597 W. Suss RO EpI/33/1597/3
Dungey, Otho, husbandman, Mawgan-in-Pydar, Corn, 1613 Cornwall RO AP/D109/2
Dungey, William, St Wenn, Corn, 1606 Cornwall RO AP/D24/3
Dungott, Edward, Besselsleigh, Berks, 1610 Berks RO D/A1/196/97C
Dungworth, Joseph, cutler, Sheffield (Whirlow Hall), Yorks, 1773 Borthwick Test C.P. 1773/4
Dunham, Gabriell, Somercoates, North, Lincs, 1639 Lincs RO Ad/Ac/26/133
Dunham, Thomas, Fulstow, Lincs, 1648 Lincs RO Ad/Ac/30/362
Duninge, James, Alford, Lincs, 1635 Lincs RO Ad/Ac/24/355
Dunke, Edward, Biddenden, Kent, 1678 CKS PRC2/38/23
Dunke, John, Cranbrook, Kent, 1617 CKS PRC2/21/137
Dunke, Thomas ygr, Hawkhurst, Kent, 1583 CKS PRC2/3/108
Dunke, William, wheelwright, Hawkhurst, Kent, 1683 CKS PRC2/40/110
Dunkin, Edward, Benenden, Kent, 1632 CKS PRC2/31/103
Dunkin, George, Dover, Kent, 1632 CKS PRC20/10/274
Dunkin, Gregorie, Whitstable, Kent, 1616 CKS PRC2/21/129
Dunkin, John, Ash next Sandwich, Kent, 1625 CKS PRC20/6/62
Dunkin, Jonathan, yeoman, Canterbury St George Martyr, Kent, 1678 CKS PRC2/38/22
Dunkin, Richard, Selling, Kent, 1622 CKS PRC2/23/94
Dunkin, Richard, Canterbury St Mary Bredin, Kent, 1640 CKS PRC19/1/39
Dunkin, Susann, widow, St Peter in Thanet, Kent, 1665 CKS PRC1/11/19
Dunkin, Thomas, Winteringham, Lincs, 1635 Lincs RO Ad/Ac/40/93
Dunkyn, Joane, widow, Boxley, Kent, 1612 CKS PRC2/16/145
Dunkyn, John, Sandwich, Kent, 1595 CKS PRC2/7/158
Dunkyn, John, Westwell, Kent, 1627 CKS PRC20/8/151
Dunkyn, Mary, widow, Canterbury, Kent, 1623 CKS PRC20/6/388
Dunlin, Margarett, widow, Crowle, Lincs, 1671 Lincs RO Ad/Ac/33/209
Dunn, Edward, Barwick, Som, 1620 Somerset RO D/D/Cta/D2
Dunn, John, miller, Elham, Kent, 1680 CKS PRC2/39/25
Dunn, William, Brent Knoll, Som, 1644 Somerset RO D/D/Cta/D21
Dunne, Richard, Wem, Shrops, 1681 LJRO/B/C/5/1681/11
Dunney, Thomas, Wittersham, Kent, 1582 CKS PRC21/6/154
Dunney, William, New Romney, Kent, 1595 CKS PRC21/14/231
Dunniclyffe, Martin, Mugginton (Weston under Wood), Derby, 1680 LJRO:cards/1680/12
Dunning, Robert, Maidstone, Kent, 1603 CKS PRC21/17/69
Dunning, William, Godmersham, Kent, 1618 CKS PRC20/4/71
Dunning, William, Bradley, North, Wilts, 1642 Wilts RO Arch. Sarum/(+ name and date)
Dunninge, Edward, Chartham, Kent, 1621 CKS PRC2/21/140
Dunnings, George, Graveney, Kent, 1688 CKS PRC2/41/119
Dunnyng, William, Staple next Wingham, Kent, 1596 CKS PRC21/14/87
Dunsby, Nicholas, yeoman, Gosberton, Lincs, 1614 Lincs RO Ad/Ac/13/10
Dunsdon, William, cordwainer/yeoman, Ardington, Berks, 1678 Berks RO D/A1/187/33A
Dunstall, Nicholas, Bramber, Sussex, 1613 W. Suss RO EpI/33/1613/26
Dunston, Gamaliell?, Ashby de la Zouch, Leics, Leics RO Administrators Accounts 1667-72 f102
Dunt, Robert, husbandman, Sulhampstead Bannister, Berks, 1683 Berks RO D/A1/187/41D
Dunton, John, Worlaby, Lincs, 1613 Lincs RO Ad/Ac/11/69
Dunton, Thomas, chandler: 'tallow chandler', St Andrew Holborn, London & Middlesex, 1679

PRO PROB32/18/108
Dunton, Walter, Shipley, Sussex, 1626 W. Suss RO EpI/33/1625/10
Dupe, Christopher, yeoman, Salisbury, Wilts, 1672 Wilts RO Miscellaneous Index to Wills (name + date)
Duport, Henry, esquire, Sheepshed, Leics, 1641 Leics RO PR/I/41A/63
Duppa, Robert, Cranbrook, Kent, 1624 CKS PRC2/23/103
Durbarne, John, Ringwould, Kent, 1613 CKS PRC2/17/278
Durber,
Som 1632 Somerset RO D/D/Cta/D39
Durburn, Thomas, widower, Stepney, London & Middlesex, 1691 PRO PROB32/30/245
Durden, Abdias, gentleman, Reading, Berks, 1625 Berks RO D/A1/186/127C
Durden/Jurden, Richard, Ash next Sandwich, Kent, 1590 CKS PRC21/10/91
Durell, Clement, Catherington, Hants, 1624 Hants RO 21M65 D8/64
Durgat, John, Yateley, Hants, 1624 Hants RO 21M65 D8/63
Durham, Ann, widow, St Giles in the Fields (Vinegar Yard), London & Middlesex, 1808 Greater London RO DL/C/567/
Durham, Thomas, brewer, Worcester, Worcs, 1610 Worcs RO 008.7 BA3585/839/486
Durholme, Thomas, Dunsby, Lincs, 1632 Lincs RO Ad/Ac/23/141
Durkin, Thomas, butcher, Linton, Kent, 1675 CKS PRC2/36/181
Durlach, Peter, York, Yorks, Borthwick Test C.P. 1753/2
Durman, William, clergy: 'clerk', Stratton on the Foss, Som, 1691 Somerset RO D/D/Cta/D40
Durnell, Edith, Camerton, Som, 1604 Somerset RO D/D/Cta/D17
Durrant, Augustine, Hessett, Suff, 1729 Suff RO(B) IC500/3/46/7
Durrant, John, Luddenham, Kent, 1605 CKS PRC2/13/164
Durrant, John, Minster in Thanet, Kent, 1616 CKS PRC2/21/124
Durrant, John, Rickmansworth, Herts, 1627 Herts RO ASA25/4842
Durrant, John, King's Lynn, Norf, 1755 Norfolk RO ANW/23/24/149C
Durrant, Thomas, Eastwell, Kent, 1598 CKS PRC2/9/361
Durston, Alexander, Lyme Regis, Dors, 1589 Wilts RO Dean Sarum (name + date)
Durtknowle, John eld, Marden, Kent, 1614 CKS PRC2/18/116
Durtnall, Alexander, fellmonger, Leeds, Kent, 1668 CKS PRC1/12/30
Durtnall, Rose, widow, Leeds, Kent, 1667 CKS PRC1/12/31
Durtnall, Susan, widow, Marden, Kent, 1672 CKS PRC2/35/127
Dustie, William, Appledore, Kent, 1600 CKS PRC2/11/409
Dutton, Lawrence, tailor, Covent Garden, St Paul, London & Middlesex, 1691 PRO PROB32/30/178
Dutton, Richard (Edward?), husbandman, Aldridge, Staffs, 1672 LJRO:cards/1672/17
Dutton, William, Bristol, Glos, Bristol RO 1728/12
Duxbury, William, dyer, Manchester, Lancs, 1788 Lancs RO (Name of Deceased) D.R.C.H. 1787-89
Duxon, Rychard, Gainsborough, Lincs, 1585 Lincs RO Ad/Ac/37/1
Duzzell, William, waterman, St Katherine by the Tower, London & Middlesex, 1675 PRO PROB32/12/41
Dyamond, Peter, Boughton Aluph, Kent, 1636 CKS PRC2/33/41
Dyche, Thomas, Watford, Herts, 1573 Herts RO ASA25/748
Dyer, Alice, widow, Woodchurch, Kent, 1614 CKS PRC20/3/138
Dyer, Henrie, Woodchurch, Kent, 1611 CKS PRC20/2/116
Dyer, Jeremy, Faversham, Kent, 1597 CKS PRC2/9/275
Dyer, John, Milton Falconbridge, Som, 1641 Somerset RO D/D/Cta/D11
Dyer, John, Stoke Climsland, Corn, 1646 Cornwall RO AP/D515/2
Dyer, John, clothier, Appledore, Kent, 1680 CKS PRC2/39/26
Dyer, John, Heytesbury, Wilts, 1737? Wilts RO Dean Sarum (name + date)
Dyer, John, yeoman, St Catherine, Som, 1740 Somerset RO D/D/Cta/D41
Dyer, Richard, Yapton (Bilsham), Sussex, 1606 W. Suss RO EpI/33/1606/3
Dyer, Richard, Avebury (West Kennett), Wilts, 1650 Wilts RO CC Sarum(+ name and date)

[Dyer:]
Dyer, Robert, husbandman, St Laurence Thanet, Kent, 1672 CKS PRC2/35/125
Dyer, Thomas, Pelynt, Corn, 1629 Cornwall RO AP/D314/2
Dyer, William, Shipley, Sussex, 1635 W. Suss RO EpI/33/1635/27
Dyke, Humphrey, Stepney, St Dunstan (Stebenhythe), London & Middlesex, 1704 PRO PROB32/47/73
Dyke, Thomas, Woodborough, Wilts, 1676 Wilts RO Miscellaneous Index to Wills (name + date)
Dykes, Jane, widow, Brigham (Cockermouth), Cumb, Borthwick Test C.P. 1756/1
Dymer, John, Overton, Wilts, 1625 Wilts RO Arch. Wilts.(name + date)
Dymersh, William, Eversley, Hants, 1672 Hants RO 21m65 D8/240
Dymocke, Edward, Haltham on Bain, Lincs, 1639 Lincs RO Ad/Ac/26/307
Dymocke, John, gentleman, Belshford, Lincs, 1670 Lincs RO Ad/Ac/32/179
Dymocke, Trothe, gentlewoman,
Lincs 1607 Lincs RO Ad/Ac/8a/169
Dyne, Edward, Teynham, Kent, 1601 CKS PRC2/12/137
Dyne, Jeames, Doddington, Kent, 1592 CKS PRC2/5/124
Dyne, Jeremy, Headcorn, Kent, 1594 CKS PRC2/7/45
Dyne, John, Godmersham, Kent, 1579 CKS PRC21/3/331
Dyne, John, Doddington, Kent, 1596 CKS PRC2/9/99
Dyne, William, Lydd, Kent, 1599 CKS PRC21/15/53
Dynes, John, Partney, Lincs, 1601 Lincs RO Ad/Ac/5/477
Dynham, Christopher, esquire, Piddington (Muswell), Oxon, 1628 Oxon RO MSS Wills 296/4/49b
Dynham, George, gentleman, Murston, Kent, 1599 CKS PRC2/11/76
Dynis, see Curtis,
Dynnis, Ellen, widow, Luddington (Garthorpe), Lincs, 1683 Lincs RO Ad/Ac/44/76
Dynnis, John, Hatton, Lincs, 1624 Lincs RO Ad/Ac/19A/87
Dynsdale, John, degrees: 'M.A.', Oxford (University), Oxon, Bodleian HYP B8/43
Dyson, Francis, Inkberrow, Worcs, 1684 Worcs RO 008.7 BA3585/837/bdl 4
Dyson, James, Tothill, Lincs, 1613 Lincs RO Ad/Ac/12/214
Dyson, Richard, Polesworth, Warks, 1672 LJRO:cards/1672/18
Dyston, John, Norton, Chipping, Oxon, 1676 Oxon RO MSS Wills 296/4/92
Dytton, Daniell, Swingfield, Kent, 1601 CKS PRC2/12/132
Dytton, Thomas, Swingfield, Kent, 1601 CKS PRC2/12/135
Dyve, Edward, Boughton under Blean, Kent, 1603 CKS PRC21/16/49
Dyve, Thomas, Bearsted, Kent, 1603 CKS PRC2/12/430
Dyvers, William, Canterbury St Mary Northgate, Kent, 1610 CKS PRC2/15/90
Eachyard, Thomas, Wigtoft, Lincs, 1619 Lincs RO Ad/Ac/15/73
Eacopp/Eacupp, William, husbandman, Billingborough, Lincs, 1668 Lincs RO Ad/Ac/33/61
Eacupp, see Eacopp,
Eager, Thomas, Aby, Lincs, 1632 Lincs RO Ad/Ac/23/9
Eagley, John, Birdham, Sussex, 1633 W. Suss RO EpI/33/1633/7
Eakin, Rowland, clothworker, Chester, Ches, 1666 Cheshire RO (Name) W.C. 1666
Ealmes, Grace, widow, Ashton, Steeple, Wilts, 1687 Wilts RO Arch. Sarum/(+ name and date)
Eames, Christabel, Greinton, Som, 1685 Somerset RO D/D/Cta/E14
Eames, William, Kirdford (Plaistow), Sussex, 1639 W. Suss RO EpIV/10/2/24
Eare, Richard, Tarvin, Ches, 1618 Cheshire RO (Name) W.C. 1618
Earl, William, staymaker, Chester, Ches, 1780 Cheshire RO (Name) W.C. 1780
Earle, Alice, spinster, Hemingford Abbots, Hunts, 1676 Hunts RO/Acc58/83(155)
Earle, Ann, Deal, Kent, 1674 CKS PRC20/12/124
Earle, Benjamin, Dover, Kent, 1717 CKS PRC19/6/61
Earle, Bennett, widow, Wittersham, Kent, 1584 CKS PRC21/7/73
Earle, Edward, Pinchbeck, Lincs, 1670s? Lincs RO Ad/Ac/32/198
Earle, Edward, Pinchbeck, Lincs, 1671 Lincs RO Ad/Ac/32/232
Earle, Elizabeth, widow, Biddenden, Kent, 1637 CKS PRC1/1/51
Earle, John, Malmesbury, Wilts, 1626 Wilts RO Arch. Wilts.(name + date)
Earle, John, clergy: 'clerk/rector', Shipham, Som, 1674 Somerset RO D/D/Cta/E15

Earle, John, Kilby, Leics, 1686 Leics RO Administrators Accounts 1682-86 f48
Earle, John, farrier, Wetherby, Yorks, 1719 Borthwick Test C.P. 1720/3
Earle, John, Middlewich (Kinderton), Ches, 1735 Cheshire RO (Name) W.C. 1735
Earle, Katherine, Cranbrook, Kent, 1624 CKS PRC2/23/113
Earle, Mary, widow, Dover, Kent, 1714 CKS PRC19/6/62
Earle, Richard, cordwainer: 'shoemaker', Wittersham, Kent, 1640 CKS PRC19/1/40
Earle, Robert, Ingham, Lincs, 1674 Lincs RO Ad/Ac/35/84
Earle, Thomas, High Halstow, Kent, 1665 CKS PRC1/11/20
Earle, Thomas, weaver: 'broad weaver', Goudhurst, Kent, 1667 CKS PRC1/12/32
Earle, William, mariner, Dover, Kent, 1679 CKS PRC20/12/301
Earles, Sarah, Ulcombe, Kent, 1677 CKS PRC2/37/140
Earlie, Anthony, Bedwin, Little, Wilts, 1625 Wilts RO Miscellaneous Index to Wills (name + date)
Earlie, Paule, weaver: 'broad weaver', Marden, Kent, 1613 CKS PRC2/16/129
Earlsfield, Robert, Hawkhurst, Kent, 1598 CKS PRC2/10/206
Earsye, James, Snave, Kent, 1616 CKS PRC2/21/110
Easday, Thomas, gentleman, Canterbury St Mary Bredin, Kent, 1626 CKS PRC2/27/46
Easly, Joseph, cutler, Faversham, Kent, 1690 CKS PRC2/41/172 and 172a
Easman, Willyam, pewterer, Lincoln, Lincs, 1633 Lincs RO Ad/Ac/23/171
Eason, Edward, St Laurence Thanet, Kent, 1667 CKS PRC1/12/33
Eason, Elizabeth, widow, St Peter in Thanet, Kent, 1620 CKS PRC2/21/94
Eason, George, Nonington, Kent, 1640 CKS PRC19/1/41
Eason, John, Throwleigh, Kent, 1640 CKS PRC1/4/31
Eason, Richard, St Peter in Thanet, Kent, 1607 CKS PRC2/15/101
Eason, Richard, St Laurence Thanet, Kent, 1668 CKS PRC1/13/33
Eason, see Randolph,
Easson, Joan, widow, Herne, Kent, 1610 CKS PRC20/2/176
Easson, William, Preston next Faversham, Kent, 1583 CKS PRC2/3/41
Easson, William, Preston next Faversham, Kent, 1594 CKS PRC2/7/23
East, James, watchmaker/bachelor, St Martin in the Fields, London & Middlesex, 1679 PRO PROB32/16/60
East, Joseph jun, clothworker, Reading, Berks, 1683 Berks RO D/A1/189/11C
East, Richard, Sutton in the Marsh, Lincs, 1612 Lincs RO Ad/Ac/11/119
East, Stephen, Keal, East, Lincs, 1638 Lincs RO Ad/Ac/25/216
East, Thomas, Aston Abbots, Bucks, 1627 Herts RO ASA25/4843
East, Thomas, Stone in Oxney, Kent, 1676 CKS PRC2/36/184
East, Thomas, Deddington, Oxon, 1806 Oxon RO MSS Wills Pec 305/9/1
East, William, Bierton, Bucks, Oxon RO MSS Wills Pec 37/4/23
East, William, carpenter, Easthamstead, Berks, 1616 Berks RO D/A1/188/42A
East, William, Tetney, Lincs, 1639 Lincs RO Ad/Ac/25/291
Easte, Christiane, widow, Appledore, Kent, 1612 CKS PRC2/17/441
Easte, Joan, widow, St Albans St Stephens, Herts, 1612 Herts RO ASA25/4794
Easter, Robert, yeoman, Ryburgh, Great, Norf, Norfolk RO ANW/23/21/43
Easterby, Edward, Humberstone, Lincs, 1627 Lincs RO Ad/Ac/20/99
Eastes, Mercie, widow, Walmer, Kent, 1640 CKS PRC1/4/32
Eastes, Richard, Deal, Kent, 1668 CKS PRC19/4/10
Eastes, Robert, Sheldwich, Kent, 1717 CKS PRC1/18/3
Eastes, Silvester, yeoman, Waldershare, Kent, 1649 CKS PRC1/8/66
Eastes, Susan, widow, Sheldwich, Kent, 1717 CKS PRC1/18/2
Eastis, Margaret, widow, Deal, Kent, 1624 CKS PRC20/6/48
Eastis, Mathewe, Deal, Kent, 1621 CKS PRC20/5/63
Eastis, Priscilla, widow, Deal, Kent, 1667 CKS PRC19/3/118
Eastis, Richard, Deal, Kent, 1627 CKS PRC20/7/60
Eastland, John, Cranbrook, Kent, 1599 CKS PRC2/10/496
Eastland, Phillip, Saltwood, Kent, 1673 CKS PRC20/12/78

[Eastman:]
Eastman, John, collar maker, Canterbury St George Martyr, Kent, 1663 CKS PRC1/9/100
Eastman, Lawrence, Alton, Hants, 1693 Hants RO 21m65 D8/356
Eastman, Thomas, Stratfield Mortimer, Berks, 1678 Berks RO D/A1/189/8C
Eastmay, Robert, Herne, Kent, 1634 CKS PRC20/10/304
Easton, Eleanor, widow, Tarring, West, Sussex, 1631 W. Suss RO EpIV/10/2/2
Easton, James, Tarring, West, Sussex, 1621 W. Suss RO EpIV/10/1/36
Easton, Paul, shopkeeper, Seaton Ross, Yorks, 1787 Borthwick Test C.P. 1787/7
Easton, Roger, Heene, Sussex, 1617 W. Suss RO EpIV/10/1/45
Easton, William, Pennard, East, Som, 1594 Somerset RO D/D/Cta/E13
Eastwood, James, baker, Wakefield, Yorks, 1788 Borthwick Test C.P. 1788/2
Eastwood, John, Whaplode Drove, Lincs, 1651 Lincs RO Ad/Ac/29/137
Eastwood/Hirst, John, butcher, Birstall (Hekmondwike), Yorks, 1805 Borthwick Test C.P. 1805/8
Eastyes, Thomas, Petham, Kent, 1683 CKS PRC2/40/112
Eatall, Robert, Winterbourne Monkton, Wilts, 1640 Wilts RO Arch. Wilts.(name + date)
Eaton, Humphrey, butcher, Worcester St Helen, Worcs, 1593 Worcs RO 008.7 BA3585/838/99
Eaton, John, Worth, Kent, 1633 CKS PRC20/10/300
Eaton, John, Bowdon, Ches, 1662 Cheshire RO (Name) W.C. 1661
Eaton, John, Birmingham, Warks, 1682 LJRO/B/C/5/1682/34
Eaton, John, Ewell, Kent, 1710 CKS PRC1/17/23
Eaton, Joseph, widower, St Albans St Peters, Herts, 1693 Herts RO ASA25/4388
Eaton, Peter, Dover, Kent, 1627 CKS PRC20/8/179
Eaton, Peter, Dover, Kent, 1633 CKS PRC20/10/310
Eaton, Samuell, Canterbury Holy Cross Westgate, Kent, 1627 CKS PRC2/28/42
Eaton, William, husbandman, Buscot, Berks, 1640 Berks RO D/A1/188/63A
Eatwell, Richard, maltster, Ashton Keynes, Wilts, 1697 Wilts RO Arch. Wilts.(name + date)
Eborn, Daniell, Langton by Wragby, Lincs, 1627 Lincs RO Ad/Ac/20b/37
Eccleshall, Humfry, Ellenhall, Staffs, 1682 LJRO/B/C/5/1681/12
Eccleston, Richard, mariner/aledraper, Liverpool, Lancs, 1742 Lancs RO (Name of Deceased) D.R.C.H. 1742
Eccleston, William, Prescot (Sutton), Lancs, 1628 Lancs RO (Name of Deceased) D.R.C.H. 1627-28
Edcox, James, Congresbury, Som, 1596 Somerset RO D/D/Cta/E12
Eddenden, Anthony, Chart, Great, Kent, 1628 CKS PRC2/29/33
Eddleston, Elizabeth, widow, Warrington, Lancs, 1687 Lancs RO (Name of Deceased) D.R.C.H. 1687
Eddone, William, Shipston on Stour, Worcs, Worcs RO 008.7 BA3585/838/76
Eddowes, Samuel, glover, Whitchurch, Shrops, 1716 LJRO/B/C/5/1716/14
Edds, Grace, widow, Brookland, Kent, 1675 CKS PRC2/36/43
Ede, John, Slinfold, Sussex, 1635 W. Suss RO EpI/33/1635/1
Eden, Judith, mrs/widow, Hawkhurst, Kent, 1680 CKS PRC2/39/34
Eden/Sampson, George, Kingston, Hants, 1600 Hants RO 1599 AD12/4
Eden/Sampson, Richard, Lymington, Hants, 1673 Hants RO 21m65 D8/259
Ederidge, Thomas, Aslackby, Lincs, 1646 Lincs RO Ad/Ac/28/188
Edes, George, New Romney, Kent, 1582 CKS PRC21/6/111
Edes, Henry, Brenzett, Kent, 1672 CKS PRC2/35/130
Edes, Henrye, New Romney, Kent, 1608 CKS PRC20/1/294
Edes, Richard, Michelmersh, Hants, 1679 Hants RO 21m65 D8/284
Edge, Thomas, Marbury (Hurstgreen, Norbury), Ches, 1669 Cheshire RO (Name) W.C. 1669
Edge, William, yeoman, Audlem (Dodcot cum Wilkesley), Ches, 1730 Cheshire RO (Name) W.C. 1730
Edge/Inyons, Robert, Pershore, Worcs, 1606 Worcs RO 008.7 BA3585/839/420
Edgell, George, Norton St Philip, Som, 1666 Somerset RO D/D/Cta/E11
Edgerden, Thomas, Faversham, Kent, 1647 CKS PRC1/7/80
Edgeworth, Richard, Warrington, Lancs, 1608 Lancs RO (Name of Deceased) D.R.C.H. 1608
Edghill, John, chandler, Wells, Som, 1725 Somerset RO D/D/Cta/E16

Edie, James, Antony, Corn, 1615 Cornwall RO AP/E47/3
Edis, Thomas, Fulham, London & Middlesex, 1706 Greater London RO DL/C/545/24
Edkyns, Thomas, yeoman, Aston Cantlow, Warks, 1600 Worcs RO 008.7 BA3585/838/174
Edleston, James, chapman, Winwick (Ashton in Makerfield), Lancs, 1751 Lancs RO (Name of Deceased) D.R.C.H. 1751
Edly, John, St Dominic, Corn, 1608 Cornwall RO AP/E34/3
Edlyn, John, yeoman, Bushey, Herts, 1576 Herts RO ASA25/899
Edmed, James, Cranbrook, Kent, 1629 CKS PRC2/30/48
Edmed, Peter, yeoman, High Halden, Kent, 1665 CKS PRC1/10/32
Edmett, John, Frittenden, Kent, 1638 CKS PRC2/34/199
Edmondes, John, gentleman, Yapton, Sussex, 1627 W. Suss RO EpI/33/1627/17
Edmondes, Richard, Canterbury, Kent, 1596 CKS PRC2/9/111
Edmonds, Francis, All Hallows London Wall, London & Middlesex, 1681 PRO PROB5/1773
Edmonds, John, Canterbury St Paul, Kent, 1606 CKS PRC2/14/166
Edmonds, John, Lydd, Kent, 1639 CKS PRC20/10/298
Edmonds, Richard, Littlehampton, Sussex, 1617 W. Suss RO EpI/33/1617/11
Edmonds, Richard, husbandman, Uffington, Berks, 1625 Berks RO D/A1/188/51A
Edmonds, Richard, clothier, Newbury, Berks, 1675 Berks RO D/A1/188/95A
Edmonds, Robert, maltster, Long Wittenham, Berks, 1687 Berks RO D/A1/189/19C
Edmonds, Stephen, Canterbury St George Martyr, Kent, 1675 CKS PRC2/36/183
Edmonds, William, Whitchurch, Hants, 1625 Hants RO 1624 AD34
Edmonds, William, Beaudesert, Warks, 1678 Worcs RO 008.7 BA3585/830/1
Edmonds/Leonard, John, Aldingbourne, Sussex, 1596 W. Suss RO EpI/33/1596/2
Edmonds, see Taylor,
Edmunds, James, Bourne, Lincs, 1626 Lincs RO Ad/Ac/20/43
Edmunds, John, Loose, Kent, 1685 CKS PRC20/13/420
Edmunds, Maskal, Tardebigge, Worcs, 1681 Worcs RO 008.7 BA3585/830/5
Edmunds, Richard, Huish, Wilts, 1635 Wilts RO CC Sarum(+ name and date)
Edmunds, Susanna, mistress/widow, Rickmansworth, Herts, 1635 Herts RO ASA25/4902
Edmunds, Thomas, Canterbury Holy Cross Westgate, Kent, 1602 CKS PRC2/12/139
Edmunds/Sawyer, John, Collingbourne Kingston, Wilts, 1634 Wilts RO Arch. Wilts.(name + date)
Edmundson, Richard, Mellor, Lancs, 1701 Lancs RO (Name of Deceased) D.R.C.H. 1701
Edmundson, William, university: 'Fellow of Queen's College, Oxford/B.D.', Oxford (Queen's College), Oxon, 1615 Bodleian HYP B8/44-45
Edmunse, John, Shadoxhurst, Kent, 1593 CKS PRC2/7/319
Edny, Nicholas, husbandman, Langford, Steeple, Wilts, 1662 Wilts RO Arch. Sarum/(+ name and date)
Edoe, William, Nuneaton, Warks, 1682 LJRO/B/C/5/1682/35
Edolph, Ann, Canterbury St Mary Bredin, Kent, 1677 CKS PRC2/37/139
Edolph, Robert, Faversham, Kent, 1677 CKS PRC2/37/143
Edridge, John, Sherrington, Wilts, 1615 Wilts RO Miscellaneous Index to Wills (name + date)
Edsaw, John, Petworth, Sussex, 1672 W. Suss RO EpI/33/1672/13
Edson, William, Backwell, Som, 1619 Somerset RO D/D/Cta/E10
Edward, Fillip, Scawby, Lincs, 1612 Lincs RO Ad/Ac/8a/347
Edward, Henry, Edington, Wilts, 1625 Wilts RO CC Sarum(+ name and date)
Edward, John, husbandman, Marsh Chapel, Lincs, 1672 Lincs RO Ad/Ac/43/61
Edward, Robert, Hagworthingham, Lincs, 1629 Lincs RO Ad/Ac/22/52
Edward, William, Merther, Corn, 1606 Cornwall RO AP/E24
Edwarde, William, maltster, St Albans, Herts, 1712 Herts RO ASA25/4635
Edwardes, Griffin, Maidstone, Kent, 1637 CKS PRC20/10/294
Edwardes, Wyllyam, Kingsnorth, Kent, 1587 CKS PRC2/4/94
Edwards, Alexander, High Halstow, Kent, 1635 CKS PRC2/32/149
Edwards, Ann, Urchfont, Wilts, 1636 Wilts RO Arch. Sarum/(+ name and date)
Edwards, Ann, St Neots, Hunts, 1685 Hunts RO/Acc58/251(243)
Edwards, Ann, widow, Birmingham, Warks, 1850 LJRO/B/C/5/1850/3

[Edwards:]
Edwards, Anne, widow, Chapel, North, Sussex, 1640 W. Suss RO EpI/33/1640/13
Edwards, Anthony, gentleman, Cowley, Oxon, 1644 Oxon RO MSS Wills 164/4/21
Edwards, Christopher, Scarborough, Yorks, 1635 Borthwick Prob. Ex. 1635/2
Edwards, Christopher, yeoman, Marden, Kent, 1682 CKS PRC2/40/24
Edwards, David, limeburner, Clifton, Glos, Bristol RO 1678/69
Edwards, Edward, Fonthill Gifford, Wilts, 1612 Wilts RO CC Sarum(+ name and date)
Edwards, Francis, Wyberton, Lincs, 1635 Lincs RO Ad/Ac/24/524
Edwards, George, Rolvenden, Kent, 1634 CKS PRC2/32/150
Edwards, George, butcher, Winteringham, Lincs, 1646 Lincs RO Ad/Ac/40/135
Edwards, Gillian, widow, Burgh le Marsh, Lincs, 1683 Lincs RO Ad/Ac/44/58
Edwards, Henry, Wittersham, Kent, 1631 CKS PRC20/9/135
Edwards, James, Arundel, Sussex, 1631 W. Suss RO EpI/33/1631/38
Edwards, James, Stockbury, Kent, 1638 CKS PRC20/10/296
Edwards, James, Urchfont (Wedhampton), Wilts, 1647 Wilts RO Arch. Sarum/(+ name and date)
Edwards, James, Rosthern (High Legh), Ches, 1773 Cheshire RO (Name) W.C. 1773-4
Edwards, Joane, widow, Northill, Beds, 1602 Lincs RO Ad/Ac/5/568
Edwards, John, Sancreed, Corn, Cornwall RO AP/E164/3
Edwards, John, yeoman, Olveston (Woodhouse), Glos, Bristol RO 1736/14
Edwards, John, Hythe St Leonard, Kent, 1589 CKS PRC21/9/230
Edwards, John, Moreton, North, Berks, 1606 Berks RO D/A1/188/36A
Edwards, John, Boughton under Blean, Kent, 1614 CKS PRC20/3/121
Edwards, John, Faversham, Kent, 1637 CKS PRC2/33/46
Edwards, John, Stanton Fitzwarren, Wilts, 1637 Wilts RO Arch. Wilts.(name + date)
Edwards, John, Bierton (Quarrendon), Bucks, 1666 Oxon RO MSS Wills Pec 37/4/27
Edwards, John, yeoman, St Mary in the Marsh, Kent, 1680 CKS PRC2/39/35
Edwards, John, Farnham, Surrey, 1739 Greater London RO DW/OP/1738/146
Edwards, John England, gentleman, Shrivenham, Berks, 1615 Berks RO D/A1/65/114E
Edwards, Jonathan, mr, Filby, Norf, 1749 Norfolk RO ANW/23/24/82
Edwards, Mary, widow, Norwich, Norf, 1730 Norfolk RO NCC INV/76C/73
Edwards, Richard, Budbrooke, Warks, Worcs RO 008.7 BA3585/838/50
Edwards, Richard, Budbrooke, Warks, 1590 Worcs RO 008.7 BA3585/838/77
Edwards, Richard, gentleman/soap manufacturer, Stoke-upon-Trent (Penkhull), Staffs, 1815 LJRO/B/C/5/1815/27
Edwards, Robaert, Quadring, Lincs, 1599 Lincs RO Ad/Ac/5/527
Edwards, Robert, clothier, Newbury, Berks, 1623 Berks RO D/A1/188/48D
Edwards, Roger, gentleman, Bolingbroke, Old, Lincs, 1619 Lincs RO Ad/Ac/15/43
Edwards, Thomas, Singleton, Sussex, 1630 W. Suss RO EpI/33/1630/19
Edwards, William, Norton Bavant, Wilts, 1639 Wilts RO Arch. Sarum/(+ name and date)
Edwards, William, university: 'Fellow of Jesus College, Oxford/M.A.', Oxford (Jesus College), Oxon, 1681 Bodleian HYP B8/46-47
Edwards, see Heath,
Edye, Hugh, yeoman, St Mabyn, Corn, Cornwall RO AP/E168/4
Eeles, Thomas, yeoman, Henley, Oxon, 1670 Oxon RO MSS Wills 164/5/4
Effard, Susann, widow, Deal, Kent, 1685 CKS PRC20/13/422
Effeild, Robert, Ashford, Kent, 1618 CKS PRC2/21/99
Effeilde, Henry, Sittingbourne, Kent, 1616 CKS PRC2/21/100
Effield, Aphra, Kingsnorth, Kent, 1680 CKS PRC2/39/32
Effield, Hammon, Brabourne, Kent, 1640 CKS PRC1/4/33
Effield, John, Brabourne, Kent, 1664 CKS PRC1/10/33
Effield, Robert, Upchurch, Kent, 1639 CKS PRC1/2/53
Egborowe, Edward, Morborne, Hunts, 1636 Hunts RO/Acc58/7(45)
Egerden, John ygr, Brook, Kent, 1606 CKS PRC2/14/170
Egerden, Robert, yeoman, Mersham, Kent, 1674 CKS PRC2/36/41
Egerden, William, Mersham, Kent, 1680 CKS PRC2/39/33
Egerton, Elizabeth, widow, Shaw, Lancs, 1663 Lancs RO (Name of Deceased) D.R.C.H. 1663

Egerton, Thomas, esquire, Berkhamsted St Peter, Herts, Herts RO AHH23/763
Eggar, Thomas, yeoman, Eversley, Hants, 1600 Hants RO 1599 AD13/2
Egginton, Thomas, Tamworth, Staffs, 1685 LJRO/B/C/5/1685/38
Egglestone, John, Kelsey, North, Lincs, 1665 Lincs RO Ad/Ac/42/21
Egleden, William, Hawkhurst, Kent, 1608 CKS PRC2/15/103
Eglestone, see Igglestone,
Eglington, Henry, gentleman, Bawdeswell, Norf, 1743 Norfolk RO ANW/23/24/18A
Eglot, William + Alice, widow, Norton Disney, Lincs, 1624 Lincs RO Ad/Ac/19A/94
Eglye, John, Selsey, Sussex, 1582 W. Suss RO EpI/33/1582/1
Ekins, Wimborne Minster, Dors, Dorset RO PE/WM CP 2/4/93
Eland, Thomas, Belshford, Lincs, 1599 Lincs RO Ad/Ac/5/411
Elbery, William, surgeon, Canterbury St Peter, Kent, 1685 CKS PRC2/41/27
Elborowe, Anne, Purton, Wilts, 1618 Wilts RO Arch. Wilts.(name + date)
Elborrough, William, butler/scholar's servant, Cambridge (St John's College), Cambs, 1618 CUL V.C.Acc./Box1/15
Eld, Thomas, Stretton en le Field, Derby, 1685 LJRO/B/C/5/1685/39
Eldred, Jane, widow, Wyberton, Lincs, 1624 Lincs RO Ad/Ac/18/73
Eldred, John, Norwich St John Maddermarket, Norf, 1688 Norfolk RO NCC INV/65A/14
Eldredge, Robert, Sturry, Kent, 1604 CKS PRC2/14/172
Eldredge, William, Tenterden, Kent, 1629 CKS PRC2/30/49
Eldridge, Anne, widow, Cholsey, Berks, 1662 Berks RO D/A1/188/72C
Eldridge, Edmund, Streatley, Berks, 1636 Berks RO D/A1/188/58A
Eldridge, Thomas, bellfounder, Wokingham, Berks, 1596 Wilts RO Miscellaneous Index to Wills (name + date)
Eldridge, Thomas, Gosberton, Lincs, 1607 Lincs RO Ad/Ac/8a/170
Eldridge, Thomas, husbandman, Hinksey, South, Berks, 1623 Berks RO D/A1/188/50A
Eldridge, Thomas, Steventon, Berks, 1629 Wilts RO CC Sarum(+ name and date)
Eldrige, Edmund, yeoman, Cholsey, Berks, 1672 Berks RO D/A1/188/91C
Eldrige, Richard, husbandman, Cholsey, Berks, 1667 Berks RO D/A1/188/92C
Elemston, Jeaferie, Rainham, Kent, 1582 CKS PRC2/2/219
Eley, Cornelius, labourer, Enford, Wilts, 1741 Wilts RO Arch. Sarum/(+ name and date)
Eley, Cornelius, labourer, Enford, Wilts, 1741 Wilts RO Miscellaneous Index to Wills (name + date)
Eley, Joseph, Wittersham, Kent, 1662 CKS PRC19/3/6
Elficke, Richard, yeoman, Wittersham, Kent, 1680 CKS PRC20/13/20
Elfine, William, Ludborough, Lincs, 1605 Lincs RO Ad/Ac/6/135
Elfinne, Abraham, Ludborough, Lincs, 1638 Lincs RO Ad/Ac/25/206
Elford, Amos, clergy: 'clerk', Martock, Som, 1625 Somerset RO D/D/Cta/E2
Elfryth, Marke, Faversham, Kent, 1626 CKS PRC2/27/48
Elgar, Edward, Canterbury St Margaret, Kent, 1597 CKS PRC2/9/107
Elgar, Elizabeth, widow, Kintbury, Berks, 1674 Berks RO D/A1/188/94A
Elgar, Francis, 1690 PRO PROB32/31/3
Elgar, John, Wootton, Kent, 1632 CKS PRC2/31/108
Elgar, John, yeoman, Kintbury, Berks, 1676 Berks RO D/A1/189/96D
Elgar, Martha, Woodnesborough, Kent, 1607 CKS PRC2/14/168
Elgar, Mary, Great Mongeham, Kent, 1678 CKS PRC2/38/25
Elgar, Thomas, clergy: 'mr/parson', Deal, Kent, 1588 CKS PRC21/9/74
Elgar, Thomas, Tilmanstone, Kent, 1631 CKS PRC2/31/29
Elgar, Thomas, Lympne, Kent, 1685 CKS PRC2/40/197
Elgar, William, Wootton, Kent, 1596 CKS PRC2/8/57
Elgar, William, Canterbury Holy Cross Westgate, Kent, 1641 CKS PRC1/4/34
Elgar/Elvar, John eld, Ripple, Kent, 1619 CKS PRC2/21/104
Elgar, see Elver & Elwere,
Elie, Ann, Mumby, Lincs, 1640 Lincs RO Ad/Ac/27/174
Elie, Thomas, Maidstone, Kent, 1586 CKS PRC21/8/67

[Eliott:]
Eliott, Richarde, Minster in Sheppey, Kent, 1597 CKS PRC2/9/109
Eliott, Thomas, St Albans, Herts, 1629 Herts RO ASA25/4860
Elkin, Thomas, Newcastle under Lyme, Staffs, 1684 LJRO/B/C/5/1684/32
Elkins, widow,
Wilts 1681 Wilts RO Arch. Sarum/(+ name and date)
Elkins, Thomas, Stainfield, Lincs, 1611 Lincs RO Ad/Ac/10/61
Elkinton, Michael, Deddington, Oxon, 1674 Oxon RO MSS Wills 79/2/30b
Ell, Thomas, Beckingham, Lincs, 1606 Lincs RO Ad/Ac/7/86
Ellaby, Samuel, gentleman, Neston, Great, Ches, 1797 Cheshire RO (Name) W.C. 1797
Ellell, Giles, wagoner, Sandwich, Kent, 1593 CKS PRC2/6/230
Ellenden/Iddenden, Richard, Whitstable, Kent, 1619 CKS PRC2/21/97
Ellerbecke, Michaell, Barton on Humber, Lincs, 1646 Lincs RO Ad/Ac/28/235
Ellerbie, Richard, Kyme, South, Lincs, 1636 Lincs RO Ad/Ac/24/333
Ellerby, Edward, labourer, Ulceby, Lincs, 1614 Lincs RO Ad/Ac/13/167
Ellet, Richard, Minster in Sheppey, Kent, 1592 CKS PRC2/5/114
Ellet, Richard, husbandman, Fairfield, Kent, 1617 CKS PRC20/4/83
Ellett, Alexander, Maidstone, Kent, 1595 CKS PRC21/14/223
Ellett, Edward, Ospringe, Kent, 1634 CKS PRC2/32/156
Ellett, Thomas, Newington next Sittingbourne, Kent, 1615 CKS PRC2/21/101
Ellett, William, Lenham, Kent, 1611 CKS PRC2/16/96
Ellgar, George, Newington next Sittingbourne, Kent, 1673 CKS PRC2/35/213
Ellice, Brigget, widow, Orlestone, Kent, 1591 CKS PRC2/6/492
Ellicet, see Ellis,
Elliffe, William, Morton, Lincs, 1633 Lincs RO Ad/Ac/23/175
Ellingham, John, Boston, Lincs, 1622 Lincs RO Ad/Ac/17/19
Ellington, Antonie, Deeping St James, Lincs, 1599 Lincs RO Ad/Ac/5/247
Ellington, Thomas, Warboys, Hunts, 1683 Hunts RO/Acc58/202(221)
Elliot, Anne, widow, Bridgewater, Som, 1728 Somerset RO D/D/Cta/E18
Elliot, Richard, Enville, Staffs, 1675 LJRO:cards/1675/20
Elliot, Robert, Eastling, Kent, 1641 CKS PRC1/5/95
Elliot, Stephen eld, Wimborne Minster, Dors, 1623 Dorset RO PE/WM CP 2/4/28
Elliot, William, Sittingbourne, Kent, 1626 CKS PRC2/27/47
Elliott, Anne, Lenham, Kent, 1683 CKS PRC2/40/26
Elliott, Bridget, spinster, Lyford, Berks, 1636 Berks RO D/A1/188/57A
Elliott, George, Minster in Sheppey, Kent, 1636 CKS PRC2/33/45
Elliott, Giles, ironmonger, Doncaster, Yorks, 1815 Borthwick Test C.P. 1815/1
Elliott, Henry, husbandman, Doddington, Kent, 1674 CKS PRC2/35/214
Elliott, Joane, widow, Minster in Sheppey, Kent, 1632 CKS PRC2/31/107
Elliott, John, Glastonbury St John, Som, 1588 Somerset RO D/D/Cta/E7
Elliott, John, Minster in Sheppey, Kent, 1629 CKS PRC2/30/47
Elliott, John, Rolvenden, Kent, 1629 CKS PRC2/30/45
Elliott, John, Deddington, Oxon, 1633 Oxon RO MSS Wills 164/4/10b
Elliott, Lawrence, gentleman/widower, St Clement Danes, London & Middlesex, 1697 Lambeth Palace Arches G46/3
Elliott, Paul, Lyford, Berks, 1610 Berks RO D/A1/188/38A
Elliott, Philip, Wells St Cuthbert, Som, 1607 Somerset RO D/D/Cta/E8
Elliott, Richard, husbandman, Harwell, Berks, 1627 Berks RO D/A1/188/52A
Elliott, Richard, Wimborne Minster (Holt), Dors, 1628 Dorset RO PE/WM CP 2/4/42
Elliott, Richard, bachelor, Amberley, Sussex, 1684 W. Suss RO EpI/33/1684/19
Elliott, Stephen, Wimborne Minster, Dors, 1639 Dorset RO PE/WM CP 2/4/58
Elliott, Thomas, Wimborne Minster, Dors, 1607 Dorset RO PE/WM CP 2/4/9
Elliott, Thomas, Winslow, Bucks, 1633 Herts RO ASA25/4892
Ellis, Anne, Gainsborough, Lincs, 1673 Lincs RO Ad/Ac/35/52
Ellis, Arnold, husbandman, Hernhill, Kent, 1642 CKS PRC19/2/14
Ellis, Christopher, Fleet, Lincs, 1612 Lincs RO Ad/Ac/11/183

Ellis, Clement, Chartham, Kent, 1667 CKS PRC1/11/116
Ellis, Edward, Whitstable, Kent, 1642 CKS PRC1/5/96
Ellis, Elizabeth, spinster, Chart, Great, Kent, 1645 CKS PRC1/7/45
Ellis, George, carpenter, Lympne, Kent, 1648 CKS PRC1/8/44
Ellis, Henry, All Hallows Lombard Street, London & Middlesex, 1712 PRO PROB5/1441
Ellis, Henry, collar maker, Thetford, Norf, 1805 Norfolk RO ANW/23/27/4
Ellis, Hester, Chart, Great, Kent, 1600 CKS PRC2/11/209
Ellis, John, Reculver, Kent, 1606 CKS PRC20/1/179
Ellis, John, Canterbury All Saints, Kent, 1623 CKS PRC2/23/108
Ellis, John, Egerton, Kent, 1623 CKS PRC20/6/384
Ellis, John, Hornblotton, Som, 1635 Somerset RO D/D/Cta/E5
Ellis, John, Stockbury, Kent, 1638 CKS PRC2/34/198
Ellis, John, cook: 'senior cook', Cambridge St Botolph, Cambs, 1658 CUL V.C. Acc./Box3/16
Ellis, John, yeoman, Farringdon (Littleworth), Berks, 1666 Berks RO D/A3/2/143B
Ellis, John, clothier, Cranbrook, Kent, 1673 CKS PRC20/12/77
Ellis, John, St Giles in the Fields, London & Middlesex, 1708 PRO PROB32/51/102
Ellis, Joseph, gentleman, Grantham, Lincs, 1632 Lincs RO Ad/Ac/23/75
Ellis, Mary, widow, Kenardington, Kent, 1676 CKS PRC2/37/30
Ellis, Mary, spinster, Herne, Kent, 1685 CKS PRC20/13/495
Ellis, Peter, yeoman, Teynham, Kent, 1679 CKS PRC2/38/122
Ellis, Richard, Thornham, Kent, 1597 CKS PRC2/9/103
Ellis, Richard, Godmersham, Kent, 1624 CKS PRC20/6/46
Ellis, Richard, Woodchurch, Kent, 1629 CKS PRC20/8/171
Ellis, Richard, yeoman, Bray, Berks, 1640 Berks RO D/A1/188/60A
Ellis, Robert, Rudston, Yorks, 1623 Borthwick Prob. Ex. 1623/1
Ellis, Roger, Bobbing, Kent, 1610 CKS PRC2/15/99
Ellis, Thomas, Kenardington, Kent, 1630 CKS PRC2/31/28
Ellis, Thomas, Grantham, Lincs, 1638 Lincs RO Ad/Ac/25/131
Ellis, Thomas, yeoman, Sellindge, Kent, 1663 CKS PRC1/9/101
Ellis, Thomas, victualler, Newington next Sittingbourne, Kent, 1674 CKS PRC2/36/42
Ellis, Thomas, Chart, Great, Kent, 1676 CKS PRC2/37/31
Ellis, Thomas, esquire, Wellingore, Lincs, 1678 Lincs RO Ad/Ac/42/76
Ellis, Thomas, clothier, Marden, Kent, 1684 CKS PRC20/13/327
Ellis, William, innkeeper, Wakefield, Yorks, 1817 Borthwick Test C.P. 1817/4
Ellis, William, farmer/bachelor, Otley (Baildon), Yorks, 1832 Borthwick Test C.P. 1830/11
Ellis, William eld, widower/yeoman, Littleworth, Berks, 1693 Berks RO D/A3/146D
Ellis, Willyam, Kenardington, Kent, 1612 CKS PRC2/16/54
Ellis/Baker, Richard, Wootton Rivers, Wilts, 1704 Wilts RO Arch. Wilts.(name + date)
Ellis/Ellicet, William, cook, Cambridge (King's College), Cambs, 1600 CUL V.C.Acc./Box1/16
Ellis, see Reynolds,
Ellison, Richard, Sandwich, Kent, 1603 CKS PRC2/14/177
Ellison, Richard, Darwen, Over, Lancs, 1784 Lancs RO (Name of Deceased) D.R.C.H. 1784
Ellnor, Emanuel, bricklayer, St Johns Thanet, Kent, 1688 CKS PRC2/41/121
Ellson, Roger, Fordwich, Kent, 1610 CKS PRC2/15/111
Ellwall, Edward, Dudley, Worcs, 1681 Worcs RO 008.7 BA3585/830/60
Ellwood, Adam, Toynton, Lincs, 1615 Lincs RO Ad/Ac/13/101
Ellye, Philip, yeoman, Ombersley, Worcs, Worcs RO 008.7 BA3585/838/142
Ellyot, George, Winslow, Bucks, 1597 Herts RO ASA25/1607
Ellyot, William, Binfield, Berks, 1634 Berks RO D/A1/188/56
Ellyott, Richard, Ringwood, Hants, 1679 Hants RO 21m65 D8/270
Ellyott, Robert, Lenham, Kent, 1678 CKS PRC2/37/141
Ellys, Anthonie, Westborough, Lincs, 1599 Lincs RO Ad/Ac/5/67
Ellys, John, Kenardington, Kent, 1592 CKS PRC21/13/13
Ellys, John, Charing, Kent, 1596 CKS PRC21/14/119
Ellys, Peter, Ash next Sandwich, Kent, 1595 CKS PRC21/14/242

[Ellys:]
Ellys, Richard, Sandhurst, Kent, 1587 CKS PRC2/4/339
Ellys, Richard, Chart, Great, Kent, 1610 CKS PRC2/15/95
Ellys, Thomas, gentleman, Kennington, Kent, 1612 CKS PRC2/17/317
Elmer, Agnes, widow, Spalding, Lincs, 1620 Lincs RO Ad/Ac/16/37
Elmer, John, yeoman, Moreley St Peter, Norf, 1763 Norfolk RO ANF/11/5/50
Elmer, Richard, Canterbury St Mary Northgate, Kent, 1618 CKS PRC2/21/107
Elmes, John, Stamford, Lincs, 1622 Lincs RO Ad/Ac/17/24
Elmes, William, husbandman, Welford (Hoe Benham), Berks, 1664 Berks RO D/A1/188/78A
Elmeston, Marian, widow, Rainham, Kent, 1614 CKS PRC2/18/10
Elmeston, Nicolas, East Sutton, Kent, 1591 CKS PRC2/5/116
Elmeston, Radulph, Rainham, Kent, 1619 CKS PRC2/21/109
Elmestone, Henrie, Appledore, Kent, 1593 CKS PRC2/6/232
Elmston, John, Boughton Malherbe, Kent, 1598 CKS PRC2/9/435
Elner, Davyd, St Laurence Thanet, Kent, 1604 CKS PRC2/14/174
Elner, Henrye, Tenterden, Kent, 1613 CKS PRC2/17/388
Elnor, Emanuell, Sturry, Kent, 1606 CKS PRC2/13/185
Elphyk, Thomas, Storrington, Sussex, 1589 W. Suss RO EpI/33/1588/1
Elsdon, Thomas, Keddington, Lincs, 1679 Lincs RO Ad/Ac/43/116
Elsegood, Daniel, butcher, Dereham, East, Norf, 1754 Norfolk RO ANF/11/5/4
Elsey, John, Canterbury St Paul, Kent, 1639 CKS PRC1/2/54
Elsham, Gregory, Grantham (Spittlegate), Lincs, 1624 Lincs RO Ad/Ac/19A/114
Elsham, Robert, Bitchfield, Lincs, 1614 Lincs RO Ad/Ac/12/186
Elsham, William, Rippingale, Lincs, 1640 Lincs RO Ad/Ac/27/59
Elsome, Richard, Winterton, Lincs, 1602 Lincs RO Ad/Ac/37/112
Elsome, Richard, Stoke, South, Lincs, 1632 Lincs RO Ad/Ac/23/104
Elson, Anne, Quadring, Lincs, 1623 Lincs RO Ad/Ac/18/6
Elson, Grace, Barnham, Sussex, 1631 W. Suss RO EpI/33/1630/20
Elson, John, Tonge, Kent, 1669 CKS PRC1/13/34
Elson, John, yeoman/gentleman, Bucklebury, Berks, 1677 Berks RO D/A1/189/4C
Elson, Ralfe, Egerton, Kent, 1606 CKS PRC20/1/136
Elson, Richard, Petworth, Sussex, 1617 W. Suss RO EpI/33/1617/1
Elson, Richarde, tailor, Quadring, Lincs, 1612 Lincs RO Ad/Ac/11/182
Elsted, Agnes, widow, Harbledown, Kent, 1600 CKS PRC2/11/215
Elsted, Thomas, Woodnesborough, Kent, 1616 CKS PRC2/21/108
Elsted, Thomas, yeoman, Hackington, Kent, 1674 CKS PRC2/36/44
Elstonne, Broughton, Brant, Lincs, 1599 Lincs RO Ad/Ac/5/560
Elsworth, Richard, Ospringe, Kent, 1631 CKS PRC20/9/133
Elsworth, Thomas, vintner, Stillington, Yorks, 1814 Borthwick Test C.P. 1814/5
Elton, Ralph, yeoman, Kingston Lisle, Berks, 1673 Berks RO D/A1/66/8A
Elton, Richard, Portsmouth, Hants, 1625 Hants RO 21M65 D8/65
Elton, Thomas, yeoman, Dorchester, Oxon, 1678 Oxon RO MSS Wills Pec 67/3/7
Eltonhed, Joan, widow, Preston next Wingham, Kent, 1597 CKS PRC2/9/431
Elvar, see Elgar,
Elver, Amye, Ewell, Kent, 1599 CKS PRC2/11/213
Elver/Elgar, Thomazine, Aldington, Kent, 1626 CKS PRC20/7/56
Elverie, John, Faversham, Kent, 1592 CKS PRC2/6/103
Elvery, Thomas, bachelor, Canterbury, Kent, 1668 CKS PRC19/4/11
Elvery, William, fellmonger, Canterbury St Mary Bredman, Kent, 1670 CKS PRC1/15/20
Elverye, John, Wittersham, Kent, 1596 CKS PRC21/14/47
Elves, Rowland, Bolton upon Dearne, Yorks, 1637 Borthwick Prob. Ex. 1637/2
Elvidge, John, yeoman, Moulton, Lincs, 1680 Lincs RO Ad/Ac/34/63
Elvidge, Matthew, Killingholme, Lincs, 1649 Lincs RO Ad/Ac/30/148
Elvie, Richard, Charing, Kent, 1598 CKS PRC21/14/577
Elvie, see Pelland,
Elvy, Edward, yeoman, Aldington, Kent, 1662 CKS PRC19/3/5

Elvy, Edward, gentleman, Ashford, Kent, 1674 CKS PRC2/36/45
Elvy, Ingram, yeoman, Lympne, Kent, 1640 CKS PRC1/2/55
Elvy, Jone, Selling, Kent, 1594 CKS PRC2/7/335
Elvy, Roger, Buckland nr Dover, Kent, 1628 CKS PRC20/8/181
Elvy, Stephen, Selling, Kent, 1580 CKS PRC2/1/296
Elvy, William eld, Selling, Kent, 1616 CKS PRC2/21/111
Elvye, John, Aldington, Kent, 1603 CKS PRC21/17/31
Elvyn, George, alderman/mr, Canterbury, Kent, 1623 CKS PRC2/23/109
Elwarde, Roger, Kirton, Lincs, 1600 Lincs RO Ad/Ac/5/133
Elwere/Elgar, Thomas, Ewell, Kent, 1593 CKS PRC2/6/242
Elwes, Thomas, widower, St Thomas Jewry, London & Middlesex, 1688 PRO PROB5/1788
Elwich, William, Haxey (Burnham), Lincs, 1679 Lincs RO Ad/Ac/43/136
Elwin, Henry ygr, gentleman, Stalisfield, Kent, 1641 CKS PRC1/4/35
Elwin, Richard, maltster/bachelor, Milton next Sittingbourne, Kent, 1666 CKS PRC1/11/117
Elwin, Zacharie, Chart, Great, Kent, 1619 CKS PRC2/21/98
Elwood, Edward, Kirby Bellars, Leics, 1642 Leics RO PR/I/41A/95
Elwood, Edward, Althorpe, Lincs, 1676 Lincs RO Ad/Ac/35/111
Elwood, Gregorye, Dover, Kent, 1606 CKS PRC20/1/120
Elwood, Richardine, Sandwich St Mary, Kent, 1627 CKS PRC2/27/49
Elwood, Susan, mrs, Dover, Kent, 1641 CKS PRC19/2/15
Elwyn, Steven, Canterbury St Paul, Kent, 1632 CKS PRC2/31/109
Elwyn, William eld, Murston, Kent, 1638 CKS PRC2/34/200
Elwyn/Brockwell, Mary, wife, Milton next Sittingbourne, Kent, 1631 CKS PRC2/31/27
Elwyne, Stephen, Stalisfield, Kent, 1622 CKS PRC2/23/105
Ely, Anne, widow, Oxford, Oxon, 1667 Oxon RO MSS Wills 79/2/25
Ely, Edward, yeoman, Bethersden, Kent, 1690 CKS PRC2/41/173
Ely, Henry, clergy: 'curate', Smarden, Kent, 1632 CKS PRC2/31/26
Ely, James, gentleman, Eastling, Kent, 1679 CKS PRC2/38/24
Ely, John, gentleman, Linton, Kent, 1684 CKS PRC2/40/198
Ely, John + Eddy, Faversham, Kent, 1627 CKS PRC2/28/43
Ely, Mary, widow, Chippenham, Wilts, 1655 Wilts RO Miscellaneous Index to Wills (name + date)
Ely, Ralf, Tenterden, Kent, 1598 CKS PRC2/11/54
Ely, Richard, innkeeper, Abingdon, Berks, 1667 Berks RO D/A1/188/85C
Ely, Thomas, cooper, Wallingford, Berks, 1663 Berks RO D/A1/188/75A
Ely, Thomas, Fiskerton, Lincs, 1683 Lincs RO Ad/Ac/44/45
Ely, William, Chippenham, Wilts, 1635 Wilts RO Arch. Wilts.(name + date)
Elye, Andrewe, Tenterden, Kent, 1611 CKS PRC2/16/34
Elye, Edward, Ormsby, North, Lincs, 1612 Lincs RO Ad/Ac/11/33
Elye, Joane, Bremhill, Wilts, 1615 Wilts RO Arch. Wilts.(name + date)
Elye, Nathaniel, Biddenden, Kent, 1615 CKS PRC2/21/102
Elye, Ralf, Tenterden, Kent, 1596 CKS PRC2/8/208
Elye, Richard, Abingdon, Berks, 1616 Berks RO D/A1/65/116D
Elye, Thomas, Mareham le Fen, Lincs, 1600 Lincs RO Ad/Ac/5/173
Elyott, John, Tenterden, Kent, 1585 CKS PRC2/3/238
Elyott, John, Hernhill, Kent, 1601 CKS PRC21/15/115
Elyott, Robert, Northchapel, Sussex, 1683 W. Suss RO EpI/33/1682/43
Em, Symon, Thorpe, Lincs, 1632 Lincs RO Ad/Ac/23/108
Emberson, John, Headcorn, Kent, 1594 CKS PRC2/7/31
Emberson, Thomas, mariner, Dover, Kent, 1681 CKS PRC20/13/129
Embrie, Toby, husbandman, Wytham, Berks, 1652 Berks RO D/A1/188/71A
Embry, Thomas, Ashton Keynes, Wilts, 1750? Wilts RO Miscellaneous Index to Wills (name + date)
Emeley, Henrie, Witham on the Hill, Lincs, 1636 Lincs RO Ad/Ac/24/329
Emenson, Thomas, Thurlby, Lincs, 1623 Lincs RO Ad/Ac/18/62

[Emerie:]
Emerie, Robert, Yapton, Sussex, 1618 W. Suss RO EpI/33/1617/12
Emerson, Frances, widow, Barnetby, Lincs, 1670 Lincs RO Ad/Ac/32/203
Emerson, Giles, yeoman, Newbury, Berks, 1633 Berks RO D/A1/188/55D
Emerson, John, Normanby le Wold, Lincs, 1651 Lincs RO Ad/Ac/29/149
Emerson, Robert, Bardsey, Yorks, 1634 Borthwick Prob. Ex. 1634/1
Emerson, Thomas, Boston, Lincs, 1606 Lincs RO Ad/Ac/7/88
Emerson, Thomas, Althorpe (Burringham), Lincs, 1630 Lincs RO Ad/Ac/39/265
Emerson, Thomas, gentleman, Caistor, Lincs, 1668 Lincs RO Ad/Ac/42/20
Emerton, Thomas, blacksmith, Milton next Sittingbourne, Kent, 1617 CKS PRC2/21/93
Emery, Thomas, Ashwick, Som, 1623 Somerset RO D/D/Cta/E4
Emiott, Alice, spinster, Boughton Monchelsea, Kent, 1624 CKS PRC2/23/110
Emley, George + Elinor, Aldrington, Wilts, 1615? Wilts RO Arch. Wilts.(name + date)
Emme, Robert, Croft, Lincs, 1639 Lincs RO Ad/Ac/26/235
Emmersonne, Johnne, Stickney, Lincs, 1579 Lincs RO Ad/Ac/2b/4
Emmery, Robert, miller, River, Kent, 1672 CKS PRC2/35/131
Emmott, George, husbandman, Holton Beckering, Lincs, 1670 Lincs RO Ad/Ac/32/186
Emotson, Thomas, gentleman, Gunby St Peter, Lincs, 1619 Lincs RO Ad/Ac/14/275
Empson, William, university: 'scholar's servant', Cambridge, Cambs, 1631 CUL V.C. Acc./Box2/23
Empsone, Roberte, Mumby, Lincs, 1597 Lincs RO Ad/Ac/4/105
Emptage, John eld, Langdon, West, Kent, 1676 CKS PRC2/37/32
Emptage, Nicholas, St Peter in Thanet, Kent, 1627 CKS PRC2/28/43
Emptage, Ralph, yeoman, St Nicholas at Wade, Kent, 1663 CKS PRC19/3/22
Emptage, Richard, St Nicholas at Wade, Kent, 1636 CKS PRC19/1/5
Emptage, Thomas, St Peter in Thanet, Kent, 1608 CKS PRC2/15/105
Emptiage, Helene, St Peter in Thanet, Kent, 1597 CKS PRC2/9/283
Emree, Robert, Sawtry St Judith, Hunts, 1668 Lincs RO Ad/Ac/43/50
Emsell, see Emson,
Emson, John, Sausthorpe, Lincs, 1645 Lincs RO Ad/Ac/28/129
Emson, William, Rainham, Kent, 1605 CKS PRC2/13/175
Emson/Emsell, Robert, salesman, St Martin in the Fields, London & Middlesex, 1685 PRO PROB32/25/114
Emyot, Nicholas, Milton next Sittingbourne, Kent, 1623 CKS PRC2/23/107
Emyott, Elizabeth, widow, Maidstone, Kent, 1616 CKS PRC20/3/456
Endall, John jun, Aldworth, Berks, 1666 Berks RO D/A1/188/74A
Enderbie, Thomas, gentleman, Lincoln St Benedict, Lincs, 1619 Lincs RO Ad/Ac/15/195
Enderby, Elizabeth, widow, Bourne, Lincs, 1637 Lincs RO Ad/Ac/25/553
Enderby, James, Blankney, Lincs, 1635 Lincs RO Ad/Ac/24/308
Engeham, Edward, Canterbury St Alphege, Kent, 1719 CKS PRC19/6/63
Engham, Anne, mrs/widow, Canterbury Christchurch, Kent, 1677 CKS PRC20/12/232
England, John, Immingham, Lincs, 1648 Lincs RO Ad/Ac/30/261
England, Johnathan, Owston, Lincs, 1683 Lincs RO Ad/Ac/44/46
England, Mary, widow, Norwich, Norf, Norfolk RO ANW/23/17/48
England, William, Wyberton, Lincs, 1664 Lincs RO Ad/Ac/43/12
England, William, Waddingham, Lincs, 1666 Lincs RO Ad/Ac/41/179
Englefield, John, joiner, Newbury, Berks, 1686 Berks RO D/A1/189/14C
English, James, Keal, West, Lincs, 1632 Lincs RO Ad/Ac/23/95
English, James, clergy: 'clerk', Bennington, Long, Lincs, 1679 Lincs RO Ad/Ac/43/103
Ente, Jane/Jacomyn, widow, Sandwich, Kent, 1624 CKS PRC2/23/111
Ente, Peter, mr, Sandwich, Kent, 1624 CKS PRC2/23/112
Entwisle, Elizabeth, widow, Bolton (Entwisle), Lancs, 1688 Lancs RO (Name of Deceased) D.R.C.H. 1688
Entwisley, Richard, gentleman, Rochdale (Hundersfield), Lancs, 1622 Lancs RO (Name of Deceased) D.R.C.H. 1622
Entwisley, Robert, Goosnargh, Lancs, 1618 Lancs RO (Name of Deceased) D.R.C.H. 1628

Epperston, Richard, Bloxholme, Lincs, 1620 Lincs RO Ad/Ac/16/36
Eppes, Chrystyan, widow, Barham, Kent, 1592 CKS PRC2/5/21
Eppes, Peter, Crundale, Kent, 1605 CKS PRC2/13/177
Eppes, Sampson, Nackington, Kent, 1587 CKS PRC2/4/333
Epps, George eld, Mersham, Kent, 1612 CKS PRC2/16/171
Epps, George eld, Mersham, Kent, 1613 CKS PRC2/16/170
Epps, Richard, Ickham, Kent, 1631 CKS PRC20/10/292
Epps, Roger, Elmsted, Kent, 1642 CKS PRC1/6/59
Epps, William, mariner, Dover St Mary, Kent, 1642 CKS PRC19/2/54
Epps, William, husbandman, Minster in Sheppey, Kent, 1646 CKS PRC1/7/81
Epsley, Stephen, St Laurence Thanet, Kent, 1599 CKS PRC2/10/500
Epsley, Stephen, St Laurence Thanet, Kent, 1632 CKS PRC2/31/106
Epsly, Gilbert, mariner, St Laurence Thanet, Kent, 1678 CKS PRC2/37/142
Epson, Robert, Spridlington, Lincs, 1665 Lincs RO Ad/Ac/41/164
Erdall, John, clergy: 'clerk', Skegness, Lincs, 1650 Lincs RO Ad/Ac/29/50
Erlam, Richard, university: 'scholar's servant', Cambridge, Cambs, 1606 CUL V.C.Acc./Box1/17
Erlidge, James, Pinchbeck, Lincs, 1612 Lincs RO Ad/Ac/11/99
Ermondinger, James, St Martin in the Fields, London & Middlesex, 1693 Greater London RO AM/PP/Box 1685-1694 pt (uncatalogued)
Ernle, William, bachelor, St Martin in the Fields, London & Middlesex, 1699 PRO PROB32/40/85
Erpe, Thomas, Fillongley, Warks, 1672 LJRO:cards/1672/19
Errington, Gerrard, Salisbury, Wilts, 1681 Wilts RO Miscellaneous Index to Wills (name + date)
Errott/Ewatt, Thomas, Owston, Lincs, 1615 Lincs RO Ad/Ac/8b/244
Erwaker, Richard, Meon, East, Hants, 1673 Hants RO 21m65 D8/241
Eryetaydge, Roge, Banbury, Oxon, 1613 Oxon RO MSS Wills Pec 37/3/14
Escott, Lawrence, Dunster, Som, 1607 Somerset RO D/D/Cta/E9
Esh, Richard, farmer, Bossall (Stubdell House), Yorks, 1812 Borthwick Test C.P. 1812/9
Essex, Humphrey, esquire, Lambourn, Berks, 1613 Berks RO D/A1/188/40A
Essex, Humphrey sen, esquire, Lambourn, Berks, 1591 Berks RO D/A1/188/26C
Essex, Lawrence, carpenter, Molash, Kent, 1663 CKS PRC1/9/102
Essex, Sara, widow, Ruckinge, Kent, 1613 CKS PRC2/17/128
Essexe, Hellen, Molash, Kent, 1589 CKS PRC2/5/112
Essington, Charles, Kington St Michael, Wilts, 1677 Wilts RO Miscellaneous Index to Wills (name + date)
Essington, Simon, Sempringham, Lincs, 1639 Lincs RO Ad/Ac/26/310
Estcourt, Ursula, widow, Bristol, Glos, Bristol RO 1678/70
Estdey, William, Sandwich, Kent, 1600 CKS PRC2/11/413
Estin, Simon, Broadwater, Sussex, 1610 W. Suss RO EpI/33/1610/9
Estman, Richard, Canterbury All Saints, Kent, 1597 CKS PRC2/11/43
Ests, John, Wingham, Kent, 1670 CKS PRC19/4/76
Etchells, Susannah, widow, Pott Shrigley, Ches, 1724 Cheshire RO (Name) W.C. 1724
Etches, John, grocer/bachelor, Leek, Staffs, 1792 LJRO/B/C/5/1792/26
Etherick, Thomas, yeoman, New Romney, Kent, 1625 CKS PRC20/7/375
Etheridge, James, Aslackby, Lincs, 1673 Lincs RO Ad/Ac/35/5
Etheridge, Michael, Dover, Kent, 1624 CKS PRC20/6/44
Etherington, Prudence, widow, Aby (Aby Grange), Lincs, 1640 Lincs RO Ad/Ac/27/1
Ettinge, John, Ingoldmels, Lincs, 1612 Lincs RO Ad/Ac/11/176
Etty, Francis, Scarborough (Falsgrave), Yorks, 1847 Borthwick Test C.P. 1847/3
Eure, Michael, gentleman, Langton by Wragby, Lincs, 1653 Lincs RO Ad/Ac/29/161
Eure, Robert, mercer, Lincoln, Lincs, 1672 Lincs RO Ad/Ac/33/180
Eustace, Henry, Bledlow, Bucks, 1682 PRO PROB32/21/256
Eustace, Rebecca, St Martin in the Fields, London & Middlesex, 1680 PRO PROB32/17/24
Eustance, John, Bremhill, Wilts, 1678 Wilts RO CC Sarum(+ name and date)
Eustis, Thomas, Kensington, London & Middlesex, 1712 Greater London RO AM/PP/Box 1711-

[Eustis:]
1714 pt (uncatalogued)
Evans,
Som 1690 Somerset RO D/D/Cta/E1
Evans, Christian, widow, Folkestone, Kent, 1596 CKS PRC2/9/105
Evans, Gawin, Quantoxhead, East, Som, 1683 Somerset RO D/D/Cta/E19
Evans, Hugh, Hythe St Leonard, Kent, 1579 CKS PRC21/4/117
Evans, Humphrey, Tew, Little, Oxon, 1635 Oxon RO MSS Wills 164/4/13
Evans, Jane, widow, Oxford St John Baptist, Oxon, 1645 Oxon RO MSS Wills 164/4/24
Evans, John, High Halstow, Kent, 1669 CKS PRC1/14/32
Evans, John, captain/citizen/merchant tailor, St Andrew Holborn, London & Middlesex, 1681 PRO PROB32/20/88
Evans, John, blacksmith, Faversham, Kent, 1686 CKS PRC2/41/65
Evans, John, collier: 'master collier', Wellington (Ketley), Shrops, 1773 LJRO/B/C/5/1773/16
Evans, Matthew, Ashford, Kent, 1633 CKS PRC2/32/40
Evans, Peter, Chichester St Bartholomew, Sussex, 1682 W. Suss RO EpIII/9/1/59
Evans, Richard, Deptford, Kent, PRO PROB32/56/4
Evans, Richard, Longstock, Hants, 1663 Hants RO 21M65 D8/167
Evans, Robert, merchant, Chester, Ches, 1574 Cheshire RO (Name) W.C. 1574
Evans, Robert, Harbury, Warks, 1672 LJRO:cards/1672/20
Evans, Thomas, Worcester St Nicholas, Worcs, 1599 Worcs RO 008.7 BA3585/838/144
Evans, Thomas, mason, Banbury, Oxon, 1619 Oxon RO MSS Wills Pec 37/3/20
Evans, Thomas, Broughton (Castlethorpe), Lincs, 1627 Lincs RO Ad/Ac/39/104
Evans, Thomas, carpenter, Oare, Kent, 1687 CKS PRC2/41/64
Evans, Thomas, farmer, Sedgley (Ettingsall), Staffs, 1804 LJRO/B/C/5/1804/13
Evans, Thomas eld, husbandman, Eynsham, Oxon, 1638 Oxon RO MSS Wills 79/2/21
Evans, William, Maidstone, Kent, 1616 CKS PRC20/3/304
Evans, William, St Andrew Undershaft, London & Middlesex, 1756 Greater London RO DL/C/554/8
Evans, see Wright,
Evanson, Thomas, Whitchurch, Shrops, 1681 LJRO/B/C/5/1681/13
Evat, Richard, clergy: 'clerk', Stamford St George, Lincs, 1622 e 23 Lincs RO Ad/Ac/17/81
Evelin, Abraham, Rickmansworth, Herts, 1634 Herts RO ASA25/4903
Evell, William, yeoman, Hallow, Worcs, Worcs RO 008.7 BA3585/839/323
Evenden, Robert, Leeds, Kent, 1665 CKS PRC1/11/21
Evenden, see Baseden,
Evenes, George, Salisbury, Wilts, 1678 Wilts RO Miscellaneous Index to Wills (name + date)
Everard, Edward, Tottenham (High Cross), London & Middlesex, 1758 Greater London RO DL/C/554/89/2
Everard, George, Naseby, Northants, 1677 Northants RO NWill A/C/54
Everard, John, Harborough, Market, Leics, 1665 Leics RO Administrators Accounts C17th f36
Everard, Thomas, maltster, Ashwell, Herts, Herts RO AHH23/766
Everat, David, Owston (West Kinnard's Ferry), Lincs, 1667 Lincs RO Ad/Ac/33/33
Everatt, Anne, Owston (Gunthorpe), Lincs, 1676 Lincs RO Ad/Ac/35/116
Everatt, Christopher, Crowle, Lincs, 1646 Lincs RO Ad/Ac/40/133
Everatt, John, Owston (Gunthorpe), Lincs, 1625 Lincs RO Ad/Ac/39/161
Everatt, John, Crowle, Lincs, 1646 Lincs RO Ad/Ac/40/139
Everatt, Richard, Messingham, Lincs, 1668 Lincs RO Ad/Ac/33/82
Everatt, Thomas, Horbling, Lincs, 1680 Lincs RO Ad/Ac/34/45
Everatt, Thomas, Luddington, Lincs, 1682 Lincs RO Ad/Ac/44/5
Everden, Christophr eld, St Mary in the Marsh, Kent, 1646 CKS PRC1/7/82
Everden, Elizabeth, Cranbrook, Kent, 1682 CKS PRC2/40/25
Everden, John, Chislet, Kent, 1639 CKS PRC1/2/56
Everden, William, yeoman, Wickhambreaux, Kent, 1648 CKS PRC1/8/45
Everest, Henry, Canterbury St Andrew, Kent, 1675 CKS PRC2/36/185
Everet, George, Heckington, Lincs, 1614 Lincs RO Ad/Ac/13/189

Everett, Christopher, Atherstone, Warks, 1672 LJRO:cards/1672/21
Everett, Millicent, Canterbury Christchurch, Kent, 1668 CKS PRC19/4/12
Everett/Randall, John, Tidcombe, Wilts, 1615 Wilts RO Arch. Wilts.(name + date)
Everett, see Webb,
Everinge, Jane, Alkham, Kent, 1629 CKS PRC2/30/46
Everinge/Reeve, Jane, widow, Alkham, Kent, 1630 CKS PRC20/9/365
Everingham, Edward, chandler, Hindley, Lancs, 1769 Lancs RO (Name of Deceased) D.R.C.H. 1769
Everington, Ambrose, Laughton, Lincs, 1602 Lincs RO Ad/Ac/37/137
Everington, Thomas, yeoman, Friskney, Lincs, 1669 Lincs RO Ad/Ac/33/147
Everitt, Edward, husbandman, Wickhambreaux, Kent, 1669 CKS PRC1/14/33
Everitt, John ygr, butcher, Atherstone, Warks, 1817 LJRO/B/C/5/1817/47b
Everitt, Richard, Welby, Lincs, 1637 Lincs RO Ad/Ac/24/258
Everitt, Richard, Gosberton, Lincs, 1714 Lincs RO Ad/Ac/45/5
Everitt, Thomas, Pickworth, Lincs, 1612 Lincs RO Ad/Ac/11/22
Everitt, Thomas, gentleman, Pickworth, Lincs, 1650 Lincs RO Ad/Ac/30/19
Evernden, Daniell, Marden, Kent, 1610 CKS PRC2/15/97
Evernden, Edmund, Dymchurch, Kent, 1680 CKS PRC2/39/31
Evernden, George, Kenardington, Kent, 1664 CKS PRC1/10/34
Evernden, Henry, carpenter, Wickhambreaux, Kent, 1675 CKS PRC2/36/182
Evernden, John, Benenden, Kent, 1587 CKS PRC2/4/86
Evernden, John, Rolvenden, Kent, 1599 CKS PRC2/11/211
Evernden, John, husbandman, Goudhurst, Kent, 1619 CKS PRC2/21/95
Evernden, John, yeoman, Wickhambreaux, Kent, 1720 CKS PRC1/18/17
Evernden, Lawrence, Benenden, Kent, 1586 CKS PRC2/4/120
Evernden, Repent, Fairfield, Kent, 1615 CKS PRC20/3/302
Evernden, Richard, Woodchurch, Kent, 1611 CKS PRC20/2/210
Evernden, Richarde, Lydd, Kent, 1590 CKS PRC21/10/158
Evernden, Thomas, Benenden, Kent, 1597 CKS PRC2/9/285
Evernden, Thomasine, widow, Benenden, Kent, 1608 CKS PRC2/15/107
Evernden, Thomasine, widow, Benenden, Kent, 1608 CKS PRC2/15/110
Evernden, William, Newchurch, Kent, 1600 CKS PRC21/16/137
Evernden, William, yeoman, Elham, Kent, 1680 CKS PRC2/38/124
Everneden, Elizabeth, widow, Woodchurch, Kent, 1620 CKS PRC20/5/65
Everneden, Mildred, Tenterden, Kent, 1616 CKS PRC2/21/96
Everott, William, Owston, Lincs, 1613 Lincs RO Ad/Ac/8b/16
Evers, John, St Laurence Thanet, Kent, 1640 CKS PRC1/4/36
Evers, John, mariner, St Laurence Thanet, Kent, 1667 CKS PRC1/12/34
Evers, John ygr, brewer/merchant, St Laurence Thanet, Kent, 1692 CKS PRC2/42/32
Evers, Stephen, St Laurence Thanet, Kent, 1639 CKS PRC2/34/197
Evers, Thomas, university: 'scholar's servant', Cambridge All Saints, Cambs, CUL V.C.Acc./Box1/18
Eversley, see Loosely,
Everynge, James, Smeeth, Kent, 1579 CKS PRC21/4/4
Evets, Edward, bookseller, St Faith under St Pauls, London & Middlesex, 1706 Lambeth Palace Arches G56/3
Evett, Henry, Cotheridge, Worcs, 1681 Worcs RO 008.7 BA3585/835/bdl 3
Evetts, William, merchant, Birmingham, Warks, 1775 LJRO/B/C/5/1775/33
Evinges, John, Walden, Kings, Herts, 1636 Herts RO AHH23/746
Evington, Maurice, gentleman, Spalding, Lincs, 1632 Lincs RO Ad/Ac/23/117
Evins, Richard, yeoman, Tew, Great, Oxon, 1678 Oxon RO MSS Wills 79/2/32
Ewatt, see Errott,
Ewell, Friswith, widow, Herne, Kent, 1606 CKS PRC20/1/195
Ewell, George, Harbledown, Kent, 1623 CKS PRC2/23/106
Ewell, Israel, bachelor, Seasalter, Kent, 1685 CKS PRC2/41/26

[Ewell:]
Ewell, John, Herne, Kent, 1592 CKS PRC21/11/179
Ewell, John, Herne, Kent, 1600 CKS PRC21/16/198
Ewell, John, Appledore, Kent, 1606 CKS PRC2/15/210
Ewell, John, Sandwich, Kent, 1625 CKS PRC2/25/50
Ewell, John, yeoman, Whitstable, Kent, 1663 CKS PRC1/9/103
Ewell, Richard, Herne, Kent, 1599 CKS PRC21/15/23
Ewell, Thomas, Reculver, Kent, 1593 CKS PRC21/12/366
Ewell, Valentine, yeoman, Reculver, Kent, 1680 CKS PRC20/13/22
Ewell, William, Herne, Kent, 1606 CKS PRC20/1/207
Ewell, William, Sandwich, Kent, 1639 CKS PRC1/2/57
Ewell, Willyam, Herne, Kent, 1626 CKS PRC20/7/62
Ewen, Joan, widow, Graffham, Sussex, W. Suss RO EpI/33/1624/7
Ewens, Richard, husbandman, Brookland, Kent, 1679 CKS PRC2/38/123
Ewens, Thomas, Bighton, Hants, 1679 Hants RO 21m65 D8/306
Ewer, Christopher,
Wilts 1688 Wilts RO Miscellaneous Index to Wills (name + date)
Ewer, Cicely, Rickmansworth, Herts, 1599 Herts RO ASA25/1670
Ewer, Cicely, widow, St Albans St Stephens, Herts, 1599 Herts RO ASA25/1715
Ewer, George, St Albans St Stephens, Herts, 1599 Herts RO ASA25/1715
Ewer, Joan, widow, Watford, Herts, 1627 Herts RO ASA25/4844
Ewer, John, mariner: 'master of a merchant ship', Stepney, St Dunstan, London & Middlesex, 1727 Lambeth Palace Arches G98/3
Ewer, William, Watford, Herts, 1602 Herts RO ASA25/4757
Ewerby, Jo, Grasby, Lincs, 1602 Lincs RO Ad/Ac/5/284
Ewins, John, yeoman, Reading St Giles (Whitley), Berks, 1677 Berks RO D/A1/189/1C
Ewstace, John + Alice, Hill, North, Corn, 1606 Cornwall RO AP/E21/3
Ewstes, Robert, Ringwould, Kent, 1619 CKS PRC2/21/105
Ewstis, John, St Thomas-by-Launceston, Corn, 1615 Cornwall RO AP/E60/2
Exon, Katherine, widow, Cambridge St Mary the Less, Cambs, 1606 CUL V.C.Acc./Box1/19
Exton, Francis, Tisbury, Wilts, 1616 Wilts RO Miscellaneous Index to Wills (name + date)
Exton, John, Surfleet, Lincs, 1612 Lincs RO Ad/Ac/11/170
Exton, Robert, Bersted, South, Sussex, 1613 W. Suss RO EpIV/10/1/8
Eyer, Robert, esquire, Boughton under Blean, Kent, 1578 CKS PRC21/3/218
Eyles, James, yeoman, Fisherton Delamere, Wilts, 1668? Wilts RO Arch. Sarum/(+ name and date)
Eyles, Robert, mercer, Southampton, Hants, 1623 Hants RO 21M65 D8/15
Eyre, Cutbert, Salisbury, Wilts, 1629 Wilts RO Miscellaneous Index to Wills (name + date)
Eyre, Ellis, Goodnestone next Wingham, Kent, 1588 CKS PRC21/9/225
Eyre, James, St Martin in the Fields, London & Middlesex, 1784 Greater London RO DL/C/560/72/2
Eyre, Robert, Castleton, Derby, 1684 LJRO/B/C/5/1683/7
Eyre, Thomas, Bromham, Wilts, 1617 Wilts RO Arch. Wilts.(name + date)
Eyres, Wimborne Minster, Dors, 1603 Dorset RO PE/WM CP 2/4/7
Eyres, Giles, yeoman, Salisbury St Edmund, Wilts, 1629 Wilts RO Miscellaneous Index to Wills (name + date)
Fabian, Gilbert, butler/privileged person, Cambridge St Mary the Great, Cambs, 1657 CUL V.C. Acc./Box3/17
Fabian, Tristram, Amport, Hants, 1678 Hants RO 21m65 D8/285
Facer, Thomas ygr, chandler, Watlington, Oxon, 1680 Oxon RO MSS Wills 79/4/2
Fagg, John, Maidstone, Kent, 1598 CKS PRC21/14/254
Fagg, John, Alkham, Kent, 1638 CKS PRC2/34/204
Fagg, Robert, Folkestone, Kent, 1620 CKS PRC2/21/92
Fagg, Stephen, Hougham, Kent, 1609 CKS PRC2/15/130
Fagg, William, Hougham, Kent, 1675 CKS PRC2/36/50
Fagge, Anne, widow, Brabourne, Kent, 1594 CKS PRC2/6/246

Fagge, John, Postling, Kent, 1617 CKS PRC2/21/62
Fagge, John, yeoman, Hougham, Kent, 1670 CKS PRC1/15/21
Fagge, Richard, yeoman, Folkestone, Kent, 1689 CKS PRC2/41/147
Fagge, Thomas, Paddlesworth, Kent, 1674 CKS PRC20/12/125
Fagge, Thomas, jurat, Folkestone, Kent, 1674 CKS PRC2/36/49
Fagge, William, Brook, Kent, 1593 CKS PRC2/6/154
Fagge, William, gentleman, Stockbury, Kent, 1668 CKS PRC1/13/35
Faggon, Agnes, Lydd, Kent, 1596 CKS PRC21/14/125
Faggon, Richard, Lydd, Kent, 1598 CKS PRC21/15/1
Fainte, Joseph, Covent Garden, St Paul, London & Middlesex, 1750 Greater London RO AM/PI pt (uncatalogued)
Fairbeard, Mary, widow, Mersham, Kent, 1720 CKS PRC1/18/18
Fairbrother, Richard, innholder, Wigan, Lancs, 1770 Lancs RO (Name of Deceased) D.R.C.H. 1770
Fairebeard, Thomas, miller, Mersham, Kent, 1686 CKS PRC2/41/51
Fairebeard, Thomas, Smeeth, Kent, 1698 CKS PRC19/5/57
Fairefaxe, George, gentleman, Bolingbroke, Old, Lincs, 1608 Lincs RO Ad/Ac/8a/171
Fairehurst, John, Prescot (Sutton), Lancs, 1625 Lancs RO (Name of Deceased) D.R.C.H. 1625
Faireman, Agnes, widow, St Laurence Thanet, Kent, 1596 CKS PRC2/8/274
Faireman, Catheryne, Boughton under Blean, Kent, 1592 CKS PRC21/11/137
Faireman, William, Ickham, Kent, 1627 CKS PRC20/8/201
Fairethorne, John, yeoman, Watchfield, Berks, 1678 Berks RO D/A1/190/87B
Faireway, Henry, Egerton, Kent, 1628 CKS PRC20/8/193
Faireway, Henry, Staplehurst, Kent, 1636 CKS PRC2/33/47
Faireway, Margaret, Benenden, Kent, 1641 CKS PRC1/4/37
Fairfax, Andrew, Barford, Warks, 1685 Worcs RO 008.7 BA3585/830/89
Fairfax, William, butcher, Birmingham, Warks, 1665 LJRO:cards/1665/3
Fairman, Nicholas, Boughton under Blean, Kent, 1625 CKS PRC20/6/36
Fairne, George, Acrise, Kent, 1615 CKS PRC2/21/64
Fairweather, Henry, Gainsborough (East Stockwith), Lincs, 1679 Lincs RO Ad/Ac/43/137
Falber, John, university: 'scholar's servant', Cambridge, Cambs, 1599 CUL V.C.Acc./Box1/20
Falconer, see Vulckenes,
Falding, Thomas, Goxhill, Lincs, 1636 Lincs RO Ad/Ac/24/411
Falkingham, John, tailor, Goldsborough, Yorks, 1854 Borthwick Test C.P. 1854/7
Falkner, Henry, Linton, Kent, 1681 CKS PRC2/39/171
Falkner, John, dyer, Sleaford, New, Lincs, 1674 Lincs RO Ad/Ac/42/22
Falkner, John, yeoman, Barford St Michael, Oxon, 1678 Oxon RO MSS Wills 79/3/32
Falkner, Mary, widow, Weston on the Green, Oxon, Oxon RO MSS Wills 79/4/3
Falkner, Robert, Somersham, Hunts, 1676 Hunts RO/Acc58/56(131)
Falkner, William, Gedney, Lincs, 1660s? Lincs RO Ad/Ac/43/6
Falkoner, Anne, Coventry, Warks, 1675 LJRO:cards/1675/22
Fall, John, bachelor/HMS Sorlings, 1714 PRO PROB32/58/194
Fall, Robert, husbandman, Hackthorne, Lincs, 1673 Lincs RO Ad/Ac/35/40
Fallows, John, butcher, Cheadle, Staffs, 1797 LJRO/B/C/5/1797/25
Fallwell, Robert, yeoman, Wittersham, Kent, 1669 CKS PRC19/4/48
Fally, Thomas, carpenter, Reading St Giles, Berks, 1678 Berks RO D/A1/190/84C
Falsbury, John, Detling, Kent, 1678 CKS PRC20/12/260
Fan or Van, Abraham, husbandman, Minster in Sheppey, Kent, 1645 CKS PRC1/7/46
Fancort, Robert, innholder, Wallingford St Mary, Berks, 1607 Berks RO D/A1/189/147A
Fancott, Robert, Ipsden, Oxon, 1684 Oxon RO MSS Wills 165/3/1
Faning, Stephen, Moorlinch, Som, 1675 Somerset RO D/D/Cta/F28
Fann, John, Wittersham, Kent, 1663 CKS PRC19/3/7
Fann, John, husbandman, Kenardington, Kent, 1667 CKS PRC1/12/35
Fanne, Henry, clothier, Appledore, Kent, 1641 CKS PRC1/4/38
Fanning, Guy, Hythe St Leonard, Kent, 1627 CKS PRC20/8/209

[Fanstone:]
Fanstone, John, Downton, Wilts, 1640 Wilts RO Arch. Sarum/(+ name and date)
Fante, John, Marden, Kent, 1607 CKS PRC2/13/195
Fanting, Robert, Chislet, Kent, 1673 CKS PRC2/35/134
Farbrace, John, Minster in Thanet, Kent, 1609 CKS PRC2/15/132
Farbrace, Rose, widow, Chartham, Kent, 1612 CKS PRC2/17/113
Farbrace, Sampson, Canterbury St Mildred, Kent, 1647 CKS PRC1/7/83
Farbrace, Thomas, yeoman, Chartham, Kent, 1669 CKS PRC1/13/36
Farby, Francis, innholder, Dover, Kent, 1685 CKS PRC20/13/499
Farden, Richard, Barley, Northants, 1683 Northants RO NWill A/C/20
Farebrace, Lawrence, Petham, Kent, 1608 CKS PRC2/15/115
Farebroke, Alice, St Laurence Thanet, Kent, 1601 CKS PRC2/12/157
Fareley, Richard, Upton on Severn, Worcs, Worcs RO 008.7 BA3585/839/433
Farforthe, Thomas, Belshford, Lincs, 1567 Lincs RO Ad/Ac/0/2
Farginson, Abia, Norton in Hales, Shrops, 1667 LJRO:cards/1667/27
Farley, John, Steventon, Berks, 1638 Berks RO D/A1/190/37B
Farley, William, Bishampton, Worcs, 1680 Worcs RO 008.7 BA3585/837/bdl 4
Farlie, Robarte, Snave, Kent, 1596 CKS PRC2/8/248
Farling, Susan, widow, Beckingham, Lincs, 1666 Lincs RO Ad/Ac/32/99
Farlly, Richard, Upton on Severn, Worcs, 1683 Worcs RO 008.7 BA3585/837/bdl 3
Farmar, Richard, Chaddleworth, Berks, 1610 Berks RO D/A1/189/153A
Farmary, John, carpenter, Marton, Lincs, 1680 Lincs RO Ad/Ac/43/143
Farme, Lawrence, New Romney, Kent, 1585 CKS PRC21/7/254
Farmer, Elizabeth, Warehorne, Kent, 1628 CKS PRC2/29/35
Farmer, George, Atherstone, Warks, 1675 LJRO:cards/1675/23
Farmer, Henry, Swindon, Wilts, 1636 Wilts RO Arch. Wilts.(name + date)
Farmer, James, innholder, Henley, Oxon, 1673 Oxon RO MSS Wills 165/2/17
Farmer, Martin, Camborne, Corn, 1605 Cornwall RO AP/F11/2
Farmer, Mary, spinster, Atherstone, Warks, 1773 LJRO/B/C/5/1773/22
Farmer, Richard, yeoman, Tenterden, Kent, 1680 CKS PRC2/39/36
Farmer, Robert, gentleman, Bix Brand, Oxon, 1668 Oxon RO MSS Wills 165/2/9
Farmer, Thomas, Warehorne, Kent, 1640 CKS PRC1/4/39
Farmer, Thomas, yeoman, Worcester St John Bedwardine (Wick Episcopi), Worcs, 1678 Worcs RO 008.7 BA3585/830/94
Farmer, William, draper: 'woollen draper', Wrawby cum Brigg (Glanford Brigg), Lincs, 1679 Lincs RO Ad/Ac/43/112
Farmer/Hasell, John, Speen, Berks, 1594 Berks RO D/A1/189/130B
Farmer/Hayward, William, yeoman, Cliffe Pypard, Wilts, 1621 Wilts RO Arch. Wilts.(name + date)
Farmer, see Smithe,
Farmerie, Anthonie, Burton, Gate, Lincs, 1627 Lincs RO Ad/Ac/39/102
Farmerie, Christopher, Northorpe, Lincs, 1661 Lincs RO Ad/Ac/41/81
Farmerie, William, Marton, Lincs, 1623 Lincs RO Ad/Ac/39/133
Farmery, George, Northorpe, Lincs, 1667 Lincs RO Ad/Ac/33/23
Farmery, William, Crowle, Lincs, 1616 Lincs RO Ad/Ac/8b/260
Farn, James, yeoman, Glossop (Mellor), Derby, 1828 LJRO/B/C/5/1829/13
Farncombe, Henry, Steyning, Sussex, 1671 W. Suss RO EpI/33/1670/1
Farncombe, Henry, Steyning, Sussex, 1671 W. Suss RO EpI/33/1670/16
Farncombe, John, labourer, Maidstone, Kent, 1674 CKS PRC19/4/101
Farncombe, Margery, widow, Tarring, West, Sussex, 1641 W. Suss RO EpIV/10/2/31
Farncombe, Thomas, Tarring, West, Sussex, 1641 W. Suss RO EpIV/10/2/32
Farnden, Stephen, Bosham, Sussex, 1611 W. Suss RO EpI/33/1611/10
Farne, Robert, Willesborough, Kent, 1670 CKS PRC1/15/22
Farne, William, Cranbrook, Kent, 1612 CKS PRC2/17/309
Farnell, John, Burghfield, Berks, 1685 Berks RO D/A1/190/115B
Farnell, Marian, Tisbury, Wilts, 1626 Wilts RO Arch. Sarum/(+ name and date)

Farnell, Robert, Knoyle, East, Wilts, 1629 Wilts RO Arch. Sarum/(+ name and date)
Farnesfield, Francis, Fulbeck, Lincs, 1599 Lincs RO Ad/Ac/5/556
Farnham, John, yeoman, Reading St Giles, Berks, 1663 Berks RO D/A1/190/63B
Farquhar, Hugh, maltster, Shrewsbury, Shrops, 1782 LJRO/B/C/5/1782/72
Farquharson, Elizabeth, widow, Birmingham, Warks, 1808 LJRO/B/C/5/1808/17
Farquharson, Elizabeth, widow, Birmingham, Warks, 1808 LJRO/B/C/5/1808/18
Farr, Ann, Barton on Humber, Lincs, 1649 Lincs RO Ad/Ac/30/186
Farr, Israell, Epworth, Lincs, 1624 Lincs RO Ad/Ac/39/134
Farr, Samuel, baker, Bath, Som, 1739 Somerset RO D/D/Cta/F29
Farra, Alice, Warfield, Berks, 1595 Berks RO D/A1/189/131A
Farran, Sarah, spinster, Kingham, Oxon, 1678 Oxon RO MSS Wills 165/2/21
Farrance, Daniell, Headcorn, Kent, 1639 CKS PRC1/2/58
Farrance, Michael, clothier, Cranbrook, Kent, 1680 CKS PRC2/38/125
Farrand, Thomas, Kingham, Oxon, 1624 Oxon RO MSS Wills 297/1/46
Farrar, William, Sefton (Little Crosby), Lancs, 1788 Lancs RO (Name of Deceased) D.R.C.H. 1787
Farre, Robarte, Whitstable, Kent, 1595 CKS PRC2/7/397
Farrer, John, Tydd St Mary, Lincs, 1602 Lincs RO Ad/Ac/5/235
Farrer, Thomas, Fleet, Lincs, 1639 Lincs RO Ad/Ac/26/175
Farrin, John, grazier, Sawtry Beaumes, Hunts, 1692 Hunts RO/Acc58/272
Farring, Thomas, Ruckinge, Kent, 1609 CKS PRC2/15/125
Farrington, Charles, yeoman, Ashton Keynes, Wilts, 1754 Wilts RO Miscellaneous Index to Wills (name + date)
Farrington, Charles, yeoman, Malpas (Bickerton), Ches, 1799 Cheshire RO (Name) W.C. 1799
Farrington, Nathaniel, St Ives, Hunts, 1684 Hunts RO/Acc58/212(203)
Farrington, William, Holbeach, Lincs, 1650 Lincs RO Ad/Ac/29/68
Farrow, Michael, Winteringham, Lincs, 1674 Lincs RO Ad/Ac/35/85
Farrow, William, Owmby by Spital, Lincs, 1617 Lincs RO Ad/Ac/8b/189
Farrow, William, wool comber, Bildeston, Suff, 1739 Suff RO(B) IC500/3/48/10
Farrow, see Cooke,
Farrowe, Humfrey, Kirkby, East, Lincs, 1602 Lincs RO Ad/Ac/5/171
Farrs, John, victualler, St Sepulchre, London & Middlesex, 1696 PRO PROB32/39/50
Farthing, Elizabeth, Moorlinch (Stawell), Som, 1699 Somerset RO D/D/Cta/F30
Fashall, Ralfe, Cranbrook, Kent, 1616 CKS PRC2/21/87
Fasham, James, fisherman, St Johns Thanet, Kent, 1683 CKS PRC2/40/114
Fassett, John, tailor, Norwich St Peter per Mountgate, Norf, Norfolk RO ANW/23/17A(i)/17
Fauchin, Edmund, university: 'Fellow of New College, Oxford/M.A.', Oxford (New College), Oxon, 1669 Bodleian HYP B8/50-51
Faukner, William, Holbeach, Lincs, 1638 Lincs RO Ad/Ac/25/63
Faulkner, Anthony, yeoman, Weston on the Green, Oxon, 1678 Oxon RO MSS Wills 79/3/30
Faulkner, Thomas, Sandwich St Bartholomew's Hospital, Kent, 1677 CKS PRC20/12/199
Faulkner, see Johnson,
Faulthorppe, John, Stamford St Mary, Lincs, 1599 Lincs RO Ad/Ac/5/39
Faunte, Edmund, Sotby, Lincs, 1620 Lincs RO Ad/Ac/16/40
Favell, Robert, Washingborough, Lincs, 1629 Lincs RO Ad/Ac/22/38
Favell, Steven, Branston, Lincs, 1612 Lincs RO Ad/Ac/11/30
Favor, Philip, Winslow, Bucks, 1600 Herts RO ASA25/1755
Fawconer, John, esquire, Kingsclere, Hants, 1625 Hants RO 21M65 D8/114
Fawde, Richard, Ulceby, Lincs, 1625 Lincs RO Ad/Ac/19B/113
Fawdlinge, John, Thornton, Lincs, 1606 Lincs RO Ad/Ac/7/169
Fawkener, see Perryn,
Fawkner, Ellen, widow, Lenton, Lincs, 1637 Lincs RO Ad/Ac/25/190
Fawkner, Knight, yeoman, Denton (Eastry hundred), Kent, 1638 CKS PRC1/1/74
Fawler, John, Chilton Foliat, Wilts, 1635? Wilts RO Arch. Wilts.(name + date)
Fawne, Christopher, Spalding, Lincs, 1622 Lincs RO Ad/Ac/17/51

[Fawnt:]
Fawnt, Anthonie, esquire, Claybrooke, Leics, 1641 Leics RO PR/I/41A/64
Fawnte, Richard, Willingham, South, Lincs, 1569 Lincs RO Ad/Ac/0/6
Fawsett, Walter, Gedney Hill, Lincs, 1790 Lincs RO Ad/Ac/45/58
Fawson, Sarah, widow, Coventry, Warks, 1764 LJRO/B/C/5/1764/61a
Faxon, Thomas, smith, Rickmansworth, Herts, 1559 Herts RO ASA25/401
Fayerman, John, Reculver, Kent, 1616 CKS PRC20/3/443
Fayerst, Richarde, Milton next Sittingbourne, Kent, 1598 CKS PRC2/11/29
Fayreman, John, Boughton under Blean, Kent, 1579 CKS PRC21/3/325
Fayreman, Jone, widow, Milton next Sittingbourne, Kent, 1598 CKS PRC2/10/74
Fayreman, Mathew, Hernhill, Kent, 1618 CKS PRC20/4/95
Fayres, Thomas, Pagham (South Mundham), Sussex, 1613 W. Suss RO EpIV/10/1/9
Fayrmainer, George, Bosham, Sussex, 1674 W. Suss RO EpI/33/1673/28
Fazacherley, Thomas, Stoke Newington, London & Middlesex, 1671 PRO PROB32/7/40
Fealps, Thomas, Keevil, Wilts, 1627 Wilts RO Arch. Sarum/(+ name and date)
Feare, Richard, Tisbury, Wilts, 1616 Wilts RO Miscellaneous Index to Wills (name + date)
Fearne, John, Murston, Kent, 1622 CKS PRC2/23/116
Fearne, John, gentleman, Faversham, Kent, 1663 CKS PRC1/9/104
Fearne, John, yeoman, Northbourne, Kent, 1669 CKS PRC1/14/34
Fearne, Robert, Murston, Kent, 1622 CKS PRC2/23/118
Fearne, William, yeoman, Mersham, Kent, 1674 CKS PRC2/36/47
Featherstone, Thomas, esquire/alderman, Canterbury, Kent, 1617 CKS PRC20/3/437
Feaver, Edmund, Kettering, Northants, 1671 Northants RO NWill A/C/119
Feazar, Thomas, Hethersett, Norf, 1766 Norfolk RO ANW/23/25/86
Feeld, John, Leverton, Lincs, 1638 Lincs RO Ad/Ac/25/65
Feepound, Edward, haberdasher of hats, Stafford, Staffs, 1783 LJRO/B/C/5/1784/32
Feest, Elizabeth, widow, Itchingfield, Sussex, 1620 W. Suss RO EpI/33/1619/11
Feild, Francis, haberdasher, Oxford All Saints, Oxon, 1635 Oxon RO MSS Wills 297/2/1
Feild, Nathaniell, Chart, Little, Kent, 1621 CKS PRC2/21/86
Feild, Richard, Benington, Lincs, 1640 Lincs RO Ad/Ac/26/27
Feild, Robert, Lambourn (East Hanney), Berks, 1611 Berks RO D/A1/189/155A
Feild, Robert, Queenborough, Kent, 1639 CKS PRC1/2/59
Feild, Thomas, Sutton Coldfield, Warks, 1675 LJRO:cards/1675/24
Feild, William, Rainham, Kent, 1637 CKS PRC2/34/52
Feild, see Anstye,
Feilde, John, Kintbury (Elcot), Berks, 1613 Berks RO D/A1/189/157A
Feilde, Margarett, widow, Lincoln, Lincs, 1646 Lincs RO Ad/Ac/28/239
Feilde, Richard, Ash next Sandwich, Kent, 1602 CKS PRC21/16/60
Feilde, Richard ygr, Bridge, Kent, 1603 CKS PRC2/14/195
Feilder, George, Storrington, Sussex, 1625 W. Suss RO EpI/33/1625/12
Feilder, George, Sutton, Sussex, 1630 W. Suss RO EpI/33/1630/21
Feilder, Robert, Storrington, Sussex, 1627 W. Suss RO EpI/33/1627/20
Feildesende, Thomas, Lincoln St Botolph, Lincs, 1597 Lincs RO Ad/Ac/4/37
Feildhouse, Joseph, Bromley, Abbots, Staffs, 1678 LJRO:cards/1678/10
Feildinge, Robert, Barrowby, Lincs, 1605 Lincs RO Ad/Ac/6/85
Feildsend, John, Waddington, Lincs, 1634 Lincs RO Ad/Ac/24/110
Feist, Jane, spinster, Shipley, Sussex, 1662 W. Suss RO EpI/33/1661/15
Feldon, Richard, Halesowen, Worcs, 1682 Worcs RO 008.7 BA3585/837/bdl 3
Feldon/Carpenter, William, Halesowen, Worcs, 1599 Worcs RO 008.7 BA3585/838/145
Fell, Robert, Binbrook St Mary, Lincs, 1612 Lincs RO Ad/Ac/12/49
Fellow, Robert, Minster in Sheppey, Kent, 1632 CKS PRC2/31/30
Fellowe, Thomas, Minster in Sheppey, Kent, 1601 CKS PRC2/12/149
Fellowe, Thomas, yeoman, Lewknor, Oxon, 1635 Oxon RO MSS Wills 297/2/2
Fellowe, Thomas, innholder, Dorchester, Oxon, 1667 Oxon RO MSS Wills Pec 68/1/15
Fellowes, John, alehouse keeper, Wimborne Minster, Dors, Dorset RO PE/WM CP 2/4/81
Fellowes, Luke, Gumley, Leics, 1687 Leics RO Administrators Accounts 1682-86 f53

Fellowes, William, St Clement Danes, London & Middlesex, 1689 PRO PROB32/28/185
Fellows, Joseph, innkeeper, Burford, Oxon, 1772 Oxon RO MSS Wills Pec 302/3/22
Fells, Mabell, Binbrook St Mary, Lincs, 1626 Lincs RO Ad/Ac/20b/103
Felps, Richard, Newnham, Kent, 1616 CKS PRC2/21/83
Feltham, John, yeoman, Fovant, Wilts, 1632 Wilts RO Arch. Sarum/(+ name and date)
Feltham, Robert, yeoman, Fovant, Wilts, 1646 Wilts RO Arch. Sarum/(+ name and date)
Feltham, William, Fovant, Wilts, 1633 Wilts RO Arch. Sarum/(+ name and date)
Fen, Richard, Canterbury St Mary-Magdalen Burgate, Kent, 1671 CKS PRC2/35/36
Fenby, William, gentleman, Wye, Kent, 1683 CKS PRC2/40/113
Fendall, Elizabeth, New Romney, Kent, 1618 CKS PRC20/4/89
Fendike, Susan, Leverton, Lincs, 1632 Lincs RO Ad/Ac/23/53
Fendowning, James, Winteringham, Lincs, 1615 Lincs RO Ad/Ac/8b/85
Fenis, John, university: 'Fellow of Magdalen College, Oxford/M.A.', Oxford (Magdalen College), Oxon, 1674 Bodleian HYP B8/52-55
Fenix, Jacob, mariner, Sandwich St Mary, Kent, 1668 CKS PRC1/13/37
Fenn, Elizabeth, widow, Kenninghall, Norf, 1730 Norfolk RO ANF/11/3/144
Fenn, John, Edenham, Lincs, 1613 Lincs RO Ad/Ac/12/112
Fenn, Thomas, mariner: 'seaman?/bachelor', Stepney, London & Middlesex, 1684 PRO PROB32/23/65
Fennar, Thomas, clothier, Boughton Malherbe, Kent, 1615 CKS PRC20/3/294
Fenner, Frances, Weston Zoyland, Som, 1600 Somerset RO D/D/Cta/F17
Fenner, Increase, yeoman, Bethersden, Kent, 1678 CKS PRC2/37/146
Fenner, John + Agnes, Weston Zoyland, Som, 1588 Somerset RO D/D/Cta/F24
Fenner, John + Agnes, Weston Zoyland, Som, 1588 Somerset RO D/D/Cta/F25
Fenney, William, Ruckinge, Kent, 1635 CKS PRC2/33/49
Fenton, George, Stone, Staffs, 1684 LJRO/B/C/5/1684/33
Fenton, John, Stoke-upon-Trent (Boothon), Staffs, 1684 LJRO/B/C/5/1684/34
Fenton, Richard, Trentham, Staffs, 1596 LJRO:cards/1596/2
Fenton, Robert, Appledore, Kent, 1587 CKS PRC2/4/109
Fenton, Thomas ygr, esquire, Wakefield, Yorks, 1815 Borthwick Test C.P. 1815/2
Fenton, Tobias, Stepney, St Dunstan, London & Middlesex, 1704 Lambeth Palace Arches G54/1
Fenton, William, Sturry, Kent, 1596 CKS PRC2/8/5
Fenton, William, Biddulph, Staffs, 1667 LJRO:cards/1667/28
Fenton/Huckell, Elizabeth, widow, Bloxham, Oxon, 1674 Oxon RO MSS Wills 79/3/25
Fereby, Hughe, Barton on Humber, Lincs, 1603 Lincs RO Ad/Ac/5/57
Feriman, Thomas, cordwainer: 'shoemaker', Burford, Oxon, 1635 Oxon RO MSS Wills 297/2/3
Fernace, Ciriacke, Graveney, Kent, 1616 CKS PRC2/21/80
Ferne, Edmund, Bonsall, Derby, 1667 LJRO:cards/1667/29
Ferne, Elizabeth, Dover, Kent, 1633 CKS PRC20/10/314
Ferne, Thomas, Wye, Kent, 1627 CKS PRC2/28/45
Ferne, William, Sudbury (Mackley, EPNS), Derby, 1667 LJRO:cards/1667/30
Ferneley, Thomas, Thrussington, Leics, 1673 Leics RO Administrators Accounts 1667-72 f139
Fernes, Nicholas, Frampton, Lincs, 1612 Lincs RO Ad/Ac/11/13
Fernhill, Hugh, Claines, Worcs, 1588 Worcs RO 008.7 BA3585/838/79
Fernihough, Samuel, Newcastle under Lyme, Staffs, 1676 LJRO:cards/1676/22
Ferrabosco, Moses, 1709 Lambeth Palace Arches G58/1
Ferrall, Peter, Hollingbourne, Kent, 1622 CKS PRC20/6/378
Ferrall, Thomas, Cranbrook, Kent, 1673 CKS PRC2/35/215
Ferrall, William, tanner, Biddenden, Kent, 1675 CKS PRC2/36/52
Ferrall/Verrall, Richard, Marden, Kent, 1634 CKS PRC2/32/152
Ferrebe, Edmund, Mildenhall (Poulton), Wilts, 1680 Wilts RO Miscellaneous Index to Wills (name + date)
Ferreit, John, Canterbury St Mary Northgate, Kent, 1611 CKS PRC2/15/118
Ferrers, Catherine, widow, Faversham, Kent, 1674 CKS PRC2/36/51
Ferrers, Julius, jurat, Faversham, Kent, 1664 CKS PRC1/9/105

[Ferriday:]
Ferriday, John, collier, Dawley (Lawley Bank), Shrops, 1750 LJRO/B/C/5/1750/195
Ferris, Edward, Ashton Keynes, Wilts, 1625 Wilts RO Arch. Wilts.(name + date)
Ferris, Robert, yeoman, Sutton Benger, Wilts, 1763 Wilts RO Miscellaneous Index to Wills (name + date)
Ferris, William, Challock, Kent, 1705 CKS PRC19/6/11
Ferron, Lawrence, gentleman, Ashford, Kent, 1619 CKS PRC2/21/78
Ferryer, see Verryer,
Ferse, Joane, Warehorne, Kent, 1605 CKS PRC2/13/188
Fessant, David, Faversham, Kent, 1663 CKS PRC1/9/106
Fessant, William, Blyton, Lincs, 1676 Lincs RO Ad/Ac/35/107
Fessante, Ann, Rodmersham, Kent, 1608 CKS PRC2/14/182
Fetherstone, Henrie, Harrietsham, Kent, 1606 CKS PRC2/14/187
Fetherstone, John, Leeds, Kent, 1593 CKS PRC2/6/228
Fetherton, John, innkeeper, Langtoft, Lincs, 1671 Lincs RO Ad/Ac/43/59
Fetrey, Adryan + Mildred, Brenzett, Kent, 1596 CKS PRC2/8/17
Fettiplace, Dorothy, widow, Letcombe Regis, Berks, 1611 Berks RO D/A1/67/135C
Fettyplace, Rebecca, widow, Stepney, London & Middlesex, 1713 PRO PROB32/57/143
Few, John, Chillenden, Kent, 1599 CKS PRC2/10/143
Fewe, William, St Johns Thanet, Kent, 1601 CKS PRC2/12/155
Fewkes, Richard?, Coston, Leics, 1665 Leics RO Administrators Accounts C17th f8
Fickus, Thomas + Elizabeth, Marston, Oxon, 1697 Oxon RO MSS Wills 79/4/18
Fidge, Augustine, Canterbury St Martin, Kent, 1613 CKS PRC20/2/400
Fidge, Edward, Whitstable, Kent, 1631 CKS PRC2/30/54
Fidge, George, Westwell, Kent, 1596 CKS PRC21/14/81
Fidge, John, Langley, Kent, 1596 CKS PRC2/9/287
Fidge, Oliver eld, Wittersham, Kent, 1636 CKS PRC20/10/344
Fidge, Robert, Wittersham, Kent, 1598 CKS PRC21/15/3
Fidler, Edward, yeoman, Morton (Woolley Moor), Derby, 1780 LJRO/B/C/5/1780/13
Fidler, George, yeoman, Pentrich, Derby, 1792 LJRO/B/C/5/1792/28
Fidler, John, butcher, Stockport, Ches, 1745 Cheshire RO (Name) W.C. 1744
Fidoe, John, Malvern, Great, Worcs, 1600 Worcs RO 008.7 BA3585/838/178
Field, Gedion, Sherbourne, Dors, 1627 Wilts RO Miscellaneous Index to Wills (name + date)
Field, Joan, widow, Watchfield, Berks, Berks RO D/A1/67/60
Field, John, husbandman, Speen, Berks, 1614 Berks RO D/A1/189/158A
Field, John, husbandman, Welford (Easton), Berks, 1628 Berks RO D/A1/190/18B
Field, John, university: 'printer', Cambridge, Cambs, 1671? PRO PROB5/1054
Field, Jonas, shopkeeper, Halifax, Yorks, 1820 Borthwick Test C.P. 1820/1
Field, Richard, husbandman, Beenham, Berks, 1627 Berks RO D/A1/190/15B
Field, Samuel, yeoman, Wickham, Berks, 1684 Berks RO D/A1/190/108
Field, Thomas, shepherd, Moreton, North, Berks, 1634 Berks RO D/A1/190/30B
Field, Thomas, Stratford-upon-Avon, Warks, 1682 Worcs RO 008.7 BA3585/837/bdl 3
Field, Thomas, husbandman, Bovingdon, Herts, 1689 Herts RO AHH23/832
Field, William, Boxley, Kent, 1616 CKS PRC2/23/117
Field, William, victualler, Redditch (Headless Cross), Worcs, 1811 Worcs RO 008.7 BA3585/835/bdl 2
Field, see Parman,
Fielden, William, innholder, Wigan, Lancs, 1787 Lancs RO (Name of Deceased) D.R.C.H. 1787
Fielders, Richard, blacksmith, Atherstone, Warks, 1812 LJRO/B/C/5/1812/30
Fieldston, William, Marton, Lincs, 1679 Lincs RO Ad/Ac/45/99
Figg, Jeremie, Tunstall, Kent, 1637 CKS PRC2/34/50
Figg, Ralph, Hucking, Kent, 1628 CKS PRC20/8/185
Figg, Robert, Stockbury, Kent, 1630 CKS PRC2/30/53
Figg, Susanna, widow, Canterbury St George Martyr, Kent, 1702 CKS PRC1/16/45
Figg, Thomas, yeoman, Ulcombe, Kent, 1668 CKS PRC1/13/38
Figge, Jeremiah, cordwainer, New Romney, Kent, 1683 CKS PRC20/13/245

Figge, Robarte, Bredgar, Kent, 1597 CKS PRC2/10/84
Figgens, Robert, gardener, Warminster, Wilts, 1680 Wilts RO Arch. Sarum/(+ name and date) w
Filcock, Arthure, Sandwich, Kent, 1597 CKS PRC2/10/61
Filcott, John, Milton next Sittingbourne, Kent, 1692 CKS PRC2/42/33
Filder, Richard, Tillington, Sussex, 1622 W. Suss RO EpI/33/1621/1
File, Anne, widow, Wye, Kent, 1680 CKS PRC2/39/38
File, Thomas, Sandwich, Kent, 1627 CKS PRC2/27/54
Filer,
Som 1663 Somerset RO D/D/Cta/F1
Filkes, John, Cranbrook, Kent, 1602 CKS PRC2/12/153
Fillcutt, George, Teynham, Kent, 1669 CKS PRC1/14/35
Filles, see Miller,
Fillingham, John, Haxey (Upperthorpe), Lincs, 1671 Lincs RO Ad/Ac/32/131
Fills, Richard, Ulcombe, Kent, 1628 CKS PRC2/29/38
Filmer, Jeames, Otterden, Kent, 1597 CKS PRC2/9/115
Filmer, Joseph, Hollingbourne, Kent, 1625 CKS PRC20/7/381
Filmer, Mary, widow, Borden, Kent, 1594 CKS PRC2/7/215
Filmer, Reginald, yeoman, Lenham, Kent, 1668 CKS PRC1/13/39
Filmer, Richard, yeoman, Wichling, Kent, 1666 CKS PRC1/11/118
Filmer, Robert, yeoman, Bobbing, Kent, 1681 CKS PRC2/39/172
Filmer, William, Hollingbourne, Kent, 1639 CKS PRC20/10/368
Fin, Hammon, Birchington, Kent, 1638 CKS PRC20/10/378
Finch, Anthony, butcher, Sandwich St Peter, Kent, 1668 CKS PRC1/13/40
Finch, Christopher, yeoman, Warfield, Berks, 1629 Berks RO D/A1/190/20C
Finch, Edward, yeoman, Kenardington, Kent, 1668 CKS PRC1/13/41
Finch, Gartrude, widow, Faversham, Kent, 1641 CKS PRC1/4/40
Finch, Heneage, Right Honourable Earl Of Winchelsea, 1692 Lambeth Palace Arches G42/1
Finch, John, gentleman, Linsted, Kent, 1601 CKS PRC2/12/143
Finch, John, Redbourn (Norringtonend), Herts, 1612 Herts RO ASA25/4795
Finch, John, labourer, Saltwood, Kent, 1641 CKS PRC19/1/42
Finch, John, cordwainer, Milton next Sittingbourne, Kent, 1695 CKS PRC2/42/80
Finch, John, Kingston, Surrey, 1742 Greater London RO DW/OP/1742/2
Finch, Mabella, dame/widow, Fordwich, Kent, CKS PRC1/15/96
Finch, Margaret, mrs, Canterbury, Kent, 1639 CKS PRC1/2/60
Finch, Nicholas, Bobbing, Kent, 1666 CKS PRC1/11/119
Finch, Peter, Alconbury, Hunts, 1682 Hunts RO/Acc58/183(162)
Finch, Richard, yeoman, Tenterden, Kent, 1614 CKS PRC2/18/137
Finch, Richard, yeoman, Bray, Berks, 1635 Berks RO D/A1/190/32C
Finch, Thomas, Faversham, Kent, 1622 CKS PRC2/23/114
Finch, Thoms, Tenterden, Kent, 1613 CKS PRC2/16/139
Finch, William, Reading St Giles, Berks, 1598 Berks RO D/A1/189/133A
Finch, William, Faversham, Kent, 1617 CKS PRC2/21/74
Finch, William, gentleman, Linsted, Kent, 1628 CKS PRC2/29/36
Finch, William, Stelling, Kent, 1638 CKS PRC2/34/201
Finche, Christofer, mayor/esquire, Faversham, Kent, 1611 CKS PRC20/2/202
Finche, Joane, Rolvenden, Kent, 1599 CKS PRC2/11/41
Finche, John, gentleman, Rolvenden, Kent, 1606 CKS PRC20/1/41
Finche, Peter, Standish (Shevington), Lancs, 1597 Lancs RO (Name of Deceased) D.R.C.H. 1597
Finche, Robert, victualler, Redbourn, Herts, 1632 Herts RO ASA25/4882
Finchurst, Edward, Woodchurch, Kent, 1672 CKS PRC20/12/47
Finckle, Joan, widow, Headcorn, Kent, 1594 CKS PRC2/7/59
Finden, John, Wield, Hants, 1679 Hants RO 21m65 D8/307
Fineux, Thomas, gentleman, Smeeth, Kent, 1618 CKS PRC20/4/91
Finham, Thomas, Salisbury, Wilts, 1687 Wilts RO Miscellaneous Index to Wills (name + date)
Finlay, John, mariner, Bristol, Glos, Bristol RO 1764/2

[Finlow:]
Finlow, Henry, brushmaker, Liverpool, Lancs, 1783 Lancs RO (Name of Deceased) D.R.C.H. 1783
Finn, Edward, Molash, Kent, 1639 CKS PRC1/2/61
Finne, George, Hothfield, Kent, 1678 CKS PRC2/38/30
Finne, Henry, Orlestone, Kent, 1683 CKS PRC2/40/27
Finne, Thomas, Egerton, Kent, 1624 CKS PRC20/6/30
Finne, Thomas, New Romney, Kent, 1641 CKS PRC19/2/16
Finne, Thomas, New Romney, Kent, 1641 CKS PRC19/2/16a
Finneux, Thomas, esquire, Dover, Kent, 1629 CKS PRC20/8/220
Finney, Henry, Castleford (Houghton), Yorks, Borthwick Test C.P. 1751/1
Finney, John, Alstonfield, Staffs, 1676 LJRO:cards/1676/23
Finneyhouse, John, Lapley, Staffs, 1680 LJRO:cards/1680/13
Finnies, Richard, Dover, Kent, 1690 CKS PRC19/4/116
Finnis, Anne, widow, Dover, Kent, 1682 CKS PRC20/13/241
Finnis, Henry, St Margarets At Cliffe, Kent, 1640 CKS PRC20/10/366
Finnis, Henry, Egerton, Kent, 1668 CKS PRC19/4/13
Finnis, John, Dover, Kent, 1634 CKS PRC20/10/320
Firman, Joseph, victualler, Bury St Edmunds, Suff, 1815 Suff RO(B) IC500/3/53/115
Firminger, Henry, Shadoxhurst, Kent, 1679 CKS PRC2/38/128
Firminger, Stephen, Bethersden, Kent, 1640 CKS PRC1/2/62
Firth, Charles, farmer, Bradford (Little Horton), Yorks, 1844 Borthwick Test C.P. 1844/9
Firth, Joseph Bagshaw, gentleman, Wadworth, Yorks, 1821 Borthwick Test C.P. 1821/1
Firth, Joseph Bagshaw, gentleman, Wadworth, Yorks, 1821 Borthwick Test C.P. 1821/6
Firth, Thomas eld, carpenter, Birstall (Birkenshaw), Yorks, 1835 Borthwick Test C.P. 1835/3
Firth, Timothy, farmer, Thornhill (Stocks Moor), Yorks, 1802 Borthwick Test C.P. 1802/2
Fish, Abraham, weaver: 'woollen weaver', Haslingden, Lancs, 1748 Lancs RO (Name of Deceased) D.R.C.H. 1748
Fish, Henry, Haxey (Graizelound), Lincs, 1667 Lincs RO Ad/Ac/33/34
Fish, John, Bowden, Great, Leics, 1666 Leics RO Administrators Accounts C17th f78
Fish, Nicholas, Hythe St Leonard, Kent, 1639 CKS PRC20/10/360
Fish, Thomas, Owston, Lincs, 1663 Lincs RO Ad/Ac/41/93
Fish, Thomas, Bowden, Great, Leics, 1668 Leics RO Administrators Accounts 1667-72 f8
Fishcocke, John, Ashford, Kent, 1604 CKS PRC2/13/193
Fishe, Robert, Wragby, Lincs, 1619 Lincs RO Ad/Ac/15/95
Fishenden, Edward, blacksmith, Milton next Sittingbourne, Kent, 1667 CKS PRC1/12/36
Fishenden, John, gentleman, Marden, Kent, 1679 CKS PRC2/38/129
Fishenden, Marie, spinster, Maidstone, Kent, 1636 CKS PRC20/10/338
Fishenden, Mary, spinster, Sandwich, Kent, 1686 CKS PRC2/41/52
Fishenden, Thomas, Sandhurst, Kent, 1646 CKS PRC19/2/96
Fisher, Adam, tailor, Salisbury, Wilts, 1640 Wilts RO Miscellaneous Index to Wills (name + date)
Fisher, Alexander, Detling, Kent, 1592 CKS PRC21/11/246
Fisher, Anne, widow, Widley, Hants, 1664 Hants RO 21M65 D8/185
Fisher, Christopher, Grantham, Lincs, 1598 Lincs RO Ad/Ac/4/67
Fisher, Christopher, Grantham, Lincs, 1646 Lincs RO Ad/Ac/28/194
Fisher, Danyel, Milton next Sittingbourne, Kent, 1614 CKS PRC2/18/72
Fisher, Edward, butcher, Wallingford St Peter, Berks, 1620 Berks RO D/A1/190/2C
Fisher, Elizabeth, Quadring, Lincs, 1624 Lincs RO Ad/Ac/19A/53
Fisher, Francis, Gainsborough, Lincs, 1606 Lincs RO Ad/Ac/37/228
Fisher, Gilberte, gentleman, Bourne, Lincs, 1634 Lincs RO Ad/Ac/24/70
Fisher, James, gentleman, Oxford St Peter le Bailey, Oxon, 1624 Oxon RO MSS Wills 297/1/42
Fisher, James, degrees: 'Doctor', Caversham, Oxon, 1679 PRO PROB5/1759
Fisher, James, Eckington, Worcs, 1682 Worcs RO 008.7 BA3585/837/bdl 3
Fisher, James, yeoman, Whatcote, Warks, 1808 Worcs RO 008.7 BA3585/829/143
Fisher, Jane, widow, Chester, Ches, 1626 Cheshire RO (Name) W.C. 1626
Fisher, Jasper, Ellington, Hunts, 1678 Hunts RO/Acc58/126(1)

Fisher, John, Sotwell, Berks, 1604 Berks RO D/A1/189/141B
Fisher, John, Wigtoft, Lincs, 1618 Lincs RO Ad/Ac/14/86
Fisher, John, Brauncewell, Lincs, 1623 Lincs RO Ad/Ac/18/50
Fisher, John, Bampton (Cote), Oxon, 1627 Oxon RO MSS Wills 297/1/49
Fisher, John, Upton, Lincs, 1627 Lincs RO Ad/Ac/39/33
Fisher, John, Northmoor, Oxon, 1628 Oxon RO MSS Wills 297/1/55
Fisher, John, Farlesthorpe, Lincs, 1637 Lincs RO Ad/Ac/24/553
Fisher, John, Sutton St Edmunds, Lincs, 1639 Lincs RO Ad/Ac/26/282
Fisher, John, Wimborne Minster (Cowgrove), Dors, 1639 Dorset RO PE/WM CP 2/4/53
Fisher, John, brickmaker, Welford, Berks, 1641 Berks RO D/A1/190/43C
Fisher, John, Wigtoft, Lincs, 1649 Lincs RO Ad/Ac/30/188
Fisher, John, Kirton, Lincs, 1677 Lincs RO Ad/Ac/34/35
Fisher, John, widower, Eckington, Worcs, 1684 Worcs RO 008.7 BA3585/837/bdl 4
Fisher, John eld, gentleman, Abingdon, Berks, 1627 Berks RO D/A1/190/17B
Fisher, Mary, widow, Coppul, Lancs, 1780 Lancs RO (Name of Deceased) D.R.C.H. 1780
Fisher, Michael, Birstall, Leics, 1639 Leics RO PR/I/41A/14
Fisher, Nathaniell, St Stephen Walbrook, London & Middlesex, 1694 PRO PROB32/34/80
Fisher, Ralph, Caverswall (Meare Lane), Staffs, 1684 LJRO/B/C/5/1684/35
Fisher, Richard, clergy: 'clerk', Snitterby, Lincs, 1615 Lincs RO Ad/Ac/8b/129
Fisher, Robert, Scampton, Lincs, 1633 Lincs RO Ad/Ac/40/61
Fisher, Samuel, Glastonbury St Benedict, Som, 1707 Somerset RO D/D/Cta/F31
Fisher, Thomas, Leverton, Lincs, 1620 Lincs RO Ad/Ac/16/41
Fisher, Thomas, innholder, St Albans, Herts, 1637 Herts RO ASA25/4938
Fisher, Thomas, Boldre, Hants, 1673 Hants RO 21m65 D8/260
Fisher, Tristram, Holbeach, Lincs, 1618 Lincs RO Ad/Ac/14/294
Fisher, William, university: 'scholar's servant', Cambridge, Cambs, 1629 CUL V.C. Acc./Box2/24
Fisher, William, bricklayer, Clewer, Berks, 1633 Berks RO D/A1/190/27B
Fisher/Lamyman, William, Grainthorpe, Lincs, 1611 Lincs RO Ad/Ac/10/21
Fishlocke, Robert, Severnake, Wilts, 1684 Wilts RO CC Sarum(+ name and date)
Fishre, Alice, widow, Fleet, Lincs, 1672 Lincs RO Ad/Ac/34/112
Fissenden, John, Shadoxhurst, Kent, 1631 CKS PRC20/9/139
Fist, Richard, Wickhambreaux, Kent, 1639 CKS PRC2/34/203
Fist, William, Wickhambreaux, Kent, 1638 CKS PRC2/34/206
Fitch, Robert, gentleman, Ashton Keynes, Wilts, 1632 Wilts RO Arch. Wilts.(name + date)
Fitch-John, John, Hamerton, Hunts, 1678 Hunts RO/Acc58/123(49)
Fittz, Elizabeth,
Norf 1716 Norfolk RO ANW/23/12/102
Fitzherbert, Henry, gentleman, Chichester, Sussex, 1669 W. Suss RO EpIII/9/1/57
Fitzwilliam, Edmund, gentleman, Grimsby, Great, Lincs, 1626 Lincs RO Ad/Ac/19B/60
Fitzwilliam, Thomas, Toynton All Saints, Lincs, 1624 Lincs RO Ad/Ac/18/104
Fiver, William, husbandman, Snargate, Kent, 1699 CKS PRC2/42/153
Flackden, Tobyas, Canterbury All Saints, Kent, 1610 CKS PRC2/15/120
Flanner, Robert, yeoman, Wixoe, Suff, 1738 Suff RO(B) IC500/3/47/37
Flaunders, Thomas, St Albans St Stephens, Herts, 1638 Herts RO ASA25/4954
Flauner, Robert,
Suff 1732 Suff RO(B) IC500/3/47/37
Flavell, William, Newton Harcourt, Leics, 1674 Leics RO Administrators Accounts 1667-72 f141
Flaxman, John, Blickling, Norf, 1741 Norfolk RO ANW/23/23/54A
Flaxman, Richard, bachelor, Bodicote, Oxon, 1650 Oxon RO MSS Wills 297/2/34
Flaxton, see Flecton,
Flayne, Margaret, Moorby, Lincs, 1586 Lincs RO Ad/Ac/2C/139
Fleate, Richard, Kirdford, Sussex, 1676 W. Suss RO EpI/33/1676/34
Flecher, John, Lea, Lincs, 1620 Lincs RO Ad/Ac/8b/449
Flecher, Rychard, Blean, Kent, 1591 CKS PRC2/5/110
Flecton, Henry, Milton next Sittingbourne, Kent, 1672 CKS PRC2/35/133

[Flecton/Flaxton:]
Flecton/Flaxton, Henry, Canterbury St Dunstan Without, Kent, 1663 CKS PRC1/9/107
Fleete, Arthur, Bosham, Sussex, 1684 W. Suss RO EpI/33/1684/39
Fleete, Edwarde, St Johns Thanet, Kent, 1610 CKS PRC2/13/183
Fleete, Henry, St Johns Thanet, Kent, 1617 CKS PRC2/21/73
Fleete, James, mariner, St Johns Thanet, Kent, 1665 CKS PRC1/11/22
Fleete, Joseph, Seasalter, Kent, 1672 CKS PRC2/35/132
Fleete, Thomas, St Johns Thanet, Kent, 1638 CKS PRC2/34/202
Fleete, Thomas, butcher, Worcester All Saints, Worcs, 1680 Worcs RO 008.7 BA3585/837/bdl 2
Fleete, Thomas eld, St Johns Thanet, Kent, 1609 CKS PRC20/2/1
Fleete/Sampson, Mary, St Peter in Thanet, Kent, 1638 CKS PRC2/34/207
Fleetwood, Jone,
Wilts 1674 Wilts RO Miscellaneous Index to Wills (name + date)
Flemhill, Edward, weaver: 'worsted weaver', Coventry, Warks, 1783 LJRO/B/C/5/1783/96
Fleming, Lewes, baker, Sandwich, Kent, 1623 CKS PRC2/23/121
Fleminge, Alice, Toynton, High, Lincs, 1613 Lincs RO Ad/Ac/12/46
Fleminge, John, degrees: 'D.D.', Oxford (University), Oxon, 1617 Bodleian HYP B8/56-59
Fleminge, Robert, Dover, Kent, 1625 CKS PRC20/7/215
Flemynge, Thomas, Madron, Corn, Cornwall RO AP/F145/1
Fleshall, Richard, Elmley Castle, Worcs, 1675 Worcs RO 008.7 BA3585/835/bdl 1
Fletcher, Edward, husbandman, Rickmansworth, Herts, 1636 Herts RO ASA25/4932
Fletcher, Edward, weaver, Pilham, Lincs, 1671 Lincs RO Ad/Ac/45/96
Fletcher, Edward, carpenter, St Andrew Holborn, London & Middlesex, 1687 PRO PROB32/26/136
Fletcher, Harman, husbandman, Asthall, Oxon, 1679 Oxon RO MSS Wills 79/4/1
Fletcher, Henry, Ewerby, Lincs, 1637 Lincs RO Ad/Ac/25/368
Fletcher, James, cotton manufacturer, Bury (Tottington Lower), Lancs, 1796 Lancs RO (Name of Deceased) D.R.C.H. 1796
Fletcher, Jeremiah, tailor, Milton next Sittingbourne, Kent, 1674 CKS PRC2/36/55
Fletcher, Joan, widow, Ascot under Wychwood, Oxon, 1684 Oxon RO MSS Wills 79/4/8
Fletcher, John, Harlaxton, Lincs, 1580 Lincs RO Ad/Ac/2b/50
Fletcher, John, Tonge, Kent, 1622 CKS PRC2/23/119
Fletcher, John, Boston, Lincs, 1627 Lincs RO Ad/Ac/20b/108
Fletcher, John, weaver, Rochdale (Peanock, Butterworth), Lancs, 1799 Lancs RO (Name of Deceased) D.R.C.H. 1799
Fletcher, Jonathan, farmer, Blyth (Barnby Moor), Notts, 1811 Borthwick Test C.P. 1811/2
Fletcher, Joseph, butcher, Woodstock, Oxon, 1661 Oxon RO MSS Wills 297/2/36
Fletcher, Joseph, Rolleston, Staffs, 1680 LJRO:cards/1680/14
Fletcher, Mathew, Somercoates, Lincs, 1645 Lincs RO Ad/Ac/28/251
Fletcher, Nathan, Whitstable, Kent, 1634 CKS PRC2/32/151
Fletcher, Richard, Spalding, Lincs, 1652 Lincs RO Ad/Ac/29/34
Fletcher, Robert, Greatford, Lincs, 1606 Lincs RO Ad/Ac/6/53
Fletcher, Samuel, Stockton, Shrops, 1685 LJRO/B/C/5/1685/40
Fletcher, Thomas, Maidstone, Kent, 1625 CKS PRC20/7/379
Fletcher, Thomas + Alice, yeoman & widow, Bourne, Lincs, 1619 Lincs RO Ad/Ac/15/117
Fletcher, William, Boston, Lincs, 1613 Lincs RO Ad/Ac/12/10
Fletcher, William, Chesterfield, Derby, 1655 LJRO:cards/1655/2
Fletcher, William, collier, Pentrich, Derby, 1789 LJRO/B/C/5/1789/17
Fletcher/Stowe, Rachaell, widow, Kirton, Lincs, 1649 Lincs RO Ad/Ac/30/231
Fletcher, see Holland & Taylor,
Flete, Thomas eld, St Johns Thanet, Kent, 1592 CKS PRC2/5/23
Flexney, Edmund, Oxford St Giles, Oxon, 1630 Oxon RO MSS Wills 297/1/60
Flexney, Elizabeth, widow, Stanton Harcourt (Sutton), Oxon, 1666 Oxon RO MSS Wills 165/2/4
Flexney, Jane, widow, Stanton Harcourt (Goldfinch), Oxon, 1666 Oxon RO MSS Wills 165/2/5
Flexney, Ralph, yeoman, Stanton Harcourt (Sutton), Oxon, 1663 Oxon RO MSS Wills 79/3/11
Flexney, Richard ygr, Garsington, Oxon, 1640 Oxon RO MSS Wills 297/2/8

Flexney, Thomas, yeoman, Stanton Harcourt, Oxon, 1625 Oxon RO MSS Wills 297/1/43
Flight, George, labourer, Lewknor, Oxon, 1637 Oxon RO MSS Wills 297/2/7
Flight, John, gentleman, Lewknor (Nethercote), Oxon, 1670 Oxon RO MSS Wills 79/3/21
Flint, Benjamin, Ashford, Kent, 1702 CKS PRC1/16/25
Flint, Henry, Bonsall, Derby, 1667 LJRO:cards/1667/31
Flintham, Thomas, yeoman, Gosberton, Lincs, 1638 Lincs RO Ad/Ac/25/112
Flintstone/Blinstone, John eld, St Margarets At Cliffe, Kent, 1613 CKS PRC20/2/418
Floar, William, Whissendine, Northants, 1809 Northants RO X954/21/67
Floate, Margaret, widow, Chislet, Kent, 1613 CKS PRC2/18/50
Flood, Edward, St Stephen by Launceston, Corn, 1650 Cornwall RO AP/F225
Flooks, Mary, spinster, Berwick St John, Wilts, 1735 Wilts RO Arch. Sarum/(+ name and date)
Florrye, William, Bedwin, Great, Wilts, 1637 Wilts RO Pec Lord Warden Savernake Forest Bundle 1/26
Flower, Edward, Lavington, Market (Easterton), Wilts, 1672 Wilts RO Arch. Sarum/(+ name and date)
Flower, John, Buckinha, Wilts, 1614 Wilts RO Arch. Sarum/(+ name and date)
Flower, John, yeoman, Sheffield, Yorks, 1813 Borthwick Test C.P. 1813/8
Flower, Priscilla, widow, Pangbourne, Berks, 1663 Berks RO D/A1/190/59C
Flower, Richard, Keevil, Wilts, 1614 Wilts RO Arch. Sarum/(+ name and date)
Flower, Thomas, Imber, Wilts, 1626 Wilts RO Arch. Sarum/(+ name and date)
Flower, Thomas, Witney (Newyatte in Hailey), Oxon, 1690 Oxon RO MSS Wills 165/3/15
Flower, Tymothy, flaxdresser, Loughborough, Leics, 1686 Leics RO Administrators Accounts 1682-86 f47
Flowerdew, William,
Suff 1803 Suff RO(B) IC500/3/53/107
Flowers, Robert, Kirton, Lincs, 1648 Lincs RO Ad/Ac/30/348
Floyd, Henry, chandler: 'tallow chandler', Stamford St Michael, Lincs, 1668 Lincs RO Ad/Ac/33/68
Floyd, James, Thornham, Kent, 1678 CKS PRC2/38/26
Floyd, John, Salisbury St Thomas, Wilts, 1633 Wilts RO Miscellaneous Index to Wills (name + date)
Floyd, William, Chichester St Andrew, Sussex, 1640 W. Suss RO EpIII/9/1/46
Floyd/Huges, Richard, Burford, Oxon, 1631 Oxon RO MSS Wills 297/1/62
Flud, Thomas, husbandman, Rainham, Kent, 1690 CKS PRC2/41/174
Fludd, Robert, yeoman, Berkeley, Glos, 1744 GRO GDR/B4/2/F52
Fludd/Lloyd, Thomas eld, Milton next Sittingbourne, Kent, 1625 CKS PRC2/23/125
Fluddyer, Henry, husbandman, Hagbourne, East, Berks, 1603 Berks RO D/A1/189/140A
Fluellin, Richard, citizen/turner, St Katherine by the Tower, London & Middlesex, 1698 PRO PROB32/36/35
Flusse, Abraham, Ashford, Kent, 1614 CKS PRC2/18/107
Flye, Roger, cook, Oxford (New College), Oxon, 1613 Bodleian HYP B8/60-65
Flynder, James, Dover, Kent, 1624 CKS PRC20/6/42
Flyntham, Fulk, Pleasley, Derby, 1663 LJRO:cards/1663/22
Foache, Joseph, Lympne, Kent, 1597 CKS PRC2/9/113
Foad, Christopher, Elham, Kent, 1600 CKS PRC2/11/417
Foard, John, Newcastle under Lyme, Staffs, 1681 LJRO/B/C/5/1682/36
Foard, Robert, Chichester St Olave, Sussex, 1616 W. Suss RO EpIII/9/1/9
Foart, Robert, Eastchurch, Sheppey, Kent, 1682 CKS PRC2/40/29
Foart, Thomas, yeoman, Minster in Sheppey, Kent, 1699 CKS PRC2/42/155
Foate, Joane, St Peter in Thanet, Kent, 1616 CKS PRC2/21/82
Foate, Valentine, Chislet, Kent, 1612 CKS PRC2/17/320
Foate, Vincent, Reculver, Kent, 1640 CKS PRC20/10/358
Foate/Foorte, Mary, Charing, Kent, 1621 CKS PRC20/5/71
Foch, William, Deal, Kent, 1615 CKS PRC20/3/182
Foche, Henrie, gentleman, Deal, Kent, 1636 CKS PRC20/10/348

[Foe:]
Foe, John, Algarkirk, Lincs, 1605 Lincs RO Ad/Ac/6/83
Fogg, George, gentleman, Harbledown, Kent, 1617 CKS PRC20/4/87
Fogg, William, butcher, Liverpool, Lancs, 1795 Lancs RO (Name of Deceased) D.R.C.H. 1795
Fogge, George, mr, Faversham, Kent, 1628 CKS PRC2/29/37
Fogge, Thomas eld, gentleman, Challock, Kent, 1635 CKS PRC20/10/330
Fogge, Whittingham eld, gentleman, Chilham, Kent, 1667 CKS PRC1/13/42a
Fogge, Whittingham eld, gentleman, Chilham, Kent, 1668 CKS PRC1/13/42
Fogger, Nicholas, Seasalter, Kent, 1604 CKS PRC2/14/189
Foggs, Richard, gentleman, Barham, Kent, 1631 CKS PRC20/9/147
Foley, John, Rowley Regis, Staffs, 1683 Worcs RO 008.7 BA3585/837/bdl 3
Follett, Robert, Sandford Orcas, Som, 1686 Somerset RO D/D/Cta/F32
Follwell, Ferdinando, Kingsclere, Hants, 1624 Hants RO 21M65 D8/66
Fones, William, Upton on Severn, Worcs, Worcs RO 008.7 BA3585/837/bdl 3
Fookes, John, carpenter, Queenborough, Kent, 1678 CKS PRC2/38/29
Foord, Catherine, Canterbury St Alphege, Kent, 1615 CKS PRC20/3/292
Foord, Elianor, Tenterden, Kent, 1574 CKS PRC2/1/118
Foord, Elizabeth, Kenardington, Kent, 1628 CKS PRC2/29/34
Foord, Elizabeth, spinster, Wargrave (Fordhouse), Berks, 1640 Berks RO D/A1/190/42C
Foord, George, St Nicholas at Wade, Kent, 1577 CKS PRC21/3/141
Foord, George, St Nicholas at Wade, Kent, 1580 CKS PRC21/4/185
Foord, George, Staplehurst, Kent, 1619 CKS PRC2/21/65
Foord, Henrie, Birchington, Kent, 1638 CKS PRC20/10/362
Foord, James, Newenden, Kent, 1583 CKS PRC21/6/236
Foord, Jane, Petworth, Sussex, 1594 W. Suss RO EpI/33/1594/10
Foord, Jane, widow, Brabourne, Kent, 1666 CKS PRC1/11/23
Foord, John, St Nicholas at Wade, Kent, 1616 CKS PRC20/3/450
Foord, John, yeoman, Broad Chalke, Wilts, 1639 Wilts RO Arch. Sarum/(+ name and date)
Foord, John, Brockenhurst, Hants, 1663 Hants RO 21M65 D8/154
Foord, John, High Halstow, Kent, 1666 CKS PRC1/11/24
Foord, Richard, Aldington, Kent, 1632 CKS PRC20/10/326
Foord, Vincent, Aldington, Kent, 1638 CKS PRC20/10/352
Foord, William, St Nicholas at Wade, Kent, 1592 CKS PRC21/12/190
Foord, William, Whitfield alias Beauxfield, Kent, 1629 CKS PRC2/30/51
Foord, William, husbandman, Langford (Little Faringdon), Oxon, 1678 Oxon RO MSS Wills Pec 78/2/32
Foorde, Henry, Barham, Kent, 1701 CKS PRC1/16/26
Foorte, see Foate,
Foot, Hannah, victualler, Bristol, Glos, Bristol RO 1773/CP
Foot, John, Whitechapel, London & Middlesex, 1696 PRO PROB32/39/254
Foote, John, Linkinhorne, Corn, 1643 Cornwall RO AP/F197/1
Footehelle, Nicholas,
Lincs 1573 Lincs RO Ad/Ac/1/7
Footehelle, Nicholas, Sleaford, Lincs, 1573 Lincs RO Ad/Ac/2C/153
Forargus, John,
Lincs 1781 Lincs RO Ad/Ac/45/44
Forbie, Henry, bachelor, Kirmington, Lincs, 1642 Lincs RO Ad/Ac/28/23
Forcet, Robert, Saleby (Thoresthorpe), Lincs, 1614 Lincs RO Ad/Ac/13/105
Ford, Alexander, Ilchester, Som, 1624 Somerset RO D/D/Cta/F6
Ford, Anne, 1664 Lancs RO (Name of Deceased) D.R.C.H. 1664
Ford, David, Maidstone, Kent, 1674 CKS PRC20/12/126
Ford, Elizabeth, Leeds, Kent, 1675 CKS PRC2/36/186
Ford, Elizabeth, Norton in the Moors, Staffs, 1676 LJRO:cards/1676/24
Ford, Elizabeth, spinster, Knightsbridge, London & Middlesex, 1815 Greater London RO DL/C/575/60
Ford, Jeremiah, St James Westminster, London & Middlesex, 1743 Greater London RO

AM/PP/Box 1739-1749 pt (uncatalogued)
Ford, John, Hagbourne, East, Berks, 1618 Berks RO D/A1/189/162A
Ford, John, Keele, Staffs, 1675 LJRO:cards/1675/25
Ford, John, gunner at Dover Castle, Bridge, Kent, 1678 CKS PRC2/38/27
Ford, John, yeoman, Sellindge, Kent, 1678 CKS PRC2/38/28
Ford, John, Horton (Damms Lane), Staffs, 1687 LJRO/B/C/5/1687/31
Ford, John, yeoman, Sutton Veny, Wilts, 1736 Wilts RO Arch. Sarum/(+ name and date)
Ford, John eld, cordwainer, Rolvenden, Kent, 1669 CKS PRC1/14/36
Ford, Marke, chandler, Hougham, Lincs, 1673 Lincs RO Ad/Ac/35/2
Ford, Mary, 1664 Lancs RO (Name of Deceased) D.R.C.H. 1664
Ford, Nicholas, yeoman, Damerham, Wilts, 1684 Wilts RO CC Sarum(+ name and date)
Ford, Thomas, Compton Martin, Som, 1612 Somerset RO D/D/Cta/F20
Ford, Thomas, Frome Selwood, Som, 1622 Somerset RO D/D/Cta/F5
Ford, Thomas, gentleman, Farrington Curney, Som, 1627 Somerset RO D/D/Cta/F7
Ford, Thomas, Orlestone, Kent, 1680 CKS PRC2/39/40
Ford, William, Stapleford, Wilts, 1770? Wilts RO Miscellaneous Index to Wills (name + date)
Ford, Willyam, Marden, Kent, 1626 CKS PRC2/27/53
Forde, Harbert, Hawkhurst, Kent, 1604 CKS PRC2/14/191
Forde, Thomas, St Nicholas at Wade, Kent, 1604 CKS PRC21/17/23
Forde, William, Slindon, Sussex, 1637 W. Suss RO EpIV/10/2/11
Forder, John, Sidlesham, Sussex, 1610 W. Suss RO EpI/33/1610/3
Forder, John, Wittering, West, Sussex, 1617 W. Suss RO EpI/33/1617/7
Fordred, Henry, yeoman, Elmsted, Kent, 1642 CKS PRC1/6/60
Fordred, John, Hythe St Leonard, Kent, 1583 CKS PRC21/6/175
Fordred, John, Elmsted, Kent, 1625 CKS PRC2/25/52
Fordred, John ygr, Elmsted, Kent, 1610 CKS PRC2/15/123
Fordred, Thomas, Elmsted, Kent, 1600 CKS PRC2/11/219
Fordred, William, Hythe St Leonard, Kent, 1593 CKS PRC21/12/271
Fordred, William, cordwainer, Hythe St Leonard, Kent, 1662 CKS PRC19/3/8
Fords, Margaret, widow, Tydd St Mary, Lincs, 1625 Lincs RO Ad/Ac/19B/48
Foreman, Arthure, Calne, Wilts, 1675 Wilts RO Miscellaneous Index to Wills (name + date)
Foreman, John, yeoman, Pidley, Hunts, 1726 Hunts RO/Acc58/317
Foreman, Robert, Stourmouth, Kent, 1605 CKS PRC2/14/179
Foremantle, Morderay, Whitechapel, London & Middlesex, Greater London RO DL/C/(Ac 73.77 pt)/Box 85/5 (uncatalogued)
Forest, James, Wimborne Minster, Dors, 1625 Dorset RO PE/WM CP 2/4/37
Forgie, Mary, widow, St Mary le Savoy, London & Middlesex, 1687 PRO PROB32/26/329
Forman, Anthony, Boston, Lincs, 1638 Lincs RO Ad/Ac/25/325
Forman, Anthony, yeoman, Bardney (Bardney Dairies), Lincs, 1673 Lincs RO Ad/Ac/35/23
Forman, Edmund, Baston, Lincs, 1614 Lincs RO Ad/Ac/13/38
Forman, Edward, Kyme, South, Lincs, 1640 Lincs RO Ad/Ac/27/148
Forman, Elizabeth, widow, Metheringham, Lincs, 1636 Lincs RO Ad/Ac/24/234
Forman, John, Alkborough, Lincs, 1612 Lincs RO Ad/Ac/8a/348
Forman, John, yeoman, Bardney (Bardney Dairies), Lincs, 1673 Lincs RO Ad/Ac/35/18
Forman, Mary, widow, Chiltington, West, Sussex, 1677 W. Suss RO EpI/33/1676/2
Forman, Richard, clergy: 'clerk', Halton, West, Lincs, 1613 Lincs RO Ad/Ac/8b/82
Forman, Ruben, yeoman, Tattershall, Lincs, 1614 Lincs RO Ad/Ac/12/215
Forman, Thomas, clergy: 'clerk', Coates, Great, Lincs, 1626 Lincs RO Ad/Ac/20/39
Forman, Thomas, gentleman, Rodbourne Cheney, Wilts, 1679 Wilts RO Miscellaneous Index to Wills (name + date)
Forman, William, Calne, Wilts, 1600 Wilts RO Miscellaneous Index (name + date)
Forman, William, Lincoln St Swithin, Lincs, 1619 Lincs RO Ad/Ac/15/109a
Forman, William, Boston, Lincs, 1781 Lincs RO Ad/Ac/36/13
Formell, Ciriack,

[Formell:]
Kent 1596 CKS PRC2/8/290
Formeston, John, Redbourn, Herts, 1637 Herts RO ASA25/4925
Forrest, Anthoney, Horningsham, Wilts, 1625 Wilts RO Dean Sarum (name + date)
Forrest, John, Halesowen, Worcs, 1675 Worcs RO 008.7 BA3585/835/bdl 3
Forrest, John, butcher, Eastry, Kent, 1686 CKS PRC20/13/549
Forrest, Joseph, Sherbourne, Dors, 1627? Wilts RO Miscellaneous Index (name + date)
Forrest, Joseph, Wimborne Minster (Barnsley), Dors, 1670 Dorset RO PE/WM CP 2/4/72
Forrest, Richard, Kenilworth, Warks, 1683 LJRO/B/C/5/1682/37
Forrest, William, St Albans St Michaels, Herts, 1626 Herts RO ASA25/2946
Forrian, Francis, Congerstone, Leics, 1666 Leics RO Administrators Accounts C17th f80
Forsett, Robert, esquire, St Marylebone, London & Middlesex, 1689 PRO PROB32/28/88
Forstall, John, St Nicholas at Wade, Kent, 1583 CKS PRC21/7/117 and 117a
Forstall, John, Wickhambreaux, Kent, 1612 CKS PRC2/16/55
Forstall, William, Langdon, East, Kent, CKS PRC2/2/86
Forster, Abraham, webster, Uttoxeter, Staffs, 1704 LJRO/B/C/5/1704/8
Forster, Abraham, webster, Uttoxeter, Staffs, 1704 LJRO/B/C/5/1794/8
Forster, Margerie, Grimsby, Great, Lincs, 1622 Lincs RO Ad/Ac/17/44
Forster, Oliver, Standish (Coppull), Lancs, 1592 Lancs RO (Name of Deceased) D.R.C.H. 1592
Forster, Thomas, butler, Huddersfield (Longwood), Yorks, 1804 Borthwick Test C.P. 1804/11
Forster, see Foster,
Fort, Jeffery, Ash next Sandwich, Kent, 1711 CKS PRC19/6/42
Forte, Henrye, Haxey (Graizelound), Lincs, 1606 Lincs RO Ad/Ac/37/224
Forte, John, Ash next Sandwich, Kent, 1582 CKS PRC21/5/212
Forte, Lucke, St Nicholas at Wade, Kent, 1600 CKS PRC21/16/188
Forte, Robert, Taunton St James, Som, 1587 Somerset RO D/D/Cta/F26
Forte, Robert, Taunton St James, Som, 1588 Somerset RO D/D/Cta/F16
Forte, Robert, Chilham, Kent, 1608 CKS PRC2/14/184
Forth, Elizabeth, Chesterfield, Derby, 1684 LJRO/B/C/5/1684/36
Forthington, Christopher, Steeping, Great, Lincs, 1624 Lincs RO Ad/Ac/19A/132
Forton, Richard, Kinnersley, Shrops, 1663 LJRO:cards/1663/23
Forty, Henry, clergy: 'priest', Abingdon, Berks, Berks RO D/A1/1/70V
Forty, John, husbandman, Kidlington, Oxon, 1644 Oxon RO MSS Wills 297/2/24
Forty, John, glover, Newbury, Berks, 1683 Berks RO D/A1/190/98C
Forty, Leonard, Ilsley, East, Berks, 1637 Berks RO D/A1/190/33B
Forward, Edward, mariner, Sandwich St Mary, Kent, 1669 CKS PRC1/14/37
Forward, Stephen, Mere, Wilts, 1640 Wilts RO Miscellaneous Index (name + date)
Forwood, John, Sandwich, Kent, 1627 CKS PRC2/28/46
Fosbury, Thomas, yeoman, Bozeat, Northants, 1676 Northants RO NWill A/C/113
Fosket, Walter, Brinkworth, Wilts, 1619 Wilts RO Arch. Wilts.(name + date)
Foskett, Joan, widow, Sawtry Moyne, Hunts, 1679 Hunts RO/Acc58/139(35)
Fossett, Christopher, Baumber, Lincs, 1623 Lincs RO Ad/Ac/18/65
Fossier, Elizabeth, widow, Canterbury, Kent, 1616 CKS PRC20/3/433
Fossier, Elizabeth, widow, Canterbury, Kent, 1617 CKS PRC20/4/85
Fostall, Richard, Wingham, Kent, 1627 CKS PRC20/8/189
Fostall, Robert, bachelor, Minster in Sheppey, Kent, 1664 CKS PRC1/10/35
Fosten, John eld, victualler, Cranbrook, Kent, 1626 CKS PRC2/27/51
Fosten, Nathaniel, victualler, Cranbrook, Kent, 1668 CKS PRC1/13/44
Foster, Anne, Winteringham, Lincs, 1632 Lincs RO Ad/Ac/39/281
Foster, Edward, Witham on the Hill, Lincs, 1662 Lincs RO Ad/Ac/32/32
Foster, Edward, Corhampton, Hants, 1684 Hants RO 21m65 D8/338
Foster, Edward, tailor, New Romney, Kent, 1685 CKS PRC20/13/501
Foster, Elizabeth, widow, Langton by Wragby, Lincs, 1679 Lincs RO Ad/Ac/43/119
Foster, Elizabethe, Cranbrook, Kent, 1586 CKS PRC2/4/174
Foster, Francis, Hollingbourne, Kent, 1664 CKS PRC19/3/23
Foster, George, Boston, Lincs, 1574 Lincs RO Ad/Ac/1/10

Foster, Henrie, clergy: 'clerk', Wainfleet All Saints, Lincs, 1606 Lincs RO Ad/Ac/7/28
Foster, Henrie, Raithby, Lincs, 1620 Lincs RO Ad/Ac/15/191
Foster, Henry, St Albans, Herts, 1590 Herts RO ASA25/1268
Foster, Henry, miller, Ingestre (Hoo Mill), Staffs, 1789 LJRO/B/C/5/1789/21
Foster, James, Minting, Lincs, 1598 Lincs RO Ad/Ac/4/53
Foster, John, Cranbrook, Kent, 1579 CKS PRC21/3/266
Foster, John, Maidstone, Kent, 1585 CKS PRC21/7/294
Foster, John, Thatcham (Crookham), Berks, 1610 Berks RO D/A1/189/156B
Foster, John, yeoman, Ashby, Lincs, 1619 Lincs RO Ad/Ac/15/284
Foster, John, yeoman, Panton, Lincs, 1619 Lincs RO Ad/Ac/15/286
Foster, John, Cranbrook, Kent, 1637 CKS PRC2/34/49
Foster, John, Winteringham, Lincs, 1662 Lincs RO Ad/Ac/41/18
Foster, John, husbandman, Holton le Clay, Lincs, 1671 Lincs RO Ad/Ac/33/190
Foster, John, jurat, Dover, Kent, 1673 CKS PRC20/12/48
Foster, John, Biddenden, Kent, 1684 CKS PRC2/40/199
Foster, Laurence, Rolvenden, Kent, 1668 CKS PRC1/14/38a
Foster, Laurence, yeoman, Rolvenden, Kent, 1669 CKS PRC1/14/38
Foster, Lawrence, Rolvenden, Kent, 1669 CKS PRC1/13/43
Foster, Libens, labourer, Newton by Toft, Lincs, 1619 Lincs RO Ad/Ac/15/297
Foster, Mary, Sandhurst, Kent, 1626 CKS PRC2/27/52
Foster, Nicholas, husbandman, Ilsley, East, Berks, 1676 Berks RO D/A1/68/149D
Foster, Richard, High Halden, Kent, 1605 CKS PRC2/14/186
Foster, Richard, saddler, Ashford, Kent, 1612 CKS PRC2/16/32
Foster, Richard, St Mary Aldermary, London & Middlesex, 1628 Lambeth Palace VH95/703
Foster, Richard, Bratoft, Lincs, 1637 Lincs RO Ad/Ac/25/465
Foster, Richard, yeoman, Barrow upon Trent, Derby, 1642 LJRO:cards/1642/2
Foster, Richard, yeoman, Rolvenden, Kent, 1671 CKS PRC2/35/35
Foster, Richard, innholder, Faversham, Kent, 1674 CKS PRC2/36/54
Foster, Richard, yeoman, Westborough, Lincs, 1680 Lincs RO Ad/Ac/34/39
Foster, Robert, Faldingworth, Lincs, 1606 Lincs RO Ad/Ac/37/229
Foster, Robert, yeoman, Ulceby, Lincs, 1614 Lincs RO Ad/Ac/13/169
Foster, Robert, husbandman, Epworth, Lincs, 1668 Lincs RO Ad/Ac/33/11
Foster, Roger, fellmonger, Maidstone, Kent, 1637 CKS PRC20/10/334
Foster, Thomas, Northaw, Herts, 1597 Herts RO ASA25/1544
Foster, Thomas, Belton, Lincs, 1602 Lincs RO Ad/Ac/37/133
Foster, Thomas, Kirmington, Lincs, 1612 Lincs RO Ad/Ac/11/91
Foster, Thomas, Tattershall, Lincs, 1614 Lincs RO Ad/Ac/13/149
Foster, Thomas, Stone in Oxney, Kent, 1621 CKS PRC2/21/106
Foster, Thomas, victualler, Windsor, New, Berks, 1638 Berks RO D/A1/190/36C
Foster, Thomas, St Neots, Hunts, 1676 Hunts RO/Acc58/67(178)
Foster, Thomas, Wells, Som, 1691 Somerset RO D/D/Cta/F10
Foster, Thomas, cordwainer, St Johns Thanet, Kent, 1691 CKS PRC2/42/5
Foster, Thomas, baker, Birmingham, Warks, 1799 LJRO/B/C/5/1799/29
Foster, Vincent, Gedney, Lincs, 1612 Lincs RO Ad/Ac/11/72
Foster, William, Bristol St Stephen, Glos, Bristol RO 1677/61
Foster, William, Bearsted, Kent, 1613 CKS PRC2/16/140
Foster, William, Ashington, Sussex, 1620 W. Suss RO EpI/33/1619/1
Foster, William, Holbeach, Lincs, 1625 Lincs RO Ad/Ac/19B/69
Foster, William, yeoman, Belton, Lincs, 1625 Lincs RO Ad/Ac/39/226
Foster, William, Kettlethorpe (Laughterton), Lincs, 1662 Lincs RO Ad/Ac/41/61
Foster, William, Biddenden, Kent, 1694 CKS PRC2/42/79
Foster/Forster, William, Dinton, Wilts, 1743 Wilts RO Arch. Sarum/(+ name and date)
Foster/Smith, Eleanor, widow, Thatcham, Berks, 1677 Berks RO D/A1/69/2C
Foster/Smith, Richard, Thatcham, Berks, 1616 Berks RO D/A1/189/161A
Foster/Smith, Richard, husbandman, Thatcham, Berks, 1677 Berks RO D/A1/190/85B

[Foster, see Smith:]
Foster, see Smith,
Foston, Christopher, Addlethorpe, Lincs, 1611 Lincs RO Ad/Ac/10/115
Fostons, Thomas, husbandman, Ulceby, Lincs, 1635 Lincs RO Ad/Ac/24/248
Fotherbie, Ellen, widow, Wrawby, Lincs, 1620 Lincs RO Ad/Ac/16/39
Fotherbie, Francis, clergy: 'mr/vicar', Linsted, Kent, 1647 CKS PRC1/8/14
Fotherbie, Robert, Grimsby, Lincs, 1600 Lincs RO Ad/Ac/5/461
Fotherby, Titus, Boston, Lincs, 1625 Lincs RO Ad/Ac/19B/62
Fotherley, James, Rickmansworth, Herts, 1589 Herts RO ASA25/1237
Foulis, Henry, degrees: 'B.D.', Oxford (Lincoln College), Oxon, 1672 Bodleian HYP B8/66-67
Fountain, Robert, Donington, Lincs, 1790 Lincs RO Ad/Ac/45/59
Fountaine, Thomas, Sapperton, Lincs, 1649 Lincs RO Ad/Ac/30/136
Fountance, Thomas, Killingholme, Lincs, 1626 Lincs RO Ad/Ac/20/73
Fountance, William, Swineshead, Lincs, 1624 Lincs RO Ad/Ac/19A/111
Fourd, Thamasine, widow,
Kent 1611 CKS PRC2/16/100
Fourneer, Peter, Dover, Kent, 1687 CKS PRC20/13/588
Fouseden, Thomas, Goudhurst, Kent, 1616 CKS PRC2/21/72
Fowcett, Thomas, Bilsby, Lincs, 1581 Lincs RO Ad/Ac/2b/62a
Fowle, Alexander, barber, Goudhurst, Kent, 1620 CKS PRC2/21/76
Fowle, Anne, widow, Canterbury Holy Cross Westgate, Kent, 1676 CKS PRC2/37/33
Fowle, Chrisogon eld, Old Romney, Kent, 1630 CKS PRC2/30/52
Fowle, Edmund, Sandhurst, Kent, 1614 CKS PRC2/18/32
Fowle, Edward, Frittenden, Kent, 1603 CKS PRC2/12/431
Fowle, Edward, Sandhurst, Kent, 1621 CKS PRC2/23/115
Fowle, James, Woodchurch, Kent, 1689 CKS PRC20/13/630
Fowle, John, Wittersham, Kent, 1604 CKS PRC21/17/19
Fowle, John, Maidstone, Kent, 1627 CKS PRC20/8/199
Fowle, John, knight, Sandhurst, Kent, 1640 CKS PRC19/1/43
Fowle, Mathew, Sturry, Kent, 1610 CKS PRC2/15/122
Fowle, Richard, Canterbury St George Martyr, Kent, 1670 CKS PRC1/15/23
Fowle, Richard, yeoman, Wittersham, Kent, 1670 CKS PRC19/4/77
Fowle, Thomas, Smarden, Kent, 1594 CKS PRC2/7/43
Fowle, Thomas, Kirton, Lincs, 1619 Lincs RO Ad/Ac/14/291
Fowle, Thomas, Frittenden, Kent, 1628 CKS PRC20/8/205
Fowle, Thomas, Wittersham, Kent, 1665 CKS PRC19/3/70
Fowler, Anne, widow, Haxey, Lincs, 1674 Lincs RO Ad/Ac/35/76
Fowler, Anthony, Theddingworth, Leics, 1666 Leics RO Administrators Accounts C17th f50
Fowler, Cleamont, Ashby de la Zouch, Leics, 1666 Leics RO Administrators Accounts C17th f69
Fowler, Edward, Barrow on Humber, Lincs, 1618 Lincs RO Ad/Ac/14/116
Fowler, Elizabeth, widow, Whitton, Lincs, 1664 Lincs RO Ad/Ac/41/138
Fowler, Francis, Whitmore, Staffs, 1682 LJRO/B/C/5/1681/14
Fowler, Henrie, Canterbury St Martin, Kent, 1596 CKS PRC21/14/39
Fowler, Henry, yeoman, Helpringham, Lincs, 1639 Lincs RO Ad/Ac/26/132
Fowler, James, husbandman, Sittingbourne, Kent, 1671 CKS PRC2/35/34
Fowler, Jeremiah, Hexton, Herts, 1685 Herts RO ASA25/4124
Fowler, Joan, Wimborne Minster (Leigh), Dors, Dorset RO PE/WM CP 2/4/46
Fowler, John, Bobbing, Kent, 1579 CKS PRC21/4/146
Fowler, John, Ashford, Kent, 1592 CKS PRC2/6/176
Fowler, John, Chart, Great, Kent, 1616 CKS PRC2/21/79
Fowler, John, Helpringham, Lincs, 1624 Lincs RO Ad/Ac/19A/112
Fowler, John, Bersted, South, Sussex, 1637 W. Suss RO EpIV/10/2/14
Fowler, John, Sutton Maddock, Shrops, 1674 LJRO:cards/1674/13
Fowler, Peter, milliner, Hallington, Lincs, 1619 Lincs RO Ad/Ac/15/19
Fowler, Richard, Halton, West, Lincs, 1635 Lincs RO Ad/Ac/40/106
Fowler, Richard, Swell, Som, 1692 Somerset RO D/D/Cta/F11

Fowler, Richerde, Woodchurch, Kent, 1587 CKS PRC21/8/368
Fowler, Robert, Spalding, Lincs, 1619 Lincs RO Ad/Ac/15/29
Fowler, Robert, husbandman, Stokenchurch, Oxon, 1624 Oxon RO MSS Wills 297/1/36
Fowler, Robert, Burton on Stather, Lincs, 1652 Lincs RO Ad/Ac/40/234
Fowler, Robert, husbandman, Messingham, Lincs, 1678 Lincs RO Ad/Ac/35/128
Fowler, Robert, Shifnal, Shrops, 1682 LJRO/B/C/5/1681/15
Fowler, Stephen, Winterton, Lincs, 1675 Lincs RO Ad/Ac/35/98
Fowler, Susan, Bottesford, Lincs, 1661 Lincs RO Ad/Ac/41/30
Fowler, Thomas, Burton on Stather, Lincs, 1632 Lincs RO Ad/Ac/39/268
Fowler, Thomas, Frodingham (Scunthorpe), Lincs, 1680 Lincs RO Ad/Ac/43/156
Fowler, William, Frodingham (Crosby), Lincs, 1630 Lincs RO Ad/Ac/39/287
Fowler, William, gentleman, Repton, Derby, 1679 LJRO:cards/1679/2
Fowler, William, yeoman, Norbury (Blakemore House), Staffs, 1819 LJRO/B/C/5/1819/68
Fowler, William, yeoman, Norbury (Blakemore House), Staffs, 1819 LJRO/B/C/5/1819/70
Fowler, see Healey,
Fowlle, Richard, Benenden, Kent, 1601 CKS PRC2/12/151
Fowse, see Phillipps,
Fowslie, Jeames, Chart, Great, Kent, 1593 CKS PRC2/6/254
Fowtrell, John, Tilmanstone, Kent, 1725 CKS PRC1/18/38
Fowtrell, Richard, Ashford, Kent, 1647 CKS PRC1/8/15
Fox, Andrew, Holme, Hunts, 1676 Hunts RO/Acc58/41(2)
Fox, Ann, Birmingham, Warks, 1794 LJRO/B/C/5/1813/60b
Fox, Anne, Chart, Little, Kent, 1640 CKS PRC1/4/41
Fox, Daniel, Ruckinge, Kent, 1682 CKS PRC2/40/28
Fox, Edward, Tatenhill (Barton), Staffs, 1776 LJRO/B/C/5/1776/27
Fox, Elizabeth, widow, Ash next Sandwich, Kent, 1685 CKS PRC20/13/497
Fox, Francis, Withern, Lincs, 1640 Lincs RO Ad/Ac/27/47
Fox, George, Eastchurch, Sheppey, Kent, 1618 CKS PRC2/21/89
Fox, George, yeoman, Eastchurch, Sheppey, Kent, 1618 CKS PRC2/21/90
Fox, George, Glen, Great, Leics, 1683 Leics RO Administrators Accounts 1682-86 f4
Fox, George, vintner, St Mary le Savoy, London & Middlesex, 1696 PRO PROB32/39/175
Fox, Henry, husbandman, Swalecliffe, Kent, 1680 CKS PRC2/39/39
Fox, John, Radnall, Ches, 1626 Cheshire RO (Name) W.C. 1625/6
Fox, John, butcher, Sandwich, Kent, 1669 CKS PRC19/4/14
Fox, John, Owston, Lincs, 1677 Lincs RO Ad/Ac/35/117
Fox, John, Deal, Kent, 1695 CKS PRC19/5/35
Fox, Laurence, clergy: 'vicar', Lenham, Kent, 1633 CKS PRC2/32/41
Fox, Margaret, widow, Seasalter, Kent, 1620 CKS PRC2/21/75
Fox, Nathaniel, St Katherine by the Tower, London & Middlesex, 1695 Lambeth Palace Arches G45/1
Fox, Nicholas, Sturry, Kent, 1626 CKS PRC2/27/63
Fox, Ralfe, Saxilby, Lincs, 1617 Lincs RO Ad/Ac/8b/197
Fox, Ralph, Kelsey, North, Lincs, 1683 Lincs RO Ad/Ac/42/93
Fox, Robert, yeoman, Irnham, Lincs, 1636 Lincs RO Ad/Ac/24/267
Fox, Robert, yeoman, Elham, Kent, 1643 CKS PRC1/6/103
Fox, Robert, Teynham, Kent, 1671 CKS PRC2/35/37
Fox, Robert, Cley next the Sea, Norf, 1743 Norfolk RO ANW/23/24/5
Fox, Robert eld, gentleman, Hutton Cranswick, Yorks, Borthwick Test C.P. 1779/6
Fox, Stephen, Elham, Kent, 1635 CKS PRC2/33/50
Fox, Thomas, Owmby, Lincs, 1664 Lincs RO Ad/Ac/43/21
Fox, Thomas, yeoman, Upper Hardres, Kent, 1665 CKS PRC1/11/25
Fox, Thomas, gentleman, Canterbury St George Martyr, Kent, 1682 CKS PRC2/39/169
Fox, William, pavier, Bristol, Glos, Bristol RO 1737/11
Fox, William, Bromfield, Kent, 1606 CKS PRC2/13/191
Fox, William, clergy: 'clerk', Donington, Lincs, 1642 Lincs RO Ad/Ac/28/55

[Fox:]
Fox, William, husbandman, Bottesford, Lincs, 1675 Lincs RO Ad/Ac/35/94
Fox, William, surgeon, Abingdon, Berks, 1680 Berks RO D/A1/190/89C
Fox, William, weaver, Shifnal, Shrops, 1711 LJRO/B/C/5/1711/12
Fox/Bickerton, Sarah, Donington, Castle, Leics, 1672 Leics RO Administrators Accounts 1667-72 f51
Fox, see Bayly & Oxen,
Foxall, John, nailer, Halesowen, Worcs, 1785 Worcs RO 008.7 BA3585/835/bdl 2
Foxe, Clement, Kelsey, South, Lincs, 1612 Lincs RO Ad/Ac/11/95
Foxe, Francis, Glentworth, Lincs, 1621 Lincs RO Ad/Ac/8c/17
Foxe, Henry, Whitstable, Kent, 1625 CKS PRC2/25/53
Foxe, Joane, Wymeswold, Leics, 1625 Lincs RO Ad/Ac/19B/89
Foxe, Robert, Hollingbourne, Kent, 1573 CKS PRC21/1/172
Foxe, Sara, Burgh le Marsh, Lincs, 1606 Lincs RO Ad/Ac/7/26
Foxe, Valentine, Birchington, Kent, 1611 CKS PRC20/2/206
Foxe, William, husbandman, Sutton in the Marsh, Lincs, 1618 Lincs RO Ad/Ac/14/112
Foxley, Thomas, Witton, Ches, 1588 Cheshire RO (Name) W.C. 1588
Foxton, Anthony, clergy: 'clerk', Canterbury Christchurch, Kent, 1633 CKS PRC20/10/322
Foxton, Francis, clergy: 'D.D.', Mersham, Kent, 1633 CKS PRC20/10/316
Foxton, Thomas, gentleman, Sandwich, Kent, 1679 CKS PRC2/38/126
Foyce, James, Horsham (Bishopric), Sussex, 1640 W. Suss RO EpIV/10/2/27
Foyles, Richard, Borden, Kent, 1615 CKS PRC2/21/71
Fracey, Robert, husbandman, Wyberton, Lincs, 1666 Lincs RO Ad/Ac/32/84
Fracie, John, Witham on the Hill, Lincs, 1635 Lincs RO Ad/Ac/24/322
Fracy, William, Hacconby, Lincs, 1648 Lincs RO Ad/Ac/30/374
Frampton, Amy, Wimborne Minster, Dors, 1668 Dorset RO PE/WM CP 2/4/70
Frampton, Christopher, Wimborne Minster (Barnsley), Dors, 1640 Dorset RO PE/WM CP 2/4/63
Frances, Ann, St Albans St Stephens, Herts, Herts RO ASA25/1671
Frances, Isabel, widow, Clutton, Som, 1666 Somerset RO D/D/Cta/F23
Frances, Margarett, widow, Hernhill, Kent, 1612 CKS PRC20/2/404
Frances, Nicholas, Wimborne Minster, Dors, 1620 Dorset RO PE/WM CP 2/4/24
Frances, Sarah, widow, Reading St Lawrence, Berks, 1632 Berks RO D/A1/190/25B
Francis, Augustine, Willoughton, Lincs, 1591 Lincs RO Ad/Ac/37/10
Francis, Edward, Willoughton, Lincs, 1633? Lincs RO Ad/Ac/40/10
Francis, Jane, widow, Grimsby, Great, Lincs, 1618 Lincs RO Ad/Ac/14/166
Francis, John, gentleman, Abingdon, Berks, 1618 Berks RO D/A1/189/164A
Francis, John, yeoman, Wisborough Green, Sussex, 1661 W. Suss RO EpI/33/1661/9
Francis, John, farmer, Harrietsham, Kent, 1672 CKS PRC2/35/135
Francis, Nicholas, Willoughton, Lincs, 1671 Lincs RO Ad/Ac/33/204
Francis, Richard, Amberley, Sussex, 1650 W. Suss RO EpI/33/1650/2
Francis, Richard, husbandman, Minster in Sheppey, Kent, 1670 CKS PRC1/14/39
Francis, Stephen, husbandman, Langford, Steeple, Wilts, 1608 Wilts RO Arch. Sarum/(+ name and date)
Francis, Thomas, Muchelney, Som, 1591 Somerset RO D/D/Cta/F27
Francis, Thomas, Liskeard, Corn, 1604 Cornwall RO AP/F5/2
Francis, Thomas, St Martin by Looe, Corn, 1612 Cornwall RO AP/F54
Francis, Thomas, Fladbury, Worcs, 1685 Worcs RO 008.7 BA3585/837/bdl 4
Francis, William, Ridge, Herts, 1638 Herts RO ASA25/4955
Francius, John, university: 'Fellow of Peterhouse College, Cambridge/Doctor of Physic/Tutor' Cambridge (Peterhouse College), Cambs, 1666 CUL V.C. Acc./Box3/18
Franck, Isaack, Birchington, Kent, 1637 CKS PRC20/10/340
Franck, see Yorck,
Francke, John, Northbourne, Kent, 1616 CKS PRC2/21/67
Francke, John, Teynham, Kent, 1677 CKS PRC2/37/145
Francke, Mary, widow, Canterbury St Mildred, Kent, 1677 CKS PRC2/37/144
Francke, Nathaniel, Ospringe, Kent, 1671 CKS PRC2/35/38

Francke, William, Boughton under Blean, Kent, 1670 CKS PRC19/4/78
Franckland, Thomas, yeoman, Kirton, Lincs, 1667 Lincs RO Ad/Ac/32/120
Franckland, William + Dorothy, Kirton, Lincs, 1624 Lincs RO Ad/Ac/19A/60
Franckleyn, Nycholas, Canterbury St Paul, Kent, 1593 CKS PRC2/6/430
Francklin, Arthur, gentleman, Badlesmere, Kent, 1676 CKS PRC2/36/189
Francklin, George, Headcorn, Kent, 1625 CKS PRC2/25/54
Francklin, James, gentleman, Faversham, Kent, 1668 CKS PRC1/13/45
Francklin, John, yeoman, Uffington, Berks, 1684 Berks RO D/A1/190/105C
Francklin, John, milliner, Sudbury, Suff, 1742 Suff RO(B) IC500/3/50/78
Francklin, Richard, Folkestone, Kent, 1646 CKS PRC1/7/47
Francklin, see Stokes,
Franckling, Nicholas, Chart nr Sutton Valence, Kent, 1601 CKS PRC2/12/145
Franckling, Nicholas, Canterbury, Kent, 1695 CKS PRC19/5/25
Francklinge, George, Sittingbourne, Kent, 1610 CKS PRC2/13/181
Francklyn, Edmund, warrener, Holton, Oxon, 1640 Oxon RO MSS Wills 297/2/17
Francklyn, Francis, yeoman, Longcot, Berks, 1681 Berks RO D/A1/190/90C
Francklyn, Joyce, widow, Abingdon, Berks, 1672 Berks RO D/A1/190/76C
Franckwell, Henrie, Boxley, Kent, 1642 CKS PRC1/6/61
Franckwell, John, High Halstow, Kent, 1640 CKS PRC20/10/370
Franke, John, Stubton, Lincs, 1606 Lincs RO Ad/Ac/7/162
Franke, Thomas, Minster in Sheppey, Kent, 1616 CKS PRC2/21/88
Frankelin, Henry, Adwell, Oxon, 1664 Oxon RO MSS Wills 79/3/12
Frankish, Robert, gentleman, Bridlington, Yorks, 1830 Borthwick Test C.P. 1830/2
Frankish, Thomas, Nettleton, Lincs, 1619 Lincs RO Ad/Ac/15/274
Frankish, William, Kirmond le Mire, Lincs, 1637 Lincs RO Ad/Ac/25/440
Frankishe, John, Hacconby, Lincs, 1607 Lincs RO Ad/Ac/8a/172
Franklin, Arthur eld, gentleman, Badlesmere, Kent, 1669 CKS PRC1/14/40
Franklin, Arthur eld, gentleman, Badlesmere, Kent, 1669 CKS PRC1/14/40a
Franklin, Edward, jurat, Dover, Kent, 1700 CKS PRC19/5/72
Franklin, George, draper: 'linen draper', York, Yorks, 1794 Borthwick Test C.P. 1794/3
Franklin, Richard, Utterby, Lincs, 1669 Lincs RO Ad/Ac/33/143
Franklin, Walter, esquire, Maidstone, Kent, 1683 CKS PRC20/13/329
Franklin/Wirge, Thomas, Fulbrook, Oxon, 1629 Oxon RO MSS Wills 297/1/57
Franklyn, John, Canterbury St Mildred, Kent, 1617 CKS PRC2/21/61
Franklyn, John, Littlebourne, Kent, 1714 CKS PRC1/17/
Franklyn, John, Littlebourne, Kent, 1714 CKS PRC1/17/55a
Franklyn, John, Littlebourne, Kent, 1714 CKS PRC1/17/55b
Franklyn, John, mr, Littlebourne, Kent, 1714 CKS PRC1/17/55
Frannces, Thomas, fishmonger, Burford, Oxon, 1638 Oxon RO MSS Wills 297/2/11
Frape, Joseph, butcher, Oxford (New College), Oxon, 1635 Bodleian HYP B8/68-71
Frape, William, Slimbridge?, Glos, 1685 GRO GDR/B4/2/F54
Frary, John, husbandman, Stone in Oxney, Kent, 1638 CKS PRC2/34/47
Frary, John, Cromer, Norf, 1750 Norfolk RO ANF/11/4/81
Fraudingham, Marie, Quadring, Lincs, 1618 Lincs RO Ad/Ac/14/228
Fraunce, Edward, husbandman, Fladbury, Worcs, 1604 Worcs RO 008.7 BA3585/839/354
Fraunces, John, Wellesbourne, Warks, 1600 Worcs RO 008.7 BA3585/838/180
Fraunces, Richard, Bushey, Herts, 1615 Herts RO ASA25/4819
Frauncis, Brise, Blyborough, Lincs, 1626 Lincs RO Ad/Ac/39/16
Frauncis, William, Itchingfield, Sussex, 1611 W. Suss RO EpI/33/1611/6
Frauncys, Wyllyam, Folkestone, Kent, 1593 CKS PRC2/6/422
Frawncis, James, Faversham, Kent, 1589 CKS PRC2/5/100
Frawncis, Michaell, Northbourne, Kent, 1590 CKS PRC2/5/106
Fraye, James, Washington, Sussex, 1622 W. Suss RO EpI/33/1622/1
Frazar, Thomas, Kerdiston, Norf, 1769 Norfolk RO ANW/23/26/14
Freake, Edith, widow, Chilthorne Domer, Som, 1619 Somerset RO D/D/Cta/F19

[Freame:]
Freame, George, Biddenden, Kent, 1629 CKS PRC2/30/50
Frear, John, Wainfleet All Saints, Lincs, 1666 Lincs RO Ad/Ac/32/112
Freaston, Thomas, Boston, Lincs, 1612 Lincs RO Ad/Ac/11/139
Frebbins, Robert, Kennett, East, Wilts, 1674 Wilts RO Miscellaneous Index (name + date)
Frebody, Thomas, Snargate, Kent, 1597 CKS PRC2/9/233
Freckleton, see Haynes,
Fred, Robert, Canterbury St Mary Northgate, Kent, 1681 CKS PRC2/39/37
Fredrick, Jasper, Maidstone, Kent, 1597 CKS PRC21/14/95
Freebody, Robert, mr, Frittenden, Kent, 1687 CKS PRC2/41/50
Freebody, Thomas, gentleman, New Romney, Kent, 1684 CKS PRC20/13/424
Freebody, William, apothecary, Canterbury St Margaret, Kent, 1700 CKS PRC2/42/154
Freed, Robert, Petham, Kent, 1665 CKS PRC1/10/36
Freeland, John, Aldingbourne, Sussex, 1631 W. Suss RO EpI/33/1631/16
Freeman, Abraham, Normanton, South, Derby, 1684 LJRO/B/C/5/1683/8
Freeman, Abraham, Normanton, South, Derby, 1693 LJRO/B/C/5/1693/61
Freeman, Danyell, Whitnash, Warks, 1683 LJRO/B/C/5/1682/38
Freeman, Donald, Scalford, Leics, 1672 Leics RO Administrators Accounts 1667-72 f48
Freeman, Edward, gentleman, Coventry?, Warks, 1681 LJRO/B/C/5/1681/16a, b
Freeman, Elizabeth, widow, Pinchbeck, Lincs, 1622 Lincs RO Ad/Ac/18/4
Freeman, Elizabeth, widow, Warmington, Northants, 1774 Northants RO X954/21/27
Freeman, George, painter, St Martin in the Fields, London & Middlesex, 1695 Greater London RO AM/PP/Box 1695-1706 pt (uncatalogued)
Freeman, Henry, Rolvenden, Kent, 1640 CKS PRC1/2/63
Freeman, John, Hernhill, Kent, 1603 CKS PRC21/16/75
Freeman, John, Pinchbeck, Lincs, 1613 Lincs RO Ad/Ac/12/62
Freeman, John, Pulborough, Sussex, 1629 W. Suss RO EpI/33/1629/34
Freeman, John, yeoman, Lockinge, East, Berks, 1673 Berks RO D/A1/190/74C
Freeman, Mathew, yeoman, Barton on Humber, Lincs, 1587 Lincs RO Ad/Ac/0/31b
Freeman, Richard, Grayingham, Lincs, 1630 Lincs RO Ad/Ac/39/247
Freeman, Richard, Swaton, Lincs, 1652 Lincs RO Ad/Ac/29/145
Freeman, Richard, yeoman, Benson, Oxon, 1665 Oxon RO MSS Wills Pec 68/1/14
Freeman, Robert, servant, Oxford St Ebbe, Oxon, 1616 Bodleian HYP B8/72-73
Freeman, Robert, grocer, Deal, Kent, 1679 CKS PRC20/12/302
Freeman, Thomas, Hinton Charterhouse, Som, 1588 Somerset RO D/D/Cta/F15
Freeman, Thomas, Ramsbury, Wilts, 1631 Wilts RO Miscellaneous Index (name + date)
Freeman, Thomas, husbandman, Ospringe, Kent, 1663 CKS PRC1/9/108
Freeman, William, yeoman, Hagnaby, Lincs, 1669 Lincs RO Ad/Ac/33/109
Freeman, William, Islington St Mary, London & Middlesex, 1756 Greater London RO DL/C/554/9/1
Freer, Daniell, Mumby, Lincs, 1622 Lincs RO Ad/Ac/17/14
Freer, John, Rasen, Middle, Lincs, 1620 Lincs RO Ad/Ac/16/38
Freestone, George, Alford, Lincs, 1593 Lincs RO Ad/Ac/3/25
Freind, Ann, spinster, Waltham, Bishops, Hants, 1672 Hants RO 21m65 D8/231
Freind, Ann, spinster, Waltham, Bishops, Hants, 1672 Hants RO 21m65 D8/231a
Freind, Ann, spinster, Waltham, Bishops, Hants, 1672 Hants RO 21m65 D8/231b
Freind, Averye, Brabourne, Kent, 1612 CKS PRC2/16/151
Freind, Cornelius, Sandwich, Kent, 1621 CKS PRC2/23/120
Freind, Edward, St Clement Danes, London & Middlesex, 1692 Greater London RO AM/PP/Box 1685-1694 pt (uncatalogued)
Freind, Mary, Wilton, Wilts, 1675 Wilts RO Arch. Sarum/(+ name and date)
Freind, Roger,
Kent 1632 CKS PRC20/9/143
Freind, Rowland, Drayton, Market (Drayton in Hales), Shrops, 1674 LJRO:cards/1674/14
Freind, Thomas, Eastry, Kent, 1597 CKS PRC21/14/31
Freind, William, Adisham, Kent, 1616 CKS PRC20/3/446

Freind, William, Great Mongeham, Kent, 1676 CKS PRC2/36/188
Freland, John, Canterbury St Mary Northgate, Kent, 1593 CKS PRC2/6/274
Freman, Richard, Kenardington, Kent, 1590 CKS PRC2/5/108
Fremaux/Parmentire, Alison, widow, Canterbury St Alphege, Kent, 1615 CKS PRC20/3/178
French, Alice, Salwarpe, Worcs, 1675 Worcs RO 008.7 BA3585/835/bdl 1
French, Anne, Tenterden, Kent, 1621 CKS PRC2/21/81
French, Anthony, Appledore, Kent, 1632 CKS PRC2/31/110
French, James, bone setter, Cowfold, Sussex, 1675 W. Suss RO EpI/33/1675/4
French, John, Wittering, East, Sussex, 1646 W. Suss RO EpI/33/1646/5
French, John, yeoman, Snargate, Kent, 1677 CKS PRC2/37/34
French, John eld, husbandman, Whitstable, Kent, 1669 CKS PRC1/14/41
French, Robert, yeoman, Stone in Oxney, Kent, 1670 CKS PRC1/15/24
French, Robert, Heene, Sussex, 1680 W. Suss RO EpIV/10/2A/21
French, Thomas, Sandwich St Peter, Kent, 1603 CKS PRC2/14/193
French, William, husbandman, Moreton, North, Berks, 1599 Berks RO D/A1/189/136A
French, William, Fairfield, Kent, 1640 CKS PRC19/1/44
French/Westridge, Thomas, Findon, Sussex, 1669 W. Suss RO EpI/33/1669/14
Frencham, Daniell, Rolvenden, Kent, 1594 CKS PRC2/7/221
Frencham, Mary, widow, Sandwich St Peter, Kent, 1616 CKS PRC2/21/66
Frencham, Thomas, Dover, Kent, 1640 CKS PRC19/1/45
Frenchborne, Andrewe, Canterbury St Mary Bredman, Kent, 1610 CKS PRC2/15/126
Frenchborne, John, Westwell, Kent, 1633 CKS PRC20/10/318
Frenchbourne, John, Faversham, Kent, 1680 CKS PRC2/38/127
Frenchbourne, Margaret, widow, Ospringe, Kent, 1628 CKS PRC2/29/39
Frenchbourne/Heneker, Ann, Boughton Malherbe, Kent, 1675 CKS PRC2/36/187
Frenche, Clare, widow, Sandwich, Kent, 1611 CKS PRC20/2/200
Frenche, John, St Johns Thanet, Kent, 1595 CKS PRC2/7/187
Frenche, Lewes, Dover, Kent, 1606 CKS PRC20/1/171
Frenche, Margarett, Canterbury, Kent, 1595 CKS PRC2/7/181
Frenche, Roger, Ruckinge, Kent, 1590 CKS PRC2/5/104
Frenche, Thomas, Redbourn, Herts, 1611 Herts RO ASA25/4791
Frenche, Thomas ygr, Tenterden, Kent, 1612 CKS PRC2/16/181
Frenche, Valentine, Canterbury St Andrew, Kent, 1599 CKS PRC2/10/226
Frend, Dionisia, Sandwich St Mary, Kent, 1624 CKS PRC2/23/122
Frend, John, Brabourne, Kent, 1615 CKS PRC2/21/59
Frend, Thomas, Folkestone, Kent, 1612 CKS PRC2/17/197
Frend, Thomas, Milton next Sittingbourne, Kent, 1622 CKS PRC20/6/382
Frere, William, degrees: 'B.D.', Cambridge (Sidney Sussex College), Cambs, 1682 CUL V.C. Acc./Box3/19
Fresh, Thomas, St George, London & Middlesex, 1749 Greater London RO DL/C/552/47/1
Freshwater, Thomas, Staughton, Great (Beetham Street), Hunts, 1676 Hunts RO/Acc58/44(136)
Fretwell, Francis, Bilton (Bickerton), Yorks, Borthwick Test C.P. 1736/4
Frevitt, Nicholas, clergy: 'clerk', Netherbury, Dors, 1638 Wilts RO Dean Sarum (name + date)
Frewen, Richard, gentleman, Hanley Castle, Worcs, Worcs RO 008.7 BA3585/838/286
Frewin, Thomas, Pamber, Hants, 1625 Hants RO 21M65 D8/115
Frewin, Willyam, Newenden, Kent, 1612 CKS PRC2/16/5
Friar, Margery, Broadwas, Worcs, 1605 Worcs RO 008.7 BA3585/839/356
Friar, Thomas, Stowting, Kent, 1599 CKS PRC2/10/222
Fricker, Henry, Tisbury, Wilts, 1638 Wilts RO Arch. Sarum/(+ name and date)
Frickle, John, Monkton, Kent, 1629 CKS PRC20/8/213
Friday, Michaell, Luddenham, Kent, 1596 CKS PRC2/8/409
Fridd, Alexander, Ulcombe, Kent, 1616 CKS PRC2/21/91
Fridd, Joane, widow, Ulcombe, Kent, 1624 CKS PRC2/23/123
Frie, Henry, Martock, Som, 1620 Somerset RO D/D/Cta/F4
Frie, William, Pennard, West, Som, 1637 Somerset RO D/D/Cta/F8

[Friend:]
Friend, Mary, Cranbrook, Kent, 1673 CKS PRC2/35/216
Friend, Robert, St Johns Thanet, Kent, 1613 CKS PRC2/16/27
Friend, Robert, Salisbury, Wilts, 1674 Wilts RO Miscellaneous Index (name + date)
Friend, see Cozens & Hayward,
Frierson, Robert, Sittingbourne, Kent, 1627 CKS PRC2/28/47
Friesby, Charles, Baumber, Lincs, 1599 Lincs RO Ad/Ac/5/471
Frieston, Thomas, husbandman, Friskney, Lincs, 1670 Lincs RO Ad/Ac/32/222
Friland, Samuel, Cranbrook, Kent, 1638 CKS PRC2/34/51
Frind, Richard, St Nicholas at Wade, Kent, 1586 CKS PRC21/8/27
Frinde, Thomas, Eastry, Kent, 1590 CKS PRC21/10/26
Frisbee, Thomas, Dorking, Surrey, 1778 Greater London RO DW/OP/1778/26
Frisby, Henry, gentleman, Sheldwich, Kent, 1681 CKS PRC2/39/170
Frisby, Jane, Marston, Lincs, 1638 Lincs RO Ad/Ac/25/324
Frith, Edmund, Fleet, Lincs, 1606 Lincs RO Ad/Ac/7/30
Frith, John, Swineshead, Lincs, 1587 Lincs RO Ad/Ac/2C/141
Frith, John, Egerton, Kent, 1617 CKS PRC20/4/97
Frith, Joseph, bricklayer, Hernhill, Kent, 1682 CKS PRC20/13/239
Frith, Luke, Sutton on the Hill, Derby, 1682 LJRO/B/C/5/1682/39
Frith, Richard, tailor, Boughton under Blean, Kent, 1625 CKS PRC20/7/377
Frith, Robert, Egerton, Kent, 1626 CKS PRC20/7/54
Frith, Robert, Altrincham, Ches, 1649 Cheshire RO (Name) W.C. 1649
Fritwell, Mary, Appleton, Berks, 1617 Berks RO D/A1/189/160A
Frogg, Thomas, Middlewich (Minshull Vernon), Ches, 1649 Cheshire RO (Name) W.C. 1649
Froggett, Thomas, labourer, Keal, East, Lincs, 1638 Lincs RO Ad/Ac/25/226
Froome, Edward, fishmonger, Newbury, Berks, 1606 Berks RO D/A1/189/146A
Frosle, see Throstle,
Frost, John, Wimborne Minster (Kingston Lacy), Dors, 1639 Dorset RO PE/WM CP 2/4/56
Frost, John, Botus Fleming, Corn, 1646 Cornwall RO AP/F210/2
Frost, Richard, Binstead, Hants, 1624 Hants RO 21M65 D8/67
Frost, Solomon, farmer, Checkley, Staffs, 1789 LJRO/B/C/5/1789/22
Frost(e), Humphrey, Seighford, Staffs, 1667 LJRO:cards/1667/32
Froth, John, labourer, Croft, Lincs, 1673 Lincs RO Ad/Ac/34/11
Froud, Nicholas, husbandman, Welford, Berks, 1676 Berks RO D/A1/190/80D
Frowd, Thomas, Sedgehill, Wilts, 1681 Wilts RO Arch. Sarum/(+ name and date)
Frowde, Elizabeth, Widley, Hants, 1666 Hants RO 21M65 D8/195
Frowde, Jeffreye, Appledore, Kent, 1602 CKS PRC2/12/141
Frowde, John, Shadoxhurst, Kent, 1581 CKS PRC2/2/19
Frowde, Thomas, Widley, Hants, 1611 Hants RO 1610 AD24/2
Frowde, Thomas, millwright, Cheriton, Kent, 1640 CKS PRC1/4/42
Frowde, William, Salisbury, Wilts, 1683 Wilts RO Miscellaneous Index (name + date)
Frowde, see Parsons,
Frowe, James, Woodchurch, Kent, 1620 CKS PRC20/5/67
Frowe, Nicholas, Biddenden, Kent, 1616 CKS PRC2/21/85
Frowyke, Henry, St Albans, Herts, 1627 Herts RO ASA25/4845
Frubbisher, Francis, gentleman, Ferriby, South, Lincs, 1637 Lincs RO Ad/Ac/25/605
Frulen, John ygr, Canterbury Holy Cross Westgate, Kent, 1624 CKS PRC2/23/124
Frusher, Anne, widow, Wroot, Lincs, 1673 Lincs RO Ad/Ac/35/51
Fry, Christopher, manciple, Oxford (St Mary Hall), Oxon, 1673 Bodleian HYP B8/74-75
Fry, Francis, Overton, Hants, 1685 Hants RO 21m65 D8/339
Fry, Henry, tanner, Abingdon, Berks, 1609 Berks RO D/A1/189/149B
Fry, Joan, widow, Berrow, Som, 1664 Somerset RO D/D/Cta/F21
Fry, John, Maidstone, Kent, 1667 CKS PRC19/3/119
Fry, Michaell, Brinkworth, Wilts, 1629 Wilts RO Arch. Wilts.(name + date)
Fry, Richard, Lea & Cleverton, Wilts, 1636 Wilts RO Arch. Wilts.(name + date)
Fry, Richard, Stepney, London & Middlesex, 1667 PRO PROB32/2/90

Fry, Thomas, yeoman, Woolhampton, Berks, 1681 Berks RO D/A1/190/92C
Fryars, William, university: 'scholar's servant', Cambridge, Cambs, 1633 CUL V.C. Acc./Box2/25
Fryday, Mary, widow, Teynham, Kent, 1722 CKS PRC1/18/39
Fryday, see Cooper,
Frydaye, John, Teynham, Kent, 1586 CKS PRC2/4/464
Frydd, Robert, yeoman, Upper Hardres, Kent, 1627 CKS PRC2/28/44
Frye, Anne, widow, Old Romney, Kent, 1608 CKS PRC20/1/374
Frye, John, Badgworth, Som, 1631 Somerset RO D/D/Cta/F14
Fryer, Dulsabella, widow, Boxley, Kent, 1663 CKS PRC1/9/109
Fryer, Edward, Alkham, Kent, 1609 CKS PRC2/14/180
Fryer, Jerome, fruiterer/citizen, St Martin Vintry, London & Middlesex, 1672? PRO PROB5/841
Fryer, John, innholder, Faversham, Kent, 1675 CKS PRC2/36/48
Fryer, John eld, Wells St Cuthbert, Som, 1664 Somerset RO D/D/Cta/F22
Fryer, Richard, Ercall, High, Shrops, 1667 LJRO:cards/1667/33
Fryer, Thomas, Tydd St Mary, Lincs, 1638 Lincs RO Ad/Ac/25/35
Fryer, Thomas, Dover St Mary, Kent, 1639 CKS PRC20/10/374
Fryland, John, Goudhurst, Kent, 1640 CKS PRC1/2/64
Fryman, George, Hawkhurst, Kent, 1637 CKS PRC2/33/48
Fryth, Thomas, Boughton under Blean, Kent, 1635 CKS PRC20/10/354
Frythe, Joane, widow, Lydd, Kent, 1583 CKS PRC21/6/345
Frytherne, Ferdinand, St Albans, Herts, Herts RO ASA25/4777
Fugar, Hugh, Eastchurch, Sheppey, Kent, 1675 CKS PRC2/36/46
Fugar, Thomas, Newington next Sittingbourne, Kent, 1585 CKS PRC2/3/333
Fuge, John, Stoke Climsland, Corn, 1614 Cornwall RO AP/F56/2
Fuggle, Thomas, Tenterden, Kent, 1632 CKS PRC2/31/111
Fulbrooke, Grace, widow, Milton, Berks, 1626 Berks RO D/A1/190/14B
Fulford, Thomas, Iffley (Hockmore Street), Oxon, 1636 Oxon RO MSS Wills 297/2/6
Fulham, Mary, widow, Stepney, London & Middlesex, 1684 PRO PROB32/23/208
Fuljames, see How,
Fullagar, Amy, widow, Otham, Kent, 1708 CKS PRC1/17/5a
Fullagar, Amy, widow, Otham, Kent, 1709 CKS PRC1/17/5
Fullcombe, John, Hythe St Leonard, Kent, 1588 CKS PRC21/9/54
Fuller, Abraham, yeoman, Warehorne, Kent, 1645 CKS PRC1/7/48
Fuller, Abraham, Warehorne, Kent, 1670 CKS PRC1/15/25
Fuller, Alice, Deal, Kent, 1606 CKS PRC20/1/152
Fuller, Alice, widow, Tilehurst, Berks, 1663 Berks RO D/A1/190/61D
Fuller, Barnaby, Wimborne Minster, Dors, 1639 Dorset RO PE/WM CP 2/4/57
Fuller, Christopher, husbandman, Eastchurch, Sheppey, Kent, 1665 CKS PRC1/11/26
Fuller, Frank, cooper, Bury St Edmunds, Suff, 1759 Suff RO(B) IC500/3/51/10
Fuller, Gervase, Cranbrook, Kent, 1599 CKS PRC2/11/72
Fuller, Henry, Wiston, Sussex, 1676 W. Suss RO EpI/33/1676/35
Fuller, James, Charing, Kent, 1630 CKS PRC20/9/151
Fuller, John, Pinchbeck, Lincs, 1595 Lincs RO Ad/Ac/5/310
Fuller, John, Horsham (Southwater), Sussex, 1611 W. Suss RO EpI/33/1611/3
Fuller, John, St Laurence Thanet, Kent, 1611 CKS PRC2/16/192
Fuller, John, Westwell, Kent, 1640 CKS PRC19/1/46
Fuller, John, university: 'porter/farmer/scholar's servant', Shelford, Great/Cambridge (Gonville and Caius College), Cambs, 1650 CUL V.C. Acc./Box3/21
Fuller, Marian, Chart nr Sutton Valence, Kent, 1635 CKS PRC20/10/342
Fuller, Mary, brewer/farmer/widow, Shelford, Great, Cambs, 1665 CUL V.C. Acc./Box3/20
Fuller, Michaell, Ruckinge, Kent, 1665 CKS PRC1/11/27
Fuller, Nicholas, Linton, Kent, 1638 CKS PRC2/34/205
Fuller, Penelope, 1704 PRO PROB32/46/29
Fuller, Peter eld, yeoman, Tilehurst, Berks, 1630 Berks RO D/A1/190/23C
Fuller, Richard eld, yeoman, Cholsey, Berks, 1621 Berks RO D/A1/190/5D

[Fuller:]
Fuller, Robert, Boughton Malherbe, Kent, 1640 CKS PRC1/4/43
Fuller, Robert, fellmonger, Canterbury St Peter, Kent, 1667 CKS PRC1/12/37
Fuller, Stephen eld, Staplehurst, Kent, 1610 CKS PRC2/13/179
Fuller, Thomas, Dover, Kent, 1595 CKS PRC21/16/1
Fuller, Thomas, Seasalter, Kent, 1617 CKS PRC2/21/69
Fuller, Thomas, Deal, Kent, 1625 CKS PRC20/6/34
Fuller, Thomas + Martha, Dover, Kent, 1595 CKS PRC21/14/191
Fuller, Thomas + Martha, Dover, Kent, 1603 CKS PRC21/16/53
Fuller, Walter, Linton, Kent, 1584 CKS PRC2/3/188
Fuller, William, Deal, Kent, 1597 CKS PRC21/14/203
Fuller, William, Tenterden, Kent, 1600 CKS PRC2/11/223
Fuller, William, Wherwell, Hants, 1669 Hants RO 21m65 D8/215
Fuller, William, Deal, Kent, 1681 CKS PRC20/13/131
Fuller, William, Deal, Kent, 1691 CKS PRC20/13/132
Fullforth, Elizabeth, widow, Hale, Great, Lincs, 1631 Lincs RO Ad/Ac/23/126
Fullicke, William, Trotton, Sussex, 1604 W. Suss RO EpI/33/1604/3
Fullin, Robert, yeoman, Rollright, Little, Oxon, 1683 Oxon RO MSS Wills 79/4/5
Fullwood, Richard, esquire, Tamworth, Warks, Worcs RO 008.7 BA3585/838/55
Fulse, Robart, St Nicholas at Wade, Kent, 1604 CKS PRC21/16/85
Fulshoe, William, Waddingworth, Lincs, 1625 Lincs RO Ad/Ac/19A/6
Fulwood, Anthony, gentleman, Stamford, Lincs, 1663 Lincs RO Ad/Ac/32/52
Funge, William, Milsted, Kent, 1594 CKS PRC2/7/87
Furborrow, Vincent, yeoman, Frowlesworth, Leics, 1670 Leics RO Administrators Accounts 1667-72 f41
Furbushe, John, Sandwich, Kent, 1583 CKS PRC2/3/73
Furley, John, Whitton, Lincs, 1635 Lincs RO Ad/Ac/40/105
Furlonger, William, Rudgwick, Sussex, 1670 W. Suss RO EpI/33/1670/2
Furminger, Stephen, Chart nr Sutton Valence, Kent, 1590 CKS PRC2/5/102
Furminger, Thomas, Faversham, Kent, 1596 CKS PRC2/8/260
Furmynger, John, Herne, Kent, 1596 CKS PRC21/14/59
Furmynger, Stephen, Chart nr Sutton Valence, Kent, 1589 CKS PRC2/4/422
Furnace, Nycholas, Hythe St Leonard, Kent, 1610 CKS PRC20/2/158
Furnell, John, Freshford, Som, 1675 Somerset RO D/D/Cta/F12
Furner, John, Marden, Kent, 1624 CKS PRC20/6/38
Furner, Margerie, widow, Marden, Kent, 1625 CKS PRC2/25/51
Furner, Robert, St Johns Thanet, Kent, 1637 CKS PRC2/34/48
Furner, Walter, Benenden, Kent, 1615 CKS PRC2/21/68
Furnesse, Henry, grocer, Sandwich, Kent, 1675 CKS PRC2/36/53
Furnesse, Rychard, Graveney, Kent, 1582 CKS PRC2/2/199
Furneys, Rychard, Graveney, Kent, 1584 CKS PRC2/3/179
Furniss, Thomas, St Anne Westminster, London & Middlesex, Greater London RO AM/PI pt (uncatalogued)
Furrs, Thomas, Canterbury St Margaret, Kent, 1606 CKS PRC2/13/190
Furser, John, St Peter in Thanet, Kent, 1618 CKS PRC2/21/115
Furser, Richard, Canterbury St Andrew, Kent, 1625 CKS PRC2/25/55
Fusse, Symon, Bearsted, Kent, 1628 CKS PRC2/29/40
Fussell, William, Bradley, West, Som, 1718 Somerset RO D/D/Cta/F13
Fuzard, Henry, Millbrook, Hants, 1678 Hants RO 21m65 D8/286
Fygge, Robert, Bredgar, Kent, 1612 CKS PRC2/17/370
Fyle, Thomas, St Thomas Isle of Harty, Kent, 1664 CKS PRC1/9/110
Fyle, Wyllyam, Northbourne, Kent, 1585 CKS PRC2/3/248
Fylkes, Richarde, Newington next Sittingbourne, Kent, 1586 CKS PRC2/4/368
Fymeux, see Lewkmer,
Fynch, Arthur, Redbourn, Herts, 1633 Herts RO ASA25/4893
Fynch, Christopher, gentleman, Borden, Kent, 1615 CKS PRC2/21/77

Fynch, Hilary, Shenley, Herts, 1639 Herts RO AHH23/806
Fynch, Katherine, St Albans St Michaels, Herts, 1635 Herts RO ASA25/4909
Fynch, Richard, Redbourn, Herts, 1626 Herts RO ASA25/2945
Fynch, Thomas, gentleman, Milton next Sittingbourne, Kent, 1626 CKS PRC2/27/50
Fynche, Nicolas, Faversham, Kent, 1595 CKS PRC2/7/185
Fynche, Nycholas, Norton, Kent, 1575 CKS PRC2/1/142
Fynche, Thomas, Faversham, Kent, 1575 CKS PRC2/1/146
Fynche, Thomas, Faversham, Kent, 1575 CKS PRC2/1/148
Fynche, Thomas, Redbourn, Herts, 1612 Herts RO ASA25/4790
Fynche, William eld, Watford, Herts, 1577 Herts RO ASA25/859
Fynche, William ygr, River, Kent, 1594 CKS PRC2/7/347
Fyneux, Rebecca, spinster, Hougham, Kent, 1618 CKS PRC2/21/60
Fynnex, Edward, yeoman, St Johns Thanet, Kent, 1620 CKS PRC2/21/63
Fynnye, Elizabeth, Minster in Sheppey, Kent, 1610 CKS PRC2/15/113
Fyshe, Peter, Holton, Oxon, 1624 Oxon RO MSS Wills 297/1/40
Fysher, Gabriell, Fordington, Dors, 1597 Wilts RO Miscellaneous Index to Wills (name + date)
Fyssher, George, Dover St James, Kent, 1595 CKS PRC21/14/213
Fytnys, Henrye, Newenden, Kent, 1618 CKS PRC2/21/84
Fyttell, Thomas, Monks Horton, Kent, 1580 CKS PRC2/1/303
Gabiter, Thomas, Skendleby, Lincs, 1619 Lincs RO Ad/Ac/15/115
Gable, John, Hunston, Sussex, 1648 W. Suss RO EpI/33/1648/10
Gabriell, William, Brookland, Kent, 1611 CKS PRC2/17/171
Gadbury, Sarah, widow, Ibstone, Oxon, 1663 Oxon RO MSS Wills 80/2/10
Gadbury, Thomas, Ibstone, Oxon, 1663 Oxon RO MSS Wills 80/2/7
Gadfar, John, Milton next Sittingbourne, Kent, 1618 CKS PRC2/21/49
Gadsaw/Godsave, John, husbandman, Fenton, Lincs, 1681 Lincs RO Ad/Ac/34/68
Gadsby, Edward, Ruckinge, Kent, 1702 CKS PRC1/16/46
Gadsby, John, Bobbing, Kent, 1675 CKS PRC2/36/58
Gadsby, Richard, victualler, Atherstone, Warks, 1790 LJRO/B/C/5/1790/23a
Gadsby, Robert, butcher, Hothfield, Kent, 1669 CKS PRC1/14/42
Gagg, Barbara, widow, Bristol, Glos, Bristol RO 1714/18
Gagg, John, soap maker, Bristol, Glos, Bristol RO 1685/CP
Gaile, William, Pershore, Worcs, 1605 Worcs RO 008.7 BA3585/839/381
Gainsborow, John, Frampton, Lincs, 1648 Lincs RO Ad/Ac/30/388
Gainsburgh, William, Yarburgh, Lincs, 1664 Lincs RO Ad/Ac/43/34
Gainsford, George, Ash next Sandwich, Kent, 1683 CKS PRC20/13/251
Gainsford, John, husbandman, Ash next Sandwich, Kent, 1669 CKS PRC19/4/49
Gale, Frideswith, Faversham, Kent, 1664 CKS PRC1/9/111
Gale, Henry, Ombersley (Borley), Worcs, 1683 Worcs RO 008.7 BA3585/837/bdl 3
Gale, John, husbandman, Ashton Keynes, Wilts, 1621 Wilts RO Arch. Wilts.(name + date)
Gale, Nicholas, Langley Burrell, Wilts, 1618 Wilts RO Arch. Wilts.(name + date)
Gale, Ralph, Sutton Benger, Wilts, 1620 Wilts RO Arch. Wilts.(name + date)
Gale, Thomas, Elcombe, Wilts, 1679 Wilts RO Miscellaneous Index (name + date)
Gale, William, Pewsey, Wilts, 1639 Wilts RO Arch. Wilts.(name + date)
Galilee, George, gentleman, Whitby, Yorks, 1818 Borthwick Test C.P. 1818/10
Gall, Robert,
Wilts 1676 Wilts RO Miscellaneous Index (name + date)
Gall, Robert, Elmswell, Suff, 1731 Suff RO(B) IC500/3/47/26
Gallant, Robert, tailor, Reading, Berks, 1632 Berks RO D/A1/191/166
Gallard, Elizabeth, widow, Wymondham, Norf, 1750 Norfolk RO ANF/11/4/82
Gallard, William, weaver, Reading, Berks, 1606 Berks RO D/A1/191/104C
Galler, George, St Katherine Creechurch, London & Middlesex, 1729 Greater London RO DL/C/548/7
Galley, Thomas, Willoughby, Silk, Lincs, 1607 Lincs RO Ad/Ac/8a/155
Galliard, Thomas, Canterbury St Paul, Kent, 1675 CKS PRC2/36/190

[Gallimore:]
Gallimore, Isaac, farmer, Caverswall (Buttfield), Staffs, 1826 LJRO/B/C/5/1826/14a
Gamber, John, Canterbury All Saints, Kent, 1666 CKS PRC1/11/28
Gamble, John, Navenby, Lincs, 1603 Lincs RO Ad/Ac/5/238
Gamble, Thomas + Anne, Burton Lazars, Leics, 1684 Leics RO Administrators Accounts 1682-86 f10
Gamboll, David, blacksmith, Malmesbury, Wilts, 1635? Wilts RO Arch. Wilts.(name + date)
Gambye, John, Stone in Oxney, Kent, 1611 CKS PRC2/13/211
Games, Thomas, Aberbran, Breck, 1644 NLW BR 1644-49 Ac
Gamlin, William,
Som Somerset RO D/D/Cta/G33
Gamlyn, Mathew, knight, Spalding, Lincs, 1619 Lincs RO Ad/Ac/15/109
Gamlyn, William, husbandman, Aller, Som, 1619 Somerset RO D/D/Cta/G18
Gamlyn, William, Aller, Som, 1636 Somerset RO D/D/Cta/C11
Gammon, John, Stelling, Kent, 1630 CKS PRC2/30/55
Gammon, John, husbandman, Marden, Kent, 1671 CKS PRC2/35/39
Gammon, John eld, Elham, Kent, 1625 CKS PRC2/23/146
Gammon, Thomas eld, yeoman, Hagbourne, East, Berks, 1693 Berks RO D/A1/192/142S
Gammon, William, Warborough, Oxon, 1626 Oxon RO MSS Wills Pec 68/3/2
Gamon, William, Sturry, Kent, 1662 CKS PRC1/9/20
Ganderton, George, Powick, Worcs, 1682 Worcs RO 008.7 BA3585/837/bdl 3
Ganderton, Samuel, Sedgeberrow, Worcs, 1685 Worcs RO 008.7 BA3585/837/bdl 4
Gandy, William, gentleman, Doncaster, Yorks, 1834 Borthwick Test C.P. 1833/5
Ganesborrowe, Ganesborrowe, John, Billingborough, Lincs, 1600 Lincs RO Ad/Ac/5/362
Gann, Thomas, Spalding, Lincs, 1614 Lincs RO Ad/Ac/13/49
Gannocke, Gregorie, Stickney, Lincs, 1620 Lincs RO Ad/Ac/16/44
Ganthery, An, widow, Biddenden, Kent, 1623 CKS PRC2/23/140
Gantlett, John, Amesbury, Wilts, 1631 Wilts RO Arch. Sarum(+ name and date)
Gape, John, St Albans St Michaels, Herts, 1626 Herts RO ASA25/2948
Garburrowe, Richard, Grimsby, Great, Lincs, 1616 Lincs RO Ad/Ac/15/300
Garbutt, James, university: 'Fellow of Sidney Sussex College, Cambridge/B.D./priest' Cambridge (Sidney Sussex College), Cambs, 1649 CUL V.C. Acc./Box3/22
Gardenar, Elizabethe, widow, Littlebourne, Kent, 1590 CKS PRC2/5/86
Gardenner, Henry, Rainham, Kent, 1631 CKS PRC20/9/155
Gardenner, Robert, Rainham, Kent, 1633 CKS PRC2/32/43
Gardiner, Frawncis, Lenham, Kent, 1606 CKS PRC2/13/200
Gardiner, George, Preston next Wingham, Kent, 1592 CKS PRC2/6/85
Gardiner, William, Salisbury, Wilts, 1674 Wilts RO Miscellaneous Index (name + date)
Gardmer, Matthew, High Halden, Kent, 1616 CKS PRC2/21/20
Gardner, Adam, chandler, Newbury, Berks, 1607 Berks RO D/A1/191/105A
Gardner, Edward, wheelwright, Oxford St Peter in the East, Oxon, Oxon RO MSS Wills 297/3/59
Gardner, Edward, husbandman, Claydon, Oxon, 1614 Oxon RO MSS Wills Pec 39/3/17
Gardner, Henrie, Maidstone, Kent, 1631 CKS PRC20/9/175
Gardner, Henry, Canterbury Christchurch, Kent, 1633 CKS PRC20/10/404
Gardner, James, gentleman, Newcastle under Lyme, Staffs, 1829 LJRO/B/C/5/1829/21
Gardner, Joan, widow, Newbury, Berks, 1642 Berks RO D/A1/192/34C
Gardner, John, Cheddar, Som, 1634 Somerset RO D/D/Cta/G10
Gardner, John, yeoman, Eythorne, Kent, 1639 CKS PRC2/34/210
Gardner, John, Worcester, Worcs, 1684 Worcs RO 008.7 BA3585/837/bdl 4
Gardner, Martha, widow, Reculver, Kent, 1668 CKS PRC19/4/15
Gardner, Mary, dame/lady/widow, Abingdon St Helen, Berks, 1641 Berks RO D/A1/192/38A
Gardner, Ralph, Leek, Staffs, 1642 LJRO:cards/1642/3
Gardner, Richard, Ombersley, Worcs, 1608 Worcs RO 008.7 BA3585/839/450
Gardner, Richard, Bonnington, Kent, 1674 CKS PRC2/36/57
Gardner, Richard, Bobbing, Kent, 1677 CKS PRC2/37/147
Gardner, Richard, gun barrel maker, Birmingham, Warks, 1814 LJRO/B/C/5/1814/16

Gardner, Robert, yeoman, Elmsted, Kent, 1667 CKS PRC1/12/38
Gardner, Samuel, Benenden, Kent, 1638 CKS PRC2/34/215
Gardner, Stephen, Charing, Kent, 1669 CKS PRC19/4/50
Gardner, Stephen, Charing, Kent, 1672 CKS PRC20/12/9
Gardner, Thomas, mariner, Faversham, Kent, 1671 CKS PRC2/35/46
Gardyner, Beniamyn, Seasalter, Kent, 1598 CKS PRC2/11/33
Gardyner, John, Deal, Kent, 1596 CKS PRC21/14/7
Gardyner, Thomas, Culworth, Northants, Northants RO X950/Box2/21a
Garfoorthe, Jane, widow, Hothfield, Kent, 1611 CKS PRC2/16/73
Garford, John,
Lincs 1771 Lincs RO Ad/Ac/45/32
Garland, Edward, grocer, Milton next Sittingbourne, Kent, 1680 CKS PRC2/39/41
Garland, Humfrey, Newbury, Berks, 1592 Berks RO D/A1/191/74C
Garland, Isabella, Epworth, Lincs, 1664 Lincs RO Ad/Ac/41/153
Garland, Simon, Willingham, Lincs, 1627 Lincs RO Ad/Ac/39/3
Garland, Thomas, Osbournby, Lincs, 1636 Lincs RO Ad/Ac/24/279
Garland, William, gentleman, Willingham, Lincs, 1633 Lincs RO Ad/Ac/40/63
Garland, William, Fiskerton, Lincs, 1682 Lincs RO Ad/Ac/44/7
Garner, Edward, Toynton, Low, Lincs, 1633 Lincs RO Ad/Ac/24/181
Garner, Henry, St Laurence Thanet, Kent, 1597 CKS PRC2/11/227
Garner, Henry, Pinchbeck, Lincs, 1649 Lincs RO Ad/Ac/30/214
Garner, James, maltster, Isham, Northants, 1671 Northants RO NWill A/C/100
Garner, Joseph, potter, Stoke-upon-Trent (Lane End), Staffs, 1793 LJRO/B/C/5/1793/16
Garner, Mary, widow, Doddington, Kent, 1695 CKS PRC2/42/100
Garner, Robert, Grafham (East Perry), Hunts, Hunts RO/Acc58/329
Garner, William, Mareham le Fen, Lincs, 1593 Lincs RO Ad/Ac/3/85
Garnett, Thomas, Prescot (Whiston), Lancs, 1627 Lancs RO (Name of Deceased) D.R.C.H. 1627
Garnett, Thomas, Wigan, Lancs, 1666 Lancs RO (Name of Deceased) D.R.C.H. 1666
Garnier, Edward, Surfleet, Lincs, 1667 Lincs RO Ad/Ac/33/1
Garrard, Anne, Cliffe Pypard, Wilts, 1638 Wilts RO Arch. Wilts.(name + date)
Garrard, Elizabeth, spinster, Lambourn (Upper Lambourn), Berks, 1641 Berks RO D/A1/192/35A
Garrard, John, gentleman, Lambourn (Upper Lambourn), Berks, 1612 Berks RO D/A1/191/120A
Garrard, Thomas, gentleman, Inkpen, Berks, 1618 Berks RO D/A1/191/131C
Garrarde, William, gentleman, Inkpen, Berks, 1614 Berks RO D/A1/191/121C
Garratt, Christopher, Newton by Toft, Lincs, 1619 Lincs RO Ad/Ac/15/205
Garratt, Elizabeth, spinster, Cookham, Berks, 1628 Berks RO D/A1/191/156A
Garratt, William, Gedney, Lincs, 1619 Lincs RO Ad/Ac/14/144
Garratt, William, Boston, Lincs, 1637 Lincs RO Ad/Ac/24/554
Garratt, William, farmer, Duffield (Turnditch), Derby, 1819 LJRO/B/C/5/1819/72
Garret, Abell, Sandwich, Kent, 1582 CKS PRC2/2/39
Garret, Ales, widow, Dover, Kent, 1596 CKS PRC21/14/97
Garrett, Christopher, Elham, Kent, 1613 CKS PRC2/17/67
Garrett, Edmond, mariner?, Stepney, London & Middlesex, 1688 PRO PROB32/27/85
Garrett, Edmund, gentleman, Barlavington, Sussex, 1661 W. Suss RO EpI/33/1661/14
Garrett, George, Boston, Lincs, 1614 Lincs RO Ad/Ac/13/125
Garrett, Henrie, Sutton, Long, Lincs, 1638 Lincs RO Ad/Ac/25/270
Garrett, James, St Peter in Thanet, Kent, 1619 CKS PRC2/21/47
Garrett, James, Wingham, Kent, 1645 CKS PRC19/2/97
Garrett, Jeames, St Peter in Thanet, Kent, 1606 CKS PRC2/14/202
Garrett, John, Goudhurst, Kent, 1613 CKS PRC2/18/66
Garrett, John, St Laurence Thanet, Kent, 1630 CKS PRC2/30/64
Garrett, John, Goudhurst, Kent, 1645 CKS PRC1/7/49
Garrett, John, Claybrooke (Ullesthorpe), Leics, 1665 Leics RO Administrators Accounts C17th f18
Garrett, Laurence, Seasalter, Kent, 1623 CKS PRC2/23/134

[Garrett:]
Garrett, Richard, mariner, Dover, Kent, 1627 CKS PRC20/8/226
Garrett, Robert, clergy: 'clerk', St Katherine by the Tower, London & Middlesex, 1701 PRO PROB32/42/212
Garrett, Stephen, St Peter in Thanet, Kent, 1621 CKS PRC2/23/131
Garrett, Thamasine, widow, Eastry, Kent, 1611 CKS PRC20/2/132
Garrett, William, Napton on the Hill, Warks, 1672 LJRO:cards/1672/22
Garter, Joan, widow, Brimpton, Berks, 1640 Berks RO D/A1/192/27A
Gartham, Elizabeth, widow, Surfleet, Lincs, 1623 Lincs RO Ad/Ac/18/75
Gartham, John, labourer, Bigby, Lincs, 1636 Lincs RO Ad/Ac/24/330
Garthwaite, Elizabeth, widow, Lincoln, Lincs, 1735 Lincs RO Ad/Ac/45/22
Garthwaite, Thomas, Harmston, Lincs, 1648 Lincs RO Ad/Ac/30/368
Gartside, Ellen, Mottram in Longdendale, Ches, 1723 Cheshire RO (Name) W.C. 1723-4
Garwell, John, Boston, Lincs, 1607 Lincs RO Ad/Ac/8a/81
Gascoyn, Clement, Canterbury Holy Cross Westgate, Kent, 1596 CKS PRC2/8/9
Gascoyne, John, sheriffs officer, Sheffield, Yorks, 1842 Borthwick Test C.P. 1842/7
Gascoyne, Thomas, yeoman, Bloxham, Oxon, 1640 Oxon RO MSS Wills 297/3/48
Gash, David, husbandman, Blankney, Lincs, 1683 Lincs RO Ad/Ac/44/103
Gaske, Marke, draper, Rasen, Middle, (Drax), Lincs, 1618 Lincs RO Ad/Ac/14/11
Gaskell, Adam, yeoman, Unsworth, Lancs, 1749 Lancs RO (Name of Deceased) D.R.C.H. 1749
Gaskell, Peter ygr, yeoman, Prestbury (Lyme Landley), Ches, 1730 Cheshire RO (Name) W.C. 1730-32
Gaskin, Henry, Bury, Hunts, 1683 Hunts RO/Acc58/196(200)
Gaskin, Richard, Bassingham, Lincs, 1639? Lincs RO Ad/Ac/26/101
Gason, John, gentleman, Sandwich, Kent, 1626 CKS PRC2/25/60
Gasp, Gyles, husbandman, Fovant, Wilts, 1588 Wilts RO Arch. Sarum(+ name and date) w
Gatcombe, Henry, butcher, Abingdon, Berks, 1617 Berks RO D/A1/191/124A
Gatcombe, William, butcher, Abingdon St Helen, Berks, 1603 Berks RO D/A1/191/95C
Gate/Bridge, Christiane, Canterbury, Kent, 1605 CKS PRC2/14/206
Gateland, Richard, thatcher, Kenardington, Kent, 1674 CKS PRC2/36/59
Gateman, Richard, Worth, Kent, 1608 CKS PRC20/1/304
Gateman, Thomas, blacksmith, Herne, Kent, 1667 CKS PRC19/3/120
Gater, Richard, Steyning, Sussex, 1611 W. Suss RO EpI/33/1611/8
Gates, Elizabeth, widow, Canterbury St Andrew, Kent, 1599 CKS PRC2/11/232
Gates, James, Sidlesham, Sussex, W. Suss RO EpI/33/1618/12
Gates, John, mercer/bailiff, Windsor, New, Berks, 1622 Berks RO D/A1/191/138A
Gates, John, Selsey, Sussex, 1627 W. Suss RO EpI/33/1627/9
Gates, John,
Leics 1639 Leics RO PR/I/41A/21
Gates, John, Smarden, Kent, 1664 CKS PRC1/10/37
Gates, John, bachelor, Bethersden, Kent, 1716 CKS PRC1/18/4
Gates, Jone, widow, Oare, Kent, 1597 CKS PRC2/9/120
Gates, Jone, widow, Oare, Kent, 1604 CKS PRC2/13/202
Gates see Yates,
Gathorne, Elizabeth, Luddington, Lincs, 1685 Lincs RO Ad/Ac/44/154
Gatland, William, Arundel, Sussex, 1683 W. Suss RO EpI/33/1682/21
Gatlye, John, Hythe St Leonard, Kent, 1626 CKS PRC20/7/48
Gattacre, Ambrose, Shifnal, Shrops, 1674 LJRO:cards/1674/16
Gauden, Nicholas, Oving, Sussex, 1632 W. Suss RO EpI/33/1632/34
Gaule, George, cordwainer: 'shoemaker', Spilsby, Lincs, 1634 Lincs RO Ad/Ac/24/532
Gaunt, Thomas, Lincoln St Peter at Gowts, Lincs, 1624 Lincs RO Ad/Ac/19A/47
Gaunt, William, farmer, Leeds St Peter (Farnley), Yorks, 1815 Borthwick Test C.P. 1815/3
Gauntlett, George, Gainsborough, Lincs, 1610 Lincs RO Ad/Ac/8a/317
Gavan, John, tailor, Covent Garden, St Paul, London & Middlesex, 1667 PRO PROB32/2/100
Gave, Roger,

Som 1633 Somerset RO D/D/Cta/G35
Gawbee, John, Bromham, Wilts, 1629 Wilts RO Arch. Wilts.(name + date)
Gawdron, Richard, Swineshead, Lincs, 1648? Lincs RO Ad/Ac/30/349
Gawen, John, Breage, Corn, 1607 Cornwall RO AP/G74
Gawler, John + Joan, husbandman, Butleigh, Som, 1591 Somerset RO D/D/Cta/G32
Gawne, Thomas, Littlehampton, Sussex, 1629 W. Suss RO EpI/33/1629/36
Gawthorpe, Matthew, corn factor, Hull (Myton), Yorks, 1778 Borthwick Test C.P. 1778/4
Gay, Henry, gentleman, Lyng, Norf, 1687 Lambeth Palace Arches G37/2
Gaye, Humfrye, Lenham, Kent, 1600 CKS PRC2/11/107
Gayler, Symon, Newchurch, Kent, 1583 CKS PRC21/6/415
Gaylor, John, Newchurch, Kent, 1602 CKS PRC21/17/78
Gayme, William, Sandwich, Kent, 1598 CKS PRC2/10/98
Gaynam, Margaret, Leighton, Shrops, 1685 LJRO/B/C/5/1685/42
Gayscoyn, John, shipwright, Stepney (Blackwall), London & Middlesex, 1690 PRO PROB32/29/92
Gaythorne, Richard, locksmith/privileged person, Cambridge, Cambs, 1668 CUL V.C. Acc./Box3/23
Gayton, John, Iwade, Kent, 1598 CKS PRC2/10/391
Geare, William, St Martin in Meneage, Corn, 1622 Cornwall RO AP/G228/2
Gearinge, John, Broadwater (Worthing), Sussex, 1614 W. Suss RO EpI/33/1613/24
Geary, Henry, Ospringe, Kent, 1681 CKS PRC2/39/175
Geast, John, yeoman, Alvechurch, Worcs, 1603 Worcs RO 008.7 BA3585/839/297
Gedney, John, husbandman, Swinefleet, Yorks, 1649 Lincs RO Ad/Ac/30/247
Gedney, Richard, university: 'Fellow of Magdalene College, Cambridge/M.A.', Cambridge, Cambs, 1608 CUL V.C.Acc./Box1/21
Gedney, Thomas, Farforth cum Maidenwell, Lincs, 1622 Lincs RO Ad/Ac/17/57
Gee, Thomas, Horbling, Lincs, 1627 Lincs RO Ad/Ac/20/112
Gee, Thomas, Horbling, Lincs, 1633 Lincs RO Ad/Ac/24/5
Geerishe, Robert, Seend, Wilts, 1634 Wilts RO CC Sarum(+ name and date)
Geery, William, butcher, Dover, Kent, 1682 CKS PRC20/13/247
Gefford, see Blagdon,
Geffrey, John, Surfleet, Lincs, 1618 Lincs RO Ad/Ac/14/170
Gelder, Jennett, widow, Glentworth, Lincs, 1637 Lincs RO Ad/Ac/25/468
Gelder, Oliver, Hemingby, Lincs, 1565 Lincs RO Ad/Ac/0/17a
Gell,
Lincs 1672 Lincs RO Ad/Ac/43/72
Gell, John, Frampton, Lincs, 1660s? Lincs RO Ad/Ac/32/45
Gelley, William eld, Chidham, Sussex, 1635 W. Suss RO EpI/33/1635/34
Gelson, Thomas, gentleman, Kirton, Lincs, 1632 Lincs RO Ad/Ac/23/130
Gelsthorpe, Edward, university: 'Fellow of Gonville and Caius College, Cambridge/Doctor of Physic' Cambridge (Gonville and Caius College), Cambs, 1672 CUL V.C. Acc./Box3/24
Gelstropp, Francis, Ponton, Great, Lincs, 1602 Lincs RO Ad/Ac/5/113
Gennings, Robert, Newchurch, Kent, 1632 CKS PRC20/10/454
Gennyngs, John, Egerton, Kent, 1618 CKS PRC20/4/113
Gennys, William, Lostwithiel, Corn, 1613 Cornwall RO AP/G138
Gent, William, Broadwater, Sussex, 1607 W. Suss RO EpI/33/1606/2
Gente, Edward, Lancing, Sussex, 1630 W. Suss RO EpI/33/1630/22
Gentle, Hamond, Washingborough, Lincs, 1612 Lincs RO Ad/Ac/10/140
Gentle, John, Yaxley, Hunts, 1636 Hunts RO/Acc58/8(46)
Gentle, Robert, Grantham, Lincs, 1568 Lincs RO Ad/Ac/0/5
Gentle, Thomas, Withcall, Lincs, 1611 Lincs RO Ad/Ac/10/112
Gentle, Thomas, Burwell, Lincs, 1649 Lincs RO Ad/Ac/30/408
Genvey, Ann, St Johns Thanet, Kent, 1665 CKS PRC1/11/29
George, Alice, spinster/widow, Woodchurch, Kent, 1675 CKS PRC20/12/170
George, Daniel, yeoman, Woodchurch, Kent, 1675 CKS PRC20/12/169

[George:]
George, Giles, yeoman, Appledore, Kent, 1633 CKS PRC20/10/422
George, John, Stone in Oxney, Kent, 1594 CKS PRC2/7/309
George, John, Pershore, Worcs, 1680 Worcs RO 008.7 BA3585/837/bdl 2
George, Thomas, Beedon, Berks, 1598 Berks RO D/A1/191/86C
George, Thomas, Wittersham, Kent, 1633 CKS PRC20/10/416
George, Tymothy, Chart, Great, Kent, 1593 CKS PRC2/6/376
George, William, Oxford St Peter in the East, Oxon, 1662 Oxon RO MSS Wills 80/2/1
George, William, Badsey, Worcs, 1684 Worcs RO 008.7 BA3585/837/bdl 4
George/Kinsham, John, yeoman, Norton by Bredon, Worcs, 1648 Worcs RO 008.7 BA3585/837/bdl 1
Geprge, John, Bethersden, Kent, 1620 CKS PRC2/21/30
Geri, Nicholas, clergy: 'mr/parson', Snargate, Kent, 1610 CKS PRC2/15/141
Gerish, William, Melksham, Wilts, 1632 Wilts RO Arch. Sarum(+ name and date)
Gerling, Lambert, Boothby Pagnell, Lincs, 1612 Lincs RO Ad/Ac/11/192
German, Phyllyppe, Canterbury Holy Cross Westgate, Kent, 1583 CKS PRC2/3/125
Germon, John, Wye, Kent, 1632 CKS PRC2/31/117
Gerrard, James, Blackburn, Lancs, 1619 Lancs RO (Name of Deceased) D.R.C.H. 1619
Gerrard, John, musician, Oxford (University), Oxon, 1636 Bodleian HYP B8/76-80
Gerrett, Stephen, Downton, Wilts, 1612 Wilts RO Arch. Sarum(+ name and date)
Gerrish, Charles, basket maker, Bristol, Glos, Bristol RO 1768/CP
Gerrish, Richard, Melksham (Shaw), Wilts, 1617? Wilts RO Miscellaneous Index (name + date)
Gervise, Charles, Beckington, Som, 1706 Somerset RO D/D/Cta/G36
Gerye, John eld, New Romney, Kent, 1608 CKS PRC20/1/390
Gesopp, Christopher, Brox-Holme, Lincs, 1618 Lincs RO Ad/Ac/8b/262
Gesse, John, Bridgewater, Som, 1666 Somerset RO D/D/Cta/G25
Gest, William, Swineshead, Lincs, 1624 Lincs RO Ad/Ac/19A/56
Geste, Jane, widow,
London & Middlesex 1555? Lambeth Palace Arches F 1A ff241-245
Gettley, William, yeoman, Donington, Castle, Leics, 1684 Leics RO Administrators Accounts 1682-86 f28
Gew, George, labourer, Knebworth, Herts, 1639 Herts RO AHH23/947
Gey, John, Tilshead, Wilts, 1673 Wilts RO CC Sarum(+ name and date)
Ghennell, Thomas, husbandman, Swineshead, Lincs, 1666 Lincs RO Ad/Ac/32/119
Ghest, William, Navenby, Lincs, 1649 Lincs RO Ad/Ac/30/131
Ghost, Henry, Eling, Hants, 1672 Hants RO 21m65 D8/242
Gibbes, Augustine, Worth, Kent, 1633 CKS PRC20/10/406
Gibbes, Edmund eld, mr, Elmstone, Kent, 1632 CKS PRC20/9/195
Gibbes, Elizabeth, widow, Folkestone, Kent, 1597 CKS PRC2/10/24
Gibbes, James, Marlborough, Wilts, 1640 Wilts RO CC Sarum(+ name and date)
Gibbes, John, Ash next Sandwich, Kent, 1581 CKS PRC21/4/321
Gibbes, John, Ash next Sandwich, Kent, 1600 CKS PRC21/15/109
Gibbes, Richard, Wimborne Minster, Dors, 1663 Dorset RO PE/WM CP 2/4/66
Gibbes, Thomas, Hastingleigh, Kent, 1594 CKS PRC2/7/51
Gibbes, Thomas, Week (Lawrence Week), Som, 1599 Somerset RO D/D/Cta/G22
Gibbins, Joan, widow, Towersey, Bucks, 1617 Oxon RO MSS Wills Pec 39/3/20
Gibbins, Ralph, Henley, Oxon, 1625 Oxon RO MSS Wills 166/1/47
Gibbon, Agnes, widow, Benenden, Kent, 1586 CKS PRC2/4/354
Gibbon, Arthur, victualler, Cranbrook, Kent, 1682 CKS PRC2/40/33
Gibbon, Edward, clothier, Hawkhurst, Kent, 1617 CKS PRC2/21/31
Gibbon, Edward, Hackington, Kent, 1670 CKS PRC1/15/26
Gibbon, Elizabeth, widow, Etchells, Ches, 1662 Cheshire RO (Name) W.C. 1662
Gibbon, Francis, draper, Grantham, Lincs, 1626 Lincs RO Ad/Ac/20/20
Gibbon, George, maltster, Shepherdswell alias Sibertswold, Kent, 1674 CKS PRC2/36/56
Gibbon, George, Dover, Kent, 1678 CKS PRC20/12/261
Gibbon, Jane, mrs/widow, Bishopsbourne, Kent, 1622 CKS PRC2/23/133

Gibbon, John, Swineshead, Lincs, 1620 Lincs RO Ad/Ac/15/280
Gibbon, John, Claypole, Lincs, 1665 Lincs RO Ad/Ac/32/59
Gibbon, Margaret, widow, Tenterden, Kent, 1624 CKS PRC2/23/143
Gibbon, Matthew, Cliffe, West, Kent, 1663 CKS PRC1/9/112
Gibbon, Phillip, Canterbury Christchurch, Kent, 1641 CKS PRC19/2/17
Gibbon, Robert, Grantham, Lincs, 1619 Lincs RO Ad/Ac/15/85
Gibbon, Thomas, clothier, Hawkhurst, Kent, 1665 CKS PRC1/11/30
Gibbon, Thomas, yeoman, Dover, Kent, 1689 CKS PRC20/13/632
Gibbon, William, yeoman, Etchells, Ches, 1662 Cheshire RO (Name) W.C. 1662
Gibbon, William, Marden, Kent, 1667 CKS PRC19/3/121
Gibbon/Morton, Alice, Sutton in the Marsh, Lincs, 1624 Lincs RO Ad/Ac/19A/71
Gibbons, Abraham, gentleman, Coventry, Warks, 1701 LJRO/B/C/5/1701/46c
Gibbons, George, Littlehampton, Sussex, 1630 W. Suss RO EpI/33/1630/23
Gibbons, John, Birmingham, Warks, 1795 LJRO/B/C/5/1795/18
Gibbons, Mary, Taunton St Mary Magdalan, Som, 1640 Somerset RO D/D/Cta/G28
Gibbons, Robert, gentleman, Saxilby, Lincs, 1670? Lincs RO Ad/Ac/32/133
Gibbons, Thomas, Bethersden, Kent, 1590 CKS PRC2/5/96
Gibbons, Thomas, Boxgrove, Sussex, 1676 W. Suss RO EpI/33/1676/14
Gibbons, Thomas, wheelwright, Newland, Glos, 1751 GRO GDR/B4/2/G68
Gibbons, William, gentleman, Cheadle (Huntley), Staffs, 1795 LJRO/B/C/5/1795/23
Gibbs, Abigall, spinster, Ash next Sandwich, Kent, 1629 CKS PRC20/8/249
Gibbs, Edmond, Fugglestone St Peter, Wilts, 1689 Wilts RO Arch. Sarum(+ name and date)
Gibbs, Elizabeth, widow, Ickham, Kent, 1598 CKS PRC21/14/571
Gibbs, Jonas, Brookland, Kent, 1628 CKS PRC2/29/45
Gibbs, Julyan, Eastry, Kent, 1592 CKS PRC21/12/182
Gibbs, Nicholas, yeoman, Littlebourne, Kent, 1719 CKS PRC1/18/19
Gibbs, Stephen, wool chapman, Wymondham, Norf, 1729 Norfolk RO ANF/11/3/79
Gibbs, Thomas, gentleman, Ash next Sandwich, Kent, 1597 CKS PRC21/16/9
Gibbs, Thomas, Publow, Som, 1637 Somerset RO D/D/Cta/G6
Gibbs, Thomas, Elmstone, Kent, 1710 CKS PRC1/17/24
Gibbs, William, Fairfield, Kent, 1615 CKS PRC20/3/264
Gibbs, William, Blisworth, Northants, 1680 Northants RO NWill A/C/41
Gibbs, William, clergy: 'clerk', Wainfleet All Saints, Lincs, 1687 PRO PROB5/809
Gibence, Thomas, Boxgrove?, Sussex, W. Suss RO EpI/33/1675/6
Giblett, Joan, widow, Meare, Som, 1611 Somerset RO D/D/Cta/G15
Giblett, Thomas, Meare, Som, 1663 Somerset RO D/D/Cta/G24
Gibon, Robarte, Hawkhurst, Kent, 1593 CKS PRC2/6/222
Gibs, Edmund, mr, Elmstone, Kent, 1629 CKS PRC2/30/59
Gibson, Elizabeth, Beverley, Yorks, 1723 Borthwick Test C.P. 1723/5
Gibson, James, Bagworth, Leics, 1672 Leics RO Administrators Accounts 1667-72 f85
Gibson, James + Mary, widow, Grantham, Lincs, 1629 Lincs RO Ad/Ac/22/14
Gibson, Jeffrey, yeoman, Stamford St Michael, Lincs, 1619 Lincs RO Ad/Ac/15/225
Gibson, Joane, widow, Biddenden, Kent, 1619 CKS PRC2/21/39
Gibson, John, Worlaby, Lincs, 1614 Lincs RO Ad/Ac/13/143
Gibson, John, Deal, Kent, 1627 CKS PRC20/8/230
Gibson, John, Congleton, Ches, 1632 Cheshire RO (Name) W.C. 1632
Gibson, John, Bagworth, Leics, 1672 Leics RO Administrators Accounts 1667-72 f53
Gibson, John, victualler, Hull, Yorks, 1794 Borthwick Test C.P. 1793/7
Gibson, Joseph, labourer, Bradford (Claydon Street), Yorks, 1855 Borthwick Test C.P. 1855/11
Gibson, Margaret, spinster, Rasen, Middle, Lincs, 1618 Lincs RO Ad/Ac/14/285
Gibson, Mary, widow, Overton, Cold, Leics, 1673 Leics RO Administrators Accounts 1667-72 f112
Gibson, Mary, widow, St Martin in the Fields, London & Middlesex, 1705 PRO PROB32/49/85
Gibson, Nevill, weaver, Syston, Lincs, 1633 Lincs RO Ad/Ac/24/116
Gibson, Nicholas, Uffington, Lincs, 1630 Lincs RO Ad/Ac/24/482

[Gibson:]
Gibson, Richard, Spalding, Lincs, 1665 Lincs RO Ad/Ac/32/60
Gibson, Robert, clergy: 'clerk', Sudbrooke, Lincs, 1613 Lincs RO Ad/Ac/12/1
Gibson, Robert, Elmsted, Kent, 1676 CKS PRC2/37/36
Gibson, Robert + Joan, clergy: 'clerk', Sedgebrook, Lincs, 1613 Lincs RO Ad/Ac/12/59
Gibson, Susan, widow, Bonnington, Kent, 1618 CKS PRC2/21/52
Gibson, Thomas, Hale, Great, Lincs, 1612 Lincs RO Ad/Ac/11/1
Gibson, Thomas, Ewerby (Ewerby Thorpe), Lincs, 1639? Lincs RO Ad/Ac/26/100
Gibson, Thomas, husbandman, Bassingham, Lincs, 1642 Lincs RO Ad/Ac/28/37
Gibson, Thomas, husbandman, Stallingborough, Lincs, 1666 Lincs RO Ad/Ac/32/63
Gibson, Thomas, Wye, Kent, 1669 CKS PRC1/13/46
Gibson, Thomas, Wye, Kent, 1669 CKS PRC1/14/43
Gibson, Tristram, Minting, Lincs, 1612 Lincs RO Ad/Ac/11/32
Gibson, William, Haxey, Lincs, 1603 Lincs RO Ad/Ac/37/161
Gibson, William, Haxey, Lincs, 1607 Lincs RO Ad/Ac/37/260
Gibson, William, university: M.A. of Peterhouse College, Cambridge, Cambridge, Cambs, 1614 CUL V.C.Acc./Box1/22
Gibson, William, St Laurence Thanet, Kent, 1635 CKS PRC2/33/51
Gibson, William, Haxey, Lincs, 1663 Lincs RO Ad/Ac/41/90
Gibson, William, husbandman, Biddulph, Staffs, 1667 LJRO:cards/1667/34
Gibson, William, yeoman, Haxey, Lincs, 1674 Lincs RO Ad/Ac/35/73
Gibson, see Hesseldine,
Gibsone, Alexander, university: 'Fellow of Gonville and Caius College, Cambridge/M.A.' Cambridge (Gonville and Caius College), Cambs, 1649 CUL V.C. Acc./Box3/25
Giddings, William, Chirton, Wilts, 1683 Wilts RO Arch. Sarum(+ name and date)
Giddion, Richard, innkeeper, Lambourn, Berks, 1680 Berks RO D/A1/192/106C
Gidley, John, Michaelstow, Corn, 1636 Cornwall RO AP/G403/2
Gifford, Edward, Southoe, Hunts, 1682 Hunts RO/Acc58/188(101)
Gifford, Matthew, Hythe West, Kent, 1640 CKS PRC1/2/65
Gifford, Thomas, Wellington, Som, Somerset RO D/D/Cta/G5
Gilbart, Jeames, Littlebourne, Kent, 1600 CKS PRC2/11/231
Gilbart, Robart, St Johns Thanet, Kent, 1585 CKS PRC2/3/315
Gilbarte, Abigall,
Kent 1595 CKS PRC2/8/125
Gilbarte, Jeames, Benenden, Kent, 1596 CKS PRC2/8/242
Gilbarte, William, Canterbury Holy Cross Westgate, Kent, 1592 CKS PRC2/5/78
Gilbert, Adrian, esquire, Wilton, Wilts, 1628 Wilts RO CC Sarum(+ name and date)
Gilbert, Alexander, Cranbrook, Kent, 1625 CKS PRC2/23/148
Gilbert, Benjamin, grocer, Derby (St Werburgh), Derby, 1825 LJRO/B/C/5/1825/12
Gilbert, Edward, Chislet, Kent, 1636 CKS PRC2/33/53
Gilbert, Elizabeth, spinster, Canterbury, Kent, 1640 CKS PRC1/4/44
Gilbert, George, Cranbrook, Kent, 1618 CKS PRC2/21/33
Gilbert, George, Ellastone (Ramsor), Staffs, 1667 LJRO:cards/1667/35
Gilbert, George, Weston-upon-Trent, Derby, 1672 LJRO:cards/1672/23
Gilbert, Henrie, fellmonger, Northbourne, Kent, 1648 CKS PRC1/8/16
Gilbert, Henry, Leeds, Kent, 1616 CKS PRC2/21/21
Gilbert, Joell, yeoman, Lenham, Kent, 1619 CKS PRC2/21/26
Gilbert, John, Loose, Kent, 1596 CKS PRC21/14/189
Gilbert, John, St Johns Thanet, Kent, 1614 CKS PRC2/18/99
Gilbert, John, Canterbury All Saints, Kent, 1624 CKS PRC2/23/144
Gilbert, John, Shipton Bellinger, Hants, 1625 Hants RO 21M65 D8/116
Gilbert, John, Sonning, Berks, 1629 Wilts RO Miscellaneous Index (name + date)
Gilbert, Mary, spinster, Canterbury, Kent, 1640 CKS PRC1/4/45
Gilbert, Nicholas, Lutterworth, Leics, 1672 Leics RO Administrators Accounts 1667-72 f86
Gilbert, Richard, Hawkhurst, Kent, 1601 CKS PRC2/12/165
Gilbert, Richard, Patney, Wilts, 1648 Wilts RO Arch. Sarum(+ name and date)

Gilbert, Robert, Canterbury St Mildred, Kent, 1624 CKS PRC2/23/139
Gilbert, Robert, husbandman, Birchington, Kent, 1682 CKS PRC20/13/253
Gilbert, Sarah, spinster, Canterbury, Kent, 1640 CKS PRC1/4/46
Gilbert, Sarah, widow, Broadwater (Worthing), Sussex, 1672 W. Suss RO EpI/33/1672/4
Gilbert, Thomas, brewer: 'beerbrewer', Canterbury, Kent, 1641 CKS PRC1/5/97
Gilbert, Thomas, Spondon (Lockhay), Derby, 1661 Lincs RO Ad/Ac/43/4a
Gilbert, Thomas, Tenterden, Kent, 1669 CKS PRC1/14/44
Gilbert, Thomas, Bethersden, Kent, 1671 CKS PRC2/35/40
Gilbert, William, Patney, Wilts, 1636 Wilts RO Arch. Sarum(+ name and date)
Gilbert, William, Benington, Lincs, 1649 Lincs RO Ad/Ac/30/101
Gilbert, William, Doulting (Prestleigh), Som, 1662 Somerset RO D/D/Cta/G23
Gilbert, William, miller, Leeds, Kent, 1669 CKS PRC1/13/48
Gilbert, William, butcher, Sandwich, Kent, 1679 CKS PRC2/38/134
Gilberte, Bryan, Shrewton, Wilts, 1628 Wilts RO Arch. Sarum(+ name and date)
Gilberte, Thomas, Biddenden, Kent, 1603 CKS PRC2/12/432
Gilberte, Thomas, Benington, Lincs, 1607 Lincs RO Ad/Ac/8a/85
Gilbertes, John, yeoman, Ingoldsby, Lincs, 1623 Lincs RO Ad/Ac/18/68
Gilberthorpe, Millicent, widow, Moulton, Lincs, 1627 Lincs RO Ad/Ac/20/109
Gilbie, Thomas, Blyton, Lincs, 1673 Lincs RO Ad/Ac/33/15
Gilbody, Rebecca, widow, Wilmslow (Hough), Ches, 1748 Cheshire RO (Name) W.C. 1748
Gilburt/Clarke, Anne, Lacock, Wilts, 1624 Wilts RO Arch. Wilts.(name + date)
Gilby, Richard, yeoman, Snelland (Swinethorpe), Lincs, 1680 Lincs RO Ad/Ac/34/58
Gilby, Thomas, Navenby, Lincs, 1576 Lincs RO Ad/Ac/2b/40
Gilby, William, Corringham, Lincs, 1670s? Lincs RO Ad/Ac/42/23
Gilden, Edward, Frieston, Lincs, 1648 Lincs RO Ad/Ac/30/331
Gilder, John, Boston, Lincs, 1662 Lincs RO Ad/Ac/32/14
Gilding, William, yeoman, Donington, Lincs, 1649 Lincs RO Ad/Ac/30/55
Gildon, Edward, Mere, Wilts, 1598? Wilts RO Miscellaneous Index (name + date)
Gildon, William, husbandman, Glentworth, Lincs, C17th? Lincs RO Ad/Ac/45/112
Giles, Alice, Upper Hardres, Kent, 1664 CKS PRC1/10/43
Giles, Anne, widow, Faversham, Kent, 1682 CKS PRC2/40/30
Giles, Daniel, Canterbury St Paul, Kent, 1664 CKS PRC1/9/113
Giles, Edmund, Sittingbourne, Kent, 1632 CKS PRC2/31/115
Giles, Henry, Bury St Edmunds, Suff, 1733 Suff RO(B) IC500/3/47/56
Giles, Jeremie, Tenterden, Kent, 1629 CKS PRC2/30/61
Giles, Jeremy, Rainham, Kent, 1670 CKS PRC1/15/27
Giles, John, Cranbrook, Kent, 1619 CKS PRC2/21/48
Giles, John, Cranbrook, Kent, 1630 CKS PRC20/9/199
Giles, John, cordwainer, Witney, Oxon, 1638 Oxon RO MSS Wills 297/3/46
Giles, John, Upper Hardres, Kent, 1664 CKS PRC1/9/114
Giles, Margaret, widow, Chaddleworth, Berks, 1610 Berks RO D/A1/191/112C
Giles, Mary, Langford, Steeple, Wilts, 1684 Wilts RO Arch. Sarum(+ name and date)
Giles, Richard, Doddington, Kent, 1597 CKS PRC2/10/521
Giles, Richarde, Westbere, Kent, 1592 CKS PRC2/5/92
Giles, Robert, Petham, Kent, 1610 CKS PRC2/15/140
Giles, Robert, yeoman, Sheldwich, Kent, 1672 CKS PRC2/35/47
Giles, Thomas, clergy: 'clerk/reverend', Worcester St Nicholas, Worcs, 1772 Worcs RO 008.7 BA3585/835/bdl 1
Giles, William, clergy: 'mr/clerk', Sutton Valence, Kent, 1639 CKS PRC1/2/66
Giles, William, yeoman, Monkton, Kent, 1663 CKS PRC19/3/24
Giles, see Randolph,
Gilford, Elizabeth, widow, Bersted, South (Bognor), Sussex, 1645 W. Suss RO EpIV/10/2A/5
Gilham, Tobias, Tonge, Kent, 1617 CKS PRC2/21/24
Gilham, Walter, Smarden, Kent, 1679 CKS PRC2/38/136
Gill, Henry, Warehorne, Kent, 1667 CKS PRC1/12/40a

[Gill:]
Gill, Henry, Warehorne, Kent, 1668 CKS PRC1/12/40
Gill, Henry, gentleman, York, Yorks, 1834 Borthwick Test C.P. 1834/5
Gill, Jacob, bachelor, Chilham, Kent, 1700 CKS PRC1/16/27
Gill, John, Bennington, Long, Lincs, 1607 Lincs RO Ad/Ac/8a/83
Gill, John, dyer, Newbury, Berks, 1622 Berks RO D/A1/191/137A
Gill, John, Canterbury St Mary Northgate, Kent, 1671 CKS PRC2/35/42
Gill, John, farmer, Whitchurch (Bubney), Shrops, 1792 LJRO/B/C/5/1792/31
Gill, Margarett, Kenardington, Kent, 1630 CKS PRC2/30/65
Gill, Nicholas, bricklayer, Westwell, Kent, 1675 CKS PRC20/12/171
Gill, Paul, Chilham, Kent, 1632 CKS PRC2/31/114
Gill, Richarde, Faversham, Kent, 1602 CKS PRC2/12/433
Gill, Robert, husbandman, Kenardington, Kent, 1682 CKS PRC2/40/31
Gill, Roger, Warehorne, Kent, 1628 CKS PRC2/29/42
Gill, Roger, Kidderminster, Worcs, 1685 Worcs RO 008.7 BA3585/837/bdl 4
Gill, Thomas, Faversham, Kent, 1597 CKS PRC2/9/353
Gill, William, Minster in Sheppey, Kent, 1639 CKS PRC1/2/67
Gill, William, Kennington, Kent, 1664 CKS PRC1/10/38
Gill, William, carpenter, Canterbury St Alphege, Kent, 1670 CKS PRC19/4/51
Gillam, John, Spalding, Lincs, 1623 Lincs RO Ad/Ac/18/77
Gillam, John, High Halden, Kent, 1624 CKS PRC2/23/142
Gillart, Claudius, saddler, Dover, Kent, 1680 CKS PRC20/13/26
Gillet, John, Hougham, Kent, 1598 CKS PRC2/10/264
Gillet, John, blacksmith, Hythe St Leonard, Kent, 1662 CKS PRC19/3/9
Gillet, William, wheelwright, Bobbing, Kent, 1624 CKS PRC2/23/145
Gillett, John eld, Glastonbury St John, Som, 1622 Somerset RO D/D/Cta/G2
Gillett, Mary, spinster, Sellindge, Kent, 1720 CKS PRC1/18/20
Gillett, Nicholas eld, Hythe St Leonard, Kent, 1634 CKS PRC20/10/410
Gillett, William, Faversham, Kent, 1631 CKS PRC20/9/193
Gillham, William, Kennington, Kent, 1638 CKS PRC1/1/75
Gilliat, Anne, Torrington, West, Lincs, 1620 Lincs RO Ad/Ac/16/46
Gilliatt, William, Barrow, Lincs, 1642 Lincs RO Ad/Ac/28/2
Gillimore, Mary, widow, Marlborough, Wilts, 1754 Wilts RO CC Sarum(+ name and date)
Gillingham, Joane, widow, Canterbury Holy Cross Westgate, Kent, 1690 CKS PRC2/41/175
Gillingham, Richard, Wimborne Minster, Dors, 1625 Dorset RO PE/WM CP 2/4/31
Gilliot, Appleby, Lincs, 1662 Lincs RO Ad/Ac/41/59
Gilliott, Roberte, Luddington, Lincs, 1606 Lincs RO Ad/Ac/37/227
Gillis, Daniel, Dover St Mary, Kent, 1694 CKS PRC19/5/20
Gillman, John, Stodmarsh, Kent, 1711 CKS PRC1/17/25
Gillman, Joseph, gentleman, Longford (Hollington), Derby, 1800 LJRO/B/C/5/1800/26
Gillow, John, Deal, Kent, 1643 CKS PRC19/2/55
Gillow, Mary, widow, St Laurence Thanet, Kent, 1684 CKS PRC19/4/108
Gillow, Mary, widow, St Laurence Thanet, Kent, 1685 CKS PRC2/40/200
Gillow, Richard, yeoman, Northbourne, Kent, 1670 CKS PRC1/15/28
Gillow, Thomas, yeoman, Walmer, Kent, 1644 CKS PRC1/6/104
Gillowe, Henry, Walmer, Kent, 1622 CKS PRC2/23/128
Gillowe, John, Walmer, Kent, 1601 CKS PRC2/12/159
Gilman, Katherine, spinster, Carlton le Moorland, Lincs, 1633 Lincs RO Ad/Ac/23/167
Gilman, William, Whitstable, Kent, 1630 CKS PRC2/30/60
Gilmer, Phillip, Canterbury St Mary Northgate, Kent, 1626 CKS PRC2/27/59
Gilmore, John, Canterbury St Paul, Kent, 1677 CKS PRC2/37/148
Gilnett, Samuell, Reculver, Kent, 1619 CKS PRC20/4/103
Gilphin, Joseph, Snargate, Kent, 1631 CKS PRC20/9/181
Gilphin, Richard, Warehorne, Kent, 1593 CKS PRC2/6/166
Gilphin, Robart, Oare, Kent, 1594 CKS PRC2/7/233
Gilphin, Robert, Dymchurch, Kent, 1638 CKS PRC2/34/213

Gilphin, Thomas, Snargate, Kent, 1599 CKS PRC2/10/452
Gilpin, George eld., innholder, Sittingbourne, Kent, 1671 CKS PRC2/35/43
Gilson, Daniel, blacksmith, Brotherton, Yorks, 1770 Borthwick Chanc C.P. 1770/3
Gilvin, William, Whitstable, Kent, 1679 CKS PRC2/38/34
Gimbard, William, cook, Cambridge St Botolph, Cambs, 1667 CUL V.C. Acc./Box3/26
Gimber, Edmund, Milton next Sittingbourne, Kent, CKS PRC2/23/138
Gimber, John, Milton next Sittingbourne, Kent, 1640 CKS PRC1/4/47
Gimber, Salomon, Baston, Lincs, 1624 Lincs RO Ad/Ac/18/92
Gimlett, Nicholas, Altarnun, Corn, 1624 Cornwall RO AP/G295/1
Ginder, George, Benenden, Kent, 1630 CKS PRC2/30/66
Ginder, John, bachelor/yeoman, Elham, Kent, 1664 CKS PRC19/3/25
Ginder, Stephen, Benenden, Kent, 1641 CKS PRC1/5/98a
Ginder, Stephen, clothier, Benenden, Kent, 1641 CKS PRC1/5/98
Ginder, Thomas, Caverswall, Staffs, 1682 LJRO/B/C/5/1681/17
Gine, Richard + Joane, Enford, Wilts, 1633 Wilts RO Arch. Sarum(+ name and date)
Gingell, Elinor, Brinkworth, Wilts, 1674 Wilts RO Miscellaneous Index (name + date)
Gingell, Ellinor, Brinkworth, Wilts, 1675 Wilts RO Miscellaneous Index (name + date)
Gingell, John, Christian Malford, Wilts, 1639 Wilts RO Arch. Wilts.(name + date)
Gingell, Wolfran, Hullavington, Wilts, 1630 Wilts RO Arch. Wilts.(name + date)
Ginn, Thomas, Stilton, Hunts, 1693 Hunts RO/Acc58/277
Gipson, Robert, husbandman, Eastry, Kent, 1680 CKS PRC20/13/24
Girdler, Phillis, widow, Salisbury St Edmund, Wilts, 1632 Wilts RO Miscellaneous Index (name + date)
Girdler, Simon, gentleman, Goudhurst, Kent, 1631 CKS PRC20/9/183
Girling, Anne, widow, St Andrew Holborn, London & Middlesex, 1670 Lambeth Palace Arches G25/1
Girlinge, Thomas, gentleman, Sutton, Long, Lincs, 1697 PRO PROB5/1368
Girney, Richard, Hundleby, Lincs, 1607 Lincs RO Ad/Ac/8a/79
Girrishe, Nichiolas, Laverton, Som, 1624 Somerset RO D/D/Cta/G1
Gisburne, John, Aston, Warks, 1683 LJRO/B/C/5/1682/40
Gisby, Thomas, Soberton, Hants, 1685 Hants RO 21m65 D8/340
Gisslingham, Thomas, butcher, Throwleigh, Kent, 1638 CKS PRC2/34/214
Gittens, Richard, Bignor, Sussex, 1632 W. Suss RO EpI/33/1632/33
Gitting, Francis, Sempringham (Pointon), Lincs, 1640 Lincs RO Ad/Ac/27/155
Gladish, George, Ebony, Kent, 1623 CKS PRC2/23/129
Gladish, Ralfe, Ivychurch, Kent, 1642 CKS PRC19/2/56
Gladish, William, Pluckley, Kent, 1677 CKS PRC2/37/37
Gladman, Mary, widow, Rickmansworth, Herts, 1629 Herts RO ASA25/4861
Gladman, Ralph, Abbots Langley, Herts, 1632 Herts RO ASA25/4874
Gladman, Thomas, Rickmansworth, Herts, 1628 Herts RO ASA25/4855
Gladman/Grene, John, Abbots Langley, Herts, 1572 Herts RO ASA25/725
Gladwin, Robert, miller, Charlbury, Oxon, 1689 Oxon RO MSS Wills 166/2/29
Gladwyne, Marie, widow, Swineshead, Lincs, 1612 Lincs RO Ad/Ac/10/164
Glanfelde/Nevell, Mary, Newnham, Herts, 1596 Herts RO ASA25/1424
Glasbrooke, Thomas, Maidstone, Kent, 1636 CKS PRC20/10/386
Glasbury, Beniamin, Bethersden, Kent, 1626 CKS PRC2/27/60
Glasbury, Mary, widow, Bethersden, Kent, 1627 CKS PRC2/28/51
Glasebury, Thomas, Bethersden, Kent, 1621 CKS PRC2/21/25
Glasier (written Blasier), Richard, Biddenden, Kent, 1675 CKS PRC2/36/192
Glasse, John, yeoman, Pewsey, Wilts, 1686 Wilts RO Arch. Wilts.(name + date)
Glassopp, William, Hethe, Oxon, 1632 Oxon RO MSS Wills 297/3/34
Glasyer, Goddarde, yeoman, Wittersham, Kent, 1614 CKS PRC20/3/119
Glasyer, Thomas, clergy: 'rector/Doctor of Law', Oxford (Exeter College), Oxon, 1592 Bodleian HYP B8/81-82
Glazier, Robert, Hawkhurst, Kent, 1670 CKS PRC1/14/45

[Gleane:]
Gleane, Christopher, Boston, Lincs, 1629 Lincs RO Ad/Ac/22/43
Gleane, John, Gayton le Marsh, Lincs, 1639? Lincs RO Ad/Ac/26/128
Gleane, John, yeoman, Willoughby, Lincs, 1673 Lincs RO Ad/Ac/34/17
Gleast, Thomas, yeoman, Ormskirk, Lancs, Lancs RO (Name of Deceased) D.R.C.H. 1635-36
Gleave, Thomas, bachelor, Temple, Inner, London & Middlesex, 1711 PRO PROB32/54/58
Gleed, John, Purton, Wilts, 1638 Wilts RO Arch. Wilts.(name + date)
Gleed, Richard, Milford, Hants, 1673 Hants RO 1672 AD52/2
Glegge, William, Heswall (Gayton), Ches, 1590 Cheshire RO (Name) W.C. 1588
Glemham, Constance, widow, Trotton, Sussex, 1635 W. Suss RO EpI/33/1635/10
Glenforth, John, Gosberton, Lincs, 1612 Lincs RO Ad/Ac/11/124
Glenn, Anne, widow, Bourne, Lincs, 1664 Lincs RO Ad/Ac/43/45
Glentforthe, Christopher, Grantham (Houghton), Lincs, 1601 Lincs RO Ad/Ac/5/29
Glew, Henry, Owston, Lincs, 1662 Lincs RO Ad/Ac/41/33
Glew, John, Heanor, Derby, 1685 LJRO/B/C/5/1685/43
Glewe, Thomas, Thoresby, North, Lincs, 1605 Lincs RO Ad/Ac/6/139
Glossop, Joseph, coal master, Chesterfield (Newbold), Derby, 1826 LJRO/B/C/5/1826/20a
Glover, Edward, Westwell, Kent, 1626 CKS PRC20/7/52
Glover, Eliz + Jarman, Bethersden, Kent, 1598 CKS PRC2/10/262
Glover, Flower, Warehorne, Kent, 1632 CKS PRC1/1/42
Glover, George, yeoman, Ebony, Kent, 1619 CKS PRC1/1/26
Glover, George, Ebony, Kent, 1620 CKS PRC1/1/26a
Glover, German, Bethersden, Kent, 1582 CKS PRC2/2/159
Glover, German, New Romney, Kent, 1618 CKS PRC20/4/109
Glover, Gyles, Witchurch, London & Middlesex, 1748 Greater London RO DL/C/551/146/1
Glover, Humfrey, Grantham, Lincs, 1586 Lincs RO Ad/Ac/2C/19
Glover, James, Bethersden, Kent, 1630 CKS PRC2/30/58
Glover, Jerman eld, Bethersden, Kent, 1597 CKS PRC2/9/130
Glover, John, bricklayer, Mersham, Kent, 1663 CKS PRC1/9/21
Glover, John, labourer, Chart, Great, Kent, 1671 CKS PRC1/15/29
Glover, John, Kettering, Northants, 1680 Northants RO NWill A/C/1
Glover, John, Sherriff Hales (Burlington), Shrops, 1709 LJRO/B/C/5/1709/31a
Glover, Mary, mrs, Lydd, Kent, 1623 CKS PRC20/6/20
Glover, Mildred, Tenterden, Kent, 1597 CKS PRC2/9/128
Glover, Richard, Cranbrook, Kent, 1607 CKS PRC2/15/134
Glover, Richard, Willesborough, Kent, 1612 CKS PRC2/16/164
Glover, Richard, Hythe St Leonard, Kent, 1631 CKS PRC20/9/153
Glover, Rychard, Lydd, Kent, 1588 CKS PRC21/9/78
Glover, Thomas, Benenden, Kent, 1579 CKS PRC2/1/224
Glover, Thomas, Kenardington, Kent, 1622 CKS PRC2/23/127
Glover, Thomas, cooper, St Johns Thanet, Kent, 1677 CKS PRC2/37/35
Glover, Thomas, Milton next Sittingbourne, Kent, 1680 CKS PRC2/39/45
Glover, Thomas, cooper, Ashford, Kent, 1684 CKS PRC2/40/115
Glover, Walter, Appledore, Kent, 1628 CKS PRC2/29/43
Glover, William, blacksmith, Rotherby, Leics, Leics RO Administrators Accounts 1667-72 f89
Glover, William, Bethersden, Kent, 1571 CKS PRC2/1/41
Glover, William, Smarden, Kent, 1571 CKS PRC2/1/51
Glover, Willyam, Smarden, Kent, 1617 CKS PRC2/21/43
Glover, see Swift,
Goakes, John, Horncastle, Lincs, 1634 Lincs RO Ad/Ac/24/197
Goard, John, carpenter, Snave, Kent, 1687 CKS PRC2/41/93
Goare, John, husbandman, Reculver, Kent, 1669 CKS PRC19/4/16
Goare, Mary, widow, Frittenden, Kent, 1666 CKS PRC1/11/32
Goare, Peter, Chislet, Kent, 1625 CKS PRC2/23/147
Goate, John, Huttoft, Lincs, 1614 Lincs RO Ad/Ac/13/107
Goately, Anthony, Challock, Kent, 1634 CKS PRC20/10/420

Goately, Margery, widow, Ospringe, Kent, 1626 CKS PRC2/25/58
Goater, Francis, gentleman, Chichester, Sussex, 1662 W. Suss RO EpIII/9/1/48
Goatley, Thomas, Marlborough, Wilts, 1763 Wilts RO CC Sarum(+ name and date)
Goatlie, Christopher, Molash, Kent, 1611 CKS PRC2/17/404
Goatly, Grygorye, St Peter in Thanet, Kent, 1616 CKS PRC2/21/42
Goatly, Peter, Ashford, Kent, 1614 CKS PRC20/2/450
Goatly, William, Tenterden, Kent, 1671 CKS PRC2/35/41
Goble, Laurence, Felpham, Sussex, 1630 W. Suss RO EpI/33/1630/24
Goble, Richard, Bosham, Sussex, 1594 W. Suss RO EpI/33/1594/3
Goble, Thomas, Petworth (Byworth), Sussex, 1632 W. Suss RO EpI/33/1632/26
Goble, Walter, Willesborough, Kent, 1667 CKS PRC1/11/120
Goborne, Thomas, blacksmith, Stanford Dingley, Berks, 1633 Berks RO D/A1/192/6A
Goby, Alice, Wimborne Minster, Dors, 1600 Dorset RO PE/WM CP 2/4/2
Goby, John, butcher, Canterbury, Kent, 1618 CKS PRC2/21/54
Gobye, John, Milton next Sittingbourne, Kent, 1601 CKS PRC2/12/167
Goddard, Alexander, gentleman, Shipton Bellinger, Hants, 1669 Hants RO 21m65 D8/216
Goddard, Anthonie, gentleman, Cliffe Pypard, Wilts, 1647? Wilts RO CC Sarum(+ name and date)
Goddard, Anthonye, minor, Wye, Kent, 1595 CKS PRC2/8/177
Goddard, Elizabeth, widow, Shaw cum Donnington, Berks, 1616 Berks RO D/A1/71/206D
Goddard, Henry, Thatcham, Berks, 1606 Berks RO D/A1/191/101A
Goddard, Henry, Glossop, Derby, 1682 LJRO/B/C/5/1682/43
Goddard, John, yeoman, Chartham, Kent, 1620 CKS PRC2/21/55
Goddard, John, yeoman, Bucklebury, Berks, 1635 Berks RO D/A1/192/10
Goddard, John, miller, Windsor, New, Berks, 1677 Berks RO D/A1/192/99C
Goddard, Jonathan, yeoman, Mersham, Kent, 1640 CKS PRC1/4/48
Goddard, Jonathan, Mersham, Kent, 1641 CKS PRC1/4/48a
Goddard, Marye, Minster in Thanet, Kent, 1601 CKS PRC2/12/175
Goddard, Philip, husbandman, Bucklebury, Berks, 1633 Berks RO D/A1/191/167E
Goddard, Richard, Hampstead Norris, Berks, 1603 Berks RO D/A1/191/93C
Goddard, Richard, Welford, Berks, 1603 Berks RO D/A1/191/96C
Goddard, Richard, Hendred, West, Berks, 1618 Berks RO D/A1/191/127A
Goddard, Robert, Fairfield, Kent, 1629 CKS PRC20/8/244
Goddard, Samuel, bellows maker, Reading St Lawrence, Berks, 1638 Berks RO D/A1/192/22A
Goddard, Thomas, Hendred, West, Berks, 1609 Berks RO D/A1/191/108A
Goddard, Thomas, Upton Lovell, Wilts, 1612 Wilts RO Arch. Sarum(+ name and date)
Goddard, Thomas, gentleman, Newbury, Berks, 1621 Berks RO D/A1/191/139A
Goddard, Thomas, husbandman, Thatcham (Henwick), Berks, 1629 Berks RO D/A1/191/160C
Goddard, Thomas, yeoman, Bucklebury, Berks, 1667 Berks RO D/A1/192/80A
Goddard, Thomas, bachelor, Cranbrook, Kent, 1668 CKS PRC1/13/49
Goddard, Thomas, yeoman, Bucklebury, Berks, 1669 Berks RO D/A1/192/81
Goddard, William, Marlborough St Peter & St Paul, Wilts, 1679 Wilts RO CC Sarum(+ name and date)
Goddarde, John, Mersham, Kent, 1585 CKS PRC2/3/278
Goddarde, John, Longcot, Berks, 1615 Berks RO D/A1/191/122A
Goddarde, Richard, Selling, Kent, 1611 CKS PRC2/16/71
Godden, Anthony, Egerton, Kent, 1628 CKS PRC20/8/240
Godden, Edward, yeoman, Thornham, Kent, 1667 CKS PRC19/3/122
Godden, Francis, Marden, Kent, 1608 CKS PRC20/1/378
Godden, Francis, Waltham, Kent, 1634 CKS PRC2/32/49
Godden, Francis, Sheldwich, Kent, 1638 CKS PRC2/34/53
Godden, Henrie, Ospringe, Kent, 1610 CKS PRC2/15/138
Godden, John, Folkestone, Kent, 1620 CKS PRC2/21/56
Godden, John, Folkestone, Kent, 1629 CKS PRC2/30/56
Godden, Nicholas, Thornham, Kent, 1633 CKS PRC2/32/46

[Godden:]
Godden, Nicholas, wheelwright, Linton, Kent, 1642 CKS PRC19/2/18
Godden, Peter, yeoman, Minster in Sheppey, Kent, 1676 CKS PRC2/36/191
Godden, Robert, Farlington, Hants, 1625 Hants RO 21M65 D8/67A
Godden, Robert, tanner, Maidstone, Kent, 1634 CKS PRC20/10/388
Godden, Robert, gentleman, Cranbrook, Kent, 1678 CKS PRC2/38/31
Godden, Sarah, Thornham, Kent, 1681 CKS PRC2/39/173
Godden, Thomas, Detling, Kent, 1637 CKS PRC20/10/450
Godden, Thomas, mason: 'freemason', Loose, Kent, 1672 CKS PRC20/12/10
Godden, William, Folkestone, Kent, 1595 CKS PRC2/7/419
Godden, William, Upchurch, Kent, 1607 CKS PRC2/15/155
Goddin, Maddington, Wilts, 1614 Wilts RO Arch. Sarum(+ name and date)
Goddin, Edward, Dorchester, Oxon, 1631 Oxon RO MSS Wills Pec 68/3/3
Goddin, Robert, clergy: 'mr/vicar', Reculver, Kent, 1675 CKS PRC20/12/127
Goddin, William, Tilehurst, Berks, 1593 Berks RO D/A1/191/77C
Goddin/Goodwyn, William, Nonington, Kent, 1594 CKS PRC21/13/24
Goddin, see Ruffin,
Goddyn, Henry, Langley Burrell, Wilts, 1620 Wilts RO Arch. Wilts.(name + date)
Godfrey, Anne, widow, Upchurch, Kent, 1633 CKS PRC2/32/42
Godfrey, Buttolph, Minster in Sheppey, Kent, 1632 CKS PRC2/31/37
Godfrey, Edmund, Tatenhill (Barton under Needwood), Staffs, 1663 LJRO:cards/1663/24
Godfrey, Edward, Brook, Kent, 1677 CKS PRC2/37/149
Godfrey, Elizabeth, widow, Harwich, Essex, 1744 Greater London RO DL/C/550/142
Godfrey, Francis, Sandwich, Kent, 1638 CKS PRC2/34/211
Godfrey, Henry, yeoman, Cumnor (Chawley), Berks, 1645 Berks RO D/A1/192/49A
Godfrey, Henry, dairyman/yeoman, Shrivenham, Berks, 1671 Berks RO D/A1/192/90C
Godfrey, John, weaver, Mells, Som, 1588 Somerset RO D/D/Cta/G31
Godfrey, John, Sandwich, Kent, 1625 CKS PRC2/25/57
Godfrey, John, Biddenden, Kent, 1627 CKS PRC2/28/55
Godfrey, John, Detling, Kent, 1636 CKS PRC20/10/382
Godfrey, John, Pinchbeck, Lincs, 1669 Lincs RO Ad/Ac/33/144
Godfrey, Peeter, Lydd, Kent, 1614 CKS PRC20/3/115
Godfrey, Richard, Luddington, Lincs, 1642 Lincs RO Ad/Ac/41/113
Godfrey, Roger, Salisbury, Wilts, 1678 Wilts RO Miscellaneous Index (name + date)
Godfrey, Thomas, blacksmith, Faversham, Kent, 1615 CKS PRC2/21/37
Godfrey, Thomas, tailor, Linsted, Kent, 1678 CKS PRC2/38/33
Godfrey, Thomas, yeoman, Hothfield, Kent, 1684 CKS PRC2/40/201
Godfrey, William, Sandhurst, Kent, 1632 CKS PRC2/31/116
Godfrey, William, Harbledown, Kent, 1672 CKS PRC2/35/137
Godfreye, Barnabye, Egerton, Kent, 1586 CKS PRC21/8/119
Godfreye, Samuell, Milton next Sittingbourne, Kent, 1594 CKS PRC2/7/361
Godfrie, William, husbandman, Morton, Abbots, Worcs, 1604 Worcs RO 008.7 BA3585/839/359
Godfry, John, Milton next Sittingbourne, Kent, 1623 CKS PRC2/23/132
Godfry, Thomas, Folkestone, Kent, 1624 CKS PRC2/23/137
Godfry, William, Boughton Aluph, Kent, 1670 CKS PRC1/14/46
Godfrye, Joan, widow, Woodstock, Oxon, 1639 Oxon RO MSS Wills 297/3/42
Godfrye, Margerye, widow, Aldington, Kent, 1600 CKS PRC21/15/151
Godfrye, Thomas, River, Kent, 1612 CKS PRC2/16/160
Godhelp, George, Rocester, Staffs, 1684 LJRO/B/C/5/1684/37
Godhelpe, Nicholas, gentleman, Grimsby, Great, Lincs, 1679 Lincs RO Ad/Ac/43/108
Godherd, John, Chislet, Kent, 1596 CKS PRC2/8/282
Godley, Blastus, St Albans, Herts, 1635 Herts RO ASA25/4910
Godman, Thomas, Rumboldswyke, Sussex, 1629 W. Suss RO EpIII/9/1/36
Godman, Thomas, Chiltington, West, Sussex, 1673 W. Suss RO EpI/33/1673/29
Godsaie, Margarett, widow, Scarle, North, Lincs, 1633 Lincs RO Ad/Ac/24/216
Godsall, Anne, widow, Nantwich, Ches, 1728 Cheshire RO (Name) W.C. 1728

Godsave, see Gadsaw,
Godsmarke, John, Ashurst, Sussex, 1614 W. Suss RO EpI/33/1613/28
Godson, John, Broughton, Lincs, 1662 Lincs RO Ad/Ac/41/16
Godstowe, Agnes, widow, St Albans, Herts, 1632 Herts RO ASA25/4875
Godwin, Annie, widow, Newbury, Berks, 1641 Berks RO D/A1/192/36C
Godwin, Joane, Weeke, Hants, 1670 Hants RO 21m65 D8/217
Godwin, John, Kingsnorth, Kent, 1669 CKS PRC1/14/47
Godwin, John, Street, Som, 1731 Somerset RO D/D/Cta/G37
Godwin, Thomas, Stanton St Bernard, Wilts, 1674 Wilts RO Miscellaneous Index (name + date)
Godwyn, Bartylmew, Cheriton, Kent, 1595 CKS PRC2/7/375
Godwyn, Richard, Kington St Michael, Wilts, 1636 Wilts RO Arch. Wilts.(name + date)
Godwyne, Richard, Tilehurst, Berks, 1584 Berks RO D/A2/C19/f156V
Gody, Anne, widow, Dover St Mary, Kent, 1631 CKS PRC20/9/187
Goff, Francis, Meare, Som, 1710 Somerset RO D/D/Cta/G38
Goffe, Charles, Martin, Wilts, 1627 Wilts RO Arch. Sarum(+ name and date)
Goffe, Gallion, Ruckinge, Kent, 1626 CKS PRC2/27/62
Goffe, Jeremiah, Arundel, Sussex, 1672 W. Suss RO EpI/33/1672/17
Goffe, Jerman, Halstock, Dors, 1631 Wilts RO Miscellaneous Index (name + date)
Goffe, Peter, Norton, Hook (Southrope), Oxon, 1626 Oxon RO MSS Wills 166/1/48
Goffe, Richard, Arundel, Sussex, 1676 W. Suss RO EpI/33/1676/12
Gofford, William, Watford, Herts, 1628 Herts RO ASA25/4856
Gofinch/Goldfinch, William, Wickhambreaux, Kent, 1629 CKS PRC2/30/57
Gofrey, Thomas, Ashford, Kent, 1617 CKS PRC2/21/29
Gofton, George, butcher, Scarborough, Yorks, 1793 Borthwick Test C.P. 1794/4
Gogar, Isaac, merchant, Sandwich, Kent, 1640 CKS PRC20/10/458
Gogar, Isaack, Sandwich, Kent, 1640 CKS PRC20/10/396
Golborne, John, bucketmaker, Stanford Dingley, Berks, 1668 Berks RO D/A1/192/74C
Gold, John, Alstonfield, Staffs, 1678 LJRO:cards/1678/11
Gold, Thomas, Donnington, Sussex, 1599 W. Suss RO EpI/33/1599/3
Gold, William, Shrewsbury Holy Cross, Shrops, 1717 LJRO/B/C/5/1717/11
Goldborowe, James, Heckington, Lincs, 1619 Lincs RO Ad/Ac/15/83
Golde, Margaret, widow, Teynham, Kent, 1609 CKS PRC2/13/213
Golde, Nicholas, Sturry, Kent, 1637 CKS PRC2/34/54
Golder, Anne, spinster, Beenham, Berks, Berks RO D/A1/192/143E
Golder, Henrie, Dover, Kent, 1616 CKS PRC20/4/117
Golder, James, Sholden, Kent, 1634 CKS PRC2/32/44
Golder, John, Eastry, Kent, 1599 CKS PRC21/16/174
Golder, John, Eastry, Kent, 1627 CKS PRC20/8/224
Golder, Richard, brewer: 'beerbrewer', Dover, Kent, 1640 CKS PRC20/10/444
Goldfinch, Edward, Chislet, Kent, 1637 CKS PRC2/34/55
Goldfinch, Edward, yeoman, Chislet, Kent, 1638 CKS PRC2/34/56
Goldfinch, Henry, Upham, Hants, 1697 Hants RO 1697 AD58
Goldfinch, John, Blean, Kent, 1668 CKS PRC1/13/50a
Goldfinch, John, Blean, Kent, 1669 CKS PRC1/13/50
Goldfinch, John, Blean, Kent, 1669 CKS PRC1/14/48
Goldfinch, John, Blean, Kent, 1669 CKS PRC1/14/48b
Goldfinch, Joseph, bachelor, Patrixbourne, Kent, 1662 CKS PRC1/9/22
Goldfinch, Nicholas, Goodnestone next Wingham, Kent, 1681 CKS PRC20/13/135
Goldfinch, Robert, yeoman, Minster in Thanet, Kent, 1664 CKS PRC1/10/39
Goldfinch, Stephen, Waltham, Kent, 1592 CKS PRC2/5/15
Goldfinch, Stephen, yeoman, Boughton under Blean, Kent, 1685 CKS PRC20/13/430
Goldfinch, Thomas, yeoman, St Laurence Thanet, Kent, 1667 CKS PRC1/12/41
Goldfinch, see Argoe & Gofinch,
Goldfinche, Roger, Bearsted, Kent, 1610 CKS PRC2/13/209
Goldfynche, Thomas, Sandwich St Bartholomew's Hospital, Kent, 1585 CKS PRC21/7/234

[Goldhill:]
Goldhill, Dorothie, Hinxhill, Kent, 1611 CKS PRC2/17/182
Goldhill, Thomas, Old Romney, Kent, 1669 CKS PRC1/13/51
Goldhill/Goldwell, Thomas, Ivychurch, Kent, 1635 CKS PRC20/10/384
Golding, Anne, widow, Watford, Herts, 1594 Herts RO ASA25/1464
Golding, Joan, widow, Godmanchester, Hunts, Hunts RO/Acc58/85(29)
Goldinge, Robert, esquire, Canterbury, Kent, 1590 CKS PRC21/10/301
Goldinge, Robert, Linton, Kent, 1665 CKS PRC1/11/33
Goldinge, William, yeoman, Stoke, South, Lincs, 1635 Lincs RO Ad/Ac/24/480
Goldsborough, John, knight, Bednall Green, London & Middlesex, 1699 PRO PROB32/38/79
Goldsmith, Harbert, cutler, Marden, Kent, 1675 CKS PRC2/36/193
Goldsmith, John, Sutton Valence, Kent, 1615 CKS PRC2/21/22
Goldsmith, John, Westwell, Kent, 1629 CKS PRC20/8/234
Goldsmith, John, Barton, Steeple, Oxon, 1632 Oxon RO MSS Wills 297/3/35
Goldsmith, John, Haxey, Lincs, 1640? Lincs RO Ad/Ac/40/270
Goldsmith, John, St Sepulchre, London & Middlesex, 1684 PRO PROB32/23/137
Goldsmith, Lucy, widow, Boxley, Kent, 1668 CKS PRC1/13/52
Goldsmith, Thomas, Hexton, Herts, 1597 Herts RO ASA25/1615
Goldsmith, William, Lenham, Kent, 1593 CKS PRC2/6/91
Goldsmith, William, Boughton under Blean, Kent, 1618 CKS PRC20/4/124
Goldsmyth, William, husbandman, Hibaldstow, Lincs, 1608 Lincs RO Ad/Ac/37/258
Goldson, An,
Kent 1631 CKS PRC2/31/31
Goldson, John, Seasalter, Kent, 1631 CKS PRC2/31/38
Goldstone, Roger, St Peter in Thanet, Kent, 1632 CKS PRC2/31/112
Goldthorp, Joseph, innkeeper, Mirfield, Yorks, 1843 Borthwick Test C.P. 1843/3
Goldwell, Henrie, Smarden, Kent, 1613 CKS PRC2/16/197
Goldwell, Henrie, Smarden, Kent, 1613 CKS PRC2/16/198
Goldwell, Henry, Smarden, Kent, 1614 CKS PRC2/18/130
Goldwell, Richard, weaver: 'linen weaver', Smarden, Kent, 1681 CKS PRC2/39/44
Goldwell, see Goldhill,
Goldwire, Richard, Chart nr Sutton Valence, Kent, 1633 CKS PRC2/31/113
Goler, Goudhurst, Kent, 1622 CKS PRC2/26/111
Golledge, William, Pylle, Som, 1623 Somerset RO D/D/Cta/G3
Gollins, John, Brockton, 1674 LJRO:cards/1674/17
Golsmith, Henrie, gentleman, Exton, Hants, 1624 Hants RO 21M65 D8/69
Golsmythe, Thomas, Hexton, Herts, 1567 Herts RO ASA25/599
Golsney, John, gentleman, Holnest, Dors, 1680 Wilts RO Dean Sarum (name + date)
Golson, Thomas ygr, Whitstable, Kent, 1631 CKS PRC2/31/36
Golsthorpe, William, St Andrew Holborn, London & Middlesex, 1668 PRO PROB32/3/115
Gonnell, Robert, husbandman, Burghfield, Berks, 1617 Berks RO D/A1/191/125C
Good, Drew, Tenterden, Kent, 1682 CKS PRC2/40/34
Good, Jane, Yatesbury, Wilts, 1664 Wilts RO CC Sarum(+ name and date)
Good, John, Stedham, Sussex, 1629 W. Suss RO EpI/33/1629/41
Good, Katherine, widow, Doddington, Lincs, 1620 Lincs RO Ad/Ac/15/193
Good, William, clergy: 'rector', Brattleby & Fillingham, Lincs, 1681 PRO PROB5/1330
Goodale, John, Allington, Wilts, 1621 Wilts RO Miscellaneous Index (name + date)
Goodall, Simon, weaver: 'broad weaver', Newbury, Berks, 1644 Berks RO D/A1/192/46C
Goodall, Thomas, Thruxton, Hants, 1623 Hants RO 21M65 D8/16
Goodbarne, Thomas, Reading, Berks, 1565 Berks RO D/A2/C5/f277V
Goodchild, Susan, widow, Horringer, Suff, 1791 Suff RO(B) IC500/3/53/78
Goodchild, William, Stoughton, Sussex, 1635 W. Suss RO EpI/33/1635/31
Gooddaile, Richard, Asterby, Lincs, 1618 Lincs RO Ad/Ac/14/90
Gooddall, see Gorham,
Goodden, Thomas, Biddenden, Kent, 1677 CKS PRC2/37/150
Gooddin, Abraham, Dover, Kent, 1610 CKS PRC20/2/110

Gooddis, Richard, Teynham, Kent, 1622 CKS PRC2/23/130
Gooddyn, James, Otterden, Kent, 1592 CKS PRC2/5/68
Gooden, Anne, St Johns Thanet, Kent, 1602 CKS PRC2/12/173
Gooden, William, Ambersham, South, Sussex, 1595 W. Suss RO EpI/33/1595
Gooderson, Francis, Leake, Lincs, 1626 Lincs RO Ad/Ac/20/68
Goodes, Thomas, St Albans, Herts, 1609 Herts RO ASA25/4770
Goodfellow, Henry, Compton Chamberlain, Wilts, 1676 Wilts RO Arch. Sarum(+ name and date)
Goodge, William, Biddenden, Kent, 1616 CKS PRC2/21/46
Goodgrome, Edward, Westwell, Kent, 1606 CKS PRC20/1/27
Goodgrome, Richard, Sheldwich, Kent, 1622 CKS PRC20/6/374
Goodgrome, William, Ebony, Kent, 1602 CKS PRC2/12/161
Goodgroome, Edwarde, Westwell, Kent, 1602 CKS PRC21/16/91
Goodhand, Charles, gentleman, Stainton le Vale, Lincs, 1618 Lincs RO Ad/Ac/14/3
Goodhand, Thomas, gentleman, Spilsby, Lincs, 1610 Lincs RO Ad/Ac/10/40
Goodheird, William, mercer, Gainsborough, Lincs, 1667 Lincs RO Ad/Ac/33/30
Goodhewe, John, yeoman, Preston next Faversham, Kent, 1607 CKS PRC1/1/5
Goodier, Margaret, widow, Minster in Thanet, Kent, 1626 CKS PRC2/28/53
Goodier, Philip, Winslow, Bucks, 1708 Herts RO ASA25/4588
Goodin, Henry, husbandman, Fleet, Lincs, 1666 Lincs RO Ad/Ac/32/73
Gooding, Edward, grocer, Pluckley, Kent, 1681 CKS PRC2/39/174
Goodinge, Humfrey, clergy: 'clerk', Hampstead, East, Berks, 1622 Wilts RO CC Sarum(+ name and date)
Goodman, Edmund, tailor, Kintbury, Berks, 1591 Berks RO D/A1/191/72C
Goodman, Margerie, widow, Walsall (Hawarden), Staffs, 1663 LJRO:cards/1663/25
Goodman, Ralph, alderman, Chester, Ches, Cheshire RO (Name) W.C. 1575
Goodman, Richard, Martin Hussingtree, Worcs, 1682 Worcs RO 008.7 BA3585/837/bdl 3
Goodman, Robert, Sandwich St Clement, Kent, 1619 CKS PRC2/21/53
Goodman, Thomas eld, Sulhampstead Abbots, Berks, 1633 Berks RO D/A1/191/162A
Goodriche, John, burgess: 'principal burgess', St Albans, Herts, 1597 Herts RO ASA25/1617
Goodridge, Thomas, St Nicholas at Wade, Kent, 1609 CKS PRC20/2/25
Goodson, Alexander, St Peter in Thanet, Kent, 1599 CKS PRC2/11/9
Goodson, Alexander, St Peter in Thanet, Kent, 1623 CKS PRC2/23/135
Goodson, Augustine, Belton, Lincs, 1611 Lincs RO Ad/Ac/10/80
Goodson, Samuel, yeoman, St Johns Thanet, Kent, 1680 CKS PRC2/39/42
Goodson, Thomas, St Johns Thanet, Kent, CKS PRC20/10/426
Goodson, Thomas, Petham, Kent, 1613 CKS PRC2/17/258
Goodsone, Richard, university: 'privileged person', Oxford (University), Oxon, 1673 Bodleian HYP B8/83-86
Goodwin, Bryan, husbandman, Stainton Waddingham, Lincs, 1669 Lincs RO Ad/Ac/33/153
Goodwin, Christopher, Aubourn, Lincs, 1620 Lincs RO Ad/Ac/15/282
Goodwin, Daniell, yeoman, Herne, Kent, 1675 CKS PRC20/12/130
Goodwin, Edward, yeoman, Trumpington, Cambs, 1750? Cambs RO 1750/Inv
Goodwin, George, esquire, Derby, Derby, 1838 LJRO/B/C/5/1838/8
Goodwin, Henry, Dover, Kent, 1636 CKS PRC20/10/394
Goodwin, John, Walsall, Staffs, 1678 LJRO:cards/1678/12
Goodwin, John, husbandman, Prestbury (Kettleshulme), Ches, 1798 Cheshire RO (Name) W.C. 1798
Goodwin, Joseph, Herne, Kent, 1709 CKS PRC19/6/38
Goodwin, Robert, grocer, Sandwich, Kent, 1622 CKS PRC2/23/136
Goodwin, Robert, husbandman, Marden, Kent, 1663 CKS PRC1/9/116
Goodwin, William, university: 'Dean of Christ Church College, Oxford/D.D.', Oxford (Christ Church College), Oxon, 1625 Bodleian HYP B8/87-88
Goodwin, William, Stockbury, Kent, 1674 CKS PRC2/36/60
Goodwine, Edmund, Winteringham, Lincs, 1624 Lincs RO Ad/Ac/8c/85
Goodwine, George, ropemaker, St Peter in Thanet, Kent, 1663 CKS PRC1/9/115

[Goodwine:]
Goodwine, Gilbert, Pinchbeck, Lincs, 1607 Lincs RO Ad/Ac/8a/156
Goodworth, William, yeoman, Belton, Lincs, 1686 Lincs RO Ad/Ac/44/148
Goodwyn, Gabriel, Tonge, Kent, 1632 CKS PRC2/31/35
Goodwyn, John, Boxley, Kent, 1596 CKS PRC2/8/149
Goodwyn, John, St Johns Thanet, Kent, 1599 CKS PRC2/11/45
Goodwyn, Richard, Bradbourne, Derby, 1680 LJRO:cards/1680/15
Goodwyn, Roberte, Willoughby, Lincs, 1599 Lincs RO Ad/Ac/5/55
Goodwyn, Symon, Fordwich, Kent, 1631 CKS PRC2/31/34
Goodwyn, Thomas, Worth, Kent, 1617 CKS PRC20/3/429
Goodwyn, William, Hogsthorpe, Lincs, 1618 Lincs RO Ad/Ac/14/273
Goodwyn, see Goddin,
Goodwyne, George, roper, St Peter in Thanet, Kent, 1679 CKS PRC2/38/133
Goodwyne, John, Stickney, Lincs, 1599 Lincs RO Ad/Ac/5/163
Goodyear, William, Ormsby, Lincs, 1603 Lincs RO Ad/Ac/5/465
Goodyn, William, Wingham, Kent, 1593 CKS PRC21/12/109
Goolde, John, Doulting, Som, 1611 Somerset RO D/D/Cta/G14
Gooler, William, Sidlesham, Sussex, 1602 W. Suss RO EpI/33/1600/16
Goore, Margerie, Staplehurst, Kent, 1593 CKS PRC2/6/138
Goore, Robert, Staplehurst, Kent, 1635 CKS PRC2/33/52
Goore, William, St Albans, Herts, 1635 Herts RO ASA25/4911
Goorely, Thomas, Bilsington, Kent, 1633 CKS PRC2/32/45
Goorly, Anne, widow, Bilsington, Kent, 1639 CKS PRC2/34/209
Goose, John, labourer, Beesby in the Marsh, Lincs, C17th? Lincs RO Ad/Ac/45/115
Gootheringe, Thomas, Redbourn, Herts, 1634 Herts RO ASA25/4904
Gore, Benjamin, bachelor, St James Garlickhithe, London & Middlesex, 1668 PRO PROB5/1661
Gore, John, Bobbing, Kent, 1618 CKS PRC2/21/44
Gore, Robert, Queenborough, Kent, 1626 CKS PRC2/27/56
Goreing, Henry, esquire, Steyning, Sussex, 1690 PRO PROB32/31/328
Gorges, Arthur, esquire, Ancaster, Lincs, 1671 Lincs RO Ad/Ac/33/192
Gorham, Augustine, Hythe St Leonard, Kent, 1703 CKS PRC19/6/12
Gorham, George, Sittingbourne, Kent, 1662 CKS PRC1/9/23
Gorham, John, Dover, Kent, CKS PRC19/1/2
Gorham, John, Gidding, Great, Hunts, Hunts RO/Acc58/207(228)
Gorham, John, Tenterden, Kent, 1614 CKS PRC2/21/40
Gorham, Mary, Worth, Kent, 1619 CKS PRC20/4/101
Gorham, Nicholas, Sittingbourne, Kent, 1602 CKS PRC2/12/171
Gorham, Richard, Headcorn, Kent, 1617 CKS PRC2/21/45
Gorham, Richard, Patrixbourne, Kent, 1632 CKS PRC2/31/33
Gorham, Robart, Ulcombe, Kent, 1594 CKS PRC2/7/97
Gorham, Thomas, Faversham, Kent, 1640 CKS PRC1/4/49
Gorham, William, Harrietsham, Kent, 1619 CKS PRC2/21/27
Gorham, Willyam, Petham, Kent, 1611 CKS PRC2/17/420
Gorham/Gooddall, Chaterine, Smarden, Kent, 1598 CKS PRC2/10/280
Gorrell, Richard, Sutterton, Lincs, 1638 Lincs RO Ad/Ac/25/133
Gorton, Henry, blacksmith, Elford, Staffs, 1666 LJRO:cards/1666/5
Gorton, Richard, Lydeard St Lawrence, Som, 1668 Somerset RO D/D/Cta/G27
Gorton, William, Sefton, Lancs, 1611 Lancs RO (Name of Deceased) D.R.C.H. 1611
Gorton, William, husbandman, Blackrod, Lancs, 1765 Lancs RO (Name of Deceased) D.R.C.H. 1765
Gorway, Agnes, widow, Hurst, Berks, 1632 Wilts RO Miscellaneous Index (name + date)
Gorway, Christopher, Alfrick, Worcs, 1681 Worcs RO 008.7 BA3585/830/62
Gorway, John, Chew Magna, Som, Somerset RO D/D/Cta/G39
Gorwill, John, Carlton, Great, Lincs, 1613 Lincs RO Ad/Ac/12/92
Gosby, Henry, Herne, Kent, 1637 CKS PRC20/10/184
Gosby, William, St Johns Thanet, Kent, 1676 CKS PRC2/37/38

Goseney, Richard, Barford, Wilts, 1628 Wilts RO CC Sarum(+ name and date)
Gosford, William,
Herts 1627 Herts RO ASA25/2950
Gosfrithe, Peeter, Ashford, Kent, 1600 CKS PRC2/11/405
Goslin, Stephen, yeoman, Wistow, Hunts, 1709 Hunts RO/Acc58/301
Gosling, Henry, Elmore, Glos, GRO GDR/B4/2/G70
Gosling, John, Collingbourne Kingston, Wilts, 1643 Wilts RO CC Sarum(+ name and date)
Gosling, John, Sutton cum Duckmanton, Derby, 1667 LJRO:cards/1667/36
Gosling, John, Mumby, Lincs, 1670 Lincs RO Ad/Ac/32/173
Gosling, Thomas, Benington, Lincs, 1649 Lincs RO Ad/Ac/30/119
Gosling, Thomas, Sellindge, Kent, 1680 CKS PRC2/39/43
Gosling, Walram, Canterbury St Mildred, Kent, 1622 CKS PRC1/1/30
Gosling, William, tailor, Kirton, Lincs, 1620 Lincs RO Ad/Ac/16/42
Goslinge, Margaret, Haxey, Lincs, 1607 Lincs RO Ad/Ac/37/234
Goslinge, William, Moorby, Lincs, 1633 Lincs RO Ad/Ac/24/193
Gosse, Edmond, Ashford, Kent, 1611 CKS PRC2/16/81
Gossewell, Ellen, Pangbourne, Berks, 1597 Berks RO D/A1/191/84A
Gosson, Thomas, Langford (Little Faringdon), Oxon, 1619 Oxon RO MSS Wills Pec 78/3/1
Gostelow, Mary, widow, Adstone, Northants, 1792 Northants RO X954/22/28
Gostilowe, Edward, Frampton, Lincs, 1612? Lincs RO Ad/Ac/10/159
Gostling, Phillip, mariner, Dover, Kent, 1682 CKS PRC20/13/249
Gostlyn, William, university: 'scholar's servant', Cambridge, Cambs, 1622 CUL V.C. Acc./Box2/26
Goswell, John, tailor: 'merchant tailor', Bristol St John, Glos, Bristol RO 1678/72
Goswell, Ralph, Hurst, Berks, 1631 Wilts RO Miscellaneous Index (name + date)
Goteley, William, Throwleigh, Kent, 1590 CKS PRC2/5/80
Goter, Thomas, Eling, Hants, 1623 Hants RO 21M65 D8/17
Gothridge, John, Ruscombe, Berks, 1675 Wilts RO Miscellaneous Index (name + date)
Gotobed, William, Langford, Beds, 1625 Lincs RO Ad/Ac/19B/105
Goudger, William, Minster in Thanet, Kent, 1619 CKS PRC2/21/23
Gough, Anthony, yeoman, Ingoldmels, Lincs, 1648 Lincs RO Ad/Ac/30/382
Gough, Edmund, Smeeth, Kent, 1634 CKS PRC20/10/434
Gough, Thomas, goldsmith, Newbury, Berks, 1669 Berks RO D/A1/192/76A
Gough, William, tailor, Oxford St Ebbe, Oxon, 1640 Oxon RO MSS Wills 297/3/53
Gould, John, husbandman, Holnest, Dors, 1610 Wilts RO Dean Sarum (name + date)
Gould, Thomas, Sittingbourne, Kent, 1610 CKS PRC2/13/207
Gould, William, yeoman, Rocester (The Banks), Staffs, 1815 LJRO/B/C/5/1815/30
Gouldbrough, Robert, plumber, Gainsborough, Lincs, 1674 Lincs RO Ad/Ac/35/43
Goulder, Henry, Dover, Kent, 1617 CKS PRC20/4/118
Goulder, Henry, Dover, Kent, 1618 CKS PRC20/4/115
Goulder, Roger, yeoman, Eastry, Kent, 1673 CKS PRC20/12/49
Goulder, William, Worth, Kent, 1615 CKS PRC20/3/286
Goulding, Edward, Farringdon, Great, Berks, 1676 Wilts RO Dean Sarum (name + date)
Goulding, John, Bray, Berks, 1640 Berks RO D/A1/192/27A
Goulding, John, Cranbrook, Kent, 1670 CKS PRC1/15/30
Goulding, Roger, St Laurence Thanet, Kent, 1646 CKS PRC1/7/84
Goulding, Stephen, St Laurence Thanet, Kent, 1667 CKS PRC1/12/42
Goulding, Thomas, Seasalter, Kent, 1664 CKS PRC1/9/117
Goulding, Thomas, Whitchurch, Shrops, 1685 LJRO/B/C/5/1685/44
Gouldinge, John, Linton, Kent, 1661 CKS PRC1/8/99
Gouldinge, William, Linton, Kent, 1664 CKS PRC1/10/40
Gouldingham, Edward, university: 'Fellow of Trinity College, Cambridge/M.A.', Cambridge, Cambs, 1614 CUL V.C.Acc./Box1/23
Gouldsborowe, Richard, tailor, Lincoln, Lincs, 1614 Lincs RO Ad/Ac/12/190
Gouldsmith, John, Brook, Kent, 1632 CKS PRC2/31/32

[Gouldsmithe:]
Gouldsmithe, William, High Halden, Kent, 1613 CKS PRC2/18/54
Goulducke, Nicholas, Didling, Sussex, 1618 W. Suss RO EpI/33/1618/14
Gouldwell, Margrett, Spalding, Lincs, 1639? Lincs RO Ad/Ac/26/99
Goulsney, Richard, husbandman, Wimborne Minster (Leigh), Dors, 1615 Dorset RO PE/WM CP 2/4/17
Goulson, Christopher, Seasalter, Kent, 1630 CKS PRC20/9/163
Goulson, Thomas, Whitstable, Kent, 1629 CKS PRC2/30/62
Goulston, Robert, gentleman, Clewer, Berks, 1620 Berks RO D/A1/191/134A
Goulston, Robert, Warden, Kent, 1647 CKS PRC1/8/17
Gourley, Thomas, mr, Dover, Kent, 1630 CKS PRC20/9/203
Gourley, William, Ickham, Kent, 1674 CKS PRC20/12/129
Gourney/Gurner, Edward, labourer, Whitstable, Kent, 1693 CKS PRC2/42/63
Gourneye, John, Throwleigh, Kent, 1612 CKS PRC2/16/19
Gover, William, Sparkford, Som, 1594 Somerset RO D/D/Cta/G11
Gover, William, husbandman, Sparkford, Som, 1594 Somerset RO D/D/Cta/G30
Govett, Robert, Kilton, Som, 1663 Somerset RO D/D/Cta/G40
Gowen, Samuel, Acle, Norf, 1778 Norfolk RO ANW/23/26/44
Gowen, William, yeoman, Gislingham, Suff, 1778 Suff RO(B) IC500/3/52/39
Gower, Edward, Canterbury Holy Cross Westgate, Kent, 1595 CKS PRC2/7/169
Gower, John, Staplehurst, Kent, 1592 CKS PRC2/6/326
Gower, John, Tytherley, East, Hants, 1626 Hants RO 21M65 D8/117
Gower, Samuel, bachelor, Inkberrow, Worcs, 1794 Worcs RO 008.7 BA3585/835/bdl 2
Gowldock, Thomazine, spinster, Hucking, Kent, 1624 CKS PRC20/6/26
Gowle, William, Stratton St Margaret, Wilts, 1597 Wilts RO Dean Sarum (name + date)
Gowrley, Jacob, Maidstone, Kent, 1615 CKS PRC20/3/290
Goxhill, Elizabeth, widow, Goxhill, Lincs, 1618 Lincs RO Ad/Ac/14/154
Goyles, George, Tenterden, Kent, 1639 CKS PRC2/34/208
Grace, Richard, innholder, Amesbury, Wilts, 1592 Wilts RO Arch. Sarum(+ name and date)
Grace, Richard, Grandborough, Bucks, 1615 Herts RO ASA25/4820
Grace, Thomas, gentleman, Desford, Leics, 1666 Leics RO Administrators Accounts C17th f66
Grace, William, cook, Abingdon, Berks, 1670 Berks RO D/A1/192/87A
Graden, Edmund, Taunton, Som, 1626 Somerset RO D/D/Cta/C4
Gradwell, Roger, Leyland, Lancs, 1598 Lancs RO (Name of Deceased) D.R.C.H. 1597
Graffton, Andrew, Preston Bagot, Warks, 1675 Worcs RO 008.7 BA3585/835/bdl 1
Grafton, Mary, widow, Salisbury, Wilts, 1677 Wilts RO Miscellaneous Index (name + date)
Grafton, Richard, Canning, Bishops, Wilts, 1632 Wilts RO Dean and Chapter B20
Grafton, Richard, Salisbury, Wilts, 1675 Wilts RO Miscellaneous Index (name + date)
Grafton, Robart, St Johns Thanet, Kent, 1596 CKS PRC2/8/399
Graie, John, Ash next Sandwich, Kent, 1609 CKS PRC20/1/346
Graie, William, clergy: 'clerk', Grainthorpe, Lincs, 1620 Lincs RO Ad/Ac/16/45
Grainge, William, husbandman, Sidlesham, Sussex, W. Suss RO EpI/33/1613/22
Grainger, George, 1679 LJRO:cards/1679/3
Grainger, Peter, husbandman, Harpswell, Lincs, 1669? Lincs RO Ad/Ac/33/168
Grainger, Thomas, husbandman, Eagle, Lincs, 1634 Lincs RO Ad/Ac/24/41
Graistocke, John, husbandman, Scarle, North, Lincs, 1627 Lincs RO Ad/Ac/20/102
Grandsden, James, Canterbury Holy Cross Westgate, Kent, 1638 CKS PRC20/10/440
Grandsden, James, tanner, Canterbury Holy Cross Westgate, Kent, 1638 CKS PRC20/10/436
Grangeman, John, Bapchild, Kent, 1596 CKS PRC2/8/467
Granger, Jane, widow, St James Westminster, London & Middlesex, 1729 Greater London RO DL/C/548/11
Granger, Richard, clergy: 'clerk', Frittenden, Kent, 1596 CKS PRC2/8/196
Grant, John, miller, Hawkhurst, Kent, 1641 CKS PRC1/4/50
Grant, John, Skidbrooke, Lincs, 1649 Lincs RO Ad/Ac/30/117
Grant, John, Hawkhurst, Kent, 1686 CKS PRC2/41/28
Grant, Nicolas, Ewell, Kent, 1639 CKS PRC2/34/212

Grant, Peter, victualler, Bristol, Glos, Bristol RO 1677/54
Grant, Richard + Mary, Hanwell, Oxon, 1678 Oxon RO MSS Wills 80/2/34
Grant, Robert, yeoman, St Nicholas at Wade, Kent, 1687 CKS PRC20/13/551
Grant, Simon, Sandhurst, Kent, 1631 CKS PRC20/9/189
Grant, Walter, Monkton Farleigh, Wilts, 1685 Wilts RO Arch. Sarum(+ name and date)
Grant, William, Sandwich St Mary, Kent, 1639 CKS PRC1/2/68
Grant, William, Sutton Valence, Kent, 1639 CKS PRC1/2/69
Grant, William, Stickney, Lincs, 1774 Lincs RO Ad/Ac/45/38
Grante, Richard, husbandman, Moulton, Lincs, 1618 Lincs RO Ad/Ac/14/104
Grante, William, Dover, Kent, 1627 CKS PRC20/8/232
Grantham, John, Milton next Sittingbourne, Kent, 1614 CKS PRC2/21/38
Grantham, Thomas, Elkington, South, Lincs, 1614 Lincs RO Ad/Ac/13/133
Grantham, William, Whaplode, Lincs, 1652 Lincs RO Ad/Ac/29/19
Grantham, William, husbandman, Faldingworth, Lincs, 1682 Lincs RO Ad/Ac/44/28
Grantham, William, mariner: 'purser', Gombroune Rd, Persia, 1701 Lambeth Palace Arches G51/1
Grantham/Wright, Frances, Owersby, Lincs, 1611 Lincs RO Ad/Ac/10/108
Grantham, see Brinsbury,
Grascombe, Nathaniel, Mancetter (Hartshill), Warks, 1675 LJRO:cards/1675/27
Grasman, Richard, Lancing, Sussex, 1671 W. Suss RO EpI/33/1671/7
Grasonne, George, Cammeringham, Lincs, 1599 Lincs RO Ad/Ac/37/84
Grathorne/Craythorne, William, yeoman, Whitstable, Kent, 1646 CKS PRC1/7/85
Gratwicke, John, Coombes, Sussex, 1634 W. Suss RO EpI/33/1634/3
Gratwicke, William, Shipley, Sussex, 1631 W. Suss RO EpI/33/1631/23
Graunt, Christopher, Holt, Wilts, 1626 Wilts RO Arch. Sarum(+ name and date)
Graunt, Gervase, Cuxwold, Lincs, 1618 Lincs RO Ad/Ac/14/224
Graunt, Isabell, widow, Sandwich St Peter, Kent, 1609 CKS PRC2/14/200
Graunt, John, St Johns Thanet, Kent, 1623 CKS PRC2/23/126
Graunt, John, yeoman, Skidbrooke, Lincs, 1640 Lincs RO Ad/Ac/27/56
Graunt, John, Hallington, Lincs, 1652 Lincs RO Ad/Ac/29/5
Graunt, John, Wolfhampcote, Warks, 1685 LJRO/B/C/5/1685/45
Graunt, Nicholas, Monkton, Kent, 1662 CKS PRC19/3/10
Graunt, Susann, widow, Lincoln, Lincs, 1627 Lincs RO Ad/Ac/20b/104
Graunt, Thomas, Grinstead, West, Sussex, 1629 W. Suss RO EpI/33/1629/13
Graunt, Thomas, Edington, Wilts, 1639 Wilts RO Arch. Sarum(+ name and date)
Graunt, Thomas,
Jamaica 1700 PRO PROB5/1148
Graunte, Alice, Benenden, Kent, 1586 CKS PRC2/4/108
Graunte, George, Wootton, Kent, 1592 CKS PRC2/6/348
Graunte, Thomas, St Peter in Thanet, Kent, 1596 CKS PRC2/8/429
Gravatt, John, Hambledon, Hants, 1697 Hants RO 1696 AD40/2
Grave, Hester, widow, Kirton, Lincs, 1627 Lincs RO Ad/Ac/20b/31
Grave, William, Kirton, Lincs, 1625 Lincs RO Ad/Ac/19B/98
Gravener, Samuel, Coventry Holy Trinity, Warks, 1684 LJRO/B/C/5/1684/38
Graves, Anne, widow, Spalding, Lincs, 1790 Lincs RO Ad/Ac/45/60
Graves, Bartholomewe + Frances, yeoman, Algarkirk, Lincs, 1620 Lincs RO Ad/Ac/16/43
Graves, Humphrey, Kirton, Lincs, 1646 Lincs RO Ad/Ac/28/249
Graves, James, Tarring, West, Sussex, 1683 W. Suss RO EpIV/10/2A/28
Graves, Rychard, Westwell, Kent, 1619 CKS PRC20/4/107
Graves, Sarah, Barham, Kent, 1678 CKS PRC2/38/32
Graves, Susan, Wickenby, Lincs, 1638 Lincs RO Ad/Ac/25/2
Graves, Thomas, Algarkirk, Lincs, 1619 Lincs RO Ad/Ac/15/7
Graves, William, innholder, Horncastle, Lincs, 1683 Lincs RO Ad/Ac/44/123
Graves, William, stationer/bookseller, Cambridge St Mary the Great, Cambs, 1712 CUL V.C. Acc./Box3/27

[Gravet:]
Gravet, Richard, Findon, Sussex, 1597 W. Suss RO EpI/33/1596/18
Grawnte, Bartholomew, cooper, Walmer, Kent, 1605 CKS PRC2/14/204
Grawnte, John, Walmer, Kent, 1610 CKS PRC2/15/159
Grawnte, Leonarde, St Peter in Thanet, Kent, 1606 CKS PRC2/13/198
Grawnte, Marckes, Sandwich St Mary, Kent, 1610 CKS PRC2/15/147
Grawson, Gregorie, carpenter, Spalding, Lincs, 1626 Lincs RO Ad/Ac/20/3
Gray, Andrew, glover, Canterbury Holy Cross Westgate, Kent, 1715 CKS PRC1/17/70
Gray, Elizabeth, Milton next Sittingbourne, Kent, 1664 CKS PRC1/10/41
Gray, George, Borden, Kent, 1617 CKS PRC2/21/34
Gray, George, Bredgar, Kent, 1672 CKS PRC2/35/44
Gray, Henry, Chisledon, Wilts, 1677 Wilts RO Miscellaneous Index (name + date)
Gray, Henry, Burcombe, Wilts, 1681 Wilts RO Arch. Sarum(+ name and date)
Gray, James, bachelor, St Christopher le Stock, London & Middlesex, 1698 PRO PROB5/1749
Gray, Jasper, Homington, Wilts, 1678 Wilts RO Dean and Chapter J60
Gray, Joane, Wilton, Wilts, 1682 Wilts RO Arch. Sarum(+ name and date)
Gray, John, Bersted, South, Sussex, 1640 W. Suss RO EpIV/10/2/33
Gray, John, Ilmington, Warks, 1680 Worcs RO 008.7 BA3585/837/bdl 2
Gray, John, Fisherton Anger, Wilts, 1760? Wilts RO Miscellaneous Index (name + date)
Gray, Mathew, clergy: 'clerk', Sturry, Kent, 1671 CKS PRC2/35/48
Gray, Ralph, Nonington, Kent, 1620 CKS PRC20/4/99
Gray, Richard, St Albans St Peters, Herts, 1605 Herts RO ASA25/4752
Gray, Richard, Wimborne Minster, Dors, 1625 Dorset RO PE/WM CP 2/4/32
Gray, Richard, Chilham, Kent, 1632 CKS PRC2/31/118
Gray, Richard, husbandman, Warfield, Berks, 1685 Berks RO D/A1/192/125D
Gray, Samuel, Southrepps, Norf, 1750 Norfolk RO ANF/11/4/79
Gray, Thomas, Sompting, Sussex, 1625 W. Suss RO EpI/33/1625/4
Gray, Thomas, Kingston, Sussex, 1629 W. Suss RO EpI/33/1629/22
Gray, Thomas, gardener, Maidstone, Kent, 1663 CKS PRC19/3/11
Gray, Thomas, Stanton upon Hine Heath, Shrops, 1667 LJRO:cards/1667/37
Gray, Thomas, innholder, Amesbury, Wilts, 1680 Wilts RO Arch. Sarum(+ name and date)
Gray, Thomas, gentleman, Stratfield Mortimer, Berks, 1682 Berks RO D/A1/192/115D
Gray, William, Kingsnorth, Kent, 1634 CKS PRC2/32/48
Gray, William, St Peter in Thanet, Kent, 1665 CKS PRC1/11/34
Gray, William, husbandman, Kintbury, Berks, 1679 Berks RO D/A1/192/105D
Gray/Crouch, Elizabeth, widow, Woodchurch, Kent, 1669 CKS PRC19/4/52
Graye, Frawncis, Oare, Kent, 1615 CKS PRC2/21/35
Graye, George, Stockbury, Kent, 1582 CKS PRC2/2/215
Graye, Richard, Stodmarsh, Kent, 1618 CKS PRC2/21/50
Graye, Richard, Bepton, Sussex, 1627 W. Suss RO EpI/33/1627/2
Graye, Richarde, Sellindge, Kent, 1596 CKS PRC2/9/117
Graye, Robert, Graveney, Kent, 1601 CKS PRC2/12/163
Graye, Rowland, Faversham, Kent, 1586 CKS PRC2/4/384
Graye, William, Canterbury St Paul, Kent, 1596 CKS PRC2/9/126
Graye, William, Benington, Lincs, 1619 Lincs RO Ad/Ac/15/69
Grayling, Alexander, Cranbrook, Kent, 1629 CKS PRC2/29/44
Graystocke, Ralfe, husbandman, Scarle, North, Lincs, 1636 Lincs RO Ad/Ac/24/561
Gready, Richard, gentleman, Wroot, Lincs, 1665 Lincs RO Ad/Ac/41/169
Greatbach, William, Chester, Ches, 1669 Cheshire RO (Name) W.C. 1669
Greathead, George, Blyton, Lincs, 1618 Lincs RO Ad/Ac/8b/294
Greatorex, John, gaoler, Derby, Derby, 1743 LJRO/B/C/5/1744/202
Greatrix, Thomas, farmer, Colton, Staffs, 1805 LJRO/B/C/5/1805/23
Greaves, James, plumber/glazier, Stoke-upon-Trent, Staffs, 1782 LJRO/B/C/5/1782/77
Greaves, John, Birstall, Leics, 1639 Leics RO PR/I/41A/13
Greaves, Jonathon, Beighton, Derby, 1682 LJRO/B/C/5/1682/41
Greaves, Richard, innkeeper, Prescot, Lancs, 1742 Lancs RO (Name of Deceased) D.R.C.H. 1742

Greaves, Robert, husbandman, Claypole, Lincs, 1614 Lincs RO Ad/Ac/12/187
Greaves, Thomas, Barnet, East, Herts, 1621 Herts RO ASA25/2721
Greaves, Thomas, labourer, Claypole, Lincs, 1638 Lincs RO Ad/Ac/27/49
Greaves, Thomas, Felkirk (Havercroft), Yorks, 1717 Borthwick Test C.P. 1717/9
Grebbie, Agnes, Leake, Lincs, 1594 Lincs RO Ad/Ac/5/517
Grediers, David, maltster, St Johns Thanet, Kent, 1650 CKS PRC1/8/67
Gree, John, Glentham, Lincs, 1681 Lincs RO Ad/Ac/42/88
Greedier, John, mariner, St Johns Thanet, Kent, 1666 CKS PRC1/11/121
Green, Edmund, yeoman, Wytham, Berks, 1684 Berks RO D/A1/192/121D
Green, Edmund, St Bride, London & Middlesex, 1702 Lambeth Palace Arches G51/4
Green, Edward, Solihull, Warks, 1681 LJRO/B/C/5/1682/44
Green, Elizabeth, widow, Sutton, Long, Lincs, 1683 Lincs RO Ad/Ac/44/86
Green, George, Brabourne, Kent, 1674 CKS PRC2/35/217
Green, Henry, bachelor, Eastchurch, Sheppey, Kent, 1672 CKS PRC2/35/139
Green, John, husbandman, Marsham, Norf, Norfolk RO ANW/23/24/136
Green, John, mariner: 'seaman', Dover, Kent, 1632 CKS PRC20/10/402
Green, John, yeoman, Rothwell, Lincs, 1676 Lincs RO Ad/Ac/34/34
Green, John, Barton, Lincs, 1683 Lincs RO Ad/Ac/44/102
Green, John, Stone, Staffs, 1684 LJRO/B/C/5/1684/39
Green, John, Lympne, Kent, 1713 CKS PRC1/17/56
Green, John, Downham Market, Norf, 1771 Norfolk RO ANF/11/5/92
Green, John, Checkley (Hollington), Staffs, 1830 LJRO/B/C/5/1830/12
Green, John, farmer, Almondbury (Yateholme), Yorks, 1836 Borthwick Test C.P. 1836/2
Green, Mary, Leeds, Kent, 1670 CKS PRC1/15/31
Green, Mary, Coleshill, Warks, 1680s LJRO/B/C/5/1682/45
Green, Mary, widow, Bury St Edmunds, Suff, 1776 Suff RO(B) IC500/3/52/21
Green, Nicholas, Scampton, Lincs, 1661 Lincs RO Ad/Ac/41/102
Green, Nicholas, Scampton, Lincs, 1668? Lincs RO Ad/Ac/33/88
Green, Phillip, brickmaker, Gloucester, Glos, 1723 GRO GDR/B4/2/G61
Green, Richard, Monks Horton, Kent, 1717 CKS PRC1/18/5
Green, Robert, Caenby, Lincs, 1664 Lincs RO Ad/Ac/41/152
Green, Robert, yeoman, Tetsworth, Oxon, 1674 Oxon RO MSS Wills Pec 39/5/20
Green, Thomas, Newington next Sittingbourne, Kent, 1672 CKS PRC2/35/45
Green, Thomas, Halesowen, Worcs, 1685 Worcs RO 008.7 BA3585/830/85
Green, Thomas, mason, Headington, Oxon, 1723 Oxon RO MSS Wills 166/4/4
Green, Thomas, Spixworth, Norf, 1768 Norfolk RO ANW/23/25/89C
Green, Walter, Stockton (Boningale), Shrops, 1696 LJRO/B/C/5/1696/20a, b
Green, Walter, Liverpool, Lancs, 1791 Lancs RO (Name of Deceased) D.R.C.H. 1790
Green, William, farmer, Combs, Suff, 1818 Suff RO(B) IC500/3/53/120
Greenbank, John, Worcester St Swithin, Worcs, 1682 Worcs RO 008.7 BA3585/830/61
Greene, Alice, widow, Epworth, Lincs, 1618 Lincs RO Ad/Ac/8b/181
Greene, Alice, widow, Epworth, Lincs, 1621? Lincs RO Ad/Ac/8c/19
Greene, Anthony, Minster in Thanet, Kent, 1609 CKS PRC2/15/153
Greene, Bushey, Swineshead, Lincs, 1611 Lincs RO Ad/Ac/10/111
Greene, Daniell, Sandwich, Kent, 1619 CKS PRC2/21/51
Greene, Edmund, Worcester St Martin, Worcs, 1598 Worcs RO 008.7 BA3585/838/147
Greene, Edmund, Malvern, Great (Newland), Worcs, 1675 Worcs RO 008.7 BA3585/835/bdl 1
Greene, Edward, Knoyle, East, Wilts, 1619 Wilts RO Arch. Sarum(+ name and date)
Greene, Edward, yeoman, Immingham, Lincs, 1627 Lincs RO Ad/Ac/20b/95
Greene, Edward, husbandman, Fyfield (Woodhouse), Berks, 1690 Berks RO D/A1/192/139D
Greene, Eleonar, widow, Portsea, Hants, 1684 Hants RO 21m65 D8/341a
Greene, Franciss, fruiterer, Faversham, Kent, 1672 CKS PRC2/35/138
Greene, Gabriel, gentleman, Maidstone, Kent, 1630 CKS PRC20/8/238
Greene, George, Hale, Great, Lincs, 1612 Lincs RO Ad/Ac/11/115
Greene, George, Amberley, Sussex, 1651 W. Suss RO EpI/33/1650/6

[Greene:]
Greene, Gilberte, yeoman, Aslackby, Lincs, 1620 Lincs RO Ad/Ac/16/109
Greene, Henrie, Pinchbeck, Lincs, 1603 Lincs RO Ad/Ac/5/389
Greene, James, Aspenden, Herts, 1685 Herts RO AHH23/981
Greene, James, Salisbury, Wilts, 1702 Wilts RO Miscellaneous Index (name + date)
Greene, John, Mundham, North, Sussex, 1606 W. Suss RO EpI/33/1606/1
Greene, John, yeoman, Stainton le Vale, Lincs, 1625 Lincs RO Ad/Ac/19A/138
Greene, John, Halton Holgate, Lincs, 1629 Lincs RO Ad/Ac/22/76
Greene, John, St Albans St Michaels, Herts, 1634 Herts RO ASA25/4894
Greene, John, Chichester All Saints, Sussex, 1638 W. Suss RO EpIV/10/2/15
Greene, John, Marden, Up, Sussex, 1640 W. Suss RO EpI/33/1640/26
Greene, John, Minety, Glos, 1640 Wilts RO Arch. Wilts.(name + date)
Greene, John, weaver, Newbury, Berks, 1644 Berks RO D/A1/192/41A
Greene, John, Bitteswell, Leics, 1665 Leics RO Administrators Accounts C17th f11
Greene, John, bachelor, Warkton, Northants, 1671 Northants RO NWill A/C/99
Greene, John, Wittersham, Kent, 1674 CKS PRC20/12/128
Greene, Johnne, Waltham, Lincs, 1581 Lincs RO Ad/Ac/2b/70
Greene, Leonard, carpenter, Abingdon, Berks, 1612 Berks RO D/A1/191/94A
Greene, Leonard,
Oxon 1624 Oxon RO MSS Wills 297/3/32
Greene, Mark, glazier, Bristol St Thomas, Glos, Bristol RO 1678/76
Greene, Martine, Thorpe, Lincs, 1579 Lincs RO Ad/Ac/2b/15
Greene, Mathew, cordwainer, Abingdon St Helen, Berks, 1626 Berks RO D/A1/191/151C
Greene, Morgan, Lyme Regis, Dors, 1636 Wilts RO Miscellaneous Index (name + date)
Greene, Philip, St Albans, Herts, 1596 Herts RO ASA25/1548
Greene, Philip, Glastonbury St John, Som, 1638 Somerset RO D/D/Cta/G7
Greene, Richard, Ranby, Lincs, 1611 Lincs RO Ad/Ac/10/85
Greene, Richard, cook, Cambridge Holy Trinity, Cambs, 1629 CUL V.C. Acc./Box2/27
Greene, Richard, Sibsey, Lincs, 1670 Lincs RO Ad/Ac/32/167
Greene, Richard, Newcastle under Lyme, Staffs, 1681 LJRO/B/C/5/1682/42
Greene, Richard, butcher, Moulton, Lincs, 1683 Lincs RO Ad/Ac/44/114
Greene, Robert, Hacconby, Lincs, 1606 Lincs RO Ad/Ac/7/134
Greene, Robert, Stapleford, Lincs, 1623 Lincs RO Ad/Ac/18/56
Greene, Robert, tailor, Algarkirk, Lincs, 1624 Lincs RO Ad/Ac/19A/92
Greene, Robert, Aston Abbots, Bucks, 1632 Herts RO ASA25/4887
Greene, Robert, Algarkirk, Lincs, 1639 Lincs RO Ad/Ac/26/263
Greene, Thomas, Ogbourne St George, Wilts, 1600? Wilts RO Miscellaneous Index (name + date)
Greene, Thomas, 1621 Wilts RO Unlisted Fragment
Greene, Thomas, husbandman, Coxwell, Great, Berks, 1621 Berks RO D/A1/191/140A
Greene, Thomas, Burgh le Marsh, Lincs, 1637 Lincs RO Ad/Ac/25/378
Greene, Thomas, Firsby, Lincs, 1651 Lincs RO Ad/Ac/29/129
Greene, Thomas, Imber, Wilts, 1672 Wilts RO Arch. Sarum(+ name and date)
Greene, Thomas, husbandman, Tonge, Kent, 1683 CKS PRC2/40/116
Greene, Thomas sen, Coleshill, Berks, 1593 Berks RO D/A1/191/78C
Greene, William, Wyberton, Lincs, 1602 Lincs RO Ad/Ac/5/33
Greene, William, Boston, Lincs, 1611 Lincs RO Ad/Ac/10/19
Greene, William, Snitterby, Lincs, 1632 Lincs RO Ad/Ac/39/329
Greene, William, Cosby, Leics, 1641 Leics RO PR/I/41A/40
Greene, William, Stretton upon Dunsmore (Princethorpe), Warks, 1675 LJRO:cards/1675/28
Greene, William, Wirksworth, Derby, 1694 LJRO/B/C/5/1694/29
Greene, Wyllyam, Sevington, Kent, 1594 CKS PRC2/7/303
Greene, see Guy,
Greeneaway, Robert, miller, Newbury, Berks, 1609 Berks RO D/A1/191/109A
Greenehill, Thomas, Ashton, Steeple, Wilts, 1614 Wilts RO Arch. Sarum(+ name and date)
Greenell, Anne, Maidstone, Kent, 1634 CKS PRC20/10/414
Greenell, John, Maidstone, Kent, 1631 CKS PRC20/9/173

Greenenge, Isabel, widow, Tetsworth, Oxon, 1630 Oxon RO MSS Wills Pec 39/4/6
Greener, William, yeoman, Waltham St Lawrence, Berks, 1640 Berks RO D/A1/192/20C
Greener, William sen, tailor, Waltham St Lawrence, Berks, 1682 Berks RO D/A1/192/114D
Greenestreate, Obediah, Ivychurch, Kent, 1631 CKS PRC20/9/157
Greenestreet, Peter, gentleman, Ospringe, Kent, 1646 CKS PRC1/7/86
Greenestreete, Roberte, Stone next Faversham, Kent, 1620 CKS PRC2/21/32
Greenewaie, Peter, yeoman, Hendred, West (East Ginge), Berks, 1609 Berks RO D/A1/191/111A
Greeneway, John, yeoman, Buckland, Berks, 1618 Berks RO D/A1/191/130A
Greeneway, Thomas, Cassington, Oxon, 1645 Oxon RO MSS Wills 297/3/68
Greenewood, Adam, Boston, Lincs, 1624 Lincs RO Ad/Ac/20/60
Greenewood, William, Trusthorpe, Lincs, 1662 Lincs RO Ad/Ac/32/5
Greenfeild, Gervas, feltmaker, Boston, Lincs, 1673 Lincs RO Ad/Ac/35/12
Greenfeild, John,
Sussex 1651 W. Suss RO EpI/33/1651/6
Greenfeild, Maurice, Shipley, Sussex, 1682 W. Suss RO EpI/33/1682/22
Greenfeild, Thomas, Billingshurst, Sussex, 1669 W. Suss RO EpI/33/1669/20
Greenfeilde, John, Biddenden, Kent, 1599 CKS PRC2/11/225
Greenfeld, Thomas, Horsham, Sussex, 1651 W. Suss RO EpI/33/1651/2
Greengrasse, Thomas, mariner: 'seaman', Faversham, Kent, 1670 CKS PRC1/14/49
Greenhall, Francis, tanner, Banbury, Oxon, 1618 Oxon RO MSS Wills Pec 39/3/22
Greenham, Richard, soap boiler, Liverpool, Lancs, 1774 Lancs RO (Name of Deceased) D.R.C.H. 1774
Greenhill, John, Westbury, Wilts, 1742 Wilts RO Miscellaneous Index (name + date)
Greenhill, Richard, Canterbury St George Martyr, Kent, 1710 CKS PRC1/17/26
Greenhill, Richard, Canterbury St George Martyr, Kent, 1710 CKS PRC1/17/26a
Greenhill, William, Chidham, Sussex, 1631 W. Suss RO EpI/33/1630/3
Greening, John, husbandman, Wotton, North, Dors, 1610? Wilts RO Dean Sarum (name + date)
Greenleafe, Timothy, Dover, Kent, 1629 CKS PRC20/8/247
Greenleif, John, Pagham, Sussex, 1617 W. Suss RO EpIV/10/1/46
Greenstead, George, Fordwich, Kent, 1611 CKS PRC2/17/173
Greenstreet, Anna, mrs/widow, Ospringe, Kent, 1648 CKS PRC1/8/18
Greenstreet, Edward, yeoman, Norton, Kent, 1626 CKS PRC2/25/59
Greenstreet, Edward, Norton, Kent, 1627 CKS PRC2/27/57
Greenstreet, Elizabeth, Doddington, Kent, 1598 CKS PRC2/10/373
Greenstreet, Monnins, gentleman, Sittingbourne, Kent, 1713 CKS PRC1/17/57
Greenstreet, Monnins, Sittingbourne, Kent, 1714 CKS PRC1/17/57b
Greenstreet, Richard, St Thomas Isle of Harty, Kent, 1649 CKS PRC1/8/68
Greenstreet, Robert, jurat/mr, Faversham, Kent, 1663 CKS PRC1/9/118
Greenstreete, Anne, mrs/spinster, Ospringe, Kent, 1662 CKS PRC1/9/24
Greenstreete, Anne, widow, Faversham, Kent, 1682 CKS PRC2/40/32
Greenstreete, Elizabeth, widow, Ospringe, Kent, 1672 CKS PRC2/35/140
Greenstreete, George, Doddington, Kent, 1596 CKS PRC2/8/393
Greenstreete, Henry, yeoman, Ospringe, Kent, 1671 CKS PRC1/15/32
Greenstreete, Isaack, Eastling, Kent, 1630 CKS PRC2/30/67
Greenstreete, James, yeoman, Faversham, Kent, 1625 CKS PRC2/25/56
Greenstreete, Simon, apothecary, Faversham, Kent, 1685 CKS PRC2/41/30
Greenstreete, Thomas, Stalisfield, Kent, 1596 CKS PRC2/8/423
Greenstreete, William, Stalisfield, Kent, 1596 CKS PRC2/9/289
Greenstrete, Peter, bachelor, Sandwich St Mary, Kent, 1670 CKS PRC1/14/50
Greentree, Thomas, Wimbledon, Surrey, 1730 Lambeth Palace VH82/96
Greenwood, John, fellmonger, Faversham, Kent, 1679 CKS PRC2/38/135
Greenwood, John, St John the Baptist Savoy, London & Middlesex, 1731 Greater London RO AM/CP Box 1720-1768 pt (uncatalogued)
Greenwood, William, miller, Calverley, Yorks, 1814 Borthwick Test C.P. 1814/1
Greenwood, William, clothier, Dewsbury, Yorks, 1817 Borthwick Test C.P. 1816/6

[Greetam:]
Greetam, Richard, Whitby (Eskdaleside), Yorks, 1719 Borthwick Test C.P. 1719/5
Greetham/Chipman, William, husbandman, Fyfield, Berks, 1594 Berks RO D/A1/71/110D
Greey, Thomas, Paxton, Little, Hunts, 1676 Hunts RO/Acc58/69(133)
Gregg, Humfrey, husbandman, Mathon, Worcs, 1599 Worcs RO 008.7 BA3585/838/149
Gregg, John, Horbling, Lincs, 1638 Lincs RO Ad/Ac/25/490
Gregg, Thomas, yeoman, Langtoft, Lincs, 1637 Lincs RO Ad/Ac/24/405
Gregge, Michaell, Billinghay, Lincs, 1579 Lincs RO Ad/Ac/2b/35
Gregge, Paulle, Pinchbeck, Lincs, 1614 Lincs RO Ad/Ac/13/41
Greggorie, Richard, Gainsborough (East Stockwith), Lincs, 1629 Lincs RO Ad/Ac/39/106
Gregorie, John, Ditcheat, Som, 1612 Somerset RO D/D/Cta/G20
Gregorie, Richard, Milton next Sittingbourne, Kent, 1613 CKS PRC2/18/58
Gregorie, Richard, Petham, Kent, 1666 CKS PRC1/11/122
Gregorie, Thomas, Brightwell, Berks, Berks RO D/A1/71/124D
Gregorie, Thomas, Linton, Kent, 1594 CKS PRC2/7/201
Gregorie, Thomas, husbandman, Baldock, Herts, 1638 Herts RO AHH23/948
Gregory, Edmond, yeoman, Severnake, Wilts, 1683 Wilts RO CC Sarum(+ name and date)
Gregory, George, Oxford St Mary Magdalene, Oxon, 1673 Oxon RO MSS Wills 80/2/22
Gregory, Jacob, haberdasher, St Lawrence Jewry, London & Middlesex, 1682 PRO PROB5/1784
Gregory, James, Charlton Horethorne, Som, 1714 Somerset RO D/D/Cta/G17
Gregory, John, gentleman, Bucklebury, Berks, 1668 Berks RO D/A1/192/79D
Gregory, John, gentleman, Islington St Mary, London & Middlesex, 1674 PRO PROB32/11/42
Gregory, John, Hernhill, Kent, 1687 CKS PRC20/13/553
Gregory, Joseph, yeoman, Youlgreave, Derby, 1801 LJRO/B/C/5/1801/25
Gregory, Paul, gentleman, Brill, Bucks, 1678 Lambeth Palace Arches G29/1
Gregory, Robert eld, Barton St David, Som, 1641 Somerset RO D/D/Cta/G29
Gregory, Thomas, labourer, Sleaford, New, Lincs, 1667? Lincs RO Ad/Ac/42/24
Gregory, William, husbandman, Moreton, North, Berks, 1635 Berks RO D/A1/72/84D
Gregory, William, yeoman, Youlgreave, Derby, 1808 LJRO/B/C/5/1808/22
Gregorye, Thomas, Ridge, Herts, 1571 Herts RO ASA25/708
Gregson, James, Edenham, Lincs, 1639 Lincs RO Ad/Ac/26/157
Gregson, Thomas, Morton, Lincs, 1638 Lincs RO Ad/Ac/25/179
Greinfeild, Michael eld, Billingshurst, Sussex, W. Suss RO EpI/33/1602
Grene, Harry, Elstree, Herts, 1567 Herts RO ASA25/641
Grene, Jane, Canterbury St John's Hospital, Kent, 1578 CKS PRC21/3/254
Grene, see Gladman,
Greneawaye, Thomas, Lydd, Kent, 1582 CKS PRC21/6/26
Grenefeild, Richard, Billingshurst, Sussex, 1620 W. Suss RO EpI/33/1619/4
Greneland, see Mussared,
Grenell, John, Borden, Kent, 1600 CKS PRC2/11/229
Grenell, Thomas, Rolvenden, Kent, 1591 CKS PRC2/5/98
Grenestrete, George, clergy: 'clerk', Chillenden, Kent, 1591 CKS PRC2/5/150
Grenfeild, William, Arundel, Sussex, 1635 W. Suss RO EpI/33/1635/21
Grenfeld, Mathew, Chichester St Andrew, Sussex, 1593 W. Suss RO EpI/33/1593/4
Grenfeld, see Hewet,
Grenfell, Edward, Lyminster, Sussex, 1671 W. Suss RO EpI/33/1671/11
Grennell, John, Frittenden, Kent, 1596 CKS PRC2/8/194
Grennell, John, Milton next Sittingbourne, Kent, 1631 CKS PRC20/9/179
Grennoay, Richard, Whitstable, Kent, 1638 CKS PRC2/34/216
Gresley, Mary, mrs, 1680 PRO PROB32/18/67
Gressam, John, waterman, Billinghay, Lincs, 1636 Lincs RO Ad/Ac/24/413
Gressom, Edward, Birchington, Kent, 1593 CKS PRC21/12/64
Grestocke, William, Claypole, Lincs, 1597 Lincs RO Ad/Ac/4/74
Greswell, Frauncis, Gainsborough (Northolme), Lincs, 1613 Lincs RO Ad/Ac/12/96
Greswell, John, Barlings, Lincs, Lincs RO Ad/Ac/2C/160
Greswell, John, Blankney, Lincs, 1623 Lincs RO Ad/Ac/17/37

Greswell, Richard, labourer, Blankney, Lincs, 1640 Lincs RO Ad/Ac/27/92
Grevet, Robert, Durrington, Sussex, 1615 W. Suss RO EpIV/10/1/54
Grevett, Richard, Broadwater (Worthing), Sussex, 1629 W. Suss RO EpI/33/1629/20
Grevett, William, Shipley, Sussex, 1620 W. Suss RO EpI/33/1619/7
Grevill, Francis, Cropredy (Mollington), Oxon, 1678 Northants RO NWill A/C/141
Grevott, John, Broadwater, Sussex, 1633 W. Suss RO EpI/33/1633/23
Grewbie, William, cordwainer: 'shoemaker', Burton on Stather, Lincs, 1664 Lincs RO Ad/Ac/41/147
Grewell, John, joiner, New Romney, Kent, 1641 CKS PRC19/1/47
Grewer, William, Faversham, Kent, 1637 CKS PRC20/10/446
Grewer, see Gruer,
Grey, Henry, St Botolph without Aldersgate, London & Middlesex, 1677 PRO PROB5/1765
Grice, Joseph, Wellington (Hadley), Shrops, 1667 LJRO:cards/1667/38
Grice, Robert, glover, Chester, Ches, 1639 Cheshire RO (Name) W.C. 1638
Grice, Roger, Dover, Kent, 1596 CKS PRC21/14/37
Grice, William, Dover, Kent, 1605 CKS PRC21/17/279
Griffin, Anne, Stilton, Hunts, 1683 Hunts RO/Acc58/198(48)
Griffin, Edwarde, Barham, Kent, 1593 CKS PRC2/6/190
Griffin, Joan, widow, Rustington, Sussex, 1682 W. Suss RO EpI/33/1682/17
Griffin, John, Chippenham, Wilts, 1667? Wilts RO Miscellaneous Index (name + date)
Griffin, John, miller, Wappenbury (Eathorpe), Warks, 1672 LJRO:cards/1672/24
Griffin, John, baker, Birmingham, Warks, 1792 LJRO/B/C/5/1791/29
Griffin, John, baker, Birmingham, Warks, 1792 LJRO/B/C/5/1792/34
Griffin, John, baker, Birmingham, Warks, 1792 LJRO/B/C/5/1792/35
Griffin, Joseph, Mersham, Kent, 1649 CKS PRC1/8/69
Griffin, Margaret, wife, Wrawby cum Brigg, Lincs, 1627 Lincs RO Ad/Ac/20/96
Griffin, Owen, mr/widower, St Martin in the Fields, London & Middlesex, 1718 Greater London RO AM/PP/Box 1715-1719 pt (uncatalogued)
Griffin, Robert, Sandwich St Bartholomew's Hospital, Kent, 1614 CKS PRC20/2/452
Griffin, Rowland, Fordwich, Kent, 1610 CKS PRC2/15/157
Griffin, Sara, Chart, Great, Kent, 1626 CKS PRC2/27/55
Griffin, Thomas, Irthlingborough, Northants, 1680 Northants RO NWill A/C/6
Griffin, Thomas, mason: 'stone mason', Birmingham, Warks, 1804 LJRO/B/C/5/1804/18
Griffin, William, Brightwell Baldwin, Oxon, 1638 Oxon RO MSS Wills 297/3/47
Griffin/Littleton, Daniel, Gomeroon, Persia, 1714 PRO PROB5/1143
Griffine, Alice, widow, Godmersham, Kent, 1608 CKS PRC20/1/386
Griffis, Paul, watchmaker, Birmingham, Warks, 1784 LJRO/B/C/5/1784/50
Griffith, James, clergy: 'clerk', Kirkby Underwood, Lincs, 1623 Lincs RO Ad/Ac/17/74
Griffith, Thomas, cordwainer, Hagbourne, Berks, 1662 Berks RO D/A1/192/67C
Griffith, Thomas, watchchain maker, Birmingham, Warks, 1788 LJRO/B/C/5/1788/29
Griffith, Thomas John, Llansbyddyd, Breck, NLW BR 1637/107 Ac
Griffith ap John, William, Llanfihangel-Nant-Bran, Breck, NLW BR 1620/43 Ac
Griffiths, Jonathan, Shrewsbury St Chad, Shrops, 1681 LJRO/B/C/5/1681/19
Griffiths, Joseph, St Michael Cornhill, London & Middlesex, 1756 Greater London RO DL/C/554/1/2
Griffyn, see Jones,
Grifte, Thomas, Glastonbury, Som, 1611 Somerset RO D/D/Cta/G16
Grig, see Mace,
Grigbye, Alexander, gentleman, Mersham, Kent, 1587 CKS PRC2/4/69
Grigg, Henrie, Barham, Kent, 1617 CKS PRC2/21/57
Grigge, Richard, Eastergate, Sussex, 1619 W. Suss RO EpI/33/1618/15
Grigge, William, Northaw, Herts, Herts RO ASA25/4939
Grigges, John, Rainham, Kent, 1596 CKS PRC2/8/477
Grigges, Peter, Bridge, Kent, 1665 CKS PRC1/10/42
Griggs, Christian, widow, Barham, Kent, 1666 CKS PRC1/11/123

[Griggs:]
Griggs, Giles, Sandwich, Kent, 1685 CKS PRC2/41/29
Griggs, John, Middlezoy, Som, 1626 Somerset RO D/D/Cta/G4
Griggs, Richard, Milton next Sittingbourne, Kent, 1639 CKS PRC1/2/70
Griggs, Stephen, glover, Faversham, Kent, 1687 CKS PRC2/41/94
Griggs, Whittingham, smith, Chartham, Kent, 1679 CKS PRC2/38/130
Grigsbie, Isaacke, gentleman, Mersham, Kent, 1605 CKS PRC2/14/197
Grigsbie, Richard, Chart, Great, Kent, 1640 CKS PRC1/4/51
Grigson, John, Elmley Lovett, Worcs, 1678 Worcs RO 008.7 BA3585/830/95
Grills, Mark, Calstock, Corn, 1605 Cornwall RO AP/G49/3
Grim, Ann, widow, Fordwich, Kent, 1624 CKS PRC2/23/141
Grimbleby, Robert, Clee (Cleethorpes), Lincs, 1648 Lincs RO Ad/Ac/30/306
Grime, Thomas, Stainfield, Lincs, 1612 Lincs RO Ad/Ac/11/186
Grime, William, yeoman, Theddlethorpe, Lincs, 1626 Lincs RO Ad/Ac/20/42
Grime/Wagstaffe, Anne,
Leics 1685 Leics RO Administrators Accounts 1682-86 f42
Grimes, James, Burmarsh, Kent, 1686 CKS PRC2/41/53
Grimeshawe, John, Horsington, Lincs, 1606 Lincs RO Ad/Ac/7/100
Grimland, see Tanner,
Grimsbye, Edward, Horkstow, Lincs, 1619 Lincs RO Ad/Ac/14/32
Grimsell, John, yeoman, Teynham, Kent, 1668 CKS PRC1/13/54
Grimsey/Grimstone, George, Boxley, Kent, 1614 CKS PRC2/18/22
Grimson, John, husbandman, Wolverhampton, Staffs, 1672 LJRO:cards/1672/25
Grimsteede, Andrew, Baltonsborough, Som, 1641 Somerset RO D/D/Cta/G21
Grimstone, Margerye, Sellindge, Kent, 1610 CKS PRC2/15/145
Grimstone, Stephen, Molash, Kent, 1627 CKS PRC2/28/48
Grimstone, see Grimsey,
Grindle, Richard, Longdon, Worcs, 1685 Worcs RO 008.7 BA3585/837/bdl 4
Grindley, Robert, Whitchurch, Shrops, 1674 LJRO:cards/1674/18
Grinhill, Worcester, Worcs, Worcs RO 008.7 BA3585/834/452
Grinnell, Hugh, Newington next Sittingbourne, Kent, 1635 CKS PRC2/33/54
Grinsbie, Ann, Horkstow, Lincs, 1639 Lincs RO Ad/Ac/26/55
Grire, William, Sandhurst, Kent, 1593 CKS PRC2/6/93
Grise, John, Pennard, West, Som, 1598 Somerset RO D/D/Cta/G26
Grist, Ann, Brookland, Kent, 1675 CKS PRC2/36/194
Grist, Thomas, Boxgrove, Sussex, 1684 W. Suss RO EpI/33/1684/35
Grivelle, Edward, gentleman, Adderbury, Oxon, 1637 Oxon RO MSS Wills 297/3/41
Groane, Peter, Croft, Lincs, 1650 Lincs RO Ad/Ac/29/99
Groggyn, John, Felpham, Sussex, 1596 W. Suss RO EpI/33/1596
Grolie, see Arnold,
Gromett, John, Berkhamsted St Peter, Herts, 1636 Herts RO AHH23/945
Gromitt, Richard, Morton/Bourne, Lincs, 1663 Lincs RO Ad/Ac/43/8
Grommett, John, Saltfleet Haven, Lincs, 1651 Lincs RO Ad/Ac/29/76
Groococke, Thomas, Laughton, Leics, 1673 Leics RO Administrators Accounts 1667-72 f128
Groome,
Som Somerset RO D/D/Cta/G12
Groome, Elinor, Shawbury, Shrops, 1674 LJRO:cards/1674/19
Grosier, Elizabeth, widow, Lissington, Lincs, 1669? Lincs RO Ad/Ac/33/112
Grosse, Erkenwall, husbandman, Pelynt, Corn, 1610 Cornwall RO AP/G108/3
Grosse, Jane, widow, Sturry, Kent, 1596 CKS PRC2/8/485
Grosse, Margaret + Daniel, Sturry, Kent, 1593 CKS PRC2/6/1
Grosvenor, Martha, Ercall, High, Shrops, 1675 LJRO:cards/1675/29
Grouse, Christopher, Spalding, Lincs, 1612 Lincs RO Ad/Ac/10/169
Grout, Chrysostome, yeoman, Hythe St Leonard, Kent, 1639 CKS PRC20/10/442
Grove, John, Maidenhead, Berks, Berks RO D/A1/1/158V
Grove, John, gentleman, Canterbury, Kent, 1635 CKS PRC19/1/4

Grove, John, Sparsholt, Berks, 1637 Berks RO D/A1/192/19C
Grove, Marie, Kirton, Lincs, 1631 Lincs RO Ad/Ac/23/85
Grove, Robert, bachelor, Salehurst (Robertsbridge), Sussex, 1690 PRO PROB5/1390
Grove, William, Appledore, Kent, 1595 CKS PRC2/8/167
Grove, William, Arborfield, Berks, 1597 Wilts RO Miscellaneous Index (name + date)
Grover, Sampson, Canterbury St Mildred, Kent, 1611 CKS PRC2/15/143
Groves, Thomas, Watford, Herts, 1753 Herts RO ASA25/4722
Growcoate, John, Hodnet, Shrops, 1681 LJRO/B/C/5/1681/18
Grub, John, St Albans, Herts, 1576 Herts RO ASA25/884
Gruer, Alyce, widow, Westwell, Kent, 1584 CKS PRC21/6/403
Gruer/Grewer, Thomas, Westwell, Kent, 1582 CKS PRC21/5/253
Grumbridge, Andrewe, Hawkhurst, Kent, 1621 CKS PRC20/5/73
Grummett, Richard, Grimoldby, Lincs, 1652 Lincs RO Ad/Ac/29/36
Grummett, Thomas, yeoman, Aslackby, Lincs, 1653 Lincs RO Ad/Ac/29/3
Grumwell, Elizabeth, widow, Westbury-on-Trym (Shirehampton), Glos, Bristol RO 1679/81b
Grundy, Edmund, butcher, Bolton-le-Moors, Lancs, 1753 Lancs RO (Name of Deceased) D.R.C.H. 1753
Grundy, John sen, yeoman, Lambourn (Isbury), Berks, 1663 Berks RO D/A1/192/68A
Gryffethe, Raffe, Hythe St Leonard, Kent, 1587 CKS PRC21/10/317
Gryffyth, John, Cauldon, Staffs, 1678 LJRO:cards/1678/13
Gryme, Symon, Fordwich, Kent, 1614 CKS PRC2/17/47
Gryme, Thomas, Sandwich St Clement, Kent, 1629 CKS PRC2/29/41
Gryme, Thomas, yeoman, Wardington, Oxon, 1631 Oxon RO MSS Wills Pec 39/4/11
Grymold, Thomas, yeoman, Whaplode, Lincs, 1614 Lincs RO Ad/Ac/13/141
Gubberd, Robert, Boxley, Kent, 1663 CKS PRC1/9/119
Gudgin, Robert, yeoman, Daventry, Northants, 1671 Northants RO NWill A/C/88
Guest, Joan, widow, Handsworth, Staffs, 1675 LJRO:cards/1675/30
Guest, Ralph, Pretwich, Lancs, 1766 Lancs RO (Name of Deceased) D.R.C.H. 1766
Guilford, Joane, widow, Linsted, Kent, 1620 CKS PRC2/21/41
Guilforde, Thomas, Linsted, Kent, 1605 CKS PRC2/15/149
Guise, Joseph, weaver/mr, Kidderminster, Worcs, 1765 Worcs RO 008.7 BA3585/836/bdl 2
Guiseing, George, Horncastle, Lincs, 1683 Lincs RO Ad/Ac/44/80
Gull, John, Billingborough, Lincs, 1623 Lincs RO Ad/Ac/18/54
Gull, Robert, tailor, Linton, Kent, 1672 CKS PRC2/35/136
Gull, Thomas, clothier, Linton, Kent, 1679 CKS PRC2/38/131
Gull, William, Linton, Kent, 1600 CKS PRC2/11/235
Gullifer, John, Wells St Cuthbert, Som, 1612 Somerset RO D/D/Cta/G19
Gulson, Maurice, clergy: 'clerk', Scartho, Lincs, 1614 Lincs RO Ad/Ac/13/175
Gumas, Margaret, Althorpe, Lincs, 1626 Lincs RO Ad/Ac/39/14
Gummas, William, Burgh le Marsh, Lincs, 1599 Lincs RO Ad/Ac/5/105
Gunby, Richard, Barkston, Lincs, 1664 Lincs RO Ad/Ac/43/36
Gundrie, John, Petherton, South, Som, 1634 Somerset RO D/D/Cta/G8
Gunn, Thomas, Lancing, Sussex, 1662 W. Suss RO EpI/33/1662/3
Gunn, Thomas, gentleman, Broadwater, Sussex, 1683 W. Suss RO EpI/33/1682/12
Gunnas, Anne, Luddington, Lincs, 1611 Lincs RO Ad/Ac/8a/333
Gunne, John, Wigtoft, Lincs, 1619 Lincs RO Ad/Ac/15/197
Gunnell, Anthony, Messingham, Lincs, 1665 Lincs RO Ad/Ac/41/166
Gunnell, John, yeoman, Wargrave, Berks, 1633 Berks RO D/A1/192/1A
Gunnill, John, Offord Cluney, Hunts, 1702 Hunts RO/Acc58/293
Gunningham, Mathew, Winscombe, Som, 1606 Somerset RO D/D/Cta/C45
Gunsley, Robert + Eliz, clergy: 'mr/clerk', Queenborough, Kent, 1638 CKS PRC1/1/76
Gunter, John, Duncton, Sussex, 1630 W. Suss RO EpI/33/1629/27
Gunter, William, Marlborough, Wilts, 1636 Wilts RO CC Sarum(+ name and date)
Gunter, see Piddington,
Gunthorpe, Edward, yeoman, Donington, Lincs, 1679 Lincs RO Ad/Ac/43/104

[Gunthorpe:]
Gunthorpe, Robert, Toynton, Lincs, 1632 Lincs RO Ad/Ac/23/134
Gurdan, William, brewer: 'beerbrewer', Hythe St Leonard, Kent, 1669 CKS PRC19/4/53
Gurden, George, yeoman, Whittlebury, Northants, 1763 Northants RO X954/21/6
Gurden, Margaret, widow, Headington, Oxon, 1633 Oxon RO MSS Wills 297/3/37
Gurdon, Richard, Headington, Oxon, 1625 Oxon RO MSS Wills 166/1/49
Gurle, Leonard, St Martin in the Fields, London & Middlesex, 1687 PRO PROB32/26/194
Gurnard, William, Sandwich, Kent, 1613 CKS PRC2/17/83
Gurner, see Gourney,
Gurney, Alice, widow, Eythorne, Kent, 1634 CKS PRC2/32/47
Gurr, Agnes, Appledore, Kent, 1627 CKS PRC2/28/49
Gurre, John, Rustington, Sussex, 1636 W. Suss RO EpI/33/1636
Gurwood, Thomas, Langton, Yorks, 1720 Borthwick Test C.P. 1721/5
Guslinge, John, yeoman, Trusthorpe, Lincs, 1646 Lincs RO Ad/Ac/28/210
Gutterd/Gutterson, Christopher, Limber Magna, Lincs, 1618 Lincs RO Ad/Ac/14/218
Gutterson, Thomas, Kirkby cum Osgodby, Lincs, 1646 Lincs RO Ad/Ac/28/168
Gutterson, see Gutterd,
Guy, Richard, Warnham, Sussex, 1598 W. Suss RO EpI/33/1598/1
Guy, William, Marlborough St Peter & St Paul, Wilts, 1621 Wilts RO CC Sarum(+ name and date)
Guy, William, Mundham, North, Sussex, 1682 W. Suss RO EpI/33/1682/23
Guy/Greene, John, Collingbourne Kingston, Wilts, 1621 Wilts RO Arch. Wilts.(name + date)
Guye, John, Dean, West, Sussex, 1610 W. Suss RO EpI/33/1610/2
Guyer, Jermaine, Beer Hackett, Dors, 1676 Wilts RO Dean Sarum (name + date)
Guyes, Nicholas, Goudhurst, Kent, 1626 CKS PRC2/27/58
Gwillam, William, Elmley Castle, Worcs, 1685 Worcs RO 008.7 BA3585/830/86
Gwines, Thomas, Sandwich St Clement, Kent, 1599 CKS PRC2/10/4
Gwinnett, George, Gloucester (Barton Street), Glos, GRO GDR/B4/2/G58
Gybbes, William, Westbere, Kent, 1583 CKS PRC2/3/69
Gybson, John, Appledore, Kent, 1613 CKS PRC2/16/153
Gybson, Thomas, Biddenden, Kent, 1614 CKS PRC2/21/36
Gybson, William, Elmsted, Kent, 1614 CKS PRC2/17/57
Gyfford, John, clergy: 'clerk', Witney, Oxon, 1631 Oxon RO MSS Wills 297/3/33
Gylbart, Arthur, Lydd, Kent, 1585 CKS PRC21/7/398
Gylbert, George, Canterbury St Mildred, Kent, 1592 CKS PRC2/5/35
Gylbert, Henry, Lyminge, Kent, 1586 CKS PRC21/8/71
Gylbert, John, Canterbury St Mildred, Kent, 1580 CKS PRC2/1/300
Gylbert, Laurence, Dover, Kent, 1625 CKS PRC20/6/24
Gylbert, Peter, Lyminge, Kent, 1608 CKS PRC20/1/306
Gylbert, Robert, Hythe St Leonard, Kent, 1580 CKS PRC21/4/144
Gylbert, Rychard, Charing, Kent, 1588 CKS PRC21/9/31
Gylbert, Stephen, Postling, Kent, 1587 CKS PRC2/4/190
Gylbye, Thomas, Navenby, Lincs, 1576 Lincs RO Ad/Ac/1/19
Gyles, Anne, Worcester All Saints, Worcs, 1680 Worcs RO 008.7 BA3585/837/bdl 2
Gyles, Elizabeth, widow, Beedon (Stanmore), Berks, 1621 Berks RO D/A1/72/2C
Gyles, Frauncis, gentleman, Sheldwich, Kent, 1611 CKS PRC20/2/196
Gyles, Gabriell eld, gentleman, Sheldwich, Kent, 1626 CKS PRC2/27/61
Gyles, John, Dover, Kent, 1624 CKS PRC20/6/28
Gyles, John, gentleman, Chislet, Kent, 1665 CKS PRC1/11/31
Gyles, John, gentleman, Chislet, Kent, 1667 CKS PRC1/12/39
Gyles, Michaell, Molash, Kent, 1613 CKS PRC2/17/121
Gyles, Richard, Goodnestone next Wingham, Kent, 1586 CKS PRC21/7/368
Gyles, Richard, Enborne, Berks, 1668 Berks RO D/A1/192/71A
Gyles, Robert, Sheldwich, Kent, 1630 CKS PRC2/30/63
Gyles, Thomas, Denton (Eastry hundred), Kent, 1612 CKS PRC2/17/115
Gyles, Thomas, Badlesmere, Kent, 1618 CKS PRC2/21/28

Gyles, Thomas, Ospringe, Kent, 1627 CKS PRC2/28/50
Gyles, Thomas eld, mason, Newbury, Berks, 1631 Berks RO D/A1/191/163A
Gyles, William, 1637 NLW BR 1637/42/Ac
Gylfyn, William, New Romney, Kent, 1597 CKS PRC21/14/161
Gyll, Chrystopher, Godmersham, Kent, 1604 CKS PRC21/16/17
Gyll, Thomas, Bushey, Herts, 1584 Herts RO ASA25/1087
Gyllam, Thomas, Biddenden, Kent, 1611 CKS PRC2/15/136
Gylles, John, Ashton Keynes, Wilts, 1631 Wilts RO Arch. Wilts.(name + date)
Gylphyn, John, Ivychurch, Kent, 1588 CKS PRC21/9/27
Gylphyn, Robarte, Brookland, Kent, 1590 CKS PRC2/5/88
Gymber, Susanna, spinster, Milton next Sittingbourne, Kent, 1664 CKS PRC1/10/44
Gymm, Anthony, Fillingham, Lincs, 1662 Lincs RO Ad/Ac/41/9
Gynes, Gilbert, Kensington, London & Middlesex, 1683 Greater London RO AM/PP/Box 1739-1749 pt (uncatalogued)
Gynmynges, John, cutler, St Albans, Herts, 1567 Herts RO ASA25/643
Gyrdler, Stephen, clothier ?, Benenden, Kent, 1593 CKS PRC2/6/402
Habbercombe, Richard,
Lincs 1603 Lincs RO Ad/Ac/5/413
Habberton, John, barber, Norwich St George at Tombland, Norf, Norfolk RO ANW/23/14/27
Hacke, Edmund, Upton Lovell, Wilts, 1690 PRO PROB32/31/258
Hacker, John, Reculver, Kent, 1585 CKS PRC21/7/185
Hacker, Margery, widow, Limington, Som, 1626 Somerset RO D/D/Cta/H16
Hackerbie, William, Woolsthorpe, Lincs, 1634 Lincs RO Ad/Ac/24/33
Hackett, Elizabeth, Stainby, Lincs, 1639 Lincs RO Ad/Ac/26/322
Hackett, Thomas, clergy: 'clerk', Orby, Lincs, 1623 Lincs RO Ad/Ac/18/19
Hackleton, John, Staverton, Northants, 1671 Northants RO NWill A/C/97
Had, Henry, gentleman, Canterbury St Alphege, Kent, 1641 CKS PRC19/1/48
Hadd, Thomas, Whitstable, Kent, 1626 CKS PRC2/27/67
Haddocke, James, yeoman, Newcastle under Lyme, Staffs, 1663 LJRO:cards/1663/26
Haddocke, see Harrock,
Haddowe, John, Sibsey, Lincs, 1652 Lincs RO Ad/Ac/29/30
Haden, Henry, Halesowen, Worcs, 1681 Worcs RO 008.7 BA3585/830/65
Haden, John, victualler, Sedgley (Gornall), Staffs, 1811 LJRO/B/C/5/1811/24
Hadley, John, gentleman, Birmingham, Warks, 1781 LJRO/B/C/5/1781/60
Hadlow, Edward, Newington next Sittingbourne, Kent, 1671 CKS PRC2/35/53
Hadlow, James, husbandman, Linton, Kent, 1667 CKS PRC1/12/43
Hadlow, James, Linton, Kent, 1678 CKS PRC2/38/40
Hadlow, John, Kenardington, Kent, 1625 CKS PRC2/25/65
Hadlow, John, Leysdown, Kent, 1681 CKS PRC2/39/183
Hadlow, Simon, Upchurch, Kent, 1678 CKS PRC2/37/155
Hadman, Sarah, Chilham, Kent, 1640 CKS PRC1/4/52
Hadman, Sarah, Chilham, Kent, 1640 CKS PRC1/4/52a
Hadnam, Mariam, Hullavington, Wilts, 1610 Wilts RO Arch. Wilts.(name + date)
Haffenden, George, mr, Brenzett, Kent, 1648 CKS PRC1/8/46
Haffenden, George, gentleman, Brenzett, Kent, 1666 CKS PRC1/11/35
Haffenden, Joane, Tenterden, Kent, 1627 CKS PRC2/27/74
Haffenden, John, Smarden, Kent, 1644 CKS PRC1/7/26
Haffenden, John, clothier, Smarden, Kent, 1672 CKS PRC20/12/12
Haffenden, Richard, Tenterden, Kent, 1677 CKS PRC2/37/160
Haffenden, Richard, yeoman/widower, Biddenden, Kent, 1680 CKS PRC2/39/49
Haffenden, Thomas, Faversham, Kent, 1586 CKS PRC2/4/168
Haffenden, Thomas, yeoman, Appledore, Kent, 1665 CKS PRC1/10/45
Haffenden, Thomas, weaver: 'linen weaver', Goudhurst, Kent, 1680 CKS PRC2/39/47
Haffenden, Thomas, Smeeth, Kent, 1707 CKS PRC19/6/29
Haffenden, Zacharie, Biddenden, Kent, 1610 CKS PRC2/13/239

[Haggard:]
Haggard, Edward, Sandford Orcas, Som, 1666 Somerset RO D/D/Cta/H47
Haggas, George, Maidstone, Kent, 1601 CKS PRC21/15/172
Hagger, Ralph, gentleman, Bedminster, Som, 1619 Somerset RO D/D/Cta/H67
Hagget, Thomas, husbandman, Hibaldstow, Lincs, 1683 Lincs RO Ad/Ac/34/104
Haggett, William, Hibaldstow, Lincs, 1662 Lincs RO Ad/Ac/41/12
Haggett/Terry, Mary, wife, Faversham, Kent, 1628 CKS PRC2/29/51
Haggott, Edward, Sandford Orcas, Som, 1666 Somerset RO D/D/Cta/H47b
Hagsten, Mathew, Stickney, Lincs, 1614 Lincs RO Ad/Ac/13/123
Haies, Marie, widow, Lydd, Kent, 1624 CKS PRC20/6/3
Haigh, John, clergy: 'clerk', Manchester, Lancs, 1786 Lancs RO (Name of Deceased) D.R.C.H. 1786-87
Haigh, Joseph, clothmaker, Batley, Yorks, 1773 Borthwick Test C.P. 1773/5
Haigh, Joseph, clothier, Almondbury (Honley), Yorks, 1804 Borthwick Test C.P. 1804/8
Haigh, Mary, widow, Thornhill (Thornhill Edge), Yorks, 1827 Borthwick Test C.P. 1827/6
Haine, John, clothworker, Newbury, Berks, 1613 Berks RO D/A1/195/51A
Haines, Ambrose, Queenborough, Kent, 1606 CKS PRC2/13/231
Haines, George, Killingholme, Lincs, 1599 Lincs RO Ad/Ac/5/70
Haines, John, haberdasher, Canterbury St Andrew, Kent, 1635 CKS PRC2/33/55
Haines, John, Southampton, Hants, 1673 Hants RO 21m65 D8/263
Haines, Margerye, widow, Queenborough, Kent, 1607 CKS PRC2/15/161
Haines, Richard, blacksmith, Stratfield Mortimer, Berks, 1676 Berks RO D/A1/197/17B
Hainsworth, John, Sutterton, Lincs, 1649 Lincs RO Ad/Ac/30/103
Hainsworth, Sarah, Swineshead, Lincs, 1637 Lincs RO Ad/Ac/25/507
Haiston, John, yeoman, Tadcaster, Yorks, 1812 Borthwick Test C.P. 1812/7
Haith, John eld, Linsted, Kent, 1601 CKS PRC2/12/206
Haiward, Alice, widow, Swallowcliffe, Wilts, 1621 Wilts RO Miscellaneous Index (name + date)
Hakeman, John, Cowbit, Lincs, 1607 Lincs RO Ad/Ac/7/70
Haksell, John, Milton next Sittingbourne, Kent, 1617 CKS PRC2/22/162
Halam, William, husbandman, Timberland, Lincs, 1649 Lincs RO Ad/Ac/30/201
Haldanby, Francis, Willoughton, Lincs, 1620 Lincs RO Ad/Ac/8b/463
Halden/Seymer, Marye, Faversham, Kent, 1613 CKS PRC2/17/390
Hale, Adam, Wye, Kent, 1588 CKS PRC2/4/458
Hale, Benet, Warehorne, Kent, 1586 CKS PRC2/4/63
Hale, Edward, esquire, Ewelme, Oxon, 1684 Oxon RO MSS Wills 167/2/42
Hale, George, husbandman, Ford, Sussex, 1633 W. Suss RO EpI/33/1633/12
Hale, Richarde, Warehorne, Kent, 1587 CKS PRC2/4/303
Hale, Roger, Wittering, East, Sussex, 1652 W. Suss RO EpI/33/1652/4
Hale, Thomas, Aldingbourne, Sussex, 1673 W. Suss RO EpI/33/1673/1
Hale, Thomas eld, yeoman, Shellingford, Berks, 1664 Berks RO D/A1/196/133A
Hale, Walter, yeoman, Birdham, Sussex, 1684 W. Suss RO EpI/33/1684/12
Hale, William, mariner, Faversham, Kent, 1680 CKS PRC2/39/52
Hale, William, Thorney, West, Sussex, 1682 W. Suss RO EpI/33/1682/47
Hale, see Salmon,
Haler, Edward, Shipley, Sussex, 1601 W. Suss RO EpI/33/1600/15
Haler, James, Grinstead, West, Sussex, 1643 W. Suss RO EpI/33/1643/5
Haler, Robert, Marden, Kent, 1596 CKS PRC2/8/141
Hales, Christian, dame/widow, Tunstall, Kent, 1641 CKS PRC1/5/99
Hales, Edward, fuller, Westbury, Wilts, 1627 Wilts RO Chantor Sarum Bundle 2/8
Hales, Edward, esquire, Faversham, Kent, 1636 CKS PRC20/10/466
Hales, John, esquire, Canterbury, Kent, 1629 CKS PRC2/30/81
Hales, John, gentleman, Boughton Malherbe, Kent, 1637 CKS PRC2/34/68
Hales, John, knight, Tunstall, Kent, 1640 CKS PRC19/1/49
Hales, John, baker, Dover, Kent, 1677 CKS PRC20/12/200
Hales, Robert, Stoke-upon-Trent, Staffs, 1684 LJRO/B/C/5/1684/40
Hales, Samuel, esquire, Davington, Kent, 1640 CKS PRC19/1/50

Hales, Thomas, Marston Bigot, Som, 1619 Somerset RO D/D/Cta/H70
Hales, Thomas, Titchmarsh, Northants, 1787 Northants RO X954/22/17
Hales, William, yeoman, Loppington, Shrops, 1674 LJRO:cards/1674/20
Halfacre, Thomas, yeoman, Clewer, Berks, Berks RO D/A1/77/208C
Halfepeney, Thomas, St Albans, Herts, 1626 Herts RO ASA25/2951
Halford, Francis, yeoman, Clipston, Northants, Northants RO NWill A/C/114
Halford, Thomas, farmer, Hartpury, Glos, 1798 GRO GDR/B4/2/H57
Halfpenny, Richard, gardener, Birmingham, Warks, 1826 LJRO/B/C/5/1826/21
Halhead, William, clergy: 'clerk', Banbury, Oxon, 1631 Oxon RO MSS Wills Pec 41/3/20
Halie, Richard, Withiel, Corn, 1614 Cornwall RO AP/H293/2
Halifax, Edward, husbandman, Belton, Lincs, 1667 Lincs RO Ad/Ac/33/20
Hall, Alice, widow, Maidstone, Kent, 1624 CKS PRC20/6/12
Hall, Anne, spinster, Manchester, Lancs, 1624 Lancs RO (Name of Deceased) D.R.C.H. 1624
Hall, Anne, Norton, Hook, Oxon, 1633 Oxon RO MSS Wills 298/1/2
Hall, Cecill, esquire, Coleby, Lincs, 1627 Lincs RO Ad/Ac/20b/96
Hall, Cecill, Boothby Graffoe, Lincs, 1647 Lincs RO Ad/Ac/28/243
Hall, Cecill, gentleman, Boothby Graffoe, Lincs, 1647 Lincs RO Ad/Ac/28/215
Hall, Christopher, Laughton, Lincs, 1613 Lincs RO Ad/Ac/8b/73
Hall, Collett, spinster, Wimborne Minster (Cowgrove), Dors, 1615 Dorset RO PE/WM CP 2/4/16
Hall, Dorothy, spinster, Pinchbeck, Lincs, 1618 Lincs RO Ad/Ac/14/194
Hall, Edward, Kirtlington, Oxon, Oxon RO MSS Wills 80/4/11
Hall, Edward, husbandman, Bushley, Worcs, Worcs RO 008.7 BA3585/838/200
Hall, Edward, Thanington, Kent, 1616 CKS PRC2/21/15
Hall, Edward, Rasen, Middle, Lincs, 1632 Lincs RO Ad/Ac/23/77
Hall, Edward, bookseller/mr, Cambridge St Mary the Great, Cambs, 1704 c. CUL V.C. Acc./Box3/28
Hall, Flory, Kilmersdon, Som, 1697 Somerset RO D/D/Cta/H80
Hall, Francis, gentleman, Burton Coggles, Lincs, 1635 Lincs RO Ad/Ac/24/563
Hall, Francis, Addlethorpe, Lincs, 1649 Lincs RO Ad/Ac/30/384
Hall, Francis, Newbury, Berks, 1694 Berks RO D/A1/197/146D
Hall, George, Queenborough, Kent, 1618 CKS PRC2/22/163
Hall, George, Manchester, Lancs, 1624 Lancs RO (Name of Deceased) D.R.C.H. 1624
Hall, George, Althorpe (Burringham), Lincs, 1663 Lincs RO Ad/Ac/41/85
Hall, George, Stickney, Lincs, 1667 Lincs RO Ad/Ac/32/115
Hall, Grigory, Petersfield, Hants, Hants RO 1577 AD15/3
Hall, Henrie, gentleman, St Mary Bourne, Hants, 1623 Hants RO 21M65 D8/18
Hall, Henry, Chilton Foliat, Wilts, 1620? Wilts RO Arch. Wilts.(name + date)
Hall, Henry, Whitstable, Kent, 1621 CKS PRC2/26/132
Hall, Henry, esquire, Baston, Lincs, 1639? Lincs RO Ad/Ac/26/284
Hall, Henry, Cubley, Derby, 1666 LJRO:cards/1666/6
Hall, Henry, Willesborough, Kent, 1673 CKS PRC2/35/144
Hall, Henry, husbandman, Newbury, Berks, 1695 Berks RO D/A1/197/135C
Hall, Henry, gentleman, Holt, Norf, 1743 Norfolk RO ANW/23/24/12
Hall, Henrye, Gosberton, Lincs, 1598 Lincs RO Ad/Ac/4/11
Hall, Hester, Althorpe (Burringham), Lincs, 1663 Lincs RO Ad/Ac/41/84
Hall, Humphrey, Radbourne, Derby, 1684 LJRO/B/C/5/1685/46
Hall, James, victualler, Reading St Mary, Berks, 1636 Berks RO D/A1/196/35C
Hall, James, Canterbury Holy Cross Westgate, Kent, 1683 CKS PRC2/40/42
Hall, Jane, widow, Challock, Kent, 1614 CKS PRC20/3/99
Hall, Joan, widow, Ashford, Kent, 1597 CKS PRC2/9/134
Hall, John, yeoman, Aldford (Buerton), Ches, Cheshire RO (Name) W.C. 1784
Hall, John, Willesborough, Kent, 1593 CKS PRC2/6/360
Hall, John, St Nicholas at Wade, Kent, 1600 CKS PRC21/16/200
Hall, John, Littlebourne, Kent, 1608 CKS PRC2/14/227
Hall, John, yeoman, Enborne, Berks, 1612 Berks RO D/A1/195/39A

[Hall:]
Hall, John, Barkston, Lincs, 1619 Lincs RO Ad/Ac/15/272
Hall, John, Blyborough, Lincs, 1626 Lincs RO Ad/Ac/39/25
Hall, John, Lydd, Kent, 1627 CKS PRC20/7/46
Hall, John, yeoman, Tilehurst, Berks, 1629 Berks RO D/A1/195/116A
Hall, John, baker, Abingdon St Helen, Berks, 1633 Berks RO D/A1/196/18C
Hall, John, labourer, Leverton, Lincs, 1634 Lincs RO Ad/Ac/24/512
Hall, John, Mullion, Corn, 1638 Cornwall RO AP/H976/2
Hall, John, Ivychurch, Kent, 1641 CKS PRC19/2/19
Hall, John, Stapenhill, Derby, 1663 LJRO:cards/1663/27
Hall, John, yeoman, St Peter in Thanet, Kent, 1665 CKS PRC1/11/36
Hall, John, husbandman, Chislet, Kent, 1669 CKS PRC1/14/51
Hall, John, Angmering, Sussex, 1670 W. Suss RO EpI/33/1669/15
Hall, John, Wishaw, Warks, 1672 LJRO:cards/1672/26
Hall, John, Ramsey, Hunts, 1676 Hunts RO/Acc58/45(168)
Hall, John, cheesemonger, Dover, Kent, 1678 CKS PRC20/12/263
Hall, John, grocer, Abingdon St Helen, Berks, 1682 Berks RO D/A1/197/55B
Hall, John, yeoman, Sutton, Long, Lincs, 1683 PRO PROB5/1394
Hall, John, Whittington, Derby, 1684 LJRO/B/C/5/1683/9
Hall, John, merchant/mr, St Dionis Backchurch, London & Middlesex, 1703 PRO PROB5/1761
Hall, John, glazier, Liverpool, Lancs, 1797 Lancs RO (Name of Deceased) D.R.C.H. 1796-97
Hall, John eld, Willesborough, Kent, 1606 CKS PRC2/14/216
Hall, John ygr, St Peter in Thanet, Kent, 1601 CKS PRC2/12/208
Hall, Joseph, victualler, Bristol, Glos, Bristol RO 1737/17
Hall, Joseph, shopkeeper, Castleton, Derby, 1808 LJRO/B/C/5/1808/25
Hall, Josiah, Burton, Gate, Lincs, 1666 Lincs RO Ad/Ac/41/171
Hall, Leonard, yeoman, Bodicote, Oxon, 1663 Oxon RO MSS Wills 298/2/36
Hall, Margaret, Aisby, Lincs, 1617 Lincs RO Ad/Ac/8b/157
Hall, Margaret, widow, Stamford, Lincs, 1629 Lincs RO Ad/Ac/22/73
Hall, Martha + Sara, Old Romney, Kent, 1622 CKS PRC1/1/31
Hall, Mary, widow, Hythe St Leonard, Kent, 1673 CKS PRC20/12/86
Hall, Michael, Kenley, Shrops, 1682 LJRO/B/C/5/1681/20
Hall, Richard, Burghfield, Berks, 1595 Berks RO D/A1/194/70A
Hall, Richard, Speen (Bagnor), Berks, 1598 Berks RO D/A1/194/90C
Hall, Richard, Old Romney, Kent, 1603 CKS PRC2/14/256
Hall, Richard, Goxhill, Lincs, 1623 Lincs RO Ad/Ac/18/31
Hall, Richard, Wittersham, Kent, 1673 CKS PRC20/12/87
Hall, Richard, gentleman, Fordwich, Kent, 1679 CKS PRC2/38/140
Hall, Richard, Grindon, Staffs, 1710 LJRO/B/C/5/1710/36
Hall, Richard, yeoman, Grappenhall, Ches, 1722 Cheshire RO (Name) W.C. 1722
Hall, Richard eld, Hothfield, Kent, 1635 CKS PRC2/33/62
Hall, Robaert, Ipswich, Suff, 1733 Lambeth Palace Arches G103/14
Hall, Robarte ygr, Ashford, Kent, 1588 CKS PRC2/4/511
Hall, Robert, Scremby, Lincs, 1618 Lincs RO Ad/Ac/14/78
Hall, Robert, Ashford, Kent, 1624 CKS PRC2/23/170
Hall, Robert, labourer, Skirbeck, Lincs, 1632 Lincs RO Ad/Ac/23/92
Hall, Robert, Melton Ross, Lincs, 1644 Lincs RO Ad/Ac/42/25
Hall, Robert, yeoman, Burton, Gate, Lincs, 1664 Lincs RO Ad/Ac/41/131
Hall, Robert, Lincoln St Mary Magdalen in the Bail, Lincs, 1668 Lincs RO Ad/Ac/42/27
Hall, Robert, husbandman, Ingham, Lincs, 1685 Lincs RO Ad/Ac/44/167
Hall, Roberte, Croft, Lincs, 1599 Lincs RO Ad/Ac/5/304
Hall, Roger, Timberland, Lincs, 1637 Lincs RO Ad/Ac/25/550
Hall, Ruth,
Leics 1685 Leics RO Administrators Accounts 1682-86 f35
Hall, Rychard, Bilsington, Kent, 1601 CKS PRC2/12/177
Hall, Sybell, widow, Lydd, Kent, 1616 CKS PRC20/3/278

Hall, Thomas, Faversham, Kent, 1588 CKS PRC2/4/434
Hall, Thomas, Langton, Lincs, 1594 Lincs RO Ad/Ac/3/133
Hall, Thomas, Candlesby, Lincs, 1606 Lincs RO Ad/Ac/7/82
Hall, Thomas, yeoman, Windsor, New, Berks, 1635 Berks RO D/A1/196/14C
Hall, Thomas, Harbledown, Kent, 1640 CKS PRC1/4/53
Hall, Thomas, Langton, Lincs, 1641 Lincs RO Ad/Ac/27/45
Hall, Thomas, Burgh le Marsh, Lincs, 1651 Lincs RO Ad/Ac/29/87
Hall, Thomas, Winterton, Lincs, 1674 Lincs RO Ad/Ac/35/81
Hall, Thomas, gentleman, Dymchurch, Kent, 1677 CKS PRC2/37/152
Hall, Thomas, cook, Oxford St Michael, Oxon, 1680 Bodleian HYP B8/89-92
Hall, Thomas, yeoman, Luddenham, Kent, 1683 CKS PRC2/40/121
Hall, William, Herne, Kent, 1614 CKS PRC20/3/109
Hall, William, Pinchbeck, Lincs, 1620 Lincs RO Ad/Ac/16/51
Hall, William, Smeeth, Kent, 1623 CKS PRC20/6/352
Hall, William, Mersham, Kent, 1636 CKS PRC2/33/60
Hall, William, Farndale, Yorks, 1638 Borthwick Prob. Ex. 1638/12
Hall, William, gentleman, Dymchurch, Kent, 1665 CKS PRC1/11/37
Hall, William, Stratfield Saye, Hants, 1669 Hants RO 21M65 D8/200
Hall, William, Ipstones, Staffs, 1676 LJRO:cards/1676/25
Hall, William, Ravensthorpe (Coaton), Northants, 1681 Northants RO NWill A/C/78
Hall, William, Salisbury Cathedral (The Close), Wilts, 1690 Wilts RO Dean Sarum (name + date)
Hall, William, carpenter, Oldham, Lancs, 1770 Lancs RO (Name of Deceased) D.R.C.H. 1769-70
Hall, William, fellmonger, Driffield, Great, Yorks, 1780 Borthwick Test C.P. 1780/3
Hall, William, attorney, Halifax, Yorks, 1814 Borthwick Test C.P. 1814/14
Hall/Wraight, Elizabeth, Faversham, Kent, 1643 CKS PRC1/6/62
Hallaley, John, yeoman, Killingholme, Lincs, 1606 e 19 Lincs RO Ad/Ac/7/80
Hallam, Matthewe, Cranbrook, Kent, 1599 CKS PRC2/11/125
Halldenby, Anthonie, gentleman, Gainsborough, Lincs, 1606 Lincs RO Ad/Ac/37/218
Halle, Joan, widow, Halesowen, Worcs, 1600 Worcs RO 008.7 BA3585/838/186
Hallelaye, William, Scotton, Lincs, 1571 Lincs RO Ad/Ac/1/25
Hallett, Edward, Stratton, Corn, 1646 Cornwall RO AP/H1222/1
Hallett, John eld, gentleman, Faversham, Kent, 1632 CKS PRC2/31/121
Hallett, Richard, St Johns Thanet, Kent, 1633 CKS PRC2/32/59
Hallett, William, Boscombe, Wilts, 1630 Wilts RO Arch. Sarum(+ name and date)
Hallett, William, Swalecliffe, Kent, 1636 CKS PRC2/33/64
Hallidaie, John, Boultham, Lincs, 1612 Lincs RO Ad/Ac/11/23
Hallidaie, Richarde, Grimoldby, Lincs, 1598 Lincs RO Ad/Ac/4/83
Halliday, Anthony, Metheringham, Lincs, 1612 Lincs RO Ad/Ac/10/128
Halliday/Moodie, Isabell, Mumby, Lincs, 1626 Lincs RO Ad/Ac/20/45
Hallifax, Edmund, Epworth, Lincs, 1679 Lincs RO Ad/Ac/43/135
Hallifax, Frances, widow, Epworth, Lincs, 1680 Lincs RO Ad/Ac/43/152
Hallifax, John, clergy: 'clerk', Springthorpe, Lincs, 1678 Lincs RO Ad/Ac/35/136
Hallifeild, Robert, Huttoft, Lincs, 1639 Lincs RO Ad/Ac/26/220
Hallifeild, William, Anderby, Lincs, 1618 Lincs RO Ad/Ac/14/160
Hallington, Edward, alderman, Grimsby, Great, Lincs, 1623 Lincs RO Ad/Ac/18/111
Halliocke, Charles, Garthorpe, Leics, 1666 Leics RO Administrators Accounts C17th f82
Halliwell, Gilbert, Sandwich, Kent, 1628 CKS PRC2/29/48
Halliwell, Henry, clergy: 'clerk', Threckingham, Lincs, 1613 Lincs RO Ad/Ac/12/165
Halliwell, Thomas, Winterton, Lincs, 1630s? Lincs RO Ad/Ac/39/239
Halliwell, Willyam, Sandwich, Kent, 1626 CKS PRC2/25/68
Halloway, James, Bilsington, Kent, 1604 CKS PRC2/13/218
Halloway, Ralph, yeoman, Stoke, North, Oxon, 1680 Oxon RO MSS Wills 298/2/54
Hallowday, Ambrose, yeoman, Knaptoft, Leics, Leics RO Administrators Accounts 1667-72 f65
Hallowes, William, Bourne, Lincs, 1624 Lincs RO Ad/Ac/19B/71
Halls, Edward, university: 'scholar's servant', Cambridge, Cambs, 1612 CUL V.C.Acc./Box1/24

[Hallywell:]
Hallywell, Bryan, husbandman, Roxby, Lincs, 1652 Lincs RO Ad/Ac/40/233
Halsey, Henry, yeoman, Watford, Herts, Herts RO ASA25/1875
Halsnoade, Ann, spinster, Sittingbourne, Kent, 1674 CKS PRC2/35/227
Halsnoade, John, Canterbury St Peter, Kent, 1677 CKS PRC2/37/151
Halsnod, John, Frittenden, Kent, 1630 CKS PRC20/9/209
Halsnod, John, threadman, Maidstone, Kent, 1668 CKS PRC19/4/17
Halsnod, Martin, Sandwich St Clement, Kent, 1616 CKS PRC2/21/2
Halsnode, Daniell, Rodmersham, Kent, 1616 CKS PRC2/22/125
Halsnode, Richard, Sandwich, Kent, 1613 CKS PRC2/17/149
Halsnode, William ygr, yeoman, Leeds, Kent, 1640 CKS PRC1/4/54
Halsnode/Halsnothe, John, Maidstone, Kent, 1605 CKS PRC20/1/29
Halsnoth, Samuel, Canterbury St Mary-Magdalen Burgate, Kent, 1630 CKS PRC2/30/90
Halsnoth, William, Whitstable, Kent, 1599 CKS PRC2/11/21
Halsnoth, see Church,
Halsnothe, Elizabethe, widow, Frittenden, Kent, 1586 CKS PRC2/5/352
Halsnothe, John, Faversham, Kent, 1590 CKS PRC2/5/346
Halsnothe, see Halsnode,
Ham, William, carpenter, Dover, Kent, 1680 CKS PRC20/13/34
Haman, John, Duncton, Sussex, 1600 W. Suss RO EpI/33/1600/2
Haman, see Jenens,
Hambledon, John, haberdasher, Milton next Sittingbourne, Kent, 1674 CKS PRC2/36/74
Hamblen, Alice, Boxley, Kent, 1629 CKS PRC2/30/77
Hambleton, Robert, fisherman, Milton next Sittingbourne, Kent, 1668 CKS PRC1/13/55
Hambleton, Robert, Milton next Sittingbourne, Kent, 1674 CKS PRC2/36/75
Hamblie, Christopher, Warbstow, Corn, 1606 Cornwall RO AP/H87/1
Hambly, John, Warbstow, Corn, 1646 Cornwall RO AP/H1223/1
Hamblye, Edward, St Ewe, Corn, 1612 Cornwall RO AP/H271b/1
Hamblye, John, Launceston, Corn, 1607 Cornwall RO AP/H114
Hambroke, Sylvester, Herne, Kent, 1598 CKS PRC21/14/522
Hambrooke, Anthony, yeoman, Hawkinge, Kent, 1691 CKS PRC2/42/6
Hambrooke, Emanuel, Lyminge, Kent, 1615 CKS PRC20/3/262
Hambrooke, John, blacksmith, Stowting, Kent, 1675 CKS PRC2/36/202
Hambrooke, William, Lympne, Kent, 1671 CKS PRC2/35/60
Hamell, Joseph, blacksmith, St Albans St Michaels, Herts, 1700 Herts RO ASA25/4507
Hamer, Abraham, yeoman, Manchester, Lancs, 1798 Lancs RO (Name of Deceased) D.R.C.H. 1798-99
Hamerton, Henry, yeoman, Thatcham, Berks, 1663 Berks RO D/A1/196/121A
Hamerton, Thomas, Horncastle, Lincs, 1613 Lincs RO Ad/Ac/12/143
Hamerton, Thomas, gentleman, Horncastle, Lincs, 1631 Lincs RO Ad/Ac/23/68
Hamerton, Thomas, Horncastle, Lincs, 1666 Lincs RO Ad/Ac/32/70
Hames, Jeames, Hawkhurst, Kent, 1598 CKS PRC2/9/355
Hames, John, Stalisfield, Kent, 1611 CKS PRC2/16/114
Hames, Peter, Wittering, East, Sussex, 1595 W. Suss RO EpI/33/1595/7
Hamidge, Daniel, Canterbury St Andrew, Kent, 1663 CKS PRC1/9/120
Hamlin, John, Broadwell (Filkins), Oxon, 1636 Oxon RO MSS Wills 298/1/23
Hamm, John, Butleigh, Som, 1638 Somerset RO D/D/Cta/H22
Hamman, Peter, bachelor, Faversham, Kent, 1667 CKS PRC1/12/44
Hamme, Jasper, Kingsdon, Som, 1640 Somerset RO D/D/Cta/H52
Hammer, Edmund, Pilham, Lincs, 1609 Lincs RO Ad/Ac/8a/308
Hammersley, Thomas, yeoman, Gawsworth, Ches, 1795 Cheshire RO (Name) W.C. 1795
Hammon, Daniell, Acrise, Kent, 1611 CKS PRC2/17/162
Hammon, Edmund, yeoman, Sandhurst, Kent, 1630 CKS PRC20/9/251
Hammon, Joan, widow, Bersted, South, Sussex, 1684 W. Suss RO EpIV/10/2A/36
Hammon, John, Bearsted, Kent, 1610 CKS PRC2/13/241
Hammon, Richard, Ospringe, Kent, 1670 CKS PRC1/15/33

Hammon, Richerde, Stourmouth, Kent, 1584 CKS PRC2/3/215
Hammon, Robert, Saltwood, Kent, 1636 CKS PRC20/10/490
Hammon, Robert, Deal, Kent, 1670 CKS PRC19/4/79
Hammon, Thomas, Hernhill, Kent, 1606 CKS PRC20/1/124
Hammon, Thomas, turner, Milton next Sittingbourne, Kent, 1670 CKS PRC2/35/59
Hammon, William, Fishbourne, Sussex, 1613 W. Suss RO EpIII/9/1/11
Hammond, Anne, widow, Bekesbourne, Kent, 1675 CKS PRC2/36/64
Hammond, John, Mundham, North, Sussex, 1682 W. Suss RO EpI/33/1682/27
Hammond, Mary, widow, Thurston, Suff, 1750 Suff RO(B) IC500/3/50/20
Hammond, Owen, esquire, Lambeth (Lambeth Marsh), Surrey, 1681 PRO PROB5/1297
Hammond, Richard, Chart nr Sutton Valence, Kent, 1617 CKS PRC2/22/139
Hammond, Richard, Chart, Great, Kent, 1680 CKS PRC2/38/144
Hammond, Thomas, yeoman, Shenstone, Staffs, 1770 LJRO/B/C/5/1769/97
Hammond, Timothy, clergy: 'vicar', Barnetby le Wold, Lincs, 1679 Lincs RO Ad/Ac/43/122
Hammond, William, Maidstone, Kent, 1605 CKS PRC21/17/21
Hamms, Stephen, haberdasher/citizen, St Anne and St Agnes, London & Middlesex, 1691 PRO PROB5/1781
Hamnell, William, husbandman, St Peter in Thanet, Kent, 1647 CKS PRC1/8/19
Hamon, Abraham, Snave, Kent, 1611 CKS PRC2/15/186
Hamon, Anne, spinster, Maidstone, Kent, 1663 CKS PRC19/3/26
Hamon, Daniel, Mundham, North, Sussex, 1619 W. Suss RO EpI/33/1619/8
Hamon, Edmund, Minster in Thanet, Kent, 1620 CKS PRC2/22/173
Hamon, George, Tilmanstone, Kent, 1621 CKS PRC2/22/147
Hamon, Hugh, Barrow on Humber, Lincs, 1626 Lincs RO Ad/Ac/20/7
Hamon, Isaack, Alkham, Kent, 1642 CKS PRC1/6/63
Hamon, John, New Romney, Kent, 1586 CKS PRC21/8/98
Hamon, John, Chart, Great, Kent, 1603 CKS PRC2/12/442
Hamon, Oliver, Deal, Kent, 1618 CKS PRC20/4/163
Hamon, Peter, gentleman, Deal, Kent, 1596 CKS PRC21/14/127
Hamon, Richard, Billingshurst, Sussex, 1579 W. Suss RO EpI/33/1579/2
Hamon, Richard, Sandwich, Kent, 1629 CKS PRC2/30/80
Hamon, Thomas, Swingfield, Kent, 1590 CKS PRC2/5/342
Hamon, Thomas, Hawkhurst, Kent, 1601 CKS PRC2/12/199
Hamon, Thomas, yeoman, Lyminge, Kent, 1620 CKS PRC20/4/139
Hamon, Thomas, Bobbing, Kent, 1637 CKS PRC2/33/57
Hamon, Thomas, husbandman, Dover, Kent, 1638 CKS PRC20/10/520
Hamon, Thomasine + Mercie + Josephe + Anne, Maidstone, Kent, 1604 CKS PRC21/16/21
Hamon, Valentine, Herne, Kent, 1613 CKS PRC20/2/376
Hamon, William, Warden, Kent, 1596 CKS PRC2/8/453
Hamon, William, Canterbury St Paul, Kent, 1623 CKS PRC1/1/33
Hamon, William, Staplehurst, Kent, 1635 CKS PRC2/33/65
Hamon, Wyllyam, Postling, Kent, 1574 CKS PRC2/1/106
Hamond, Agnes, Waltham, Kent, 1594 CKS PRC2/7/65
Hamond, Amy, Walton, Wood, Hunts, 1687 Hunts RO/Acc58/266(262)
Hamond, John, Faversham, Kent, 1681 CKS PRC2/39/184
Hamond, Percival, Westbourne, Sussex, 1594 W. Suss RO EpI/33/1593/3
Hamond, Simon, surgeon, Bearsted, Kent, 1710 CKS PRC1/17/27
Hamond, Thomas, Staplehurst, Kent, 1619 CKS PRC2/22/178
Hamond, William, yeoman, St Johns Thanet, Kent, 1616 CKS PRC2/22/142
Hamper, George, Tarring, West, Sussex, 1631 W. Suss RO EpIV/10/2/3
Hamper, John, Tarring, West, Sussex, 1645 W. Suss RO EpI/33/1645/2
Hampson, James, yeoman, Crowland, Lincs, 1674 Lincs RO Ad/Ac/45/111
Hampton, Francis, Cranbrook, Kent, 1616 CKS PRC2/22/140
Hampton, Francis, Itchenor, West, Sussex, 1627 W. Suss RO EpI/33/1627/16
Hampton, John, East Sutton, Kent, 1614 CKS PRC2/18/45

[Hampton:]
Hampton, John, Sandwich St Bartholomew's Hospital, Kent, 1623 CKS PRC20/6/6
Hampton, John, whitesmith, Blean, Kent, 1679 CKS PRC2/38/146
Hampton, Randle, mercer, Nantwich, Ches, Cheshire RO (Name) W.C. 1662
Hampton, William, Hartlip, Kent, 1630 CKS PRC20/9/207
Hamson, William, Chorlton, Lancs, 1625 Lancs RO (Name of Deceased) D.R.C.H. 1625
Hamvell, Richard, Tenterden, Kent, 1606 CKS PRC2/13/215
Hanadowne, Charles, Waddington, Lincs, 1596 Lincs RO Ad/Ac/5/308
Hanbury, Walter, gentleman, Feckenham, Worcs, 1593 Worcs RO 008.7 BA3585/838/101
Hancock, Ambrose, Wroughton, Wilts, 1629 Wilts RO Arch. Wilts.(name + date)
Hancock, Christopher, Wiveliscombe, Som, 1626 Somerset RO D/D/Cta/H15
Hancock, James, Ryde, Hants, 1665 Hants RO 1665 AD50/3
Hancock, James, Newchurch, Hants, 1668 Hants RO 21M65 D8/201
Hancock, Margaret, widow, Reading, Berks, 1684 Berks RO D/A1/197/71C
Hancock, Richard, Dassett, Burton, Warks, 1672 LJRO:cards/1672/27
Hancock, Thomas, St Neots, Hunts, 1687 Hunts RO/Acc58/263(259)
Hancock, Thomas, 1691 Lancs RO (Name of Deceased) D.R.C.H. 1691
Hancock, Thomas, labourer, Shrewsbury, Shrops, 1736 LJRO/B/C/5/1735/33
Hancocke, Jeremye, Hythe St Leonard, Kent, 1606 CKS PRC20/1/53
Hancocke, John, Bodmin, Corn, 1608 Cornwall RO AP/H174
Hancocke, John, Boxley, Kent, 1643 CKS PRC1/6/105
Hancocke, Richard, Dassett, Burton, Warks, 1670 LJRO:cards/1670/32
Hancocke, Robert, Maker, Corn, 1615 Cornwall RO AP/H354/2
Hancocke, Robert, St Andrew Holborn, London & Middlesex, 1673 PRO PROB32/10/186
Hancocke, Thomas, husbandman, Shinfield, Berks, 1630 Berks RO D/A1/195/120A
Hancocks, Mary, spinster, Cirencester, Glos, 1748 GRO GDR/B4/2/H67
Hancox, Thomas, Myddle, Shrops, 1675 LJRO:cards/1675/31
Handcocke, Edward, Hernhill, Kent, 1601 CKS PRC21/16/170
Handcocke, Richard, Kingsnorth, Kent, 1597 CKS PRC2/9/245
Handes, Thomas, butcher, Witney, Oxon, 1630 Oxon RO MSS Wills 297/5/24
Handfeelde, Stephen, Lower Hardres, Kent, 1594 CKS PRC2/7/15
Handfeild, Anne, widow, Stockbury, Kent, 1677 CKS PRC2/37/159
Handfeild, John, Bredgar, Kent, 1679 CKS PRC2/38/35
Handfeild, Thomas, Linsted, Kent, 1701 CKS PRC1/16/28
Handfield, James, gentleman, Sutton Valence, Kent, 1634 CKS PRC2/32/58
Handley, Amye, Kirton, Lincs, 1638 Lincs RO Ad/Ac/25/72
Handley, Thomas, husbandman, Kirton, Lincs, 1633 Lincs RO Ad/Ac/24/187
Handley, Thomas, Hallam, West, Derby, 1682 LJRO/B/C/5/1682/46
Handly, Olyver, Hernhill, Kent, 1594 CKS PRC21/12/405
Hands, Cornelius, buttonmaker, Birmingham, Warks, 1806 LJRO/B/C/5/1806/20
Hands, Nicholas, Wick, Worcs, 1638 Worcs RO 008.7 BA3585/837/bdl 1
Hands, Sarah, spinster, Chilvers Coton, Warks, 1797 LJRO/B/C/5/1797/28
Hanes, Edward, cook, Oxford (University), Oxon, 1672 Bodleian HYP B8/99-100
Haninge, John, Lympne, Kent, 1596 CKS PRC2/9/136
Hankey, Thomas, Chester, Ches, 1648 Cheshire RO (Name) W.C. 1648
Hankin, see Pope,
Hankrie?, William, Countesthorpe, Leics, 1641 Leics RO PR/I/41A/78
Hanley, Edward, husbandman, Sutton, Kings, Northants, 1620 Oxon RO MSS Wills Pec 41/2/40
Hanly, Jane, widow, Seasalter, Kent, 1623 CKS PRC2/23/162
Hanly, John, Whitstable, Kent, 1664 CKS PRC1/9/121
Hanmell, William, St Johns Thanet, Kent, 1682 CKS PRC2/40/45
Hanmer/Merth, Thomas, Upchurch, Kent, 1610 CKS PRC2/13/237
Hannah, Edward, Alvingham, Lincs, 1670 Lincs RO Ad/Ac/32/180
Hannah, Henry, Hibaldstow, Lincs, 1662 Lincs RO Ad/Ac/41/5
Hannam, Elnathan, surgeon/gentleman, Deal, Kent, 1679 CKS PRC20/12/306
Hannam, Henry, Compton Pauncefoot, Som, 1641 Somerset RO D/D/Cta/H57

Hannam, John eld, Dundry (Littleton), Som, 1635 Somerset RO D/D/Cta/H19
Hanney, Edward, mariner, Yarmouth, Great, Norf, 1758 Norfolk RO ANW/23/25/29A
Hanney, William, Hibaldstow, Lincs, 1600 Lincs RO Ad/Ac/5/487
Hannington, Simon, Lydd, Kent, 1630 CKS PRC20/8/283
Hannington, William, gentleman, Thatcham, Berks, 1783 Berks RO D/A1/197/59C
Hanscombe, Robert, Tewin, Herts, 1635 Herts RO AHH23/1079
Hanserd, Ralphe, gentleman, Swallow, Lincs, 1620 Lincs RO Ad/Ac/15/133
Hanserd, William, gentleman, Humberstone, Lincs, 1627 Lincs RO Ad/Ac/20b/26
Hanshard, William, gentleman, Biscathorpe, Lincs, 1606 Lincs RO Ad/Ac/7/102
Hanshawe, John, Barton on Humber, Lincs, 1613 Lincs RO Ad/Ac/12/157
Hanson, Bartholomew, All Hallows The Great, London & Middlesex, 1667 PRO PROB5/1771
Hanson, Bethel, ironfounder, Halifax, Yorks, 1848 Borthwick Test C.P. 1848/6
Hanson, Catherine, Worcester St Helen, Worcs, 1682 Worcs RO 008.7 BA3585/837/bdl 3
Hanson, Christopher, widower, Harewood (Alwoodley), Yorks, 1824 Borthwick Test C.P. 1829/9
Hanson, Isaac, Feckenham, Worcs, 1680 Worcs RO 008.7 BA3585/837/bdl 2
Hanson, John, Grantham, Lincs, 1623 Lincs RO Ad/Ac/18/17
Hanson, John, Grantham, Lincs, 1636 Lincs RO Ad/Ac/24/266
Hanson, John, clergy: 'clerk', Grantham, Lincs, 1670 Lincs RO Ad/Ac/32/169
Hanson, John, labourer, Burgh, Lincs, 1680 Lincs RO Ad/Ac/34/56
Hanson, Michaell, butcher, Grantham, Lincs, 1599 Lincs RO Ad/Ac/5/117
Hanson, Robert, Wakefield, Yorks, Borthwick Test C.P. 1757/2
Hanson, Robert, knight/alderman,
London & Middlesex 1683 PRO PROB32/24/114
Hanson, Thomas, Ludford, Lincs, 1601 Lincs RO Ad/Ac/5/103
Hanson, William, clergy: 'vicar', Twerton, Som, 1646 Somerset RO D/D/Cta/H51
Hanson, William, shopkeeper/glover?, Birmingham, Warks, 1736 LJRO/B/C/5/1736/31
Hanson/Mountague, Susanna, wife, Warfield, Berks, 1610s Berks RO D/A1/203/281B
Hanwell, Edmund, wheeler, Cumnor, Berks, 1619 Berks RO D/A1/195/81A
Haram, Henry, Broughton, Lincs, 1632 Lincs RO Ad/Ac/39/319
Harbar, Joel, Milton next Sittingbourne, Kent, 1592 CKS PRC2/6/256
Harbard, John, Waddington, Lincs, 1572 Lincs RO Ad/Ac/1/3
Harbe, see Horbey,
Harber, William, Bilsington, Kent, 1616 CKS PRC2/21/1
Harbert, Edward, Lincoln (Bail), Lincs, 1652 Lincs RO Ad/Ac/29/13
Harbert, George, Hillmorton, Warks, 1675 LJRO:cards/1675/32
Harbert, Julyan, widow, Mathon, Worcs, 1602 Worcs RO 008.7 BA3585/838/244
Harbert, Mary, widow, Chieveley (Curridge), Berks, Berks RO D/A1/80/55
Harbert, Simon, tailor, St Stephens by Saltash, Corn, 1608 Cornwall RO AP/H123/4
Harbie, Edward, tanner, Bourne, Lincs, 1638 Lincs RO Ad/Ac/25/239
Harbie, Thomas, weaver, Willoughby, Silk, Lincs, 1637 Lincs RO Ad/Ac/25/457
Harby, John, Harby, Leics, 1684 Leics RO Administrators Accounts 1682-86 f25
Harby, William, Moulton, Lincs, 1612 Lincs RO Ad/Ac/11/114
Hardcastle, Elizabeth, widow, Wakefield, Yorks, 1812 Borthwick Test C.P. 1812/4
Harde, John, Cockerington, North, Lincs, 1599 Lincs RO Ad/Ac/5/183
Harde, Walter, Canterbury St Andrew, Kent, 1610 CKS PRC2/15/167
Hardell, Daniell, Colsterworth, Lincs, 1632 Lincs RO Ad/Ac/23/2
Hardham, Henry, Tillington, Sussex, 1613 W. Suss RO EpI/33/1613/6
Hardham, Joan, widow, Tillington, Sussex, W. Suss RO EpI/33/1618/3
Hardham, Joan, widow, Yapton, Sussex, 1673 W. Suss RO EpI/33/1673/16
Hardick, Sydrach, Shepton Mallet, Som, 1625 Somerset RO D/D/Cta/H10
Hardie, Bryan, Skidbrooke, Lincs, 1612 Lincs RO Ad/Ac/11/28
Hardie, John, Thornton Curtis, Lincs, 1597 Lincs RO Ad/Ac/4/127
Hardie, Paull, Sibsey, Lincs, 1639 Lincs RO Ad/Ac/26/265
Hardie, Richard, Stickney, Lincs, 1640 Lincs RO Ad/Ac/26/189
Hardie, Robert, esquire, Fenton, Lincs, 1625 Lincs RO Ad/Ac/19B/84

[Hardie:]
Hardie, William, Hemingby, Lincs, 1624 Lincs RO Ad/Ac/18/107
Hardiman, William, Bowerchalke, Wilts, 1620 Wilts RO CC Sarum(+ name and date)
Hardiman, William, Graveney, Kent, 1625 CKS PRC2/25/72
Hardin, Simon, Milton next Sittingbourne, Kent, 1633 CKS PRC2/32/62
Harding, George, Cranbrook, Kent, 1607 CKS PRC2/14/219
Harding, James, farmer, Lythe, Yorks, 1805 Borthwick Test C.P. 1805/1
Harding, John, Oare, Kent, 1670 CKS PRC1/15/34
Harding, John eld, yeoman, Ashbury, Berks, Berks RO D/A1/196/33A
Harding, Laurence, Woodchurch, Kent, 1664 CKS PRC19/3/27
Harding, Mary, widow, Biddenden, Kent, 1668 CKS PRC1/13/56
Harding, Richard, bachelor, Nutley, Hants, 1662 Hants RO 21M65 D8/155
Harding, Richard, baker/citizen, St Ethelburga, London & Middlesex, 1667 Lambeth Palace Arches GG22/3
Harding, Robert, tanner, Pickering, Yorks, Borthwick Test C.P. 1731/3
Harding, Robert, Tenterden, Kent, 1667 CKS PRC1/12/45
Harding, Robert, Crudwell, Wilts, 1676 Wilts RO Miscellaneous Index (name + date)
Harding, Thomas, yeoman, Shrivenham, Berks, 1615 Berks RO D/A1/195/58A
Harding, Thomas, Holybourne, Hants, 1623 Hants RO 21M65 D8/19
Harding, Thomas, Woodchurch, Kent, 1646 CKS PRC19/2/106
Harding, William, Mere, Wilts, 1685 Wilts RO Dean Sarum (name + date)
Harding, William, yeoman, Hampton in Arden, Warks, 1736 LJRO/B/C/5/1735/37
Harding/North, Robert, Ashbury, Berks, 1600 Berks RO D/A1/194/103A
Harding/North, Robert, yeoman, Chisledon, Wilts, 1632 Wilts RO Arch. Wilts.(name + date)
Hardinge, Francis, yeoman, Spalding, Lincs, 1668 Lincs RO Ad/Ac/33/43
Hardinge, John, yeoman, Winterbourne Bassett, Wilts, 1639 Wilts RO Arch. Wilts.(name + date)
Hardinge, Nicholas, Maidstone, Kent, 1598 CKS PRC21/14/579
Hardinge, Richard, Avebury, Wilts, 1627 Wilts RO Arch. Wilts.(name + date)
Hardinge, William, Chisledon, Wilts, 1632 Wilts RO Arch. Wilts.(name + date)
Hardinge, William,
Wilts 1679? Wilts RO Arch. Sarum(+ name and date)
Hardman, Charles, Turton, Lancs, 1690 Lancs RO (Name of Deceased) D.R.C.H. 1690
Hardman, Henry, whitster, Manchester (Broughton, Kersal), Lancs, 1769 Lancs RO (Name of Deceased) D.R.C.H. 1769
Hardman, John, carpenter, Rochdale, Lancs, 1799 Lancs RO (Name of Deceased) D.R.C.H. 1799
Hardowle, Nicholas, Newington next Sittingbourne, Kent, 1607 CKS PRC20/1/205
Hardwick, John,
Som 1592 Somerset RO D/D/Cta/H5
Hardwick, John, Pattingham, Staffs, 1710 LJRO/B/C/5/1710/37
Hardwick, Thomas, Bourne (Cawthorpe), Lincs, 1670 Lincs RO Ad/Ac/32/214
Hardwicke, Roger, Butterwick, Lincs, 1624 Lincs RO Ad/Ac/19A/18
Hardwin, Augustine, yeoman, High Halstow, Kent, 1663 CKS PRC1/9/122
Hardwitch, Robert, Burnham, Som, 1611 Somerset RO D/D/Cta/H72
Hardwyck, Richard, yeoman, Worcester St Martin, Worcs, Worcs RO 008.7 BA3585/838/90
Hardy, Edward, Coningsby, Lincs, 1679 Lincs RO Ad/Ac/43/110
Hardy, John, husbandman, Goxhill, Lincs, 1669 Lincs RO Ad/Ac/33/104
Hardy, John, farmer, Scoulton, Norf, 1816 Norfolk RO ANW/23/27/18
Hardy, Joseph, Barrowby, Lincs, 1717 Lincs RO Ad/Ac/45/6
Hardy, Richard, yeoman, Skidbrooke, Lincs, 1672 Lincs RO Ad/Ac/43/76
Hardy, Thomas, husbandman, Fishtoft, Lincs, 1683 Lincs RO Ad/Ac/44/81
Hardy, Walter, St Anne Westminster, London & Middlesex, 1727 Greater London RO AM/PP/Box 1726-1732 pt (uncatalogued)
Hardy, William, Steeping, Little, Lincs, 1637 Lincs RO Ad/Ac/25/577
Hardy, William, gentleman, Middlewich, Ches, 1789 Cheshire RO (Name) W.C. 1789
Hardy, Wyllyam, Selling, Kent, 1591 CKS PRC2/5/340
Hardye, Christopher, Heapham, Lincs, 1681 Lincs RO Ad/Ac/34/98

Hardyman, George, Elmsted, Kent, 1623 CKS PRC2/23/160
Hardyman, Thomas, Leicester St Mary, Leics, 1641 Leics RO PR/I/41A/82
Hare, Charles, Thurlby, Lincs, 1632 Lincs RO Ad/Ac/23/82
Hare, George, Cadney, Lincs, 1633 Lincs RO Ad/Ac/24/177
Hare, Richard, yeoman, Billingborough, Lincs, 1623 Lincs RO Ad/Ac/18/40
Hare, Richard, Pershore, Worcs, 1685 Worcs RO 008.7 BA3585/830/13
Hare, Robert, mariner, Blakeney, Norf, 1749 Norfolk RO ANW/23/24/77
Hare, Stephen, Dover, Kent, 1618 CKS PRC20/4/173
Hare, William, Crowle, Lincs, 1675 Lincs RO Ad/Ac/35/93
Hare, William eld, Folkestone, Kent, 1626 CKS PRC2/27/71
Harebie, John, Kirkby, East, Lincs, 1606 Lincs RO Ad/Ac/6/26
Harewell, Thomas, Evesham, Worcs, 1681 Worcs RO 008.7 BA3585/837/bdl 2
Harfleete, Charles, clergy: 'clerk', Newington next Hythe, Kent, 1673 CKS PRC2/35/221
Harflete, Dorothy, dame, Canterbury St Margaret, Kent, 1620 CKS PRC20/5/113
Harflete, Edward, Petham, Kent, 1597 CKS PRC2/9/235
Harford, Gyles, Bishopstone, Wilts, 1640 Wilts RO Arch. Sarum(+ name and date)
Harford, John, mariner, Bristol, Glos, Bristol RO 1714/20
Harforde, Nicholas, Whitstable, Kent, 1607 CKS PRC2/14/214
Hargate, William, Cowbit, Lincs, 1618 Lincs RO Ad/Ac/14/248
Hargoll, George, Fisherton Anger, Wilts, 1625 Wilts RO Miscellaneous Index (name + date)
Hargrave, Ann, widow, Lambeth, Surrey, 1692 PRO PROB5/1274
Hargrave, James, Spalding, Lincs, 1612 Lincs RO Ad/Ac/11/83
Hargrave, William, St James in the Fields, London & Middlesex, 1688 PRO PROB32/27/295
Hargraves, Francis, Leeds, Yorks, 1617 Borthwick Prob. Ex. 1617/1
Hargreave, James, Oxford St Aldate, Oxon, 1786 Oxon RO MSS Wills 302/5/96
Hargreaves, Thomas, yeoman, Haslingden (Higher Lane), Lancs, 1788 Lancs RO (Name of Deceased) D.R.C.H. 1788
Harhord?, Ursuley?, widow, Swinford, Leics, 1642 Leics RO PR/I/41A/94
Harison, George, Loughborough, Leics, 1666 Leics RO Administrators Accounts C17th f83
Harison, Mary, widow, St Ives, Hunts, 1679 Hunts RO/Acc58/133(186)
Harker, Bartholomewe, Sibsey, Lincs, 1620 Lincs RO Ad/Ac/16/50
Harker, John ygr, Whitstable, Kent, 1598 CKS PRC2/10/309
Harker, Richard, Whitstable, Kent, 1600 CKS PRC2/11/135
Harkett, Thomas, Ashby de la Zouch, Leics, 1668 Leics RO Administrators Accounts 1667-72 f11
Harlackenden, John, gentleman, New Romney, Kent, 1584 CKS PRC21/7/9
Harland, Ralph, Farndale, Yorks, 1638 Borthwick Prob. Ex. 1638/1
Harle, Bartholmew, Horsington, Lincs, 1640 Lincs RO Ad/Ac/27/82
Harlestone, see Tritton,
Harley, Thomas, Ashford, Kent, 1608 CKS PRC2/14/232
Harley, Thomas, Ashford, Kent, 1638 CKS PRC1/1/77
Harlie, Elizabeth, Ruckinge, Kent, 1613 CKS PRC2/17/207
Harlie, Richard, Egerton, Kent, 1612 CKS PRC20/2/388
Harloe, Mary, Faversham, Kent, 1632 CKS PRC2/31/122
Harlow, Gregory, Worth, Kent, 1592 CKS PRC21/11/272
Harlow, John, Worth, Kent, 1687 CKS PRC20/13/590
Harlowe, Alice, widow, Worth, Kent, 1592 CKS PRC21/12/172
Harlswoorthe, Robert, Ewell, Kent, 1613 CKS PRC2/17/55
Harman, Elizabeth, spinster, St Katherine Coleman, London & Middlesex, 1732 Greater London RO DL/C/548/88
Harman, Helen, spinster, Cranbrook, Kent, 1623 CKS PRC2/23/165
Harman, John, Pluckley, Kent, 1602 CKS PRC2/12/185
Harman, John, Cranbrook, Kent, 1623 CKS PRC2/23/163
Harman, Stephen, yeoman, Headcorn, Kent, 1691 CKS PRC2/41/177
Harman, Thomas, Cranbrook, Kent, 1607 CKS PRC2/14/221
Harman, Thomas, Bromfield, Kent, 1637 CKS PRC2/34/58

[Harman:]
Harman, Thomas, yeoman, Appledore, Kent, 1678 CKS PRC2/38/38
Harmer, William, Chippenham, Wilts, 1626 Wilts RO Arch. Wilts.(name + date)
Harmon, John, clothier, Headcorn, Kent, 1665 CKS PRC1/11/38
Harmond, Roberte, Goudhurst, Kent, 1600 CKS PRC2/11/137
Harnbie, John, Canterbury, Kent, 1598 CKS PRC2/10/228
Harnden, Bartholomew, Mersham, Kent, 1668 CKS PRC1/13/57
Harnden, Nathaniel, Marden, Kent, 1671 CKS PRC2/35/55
Harneden, John, cordwainer: 'shoemaker', Tenterden, Kent, 1629 CKS PRC20/8/271
Harneden, William, Smarden, Kent, 1613 CKS PRC2/16/119
Harnes, John, yeoman, Laceby, Lincs, 1620 Lincs RO Ad/Ac/16/47
Harnes, William, Leverton, Lincs, 1632 Lincs RO Ad/Ac/23/42
Harnesse, William, Sutton in the Marsh, Lincs, 1640 Lincs RO Ad/Ac/27/3
Harnet, William ygr, Sandwich, Kent, 1626 CKS PRC2/27/69
Harnett, Edward, Aldington, Kent, 1675 CKS PRC20/12/131
Harnett, Elizabeth, spinster, Minster in Thanet, Kent, 1712 CKS PRC1/17/28
Harnett, Henry, yeoman, St Laurence Thanet, Kent, 1686 CKS PRC2/41/55
Harnett, Margaret, widow, Canterbury, Kent, 1624 CKS PRC2/23/167
Harpam, William, Fiskerton, Lincs, 1592 Lincs RO Ad/Ac/37/13
Harpe, Christofer, Lenham, Kent, 1597 CKS PRC2/9/132
Harpe, James, St Thomas Isle of Harty, Kent, 1627 CKS PRC2/28/52
Harpe, Solomon, Doddington, Kent, 1632 CKS PRC2/31/43
Harper, Henry, watchmaker?/widower, Islington St Mary, London & Middlesex, 1710 PRO PROB32/53/43
Harper, Michael, clothier, Cranbrook, Kent, 1676 CKS PRC2/37/42
Harper, Timothy, Skirbeck, Lincs, 1641? Lincs RO Ad/Ac/27/220
Harper, William, Lenham, Kent, 1628 CKS PRC2/29/49
Harpley, William, baker, Wymondham, Norf, 1765 Norfolk RO ANF/11/5/58
Harpur, Edward, Stockport, Ches, 1665 Cheshire RO (Name) W.C. 1651-64
Harpur, Henry, Shustoke, Warks, 1680 LJRO/B/C/5/1682/49
Harpur, John, Whitchurch, Shrops, 1682 LJRO/B/C/5/1681/21
Harpur, Richard, Daresbury (Moore), Ches, 1612 Cheshire RO (Name) W.C. 1612
Harr, Francis, Welton le Marsh (Boothby), Lincs, 1626 Lincs RO Ad/Ac/20/64
Harr, Jone, widow, Addlethorpe, Lincs, 1666 Lincs RO Ad/Ac/32/80
Harrap, Richard, farmer, Dewsbury, Yorks, 1804 Borthwick Test C.P. 1804/3
Harrden, Elizabeth, spinster, Grinstead, West, Sussex, 1674 W. Suss RO EpI/33/1674/8
Harres, William, Glastonbury St John, Som, 1596 Somerset RO D/D/Cta/H36
Harrett, Nicholas, Chilham, Kent, 1610 CKS PRC2/15/184
Harrey, Jane, Hawkhurst, Kent, 1639 CKS PRC19/1/17
Harriatt, Francis, Wellingborough, Northants, 1679 Northants RO NWill A/C/43
Harrice, Elizabeth, Haxey, Lincs, 1674 Lincs RO Ad/Ac/35/77
Harriden, William, carpenter, Thakeham, Sussex, 1598 W. Suss RO EpI/33/1597/9
Harrie, John, Lanreath, Corn, 1614 Cornwall RO AP/H318
Harriet, Stephen, Faversham, Kent, 1628 CKS PRC2/29/46
Harrington, Christopher, Keddington, Lincs, 1605 Lincs RO Ad/Ac/6/14
Harrington, Mary, widow, Westley, Suff, 1781 Suff RO(B) IC500/3/52/80
Harrington, Richard, glover, Gainsborough, Lincs, 1604 Lincs RO Ad/Ac/37/176
Harrington, Robarte, esquire, Witham on the Hill, Lincs, 1602 Lincs RO Ad/Ac/5/393
Harrington, Thomas, physician: 'practitioner of physic', Bagworth, Leics, 1686 Leics RO Administrators Accounts 1682-86 f50
Harriotts, Francis, Stockton, Warks, 1682 LJRO/B/C/5/1682/48
Harris, Adam, Whitstable, Kent, 1695 CKS PRC2/42/102
Harris, Alexander, yeoman, Molash, Kent, 1626 CKS PRC2/27/72
Harris, Ann, widow, Canterbury St Mary Northgate, Kent, 1624 CKS PRC2/23/169
Harris, Anne, widow, Faversham, Kent, 1663 CKS PRC1/9/123
Harris, Arnold, Preston next Faversham, Kent, 1603 CKS PRC2/14/240

Harris, Benjamin, gentleman, Appledore, Kent, 1674 CKS PRC2/36/69
Harris, Charles, Winslow, Bucks, 1676 Herts RO ASA25/3953
Harris, Christopher, dyer, Faversham, Kent, 1671 CKS PRC1/15/35
Harris, Daniel, Weston Favell, Northants, 1680 Northants RO NWill A/C/3
Harris, Edward, Goudhurst, Kent, 1605 CKS PRC2/14/238
Harris, Edward, Birchington, Kent, 1621 CKS PRC20/5/77
Harris, George, husbandman, Marden, Kent, 1649 CKS PRC1/8/70
Harris, George, Damerham, Wilts, 1670 Wilts RO Arch. Sarum(+ name and date)
Harris, Henry, Salford Priors, Warks, 1684 Worcs RO 008.7 BA3585/837/bdl 4
Harris, Jane, spinster, Swineshead, Lincs, 1632 Lincs RO Ad/Ac/23/21
Harris, Joan, spinster, Garston, East, Berks, 1623 Berks RO D/A1/78/152B
Harris, John, Throwleigh, Kent, 1596 CKS PRC2/8/77
Harris, John, Pluckley, Kent, 1599 CKS PRC2/10/155
Harris, John, Bethersden, Kent, 1602 CKS PRC2/12/218
Harris, John, Appledore, Kent, 1610 CKS PRC20/2/112
Harris, John, Frampton, Lincs, 1612 Lincs RO Ad/Ac/11/15
Harris, John, St Blazey, Corn, 1615 Cornwall RO AP/H357
Harris, John, Milton next Sittingbourne, Kent, 1616 CKS PRC2/22/176
Harris, John, Coker, East, Som, 1624 Somerset RO D/D/Cta/H28
Harris, John, Canterbury St Margaret, Kent, 1625 CKS PRC2/25/66
Harris, John, Martin, Wilts, 1632 Wilts RO Arch. Sarum(+ name and date)
Harris, John, yeoman, Ashton, Steeple, Wilts, 1638 Wilts RO Arch. Sarum(+ name and date)
Harris, John, Welton, Northants, 1680 Northants RO NWill A/C/28
Harris, John, Kingsbury, Warks, 1682 LJRO/B/C/5/1682/50
Harris, John eld, husbandman, Harrietsham, Kent, 1665 CKS PRC1/11/39
Harris, John jun, Donnington, Sussex, 1676 W. Suss RO EpI/33/1676/9
Harris, Joseph, bachelor: 'singleman', Somerton, East, Norf, 1711 Norfolk RO ANW/23/10/36
Harris, Josias, mariner, Dover, Kent, 1676 CKS PRC20/12/202
Harris, Leonard, Bagborough, West, Som, 1687 Somerset RO D/D/Cta/H82
Harris, Luke, mariner, Dover, Kent, 1681 CKS PRC20/13/145
Harris, Margaret, Minster in Sheppey, Kent, 1618 CKS PRC2/22/170
Harris, Margaret, Minster in Sheppey, Kent, 1631 CKS PRC2/30/83
Harris, Margaret, Minster in Sheppey, Kent, 1641 CKS PRC1/4/55
Harris, Nicholas, Queenborough, Kent, 1596 CKS PRC2/8/441
Harris, Oliver, carpenter, Benenden, Kent, 1682 CKS PRC2/40/39
Harris, Paul, Chislet, Kent, 1669 CKS PRC1/13/58
Harris, Philip, Westbourne, Sussex, 1613 W. Suss RO EpI/33/1613/20
Harris, Reginald, Hernhill, Kent, 1672 CKS PRC20/12/52
Harris, Richard, yeoman, Bampton (Shifford), Oxon, Oxon RO MSS Wills 131/5/22
Harris, Richard, St Veep, Corn, 1607 Cornwall RO AP/H145
Harris, Richard, Bethersden, Kent, 1613 CKS PRC2/18/8
Harris, Richard, Donnington, Sussex, 1627 W. Suss RO EpI/33/1627/11
Harris, Richard, Marden, Kent, 1628 CKS PRC2/29/53
Harris, Richard, gentleman, Damerham, South, Wilts, 1641 Wilts RO Arch. Sarum(+ name and date)
Harris, Robert, Maidstone, Kent, 1599 CKS PRC21/15/37
Harris, Robert, gentleman, Reading St Lawrence, Berks, 1606 Berks RO D/A1/195/17C
Harris, Robert, brewer's servant/labourer, Reading St Giles, Berks, 1679 Berks RO D/A1/197/38B
Harris, Robert + Mary, Bremhill (Foxham), Wilts, 1637 Wilts RO Arch. Wilts.(name + date)
Harris, Samuel, gentleman, Sutton (Lutton), Lincs, 1679 Lincs RO Ad/Ac/43/100
Harris, Simon, Wimborne Minster, Dors, 1676 Dorset RO PE/WM CP 2/4/82
Harris, Thomas, yeoman, Chart, Great, Kent, 1623 CKS PRC2/23/150
Harris, Thomas, Teynham, Kent, 1626 CKS PRC2/27/66
Harris, Thomas, husbandman, Charlbury (Chilson), Oxon, 1628 Oxon RO MSS Wills 297/5/11
Harris, Thomas, Orcheston St George, Wilts, 1663 Wilts RO Arch. Sarum(+ name and date)

[Harris:]
Harris, Thomas, clothier, Witney, Oxon, 1663 Oxon RO MSS Wills 80/4/27
Harris, Thomas, Wellow, East, Hants, 1669 Hants RO 21M65 D8/202
Harris, Thomas, Bidford, Warks, 1685 Worcs RO 008.7 BA3585/830/83
Harris, Thomas, Whaddon, Glos, 1685 GRO GDR/B4/2/H175
Harris, William, Kennington, Kent, 1614 CKS PRC2/18/85
Harris, William, waterman, Spalding, Lincs, 1618 Lincs RO Ad/Ac/14/38
Harris, William, butcher, Faversham, Kent, 1624 CKS PRC2/23/164
Harris, William, Bridge, Kent, 1625 CKS PRC2/25/63
Harris, William, husbandman, Bedwin, Great, Wilts, 1637 Wilts RO Pec Lord Warden Savernake Forest Bundle 1/25
Harris, William, Fisherton Anger, Wilts, 1638? Wilts RO CC Sarum(+ name and date)
Harris, William, Dalby, Great, Leics, 1639 Leics RO PR/I/41A/17
Harris, William, Chartham, Kent, 1641 CKS PRC1/5/100
Harris, William, yeoman, Bourton on Dunsmore, Warks, 1675 LJRO:cards/1675/33
Harris, William, Stapleford, Wilts, 1690 Wilts RO Arch. Sarum(+ name and date)
Harris, Wylliam, Canterbury St Dunstan Without, Kent, 1597 CKS PRC2/9/501
Harris/Combes, Katherine, Wimborne Minster (Hound Hill), Dors, 1663 Dorset RO PE/WM CP 2/4/68
Harrison, Boston, Lincs, 1648 Lincs RO Ad/Ac/30/346
Harrison, Agnes, Luccombe, Som, 1597 Somerset RO D/D/Cta/H34
Harrison, Alexander, New Romney, Kent, 1667 CKS PRC19/3/123
Harrison, Andrew, yeoman, Chilham, Kent, 1693 CKS PRC2/42/66
Harrison, Anne, widow, Belton, Lincs, 1670 Lincs RO Ad/Ac/32/130
Harrison, Basil, yeoman, Chislet, Kent, 1689 CKS PRC2/41/124
Harrison, Charles, esquire, Ripon, Yorks, 1831 Borthwick Test C.P. 1831/1
Harrison, Clement, Eastry, Kent, 1609 CKS PRC20/1/360
Harrison, Daniell, husbandman, Breedon on the Hill, Leics, 1671 Leics RO Administrators Accounts 1667-72 f34
Harrison, Edward, Cheriton, Kent, 1606 CKS PRC20/1/108
Harrison, Elizabeth, Whitton, Lincs, 1609 Lincs RO Ad/Ac/8a/309
Harrison, Francis, gentleman, Burton on Stather, Lincs, 1623 Lincs RO Ad/Ac/8c/33
Harrison, Gawin, Donnington, Sussex, 1632 W. Suss RO EpI/33/1632/29
Harrison, George, Mareham le Fen, Lincs, 1607 Lincs RO Ad/Ac/8a/87
Harrison, George, Hollingbourne, Kent, 1682 CKS PRC20/13/141
Harrison, George, Godmersham, Kent, 1683 CKS PRC20/13/337
Harrison, George, Charing, Kent, 1724 CKS PRC19/6/72
Harrison, Hugh, Dymchurch, Kent, 1699 CKS PRC2/42/156
Harrison, Isabell, Haxey, Lincs, 1619 Lincs RO Ad/Ac/8b/417
Harrison, Jacob, university: 'Fellow of Christ's College, Cambridge/B.D.', Cambridge, Cambs, 1613 CUL V.C.Acc./Box1/25
Harrison, James, yeoman, Haxey (Burnham), Lincs, 1669 Lincs RO Ad/Ac/33/158
Harrison, James, husbandman, Ruckinge, Kent, 1681 CKS PRC2/39/192
Harrison, Joan, widow, Easebourne, Sussex, 1625 W. Suss RO EpI/33/1624/2
Harrison, John, Holton Beckering, Lincs, 1593 Lincs RO Ad/Ac/3/61
Harrison, John, Grantham, Lincs, 1605 Lincs RO Ad/Ac/6/145
Harrison, John, Fleet, Lincs, 1607 Lincs RO Ad/Ac/8a/95
Harrison, John, brother, Canterbury St John's Hospital, Kent, 1622 CKS PRC20/5/97
Harrison, John, Sandwich, Kent, 1632 CKS PRC2/31/39
Harrison, John, Belshford, Lincs, 1662 Lincs RO Ad/Ac/32/30a
Harrison, John, Mablethorpe, Lincs, 1664 Lincs RO Ad/Ac/43/49
Harrison, John, cheesemonger/bachelor, Dover, Kent, 1667 CKS PRC19/3/95
Harrison, John, cordwainer, Saltfleetby, Lincs, 1669 Lincs RO Ad/Ac/32/194
Harrison, John, innholder, Louth, Lincs, 1670 Lincs RO Ad/Ac/42/107
Harrison, John, yeoman, Canwick, Lincs, 1670 Lincs RO Ad/Ac/43/54
Harrison, John, 1682 Lancs RO (Name of Deceased) D.R.C.H. 1681-82

Harrison, John, Chart, Great, Kent, 1683 CKS PRC2/40/119
Harrison, Joseph, plasterer, Manchester, Lancs, 1799 Lancs RO (Name of Deceased) D.R.C.H. 1799
Harrison, Katherine, spinster, Oxford St Peter in the East, Oxon, 1637 Oxon RO MSS Wills 298/1/25
Harrison, Magdalen, widow, Toynton, Lincs, 1652 Lincs RO Ad/Ac/29/16
Harrison, Margery, Woodnesborough, Kent, 1599 CKS PRC2/10/218
Harrison, Mary, Dymchurch, Kent, 1690 CKS PRC2/41/176
Harrison, Richard, yeoman, Wainfleet All Saints, Lincs, 1629 Lincs RO Ad/Ac/22/118
Harrison, Richard, Oxford (University), Oxon, 1633 Bodleian HYP B8/96-97
Harrison, Richard, Gedney, Lincs, 1634 Lincs RO Ad/Ac/24/250
Harrison, Richard, Earl Shilton, Leics, 1666 Leics RO Administrators Accounts C17th f62
Harrison, Richard, Blore, Staffs, 1702 LJRO/B/C/5/1702/12
Harrison, Robert, Herne, Kent, 1623 CKS PRC20/6/372
Harrison, Robert, Wroot, Lincs, 1631 Lincs RO Ad/Ac/39/251
Harrison, Robert, Alford, Lincs, 1639? Lincs RO Ad/Ac/26/148
Harrison, Robert, Glentham, Lincs, 1674 Lincs RO Ad/Ac/42/28
Harrison, Robert, Orton Water Ville, Hunts, 1684 Hunts RO/Acc58/210
Harrison, Rose, university: 'privileged person/widow', Cambridge, Cambs, 1647 c. CUL V.C. Acc./Box2/28
Harrison, Rowland, Cauldon, Staffs, 1676 LJRO:cards/1676/26
Harrison, Samuel, bachelor, Stainton by Langworth, Lincs, 1668 Lincs RO Ad/Ac/33/51
Harrison, Sarles, Chislet, Kent, 1680 CKS PRC2/38/139
Harrison, Searles, Chislet, Kent, 1681 CKS PRC1/15/97
Harrison, Stephen, Woodnesborough, Kent, 1635 CKS PRC2/33/59
Harrison, Thomas, Broughton, Lincs, 1610 Lincs RO Ad/Ac/8a/326
Harrison, Thomas, Stratfield Mortimer, Berks, 1612 Berks RO D/A1/195/47A
Harrison, Thomas, Sandwich, Kent, 1618 CKS PRC1/1/24
Harrison, Thomas, Sandwich, Kent, 1618 CKS PRC1/1/24a
Harrison, Thomas, university: 'Vice-Master of Trinity College, Cambridge/B.D.' Cambridge (Trinity College), Cambs, 1631 c. CUL V.C. Acc./Box2/29
Harrison, Thomas, Coldred, Kent, 1638 CKS PRC2/34/217
Harrison, Thomas, St Albans St Peters, Herts, 1638 Herts RO ASA25/4940
Harrison, Thomas, labourer, Edlington, Lincs, 1639 Lincs RO Ad/Ac/26/200
Harrison, Thomas, Hemingby, Lincs, 1639? Lincs RO Ad/Ac/26/106
Harrison, Thomas, Stourmouth, Kent, 1669 CKS PRC1/14/52
Harrison, Thomas, Canterbury St Andrew, Kent, 1678 CKS PRC2/38/36
Harrison, Thomas, Guston, Kent, 1708 CKS PRC19/6/30
Harrison, Thomas, Landrax, Yorks, 1720 Borthwick Test C.P. 1720/4
Harrison, Thomas, Height, Lancs, 1767 Lancs RO (Name of Deceased) D.R.C.H. 1767
Harrison, Walter, Sturry, Kent, 1620 CKS PRC2/22/146
Harrison, William, Wigtoft, Lincs, 1618 Lincs RO Ad/Ac/14/276
Harrison, William, Haxey, Lincs, 1619 Lincs RO Ad/Ac/8b/447
Harrison, William, Kirton, Lincs, 1619 Lincs RO Ad/Ac/15/260
Harrison, William, Wickhambreaux, Kent, 1619 CKS PRC2/22/155
Harrison, William, Minster in Thanet, Kent, 1620 CKS PRC1/1/27
Harrison, William, Caistor, Lincs, 1624 Lincs RO Ad/Ac/39/137
Harrison, William, yeoman, Tonge, Kent, 1626 CKS PRC2/27/68
Harrison, William, Tattell, Lincs, 1662 Lincs RO Ad/Ac/32/39
Harrison, William, yeoman, Stourmouth, Kent, 1671 CKS PRC2/35/52
Harrison, William, St Martin in the Fields, London & Middlesex, 1674 Greater London RO AM/PP/Box 1670-1678 pt (uncatalogued)
Harrison, William, gentleman, Canterbury St Paul, Kent, 1675 CKS PRC2/36/65
Harrison, William, farmer, Chellaston, Derby, 1809 LJRO/B/C/5/1809/31b
Harrison, Woodthorpe, Fulletby, Lincs, 1680 Lincs RO Ad/Ac/34/52

[Harrison, see Hey:]
Harrison, see Hey,
Harrisonne, Ambrose, Spalding, Lincs, 1627 Lincs RO Ad/Ac/20b/10
Harrock/Haddocke, draper,
Worcs Worcs RO 008.7 BA3585/834/441
Harrold, Ralfe, Marlborough, Wilts, 1629 Wilts RO CC Sarum(+ name and date)
Harrold, Thomas, Pirton, Wilts, 1621 Wilts RO CC Sarum(+ name and date)
Harrolde, Thomas, Bedwin, Great, Wilts, 1597 Wilts RO Miscellaneous Index (name + date)
Harrwood, Henry, Hacconby (Stainfield), Lincs, 1649 Lincs RO Ad/Ac/30/40
Harry, Anthony, Marden, Kent, 1627 CKS PRC2/28/63
Harry, Roberte, St Laurence Thanet, Kent, 1591 CKS PRC2/5/332
Harryden, Edward, Thakeham, Sussex, 1635 W. Suss RO EpI/33/1635/22
Harryman, James, gentleman, Hemingby, Lincs, 1680 Lincs RO Ad/Ac/34/38
Harryman, William, Donington, Lincs, 1584? Lincs RO Ad/Ac/1/27
Harrys, Christopher, Minster in Sheppey, Kent, 1582 CKS PRC21/6/87
Harrys, Edward, joiner, Faversham, Kent, 1580 CKS PRC2/1/269
Harrys, John + Cassandra, Tydd St Mary, Lincs, 1607 Lincs RO Ad/Ac/8a/91
Harrys, Margarett, widow, Appledore, Kent, 1592 CKS PRC2/6/448
Harrys, William, Lelant, Corn, 1610 Cornwall RO AP/H224
Harryson, Robert, Belshford, Lincs, 1645 Lincs RO Ad/Ac/28/119
Harryson, William, Watford, Herts, 1581 Herts RO ASA25/1010
Harryson, see Marchall,
Harse, Richard,
Som 1689 Somerset RO D/D/Cta/H83
Harsenett, Thomas, butcher, Linton, Kent, 1682 CKS PRC2/39/186
Harsnet, Henry, Orlestone, Kent, 1619 CKS PRC2/22/156
Hart, Christopher, yeoman, Clewer, Berks, 1647 Berks RO D/A1/196/71A
Hart, Christopher, Bredgar, Kent, 1649 CKS PRC1/8/71
Hart, Daniell, Egerton, Kent, 1624 CKS PRC20/6/10
Hart, Edmund, Chilham, Kent, 1631 CKS PRC2/30/88
Hart, Edward, Smeeth, Kent, 1622 CKS PRC20/6/356
Hart, George, Wittersham, Kent, 1629 CKS PRC20/8/279
Hart, Henry, Wye, Kent, 1664 CKS PRC1/10/46
Hart, Henry, Sellindge, Kent, 1678 CKS PRC2/38/39
Hart, Henry eld, gentleman, Sellindge, Kent, 1677 CKS PRC2/37/153
Hart, Henry ygr, gentleman, Sellindge, Kent, 1676 CKS PRC2/37/40
Hart, John, Reculver, Kent, 1609 CKS PRC20/2/41
Hart, Katherin, widow, Ruckinge, Kent, 1617 CKS PRC2/22/161
Hart, Priscilla, widow, Langdon, East, Kent, 1622 CKS PRC2/23/153
Hart, Richard, Ivychurch, Kent, 1639 CKS PRC20/10/536
Hart, Richard, maltster, Sandwich St Peter, Kent, 1669 CKS PRC1/14/53
Hart, Richard, Canterbury St Mary Northgate, Kent, 1679 CKS PRC2/38/137
Hart, Robert, Molash, Kent, 1617 CKS PRC2/21/3
Hart, Susanna, shopkeeper, Wheatley, Oxon, 1725 Oxon RO MSS Wills 134/1/29
Hart, Thomas, Dover, Kent, 1607 CKS PRC20/1/193
Hart, Thomas, Folkestone, Kent, 1622 CKS PRC2/23/154
Hart, Thomas, New Romney, Kent, 1669 CKS PRC19/4/18
Hart, Thomas, Melksham, Wilts, 1770 Wilts RO Miscellaneous Index (name + date)
Hart, Tobias, Nailsea, Som, 1707 Somerset RO D/D/Cta/H92
Hart, William, Whitstable, Kent, 1635 CKS PRC2/33/66
Hart, William, yeoman, Seend, Wilts, 1639 Wilts RO CC Sarum(+ name and date)
Hart, Wylliam, Spalding, Lincs, 1580 Lincs RO Ad/Ac/2b/55
Harte, George, Goodnestone next Wingham, Kent, 1616 CKS PRC20/3/272
Harte, Giles, Snave, Kent, 1605 CKS PRC2/14/217
Harte, Henry, Ebony, Kent, 1595 CKS PRC2/7/457
Harte, James, Westwell, Kent, 1621 CKS PRC20/5/86

Harte, James, Charing, Kent, 1635 CKS PRC20/10/486
Harte, James, Cammeringham, Lincs, 1649 Lincs RO Ad/Ac/40/186
Harte, James eld, Westwell, Kent, 1621 CKS PRC20/5/91
Harte, Joan, widow, St Nicholas at Wade, Kent, 1604 CKS PRC21/15/338
Harte, Joane, widow, Smeeth, Kent, 1634 CKS PRC20/10/578
Harte, John, Dover, Kent, 1587 CKS PRC21/8/375
Harte, John, Charing, Kent, 1597 CKS PRC21/14/155
Harte, John,
Kent 1612 CKS PRC2/17/189
Harte, John, St Albans St Stephens, Herts, 1650 Herts RO ASA25/3563
Harte, John eld, Charing, Kent, 1696 CKS PRC19/5/43
Harte, Nicholas, Hollingbourne, Kent, 1663 CKS PRC19/3/28
Harte, Paule, Selling, Kent, 1634 CKS PRC2/32/52
Harte, Richard, husbandman, Leigh, Worcs, 1604 Worcs RO 008.7 BA3585/839/301
Harte, Symon, Eastwell, Kent, 1597 CKS PRC2/10/327
Harte, Thomas, Stanford, Kent, 1585 CKS PRC21/7/250
Harte, Thomas, Davington, Kent, 1597 CKS PRC2/9/497
Harte, Thomas, Smeeth, Kent, 1605 CKS PRC20/1/37
Harte, Thomas, Swalecliffe, Kent, 1605 CKS PRC2/15/178
Harte, Thomas, Stanford, Kent, 1619 CKS PRC20/4/126
Harte, Thomas, Chart, Little, Kent, 1627 CKS PRC2/28/62
Harte, Thomas, Chichester (Pallant), Sussex, 1639 W. Suss RO EpIV/10/2/22
Harte, Vincent, Stanford, Kent, 1632 CKS PRC20/9/237
Harte, see Lucas & Paine,
Hartey, Jeremy, Birchington, Kent, 1620 CKS PRC20/5/95
Hartfield, Andrew, Shalbourne, Berks, 1681 Wilts RO Dean Sarum (name + date)
Hartford, John, shopkeeper, Dauntsey, Wilts, 1750 Wilts RO Arch. Wilts.(name + date)
Hartfordshire, Margaret, widow, Bristol St Stephen, Glos, Bristol RO 1678/78
Hartgrave, Francis, Coningsby, Lincs, 1640 Lincs RO Ad/Ac/27/112
Hartley, Elizabeth, Washingborough (Heighington), Lincs, 1624 Lincs RO Ad/Ac/19A/122
Hartley, Henry, Corringham, Lincs, 1684 Lincs RO Ad/Ac/42/96
Hartley, James, Gainsborough, Lincs, 1663 Lincs RO Ad/Ac/41/100
Hartley, Joseph, Eartham, Sussex, 1625 W. Suss RO EpI/33/1625/5
Hartley, Thomas, Bristol St James, Glos, Bristol RO 1678/73
Hartley, Thomas, yeoman, Aldingbourne, Sussex, 1682 W. Suss RO EpI/33/1682/11
Hartnup, Mathew, Headcorn, Kent, 1682 CKS PRC2/39/178
Hartopp, Thomas, Grantham, Lincs, 1619 Lincs RO Ad/Ac/15/89
Hartridge, William, gentleman, Canterbury St Augustine's Monastery, Kent, 1680 CKS PRC20/13/30
Hartrop, Stephen, yeoman, Boxley, Kent, 1618 CKS PRC20/4/165
Hartrop, William, Newington next Sittingbourne, Kent, 1618 CKS PRC2/22/174
Hartsole, Peter, clothier, Hawkhurst, Kent, 1614 CKS PRC2/18/43
Hartt/Barrom, Elizabeth, widow, Smeeth, Kent, 1636 CKS PRC20/10/574
Hartte, Nicholas, Brabourne, Kent, 1592 CKS PRC2/6/511
Hartup/Virgin, Elizabeth, widow, East Sutton, Kent, 1676 CKS PRC2/37/43
Hartupp, Robert, yeoman, East Sutton, Kent, 1675 CKS PRC2/36/199
Hartupp, William, Kirton, Lincs, 1631 Lincs RO Ad/Ac/23/65
Hartwell, Edward, Titchfield, Hants, 1662 Hants RO 21M65 D8/156
Hartwell, John, St Dunstan in the East, London & Middlesex, 1632 Lambeth Palace VH95/894
Hartwell, Toby, Swalcliffe, Oxon, 1628 Oxon RO MSS Wills 297/5/17
Harvard, John, Isle Abbots, Som, 1714 Somerset RO D/D/Cta/H68
Harvet, Richard, Bersted, South (Bognor), Sussex, 1676 W. Suss RO EpIV/10/2A/14
Harvey, Frances, widow, Winchcombe, Glos, 1702 GRO GDR/B4/2/H84
Harvey, Francis, carpenter/privileged person, Cambridge Holy Trinity, Cambs, 1632 CUL V.C. Acc./Box2/33

[Harvey:]
Harvey, James, husbandman, Blankney, Lincs, 1672 Lincs RO Ad/Ac/43/71
Harvey, Joan, widow, Bersted, South (Bognor), Sussex, 1639 W. Suss RO EpIV/10/2/23
Harvey, John, Holbeach, Lincs, 1619 Lincs RO Ad/Ac/14/278
Harvey, John, cook, Oxford (University), Oxon, 1638 Bodleian HYP B8/97-98
Harvey, John, Niton, Hants, 1668 Hants RO 21M65 D8/203
Harvey, John, Measham, Derby, 1679 LJRO:cards/1679/4
Harvey, John, bachelor, Connington, Hunts, 1682 Hunts RO/Acc58/184(28)
Harvey, John, bucklemaker, Birmingham, Warks, 1754 LJRO/B/C/5/1754/127a
Harvey, John, Wymondham, Norf, 1764 Norfolk RO ANF/11/5/52
Harvey, Richard, Eling, Hants, 1672 Hants RO 21m65 D8/243
Harvey, Richard, Cranbrook, Kent, 1675 CKS PRC2/36/71
Harvey, Robert, Buckland nr Dover, Kent, 1617 CKS PRC20/4/157
Harvey, Robert, Kyme, South, Lincs, 1618 Lincs RO Ad/Ac/14/277
Harvey, Robert, St Buryan, Corn, 1644 Cornwall RO AP/DSB/8/2
Harvey, Robert, yeoman, Foulden, Norf, 1763 Norfolk RO ANF/11/5/51
Harvey, Sarah, spinster, Cauldon, Staffs, 1799 LJRO/B/C/5/1799/46
Harvey, Thomas, Milton next Sittingbourne, Kent, 1665 CKS PRC1/10/47
Harvey, Thomas, Kingstone, Staffs, 1680 LJRO:cards/1680/17
Harvey, Valentine, Hougham, Kent, 1632 CKS PRC2/31/123
Harvey, William, Pidley, Hunts, 1676 Hunts RO/Acc58/57(20)
Harvey, William, clergy: 'clerk', Metheringham, Lincs, 1720 Lincs RO Ad/Ac/45/12
Harveye, Thomas, Dover, Kent, 1614 CKS PRC20/3/107
Harvie, Henry, Belton, Lincs, 1662 Lincs RO Ad/Ac/32/9
Harvie, John, St Minver, Corn, 1612 Cornwall RO AP/H245
Harvie, Robert, Coleby, Lincs, 1624 Lincs RO Ad/Ac/8c/49
Harvie, Rose, Lympne, Kent, 1602 CKS PRC2/12/193
Harvie, William, Swingfield, Kent, 1594 CKS PRC2/6/136
Harvie, William, yeoman, Foston, Lincs, 1637 Lincs RO Ad/Ac/25/406
Harvie, William, Pinchbeck, Lincs, 1638 Lincs RO Ad/Ac/25/17
Harvill, William, High Halden, Kent, 1598 CKS PRC2/10/334
Harvord, John, Aller, Som, 1665 Somerset RO D/D/Cta/H77
Harvy, Henry, Swingfield, Kent, 1639 CKS PRC1/2/71
Harvy, Samuel, Benenden, Kent, 1685 CKS PRC2/41/31
Harvy, Thomas, gentleman, Northwood, Hants, Hants RO 1582 AD15/5
Harvy, William, yeoman, Kirton, Lincs, 1613 Lincs RO Ad/Ac/12/98
Harvye, Robart, Northbourne, Kent, 1602 CKS PRC2/12/187
Harwar, Thomas, gentleman, Congleton, Ches, 1797 Cheshire RO (Name) W.C. 1797
Harward, Paul, mr/gentleman, St Martin in the Fields, London & Middlesex, 1675 PRO PROB32/12/80
Harward, Thomas, clergy: 'clerk', Herne, Kent, 1622 CKS PRC20/6/344
Harwood, Alice, widow, Dover, Kent, 1621 CKS PRC20/5/105
Harwood, Androw, Sandwich, Kent, 1596 CKS PRC2/8/320
Harwood, Arthur, Milford, Hants, 1672 Hants RO 21m65 D8/244
Harwood, George, Swinderby, Lincs, 1637 Lincs RO Ad/Ac/25/527
Harwood, Goddard, New Romney, Kent, 1597 CKS PRC21/14/163
Harwood, Henry, fishmonger, Dover, Kent, 1620 CKS PRC20/4/143
Harwood, John, Sholden, Kent, 1619 CKS PRC2/21/4
Harwood, John, tailor, Spilsby, Lincs, 1668 Lincs RO Ad/Ac/33/45
Harwood, Margaret, widow, Kirton, Lincs, 1670 Lincs RO Ad/Ac/32/150
Harwood, Richard, gentleman, Winchester, Hants, 1654 Hants RO 1638 A79/2
Harwood, Thomas, Sandwich St Mary, Kent, 1594 CKS PRC2/6/352
Harwood, Thomas, Shadoxhurst, Kent, 1626 CKS PRC2/27/79
Harwood, Thomas, Climping, Sussex, 1630 W. Suss RO EpI/33/1630/25
Harwood, Thomas, Houghton, Sussex, 1632 W. Suss RO EpI/33/1632/30
Harwood, Thomas, Pulborough, Sussex, 1640 W. Suss RO EpI/33/1640/5

Harwood, Thomas, High Halden, Kent, 1681 CKS PRC2/39/190
Harwood, Thomas, Waltham, Bishops, Hants, 1689 Hants RO 21m65 D8/354
Harwood, William, Shadoxhurst, Kent, 1595 CKS PRC2/7/439
Harwood, William, Thurlby, Lincs, 1602 Lincs RO Ad/Ac/5/457
Harwood, William, Dover, Kent, 1629 CKS PRC20/8/277
Hasel, John, Bethersden, Kent, 1620 CKS PRC2/22/143
Haselden, John, Biddenden, Kent, 1590 CKS PRC2/5/334
Haseler, Roger, Fareham, Hants, 1684 Hants RO 21m65 D8/341b
Haselherst, Augustine, Burmarsh, Kent, 1621 CKS PRC2/22/144
Haselhurst, John, Bonnington, Kent, 1618 CKS PRC2/21/5
Hasell, Richard, Welford, Berks, 1594 Berks RO D/A1/194/69B
Hasell, Richard eld, yeoman, Shefford, Great, Berks, 1677 Berks RO D/A1/197/27D
Hasell, Robert, Yateley, Hants, 1663 Hants RO 21M65 D8/168
Hasell, Thomas, blacksmith, Kintbury, Berks, 1634 Berks RO D/A1/196/28A
Hasell, see Farmer,
Haselupp, George, Ickham, Kent, 1614 CKS PRC20/2/444
Haselwood, Isaac, Doddington, Kent, 1633 CKS PRC2/32/60
Haselwood, Richard, mariner: 'seafaring man', Dover, Kent, 1637 CKS PRC20/10/518
Hasker, Stephen, Sherfield Upon Loddon, Hants, 1623 Hants RO 21M65 D8/20
Haslam, Christopher, Gainsborough, Lincs, 1631? Lincs RO Ad/Ac/39/238
Haslam, Joshua, mariner, Liverpool, Lancs, 1762 Lancs RO (Name of Deceased) D.R.C.H. 1762
Haslam, William, Maidstone, Kent, 1604 CKS PRC21/17/138
Hasland, Adam, Cranbrook, Kent, 1595 CKS PRC2/7/445
Hasleby, George, Walmer, Kent, 1641 CKS PRC1/5/101
Haslegrove, Richard, Hothfield, Kent, 1637 CKS PRC2/34/69
Hasleham, George, miner: 'lead miner', Linton (Grassington), Yorks, 1794 Borthwick Test C.P. 1794/5
Hasleham, John, Goudhurst, Kent, 1637 CKS PRC2/34/59
Haslehurst, Thomas, yeoman, Drayton, Market (Sutton), Shrops, 1674 LJRO:cards/1674/21
Haslen, John, Headcorn, Kent, 1625 CKS PRC2/25/67
Haslewood, Peter, Lincoln, Lincs, 1719 Lincs RO Ad/Ac/45/10
Haslewood, Thomas, pilot, Deal, Kent, CKS PRC19/4/109
Haslipp, Thomas, Steyning, Sussex, 1673 W. Suss RO EpI/33/1673/17
Hassell, Edward, Ashendon (Pollicott), Bucks, 1682 PRO PROB5/1028
Hassell, Henry, Norwich, Norf, 1781? Lincs RO Ad/Ac/45/43
Hasslewood, John, Rippingale, Lincs, 1576 Lincs RO Ad/Ac/1/20
Hasslewood, John, esquire, Rippingale, Lincs, 1576 Lincs RO Ad/Ac/2b/45
Hasted, William, Luddenham, Kent, 1615 CKS PRC20/3/282
Haswold, William, Halesowen, Worcs, 1608 Worcs RO 008.7 BA3585/839/454
Hasyll, Henry, Teynham, Kent, 1586 CKS PRC2/4/1
Hatch, Andrew, Sandwich, Kent, 1628 CKS PRC2/29/47
Hatch, John, Wormshill, Kent, 1629 CKS PRC2/30/68
Hatch, John, Chichester, Sussex, 1669 W. Suss RO EpIII/9/1/56
Hatch, Robert, Barton Stacey, Hants, 1668 Hants RO 21M65 D8/204
Hatch, Robert, Leeds, Kent, 1690 CKS PRC2/41/149
Hatch, Thomas, yeoman, Lydd, Kent, 1680 CKS PRC20/13/28
Hatch, William, Bredgar, Kent, 1627 CKS PRC2/28/58
Hatche, Bartholomewe, Ickham, Kent, 1613 CKS PRC20/2/448
Hatche, George, Linton, Kent, 1612 CKS PRC2/16/16
Hatche, John, Mersham, Kent, 1594 CKS PRC2/7/69
Hatche, Rychard, Ruckinge, Kent, 1594 CKS PRC2/7/315
Hatche, Walter, Bapchild, Kent, 1605 CKS PRC2/13/233
Hatcher, Henry, Ash next Sandwich, Kent, 1700 CKS PRC19/5/73
Hatcher, John, Herne, Kent, 1601 CKS PRC21/16/143
Hatcher, John, Whitstable, Kent, 1626 CKS PRC2/27/78

[Hatcher:]
Hatcher, Richard, St Nicholas at Wade, Kent, 1680 CKS PRC19/4/110
Hatcher, Richard, yeoman, St Peter in Thanet, Kent, 1693 CKS PRC2/42/38
Hatcher, Thomas, Bobbing, Kent, 1613 CKS PRC2/18/69
Hatcher, Thomas, Ferring, Sussex, 1613 W. Suss RO EpI/33/1612/6
Hatcher, Thomas, Staple next Wingham, Kent, 1621 CKS PRC20/5/109
Hatcher, Thomas, Birchington, Kent, 1675 CKS PRC20/12/173
Hatchet, see Archard,
Hatchett, Alice, widow, Wellow, East, Hants, 1666 Hants RO 21M65 D8/196
Hatchett, Thomas, tailor, Brinkworth, Wilts, 1674 Wilts RO Miscellaneous Index (name + date)
Hatchman, John, Netheravon, Wilts, 1676 Wilts RO Dean Sarum (name + date)
Hatchman, William, Fawley, Berks, 1618 Berks RO D/A1/195/78A
Hatfeelde, Thomas, Lympne, Kent, 1612 CKS PRC2/16/168
Hatfeild, Humphry, Cheadle, Staffs, 1685 LJRO/B/C/5/1684/41
Hatfeild, Reginald, clergy: 'clerk', Tathwell, Lincs, 1651 Lincs RO Ad/Ac/29/48
Hatfeild, William, Ticknall, Derby, 1683 LJRO/B/C/5/1682/51
Hatfield, John, Newark on Trent, Notts, 1793 Borthwick Test C.P. 1793/8
Hatfield, Thomas, Caenby, Lincs, 1666 Lincs RO Ad/Ac/41/174
Hathaway, Thomas, mason, Fulbrook, Oxon, 1680 Oxon RO MSS Wills 81/2/4
Hatherell, Elizabeth, widow, Langley Burrell, Wilts, 1618 Wilts RO Arch. Wilts.(namc + date)
Hatherell, James, Sutton Benger, Wilts, 1736 Wilts RO CC Sarum(+ name and date)
Hatherley, Francis, husbandman, Ashley, Staffs, 1744 LJRO/B/C/5/1744/214
Hathersi(t)ch, Ralph, Tixall, Staffs, 1676 LJRO:cards/1676/27
Hathorne, Martha, St Giles without Cripplegate, London & Middlesex, 1668 PRO PROB32/3/12
Hathorne, Thomas, yeoman, Bray, Berks, 1680 Berks RO D/A1/197/50B
Hathwaie, John, Banbury, Oxon, 1614 Oxon RO MSS Wills Pec 41/2/20
Haton, Robert jun, Port Royal, Jamaica, 1688 PRO PROB5/1561
Hatt, Henry, yeoman, Chieveley (Snelsmore), Berks, 1605 Berks RO D/A1/194/115C
Hatt, John, brewer, Reading, Berks, 1606 Berks RO D/A1/195/21A
Hatt, Thomas, husbandman, Waltham, White, Berks, 1639 Berks RO D/A1/196/48A
Hattlie, Edward, Snarford, Lincs, 1633 Lincs RO Ad/Ac/40/37
Hatton, Edward, Lympsham, Som, 1640 Somerset RO D/D/Cta/H2
Hatton, Elizabeth, Cricklade St Mary, Wilts, 1626 Wilts RO Arch. Wilts.(+ name and date)
Hatton, Simon, Wittersham, Kent, 1626 CKS PRC20/7/3
Hatton, Sybil, Hilton, Hunts, 1684 Hunts RO/Acc58/228(233)
Hatton, Thomas, gentleman, Noke, Oxon, 1631 Oxon RO MSS Wills 297/5/39
Hatton, Thomas, yeoman, Monks Horton, Kent, 1684 CKS PRC2/40/204
Haucon, Thomas, Epworth, Lincs, 1668? Lincs RO Ad/Ac/33/87
Haugh, Humfrey, Drayton, Fen, Cambs, 1627 c. CUL V.C. Acc./Box2/34
Haukes, George, clergy: 'mr/vicar', Stockbury, Kent, 1612 CKS PRC2/16/35
Haukes, Robert, Cassington, Oxon, 1639 Oxon RO MSS Wills 298/1/34
Haull, John, Challock, Kent, 1595 CKS PRC21/14/117
Haull, Robert, Herne, Kent, 1580 CKS PRC21/4/283
Haunch, Simon, Kirkby on Bain, Lincs, 1612 Lincs RO Ad/Ac/11/168
Hauthorne, John, Binfield, Berks, 1616 Berks RO D/A1/195/66A
Hauvill, see Wolgar,
Havart, William, Bonnington, Kent, 1612 CKS PRC1/1/19
Havarte, William, Bonnington, Kent, 1615 CKS PRC2/21/9
Haveioy, Wyllyam, Graveney, Kent, 1592 CKS PRC2/6/386
Haveland, James, Ashford, Kent, 1630 CKS PRC20/9/221
Haveland, James, Ashford, Kent, 1635 CKS PRC2/33/63
Havenagle, see Watelyer,
Haverdine, Augustus,
Lincs 1806 Lincs RO Ad/Ac/45/73
Haverlyn, Thomas, yeoman, Sulhampstead Abbots, Berks, 1683 Berks RO D/A1/197/78F
Havert/Kyte, Isabell, widow, Bonnington, Kent, 1617 CKS PRC2/22/160

Haverte, Isabell, widow, Bonnington, Kent, 1616 CKS PRC2/21/12
Haward, John, Brookland, Kent, 1617 CKS PRC2/22/169
Haward, John, gentleman, Mareham le Fen, Lincs, 1622 Lincs RO Ad/Ac/17/17
Haward, Samuel, gentleman, Faversham, Kent, 1635 CKS PRC20/10/554
Haward, William, Canterbury St Mildred, Kent, 1668 CKS PRC1/13/59
Hawarden, William, Mareham le Fen, Lincs, 1637 Lincs RO Ad/Ac/25/504
Hawe, Robert, Frampton, Lincs, 1649 Lincs RO Ad/Ac/30/68
Hawe, William, Wigtoft, Lincs, 1649 Lincs RO Ad/Ac/30/120
Hawes, Robert, Stoke Rochford (North Stoke), Lincs, 1618 Lincs RO Ad/Ac/14/192
Hawes, Thomas, Legbourne, Lincs, 1632 Lincs RO Ad/Ac/23/16
Hawes, Thomas, Oxford (Holywell), Oxon, 1644 Oxon RO MSS Wills 298/2/12
Hawford, Robert, husbandman, Ashbourne, Derby, 1747 LJRO/B/C/5/1747/184
Hawford, Thomas, Bampton (Cote), Oxon, 1635 Oxon RO MSS Wills 298/1/15
Hawgood, John, St Albans St Michaels, Herts, 1582 Herts RO ASA25/1126
Hawgood, John, St Albans St Michaels, Herts, 1632 Herts RO ASA25/4883
Hawgood, Robert, yeoman, Harrowden, Little, Northants, 1678 Northants RO NWill A/C/84
Hawioye, Roger, Minster in Thanet, Kent, 1598 CKS PRC2/10/412
Hawis, Alexander, baker, Cambridge All Saints, Cambs, 1625 c. CUL V.C. Acc./Box2/35
Hawke, Edward, butcher, Sheffield (Leavygreave), Yorks, 1785 Borthwick Test C.P. 1785/3
Hawke, John, Canterbury St Peter, Kent, 1669 CKS PRC1/14/54
Hawke, Richard, Aldington, Kent, 1605 CKS PRC20/1/71
Hawke, Richard, 1638 CKS PRC2/34/
Hawke, Richard, Aldington, Kent, 1638 CKS PRC20/10/522
Hawke, Richard, Hernhill, Kent, 1670 CKS PRC19/4/80
Hawke, Samuell, Smarden, Kent, 1619 CKS PRC2/22/172
Hawke, Thomas, Harbledown, Kent, 1634 CKS PRC20/10/558
Hawkens, Francis, Newton, Water, Hunts, 1680 Hunts RO/Acc58/144(175)
Hawker, John, Ash next Sandwich, Kent, 1622 CKS PRC20/6/364
Hawker, Margery, Dymchurch, Kent, 1586 CKS PRC2/4/50
Hawker, Richard + Parnell, St Johns Thanet, Kent, 1580 CKS PRC2/2/249
Hawker, Robart, Dymchurch, Kent, 1602 CKS PRC2/12/189
Hawker, Thomas, gentleman, Challock, Kent, 1639 CKS PRC20/10/506
Hawker, William, Borden, Kent, 1597 CKS PRC2/9/253
Hawkes, Christopher, gentleman, Hackney, London & Middlesex, 1684 PRO PROB32/23/99
Hawkes, Isaac, Canterbury St Mary Bredman, Kent, 1665 CKS PRC1/11/40
Hawkes, John, Stoneham, South (Bittern), Hants, 1632 Hants RO 1631 ND1
Hawkes, John, St Johns Thanet, Kent, 1637 CKS PRC2/34/60
Hawkes, Michael, Birchington, Kent, 1673 CKS PRC20/12/79
Hawkes, Richard, Canterbury All Saints, Kent, 1673 CKS PRC2/35/228
Hawkes, Richard, Stepney, London & Middlesex, 1694 PRO PROB32/32/135
Hawkes, Robert, Shutford, Oxon, 1634 Oxon RO MSS Wills 298/1/10
Hawkes, Ryuchard, Bilsington, Kent, 1585 CKS PRC2/3/303
Hawkes, Samuel, Sandwich, Kent, 1687 CKS PRC2/41/96
Hawkes, Thomas eld, husbandman, Swalcliffe (Sibford Gower), Oxon, 1630 Oxon RO MSS Wills 297/5/12
Hawkes, William, victualler, Birmingham, Warks, 1809 LJRO/B/C/5/1809/34
Hawkes, see Stevens,
Hawkesford, Thomas, yeoman, Fillongley, Warks, 1807 LJRO/B/C/5/1807/39
Hawkesworth, John, bootmaker, Burton on Stather, Lincs, 1608 Lincs RO Ad/Ac/37/263
Hawkin, Sarah, Butterwick, Lincs, 1679 Lincs RO Ad/Ac/43/82
Hawking, Humphrey, yeoman, Marcham, Berks, 1689 Berks RO D/A1/197/84C
Hawkins, Anne, widow, Marcham, Berks, 1663 Berks RO D/A1/196/115C
Hawkins, Anne, Stone, Staffs, 1685 LJRO/B/C/5/1684/42
Hawkins, Dennis, widow, Marcham, Berks, 1626 Berks RO D/A1/195/108A
Hawkins, Edward, Deeping, Market, Lincs, 1618 Lincs RO Ad/Ac/14/288

[Hawkins:]
Hawkins, Henry, yeoman, Edenham, Lincs, 1618 Lincs RO Ad/Ac/14/240
Hawkins, Henry, coal burner, Pyrton, Oxon, 1684 Oxon RO MSS Wills 81/2/24
Hawkins, Isabel, Kingham, Oxon, 1634 Oxon RO MSS Wills 298/1/8
Hawkins, John, Sittingbourne, Kent, 1597 CKS PRC2/9/249
Hawkins, John, Digswell, Herts, 1635 Herts RO AHH23/1080
Hawkins, John, victualler/alehouse keeper, Winkfield, Berks, 1637 Berks RO D/A1/196/40A
Hawkins, John, shepherd, Wootton, Oxon, 1667 Oxon RO MSS Wills 80/5/13
Hawkins, John, yeoman, Corse, Glos, 1741 GRO GDR/B4/2/H90
Hawkins, John eld, yeoman, Marcham, Berks, 1646 Berks RO D/A1/196/76A
Hawkins, Lawrence, Luckington, Wilts, 1648 Wilts RO CC Sarum(+ name and date)
Hawkins, Osmund, Wilsford, Wilts, 1637 Wilts RO Arch. Sarum(+ name and date)
Hawkins, Peter, yeoman, Thatcham (Midgham), Berks, 1634 Berks RO D/A1/195/131A
Hawkins, Ralph, alderman/mr, Canterbury, Kent, 1629 CKS PRC2/31/47
Hawkins, Richard eld, yeoman, Marcham, Berks, 1635 Berks RO D/A1/196/24C
Hawkins, Simon, husbandman, Marcham, Berks, 1616 Berks RO D/A1/195/65A
Hawkins, Simon, gentleman, Abingdon, Berks, 1698? PRO PROB5/974
Hawkins, Thomas, husbandman/widower, Thatcham (Midgham), Berks, 1663 Berks RO D/A1/196/118C
Hawkins, Thomas, yeoman, Old Romney, Kent, 1664 CKS PRC1/10/48
Hawkins, Thomas, gentleman, Boughton under Blean, Kent, 1680 CKS PRC20/12/307
Hawkins, Thomas, bachelor, Lydd, Kent, 1681 CKS PRC20/13/143
Hawkins, Thomas, gentleman, King's Lynn, Norf, 1789 Norfolk RO ANW/23/26/78C
Hawkins, see Arneway,
Hawks, Ann, spinster, Canterbury, Kent, 1641 CKS PRC1/5/102
Hawks, John, Hernhill, Kent, 1637 CKS PRC20/10/470
Hawks, Samuell, Smarden, Kent, 1622 CKS PRC2/23/158
Hawksford, Nicholas, yeoman, Birmingham, Warks, 1744 LJRO/B/C/5/1744/217
Hawksworth, John, husbandman, Saxilby, Lincs, 1686 Lincs RO Ad/Ac/44/153
Hawksworth, Thomas, Newton on Trent, Lincs, 1682 Lincs RO Ad/Ac/44/13
Hawksworth, William, St Albans St Peters, Herts, 1639 Herts RO ASA25/4956
Hawkyns, Martha, Canterbury All Saints, Kent, 1613 CKS PRC2/16/159
Hawkyns, Richard, Cotheridge, Worcs, 1608 Worcs RO 008.7 BA3585/834/429
Hawkyns, Walter, Winslow, Bucks, 1582 Herts RO ASA25/1036
Hawlet, Jeames, Minster in Thanet, Kent, 1597 CKS PRC2/10/377
Hawlett, George, Reculver, Kent, 1610 CKS PRC20/2/170
Hawlett, John, Herne, Kent, 1612 CKS PRC20/2/382
Hawlett, Thomas, Canterbury St Andrew, Kent, 1610 CKS PRC20/2/73
Hawley, Edward, citizen/alderman, Lincoln, Lincs, 1627 Lincs RO Ad/Ac/20/98
Hawnby, William, Grimoldby, Lincs, 1646 Lincs RO Ad/Ac/28/145
Haworth, Edmund, Rochdale (Whitworth), Lancs, 1617 Lancs RO (Name of Deceased) D.R.C.H. 1617
Haworth, Jonathan, innkeeper, Rochdale, Lancs, 1794 Lancs RO (Name of Deceased) D.R.C.H. 1794
Haworth, Richard, Wellingborough, Northants, 1681 Northants RO NWill A/C/75
Haworth, Robert, Laughton, Lincs, 1650 Lincs RO Ad/Ac/40/222
Hawse, William, Wokingham, Berks, 1676 Wilts RO Dean Sarum (name + date)
Hawstead, John, victualler, Bristol, Glos, Bristol RO 1724/8
Hawthorne, John, Warfield, Berks, 1612 Berks RO D/A1/195/48A
Hawthorne, William, St Martin in the Fields, London & Middlesex, 1668 PRO PROB32/3/97
Hawtin, Anthony, Stoke Lyne, Oxon, 1671 Oxon RO MSS Wills 80/5/29
Hawtin, Frances, widow, Bermondsey St Mary Magdalen, Surrey, 1679 PRO PROB32/18/42
Hawtree, William, Leake, Lincs, 1624 Lincs RO Ad/Ac/19A/78
Hawtwine, George, Malmesbury, Wilts, 1622 Wilts RO Arch. Wilts.(name + date)
Hawxe, John, St Albans St Stephens, Herts, 1615 Herts RO ASA25/4821
Hay, John, Ombersley, Worcs, 1681 Worcs RO 008.7 BA3585/830/67

Hay, John, Alvechurch, Worcs, 1684 Worcs RO 008.7 BA3585/837/bdl 4
Hay, Pattericke, clergy: 'clerk', Belleau, Lincs, 1632 Lincs RO Ad/Ac/23/137
Haycock, Francis, Hacconby, Lincs, 1607 Lincs RO Ad/Ac/8a/159
Hayden, Mary, spinster, Bristol, Glos, Bristol RO 1730/27
Hayden, Stephen, Milton next Sittingbourne, Kent, 1692 CKS PRC2/42/35
Hayden, William, Norton, Chipping, Oxon, 1629 Oxon RO MSS Wills 297/5/18
Haydon, Thomas, Uphill, Som, 1662 Somerset RO D/D/Cta/H96
Haye, David, Yarlington, Som, 1616 Somerset RO D/D/Cta/H69
Hayes, Anne, widow, Newbury, Berks, Berks RO D/A1/194/96A
Hayes, Joan, widow, Cambridge, Cambs, 1620 CUL V.C.Acc./Box1/26
Hayes, John, Milton next Sittingbourne, Kent, 1615 CKS PRC2/22/123
Hayes, John, Mere, Wilts, 1635 Wilts RO Dean Sarum (name + date)
Hayes, John, Stow on the Wold, Glos, 1685 GRO GDR/B4/2/H176
Hayes, John, butcher, Sherston Magna, Wilts, 1687 Wilts RO Arch. Wilts.(name + date)
Hayes, John, feltmaker, Norwich, Norf, 1742 Norfolk RO ANW/23/23/73B
Hayes, Richard, Bourne, Lincs, 1612 Lincs RO Ad/Ac/11/21
Hayes, Richard, vintner, St Martin in the Fields, London & Middlesex, 1701 PRO PROB32/43/58
Hayes, Thomas, Wilton, Wilts, 1613 Wilts RO CC Sarum(+ name and date)
Hayes, Thomas, yeoman, Skellingthorpe, Lincs, 1679 Lincs RO Ad/Ac/43/129
Hayes, Thomas, gentleman, Derby, Derby, 1723 LJRO/B/C/5/1723/10
Hayes, William, Howell, Lincs, 1623 Lincs RO Ad/Ac/17/69
Hayes, William, Broad Chalke, Wilts, 1630 Wilts RO Arch. Sarum(+ name and date)
Hayes, William, yeoman, Inkpen, Berks, 1641 Berks RO D/A1/196/58C
Hayfeild, Anne, Appleby, Leics, 1666 Leics RO Administrators Accounts C17th f44
Hayfeild, William, husbandman, Aslackby, Lincs, 1666 Lincs RO Ad/Ac/32/126
Hayle, Thomas, St Albans St Peters, Herts, 1636 Herts RO ASA25/4926
Hayles, Christopher, Lea, Lincs, 1606 Lincs RO Ad/Ac/37/221
Hayles, Giles, Godshill, Hants, 1640 Hants RO 1639 A116/1
Haylor, John, Rudgwick, Sussex, 1595 W. Suss RO EpI/33/1595/2
Haylor, John, Billingshurst, Sussex, 1672 W. Suss RO EpI/33/1672/14
Haym, Francis Nicholas, St Anne Westminster, London & Middlesex, 1730 Greater London RO AM/PP/Box 1726-1732 pt (uncatalogued)
Hayman, William, Stratton, Corn, 1638 Cornwall RO AP/R588/3
Haymes, John, cordwainer: 'shoemaker', Glastonbury St John, Som, 1606 Somerset RO D/D/Cta/H76
Hayne, Edward, Warden, Kent, 1574 CKS PRC2/1/160
Haynes, Ambrose, yeoman, Windsor, New, Berks, 1639 Berks RO D/A1/196/49A
Haynes, Anna, widow, Frampton on Severn, Glos, GRO GDR/B4/2/M47
Haynes, James, Ampney Crucis, Glos, 1708 GRO GDR/B4/2/H55
Haynes, James, Ampney Crucis, Glos, 1713 GRO GDR/B4/2/H55
Haynes, Thomas, Boxford, Berks, 1593 Berks RO D/A1/77/81D
Haynes/Freckleton, Margery, widow, Wasperton, Warks, 1605 Worcs RO 008.7 BA3585/839/398
Hayse, Elizabeth, Hutton, Som, 1723 Somerset RO D/D/Cta/H84
Haysome, John, Martin, Wilts, 1662 Wilts RO Arch. Sarum(+ name and date)
Haystings, Richard, Alford, Lincs, 1602 Lincs RO Ad/Ac/5/99
Hayte, Simon, Linsted, Kent, 1665 CKS PRC1/10/49
Hayter,
 Wilts 1650 c. Wilts RO Miscellaneous Index (name + date)
Hayter, Henry, Clarendon Park, Wilts, 1670 Wilts RO Miscellaneous Index (name + date)
Hayter, Henry eld, Wimborne Minster (Grange), Dors, 1664 Dorset RO PE/WM CP 2/4/69
Hayter, John, Downton, Wilts, 1637 Wilts RO Arch. Sarum(+ name and date)
Hayter, John, Barford St Martin, Wilts, 1671 Wilts RO Arch. Sarum(+ name and date)
Hayter, Robert, Wimborne Minster (Grange), Dors, 1640 Dorset RO PE/WM CP 2/4/62
Hayter, Thomas, yeoman, Wishford, Great, Wilts, 1681 Wilts RO Arch. Sarum(+ name and date)
Hayward, Christopher, Chilham, Kent, 1610 CKS PRC2/15/172

[Hayward:]
Hayward, Edward, Snargate, Kent, 1593 CKS PRC2/6/394
Hayward, Edward, Sandwich, Kent, 1633 CKS PRC2/32/56
Hayward, George, blacksmith, Ospringe, Kent, 1679 CKS PRC2/38/138
Hayward, Henrie, Birchington, Kent, 1637 CKS PRC20/10/478
Hayward, James, Abbots Langley, Herts, 1566 Herts RO ASA25/624
Hayward, James, husbandman, Hothfield, Kent, 1624 CKS PRC2/23/166
Hayward, Joan, Sutton, Long, Som, 1590 Somerset RO D/D/Cta/H38
Hayward, John, Milton next Sittingbourne, Kent, 1613 CKS PRC2/18/60
Hayward, John, miller, Aldermaston, Berks, 1631 Berks RO D/A1/195/134A
Hayward, John, Thakeham, Sussex, 1633 W. Suss RO EpI/33/1633/18
Hayward, Roger, Watford, Herts, Herts RO ASA25/4778
Hayward, Stephen, gentleman, Faversham, Kent, 1614 CKS PRC2/18/25
Hayward, Thomas, St Thomas Isle of Harty, Kent, 1599 CKS PRC2/10/494
Hayward, Thomas, Sittingbourne, Kent, 1625 CKS PRC20/7/393
Hayward, Thomas, yeoman, Sittingbourne, Kent, 1625 CKS PRC20/7/387
Hayward, Thomas, gentleman, Faversham, Kent, 1631 CKS PRC2/31/42
Hayward, Thomas, Appledore, Kent, 1668 CKS PRC1/13/60
Hayward, William, Maidstone, Kent, 1641 CKS PRC19/2/20
Hayward, William, yeoman, Garford, Berks, 1644 Berks RO D/A1/196/70C
Hayward, William, Newnton, North, Wilts, 1677 Wilts RO Miscellaneous Index (name + date)
Hayward, William, butcher, Aston Tirrold, Berks, 1684 Berks RO D/A1/197/72C
Hayward, William eld, Bethersden, Kent, 1629 CKS PRC2/30/71
Hayward, William ygr, Ridge, Herts, Herts RO ASA25/4971
Hayward, William ygr, Ridge, Herts, 1686 Herts RO ASA25/4970
Hayward/Friend, John, Westwood, Wilts, 1616 Wilts RO Miscellaneous Index (name + date)
Hayward/Howard, Richard, Dover, Kent, 1599 CKS PRC21/15/57
Hayward, see Farmer & Symmes,
Haywarde, Margaret, Milton next Sittingbourne, Kent, 1586 CKS PRC2/4/362
Haywards, Richard, Sandwich, Kent, 1669 CKS PRC1/14/55
Haywood, Alice, widow, St Giles in the Fields, London & Middlesex, 1677 PRO PROB32/14/95
Haywood, John, Ombersley, Worcs, 1675 Worcs RO 008.7 BA3585/835/bdl 1
Haywood, John, gentleman, Darfield (Milnehouse), Yorks, 1842 Borthwick Test C.P. 1842/5
Haywood, Thomas, Smeeth, Kent, 1596 CKS PRC21/14/137
Hayword, John, Faversham, Kent, 1641 CKS PRC1/5/103
Hazard, James, Deal, Kent, 1691 CKS PRC19/5/2
Hazard, Ralphe, Deal, Kent, 1674 CKS PRC20/12/84
Hazell, John, husbandman, Woodchurch, Kent, 1666 CKS PRC19/3/71
Hazlehurst, Godfry, gentleman, Normanton, South, Derby, 1692 LJRO/B/C/5/1692/35
Hazlehurst, Godfry, gentleman, Normanton, South, Derby, 1692 LJRO/B/C/5/1692/36
Heach, Thomas, clergy: 'mr/clerk', Ewell, Kent, 1627 CKS PRC20/7/17
Head, Christopher, husbandman, Dymchurch, Kent, 1670 CKS PRC1/14/56
Head, Edward, Kennington, Kent, 1678 CKS PRC2/38/147
Head, Edward, Bilsington, Kent, 1709 CKS PRC1/17/6
Head, Eliazer, Ospringe, Kent, 1639 CKS PRC20/10/540
Head, Elizabeth + John, St Thomas Isle of Harty, Kent, 1613 CKS PRC2/16/133
Head, Henry, yeoman, Boxford, Berks, 1622 Berks RO D/A1/195/88A
Head, Henry, yeoman, Leckhamstead, Berks, 1663 Berks RO D/A1/196/106C
Head, Margery, Faversham, Kent, 1639 CKS PRC1/2/72
Head, Robert, Bobbing, Kent, 1668 CKS PRC1/13/61
Head, Samuel, yeoman, Kenardington, Kent, 1674 CKS PRC2/36/61
Head, Stephen, Bilsington, Kent, 1677 CKS PRC2/37/157
Head, Thomas, Ruckinge, Kent, 1615 CKS PRC2/22/165
Head, Thomas, yeoman, Bobbing, Kent, 1677 CKS PRC2/37/161
Head, Thomas, Collingbourne Kingston, Wilts, 1702 Wilts RO Arch. Wilts.(name + date)
Head, William, Newnham, Herts, 1636 Herts RO ASA25/4927

Head, William, gentleman, Reading St Giles, Berks, 1675 Berks RO D/A1/197/11B
Headach, Thomas, husbandman, Tidmarsh, Berks, 1622 Berks RO D/A1/195/87A
Headach, William, husbandman, Bradfield, Berks, 1642 Berks RO D/A1/196/56A
Headach, see Thomas,
Heade, William, Stoke, South, Lincs, 1612 Lincs RO Ad/Ac/11/88
Headen, Crowle, Lincs, 1663 Lincs RO Ad/Ac/41/101
Headland, Thomas, yeoman, Shinfield, Berks, 1685 Berks RO D/A1/197/79C
Headley, William, Easingwold, Yorks, 1765 Borthwick Test C.P. 1765/2
Heake, Agnes, widow, Upchurch, Kent, 1598 CKS PRC2/10/336
Heald, Margey, widow, Liverpool, Lancs, 1670 Lancs RO (Name of Deceased) D.R.C.H. 1670
Heale, William, husbandman, Mildenhall, Wilts, 1633 Wilts RO Arch. Wilts.(name + date)
Healey, John, carpenter, Wilsford, Lincs, 1669 Lincs RO Ad/Ac/33/129
Healey, Richard, Bottesford (East Butterwick), Lincs, 1602 Lincs RO Ad/Ac/37/124
Healey, Thomas, gentleman, Althorpe (Burringham), Lincs, 1683 Lincs RO Ad/Ac/44/44
Healey, William, bachelor: 'singleman', Roxby, Lincs, 1684 Lincs RO Ad/Ac/44/128
Healey/Fowler, Anne, Tealby, Lincs, 1663 Lincs RO Ad/Ac/41/95
Heanes, Leonard, Tong, Shrops, 1674 LJRO:cards/1674/22
Heapy, John, chapman, Alstonfield (Adders Green), Staffs, 1764 LJRO/B/C/5/1764/66
Heard, Thomas, St Margaret Westminster, London & Middlesex, 1700 PRO PROB32/41/70
Heard, William, St Cleer, Corn, 1621 Cornwall RO AP/H508/1
Heardie, Francis, Stoke, South, Lincs, 1626 Lincs RO Ad/Ac/20b/44
Heardson, Thomas, Saxilby, Lincs, 1652 Lincs RO Ad/Ac/40/232
Hearne, Edward, husbandman, Hethe, Oxon, 1675 Oxon RO MSS Wills 33/4/34
Hearne, John, feltmaker, Kingsclere, Hants, 1638 Hants RO 1638 A84/4
Hearne, Thomas, Barrow, Lincs, 1662 Lincs RO Ad/Ac/32/26
Hearne, Thomas, mariner: 'seafaring man', Milton next Sittingbourne, Kent, 1670 CKS PRC1/15/36
Hearner, Toby, Cookham (Northtown), Berks, 1611 Berks RO D/A1/195/38A
Hearsey, John, Fernhurst, Sussex, 1684 W. Suss RO EpI/33/1684/28
Hearson, John, bachelor, Alford, Lincs, 1633 Lincs RO Ad/Ac/24/122
Hearsy, Margaret, widow, Tonge, Kent, 1646 CKS PRC1/7/50
Heath, Andrew, Benenden, Kent, 1628 CKS PRC2/29/54
Heath, Edward, Ranworth, Norf, 1753 Norfolk RO ANW/23/24/137
Heath, George, husbandman, Stevenage, Herts, 1639 Herts RO AHH23/1102
Heath, James, gentleman, Preston next Faversham, Kent, 1669 CKS PRC1/14/57
Heath, John, Hinksey, South, Berks, 1595 Berks RO D/A1/194/75B
Heath, John, husbandman/labourer, Long Wittenham, Berks, 1621 Berks RO D/A1/195/90A
Heath, John, Selborne, Hants, 1624 Hants RO 21M65 D8/21
Heath, John, Marlborough, Wilts, 1637? Wilts RO CC Sarum(+ name and date)
Heath, John, blacksmith, Newbury, Berks, 1694 Berks RO D/A1/197/152C
Heath, Margaret, widow, Oxford St Michael, Oxon, 1641 Oxon RO MSS Wills 298/1/47
Heath, Mary, Shrewsbury, Shrops, 1685 LJRO/B/C/5/1685/47
Heath, Read, grocer, Newbury, Berks, 1684 Berks RO D/A1/197/76B
Heath, Richard, Wallop, Nether, Hants, Hants RO 1632 AD52/5
Heath, Richard, Yarnton, Oxon, 1628 Oxon RO MSS Wills 297/5/16
Heath, Richard, Chipping Warden, Northants, 1672 Northants RO NWill A/C/103
Heath, Robert, Stratton St Margaret, Wilts, 1679 Wilts RO Miscellaneous Index (name + date)
Heath, Samuel, yeoman, Warwick, Warks, 1682 Worcs RO 008.7 BA3585/837/bdl 3
Heath, Thomas,
Wilts 1677 Wilts RO Miscellaneous Index (name + date)
Heath, Thomas, carpenter, Reculver, Kent, 1682 CKS PRC20/13/255
Heath, William, yeoman, Twyning, Glos, 1799 GRO GDR/B4/2/H99
Heath/Ledger/Edwards, Elizabeth, Boughton under Blean, Kent, 1662 CKS PRC19/3/12
Heathcock, Hugh, St Albans St Michaels, Herts, 1640 Herts RO ASA25/4966
Heathe, Jeffrey, Chipping Barnet, Herts, 1616 Herts RO ASA25/4825

[Heathe:]
Heathe, Katharine, Sevenhampton, Wilts, 1628 Wilts RO Miscellaneous Index (name + date)
Heathe, see Shorie,
Heather, Benjamin eld, St Martin in the Fields, London & Middlesex, 1692 PRO PROB32/32/306
Heather, Henry, Havant, Hants, 1675 Hants RO 21m65 D8/269
Heather, Nicholas, Tenterden, Kent, 1624 CKS PRC2/23/173
Heaton, Elizabeth, spinster, Grimsby, Great, Lincs, 1679 Lincs RO Ad/Ac/43/109
Heaton, George, clothdresser, Birstall (Liversedge), Yorks, 1801 Borthwick Test C.P. 1802/7
Heaton, James, yeoman, Coates, Great, Lincs, 1612 Lincs RO Ad/Ac/11/135
Heaton, John, gentleman, Langton, Lincs, 1666 Lincs RO Ad/Ac/32/64
Heaton, Thomas, Standish (Adlington), Lancs, 1662 Lancs RO (Name of Deceased) D.R.C.H. 1662-63
Heaward, Alexander, yeoman, Lenton, Lincs, 1638 Lincs RO Ad/Ac/25/165
Heaward, Edmund eld, 1628 Lancs RO (Name of Deceased) D.R.C.H. 1628
Heaward, Mary, spinster, Stockport (Woodley), Ches, 1780 Cheshire RO (Name) W.C. 1780
Hebb, Samuel, gentleman, Loughborough, Leics, 1673 Leics RO Administrators Accounts 1667-72 f108
Hebdich, Thomas, Sherbourne, Dors, 1639 Wilts RO Miscellaneous Index (name + date)
Hebdiche, Henry eld, Sparkford, Som, 1634 Somerset RO D/D/Cta/H21
Hebditch, Richard, Mere, Wilts, 1681 Wilts RO Dean Sarum (name + date)
Heberden, John, Angmering, Sussex, 1669 W. Suss RO EpI/33/1669/16
Heblethwayte, William, New Romney, Kent, 1619 CKS PRC20/4/137
Heblithwaite, Josua, New Romney, Kent, 1607 CKS PRC20/1/261
Heburne, John, Windsor, Old, Berks, 1615 Berks RO D/A1/195/59A
Hed, Anthony, Welford, Berks, 1605 Berks RO D/A1/195/1A
Hedgcocke, John, bricklayer, Aldington, Kent, 1670 CKS PRC19/4/81
Hedgcocke, William, Folkestone, Kent, 1680 CKS PRC2/39/54
Hedge, Robert, Appleby, Lincs, 1615 Lincs RO Ad/Ac/8b/230
Hedgecocke, James, St Johns Thanet, Kent, 1634 CKS PRC2/32/153
Hedgeman, Robert, gardener, Newbury, Berks, Berks RO D/A1/195/77A
Hedger, Thomas, Beauworth, Hants, 1624 Hants RO 21M65 D8/22
Hedges,
Som Somerset RO D/D/Cta/H85
Hedges, John, Buttermere, Wilts, 1612? Wilts RO Arch. Wilts.(name + date)
Hedges, Richard, cook/privileged person, Oxford (University), Oxon, 1658 Bodleian HYP B8/101-102
Hedges, Richard, butcher, Oxford St Thomas, Oxon, 1768 Oxon RO MSS Wills 302/5/59
Hedges, Thomas, Cumnor (Whitley), Berks, 1615 Berks RO D/A1/195/62A
Hedges, Thomas, Cassington (Worton), Oxon, 1628 Oxon RO MSS Wills 297/5/15
Hedges, William ygr, Charlbury (Fawler), Oxon, 1641 Oxon RO MSS Wills 298/2/6
Heele, see Hylde,
Heeler, Caleb, Goodnestone next Faversham, Kent, 1627 CKS PRC2/28/57
Heeler, Jervace, Goodnestone next Faversham, Kent, 1643 CKS PRC1/6/106
Heeler, John, Hernhill, Kent, 1583 CKS PRC21/6/401
Heely, Jarvis, gentleman, Maidstone, Kent, 1675 CKS PRC20/12/174
Heely, Richard, Canterbury St Paul, Kent, 1676 CKS PRC2/37/44
Heelye, Richard, Maidstone, Kent, 1614 CKS PRC20/3/95
Hefford, John, chandler: 'tallow chandler', Rugby, Warks, 1683 LJRO/B/C/5/1682/53
Heighfeild, Richard, Newton, Lincs, 1622 Lincs RO Ad/Ac/17/41
Heintz, Emanuel, Oxford St Mary, Oxon, 1645 Oxon RO MSS Wills 298/2/13
Heirsey, William, Liss, Hants, 1669 Hants RO 21m65 D8/310
Heite, Humphrey, university: 'scholar's servant/privileged person', Cambridge (Trinity College), Cambs, 1639 CUL V.C. Acc./Box2/36
Heldrethe, Christopher, Nettleton, Lincs, 1605 Lincs RO Ad/Ac/6/125
Helfoord, Richard, St Stephen in Brannel, Corn, 1621 Cornwall RO AP/E93/3
Helland, Peter, Calstock, Corn, 1616 Cornwall RO AP/H331/2

Helliar, John, Minety, Wilts, 1621 Wilts RO Arch. Wilts.(name + date)
Helliar, John, Salisbury, Wilts, 1622? Wilts RO Miscellaneous Index (name + date)
Hellier, Anthony, Wootton Rivers, Wilts, 1677 Wilts RO Miscellaneous Index (name + date)
Hellier, John, yeoman, Wokingham, Berks, 1611 Wilts RO Dean Sarum (name + date)
Hellier, see Chiselden,
Hellingbridge, Gyles, Spilsby, Lincs, 1599 Lincs RO Ad/Ac/5/417
Hellinges, Robert, husbandman, Tenterden, Kent, 1617 CKS PRC2/22/127
Hellings, George, Tenterden, Kent, 1614 CKS PRC2/18/41
Hellman, Alexander, Hernhill, Kent, 1618 CKS PRC20/4/155
Hellyard, Alexander, husbandman, Buckland, Berks, 1625 Berks RO D/A1/195/105A
Hellyer, Anne, widow, Fareham, Hants, 1692 Hants RO 21M65 D3/269
Helman, Nicholas, Lanhydrock, Corn, 1609 Cornwall RO AP/H206/2
Helman, William, Eastchurch, Sheppey, Kent, 1603 CKS PRC2/12/440
Helme, John, plumber/glazier, Huddersfield, Yorks, 1820 Borthwick Test C.P. 1820/16
Helps, William, Rowde, Wilts, 1681 Wilts RO Miscellaneous Index (name + date)
Helsby, Henry, shopkeeper, Ormskirk, Lancs, 1728 Lancs RO (Name of Deceased) D.R.C.H. 1729
Helstone, Marke, Sholden, Kent, 1608 CKS PRC2/14/223
Helvis, Joseph, Canterbury, Kent, 1599 CKS PRC2/11/97
Helwis, Marie, widow, Worlaby, Lincs, 1637 Lincs RO Ad/Ac/25/541
Helwys, Nicholas, esquire/alderman, Norwich, Norf, Norfolk RO NCC INV/74A/256
Hely, Robert, Deeping, West, Lincs, 1638 Lincs RO Ad/Ac/25/167
Heman, Richard, Tintagel, Corn, 1621 Cornwall RO AP/H507/2
Hembrowgh, William, yeoman, Winterton, Lincs, 1610 Lincs RO Ad/Ac/8a/310
Hemesley, William, Cadney, Lincs, 1599 Lincs RO Ad/Ac/5/525
Hemings, Wilts RO Unlisted Fragment
Hemings, James, Eton, Bucks, 1731 Lambeth Palace Arches G103/3
Hemingway, David, clothier, Dewsbury (Daw Green), Yorks, 1815 Borthwick Test C.P. 1814/7
Hemingway, Joseph, clothier, Dewsbury, Yorks, 1840 Borthwick Test C.P. 1840/7
Hemingway, Joshua, clergy: 'clerk', St Ives, Hunts, 1678 Hunts RO/Acc58/128(182)
Hemley, Joan, Alderton, Wilts, 1621 Wilts RO CC Sarum(+ name and date)
Hemming, Samuel, Alne, Great, Warks, 1755 Worcs RO 008.7 BA3585/835/bdl 1
Hempstock, Robert, Boston, Lincs, 1683 Lincs RO Ad/Ac/44/53
Hemseley, Thomas, glover, Gainsborough, Lincs, 1609 Lincs RO Ad/Ac/8a/307
Hemsly, William, yeoman, Bethersden, Kent, 1684 CKS PRC2/40/202
Hemwood, Henry, tucker, Garston, East, Berks, 1608 Berks RO D/A1/195/23D
Henden, John, gentleman, Benenden, Kent, 1676 CKS PRC2/37/46
Henden, Simon, Sandhurst, Kent, CKS PRC1/1/78
Henden, Simon, Sandhurst, Kent, 1638 CKS PRC1/1/78a
Henden, Simon, Sandhurst, Kent, 1640 CKS PRC1/4/56
Hendlie, Henrie, Cranbrook, Kent, 1613 CKS FRC2/18/90
Hendly, Jervase, Wye, Kent, 1610 CKS PRC2/15/170
Hendly, William, husbandman, Woodchurch, Kent, 1672 CKS PRC20/12/13
Hendry, Thomas, cabinet maker, Brancaster, Norf, 1791 Norfolk RO ANF/11/5/119
Heneage, George, knight, Ludford, Lincs, 1632 Lincs RO Ad/Ac/23/56
Heneker, John, Davington, Kent, 1673 CKS PRC2/35/220
Heneker, John, yeoman, Pluckley, Kent, 1677 CKS PRC2/37/154
Heneker, Robert, yeoman, Detling, Kent, 1617 CKS PRC20/4/200
Heneker, Thomas, Iwade, Kent, 1632 CKS PRC2/31/41
Heneker, Thomazine, Sandwich, Kent, 1634 CKS PRC2/32/50
Heneker, William, Milton next Sittingbourne, Kent, 1633 CKS PRC2/31/119
Heneker, see Frenchbourne,
Henley, Jeffery, yeoman, Brinkworth, Wilts, 1639 Wilts RO Arch. Wilts.(name + date)
Henly, Alexander, Brinkworth, Wilts, 1680? Wilts RO Miscellaneous Index (name + date)
Henly, Andrew, painter, Faversham, Kent, 1680 CKS PRC2/39/53

[Henly:]
Henly, Grygory, Tenterden, Kent, 1620 CKS PRC2/26/112
Henly, John, grocer, Ash next Sandwich, Kent, 1684 CKS PRC20/13/432
Henly, Thomas, servant, Pyrton, Oxon, 1673 Oxon RO MSS Wills 167/2/18
Henman, Adam, yeoman, Whitstable, Kent, 1672 CKS PRC2/35/143
Henman, Alane, Queenborough, Kent, 1582 CKS PRC2/2/186
Henman, Alane, Doddington, Kent, 1588 CKS PRC2/4/279
Henman, Alexander, Upchurch, Kent, 1641 CKS PRC1/4/57
Henman, Allen, Lenham, Kent, 1677 CKS PRC2/37/162
Henman, Arthur, Ospringe, Kent, 1697 CKS PRC2/42/128
Henman, Henry, Tonge, Kent, 1634 CKS PRC2/32/155
Henman, James, Whitstable, Kent, 1629 CKS PRC2/30/70
Henman, Joane, Lenham, Kent, 1611 CKS PRC2/16/93
Henman, John, Boughton under Blean, Kent, CKS PRC20/10/544
Henman, John, Sandwich, Kent, 1612 CKS PRC2/16/161
Henman, John, yeoman, Murston, Kent, 1616 CKS PRC2/22/141
Henman, John, Ospringe, Kent, 1642 CKS PRC1/5/104
Henman, John, yeoman, Herne, Kent, 1676 CKS PRC20/12/172
Henman, Peter, Whitstable, Kent, 1593 CKS PRC2/6/500
Henman, Rafe, Murston, Kent, 1602 CKS PRC2/12/214
Henman, Solomon, Whitstable, Kent, 1611 CKS PRC2/13/235
Henman, Thomas, Upchurch, Kent, 1627 CKS PRC2/27/76
Henman, Thomas, minor, Upchurch, Kent, 1627 CKS PRC2/28/64
Henman, William, Lenham, Kent, 1592 CKS PRC2/6/121
Henman, William, Maidstone, Kent, 1610 CKS PRC20/2/164
Henman, William, Lenham, Kent, 1674 CKS PRC2/36/62
Henn, William, Launton, Oxon, 1640 Oxon RO MSS Wills 298/1/45
Hennant, Thomas, clergy: 'vicar', Thame, Oxon, 1667 Oxon RO MSS Wills Pec 41/4/13
Henneker, Francis, Harrietsham, Kent, 1638 CKS PRC2/34/67
Henneker, Henry, Bredhurst, Kent, 1629 CKS PRC20/8/287
Henneker, Nicholas, Hythe St Leonard, Kent, 1682 CKS PRC20/13/139
Henneker, Richard, High Halden, Kent, 1682 CKS PRC2/40/35
Henneker, Robart, Biddenden, Kent, 1613 CKS PRC2/16/178
Henneker, Thomas, Sandwich, Kent, 1626 CKS PRC20/7/42
Henneker, William, Rainham, Kent, 1600 CKS PRC2/12/201
Henneker, William, Bobbing, Kent, 1609 CKS PRC2/13/247
Henneker, William, Bredhurst, Kent, 1626 CKS PRC20/7/38
Henneker, Wylliam, Bredhurst, Kent, 1601 CKS PRC21/15/227
Henney, Peter, husbandman, Washingborough (Heighington), Lincs, 1673 Lincs RO Ad/Ac/34/113
Hennom, John, Canterbury Holy Cross Westgate, Kent, 1626 CKS PRC2/27/64
Henry, John, bachelor, St Martin Orgar, London & Middlesex, 1682 PRO PROB5/797
Henshall, John, Budworth, Great (Plumley), Ches, 1597 Cheshire RO (Name) W.C. 1596/7
Henshall, Ralph, hatband maker, Stockport, Ches, 1669 Cheshire RO (Name) W.C. 1667/8
Henshall, William, shopkeeper, Knutsford, Ches, 1786 Cheshire RO (Name) W.C. 1786
Henshaw, William, cordwainer, Manchester, Lancs, 1764 Lancs RO (Name of Deceased) D.R.C.H. 1765
Hensley, Arthur, husbandman, Tydd St Mary, Lincs, 1633 Lincs RO Ad/Ac/24/4
Henslow, Mary, mistress/widow, Brimpton, Berks, 1678 Berks RO D/A1/197/28B
Henslye, Joseph, Fyfield (Netherton), Berks, 1671 Berks RO D/A1/196/169C
Hensman, Richard, Dover St Mary, Kent, 1620 CKS PRC20/4/141
Henson, Ellen, wife, Folksworth, Hunts, Hunts RO/Acc58/86(161)
Henson, John, Staughton, Great, Hunts, 1684 Hunts RO/Acc58/227(217)
Henson, Thomas, farmer, Hanbury, Staffs, 1826 LJRO/B/C/5/1826/23b
Henth, Thomas, clergy: 'clerk', NLW BR 1634/13 Ac
Henton, George, university: 'Fellow of Trinity College, Cambridge/M.A.', Cambridge (Trinity College), Cambs, 1636 CUL V.C. Acc./Box2/37

Henton, John, Hollingbourne, Kent, 1619 CKS PRC20/4/151
Hentson, Henrie, husbandman, Bluntisham, Hunts, 1602 Lincs RO Ad/Ac/5/570
Henwood, Richard, yeoman, Steventon, Berks, 1637 Berks RO D/A1/196/30A
Hepburne, John, clergy: 'vicar', Bethersden, Kent, 1613 CKS PRC2/18/59
Heppenstall, Edward, Rasen, Middle, Lincs, 1624 Lincs RO Ad/Ac/19A/66
Heptenshall, William, Flixborough, Lincs, 1680 Lincs RO Ad/Ac/43/163
Hepworth, Francis, yeoman, Wakefield, Yorks, 1784 Borthwick Test C.P. 1784/1
Hepworth, John, Stone in Oxney, Kent, 1665 CKS PRC1/11/41
Herbert, Edward, husbandman, Chieveley (Curridge), Berks, 1633 Berks RO D/A1/196/19A
Herbert, George, gentleman, Eton, Bucks, 1713? PRO PROB5/1013
Herbert, Henry, Cirencester, Glos, 1685 GRO GDR/B4/2/H177
Herbert, John, victualler/wool comber, Atherstone, Warks, 1796 LJRO/B/C/5/1796/57
Herbert, Robert, Cuxham, Oxon, 1677 Oxon RO MSS Wills 167/2/27
Herbert, Robert, innholder, Northampton, Northants, 1677 Northants RO NWill A/C/70
Herbert, Walter, 1634 NLW BR 1634/78 Ac
Herberte, Walter, clergy: 'clerk', Hendred, East, Berks, 1606 Berks RO D/A1/195/14A
Herenden, John, Smarden, Kent, 1599 CKS PRC2/10/298
Herenden, John, Elham, Kent, 1601 CKS PRC2/12/212
Heritage, Robert, Buckland nr Dover, Kent, 1619 CKS PRC20/4/81
Herman, Richard, Hendred, East, Berks, 1620 Berks RO D/A1/195/80A
Hernden, Aymer, Boughton Monchelsea, Kent, 1629 CKS PRC20/8/269
Hernden, John, yeoman, Bethersden, Kent, 1627 CKS PRC2/28/60
Herne, Anthony, Linton, Kent, 1632 CKS PRC2/31/120
Herne, Anthony, husbandman, Linton, Kent, 1670 CKS PRC1/14/58
Herne, Peter, tailor, Wantage, Berks, 1649 Oxon RO MSS Wills Pec 83/3/39
Herne, Thomas,
Oxon 1647 Oxon RO MSS Wills 298/2/21
Herne/Storre, Anthony, Bremhill, Wilts, 1621 Wilts RO Arch. Wilts.(name + date)
Herrin, Jonathan, Adwick, Yorks, Borthwick Test C.P. 1734/4
Herring, Emanuell, St Clement Danes, London & Middlesex, 1682 PRO PROB32/19/
Herring, Nathaniel, Canterbury, Kent, 1712 CKS PRC19/6/43
Herring, Reynold, Stratton St Margaret, Wilts, 1638 Wilts RO Arch. Wilts.(name + date)
Herris, William, Weston, Lincs, 1641 Lincs RO Ad/Ac/27/261
Herritage, Edward, Mersham, Kent, 1681 CKS PRC2/39/181
Herst, Thomas, Cheriton, Kent, 1629 CKS PRC2/30/79
Heselop, Valentine, Sturry, Kent, 1650 CKS PRC1/8/72
Heseman, Nicholas, Tenterden, Kent, 1618 CKS PRC2/22/138
Hesketh, Bartholemew, Gainsborough, Lincs, 1681 Lincs RO Ad/Ac/34/96
Hesketh, Robert, esquire, Rufford, Lancs, 1621 Lancs RO (Name of Deceased) D.R.C.H. 1620-21
Hesketh, Robert sen, esquire, Rufford, Lancs, 1621 Lancs RO (Name of Deceased) D.R.C.H. 1620-21
Heslewood, Henry, Epworth, Lincs, 1676 Lincs RO Ad/Ac/35/104
Heslop, Robert, blacksmith, Donington, Lincs, 1614 Lincs RO Ad/Ac/13/65
Hessel, John, Sandwich, Kent, 1625 CKS PRC2/25/64
Hesseldine/Gibson, Joane, widow, Caythorpe, Lincs, 1649 Lincs RO Ad/Ac/30/134
Hessell, Lambert, weaver, Sandwich, Kent, 1637 CKS PRC2/34/65
Hessell, Thomas, baker, York, Yorks, 1720 Borthwick Test C.P. 1720/6
Hethar, Bartholomew, Mudford, Som, 1693 Somerset RO D/D/Cta/H86
Hethe, George, Boxley, Kent, 1664 CKS PRC1/10/50
Hevar, Lawrence, Ivychurch, Kent, 1583 CKS PRC21/6/250
Hevell, Elizabeth, widow, Edington, Wilts, 1687 Wilts RO Arch. Sarum(+ name and date)
Hevill, Deanes, Langford, Steeple, Wilts, 1627 Wilts RO Arch. Sarum(+ name and date)
Hevill, John, Edington, Wilts, 1611 Wilts RO Arch. Sarum(+ name and date)
Hewel, John, Waltham St Lawrence, Berks, 1612 Berks RO D/A1/195/46C
Hewes, Richard, husbandman, Ducklington (Hardwick), Oxon, 1631 Oxon RO MSS Wills

[Hewes:]
297/5/37
Hewes, Richard, Pluckley, Kent, 1680 CKS PRC2/39/51
Hewes, Thomas, Compton, Long, Warks, Worcs RO 008.7 BA3585/839/305
Hewes, Thomas, Rogate, Sussex, 1645 W. Suss RO EpI/33/1645/6
Hewess, John, Tenterden, Kent, 1725 CKS PRC1/18/40
Hewet, Elizabethe, Alkham, Kent, 1598 CKS PRC2/9/417
Hewet, Mathew, Linsted, Kent, 1582 CKS PRC2/2/183
Hewet, Paule, St Johns Thanet, Kent, 1639 CKS PRC1/2/73
Hewet, Thomas, Northmoor, Oxon, 1641 Oxon RO MSS Wills 298/2/8
Hewet/Grenfeld, Joan, Tenterden, Kent, 1595 CKS PRC2/7/261
Hewet, see Troward,
Hewetson, Michael, Watford, Herts, 1630 Herts RO ASA25/4867
Hewett, Ambrose, yeoman, Chislet, Kent, 1666 CKS PRC1/11/124
Hewett, Edward, carpenter, Bristol, Glos, Bristol RO 1678/67
Hewett, John, Lodsworth, Sussex, 1683 W. Suss RO EpI/33/1682/6
Hewett, Robert, Bonnington, Kent, 1610 CKS PRC2/15/182
Hewett, Samuel, Norwich, Norf, 1733 Norfolk RO ANW/23/21/25
Hewett, Thomas, Hoath, Kent, 1620 CKS PRC20/5/75
Hewett, William, clergy: 'clerk', Ashley, Hants, Hants RO 1591 B35/7
Hewins, Thomas, Graveney, Kent, 1611 CKS PRC2/16/99
Hewit, Thomas, Stoke-upon-Trent, Staffs, 1667 LJRO:cards/1667/43
Hewitson, John, Sutterton, Lincs, 1614 Lincs RO Ad/Ac/12/192
Hewitt, John, Ansley, Warks, 1672 LJRO:cards/1672/28
Hewitt, Randle, Waverton (Hatton Hall), Ches, 1796 Cheshire RO (Name) W.C. 1796
Hewitt, William, Hemswell, Lincs, 1682 Lincs RO Ad/Ac/44/17
Hewkenes, Thomas, Chilham, Kent, 1619 CKS PRC2/21/6
Hewson, Richard, butcher, Owersby, Lincs, 1666 Lincs RO Ad/Ac/32/69
Hewytt, John, Surfleet, Lincs, 1612 Lincs RO Ad/Ac/11/85
Hey, Ralph, Farnworth (Penketh), Lancs, 1602 Lancs RO (Name of Deceased) D.R.C.H. 1602
Hey/Harrison, Thomas, Warrington (Little Sankey), Lancs, 1609 Lancs RO (Name of Deceased) D.R.C.H. 1609/11
Heycocke, Stephen, Petworth, Sussex, 1633 W. Suss RO EpI/33/1632/28
Heycroft, John, Catherington, Hants, 1597 Hants RO 1588 A32/3
Heyden, Mary, widow, Broadway, Worcs, 1781 Worcs RO 008.7 BA3585/835/bdl 2
Heydon, Elizabeth, widow, Lenham, Kent, 1687 CKS PRC2/41/95
Heydon, Francis, esquire, Watford, Herts, 1608 Herts RO ASA25/4767
Heydon, Richard, surgeon, Minster in Sheppey, Kent, 1681 CKS PRC2/39/187
Heydon, William, Lenham, Kent, 1685 CKS PRC2/41/35
Heyfeild, George + Elizabeth, Bourne, Lincs, 1607 Lincs RO Ad/Ac/8a/89
Heyman, Ann, Elham, Kent, 1681 CKS PRC2/39/191
Heyman, Emlyn, mrs, Canterbury Christchurch, Kent, 1581 CKS PRC21/5/98
Heyman, Rebecca ygr, mrs/spinster, Canterbury St Alphege, Kent, 1626 CKS PRC20/7/13
Heymis, John, Hendred, East, Berks, 1608 Berks RO D/A1/195/27A
Heynes, Edward, Mollington, Oxon, 1614 Oxon RO MSS Wills Pec 41/2/22
Heys, George, Ivychurch, Kent, 1573 CKS PRC21/2/113
Heysham, Henry, yeoman, Frome Selwood, Som, 1604 Somerset RO D/D/Cta/H75
Heyter, Leonard, Wishford, Great, Wilts, 1616 Wilts RO Miscellaneous Index (name + date)1
Heyward, Edmund, Rochdale (Chadwick), Lancs, 1621 Lancs RO (Name of Deceased) D.R.C.H. 1621-3
Heyward, John ygr, Birchington, Kent, 1618 CKS PRC20/4/181
Heyward, John ygr, Sandridge, Herts, 1626 Herts RO ASA25/2834
Heyward, Robert, Warrington, Lancs, 1634 Lancs RO (Name of Deceased) D.R.C.H. 1634-35
Heyward, William, Redbourn, Herts, 1632 Herts RO ASA25/4884
Hibbard, Elias, Wilton, Wilts, 1678 Wilts RO Arch. Sarum(+ name and date)
Hibbard, James, Wilton, Wilts, 1681? Wilts RO Arch. Sarum(+ name and date)

Hibberden, Rooke, Slindon, Sussex, 1630 W. Suss RO EpIV/10/1/14
Hibbert, Joseph, farmer, Barrow upon Trent, Derby, 1818 LJRO/B/C/5/1818/16
Hibble, James, Melford, Long, Suff, 1750 Suff RO(B) IC500/3/50/16
Hiberd, Christopher, Barford St Martin, Wilts, 1619 Wilts RO Miscellaneous Index (name + date)
Hiberden, Joyce, widow, Bersted, South, Sussex, 1642 W. Suss RO EpIV/10/2/30
Hibling, Mary, Hibaldstow, Lincs, 1683 Lincs RO Ad/Ac/44/43
Hiccock, see Hiccocks,
Hiccocks/Hiccock, John, Bilton, Warks, 1663 LJRO:cards/1663/29
Hick, David, Cawood, Yorks, 1780 Borthwick D/C C.P. 1780/1
Hick, Leonard, Walton, Yorks, 1716 Borthwick Test C.P. 1717/10
Hicke, Sidracke, Dover, Kent, 1596 CKS PRC21/14/103
Hickes, Alexander, Herne, Kent, 1603 CKS PRC21/15/174
Hickes, Alice, Charing, Kent, 1587 CKS PRC21/8/268
Hickes, Elizabeth, Coventry, Warks, 1675 LJRO:cards/1675/34
Hickes, George, Condover, Shrops, 1674 LJRO:cards/1674/23
Hickes, Jane, Theddlethorpe All Saints, Lincs, 1632 Lincs RO Ad/Ac/23/15
Hickes, Nichalaus, Scotter, Lincs, 1615 Lincs RO Ad/Ac/8b/250
Hickes, Thomas, Charing, Kent, 1583 CKS PRC21/6/434
Hickes, Thomas, Herne, Kent, 1584 CKS PRC21/6/527
Hickes, Thomas, Dover, Kent, 1596 CKS PRC21/14/43
Hickles, John, St Laurence Thanet, Kent, 1593 CKS PRC2/6/478
Hicklin, Edward, butcher, Gainsborough, Lincs, 1681 Lincs RO Ad/Ac/34/78
Hicklinge, William, Clawson, Long, Leics, Leics RO PR/I/41A/8
Hickman, Alice, spinster, St Ives, Hunts, 1684 Hunts RO/Acc58/213(202)
Hickman, Edward, Frodesley, Shrops, 1674 LJRO:cards/1674/24
Hickman, George, Bushey, Herts, 1635 Herts RO ASA25/4912
Hickman, Henry, Bushey, Herts, Herts RO ASA25/4895
Hickman, Henry, Watford (Bushey Warren), Herts, 1598 Herts RO ASA25/1621
Hickman, John, Watford (Bushey Warren), Herts, 1599 Herts RO ASA25/1725
Hickman, Robert, Saleby, Lincs, 1641 Lincs RO Ad/Ac/27/158
Hickman, Thomas, Hursley, Hants, 1688 Hants RO 1688 AD52/2
Hickman, William, Bulford, Wilts, 1736 Wilts RO Arch. Sarum(+ name and date)
Hickmans, William, Sedgley, Staffs, 1685 LJRO/B/C/5/1685/48
Hickmans, William, Sedgley (Coseley), Staffs, 1691 LJRO/B/C/5/1691/43
Hickmot, Francis, mercer, Headcorn, Kent, 1662 CKS PRC1/8/100
Hicks, Arthur, yeoman, Longcot, Berks, 1632 Berks RO D/A1/196/10A
Hicks, Digory, Menheniot, Corn, 1639 Cornwall RO AP/H1018/1
Hicks, Jeffrey, Ashton, Steeple, Wilts, 1646 Wilts RO Arch. Sarum(+ name and date)
Hicks, John, Milton, Oxon, 1673 Oxon RO MSS Wills 167/2/21
Hicks, John, shepherd, Fritwell, Oxon, 1674 Oxon RO MSS Wills 81/1/2
Hicks, John, victualler, Faversham, Kent, 1675 CKS PRC2/36/204
Hicks, Joseph, Rochester, Kent, 1732 Lambeth Palace Arches G103/1
Hicks, Ralph, yeoman, St Minver, Corn, 1638 Cornwall RO AP/H929/3
Hicks, Thomas, Milford, Hants, 1678 Hants RO 21m65 D8/287
Hicks, Timothy, yeoman, Glympton, Oxon, 1675 Oxon RO MSS Wills 81/1/11
Hickson, Anthony, Sandwich, Kent, 1619 CKS PRC2/22/159
Hickson, Gibbs, cooper: 'wine cooper', Dover, Kent, 1678 CKS PRC20/12/262
Hickson, Richard, gentleman, Dunton Bassett, Leics, 1672 Leics RO Administrators Accounts 1667-72 f79
Hickson, Robert, yeoman, Spalding, Lincs, 1618 Lincs RO Ad/Ac/14/255
Hickson, William, cordwainer: 'shoemaker', Grantham, Lincs, 1626 Lincs RO Ad/Ac/20/36
Hickson, William, Donington, Lincs, 1666 Lincs RO Ad/Ac/32/81
Hide, Edward, gentleman, Hendred, East, Berks, 1674 Berks RO D/A1/196/183C
Hide, Edward, gentleman, Aldworth (Bower), Berks, 1684 Berks RO D/A1/197/73C
Hide, Elizabeth, dame, Cumnor (Blagrove), Berks, 1633 Berks RO D/A1/196/1E

[Hide:]
Hide, John, New Romney, Kent, 1645 CKS PRC19/2/98
Hide, Peter, Sherbourne, Dors, 1627 Wilts RO Miscellaneous Index (name + date)
Hide, Robert, Warminghurst, Sussex, 1631 W. Suss RO EpI/33/1631/24
Hide, Rowland, husbandman, Newnham, Herts, 1631 Herts RO ASA25/4876
Hide, Silvester, Pershore, Worcs, 1681 Worcs RO 008.7 BA3585/830/63
Hide, Thomas, clothier, Newbury, Berks, 1591 Berks RO D/A1/194/59J
Hide, William, esquire, Kingston Lisle, Berks, 1600 Berks RO D/A1/194/100C
Hide, William, Canterbury, Kent, 1618 CKS PRC2/22/151
Hider, Henry, Yapton, Sussex, 1678 W. Suss RO EpI/33/1678/8
Hider, John, Ashford, Kent, 1643 CKS PRC1/6/64
Hider, John, clothier, Ashford, Kent, 1679 CKS PRC2/38/145
Hider, John, yeoman, Hawkhurst, Kent, 1683 CKS PRC2/40/118
Hieron, William, Malmesbury, Wilts, 1677 Wilts RO Miscellaneous Index (name + date)
Higbee, Thomas, innholder, Stilton, Hunts, 1731 Hunts RO/Acc58/320
Higden, Luke, Hagnaby, Lincs, 1611 Lincs RO Ad/Ac/10/33
Higdon, Thomas, Stallingborough, Lincs, 1614 Lincs RO Ad/Ac/13/26
Higdon, Thomas, Bradley, West, Som, 1667 Somerset RO D/D/Cta/H49
Higgens, John, Yarlington, Som, 1664 Somerset RO D/D/Cta/H48
Higges, Richard, Cropthorne (Charlton), Worcs, Worcs RO 008.7 BA3585/839/303
Higges, William, husbandman, Swallowfield, Berks, 1614 Berks RO D/A1/78/41B
Higginbotham, George, Chesterfield, Derby, 1684 LJRO/B/C/5/1685/49
Higgins, Dunstane, Canterbury All Saints, Kent, 1665 CKS PRC1/10/51
Higgins, Edward, university: 'Fellow of Brasenose College, Oxford/M.A.', Oxford (Brasenose College), Oxon, 1588 Bodleian HYP B8/103-104
Higgins, Ephrain, grocer, Gloucester, Glos, 1750 GRO GDR/B4/2/H112
Higgins, John, glover, Milton next Sittingbourne, Kent, 1641 CKS PRC1/5/105
Higgins, Margery, spinster, Nettleton, Wilts, 1640 Wilts RO Arch. Wilts.(name + date)
Higgins, Richard eld, yeoman, Marcham, Berks, 1627 Berks RO D/A1/195/109A
Higgins, Thomas, Shifnal, Shrops, 1675 LJRO:cards/1675/35
Higgins, Thomas, Hasfield, Glos, 1685 GRO GDR/B4/2/H178
Higginson, Edward, gentleman, Sowe (Hawkesbury), Warks, 1740 LJRO/B/C/5/1740/253
Higginson, Richard, Adderley, Shrops, 1685 LJRO/B/C/5/1685/50
Higginson, William, Myddle, Shrops, 1667 LJRO:cards/1667/44
Higginson/Cooper, Alice, spinster, Drayton (Betton), Staffs, 1693 LJRO/B/C/5/1693/45
Higginson/Cooper, Alice, spinster, Drayton (Betton), Staffs, 1694 LJRO/B/C/5/1693/50
Higgs, Edward, gentleman, Basildon, Berks, 1624 Berks RO D/A1/195/97C
Higgs, Mary, spinster, Thatcham (Henwick), Berks, 1666 Berks RO D/A1/196/143C
Higgs, Nicholas, yeoman, Thatcham (Henwick), Berks, 1663 Berks RO D/A1/80/111D
Higgs, Nicholas, yeoman, Swallowfield, Berks, 1673 Berks RO D/A1/196/170C
Higgs, Samuel, draper: 'linen draper', Reading St Lawrence, Berks, 1683 Berks RO D/A1/197/64C
Higgs, Thomas, Ashampstead, Berks, 1600 Berks RO D/A1/77/131D
Higgs, Thomas, Marston on Dove, Derby, 1663 LJRO:cards/1663/30
Higgs, Thomas, Faversham, Kent, 1712 CKS PRC1/17/29
Higgs, Thomas, miller, Almondsbury (Over), Glos, 1750 GRO GDR/B4/2/H172
Higgs, William, yeoman, Wargrave, Berks, 1663 Berks RO D/A1/196/99A
Higgs, William, Uttoxeter, Staffs, 1682 LJRO/B/C/5/1681/22
Higgyns, James, Thorney, West, Sussex, 1594 W. Suss RO EpI/33/1594/8
Higham, George, Sittingbourne, Kent, 1609 CKS PRC2/13/252
Higham, George, Sittingbourne, Kent, 1615 CKS PRC2/22/120
Higham, John, Boxley, Kent, 1597 CKS PRC2/9/255
Higham, Richard eld, weaver: 'broad weaver', Biddenden, Kent, 1637 CKS PRC1/1/52
Higham, Robert, Brimpton, Berks, 1594 Berks RO D/A1/194/32A
Higham, Thomas, Goudhurst, Kent, 1626 CKS PRC20/7/19
Higham, Thomas, Thornham, Kent, 1631 CKS PRC20/9/235

Highnam, Thomas, Camely, Som, 1634 Somerset RO D/D/Cta/H20
Highway, Robert, Alconbury, Hunts, 1685 Hunts RO/Acc58/256(254)
Highwood, Richard, Canterbury St George Martyr, Kent, 1612 CKS PRC20/2/378
Hignell, Robert, innholder, Ilsley, East, Berks, 1673 Berks RO D/A1/196/160A
Higson, Thomas, Asterby, Lincs, 1612 Lincs RO Ad/Ac/11/92
Hiland, Richard, Dover St Mary, Kent, 1646 CKS PRC19/2/99
Hild, John, pilot, Deal, Kent, 1674 CKS PRC20/12/80
Hilde, Bartholomew, Worth, Kent, 1619 CKS PRC20/4/171
Hilde, Elizabeth, Eastry, Kent, 1602 CKS PRC21/16/105
Hilde, Jane, widow, Elham, Kent, 1640 CKS PRC1/2/74
Hilde, Jeames, Sholden, Kent, 1600 CKS PRC2/11/139
Hilde, John, Eastry, Kent, 1588 CKS PRC21/9/84
Hilde, Katherine, widow, Sholden, Kent, 1617 CKS PRC2/21/11
Hilde, Thomas, Worth, Kent, 1627 CKS PRC20/8/265
Hilde, William, Worth, Kent, 1626 CKS PRC20/7/34
Hilder, Thomas, Sutton Valence, Kent, 1619 CKS PRC2/22/158
Hile, William, Deal, Kent, 1673 CKS PRC20/12/85
Hiley, Peter, merchant, Poole, Dors, 1673 PRO PROB5/1092
Hilkes, Sidrack, Milton next Sittingbourne, Kent, 1679 CKS PRC2/38/143
Hill, Abraham, Abingdon St Nicholas, Berks, 1604 Berks RO D/A1/194/119A
Hill, Agnes, Epworth, Lincs, 1611 Lincs RO Ad/Ac/8a/338
Hill, Alexander, yeoman, Epworth, Lincs, 1610 Lincs RO Ad/Ac/8a/327
Hill, Alexander, cordwainer, Oxford St Aldate, Oxon, 1639 Oxon RO MSS Wills 298/1/44
Hill, Edward, Nuthurst, Sussex, 1634 W. Suss RO EpI/33/1633/10
Hill, Edward, Halton, Bucks, 1678 Bucks R.O. MSS Wills Pec 79/6/17
Hill, Edward, Lapworth, Worcs, 1684 Worcs RO 008.7 BA3585/837/bdl 4
Hill, Edward, goldsmith/silversmith?, St Botolph without Aldersgate, London & Middlesex, 1685 PRO PROB32/25/212
Hill, Elizabeth, Horsington, Lincs, 1634 Lincs RO Ad/Ac/24/26
Hill, Elizabeth, Oxford St Peter in the East, Oxon, 1669 Oxon RO MSS Wills 33/2/18
Hill, Eurias, Pilham, Lincs, 1632 Lincs RO Ad/Ac/40/6
Hill, Francis, Stowting, Kent, 1609 CKS PRC2/15/195
Hill, Francis, yeoman, Windsor, New, Berks, 1639 Berks RO D/A1/196/43A
Hill, George, Graffham, Sussex, 1646 W. Suss RO EpI/33/1645/1
Hill, Humfrey, Uttoxeter, Staffs, 1700 LJRO/B/C/5/1700/28
Hill, Joan, widow, Winterbourne (Sturdon House), Glos, Bristol RO 1708/19
Hill, Joan, widow, Risborough, Monks, Bucks, 1617 Bucks R.O. MSS Wills Pec 79/6/5
Hill, John, brickmaker, Bristol St Philip & St Jacob, Glos, Bristol RO 1737/17
Hill, John, Broughton, Lincs, 1617 Lincs RO Ad/Ac/8b/185
Hill, John, Langford, Steeple, Wilts, 1617 Wilts RO Miscellaneous Index (name + date)
Hill, John, husbandman, Wargrave, Berks, 1617 Berks RO D/A1/195/64A
Hill, John, gentleman, Chard, Som, 1620 Somerset RO D/D/Cta/H26
Hill, John, Boston, Lincs, 1623 Lincs RO Ad/Ac/18/81
Hill, John, Horncastle, Lincs, 1627 Lincs RO Ad/Ac/20b/35
Hill, John, Folkingham, Lincs, 1650 Lincs RO Ad/Ac/29/119
Hill, John, Eyam, Derby, 1682 LJRO/B/C/5/1682/52
Hill, John, Kimbolton, Hunts, 1682 Hunts RO/Acc58/174(21)
Hill, John, farmer, Sheffield (Hill Top), Yorks, 1801 Borthwick Test C.P. 1801/5
Hill, John sen, yeoman, Basildon, Berks, 1678 Berks RO D/A1/197/30B
Hill, Judith, widow, Winford, Som, 1738 Somerset RO D/D/Cta/H87a
Hill, Lawrence, Donington, Lincs, 1600 Lincs RO Ad/Ac/5/115
Hill, Lawrence, Wells St Cuthbert, Som, 1621 Somerset RO D/D/Cta/H27
Hill, Lewie, Grantham, Lincs, 1605 Lincs RO Ad/Ac/6/25
Hill, Marie, Grantham, Lincs, 1605 Lincs RO Ad/Ac/6/28
Hill, Martha, widow, Stourmouth, Kent, 1631 CKS PRC20/9/223

[Hill:]
Hill, Mary, Watford, Herts, 1596 Herts RO ASA25/1554
Hill, Ralph, Watford (Fortunes), Herts, 1610 Herts RO ASA25/4779
Hill, Richard, Scothorne, Lincs, 1629 Lincs RO Ad/Ac/40/91
Hill, Richard, bachelor, Grinstead, West, Sussex, 1672 W. Suss RO EpI/33/1672/15
Hill, Richard, Malvern, Great, Worcs, 1677 Worcs RO 008.7 BA3585/830/96
Hill, Robert, Mumby, Lincs, 1632 Lincs RO Ad/Ac/23/19
Hill, Robert, Petworth, Sussex, 1635 W. Suss RO EpI/33/1635/25
Hill, Robert, Appleby, Lincs, 1650 Lincs RO Ad/Ac/40/204
Hill, Robert, Uttoxeter, Staffs, 1684 LJRO/B/C/5/1684/43
Hill, Roger, Gayton le Marsh, Lincs, 1607 Lincs RO Ad/Ac/8a/158
Hill, Simon, Pulborough, Sussex, 1669 W. Suss RO EpI/33/1669/19
Hill, Sybil, widow, Wembdon, Som, 1592 Somerset RO D/D/Cta/H79
Hill, Thomas, Brompton Regis, Som, Somerset RO D/D/Cta/H63
Hill, Thomas, Sutton (Lutton), Lincs, 1611 Lincs RO Ad/Ac/10/100
Hill, Thomas, Cumnor (Whitley), Berks, 1615 Berks RO D/A1/195/60A
Hill, Thomas, Springthorpe, Lincs, 1622 Lincs RO Ad/Ac/8c/92
Hill, Thomas, Donington, Lincs, 1623 Lincs RO Ad/Ac/18/23
Hill, Thomas, yeoman, Stoke-upon-Trent (Shelton), Staffs, 1663 LJRO:cards/1663/31
Hill, Thomas, mr, St Martin in the Fields, London & Middlesex, 1704 PRO PROB32/47/35
Hill, Thomasin, widow, Sutton, Long, Lincs, 1628 Lincs RO Ad/Ac/20b/55
Hill, Wilfrid, Crowle, Lincs, 1650 Lincs RO Ad/Ac/40/205
Hill, William, gentleman, Longdon, Worcs, 1604 Worcs RO 008.7 BA3585/839/362
Hill, William, yeoman, Marsh Chapel, Lincs, 1623 Lincs RO Ad/Ac/18/51
Hill, William, Boston, Lincs, 1630? Lincs RO Ad/Ac/40/99
Hill, William, Staunton, Worcs, 1680 Worcs RO 008.7 BA3585/837/bdl 2
Hill, William, farmer, Gaywood, Norf, 1762 Norfolk RO ANW/23/25/57
Hill/Andrew, William, Kirdford, Sussex, 1669 W. Suss RO EpI/33/1669/17
Hill/Huband, Mary, wife, Inkberrow, Worcs, 1680 Worcs RO 008.7 BA3585/837/bdl 2
Hillary, Richard, cordwainer: 'shoemaker', Salisbury, Wilts, 1672 Wilts RO Miscellaneous Index (name + date)
Hiller, Francis, Beechingstoke, Wilts, 1678 Wilts RO Miscellaneous Index (name + date)
Hiller, John, Pagham, Sussex, 1637 W. Suss RO EpIV/10/2/12
Hiller, see Clarke,
Hilles, Agnes, Iwade, Kent, 1611 CKS PRC2/16/106
Hilles, Averie, Badlesmere, Kent, 1594 CKS PRC2/7/393
Hilles, Catherine, widow, Hinxhill, Kent, 1611 CKS PRC2/17/166
Hilles, Christopher, Smeeth, Kent, 1610 CKS PRC20/2/53
Hilles, Joane, widow, Headcorn, Kent, 1618 CKS PRC2/22/135
Hilles, John, Goudhurst, Kent, 1614 CKS PRC2/18/105
Hilles, John, St Laurence Thanet, Kent, 1664 CKS PRC1/10/52
Hilles, Lawrence, Sandwich St Peter, Kent, 1616 CKS PRC2/21/4
Hilles, Michaell, Badlesmere, Kent, 1601 CKS PRC2/12/195
Hilles, Nicholas, Maidstone, Kent, 1603 CKS PRC21/17/25
Hilles, Peter, Chislet, Kent, 1627 CKS PRC2/28/65
Hilles, Richard, Kenardington, Kent, 1630 CKS PRC2/30/87
Hilles, Thomas, High Halden, Kent, 1599 CKS PRC2/10/523
Hilles, Thomas, Iwade, Kent, 1606 CKS PRC2/13/229
Hilles, Thomas, husbandman, Spalding, Lincs, 1620 Lincs RO Ad/Ac/16/52
Hilles, Thomas, Faversham, Kent, 1662 CKS PRC1/9/25
Hilles, Thomas, Faversham, Kent, 1662 CKS PRC1/9/25a
Hilles, William eld, Goudhurst, Kent, 1639 CKS PRC1/2/75
Hillhowse, Edmund, yeoman, Congresbury, Som, 1619 Somerset RO D/D/Cta/H66
Hilliard, Henry, Brenzett, Kent, 1621 CKS PRC2/23/156
Hilliard, Henry, St Thomas Isle of Harty, Kent, 1634 CKS PRC2/32/54
Hillier, Thomas, Maidenhead, Berks, 1613 Berks RO D/A1/195/52A

Hillman, Thomas, Kinver, Staffs, 1685 LJRO/B/C/5/1685/51
Hills, Agnes, Staplehurst, Kent, 1616 CKS PRC2/22/177
Hills, Anthonie, Horbling, Lincs, 1637 Lincs RO Ad/Ac/25/471
Hills, Edward, Boughton Monchelsea, Kent, 1629 CKS PRC2/29/50
Hills, Elizabeth, widow, Rainham, Kent, 1675 CKS PRC2/36/197
Hills, Elizabeth, widow, Sheldwich, Kent, 1680 CKS PRC2/39/50
Hills, George, Fordwich, Kent, 1639 CKS PRC2/34/219
Hills, George, husbandman, Smarden, Kent, 1675 CKS PRC2/36/200
Hills, Henrie, Ashford, Kent, 1632 CKS PRC2/31/40
Hills, Henry, Minster in Sheppey, Kent, 1639 CKS PRC1/1/79
Hills, John, Headcorn, Kent, 1637 CKS PRC2/34/64
Hills, John, Egerton, Kent, 1639 CKS PRC20/10/526
Hills, John, husbandman, Chislet, Kent, 1641 CKS PRC1/4/58
Hills, John, Ramsey, Hunts, 1679 Hunts RO/Acc58/132(8)
Hills, John, blacksmith, Sellindge, Kent, 1680 CKS PRC2/39/56
Hills, John, Kingsnorth, Kent, 1681 CKS PRC2/39/176
Hills, John, St Laurence Thanet, Kent, 1682 CKS PRC2/39/177
Hills, John, blacksmith, St Johns Thanet, Kent, 1682 CKS PRC2/40/37
Hills, John, Newnham, Kent, 1692 CKS PRC2/42/34
Hills, Martha, widow, Sturry, Kent, 1712 CKS PRC1/17/59
Hills, Mathew, Wingham, Kent, 1682 CKS PRC20/13/257
Hills, Michael, Chilham, Kent, 1689 CKS PRC2/41/123
Hills, Reginold, Mersham, Kent, 1675 CKS PRC2/36/207
Hills, Richard, Deal, Kent, 1598 CKS PRC21/14/270
Hills, Richard, Shadoxhurst, Kent, 1643 CKS PRC1/6/107
Hills, Richard, tanner, Canterbury Holy Cross Westgate, Kent, 1671 CKS PRC2/35/54
Hills, Richard, tanner, Sutton Valence, Kent, 1673 CKS PRC2/35/218
Hills, Robert, Staplehurst, Kent, 1609 CKS PRC2/13/245
Hills, Sarles, Teynham, Kent, 1682 CKS PRC2/40/38
Hills, Simon, yeoman, Kingsnorth, Kent, 1672 CKS PRC2/35/145
Hills, Stephen, yeoman, Eastchurch, Sheppey, Kent, 1618 CKS PRC2/22/130
Hills, Stephen, Eastchurch, Sheppey, Kent, 1619 CKS PRC20/4/130
Hills, Thomas, Ashford, Kent, 1597 CKS PRC2/9/237
Hills, Thomas, Warehorne, Kent, 1616 CKS PRC2/21/10
Hills, Thomas, Minster in Sheppey, Kent, 1617 CKS PRC2/22/167
Hills, Thomas, Hothfield, Kent, 1619 CKS PRC2/22/164
Hills, Thomas, Minster in Sheppey, Kent, 1625 CKS PRC2/25/74
Hills, Thomas, Milton next Sittingbourne, Kent, 1633 CKS PRC2/32/61
Hills, Thomas, tanner, Hythe St Leonard, Kent, 1671 CKS PRC20/12/11
Hills, Thomas, husbandman, Pluckley, Kent, 1674 CKS PRC2/36/78
Hills, Thomas, Charing, Kent, 1681 CKS PRC20/13/147
Hills, Thomas, Kingsnorth, Kent, 1683 CKS PRC2/40/43
Hills, Thomas, widower, Murston, Kent, 1683 CKS PRC2/40/117
Hills, Walter, maltster, Maidstone, Kent, 1670 CKS PRC19/4/54
Hills, William, Maidstone, Kent, 1604 CKS PRC21/17/5
Hills, William, Bersted, South, Sussex, 1617 W. Suss RO EpIV/10/1/49
Hills, William, Milton next Sittingbourne, Kent, 1623 CKS PRC2/23/155
Hills, William, blacksmith, Thanington, Kent, 1676 CKS PRC2/37/45
Hills, see Vidian,
Hilpes, John, Holt, Wilts, 1610 Wilts RO Arch. Sarum(+ name and date)
Hilsdon/Burdge, John, Warminster, Wilts, 1632 Wilts RO Arch. Sarum(+ name and date)
Hilton, Jo.,
    Wilts 1633 Wilts RO Arch. Sarum(+ name and date)
Hilton, John, degrees: 'B.Mus.', Cambridge, Cambs, 1608 CUL V.C.Acc./Box1/27
Hilton, Richard, Manchester, Lancs, 1625 Lancs RO (Name of Deceased) D.R.C.H. 1625

[Hilton:]
Hilton, Thomas, Eastchurch, Sheppey, Kent, 1602 CKS PRC2/12/434
Hilton, William, Burwell, Lincs, 1612 Lincs RO Ad/Ac/11/161
Hilton, William, carpenter: 'ships carpenter', Deptford, Kent, 1699 PRO PROB5/1106
Hinckley, Henry, Longdon (Brereton), Staffs, 1711 LJRO/B/C/5/1711/29
Hinckley, Hester, widow, Salisbury, Wilts, 1669 Wilts RO Miscellaneous Index (name + date)
Hinckley, Isaac, Ulcombe, Kent, 1637 CKS PRC2/34/66
Hinckley, Isaac, Harrietsham, Kent, 1662 CKS PRC1/9/26
Hinckley, James, yeoman, Doddington, Kent, 1682 CKS PRC2/40/44
Hinckley, John, Cottesbrooke, Northants, 1671 Northants RO NWill A/C/132
Hinckley, John, Hawkhurst, Kent, 1676 CKS PRC2/37/47
Hinckley, Stephen, Milton next Sittingbourne, Kent, 1631 CKS PRC2/30/82
Hincklin, Mysaac, Borden, Kent, 1617 CKS PRC2/22/137
Hincksell, Clement, Headcorn, Kent, 1613 CKS PRC2/18/51
Hind, Gylbert, Marden, Kent, 1625 CKS PRC2/23/172
Hind, Margerie, widow, Morton, Lincs, 1626 Lincs RO Ad/Ac/20/15
Hind, Nichalas, Blyborough, Lincs, 1649 Lincs RO Ad/Ac/40/167
Hinde, Ellene, widow, Eccleston, Ches, 1636 Cheshire RO (Name) W.C. 1636
Hinde, Henrye, Marden, Kent, 1602 CKS PRC2/12/439
Hinde, John, tanner, Alconbury Weston, Hunts, 1683 Hunts RO/Acc58/201(43)
Hinde, Percevall, gentleman, Smeeth, Kent, 1617 CKS PRC20/4/183
Hinde, William, husbandman, Willoughton, Lincs, 1608 Lincs RO Ad/Ac/37/256
Hinde, William, Wrangle, Lincs, 1611 Lincs RO Ad/Ac/11/31
Hinde, William, Wickhambreaux, Kent, 1666 CKS PRC1/11/125
Hinde, William, clergy: 'clerk/vicar', Fittleworth, Sussex, 1670 W. Suss RO EpI/33/1669/22
Hindley, Francis, Martin, Lincs, 1670 Lincs RO Ad/Ac/32/137
Hindmarsh, George, butcher, Grimsby, Great, Lincs, 1669 Lincs RO Ad/Ac/33/92
Hinds, William, Canterbury Holy Cross Westgate, Kent, 1702 CKS PRC1/16/47b
Hinds, William, yeoman, Canterbury Holy Cross Westgate, Kent, 1702 CKS PRC1/16/47
Hinksell, Christopher, Brabourne, Kent, 1618 CKS PRC2/22/150
Hinman, Zacharie, Donington, Lincs, 1623 Lincs RO Ad/Ac/18/46
Hinstocke, William, Stoke upon Tern, Shrops, 1674 LJRO:cards/1674/25
Hinton, John, Charlton on Otmoor, Oxon, 1772 Oxon RO MSS Wills 302/5/67
Hinton, Stephen, Sutton Veny, Wilts, 1628 Wilts RO Arch. Sarum(+ name and date)
Hinton, Thomas, gentleman, Shrivenham (Bourton), Berks, 1677 Berks RO D/A1/197/25C
Hinton, Walter, Cumnor, Berks, 1596 Berks RO D/A1/194/78A
Hinton, William, Warminster, Wilts, 1620 Wilts RO Miscellaneous Index (name + date)
Hinxhill, Nicholas, Frittenden, Kent, 1597 CKS PRC2/9/251
Hinxill, see Hynckcell,
Hiorns, Thomas, yeoman, Itchington, Long, Warks, 1791 LJRO/B/C/5/1791/38
Hipkin, John, Westbourne (Inlands?), Sussex, 1640 W. Suss RO EpI/33/1640/29
Hippisley, Christopher, gentleman, St Mary Abchurch, London & Middlesex, 1712 PRO PROB5/1448
Hipplethwayt, Stephen, yeoman, Tilmanstone, Kent, 1619 CKS PRC2/22/149
Hipwell, Thomas, yeoman, Monks Kirby, Warks, 1809 LJRO/B/C/5/1809/36
Hird, Michaell, Fiskerton, Lincs, 1639 Lincs RO Ad/Ac/40/276
Hird, Robert, Barlings, Lincs, 1619 Lincs RO Ad/Ac/8b/328
Hird, Robert, Ingham, Lincs, 1632 Lincs RO Ad/Ac/39/291
Hiron, John, Pillerton Priors, Warks, 1681 Worcs RO 008.7 BA3585/830/68
Hirst, Abraham, Mickleover, Derby, 1760 LJRO/B/C/5/1760/189
Hirst, Edmund, yeoman, Milton next Sittingbourne, Kent, 1686 CKS PRC2/41/56
Hirst, John, engineer, Almondbury (South Crossland), Yorks, 1840 Borthwick Test C.P. 1840/4
Hirst, Susan + Edward, clergy: 'clerk', Linsted, Kent, 1626 CKS PRC2/25/62
Hirst, see Eastwood,
Hiscock, John, yeoman, Wilcot, Wilts, 1612 Wilts RO Arch. Wilts.(name + date)
Hiscock, John, mercer, Pewsey, Wilts, 1685 Wilts RO Arch. Wilts.(name + date)

Hiscocks, John, Hilmarton, Wilts, 1675 Wilts RO Miscellaneous Index (name + date)
Hiscocks, Richard, Barford, Wilts, 1641 Wilts RO Arch. Sarum(+ name and date)
Hiscox, John, Somerford, Little, Wilts, 1632 Wilts RO Arch. Wilts.(name + date)
Hiscox, Stephen, Frome Selwood, Som, 1590 Somerset RO D/D/Cta/H39
Hissey, John, yeoman, Longworth (Draycott-Moore), Berks, 1680 Berks RO D/A1/197/46B
Hitch, John, gentleman, Wendlebury, Oxon, 1634 Oxon RO MSS Wills 298/1/5
Hitchcock, Edward, Chichester, Sussex, 1669 W. Suss RO EpIII/9/1/55
Hitchcocke, Christopher, Sittingbourne, Kent, 1618 CKS PRC2/22/153
Hitchcocke, Peeter, Leysdown, Kent, 1592 CKS PRC2/5/376
Hitchcocke, William, Eastchurch, Sheppey, Kent, 1678 CKS PRC2/38/37
Hitchcocke, Zendby, widow, Preshute, Wilts, 1674 Wilts RO CC Sarum(+ name and date)
Hitchens, Kezekiah, Horsley, Glos, 1718 GRO GDR/B4/2/H169
Hitchfild, William, Petherton, North, Som, 1587 Somerset RO D/D/Cta/H44
Hitchington, William, Thame, Oxon, 1626 Oxon RO MSS Wills Pec 41/2/55
Hitchins, Jonathan, Westminster (Millbank), London & Middlesex, 1813 Greater London RO DL/C/572/125
Hitt, Christoper, turner, Donington, Lincs, 1638 Lincs RO Ad/Ac/25/188
Hix, John, Harptree, West, Som, 1601 Somerset RO D/D/Cta/H74
Hix, John, Deal, Kent, 1634 CKS PRC20/10/572
Hixe, Edmund, husbandman, Pennard, West, Som, 1625 Somerset RO D/D/Cta/H12
Hixe, John, Minster in Sheppey, Kent, 1608 CKS PRC2/15/193
Hixe, John ygr, Mark, Som, 1582 Somerset RO D/D/Cta/H7
Hixon, Robert, Coningsby, Lincs, 1636 Lincs RO Ad/Ac/24/468
Hixson, Thomas, Swalecliffe, Kent, 1609 CKS PRC2/15/176
Hoad, James, Borden, Kent, 1630 CKS PRC2/30/84
Hoad, William, husbandman, Boxley, Kent, 1680 CKS PRC2/38/141
Hoadley, William, Hawkhurst, Kent, 1683 CKS PRC2/40/124
Hoadley, William, Hawkhurst, Kent, 1683 CKS PRC2/40/125
Hoadly, John, Rolvenden, Kent, 1673 CKS PRC2/35/222
Hoare, Awdrie, Christian Malford, Wilts, 1628 Wilts RO Arch. Wilts.(name + date)
Hoare, Christopher, yeoman, Maidenhead, Berks, 1663 Berks RO D/A1/196/126A
Hoare, Francis, yeoman, Coxwell, Little, Berks, 1671 Berks RO D/A3/3/70B
Hoare, John, innholder, Sittingbourne, Kent, 1661 CKS PRC1/8/101
Hoare, Josias, Staplehurst, Kent, 1593 CKS PRC2/6/202
Hoare, William, Brookland, Kent, 1669 CKS PRC1/14/59
Hobbe, Reginald, Lanivet, Corn, 1606 Cornwall RO AP/H128
Hobbell, Marten, Sandwich, Kent, 1597 CKS PRC2/9/509
Hobbes, Edward, Letcombe Bassett, Berks, 1598 Berks RO D/A1/194/92D
Hobbes, Elizabeth, Selsey, Sussex, 1675 W. Suss RO EpI/33/1675/2
Hobbes, Richard, innholder, Abingdon, Berks, 1625 Berks RO D/A1/195/107A
Hobbes, Robert, Alverstoke, Hants, 1665 Hants RO 1665 P25
Hobbes, Stephen, Warminster, Wilts, 1616 Wilts RO CC Sarum(+ name and date)
Hobbes, Thomas, Letcombe Bassett, Berks, 1598 Berks RO D/A1/194/92C
Hobbs, Alice, widow, Othery, Som, 1619 Somerset RO D/D/Cta/H64
Hobbs, Edward, Wimborne Minster, Dors, Dorset RO PE/WM CP 2/4/49
Hobbs, John, Selsey, Sussex, 1630 W. Suss RO EpI/33/1630/28
Hobbs, John, innholder, Abingdon, Berks, 1670 Berks RO D/A1/196/177B
Hobbs, John eld, yeoman, Buckland, Berks, 1678 Berks RO D/A1/197/34C
Hobbs, Richard, Deal, Kent, 1632 CKS PRC20/10/550
Hobbs, Thomas, Boughton under Blean, Kent, 1629 CKS PRC20/8/275
Hobbs, Thomas, Charlton Horethorne, Som, 1667 Somerset RO D/D/Cta/H50
Hobbs, Thomas, university: 'Fellow of Magdalen College, Oxford/B.D.', Oxford (Magdalen College), Oxon, 1672 Bodleian HYP B8/105-106
Hobby, Jane, Wylye, Wilts, 1674 Wilts RO Arch. Sarum(+ name and date)
Hobcrofte, Roger, St Johns Thanet, Kent, 1615 CKS PRC2/22/121

[Hobday:]
Hobday, Alice, widow, Elham, Kent, 1613 CKS PRC2/17/148
Hobday, Elizabeth, widow, Folkestone, Kent, 1626 CKS PRC2/25/70
Hobday, Hercules, Lydd, Kent, 1630 CKS PRC20/9/229
Hobday, James, Hythe St Leonard, Kent, 1631 CKS PRC20/9/239
Hobday, Joseph, Aldington, Kent, 1606 CKS PRC20/1/65
Hobday, Joseph, Ringwould, Kent, 1690 CKS PRC2/41/148
Hobday, Nicholas, Lydden, Kent, 1621 CKS PRC2/22/171
Hobday, Richard, Folkestone, Kent, 1626 CKS PRC2/25/71
Hobday, Richard eld, Barham, Kent, 1698 CKS PRC2/42/142
Hobday, Robert, gentleman, Cheriton, Kent, 1643 CKS PRC1/6/108
Hobday, Thomas, blacksmith, Elmsted, Kent, 1693 CKS PRC2/42/36
Hobday, Thomazine, spinster, Bishopsbourne, Kent, 1633 CKS PRC2/32/63
Hobday, William, innholder, Tetsworth, Oxon, 1675 Oxon RO MSS Wills Pec 41/4/36
Hobday, William, Lydden, Kent, 1676 CKS PRC2/36/195
Hobday, William, shipwright, Dover, Kent, 1677 CKS PRC20/12/203
Hobdey, Henry, Lyminge, Kent, 1596 CKS PRC21/14/29
Hobdeye, John, Dover, Kent, 1573 CKS PRC21/2/1
Hobell, Malliart, Sandwich, Kent, 1626 CKS PRC2/27/77
Hoben, Henrie, Ruckinge, Kent, 1629 CKS PRC2/29/52
Hobes, William, miller, Stanton St John, Oxon, 1663 Oxon RO MSS Wills 32/4/15
Hobey, William, Woodhurst, Hunts, Hunts RO/Acc58/192(23)
Hobjohn, John, Lyminster, Sussex, 1598 W. Suss RO EpI/33/1598/12
Hoblocke, John, labourer, Dover, Kent, 1618 CKS PRC20/4/177
Hoblyn, Ephne, widow, St Stephen in Brannel, Corn, 1644 Cornwall RO AP/H1183
Hobs, Gregory, Ringwould, Kent, 1612 CKS PRC2/17/136
Hobson, Christopher, Somersham, Hunts, 1676 Hunts RO/Acc58/70(4)
Hobson, John, Herne, Kent, 1607 CKS PRC20/1/233
Hobson, John, Chidham, Sussex, 1679 W. Suss RO EpI/33/1678/5
Hobson, John, labourer, Sandwich, Kent, 1695 CKS PRC2/42/81
Hobson, Katherine, mistress, Kintbury (Wallingtons), Berks, 1663 Berks RO D/A1/196/116A
Hobson, Martin, Kintbury (Elcot), Berks, 1609 Berks RO D/A1/195/33A
Hobson, Richard, tailor, Boston, Lincs, 1612 Lincs RO Ad/Ac/11/144
Hobson, Richard, Boxgrove (Halnaker), Sussex, 1631 W. Suss RO EpI/33/1631/22
Hobson, Thomas, Althorpe (Burringham), Lincs, 1602 Lincs RO Ad/Ac/37/128
Hobson, Thomas, Wellingborough, Northants, 1675 Northants RO NWill A/C/55
Hobson, Thomas, Somersham, Hunts, 1676 Hunts RO/Acc58/87(5)
Hobson, Toby, Ridge, Herts, 1627 Herts RO ASA25/4846
Hobster, William, husbandman, Croft, Lincs, 1670 Lincs RO Ad/Ac/32/221
Hoby, Thomas, esquire, Bickerton, Hants, 1720 PRO PROB5/796A
Hocker, John, Canterbury St George Martyr, Kent, 1608 CKS PRC2/15/192
Hockerston, John, husbandman, Morton, Lincs, 1671 Lincs RO Ad/Ac/33/174
Hockerstone, George, Dowsby, Lincs, 1639 Lincs RO Ad/Ac/26/203
Hockin, Margaret, widow, Pillaton, Corn, 1624 Cornwall RO AP/H373/3
Hockley, James, yeoman, Ufton Nervet, Berks, 1664 Berks RO D/A1/196/134C
Hocknell, Toby, Cadbury, North, Som, 1639 Somerset RO D/D/Cta/H3
Hodds, John, Portishead, Som, 1662 Somerset RO D/D/Cta/H45
Hodge, Benjamin, yeoman, Antony, Corn, 1614 Cornwall RO AP/H610/2
Hodge, Edward, Pillaton, Corn, 1609 Cornwall RO AP/H192/1
Hodge, George, Dover, Kent, 1626 CKS PRC20/7/213
Hodge, John, Altarnun, Corn, 1619 Cornwall RO AP/H486
Hodge, John, Lanreath, Corn, 1622 Cornwall RO AP/H550/2
Hodge, Mathew, clothier, Goudhurst, Kent, 1676 CKS PRC2/37/41
Hodge, Richard, New Romney, Kent, 1623 CKS PRC20/6/362
Hodgekinson, John, St Albans St Peters, Herts, Herts RO ASA25/4809
Hodgekynm, Thomas, Sandwich St Peter, Kent, 1574 CKS PRC2/1/104

Hodgeman, William, Selling, Kent, 1586 CKS PRC2/4/178
Hodges, Arthure, Charing, Kent, 1620 CKS PRC20/5/107
Hodges, Bartholomew, Stogursey, Som, 1687 Somerset RO D/D/Cta/H88
Hodges, Daniel, tailor, Covent Garden, St Paul, London & Middlesex, 1698 PRO PROB32/31/127
Hodges, Francis, Faversham, Kent, 1704 CKS PRC1/16/48
Hodges, John, Muchelney, Som, 1641 Somerset RO D/D/Cta/H58
Hodges, John, Wedmore, Som, 1641 Somerset RO D/D/Cta/H56
Hodges, Joshua, Dogmersfield, Hants, 1679 Hants RO 21m65 D8/289
Hodges, Moses, Sandwich, Kent, 1634 CKS PRC2/32/51
Hodges, Ralph, Oxford St Ebbe, Oxon, 1636 Oxon RO MSS Wills 298/1/17
Hodges, Robert, husbandman, Harbury, Warks, 1688 LJRO/B/C/5/1688/15a
Hodges, Thomas, Smeeth, Kent, 1588 CKS PRC21/9/190
Hodges, Thomas, Netherhampton, Dors, 1615 Wilts RO Miscellaneous Index (name + date)
Hodges, Thomas, innholder, Faversham, Kent, 1666 CKS PRC1/11/126
Hodges, Thomas, Midhurst, Sussex, 1676 W. Suss RO Epl/33/1676/8
Hodges, Thomas, St Johns Thanet, Kent, 1680 CKS PRC2/39/48
Hodges, Thomas, tanner, Benenden, Kent, 1686 CKS PRC2/41/34
Hodges, Thomas, Lavington, Market, Wilts, 1762? Wilts RO Miscellaneous Index (name + date)
Hodges, Thomas eld, Goudhurst, Kent, 1612 CKS PRC20/2/384
Hodges, Thomas jun, gentleman, Shipton Moyne, Glos, 1680 PRO PROB5/1301
Hodges, Walter, East Sutton, Kent, 1629 CKS PRC2/30/76
Hodges, William, gentleman, Yeovilton (Specklington), Som, 1647 Somerset RO D/D/Cta/H60
Hodges, see Brookes,
Hodgeskyn, Thomas eld, Littlebourne, Kent, 1584 CKS PRC21/7/380
Hodgetts, John, Aldridge (Great Barr), Staffs, 1720 LJRO/B/C/5/1720/26
Hodgkin, Anthony, Saughton, Ches, 1691 Cheshire RO (Name) W.C. 1691
Hodgkins, Jonathan, brushmaker, Birmingham, Warks, 1772 LJRO/B/C/5/1772/46
Hodgkinson, Francis, miller, Eckington (Millne Lane), Derby, 1663 LJRO:cards/1663/32
Hodgkinson, George, husbandman, Ashover, Derby, 1672 LJRO:cards/1672/30
Hodgkinson, Thomas, gentleman, Aston, Warks, 1815 LJRO/B/C/5/1815/33
Hodgkyne, Alice, spinster, Fladbury (Moor), Worcs, 1602 Worcs RO 008.7 BA3585/838/206
Hodgman, Edward, Hougham, Kent, 1712 CKS PRC19/6/53
Hodgskin, Thomas, Hackleton, Northants, 1679 Northants RO NWill A/C/38
Hodgson, Edmund, Metheringham, Lincs, 1632 Lincs RO Ad/Ac/23/132
Hodgson, Edward, butcher, Grimsby, Great, Lincs, 1612 Lincs RO Ad/Ac/11/157
Hodgson, George, mariner, Deal, Kent, 1683 CKS PRC20/13/335
Hodgson, George, Boston, Lincs, 1684 Lincs RO Ad/Ac/44/140
Hodgson, Henry, Spridlington, Lincs, 1662 Lincs RO Ad/Ac/41/42
Hodgson, James, Stone, Staffs, 1689 LJRO/B/C/5/1689/14
Hodgson, John, Bolingbroke, Old, Lincs, 1607 Lincs RO Ad/Ac/8a/93
Hodgson, John, Sutton, Long, Lincs, 1611 Lincs RO Ad/Ac/10/91
Hodgson, John, yeoman, Kirton, Lincs, 1684 Lincs RO Ad/Ac/44/69
Hodgson, Michael, Greetwell, Lincs, 1617 Lincs RO Ad/Ac/8b/145
Hodgson, Michael, Wyberton, Lincs, 1624 Lincs RO Ad/Ac/19A/97
Hodgson, Philipp, gentleman, Bardney, Lincs, 1623 Lincs RO Ad/Ac/18/35
Hodgson, Thomas, Frampton, Lincs, 1606 Lincs RO Ad/Ac/7/78
Hodgson, Thomas, Wragby, Lincs, 1611 Lincs RO Ad/Ac/10/34
Hodgson, Thomas, gentleman, Bardney, Lincs, 1623 Lincs RO Ad/Ac/17/1
Hodgson, William, yeoman, Spridlington, Lincs, 1607 Lincs RO Ad/Ac/37/245
Hodgson, William, Kirkstead, Lincs, 1619 Lincs RO Ad/Ac/15/53
Hodgson, William, Alkborough, Lincs, 1623 Lincs RO Ad/Ac/8c/57
Hodgson, see Wright,
Hodsden, Edward, husbandman, Watford, Herts, 1596 Herts RO ASA25/1476
Hodsden, Richard, Watford, Herts, 1636 Herts RO ASA25/4928
Hodsdon, John, Watford, Herts, Herts RO ASA25/4957

[Hodsham:]
Hodsham, Thomas, Walesby, Lincs, 1606 Lincs RO Ad/Ac/7/68
Hodskin, David, yeoman, Bredhurst, Kent, 1663 CKS PRC19/3/29
Hodskins, Richard, Ashford, Kent, 1716 CKS PRC1/18/6
Hodsoll, John, Boughton under Blean, Kent, 1665 CKS PRC19/3/53
Hoegson, Isabell, widow, Tealby, Lincs, 1619 Lincs RO Ad/Ac/8b/401
Hofer, Mercy, Sutton Valence, Kent, 1664 CKS PRC1/10/53
Hofer, Thomas, Sutton Valence, Kent, 1680 CKS PRC2/39/46
Hoford, Sarah, widow, Sutton Valence, Kent, 1683 CKS PRC2/40/123
Hogan, Joseph jun, mr, Roughton, Norf, 1762 Norfolk RO ANW/23/25/62
Hogbean, Thomazin, Barham, Kent, 1622 CKS PRC2/23/152
Hogbeane, John, Folkestone, Kent, 1603 CKS PRC2/14/252
Hogben, Alice, widow, Hythe St Leonard, Kent, 1682 CKS PRC20/13/137
Hogben, Ann, widow, Sellindge, Kent, 1682 CKS PRC2/40/41
Hogben, David, Stanford, Kent, 1690 CKS PRC19/4/117
Hogben, Edward, Deal, Kent, 1629 CKS PRC20/8/257
Hogben, Edward, River, Kent, 1662 CKS PRC1/9/27
Hogben, Edward, cordwainer, Sandwich, Kent, 1677 CKS PRC2/37/164
Hogben, Henry, gentleman, Challock, Kent, 1626 CKS PRC20/7/383
Hogben, Henry, ropemaker, St Peter in Thanet, Kent, 1639 CKS PRC1/2/76
Hogben, Henry, yeoman, Brenzett, Kent, 1662 CKS PRC1/9/28
Hogben, Henry, Brookland, Kent, 1674 CKS PRC2/35/224
Hogben, Jane, widow, Swingfield, Kent, 1614 CKS PRC2/18/20
Hogben, John, gentleman, Elham, Kent, 1677 CKS PRC2/37/156
Hogben, Margaret, widow, Folkestone, Kent, 1681 CKS PRC2/39/195
Hogben, Nicholas, Lydd, Kent, 1618 CKS PRC20/4/189
Hogben, Richard, Elham, Kent, 1623 CKS PRC2/23/151
Hogben, Stephen, Elham, Kent, 1615 CKS PRC2/21/7
Hogben, Stephen, yeoman, Selling, Kent, 1672 CKS PRC2/35/142
Hogben, Stephen, maltster, Brabourne, Kent, 1679 CKS PRC2/38/142
Hogben, Thomas, Acrise, Kent, 1664 CKS PRC1/10/54
Hogben, William, Elham, Kent, 1629 CKS PRC2/30/69
Hogben, William, jurat/mr, Folkestone, Kent, 1629 CKS PRC2/30/78
Hogben, William, clothier, Headcorn, Kent, 1641 CKS PRC19/2/21
Hogben, William, tailor, Elham, Kent, 1673 CKS PRC2/35/225
Hogben, William, yeoman, Lyminge, Kent, 1674 CKS PRC20/12/83
Hogbin, David, Lyminge, Kent, 1594 CKS PRC21/13/9
Hogbine, William, Ewell, Kent, 1608 CKS PRC2/15/188
Hogbyne, Robert, Lyminge, Kent, 1620 CKS PRC20/5/102
Hogg, Barnard, Winslow, Bucks, 1621 Herts RO ASA25/2536
Hogg, James, yeoman, Swineshead, Lincs, 1613 Lincs RO Ad/Ac/12/126
Hogg, John, Bagby, Yorks, 1637 Borthwick Prob. Ex. 1637/5
Hogge, Richard, Skirbeck, Lincs, 1638 Lincs RO Ad/Ac/25/44
Hogge, Robert, victualler, Holton le Clay, Lincs, 1620 Lincs RO Ad/Ac/16/49
Hogge, Thomas, gentleman, Stainton le Vale, Lincs, 1668 Lincs RO Ad/Ac/33/53
Hoggerston, Jeffery, Bassingthorpe, Lincs, 1650 Lincs RO Ad/Ac/30/23
Hoggesfleshe, Richard, Fernhurst, Sussex, 1618 W. Suss RO EpI/33/1618/11
Hogsflesh, Edward, maltster, Tenterden, Kent, 1671 CKS PRC2/35/49
Hoies, Barnard, yeoman, Claypole, Lincs, 1627 Lincs RO Ad/Ac/20/115
Holbache, Amilion, Warwick, Warks, 1603 Worcs RO 008.7 BA3585/839/363
Holbourne, Ralph, St Martin in the Fields, London & Middlesex, 1683 PRO PROB32/22/71
Holbrooke, George, gentleman, Newington next Sittingbourne, Kent, 1635 CKS PRC20/10/494
Holbrooke, John, Chichester, Sussex, 1627 W. Suss RO EpIII/9/1/29
Holbrooke, John, Calbourne, Hants, 1672 Hants RO 21m65 D8/245
Holcombe, William, Cranbrook, Kent, 1637 CKS PRC2/33/56
Holcroft, Sarah, dame/widow, St James Westminster, London & Middlesex, 1706 PRO

PROB32/49/113
Holcroft, Thomas, gentleman, Hurst, Lancs, 1637 Lancs RO (Name of Deceased) D.R.C.H. 1636
Holden, Bennett, Stickney, Lincs, 1611 Lincs RO Ad/Ac/10/106
Holden, Edward, Faversham, Kent, 1588 CKS PRC2/4/285
Holden, Edward, Stone in Oxney, Kent, 1617 CKS PRC2/22/133
Holden, Francis, Harrington, Lincs, 1668 Lincs RO Ad/Ac/33/56
Holden, Francis, husbandman, Boxford, Berks, 1677 Berks RO D/A1/197/22A
Holden, James, clothier, Cranbrook, Kent, 1606 CKS PRC2/14/225
Holden, John, yeoman, Bethersden, Kent, 1623 CKS PRC2/23/161
Holden, John, Whitechapel, London & Middlesex, 1674 PRO PROB32/11/28
Holden, John eld, Hawkhurst, Kent, 1634 CKS PRC2/32/154
Holden, Mary, widow, Cranbrook, Kent, 1612 CKS PRC2/13/250
Holden, Peeter, Cranbrook, Kent, 1639 CKS PRC1/2/77
Holden, Richard, St Albans, Herts, 1585 Herts RO ASA25/1091
Holden, Richard, Cranbrook, Kent, 1634 CKS PRC2/32/55
Holden, Thomas, Cranbrook, Kent, 1611 CKS PRC2/16/205
Holden, William, Ferring, Sussex, 1672 W. Suss RO EpI/33/1672/16
Holder, John, Frampton on Severn, Glos, 1740 GRO GDR/B4/2/H130
Holderness, William, husbandman, Gonerby, Lincs, 1671 Lincs RO Ad/Ac/33/189
Holdernesse, William, Boston, Lincs, 1637? Lincs RO Ad/Ac/25/547
Holdin, John, citizen/weaver, Stepney, St Dunstan, London & Middlesex, 1693 PRO PROB32/35/93
Holdin, Thomas, carpenter, Strumpshaw, Norf, Norfolk RO ANW/23/24/139
Holding, John, innholder, Nettlebed, Oxon, 1666 Oxon RO MSS Wills Pec 69/1/30
Holdippe, Christopher, husbandman, Welford (Benham Hoe), Berks, 1633 Berks RO D/A1/196/3C
Holdship, George, Upton Snodsbury, Worcs, Worcs RO 008.7 BA3585/838/247
Holdship, James, Maidstone, Kent, 1679 CKS PRC20/12/303
Holdstocke, Mary, widow, Althorpe (Burringham), Lincs, 1679 Lincs RO Ad/Ac/43/132
Holdsworth, Bryan, labourer, Deeping, Market, Lincs, 1627 Lincs RO Ad/Ac/20b/81
Holdsworth, Richard, shopkeeper, Mirfield, Yorks, 1840 Borthwick Test C.P. 1840/3
Holdsworth, Thomas, Mirfield (Wellhouse), Yorks, Borthwick Test C.P. 1719/7
Holdsworth, William, gentleman, Bilbrough, Yorks, 1850 Borthwick Test C.P. 1850/10
Holdway, John, St Mary Bourne, Hants, 1678 Hants RO 21m65 D8/288
Hole, Christofer, Ash next Sandwich, Kent, 1598 CKS PRC21/15/31
Hole, Edward, Castle Cary, Som, 1683 Somerset RO D/D/Cta/H89
Hole, John, Heckington, Lincs, 1619 Lincs RO Ad/Ac/15/137
Hole, Nicholas, Spondon, Derby, 1667 LJRO:cards/1667/45
Holesforth, Joseph, St Laurence Thanet, Kent, 1597 CKS PRC2/9/259
Holford, James, esquire, Newbrough, Ches, 1669 Cheshire RO (Name) W.C. 1668
Holford, John, gentleman, Davenham (Moulton), Ches, 1667 Cheshire RO (Name) W.C. 1666/7
Holford, Richard, Cranbrook, Kent, 1612 CKS PRC2/16/45
Holford, Thomas, Nuthurst, Sussex, 1672 W. Suss RO EpI/33/1672/10
Holford, Thomas, wool comber/shopkeeper, Wilmslow, Ches, 1771 Cheshire RO (Name) W.C. 1771
Holgate, Thomas, Deeping, Market, Lincs, 1627 Lincs RO Ad/Ac/20b/106
Holiday, Robart, Folkestone, Kent, 1593 CKS PRC2/6/470
Holker, Nicholas, Whalley (Read), Lancs, 1625 Lancs RO (Name of Deceased) D.R.C.H. 1625
Hollam, Elizabeth, widow, Stourmouth, Kent, 1619 CKS PRC2/21/8
Hollam, Thomas, Sandwich, Kent, 1606 CKS PRC2/13/225
Hollam, Thomas, Monkton, Kent, 1614 CKS PRC20/3/101
Holland, Anne, widow, Sempringham, Lincs, 1619 Lincs RO Ad/Ac/15/237
Holland, Brian, clergy: 'clerk/minister', Long Wittenham, Berks, 1674 Berks RO D/A1/196/184C
Holland, Edward, Halton, East, Lincs, 1637 Lincs RO Ad/Ac/25/404
Holland, Francis, innholder, Hemswell (Spital in the Street), Lincs, 1677 Lincs RO Ad/Ac/35/119
Holland, George, Helpringham, Lincs, 1624 Lincs RO Ad/Ac/19A/118

[Holland:]
Holland, George, High Halden, Kent, 1627 CKS PRC2/28/66
Holland, George, Bushey, Herts, 1638 Herts RO ASA25/4958
Holland, Joan, widow, Arundel, Sussex, 1625 W. Suss RO EpI/33/1624/6
Holland, John, Whitstone, Corn, 1607 Cornwall RO AP/H130/2
Holland, John, carrier, Cranbrook, Kent, 1620 CKS PRC20/4/145
Holland, John, Petworth, Sussex, 1633 W. Suss RO EpI/33/1633/9
Holland, John, Owston (West Kinnard's Ferry), Lincs, 1649 Lincs RO Ad/Ac/40/162
Holland, John, Wigtoft, Lincs, 1649 Lincs RO Ad/Ac/30/122
Holland, John, soldier, Denton, Lancs, 1650 Lancs RO (Name of Deceased) D.R.C.H. 1650
Holland, Kristian, Wainfleet St Mary, Lincs, 1581 Lincs RO Ad/Ac/2C/34
Holland, Margaret, spinster, Leverton, Lincs, 1630 Lincs RO Ad/Ac/22/88
Holland, Richard, Burton, Gate, Lincs, 1626 Lincs RO Ad/Ac/39/61
Holland, Thomas, clergy: 'parson', Coombes, Sussex, 1598 W. Suss RO EpI/33/1598/5
Holland, Thomas, Lydd, Kent, 1632 CKS PRC20/10/562
Holland, Thomas, yeoman, Grimoldby, Lincs, 1671 Lincs RO Ad/Ac/33/170
Holland, Thomas, mercer, Worcester, Worcs, 1682 Worcs RO 008.7 BA3585/837/bdl 3
Holland/Fletcher, Elizabeth, Chesterfield, Derby, 1663 LJRO:cards/1663/33
Hollande, Edward, Firsby, Lincs, 1597 Lincs RO Ad/Ac/4/95
Hollande, John, clergy: 'clerk', Ashford, Kent, 1596 CKS PRC2/8/73
Hollande, John, Dowsby (Graby), Lincs, 1611 Lincs RO Ad/Ac/10/65
Hollands, John, yeoman, Sandhurst, Kent, 1668 CKS PRC19/4/19
Hollands, John, yeoman, Sandhurst, Kent, 1675 CKS PRC2/36/196
Hollaway, Robert, Kington St Michael, Wilts, 1680 Wilts RO Miscellaneous Index (name + date)
Hollender, John, Donington, Lincs, 1637 Lincs RO Ad/Ac/25/422
Hollford, John, Fawley, Hants, 1598 Hants RO 1589 B30/4
Holliarde, Edmund, Arundel, Sussex, 1578 W. Suss RO EpI/33/1577
Holliday, Richard, Warningcamp, Sussex, 1635 W. Suss RO EpI/33/1635/11
Holliday, Robert, husbandman, Shrivenham (Fernham), Berks, 1615 Berks RO D/A1/78/47
Hollier, John ygr, yeoman, Deddington, Oxon, 1662 Oxon RO MSS Wills 167/2/6
Hollinder, George, Wigtoft, Lincs, 1618 Lincs RO Ad/Ac/14/212
Hollingbury, Richard, husbandman, Northbourne, Kent, 1639 CKS PRC2/34/218
Hollingedge, Robert, clergy: 'clerk', Horncastle, Lincs, 1634 Lincs RO Ad/Ac/24/199
Hollingham, John, Clapham, Sussex, 1670 W. Suss RO EpI/33/1670/3
Hollingham, Richard, Angmering, Sussex, 1684 W. Suss RO EpI/33/1684/37
Hollinghedge, Richard, Spalding, Lincs, 1587 Lincs RO Ad/Ac/2C/36
Hollingsheade, William, Tattershall, Lincs, 1629 Lincs RO Ad/Ac/22/72
Hollingsworth, William, Staveley, Derby, 1680 LJRO:cards/1680/19
Hollingworth, Rodolph, degrees: 'D.D.', Fillingham, Lincs, 1662 Lincs RO Ad/Ac/41/2
Hollingworthe, Richard, Brant Broughton, Lincs, 1601 Lincs RO Ad/Ac/5/43
Hollins, William, university: 'privileged person', Oxford (University), Oxon, Bodleian HYP B8/107-108
Hollinworth, George, Mottram (Tintwistle), Ches, 1624 Cheshire RO (Name) W.C. 1624
Hollis, Thomas, labourer, Ercall, High, Shrops, 1811 LJRO/B/C/5/1811/52
Hollis, William, Selsey, Sussex, 1672 W. Suss RO EpI/33/1672/12
Hollister, Edward, Compton Greenfield, Glos, Bristol RO 1680/66
Hollister, Thomas, Compton Greenfield, Glos, Bristol RO 1680/64
Hollister, Thomas, Cubled, Som, 1698 Somerset RO D/D/Cta/H90
Hollister, Timothy, chandler, Lacock, Wilts, 1679 Wilts RO Miscellaneous Index (name + date)
Hollman, Robert, Woodchurch, Kent, 1572 CKS PRC21/1/135
Hollmes, James, Ruskington, Lincs, 1648 Lincs RO Ad/Ac/30/255
Hollmes, Robert, Hacconby, Lincs, 1602 Lincs RO Ad/Ac/5/405
Hollome, Anne, widow, Grainthorpe, Lincs, 1674 Lincs RO Ad/Ac/34/110
Holloway, Corsley, Wilts, 1600 c. Wilts RO Miscellaneous Index (name + date)
Holloway, Bennet/Benedict, St Nicholas at Wade, Kent, 1638 CKS PRC20/10/510
Holloway, Catherine, widow, Bucklebury, Berks, 1622 Berks RO D/A1/78/102C

Holloway, John, Purton, Wilts, 1621 Wilts RO Arch. Wilts.(name + date)
Holloway, John, yeoman, Pangbourne, Berks, 1627 Berks RO D/A1/195/113A
Holloway, John, husbandman, Tidmarsh, Berks, 1632 Berks RO D/A1/195/136A
Holloway, John, Worcester St Clement, Worcs, 1776 Worcs RO 008.7 BA3585/835/bdl 2
Holloway, John eld, yeoman, Tilehurst, Berks, 1627 Berks RO D/A1/195/12A
Holloway, Richard eld, yeoman, Wroxton, Oxon, 1663 Oxon RO MSS Wills 80/4/24
Holloway, Thomas, husbandman, Broadfield, Berks, 1635 Wilts RO CC Sarum(+ name and date)
Holloway, Thomas, tailor, Oxford St Peter in the East, Oxon, 1646 Oxon RO MSS Wills 298/2/16
Holloway, William, Herne, Kent, 1607 CKS PRC20/1/229
Holloway, William, St Nicholas at Wade, Kent, 1636 CKS PRC20/10/474
Holloway, William, Hilmarton, Wilts, 1637 Wilts RO Arch. Wilts.(name + date)
Holloway, William, Kidlington (Water Eaton), Oxon, 1679 Oxon RO MSS Wills 167/2/32
Holloway, William, yeoman, Tilehurst, Berks, 1680 Berks RO D/A1/197/43C
Hollowaye, Anne, Bilsington, Kent, 1605 CKS PRC2/14/234
Hollowell, Edward, Faxton, Northants, 1680 Northants RO NWill A/C/29
Hollway, Agnes, Weston Zoyland, Som, 1622 Somerset RO D/D/Cta/H29
Hollway, James, Wimborne Minster, Dors, 1700 Dorset RO PE/WM CP 2/4/98
Hollway, see Hollwell,
Hollwell, John, yeoman, Othery, Som, 1610 Somerset RO D/D/Cta/H71
Hollwell/Hollway, William, Camerton, Som, 1620 Somerset RO D/D/Cta/H25
Hollywood, Stephan, St Nicholas at Wade, Kent, 1624 CKS PRC20/6/8
Holman, Constance, Wittersham, Kent, 1640 CKS PRC20/10/528
Holman, Elizabeth, widow, Newington next Sittingbourne, Kent, 1597 CKS PRC2/9/495
Holman, Enoch, yeoman, Marden, Kent, 1671 CKS PRC2/35/50
Holman, Francis, spinster, Boyton, Corn, 1642 Cornwall RO AP/H1104/2
Holman, John, Wittersham, Kent, CKS PRC20/9/216
Holman, John, High Halstow, Kent, 1591 CKS PRC2/5/354
Holman, John, Newenden, Kent, 1599 CKS PRC2/10/151
Holman, John, Egloskerry, Corn, 1606 Cornwall RO AP/H103/1
Holman, John, Aldington, Kent, 1607 CKS PRC20/1/144
Holman, John, Wittersham, Kent, 1631 CKS PRC20/9/217
Holman, Margerie, widow, Upchurch, Kent, 1612 CKS PRC2/16/36
Holman, Ralfe, Borden, Kent, 1596 CKS PRC2/8/198
Holman, Richard, Brixworth, Northants, 1682 Northants RO NWill A/C/74
Holman, Robert, Tenterden, Kent, 1576 CKS PRC2/1/158
Holman, Stephen, Ickham, Kent, 1629 CKS PRC20/8/289
Holman, Stephen, cooper, St Laurence Thanet, Kent, 1693 CKS PRC2/42/142
Holman, Thomas, Deal, Kent, 1631 CKS PRC20/9/233
Holman, Thomas, Tonge, Kent, 1706 CKS PRC19/6/19
Holman, Windebancke, yeoman, St Laurence Thanet, Kent, 1627 CKS PRC2/28/59
Holme, Edmund, esquire, Maghull, Lancs, 1588 Lancs RO (Name of Deceased) D.R.C.H. 1588
Holmer, Robert, Bere Regis, Dors, 1631 Wilts RO Miscellaneous Index (name + date)
Holmes, Anthonie, Owmby by Spital, Lincs, 1612 Lincs RO Ad/Ac/8a/346
Holmes, Bartholomew, Pinchbeck, Lincs, 1619 Lincs RO Ad/Ac/15/21
Holmes, Bryan, Maidstone, Kent, 1667 CKS PRC19/3/124
Holmes, Christopher, gentleman, Alfreton, Derby, 1778 LJRO/B/C/5/1778/34
Holmes, Edward, Barkwith, West, Lincs, 1613 Lincs RO Ad/Ac/12/120
Holmes, Edward, Saxilby, Lincs, 1680 Lincs RO Ad/Ac/43/159
Holmes, Evan, farmer, Halifax (Soyland), Yorks, 1815 Borthwick Test C.P. 1814/8
Holmes, Faith, spinster, Grainsby, Lincs, 1664 Lincs RO Ad/Ac/43/10
Holmes, Francis, Scampton, Lincs, 1662 Lincs RO Ad/Ac/41/157
Holmes, Francis, Scampton, Lincs, 1663? Lincs RO Ad/Ac/41/87
Holmes, Henry, collar maker, Ewell, Kent, 1682 CKS PRC2/40/36
Holmes, Jane, widow, Nonington, Kent, 1668 CKS PRC19/3/125

[Holmes:]
Holmes, John, Willoughby, Silk, Lincs, 1608 Lincs RO Ad/Ac/8a/144
Holmes, John, Wilsthorpe, Lincs, 1618 Lincs RO Ad/Ac/14/102
Holmes, John, Horbling (Bridgend), Lincs, 1625 Lincs RO Ad/Ac/19B/103
Holmes, John, husbandman, Stoke, North, Oxon, 1637 Oxon RO MSS Wills 298/1/30
Holmes, John, Claypole, Lincs, 1649 Lincs RO Ad/Ac/30/154
Holmes, John, yeoman, Shalbourne, Berks, 1681 Wilts RO Dean Sarum (name + date)
Holmes, John, Langtoft, Lincs, 1728? Lincs RO Ad/Ac/36/3
Holmes, John + Mary, banker & widow, York St Sampson, Yorks, 1793 Borthwick Test C.P. 1782/3
Holmes, Joseph, Smisby, Derby, 1682 LJRO/B/C/5/1682/54
Holmes, Michael, university: 'scholar's servant', Cambridge, Cambs, 1626 CUL V.C. Acc./Box2/39
Holmes, Nicholas, Manton, Lincs, 1629 Lincs RO Ad/Ac/39/112
Holmes, Peter, husbandman, Whitchurch, Oxon, 1641 Oxon RO MSS Wills 298/1/54
Holmes, Ralph, Goodnestone next Wingham, Kent, 1683 CKS PRC20/13/331
Holmes, Richard, husbandman, Whitchurch, Oxon, 1683 Oxon RO MSS Wills 167/2/41
Holmes, Richard, Wittering, West, Sussex, 1684 W. Suss RO EpI/33/1684/24
Holmes, Robert, Grainthorpe, Lincs, 1605 Lincs RO Ad/Ac/6/27
Holmes, Robert, husbandman, Ulceby, Lincs, 1683 Lincs RO Ad/Ac/44/71
Holmes, Robert, yeoman, Markby, Lincs, 1684 Lincs RO Ad/Ac/44/100
Holmes, Simon, Glastonbury, Som, 1588 Somerset RO D/D/Cta/H35
Holmes, Thomas, Normanby, Lincs, 1610 Lincs RO Ad/Ac/8a/325
Holmes, Thomas, yeoman, Chieveley, Berks, 1648 Berks RO D/A1/196/87A
Holmes, Thomas, St Giles in the Fields, London & Middlesex, 1687 PRO PROB32/26/162
Holmes, Thomas, Bethersden, Kent, 1691 CKS PRC2/42/37
Holmes, William, Frampton, Lincs, 1595 Lincs RO Ad/Ac/5/509
Holmes, William, Chipping Barnet, Herts, 1612 Herts RO ASA25/4796
Holmes, William, victualler, Maidstone, Kent, 1618 CKS PRC20/4/161
Holmes, William, Sibsey, Lincs, 1638 Lincs RO Ad/Ac/25/61
Holmes, William, Normanby, Lincs, 1662 Lincs RO Ad/Ac/41/28
Holmes, William, husbandman, Eastchurch, Sheppey, Kent, 1671 CKS PRC2/35/56
Holms, William, husbandman, Enborne, Berks, 1680 Berks RO D/A1/197/41C
Holneis, John, Headcorn, Kent, 1602 CKS PRC2/12/438
Holnes, Elinor, widow, Appledore, Kent, 1587 CKS PRC2/4/128
Holnes, John, Sandhurst, Kent, 1593 CKS PRC2/6/516
Holnes, Mary, widow, Benenden, Kent, 1688 CKS PRC2/41/122
Holnes, Percyvall, Bethersden, Kent, 1583 CKS PRC2/2/271
Holnes, Peter, Bethersden, Kent, 1587 CKS PRC2/4/327
Holnes, Robert, clothier, Benenden, Kent, 1675 CKS PRC2/36/203
Holnes, Thomas, husbandman, Kenardington, Kent, 1669 CKS PRC1/14/60
Holnes, Thomas, yeoman, Chislet, Kent, 1679 CKS PRC2/38/41
Holnes, Thomas, yeoman, Ickham, Kent, 1686 CKS PRC20/13/555
Holnes, William, Canterbury Holy Cross Westgate, Kent, 1682 CKS PRC2/40/40
Holnest, John, Bethersden, Kent, 1631 CKS PRC20/9/219
Holnest, Richard, Benenden, Kent, 1591 CKS PRC2/5/336
Holneys, Robarte, Bethersden, Kent, 1603 CKS PRC2/12/441
Holroyd, Eliza, widow, Halifax (Barkisland), Yorks, 1846 Borthwick Test C.P. 1846/2
Holsforth, Thomas, Hollingbourne, Kent, 1608 CKS PRC20/1/356
Holsted, John, Bobbing, Kent, 1669 CKS PRC1/14/61
Holstock, Gregory, Harbledown, Kent, 1606 CKS PRC2/14/212
Holt, George, butcher, Stockport, Ches, 1729 Cheshire RO (Name) W.C. 1729
Holt, Hugh, Sonning, Berks, 1635 Wilts RO Dean Sarum (name + date)
Holt, John, Frittenden, Kent, 1611 CKS PRC2/16/202
Holt, John, Frittenden, Kent, 1612 CKS PRC2/16/201 and unnumbered
Holt, Richard, husbandman, Heaton Wood Green, Lancs, 1651 Lancs RO (Name of Deceased)

D.R.C.H. 1651
Holt, Saker/Zachary, Faversham, Kent, 1686 CKS PRC2/41/54
Holt, Thomas, Chilham, Kent, 1603 CKS PRC2/14/250
Holt, Thomas, yeoman, Cogges, Oxon, 1672 Oxon RO MSS Wills 80/5/31
Holte, George, mariner: 'sailor', St Thomas Isle of Harty, Kent, 1620 CKS PRC2/22/175
Holte, John, Teynham, Kent, 1602 CKS PRC2/12/436
Holte, John, Cliffe, West, Kent, 1616 CKS PRC2/21/17
Holte, Symon, husbandman, Burgh le Marsh, Lincs, 1619 Lincs RO Ad/Ac/15/1
Holtham, Thomas, Tewkesbury, Glos, 1618 GRO GDR/B4/2/H170
Holton, Robert, Sandwich, Kent, 1682 CKS PRC2/39/180
Holton, William, Barrow, Lincs, 1639 Lincs RO Ad/Ac/26/63
Holwell, Anne, widow, Weston Zoyland, Som, 1622 Somerset RO D/D/Cta/H31
Holyday, Daniel, Acrise, Kent, 1692 CKS PRC2/42/40
Holyman, Elizabeth, widow, Marden, Kent, 1596 CKS PRC2/8/189
Holystar, Jervis, Deal, Kent, 1639 CKS PRC20/10/464
Homan, Thomas, brewer, Windsor, New, Berks, 1633 Berks RO D/A1/196/5A
Homer, John, Wimborne Minster, Dors, 1667 Dorset RO PE/WM CP 2/4/71
Homer, John, yeoman, Penn, Staffs, 1802 LJRO/B/C/5/1802/37
Homer, Thomas, gentleman, Kingswinford, Staffs, 1772 LJRO/B/C/5/1772/50
Homersham, Arthur, Linsted, Kent, 1625 CKS PRC2/23/171
Homersham, Sarah, spinster, Ospringe, Kent, 1693 CKS PRC2/42/67
Homersham, William, millwright, Ospringe, Kent, 1692 CKS PRC2/42/39
Homes, Thomas, Canterbury, Kent, 1631 CKS PRC2/30/86
Homes, William, Warehorne, Kent, 1716 CKS PRC1/17/71
Homesbie, John, Ripple, Kent, 1678 CKS PRC2/37/158
Homesbie, Thomas, Willesborough, Kent, 1600 CKS PRC2/11/131
Homesby, Susanna, spinster, Norton, Kent, 1695 CKS PRC2/42/103
Homewood, James, husbandman, Smarden, Kent, 1677 CKS PRC2/37/39
Homewood, John, Sutton by Dover, Kent, 1592 CKS PRC2/5/338
Homewood, Robert, Hartlip, Kent, 1631 CKS PRC2/31/46
Homewoode, Richerde, Herne, Kent, 1585 CKS PRC21/7/400
Homsby, Alexander, Biddenden, Kent, 1685 CKS PRC2/40/205
Homsby, Alexander, mercer, Biddenden, Kent, 1693 CKS PRC2/42/65
Honey, Henry, yeoman, Bethersden, Kent, 1681 CKS PRC2/39/182
Honey, John, fisherman, Tenterden, Kent, 1681 CKS PRC2/39/188
Honey, Oliver, Whitechapel, London & Middlesex, 1670 PRO PROB32/8/48
Honey, Peter, yeoman, Appledore, Kent, 1681 CKS PRC2/39/189
Honiborne, Sarah, spinster, Sittingbourne, Kent, 1675 CKS PRC2/36/205
Honifold, William, Monks Horton, Kent, 1633 CKS PRC2/32/65
Honiman, Robert, clergy: 'clerk/M.A.', Oxford (Magdalen College), Oxon, 1617 Bodleian HYP B8/109-110
Honiwood, Christopher, Hythe St Leonard, Kent, 1599 CKS PRC21/15/155
Honner, William, labourer, Clent, Worcs, 1606 Worcs RO 008.7 BA3585/839/397
Honnyborne, Peter, Newington next Sittingbourne, Kent, 1626 CKS PRC2/27/65
Honour, Gabriel, Sonning, Berks, 1685 Wilts RO Dean Sarum (name + date)
Honour, John, mariner: 'sailor', Faversham, Kent, 1642 CKS PRC1/6/65
Hony, Edward, Marden, Kent, 1670 CKS PRC1/14/62
Hony, John, St Austell, Corn, 1615 Cornwall RO AP/H377/2
Hony, John, mariner: 'seaman, RN?', Deptford, Kent, 1685 PRO PROB32/25/397
Hood, Francis, merchant, Boston, Lincs, 1577 Lincs RO Ad/Ac/2b/24
Hood, Henry, clergy: 'clerk', Cowbit, Lincs, 1618 Lincs RO Ad/Ac/14/7
Hood, William, Newton Regis, Warks, 1683 LJRO/B/C/5/1682/55
Hoode, Thomas, St Albans, Herts, 1613 Herts RO ASA25/4797
Hooge, Otto, gentleman, Oxford (University), Oxon, 1640 Bodleian HYP B8/111
Hooke, Arthur, gentleman, Lydd, Kent, 1686 CKS PRC20/13/559

[Hooke:]
Hooke, Henery, Hythe St Leonard, Kent, 1623 CKS PRC20/6/368
Hooke, John, Dover, Kent, CKS PRC19/1/3
Hooke, John, Hythe St Leonard, Kent, 1607 CKS PRC20/1/251
Hooke, John, yeoman, Deeping St James, Lincs, 1649 Lincs RO Ad/Ac/30/137
Hooke, Leonard, Sonning, Berks, 1628 Wilts RO Miscellaneous Index (name + date)
Hooke, Thomas, Brookland, Kent, 1621 CKS PRC2/23/157
Hooke, Thomas, Rendcombe, Glos, 1666 GRO GDR/B4/2/H173
Hooke, Wyllyam, Sandwich St Peter, Kent, 1582 CKS PRC2/2/206
Hooker, Alice, Newton on Trent, Lincs, 1681 Lincs RO Ad/Ac/34/84
Hooker, Clement, Charing, Kent, 1600 CKS PRC21/16/168
Hooker, Dorothy, spinster, Boughton Malherbe, Kent, 1662 CKS PRC1/9/29
Hooker, Henry, Brabourne, Kent, 1596 CKS PRC2/8/389
Hooker, John, Hambledon, Hants, 1623 Hants RO 21M65 D8/23
Hooker, John, Fishbourne, Sussex, 1628 W. Suss RO EpIII/9/1/30
Hooker, John, kerseymaker, Boughton Malherbe, Kent, 1643 CKS PRC1/6/66
Hooker, Mary, widow, Deal, Kent, 1676 CKS PRC20/12/201
Hooker, Richard, butcher?, Sandwich, Kent, 1680 CKS PRC2/39/58
Hooker, Robert, husbandman, Seasalter, Kent, 1678 CKS PRC2/38/42
Hooker, Thomas, Hythe St Leonard, Kent, 1598 CKS PRC21/14/530
Hooker, Thomas, Hythe St Leonard, Kent, 1611 CKS PRC20/2/194
Hooker, Thomas, Newton on Trent, Lincs, 1616 Lincs RO Ad/Ac/8b/238
Hooker, Thomas, Newton on Trent, Lincs, 1616 Lincs RO Ad/Ac/8b/248
Hooker, William, Lincoln St Benedict, Lincs, 1640 Lincs RO Ad/Ac/27/128
Hooker/Withers, Alice, St Johns Thanet, Kent, 1637 CKS PRC2/34/148
Hoolgreave, Ellen, widow, Childwall (Halewood), Lancs, 1626 Lancs RO (Name of Deceased) D.R.C.H. 1626-27
Hooper, Elizabeth, widow, Stockton, Wilts, 1614 Wilts RO Arch. Sarum(+ name and date)
Hooper, John, St Dennis, Corn, 1611 Cornwall RO AP/H237/2
Hooper, John, Sonning, Berks, 1676 Wilts RO Dean Sarum (name + date)
Hooper, John, Hill, Glos, 1734 GRO GDR/B4/2/H138
Hooper, Robert, Kinnersley, Shrops, 1667 LJRO:cards/1667/46
Hooper, Roger, St Laurence Thanet, Kent, 1627 CKS PRC2/28/61
Hooper, Thomas, St Mewan, Corn, 1622 Cornwall RO AP/H521/2
Hooper, William, yeoman, Corsley, Wilts, 1683 Wilts RO Arch. Sarum(+ name and date)
Hooper, see Cherrington & Rosier,
Hoore, John, yeoman, Childrey, Berks, 1678 Berks RO D/A1/197/23C
Hoore, Thomas, Staplehurst, Kent, 1582 CKS PRC2/2/104
Hootham/Baldon, Margaret,
Lincs 1620 Lincs RO Ad/Ac/8b/445
Hooton, Edward, Deeping, Lincs, 1779 Lincs RO Ad/Ac/45/41
Hooton, Ralph, Edlington, Lincs, 1652 Lincs RO Ad/Ac/29/127
Hope, Christopher, Sevington, Kent, 1620 CKS PRC2/22/145
Hope, Edmond, shipwright, Dover, Kent, 1679 CKS PRC20/12/304
Hope, Edmund, Sevington, Kent, 1616 CKS PRC2/21/14
Hope, Edmund, butcher, Maidstone, Kent, 1680 CKS PRC20/13/36
Hope, Edward, gentleman, Navenby, Lincs, 1634 Lincs RO Ad/Ac/24/3
Hope, Edward, Maidstone, Kent, 1688 CKS PRC20/13/610
Hope, Elizabeth, widow, St Bride, London & Middlesex, 1703 Lambeth Palace Arches G53/1
Hope, John, Maidstone, Kent, 1599 CKS PRC21/16/129
Hope, John, Ebony, Kent, 1601 CKS PRC2/12/183
Hope, John, Warehorne, Kent, 1617 CKS PRC2/21/18
Hope, John, Cumberworth, Lincs, 1639 Lincs RO Ad/Ac/26/303
Hope, John, Middleton, Lancs, 1676 Lancs RO (Name of Deceased) D.R.C.H. 1675-6
Hope, John, yeoman, Charing, Kent, 1688 CKS PRC20/13/593
Hope, Richard, Egerton, Kent, CKS PRC20/9/211

Hope, Richard, Egerton, Kent, 1631 CKS PRC20/9/212
Hope, Richard, Kingsnorth, Kent, 1639 CKS PRC1/2/78
Hope, Richard, Aldington, Kent, 1640 CKS PRC19/1/51
Hope, Richard, Kingsnorth, Kent, 1641 CKS PRC1/4/59
Hope, Richard, Cranbrook, Kent, 1683 CKS PRC20/13/333
Hope, Robert, husbandman, Ulcombe, Kent, 1643 CKS PRC1/6/67
Hope, Robert, yeoman, Queenborough, Kent, 1681 CKS PRC2/39/185
Hope, Thomas, Kingsnorth, Kent, 1590 CKS PRC2/5/366
Hope, Valentine, Sevington, Kent, 1604 CKS PRC2/14/244
Hope, William, Ulcombe, Kent, 1612 CKS PRC2/17/311
Hopgood, William, Stoneham, North, Hants, 1623 Hants RO 21M65 D8/24
Hopken, William, yeoman, Littlebourne, Kent, 1617 CKS PRC2/21/16
Hopkin, Edward, gentleman, Algarkirk, Lincs, 1623 Lincs RO Ad/Ac/18/47
Hopkin, Stephen, Amberley, Sussex, 1618 W. Suss RO EpI/33/1618/20
Hopkine, Thomas, Kingston, Kent, 1594 CKS PRC2/7/13
Hopkins, Bartholomewe, Dover, Kent, 1623 CKS PRC20/6/348
Hopkins, Benjamin, Westwell, Kent, 1672 CKS PRC20/12/51
Hopkins, Clement, victualler, Bristol, Glos, Bristol RO 1739/8
Hopkins, Elizabeth, widow, Sibford Gower, Oxon, 1676 Oxon RO MSS Wills 81/1/16
Hopkins, Henry, Amberley, Sussex, 1651 W. Suss RO EpI/33/1650/5
Hopkins, John, Burton Latimer, Northants, Northants RO NWill A/C/148
Hopkins, John, Staplehurst, Kent, 1600 CKS PRC2/11/129
Hopkins, John, Hinton Waldrist (Duxford), Berks, 1637 Berks RO D/A1/196/39A
Hopkins, John, Bishopsbourne, Kent, 1674 CKS PRC2/36/70
Hopkins, John, Norton, Northants, 1680 Northants RO NWill A/C/39
Hopkins, John, Kington St Michael, Wilts, 1765 Wilts RO Arch. Wilts.(name + date)
Hopkins, John, baker/maltster, Wednesbury, Staffs, 1795 LJRO/B/C/5/1795/43
Hopkins, Peter, hatter, Christchurch, Glos, Bristol RO 1768/CP
Hopkins, Richard, Aston Cantlow, Warks, 1685 Worcs RO 008.7 BA3585/830/84
Hopkins, Richard, Churcham, Glos, 1685 GRO GDR/B4/2/H179
Hopkins, Robert, Boxley, Kent, 1613 CKS PRC2/17/386
Hopkins, Robert, Aston Cantlow, Warks, 1676 Worcs RO 008.7 BA3585/830/97
Hopkins, Thomas, Warwick, Warks, 1589 Worcs RO 008.7 BA3585/838/105
Hopkins, Thomas, Ash next Sandwich, Kent, 1621 CKS PRC20/5/79
Hopkins, Thomas, Maidstone, Kent, 1622 CKS PRC20/5/83
Hopkins, Thomas, yeoman, Hackington, Kent, 1664 CKS PRC1/10/55
Hopkins, Thomas, Wednesbury, Staffs, 1676 LJRO:cards/1676/31
Hopkins, William, Worcester All Saints, Worcs, 1602 Worcs RO 008.7 BA3585/838/249
Hopkins, William, Stapleford, Wilts, 1683 Wilts RO Arch. Sarum(+ name and date)
Hopkinson, Anthony, Skendleby, Lincs, 1662 Lincs RO Ad/Ac/32/10
Hopkinson, John, Tetney, Lincs, 1599 Lincs RO Ad/Ac/5/47
Hopkinson, John, Kirmington, Lincs, 1614 Lincs RO Ad/Ac/13/29
Hopkinson, Robert, Maltby le Marsh, Lincs, 1600 Lincs RO Ad/Ac/5/431
Hopkinson, Silvester, Boston, Lincs, 1606 Lincs RO Ad/Ac/7/72
Hopkinson, Walter, Billinghay, Lincs, 1612 Lincs RO Ad/Ac/11/127
Hopkott, Ciprian, Pershore, Worcs, 1681 Worcs RO 008.7 BA3585/837/bdl 2
Hopkyn, Thomas,
Kent 1596 CKS PRC2/8/489
Hopkyns, John, Warwick, Warks, 1589 Worcs RO 008.7 BA3585/838/84
Hopkyns, William, Steventon, Berks, Berks RO D/A1/1/84V
Hopkyns/Piper, Thomas, Aston Cantlow, Warks, Worcs RO 008.7 BA3585/838/103
Hopper, Alexander, Canterbury St Mary Northgate, Kent, 1640 CKS PRC1/4/60
Hopper, Elizabeth, widow, Woodchurch, Kent, 1641 CKS PRC19/1/52
Hopper, John, Appledore, Kent, 1598 CKS PRC2/10/238
Hopper, John, Smarden, Kent, 1598 CKS PRC2/10/214

[Hopper:]
Hopper, John, Chart nr Sutton Valence, Kent, 1642 CKS PRC1/5/106
Hopper, Joseph, Appledore, Kent, 1627 CKS PRC2/28/54
Hopper, Richerde, Woodchurch, Kent, 1585 CKS PRC21/8/75
Hopper, Robarte, Headcorn, Kent, 1590 CKS PRC2/5/356
Hopper, Robert, Boughton Monchelsea, Kent, 1628 CKS PRC20/8/261
Hopper, Thomas, Donington, Lincs, 1625 Lincs RO Ad/Ac/19B/99
Hopper, Thomas, Ivychurch, Kent, 1625 CKS PRC20/6/14
Hopper, Thomas, mariner, Bridlington (Bridlington Quay), Yorks, 1849 Borthwick Test C.P. 1849/4
Hopper, Timothy, Alkerton, Oxon, 1629 Oxon RO MSS Wills 297/5/19
Hopper, Tobias, Staplehurst, Kent, 1610 CKS PRC2/13/243
Hopper, William, Smarden, Kent, 1615 CKS PRC2/22/122
Hopster, Richard, Leake, Lincs, 1641 Lincs RO Ad/Ac/27/200
Hopwood, Alice, widow, Osbournby, Lincs, 1636 Lincs RO Ad/Ac/24/259
Hopwood, Edmund, esquire, Middleton (Hopwood), Lancs, 1684 Lancs RO (Name of Deceased) D.R.C.H. 1684-85
Hopwood, John, Burgh le Marsh, Lincs, 1668 Lincs RO Ad/Ac/33/46
Hopwood, Robert, saddler, Boston, Lincs, 1664 Lincs RO Ad/Ac/43/38
Horbey/Harbe, William, Detling, Kent, 1698 CKS PRC19/5/54
Horden, Agnes, spinster, Biddenden, Kent, 1614 CKS PRC2/18/35
Horden, Jeames, Biddenden, Kent, 1614 CKS PRC2/18/34
Horden, John, Cranbrook, Kent, 1620 CKS PRC2/22/136
Horden, John, Hollingbourne, Kent, 1629 CKS PRC20/8/281
Horden, Symon, yeoman, Chart nr Sutton Valence, Kent, 1646 CKS PRC1/7/51
Horderne, Edward, husbandman, Stone, Staffs, 1667 LJRO:cards/1667/47
Hore, John, Fairfield, Kent, 1618 CKS PRC20/4/187
Hore, Josias, Biddenden, Kent, 1621 CKS PRC2/23/159
Hore, Nicholas, Stratton, Corn, 1642 Cornwall RO AP/H1060/2
Hore, Thomas, yeoman/husbandman, Maidenhead, Berks, 1640 Berks RO D/A1/196/45C
Horley, James, Sompting, Sussex, 1670 W. Suss RO EpI/33/1670/4
Horlocke, Anthonie, husbandman, Trowbridge, Wilts, 1636? Wilts RO CC Sarum(+ name and date)
Horly, John, Steyning, Sussex, 1629 W. Suss RO EpI/33/1629/38
Hormebie, Matthewe, Croft, Lincs, 1612/13? Lincs RO Ad/Ac/11/121
Horn, Joseph, St Martin in the Fields, London & Middlesex, 1742 Greater London RO AM/PP/Box 1739-1749 pt (uncatalogued)
Horn, William, weaver: 'stuff weaver', Wakefield, Yorks, 1809 Borthwick Test C.P. 1809/3
Hornbie, Mathew, Rasen, West, Lincs, 1640 Lincs RO Ad/Ac/27/142
Hornbie, William, Scotter, Lincs, 1636 Lincs RO Ad/Ac/40/85
Hornbsy, Robert, Canterbury St Paul, Kent, 1718 CKS PRC1/18/21
Hornby, John, Wittersham, Kent, 1581 CKS PRC21/5/156
Hornby, Mary, widow, Pilham, Lincs, 1684 Lincs RO Ad/Ac/44/127
Horncastle, Jeffrey, Skidbrooke, Lincs, 1618 Lincs RO Ad/Ac/14/24
Horncliffe, Francis, Keyingham, Yorks, 1640 Borthwick Prob. Ex. 1640/2
Horne, Anthony, weaver: 'linen weaver', Stowting, Kent, 1662 CKS PRC1/8/102
Horne, Anthony, joiner, Bicester, Oxon, 1675 Oxon RO MSS Wills 298/2/50
Horne, Charles, Ash next Sandwich, Kent, 1663 CKS PRC19/3/30
Horne, Christopher, Waltham, Lincs, 1598 Lincs RO Ad/Ac/4/25
Horne, George, Newchurch, Kent, 1623 CKS PRC20/6/360
Horne, John, Hythe West, Kent, 1606 CKS PRC2/13/223
Horne, John, Tidworth, North, Wilts, 1624 Wilts RO CC Sarum(+ name and date)
Horne, John, Hurst, Berks, 1635 Wilts RO Dean Sarum (name + date)
Horne, John, yeoman, Deal, Kent, 1678 CKS PRC20/12/264
Horne, Martha, Little Mongeham, Kent, 1633 CKS PRC2/32/64
Horne, Moses, scrivener/penioner/gentleman, Cambridge (Gonville and Caius College), Cambs,

1664 CUL V.C. Acc./Box3/29
Horne, Peter, Ickham, Kent, 1580 CKS PRC21/4/86
Horne, Peter, clothier, Reading, Berks, 1666 Berks RO D/A1/80/122D
Horne, Peter, yeoman, Warehorne, Kent, 1668 CKS PRC1/12/46
Horne, Richard, Wellow, Som, 1587 Somerset RO D/D/Cta/H41
Horne, Richard, yeoman, Deal, Kent, 1646 CKS PRC19/2/107
Horne, Stephen, Lympne, Kent, 1669 CKS PRC1/14/63
Horne, Stephen, Burmarsh, Kent, 1683 CKS PRC2/40/120
Horne, William, Monks Horton, Kent, 1634 CKS PRC2/32/53
Horne, William, Newchurch, Kent, 1639 CKS PRC20/10/532
Horne, William, weaver: 'linen weaver', Stowting, Kent, 1680 CKS PRC2/39/55
Horne, William, yeoman, Deal, Kent, 1682 CKS PRC20/13/259
Hornecastle, Samuell, Hull, Yorks, 1637 Borthwick Prob. Ex. 1637/7
Horner, Frances, Orby, Lincs, 1639 Lincs RO Ad/Ac/25/13
Horner, John, Deeping St James, Lincs, 1652 Lincs RO Ad/Ac/29/9
Horner, Thomas, Ruckinge, Kent, 1626 CKS PRC2/27/70
Hornsey, Robert, Hale, Great (Little Hale), Lincs, 1646 Lincs RO Ad/Ac/28/174
Horrell, Robert, Yarmouth, Hants, 1624 Hants RO 21M65 D8/70
Horroad, Richard, Ambrosden (Arncott), Oxon, 1676 Oxon RO MSS Wills 81/1/12
Horrockes, Samuell, yeoman, Bolton (Sharples), Lancs, 1683 Lancs RO (Name of Deceased) D.R.C.H. 1683
Horscroft, Silvester, Lyminster, Sussex, 1619 W. Suss RO EpI/33/1618/13
Horsecroft, Richard, Tortington, Sussex, 1635 W. Suss RO EpI/33/1635/12
Horsefeild/Maeuse, Thomas, cooper, Sandwich, Kent, 1693 CKS PRC2/42/64
Horseman, Peter, Leeds (Great Woodhouse), Yorks, 1719 Borthwick Test C.P. 1719/8
Horsett, William, Alvingham, Lincs, 1612 Lincs RO Ad/Ac/11/125
Horsey, William, Bedminster, Som, 1722 Somerset RO D/D/Cta/H91
Horsfield, Elizabeth, widow, Barham, Kent, 1643 CKS PRC1/6/68
Horsham, Richard, Aldingbourne, Sussex, 1632 W. Suss RO EpI/33/1632/35
Horsington, William, Compton Dando, Som, 1593 Somerset RO D/D/Cta/H37
Horsley, Elinor, widow, Didcot, Berks, 1634 Berks RO D/A1/79/67A
Horsley, William, gentleman, Beckhouse, Yorks, 1639 Borthwick Prob. Ex. 1638/4
Horsley/Bowle, Margaret, widow, Longcot, Berks, 1620 Berks RO D/A1/195/82A
Horsnell, Christopher, yeoman, Warfield, Berks, 1683 Berks RO D/A1/197/48C
Hort, Anthony, Westbury-on-Trym, Glos, Bristol RO 1677/58
Hort, Joan, Almondsbury, Glos, Bristol RO 1680/65
Hort, Robert, Winscombe, Som, 1646 Somerset RO D/D/Cta/H61
Hort, Thomas, Henbury, Glos, Bristol RO 1729/21
Hort, William, Compton Dando, Som, 1642 Somerset RO D/D/Cta/H54
Horte, Robert, Wraxall, North, Wilts, 1617 Wilts RO Arch. Wilts.(name + date)
Hortell, Gilbert, scythe grinder, Belbroughton, Worcs, 1608 Worcs RO 008.7 BA3585/839/452
Horton, Anne, Pensford, Som, 1709 Somerset RO D/D/Cta/H93
Horton, George, miller, Appledore, Kent, 1675 CKS PRC2/36/63
Horton, Isaac, butcher, Witley, Great, Worcs, 1822 Worcs RO 008.7 BA3585/835/bdl 2
Horton, John, gentleman, Calne, Wilts, 1604 Wilts RO Dean Sarum (name + date)
Horton, John, Dover, Kent, 1636 CKS PRC20/10/484
Horton, John, clergy: 'clerk/vicar', Kirdford, Sussex, 1639 W. Suss RO EpIII/9/1/41
Horton, John, butcher, Ashford, Kent, 1665 CKS PRC1/10/56
Horton, John, victualler, Chislet, Kent, 1672 CKS PRC2/35/141
Horton, Michelbourne, Capel le Ferne, Kent, 1630 CKS PRC2/30/89
Horton, Thomas, Bonnington, Kent, 1677 CKS PRC2/37/163
Horwell, John, St Stephen by Launceston, Corn, 1606 Cornwall RO AP/H108
Horwood, John, Stoke, North, Sussex, 1632 W. Suss RO EpI/33/1632/36
Horwood, Thomas, yeoman, Badsey, Worcs, 1598 Worcs RO 008.7 BA3585/838/150
Horwood (Horroad), William, yeoman, Bicester, Oxon, 1676 Oxon RO MSS Wills 81/1/13

[Hose:]
Hose, William, Walton on the Wolds, Leics, 1667 Leics RO Administrators Accounts 1667-72 f2
Hosier, see Walter,
Hoskinge, Richard, Sancreed, Corn, 1611 Cornwall RO AP/H267/1
Hoskins, John, Chelvey, Som, 1619 Somerset RO D/D/Cta/H78
Hoskins, John, yeoman, Chewton Mendip, Som, 1619 Somerset RO D/D/Cta/H65
Hoskins, William, yeoman, Melksham, Wilts, 1681 Wilts RO Arch. Sarum(+ name and date)
Hoskins, William, Overton, Wilts, 1741? Wilts RO Arch. Wilts.(name + date)
Hoskins, William, Overton, Wilts, 1743? Wilts RO Miscellaneous Index (name + date)
Hoskyn, Agnes, widow, Birchington, Kent, 1619 CKS PRC20/4/149
Hoskyns, Richard, Lavington, Wilts, 1580 Wilts RO Arch. Sarum(+ name and date) w
Hosmar, John, Godmersham, Kent, 1635 CKS PRC20/10/482
Hosmer, Joseph, Staplehurst, Kent, 1612 CKS PRC2/16/1
Hotchkiss, Edward, labourer, Uppington, Shrops, 1818 LJRO/B/C/5/1818/23
Hotham, Thomas, York St Margaret, Yorks, 1720 Borthwick Test C.P. 1720/7
Hothorne, William eld, Stratfield Mortimer, Berks, 1605 Berks RO D/A1/195/2C
Hough, John, Radbourne, Derby, 1667 LJRO:cards/1667/48
Hough, John, Betley, Staffs, 1672 LJRO:cards/1672/31
Hough, Thomas, Edmondthorpe, Leics, 1684 Leics RO Administrators Accounts 1682-86 f15
Hough, Thomas, Swinehead, Ches, 1692 Cheshire RO (Name) W.C. 1692
Hougham, Henry, yeoman, Graveney, Kent, 1676 CKS PRC2/36/201
Hougham, Michael, gentleman, Goodnestone next Faversham, Kent, 1696 CKS PRC2/42/115
Houghton, Anne, widow, Newbury, Berks, 1663 Berks RO D/A1/196/122C
Houghton, Grace, widow, Broughton Astley (Primethorpe), Leics, Leics RO Administrators Accounts 1682-86 f33
Houghton, Joseph, Measham, Derby, 1685 LJRO/B/C/5/1684/44
Houghton, Samuel, Lincoln, Lincs, 1632 Lincs RO Ad/Ac/23/62
Houlden, Christopher, Liverpool, Lancs, 1598 Lancs RO (Name of Deceased) D.R.C.H. 1598
Houlder, William, Gosberton, Lincs, 1600 Lincs RO Ad/Ac/5/439
Houldin, John, yeoman, Mickleover, Derby, 1822 LJRO/B/C/5/1822/13
Houldway, Gregory, yeoman, Inkpen, Berks, 1632 Berks RO D/A1/195/125A
Houlton, Alane, Ashby cum Fenby, Lincs, 1594 Lincs RO Ad/Ac/3/137
Houlton, Samuel, Clifton upon Dunsmore, Warks, 1665 LJRO:cards/1665/4
House, John, yeoman, Thatcham (Crookham), Berks, 1676 Berks RO D/A1/197/10D
House, Thomas, Rochdale, Lancs, 1625 Lancs RO (Name of Deceased) D.R.C.H. 1625
Household, Thomas, Ramsey, Hunts, 1676 Hunts RO/Acc58/49(72)
Hovenden, Giles, Cranbrook, Kent, 1604 CKS PRC2/13/227
Hovenden, John, Hawkhurst, Kent, 1612 CKS PRC2/17/342
Hovenden, John, clothier, Marden, Kent, 1685 CKS PRC2/41/32
Hovenden, Magdalene, widow, Challock, Kent, 1618 CKS PRC20/4/185
Hovenden, Nicholas, Canterbury St Dunstan Without, Kent, 1600 CKS PRC2/11/133
Hovenden, Richard, Hawkhurst, Kent, 1598 CKS PRC2/10/398
Hovenden, Richard, Challock, Kent, 1635 CKS PRC20/10/568
Hovenden, Richard, Rolvenden, Kent, 1637 CKS PRC2/34/62
Hovenden, Robert, Marden, Kent, 1631 CKS PRC2/31/45
Hovenden, Robert eld, clothier, Cranbrook, Kent, 1662 CKS PRC1/8/103
Hovenden, Samuel, gentleman, Cranbrook, Kent, 1662 CKS PRC1/9/30
Hovenden, Stephen, Canterbury St Mary-Magdalen Burgate, Kent, 1602 CKS PRC2/14/259
Hovenden, Stephen, Canterbury St Mary-Magdalen Burgate, Kent, 1603 CKS PRC2/14/254
Hovenden, William, Cranbrook, Kent, 1599 CKS PRC2/11/50
Hoverland, William, Sandwich St Clement, Kent, 1617 CKS PRC2/22/148
How, Thomas, Ospringe, Kent, 1618 CKS PRC2/22/168
How/Fuljames, Tristram, Pawlett, Som, 1631 Somerset RO D/D/Cta/F9
Howard, George, husbandman, Marston, Lincs, 1670 Lincs RO Ad/Ac/32/145
Howard, Henry, husbandman, Bradfield, Berks, 1663 Berks RO D/A1/196/108D
Howard, John, Bolingbroke, Old, Lincs, 1684 Lincs RO Ad/Ac/44/142

Howard, see Hayward,
Howdle, Elizabeth, widow, Hemingbrough, Yorks, 1855 Borthwick Test C.P. 1853/10
Howe, Anthonie, Canterbury All Saints, Kent, 1605 CKS PRC2/13/220
Howe, Edmund, St Albans St Peters, Herts, 1627 Herts RO ASA25/2954
Howe, Francis, husbandman, Northchurch, Herts, 1632 Herts RO AHH23/1077
Howe, John, Gwennap, Corn, 1604 Cornwall RO AP/H78
Howe, Richard, St Helens, Hants, 1672 Hants RO 21m65 D8/246
Howe, Richard, knight/alderman, Christchurch, London & Middlesex, 1685 PRO PROB5/1310
Howe, Richard, knight/alderman, Christchurch, London & Middlesex, 1685 PRO PROB5/1311
Howe, Robert, Brading, Hants, 1679 Hants RO 21m65 D8/311
Howe, Thomas, St Laurence Thanet, Kent, 1667 CKS PRC1/12/47
Howe, William, Wye, Kent, 1601 CKS PRC2/12/179
Howel, Sarah, Saxby, Lincs, 1680 Lincs RO Ad/Ac/43/147
Howell, Christopher, Bradford on Avon, Wilts, 1619 Wilts RO Miscellaneous Index (name + date)
Howell, Edward, Sompting, Sussex, 1669 W. Suss RO EpI/33/1669/21
Howell, Hugh, Dean, East, Sussex, 1598 W. Suss RO EpI/33/1597/12
Howell, John, Oare, Kent, 1640 CKS PRC1/4/61
Howell, John, weaver, Canterbury St Mildred, Kent, 1682 CKS PRC2/39/179
Howell, Joseph, yeoman, Monkton Deverill, Wilts, 1733 Wilts RO Arch. Sarum(+ name and date)
Howell, Richard, Snargate, Kent, 1612 CKS PRC2/17/436
Howell, Richard, Dodleston, Ches, 1635 Cheshire RO (Name) W.C. 1634
Howell, Richard, Sittingbourne, Kent, 1678 CKS PRC2/38/44
Howell, Thomas, husbandman, Hinksey, North, Berks, 1618 Berks RO D/A1/195/74A
Howell, William, Monkton Deverill, Wilts, 1634 Wilts RO Arch. Sarum(+ name and date)
Howell, William, Wraxall, South, Wilts, 1637 Wilts RO Arch. Sarum(+ name and date)
Howell, William, Camerton (Carlingcott), Som, 1664 Somerset RO D/D/Cta/H46
Howell, William, tailor, Oxford St Michael, Oxon, 1670 Oxon RO MSS Wills 80/5/24
Howen, George, Deeping St James, Lincs, 1612 Lincs RO Ad/Ac/10/145
Howes, Gregorie, Bennington, Long, Lincs, 1605 Lincs RO Ad/Ac/6/122
Howes, Henry, university: 'privileged person', Cambridge St Michael, Cambs, 1646 c. CUL V.C. Acc./Box2/40
Howes, Thomas, Boughton under Blean, Kent, 1627 CKS PRC20/8/263
Howett, John, clergy: 'clerk', Bassingthorpe, Lincs, 1637 Lincs RO Ad/Ac/25/241
Howett, Richard, Heckington, Lincs, 1637 Lincs RO Ad/Ac/25/364
Howett/Saule, Francys, Heckington, Lincs, 1636 Lincs RO Ad/Ac/24/389
Howgill, George, Sandwich St Mary, Kent, 1696 CKS PRC2/42/101
Howis, Ann, Boughton under Blean, Kent, 1616 CKS PRC20/3/427
Howis, Richard, Boughton under Blean, Kent, 1614 CKS PRC20/3/105
Howit, George, baker, Gonerby, Lincs, 1673 Lincs RO Ad/Ac/34/13
Howkins, George, Pusey, Berks, 1620 Berks RO D/A1/195/84A
Howland, John, Canterbury, Kent, 1633 CKS PRC2/32/66
Howland, Leonard, Dymchurch, Kent, 1700 CKS PRC1/16/30
Howlde, William, Appleby, Lincs, 1599 Lincs RO Ad/Ac/37/80
Howlden, Margaret, widow, Blackrod, Lancs, 1609 Lancs RO (Name of Deceased) D.R.C.H. 1609
Howldesworthe, Roberte, Clee, Lincs, 1594 Lincs RO Ad/Ac/3/119
Howlen, Anthony, labourer, Goodnestone next Wingham, Kent, 1633 CKS PRC20/10/556
Howlen, Jasper, Warehorne, Kent, 1614 CKS PRC2/18/18
Howlen, Jeames + Mgt, Hastingleigh, Kent, 1597 CKS PRC2/9/293
Howlen, John, Mersham, Kent, 1614 CKS PRC2/22/119
Howlen, Robarte, Woodchurch, Kent, 1584 CKS PRC21/6/355
Howlen, Wyllyam, Woodchurch, Kent, 1591 CKS PRC21/11/1
Howlet, Henry, victualler, York, Yorks, 1811 Borthwick Test C.P. 1811/6
Howlet, John, Hawkhurst, Kent, 1597 CKS PRC2/9/507

[Howlett:]
Howlett, Joseph, yeoman, Emington, Oxon, 1676 Oxon RO MSS Wills 298/2/49
Howlett, William, Stelling, Kent, 1665 CKS PRC1/11/42
Howlin, Robarte, Whitfield alias Beauxfield, Kent, 1589 CKS PRC2/4/527
Howlte, Edwarde, Hawkhurst, Kent, 1597 CKS PRC2/10/40
Howlte, John, Faversham, Kent, 1597 CKS PRC2/9/241
Howlton, George + Ursula, Ditton, Fen, Cambs, CUL V.C.Acc./Box1/28
Howman, Robert, Tenterden, Kent, 1597 CKS PRC2/10/38
Hows, Thomas, Stilton, Hunts, 1676 Hunts RO/Acc58/71(6)
Howse, Richard, Dundry, Som, 1638 Somerset RO D/D/Cta/H1
Howse, Solomon, yeoman, Cropredy, Oxon, 1692 Oxon RO MSS Wills Pec 42/1/38
Howse, William, yeoman, Bray, Berks, 1628 Berks RO D/A1/195/115A
Howsen, Charles, Wellington, Som, 1625 Somerset RO D/D/Cta/H13
Howson, Mary, widow, Nonington, Kent, 1662 CKS PRC19/3/13
Howson, Robert, yeoman, Sutterton, Lincs, 1605 Lincs RO Ad/Ac/6/131
Howson, William, Sutterton, Lincs, 1634 Lincs RO Ad/Ac/24/237
Howson, William, yeoman, Herne, Kent, 1640 CKS PRC19/1/53
Howten, Edward, Burmarsh, Kent, 1626 CKS PRC2/25/73
Howting, Nicholas, Wormshill, Kent, 1603 CKS PRC2/12/437
Howting, Thomas, victualler, Maidstone, Kent, 1671 CKS PRC19/4/82
Howting, Thomas, yeoman, Queenborough, Kent, 1672 CKS PRC2/35/51
Howtinge, Walter, Hollingbourne, Kent, 1630 CKS PRC20/9/247
Howton, William, Stallingborough, Lincs, Lincs RO Ad/Ac/1/34
Hoy, William, Wittersham, Kent, 1672 CKS PRC20/12/50
Hoyes, Robert, Claypole, Lincs, 1613 Lincs RO Ad/Ac/12/80
Hoyse, Thomas, Westborough, Lincs, 1626 Lincs RO Ad/Ac/20/78
Hoyse, William,
Lincs 1648 Lincs RO Ad/Ac/30/401
Hoysted, Thomas, Tonge, Kent, 1635 CKS PRC2/33/58
Hoysted, William, High Halstow, Kent, 1613 CKS PRC2/17/396
Huband, see Hill,
Hubart, James, Tunstall, Kent, 1713 CKS PRC1/17/60
Hubbard, Michaell, yeoman, Doddington, Kent, 1626 CKS PRC2/27/75
Hubbard, Michaell, St Laurence Thanet, Kent, 1705 CKS PRC1/16/64
Hubbard, Robarte, Selling, Kent, 1592 CKS PRC2/5/360
Hubbard, Thomas, Tunstall, Kent, CKS PRC1/15/115
Hubbard, Thomas, Tunstall, Kent, 1680 CKS PRC2/39/59
Hubbard, William, High Halden, Kent, 1673 CKS PRC2/35/219
Hubbard, William, yeoman, Mareham le Fen, Lincs, 1684 Lincs RO Ad/Ac/44/119
Hubbard/Hubbert, Thomas, Tunstall, Kent, 1693 CKS PRC1/15/115b
Hubbarde, Humphrey, Kirkby, East, Lincs, 1607 Lincs RO Ad/Ac/8a/143
Hubbarde, William, Colsterworth, Lincs, 1605 Lincs RO Ad/Ac/6/29
Hubbart, John, Sittingbourne, Kent, 1619 CKS PRC2/22/129
Hubberd, Ezechiell, Adisham, Kent, 1626 CKS PRC20/7/30
Hubberd, John, Canterbury St Mildred, Kent, 1675 CKS PRC2/36/67
Hubberd, William, Kirkby, East, Lincs, 1579 Lincs RO Ad/Ac/2b/19
Hubberde, Rycharde, Goudhurst, Kent, 1589 CKS PRC2/4/494
Hubbersley, Walter, Boston, Lincs, 1622 Lincs RO Ad/Ac/17/23
Hubbert, Henry, knacker, Sibsey, Lincs, 1669 Lincs RO Ad/Ac/33/116
Hubbert, John, clergy: 'mr/clerk', New Romney, Kent, 1624 CKS PRC20/6/16
Hubbert, Michaell, Goodnestone next Wingham, Kent, 1617 CKS PRC20/3/425
Hubbert, see Hubbard,
Hubbing, John, St Laurence Thanet, Kent, 1674 CKS PRC2/36/66
Hublethorne, John, Stainton, Market, Lincs, 1599 Lincs RO Ad/Ac/5/547
Huchon, Adam, Canterbury, Kent, 1614 CKS PRC20/3/174
Huchon, Adam, Canterbury St Alphege, Kent, 1615 CKS PRC20/3/170

Huchon, Adam, Canterbury St Alphege, Kent, 1615 CKS PRC20/3/274
Huchon, Peeter ygr, Canterbury St Alphege, Kent, 1615 CKS PRC20/3/280
Hucke, George, husbandman, Digby, Lincs, 1611 Lincs RO Ad/Ac/10/49
Huckell, see Fenton,
Huckle, Robert, Toseland, Hunts, Hunts RO/Acc58/119
Hucklebridge, George, Middlezoy, Som, 1697 Somerset RO D/D/Cta/H95
Huckneale, Mark, husbandman, Enstone, Church (Neat Enstone), Oxon, 1666 Oxon RO MSS Wills 298/2/39
Hucks, John, shepherd, Broadwell (Filkins), Oxon, 1669 Oxon RO MSS Wills 80/4/15
Huckstep, Nicholas, Appledore, Kent, 1617 CKS PRC2/22/132
Huckstep, Thomas, Appledore, Kent, 1609 CKS PRC2/15/174
Huckstepp, Elizabeth, Tenterden, Kent, 1675 CKS PRC2/36/206
Huckstepp, John, haberdasher, Tenterden, Kent, 1665 CKS PRC1/11/43
Huckstepp, William, yeoman, Tenterden, Kent, 1668 CKS PRC1/13/62
Hud, John, yeoman, Spalding (Wykeham), Lincs, 1674 Lincs RO Ad/Ac/34/31
Huddleston, Robert, Fulbeck, Lincs, 1642 Lincs RO Ad/Ac/27/321
Huddleston, William, Baumber, Lincs, 1638 Lincs RO Ad/Ac/26/15
Huddy, Abraham, yeoman, Probus, Corn, 1642 Cornwall RO AP/H1089/2
Hudgeboute, Abraham, Shoreditch St Leonard, London & Middlesex, 1692 PRO PROB32/32/191
Hudleston, George, Louth, Lincs, 1649 Lincs RO Ad/Ac/42/26
Hudnall, John, Berkhamsted St Peter, Herts, 1621 Herts RO AHH23/1076
Hudson, Ann, widow, Hythe St Leonard, Kent, 1605 CKS PRC20/1/83
Hudson, Anne, widow, Woolpit, Suff, 1733 Suff RO(B) IC500/3/47/23
Hudson, Christopher, Ingoldmels, Lincs, 1611 Lincs RO Ad/Ac/10/68
Hudson, Dorothy, widow, Canterbury St Alphege, Kent, 1639 CKS PRC20/10/462
Hudson, Edward, clergy: 'vicar', Charing, Kent, 1596 CKS PRC21/14/83
Hudson, Edward, Owston, Lincs, 1662 Lincs RO Ad/Ac/41/45
Hudson, James, chapman, Stockport, Ches, 1735 Cheshire RO (Name) W.C. 1734-5
Hudson, John, Sittingbourne, Kent, 1611 CKS PRC2/16/109
Hudson, John, Hythe St Leonard, Kent, 1613 CKS PRC20/2/446
Hudson, John, Ospringe, Kent, 1619 CKS PRC2/22/124
Hudson, John, Barrow, Lincs, 1651 Lincs RO Ad/Ac/29/153
Hudson, John, Oxford St Aldate, Oxon, 1668 Oxon RO MSS Wills 80/5/17
Hudson, John, Upton on Severn, Worcs, 1682 Worcs RO 008.7 BA3585/830/66
Hudson, John, Sparham, Norf, 1737 Norfolk RO ANW/23/22A/39
Hudson, John, farmer, Garforth, Church, Yorks, 1795 Borthwick Test C.P. 1794/7
Hudson, John sen, Woolpit, Suff, 1724 Suff RO(B) IC500/3/46/49
Hudson, Leonard, St Albans St Stephens, Herts, 1635 Herts RO ASA25/4913
Hudson, Mary, Leeds, Kent, 1598 CKS PRC2/9/419
Hudson, Peeter, Hythe St Leonard, Kent, 1611 CKS PRC20/2/190
Hudson, Robert, Stalisfield, Kent, 1611 CKS PRC2/16/103
Hudson, Robert, yeoman, Clee (Thrunscoe), Lincs, 1624 Lincs RO Ad/Ac/19A/119
Hudson, Robert, Stepney, London & Middlesex, 1680 PRO PROB32/17/73
Hudson, Stephen, Warehorne, Kent, 1649 CKS PRC1/8/47
Hudson, Thomas, university: 'scholar's servant', Cambridge, Cambs, CUL V.C.Acc./Box1/29
Hudson, Thomas, Faversham, Kent, 1611 CKS PRC2/16/206
Hudson, Thomas, clergy: 'clerk', Hameringham, Lincs, 1620 Lincs RO Ad/Ac/16/48
Hudson, Thomas, Selsey, Sussex, 1632 W. Suss RO EpI/33/1632/27
Hudson, Thomas, Branston, Lincs, 1648 Lincs RO Ad/Ac/30/372
Hudson, Thomas, yeoman, Leake, Lincs, 1662? Lincs RO Ad/Ac/32/2
Hudson, Thomas, husbandman, Melton Ross, Lincs, 1681 Lincs RO Ad/Ac/42/83
Hudson, Thomas, St Clement Danes, London & Middlesex, 1692 Greater London RO AM/PP/Box 1685-1694 pt (uncatalogued)
Hudson, William, carpenter, Oxford St Giles, Oxon, 1636 Oxon RO MSS Wills 298/1/12
Hudson, William, Kirkstead, Lincs, 1640 Lincs RO Ad/Ac/27/65

[Hudson:]
Hudson, William, merchant, Dover, Kent, 1641 CKS PRC19/2/22
Hudson, William, Muckton, Lincs, 1669 Lincs RO Ad/Ac/33/106
Hudson, William + Elizabeth, St Albans, Herts, 1579 Herts RO ASA25/909
Hudswell, Thomas, Bethersden, Kent, 1619 CKS PRC2/22/128
Huffam, Brooke, Challock, Kent, 1598 CKS PRC21/14/153
Huffam, Henry, Preston next Wingham, Kent, 1586 CKS PRC2/4/241
Huffam, Michaell, Stourmouth, Kent, 1602 CKS PRC2/14/245
Huffington, George, wine & spirit: 'wine merchant'?, St Andrew Holborn, London & Middlesex, 1684 PRO PROB32/23/259
Huffington, William + Alice, Birchington, Kent, 1627 CKS PRC20/7/27
Hugben, Peter, surgeon: 'barber-surgeon', Deal, Kent, 1677 CKS PRC20/12/233
Hugbon, Thomas, Eastry, Kent, 1630 CKS PRC20/9/241
Hugbone, Ingram, Eastry, Kent, 1610 CKS PRC20/2/106
Hugbone, John, Langdon, East, Kent, 1590 CKS PRC2/5/370
Hugbone, William, Ewell, Kent, 1595 CKS PRC2/7/461
Hugden, George, Swineshead, Lincs, 1638 Lincs RO Ad/Ac/25/88
Huges, see Floyd,
Hugessen, Aletheia, Linsted, Kent, 1671 CKS PRC2/35/58
Hugesson, Cornelius, gentleman, Dover, Kent, 1627 CKS PRC20/8/267
Huggard, Henry, tanner, Grimsby, Great, Lincs, 1669 Lincs RO Ad/Ac/33/119
Huggard, Thomas, Lincoln, Lincs, 1605 Lincs RO Ad/Ac/6/129
Huggard, William, labourer, Stickford, Lincs, 1639 Lincs RO Ad/Ac/25/212
Huggate, Michaell, Gainsborough, Lincs, 1674 Lincs RO Ad/Ac/35/83
Huggens, Robert, yeoman, Throwleigh, Kent, 1630 CKS PRC2/30/85
Huggens, Robert, Lenham, Kent, 1641 CKS PRC1/5/107
Huggett, Agnes, Ivychurch, Kent, 1596 CKS PRC21/14/67
Huggett, Anne, Hoath, Kent, CKS PRC19/1/7a
Huggett, Anne, widow, Hoath, Kent, 1638 CKS PRC19/1/7
Huggett, David, mariner, Dover, Kent, 1674 CKS PRC20/12/133
Huggett, Elizabeth, widow, Whitstable, Kent, 1674 CKS PRC2/35/223
Huggett, Robert, Dover, Kent, 1685 CKS PRC20/13/505
Huggett, Thomas, Sutton Valence, Kent, 1668 CKS PRC1/13/63
Huggett, William, Pluckley, Kent, 1615 CKS PRC20/3/268
Huggin, Geffrey, Minster in Thanet, Kent, 1589 CKS PRC2/4/493
Huggin, John, Boxley, Kent, 1617 CKS PRC2/22/154
Huggin, William, Metheringham, Lincs, 1605 Lincs RO Ad/Ac/6/30
Huggins, Elizabeth, widow, Throwleigh, Kent, 1596 CKS PRC2/8/417
Huggins, Richard, Upchurch, Kent, 1613 CKS PRC2/16/29
Hugh, ap, Owen, Llandwrog (Modryn), Caern, NLW B 1682-44 Ac
Hughes, Andrew, gentleman, Woodnesborough, Kent, 1683 CKS PRC2/40/122
Hughes, Ann, mrs, Woodnesborough, Kent, 1645 CKS PRC1/7/52
Hughes, Elizabeth, widow, Chilham, Kent, 1613 CKS PRC2/17/295
Hughes, Griffith, St Anne Westminster, London & Middlesex, 1712 PRO PROB32/55/29
Hughes, John, Chilham, Kent, 1603 CKS PRC2/14/248
Hughes, John, Windsor, New, Berks, 1618 Berks RO D/A1/195/76C
Hughes, John, clergy: 'clerk', Cawkwell, Lincs, 1637 Lincs RO Ad/Ac/25/409
Hughes, John, carpenter, Ashford, Kent, 1674 CKS PRC2/36/73
Hughes, Richard, Melton Mowbray, Leics, 1672 Leics RO Administrators Accounts 1667-72 f73
Hughes, Robert, husbandman, Barford St John, Oxon, 1663 Oxon RO MSS Wills 32/4/13
Hughes, Thomas, weaver: 'broad weaver', Staplehurst, Kent, 1671 CKS PRC2/35/57
Hughes, Thomas, New Romney, Kent, 1698 CKS PRC19/5/58
Hughes, William, Sutton Maddock, Shrops, 1677 LJRO:cards/1677/5
Hughes/Williams, John, clergy: 'clerk', Easton, Wilts, 1632 Wilts RO Arch. Wilts.(name + date)
Hughes, see Calcott,
Hughson, John, Budworth, Great (Dutton), Ches, 1617 Cheshire RO (Name) W.C. 1616

Huglin, Alice, Lydd, Kent, 1629 CKS PRC20/8/285
Huishe, John, gentleman, Cleeve, Old, Som, 1625 Somerset RO D/D/Cta/H23
Huitson, William, Kirton, Lincs, 1624 Lincs RO Ad/Ac/39/146
Hulbert, Abraham, cordwainer, Reading St Mary, Berks, 1640 Berks RO D/A1/196/44A
Hulcottes, John, Abingdon St Helen, Berks, 1608 Berks RO D/A1/195/25
Hulcottes, Margaret, widow, Abingdon, Berks, 1609 Berks RO D/A1/195/32A
Hulcotts, Thomas, yeoman, Hendred, East, Berks, 1633 Berks RO D/A1/196/13A
Hulett, Margaret, widow, Sherbourne, Dors, 1627 Wilts RO Miscellaneous Index (name + date)
Hulett, Richard, Heytesbury, Wilts, 1599 Wilts RO Miscellaneous Index (name + date)
Hulett, Robert, clergy: 'clerk/minister', Streatley, Berks, 1672 Berks RO D/A1/196/179A
Hulke, Benjamin, Deal, Kent, 1678 CKS PRC20/12/265
Hulke, John, Deal, Kent, 1682 CKS PRC19/4/111
Hulke, William, blacksmith, Deal, Kent, 1681 CKS PRC20/13/32
Hulkes, Joanne, widow, Doddington, Kent, 1633 CKS PRC2/32/57
Hull, Ann, widow, Stadhampton, Oxon, 1760 Oxon RO MSS Wills 302/5/46
Hull, Edward, Sherbourne, Dors, 1627 Wilts RO Miscellaneous Index (name + date)
Hull, Francis, Ramsey, Hunts, 1679 Hunts RO/Acc58/136(185)
Hull, George, Mere, Wilts, 1636 Wilts RO Miscellaneous Index (name + date)
Hull, George, Mere, Wilts, 1680 Wilts RO Dean Sarum (name + date)
Hull, Gilbert, Ash next Sandwich, Kent, 1674 CKS PRC20/12/82
Hull, Jane, Aldingbourne, Sussex, 1669 W. Suss RO EpI/33/1669/26
Hull, John, Deal, Kent, 1600 CKS PRC21/15/149
Hull, Richard, Christian Malford, Wilts, 1622 Wilts RO Arch. Wilts.(name + date)
Hull, Richard, Deverill, Hill, Wilts, 1670 Wilts RO Miscellaneous Index (name + date)
Hull, Toby, Boxgrove, Sussex, 1617 W. Suss RO EpI/33/1617/6
Hull/Billingshurst, Agnes, Funtington, Sussex, 1613 W. Suss RO EpI/33/1613/21
Hulley, Robert, university: 'Fellow of Merton College, Oxford', Oxford (Merton College), Oxon, 1655 Bodleian HYP B8/112
Hulme, Hugh, gentleman, Coddington, Ches, 1574 Cheshire RO (Name) W.C. 1573/4
Hulme, Margaret, widow, Heaton Norris (Shaw Fold), Lancs, 1626 Lancs RO (Name of Deceased) D.R.C.H. 1626
Hulme, Sarah, Wolstanton, Staffs, 1676 LJRO:cards/1676/33
Hulme, William, yeoman, Derby, West, Lancs, 1679 Lancs RO (Name of Deceased) D.R.C.H. 1679
Hulse, Charles, gentleman, Chartham, Kent, 1680 CKS PRC2/39/57
Hulse, John, gentleman, Chartham, Kent, 1685 CKS PRC2/41/33
Hulse, Matthew, Cossington, Leics, 1665 Leics RO Administrators Accounts C17th f14
Hulton, Henry, Warrington, Lancs, 1663 Lancs RO (Name of Deceased) D.R.C.H. 1663
Hulton, Ralph, yeoman, Hurley, Berks, 1595 Berks RO D/A1/194/72A
Humber, Mark, Wootton Bassett, Wilts, 1629 Wilts RO Arch. Wilts.(name + date)
Humberston, John, Walkern, Herts, 1622 Lincs RO Ad/Ac/17/103
Humberston, Thomas, Usselby, Lincs, 1640 Lincs RO Ad/Ac/27/153
Humble, Edward, Welton le Wold, Lincs, 1640 Lincs RO Ad/Ac/26/243
Humbletoft, Richard, Sleaford, New, Lincs, 1677 Lincs RO Ad/Ac/42/101
Humby, Robert, Downton, Wilts, 1632 Wilts RO Arch. Sarum(+ name and date)
Hume, John, clergy: 'clerk', Offord Cluney, Hunts, 1694 Hunts RO/Acc58/279
Humerdine, Robert, butcher, Dover, Kent, 1642 CKS PRC19/2/57
Humerston, John ygr, St Albans St Peters, Herts, 1638 Herts RO ASA25/4959
Humfery, William, husbandman, Westbury, Wilts, 1675 Wilts RO Chantor Sarum Bundle 10/7
Humfreston, Robert, Ercall, High, Shrops, 1674 LJRO:cards/1674/26
Humfrey, Edward jun, Sulgrave, Northants, 1680 Northants RO NWill A/C/13
Humfrey, George, weaver: 'broad weaver', Cranbrook, Kent, 1616 CKS PRC2/22/126
Humfrey, Richard, Minster in Sheppey, Kent, 1614 CKS PRC2/18/23
Humfrey, Thomas, Walmer, Kent, 1617 CKS PRC2/22/166
Humfreys, Charles, St Alban, London & Middlesex, 1703 PRO PROB5/1454

[Humfrie:]
Humfrie, William, Canterbury St Dunstan Without, Kent, 1610 CKS PRC2/15/165
Humfry, Henry, Stanground, Hunts, 1677 Hunts RO/Acc58/93(24)
Humfry, John, Ferring, Sussex, 1631 W. Suss RO EpI/33/1631/35
Humfry, John, Stourton, Wilts, 1674 Wilts RO Arch. Sarum(+ name and date)
Humfry, Lennard, husbandman, Maiden Bradley, Wilts, 1639 Wilts RO Arch. Sarum(+ name and date)
Humfry, Michael, husbandman, Mere, Wilts, 1640 Wilts RO Dean Sarum (name + date)
Humfry, Richard, clergy: 'clerk/vicar', Angmering, Sussex, 1595 W. Suss RO EpI/33/1595/6
Humfry, Richard, Yatton Keynell, Wilts, 1678 Wilts RO Miscellaneous Index (name + date)
Humfry, Thomas, yeoman, Aldingbourne, Sussex, 1682 W. Suss RO EpI/33/1682/40
Humfrye, Thomas, Luddenham, Kent, 1603 CKS PRC2/12/435
Humpherie, William, Immingham, Lincs, 1633 Lincs RO Ad/Ac/24/78
Humphery, Francis, innholder, Northampton, Northants, 1768 Northants RO X954/21/10
Humphrey, John, Hythe St Leonard, Kent, 1638 CKS PRC20/10/514
Humphrey, Stephen, Woodchurch, Kent, 1665 CKS PRC19/3/72
Humphrey, Thomas, Pulborough, Sussex, 1681 W. Suss RO EpI/33/1681/4
Humphreyes, Tustram, Hanborough, Oxon, 1627 Oxon RO MSS Wills 297/5/4
Humphreys, Sarah, Andover, Hants, 1689 Hants RO 21m65 D8/355
Humphreys, William, Eastchurch, Sheppey, Kent, 1706 CKS PRC19/6/20
Humphries, Mary, Broad Hinton, Wilts, 1677 Wilts RO Miscellaneous Index (name + date)
Humphris, John, Latton, Wilts, 1745 Wilts RO Arch. Wilts.(name + date)
Humphry, Richard, Saltwood, Kent, 1636 CKS PRC20/10/472
Humphry, William, Sittingbourne, Kent, 1668 CKS PRC1/13/64
Humphrys, Ambrose, Coleshill, Berks, 1678 Berks RO D/A1/197/33B
Hun, Marie, Algarkirk, Lincs, 1612 Lincs RO Ad/Ac/10/130
Hun, Robert, Wigtoft, Lincs, 1605 Lincs RO Ad/Ac/6/13
Hundlebie, Dorothy, widow, Trusthorpe, Lincs, 1623 Lincs RO Ad/Ac/18/10
Hundleby, Thomas, Theddlethorpe, Lincs, 1638 Lincs RO Ad/Ac/25/94
Hungerford, John, clergy: 'clerk', Warren, Upper, Oxon, 1664 Oxon RO MSS Wills 80/5/6
Hungerforde, George, Ashton Keynes, Wilts, 1631 Wilts RO Arch. Wilts.(name + date)
Hunn, David, Gosberton, Lincs, 1649 Lincs RO Ad/Ac/30/105
Hunn, William, Yarmouth, Great, Norf, 1750 Norfolk RO ANW/23/24/92
Hunne, William, Broadwater, Sussex, 1627 W. Suss RO EpI/33/1627/12
Hunne, William, Broadwater, Sussex, 1627 W. Suss RO EpI/33/1627/13
Hunnings, George, husbandman, Whaplode, Lincs, 1683 Lincs RO Ad/Ac/44/120
Hunnings, John, gentleman, Holbeach, Lincs, 1802 Lincs RO Ad/Ac/45/68
Hunslie, John, Appleby, Lincs, 1622 Lincs RO Ad/Ac/8c/83
Hunston, Thomas, gentleman, Croft, Lincs, 1668 Lincs RO Ad/Ac/33/64
Hunt,
Som Somerset RO D/D/Cta/H6
Hunt, Ambrose, Fordington, Dors, 1682 Wilts RO Miscellaneous Index (name + date)
Hunt, Aquilla, saddler, Ashford, Kent, 1674 CKS PRC2/36/68
Hunt, Benjamin, Hythe St Leonard, Kent, 1679 CKS PRC20/12/266
Hunt, Danyell, Boughton Monchelsea, Kent, 1608 CKS PRC2/14/229
Hunt, Edith, Salisbury Cathedral (The Close), Wilts, 1681 Wilts RO Dean Sarum (name + date)
Hunt, Edward, St Johns Thanet, Kent, 1606 CKS PRC2/14/236
Hunt, Edward, Bearsted, Kent, 1621 CKS PRC2/23/149
Hunt, Edward, Charlbury (Fawler), Oxon, 1647 Oxon RO MSS Wills 298/2/23
Hunt, Edward, mercer, Oxford St Michael, Oxon, 1675 Oxon RO MSS Wills 298/2/45
Hunt, Edward, Chisledon, Wilts, 1677 Wilts RO Miscellaneous Index (name + date)
Hunt, Elizabeth, widow, Westborough, Lincs, 1685 Lincs RO Ad/Ac/44/172
Hunt, Henry, Fordwich, Kent, 1710 CKS PRC1/17/30
Hunt, Isaac, Hythe St Leonard, Kent, 1602 CKS PRC21/16/95
Hunt, Isaac, yeoman, Bethersden, Kent, 1661 CKS PRC1/8/104
Hunt, Isaack, Woodchurch, Kent, 1618 CKS PRC20/4/167

Hunt, John, Stanford, Kent, 1592 CKS PRC21/11/311
Hunt, John, Liskeard, Corn, 1604 Cornwall RO AP/H270
Hunt, John, Frittenden, Kent, 1618 CKS PRC2/22/157
Hunt, John, Potterne, Wilts, 1618 Wilts RO CC Sarum(+ name and date)
Hunt, John, maltster, Henley, Oxon, 1639 Oxon RO MSS Wills 298/1/36
Hunt, John, Dunton Bassett, Leics, 1671 Leics RO Administrators Accounts 1667-72 f33
Hunt, John, Chisledon, Wilts, 1674 Wilts RO Miscellaneous Index (name + date)
Hunt, John, husbandman, Cheriton, Kent, 1678 CKS PRC2/38/43
Hunt, John, harness maker?, coach/freeman of London, St Giles in the Fields, London & Middlesex, 1701 PRO PROB32/43/131
Hunt, Margaret + Thomas, Hythe St Leonard, Kent, 1640 CKS PRC20/10/498
Hunt, Mary, Hythe St Leonard, Kent, 1630 CKS PRC20/9/245
Hunt, Michael, Aston, Warks, 1663 LJRO:cards/1663/34
Hunt, Nicholas, Folkestone, Kent, 1597 CKS PRC2/9/499
Hunt, Nicholas, Canterbury St Alphege, Kent, 1619 CKS PRC20/4/135
Hunt, Nicholas, Chart nr Sutton Valence, Kent, 1639 CKS PRC20/10/530
Hunt, Nicholas, carpenter, Sellindge, Kent, 1674 CKS PRC2/36/77
Hunt, Nicholas, Cheriton, Kent, 1702 CKS PRC1/16/49
Hunt, Richard, maltster/currier, Newark on Trent, Notts, Borthwick Test C.P. 1764/2
Hunt, Richard, Pluckley, Kent, 1609 CKS PRC2/15/180
Hunt, Richard, Piddle, North, Worcs, 1683 Worcs RO 008.7 BA3585/837/bdl 3
Hunt, Robert, Mersham, Kent, 1596 CKS PRC2/9/9
Hunt, Robert, Spalding, Lincs, 1648 Lincs RO Ad/Ac/30/277
Hunt, Silvester, Watford, Herts, 1621 Herts RO ASA25/2696
Hunt, Stephen, Bethersden, Kent, 1631 CKS PRC2/31/44
Hunt, Stephen, yeoman, St Laurence Thanet, Kent, 1649 CKS PRC1/8/73
Hunt, Stephen, husbandman, Eastchurch, Sheppey, Kent, 1665 CKS PRC1/11/44
Hunt, Symon, Boughton Monchelsea, Kent, 1591 CKS PRC2/5/344
Hunt, Thomas, husbandman, Damerham, South, Wilts, Wilts RO Arch. Sarum(+ name and date)
Hunt, Thomas, Maidstone, Kent, 1596 CKS PRC21/14/121
Hunt, Thomas, Canterbury St Mary Northgate, Kent, 1599 CKS PRC2/10/145
Hunt, Thomas, Wingham, Kent, 1600 CKS PRC21/15/129
Hunt, Thomas, husbandman, Drayton, Berks, 1606 Berks RO D/A1/195/16C
Hunt, Thomas, Milton next Sittingbourne, Kent, 1609 CKS PRC2/15/190
Hunt, Thomas, Harbledown, Kent, 1610 CKS PRC2/15/163
Hunt, Thomas, Dundry, Som, 1640 Somerset RO D/D/Cta/H55
Hunt, Thomas, husbandman, Damerham, South, Wilts, 1667 Wilts RO Arch. Sarum(+ name and date)
Hunt, Thomas, husbandman, Damerham, South, Wilts, 1668 Wilts RO Arch. Sarum(+ name and date)
Hunt, Thomas, yeoman, Upchurch, Kent, 1674 CKS PRC2/36/76
Hunt, Thomas, husbandman, Eastchurch, Sheppey, Kent, 1681 CKS PRC2/39/193
Hunt, Thomazine, widow, Sittingbourne, Kent, 1667 CKS PRC1/12/48
Hunt, Vertue, mr, Wells, Som, 1634 Somerset RO D/D/Cta/H17
Hunt, Walter, husbandman, Bobbing, Kent, 1684 CKS PRC2/40/203
Hunt, William, Dymchurch, Kent, 1618 CKS PRC2/22/152
Hunt, William, Barrow Gurney, Som, 1622 Somerset RO D/D/Cta/H24
Hunt, William, Swineshead, Lincs, 1627 Lincs RO Ad/Ac/20b/32
Hunt, William, Deverill, Longbridge, Wilts, 1639 Wilts RO Arch. Sarum(+ name and date)
Hunt, William, Woodton, Norf, 1755 Norfolk RO ANF/11/5/12
Hunte, Barbara, widow, Headcorn, Kent, 1597 CKS PRC2/9/503
Hunte, Crispiane, Stone in Oxney, Kent, 1572 CKS PRC2/1/57
Hunte, John, Ashton, Long, Som, 1590 Somerset RO D/D/Cta/H40
Hunte, John, Inckberrow, Worcs, 1606 Worcs RO 008.7 BA3585/839/404
Hunte, Margaret, widow, Kirton, Lincs, 1623 Lincs RO Ad/Ac/18/14

[Hunte:]
Hunte, Nicholas, Langley, Kent, 1602 CKS PRC2/12/443
Hunte, Stephen, Smarden, Kent, 1598 CKS PRC2/9/349
Hunte, Stephen, Woodchurch, Kent, 1614 CKS PRC20/2/456
Hunte, Thomas, Tenterden, Kent, 1612 CKS PRC2/17/359
Hunte, William, Petworth, Sussex, 1630 W. Suss RO EpI/33/1630/26
Hunte, see Tompson,
Hunter, George, Bedminster, Som, 1644 Somerset RO D/D/Cta/H59
Hunter, John, Ribston, Yorks, 1638 Borthwick Prob. Ex. 1638/3
Hunter, Thomas, Wokingham, Berks, 1596 Wilts RO Miscellaneous Index (name + date)
Hunter, Thomas, mason, Ripon, Yorks, 1778 Borthwick Test C.P. 1778/6
Huntington, John, Theddlethorpe All Saints, Lincs, 1623 Lincs RO Ad/Ac/18/82b
Huntington, Robert, esquire, Hackney, London & Middlesex, 1687 PRO PROB32/26/72
Huntington, Thomas, Ulcombe, Kent, 1590 CKS PRC2/5/364
Huntley, John, Chitterne St Mary, Wilts, 1779 Wilts RO Arch. Sarum(+ name and date)
Huntley, Philip, Wells, Som, 1611 Somerset RO D/D/Cta/H53
Huntmill, John, Stelling, Kent, 1635 CKS PRC2/33/61
Huntsmell, Richard eld, victualler, Sittingbourne, Kent, 1675 CKS PRC2/36/72
Hunyettes, William, husbandman, Peopleton, Worcs, Worcs RO 008.7 BA3585/838/152
Hurd, widow, Stowey, Som, 1692 Somerset RO D/D/Cta/H94
Hurd, James, mr, St James Westminster, London & Middlesex, 1687 PRO PROB32/26/222
Hurd, Nicholas, Willoughton, Lincs, 1631 Lincs RO Ad/Ac/39/285
Hurd, Robert, Hogsthorpe, Lincs, 1640 Lincs RO Ad/Ac/27/54
Hurd, Robert, Irby, Lincs, 1680 Lincs RO Ad/Ac/34/51
Hurd, Robert, Hose, Leics, 1685 Leics RO Administrators Accounts 1682-86 f40
Hurd, William, Harpswell, Lincs, 1673 Lincs RO Ad/Ac/35/58
Hurd, see Peirce,
Hurde, Roger, Kingston Deverill, Wilts, 1636 Wilts RO Arch. Sarum(+ name and date)
Hurdman, John, Gayton le Marsh, Lincs, 1629 Lincs RO Ad/Ac/22/40
Hurelstone, Humphrey, Ilmington, Warks, 1681 Worcs RO 008.7 BA3585/830/64
Hurlbirt, butcher, Worcester St Margaret, Worcs, 1606 Worcs RO 008.7 BA3585/839/426a
Hurle, Roger, Knoyle, West, Wilts, 1612 Wilts RO Arch. Sarum(+ name and date)
Hurles, Elizabeth, widow, Chiswick (Turnham Green), London & Middlesex, 1713 PRO PROB32/57/37
Hurleston, Helen, widow, Sandwich, Kent, 1613 CKS PRC2/17/256
Hurleston, Josua, mariner, Sandwich, Kent, 1618 CKS PRC2/21/19
Hurleston, see Turner,
Hurlestone, John, gentleman, Ickham, Kent, 1611 CKS PRC20/2/188
Hurlestone, Richard, mariner, Sandwich, Kent, 1676 CKS PRC2/37/48
Hurlestone, Thomas, mariner, Deal, Kent, 1640 CKS PRC19/1/54
Hurley, Thomas, Uffculme, Devon, 1627 Wilts RO Preb Court Uffculme Bundle 1/12
Hurley, Thomas, Uffculme, Devon, 1631 Wilts RO Miscellaneous Index (name + date)
Hurlocke, Anthony, yeoman/gentleman, Kennington, Berks, 1644 Berks RO D/A1/196/68A
Hurlocke, John, clergy: 'clerk/vicar', Benson, Oxon, 1630 Oxon RO MSS Wills Pec 69/1/14
Hurlocke, William, Havant, Hants, 1665 Hants RO 21M65 D8/186
Hurlstone, Nicholas, Sandwich, Kent, 1625 CKS PRC2/25/61
Hurlstone, Thomas, Sandwich, Kent, 1625 CKS PRC2/25/69
Hurrey, Henry, Horningsea, Cambs, 1633 c. CUL V.C. Acc./Box3/64
Hurst, Andrew, St Peter in Thanet, Kent, 1669 CKS PRC1/13/65
Hurst, Ann, widow, St Peter in Thanet, Kent, 1674 CKS PRC2/35/226
Hurst, Edward, Chesterfield, Derby, 1680 LJRO:cards/1680/20
Hurst, Jane, widow, Westbourne, Sussex, 1618 W. Suss RO EpI/33/1618/19
Hurst, John, Queenborough, Kent, 1626 CKS PRC2/27/73
Hurst, Ralph, husbandman, Inkpen, Berks, 1622 Berks RO D/A1/195/71A
Hurst, Richard, Shipley, Sussex, 1631 W. Suss RO EpI/33/1630/7
Hurst, William, Broughton, Hants, 1680 Hants RO 21m65 D8/323

Hurstwait, Ann, widow, Bythorn, Hunts, 1744 Hunts RO/Acc58/323
Hurt, John, clergy: 'clerk', Milton next Sittingbourne, Kent, 1675 CKS PRC2/36/198
Hurt, Nicholas, Ilam (Castern), Staffs, 1678 LJRO:cards/1678/16
Hurt, Thomas, Chartham, Kent, 1594 CKS PRC2/7/17
Hurte, James, Newbury, Berks, 1610 Berks RO D/A1/195/37A
Hurte, Jeremie, East Sutton, Kent, 1627 CKS PRC2/28/56
Hurte, Michaell, Bitchfield, Lincs, 1619 Lincs RO Ad/Ac/15/155
Hurte, Robert, Milton next Sittingbourne, Kent, 1643 CKS PRC1/6/69
Hurton, Nicholas, Stone in Oxney, Kent, 1610 CKS PRC2/15/168
Huse, Christian, Longstock, Hants, 1632 Hants RO 1632 ND6
Huse, George, Brinkworth, Wilts, 1618 Wilts RO Arch. Wilts.(name + date)
Husen, Ralph, Horsington, Som, 1623 Somerset RO D/D/Cta/H30
Huson, Marion, widow, Sandwich St Clement, Kent, 1598 CKS PRC2/9/421
Husse, Stephen, Sittingbourne, Kent, 1630 CKS PRC2/30/91
Hussey, Andrew, Preston Gubbals, Shrops, 1664 LJRO:cards/1664/6
Hussey, Gregory, baker, Reading St Lawrence, Berks, 1605 Berks RO D/A1/195/11C
Hussey, James, yeoman, Farnborough, Berks, 1635 Berks RO D/A1/196/29A
Hussey, John, Landford, Wilts, 1636 Wilts RO Arch. Sarum(+ name and date)
Hussey, Richard, shepherd, Ilsley, West, Berks, 1665 Berks RO D/A1/196/13/A
Hustat or Hustwaite, Thomas, husbandman, Bythorn, Hunts, 1676 Hunts RO/Acc58/73(165)
Hutchens, John, Faversham, Kent, 1613 CKS PRC2/16/195
Hutchens, Susan, widow, Dover, Kent, 1673 CKS PRC20/12/81
Hutchin, Rebecca, Canterbury St Mildred, Kent, 1645 CKS PRC1/7/53
Hutchin, Thomas, Deal, Kent, 1674 CKS PRC20/12/132
Hutchings, Jeremiah, Kington, Worcs, Worcs RO 008.7 BA3585/837/bdl 2
Hutchingson, William, Carlton, Castle, Lincs, 1612 Lincs RO Ad/Ac/11/82
Hutchins, Christopher, Glastonbury St John, Som, 1588 Somerset RO D/D/Cta/H42
Hutchins, Christopher, Glastonbury St John, Som, 1588 Somerset RO D/D/Cta/H43
Hutchins, Rebecca, widow, Faversham, Kent, 1637 CKS PRC2/34/57
Hutchins, Robert, yeoman, Hendred, West, Berks, 1631 Berks RO D/A1/195/126C
Hutchins, Robert + Margaret, yeoman, Hendred, West, Berks, 1631 Berks RO D/A1/195/126A
Hutchins, Thomas, Brinkworth, Wilts, 1631 Wilts RO Arch. Wilts.(name + date)
Hutchins, Thomas, Madron, Corn, 1636 Cornwall RO AP/H934/2
Hutchins, Thomas, Dover, Kent, 1679 CKS PRC20/12/305
Hutchinson, Christopher, Winteringham, Lincs, 1618 Lincs RO Ad/Ac/8b/292
Hutchinson, Christopher, Horncastle, Lincs, 1632 Lincs RO Ad/Ac/23/96
Hutchinson, Edward, Alford, Lincs, 1632 Lincs RO Ad/Ac/23/39
Hutchinson, Elizabeth, widow, Halifax, Yorks, 1820 Borthwick Test C.P. 1820/5
Hutchinson, John, yeoman, Hunmanby (Fordon), Yorks, 1773 Borthwick Test C.P. 1770/1
Hutchinson, Matthew, maltster, Pontefract, Yorks, 1811 Borthwick Test C.P. 1807/2
Hutchinson, Richard, weaver, Lincoln St Peter at Gowts, Lincs, 1639 Lincs RO Ad/Ac/26/59
Hutchinson, Stephen, Broughton, Brant, Lincs, 1634 Lincs RO Ad/Ac/24/508
Hutchinson, Thomas, Croft, Lincs, 1632 Lincs RO Ad/Ac/23/11
Hutchinson, Thomas, labourer, Sibsey, Lincs, 1638 Lincs RO Ad/Ac/25/181
Hutchinson, Thomas, Leeds St John (Hollinghall), Yorks, 1750 Borthwick Test C.P. 1751/5
Hutchinson, Thomas, farmer, Cave, South (Faxfeet), Yorks, 1837 Borthwick Test C.P. 1837/2
Hutchinson, William, Milton next Sittingbourne, Kent, 1599 CKS PRC2/10/517
Hutsoll, Thomas, Warehorne, Kent, 1624 CKS PRC2/23/168
Hutson, John sen, Upton on Severn, Worcs, 1682 Worcs RO 008.7 BA3585/837/bdl 3
Hutson, Robert, fisherman, Dover, Kent, 1668 CKS PRC19/4/20
Hutson, Thomas ygr, Hythe St Leonard, Kent, 1631 CKS PRC20/9/225
Hutt, Simon, yeoman, Abingdon St Helen (Shippon), Berks, 1641 Berks RO D/A1/196/61C
Hutton, Anthony, Halton, West, Lincs, 1621 Lincs RO Ad/Ac/8c/2
Hutton, Felix, Sparsholt, Berks, 1605 Berks RO D/A1/195/20A
Hutton, John, mariner, Sandwich, Kent, 1640 CKS PRC1/4/62

[Hutton:]
Hutton, William, clothier, Bradford (Eccleshill), Yorks, 1841 Borthwick Test C.P. 1841/1
Huttson, Thomas, husbandman, Appledore, Kent, 1695 CKS PRC1/16/7
Huttsun, James, Canterbury Christchurch, Kent, 1666 CKS PRC19/3/96
Hyat, Thomas, Compton, Long, Warks, 1757 Worcs RO 008.7 BA3585/835/bdl 1
Hyatt, Richard, husbandman, Hailey, Oxon, 1675 Oxon RO MSS Wills 298/2/48
Hychcock, Gilbert, husbandman, Norton (Hatfield), Worcs, 1598 Worcs RO 008.7 BA3585/838/154
Hyde, Charles, manufacturer, Stockport, Ches, 1790 Cheshire RO (Name) W.C. 1790
Hyde, Margarett, spinster, Romsey, Hants, 1664 Hants RO 21M65 D8/169
Hyde, Nicholas, Chipping Barnet, Herts, 1612 Herts RO ASA25/4798
Hyde, Robert, esquire, Sandon, Herts, 1636 Herts RO AHH23/1081
Hyde, Thomas, Bubwith (Foggathorpe), Yorks, 1638 Borthwick Prob. Ex. 1638/9
Hyde, William, husbandman, Northaw (Cuffley), Herts, 1577 Herts RO ASA25/863
Hyden, Edward, St Columb Major, Corn, 1608 Cornwall RO AP/H181
Hyden, John, St Columb Major, Corn, 1608 Cornwall RO AP/H180
Hyder, Edward, Staplehurst, Kent, 1617 CKS PRC2/22/134
Hyder, William, Woodchurch, Kent, 1611 CKS PRC20/2/184
Hydes, John, Broughton (Castlethorpe), Lincs, 1681 Lincs RO Ad/Ac/34/83
Hydes, Mary, widow, Scawby, Lincs, 1683 Lincs RO Ad/Ac/44/42
Hydes, Thomas, Firsby, Lincs, 1644 Lincs RO Ad/Ac/28/94
Hyland, James, Cranbrook, Kent, 1638 CKS PRC2/34/63
Hylde/Heele, Davyd, Herne, Kent, 1588 CKS PRC21/9/106
Hyle, William, Northbourne, Kent, 1615 CKS PRC2/21/13
Hylhouse, Richard, Burrington, Som, 1611 Somerset RO D/D/Cta/H73
Hyll, Richard, Watford, Herts, 1619 Herts RO ASA25/4834
Hyll, Thomas, Watford (Fortunes), Herts, 1602 Herts RO ASA25/1836
Hylles, John, St Laurence Thanet, Kent, 1604 CKS PRC2/14/242
Hylles, Symon, Shadoxhurst, Kent, 1586 CKS PRC2/4/33
Hynard, Robert, yeoman, Rougham, Suff, 1732 Suff RO(B) IC500/3/47/31
Hynckcell/Hinxill, Thomas, Smarden, Kent, 1597 CKS PRC2/9/239
Hynde, Ralph, labourer, Ippollitts, Herts, 1638 Herts RO AHH23/1099
Hynde, Richard, mercer/draper, Newbury, Berks, 1613 Berks RO D/A1/195/55A
Hyott, William, carpenter, Ramsbury, Wilts, 1666 Wilts RO Dean Sarum (name + date)
Hyssey, Robert, Buckland, Berks, 1618 Berks RO D/A1/195/67A
Hysted, William, husbandman, Canterbury St Mary Bredin, Kent, 1684 CKS PRC2/40/206
Hyte, Thomas, labourer, Catworth, Great, Hunts, 1762 Hunts RO/Acc58/328
Ibbott, Edmond, clergy: 'mr/rector', Deal, Kent, 1679 CKS PRC20/12/308
Ibbott/Quintin, Elizabeth, widow, Faversham, Kent, 1682 CKS PRC2/40/47
Ible, William, Abingdon St Helen, Berks, 1612 Berks RO D/A1/199/68C
Ickham, Nicolas, Bonnington, Kent, 1585 CKS PRC2/4/51
Icoffe, Thomas, Grandborough, Bucks, 1559 Herts RO ASA25/419
Iddenborow, William + Agnes, Frittenden, Kent, 1597 CKS PRC2/9/231
Iddenden, Agnes, Cranbrook, Kent, 1602 CKS PRC2/12/444
Iddenden, Jeames, Cranbrook, Kent, 1602 CKS PRC2/12/446
Iddenden, Joan, widow, Cranbrook, Kent, 1595 CKS PRC2/7/273
Iddenden, Thomas, yeoman, Sturry, Kent, 1642 CKS PRC1/5/108
Iddenden, see Ellenden,
Ide, Edward, Lavant, Mid, Sussex, 1594 W. Suss RO EpI/33/1594/11
Ide, Henry, Lavant, Mid, Sussex, 1617 W. Suss RO EpI/33/1617/40
Ide, John,
Sussex W. Suss RO EpI/33/1675/1
Iden, Frauncis, Sandwich, Kent, 1616 CKS PRC2/22/115
Iden, James, yeoman, Linton, Kent, 1682 CKS PRC2/40/48
Iden, Reynold, Chart, Great, Kent, 1591 CKS PRC2/5/348
Iden, Thomas, gentleman, Egerton, Kent, 1681 CKS PRC20/13/38

Iden, William, Boughton Monchelsea, Kent, 1622 CKS PRC20/6/336
Idenden, Edmond, Cranbrook, Kent, 1599 CKS PRC2/10/147
Idenden, Thomas, Benenden, Kent, 1597 CKS PRC2/9/471
Idenn, Thomas, Benenden, Kent, 1629 CKS PRC2/30/73
Idiens, William, farmer, Trysull/Seisdon, Staffs, 1788 LJRO/B/C/5/1788/46
Idlei, see Robins,
Idley, William, gentleman, Eastry, Kent, 1618 CKS PRC20/4/206
Idon, Nicholas, Spalding, Lincs, 1607 Lincs RO Ad/Ac/8a/97
Idsworth, John, Wittering, East (Somerly), Sussex, 1632 W. Suss RO EpI/33/1632/10
Ifield, John, major/widower, Wapping, London & Middlesex, 1698 PRO PROB32/36/224
Iggleden, Constance, Bethersden, Kent, 1617 CKS PRC2/21/103
Iggleden, Daniel, Appledore, Kent, 1607 CKS PRC2/14/271
Iggleden, Edward, weaver: 'linen weaver', Smarden, Kent, 1665 CKS PRC1/11/45
Iggleden, Joan, Rodmersham, Kent, 1597 CKS PRC2/9/138
Iggleden, John, Frittenden, Kent, 1601 CKS PRC2/12/226
Iggleden, Josias, Tenterden, Kent, 1622 CKS PRC2/23/195
Igglestone/Eglestone, Thomas eld, yeoman, Ash next Sandwich, Kent, 1629 CKS PRC20/8/175
Igleden, John, clergy: 'vicar', Milton next Sittingbourne, Kent, 1585 CKS PRC2/3/305
Igulden, Walter, Ebony, Kent, 1593 CKS PRC2/7/139
Ilbery, Thomas, joiner, Forest Hill, Oxon, 1633 Oxon RO MSS Wills 298/3/16
Ilbury, Nicholas eld, Blewbury, Berks, 1665 Lambeth Palace Arches G19/5
Ilden, John, Wittersham, Kent, 1683 CKS PRC20/13/339
Ilent, Mildred, Chartham, Kent, 1682 CKS PRC2/40/46
Iler, William, Molash, Kent, 1639 CKS PRC1/2/79
Ilesley, William, Beenham, Berks, 1594 Berks RO D/A1/199/46C
Ilett, Thomas, Great Stukeley, Hunts, 1687 Hunts RO/Acc58/265(260)
Ilife?, Henry, Kilby, Leics, 1674 Leics RO Administrators Accounts 1667-72 f144
Illarie, John, Closworth, Som, 1588 Somerset RO D/D/Cta/I4
Illary, Thomas, St Stephen in Brannel, Corn, 1612 Cornwall RO AP/I10/1
Ille, William,
Som 1600 Somerset RO D/D/Cta/I1
Illenden, Joseph, Benenden, Kent, 1642 CKS PRC1/6/70
Illenden, Wyllyam, Sandhurst, Kent, 1586 CKS PRC2/4/3
Illidge, John, Shrewsbury St Chad, Shrops, 1685 LJRO/B/C/5/1685/53
Illingworth, Joseph, clothier, Dewsbury (Gawthorpe), Yorks, 1777 Borthwick Test C.P. 1777/4
Ilsley, John, Aldermaston, Berks, 1593 Berks RO D/A1/199/42B
Ilsley, Richard ygr, maltster, Wallingford, Berks, 1681 Berks RO D/A1/199/137C
Imber, Edward, Deptford, Wilts, 1611 Wilts RO Miscellaneous Index (name + date)
Imingham, Richard, yeoman, Friskney, Lincs, 1611 Lincs RO Ad/Ac/10/39
Immingham, Vincente,
Lincs Lincs RO Ad/Ac/4/1
Impett, Michael, yeoman, Ash next Sandwich, Kent, 1682 CKS PRC20/13/263
Impett, Peter, fellmonger, Snave, Kent, 1693 CKS PRC2/42/68
Impett, Richard, Elham, Kent, 1604 CKS PRC2/14/277
Impett, Stephen, fellmonger, New Romney, Kent, 1682 CKS PRC20/13/261
Impey, Thomas, Gaddesden, Great, Herts, 1675 Herts RO AHH23/1352
Impitt, John, Elmsted, Kent, 1617 CKS PRC2/22/114
Ince, Richard, Maidstone, Kent, 1587 CKS PRC21/8/230
Ince, Samuell, Chester, Ches, 1663 Cheshire RO (Name) W.C. 1662
Incent, William, miller, Charing, Kent, 1643 CKS PRC19/2/73
Inckley, John, Carlby, Lincs, 1602 Lincs RO Ad/Ac/11/195
Inckpett, Dionise, widow, Lyminge, Kent, 1610 CKS PRC20/2/168
Inckpett, John, Lyminge, Kent, 1607 CKS PRC20/1/245
Inge, George, yeoman, Smeeth, Kent, 1671 CKS PRC20/12/14
Inge, Richard, Bishopsbourne, Kent, 1612 CKS PRC2/16/149

[Inge:]
Inge, William, esquire, Thorpe Constantine, Staffs, 1673 Leics RO Administrators Accounts 1667-72 f119
Ingham, Joshua eld, banker, Mirfield (Blake Hall), Yorks, 1822 Borthwick Test C.P. 1822/5
Ingleby, Thomas, Somercoates, South, Lincs, 1599 Lincs RO Ad/Ac/5/201
Inglefield, Peter, Bebington (Storeton), Ches, 1618 Cheshire RO (Name) W.C. 1618
Inglett, Thomas, Brookland, Kent, 1619 CKS PRC2/22/131
Inglett, William, Brookland, Kent, 1606 CKS PRC2/13/254
Ingneham, Richard, Compton, Long, Warks, 1604 Worcs RO 008.7 BA3585/839/302
Ingram, John, Bucknall, Lincs, 1582 Lincs RO Ad/Ac/1/26
Ingram, John, butcher, Holbeach, Lincs, 1619 Lincs RO Ad/Ac/15/199
Ingram, John, Saltfleetby St Peter, Lincs, 1623 Lincs RO Ad/Ac/17/20
Ingram, John, yeoman, Codford St Peter, Wilts, 1747 Wilts RO CC Sarum(+ name and date)
Ingram, John + Susan, Dover, Kent, 1627 CKS PRC20/8/251
Ingram, Marie, widow, Sutton, Long, Lincs, 1639? Lincs RO Ad/Ac/26/105
Ingram, Phillip, Codford St Peter, Wilts, 1682 Wilts RO Arch. Sarum(+ name and date)
Ingram, Raphe, Folkestone, Kent, 1586 CKS PRC2/3/331
Ingram, Richard, Compton, Long, Warks, 1610 Worcs RO 008.7 BA3585/839/481
Ingram, Richard, fisherman, Folkestone, Kent, 1618 CKS PRC2/22/104
Ingram, Richard, husbandman, Fosdyke, Lincs, 1667 Lincs RO Ad/Ac/33/4
Ingram, Thomas, St Ives, Hunts, 1676 Hunts RO/Acc58/58(145)
Ingram, William, husbandman, Oxford St Peter le Bailey, Oxon, 1664 Oxon RO MSS Wills 168/3/10
Ingram, William, blacksmith, St Johns Thanet, Kent, 1690 CKS PRC2/41/178
Ingrame, John, Bucknall, Lincs, 1587 Lincs RO Ad/Ac/2C/28
Inkbarrow, Richard, Broughton Hackett, Worcs, Worcs RO 008.7 BA3585/839/306
Inkersall, Richard, Bassingham, Lincs, 1620 Lincs RO Ad/Ac/16/54
Inkersall, Inkersall, John, husbandman, Staughton, Great (West Perry), Hunts, 1602 Lincs RO Ad/Ac/5/564
Inkson, George, butcher, King's Lynn, Norf, 1754 Norfolk RO ANW/23/24/150
Inman, John, milliner, Steeping, Little, Lincs, 1626 Lincs RO Ad/Ac/20/14
Inman, John, Boston, Lincs, 1627 Lincs RO Ad/Ac/20b/11
Inman, Michael, Redbourne, Lincs, 1663 Lincs RO Ad/Ac/41/94
Inman, William, bookseller, Doncaster, Yorks, Borthwick Test C.P. 1735/8
Inmeth, Edmund, yeoman, Ruckinge, Kent, 1640 CKS PRC1/4/63
Inmeth, Thomas, Folkestone, Kent, 1606 CKS PRC2/14/265
Inmeth, Thomas, jurat/mr, Folkestone, Kent, 1663 CKS PRC1/9/31
Inmeth/Jumeth, John, gentleman, Folkestone, Kent, 1669 CKS PRC1/14/64
Inmith, Idden, widow, Folkestone, Kent, 1627 CKS PRC2/28/69
Inmythe, John, Folkestone, Kent, 1603 CKS PRC2/14/281
Inniotts/Bradburie, Frances, Lyneham, Wilts, 1627 Wilts RO Arch. Wilts.(name + date)
Inold, Elizabeth, widow, Coningsby, Lincs, 1627 Lincs RO Ad/Ac/20b/76
Inott, Richard, Thame (Moreton), Oxon, 1665 Oxon RO MSS Wills Pec 37/4/16
Inse, Edward, Luddenham, Kent, 1638 CKS PRC2/34/223
Insent, Andrewe, High Halden, Kent, 1612 CKS PRC2/17/315
Intnapp, Mary, widow, Selsey, Sussex, 1651 W. Suss RO EpI/33/1651/5
Inwood, Nicholas, bachelor, Broadwater, Sussex, 1683 W. Suss RO EpI/33/1682/3
Inyons, see Edge,
Irby, Anthony, esquire, Boston, Lincs, 1627 Lincs RO Ad/Ac/20b/16
Irchenett, William, Lincoln, Lincs, 1524 Lincs RO Ad/Ac/0/1
Ireland, Edward, Birdham, Sussex, 1650 W. Suss RO EpI/33/1650/3
Ireland, Joan, widow, Wittering, East, Sussex, 1635 W. Suss RO EpI/33/1635/5
Ireland, John, yeoman, Westmill, Herts, 1638 Herts RO AHH23/1344
Ireland, John, Lyminster, Sussex, 1676 W. Suss RO EpI/33/1676/21
Ireland, John, brewer, Chester, Ches, 1790 Cheshire RO (Name) W.C. 1790
Ireland, Richard, stationer/privileged person, Cambridge St Mary the Great, Cambs, 1657 CUL

[Ireland:]
V.C. Acc./Box3/30
Ireland, Thomas, Blunsdon St Andrew, Wilts, 1614? Wilts RO Arch. Wilts.(name + date)
Ireland, Thomas, wheelwright, Saltwood, Kent, 1669 CKS PRC19/4/21
Ireland/Waddell, Joane, widow, Lyminge, Kent, 1666 CKS PRC19/3/97
Iremonger, Agnes, widow, Thatcham (Henwick), Berks, 1633 Berks RO D/A1/199/97C
Iremonger, John, Thatcham (Henwick), Berks, 1631 Berks RO D/A1/199/96C
Iremonger, Nicholas, yeoman, Mapledurham, Oxon, 1666 Oxon RO MSS Wills 82/1/13
Iremonger, Stephen, shearman, Reading St Lawrence, Berks, 1625 Berks RO D/A1/199/90C
Iremonger, Thomas, Romsey, Hants, 1679 Hants RO 21m65 D8/312
Ireson, Robert, Faversham, Kent, 1674 CKS PRC2/36/81
Irishe, John, Harting (West Harting), Sussex, 1633 W. Suss RO Epl/33/1633/4
Ironmonger, Thomas, Tatenhill, Staffs, 1685 LJRO/B/C/5/1685/54
Ironmonger, William, Gaddesden, Little, Herts, 1687 Herts RO AHH23/1357
Irons, George, Kennington, Kent, 1623 CKS PRC2/23/199
Isaack, Francis, Oxford (Corpus Christi College), Oxon, 1673 Bodleian HYP B9/1-2
Isack, John + John, Cuby, Corn, 1605 Cornwall RO AP/I5
Isacke, Andrew, Huntspill, Som, 1662 Somerset RO D/D/Cta/I5
Isard, John, Kiddington, Oxon, 1630 Oxon RO MSS Wills 298/3/11
Isard, Robert, Fladbury, Worcs, 1605 Worcs RO 008.7 BA3585/839/364
Isgar, John,
Som Somerset RO D/D/Cta/I2
Isgar, John, Huntspill, Som, Somerset RO D/D/Cta/I6
Isgar, Robert, Brent, East, Som, 1639 Somerset RO D/D/Cta/I3
Isgrave, Richard, Welton, Lincs, 1598 Lincs RO Ad/Ac/4/135
Isles, George, Faversham, Kent, 1671 CKS PRC2/35/62
Isles, William, mariner, Faversham, Kent, 1670 CKS PRC1/15/37
Isley, Tobias, yeoman, Hampstead Marshall, Berks, 1683 Berks RO D/A1/199/139C
Issard, Richard, Charlton nr Dover, Kent, 1619 CKS PRC2/22/103
Isted, Edward, husbandman, Smarden, Kent, 1674 CKS PRC2/36/82
Ithell, Leonard, clergy: 'clerk', Bratoft, Lincs, 1637 Lincs RO Ad/Ac/25/532
Ittenburie, Thomas, Loose, Kent, 1608 CKS PRC20/1/348
Ivary, Mathew, university: 'Fellow of New College, Oxford/B.A.', Oxford (New College), Oxon, 1681 Bodleian HYP B8/48-49
Ivatt, Robert, Hemingford Grey, Hunts, 1682 Hunts RO/Acc58/173(107)
Ive, Ayloffe, St Laurence Thanet, Kent, 1715 CKS PRC1/17/72
Ivers, Jhon, husbandman, Elton, Hunts, 1597 Lincs RO Ad/Ac/0/13
Ivers, Robert, Sandwich, Kent 1625 CKS PRC2/25/76
Ivers, William, St Laurence Thanet, Kent, 1593 CKS PRC2/6/49
Ives, Thomas, yeoman, Milton next Sittingbourne, Kent, 1689 CKS PRC2/41/152
Ivet, Francis, yeoman, Linsted, Kent, 1697 CKS PRC2/42/130
Ivie, Alice, widow, Chieveley, Berks, 1663 Berks RO D/A1/199/121C
Izard/Shillingford, Martha, Oddington, Oxon, Oxon RO MSS Wills 298/3/23
Izern, William, St Mary Bourne, Hants, 1625 Hants RO 21M65 D8/71
Jacka, Henry, tinner, Lelant, Corn, 1622 Cornwall RO AP/J264/3
Jackett, Adam, Cranbrook, Kent, 1611 CKS PRC2/15/197
Jackett, William, Lympne, Kent, 1638 CKS PRC2/34/221
Jacklin, Richard, Thoresway, Lincs, 1602 Lincs RO Ad/Ac/5/97
Jacklin, Robert, husbandman, Withern, Lincs, 1668 Lincs RO Ad/Ac/33/59
Jacklyne, Thomas, Lincoln St Peter at Arches, Lincs, 1619 Lincs RO Ad/Ac/15/149
Jackman, Richard, Wellow, East, Hants, 1624 Hants RO 21M65 D8/25
Jackman, Robert, Kirdford, Sussex, 1635 W. Suss RO Epl/33/1635/26
Jackson, Alice, widow, Barlings, Lincs, 1662 Lincs RO Ad/Ac/41/11
Jackson, Anne, widow, Owston, Lincs, 1625 Lincs RO Ad/Ac/39/204
Jackson, Christopher, Barkwith, East, Lincs, 1624 Lincs RO Ad/Ac/19A/82
Jackson, Christopher, Mareham le Fen, Lincs, 1650 Lincs RO Ad/Ac/30/2

[Jackson:]
Jackson, Dunstan, yeoman, Windsor, New, Berks, 1619 Berks RO D/A1/199/83C
Jackson, Edith, widow, Derby, Derby, 1663 LJRO:cards/1663/35
Jackson, Elizabeth, widow, Bristol St Augustine the Less, Glos, Bristol RO 1686/CP
Jackson, Elizabeth, widow, Aslackby, Lincs, 1612 Lincs RO Ad/Ac/10/165
Jackson, George, Burton by Lincoln, Lincs, 1676? Lincs RO Ad/Ac/35/113
Jackson, Gervase, gentleman, Harston, Leics, 1673 Leics RO Administrators Accounts 1667-72 f107
Jackson, Humanity ygr, Pillerton Hersey, Warks, 1685 Worcs RO 008.7 BA3585/830/6
Jackson, James, Ormskirk, Lancs, 1613 Lancs RO (Name of Deceased) D.R.C.H. 1613
Jackson, John, pumpmaker, Bicester, Oxon, Oxon RO MSS Wills 168/4/36
Jackson, John, Grimsby, Lincs, 1598 Lincs RO Ad/Ac/4/33
Jackson, John, gentleman, Spalding, Lincs, 1607 Lincs RO Ad/Ac/8a/99
Jackson, John, clergy: 'clerk', Bourne, Lincs, 1614 Lincs RO Ad/Ac/13/74
Jackson, John, Surfleet, Lincs, 1619 Lincs RO Ad/Ac/15/40
Jackson, John, Toynton All Saints, Lincs, 1624 Lincs RO Ad/Ac/18/106
Jackson, John, Ashford, Kent, 1635 CKS PRC2/32/158
Jackson, John, Leverton, Lincs, 1639 Lincs RO Ad/Ac/25/82
Jackson, John, Sutton, Long, Lincs, 1644 Lincs RO Ad/Ac/28/86
Jackson, John, Maidstone, Kent, 1663 CKS PRC19/3/31
Jackson, John, butcher, Sittingbourne, Kent, 1663 CKS PRC19/3/32
Jackson, John, Gainsborough, Lincs, 1680 Lincs RO Ad/Ac/43/150
Jackson, John, Shenstone (Chesterfield), Staffs, 1685 LJRO/B/C/5/1685/55
Jackson, John, Halton, East, Lincs, 1785 Lincs RO Ad/Ac/45/48
Jackson, Jonathan, wine & spirit: 'wine & spirit merchant', Wensley (Leyburn), Yorks, 1825 Borthwick Test C.P. 1825b/2
Jackson, Laurence, Lenham, Kent, 1689 CKS PRC2/41/150
Jackson, Marie, widow, Ashford, Kent, 1597 CKS PRC2/10/355
Jackson, Mary, spinster, Whitby, Yorks, 1811 Borthwick Test C.P. 1811/7
Jackson, Michaell, Wynebe, Lincs, 1574 Lincs RO Ad/Ac/1/14
Jackson, Nicholas, carpenter, Saltwood, Kent, 1662 CKS PRC19/3/14
Jackson, Richard, Seasalter, Kent, 1632 CKS PRC20/11/5
Jackson, Richard, Scampton, Lincs, 1681 Lincs RO Ad/Ac/34/86
Jackson, Richard, farmer, Wilton, Yorks, 1811 Borthwick Test C.P. 1811/8
Jackson, Robert, Haltham on Bain, Lincs, 1639 Lincs RO Ad/Ac/26/49
Jackson, Robert, Faversham, Kent, 1640 CKS PRC1/4/64
Jackson, Robert, brewster, Gainsborough, Lincs, 1668 Lincs RO Ad/Ac/33/16
Jackson, Robert, Hinckley, Leics, 1683 Leics RO Administrators Accounts 1682-86 f22
Jackson, Sarah, widow, Gresley (Castle), Derby, 1674 LJRO:cards/1674/27
Jackson, Sarah, widow, Birmingham, Warks, 1842 LJRO/B/C/5/1842/9
Jackson, Thomas, clergy: 'clerk', Leysdown, Kent, 1582 CKS PRC2/2/178
Jackson, Thomas, Asterby, Lincs, 1600 Lincs RO Ad/Ac/5/41
Jackson, Thomas, tailor, Cambridge, Cambs, 1620 CUL V.C.Acc./Box1/30
Jackson, Thomas, gentleman, Minting, Lincs, 1674 Lincs RO Ad/Ac/34/29
Jackson, Thomas, husbandman, Ibstock, Leics, 1683 Leics RO Administrators Accounts 1682-86 f16a
Jackson, Thomas, cooper, Halton, Ches, 1771 Cheshire RO (Name) W.C. 1771-2
Jackson, Thomas?, Frampton, Lincs, 1640 Lincs RO Ad/Ac/27/21
Jackson, Tobias, gentleman, Bath, Som, 1644 Somerset RO D/D/Cta/J1
Jackson, William, Bray, Berks, 1612 Berks RO D/A1/199/69C
Jackson, William, Luddington, Lincs, 1615 Lincs RO Ad/Ac/8b/107
Jackson, William, yeoman, Orby, Lincs, 1620 Lincs RO Ad/Ac/16/55
Jackson, William, carpenter, Horncastle, Lincs, 1632 Lincs RO Ad/Ac/23/13
Jackson, William, Gainsborough, Lincs, 1634 Lincs RO Ad/Ac/40/41
Jackson, William, Alfreton, Derby, 1663 LJRO:cards/1663/36
Jackson, William, Frodingham (Crosby), Lincs, 1667 Lincs RO Ad/Ac/33/25

Jackson, William, Caistor, Lincs, 1669 Lincs RO Ad/Ac/42/30
Jackson, William, Barkston, Lincs, 1830 Lincs RO Ad/Ac/45/83
Jackson, Williamson, yeoman, Wistow, Yorks, 1834 Borthwick Test C.P. 1834/6
Jacksone, Thomas, Bicker, Lincs, 1598 Lincs RO Ad/Ac/5/314
Jacksonne, George, Elsham, Lincs, 1580 Lincs RO Ad/Ac/2b/59
Jacob, Caleb, mr, Sandwich, Kent, 1630 CKS PRC20/8/295
Jacob, Christopher, Whitstable, Kent, 1613 CKS PRC2/18/92
Jacob, Elizabeth, mrs/widow, Sandwich, Kent, 1633 CKS PRC20/11/15
Jacob, James, Queenborough, Kent, 1647 CKS PRC1/8/20
Jacob, James, Salisbury, Wilts, 1827 Wilts RO Miscellaneous Index (name + date)
Jacob, John, Sandwich, Kent, 1631 CKS PRC20/9/255
Jacob, John, Dauntsey, Wilts, 1681 Wilts RO Miscellaneous Index (name + date)
Jacob, John eld, Cheriton, North, Som, 1632 Somerset RO D/D/Cta/J8
Jacob, Richard, Hinksey, South, Berks, 1595 Berks RO D/A1/199/48B
Jacob, Richard, Lydiard Tregoze, Wilts, 1674 Wilts RO Miscellaneous Index (name + date)
Jacob, Stephen, Hythe St Leonard, Kent, 1617 CKS PRC20/4/214
Jacob, Thomas, Dover St James, Kent, 1616 CKS PRC20/3/411
Jacob, William, Folkestone, Kent, 1585 CKS PRC2/3/225
Jacob, William, Folkestone, Kent, 1592 CKS PRC2/6/63
Jacob, William, Minster in Sheppey, Kent, 1632 CKS PRC2/31/124
Jacob, William, Ditcheat (Alhampton), Som, 1638 Somerset RO D/D/Cta/J4
Jacob/Arnot, Richard, Dorchester, Oxon, 1685 Oxon RO MSS Wills Pec 69/3/9
Jacobb, Hellen, Bobbing, Kent, 1601 CKS PRC2/12/232
Jacobb, John, Cheriton, Kent, 1601 CKS PRC2/12/222
Jacobb, Thomas, Cucklington, Som, 1598 Somerset RO D/D/Cta/J9
Jacobb, William, Folkestone, Kent, 1604 CKS PRC2/14/279
Jacobbe, Cyriack, yeoman, Boughton under Blean, Kent, 1614 CKS PRC20/2/565
Jacobe, William, Queenborough, Kent, 1620 CKS PRC2/22/113
Jacques, Francis, baker, Bristol, Glos, Bristol RO 1783/CP
Jagger, Henry, Lurgashall, Sussex, 1682 W. Suss RO EpI/33/1682/35
Jagow, Peter, gentleman, St Ives, Corn, 1627 Cornwall RO AP/J323/1
Jaineson, Arthur, Davenham (Wharton), Ches, 1596 Cheshire RO (Name) W.C. 1596
James, Allan, husbandman, Queenborough, Kent, 1666 CKS PRC1/11/127
James, Christopher, Wincanton, Som, 1663 Somerset RO D/D/Cta/J3
James, Edward, carpenter, Finchampstead, Berks, 1632 Berks RO D/A1/199/99C
James, Elizabeth, Colton, Staffs, 1731 LJRO/B/C/5/1732/51
James, George, Calne, Wilts, 1639 Wilts RO Miscellaneous Index (name + date)
James, Jane, spinster, Lambourn (East Hanney), Berks, 1620 Berks RO D/A1/199/84C
James, Joan, mercer/widow, Wallingford, Berks, 1621 Berks RO D/A1/199/85D
James, John, butter merchant, Bristol, Glos, Bristol RO 1780/CP
James, John, yeoman, Shepton Mallet, Som, 1606 Somerset RO D/D/Cta/J10
James, John, Gorran, Corn, 1614 Cornwall RO AP/J131/2
James, John, butcher, Stanton, Fen, Hunts, 1752 Hunts RO/Acc58/326
James, John eld, Tetsworth, Oxon, 1626 Oxon RO MSS Wills Pec 43/3/27
James, Margaret, widow, Westport St Mary, Wilts, 1629 Wilts RO Arch. Wilts.(name + date)
James, Mary, widow, Ramsey, Hunts, 1679 Hunts RO/Acc58/142(10)
James, Richard, yeoman, Sulhampstead Bannister, Berks, 1668 Berks RO D/A1/199/125D
James, Richard, Mucclestone, Staffs, 1682 LJRO/B/C/5/1681/23
James, Roger, Maidstone, Kent, 1610 CKS PRC20/2/69
James, Roger, Willingham, North, Lincs, 1644 Lincs RO Ad/Ac/28/85
James, Thomas, Filton, Glos, Bristol RO 1639/57B
James, Thomas, yeoman, Enborne, Berks, 1640 Berks RO D/A1/86/179D
James, William, Gwinear, Corn, 1607 Cornwall RO AP/J80
James, William, labourer, Burghfield, Berks, 1615 Berks RO D/A1/199/73C
James, William, gentleman, Trallong, Breck, 1630 NLW BR 1630/104 Ac

[James:]
James, William, Eastchurch, Sheppey, Kent, 1637 CKS PRC2/34/74
James, William, Barkby, Leics, 1665 Leics RO Administrators Accounts C17th f27
James, William, butcher, Marlow, Great, Bucks, 1678? PRO PROB5/1031
James/Butcher, Richard, husbandman, Speen, Berks, 1617 Berks RO D/A1/199/77C
James, see Armested,
Jameson, William, mariner: 'captain/commander', St Martin in the Fields, London & Middlesex, 1710 Lambeth Palace Arches G59/3
Jancocke, John, Minster in Thanet, Kent, 1583 CKS PRC2/3/131
Jancocke, Robert, yeoman, Alkham, Kent, 1619 CKS PRC2/22/101
Jane, Edward, Kenwyn, Corn, 1612 Cornwall RO AP/J134/1
Janes, Daniel, butler, Oxford (All Souls College), Oxon, 1663 Bodleian HYP B9/3-4
Janney, Charles, Ipstones, Staffs, 1667 LJRO:cards/1667/49
Jansone, John, Bilsington, Kent, 1613 CKS PRC2/17/280
Japp, Thomas, Offord Cluney, Hunts, Hunts RO/Acc58/338
Jaques, Michaell, Haxey (Graizelound), Lincs, 1625 Lincs RO Ad/Ac/39/56
Jaques, Robert, Bicker, Lincs, 1642 Lincs RO Ad/Ac/28/22
Jaques, Robert, butcher, Reading, Berks, 1644 Berks RO D/A1/199/106C
Jarman, George, brewer: 'beerbrewer', Canterbury Holy Cross Westgate, Kent, 1665 CKS PRC1/11/46
Jarman, John, St Laurence Thanet, Kent, 1706 CKS PRC1/16/65
Jarman, John, mariner, St Laurence Thanet, Kent, 1706 CKS PRC1/16/65a
Jarman, Phillip, Appledore, Kent, 1680 CKS PRC2/39/60
Jarman, Stephen, Whitstable, Kent, 1667 CKS PRC1/12/49
Jarman, William, bachelor, Chilham, Kent, 1677 CKS PRC2/37/167
Jarrard, Thomas, Old Romney, Kent, 1585 CKS PRC2/3/272
Jarratt, Marian, Lodsworth, Sussex, 1629 W. Suss RO EpI/33/1629/5
Jarsye, Nicholas, Canterbury St Peter, Kent, 1622 CKS PRC2/23/189
Jarvice, Daniel, yeoman, Elmstone, Kent, 1685 CKS PRC2/40/208
Jarvild, Thomas, Bray, Berks, 1602 Berks RO D/A1/199/55C
Jarvis, George, Woodchurch, Kent, 1603 CKS PRC21/17/27
Jarvis, James, yeoman, Tenterden, Kent, 1679 CKS PRC2/38/47
Jarvis, John, Murston, Kent, 1605 CKS PRC2/13/258
Jarvis, John, Dover St Mary, Kent, 1610 CKS PRC20/2/130
Jarvis, John, Reculver, Kent, 1633 CKS PRC20/11/23
Jarvis, Simon, Charlton, Wilts, 1679 Wilts RO Miscellaneous Index (name + date)
Jarvis, Thomas, collier, Pyrton (Assendon), Oxon, 1629 Oxon RO MSS Wills 298/3/10
Jarvis, Thomas, Upavon, Wilts, 1642 Wilts RO Arch. Sarum(+ name and date)
Jarvis, William, yeoman, Sheffield, Yorks, 1772 Borthwick Test C.P. 1772/1
Jarvise, Matthew, Sandwich, Kent, 1629 CKS PRC2/30/72
Jasper, Valintine, Canterbury St Peter, Kent, 1680 CKS PRC2/39/61
Jayes, John, Orton Longueville, Hunts, 1677 Hunts RO/Acc58/99(21)
Jayne, Ann, widow, Henbury, Glos, Bristol RO 1773/CP
Jaynes, Richard, Epworth, Lincs, 1682 Lincs RO Ad/Ac/34/91
Jeakin, Henrie, mariner: 'seafaring man', Sandwich, Kent, 1637 CKS PRC2/34/71
Jeakin, see Bateman,
Jeakins, John, Ospringe, Kent, 1598 CKS PRC2/10/389
Jeakins, Thomazine, widow, Ospringe, Kent, 1634 CKS PRC2/32/67
Jeames, John, Calne, Wilts, 1594 Wilts RO Miscellaneous Index (name + date)
Jeames, John, Eastchurch, Sheppey, Kent, 1608 CKS PRC2/14/268
Jeames, John, Itchenor, West, Sussex, 1631 W. Suss RO EpI/33/1631/19
Jeames, William, Martock, Som, 1679 Somerset RO D/D/Cta/J15
Jeameson, John, St Pauls Walden, Herts, 1595 Herts RO ASA25/1518
Jeanes, Robert, Moorlinch, Som, 1592 Somerset RO D/D/Cta/J13
Jeans, Christopher, Chinnock, East, Som, 1735 Somerset RO D/D/Cta/J14
Jeans, Edmund, Middlezoy, Som, 1737 Somerset RO D/D/Cta/J16

Jeans, Richard, Donhead St Mary, Wilts, 1703 Wilts RO Arch. Sarum(+ name and date)
Jebb, Walter, labourer, Deeping St James, Lincs, 1668 Lincs RO Ad/Ac/33/49
Jebson, Thomas, milliner, Worlaby, Lincs, 1614 Lincs RO Ad/Ac/13/165
Jecoxe, George, Burford, Warks, 1604 Worcs RO 008.7 BA3585/839/379
Jee, George, farmer, Bulkington, Warks, 1791 LJRO/B/C/5/1791/40
Jeekey, John, innholder, Speen (Speenhamland), Berks, 1610 Berks RO D/A1/199/67C
Jefery, Thomas, St Nicholas at Wade, Kent, 1616 CKS PRC20/3/414
Jefferie, John, gentleman, Gloucester, Glos, 1706 GRO GDR/B4/2/J16
Jefferie, Richard, Maiden Bradley, Wilts, 1597 Wilts RO Miscellaneous Index (name + date)
Jefferie, William, Redbourn, Herts, 1633 Herts RO ASA25/4896
Jefferies, Mary, Kilmington, Som, 1616 Somerset RO D/D/Cta/J11
Jefferies, Nicholas, Beer Hackett, Dors, 1637 Wilts RO Unlisted Fragment
Jefferies, Robert, husbandman, Frittenden, Kent, 1664 CKS PRC1/10/57
Jefferis, Amy, widow, Deal, Kent, 1670 CKS PRC19/4/83
Jefferson, Thomas, Haxey (Burnham), Lincs, 1681 Lincs RO Ad/Ac/34/79
Jeffery, George, Frinstead, Kent, 1681 CKS PRC2/39/62
Jeffery, Henry, Gwithian, Corn, 1600 Cornwall RO AP/J122/1
Jeffery, Henry, Bremhill, Wilts, 1633 Wilts RO Arch. Wilts.(name + date)
Jeffery, James eld, Cookham (Northrow), Berks, 1637 Berks RO D/A1/199/103C
Jeffery, Joane, widow, Maidstone, Kent, 1685 CKS PRC20/13/434
Jeffery, John, Canterbury St Paul, Kent, 1625 CKS PRC2/25/77
Jeffery, John, St Nicholas at Wade, Kent, 1639 CKS PRC20/11/1
Jeffery, John, Minster in Sheppey, Kent, 1640 CKS PRC1/2/80
Jeffery, John, gentleman, Boughton Monchelsea, Kent, 1673 CKS PRC2/35/229
Jeffery, John, husbandman, Sherbourne, Dors, 1720 Wilts RO Miscellaneous Index (name + date)
Jeffery, John eld, Rolvenden, Kent, 1671 CKS PRC20/12/16
Jeffery, Peter, Ebbesbourne Wake, Wilts, 1616? Wilts RO Miscellaneous Index (name + date)
Jeffery, Richard, weaver: 'broad weaver', Cranbrook, Kent, 1616 CKS PRC2/22/105
Jeffery, Richard, Preston, East, Sussex, 1684 W. Suss RO EpI/33/1684/11
Jeffery, Robert, Huntspill, Som, 1676 Somerset RO D/D/Cta/J17
Jeffery, Stephen, husbandman, Minster in Sheppey, Kent, 1678 CKS PRC2/38/45
Jeffery, Timothy, Salisbury St Thomas, Wilts, 1671 Wilts RO Miscellaneous Index (name + date)
Jeffery, William, gentleman, Box, Wilts, 1678 Wilts RO Miscellaneous Index (name + date)
Jefferye, David, Blean, Kent, 1607 CKS PRC20/1/265
Jefferys, Henry, Woodstock, Oxon, 1684 Oxon RO MSS Wills 82/2/4
Jefford, Henry, Ash next Sandwich, Kent, 1629 CKS PRC20/8/291
Jefford, Robert, Woodnesborough, Kent, 1677 CKS PRC2/37/49
Jeffraye, Margerye, widow, Stalisfield, Kent, 1604 CKS PRC2/14/275
Jeffrey, Henry, weaver, Rickmansworth, Herts, 1602 Herts RO ASA25/4759
Jeffrey, John, Chieveley, Berks, 1607 Berks RO D/A1/199/60C
Jeffrey, John, bachelor, Moulton, Lincs, 1639 Lincs RO Ad/Ac/26/296
Jeffrey, Peeter, Sheldwich, Kent, 1600 CKS PRC2/11/237
Jeffreye, John, Otterden, Kent, 1616 CKS PRC2/22/179
Jeffreys, Anne, Hameringham, Lincs, 1626 Lincs RO Ad/Ac/20/85
Jeffreys, Thomas, Brecon, Breck, 1639 NLW BR 1638/8 Ac
Jeffrie, William, Hagbourne (Ginge), Oxon, 1593 Berks RO D/A1/199/44C
Jeffries, Anne, Hameringham, Lincs, 1626 Lincs RO Ad/Ac/20/117
Jeffry, William, tanner, Bradfield, Berks, 1687 Berks RO D/A1/199/143C
Jeffrys, James, labourer, Snelston, Derby, 1726 LJRO/B/C/5/1726/44
Jeffs, John, Aynho, Northants, 1680 Northants RO NWill A/C/9
Jekin, William, Hawkhurst, Kent, 1635 CKS PRC2/33/67
Jekins, Thomas, Boxley, Kent, 1667 CKS PRC1/11/128
Jell, John, Billingford, Norf, 1710 Norfolk RO ANW/23/10/63
Jelleflower, Richard, chapman: 'petty chapman', Maidstone, Kent, 1601 CKS PRC21/16/186
Jelliman, Robert, husbandman, Drayton, Berks, 1603 Berks RO D/A1/199/56C

[Jellings:]
Jellings, John, Stanton, Fen, Hunts, 1677 Hunts RO/Acc58/107(35)
Jellion, Catherine, Woodhall, Lincs, 1636 Lincs RO Ad/Ac/24/260
Jellow, Richard, husbandman, Holbeach, Lincs, 1623 Lincs RO Ad/Ac/19A/110
Jellowe, Richard, husbandman, Holbeach, Lincs, 1623 Lincs RO Ad/Ac/18/1
Jellowes, Alexander, Deeping, Market, Lincs, 1612 Lincs RO Ad/Ac/11/147
Jellowes, John, Moulton, Lincs, 1614 Lincs RO Ad/Ac/13/77
Jelly, Richard + Mercie, Salisbury St Edmund, Wilts, 1631 Wilts RO Miscellaneous Index (name + date)
Jelson, Christopher, Fleet, Lincs, 1625? Lincs RO Ad/Ac/19B/100
Jematt, William, Reading St Giles, Berks, 1610 Berks RO D/A1/199/63C
Jemmat, Thomas, Newbury, Berks, 1610 Berks RO D/A1/199/61C
Jemmet, John, butcher, Boughton Aluph, Kent, 1623 CKS PRC2/23/194
Jemmett, John, Linsted, Kent, 1626 CKS PRC2/27/82
Jemmett, Michaell, Warehorne, Kent, 1610 CKS PRC2/15/200
Jemmett, Thomas, Whitstable, Kent, 1617 CKS PRC2/22/106
Jemmett, Warham, Canterbury St Paul, Kent, 1626 CKS PRC2/27/83
Jemmett, Warham eld, Canterbury St Paul, Kent, 1617 CKS PRC2/22/109
Jemmett, Warham eld, gentleman, Canterbury St Paul, Kent, 1617 CKS PRC2/22/99
Jenckes, Thomas, Warwick, Worcs, Worcs RO 008.7 BA3585/834/435
Jenens/Haman, Richard, Harwell, Berks, 1583 Berks RO D/A2/C19/f80-1
Jenifer, John, Dover, Kent, 1665 CKS PRC19/3/54
Jenings, Joane, widow, Kingsnorth, Kent, 1665 CKS PRC1/11/47
Jenings, William, husbandman, Bourne, Lincs, 1683 Lincs RO Ad/Ac/44/96
Jenings/Marchant, Thomas, bachelor: 'singleman', Burghfield, Berks, 1610 Berks RO D/A1/191/115A
Jenken, Christopher, Folkestone, Kent, 1616 CKS PRC2/22/100
Jenken, Henry, Lyminge, Kent, 1625 CKS PRC20/7/391
Jenken, John, Chislet, Kent, 1635 CKS PRC2/33/70
Jenken, William, Luddenham, Kent, 1637 CKS PRC2/33/68
Jenkens, Benjamin, Wimborne Minster, Dors, 1640 Dorset RO PE/WM CP 2/4/59
Jenkin, An, widow, Maidstone, Kent, 1623 CKS PRC20/6/340
Jenkin, John, Folkestone, Kent, 1620 CKS PRC2/22/117
Jenkin, Mathew, gentleman, Folkestone, Kent, 1631 CKS PRC2/31/48
Jenkin, Michaell, St Peter in Thanet, Kent, 1626 CKS PRC2/27/81
Jenkin, Stephen, St Peter in Thanet, Kent, 1623 CKS PRC2/23/197
Jenkine, John, Lympne, Kent, 1605 CKS PRC2/14/261
Jenkins, Clement, Shoreham, Old (Erringham), Sussex, 1606 W. Suss RO EpI/33/1606/9
Jenkins, John, St Ives, Hunts, 1694 Hunts RO/Acc58/278
Jenkins, Mary, widow, St Martin in the Fields, London & Middlesex, 1685 PRO PROB32/25/30
Jenkins, Richard, St Laurence Thanet, Kent, 1599 CKS PRC2/10/473
Jenkins, Thomas, hooper, Bristol, Glos, Bristol RO 1778/CP
Jenkins, Thomas, Nailsea, Som, 1695 Somerset RO D/D/Cta/J18
Jenkinson, George, Frampton, Lincs, 1641 Lincs RO Ad/Ac/27/216
Jenkinson, Henry, Witham, South, Lincs, 1663 Lincs RO Ad/Ac/43/7
Jenkinson, John, yeoman, Brotherton, Yorks, 1840 Borthwick Test C.P. 1840/8
Jenkinson, Matthew, St Johns Thanet, Kent, 1637 CKS PRC2/34/72
Jenkinson, Peeter, Wickhambreaux, Kent, 1610 CKS PRC2/15/202
Jenkinson, Robarte, clergy: 'clerk/vicar', St Johns Thanet, Kent, 1603 CKS PRC2/12/447
Jenkyn, Margarett, widow, St Peter in Thanet, Kent, 1617 CKS PRC2/22/111
Jenkyn, Richard, Lyminge, Kent, 1596 CKS PRC21/14/63
Jenkyn, William, Gwinear, Corn, 1606 Cornwall RO AP/J53
Jenkynson, Wyllyam, Canterbury St Andrew, Kent, 1572 CKS PRC2/1/61
Jenman, Nicholas, Marden, East, Sussex, 1632 W. Suss RO EpI/33/1631/13
Jenman, William, Marden, East, Sussex, 1613 W. Suss RO EpI/33/1613/7
Jenman, William, Marden, East, Sussex, 1613 W. Suss RO EpI/33/1613/25

[Jenner:]
Jenner, Anne, widow, St Peter le Poor, London & Middlesex, 1686 Lambeth Palace Arches GG36/1
Jennett, Thomas, Newbury, Berks, 1623 Wilts RO CC Sarum(+ name and date)
Jennett, Thomas, Ashford, Kent, 1685 CKS PRC2/40/209
Jenninges, Richard, Biddenden, Kent, 1602 CKS PRC2/12/230
Jennings, Budworth, Great (Over Whitley), Ches, 1604 Cheshire RO (Name) W.C. 1604
Jennings, Anne, Bonnington, Kent, 1634 CKS PRC2/32/68
Jennings, Anthony, yeoman, Swallowfield, Berks, 1623 Berks RO D/A1/199/87C
Jennings, Benjamin, Alcester, Warks, 1684 Worcs RO 008.7 BA3585/837/bdl 4
Jennings, Edward, weaver, East Sutton, Kent, 1675 CKS PRC2/36/80
Jennings, Gabriel, lath cleaver, Pluckley, Kent, 1691 CKS PRC2/42/7
Jennings, John, Wedmore, Som, 1625 Somerset RO D/D/Cta/J6
Jennings, John, tailor, Tew, Great, Oxon, 1627 Oxon RO MSS Wills 37/3/15
Jennings, John, miller, Faversham, Kent, 1663 CKS PRC1/9/32
Jennings, John, Beaulieu, Hants, 1674 Hants RO 21m65 D8/267
Jennings, John, Mucclestone, Staffs, 1680 LJRO:cards/1680/21
Jennings, John, Rotherfield Greys, Oxon, 1684 Oxon RO MSS Wills 168/3/20
Jennings, John, mariner, Dover, Kent, 1684 CKS PRC20/13/436
Jennings, Jonas, miller: 'corn miller', Bradford, Yorks, 1811 Borthwick Test C.P. 1811/4
Jennings, Robert, Harwell, Berks, Berks RO D/A1/86/148
Jennings, Ruth, widow, Tattershall, Lincs, 1670 Lincs RO Ad/Ac/32/200
Jennings, Samuel, weaver: 'linen weaver', Kingsnorth, Kent, 1670 CKS PRC1/15/38
Jennings, Thomas, Biddenden, Kent, 1612 CKS PRC2/17/323
Jennings, Thomas, Farcet, Hunts, 1677 Hunts RO/Acc58/97(44)
Jennings, Thomas, Farcet, Hunts, 1678 Hunts RO/Acc58/122(52)
Jennings, Timothy, Linton, Kent, 1698 CKS PRC2/42/143
Jennings, William, Melksham, Wilts, 1616 Wilts RO Miscellaneous Index (name + date)
Jennings, William, Wantage, Berks, 1679 Wilts RO Dean Sarum (name + date)
Jennings, William, Alfrick, Worcs, 1682 Worcs RO 008.7 BA3585/837/bdl 3
Jennings/Merchant, Thomas, yeoman, Reading St Giles (Whitley), Berks, 1640 Berks RO D/A1/86/177E
Jennynges, Thomas, Easton Grey, Wilts, 1616 Wilts RO Arch. Wilts.(name + date)
Jennyson, Frauncys, Theddlethorpe, Lincs, 1612 Lincs RO Ad/Ac/11/19
Jennyson, Margaret, Elsham, Lincs, 1611 Lincs RO Ad/Ac/10/107
Jenyngs, William, St Johns Thanet, Kent, 1596 CKS PRC2/8/29
Jeofferie, John, husbandman, Drayton, Berks, 1646 Berks RO D/A1/199/109C
Jephcoate, Thomas, Ryton on Dunsmore, Warks, 1675 LJRO:cards/1675/36
Jerman, Jane, Faversham, Kent, 1639 CKS PRC1/2/81
Jerman, Michael, Faversham, Kent, 1627 CKS PRC2/28/71
Jerman, William, Canterbury Holy Cross Westgate, Kent, 1627 CKS PRC2/28/70
Jerom, see Lyarde,
Jerome, William, miller, Abingdon, Berks, 1641 Berks RO D/A1/199/104
Jerrard, Christopher, Wimborne Minster, Dors, 1663 Dorset RO PE/WM CP 2/4/65
Jerrom, Bartholomew, Faversham, Kent, 1627 CKS PRC2/28/68
Jerum, Israell, Faversham, Kent, 1639 CKS PRC1/2/82
Jervice, John, High Halden, Kent, 1622 CKS PRC2/23/193
Jervice, Jone, High Halden, Kent, 1622 CKS PRC2/23/192
Jervice, Robert + Sybill, Minster in Thanet, Kent, 1637 CKS PRC2/34/70
Jervice, William, yeoman, Chesterton, Oxon, 1676 Oxon RO MSS Wills 82/1/20
Jervis, Edward, Tenterden, Kent, 1619 CKS PRC2/22/110
Jervis, John, Milton next Sittingbourne, Kent, 1622 CKS PRC2/23/191
Jervis, John, Huntspill, Som, 1703 Somerset RO D/D/Cta/J19
Jervis, Lydia, spinster, Canterbury St Alphege, Kent, 1612 CKS PRC20/2/374
Jervis, Robert, Luddenham, Kent, 1641 CKS PRC1/4/65
Jervis, William, Blockley, Worcs, 1596 Worcs RO 008.7 BA3585/838/119

[Jervys:]
Jervys, John, Ivychurch, Kent, 1580 CKS PRC21/4/236
Jervys, John, High Halden, Kent, 1600 CKS PRC2/11/239
Jervys, Katheryn, Lydd, Kent, 1582 CKS PRC21/6/39
Jesop, Alexander, Rand, Lincs, 1611 Lincs RO Ad/Ac/10/83
Jesop, Cutbeard, Maidstone, Kent, 1616 CKS PRC20/3/417
Jesopp, Cutbeard, Maidstone, Kent, 1618 CKS PRC20/4/208
Jesopp, Cutberd, Maidstone, Kent, 1622 CKS PRC20/6/338
Jesopp, John, Asgarby, Lincs, 1641? Lincs RO Ad/Ac/27/339
Jesopp, Richard, Quadring, Lincs, 1614 Lincs RO Ad/Ac/13/203
Jessett/Wing?, Andrew?,
Berks 1599 Berks RO D/A1/199/53
Jessop, Edward, Rauceby, Lincs, 1648 Lincs RO Ad/Ac/30/305
Jessop, Robert, yeoman, Witham on the Hill, Lincs, 1648 Lincs RO Ad/Ac/30/265
Jessope, Esay, Aldington, Kent, 1616 CKS PRC20/3/421
Jessopp, Richard, Horsington, Lincs, 1632 Lincs RO Ad/Ac/23/51
Jessopp, Thomas, Swarby, Lincs, 1601 Lincs RO Ad/Ac/5/157
Jessopp, Thomas, Ruckinge, Kent, 1662 CKS PRC1/8/105
Jetter, Thomas, brazier, Maidstone, Kent, 1676 CKS PRC20/12/204
Jevins, William, Aston, Warks, 1663 LJRO:cards/1663/37
Jevon, Paul, farmer, Sedgley (Lower Gornall), Staffs, 1821 LJRO/B/C/5/1821/28
Jew, John, Feckenham, Worcs, 1682 Worcs RO 008.7 BA3585/837/bdl 3
Jew, Robert, Grafton Flyford, Worcs, 1604 Worcs RO 008.7 BA3585/839/366
Jewell, Elizabeth, widow, Marden, Kent, 1616 CKS PRC2/22/112
Jewell, John, Marden, Kent, 1610 CKS PRC2/15/199
Jewell, John, Marden, Kent, 1640 CKS PRC1/4/66
Jewell, Roger, Birchington, Kent, 1597 CKS PRC21/14/151
Jewer, Anne, Midhurst, Sussex, 1676 W. Suss RO EpI/33/1676/6
Jewer, Elizabeth, widow, Easebourne, Sussex, 1672 W. Suss RO EpI/33/1672/3
Jewett, Henry, butcher, Queenborough, Kent, 1670 CKS PRC1/15/39
Jewkes, William, Worcester, Worcs, 1601 Worcs RO 008.7 BA3585/838/201
Jewyll, James, Norton Disney, Lincs, 1614 Lincs RO Ad/Ac/13/159
Jezard, Mary, widow, Sturry, Kent, 1711 CKS PRC1/17/31
Jinking, John, St Enoder, Corn, 1606 Cornwall RO AP/J72
Jinking/Peller, Benedict, tailor, Breage, Corn, 1610 Cornwall RO AP/J123/2
Joad, John, Stourmouth, Kent, 1598 CKS PRC2/9/464
Joade, Andrew, yeoman, Chislet, Kent, 1675 CKS PRC2/36/208
Joade, Andrew, Chislet, Kent, 1678 CKS PRC2/38/46
Joade, Mary eld, widow, Stourmouth, Kent, 1633 CKS PRC2/32/71
Joade, Richard, mariner, St Peter in Thanet, Kent, 1716 CKS PRC1/18/8
Joade, Robert, St Peter in Thanet, Kent, 1674 CKS PRC1/15/85
Joanes, Griffine, Deal, Kent, 1606 CKS PRC20/1/177
Joanes, Isaac, Egerton, Kent, 1682 CKS PRC19/4/112
Joanes, James, Minster in Thanet, Kent, 1627 CKS PRC2/28/67
Joanes, Robert, yeoman, Faversham, Kent, 1641 CKS PRC1/4/67
Joanes, Thomas, Ospringe, Kent, 1605 CKS PRC2/13/253
Joanes, Walter, innholder, Benenden, Kent, 1681 CKS PRC2/39/196
Joanns?, Thomas, Ruckinge, Kent, 1674 CKS PRC2/36/79
Joberns, Joseph, farmer, Shenstone (Wood End), Staffs, 1801 LJRO/B/C/5/1801/34
Jobson, William, Dover, Kent, 1623 CKS PRC20/6/334
Joce, Reginold, husbandman, Lanteglos-by-Camelford, Corn, 1610 Cornwall RO AP/J63/2
Jode, William, Stourmouth, Kent, 1599 CKS PRC2/10/175
John, James, Madron, Corn, 1636 Cornwall RO AP/J413/3
John, Richard, Constantine, Corn, 1606 Cornwall RO AP/J56
John, Thomas, Blisland, Corn, 1640 Cornwall RO AP/J452/3
John/Trevewha, John, Crowan, Corn, Cornwall RO AP/J75/2

Johncocke, John, Minster in Thanet, Kent, 1608 CKS PRC2/14/263
Johncocke, Richard, Capel le Ferne, Kent, 1639 CKS PRC1/2/83
Johncocke, Robert, Cheriton, Kent, 1638 CKS PRC2/34/222
Johncocke, Thomas, Elham, Kent, 1597 CKS PRC2/10/8
Johncocke, Thomas, husbandman, Sturry, Kent, 1686 CKS PRC2/41/57
Johnes, Thomas, clergy: 'vicar', Sturry, Kent, 1683 CKS PRC1/15/98
Johns, Lewes, St Nicholas at Wade, Kent, 1583 CKS PRC21/6/351
Johns, Nicholas, husbandman, Eastchurch, Sheppey, Kent, 1672 CKS PRC2/35/146
Johns, Thomas, Hernhill, Kent, 1586 CKS PRC21/8/82
Johnson, Abraham, Sandwich St Peter, Kent, 1667 CKS PRC1/12/50
Johnson, Abraham, merchant, Dover, Kent, 1681 CKS PRC20/13/149
Johnson, Andrewe, Smeeth, Kent, 1596 CKS PRC21/14/23
Johnson, Anne, Chester, Ches, 1631 Cheshire RO (Name) W.C. 1629/30
Johnson, Anne, Gainsborough, Lincs, 1673 Lincs RO Ad/Ac/35/61
Johnson, Anne, widow, Haxey, Lincs, 1674 Lincs RO Ad/Ac/35/74
Johnson, Arthur, Maidstone, Kent, 1590 CKS PRC21/10/74
Johnson, Arthure, Bonnington, Kent, 1620 CKS PRC2/22/118
Johnson, Benjamine, Sutterton, Lincs, 1627 Lincs RO Ad/Ac/20b/64
Johnson, Brian, Bottesford, Lincs, 1628 Lincs RO Ad/Ac/39/11
Johnson, Charles, labourer, Lenton, Lincs, 1670 Lincs RO Ad/Ac/32/201
Johnson, Clemens, spinster, Lympne, Kent, 1592 CKS PRC2/5/326
Johnson, Edmund, Burmarsh, Kent, 1625 CKS PRC2/25/78
Johnson, Edmund, Bishopsbourne, Kent, 1628 CKS PRC2/29/56
Johnson, Edmund, butcher, Irnham, Lincs, 1637 Lincs RO Ad/Ac/25/411
Johnson, Edward, Barton on Humber, Lincs, 1632 Lincs RO Ad/Ac/23/178
Johnson, Edward, Maker, Corn, 1637 Cornwall RO AP/J415/2
Johnson, Edward, mercer, Heckington, Lincs, 1680 Lincs RO Ad/Ac/34/53
Johnson, Edward, Alcester, Warks, 1684 Worcs RO 008.7 BA3585/837/bdl 4
Johnson, Elias, Sandwich, Kent, 1640 CKS PRC1/4/68
Johnson, Elias, Sandwich, Kent, 1641 CKS PRC1/5/109
Johnson, Elizabeth, Woodchurch, Kent, 1620 CKS PRC20/4/202
Johnson, Elizabeth, widow, Faversham, Kent, 1624 CKS PRC2/23/200
Johnson, Elizabeth, Yarburgh, Lincs, 1641 Lincs RO Ad/Ac/27/24
Johnson, Esdras, Canterbury St Andrew, Kent, 1598 CKS PRC2/10/51
Johnson, Francis, Boston, Lincs, 1607 Lincs RO Ad/Ac/8a/101
Johnson, George, Leicester St Mary, Leics, 1641 Leics RO PR/I/41A/79
Johnson, Godferye, Wye, Kent, 1599 CKS PRC2/11/111
Johnson, Henrie, Bigby, Lincs, 1627 Lincs RO Ad/Ac/20/114
Johnson, Henry, Hurst, Berks, 1631 3 7 Wilts RO Miscellaneous Index (name + date)
Johnson, Henry, Bury, Hunts, 1676 Hunts RO/Acc58/23(147)
Johnson, Henry, coachman, St Martin in the Fields, London & Middlesex, 1679 Greater London RO AM/PP/Box 1679-1684 pt (uncatalogued)
Johnson, Hugh, Hale, Great (Little Hale), Lincs, 1642 Lincs RO Ad/Ac/28/35
Johnson, Issable, Thimbleby, Lincs, 1611 Lincs RO Ad/Ac/10/42
Johnson, Jane, widow, Sandwich St Peter, Kent, 1599 CKS PRC2/10/458
Johnson, Jane, Gedney, Lincs, 1606 Lincs RO Ad/Ac/7/136
Johnson, Jane, widow, Steeping, Great, Lincs, 1633 Lincs RO Ad/Ac/24/125
Johnson, Joan, widow, Newport, Shrops, 1765 LJRO/B/C/5/1765/87
Johnson, Joane, widow, Stone in Oxney, Kent, 1617 CKS PRC2/22/116
Johnson, John, yeoman, Bradfield, Berks, 1619 Berks RO D/A1/199/79C
Johnson, John, Deal, Kent, 1626 CKS PRC20/7/397
Johnson, John, Sempringham (Pointon), Lincs, 1629 Lincs RO Ad/Ac/22/6
Johnson, John, Preston next Wingham, Kent, 1632 CKS PRC20/11/19
Johnson, John, Drayton, Berks, 1633 Berks RO D/A1/199/98C
Johnson, John, Upton (Kexby), Lincs, 1649 Lincs RO Ad/Ac/40/159

[Johnson:]
Johnson, John, mariner, St Johns Thanet, Kent, 1661 CKS PRC1/8/106
Johnson, John, miller, Hanborough, Oxon, 1662 Oxon RO MSS Wills 168/3/7
Johnson, John, Belton All Saints, Lincs, 1663 Lincs RO Ad/Ac/41/89
Johnson, John, Angmering, Sussex, 1669 W. Suss RO EpI/33/1669/13
Johnson, John, ropemaker, Sellindge, Kent, 1679 CKS PRC2/38/148
Johnson, John, yeoman, Kenardington, Kent, 1680 CKS PRC2/39/64
Johnson, John, Morton, Lincs, 1682 Lincs RO Ad/Ac/34/90
Johnson, John, Murston, Kent, 1700 CKS PRC19/5/74
Johnson, John, Appledore, Kent, 1712 CKS PRC19/6/54
Johnson, John, St Bride, London & Middlesex, 1743 Greater London RO DL/C/550/72
Johnson, Jonathan, carpenter, Birmingham, Warks, 1744 LJRO/B/C/5/1744/221
Johnson, Joseph eld, Houghton, Great, Northants, 1770 Northants RO X954/21/21
Johnson, Joseph eld, Houghton, Great, Northants, 1771 Northants RO X954/21/22
Johnson, Judith, mrs, St Laurence Thanet, Kent, 1633 CKS PRC2/32/69
Johnson, Katherine, 1584 Lancs RO (Name of Deceased) D.R.C.H. 1583
Johnson, Katherine, Epworth, Lincs, 1662 Lincs RO Ad/Ac/41/77
Johnson, Lawrence, Huttoft, Lincs, 1626 Lincs RO Ad/Ac/20/5
Johnson, Leonard, labourer, Orby, Lincs, 1637 Lincs RO Ad/Ac/25/453
Johnson, Margarett, widow, Huttoft, Lincs, 1626 Lincs RO Ad/Ac/20/19
Johnson, Mary, widow, Frieston, Lincs, 1626 Lincs RO Ad/Ac/20/59
Johnson, Mary, Broughton, Northants, 1681 Northants RO NWill A/C/67
Johnson, Mathewe, Hurst, Kent, 1605 CKS PRC2/14/266
Johnson, Nicholas, Hythe West, Kent, 1589 CKS PRC2/5/350
Johnson, Ralph, husbandman, Brereton, Ches, 1588 Cheshire RO (Name) W.C. 1588
Johnson, Ralph, gentleman, Pilham, Lincs, 1665 Lincs RO Ad/Ac/41/170
Johnson, Raphe, Torksey, Lincs, 1587 Lincs RO Ad/Ac/37/5
Johnson, Richard, Bishopthorpe, Yorks, Borthwick Test C.P. 1762/1
Johnson, Richard, Thorpe on the Hill, Lincs, Lincs RO Ad/Ac/4/93
Johnson, Richard, Upton (Kexby), Lincs, 1623 Lincs RO Ad/Ac/8c/53
Johnson, Richard, Barnoldby le Beck, Lincs, 1626 Lincs RO Ad/Ac/20/67
Johnson, Richard, Snargate, Kent, 1630 CKS PRC20/9/259
Johnson, Richard, Hythe St Leonard, Kent, 1639 CKS PRC20/11/25
Johnson, Richard, husbandman, Dover, Kent, 1641 CKS PRC19/2/23
Johnson, Robert, Humberstone, Lincs, 1605 Lincs RO Ad/Ac/6/18
Johnson, Robert, yeoman, Reading St Lawrence, Berks, 1609 Berks RO D/A1/86/103F
Johnson, Robert, Apley (Kingthorpe), Lincs, 1612 Lincs RO Ad/Ac/10/124
Johnson, Robert, Otterden, Kent, 1617 CKS PRC2/22/107
Johnson, Robert, Sandwich, Kent, 1625 CKS PRC2/25/75
Johnson, Robert, Preston next Wingham, Kent, 1630 CKS PRC2/30/92
Johnson, Robert, Leake, Lincs, 1641 Lincs RO Ad/Ac/27/299
Johnson, Robert, Lea, Lincs, 1646 Lincs RO Ad/Ac/40/127
Johnson, Robert, Desford, Leics, 1666 Leics RO Administrators Accounts C17th f63
Johnson, Robert, Sonning, Berks, 1675 Wilts RO Miscellaneous Index (name + date)
Johnson, Robert, Beckley, Oxon, 1684 Oxon RO MSS Wills 168/3/21
Johnson, Ruthe, widow, Wellingore, Lincs, 1652 Lincs RO Ad/Ac/42/29
Johnson, Simon, glover, Newbury, Berks, 1618 Berks RO D/A1/199/80C
Johnson, Thomas, Barwell, Leics, Leics RO Administrators Accounts 1667-72 f87
Johnson, Thomas, Hawkhurst, Kent, 1598 CKS PRC2/10/340
Johnson, Thomas, Faversham, Kent, 1613 CKS PRC2/18/80
Johnson, Thomas, St Mary in the Marsh, Kent, 1615 CKS PRC2/22/102
Johnson, Thomas, clergy: 'clerk', Old Romney, Kent, 1623 CKS PRC2/23/196
Johnson, Thomas, Potter Hanworth, Lincs, 1629 Lincs RO Ad/Ac/22/69
Johnson, Thomas, clergy: 'clerk', Huttoft, Lincs, 1629 Lincs RO Ad/Ac/22/56
Johnson, Thomas, 1639? Lincs RO Ad/Ac/40/286
Johnson, Thomas, yeoman, Gedney, Lincs, 1666 Lincs RO Ad/Ac/32/90

Johnson, Thomas, yeoman, Friskney, Lincs, 1667 Lincs RO Ad/Ac/33/3
Johnson, Thomas, Tarring, West, Sussex, 1671 W. Suss RO EpIV/10/2A/12
Johnson, Thomas, butcher, Sandwich, Kent, 1673 CKS PRC2/35/230
Johnson, Thomas, clergy: 'clerk', Lincoln St Margaret in the Close, Lincs, 1677 Lincs RO Ad/Ac/42/73
Johnson, Thomas, gentleman, Fordwich, Kent, 1677 CKS PRC2/37/50
Johnson, Thomas, preacher: 'gospel preacher', Birstall, Yorks, 1804 Borthwick Test C.P. 1804/14
Johnson, William, husbandman, Tetney, Lincs, 1606 Lincs RO Ad/Ac/7/90
Johnson, William, Claxby Pluckacre, Lincs, 1607 Lincs RO Ad/Ac/8a/103
Johnson, William, Faldingworth, Lincs, 1607 Lincs RO Ad/Ac/37/231
Johnson, William, Gawsworth, Ches, 1609 Cheshire RO (Name) W.C. 1609
Johnson, William, cardmaker, Reading, Berks, 1615 Berks RO D/A1/199/72C
Johnson, William, Preston next Wingham, Kent, 1625 CKS PRC2/25/79
Johnson, William, Gosberton, Lincs, 1627 Lincs RO Ad/Ac/20b/83
Johnson, William, tailor, Hykeham, North, Lincs, 1668 Lincs RO Ad/Ac/33/55
Johnson, William, Ludford, Lincs, 1670 Lincs RO Ad/Ac/32/224
Johnson, William, Crowle, Lincs, 1672 Lincs RO Ad/Ac/35/42
Johnson, William, cordwainer, Horncastle, Lincs, 1673 Lincs RO Ad/Ac/35/32
Johnson, William, yeoman, Frodingham (Brumby), Lincs, 1675 Lincs RO Ad/Ac/35/87
Johnson, William, clergy: 'clerk', Brabourne, Kent, 1677 CKS PRC2/37/165
Johnson, William, Leek, Staffs, 1685 LJRO/B/C/5/1684/45
Johnson, William, husbandman, Astbury (Smallwood), Ches, 1773 Cheshire RO (Name) W.C. 1773
Johnson, William, gentleman, Hull (Paradise Place), Yorks, 1830 Borthwick Test C.P. 1830/1
Johnson/Browne, Browne/John, Dover, Kent, 1574 CKS PRC21/2/141
Johnson/Cookloe, Cornelius, Sandwich, Kent, 1626 CKS PRC2/27/80
Johnson/Faulkner, Margaret, Stretton, Lancs, 1622 Lancs RO (Name of Deceased) D.R.C.H. 1622
Johnson/Widdowes, Jane, widow, Lowton, Lancs, 1634 Lancs RO (Name of Deceased) D.R.C.H. 1634
Johnston, Samuel, vintner, St Martin in the Fields, London & Middlesex, 1707 PRO PROB32/50/25
Joice, Elizabeth, Sandwich, Kent, 1628 CKS PRC2/29/55
Joie, George, clergy: 'clerk', Elmstone, Kent, 1602 CKS PRC2/12/224
Jolland, Marke, Rasen, Middle, Lincs, 1632 Lincs RO Ad/Ac/23/20
Jollands, William, Gainsborough, Lincs, 1619 Lincs RO Ad/Ac/8b/393
Jollands/Richardson, Isabell, Scothorne, Lincs, 1627 Lincs RO Ad/Ac/39/60
Jolley, John, university: 'scholar's servant/privileged person', Cambridge St Mary the Great, Cambs, 1639 CUL V.C. Acc./Box2/41
Jolley, William, Derby St Peter, Derby, 1685 LJRO/B/C/5/1685/56
Jollie, Thomas, yeoman, Mumby, Lincs, 1627 Lincs RO Ad/Ac/20/95
Jollie, William, Cambridge, Cambs, 1611 CUL V.C.Acc./Box1/31
Jollvord, Gilbert, Meare, Som, 1623 Somerset RO D/D/Cta/J7
Jollye, James, yeoman, Kirkby on Bain, Lincs, 1612 Lincs RO Ad/Ac/11/27
Jones, Anne, widow, Newbury, Berks, 1584 Berks RO D/A2/C19/f149
Jones, Anne, widow, Wingham, Kent, 1616 CKS PRC20/3/250
Jones, Catherine, Tardebigge, Worcs, 1682 Worcs RO 008.7 BA3585/837/bdl 3
Jones, David, Canterbury St Martin, Kent, 1640 CKS PRC19/1/55
Jones, Edmund, Rainham, Kent, 1618 CKS PRC2/22/108
Jones, Edward, university: 'scholar's servant', Cambridge St Benedict, Cambs, 1634 CUL V.C. Acc./Box2/42
Jones, Edward, Benenden, Kent, 1677 CKS PRC2/37/166
Jones, Edward, Leebotwood, Shrops, 1685 LJRO/B/C/5/1685/57
Jones, Elizabeth, widow, Wells, Som, 1668 Somerset RO D/D/Cta/J12
Jones, Gryffyn, Hythe St Leonard, Kent, 1596 CKS PRC21/14/79
Jones, Henrye, St Johns Thanet, Kent, 1599 CKS PRC2/11/60

[Jones:]
Jones, James, Kenardington, Kent, 1680 CKS PRC2/39/63
Jones, James, Oxford St Peter le Bailey, Oxon, 1701 Oxon RO MSS Wills 168/4/1
Jones, Johannes, gentleman, Lyme Regis, Dors, 1714 PRO PROB5/1097
Jones, John, bachelor/yeoman, Stanford, Kent, 1668 CKS PRC19/3/126
Jones, John, innholder, Gloucester St Catherine (Longford), Glos, 1728 GRO GDR/B4/2/W144
Jones, John, cordwainer, Shrewsbury St Chad, Shrops, 1739 LJRO/B/C/5/1739/246
Jones, John eld, yeoman, Ambrosden (Blackthorn), Oxon, 1634 Oxon RO MSS Wills 298/3/15
Jones, Joseph, St Helen, London & Middlesex, 1703? PRO PROB5/800
Jones, Joshua, St Giles in the Fields, London & Middlesex, 1749 Greater London RO DL/C/552/44/1
Jones, Katheryn, Sandwich St Peter, Kent, 1596 CKS PRC2/9/142
Jones, Mary, widow, Bradley, North, Wilts, 1626 Wilts RO Arch. Sarum(+ name and date)
Jones, Owen, Whitstable, Kent, 1612 CKS PRC2/16/42
Jones, Philip, weaver, Worcester, Worcs, 1599 Worcs RO 008.7 BA3585/838/156
Jones, Richard, Crowle, Worcs, Worcs RO 008.7 BA3585/838/202
Jones, Richard, gunsmith, Bristol, Glos, Bristol RO 1714/27
Jones, Richard, Sandwich St Peter, Kent, 1596 CKS PRC2/8/330
Jones, Richard, Congresbury, Som, 1627 Somerset RO D/D/Cta/J5
Jones, Robert, gentleman, Chester, Ches, 1719 Cheshire RO (Name) W.C. 1718
Jones, Thomas, schoolmaster, Bristol St James, Glos, Bristol RO 1776/CP
Jones, Thomas, wheelwright, Baschurch (Weston Common), Shrops, 1800 LJRO/B/C/5/1800/32
Jones, Thomas, waterman, Holywell, Hunts, 1815 Hunts RO/Acc58/335
Jones, Thomazyn, widow, Birchington, Kent, 1590 CKS PRC21/10/112
Jones, Watts, Biddenden, Kent, 1639 CKS PRC2/34/220
Jones, William, Llanelli, Breck, NLW BR 1633/55 Ac
Jones, William, miller, Abingdon St Nicholas, Berks, 1618 Berks RO D/A1/199/81D
Jones, William, Mildenhall, Wilts, 1630 Wilts RO Arch. Wilts.(name + date)
Jones, William, fishmonger/citizen,
London & Middlesex 1663 Lambeth Palace Arches G18/4
Jones, William, Kidderminster, Worcs, 1681 Worcs RO 008.7 BA3585/830/69
Jones, William, draper, Oxford St Clement, Oxon, 1800 Oxon RO MSS Wills 303/1/30
Jones/Griffyn, Robert, St Dominic, Corn, 1627 Cornwall RO AP/J319/2
Jonson, Jarratt, Uffington, Lincs, 1599 Lincs RO Ad/Ac/5/223
Jonson, William, Burton by Lincoln, Lincs, 1582 Lincs RO Ad/Ac/0/30
Jonsonne, Jonsonne, Mathewe, Grainthorpe, Lincs, 1593 Lincs RO Ad/Ac/3/15
Jonys, John, Southampton, Hants, 1569 Hants RO 21M65 D8/1
Joones, Christian, widow, Dover St Mary, Kent, 1596 CKS PRC21/14/15
Joones, Thomas, Smarden, Kent, 1599 CKS PRC2/10/475
Jordaine, Henry, mealman, Bushey, Herts, 1583 Herts RO ASA25/1062
Jordan, Adam, carpenter, Bourne, Lincs, 1632 Lincs RO Ad/Ac/25/102
Jordan, Edward, degrees: 'Doctor',
Som Somerset RO D/D/Cta/J20
Jordan, Heartoake, university: 'Fellow of Magdalene College, Cambridge/LL.B.' Cambridge (Magdalene College), Cambs, 1690 c. CUL V.C. Acc./Box3/31
Jordan, Lawrence, Nonington, Kent, 1614 CKS PRC20/2/575
Jordane, Alice, widow, Chinnock, East, Som, 1621 Somerset RO D/D/Cta/J22
Jordeine, Elizabeth, university: 'scholar's servant', Cambridge, Cambs, 1599 CUL V.C.Acc./Box1/32
Jorden, Edward, High Halden, Kent, 1683 CKS PRC2/40/126
Jorden, Henrie + Sara, Ickham, Kent, 1613 CKS PRC20/2/569
Jorden, James, Bonnington, Kent, 1696 CKS PRC2/42/116
Jorden, John, High Halden, Kent, 1596 CKS PRC2/8/109
Jorden, Robert, High Halden, Kent, 1613 CKS PRC2/16/179
Jorden, Robert, Stamford All Saints, Lincs, 1635 c. Lincs RO Ad/Ac/24/484
Jorden, Robert, High Halden, Kent, 1670 CKS PRC1/15/40

Jorden, Robert, Lenham, Kent, 1674 CKS PRC2/35/231
Jorden, Thomas, gentleman, High Halden, Kent, 1668 CKS PRC1/13/66
Jorden, Thomas, Kingham, Oxon, 1669 Oxon RO MSS Wills 168/3/12
Jorden, William, mariner, Sandwich, Kent, 1697 CKS PRC2/42/129
Jorey, Henry, Blisland, Corn, 1617 Cornwall RO AP/J226/3
Jorye, Randolph, gentleman commoner, Oxford (St John's College), Oxon, 1704 Bodleian HYP B9/5-6
Jorye, Robert, Blisland, Corn, 1608 Cornwall RO AP/J109/1
Jose, Henry jnr, yeoman, Endellion, Corn, 1631 Cornwall RO AP/J375/3
Joseph, John, St Just in Roseland, Corn, 1612 Cornwall RO AP/J159/1
Josephe, Thomas, Veryan, Corn, 1612 Cornwall RO AP/J160
Jowle, Ingram, Folkestone, Kent, 1603 CKS PRC2/14/282
Joy, Bartholomew, Eastry, Kent, 1634 CKS PRC20/11/9
Joy, Bartholomew, Wickhambreaux, Kent, 1685 CKS PRC2/40/207
Joy, Elizabeth, New Romney, Kent, 1634 CKS PRC20/11/3
Joy, James, Langley, Kent, 1640 CKS PRC1/4/69
Joy, John, Milton next Sittingbourne, Kent, 1676 CKS PRC2/37/51
Joy, Marie, widow, Chart nr Sutton Valence, Kent, 1603 CKS PRC2/12/445
Joy, Thomas, Midley, Kent, 1627 CKS PRC2/27/84
Joy, Thomas, Herne, Kent, 1629 CKS PRC20/8/255
Joy, William, Chislet, Kent, 1621 CKS PRC2/23/190
Joy, William, Boughton Monchelsea, Kent, 1667 CKS PRC1/12/51
Joyce, Elizabeth, spinster, Whitchurch, Shrops, 1800 LJRO/B/C/5/1800/33
Joyce, Hosea, Norton Juxta Twycross, Leics, 1672 Leics RO Administrators Accounts 1667-72 f67
Joyce, John, fellmonger, Sittingbourne, Kent, 1672 CKS PRC2/35/147
Joyce, Nicholas, Sandwich, Kent, 1599 CKS PRC2/10/462
Joyce, Richard, Hargrave, Northants, 1677 Northants RO NWill A/C/152
Joyce, Robert, Orton Longueville (Bottlebridge), Hunts, 1685 Hunts RO/Acc58/247(241)
Joye, John, Chart nr Sutton Valence, Kent, 1624 CKS PRC2/23/201
Joye, Robert, yeoman, Ash next Sandwich, Kent, 1672 CKS PRC20/12/15
Joye, Thomas, Herne, Kent, 1638 CKS PRC20/10/256
Joyes, Jane, widow, Spalding, Lincs, 1641 Lincs RO Ad/Ac/27/344
Joyner, Alice, Compton, Long, Warks, 1602 Worcs RO 008.7 BA3585/838/251
Joyner, Anthony, yeoman, Charlbury, Oxon, 1638 Oxon RO MSS Wills 298/3/29
Joyner, Joane, Graveney, Kent, 1633 CKS PRC2/32/70
Joyner, John, Hernhill, Kent, 1690 CKS PRC19/4/118
Joyner, Richard, Hackthorne, Lincs, 1632 Lincs RO Ad/Ac/39/325
Joyner/Roberts, William, Burnham, Som, 1630 Somerset RO D/D/Cta/J21
Jubb, Thomas, sergeant, Sheffield, Yorks, 1809 Borthwick Test C.P. 1809/4
Juce, Richard, clergy: 'vicar', Petham, Kent, 1644 CKS PRC1/6/109
Judd, Henry, Cranbrook, Kent, 1634 CKS PRC2/32/157
Judd, John, Raveley, Great, Hunts, 1678 Hunts RO/Acc58/121(37)
Judd, Josias, weaver: 'broad weaver', Cranbrook, Kent, 1671 CKS PRC2/35/61
Judd, Sara, spinster, St James Westminster, London & Middlesex, 1707 Lambeth Palace Arches G57/3
Judd, Stephen, weaver: 'broad weaver', Tenterden, Kent, 1644 CKS PRC1/7/27
Juddery, Rowland, Dover, Kent, 1598 CKS PRC21/15/19
Juddery, Stephen, Whitstable, Kent, 1666 CKS PRC1/11/129
Judgson, John, brickmaker, Wellington, Shrops, 1795 LJRO/B/C/5/1795/45
Judkins, William, Everdon, Northants, 1670 Northants RO NWill A/C/127
Judson, Henry, Loughborough, Leics, 1642 Leics RO PR/I/41A/89
Juell, John, Tintagel, Corn, 1621 Cornwall RO AP/J260/3
Jugge, Richard, husbandman, Helpringham, Lincs, 1636 Lincs RO Ad/Ac/24/281
Juice, John, Faversham, Kent, 1624 CKS PRC2/23/202

[Jukes:]
Jukes, Richard, Myddle, Shrops, 1675 LJRO:cards/1675/37
Jull, Andrewe, mercer, Maidstone, Kent, 1613 CKS PRC20/2/571
Jull, John, victualler, Deal, Kent, 1688 CKS PRC20/13/595
Jull, Robart, Denton (Eastry hundred), Kent, 1598 CKS PRC2/9/469
Jull, Robert, Chilham, Kent, 1690 CKS PRC2/41/151
Jullow, Peter, Appledore, Kent, 1640 CKS PRC1/4/70
Julyan, John, clergy: 'clerk/vicar', Elsham, Lincs, 1601 Lincs RO Ad/Ac/5/467
Jumeth, see Inmeth,
Jumpe, Thomas, Lancs RO (Name of Deceased) D.R.C.H. (Undated)
Jumyth, Robert, Cheriton, Kent, 1624 CKS PRC2/23/198
Jupp/Mersh, Mary, Steyning, Sussex, 1674 W. Suss RO EpI/33/1673/18
Jurdan, Agnes, spinster, Martock, Som, 1669 Somerset RO D/D/Cta/J2
Jurden, Ciprian, Stourmouth, Kent, 1590 CKS PRC2/5/167
Jurden, James, Cranbrook, Kent, 1596 CKS PRC2/9/140
Jurden, Thomas, Sandwich St Clement, Kent, 1607 CKS PRC2/14/273
Jurden, see Churden & Durden,
Justice, John, yeoman, Pangbourne, Berks, 1668 Berks RO D/A1/199/127C
Justice, William, Folkestone, Kent, 1637 CKS PRC2/34/73
Justiss, John, cutler, Sheffield, Yorks, Borthwick Test C.P. 1733/6
Jutton, Anthony, Greatham, Sussex, 1606 W. Suss RO EpI/33/1606/10
Juxon, Elias, clergy: 'mr/rector', Aldington, Kent, 1667 CKS PRC19/3/127
Jynkenes, Richard, Wimborne Minster, Dors, 1603 Dorset RO PE/WM CP 2/4/6
Jynnet, Agnes, widow, Maidstone, Kent, 1586 CKS PRC21/7/390
Jynnings, Robert, High Halden, Kent, 1596 CKS PRC2/8/397